© Reed Elsevier (UK) Ltd 2013

Published by LexisNexis

ISBN for this volume: 9780754546818

Visit LexisNexis at www.lexisnexis.co.uk

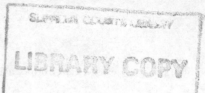

Tolley's Employment Handbook

by

Mrs Justice Slade DBE

High Court Judge,
A Recorder of the Crown Court,
A Master of the Bench of the Inner Temple,
Honorary Vice-President of the
Employment Law Bar Association

Twenty-Seventh Edition
by

members of
11 KBW Chambers
and

Sarah Bradford
Director of Writetax Ltd

Prof Dominic Regan
City Law School London, Solicitor

Stephen Barc
Solicitor

 LexisNexis®

Preface

If there was one Employment Law Reform my fellow contributing editors and I could wholeheartedly endorse it was the Government's former practice of introducing legislative changes at two fixed points each year. The present administration's determination to leave its mark on Employment Law has meant a new timetable. The easiest way of describing it is that developments are introduced just after the point it becomes possible to incorporate them into this edition.

Amongst the most recent developments that readers should be aware of but which it has not been possible to cover in depth are the new Tribunal Rules which have been developed as a result of Lord Justice Underhill's review. The Employment Appeal Tribunal has chipped in with a potentially momentous decision: *Usdaw v Ethel Austin Ltd (In Administration)* (UKEAT/0547/12) which has decided that:

> "Purposive construction of *Trade Union and Labour Relations (Consolidation) Act 1992, s 188* so as to give effect to a Directive required the court to delete the words 'at one establishment' thereby allowing protective awards to be made to employees whose employer was to dismiss 20 employees as redundant in 90 days."

The pace of development has remained brisk. Tribunal fees are about to be introduced and the Tribunal system is holding its breath and waiting to see what the effect will be. Liability for third party harassment under the *Equality Act 2010* will be gone by October 2013 and the Government has published draft legislation that will abolish the comparatively recently granted power for a Tribunal to make wider recommendations in discrimination cases. There are changes to the rules regarding settlement agreements and substantial legislative developments in the law relating to whistleblowing, including the introduction of a requirement that the employee should have a reasonable belief that the disclosure is in the public interest in the disclosure and the concomitant abolition of a requirement that the disclosure should have been made in good faith. Draft legislation amending the *Transfer of Undertakings Regulations* is expected consultation having closed in April 2013 which may abolish the Service Provision Change provisions as well as making other alterations to the existing regime. The *Trade Union and Labour Relations (Consolidation) Act 1992* has been amended to provide that the terminations of fixed term contracts on expiry of term, completion of the contract's specific task or the occurrence or non-occurrence of a specified event do not count for the purposes of determining whether an employer owes an obligation under *s 188* collectively to consult.

The Government also appears to be determined to introduce the Chancellor's somewhat "eccentric" idea for Employee Owner Status. In essence it allows employees to forgo their entitlements to unfair dismissal protection and a redundancy payment in return for an allocation of shares. The prospect of allowing employment rights to be bought out in return for an illiquid asset of uncertain value did not exactly wow the world of business. The consultation response indicated that over 98% of respondents had no interest in implementing the new status. Of the three respondents who expressed an interest in doing so, two were not actually employers. As the value of the shares allocated on recruitment may determine whether or not the Tribunal has jurisdiction in claims brought by employee owners, the delightful vista opens up of tribunals having to perform historic company valuations at preliminary hearings.

As ever, there has been too much interesting case law to summarise it all here. However, amongst the highlights is the European Court of Human Right's decision in *Eweida and Others v UK*. In the lead case an employee complained about how she had been treated when her employer, an airline, refused her to wear a crucifix on a chain so that it was visible over her uniform. The claim failed in the domestic proceedings because it was treated as a complaint of indirect discrimination and, as the Claimant could not show that anyone else shared her belief she could not establish the necessary group disadvantage.

Preface

The ECtHR paid no attention to this substantial technical difficulty and focussed instead on the question whether the airline's policy on corporate image could justify a restriction on the employee's right to manifest her religion. The Court decided that it could not. Health and safety concerns, however, did provide a sufficient justification in the joined case of *Chaplin*. In *Ladele* and *MacFarlane* the Court decided that the State was within its margin of appreciation in seeking to ensure equality of those with minority sexual orientations in a manner that meant that no remedy was available to employees who complained they had been less favourably treated as a result of not wishing to provide services (in the first case, performing civil partnership ceremonies and, in the latter providing psycho-sexual counselling) to same sex couples.

The ECtHR also decided the case of *Redfearn v UK* [2012] ECHR 1878. Before the Domestic courts the case of the BNP member sacked from his job as a bus driver had been run as a case of race discrimination. The ECtHR decided that there had been a breach of the employee's right to Freedom of Association under *Art 11* of the *Convention*. This has led to the amendment of the *Employment Rights Act 1996, s 108* to remove the need for a minimum period of qualifying employment where an employee is dismissed for a reason relating to the employee's political opinions or affiliation.

The re-writing of domestic legislation so as to have it conform with European legislation has been an emerging theme this year. In addition to the *Usdaw* case above, the courts have been prepared to take that step in the context of post-employment victimisation (*Onu v Akwiwu* [2013 IRLR 523), rolling over entitlement to paid holiday from periods of employee sickness (*NHS Leeds v Larner* [2012] EWCA Civ 1034; [2012] IRLR 825) and the rule precluding applications for trade union recognition where another union is already recognised (*Pharmacists' Defence Association v Boots Management Services Ltd* [2013] IRLR 262).

Joining us as contributing editors for the first time in this edition are Charles Bourne, Marcus Pilgerstorfer and Hannah Slarks all of whom are very welcome. We also have a new content developer: Cerys Owen, whose patience and good humour have been a blessing. I hope I will be forgiven taking a moment to pay tribute to Alistair McGregor QC (contributing editor of the chapter on Restraint of Trade). Alistair has retired from Chambers leaving a hole that simply cannot be filled. Alistair is a great mind, a vivid personality, the most convivial of companions and the most loyal of friends. We wish him and his wife Charlotte every happiness.

Seán Jones QC

List of Contributors

Members of 11 King's Bench Walk Chambers

Joseph Barrett, LLB, LLM (Harvard), barrister - Contract of Employment (7), Employee, Self-Employed or Worker? (14), References (38)

Andrew Blake BA, LLM, barrister - Holidays (27)

Charles Bourne, barrister - Discrimination and Equal Opportunities III (12)

Edward Capewell, MA, MPhil, barrister - Unfair Dismissal I, III (51), (53)

Akhlaq Choudhury, BSc, LLB (London), barrister - Government Proposals (24)

Simon Forshaw, barrister - Equal Pay (21)

Paul Greatorex, barrister - Probationary Employees (34), Time Off Work (47)

Patrick Halliday MA (Cantab), barrister - European Union Law (22)

Harini Iyengar, barrister - Insolvency (29)

Seán Jones QC, BA, BCL (Oxon), barrister - Discrimination and Equal Opportunities I (10)

Christopher Knight MA (Cantab), BCL (Oxon) barrister - Engagement of Employees (20), Maternity Rights (31)

Michael Lee MA (Cantab), barrister - Unfair Dismissal II (52)

Richard Leiper LLB, MJuris, barrister - Transfer of Undertakings (50)

Alistair McGregor QC, LLB (London), barrister - Restraint of Trade (39)

Julian Milford MA, barrister - Continuous Employment (6), Redundancy I and II (36, 37)

Marcus Pilgerstorfer , barrister - Employment Tribunals I, II (17, 18)

Nigel Porter MA (Cantab), LLM (Cantab), barrister - Introduction (1), Advisory, Concili-ation and Arbitration Service (2), Codes of Practice (4), Disclosure of Information (9), Employees' Past Criminal Convictions (16), Human Rights (28), Pay I and II (32, 33), Temporary and Seasonal Employees (45)

Anya Proops MA (Cantab), PhD, barrister - Foreign Employees (23), Vicarious Liability (54)

Amy Rogers, BA (Cantab), DipLaw, barrister - Employee Participation (15), Part-Time Workers (30)

Clive Sheldon QC, BA (Cantab), LLM, barrister - Sickness and Sick Pay (42), Termination of Employment (46), Wrongful Dismissal (56)

Hannah Slarks, barrister - Public Sector Employees (35)

Daniel Stilitz QC, BA, MA, barrister - Strikes and Industrial Action (43), Trade Unions I and II (48, 49)

Judy Stone BA (Hons) Oxon, barrister - Directors (8), Retirement (40)

Holly Stout MA (Cantab), DipLaw, barrister - Discrimination and Equal Opportunities II (11), Equal Pay (21), Restraint of Trade (39)

List of Contributors

Peter Wallington QC, MA, LLM, barrister - Collective Agreements (5), Employment Tribunals III (19), Working Time (55)

Other Contributors

Stephen Barc LLB, solicitor (non-practising), Technical Editor/Writer, LexisNexis -

Children and Young Persons (3), Education and Training (13), Service Lettings (41)

Sarah Bradford BA (Hons), ACA, CTA (Fellow), Director of Writetax Ltd - Taxation (44)

Prof Dominic Regan, City Law School London, Solicitor - Health and Safety at Work I and II (25, 26)

Contents

Abbreviations and References		ix
Table of Statutes		xi
Table of EU Legislation		xxxv
Table of Statutory Instruments		xxxix
Table of Cases		lix
1	Introduction	1
2	Advisory, Conciliation and Arbitration Service (ACAS)	9
3	Children and Young Persons	17
4	Codes of Practice	27
5	Collective Agreements	37
6	Continuous Employment	45
7	Contract of Employment	57
8	Directors	91
9	Disclosure of Information	119
10	Discrimination and Equal Opportunities – I	137
11	Discrimination and Equal Opportunities – II	207
12	Discrimination and Equal Opportunities – III	285
13	Education and Training	335
14	Employee, Self-Employed or Worker?	347
15	Employee Participation	363
16	Employee's Past Criminal Convictions	399
17	Employment Tribunals – I	407
18	Employment Tribunals – II	461
19	Employment Tribunals – III	553
20	Engagement of Employees	583
21	Equal Pay	587
22	European Union Law	651
23	Foreign Employees	665
24	Government Proposals	681
25	Health and Safety at Work – I	691
26	Health and Safety at Work – II	719
27	Holidays	741
28	Human Rights	757
29	Insolvency of Employer	773
30	Part-Time Workers	783
31	Maternity and Parental Rights	801
32	Pay – I	827
33	Pay – II	857
34	Probationary Employees	863
35	Public Sector Employees	865
36	Redundancy – I	873
37	Redundancy – II	885
38	References	897
39	Restraint of Trade and Confidential Information	903
40	Retirement	941
41	Service Lettings	971
42	Sickness and Sick Pay	981
43	Strikes and Industrial Action	989
44	Taxation	1009
45	Temporary and Seasonal Employees	1035
46	Termination of Employment	1055

Contents

47 Time Off Work   1067
48 Trade Unions – I   1081
49 Trade Unions – II   1103
50 Transfer of Undertakings   1119
51 Unfair Dismissal – I   1143
52 Unfair Dismissal – II   1163
53 Unfair Dismissal – III   1203
54 Vicarious Liability   1227
55 Working Time   1235
56 Wrongful Dismissal   1267

Index   1291

Abbreviations – General

ACAS	=	Advisory, Conciliation and Arbitration Service
ERRB	=	Enterprise and Regulatory Reform Bill
CA	=	Court of Appeal
CAC	=	Central Arbitration Committee
COET	=	Central Office of the Employment Tribunals
CRE	=	Commission for Racial Equality
DfEE	=	Department for Education and Employment
DRC	=	Disability Rights Commission
DSS	=	Department of Social Security
DTI	=	Department of Trade and Industry
EAT	=	Employment Appeal Tribunal
EEC	=	European Economic Community
EC	=	European Community
ECJ	=	European Court of Justice
EOC	=	Equal Opportunities Commission
HL	=	House of Lords
Pt	=	Part
Sch	=	Schedule
SI	=	Statutory Instrument
SR & O	=	Statutory Rules and Orders

Abbreviations – Statutes

DDA	=	Disability Discrimination Act 1995
DRCA	=	Disability Rights Commission Act 1999
EA	=	Employment Act (with date)
EPA	=	Employment Protection Act 1975
EPCA	=	Employment Protection (Consolidation) Act 1978
ETA	=	Employment Tribunals Act 1996
EqA	=	Equality Act 2010
EqPA	=	Equal Pay Act 1970
ERA 1996	=	Employment Rights Act 1996
ERA 1999	=	Employment Relations Act 1999
FA	=	Finance Act (with date)
HSWA	=	Health and Safety at Work etc. Act 1974
HRA	=	Human Rights Act 1998
ICTA	=	Income and Corporation Taxes Act 1988
OLA	=	Occupiers' Liability Act 1957
OSRPA	=	Offices, Shops and Railway Premises Act 1963
PIDA	=	Public Interest Disclosure Act 1998
RRA	=	Race Relations Act 1976
SBA	=	Supplementary Benefits Act 1976
SDA	=	Sex Discrimination Act 1975
SDA 1986	=	Sex Discrimination Act 1996
SSA	=	Social Security Act 1975
SSA 1986	=	Social Security Act 1986
SSAA	=	Social Security Administration Act 1992

Abbreviations and References

SSCBA	=	Social Security Contributions and Benefits Act 1992
SSHBA	=	Social Security and Housing Benefits Act 1982
SSPA	=	Social Security Pensions Act 1975
TUA	=	Trade Union Act 1984
TULRA	=	Trade Union and Labour Relations Act 1974
TULR(A)A	=	Trade Union and Labour Relations (Amendment) Act 1976
TULRCA	=	Trade Union and Labour Relations (Consolidation) Act 1992
TURERA	=	Trade Union Reform and Employment Rights Act 1993
UCTA	=	Unfair Contract Terms Act 1977
WA	=	Wages Act 1986

Law reports – Series referred to

AC	=	Law Reports, Appeal Cases
All ER	=	All England Law Reports
ATC	=	Annotated Tax Cases
BCLC	■	Butterworths Company Law Cases
Ch	=	Law Reports, Chancery Division
CMLR	=	Common Market Law Reports
Cr App Rep	=	Criminal Appeal Reports
FSR	=	Fleet Street Reports
ICR	=	Law Reports, Industrial Cases Reports
IDS	=	Incomes Data Services
IRLB	=	Industrial Relations Law Bulletin
IRLR	=	Industrial Relations Law Reports
ITR	=	Industrial Tribunal Reports
LJKB	=	Law Journal Reports, New Series, King's Bench (ended 1949)
Lloyd's Rep	=	Lloyd's List Law Reports
LS Gaz	=	Law Society's Gazette
PCC	=	Palmer's Company Cases
QB/KB	=	Law Reports, Queen's (King's) Bench Division
TLR	=	Times Law Reports (last year of publication 1952)
WLR	=	Weekly Law Reports

Table of Statutes

A

Access to Health Records Act 1990
.... 9.1, 52.8
s 2–6 .... 9.14
8 .... 9.14
Access to Medical Reports Act 1988
.... 9.1, 52.8
s 1 .... 9.14
3(1) 9.14
4 .... 9.14
5(1), (2) 9.14
8 .... 9.14
Administration of Justice Act 1982
s 10(i) 42.15
Agriculture (Safety, Health and Welfare Provisions) Act 1956
s 3 .... 26.29
5 .... 26.29
25(3) 26.29
(6) 26.29
Agricultural Wages Act 1948
s 3, 4 .... 27.7
11 .... 27.7
Apportionment Act 1870 .... 27.9
s 2 .... 32.22
5 .... 32.22
7 .... 32.22
Apprenticeships, Skills, Children and Learning Act 2009 .... 13.1, 13.10
Pt 1, Ch 1 (ss 1–39) 13.9, 13.11
s 32 .... 13.2, 13.7
35 .... 13.2
Pt 2, Ch 2 (s 40) 13.9
s 40 .... 13.12
83A, 83B 13.10
Arbitration Act 1950
Pt I (ss 1–34) 2.7
Arbitration Act 1996
s 9(4) 56.38
Armed Forces Act 1966 .... 35.3
Armed Forces Act 1991 .... 35.3
Armed Forces Act 1996 .... 21.2, 35.3
Armed Forces Act 2001 .... 35.3
Armed Forces Act 2006 .... 30.1, 35.3
s 334 .... 12.2
Army Act 1955 .... 35.3
Asylum and Immigration Act 1996
.... 9.1
s 8 .... 23.5
Attachment of Earnings Act 1971
.... 33.10, 33.11
s 1(1)–(3) 33.1
5(1) 33.1
6 .... 33.3

Attachment of Earnings Act 1971 – *cont.*
s 6(2) 33.1
7(1) 33.6
(2) 33.7
(4)(a), (b) 33.9
8 .... 33.9
9 .... 33.9
(2) 33.6
12(3) 33.6
14(1)(b) 33.7
15(c) 33.7
16(1)–(3) 33.2
23(5) 33.8
24(1), (2) 33.2
Sch 3
Pt.1 .... 33.4
Pt 2
para 7, .8 .... 33.5

B

Betting, Gaming and Lotteries Act 1963
.... 7.7
Sch 5A 7.48

C

Care Standards Act 2000
Pt VII (ss 80–104) 28.7
Child Support Act 1991 .... 33.1, 33.11
Child Support, Pensions and Social Security Act 2000 .... 33.1, 33.11
s 74, 75 .... 44.17
Children and Young Persons Act 1933
s 18(1) 3.2, 55.3
(2) 3.3
(2A) 3.2
21 .... 3.3
23–26 .... 3.4
Children and Young Persons Act 1963
.... 3.2, 3.3
s 37–42 .... 3.4
Children and Young Persons Act 1969
.... 3.3
Children and Young Persons (Scotland) Act 1937
.... 55.3
Chiropractors Act 1994
s 40(2) 16.4
(4) 16.4
Civil Jurisdiction and Judgments Act 1982
.... 23.8
Civil Jurisdiction and Judgments Act 1991
.... 23.8
Civil Liability (Contribution) Act 1978
.... 18.23, 25.10

Table of Statutes

Civil Liability (Contribution) Act 1978 – *cont.*
s 1(1) 54.3
2 .... 54.3
Civil Partnership Act 2004 .... 40.9
s 1 .... 10.19
212–218 .... 11.14
246, 247 .... 36.10
Sch 20 .... 11.14
Sch 21 .... 36.10
Companies Act 2006 .... 8.1, 8.16, 8.27
s 168(2) 8.36
(5) 8.36
169 .... 8.36
170 .... 15.2
(2)(a), (b) 8.24
(3), (4) 8.17
171 .... 8.17, 8.18
172 .... 8.17
(1) 8.19, 15.2
(3) 8.19
173 .... 8.17, 8.20
174 .... 8.17
(1), (2) 8.21
175 .... 8.17, 8.24
(2) 8.22
(4) 8.22
(5)(a), (b) 8.22
(6) 8.22
176 .... 8.17, 8.24
(3), (4) 8.23
177 .... 8.17
(1) 8.12
(4) 8.12
(6) 8.12
178 .... 8.17
182 .... 8.12
184, 185 .... 8.12
188 .... 7.3, 8.13, 56.14
(2), (3) 8.14
(5) 8.14
189 .... 7.3, 8.14
217 .... 8.37
218 .... 8.40
219 .... 8.41
220 .... 8.40, 8.41
(1) 8.37
221 .... 8.37, 8.40
222(2) 8.40
(3) 8.41
227 .... 8.7
228(3)–(6) 8.8
229(1) 8.8
(5) 8.8
231 .... 8.9
232(2)(b) 8.25
233 .... 8.25
234–238 .... 8.25
260 .... 15.2
317 .... 8.12
382 .... 8.32
383(1) 8.32

Companies Act 2006 – *cont.*
s 384(1), (2) 8.32
412(5), (6) 8.31
415, 416 .... 15.3
420 .... 8.31
661(3), (4) 8.25
1157(2), (3) 8.25, 8.26
Company Directors Disqualification Act 1986
s 2(1) 25.38
Compensation Act 2006 .... 19.28
s 3 .... 25.8
Pt 2 (ss 4–15) 18.40
Competition Act 1998
Pt I (ss 1–60) 39.1
Constitutional Reform Act 2005
.... 17.7
Contempt of Court Act 1981 .... 28.5
Contracts (Applicable Law) Act 1990
s 2(2) 23.7
Corporate Manslaughter and Corporate Homicide Act 2007
s 1(1) 25.42
(3) 25.42
(4)(b) 25.42
County Courts Act 1984
s 69 .... 56.31
Courts, Tribunals and Enforcement Act 2007
s 42 .... 19.9
Crime and Disorder Act 1998
s 31, 32 .... 26.28
Criminal Justice Act 1982
s 37(2) 1.10
Criminal Justice Act 1991
s 17 .... 1.10
18 .... 1.10
Criminal Justice Act 1993
s 65 .... 1.10
Criminal Justice and Public Order Act 1994
.... 10.39
Sch 9
para 11(2) 16.6
Criminal Law Act 1977
s 32(1) 1.10
Crown Proceedings Act 1947 .... 11.36

D

Data Protection Act 1984 ...... 9.1, 9.12, 9.14
s 5(1), (2) 9.11
21–23 .... 9.11
Sch 1
Pt 1
para 7 .... 9.11
Data Protection Act 1998 .... 9.1, 20.7
s 1(1) 9.13
Pt II (ss 7–15) 9.13
s 7 .... 4.17, 9.13
8 .... 16.7

Data Protection Act 1998 – *cont.*
s 10 .... 9.13
  12–14 .... 9.13
  51(3)(b) 4.17
  55A, 55B 9.13
  Sch 1 .... 9.13
  Sch 3 .... 9.13, 16.10
  Sch 8 .... 9.12
Deregulation and Contracting Out Act 1994
  .... 17.11, 49.20, 52.3
Disability Discrimination Act 1995
  . 1.6, 11.2, 11.9A, 11.10, 12.3, 12.4, 12.7,
        12.11, 14.3, 17.11, 40.6, 52.8
  Pt II (ss 3A–18D) 12.24
  s 4(2A) 11.16
   (3), (4) 11.16
   (6) 11.16, 23.9
   4A 10.37
   4B 11.24
   4C(1)(a) 11.25
    (3)(a), (b) 11.25
    (4)(b) 11.25
    (5) 11.25
   4D(1) 11.25
    (3)(c) 11.25
    (4) 11.25
    (7) 11.25
   4F(1), (2) 11.25
   4G(1)(b) 11.35
    (2) 11.35
    (4), (5) 11.35
   4H 11.35
    (1) 10.37
   4I(1) 12.22
   4J(1)(C) 12.22
    (4) 11.35
   6(1) 10.37
   6A(1), (2) 11.28
    (4) 11.28
   6C(2) 11.28
   7A(1)–(5) 11.27
   7C 11.27
   13(1)–(4) 11.29
   14A(1) 11.30
    (3) 11.30
    (5) 11.30
   16A 12.22
   16B 12.30
   16C 12.30
   17A 12.14
    (1A) 11.30, 12.2
    (2)(a)–(c) 12.12
    (4) 12.16
    (5) 11.35, 12.21
   17C 12.32, 12.33
   18B(6) 10.37
   18C 11.16
   Pt III (ss 19–28) 12.23, 12.30, 17.13
   s 19(1) 11.31
    20 .... 11.31
    21A(1)(a), (b) 11.31

Disability Discrimination Act 1995 – *cont.*
  s 21a(1)(c) 11.32
   (2) 11.31, 11.32, 11.33
   Pt IV (ss 28A–31C) 12.24
  s 49A(2) 11.37
   53 .... 4.11
   53A 4.11, 4.13
    (8), (8A) 4.12
   56(3)(b) 12.9
   57 .... 12.2
    (2) 10.58
   58 .... 12.2
   59(1) 11.21
    (2A) 11.22
   64(2) 11.36
    (7) 11.16
   64A(1)–(8) 11.26
   65 .... 11.36
   68 .... 23.9
    (2) 11.18, 11.36
    (4A) 11.18
   Sch 1
    para 4(1) 10.26
   Sch 3
    para 2(1) 12.1
     (2) 12.1, 12.22
     3(1) 12.4
      (3), (4) 12.4
   Sch 3A
    Pt 1
     para 1(1) 12.22
Disability Discrimination Act 2005
  s 18 .... 10.26

Education Act 1996
  s 8 .... 3.1
   558 .... 3.1
   559(1)–(4) 3.3
   560(4), (5) 3.2
   560A(2) 3.7
   579(1) 3.1
Education Act 2002
  s 119–130 .... 35.5
Education and Skills Act 2008
  Pt 1 (ss 1–67) 3.8, 13.1, 13.13
  s 27, 28 .... 52.3
   29 .... 13.13
   173(10) 3.8, 13.1
Employment Act 1980 .... 31.1, 49.3
Employment Act 1982 .... 49.3
Employment Act 1988 .... 49.3
Employment Act 1989
  s 3(3) 11.21
   8 .... 11.10
   10(1) 3.5
    (3)(b), (c) 3.5
    (4) 3.5
   11(1), (2) 11.13

Table of Statutes

Employment Act 1989 – *cont.*
s 11(5) 26.4
12 .... 11.13
    (1), (2) 26.4
Employment Act 1990 .... 49.3
Employment Act 2002 .... 17.15, 17.18, 17.20,
                17.25, 18.34, 31.1, 31.52,
                52.4, 52.10, 53.10
Pt II (ss 22–28) 17.1
s 21(1), (2) 31.44
24 .... 17.2
29 .... 12.4, 12.9, 17.19, 53.13
30 .... 12.4, 12.9, 17.19, 52.3, 53.13
    (3) 52.3
31 .... 17.2, 17.19, 18.63, 56.30
    (2) 53.13k
    (3) 12.15, 53.13k
    (4) 53.13k
    (6) 53.13
32 ..... 12.4, 12.9, 17.2, 17.5, 17.19, 17.34,
            18.27, 21.21, 51.2, 53.13, 56.30
    (2)–(4) 51.15
    (6) 51.15
33 .... 12.4, 12.9, 17.2, 17.19, 53.13
34 .... 12.9
38 .... 7.11, 53.16
    (2), (3) 53.13
    (5) 53.13
Sch 2 .... 12.9, 21.21, 51.15, 56.30
    Pt.1............................ 12.4
    Pt.2............................ 12.4
    para.6........................... 51.7
    .7........................... 51.7
    .8........................... 51.7
    .9........................... 51.7
Sch 3 .... 12.4, 12.9
Sch 4 .... 12.4, 12.9
Sch 5 .... 7.11
Employment Act 2008 ... 2.4, 4.2, 17.2, 32.13,
                                    45.3
s 1 .... 12.9, 51.2, 53.13
    3(1), (2) 4.3
4 .... 17.10
15, 16 .... 45.3
18 .... 45.3, 45.6
Employment Agencies Act 1973
    .... 32.13
s 3–3D 45.3
    5(2) 45.5
6 .... 45.3
9 .... 45.3
13 .... 14.3
    (2), (3) 45.5
Employment and Training Act 1973
s 2 .... 11.33
8, 9 .... 13.5
10 .... 11.33, 13.5
10A–10B 13.5
Employment of Women, Young Persons and Chil-
    dren Act 1920

Employment of Women, Young Persons and
    Children Act 1920 – *cont.*
s 1(1) 3.4
    3(2) 3.4
Schedule 3.4
Employment Protection Act 1975
    .... 2.1, 15.1, 31.1, 32.23, 48.4, 48.19
Sch 11 .... 5.1
Employment Protection (Consolidation) Act 1978
    .... 22.7, 31.1, 51.1, 52.3
s 140(1) 51.19
151 .... 6.1
    (3) 6.3
Sch 13 .... 6.1
    para 9(1)(b), (c)...................... 6.7
Employment Relations Act 1999
    .... 15.1, 31.1, 36.1, 45.3, 50.1
s 1(2) 52.3, 52.11
3, 4 .... 49.10
5 .... 48.38
10 .... 19.3, 51.11, 52.10
    (4)–(6) 49.21
11 .... 17.11, 52.3, 52.10
    (1), (2) 49.21
12 .... 49.21, 52.3
    (4) 51.11
13 .... 52.3
    (4) 49.21
16 .... 52.3
19 .... 30.1
20, 21 .... 30.2
22 .... 32.10
23 .... 51.3
30 .... 15.64
34 .... 53.7
    (1) 53.16
    (4) 53.10
37 .... 52.3
    (1) 53.10, 53.16
38 .... 35.2, 52.1
39 .... 32.13
80 .... 2.4
Sch 1 .... 48.19, 48.25, 52.3, 52.11
Sch 5 .... 52.3
Employment Relations Act 2004
    .... 4.4, 51.17
s 9 .... 28.4
38 .... 19.3
42 .... 15.4, 15.40
Employment Rights Act 1996 . 1.6, 7.39, 11.18,
                11.37, 12.19, 19.31,
                22.7, 23.9, 25.1,
                26.7, 29.1, 31.26,
                32.11, 32.14, 32.23,
                35.5, 36.1, 51.1,
                51.6, 52.8, 55.6,
                55.31
s 1 .... 7.9, 7.11, 8.6, 8.8, 50.22
    (1) 7.6
    (3) 7.7
    (4) 7.7

Employment Rights Act 1996 – *cont.*
s 1(4)(d)(i) 27.9
    (ii) 7.8
    (e) 7.8
  (5) 7.7
2 .... 8.6
  (1) 7.7
  (2), (3) 7.8
  (4)–(6) 7.6
3 .... 7.6, 8.6
  (1) 7.7
  (2) 7.7, 7.44
  (5) 7.7
3A 17.1
4 .... 7.11, 8.6, 17.5, 55.22
  (1) 7.9, 36.12
  (3) 7.9
  (6) 7.9
  (8) 7.9
5 .... 8.6
  (1) 7.10
6 .... 8.6, 55.13
7 .... 7.7
7A(1)(c) 7.6
7B 7.6
8 .... 32.16
9(1)–(4) 32.17
10(2B), (2C) 49.21
  (4), (5) 49.21
  (6) 47.2
11 .... 17.9, 32.20
  (1) 7.11, 32.19
    (a) 18.19
  (2) 7.11, 18.18, 32.19
  (4) 7.11
    (b) 32.19
  (6) 12.11, 18.18
12(1), (2) 12.11, 7.11
  (3) 18.18, 32.20
  (4), (5) 32.20
  (7) 12.11
Pt II (ss 13–27) 7.26, 7.35, 17.9, 17.11,
    17.31, 32.2, 32.12, 49.20, 55.22
s 13 .... 7.11, 27.9, 46.11
  (1) 32.6, 32.8, 32.12
  (2)–(4) 32.6
14 .... 7.11, 46.11
  (3) 32.6
15 .... 7.11, 46.11
  (1) 32.6, 32.8
  (2) 32.6
  (5) 32.6
16 .... 7.11, 46.11, 49.2
17 .... 7.11, 46.11
  (1)–(3) 32.7
18 .... 7.11, 46.11
  (1)–(3) 18.29, 32.7, 32.8
  (7) 18.13, 18.29
19 .... 7.11, 46.11
  (1) 32.7
20 .... 7.11, 46.11

Employment Rights Act 1996 – *cont.*
s 20(1) 32.7, 32.8
  (2), (3) 32.7
  (5) 32.7
21 .... 7.11, 19.1, 46.11
  (1) 32.7, 32.8
  (3) 32.7
22 .... 7.11, 46.11
  (4) 32.7
23 .... 7.11, 17.9, 32.20, 46.11
  (1) 32.8
  (3) 17.31, 27.6, 32.8
  (4) 17.31
24 .... 7.11, 32.8, 32.20, 46.11
25 .... 7.11, 32.20, 46.11
  (1), (2) 32.8
  (3) 32.6, 32.8
  (4), (5) 32.8
26 .... 7.11, 32.8, 46.11
27 .... 7.11, 31.43, 32.12, 44.8, 46.11
  (1)–(3) 32.6
  (5) 32.6
Pt III (ss 28–35) 29.2, 29.5
s 28(1)–(5) 32.24
29(1), (2) 32.25
  (3) (5) 32.26
30 .... 49.2
  (1) 32.24, 32.27
  (2) 32.27
  (3) 19.1, 32.27
  (4), (5) 32.27
31, 32 .... 32.27
34 .... 17.9
  (1)–(3) 32.28
35 .... 32.27
36–39 .... 7.48, 55.1
40 .... 55.1
41 .... 55.1
  (2), (3) 7.48
42 .... 55.1
  (2) 7.48
43 .... 7.48, 55.1
Pt IVA (ss 43A–43L) 14.8, 38.4
s 43A 15.19, 15.21, 15.28, 51.11, 52.3
43B 9.18, 26.9, 51.11, 52.3
  (1)–(4) 9.17
43C–43F 9.17, 26.9, 51.11, 52.3
43G 26.9, 51.11, 52.3
  (2)(a)–(c) 9.17
  (3), (4) 9.17
43H 9.17, 26.9, 51.11, 52.3
43I 51.11, 52.3
43J 9.17, 51.11, 52.3
43K 9.17, 14.1, 26.9, 51.11, 52.3
43KA 35.4, 51.11
43L 51.11, 52.3
Pt V (ss 43M–49A) 17.33
s 43M 47.4
44(2), (3) 26.8
45(1)–(8) 7.48
45A 55.23, 55.24

Table of Statutes

Employment Rights Act 1996 – *cont.*
s 45B 55.23
46 .... 40.15
47 .... 50.23
47A 3.10, 31.18
47B 9.16, 26.9, 38.4
47C 31.48, 31.60
47E 47.17
48 .... 3.10, 7.48, 31.19
  (1), (1A) 26.10
  (2) 9.17, 26.10, 55.23
  (3) 26.10
    (b) 17.33
  (4) 26.10
49 .... 15.29, 26.10, 31.19, 55.23
50(4) 47.4
51(1)–(3) 47.5
52(1), (2) 47.6
53 .... 29.2
  (1) (3) 47 6
  (4) 47.7
  (5) 47.6, 47.7
  (6), (7) 47.7
54(1), (2) 47.7
  (4) 47.7
55(1) 31.6, 31.7, 31.9
  (2), (3) 31.7
  (5) 31.7
56 .... 29.2
  (1) 31.6, 31.7, 31.9
  (2)–(4) 31.8
  (5), (6) 31.8, 31.9
57(1) 31.6, 31.9
  (2)–(5) 31.9
57ZA–57ZD 31.10
57A 31.16, 31.18, 47.16, 52.3
  (1)–(6) 47.15
57B(1)–(4) 47.16
58 .... 40.15
  (1), (2) 47.10
59 .... 40.15
  (1)–(4) 47.10
  (6) 47.11
60 .... 40.15
  (1)–(5) 47.11
61 .... 47.12, 50.23
62 .... 50.23, 49.2
  (1) 47.12
63 .... 50.23
63A 13.13
  (1) 3.8, 3.10
  (2)(c) 3.8
  (3) 3.8, 3.10
  (4), (5) 3.8
  (7) 3.8
63B(1)–(4) 3.8, 3.10
63C 3.8
  (1)–(5) 3.9
Pt VIA (ss 63D–63K) 13.12
s 63D 13.14, 13.15, 13.16, 13.17, 13.18,
                     13.19, 52.3

Employment Rights Act 1996 – *cont.*
s 63d(1) 13.13
  (4), (5) 13.13
  (7), (8) 13.13
63E(1)–(3) 13.14
  (4)(a) 13.14, 13.16
   (b) 13.14
63F 52.3
  (1) 13.15, 13.19
  (4)–(7) 13.15, 13.17
63H 13.16
63I 13.18, 13.19, 52.3
  (1)–(3) 1416
  (5), (6) 1416
63J(1)–(4) 13.18
Pt VII (ss 64–70) 29.2
s 64(3) 32.29
  (5) 32.29
65(1), (2) 32.29
  (3) 32.30
  (4)(a), (b) 32.30
66 .... 21.4, 31.11
  (2) 31.16, 31.18
67 .... 21.4, 26.17
  (1), (2) 31.12
68 .... 21.4, 31.13
68A–68D 31.14
69 .... 21.4, 49.2
  (1)–(3) 31.13, 32.32
69A 31.14
70 .... 17.9, 21.4
  (1)–(3) 31.13, 32.33
  (4)–(7) 31.12
70A 31.14
Pt VII (ss 71–75) 31.20
s 71 .... 6.6, 31.18, 31.21, 51.4
  (1) 10.31
  (4), (5) 40.13
72(1) 10.31
  (5) 31.27
73 .... 6.6, 31.18
  (1) 10.31
75A, 75B 6.6
76 .... 6.6
77 .... 6.6, 31.51
80(1) 31.47
80c(1) 6.6
80F–80G 2.8, 52.3
80H 2.8, 47.17, 52.3
80I 2.8
86 .... 29.5, 51.13, 56.27, 52.3
  (1) 46.7
  (2) 46.17
  (3) 46.7, 56.16, 56.21
  (5) 46.8
  (6) 36.4
87(1) 56.27
  (4) 56.27
88–90 .... 56.27
91(5) 56.27
92 .... 30.23, 46.15

Employment Rights Act 1996 – *cont.*

s 92(1) 46.14, 46.15
  (4) 31.36, 46.14
  (7) 6.6, 53.7
93(1)–(3) 46.15
Pt X (ss 94–138) ... 11.15, 13.19, 30.25, 45.9
s 94(1) 51.3
95 .... 37.4, 50.25
  (1) 46.18, 51.4
    (c) 26.11
  (2) 51.5
96 .... 38.8
97 .... 31.60
  (1) 17.23, 36.4, 51.13, 53.13
  (2) 6.6, 51.13, 53.13
  (4) 51.13, 53.7, 53.13
98 .... 40.2, 51.14
  (1) 52.1, 52.2
    (b) 45.7, 52.13, 52.14
  (2)(ba) 40.3, 40.4, 52.2, 52.13, 52.14
  (3) 52.5
  (3A) 52.4
  (4) 18.59, 28.7, 30.25, 34.2, 39.1,
            40.452.4, 52.9, 52.11, 52.14
    (b) 45.7
  (6) 34.2
98A(1) 52.3, 53.13
  (2) 52.11, 53.13
98B 47.4, 51.18, 52.3
  (1), (2) 52.11
98ZA–98ZF 40.3, 40.4, 51.14
98ZG 40.4, 51.14, 52.4
98ZH 40.3, 40.4, 51.14
99 .. 31.16, 31.17, 31.48, 31.60, 51.18, 52.3,
                                      52.11
100 ...... 51.15, 51.18, 52.11, 53.10, 55.10,
                            55.16, 55.24
  (1)(a), (b) 53.8, 53.9, 53.16
    (d), (e) 52.3
  (2), (3) 52.3
101 .... 52.3, 52.11
  (1)–(3) 7.48
101A 52.3, 52.11, 55.24
  (1)(d) 51.18, 53.8, 53.9, 53.16
101B 52.3
102 .... 40.15, 52.3
  (1) 52.11, 53.8, 53.9, 53.16
103 ... 50.23, 51.18, 52.3, 52.11, 53.8, 53.9,
                                      53.16
103A . 9.17, 18.8, 51.15, 51.18, 52.3, 52.11,
                            53.10, 53.16
104 .... 31.48, 32.6, 51.18, 52.11, 55.24
  (1) 52.3, 52.11
  (2), (3) 52.3
  (4) 7.48
104A 32.12, 52.3, 52.11
104B 52.3, 52.11
104C 47.17, 51.18, 52.3
104D 40.11, 52.3
104E 13.19, 52.3, 52.11
104F 49.10, 52.3

Employment Rights Act 1996 – *cont.*

s 104f(1)(a), (b) 52.11
105(1) 7.48
  (c) 52.3
  (3) 53.10, 53.16
  (4) 7.48
  (6A) 52.3, 53.10, 53.16
  (7D) 52.3
  (7H) 15.21
106 .... 31.36, 45.7
107 .... 52.16
108 .... 10.20
  (1), (2) 51.11
  (3) 7.10, 15.21, 31.17
    (aa) 51.11
    (b)–(i) 51.11
    (j) 45.9, 51.11
    (k)–(o) 51.11
    (q) 51.11
109 .... 11.9, 51.14
  (2) 7.48
111 .... 24.3
  (2) 51.2
  (3) 17.24, 17.29, 17.32
112(1) 53.1
  (2) 53.4
114(1) 53.2
  (3) 53.2
  (4) 53.4
115(1), (2) 53.3
  (3) 53.4
116(1) 53.2
  (2) 53.3
  (4) 53.3
  (5), (6) 53.4
117 .... 53.14
  (1) 53.4
  (2) 53.4, 53.5
  (3), (4) 53.4, 53.5
  (7) 53.5
118(1) 53.6
119(2), (3) 53.7
120 .... 53.9
  (1) 53.8
  (1A), (1B) 53.8
  (1C) 49.10
121 .... 53.8
122(1)–(3) 53.9
  (3A), (4) 53.9
123(1) 53.11, 53.13
  (2), (3) 53.11
  (6), (7) 53.13
124 .... 49.16
  (1A) 9.17, 52.3, 53.16
  (3) 53.4
  (4), (5) 53.10
124A 53.13
127B 9.17
128 .... 9.17, 17.9, 17.18, 53.18
  (2), (3) 53.18
  (4) 18.6, 18.39, 53.18

Table of Statutes

Employment Rights Act 1996 – *cont.*
s 128(5) 18.39, 53.18
129 .... 9.17, 17.9, 17.18, 53.18
130–132 .... 17.9, 17.18, 53.18
Pt XI (ss 135–181) 29.3
s 135 .... 11.15, 36.2
136 .... 36.12
(1) 46.18
(2), (3) 36.6
(5) 36.6
138(1) 6.6, 36.6, 53.8
(2) 36.6, 36.12
(3) 36.6
(4) 36.6, 36.12
(5) 36.6
(6) 36.6, 36.12
139(1)(b) 36.7
141 .... 53.8
(1) 36.10, 36.12
(?) 36.10
(3), (4) 36.10, 36.12
142(1), (2) 36.6
145 .... 17.27
(5) 6.6, 36.4
145A, 145B 52.3
146(1) 36.6
(2) 36.11
147(2) 36.8
148 .... 36.8, 36.9
149 .... 36.9
150(1) 36.8
(3) 36.8
152(1)(b) 36.9
155 .... 36.2, 36.4
156 .... 11.9
157 .... 29.4, 29.4, 36.10
159 .... 35.2, 36.10
160, 161 .... 36.10
162(1)–(3) 11.15, 36.13
163 .... 17.9
(1) 36.14
(2) 36.7
164 .... 17.22, 29.4
(1), (2) 17.27, 36.11
(3) 17.27
Pt XI, Ch VI (ss 166–170) 50.11
s 166 .... 29.5
(5)–(8) 29.4
167 .... 6.12
(3), (4) 29.4
168, 169 .... 29.4
170 .... 17.9, 29.4
Pt XII (ss 182–190) 29.3, 29.4, 29.7
s 182 .... 14.3, 29.5
183 .... 29.5
184 .... 50.11
(1)(a) 29.5
(2) 29.5
185–187 .... 29.5
188 .... 17.9, 29.6
189, 190 .... 29.5

Employment Rights Act 1996 – *cont.*
s 191 .... 35.2, 47.4, 56.43
192 .... 35.3
193 .... 35.7
194, 195 .... 47.4
196(1) 46.8
(2), (3) 32.8
(5) 51.15
197 .... 51.15
198 .... 7.6, 7.10
199 .... 46.8, 47.4
(2) 32.18, 36.10, 51.15
(4) 32.18
200 .... 47.4, 51.15
(1) 32.18, 35.4
201 .... 51.15
202 .... 35.7
203 .. 7.48, 18.33, 18.34, 18.35, 30.29, 45.9,
46.7, 53.19
(1) ,,, 2.4, 7.26, 18.32, 32.8, 36.15, 46.2,
51.19
(2) .. 2.4, 7.26, 32.8, 36.15, 51.15, 51.19
205(2) 32.8
206(4) 17.9
207A 47.5, 47.7, 47.11, 47.13, 47.16
Pt XIV, Ch 1 (ss 210–219) 45.9
s 210 .... 6.1, 36.13, 51.12
(1)–(3) 6.2
(4) 6.5, 6.12
(5) 6.5
211 .... 6.1, 36.13, 51.12
(1), (2) 6.3
(3) 6.3, 6.11
212 .... 6.1, 36.13, 51.12
(1) 6.6
(3) 6.6
(a) 6.7
(b) 6.7, 45.8
(c) 6.7
(4) 6.6
213 .... 6.1, 36.13, 51.12
214 .... 6.1, 6.12, 51.12
(2) 36.13
215 .... 6.1, 6.5, 6.12, 36.13, 51.12
(1)(a) 6.10
(2)(a), (b) 6.10
216 .... 6.1, 6.5, 6.12, 36.13, 51.12
(1)–(3) 6.10
217 .... 6.1, 6.5, 6.12, 36.13, 51.12
218 .... 6.1, 11.15, 36.13, 51.12
(2) 6.9
(4)–(10) 6.9
219 .... 6.1, 6.6, 36.13, 51.12, 53.4
220 .... 32.32
221 . 27.4, 32.12, 32.32, 32.33, 36.13, 46.15,
53.7
(2), (3) 32.35, 32.36
222 . 27.4, 32.12, 32.32, 32.34, 32.35, 36.13,
46.15, 53.7
223 . 27.4, 32.12, 32.32, 32.34, 36.13, 46.15,
53.7

Employment Rights Act 1996 – *cont.*
s 223(1), (2) 32.35
  (3) 32.36
224 . 27.4, 32.12, 32.32, 32.34, 32.37, 36.13,
                    46.15, 53.7
225 ...... 32.12, 32.32, 32.34, 32.38, 36.13,
                    46.15, 53.7
  (3) 31.8
226 .... 32.12, 32.32, 32.34, 36.13, 53.7
  (2) 46.15
227 ..... 32.12, 32.32, 32.34, 36.13, 46.15,
                    49.16
  (1) 49.21, 53.7
    (b) 40.3
228, 229 . 32.12, 32.32, 32.34, 36.13, 46.15,
                    53.7
230 .... 9.17, 14.1, 14.9, 40.11, 51.3
  (1) 7.1, 7.2, 36.3
  (2) 13.2, 14.2
  (3) 30.4, 32.6, 32.12, 52.3
231 .... 6.9, 32.38
232(1) 7.48
  (3) 7.48
  (6) 7.48
233(1), (2) 7.48
234(1)–(3) 32.36
235 .... 6.5
  (1) 31.34, 53.3
240 .... 33.4
Sch 1 .... 49.17
  para 3 .... 33.4
Sch 2
  Pt 3 .... 52.3
  para 16 .... 35.3
Employment Rights (Dispute Resolution) Act
    1998 .... 17.1, 17.8, 18.33
s 7 .... 18.37
Employment Tribunals Act 1996
                  1.6, 17.6, 18.31
s 3 .... 56.38
  4(2) 17.9
    (3)(c) 24.3
    (5) 17.3, 17.9
    (6A) 17.10
  5 .... 24.3
  6 .... 18.55
  7(3A) 17.10
    (4) 18.4
  10, 10A 35.7
  12 .... 18.18
  12A(1)–(3) 21.19D
    (5)–(7) 21.19D
    (9), (10) 21.19D
  18 .... 6.6
    (1) 12.10
      (a)–(v) 2.4
    (2), (3) 2.4, 12.10
    (4), (5) 2.4
    (7) 2.4, 12.10
  18A 2.5
  19A 18.66

Employment Tribunals Act 1996 – *cont.*
s 21 .... 19.2
  22(1)(c) 19.4
  28(3), (4) 19.5
  29(1) 19.28
    (2) 19.41
  30 .... 19.6
    (1) 18.63
    (3) 19.26
  31 .... 19.26
  32 .... 18.18
  33 .... 18.77, 28.7
  35 .... 19.41
    (1) 19.22
  37(1), (2) 19.47
  117(3)–(5) 18.66
Employers' Liability (Defective Equipment) Act
    1969
s 1(3) 25.6
  2(2)(a) 26.16
Enterprise Act 2002 .... 39.1
Enterprise and New Towns (Scotland) Act 1990
s 2(3) 11.33
Enterprise and Regulatory Reform Act 2013
                      25.1
Equal Pay Act 1970 ..... 1.6, 4.9, 4.10, 7.22G,
           7.26, 11.9, 11.11, 11.37,
           12.18, 12.24, 12.33, 17.9,
           17.11, 17.28, 21.1, 21.22,
           22.2, 30.1, 30.14, 50.19
s 1 .... 21.23, 23.9
  (1) 21.4
  (2) 21.5
    (c) 21.8
    (d)–(f) 21.14
  (3) 21.5, 21.11, 21.12, 21.21
    (a), (b) 21.10
  (4) 21.6, 30.18
  (5) 21.7
  (6)(c) 21.9
  (6A)–(6C) 21.4
  (11) 21.4
  (13) 21.4
  2 .... 12.33, 21.14
  (1) 21.5, 21.19
  (2) 21.19
  (3) 21.19, 21.19F
  (4) 21.13, 21.18, 21.19A
  (5) 21.9, 21.19
  2ZA 21.19A
  2ZB 21.19B
  2A 21.14
  (1) 21.21
  (2) 21.8, 21.21
  (2A) 21.21
  5 .... 21.20
  5A, 5B 21.14
  6 .... 21.18
  (6) 21.5
  7B 21.21

Table of Statutes

Equality Act 2006 .... 4.9, 4.11, 11.37, 12.1
  Pt I (ss 1–43) 12.23, 12.24
  s 1–5 .... 12.24
    6(1)–(3) 12.27
    (6) 12.27
    8 .... 12.25, 12.31
    (1) 12.24
    9 .... 12.25, 12.31
    (4) 12.24
    10 .... 12.25, 12.31
    11(3)(c) 12.24
    12 .... 12.24
    14(1) 4.14, 12.24
    (6), (7) 12.24
    15(4) 12.3, 12.24
    (b) 4.8, 4.10, 4.12, 4.14
    16 .... 12.27
    (1), (2) 12.25
    17 .... 12.31
    20 .... 12.27, 12.28, 12.30
    (1)–(5) 12.25
    21 .... 12.25, 12.27, 12.30, 17.11
    (1), (2) 12.28
    (4)–(7) 12.28
    22 .... 12.30
    (2)–(5) 12.28
    (6)(b), (c) 12.28
    (7) 12.28
    (9) 12.28
    23 .... 12.25, 12.27, 12.29, 12.30
    (1) 12.28
    24 .... 12.27, 12.30
    (1)–(3) 12.29
    24A(1)–(4) 12.30
    25 .... 12.27, 12.30, 17.11
    (1)–(6) 12.30
    26 .... 12.30
    (1)–(3) 12.30
    28(1) 12.31
    (4) 12.31
    (6), (7) 12.31
    (12), (13) 12.31
    29 .... 12.31
    30 .... 12.24
    31, 32 .... 11.38, 12.27
    33(1) 12.24
    34 .... 12.24
    36 .... 12.23
    37, 38 .... 12.23
    40 .... 12.23
    42(3) 12.24
  Pt II (ss 44–80) 12.2, 12.24, 12.30
  s 54, 55 .... 12.30
  Pt III (ss 81–82) 12.24, 12.30
  Sch 1
    para 32 .... 12.24
  Sch 2
    para 2, 3 .... 12.25
    6–8 .... 12.25
    9–11 .... 12.26
    12(2) 12.26

Equality Act 2006 – *cont.*
  para 13 .... 12.26
    15, 16 .... 12.27
    18, 19 .... 12.27
  Sch 3 .... 12.23
Equality Act 2010 .... 1.6, 4.7, 4.9, 4.14, 10.1,
        10.2, 10.12, 11.1, 11.4, 11.8,
        11.31, 11.32, 11.36, 12.19,
        12.24, 12.31, 17.24, 21.1, 21.15,
        21.16, 21.20, 23.9, 30.14, 31.1,
        31.2, 34.2, 40.1, 40.2, 40.6,
        40.14, 40.17, 55.13
  s 1(1) 11.37
    2A(2) 21.8
    3(6)(b) 10.3
    3A(5) 10.15
    4 ... 10.3, 10.4, 10.5, 10.6, 10.7, 10.8, 10.9,
    10.10, 10.11, 10.15, 10.30, 10.34, 21.2, 21.13,
        31.5, 40.3
    5 .... 10.25
    6(1) 10.26
    (4) 10.26
    (5) 4.12
    7 .... 21.13
    (1) 10.15, 10.21
    (2) 10.21
    8 .... 10.19
    (2) 10.4
    9(1) 10.20
    (2)(a) 10.20
    (3)–(5) 10.20
    10 .... 10.7, 10.8, 10.44
    (2), (3) 10.22
    11 .... 10.18
    12 .... 10.18
    (1) 10.23
  Pt 2, Ch 2 (ss 13–27) 21.13
  s 13 . 10.15, 10.17, 10.24, 10.28, 10.31, 10.38,
    10.39, 10.43, 10.51, 11.11, 12.30, 31.5, 40.3,
        40.12
    (1) 10.13, 10.30
    (2) 11.9
    (3) 11.10
    (4) 10.27
    (5) 10.14
    (6)(b) 11.10
    14 .... 10.29, 11.11, 12.3, 12.30, 31.5
    15 .... 10.33, 12.30, 40.12
    (1) 10.33
    (b) 11.9
    (2) 11.9A
    16 .... 12.30
    (2)(a), (b) 10.15
    (3) 10.15
    17 .... 12.30
    18(2) 10.30, 10.31
    (b) 10.24, 10.32
    (3), (4) 10.31
    (5), (6) 10.30, 31.5
    (7) 10.15, 10.30, 31.5
    (a) 10.32

Equality Act 2010 – *cont.*

s 18(7)(b)	10.31
19	12.30, 31.5, 40.12
(1)	10.34
(2)	11.9
(3)	10.34
20	22.6, 40.12
(1)–(7)	10.37
(9)–(11)	10.37
23(1)–(3)	10.15
24(1)	10.15
25	10.15
26	31.5, 40.12
(1)–(4)	10.39
(5)	10.51
27	40.12
(1)–(5)	10.38
Pt 3 (ss 28–31)	10.53, 11.20
Pt 4 (ss 32–38)	10.53
Pt 5 (ss 39–83)	10.53, 20.2, 31.5, 35.2, 35.3, 35.4
Pt 5, Ch 1 (ss 39–60)	21.2, 21.9
s 39	10.44, 20.1, 54.1
(1)(b)	10.46
(2)	10.46, 10.48, 11.16
(b)	10.47
(c)	10.49
(d)	10.50
(5)	22.6
(7), (8)	10.49
40	10.51, 10.57, 20.1
(2)–(4)	10.39
41(1) (3)	11.24
(5)	11.24
42	10.41, 35.4
(1)	10.54
(2)–(6)	11.26
43(4)–(7)	11.26
44(3)–(6)	11.28
(8)	11.28
45	11.28
46	11.28
47(1)–(4)	11.27
(6)	11.27
(8), (9)	11.27
48	11.27
49	11.25, 21.4
50(2)	21.4
51	11.25
52(4), (5)	11.25
53(1)–(5)	11.30
54(2), (3)	11.30
55(1)–(5)	11.34
56(2)–(6)	11.34
(8)	11.34
57(2), (3)	11.29
(7)	11.29
58(2)–(4)	11.35A
(6)	11.35A
59(4)	11.35A
60(1)–(3)	10.44, 12.30, 20.2

Equality Act 2010 – *cont.*

s 60(6)	10.44, 20.2
(8)	10.44
(10)	10.44
(12)	10.44
(14)	10.44, 11.22
61	11.11, 21.18
(1), (2)	11.35, 40.12
(4)	11.35, 40.12
(5), (6)	11.35
62, 63	11.11, 11.35
Pt 5, Ch 3 (ss 64–80)	12.18, 21.2, 21.4, 22.2
s 64	11.11
(1), (2)	21.12
65	11.11, 21.5
(1)(b)	21.7
(2)	21.6, 21.7
(3)	21.6
(4), (5)	21.7
(6)	21.8
66	11.11
(1), (2)	21.5
67	11.11
(9), (10)	21.18
68	11.11, 21.18
69	21.5
(1)(a), (b)	21.10, 21.12
(2)	21.10, 21.12
(3)	21.12
70	11.11, 21.5
71	11.11, 21.5, 21.12
72	11.11, 21.4, 31.5
(1)	21.14
73	11.11, 21.4, 31.5
74	11.11, 31.5
75	11.11, 21.4, 21.9, 21.14, 31.5
76	11.11, 31.5
77	21.2
(1), (2)	21.11
(4), (5)	21.11
78	21.2, 21.11
79(3)–(8)	21.9
80	21.10
81, 82	10.42, 11.18
83	11.8
(2)	13.2, 35.2
(a)	14.1
(c)	10.41
(3)	10.41, 21.4, 35.3
(4)	10.41
(5)	35.2
Pt 6 (ss 84–99)	10.53
s 96(7)–(9)	11.30
Pt 7 (ss 100–107)	10.53
s 106	12.30
108	12.2
(1), (2)	10.52, 10.53, 10.58
(3)	10.52
(7)	10.52
109(1)	10.54, 54.1
(2)	10.56

Table of Statutes

Equality Act 2010 – *cont.*

s 109(3)	10.54, 10.56
(4)	10.55
(5)	10.54
110(1)	10.54, 10.57
(2)	10.54
(3)	10.54, 10.57
(5)	10.54, 10.57
111	12.2, 12.30
(1)–(6)	10.53
(8)	10.53
112	12.2, 12.30
(1)	10.53
(2)–(4)	10.57
Pt 9 (ss 113–141)	12.1, 12.2
s 113(1)–(5)	12.1
120	12.11, 17.11, 17.22
(1)	12.22, 17.29, 21.19C
(2)–(5)	12.2
(8)	12.2
121	12.2
122	17.11
123(1)	17.29
(a)	12.4
(b)	12.4, 12.7
(3)	12.4, 17.29, 17.30
124(1)	12.22
(a), (b)	12.12
(c)	12.12, 12.21, 21.19C
(2)(b)	12.22
(3)	12.12, 12.21
(4)	12.14
(5)	12.14, 12.16
(6)	12.12
(7)	12.21, 12.22, 18.66, 21.19B
126(2)–(4)	12.22
127	17.11
(1)	21.19
(3)	21.19
(4)	21.18A, 21.19
(9)	21.18A, 21.19E
(10)	21.19E
128	17.11, 17.22
(2)	21.19, 21.19E
129	21.19A
(3)	17.28
130(2)	12.1
(3), (4)	12.1, 17.28, 21.19A
(5)	12.1, 21.19A
(6)	21.19A
(7)	17.28, 21.19A
(8), (9)	21.19A
131(2)	21.21
(6)	21.21
132	21.19C
133	21.18
(3)	11.10
134	21.18
(2)	21.18A
(4), (5)	21.18A
135	21.19

Equality Act 2010 – *cont.*

s 136(1)–(3)	12.3, 21.21
(4)	21.21
137(1), (2)	12.2
138	21.21
(4)	12.9, 18.9
(5)	12.9
(7)	12.9
139(1)	12.20
(2)	21.19A
139A(2), (3)	21.19C
(5), (6)	21.19C
(8)	21.19C
140(1)–(5)	12.2
140A(1)	12.4
(5), (6)	12.4
(13)	12.4
Pt 10 (ss 142–148)	12.1
s 142	21.22, 40.7
(1)	12.32
(1)	12.32
(2)	12.32
143	7.27, 21.22
144	7.26, 21.22
(1)	12.33
(4)	12.33
145	5.15, 7.27, 21.22
(1)	21.23
146	5.15, 21.22
(1)–(3)	12.32
(5), (6)	12.32
147	18.33, 21.22, 24.5
(3)	12.33
(4)(a)–(c)	12.33
(5)(a)	12.33
(6)	12.33
(8)	12.33
149	12.32
(1)–(3)	11.37
(5), (6)	11.37
150–152	11.37
153, 154	12.32
155	11.37
156	11.38
157	11.37
158	10.44, 20.2
(1), (2)	11.10
(4)(a)	11.10
159	20.2
(1), (2)	11.10
(4)(a)–(c)	11.10
(7)	11.37
191, 192	11.21
193(1)–(5)	11.10A
(7)	11.10A
(9), (10)	11.10A
195	11.11
(1)	11.3
(3)	11.3
(5), (6)	11.12
211	12.30

Equality Act 2010 – *cont.*
s 212(1) 10.26, 10.39
   (5) 10.39, 10.51
213(3), (4) 10.31
313(7) 10.31
Sch 1
  para 2(2)......................... 10.26
    .3........................... 10.26
    5(2)......................... 10.26
    6–9......................... 10.26
    .12......................... 10.26
Sch 2
  para 6(4)......................... 40.12
Sch 3
  para .3........................... 17.13
Sch 6
  para .1........................... 11.25
    .2........................... 11.25
    .3........................... 11.25
Sch 7
  para .2...................... 21.4, 31.34
Sch 8
  para .18........................ 11.35A
Sch 9
  para 1(2)......................... 11.2
    (b)......................... 11.24
    (c), (d)................... 11.28
    (e)–(g)................... 11.25
    2(1).............. 11.3, 11.5, 11.7
    (4)(c)–(e)................. 11.3
    (5)............... 11.3, 11.5, 11.7
    (6)............... 11.3, 11.5, 11.7
    .3......................... 11.6
    .4............... 11.5, 11.11, 35.3
    (3)....................... 11.16
    5(3)–(5)................... 11.34
    .8................. 11.15, 40.4
    (1)....................... 40.3
    .9......................... 40.4
    10(3)..................... 11.15
    (6), (7)................... 11.15
    11–14..................... 11.15
    15(3), (4)................. 11.15
    .16....................... 11.15
    17(1)............... 10.46, 10.48
    (2)....................... 10.46
    (4)....................... 10.46
    (6)....................... 10.46
    .18................ 11.14, 40.9
    (1), (2)................... 10.36
    .19................ 11.16, 11.21
    (1)....................... 10.47
    (3)....................... 10.47
    (5), (6)................... 10.47
Sch 22
  para .1........................... 11.21
    .5........................... 35.2
Sch 23
  para .1........................... 11.21
    3(1)–(5)..................... 11.11
    (6)(c)....................... 11.11

Equality Act 2010 – *cont.*
  para 3(7)(a), (b).................... 11.11
    (8)......................... 11.11
    .4................... 11.10, 11.12
Sch 26
  para .6........................... 12.30
    14, .15..................... 12.30
Sch 27
  para .5........................... 11.13
European Communities Act 1972
s 2 .... 30.1, 30.21
  (1) 22.2
  (?) 15.23, 15.40, 22.2, 50.1
  (4) 22.2
3 .... 22.2

F

Factories Act 1961
s 1–7 .... 26.29
18 .... 26.29
28 .... 26.29
29 .... 26.19, 26.29
57–60 .... 26.29
69 .... 26.29
175(5) 26.29
Fair Employment (Northern Ireland) Act 1976
.... 10.34
Family Law Reform Act 1969
s 1 .... 3.1
Finance Act 2000
s 47 .... 44.31
62 .... 44.32
Sch 8 .... 44.31
Sch 12 .... 44.34
Sch 14 .... 44.32
Finance Act 2004
s 78 .... 44.23
Pt 4 (ss 149–284) 11.35
Pt 4, Ch 2 (ss 153–159) 40.11
Sch 13 .... 44.23
Finance Act 2007
s 25 .... 44.35
Sch 3 .... 44.35
Financial Services Act 1986
s 189 .... 16.4
Sch 14 .... 16.4
Fire Precautions Act 1971 .... 25.38
s 23 .... 26.13
Freedom of Information Act 2000
.... 17.5, 17.34

G

Gender Recognition Act 2004 .... 21.13
s 1(1) 10.21
9 .... 11.5

Table of Statutes

H

Health and Safety at Work etc Act 1974
...... 9.1, 15.1, 17.4, 25.16, 25.25, 54.1,
55.20, 55.21
Pt I (ss 1–54) 25.17, 25.29
s 1(1) 25.17
2 .... 25.28, 25.37, 25.43, 26.2, 26.28
  (1) 25.18
  (2) 25.18
    (c) 9.7
  (3) 9.7, 25.18
  (4) 26.21
  (6) 9.8, 26.21
3 .... 25.28, 25.43
  (1) 25.19, 25.37
  (2), (3) 25.19
4 .... 25.20, 25.28, 25.37, 25.43
5 .... 25.28, 25.37, 25.43
6 .... 25.28, 25.37, 25.43
  (8), (8A) 25.21
7 .... 25.22, 25.28, 25.37, 25.43
8 .... 25.23, 25.43
9 .... 25.24, 26.12
10 .... 25.26
14(1) 25.26
  (2) 25.26
    (a), (b) 25.40
16 .... 4.15, 25.28, 31.11
17 .... 4.16
  (2) 25.37
20(2)(a)–(i) 25.30
  (4) 25.30
  (7), (8) 25.30
21 .... 25.31, 25.32
22 .... 25.32
23(2)(a) 25.32
  (5) 25.33
24(2) 25.34
  (3)(a), (b) 25.35
  (4) 25.34
25(1) 25.30
27 .... 25.27
33(1) 9.7
    (a) 25.37
    (b) 25.23
    (c) 25.37
    (g) 25.37, 25.41
    (h) 25.37
    (o) 25.39
  (1A) 9.7, 25.37
  (2) 25.37
  (2A) 25.37, 25.39
  (3) 9.7, 25.37
    (b) 25.23
  (4) 25.37
34(1)–(3) 25.40
37 .... 25.38
40 .... 25.41
42(1), (2) 25.39
  (4) 25.37

Health and Safety at Work etc Act 1974 – *cont.*
s 47 .... 25.1
  (1)(a) 25.43
  (2) 25.43
  (5) 25.43
  53(1) 25.29
  Sch 1 .... 25.17, 25.22, 25.29, 25.38
Highways Act 1980
  s 137(1) 43.12
Housing Act 1985 .... 41.1
  Sch 1
    para 2(1)–(3) 41.7
      5(1) 41.7
Housing Act 1980
  s 52 .... 43.5
  55 .... 43.6
Housing Act 1988 .... 41.1
  s 1 .... 41.5
  7 .... 41.6
  9 .... 41.6
  13, 14 .... 41.8
  19A 41.5
  20, 20A 41.5
  21 .... 41.6
  22 .... 41.8
  24, 25 .... 41.9
  27 .... 41.3
  Sch 2
    Ground 9 .... 41.6
    16 .... 41.6
  Sch 2A 41.5
Human Rights Act 1998 . 1.7, 2.8, 9.13, 11.37,
12.24, 16.7, 18.16, 25.37,
26.3, 28.1, 28.5, 28.7
  s 2 .... 28.6
  3 .... 28.6, 28.7
  4 .... 19.1, 28.6
    (5) 28.7
  6 .... 17.13, 17.16, 18.51
    (3) 28.6
  7 .... 17.13, 28.6
  8 .... 28.6
  10 .... 28.6
  19 .... 28.6
  Sch 1 .... 28.6

I

Immigration, Asylum and Nationality Act 2006
.... 9.1, 23.5
  s 15 .... 4.6, 10.45, 23.6
  16–18 .... 23.6
  19 .... 4.6, 23.6
  20 .... 23.6
  21 .... 4.6, 23.6
  22(2) 23.6
  23 .... 4.6, 23.6
  24–26 .... 23.6
Income and Corporation Taxes Act 1988
.... 14.1

Income and Corporation Taxes Act 1988 – *cont.*
s 150 .... 42.6
Income Tax (Earnings and Pensions) Act 2003
.... 44.1
s 7 .... 44.2
44–47 .... 44.2
48–61 .... 44.2, 44.34
62 .... 44.2
63 .... 44.2, 44.3
64–66 .... 44.2
67, 68 .... 44.2, 44.3
69 .... 44.2
70–83 .... 44.2, 44.21
81 .... **44.2, 44.21**
(2A) 44.23
85–98 .... 44.2, 44.21
99, 100 .... 44.2, 44.21, 44.23
101–113 .... 44.2, 44.21
114–148 .... 44.2, 44.21, 44.25
149–153 .... 44.2, 44.21, 44.26
154 .... 44.2, 44.21
155–170 .... 44.2, 44.21, 44.27
171–200 .... 44.2, 44.21
201, 202 .... 44.2
203, 204 .... 44.2, 44.2, 44.21
205 .... 44.2, 44.21
206–215 .... 44.2
216–220 .... 44.2, 44.3
221–223 .... 44.2
225, 226 .... 44.2
229–232 .... 44.21
235, 236 .... 44.21
237 .... 44.23
242–248 .... 44.23
248A 44.27
250–264 .... 44.23
270A 44.23
271–289 .... 44.21, 44.23
313 .... 44.23
316, 317 .... 44.23
318–318D 44.23
319 .... 44.23
325 .... 44.21, 44.23
333–336 .... 44.28
Pt 6 (ss 386–416) 56.32
s 386–400 .... 44.2
401 .... 44.2, 44.8, 46.10
402 .... 44.2, 44.8
403 .... 44.2, 44.8, 46.10
404–417 .... 44.2
418 .... 44.2, 44.31
419–487 .... 44.2
488–515 .... 44.2, 44.31
516–520 .... 44.2, 44.29
521–526 .... 44.2, 44.30
527–541 .... 44.2, 44.32
542–554 .... 44.2
684 .... 44.4
686 .... 44.4
708 .... 44.4
Sch 2 .... 44.31

Income Tax (Earnings and Pensions) Act 2003 – *cont.*
Sch 3 .... 44.29
Sch 4 .... 44.30
Sch 5 .... 44.32
Industrial Courts Act 1919 .... 48.6
Industrial Relations Act 1971 .... 4.1, 5.3, 5.4, 49.3, 51.1
s 134 .... 43.10
Industrial Training Act 1982
s 5(1), (2) 13.4
(4) 13.4
6(1) 13.4
11 .... 13.4
Infants Relief Act 1874 .... 3.11
Insolvency Act 1986 .... 29.1
s 19 .... 29.11
29(2) 29.11
44(2) 29.11
386 .... 29.2
Sch B1 .... 29.10, 50.11
para 9(5)(a) 29.11
.10 .... 29.11
.14 .... 29.11
.22 .... 29.11
Sch 6
para 9–15 .... 29.2

J

Judgments Act 1838 .... 18.67

L

Law of Property Act 1925
s 146 .... 43.5
Law Reform (Contributory Negligence) Act 1945
s 1(1) 25.44
Law Reform (Frustrated Contracts) Act 1943
s 1(3) 46.3
Legal Aid, Sentencing and Punishment of Offenders Act 2012 .... 55.21
s 85 .... 1.10, 37.7
86, 87 .... 1.10, 33.8
Legal Services Act 2007 .... 12.25, 12.33
Limitation Act 1980
s 5 .... 56.40
33 .... 17.30
(3) 12.7
Limited Liability Partnerships Act 2000
s 4(4) 14.3
Local Government Act 1972 .... 47.4
s 112 .... 35.5
116 .... 35.5
222 .... 35.7
Local Government Act 1988
s 17(1) 12.32
Local Government and Housing Act 1989
s 1–3 .... 35.5

Table of Statutes

Local Government and Housing Act 1989 – *cont.*
s 7 .... 35.5
10 .... 47.4
12 .... 35.5
Localism Act 2011
s 41 .... 35.5

M

Magistrates' Courts Act 1980
s 32(2) 9.7
Merchant Shipping Act 1995
s 55(1A) 3.4
85 .... 55.32, 55.33
Minors' Contracts Act 1987
s 1 .... 3.11
Misuse of Drugs Act 1971
s 8 .... 26.2

N

National Health Service and Community Care
Act 1990
s 6(1) 7.22E
National Minimum Wage Act 1998
.... 14.1, 22.14, 51.11, 52.11, 55.22
s 2, 3 .... 32.10
5–8 .... 32.10
9, 10 .... 32.11
11(2) 32.11
12 .... 32.11
13(1)(b) 32.13
14 .... 32.13
15 .... 32.13
17 .... 17.31, 32.12, 32.13
18 .... 17.31, 32.12
19(1) 32.13
(6), (7) 32.13
19A–19H 32.13
22 .... 17.11
23 .... 32.12
24 .... 17.11, 32.12
25 .... 32.12, 54.3
27 .... 32.12
28 .... 32.10, 32.12
31(1)–(5) 32.13
(9) 32.13
32 .... 32.13
34 .... 32.10, 45.6
35–37A 32.10
38–44A 32.10
45 .... 32.10
54 .... 32.9
(3) 32.12, 45.6
(b) 32.10
Sch 1 .... 32.10
National Minimum Wage (Enforcement Notices)
Act 2003 .... 32.13

O

Occupiers' Liability Act 1957 ..... 25.1, 25.12
s 2(2), (3) 25.14
(4)(b) 25.15
Occupiers' Liability Act 1984 ..... 25.1, 25.12
Offshore Safety (Protection against Victimisation)
Act 1992 .... 52.3
Osteopaths Act 1993
s 39(2) 16.4
(4) 16.4

P

Partnership Act 1890
s 2(3) 14.3
Payment of Wages Act 1960
s 1 .... 32.4
11 .... 32.3
Pension Schemes Act 1993 .... 17.11
s 124(1)–(3A) 29.7
(4)–(6) 29.7
126 .... 17.9, 29.7
127(1) 29.7
145–151 .... 40.17
181 .... 40.9
181A, 181B 40.9
190 .... 33.2
Sch 8
para 4 .... 33.2
Pensions Act 1995 ... 11.35, 21.2, 21.15, 21.18,
40.1, 40.9
s 10 .... 40.10
46(5) 52.3
50–50B 40.17
62 .... 11.35, 21.18
(1)–(4) 21.16
(6) 21.16
63(1), (2) 21.16
(4) 21.16
(6) 21.16
64 .... 11.11
(2), (3) 21.16
65 .... 21.18
124(1) 12.22
126 .... 21.16
Pensions Act 2004 ..... 29.1, 29.9, 40.9, 40.17
Pt II Ch III (ss 126–181) 29.8
s 241, 242 .... 40.15
257, 258 .... 50.19
286 .... 29.7, 29.8
Sch 7 .... 29.8
Pensions Act 2007 .... 40.9
Pensions Act 2008 .... 40.9, 40.10
s 1–8 .... 40.11
10 .... 40.11
13(1), (2) 40.11
20–28 .... 40.11
45–47 .... 40.11
50(1) 40.11

Pensions Act 2008 – *cont.*
s 55(2) 40.11
  56(3), (4) 40.11
  58 .... 40.11
  88(1) 40.11
    (3), (4) 40.11
  89 .... 40.11
Pensions Act 2011 .... 40.9
Police Act 1996
s 3 .... 47.4
  64 .... 35.4
  88 .... 54.2
  91 .... 35.4
Police Act 1997
Pt V (ss 112–127) 16.7
s 112 .... 16.7
  113(2)–(5) 16.7
  113B 20.4
  114 .... 16.7
  115(2)–(4) 16.7
    (5)(a)–(g) 16.7
    (7)–(9) 16.7
  116–121 .... 16.7
  122(1), (2) 16.7
  123–127 .... 16.7
Police (Complaints and Conduct) Act 2012
  .... 35.4
Police and Criminal Evidence Act 1984
s 54(9) 11.5
Police Reform Act 2002 .... 35.4
Police Reform and Social Responsibility Act 2002
  .... 35.4
Powers of Criminal Courts Act 1973
s 30 .... 1.10
Private International Law (Miscellaneous Provisions) Act 1995
s 11(1) 23.7
  12(1) 23.7
Protection of Freedoms Act 2012
  .... 16.8
s 64–67 .... 16.9
  70–72 .... 16.9
  87 .... 16.9
Sch 8 .... 16.9
Protection from Eviction Act 1977
s 1(2)–(3B) 41.3
  2 .... 41.3
  3(1) 41.3
  5 .... 41.5
    (1A) 41.4
  8(2) 41.3
Protection from Harassment Act 1997
  .... 26.28
s 3 .... 26.25
Public Interest Disclosure Act 1998
  .... 9.1, 9.17, 17.11, 19.7, 26.9
s 1 .... 52.3
  5 .... 9.16, 52.3
  7 .... 9.16

Public Interest Disclosure Act 1998 – *cont.*
s 11 .... 9.16
  13 .... 9.16
Public Health Act 1936
s 205 .... 31.27
Public Order Act 1986
s 4A 26.28
Pt II (ss 11–16) 43.12

R

Race Relations Act 1976 ..... 1.6, 10.5, 10.14,
                        10.20, 10.39, 11.1, 11.4,
                        11.6, 12.3, 12.19, 17.11,
                        23.9, 28.7, 54.1
s 1(1)(a) 30.14
    (b)(ii) 11.9
    (1a)(c) 11.9
  2 .... 12.2, 12.3
  4 .... 11.18, 22.4
    (2)(b) 11.20
    (c) 10.50
    (3) 11.12
    (4) 11.20
  4A(2)(a) 11.4
  5(2)(d) 11.4
    (3)–(4) 11.4
  6 .... 11.12
  7(1) 11.24
    (2)(a) 11.25
    (3), (3A) 11.24
    (5) 11.24
  8(1) 11.18, 22.4
    (1A) 11.18
    (3) 11.18
    (5) 11.18
  9(1) 11.12
    (3) 11.12
    (5) 11.12
  10(1)–(1B) 11.28
    (2)–(6) 11.28
Pt II (ss 11–16) 12.24, 12.30
s 11 .... 11.30
    (1)–(4) 11.29
  12 .... 12.2
    (1), (1A) 11.30
    (2) 11.30
  13(1)–(3) 11.31
  14(1) 11.32
    (2) 11.33
    (3)–(6) 11.32
  15(1), (1A) 11.33
    (2) 11.33
Pt III (ss 17–27) 12.24
s 25 .... 11.30
  26A(1)–(3A) 11.27
    (4) 11.27
  26B 11.27
Pt IV (ss 27A–33) 12.24
s 27A(1) 11.37

Table of Statutes

Race Relations Act 1976 – *cont.*
s 27A(2) 11.37
 (3) 11.37
28(3) 11.40
29 .... 12.30
30 .... 12.30
31 .... 12.30
32 .... 10.58, 12.2
 (1) 11.26, 54.2
33 .... 12.2
 (1) 10.58
35 .... 11.10
37(3) 11.10
38(1)–(5) 11.10
39 .... 11.12
41(1), (1A) 11.21
 (2)(d), (e) 11.21
42 .... 11.22
43 .... 12.23
44–46 .... 12.33
47 .... 4.7, 4.14, 12.23
 (10) 4.8
48 .... 12.23
49 .... 12.23
50 .... 12.23
51 .... 12.23
52 .... 12.23
53(1), (2) 12.1
54(1) 12.2
 (2) 11.30, 12.2
54A 12.3
56(1)(a), (b) 12.12
 (c) 12.12
 (2) 12.13
 (4)(a), (b) 12.21
57(3) 12.14
 (4) 12.16
58 .... 12.23
59 .... 12.23
60 .... 12.2
61 .... 12.23
62 .... 12.23
63 .... 12.23
64 .... 12.23
65(2)(a) 12.9
 (b) 12.9
68(1) 12.4
 (6) 12.7, 17.30
 (7) 12.4
 (b) 12.6
71 .... 12.24
 (1) 11.37
71A 11.37
71C 11.37
72(1) 12.32
 (3) 12.32
 (4) 12.33
 (a) 2.4
 (5) 12.32
72A 12.17
75(2)–(9B) 11.36

Race Relations Act 1976 – *cont.*
s 75A, 75B 11.36
76(2)–(9) 11.25
76ZA(1)–(6) 11.25
 (7)(b) 11.25
 (8)(c) 11.25
 (9)(a), (b) 11.25
76A(2) 11.26
 (3)(b) 11.26
 (4)–(6) 11.26
76B(3) 11.26
78(1) 11.29, 11.38
 (4) 11.37
Race Relations (Amendment) Act 2000
.... 11.37
Race Relations (Remedies) Act 1994
.... 12.13
Railways and Transport Safety Act 2003
.... 26.26
Railways Act 2005
Sch 3 .... 26.26
Redundancy Payments Act 1965
.... 38.1
Rehabilitation of Offenders Act 1974
.... 16.5, 20.4
s 1(1) 16.1
 4(1) 16.2
 (2) 16.2, 16.4
 (a), (b) 16.7
 (3) 16.4
 (a) 16.2
 (b) 16.3
 (6) 16.2
 5 .... 16.6
 (1) 16.1
 8(3) 16.2
 (5) 16.2
Rent Act 1977 .... 41.1, 41.5
s 1 .... 41.3
 44 .... 41.8
Pt IV (ss 62–75) 41.8
s 98(2) 41.6
 100 .... 41.6
Sch 15
 Pt I
 Case.8 .... 41.6
 .19 .... 41.6
 Pt.II 41.6
Rent (Agriculture) Act 1976 .... 41.9
Reserve Forces Act 1980
s 38 .... 30.5
 40, 41 .... 30.5
Reserve Forces Act 1996 .... 33.2
s 4 .... 30.5
 22 .... 30.5
 27 .... 30.5
Pt XI (ss 110–119) 30.5
Reserve Forces (Safeguard of Employment) Act
 1985 .... 47.18
s 1(2) 47.19

Reserve Forces (Safeguard of Employment) Act
  1985 – *cont.*
  s 3–5 .... 47.19
  7–10 .... 47.19
Road Safety Act 2005 .... 26.1

S

Safeguarding of Vulnerable Groups Act 2006
  .... 16.4, 16.8
  s 34ZA 16.9
Senior Courts Act 1981
  s 31 .... 11.30
  35A 56.31
  42(1A) 18.77
Serious Organised Crime and Police Act 2005
  s 56 .... 11.26
  173 .... 30.1
Sex Discrimination Act 1975 . 1.6, 10.3, 10.23,
                              10.24, 10.34, 10.38,
                              11.1, 11.7, 12.3,
                              14.8, 17.11, 21.9,
                              21.11, 22.2, 22.6,
                              30.1, 31.2, 38.4
  s 1(1) 10.21
     (a) 30.14
     (2) 11.9
        (b)(ii) 11.9
  2(2) 11.10
  2A 11.28, 21.2, 21.13
  3 .... 11.10
  3A(3)(b) 10.32
  3A(5) 10.15
  4 .... 12.3
     (4)–(6) 21.2
     (8) 21.2
  Pt II (ss 6–20A) 12.24, 12.30
  s 6 .... 11.37, 23.9
     (1) 11.18, 21.13
     (2)(a) 10.30, 11.20
     (2B) 10.39
     (4) 11.11, 21.16
     (4A) 21.16
     (5) 11.11
     (6) 21.5
     (7) 11.20
     (8) 11.11
  7(2), (3) 11.3
     (4) 11.3, 11.5
  7A(1)(b) 11.5
     (3), (4) 11.5
  7B(1)(a) 11.5
     (3) 11.5
  9(2), (2A) 11.24
     (3)–(3B) 11.24
     (4) 11.24
  10 .... 21.4, 23.9
     (1) 11.18, 21.13
     (2)(a), (b) 11.18
     (3) 11.18

Sex Discrimination Act 1975 – *cont.*
  s 10(5) 11.18
  10A(2)–(5) 11.25
  10B(1)–(9) 11.25
     (11) 11.25
  11(1), (2) 11.28
     (2A) 11.28
     (3)–(3B) 11.28
     (4)–(6) 11.28
  12(1)–(4) 11.29
  13(1), (1A) 11.30
     (2), (3) 11.30
  14(1)(a) 11.31
     (1A), (1B) 11.31
     (2) 11.31
  15(1) 11.32
     (2) 11.33
     (3)–(6) 11.32
  16(1), (1A) 11.33
     (2) 11.33
  17(1) 11.26
     (1A)(b) 11.26
     (2), (3) 11.11
     (4)–(5A) 11.26
     (6), (7) 11.26
     (9) 11.26
  18(1), (2) 11.11
  19(1) 11.11
     (3), (4) 11.11
  Pt III (ss 21A–36) 12.24
  s 35A(1)–(4) 11.27
  35B 11.27
  Pt IV (ss 37–42) 12.24
  s 38 .... 12.30
  39 .... 12.30
  40 .... 12.30
  41 .... 12.2, 12.3
  42 .... 12.2, 12.3
     (1) 10.58
  44 .... 11.10
  46(3)–(6) 11.10
  47(4) 11.10
  48(1)–(3) 11.10
  49(1), (2) 11.10
  51(1)(c)(ii) 11.21
  52(1), (2) 11.22
  53 .... 12.23
  55, 56 .... 12.23
  56A 4.9, 4.10, 4.14, 12.23
     (10) 12.3
  57 .... 12.23
  58 .... 12.23
  59 .... 12.23
  60 .... 12.23
  61 .... 12.23
  62(1), (2) 12.1
  63(1) 12.2, 17.29
     (2) 11.30, 12.2
  63A 10.15, 12.2
     (2) 12.3
  65(1)(a) 12.12

Table of Statutes

Sex Discrimination Act 1975 – *cont.*
s 65(1)(b) 12.12
    (c) 12.12
    (1B) 12.14
    (3)(a), (b) 12.22
  66(4) 12.16
  67–71 .... 12.23
  72 .... 12.23
  73 .... 12.23
  74 .... 12.9
    (2)(a) 12.9
    (b) 12.3, 12.9
  75(2) 12.2, 12.9
    (2A) 12.9
  76 .... 12.6
    (1) 12.4, 17.29, 21.13
    (5) 12.7, 21.13
    (6) 12.4
    (c) 12.5
  76A 12.21
    (1) 11.37
    (5) 11.37
    (6) 11.37, 11.38
  76B 11.37, 12.24
  76C 12.24
  76E 11.37
    (1) 4.9
  76ZA 12.4
  77 .... 7.26, 21.23
    (1) 12.32
    (3) 12.32, 21.22
    (4)(a) 2.4
    (aa) 12.33, 21.22
    (4A) 21.22
    (5) 12.32
  82(1) 10.41, 11.29, 21.13
  85(2) 11.36
    (4) 11.11, 11.36
    (5) 11.11
    (7)–(9E) 11.36
  85A, 85B 11.36
  86(1), (2) 11.25
  Sch 3 .... 12.23
Sex Discrimination Act 1986 .... 21.2, 35.8
  s 2(1) 21.16
  6 .... 12.32
    (4A) 21.23
  9 .... 21.23
Shops Act 1950 .... 55.1
Social Security Act 1975 .... 33.10
Social Security Act 1989 .... 31.38
  Sch 5 .... 21.17
    para .2 .... 31.1
      .5 .... 21.16, 31.1
      5A, 5B 40.13
      .6 .... 21.16, 31.1
Social Security Administration Act 1992
  s 5(1) 11.35
  14(3) 42.8
  15 .... 31.40
    (2) 31.43

Social Security Administration Act 1992 – *cont.*
  s 21(2) 31.45
  130 .... 42.5
Social Security Contributions and Benefits Act
  1992 .... 6.10, 31.1, 31.38
  s 4(1) 42.6
  10 .... 44.17
  10ZA 44.17
  151(2) 42.3
  152 .... 42.3, 42.5
  153(2) 42.5
    (12) 42.5
  155(1), (2) 42.5
  156 .... 42.3
  157(1) 42.6
  161(2) 31.39
  164(1), (2) 31.39
    (4), (5) 31.40
    (6) 31.39
  165(4) 31.41
  166(1)(b) 31.42
    (2) 31.42
  167 .... 31.44
  171(1) 31.39
  Sch 11 .... 42.4
    para .2 .... 42.9
      (c) 42.6
  Sch 12 .... 42.5
  Sch 13
    para .3 .... 31.42
State Immunity Act 1978 .... 11.1, 28.4
  s 5 .... 12.2
  16(1)(a) 11.23
Statutory Sick Pay Act 1994 .... 42.6
Sunday Trading Act 1994 .... 7.7, 52.3
  s 4 .... 7.48
  Sch 4 .... 7.48
Superannuation Act 1972 .... 35.5, 40.9
Supreme Court Act 1981
  s 42(1A) 18.78

T

Tax Credits Act 1999 .... 51.11, 52.3
Tax Credits Act 2002 .... 33.2, 51.11, 52.11
Trade Descriptions Act 1968 .... 25.38
Trade Disputes Act 1906
  s 3 .... 43.1
Trade Union Reform and Employment Rights
  Act 1993 . 17.1, 18.33, 22.2, 31.1, 37.2, 50.1
  s 14 .... 49.11
Trade Union and Labour Relations Act 1974
  s 18 .... 5.4
Trade Union and Labour Relations
  (Consolidation) Act 1992 1.6, 9.1, 17.22, 43.1,
                     43.13, 49.3
  s 1 .... 48.1, 49.21
  2 .... 48.21
  5 .... 48.22

Trade Union and Labour Relations (Consolidation) Act 1992 – *cont.*

s 6	48.26
(1)	48.21
(3)	48.21
(4)	48.23
7(1)	48.24
9	48.24
10(1)	48.2
12(1)	48.2
(2)	48.17
15	43.16
(2), (3)	48.18
(5)	48.18
20	43.17
(1)	48.16
(2)	43.14, 48.16, 51.18
(3)	48.16
21	51.18
(1)–(6)	48.16
22(2), (3)	48.17
23(1), (2)	48.17
24	48.12
(3)	48.13
25(5A)	48.13
26(4)	48.13
27, 28	48.12
32, 32A	48.12
33	48.12
37A–37E	48.3
40	48.12
43(1)	2.1
45	48.3
45A	48.3
45B	48.14
45C(5A)	48.14
45D	48.13, 48.14
46	48.12
(1)	48.14
(3), (4)	48.14
(4A)	48.14
47–50	48.14
51(6)	48.14
54	48.14
55(2), (3)	48.14
(5A)	48.14
56(3), (4)	48.14
56A	48.14
62	43.18
(2), (3)	43.17
(5), (6)	43.17
(8)	43.17
63(1)–(4)	49.15
64(1), (2)	49.16
(4), (5)	49.16
65	49.13
(2)	49.9, 49.16
(3)–(6)	49.16
66	49.14
(1)–(3)	49.16
67(1)	49.16

Trade Union and Labour Relations (Consolidation) Act 1992 – *cont.*

s (3)	49.16
(5)–(9)	49.16
68(1)–(4)	49.20
68A	17.9, 47.3
(1)–(3)	49.20
70A	15.63, 48.11
70B	2.1, 48.38, 49.1
(4)	15.63
(4A)	15.63
71	48.12, 48.15
72, 72A	48.15
73–81	48.15
82(2), (3)	48.15
84(1), (2)	48.15
86	48.15, 52.3
87	48.15
97–105	48.39
108A–108C	48.3
117	48.2
119	48.14, 48.16, 49.21
128(2)	18.6
137(1)(b)	49.4
(3)–(6)	49.4
(7)(a), (b)	49.4
138	49.4
138A	51.11
139(1)	49.4
140(1)(b)	49.4
(2), (3)	49.4
141, 142	49.4
143(?)–(4)	49.4
144	43.7, 49.19
145	43.7
(1)–(5)	49.19
145A, 145B	49.17, 52.3, 53.15
145C–145F	49.17
146	47.5, 52.3
(1)	49.17
(a)	28.4
(c)	49.8
(3)	49.8, 49.17
(5)	49.8, 49.18
147	49.18
148	49.17
(1), (2)	49.18
149, 150	49.18
152	52.3, 53.8, 53.16
(1)(c)	49.5
(2)	52.3
(3)	49.6, 53.15
(4)	49.5
153	49.5, 53.8, 53.9, 53.15, 53.16
154	49.5, 51.11, 52.3
155	49.7, 53.15
156	49.7
(1)	53.8, 53.9
(2)	53.9
160	49.7, 52.16
(1), (2)	18.23, 53.17

Table of Statutes

Trade Union and Labour Relations (Consolidation) Act 1992 – *cont.*

s 160(3) 53.17
161 .... 17.9, 17.18, 17.19
  (1)–(3) 53.18
162 .... 17.18
  (1) 53.18
  (2) 18.39
  (3) 53.18
  (4) 18.39, 53.18
163 .... 9.17, 17.18, 53.18
164 .... 53.18
165, 166 .... 17.9, 53.18
168 .... 52.3
  (1)–(3) 47.2
  (4) 47.5
168A 47.2, 52.3, 54.3
  (9) 47.5
169 .... 21.3, 29.2, 52.3
  (4) 17.2
  (5) 47.5
170 .... 50.21, 52.3
  (1)–(3) 47.3
  (4) 47.5
171 .... 47.5
172(1) 47.5
  (2) 47.5, 49.13
  (3) 47.5
174 .... 49.11
  (1)–(3) 49.13
  (4) 49.13, 49.14
175 .... 49.13, 49.14
176 .... 49.13
  (1)–(3) 49.14
  (5) 49.14
  (6A) 49.16
177(2) 49.13
  (5) 49.13
Pt IV (ss 178–218) 48.19, 50.22
Pt IV, Ch I (ss 178–187) 9.2
s 178 .... 5.2, 48.27
  (1) 37.4, 48.20
  (2) 37.4, 47.2, 48.20, 55.4
  (3) 37.4, 48.20
179 .... 50.20
  (3) 5.3
180 .... 5.13
181 .... 2.11, 9.3, 48.6, 48.8, 48.19
  (2)(b) 4.2
  (4) 4.2
182 .... 2.11, 4.2
  (1), (2) 9.3
183 .... 48.6
  (1) 9.3
  (2) 2.6, 9.3, 48.8
  (3)–(5) 9.3, 48.8
184 .... 9.3
  (2) 48.8
  (4) 48.8
185 .... 48.9
  (1) 9.3

Trade Union and Labour Relations (Consolidation) Act 1992 – *cont.*

s 185(2)–(5) 9.3, 48.8
186 .... 43.7, 49.19
187 .... 43.7
  (3) 49.19
Pt IV Ch II (ss 188–198) .. 35.2, 37.3, 47.12,
                          52.3, 53.18
s 188 ... 15.15, 15.61, 17.33, 37.3, 37.7, 47.2,
              50.23, 52.3, 52.11
  (1)–(2) 37.4
  (4) 24.7, 37.6
  (7), (7A) 37.6
  (7B) 37.4
188A 37.4
  (1), (2) 37.5
189 .... 15.15, 17.9, 29.2
  (1A) 37.6
  (2) 37.6
  (4) 37.6
  (5) 17.33
  (7) 37.6
190 .... 15.15
  (1)–(3) 37.6
  (5) 37.6
191 .... 15.15
  (1)–(7) 37.6
192 .... 15.15, 17.9
  (1)–(3) 37.6
193 .... 37.2
  (1), (2) 37.7
  (4) 37.7
  (6), (7) 37.7
194(1) 37.7
195(1), (2) 37.3
196(2) 37.4
199 .... 2.11, 4.18
200 .... 4.2
201 .... 4.2, 4.18
202 .... 4.18
203 .... 4.4, 4.18, 43.14, 48.14, 48.32
204 .... 4.4, 43.14, 48.14, 48.32
205, 206 .... 4.18
207(1) 4.2, 4.3, 4.5
  (2) 4.2, 4.3
  (3) 4.5
207A 17.2, 18.60, 18.63, 53.13
  (2) 4.3
  (3), (4) 4.3
208(2) 4.4
209 .... 2.1
210 .... 2.3
210A(2) 2.3
  (4) 2.3
  (8), (9) 2.3
211 .... 2.4
212(1) 2.7
  (b) 48.7
  (2), (3) 2.7
  (4)(b) 2.7
  (5) 2.7

Trade Union and Labour Relations (Consolidation) Act 1992 – *cont.*

s 212A 2.8, 2.45, 18.37
213 .... 2.9
214(1), (2) 2.10
Pt V (ss 219–231) 28.7, 43.14
s 219 ... 43.3, 43.4, 43.6, 43.16, 43.20, 48.16, 51.17
  (3) 43.9
220 .... 43.9, 43.10, 43.12, 43.16
  (1)(b) 43.6, 43.9
221(1), (2) 43.16
222(1), (3) 43.7
223 .... 43.8
224(1) 43.6, 43.9
  (2) 43.6
  (3) 43.9
  (4)–(6) 43.6
225 .... 43.7
226(1) 43.14
  (2)(b) 43.14
  (3) 43.14
226A 43.14
226B, 226C 43.14, 43.17
227 .... 43.17
  (1) 43.14, 48.38
228 .... 43.17
  (4) 43.14
228A 43.14, 43.17
229 .... 43.17
  (1A) 43.14
  (2) 43.14
  (4) 43.14
230 .... 43.17
  (1), (2) 43.14
  (4)(a) 43.14
231 .... 43.14, 43.17
231A 43.17
  (1) 43.14
231B 43.14, 43.17
232 .... 43.14, 43.17
232A(C) 43.14
232B 43.14
233 .... 43.14, 43.17
  (3)(a) 43.15
234(1) 43.15, 43.17
  (2)–(6) 43.15
234A 43.15
235A(1)–(5) 43.18
236 .... 5.13, 7.47C, 43.16
237 .... 43.8, 43.16
  (2)–(6) 51.18
238 .... 43.16, 51.17, 51.18
238A 43.16, 52.3
  (2)–(5) 52.11
  (7) 51.17
239(4) 51.17
240(1) 43.20
  (3) 43.20
241(1)(d) 43.12
  (2) 43.12

Trade Union and Labour Relations (Consolidation) Act 1992 – *cont.*

s 244(1) 43.4
  (2) 35.2
  (3) 43.4
  (5) 43.4
245 .... 35.2, 43.2
247 .... 2.1
248 .... 2.2
251A 2.1
251B 2.5
254 .... 48.3
258 .... 48.3
259 .... 48.4
260 .... 48.5, 48.25
273 .... 35.2
282 .... 37.3
288 .... 7.26, 18.33, 48.9
296(1) 48.26
Sch A1 ..... 5.2, 15.63, 48.11, 48.19, 48.20, 48.38, 49.1
  para 1–4 .... 48.27
  5, 6 .... 48.29
  7 .... 48.29
    (1) 48.26
  8 .... 48.28, 48.29
  9 .... 48.29
  10 .... 48.28
  11, 12 .... 48.29
  15 .... 48.29
  18 .... 48.29
  19 .... 48.29, 48.30
  20 .... 48.30, 48.31
  21–24 .... 48.31
  25–29 .... 48.32
  30 .... 5.4, 48.33
  31 .... 48.33
    (6) 5.4
  32 .... 48.33
  33–42 .... 48.29, 48.30
  43–50 .... 48.30
  52 .... 48.34
  55, 56 .... 48.34
  58–63 .... 48.34
  64–89 .... 48.35
  99–153 .... 48.36
  156 .... 2.4, 48.37
  157–159 .... 48.37
  161 .... 48.37, 52.3
  162 .... 48.37, 51.11
  163–165 .... 48.37
  171 .... 48.25
Sch 3
  para 7 .... 48.6
Trade Union Reform and Employment Rights Act 1993
s 28 .... 52.3
29 .... 52.3
34 .... 52.11
Sch 5 .... 52.3
Transport and Works Act 1992 .... 26.2

Table of Statutes

Tribunals, Courts and Enforcement Act 2007
.... 17.1, 17.6
  s 42 .... 24.6
Truck Act 1831
  s 1 .... 32.3
   3 .... 32.4
   9 .... 32.4
   20 .... 32.5
   23 .... 32.5
Truck Amendment Act 1887
  s 4 .... 32.5

U

Unfair Contract Terms Act 1977
.... 56.37

Unfair Contract Terms Act 1977 – *cont.*
  s 2(2) 38.5
   11 .... 7.30
    (3) 38.5

W

Wages Act 1986 .... 17.11, 32.2
  s 11 .... 32.3
Water Act 1989 .... 35.8
Water Industry Act 1991 .... 35.8
Welfare Reform and Pensions Act 1999
  Pt I (ss 1–8) 40.9
  s 3(8) 40.10
   75 .... 44.34
Work and Families Act 2006 ...... 31.1, 31.52

Table of EU Legislation

Primary Legislation

Treaties Agreements and Conventions

European Convention for the Protection of
Human Rights and Fundamental Freedoms
(Rome, 4 November 1950)
art 1 .... 40.9
3 .... 28.4
6 .. 17.7, 17.13, 18.2, 18.16, 18.42, 18.56,
28.6, 35.6, 41.3
(1) 11.23, 28.4, 28.7
(2) 28.7
8 .. 16.6, 16.7, 17.13, 18.18, 18.51, 19.26,
20.4, 28.6
(1), (2) 28.4, 28.7
9 .... 11.9
(1) 10.22
(2) 10.22, 28.7
10 .... 28.4, 28.6, 28.7
11 .. 10.20, 28.6, 28.7, 43.1, 48.26, 48.29,
49.16
(1) 28.4, 43.4, 43.20
(2) 28.4, 28.7, 43.4
12 .... 10.19, 28.4
13 .... 28.4
14 .... 11.9, 28.4, 28.6
17 .... 28.7
First Protocol
art 1 .... 28.7
Rome Convention on the Law Applicable
to Contractual Obligations (Rome, 19 June
1980)
art 3 .... 10.42
(1) 23.7
(3) 23.7
4(2), (3) 23.7
5 .... 23.7
6(1), (2) 23.7
7(1) 10.42, 23.7
8–13 .... 23.7
16, 17 .... 23.7
Single European Act 1986 .... 22.1
Treaty Establishing the European
Economic Community (EEC Treaty) (Rome,
25 March 1957) 22.1
art 6(1) 22.1
13 .... 22.1, 22.6
39 .... 22.4
40, 41 .... 22.4
42 .... 22.4, 22.5

Treaty Establishing the European Economic Community (EEC Treaty) (Rome, 25 March 1957)
– cont.
art 48 .... 22.4, 23.2
49 .... 43.1
94 .... 22.1
95 .... 22.1
118A 55.1
119 .... 10.3
136 .... 22.1
137 .... 22.1, 25.25
138–140 .... 22.1
141 .... 6.1, 17.12, 21.1, 21.3, 21.5, 21.6,
21.9, 21.12,21.13, 21.14, 21.15, 21.16,
21.17, 21.18, 22.1, 22.2, 28.5, 40.1, 40.9
(1) 11.10
(4) 11.10
226, 227 .... 22.2
234 .... 19.48, 22.2
251 .... 22.1
302 .... 22.1
Treaty of Amsterdam (Amsterdam, 2 October
1997) 22.1
Treaty of Nice (Nice, 26 February 2001)
.... 22.1
art 49 .... 23.3
Treaty on European Union (Maastricht Treaty,
1 November 1993) 22.1
Treaty on the Functioning of the European
Union (Lisbon, 13 December 2007)
art 19 .... 10.5
(1) 10.7
101 .... 39.1
157 .... 10.3, 21.19B

Secondary Legislation

Directives

Council Directive 68/360/EEC (Abolition of
Restrictions on Movement and Residence
Directive) 23.2
Council Directive 75/117/EEC (Equal Pay
Directive) 21.1, 21.3, 22.6
Council Directive 75/129/EEC (Collective
Redundancy Directive) 22.8, 37.2, 37.4
Council Directive 76/207/EEC (Equal Treatment
Directive) ... 10.4, 10.21, 10.30, 10.41, 12.1,
22.5, 22.6, 23.9, 31.51, 31.58, 35.8

Table of EU Legislation

Council Directive 76/207/EEC (Equal Treatment Directive) – *cont.*
art 2(2) 11.9, 11.11
(4) 11.10
5(1) 10.31, 21.3
6 .... 11.22
Council Directive 77/187/EEC (Acquired Rights Directive) 22.9, 40.6
art 1–7 .... 50.1
Council Directive 79/7/EEC (Social Security Directive) 10.30, 22.5
Council Directive 80/987/EEC (Insolvency Protection Directive) 22.15
art 8 .... 29.7
Council Directive 83/189/EEC (Provision of Information in the Field of Technical Standards and Regulations Directive) 22.2
Council Directive 86/378/EEC (Principle of Equal Treatment for Men and Women in Occupational Social Security Schemes) 21.3, 21.17, 31.1
Council Directive 89/391/EEC (Health and Safety Framework Directive) .. 22.10, 26.17
art 3(a) 55.30
5(4) 25.25
7 .... 55.2
Council Directive 89/654/EEC (Minimum Safety and Health Requirements for the Workplace) 22.10, 25.25, 26.29
Annex II 26.14
Council Directive 89/655/EEC (Directive Relating to the use of Machines and Equipment) 25.25, 26.12
Council Directive 89/656/EEC (Minimum health and safety requirements for the use by workers of personal protective equipment at the workplace) 25.25, 26.12
Council Directive 90/269/EEC (Minimum Health and Safety Requirements for the Manual Handling of Loads) 25.25
Annex II 26.18
Council Directive 90/270/EEC (Directive Relating to the Use of Display Screen Equipment) 25.25
art 2(a) 26.5
Council Directive 90/364/EEC (Right of Residence Directive) 23.2
Council Directive 90/365/EEC (Right of Residence for Employees and Self-Employed Persons who Have Ceased their Occupational Activity) 23.2
Council Directive 90/394/EEC (Protection of Workers from the Risks Related to Exposure to Carcinogens at Work) 25.25

Council Directive 90/679/EEC (Protection of Workers from Risks Related to Exposure to Biological Agents at Work) 25.25
Council Directive 91/383/EEC (Temporary Workers' Directive) 26.17
Council Directive 91/533/EEC (Information on Conditions of Employment Directive) 22.7
Council Directive 92/56/EEC (Amending 75/129) 37.2
Council Directive 92/57/EEC (Minimum Safety and Health Requirements at Temporary or Mobile Work Sites) 25.25, 26.4
Council Directive 92/58/EEC (Minimum Requirements for the Provision of Safety and/or Health Signs at Work) . 25.25, 26.30
Council Directive 92/85/EEC (Pregnant Workers Directive) ... 22.6, 25.25, 26.17, 27.3a, 27.4, 31.4, 31.6, 31.38, 40.13
art 10 .... 10.31
11 .... 31.15
(2)(b) 21.14
Annex I, II 10.30
Council Directive 93/104/EC (Working Time Directive) 26.15, 27.3B, 55.1
art 1(3) 55.3
(4) 55.30
6(b) 55.21
7 .... 16.21, 27.2, 27.3A
(1) 22.11
13 .... 55.18
Council Directive 94/33/EC (Young Workers Directive on the Protection of Young People at Work) ... 3.2, 3.5, 4.6, 26.15, 26.17, 55.2, 55.3
Council Directive 94/45/EC (European Works Council Directive) 15.22
Council Directive 95/46/EC (Data Protection Directive) 9.11, 9.12
Council Directive 95/63/EC (amending 89/655) 26.12
Council Directive 96/34/EC (Directive on Parental Leave) 15.1
Council Directive 96/71/EC (Directive on the Posting of Workers) 11.18, 22.14
art 1 .... 23.3
3 .... 23.3
6 .... 23.3
Council Directive 96/96/EC (Amending 77/388) 21.3, 21.17
Council Directive 97/42/EC (Amending 90/394) 25.25
Council Directive 97/74/EC (Extending to the UK and Northern Ireland, 94/45) 15.22

Council Directive 97/74/EC (Extending to the UK and Northern Ireland, 94/45) – *cont.*
art 4(2) 15.24

Council Directive 97/80/EC (Burden of Proof Directive) 12.3, 21.13

Council Directive 97/81/EC (Framework Agreement) ... 22.6, 30.1, 30.3, 30.12, 30.26
recital 16 .... 30.5
cl 2(1) 30.6
(2) 30.5
3 .... 30.15
4 .... 30.21, 45.9
(1) 30.3, 30.21
(2) 30.3, 30.9, 30.11

Council Directive 98/23/EC (Part Time Work Directive) 30.1

Council Directive 98/59/EC (Approximation of the Laws of the Member States Relating to Collective Redundancies) 22.8, 37.4

Council Directive 99/38/EC 25.25

Council Directive 99/63/EC (Hearings provided for in 17/62) 22.11, 55.1, 55.3, 55.31

Council Directive 99/70/EC (Directive on Fixed-term Contracts) ... 19.12, 22.16, 45.9

Council Directive 99/95/EC (Seafarers' Hours of Work) 55.31

Council Directive 2000/43/EC (Race Discrimination Framework Directive)
.... 11.1, 11.6, 22.11
art 2(5) 11.9
3(2) 11.10, 22.6
5 .... 10.5
6 .... 22.6
(1) 11.9

Council Directive 2000/78/EC (Equal Treatment in Employment and Occupation Directive)
... 10.5, 10.10, 10.41, 11.1, 11.4, 11.9, 12.1, 22.6
recital 2 .... 11.14
art 2(5) 40.5
3(1)(c) 10.37
4(1) 11.7
6(1) 40.5
7 .... 11.10

Council Directive 2000/79/EC (Mobile Workers in Civil Aviation and its Domestic Implementation) 27.8, 55.1, 55.3, 55.33, 55.34

Council Directive 2001/23/EC (Transfers Directive) 22.9
art 1(1)(b) 50.1
(c) 50.9
3(1) 5.4

Council Directive 2001/86/EC (Directive on Worker Involvement) 15.1, 15.30

Council Directive 2002/14/EC (Information and Consultation Directive) 9.10, 16.4, 22.12

Council Directive 2002/15/EC (Organisation of the Working Time of Persons Performing Mobile Road Transport Activities)
.... 55.1, 55.3, 55.34
art 2(1) 55.35

Council Directive 2002/44/EC (European Physical Agents (Vibration) Directive)
.... 26.27

Council Directive 2002/73/EC (Amending 76/207)
art 2(8) 11.10

Council Directive 2002/74/EC (Amending 80/987) 29.7

Council Directive 2003/72/EC
.... 15.1, 16.39

Council Directive 2003/88/EC (Organisation of Working Time Directive) . 22.11, 23.9, 28.2, 55.1

Council Directive 2005/36/EC (mutual recognition of professional qualification)
.... 22.4

Council Directive 2005/56/EC (on cross-border mergers between limited liability companies)
.... 15.1, 15.49

Council Directive 2006/54/EC (on the implementation of the principle of equal opportunities and equal treatment of men and women in matters of employment and occupation) . 10.30, 10.31, 11.1, 17.12, 22.5, 22.6
art 14 .... 21.3

Council Directive 2008/52/EC
art 8(1) 12.4

Council Directive 2008/94/EC
.... 22.7, 29.1, 29.3

Council Directive 2008/104/EC (temporary agency work) 22.13
art 5 .... 45.2d

European Parliament and Council Directive 2009/38/EC (European Works Council)
.... 15.1, 15.22, 22.12

European Parliament and Council Directive 2009/104/EC (minimum safety and health requirements) Regulations 22.10

European Parliament and Council Directive 2010/18/EU 22.6, 31.46

European Parliament and Council Directive 2010/41/EU 31.4

Regulations

Council Regulation (EEC) No 1612/68 (Freedom of movement for Workers within the Community) 23.2

Table of EU Legislation

Council Regulation (EEC) No 1251/70 (Right of
  Workers to Remain in the Territory of a
  Member State after having been Employed
  in that State) 23.2
Council Regulation (EEC) No 3820/85 (Drivers'
  Hours Regulations) 55.1, 55.35
Council Regulation (EC) No 44/2001 (Brussels I
  Regulation)
  art 2(1) 23.8
     5(3) 23.8
     6(1) 23.8
     18(2) 23.8
     19 .... 10.42, 23.8
     20 .... 23.8
     21 .... 10.42
       (1) 23.8
     27, 28 .... 23.8

Council Regulation (EC) No 2157/2001
  (Regulation establishing a
  European Company Statute) ... 15.1, 15.30,
                                       15.31
Council Regulation (EEC) No 1435/03
  .... 15.1, 15.39
  art 1(3) 15.40
Council Regulation (EC) No 883/2005
  .... 22.5
Council Regulation (EC) No 561/2006
  .... 55.35
Council Regulation (EC) No 864/2007
  .... 23.7
Council Regulation (EC) No 593/2008
  .... 23.7
Council Regulation (EC) No 987/2009
  .... 22.5

Table of Statutory Instruments

A

ACAS Arbitration Scheme (Great Britain) Order 2004, SI 2004/753

ACAS (Flexible Working) Arbitration Scheme (England and Wales) Order 2003, SI 2003/694 .... 2.8

Act of Sederunt (Interest on Sheriff Court Decrees or Extracts) 1975, SI 1975/948 .... 12.20, 21.20

Additional Paternity Leave Regulations 2010, SI 2010/1055 .... 31.52
reg 3 .... 31.56
4(2)(c), (d) 31.57
(4) 31.56
(5) 31.57
5(4) 31.57
6 .... 31.56
(1) 31.57
(2)(c) 31.57
(3), (4) 31.57
7 .... 31.56
(1) 31.57
8(1), (2) 31.57
9 .... 31.57
23 .... 31.60
24 .... 31.57
25 .... 31.56
26, 27 .... 31.58
28 .... 31.58, 31.60
29, 30 .... 31.57
31(1), (2) 31.58
32 .... 31.58
33, 34 .... 31.60
35 .... 31.58

Additional Paternity Leave (Adoptions from Overseas) Regulations 2010, SI 2010/1059 .... 31.59

Additional Statutory Paternity Pay (Adoptions from Overseas) Regulations 2010, SI 2010/1057 .... 31.61

Additional Statutory Paternity Pay (Birth, Adoption and Adoptions from Overseas) (Administration) Regulations 2010, SI 2010/154 .... 31.61

Additional Statutory Paternity Pay (General) Regulations 2010, SI 2010/1056 .... 31.61

Additional Statutory Paternity Pay (National Health Service Employees) Regulations 2010, SI 2010/152 .... 31.61

Additional Statutory Paternity Pay (Weekly Rates) Regulations 2010, SI 2010/1060 .... 31.61

Agency Workers Regulations 2010, SI 2010/93 .... 14.3
reg 2 .... 45.2d
3 .... 45.2d, 55.37
3A 15.5
4 .... 45.2d
5(1) 45.2d
6(2), (3) 45.2d
(5) 45.2d
7 .... 31.10, 31.14
(3)–(12) 45.2d
8(a) 45.2d
9(4) 45.2d
10(1)(a) 45.2d
(c) 45.2d
11 .... 45.2d
12(3), (4) 45.2d
13, 14 .... 45.2d
16 .... 18.9, 52.3
(9) 45.2d
17 .... 45.2d, 51.11, 52.3
(3) 52.11
18 .... 17.11
(4), (5) 45.2d
(14), (15) 45.2d
Sch 2 .... 45.2d

Apprenticeship Sectors (Specification) Order 2011, SI 2011/220 .... 13.11

Apprenticeships (Alternative English Completion Conditions) Regulations 2012, SI 2012/1199 .... 13.7, 13.11

Apprenticeships (Form of Appprenticeship Agreement) Regulations 2012, SI 2012/844 .... 13.7, 13.11

Apprenticeships (Modifications to the Specification of Apprenticeship Standards for England) Order 2013, SI 2013/575 .... 13.11

Apprenticeships (Specification of Apprenticeship Standards for England) Order 2011, SI 2011/219 .... 13.11

Apprenticeships (Issue of Apprenticeship Certificates) (England) Regulations 2011, SI 2011/900 .... 13.11

Apprenticeships (the Appprenticeship Offer) (Prescribed Persons) Regulations 2013, SI 2013/560 .... 13.10

Apprenticeships, Skills, Children and Learning Act 2009 (Commencement No 2 and Transitional and Saving Provisions) Order 2010, SI 2010/303 .... 13.10
Sch 3
col 2 .... 13.12

Table of Statutory Instruments

Apprenticeships, Skills, Children and Learning
   Act 2009 (Commencement No 4) Order
   2010, SI 2010/2374 .... 13.11
Apprenticeships, Skills, Children and Learning
   Act 2009 (Commencement No 5) Order
   2011, SI 2011/200 .... 13.11
Apprenticeships (Transitional Provision for
   Existing Vocational Specifications) (England)
   Order 2011, SI 2011/901 .... 13.11
Armed Forces (Redress of Individual Grievances)
   Regulations 2007, SI 2007/3353
   .... 35.3
Armed Forces (Redundancy, Resettlement and
   Gratuity Earnings Schemes) (No 2) Order
   2010, SI 2010/832 .... 35.3
Armed Forces Redundancy Scheme Order 2006,
   SI 2006/55 .... 35.3
Attachment of Earnings (Employer's Deduction)
   Order 1991, SI 1999/356
   art 2 .... 33.9

C

Chemicals (Hazard Information and Packaging for
   Supply) Regulations 1994, SI 1994/3247
   .... 26.26
Child Support (Collection and Enforcement)
   Regulations 1992, SI 1992/1989
   reg 16(1)–(3) 33.7
   24 .... 33.11
Child Support (Information, Evidence and
   Disclosure) Regulations 1992, SI 1992/1812
   .... 33.7
Children (Protection at Work) (No 2) Regulations
   2000, SI 2000/2548 .... 3.2
Children (Protection at Work) Regulations 1998,
   SI 1998/276 .... 3.2
Children (Protection at Work) Regulations 2000,
   SI 2000/1333 .... 3.2
Civil Aviation (Working Time) Regulations 2004,
   SI 2004/756 .... 27.4, 27.8, 55.33
Civil Jurisdiction and Judgments Order 2001, SI
   2001/3929 .... 23.8
Civil Jurisdiction (Offshore Activities) Order
   1987, SI 1987/2197 .... 10.42
Civil Procedure Rules 1998, SI 1998/3132
   .... 18.1, 18.71
   Pt 3
   r 3.9 .... 18.16
   3.11 .... 18.77
   Pt 6
   PD 6B
   para 3.1 .... 23.8
   Pt 14 .... 18.52
   Pt 23 .... 39.17
   Pt 24 .... 18.15, 18.17, 56.41
   Pt 25 .... 39.17

Civil Procedure Rules 1998, SI 1998/3132 – *cont.*
   r 26.6 .... 56.41
   Pt 31 .... 18.11
   Pt 36 .... 56.41
   Pt 52
   r 52.3 .... 19.47
   52.9A 19.47
   Pt 54 .... 35.6
Code of Practice on Equal Pay Order 2003, SI
   2003/2865 .... 4.14
Collective Redundancies and Transfer of
   Undertakings (Protection of Employment)
   (Amendment) Regulations 1995, SI
   1995/2587 .... 22.8, 22.9
Companies (Cross-Border Mergers) Regulations
   2007, SI 2007/2974 .... 51.11, 52.3
   reg 2 .... 15.49
   (2)–(4) 15.50
   3 .... 15.49, 15.51
   (1) 15.52
   (b) 15.57
   5 .... 15.49
   7(2)(j) 15.53
   8–10 .... 15.53
   12–16 .... 15.53
   17 .... 15.57, 15.58
   22(1)–(3) 15.51
   23(1)–(3) 15.54
   24(1), (2) 15.54
   25(1), (2) 15.55
   26(4), (5) 15.55
   27(1)–(6) 15.55
   28(2) 15.56
   (3) 15.56, 15.57
   29(1)–(3) 15.56
   30(1)–(7) 15.56
   31 .... 15.57
   (1) 15.56
   32(1)–(3) 15.56
   33–35 .... 15.55
   36 .... 15.54, 15.57
   37(1)–(4) 15.57
   38 .... 15.56
   (5) 15.57
   39, 40 .... 15.57
   41, 42 .... 15.59
   43 .... 15.60, 47.12
   44 .... 15.60, 47.12
   45 .... 15.60, 47.12
   46 .... 15.60
   (2)–(4) 52.11
   47 .... 15.60
   (2) 52.11
   49–51 .... 15.60
   53(1)–(7) 15.58
   (9) 15.58
   54(1)–(7) 15.58
   55 .... 15.58
Companies (Model Articles) Regulations 2008, SI
   2008/3229 .... 8.1

Companies (Model Articles) Regulations 2008, SI
2008/3229 – cont.
Sch 1
para 19 .... 8.2, 8.27, 8.35
    20 .... 8.25
Sch 2
para 10 .... 8.27
    19 .... 8.2, 8.35
    20 .... 8.25
Sch 3
para 23 .... 8.2, 8.27, 8.35
    24 .... 8.25
Companies (Tables A to F) Regulations 1985, SI
1985/805
Schedule
Table A 8.1
art 82 .... 8.27
    83 .... 8.25
    84 .... 8.2, 8.27
    87 .... 8.35
Compensation (Exemptions) Order 2007, SI
2007/209 .... 18.40
Compromise Agreements (Description of Person)
Order 2004, SI 2004/754 .... 12.33
Compromise Agreements (Description of Person)
Order 2005, SI 2005/2364 .... 12.33
Conduct of Employment Agencies and
Employment Businesses Regulations 1976,
SI 1976/715 .... 45.3, 45.4
Conduct of Employment Agencies and
Employment Businesses Regulations 2003,
SI 2003/3319 .... 45.3, 45.4
reg 2 .... 45.5
    5(2), (3) 45.5
    6–8 .... 45.5
    10–12 .... 45.5
    13(1)(b) 45.5
    14 .... 14.3
      (2) 45.5
      (4)–(6) 45.5
    15 .... 14.3, 45.5
    17–19 .... 45.5
    20 .... 31.14
      (2)–(6) 45.5
    21(1)(a)(i) 45.5
      (4), (5) 45.5
    22 .... 45.5
    26(1) 45.5
      (3) 45.5
      (5)(d) 45.5
      (6) 45.5
    28 .... 45.5
    30(1) 45.5
    31(1), (2) 45.5
    32(1) 45.5
      (9) 45.5
      (12) 45.5
Sch 3 .... 45.5

Conduct of Employment Agencies and
Employment Businesses (Amendment)
Regulations 2010, SI 2010/1782
.... 45.4, 45.5
Construction (Design and Management)
Regulations 1994, SI 1994/3140
.... 26.4
Construction (Head Protection) Regulations 1989,
SI 1989/2209 .... 26.4
Construction (Health, Safety and Welfare)
Regulations 1996, SI 1996/1592
.... 26.4
Control of Asbestos at Work Regulations 1987, SI
1987/2115 .... 26.26
Control of Asbestos at Work Regulations 2002, SI
2002/2675 .... 25.17
Control of Industrial Major Accident Hazards
Regulations 1984, SI 1984/1902
.... 25.20
Control of Lead at Work Regulations 1980, SI
1980/1248
reg 16 .... 32.29
Control of Lead at Work Regulations 1998, SI
1998/543 .... 26.26
Control of Major Accident Hazards Regulations
1999, SI 1999/743 .... 25.20, 26.1
Control of Substances Hazardous to Health
Regulations 1988, SI 1988/1657
.... 25.17
reg 11 .... 32.29
Control of Substances Hazardous to Health
Regulations 2002, SI 2002/2677
.... 22.10
reg 2(1) 26.26
    3 .... 26.26
    4 .... 26.26
    6 .... 26.26
    7(1)–(4) 26.26
    8(1), (2) 26.26
    9–12 .... 26.26
    14 .... 26.26
    20 .... 26.26
Control of Vibration at Work Regulations 2005,
SI 2005/1093 .... 26.27
Council Tax (Administration and Enforcement)
Regulations 1992, SI 1992/613
reg 32(1) 33.10
    34 .... 33.10
    37(1)–(3) 33.10
    38 .... 33.10
    39(1)–(4) 33.10
      (6) 33.10
    40, 42 .... 33.10
    56(2) 33.10
Sch 4 .... 33.10
Court Funds Rules 1987, SI 1987/821
r 27(1) 12.20, 18.67, 21.19B

Table of Statutory Instruments

Criminal Justice and Public Order Act 1994
(Commencement No 5 and Transitional
Provisions) Order 1995, SI 1995/127
.... 16.6

Cross-border Railway Services (Working Time)
Regulations 2008, SI 2008/1660
.... 55.36

D

Damages-Based Agreements Regulations 2010,
2010/1206 .... 18.40

Dangerous Substances (Notification and Markings
of Sites) Regulations 1990, SI 1990/304
.... 26.26

Deregulation (Deduction from Pay of Union
Subscriptions) Order 1998, SI 1998/1529
reg 3(1)–(3) 49.20

Disability Discrimination Act 1995 (Amendment)
Regulations 2003, SI 2003/1673
reg 6 .... 11.16

Disability Discrimination Act 1995 (Pensions)
Regulations 2003, SI 2003/2770
.... 10.37

Disability Discrimination Codes of Practice
(Employment and Occupation, and Trade
Organisations and Qualifications Bodies)
Appointed Day Order 2004, SI 2004/2302
.... 4.14

Disability Discrimination Code of Practice
(Services, Public Functions, Private Clubs
and Premises) (Appointed Day) Order 2006,
SI 2006/1967 .... 4.14

Disability Discrimination (Employment Field)
(Leasehold Premises) Regulations 2004, SI
2004/153
reg 3 .... 11.35

Disability Discrimination (Questions and Replies)
Order 2004, SI 2004/1168
art 4 .... 12.9
Sch 2 .... 12.9

E

Ecclesiastical Offices (Terms of Service)
Directions 2010, SI 2010/1923
.... 31.20

Ecclesiastical Offices (Terms of Service)
Regulations 2009, SI 2009/2108
.... 47.4, 55.38
reg 23 .... 31.20

Education (Modification of Enactments Relating
to Employment) Order 2003, SI 2003/1964
.... 35.5

Electricity at Work Regulations 1989, SI
1989/635 .... 25.17
reg 4 .... 26.6
6–9 .... 26.6

Electricity at Work Regulations 1989, SI 1989/635
– cont.
reg 12–16 .... 26.6

Employee Study and Training (Eligibility,
Complaints and Remedies) Regulations 2010,
SI 2010/156 .... 13.14
reg 5 .... 13.17
6 .... 13.18

Employee Study and Training (Procedural
Requirements) Regulations 2010, SI
2010/155 .... 13.15, 13.18
reg 16(2), (3) 13.17
(5) 13.17
17 .... 13.17
20 .... 13.16

Employers' Health and Safety Policy Statements
(Exception) Regulations 1975, SI 1975/1584
.... 25.18

Employers' Liability (Compulsory Insurance)
Regulations 1998, SI 1998/2573
.... 26.16

Employment Act 1989 (Amendments and
Revocations) Order 1989, SI 1989/2311
.... 3.5

Employment Act 2002 (Dispute Resolution)
Regulations 2004, SI 2004/752
.... 53.13
reg 6 .... 51.7
7 .... 51.7
8 .... 51.7
9 .... 51.7
10 .... 51.7
14 .... 12.9
15 .... 12.4, 12.9, 51.2

Employment Act 2008 (Commencement No 1,
Transitional Provisions and Savings) Order
2008, SI 2008/3232 .... 9.17, 17.2
art 3 .... 12.9
Schedule 12.9

Employment Appeal Tribunal Rules 1993, SI
1993/2854 .... 19.6
r 3(1) 19.12
(3) 19.11
(7) 19.15, 19.17, 19.18, 19.46
(8) 19.17, 19.46
(9) 19.17
(10) 19.15, 19.17, 19.27, 19.41, 19.46
6(12) 19.15
(14)–(16) 19.15
19 .... 19.17
(1) 23.9
20 .... 19.17
21 .... 19.14, 19.17
23 .... 18.18
(2), (3) 12.11, 19.26
(5), (5A) 12.11, 19.26
(5B), (5C) 19.26
23A 18.18
24, 25 .... 19.19

Employment Appeal Tribunal Rules 1993, SI
  1993/2854 – *cont.*
  r 30A 35.7
  33 .... 19.46
  34(3) 19.43
    (4)–(6) 19.42
  34A 19.42, 19.44
    (1)–(3) 19.43
  34B 19.42, 19.44
    (1), (2) 19.43
  34C 19.42, 19.45
  34D 19.42
    (2)–(5) 19.44
    (7) 19.44
  37(1A) 19.11
  39 .... 19.19
  Schedule
  Form 1 .... 19.12
Employment Appeal Tribunal (Amendment) Rules
  2004, SI 2004/2526 .... 19.7
Employment Code of Practice (Access and Unfair
  Practices during Recognition and
  Derecognition Ballots) Order 2005, SI
  2005/2421 .... 48.32
Employment Code of Practice (Industrial Action
  Ballots and Notice to Employers) Order
  2005, SI 2005/2420 .... 43.14
Employment Code of Practice (Picketing) Order
  1992, SI 1992/476 .... 43.11
Employment Equality (Age) Regulations 2006, SI
  2006/1031 .... 11.1, 11.8, 11.9, 12.3, 17.11,
                  18.22, 40.1, 40.2
  reg 2 .... 12.24
  3 .... 12.24
    (1) 40.3
  Pt II (regs 7–24)
  reg 7(6) 11.20
  9(1)–(4) 11.24
  10 .... 23.9
    (1), (2) 11.18
    (3)(b) 11.18
    (4), (5) 11.18
  11(1), (2) 11.35
  12(1)–(7) 11.25
    (8)(b) 11.25
    (9) 11.25
    (10)(a)–(e) 11.25
    (1)–(7) 11.26
  15(1), (2) 11.27
    (4), (5) 11.27
  16 .... 11.27
  17(1), (2) 11.28
    (4) 11.28
    (6) 11.28
    (8) 11.28
  18(1)–(4) 11.29
  19(1)–(3) 11.30
  20(1)(a) 11.31
    (2)–(4) 11.31

Employment Equality (Age) Regulations 2006, SI
  2006/1031 – *cont.*
  reg 21(1)–(6) 11.32
  22(1)–(3) 11.33
  Pt III (regs 24–26)
  reg 24 .... 12.22
  25 .... 12.2
  26 .... 12.2
  27 .... 11.21, 11.22
  29(1)–(3) 11.10
  30(1) 40.3
    (2) 11.15, 40.3
  31 .... 11.15
  32(1)–(3) 11.15
    (4)(a)–(c) 11.15
    (7) 11.15
  33(1)(a) 11.15
    (4)(a)–(c) 11.15
  34(1), (2) 11.15
  35(1) 12.1
    (2) 12.1, 12.22
  36(2) 11.30
  38 .... 12.14
    (1)(a) 12.12
    (b) 12.12, 12.16
    (c) 12.12
    (3) 12.21
  39(3) 12.16
  41(2) 12.9
    (4) 12.9
  42(1) 12.4
    (3) 12.7, 17.30
    (4) 12.4
  43 .... 12.33
  44(1) 11.36
    (4) 12.2
    (5) 11.36
  45 .... 11.36
  46 .... 12.32
  Sch 2
  Pt 1
  para 1 .... 11.35
    2 .... 12.33
    (1), (2) 11.35
    (3), (4) 11.35
    5 .... 12.22
    6(1)(b) 12.22
  Pt 2
  para 3A(2) 11.35
    7(a), (b) 11.35
    8, 9 .... 11.35
    10(a)–(c) 11.35
    11–29 .... 11.35
  Pt 3 .... 11.35
  Sch 4 .... 12.9
  Sch 5
  para 1 .... 40.7
    (1), (2) 12.32
    (3) 12.32
  3(1) 12.32

Table of Statutory Instruments

Employment Equality (Age) Regulations 2006, SI 2006/1031 – *cont.*
Sch 5 – *cont.*
Pt 2 .... 12.32
Sch 6 .... 52.4
para 2 .... 40.4
　(1) 40.3
　4 .... 40.3, 40.4
　5 .... 40.3
　6–8 .... 40.3
　11 .... 40.3
Employment Equality (Religion or Belief) Regulations 2003, SI 2003/1660
　.... 10.41, 11.1, 11.4, 11.7, 12.3, 28.7, 38.4
reg 2(1) 10.22
　3(1)(a) 10.22
　　(b)(iii) 11.9
Pt II (regs 6–21) 12.24
reg 6(2)(b) 11.20
　(4) 11.20
　7(2)(b), (c) 11.6
　(3)(b), (c) 11.6
　8(1)–(4) 11.24
　9 .... 23.9
　(1), (2) 11.18
　(3)(a) 11.18
　　(b) 11.18
　(4), (5) 11.18
　9A(1), (2) 11.35
　(4) 12.22
　10(1)–(6) 11.25
　(8)(a), (b) 11.25
　(9) 11.25
　(10)(a)–(d) 11.25
　11(1)–(8) 11.26
　12(1)–(5) 11.27
　13 .... 11.27
　14(1)–(6) 11.28
　(8) 11.28
　15(1)–(4) 11.29
　16(1)–(3) 11.30
　17(1)(aa) 11.31
　(2)–(4) 11.31
　18(1)–(6) 11.32
　19(1)–(3) 11.33
　21 .... 12.22
Pt III (regs 22–23) 12.24
reg 22 .... 12.2
　23 .... 12.2
　24 .... 11.22
　25(1)–(3) 11.10
　26(1)–(4) 11.13
　27(1), (2) 12.1
　28(1) 12.2
　(2) 11.30
　　(a) 12.2
　30 .... 12.14
　(1)(a)–(c) 12.12
　(3) 12.21
　33(3), (4) 12.9
　34(1) 12.4

Employment Equality (Religion or Belief) Regulations 2003, SI 2003/1660 – *cont.*
reg 34(1A) 12.4
　(3) 12.7, 17.30
　(4) 12.4
　35 .... 12.32, 12.33
　36 .... 11.11
　(2) 11.36
　(4) 11.36
　(7)–(10) 11.36
　37, 38 .... 11.36
Sch 1A
para 1–4 .... 11.35
　6 .... 12.22
　7(1)(b) 12.22
Sch 3 .... 12.9
Sch 4
Pt 1
para 1(1) 12.32
　(3) 12.32
　2 .... 12.33
　3(1) 12.32
Pt 2 .... 12.32
Employment Equality (Religion or Belief) (Amendment) Regulations 2003, SI 2003/2828 .... 12.22
Employment Equality (Religion or Belief) Regulations 2003 (Amendment) (No 2) Regulations 2004, SI 2004/2520
　.................................. 12.33
Employment Equality (Repeal of Retirement Age Provisions) Regulations 2011, SI 2011/1069
　.......................... 11.15, 17.11
reg 2(2), (3) 40.4
　5(1) 40.4
　(4) 40.4
　(6) 40.4
Employment Equality (Sex Discrimination) Regulations 2005, SI 2005/2467
　.......................... 21.2, 31.16
reg 34 .... 11.11
　36 .... 21.14
Employment Equality (Sexual Orientation) (Amendment) Regulations 2003, SI 2003/2827 .... 12.22
Employment Equality (Sexual Orientation) Regulations 2003, SI 2003/1661
　.................. 11.1, 11.4, 12.3, 38.4
reg 3(1)(b)(iii) 11.9
Pt II (regs 6–21) 12.24
reg 6(2)b) 11.20
　(4) 11.20
　7(2) 11.7
　(3)(a), (c) 11.7
　8(1) 11.24
　(2) 11.7, 11.24
　(3), (4) 11.24
　9(1)–(5) 11.18
　9A(1), (2) 11.35

Employment Equality (Sexual Orientation) Regulations 2003, SI 2003/1661 – *cont.*
reg 9A(4) 12.22
 10(1)–(6) 11.25
  (8)(a), (b) 11.25
  (9) 11.25
  (10)(a)–(d) 11.25
 11(1)–(8) 11.26
 12(1)–(5) 11.27
 13 .... 11.27
 14(1)–(6) 11.28
  (8) 11.28
 15(1)–(4) 11.29
 16(1)–(3) 11.30
 17(1)(aa) 11.31
  (2)–(4) 11.31
 18(1)–(6) 11.32
 19(1)–(3) 11.33
 21 .... 12.22
Pt III (regs 22–23) 12.24
reg 22 .... 12.2
 23 .... 12.2
 24 .... 11.22
 25 .... 11.14, 40.9
 26(1)–(3) 11.10
 27(1), (2) 12.1
 28(1) 12.2
  (2) 11.30
   (a) 12.2
 30 .... 12.14
  (1)(a)–(c) 12.12
  (3) 12.21
 33(2) 12.9
  (4) 12.9
 34(1) 12.4
  (1A) 12.4
  (3) 12.7, 17.30
  (4) 14.2
 35 .... 12.32, 12.33
 36 .... 11.11
  (2) 11.36
  (4) 11.36
  (7)–(10) 11.36
 37, 38 .... 11.36
Sch 1A
para 1–4 .... 11.35
 6 .... 12.22
 7(1)(b) 12.22
Sch 2 .... 12.9
Sch 4
Pt 1
para 1(1) 12.32
 (2) 12.32
 2 .... 12.33
 3(1) 12.32
Pt 2 .... 12.32
Employment Equality (Sexual Orientation) Regulations 2003 (Amendment) Regulations 2004, SI 2004/2519 .... 12.33

Employment Protection Code of Practice (Time Off for Trade Union Duties and Activities) Order 2009, SI 2009/3223 .... 2.11, 4.2
Employment Protection (Continuity of Employment) Regulations 1996, SI 1996/3147 .... 6.6, 6.12, 53.4
Employment Protection (National Health Service) Order 1996, SI 1996/638 .... 6.9
Employment Protection (Part-time Employees) Regulations 1995, SI 1995/31 .... 6.1
Employment Protection (Recoupment of Jobseeker's Allowance and Income Support) Regulations 1996, SI 1996/2349 .... 18.68, 53.6
Employment Relations Act 1999 (Blacklists) Regulations 2010, SI 2010/493
reg 3 .... 7.13, 49.10, 52.3
 5, 6 .... 17.11, 49.10
 8(3) 49.10
 9 .... 17.11, 49.10
 12 .... 49.10
Employment Rights Act 1996 (Application of Section 80BB to Adoptions from Overseas) Regulations 2010, SI 2010/1058
.... 31.59
Employment Rights (Increase of Limits) Order 2012, SI 2012/3007 .... 32.27, 32.32, 32.39, 36.13, 49.4, 53.7, 53.10
Employment Tribunals Act 1996 (Tribunal Composition) Order 2012, SI 2012/988
reg 3 .... 17.3
Employment Tribunals (Constitution and Rules of Procedure) Regulations 1993, SI 1993/2687
.... 18.18
Employment Tribunals (Constitution and Rules of Procedure) Regulations 2001, SI 2001/1171
.... 17.1
Sch 1
r 15(1) 18.18
 19(3) 18.24
Sch 5 .... 25.31
r 2(1), (2) 25.34
Employment Tribunals (Constitution and Rules of Procedure) Regulations 2004, SI 2004/1861
reg 2(2) 18.71
 3 .... 17.14, 18.1, 21.21
 4 .... 17.6
 6, 7 .... 17.6
 8(5) 17.7
 9(3) 17.8
 10 .... 17.7
 11 .... 17.7, 35.7
 12 .... 35.7
 14 .... 17.15
  (1)(c) 17.16
 15(5) 18.38
  (6) 18.15

Table of Statutory Instruments

Employment Tribunals (Constitution and Rules of
  Procedure) Regulations 2004, SI 2004/1861 –
  cont.
reg 17 .... 18.65
  19 .... 17.11, 23.8
    (1) 11.18
  20 .... 21.21
    (2)–(5) 18.69
  61(4)(h) 23.9
Sch 1 .... 12.2, 17.1, 17.4, 18.78
r 1 .... 21.21
  (1), (2) 17.21
  (3) 17.16
  (4) 17.15
  (7) 17.15
  2(1) 17.16
  (2) 17.16, 17.34
  3(1) 17.16
  (5) 17.34
  (10) 19.5
  4 .... 21.21
  (1), (2) 17.35
  (4) 17.36, 17.37, 18.21
  (4A)–(4E) 17.36
  (5), (6) 17.35
  6(1) 17.35
  (2), (3) 17.37
  7 .... 17.32
  8(1) 17.38
  (1A), (1B) 17.38
  (2A) 17.38
  (3), (4) 17.38
  (6) 17.38
  9 .... 17.10, 17.37
  10(1) 18.20
    (2)(c) 18.4
    (d) 18.4, 18.11
    (e) 18.21
    (g) 18.2
    (h) 18.22
    (j) 18.24
    (k), (l) 18.23
    (n) 18.7, 18.15
    (r) 18.23
  (7) 18.24
  (8) 18.3
  11(2) 18.3
  (3) 18.8
  (4) 18.3, 18.21
  (4A) 18.3
  (5) 18.3
  12(2) 18.3
  (3) 18.3, 18.41
  13 .... 18.6, 18.75
  (1) 18.4, 18.71
    (b) 18.16
  (2) 18.4, 18.16
  14 .... 17.34
  (2) 18.6, 18.52
  (3) 18.6, 18.18, 18.20, 18.52, 18.56
  (4) 18.6, 18.38, 18.39

Employment Tribunals (Constitution and Rules of
  Procedure) Regulations 2004, SI 2004/1861 –
  cont.
Sch 1 – *cont.*
r 14(5) 18.6, 18.46, 18.47
  (6) 18.47
  15 .... 18.6
  16(1), (2) 18.51
  17(1) 18.2, 18.51
  (2) 18.2, 18.5, 18.16, 18.18, 18.70
  18 .... 18.5
  (1) 18.6, 18.51
  (2) 17.18
    (c) 17.5, 18.15
  (3) 17.9, 18.6
  (5) 18.6
  (6) 18.6
  (7) 18.27, 18.55
    (a) 18.23
    (b)–(d) 18.6, 18.17
    (e) 18.6
    (f) 18.6, 18.17
    (g) 18.18
  (8) 18.6
  (9) 18.15
  18A 18.6, 18.39
  19(1) 18.6, 18.16
  20 .... 19.5
  (1)–(5) 18.15
  21 .... 18.25
  25 .... 18.75
  (3) 12.11, 18.28
  (4) 17.10, 18.28
  (5) 18.28
  25A 17.10, 18.28
  26(3) 18.51
  27(2) 18.56
  (3) 18.49
  (4) 18.57
  (5) 17.10, 18.54
  (6) 18.54
  28 .... 18.2, 18.6
  (1)(a) 18.75
  (2) 17.10
  (4) 18.62
  30(1) 18.3
    (b) 18.62
  (2) 18.3
  (3) 18.3
    (b) 18.63, 19.22
  (5) 18.62
  (6) 17.13, 18.63, 19.36
  31(1), (2) 18.65
  33(2)–(3) 17.38
  (5)–(7) 17.38
  34 .... 17.37, 18.15, 18.16
  (1)(b) 18.75
  (3) 17.14, 17.34, 18.75
    (e) 18.76
  (4) 17.34
  (5) 18.75

Employment Tribunals (Constitution and Rules of
Procedure) Regulations 2004, SI 2004/1861 –
cont.
Sch 1 – *cont.*
r 35(1), (2) 17.34, 18.75
   (3) 18.75
36(2) 18.75
   (3) 17.34, 18.75
37 .... 18.76, 19.14
   (1) 18.64
   (2) 17.25
38(1)(a) 18.70
    (b) 18.71
    (c) 18.57
   (2) 18.70, 18.71
   (5) 18.70
   (7)–(10) 18.71
39 .... 18.71, 53.4
40(1)–(3) 18.71
41(1) 18.71
   (3) 18.71
42–44 .... 18.73
45(2)–(4) 18.73
46(1) 18.70
   (2) 18.71
47 .... 18.71
48 .... 19.45
   (1)–(6) 18.74
   (9) 18.74
49 .... 12.11, 18.19, 18.65, 19.26
50 .... 18.5, 19.26
   (1) 12.11
    (b) 18.18
   (2)–(6) 12.11, 18.18
   (7) 18.18
   (8)(a)–(c) 18.18
   (9) 12.11
   (11) 12.11
51 .... 18.18
54 .... 35.7
   (1)(a) 18.51
55 .... 18.22
57 .... 17.11
60(1) 18.18, 18.20, 18.52
61(4)(h) 23.8
Sch 2 .... 18.51, 18.78, 19.9
Sch 6 .... 17.9, 18.14, 18.78
r 3 .... 21.21
4(4) 21.21
5 .... 21.21
6(2) 21.21
7(3)–(6) 21.21
9(1)–(3) 21.21
10(1) 21.21
   (3)–(6) 21.21
11(1)–(6) 21.21
12(4), (5) 21.21
13(2) 21.21
14 .... 21.21
Employment Tribunals (Constitution and Rules of
Procedure) (Amendment) Regulations 2004,

Employment Tribunals (Constitution and Rules of
Procedure) (Amendment) Regulations 2004,
– *cont.*
SI 2004/2351 .... 21.21
Employment Tribunals (Constitution and Rules of
Procedure) (Amendment) Regulations 2010,
SI 2010/131 .... 9.17
Employment Tribunals (Constitution and Rules of
Procedure) (Amendment) Regulations 2012,
SI 2012/468
reg 2(4) 24.3
   (8) 24.3
  3 .... 18.15
Employment Tribunals (Constitution and Rules of
Procedure) (Scotland) Regulations 2001, SI
2001/1170 .... 17.1
Employment Tribunals Extension of Jurisdiction
(England and Wales) Order 1994, SI
1994/1623 .... 17.9, 17.11, 39.1, 40.17
art 3 .... 23.8
   (c) 7.44
  4 .... 7.44, 56.38
  5 .... 7.44
  7 .... 7.44, 17.32, 56.40
  8 .... 7.44, 17.32
  10 .... 7.45
Employment Tribunals Extension of Jurisdiction
(Scotland) Order 1994, SI 1994/1624
.... 56.38
art 7 .... 56.40
Employment Tribunals (Increase of Maximum
Deposit) Order 2012, SI 2012/149
.... 24.3
Employment Tribunals (Interest on Awards in
Discrimination Cases) Regulations 1996, SI
1996/2803 .... 12.13
reg 2(1)(b) 18.67
  3(1) 12.20, 21.19B
   (2) 12.20, 18.67, 21.19B
   (3) 12.20, 18.67
  4 .... 12.20, 21.19B
  6 .... 18.67
   (1)(a) 12.20, 21.19B
    (b) 12.20, 21.19B
   (2) 12.20, 21.19B
   (3) 21.19B
  7 .... 18.63
  8 .... 18.67
Employment Tribunals (Interest) Order 1990, SI
1990/479 .... 18.67
Equal Opportunities (Employment Legislation)
(Territorial Limits) Regulations 1999, SI
1999/3163 .... 21.4
Equal Pay Act 1970 (Amendment) Regulations
2003, SI 2003/1656 .... 21.2
Equal Pay (Amendment) Regulations 1983, SI
1983/1794 .... 21.2, 21.9

Table of Statutory Instruments

Equal Pay (Questions and Replies) Order 2003,
SI 2003/722 .... 21.2, 21.10, 21.21

Equality Act (Age Exceptions for Pension
Schemes) Order 2010, SI 2010/2133
reg 6 .... 11.35
Sch 1 .... 40.14

Equality Act 2006 (Commencement No 3 and
Savings) Order 2007, SI 2007/2603
art 2, 3 .... 12.23

Equality Act 2006 (Dissolution of Commissions
and Consequential and Transitional
Provisions) Order 2007, SI 2007/2602
art 3 .... 12.23
5 .... 12.23

Equality Act 2010 (Amendment) Order 2012, SI
2012/334 .... 18.34

Equality Act 2010 (Commencement No 4,
Savings, Consequential, Transitional,
Transitory and Incidental Provisions and
Revocation) Order 2010 .... 1.6

Equality Act 2010 (Commencement No 5) Order
2011, SI 2011/96
art 3 .... 11.10

Equality Act 2010 (Disability) Regulations 2010,
SI 2010/2128
reg 3(1), (2) 10.26
4(1)–(3) 10.26
5–7 .... 10.26

Equality Act 2010 (General Qualifications Bodies)
(Appropriate Regulator and Relevant
Qualifications) Regulations 2010, SI
2010/2245 .... 11.30

Equality Act 2010 (General Qualifications Bodies
Regulator and Relevant Qualifications)
(Wales) Regulations 2010, SI 2010/2217
.... 11.30

Equality Act 2010 (Guidance on the Definition of
Disability) Appointed Day Order 2011, SI
2011/1159 .... 4.12, 10.26

Equality Act 2010 (Obtaining Information) Order
2010, SI 2010/2194 .... 12.9, 18.9

Equality Act 2010 (Offshore Work) Order 2010,
SI 2010/1835 .... 10.42, 11.18

Equality Act 2010 (Qualifications Body Regulator
and Relevant Qualifications) (Scotland)
Regulations 2010, SI 2010/315
.... 11.30

Equality Act 2010
(Qualifying Compromise Contract Specified
Person) Order 2010, SI 2010/2192
.... 12.33

Equality Act (Sexual Orientation) Regulations
2007, SI 2007/1263 .... 11.9, 12.2

European Cooperative Society (Involvement of
Employees) Regulations 2006, SI 2006/2059
.... 51.11
reg 3 .... 15.40

European Cooperative Society (Involvement of
Employees) Regulations 2006, SI 2006/2059 –
cont.
reg 4(2)–(4) 15.40
5(1)–(4) 15.40
6 .... 15.40
7(1)–(3) 15.41
8(1), (2) 15.41
9 .... 15.42
10(1) 15.42
(5) 15.42
11(1)–(4) 15.42
12(4) 15.42
13 .... 15.42
14(1) 15.42
(2)(a), (b) 15.42
(3) 15.42
(5)–(8) 15.42
16(2) 15.43
(3) 15.43, 15.44
17(2)(h) 47.12
(3), (4) 15.43
(6) 15.43
18 .... 15.43
19 .... 15.43
(2)–(4) 15.45
20(1), (2) 15.43
21(3)–(5) 15.44
22(1), (2) 15.46
(4)–(9) 15.46
23 .... 15.46
(5) 15.42
24(1), (2) 15.46
(3)(b) 15.46
26, 27 .... 15.47
28–30 .... 15.48, 47.12
31 .... 15.48, 52.3, 53.11
(3) 52.11
(6) 52.11
32–34 .... 15.48
43 .... 15.40
Sch 1
para 11(2)(h) 47.12
Sch 2
para 7(4) 47.12

European Public Limited Liability Company
Regulations 2004, SI 2004/2326
.... 51.11
reg 42 .... 52.3
(3), (4) 52.11

European Public Limited-Liability Company
(Amendment) Regulations 2009, SI
2009/2400
reg 2 .... 15.31
Sch 2 .... 15.31

European Public Limited-Liability Company
(Employee Involvement) (Great Britain)
Regulations 2009, 2009/2401
reg 4(1)–(3) 15.31
5(1)–(3) 15.32

European Public Limited-Liability Company (Employee Involvement) (Great Britain) Regulations 2009, 2009/2401 – *cont.*

reg 6(1), (2)	15.32
7	15.34
8(1)–(6)	15.33
9(1)–(4)	15.33
10(4), (5)	15.33
11	15.33
12(1)–(9)	15.33
14(2)	15.34
(3)	15.34, 15.35
15(3A)	15.34
(4)	15.34
16(1)–(6)	15.34
17(1)–(4)	15.36
18(1), (2)	15.34
19	15.35
20(1), (2)	15.37
(4)–(6)	15.37
21(3)	15.37
26, 27	15.38, 47.12
28	15.38
29	15.38
(3)	52.11
(6)	52.11
30–32	15.38
Schedule	
para 2	15.35
8A	15.35

F

Fair Employment and Treatment (Northern Ireland) Order 1998 SI 1998/3162	10.22, 10.34
Financial Assistance Scheme (Miscellaneous Amendments) Regulations 2007, SI 2007/3581	29.7
Fire Precautions (Workplace) Regulations 1997, SI 1997/1840	26.13
Fishing Vessels (Working Time: Sea fishermen) Regulations 2004, SI 2004/1713	27.8, 52.3, 55.23, 55.31
Fixed-term Employees (Prevention of Less Favourable Treatment) Regulations 2002, SI 2002/2034	17.29, 19.2, 23.9, 30.15, 45.1, 45.7, 45.8, 51.11
reg 1	45.9, 51.6
2	45.9
3(2), (3)	45.9
(5)–(7)	45.9
4	45.9
5	18.9
(1)–(3)	45.9
6	52.3
(2)	45.9
(3)	45.9, 52.11
7	17.11, 17.22

Fixed-term Employees (Prevention of Less Favourable Treatment) Regulations 2002, SI 2002/2034 – *cont.*

reg 7(2), (3)	45.9
(6)	45.9
(7)(c)	45.9
(8)–(10)	45.9
(13)	45.9
8	17.30, 18.33
(2)	45.9
(4), (5)	45.9
9(1)–(4)	45.9
(5)	17.11, 45.9
(6)	17.33
(a), (b)	45.9
11	51.15
12(1)–(3)	45.9
14	45.9
18	45.9
19(3)	45.9
20	45.9
Sch 2	
Pt 1	
para 3(1)	51.15
(15)	51.15
Sch 2	
Pt 2	
para 5	51.15
Flexible Working (Eligibility, Complaints and Remedies) Regulations 2002, SI 2002/3236	47.17
Flexible Working (Procedural Requirements) Regulations 2002, SI 2002/3207	47.17

H

Health and Safety (Consultation with Employees) Regulations 1996, SI 1996/1513	9.8, 15.61, 22.10, 26.8, 26.20, 47.8, 52.3
reg 4–8	26.22
Sch 2	
para 2–5	47.9
Health and Safety (Display Screen Equipment) Regulations 1992, SI 1992/2792	26.31
reg 1(2)	26.5
3	26.5
Health and Safety (Enforcing Authority) Regulations 1989, SI 1989/1903	25.29
reg 3	53.16
Health and Safety (Enforcing Authority) Regulations 1998, SI 1998/494	
Sch 1	25.29
Health and Safety (First-Aid) Regulations 1981, SI 1981/917	25.17
reg 2–4	26.14

Table of Statutory Instruments

Health and Safety Information for Employees
(Modifications and Repeals) Regulations
1995, SI 1995/2923 .... 25.18

Health and Safety Information for Employees
Regulations 1989, SI 1989/682
.... 25.18

Health and Safety Inquiries (Procedure)
(Amendment) Regulations 1976, SI
1976/246 .... 25.26

Health and Safety Inquiries (Procedure)
Regulations 1975, SI 1975/335
.... 25.26

Health and Safety (Miscellaneous Amendments)
Regulations 2002, SI 2002/2174
.... 26.17
    reg 4 .... 26.18

Health and Safety (Safety Signs and Signals)
Regulations 1996, SI 1996/341
.... 26.30

Health and Safety (Training for Employment)
Regulations 1990, SI 1990/1380
.... 13.7, 25.17

Health and Safety (Young Persons) Regulations
1997, SI 1997/135 .... 3.5

I

Immigration (European Economic Area)
Regulations 2006, SI 2006/1003
.... 23.1, 23.2

Immigration (Restrictions on Employment) Order
2004, SI 2007/3290 .... 23.6
    art 8(1)(a) 10.45

Income Tax (Benefits in Kind) (Exemption for
Welfare Counselling) Regulations 2000, SI
2000/2080 .... 44.23

Income Tax (Exemption of Minor Benefits)
Regulations 2002, SI 2002/205
.... 44.23

Income Tax (Pay As You Earn) Regulations 2003,
SI 2003/2682 .... 44.1
    reg 41, 42 .... 44.14
    70 .... 44.14
    80 .... 44.14
    82, 83 .... 44.14
    91–93 .... 56.32

Industrial Training Levy (Construction Industry
Training Board) Order 2012, SI 2012/958
.... 13.4

Industrial Training Levy
(Engineering Construction Industry Training
Board) Order 2012, SI 2012/959
.... 13.4

Information and Consultation of Employees
Regulations 2004, SI 2004/3426
.... 15.1, 15.4, 15.8, 37.4, 48.6, 51.11
    reg 2 .... 15.6

Information and Consultation of Employees Regulations 2004, SI 2004/3426 – cont.
    reg 3 .... 15.5, 15.6
        .... 15.5
    5 .... 15.21
        (3) 15.7
    6(2) 15.7
    7(1)–(6) 15.10
    8(1)(b), (c) 9.10, 15.18
        (2)–(4) 11.11, 15.17
        (5)(b), (c) 15.17
        (6)–(9) 15.17
    8A 15.17
    9(1)–(3) 15.17
    10(1), (2) 15.17
        (3)(a), (b) 15.17
        (c)(i) 15.17
    11(1), (2) 15.9
    12(1), (2) 15.11
    13(1)–(3) 15.11
    14 .... 9.10
        (1), (2) 15.12
        (3)–(5) 15.14
        (6) 15.11
    15(1), (2) 15.13
    16(1) 9.10, 15.14
        (2) 9.10
        (3)–(6) 15.14
    17(1), (2) 15.14
    18(1) 15.15
        (2) 15.11
    19(1) 15.16
        (3)–(6) 15.16
    20(1)–(5) 15.15
    21 .... 15.14
    22(1)–(7) 15.20
    23(3) 9.10, 15.20
    25 .... 9.10
        (1)–(8) 15.19
    26 .... 9.10
        (1)–(4) 15.19
    27, 28 .... 15.21, 47.12
    29(1) 15.21
        (2)(a) 15.21
        (3)–(5) 15.21
    30 .... 52.3, 52.11
        (4) 15.21
    32(4) 15.21
    33 .... 15.21
    Sch 1 .... 15.5
    Sch 2 .... 15.16

Insolvency Proceedings (Monetary Limits) Order
1986, SI 1986/1996
    art 4 .... 29.2

Insolvency Rules 1986, SI 1986/1925
.... 29.2

Ionising Radiations Regulations 1985, SI
1985/1333
    reg 16 .... 32.29

J

Jobseeker's Allowance Regulations 1996, SI
1996/207 .... 10.30, 11.9

L

Large and Medium-sized Companies and Groups
(Accounts and Reports) Regulations 2008, SI
2008/410
reg 8 .... 8.31
10 .... 15.3
Sch 5
para 1(1) 8.31
(3) 8.31
2(1) 8.31
3 .... 8.31, 8.35
4, 5 .... 8.31
Sch 7
para 11 .... 15.3
Sch 8 .... 8.31
para 13, 14 .... 8.35
15 .... 8.37
Lifting Operations and Lifting Equipment
Regulations 1998, SI 1998/2307
.... 26.12
Local Authorities (Standing Orders) (England)
Regulations 2001, SI 2001/3384
.... 35.5
Local Authorities (Standing Orders) Regulations
1993, SI 1993/202 .... 35.5
Local Government Officers (Political Restrictions)
Regulations 1990, SI 1990/851
.... 35.5
Local Government Pension Scheme Regulations
1997, SI 1997/578 .... 40.9

M

Management of Health and Safety at Work
Regulations 1992, SI 1992/2051
.... 26.2
reg 13A(3) 31.11
Management of Health and Safety at Work
Regulations 1999, SI 1999/3242
.... 3.1, 10.30, 22.10, 25.18, 55.11
reg 2 .... 3.5
3 .... 26.17
(5) 3.5
4–9 .... 26.17
10 .... 26.17
(2) 3.4
11–15 .... 26.17
16 .... 26.17, 31.11
17 .... 26.17, 55.13
19 .... 26.17
(1)–(3) 3.5
21, 22 .... 26.17
Sch 1 .... 28.17

Manual Handling Operations Regulations 1992,
SI 1992/2793
reg 4(3) 26.18
Sch 1 .... 26.18
Maternity and Parental Leave etc and the
Paternity and Adoption Leave (Amendment)
Regulations 2006, SI 2006/2014
.... 31.46
Maternity and Parental Leave etc and the
Paternity and Adoption Leave (Amendment)
Regulations 2008, SI 2008/1966
.... 31.46
Maternity and Parental Leave etc Regulations
1999, SI 1999/3312 .... 5.14, 22.6, 31.1
reg 2(1) 31.23, 31.25
4 .... 31.28
(1) 31.22
(a)(iii) 31.28
(2) 31.22
(3) 31.22
(b) 31.28
(4) 31.22
(b) 31.28
6(1) 31.23
(b) 31.22
(2) 31.22, 31.23
(3) 31.28
7 .... 31.24
(4) 31.28
(6), (7) 31.28
8 .... 31.27
9 .... 6.6
(3) 31.21, 40.13
10 .... 31.16
(2), (3) 31.34
11(1)–(5) 31.29
12 .... 31.29
12A 31.16
(1)–(4) 31.37
(6), (7) 31.37
13(1), (2) 31.47
14(1) 31.47
(1A) 31.47
15(1)(a) 31.47
(2), (3) 31.47
16 .... 31.47
17 .... 6.6, 31.49, 31.51, 51.4
18 .... 31.25
(1) 31.50
(2) 31.31, 31.50
18A 31.25, 31.31
(1) 31.50
19 .... 31.18
(2) 31.48
20 .... 52.3, 52.11
(1)(b) 31.16
(2) 31.16
(3) 31.48
(7), (8) 31.16
21 .... 31.26, 31.33

Table of Statutory Instruments

Maternity and Parental Leave etc Regulations 1999,
SI 1999/3312 – *cont.*
Sch 2
para 1–5 .... 31.47
    7–9 .... 31.47
Maternity and Parental Leave (Amendment)
Regulations 2001, SI 2001/4010
.... 22.6, 31.46
Maternity and Parental Leave (Amendment)
Regulations 2002, SI 2002/2789
.... 31.46
Merchant Shipping and Fishing Vessels (Health
and Safety at Work) Regulations 1997, SI
1997/2962
reg 8(3) 31.11
    9(2) 31.11
Merchant Shipping and Fishing Vessels (Health
and Safety at Work) (Employment of Young
Persons) Regulations 1998, SI 1998/2411
.... 3.5
reg 6 .... 3.6
Merchant Shipping and Fishing Vessels (Manual
Handling Operations) Regulations 1998, SI
1998/2857 .... 26.18
Merchant Shipping and Fishing Vessels (Personal
Protective Equipment) Regulations 1999, SI
1999/2205 .... 26.12
Merchant Shipping (Hours of Work: Inland
Waterways) Regulations 2003, SI 2003/3049
.... 27.8, 55.32
Merchant Shipping (Hours of Work) Regulations
2002, SI 2002/2125 .... 27.8, 55.31
reg 3(1) 55.31
    18(1) 55.31
Merchant Shipping (Working Time: Inland
Waterways) Regulations 2003, SI 2003/3049
.... 52.3, 55.23

N

National Minimum Wage (Offshore Employment)
Order 1999, SI 1999/1128 .... 32.10
National Minimum Wage Regulations 1999, SI
1999/584 .... 55.5
reg 2(2) 32.10
    3–6 .... 32.9
    9 .... 32.9
    10 .... 32.9
    12(2) 13.2, 32.10
    (4A) 32.9
    (7)–(16) 32.9
    13 .... 13.7
    (1)–(3) 32.9
    15(1A) 32.12
    16(1A) 32.12
    28 .... 32.12
    30–37 .... 32.9
    38(1), (2) 32.11

National Minimum Wage Regulations 1999
(Amendment) Regulations 2000, SI
2000/1989
reg 31 .... 32.12
Noise at Work Regulations 1989, SI 1989/1790
.... 26.19
Notices to Quit, etc (Prescribed Information)
Regulations 1988, SI 1988/2201
.... 41.4, 41.5
Notification of New Substances Regulations 1993,
SI 1993/3050 .... 26.26

O

Occupational and Personal Pension Schemes
(Consultation by Employers and
Miscellaneous Amendment) Regulations
2006, SI 2006/349 .... 51.11
reg 12(2)(a) 47.12
    (3) 47.12
    13(2) 47.12
Schedule
para 2, 3 .... 47.12
    5 .... 52.3
    (3) 52.11
    (5), (6) 52.11
Occupational Pension Schemes (Automatic
Enrolment) Regulations 2010, SI 2010/772
reg 9 .... 40.11
    17 .... 40.11
Occupational Pension Schemes (Disclosure of
Information) Regulations 1986, SI
1986/1046 .... 9.1
Occupational Pension Schemes (Disclosure of
Information) Regulations 1996, SI
1996/1655
reg 3–6 .... 9.9
Sch 1 .... 9.9
Sch 2 .... 9.9
Sch 3 .... 9.9
Occupational Pension Schemes (Equal Access to
Membership) Amendment Regulations 1995,
SI 1995/1215 .... 21.15, 21.16
Occupational Pension Schemes (Equal Treatment)
Regulations 1995, SI 1995/3183
.... 21.18A
reg 3–7 .... 21.16
    9–12 .... 21.16
Occupational Pension Schemes (Member-
nominated Trustees and Directors)
Regulations 2006, SI 2006/714
.... 40.14, 47.10
Ordinary Statutory Paternity Pay (Adoption),
Additional Statutory Paternity Pay
(Adoption) and Statutory Adoption Pay
(Adoptions from Overseas) (Persons Abroad
and Mariners) Regulations 2010, SI
2010/150 .... 31.61

P

Parental Leave (EU Directive) Regulations 2013,
   SI 2013/283 .... 31.46

Part-time Workers (Prevention of Less Favourable
   Treatment) Regulations 2000, SI 2000/1551
   ... 11.9, 17.29, 17.33, 21.2, 22.6, 30.1, 45.1,
                                         51.11
reg 1(2) 30.4, 30.9
   (3) 30.9
   2(1) 30.15, 30.20
   (2) ,,,......................... 30.15
   (3) 30.15
      (a)–(c) 30.17
      (d) 30.17
   (4) 30.14
      (b) 32.16
   3 .... 30.13, 30.27
   (2) 30.20
   4 .... 30.13, 30.27
   (1), (2) 30.20
   5 ...... 30.23, 30.26, 30.27, 30.28, 32.18
   (1) 30.8
   (2) 30.8
      (a) 30.21
      (b) 30.22
   (3) 30.9
   (4) 30.10
   6 .... 18.9, 30.24, 30.25
   (3) 30.23
   7 .... 52.3
   (1) 30.4, 30.5, 30.24, 30.25
   (2) 30.24, 30.26, 30.27
   (3) 30.24, 52.11
   (4) 30.24
   8 .... 17.11, 17.22, 17.30
   (1) 30.26
   (2)–(5) 30.27
   (6) 30.26
   (7)(a)–(c) 30.28
   (9)–(14) 30.28
   9 .... 18.33
   11(1)–(3) 30.30
   12 .... 30.4
   13(1)–(6) 30.5
   14–16 .... 30.4
   16(1A), (1B) 30.4
   17 .... 30.6
Paternity and Adoption Leave Regulations 2002,
   SI 2002/2788 .... 31.52
reg 4(1) 31.54
   (2)(b), (c) 31.54
   (3) 31.53
   (5) 31.53
   5(1)–(4) 31.54
   6 .... 31.53
   (1)–(8) 31.54
   8–11 .... 31.59
   12 .... 6.6, 31.55, 31.59
   13 .... 31.59

Paternity and Adoption Leave Regulations 2002, SI
   2002/2788 – cont.
reg 13(1), (2) 31.55
   14 .... 31.55, 31.59
   15–17 .... 31.59
   18 .... 31.59
   19 .... 6.6, 31.59
   20 .... 31.59
   21 .... 6.6, 31.59
   22–27 .... 31.59
   29 .... 31.60, 52.3
Pension Protection Fund (Compensation)
   Regulations 2005, SI 2005/670
   .... 29.8
Pension Protection Fund and Occupational
   Pension Scheme (Levy Ceiling
   and Compensation Cap) Order 2013, SI
   2013/105 .... 29.8
Personal and Occupational Pensions Schemes
   (Pensions Ombudsman) Regulations 1996, SI
   1996/2475
reg 5 .... 40.17
Personal Protective Equipment at Work
   Regulations 1992, SI 1992/2966
reg 4 .... 26.12
   7(1) 26.12
Protection from Harassment Act 1997
   (Commencement) (No. 1) Order 1997, SI
   1997/1418 .... 10.39
Provision and Use of Work Equipment
   Regulations 1998, SI 1998/2306
reg 4 .... 26.12
   5(1) 26.12
   6–24 .... 26.12
Public Interest Disclosure (Compensation)
   Regulations 1999, SI 1999/1548
   .... 9.17
Public Interest Disclosure (Prescribed Persons)
   Order 1999, SI 1999/1549 .... 9.17

R

Race Relations Code of Practice relating to
   Employment (Appointed Day) Order 2006,
   SI 2006/630 .... 4.14
Race Relations (Complaints to Employment
   Tribunals) (Armed Forces) Regulations 1997,
   SI 1997/2161 .... 11.11
Race Relations (Prescribed Public Bodies) (No 2)
   Regulations 1994, SI 1994/1986
   .... 35.2
Race Relations (Questions and Replies) Order
   1977, SI 1977/842
   art 5 .... 12.9
   Sch 1 .... 12.9
   Sch 2 .... 12.9

Table of Statutory Instruments

Recognition and Derecognition Ballots (Qualified Persons) Order 2000, SI 2000/1306
.... 48.32

Rehabilitation of Act 1974 (Exceptions) Order 1975, SI 1975/1023 .... 16.4, 16.7
art 3, 4 .... 20.4

Rehabilitation of Offenders Act 1974 (Exceptions) (Amendment) (England and Wales) Order 2008, SI 2008/3259 .... 16.4

Rehabilitation of Offenders Act 1974 (Exceptions) (Amendment) (England and Wales) Order 2010, SI 2010/1153 .... 16.4

Reinstatement in Civil Employment (Procedure) Regulations 1944, SR & O 1944/880
.... 47.19

Reporting of Injuries, Diseases and Dangerous Occurrences Regulations 1995, SI 1995/3163
.... 25.17
reg 3–7 .... 26.1
10 .... 26.1
Sch 1 .... 26.1
Sch 2 .... 26.1
Sch 3 .... 26.1
Sch 4 .... 26.1

Right to Time Off for Study or Training Regulations 1999, SI 1999/986
.... 3.8

Right to Time Off for Study or Training Regulations 2001, SI 2001/2801
Schedule 3.8

Road Transport (Working Time) Regulations 2005, SI 2005/639 .... 55.35

Road Transport (Working Time) (Amendment) Regulations 2012, SI 2012/991
.... 55.35

S

Safeguarding Vulnerable Groups Act 2006 (Commencement No 6, Transitional Provisions and Savings) Order 2009, SI 2009/2611 .... 16.8

Safety Representatives and Safety Committees Regulations 1977, SI 1977/500
.... 4.15, 15.61, 26.20, 47.8, 47.11
reg 4(1), (2) 26.21
4A 26.21
7(1)–(3) 9.8
8(2) 26.21
9 .... 26.21
11(1)–(4) 47.9

Sex Discrimination (Amendment) Order 1988, SI 1988/249 .... 11.22

Sex Discrimination and Equal Pay (Remedies) Regulations 1993, SI 1993/2798
.... 21.2

Sex Discrimination Code of Practice Order 1985, SI 1985/387 .... 4.14

Sex Discrimination (Complaints to Employment Tribunals) (Armed Forces) Regulations 1997, SI 1997/2163 .... 11.11, 12.2

Sex Discrimination (Gender Reassignment) Regulations 1999, SI 1999/1102
.... 21.2

Sex Discrimination (Questions and Replies) Order 1975, SI 1975/2048
art 5 .... 12.9
Sch 1 .... 12.9
Sch 2 .... 12.9

Small Companies and Groups (Accounts and Directors' Report) Regulations 2008, SI 2008/409
Sch 3 .... 8.32

Social Security Act 1989 (Commencement No 5) Order 1994, SI 1994/1661 .... 31.1

Social Security (Claims and Payments) Regulations 1979, SI 1979/628
reg 25 .... 26.1

Social Security Contributions (Intermediaries) Regulations 2000, SI 2000/727
.... 44.34

Social Security Contributions (Managed Service Companies) Regulations 2007, SI 2007/2070 .... 44.35

Social Security Contributions, Statutory Maternity Pay and Statutory Sick Pay (Miscellaneous Amendments) Regulations 1996, SI 1996/777
reg 2 .... 42.7
3 .... 42.3

Stakeholder Pensions Scheme Regulations 2000, SI 2000/1403 .... 40.10

Statutory Maternity Pay (Compensation of Employers) and Miscellaneous Amendment Regulations 1994, SI 1994/1882
reg 5 .... 31.44

Statutory Maternity Pay (General) Regulations 1986, SI 1986/1960
reg 2(1), (2) 31.41
3 .... 31.39
4 .... 31.39
(3) 31.42
6 .... 31.42
7 .... 29.9, 31.43
9 .... 31.39
17 .... 31.39
21(7) 31.42
22, 23 .... 31.40
25A 31.43
27 .... 31.42
29 .... 31.42
30 .... 29.9, 31.43

Statutory Maternity Pay (Persons Aboard and Mariners) Regulations 1987, SI 1987/418
.... 31.39

Statutory Maternity Pay (Medical Evidence)
Regulations 1987, SI 1987/235
.... 31.40

Statutory Paternity Pay and Statutory Adoption
Pay (Weekly Rates) Regulations 2002, SI
2002/2818 .... 31.61

Statutory Paternity Pay and Statutory Adoption
Pay (General) Regulations 2002, SI
2002/2822 .... 31.61
reg 43 .... 29.9

Statutory Sick Pay and Statutory Maternity Pay
(Decisions) Regulations 1999, SI 1999/776
.... 31.43, 42.8

Statutory Sick Pay (General) Regulations 1982,
SI 1982/894
reg 3(3) 42.5
7 .... 42.3
9B 29.9
13 .... 42.7
15 .... 42.4, 42.5

Statutory Sick Pay (General) Amendment
Regulations 1985, SI 1985/126
.... 42.5

Statutory Sick Pay (General) Amendment
Regulations 1986, SI 1986/477
.... 42.5
reg 5 .... 45.7

Statutory Sick Pay (General) Amendment
Regulations 1996, SI 1996/3042
reg 2 .... 42.7

Statutory Sick Pay (Medical Evidence)
Regulations 1985, SI 1985/1604
.... 42.3, 42.8

Statutory Sick Pay (Small Employers' Relief)
Regulations 1991, SI 1991/428
.... 42.6

Suspension from Work (on Maternity Grounds)
Order 1994, SI 1994/2930 .... 31.11

Suspension from Work on Maternity Grounds
(Merchant Shipping and Fishing Vessels)
Order 1998 .... 1998/587 31.11

T

Teachers (Compensation for Redundancy and
Premature Retirement) Regulations 1997, SI
1997/311 .... 35.5

Teaching and Higher Education Act 1998
(Commencement No 5) Order 1999, SI
1999/987 .... 3.8

Trade Union Ballots and Elections (Independent
Scrutineer Qualifications) Order 1993, SI
1993/1909 .... 43.14, 48.14

Trade Union Recognition (Method of Collective
Bargaining) Order 2000, SI 2000/1300
.... 48.33, 48.34

Trade Unions and Employers' Association
(Amalgamations, etc) Regulations 1975, SI
1975/536 .... 48.39

Transfer of Employment (Pension Protection)
Regulations 2005, SI 2005/649
.... 50.19

Transfer of Undertakings (Protection of
Employment) Regulations 1981, SI
1981/1794 ... 12.2, 15.6, 17.28, 18.33, 37.6,
51.20, 52.3
reg 5(1) 39.3
10, 11 .... 53.18

Transfer of Undertakings (Protection of
Employment) Regulations 2006, SI 2006/246
. 5.12, 7.31, 8.42, 9.1, 12.2, 18.6, 22.2, 22.9,
24.7, 46.1, 47.2, 48.19, 50.1, 51.20, 52.3
reg 2(1) 50.3, 50.13
3(1)(a) 50.3, 50.5
(b) 50.3
(3)(a), (b) 50.3
(4)(a), (b) 50.6
(5) 35.2, 35.5, 50.9
(6)(a) 50.7
(b) 50.8
4 .... 50.11, 50.15
(1) 39.3, 50.14
(2) 50.18
(a) 36.5
(3) 50.12, 50.14
(4), (5) 50.29
(6) 50.19
(7) 39.3, 50.16
(8) 50.16
(9) 50.16, 50.25
(10) 50.16
(11) 50.16, 50.25
5(b) 50.20
6 .... 50.21
7 .... 50.11, 50.14
(1)(a), (b) 50.26, 52.3
(3) 50.26
(b) 52.14
(4) 50.26
8(1), (2) 50.11
(3) 29.10, 50.11
(4), (5) 50.11
(6) 29.10, 50.11
(7) 6.9, 19.2, 29.10, 50.11
9 .... 29.10
10 .... 40.5, 50.19
11 .... 9.6, 29.10
(4) 50.22
(5) 17.9
(6) 50.22
12 .... 9.6, 17.11, 29.10, 50.22
13 .. 9.6, 15.15, 15.61, 29.10, 47.12, 50.22
(1) 50.23
(2) 50.23
(2A) 50.23
(3)(b) 50.23

Table of Statutory Instruments

Transfer of Undertakings (Protection of
Employment) Regulations 2006, SI 2006/246
– *cont.*

reg 13(4) 18.23, 50.23
(5), (6) 50.23
(9) 50.23
(11) 50.23
14 .... 9.6, 15.15, 47.12, 50.22
15 .... 9.6, 15.15, 17.11, 47.12, 50.22
(1) 50.23
(3), (4) 50.23
(5) 18.23, 50.23
(7) 50.23
(9), (10) 50.23
(12) 17.33, 50.23
16 .... 9.6, 15.15, 50.22
(3) 50.23
18 .... 18.33, 50.28

Sch 5
para 1 .... 40.5

Transnational Information and Consultation of
Employees Regulations 1999, SI 1999/3323
.... 51.11

reg 5(1) 15.25
6(1)(b) 15.24
(2)–(4) 15.24
7 .... 15.24, 15.29
8 .... 15.24
9(1)–(3) 15.25
(5) 17.25
10 .... 15.25
11 .... 15.26
12(2) 15.26
(4) 15.26
13–15 .... 15.26
16(1) 15.26
(1A) 15.26
(2), (3) 15.26
17(1) 15.26
(3)–(6) 15.27
(9) 15.27
18, 18A 15.27
19A 15.27
19B 15.27, 47.14
19C–19F 15.27
20, 21 .... 15.27
22(2) 15.27
23(1)–(7) 15.28
24 .... 15.28
25 .... 15.27, 15.29, 47.14
26, 27 .... 15.29, 47.14
28 .... 15.29
(3) 52.11
(6) 52.3, 52.11
31(5), (6) 15.29
32 .... 15.29
38(8) 15.27
39(1) 15.27
41 .... 15.29
44–45A 15.23

Transnational Information and Consultation of Employees Regulations 1999, SI 1999/3323 –
cont.
Schedule
para 7(3), (4) 15.27

Transnational Information and Consultation of
Employees (Amendment) Regulations 2010,
SI 2010/1088 .... 15.23, 22.12

U

Unfair Dismissal and Statement of Reasons for
Dismissal (Variation of Qualifying Period)
Order 1999, SI 1999/1436 .... 6.1

Unfair Dismissal and Statement of Reasons for
Dismissal (Variation of Qualifying Period)
Order 2012, SI 2012/989 .. 6.1, 24.3, 46.14,
51.11

Unregistered Companies Regulations 2009, SI
2009/2436 .... 8.31

W

Wages Act 1986 (Commencement) Order 1986, SI
1986/1998 .... 32.3

Welfare Reform and Pensions Act 1999
(Commencement No 2) Order 1999, SI
1999/3420 .... 44.35

Working Time Regulations 1998, SI 1998/1833
. 4.6, 5.14, 7.26, 14.1, 14.4, 14.6, 14.9, 19.2,
22.14, 23.3, 23.9, 26.15, 27.1, 27.3B, 27.8,
27.9, 32.6, 52.11, 55.24, 55.27, 55.38

reg 2(1) ... 27.2, 55.3, 55.4, 55.5, 55.9, 55.14, 55.33
4(1) 55.6, 55.7, 55.8, 55.21
(2) 55.6, 55.7, 55.21, 55.23
(3), (4) 55.6
(5) 55.6, 55.29
(6), (7) 55.6
5 .... 55.37
5(2), (3) 55.7
5A 3.6
(2) 55.6
(4) 55.21
6(1) 55.10, 55.37
(2) 55.10, 55.21
(3)–(5) 55.10
(7) 55.11, 55.21
(8) 55.11
6A 3.6, 55.10
7 .... 55.37
(1) 55.12, 55.21
(2) 3.6, 55.12, 55.21
(4), (5) 55.12
(6) 55.13, 55.21
8 .... 55.18, 55.21
9 .... 55.7, 57.8, 55.13, 55.21
10(1) 55.15, 55.22
(2) 3.6, 55.15, 55.22

Working Time Regulations 1998, SI 1998/1833 –
  cont.
reg 10(3) 55.15
  11(1), (2) 55.16, 55.22
  (3) 3.6, 55.16, 55.22
  (4) 55.16
  (6)–(8) 55.16
  12 .... 55.18, 55.29
  (1)–(3) 55.17
  (4) 3.6, 55.17, 55.22
  (5) 55.6, 55.17
  13 .... 3.2, 27.6, 55.19
  (1) 27.2, 55.22
  (3) 27.3
  (5) 27.3
  (7), (8) 27.2
  (9) 27.3A
  (a), (b) 27.3
  13A 27.3A
  (2), (3) 27.3
  (5), (6) 27.3
  (7) 27.3, 27.6
  14(2) 55.22
  (3), (4) 27.4a
  (5) **27.4a**
  15(1) 27.3A, 27.5
  15(2)–(5) 27.5
  16 .... 27.4a
  (1) 55.22
  (4), (5) 27.4
  18 .... 55.3
  (1)(b) 55.31
  (c) 55.32
  (2)(b) 55.33
  19 .... 3.6, 55.30
  20(1) 55.28
  (2) 28.15, 55.2, 55.6, 55.28
  21 ...... 55.15, 55.16, 55.17, 55.29, 55.36
  22(1) 55.16
  (a) 55.15
  (c) 55.15
  23 ...... 55.10, 55.11, 55.15, 55.16, 55.17
  (b) 57.6
  24 ...... 55.4, 55.15, 55.16, 55.21, 55.22,
                                  55.34

Working Time Regulations 1998, SI 1998/1833 –
  cont.
reg 24(b) 55.17
  24A 55.16, 55.21, 55.22, 55.29, 55.34
  (3) 55.15
  25 .... 55.22
  (2), (3) 3.6
  25A, 25B 55.6
  26A 27.3
  27 .... 55.15, 55.17, 55.22
  (2) 3.6
  27A 55.10
  (1)–(3) 3.6
  (4)(a) 55.21
  (b) 3.6
  28 .... 55.20
  29 .... 55.21
  29A–29E 55.20, 55.21
  30 ... 3.6, 17.9, 17.11, 17.31, 55.22, 55.35
  (1)(a), (b) 27.6, 55.22
  (2), (3) 27.6
  (4), (5) 27.4a, 27.6
  31 .... 17.11
  32 .... 17.11
  35 .... 18.33, 55.25
  (1)(a) 27.4a
  35A 55.1, 55.26
  36 .... 55.3, 55.37
  37–42 .... 55.3
  43 .... 55.19
  Sch 1 .... 52.3, 53.18
  para 3 .... 55.4
  Sch 2 .... 55.19
  Sch 3 .... 55.20, 55.21

Working Time (Amendment) Regulations 2002,
  SI 2002/3128 .... 3.6
Working Time (Amendment) Regulations 2006,
  SI 2006/99 .... 55.2
Working Time (Amendment No 2) Regulations
  2006, SI 2006/2389 .... 55.3
Workplace (Health, Safety and Welfare)
  Regulations 1992, SI 1992/3004
                                    22.10
reg 4–25 .... 26.29

Table of Cases

A

A v B [2003] IRLR 405, [2003] All ER (D) 184 (May), EAT 52.10
A v B (UKEAT/0206/09/SM) [2010] ICR 849, [2010] IRLR 844, [2010] All ER (D) 40 (Nov)
.... 12.11, 18.18, 18.19, 19.26, 28.7
A v B and C (employment appeal: strike out) [2010] EWCA Civ 1378, [2011] ICR D9, [2010] All ER
(D) 101 (Dec) 12.8, 18.17
A v Chief Constable of West Yorkshire Police [2002] EWCA Civ 1584, [2003] 1 All ER 255,
[2003] 1 CMLR 782, [2003] ICR 161, [2003] IRLR 32, [2002] 3 FCR 751, [2003] 1 FLR 223,
[2003] Fam Law 98, [2003] 01 LS Gaz R 24, (2002) Times, 14 November, 146 Sol Jo LB 254,
[2002] All ER (D) 50 (Nov); affd on other grounds [2004] UKHL 21, [2005] 1 AC 51, [2004]
3 All ER 145, [2004] 2 WLR 1209, [2004] 2 CMLR 884, [2004] ICR 806, [2004] IRLR 573,
[2004] 2 FCR 160, [2004] 20 LS Gaz R 34, [2004] NLJR 734, (2004) Times, 7 May, 148 Sol Jo LB
572, 17 BHRC 585, [2004] All ER (D) 47 (May) 10.21, 11.5, 28.4
A v Company B Ltd [1997] IRLR 405, 577 IRLB 8 .... 7.46
A & G Tuck Ltd v Bartlett [1994] ICR 379, [1994] IRLR 162, EAT 50.14
A Dakri & Co Ltd v Tiffen [1981] ICR 256, [1981] IRLR 57, EAT 36.8
A Schroeder Music Publishing Co Ltd v Macaulay [1974] 3 All ER 616, [1974] 1 WLR 1308, 118
Sol Jo 734, HL 39.9, 39.10
A T Poeton (Gloucester Plating) Ltd v Horton [2001] FSR 169, [2000] ICR 1208, [2000] IP & T
1064, [2000] All ER (D) 748, CA 39.13
AB v CD [2001] IRLR 808, [2001] All ER (D) 354 (May) 48.14
AB v Ministry of Defence (UKEAT/0101/09) [2010] ICR 54, [2009] All ER (D) 135 (Sep) 18.51,
35.7
AB v South West Water Services Ltd [1993] QB 507, [1993] 1 All ER 609, [1993] 2 WLR 507,
[1993] NLJR 235, [1993] PIQR P 167, CA 12.18
ABN AMRO Management Services Ltd v Hogben (UKEAT/0266/09/DM) (20 November 2009,
unreported) 18.17
ADI (UK) Ltd v Willer [2001] EWCA Civ 971, [2001] 3 CMLR 139, [2001] IRLR 542,
[2001] All ER (D) 237 (Jun) 50.5
AGCO Ltd v Massey Ferguson Works Pension Trust Ltd [2003] EWCA Civ 1044, [2004] ICR 15,
[2003] IRLR 783, [2003] 35 LS Gaz R 37, (2003) Times, 24 July, 147 Sol Jo LB 1085, [2003]
OPLR 199, [2003] All ER (D) 292 (Jul) 40.1
AGR Regeling v Bestuur van der Bedrijfsvereniging voor de Metaallnijverheid: C-125/97
[1998] ECR I-4493, [1999] 1 CMLR 1410, [1999] ICR 605, [1999] IRLR 379, [1998] All ER (D)
336, ECJ 29.5
ALM Medical Services Ltd v Bladon [2002] EWCA Civ 1085, [2002] ICR 1444, [2002] IRLR 807,
(2002) Times, 29 August, [2002] All ER (D) 400 (Jul) 18.7
Aalders v M-Choice UK Ltd (UKEAT/0227/11/DA) [2011] All ER (D) 145 (Oct) 17.23
Abadeh v British Telecommunications plc [2001] ICR 156, [2000] All ER (D) 1456, EAT 10.26
Abbey Life Assurance Co Ltd v Tansell. See MHC Consulting Services Ltd v Tansell
Abbey National plc v Formoso [1999] IRLR 222, EAT 10.31, 12.15
Abbott v Cheshire & Wirral Partnership NHS Trust [2006] EWCA Civ 523, [2006] ICR 1267,
[2006] IRLR 546, (2006) Times, 10 May, 150 Sol Jo LB 471, [2006] All ER (D) 32 (Apr) . 10.34, 21.11
Abdoulaye v Régie nationale des usines Renault SA: C-218/98 [1999] ECR I-5723, [2001] 2 CMLR
372, [2001] ICR 527, [1999] IRLR 811, [1999] All ER (D) 1014, ECJ 21.14
Abdulla v Birmingham City Council [2010] EWHC 3303 (QB), [2011] IRLR 309, [2010] All ER (D)
217 (Dec); affd [2011] EWCA Civ 1412, [2012] 2 All ER 591, [2012] ICR 20, [2012] IRLR 116,
[2011] NLJR 1706, 155 Sol Jo (no 46) 31, [2011] All ER (D) 210 (Nov); affd [2012] UKSC 47,
[2013] 1 All ER 649, [2012] ICR 1419, [2012] NLJR 1377, (2012) Times, 05 November,
[2012] All ER (D) 229 (Oct) 17.28, 21.19E
Abegaze v Shrewsbury College of Arts and Technology [2009] EWCA Civ 96, [2010] IRLR 238,
[2009] All ER (D) 209 (Feb) 12.16, 18.17, 18.54

Table of Cases

Abegaze v South East Essex College [2006] ICR 468, [2005] All ER (D) 49 (Nov), EAT 12.7
Abellio London Ltd (formerly Travel London Ltd) v Musse (UKEAT/0283/11/CEA, UKEAT/0631/11/CEA) [2012] IRLR 360, EAT 50.16
Abels v Administrative Board of the Bedrijfsvereniging voor de Metaalindustrie en de Electrotechnische Industrie: 135/83 [1985] ECR 469, [1987] 2 CMLR 406, ECJ 50.11
Abendshine v Sunderland City Council [2012] ICR 1087 .... 21.21
Abercrombie v Aga Rangemaster Ltd [2013] ICR 213, [2013] IRLR 13, [2012] NLJR 1401, [2012] All ER (D) 334 (Oct), EAT 32.24
Aberdeen Steak Houses Group plc v Ibrahim [1988] ICR 550, [1988] IRLR 420, [1988] NLJR 151, EAT 18.52
Abernethy v Mott, Hay and Anderson [1974] ICR 323, [1974] IRLR 213, 118 Sol Jo 294, CA 52.1
Abler v Sodexho MM Catering Betriebsgesellschaft mbH: C-340/01 [2003] ECR I-14023, [2004] IRLR 168, [2003] All ER (D) 277 (Nov), ECJ 50.5
Abrahams v Performing Rights Society [1995] ICR 1028, [1995] IRLR 486, CA 46.9, 56.21, 56.26
Abrahamsson v Fogelqvist: C-407/98 [2000] ECR I-5539, [2002] ICR 932, [2000] IRLR 732, ECJ 11.10
Accurist Watches Ltd v Wadher [2009] All ER (D) 189 (Apr), EAT 17.30
Ackinclose v Gateshead Metropolitan Borough Council [2005] IRLR 79, [2004] All ER (D) 397 (Oct), EAT 50.20
Adams v British Airways plc [1996] IRLR 574, CA 5.9
Adams v Hackney London Borough Council [2003] IRLR 402, [2003] All ER (D) 54 (Feb), EAT 48.37, 49.14, 49.18
Adams v Harwich International Port Ltd (ET/1503084/10), unreported 27.3A
Adams v Lancashire County Council [1997] ICR 834, sub nom Adams v Lancashire County Council and Bet Catering Services Ltd [1997] IRLR 436, CA 50.19
Adams and Raynor v West Sussex County Council [1990] ICR 546, [1990] IRLR 215, [1990] 17 LS Gaz R 32, EAT 19.38
Adamson v B & L Cleaning Services Ltd [1995] IRLR 193, EAT 7.16
Adamson v Swansea University (UKEAT/0486/09/ZT) [2010] All ER (D) 38 (May) 18.50, 19.24
Adcock v Coors Brewers Ltd [2007] EWCA Civ 19, [2007] ICR 983, [2007] All ER (D) 190 (Jan), sub nom Coors Brewers Ltd v Adcock [2007] IRLR 440 .... 17.11, 32.6
Addis v Gramophone Co Ltd [1909] AC 488, 78 LJKB 1122, [1908–10] All ER Rep 1, 101 LT 466, HL 53.12, 56.29
Addison v Babcock FATA Ltd [1988] QB 280, [1987] 2 All ER 784, [1987] 3 WLR 122, [1987] ICR 805, 131 Sol Jo 538, [1987] LS Gaz R 1409, sub nom Babcock FATA Ltd v Addison [1987] IRLR 173, [1987] 1 FTLR 505, CA 53.13
Addison v Denholm Ship Management (UK) Ltd [1997] ICR 770, [1997] IRLR 389, EAT 51.15
Adebayo v Dresdner Kleinwort Wasserstein Ltd [2005] IRLR 514, [2005] All ER (D) 371 (Mar), EAT 12.3
Adegbuji v Meteor Parking Ltd (2011) UKEATPA/1570/09/LA, [2011] All ER (D) 39 (Dec) 18.76, 19.34
Adekeye v Post Office [1993] ICR 464, [1993] IRLR 324, EAT 12.6
Adekeye v Post Office (No 2). See Post Office v Adekeye
Adeneler v Ellinikos Organismos Galaktos: C-212/04 [2006] ECR I-6057, [2007] All ER (EC) 82, [2006] 3 CMLR 867, [2006] IRLR 716, [2006] All ER (D) 25 (Jul), ECJ 22.2, 45.9
Aderemi v London and South Eastern Railway Ltd (2012) UKEAT/0316/12/KN, [2013] ICR 591, [2013] EqLR 198, [2013] All ER (D) 201 (Feb), EAT 10.26
Adin v Sedco Forex International Resources Ltd [1997] IRLR 280, Ct of Sess 7.22b
Adlington v British Bakeries (Northern) Ltd. See British Bakeries (Northern) Ltd v Adlington
Adult Learning Inspectorate v Beloff (UKEAT/0238/07/RN) [2008] All ER (D) 254 (Jan) 35.2
Advantage Business Systems Ltd v Hopley (James) [2007] EWHC 1783 (QB), [2007] All ER (D) 399 (Jul) 39.7, 39.8
Affleck v Newcastle Mind [1999] ICR 852, [1999] IRLR 405, EAT 18.24
Afolabi v Southwark London Borough Council [2003] EWCA Civ 15, [2003] ICR 800, [2003] IRLR 220, [2003] 11 LS Gaz R 32, (2003) Times, 30 January, 147 Sol Jo LB 115, [2003] All ER (D) 217 (Jan) 12.7, 17.30
Afolayan v MRCS Ltd [2009] EWCA Civ 796, [2009] All ER (D) 256 (Jul) 19.43
Agard v Westminster Kingsway College (UKEATPA/0767/10/SM) (14 December 2010, unreported) 32.35
Agrico UK Ltd v Ireland (EATS/0042/05) (25 November 2005, unreported) 17.25

Ahmed v Amnesty International [2009] ICR 1450, [2009] NLJR 1400, [2009] All ER (D) 140 (Sep),
  sub nom Amnesty International v Ahmed [2009] IRLR 884, (2009) Times, 6 October, EAT . 10.17, 51.7
Ahmed v United Kingdom (Application 22954/93) (1998) 29 EHRR 1, [1999] IRLR 188, (1998)
  Times, 2 October, 5 BHRC 111, ECtHR 35.5
Ahsan v Watt (formerly Carter). See Watt (formerly Carter) v Ahsan
Ainsworth v Glass Tubes and Components Ltd [1977] ICR 347, [1977] IRLR 74, EAT 21.9
Ainsworth v IRC [2005] EWCA Civ 441, [2005] IRLR 465, [2005] NLJR 744, (2005) Times, 16 May
  , [2005] All ER (D) 328 (Apr), sub nom IRC v Ainsworth [2005] ICR 1149; revsd sub nom
  Revenue and Customs Comrs v Stringer (sub nom Ainsworth v IRC) [2009] UKHL 31, [2009]
  4 All ER 1205, [2009] ICR 985, [2009] IRLR 677, (2009) Times, 15 June, [2009] All ER (D) 168
  (Jun) 17.9, 17.31, 27.6, 32.6, 55.22
Air Canada v Secretary of State for Trade [1983] 2 AC 394, [1983] 2 WLR 494, 126 Sol Jo 709, sub
  nom Air Canada v Secretary of State for Trade (No 2) [1983] 1 All ER 161, CA; affd [1983] 2 AC
  394, [1983] 1 All ER 910, sub nom Air Canada v Secretary of State for Trade [1983] 2 WLR 494,
  127 Sol Jo 205, HL 35.7
Airfix Footwear Ltd v Cope [1978] ICR 1210, [1978] IRLR 396, 13 ITR 513, EAT 14.3
Aitken v Comr of Police of the Metropolis [2011] EWCA Civ 582, [2012] ICR 78, (2011) Times,
  24 June, [2011] All ER (D) 165 (May) 10.15
Ajayi v Aitch Care Homes (London) Ltd (2012) UKEAT/0464/11/JOJ, [2012] All ER (D) 73 (Jun),
  EAT 55.24
Akavan Erityisalojen Keskusliitto AEK ry v Fujitsu Siemens Computers Oy: C-44/08
  [2010] 1 CMLR 309, [2010] ICR 444, [2009] IRLR 944, [2009] All ER (D) 69 (Sep), ECJ 37.4
Akinmolasire v Camden and Islington Mental Health & Social Care Trust [2004] EWCA Civ 1351,
  [2004] All ER (D) 59 (Oct) 12.8
Ako v Rothschild Asset Management Ltd [2002] EWCA Civ 236, [2002] 2 All ER 693, [2002] ICR
  899, [2002] IRLR 348, [2002] 17 LS Gaz R 36, (2002) Times, 2 April, [2002] All ER (D) 07
  (Mar) 7.45, 18.27
Akrif v Alitalia Airport Spa. See Alitalia Airport Spa v Akhrif
Al Jumard v Clywd Leisure Ltd [2008] IRLR 345, [2008] All ER (D) 231 (Feb), EAT 12.16
Alabaster v Woolwich plc [2000] ICR 1037, [2000] All ER (D) 507, EAT; revsd sub nom Alabaster
  v Barclays Bank plc and Secretary of State for Social Security [2005] EWCA Civ 508, [2005]
  IRLR 576, (2005) Times, 27 May, 149 Sol Jo LB 579, [2005] All ER (D) 02 (May), sub nom
  Alabaster v Barclays Bank plc (formerly Woolwich plc) [2005] ICR 1246; refd Alabaster v
  Woolwich plc and Secretary of State for Social Security: C-147/02 [2004] ECR I-3101,
  [2005] All ER (EC) 490, [2004] 2 CMLR 186, [2005] ICR 695, [2004] IRLR 486, [2004] All ER
  (D) 558 (Mar), ECJ 21.9, 21.14, 22.2
Alade v Secretary of State for Trade and Industry [2007] All ER (D) 08 (May), EAT 29.4
Alam v Secretary of State for the Department for Work and Pensions [2010] ICR 665, [2010] IRLR
  283, [2009] All ER (D) 174 (Nov), EAT 11.9A
Alamo Group (Europe) Ltd v Tucker [2003] ICR 829, [2003] IRLR 266, [2003] All ER (D) 367
  (Apr), EAT 37.6
Albion Hotel (Freshwater) Ltd v Maia E Silva [2002] IRLR 200, [2001] All ER (D) 265 (Nov),
  EAT 18.52
Alboni v Ind Coope Retail Ltd [1998] IRLR 131, CA 52.14
Albron Catering BV v FNV Bondgenoten: C-242/09 [2011] 1 CMLR 1267, [2011] ICR 373, [2011]
  IRLR 76, [2010] All ER (D) 161 (Nov), ECJ 50.6
Alcan Extrusions v Yates [1996] IRLR 327, EAT 7.34, 46.1, 51.5
Alcock v Chief Constable of South Yorkshire Police [1992] 1 AC 310, [1991] 4 All ER 907, [1991] 3
  WLR 1057, 8 BMLR 37, [1992] 3 LS Gaz R 34, 136 Sol Jo LB 9, HL 25.8
Alderson v Secretary of State for Trade and Industry [2003] EWCA Civ 1767, [2004] 1 All ER 1148,
  [2004] 1 CMLR 1180, [2004] LGR 389, [2004] ICR 512, [2004] 03 LS Gaz R 33, (2003) Times,
  12 December, 147 Sol Jo LB 784, [2003] All ER (D) 137 (Dec) 50.4
Aldred v Nacanco [1987] IRLR 292, CA 54.2
Alemo-Herron v Parkwood Leisure Ltd [2010] EWCA Civ 24, [2010] 2 CMLR 1221, [2010] ICR
  793, [2010] IRLR 298, (2010) Times, 15 February, 154 Sol Jo (no 5) 28, [2010] All ER (D) 193
  (Jan); on appeal sub nom Parkwood Leisure Ltd v Alemo-Herron [2011] UKSC 26, [2011]
  4 All ER 800, [2011] ICR 920, [2011] IRLR 696, [2011] All ER (D) 86 (Jun) 5.12, 50.20
Alexander v Home Office [1988] 2 All ER 118, [1988] 1 WLR 968, [1988] ICR 685, [1988] IRLR
  190, 132 Sol Jo 1147, CA 12.13
Alexander v Jarvis Hotels plc (EATS/0062/05) (30 May 2006, unreported) 55.5
Alexander v Standard Telephones and Cables Ltd (No 2) [1991] IRLR 286 . . . . 5.7, 56.19, 56.25

Table of Cases

Alexander v Standard Telephones and Cables plc [1990] ICR 291, [1990] IRLR 55 .... 7.42, 7.43
Alexanders Holdings Ltd v Methven (EAT/782/93) (17 February 1994, unreported) 17.25
Algemene Transport-en Expeditie Onderneming van Gend en Loos NV v Nederlandse
  Belastingadministratie: 26/62 [1963] ECR 1, [1963] CMLR 105, ECJ 22.2
Ali v Christian Salvesen Food Services Ltd [1997] 1 All ER 721, [1997] ICR 25, [1997] IRLR 17,
  140 Sol Jo LB 231, sub nom Christian Salvesen Food Services Ltd v Ali [1996] 41 LS Gaz R 29,
  CA 5.10
Ali v Office of National Statistics [2004] EWCA Civ 1363, [2005] IRLR 201, 148 Sol Jo LB 1250,
  [2004] All ER (D) 274 (Oct) 12.8, 17.17, 18.10
Ali v Southwark London Borough Council [1988] ICR 567, [1988] IRLR 100 .... 7.42
Alidair Ltd v Taylor [1978] ICR 445, sub nom Taylor v Alidair Ltd [1978] IRLR 82, 13 ITR 180, 121
  Sol Jo 758, CA 52.6
Allan v Newcastle-upon-Tyne City Council [2005] ICR 1170, [2005] IRLR 504, [2005] NLJR 619,
  [2005] All ER (D) 197 (Apr), EAT 12.18, 17.28
Allan Janes LLP v Johal (Balraj) [2006] EWHC 286 (Ch), [2006] ICR 742, [2006] IRLR 599, [2006]
  NLJR 373, [2006] All ER (D) 345 (Feb) 39.3, 39.5, 39.8
Allaway v Reilly [2007] IRLR 864 .... 10.58, 12.2
Allders Department Stores Ltd, Re [2005] EWHC 172 (Ch), [2005] 2 All ER 122, [2005] ICR 867,
  [2006] 2 BCLC 1, [2005] DCC 209, (2005) Times, 2 March, [2005] All ER (D) 231 (Feb) 29.11
Allen v Amalgamated Construction Co Ltd: C-234/98 [2000] All ER (EC) 97, [1999] ECR I-8643,
  [2000] 1 CMLR 1, [2000] IRLR 119, 632 IRLB 2, ECJ 50.6
Allen v GMB [2008] EWCA Civ 810, [2008] ICR 1407, [2008] IRLR 690, (2008) Times,
  1 September, 152 Sol Jo (no 29) 30, [2008] All ER (D) 207 (Jul) 11.9, 21.12, 49.2
Allen v National Australia Group Europe Ltd [2004] IRLR 847, [2004] All ER (D) 13 (Sep) 45.9
Allied Business and Financial Consultants Ltd, Re (sub nom O'Donnell v Shanahan) [2009] EWCA
  Civ 751, [2009] 2 BCLC 666, [2009] BCC 822, (2009) Times, 21 August, [2009] All ER (D) 253
  (Jul) 8.19
Allied Dunbar (Frank Weisinger) Ltd v Weisinger [1988] IRLR 60 .... 39.8, 39.10
Allma Construction Ltd v Bonner (UKEATS/0060/09) [2011] IRLR 204 .... 2.4, 12.10, 18.32
Allonby v Accrington and Rossendale College [2001] EWCA Civ 529, [2001] 2 CMLR 559, [2001]
  ICR 1189, [2001] IRLR 364, [2001] ELR 679, [2001] All ER (D) 285 (Mar); refd: C-256/01
  [2004] ECR I-873, [2005] All ER (EC) 289, [2004] 1 CMLR 1141, [2004] ICR 1328, [2004] IRLR
  224, [2004] All ER (D) 47 (Jan), ECJ 10.34, 11.9, 11.24, 21.9, 21.16, 21.18, 22.2
Allsop v Christiani & Neilsen Ltd (UKEAT/0241/11), unreported 32.6
Alvarez v Sesa Start Espana ETT SA: C-104/09 [2010] ECR I-8661, [2011] All ER (EC) 253,
  [2011] 1 CMLR 861, [2010] NLJR 1531, [2010] All ER (D) 277 (Oct), ECJ 31.51, 31.52, 31.58
Amber Size and Chemical Co Ltd v Menzel [1913] 2 Ch 239, 82 LJ Ch 573, 30 RPC 433, 57 Sol Jo
  627, 109 LT 520, 29 TLR 590 .... 39.13
American Cyanamid Co v Ethicon Ltd [1975] AC 396, [1975] 1 All ER 504, [1975] 2 WLR 316,
  [1975] FSR 101, [1975] RPC 513, 119 Sol Jo 136, HL 7.43, 39.17
Amery v. Perth and Kinross Council [2012] CSIH 11 .... 21.21
Amey Services Ltd v Cardigan [2008] IRLR 279 .... 18.8, 21.21
Amicus v City Building (Glasgow) LLP [2009] IRLR 253, EAT 50.23
Amicus v Dynamex Friction Ltd [2008] EWCA Civ 381, [2009] ICR 511, [2008] IRLR 515,
  [2008] All ER (D) 251 (Apr) 50.26
Amicus v GBS Tooling Ltd (in administration) [2005] IRLR 683, [2005] All ER (D) 267 (Jun),
  EAT 37.6
Amicus v Macmillan Publishers Ltd [2007] IRLR 378 .... 9.10, 15.20
Amicus v Macmillan Publishers Ltd [2007] IRLR 885, [2007] All ER (D) 121 (Aug), EAT . 9.10, 15.20
Amnesty International v Ahmed. See Ahmed v Amnesty International
Anandarajah v Lord Chancellor's Department [1984] IRLR 131, EAT 34.2
Anar v Dresdner Kleinwort Ltd [2011] EWCA Civ 229, [2011] All ER (D) 88 (Mar) 7.2, 7.13
Anderson v Dalkeith Engineering Ltd [1985] ICR 66, [1984] IRLR 429, EAT 50.26
Anderson v London Fire and Emergency Planning Authority [2013] EWCA Civ 321, [2013] All ER
  (D) 47 (Apr) 5.9
Anderson v Pringle of Scotland Ltd [1998] IRLR 64, 1998 SLT 754, OH 7.42
Anderson v South Tyneside Metropolitan Borough Council [2007] All ER (D) 410 (Mar), EAT; affd
  sub nom South Tyneside Metropolitan Borough Council v Anderson [2007] EWCA Civ 654,
  [2008] LGR 507, [2007] ICR 1581, [2007] IRLR 715, [2007] All ER (D) 373 (Jun) . 21.9, 21.12, 21.19B,
                                                                                        35.5

Andreou v Lord Chancellor's Department [2002] EWCA Civ 1192, [2002] IRLR 728, [2002] All ER
    (D) 309 (Jul) 18.54, 28.7
Andrew v Eden College (UKEAT/0438/10) [2011] All ER (D) 08 (Oct) 18.73
Andrews v Cunningham [2007] EWCA Civ 762, [2008] HLR 185, [2007] All ER (D) 343 (Jul)
    .... 41.5
Andrews v King (Inspector of Taxes) [1991] STC 481, [1991] ICR 846, 135 Sol Jo LB 84 .... 7.4, 14.3
Andrews v Kings College Hospital NHS Foundation Trust [2012] EqLR 1032 .... 21.18
Andrews v Software 2000 Ltd [2007] ICR 825, [2007] IRLR 568, [2007] All ER (D) 221 (Jan),
    EAT 53.13
Angestelltenbetriebsrat der Wiener Gebietskrankenkasse v Wiener Gebietskrankenkasse: C-309/97
    [1999] ECR I-2865, [1999] 2 CMLR 1173, [1999] IRLR 804, [1999] All ER (D) 483, ECJ . 21.6, 21.12
Anglian Home Improvements Ltd v Kelly [2004] EWCA Civ 901, [2005] ICR 242, [2004] IRLR
    793, [2004] 28 LS Gaz R 33, 148 Sol Jo LB 760, [2004] All ER (D) 149 (Jun) 18.62
Angus Council v Edgley (EAT/289/99) (28 June 1999, unreported) 26.2
Angus Jowett & Co Ltd v National Union of Tailors and Garment Workers [1985] ICR 646, [1985]
    IRLR 326, EAT 37.6
Aniagwu v Hackney London Borough Council [1999] IRLR 303, EAT 12.7, 17.30
Ankers v Clearsprings Management Ltd [2009] All ER (D) 261 (Feb), EAT 50.3
Annabel's (Berkeley Square) Ltd v Revenue and Customs Comrs [2009] EWCA Civ 361, [2009]
    4 All ER 55, [2009] STC 1551, [2009] ICR 1123, (2009) Times, 13 May, [2009] All ER (D) 54
    (May) 32.9
Annandale Engineering v Samson [1994] IRLR 59, EAT 7.24
Ansar v Lloyds TSB Bank plc [2006] EWCA Civ 1462, [2007] IRLR 211, [2006] All ER (D) 88
    (Oct) 18.50, 19.24
Anstey v G4S Justice Services (UK) Ltd [2006] IRLR 588, [2006] All ER (D) 22 (Jun), EAT
    .... 50.14
Antal International Ltd, Re [2003] EWHC 1339 (Ch), [2003] 2 BCLC 406, [2003] BPIR 1067,
    [2003] All ER (D) 56 (May) 29.11
Antclizo, The. See Food Corpn of India v Antclizo Shipping Corpn, The Antclizo
Anya v University of Oxford [2001] EWCA Civ 405 , [2001] ICR 847, [2001] IRLR 377,
    [2001] All ER (D) 266 (Mar) 12.3, 18.63
Anyanwu v South Bank Student's Union (Commission for Racial Equality, interveners) [2001]
    UKHL 14, [2001] 2 All ER 353, [2001] 1 WLR 638, [2001] ICR 391, [2001] IRLR 305, [2001]
    21 LS Gaz R 39, 151 NLJ 501, [2001] All ER (D) 272 (Mar) 10.58, 18.17
Aon Training Ltd (formerly Totalamber plc) v Dore. See Dore v Aon Training Ltd (formerly
    Totalamber plc)
Aparau v Iceland Frozen Foods plc [1996] IRLR 119, EAT; revsd [2000] 1 All ER 228, [2000] IRLR
    196, [1999] 45 LS Gaz R 31, CA 7.22e, 7.32, 19.39, 40.7
Apelogun–Gabriels v Lambeth London Borough Council [2001] EWCA Civ 1853, [2002] ICR 713,
    [2002] IRLR 116, [2001] All ER (D) 350 (Nov) 12.7, 17.30
Appiah v Bishop Douglass Roman Catholic High School [2007] EWCA Civ 10, [2007] ICR 897,
    [2007] IRLR 264, [2007] All ER (D) 240 (Jan) 12.3
Apple Corpn Ltd v Apple Computer Inc [1992] FSR 431 .... 39.9
Appleyard v F M Smith (Hull) Ltd [1972] IRLR 19, Ind Trib 52.7
Arafa v Potter. See Potter v Arafa
Arbeiterwohlfahrt der Stadt Berlin e V v Bötel: C-360/90 [1992] ECR I-3589, [1992] 3 CMLR 446,
    [1992] IRLR 423, [1993] 21 LS Gaz R 45, ECJ 21.3, 21.11
Arbuthnot Fund Managers Ltd v Rawlings [2003] EWCA Civ 518, [2003] All ER (D) 181 (Mar)
    .... 39.17
Archer v Marsh (1837) 6 Ad & El 959, 6 LJKB 244, 2 Nev & PKB 562, Will Woll & Dav 641
    .... 39.10
Archibald v Fife Council [2004] UKHL 32, [2004] 4 All ER 303, [2004] ICR 954, [2004] IRLR 651,
    [2004] 31 LS Gaz R 25, 148 Sol Jo LB 826, [2004] All ER (D) 32 (Jul) 10.37
Argyll Coastal Services Ltd v Stirling (UKEATS/0012/11) (15 February 2012, unreported) 50.3
Argyll Training Ltd v Sinclair [2000] IRLR 630, EAT 50.5
Armitage v Weir Valves and Controls (UK) Ltd [2004] ICR 371, [2003] All ER (D) 80 (Dec),
    EAT 18.16
Armour v Skeen [1977] IRLR 310, 1977 JC 15, 1977 SLT 71, HC of Justiciary (Sc) 25.38
Armstrong v Newcastle Upon Tyne NHS Hospital Trust [2005] EWCA Civ 1608, [2006] IRLR 124,
    [2005] All ER (D) 341 (Dec) 21.5, 21.9, 21.10, 21.11, 21.12
Arnold v Barnfield College [2004] All ER (D) 63 (Jul), EAT 11.10

Table of Cases

Arnold v Beecham Group Ltd [1982] ICR 744, [1982] IRLR 307, EAT 21.7
Arora v Rockwell Automation Ltd [2006] All ER (D) 112 (May), EAT 32.8
Arriva London South Ltd v Nicolaou (UKEAT/0280/10/DA) (22 November 2010, unreported)
.... 55.23
Arriva London South Ltd v Nicolaou (No 2) [2012] ICR 510, EAT 55.6, 55.8, 55.23
Arrowsmith v Nottingham Trent University [2011] EWCA Civ 797, [2012] ICR 159 .... 18.72
Arthur v A-G [1999] ICR 631, EAT 11.30
Arthur v London Eastern Rly Ltd (t/a One Stansted Express) [2006] EWCA Civ 1358, [2007] ICR
  193, [2007] IRLR 58, [2006] All ER (D) 300 (Oct) 12.6
Arthur Guinness Son & Co (Great Britain) Ltd v Green [1989] ICR 241, [1989] IRLR 288, EAT
  .... 18.64, 53.12
Arthur H Wilton Ltd v Peebles (EAT/835/93) (26 July 1994, unreported) 17.31
Artisan Press Ltd v Srawley and Parker [1986] ICR 328, [1986] IRLR 126, EAT 53.4
Aryeetey v Tuntum Housing Association [2007] All ER (D) 174 (Oct), EAT 17.25
Asda Stores Ltd v Thompson [2002] IRLR 245, [2002] All ER (D) 32 (Feb), EAT 18.12
Asda Stores Ltd v Thompson (No 2) [2004] IRLR 598, [2003] All ER (D) 434 (Nov), EAT 18.12,
  52.10
Ashburn Anstalt v Arnold [1989] Ch 1, [1988] 2 All ER 147, [1988] 2 WLR 706, 55 P & CR 137,
  [1987] 2 EGLR 71, 284 Estates Gazette 1375, [1988] 16 LS Gaz R 43, 132 Sol Jo 416, CA 41.2
Ashby v Addison (t/a Brayton News) [2003] ICR 667, [2003] IRLR 211, [2003] NLJR 145, (2003)
  Times, 24 January, [2003] All ER (D) 98 (Jan), EAT 3.2, 27.2, 55.3
Ashby v Birmingham City Council [2011] EWHC 424 (QB), [2011] IRLR 473, [2011] NLJR 405,
  (2011) Times, 18 March, [2011] All ER (D) 48 (Mar) 21.19E
Ashby v Monterry Designs Ltd (UKEAT/0226/08/CEA) (18 December 2009, unreported) 8.4
Ashcroft v Haberdashers Aske's Boys School [2008] ICR 613, [2008] IRLR 375, [2008] All ER (D)
  186 (Feb), EAT 17.25
Ashley v Ministry of Defence [1984] ICR 298, [1984] IRLR 57, EAT 47.2
Ashmore v British Coal Corpn [1990] 2 QB 338, [1990] 2 All ER 981, [1990] 2 WLR 1437, [1990]
  ICR 485, [1990] IRLR 283, CA 18.24
Ashton v Chief Constable of West Mercia Constabulary [2001] ICR 67, EAT 10.21
Asim v Nazir (UKEAT/0332/09/RN) [2010] ICR 1225, [2010] All ER (D) 113 (Aug) .. 7.4, 12.2, 12.3
Askew v Governing Body of Clifton Middle School. See Clifton Middle School Governing Body v
  Askew
Aslam v Barclays Capital Services Ltd (UKEAT/0405/10/ZT) (3 February 2011, unreported)
  .... 18.11
Aslan v Murphy [1989] 3 All ER 130, [1990] 1 WLR 766, 59 P & CR 407, 21 HLR 532,
  [1989] 2 EGLR 57, [1989] 38 EG 109, [1989] NLJR 936, CA 41.2
Asociacion Nacional de Grandes Empresas de Distribucion v Federacion de Asociaciones Sindicales:
  C-78/11 [2012] ICR 1211, [2012] IRLR 779, [2012] NLJR 912, [2012] All ER (D) 228 (Jun),
  ECJ 27.3A
Aspden v Webbs Poultry & Meat Group (Holdings) Ltd [1996] IRLR 521 .. 7.22b, 40.16, 42.13, 56.19,
  56.33
Associated British Ports v Bridgeman [2012] IRLR 639 .... 55.29
Associated British Ports v Palmer [1995] 2 AC 454, [1995] 2 All ER 100, [1995] 2 WLR 354, [1995]
  ICR 406, [1995] IRLR 258, [1995] 17 LS Gaz R 48, [1995] NLJR 417, HL 49.17
Associated Foreign Exchange Ltd v International Foreign Exchange (UK) Ltd [2010] EWHC 1178
  (Ch), [2010] IRLR 964, [2010] All ER (D) 259 (May) 7.47c, 39.8
Associated Newspapers Ltd v Wilson [1995] 2 AC 454, [1995] 2 All ER 100, [1995] 2 WLR 354,
  [1995] ICR 406, [1995] IRLR 258, [1995] 17 LS Gaz R 48, [1995] NLJR 417, HL 49.17
Associated Society of Locomotive Engineers and Firemen v United Kingdom (Application No
  11002/05) (2007) 45 EHRR 793, [2007] IRLR 361, (2007) Times, 9 March, 22 BHRC 140,
  [2007] All ER (D) 348 (Feb), ECtHR 28.4, 49.13
Association belge des Consommateurs Test-Achats ASBL v Conseil des ministres: C-236/09 [2011]
  NLJR 363, [2011] Pens LR 145, [2011] All ER (D) 07 (Mar), ECJ 40.9
Assoukou v Select Services Partners Ltd [2006] EWCA Civ 1442, [2006] All ER (D) 122 (Oct)
  .... 12.16
Astbury v Gist Ltd [2007] All ER (D) 480 (Mar), EAT 45.2c
Astle v Cheshire County Council [2005] IRLR 12, [2004] All ER (D) 134 (Jun), EAT 50.5
Astles v A G Stanley Ltd (EAT/1275/95) IDS Brief 588 .... 18.54

Astley v Celtec Ltd [2002] EWCA Civ 1035, [2002] 3 CMLR 366, [2002] ICR 1289, [2002] IRLR
629, [2002] 37 LS Gaz R 38, (2002) Times, 9 August, [2002] All ER (D) 287 (Jul); affd [2006]
UKHL 29, [2006] IRLR 635, [2006] NLJR 1061, (2006) Times, 23 June, 150 Sol Jo LB 856,
[2006] All ER (D) 219 (Jun), sub nom Astley v North Wales Training and Enterprise Council (t/a
CELTEC Ltd) [2006] 4 All ER 27, sub nom North Wales Training and Enterprise Council (t/a
CELTEC Ltd) v Astley [2006] 1 WLR 2420, [2006] ICR 992 .... 6.9, 50.12
Athinaiki Chartopoiia AE v Panagiotidis: C-270/05 [2007] ECR I-1499, [2007] IRLR 284,
[2007] All ER (D) 186 (Feb), ECJ 37.4
Atkins v Coyle Personnel plc [2008] IRLR 420, [2008] All ER (D) 108 (Feb), EAT .. 31.16, 31.60, 52.3
Atos Origin IT Services UK Ltd v Haddock [2005] ICR 277, [2005] IRLR 20, [2004] All ER (D)
369 (Oct), EAT 19.10
A-G v Barker [2000] 2 FCR 1, [2000] 1 FLR 759, [2000] 10 LS Gaz R 37, DC 18.72
A-G v Blake (Jonathan Cape Ltd third party) [2001] 1 AC 268, [2000] 4 All ER 385, [2000] 2 All ER
(Comm) 487, [2000] 3 WLR 625, [2001] IRLR 36, [2000] IP & T 1261, 144 Sol Jo LB 242, [2000]
32 LS Gaz R 37, [2000] NLJR 1230, [2000] EMLR 949, [2001] 1 LRC 260, [2000] All ER (D)
1074, HL 7.47d, 39.20
A-G v Roberts [2005] All ER (D) 138 (Jul), EAT 18.72, 18.77
A-G v Wheen [2000] IRLR 461, [2000] All ER (D) 767, EAT; affd [2001] IRLR 91, [2000] All ER
(D) 2186, CA 18.77, 28.7
A-G of Commonwealth of Australia v Adelaide Steamship Co Ltd [1913] AC 781, 83 LJPC 84, 12
Asp MLC 361, [1911–13] All ER Rep 1120, 109 LT 258, 29 TLR 743, PC 39.5
Attridge Law (a firm) v Coleman. See Coleman v Attridge Law (a firm)
Attrill v Dresdner Kleinwort Ltd; Anar v same [2012] EWHC 1189 (QB), [2012] All ER (D) 97
(May) 7.13, 7.32
Attwood v Lamont [1920] 3 KB 571, 90 LJKB 121, [1920] All ER Rep 55, 65 Sol Jo 25, 124 LT 108,
36 TLR 895, CA 39.7
Attwood Holdings Ltd v Woodward [2009] EWHC 1083 (Ch) 8.19
Auguste Noel Ltd v Curtis [1990] ICR 604, [1990] IRLR 326, EAT 52.9
Austin Knight (UK) Ltd v Hinds [1994] FSR 52 .... 39.8
Austin Rover Group Ltd v HM Inspector of Factories [1990] 1 AC 619, [1989] 3 WLR 520, [1990]
ICR 133, [1989] IRLR 404, sub nom Mailer v Austin Rover Group plc [1989] 2 All ER 1087,
HL 25.20
Australian Commercial Research and Development Ltd v ANZ McCaughan Merchant Bank Ltd
[1989] 3 All ER 65 .... 7.45
Autoclenz Ltd v Belcher. See Belcher v Autoclenz Ltd
Automatic Switching Ltd v Brunet [1986] ICR 542, EAT 18.22
Automotive Products Ltd v Peake. See Peake v Automotive Products Ltd
Avon County Council v Foxall [1989] ICR 407, [1989] IRLR 435, EAT 21.8
Avon County Council v Howlett [1983] 1 All ER 1073, [1983] 1 WLR 605, 81 LGR 555, [1983]
IRLR 171, 127 Sol Jo 173, 133 NLJ 377, CA 32.15
Avonmouth Construction Co Ltd v Shipway [1979] IRLR 14, EAT 52.11
Awotona v South Tyneside Healthcare NHS Trust [2005] EWCA Civ 217, [2005] ICR 958,
[2005] All ER (D) 221 (Feb) 53.5
Aylott v Stockton-on-Tees Borough Council (UKEAT/0401/08/CEA) [2009] ICR 872, [2009]
IRLR 533, [2009] All ER (D) 186 (Apr); revsd in part [2010] EWCA Civ 910, [2010] ICR 1278,
[2010] IRLR 994, [2010] All ER (D) 316 (Jul) 10.15, 10.37, 12.8
Aylward v Glamorgan Holiday Homes Ltd (UKEAT/167/02), unreported 36.7
Aziz v Bethnal Green City Challenge Co Ltd [2000] IRLR 111, CA 19.14
Aziz v FDA [2010] EWCA Civ 304, 154 Sol Jo (no 14) 29 .... 12.6, 17.29
Aziz v Trinity Street Taxis Ltd [1989] QB 463, [1988] 2 All ER 860, [1988] 3 WLR 79, [1988] ICR
534, [1988] IRLR 204, 132 Sol Jo 898, [1988] 26 LS Gaz R 42, CA 10.38
Azmi v Kirklees Metropolitan Borough Council [2007] ICR 1154, [2007] IRLR 484, (2007) Times,
17 April, [2007] All ER (D) 528 (Mar), EAT 10.15, 10.22, 11.9

B

B v A [2007] IRLR 576, EAT 10.17
B and C v A [2010] IRLR 400, [2009] All ER (D) 149 (Sep), EAT 12.3, 12.11, 18.18, 19.26, 28.7
BBC Scotland v Souster [2001] IRLR 150, Ct of Sess 10.20

Table of Cases

BCCI SA (in liq) v Ali (No 3) [2002] EWCA Civ 82, [2002] 3 All ER 750, [2002] ICR 1258, [2002] IRLR 460, (2002) Times, 15 February, [2002] All ER (D) 308 (Jan) 7.38
BFCA Ltd v Butt (8 February 2013, unreported) 39.4
BG plc v O'Brien [2001] IRLR 496, [2001] All ER (D) 169 (May), EAT; affd sub nom O'Brien v Transco plc (formerly BG plc) [2002] EWCA Civ 379, [2002] ICR 721, [2002] IRLR 444, [2002] All ER (D) 80 (Mar) 51.7
BGC Capital Markets (Switzerland) LLC v Rees [2011] EWHC 2009 (QB), [2011] All ER (D) 51 (Aug) 39.12
BHS Ltd v Walker (2005) IDS Brief No 787 .... 12.6
BL Cars Ltd v Brown [1983] ICR 143, [1983] IRLR 193, 80 LS Gaz R 94, EAT 10.50
BNP Paribas v Mezzotero [2004] IRLR 508, 148 Sol Jo LB 666, [2004] All ER (D) 226 (Apr), EAT 12.9, 18.13, 53.19
BP Chemicals Ltd v Gillick [1995] IRLR 128, EAT 11.24
BP plc v Elstone (UKEAT/141/09) [2011] 1 All ER 718, [2010] ICR 879, [2010] IRLR 558, [2010] All ER (D) 140 (May) 9.17
BSC Sports and Social Club v Morgan [1987] IRLR 391, EAT 46.5, 56.1
BSG Property Services v Tuck [1996] IRLR 134, EAT 50.5, 50.26
BT Fleet Ltd v McKenna [2005] EWHC 387 (Admin), (2005) Times, 5 April, [2005] All ER (D) 284 (Mar) 25.32
Babcock FATA Ltd v Addison. See Addison v Babcock FATA Ltd
Babula v Waltham Forest College [2007] EWCA Civ 174, [2007] ICR 1026, [2007] IRLR 346, (2007) Times, 17 April, 151 Sol Jo LB 396, [2007] All ER (D) 98 (Mar) 9.17
Bache v Essex County Council [2000] 2 All ER 847, [2000] IRLR 251, [2000] 05 LS Gaz R 33, [2000] NLJR 99, CA 18.40, 18.55, 18.56, 19.25, 28.7
Bachnak v Emerging Markets Partnership (Europe) Ltd (0288/05) (2006) 150 Sol Jo LB 435, [2006] All ER (D) 211 (Jan), EAT 9.17
Bacica v Muir [2006] IRLR 35, EAT 14.9
Bahl v Law Society (2003) 147 Sol Jo LB 994, [2003] All ER (D) 570 (Jul), sub nom Law Society v Bahl [2003] IRLR 640, EAT; affd sub nom Bahl v Law Society [2004] EWCA Civ 1070, [2004] IRLR 799, [2004] NLJR 1292, 148 Sol Jo LB 976, [2003] All ER (D) 570 (Jul) 10.14, 12.3, 18.63
Bahous v Pizza Express Resturant Ltd (UKEAT/0029/11/DA) (2012) IDS Brief 17, [2012] EqLR 4, [2012] All ER (D) 191 (Jan), EAT 12.7, 17.30
Bailey v BP Oil (Kent Refinery) Ltd [1980] ICR 642, [1980] IRLR 287, CA 52.10
Bailey v Home Office [2005] EWCA Civ 327, [2005] ICR 1057, [2005] IRLR 369, (2005) Times, 8 April, [2005] All ER (D) 356 (Mar) 21.11
Bailey (by her father and litigation friend) v Ministry of Defence [2008] EWCA Civ 883, [2009] 1 WLR 1052, 103 BMLR 134, (2008) Times, 26 August, [2008] All ER (D) 382 (Jul) 26.25
Bailey v R & R Plant (Peterborough) Ltd [2012] EWCA Civ 410, [2012] IRLR 503, [2012] All ER (D) 37 (Apr) 40.3
Bainbridge v Circuit Foil UK Ltd [1997] ICR 541, [1997] IRLR 305, CA 42.12
Bainbridge v Redcar and Cleveland Borough Council. See Redcar and Cleveland Borough Council v Bainbridge
Baines v Blackpool Borough Council [2008] All ER (D) 95 (Jan), EAT 21.21
Baker v Metropolitan Police Comr (UKEAT/0201/09/CEA) (2010) 899 IDS Brief 9, [2010] All ER (D) 17 (Apr) 12.8
Baker v Quantum Clothing Group Ltd [2011] UKSC 17, [2011] 17 LS Gaz R 13, 155 Sol Jo (no 15) 38, [2011] All ER (D) 137 (Apr) 26.19
Bakers' Union v Clarks of Hove Ltd. See Clarks of Hove Ltd v Bakers' Union
Balamoody v UK Central Council for Nursing, Midwifery and Health Visiting [2001] EWCA Civ 2097, [2002] ICR 646, [2002] IRLR 288, [2001] All ER (D) 80 (Dec) 10.15, 18.17
Baldwin v Brighton and Hove City Council [2007] ICR 680, [2007] IRLR 232, [2006] All ER (D) 220 (Dec), EAT 7.22d
Balfour v Foreign and Commonwealth Office [1994] 2 All ER 588, [1994] 1 WLR 681, [1994] ICR 277, [1994] 2 LRC 48, CA 18.13
Balfour Beatty Power Networks Ltd v Wilcox [2006] EWCA Civ 1240, [2007] IRLR 63, [2006] All ER (D) 275 (Jul) 18.63, 19.36, 50.5
Balfron Trustees Ltd v Peterson [2001] IRLR 758, [2002] Lloyd's Rep PN 1, [2001] NLJR 1180, [2001] All ER (D) 103 (Jul) 54.2
Balgobin v Tower Hamlets London Borough Council [1987] ICR 829, [1987] IRLR 401, [1987] LS Gaz R 2530, EAT 10.14
Ball v Street [2005] EWCA Civ 76, [2005] All ER (D) 73 (Feb) 26.12

Balls v Downham Market High School and College (UKEAT/0343/10/DM) [2011] IRLR 217,
  [2010] All ER (D) 318 (Nov) 18.17
Balston Ltd v Headline Filters Ltd [1987] FSR 330 .... 39.13
Balston Ltd v Headline Filters Ltd [1990] FSR 385 .... 7.16
Bamsey v Albion Engineering and Manufacturing plc [2004] EWCA Civ 359, [2004] 2 CMLR 1353,
  [2004] ICR 1083, [2004] IRLR 457, [2004] 17 LS Gaz R 31, (2004) Times, 15 April, 148 Sol Jo
  LB 389, [2004] All ER (D) 482 (Mar) 27.4
Bangs v Connex South Eastern Ltd [2005] EWCA Civ 14, [2005] 2 All ER 316, [2005] IRLR 389,
  (2005) Times, 15 February, 149 Sol Jo LB 148, [2005] All ER (D) 263 (Jan), sub nom Connex
  South Eastern Ltd v Bangs [2005] ICR 763 .... 17.13, 18.62, 19.37
Bank of Credit and Commerce International SA, Re [1994] IRLR 282 .... 32.14, 32.22
Bank of Credit and Commerce International SA (in liq) v Ali [1999] 4 All ER 83, [1999] IRLR 508,
  [1999] 30 LS Gaz R 28; affd [2002] EWCA Civ 82, [2002] 3 All ER 750, [2002] ICR 1258, [2002]
  IRLR 460, (2002) Times, 15 February, [2002] All ER (D) 308 (Jan) 56.29
Banking Insurance and Finance Union v Barclays Bank plc [1987] ICR 495, [1987] LS Gaz R 901,
  EAT 50.23
Banks v Lavin IDS Brief No 410, EAT 46.15
Banks v Tesco Stores Ltd [2000] 1 CMLR 400, [1999] ICR 1141, EAT 21.14
Barber v Guardian Royal Exchange Assurance Group: C-262/88 [1991] 1 QB 344, [1990] 2 All ER
  660, [1990] ECR I-1889, [1991] 2 WLR 72, [1990] 2 CMLR 513, [1990] ICR 616, [1990] IRLR
  240, [1990] NLJR 925, ECJ 21.3, 21.5, 21.15, 21.16, 21.17, 21.18a, 22.2, 40.1, 40.7
Barber v RJB Mining (UK) Ltd [1999] 2 CMLR 833, [1999] ICR 679, [1999] IRLR 308, 143 Sol Jo
  LB 141, [1999] All ER (D) 244 .... 55.8, 55.21, 55.22
Barber v Staffordshire County Council [1996] 2 All ER 748, [1996] ICR 364, [1996] IRLR 209,
  [1996] 06 LS Gaz R 26, sub nom Staffordshire County Council v Barber [1996] ICR 379, CA
  .... 7.45, 17.12, 18.17, 18.27, 22.2
Barclay v City of Glasgow District Council [1983] IRLR 313, EAT 46.5, 51.10
Barclays Bank plc v Kapur [1989] ICR 142, [1989] IRLR 57, [1989] 5 LS Gaz R 41, EAT; revsd
  [1989] ICR 753, [1989] IRLR 387, [1989] 31 LS Gaz R 44, CA; affd [1991] 2 AC 355, [1991]
  1 All ER 646, [1991] 2 WLR 401, [1991] ICR 208, [1991] IRLR 136, HL 10.50, 12.6, 17.29
Barclays Bank plc v O'Brien. See O'Brien v Barclays Bank plc
Barke v SEETEC Business Technology Centre Ltd [2005] EWCA Civ 578, [2005] ICR 1373, [2005]
  IRLR 633, (2005) Times, 26 May, [2005] All ER (D) 216 (May) 18.63, 19.22
Barking and Dagenham London Borough Council v Oguoko [2000] IRLR 179, EAT 18.58
Barlow v Stone (2012) UKEAT/0049/12/MAA, [2012] IRLR 898, [2012] All ER (D) 237 (Jun),
  EAT 10.54
Barnsley Metropolitan Borough Council v Prest [1996] ICR 85, EAT 53.9
Barracks v Coles (Secretary of State for the Home Department intervening) [2006] EWCA Civ 1041,
  [2007] ICR 60, [2007] IRLR 73, (2006) Times, 7 August, [2006] All ER (D) 310 (Jul) . 12.9, 18.12, 28.7
Barralet v A-G [1980] 3 All ER 918, sub nom South Place Ethical Society, Re, Barralet v A-G [1980]
  1 WLR 1565, 54 TC 446, [1980] TR 217, 124 Sol Jo 744 .... 10.22
Barros D'Sa v University Hospital and Warwickshire NHS Trust [2001] EWCA Civ 983, [2001]
  IRLR 691, 62 BMLR 39, [2001] All ER (D) 173 (Jun) 7.42
Barry v Midland Bank plc [1998] 1 All ER 805, [1999] ICR 319, [1998] IRLR 138, CA; affd [1999]
  3 All ER 974, [1999] 1 WLR 1465, [1999] ICR 859, [1999] IRLR 581, [1999] 31 LS Gaz R 36,
  [1999] NLJR 1253, 143 Sol Jo LB 221, HL 10.34, 21.11, 21.12
Bartholomew v Hackney London Borough Council [1999] IRLR 246, CA 38.4
Barton v Investec Henderson Crosthwaite Securities Ltd [2003] ICR 1205, [2003] IRLR 332, [2003]
  22 LS Gaz R 29, (2003) Times, 16 April, [2003] All ER (D) 61 (Apr), EAT 10.17, 12.3, 21.12
Bartsch v Bosch und Siemens Hausgerate (BSH) Altersfursorge GmbH: C-427/06 [2008] ECR I-
  7245, [2009] All ER (EC) 113, [2009] 1 CMLR 163, [2008] All ER (D) 29 (Oct), ECJ 10.10
Bascetta v Santander UK plc [2010] EWCA Civ 351, [2010] All ER (D) 219 (Oct) 52.11
Base Metal Trading Ltd v Shamurin [2003] EWHC 2419 (Comm), [2004] 1 All ER (Comm) 159,
  [2003] All ER (D) 364 (Oct); affd [2004] EWCA Civ 1316, [2005] 1 All ER (Comm) 17, [2005] 1
  WLR 1157, [2005] 2 BCLC 171, [2005] BCC 325, (2004) Times, 1 November, 148 Sol Jo LB
  1281, [2004] All ER (D) 178 (Oct) 23.7
Bass Leisure Ltd v Thomas [1994] IRLR 104, EAT 7.22e, 19.46, 36.7, 37.4
Bass Taverns Ltd v Burgess [1995] IRLR 596, CA 52.3
Batchelor v British Railways Board [1987] IRLR 136, CA 51.13
Bateman v Asda Stores Ltd (UKEAT/0221/09/ZT) [2010] IRLR 370, [2010] All ER (D) 277
  (Feb) 7.13

Table of Cases

Bates van Winkelhof v Clyde & Co LLP [2012] EWCA Civ 1207, [2013] 1 All ER 844, [2012] IRLR 992, [2012] 38 LS Gaz R 19, 156 Sol Jo (no 37) 31, [2012] All ER (D) 164 (Sep) . . . 9.17, 10.42, 11.18, 14.3, 23.9

Battersby v Campbell (Inspector of Taxes) (SpC 287) [2001] STC (SCD) 189 . . . . 44.34

Baxter v Harland & Wolff plc [1990] IRLR 516, NI CA 25.2

Baynham v Philips Electronics (UK) Ltd (1995) IDS Brief No 551 . . . . 40.8

Baynton v South West Trains Ltd [2005] ICR 1730, [2005] All ER (D) 253 (Jun), EAT 12.6, 12.7

Beacard Property Management and Construction Co Ltd v Day [1984] ICR 837, EAT 18.16

Beasley v National Grid [2008] EWCA Civ 742, [2007] All ER (D) 110 (Aug) 17.21

Beattie v Leicester City Council (UKEAT0386/09/SM) (20 January 2010, unreported) 7.2

Beaumont v Amicus MSF (2004) 148 Sol Jo LB 1063, [2004] All ER (D) 34 (Aug), EAT 49.14

Bebbington v Palmer (t/a Sturry News) (UKEAT/0371/09/DM) [2010] All ER (D) 47 (Sep)
. . . . 3.2

Beck v Camden London Borough Council (UKEAT/0121/08/ZT) [2008] All ER (D) 09 (Sep)
. . . . 14.3

Beck v Canadian Imperial Bank of Commerce [2009] EWCA Civ 619, 153 Sol Jo (no 26) 28, [2009] All ER (D) 279 (Jun), sub nom Canadian Imperial Bank of Commerce v Beck [2009] IRLR 740 . . . . 12.9, 18.12

Beckett Investment Management Group Ltd v Hall [2007] EWCA Civ 613, [2007] ICR 1339, [2007] IRLR 793, (2007) Times, 11 July, 151 Sol Jo LB 891, [2007] All ER (D) 375 (Jun) 39.4, 39.6, 39.7

Beckmann v Dynamco Whicheloe MacFarlane Ltd: C-164/00 [2002] ECR I-4893, [2002] All ER (EC) 865, [2002] 2 CMLR 1152, [2003] ICR 50, [2002] IRLR 578, (2002) Times, 17 June, [2002] All ER (D) 05 (Jun), ECJ 40.6, 50.19

Beddoes v Birmingham City Council [2011] EqLR 838, [2011] 3 CMLR 1151, EAT 21.9

Belcher v Autoclenz Ltd [2009] EWCA Civ 1046, [2010] IRLR 70, (2009) Times, 16 October, [2009] All ER (D) 134 (Oct); affd sub nom Autoclenz Ltd v Belcher [2011] UKSC 41, [2011] 4 All ER 745, [2011] ICR 1157, [2011] IRLR 820, [2011] NLJR 1099, (2011) Times, 05 August, [2011] All ER (D) 251 (Jul) 7.12, 14.3, 25.2, 45.2c

Bell v Department of Health and Social Security (1989) Times, 13 June 25.3

Bell v Lever Bros Ltd [1932] AC 161, 101 LJKB 129, 37 Com Cas 98, [1931] All ER Rep 1, 76 Sol Jo 50, 146 LT 258, 48 TLR 133, HL 56.42

Bell v Stuart Peters Ltd [2009] EWCA Civ 938, [2010] 1 All ER 775, [2010] 1 WLR 10, [2009] ICR 1556, (2009) Times, 7 October, [2009] All ER (D) 54 (Oct), sub nom Stuart Peters Ltd v Bell [2009] IRLR 941 . . . . 53.12

Bennett v London Probation Service (UKEAT/0194/09) (17 June 2009, unreported) 18.16

Bennett v Southwark London Borough Council [2002] EWCA Civ 223, [2002] ICR 881, [2002] IRLR 407, (2002) Times, 28 February, 146 Sol Jo LB 59, [2002] All ER (D) 297 (Feb) . . . 18.16, 18.17, 18.40, 18.50, 18.55, 19.24

Benson v Land Registry (2012) UKEAT/0197/11/RN, [2012] ICR 627, [2012] IRLR 373, [2012] All ER (D) 135 (Mar), EAT 11.9, 40.6

Benson v Secretary of State for Trade and Industry [2003] ICR 1082, [2003] IRLR 748, [2003] All ER (D) 113 (May), EAT 29.5

Benteler Automotive UK and ISTC, Re (2000) IDS Brief No 677 . . . . 48.30

Bentley Engineering Co Ltd v Mistry [1979] ICR 47, [1978] IRLR 437, EAT 52.10

Benton v Sanderson Kayser Ltd [1989] ICR 136, [1989] IRLR 19, CA 36.12

Bentwood Bros (Manchester) Ltd v Shepherd [2003] EWCA Civ 380, [2003] ICR 1000, [2003] IRLR 364, [2003] All ER (D) 398 (Feb) 12.15, 12.20, 53.12

Benveniste v University of Southampton [1989] ICR 617, [1989] IRLR 122, CA 21.12

Beresford v Sovereign House Estates (UKEAT/0405/11/SM) [2012] ICR D9, [2012] All ER (D) 159 (Jan), EAT 12.2, 18.23

Berg and Busschers v Besselsen: 144/87 and 145/87 [1988] ECR 2559, [1989] 3 CMLR 817, [1990] ICR 396, [1989] IRLR 447, ECJ 50.6, 50.18

Bernadone v Pall Mall Services Group Ltd [2001] ICR 197 . . . . 50.18

Bernard v A-G of Jamaica [2004] UKPC 47, [2005] IRLR 398, 148 Sol Jo LB 1281, [2005] 2 LRC 561, [2004] All ER (D) 96 (Oct) 54.2

Bernstein v Immigration Appeal Tribunal and Department of Employment [1988] Imm AR 449, CA 22.2

Berriman v Delabole Slate Ltd [1985] ICR 546, sub nom Delabole Slate Ltd v Berriman [1985] IRLR 305, CA 50.26

Berwick Salmon Fisheries Co Ltd v Rutherford [1991] IRLR 203, EAT 6.7

Best v Tyne and Wear Passenger and Transport Executive (t/a Nexus) [2007] ICR 523, [2006] All ER (D) 362 (Dec), EAT 21.11

Bestuur van het Algemeen Burgerlijk Pensioenfonds v Beune: C-7/93 [1995] All ER (EC) 97, [1994] ECR I-4471, [1995] 3 CMLR 30, [1995] IRLR 103, ECJ 21.17

Beswick Paper Ltd v Britton (UKEAT/0104/09/RN) (9 October 2009, unreported) 18.54

Betriebsrat der Bofrost Josef H Boquoi Deutschland West GmbH & Co KG v Bofrost Josef H Boquoi Deutschland West GmbH & Co KG: C-62/99 [2001] ECR I-2579, [2004] 2 CMLR 1223, [2001] IRLR 403, [2001] All ER (D) 350 (Mar), ECJ 15.24

Betriebsrat der Firma ADS Anker GmbH v ADS Anker GmbH: C-349/01 [2004] ECR I-6803, [2004] 3 CMLR 299, (2004) IDS Brief No 763, [2004] All ER (D) 270 (Jul), ECJ 15.24

Betts v Brintel Helicopters Ltd (t/a British International Helicopters) [1997] 2 All ER 840, [1997] ICR 792, [1997] IRLR 361, [1997] NLJR 561, sub nom Betts v Brintel Helicopters Ltd and KLM ERA Helicopters (UK) Ltd [1998] 2 CMLR 22, CA 50.5

Beveridge v KLM UK Ltd [2000] IRLR 765, EAT 32.6

Bewley v HM Prison Service [2004] ICR 422, (2004) Times, 4 February, [2004] All ER (D) 22 (Mar), EAT 55.4

Beynon v Scadden [1999] IRLR 700 , EAT 18.71

Bick v Royal West of England Residential School for the Deaf [1976] IRLR 326, Ind Trib 10.19

Biffa Waste Services Ltd v Maschinenfabrik Ernst Hese GMBH [2008] EWCA Civ 1257, [2009] 3 WLR 324, [2009] Bus LR 696, 122 ConLR 1, [2009] BLR 1, (2008) Times, 21 November, 152 Sol Jo (no 45) 25, [2008] All ER (D) 110 (Nov) 54.1, 54.3

Biggs v Somerset County Council [1995] ICR 811, [1995] IRLR 452, EAT; affd [1996] 2 All ER 734, [1996] 2 CMLR 292, [1996] ICR 364, [1996] IRLR 203, [1996] 06 LS Gaz R 27, [1996] NLJR 174, 140 Sol Jo LB 59, CA 17.12, 17.25, 17.30, 22.2

Bilka-Kaufhaus GmbH v Weber von Hartz: 170/84 [1986] ECR 1607, [1986] 2 CMLR 701, [1987] ICR 110, [1986] IRLR 317, ECJ 10.35, 11.9, 21.3, 21.11, 21.12

Bingham v Hobourn Engineering Ltd [1992] IRLR 298, EAT 19.34, 53.12

Birch v University of Liverpool [1985] ICR 470, [1985] IRLR 165, 129 Sol Jo 245, CA 46.2, 51.8

Birch (D M) v Walsall Metropolitan Borough Council (UKEAT/0376/10/JOJ) (17 February 2011, unreported) 18.10, 18.23

Bird v Sylvester [2007] EWCA Civ 1052, [2008] ICR 208, [2008] IRLR 232, 151 Sol Jo LB 1297, [2008] All ER (D) 81 (Jan) 10.58

Birds Eye Walls Ltd v Harrison [1985] ICR 278, [1985] IRLR 47, EAT 18.11

Birds Eye Walls Ltd v Roberts: C-132/92 [1993] ECR I-5579, [1993] 3 CMLR 822, [1994] IRLR 29, sub nom Roberts v Birds Eye Walls Ltd [1994] ICR 338, ECJ 21.16, 21.17

Birkett v James [1978] AC 297, [1977] 2 All ER 801, [1977] 3 WLR 38, 121 Sol Jo 444, HL 18.17

Birmingham City Council v Akhtar [2011] 3 CMLR, [2011] EqLR 838 .... 35.5

Birmingham City Council v Equal Opportunities Commission [1989] AC 1155, [1989] 2 WLR 520, 87 LGR 557, [1989] IRLR 173, 133 Sol Jo 322, [1989] 15 LS Gaz R 36, [1989] NLJR 292, sub nom Equal Opportunities Commission v Birmingham City Council [1989] 1 All ER 769, HL
.... 10.14

Birmingham Optical Group plc v Johnson [1995] ICR 459, EAT 17.25

Blackburn v Chief Constable of West Midlands Police [2008] EWCA Civ 1208, [2009] IRLR 135, [2008] NLJR 1603, [2008] All ER (D) 50 (Nov) 11.9, 21.12

Blaik v Post Office [1994] IRLR 280, EAT 18.17

Blakley v South Eastern Health & Social Services Trust [2009] NICA 62 .... 55.5

Bleuse v MBT Transport Ltd [2008] ICR 488, [2008] IRLR 264, [2007] All ER (D) 392 (Dec), EAT 23.9, 51.15, 55.3

Bliss v South East Thames Regional Health Authority [1987] ICR 700, [1985] IRLR 308, CA
.... 51.7, 53.12

Blitz v Equant Integration Services Ltd (t/a Orange Business Services) [2008] All ER (D) 203 (Jan), EAT 18.58

Blockleys plc v Miller [1992] ICR 749, [1992] 34 LS Gaz R 39, EAT 19.46

Blue Chip Trading Ltd v Helbawi (A) (UKEAT/0397/08/LA) [2009] IRLR 128, [2009] All ER (D) 49 (Jan) 7.24, 11.19, 23.6, 32.12

Blue Circle Staff Association v Certification Officer [1977] 2 All ER 145, [1977] 1 WLR 239, [1977] ICR 224, [1977] IRLR 20, 121 Sol Jo 52, EAT 48.23

Blundell v Governing Body of St Andrews Catholic Primary School [2007] ICR 1451, [2007] IRLR 652, [2007] All ER (D) 159 (May), EAT 10.31, 31.25, 31.31

Blundell v Governing Body of St Andrew's Catholic Primary School [2011] EWCA Civ 427, [2011] All ER (D) 132 (Apr) 12.17

Table of Cases

Boardman v The Governing Body of Clarence High School and Nugent Care Society [2013] EWCA
  Civ 198, [2013] All ER (D) 146 (Mar) 59.2
Bodhu v Hampshire Area Health Authority [1982] ICR 200, EAT 17.25
Bolch v Chipman [2004] IRLR 140, [2003] All ER (D) 122 (Nov), EAT 18.17
Bolkiah v KPMG (a firm) [1999] 2 AC 222, [1999] 1 All ER 517, [1999] 2 WLR 215, [1999] 1 BCLC
  1, [1999] NLJR 16, 143 Sol Jo LB 35, [1999] PNLR 220, [1999] 3 LRC 568, HL 39.13
Bolton School v Evans. See Evans v Bolton School
Bombardier Aerospace/Short Brothers plc v McConnell [2007] NICA 27, [2008] IRLR 51 ...... 53.18
Bombardier Aerospace/Short Brothers plc v McConnell (No 2) [2008] NICA 50, [2009] IRLR 201,
  NI CA 53.18
Bond v CAV Ltd [1983] IRLR 360 .... 7.15
Bone v Fabcon Projects Ltd [2007] 1 All ER 1071, [2006] ICR 1421, [2006] IRLR 908,
  [2006] All ER (D) 167 (Oct), EAT 17.35, 17.36
Bone v Newham London Borough Council [2008] EWCA Civ 435, [2008] ICR 923, [2008] IRLR
  546, [2008] All ER (D) 414 (Apr) 18.64, 18.76
Bonner v H Gilbert Ltd [1989] IRLR 475, EAT 36.10
Boorman v Allmakes Ltd [1995] ICR 842, [1995] IRLR 553, CA 53.9
Boote v Ministry of Defence (3 March 2004, unreported), Ch D 11.9
Booth v United States of America [1999] IRLR 16, 611 IRLB 9, EAT 6.7
Borders Regional Council v Maule [1993] IRLR 199, EAT 17.2, 17.4
Bossa v Nordstress Ltd [1998] ICR 694, [1998] IRLR 284, EAT 11.18, 22.4
Bostock v Bryant (1990) 61 P & CR 23, 22 HLR 449, [1990] 2 EGLR 101, [1990] 39 EG 64, CA
  .... 41.2
Boston Deep Sea Fishing and Ice Co v Ansell (1888) 39 Ch D 339, [1886–90] All ER Rep 65, 59 LT
  345, CA 45.6, 56.6, 56.20
Botham v Ministry of Defence [2006] UKHL 3, [2006] 1 All ER 823, [2006] ICR 250, [2006]
  06 LS Gaz R 36, [2006] NLJR 184, 150 Sol Jo LB 131, [2006] All ER (D) 184 (Jan) 23.9
Botham v Ministry of Defence [2011] UKSC 58, [2012] 2 All ER 278, [2012] 2 WLR 55, [2012] ICR
  201, [2012] IRLR 129, 124 BMLR 51, [2012] 02 LS Gaz R 17, [2011] NLJR 30, (2012) Times,
  23 January, 155 Sol Jo (no 48) 31, [2011] All ER (D) 101 (Dec) 7.39
Botzen v Rotterdamsche Droogdok Maatschappij BV: 186/83 [1985] ECR 519, [1986] 2 CMLR 50,
  ECJ 50.15
Bouchaala v Trusthouse Forte Hotels Ltd [1980] ICR 721, [1980] IRLR 382, EAT 52.13
Boulding v Land Securities Trillium (Media Services) Ltd [2006] All ER (D) 158 (Nov), EAT
  .... 18.17
Bouzir v Country Style Foods Ltd [2011] EWCA Civ 1519, [2012] EqLR 163, [2011] All ER (D) 59
  (Dec) 12.3
Bowater plc v Charlwood [1991] ICR 798, [1991] IRLR 340, EAT 18.22
Bowden v Tuffnells Parcels Express Ltd: C-133/00 [2001] ECR I-7031, [2001] All ER (EC) 865,
  [2001] 3 CMLR 1342, [2001] IRLR 838, [2001] All ER (D) 32 (Oct), ECJ 55.3
Bower v Stevens [2004] ICR 1582 .... 6.9
Bowman v Harland and Wolff plc [1992] IRLR 349 .... 25.2
Boxfoldia Ltd v National Graphical Association [1988] ICR 752, [1988] IRLR 383 .... 48.17
Boyle v Equal Opportunities Commission: C-411/96 [1998] ECR I-6401, [1998] All ER (EC) 879,
  [1998] 3 CMLR 1133, [1999] ICR 360, [1998] IRLR 717, [1999] 1 FCR 581, [1999] 1 FLR 119,
  52 BMLR 169, 608 IRLB 5, [1998] All ER (D) 500, ECJ 21.14, 40.13
Boyle v SCA Packaging Ltd (Equality and Human Rights Commission intervening) [2009] UKHL
  37, [2009] NI 317, [2009] 4 All ER 1181, [2009] ICR 1056, 109 BMLR 53, (2009) Times, 6 July,
  153 Sol Jo (no 26) 27, [2009] All ER (D) 05 (Jul), sub nom SCA Packaging Ltd v Boyle [2009]
  IRLR 746 .... 10.26, 17.30, 18.6
Boyo v Lambeth London Borough Council [1994] ICR 727, [1995] IRLR 50, CA 7.36, 51.9, 56.18,
  56.25
Boys and Girls Welfare Society v Macdonald [1997] ICR 693, EAT 52.9
Brace v Calder [1895] 2 QB 253, 59 JP 693, 64 LJQB 582, 14 R 473, [1895–9] All ER Rep 1196, 72
  LT 829, 11 TLR 450, CA 56.8
Bradford City Metropolitan Council v Arora [1991] 2 QB 507, [1991] 3 All ER 545, [1991] 2 WLR
  1377, [1991] ICR 226, [1991] IRLR 165, CA 12.18
Bradford Hospitals NHS Trust v Al-Shabib [2003] IRLR 4, [2002] All ER (D) 68 (Oct), EAT
  .... 10.20
Bradley v National and Local Government Officers Association [1991] ICR 359, [1991] IRLR 159,
  EAT 49.14

Bradley v Secretary of State for Employment [1989] ICR 69, [1989] 3 LS Gaz R 43, EAT 29.4
Brandeaux Advisers (UK) Ltd v Chadwick [2010] EWHC 3241 (QB), [2011] IRLR 224,
    [2010] All ER (D) 235 (Dec) 8.19, 39.11, 39.13
Brash-Hall v Getty Images Ltd [2006] EWCA Civ 531, (2006) 811 IDS Brief 5, [2006] All ER (D)
    111 (May) 12.15
Brasserie du Pecheur SA v Germany: C-46/93 [1996] QB 404, [1996] ECR I-1029, [1996] All ER
    (EC) 301, [1996] 2 WLR 506, [1996] 1 CMLR 889, [1996] IRLR 267, ECJ 22.2
Bray v Monarch Personnel Refuelling (UK) Ltd (ET/1801581/2012), unreported 45.2d
Breach v Epsylon Industries Ltd [1976] ICR 316, [1976] IRLR 180, EAT 7.21, 56.21
Bremer Vulkan Schiffbau und Maschinenfabrik v South India Shipping Corpn Ltd [1981] AC 909,
    [1981] 1 All ER 289, [1981] 2 WLR 141, [1981] 1 Lloyd's Rep 253, [1981] Com LR 19, 125 Sol
    Jo 114, HL 39.11
Brennan v J H Dewhurst Ltd [1984] ICR 52, [1983] IRLR 357, EAT 10.44
Brennan v Sunderland City Council (UKEAT/0286/11/SM) (2 May 2012, unreported) 12.13
Brent London Borough Council v Charles (1997) 29 HLR 876, CA 41.7
Bridge v Deacons (a firm) [1984] AC 705, [1984] 2 WLR 837, 128 Sol Jo 263, [1984] LS Gaz R
    1291, 134 NLJ 723, sub nom Deacons (a firm) v Bridge [1984] 2 All ER 19, PC 39.5, 39.8
Bridge Trustees Ltd v Houldsworth (Secretary of State for Work and Pensions, intervener) [2011]
    UKSC 42, [2012] 1 All ER 659, [2011] 1 WLR 1912, [2011] ICR 1069, (2011) Times, 09 August,
    [2011] All ER (D) 252 (Jul) 40.9
Bridgen v Lancashire County Council [1987] IRLR 58, CA 51.7
Briggs v North Eastern Education and Library Board [1990] IRLR 181, NI CA 10.34
Briggs v Nottingham University Hospitals NHS Trust [2010] EWCA Civ 264, [2010] IRLR 504,
    [2010] All ER (D) 152 (Mar) 5.9
Briggs v Oates [1991] 1 All ER 407, [1990] ICR 473, [1990] IRLR 472, [1990] NLJR 208 ... 46.1, 56.8
Brill v Interactive Business Communications Ltd [2010] EWCA Civ 1604, [2010] All ER (D) 139
    (Dec) 12.8
Brind v Secretary of State for the Home Department. See R v Secretary of State for the Home
    Department, ex p Brind
Brindle v H W Smith (Cabinets) Ltd [1973] 1 All ER 230, sub nom H W Smith (Cabinets) Ltd v
    Brindle [1972] 1 WLR 1653, [1973] ICR 12, [1972] IRLR 125, 116 Sol Jo 967, CA 17.24
Brink's Global Services Inc v Igrox Ltd [2010] EWCA Civ 1207, [2011] IRLR 343, [2010] All ER
    (D) 260 (Oct) 54.1, 54.2
Briscoe v Lubrizol Ltd [2002] EWCA Civ 508, [2002] IRLR 607, [2002] All ER (D) 190 (Apr)
    .... 42.12, 42.13, 56.17
Bristol and West Building Society v Mothew (t/a Stapley & Co) [1998] Ch 1, [1996] 4 All ER 698,
    [1997] 2 WLR 436, [1996] NLJR 1273, 140 Sol Jo LB 206, [1997] PNLR 11, sub nom Mothew
    v Bristol & West Building Society 75 P & CR 241, CA 8.22
British Aerospace plc v Green [1995] ICR 1006, [1995] IRLR 433, CA 18.12, 52.11
British Aircraft Corpn v Austin [1978] IRLR 332, EAT 25.1, 25.18, 26.11
British Airways Engine Overhaul Ltd v Francis [1981] ICR 278, [1981] IRLR 9, EAT 52.3
British Airways (European Operations at Gatwick) Ltd v Moore [2000] ICR 678, [2000] IRLR 296,
    EAT 21.4, 31.12
British Airways plc v Mak (UKEAT/0055/09/SM) [2010] All ER (D) 162 (Jan); affd [2011] EWCA
    Civ 184, [2011] All ER (D) 256 (Feb) 11.18, 23.9
British Airways plc v Noble [2006] EWCA Civ 537, [2006] ICR 1227, [2006] IRLR 533,
    [2006] All ER (D) 110 (May) 27.4
British Airways plc v Williams [2012] UKSC 43, [2013] 1 All ER 443, [2013] 1 CMLR 934, [2012]
    ICR 1375, [2012] IRLR 1014, (2012) Times, 02 November, [2012] All ER (D) 162 (Oct) .. 27.4, 55.19,
                                                                                         55.33
British Airways plc v Williams. See Williams v British Airways plc
British Association of Advisers and Lecturers in Physical Education v National Union of Teachers
    [1986] IRLR 497, CA 48.1
British Bakeries (Northern) Ltd v Adlington [1989] ICR 438, sub nom Adlington v British Bakeries
    (Northern) Ltd [1989] IRLR 218, CA 47.2
British Coal Corpn v British Coal Staff Superannuation Scheme Trustees Ltd [1995] 1 All ER 912,
    [1994] ICR 537 .... 40.16
British Coal Corpn v Cheesbrough [1990] 2 AC 256, [1990] 1 All ER 641, [1990] 2 WLR 407, [1990]
    ICR 317, [1990] IRLR 148, 134 Sol Jo 661, [1990] 11 LS Gaz R 39, HL 32.36, 32.39
British Coal Corpn v Keeble [1997] IRLR 336, EAT 12.7, 17.30

Table of Cases

British Coal Corpn v Smith [1996] 3 All ER 97, [1996] ICR 515, [1996] IRLR 404, [1996] NLJR
  843, HL 21.9
British Gas plc v McCarrick [1991] IRLR 305, CA 19.35
British Gas plc v Sharma [1991] ICR 19, [1991] IRLR 101, EAT 12.21, 18.59
British Gas Services Ltd v McCaull [2001] IRLR 60 .... 10.37, 17.29, 52.8
British Heart Condition v Harrison (EAT/1354/96) unreported 34.2
British Home Stores Ltd v Burchell [1980] ICR 303n, [1978] IRLR 379, 13 ITR 560, EAT . 38.4, 52.8,
                                                                                      52.9, 52.10
British Judo Association v Petty [1981] ICR 660, [1981] IRLR 484, EAT 11.30
British Leyland (UK) Ltd v Swift [1981] IRLR 91, CA 52.4
British Nursing Association v Inland Revenue (National Minimum Wage Compliance Team) [2002]
  EWCA Civ 494, [2003] ICR 19, [2002] IRLR 480, [2002] All ER (D) 419 (Mar) 32.12
British Publishing Co Ltd v Fraser [1987] ICR 517, EAT 19.40
British Reinforced Concrete Engineering Co Ltd v Schelff [1921] 2 Ch 563, 91 LJ Ch 114,
  [1921] All ER Rep 202, 126 LT 230 .... 39.7
British Road Services Ltd v Loughran [1996] NI 181, [1997] IRLR 92, CA 21.11, 21.12
British Telecommunications plc v Grant (1994) IDS Brief No 518, EAT 10.38
British Telecommunications plc v Reid [2003] EWCA Civ 1675, [2004] IRLR 327, [2003] 41 LS Gaz
  R 33, (2003) Times, 9 October, [2003] All ER (D) 91 (Oct) 12.16, 12.18
British Telecommunications plc v Roberts [1996] ICR 625, [1996] IRLR 601, EAT 10.33, 31.31
British Telecommunications plc v Royal Mail Group Ltd [2010] EWHC 8 (QB), [2010] All ER (D)
  10 (Jan) 35.2
British Telecommunications plc v Sheridan [1990] IRLR 27, CA 19.35
British Telecommunications plc v Ticehurst [1992] ICR 383, [1992] 15 LS Gaz R 32, 136 Sol Jo LB
  96, sub nom Ticehurst and Thompson v British Telecommunications plc [1992] IRLR 219, CA
  .... 7.17, 7.47, 32.14
Brodie v Ward (t/a First Steps Nursery) [2008] All ER (D) 115 (Feb), EAT 18.13
Bromley v H & J Quick Ltd [1988] 2 CMLR 468, [1988] ICR 623, [1988] IRLR 249, CA 21.7
Bromley v Smith [1909] 2 KB 235, 78 LJKB 745, [1908–10] All ER Rep 384, 100 LT 731 .... 3.11
Brompton v AOC International Ltd [1997] IRLR 639, CA 7.22b, 40.16, 56.7
Brook v Haringey London Borough Council [1992] IRLR 478, EAT 10.15
Brook Lane Finance Co Ltd v Bradley [1988] ICR 423, [1988] IRLR 283, [1988] 15 LS Gaz R 35,
  EAT 50.12
Brooker v Charrington Fuel Oils Ltd [1981] IRLR 147, Cty Ct 32.4
Brookes v Borough Care Services and CLS Care Services Ltd [1998] ICR 1198, [1998] IRLR 636,
  EAT 50.10
Brown v Baxter (t/a Careham Hall) (UKEAT/0354/09/SM) (7 July 2010, unreported) 38.4
Brown v Croydon London Borough Council [2007] EWCA Civ 32, [2007] ICR 909, [2007] IRLR
  259, [2007] All ER (D) 239 (Jan) 10.15, 12.3
Brown v G4 Security (Cheltenham) (UKEAT/0526/09/RN) [2010] All ER (D) 84 (Aug) .. 9.10, 15.20
Brown v JBD Engineering Ltd [1993] IRLR 568, EAT 51.7, 56.22
Brown v Knowsley Borough Council [1986] IRLR 102, EAT 51.10
Brown v Merchant Ferries Ltd [1998] IRLR 682, NI CA 51.7
Brown v Rentokil Ltd: C-394/96 [1998] ECR I-4185, [1998] All ER (EC) 791, [1998] 2 CMLR
  1049, [1998] ICR 790, [1998] IRLR 445, [1999] 1 FCR 49, [1998] 2 FLR 649, [1998] Fam Law
  597, 48 BMLR 126, [1998] 34 LS Gaz R 34, [1998] All ER (D) 313, ECJ 10.32
Brown v Southall and Knight [1980] ICR 617, [1980] IRLR 130, EAT 51.13, 56.5
Brownbill v St Helens and Knowsley Hospitals NHS Trust [2011] EWCA Civ 903, [2012] 1 CMLR
  409, [2012] ICR 68, [2011] IRLR 815, [2011] NLJR 1141, [2011] All ER (D) 274 (Jul) 21.5
Bruce v Wiggins Teape (Stationery) Ltd [1994] IRLR 536, EAT 32.6, 56.24
Brumder v Motornet Service and Repairs Ltd [2013] EWCA Civ 195, [2013] NLJR 26,
  [2013] All ER (D) 159 (Mar) 25.44
Brunel University v Vaseghi. See Vaseghi v Brunel University
Brunnhofer v Bank der österreichischen Postsparkasse AG: C-381/99 [2001] ECR I-4961,
  [2001] All ER (EC) 693, [2001] 3 CMLR 173, [2001] IRLR 571, (2001) Times, 9 July,
  [2001] All ER (D) 273 (Jun), ECJ 21.6, 21.10, 21.12
Bruton v London and Quadrant Housing Trust [2000] 1 AC 406, [1999] 3 All ER 481, [1999] 3
  WLR 150, 78 P & CR D21, 31 HLR 902, [1999] NLJR 1001, [1999] 2 EGLR 59, [1999] 30 EG
  91, [1999] EGCS 90, HL 41.2
Bryant v Housing Corpn. See Housing Corpn v Bryant

Buchanan-Smith v Schleicher & Co International Ltd [1996] ICR 613, [1996] IRLR 547, EAT
.... 50.15
Buckland v Bournemouth University Higher Education Corpn [2010] EWCA Civ 121, [2011] QB
  323, [2010] 4 All ER 186, [2010] 3 WLR 1664, [2010] ICR 908, [2010] IRLR 445, (2010) Times,
  3 May, [2010] All ER (D) 299 (Feb) 19.38, 51.7, 52.14
Budd v Scotts Co (UK) Ltd [2004] ICR 299, [2003] IRLR 145, [2002] All ER (D) 58 (Nov),
  EAT 46.12, 56.27
Budgen & Co v Thomas [1976] ICR 344, [1976] IRLR 174, EAT 52.10
Bull v Nottingham and Nottinghamshire Fire and Rescue Authority [2007] EWCA Civ 240, [2007]
  LGR 439, [2007] ICR 1631, (2007) Times, 12 March, [2007] All ER (D) 372 (Feb) 5.9
Bullimore v Pothecary Witham Weld Solicitors (UKEAT/0189/10/JOJ) [2011] IRLR 18,
  [2010] All ER (D) 269 (Dec) 12.15, 12.16, 38.4
Bullock v Alice Ottley School (1993) 91 LGR 32, [1993] ICR 138, [1992] IRLR 564, CA .. 10.15, 21.16
Bulwick v Mills & Allen Ltd (8 June 2000, unreported), EAT 37.4
Bunce v Postworth Ltd (t/a Skyblue) [2005] EWCA Civ 490, [2005] IRLR 557, 149 Sol Jo LB 578,
  [2005] All ER (D) 38 (May) 14.3, 45.2c
Burke v The College of Law (UKEAT/0301/10/SM) [2011] EqLR 804, [2011] All ER (D) 238
  (Mar), EAT; affd [2012] EWCA Civ 37, [2012] All ER (D) 29 (Feb) 10.37, 11.30
Burlo v Langley [2006] EWCA Civ 1778, [2007] 2 All ER 462, [2007] ICR 390, [2007] IRLR 145,
  [2006] All ER (D) 366 (Dec) 53.12, 53.13
Burns v Royal Mail Group plc (formerly Consignia plc) [2004] ICR 1103, sub nom Burns
  v Consignia plc (No 2) [2004] IRLR 425, (2004) Times, 24 June, [2004] All ER (D) 453 (Mar),
  EAT 18.63, 19.22
Burrett v West Birmingham Health Authority [1994] IRLR 7, EAT 10.14
Burrow Down Support Services Ltd v Rossiter (UKEAT/0592/07/LA) [2008] ICR 1172,
  [2008] All ER (D) 49 (Oct) 32.12
Burton Group Ltd v Smith [1977] IRLR 351, EAT 46.5, 56.5
Bury Metropolitan Borough Council v Hamilton (UKEAT/0413-5/09/ZT) [2011] IRLR 358,
  [2011] All ER (D) 85 (Mar) 21.10, 21.11, 21.12
Busch v Klinikum Neustadt GmbH & Co Betriebs-KG: C-320/01 [2003] ECR I-2041,
  [2003] All ER (EC) 985, [2003] 2 CMLR 481, [2003] IRLR 625, [2004] 1 FCR 54, [2003] All ER
  (D) 394 (Feb), ECJ 10.30
Business Seating (Renovations) Ltd v Broad [1989] ICR 729 .... 39.8
Butlins Skyline Ltd v Beynon [2007] ICR 121 .... 17.16, 17.37, 19.10
Butt v Bradford Metropolitan District Council (UKEAT/0210/10/ZT) [2010] All ER (D) 92
  (Oct) 35.5
Bux v Slough Metals Ltd [1974] 1 All ER 262, [1973] 1 WLR 1358, [1974] 1 Lloyd's Rep 155, 117
  Sol Jo 615, CA 25.5, 25.44
Byrne v Birmingham City District Council (1987) 85 LGR 729, [1987] ICR 519, [1987] IRLR 191,
  CA 6.7
Byrne v Financial Times Ltd [1991] IRLR 417, EAT 18.8
Byrne Bros (Formwork) Ltd v Baird [2002] ICR 667, [2002] IRLR 96, [2001] All ER (D) 321 (Nov),
  EAT 14.9, 55.3
Byrnell v British Telecommunications plc [2009] EWHC 727 (QB); affd [2009] EWCA Civ 1066
  .... 38.4

C

CEF Holdings Ltd v Mundey [2012] EWHC 1524 (QB), [2012] FSR 929, [2012] IRLR 912 ..... 39.17
CIA Security International SA v Signalson: C-194/94 [1996] ECR I-2201, [1996] All ER (EC) 557,
  [1996] 2 CMLR 781, ECJ 22.2
CK Heating Ltd v Doro (UKEAT/43/09) [2010] ICR 1449 .... 18.64, 18.75
CLECE SA v Valor: C-463/09 [2011] IRLR 251, [2011] All ER (D) 156 (Jan), ECJ 50.5
CMC Group plc v Zhang [2006] EWCA Civ 408, [2006] All ER (D) 197 (Mar) 7.41
CMS Dolphin Ltd v Simonet [2001] 2 BCLC 704, [2002] BCC 600, [2001] All ER (D) 294
  (May) 8.24
CPL Distribution Ltd v Evans [2002] EWCA Civ 1481, [2002] All ER (D) 100 (Oct), sub nom CPL
  Distribution Ltd v Todd [2003] IRLR 28 .... 50.15
CPS Recruitment Ltd v Bowen and Secretary of State for Employment [1982] IRLR 54, EAT
  .... 36.6

Table of Cases

Cable & Wireless plc v Muscat [2006] EWCA Civ 220, [2006] ICR 975, [2006] IRLR 354, 150 Sol Jo LB 362, [2006] All ER (D) 127 (Mar), sub nom Muscat v Cable & Wireless plc (2006) Times, 10 April 7.2, 14.3, 45.2b, 45.2c

Cable Realisations Ltd v GMB Northern [2010] IRLR 42, sub nom GMB Northern v Cable Realisations Ltd [2009] All ER (D) 179 (Nov) 50.23

Cadman v Health and Safety Executive [2004] EWCA Civ 1317, [2005] ICR 1546, [2004] IRLR 971, 148 Sol Jo LB 1246, [2004] All ER (D) 191 (Oct) 11.9, 21.12

Cadman v Health and Safety Executive: C-17/05 [2006] ECR I-9583, [2007] All ER (EC) 1, [2007] 1 CMLR 530, [2006] ICR 1623, [2006] IRLR 969, (2006) Times, 6 October, [2006] All ER (D) 17 (Oct), ECJ 11.9, 21.12

Cadoux v Central Regional Council [1986] IRLR 131, 1986 SLT 117, Ct of Sess 5.12

Cain v Leeds Western Health Authority [1990] ICR 585, [1990] IRLR 168, EAT 52.9

Cairns v Visteon UK Ltd [2007] ICR 616, [2007] IRLR 175, [2007] All ER (D) 39 (Jan), EAT 14.3, 45.2c

Caisse Nationale d'Assurance Vieillesse des Travailleurs Salaries v Thibault: C-136/95 [1998] ECR I-2011, [1998] All ER (EC) 385, [1998] 2 CMLR 516, [1998] IRLR 399, [1998] All ER (D) 167, sub nom Thibault v Caisse Nationale d'Assurance Vieillesse des Travailleurs Salaries (CNAVTS) [1999] ICR 160, ECJ 10.31

Calder v James Finlay Corpn Ltd [1989] ICR 157n, [1989] IRLR 55, EAT 12.4, 12.11

Calder v Rowntree Mackintosh Confectionery Ltd [1993] ICR 811, [1993] IRLR 212, CA 21.12

Calder v Secretary of State for Work and Pensions (UKEAT/0512/08/LA) [2009] All ER (D) 106 (Aug) 47.8

Caledonia Bureau Investment and Property v Caffrey [1998] ICR 603, [1998] IRLR 110, 591 IRLB 6, EAT 10.32, 31.16

Caledonian Mining Co Ltd v Bassett [1987] ICR 425, [1987] IRLR 165, EAT 46.2

Callagan v Glasgow City Council [2001] IRLR 724, [2001] All ER (D) 101 (Aug), EAT 10.37

Cambridge and District Co-operative Society Ltd v Ruse [1993] IRLR 156, EAT 36.12

Cambridge and Peterborough Foundation NHS Trust v Crouchman [2009] ICR 1306, [2009] All ER (D) 96 (May), EAT 17.25

Camelot Group plc v Centaur Communications Ltd [1999] QB 124, [1998] 1 All ER 251, [1998] 2 WLR 379, [1998] IRLR 80, [1997] 43 LS Gaz R 30, [1997] NLJR 1618, 142 Sol Jo LB 19, [1998] EMLR 1, CA 28.5

Camelot Group plc v Hogg (UKEATS/0019/10/BI) (13 October 2011, unreported) 52.11

Campbell v Dunoon and Cowal Housing Association Ltd [1992] IRLR 528, 1992 SLT 1136n, Ct of Sess 19.47

Campbell v Dunoon and Cowal Housing Association Ltd [1993] IRLR 496, Ct of Sess 52.11

Campbell v Frisbee [2002] EWHC 328 (Ch), [2002] EMLR 656, [2002] All ER (D) 211 (Mar); revsd [2002] EWCA Civ 1374, [2003] ICR 141, [2003] IP & T 86, 146 Sol Jo LB 233, [2003] EMLR 76, [2002] All ER (D) 178 (Oct) 39.11

Campbell and Cosans v United Kingdom (Art 50) (Application 7511/76) (1983) 13 EHRR 441, ECtHR; refd sub nom Campbell and Cosans v United Kingdom (Application 7511/76) (1982) 4 EHRR 293, ECtHR 10.22

Campbell & Smith Construction Group Ltd v Greenwood [2001] IRLR 588, [2001] All ER (D) 240 (May), EAT 32.6

Campion v Hamworthy Engineering Ltd [1987] ICR 966, CA 19.47

Canada Life Ltd v Gray [2004] ICR 673, sub nom Gray v Canada Life Ltd [2004] All ER (D) 36 (Jan), EAT 27.6

Canadian Imperial Bank of Commerce v Beck [2009] IRLR 74. See Beck v Canadian Imperial Bank of Commerce

Canadian Imperial Bank of Commerce v Beck (2010) 912 IDS Brief 10, EAT 12.3

Canadian Imperial Bank of Commerce v Beck (UKEAT/0141/10/RN) [2011] 2 CMLR 82, [2010] All ER (D) 102 (Sep) 20.1

Caparo Industries plc v Dickman [1990] 2 AC 605, [1990] 1 All ER 568, [1990] 2 WLR 358, [1990] BCLC 273, [1990] BCC 164, 11 LDAB 563, 134 Sol Jo 494, [1990] 12 LS Gaz R 42, [1990] NLJR 248, [1991] LRC (Comm) 460, HL 38.4

Capek v Lincolnshire County Council [2000] ICR 878, [2000] IRLR 590, [2000] 24 LS Gaz R 39, CA 7.44, 17.32

Capita Hartshead Ltd v Byard (UKEAT/0445/11/RN) (20 February 2012, unreported) 52.11

Capita Health Solutions Ltd v McLean [2008] IRLR 595, EAT 50.16

Capper Pass Ltd v Lawton [1977] QB 852, [1977] 2 All ER 11, [1977] 2 WLR 26, [1977] ICR 83, [1976] IRLR 366, 11 ITR 316, 120 Sol Jo 768, EAT 21.6

Table of Cases

Carclo Technical Plastics Ltd v Jeyanthikumar (UKEAT/0129/10/CEA) [2010] All ER (D) 67
(Oct) 52.11
Carden v Pickerings Europe Ltd [2005] IRLR 720, [2005] All ER (D) 145 (May), EAT 10.26
Carl v University of Sheffield [2009] 3 CMLR 846, [2009] ICR 1286, [2009] IRLR 616,
[2009] All ER (D) 86 (Jun), EAT 19.2, 30.13, 30.20
Carlisle-Morgan v Cumbria County Council [2007] IRLR 314, [2007] All ER (D) 248 (Jan), EAT
.... 9.17, 54.1
Carmichael v National Power plc [1999] 4 All ER 897, [1999] 1 WLR 2042, [1999] ICR 1226, [2000]
IRLR 43, [1999] 46 LS Gaz R 38, 143 Sol Jo LB 281, 632 IRLB 18, HL 7.12, 14.3
Carpenter v City of Edinburgh Council (EATS/0038/07) (4 April 2008, unreported) 18.62
Carrington v Harwich Dock Co Ltd [1998] ICR 1112, [1998] IRLR 567, EAT 6.6
Carrington v Helix Lighting Ltd [1990] ICR 125, [1990] IRLR 6, [1990] 1 LS Gaz R 30, EAT
.... 12.9, 18.12
Carroll v Manek (1999) 79 P & CR 173, [1999] All ER (D) 813 .... 41.4
Carruthers v London School of Economics Students Union (UKEAT/0183/10/Z) [2011] All ER
(D) 51 (May) 18.72
Carter v Credit Change Ltd [1980] 1 All ER 252, [1979] ICR 908, [1979] IRLR 361, 123 Sol Jo 604,
CA 18.22
Carter v Prestige Nursing Ltd (UKEAT/0014/12), (11 May 2012, unreported) 55.15, 55.22
Carter v Reiner Moritz Associates Ltd [1997] ICR 881, EAT 18.32, 18.66
Cartwright v G Clancey Ltd [1983] ICR 552, [1983] IRLR 355, EAT 32.27
Caruana v Manchester Airport plc [1996] IRLR 378, EAT 10.31
Carver (née Mascarenhas) v Saudi Arabian Airlines [1999] 3 All ER 61, [1999] ICR 991, [1999]
IRLR 370, 615 IRLB 4, CA 11.18
Case FS50080369 (2 October 2008, made under Freedom of Information Act 2000) 17.5
Casella London Ltd v Banai [1990] ICR 215, [1990] 4 LS Gaz R 39, EAT 18.64
Cast v Croydon College [1998] ICR 500, [1998] IRLR 318, [1998] 16 LS Gaz R 26, 142 Sol Jo LB
119, CA 12.6, 17.29
Caston v Chief Constable of Lincolnshire Police [2009] EWCA Civ 1298, (2010) Times, 26 January,
[2009] All ER (D) 72 (Dec), sub nom Chief Constable of Lincolnshire Police v Caston [2010]
IRLR 327 .... 12.7, 17.30
Catamaran Cruisers Ltd v Williams [1994] IRLR 386, EAT 14.3, 52.14
Caterpillar Logistics Services (UK) Ltd v de Crean [2012] EWCA Civ 156, [2012] ICR 981, [2012]
IRLR 410, [2012] All ER (D) 131 (Feb) 39.4, 39.13, 39.16
Catherall v Michelin Tyres plc [2003] ICR 28, [2003] IRLR 61, [2002] All ER (D) 300 (Oct),
EAT 17.29
Catherine Haigh Harlequin Hair Design v Seed [1990] IRLR 175, EAT 46.15
Catholic Child Welfare Society v Various Claimants (FC) [2012] UKSC 56, [2013] 1 All ER 670,
[2012] 3 WLR 1319, [2013] IRLR 219, [2012] NLJR 1504, (2012) Times, 18 December, 156 Sol
Jo (no 45) 31, [2012] All ER (D) 238 (Nov) 25.7, 54.1, 54.2, 54.3
Caulfield v Marshalls Clay Products Ltd. See Marshalls Clay Products Ltd v Caulfield
Cave v Portsmouth City Council [2008] All ER (D) 313 (May), EAT 45.2c
Cavenagh v William Evans Ltd [2012] EWCA Civ 697, [2013] 1 WLR 238, [2012] ICR 1231, [2012]
IRLR 679, 156 Sol Jo (no 23) 35, [2012] All ER (D) 225 (May) 46.5, 46.9
Celebi v Scolarest Compass Group UK & Ireland Ltd (UKEAT/0032/10/LA) [2010] All ER (D)
136 (Sep) 52.10
Celtec Ltd v Astley: C-478/03 [2005] ECR I-4389, [2005] ICR 1409, [2005] IRLR 647, (2005)
Times, 9 June, [2005] All ER (D) 400 (May), ECJ 6.9, 50.12
Centrum voor gelijkheid van kansen en voor Racismebestrijding v Firma Feryn NV: C-54/07
[2008] ECR I-5187, [2008] All ER (EC) 1127, [2008] 3 CMLR 695, [2008] ICR 1390, [2008]
IRLR 732, (2008) Times, 16 July, [2008] All ER (D) 139 (Jul), ECJ 10.43
Cerberus Software Ltd v Rowley [2000] ICR 35, [1999] IRLR 690, EAT; revsd sub nom Rowley v
Cerberus Software Ltd [2001] EWCA Civ 78, [2001] ICR 376, [2001] IRLR 160, (2001) Times,
20 February, (2001) Independent, 18 January, [2001] All ER (D) 80 (Jan) 53.13, 56.16, 56.21
Chadwick v Bayer plc [2002] All ER (D) 88 (Jun), EAT 18.10
Chagger v Abbey National plc [2009] ICR 624, [2009] IRLR 86, [2008] All ER (D) 157 (Oct), EAT;
revsd in part [2009] EWCA Civ 1202, [2010] ICR 397, [2010] IRLR 47, 153 Sol Jo (no 44) 34,
[2009] All ER (D) 168 (Nov) 7.40, 12.3, 12.8, 12.15, 38.4, 53.13
Chairman and Governors of Amwell View School v Dogherty. See Dogherty v Chairman and
Governors of Amwell View School
Chambers-Mills v Allied Bakeries [2011] EWCA Civ 277, [2011] All ER (D) 214 (Feb) 12.9

Table of Cases

Chan v Hackney London Borough Council [1997] ICR 1014, EAT 12.15
Chancerygate (Business Centre) Ltd v Jenkins (UKEAT/0212/10/DM) (22 April 2010, unreported) 18.38
Chandler v Cape plc [2012] EWCA Civ 525, [2012] NLJR 621, [2012] All ER (D) 123 (Apr) 25.8
Chang Tave v Haydon School (UKEAT/0153/10/CEA) (2 September 2010, unreported) .. 18.54, 28.7
Chaplin v H J Rawlinson Ltd [1991] ICR 553, EAT 53.13
Chaplin v Leslie Frewin (Publishers) Ltd [1966] Ch 71, [1965] 3 All ER 764, [1966] 2 WLR 40, 109 Sol Jo 871, CA 3.11
Chapman v Letheby and Christopher Ltd [1981] IRLR 440, EAT 17.24
Chapman v Simon [1994] IRLR 124, CA 12.8, 17.17
Chapman and Elkin v CPS Computer Group plc [1987] IRLR 462, CA 50.17
Charlton v Forrest Printing Ink Co Ltd [1980] IRLR 331, CA 25.8
Chatwal v Wandsworth (UKEAT/0487/10/JOJ) [2011] All ER (D) 69 Aug, EAT 12.3
Chaudhary v British Medical Association [2007] EWCA Civ 788, [2007] IRLR 800, 97 BMLR 15, [2007] All ER (D) 455 (Jul) 10.34
Chaudhary v Specialist Training Authority Appeal Panel [2005] EWCA Civ 282, [2005] ICR 1086, [2005] All ER (D) 256 (Mar) 11.30, 12.2
Cheesman v R Brewer Contracts Ltd [2001] IRLR 144, [2000] All ER (D) 2047, EAT 50.5
Chelminski v Gdynia America Shipping Lines (London) Ltd [2004] EWCA Civ 871, [2004] 3 All ER 666, [2004] IRLR 725, [2004] All ER (D) 83 (Jul), sub nom Gdynia America Shipping Lines (London) Ltd v Chelminski [2004] ICR 1523, 148 Sol Jo LB 877 .... 19.11
Chelsea Football Club and Athletic Co Ltd v Heath [1981] ICR 323, [1981] IRLR 73, EAT 53.9
Cheltenham Borough Council v Laird [2009] EWHC 1253 (QB), [2009] IRLR 621, [2009] All ER (D) 188 (Jun); affd [2010] EWCA Civ 847, [2010] All ER (D) 50 (Feb) 7.3, 7.47b, 20.2
Chenge v Treasury Solicitors Department [2007] IRLR 386, [2007] All ER (D) 203 (Feb), EAT 11.31
Cherfi v G4S Security Services Ltd (UKEAT/0379/10/DM) [2011] EqLR 825 .... 11.9
Chessington World of Adventures Ltd v Reed. See A v B, ex p News Group Newspapers Ltd
Chief Constable of Avon and Somerset Constabulary v Chew (2002) IDS Brief No 701, [2001] All ER (D) 101 (Sep) 10.34
Chief Constable of Bedfordshire Police v Liversidge [2002] EWCA Civ 894, [2002] ICR 1135, [2002] IRLR 651, [2002] All ER (D) 395 (May) 11.26
Chief Constable of Cumbria v McGlennon [2002] ICR 1156, [2002] All ER (D) 231 (Jul), EAT 11.26
Chief Constable of Dumfries & Galloway Constabulary v Adams (UKEATS/0046/08/BI) [2009] ICR 1034, [2009] IRLR 612 .... 10.26
Chief Constable of Greater Manchester Police v Hope [1999] ICR 338, EAT 12.15
Chief Constable of Lincolnshire Police v Caston. See Caston v Chief Constable of Lincolnshire Police
Chief Constable of Lincolnshire Police v Stubbs [1999] ICR 547, [1999] IRLR 81, EAT 10.54
Chief Constable of Lothian and Borders Police v Cumming [2010] IRLR 109, EAT 10.26
Chief Constable of South Yorkshire Police v Jelic (UKEAT/0491/09/CEA) [2010] IRLR 744, [2010] All ER (D) 141 (May) 10.37
Chief Constable of Thames Valley Police v Kellaway [2000] IRLR 170, EAT 19.16
Chief Constable of the Bedfordshire Constabulary v Graham [2002] IRLR 239, [2001] All ER (D) 89 (Sep), EAT 10.19
Chief Constable of the West Yorkshire Police v A [2001] ICR 128, [2000] IRLR 465, EAT 12.11, 17.12, 18.18, 19.26
Chief Constable of West Yorkshire v Vento [2001] IRLR 124, EAT 10.15
Chief Constable of West Yorkshire Police v Khan [2001] UKHL 48, [2001] 1 WLR 1947, [2001] ICR 1065, [2001] IRLR 830, [2001] 42 LS Gaz R 37, 145 Sol Jo LB 230, [2001] All ER (D) 158 (Oct), sub nom Khan v Chief Constable of West Yorkshire Police [2001] 4 All ER 834 .... 10.17, 10.38
Chief Constable of West Yorkshire Police v Vento [2002] IRLR 177, [2001] All ER (D) 20 (Dec), EAT; revsd sub nom Vento v Chief Constable of West Yorkshire Police (No 2) [2002] EWCA Civ 1871, [2003] ICR 318, [2003] IRLR 102, [2003] 10 LS Gaz R 28, (2002) Times, 27 December, 147 Sol Jo LB 181, [2002] All ER (D) 363 (Dec) 9.17, 12.15, 12.16, 12.21, 49.16
Chohan v Derby Law Centre [2004] IRLR 685, [2004] All ER (D) 132 (Apr), EAT 12.7, 17.30
Chorion plc v Lane (1999) Times, 7 April, [1999] All ER (D) 194 .... 18.22
Chouafi v London United Busways Ltd [2006] EWCA Civ 689, [2006] All ER (D) 33 (May) 12.7

Table of Cases

Choudhry v Triesman [2003] EWHC 1203 (Ch), [2003] 22 LS Gaz R 29, (2003) Times, 2 May,
  [2003] All ER (D) 20 (Apr) 7.12
Chowles (t/a Granary Pine) v West (UKEAT/0473/08) (8 January 2009, unreported) 17.35, 17.36,
  17.38
Christian Salvesen Food Services Ltd v Ali. See Ali v Christian Salvesen Food Services Ltd
Christie v Carmichael (UKEATS/0064/09/BI) [2010] IRLR 1016, [2010] All ER (D) 57 (Nov)
  .... 7.21
Christie v Department for Constitutional Affairs [2007] ICR 1553, (2007) Times, 4 September,
  [2007] All ER (D) 355 (Jul), EAT 30.5, 30.22
Christie v Department for Work and Pensions [2007] ICR 1553, (2007) Times, 4 September,
  [2007] All ER (D) 355 (Jul), EAT 30.5, 30.22
Christie v John E Haith Ltd [2003] IRLR 670, [2003] All ER (D) 267 (Jul), EAT 21.12
Church v West Lancashire NHS Trust [1998] ICR 423, [1998] IRLR 4, 588 IRLB 7, EAT ... 36.7
Churchill Dulwich Ltd (in liq) v Metropolitan Resources Ltd [2009] ICR 1380, [2009] All ER (D)
  316 (Jul), sub nom Metropolitan Resources Ltd v Churchill Dulwich Ltd (in liq) [2009] IRLR
  700, EAT 50.3
Chweidan v JP Morgan Europe Ltd [2011] EWCA Civ 648, [2012] ICR 268, [2011] IRLR 673,
  [2011] All ER (D) 285 (May) 10.15
City and Hackney Health Authority v Crisp [1990] ICR 95, [1990] IRLR 47, EAT 53.4
City Equitable Fire Insurance Co Ltd, Re [1925] Ch 407, 94 LJ Ch 445, [1925] B & CR 109,
  [1924] All ER Rep 485, 133 LT 520, 40 TLR 853, CA 8.21
City of Edinburgh Council v Lauder (UK EATS/0048/11), unreported 32.12
City of Edinburgh Council v Wilkinson [2011] CSIH 70, [2012] IRLR 202, 2012 SLT 211 .... 21.9
Civil Service Union v Central Arbitration Committee [1980] IRLR 274 .... 9.3
Civilian War Claimants Association Ltd v R [1932] AC 14, 101 LJKB 105, [1931] All ER Rep 432,
  75 Sol Jo 813, 146 LT 169, 48 TLR 83, HL 22.2
Clancy v Cannock Chase Technical College [2001] IRLR 331, [2001] All ER (D) 36 (Mar), EAT
  .... 12.19, 53.2, 53.12
Clapson v British Airways plc [2001] IRLR 184, EAT 18.14, 18.57
Claridge v Daler Rowney Ltd [2008] ICR 1267, [2008] IRLR 672, [2008] All ER (D) 435 (Jul),
  EAT 7.22d
Clark v BET plc [1997] IRLR 348 .... 56.25
Clark v Civil Aviation Authority [1991] IRLR 412, EAT 52.4
Clark v Clark Construction Initiatives [2008] ICR 635, [2008] IRLR 364, [2008] All ER (D) 440
  (Feb), EAT; affd sub nom Clark v Clark Construction Initiatives Ltd [2008] EWCA Civ 1446,
  [2009] ICR 718, [2008] All ER (D) 191 (Dec) 8.4, 17.11, 18.52, 19.37
Clark v Midland Packaging Ltd [2005] 2 All ER 266, [2005] All ER (D) 10 (Mar), EAT 19.2
Clark v Newsquest Media [2011] EqLR 932 .... 10.37
Clark v Nomura International plc [2000] IRLR 766 .... 7.22c, 32.6, 56.28, 56.30
Clark v Novacold Ltd [1999] 2 All ER 977, [1999] ICR 951, [1999] IRLR 318, 48 BMLR 1, CA
  .... 10.33, 10.37
Clark v Oxfordshire Health Authority [1998] IRLR 125, 41 BMLR 18, CA 14.3
Clark v Secretary of State for Employment. See Secretary of State for Employment v Clark
Clark & Tokeley Ltd (t/a Spellbrook) v Oakes [1998] 4 All ER 353, [1999] ICR 276, [1998] IRLR
  577, 142 Sol Jo LB 253, [1998] All ER (D) 376, CA 6.9
Clarke v Eley (IMI) Kynoch Ltd [1983] ICR 165, [1982] IRLR 482, EAT 10.35
Clarke v Fahrenheit 451 (Communications) Ltd (EAT/591/99) IDS Brief 666, p. 11 .... 46.6
Clarke v Hampshire Electro-Plating Co Ltd [1992] ICR 312, [1991] IRLR 490, EAT 12.6
Clarke v Newland [1991] 1 All ER 397, CA 39.6
Clarke v Redcar and Cleveland Borough Council [2006] ICR 897, [2006] IRLR 324, [2006] All ER
  (D) 309 (Feb), EAT 2.4, 12.10, 12.33, 18.29, 18.32
Clarke v Watford Borough Council (EAT/43/99) (4 May 2000, unreported) 18.59
Clarke v Yorke (1882) 52 LJ Ch 32, 31 WR 62, 47 LT 381 .... 7.45
Clarks of Hove Ltd v Bakers' Union [1979] 1 All ER 152, [1978] 1 WLR 1207, [1978] ICR 1076, 13
  ITR 356, sub nom Bakers' Union v Clarks of Hove Ltd [1978] IRLR 366, 122 Sol Jo 643, CA
  .... 37.6
Clayton v Vigers [1989] ICR 713, [1990] IRLR 177, EAT 31.16
Clayton (Herbert) & Jack Waller Ltd v Oliver [1930] AC 209, 99 LJKB 165, [1930] All ER Rep 414,
  74 Sol Jo 187, 142 LT 585, 46 TLR 230, HL 56.29
Clemens v Richards Ltd [1977] IRLR 332, EAT 32.24

Table of Cases

Clements v London and North Western Rly Co [1894] 2 QB 482, 58 JP 818, 63 LJQB 837, 9 R 641,
  42 WR 663, 38 Sol Jo 562, 70 LT 896, 10 TLR 539, [1891–4] All ER Rep Ext 1461, CA 3.11
Cleveland Ambulance NHS Trust v Blane [1997] ICR 851, [1997] IRLR 332, EAT 49.18
Cleveland County Council v Springett [1985] IRLR 131, EAT 48.20
Clifford v Union of Democratic Mineworkers [1991] IRLR 518, CA 7.4
Clifton Middle School Governing Body v Askew [2000] LGR 96, [2000] ICR 286, [1999] ELR 425,
  [1999] 33 LS Gaz R 30, sub nom Askew v Governing Body of Clifton Middle School [1999] IRLR
  708, [1999] All ER (D) 825, CA 50.13
Close v Rhondda Cynon Taff Borough Council. See Rhondda Cynon Taff Borough Council v Close
Clyde & Co LLP v Bates Van Winkelhof [2011] EWHC 668 (QB), [2011] IRLR 467, [2011] NLJR
  475, (2011) Times, 13 June, 155 Sol Jo (no 12) 30, [2011] All ER (D) 270 (Mar) 12.33, 18.32
Clymo v Wandsworth London Borough Council [1989] 2 CMLR 577, [1989] ICR 250, [1989] IRLR
  241, [1989] 19 LS Gaz R 41, EAT 10.35
Coaches v Cook (2012) UKEATS/0025/12/BI, [2013] ICR 547 .... 50.3
Coats v Strathclyde Fire Board (UKEATS/0022/09/BI) (3 November 2009, unreported) 47.8
Cobbetts LLP v Hodge [2009] EWHC 786 (Ch), [2010] 1 BCLC 30, 153 Sol Jo (no 17) 29,
  [2009] All ER (D) 156 (Apr) 7.16
Cobley v Forward Technology Industries plc [2003] EWCA Civ 646, [2003] ICR 1050, [2003] IRLR
  706, [2003] 29 LS Gaz R 36, (2003) Times, 15 May, 147 Sol Jo LB 696, [2003] All ER (D) 175
  (May) 52.14
Cocking v Sandhurst (Stationers) Ltd [1974] ICR 650, [1975] ITR 6, NIRC 18.10
Cofone v Spaghetti House Ltd [1980] ICR 155, EAT 32.16
Cokayne v British Association of Shooting and Conservation [2008] ICR 185, [2007] All ER (D) 290
  (Oct), EAT 18.27, 18.28
Coker v Lord Chancellor. See Lord Chancellor v Coker and Osamor
Cold Drawn Tubes Ltd v Middleton [1992] ICR 318, [1992] IRLR 160, EAT 53.2
Coldridge v HM Prison Service (UKEAT/0728/04/TM) (20 April 2005, unreported) 17.25
Coleman v Attridge Law (a firm) [2007] ICR 654, (2007) Times, 12 January, [2006] All ER (D) 326
  (Dec), sub nom Attridge Law (a firm) v Coleman [2007] IRLR 88, EAT 19.48
Coleman v Attridge Law: C-303/06 [2008] ECR I-5603, [2008] All ER (EC) 1105, [2008] 3 CMLR
  777, [2008] ICR 1128, [2008] IRLR 722, (2008) Times, 29 July, [2008] All ER (D) 245 (Jul),
  ECJ 19.48
Coleman v EBR Attridge Law LLP [2010] 1 CMLR 846, [2010] ICR 242, (2009) Times,
  5 November, 153 Sol Jo (no 42) 28, [2009] All ER (D) 14 (Nov), sub nom EBR Attridge Law LLP
  v Coleman [2010] IRLR 10, EAT 17.12
Coleman v Skyrail Oceanic Ltd (t/a Goodmos Tours). See Skyrail Oceanic Ltd v Coleman
Coleman and Stephenson v Magnet Joinery Ltd [1974] ICR 25, [1973] IRLR 361, 17 KIR 11, 9 ITR
  74, NIRC; affd [1975] ICR 46, [1974] IRLR 343, [1975] KILR 139, CA 53.2
Colen v Cebrian (UK) Ltd [2003] EWCA Civ 1676, [2004] ICR 568, [2004] IRLR 210, [2004]
  02 LS Gaz R 27, (2003) Times, 27 November, [2003] All ER (D) 294 (Nov) 7.24, 11.19, 51.16
College of Ripon and York St John v Hobbs [2002] IRLR 185, [2001] All ER (D) 259 (Nov),
  EAT 10.26
Collier v Sunday Referee Publishing Co Ltd [1940] 2 KB 647, [1940] 4 All ER 234, 109 LJKB 974,
  84 Sol Jo 538, 164 LT 10, 57 TLR 2 .... 56.21
Collino v Telecom Italia SpA: C-343/98 [2000] ECR I-6659, [2001] All ER (EC) 405,
  [2002] 3 CMLR 997, [2002] ICR 38, [2000] IRLR 788, [2000] All ER (D) 1196, ECJ 15.6, 50.9
Collins v John Ansell & Partners Ltd IDS Brief No 659 .... 50.26
Collins v National Trust (2507255/05) (17 January 2006, unreported), EAT 9.17
Collison v BBC [1998] ICR 669, [1998] IRLR 238, EAT 6.5
Coloroll Pension Trustees Ltd v Russell: C-200/91 [1994] ECR I-4389, [1995] All ER (EC) 23,
  [1995] 2 CMLR 357, [1995] ICR 179, [1994] IRLR 586, [1995] 42 LS Gaz R 23, (1994) Times,
  30 November, ECJ 21.17, 40.9
Colour Quest Ltd v Total Downstream UK plc [2009] EWHC 540 (Comm), [2009] 2 Lloyd's Rep 1,
  153 Sol Jo (no 12) 29, [2009] All ER (D) 311 (Mar); affd [2010] EWCA Civ 180, [2011] QB 86,
  [2010] 3 All ER 793, [2010] 3 WLR 1192, [2010] 2 Lloyd's Rep 467, 129 ConLR 104, (2010)
  Times, 30 March, [2010] All ER (D) 09 (Apr) 54.1
Coltman v Bibby Tankers Ltd, The Derbyshire [1988] AC 276, [1987] 3 All ER 1068, [1987] 3 WLR
  1181, [1988] 1 Lloyd's Rep 109, [1988] ICR 67, 131 Sol Jo 1658, [1988] 3 LS Gaz R 36, [1987]
  NLJ Rep 1157, 1 S & B AvR I/165, HL 25.6
Commercial Motors (Wales) Ltd v Howley (UKEAT/0491/11/ZT) (24 February 2012,
  unreported) 50.12

Commercial Plastics Ltd v Vincent [1965] 1 QB 623, [1964] 3 All ER 546, [1964] 3 WLR 820, 108 Sol Jo 599, CA 39.3, 39.5, 39.6, 39.8, 39.13

Commerzbank AG v Keen. See Keen v Commerzbank AG

Commission for Racial Equality v Amari Plastics Ltd [1982] QB 265, [1981] 3 WLR 511, [1981] ICR 767, [1981] IRLR 340, 125 Sol Jo 694, EAT; affd [1982] QB 1194, [1982] 2 All ER 499, [1982] 2 WLR 972, [1982] ICR 304, [1982] IRLR 252, 126 Sol Jo 227, CA 12.28

Commission for Racial Equality v Dutton [1989] QB 783, [1989] 1 All ER 306, [1989] 2 WLR 17, [1989] IRLR 8, 133 Sol Jo 19, [1989] 1 LS Gaz R 38, CA 10.20

Commission for Racial Equality v Imperial Society of Teachers of Dancing [1983] ICR 473, [1983] IRLR 315, EAT 10.53

Comr of Police of the Metropolis v Osinaike (2010) 907 IDS Brief 15, EAT 12.3

Common Services Agency v Scottish Information Comr [2008] UKHL 47, [2008] 4 All ER 851, [2008] 1 WLR 1550, [2009] IP & T 23, 103 BMLR 170, (2008) Times, 14 July, 2008 SLT 901, 2008 SCLR 672, 27 BHRC 345, [2008] All ER (D) 120 (Jul) 9.13

Commotion Ltd v Rutty [2006] ICR 290, sub nom Rutty v Commotion Ltd [2006] IRLR 171, [2006] All ER (D) 122 (Jan), EAT 47.17

Communication Workers Union v Royal Mail Group Ltd [2009] ICR 357, [2009] IRLR 108, 152 Sol Jo (no 47) 30, [2009] All ER (D) 07 (Jan), EAT; affd [2009] EWCA Civ 1045, [2010] 2 All ER 823, [2010] ICR 83, (2009) Times, 16 October, [2009] All ER (D) 141 (Oct), sub nom Royal Mail Group Ltd v Communication Workers Union [2009] IRLR 1046 .... 9.6, 50.15, 50.23

Community Dental Centres Ltd v Sultan-Darmon (UKEAT/0532/09/DA) [2010] IRLR 1024, [2010] All ER (D) 99 (Sep) 14.3, 14.9

Compass Group plc v Ayodele (UKEAT/0484/10/SM) [2011] IRLR 802, [2011] ICR D25, [2011] All ER (D) 121 (Aug), EAT 40.3, 53.13

Conlin v United Distillers [1994] IRLR 169, Ct of Sess 18.63

Conn v Sunderland City Council [2007] EWCA Civ 1492, [2008] IRLR 324, [2007] All ER (D) 99 (Nov) 26.25

Connex South Eastern Ltd v Bangs. See Bangs v Connex South Eastern Ltd

Connolly v Whitestone Solicitors (UKEAT/0445/10/ZT) [2011] All ER (D) 166 (Oct), EAT 7.24

Consistent Group Ltd v Kalwak [2008] EWCA Civ 430, [2008] IRLR 505, [2008] All ER (D) 394 (Apr) 14.3, 45.2c

Constantine v McGregor Cory Ltd [2000] ICR 938, EAT 53.1

Construction Industry Training Board v Labour Force Ltd [1970] 3 All ER 220, 114 Sol Jo 704, DC 14.3

Construction Industry Training Board v Leighton [1978] 2 All ER 723, [1978] IRLR 60, sub nom Leighton v Construction Industry Training Board [1978] ICR 577, EAT 7.11

Conteh v Parking Partners Ltd (UKEAT/0288/10) [2011] ICR 341, [2011] All ER (D) 223 (Feb) 10.39

Conway v Rimmer [1968] AC 910, [1968] 1 All ER 874, [1968] 2 WLR 998, 112 Sol Jo 191, HL. 35.7

Cook v Square D Ltd [1992] ICR 262, [1992] PIQR P33, 135 Sol Jo LB 180, sub nom Square D Ltd v Cook [1992] IRLR 34, CA 25.3

Cooke v Glenrose Fish Co [2004] ICR 1188, [2004] IRLR 866, [2004] All ER (D) 19 (Jun), EAT 18.54

Cooksey (GMB Claimants) v Trafford BC [2012] Eq LR 744 .... 21.10, 21.11

Coombes v Waltham Forest London Borough Council. See R (on the application of Coombes) v Secretary of State for Communities and Local Government

Coombs & Holder v GE Aviation Systems Ltd (2012), unreported 15.4, 15.6

Cooper v Isle of Wight College [2007] EWHC 2831 (QB), [2008] IRLR 124, [2007] All ER (D) 474 (Nov) 7.47, 32.14

Coors Brewers Ltd v Adcock. See Adcock v Coors Brewers Ltd

Coote v Granada Hospitality Ltd: C-185/97 [1998] ECR I-5199, [1998] All ER (EC) 865, [1998] 3 CMLR 958, [1999] ICR 100, [1998] IRLR 656, [1998] All ER (D) 423, ECJ; apld Coote v Granada Hospitality Ltd (No 2) [1999] 3 CMLR 334, [1999] ICR 942, [1999] IRLR 452, EAT 38.4

Copland v UK (Application 62617/00) [2007] 45 EHRR 37, [2007] IP & T 600, (2007) Times, 24 April, 25 BHRC 216, [2007] All ER (D) 32 (Apr), ECtHR 28.4

Copple v Littlewoods plc (UKEAT/0116/10/ZT) [2011] ICR 296, [2011] All ER (D) 18 (Jan), EAT; affd [2011] EWCA Civ 1281, [2012] 2 All ER 97, [2012] 1 CMLR 1025, [2012] ICR 354, [2012] IRLR 121, [2011] All ER (D) 186 (Nov) 12.22, 21.18, 21.19B, 30.1, 40.13

Table of Cases

Copsey v WWB Devon Clays Ltd [2005] EWCA Civ 932, [2005] ICR 1789, [2005] IRLR 811, [2005] NLJR 1484, (2005) Times, 25 August, [2005] All ER (D) 350 (Jul) 28.7

Coral Leisure Group Ltd v Barnett [1981] ICR 503, [1981] IRLR 204, 125 Sol Jo 374, EAT 7.24

Cordell v Foreign and Commonwealth Office (UKEAT/0016/11/SM) [2012] ICR 280, [2012] All ER (D) 97 (Mar), EAT 10.15, 11.9

Cornell (Lynne) v Revenue and Customs Comrs (TC00108) [2009] UKFTT 140 (TC), [2009] STI 2199 .... 34.3

Corner v Buckinghamshire County Council (1978) 77 LGR 268, [1978] ICR 836, [1978] IRLR 320, 13 ITR 421, EAT 47.5

Cornwall County Care Ltd v Brightman [1998] ICR 529, [1998] IRLR 228, EAT 50.29

Corporate Express Ltd v Day [2004] EWHC 2943 (QB), [2004] All ER (D) 290 (Dec) 39.17, 39.18

Corr (Administratrix of Corr dec'd) v IBC Vehicles Ltd [2008] UKHL 13, [2008] 1 AC 884, [2008] 2 All ER 943, [2008] 2 WLR 499, [2008] ICR 372, 152 Sol Jo (no 9) 30, [2008] PIQR P207, (2008) Times, 28 February, [2008] 5 LRC 124, [2008] All ER (D) 386 (Feb) 25.8

Cortest Ltd v O'Toole v (UKEAT/0470/07/LA) [2008] All ER (D) 220 (May) 47.15

Costa v ENEL: 6/64 [1964] ECR 585, [1964] CMLR 425, ECJ 22.2

Costain Building and Civil Engineering Ltd v Smith [2000] ICR 215, EAT 14.3, 45.2a

Cotswold Developments Construction Ltd v Williams [2006] IRLR 181, [2005] All ER (D) 355 (Dec), EAT 14.3, 14.9

Council of Civil Service Unions v Minister for the Civil Service [1985] AC 374, [1984] 3 All ER 935, [1984] 3 WLR 1174, [1985] ICR 14, 128 Sol Jo 837, [1985] LS Gaz R 437, [1985] LRC (Const) 948, sub nom R v Secretary of State for Foreign and Commonwealth Affairs, ex p Council of Civil Service Unions [1985] IRLR 28, HL 35.2, 35.7

Council of the City of Newcastle Upon Tyne v Marsden (UKEAT/393/09) [2010] ICR 743, sub nom Marsden v Council of the City of Newcastle Upon Tyne [2010] All ER (D) 74 (Feb) 18.76

Council of the City Sunderland v Brennan [2012] EWCA Civ 413, [2012] ICR 1216, [2012] IRLR 507, [2012] All ER (D) 172 (Apr) 21.10, 21.12

Countrywide Assured Financial Services Ltd v Smart [2004] EWHC 1214 (Ch) 39.4, 39.5, 39.8

Courage Take Home Trade Ltd v Keys [1986] ICR 874, [1986] IRLR 427, EAT 53.19

Courtaulds Northern Spinning Ltd v Sibson [1988] ICR 451, [1988] IRLR 305, 132 Sol Jo 1033, CA 7.22e

Coutinho v Vision Information Services (UK) Ltd [2008] All ER (D) 244 (Feb), EAT 12.2

Coutts & Co plc v Cure [2005] ICR 1098, (2004) Times, 25 October, [2004] All ER (D) 393 (Oct), EAT 17.18

Coventry City Council v Nicholls [2009] IRLR 345, [2009] All ER (D) 15 (Mar), EAT 21.12

Cowan v Scargill [1985] Ch 270, [1984] 2 All ER 750, [1984] 3 WLR 501, [1984] ICR 646, [1984] IRLR 260, 128 Sol Jo 550 .... 40.15

Cowen v Haden Ltd [1983] ICR 1, 126 Sol Jo 725, sub nom Haden Ltd v Cowen [1982] IRLR 314, CA 36.7

Cowley v Manson Timber Ltd [1995] ICR 367, [1995] IRLR 153, CA 53.1

Cox v Sun Alliance Life Ltd [2001] EWCA Civ 649, [2001] IRLR 448, [2001] All ER (D) 108 (May) 38.4

Coxall v Goodyear Great Britain Ltd [2002] EWCA Civ 1010, [2003] 1 WLR 536, [2003] ICR 152, [2002] IRLR 742, (2002) Times, 5 August, [2002] All ER (D) 303 (Jul) 25.8

Cranswick Country Foods plc v Beall [2007] ICR 691, [2006] All ER (D) 315 (Dec), EAT 37.6

Crawford v Secretary of State for Employment [1995] IRLR 523, EAT 17.27, 29.4

Crawford v Suffolk Mental Health Partnership NHS Trust [2012] EWCA Civ 138, [2012] IRLR 402, [2012] All ER (D) 132 (Feb) 51.7, 52.10

Crawford v Swinton Insurance Brokers Ltd [1990] ICR 85, [1990] IRLR 42, EAT 50.26

Credit Suisse Asset Management Ltd v Armstrong [1996] ICR 882, [1996] IRLR 450, [1996] 23 LS Gaz R 36, 140 Sol Jo LB 140, CA 39.14, 56.21

Credit Suisse First Boston (Europe) Ltd v Lister [1999] ICR 794, [1998] IRLR 700, [1998] 44 LS Gaz R 35, 142 Sol Jo LB 269, [1998] All ER (D) 462, CA 39.3

Credit Suisse First Boston (Europe) Ltd v Padiachy, Winram and Cracknell [1998] 2 CMLR 1322, [1999] ICR 569, [1998] IRLR 504 .... 39.14

Crees v Royal London Mutual Insurance Society Ltd [1998] ICR 848, [1998] IRLR 245, [1998] 15 LS Gaz R 33, 142 Sol Jo LB 94, 590 IRLB 11, CA 31.32

Cresswell v Inland Revenue Board [1984] 2 All ER 713, [1984] ICR 508, [1984] IRLR 190, 128 Sol Jo 431 .... 7.17

Criddle v Epcot Leisure Ltd [2005] All ER (D) 89 (Aug), EAT 18.71

Croft v Royal Mail Group plc [2003] EWCA Civ 1045, [2003] ICR 1425, [2003] IRLR 592, (2003) Times, 24 July, 147 Sol Jo LB 904, [2002] All ER (D) 179 (Sep) 10.14
Crofton v Yeboah [2002] EWCA Civ 794, (2002) Times, 20 June, [2002] All ER (D) 512 (May), sub nom Yeboah v Crofton [2002] IRLR 634 .... 10.58, 19.16, 19.35
Crofts v Cathay Pacific Airways Ltd [2005] EWCA Civ 599, [2005] ICR 1436, [2005] IRLR 624, (2005) Times, 31 May, [2005] All ER (D) 305 (May); affd sub nom Crofts v Veta Ltd [2006] UKHL 3, [2006] 1 All ER 823, [2006] ICR 250, [2006] 06 LS Gaz R 36, [2006] NLJR 184, 150 Sol Jo LB 131, [2006] All ER (D) 184 (Jan) 23.8, 23.9, 51.15
Cromie v Moroak (t/a Blake Envelopes). See Moroak (t/a Blake Envelopes) v Cromie
Crosbie v Secretary of State for Defence [2011] EWHC 879 (Admin), [2011] 19 LS Gaz R 20, [2011] All ER (D) 64 (Apr) 35.3, 35.6
Cross v British Airways plc [2005] IRLR 423, [2005] All ER (D) 10 (Apr), EAT; affd [2006] EWCA Civ 549, [2006] ICR 1239, [2006] IRLR 804, [2006] 21 LS Gaz R 24, (2006) Times, 5 June, [2006] All ER (D) 148 (May) 11.9, 21.12, 50.17
Cross v Highlands and Islands Enterprise [2001] IRLR 336, 2001 SLT 1060, 2001 SCLR 547, OH 25.8
Cross v Redpath Dorman Long (Contracting) Ltd [1978] ICR 730, EAT 45.2
Crossland v Corps of Commissionaires Management Ltd (UKEAT/0014/10/LA) (18 August 2010, unreported) 27.4
Crossley v Faithful & Gould Holdings Ltd [2004] EWCA Civ 293, [2004] 4 All ER 447, [2004] ICR 1615, [2004] IRLR 377, [2004] NLJR 653, (2004) Times, 29 March, 148 Sol Jo LB 356, [2004] All ER (D) 295 (Mar) 7.22a
Crosville Motor Services Ltd v Ashfield [1986] IRLR 475, EAT 49.5
Crosville Wales Ltd v Tracey (No 2). See Tracey v Crosville Wales Ltd
Crouch v British Rail Engineering Ltd [1988] IRLR 404, CA 25.5
Crown Estate Comrs v Dorset County Council [1990] Ch 297, [1990] 1 All ER 19, [1990] 2 WLR 89, 88 LGR 132, 60 P & CR 1 .... 18.22
Crown Suppliers (Property Services Agency) v Dawkins [1993] ICR 517, sub nom Dawkins v Department of the Environment [1993] IRLR 284, CA 10.20
Crowson Fabrics Ltd v Rider [2007] EWHC 2942 (Ch), [2008] FSR 424, [2008] IRLR 288, [2007] All ER (D) 338 (Dec) 8.19, 39.13
Crowther & Nicholson Ltd, Re (1981) Times, 10 June 56.28
Croydon Health Authority v Jaufurally [1986] ICR 4, EAT 17.25
Cruickshank v VAW Motorcast Ltd [2002] ICR 729, [2002] IRLR 24, [2001] All ER (D) 372 (Oct), EAT 10.26
Crystal Palace FC (2000) Ltd v Dowie [2007] EWHC 1392 (QB), [2007] IRLR 682, [2007] All ER (D) 135 (Jun) 18.34
Cullinane v Balfour Beatty Engineering Services Ltd (UKEAT/0537/10/DA) (5 April 2011, unreported) 17.25, 17.26
Cumbria County Council v Dow (No 1) [2008] IRLR 91, [2007] All ER (D) 178 (Nov), EAT 21.12
Cumbria County Council v Dow (No 2) [2008] IRLR 109, [2007] All ER (D) 179 (Nov), EAT 7.32, 7.34, 21.19A
Curling v Securicor Ltd [1992] IRLR 549, EAT 7.22e
Curr v Marks & Spencer plc [2002] EWCA Civ 1852, [2003] ICR 443, [2003] IRLR 74, (2003) Times, 30 January, [2002] All ER (D) 205 (Dec) 6.7
Customer Systems PLC v Ranson [2011] EWHC 3304 (QB), [2011] All ER (D) 129 (Dec); revsd [2012] EWCA Civ 841, [2012] IRLR 769, [2012] All ER (D) 186 (Jun) 8.19, 39.8
Cyril Leonard & Co v Simo Securities Trust Ltd [1971] 3 All ER 1313, [1972] 1 WLR 80, 115 Sol Jo 911, CA 56.20

D

DB Schenker Rail (UK) Ltd v Doolan (UKEATS/0053/09/BI) (13 April 2011, unreported) 52.8
DJM International Ltd v Nicholas [1996] ICR 214, [1996] IRLR 76, EAT 50.18
Da'Bell v National Society for Prevention of Cruelty to Children (NSPCC) [2010] IRLR 19, [2009] All ER (D) 219 (Nov), EAT 12.16, 46.19
Dacas v Brook Street Bureau (UK) Ltd [2003] IRLR 190, [2003] All ER (D) 241 (Jan), EAT; revsd [2004] EWCA Civ 217, [2004] ICR 1437, [2004] IRLR 358, (2004) Times, 19 March, [2004] All ER (D) 125 (Mar) 7.2, 14.3, 45.2b, 45.2c

Table of Cases

Dairy Crest Ltd v Pigott [1989] ICR 92, CA 39.8
Daleside Nursing Home Ltd v Mathew (UKEAT/0519/08/RN) (18 February 2009, unreported)
.... 18.72
Daley v A E Dorsett (Almar Dolls) Ltd [1982] ICR 1, [1981] IRLR 385, EAT 53.12, 53.13
Daley v Allied Suppliers Ltd [1983] ICR 90, [1983] IRLR 14, EAT 10.41
Daley v Strathclyde Regional Council [1977] IRLR 414, Ind Trib 32.24
Dalgleish v Lothian and Borders Police Board [1991] IRLR 422, 1992 SLT 721, Ct of Sess 9.15
Dandpat v University of Bath (UKEAT/408/09) (10 November 2009, unreported) 9.17, 53.18
Danske Slagterier v Bundesrepublik Deutschland: C-445/06 [2010] All ER (EC) 74,
   [2009] 3 CMLR 311, [2009] All ER (D) 272 (Mar), ECJ 22.2
Darnton v Bournemouth University [2009] IRLR 4; affd (UKEAT/391/09) [2010] ICR 524, [2010]
   IRLR 294 .... 9.10, 15.4, 15.12
Darnton v Bournemouth University (IC/22/2009) (20 May 2009, unreported), CAC 15.14
Darnton v Bournemouth University (No 2) (UKEAT/0391/09/RN) (4 March 2010, unreported)
   .... 15.20
Darr v LRC Products Ltd [1993] IRLR 257, EAT 53.14
Da Silva Junior v Composite Mouldings & Design Ltd (UKEAT/0241/08/MAA) [2009] ICR 416,
   [2008] All ER (D) 157 (Aug) 6.9
Dathi v South London and Maudsley NHS Trust. See South London and Maudsley NHS Trust v
   Dathi
Dattani v Chief Constable of West Mercia Police [2005] IRLR 327, [2005] All ER (D) 95 (Feb),
   EAT 12.3, 12.9, 18.9
Dave v Robinska [2003] ICR 1248, [2003] NLJR 921, [2003] All ER (D) 35 (Jun), EAT 11.28
David-John v North Essex Health Authority [2004] ICR 112, [2003] All ER (D) 84 (Aug), EAT
   .... 11.24, 14.3
Davidson v City Electrical Factors Ltd [1998] IRLR 435a 19.2
Davidson v Dallas McMillan [2009] CSIH 70, [2010] IRLR 439, 2010 SC 100, 2009 SLT 1009
   .... 12.11, 18.18
Davidson-Hogg v Davis Gregory Solicitors and Howarth (UKEAT/0512/09/ZT) (15 November
   2010, unreported) 34.2
Davies v Asda Stores Ltd (IDS Brief 801) 49.17
Davies v Davies (1887) 36 Ch D 359, 56 LJ Ch 962, 36 WR 86, 58 LT 209, 3 TLR 839, CA
   .... 39.7
Davies v Farnborough College of Technology [2008] IRLR 14, [2007] All ER (D) 288 (Nov),
   EAT 52.11
Davies v M J Wyatt (Decorators) Ltd [2000] IRLR 759, EAT 32.6
Davies v McCartneys [1989] ICR 705, [1989] IRLR 439, EAT 21.12
Davies v Neath Port Talbot County Borough Council [1999] ICR 1132, [1999] IRLR 769, EAT
   .... 21.3, 47.2
Davies v Presbyterian Church of Wales [1986] 1 All ER 705, [1986] 1 WLR 323, [1986] ICR 280,
   [1986] IRLR 194, 130 Sol Jo 203, HL 14.3
Dawkins v Department of the Environment. See Crown Suppliers (Property Services Agency) v
   Dawkins
Dawnay, Day & Co Ltd v de Braconier d'Alphen [1997] IRLR 285; affd [1998] ICR 1068, [1997]
   IRLR 442, [1997] 26 LS Gaz R 30, 141 Sol Jo LB 129, CA 39.4, 39.8
Day v Haine [2008] EWCA Civ 626, [2008] ICR 1102, [2008] IRLR 642, [2008] 2 BCLC 517,
   [2008] BCC 845, (2008) Times, 22 July, [2008] BPIR 1343, [2008] All ER (D) 121 (Jun) 29.2
Day v T Pickles Farms Ltd [1999] IRLR 217, EAT 26.17
Daynecourt Insurance Brokers Ltd v Iles [1978] IRLR 335, EAT 46.15
Days Medical Aids Ltd v Pihsiang Machinery Manufacturing Co Ltd [2004] EWHC 44 (Comm),
   [2004] 1 All ER (Comm) 991, [2004] All ER (D) 282 (Jan) 39.1
Deacons (a firm) v Bridge. See Bridge v Deacons (a firm)
Dean & Dean v Dionissiou-Moussaoui [2011] EWCA Civ 1332, [2011] All ER (D) 142 (Nov)
   .... 18.72
Deane v Ealing London Borough Council [1993] ICR 329, [1993] IRLR 209, EAT 10.58, 12.18
De'Antiquis v Key2Law (Surrey) LLP [2011] EWCA Civ 1567, [2012] ICR 881, [2012] IRLR 212,
   [2011] All ER (D) 194 (Dec) 19.2, 29.10, 50.11
Deary (HM Inspector of Factories) v Mansion Hide Upholstery Ltd [1983] ICR 610, [1983] IRLR
   195, 147 JP 311 .... 25.41
Deaway Trading Ltd v Calverley [1973] 3 All ER 776, [1973] ICR 546, NIRC 29.10

De Belin v Eversheds Legal Services Ltd (UKEAT/0352/10/JOJ, UKEAT/0444/10/JOJ) [2011] ICR 1137, [2011] IRLR 448, [2011] 16 LS Gaz R 18, [2011] NLJR 661, [2011] All ER (D) 16 (May), EAT 10.3, 11.10, 12.15, 12.19, 31.16, 31.34, 53.13

DeBique v Ministry of Defence (No 2) (2012) 941 IDS Brief 7, EAT 12.15

Decision D/3/89 (17 August 1989), Certification Officer 48.14

De Clare Johnson v MYA Consulting Ltd [2007] All ER (D) 58 (Dec), EAT 54.1

Dedman v British Building and Engineering Appliances Ltd [1974] 1 All ER 520, [1974] 1 WLR 171, [1974] ICR 53, [1973] IRLR 379, 16 KIR 1, 9 ITR 100, 117 Sol Jo 938, CA .. 17.23, 17.25, 51.13

Deer v Walford (UKEAT/0283/10/JOJ) [2011] All ER (D) 58 (May) 18.9, 18.71, 18.72

De Francesco v Barnum (1890) 45 Ch D 430, 60 LJ Ch 63, 39 WR 5, [1886–90] All ER Rep 414, 63 LT 438, 6 TLR 463 .... 3.11

Defrenne v Sabena: 43/75 [1981] 1 All ER 122, [1976] ECR 455, [1976] 2 CMLR 98, [1976] ICR 547, ECJ 21.9, 21.17, 21.18, 21.18a, 21.19B, 22.2

Degnan v Redcar and Cleveland Borough Council [2005] EWCA Civ 726, [2005] IRLR 615, [2005] All ER (D) 167 (Jun) 21.5, 21.12

Degnan v Redcar and Cleveland Borough Council [2005] ICR 1170, [2005] IRLR 504, [2005] NLJR 619, [2005] All ER (D) 197 (Apr), EAT 21.19A, 21.19B

De Grasse v Stockwell Tools Ltd [1992] IRLR 269, EAT 52.11

De Haney v Brent Mind [2003] EWCA Civ 1637, [2004] ICR 348, [2003] 45 LS Gaz R 29, (2003) Times, 11 November, 147 Sol Jo LB 1275, [2003] All ER (D) 444 (Oct) 17.8, 19.5

De Keyser Ltd v Wilson [2001] IRLR 324, [2001] All ER (D) 237 (Mar), EAT 10.26, 18.14, 28.7

Dekker v Stichting Vormingscentrum voor Jong Volwassenen (VJV-Centrum) Plus: C-177/88 [1990] ECR I-3941, [1992] ICR 325, [1991] IRLR 27, ECJ 10.15, 10.31

Del Cerro Alonso v Osakidetza-Servicio Vasco de Salud: C-307/05 [2007] ECR I-7109, [2007] 3 CMLR 1492, [2008] ICR 145, [2007] IRLR 911, [2007] All ER (D) 87 (Sep), ECJ 45.9

Delabole Slate Ltd v Berriman. See Berriman v Delabole Slate Ltd

Delaney v Staples (RJ) (t/a De Montfort Recruitment) [1991] 2 QB 47, [1991] 1 All ER 609, [1991] 2 WLR 627, [1991] ICR 331, [1991] IRLR 112, CA; affd [1992] 1 AC 687, [1992] 1 All ER 944, [1992] 2 WLR 451, [1992] ICR 483, [1992] IRLR 191, [1992] 15 LS Gaz R 32, 136 Sol Jo LB 91, HL 29.11, 32.6, 44.8, 46.9, 46.10

Dellas v Premier Ministre: C-14/04 [2006] IRLR 225, [2005] All ER (D) 19 (Dec), ECJ 55.5

Demir v Turkey (Application No 34503/97) (2008) 48 EHRR 1272, [2009] IRLR 766, [2008] ECHR 34503/97, ECtHR 28.4, 48.19

Dench v Flynn & Partners [1998] IRLR 653, CA 53.12

Denham v Midland Employers' Mutual Assurance Ltd [1955] 2 QB 437, [1955] 2 All ER 561, [1955] 3 WLR 84, [1955] 1 Lloyd's Rep 467, 99 Sol Jo 417, CA 45.2

Dentmaster (UK) Ltd v Kent [1997] IRLR 636, CA 39.8

Department for Work and Pensions v Thompson [2004] IRLR 348, EAT 10.14

Department for Work and Pensions v Webley [2004] EWCA Civ 1745, [2005] ICR 577, [2005] IRLR 288, (2005) Times, 17 January, [2004] All ER (D) 368 (Dec) 45.9

Department of Constitutional Affairs v Jones. See Jones v Department For Constitutional Affairs

Department of Education and Science v Taylor [1992] IRLR 308 .... 18.17, 18.24

Department of Transport v Gallacher [1994] ICR 967, [1994] IRLR 231, CA 49.17

Depledge v Pye Telecommunications Ltd [1981] ICR 82, [1980] IRLR 390, EAT 47.2

Depner v General Medical Council (2013) UKEAT/0457/11/KN, [2013] All ER (D) 361 (Feb), EAT 11.30

Derby Daily Telegraph Ltd v Foss, IDS Brief No 471 .... 53.18

Derby Daily Telegraph Ltd v Pensions Ombudsman [1999] ICR 1057, [1999] IRLR 476, [1999] All ER (D) 300 .... 40.6

Derby Specialist Fabrication Ltd v Burton [2001] 2 All ER 840, [2001] ICR 833, [2001] IRLR 69, [2000] All ER (D) 1348, EAT 17.29

Derbyshire v St Helens Metropolitan Borough Council [2007] UKHL 16, [2007] 3 All ER 81, [2007] ICR 841, [2007] IRLR 540, [2007] NLJR 635, (2007) Times, 27 April, 151 Sol Jo LB 573, [2007] All ER (D) 207 (Apr) 10.38

Derbyshire County Council v Times Newspapers Ltd [1993] AC 534, [1993] 1 All ER 1011, [1993] 2 WLR 449, 91 LGR 179, [1993] 14 LS Gaz R 46, [1993] NLJR 283, 137 Sol Jo LB 52, 81, HL 28.5

Derbyshire, The. See Coltman v Bibby Tankers Ltd, The Derbyshire

Deria v General Council of British Shipping [1986] 1 WLR 1207, [1986] ICR 172, [1986] IRLR 108, 130 Sol Jo 649, [1986] LS Gaz R 2996, CA 11.18

Desmond v Cheshire West and Chester Council (UKEATPA/0027/12), unreported 19.12, 19.14

Table of Cases

Desmond v Chief Constable of Nottinghamshire Police [2011] EWCA Civ 3, [2011] PTSR 1369, [2011] 1 FLR 1361, [2011] Fam Law 358, [2011] NLJR 102, 175 CL&J 30, [2011] All ER (D) 37 (Jan) 16.7
De Souza v Automobile Association [1986] ICR 514, [1986] IRLR 103, 130 Sol Jo 110, [1986] LS Gaz R 288, CA 10.50
Deutsche Telekom AG v Schröder: C-50/96 [2000] ECR I-743, [2002] 2 CMLR 583, [2000] IRLR 353, ECJ 21.17
Devenney v United Kingdom (Application 24265/94) (2002) Times, 11 April, ECtHR 28.4
Devine v Designer Flowers Wholesale Florist Sundries Ltd [1993] IRLR 517, EAT 53.12
Devlin v United Kingdom (Application 29545/95) (2001) 34 EHRR 1029, [2002] IRLR 155, (2001) Times, 9 November, [2001] ECHR 29545/95 , ECtHR 28.4
Devon and Somerset Fire and Rescue Service v Tilke [2010] EWCA Civ 1402, [2010] All ER (D) 197 (Dec) 19.38
Devon and Somerset Fire and Rescue Service v Tilke (UKEAT/0303/09/RN) (25 January 2010, unreported) 7.22d
Devon County Council v Cook [1977] IRLR 188, EAT 56.5
Devonald v Rosser & Sons [1906] 2 KB 728, 75 LJKB 688, [1904–7] All ER Rep 988, 50 Sol Jo 616, 95 LT 232, 22 TLR 682, CA 56.21
Devonshire v Trico-Folberth Ltd [1989] ICR 747, sub nom Trico-Folberth Ltd v Devonshire [1989] IRLR 396, CA 53.13
Dewhirst Group v GMB Trade Union [2003] All ER (D) 175 (Dec), EAT 37.4
Dhaliwal v British Airways Board [1985] ICR 513, EAT 52.9
Dhatt v McDonalds Hamburgers Ltd [1991] 3 All ER 692, [1991] 1 WLR 527, [1991] ICR 238, [1991] IRLR 130, CA 10.15, 11.21
Dhunna v Creditsights Ltd (2013) UKEAT/0246/12/LA, [2013] NLJR 21, [2013] All ER (D) 133 (May), EAT 23.9, 55.3
Diamond v Park Lane College (UKEAT/0249/05/LA) (25 July 2005, unreported) 47.2
Diamond Resorts (Europe) Ltd, Re [2012] EWHC 3576 (Ch) 15.49
Dibro Ltd v Hore [1990] ICR 370, [1990] IRLR 129, [1990] 13 LS Gaz R 43, EAT 21.8
Dick v Boots the Chemist Ltd IDS Brief No 451 .... 52.11
Dick v University of Glasgow [1993] IRLR 581, Ct of Sess 52.4
Dickins v O2 plc [2008] EWCA Civ 1144, [2009] IRLR 58, [2008] All ER (D) 154 (Oct) 25.8
Diem v Crystal Services plc [2006] All ER (D) 84 (Feb), EAT 18.52, 19.24
Dietman v Brent London Borough Council [1987] ICR 737, [1987] IRLR 259; affd [1988] ICR 842, [1988] IRLR 299, CA 7.42, 56.17, 56.18
Dietrich v Westdeutscher Rundfunk: C-11/99 [2000] ECR I-5589, ECJ 26.5
Dietz v Stichting Thuiszorg Rotterdam: C-435/93 [1996] ECR I-5223, [1997] 1 CMLR 199, [1996] IRLR 692, 563 IRLB 13, ECJ 21.16, 21.17
Digby v East Cambridgeshire District Council [2007] IRLR 585, [2007] All ER (D) 24 (Mar), EAT 18.56
Diggins v Condor Marine Crewing Services Ltd [2009] EWCA Civ 1133, [2010] ICR 213, [2010] IRLR 119 .... 51.15, 55.31
Digital Equipment Co Ltd v Clements (No 2) [1997] ICR 237, [1997] IRLR 140, EAT; revsd [1998] ICR 258, [1998] IRLR 134, [1998] 03 LS Gaz R 24, CA 12.15, 19.46, 53.13
Dignity Funerals v Bruce [2005] IRLR 189, 2004 SLT 1223, 148 Sol Jo LB 1313, [2005] All ER (D) 427 (Apr), Ct of Sess 53.12
Dillenkofer v Germany: C-178/94, C-179/94, C-188/94, C-189/94 and C-190/94 [1997] QB 259, [1996] ECR I-4845, [1996] All ER (EC) 917, [1997] 2 WLR 253, [1996] 3 CMLR 469, [1997] IRLR 60, ECJ 22.2
Dillon v Todd (UKEATS/0010/11/BI) (21 September 2011, unreported) 17.33
Dimtsu v Westminster City Council [1991] IRLR 450, EAT 12.6
Dines v Initial Health Care Services Ltd [1995] ICR 11, [1994] IRLR 336, CA 50.5
Diosynth Ltd v Thomson [2006] CSIH 5, [2006] IRLR 284, 2006 SLT 323, [2006] All ER (D) 165 (Feb) 52.9
DPP v Marshall [1998] ICR 518, EAT 12.7, 17.30
Discount Tobacco and Confectionery Ltd v Armitage [1990] IRLR 15, [1995] ICR 431n, EAT 52.3
Discount Tobacco and Confectionery Ltd v Williamson [1993] ICR 371, [1993] IRLR 327, EAT 32.6
Dispatch Management Services (UK) Ltd v Douglas [2002] IRLR 389, [2001] All ER (D) 26 (Dec), EAT 18.55, 28.7

Table of Cases

Divine-Bortey v Brent London Borough Council [1998] ICR 886, [1998] IRLR 525, [1998] 22 LS Gaz R 29, 142 Sol Jo LB 152, CA 12.8, 18.26

Dixon v BBC [1979] QB 546, [1979] 2 All ER 112, [1979] 2 WLR 647, [1979] ICR 281, [1979] IRLR 114, 122 Sol Jo 713, CA 51.6

Dixon and Shaw v West Ella Developments Ltd [1978] ICR 856, [1978] IRLR 151, 13 ITR 235, EAT 52.3

Dixon Stores Group v Arnold (EAT/772/93) (23 February 1994, unreported) 17.25

Dobie v Burns International Security Services (UK) Ltd [1984] 3 All ER 333, [1985] 1 WLR 43, [1984] ICR 812, [1984] IRLR 329, 128 Sol Jo 872, CA 19.38

Dodd v Bank of Tokyo-Mitsubishi [2005] All ER (D) 74 (Dec), EAT 19.11, 19.14

Dogherty v Chairman and Governors of Amwell View School [2007] ICR 135, (2006) Times, 5 October, [2006] All ER (D) 112 (Sep), sub nom Chairman and Governors of Amwell View School v Dogherty [2007] IRLR 190, EAT 17.13, 20.7, 52.10

Doherty v British Midland Airways Ltd [2006] IRLR 90, [2005] All ER (D) 12 (Apr), EAT 7.22d

Dolland v Trustees of BTG Pension Fund [2011] NLJR 636, [2011] All ER (D) 247 (Apr) 40.17

Dominguez v Centre Informatique Du Centre Ouest Atlantique: C-282/10 [2012] IRLR 321, ECJ 17.12, 22.11, 27.3A, 55.2

Donaldson v Perth and Kinross Council [2004] ICR 667, [2004] IRLR 121, [2003] All ER (D) 416 (Dec) 50.11

Donnelly v Kelvin International Services [1992] IRLR 496, EAT 6.7

Doolan v United Kingdom [2002] IRLR 568, ECtHR 28.4

Dore v Aon Training Ltd (formerly Totalamber plc) [2005] EWCA Civ 411, [2005] All ER (D) 328 (Mar), sub nom Aon Training Ltd (formerly Totalamber plc) v Dore [2005] IRLR 891 .... 12.15, 53.13

Doshoki v Draeger Ltd [2002] IRLR 340, [2002] All ER (D) 139 (Mar), EAT 12.16

Doughty v Rolls-Royce plc [1992] 1 CMLR 1045, [1992] IRLR 126, sub nom Rolls-Royce plc v Doughty [1992] ICR 538, CA 35.8

Dowson v Chief Constable of Northumbria Police [2010] EWHC 2612 (QB), [2010] All ER (D) 191 (Oct) 26.25

Doyle v ESB International Ltd [2013] 1 CMLR 48 .... 40.5

Doyle v North West London Hospitals Trust (UKEAT/0271/11/RN) (20 April 2012, unreported) 18.71

Doyle v White City Stadium Ltd [1935] 1 KB 110, 104 LJKB 140, [1934] All ER Rep 252, 78 Sol Jo 601, 152 LT 32, CA 3.11

Drage v Governors of Greenford High School [2000] ICR 899, [2000] IRLR 314, 144 Sol Jo LB 165, [2000] All ER (D) 343, CA 17.23

Dranez Anstalt v Hayek (Zamir) [2002] EWCA Civ 1729, [2003] FSR 561, [2003] 1 BCLC 278, (2002) Times, 3 December, 146 Sol Jo LB 273, [2002] All ER (D) 377 (Nov) 39.5

Drew v St Edmundsbury Borough Council [1980] ICR 513, [1980] IRLR 459, EAT 52.3

Drinkwater Sabey Ltd v Burnett [1995] ICR 328, [1995] IRLR 238, EAT 18.10

Driskel v Peninsula Business Services Ltd [2000] IRLR 151, EAT 10.51

D'Silva v Manchester Metropolitan University (UKEAT/0336/09/LA) [2011] All ER (D) 05 (May) 18.54

D'Silva v NATFHE [2008] IRLR 412, [2008] All ER (D) 163 (Mar), EAT 12.9, 18.9

D'Souza v Lambeth London Borough Council [1997] IRLR 677, EAT; revsd sub nom Lambeth London Borough Council v D'Souza [1999] IRLR 240, CA 12.19

D'Souza v Lambeth London Borough Council [2003] UKHL 33, [2003] 4 All ER 1113, [2003] 2 CMLR 1329, [2003] ICR 867, [2003] IRLR 484, 74 BMLR 109, [2003] 30 LS Gaz R 30, (2003) Times, 23 June, 147 Sol Jo LB 782, [2003] All ER (D) 258 (Jun) 10.52

Duarte v Black and Decker Corpn [2007] EWHC 2720 (QB), [2008] 1 All ER (Comm) 401, [2007] All ER (D) 378 (Nov) 23.7, 39.7, 39.8, 39.12

Dudley Bower Building Services Ltd v Lowe [2003] ICR 843, [2003] IRLR 260, [2003] All ER (D) 243 (Feb), EAT 50.5

Duffy v Yeomans & Partners Ltd [1993] ICR 862, [1993] IRLR 368, EAT; affd [1995] ICR 1, [1994] IRLR 642, CA 18.60, 52.4, 52.11

Dugdale v Kraft Foods Ltd [1977] 1 All ER 454, [1976] 1 WLR 1288, [1977] ICR 48, [1976] IRLR 368, 11 ITR 309, 120 Sol Jo 780, EAT 21.6

Dugmore v Swansea NHS Trust [2002] EWCA Civ 1689, [2003] 1 All ER 333, [2003] ICR 574, [2003] IRLR 164, 72 BMLR 22, [2003] 05 LS Gaz R 30, (2002) Times, 9 December, 146 Sol Jo LB 271, [2002] All ER (D) 307 (Nov) 26.26

Table of Cases

Duke v GEC Reliance Ltd (formerly Reliance Systems Ltd) [1988] AC 618, [1988] 1 All ER 626,
  [1988] 2 WLR 359, [1988] 1 CMLR 719, [1988] ICR 339, [1988] IRLR 118, 132 Sol Jo 226,
  [1988] 11 LS Gaz R 42, HL 22.2
Dumfries and Galloway Council v North (UKEATS/0047/08/BI) [2009] ICR 1363, [2009] IRLR
  915; revsd sub nom North v Dumfries and Galloway Council [2011] CSIH 2, [2011] IRLR 239,
  2011 SLT 203 .... 21.9, 35.5
Duncan Web Offset (Maidstone) Ltd v Cooper [1995] IRLR 633, EAT 50.15
Duncombe v Department for Education and Skills [2008] All ER (D) 343 (Apr), EAT; revsd in part
  sub nom Duncombe v Secretary of State for Children, Schools and Families; Fletcher v same
  [2009] EWCA Civ 1355, [2010] 4 All ER 335, [2010] 2 CMLR 367, [2010] ICR 815, [2010] IRLR
  331, (2010) Times, 7 January, [2009] All ER (D) 134 (Dec); revsd sub nom Duncombe v Secretary
  of State for Children, Schools and Families [2011] UKSC 14, [2011] 2 All ER 417, [2011] ICR
  495, [2011] IRLR 498, (2011) Times, 1 April, [2011] All ER (D) 332 (Mar)[2011] UKSC 36,
  [2011] ICR 1312, [2011] IRLR 840, (2011) Times, 01 August, [2011] All ER (D) 138 (Jul) .. 23.9, 45.9,
                                                                                        51.15, 55.3
Dundon v GPT Ltd [1995] IRLR 403, EAT 52.3
Dunedin Canmore Housing Association Ltd v Donaldson (UKEATS/0014/09/BI) (8 July 2009,
  unreported) 18.72
Dunham v Ashford Windows [2005] ICR 1584, [2005] IRLR 608, [2005] All ER (D) 104 (Jun),
  EAT 10.20
Dunk v George Waller & Son Ltd [1970] 2 QB 163, [1970] 2 All ER 630, [1970] 2 WLR 1241, 114
  Sol Jo 356, CA 13.2, 56.29
Dunlop Pneumatic Tyre Co Ltd v New Garage and Motor Co Ltd [1915] AC 79, 83 LJKB 1574,
  [1914–15] All ER Rep 739, 111 LT 862, 30 TLR 625, HL 56.26
Dunlop Tyres Ltd v Blows [2001] EWCA Civ 1032, [2001] IRLR 629, [2001] All ER (D) 179
  (Jun) 5.9, 7.12, 32.6
Dunn v Institute of Cemetery and Crematorium Management (UKEAT/0531/10/DA) [2012]
  11 LS Gaz R 20, [2012] NLJR 363, [2012] All ER (D) 173 (Feb), EAT 10.4
Dunn v R [1896] 1 QB 116, 60 JP 117, 65 LJQB 279, 44 WR 243, [1895–9] All ER Rep 907, 40 Sol
  Jo 129, 73 LT 695, 12 TLR 101, CA 35.2
Dunnachie v Kingston-upon-Hull City Council [2004] EWCA Civ 84, [2004] 2 All ER 501, [2004]
  ICR 481, [2004] IRLR 287, [2004] NLJR 248, (2004) Times, 26 February, 148 Sol Jo LB 233,
  [2004] All ER (D) 185 (Feb); revsd [2004] UKHL 36, [2005] 1 AC 226, [2004] 3 All ER 1011,
  [2004] 3 WLR 310, [2004] ICR 1052, [2004] IRLR 727, [2004] 33 LS Gaz R 34, [2004] NLJR
  1156, 148 Sol Jo LB 909, [2004] All ER (D) 251 (Jul) 7.39, 9.17, 53.12, 56.29
Durant v Financial Services Authority [2003] EWCA Civ 1746, [2004] FSR 573, [2004] IP & T 814,
  (2004) Times, 2 January, [2003] All ER (D) 124 (Dec) 9.13
Durant and Cheshire v Clariston Clothing Co Ltd [1974] IRLR 360, Ind Trib 52.14
D'Urso v Ercole Marelli Elettromeccanica Generale SpA: C-362/89 [1991] ECR I-4105,
  [1993] 3 CMLR 513, [1992] IRLR 136, ECJ 50.26, 50.28
Duru v Granada Retail Catering Ltd [2001] All ER (D) 97 (Jul), EAT 18.32
Duthie v Bath & North East Somerset Council [2003] ICR 1405, [2003] 26 LS Gaz R 37, (2003)
  Times, 16 May, [2003] All ER (D) 358 (Apr), EAT 47.8
Dutton v Hawker Siddeley Aviation Ltd [1978] ICR 1057, [1978] IRLR 390, EAT 47.6
Dutton v Jones t/a Llandow Metals (2012) UKEAT/0236/12/ZT, [2013] ICR 559, [2013] All ER
  (D) 317 (Feb), EAT 36.13
Dutton & Clark Ltd v Daly [1985] ICR 780, [1985] IRLR 363, EAT 7.19, 26.28
Dyke v Hereford and Worcester County Council [1989] ICR 800, EAT 52.11
Dyson Technology Ltd v Strutt [2005] EWHC 2814 (Ch), [2005] All ER (D) 355 (Nov) 39.6
Dziennik v CTO Gesellschaft Fur Containertransport MBH [2006] EWCA Civ 1456, [2006] All ER
  (D) 157 (Nov) 25.44

E

E Green & Son (Castings) Ltd v Association of Scientific, Technical and Managerial Staffs [1984]
  ICR 352, [1984] IRLR 135, EAT 37.4, 37.6
E T Marler Ltd v Robertson [1974] ICR 72, NIRC 18.72
E Worsley & Co Ltd v Cooper [1939] 1 All ER 290 .... 39.13
EB v BA [2006] EWCA Civ 132, [2006] IRLR 471, [2006] All ER (D) 300 (Feb) 12.3
EBR Attridge Law LLP v Coleman. See Coleman v EBR Attridge Law LLP

EC Commission v Belgium: C-229/89 [1991] ECR I-2205, [1993] 2 CMLR 403, [1991] IRLR 393,
ECJ 11.9
EC Commission v Belgium: C-173/91 [1993] IRLR 404, ECJ 21.3
EC Commission v Germany: C-341/02 [2005] ECR I-2733, [2005] All ER (D) 172 (Apr), ECJ
.... 23.3
EC Commission v United Kingdom: C-382/92 [1994] ECR I-2435, [1995] 1 CMLR 345, [1994]
ICR 664, [1994] IRLR 392, ECJ 22.2, 22.9
EC Commission v United Kingdom: C-383/92 [1994] ECR I-2479, [1995] 1 CMLR 345, [1994]
ICR 664, [1994] IRLR 412, ECJ 22.8
EC Commission v United Kingdom: C-484/04 [2006] ECR I-7471, [2006] 3 CMLR 1322, [2007]
ICR 592, [2006] IRLR 888, (2006) Times, 21 September, [2006] All ER (D) 32 (Sep), ECJ 22.11,
55.2, 55.15, 55.26
EC Commission v United Kingdom of Great Britain and Northern Ireland: 61/81 [1982] ECR
2601, [1982] 3 CMLR 284, [1982] ICR 578, [1982] IRLR 333, ECJ 22.6
ECM (Vehicle Delivery Service) v Cox [1999] 4 All ER 669, [2000] 1 CMLR 224, [1999] ICR 1162,
[1999] IRLR 559, [1999] All ER (D) 838, CA 50.5
EDF Energy Powerlink Ltd v National Union of Rail, Maritime and Transport Workers [2009]
EWHC 2852 (QB), [2010] IRLR 114 .... 28.7
EFTA Surveillance Authority v Norway: E-1/02 [2003] 1 CMLR 725, [2003] IRLR 318, EFTA
Ct 11.10
EMI Group Electronics Ltd v Coldicott (Inspector of Taxes) [2000] 1 WLR 540, [1999] STC 803,
71 TC 455, [1999] IRLR 630, [1999] 32 LS Gaz R 34, 143 Sol Jo LB 220, [1999] All ER (D) 803,
CA 44.8, 46.10, 56.21
EPI Coaches Ltd v Lafferty [2009] All ER (D) 81 (Apr), EAT 18.16
Eagland v British Telecommunications plc [1993] ICR 644, [1992] IRLR 323, CA 7.11
Eagle Place Services Ltd v Rudd [2010] IRLR 486, [2009] All ER (D) 184 (Oct), EAT 10.14, 12.3
Ealing London Borough v Race Relations Board [1972] AC 342, [1972] 1 All ER 105, [1972] 2 WLR
71, 116 Sol Jo 60, HL 10.20
East Berkshire Health Authority v Matadeen [1992] ICR 723, [1992] IRLR 336, [1992] 29 LS Gaz
R 24, EAT 19.16, 19.35
East Lindsey District Council v Daubney [1977] ICR 566, [1977] IRLR 181, 12 ITR 359, EAT
.... 52.8
Eastbourne Borough Council v Foster [2001] EWCA Civ 1091, [2001] LGR 529, [2002] ICR 234,
[2001] 31 LS Gaz R 30, (2001) Times, 17 August, 145 Sol Jo LB 182, [2001] All ER (D) 135
(Jul) 7.2
Eastham v Newcastle United Football Club Ltd [1964] Ch 413, [1963] 3 All ER 139, [1963] 3 WLR
574, 107 Sol Jo 574, Aus HC 39.5
Eastwood v Magnox Electric plc [2004] UKHL 35, [2005] 1 AC 503, [2004] 3 All ER 991, [2004] 3
WLR 322, [2004] ICR 1064, [2004] IRLR 733, [2004] NLJR 1155, 148 Sol Jo LB 909,
[2004] All ER (D) 268 (Jul) 7.22d, 7.39, 51.7
Eaton v Robert Eaton Ltd [1988] ICR 302, [1988] IRLR 83, EAT 29.2
Eaton v Spencer (t/a Wiggles Experience) [2012] ICR D7, EAT 12.8, 17.38
Eaton Ltd v Nuttall [1977] 3 All ER 1131, [1977] 1 WLR 549, [1977] ICR 272, [1977] IRLR 71, 12
ITR 197, 121 Sol Jo 353, EAT 21.6, 21.7
Ebac Ltd v Wymer [1995] ICR 466, EAT 36.12
Ecclestone v National Union of Journalists [1999] IRLR 166 .... 48.14
Eddie Stobart Ltd v Moreman (2012) UKEAT/0223/11/ZT, [2012] ICR 919, [2012] IRLR 356,
EAT 50.3
Edge v Pensions Ombudsman [2000] Ch 602, [1999] 4 All ER 546, [2000] 3 WLR 79, [2000] ICR
748, [1999] PLR 215, [1999] 35 LS Gaz R 39, [1999] NLJR 1442, CA 40.17
Edinburgh City Council v Wilkinson [2010] IRLR 756 .... 21.9
Edinburgh Home-Link Partnership v The City of Edinburgh Council (UKEATS/0061/11) (10 July
2012, unreported) 50.3
Edmonds v Lawson [2000] IRLR 18, [1999] 39 LS Gaz R 38, 143 Sol Lo LB 234, [1999] All ER (D)
1035; revsd [2000] QB 501, [2000] 2 WLR 1091, [2000] ICR 567, [2000] IRLR 391, 144 Sol Jo LB
151, [2000] All ER (D) 312, CA 13.2, 32.10
Edmund Nuttall Ltd v Butterfield [2005] IRLR 751, [2005] All ER (D) 488 (Jul), EAT 10.26
Edozie v Group 4 Securicor plc (UKEAT/0124/09/ZT) (2010) 894 IDS Brief 7, [2010] All ER (D)
07 (Jan) 12.3

Table of Cases

Edwards v Chesterfield Royal Hospital NHS Foundation Trust [2010] EWCA Civ 571, [2011] QB
339, [2010] 3 WLR 1285, [2010] ICR 1181, [2010] IRLR 702, 154 Sol Jo (no 21) 28, [2010]
23 LS Gaz R 19, [2010] NLJR 806, [2010] All ER (D) 247 (May); revsd [2011] UKSC 58, [2012]
2 All ER 278, [2012] 2 WLR 55, [2012] ICR 201, [2012] IRLR 129, 124 BMLR 51, [2012]
02 LS Gaz R 17, [2011] NLJR 30, (2012) Times, 23 January, 155 Sol Jo (no 48) 31, [2011] All ER
(D) 101 (Dec) 7.39, 51.7, 56.25
Edwards v Derby City Council [1999] ICR 114, EAT 21.14
Edwards v Governors of Hanson School [2001] IRLR 733, [2001] All ER (D) 05 (Jan), EAT 52.8
Edwards v National Coal Board [1949] 1 KB 704, [1949] 1 All ER 743, 93 Sol Jo 337, 65 TLR 430,
CA 25.5
Edwards v Skyways Ltd [1964] 1 All ER 494, [1964] 1 WLR 349, 108 Sol Jo 279 .... 5.6
Edwards v Society of Graphical and Allied Trades [1971] Ch 354, [1970] 3 All ER 689, [1970] 3
WLR 713, 114 Sol Jo 618, CA 49.12
Edwards v Worboys [1984] AC 724n, [1984] 2 WLR 850n, [1983] Com LR 151, 127 Sol Jo 287,
CA 39.5
Egg Stores (Stamford Hill) Ltd v Leibovici [1977] ICR 260, [1976] IRLR 376, 11 ITR 289, EAT
.... 46.3
Eidesund v Stavanger Catering A/S: E-2/95 [1997] 2 CMLR 672, [1996] IRLR 684, EFTA Ct
.... 50.19
Ekpe v Metropolitan Police Comr [2001] ICR 1084, [2001] IRLR 605, [2001] All ER (D) 353 (May),
EAT 10.26
Elkouil v Coney Island Ltd [2002] IRLR 174, [2001] All ER (D) 181 (Nov), EAT 53.13
Elliott Turbomachinery Ltd v Bates [1981] ICR 218, EAT 36.7
Ellis v M&P Steelcraft Ltd. See M&P Steelcraft Ltd v Ellis
Elsner–Lakeberg v Land Nordrhein-Westfalen: C-285/02 [2004] ECR I-5861, [2004] 2 CMLR 874,
[2005] IRLR 209, [2004] All ER (D) 423 (May), ECJ 21.5
Eltek (UK) Ltd v Thomson [2000] ICR 689, EAT 18.10
Elvidge v Coventry City Council [1994] QB 241, [1993] 4 All ER 903, [1993] 3 WLR 976, [1994]
ICR 68, 26 HLR 281, CA 41.7
Ely v YKK Fasteners (UK) Ltd [1994] ICR 164, [1993] IRLR 500, CA 52.1
Emmott v Minister for Social Welfare and A-G: C-208/90 [1991] ECR I-4269, [1991] 3 CMLR 894,
[1993] ICR 8, [1991] IRLR 387, ECJ 22.2
Employment Service v Nathan EAT/1316/95, IDS Brief No 568 .... 18.38
Enderby v Frenchay Health Authority (No 2) [2000] ICR 612, [2000] IRLR 257, CA 21.5, 21.9
Enderby v Frenchay Health Authority and Secretary of State for Health [1991] 1 CMLR 626, [1991]
ICR 382, [1991] IRLR 44, EAT; on appeal [1994] ICR 112, [1992] IRLR 15, CA; refd sub nom
Enderby v Frenchay Health Authority: C-127/92 [1994] 1 All ER 495, [1993] ECR I-5535,
[1994] 1 CMLR 8, [1994] ICR 112, [1993] IRLR 591, ECJ 19.48, 21.10, 21.11, 21.12
English v Emery Reimbold & Strick Ltd [2002] EWCA Civ 605, [2002] 3 All ER 385, [2002] 1 WLR
2409, [2003] IRLR 710, (2002) Times, 10 May, [2002] All ER (D) 302 (Apr) 18.63, 19.22
English v Thomas Sanderson Blinds Ltd [2008] EWCA Civ 1421, [2009] 2 All ER 468,
[2009] 2 CMLR 437, [2009] ICR 543, [2009] IRLR 206, (2009) Times, 5 January, 153 Sol Jo (no
1) 31, [2008] All ER (D) 219 (Dec) 10.20, 10.23, 10.39
English v UNISON (2000) IDS Brief No 668 .... 49.21
Enterprise Liverpool Ltd v Jonas (UKEAT/0112/09/CEA) [2009] All ER (D) 115 (Aug) . 18.10, 18.23
Enterprise Managed Services Ltd v Dance (UKEAT/0200/11/DM) unreported 50.29
Enterprise Management Services Ltd v Connect-Up Ltd (2011) UKEAT/0462/10/CEA, [2012]
IRLR 190, [2012] All ER (D) 15 (Jan), EAT 50.3
Environment Agency v Rowan [2008] IRLR 20, [2008] ICR 218, [2007] All ER (D) 22 (Nov),
EAT 10.37
Equal Opportunities Commission v Birmingham City Council. See Birmingham City Council v
Equal Opportunities Commission
Equal Opportunities Commission v Secretary of State for Employment. See R v Secretary of State
for Employment, ex p Equal Opportunities Commission
Equal Opportunities Commission v Secretary of State for Trade and Industry [2007] EWHC 483
(Admin), [2007] 2 CMLR 1351, [2007] ICR 1234, [2007] IRLR 327, [2007] All ER (D) 183
(Mar) 10.51, 22.2, 22.6
Essa v Laing Ltd [2003] ICR 1110, [2003] IRLR 346, [2003] 18 LS Gaz R 34, (2003) Times, 7 April,
[2003] All ER (D) 215 (Feb), EAT; affd [2004] EWCA Civ 02, [2004] ICR 746, [2004] IRLR 313,
(2004) Times, 29 January, 148 Sol Jo LB 146, [2004] All ER (D) 155 (Jan) 12.17

Esso Petroleum Co Ltd v Harper's Garage (Stourport) Ltd [1968] AC 269, [1967] 1 All ER 699, [1967] 2 WLR 871, 111 Sol Jo 174, 201 Estates Gazette 1043, HL 39.3, 39.5, 39.10
Esso Petroleum Co Ltd v Jarvis [2002] All ER (D) 112 (Jan), EAT 45.2a
Etam plc v Rowan [1989] IRLR 150, EAT 11.3
Euro–Diam Ltd v Bathurst [1990] 1 QB 1, [1988] 2 All ER 23, [1988] 2 WLR 517, [1988] 1 Lloyd's Rep 228, 132 Sol Jo 372, [1988] 9 LS Gaz R 45, CA 7.24
Euro Hotels (Thornton Heath) Ltd v Alam (UKEAT/0006/09) [2009] All ER (D) 198 (Aug) 18.54
Euroguard Ltd v Rycroft IDS Brief No 498 .... 52.11
European Commission v Hungary: C-286/12 [2013] 1 CMLR 1243, [2012] All ER (D) 345 (Nov), ECJ 40.5
Europièces SA (in liq) v Sanders: C-399/96 [1998] ECR I-6965, [1999] All ER (EC) 831, [2001] 1 CMLR 667, [1998] All ER (D) 574, ECJ 50.11
Evans v Bolton School [2006] EWCA Civ 1653, [2007] ICR 641, 150 Sol Jo LB 1532, [2006] All ER (D) 198 (Nov), sub nom Bolton School v Evans [2007] IRLR 140 .... 9.17
Evans v Malley Organisation Ltd (t/a First Business Support) [2002] EWCA Civ 1834, [2003] ICR 432, [2003] IRLR 156, (2003) Times, 23 January, [2002] All ER (D) 397 (Nov) 27.4
Evans v Metropolitan Police Comr [1993] ICR 151, [1992] IRLR 570, CA 18.17
Evans v Parasol Ltd (UKEAT/0536/08/RN) [2009] All ER (D) 52 (Dec); affd Evans v RSA Consulting Ltd [2010] EWCA Civ 866, [2011] ICR 37, [2010] All ER (D) 240 (Jul) 14.3
Evans v University of Oxford (UKEATPA/1510/09) (23 April 2010, unreported) 19.16
Evening Standard Co Ltd v Henderson [1987] ICR 588, [1987] IRLR 64, CA 7.47c
Evershed v New Star Asset Management (UKEAT/0249/09/CEA) (31 July 2009, unreported) 18.10
Evershed v New Star Asset Management Holdings Ltd [2010] EWCA Civ 870, [2010] All ER (D) 322 (Jul) 18.10
Eversheds LLP v Gray (UKEAT/0585/11/CEA) (29 November 2011, unreported) 18.51
Everson and Barrass v Secretary of State for Trade and Industry and Bell Lines Ltd: C-198/98 [1999] ECR I-8903, [2000] All ER (EC) 29, [2000] 1 CMLR 489, [2000] IRLR 202, ECJ 29.3
Eweida v British Airways plc [2009] ICR 303, [2009] IRLR 78, 152 Sol Jo (no 47) 31, [2008] All ER (D) 13 (Dec), EAT; affd [2010] EWCA Civ 80, [2010] ICR 890, [2010] IRLR 322, [2010] 09 LS Gaz R 19, (2010) Times, 18 February, 154 Sol Jo (no 7) 36, [2010] All ER (D) 144 (Feb) 10.22, 10.34, 11.9, 28.7
Eweida v United Kingdom ((Application Nos 48420/10, 59842/10, 51671/10 and 36516/10) [2013] IRLR 231, [2013] NLJR 70, (2013) Times, 04 February, [2013] ECHR 48420/10, [2013] All ER (D) 69 (Jan), ECtHR 10.2, 11.9
Export Credits Guarantee Department v Universal Oil Products Co [1983] 2 All ER 205, [1983] 1 WLR 399, [1983] 2 Lloyd's Rep 152, 127 Sol Jo 408, 23 BLR 106, 133 NLJ 662, HL 56.26
Express and Echo Publications Ltd v Tanton [1999] ICR 693, [1999] IRLR 367, [1999] 14 LS Gaz R 31, [1999] All ER (D) 256, CA 14.3
Express and Star Ltd v National Graphical Association [1985] IRLR 455; affd [1986] ICR 589, [1986] IRLR 222, [1986] LS Gaz R 2083, CA 48.16
Ezsias v North Glamorgan NHS Trust [2007] EWCA Civ 330, [2007] 4 All ER 940, [2007] ICR 1126, [2007] IRLR 603, (2007) Times, 19 March, [2007] All ER (D) 104 (Mar) 18.17
Ezsias v North Glamorgan NHS Trust (UKEAT/0399/09/CEA) (18 March 2011, unreported) 52.14

F

F v G (UKEAT/0042/11/DA) [2012] ICR 246, [2011] All ER (D) 42 (Dec), EAT . 12.11, 18.18, 18.19, 19.26
F C Shepherd & Co Ltd v Jerrom [1987] QB 301, [1986] 3 All ER 589, [1986] 3 WLR 801, [1986] ICR 802, [1986] IRLR 358, 130 Sol Jo 665, CA 46.3
FS Consulting Ltd v McCaul (Inspector of Taxes) (SpC 305) [2002] STC (SCD) 138 .... 44.34
FW Farnsworth Ltd v McCoid [1998] IRLR 362, EAT; affd [1999] ICR 1047, [1999] IRLR 626, [1999] 16 LS Gaz R 35, CA 49.17
Faccenda Chicken Ltd v Fowler [1985] 1 All ER 724, [1985] FSR 105, [1984] ICR 589, [1984] IRLR 61; affd [1987] Ch 117, [1986] 1 All ER 617, [1986] 3 WLR 288, [1986] FSR 291, [1986] ICR 297, [1986] IRLR 69, 130 Sol Jo 573, CA 39.11, 39.13

Table of Cases

Faccini Dori v Recreb Srl: C-91/92 [1994] ECR I-3325, [1995] All ER (EC) 1, [1995] 1 CMLR 665, ECJ 22.2

Facey v Midas Retail Security [2001] ICR 287, [2000] IRLR 812, [2000] All ER (D) 1306, EAT 19.23

Factortame Ltd v Secretary of State for Transport (No 2). See R v Secretary of State for Transport, ex p Factortame Ltd (No 2)

Fadipe v Reed Nursing Personnel [2001] EWCA Civ 1885, [2005] ICR 1760, [2001] All ER (D) 23 (Dec) 9.17

Fairchild v Glenhaven Funeral Services Ltd [2001] EWCA Civ 1881, [2002] 1 WLR 1052, [2002] ICR 412, [2002] IRLR 129, (2001) Times, 13 December, [2001] All ER (D) 125 (Dec); revsd [2002] UKHL 22, [2003] 1 AC 32, [2002] 3 All ER 305, [2002] ICR 798, [2002] IRLR 533, 67 BMLR 90, [2002] NLJR 998, (2002) Times, 21 June, [2003] 1 LRC 674, [2002] All ER (D) 139 (Jun) 25.8, 25.14

Fairfield Ltd v Skinner [1992] ICR 836, [1993] IRLR 4, [1992] 34 LS Gaz R 39, EAT 32.6

Fairhurst Ward Abbotts Ltd v Botes Building Ltd [2004] EWCA Civ 83, [2004] ICR 919, [2004] IRLR 304, 148 Sol Jo LB 235, [2004] All ER (D) 225 (Feb) 50.4

Fantask A/S v Industriministeriet (Erhvervsministeriet): C-188/95 [1998] All ER (EC) 1, [1997] ECR I-6783, [1998] 1 CMLR 473, ECJ 22.2

Farooq v Comr of Police of the Metropolis [2008] All ER (D) 187 (Jun), EAT 18.51

Farrant v Woodroffe School [1998] ICR 184, [1998] IRLR 176, EAT 52.9

Farrell Matthews & Weir (a firm) v Hansen [2005] ICR 509, [2005] IRLR 160, [2004] All ER (D) 365 (Oct), EAT 32.6

Farrow v Wilson (1869) LR 4 CP 744, 38 LJCP 326, 18 WR 43, [1861–73] All ER Rep 846, 20 LT 810 .... 56.8

Fassihi v Item Software (UK) Ltd. See Item Software (UK) Ltd v Fassihi

Faust v Power Packing Casemakers Ltd. See Power Packing Casemakers Ltd v Faust

Fay v North Yorkshire County Council (1986) 85 LGR 87, [1986] ICR 133, sub nom North Yorkshire County Council v Fay [1985] IRLR 247, CA 45.7, 52.14

Fecitt v NHS Manchester (2010) UKEAT/0150/10/CEA, [2011] ICR 476, [2011] IRLR 111, [2010] All ER (D) 320 (Nov), EAT; revsd [2011] EWCA Civ 1190, [2012] ICR 372, [2012] IRLR 64, [2011] 43 LS Gaz R 20, [2011] All ER (D) 208 (Oct) 9.18, 54.1, 55.23

Federación de Servicios Públicos de la UGT (UGT-FSP) v Ayuntamiento de La Línea de la Concepción: C-151/09 [2010] ICR 1248, [2010] All ER (D) 30 (Dec), ECJ 50.21

Federatie Nederlandse Vakbeweging v Netherlands State: C-124/05 [2006] ECR I-3423, [2006] All ER (EC) 913, [2006] ICR 962, [2006] IRLR 561, [2006] All ER (D) 69 (Apr), ECJ 27.3

Feist v First Hampshire & Dorset Ltd [2007] All ER (D) 180 (Feb), EAT 55.3, 55.15, 55.29, 55.34

Fellowes & Son v Fisher [1976] QB 122, [1975] 2 All ER 829, [1975] 3 WLR 184, 119 Sol Jo 390, CA 39.8

Fennelly v Connex South Eastern Ltd [2001] IRLR 390, [2000] All ER (D) 2233, CA 54.2

Fentiman v Fluid Engineering Products Ltd [1991] ICR 570, [1991] IRLR 150, EAT 53.12

Fenton v Stablegold Ltd (t/a Chiswick Court Hotel) [1986] ICR 236, [1986] IRLR 64, EAT 53.7

Ferenc-Batchelor v London Underground Ltd [2003] ICR 656, [2003] IRLR 252, [2003] All ER (D) 252 (Mar), EAT 49.21

Ferguson v British Gas Trading Ltd [2009] EWCA Civ 46, [2009] 3 All ER 304, [2010] 1 WLR 785, 153 Sol Jo (no 7) 34, [2009] 8 LS Gaz R 18, [2009] All ER (D) 80 (Feb) 26.25

Ferguson v Gateway Training Centre Ltd [1991] ICR 658, EAT 18.60

Ferguson v John Dawson & Partners (Contractors) Ltd [1976] 3 All ER 817, [1976] 1 WLR 1213, [1976] 2 Lloyd's Rep 669, [1976] IRLR 346, 120 Sol Jo 603, 8 BLR 38, CA 20.5

Ferguson v Prestwick Circuits Ltd [1992] IRLR 266, EAT 52.11

Ferguson v Welsh [1987] 3 All ER 777, [1987] 1 WLR 1553, 86 LGR 153, [1988] IRLR 112, 131 Sol Jo 1552, [1987] LS Gaz R 3581, [1987] NLJ Rep 1037, HL 25.15

Fernandez v McDonald [2003] EWCA Civ 1219, [2003] 4 All ER 1033, [2004] 1 WLR 1027, [2004] HLR 189, [2003] 42 EG 128, [2003] 34 LS Gaz R 33, (2003) Times, 9 October, 147 Sol Jo LB 995, [2003] All ER (D) 94 (Aug) 41.6

Fernandez v Office of the Parliamentary Comr for Administration and the Health Service Comr [2006] All ER (D) 460 (Jul), EAT 12.3

Finalarte Sociedade de Construção Civil Lda v Urlaubs- und Lohnausgleichskasse der Bauwirtschaft: C-49/98, C-50/98, C-52/98 to C-54/98 and C-68/98 to C-71/98 [2001] ECR I-7831, [2003] 2 CMLR 333, [2001] All ER (D) 361 (Oct), ECJ 23.3

Financial Techniques (Planning Services) Ltd v Hughes [1981] IRLR 32, CA 51.7

Financial Times Ltd v Byrne (No 2) [1992] IRLR 163, EAT 21.12
Finlay v Cyron (UKEAT/0121/11/RN) (14 October 2011, unreported) 18.23
Fire Brigades Union v Fraser [1998] IRLR 697, Ct of Sess 11.29
First Castle Electronics Ltd v West [1989] ICR 72, EAT 18.22
First Point International Ltd v Department of Trade and Industry (1999) 164 JP 89, [1999] All ER
  (D) 898, DC 45.3
First West Yorkshire Ltd (t/a First Leeds) v Haigh [2008] IRLR 182, [2008] All ER (D) 207 (Jan),
  EAT 52.8
Fisher v Brooker [2009] UKHL 41, [2009] 4 All ER 789, [2009] 1 WLR 1764, [2009] Bus LR 1334,
  [2009] FSR 919, [2010] IP & T 1, (2009) Times, 12 August, 153 Sol Jo (no 31) 29, [2010] 3 LRC
  38, [2009] All ER (D) 338 (Jul) 3.11
Fisher-Karpark Industries Ltd v Nichols [1982] FSR 351 .... 39.15
Fisscher v Voorhuis Hengelo BV: C-128/93 [1994] ECR I-4583, [1995] All ER (EC) 193,
  [1995] 1 CMLR 881, [1995] ICR 635, [1994] IRLR 662, ECJ 17.12, 21.17, 22.2
Fitch v Dewes [1921] 2 AC 158, 90 LJ Ch 436, [1921] All ER Rep 13, 65 Sol Jo 626, 125 LT 744,
  37 TLR 784, HL 39.8
Fitzgerald v Hall, Russell & Co Ltd [1970] AC 984, [1969] 3 All ER 1140, [1969] 3 WLR 868, [1969]
  2 Lloyd's Rep 514, 7 KIR 263, 5 ITR 1, 113 Sol Jo 899, 1970 SC 1, 1970 SLT 37, HL 45.8
Fitzgerald v University of Kent at Canterbury [2004] EWCA Civ 143, [2004] ICR 737, [2004] IRLR
  300, [2004] 11 LS Gaz R 34, (2004) Times, 4 March, 148 Sol Jo LB 237, [2004] All ER (D) 262
  (Feb) 17.23, 51.13
Fitzpatrick v British Railways Board [1992] ICR 221, [1991] IRLR 376, CA 52.3
Flack v Kodak Ltd [1986] 2 All ER 1003, [1987] 1 WLR 31, [1986] ICR 775, [1986] IRLR 255, 130
  Sol Jo 713, [1986] LS Gaz R 2238, CA 6.7
Fletcher v Blackpool Fylde & Wyre Hospitals NHS Trust. See Fletcher v NHS Pensions Agency
Fletcher v Ministry of Defence. See Ministry of Defence v Fletcher
Fletcher v NHS Pensions Agency [2005] ICR 1458, sub nom Fletcher v Blackpool Fylde & Wyre
  Hospitals NHS Trust [2005] IRLR 689, [2005] All ER (D) 57 (Jun), EAT 10.15, 11.31
Flett v Matheson [2005] ICR 1134, [2005] IRLR 412, [2005] All ER (D) 188 (Apr), EAT; revsd
  [2006] EWCA Civ 53, [2006] ICR 673, [2006] IRLR 277, [2006] All ER (D) 88 (Feb) 13.2, 14.3,
                                                                                32.10, 56.15
Flintshire County Council v Moore (UKEAT/0379/11/DA) (15 September 2011, unreported)
  .... 52.11
Fogarty v United Kingdom (Application 37112/97) (2001) 34 EHRR 302, [2002] IRLR 148,
  12 BHRC 132, (2001) Times, 26 November, [2001] ECHR 37112/97, ECtHR 11.23, 28.4
Folami v Nigerline (UK) Ltd [1978] ICR 277, EAT 8.4
Foley v NHS Greater Glasgow & Clyde (2012) UKEATS/0007/12/BI, UKEATS/0008/12/BI,
  [2013] ICR 342 .... 21.18
Food Corpn of India v Antclizo Shipping Corpn, The Antclizo [1988] 2 All ER 513, [1988] 1 WLR
  603, [1988] 2 Lloyd's Rep 93, 132 Sol Jo 752, [1988] NLJR 135, HL 39.11
Forbouys Ltd v Rich (EAT/144/01) [2002] All ER (D) 156 (Apr) 55.22
Force One Utilities Ltd v Hatfield [2009] IRLR 45, [2008] All ER (D) 130 (May), EAT 18.17
Ford v Milthorn Toleman Ltd [1980] IRLR 30, CA 51.7
Ford v Stakis Hotels and Inns Ltd [1987] ICR 943, [1988] IRLR 46, [1987] LS Gaz R 2192,
  EAT 17.21
Ford v Warwickshire County Council [1983] 2 AC 71, [1983] 1 All ER 753, [1983] 2 WLR 399, 81
  LGR 326, [1983] ICR 273, [1983] IRLR 126, 127 Sol Jo 154, HL 6.7, 45.8
Ford Motor Co Ltd v Amalgamated Union of Engineering and Foundry Workers [1969] 2 QB 303,
  [1969] 2 All ER 481, [1969] 1 WLR 339, 113 Sol Jo 203 .... 5.3
Foreningen af Arbejdsledere i Danmark v Daddy's Dance Hall A/S: 324/86 [1988] ECR 739,
  [1989] 2 CMLR 517, [1988] IRLR 315, ECJ 50.6, 50.29
Forshaw v Archcraft Ltd [2006] ICR 60, [2005] IRLR 600, [2005] All ER (D) 105 (May), EAT
  .... 39.1
Forster v Cartwright Black [2004] ICR 1728, [2004] IRLR 781, [2004] All ER (D) 93 (Aug), EAT
  .... 47.15
Fosca Services (UK) Ltd v Birkett [1996] IRLR 325, EAT 7.36, 56.25
Foster v Bon Groundwork Ltd (UKEAT/0382/10/SM) [2011] ICR 1122, [2011] IRLR 645, EAT;
  affd [2012] EWCA Civ 252, [2012] IRLR 517, [2012] All ER (D) 107 (Mar) . 17.27, 18.22, 18.26, 18.27

Table of Cases

Foster v British Gas plc: C-188/89 [1991] 1 QB 405, [1990] 3 All ER 897, [1990] ECR I-3313, [1991] 2 WLR 258, [1990] 2 CMLR 833, [1991] ICR 84, [1990] IRLR 353, ECJ; apld [1991] 2 AC 306, [1991] 2 All ER 705, [1991] 2 WLR 1075, [1991] 2 CMLR 217, [1991] ICR 463, [1991] IRLR 268, [1991] 18 LS Gaz R 34, HL 22.2, 35.8

Foster v D & H Travel Ltd [2006] ICR 1537, [2006] All ER (D) 15 (Aug), EAT 17.38, 18.16

Foster v South Glamorgan Health Authority [1988] ICR 526, [1988] IRLR 277, [1988] 15 LS Gaz R 37, EAT 17.30

Foster Bryant Surveying Ltd v Bryant [2007] EWCA Civ 200, [2007] Bus LR 1565, [2007] IRLR 425, [2007] 2 BCLC 239, [2007] BCC 804, [2007] All ER (D) 213 (Mar) 7.16, 8.19, 8.24

Foster Clark Ltd's Indenture Trusts, Re, Loveland v Horscroft [1966] 1 All ER 43, [1966] 1 WLR 125, 110 Sol Jo 108 .... 29.10, 56.9

Four Seasons Healthcare Ltd (formerly Cotswold Spa Retirement Hotels Ltd) v Maughan [2005] IRLR 324, [2005] All ER (D) 24 (Jan), EAT 46.3

Fowler v British School of Motoring [2006] All ER (D) 93 (May), EAT 19.43

Fox v North Cumbria University Hospitals NHS Trust. See Potter v North Cumbria Acute Hospitals NHS Trust

Fox v Rangecroft [2006] EWCA Civ 1112 .... 12.3

Fox Cross Claimants v Glasgow City Council (UKEATS/0027/12/BI), unreported 21.9

Frames Snooker Centre v Boyce [1992] IRLR 472, EAT 52.9

Framlington Group Ltd v Barnetson [2007] EWCA Civ 502, [2007] 3 All ER 1054, [2007] 1 WLR 2443, [2007] ICR 1439, [2007] IRLR 598, (2007) Times, 11 June, [2007] All ER (D) 429 (May) 18.13

Francis v Elizabeth Claire Care Management Ltd [2005] IRLR 858, [2005] All ER (D) 244 (Jun), EAT 32.6

Francois v Castle Rock Properties Ltd (t/a Electric Ballroom) (UKEAT/0260/10/SM) (5 April 2011, unreported) 18.72

Francotype-Postalia Ltd v Whitehead [2011] EWHC 367 (Ch), [2011] All ER (D) 278 (Feb) 39.7

Francovich and Bonifaci v Italy: C-6/90 and C-9/90 [1991] ECR I-5357, [1993] 2 CMLR 66, [1995] ICR 722, [1992] IRLR 84, ECJ 22.2, 27.8

Frank Wright & Co (Holdings) Ltd v Punch [1980] IRLR 217, EAT 56.22

Franks v Reuters Ltd [2003] EWCA Civ 417, [2003] ICR 1166, [2003] IRLR 423, [2003] 25 LS Gaz R 45, (2003) Times, 23 April, 147 Sol Jo LB 474, [2003] All ER (D) 160 (Apr) 7.2, 14.3, 45.2b

Fraser v HLMAD Ltd [2006] EWCA Civ 738, [2007] 1 All ER 383, [2006] ICR 1395, [2006] IRLR 687, 150 Sol Jo LB 809, [2006] All ER (D) 152 (Jun) 7.45, 18.26, 56.39

Fraser v Southwest London St George's Mental Health Trust (UKEAT/0456/10/DA) [2012] ICR 403, [2012] IRLR 100, [2012] All ER (D) 08 (Jan), EAT 27.3A, 27.6

Freeman v Sovereign Chicken Ltd [1991] ICR 853, [1991] IRLR 408, EAT 18.32

Freeman v Ultra Green Group Ltd (UKEAT/0239/11/CEA) (9 August 2011, unreported) 40.3

Freer v Glover [2005] EWHC 3341 (QB), [2006] IRLR 521, [2005] All ER (D) 271 (Dec) 2.4

French v Barclays Bank plc [1998] IRLR 646, CA 53.12

French v MITIE Management Services Ltd [2002] IRLR 512, [2002] All ER (D) 150 (Sep), EAT 50.18

Freud v Bentalls Ltd [1983] ICR 77, [1982] IRLR 443, EAT 52.11

Friend v Institution of Professional Managers and Specialists [1999] IRLR 173 .... 49.22

Frost v Chief Constable of South Yorkshire Police [1998] QB 254, [1997] 1 All ER 540, [1997] 3 WLR 1194, [1997] IRLR 173, 33 BMLR 108, [1996] NLJR 1651, CA; revsd sub nom White v Chief Constable of South Yorkshire Police [1999] 2 AC 455, [1999] 1 All ER 1, [1998] 3 WLR 1509, [1999] ICR 216, [1999] IRLR 110, 45 BMLR 1, [1999] 02 LS Gaz R 28, [1998] NLJR 1844, [1999] 3 LRC 644, sub nom Frost v Chief Constable of South Yorkshire Police 143 Sol Jo LB 51, HL 25.8

Fry v Foreign and Commonwealth Office [1997] ICR 512, EAT 18.51

Fub v Stadt Halle (No 2): C-429/09 [2011] 2 CMLR 305, [2011] IRLR 176, [2010] All ER (D) 24 (Dec), ECJ 55.8, 55.15, 55.21, 55.22

Fuchs and Kohler v Land Hessen: C-159/10 and C-160/10 [2011] 3 CMLR 1299, [2012] ICR 93, [2011] IRLR 1043, (2011) Times, 27 August, [2011] All ER (D) 97 (Sep), ECJ 11.9, 40.5

Fulcrum Pharma (Europe) Ltd v Bonassera (UKEAT/0198/10/DM) (22 October 2010, unreported) 52.11

Fullarton Computer Industries Ltd v Central Arbitration Committee [2001] IRLR 752, Ct of Sess 48.10, 48.31

Fuller v Brent London Borough Council [2011] EWCA Civ 267, [2011] ICR 806, [2011] IRLR 414, [2011] All ER (D) 162 (Mar) 52.9

Fuller v Lloyds Bank plc [1991] IRLR 336, EAT 52.4
Fyfe v Scientific Furnishings Ltd [1989] ICR 648, [1989] IRLR 331, EAT 53.13, 56.30
Fytche v Wincanton Logistics plc [2004] UKHL 31, [2004] 4 All ER 221, [2004] ICR 975, [2004]
    IRLR 817, [2004] 31 LS Gaz R 25, (2004) Times, 2 July, 148 Sol Jo LB 825, [2004] All ER (D)
    07 (Jul) 26.12

G

G (by his litigation friend) v Head Teacher and Governors of St Gregory's Catholic Science College
    [2011] EWHC 1452 (Admin), [2011] NLJR 884, [2011] All ER (D) 113 (Jun) 11.9
G F Sharp & Co Ltd v McMillan [1998] IRLR 632, EAT 46.3
G W Plowman & Son Ltd v Ash [1964] 2 All ER 10, [1964] 1 WLR 568, 108 Sol Jo 216, CA
    .... 39.6, 39.8
GEC Ferranti Defence Systems Ltd v MSF [1993] IRLR 101, EAT 37.4
GFI Group Inc v Eaglestone [1994] IRLR 119 .... 39.14
GFI Holdings Ltd v Camm [2008] All ER (D) 74 (Sep), EAT 18.22
G4S Security Services (UK) v Rondeau (UKEAT/0207/09/DA) (13 October 2009, unreported)
    .... 18.72, 19.43
GHLM Trading Ltd v Maroo [2012] EWHC 61 (Ch), [2012] 07 LS Gaz R 18, [2012] NLJR 213,
    [2012] All ER (D) 172 (Jan) 7.17, 8.19
GKN Sankey Ltd v National Society of Motor Mechanics [1980] ICR 148, [1980] IRLR 8, EAT
    .... 37.4
GMB v Hamm (EAT/246/00) [2000] All ER (D) 1830 .... 17.25
GMB v Lambeth Service Team Ltd [2005] All ER (D) 153 (Jul), EAT 37.6
GMB v MAN Truck and Bus UK Ltd [2000] ICR 1101, [2000] IRLR 636, EAT 37.3
GMB v Susie Radin Ltd [2004] EWCA Civ 180, [2004] 2 All ER 279, [2004] ICR 893, [2004]
    11 LS Gaz R 34, 148 Sol Jo LB 266, [2004] All ER (D) 353 (Feb), sub nom Susie Radin Ltd v
    GMB [2004] IRLR 400, (2004) Times, 16 March 37.6, 50.23
GMB and Amicus v Beloit Walmsley Ltd [2003] ICR 1396, [2004] IRLR 18, [2003] All ER (D) 29
    (Sep), EAT 37.6
GMB Northern v Cable Realisations Ltd. See Cable Realisations Ltd v GMB Northern
GMB Union v Corrigan [2008] ICR 197, [2007] All ER (D) 288 (Oct), EAT 48.14
Gale v Northern General Hospital NHS Trust. See Northern General Hospital NHS Trust v Gale
Gallagher v Alpha Catering Services Ltd (t/a Alpha Flight Services) [2004] EWCA Civ 1559, [2005]
    ICR 673, [2005] IRLR 102, [2004] All ER (D) 121 (Nov) 55.5, 55.17, 55.29
Galloway v Barnet Enfield and Haringey Mental Health NHS Trust [2010] EWCA Civ 1368,
    [2010] All ER (D) 120 (Dec) 19.24
Garcia-Bello v Aviance UK Ltd [2007] All ER (D) 318 (Dec), EAT 11.9
Gardiner v London Borough of Merton. See Merton London Borough Council v Gardiner
Gardiner-Hill v Roland Beiger Technics Ltd [1982] IRLR 498, EAT 53.13, 56.30
Gardner v Chief Constable of West Midlands Police (UKEAT/0174/11/DA) [2012] EqLR 20,
    [2012] All ER (D) 39 (Mar), EAT 12.19
Garland v British Rail Engineering Ltd: 12/81 [1983] 2 AC 751, [1982] 2 All ER 402, [1982] ECR
    359, [1982] 2 WLR 918, [1982] 1 CMLR 696, [1982] ICR 420, [1982] IRLR 111, ECJ; apld [1983]
    2 AC 751, [1982] 2 All ER 402, [1982] 2 WLR 918, [1982] 2 CMLR 174, [1982] ICR 420, [1982]
    IRLR 257, 126 Sol Jo 309, HL 40.8
Garratt v Mirror Group Newspapers Ltd [2011] EWCA Civ 425, [2011] All ER (D) 149 (Apr)
    .... 5.10, 7.15
Garrett v Camden London Borough Council [2001] EWCA Civ 395, [2001] All ER (D) 202
    (Mar) 26.25
Garside and Laycock Ltd v Booth (UKEAT/0003/11/CEA) (27 May 2011, unreported) 52.14
Gascol Conversions Ltd v Mercer [1974] ICR 420, [1974] IRLR 155, [1975] KILR 149, 9 ITR 282,
    118 Sol Jo 219, CA 32.36
Gassmayr v Bundesminister Fur Wissenschaft und Forschung: C-194/08 [2010] ECR I-6281,
    [2011] 1 CMLR 175, ECJ 31.11, 31.15
Gate Gourmet London Ltd v Transport and General Workers Union [2005] EWHC 1889 (QB),
    [2005] IRLR 881, [2005] 35 LS Gaz R 41, [2005] All ER (D) 117 (Aug) 28.7
Gateway Hotels Ltd v Stewart [1988] IRLR 287, EAT 50.26
Gavieiro Gavieiro v Conselleria de Educacion e Ordenacion Universitaria de la Xunta de Galicia:
    C-444/09 [2011] IRLR 504, [2011] All ER (D) 05 (Jan), ECJ 45.9

Table of Cases

Gayle v Sandwell and West Birmingham Hospitals NHS Trust [2011] EWCA Civ 924, [2011] IRLR 810, [2012] ICR D3, [2011] All ER (D) 268 (Jul) 47.5
Gbaja-Biamila v DHL International (UK) Ltd [2000] ICR 730, EAT 12.13, 12.18
Gdynia America Shipping Lines (London) Ltd v Chelminski. See Chelminski v Gdynia America Shipping Lines (London) Ltd
Geduld v Cavendish Munro Professional Risks Management Ltd [2010] ICR 325, [2010] IRLR 38, [2009] All ER (D) 15 (Nov), EAT 9.17
Gee v Shell UK Ltd [2002] EWCA Civ 1479, [2003] IRLR 82, [2002] 49 LS Gaz R 19, (2002) Times, 4 November, 146 Sol Jo LB 245, [2002] All ER (D) 350 (Oct) 18.61
General Billposting Co Ltd v Atkinson [1909] AC 118, 78 LJ Ch 77, [1908–10] All ER Rep 619, 99 LT 943, 25 TLR 178, HL 39.11, 56.34
General Cleaning Contractors Ltd v Christmas [1953] AC 180, [1952] 2 All ER 1110, [1953] 2 WLR 6, 51 LGR 109, 97 Sol Jo 7, HL 25.3, 25.5
General Engineering Services Ltd v Kingston and St Andrew Corpn [1988] 3 All ER 867, [1989] 1 WLR 69, [1989] ICR 88, [1989] IRLR 35, 133 Sol Jo 20, [1989] 4 LS Gaz R 44, PC 54.2
General Mills (Berwick) Ltd v Glowacki (UKEAT/0139/11/ZT) (22 September 2011, unreported) 52.9
General of the Salvation Army v Dewsbury [1984] ICR 498, [1984] IRLR 222, EAT   ... 6.3, 20.5, 51.11
General Rolling Stock Co, Re, Chapman's Case (1866) LR 1 Eq 346, 35 Beav 207, 12 Jur NS 44 .... 29.10, 30.9
Generics (UK) Ltd v Yeda Research & Development Co Ltd [2012] EWCA Civ 726, [2012] CP Rep 39, [2012] All ER (D) 01 (Jun) 39.4, 39.13
Genower v Ealing, Hammersmith and Hounslow Area Health Authority [1980] IRLR 297, EAT 52.14
George v Luton Borough Council (UKEAT/0311/03/RN) (16 September 2003, unreported) 17.23
Georgiev v Tehnicheski universitet – Sofia, filial Plovdiv: C-250/09 and C-268/09 [2011] 2 CMLR 179, [2010] All ER (D) 25 (Dec), ECJ 40.5
Georgiou v Colman Coyle (2002) IDS Brief No 705   .... 10.35
Gerster v Freistaat Bayern: C-1/95 [1997] ECR I-5253, [1998] 1 CMLR 303, [1998] ICR 327, [1997] IRLR 699, ECJ 21.3, 21.12
Gesamtbetriebsrat Der Kühne & Nagel AG & Co KG v Kühne & Nagel AG & Co KG: C-440/00 [2004] ECR I-787, [2004] 2 CMLR 1242, [2004] IRLR 332, [2004] All ER (D) 31 (Jan), ECJ 15.24
Geys v Societe Generale, London Branch [2010] EWHC 648 (Ch), [2010] IRLR 950, [2010] All ER (D) 272 (Mar); revsd in part [2011] EWCA Civ 307, [2011] IRLR 482, [2011] All ER (D) 350 (Mar); revsd [2012] UKSC 63, [2013] AC 523, [2013] 1 All ER 1061, [2013] 2 WLR 50, [2013] ICR 117, (2013) Times, 28 January, [2012] All ER (D) 196 (Dec) . 17.23, 46.5, 46.19, 51.9, 51.13, 56.7, 56.21
Gibb v Maidstone and Tunbridge Wells NHS Trust [2009] EWHC 862 (QB), [2009] IRLR 707, [2009] All ER (D) 209 (Apr); revsd [2010] EWCA Civ 678, [2010] IRLR 786, [2010] NLJR 942, [2010] All ER (D) 229 (Jun) 35.7, 56.29
Gibbons v Associated British Ports [1985] IRLR 376   .... 5.11
Gibson v East Riding of Yorkshire Council [2000] ICR 890, [2000] IRLR 598, [2000] All ER (D) 846, CA 27.2
Gibson v Motortune Ltd [1990] ICR 740, EAT 6.9
Gibson v Scottish Ambulance Service (EATS/0052/04) (16 December 2004, unreported)   .. 30.7, 30.20
Gibson v Sheffield City Council [2010] EWCA Civ 63, [2010] ICR 708, [2010] IRLR 311, (2010) Times, 19 March, 154 Sol Jo (no 7) 36, [2010] All ER (D) 117 (Feb) 21.10, 21.11, 21.12
Gilbank v Miles (2005) Times, 16 November, [2005] All ER (D) 355 (Oct), sub nom Miles v Gilbank [2006] ICR 12, EAT; affd sub nom Gilbank v Miles [2006] EWCA Civ 543, [2006] ICR 1297, [2006] IRLR 538, [2006] All ER (D) 160 (May) 10.58, 12.13, 12.16, 18.23
Gilbert v Barnsley Metropolitan Borough Council (UKEAT/674/00) [2002] All ER (D) 45 (Apr) 32.35
Gilbert v Kembridge Fibres Ltd [1984] ICR 188, [1984] IRLR 52, EAT 2.4
Gilford Motor Co Ltd v Horne [1933] Ch 935, 102 LJ Ch 212, [1933] All ER Rep 109, 149 LT 241, CA 39.8
Gilham v Kent County Council [1985] IRLR 16. See Kent County Council v Gilham
Gilham v Kent County Council (No 2) [1985] ICR 233, [1985] IRLR 18, CA 52.4
Gilham v Kent County Council (No 3) [1986] ICR 52, [1986] IRLR 56, EAT 53.12
Gill v Cremadez [2000] CLY 3876   .... 41.5

Gill v Ford Motor Co Ltd [2004] IRLR 840, [2004] 33 LS Gaz R 34, (2004) Times, 30 August, [2004] All ER (D) 131 (Jul), EAT 32.6
Gill v Humanware Europe Ltd (UKEAT/0312/08) [2009] All ER (D) 77 (Aug) 18.52, 19.24
Gill v Humanware Europe Ltd [2010] EWCA Civ 799, [2010] ICR 1343, [2010] IRLR 877, [2010] All ER (D) 38 (Feb) 18.74, 19.45
Gillespie v Northern Health and Social Services Board: C-342/93 [1996] ECR I-475, [1996] All ER (EC) 284, [1996] ECR I-475, [1996] 2 CMLR 969, [1996] ICR 498, [1996] IRLR 214, ECJ 21.14, 31.42, 40.13
Gillespie v Northern Health and Social Services Board (No 2) [1997] NI 190, [1997] IRLR 410, NI CA 21.14
Ging v Ellward Lancs Ltd [1991] ICR 222n, 13 ITR 265, EAT 53.12
Ginn v Tesco Stores Ltd [2005] All ER (D) 259 (Oct), EAT 10.26
Giraud UK Ltd v Smith [2000] IRLR 763, EAT 7.47b, 13.3, 46.16, 56.26
Grisda Cyf v Barratt [2010] UKSC 41, [2010] 4 All ER 851, [2010] ICR 1475, [2010] IRLR 1073, [2010] NLJR 1457, (2010) Times, 19 October, 154 Sol Jo (no 39) 30, [2010] All ER (D) 124 (Oct) 17.18, 17.23, 51.5, 51.13
Gladwell v Secretary of State for Trade and Industry [2007] ICR 264, [2006] All ER (D) 154 (Nov), EAT 17.9
Glasgow City Council v McNab [2007] IRLR 476, EAT 11.6, 12.16
Glasgow City Council v Marshall [2000] 1 All ER 641, [2000] 1 WLR 333, [2000] LGR 229, [2000] ICR 196, [2000] IRLR 272, [2000] 07 LS Gaz R 39, 2000 SC (HL) 67, 2000 SLT 429, [2000] All ER (D) 119, HL 21.10, 21.12
Glasgow City Council v Zafar [1998] 2 All ER 953, [1997] 1 WLR 1659, [1998] ICR 120, [1997] 48 LS Gaz R 29, 1998 SC (HL) 27, 1998 SLT 135, 142 Sol Jo LB 30, sub nom Zafar v Glasgow City Council [1998] IRLR 36, HL 10.14, 12.3
Glaxosmithkline v Rouard: C-462/06 [2008] ECR I-3965, [2008] ICR 1375, [2008] All ER (D) 312 (May), ECJ 23.8
Gledhow Autoparts Ltd v Delaney [1965] 3 All ER 288, [1965] 1 WLR 1366, 109 Sol Jo 571, CA 39.3
Glenboig Union Fireclay Co Ltd v Stewart (1971) 6 ITR 14, Ct of Sess 56.8
Glendale Managed Services v Graham [2003] EWCA Civ 773, [2003] IRLR 465, (2003) Times, 4 June, [2003] All ER (D) 225 (May) 50.18
Glennie v Independent Magazines (UK) Ltd [1999] IRLR 719, [1999] All ER (D) 637, CA 19.33
Glenrose (Fish Merchants) Ltd v Chapman IDS Brief No 438 .... 51.17
Gloystarne & Co Ltd v Martin [2001] IRLR 15, EAT 18.32
Godfrey Morgan Solicitors Ltd v Cobalt Systems Ltd (UKEAT/0608/10/LA) [2012] ICR 305, 155 Sol Jo (no 34) 31, [2011] All ER (D) 29 (Oct), EAT 18.74
Godfrey Morgan Solicitors Ltd v Marzan (UKEAT/0465/11/DM) (15 February 2012, unreported) 18.72
Gogay v Hertfordshire County Council [2000] IRLR 703, [2001] 1 FCR 455, [2000] Fam Law 883, [2000] All ER (D) 1057, CA 7.22d, 7.39
Goldman Sachs Services Ltd v Montali [2002] ICR 1251, CA 18.3, 18.7
Gomez (Merino) v Continental Industrias del Caucho SA: C-342/01 [2004] ECR I-2605, [2004] 2 CMLR 38, [2005] ICR 1040, [2004] IRLR 407, [2004] All ER (D) 350 (Mar), ECJ 27.3A, 27.5, 31.21
Gomez v Glaxosmithkline Services Unlimited [2011] EqLR 804 .... 10.37
Goode v Marks and Spencer plc (UKEAT/0442/09/DM) [2010] All ER (D) 63 (Sep) 9.17, 26.9
Goodwin v Cabletel UK Ltd [1998] ICR 112, [1997] IRLR 665, EAT 26.8, 52.3
Goodwin v Patent Office [1999] ICR 302, [1999] IRLR 4, EAT 10.26
Goodwin v United Kingdom (Application 17488/90) (1996) 22 EHRR 123, 1 BHRC 81, ECtHR 28.5
Goodwin v United Kingdom (Application 28957/95) [2002] IRLR 664, [2002] 2 FCR 577, [2002] 2 FLR 487, [2002] Fam Law 738, 35 EHRR 447, 13 BHRC 120, 67 BMLR 199, [2002] NLJR 1171, (2002) Times, 12 July, [2002] All ER (D) 158 (Jul), ECtHR 10.21, 21.13, 28.4
Gorictree Ltd v Jenkinson [1985] ICR 51, [1984] IRLR 391, EAT 50.27
Goring v British Actors Equity Association [1987] IRLR 122 .... 49.12, 49.15
Gothard v Mirror Group Newspapers Ltd [1988] ICR 729, [1988] IRLR 396, CA 46.11, 56.21
Gover v Mindimaxnox LLP (UKEAT/0225/10/DQ) [2011] All ER (D) 146 (May) 18.22, 19.38
Gover v Propertycare Ltd [2006] EWCA Civ 286, [2006] All ER (D) 408 (Mar) 19.47
Governing Body of Addey and Stanhope School v Vakante [2003] ICR 290, [2002] All ER (D) 79 (Oct), EAT 11.19

Table of Cases

Governing Body of Wishmorecross School v Balado (UKEAT/0199/11/CEA) [2011] ICR D31, EAT 17.24

Governing Body of St Albans Girls' School v Neary (No 2) [2009] EWCA Civ 1214, [2010] IRLR 124 .... 19.47

Government Communications Staff Federation v Certification Officer [1993] ICR 163, [1993] IRLR 260, [1993] 5 LS Gaz R 41, EAT 48.22

Graf v Filzmoser Maschinenbau GmbH: C-190/98 [2000] ECR I-493, [2000] All ER (EC) 170, [2000] 1 CMLR 741, ECJ 23.2

Grainger plc v Nicholson. See Nicholson v Grainger plc

Grant v In 2 Focus Sales Development Services Ltd [2007] All ER (D) 281 (Jan), EAT .. 17.16, 17.34, 19.10

Grant v HM Land Registry [2011] EWCA Civ 769, [2011] ICR 1390, [2011] IRLR 748, [2011] All ER (D) 21 (Jul) 10.39

Grant v South-West Trains Ltd: C-249/96 [1998] ECR I-621, [1998] All ER (EC) 193, [1998] 1 CMLR 993, [1998] ICR 449, [1998] IRLR 206, [1998] 1 FCR 377, [1998] 1 FLR 839, [1998] Fam Law 392, 3 BHRC 578, ECJ 28.5

Graphical, Paper and Media Union v Derry Print Ltd [2002] IRLR 380 .... 48.30

Gravil v Carroll [2008] EWCA Civ 689, [2008] ICR 1222, [2008] IRLR 829, [2008] NLJR 933, (2008) Times, 22 July, [2008] All ER (D) 231 (Jun) 54.1

Gray v Canada Life Ltd. See Canada Life Ltd v Gray

Greater Glasgow Health Board v Lamont (UKEATS/0019/12), unreported 36.7

Greater Manchester Police Authority v Lea [1990] IRLR 372, EAT 10.34

Green v DB Group Services (UK) Ltd [2006] EWHC 1898 (QB), [2006] IRLR 764, [2006] All ER (D) 02 (Aug) 26.25, 26.28

Green v Hampshire County Council [1979] ICR 861 .... 7.45

Greenaway Harrison Ltd v Wiles [1994] IRLR 380, 501 IRLIB 2, EAT 51.7

Greenhof v Barnsley Metropolitan Borough Council [2006] IRLR 98, [2006] ICR 1514, [2005] All ER (D) 347 (Oct), EAT 7.22d, 10.37, 12.19

Greenwood v NWF Retail Ltd (UKEAT/0409/09/JOJ) [2011] ICR 896, EAT 18.63, 19.36

Greg May (Carpet Fitters and Contractors) Ltd v Dring [1990] ICR 188, [1990] IRLR 19, EAT 32.6

Gregory v Tudsbury Ltd [1982] IRLR 267, Ind Trib 31.7

Gregory v Wallace [1998] IRLR 387, CA 56.21

Greig v Insole [1978] 3 All ER 449, [1978] 1 WLR 302, 122 Sol Jo 163 .... 39.5

Grey v Eastern and Coastal Kent plc [2009] IRLR 429, [2009] All ER (D) 171 (Jan), EAT 10.37, 11.9A

Griffin v London Pensions Fund Authority [1993] 2 CMLR 571, [1993] ICR 564, [1993] IRLR 248, [1993] 11 LS Gaz R 44, EAT 21.17

Griffin v South West Water Services Ltd [1995] IRLR 15 .... 35.8, 37.4

Griffiths v Secretary of State for Social Services [1974] QB 468, [1973] 3 All ER 1184, [1973] 3 WLR 831, 117 Sol Jo 873 .... 29.10, 56.9

Griffiths-Henry v Network Rail Infrastructure Ltd [2006] IRLR 865, [2006] All ER (D) 15 (Jul), EAT 12.3

Grimaldi v Fonds des Maladies Professionnelles: 2 [1989] ECR 4407, [1991] 2 CMLR 265, [1990] IRLR 400, ECJ 22.1

Grimmer v KLM Cityhopper UK Ltd [2005] IRLR 596, [2005] All ER (D) 218 (May), EAT 17.16

Grosvenor v Governing Body of Aylesford School (UKEAT/0001/08) (10 June 2008, unreported) 19.37

Group 4 Nightspeed Ltd v Gilbert [1997] IRLR 398, 574 IRLB 13, EAT 17.31, 32.8

Gruber v Silhouette International Schmied GmbH & Co KG: C-249/97 [1999] ECR I-5295, [1999] All ER (D) 1013, ECJ 21.14

Grundy v British Airways plc [2005] All ER (D) 94 (Aug), EAT; revsd [2007] EWCA Civ 1020, [2008] IRLR 74, [2007] All ER (D) 345 (Oct); on appeal [2008] EWCA Civ 875, [2008] IRLR 815, [2008] All ER (D) 350 (Jul) 10.34, 11.9, 21.5, 21.11, 21.12

Grundy (Teddington) Ltd v Plummer [1983] ICR 367, [1983] IRLR 98, EAT 52.11

Gryf-Lowczowski (Jan) v Hinchingbrooke Healthcare NHS Trust [2005] EWHC 2407 (QB), [2006] ICR 425, [2006] IRLR 100, 87 BMLR 46, [2005] All ER (D) 21 (Nov) 46.3, 56.23

Guinness plc v Saunders [1990] 2 AC 663, [1990] 1 All ER 652, [1990] 2 WLR 324, [1990] BCLC 402, 134 Sol Jo 457, [1990] 9 LS Gaz R 42, HL 8.3, 56.36

Table of Cases

Guney-Gorres v Securicor Aviation (Germany) Ltd: C-232/04 and C-233/04 [2005] ECR I-11237,
  [2006] IRLR 305, [2005] All ER (D) 230 (Dec), ECJ 50.5
Gunning v Mirror Group Newspapers Ltd [1986] 1 All ER 385, sub nom Mirror Group
  Newspapers Ltd v Gunning [1986] 1 WLR 546, [1986] ICR 145, [1986] IRLR 27, 130 Sol Jo 242,
  CA 10.41
Gunton v Richmond-upon-Thames London Borough Council [1981] Ch 448, [1980] 3 All ER 577,
  [1980] 3 WLR 714, 79 LGR 241, [1980] ICR 755, [1980] IRLR 321, CA 51.9, 56.18, 56.25
Gutridge v Sodexo Ltd. See Sodexo Ltd v Gutridge
Gutzmore v J Wardley (Holdings) Ltd [1993] ICR 581, CA 18.64

H

H J Heinz Co Ltd v Kenrick [2000] ICR 491, [2000] IRLR 144, 635 IRLB 10, EAT 11.9A, 52.8
H W Smith (Cabinets) Ltd v Brindle. See Brindle v H W Smith (Cabinets) Ltd
HM Land Registry v Grant (UKEAT/0232/09/DA) [2010] IRLR 583, [2010] All ER (D) 230
  (Jun) 10.39
HM Land Registry v S M Benson (UKEAT/0197/11/RN) (26 March 2012, unreported) 11.9
HM Land Registry v Wakefield [2009] All ER (D) 205 (Feb), EAT 10.37
HM Prison Service v Beart (No 2) [2005] IRLR 171, [2004] All ER (D) 370 (Oct), EAT; affd sub
  nom HM Prison Service v Beart [2005] EWCA Civ 467, [2005] ICR 1206, [2005] IRLR 568,
  [2005] All ER (D) 369 (Apr) 12.19
HM Prison Service v Davis (2000) IDS Brief No 666, EAT 10.54
HM Prison Service v Dolby [2003] IRLR 694, [2003] All ER (D) 156 (Jul), EAT 18.15, 18.17
HM Prison Service v Ibimidun [2008] IRLR 940, sub nom Ibimidun v HM Prison Service
  [2008] All ER (D) 436 (Apr), EAT 10.38
HM Prison Service v Johnson [1997] ICR 275, [1997] IRLR 162, 567 IRLB 13, EAT 12.16, 12.18
HM Prison Service v Salmon [2001] IRLR 425, [2001] All ER (D) 154 (Apr), EAT 12.17
HM Revenue and Customs v Stringer: C-520/06 [2009] All ER (EC) 906, [2009] 2 CMLR 657,
  [2009] ICR 932, [2009] IRLR 214, (2009) Times, 28 January, [2009] All ER (D) 147 (Jan), ECJ
  .... 27.3A
HSBC Asia Holdings BV v Gillespie (UKEAT/0417/10/DA) [2011] ICR 192, [2011] IRLR 209,
  [2011] All ER (D) 78 (Mar) 12.8, 17.29, 18.45, 18.56
HSBC Bank plc (formerly Midland Bank plc) v Madden [2001] 1 All ER 550, [2000] ICR 1283,
  [2000] IRLR 827, [2000] All ER (D) 1137, CA 52.4, 52.9
Hackney London Borough Council v Sivanandan (UKEAT/0075/10/CEA) [2011] ICR 1374,
  [2011] IRLR 740, EAT 12.13, 12.16, 18.23
Haddon v Van den Bergh Foods Ltd [1999] ICR 1150, [1999] IRLR 672, 628 IRLB 3, EAT 52.4
Haden Ltd v Cowen. See Cowen v Haden Ltd
Hadfield v Health and Safety Executive (UKEATS/0013/10/BI) (5 November 2010, unreported)
  .... 11.35, 18.17
Hadjioannous v Coral Casinos Ltd [1981] IRLR 352, EAT 52.9
Hair Colour Consultants Ltd v Mena [1984] ICR 671, [1984] IRLR 386, [1984] LS Gaz R 2147,
  EAT 6.9
Hair Division Ltd v Macmillan (12 October 2012, unreported), EAT 31.43
Hairsine v Kingston upon Hull City Council [1992] ICR 212, [1992] IRLR 211, EAT 47.2
Hakim v Italia Conti Academy of Theatre Arts (UKEATPA/1444/08) (20 May 2009, unreported)
  .... 19.14
Halford v Sharples [1992] ICR 146, EAT; affd [1992] 3 All ER 624, [1992] 1 WLR 736, [1992] ICR
  583, CA 18.13, 18.50
Halford v United Kingdom (Application 20605/92) (1997) 24 EHRR 523, [1997] IRLR 471, [1998]
  Crim LR 753, [1997] 94 LS Gaz R 24, 3 BHRC 31, ECtHR 28.4
Halfpenny v IGE Medical Systems Ltd [1999] ICR 834, [1999] IRLR 177, [1999] 1 FLR 944,
  52 BMLR 153, 143 Sol Jo LB 38, [1998] All ER (D) 769, CA; revsd [2001] ICR 73, [2001] IRLR
  96, [2000] All ER (D) 2284, HL 31.32
Hall (Inspector of Taxes) v Lorimer [1994] 1 All ER 250, [1994] 1 WLR 209, [1994] STC 23, 66 TC
  349, [1994] ICR 218, [1994] IRLR 171, [1993] 45 LS Gaz R 45, 137 Sol Jo LB 256, CA 14.3
Hall v Woolston Hall Leisure Ltd [2000] 4 All ER 787, [2001] 1 WLR 225, [2001] ICR 99, [2000]
  IRLR 578, [2000] 24 LS Gaz R 39, [2000] NLJR 833, CA 7.24, 11.19

Table of Cases

Hallam v Avery [2000] 1 WLR 966, [2000] LGR 452, [2000] ICR 583, [2000] 01 LS Gaz R 23, 144
  Sol Jo LB 32; affd [2001] UKHL 15, [2001] 1 WLR 655, [2001] LGR 278, [2001] ICR 408, [2001]
  IRLR 312, [2001] 21 LS Gaz R 39, 145 Sol Jo LB 116, [2001] All ER (D) 273 (Mar) 10.58
Hallam Diocese Trustee v Connaughton [1996] ICR 860, [1996] IRLR 505, EAT 21.9
Halstead v Paymentshield Group Holdings Ltd. See Paymentshield Group Holdings Ltd v Halstead
Hameed v Central Manchester University Hospitals NHS Foundation Trust [2010] EWHC 2009
  (QB), [2011] All ER (D) 11 (May) 28.7
Hamilton v Futura Floors Ltd [1990] IRLR 478, OH 5.5
Hamilton v GMB (Northern Region) [2007] IRLR 391, [2006] All ER (D) 412 (Nov), EAT 18.50
Hamlet v General Municipal Boilermakers and Allied Trades Union [1987] 1 All ER 631, [1987] 1
  WLR 449, [1987] ICR 150, [1986] IRLR 293, 131 Sol Jo 470, [1987] LS Gaz R 1327 ..... 49.12, 49.15
Hamling v Coxlease School Ltd [2007] ICR 108, [2007] IRLR 8, [2006] All ER (D) 172 (Nov),
  EAT 17.16, 17.34
Hampson v Department of Education and Science [1990] 2 All ER 25, [1989] ICR 179, [1989] IRLR
  69, 133 Sol Jo 151, [1989] 13 LS Gaz R 43, CA; revsd [1991] 1 AC 171, [1990] 2 All ER 513,
  [1990] 3 WLR 42, [1990] ICR 511, [1990] IRLR 302, 134 Sol Jo 1123, [1990] 26 LS Gaz R 39,
  [1990] NLJR 853, HL 11.9, 11.21
Hampton v Lord Chancellor [2008] IRLR 258 .... 11.9, 40.5
Hancill v Marcon Engineering Ltd [1990] ICR 103, [1990] IRLR 51, EAT 6.9
Hancocks v Cambian Education Services Ltd (UKEATPA/0824/10/CEA) [2011] All ER (D) 64
  (May) 19.14
Handels-og Kontorfunktionaerernes Forbund i Danmark v Dansk Arbejdsgiverforening, acting on
  behalf of Danfoss: 109/88 [1989] ECR 3199, [1991] 1 CMLR 8, [1991] ICR 74, [1989] IRLR 532,
  ECJ 11.9, 21.12
Handels-og Kontorfunktionaerernes Forbund i Danmark (acting on behalf of Hoj Pedersen) v
  Faellesforeningen for Danmarks Brugsforeninger (acting on behalf of Kvickly Skive): C-66/96
  [1998] ECR I-7327, [1999] 2 CMLR 326, [1999] IRLR 55, sub nom Pedersen v Kvickly Skive
  [1999] All ER (EC) 138, [1998] All ER (D) 614, ECJ 21.14
Haniff v Robinson [1993] QB 419, [1993] 1 All ER 185, [1992] 3 WLR 875, 26 HLR 386,
  [1992] 2 EGLR 111, [1992] 45 EG 145, CA 41.3
Hannah Blumenthal, The. See Paal Wilson & Co A/S v Partenreederei Hannah Blumenthal, The
  Hannah Blumenthal
Hannan v TNT-IPEC (UK) Ltd [1986] IRLR 165, EAT 52.1
Hanover Insurance Brokers Ltd v Schapiro [1994] IRLR 82, CA 39.8
Haq v Audit Commission [2012] EWCA Civ 1621, [2013] IRLR 206, [2012] All ER (D) 59 (Dec)
  .... 21.11, 21.12
Harada Ltd (t/a Chequepoint UK) v Turner [2001] EWCA Civ 599, [2001] All ER (D) 82 (Apr)
  .... 23.8
Harding v Vehicle and Operator Services Agency [2010] EWHC 713 (Admin) 55.35
Harding v Wealands [2006] UKHL 32, [2007] 2 AC 1, [2006] 4 All ER 1, [2006] 3 WLR 83, [2006]
  RTR 422, [2006] NLJR 1136, (2006) Times, 6 July, [2006] All ER (D) 40 (Jul) 23.7
Hardman v Mallon (t/a Orchard Lodge Nursing Home) [2002] IRLR 516, [2002] All ER (D) 439
  (May), EAT 10.30
Hardy v Polk (Leeds) Ltd [2004] IRLR 420, [2004] All ER (D) 282 (Mar), EAT 53.13, 56.21
Hardy v Tourism South East [2005] IRLR 242, [2005] All ER (D) 201 (Jan), EAT 37.4
Hardys & Hansons plc v Lax [2005] EWCA Civ 846, [2005] ICR 1565, [2005] IRLR 726, (2005)
  Times, 26 July, [2005] All ER (D) 83 (Jul) 11.9, 31.31
Harford v Swiftrim Ltd [1987] ICR 439, [1987] IRLR 360, [1987] LS Gaz R 820, EAT 6.9
Haritaki v South East England Development Agency [2008] IRLR 945, EAT 19.17
Harland and Wolff Pension Trustees Ltd v Aon Consulting Financial Services Ltd [2006] EWHC
  1778 (Ch), [2007] ICR 429, [2006] All ER (D) 216 (Jul) 21.17
Harmer v Cornelius (1858) 22 JP 724, 5 CBNS 236, 28 LJCP 85, 4 Jur NS 1110, 6 WR 749, 141 ER
  94, [1843–60] All ER Rep 624, 32 LTOS 62 .... 8.21, 56.17
Harmony Healthcare plc v Drewery (EAT/866/00) (21 July 2000, unreported) 18.17
Harold Holdsworth & Co (Wakefield) Ltd v Caddies [1955] 1 All ER 725, [1955] 1 WLR 352, 99 Sol
  Jo 234, HL 8.5
Harper v Virgin Net Ltd [2004] EWCA Civ 271, [2005] ICR 921, [2004] IRLR 390, (2004) Times,
  16 March, 148 Sol Jo LB 353, [2004] All ER (D) 184 (Mar) 7.37, 51.11, 56.33
Harris v Courage (Eastern) Ltd [1982] ICR 530, [1982] IRLR 509, CA 52.9
Harris v Shuttleworth (Lord) [1994] ICR 991, [1994] IRLR 547, CA 40.6, 40.17

Harris & Russell Ltd v Slingsby [1973] 3 All ER 31, [1973] ICR 454, [1973] IRLR 221, 15 KIR 157,
  8 ITR 433, NIRC 51.5
Harrison v Kent County Council [1995] ICR 434, EAT 49.4
Harrison v Norwest Holst Group Administration Ltd. See Norwest Holst Group
  Administration Ltd v Harrison
Harrison v Royal Bank of Scotland plc [2009] ICR 116, [2009] IRLR 28, [2008] All ER (D) 126
  (Oct), EAT 47.15
Harrison Bowden Ltd v Bowden [1994] ICR 186, EAT 50.14
Harrods Ltd v Remick [1998] 1 All ER 52, [1998] ICR 156, [1997] IRLR 583, CA 11.24
Harrow London Borough Council v Cunningham [1996] IRLR 256, EAT 52.9
Hart v A R Marshall & Sons (Bulwell) Ltd [1978] 2 All ER 413, [1977] 1 WLR 1067, [1977] ICR
  539, [1977] IRLR 51, 12 ITR 190, 121 Sol Jo 677, EAT 46.3
Hart v English Heritage (Historic Buildings and Monuments Commission for England) [2006] ICR
  655, [2006] IRLR 915, [2006] All ER (D) 343 (Feb), EAT 18.2, 18.3, 18.7, 18.16, 18.75
Hartlebury Printers Ltd (in liq), Re [1993] 1 All ER 470, [1992] ICR 559, [1992] IRLR 516,
  [1993] BCLC 902, [1992] BCC 428 .... 22.2, 37.2, 37.4, 37.6
Hartlepool Borough Council v Dolphin [2009] IRLR 168, 152 Sol Jo (no 38) 30, [2008] All ER (D)
  73 (Sep), EAT 21.12
Hartlepool Borough Council v Llewellyn. See Llewellyn v Hartlepool Borough Council
Hartwell v A-G of the British Virgin Islands [2004] UKPC 12, [2004] 1 WLR 1273, (2004) Times,
  27 February, 148 Sol Jo LB 267, [2004] All ER (D) 372 (Feb) 54.2
Harvest Press Ltd v McCaffrey [1999] IRLR 778, EAT 26.8, 52.3
Harvest Town Circle Ltd v Rutherford [2001] 3 CMLR 691, [2002] ICR 123, [2001] IRLR 599,
  [2001] All ER (D) 112 (Jul), EAT 10.34
Harvey v Port of Tilbury (London) Ltd [1999] ICR 1030, [1999] IRLR 693, EAT 18.10
Harvey's Household Linens Ltd v Benson [1974] ICR 306, 16 KIR 228, 9 ITR 234, NIRC 17.25
Haseltine Lake & Co v Dowler [1981] ICR 222, [1981] IRLR 25, EAT 51.5, 51.8, 56.5
Hashman v Orchard Park Garden Centre unreported, UKEAT 10.22
Hashwani v Jivraj [2010] EWCA Civ 712, [2011] 1 All ER 50, [2011] 1 All ER (Comm) 33, [2010]
  Bus LR 1683, [2010] 2 Lloyd's Rep 534, [2010] ICR 1435, [2010] All ER (D) 202 (Jun); revsd sub
  nom Jivraj v Hashwani [2011] UKSC 40, [2012] 1 All ER 629, [2011] 1 WLR 1872,
  [2012] 1 CMLR 307, [2011] Bus LR 1182, [2011] 2 Lloyd's Rep 513, [2011] ICR 1004, [2011]
  IRLR 827, [2011] NLJR 1100, (2011) Times, 04 August, [2011] All ER (D) 246 (Jul) 14.9, 10.41,
                                                                                          12.32
Hasley v Fair Employment Agency [1989] IRLR 106, NI CA 6.9
Hatton v Sutherland [2002] EWCA Civ 76, [2002] 2 All ER 1, [2002] ICR 613, 68 BMLR 115,
  (2002) Times, 11 February, [2002] All ER (D) 53 (Feb), sub nom Sutherland v Hatton [2002]
  IRLR 263 .... 26.25
Hawkes v Southwark London Borough Council (20 February 1998, unreported), CA 26.18
Hawkins v Atex Group Ltd (2012) UKEAT/0302/11/LA, [2012] ICR 1315, [2012] NLJR 578,
  [2012] All ER (D) 71 (Apr), EAT 10.19
Hawkins v Ball and Barclays Bank plc [1996] IRLR 258, EAT 12.7, 17.30, 19.21, 19.29
Hawley v Luminar Leisure Ltd [2006] EWCA Civ 18, [2006] Lloyd's Rep IR 307, [2006] IRLR 817,
  150 Sol Jo LB 163, [2006] All ER (D) 158 (Jan) 54.1, 54.3
Hay v George Hanson (Building Contractors) Ltd [1996] IRLR 427, EAT 50.16
Hay v Surrey County Council [2007] EWCA Civ 93, [2007] All ER (D) 199 (Feb) 10.37
Haynes v Doman [1899] 2 Ch 13, 68 LJ Ch 419, 43 Sol Jo 553, 80 LT 569, 15 TLR 354,
  [1895–9] All ER Rep Ext 1468, CA 39.6, 39.8
Hayward v Cammell Laird Shipbuilders Ltd [1988] AC 894, [1988] 2 All ER 257, [1988] 2 WLR
  1134, [1988] ICR 464, [1988] IRLR 257, 132 Sol Jo 750, [1988] NLJR 133, HL 21.5, 21.8, 30.18
Hazelwood v Eagle [2009] All ER (D) 55 (May), EAT 18.16
Healey v Française Rubastic SA [1917] 1 KB 946, 86 LJKB 1254, 117 LT 92, 33 TLR 300 ...... 8.19,
                                                                                     39.11, 56.28
Health Development Agency v Parish [2004] IRLR 550, [2004] All ER (D) 106 (Jan), EAT 18.70
Heartland (Midlands) Ltd v Marcroft [2011] EWCA Civ 438, [2011] IRLR 599, [2011] All ER (D)
  154 (Apr) 50.13
Heasmans v Clarity Cleaning Co Ltd [1987] ICR 949, [1987] IRLR 286, [1987] BTLC 174, [1987]
  NLJ Rep 101, CA 54.2
Heath v Metropolitan Police Comr [2004] EWCA Civ 943, [2005] ICR 329, [2005] IRLR 270, 148
  Sol Jo LB 913, [2004] All ER (D) 359 (Jul) 12.2

Table of Cases

Heatherwood and Wexham Park Hospitals NHS Trust v Kulubowila [2007] All ER (D) 496 (Mar), EAT 45.2c

Heathmill Multimedia ASP Ltd v Jones [2003] IRLR 856, [2003] All ER (D) 440 (Oct), EAT 49.21

Hedley Byrne & Co Ltd v Heller & Partners Ltd [1964] AC 465, [1963] 2 All ER 575, [1963] 3 WLR 101, [1963] 1 Lloyd's Rep 485, 107 Sol Jo 454, HL 38.5

Heggie v Uniroyal Englebert Tyres Ltd [1998] IRLR 425, EAT; revsd [1999] IRLR 802, Ct of Sess 53.13

Heimann v Kaiser GmbH: C-229/11 and C-230/11 [2013] 1 CMLR 1425, [2013] ICR D11, [2012] All ER (D) 179 (Nov), ECJ 27.3B, 30.11

Heinisch v Germany (Application No 28274/08) [2011] IRLR 922, 32 BHRC 252, ECtHR 28.4

Hellyer Bros Ltd v Atkinson and Dickinson [1992] IRLR 540, EAT; revsd [1994] IRLR 88, CA 46.2

Hellyer Bros Ltd v McLeod [1987] 1 WLR 728, [1987] ICR 526, 131 Sol Jo 805, [1987] LS Gaz R 1056, sub nom McLeod v Hellyer Bros Ltd [1987] IRLR 232, CA 14.3, 45.8

Helmet Integrated Systems Ltd v Tunnard [2006] EWCA Civ 1735, [2007] FSR 437, [2007] IRLR 126, [2006] All ER (D) 228 (Dec) 7.16, 8.19, 39.13

Helow v Secretary of State for the Home Department [2008] UKHL 62, [2009] 2 All ER 1031, [2000] 1 WLR 2116, (2008) Times, 5 November, 2009 SC (HL) 1, 2008 SLT 967, 2008 SCLR 830, 152 Sol Jo (no 41) 29, [2008] All ER (D) 222 (Oct) 19.24

Hely-Hutchinson v Brayhead Ltd [1968] 1 QB 549, [1967] 3 All ER 98, [1967] 3 WLR 1408, 111 Sol Jo 830, CA 8.12

Hempell v W H Smith & Sons Ltd [1986] ICR 365, [1986] IRLR 95, EAT 36.12

Henderson v Henderson (1843) 3 Hare 100, 67 ER 313, [1843–60] All ER Rep 378, 1 LTOS 410 .... 12.8, 18.26, 21.19

Hendricks v Metropolitan Police Comr [2002] EWCA Civ 1686, [2003] 1 All ER 654, [2003] ICR 530, [2003] IRLR 96, [2003] 05 LS Gaz R 30, (2002) Times, 6 December, 146 Sol Jo LB 274, [2002] All ER (D) 407 (Nov); affd Metropolitan Police Comr v Hendricks [2003] ICR 999, HL 11.18, 12.6, 17.29

Hendry v Scottish Liberal Club [1977] IRLR 5, Ind Trib 16.3

Henke v Gemeinde Schierke and Verwaltungsgemeinschaft Brocken: C-298/94 [1996] ECR I-4989, [1997] All ER (EC) 173, [1997] 1 CMLR 373, [1997] ICR 746, [1996] IRLR 701, ECJ 15.6, 50.9

Hennessy v Craigmyle & Co Ltd [1986] ICR 461, [1986] IRLR 300, 130 Sol Jo 633, [1986] LS Gaz R 2160, CA 2.4, 19.47

Hennigs v Eisenbahn-Bundesamt; Land Berlin v Mai: C-297/10 and C-298/10 [2012] 1 CMLR 484, [2012] IRLR 83, [2011] All ER (D) 72 (Oct), ECJ 11.9

Henry v London General Transport Services Ltd [2002] EWCA Civ 488, [2002] ICR 910, [2002] IRLR 472, [2002] All ER (D) 322 (Mar) 5.8, 7.15, 7.32, 32.6

Henry Leetham & Sons Ltd v Johnstone-White [1907] 1 Ch 322, 76 LJ Ch 304, 14 Mans 162, 96 LT 348, 23 TLR 254, CA 39.4

Herbert Morris Ltd v Saxelby [1916] 1 AC 688, 85 LJ Ch 210, [1916–17] All ER Rep 305, 60 Sol Jo 305, 114 LT 618, 32 TLR 297, HL 39.4, 39.5, 39.8, 39.13

Hereford and Worcester County Council v Neale. See Neale v Hereford and Worcester County Council

Heron v Citilink-Nottingham [1993] IRLR 372, EAT 52.11

Heron Corpn Ltd v Commis [1980] ICR 713, EAT 11.12

Herrero (Sarkatzis) v Instituto Madrileno de la Salud (Imsalud): C-294/04 [2006] ECR I-1513, [2006] IRLR 296, [2006] All ER (D) 220 (Feb), ECJ 10.31

Hertaing v Benoidt: C-305/94 [1996] ECR I-5927, [1997] All ER (EC) 40, [1997] 1 CMLR 329, [1997] IRLR 127, ECJ 50.13

Hewage v Grampian Health Board [2012] UKSC 37, [2012] 4 All ER 447, [2012] ICR 1054, [2012] IRLR 870, [2012] NLJR 1028, (2012) Times, 29 October, [2012] All ER (D) 253 (Jul) 10.15

Hewcastle Catering Ltd v Ahmed and Elkamah [1992] ICR 626, [1991] IRLR 473, CA 7.24

Hewlett Packard Ltd v O'Murphy [2002] IRLR 4, [2001] All ER (D) 91 (Sep), EAT 14.3, 45.2a

Hibbins v Hesters Way Neighbourhood Project [2009] 1 All ER 949, [2009] ICR 319, [2009] IRLR 198, [2008] All ER (D) 145 (Oct), EAT 9.17

High Table Ltd v Horst [1998] ICR 409, [1997] IRLR 513, sub nom Horst v High Table Ltd [1997] 28 LS Gaz R 25, 141 Sol Jo LB 161, CA 7.22e, 18.63, 36.7

Higham v Meurig Lestyn Horton. See Horton v Horton

Hill v Chapell [2003] IRLR 19, [2002] All ER (D) 461 (May), EAT 27.4a, 27.9

Hill v General Accident Fire and Life Assurance Corpn plc [1998] IRLR 641, 1999 SLT 1157, 1998 SCLR 1030, 609 IRLB 8, OH 7.22b, 7.22d, 40.16, 42.13, 56.19
Hill v Governing Body of Great Tey Primary School [2013] IRLR 274 .... 28.7
Hill v Revenue Comrs and Department of Finance: C-243/95 [1998] ECR I-3739, [1998] All ER (EC) 722, [1998] 3 CMLR 81, [1999] ICR 48, [1998] IRLR 466, [1998] 34 LS Gaz R 33, [1998] All ER (D) 277, ECJ 21.3
Hillier v Hamilton House Medical Ltd (UKEAT/0246/09/CEA) [2009] All ER (D) 319 (Nov) 32.9
Hillingdon London Borough Council v Commission for Racial Equality [1982] AC 779, [1982] 3 WLR 159, 80 LGR 737, [1982] IRLR 424, 126 Sol Jo 449, HL 12.25, 12.28
Hillman v London General Transport Services Ltd (14 April 1999, unreported), EAT 35.8
Hills v Co-operative Wholesale Society Ltd [1940] 2 KB 435, [1940] 3 All ER 233, 109 LJKB 972, 84 Sol Jo 658, 163 LT 167, 56 TLR 875, CA 7.45
Hillsdown Holdings plc v Pensions Ombudsman [1997] 1 All ER 862, [1996] PLR 427 .... 40.16
Hilton v Shiner Ltd Builders Merchants [2001] IRLR 727, [2001] All ER (D) 316 (May), EAT 7.22d
Hilton International Hotels (UK) Ltd v Faraji [1994] ICR 259, [1994] IRLR 267, EAT ... 53.12, 53.13
Hilton International Hotels (UK) Ltd v Protopapa [1990] IRLR 316, EAT 51.7
Hilton UK Hotels Ltd v McNaughton [2006] All ER (D) 327 (May), EAT 12.33, 18.34
Hindle Gears Ltd v McGinty [1985] ICR 111, [1984] IRLR 477, EAT 51.5, 56.5
Hine v Talbot (UKEATPA/1783/10/SM) (27 June 2011, unreported) 19.12, 19.14
Hinton v University of East London [2005] EWCA Civ 532, [2005] ICR 1260, [2005] IRLR 552, [2005] NLJ 827, 149 Sol Jo LB 637, [2005] All ER (D) 83 (May) 18.34, 51.20, 53.19
Hitchcock v Coker (1837) 1 JP 215, 6 Ad & El 438, 6 LJ Ex 266, 2 Har & W 464, 1 Nev & PKB 796, 112 ER 167, [1835–42] All ER Rep 452, Ex Ch 39.10
Hitchcock v Post Office [1980] ICR 100, EAT 14.3
Hivac Ltd v Park Royal Scientific Instruments Ltd [1946] Ch 169, [1946] 1 All ER 350, 115 LJ Ch 241, 90 Sol Jo 175, 174 LT 422, 62 TLR 231, CA 8.19
Hockenjos v Secretary of State for Social Security [2004] EWCA Civ 1749, [2005] IRLR 471, [2005] 1 FCR 286, (2005) Times, 4 January, [2004] All ER (D) 331 (Dec) 11.9
Hodgson v Scarlett (1818) 1 B & Ald 232 .... 38.4
Hoeffler v Kwik Save Stores Ltd (EAT/803/97) (17 November 1997, unreported) 18.35
Hogg v Dover College [1990] ICR 39, EAT 7.34, 46.1, 46.5
Holc-Gale v Makers UK Ltd [2006] ICR 462, [2006] IRLR 178, [2005] All ER (D) 361 (Dec), EAT 12.9
Holis Metal Industries Ltd v GMB and Newell Ltd [2008] ICR 464, [2008] IRLR 187, [2007] All ER (D) 304 (Dec), EAT 23.9, 50.6
Holland v Glendale Industries Ltd [1998] ICR 493, EAT 46.19, 51.7
Hollis & Co v Stocks [2000] IRLR 712 .... 39.6
Hollister v National Farmers' Union [1979] ICR 542, [1979] IRLR 238, CA 52.14
Holmes v Greater Glasgow Health Board (UKEATS/0045/11/BI) (8 March 2012, unreported) 18.27
Holmes v South Yorkshire Police Authority [2008] EWCA Civ 51, [2008] HLR 532, [2008] All ER (D) 93 (Feb) 41.7
Holst v Dansk Arbejdsgiverforening: C-405/08 [2010] 2 CMLR 49, ECJ 15.4, 15.21
Homan v A1 Bacon Co Ltd [1996] ICR 721, EAT 53.6
Home Counties Dairies Ltd v Skilton [1970] 1 All ER 1227, [1970] 1 WLR 526, 114 Sol Jo 107, CA 39.3, 39.6
Home Office v Ayres [1992] ICR 175, [1992] IRLR 59, EAT 32.6
Home Office v Bailey [2005] IRLR 757, [2005] All ER (D) 499 (Jul), EAT 21.7, 21.12
Home Office v Coyne [2000] ICR 1443, [2000] IRLR 838, [2000] All ER (D) 1081, CA 10.39
Home Office v Tariq. See Tariq v Home Office
Homer v Chief Constable of West Yorkshire [2010] EWCA Civ 419, [2010] ICR 987, [2010] IRLR 619, [2010] 19 LS Gaz R 24, 154 Sol Jo (no 17) 29, [2010] All ER (D) 189 (Apr); revsd sub nom Homer v Chief Constable of West Yorkshire Police [2012] UKSC 15, [2012] ICR 704, [2012] IRLR 601, 156 Sol Jo (no 17) 31, [2012] NLJR 652, [2012] All ER (D) 122 (Apr) 10.34, 11.9
Hone v Six Continents Retail Ltd [2005] EWCA Civ 922, [2006] IRLR 49 .... 55.21
Honey v City and County of Swansea (UKEAT/0465/09/JOJ) (16 April 2010, unreported) . 28.7, 52.9
Honey v Swansea City Council [2008] All ER (D) 311 (Nov), EAT 18.50, 19.24
Honeywill & Stein Ltd v Larkin Bros (London's Commercial Photographers) Ltd [1934] 1 KB 191, 103 LJKB 74, [1933] All ER Rep 77, 150 LT 71, 50 TLR 56, CA 54.1

Table of Cases

Hooper v British Railways Board [1988] IRLR 517, CA 7.12, 52.4
Hoover Ltd v Forde [1980] ICR 239, EAT 53.13
Hopkins v Norcros plc [1994] ICR 11, [1994] IRLR 18, CA 53.13, 56.30
Hopley-Dodd v Highfield Motors (Derby) Ltd (1969) 4 ITR 289 .... 56.9
Horcal Ltd v Gatland [1984] IRLR 288, [1984] BCLC 549, CA 8.19
Horizon Recruitment Ltd v Vincent [2010] ICR 491, sub nom Industrious Ltd v Horizon
    Recruitment Ltd (in liq) [2010] IRLR 204, sub nom Industrious Ltd v Vincent (2010) Times,
    11 January, EAT 12.33, 18.34, 51.20, 53.19
Horkulak v Cantor Fitzgerald International [2004] EWCA Civ 1287, [2005] ICR 402, [2004] IRLR
    942, 148 Sol Jo LB 1218, [2004] All ER (D) 170 (Oct) 7.22c, 51.7, 56.25, 56.28
Hornfeldt v Posten Meddelande AB: C-141/11 [2012] 3 CMLR 37, [2013] All ER (EC) 593, [2012]
    IRLR 785, [2012] NLJR 962, [2012] EqLR 892, [2012] All ER (D) 63 (Jul), ECJ 11.9, 40.5
Horst v High Table Ltd. See High Table Ltd v Horst
Horton v Higham [2004] EWCA Civ 941, [2004] 3 All ER 852, [2004] All ER (D) 261 (Jul), sub
    nom 1 Pump Court Chambers v Horton [2004] 33 LS Gaz R 34, sub nom Higham v Meurig
    Lestyn Horton [2005] ICR 292, 148 Sol Jo LB 911 .... 11.10
Horton v Taplin Contracts Ltd [2002] EWCA Civ 1604, [2003] ICR 179, [2003] 01 LS Gaz R 24,
    [2003] PIQR P180, [2003] BLR 74, (2002) Times, 25 November, 146 Sol Jo LB 256,
    [2002] All ER (D) 122 (Nov) 26.12
Horwood v Lincolnshire County Council (UKEAT/0462/11/RN) (3 April 2012, unreported)
    .... 17.23
Hospice of St Mary of Furness v Howard [2007] IRLR 944, [2007] All ER (D) 305 (May), EAT
    .... 10.26, 18.14
Hosso v European Credit Management Ltd [2011] EWCA Civ 1589, [2012] ICR 547, [2012] IRLR
    235, [2011] All ER (D) 158 (Dec) 12.4, 21.5
Hotson v Wisbech Conservative Club [1984] ICR 859, [1984] IRLR 422, EAT 17.35
Hough v Leyland DAF Ltd [1991] ICR 696, [1991] IRLR 194, EAT 19.35, 37.2, 37.4, 52.11
Hougna v Allen (UKEAT/0326/10/LA) [2011] All ER (D) 250 (Apr) 7.24
Hounga v Allen [2012] EWCA Civ 609, [2012] IRLR 685, [2012] All ER (D) 132 (May) 11.19
Housing Corpn v Bryant [1999] ICR 123, sub nom Bryant v Housing Corpn [1998] 26 LS Gaz R 31,
    142 Sol Jo LB 181, CA 12.8, 18.10
Hovell v Ashford and St Peter's Hospital NHS Trust [2009] EWCA Civ 670, [2009] ICR 1545,
    [2009] IRLR 734, (2009) Times, 5 October, [2009] All ER (D) 95 (Jul) 21.8
Howard v Campbell's Caravans Ltd (UKEAT/0609/10/LA) unreported 40.3
Howard v Millrise Ltd (t/a Colourflow) (in liq) [2005] ICR 435, [2005] IRLR 84, [2004] All ER (D)
    436 (Nov), EAT 50.23
Howard v Pickford Tool Co Ltd [1951] 1 KB 417, 95 Sol Jo 44, CA 39.11
Howes v Hinckley and Bosworth Borough Council [2008] All ER (D) 112 (Aug), EAT 18.13
Howlett Marine Services Ltd v Bowlam [2001] ICR 595, [2001] IRLR 201, [2000] All ER (D) 2494,
    EAT 17.25, 17.26, 17.33, 37.6
Howman & Son v Blyth [1983] ICR 416, [1983] IRLR 139, EAT 42.2
Hoyland v Asda Stores Ltd [2005] ICR 1235, [2005] IRLR 438, [2005] All ER (D) 219 (Apr); affd
    [2006] CSIH 21, [2006] IRLR 468, 2006 SLT 524, [2006] All ER (D) 133 (Apr) 21.5, 21.14, 31.18
Huddersfield Fine Worsteds Ltd, Re, Krasner v McMath [2005] EWCA Civ 1072, [2005] 4 All ER
    886, [2006] ICR 205, [2005] IRLR 995, [2006] 2 BCLC 160, [2005] BCC 915, [2005] NLJR 1355,
    (2005) Times, 26 September, [2005] All ER (D) 65 (Aug) 29.11
Hudson v Department for Work and Pension [2013] IRLR 32 .... 45.9
Hudson v GMB [1990] IRLR 67 .... 49.12
Hudson v Ridge Manufacturing Co Ltd [1957] 2 QB 348, [1957] 2 All ER 229, [1957] 2 WLR 948,
    101 Sol Jo 409 .... 25.7
Hudson v University of Oxford [2007] EWCA Civ 336, [2007] All ER (D) 356 (Feb) 30.14
Hugh-Jones v St John's College Cambridge [1979] ICR 848, 123 Sol Jo 603, EAT 11.21
Hughes v Corps of Commissionaires Management Ltd (No 1) [2009] ICR 345, [2009] IRLR 122,
    [2008] All ER (D) 225 (Oct), EAT 55.17
Hughes v Corps of Commissionaires Management Ltd (UKEAT/0173/10/SM) [2011] IRLR 100,
    [2011] ICR D2, EAT; affd [2011] EWCA Civ 1061, [2012] 1 CMLR 649, [2011] IRLR 915, [2011]
    39 LS Gaz R 19, [2011] All ER (D) 123 (Sep) 55.17, 55.29
Hughes v Graham (t/a Graylyns Residential Home) (UKEA/T/0159/08MAA) [2008] All ER (D)
    137 (Oct) 55.5

Hughes v Greenwich London Borough Council [1994] 1 AC 170, [1993] 4 All ER 577, [1993] 3 WLR 821, 92 LGR 61, 69 P & CR 487, [1994] ICR 48, 26 HLR 99, [1993] 46 LS Gaz R 38, [1993] NLJR 1571n, 137 Sol Jo LB 244, HL 41.7
Hughes v Southwark London Borough Council [1988] IRLR 55 .... 7.42
Huke v Department for Education (2012) UKEAT/0080/12/LA, [2012] All ER (D) 61 (Nov), EAT 50.3
Humphreys v Norilsk Nickel International (UK) Ltd [2010] EWHC 1867 (QB), [2010] IRLR 976, [2010] All ER (D) 235 (Jul) 7.22c
Hunt v United Airlines Inc [2008] ICR 934, [2008] All ER (D) 35 (Apr), EAT 23.9
Hunter v British Coal Corpn [1999] QB 140, [1998] 2 All ER 97, [1998] 3 WLR 685, [1999] ICR 72, [1998] 12 LS Gaz R 27, 142 Sol Jo LB 85, CA 25.8
Hunter v McCarrick. See McCarrick v Hunter
Hunter Kane Ltd v Watkins [2003] EWHC 186 (Ch), [2003] All ER (D) 144 (Feb) 8.24
Hurley v Mustoe (No 2) [1983] ICR 422, EAT 12.12
Hurst v Suffolk Mental Health Partnership NHS Trust [2009] EWCA Civ 309, [2009] ICR 1011, [2009] IRLR 452, (2009) Times, 28 April, [2009] All ER (D) 73 (Apr) 21.21
Hurt v Sheffield Corpn (1916) 85 LJKB 1684 .... 27.9
Hussain v Acorn Independent College Ltd (UKEAT/0199/10/SM) [2011] IRLR 463, [2010] All ER (D) 137 (Sep), EAT 6.7
Hussain v Surrey and Sussex Healthcare NHS Trust [2011] EWHC 1670 (QB), [2011] All ER (D) 91 (Jul) 5.8, 7.13
Hussain v Elonex plc [1999] IRLR 420, CA 52.10
Hussain v New Taplow Paper Mills Ltd [1987] 1 All ER 417, [1987] 1 WLR 336, [1987] ICR 28, 131 Sol Jo 358, [1987] LS Gaz R 1242, CA; affd [1988] AC 514, [1988] 1 All ER 541, [1988] 2 WLR 266, [1988] ICR 259, [1988] IRLR 167, 132 Sol Jo 226, [1988] 10 LS Gaz R 45, [1988] NLJR 45, HL 42.9
Hussman Manufacturing Ltd v Weir [1998] IRLR 288, 599 IRLB 5, EAT 32.6
Hutchins v Permacell Finesse Ltd (In Administration) [2008] All ER (D) 112 (Jan), EAT 37.6
Hutchinson v Westward Television Ltd [1977] ICR 279, [1977] IRLR 69, 12 ITR 125, EAT 17.30
Hutchinson 3G UK Ltd v Francois [2009] EWCA Civ 405, [2009] ICR 1323, [2009] All ER (D) 127 (May) 17.21
Hutton v Parker (1839) 7 Dowl 739 .... 39.10
Hyde v Lehman Bros Ltd [2004] All ER (D) 40 (Aug), EAT 17.31
Hyde-Walsh v Ashby [2008] All ER (D) 225 (Feb), EAT 18.52
Hydra plc v Anastasi [2005] EWHC 1559 (QB), [2005] All ER (D) 276 (Jul) 39.8
Hynd v Armstrong [2007] CSIH 16, [2007] IRLR 338, 2007 SC 409 .... 50.26

I

ICTS (UK) Ltd v Tchoula [2000] IRLR 643, [2000] All ER (D) 614, EAT 12.16, 12.18
Ibe v McNally [2005] EWHC 1551 (Ch), [2005] STC 1426, sub nom Redundant Employee v McNally (Inspector of Taxes) [2005] All ER (D) 389 (Mar) 44.8
Ibex Trading Co Ltd v Walton [1994] ICR 907, [1994] IRLR 564, [1994] BCC 982, EAT 50.26
Ibimidun v HM Prison Service. See HM Prison Service v Ibimidun
Iceland Frozen Foods Ltd v Jones [1983] ICR 17, [1982] IRLR 439, EAT 52.4
Igbo v Johnson Matthey Chemicals Ltd [1986] ICR 505, [1986] IRLR 215, 130 Sol Jo 524, [1986] LS Gaz R 2089, CA 51.19
Iggesund Converters Ltd v Lewis [1984] ICR 544, [1984] IRLR 431, EAT 18.60
Imam-Sadeque v Bluebay Asset Management (Services) Ltd [2012] EWHC 3511 (QB), [2012] All ER (D) 78 (Dec) 13.3, 39.3, 39.13
Impact v Minister for Agriculture and Food: C-268/06 [2008] ECR I-2483, [2009] All ER (EC) 306, [2008] 2 CMLR 1265, [2008] IRLR 552, [2008] All ER (D) 194 (Apr), ECJ 17.12, 22.2, 45.9
Imperial Group Pension Trust Ltd v Imperial Tobacco Ltd [1991] 2 All ER 597, [1991] 1 WLR 589, [1991] ICR 524, [1991] IRLR 66 .... 40.16
Income Tax Special Purposes Comrs v Pemsel [1891] AC 531, 3 TC 53, 55 JP 805, 61 LJQB 265, [1891–4] All ER Rep 28, 65 LT 621, 7 TLR 657, HL 10.22
Incorporated Trustees of the National Council on Ageing (Age Concern England) v Secretary of State for Business, Enterprise and Regulatory Reform: C-388/07 [2009] All ER (EC) 619, [2009] 3 CMLR 105, [2009] ICR 1080, [2009] IRLR 373, (2009) Times, 9 March, [2009] All ER (D) 51 (Mar), ECJ 11.9

Table of Cases

Independent Insurance Co Ltd (in provisional liq) v Aspinall (UKEAT/0051/11/CEA) [2011] ICR 1234, [2011] IRLR 716, [2011] All ER (D) 136 (Aug), EAT 37.6
Independent Research Services Ltd v Catterall [1993] ICR 1, EAT 18.13
Industrial Accoustics Ltd v Crowhurst (5 May 2011, unreported), Ch 40.1
Industrial and Commercial Maintenance Ltd v Briffa [2008] All ER (D) 105 (Sep), EAT 27.5
Industrial Rubber Products v Gillon [1977] IRLR 389, 13 ITR 100, EAT 51.7
Industrious Ltd v Horizon Recruitment Ltd (in liq). See Horizon Recruitment Ltd v Vincent
Industrious Ltd v Vincent. See Horizon Recruitment Ltd v Vincent
Ingeniorforeningen i Danmark, acting on behalf of Ole Andersen v Region Syddanmark: C-499/08 [2012] All ER (EC) 342, [2011] 1 CMLR 1140, [2010] All ER (D) 99 (Oct), ECJ 11.9, 40.5
Ingram v Foxon [1984] ICR 685, [1985] IRLR 5, EAT 6.7
Initial Electronic Security Systems Ltd v Avdic [2005] IRLR 671, [2005] All ER (D) 335 (Jul), EAT 17.25
Initial Supplies Ltd v McCall 1992 SLT 67 .... 50.10
IRC v Ainsworth. See Ainsworth v IRC
IRC v Bebb Travel plc [2002] 4 All ER 534, [2003] ICR 201, [2002] IRLR 783, [2002] NLJR 1350, (2002) Times, 30 October, [2002] All ER (D) 105 (Aug), EAT; affd [2003] EWCA Civ 563, [2003] 3 All ER 546, [2003] ICR 1271, [2003] NLJR 633, (2003) Times, 25 April, 147 Sol Jo LB 505, [2003] All ER (D) 291 (Apr) ,,, 32.13
IRC v Mills. See Mills v IRC
IRC v Post Office Ltd [2003] ICR 546, [2003] IRLR 199, [2002] All ER (D) 282 (Dec), EAT 32.10
Insaidoo v Metropolitan Resources North West Ltd (UKEAT/0365/10/DA) [2011] All ER (D) 04 (May) 17.9
Insitu Cleaning Co Ltd v Heads [1995] IRLR 4, EAT 10.51
Institution of Professional Civil Servants v Secretary of State for Defence [1987] 3 CMLR 35, [1987] IRLR 373 .... 50.23
International Computers Ltd v Kennedy [1981] IRLR 28, EAT 56.5
International Consulting Services (UK) Ltd v Hart [2000] IRLR 227 .... 39.8
International Packaging Corpn (UK) Ltd v Balfour [2003] IRLR 11, [2002] All ER (D) 146 (Nov) 32.6
International Sports Co Ltd v Thomson [1980] IRLR 340, EAT 52.8
Investors' Compensation Scheme Ltd v West Bromwich Building Society [1998] 1 All ER 98, [1998] 1 WLR 896, [1998] 1 BCLC 493, [1997] NLJR 989, [1997] CLC 1243, [1997] PNLR 541, HL 5.9, 7.12, 39.6
Irani v Southampton and South West Hampshire Health Authority [1985] ICR 590, [1985] IRLR 203 .... 7.42
Iron and Steel Trades Confederation v ASW Ltd (in liq) [2004] IRLR 926, [2004] All ER (D) 101 (Sep), EAT 19.43
Ironmonger v Movefield Ltd (t/a Deering Appointments) [1988] IRLR 461, EAT 14.3, 45.2
Ironsides Ray & Vials v Lindsay [1994] ICR 384, [1994] IRLR 318, EAT 17.18, 18.76
Irving v GMB [2008] IRLR 202, [2007] All ER (D) 192 (Oct), EAT 48.3
Iske v P & O European Ferries (Dover) Ltd [1997] IRLR 401, EAT 10.30, 21.14
Isles of Scilly Council v Brintel Helicopters Ltd [1995] ICR 249, [1995] IRLR 6, EAT 50.5
Islington London Borough Council v Ladele. See Ladele v Islington London Borough Council
Istituto Nazionale Della Previdenza Sociale (Inps) v Bruno: C-395/08 [2010] 3 CMLR 1225, [2010] IRLR 890, ECJ 30.1, 30.11
Istituto Nazionale Della Previdenza Sociale (Inps) v Lotti: C-396/08 [2010] 3 CMLR 1225, [2010] IRLR 890, ECJ 30.1, 30.11
Itau BBA International Ltd, Re [2012] EWHC 1783 (Ch), [2013] Bus LR 490, (2012) Times, 11 September, [2012] All ER (D) 206 (Jun) 15.49
Item Software (UK) Ltd v Fassihi [2002] EWHC 3116 (Ch), [2003] IRLR 769, [2003] 2 BCLC 1, [2003] BCC 858, [2002] All ER (D) 62 (Dec); revsd in part [2004] EWCA Civ 1244, [2005] ICR 450, [2004] IRLR 928, [2005] 2 BCLC 91, [2004] 39 LS Gaz R 34, (2004) Times, 21 October, 148 Sol Jo LB 1153, [2004] All ER (D) 187 (Sep), sub nom Fassihi v Item Software (UK) Ltd [2004] BCC 994 .... 7.17, 8.19, 32.22, 56.20, 56.28
Ivory v Palmer [1975] ICR 340, 119 Sol Jo 405, CA 41.4
Iwanuszezak v General Municipal Boilermakers and Allied Trades Union [1988] IRLR 219, CA 49.2
Ixora Trading Inc v Jones [1990] FSR 251 .... 7.16

J

J v DLA Piper UK LLP (UKEAT/0263/09/RN) [2010] ICR 1052, [2010] IRLR 936, 115 BMLR
    107, 154 Sol Jo (no 24) 37, [2010] All ER (D) 112 (Aug) 10.26, 10.28
J A Mont (UK) Ltd v Mills [1993] FSR 577, [1993] IRLR 172, CA . 39.1, 39.3, 39.6, 39.7, 39.8, 39.10,
    39.14
J Sainsbury Ltd v Savage [1981] ICR 1, [1980] IRLR 109, CA 17.23, 51.13, 52.15
J Sainsbury plc v Moger [1994] ICR 800, EAT 19.40
JH Walker Ltd v Hussain [1996] ICR 291, [1996] IRLR 11, EAT 12.14
JMCC Holdings Ltd v Conroy [1990] ICR 179, EAT 18.22
Jackson v Computershare Investor Services plc [2007] EWCA Civ 1065, [2008] ICR 341, [2008]
    IRLR 70, 151 Sol Jo LB 1434, [2007] All ER (D) 448 (Oct) 50.17
Jackson v Ghost Ltd [2003] IRLR 824, [2003] All ER (D) 17 (Sep), EAT 51.15
Jackson v Invicta Plastics Ltd [1987] BCLC 329 .... 56.17
Jackson v Liverpool City Council [2011] EWCA Civ 1068, [2011] IRLR 1009, [2011] All ER (D) 89
    (Jun) 38.4
Jaffrey v Department of the Environment Transport, and the Regions [2002] IRLR 688,
    [2002] All ER (D) 111 (Jul), EAT 10.34
Jakeman v South West Thames Regional Health Authority and London Ambulance Service [1990]
    IRLR 62 .... 7.43, 32.14
James v Blockbuster Entertainment Ltd [2006] EWCA Civ 684, [2006] IRLR 630, [2006] All ER (D)
    360 (May) 18.16, 18.17
James v Eastleigh Borough Council [1990] 2 AC 751, [1990] 2 All ER 607, [1990] 3 WLR 55, 88
    LGR 756, [1990] ICR 554, [1990] IRLR 288, [1990] 27 LS Gaz R 41, [1990] NLJR 926, HL
    .... 10.17
James v Gina Shoes Ltd (UKEAT/0384/11/DM) [2012] All ER (D) 166 (Mar), EAT 12.3
James v Great North Eastern Railways [2005] All ER (D) 15 (Mar), EAT 30.8, 30.9
James v Greenwich London Borough Council [2007] ICR 577, [2007] IRLR 168, [2007] All ER (D)
    12 (Jan), EAT; affd sub nom James v London Borough of Greenwich [2008] EWCA Civ 35,
    [2008] ICR 545, [2008] IRLR 302, [2008] All ER (D) 54 (Feb) 14.3, 45.2, 45.2c
James v Redcats (Brands) Ltd [2007] ICR 1006, [2007] IRLR 296, [2007] All ER (D) 270 (Feb),
    EAT 14.3, 14.9, 27.2, 32.10
James v Waltham Holy Cross UDC [1973] ICR 398, [1973] IRLR 202, 14 KIR 576, 8 ITR 467,
    NIRC 52.6
James W Cook & Co (Wivenhoe) Ltd (in liq) v Tipper [1990] ICR 716, [1990] IRLR 386, CA
    .... 17.26, 52.11, 53.13
Jämställdhetsombudsmannen v Örebro läns landsting: C-236/98 [2000] ECR I-2189,
    [2000] 2 CMLR 708, [2001] ICR 249, [2000] IRLR 421, ECJ 21.5
Janata Bank v Ahmed [1981] ICR 791, [1981] IRLR 457, CA 7.18, 7.47b
Janciuk v Winerite Ltd [1998] IRLR 63, EAT 7.36, 56.25
Janes Solicitors v Lamb-Simpson (1996) 541 IRLB 15, EAT 27.9
Jansen Van Resnburg v Royal Borough of Kingston-upon-Thames (UKEAT/0096/07) (16 October
    2007, unreported) 18.15
Jenvey v Australian Broadcasting Corp [2002] EWHC 927 (QB), [2003] ICR 79, [2002] IRLR 520,
    [2002] All ER (D) 179 (Apr) 56.19
Joao v Jurys Hotel Management UK Ltd (UKEAT/0210/11/SM) (11 October 2011, unreported)
    .... 26.7, 52.3, 55.24
Jarretts Motors Ltd v Wells (UKEAT/0327/08/DA) [2009] All ER (D) 350 (Jul) 17.35, 17.38
Jean Sorelle Ltd v Rybak. See Rybak v Jean Sorelle Ltd
Jeetle v Elster [1985] ICR 389, [1985] IRLR 227, EAT 6.9, 50.4
Jenkins v Kingsgate (Clothing Production) Ltd [1981] 1 WLR 1485, [1980] 1 CMLR 81, [1981] ICR
    715, [1980] IRLR 6, 125 Sol Jo 587, EAT 21.11
Jenkins v P & O European Ferries (Dover) Ltd [1991] ICR 652, EAT 19.46
Jenvey v Australian Broadcasting Corpn [2002] EWHC 927 (QB), [2003] ICR 79, [2002] IRLR 520,
    [2002] All ER (D) 179 (Apr) 7.22b
Jeremiah v Ministry of Defence. See Ministry of Defence v Jeremiah
Jiad v Byford [2003] EWCA Civ 135, [2003] IRLR 232, [2003] All ER (D) 299 (Jan) 10.50
Jilley v Birmingham and Solihull Mental Health NHS Trust [2008] All ER (D) 35 (Feb), EAT
    .... 18.71
Jiménez Melgar v Ayuntamiento de Los Barrios: C-438/99 [2001] ECR I-6915, [2003] 3 CMLR 67,
    [2004] ICR 610, [2001] IRLR 848, [2001] All ER (D) 42 (Oct), ECJ 10.31

Table of Cases

Jiminez v Southwark London Borough Council [2003] EWCA Civ 502, [2003] ICR 1176, [2003]
 IRLR 477, [2003] 23 LS Gaz R 37, (2003) Times, 1 May, 147 Sol Jo LB 476, [2003] All ER (D)
 123 (Apr) 18.61
Jivraj v Hashwani. See Hashwani v Jivraj
Johanson (T/A Kaleidascope Child Care) v Yeo (UKEAT/0541/10/CEA) (7 April 2011,
 unreported) 18.56
John v Rees [1970] Ch 345, [1969] 2 All ER 274, [1969] 2 WLR 1294, 113 Sol Jo 487 .... 53.13
John Brown Engineering Ltd v Brown [1997] IRLR 90, EAT 52.11
John Lewis Partnership v Charman (UKEAT/0079/11/ZT) (24 March 2011, unreported) 17.25
John Lewis plc v Coyne [2001] IRLR 139, EAT 52.9
John Michael Design plc v Cooke [1987] 2 All ER 332, [1987] ICR 445, 131 Sol Jo 595,
 [1987] LS Gaz R 1492, CA 39.8
Johns v Solent SD Ltd [2008] IRLR 88, [2007] All ER (D) 228 (Dec), EAT; affd [2008] EWCA Civ
 790, [2008] IRLR 820, (2008) Times, 27 June, [2008] All ER (D) 158 (Jun) 18.22
Johnson v Chief Adjudication Officer (No 2): C-410/92 [1994] ECR I-5483, [1995] All ER (EC) 258,
 [1995] 1 CMLR 725, [1995] ICR 375, [1995] IRLR 157, ECJ 22.2
Johnson v Coventry Churchill International Ltd [1992] 3 All ER 14 .... 23.7
Johnson v Edwardian International Hotels Ltd [2008] All ER (D) 23 (May), EAT 18.55
Johnson v Gore Wood & Co (a firm) [2002] 2 AC 1, [2001] 1 All ER 481, [2001] 2 WLR 72,
 [2001] 1 BCLC 313, 150 NLJ 1889, [2000] All ER (D) 2293, HL 18.26
Johnson v Ryan [2000] ICR 236, EAT 14.8
Johnson v Unisys Ltd [2001] UKHL 13, [2003] 1 AC 518, [2001] 2 All ER 801, [2001] 2 WLR 1076,
 [2001] ICR 480, [2001] IRLR 279, [2001] All ER (D) 274 (Mar) 7.22d, 7.39, 53.12, 56.18, 56.29
Johnson Controls Ltd v Campbell (UKEAT/0041/12/JOJ) (14 February 2012, unreported) 50.3
Johnson Underwood Ltd v Montgomery [2001] EWCA Civ 318, [2001] ICR 819, [2001] IRLR 269,
 [2001] 20 LS Gaz R 40, [2001] All ER (D) 101 (Mar) 14.1, 14.3, 45.2a
Johnston v Chief Constable of the Royal Ulster Constabulary: 222/84 [1987] QB 129, [1986]
 3 All ER 135, [1986] ECR 1651, [1986] 3 WLR 1038, [1986] 3 CMLR 240, [1987] ICR 83, [1986]
 IRLR 263, 130 Sol Jo 953, [1987] LS Gaz R 188, ECJ 11.22
Johnstone v Bloomsbury Health Authority [1992] QB 333, [1991] 2 All ER 293, [1991] 2 WLR 1362,
 [1991] ICR 269, [1991] IRLR 118, [1991] 2 Med LR 38, CA 7.17, 7.19
Jones v Associated Tunnelling Co Ltd [1981] IRLR 477, EAT 7.22e, 7.32
Jones v Corbin (t/a Boo) (UKEAT/0504/10/RN) (7 September 2011, unreported) 18.52
Jones v DAS Legal Expenses Insurance Co Ltd [2003] EWCA Civ 1071, [2004] IRLR 218, 147 Sol
 Jo LB 932, [2003] All ER (D) 425 (Jul) 18.50, 19.24, 28.7
Jones v Department For Constitutional Affairs [2006] All ER (D) 345 (Nov), EAT; affd sub nom
 Department of Constitutional Affairs v Jones [2007] EWCA Civ 894, [2008] IRLR 128,
 [2008] All ER (D) 43 (Jan) 12.7, 17.30
Jones v Friends Provident Life Office [2004] IRLR 783, NI CA 11.24
Jones v Governing Body of Burdett Coutts School [1997] ICR 390, 571 IRLB 9, EAT; revsd [1999]
 ICR 38, [1998] IRLR 521, [1998] 18 LS Gaz R 32, 142 Sol Jo LB 142, CA 19.33, 36.12
Jones v Gwent County Council [1992] IRLR 521 .... 7.43
Jones v Merton London Borough Council [2008] EWCA Civ 660, [2008] 4 All ER 287, [2009] 1 P
 & CR 63, [2008] 2 P & CR D26, [2008] 33 EG 74, (2008) Times, 3 July, [2008] All ER (D) 185
 (Jun), sub nom Merton London Borough Council v Jones [2009] 1 WLR 1269 .... 41.3
Jones v Mid-Glamorgan County Council [1997] ICR 815, [1997] IRLR 685, CA 51.8
Jones v Post Office [2001] EWCA Civ 558, [2001] ICR 805, [2001] IRLR 384, [2001] All ER (D) 133
 (Apr) 11.9
Jones v Ruth [2011] EWCA Civ 804, [2012] 1 All ER 490, [2011] NLJR 1027, [2011] All ER (D) 112
 (Jul) 26.25
Jones v Secretary of State for Employment [1982] ICR 389, EAT 29.4
Jones v Thornton (UKEAT/0068/11/SM) [2011] NLJR 1335, [2011] All ER (D) 122 (Sep),
 EAT 17.37, 17.38
Jones v Tower Boot Co Ltd. See Tower Boot Co Ltd v Jones
Jones v University of Manchester [1993] ICR 474, [1993] IRLR 218, [1993] 10 LS Gaz R 33, 137
 Sol Jo LB 14, CA 10.34, 11.9
Jooste v General Medical Council [2012] Eq LR 1049, EAT 11.30
Jørgensen v Foreningen af Speciallæger and Sygesikringens Forhandlingsudvalg: C-226/98
 [2000] ECR I-2447, [2002] 1 CMLR 1151, [2000] IRLR 726, ECJ 11.9
Joshua Wilson & Bros Ltd v Union of Shop, Distributive and Allied Workers [1978] 3 All ER 4,
 [1978] ICR 614, [1978] IRLR 120, 13 ITR 229, EAT 48.20

Jouini v Princess Personal Service GmbH (PPS): C-458/05 [2007] 3 CMLR 1472, [2008] ICR 128, [2007] IRLR 1005, [2007] All ER (D) 84 (Sep), ECJ 50.5
Jowitt v Pioneer Technology (UK) Ltd [2003] EWCA Civ 411, [2003] ICR 1120, [2003] IRLR 356, [2003] All ER (D) 263 (Mar) 42.12, 42.15
Judge v Crown Leisure Ltd [2005] EWCA Civ 571, [2005] IRLR 823, [2005] All ER (D) 283 (Apr) 7.2, 7.32
Jules Dethier Equipement SA v Dassy and Sovam SPRL (in liq): C-319/94 [1998] ECR I-1061, [1998] All ER (EC) 346, [1998] 2 CMLR 611, [1998] ICR 541, [1998] IRLR 266, ECJ 50.11, 50.26
Julio v Jose (UKEAT/0553/10/DM) [2012] IRLR 180, [2012] NLJR 137, [2012] All ER (D) 100 (Jan), EAT 32.10
Junk v Kuhnel: C-188/03 [2005] ECR I-885, [2005] IRLR 310, [2005] All ER (D) 264 (Jan), ECJ 37.4
Jupiter General Insurance Co Ltd v Shroff [1937] 3 All ER 67, PC 56.17
Jurkowska v Hlmad Ltd [2008] EWCA Civ 231, [2008] ICR 841, [2008] IRLR 430, [2008] All ER (D) 283 (Mar) 19.14
Justfern Ltd v D'Ingerthorpe [1994] ICR 286, [1994] IRLR 164, EAT 53.13

K

KB v National Health Service Pensions Agency: C-117/01 [2004] ECR I-541, [2004] All ER (EC) 1089, [2004] 1 CMLR 931, [2004] ICR 781, [2004] IRLR 240, [2004] 1 FLR 683, (2004) Times, 15 January, [2004] All ER (D) 03 (Jan), ECJ 21.13
KHS AG v Schulte: C-214/10 [2012] 1 CMLR 1352, [2012] IRLR 156, [2012] ICR D19, ECJ 27.3A, 27.6
Kachelmann v Bankhaus Hermann Lampe KG: C-322/98 [2000] ECR I-7505, [2002] 1 CMLR 155, [2001] IRLR 49, ECJ 10.35
Kalac v Turkey (Application 20704/92) (1997) 27 EHRR 552, ECtHR 28.7
Kalanke v Freie Hansestadt Bremen: C-450/93 [1995] ECR I-3051, [1996] All ER (EC) 66, [1996] 1 CMLR 175, [1996] ICR 314, [1995] IRLR 660, ECJ 11.10
Kalliope Schöning-Kougebetopoulou v Freie und Hansestadt Hamburg. See Schöning-Kougebetopoulou v Freie und Hansestadt Hamburg
Kapadia v Lambeth London Borough Council [2000] IRLR 14, EAT; affd [2000] IRLR 699, 57 BMLR 170, [2000] All ER (D) 785, CA 10.26
Kapfunde v Abbey National plc and Daniel [1999] ICR 1, [1998] IRLR 583, 46 BMLR 176, CA 38.7
Kapur v Shields [1976] 1 All ER 873, [1976] 1 WLR 131, [1976] ICR 26, 120 Sol Jo 96 .... 51.15
Katsikas v Konstantinidis: C-132/91, C-138/91 and C-139/91 [1992] ECR I-6577, [1993] 1 CMLR 845, [1993] IRLR 179, ECJ 50.16
Kaur v MG Rover Group Ltd [2004] EWCA Civ 1507, [2005] ICR 625, [2005] IRLR 40, (2004) Times, 6 December, [2004] All ER (D) 273 (Nov) 5.7
Kauser v Asda Stores Ltd [2007] All ER (D) 195 (Oct), EAT 17.25
Kavanagh v Crystal Palace FC (2000) Ltd (2012) UKEAT/0354/12/SM, [2013] All ER (D) 122 (Mar), EAT 50.26
Keefe v Isle of Man Steam Packet Co Ltd [2010] EWCA Civ 683, [2010] All ER (D) 137 (Jun) 26.19
Keeley v Fosroc International Ltd [2006] EWCA Civ 1277, [2006] IRLR 961, [2006] 40 LS Gaz R 33, 150 Sol Jo LB 1328, [2006] All ER (D) 65 (Oct) 7.13
Keen v Commerzbank AG [2006] EWCA Civ 1536, [2007] ICR 623, [2006] All ER (D) 239 (Nov), sub nom Commerzbank AG v Keen [2007] IRLR 132 .... 7.22c, 7.30, 56.37
Kells v Pilkington plc [2002] IRLR 693, [2002] All ER (D) 33 (May), EAT 21.9
Kelly v Northern Ireland Housing Executive [1999] 1 AC 428, [1998] 3 WLR 735, [1998] ICR 828, [1998] IRLR 593, [1998] 36 LS Gaz R 31, 142 Sol Jo LB 254, HL 10.41
Kelly v Upholstery and Cabinet Works (Amesbury) Ltd [1977] IRLR 91, EAT 37.4
Kelly-Madden v Manor Surgery [2007] ICR 203, [2007] IRLR 17, [2006] All ER (D) 232 (Oct), EAT 52.11, 53.13
Kelman v Care Contract Services Ltd [1995] ICR 260, EAT 50.5
Kennaugh v Lloyd Jones (t/a Cheshire Tree Surgeons) [2006] All ER (D) 363 (Nov), EAT 18.64
Kenneth MacRae & Co Ltd v Dawson [1984] IRLR 5, EAT 36.8
Kenny v Hampshire Constabulary [1998] ICR 27, [1999] IRLR 76, EAT 10.37

Table of Cases

Kenny v Ministry for Justice, Equality and Law Reform: C-427/11 [2013] All ER (D) 37 (Mar),
ECJ 21.12
Kenny v South Manchester College [1993] ICR 934, [1993] IRLR 265 .... 50.5
Kent County Council v Gilham [1985] ICR 227, sub nom Gilham v Kent County Council [1985]
IRLR 16, CA 46.14
Kent Management Services Ltd v Butterfield [1992] ICR 272, [1992] IRLR 394, EAT 32.6
Kerr v Ernst & Young Services Ltd (UKEAT/0567/10/RN) [2011] ICR D13, [2011] All ER (D)
146 (Feb) 12.6, 18.2, 18.5
Kerr v Morris [1987] Ch 90, [1986] 3 All ER 217, [1986] 3 WLR 662, 130 Sol Jo 665, [1986] LS Gaz
R 2570, CA 39.5
Kerr v Sweater Shop (Scotland) Ltd [1996] IRLR 424, EAT 32.6
Kerry Foods Ltd v Creber [2000] ICR 556, [2000] IRLR 10, EAT 37.6, 50.26
Kerry Foods Ltd v Lynch [2005] IRLR 680, [2005] All ER (D) 351 (Jun), EAT 51.7
Keywest Club Ltd (t/a Veeraswamys Restaurant) v Choudhury [1988] IRLR 51, EAT 32.35
Khan v Chief Constable of West Yorkshire Police. See Chief Constable of West Yorkshire Police v
Khan
Khan v General Medical Council [1996] ICR 1032, [1994] IRLR 646, CA 11.30, 12.2
Khan v Heywood & Middleton Primary Care Trust [2006] EWCA Civ 1087, [2007] ICR 24, [2006]
IRLR 793, 150 Sol Jo LB 1021, [2006] All ER (D) 424 (Jul) 7.45, 18.28
Khan v Landskerr Childcare Ltd (UKEAT/0036/12/DM), unreported 39.13
Khan v Martin McColl (ET/1702926/09) (22 March 2010, unreported) 27.6
Khan v Trident Safeguards Ltd [2004] EWCA Civ 624, [2004] ICR 1591, [2004] IRLR 961, (2004)
Times, 28 May, 148 Sol Jo LB 634 .... 12.2
Khan v Vignette Europe Ltd (UKEAT/0350/08) (1 December 2008, unreported) 19.46
Khan v Vignette Europe Ltd (UKEAT/0134/09/CEA) (14 January 2010, unreported) 18.56
Khan & King v The Home Office (EAT/0026/06/LA and EAT/0250/06/LA) [2007] All ER (D)
54 (Feb); affd [2008] EWCA Civ 578, (2008) 858 IDS Brief 16, [2008] All ER (D) 323 (May)
.... 12.3
Khanum v Mid-Glamorgan Area Health Authority [1979] ICR 40, [1978] IRLR 215, 13 ITR 303,
EAT 52.10
Khatri v Co-operative Centrale Raiffeisen-Boerenleenbank BA [2010] EWCA Civ 397, [2010] IRLR
715, [2010] All ER (D) 158 (Apr) 7.32
Khetab v AGA Medical Ltd (UKEAT/0313/10/RN) (21 October 2010, unreported) 17.29
Khetab v AGA Medical Ltd (2011) 922 IDS Brief 9, EAT 12.6
Khudados v Leggate [2005] ICR 1013, [2005] IRLR 540, [2005] All ER (D) 241 (Feb), EAT 19.27
Kidd v Axa Equity and Law Life Assurance Society plc [2000] IRLR 301 .... 38.4
Kidd v DRG (UK) Ltd [1985] ICR 405, [1985] IRLR 190, EAT 10.35
Kimberley Group Housing Ltd v Hambley [2008] ICR 1030, [2008] IRLR 682, [2008] All ER (D)
408 (Jun), EAT 50.3, 50.15
King v Eaton Ltd [1996] IRLR 199, 1997 SLT 654, Ct of Sess 18.12
King v Eaton Ltd (No 2) [1998] IRLR 686, 1999 SLT 656, Ct of Sess 53.13
King v Great Britain-China Centre [1992] ICR 516, [1991] IRLR 513, CA 12.3
King v Royal Bank of Canada Europe Ltd [2012] IRLR 280, EAT 19.27, 53.4
King v Smith [1995] ICR 339, CA 25.5
King's College London v Clark (2003) IDS Brief No 747 .... 21.10, 21.12
Kingston v British Railways Board [1982] ICR 392, [1982] IRLR 274, EAT; affd [1984] ICR 781,
[1984] IRLR 146, CA 52.14
Kingston Upon Hull City Council v Schofield (2012) UKEAT/0616/11/DM, [2012] All ER (D)
342 (Nov), EAT 32.6
Kirby v National Probation Service for England and Wales (Cumbria Area) [2006] IRLR 508,
[2006] All ER (D) 111 (Mar), EAT 10.38
Kirklees Metropolitan Borough Council v Radecki. See Radecki v Kirklees Metropolitan
Borough Council
Kirton v Tetrosyl Ltd [2003] EWCA Civ 619, [2003] ICR 1237, [2003] IRLR 353, (2003) Times,
28 April, 147 Sol Jo LB 474, [2003] All ER (D) 190 (Apr) 10.26
Klarenberg v Ferrotron Technologies GmbH: C-466/07 [2009] ICR 1263, [2009] IRLR 301,
[2009] All ER (D) 133 (Feb), ECJ 50.4
Kleist v Pensionsversicherungsanstalt: C-356/09 [2010] All ER (D) 37 (Dec), ECJ 40.1
Knapton v ECC Card Clothing Ltd [2006] ICR 1084, [2006] IRLR 756, EAT 53.12
Knight v Central London Bus Co Ltd (EAT/443/00) (18 October 2001, unreported) 19.23

Knight v Department of Social Security [2002] IRLR 249, [2001] All ER (D) 473 (Nov), EAT
.... 18.12
Knowles v Liverpool City Council [1993] 4 All ER 321, [1993] 1 WLR 1428, 91 LGR 629, [1994]
  1 Lloyd's Rep 11, [1994] ICR 243, [1993] IRLR 588, [1993] NLJR 1479n, [1994] PIQR P8,
  HL 25.6
Komeng v Sandwell MBC [2011] EqLR 1053 .... 30.21
Konski v Peet [1915] 1 Ch 530, 84 LJ Ch 513, 59 Sol Jo 383, 112 LT 1107 .... 39.8
Kopel v Safeway Stores plc [2003] IRLR 753, [2003] All ER (D) 05 (Sep), EAT ... 18.36, 18.72, 53.19
Korashi v Abertawe Bro Morgannwg University Local Health Board [2011] EWCA Civ 187,
  [2011] All ER (D) 09 (Mar) 18.63, 19.34
Korashi v Abertawe Bro Morgannwg University Local Health Board (UKEAT/0424/09/JOJ)
  [2012] IRLR 4, [2012] 01 LS Gaz R 15, [2011] All ER (D) 40 (Dec), EAT 9.17, 18.76
Kording v Senator für Finanzen: C-100/95 [1997] ECR I-5289, [1998] 1 CMLR 395, [1997] IRLR
  710, ECJ 21.3
Kores Manufacturing Co Ltd v Kolok Manufacturing Co Ltd [1957] 3 All ER 158, [1957] 1 WLR
  1012, [1957] RPC 431, 101 Sol Jo 799, [1957] CLY 1285; affd [1959] Ch 108, [1958] 2 All ER 65,
  [1958] 2 WLR 858, [1958] RPC 200, 102 Sol Jo 362, 1958 SLT 221, [1958] JBL 306, CA ... 39.5, 39.8
Kovacs v Queen Mary and Westfield College [2002] EWCA Civ 352, [2002] ICR 919, [2002] IRLR
  414, [2002] 19 LS Gaz R 29, (2002) Times, 12 April, 146 Sol Jo LB 91, [2002] All ER (D) 368
  (Mar) 18.36, 18.71, 18.73
Kovats v TFO Management LLP [2009] ICR 1140, [2009] All ER (D) 116 (May), EAT 14.3
Kowalska v Freie und Hansestadt Hamburg: C-33/89 [1990] ECR I-2591, [1992] ICR 29, [1990]
  IRLR 447, ECJ 21.22, 21.23
Kraft Foods Ltd v Hastie (UKEAT/0024/10/ZT) [2010] ICR 1355, [2010] All ER (D) 100
  (Aug) 11.9, 40.5
Kraus v Penna plc [2004] IRLR 260, [2003] All ER (D) 275 (Nov), EAT 9.17
Kuddus v Chief Constable of Leicestershire Constabulary [2001] UKHL 29, [2002] 2 AC 122,
  [2001] 3 All ER 193, [2001] 2 WLR 1789, [2001] 28 LS Gaz R 43, [2001] NLJR 936, 145 Sol Jo
  LB 166, [2001] All ER (D) 30 (Jun) 12.13, 12.18
Kudjodji v Lidl Ltd (UKEAT/0054/11) [2011] 31 LS Gaz R 20, [2011] ICR D23, [2011] All ER
  (D) 165 (Jul), EAT 17.11, 17.18
Kulikaoskas v Macduff Shellfish Ltd (UKEATS/62/09) [2011] ICR 48 .... 17.34, 31.2
Kulkarni v Milton Keynes Hospital NHS Trust [2009] EWCA Civ 789, [2010] ICR 101, [2009]
  IRLR 829, 109 BMLR 133, (2009) Times, 6 August, [2009] All ER (D) 248 (Jul) 28.7, 52.10
Kulkarni v NHS Education Scotland [2013] Eq LR 34, EAT 11.30
Kuratorium für Dialyse und Nierentransplantation eV v Lewark: C-457/93 [1996] ECR I-243,
  [1996] IRLR 637, ECJ 21.3
Kutz-Bauer v Freie und Hansestadt Hamburg: C-187/00 [2003] ECR I-2741, [2003] IRLR 368,
  [2003] All ER (D) 327 (Mar), ECJ 11.9
Kuzel v Roche Products Ltd [2008] EWCA Civ 380, [2008] ICR 799, [2008] IRLR 530,
  [2008] All ER (D) 234 (Apr) 9.17, 52.2
Kwamin v Abbey National plc [2004] ICR 841, [2004] IRLR 516, [2004] NLJR 418, [2004] All ER
  (D) 189 (Mar), EAT 17.13, 18.62, 28.7
Kwik-Fit (GB) Ltd v Lineham [1992] ICR 183, [1992] IRLR 156, [1992] 4 LS Gaz R 31, EAT
  .... 46.5
Kwik Save Stores Ltd v Swain [1997] ICR 49, EAT 17.37, 17.38

L

LMC Drains Ltd v Waugh [1991] 3 CMLR 172, EAT 50.6
Labour Party v Oakley [1988] ICR 403, sub nom Oakley v Labour Party [1988] IRLR 34, CA
  .... 52.14
Ladbrokes Racing v Traynor (UKEATS/0067/06) (3 October 2007, unreported) 18.10
Ladd v Marshall [1954] 3 All ER 745, [1954] 1 WLR 1489, 98 Sol Jo 870, CA 19.34
Ladele v Islington London Borough Council [2009] ICR 387, [2009] All ER (D) 100 (Jan), sub nom
  Islington London Borough Council v Ladele [2009] LGR 305, [2009] IRLR 154, EAT; affd sub
  nom Ladele v Islington London Borough Council [2009] EWCA Civ 1357, [2010] 1 WLR 955,
  [2010] LGR 690, [2010] ICR 532, [2010] IRLR 211, [2010] PTSR 982, (2010) Times, 1 January,
  [2009] All ER (D) 148 (Dec) 10.22, 11.9, 12.3, 28.7
Laher v Hammersmith and Fulham London Borough EAT/215/91, IDS Brief No 531 .... 18.52

Table of Cases

Laing v Manchester City Council [2006] ICR 1519, [2006] IRLR 748, [2006] All ER (D) 452 (Jul),
  EAT 10.15, 12.3
Laird v A K Stoddart Ltd [2001] IRLR 591, [2001] All ER (D) 261 (Jan), EAT 32.12
Lairikyengbam v Shrewsbury and Telford Hospital NHS Trust [2010] ICR 66, [2009] All ER (D)
  271 (Oct), EAT 7.2
Lake v British Transport Police [2007] ICR 47, [2006] All ER (D) 04 (Oct), EAT; revsd [2007]
  EWCA Civ 424, [2007] ICR 1293, [2007] All ER (D) 77 (May) 12.2, 35.4
Lambeth London Borough Council v Commission for Racial Equality (1989) 87 LGR 862, [1989]
  ICR 641, [1989] IRLR 379, [1989] 29 LS Gaz R 44, EAT; affd [1990] ICR 768, [1990] IRLR 231,
  CA 10.20, 11.4, 11.10, 11.17
Lambeth London Borough Council v D'Souza. See D'Souza v Lambeth London Borough Council
Lamont v Fry's Metals Ltd [1985] ICR 566, [1985] IRLR 470, CA 18.64
Lana v Positive Action Training In Housing (London) Ltd [2001] IRLR 501, [2001] All ER (D) 23
  (Jun), EAT 10.56
Lancashire Fire Ltd v SA Lyons & Co Ltd [1997] IRLR 113, CA 39.13
Lancaster v DEK Printing Machines Ltd (EAT/623/99) (14 April 2000, unreported) 17.25
Land Brandenburg v Sass: C-284/02 [2005] IRLR 147, [2004] All ER (D) 310 (Nov), ECJ 10.31
Land Securities Trillium Ltd v Thornley [2005] IRLR 765, [2005] All ER (D) 194 (Jun), EAT
  .... 51.7
Landeshauptstadt Kiel v Jaeger: C-151/02 [2003] ECR I-8389, [2004] All ER (EC) 604,
  [2003] 3 CMLR 493, [2004] ICR 1528, [2003] IRLR 804, 75 BMLR 201, [2003] All ER (D) 72
  (Sep), ECJ 55.5, 55.14, 55.15, 55.17
Landmark Brickwork Ltd v Sutcliffe [2011] EWHC 1239 (QB), [2011] IRLR 976, [2011] All ER (D)
  160 (May) 39.4, 39.8, 39.17
Landon v Lill (EAT/1486/00) (9 October 2002, unreported) 17.18
Lane v Shire Roofing Co (Oxford) Ltd [1995] IRLR 493, [1995] PIQR P417, CA 25.2
Lange v Georg Schünemann GmbH: C-350/99 [2001] ECR I-1061, [2001] All ER (EC) 481, [2001]
  IRLR 244, [2001] All ER (D) 90 (Feb), ECJ 7.11
Langston v Amalgamated Union of Engineering Workers [1974] 1 All ER 980, [1974] 1 WLR 185,
  [1974] ICR 180, [1974] IRLR 15, 16 KIR 139, 118 Sol Jo 97, CA 7.21, 56.21
Lansing Linde Ltd v Kerr [1991] 1 All ER 418, [1991] 1 WLR 251, [1991] ICR 428, [1991] IRLR
  80, [1990] NLJR 1458, CA 7.43, 39.13, 39.17
Lanton Leisure Ltd v White and Gibson [1987] IRLR 119, EAT 51.13
Larner v NHS Leeds (2011) UKEAT/0088/11/CEA, [2011] IRLR 894, [2011] NLJR 1182, [2011]
  ICR D27, [2011] All ER (D) 119 (Aug), EAT; affd [2012] EWCA Civ 1034, [2012] 4 All ER 1006,
  [2012] 3 CMLR 1101, [2012] ICR 1389, [2012] IRLR 825, 156 Sol Jo (30) 31, [2012] All ER (D)
  273 (Jul) 27.2, 27.3A
Larsen v Henderson [1990] IRLR 512, sub nom Larsen's Executrix v Henderson 1990 SLT 498, Ct
  of Sess 29.11
Lasertop Ltd v Webster [1997] ICR 828, [1997] IRLR 498, 572 IRLB 14, EAT 11.3
Latchman v Reed Business Information Ltd [2002] ICR 1453 .... 10.26
Latif v Project Management Institute [2007] All ER (D) 148 (May), sub nom Project Management
  Institute v Latif [2007] IRLR 579, EAT 12.3
Lauffer v Barking, Havering and Redbridge University Hospitals NHS Trust [2009] EWHC 2360
  (QB), [2010] Med LR 68 .... 7.43
Launahurst Ltd v Larner (Nigel) [2010] EWCA Civ 334, [2010] All ER (D) 282 (Mar) .. 18.52, 18.60,
  19.37
Laurie v Holloway [1994] ICR 32, EAT 18.52
Lavarack v Woods of Colchester Ltd [1967] 1 QB 278, [1966] 3 All ER 683, [1966] 3 WLR 706, 1
  KIR 312, 110 Sol Jo 770, CA 56.25
Law Hospital NHS Trust v Rush [2001] IRLR 611, Ct of Sess 10.26
Law Society v Bahl. See Bahl v Law Society
Law Society v Otobo (20 April 2011, unreported), Ch D 18.77
Law Society of England and Wales v Secretary of State for Justice [2010] EWHC 352 (QB), [2010]
  IRLR 407, [2010] All ER (D) 10 (Mar) 50.9
Lawal v Northern Spirit Ltd [2003] UKHL 35, [2004] 1 All ER 187, [2003] ICR 856, [2003] IRLR
  538, [2003] 28 LS Gaz R 30, [2003] NLJR 1005, (2003) Times, 27 June, 147 Sol Jo LB 783,
  [2003] All ER (D) 255 (Jun) 28.7
Lawrence v HM Prison Service [2007] IRLR 468, [2007] All ER (D) 119 (Jul), EAT 12.4
Lawrence v Regent Office Care Ltd: C-320/00 [2002] ECR I-7325, [2002] 3 CMLR 761, [2003] ICR
  1092, [2002] IRLR 822, (2002) Times, 10 October, [2002] All ER (D) 84 (Sep), ECJ 21.9

Lawrence David Ltd v Ashton [1991] 1 All ER 385, [1989] ICR 123, [1989] IRLR 22, CA . . . 39.8, 39.17
Lawrie-Blum v Land Baden-Württemberg: 66/85 [1986] ECR 2121, [1987] 3 CMLR 389, [1987]
  ICR 483, ECJ 21.4
Laws v London Chronicle (Indicator Newspapers) Ltd [1959] 2 All ER 285, [1959] 1 WLR 698, 103
  Sol Jo 470, CA 56.17
Lawson v Serco Ltd [2004] EWCA Civ 12, [2004] 2 All ER 200, [2004] ICR 204, [2004] IRLR 206,
  (2004) Times, 30 January, 148 Sol Jo LB 148, [2004] All ER (D) 217 (Jan); revsd [2006] UKHL
  3, [2006] 1 All ER 823, [2006] ICR 250, [2006] IRLR 289, [2006] 06 LS Gaz R 36, [2006] NLJR
  184, 150 Sol Jo LB 131, [2006] All ER (D) 184 (Jan) 10.42, 11.18, 23.3, 23.9, 45.9, 51.15
Leach v Office of Communications [2012] EWCA Civ 959, [2012] ICR 1269, [2012] IRLR 839,
  [2012] All ER (D) 148 (Jul) 28.7
Learoyd v Brook [1891] 1 QB 431, 55 JP 265, 60 LJQB 373, 39 WR 480, 64 LT 458, 7 TLR 236
  . . . . 56.44
Ledernes Hovedorganisation (acting for Rygard) v Dansk Arbejdsgiverforening (acting for Sto Molle
  Akustik A/S): C-48/94 [1995] ECR I-2745, [1996] 3 CMLR 45, [1996] ICR 333, [1996] IRLR 51,
  ECJ 50.5
Lee v Chassis & Cab Specialists Ltd (UKEAT/0268/10/JOJ) [2011] All ER (D) 178 (Feb) . 13.2, 32.10
Lee v GEC Plessey Telecommunications [1993] IRLR 383 . . . . 5.11, 7.32
Lee v Showmen's Guild of Great Britain [1952] 2 QB 329, [1952] 1 All ER 1175, 96 Sol Jo 296,
  [1952] 1 TLR 1115, CA 49.12
Lee Ting Sang v Chung Chi-Keung [1990] 2 AC 374, [1990] 2 WLR 1173, [1990] ICR 409, [1990]
  IRLR 236, 134 Sol Jo 909, [1990] 13 LS Gaz R 43, PC 14.3, 14.9
Leech v Preston Borough Council [1985] ICR 192, [1985] IRLR 337, EAT 51.13
Leeds City Council v Woodhouse. See Woodhouse v Leeds City Council
Leeds Private Hospital Ltd v Parkin [1992] ICR 571, EAT 10.15
Leeds United Association Football Club Ltd, Re [2007] EWHC 1761 (Ch), [2007] Bus LR 1560,
  [2007] ICR 1688, [2008] BCC 11, (2007) Times, 4 September, [2007] All ER (D) 385 (Jul) 29.2
Leefe v NSM Music Ltd [2006] ICR 450, 150 Sol Jo LB 400, [2006] All ER (D) 57 (Feb), EAT
  . . . . 17.37
Legal & General Assurance Ltd v Kirk [2001] EWCA Civ 1803, [2002] IRLR 124, [2001] All ER
  (D) 212 (Nov) 28.7
Legal & General Assurance Society Ltd v Pensions Ombudsman [2000] 2 All ER 577, [2000] 1 WLR
  1524, [1999] 46 LS Gaz R 40, [1999] NLJR 1733, 144 Sol Jo LB 8 . . . . 40.17
Lehman Brothers Ltd v Smith [2005] All ER (D) 177 (Oct), EAT 18.10
Leicester University v A [1999] ICR 701, [1999] IRLR 352, EAT 12.11, 18.18
Leighton v Charalambous [1995] ICR 1091, [1996] IRLR 67, EAT 7.24
Leighton v Construction Industry Training Board. See Construction Industry Training Board v
  Leighton
Leighton v Michael [1995] ICR 1091, [1996] IRLR 67, EAT 7.24, 11.19
Leisure Employment Services Ltd v Revenue and Customs Comrs [2007] EWCA Civ 92, [2007]
  ICR 1056, [2007] IRLR 450, (2007) Times, 7 March, [2007] All ER (D) 202 (Feb) 32.9
Leisure Leagues UK Ltd v Maconnachie [2002] IRLR 600, (2002) Times, 3 May, [2002] All ER (D)
  223 (Mar), EAT 27.9, 32.14, 32.22
Lennon v Birmingham City Council [2001] EWCA Civ 435, [2001] IRLR 826, [2001] All ER (D)
  321 (Mar) 7.45, 18.27
Leonard v Southern Derbyshire Chamber of Commerce [2001] IRLR 19, [2000] All ER (D) 1327,
  EAT 10.26
Leonard v Strathclyde Buses Ltd [1998] IRLR 693, 1999 SC 57, 1999 SLT 734, 606 IRLB 8, Ct of
  Sess 53.13
Letheby & Christopher Ltd v Bond [1988] ICR 480, EAT 6.7
Leverton v Clwyd County Council [1989] AC 706, [1989] 2 WLR 47, [1988] 2 CMLR 811, 87 LGR
  269, [1989] ICR 33, [1988] IRLR 239, CA; affd [1989] AC 706, [1989] 1 All ER 78, [1989] 2 WLR
  47, 87 LGR 269, [1989] ICR 33, [1989] IRLR 28, 133 Sol Jo 45, [1989] 19 LS Gaz R 41, HL
  . . . . 21.7, 21.9, 21.12
Levez v T H Jennings (Harlow Pools) Ltd: C-326/96 [1998] ECR I-7835, [1999] All ER (EC) 1,
  [1999] 2 CMLR 363, [1999] ICR 521, [1999] IRLR 36, 608 IRLB 3, [1998] All ER (D) 662,
  ECJ 17.12
Lewen v Denda: C-333/97 [1999] ECR I-7243, [2000] All ER (EC) 261, [2000] 2 CMLR 38, [2000]
  IRLR 67, ECJ 21.14
Lewicki v Brown & Root Wimpey Highland Fabricators Ltd [1996] STC 145, [1996] IRLR 565,
  OH 42.14

Table of Cases

Lewis v Motorworld Garages Ltd [1986] ICR 157, [1985] IRLR 465, CA 51.7
Lewis and Britton v E Mason & Sons [1994] IRLR 4, EAT 51.17
Lewis Woolf Griptight Ltd v Corfield [1997] IRLR 432, EAT 10.31
Lewisham and Guys Mental Health NHS Trust v Andrews [2000] ICR 707, CA 12.2
Lewisham London Borough Council v Malcolm [2008] UKHL 43, [2008] 1 AC 1399, [2008]
    4 All ER 525, [2008] 3 WLR 194, [2008] LGR 549, [2008] 2 P & CR 358, [2008] IRLR 700,
    102 BMLR 170, (2008) Times, 26 June, 152 Sol Jo (no 26) 29, [2008] All ER (D) 342 (Jun) 10.33,
                                                                                11.9, 11.9A, 40.6
Leyland DAF Ltd, Re. See Talbot v Cadge
Leyland DAF Ltd (No 2), Re. See Talbot v Cadge
Leyland Daf Ltd, Re, Talbot v Cadge. See Talbot v Cadge
Leyland Vehicles Ltd v Jones [1981] ICR 428, [1981] IRLR 269, EAT 49.5
Libyan Arab Foreign Bank v Bankers Trust Co [1989] QB 728, [1989] 3 All ER 252, [1989] 3 WLR
    314, [1988] 1 Lloyd's Rep 259, 133 Sol Jo 568 .... 56.15
Lightfoot v D & J Sporting Ltd [1996] IRLR 64, EAT 7.24
Lightways (Contractors) Ltd v Associated Holdings Ltd [2000] IRLR 247, Ct of Sess 50.5
Linbourne v Constable [1993] ICR 698, EAT 18.10
Lincoln v Daniels [1962] 1 QB 237, [1961] 3 All ER 740, [1961] 3 WLR 866, 105 Sol Jo 647, CA
                                                                                        2.4
Lincoln Mills (Australia) Ltd v Gough [1964] VR 193 .... 8.37
Linfood Cash and Carry Ltd v Thomson [1989] ICR 518, [1989] IRLR 235, EAT 52.10
Lionel Leventhal Ltd v North (UKEAT/0265/04) (27 October 2004, unreported) 52.11
Lipkin Gorman (a firm) v Karpnale Ltd [1991] 2 AC 548, [1992] 4 All ER 512, [1991] 3 WLR 10,
    [1991] NLJR 815, 135 Sol Jo LB 36, HL 32.15
Lipscombe v Forestry Commission [2007] EWCA Civ 428, [2007] All ER (D) 132 (May) 19.33
Lisk-Carew v Birmingham City Council [2004] EWCA Civ 565, [2004] 20 LS Gaz R 35, (2004)
    Times, 7 June, [2004] All ER (D) 215 (Apr) 12.19
List Design Group Ltd v Douglas [2002] ICR 686, [2003] IRLR 14, [2002] All ER (D) 215 (Mar),
    EAT 32.6
Lister v Hesley Hall Ltd [2001] UKHL 22, [2002] 1 AC 215, [2001] 2 All ER 769, [2001] 1 WLR
    1311, [2001] ICR 665, [2001] IRLR 472, [2001] 2 FCR 97, [2001] 2 FLR 307, [2001] Fam Law
    595, [2001] ELR 422, [2001] NPC 89, [2001] NLJR 728, (2001) Times, 10 May, 145 Sol Jo LB
    126, [2001] All ER (D) 37 (May) 10.54, 25.9, 54.2
Lister v Romford Ice and Cold Storage Co Ltd [1957] AC 555, [1957] 1 All ER 125, [1957] 2 WLR
    158, [1956] 2 Lloyd's Rep 505, 121 JP 98, 101 Sol Jo 106, HL 7.18, 8.21, 54.1
Litster v Forth Dry Dock and Engineering Co Ltd [1990] 1 AC 546, [1989] 1 All ER 1134, [1989]
    2 WLR 634, [1989] ICR 341, [1989] IRLR 161, 133 Sol Jo 455, [1989] NLJR 400, 1989 SC (HL)
    96, HL 6.9, 22.2, 50.6, 50.12, 50.14, 50.26
Little v Charterhouse Magna Assurance Co Ltd [1980] IRLR 19, EAT 7.22e
Littlewoods Organisation Ltd v Harris [1978] 1 All ER 1026, [1977] 1 WLR 1472, 121 Sol Jo 727,
    CA 39.6, 39.8
Littlewoods Organisation plc v Traynor [1993] IRLR 154, EAT 12.6
Liverpool City Council v Irwin [1977] AC 239, [1976] 2 All ER 39, [1976] 2 WLR 562, 74 LGR 392,
    32 P & CR 43, 13 HLR 38, 120 Sol Jo 267, 238 Estates Gazette 879, 963, HL 7.15
Living Design (Home Improvements) Ltd v Davidson [1994] IRLR 69, Ct of Sess 39.7
Livingstone v Hepworth Refractories Ltd [1992] 3 CMLR 601, [1992] ICR 287, [1992] IRLR 63,
    [1992] 5 LS Gaz R 31, EAT 2.4, 17.12
Llewellyn v Hartlepool Borough Council [2009] ICR 1426, (2009) Times, 9 July, [2009] All ER (D)
    211 (Aug), sub nom Hartlepool Borough Council v Llewellyn [2009] IRLR 796, EAT 21.5, 21.9
Lloyd v BCQ Ltd (2012) UKEAT/0148/12/KN, [2013] 1 CMLR 1166, [2012] All ER (D) 343
    (Nov), EAT 42.13
Lloyd v Grace, Smith & Co [1912] AC 716, 81 LJKB 1140, [1911–13] All ER Rep 51, 56 Sol Jo 723,
    107 LT 531, 28 TLR 547, HL 54.2
Lloyd v Taylor Woodrow Construction [1999] IRLR 782, EAT 52.11
Locabail (UK) Ltd v Bayfield Properties Ltd [2000] QB 451, [2000] 1 All ER 65, [2000] 2 WLR 870,
    [2000] IRLR 96, [2000] 3 LRC 482, 7 BHRC 583, [1999] All ER (D) 1279, CA 18.50
Lock v Cardiff Rly Co [1998] IRLR 358, 599 IRLB 6, EAT 52.4, 52.10
Lock v Connell Estate Agents [1994] ICR 983, [1994] IRLR 444, EAT 53.9, 53.13, 56.30
Locke v Candy and Candy Ltd [2010] EWCA Civ 1350, [2011] IRLR 163 .... 7.36, 56.21
Lockwood v Crawley Warren Group Ltd (2001) IDS Brief No 680 .... 10.35

Table of Cases

Lockwood v Department of Work and Pensions (2013) UKEAT/0094/12/RN,[2013] EqLR 206, [2013] All ER (D) 338 (Feb), EAT 10.5, 11.9

Lodwick v Southwark London Borough Council [2004] EWCA Civ 306, [2004] ICR 884, [2004] IRLR 554, (2004) Times, 9 April, 148 Sol Jo LB 385, [2004] All ER (D) 349 (Mar) 18.70, 18.71, 19.23, 19.24

Logan v Customs and Excise Comrs [2003] EWCA Civ 1068, [2004] ICR 1, [2004] IRLR 63, [2003] 37 LS Gaz R 31, (2003) Times, 4 September, [2003] All ER (D) 388 (Jul) 18.59

Lommers v Minister van Landbouw, Natuurbeheer en Visserij: C-476/99 [2002] ECR I-2891, [2004] 2 CMLR 1141, [2002] IRLR 430, [2002] All ER (D) 280 (Mar), ECJ 21.3

London Ambulance Service v Charlton [1992] ICR 773, [1992] IRLR 510, EAT 47.2

London Ambulance Service NHS Trust v Small. See Small v London Ambulance Service NHS Trust

London and Birmingham Railway Ltd (t/a London Midland v Associated Society of Locomotive Engineers and Firemen) [2011] EWCA Civ 226, [2011] 3 All ER 913, [2011] ICR 848, [2011] IRLR 399, [2011] NLJR 405, [2011] All ER (D) 65 (Mar) 43.14

London and Mashonaland Exploration Co Ltd v New Mashonaland Exploration Co Ltd [1891] WN 165 .... 8.19

London Fire and Civil Defence Authority v Betty [1994] IRLR 384, EAT 52.8

London Fire and Civil Defence Authority v Samuels EAT/450/00, IDS Brief No 669 (22 June 2000, unreported) 18.38, 18.42

London International College v Sen [1993] IRLR 333, CA 17.25

London Probation Board v Kirkpatrick [2005] ICR 965, [2005] IRLR 443, [2005] All ER (D) 148 (Feb), EAT 6.7, 17.23

London Transport Executive v Clarke [1981] ICR 355, [1981] IRLR 166, CA 51.9

London Underground Ltd v Associated Society of Locomotive Engineers and Firemen [2011] EWHC 3506 (QB), [2012] IRLR 196, [2012] NLJR 68, [2011] All ER (D) 200 (Dec) 43.14

London Underground Ltd v Edwards [1995] ICR 574, [1995] IRLR 355, EAT 10.34, 12.14

London Underground Ltd v Edwards (No 2) [1999] ICR 494, [1998] IRLR 364, [1998] 25 LS Gaz R 32, [1998] NLJR 905, 142 Sol Jo LB 182, [1998] All ER (D) 231, CA 10.34

London Underground Ltd v Noel [2000] ICR 109, [1999] IRLR 621, sub nom Noel v London Underground [1999] 31 LS Gaz R 38, CA 17.25

Longden v Ferrari Ltd [1994] ICR 443, [1994] BCC 250, sub nom Longden and Paisley v Ferrari Ltd and Kennedy International Ltd [1994] IRLR 157, EAT 50.11

Lonmar Global Risks Ltd (formerly SBJ Global Risks Ltd) v West [2010] EWHC 2878 (QB), [2011] IRLR 138, [2010] All ER (D) 118 (Nov) 39.11

Lord Chancellor v Coker and Osamor [2001] ICR 507, [2001] IRLR 116, [2001] All ER (D) 68 (Jan), EAT; affd sub nom Coker v Lord Chancellor [2001] EWCA Civ 1756, [2002] ICR 321, [2002] IRLR 80, (2001) Times, 3 December, 145 Sol Jo LB 268, [2001] All ER (D) 334 (Nov) 10.34

Louies v Coventry Hood and Seating Co Ltd [1990] ICR 54, [1990] IRLR 324, EAT 52.10

Loveridge v Mayor and Burgesses of the London Borough of Lambeth [2013] EWCA Civ 494, [2013] All ER (D) 110 (May) 41.3

Lowe v Cabinet Office [2011] EqLR 803 .... 10.37

Loxley v BAE Systems Land Systems (Munitions and Ordnance) Ltd [2008] ICR 1348, [2008] IRLR 853, [2008] All ER (D) 82 (Aug), EAT 11.9, 11.15

Lubbe v Cape plc [2000] 4 All ER 268, [2000] 1 WLR 1545, [2000] 2 Lloyd's Rep 383, 144 Sol Jo LB 250, [2000] 5 LRC 605, HL 23.8

Luce v Bexley London Borough Council (1990) 88 LGR 909, [1990] ICR 591, [1990] IRLR 422, [1990] 27 LS Gaz R 41, EAT 47.3

Lucy v British Airways plc (UKEAT/0033/08/LA) [2009] All ER (D) 58 (Jan) 32.6

Luke v Stoke-on-Trent City Council [2007] EWCA Civ 761, [2007] ICR 1678, [2007] IRLR 777, [2007] All ER (D) 380 (Jul) 7.47, 32.14

Lunt v Merseyside Tec Ltd [1999] ICR 17, [1999] IRLR 458, EAT 12.33, 18.34

Lycee Charles de Gaulle v Delambre [2011] EqLR 948, EAT 12.21

Lyddon v Englefield Brickwork Ltd [2008] IRLR 198, [2007] All ER (D) 198 (Nov), EAT 27.4

Lyfar v Brighton and Sussex University Hospitals Trust [2006] EWCA Civ 1548, [2006] All ER (D) 182 (Nov) 12.6, 17.29

Lynch v East Dunbartonshire Council [2010] ICR 1094, EAT 18.27

Lynch v Royal Mail Group plc [2003] All ER (D) 11 (Sep), EAT 30.13

Lynock v Cereal Packaging Ltd [1988] ICR 670, [1988] IRLR 510, EAT 52.8

Lyons v Mitie Security Ltd [2010] ICR 628, [2010] IRLR 288, EAT 27.5

Lytlarch Ltd v Reid [1991] ICR 216, EAT 53.12

Table of Cases

M

M v Vincent [1998] ICR 73, EAT 18.18
M&P Steelcraft Ltd v Ellis [2008] ICR 578, sub nom Ellis v M&P Steelcraft Ltd [2008] IRLR 355, [2008] All ER (D) 353 (Feb), EAT 14.3
M and S Drapers (a firm) v Reynolds [1956] 3 All ER 814, [1957] 1 WLR 9, 101 Sol Jo 44, CA 39.8, 39.10
MBA v Mayor and Burgesses of the London Borough of Merton (2012) UKEAT/0332/12/SM, 157 Sol Jo (no 3) 31, [2013] EqLR 209, [2013] All ER (D) 68 (Jan), EAT 11.9
MHC Consulting Services Ltd v Tansell [1999] ICR 1211, [1999] IRLR 677, EAT; affd [2000] ICR 789, 144 Sol Jo LB 205, sub nom Abbey Life Assurance Co Ltd v Tansell [2000] IRLR 387, [2000] All ER (D) 483, CA 11.24
MPB Structure Ltd v Munro [2002] IRLR 601, [2002] All ER (D) 264 (Apr); affd sub nom Munro v MPB Structures Ltd [2004] 2 CMLR 1032, [2004] ICR 430, [2003] IRLR 350, (2003) Times, 24 April, 2003 SLT 551, 2003 SCLR 542 .... 19.2, 27.4, 55.25
MSF v Refuge Assurance plc [2002] ICR 1365, [2002] IRLR 324, [2002] All ER (D) 209 (Feb), EAT 37.4
Ma v Merck Sharp & Dohme Ltd [2008] EWCA Civ 1426, [2008] All ER (D) 158 (Dec) 12.6
Mabey Plant Hire Ltd v Richens IDS Brief No 495 .... 53.12
Mabliizi v National Hospital for Nervous Diseases [1990] ICR 781, [1990] IRLR 133, EAT 53.5
McAdie v Royal Bank of Scotland [2007] EWCA Civ 806, [2008] ICR 1087, [2007] IRLR 895, [2007] NLJR 1355, [2007] All ER (D) 477 (Jul) 52.8
Macari v Celtic Football & Athletic Co Ltd [1999] IRLR 787, 2000 SLT 80, 2000 SCLR 209 .... 56.17
Macarthys Ltd v Smith [1981] QB 180, [1981] 1 All ER 111, [1980] 3 WLR 929, [1980] 2 CMLR 217, [1980] ICR 672, [1980] IRLR 210, 124 Sol Jo 808, CA 21.9
McAuley v Eastern Health and Social Services Board [1991] IRLR 467, NI CA 21.8
McBrearty v Thomson IDS Brief No 450 .... 46.15
McBride v Standards Board for England (UKEAT/0092/09/MAA) [2009] All ER (D) 165 (Jun) 18.14, 18.51
McCabe v Cornwall County Council [2004] UKHL 35, [2005] 1 AC 503, [2004] 3 All ER 991, [2004] 3 WLR 322, [2004] ICR 1064, [2004] IRLR 733, [2004] NLJR 1155, 148 Sol Jo LB 909, [2004] All ER (D) 268 (Jul) 7.22d, 7.39, 56.29
McCammon v Gillingham Football Club (UKEAT/0625/11/RN) [2012] All ER (D) 218 (May), EAT 19.38
McCarrick v Hunter (2011) UKEAT/0617/10/DA, [2012] ICR 533, [2012] IRLR 274, [2012] All ER (D) 86 (Feb), EAT; affd sub nom Hunter v McCarrick [2012] EWCA Civ 1399, [2013] ICR 235, [2012] All ER (D) 315 (Oct) 50.3
McCarthy v Basildon District Council (Equality and Human Rights Commission intervening). See R (on the application of McCarthy) v Basildon District Council
McCarthy v British Insulated Callenders Cables plc [1985] IRLR 94, EAT 53.10
MacCartney v Oversley House Management [2006] ICR 510, [2006] IRLR 514, [2006] All ER (D) 246 (Jan), EAT 32.12, 55.5, 55.17
McCausland v Dungannon District Council [1993] IRLR 583, NI CA 10.34
McClaren v Home Office [1990] ICR 824, [1990] IRLR 338, CA 35.2, 35.6
McClelland v Northern Ireland General Health Services Board [1957] 2 All ER 129, [1957] 1 WLR 594, 55 LGR 281, [1957] NI 100, 101 Sol Jo 355, HL 56.15
McClintock v Department of Constitutional Affairs [2008] IRLR 29, (2007) Times, 5 December, [2007] All ER (D) 25 (Nov), EAT 10.22, 28.7
McClory v Post Office [1993] 1 All ER 457, [1992] ICR 758, [1993] IRLR 159 .... 7.22
McConkey v Simon Community Northern Ireland [2009] UKHL 24, [2009] NI 297, [2009] ICR 787, [2009] IRLR 757, (2009) Times, 26 May 10.22
McConnell v Police Authority for Northern Ireland [1997] IRLR 625, NI CA 12.18
McCook v Lobo [2002] EWCA Civ 1760, [2003] ICR 89, [2002] All ER (D) 272 (Nov) 25.2
MacCulloch v Imperial Chemical Industries plc [2008] ICR 1334, [2008] IRLR 846, 152 Sol Jo (no 34) 31, [2008] All ER (D) 81 (Aug), EAT 11.9, 11.15
McDermid v Nash Dredging and Reclamation Co Ltd [1987] AC 906, [1987] 2 All ER 878, [1987] 3 WLR 212, [1987] 2 Lloyd's Rep 201, [1987] ICR 917, [1987] IRLR 334, 131 Sol Jo 973, [1987] LS Gaz R 2458, HL 25.3, 54.1
McDonagh and Triesman v Ali [2002] EWCA Civ 93, [2002] ICR 1026, [2002] IRLR 489, (2002) Times, 11 March, [2002] All ER (D) 87 (Feb) 11.30

Macdonald v Advocate General for Scotland [2003] UKHL 34, [2004] 1 All ER 339, [2003] ICR
937, [2003] IRLR 512, [2003] ELR 655, [2003] 29 LS Gaz R 36, (2003) Times, 20 June, 2003 SLT
1158, 2003 SCLR 814, 147 Sol Jo LB 782, [2004] 2 LRC 111, [2003] All ER (D) 259 (Jun) 10.15,
10.23
McDougall v Richmond Adult Community College [2008] EWCA Civ 4, [2008] ICR 431, [2008]
IRLR 227, (2008) Times, 22 February, 152 Sol Jo LB 30, [2008] All ER (D) 54 (Jan) 10.26
Macer v Abafast Ltd [1990] ICR 234, [1990] IRLR 137, EAT 6.9, 50.12, 50.14
McFadden v Greater Glasgow Passenger Transport Executive [1977] IRLR 327, Ind Trib 31.16
McFarlane v Glasgow City Council [2001] IRLR 7, EAT 14.3
McFarlane v Relate Avon Ltd (UKEAT/0106/09/DA) [2010] ICR 507, [2010] IRLR 196,
[2009] All ER (D) 233 (Dec); affd [2010] EWCA Civ 880, [2010] IRLR 872, 29 BHRC 249 ..... 10.22,
11.9, 28.7
McFadyen v PB Recovery Ltd (UKEATS/0072/08) (31 July 2009, unreported) 17.11, 17.21, 18.25
McGhee v Midlands British Road Services Ltd [1985] ICR 503, [1985] IRLR 198, EAT 49.13
McGowan v Scottish Water [2005] IRLR 167, [2004] All ER (D) 130 (Nov) 28.7
McGuigan v T G Boynes & Sons (1999) IDS Brief No 633, EAT 10.15
Machine Tool Industry Research Association v Simpson [1988] ICR 558, [1988] IRLR 212, CA
.... 17.25
McHugh v Hempsall Bulk Transport Ltd IDS Brief No 480 .... 36.12
McIntosh v John Brown Engineering Ltd IDS Brief No 441 .... 9.14
Mack Trucks (Britain) Ltd, Re [1967] 1 All ER 977, [1967] 1 WLR 780, 111 Sol Jo 435 ... 29.10, 56.9
McKechnie v UBM Building Supplies (Southern) Ltd [1991] 2 CMLR 668, [1991] ICR 710, [1991]
IRLR 283, EAT 21.3
McKie v Swindon College [2011] EWHC 469 (QB), [2011] IRLR 575, [2011] All ER (D) 128
(May) 38.4
McKindless Group v McLaughlin [2008] IRLR 678, EAT 53.13
McKinson v Hackney Community College (UKEAT/0237/11/JOJ) (2012) 942 IDS Brief 16,
[2011] EqLR 1114, [2012] All ER (D) 128 (Jan), EAT 12.8, 18.7
Maclaine v Prudential Assurance Co Ltd [2006] EWHC 2037 (Ch) 40.17
McLean v TLC Marketing plc (UKEAT/0429/08) [2009] All ER (D) 144 (Aug) 18.32
McLeod v Hellyer Bros Ltd. See Hellyer Bros Ltd v McLeod
McManus v Daylay Foods Ltd (EAT/82/95) unreported 22.2
McMaster v Manchester Airport plc [1998] IRLR 112, 593 IRLB 17, EAT 17.23, 51.13
McMeechan v Secretary of State for Employment [1997] ICR 549, [1997] IRLR 353, CA ... 14.3, 45.2,
45.2c
McMenemy v Capita Business Services Ltd [2006] IRLR 761, EAT; affd [2007] CSIH 25, [2007]
IRLR 400, 2007 SC 492 .... 19.2, 30.8, 30.13, 30.20
Macmillan v Ministry of Defence (11 November 2003, unreported), EAT 11.9
Macmillan Inc v Bishopsgate Investment Trust plc [1993] 4 All ER 998, [1993] 1 WLR 837, [1993]
IRLR 393, [1993] 11 LS Gaz R 44, sub nom Macmillan Inc v Bishopsgate Investment Trust plc
(No 2) [1993] ICR 385; affd sub nom Macmillan Inc v Bishopsgate Investment Trust plc [1993]
4 All ER 998, [1993] 1 WLR 1372, [1993] 31 LS Gaz R 39, CA 7.17
McNicol v Balfour Beatty Rail Maintenance Ltd [2002] EWCA Civ 1074, [2002] ICR 1498, [2002]
IRLR 711, 71 BMLR 1, (2002) Times, 26 August, [2002] All ER (D) 407 (Jul) 10.26, 18.52
McPherson v BNP Paribas (London Branch) [2004] EWCA Civ 569, [2004] 3 All ER 266, [2004]
IRLR 558, (2004) Times, 31 May, [2004] All ER (D) 175 (May) 18.17, 18.72
MacPherson v Lambeth London Borough Council [1988] IRLR 470 .... 7.42, 32.14
McVeigh v Livingstone (UKEATS/0027/08/BI) (16 June 2009, unreported) 7.4
McVitae v UNISON [1996] IRLR 33 .... 49.15
McWilliam Glasgow City Council (UKEATS/0036/10/BI) [2011] IRLR 568, EAT 12.33, 18.34
Madarassy v Nomura International plc [2007] EWCA Civ 33, [2007] ICR 867, [2007] IRLR 246,
[2007] All ER (D) 226 (Jan) 10.30, 12.3, 21.10
Madden v Preferred Technical Group CHA Ltd [2004] EWCA Civ 1178, [2005] IRLR 46, 148 Sol
Jo LB 1064, [2004] All ER (D) 153 (Aug) 10.15
Maga v Roman Catholic Archdiocese of Birmingham [2009] EWHC 780 (QB), [2009] All ER (D)
176 (Apr); affd [2010] EWCA Civ 256, [2010] 1 WLR 1441, [2010] PTSR 1618, 154 Sol Jo (no 11)
28, (2010) Times, 25 March, [2010] All ER (D) 141 (Mar) 25.9, 54.1, 54.2
Magorrian v Eastern Health and Social Services Board: C-246/96 [1997] ECR I-7153, [1998] All ER
(EC) 38, [1998] ICR 979, [1998] IRLR 86, ECJ 17.12
Mahlburg v Land Mecklenburg-Vorpommern: C-207/98 [2000] ECR I-549, [2001] 3 CMLR 887,
[2001] ICR 1032, [2000] IRLR 276, [2000] All ER (D) 116, ECJ 10.30

Table of Cases

Mahood v Irish Centre Housing (UKEAT/0228/10/ZT) unreported 54.1
Mailer v Austin Rover Group plc. See Austin Rover Group Ltd v HM Inspector of Factories
Mailway (Southern) Ltd v Willsher [1978] ICR 511, [1978] IRLR 322, 122 Sol Jo 79, EAT 32.24
Majrowski v Guy's and St Thomas' NHS Trust [2006] UKHL 34, [2007] 1 AC 224, [2006] 4 All ER
    395, [2006] 3 WLR 125, [2006] ICR 1199, [2006] IRLR 695, 91 BMLR 85, [2006] NLJR 1173,
    (2006) Times, 13 July, 150 Sol Jo LB 986, [2006] All ER (D) 146 (Jul) 9.17, 54.1
Malcolm v Dundee City Council [2012] CSIH 13, [2012] EqLR 363 .... 12.7
Malik v BCCI SA (in liq) [1998] AC 20, [1997] 3 All ER 1, [1997] 3 WLR 95, [1997] ICR 606,
    [1997] IRLR 462, [1997] 94 LS Gaz R 33, [1997] NLJR 917, HL . 7.22d, 7.38, 7.39, 51.7, 53.12, 56.29
Malik v Post Office Counters Ltd [1993] ICR 93, EAT 11.30
Malone v British Airways plc [2010] EWHC 302 (QB), [2010] IRLR 431, [2010] All ER (D) 220
    (Feb); affd sub nom Malone v British Airways [2010] EWCA Civ 1225, [2011] ICR 125, [2011]
    IRLR 32, [2010] All ER (D) 32 (Nov) 5.7, 7.14, 7.33
Mamedu v Hatten Wyatt Solicitors [2008] All ER (D) 76 (Apr), EAT 20.8
Manchester College v Cocliff (UKEAT/0035/10/CEA) [2010] All ER (D) 92 (Sep) 45.9
Manchester College v Hazel (2012) UKEAT/0642/11/RN, [2012] All ER (D) 46 (Sep), EAT
    .... 50.26
Manchester College v Hazel [2013] EWCA Civ 281 .... 19.47
Mandla v Dowell Lee [1983] 2 AC 548, [1983] 1 All ER 1062, [1983] 2 WLR 620, [1983] ICR 385,
    [1983] IRLR 209, 127 Sol Jo 242, HL 10.20
Manel v Memon (2000) 33 HLR 235, [2000] 2 EGLR 40, [2000] 33 EG 74, 80 P & CR D22,
    [2000] All ER (D) 481, CA 41.5
Mangold v Helm: C-144/04 [2005] ECR I-9981, [2006] All ER (EC) 383, [2006] IRLR 143,
    [2005] All ER (D) 287 (Nov), ECJ 10.10, 11.9, 17.12, 22.2, 40.5
Mann v Secretary of State for Employment. See Secretary of State for Employment v Mann
Manor Bakeries Ltd v Nazir [1996] IRLR 604, EAT 21.3
Manpower Ltd v Hearne [1983] ICR 567, [1983] IRLR 281, EAT 53.12
Maresca v Motor Insurance Repair Research Centre [2004] 4 All ER 254, [2005] ICR 197,
    [2004] All ER (D) 20 (Mar), EAT 18.16, 18.76
Margarot Forrest Care Management v Kennedy (UKEAT/0023/10/BI) (26 November 2010,
    unreported) 18.10
Marion White Ltd v Francis [1972] 3 All ER 857, [1972] 1 WLR 1423, 116 Sol Jo 822, CA 39.16
Market Force (UK) Ltd v Hunt [2002] IRLR 863, [2002] All ER (D) 06 (Jul), EAT 18.60
Market Investigations Ltd v Minister of Social Security [1969] 2 QB 173, [1968] 3 All ER 732,
    [1969] 2 WLR 1, 112 Sol Jo 905 .... 14.3
Marks & Spencer plc v Williams-Ryan [2005] EWCA Civ 470, [2005] ICR 1293, [2005] IRLR 562,
    149 Sol Jo LB 511, [2005] All ER (D) 248 (Apr) 17.25
Marleasing SA v La Comercial Internacional de Alimentacion SA: C-106/89 [1990] ECR I-4135,
    [1992] 1 CMLR 305, [1993] BCC 421, 135 Sol Jo 15, ECJ 22.2
Marley v Forward Trust Group Ltd [1986] ICR 891, [1986] IRLR 369, CA 5.5
Marley (UK) Ltd v Anderson [1996] ICR 728, [1996] IRLR 163, [1996] 02 LS Gaz R 28, 140 Sol
    Jo LB 26, CA 17.25, 17.26
Marley Tile Co Ltd v Johnson [1982] IRLR 75, CA 39.8
Marley Tile Co Ltd v Shaw [1980] ICR 72, [1980] IRLR 25, 123 Sol Jo 803, CA 52.3
Marlow v East Thames Housing Group Ltd [2002] IRLR 798, [2002] All ER (D) 393 (May) 7.22b,
    42.12
Marriott v Oxford and District Co-operative Society Ltd (No 2) [1970] 1 QB 186, [1969] 3 All ER
    1126, [1969] 3 WLR 984, 113 Sol Jo 655, CA 46.19
Marschall v Land Nordrhein-Westfalen: C-409/95 [1997] ECR I-6363, [1997] All ER (EC) 865,
    [1998] 1 CMLR 547, [2001] ICR 45, [1998] IRLR 39, ECJ 11.10
Marsden v Council of the City of Newcastle Upon Tyne. See Council of the City of Newcastle
    Upon Tyne v Marsden
Marsh v National Autistic Society [1993] ICR 453 .... 46.19
Marsh & McLennan Companies UK Ltd v Pensions Ombudsman [2001] IRLR 505, [2001] PLR 51,
    [2001] All ER (D) 299 (Feb) 40.17
Marshall v Harland & Wolff Ltd [1972] 2 All ER 715, [1972] 1 WLR 899, [1972] ICR 101, [1972]
    IRLR 90, 7 ITR 150, 116 Sol Jo 484, NIRC 46.3
Marshall v Harland & Wolff Ltd (No 2) (Practice Note) [1972] ICR 97, 7 ITR 132, NIRC 19.14
Marshall v NM Financial Management Ltd [1995] 4 All ER 785, [1995] 1 WLR 1461, [1995] ICR
    1042, [1996] IRLR 20; on appeal [1997] 1 WLR 1527, [1997] ICR 1065, [1997] IRLR 449, CA
    .... 39.3, 39.7

Marshall v Southampton and South West Hampshire Area Health Authority (Teaching): 152/84
 [1986] QB 401, [1986] 2 All ER 584, [1986] ECR 723, [1986] 2 WLR 780, [1986] 1 CMLR 688,
 [1986] ICR 335, [1986] IRLR 140, 130 Sol Jo 340, [1986] LS Gaz R 1720, ECJ 17.12, 35.8
Marshall v Southampton and South West Hampshire Area Health Authority (No 2): C-271/91
 [1994] QB 126, [1993] 4 All ER 586, [1993] ECR I-4367, [1993] 3 WLR 1054, [1993] 3 CMLR
 293, [1993] ICR 893, [1993] IRLR 445, ECJ; apld sub nom Marshall v Southampton and South-
 West Hampshire Area Health Authority (Teaching) (No 2) [1994] 1 AC 530n, [1994] 1 All ER
 736n, [1994] 2 WLR 392, [1994] ICR 242n, HL 12.13, 17.12, 18.67
Marshall (Cambridge) Ltd v Hamblin [1994] ICR 362, [1994] IRLR 260, EAT 7.22, 51.5, 56.21
Marshalls Clay Products Ltd v Caulfield [2004] ICR 436, (2003) Times, 25 August, sub nom
 Caulfield v Marshalls Clay Products Ltd [2003] IRLR 552, [2003] All ER (D) 478 (Jul), EAT;
 revsd sub nom Caulfield v Marshalls Clay Products Ltd [2004] EWCA Civ 422, [2004] 2 CMLR
 1040, [2004] ICR 1502, [2004] IRLR 564, 148 Sol Jo LB 539, [2004] All ER (D) 292 (Apr)   19.2, 27.1,
    55.25
Martin v British Railways Board [1989] ICR 24, [1989] IRLR 198, EAT 19.12
Martin v Devonshires Solicitors (UKEAT/0086/10) [2011] ICR 352, [2011] All ER (D) 345
 (Mar) 10.17, 10.38
Martin v Glynwed Distribution Ltd [1983] ICR 511, sub nom Martin v MBS Fastings (Glynwed)
 Distribution Ltd [1983] IRLR 198, CA 51.8
Martin v Lancehawk Ltd (t/a European Telecom Solutions) [2004] All ER (D) 400 (Mar), EAT
 . . . . 10.17
Martin v South Bank University: C-4/01 [2003] ECR I-12859, [2004] 1 CMLR 472, [2004] ICR
 1234, [2004] IRLR 74, [2003] OPLR 317, [2003] All ER (D) 85 (Nov), ECJ 40.6, 50.19, 50.29
Martin v Southern Health and Social Care Trust [2010] NICA 31, [2010] IRLR 1048 . . . . . 55.17, 55.29
Martin v Yeoman Aggregates Ltd [1983] ICR 314, [1983] IRLR 49, EAT 46.20, 51.10
Martin v Yorkshire Imperial Metals Ltd [1978] IRLR 440, EAT 25.23, 26.11
Martins v Marks & Spencer plc [1998] ICR 1005, [1998] IRLR 326, CA 10.14, 18.7
Maruko v Versorgungsanstalt der deutschen Buhnen: C-267/06 [2008] ECR I-1757, [2008] All ER
 (EC) 977, [2008] IRLR 450, [2008] All ER (D) 07 (Apr), ECJ 10.36, 11.14
Masiak v City Restaurants (UK) Ltd [1999] IRLR 780, EAT 26.8, 52.3, 56.16
Mason v Provident Clothing and Supply Co Ltd [1913] AC 724, 82 LJKB 1153, [1911–13] All ER
 Rep 400, 57 Sol Jo 739, 109 LT 449, 29 TLR 727, HL 39.4, 39.6, 39.7
Massey v Crown Life Insurance Co Ltd [1978] 2 All ER 576, [1978] 1 WLR 676, [1978] ICR 590,
 [1978] IRLR 31, 13 ITR 5, 121 Sol Jo 791, CA 14.3
Massey v UNIFI [2007] EWCA Civ 800, [2008] ICR 62, [2007] IRLR 902, [2007] All ER (D) 500
 (Jul) 12.16, 49.16
Matthews v Kent and Medway Towns Fire Authority [2004] ICR 257, [2003] IRLR 732,
 [2003] All ER (D) 90 (Aug), EAT; affd [2004] EWCA Civ 844, [2004] 3 All ER 620, [2005] ICR
 84, [2004] IRLR 697, (2004) Times, 8 July, 148 Sol Jo LB 876, [2004] All ER (D) 47 (Jul); revsd
 in part [2006] UKHL 8, [2006] 2 All ER 171, [2006] ICR 365, [2006] IRLR 367, [2006] NLJR
 420, (2006) Times, 2 March, [2006] All ER (D) 15 (Mar) 30.8, 30.16, 30.17, 30.18
Mattis v Pollock (t/a Flamingos Nightclub) [2003] EWCA Civ 887, [2004] 4 All ER 85, [2003] 1
 WLR 2158, [2003] ICR 1335, [2003] IRLR 603, (2003) Times, 16 July, 147 Sol Jo LB 816,
 [2003] All ER (D) 10 (Jul) 54.2
Mattu v University Hospitals of Coventry and Warwickshire NHS Trust [2012] EWCA Civ 641,
 [2012] IRLR 661, [2012] All ER (D) 153 (May) 28.7
Matuszowicz v Kingston-Upon-Hull City Council [2009] EWCA Civ 22, [2009] 3 All ER 685,
 [2009] ICR 1170, [2009] IRLR 288, [2009] All ER (D) 93 (Feb) 12.6, 17.29
Mau v Bundesanstalt fur Arbeit: C-160/01 [2003] ECR I-4791, [2004] 1 CMLR 1113, [2003] All ER
 (D) 197 (May), ECJ 29.5
Maund v Penwith District Council [1984] ICR 143, [1984] IRLR 24, 134 NLJ 147, CA 52.1, 52.3
Maxwell Fleet and Facilities Management Ltd (in administration) (No 2), Re [2000] 2 All ER 860,
 [2000] 2 BCLC 155, [2000] ICR 717, [2000] 06 LS Gaz R 35 . . . . 50.7
May v Greenwich Council (UKEAT/0102/10/LA) [2010] All ER (D) 105 (May) 17.16, 17.34
May & Baker Ltd (t/a Sanofi-Aventis Pharma) v Okerago (UKEAT/0278/09/ZT) [2010] IRLR
 394, sub nom Okerago v May & Baker Ltd (t/a Sanofi-Aventis Pharma) [2010] All ER (D) 79
 (Mar) 10.58
Mayeur v Association Promotion de l'Information Messine (APIM): C-175/99 [2002] ICR 1316,
 [2000] IRLR 783, ECJ 15.6, 50.9
Mayhew v Suttle (1854) 19 JP 38, 4 E & B 347, 24 LJQB 54, 1 Jur NS 303, 3 WR 108, 3 CLR 59,
 24 LTOS 159, Ex Ch 41.2

Table of Cases

Mayo-Deman v University of Greenwich [2005] IRLR 845, [2005] All ER (D) 101 (Sep), EAT
.... 12.33, 18.32
Mayr v Backerei und Konditorei Gerhard Flockner OHG: C-506/06 [2008] All ER (EC) 613,
    [2008] ECR I-1017, [2008] 2 CMLR 759, [2008] IRLR 387, [2008] 3 FCR 44, [2008] 1 FLR 1242,
    [2008] Fam Law 381, [2008] Fam Law 512, (2008) Times, 12 March, [2008] All ER (D) 370 (Feb),
    ECJ 10.30, 31.2
Mazzoleni (criminal proceedings against): C-165/98 [2001] ECR I-2189, ECJ 23.3
Meacham v Amalgamated Engineering and Electrical Union [1994] IRLR 218 .... 49.15
Meade-Hill and National Union of Civil and Public Servants v British Council [1996] 1 All ER 79,
    [1995] ICR 847, [1995] IRLR 478, CA 5.15, 10.35
Meadows v Faithful Overalls Ltd [1977] IRLR 330, Ind Trib 32.26
Mears v Safecar Security Ltd [1983] QB 54, [1982] 2 All ER 865, [1982] 3 WLR 366, [1982] ICR
    626, [1982] IRLR 183, 126 Sol Jo 496, [1982] LS Gaz R 921, CA 7.11, 42.2
Mears v Salt (UKEAT/0522/11), unreported, EAT 32.6
Measures Bros Ltd v Measures [1910] 2 Ch 248, 79 LJ Ch 707, 18 Mans 40, 54 Sol Jo 521, 102 LT
    794, 26 TLR 488, [1908–10] All ER Rep Ext 1188, CA 29.10, 56.9
Medical Protection Society v Sadek. See Sadek v Medical Protection Society
Meek v City of Birmingham District Council [1987] IRLR 250, CA 18.63, 19.36
Meerts v Proost NV: C-116/08 [2010] All ER (EC) 1085, [2009] All ER (D) 259 (Oct), ECJ 30.1,
                                                                                         31.51
Mehta v Child Support Agency (UKEAT/0127/10/CEA) [2011] IRLR 305, [2011] ICR D7,
    [2011] All ER (D) 177 (Mar) 18.46, 18.57
Meikle v Nottinghamshire County Council [2004] EWCA Civ 859, [2004] 4 All ER 97, [2005] ICR
    1, [2004] IRLR 703, (2004) Times, 15 July, [2004] All ER (D) 123 (Jul), sub nom
    Nottinghamshire County Council v Meikle 80 BMLR 129, 148 Sol Jo LB 908 ...... 7.22d, 12.6, 17.29
Meister v Speech Design Carrier Systems GmbH: C-415/10 [2012] 2 CMLR 1119, [2012] ICR
    1006, (2012) Times, 20 August, ECJ 10.44, 12.9
Melhuish v Redbridge Citizens Advice Bureau [2005] IRLR 419, [2004] All ER (D) 116 (Aug),
    EAT 14.3
Melia v Magna Kansei Ltd [2005] EWCA Civ 1547, [2006] ICR 410, [2006] IRLR 117, (2005)
    Times, 14 November, [2005] All ER (D) 75 (Nov) 18.67, 53.13
Mennell v Newell & Wright (Transport Contractors) Ltd [1997] ICR 1039, [1997] IRLR 519, [1997]
    33 LS Gaz R 26, CA 32.6, 52.3
Mensah v East Hertfordshire NHS Trust [1998] IRLR 531, [1998] All ER (D) 260, CA 12.8, 18.52
Merckx v Ford Motors Co Belgium SA: C-171/94 and C-172/94 [1996] ECR I-1253, [1996] All ER
    (EC) 667, [1997] ICR 352, [1996] IRLR 467, ECJ 50.5, 50.16
Mersey Docks and Harbour Board v Coggins & Griffiths (Liverpool) Ltd [1947] AC 1, [1946]
    2 All ER 345, 115 LJKB 465, 90 Sol Jo 466, 175 LT 270, 62 TLR 533, HL 45.2, 54.3
Merseyside and North Wales Electricity Board v Taylor [1975] ICR 185, [1975] IRLR 60, 10 ITR 52,
    119 Sol Jo 272 .... 52.8
Merton London Borough Council v Gardiner [1981] QB 269, [1981] 2 WLR 232, 79 LGR 374,
    [1981] ICR 186, sub nom Gardiner v London Borough of Merton [1980] IRLR 472, 125 Sol Jo
    97, CA 6.9
Merton London Borough Council v Jones. See Jones v Merton London Borough Council
Meter U Ltd v Ackroyd (2012) UKEAT/0206/11/CEA, UKEAT/0207/11/CEA, [2012] ICR 834,
    [2012] IRLR 367, EAT 50.26
Meteorological Office v Edgar [2002] ICR 149, (2001) Times, 15 August, [2001] All ER (D) 06
    (Aug), EAT 9.17
Methuen v Community Law Clinic Solicitors (judgment delivered extempore) [2012] EWCA Civ
    571, [2012] All ER (D) 23 (Apr) 12.8
Metrobus Ltd v Unite the Union [2009] EWCA Civ 829, [2010] ICR 173, [2009] IRLR 851,
    [2009] All ER (D) 03 (Aug) 28.7
Metroline Travel Ltd v Unite [2012] EWHC 1778 (QB), [2012] IRLR 749, [2012] All ER (D) 185
    (Jun) 43.14
Metropolitan Police Comr v Harley [2001] ICR 927, [2001] IRLR 263, [2001] All ER (D) 216 (Feb),
    EAT 17.29
Metropolitan Police Comr v Hendricks (2002) IDS Brief No 707 .... 12.6
Metropolitan Police Comr v Hendricks [2003] ICR 999. See Hendricks v Metropolitan Police Comr
Metropolitan Police Comr v Lowrey-Nesbitt [1999] ICR 401, EAT 35.4
Metropolitan Police Service v Shoebridge (UKEAT/0234/03/TM) [2004] ICR 1680 .... 38.4

Metropolitan Resources Ltd v Churchill Dulwich Ltd (in liq). See Churchill Dulwich Ltd (in liq) v Metropolitan Resources Ltd

Mettoy Pension Trustees Ltd v Evans [1991] 2 All ER 513, [1990] 1 WLR 1587 .... 40.16

Meyers v Adjudication Officer: C-116/94 [1995] All ER (EC) 705, [1995] ECR I-2131, [1996] 1 CMLR 461, [1995] IRLR 498, ECJ 22.5

Mezey v South West London and St George's Mental Health NHS Trust [2007] EWHC 62 (QB), [2007] IRLR 237; affd Mezey v South West London & St George's Mental Health NHS Trust [2010] EWCA Civ 293, [2010] IRLR 512, 154 Sol Jo (no 13) 28, [2010] All ER (D) 290 (Mar) 7.42, 7.43

Michael Peters Ltd v Farnfield [1995] IRLR 190, EAT 50.15

Midas IT Services Ltd v Opus Portfolios Ltd (21 December 1999, unreported), Ch D 39.15

Middlebrook Mushrooms Ltd v Transport and General Workers' Union [1993] ICR 612, [1993] IRLR 232, CA 28.4

Middlesbrough Borough Council v Surtees (No 2) [2008] ICR 349, [2007] IRLR 981, [2007] All ER (D) 278 (Oct), EAT 21.21

Middlesbrough Borough Council v Transport and General Workers Union [2002] IRLR 332, [2001] All ER (D) 79 (May), EAT 37.4

Midland Bank plc v Madden [2000] IRLR 288, EAT 52.4

Midland Counties District Bank Ltd v Attwood [1905] 1 Ch 357, 74 LJ Ch 286, 12 Mans 20, [1904–7] All ER Rep 648, 92 LT 360, 21 TLR 175 .... 29.10, 56.9

Mid-Staffordshire General Hospitals NHS Trust v Cambridge [2003] IRLR 566, [2003] All ER (D) 06 (Sep), EAT 10.37

Mihlenstedt v Barclays Bank International Ltd and Barclays Bank plc [1989] IRLR 522, [1989] PLR 124, CA 40.6, 40.16

Mikeover Ltd v Brady [1989] 3 All ER 618, 59 P & CR 218, 21 HLR 513, [1989] 2 EGLR 61, [1989] 40 EG 92, CA 41.2

Miles v Gilbank. See Gilbank v Miles

Miles v Linkage Community Trust Ltd [2008] IRLR 602, [2008] All ER (D) 144 (May), EAT 55.15, 55.22

Miles v Wakefield Metropolitan District Council [1987] AC 539, [1987] 1 All ER 1089, [1987] 2 WLR 795, 85 LGR 649, [1987] ICR 368, [1987] IRLR 193, 131 Sol Jo 408, [1987] LS Gaz R 1239, [1987] NLJ Rep 266, HL 7.47, 32.14

Millam v Print Factory (London) 1991 Ltd [2007] EWCA Civ 322, [2007] ICR 1331, [2007] IRLR 526, [2008] BCC 169, [2007] All ER (D) 132 (Apr) 50.10

Miller v Community Links Trust Ltd [2007] All ER (D) 196 (Nov), EAT 17.21, 18.40

Miller v Harry Thornton (Lollies) Ltd [1978] IRLR 430, Ind Trib 32.24

Miller v Inserverve Industrial Services Ltd (UKEAT/0244/12/SM), unreported 49.4, 49.10

Miller v Karlinski (1945) 62 TLR 85, CA 7.24

Miller Bros and F P Butler Ltd v Johnston [2002] ICR 744, [2002] IRLR 386, (2002) Times, 18 April, [2002] All ER (D) 220 (Mar), EAT 7.44, 17.32, 18.35

Milligan v Securicor Cleaning Ltd [1995] ICR 867, [1995] IRLR 288, EAT 6.13

Mills v Dunham [1891] 1 Ch 576, 60 LJ Ch 362, 39 WR 289, 64 LT 712, 7 TLR 238, CA 39.6

Mills v IRC [1973] Ch 225, [1972] 3 All ER 977, [1972] 3 WLR 980, [1973] STC 1, 49 TC 367, 51 ATC 263, [1972] TR 245, 116 Sol Jo 802, L(TC) 2467, CA; revsd sub nom IRC v Mills [1975] AC 38, [1974] 1 All ER 722, [1974] 2 WLR 325, [1974] STC 130, 53 ATC 34, [1974] TR 39, 118 Sol Jo 205, L(TC) 2506, HL 3.11

Milsom v Leicestershire County Council [1978] IRLR 433, Ind Trib 32.20

Mingeley v Pennock and Ivory (t/a Amber Cars) [2004] EWCA Civ 328, [2004] ICR 727, [2004] IRLR 373, [2004] 11 LS Gaz R 33, (2004) Times, 4 March, [2004] All ER (D) 132 (Feb) 10.41

Mining Supplies (Longwall) Ltd v Baker [1988] ICR 676, [1988] IRLR 417, EAT 53.13

Ministry of Defence v Anderson [1996] IRLR 139, EAT 12.16

Ministry of Defence v Armstrong [2004] IRLR 672, [2004] All ER (D) 146 (Apr), EAT 21.11

Ministry of Defence v Cannock [1995] 2 All ER 449, [1994] ICR 918, [1994] IRLR 509, EAT 12.15, 12.16

Ministry of Defence v DeBique [2010] IRLR 471, EAT 10.34, 12.3

Ministry of Defence v Fletcher [2010] IRLR 25, sub nom Fletcher v Ministry of Defence [2009] All ER (D) 187 (Nov), EAT 12.18

Ministry of Defence v Guellard (UKEAT/0210/09 & UKEAT/0337/09) [2009] All ER (D) 50 (Dec) 7.20

Ministry of Defence v Hay [2008] ICR 1247, [2008] IRLR 928, [2008] All ER (D) 269 (Jul), EAT 10.26

Table of Cases

Ministry of Defence v Hunt [1996] ICR 544, EAT 12.15
Ministry of Defence v Jeremiah [1980] QB 87, [1979] 3 All ER 833, [1979] 3 WLR 857, [1980] ICR
   13, 123 Sol Jo 735, sub nom Jeremiah v Ministry of Defence [1979] IRLR 436, CA 10.50
Ministry of Defence v Meredith [1995] IRLR 539, EAT 12.18, 18.12
Ministry of Defence v O'Hare (No 2) [1997] ICR 306, EAT 12.16
Ministry of Defence v Pope [1997] ICR 296, EAT 10.30
Ministry of Defence v Wallis and Grocott. See Wallis v Ministry of Defence
Ministry of Defence v Wheeler [1998] 1 All ER 790, [1998] 1 WLR 637, [1998] ICR 242, [1998]
   IRLR 23, [1997] 45 LS Gaz R 27, 142 Sol Jo LB 13, CA 12.15, 53.13
Ministry of Defence HQ Defence Dental Service v Kettle (UKEAT/0308/06/LA) [2007] All ER
   (D) 301 (Jan) 14.3
Ministry of Justice (formerly Department for Constitutional Affairs) v O'Brien (Council of
   Immigration Judges intervening) [2013] UKSC 6, [2013] 2 All ER 1, [2013] 1 WLR 522, [2013]
   ICR 499, (2013) Times, 22 February, [2013] All ER (D) 48 (Feb) 11.9, 30.4, 30.6
Ministry of Justice v Prison Officers Association [2008] EWHC 239 (QB), [2008] ICR 702, [2008]
   IRLR 380, (2008) Times, 31 March, [2008] All ER (D) 246 (Feb) 28.7
Miriki v General Council of the Bar [2001] EWCA Civ 1973, [2002] ICR 505, (2002) Times,
   22 January, [2001] All ER (D) 364 (Dec) 19.19
Mirikwe v Wilson & Co Solicitors (UKEAT/0025/11/RN) (11 May 2011, unreported) 18.71
Mirror Group Newspapers Ltd v Gunning. See Gunning v Mirror Group Newspapers Ltd
Mitchell v Arkwood Plastics (Engineering) Ltd [1993] ICR 471, EAT 52.8
Mitchell v Barratt Homes (Leeds) Ltd (UKEATPA/0903/08) (13 March 2009, unreported) 19.17
Mitchells Solicitors v Funkwerk Information Technologies York Ltd [2008] PNLR 717,
   [2008] All ER (D) 99 (Apr), EAT 18.74
Mitre Plastics v Revenue and Customs Comrs (TC00720) [2010] UKFTT 455 (TC) 42.8
Mock v IRC [1999] IRLR 785, EAT 19.14
Moenich v Fenestre (1892) 61 LJ Ch 737, 2 R 102, 67 LT 602, 8 TLR 804, CA 39.6
Mohmed v West Coast Trains Ltd (2006) 814 IDS Brief 7, EAT 12.3
Molaudi v Ministry of Defence (UKEAT/0463/10) [2011] ICR D19, (2011), 939 IDS Brief 21,
   [2011] All ER (D) 72 (May), EAT 12.2
Monie v Coral Racing Ltd [1981] ICR 109, [1980] IRLR 464, CA 52.9
Mono Pumps Ltd v Froggatt and Radford [1987] IRLR 368, EAT 53.12
Moonsar v Fiveways Express Transport Ltd [2005] IRLR 9, [2004] All ER (D) 110 (Nov), EAT
   .... 12.16
Moore v Duport Furniture Products Ltd [1982] ICR 84, [1982] IRLR 31, 126 Sol Jo 98, HL
   .... 2.4, 18.32
Moore v President of the Methodist Conference (UKEAT/0219/10/DM) (15 March 2011,
   unreported) 7.2
Moore's (Wallisdown) Ltd v Pensions Ombudsman [2002] 1 All ER 737, [2002] 1 WLR 1649, [2002]
   ICR 773, (2002) Times, 1 March, [2001] All ER (D) 372 (Dec) 40.17
Moores v Bude Stratton Town Council [2001] LGR 129, [2001] ICR 271, [2000] IRLR 676,
   [2000] All ER (D) 404, EAT 7.22d, 54.1
Morgan v Electrolux Ltd [1991] ICR 369, [1991] IRLR 89, CA 19.38
Morgan v Greater Glasgow Health Board (UKEATS/0044/11), unreported 19.43
Morgan v Staffordshire University [2002] ICR 475, [2002] IRLR 190, [2001] All ER (D) 119 (Dec),
   EAT 10.26
Morgan v Welsh Rugby Union [2011] IRLR 376, EAT 52.11
Morgan v West Glamorgan County Council [1995] IRLR 68, EAT 32.6
Morganite Electrical Carbon Ltd v Donne [1988] ICR 18, [1987] IRLR 363, EAT 53.14
Morgans v Alpha Plus Security Ltd [2005] 4 All ER 655, [2005] ICR 525, [2005] IRLR 234,
   [2005] All ER (D) 229 (Jan), EAT 53.13
Morley v Heritage plc [1993] IRLR 400, CA 7.7, 27.9
Moroak (t/a Blake Envelopes) v Cromie [2005] ICR 1226, sub nom Cromie v Moroak (t/a Blake
   Envelopes) [2005] IRLR 535, [2005] All ER (D) 233 (May), EAT 17.37, 17.38, 18.21
Moroni v Collo GmbH: C-110/91 [1993] ECR I-6591, [1995] 2 CMLR 357, [1995] ICR 137, [1994]
   IRLR 130, [1995] 42 LS Gaz R 23, ECJ 21.17
Morris v Acco Ltd [1985] ICR 306, EAT 53.13
Morris v Breaveglen Ltd (t/a Anzac Construction Co) [1993] ICR 766, [1993] IRLR 350, [1993]
   PIQR P294, 137 Sol Jo LB 13, CA 54.3
Morris v C W Martin & Sons Ltd [1966] 1 QB 716, [1965] 2 All ER 725, [1965] 3 WLR 276, [1965]
   2 Lloyd's Rep 63, 109 Sol Jo 451, CA 54.2

Morris v John Grose Group Ltd [1998] ICR 655, [1998] IRLR 499, EAT 50.26
Morris v Secretary of State for Employment [1985] ICR 522, [1985] IRLR 297, EAT 29.5
Morris v Walsh Western UK Ltd [1997] IRLR 562, EAT 6.7
Morris Angel & Son Ltd v Hollande [1993] 3 All ER 569, [1993] ICR 71, [1993] IRLR 169, CA
.... 39.3, 50.13, 50.17
Morrison v Amalgamated Transport and General Workers Union [1989] IRLR 361, NI CA 52.10,
                                                                                        53.13
Morrison v Hillcrest Care Ltd [2005] EWCA Civ 1378 .... 19.17
Morrow v Safeway Stores plc [2002] IRLR 9, [2001] All ER (D) 63 (Sep), EAT 7.22d, 51.7, 56.6
Morse v Wiltshire County Council [1998] ICR 1023, [1998] IRLR 352, 44 BMLR 58, EAT 10.37
Morton Sundour Fabrics Ltd v Shaw (1966) 2 KIR 1, 2 ITR 84, DC 46.5, 56.5
Mossman v Bray Management Ltd [2005] All ER (D) 06 (Apr), EAT 17.21
Mothew v Bristol & West Building Society. See Bristol and West Building Society v Mothew
  (t/a Stapley & Co)
Motorola Ltd v Davidson and Melville Craig [2001] IRLR 4, EAT 14.3, 45.2a
Mouteng v Select Services Partner Ltd [2008] All ER (D) 25 (Jun), EAT 18.10
Mowat-Brown v University of Surrey [2002] IRLR 235, [2001] All ER (D) 115 (Dec), EAT 10.26
Mowlem Northern Ltd v Watson [1990] ICR 751, [1990] IRLR 500, EAT 46.5
Moxam v Visible Changes Ltd (2012) 946 IDS Brief 13 .... 12.6
Moyhing v Barts and London NHS Trust [2006] IRLR 860, [2006] All ER (D) 64 (Jun), EAT
.... 12.16
Moyling v Homerton University Hospitals NHS Trust, City University (25 August 2005,
  unreported), EAT 11.31
Mugford v Midland Bank plc [1997] ICR 399, [1997] IRLR 208, EAT 52.11
Mulox IBC Ltd v Geels: C-125/92 [1993] ECR I-4075, [1994] IRLR 422, ECJ 23.8
Munchkins Restaurant Ltd v Karmazyn (UKEAT/0359/09/LA) (2010) 907 IDS Brief 7,
  [2010] All ER (D) 76 (Jun) 12.13, 12.16
Munir v Jang Publications [1989] ICR 1, [1989] IRLR 224, CA 18.22
Munro v MPB Structures Ltd. See MPB Structure Ltd v Munro
Murphy v A Birrell & Sons Ltd [1978] IRLR 458, EAT 6.7
Murphy v Bord Telecom Eireann: 157/86 [1988] ECR 673, [1988] 1 CMLR 879, [1988] ICR 445,
  [1988] IRLR 267, (1988) Times, 6 February, ECJ 21.6, 21.8
Murphy v Slough Borough Council [2005] EWCA Civ 122, [2005] ICR 721, [2005] IRLR 382,
  (2005) Times, 6 April, [2005] All ER (D) 244 (Feb) 35.5
Murray v Foyle Meats Ltd [2000] 1 AC 51, [1999] 3 All ER 769, [1999] 3 WLR 356, [1999] ICR
  827, [1999] IRLR 562, [1999] 31 LS Gaz R 36, 143 Sol Jo LB 214, HL 36.7
Murray v Leisureplay plc [2005] EWCA Civ 963, [2005] IRLR 946, [2005] All ER (D) 428 (Jul)
.... 7.41, 7.47b, 8.37, 56.26
Murray v Powertech (Scotland) Ltd [1992] IRLR 257, EAT 12.16
Muscat v Cable & Wireless plc. See Cable & Wireless plc v Muscat
Muschett v HM Prison Service [2010] EWCA Civ 25, [2010] IRLR 451, [2010] All ER (D) 18
  (Feb) 45.2c
Muschett v Hounslow London Borough Council [2009] ICR 424, 151 Sol Jo LB 1262, EAT 19.14
Musse v Abellio London Ltd (formerly Travel London Ltd) (2012) UKEAT/0283/11/CEA,
  UKEAT/0631/11/CEA, [2012] IRLR 360, [2012] All ER (D) 205 (Jan), EAT 50.25

N

N v Chief Constable of Merseyside Police [2006] EWHC 3041 (QB), [2006] All ER (D) 421
  (Nov) 54.2
N v Lewisham London Borough Council (UKEAT/156/09) [2009] ICR 1538, [2009] All ER (D) 74
  (Aug) 34.3
NACODS v Gluchowski [1996] IRLR 252, EAT 49.13
NALGO v Secretary of State for the Environment (1992) 5 Admin LR 785 .... 28.4
NRG Victory Reinsurance Ltd v Alexander [1992] ICR 675, EAT 53.1
NUMAST v P & O Scottish Ferries [2005] ICR 1270, sub nom National Union of Maritime
  Aviation and Shipping Transport v P & O Scottish Ferries [2005] All ER (D) 27 (Apr), EAT
.... 50.5

Table of Cases

Nagarajan v London Regional Transport [1998] IRLR 73, CA; revsd [2000] 1 AC 501, [1999] 4 All ER 65, [1999] 3 WLR 425, [1999] ICR 877, [1999] IRLR 572, [1999] 31 LS Gaz R 36, 143 Sol Jo LB 219, HL 10.17, 17.17, 21.10

Nagle v Feilden [1966] 2 QB 633, [1966] 1 All ER 689, [1966] 2 WLR 1027, 110 Sol Jo 286, CA 49.12

Nairne v Highland and Islands Fire Brigade [1989] IRLR 366, 1989 SLT 754, Ct of Sess 53.13

Nambalat v Tayeb [2012] EWCA Civ 1249, [2012] IRLR 1004, [2012] All ER (D) 62 (Oct) 32.10

Nascimento v British Bakeries Ltd [2005] All ER (D) 20 (Sep), EAT 17.9

National and Local Government Officers' Association v Killorn and Simm [1991] ICR 1, [1990] IRLR 464, EAT 49.16

National Centre for Young People with Epilepsy v Boateng (UKEAT/0440/10/CEA) (27 October 2010, unreported) 18.13

National Coal Board v National Union of Mineworkers [1986] ICR 736, [1986] IRLR 439 ..... 5.3, 5.7

National Coal Board v Sherwin [1978] ICR 700, [1978] IRLR 122, EAT 21.6

National Dock Labour Board v Pinn & Wheeler Ltd [1989] BCLC 647, 5 BCC 75; revsd (1989) Times, 5 April, CA 6.9

National Federation of Self-Employed and Small Businesses Ltd v Philpott [1997] ICR 518, [1997] IRLR 340, EAT 11.29

National Grid Co plc v Mayes [2001] UKHL 20, [2001] 2 All ER 417, [2001] 1 WLR 864, [2001] ICR 544, [2001] IRLR 394, [2001] NLJR 572, (2001) Times, 10 April, 145 Sol Jo LB 98, [2001] All ER (D) 28 (Apr) 40.16

National Union of Gold, Silver and Allied Trades v Albury Bros Ltd [1979] ICR 84, [1978] IRLR 504, 122 Sol Jo 662, CA 37.4, 48.20

National Union of Maritime Aviation and Shipping Transport v P & O Scottish Ferries. See NUMAST v P & O Scottish Ferries

National Union of Mineworkers (Yorkshire Area) v Millward [1995] ICR 482, [1995] IRLR 411, EAT 48.39

National Union of Teachers v Avon County Council (1978) 76 LGR 403, [1978] ICR 626, [1978] IRLR 55, EAT 37.4, 52.11

National Union of Teachers v St Mary's Church of England Aided Junior School (Governing Body) [1997] ICR 334, [1997] IRLR 242, [1997] ELR 169, CA 22.2, 35.8

Nationwide Building Society v Benn (UKEAT/0273/09) [2010] IRLR 922, [2010] All ER (D) 104 (Aug) 50.26

Navas (Chacon) v Eurest Colectividades SA: C-13/05 [2006] ECR I-6467, [2007] All ER (EC) 59, [2006] 3 CMLR 1123, [2007] ICR 1, [2006] IRLR 706, (2006) Times, 9 August, [2006] All ER (D) 132 (Jul), ECJ 22.6

Neale v Hereford and Worcester County Council [1986] ICR 471, sub nom Hereford and Worcester County Council v Neale [1986] IRLR 168, CA 19.35, 52.4

Neary v Dean of Westminster [1999] IRLR 288, SCD 56.17

Neary v Governing Body of St Albans Girls' School [2009] All ER (D) 30 (Jan), EAT; revsd [2009] EWCA Civ 1190, [2010] ICR 473, [2010] IRLR 124, (2009) Times, 23 November, [2009] All ER (D) 144 (Nov) 18.16, 18.75

Neary v Service Children's Education (UKEAT/0101/10/DA) [2010] ICR 1083, [2010] IRLR 1030, [2010] All ER (D) 70 (Aug) 11.18

Neath v Hugh Steeper Ltd: C-152/91 [1994] 1 All ER 929, [1993] ECR I-6935, [1995] 2 CMLR 357, [1995] ICR 158, [1994] IRLR 91, [1995] 42 LS Gaz R 23, ECJ 19.48, 21.17

Neidel v Stadt Frankfurt am Main: C-337/10 [2012] 3 CMLR 92, [2012] ICR 1201, [2012] IRLR 607, ECJ 27.3A

Neil v Strathclyde Borough Council. See Strathclyde Regional Council v Neil

Nelhams v Sandells Maintenance Ltd (1995) Times, 15 June, CA 25.10

Nelson v BBC (No 2) [1980] ICR 110, [1979] IRLR 346, 123 Sol Jo 552, CA 53.13

Nelson v Carillion Services Ltd [2003] EWCA Civ 544, [2003] ICR 1256, [2003] IRLR 428, [2003] 26 LS Gaz R 36, (2003) Times, 2 May, 147 Sol Jo LB 504, [2003] All ER (D) 253 (Apr) 21.21

Nelson v James Nelson & Sons Ltd [1914] 2 KB 770, 83 LJKB 823, 110 LT 888, 30 TLR 368, CA 8.3

Nelson v Newry and Mourne District Council [2009] NICA 24, [2009] IRLR 548, NI CA . 10.14, 12.3

Nerva v RL & G Ltd [1997] ICR 11, [1996] IRLR 461, [1996] 23 LS Gaz R 35, 140 Sol Jo LB 140, CA 32.21

Nerva v United Kingdom (Application 42295/98) (2002) 36 EHRR 31, [2002] IRLR 815, 13 BHRC 246, (2002) Times, 10 October, [2002] ECHR 42295/98, [2002] All ER (D) 137 (Sep), ECtHR 28.7, 32.9, 32.21

Nethermere (St Neots) Ltd v Gardiner [1984] ICR 612, sub nom Nethermere (St Neots) Ltd v
  Taverna and Gardiner [1984] IRLR 240, CA 14.3
Netjets Management Ltd v Central Arbitration Committee [2012] EWHC 2685 (Admin), [2013]
  1 All ER 288, [2012] IRLR 986, [2012] NLJR 1323, [2012] All ER (D) 57 (Oct) 48.26
New Century Cleaning Co Ltd v Church [2000] IRLR 27, [1999] All ER (D) 345, CA 32.6
New ISG Ltd v Vernon [2007] EWHC 2665 (Ch), [2008] ICR 319, [2008] IRLR 115, (2007) Times,
  12 December, [2007] All ER (D) 220 (Nov) 39.3, 50.16
New Southern Railway Ltd v Quinn [2006] ICR 761, [2006] IRLR 266, [2005] All ER (D) 367
  (Nov), EAT 10.30, 31.11
New Southern Railways Ltd (formerly South Central Trains Ltd) v Rodway [2005] EWCA Civ 443,
  [2005] ICR 1162, sub nom Rodway v New Southern Railways Ltd [2005] IRLR 583, (2005)
  Times, 21 April, [2005] All ER (D) 216 (Apr) 31.47, 31.48
New Testament Church of God v Stewart. See Stewart v New Testament Church of God
New Victoria Hospital v Ryan [1993] ICR 201, [1993] IRLR 202, [1993] 5 LS Gaz R 41, EAT
  .... 18.13
Newcastle-upon-Tyne NHS Hospitals Trust v Armstrong (UKEAT/0069/09/JOJ) [2010] ICR 674,
  [2010] All ER (D) 215 (Mar) 21.10
Newell v Gillingham Corpn [1941] 1 All ER 552, 39 LGR 191, 165 LT 184 .... 56.44
Newham London Borough Council v Skingle [2003] EWCA Civ 280, [2003] 2 All ER 761, [2003]
  ICR 1008, [2003] IRLR 359, 147 Sol Jo LB 300, [2003] All ER (D) 287 (Feb) 40.9
Newland v Simons and Willer (Hairdressers) Ltd [1981] ICR 521, [1981] IRLR 359, EAT 7.24
Newman v Polytechnic of Wales Students Union [1995] IRLR 72, EAT 17.23
Newns v British Airways plc [1992] IRLR 575, CA 50.25
News Group Newspapers Ltd v Society of Graphical and Allied Trades '82 (No 2) [1987] ICR 181,
  [1986] IRLR 337 .... 48.1
Nicholls v Corin Tech Ltd (UKEAT/0290/07) unreported 18.57
Nicholson v Grainger plc [2010] 2 All ER 253, [2010] ICR 360, [2009] NLJR 1582, [2009] All ER
  (D) 59 (Nov), sub nom Grainger plc v Nicholson [2010] IRLR 4, (2009) Times, 11 November,
  EAT 10.22
Nicoll v Cutts [1985] BCLC 322, 1 BCC 99,427, [1985] PCC 311, CA 29.10
Nicolson Highlandwear Ltd v Nicolson [2010] IRLR 859, EAT 18.17, 18.72
Nimz v Freie und Hansestadt Hamburg: C-184/89 [1991] ECR I-297, [1992] 3 CMLR 699, [1991]
  IRLR 222, ECJ 21.3, 21.12, 21.22, 21.23
Noel v London Underground Ltd. See London Underground Ltd v Noel
Nolan v Balfour Beatty Engineering Services (UKEAT/0109/11/SM) [2011] NLJR 1558,
  [2011] All ER (D) 09 (Nov), EAT 17.26
Noone v North West Thames Regional Health Authority (No 2). See North West Thames Regional
  Health Authority v Noone
Noor v Foreign & Commonwealth Office (2011) UKEAT/0470/10/SM, [2011] ICR 695, EAT
  .... 10.37
Noorani v Merseyside Tec Ltd [1999] IRLR 184, CA 18.14
Norbrook Laboratories (GB) Ltd v Adair [2008] EWHC 978 (QB), [2008] IRLR 878, [2008] All ER
  (D) 49 (May) 39.8, 39.10, 39.17
Nordenfelt v Maxim Nordenfelt Guns and Ammunition Co Ltd [1894] AC 535, 63 LJ Ch 908, 11
  R 1, [1891–4] All ER Rep 1, 71 LT 489, 10 TLR 636, HL 39.2, 39.5, 39.9, 39.10
Norman v Yellow Pages [2010] EWCA Civ 1395, [2010] All ER (D) 272 (Dec) 12.16
Norouzi v Sheffield City Council (2011) UKEAT/0497/10/RN, [2011] IRLR 897, [2011] All ER
  (D) 77 (Aug), EAT 10.39
Norris v Checksfield [1991] 4 All ER 327, [1991] 1 WLR 1241, 63 P & CR 38, [1991] ICR 632, 23
  HLR 425, [1992] 1 EGLR 159, [1991] NLJR 707, [1992] 01 EG 97, CA 41.2, 41.4
North v Dumfries and Galloway Council. See Dumfries and Galloway Council v North
North Cumbria Acute Hospitals NHS Trust v Potter [2009] IRLR 176, EAT 21.9
North East Midlands Co-operative Society Ltd v Allen [1977] IRLR 212, EAT 37.4
North Tyneside Primary Care Trust v Aynsley [2009] ICR 1333, [2009] All ER (D) 125 (May),
  EAT 18.7, 18.16, 18.75
North Wales Training and Enterprise Council (t/a CELTEC Ltd) v Astley. See Astley v Celtec Ltd
North West Thames Regional Health Authority v Noone [1988] ICR 813, sub nom Noone v North
  West Thames Regional Health Authority (No 2) [1988] IRLR 530, CA 12.13, 12.21
North Yorkshire County Council v Fay. See Fay v North Yorkshire County Council

Table of Cases

North Yorkshire County Council v Ratcliffe [1994] ICR 810, [1994] IRLR 342, CA; revsd sub nom
Ratcliffe v North Yorkshire County Council [1995] 3 All ER 597, 93 LGR 571, 159 LG Rev 1009,
[1995] IRLR 439, [1995] 30 LS Gaz R 34, [1995] NLJR 1092, 139 Sol Jo LB 196, sub nom North
Yorkshire County Council v Ratcliffe [1995] ICR 833, HL 21.9, 21.10, 21.12
Northamptonshire County fCouncil v Entwhistle (UKEAT/0540/09/ZT) [2010] IRLR 740,
[2010] All ER (D) 35 (Sep) 17.25
Northern General Hospital NHS Trust v Gale [1994] ICR 426, sub nom Gale v Northern General
Hospital NHS Trust [1994] IRLR 292, CA 6.9, 7.22e, 50.15
Northern Joint Police Board v Power [1997] IRLR 610, EAT 10.20
Northgate HR Ltd v Mercy [2007] EWCA Civ 1304, [2008] ICR 410, [2008] IRLR 222,
[2007] All ER (D) 196 (Dec) 37.6, 52.11
Norton Tool Co Ltd v Tewson [1973] 1 All ER 183, [1973] 1 WLR 45, [1972] ICR 501, [1972] IRLR
86, 117 Sol Jo 33, NIRC 53.12
Norwest Holst Group Administration Ltd v Harrison [1985] ICR 668, sub nom Harrison v Norwest
Holst Group Administration Ltd [1985] IRLR 240, CA 51.7, 51.8
Norwich Pharmacal Co v Customs and Excise Comrs [1974] AC 133, [1972] 3 All ER 813, [1972] 3
WLR 870, [1972] RPC 743, 116 Sol Jo 823, CA; revsd [1974] AC 133, [1973] 2 All ER 943, [1973]
3 WLR 164, [1973] FSR 365, [1974] RPC 101, 117 Sol Jo 567, HL 7.46
Notcutt v Universal Equipment Co (London) Ltd [1986] 3 All ER 582, [1986] 1 WLR 641, [1986]
ICR 414, [1986] IRLR 218, 130 Sol Jo 392, [1986] LS Gaz R 1314, [1986] NLJ Rep 393, CA
.... 46.3
Notting Hill Housing Trust v Roomus [2006] EWCA Civ 407, [2006] 1 WLR 1375, [2006] All ER
(D) 432 (Mar) 41.6
Nottingham University v Fishel [2000] ICR 1462, [2000] IRLR 471, [2000] ELR 385, [2001] RPC
367, [2000] All ER (D) 269 .... 7.17
Nottinghamshire County Council v Bowly [1978] IRLR 252, EAT 52.9
Nottinghamshire County Council v Meikle. See Meikle v Nottinghamshire County Council
Nowicka-Price v Chief Constable of Gwent Constabulary (UKEAT/0268/09/ZT) (3 August 2009,
unreported) 18.52
Nu-Swift International Ltd v Mallinson [1979] ICR 157, [1978] IRLR 537, 122 Sol Jo 744, EAT
.... 31.9
Nunn v Royal Mail Group Ltd (UKEAT/0530/09/DM) [2011] ICR 162 .... 52.9

O

OCS Group Ltd v Jones (UKEAT/0038/09) (4 August 2009, unreported) 50.3
OTG Ltd v Barke (UKEAT/0320/09/RN) [2011] IRLR 272, [2011] All ER (D) 241 (Mar) 19.2, 29.10
Oakland v Wellswood (Yorkshire) Ltd [2009] IRLR 250, [2009] All ER (D) 12 (Jan), EAT; revsd
[2009] EWCA Civ 1094, [2010] ICR 902, [2010] IRLR 82, [2009] All ER (D) 11 (Nov) . 6.9, 19.2, 51.12
Oakley v Labour Party. See Labour Party v Oakley
O'Brien v Associated Fire Alarms Ltd [1969] 1 All ER 93, [1968] 1 WLR 1916, 3 KIR 223, 3 ITR
182, 112 Sol Jo 232, CA 7.22e
O'Brien v Barclays Bank plc [1995] 1 All ER 438, sub nom Barclays Bank plc v O'Brien [1994] ICR
865, [1994] IRLR 580, CA 40.3
O'Brien v Department for Constitutional Affairs [2008] EWCA Civ 1448, [2009] 2 CMLR 389,
[2009] ICR 593, [2009] IRLR 294, [2009] NLJR 74, [2008] All ER (D) 224 (Dec); revsd O'Brien
v Ministry of Justice [2010] UKSC 34, [2010] 4 All ER 62, [2011] 1 CMLR 1172, [2010] IRLR
883, (2010) Times, 11 November, [2010] All ER (D) 297 (Jul) 10.41, 30.5
O'Brien (Dermod Patrick) v Ministry of Justice: C-393/10 [2012] All ER (EC) 757, [2012] 2 CMLR
728, [2012] ICR 955, [2012] IRLR 421, ECJ 10.41, 14.8, 30.3, 30.5, 30.15, 30.21, 30.22
O'Brien v Pacitti Jones (a firm) [2005] CSIH 56, [2005] IRLR 888, [2005] All ER (D) 141 (Jul)
.... 6.3, 51.11
O'Brien v Sim-Chem Ltd [1980] 3 All ER 132, [1980] 1 WLR 1011, [1980] ICR 573, [1980] IRLR
373, 124 Sol Jo 560, HL 21.7
O'Brien v Transco plc (formerly BG plc). See BG plc v O'Brien
O'Cathail v Transport for London (UKEAT/0247/11/MAA) (13 January 2012, unreported) 18.54
O'Cathail v Transport for London [2012] EWCA Civ 1004, [2012] IRLR 1011, [2013] ICR D2,
[2012] All ER (D) 355 (Jul) 19.14
Oceanrose Investments Ltd, Re [2008] EWHC 3475 (Ch), [2009] Bus LR 947 .... 15.49

Octavius Atkinson & Sons Ltd v Morris [1989] ICR 431, [1989] IRLR 158, CA 46.13, 51.13
Ocular Sciences Ltd v Aspect Vision Care Ltd [1997] RPC 289 .... 39.16
O'Dea v ISC Chemicals Ltd (t/a as Rhône-Poulenc Chemicals) [1996] ICR 222, [1995] IRLR 599,
    CA 53.13
O'Donnell v Shanahan. See Allied Business and Financial Consultants Ltd, Re
O'Donoghue v Redcar and Cleveland Borough Council [2001] EWCA Civ 701, [2001] IRLR 615,
    [2001] All ER (D) 192 (May) 12.15, 12.16, 53.13
Office Angels Ltd v Rainer-Thomas and O'Connor [1991] IRLR 214, (1991) Times, 11 April, CA
    .... 39.4, 39.8
Ogbonna v Republic of Nigeria (UKEAT/0585/10) [2012] 1 WLR 139, [2012] ICR 32,
    [2011] All ER (D) 19 (Oct), EAT 12.2
O'Hanlon v Revenue and Customs Comrs [2006] ICR 1579, [2006] IRLR 840, [2006] All ER (D) 53
    (Aug), EAT; affd [2007] EWCA Civ 283, [2007] ICR 1359, [2007] IRLR 404, (2007) Times,
    20 April, [2007] All ER (D) 516 (Mar) 10.37, 11.9
Ojutiku v Manpower Services Commission [1982] ICR 661, [1982] IRLR 418, CA 11.9
O'Kelly v Trusthouse Forte plc [1984] QB 90, [1983] 3 All ER 456, [1983] 3 WLR 605, [1983] ICR
    728, [1983] IRLR 369, 127 Sol Jo 632, [1983] LS Gaz R 2367, CA 14.3
Okerago v May & Baker Ltd (t/a Sanofi-Aventis Pharma). See May & Baker Ltd (t/a Sanofi-Aventis
    Pharma) v Okerago
Okonu v G4S Services (UK) Ltd [2008] ICR 598, [2008] All ER (D) 133 (Feb), EAT 12.3, 12.8
O'Laoire v Jackel International Ltd (No 2) [1991] ICR 718, [1991] IRLR 170, CA, CA 56.33
Oliver v J P Malnick & Co [1983] 3 All ER 795, [1983] ICR 708, [1983] IRLR 456, 127 Sol Jo 646,
    EAT 13.2
Omar v Worldwide News Inc (t/a United Press International) [1998] IRLR 291, EAT 18.71
Omilaju v Waltham Forest London Borough Council [2004] EWCA Civ 1493, [2005] 1 All ER 75,
    [2005] ICR 481, 148 Sol Jo LB 1370, (2004) Times, 26 November, [2004] All ER (D) 174 (Nov),
    sub nom Waltham Forest London Borough Council v Omilaju [2005] IRLR 35 .... 51.7
1 Pump Court Chambers v Horton. See Horton v Higham
O'Neill v Buckinghamshire County Council (UKEAT/0020/09/JOJ) [2010] IRLR 384,
    [2010] All ER (D) 15 (Feb) 10.30, 31.3
O'Neill v DSG Retail Ltd [2002] EWCA Civ 1139, [2003] ICR 222, [2002] 40 LS Gaz R 32, (2002)
    Times, 9 September, [2002] All ER (D) 500 (Jul) 26.18
O'Neill v Governors of St Thomas More RCVA Upper School [1997] ICR 33, [1996] IRLR 372,
    EAT 10.30
Oni v NHS Leicester City (2012) UKEAT/0144/12/LA, [2013] ICR 91, [2012] All ER (D) 05
    (Oct), EAT 19.24
Onwuka v Spherion Technology UK Ltd [2005] ICR 567, [2004] All ER (D) 153 (Dec), EAT
    .... 18.3, 18.7, 18.75
Onyango v Berkley (t/a Berkley Solicitors) (2013) (UKEAT/0407/12/ZT), unreported 9.17
Optare Group Ltd v Transport and General Workers Union [2007] IRLR 931, [2007] All ER (D)
    135 (Jul), EAT 37.4, 46.2
Optical Express Ltd v Williams [2008] ICR 1, [2007] IRLR 936, [2007] All ER (D) 416 (Oct),
    EAT 36.12
Optikinetics Ltd v Whooley [1999] ICR 984 .... 53.13
O'Reilly v Mackman [1983] 2 AC 237, [1982] 3 All ER 680, [1982] 3 WLR 604, 126 Sol Jo 311;
    revsd [1983] 2 AC 237, [1982] 3 All ER 680, [1982] 3 WLR 604, 126 Sol Jo 578, CA; affd [1983]
    2 AC 237, [1982] 3 All ER 1124, [1982] 3 WLR 1096, 126 Sol Jo 820, HL 35.6
Orlando v Didcot Power Station Sports and Social Club [1996] IRLR 262, EAT 12.16
Orphanos v Queen Mary College [1985] AC 761, [1985] 2 All ER 233, [1985] 2 WLR 703,
    [1986] 2 CMLR 73, [1985] IRLR 349, 129 Sol Jo 284, [1985] LS Gaz R 1787, HL 11.9
Orr v Milton Keynes Council [2011] EWCA Civ 62, [2011] 4 All ER 1256, [2011] ICR 704, [2011]
    IRLR 317, (2011) Times, 13 April, [2011] All ER (D) 20 (Feb) 52.4, 52.10
Orthet Ltd v Vince-Cain [2005] ICR 374, [2004] IRLR 857, [2004] All ER (D) 143 (May), EAT
    .... 12.16, 12.19
Osborn & Co Ltd v Dior [2003] EWCA Civ 281, [2003] HLR 649, [2003] 05 EG 144 (CS),
    [2003] All ER (D) 185 (Jan) 41.5
Osborne v Premium Care Homes Ltd [2006] All ER (D) 272 (Oct), EAT 18.16
Osborne v Valve (Engineering) Services Ltd (24 November 2000, unreported), EAT 7.45
Osborne Clarke Services v Purohit [2009] IRLR 341, [2009] All ER (D) 122 (Feb), EAT ... 10.45, 11.9

Table of Cases

Osei-Bonsu v Wandsworth London Borough Council [1999] 1 All ER 265, [1999] 1 WLR 1011, sub nom Wandsworth London Borough Council v Osei-Bonsu [1999] 3 FCR 1, [1999] 1 FLR 276, 31 HLR 515, [1999] 1 EGLR 26, [1998] 42 LS Gaz R 34, [1998] NLJR 1641, [1999] 11 EG 167, [1998] EGCS 148, 143 Sol Jo LB 12, CA 41.3
Osterreichischer Gewerkschaftsbund v Wirtschaftskammer Osterreich (2004) IDS Brief No 760 .... 21.14
Oswald Hickson Collier & Co v Carter-Ruck [1984] AC 720n, [1984] 2 All ER 15, [1984] 2 WLR 847n, 126 Sol Jo 120, CA 39.5
Oti-Obihara v Revenue and Customs Comrs [2010] UKFTT 568 (TC), [2011] SFTD 202, [2011] IRLR 386, [2011] SWTI 415 .... 12.16
Oudahar v Esporta Group Ltd (UKEAT/0566/10/DA) [2011] ICR 1406, [2011] IRLR 730, [2011] All ER (D) 137 (Aug), EAT 26.7, 52.3
Outram v Academy Plastics [2001] ICR 367, [2000] IRLR 499, CA 40.16
Owusu v Jackson (t/a Villa Holidays Bal-Inn Villas): C-281/02 [2005] QB 801, [2005] ECR I-1383, [2005] 2 All ER (Comm) 577, [2005] 2 WLR 942, [2005] 1 Lloyd's Rep 452, (2005) Times, 9 March, [2005] All ER (D) 47 (Mar), ECJ 23.8
Owusu v London Fire and Civil Defence Authority [1995] IRLR 574, EAT 12.6, 17.29
Oxford v Department of Health and Social Security [1977] ICR 884, [1977] IRLR 225, 12 ITR 436, EAT 12.9
Oy Liikenne Ab v Liskojärvi: C-172/99 [2001] ECR I 745, [2001] All ER (EC) 544, [2001] 3 CMLR 807, [2002] ICR 155, [2001] IRLR 171, [2001] All ER (D) 168 (Jan), ECJ 50.5
Oyarce v Cheshire County Council [2007] ICR 1693, [2007] All ER (D) 101 (Aug), EAT; affd [2008] EWCA Civ 434, [2008] 4 All ER 907, [2008] ICR 1179, [2008] IRLR 653, [2008] All ER (D) 24 (May) 12.3, 12.24

P

P v Nottinghamshire County Council [1992] ICR 706, [1992] IRLR 362, CA 52.9
P v S and Cornwall County Council: C-13/94 [1996] ECR I-2143, [1996] All ER (EC) 397, [1996] 2 CMLR 247, [1996] ICR 795, [1996] IRLR 347, [1997] 2 FCR 180, [1996] 2 FLR 347, ECJ 10.18, 19.48, 21.2
P & O European Ferries (Dover) Ltd v Iverson (1999) IDS Brief No 640 .... 21.14
P & O Property Ltd v Allen [1997] ICR 436, EAT 50.16
P & O Trans European Ltd v Initial Transport Service Ltd [2003] IRLR 128, sub nom P&O Trans European Ltd v Initial Transport Service Ltd [2002] All ER (D) 116 (Nov), EAT 50.5
P Bork International A/S v Foreningen af Arbejdsledere i Danmark: 101/87 [1988] ECR 3057, [1990] 3 CMLR 701, [1989] IRLR 41, ECJ 50.6, 50.14
PSM International plc v Whitehouse [1992] FSR 489, [1992] IRLR 279, CA 39.15
Paal Wilson & Co A/S v Partenreederei Hannah Blumenthal, The Hannah Blumenthal [1983] 1 AC 854, [1982] 3 All ER 394, [1982] 3 WLR 49, [1982] 1 Lloyd's Rep 582, 126 Sol Jo 292, CA; varied [1983] 1 AC 854, [1983] 1 All ER 34, [1982] 3 WLR 1149, [1983] 1 Lloyd's Rep 103, 126 Sol Jo 835, HL 46.3
Packman (t/a Packman Lucas Associates) v Fauchon (2012) UKEAT/0017/12/LA, [2012] ICR 1362, [2012] IRLR 721, EAT 36.7
Page v Freight Hire (Tank Haulage) Ltd [1981] 1 All ER 394, [1981] ICR 299, [1981] IRLR 13, EAT 11.21
Page v Hull University Visitor. See R v Hull University Visitor, ex p Page
Paggetti v Cobb [2002] IRLR 861, (2002) Times, 12 April, [2002] All ER (D) 394 (Mar), EAT 32.12
Paine v Colne Valley Electricity Supply Co Ltd and British Insulated Cables Ltd [1938] 4 All ER 803, 37 LGR 200, 83 Sol Jo 115, 160 LT 124, 55 TLR 181 .... 25.3
Pakenham-Walsh v Connell Residential [2006] EWCA Civ 90, [2006] 11 LS Gaz R 25, [2006] All ER (D) 275 (Feb) 55.21
Palacios de la Villa v Cortefiel Servicios SA: C-411/05 [2007] ECR I-8531, [2008] All ER (EC) 249, [2008] 1 CMLR 385, [2009] ICR 1111, [2007] IRLR 989, (2007) Times, 23 October, [2007] All ER (D) 207 (Oct), ECJ 10.10, 11.9, 22.2, 40.5
Palfrey v Greater London Council [1985] ICR 437 .... 42.9
Palfrey v Transco plc [2004] IRLR 916, [2004] All ER (D) 150 (Jul), EAT 46.5, 51.5
Palihakkara v British Telecommunications plc (2007) 823 IDS Brief 18, [2007] All ER (D) 131 (Jan), EAT 12.33, 18.34

Palmer v Southend-on-Sea Borough Council [1984] 1 All ER 945, [1984] 1 WLR 1129, [1984] ICR 372, [1984] IRLR 119, 128 Sol Jo 262, CA 17.25
Palmer, Wyeth and National Union of Rail, Maritime and Transport Workers v United Kingdom [2002] IRLR 568, ECtHR 28.4
Parmar v East Leicester Medical Practice (UKEAT/0490/10/JOJ) [2011] IRLR 641, [2011] All ER (D) 92 (Apr), EAT 12.2, 18.57
Pambakian v Brentford Nylons Ltd [1978] ICR 665, 122 Sol Jo 177, EAT 29.10
Panama v Hackney London Borough Council [2003] EWCA Civ 273, [2003] IRLR 278, [2003] All ER (D) 224 (Feb) 52.9
Pannu v Geo W King Ltd (in liq) (2011) UKEAT/0021/11/DA, [2012] IRLR 193, [2012] All ER (D) 79 (Jan), EAT 50.3
Paquay v Societe d'architectes Hoet + Minne SPRL: C-460/06 [2008] 1 CMLR 263, [2008] ICR 420, [2007] All ER (D) 137 (Oct), ECJ 10.30
Paragon Finance plc (formerly National Home Loans Corpn) v Nash [2001] EWCA Civ 1466, [2002] 2 All ER 248, [2001] 2 All ER (Comm) 1025, [2002] 1 WLR 685, [2002] 1 P & CR D22, [2002] 2 P & CR 279, [2001] 44 LS Gaz R 36, (2001) Times, 24 October, 145 Sol Jo LB 244, [2001] All ER (D) 202 (Oct) 7.22c
Parfett v John Lamb Partnership Ltd (UKEAT/0111/08) [2008] All ER (D) 22 (Jul) 17.9
Parker v Clifford Dunn Ltd [1979] ICR 463, [1979] IRLR 56, EAT 52.10
Parker v Northumbrian Water (2011) UKEAT/0221/10/CEA, [2011] ICR 1172, [2011] IRLR 652, [2011] All ER (D) 56 (May), EAT 18.26
Parker, Rhodes, Hickmotts Solicitors v Harvey (UKEAT/0455/11/SM) (9 February 2012, unreported) 17.23
Parkins v Sodexho Ltd [2002] IRLR 109, [2001] All ER (D) 377 (Jun), EAT 9.17
Parkinson v March Consulting Ltd [1998] ICR 276, [1997] IRLR 308, CA 52.1
Parkwood Leisure Ltd v Alemo-Herron. See Alemo-Herron v Parkwood Leisure Ltd
Parliamentary Comr for Administration v Fernandez [2004] 2 CMLR 59, [2004] ICR 123, [2004] IRLR 22, [2003] All ER (D) 115 (Oct), EAT 21.10, 21.12
Parr v Whitbread & Co plc [1990] ICR 427, [1990] IRLR 39, EAT 52.9
Parry v Ministry of Justice (2012) UKEAT/0068/12/ZT, [2013] ICR 311, [2013] All ER (D) 33 (Mar), EAT 53.13
Parry v National Westminster Bank plc [2004] EWCA Civ 1563, [2005] ICR 396, [2005] IRLR 193, (2004) Times, 4 November, 148 Sol Jo LB 1314, [2004] All ER (D) 22 (Nov) 53.5
Parsons v Albert J Parsons & Sons Ltd [1979] FSR 254, [1979] ICR 271, [1979] IRLR 117, 122 Sol Jo 812, CA 8.4, 14.3
Parsons v BNM Laboratories Ltd [1964] 1 QB 95, [1963] 2 All ER 658, [1963] 2 WLR 1273, 42 ATC 200, [1963] TR 183, 107 Sol Jo 294, CA 56.30
Parviainen v Finnair Oyj: C-471/08 [2011] 1 CMLR 209, [2011] ICR 99, ECJ 31.15
Patefield v Belfast City Council [2000] IRLR 664, NI CA 11.24
Patel v Marquette Partners (UK) Ltd [2009] ICR 569, [2009] IRLR 425, [2009] All ER (D) 175 (Feb), EAT 32.6, 32.8
Patel v Nagesan [1995] ICR 989, [1995] IRLR 370, CA 17.23
Patel v Oldham Metropolitan Borough Council [2010] ICR 603, [2010] IRLR 280, EAT 10.26
Patel v Pirabakaran [2006] EWCA Civ 685, [2006] 4 All ER 506, [2006] 1 WLR 3112, [2006] 2 P & CR 577, [2006] HLR 742, [2006] 23 EG 165 (CS), (2006) Times, 19 July, 150 Sol Jo LB 743, [2006] All ER (D) 380 (May) 41.3
Patel v RCMS Ltd [1999] IRLR 161, EAT 17.32
Patel v South Tyneside Council (UKEATPA/0917/11/ZT) (28 November 2011, unreported)
. . . . 17.21, 19.11
Paterson (KD) v Islington London Borough Council (23 April 2004, unreported), EAT 21.7
Paterson v Metropolitan Police Comr [2007] ICR 1522, [2007] IRLR 763, (2007) Times, 22 August, [2007] All ER (D) 346 (Jul), EAT 10.26
Patsystems Holdings Ltd v Neilly [2012] EWHC 2609 (QB), [2012] IRLR 979, [2012] All ER (D) 138 (Jun) 39.3, 39.8
Patterson v Legal Services Commission [2003] EWCA Civ 1558, [2004] ICR 312, [2004] IRLR 153, [2004] 02 LS Gaz R 28, (2003) Times, 20 November, 147 Sol Jo LB 1364, [2003] All ER (D) 140 (Nov) 10.41, 11.30
Paul v East Surrey District Health Authority [1995] IRLR 305, 30 BMLR 41, CA 52.9
Paul v National and Local Government Officers' Association [1987] IRLR 43 . . . . 48.12
Paul v National Probation Service [2004] IRLR 190, [2003] All ER (D) 177 (Nov), EAT 10.37
Paul v Visa International Service Association. See Visa International Service Association v Paul

Table of Cases

Paw v Revenue and Customs Comrs (UKEATPA/0703/11) (23 November 2011, unreported)
.... 19.3
Pay v Lancashire Probation Service [2004] ICR 187, [2004] IRLR 129, (2003) Times, 27 November,
[2003] All ER (D) 468 (Oct), EAT 28.7
Pay v United Kingdom (Application 32792/05) [2009] IRLR 139, ECtHR 28.4
Paymentshield Group Holdings Ltd v Halstead (UKEAT/0470/11/DM) [2012] ICR D5; revsd sub
nom Halstead v Paymentshield Group Holdings Ltd [2012] EWCA Civ 524, [2012] All ER (D)
161 (Apr) 18.22
Payne v Enfield Technical Services Ltd [2008] EWCA Civ 393, [2008] ICR 1423, [2008] IRLR 500,
(2008) Times, 2 June, [2008] All ER (D) 300 (Apr) 7.24
Payne v Secretary of State for Employment [1989] IRLR 352, CA 6.9
Peace v City of Edinburgh Council [1999] IRLR 417, 1999 SLT 712, OH 7.42
Peach Grey & Co (a firm) v Sommers [1995] 2 All ER 513, [1995] ICR 549, [1995] IRLR 363, [1995]
13 LS Gaz R 31 .... 18.14
Peake v Automotive Products Ltd [1977] QB 780, [1977] 2 WLR 751, [1977] ICR 480, [1977] IRLR
105, 12 ITR 259, 121 Sol Jo 222, EAT; revsd [1978] QB 233, [1978] 1 All ER 106, [1977] 3 WLR
853, [1977] ICR 968, 121 Sol Jo 644, sub nom Automotive Products Ltd v Peake [1977] IRLR 365,
12 ITR 428, CA 21.5
Pearson v Kent County Council [1993] IRLR 165, CA 6.7
Pedersen v Camden London Borough Council [1981] ICR 674, [1981] IRLR 173, CA 51.7
Pedersen v Kvickly Skive See Handels-og Kontorfunktionaerernes Forbund i Danmark (acting on
behalf of Hoj Pedersen) v Faellesforeningen for Danmarks Brugsforeninger (acting on behalf of
Kvickly Skive)
Peixoto v British Telecommunications plc [2008] All ER (D) 240 (May), EAT 18.17
Pendragon plc (t/a CD Bramall Bradford) v Copus [2005] ICR 1671, [2005] All ER (D) 42 (Aug),
EAT 17.37, 17.38
Peninsula Business Services Ltd v Rees (UKEAT/0335/08) [2009] All ER (D) 134 (Sep) . 18.50, 19.24
Peninsula Business Services Ltd v Sweeney [2004] IRLR 49, [2003] All ER (D) 06 (Apr), EAT
.... 7.44, 39.1, 39.3
Pennwell Publishing (UK) Ltd v Ornstien [2007] EWHC 1570 (QB), [2007] IRLR 700,
[2007] All ER (D) 180 (Jun) 39.13
Penrose v Fairey Surveys Ltd [1973] ICR 26, NIRC 17.24
Pepper (Inspector of Taxes) v Hart [1993] AC 593, [1993] 1 All ER 42, [1992] 3 WLR 1032, [1992]
STC 898, 65 TC 421, [1993] ICR 291, [1993] IRLR 33, [1993] NLJR 17, [1993] RVR 127, (1992)
Times, 30 November, HL 44.21
Pepper v Lancashire County Council [2008] All ER (D) 122 (Jan) 21.18
Perceval-Price v Department of Economic Development [2000] NI 141, [2000] IRLR 380, (2000)
Times, 28 April, NI CA 21.4, 22.2
Percy v Board of National Mission of the Church of Scotland [2005] UKHL 73, [2006] 2 AC 28,
[2006] 4 All ER 1354, [2006] 2 WLR 353, [2006] ICR 134, [2006] IRLR 195, (2005) Times,
16 December, 2006 SLT 11, 150 Sol Jo LB 30, [2005] All ER (D) 229 (Dec) .. 10.41, 11.11, 14.3, 14.8
Pereda v Madrid Movilidad SA: C-277/08 [2010] 1 CMLR 103, [2009] IRLR 959, [2009] NLJR
1323, (2009) Times, 8 October, [2009] All ER (D) 88 (Sep), ECJ 27.3A, 27.5
Perkin v St George's Healthcare NHS Trust [2005] EWCA Civ 1174, [2006] ICR 617, [2005] IRLR
934, [2005] All ER (D) 112 (Oct) 52.14
Perkins v Southern Cross Healthcare Co Ltd [2010] EWCA Civ 1442, [2011] IRLR 247, (2011)
Times, 28 February, [2010] All ER (D) 199 (Dec), sub nom Southern Cross Healthcare Co Ltd v
Perkins [2011] ICR 285 .... 7.11, 17.11
Personalrat der Feuerwehr Hamburg v Leiter der Feuerwehr Hamburg: C-52/04 (14 July 2005,
unreported), ECJ 55.3
Pervez v Macquarie Bank Ltd (London Branch) (UKEAT/0246/10/CEA) [2011] ICR 266, [2011]
IRLR 284, [2011] All ER (D) 158 (Feb) 11.18, 17.11, 23.9, 51.15
Pestle and Mortar v Turner (UKEAT/0652/05/ZT) (9 December 2005, unreported) 17.38
Petch v Customs and Excise Comrs [1993] ICR 789, 137 Sol Jo LB 120, CA 40.16
Peter Simper & Co Ltd v Cooke [1986] IRLR 19, EAT 19.25
Peters v Sat Katar Co Ltd [2003] ICR 1574, [2003] IRLR 574, [2003] 33 LS Gaz R 28, (2003)
Times, 1 July, [2003] All ER (D) 271 (Jun), CA 19.14
Petersen v Berufungsausschuss fur Zahnarzte fur den Bezirk Westfalen-Lippe: C-341/08 [2010]
IRLR 254, sub nom Peterson v Berufungsausschuss fur Zahnarzte fur den Bezirk Westfalen-
Lippe: C-341/08 [2010] All ER (D) 233 (Feb), ECJ 11.9, 40.5

Petrofina (Great Britain) Ltd v Martin [1966] Ch 146, [1966] 1 All ER 126, [1966] 2 WLR 318, 109
Sol Jo 126, [1966] Brewing Tr Rev 145, CA 39.16
Pfaffinger v City of Liverpool Community College [1997] ICR 142, [1996] IRLR 508, EAT . 36.7, 51.7
Pfeiffer v Deutsches Rotes Kreuz, Kreisverband Waldshut eV: C-397/01 to C-403/01 [2005] ICR
1307, [2005] IRLR 137, [2004] All ER (D) 52 (Oct), ECJ 55.2, 55.3, 55.8
Pharmacists' Defence Association v Boots Management Services Ltd [2013] IRLR 262 .... 48.29
Phillips v Xtera Communications Ltd (UKEAT/0244/10/DM) [2012] ICR 171, [2011] IRLR 724,
EAT 37.5
Phoenix Partners Group LLP v Asoyag (Maurice) [2010] EWHC 846 (QB), [2010] IRLR 594,
[2010] All ER (D) 129 (Apr) 39.3, 39.4
Photo Production Ltd v Securicor Transport Ltd [1980] AC 827, [1980] 1 All ER 556, [1980] 2
WLR 283, [1980] 1 Lloyd's Rep 545, 124 Sol Jo 147, 130 NLJ 188, HL 39.11
Photostatic Copiers (Southern) Ltd v Okuda and Japan Office Equipment Ltd (in liq) [1995] IRLR
11, EAT 50.13
Pickford v Imperial Chemical Industries plc [1998] 3 All ER 462, [1998] 1 WLR 1189, [1998] ICR
673, [1998] IRLR 435, [1998] 31 LS Gaz R 36, [1998] NLJR 978, 142 Sol Jo LB 198,
[1998] All ER (D) 302, HL 26.31
Pickstone v Freemans plc [1989] AC 66, [1987] 3 All ER 756, [1987] 3 WLR 811, [1987] 2 CMLR
572, [1987] ICR 867, [1987] IRLR 218, 131 Sol Jo 538, [1987] LS Gaz R 1409, [1987] NLJ Rep
315, CA; affd [1989] AC 66, [1988] 2 All ER 803, [1988] 3 WLR 265, [1988] 3 CMLR 221, [1988]
ICR 697, [1988] IRLR 357, 132 Sol Jo 994, [1988] NLJR 193, HL 17.12, 21.8
Pickwell v Lincolnshire County Council (1993) 91 LGR 509, [1993] ICR 87, [1992] 41 LS Gaz R
36, EAT 36.6, 50.18
Pieretti v Enfield London Borough Council [2010] EWCA Civ 1104, [2011] 2 All ER 642, [2010]
LGR 944, [2011] PTSR 565, [2011] HLR 46, [2010] NLJR 1458, [2010] All ER (D) 96 (Oct)
.... 11.37
Pierre-Davis v North West London Hospitals NHS Trust (UKEATPA/1496/08/LA) (14 July 2009,
unreported) 19.11
Piggott Bros & Co Ltd v Jackson [1992] ICR 85, [1991] IRLR 309, CA 19.16, 19.29, 19.35, 26.11
Pike v Somerset County Council [2009] EWCA Civ 808, [2010] ICR 46, [2009] IRLR 870, [2009]
ELR 559, [2009] All ER (D) 284 (Jul) 21.11, 30.1
Pinfold North Ltd v Humberside Fire Authority [2010] EWHC 2944 (QB) 35.5
Pinkney v Sandpiper Drilling Ltd [1989] ICR 389, [1989] IRLR 425, EAT 6.9
Pinnington v City and Council of Swansea [2005] EWCA Civ 135, [2005] ICR 685, [2005] All ER
(D) 58 (Feb), sub nom Pinnington v Swansea City Council (2005) Times, 9 March 9.17, 26.9
Pinochet Ugarte, Re. See R v Bow Street Metropolitan Stipendiary Magistrate, ex p Pinochet
Ugarte (No 2)
Pioneer GB Ltd v Webb [2011] EWHC 2683 (Ch) 40.1
Pipe v Hendrickson Europe Ltd [2003] All ER (D) 280 (Apr), EAT 30.25
Pirelli General Cable Works Ltd v Murray [1979] IRLR 190, EAT 53.3
Pitts v Hunt [1991] 1 QB 24, [1990] 3 All ER 344, [1990] 3 WLR 542, [1990] RTR 290, 134 Sol Jo
834, [1990] 27 LS Gaz R 43, CA 25.44
Plank v Atkins Ltd (UKEATPA/0799/09/JOJ) (20 January 2010, unreported) 19.17
Polentarutti v Autokraft Ltd [1991] ICR 757, [1991] IRLR 457, EAT 53.13
Police Comr v Rixon (UKEAT/0126/10/SM) [2010] All ER (D) 75 (May) 17.16, 17.34
Polkey v A E Dauton (or Dayton) Services Ltd [1988] AC 344, [1987] 3 All ER 974, [1987] 3 WLR
1153, [1988] ICR 142, [1987] IRLR 503, 131 Sol Jo 1624, [1988] 1 LS Gaz R 36, [1987] NLJ Rep
1109, HL 12.15, 18.60, 37.4, 52.4, 52.11, 53.13
Porcelli v Strathclyde Regional Council [1986] ICR 564, sub nom Strathclyde Regional Council v
Porcelli [1986] IRLR 134, Ct of Sess 10.51
Port of London Authority v Payne [1994] ICR 555, [1994] IRLR 9, CA 53.2, 53.5
Porter v Bandridge Ltd [1978] 1 WLR 1145, [1978] ICR 943, [1978] IRLR 271, 13 ITR 340, 122 Sol
Jo 592, CA 17.25
Porter v Cannon Hygiene Ltd [1993] IRLR 329, NI CA 22.2
Porter v Magill [2001] UKHL 67, [2002] 2 AC 357, [2002] 1 All ER 465, [2002] 2 WLR 37, [2002]
LGR 51, (2001) Times, 14 December, [2001] All ER (D) 181 (Dec) 19.24, 28.7
Porter and Nanyakkara v Queen's Medical Centre (Nottingham University Hospital) [1993] IRLR
486 .... 50.26
Portsea Island Mutual Co-operative Society Ltd v Leyland (1978) 77 LGR 164, [1978] ICR 1195,
[1978] IRLR 556, [1978] Crim LR 554, 122 Sol Jo 486, DC 3.3

Table of Cases

Post Office v Adekeye [1997] ICR 110, 140 Sol Jo LB 262, sub nom Adekeye v Post Office (No 2)
  [1997] IRLR 105, CA 10.44, 38.4
Post Office v Fennell [1981] IRLR 221, CA 52.9
Post Office v Foley [2001] 1 All ER 550, [2000] ICR 1283, [2000] IRLR 827, [2000] All ER (D)
  1137, CA 52.4, 52.9
Post Office v Footitt [2000] IRLR 243 .... 26.29
Post Office v Marney [1990] IRLR 170, EAT 52.4, 52.9
Post Office v Moore [1981] ICR 623, EAT 17.21
Post Office v Mughal [1977] ICR 763, [1977] IRLR 178, 12 ITR 130, EAT 34.2
Post Office v Roberts [1980] IRLR 347, EAT 7.22d
Post Office v Strange [1981] IRLR 515, EAT 51.7
Postcastle Properties Ltd v Perridge (1985) 18 HLR 100, [1985] 2 EGLR 107, 276 Estates Gazette
  1063, CA 41.2
Pothecary Witham Weld v Bullimore (UKEAT/0158/09/JOJ) [2010] ICR 1008, [2010] IRLR 572,
  [2010] All ER (D) 72 (Aug) 12.3
Potter v Arafa [1995] IRLR 316, sub nom Arafa v Potter [1994] PIQR Q73, CA 56.30
Potter v Hunt Contracts Ltd [1992] ICR 337, [1992] IRLR 108, EAT 32.6, 32.8
Potter v North Cumbria Acute Hospitals NHS Trust [2008] ICR 910, [2009] IRLR 22,
  [2008] All ER (D) 236 (Apr), EAT 18.10, 21.8, 21.21
Potter v North Cumbria Acute Hospitals NHS Trust [2009] IRLR 900, [2009] All ER (D) 24 (May),
  EAT; affd on other grounds sub nom Fox v North Cumbria University Hospitals NHS Trust
  [2010] EWCA Civ 729, [2010] IRLR 804, [2010] All ER (D) 267 (Jun) 7.34, 21.19A, 21.21
Potter v R J Temple plc (in liq) (UKEAT/0478/03) (2004) Times, 11 February, [2003] All ER (D)
  327 (Dec), EAT 17.23
Powdrill v Watson [1995] 2 AC 394, [1995] 2 All ER 65, [1995] 2 WLR 312, [1995] ICR 1100,
  [1995] 1 BCLC 386, [1995] NLJR 449, [1995] 17 LS Gaz R 47, sub nom Powdrill and Atkinson
  (as joint administrators of Paramount Airways Ltd) v Watson [1995] IRLR 269, sub nom Powdrill
  v Watson (Paramount Airways Ltd) [1995] BCC 319, HL 29.11
Powell v Brent London Borough Council [1988] ICR 176, [1987] IRLR 466, CA 7.42
Power v Greater Manchester Police Authority (UKEAT/0087/10) (29 April 2010, unreported)
  .... 17.13, 18.56
Power v Panasonic (UK) Ltd [2005] All ER (D) 130 (Jul), EAT 18.72
Power v Panasonic UK Ltd [2003] IRLR 151, 72 BMLR 1, [2002] All ER (D) 297 (Nov), EAT
  .... 10.26
Power v Regent Security Services Ltd [2007] EWCA Civ 1188, [2008] 2 All ER 977, [2008] ICR 442,
  [2008] IRLR 66, [2007] All ER (D) 298 (Nov) 50.29
Power v Trustees of the Open Text (UK) Ltd Group Life Assurance Scheme [2009] EWHC 3064
  (Ch), [2010] SWTI 567, [2009] All ER (D) 236 (Dec) 40.16
Power Packing Casemakers Ltd v Faust [1983] QB 471, [1983] 2 All ER 166, [1983] 2 WLR 439,
  [1983] ICR 292, 127 Sol Jo 187, sub nom Faust v Power Packing Casemakers Ltd [1983] IRLR
  117, CA 51.17
Powerhouse Retail Ltd v Burroughs. See Preston v Wolverhampton Healthcare Trust (No 2)
Practice Direction (Employment Appeal Tribunal Procedure) [2005] IRLR 94 .... 19.7
Practice Direction (Employment Appeal Tribunal Procedure) [2008] IRLR 621 .... 19.7
Practice Statement [2005] IRLR 189a 19.12
Prakash v Wolverhampton City Council [2006] All ER (D) 71 (Nov), EAT 18.10
Prater v Cornwall County Council [2006] EWCA Civ 102, [2006] 2 All ER 1013, [2006] LGR 479,
  [2006] ICR 731, [2006] IRLR 362, [2006] NLJR 372, [2006] All ER (D) 358 (Feb) 14.3, 45.8
Premier Model Management Ltd v Bruce [2012] EWHC 3509 (QB), [2012] NLJR 1564, [2012]
  Lexis Citation 102, [2012] All ER (D) 05 (Dec) 39.8
Premier Motors (Medway) Ltd v Total Oil Great Britain Ltd [1984] 1 WLR 377, [1984] ICR 58,
  [1983] IRLR 471, 128 Sol Jo 151, EAT 50.25
Premier Waste Management Ltd v Towers [2011] EWCA Civ 923, [2012] IRLR 73, [2012] 1 BCLC
  67, [2011] All ER (D) 282 (Jul) 8.17, 8.22, 8.26
Prescription Pricing Authority v Ferguson [2005] CSIH 5, [2005] IRLR 464, 2005 SLT 63,
  2006 SCLR 1, [2005] All ER (D) 355 (Feb) 17.11
Presley v Llanelli Borough Council [1979] ICR 419, [1979] IRLR 381, EAT 17.24
Pressure Coolers Ltd v Molloy (2011) UKEAT/0272/10/RN, UKEAT/0479/10/RN,
  UKEAT/0480/10/RN, [2012] ICR 51, [2011] IRLR 630, EAT 29.10, 50.11
Prest v Mouchel Business Services Ltd (UKEAT/0604/10/DA) [2011] ICR 1345, EAT 21.19B

Prestige Group plc, Re, Commission for Racial Equality v Prestige Group plc [1984] 1 WLR 335, [1984] ICR 473, [1984] IRLR 166, 128 Sol Jo 131, HL 12.25

Preston v President of the Methodist Church [2011] EWCA Civ 1581, [2012] 2 All ER 934, [2012] ICR 432, [2012] IRLR 229, [2012] 03 LS Gaz R 16, [2012] NLJR 67, [2011] All ER (D) 155 (Dec) 7.2

Preston v Wolverhampton Healthcare NHS Trust and Secretary of State for Health [1996] IRLR 484, EAT; affd sub nom Preston v Wolverhampton Healthcare NHS Trust and Secretary of State for Health [1997] 2 CMLR 754, [1997] ICR 899, [1997] IRLR 233, CA; on appeal [1998] 1 All ER 528, [1998] 1 WLR 280, [1998] ICR 227, [1998] IRLR 197, [1998] 08 LS Gaz R 33, 142 Sol Jo LB 82, 566 IRLB 12, HL; refd sub nom Preston v Wolverhampton Healthcare NHS Trust: C-78/98 [2001] 2 AC 415, [2000] ECR I-3201, [2000] All ER (EC) 714, [2001] 2 WLR 408, [2000] 2 CMLR 837, [2000] ICR 961, [2000] IRLR 506, [2000] All ER (D) 663, ECJ; apld sub nom Preston v Wolverhamptom Healthcare NHS Trust (No 2) [2001] UKHL 5, [2001] 2 AC 455, [2001] 3 All ER 947, [2001] 2 WLR 448, [2001] ICR 217, [2001] IRLR 237, (2001) Times, 8 February, 145 Sol Jo LB 55, [2001] All ER (D) 99 (Feb) 17.28, 21.18, 21.19A, 21.19B, 22.2

Preston v Wolverhampton Healthcare Trust (No 2) [2004] EWCA Civ 1281, [2005] ICR 222, (2004) Times, 27 October, 148 Sol Jo LB 1212, [2004] All ER (D) 73 (Oct), sub nom Powerhouse Retail Ltd v Burroughs [2004] IRLR 979; affd sub nom Preston v Wolverhampton Healthcare NHS Trust [2006] UKHL 13, [2006] 3 All ER 193, [2006] ICR 606, (2006) Times, 13 March, [2006] All ER (D) 102 (Mar), sub nom Powerhouse Retail Ltd v Burroughs [2007] 2 CMLR 980, [2006] IRLR 381, 150 Sol Jo LB 364 .... 17.28, 21.18, 50.19

Prestwick Circuits Ltd v McAndrew [1990] IRLR 191, 1990 SLT 654, Ct of Sess 7.22e

Price v Civil Service Commission (No 2) [1978] IRLR 3, Ind Trib 10.35

Price v Surrey County Council (UKEAT/0450/10/SM) (13 September 2011, unreported) 18.56

Prigge v Deutsche Lufthansa AG: C-447/09 [2011] IRLR 1052, [2011] 38 LS Gaz R 19, [2011] All ER (D) 102 (Sep), ECJ 40.5

Printers and Finishers Ltd v Holloway [1964] 3 All ER 54n, [1965] 1 WLR 1, [1965] RPC 239, 108 Sol Jo 521 .... 39.8, 39.13

Prison Officers' Association and Securicor Custodial Services Ltd, Re (2000) IDS Brief 670 ..... 48.29

Procter & Gamble Co v Svenska Cellulosa Aktiebolaget SCA [2012] EWHC 1257 (Ch), [2012] IRLR 733, [2012] All ER (D) 133 (May) 40.6, 50.19

Proform Sports Management Ltd v Proactive Sports Management Ltd [2006] EWHC 2812 (Ch), [2007] 1 All ER 542, [2007] 1 All ER (Comm) 356, [2007] Bus LR 93, [2006] NLJR 1723, (2006) Times, 13 November, [2006] All ER (D) 38 (Nov) 3.11

Project Management Institute v Latif. See Latif v Project Management Institute

Property Guards Ltd v Taylor and Kershaw [1982] IRLR 175, EAT 16.3

Prosecution Appeal (No 28 of 2007), R v Harris [2008] All ER (D) 190 (Feb), CA 41.3

Protectacoat Firthglow Ltd v Szilagyi [2009] EWCA Civ 98, [2009] ICR 835, [2009] IRLR 365, sub nom Szilagyi v Protectacoat Firthglow Ltd [2009] All ER (D) 208 (Feb) 7.12, 14.3, 45.2c

Provident Financial Group plc and Whitegates Estate Agency Ltd v Hayward [1989] 3 All ER 298, [1989] ICR 160, [1989] IRLR 84, CA 7.47c, 39.3, 39.7, 39.14

Prowse-Piper v Anglian Windows Ltd [2010] EWCA Civ 428, [2010] All ER (D) 74 (Nov) 12.8

Pruden v Cunard Ellerman Ltd [1993] IRLR 317, EAT 17.18

Prudential Assurance Co Ltd v London Residuary Body [1992] 2 AC 386, [1992] 3 All ER 504, [1992] 3 WLR 279, 64 P & CR 193, [1992] 2 EGLR 56, [1992] 33 LS Gaz R 36, [1992] NLJR 1087, [1992] 36 EG 129, 136 Sol Jo LB 229, HL 41.2

Prudential Staff Pensions Ltd v The Prudential Assurance Co Ltd [2011] EWHC 960 (Ch), [2011] NLJR 597, [2011] All ER (D) 142 (Apr) 40.16

Przybylska v Modus Telecom Ltd (UKEAT/0566/06/CEA) [2007] All ER (D) 06 (May) 34.3

Public and Commercial Services Union v Minister for the Civil Service [2011] EWHC 2041 (Admin), [2011] IRLR 903, [2011] All ER (D) 56 (Aug), sub nom R (on the application Public and Commercial Services Union) v Minister for the Civil Service [2012] 1 All ER 985 ...... 35.2, 40.9

Puglia v James & Sons [1996] ICR 301, [1996] IRLR 70, EAT 53.12, 53.13

Pulham v Barking and Dagenham London Borough Council [2010] ICR 333, [2010] IRLR 184, [2009] All ER (D) 221 (Dec), EAT 11.9, 21.12

Purdy v Willowbrook International Ltd [1977] IRLR 388, Ind Trib 32.26

Puttick v Eastbourne Borough Council (COIT 3106/2) (1995) unreported 10.35

Table of Cases

Q

QBE Management Services (UK) Ltd v Dymoke [2012] EWHC 80 (QB), [2012] EWHC 116 (QB),
[2012] IRLR 458, [2012] NLJR 180, [2012] All ER (D) 156 (Jan) 8.19, 39.8, 39.14, 39.15
Qua v John Ford Morrison Solicitors [2003] ICR 482, [2003] IRLR 184, (2003) Times, 6 February,
[2003] NLJR 95, [2003] All ER (D) 29 (Jan), EAT 47.15
Quadrant Catering Ltd v Smith (UKEAT/0362/10/RN) (10 December 2010, unreported) 52.9
Qualcast (Wolverhampton) Ltd v Haynes [1959] AC 743, [1959] 2 All ER 38, [1959] 2 WLR 510,
103 Sol Jo 310, HL 25.5
Quarcoopome v Sock Shop Holdings Ltd [1995] IRLR 353, EAT 12.8, 18.10
Quashie v Stringfellows Restaurants Ltd [2012] EWCA Civ 1735, [2013] NLJR 21, 157 Sol Jo (no
1) 31, [2012] All ER (D) 229 (Dec) 14.3
Quashie v Methodist Homes Housing Association (UKEAT/0422/11/DM) [2012] All ER (D) 74
(May), EAT 18.54, 18.58
Quirk v Burton Hospital NHS Trust [2002] EWCA Civ 149, [2002] IRLR 353, (2002) Times,
19 February, [2002] All ER (D) 149 (Feb) 21.17

R

R v Associated Octel Co Ltd [1996] 4 All ER 846, [1996] 1 WLR 1543, [1996] ICR 972, [1997]
IRLR 123, [1997] Crim LR 355, [1996] NLJR 1685, HL 25.19
R v A-G for Northern Ireland, ex p Burns [1999] IRLR 315 .... 17.12, 55.9
R (on the application of McCarthy) v Basildon District Council [2008] EWHC 987 (Admin),
[2008] All ER (D) 118 (May); revsd sub nom McCarthy v Basildon District Council (Equality and
Human Rights Commission intervening) [2009] EWCA Civ 13, [2009] LGR 1013, [2009] BGLR
1013, [2009] All ER (D) 160 (Jan) 11.37, 12.24
R v Boal [1992] QB 591, [1992] 3 All ER 177, [1992] 2 WLR 890, 95 Cr App Rep 272, [1992] ICR
495, [1992] IRLR 420, 156 JP 617, [1992] BCLC 872, [1992] 21 LS Gaz R 26, 136 Sol Jo LB 100,
CA 25.38, 26.13
R v Bow Street Metropolitan Stipendiary Magistrate, ex p Pinochet Ugarte (No 2) [2000] 1 AC 119,
[1999] 1 All ER 577, [1999] 2 WLR 272, 6 BHRC 1, [1999] 1 LRC 1, sub nom Pinochet Ugarte,
Re [1999] NLJR 88, [1999] All ER (D) 18, HL 19.24
R (on the application of Puri) v Bradford Teaching Hospitals NHS Foundation Trust [2011] EWHC
970 (Admin), [2011] IRLR 582, [2011] All ER (D) 156 (Apr) 28.7
R v BBC, ex p Lavelle [1983] 1 All ER 241, [1983] 1 WLR 23, [1983] ICR 99, [1982] IRLR 404, 126
Sol Jo 836 .... 7.42, 56.18
R v British Coal Corpn, ex p Vardy [1993] 1 CMLR 721, [1993] ICR 720, sub nom R v
British Coal Corpn and Secretary of State for Trade and Industry, ex p Vardy [1993] IRLR 104
.... 37.4
R v British Coal Corpn and Secretary of State for Trade and Industry, ex p Price [1994] IRLR 72,
DC 37.4, 52.11
R v British Steel plc [1995] 1 WLR 1356, [1995] ICR 586, [1995] IRLR 310, [1995] Crim LR 654,
CA 25.19, 25.38
R v Burke [1991] 1 AC 135, [1990] 2 All ER 385, [1990] 2 WLR 1313, 90 Cr App Rep 384, 154 JP
798, [1990] Crim LR 877, 22 HLR 433, 134 Sol Jo 1106, [1990] 24 LS Gaz R 43, [1990] NLJR
742, HL 41.3
R (on the application of Cable and Wireless Services UK Ltd) v Central Arbitration Committee
[2008] EWHC 115 (Admin), [2008] ICR 693, [2008] IRLR 425, [2008] All ER (D) 22 (Feb) 48.30
R (on the application of Kwik-Fit (GB) Ltd) v Central Arbitration Committee [2002] EWCA Civ
512, [2002] ICR 1212, [2002] IRLR 395, (2002) Times, 29 March, [2002] All ER (D) 272
(Mar) 48.30
R (on the application of National Union of Journalists) v Central Arbitration Committee [2005]
EWCA Civ 1309, [2006] ICR 1, [2006] IRLR 53, [2005] All ER (D) 299 (Jul) 48.29
R (on the application of the BBC) v Central Arbitration Committee [2003] EWHC 1375 (Admin),
[2003] ICR 1542, [2003] IRLR 460, (2003) Times, 12 June, [2003] All ER (D) 71 (Jun) 48.26
R (on the application of Ultraframe (UK) Ltd) v Central Arbitration Committee [2005] EWCA Civ
560, [2005] ICR 1194, [2005] IRLR 641, (2005) Times, 11 May, [2005] All ER (D) 326 (Apr)
.... 48.32
R v Central Arbitration Committee, ex p BTP Tioxide Ltd [1981] ICR 843, [1982] IRLR 60 . 9.3, 48.8

R v Certification Officer for Trade Unions and Employers' Associations, ex p Electrical Power Engineers' Association [1990] ICR 682, [1990] IRLR 398, HL 48.14

R (on the application T) v Chief Constable of Greater Manchester Police [2012] EWHC 147 (Admin), [2012] 2 Cr App Rep 16, [2012] Crim LR 883, [2012] All ER (D) 154 (Feb); revsd sub nom R (on the application of T) v Chief Constable of Greater Manchester [2013] EWCA Civ 25, [2013] 1 Cr App Rep 344, [2013] All ER (D) 212 (Jan) 16.6, 16.7, 20.4

R (on the application of Pinnington) v Chief Constable of Thames Valley Police [2008] EWHC 1870 (Admin), [2008] All ER (D) 405 (Jul) 16.7

R (on the application of X) v Chief Constable of the West Midlands Police [2004] EWCA Civ 1068, [2005] 1 All ER 610, [2005] 1 WLR 65, [2004] 35 LS Gaz R 34, (2004) Times, 18 August, 148 Sol Jo LB 1119, [2004] All ER (D) 576 (Jul) 16.7

R (on the application of W) v Chief Constable of Warwickshire Police [2012] EWHC 406 (Admin), [2012] All ER (D) 38 (Mar) 20.4

R v Chief Constable of West Midlands Police, ex p Wiley [1995] 1 AC 274, [1994] 3 All ER 420, [1994] 3 WLR 433, 159 LG Rev 181, [1995] 1 Cr App Rep 342, [1994] 40 LS Gaz R 35, [1994] NLJR 1008, 138 Sol Jo LB 156, HL 18.13, 35.7

R v Civil Service Appeal Board, ex p Bruce [1988] 3 All ER 686, [1988] ICR 649, DC; affd sub nom R v Civil Service Appeal Board, ex p Bruce (A–G intervening) [1989] 2 All ER 907, [1989] ICR 171, CA 35.2, 35.6

R v Civil Service Appeal Board, ex p Cunningham [1991] 4 All ER 310, [1992] ICR 816, [1991] IRLR 297, [1991] NLJR 455, CA 35.6

R v Commission for Racial Equality, ex p Cottrell and Rothon [1980] 3 All ER 265, [1980] 1 WLR 1580, 124 Sol Jo 882, 255 Estates Gazette 783 .... 12.25

R v Commission for Racial Equality, ex p Westminster City Council [1984] ICR 770, [1984] IRLR 230; affd [1985] ICR 827, [1985] IRLR 426, CA 10.17, 12.28

R v Davies (David Janway) [2002] EWCA Crim 2949, [2003] ICR 586, [2003] IRLR 170, 147 Sol Jo LB 29, [2003] 09 LS Gaz R 27, (2002) Times, 27 December, [2002] All ER (D) 275 (Dec) 25.37

R v Department of Health, ex p Gandhi [1991] 4 All ER 547, [1991] 1 WLR 1053, [1991] ICR 805, [1991] IRLR 431, DC 11.30, 12.2

R (on the application of Corner House Research) v Director of the Serious Fraud Office (BAE Systems plc, interested party) [2008] UKHL 60, [2009] AC 756, [2008] 4 All ER 927, [2009] Crim LR 47, [2008] NLJR 1149, (2008) Times, 31 July, 152 Sol Jo (no 32) 29, [2009] 1 LRC 343, [2008] All ER (D) 399 (Jul) 35.7

R v Durham County Council, ex p Huddleston [2000] 1 WLR 1484, [2000] 2 CMLR 229, [2000] 1 PLR 122, [2000] 13 LS Gaz R 43, [2000] EGCS 39, [2000] JPL 1125, [2000] All ER (D) 297, CA 22.2

R v F Howe & Son (Engineers) Ltd [1999] 2 All ER 249, [1999] 2 Cr App Rep (S) 37, [1999] IRLR 434, 163 JP 359, [1999] Crim LR 238, [1998] 46 LS Gaz R 34, [1998] All ER (D) 552, CA 25.37

R (on the application of Unison) v First Secretary of State [2006] EWHC 2373 (Admin), [2007] LGR 188, [2006] IRLR 926, [2006] All ER (D) 127 (Sep) 11.9

R v Gateway Foodmarkets Ltd [1997] 3 All ER 78, [1997] 2 Cr App Rep 40, [1997] ICR 382, [1997] IRLR 189, [1997] Crim LR 512, [1997] 03 LS Gaz R 28, 141 Sol Jo LB 28, CA 25.18

R (on the application of Bonhoeffer) v General Medical Council [2011] EWHC 1585 (Admin), [2012] IRLR 37, [2011] All ER (D) 141 (Jun) 28.7

R v Ghosh [1982] QB 1053, [1982] 2 All ER 689, [1982] 3 WLR 110, 75 Cr App Rep 154, 146 JP 376, [1982] Crim LR 608, 126 Sol Jo 429, CA 52.9

R (on the application of Watkins-Singh) v Governing Body of Aberdare Girls' High School [2008] EWHC 1865 (Admin), [2008] 3 FCR 203, [2008] ELR 561, [2008] All ER (D) 376 (Jul) 11.9

R (on the application of E) v Governing Body of JFS (Secretary of State for Children, School and Families, interested parties) (United Synagogue intervening) [2009] UKSC 15, [2010] 2 AC 728, [2010] 1 All ER 319, [2010] 2 WLR 153, [2010] IRLR 136, [2010] PTSR 147, [2010] ELR 26, [2010] NLJR 29, (2009) Times, 17 December, 153 Sol Jo (no 48) 32, 27 BHRC 656, [2009] All ER (D) 163 (Dec) 10.17, 10.20

R (on the application of G) v Governors of X School [2010] EWCA Civ 1, [2010] 2 All ER 555, [2010] 1 WLR 2218, [2010] LGR 207, [2010] IRLR 222, [2010] PTSR 1435, [2010] ELR 235, (2010) Times, 23 February, [2010] All ER (D) 118 (Jan); revsd [2011] UKSC 30, [2012] AC 167, [2011] 4 All ER 625, [2011] 3 WLR 237, [2011] LGR 849, [2011] ICR 1033, [2011] IRLR 756, [2011] PTSR 1230, [2011] NLJR 953, (2011) Times, 4 July, 155 Sol Jo (no 26) 27, [2011] All ER (D) 220 (Jun) 28.7, 52.10

R (on the application of Greenwich Community Law Centre) v Greenwich London Borough Council [2012] EWCA Civ 496, [2012] All ER (D) 157 (May) 11.37

Table of Cases

R (on the application of Domb) v Hammersmith and Fulham London Borough Council [2009] EWCA Civ 941, [2009] LGR 843, 153 Sol Jo (no 34) 30, [2009] BGLR 843, [2009] All ER (D) 42 (Sep) 11.37

R v Hammersmith and Fulham London Borough Council, ex p NALGO [1991] IRLR 249, [1991] COD 397 .... 35.6

R (on the application of Harris) v Haringey London Borough Council (Equality and Human Rights Commission intervening) [2010] EWCA Civ 703, [2010] LGR 713, [2010] EqLR 98, [2010] All ER (D) 177 (Jun) 11.37

R v Hull University Visitor, ex p Page [1991] 4 All ER 747, [1991] 1 WLR 1277, [1992] ICR 67, CA; on appeal sub nom R v Lord President of the Privy Council, ex p Page [1993] AC 682, [1992] 3 WLR 1112, [1993] ICR 114, [1993] 10 LS Gaz R 33, 137 Sol Jo LB 45, sub nom Page v Hull University Visitor [1993] 1 All ER 97, [1993] NLJR 15, HL 7.14

R (on the application of Professional Contractors Group Ltd) v IRC [2001] EWCA Civ 1945, [2002] STC 165, 74 TC 393, 4 ITLR 483, [2002] 09 LS Gaz R 31, 146 Sol Jo LB 21, [2001] All ER (D) 356 (Dec) 44.34

R v Islington London Borough Council, ex p Building Employers' Confederation [1989] IRLR 382, 45 BLR 45, DC 12.32

R v Kirk: 63/83 [1985] 1 All ER 453, [1984] ECR 2689, [1984] 3 CMLR 522, ECJ 28.5

R (on the application of Lock) v Leicester City Council [2012] EWHC 2058 (Admin) 35.6

R v Local Authority and Police Authority in the Midlands, ex p LM [2000] 1 FCR 736, [2000] 1 FLR 612, [2000] Fam Law 83 .... 16.7

R v London (North) Industrial Tribunal, ex p Associated Newspapers Ltd [1998] ICR 1212, [1998] IRLR 569, [1998] All ER (D) 181 .... 12.11, 18.18, 18.51

R v Lord Chancellor's Department, ex p Nangle [1992] 1 All ER 897, [1991] ICR 743, [1991] IRLR 343 .... 35.2

R v Lord President of the Privy Council, ex p Page. See R v Hull University Visitor, ex p Page

R v Mara [1987] 1 All ER 478, [1987] 1 WLR 87, [1987] ICR 165, [1987] IRLR 154, 131 Sol Jo 132, [1986] LS Gaz R 3751, CA 25.19, 25.38

R (on the application of L) v Metropolitan Police Comr [2006] EWHC 482 (Admin), [2006] All ER (D) 262 (Mar); affd [2007] EWCA Civ 168, [2007] 4 All ER 128, [2008] 1 WLR 681, (2007) Times, 28 March, [2007] All ER (D) 19 (Mar); affd [2009] UKSC 3, [2010] 1 AC 410, [2010] 1 All ER 113, [2009] 3 WLR 1056, [2010] PTSR 245, [2010] 2 FCR 25, [2010] 1 FLR 643, [2010] Fam Law 21, [2009] NLJR 1549, 153 Sol Jo (no 42) 30, 28 BHRC 391, [2009] All ER (D) 296 (Oct) 16.7

R (on the application of Kirk) v Middlesbrough Borough Council [2010] EWHC 1035 (Admin), [2010] IRLR 699, [2010] 2 FLR 1144, [2010] Fam Law 799 .... 28.7, 35.6

R (on the application Public and Commercial Services Union) v Minister for the Civil Service [2010] EWHC 1027 (Admin), [2010] ICR 1198, (2010) Times, 24 May, [2010] All ER (D) 70 (May) 35.2

R (on the application Public and Commercial Services Union) v Minister for the Civil Service [2011] EWHC 2041. See Public and Commercial Services Union v Minister for the Civil Service

R (on the application of Manson (Finian)) v Ministry of Defence [2005] EWHC 427 (Admin), [2005] All ER (D) 270 (Feb); affd [2005] EWCA Civ 1678, [2006] ICR 355, [2005] All ER (D) 69 (Nov) 22.2, 30.4, 30.22, 30.26

R (on the application of the British Gurkha Welfare Society) v Ministry of Defence [2010] EWCA Civ 1098, [2010] 1 WLR 1067, [2010] All ER (D) 131 (Oct) 11.9

R v Nelson Group Services (Maintenance) Ltd [1998] 4 All ER 331, [1999] 1 WLR 1526, [1999] ICR 1004, [1999] IRLR 646, CA 25.19

R (on the application of Shoesmith) v Ofsted [2010] EWHC 852 (Admin), [2011] PTSR D13, 154 Sol Jo (no 17) 27, [2010] All ER (D) 162 (Apr); revsd in part [2011] EWCA Civ 64, [2011] All ER (D) 293 (May) 35.6

R (on the application of Davies) v Pennine Acute Hospitals [2010] EWHC 2887 (Admin) 35.6

R v Registrar General, ex p Segerdal [1970] 2 QB 697, [1970] 3 All ER 886, [1970] 3 WLR 479, [1970] RA 439, 114 Sol Jo 703, CA 10.22

R v Rhone-Poulenc Rorer Ltd [1996] ICR 1054, [1996] Crim LR 656, [1996] 02 LS Gaz R 27, 140 Sol Jo LB 39, CA 25.19

R v Rollco Screw and Rivet Co Ltd [1999] 2 Cr App Rep (S) 436, [1999] IRLR 439, CA . 25.37, 25.38

R v Science Museum (Board of Trustees) [1994] IRLR 25, 158 JP 39, CA 25.19

R (on the application of Age UK) v Secretary of State for Business, Innovation & Skills [2009] EWHC 2336 (Admin), [2010] 1 CMLR 671, [2010] ICR 260, [2009] IRLR 1017, [2009] NLJR 1401, (2009) Times, 8 October, 153 Sol Jo (no 37) 36, [2009] All ER (D) 141 (Sep) .. 11.9, 11.15, 40.3, 40.5

R (on the application of Baker) v Secretary of State for Communities and Local Government [2008] EWCA Civ 141, [2008] LGR 239, [2008] All ER (D) 412 (Feb) 11.37

R (on the application of Coombes) v Secretary of State for Communities and Local Government [2010] EWHC 666 (Admin), [2010] 2 All ER 940, [2010] 11 EG 120 (CS), (2010) Times, 11 May, sub nom Coombes v Waltham Forest London Borough Council [2010] 2 All ER (D) 940 (Mar)
.... 41.3

R (on the application of Elias) v Secretary of State for Defence [2006] EWCA Civ 1293, [2006] 1 WLR 3213, [2006] IRLR 934, (2006) Times, 17 October, [2006] All ER (D) 104 (Oct) 10.34, 11.9, 12.16, 12.18

R (on the application of Mohammed) v Secretary of State for Defence [2007] EWCA Civ 1023, (2007) Times, 9 May, 151 Sol Jo LB 610, [2007] All ER (D) 09 (May) 11.21

R (on the application of Williamson) v Secretary of State for Education and Employment [2001] EWHC 960 (Admin), [2002] 1 FLR 493, [2002] Fam Law 257, [2002] ELR 214, [2001] All ER (D) 405 (Nov); affd [2002] EWCA Civ 1926, [2003] QB 1300, [2003] 1 All ER 385, [2003] 3 WLR 482, [2003] 1 FCR 1, [2003] 1 FLR 726, [2003] ELR 176, [2003] 09 LS Gaz R 27, (2002) Times, 18 December, [2002] All ER (D) 192 (Dec); affd on other grounds [2005] UKHL 15, [2005] 2 AC 246, [2005] 2 All ER 1, [2005] 2 WLR 590, [2005] 1 FCR 498, [2005] 2 FLR 374, [2005] NLJR 324, (2005) Times, 25 February, 149 Sol Jo LB 266, 19 BHRC 99, [2005] 5 LRC 670, [2005] All ER (D) 380 (Feb) 10.22

R v Secretary of State for Employment, ex p Equal Opportunities Commission [1993] 1 All ER 1022, [1993] 1 WLR 872, [1993] 1 CMLR 915, [1993] ICR 251, [1993] IRLR 10, [1993] NLJR 332n, CA; on appeal [1995] 1 AC 1, [1994] 2 WLR 409, [1995] 1 CMLR 391, 92 LGR 360, [1994] IRLR 176, [1994] 18 LS Gaz R 43, [1994] NLJR 358, sub nom Equal Opportunities Commission v Secretary of State for Employment [1994] 1 All ER 910, [1994] ICR 317, HL 6.1, 10.35, 12.24, 21.12, 22.2

R v Secretary of State for Employment, ex p Seymour-Smith and Perez [1996] All ER (EC) 1, [1995] ICR 889, [1995] IRLR 464, CA; revsd sub nom R v Secretary of State for Employment, ex p Seymour-Smith [1997] 2 All ER 273, [1997] 1 WLR 473, [1997] 2 CMLR 904, [1997] ICR 371, 566 IRLB 15, sub nom R v Secretary of State for Employment, ex p Seymour-Smith and Perez [1997] IRLR 315, HL; refd sub nom R v Secretary of State for Employment, ex p Seymour-Smith: C-167/97 [1999] 2 AC 554, [1999] ECR I-623, [1999] All ER (EC) 97, [1999] 3 WLR 460, [1999] 2 CMLR 273, [1999] ICR 447, [1999] IRLR 253, ECJ; apld sub nom R v Secretary of State for Employment, ex p Seymour-Smith (No 2) [2000] 1 All ER 857, [2000] 1 WLR 435, [2000] 1 CMLR 770, [2000] ICR 244, [2000] IRLR 263, [2000] 09 LS Gaz R 40, HL 10.34, 11.9, 21.3, 21.11, 22.2, 51.11

R (on the application of Mohamed) v Secretary of State for Foreign and Commonwealth Affairs [2010] EWCA Civ 65, [2010] 4 All ER 91, [2010] 3 WLR 554, (2010) Times, 16 February, [2010] All ER (D) 118 (Feb) 35.7

R v Secretary of State for Foreign and Commonwealth Affairs, ex p Council of Civil Service Unions. See Council of Civil Service Unions v Minister for the Civil Service

R (on the application of Cockburn) v Secretary of State for Health [2011] EWHC 2095 (Admin), [2011] All ER (D) 18 (Aug) 40.9

R (on the application of Wright) v Secretary of State for Health [2009] UKHL 3, [2009] AC 739, [2009] 2 All ER 129, [2009] 2 WLR 267, [2009] PTSR 401, 106 BMLR 71, (2009) Times, 23 January, 153 Sol Jo (no 4) 30, 26 BHRC 269, [2009] All ER (D) 150 (Jan) 28.7

R (on the application of Low) v Secretary of State for the Home Department [2009] EWHC 35 (Admin), [2009] 2 CMLR 539, [2009] All ER (D) 175 (Jan); affd [2010] EWCA Civ 4, [2010] 2 CMLR 909, [2010] ICR 755, [2010] All ER (D) 66 (Jan) 23.3

R (on the application of the Royal College of Nursing) v Secretary of State for the Home Department [2010] EWHC 2761 (Admin), [2011] Fam Law 231, 154 Sol Jo (no 46) 30, 117 BMLR 10, [2010] All ER (D) 103 (Nov) 16.8

R v Secretary of State for the Home Department, ex p Brind [1991] 1 AC 696, [1991] 2 WLR 588, 135 Sol Jo 250, sub nom Brind v Secretary of State for the Home Department [1991] 1 All ER 720, HL 28.5

R v Secretary of State for the Home Department, ex p Narin [1990] 2 CMLR 233, [1990] Imm AR 403, [1990] COD 417, CA 23.2

Table of Cases

R (on the application of B) v Secretary of State for the Home Department and Metropolitan Police Comr [2006] EWHC 579 (Admin), [2006] All ER (D) 370 (Mar) 16.7

R (on the application of Amicus – MSF section) v Secretary of State for Trade and Industry [2004] EWHC 860 (Admin), [2007] ICR 1176, [2004] IRLR 430, [2004] ELR 311, [2004] All ER (D) 238 (Apr) 11.7, 11.14, 28.7

R (on the application of the Broadcasting, Entertainment, Cinematographic and Theatre Union) v Secretary of State for Trade and Industry: C-173/99 [2001] ECR I-4881, [2001] All ER (EC) 647, [2001] 1 WLR 2313, [2001] 3 CMLR 109, [2001] ICR 1152, [2001] IRLR 559, [2001] All ER (D) 272 (Jun), ECJ 22.11, 27.2

R v Secretary of State for Trade and Industry, ex p Trades Union Congress [2001] 1 CMLR 5, [2000] Eu LR 698, [2000] IRLR 565; affd [2001] 1 CMLR 8, CA 22.6

R v Secretary of State for Trade and Industry, ex p UNISON [1997] 1 CMLR 459, [1996] ICR 1003, [1996] IRLR 438 .... 37.6

R (on the application of United Road Transport Union) v Secretary of State for Transport [2012] EWHC 1909 (Admin), [2012] IRLR 941, [2012] All ER (D) 156 (Jul) 55.35

R v Secretary of State for Transport, ex p Factortame Ltd (No 2) [1991] 1 AC 603, [1990] 3 WLR 818, [1990] 3 CMLR 375, [1990] 2 Lloyd's Rep 365n, [1991] 1 Lloyd's Rep 10, 134 Sol Jo 1189, [1990] 41 LS Gaz R 36, [1990] NLJR 1457, sub nom Factortame Ltd v Secretary of State for Transport (No 2) [1991] 1 All ER 70, HL 22.2

R v Securities and Futures Authority Ltd, ex p Fleurose [2001] EWCA Civ 2015, [2002] IRLR 297, (2002) Times, 15 January, [2001] All ER (D) 361 (Dec) 28.7

R v Southampton Industrial Tribunal, ex p INS News Group Ltd [1995] IRLR 247 ...... 18.18, 18.51

R v Transco [2006] EWCA Crim 838, [2006] 2 Cr App Rep (S) 740, [2006] All ER (D) 416 (Mar), CA 25.38

R (on the application of Malik) v Waltham Forest Primary Care Trust [2006] EWHC 487 (Admin), [2006] 3 All ER 71, [2006] ICR 1111, [2006] IRLR 526, 90 BMLR 49,1 (2006) Times, 26 May, [2006] All ER (D) 260 (Mar); revsd sub nom R (on the application of Malik) v Waltham Forest NHS Primary Care Trust (Secretary of State for Health, interested party) [2007] EWCA Civ 265, [2007] 4 All ER 832, [2007] 1 WLR 2092, [2007] ICR 1101, [2007] IRLR 529, (2007) Times, 10 April , [2007] All ER (D) 462 (Mar) 28.7

RCO Support Services Ltd v UNISON [2000] ICR 1502, [2000] IRLR 624, EAT; affd [2002] EWCA Civ 464, [2002] ICR 751, [2002] IRLR 401, [2002] All ER (D) 50 (Apr) 50.5

RDF Media Group plc v Clements [2007] EWHC 2892 (QB), [2008] IRLR 207, [2007] All ER (D) 53 (Dec) 39.11, 56.6

RS Components Ltd v Irwin [1974] 1 All ER 41, [1973] ICR 535, [1973] IRLR 239, NIRC 52.14

Rabahallah v British Telecommunications plc [2005] ICR 440, [2005] IRLR 184, [2004] All ER (D) 411 (Nov), EAT 17.8

Radakovits v Abbey National plc [2009] EWCA Civ 1346, [2010] IRLR 307, [2010] All ER (D) 16 (Mar) 17.11

Radecki v Kirklees Metropolitan Borough Council [2009] EWCA Civ 298, [2009] ICR 1244, [2009] All ER (D) 109 (Apr), sub nom Kirklees Metropolitan Borough Council v Radecki [2009] IRLR 555 .... 17.23, 51.5, 51.13

Rahman v Comr of Police of the Metropolis (UKEATPA/0076/09/RN) (25 April 2012, unreported) 35.7

Rai v Somerfield Stores Ltd [2004] ICR 656, [2004] IRLR 124, EAT 17.24, 46.5

Rainey v Greater Glasgow Health Board [1987] AC 224, [1987] 1 All ER 65, [1986] 3 WLR 1017, [1987] 2 CMLR 11, [1987] ICR 129, [1987] IRLR 26, 130 Sol Jo 954, [1987] LS Gaz R 188, [1986] NLJ Rep 1161, 1987 SC (HL) 1, 1987 SLT 146, HL 11.9, 21.12

Raja v Secretary of State for Justice (UKEAT/0364/09/CEA) [2010] All ER (D) 134 (Mar) . 9.17, 18.6

Ralton v Havering College of Further and Higher Education [2001] 3 CMLR 1452, [2001] IRLR 738, [2001] All ER (D) 297 (Jun), EAT 50.29

Ramdoolar v Bycity Ltd [2005] ICR 368, [2004] All ER (D) 21 (Nov), EAT 31.16

Ramsay v Bowercross Construction Ltd (UKEAT/0534/07) [2008] All ER (D) 131 (Aug) 18.70

Ramsden v David Sharratt & Sons Ltd (1930) 35 Com Cas 314, HL 39.11

Rance v Secretary of State for Health [2007] IRLR 665, [2007] All ER (D) 81 (May), EAT 19.33, 21.19A

Rank Nemo (DMS) Ltd v Coutinho [2009] EWCA Civ 454, [2009] ICR 1296, [2009] IRLR 672, (2009) Times, 8 June 12.2, 18.66

Rank Xerox Ltd v Churchill [1988] vIRLR 280, EAT 7.22e

Rank Xerox (UK) Ltd v Stryczek [1995] IRLR 568, EAT 53.3

Rankin v British Coal Corpn [1995] ICR 774, [1993] IRLR 69, EAT 22.2

Rao v Civil Aviation Authority [1994] ICR 495, [1994] IRLR 240, CA 53.13
Rask and Christensen v ISS Kantineservice A/S: C-209/91 [1992] ECR I-5755, [1993] IRLR 133,
ECJ 50.5
Ratcliffe v North Yorkshire County Council. See North Yorkshire County Council v Ratcliffe
Ravat v Halliburton Manufacturing & Services Ltd [2008] All ER (D) 82 (Dec), EAT; revsd [2010]
CSIH 52, [2010] IRLR 1053, 2010 SC 698, 2011 SLT 44, 2010 SCLR 718, Ct of Sess; affd sub
nom Ravat v Halliburton Manufacturing and Services Ltd [2012] UKSC 1, [2012] 2 All ER 905,
[2012] ICR 389, [2012] IRLR 315, 156 Sol Jo (no 6) 31, [2012] 08 LS Gaz R 19, [2012] NLJR
262, (2012) Times, 15 February, [2012] All ER (D) 49 (Feb) 11.18, 23.9, 51.15
Ravenseft Properties Ltd v Hall [2001] EWCA Civ 2034, [2002] HLR 624, [2002] 11 EG 156, (2002)
Times, 15 January, [2001] All ER (D) 318 (Dec) 41.5
Rawlings v Direct Garage Door Co Ltd (ET/2800547/06) unreported 27.6
Read v Astoria Garage (Streatham) Ltd [1952] Ch 637, [1952] 2 All ER 292, [1952] 2 TLR 130,
CA 8.3, 56.10
Read v Phoenix Preservation Ltd [1985] ICR 164, [1985] IRLR 93, [1985] LS Gaz R 43, EAT
.... 52.9
Readman v Devon Primary Care Trust (UKEAT/0116/11/ZT) (1 December 2011, unreported)
.... 19.17, 19.27
Readman v Devon Primary Care Trust [2013] All ER (D) 100 (Feb), CA 36.12
Ready Mixed Concrete (South East) Ltd v Minister of Pensions and National Insurance [1968] 2 QB
497, [1968] 1 All ER 433, [1968] 2 WLR 775, 112 Sol Jo 14 .... 14.3
Red Bank Manufacturing Co Ltd v Meadows [1992] ICR 204, [1992] IRLR 209, EAT 19.25, 53.13
Reda v Flag Ltd [2002] UKPC 38, [2002] IRLR 747, [2002] All ER (D) 201 (Jul) . 7.22d, 7.22e, 42.13,
46.6, 56.15
Redcar and Cleveland Borough Council v Bainbridge [2008] ICR 249, [2007] IRLR 91,
[2006] All ER (D) 197 (Nov), EAT; affd sub nom Bainbridge v Redcar and Cleveland
Borough Council [2007] IRLR 494, [2007] All ER (D) 409 (Mar), EAT; revsd in part [2008]
EWCA Civ 885, [2009] ICR 133, [2008] IRLR 776, [2008] All ER (D) 386 (Jul) 11.9, 12.24, 12.33,
21.8, 21.10, 21.12, 21.19, 21.19B, 21.21
Reddington v Straker & Sons Ltd [1994] ICR 172, EAT 18.3, 18.10, 18.41
Redfearn v Serco Ltd (t/a West Yorkshire Transport Service) [2005] IRLR 744, [2005] All ER (D)
98 (Sep), EAT; revsd [2006] EWCA Civ 659, [2006] ICR 1367, [2006] IRLR 623, (2006) Times,
27 June, 150 Sol Jo LB 703, [2006] All ER (D) 366 (May) 10.20, 11.9, 28.7
Redfearn v United Kingdom (Application 47335/06) [2013] IRLR 15, [2012] NLJR 1466, (2013)
Times, 10 January, 33 BHRC 713, [2012] ECHR 47335/06, [2012] All ER (D) 112 (Nov),
ECtHR 28.4, 28.7, 51.11
Redmond (Dr Sophie) Stichting v Bartol: C-29/91 [1992] ECR I-3189, [1994] 3 CMLR 265, [1992]
IRLR 366, ECJ 50.4, 50.5
Redrow Homes (Yorkshire) Ltd v Buckborough & Sewell [2009] IRLR 34, [2008] All ER (D) 186
(Nov), EAT 7.12, 14.3
Redundant Employee v McNally (Inspector of Taxes). See Ibe v McNally
Reed and Bull Information Systems Ltd v Stedman [1999] IRLR 299, EAT 10.39, 10.51
Reed in Partnership Ltd v Fraine (UKEAT/0520/10/DA) (8 April 2011, unreported) 17.25
Rees v Apollo Watch Repairs plc [1996] ICR 466, EAT 10.31
Refreshment Systems Ltd (t/a Northern Vending Services) v Wolstenholme (UKEAT/608/03)
(2004) Times, 2 March, sub nom Wolstenholme v Refreshment Systems Ltd (t/a Northern
Vending Services) [2004] All ER (D) 185 (Mar) 19.3
Regent Security Services Ltd v Power [2007] EWCA Civ 1188, [2008] 2 All ER 977, [2008] ICR 442,
[2008] IRLR 66, [2007] All ER (D) 298 (Nov) 40.7
Reid v Camphill Engravers [1990] ICR 435, [1990] IRLR 268, EAT 17.31, 32.8
Reid v Explosives Co Ltd (1887) 19 QBD 264, 56 LJQB 388, 35 WR 509, [1886-90] All ER Rep
712, 57 LT 439, 3 TLR 588, CA 29.10, 56.9
Reid v Rush & Tompkins Group plc [1989] 3 All ER 228, [1990] 1 WLR 212, [1990] RTR 144,
[1989] 2 Lloyd's Rep 167, [1990] ICR 61, [1989] IRLR 265, CA 26.16
Relaxion Group plc v Rhys-Harper [2003] UKHL 33, [2003] 4 All ER 1113, [2003] 2 CMLR 1329,
[2003] ICR 867, [2003] IRLR 484, 74 BMLR 109, [2003] 30 LS Gaz R 30, (2003) Times, 23 June,
147 Sol Jo LB 782, [2003] All ER (D) 258 (Jun) 9.17, 10.50, 12.6, 38.4
Renfrewshire Council v Educational Institute of Scotland (2012) UKEATS/18/12, [2013] ICR
172 .... 37.4
Rentokil Ltd v Mackin [1989] IRLR 286, EAT 52.9

Table of Cases

Retarded Children's Aid Society Ltd v Day [1978] 1 WLR 763, [1978] ICR 437, [1978] IRLR 128,
122 Sol Jo 385, CA 19.35
Revenue and Customs Comrs v Stringer. See Ainsworth v IRC
Revenue and Customs Comrs v Thorn Baker Ltd [2007] EWCA Civ 626, 79 TC 1, [2008] ICR 46,
(2007) Times, 27 July, 151 Sol Jo LB 890, [2007] All ER (D) 319 (Jun) 42.4, 45.9
Rewe-Zentralfinanz GmbH v Landwirtschaftskammer für Saarland: 33/76 [1976] ECR 1989,
[1977] 1 CMLR 533, CMR 8382, ECJ 22.2
Rex Stewart Jeffries Parker Ginsberg Ltd v Parker [1988] IRLR 483, CA 56.21
Reyners v Belgium: 2/74 [1974] ECR 631, [1974] 2 CMLR 305, ECJ 22.2
Rhondda Cynon Taff Borough Council v Close [2008] IRLR 868, sub nom Close v Rhondda Cynon
Taff Borough Council [2008] All ER (D) 278 (Jun), EAT 52.9
Richardson (HM Inspector of Taxes) v Delaney [2001] STC 1328, 74 TC 167, [2001] IRLR 663,
(2001) Times, 11 July, [2001] All ER (D) 74 (Jun) 46.10
Richardson v Koefod [1969] 3 All ER 1264, [1969] 1 WLR 1812, 113 Sol Jo 898, CA 56.15
Richardson v U Mole Ltd [2005] ICR 1664, [2005] IRLR 668, [2005] All ER (D) 80 (Jul), EAT
.... 17.16, 17.34, 19.10
Richmond Pharmacology Ltd v Dhaliwal [2009] IRLR 336, [2009] All ER (D) 158 (Feb), EAT
.... 10.39
Richmond Precision Engineering Ltd v Pearce [1985] IRLR 179, EAT 52.14
Rickard v PB Glass Supplies Ltd [1990] ICR 150, CA 32.8
Ridehalgh v Horsefield [1994] Ch 205, [1994] 3 All ER 848, [1994] 3 WLR 462, [1994] 2 FLR 194,
[1994] Fam Law 560, [1994] BCC 390, CA 18.74
Ridout v T C Group [1998] IRLR 628, EAT 10.37
Rigby v Ferodo Ltd [1988] ICR 29, [1987] IRLR 516, HL 56.24
Riley v Tesco Stores Ltd [1980] ICR 323, [1980] IRLR 103, CA 17.25
Riley-Williams v Argos Ltd (EAT/811/02) (2003) 147 SJLB 695, [2003] All ER (D) 58 (Jul)
.... 47.4
Rinner-Kühn v FWW Spezial-Gebäudereinigung GmbH & Co KG: 171/88 [1989] ECR 2743,
[1993] 2 CMLR 932, [1989] IRLR 493, ECJ 21.3, 21.11
Riordan v War Office [1959] 3 All ER 552, [1959] 1 WLR 1046, 103 Sol Jo 921; affd [1960] 3 All ER
774n, [1961] 1 WLR 210, CA 46.20, 51.5, 51.10, 56.5, 56.43
Roach v CSB (Moulds) Ltd [1991] ICR 349, [1991] IRLR 200, EAT 6.6
Roach v Home Office [2009] EWHC 312 (QB), [2010] QB 256, [2009] 3 All ER 510, [2010] 2 WLR
746, [2009] NLJR 474, [2009] 2 Costs LR 287, [2009] All ER (D) 164 (Mar) 25.47
Robb v Green [1895] 2 QB 1, 59 JP 695, 64 LJQB 593, 44 WR 26, 39 Sol Jo 382, 72 LT 686, 11 TLR
330; affd [1895] 2 QB 315, 59 JP 695, 64 LJQB 593, 14 R 580, 44 WR 25, [1895–9] All ER Rep
1053, 39 Sol Jo 653, 73 LT 15, 11 TLR 517, CA 39.13
Robb v Hammersmith and Fulham London Borough Council [1991] ICR 514, [1991] IRLR 72
.... 7.42
Robert Cort & Son Ltd v Charman [1981] ICR 816, [1981] IRLR 437, EAT 46.9, 51.13
Roberts v Acumed Ltd (UKEAT/0466/09/DA) (25 November 2010, unreported) 52.14
Roberts v Birds Eye Walls Ltd. See Birds Eye Walls Ltd v Roberts
Roberts v Carling (UKEAT/0183/09) (8 October 2009, unreported) 19.23
Roberts v Skelmersdale College [2003] EWCA Civ 954, [2003] ICR 1127, [2004] IRLR 69,
[2003] All ER (D) 272 (Jun) 18.54
Roberts v West Coast Trains Ltd [2004] EWCA Civ 900, [2005] ICR 254, [2004] IRLR 788, [2004]
28 LS Gaz R 33, (2004) Times, 25 June, [2004] All ER (D) 147 (Jun) 53.2
Robertson v Bexley Community Centre (t/a Leisure Link) [2003] EWCA Civ 576, [2003] IRLR 434,
[2003] All ER (D) 151 (Mar) 12.7, 17.29, 17.30
Robertson v Blackstone Franks Investment Management Ltd [1998] IRLR 376, CA 32.6, 32.8
Robertson v British Gas Corpn [1983] ICR 351, [1983] IRLR 302, CA 5.11, 7.6
Robertson v Department for Environment Food and Rural Affairs [2005] EWCA Civ 138, [2005]
ICR 750, [2005] IRLR 363, (2005) Times, 2 March, [2005] All ER (D) 335 (Feb) 21.9
Robertson v Magnet Ltd (Retail Division) [1993] IRLR 512, EAT 53.13
Robertson and Rough v Forth Road Bridge Joint Board [1995] IRLR 251, Ct of Sess 25.8
Robins v Secretary of State for Work and Pensions: C-278/05 [2007] ECR I-1053, [2007] All ER
(EC) 648, [2007] 2 CMLR 269, [2007] ICR 779, [2007] IRLR 270, (2007) Times, 30 January,
[2007] All ER (D) 195 (Jan), ECJ 29.7
Robinson v Oddbins Ltd [1996] 27 DCLD 1 .... 10.35
Robinson v Post Office [2000] IRLR 804, [2000] All ER (D) 1304, EAT 12.7, 17.30
Robinson v Tescom Corpn [2008] IRLR 408, [2008] All ER (D) 10 (Mar), EAT 51.5, 51.7

Robinson v Ulster Carpet Mills Ltd [1991] IRLR 348, NI CA 52.4
Robinson-Steele v RD Retail Services Ltd: C-131/04 [2006] ECR I-2531, [2006] All ER (EC) 749,
 [2006] ICR 932, [2006] IRLR 386, (2006) Times, 22 March, [2006] All ER (D) 238 (Mar), ECJ
 .... 19.2, 19.48, 27.4, 55.25
Rock-it Cargo Ltd v Green [1997] IRLR 581, EAT 7.44, 18.35
Rock Refrigeration Ltd v Jones and Seward Refrigeration Ltd [1997] 1 All ER 1, [1997] ICR 938,
 [1996] IRLR 675, [1996] 41 LS Gaz R 29, 140 Sol Jo LB 226, CA 39.11, 56.34
Rockfon A/S v Specialarbejderforbundet i Danmark: C-449/93 [1995] ECR I-4291, [1996] ICR 673,
 [1996] IRLR 168, ECJ 37.4
Roebuck v National Union of Mineworkers (Yorkshire Area) [1977] ICR 573, 121 Sol Jo 709 .... 49.15
Roger Bullivant Ltd v Ellis [1987] FSR 172, [1987] ICR 464, [1987] IRLR 491, CA 39.15
Rolls-Royce Ltd v Walpole [1980] IRLR 343, EAT 52.8
Rolls-Royce Motor Cars Ltd v Price [1993] IRLR 203, EAT ,,,,,,,,,,,,,,,,, 52.11
Rolls-Royce Motors Ltd v Dewhurst [1985] ICR 869, [1985] IRLR 184, EAT 52.11
Rolls-Royce plc v Doughty. See Doughty v Rolls-Royce plc
Rolls Royce plc v Riddle [2008] IRLR 873, EAT 18.17, 18.54
Rolls-Royce plc v Unite the Union [2009] EWCA Civ 387, [2010] 1 WLR 318, [2010] ICR 1, [2009]
 IRLR 576, [2009] 21 LS Gaz R 15, (2009) Times, 27 May, 153 Sol Jo (no 20) 38, [2009] All ER
 (D) 131 (May) 11.9, 11.15
Romer v Freie und Hansestadt Hamburg: C-147/08 [2013] 2 CMLR 259, [2011] All ER (D) 212
 (May), ECJ 11.14
Rookes v Barnard [1964] AC 1129, [1964] 1 All ER 367, [1964] 2 WLR 269, [1964] 1 Lloyd's Rep
 28, 108 Sol Jo 93, HL 12.18
Ros and Angel v Fanstone (UKEAT/0372/07) unreported 38.2
Rose v Plenty [1976] 1 All ER 97, [1976] 1 WLR 141, [1976] 1 Lloyd's Rep 263, [1975] ICR 430,
 [1976] IRLR 60, 119 Sol Jo 592, CA 54.2
Rosenbladt (Gisela) v Oellerking Gebaudereinigungsges mbH: C-45/09 [2011] 1 CMLR 1011,
 [2011] IRLR 51, [2010] All ER (D) 101 (Oct), ECJ 11.9, 40.5
Ross v Delrosa Caterers Ltd [1981] ICR 393, EAT 6.12
Ross v Eddie Stobart Ltd (UKEAT/0085/10/CEA) (16 May 2011, unreported) 55.24
Ross v Parkyns (1875) LR 20 Eq 331, 44 LJ Ch 610, 24 WR 5 .... 14.3
Rousillon v Rousillon (1880) 14 Ch D 351, 44 JP 663, 49 LJ Ch 338, 28 WR 623, 42 LT 679
 .... 39.12
Rovenska v General Medical Council [1998] ICR 85, [1997] IRLR 367, CA 12.6, 17.29
Rowan v Machinery Installations (South Wales) Ltd [1981] ICR 386, [1981] IRLR 122, EAT
 .... 6.12
Rowell v Hubbard Group Services Ltd [1995] IRLR 195, EAT 52.11
Rowley v Cerberus Software Ltd. See Cerberus Software Ltd v Rowley
Rowstock Ltd v Jessemy (26 September 2012, unreported), EAT 40.3
Roy v Kensington and Chelsea and Westminster Family Practitioner Committee [1992] 1 AC 624,
 [1992] 1 All ER 705, [1992] 2 WLR 239, [1992] IRLR 233, 8 BMLR 9, [1992] 17 LS Gaz R 48,
 136 Sol Jo LB 62, HL 35.6
Royal Bank of Scotland v Donaghay (UKEATS/0049/10/BI) (11 November 2011, unreported)
 .... 52.9
Royal Bank of Scotland v Nwosuagwu-Ibe (UKEAT/0594/10/ZT) (22 September 2011,
 unreported) 52.9
Royal Mail Group Ltd v Communication Workers Union. See Communication Workers Union v
 Royal Mail Group Ltd
Royal National Lifeboat Institution v Bushaway [2005] IRLR 674, [2005] All ER (D) 307 (Apr),
 EAT 14.3, 45.2c
Royal National Orthopaedic Hospital Trust v Howard [2002] IRLR 849, [2002] All ER (D) 54 (Aug),
 EAT 18.32
Royal Philanthropic Society v County (1985) 18 HLR 83, 129 Sol Jo 854, [1985] 2 EGLR 109, 276
 Estates Gazette 1068, CA 41.2
Royal Society for the Prevention of Cruelty to Animals v Cruden [1986] ICR 205, [1986] IRLR 83,
 EAT 52.10
Royal Society for the Protection of Birds v Croucher [1984] ICR 604, [1984] IRLR 425, EAT
 .... 52.10
Rubenstein and Roskin (t/a McGuffics Dispensing Chemists) v McGloughlin [1997] ICR 318,
 [1996] IRLR 557, EAT 19.46, 53.13

Table of Cases

Ruffert (Dirk) v Land Niedersachsen: C-346/06 [2008] ECR I-1989, [2008] All ER (EC) 902, [2008] IRLR 467, [2008] All ER (D) 37 (Apr), ECJ 23.3
Rugamer v Sony Music Entertainment UK Ltd [2002] ICR 381, [2001] IRLR 644, [2001] All ER (D) 404 (Jul), EAT; affd [2002] EWCA Civ 1074, [2002] ICR 1498, [2002] IRLR 711, 71 BMLR 1, (2002) Times, 26 August, [2002] All ER (D) 407 (Jul) 10.26
Ruhaza v Alexander Hancock Recruitment Ltd [2012] EqLR 9, EAT 12.6, 12.30
Rummler v Dato-Druck GmbH: 237/85 [1987] ICR 774, [1987] IRLR 32, ECJ 21.7
Runciman v Walter Runciman plc [1992] BCLC 1084, [1993] BCC 223 .... 8.12, 56.28, 56.36
Rushton v Harcros Timber and Building Supplies Ltd [1993] ICR 230, [1993] IRLR 254, [1993] 8 LS Gaz R 40, EAT 53.13
Russell v Elmdon Freight Terminal Ltd [1989] ICR 629, EAT 6.9
Russell v Transocean International Resources Ltd (Case S/104056/04) (May 2005, unreported) 55.5
Russell v Transocean International Resources Ltd [2011] UKSC 57, [2012] 2 All ER 166, [2012] 1 CMLR 1527, [2012] ICR 185, [2012] IRLR 149, [2012] 01 LS Gaz R 15, [2011] NLJR 1743, (2011) Times, 08 December, 2012 SLT 239, 2012 SCLR 238, 155 Sol Jo (no 47) 31, [2011] All ER (D) 53 (Dec) 27.5, 55.5, 55.14
Rutherford v Radio Rentals Ltd 1993 SLT 221 .... 42.12
Rutherford v Secretary of State for Trade and Industry [2003] 3 CMLR 933, [2003] IRLR 858, [2003] 42 LS Gaz R 31, [2003] NLJR 1633, (2003) Times, 8 October, [2003] All ER (D) 67 (Oct), EAT; on appeal [2004] EWCA Civ 1186, [004] 3 CMLR 1158, [2004] IRLR 892, (2004) Times, 4 November, [2004] All ER (D) 23 (Sep), sub nom Secretary of State for Trade and Industry v Rutherford (No 2) [2005] ICR 119, sub nom Rutherford v Towncircle Ltd 148 Sol Jo LB 1065; affd sub nom Rutherford v Secretary of State for Trade and Industry [2006] UKHL 19, [2006] ICR 785, [2006] IRLR 551, (2006) Times, 8 May, [2006] All ER (D) 30 (May), sub nom Secretary of State for Trade and Industry v Rutherford [2006] 4 All ER 577 .... 10.34, 11.9, 21.11, 40.2
Rutherford v Seymour Pierce Ltd [2010] EWHC 375 (QB), [2010] IRLR 606, [2010] All ER (D) 15 (Jun) 7.36
Rutten v Cross Medical Ltd: C-383/95 [1997] ECR I-57, [1997] All ER (EC) 121, [1997] ICR 715, [1997] IRLR 249, ECJ 23.8
Rutty v Commotion Ltd. See Commotion Ltd v Rutty
Ryan v Shipboard Maintenance Ltd [1980] ICR 88, [1980] IRLR 16, EAT 51.10
Rybak v Jean Sorelle Ltd [1991] ICR 127, sub nom Jean Sorelle Ltd v Rybak [1991] IRLR 153, EAT 17.25
Ryford Ltd v Drinkwater [1996] IRLR 16, EAT 47.2, 47.5

S

S & U Stores Ltd v Wilkes [1974] 3 All ER 401, [1974] ICR 645, [1974] IRLR 283, [1975] KILR 117, 9 ITR 415, NIRC 32.39
S H Muffett Ltd v Head [1987] ICR 1, [1986] IRLR 488, [1986] LS Gaz R 2653, EAT 53.12
SBJ Stephenson Ltd v Mandy [2000] FSR 286, [2000] IRLR 233 .... 39.13, 39.19, 56.21
SCA Packaging Ltd v Boyle. See Boyle v SCA Packaging Ltd (Equality and Human Rights Commission intervening)
SG&R Valuation Service Co LLC v Boudrais [2008] EWHC 1340 (QB), [2008] IRLR 770, [2008] All ER (D) 141 (May) 7.21, 7.47c, 56.21
SIP Industrial Products Ltd v Swinn [1994] ICR 473, sub nom SIP (Industrial Products) Ltd v Swinn [1994] IRLR 323, EAT 32.6
SNR Denton UK LLP v Kirwan (2012) UKEAT/0158/12/ZT, [2013] ICR 101, [2012] IRLR 966, [2012] All ER (D) 215 (Oct), EAT 50.3
ST v North Yorkshire County Council. See Trotman v North Yorkshire County Council
Sabeh El Leil v France (Application No 34869/05) [2011] IRLR 781, ECtHR 28.4
Saddington v F & G Cleaners Ltd (2012) UKEAT/0140/11/JOJ, [2012] IRLR 892, [2012] All ER (D) 159 (Aug), EAT 50.26
Sadek v Medical Protection Society [2004] EWCA Civ 865, [2004] 4 All ER 118, [2005] IRLR 57, (2004) Times, 2 September, [2004] All ER (D) 163 (Jul), sub nom Medical Protection Society v Sadek [2004] ICR 1263, 148 Sol Jo LB 878 .... 11.29
Sadler v Imperial Life Assurance Co of Canada Ltd [1988] IRLR 388 .... 39.3, 39.7
Safetynet Security Ltd v Coppage [2012] Lexis Citation 104, [2012] All ER (D) 57 (Dec) 39.8
Safeway Stores plc v Burrell [1997] ICR 523, [1997] IRLR 200, 567 IRLB 8, EAT 36.7

Saggar v Ministry of Defence [2004] ICR 1708, [2004] All ER (D) 54 (Jul), EAT; revsd [2005] EWCA Civ 413, [2005] ICR 1073, [2005] IRLR 618, (2005) Times, 9 May, [2005] All ER (D) 382 (Apr) 11.18, 23.9

Sahota v Home Office (UKEAT/342/09) [2010] 2 CMLR 771, [2010] ICR 772 .... 10.24, 31.2

Saiger v North Cumbria Acute Hospitals NHS Trust (UKEAT/0325/10/CEA) (14 December 2010, unreported) 18.72

Saini v All Saints Haque Centre [2009] IRLR 74, [2008] All ER (D) 250 (Oct), EAT 10.39

Saini v Bungay (UKEAT/0331/10/CEA) (2011) 938 IDS Brief 13, [2011] EqLR 1130, [2012] All ER (D) 40 (Mar), EAT 12.13, 12.18

Sainsbury's Supermarkets Ltd v Hitt [2002] EWCA Civ 1588, [2003] ICR 111, [2003] IRLR 23, (2002) Times, 14 November, 146 Sol Jo LB 238, [2002] All ER (D) 259 (Oct) 52.9

St Alphonsus RC Primary School v Blenkinsop (UKEAT/0082/09) [2009] All ER (D) 54 (Aug) 31.22

St Anne's Board Mill Co Ltd v Brien [1973] ICR 444, [1973] IRLR 309, NIRC 52.10

St Christopher's Fellowship v Walters-Ennis [2010] EWCA Civ 921, [2010] All ER (D) 03 (Aug) 12.3

St Ives Plymouth Ltd v Haggerty [2008] All ER (D) 317 (May), EAT 14.3

St John of God (Care Services) Ltd v Brooks [1992] ICR 715, [1992] IRLR 546, [1992] 29 LS Gaz R 24, EAT 52.14

Sajid v Sussex Muslim Society [2001] EWCA Civ 1684, [2002] IRLR 113, [2001] All ER (D) 19 (Oct) 7.45, 18.27, 56.39

Sakharkar v Northern Foods Grocery Group Ltd (t/a Fox's Biscuits) (UKEAT/0442/10/ZT) [2011] All ER (D) 61 (Apr) 52.9

Salford Royal NHS Foundation Trust v Roldan [2010] EWCA Civ 522, [2010] ICR 1457, [2010] IRLR 721, 114 BMLR 152, [2010] All ER (D) 110 (May) 52.10

Salgueiro da Silva Moura v Portugal [2001] 1 FCR 653, ECtHR 28.4

Salinas v Bear Stearns International Holdings Inc [2005] ICR 1117, [2004] All ER (D) 296 (Oct), EAT 18.72

Salton (Logan) v Durham County Council [1989] IRLR 99, EAT 51.19

Salvesen v Simons [1994] ICR 409, [1994] IRLR 52, EAT 7.24

Samengo-Turner v J & H Marsh & McLennan (Services) Ltd [2007] EWCA Civ 723, [2007] 2 All ER (Comm) 813, [2008] ICR 18, [2008] IRLR 237, [2007] All ER (D) 196 (Jul) 23.8

Sampson v Wilson [1996] Ch 39, [1995] 3 WLR 455, 70 P & CR 359, 29 HLR 18, CA 41.3

Samsung Electronics (UK) Ltd v Monte-D'Cruz (UKEAT/0039/11/DM) (1 March 2012, unreported) 52.11

Samsung Semiconductor Europe Ltd v Docherty [2011] CSOH 32, 2011 Scot (D) 9/3 .... 7.16

San Ling Chinese Medicine Centre v Lian Wei Ji (UKEAT/0370/09/ZT) (25 January 2010, unreported) 7.24, 23.6

Sanchez Hidalgo v Asociacion de Servicios Aser and Sociedad Cooperativa Minerva: C-173/96 [1998] ECR I-8237, [2002] ICR 73, [1999] IRLR 136, ECJ 50.5

Sandhu v Jan De Rijk Transport Ltd [2007] EWCA Civ 430, [2007] ICR 1137, [2007] IRLR 519, 151 Sol Jo LB 672, [2007] All ER (D) 167 (May) 46.2, 51.8

Sands-Ellison v One Call Insurance [2003] All ER (D) 389 (Mar), EAT 13.3

Santamera v Express Cargo Forwarding (t/a IEC Ltd) [2003] IRLR 273, (2003) Times, 13 January, [2002] All ER (D) 379 (Nov), EAT 52.10

Sarfraz v Ministry of Justice (2011) UKEAT/0578/10/Z, [2011] IRLR 562, [2011] All ER (D) 141 (May), EAT 9.17

Sarkar v West London Mental Health NHS Trust [2010] EWCA Civ 289, [2010] IRLR 508, [2010] All ER (D) 211 (Mar) 52.4, 52.10

Sarker v South Tees Acute Hospitals NHS Trust [1997] ICR 673, [1997] IRLR 328, EAT ... 7.36, 20.8

Sarti (Sauchiehall St) Ltd v Polito [2008] ICR 1279 .... 42.8

Saunders v Home Office [2006] ICR 318, (2005) Times, 2 December, [2005] All ER (D) 83 (Nov), EAT 10.15

Saunders v Richmond-upon-Thames London Borough Council [1978] ICR 75, [1977] IRLR 362, 12 ITR 488, EAT 10.44

Savage v British India Steam Navigation Co Ltd (1930) 46 TLR 294 .... 56.17

Savoia v Chiltern Herb Farms Ltd [1982] IRLR 166, CA 51.7

Sawyer v Ahsan [2000] ICR 1, [1999] IRLR 609, EAT 11.30

Sayers v Cambridgeshire County Council [2006] EWHC 2029 (QB), [2007] IRLR 29 ..... 26.25, 55.21

Sayers v International Drilling Co NV [1971] 3 All ER 163, [1971] 1 WLR 1176, [1971] 2 Lloyd's Rep 105, 115 Sol Jo 466, CA 23.7

Table of Cases

Scally v Southern Health and Social Services Board [1992] 1 AC 294, [1991] 4 All ER 563, [1991] 3 WLR 778, [1991] ICR 771, [1991] IRLR 522, 135 Sol Jo LB 172, HL . 7.11, 7.15, 7.22a, 21.18, 40.16

Scanfuture UK Ltd v Secretary of State for the Department of Trade and Industry [2001] ICR 1096, [2001] IRLR 416, [2001] All ER (D) 296 (Mar), EAT 28.7

Scattolon v Ministero Dell'istruzione, Dell'università E Della Ricerca: C-108/10 [2012] 1 CMLR 432, [2012] ICR 740, [2011] IRLR 1020, ECJ 50.9

Schmidt v Austicks Bookshops Ltd [1978] ICR 85, [1977] IRLR 360, EAT 10.14

Schmidt v Spar und Leihkasse der früheren Amter Bordesholm, Kiel und Cronshagen: C-392/92 [1994] ECR I-1311, [1995] 2 CMLR 331, [1995] ICR 237, [1994] IRLR 302, ECJ 50.5

Schönheit (Hilde) v Stadt Frankfurt am Main: C-4/02 and C-5/02 [2003] ECR I-12575, [2004] IRLR 983, [2003] All ER (D) 401 (Oct), ECJ 11.9, 21.12, 40.13

Schöning-Kougebetopoulou v Freie und Hansestadt Hamburg: C-15/96 [1998] All ER (EC) 97, [1998] 1 CMLR 931, sub nom Kalliope Schöning-Kougebetopoulou v Freie und Hansestadt Hamburg [1998] ECR I-47, ECJ 23.2

Schuler-Zgraggen v Switzerland (Application 14518/89) (1993) 16 EHRR 405, [1994] 1 FCR 453, ECtHR 28.4

Schultz v Esso Petroleum Ltd [1999] 3 All ER 338, [1999] ICR 1202, [1999] IRLR 488, CA 17.25

Schultz-Hoff v Deutsche Rentenversicherung Bund: C-350/06 [2009] All ER (EC) 906, [2009] 2 CMLR 657, [2009] ICR 932, [2009] IRLR 214, (2009) Times, 28 January, [2009] All ER (D) 147 (Jan), ECJ 27.3A

Science Research Council v Nassé [1980] AC 1028, [1979] 3 All ER 673, [1979] 3 WLR 762, [1979] IRLR 465, [1979] ICR 921, 123 Sol Jo 768, HL 12.9, 18.12

Scope v Thornett. See Thornett v Scope

Scorer v Seymour-Johns [1966] 3 All ER 347, [1966] 1 WLR 1419, 1 KIR 303, 110 Sol Jo 526, CA 39.8

Scotch Premier Meat Ltd v Burns [2000] IRLR 639, EAT 37.4

Scott v Coalite Fuels and Chemicals Ltd [1988] ICR 355, [1988] IRLR 131, EAT 46.2, 51.19

Scott v Creager [1979] ICR 403, [1979] IRLR 162, EAT 32.20

Scott v IRC [2004] EWCA Civ 400, [2004] IRLR 713, (2004) Times, 19 April, 148 Sol Jo LB 474, [2004] All ER (D) 46 (Apr) 12.18, 18.11

Scottbridge Construction Ltd v Wright [2003] IRLR 21, Ct of Sess 32.12

Scotthorne v Four Seasons Conservatories (UK) Ltd (UKEAT/0178/10/ZT) [2010] All ER (D) 17 (Sep) 18.13, 18.74

Scottish Ambulance Service v Truslove (UKEATS/0028/11/BI) (12 January 2012, unreported) 55.22

Scullard v Knowles and Southern Regional Council for Education and Training [1996] ICR 399, [1996] IRLR 344, EAT 21.3, 21.9, 22.2, 22.6

Scully UK Ltd v Lee [1998] IRLR 259, CA 39.7, 39.8

Sealy v Consignia plc [2002] EWCA Civ 878, [2002] 3 All ER 801, [2002] ICR 1193, [2002] IRLR 624, (2002) Times, 3 July, [2002] All ER (D) 129 (Jun) 17.21, 17.25

Seawell Ltd v Ceva Freight (Uk) Ltd [2012] IRLR 802, EAT 50.3

Secretary of State for Business, Enterprise and Regulatory Reform v Howe (Keith) [2009] EWCA Civ 280, [2009] IRLR 475, (2009) Times, 10 April, [2009] All ER (D) 40 (Apr) 14.3

Secretary of State for Business, Enterprise and Regulatory Reform v Neufeld (Richard) [2009] EWCA Civ 280, [2009] 3 All ER 790, [2009] ICR 1183, [2009] IRLR 475, [2009] 2 BCLC 273, (2009) Times, 10 April, [2009] BPIR 909, [2009] All ER (D) 40 (Apr) 8.4, 14.3, 29.4

Secretary of State for Children Schools and Families v Fletcher (UKEAT/0095/08/RN) [2008] 3 CMLR 1462, [2009] ICR 102, [2008] All ER (D) 133 (Oct) 45.9

Secretary of State for Employment v Associated Society of Locomotive Engineers and Firemen (No 2) [1972] 2 QB 455, [1972] 2 All ER 949, [1972] 2 WLR 1370, [1972] ICR 19, 13 KIR 1, 116 Sol Jo 467, CA 7.17

Secretary of State for Employment v Banks [1983] ICR 48, EAT 36.11

Secretary of State for Employment v Chapman [1989] ICR 771, CA 6.9

Secretary of State for Employment v Clark [1997] 1 CMLR 613, sub nom Clark v Secretary of State for Employment [1997] ICR 64, [1996] IRLR 578, CA 21.3, 21.14

Secretary of State for Employment v Cooper [1987] ICR 766, EAT 29.5

Secretary of State for Employment v Doulton Sanitaryware Ltd [1981] ICR 477, [1981] IRLR 365, EAT 31.39

Secretary of State for Employment v Globe Elastic Thread Co Ltd [1980] AC 506, [1979] 2 All ER 1077, [1979] 3 WLR 143, [1979] ICR 706, [1979] IRLR 327, 123 Sol Jo 504, HL 6.5, 6.7, 36.13

Secretary of State for Employment v Helitron Ltd [1980] ICR 523, EAT 37.7

Secretary of State for Employment v John Woodrow & Sons (Builders) Ltd [1983] ICR 582, [1983] IRLR 11, EAT 32.39

Secretary of State for Employment v McGlone [1997] BCC 101, EAT 29.4

Secretary of State for Employment v Mann [1996] ICR 197, [1996] IRLR 4, EAT; revsd [1997] ICR 209, [1997] IRLR 21, CA; affd on other grounds sub nom Mann v Secretary of State for Employment [1999] ICR 898, [1999] IRLR 566, [1999] All ER (D) 791, HL 17.12, 22.2, 29.5

Secretary of State for Employment v Reeves [1993] ICR 508, EAT 29.6

Secretary of State for Employment v Spence [1987] QB 179, [1986] 3 All ER 616, [1986] 3 WLR 380, [1986] 3 CMLR 647, [1986] ICR 651, [1986] IRLR 248, 130 Sol Jo 407, [1986] LS Gaz R 2084, CA 50.12

Secretary of State for Employment v Staffordshire County Council. See Staffordshire County Council v Secretary of State for Employment

Secretary of State for Employment v Stewart [1996] IRLR 334, EAT 29.5

Secretary of State for Employment v Wilson [1997] ICR 408, [1996] IRLR 330, EAT 29.5

Secretary of State for Justice (sued as national offenders management service) v Bowling (UKEAT/0297/11/SM) [2012] IRLR 382, [2012] All ER (D) 13 (Jan), EAT 21.12

Secretary of State for Scotland v Taylor [2000] 3 All ER 90, [2000] ICR 595, (2000) Times, 12 May, 2000 SC (HL) 139, 2000 SLT 708, sub nom Taylor v Secretary of State for Scotland [2000] IRLR 502, HL 7.13, 40.2

Secretary of State for Scotland and Greater Glasgow Health Board v Wright and Hannah [1993] 2 CMLR 257, [1991] IRLR 187, EAT 22.2

Secretary of State for Trade and Industry v Cook [1997] 3 CMLR 1465, [1997] ICR 288, [1997] IRLR 150, 562 IRLB 12, EAT 50.13

Secretary of State for Trade and Industry v Forde [1997] ICR 231, [1997] IRLR 387, EAT 29.4

Secretary of State for Trade and Industry v Lassman (Pan Graphics Industries Ltd, in receivership) [2000] ICR 1109, [2000] IRLR 411, CA 6.12

Secretary of State for Trade and Industry v Rutherford. See Rutherford v Secretary of State for Trade and Industry

Secretary of State for Trade and Industry v Slater [2008] ICR 54, [2007] IRLR 928, [2008] BCC 70, [2007] All ER (D) 349 (Jun), EAT 29.10, 50.11

Secretary of State for Trade and Industry v Walden [2000] IRLR 168, EAT 29.4

Secretary of State for Work and Pensions (Jobcentre Plus) v Constable (UKEAT/0156/10/JOJ) [2010] All ER (D) 190 (Nov) 18.8

Secretary of State for Work and Pensions v McCarthy (2010) 908 IDS Brief 11, EAT 12.3

Securicor Guarding Ltd v R [1994] IRLR 633, EAT 18.18

Securicor Omega Express Ltd v GMB [2004] IRLR 9, [2003] All ER (D) 181 (Sep), EAT 37.4

Seda Kucukdeveci v Swedex GmbH & Co KG: C-555/07 [2010] All ER (EC) 867, [2010] 2 CMLR 874, [2010] IRLR 346, [2010] All ER (D) 126 (Feb), ECJ 10.10, 11.9, 17.12, 22.2

Sefton Metropolitan Borough Council v Hincks (UKEAT/0092/11/SM) [2011] ICR 1357, [2011] All ER (D) 122 (Aug), EAT 21.21

Segor v Goodrich Actuation Systems Ltd (UKEAT/0145/11/DM) (10 February 2012, unreported) 18.28, 18.56

Sehmi v Gate Gourmet London Ltd [2009] IRLR 807, [2009] All ER (D) 46 (Aug), EAT 51.18

Seide v Gillette Industries [1980] IRLR 427, EAT 10.20

Seldon v Clarkson Wright & Jakes [2009] 3 All ER 435, [2009] IRLR 267, [2009] All ER (D) 180 (Feb), EAT; affd [2010] EWCA Civ 899, [2011] 1 All ER 770, [2011] 1 CMLR 143, [2011] ICR 60, [2010] IRLR 865, [2010] All ER (D) 309 (Jul); affd sub nom Seldon v Clarkson Wright and Jakes [2012] UKSC 16, [2012] ICR 716, [2012] IRLR 590, [2012] NLJR 653, 156 Sol Jo (no 17) 31, [2012] All ER (D) 121 (Apr) 11.9, 11.15, 12.24, 40.5

Selfridges Ltd v Malik [1998] ICR 268, [1997] IRLR 577, EAT 53.5

Selkent Bus Co Ltd v Moore [1996] ICR 836, [1996] IRLR 661, EAT 18.10, 18.41

Senior Heat Treatment Ltd v Bell [1997] IRLR 614, EAT 6.12, 50.16

Serco Ltd t/a Serco Docklands v National Union of Rail, Maritime and Transport Workers [2011] EWCA Civ 226, [2011] 3 All ER 913, [2011] ICR 848, [2011] IRLR 399, [2011] NLJR 405, [2011] All ER (D) 65 (Mar) 43.14

Setiya v East Yorkshire Health Authority [1995] ICR 799, [1995] IRLR 348, EAT 19.14

Sevince v Staatssecretaris van Justitie: C-192/89 [1990] ECR I-3461, [1992] 2 CMLR 57, ECJ 23.2

Shamoon v Chief Constable of the Royal Ulster Constabulary (Northern Ireland) [2003] UKHL 11, [2003] 2 All ER 26, [2003] ICR 337, [2003] IRLR 285, (2003) Times, 4 March, 147 Sol Jo LB 268, [2003] All ER (D) 410 (Feb) 10.13, 10.15, 10.17, 10.50

Table of Cases

Shanahan Engineering Ltd v Unite the Union (UKEAT/0411/09/DM) [2010] All ER (D) 108
(Mar) 37.6
Sharifi v Strathclyde Regional Council [1992] IRLR 259, EAT 12.13
Sharma v Hindu Temple IDS Brief No 464 .... 7.24
Sharma v Manchester City Council [2008] ICR 623, [2008] IRLR 336, [2008] All ER (D) 37 (Mar),
EAT 19.2, 30.7, 30.20
Sharp v Caledonia Group Services Ltd [2006] ICR 218, [2006] IRLR 4, [2005] All ER (D) 09 (Nov),
EAT 21.10
Shaw v CCL Ltd [2008] IRLR 284, [2008] All ER (D) 123 (Jan), EAT 10.49, 51.7
Shaw v Metropolitan Police Comr (UKEAT/0125/11/ZT) [2012] ICR 464, [2012] IRLR 291,
[2012] All ER (D) 32 (Feb), EAT 9.17, 12.18
Shawkat v Nottingham City Hospital NHS Trust (No 2) [2001] EWCA Civ 954, [2002] ICR 7,
[2001] IRLR 555, [2001] All ER (D) 214 (Jun)v 36.7
Sheffield v Oxford Controls Co Ltd [1979] ICR 396, [1979] IRLR 133, EAT 46.2, 51.8
Sheffield Forgemasters International Ltd v Fox [2009] ICR 333, [2009] IRLR 192 .... 12.15, 53.13
Sheikh v Chief Constable of Greater Manchester Police [1990] 1 QB 637, [1989] 2 All ER 684,
[1989] 2 WLR 1102, [1989] ICR 373, 133 Sol Jo 784, CA 10.41
Sheiky v Argos Distributors Ltd (1997) 597 IDS Brief 16 .... 10.45
Shepherd v North Yorkshire County Council [2006] IRLR 190, [2005] All ER (D) 354 (Dec),
EAT 10.58
Shepherds Investments Ltd v Walters [2006] EWHC 836 (Ch), [2007] FSR 395, [2007] IRLR 110,
[2007] 2 BCLC 202, [2006] All ER (D) 213 (Apr) 7.16, 7.17, 8.19
Sheridan v Stanley Cole (Wainfleet) Ltd [2003] ICR 297, [2003] IRLR 52, [2002] All ER (D) 11
(Nov), EAT; affd [2003] EWCA Civ 1046, [2003] 4 All ER 1181, [2003] ICR 1449, [2003]
38 LS Gaz R 33, (2003) Times, 5 September, sub nom Stanley Cole (Wainfleet) Ltd v Sheridan
[2003] IRLR 885 .... 18.52, 19.37, 51.7
Sheriff v Klyne Tugs (Lowestoft) Ltd [1999] ICR 1170, [1999] IRLR 481, 625 IRLB 6,
[1999] All ER (D) 666, CA 12.17, 18.26
Shestak v Royal College of Nursing (2008) 152 Sol Jo (no 37) 30, [2008] All ER (D) 193 (Oct),
EAT 12.8
Shields Automotive Ltd v Greig (UKEATS/0024/10/BI) (15 July 2011, unreported) 18.71
Shillcock v Uppingham School [1997] Pens LR 207 .... 21.16
Shillito v Van Leer (UK) Ltd [1997] IRLR 495, EAT 26.8
Simpson v Endsleigh Insurance Services Ltd (UKEAT/0544/09/DA) [2011] ICR 75, [2010] All ER
(D) 95 (Sep) 31.16, 31.34
Simpson v Chief Constable, Strathclyde Police (UKEATS/0030/11/BI) (10 January 2012,
unreported) 18.15
Sharma v New College Nottingham (UKEAT/0287/11) (1 December 2012, unreported) 18.15
Shindler v Northern Raincoat Co Ltd [1960] 2 All ER 239, [1960] 1 WLR 1038, 104 Sol Jo 806
.... 8.3, 56.10, 56.30
Shomer v B & R Residential Lettings Ltd [1992] IRLR 317, CA 10.15
Shove v Downs Surgical plc [1984] 1 All ER 7, [1984] ICR 532, [1984] IRLR 17 .. 53.12, 56.28, 56.32
Showboat Entertainment Centre Ltd v Owens [1984] 1 All ER 836, [1984] 1 WLR 384, [1984] ICR
65, [1984] IRLR 7, 128 Sol Jo 152, [1983] LS Gaz R 3002, 134 NLJ 37, EAT 10.20
Sibson v United Kingdom (Application 14327/88) (1993) 17 EHRR 193, ECtHR 28.4
Sidhu v Aerospace Composite Technology Ltd [2001] ICR 167, [2000] IRLR 602, [2000] 25 LS Gaz
R 38, [2000] All ER (D) 744, CA 10.20, 10.54, 54.2
Sienkiewicz v Greif (UK) Ltd [2011] UKSC 10, [2011] ICR 391, (2011) Times, 10 March, 155 Sol
Jo (no 10) 30, [2011] All ER (D) 107 (Mar) 25.8
Sigurjonsson v Iceland (Application 16130/90) (1993) 16 EHRR 462, ECtHR 28.4
Sillars v Charringtons Fuels Ltd [1989] ICR 475, [1989] IRLR 152, CA 6.7, 45.8
Silvey v Pendragon plc [2001] EWCA Civ 784, [2001] IRLR 685 .... 7.36, 56.21
Sim v Rotherham Metropolitan Borough Council [1987] Ch 216, [1986] 3 All ER 387, [1986] 3
WLR 851, 85 LGR 128, [1986] ICR 897, [1986] IRLR 391, 130 Sol Jo 839, [1986] LS Gaz R
3746 .... 7.47, 32.14
Sime v Sutcliffe Catering Scotland Ltd [1990] IRLR 228, 1990 SLT 687n, Ct of Sess 54.3
Simmons v Hoover Ltd [1977] QB 284, [1977] 1 All ER 775, [1976] 3 WLR 901, [1977] ICR 61,
[1976] IRLR 266, 10 ITR 234, 120 Sol Jo 540, EAT 56.17
Simms v Transco plc [2001] All ER (D) 245 (Jan), EAT 12.7
Simon v Brimham Associates [1987] ICR 596, [1987] IRLR 307, CA 10.20

Simpson v Intralinks Ltd (2012) UKEAT/0593/11/RN, [2012] ICR 1343, [2012] All ER (D) 215
(Jun), EAT 10.42
Simrad Ltd v Scott [1997] IRLR 147, EAT 53.13
Sinclair Roche & Temperley v Heard [2004] IRLR 763, [2004] All ER (D) 432 (Jul), EAT 10.35,
10.58, 12.3, 18.58, 19.38
Sindicato de Médicos de Asistencia Pública (Simap) v Conselleria de Sanidad y Consumo de la
Generalidad Valenciana: C-303/98 [2000] ECR I-7963, [2001] All ER (EC) 609, [2001] 3 CMLR
932, [2001] ICR 1116, [2000] IRLR 845, [2000] All ER (D) 1236, ECJ 55.5, 55.7
Singh v British Rail Engineering Ltd [1986] ICR 22, EAT 11.9
Singh v Guru Nanak Gurdwara [1990] ICR 309, CA 14.3
Singh-Rathour v Taylor (UKEATPA/0879/10/SM) [2011] All ER (D) 64 (May) 19.12
Sir W C Leng & Co Ltd v Andrews [1909] 1 Ch 763, 78 LJ Ch 80, 100 LT 7, 25 TLR 93, CA
.... 39.5
Sirdar v Army Board and Secretary of State for Defence. C-273/97 [1999] ECR I-7403,
[1999] All ER (EC) 928, [1999] 3 CMLR 559, [2000] ICR 130, [2000] IRLR 47, 7 BHRC 459,
[1999] All ER (D) 1156, ECJ 11.11, 11.22
Sisley v Britannia Security Systems Ltd [1983] ICR 628, [1983] IRLR 404, EAT 11.3
Sita (GB) Ltd v Burton [1998] ICR 17, [1997] IRLR 501, EAT 50.25
Skiggs v South West Trains Ltd [2005] IRLR 459, [2005] All ER (D) 96 (Mar), EAT 47.5, 49.21
Skills Development Scotland Co Ltd v Buchanan (UKEATS/0042/10/BI) (25 May 2011,
unreported) 21.12
Skyrail Oceanic Ltd v Coleman [1981] ICR 864, sub nom Coleman v Skyrail Oceanic Ltd (t/a
Goodmos Tours) [1981] IRLR 398, 125 Sol Jo 638, CA 10.35, 12.16
Slack v Cumbria County Council (Equality and Human Rights Commission intervening) [2009]
EWCA Civ 293, [2009] 3 CMLR 267, [2009] ICR 1217, [2009] IRLR 463, (2009) Times, 14 April,
153 Sol Jo (no 14) 29, [2009] All ER (D) 54 (Apr) 12.24, 17.28, 21.19A
Slack v Greenham (Plant Hire) Ltd [1983] ICR 617, [1983] IRLR 271, EAT 2.4
Slater v Leicestershire Health Authority [1989] IRLR 16, CA 52.10
Slaughter v C Brewer & Sons Ltd [1990] ICR 730, [1990] IRLR 426, EAT 53.13
Slaven v Thermo Engineers Ltd [1992] ICR 295, HC 47.19
Slingsby v Griffith Smith Solicitors (a firm) [2009] All ER (D) 150 (Feb), EAT 19.15
Small v Boots Co plc (UKEAT/0248/08/MAA) [2009] IRLR 328, [2009] All ER (D) 200 (Jan)
.... 7.22c, 50.23
Small v London Ambulance Service NHS Trust [2009] EWCA Civ 220, [2009] All ER (D) 179
(Mar), sub nom London Ambulance Service NHS Trust v Small [2009] IRLR 563 .. 18.63, 52.9, 53.13
Smith v A J Morrisroes & Sons Ltd [2005] ICR 596, [2005] IRLR 72, [2004] All ER (D) 291 (Dec),
EAT 27.4
Smith v Avdel Systems Ltd: C-408/92 [1994] ECR I-4435, [1995] All ER (EC) 132, [1995] 3 CMLR
543, [1995] ICR 596, [1994] IRLR 602, ECJ 19.48, 21.17, 40.7
Smith v Bexley London Borough Council IDS Brief No 448 .... 32.14
Smith v Chelsea Football Club plc [2010] EWHC 1168 (QB), [2010] All ER (D) 205 (Apr) 7.45
Smith v Cherry Lewis Ltd [2005] IRLR 86, [2004] All ER (D) 165 (Nov), EAT 37.6
Smith v Churchills Stairlifts plc [2005] EWCA Civ 1220, [2006] ICR 524, [2006] IRLR 41,
[2005] All ER (D) 318 (Oct) 10.37
Smith v City of Glasgow District Council [1987] ICR 796, [1987] IRLR 326, 1987 SC (HL) 175,
1987 SLT 605, HL 52.4
Smith v Gardner Merchant Ltd [1998] 3 All ER 852, [1999] ICR 134, [1998] IRLR 510, [1998]
32 LS Gaz R 29, 142 Sol Jo LB 244, [1998] All ER (D) 338, CA 10.15
Smith v Greenwich Council (UKEAT/0113/10/JOJ and UKEAT/0114/10/JOJ) [2011] ICR 277
.... 18.28
Smith v Gwent District Health Authority [1996] ICR 1044, EAT 18.41
Smith v Hayle Town Council [1978] ICR 996, [1978] IRLR 413, 77 LGR 52, 122 Sol Jo 642, CA
.... 52.3
Smith v London Metropolitan University (2011) UKEAT/0364/10/DM, [2011] IRLR 884,
[2011] All ER (D) 19 (Sep), EAT 9.17
Smith v Northamptonshire County Council [2009] UKHL 27, [2009] 4 All ER 557, [2009] ICR 734,
110 BMLR 15, 153 Sol Jo (no 20) 39, [2009] PIQR P292, (2009) Times, 21 May, [2009] All ER
(D) 170 (May) 26.12
Smith v Oxfordshire Learning Disability NHS Trust (UKEAT/0176/09) [2009] ICR 1395,
[2009] All ER (D) 170 (Aug) 32.9
Smith v Safeway plc [1996] ICR 868, [1996] IRLR 456, CA 10.14

Table of Cases

Smith v Secretary of State for Trade and Industry [2000] ICR 69, [2000] IRLR 6, EAT 28.7
Smith v Seghill Overseers (1875) LR 10 QB 422, 40 JP 228, 44 LJMC 114, 23 WR 745,
  [1874–80] All ER Rep 373, 32 LT 859 .... 41.2
Smith v Stages [1989] AC 928, [1989] 1 All ER 833, [1989] 2 WLR 529, [1989] ICR 272, [1989]
  IRLR 177, 133 Sol Jo 324, [1989] 15 LS Gaz R 42, [1989] NLJR 291, HL 54.2
Smith v Trafford Housing Trust [2013] IRLR 86 .... 46.1, 46.5
Smith v Trustees of Brooklands College (UKEAT/0128/11/ZT) (5 September 2011, unreported)
  .... 50.29
Smith v Zeneca (Agrochemicals) Ltd [2000] ICR 800, [2000] All ER (D) 163, EAT 12.8, 18.10
Smith and Grady v United Kingdom (Applications 33985/96 and 33986/96) (1999) 29 EHRR 493,
  [1999] IRLR 734, 11 Admin LR 879, ECtHR 10.23, 28.4
Smiths Industries Aerospace and Defence Systems v Rawlings [1996] IRLR 656, EAT 52.11
Sodexho Ltd v Gibbons [2005] ICR 1647, [2005] IRLR 836, [2005] All ER (D) 477 (Jul), EAT
  .... 17.10, 17.14, 17.34, 17.37, 18.6, 18.7, 18.15, 18.75, 18.76
Sodexo Health Care Services Ltd v Harmer (UKEATS/0079/08) (10 July 2009, unreported)
  .... 17.22
Sodexo Ltd v Gutridge [2009] ICR 70, [2008] IRLR 752, 152 Sol Jo (no 34) 30, [2008] All ER (D)
  70 (Aug), EAT; affd sub nom Gutridge v Sodexo Ltd [2009] EWCA Civ 729, [2009] ICR 1486,
  [2009] IRLR 721, (2009) Times, 6 October, [2009] All ER (D) 132 (Jul) 17.28, 21.9, 21.18, 50.19
Sogbetun v Hackney London Borough Council [1998] ICR 1264, [1998] IRLR 676, EAT 17.9
Solectron Scotland Ltd v Roper [2004] IRLR 4, EAT 7.15, 7.32, 50.28
Somjee v United Kingdom (Application 42116/98) (2002) 36 EHRR 228, [2002] IRLR 886,
  [2002] ECHR 42116/98, [2002] All ER (D) 214 (Oct), ECtHR 17.13, 28.4
Soros v Davison [1994] ICR 590, [1994] IRLR 264, EAT 53.13
Soteriou v Ultrachem Ltd [2004] EWHC 983 (QB), [2004] IRLR 870, [2004] All ER (D) 278
  (Apr) 18.16, 18.22, 28.7
Sothern v Franks Charlesly & Co [1981] IRLR 278, CA 46.5, 51.10
Sougrin v Haringey Health Authority [1992] ICR 650, [1992] IRLR 416, CA 12.6
South Ayrshire Council v Morton [2001] IRLR 28, [2000] All ER (D) 1899, EAT; affd [2002] IRLR
  256, (2002) Times, 1 March, Ct of Sess 21.9
South Durham Health Authority v UNISON [1995] ICR 495, [1995] IRLR 407, EAT 17.33, 50.23
South London and Maudsley NHS Trust v Dathi [2008] IRLR 350, sub nom Dathi v South
  London and Maudsley NHS Trust [2008] All ER (D) 240 (Feb), EAT 10.38, 12.2, 18.3
South Manchester Abbeyfield Society Ltd v Hopkins (UKEAT/0079/10/ZT) [2011] ICR 254,
  [2011] IRLR 300, [2011] All ER (D) 72 (Mar) 32.12
South Place Ethical Society, Re, Barralet v A-G. See Barralet v A-G
South Tyneside Council v Ward (UKEAT/0358/10/RN) (12 July 2011, unreported) 52.4
South Tyneside Metropolitan Borough Council v Anderson. See Anderson v South Tyneside
  Metropolitan Borough Council
South Tyneside Metropolitan Borough Council v Toulson [2003] 1 CMLR 867, [2002] All ER (D)
  437 (Nov), EAT 27.2
South West Launderettes Ltd v Laidler [1986] ICR 455, [1986] IRLR 305, CA 6.9
Southampton City College v Randall [2006] IRLR 18, [2005] All ER (D) 87 (Nov), EAT 10.37
Southern Cross Healthcare Co Ltd v Perkins. See Perkins v Southern Cross Healthcare Co Ltd
Southern Foundries (1926) Ltd v Shirlaw [1940] AC 701, [1940] 2 All ER 445, 109 LJKB 461, 84
  Sol Jo 464, 164 LT 251, 56 TLR 637, HL 8.3, 56.10
Southwark London Borough Council v Bartholomew [2004] ICR 358, [2003] All ER (D) 190 (Dec),
  EAT 18.54, 18.76
Southwark London Borough Council v O'Brien [1996] IRLR 420, EAT 32.6
Sovereign Distribution Services Ltd v Transport and General Workers' Union [1990] ICR 31, [1989]
  IRLR 334, EAT 37.4, 37.6
Sovereign House Security Services Ltd v Savage [1989] IRLR 115, CA 46.5, 56.5
Spaceright Europe Ltd v Baillavoine [2011] EWCA Civ 1565, [2012] 2 All ER 812, [2012] ICR 520,
  [2012] IRLR 111, [2012] NLJR 68, [2011] All ER (D) 106 (Dec) 50.26
Spackman v London Metropolitan University [2007] IRLR 744, Cty Ct 7.47, 32.14
Spafax Ltd v Harrison [1980] IRLR 442, CA 39.8
Spano v Fiat Geotech SpA and Fiat Hitachi Excavators SpA: C-472/93 [1995] ECR I-4321, ECJ
  .... 50.28
Specialarbejderforbundet i Danmark v Dansk Industri acting for Royal Copenhagen A/S: C-400/93
  [1995] ECR I-1275, [1995] All ER (EC) 577, [1996] 1 CMLR 515, [1996] ICR 51, [1995] IRLR
  648, ECJ 21.11

Speciality Care plc v Pachela [1996] ICR 633, [1996] IRLR 248, EAT 52.3
Spence v British Railways Board [2001] ICR 232, [2000] All ER (D) 1956, EAT 51.15
Spencer v Marchington [1988] IRLR 392 .... 7.21, 39.8, 56.21
Spencer v Paragon Wallpapers Ltd [1977] ICR 301, [1976] IRLR 373, EAT 52.8
Spencer and Griffin v Gloucestershire County Council [1985] IRLR 393, CA 36.12
Spicer v Government of Spain [2004] EWCA Civ 1046, [2005] ICR 213, (2004) Times,
    10 September, [2004] All ER (D) 526 (Jul) 10.15
Spijkers v Gebroeders Benedik Abbatoir CV and Alfred Benedik en Zonen BV: 24/85 [1986] ECR
    1119, [1986] 2 CMLR 296, ECJ 50.5
Spiliada Maritime Corpn v Cansulex Ltd, The Spiliada [1987] AC 460, [1986] 3 All ER 843, [1986]
    3 WLR 972, [1987] 1 Lloyd's Rep 1, 130 Sol Jo 925, [1987] LS Gaz R 113, [1986] NLJ Rep 1137,
    [1987] LRC (Comm) 356, HL 23.8
Spillers-French (Holdings) Ltd v Union of Shop, Distributive and Allied Workers [1980] 1 All ER
    231, [1980] ICR 31, [1979] IRLR 339, 123 Sol Jo 651, EAT 37.6
Sports Club v HM Inspector of Taxes (SpC 253) [2000] STC (SCD) 443 .... 44.34
Spring v Guardian Assurance plc [1995] 2 AC 296, [1994] 3 All ER 129, [1994] 3 WLR 354, [1994]
    ICR 596, [1994] IRLR 460, [1994] 40 LS Gaz R 36, [1994] NLJR 971, 138 Sol Jo LB 183, HL
    .... 38.4, 40.16
Spring Grove Service Group plc v Hickinbottom [1990] ICR 111, EAT 18.64
Springboard Sunderland Trust v Robson [1992] ICR 554, [1992] IRLR 261, EAT 21.7
Square D Ltd v Cook. See Cook v Square D Ltd
Squibb UK Staff Association v Certification Officer [1979] 2 All ER 452, [1979] 1 WLR 523, [1979]
    ICR 235, [1979] IRLR 75, 123 Sol Jo 352, CA 48.22, 48.23
Sridhar v East Living Ltd (UKEAT/0476/07/RN) [2008] All ER (D) 290 (Nov) 14.3
Stacey v Babcock Power Ltd [1986] QB 308, [1986] 2 WLR 207, [1986] ICR 221, [1986] IRLR 3,
    130 Sol Jo 71, EAT 52.11
Stadt Lengerich v Helmig: C-399/92, C-409/92, C-425/92, C-34/93, C-50/93, and C-78/93
    [1994] ECR I-5727, [1995] 2 CMLR 261, [1996] ICR 35, [1995] IRLR 216, ECJ 21.12, 30.9
Staffordshire County Council v Barber. See Barber v Staffordshire County Council
Staffordshire County Council v Secretary of State for Employment [1989] ICR 664, sub nom
    Secretary of State for Employment v Staffordshire County Council [1989] IRLR 117, CA 51.13
Staffordshire Sentinel Newspapers Ltd v Potter [2004] IRLR 752, [2004] All ER (D) 131 (May),
    EAT 11.3
Stamp v South Holland District Council [2003] All ER (D) 19 (Jun), EAT 55.5
Standard Life Bank Ltd v Wilson (2008) 851 IDS Brief 5, EAT 12.8
Standard Life Health Care Ltd v Gorman [2009] EWCA Civ 1292, [2010] IRLR 233, [2009] All ER
    (D) 105 (May) 7.21, 7.47c
Stankovic v City of Westminster [2001] All ER (D) 340 (Oct), EAT 36.7
Stanley Cole (Wainfleet) Ltd v Sheridan. See Sheridan v Stanley Cole (Wainfleet) Ltd
Stannard v Fisons Pension Trust Ltd [1992] IRLR 27, [1991] PLR 225, CA 40.16
Stannard & Co (1969) Ltd v Wilson [1983] ICR 86, EAT 19.46
Stansbury v Datapulse plc [2003] EWCA Civ 1951, [2004] ICR 523, [2004] IRLR 466, [2004]
    06 LS Gaz R 32, (2004) Times, 28 January, 148 Sol Jo LB 145, [2003] All ER (D) 264 (Dec)
    .... 18.52, 18.56, 19.25
Stapp v Shaftesbury Society [1982] IRLR 326, CA 51.13
Stark v Post Office [2000] ICR 1013, 144 Sol Jo LB 150, [2000] 14 LS Gaz R 41, [2000] PIQR P105,
    CA 26.12
Starmer v British Airways plc [2005] IRLR 862, [2005] All ER (D) 323 (Jul), EAT 10.34, 11.9
Stedman v United Kingdom [1997] 23 EHRR CD 168 .... 28.7
Steel Stockholders (Birmingham) Ltd v Kirkwood [1993] IRLR 515, EAT 53.13
Steenhorst-Neerings v Bestuur van de Bedrijfsvereniging voor Detailhandel, Ambachten en
    Huisvrouwen: C-338/91 [1993] ECR I-5475, [1995] 3 CMLR 323, [1994] IRLR 244, ECJ 22.2
Steinicke v Bundesanstalt fur Arbeit: C-77/02 [2003] ECR I-9027, [2003] IRLR 892, [2003] All ER
    (D) 87 (Sep), ECJ 21.3
Stekel v Ellice [1973] 1 All ER 465, [1973] 1 WLR 191, 117 Sol Jo 126 .... 14.3
Stenhouse Australia Ltd v Phillips [1974] AC 391, [1974] 1 All ER 117, [1974] 2 WLR 134, [1974]
    1 Lloyd's Rep 1, 117 Sol Jo 875, PC 39.3, 39.4, 39.8
Stephenson v Delphi Diesel Systems Ltd [2003] ICR 471, [2003] All ER (D) 84 (Mar), EAT
    .... 14.3
Sterling Developments (London) Ltd v Pagano [2007] IRLR 471, [2007] All ER (D) 01 (May),
    EAT 17.9

Table of Cases

Stevedoring and Haulage Services Ltd v Fuller [2001] EWCA Civ 651, [2001] IRLR 627,
[2001] All ER (D) 106 (May) 14.3
Stevens v Bexley Health Authority [1989] ICR 224, [1989] IRLR 240, EAT 12.7, 22.2
Stevenson v United Road Transport Union [1977] 2 All ER 941, [1977] ICR 893, CA 49.15
Stevenson (or Stephenson) Jordan and Harrison Ltd v MacDonald and Evans (1952) 69 RPC 10,
[1952] 1 TLR 101, CA 8.4
Stewart v Cleveland Guest (Engineering) Ltd [1994] ICR 535, [1994] IRLR 440, EAT 19.35
Stewart v Glentaggart (1963) 42 ATC 318, [1963] TR 345, 1963 SC 300, 1963 SLT 119, Ct of
Sess 56.32
Stewart (J) v Moray Council [2006] ICR 1253, [2006] IRLR 592, EAT 9.10, 15.18
Stewart v New Testament Church of God [2007] EWCA Civ 1004, [2008] ICR 282, [2007] All ER
(D) 285 (Oct), sub nom New Testament Church of God v Stewart [2008] IRLR 134 .. 11.11, 14.3, 14.8
Stocker v Lancashire County Council [1992] IRLR 75, CA 52.4, 52.10
Stokes v Guest, Keen and Nettlefold (Bolts and Nuts) Ltd [1968] 1 WLR 1776, 5 KIR 401, 112 Sol
Jo 821 .... 25.8
Stolt Offshore Ltd v Miklaszewicz [2002] IRLR 344, 2002 SC 232, 2002 SLT 103, 2002 SCLR
455 .... 9.17, 52.3
Stonehill Furniture Ltd v Phillippo [1983] ICR 556, EAT 18.75
Storer v British Gas plc [2000] 2 All ER 440, [2000] 1 WLR 1237, [2000] ICR 603, [2000] IRLR
495, CA 17.8, 18.51
Stowe v Voith Turbo Ltd [2005] ICR 543, [2005] All ER (D) 152 (Jan), sub nom Voith Turbo Ltd
v Stowe [2005] IRLR 228, EAT 12.16, 53.13
Strange (SW) Ltd v Mann [1965] 1 All ER 1069, [1965] 1 WLR 629, 109 Sol Jo 352 .... 39.5
Strathclyde Regional Council v Neil [1984] IRLR 11, Sh Ct; affd sub nom Neil v Strathclyde
Borough Council [1984] IRLR 14, 1983 SLT (Sh Ct) 89 .... 13.3
Strathclyde Regional Council v Porcelli. See Porcelli v Strathclyde Regional Council
Strathclyde Regional Council v Wallace [1998] 1 All ER 394, [1998] 1 WLR 259, [1998] ICR 205,
[1998] IRLR 146, [1998] 07 LS Gaz R 32, 1998 SC (HL) 72, 142 Sol Jo LB 83, sub nom West
Dunbartonshire Council v Wallace 1998 SLT 421, HL 21.10, 21.12
Street v Derbyshire Unemployed Workers' Centre [2004] EWCA Civ 964, [2004] 4 All ER 839,
[2005] ICR 97, [2004] IRLR 687, (2004) Times, 6 September, [2004] All ER (D) 377 (Jul) .. 9.17, 26.9
Street v Mountford [1985] AC 809, [1985] 2 All ER 289, [1985] 2 WLR 877, 50 P & CR 258, 17
HLR 402, 129 Sol Jo 348, [1985] 1 EGLR 128, [1985] LS Gaz R 2087, [1985] NLJ Rep 460, 274
Estates Gazette 821, HL 41.2
Stribling v Wickham (1989) 21 HLR 381, [1989] 2 EGLR 35, [1989] 27 EG 81, CA 41.2
Strouthos v London Underground Ltd [2004] EWCA Civ 402, [2004] IRLR 636, [2004] All ER (D)
366 (Mar) 52.9, 52.10
Strudwick v Iszatt Bros Ltd (or IBL) [1988] ICR 796, [1988] IRLR 457, EAT 6.9
Stuart Peters Ltd v Bell. See Bell v Stuart Peters Ltd
Suffritti v Istituto Nazionale della Previdenza Sociale (INPS): C-140/91, C-141/91, C-278/91 and
C-279/91 [1992] ECR I-6337, [1993] IRLR 289, ECJ 22.2
Sumsion v BBC (Scotland) [2007] IRLR 678, EAT 27.5
Sun Alliance and London Insurance Ltd v Dudman [1978] ICR 551, [1978] IRLR 169, EAT
.... 21.5
Sunderland Polytechnic v Evans [1993] ICR 392, [1993] IRLR 196, EAT 32.6
Sunley Turriff Holdings Ltd v Thomson [1995] IRLR 184, EAT 50.15
Surrey County Council v Lamond (1998) 78 P & CR D3, 31 HLR 1051, [1999] 1 EGLR 32, [1999]
12 EG 170, [1998] EGCS 185, CA 41.7
Surtees v Middlesbrough Borough Council [2007] ICR 1644, [2007] IRLR 869, [2007] All ER (D)
249 (Jul), EAT; revsd in part [2008] EWCA Civ 885, [2009] ICR 133, [2008] IRLR 776,
[2008] All ER (D) 386 (Jul) 21.10, 21.12
Susie Radin Ltd v GMB. See GMB v Susie Radin Ltd
Sutcliffe v Big C's Marine Ltd [1998] ICR 913, [1998] IRLR 428, EAT 17.9, 17.18, 19.20
Sutherland v British Telecommunications plc (1989) Times, 30 January 38.4
Sutherland v Hatton. See Hatton v Sutherland
Sutherland v Network Appliance Ltd [2001] IRLR 12, [2000] All ER (D) 1000, EAT 18.35, 56.42
Sutton v The Ranch Ltd [2006] ICR 1170, [2006] All ER (D) 195 (Jun), EAT 18.70, 19.43
Suzen v Zehnacker Gebaudereinigung GmbH Krankenhausservice: C-13/95 [1997] All ER (EC)
289, [1997] ECR I-1259, [1997] 1 CMLR 768, [1997] ICR 662, [1997] IRLR 255, ECJ 50.5
Swain v Denso Marston Ltd [2000] ICR 1079, [2000] PIQR P129, CA 26.18
Swain v Hillman [2001] 1 All ER 91, [2000] PIQR P51, (1999) Times, 4 November, CA .. 18.15, 18.17

Swainston v Hetton Victory Club Ltd [1983] 1 All ER 1179, [1983] ICR 341, [1983] IRLR 164, 127
Sol Jo 171, CA 17.21
Swallow Security Services Ltd v Millicent [2009] All ER (D) 299 (Mar), EAT 18.60
Sweater Shop (Scotland) Ltd v Park [1996] IRLR 424, EAT 32.6
Sweden v Holmqvist: C-310/07 [2008] ECR I-7871, [2009] ICR 675, [2008] IRLR 970,
[2008] All ER (D) 265 (Oct), ECJ 29.3
Sweeny v Aer Lingus TEO [2013] 1 CMLR 51 .... 40.5
Sweeney v J & S Henderson (Concessions) Ltd [1999] IRLR 306, EAT 6.6
Sweetin v Coral Racing [2006] IRLR 252, [2006] All ER (D) 74 (Mar) 50.23
Sweetlove v Redbridge and Waltham Forest Area Health Authority [1979] ICR 477, [1979] IRLR
195, EAT 53.13
Swift v Chief Constable of Wiltshire Constabulary [2004] ICR 909, [2004] IRLR 540, [2004] All ER
(D) 299 (Feb), EAT 10.26
Swithland Motors plc v Clarke [1994] ICR 231, [1994] IRLR 275, EAT 12.3, 17.29
Sybron Corpn v Rochem Ltd [1984] Ch 112, [1983] 2 All ER 707, [1983] 3 WLR 713, [1983] ICR
801, [1983] IRLR 253, [1983] BCLC 43, 127 Sol Jo 391, CA 7.17, 8.19
Symbian Ltd v Christensen [2001] IRLR 77 .... 39.3, 39.8, 39.14
System Floors (UK) Ltd v Daniel [1982] ICR 54, [1981] IRLR 475, EAT 7.6
Systems Reliability Holdings plc v Smith [1990] IRLR 377 .... 39.8, 39.13
Szilagyi v Protectacoat Firthglow Ltd. See Protectacoat Firthglow Ltd v Szilagyi
Szima v Hungary [2013] IRLR 59 .... 28.4

T

T v North Yorkshire County Council. See Trotman v North Yorkshire County Council
T C Harrison (Newcastle-under-Lyme) Ltd v Ramsey (K) (HM Inspector) [1976] IRLR 135, Ind
Trib 25.36
T Lucas & Co Ltd v Mitchell [1974] Ch 129, [1972] 3 All ER 689, [1972] 3 WLR 934, 116 Sol Jo
711, CA 39.7
T Mobile (UK) Ltd v Singleton (UKEAT/0410/10/ZT) [2011] All ER (D) 12 (May) 17.25
TDG Chemical Ltd v Benton (UKEAT/0166/10/DM) (10 September 2010, unreported) 52.10
TFS Derivatives Ltd v Morgan [2004] EWHC 3181 (QB), [2005] IRLR 246, [2004] All ER (D) 236
(Nov) 39.6, 39.8, 39.9, 39.14
TGWU v Lambeth Service Team Ltd [2005] All ER (D) 153 (Jul), EAT 37.6
TNT Express (UK) Ltd v Downes [1994] ICR 1, [1993] IRLR 432, EAT 53.13
TSB Bank plc v Harris [2000] IRLR 157, EAT 38.4, 46.19
TSC Europe (UK) Ltd v Massey [1999] IRLR 22 .... 39.8
Taddese v Abusabib (2012) UKEAT/0424/11/ZT, [2013] ICR 603, [2013] All ER (D) 121 (Mar),
EAT 11.23
Tagro v Cafane [1991] 2 All ER 235, [1991] 1 WLR 378, 23 HLR 250, [1991] 1 EGLR 279, CA
.... 41.3
Talbot v Cadge [1995] 2 AC 394, [1995] 2 WLR 312, [1995] ICR 1100, sub nom Leyland DAF Ltd,
Re [1994] 4 All ER 300, [1994] NLJR 1311; sub nom Leyland DAF Ltd (No 2), Re
[1994] 2 BCLC 760, sub nom Leyland Daf Ltd, Re, Talbot v Cadge [1994] BCC 658; on appeal
sub nom Talbot v Grundy [1995] 2 AC 394, [1995] 2 WLR 312, [1995] ICR 1100, [1995] IRLR
269, [1995] 17 LS Gaz R 47, sub nom Leyland DAF Ltd, Re [1995] 2 All ER 65, [1995] NLJR
449, sub nom Leyland DAF Ltd (No 2), Re [1995] 1 BCLC 386, sub nom Talbot v Cadge
(Leyland DAF Ltd) [1995] BCC 319, HL 29.10
Tan v Sitkowski [2007] EWCA Civ 30, [2007] 1 WLR 1628, (2007) Times, 15 February,
[2007] All ER (D) 16 (Feb) 41.3
Tanna v Post Office [1981] ICR 374, EAT 10.41
Tanner v D T Kean Ltd [1978] IRLR 110, EAT 56.5
Tapere v South London and Maudsley NHS Trust [2009] ICR 1563, [2009] IRLR 972,
[2009] All ER (D) 155 (Sep), EAT 50.16, 50.18, 50.25
Taplin v C Shippam Ltd [1978] ICR 1068, [1978] IRLR 450, 13 ITR 532, EAT 9.17, 53.18
Tarbuck v Sainsbury Supermarkets Ltd [2006] IRLR 664, [2006] All ER (D) 50 (Jun), EAT 10.37
Tariq v Home Office [2010] EWCA Civ 462, [2010] ICR 1034, [2010] IRLR 1065, [2010] NLJR 696,
[2010] All ER (D) 08 (May); revsd sub nom Home Office v Tariq [2011] UKSC 35, [2012] AC
452, [2012] 1 All ER 58, [2011] 3 WLR 322, [2012] 1 CMLR 14, [2011] ICR 938, [2011] IRLR
843, [2011] NLJR 1027, (2011) Times, 18 July, [2011] All ER (D) 108 (Jul) 17.13, 18.51, 28.7, 35.7

Table of Cases

Tariquez-Zaman v Genaral Medical Council (UKEAT/0292/06), unreported 11.30
Tariquez-Zaman v University of London [2010] EWHC 908 (QB), [2010] All ER (D) 181 (Apr)
.... 7.45
Tarling v Wisdom Toothbrushes Ltd (COIT 1500148/97) (24 June 1997, unreported) 10.37
Tarmac Roadstone Holdings Ltd v Peacock [1973] 2 All ER 485, [1973] 1 WLR 594, [1973] ICR
273, [1973] IRLR 157, 14 KIR 277, 8 ITR 300, 117 Sol Jo 186, CA 32.36
Tasneem v Dudley Group of Hospitals NHS Trust (UKEAT/0232/10/CEA) (29 June 2011,
unreported) 52.14
Tattari v Private Patients Plan Ltd [1998] ICR 106, [1997] IRLR 586, 38 BMLR 24, CA 11.30
Taupo Totara Timber Co Ltd v Rowe [1978] AC 537, [1977] 3 All ER 123, [1977] 3 WLR 466, 121
Sol Jo 692, [1977] 2 NZLR 453, PC 8.37
Taylor v Alidair Ltd. See Alidair Ltd v Taylor
Taylor v Connex South Eastern Ltd IDS Brief No 670 .... 50.26
Taylor v East Midlands Offender Employment [2000] IRLR 760, EAT 27.9
Taylor v National Union of Mineworkers (Derbyshire Area) [1984] IRLR 440 .... 49.15
Taylor v OCS Group Ltd [2006] EWCA Civ 702, [2006] ICR 1602, [2006] IRLR 613, (2006) Times,
12 July, 150 Sol Jo LB 810, [2006] All ER (D) 51 (Aug) 52.10, 52.11
Taylor v Secretary of State for Scotland. See Secretary of State for Scotland v Taylor
Taylor v Serviceteam Ltd [1998] PIQR P201 .... 50.18
Taylor v XLN Telecom (UKEAT/0385/09/ZT) [2010] ICR 656, [2010] IRLR 499, [2010] All ER
(D) 44 (May) 12.18
Taylor Gordon & Co Ltd (t/a Plan Personnel) v Timmons [2004] IRLR 180, [2003] 44 LS Gaz R
32, (2003) Times, 7 November, [2003] All ER (D) 05 (Oct), EAT 17.11, 31.43, 32.6. 42.8
Taylor Stuart & Co v Croft (Timothy) (1998) 606 IRLB 15 .... 39.8
Taylorplan Services Ltd v Jackson [1996] IRLR 184, EAT 17.31, 32.8
Taymech Ltd v Ryan (UKEAT/663/94) (15 November 1994, unreported) 52.11
Tehrani v United Kingdom Central Council for Nursing, Midwifery and Health Visiting [2001]
IRLR 208, 2001 SLT 879, Ct of Sess 28.7
Teinaz v Wandsworth London Borough Council [2002] EWCA Civ 1040, [2002] ICR 1471, [2002]
IRLR 721, (2002) Times, 21 August, [2002] All ER (D) 238 (Jul) 18.54, 28.7
Tejani v Superintendent Registrar for the District of Peterborough [1986] IRLR 502, CA 10.20
Tele Danmark A/S v Handels- og Kontorfunktionærernes Forbund i Danmark (HK): C-109/00
[2001] ECR I-6993, [2001] All ER (EC) 941, [2002] 1 CMLR 105, [2004] ICR 610, [2001] IRLR
853, [2001] All ER (D) 37 (Oct), ECJ 10.31
Tele-Trading Ltd v Jenkins [1990] IRLR 430, CA 53.13
Telephone Information Services Ltd v Wilkinson [1991] IRLR 148, EAT 18.17, 18.72, 53.1
Temco Service Industries SA v Imzilyen: C-51/00 [2002] ECR I-969, [2004] 1 CMLR 877, [2002]
IRLR 214, [2002] All ER (D) 199 (Jan), ECJ 50.7
Ten Oever v Stichting Bedrijfspensioenfonds voor het Glazenwassers- en Schoonmaakbedrijf:
C-109/91 [1993] ECR I-4879, [1995] 2 CMLR 357, [1995] ICR 74, [1993] IRLR 601, [1995]
42 LS Gaz R 23, ECJ 21.17
Terry v East Sussex County Council [1977] 1 All ER 567, 75 LGR 111, [1976] ICR 536, [1976]
IRLR 332, 12 ITR 265, EAT 45.7, 52.14
Terry Ballard & Co (a firm) v Stonestreet (UKEAT/0568/06/DA) [2007] All ER (D) 176 (Mar)
.... 17.38
Tesco Stores Ltd v Pook [2003] EWHC 823 (Ch), [2004] IRLR 618, [2003] All ER (D) 233 (Apr)
.... 7.17, 8.19
Tesco Supermarkets Ltd v Nattrass [1972] AC 153, [1971] 2 All ER 127, [1971] 2 WLR 1166, 69
LGR 403, 135 JP 289, 115 Sol Jo 285, HL 25.38
Teva (UK) Ltd v Heslip (UKEAT/0008/09) [2009] All ER (D) 277 (Jul) 17.24
Thaine v London School of Economics (UKEAT/144/10) [2010] ICR 1422, [2010] All ER (D) 105
(Sep) 12.17
Thames Water Utilities v Reynolds [1996] IRLR 186, EAT 27.9, 32.14, 32.22
Theobald v The Royal Bank of Scotland plc (EAT/0444/06) [2007] All ER (D) 04 (Jan) .. 17.25, 17.26
Thermasacan v Norman [2009] EWCA Civ 3694 (Civ), [2011] BCC 535 .... 8.24
Thibault v Caisse Nationale d'Assurance Viellesse des Travailleurs Salaries (CNAVTS). See Caisse
Nationale d'Assurance Vieillesse des Travailleurs Salaries v Thibault
Thind v Salvesen Logistics Ltd (UKEAT/0487/09/DA) (13 January 2010, unreported) 18.16
Thoburn v Sunderland City Council [2002] EWHC 195 (Admin), [2003] QB 151, [2002] 4 All ER
156, [2002] 3 WLR 247, 166 JP 257, [2002] 15 LS Gaz R 35, [2002] NLJR 312, (2002) Times,
22 February, [2002] All ER (D) 223 (Feb) 22.2

Thomas v Bristol Aeroplane Co Ltd [1954] 2 All ER 1, [1954] 1 WLR 694, 52 LGR 292, 98 Sol Jo
302, CA 25.3
Thomas v Devon County Council [2008] All ER (D) 236 (Feb), EAT 18.26
Thomas v Farr plc [2007] EWCA Civ 118, [2007] ICR 932, [2007] IRLR 419, (2007) Times,
27 February, [2007] All ER (D) 240 (Feb) 39.8, 39.13
Thomas v National Coal Board [1987] ICR 757, [1987] IRLR 451, [1987] LS Gaz R 2045, EAT
.... 21.6
Thomas v National Union of Mineworkers (South Wales Area) [1986] Ch 20, [1985] 2 All ER 1,
[1985] 2 WLR 1081, [1985] ICR 886, [1985] IRLR 136, 129 Sol Jo 416, [1985] LS Gaz R 1938
.... 4.5
Thomas & Betts Manufacturing Ltd v Harding [1980] IRLR 255, CA 52.11
Thomas Marshall (Exports) Ltd v Guinle [1979] Ch 227, [1978] 3 All ER 193, [1978] 3 WLR 116,
[1979] FSR 208, [1978] ICR 905, [1978] IRLR 174, 122 Sol Jo 295 .... 8.19, 51.9
Thompson v Northumberland County Council [2007] All ER (D) 95 (Sep), EAT 17.26
Thompson v SCS Consulting Ltd [2001] IRLR 801, [2001] All ER (D) 03 (Sep), EAT 50.26
Thompson v Walon Car Delivery [1997] IRLR 343, EAT 51.20
Thornett v Scope [2006] EWCA Civ 1600, [2007] ICR 236, [2006] All ER (D) 357 (Nov), sub nom
Scope v Thornett [2007] IRLR 155 .... 53.12, 53.13
Thorpe v Dul [2003] ICR 1556, [2003] All ER (D) 14 (Jul), EAT 13.2
Threlfall v Hull City Council [2010] EWCA Civ 1147, [2011] ICR 209, [2010] 42 LS Gaz R 18,
(2011) Times, 04 March, [2010] All ER (D) 184 (Oct) 26.12
Thurstan Hoskin & Partners v Jewill Hill & Bennett [2002] EWCA Civ 249, [2002] All ER (D) 62
(Feb) 39.8
Tice v Cartwright [1999] ICR 769, EAT 6.9
Ticehurst and Thompson v British Telecommunications plc. See British Telecommunications plc v
Ticehurst
Tiffin v Lester Aldridge LLP [2011] IRLR 105, EAT 14.3
Tilson v Alstom Transport [2010] EWCA Civ 1308, [2011] IRLR 169, [2010] All ER (D) 281
(Nov) 14.3, 19.38, 45.2c
Tipper v Roofdec Ltd [1989] IRLR 419, EAT 6.5
Tisson v Telewest Communications Group Ltd [2008] All ER (D) 42 (May), EAT 18.75
Titchener v Secretary of State for Trade and Industry [2002] ICR 225, [2002] IRLR 195,
[2001] All ER (D) 93 (Sep), EAT 29.5
Tocher v General Motors Scotland Ltd [1981] IRLR 55, EAT 5.5
Todd v British Midland Airways Ltd [1978] ICR 959, [1978] IRLR 370, 13 ITR 553, 122 Sol Jo 661,
CA 51.15
Todd v Strain (UKEATS/0057/10) [2011] IRLR 11, [2010] All ER (D) 108 (Oct) 50.23
Tottenham Green Under Fives' Centre v Marshall [1989] ICR 214, [1989] IRLR 147, [1989]
15 LS Gaz R 39, EAT 11.4
Tottenham Green Under Fives' Centre v Marshall (No 2) [1991] ICR 320, [1991] IRLR 162,
EAT 11.4
Tower Boot Co Ltd v Jones [1995] IRLR 529, EAT; revsd sub nom Jones v Tower Boot Co Ltd
[1997] 2 All ER 406, [1997] ICR 254, [1997] IRLR 168, [1997] NLJR 60, CA 10.54, 54.1
Tower Hamlets Health Authority v Anthony [1989] ICR 656, [1989] IRLR 394, CA 52.9
Towry EJ Ltd v Bennett [2012] EWHC 224 (QB), [2012] All ER (D) 148 (Feb) 39.4, 39.8
Tracey v Crosville Wales Ltd [1998] AC 167, [1997] 4 All ER 449, [1997] 3 WLR 800, [1997] ICR
862, [1997] 41 LS Gaz R 28, [1997] NLJR 1582, sub nom Crosville Wales Ltd v Tracey (No 2)
[1997] IRLR 691, HL 53.13
Tradewinds Airways Ltd v Fletcher [1981] IRLR 272, EAT 53.12
Tradition Securities and Futures SA v Mouradian [2009] EWCA Civ 60, [2009] All ER (D) 100
(Feb) 32.6
Tradition Securities and Futures SA v Times Newspaper Ltd [2009] IRLR 354, [2008] All ER (D)
90 (Dec), EAT 12.11, 18.18
Tradition Securities and Futures SA v X and Y [2009] ICR 88, [2008] IRLR 934, [2008] All ER (D)
103 (Aug), EAT 11.18, 23.9
Trafford v Sharpe & Fisher (Building Supplies) Ltd [1994] IRLR 325, EAT 50.26
Trafford Carpets Ltd v Barker IDS Brief No 440 .... 2.4
Tran (Kien) v Greenwich Vietnam Community Project [2002] EWCA Civ 553, [2002] ICR 1101,
[2002] IRLR 735, [2002] 21 LS Gaz R 31, [2002] All ER (D) 238 (Apr) 18.63, 19.22
Transco plc (formerly BG plc) v O'Brien [2002] EWCA Civ 379, [2002] ICR 721, [2002] IRLR 444,
[2002] All ER (D) 80 (Mar) 7.22d, 51.7

Table of Cases

Transocean International Resources Ltd v Russell (UKEATS/0074/05) (4 October 2006, unreported) 55.3
Transocean Maritime Agencies SA Monegasque v Pettit 1997 SCLR 534 .... 13.3
Transport and General Workers' Union v Asda [2004] IRLR 836 .... 48.29
Transport and General Workers' Union v Brauer Coley Ltd (in administration) [2007] ICR 226, [2007] IRLR 207, [2006] All ER (D) 254 (Nov), EAT 37.6
Transport and General Workers' Union v Howard [1992] ICR 106, [1992] IRLR 170, EAT . 49.7, 53.15
Transport and General Workers' Union v Ledbury Preserves (1928) Ltd [1985] IRLR 412, EAT
.... 37.4
Transport and General Workers' Union v Ledbury Preserves (1928) Ltd [1986] ICR 855, [1986] IRLR 492, EAT 37.6
Transport and General Workers' Union v McKinnon [2001] ICR 1281, [2001] IRLR 597, [2001] All ER (D) 275 (Jun) 37.6
Transport & General Workers Union v Safeway Stores Ltd [2007] All ER (D) 14 (Jun), EAT
.... 18.10
Transport & General Workers Union v Swissport (UK) Ltd (in administration) [2007] ICR 1593, [2007] All ER (D) 329 (Jun), EAT 50.4, 50.11
Transport and General Workers' Union v Webber [1990] ICR 711, [1990] IRLR 462, [1990] 27 LS Gaz R 40, EAT 49.16
Treganowan v Robert Knee & Co Ltd [1975] ICR 105, [1975] IRLR 247, 10 ITR 121, 119 Sol Jo 490 .... 46.5, 56.1
Trego v Hunt [1896] AC 7, 65 LJ Ch 1, 44 WR 225, [1895–9] All ER Rep 804, 73 LT 514, 12 TLR 80, HL 39.8, 39.11
Trevelyans (Birmingham) Ltd v Norton [1991] ICR 488, EAT 17.25
Trico-Folberth Ltd v Devonshire. See Devonshire v Trico-Folberth Ltd
Triggs v GAB Robins (UK) Ltd [2008] EWCA Civ 17, [2008] STC 529, [2008] ICR 529, [2008] IRLR 317, (2008) Times, 5 March, [2008] All ER (D) 266 (Jan) 51.7, 51.9, 52.8, 53.12
Trimble v North Lanarkshire Council (UKEATS/0048/12/BI), unreported 21.18
Trimble v Supertravel Ltd [1982] ICR 440, [1982] IRLR 451, EAT 17.14, 18.76, 53.13
Trotman v North Yorkshire County Council [1999] LGR 584, [1998] 32 LS Gaz R 29, 142 Sol Jo LB 218, sub nom ST v North Yorkshire County Council [1999] IRLR 98, sub nom T v North Yorkshire County Council 49 BMLR 150, CA 54.2
Trotter v Forth Ports Authority [1991] IRLR 419, Ct of Sess 46.7
Trussed Steel Concrete Co Ltd v Green [1946] Ch 115, 44 LGR 263, 110 JP 144, 115 LJ Ch 123, 90 Sol Jo 80, 174 LT 122, 62 TLR 128 .... 8.4
Trustees of Uppingham School Retirement Benefit Scheme for Non-Teaching Staff v Shillcock [2002] EWHC 641 (Ch), [2002] IRLR 702, [2002] All ER (D) 147 (Apr) 21.16, 21.17
Tucker v British Leyland Motor Corpn Ltd [1978] IRLR 493, Cty Ct 27.9
Tullett Prebon Group Ltd v El-Hajjali [2008] EWHC 1924 (QB), [2008] IRLR 760, [2008] All ER (D) 427 (Jul) 7.41, 7.47b, 13.3
Tullett Prebon plc v BGC Brokers LP [2010] EWHC 484 (QB), [2010] IRLR 648, 154 Sol Jo (no 12) 37, [2010] All ER (D) 186 (Mar); affd [2011] EWCA Civ 131, [2011] IRLR 420, [2011] All ER (D) 227 (Feb) 7.22d, 20.8, 39.7, 39.11, 39.14, 39.15, 51.7
Tunstall v Condon [1980] ICR 786, EAT 56.8
Turner v Commonwealth & British Minerals Ltd [2000] IRLR 114, [1999] All ER (D) 1097, CA
.... 39.6, 39.8
Turner v East Midlands Trains Ltd [2012] EWCA Civ 1470, [2013] ICR 525, [2012] All ER (D) 196 (Nov) 28.7
Turner v Grovit: C-159/02 [2005] 1 AC 101, [2004] ECR I-3565, [2004] 2 All ER (Comm) 381, [2004] All ER (EC) 485, [2004] 3 WLR 1193, [2004] 2 Lloyd's Rep 169, [2005] ICR 23, [2004] IRLR 899, (2004) Times, 29 April, [2004] All ER (D) 259 (Apr), ECJ 23.8
Turner v Turner (ET/2401702/04) unreported 10.19
Turvey v C W Cheyney & Son Ltd [1979] ICR 341, [1979] IRLR 105, EAT 36.12
20:20 London Ltd v Riley [2012] EWHC 1912 (Ch), [2012] All ER (D) 134 (Jul) 39.3
Tyagi v BBC World Service [2001] EWCA Civ 549, [2001] IRLR 465, [2001] All ER (D) 86 (Mar) 12.6, 17.29
Tyldesley v TML Plastics Ltd [1996] ICR 356, [1996] IRLR 395, EAT 21.10, 21.12
Tyne and Wear Autistic Society v Smith [2005] ICR 663, [2005] IRLR 336, EAT 17.21
Tyrolean Airways Tiroler Luftfahrt Gesellschaft mbH v Betriebsrat Bord der Tyrolean Airways Tiroler Luftfahrt Gesellschaft mbH: C-132/11 [2012] 3 CMLR 464, [2013] ICR 71, [2012] IRLR 781, (2012) Times, 25 July, [2012] All ER (D) 38 (Jul), ECJ 10.34

Tyson v Concurrent Systems Inc Ltd [2003] All ER (D) 09 (Sep), EAT 30.13, 30.28

U

UBS Wealth Management (UK) Ltd v Vestra Wealth LLP [2008] EWHC 1974 (QB), [2008] IRLR
965 .... 39.15
UK Coal Mining Ltd v National Union of Mineworkers (Northumberland Area) [2008] ICR 163,
[2008] IRLR 4, [2007] All ER (D) 315 (Oct), EAT 37.4
UNIFI v Union Bank of Nigeria [2001] IRLR 713 .... 48.27
UNISON v Brennan [2008] ICR 955, [2008] IRLR 492, 152 Sol Jo (no 13) 28, [2008] All ER (D) 29
(Apr), EAT 12.32, 21.23, 22.2
UNISON v Gallagher (2005) IDS Brief No 791 .... 18.3
Unison v Kelly (2012) UKEAT/0188/11/SM, [2012] IRLR 442, EAT; revsd [2012] EWCA Civ
1148, [2012] IRLR 951 .... 49.16
UNISON v Leicestershire County Council [2005] IRLR 920, [2005] 42 LS Gaz R 24, [2005] All ER
(D) 175 (Sep), EAT; revsd in part [2006] EWCA Civ 825, [2007] LGR 208, [2006] IRLR 810,
[2006] All ER (D) 339 (Jun) 19.33, 37.4
UNISON v National Probation Service South Yorkshire (UKEAT/0339/09/SM) [2010] IRLR 930,
[2010] All ER (D) 08 (Mar) 17.16
UNISON v Somerset County Council (UKEAT/0043/09/DA) [2010] ICR 498, [2010] IRLR 207,
[2010] All ER (D) 09 (Feb) 50.23
UNISON v United Kingdom [2002] IRLR 497, ECtHR 28.4, 28.7
UPS Ltd v Harrison (UKEAT/0038/11/RN) (16 January 2012, unreported) 52.4
Union Nationale des Entraîneurs et Cadres Techniques Professionnels du Football (UNECTEF) v
Heylens: 222/86 [1987] ECR 4097, [1989] 1 CMLR 901, ECJ 22.4
Union syndicale Solidaires Isère v Premier ministre: C-428/09 [2011] 1 CMLR 1206, [2011] IRLR
84, [2010] All ER (D) 172 (Nov), ECJ 55.3, 55.15, 55.17, 55.28
Unite the Union v Nortel Networks UK Ltd (in administration) [2010] EWHC 826 (Ch), [2010]
IRLR 1042, [2010] 2 BCLC 674, (2010) Times, 18 May, [2010] BPIR 1003, [2010] All ER (D) 164
(Apr) 29.10
United Arab Emirates v Abdelghafar [1995] ICR 65, [1995] IRLR 243, EAT 19.14
United Bank Ltd v Akhtar [1989] IRLR 507, EAT 7.22e, 56.22
United Closures and Plastics Ltd, petitioner [2011] CSOH 114, [2012] IRLR 29, 2011 SLT 1105, Ct
of Sess 43.14
United Kingdom v EU Council: C-84/94 [1996] ECR I-5755, [1996] All ER (EC) 877,
[1996] 3 CMLR 671, [1997] ICR 443, [1997] IRLR 30, ECJ 22.11, 55.1
United States of America v Nolan (Christine) [2010] EWCA Civ 1223, [2011] IRLR 40,
[2010] All ER (D) 87 (Nov) 37.4
United States of America v Nolan: C-583/10 [2013] 1 CMLR 961, [2013] ICR 193, [2012] IRLR
1020, (2012) Times, 26 December, [2012] All ER (D) 210 (Oct), ECJ 37.4
University College of Swansea v Cornelius [1988] ICR 735, EAT 18.50
University of Cambridge v Murray [1993] ICR 460, EAT 17.18
University of Huddersfield v Wolff [2004] ICR 828, [2004] IRLR 534, [2003] All ER (D) 245 (Oct),
EAT 12.3
University of Nottingham v Eyett [1999] 2 All ER 437, [1999] 1 WLR 594, [1999] ICR 721, [1999]
IRLR 87, [1999] ELR 141, [1999] 01 LS Gaz R 24, [1998] All ER (D) 584 .... 7.22d, 40.16
University of Oxford (Chancellor, Master and Scholars) v Humphreys [2000] 1 All ER 996,
[2000] 1 CMLR 647, [2000] ICR 405, [2000] IRLR 183, CA 50.16, 50.25
University of Stirling v University and College Union (2011) UKEATS/0001/11/BI, [2012] IRLR
266, EAT 37.3
University of Westminister v Bailey (UKEAT/0345/09) [2009] All ER (D) 47 (Nov) 17.30
Uratemp Ventures Ltd v Collins [2001] UKHL 43, [2002] 1 AC 301, [2002] 1 All ER 46, [2001] 3
WLR 806, [2002] 1 P & CR D28, 33 HLR 972, [2001] 43 EGCS 186, [2001] All ER (D) 154
(Oct) 41.5
Uyanwa-Odu v Schools Office Services Ltd (UKEAT/0294/05) (4 July 2008, unreported) 18.16

Table of Cases

V

VMI (Blackburn) Ltd v Camm (UKEAT/0011/11/JOJ) (2 June 2011, unreported) 17.37
Vakante v Governing Body of Addey and Stanhope School [2004] ICR 279, [2003] All ER (D) 352 (Dec), EAT; affd [2004] EWCA Civ 1065, [2004] 4 All ER 1056, [2005] 1 CMLR 62, [2005] ICR 231, [2004] 36 LS Gaz R 33, (2004) Times, 28 September, [2004] All ER (D) 561 (Jul) 7.24, 11.19, 23.6
Validity of Regulation 1435/2003, Re: European Parliament v EU Council: C-436/03 [2006] ECR I-3733, [2006] 3 CMLR 3, [2006] All ER (D) 12 (May), ECJ 15.39
Vaseghi v Brunel University (2006) 818 IDS Brief 10, [2006] All ER (D) 163 (Oct), EAT; affd [2007] EWCA Civ 482, 151 Sol Jo LB 709, [2007] All ER (D) 377 (May), sub nom Brunel University v Vaseghi [2007] IRLR 592 .... 12.9, 18.13
Vatish v Crown Prosecution Service (UKEAT/0164/11/DA) (18 April 2011, unreported) 18.18
Vauxhall Motors Ltd v Ghafoor [1993] ICR 376, EAT 52.10
Vauxhall Motors Ltd v Transport and General Workers Union [2006] IRLR 674, [2006] All ER (D) 214 (Apr), EAT 37.7
Vehicle & Operator Services Agency v Wright [2011] EWHC 1389 (Admin), [2011] RTR 387, [2011] NLJR 811, [2011] All ER (D) 09 (Jun) 55.35
Venables v Hornby (Inspector of Taxes) [2003] UKHL 65, [2004] 1 All ER 627, [2003] 1 WLR 3022, [2004] STC 84, [2004] ICR 42, (2003) Times, 5 December, 147 Sol Jo LB 1431, [2004] OPLR 19, [2003] All ER (D) 86 (Dec) 40.1
Vento v Chief Constable of West Yorkshire Police (No 2). See Chief Constable of West Yorkshire Police v Vento
Verdin v Harrods Ltd [2006] ICR 396, [2006] IRLR 339, [2005] All ER (D) 349 (Dec), EAT 18.28
Verholen v Sociale Versekeringsbank Amsterdam: C-87/90, C-99/90, and C-89/90 [1991] ECR I-3757, [1994] 1 CMLR 157, [1992] IRLR 38, ECJ 22.2
Viasystems (Tyneside) Ltd v Thermal Transfer (Northern) Ltd [2005] EWCA Civ 1151, [2006] QB 510, [2005] 4 All ER 1181, [2006] 2 WLR 428, [2006] ICR 327, [2005] IRLR 983, [2005] 44 LS Gaz R 31, [2005] All ER (D) 93 (Oct) 54.1, 54.3
Vicary v British Telecommunications plc [1999] IRLR 680, EAT 10.26
Victoria and Albert Museum v Durrant (UKEAT/0381/09/DM) [2011] IRLR 290, [2011] All ER (D) 19 (Jan) 31.35
Vidal-Hall v Hawley (UKEAT/0462/07/DA) (21 February 2008, unreported) 11.24
Vidal (Francisco Hernandez) SA v Perez: C-127/96, C-229/96 and C-74/97 [1998] ECR I-8179, [1999] IRLR 132, ECJ 50.5
Vidler v UNISON [1999] ICR 746 .... 18.77
Viggosdottir v Islandspostur HF [2002] IRLR 425 .... 50.9
Villalba v Merrill Lynch & Co Inc [2007] ICR 469, [2006] IRLR 437, 150 Sol Jo LB 742, [2006] All ER (D) 486 (Mar), EAT 10.17, 21.10, 21.12
Villella v MFI Furniture Centres Ltd [1999] IRLR 468 .... 7.22b, 40.16, 42.12, 56.19
Virdi v Metropolitan Police Comr [2007] IRLR 24, [2006] All ER (D) 214 (Oct), EAT 12.6, 12.7
Virdi v Metropolitan Police Comr [2009] EWCA Civ 477, [2009] All ER (D) 62 (Jun) 12.3
Virgo Fidelis Senior School v Boyle [2004] ICR 1210, [2004] IRLR 268, (2004) Times, 26 February, [2004] All ER (D) 214 (Jan), EAT 9.17, 12.18
Visa International Service Association v Paul [2004] IRLR 42, sub nom Paul v Visa International Service Association [2003] All ER (D) 265 (May), EAT 12.15, 51.7
Vogt v Germany (Application 17851/91) (1995) 21 EHRR 205, [1996] ELR 232, ECtHR 28.4
Voith Turbo Ltd v Stowe. See Stowe v Voith Turbo Ltd
Vokes Ltd v Bear [1974] ICR 1, [1973] IRLR 363, 15 KIR 302, 9 ITR 85, NIRC 52.11
Vorel v Nemocnice Cesky Krumlov: C-437/05 [2007] ECR-I 331 .... 55.5
Voss v Land Berlin: C-300/06 [2007] ECR I-10573, [2008] 1 CMLR 1313, [2007] All ER (D) 87 (Dec), ECJ 30.1
Voteforce Associates Ltd v Quinn [2002] ICR 1, [2001] All ER (D) 483 (Jul), EAT 27.2
Vroege v NCIV Instituut voor Volkshuisvesting BV: C-57/93 [1994] ECR I-4541, [1995] All ER (EC) 193, [1995] 1 CMLR 881, [1995] ICR 635, [1994] IRLR 651, [1995] 42 LS Gaz R 23, ECJ 21.11

W

W A Armstrong & Sons v Borril [2000] ICR 367, EAT 32.39

W A Goold (Pearmak) Ltd v McConnell [1995] IRLR 516, EAT 7.20
W & M Roith Ltd, Re [1967] 1 All ER 427, [1967] 1 WLR 432, 110 Sol Jo 963 .... 56.36
W Devis & Sons Ltd v Atkins [1977] AC 931, [1977] 2 All ER 321, [1977] 2 WLR 70, [1977] ICR
    377, [1976] IRLR 428, 12 ITR 12, 121 Sol Jo 52, CA; affd [1977] AC 931, [1977] 3 All ER 40,
    [1977] 3 WLR 214, [1977] ICR 662, [1977] IRLR 314, 13 ITR 71, 121 Sol Jo 512, 8 BLR 57,
    HL 4.3, 52.1, 52.10, 53.13
W E Cox Toner (International) Ltd v Crook [1981] ICR 823, [1981] IRLR 443, EAT 51.7
W Gimber & Sons Ltd v Spurrett (1967) 2 ITR 308, DC 36.7
WRN Ltd v Ayris [2008] EWHC 1080 (QB), [2008] IRLR 889, [2008] All ER (D) 276 (May)
    .... 39.10
Wadcock v London Borough of Brent [1990] IRLR 223 .... 7.42
Waddington v Leicester Council for Voluntary Services [1977] 2 All ER 633, [1977] 1 WLR 544,
    [1977] ICR 266, [1977] IRLR 32, 12 ITR 65, 121 Sol Jo 84, EAT 21.6
Wade v North Yorkshire Police Authority [2011] IRLR 393 .... 31.38, 31.41
Wadman v Carpenter Farrer Partnership [1993] 3 CMLR 93, [1993] IRLR 374, EAT 22.1
Wain v Guernsey Ship Management Ltd [2007] EWCA Civ 294, [2007] ICR 1350, [2007] All ER
    (D) 35 (Apr) 50.4
Waite v South East Coast Ambulance Services NHS Trust [2009] All ER (D) 43 (Jan), EAT 9.17
Wakeman v Quick Corpn [1999] IRLR 424, [1999] All ER (D) 158, CA 10.15
Waldemar Hudzinski v Agentur Fur Arbeit Wesel-Familienkasse: C-611/10 and C-612/10
    [2012] 3 CMLR 500, [2012] All ER (D) 43 (Sep), ECJ 23.3
Walden Engineering Co Ltd v Warrener [1993] 3 CMLR 179, [1993] ICR 967, [1993] IRLR 420,
    [1992] OPLR 1, EAT 50.19
Walker v Innospec Ltd [2013] Pens L R 21 .... 11.14
Walker v Josiah Wedgwood & Sons Ltd [1978] ICR 744, [1978] IRLR 105, 13 ITR 271, EAT
    .... 51.7
Walker v North Tees and Hartlepool NHS Trust (UKEAT/0563/07/RN) [2008] All ER (D) 55
    (Oct) 47.8
Walker v Northumberland County Council [1995] 1 All ER 737, [1995] ICR 702, [1995] IRLR 35,
    [1995] ELR 231, [1994] NLJR 1659 .... 7.19, 25.8
Wallace v C A Roofing Services Ltd [1996] IRLR 435 .... 13.2, 56.44
Wallace Bogan & Co v Cove [1997] IRLR 453, CA 39.11
Wallbank v Wallbank Fox Designs Ltd [2012] EWCA Civ 25, [2012] IRLR 307, [2012] All ER (D)
    01 (Feb) 25.7, 54.1, 54.2
Waller v Bromsgrove District Council (UKEATPA/0019/07) (14 July 2009, unreported) 19.14
Wallis v Ministry of Defence (UKEAT/0546/08) [2011] CMLR 1250, [2010] ICR 1301, [2010]
    IRLR 1035, [2010] All ER (D) 101 (Aug); affd sub nom Ministry of Defence v Wallis and Grocott
    [2011] EWCA Civ 231, [2011] ICR 617, [2011] All ER (D) 97 (Mar) 11.18, 23.9, 51.15
Walls Meat Co Ltd v Khan [1979] ICR 52, [1978] IRLR 499, 122 Sol Jo 759, CA 17.25
Walls Meat Co Ltd v Selby [1989] ICR 601, CA 52.11
Walmsley v C & R Ferguson Ltd [1989] IRLR 112, 1989 SLT 258, Ct of Sess 46.16
Walter v Secretary of State for Social Security [2001] EWCA Civ 1913, [2002] ICR 540, (2001)
    Times, 13 December, [2001] All ER (D) 71 (Dec) 10.30
Walter Braund (London) Ltd v Murray [1991] ICR 327, [1991] IRLR 100, EAT 53.10
Waltham Forest London Borough Council v Omilaju. See Omilaju v Waltham Forest London
    Borough Council
Walton v Airtours plc [2002] EWCA Civ 1659, [2004] Lloyd's Rep IR 69, [2003] IRLR 161,
    [2002] All ER (D) 34 (Nov) 42.15
Walton v Independent Living Organisation Ltd [2003] EWCA Civ 199, [2003] ICR 688, [2003]
    IRLR 469, (2003) Times, 27 February, 147 Sol Jo LB 266, [2003] All ER (D) 373 (Feb) 32.12
Walton Centre for Neurology and Neurosurgery NHS Trust v Bewley [2008] ICR 1047, [2008]
    IRLR 588, [2008] All ER (D) 341 (May), EAT 21.9
Waltons and Morse v Dorrington [1997] IRLR 488, EAT 7.19, 26.23, 51.7
Wandsworth Borough Council v Covent Garden Market Authority [2011] EWHC 1245 (QB),
    [2011] All ER (D) 173 (May) 17.25
Wandsworth London Borough Council v D'Silva [1998] IRLR 193, CA 7.13, 7.33
Wandsworth London Borough Council v Osei-Bonsu. See Osei-Bonsu v Wandsworth London
    Borough Council
Wang v Beijing Ton Ren Tang (UK) Ltd (UKEAT/0024/09/DA) [2010] All ER (D) 84 (Jan)
    .... 27.9

Table of Cases

Wang v University of Keele (UKEAT/0223/10/CEA) [2011] ICR 1251, [2011] IRLR 542, [2011] All ER (D) 88 (May), EAT 17.24

Ward Hadaway Solicitors v Love (UKEAT/0471/09) (25 March 2010, unreported) 50.3

Wardle v Crédit Agricole Corporate and Investment Bank [2011] EWCA Civ 545, [2011] ICR 1290, [2011] IRLR 604, [2011] NLJR 743, [2011] All ER (D) 101 (May) 12.15, 53.12, 53.13

Wardle v Crédit Agricole Corporate and Investment Bank (No. 2) [2011] EWCA Civ 770, [2011] IRLR 819 .... 12.15

Warner v Adnet Ltd [1998] ICR 1056, [1998] IRLR 394, CA 50.26, 52.11

Warnes v Trustees of Cheriton Oddfellows Social Club [1993] IRLR 58, EAT 51.5, 51.7

Warnock v Scarborough Football Club [1989] ICR 489, EAT 17.26, 18.22

Warren v Mendy [1989] 3 All ER 103, [1989] 1 WLR 853, [1989] ICR 525, [1989] IRLR 210, CA 7.21, 7.47c

Watson v Durham University [2008] EWCA Civ 1266, [2008] All ER (D) 249 (Oct) 7.22

Waters v Metropolitan Police Comr [1997] ICR 1073, [1997] IRLR 589, CA; revsd [2000] 4 All ER 934, [2000] 1 WLR 1607, [2000] ICR 1064, [2000] IRLR 720, HL 7.22d, 10.38, 10.54

Watkins v Crouch (t/a Temple Bird Solicitors) (UKEAT/0145/10ZT) [2011] IRLR 382, [2010] All ER (D) 87 (Sep) 52.11

Watt (formerly Carter) v Ahsan [2007] UKHL 51, [2008] 1 AC 696, [2008] 2 WLR 17, [2008] ICR 82, [2007] NLJR 1694, (2007) Times, 27 November, [2007] All ER (D) 334 (Nov), sub nom Ahsan v Watt (formerly Carter) [2008] 1 All ER 869, [2008] IRLR 243 .... 11.30, 12.2, 18.27

Watts v High Quality Lifestyles Ltd [2006] IRLR 850, [2006] All ER (D) 216 (Apr), EAT 10.15

Watts v Rubery Owen Conveyancer Ltd [1977] 2 All ER 1, [1977] ICR 429, [1977] IRLR 112, 12 ITR 60, 121 Sol Jo 34, EAT 17.27

Way v Crouch [2005] ICR 1362, [2005] IRLR 603, [2005] NLJR 937, [2005] All ER (D) 40 (Jun), EAT 12.13

Way v Powercraft Retail Ltd [2008] All ER (D) 151 (Aug), EAT 18.5, 18.16

Weathersfield Ltd (t/a Van and Truck Rentals) v Sargent [1999] ICR 425, [1999] IRLR 94, 143 Sol Jo LB 39, CA 10.53, 46.19

Webb v Airbus UK Ltd [2008] EWCA Civ 49, [2008] ICR 561, [2008] IRLR 309, (2008) Times, 26 February, [2008] All ER (D) 94 (Feb) 52.9

Webb v EMO Air Cargo (UK) Ltd [1992] 4 All ER 929, [1993] 1 WLR 49, [1993] 1 CMLR 259, [1993] ICR 175, [1993] IRLR 27, [1993] 9 LS Gaz R 44, 137 Sol Jo LB 48, HL; refd: C-32/93 [1994] QB 718, [1994] 4 All ER 115, [1994] ECR I-3567, [1994] 3 WLR 941, [1994] 2 CMLR 729, [1994] ICR 770, [1994] IRLR 482, [1994] NLJR 1278, ECJ; apld sub nom Webb v EMO Air Cargo (UK) Ltd (No 2) [1995] 4 All ER 577, [1995] 1 WLR 1454, [1996] 2 CMLR 990, [1995] ICR 1021, [1995] IRLR 645, [1995] 42 LS Gaz R 24, 140 Sol Jo LB 9, HL 10.15, 22.2

Weber v Universal Ogden Services Ltd: C-37/00 [2002] QB 1189, [2002] ECR I-2013, [2002] All ER (EC) 397, [2002] 3 WLR 931, [2002] ICR 979, [2002] IRLR 365, [2002] All ER (D) 377 (Feb), ECJ 23.8

Webster v Woodhouse School [2009] EWCA Civ 91, [2009] ICR 818, [2009] All ER (D) 184 (Feb), sub nom Woodhouse School v Webster [2009] IRLR 568 .... 18.63, 19.22

Weddall v Barchester Healthcare Ltd [2012] EWCA Civ 25, [2012] IRLR 307, [2012] All ER (D) 01 (Feb) 25.7, 54.1, 54.2

Weedon v Pinnacle Entertainment Ltd (UKEAT/0217/11/LA) [2012] All ER (D) 109 (Jan) 17.9

Weir v Bettison (sued as Chief Constable of Merseyside Police) [2003] EWCA Civ 111, [2003] ICR 708, [2003] 12 LS Gaz R 32, (2003) Times, 4 February, 147 Sol Jo LB 145, [2003] All ER (D) 273 (Jan) 54.2

Wellcome Foundation v Darby [1996] IRLR 538, EAT 17.18

Welsh v Cowdenbeath Football Club Ltd [2009] CSOH 16, [2009] IRLR 362, OH 56.20

Welton v Deluxe Retail Ltd (t/a Madhouse) (2012) UKEAT/0266/12/ZT, [2013] ICR 428, [2013] IRLR 166, [2013] All ER (D) 135 (Feb), EAT 6.7

Werhof v Freeway Traffic Systems GmbH & Co KG: C-499/04 [2005] ECR I-2397, [2006] IRLR 400, [2006] All ER (D) 145 (Mar), ECJ 5.12, 50.20

Wessex Dairies Ltd v Smith [1935] 2 KB 80, 104 LJKB 484, [1935] All ER Rep 75, 153 LT 185, 51 TLR 439, CA 39.8

West v Kneels Ltd [1987] ICR 146, [1986] IRLR 430, [1986] LS Gaz R 2488, EAT 51.13, 56.5

West Dunbartonshire Council v Wallace. See Strathclyde Regional Council v Wallace

West Midland Co-operative Society Ltd v Tipton [1986] AC 536, [1986] 1 All ER 513, [1986] 2 WLR 306, [1986] ICR 192, [1986] IRLR 112, 130 Sol Jo 143, [1986] LS Gaz R 780, [1986] NLJ Rep 163, HL 51.13, 52.4, 52.10, 52.15

West Midlands Passenger Executive v Singh [1988] 2 All ER 873, sub nom West Midlands Passenger Transport Executive v Singh [1988] 1 WLR 730, [1988] ICR 614, [1988] IRLR 186, 132 Sol Jo 933, CA 12.9, 18.12
WestLB AG London Branch v Pan (UKEAT/0308/11/DM) (19 July 2011, unreported) 18.50
Western Excavating (ECC) Ltd v Sharp [1978] QB 761, [1978] 1 All ER 713, [1978] 2 WLR 344, [1978] ICR 221, [1978] IRLR 27, 121 Sol Jo 814, CA 51.7
Westminster City Council v Cabaj [1996] ICR 960, [1996] IRLR 399, CA 52.10, 56.1
Westminster City Council v Haywood [1998] Ch 377, [1997] 2 All ER 84, [1997] 3 WLR 641, [1998] ICR 920, CA 40.17
Weston v Vega Space Systems Engineering Ltd [1989] IRLR 429, EAT 51.15
Westwood v Secretary of State for Employment [1985] AC 20, [1984] 1 All ER 874, [1984] 2 WLR 418, [1985] ICR 209, [1984] IRLR 209, 128 Sol Jo 221, [1984] LS Gaz R 1443, HL . 29.5, 56.27, 56.30
Wheeler v Patel [1987] ICR 631, [1987] IRLR 211, [1987] LS Gaz R 1240, EAT 50.12, 50.26
Whelan (t/a Cheers Off Licence) v Richardson [1998] ICR 318, [1998] IRLR 114, EAT 53.12
Whent v T Cartledge Ltd [1997] IRLR 153, EAT 5.12, 50.20
Whiffen v Milham Ford Girls' School [2001] EWCA Civ 385, [2001] LGR 309, [2001] ICR 1023, [2001] IRLR 468, [2001] All ER (D) 256 (Mar) 11.9
Whitbread & Co plc v Thomas [1988] ICR 135, [1988] IRLR 43, [1987] LS Gaz R 3500, EAT 52.9
Whitbread plc (t/a Whitbread Medway Inns) v Hall [2001] EWCA Civ 268, [2001] ICR 699, [2001] IRLR 275, [2001] 16 LS Gaz R 32, 145 Sol Jo LB 77, [2001] All ER (D) 338 (Feb) 52.4
Whitbread West Pennines Ltd v Reedy [1988] ICR 807, 20 HLR 642, CA 41.4
White v Bristol Rugby Ltd [2002] IRLR 204 .... 46.19
White v Chief Constable of South Yorkshire Police. See Frost v Chief Constable of South Yorkshire Police
White v Holbrook Precision Castings [1985] IRLR 215, CA 25.2
White v Knowsley Housing Trust [2008] UKHL 70, [2009] AC 636, [2009] 2 All ER 829, [2009] 2 WLR 78, [2009] 1 P & CR 519, [2009] PTSR 281, [2008] 50 EG 73 (CS), (2008) Times, 15 December, 153 Sol Jo (no 1) 32, [2008] All ER (D) 115 (Dec) 41.6
White v London Transport Executive [1982] QB 489, [1982] 1 All ER 410, [1982] 2 WLR 791, [1981] IRLR 261, 126 Sol Jo 277 .... 34.1
White v Reflecting Roadstuds Ltd [1991] ICR 733, [1991] IRLR 331, EAT 7.17, 7.22e
White v South London Transport Ltd [1998] ICR 293, EAT 52.11
Whitefield v General Medical Council [2002] UKPC 62, [2003] IRLR 39, 72 BMLR 7, (2002) Times, 29 November, [2002] All ER (D) 220 (Nov) 28.7
Whitehouse v Blatchford & Sons Ltd [2000] ICR 542 .... 50.26
Whitelock and Storr v Khan (UKEAT/0017/10/RN) (26 October 2010, unreported) 52.2
Whitely v Marton Electrical Ltd [2003] ICR 495, [2003] IRLR 197, (2003) Times, 2 January, [2002] All ER (D) 370 (Nov), EAT 13.2, 14.3
Whitewater Leisure Management Ltd v Barnes [2000] ICR 1049, [2000] IRLR 456, [2000] All ER (D) 568, EAT 50.5
Whittaker v Watson (P & D) (t/a P & M Watson Haulage) [2002] ICR 1244, 67 BMLR 28, (2002) Times, 26 March, [2002] All ER (D) 424 (Feb), EAT 17.13, 19.1, 28.7
Wickens v Champion Employment [1984] ICR 365, 134 NLJ 544, EAT 45.2
Wigan Borough Council v Davies [1979] ICR 411, [1979] IRLR 127, EAT 51.7
Wiggle Ltd v Burge (9 May 2012, unreported) 39.6
Wignall v British Gas Corpn [1984] ICR 716, [1984] IRLR 493, EAT 47.2
Wilcox v Birmingham CAB Services Ltd (UKEAT/0293/10/DM) [2011] EqLR 810, [2011] All ER (D) 73 (Aug), EAT 10.37, 11.9A
Wilding v British Telecommunications plc [2002] EWCA Civ 349, [2002] ICR 1079, [2002] IRLR 524, [2002] All ER (D) 278 (Mar) 53.5, 53.13
Wileman v Minilec Engineering Ltd [1988] ICR 318, [1988] IRLR 144, EAT 12.16, 18.76, 19.34
William B Morrison & Son Ltd (1999) IDS Brief No 648 .... 10.32
William Hill Organisation Ltd v Tucker [1999] ICR 291, [1998] IRLR 313, [1998] 20 LS Gaz R 33, 142 Sol Jo LB 140, CA 7.21, 7.47c, 56.21
Williams v British Airways plc [2008] ICR 779, [2008] All ER (D) 409 (Feb), EAT; revsd [2009] EWCA Civ 281, [2009] ICR 906, [2009] IRLR 491, (2009) Times, 28 April, [2009] All ER (D) 46 (Apr); on appeal sub nom British Airways plc v Williams [2010] UKSC 16, [2010] 2 All ER 1053n, [2010] 3 CMLR 544, [2010] IRLR 541, [2010] All ER (D) 237 (Mar) 55.19, 55.33
Williams v British Airways plc C-155/10 [2012] 1 CMLR 591, [2011] IRLR 948, [2011] NLJR 1292, [2011] All ER (D) 65 (Sep), ECJ 27.4, 27.8

Table of Cases

Williams v Cater Link Ltd (UKEAT/0393/08) [2009] All ER (D) 70 (Aug) 18.50, 19.24
Williams v Channel 5 Engineering Services Ltd IDS Brief No 609 .... 10.37
Williams v Compair Maxam Ltd [1982] ICR 156, [1982] IRLR 83, EAT 52.11
Williams v Ferrosan Ltd [2004] IRLR 607, [2004] All ER (D) 272 (May), EAT 17.14, 18.76, 19.46
Williams v J Walter Thompson Group Ltd [2005] EWCA Civ 133, [2005] IRLR 376, (2005) Times,
  5 April, 149 Sol Jo LB 237, [2005] All ER (D) 261 (Feb) 10.37, 11.9
Williams v Redcar and Cleveland Borough Council [2007] IRLR 494, [2007] All ER (D) 409 (Mar),
  EAT 12.33
Williams v University of Birmingham [2011] EWCA Civ 1242, [2011] All ER (D) 25 (Nov) 25.2
Williams v University of Nottingham [2007] IRLR 660, [2007] All ER (D) 304 (Jun), EAT . 23.9, 51.15
Williams v Watsons Luxury Coaches Ltd [1990] ICR 536, [1990] IRLR 164, EAT 46.3
Williams-Drabble v Pathway Care Solutions Ltd IDS Brief No 776 .... 11.9
Willment Bros Ltd v Oliver [1979] ICR 378 .... 53.12
Willoughby v CF Capital plc [2011] EWCA Civ 1115, [2011] IRLR 985, [2011] All ER (D) 132
  (Oct) 46.5, 46.20, 51.5
Willow Oak Developments Ltd (t/a Windsor Recruitment) v Silverwood [2006] EWCA Civ 660,
  [2006] IRLR 607, [2006] All ER (D) 351 (May) 39.1, 52.14
Wilson (HM Inspector of Taxes) v Clayton [2004] EWHC 898 (Ch), [2004] STC 1022, [2004] IRLR
  611, [2004] 19 LS Gaz R 29, (2004) Times, 7 June, [2004] All ER (D) 313 (Apr); affd [2004]
  EWCA Civ 1657, [2005] STC 157, 77 TC 1, [2005] IRLR 108, (2005) Times, 12 January, 149 Sol
  Jo LB 24, [2004] All ER (D) 94 (Dec) 53.19
Wilson v Ethicon Ltd [2000] IRLR 4, EAT 52.4
Wilson v Exel UK Ltd (t/a Exel) [2010] CSIH 35, 2010 SLT 671 .... 54.1, 54.2
Wilson v Health and Safety Executive (Equality and Human Rights Commission intervening) [2009]
  EWCA Civ 1074, [2010] 1 CMLR 772, [2010] ICR 302, [2010] IRLR 59, (2009) Times,
  26 October, 153 Sol Jo (no 40) 36, [2009] All ER (D) 200 (Oct) 11.9, 21.12
Wilson v Maynard Shipbuilding Consultants AB [1978] QB 665, [1978] 2 All ER 78, [1978] 2 WLR
  466, [1978] ICR 376, [1977] IRLR 491, 13 ITR 23, 121 Sol Jo 792, CA 51.15
Wilson v Post Office [2000] IRLR 834 .... 52.2
Wilson v Racher [1974] ICR 428, [1974] IRLR 114, 16 KIR 212, CA 56.17
Wilson v St Helens Borough Council [1999] 2 AC 52, [1998] 4 All ER 609, [1998] 3 WLR 1070,
  [1999] 1 CMLR 918, [1999] LGR 255, [1998] ICR 1141, [1998] IRLR 706, [1998] All ER (D)
  516, HL 50.26
Wilsons Solicitors v Johnson (UKEAT/515/10) [2011] ICR D21, EAT 18.74
Wilson and National Union of Journalists v United Kingdom (Applications 30668/96, 30679/61 and
  30678/96) [2002] IRLR 568, 13 BHRC 39, (2002) Times, 5 July, [2002] All ER (D) 35 (Jul),
  ECtHR 28.4, 48.19, 49.17
Wiltshire Police Authority v Wynn [1981] QB 95, [1980] 3 WLR 445, 79 LGR 591, [1980] ICR 649,
  124 Sol Jo 463, CA 14.3
Wiltshire County Council v National Association of Teachers in Further and Higher Education
  (1980) 78 LGR 445, [1980] ICR 455, [1980] IRLR 198, CA 51.6
Wiluszynski v Tower Hamlets London Borough Council (1989) 88 LGR 14, [1989] ICR 493, [1989]
  IRLR 259, 133 Sol Jo 628, CA 7.47, 32.14
Wincanton Ltd v Cranny [2000] IRLR 716 .... 39.1
Wincanton plc v Atkinson (UKEAT/0040/11/DM) (19 July 2011, unreported) 52.9
Winder v Aston University (UKEAT/0025-6/07/ZT) [2007] All ER (D) 45 (Nov) 21.19A
Winfield v London Philharmonic Orchestra Ltd [1979] ICR 726, EAT 14.3
Wippel v Peek & Cloppenburg Gmbh & Co Kg: C-313/02 [2004] ECR I-9483, [2005] ICR 1604,
  [2005] IRLR 211, ECJ 10.41, 30.4, 30.13, 30.16
Wise v Union of Shop, Distributive and Allied Workers [1996] ICR 691, [1996] IRLR 609 ...... 48.14
Wise Group v Mitchell [2005] ICR 896, [2005] All ER (D) 168 (Feb), EAT 56.25, 56.33
Wishart v National Association of Citizens Advice Bureaux Ltd [1990] ICR 794, [1990] IRLR 393,
  CA 7.42, 20.5, 38.9
Witley and District Men's Club v Mackay [2001] IRLR 595, [2001] All ER (D) 31 (Jun), EAT
  .... 27.4a
Wolf v Stadt Frankfurt Am Main: C-229/08 [2010] IRLR 244, [2010] All ER (D) 239 (Feb), ECJ
  .... 11.8
Wolstenholme v Post Office Ltd [2003] ICR 546, EAT 14.3
Wolstenholme v Refreshment Systems Ltd (t/a Northern Vending Services). See Refreshment
  Systems Ltd (t/a Northern Vending Services) v Wolstenholme

Wong v BAE Systems Operations Ltd [2004] IRLR 840, [2004] 33 LS Gaz R 34, (2004) Times,
    30 August, [2004] All ER (D) 131 (Jul), EAT 32.6
Wong v Igen Ltd (Equal Opportunities Commission intervening) [2005] EWCA Civ 142, [2005]
    3 All ER 812, [2005] ICR 931, [2005] IRLR 258, (2005) Times, 3 March, 149 Sol Jo LB 264,
    [2005] All ER (D) 300 (Feb) 9.17, 10.14, 10.17, 12.3, 55.23
Wood v Coverage Care Ltd [1996] IRLR 264, EAT 16.4, 52.11
Wood v Cunard Line Ltd [1991] ICR 13, [1990] IRLR 281, CA 51.11, 51.15
Wood v National Grid Electricity Transmission plc [2007] All ER (D) 358 (Oct), EAT 45.2c
Wood DIY Ltd, Re [2011] EWHC 3089 (Ch), [2012] BCC 67 .... 15.49
Wood Group Engineering Ltd v Robertson (UKEAT/0081/06) (6 July 2007, unreported) 45.2c
Wood Group Heavy Industrial Turbines Ltd v Crossan [1998] IRLR 680, EAT 53.2
Woodcock v Cumbria Primary Care Trust (UKEAT/0489/09/RN) [2011] ICR 143, [2011] IRLR
    119; affd [2012] EWCA Civ 330 .... 10.25, 11.9, 21.12
Woodhouse v Leeds City Council [2010] EWCA Civ 110, [2010] All ER (D) 208 (Jul), sub nom
    Leeds City Council v Woodhouse [2010] IRLR 625 .... 11.24
Woodhouse School v Webster. See Webster v Woodhouse School
Woodrup v Southwark London Borough Council [2002] EWCA Civ 1716, [2003] IRLR 111, 146 Sol
    Jo LB 263, [2002] All ER (D) 181 (Nov) 10.26, 17.13
Woods v Pasab Ltd [2012] EWCA Civ 1578, [2013] IRLR 305 .... 10.38
Woods v Suffolk Mental Health Partnership NHS Trust (UKEATPA/0360/06) unreported; affd
    [2007] EWCA Civ 1180 .... 19.12
Woods v WM Car Services (Peterborough) Ltd [1982] ICR 693, [1982] IRLR 413, [1982] Com LR
    208, CA 51.7
Woodward v Abbey National plc [2005] 4 All ER 1346, [2005] ICR 1702, [2005] IRLR 782,
    [2005] All ER (D) 64 (Aug), EAT; revsd [2006] EWCA Civ 822, [2006] 4 All ER 1209, [2006] ICR
    1436, [2006] IRLR 677, (2006) Times, 11 July, 150 Sol Jo LB 857, [2006] All ER (D) 253 (Jun)
    .... 9.17, 17.21, 19.2, 19.11, 19.14, 38.4, 55.23
Woodward v Santander UK plc (formerly Abbey National plc) (UKEAT/0250/09/ZT) [2010]
    IRLR 834, 154 Sol Jo (no 25) 41 .... 12.8, 12.9, 18.13
Wooster v Mayor and Burgesses of the London Borough of Tower Hamlets [2010] LGR 268, [2009]
    IRLR 980, [2009] All ER (D) 160 (Oct), EAT 10.25, 12.15
Worrall v Wilmott Dixon Partnerships Ltd (UKEAT/0521/09/DM) [2010] All ER (D) 107 (Jul)
    .... 5.8, 5.12
Wragg v Surrey County Council [2008] EWCA Civ 19, [2008] HLR 464, [2008] All ER (D) 09
    (Feb) 41.7
Wray v J W Lees & Co (Brewers) Ltd (UKEAT/0102/11/CEA) [2012] ICR 43, [2011] 39 LS Gaz
    R 19, [2011] All ER (D) 124 (Sep), EAT 55.5
Wright v London General Omnibus Co (1877) 2 QBD 271, 41 JP 486, 46 LJQB 429, 25 WR 647,
    36 LT 590, [1874–80] All ER Rep Ext 1721 .... 7.45
Wright v Redrow Homes (Yorkshire) Ltd [2004] EWCA Civ 469, [2004] 3 All ER 98, [2004] ICR
    1126, [2004] IRLR 720, 148 Sol Jo LB 666, [2004] All ER (D) 221 (Apr) 14.9, 55.3
Wright v Wolverhampton City Council (UKEAT/0117/08) [2009] All ER (D) 179 (Feb) 17.30
Wyatt v Kreglinger and Fernau [1933] 1 KB 793, 102 LJKB 325, [1933] All ER Rep 349, 148 LT
    521, 49 TLR 261, CA 39.4, 39.7
Wynnwith Engineering Co Ltd v Bennett [2002] IRLR 170, [2001] All ER (D) 134 (Dec), EAT
    .... 50.4

X

X v Citizens Advice Bureau (Equality and Human Rights Commission intervening) [2011] EWCA
    Civ 28, [2011] 2 CMLR 436, [2011] ICR 460, [2011] IRLR 335, 155 Sol Jo (no 4) 39, 118 BMLR
    147, [2011] All ER (D) 193 (Jan); affd sub nom X v Mid Sussex Citizens Advice Bureau [2012]
    UKSC 59, [2013] 1 All ER 1038, [2013] ICR 249, [2013] IRLR 146, 156 Sol Jo (no 48) 31,
    [2012] All ER (D) 97 (Dec) 10.41, 14.9, 10.41, 11.31
X v Metropolitan Police Comr [2003] ICR 1031, [2003] NLJR 719, [2003] All ER (D) 374 (Apr),
    sub nom X v Stevens [2003] IRLR 411, EAT 12.11, 18.18, 19.1, 19.26
X v United Kingdom (1977) 11 DR 55 .... 10.22
X v Y [2004] EWCA Civ 662, [2004] ICR 1634, [2004] IRLR 625, (2004) Times, 16 June, 148 Sol
    Jo LB 697, [2004] All ER (D) 449 (May) 17.13, 28.7, 52.9
X v Z Ltd [1998] ICR 43, CA 18.18

Table of Cases

X and Church of Scientology v Sweden (Application 7805/77) (1979) 16 DR 68, EComHR 10.22
XXX v YYY [2004] IRLR 137, [2003] All ER (D) 07 (Sep), EAT; revsd [2004] EWCA Civ 231,
    [2004] IRLR 471, [2004] All ER (D) 144 (Feb) 18.51, 28.7

Y

YKK Europe Ltd v Heneghan (UKEAT/0271/09/ZT) [2010] ICR 611, [2010] IRLR 563,
    [2010] All ER (D) 13 (Jun) 11.18
Yarrow v Edwards Chartered Accountants [2007] All ER (D) 118 (Aug), EAT 27.9
Yeboah v Crofton. See Crofton v Yeboah
Yell Ltd v Garton [2004] EWCA Civ 87, (2004) Times, 26 February, 148 Sol Jo LB 180,
    [2004] All ER (D) 80 (Feb) 19.30
Yellow Pages Sales Ltd v Davie (UKEATS/0017/11/BI) [2012] ICR D11 .... 17.21
Yemm v British Steel plc [1994] IRLR 117, EAT 32.6
Yenula Properties Ltd v Naidu [2002] EWCA Civ 719, [2003] HLR 229, [2002] 42 EG 162, [2002]
    27 LS Gaz R 34, [2002] 23 EGCS 121, (2002) Times, 5 June, [2002] All ER (D) 366 (May) 41.5
Yerrakalva v Barnsley Metropolitan Borough Council [2011] EWCA Civ 1255, [2012] 2 All ER 215,
    [2012] ICR 420, [2012] IRLR 78, [2011] NLJR 1595, [2011] All ER (D) 39 (Nov) 18.70, 18.72
York and Reynolds v Colledge Hosiery Co Ltd [1978] IRLR 53, Ind Trib 32.24
York Trailer Co Ltd v Sparkes [1973] ICR 518, NIRC 53.12
York Truck Equipment Ltd, Re IDS Brief No 439 .... 10.37
Yorkshire Blood Transfusion Service v Plaskitt [1994] ICR 74, EAT 21.10, 21.12
Young v Charles Church (Southern) Ltd (1997) 33 BMLR 101, CA 25.8
Young v Hexion Speciality Chemicals UK Ltd (UKEATS/0023/09/BI) (27 October 2009,
    unreported) 17.34
Young v National Power plc [2001] 2 All ER 339, [2001] ICR 328, [2001] IRLR 32, (2000) Times,
    23 November, [2000] All ER (D) 1727, CA 17.28
Young v Timmins (1831) 1 Cr & J 331, 9 LJOS Ex 68, 1 Tyr 226 .... 39.3
Young & Woods Ltd v West [1980] IRLR 201, CA 14.3
Young, James and Webster v United Kingdom (Applications 7601/76, 7806/77) (1981) 4 EHRR 38,
    [1981] IRLR 408, ECtHR 28.4
Young, James and Webster v United Kingdom [1983] IRLR 35 .... 28.4

Z

Zafar v Glasgow City Council. See Glasgow City Council v Zafar
Zaiwalla & Co v Walia [2002] IRLR 697, (2002) Times, 1 August, [2002] All ER (D) 103 (Aug),
    EAT 12.16, 12.18
Zaman v Kozee Sleep Products Ltd (t/a Dorlux Beds UK) (UKEAT/0312/10/CEA) [2011] IRLR
    196, [2011] ICR D5, [2011] All ER (D) 27 (Jan) 50.23
Zarb and Samuels v British and Brazilian Produce Co (Sales) Ltd [1978] IRLR 78, EAT 6.9
Zarkasi v Anindita (UKEAT/0400/11/JOJ) (18 January 2012, unreported) 7.24
Zentralbetriebsrat der Landeskrankenhauser Tirols v Land Tirol: C-486/08 [2010] IRLR 631,
    [2010] All ER (D) 172 (Apr), ECJ 27.3, 27.3A, 27.5, 30.10, 30.22, 31.51, 45.9
Zinda v Governing Body of Barn Hill Community High (UKEATPA/1146/09/LA) [2011] ICR
    174 .... 19.7, 19.17, 19.46
Zoi Chatzi v Ipourgos Ikonomikon: C-149/10 [2010] ECR I-8489, [2010] NLJR 1299, [2010] All ER
    (D) 84 (Sep), ECJ 31.51
Zurich Insurance Co v Gulson [1998] IRLR 118, EAT 18.56

Decisions of the European Court of Justice are listed below numerically. These decisions are also listed alphabetically in the preceding Table of Cases.

43/75: Defrenne v Sabena [1981] 1 All ER 122, [1976] ECR 455, [1976] 2 CMLR 98, [1976] ICR
    547, ECJ 21.9, 21.17, 21.18, 21.18a, 21.19, 22.2
33/76: Rewe-Zentralfinanz GmbH v Landwirtschaftskammer für Saarland [1976] ECR 1989,
    [1977] 1 CMLR 533, CMR 8382, ECJ 22.2

Table of Cases

12/81: Garland v British Rail Engineering Ltd [1983] 2 AC 751, [1982] 2 All ER 402, [1982] ECR 359, [1982] 2 WLR 918, [1982] 1 CMLR 696, [1982] ICR 420, [1982] IRLR 111, ECJ; apld [1983] 2 AC 751, [1982] 2 All ER 402, [1982] 2 WLR 918, [1982] 2 CMLR 174, [1982] ICR 420, [1982] IRLR 257, 126 Sol Jo 309, HL 40.8
61/81: EC Commission v United Kingdom of Great Britain and Northern Ireland [1982] ECR 2601, [1982] 3 CMLR 284, [1982] ICR 578, [1982] IRLR 333, ECJ 22.6
165/82: EC Commission v United Kingdom [1984] 1 All ER 353, [1983] ECR 3431, [1984] 1 CMLR 44, [1984] ICR 192, [1984] IRLR 29, ECJ 22.6
63/83: R v Kirk [1985] 1 All ER 453, [1984] ECR 2689, [1984] 3 CMLR 522, ECJ 28.5
135/83: Abels v Administrative Board of the Bedrijfsvereniging voor de Metaalindustrie en de Electrotechnische Industrie [1985] ECR 469, [1987] 2 CMLR 406, ECJ 50.11
186/83: Botzen v Rotterdamsche Droogdok Maatschappij BV [1985] ECR 519, [1986] 2 CMLR 50, ECJ 50.13
152/84: Marshall v Southampton and South West Hampshire Area Health Authority (Teaching) [1986] QB 401, [1986] 2 All ER 584, [1986] ECR 723, [1986] 2 WLR 780, [1986] 1 CMLR 688, [1986] ICR 335, [1986] IRLR 140, 130 Sol Jo 340, [1986] LS Gaz R 1720, ECJ 17.12, 22.6, 35.8
170/84: Bilka-Kaufhaus GmbH v Weber von Hartz [1986] ECR 1607, [1986] 2 CMLR 701, [1987] ICR 110, [1986] IRLR 317, ECJ 10.35, 11.9, 21.3, 21.11, 21.12
222/84: Johnston v Chief Constable of the Royal Ulster Constabulary [1987] QB 129, [1986] 3 All ER 135, [1986] ECR 1651, [1986] 3 WLR 1038, [1986] 3 CMLR 240, [1987] ICR 83, [1986] IRLR 263, 130 Sol Jo 953, [1987] LS Gaz R 188, ECJ 11.22, 22.6
24/85: Spijkers v Gebroeders Benedik Abbatoir CV and Alfred Benedik en Zonen BV [1986] ECR 1119, [1986] 2 CMLR 296, ECJ 50.5
66/85: Lawrie-Blum v Land Baden-Württemberg [1986] ECR 2121, [1987] 3 CMLR 389, [1987] ICR 483, ECJ 21.4
237/85: Rummler v Dato-Druck GmbH [1987] ICR 774, [1987] IRLR 32, ECJ 21.7
157/86: Murphy v Bord Telecom Eireann [1988] ECR 673, [1988] 1 CMLR 879, [1988] ICR 445, [1988] IRLR 267, (1988) Times, 6 February, ECJ 21.6, 21.8
222/86: Union Nationale des Entraîneurs et Cadres Techniques Professionnels du Football (UNECTEF) v Heylens [1987] ECR 4097, [1989] 1 CMLR 901, ECJ 22.4
324/86: Foreningen af Arbejdsledere i Danmark v Daddy's Dance Hall A/S [1988] ECR 739, [1989] 2 CMLR 517, [1988] IRLR 315, ECJ 50.6, 50.29
101/87: P Bork International A/S v Foreningen af Arbejdsledere i Danmark [1988] ECR 3057, [1990] 3 CMLR 701, [1989] IRLR 41, ECJ 50.6, 50.14
144/87 and 145/87: Berg and Busschers v Besselsen [1988] ECR 2559, [1989] 3 CMLR 817, [1990] ICR 396, [1989] IRLR 447, ECJ 50.6, 50.18
109/88: Handels-og Kontorfunktionaerernes Forbund i Danmark v Dansk Arbejdsgiverforening, acting on behalf of Danfoss [1989] ECR 3199, [1991] 1 CMLR 8, [1991] ICR 74, [1989] IRLR 532, ECJ 11.9, 21.12
171/88: Rinner-Kühn v FWW Spezial-Gebäudereinigung GmbH & Co KG [1989] ECR 2743, [1993] 2 CMLR 932, [1989] IRLR 493, ECJ 21.3, 21.11
C-177/88: Dekker v Stichting Vormingscentrum voor Jong Volwassenen (VJV-Centrum) Plus [1990] ECR I-3941, [1992] ICR 325, [1991] IRLR 27, ECJ 10.15, 10.31
C-262/88: Barber v Guardian Royal Exchange Assurance Group [1991] 1 QB 344, [1990] 2 All ER 660, [1990] ECR I-1889, [1991] 2 WLR 72, [1990] 2 CMLR 513, [1990] ICR 616, [1990] IRLR 240, [1990] NLJR 925, ECJ 21.3, 21.5, 21.15, 21.16, 21.17, 21.18a, 22.2, 40.1, 40.7
322/88: Grimaldi v Fonds des Maladies Professionnelles [1989] ECR 4407, [1991] 2 CMLR 265, [1990] IRLR 400, ECJ 22.1
C-33/89: Kowalska v Freie und Hansestadt Hamburg [1990] ECR I-2591, [1992] ICR 29, [1990] IRLR 447, ECJ 21.22, 21.23
C-106/89: Marleasing SA v La Comercial Internacional de Alimentacion SA [1990] ECR I-4135, [1992] 1 CMLR 305, [1993] BCC 421, 135 Sol Jo 15, ECJ 22.2
C-184/89: Nimz v Freie und Hansestadt Hamburg [1991] ECR I-297, [1992] 3 CMLR 699, [1991] IRLR 222, ECJ 21.3, 21.12, 21.22, 21.23
C-188/89: Foster v British Gas plc [1991] 1 QB 405, [1990] 3 All ER 897, [1990] ECR I-3313, [1991] 2 WLR 258, [1990] 2 CMLR 833, [1991] ICR 84, [1990] IRLR 353, ECJ; apld [1991] 2 AC 306, [1991] 2 All ER 705, [1991] 2 WLR 1075, [1991] 2 CMLR 217, [1991] ICR 463, [1991] IRLR 268, [1991] 18 LS Gaz R 34, HL 22.2, 35.8
C-192/89: Sevince v Staatssecretaris van Justitie [1990] ECR I-3461, [1992] 2 CMLR 57, ECJ 23.2

Table of Cases

C-229/89: EC Commission v Belgium [1991] ECR I-2205, [1993] 2 CMLR 403, [1991] IRLR 393,
ECJ 11.9
C-362/89: d'Urso v Ercole Marelli Elettromeccanica Generale SpA [1991] ECR I-4105,
[1993] 3 CMLR 513, [1992] IRLR 136, ECJ 50.26, 50.28
C-6/90 and C-9/90: Francovich and Bonifaci v Italy [1991] ECR I-5357, [1993] 2 CMLR 66, [1995]
ICR 722, [1992] IRLR 84, ECJ 22.2, 27.8
C-87/90, C-99/90, and C-89/90: Verholen v Sociale Versekeringsbank Amsterdam [1991] ECR I-
3757, [1994] 1 CMLR 157, [1992] IRLR 38, ECJ 22.2
C-208/90: Emmott v Minister for Social Welfare and A-G [1991] ECR I-4269, [1991] 3 CMLR 894,
[1993] ICR 8, [1991] IRLR 387, ECJ 22.2
C-360/90: Arbeiterwohlfahrt der Stadt Berlin e V v Bötel [1992] ECR I-3589, [1992] 3 CMLR 446,
[1992] IRLR 423, [1993] 21 LS Gaz R 45, ECJ 21.3, 21.11
C-29/91: Redmond (Dr Sophie) Stichting v Bartol [1992] ECR I-3189, [1994] 3 CMLR 265, [1992]
IRLR 366, ECJ 50.4, 50.5
C-109/91: Ten Oever v Stichting Bedrijfspensioenfonds voor het Glazenwassers- en
Schoonmaakbedrijf [1993] ECR I-4879, [1995] 2 CMLR 357, [1995] ICR 74, [1993] IRLR 601,
[1995] 42 LS Gaz R 23, ECJ 21.17
C-110/91: Moroni v Collo GmbH [1993] ECR I-6591, [1995] 2 CMLR 357, [1995] ICR 137, [1994]
IRLR 130, [1995] 12 LS Gaz R 23, ECJ 21.17
C-132/91, C-138/91 and C-139/91: Katsikas v Konstantinidis [1992] ECR I-6577, [1993] 1 CMLR
845, [1993] IRLR 179, ECJ 50.16
C-140/91, C-141/91, C-278/91 and C-279/91: Suffritti v Istituto Nazionale della Previdenza
Sociale (INPS) [1992] ECR I-6337, [1993] IRLR 289, ECJ 22.2
C-152/91: Neath v Hugh Steeper Ltd [1994] 1 All ER 929, [1993] ECR I-6935, [1995] 2 CMLR
357, [1995] ICR 158, [1994] IRLR 91, [1995] 42 LS Gaz R 23, ECJ 19.48, 21.17
C-173/91: EC Commission v Belgium [1993] IRLR 404, ECJ 21.3
C-200/91: Coloroll Pension Trustees Ltd v Russell [1994] ECR I-4389, [1995] All ER (EC) 23,
[1995] 2 CMLR 357, [1995] ICR 179, [1994] IRLR 586, [1995] 42 LS Gaz R 23, (1994) Times,
30 November, ECJ 21.17, 40.9
C-209/91: Rask and Christensen v ISS Kantineservice A/S [1992] ECR I-5755, [1993] IRLR 133,
ECJ 50.5
C-271/91: Marshall v Southampton and South West Hampshire Area Health Authority (No 2)
[1994] QB 126, [1993] 4 All ER 586, [1993] ECR I-4367, [1993] 3 WLR 1054, [1993] 3 CMLR
293, [1993] ICR 893, [1993] IRLR 445, ECJ; apld sub nom Marshall v Southampton and South-
West Hampshire Area Health Authority (Teaching) (No 2) [1994] 1 AC 530n, [1994] 1 All ER
736n, [1994] 2 WLR 392, [1994] ICR 242n, HL 12.13, 17.12, 18.67, 22.6
C-338/91: Steenhorst-Neerings v Bestuur van de Bedrijfsvereniging voor Detailhandel, Ambachten
en Huisvrouwen [1993] ECR I-5475, [1995] 3 CMLR 323, [1994] IRLR 244, ECJ 22.2
C-91/92: Faccini Dori v Recreb Srl [1994] ECR I-3325, [1995] All ER (EC) 1, [1995] 1 CMLR 665,
ECJ 22.2
C-125/92: Mulox IBC Ltd v Geels [1993] ECR I-4075, [1994] IRLR 422, ECJ 23.8
C-127/92: Enderby v Frenchay Health Authority [1994] 1 All ER 495, [1993] ECR I-5535,
[1994] 1 CMLR 8, [1994] ICR 112, [1993] IRLR 591, ECJ 19.48, 21.10, 21.11, 21.12
C-132/92: Birds Eye Walls Ltd v Roberts [1993] ECR I-5579, [1993] 3 CMLR 822, [1994] IRLR 29,
sub nom Roberts v Birds Eye Walls Ltd [1994] ICR 338, ECJ 21.16, 21.17
C-382/92: EC Commission v United Kingdom [1994] ECR I-2435, [1995] 1 CMLR 345, [1994]
ICR 664, [1994] IRLR 392, ECJ 22.2, 22.9
C-383/92: EC Commission v United Kingdom [1994] ECR I-2479, [1995] 1 CMLR 345, [1994]
ICR 664, [1994] IRLR 412, ECJ 22.8
C-392/92: Schmidt v Spar und Leihkasse der früheren Amter Bordesholm, Kiel und Cronshagen
[1994] ECR I-1311, [1995] 2 CMLR 331, [1995] ICR 237, [1994] IRLR 302, ECJ 50.5
C-399/92, C-409/92, C-425/92, C-34/93, C-50/93, and C-78/93: Stadt Lengerich v Helmig
[1994] ECR I-5727, [1995] 2 CMLR 261, [1996] ICR 35, [1995] IRLR 216, ECJ 21.12, 30.9
C-408/92: Smith v Avdel Systems Ltd [1994] ECR I-4435, [1995] All ER (EC) 132, [1995] 3 CMLR
543, [1995] ICR 596, [1994] IRLR 602, ECJ 19.48, 21.17, 40.7
C-410/92: Johnson v Chief Adjudication Officer (No 2) [1994] ECR I-5483, [1995] All ER (EC) 258,
[1995] 1 CMLR 725, [1995] ICR 375, [1995] IRLR 157, ECJ 22.2
C-7/93: Bestuur van het Algemeen Burgerlijk Pensioenfonds v Beune [1994] ECR I-4471,
[1995] All ER (EC) 97, [1995] 3 CMLR 30, [1995] IRLR 103, ECJ 21.17

Table of Cases

C-32/93: Webb v EMO Air Cargo (UK) Ltd [1994] QB 718, [1994] 4 All ER 115, [1994] 3 WLR
941, [1994] ECR I-3567, [1994] 2 CMLR 729, [1994] ICR 770, [1994] IRLR 482, [1994] NLJR
1278, ECJ; apld sub nom Webb v EMO Air Cargo (UK) Ltd (No 2) [1995] 4 All ER 577, [1995]
1 WLR 1454, [1996] 2 CMLR 990, [1995] ICR 1021, [1995] IRLR 645, [1995] 42 LS Gaz R 24,
140 Sol Jo LB 9, HL 10.15
C-46/93: Brasserie du Pecheur SA v Germany [1996] QB 404, [1996] ECR I-1029, [1996] All ER
(EC) 301, [1996] 2 WLR 506, [1996] 1 CMLR 889, [1996] IRLR 267, ECJ 22.2
C-57/93: Vroege v NCIV Instituut voor Volkshuisvesting BV [1994] ECR I-4541, [1995] All ER (EC)
193, [1995] 1 CMLR 881, [1995] ICR 635, [1994] IRLR 651, [1995] 42 LS Gaz R 23, ECJ 21.11
C-128/93: Fisscher v Voorhuis Hengelo BV [1994] ECR I-4583, [1995] All ER (EC) 193,
[1995] 1 CMLR 881, [1995] ICR 635, [1994] IRLR 662, ECJ 17.12, 21.17, 22.2
C-342/93: Gillespie v Northern Health and Social Services Board [1996] ECR I-475, [1996] All ER
(EC) 284, [1996] ECR I-475, [1996] 2 CMLR 969, [1996] ICR 498, [1996] IRLR 214, ECJ 21.14,
31.42, 40.13
C-400/93: Specialarbejderforbundet i Danmark v Dansk Industri acting for Royal Copenhagen A/S
[1995] ECR I-1275, [1995] All ER (EC) 577, [1996] 1 CMLR 515, [1996] ICR 51, [1995] IRLR
648, ECJ 21.11
C-435/93: Dietz v Stichting Thuiszorg Rotterdam [1996] ECR I-5223, [1997] 1 CMLR 199, [1996]
IRLR 692, 563 IRLB 13, ECJ 21.16, 21.17
C-449/93: Rockfon A/S v Specialarbejderforbundet i Danmark [1995] ECR I-4291, [1996] ICR 673,
[1996] IRLR 168, ECJ 37.4
C-450/93: Kalanke v Freie Hansestadt Bremen [1995] ECR I-3051, [1996] All ER (EC) 66,
[1996] 1 CMLR 175, [1996] ICR 314, [1995] IRLR 660, ECJ 11.10
C-457/93: Kuratorium für Dialyse und Nierentransplantation eV v Lewark [1996] ECR I-243,
[1996] IRLR 637, ECJ 21.3
C-472/93: Spano v Fiat Geotech SpA and Fiat Hitachi Excavators SpA [1995] ECR I-4321, ECJ
.... 50.28
C-13/94: P v S and Cornwall County Council [1996] ECR I-2143, [1996] All ER (EC) 397,
[1996] 2 CMLR 247, [1996] ICR 795, [1996] IRLR 347, [1997] 2 FCR 180, [1996] 2 FLR 347,
ECJ 10.18, 19.48, 21.2
C-48/94: Ledernes Hovedorganisation (acting for Rygard) v Dansk Arbejdsgiverforening (acting
for Sto Molle Akustik A/S) [1995] ECR I-2715, [1996] 3 CMLR 45, [1996] ICR 333, [1996]
IRLR 51, ECJ 50.5
C-84/94: United Kingdom v EU Council [1996] ECR I-5755, [1996] All ER (EC) 877,
[1996] 3 CMLR 671, [1997] ICR 443, [1997] IRLR 30, ECJ 22.11, 55.1
C-116/94: Meyers v Adjudication Officer [1995] All ER (EC) 705, [1995] ECR I-2131,
[1996] 1 CMLR 461, [1995] IRLR 498, ECJ 22.5
C-171/94 and C-172/94: Merckx v Ford Motors Co Belgium SA [1996] ECR I-1253, [1996] All ER
(EC) 667, [1997] ICR 352, [1996] IRLR 467, ECJ 50.5, 50.16
C-178/94, C-179/94, C-188/94, C-189/94 and C-190/94: Dillenkofer v Germany [1997] QB 259,
[1996] ECR I-4845, [1996] All ER (EC) 917, [1997] 2 WLR 253, [1996] 3 CMLR 469, [1997]
IRLR 60, ECJ 22.2
C-194/94: CIA Security International SA v Signalson [1996] ECR I-2201, [1996] All ER (EC) 557,
[1996] 2 CMLR 781, ECJ 22.2
C-298/94: Henke v Gemeinde Schierke and Verwaltungsgemeinschaft Brocken [1996] ECR I-4989,
[1997] All ER (EC) 173, [1997] 1 CMLR 373, [1997] ICR 746, [1996] IRLR 701, ECJ 15.6, 50.9
C-305/94: Hertaing v Benoidt [1996] ECR I-5927, [1997] All ER (EC) 40, [1997] 1 CMLR 329,
[1997] IRLR 127, ECJ 50.13
C-319/94: Jules Dethier Equipement SA v Dassy and Sovam SPRL (in liq) [1998] ECR I-1061,
[1998] All ER (EC) 346, 1998] 2 CMLR 611, [1998] ICR 541, [1998] IRLR 266, ECJ 50.11, 50.26
C-1/95: Gerster v Freistaat Bayern [1997] ECR I-5253, [1998] 1 CMLR 303, [1998] ICR 327, [1997]
IRLR 699, ECJ 21.3, 21.12
E-2/95: Eidesund v Stavanger Catering A/S: [1997] 2 CMLR 672, [1996] IRLR 684, EFTA Ct
.... 50.19
C-13/95: Suzen v Zehnacker Gebaudereinigung GmbH Krankenhausservice [1997] All ER (EC)
289, [1997] ECR I-1259, [1997] 1 CMLR 768, [1997] ICR 662, [1997] IRLR 255, ECJ 50.5
C-100/95: Kording v Senator für Finanzen [1997] ECR I-5289, [1998] 1 CMLR 395, [1997] IRLR
710, ECJ 21.3

Table of Cases

C-136/95: Caisse Nationale d'Assurance Vieillesse des Travailleurs Salaries v Thibault [1998] ECR
I-2011, [1998] All ER (EC) 385, [1998] 2 CMLR 516, [1998] IRLR 399, [1998] All ER (D) 167,
sub nom Thibault v Caisse Nationale d'Assurance Viellesse des Travailleurs Salaries (CNAVTS)
[1999] ICR 160, ECJ 10.31
C-188/95: Fantask A/S v Industriministeriet (Erhvervsministeriet) [1998] All ER (EC) 1,
[1997] ECR I-6783, [1998] 1 CMLR 473, ECJ 22.2
C-243/95: Hill v Revenue Comrs and Department of Finance [1998] ECR I-3739, [1998] All ER
(EC) 722, [1998] 3 CMLR 81, [1999] ICR 48, [1998] IRLR 466, [1998] 34 LS Gaz R 33,
[1998] All ER (D) 277, ECJ 21.3
C-383/95: Rutten v Cross Medical Ltd [1997] ECR I-57, [1997] All ER (EC) 121, [1997] ICR 715,
[1997] IRLR 249, ECJ 23.8
C-409/95: Marschall v Land Nordrhein-Westfalen [1997] ECR I-6363, [1997] All ER (EC) 865,
[1998] 1 CMLR 547, [2001] ICR 45, [1998] IRLR 39, ECJ 11.10
C-15/96: Schöning-Kougebetopoulou v Freie und Hansestadt Hamburg: [1998] All ER (EC) 97,
[1998] 1 CMLR 931, sub nom Kalliope Schöning-Kougebetopoulou v Freie und Hansestadt
Hamburg [1998] ECR I-47, ECJ 23.2
C-50/96: Deutsche Telekom AG v Schröder [2000] ECR I-743, [2002] 2 CMLR 583, [2000] IRLR
353, ECJ 21.17
C-66/96: Handels-og Kontorfunktionaerernes Forbund i Danmark (acting on behalf of Hoj
Pedersen) v Faellesforeningen for Danmarks Brugsforeninger (acting on behalf of Kvickly Skive)
[1998] ECR I-7327, [1999] 2 CMLR 326, [1999] IRLR 55, sub nom Pedersen v Kvickly Skive
[1999] All ER (EC) 138, [1998] All ER (D) 614, ECJ 21.14
C-127/96, C-229/96 and C-74/97: Vidal (Francisco Hernandez) SA v Perez [1998] ECR I-8179,
[1999] IRLR 132, ECJ 50.5
C-173/96: Sanchez Hidalgo v Asociacion de Servicios Aser and Sociedad Cooperativa Minerva
[1998] ECR I-8237, [2002] ICR 73, [1999] IRLR 136, ECJ 50.5
C-246/96: Magorrian v Eastern Health and Social Services Board [1997] ECR I-7153, [1998] All ER
(EC) 38, [1998] ICR 979, [1998] IRLR 86, ECJ 17.12
C-249/96: Grant v South-West Trains Ltd [1998] ECR I-621, [1998] All ER (EC) 193,
[1998] 1 CMLR 993, [1998] ICR 449, [1998] IRLR 206, [1998] 1 FCR 377, [1998] 1 FLR 839,
[1998] Fam Law 392, 3 BHRC 578, ECJ 28.5
C-326/96: Levez v T H Jennings (Harlow Pools) Ltd [1998] ECR I-7835, [1999] All ER (EC) 1,
[1999] 2 CMLR 363, [1999] ICR 521, [1999] IRLR 36, 608 IRLB 3, [1998] All ER (D) 662,
ECJ 17.12
C-394/96: Brown v Rentokil Ltd [1998] ECR I-4185, [1998] All ER (EC) 791, [1998] 2 CMLR
1049, [1998] ICR 790, [1998] IRLR 445, [1999] 1 FCR 49, [1998] 2 FLR 649, [1998] Fam Law
597, 48 BMLR 126, [1998] 34 LS Gaz R 34, [1998] All ER (D) 313, ECJ 10.32
C-399/96: Europièces SA (in liq) v Sanders [1998] ECR I-6965, [1999] All ER (EC) 831,
[2001] 1 CMLR 667, [1998] All ER (D) 574, ECJ 50.11
C-411/96: Boyle v Equal Opportunities Commission [1998] ECR I-6401, [1998] All ER (EC) 879,
[1998] 3 CMLR 1133, [1999] ICR 360, [1998] IRLR 717, [1999] 1 FCR 581, [1999] 1 FLR 119,
52 BMLR 169, 608 IRLB 5, [1998] All ER (D) 500, ECJ 21.14, 40.13
C-125/97: AGR Regeling v Bestuur van der Bedrijfsvereniging voor de Metaallnijverheid
[1998] ECR I-4493, [1999] 1 CMLR 1410, [1999] ICR 605, [1999] IRLR 379, [1998] All ER (D)
336, ECJ 29.5
C-167/97: R v Secretary of State for Employment, ex p Seymour-Smith [1999] 2 AC 554,
[1999] All ER (EC) 97, [1999] 3 WLR 460, [1999] ECR I-623, [1999] 2 CMLR 273, [1999] ICR
447, [1999] IRLR 253, ECJ; apld sub nom R v Secretary of State for Employment, ex p Seymour-
Smith (No 2) [2000] 1 All ER 857, [2000] 1 WLR 435, [2000] 1 CMLR 770, [2000] ICR 244,
[2000] IRLR 263, [2000] 09 LS Gaz R 40, HL 6.1, 11.9, 21.3, 21.11, 22.2, 51.11
C-185/97: Coote v Granada Hospitality Ltd [1998] ECR I-5199, [1998] All ER (EC) 865,
[1998] 3 CMLR 958, [1999] ICR 100, [1998] IRLR 656, [1998] All ER (D) 423, ECJ; apld Coote
v Granada Hospitality Ltd (No 2) [1999] 3 CMLR 334, [1999] ICR 942, [1999] IRLR 452,
EAT 38.4
C-249/97: Gruber v Silhouette International Schmied GmbH & Co KG [1999] ECR I-5295,
[1999] All ER (D) 1013, ECJ 21.14
C-273/97: Sirdar v Army Board and Secretary of State for Defence [1999] ECR I-7403,
[1999] All ER (EC) 928, [1999] 3 CMLR 559, [2000] ICR 130, [2000] IRLR 47, 7 BHRC 459,
[1999] All ER (D) 1156, ECJ 11.11, 11.22
C-309/97: Angestelltenbetriebsrat der Wiener Gebietskrankenkasse v Wiener Gebietskrankenkasse
[1999] ECR I-2865, [1999] 2 CMLR 1173, [1999] IRLR 804, [1999] All ER (D) 483, ECJ 21.6

Table of Cases

C-333/97: Lewen v Denda [2000] All ER (EC) 261, [1999] ECR I-7243, [2000] 2 CMLR 38, [2000] IRLR 67, ECJ 21.14
C-49/98, C-50/98, C-52/98 to C-54/98 and C-68/98 to C-71/98: Finalarte Sociedade de Construção Civil Lda v Urlaubs- und Lohnausgleichskasse der Bauwirtschaft [2001] ECR I-7831, [2003] 2 CMLR 333, [2001] All ER (D) 361 (Oct), ECJ 23.3
C-78/98: Preston v Wolverhampton Healthcare NHS Trust: [2001] 2 AC 415, [2000] ECR I-3201, [2000] All ER (EC) 714, [2001] 2 WLR 408, [2000] 2 CMLR 837, [2000] ICR 961, [2000] IRLR 506, [2000] All ER (D) 663, ECJ; apld sub nom Preston v Wolverhamptom Healthcare NHS Trust (No 2) [2001] UKHL 5, [2001] 2 AC 455, [2001] 3 All ER 947, [2001] 2 WLR 448, [2001] ICR 217, [2001] IRLR 237, (2001) Times, 8 February, 145 Sol Jo LB 55, [2001] All ER (D) 99 (Feb) 21.18, 21.19, 22.2
C-165/98: Mazzoleni (criminal proceedings against) [2001] ECR I-2189, ECJ 23.3
C-190/98: Graf v Filzmoser Maschinenbau GmbH [2000] ECR I-493, [2000] All ER (EC) 170, [2000] 1 CMLR 741, ECJ 23.2
C-198/98: Everson and Barrass v Secretary of State for Trade and Industry and Bell Lines Ltd [1999] ECR I-8903, [2000] All ER (EC) 29, [2000] 1 CMLR 489, [2000] IRLR 202, ECJ 29.3
C-207/98: Mahlburg v Land Mecklenburg-Vorpommern [2000] ECR I-549, [2001] 3 CMLR 887, [2001] ICR 1032, [2000] IRLR 276, [2000] All ER (D) 116, ECJ 10.30
C-218/98: Abdoulaye v Régie nationale des usines Renault SA [1999] ECR I-5723, [2001] 2 CMLR 372, [2001] ICR 527, [1999] IRLR 811, [1999] All ER (D) 1014, ECJ 21.14
C-226/98: Jørgensen v Foreningen af Speciallæger and Sygesikringens Forhandlingsudvalg [2000] ECR I-2447, [2002] 1 CMLR 1151, [2000] IRLR 726, ECJ 11.9
C-234/98: Allen v Amalgamated Construction Co Ltd [1999] ECR I-8643, [2000] All ER (EC) 97, [2000] 1 CMLR 1, [2000] IRLR 119, 632 IRLB 2, ECJ 50.6
C-236/98: Jämställdhetsombudsmannen v Örebro läns landsting [2000] ECR I-2189, [2000] 2 CMLR 708, [2001] ICR 249, [2000] IRLR 421, ECJ 21.5
C-303/98: Sindicato de Médicos de Asistencia Pública (Simap) v Conselleria de Sanidad y Consumo de la Generalidad Valenciana [2000] ECR I-7963, [2001] All ER (EC) 609, [2001] 3 CMLR 932, [2001] ICR 1116, [2000] IRLR 845, [2000] All ER (D) 1236, ECJ 55.5, 55.7
C-322/98: Kachelmann v Bankhaus Hermann Lampe KG [2000] ECR I-7505, [2002] 1 CMLR 155, [2001] IRLR 49, ECJ 10.35
C-343/98: Collino v Telecom Italia SpA [2000] ECR I-6659, [2001] All ER (EC) 405, [2002] 3 CMLR 997, [2002] ICR 38, [2000] IRLR 788, [2000] All ER (D) 1196, ECJ 15.6, 50.9
C-407/98: Abrahamsson v Fogelqvist [2000] ECR I-5539, [2002] ICR 932, [2000] IRLR 732, ECJ 11.10
C-11/99: Dietrich v Westdeutscher Rundfunk [2000] ECR I-5589, ECJ 26.5
C-62/99: Betriebsrat der Bofrost Josef H Boquoi Deutschland West GmbH & Co KG v Bofrost Josef H Boquoi Deutschland West GmbH & Co KG [2001] ECR I-2579, [2004] 2 CMLR 1223, [2001] IRLR 403, [2001] All ER (D) 350 (Mar), ECJ 15.24
C-172/99: Oy Liikenne Ab v Liskojärvi [2001] ECR I-745, [2001] All ER (EC) 544, [2001] 3 CMLR 807, [2002] ICR 155, [2001] IRLR 171, [2001] All ER (D) 168 (Jan), ECJ 50.5
C-173/99: R (on the application of the Broadcasting, Entertainment, Cinematographic and Theatre Union) v Secretary of State for Trade and Industry [2001] ECR I-4881, [2001] All ER (EC) 647, [2001] 1 WLR 2313, [2001] 3 CMLR 109, [2001] ICR 1152, [2001] IRLR 559, [2001] All ER (D) 272 (Jun), ECJ 22.11, 27.2
C-175/99: Mayeur v Association Promotion de l'Information Messine (APIM): [2002] ICR 1316, [2000] IRLR 783, ECJ 15.6, 50.9
C-350/99: Lange v Georg Schünemann GmbH [2001] All ER (EC) 481, [2001] ECR I-1061, [2001] IRLR 244, [2001] All ER (D) 90 (Feb), ECJ 7.11
C-381/99: Brunnhofer v Bank der österreichischen Postsparkasse AG [2001] All ER (EC) 693, [2001] ECR I-4961, [2001] 3 CMLR 173, [2001] IRLR 571, (2001) Times, 9 July, [2001] All ER (D) 273 (Jun), ECJ 21.6, 21.10, 21.12
C-438/99: Jiménez Melgar v Ayuntamiento de Los Barrios [2001] ECR I-6915, [2003] 3 CMLR 67, [2004] ICR 610, [2001] IRLR 848, [2001] All ER (D) 42 (Oct), ECJ 10.31
C-476/99: Lommers v Minister van Landbouw, Natuurbeheer en Visserij [2002] ECR I-2891, [2004] 2 CMLR 1141, [2002] IRLR 430, [2002] All ER (D) 280 (Mar), ECJ 21.3
C-37/00: Weber v Universal Ogden Services Ltd [2002] QB 1189, [2002] ECR I-2013, [2002] All ER (EC) 397, [2002] 3 WLR 931, [2002] ICR 979, [2002] IRLR 365, [2002] All ER (D) 377 (Feb), ECJ 23.8
C-51/00: Temco Service Industries SA v Imzilyen [2002] ECR I-969, [2004] 1 CMLR 877, [2002] IRLR 214, [2002] All ER (D) 199 (Jan), ECJ 50.7

clxv

Table of Cases

C-109/00: Tele Danmark A/S v Handels- og Kontorfunktionærernes Forbund i Danmark (HK) [2001] ECR I-6993, [2001] All ER (EC) 941, [2002] 1 CMLR 105, [2004] ICR 610, [2001] IRLR 853, [2001] All ER (D) 37 (Oct), ECJ 10.31

C-133/00: Bowden v Tuffnells Parcels Express Ltd [2001] All ER (EC) 865, [2001] ECR I-7031, [2001] 3 CMLR 1342, [2001] IRLR 838, [2001] All ER (D) 32 (Oct), ECJ 55.3

C-164/00: Beckmann v Dynamco Whicheloe MacFarlane Ltd [2002] ECR I-4893, [2002] All ER (EC) 865, [2002] 2 CMLR 1152, [2003] ICR 50, [2002] IRLR 578, (2002) Times, 17 June, [2002] All ER (D) 05 (Jun), ECJ 40.6, 50.19

C-187/00: Kutz-Bauer v Freie und Hansestadt Hamburg [2003] ECR I-2741, [2003] IRLR 368, [2003] All ER (D) 327 (Mar), ECJ 11.9

C-320/00: Lawrence v Regent Office Care Ltd [2002] ECR I-7325, [2002] 3 CMLR 761, [2003] ICR 1092, [2002] IRLR 822, (2002) Times, 10 October, [2002] All ER (D) 84 (Sep), ECJ 21.9

C-440/00: Gesamtbetriebsrat Der Kühne & Nagel AG & Co KG v Kühne & Nagel AG & Co KG [2004] ECR I-787, [2004] 2 CMLR 1242, [2004] IRLR 332 , [2004] All ER (D) 31 (Jan), ECJ 15.24

C-4/01: Martin v South Bank University [2003] ECR I-12859, [2004] 1 CMLR 472, [2004] ICR 1234, [2004] IRLR 74, [2003] OPLR 317, [2003] All ER (D) 85 (Nov), ECJ 40.6, 50.19, 50.29

C-117/01: KB v National Health Service Pensions Agency [2004] ECR I-541, [2004] All ER (EC) 1089, [2001] 1 CMLR 931, [2004] ICR 781, [2004] IRLR 240, [2004] 1 FLR 683, (2004) Times, 15 January, [2004] All ER (D) 03 (Jan), ECJ 21.13

C-160/01: Mau v Bundesanstalt fur Arbeit [2003] ECR I-4791, [2004] 1 CMLR 1113, [2003] All ER (D) 197 (May), ECJ 29.5

C-256/01: Allonby v Accrington and Rossendale College [2004] ECR I-873, [2005] All ER (EC) 289, [2004] 1 CMLR 1141, [2004] ICR 1328, [2004] IRLR 224, [2004] All ER (D) 47 (Jan), ECJ 21.9, 21.16, 21.18, 22.2

C-320/01: Busch v Klinikum Neustadt GmbH & Co Betriebs-KG [2003] ECR I-2041, [2003] All ER (EC) 985, [2003] 2 CMLR 481, [2003] IRLR 625, [2004] 1 FCR 54, [2003] All ER (D) 394 (Feb), ECJ 10.30

C-340/01: Abler v Sodexho MM Catering Betriebsgesellschaft mbH [2003] ECR I-14023, [2004] IRLR 168, [2003] All ER (D) 277 (Nov), ECJ 50.5

C-342/01: Gomez (Merino) v Continental Industrias del Caucho SA [2004] ECR I-2605, [2004] 2 CMLR 38, [2005] ICR 1040, [2004] IRLR 407, [2004] All ER (D) 350 (Mar), ECJ 27.3a, 27.5, 31.21

C-349/01: Betriebsrat der Firma ADS Anker GmbH v ADS Anker GmbH [2004] ECR I-6803, [2004] 3 CMLR 299, (2004) IDS Brief No 763, [2004] All ER (D) 270 (Jul), ECJ 15.24

C-397/01 to C-403/01: Pfeiffer v Deutsches Rotes Kreuz, Kreisverband Waldshut eV [2005] ICR 1307, [2005] IRLR 137, [2004] All ER (D) 52 (Oct), ECJ 55.2, 55.3, 55.8

E-1/02: EFTA Surveillance Authority v Norway [2003] 1 CMLR 725, [2003] IRLR 318, EFTA Ct 11.10

C-4/02 and C-5/02: Schönheit (Hilde) v Stadt Frankfurt am Main [2003] ECR I-12575, [2004] IRLR 983, [2003] All ER (D) 401 (Oct), ECJ 11.9, 21.12, 40.13

C-77/02: Steinicke v Bundesanstalt fur Arbeit [2003] ECR I-9027, [2003] IRLR 892, [2003] All ER (D) 87 (Sep), ECJ 21.3

C-147/02: Alabaster v Woolwich plc and Secretary of State for Social Security [2004] ECR I-3101, [2005] All ER (EC) 490, [2004] 2 CMLR 186, [2005] ICR 695, [2004] IRLR 486, [2004] All ER (D) 558 (Mar), ECJ 21.14, 31.42

C-151/02: Landeshauptstadt Kiel v Jaeger [2003] ECR I-8389, [2004] All ER (EC) 604, [2003] 3 CMLR 493, [2004] ICR 1528, [2003] IRLR 804, 75 BMLR 201, [2003] All ER (D) 72 (Sep), ECJ 55.5, 55.14, 55.15, 55.17

C-159/02: Turner v Grovit [2005] 1 AC 101, [2004] ECR I-3565, [2004] 2 All ER (Comm) 381, [2004] All ER (EC) 485, [2004] 3 WLR 1193, [2004] 2 Lloyd's Rep 169, [2005] ICR 23, [2004] IRLR 899, (2004) Times, 29 April, [2004] All ER (D) 259 (Apr), ECJ 23.8

C-281/02: Owusu v Jackson (t/a Villa Holidays Bal-Inn Villas) [2005] QB 801, [2005] ECR I-1383, [2005] 2 All ER (Comm) 577, [2005] 2 WLR 942, [2005] 1 Lloyd's Rep 452, (2005) Times, 9 March, [2005] All ER (D) 47 (Mar), ECJ 23.8

C-284/02: Land Brandenburg v Sass [2005] IRLR 147, [2004] All ER (D) 310 (Nov), ECJ 10.31

C-285/02: Elsner-Lakeberg v Land Nordrhein-Westfalen [2004] ECR I-5861, [2004] 2 CMLR 874, [2005] IRLR 209, [2004] All ER (D) 423 (May), ECJ 21.5

C-313/02: Wippel v Peek & Cloppenburg Gmbh & Co Kg [2004] ECR I-9483, [2005] ICR 1604, [2005] IRLR 211, ECJ 10.41, 30.4, 30.13, 30.16

Table of Cases

C-341/02: EC Commission v Germany [2005] ECR I-2733, [2005] All ER (D) 172 (Apr), ECJ
.... 23.3
C-188/03: Junk v Kuhnel [2005] ECR I-885, [2005] IRLR 310, [2005] All ER (D) 264 (Jan), ECJ
.... 37.4
C-436/03: Validity of Regulation 1435/2003, Re: European Parliament v EU Council [2006] ECR I-3733, [2006] 3 CMLR 3, [2006] All ER (D) 12 (May), ECJ 15.39
C-478/03: Celtec Ltd v Astley [2005] ECR I-4389, [2005] ICR 1409, [2005] IRLR 647, (2005) Times, 9 June, [2005] All ER (D) 400 (May), ECJ 6.9, 50.12
C-14/04: Dellas v Premier Ministre [2006] IRLR 225, [2005] All ER (D) 19 (Dec), ECJ 55.5
C-52/04: Personalrat der Feuerwchr Hamburg v Leiter der Feuerwehr Hamburg (14 July 2005, unreported), ECJ 55.3
C-131/04: Robinson-Steele v RD Retail Services Ltd [2006] ECR I-2531, [2006] All ER (EC) 749, [2006] ICR 932, [2006] IRLR 386, (2006) Times, 22 March, [2006] All ER (D) 238 (Mar), ECJ
.... 19.2, 19.48, 27.4, 27.8, 55.25
C-144/04: Mangold v Helm [2005] ECR I-9981, [2006] All ER (EC) 383, [2006] IRLR 143, [2005] All ER (D) 287 (Nov), ECJ 10.10, 11.9, 17.12, 22.2
C-212/04: Adeneler v Ellinikos Organismos Galaktos [2006] ECR I-6057, [2007] All ER (EC) 82, [2006] 3 CMLR 867, [2006] IRLR 716, [2006] All ER (D) 25 (Jul), ECJ 22.2, 45.9
C-232/04 and C-233/04: Guney-Gorres v Securicor Aviation (Germany) Ltd: [2005] ECR I-11237, [2006] IRLR 305, [2005] All ER (D) 230 (Dec), ECJ 50.5
C-294/04: Herrero (Sarkatzis) v Instituto Madrileno de la Salud (Imsalud) [2006] ECR I-1513, [2006] IRLR 296, [2006] All ER (D) 220 (Feb), ECJ 10.31
C-484/04: EC Commission v United Kingdom [2006] ECR I-7471, [2006] 3 CMLR 1322, [2007] ICR 592, [2006] IRLR 888, (2006) Times, 21 September, [2006] All ER (D) 32 (Sep), ECJ 22.11, 55.2, 55.15, 55.26
C-499/04: Werhof v Freeway Traffic Systems GmbH & Co KG [2005] ECR I-2397, [2006] IRLR 400, [2006] All ER (D) 145 (Mar), ECJ 5.12, 50.20
C-13/05: Navas (Chacon) v Eurest Colectividades SA [2006] ECR I-6467, [2007] All ER (EC) 59, [2. 006] 3 CMLR 1123, [2007] ICR 1, [2006] IRLR 706, (2006) Times, 9 August, [2006] All ER (D) 132 (Jul), ECJ22.6
C-17/05: Cadman v Health and Safety Executive [2006] ECR I-9583, [2007] All ER (EC) 1, [2007] 1 CMLR 530, [2006] ICR 1623, [2006] IRLR 969, (2006) Times, 6 October, [2006] All ER (D) 17 (Oct), ECJ 11.9, 21.12
C-124/05: Federatie Nederlandse Vakbeweging v Netherlands State [2006] ECR I-3423, [2006] All ER (EC) 913, [2006] ICR 962, [2006] IRLR 561, [2006] All ER (D) 69 (Apr), ECJ
.... 27.3
C-270/05: Athinaiki Chartopoiia AE v Panagiotidis [2007] ECR I-1499, [2007] IRLR 284, [2007] All ER (D) 186 (Feb), ECJ 37.4
C-278/05: Robins v Secretary of State for Work and Pensions [2007] ECR I-1053, [2007] All ER (EC) 648, [2007] 2 CMLR 269, [2007] ICR 779, [2007] IRLR 270, (2007) Times, 30 January, [2007] All ER (D) 195 (Jan), ECJ 22.2, 29.7
C-307/05: Del Cerro Alonso v Osakidetza-Servicio Vasco de Salud [2007] ECR I-7109, [2007] 3 CMLR 1492, [2008] ICR 145, [2007] IRLR 911, [2007] All ER (D) 87 (Sep), ECJ 45.9
C-411/05: Palacios de la Villa v Cortefiel Servicios SA [2007] ECR I-8531, [2008] All ER (EC) 249, [2008] 1 CMLR 385, [2009] ICR 1111, [2007] IRLR 989, (2007) Times, 23 October, [2007] All ER (D) 207 (Oct), ECJ 10.10, 11.9, 22.2, 40.5
C-437/05: Vorel v Nemocnice Cesky Krumlov [2007] ECR-I 331 .... 55.5
C-458/05: Jouini v Princess Personal Service GmbH (PPS) [2007] 3 CMLR 1472, [2008] ICR 128, [2007] IRLR 1005, [2007] All ER (D) 84 (Sep), ECJ 50.5
C-267/06: Maruko v Versorgungsanstalt der deutschen Buhnen [2008] ECR I-1757, [2008] All ER (EC) 977, [2008] IRLR 450, [2008] All ER (D) 07 (Apr), ECJ 10.36, 11.14
C-268/06: Impact v Minister for Agriculture and Food [2008] ECR I-2483, [2009] All ER (EC) 306, [2008] 2 CMLR 1265, [2008] IRLR 552, [2008] All ER (D) 194 (Apr), ECJ 17.12, 22.2, 45.9
C-300/06: Voss v Land Berlin [2007] ECR I-10573, [2008] 1 CMLR 1313, [2007] All ER (D) 87 (Dec), ECJ 30.1
C-303/06: Coleman v Attridge Law [2008] ECR I-5603, [2008] All ER (EC) 1105, [2008] 3 CMLR 777, [2008] ICR 1128, [2008] IRLR 722, (2008) Times, 29 July, [2008] All ER (D) 245 (Jul), ECJ 19.48
C-346/06: Ruffert (Dirk) v Land Niedersachsen [2008] ECR I-1989, [2008] All ER (EC) 902, [2008] IRLR 467, [2008] All ER (D) 37 (Apr), ECJ 23.3

Table of Cases

C-350/06: Schultz-Hoff v Deutsche Rentenversicherung Bund [2009] All ER (EC) 906, [2009] 2 CMLR 657, [2009] ICR 932, [2009] IRLR 214, (2009) Times, 28 January, [2009] All ER (D) 147 (Jan), ECJ 27.3

C-427/06: Bartsch v Bosch und Siemens Hausgerate (BSH) Altersfursorge GmbH [2008] ECR I-7245, [2009] All ER (EC) 113, [2009] 1 CMLR 163, [2008] All ER (D) 29 (Oct), ECJ 10.10

C-445/06: Danske Slagterier v Bundesrepublik Deutschland [2010] All ER (EC) 74, [2009] 3 CMLR 311, [2009] All ER (D) 272 (Mar), ECJ 22.2

C-460/06: Paquay v Societe d'architectes Hoet + Minne SPRL [2008] 1 CMLR 263, [2008] ICR 420, [2007] All ER (D) 137 (Oct), ECJ 10.30

C-462/06: Glaxosmithkline v Rouard [2008] ECR I-3965, [2008] ICR 1375, [2008] All ER (D) 312 (May), ECJ 23.8

C-506/06: Mayr v Backerei und Konditorei Gerhard Flockner OHG [2008] All ER (EC) 613, [2008] ECR I-1017, [2008] 2 CMLR 759, [2008] IRLR 387, [2008] 3 FCR 44, [2008] 1 FLR 1242, [2008] Fam Law 381, [2008] Fam Law 512, (2008) Times, 12 March, [2008] All ER (D) 370 (Feb), ECJ 10.30, 31.2

C-520/06: HM Revenue and Customs v Stringer [2009] All ER (EC) 906, [2009] 2 CMLR 657, [2009] ICR 932, [2009] IRLR 214, (2009) Times, 28 January, [2009] All ER (D) 147 (Jan), ECJ 27.3

C-54/07. Centrum voor gelijkheid van kansen en voor Racismebestrijding v Firma Feryn NV [2008] ECR I-5187, [2008] All ER (EC) 1127, [2008] 3 CMLR 695, [2008] ICR 1390, [2008] IRLR 732, (2008) Times, 16 July, [2008] All ER (D) 139 (Jul), ECJ 10.43

C-310/07: Sweden v Holmqvist [2008] ECR I-7871, [2009] ICR 675, [2008] IRLR 970, [2008] All ER (D) 265 (Oct), ECJ 29.3

C-388/07: Incorporated Trustees of the National Council on Ageing (Age Concern England) v Secretary of State for Business, Enterprise and Regulatory Reform [2009] All ER (EC) 619, [2009] 3 CMLR 105, [2009] ICR 1080, [2009] IRLR 373, (2009) Times, 9 March, [2009] All ER (D) 51 (Mar), ECJ 11.9

C-466/07: Klarenberg v Ferrotron Technologies GmbH [2009] ICR 1263, [2009] IRLR 301, [2009] All ER (D) 133 (Feb), ECJ 50.4

C-555/07: Seda Kucukdeveci v Swedex GmbH & Co KG [2010] All ER (EC) 867, [2010] 2 CMLR 874, [2010] IRLR 346, [2010] All ER (D) 126 (Feb), ECJ 10.10, 11.9, 17.12, 22.2

C-44/08: Akavan Erityisalojen Keskusliitto AEK ry v Fujitsu Siemens Computers Oy [2010] 1 CMLR 309, [2010] ICR 444, [2009] IRLR 944, [2009] All ER (D) 69 (Sep), ECJ 37.4

C-116/08: Meerts v Proost NV [2010] All ER (EC) 1085, [2009] All ER (D) 259 (Oct), ECJ 30.1, 31.51

C-194/08: Gassmayr v Bundesminister Fur Wissenschaft und Forschung [2010] ECR I-6281, [2011] 1 CMLR 175, ECJ 31.11, 31.15

C-229/08: Wolf v Stadt Frankfurt Am Main [2010] IRLR 244, [2010] All ER (D) 239 (Feb), ECJ 11.8

C-277/08: Pereda v Madrid Movilidad SA [2010] 1 CMLR 103, [2009] IRLR 959, [2009] NLJR 1323, (2009) Times, 8 October, [2009] All ER (D) 88 (Sep), ECJ 27.3a, 27.5

C-341/08: Petersen v Berufungsausschuss fur Zahnarzte fur den Bezirk Westfalen-Lippe: C-341/08 [2010] IRLR 254, sub nom Peterson v Berufungsausschuss fur Zahnarzte fur den Bezirk Westfalen-Lippe [2010] All ER (D) 233 (Feb), ECJ 11.9, 40.5

C-395/08: Istituto Nazionale Della Previdenza Sociale (Inps) v Bruno [2010] 3 CMLR 1225, [2010] IRLR 890, ECJ 30.1, 30.11

C-396/08: Istituto Nazionale Della Previdenza Sociale (Inps) v Lotti [2010] 3 CMLR 1225, [2010] IRLR 890, ECJ 30.1, 30.11

C-405/08: Holst v Dansk Arbejdsgiverforening [2010] 2 CMLR 49, ECJ 15.4, 15.21

C-471/08: Parviainen v Finnair Oyj [2011] 1 CMLR 209, [2011] ICR 99, ECJ 31.15

C-486/08: Zentralbetriebsrat der Landeskrankenhäuser Tirols v Land Tirol [2010] IRLR 631, [2010] All ER (D) 172 (Apr), ECJ 27.3, 27.3a, 27.5, 30.10, 30.22, 31.51, 45.9

C-499/08: Ingeniorforeningen i Danmark, acting on behalf of Ole Andersen v Region Syddanmark [2011] 1 CMLR 1140, [2010] All ER (D) 99 (Oct), ECJ 11.9

C-45/09: Rosenbladt (Gisela) v Oellerking Gebaudereinigungsges mbH [2011] 1 CMLR 1011, [2011] IRLR 51, [2010] All ER (D) 101 (Oct), ECJ 11.9, 40.5

C-104/09: Pedro Manuel Roca Alvarez v Sesa Start Espana ETT SA [2011] All ER (EC) 253, [2011] 1 CMLR 861, [2010] NLJR 1531, [2010] All ER (D) 277 (Oct), ECJ 31.51, 31.52

C-151/09: Federación de Servicios Públicos de la UGT (UGT-FSP) v Ayuntamiento de La Línea de la Concepción [2010] ICR 1248, [2010] All ER (D) 30 (Dec), ECJ 50.21

Table of Cases

C-236/09: Association belge des Consommateurs Test-Achats ASBL v Conseil des ministres [2011] NLJR 363, [2011] Pens LR 145, [2011] All ER (D) 07 (Mar), ECJ 40.9
C-242/09: Albron Catering BV v FNV Bondgenoten [2011] 1 CMLR 1267, [2011] ICR 373, [2011] IRLR 76, [2010] All ER (D) 161 (Nov), ECJ 50.6
C-250/09 and C-268/09: Georgiev v Tehnicheski universitet – Sofia, filial Plovdiv [2011] 2 CMLR 179, [2010] All ER (D) 25 (Dec), ECJ 11.9, 40.5
C-356/09: Kleist v Pensionsversicherungsanstalt [2010] All ER (D) 37 (Dec), ECJ 40.1
C-428/09: Union syndicale Solidaires Isère v Premier ministre [2011] 1 CMLR 1206, [2011] IRLR 84, [2010] All ER (D) 172 (Nov), ECJ 55.3, 55.15, 55.17, 55.28
C-429/09: Fub v Stadt Halle (No 2) [2011] 2 CMLR 305, [2011] IRLR 176, [2010] All ER (D) 24 (Dec), ECJ 55.8, 55.15, 55.21, 55.22
C-444/09: Gavieiro Gavieiro v Conselleria de Educacion e Ordenacion Universitaria de la Xunta de Galicia [2011] IRLR 504, [2011] All ER (D) 05 (Jan), ECJ 45.9
C-447/09: Prigge v Deutsche Lufthansa AG [2011] IRLR 1052, [2011] 38 LS Gaz R 19, [2011] All ER (D) 102 (Sep), ECJ 11.9, 40.5
C-463/09: CLECE SA v Valor [2011] IRLR 251, [2011] All ER (D) 156 (Jan), ECJ 50.5
C-108/10: Scattolon v Ministero Dell'istruzione, Dell'università E Della Ricerca [2012] 1 CMLR 432, [2011] IRLR 1020, ECJ 50.9
C-149/10: Zoi Chatzi v Ipourgos Ikonomikon [2010] ECR I-8489, [2010] NLJR 1299, [2010] All ER (D) 84 (Sep), ECJ 31.51
C-155/10: Williams v British Airways plc: C-155/10 [2012] 1 CMLR 591, [2011] IRLR 948, [2011] NLJR 1292, [2011] All ER (D) 65 (Sep), ECJ 27.4, 27.8
C-159/10 and C-160/10: Fuchs and Kohler v Land Hessen [2011] 3 CMLR 1299, [2012] ICR 93, [2011] IRLR 1043, (2011) Times, 27 August, [2011] All ER (D) 97 (Sep), ECJ 11.9, 40.5
C-214/10: KHS AG v Schulte [2012] 1 CMLR 1352, [2012] IRLR 156, ECJ 27.3a
C-282/10: Dominguez v Centre Informatique Du Centre Ouest Atlantique [2012] IRLR 321, ECJ 17.12, 22.11, 27.3a, 55.2
C-297/10 and C-298/10: Hennigs v Eisenbahn-Bundesamt; Land Berlin v Mai [2012] 1 CMLR 484, [2012] IRLR 83, [2011] All ER (D) 72 (Oct), ECJ 11.9
C-337/10: Neidel v Stadt Frankfurt am Main (3 May 2012, unreported), ECJ 27.3a
C-393/10: O'Brien (Dermod Patrick) v Ministry of Justice [2012] IRLR 421, ECJ 14.8, 30.3, 30.5, 30.15, 30.21
C-415/10: Meister v Speech Design Carrier Systems GmbH (19 April 2010, unreported), ECJ 12.9

1   Introduction

1.1   SCOPE AND AIMS OF THIS BOOK

Employment law is fully recognised today as a subject of the greatest importance. Legislation passed in recent years has transformed the law and created important new statutory rights and obligations. Employment law continues to develop at a rapid pace, with new domestic legislation creating or modifying statutory rights being enacted each year. Further, EC legislation and decisions of the European Court have had, and will continue to have, an important impact on certain areas of domestic employment law. Inevitably, a wealth of reported tribunal and court decisions on the meaning and effect of these new provisions has also built up.

This handbook seeks to explain the legislation in its context, along with the common law and the EC law on employment matters. It is intended as a reference guide for the employer, company secretary, manager or personnel officer involved daily in decisions concerning the rights of employees. It is also intended to serve as a comprehensive handbook on employment law for solicitors, employees, trade union officials, and all kinds of advisers and professional people.

The remainder of this chapter serves as an introduction to the subject by examining a number of fundamental aspects of current employment law. It concludes with a checklist of the areas of law relevant to the various stages of employment and a brief explanation of the standard scale of maximum fines which may be imposed upon conviction of an adult of a summary offence.

Employment law and trade union law. The main emphasis of this book is on the law affecting the individual employment relationship, ie directly applying to employers and their employees. It therefore provides detailed coverage of the law governing the contract of employment, termination of employment, redundancy, unfair dismissal, equal pay, the various forms of unlawful discrimination relevant to employment and numerous other individual employment rights. The importance of trade unions is nonetheless fully recognised, and the status, functions and liabilities of trade unions and the law relating to trade union membership are considered in appropriate chapters.

1.2   WHAT CONSTITUTES EMPLOYMENT?

One of the most fundamental questions asked is whether a particular worker is an employee or not. An employee is a person who agrees to work for another person pursuant to a *contract of employment* (or 'contract of service' to use the more traditional term). It is important to be able to distinguish a contract of employment from other types of agreement under which services are rendered. There are a number of characteristics which enable a contract of employment to be identified. One problem which can often arise is deciding whether a particular person doing work for another is working as an employee, ie under a contract of employment, or as an independent contractor (or 'self-employed' person) under a *contract for services*. These matters are discussed further in EMPLOYEE, SELF-EMPLOYED OR WORKER? (14).

1.3   The contract of employment

The most important matters to be borne in mind are the following.

(a)   In general, the parties are free to agree whatever contractual terms they wish – this means, among other things, that they may agree that work is to be done either by an employee or by an independent contractor.

1

1.3 Introduction

(b) However, *all the terms* of the contract, and the way in which it is performed, will be looked at in deciding whether it is in substance a contract of employment or not, so it will not be sufficient merely to state that the contract is a contract for services and not a contract of employment.

(c) Whether or not the contract is a contract of employment, certain further terms may be implied, if not expressly agreed.

(d) If the contract *is* a contract of employment, all the statutory employment rights are capable of applying, if the relevant pre-conditions are satisfied, and (subject to limited exceptions) any term of the contract excluding these rights is usually *ineffective*.

(e) If the contract *is not* a contract of employment, the main statutory employment rights cannot apply, because they apply only for the benefit of people working under a contract of employment. However, there are some important statutory provisions which also apply to self-employed persons and/or 'workers' as defined in the relevant legislation.

For further details, see CONTRACT OF EMPLOYMENT (7) and EMPLOYEE, SELF-EMPLOYED OR WORKER? (14).

1.4 SOURCES OF EMPLOYMENT LAW

The legal rules governing employment law are derived from three principal sources:

(a) the common law, including the law of contract pursuant to which the contract of employment is enforced, and the law of torts (wrongful acts which cause damage or loss) which governs (for example) an employer's liability for acts of his employees, civil liability for industrial accidents and for strikes and other forms of industrial action;

(b) statute law, ie Acts of Parliament and Regulations, which operate outside the contract (eg the law on unfair dismissal); and

(c) European legislation and judgments of the European Court of Justice ('ECJ').

Some elements of these three sources are considered briefly below.

1.5 Terms of the contract of employment

Generally, the employer and employee are free to agree whatever terms they wish. Therefore, the most basic legal rules governing the employment relationship are those agreed by the parties themselves, for example, the type of work to be done, place of work, rate of pay, etc. In practice, the more detailed terms and conditions of the contract are often not discussed and agreed individually with each employee. Many employers have written standard terms and conditions of employment for all employees, sometimes drawn up and agreed in consultation with officials of recognised trade unions.

In cases where a disagreement arises, the main problem is often evidential. If an employer does not provide written particulars of the terms and conditions of employment, or if a particular matter was agreed orally but never put in writing, years later memories will have faded and there may be no reliable evidence of precisely what was agreed. This is one reason why employers are under a statutory obligation to provide a written summary of the main contractual terms to each employee within a short time after he begins his job. They must notify changes in the same way. (See 7.7 CONTRACT OF EMPLOYMENT.)

1.6   Domestic employment legislation

The main statutory employment rights are found in the *Employment Rights Act 1996*, as amended.

In relation to discrimination in employment, the protection afforded to employees and applicants for employment was, prior to 1 October 2010, found in a substantial body of anti-discrimination legislation, both primary and secondary. The main domestic statutory provisions prohibiting discrimination were:

(a)   *Equal Pay Act 1970*, as amended.

(b)   *Sex Discrimination Act 1975*, as amended.

(c)   *Race Relations Act 1976*, as amended.

(d)   *Disability Discrimination Act 1995*, as amended.

These statutes will remain relevant to any ongoing cases involving discrimination matters predating October 2011.

The Equality Act 2010

For matters arising after 1 October 2011, the law in relation to all strands of discrimination is now harmonised in the *Equality Act 2010*, which received the Royal Assent on 8 April 2010. Under the *Equality Act 2010* the various grounds of discrimination are drawn together as "protected characteristics". The principal commencement order under the *Equality Act* (the *Equality Act 2010 (Commencement No 4, Savings, Consequential, Transitional, Transitory and Incidental Provisions and Revocation) Order 2010, SI 2010/2317*) brought into force the majority of the employment related provisions with effect from 1 October 2011.

The main Act governing trade unions and trade disputes is the *Trade Union and Labour Relations (Consolidation) Act 1992*, as amended.

The Act governing the presentation of complaints to an employment tribunal is the *Employment Tribunals Act 1996*.

In addition to the primary legislation a substantial number of statutory instruments provide important and specific rights in relation to employment and are considered, where relevant, in the chapters of the book.

This book provides an account of the effect of all of these main legislative provisions, with references to the specific provisions and to decided cases. However, a reader who is called upon to consider the law in detail would probably be well advised to obtain copies of the Acts themselves in addition. The Acts are obtainable from the Stationery Office or through bookshops. The majority of relevant legislation, including Statutory Instruments, is available online from the legislation website (www.legislation.gov.uk). For those requiring a complete reprint of all the relevant legislation, compendia of employment legislation are published commercially by a number of law publishers. In a particular case of doubt or difficulty the reader should always consult a professional adviser.

1.7   European law

European legislative instruments. Where English domestic legislation has failed fully to implement EC Treaty obligations, individuals may rely in the English courts upon the EC Treaty, and, where the employer is the State, upon certain EC directives. (See EUROPEAN UNION LAW (22).)

In the employment context, this has been done in particular to establish claims for equal pay and equal treatment (see EQUAL PAY (21)).

1.7 Introduction

EC legislation is also important where a business is transferred from one employer to another (see Transfer of Undertakings (50)). Other areas influenced by EC legislation include Health and Safety at Work – II (26), Holidays (27), the rules on written particulars of employment (see 7.4 Contract of Employment) and requirements for consultation in redundancy situations (see 37.2 Redundancy – II).

Judgments of the European Court. The ECJ is the final arbiter in matters of interpretation of European legislation. Thus, its judgments are of importance in interpreting directly applicable European legislative instruments and also domestic legislation which implements European law obligations.

The *European Convention on Human Rights* is also relevant; the *Human Rights Act 1998* requires the court to interpret United Kingdom law in accordance with the Convention. This has clear implications in the employment context (see Human Rights (28)).

1.8 GEOGRAPHICAL SCOPE OF THIS BOOK

This book seeks to explain the law applying in England and Wales. Much of the relevant legislation applies, without significant differences, to *Scotland*. However, Scotland has a quite different legal system from that of England and Wales, and different legal traditions. It also has a separate system of courts and tribunals. This book should not be regarded as authoritative on the law applying in Scotland because specific matters of Scottish law have not been taken into consideration. For example, the explanation of attachment of earnings for payment of debts (Pay – II (33)) relates to England and Wales only: different procedures apply in Scotland.

The legal system and legal traditions of *Northern Ireland* are much more similar to those of England and Wales than are those of Scotland, but the legislation discussed in this book generally does not apply to Northern Ireland. It has a separate legislative code, although on employment law its provisions are co-ordinated with those of Great Britain. Northern Ireland also has a separate system of courts and tribunals. Therefore, while the law will often be similar, this book is not authoritative on Northern Ireland employment law and any reader in Northern Ireland is advised to consult the specific Northern Ireland legal sources on any particular issue.

This book does not contain an account of the laws relating to employment applying in the Channel Islands or the Isle of Man, nor of those foreign systems of law which may apply where an English employee is sent to work abroad. For the rules determining which system of law governs an employment relationship with international elements, see 26.9 Foreign Employees.

1.9 STAGES OF EMPLOYMENT – CHECKLIST

The chapters of this book are arranged in alphabetical order to assist the reader in tracing all the areas of law that may relate to a particular problem. The following checklist sets out the chronological stages of employment, from selection for appointment to termination, and beyond, together with a list of chapters relevant to each stage.

All stages	
General	Contract of Employment (7)
	Employee, Self-Employed or Worker? (14)
Discrimination	Equal Pay (21)
	Discrimination and Equal Opportunities– I, II and III (10, 11, 12)

	EUROPEAN UNION LAW (22)
Statutory rights	CONTINUOUS EMPLOYMENT (6)
	PAY – I (32)
Chronological stages	
Selection for appointment	CHILDREN AND YOUNG PERSONS (3)
	EMPLOYEE'S PAST CRIMINAL CONVICTIONS (17)
	FOREIGN EMPLOYEES (23)
Terms of engagement	CONTRACT OF EMPLOYMENT (7)
	EMPLOYEE, SELF-EMPLOYED OR WORKER? (14)
	ENGAGEMENT OF EMPLOYEES (20)
	PROBATIONARY EMPLOYEES (34)
Duration of employment	CONTINUOUS EMPLOYMENT (6)
	TEMPORARY AND SEASONAL EMPLOYEES (45)
	TRANSFER OF UNDERTAKINGS (50)
Pay, etc	EQUAL PAY (21)
	PAY – I AND II (32, 33)
	SICKNESS AND SICK PAY (42)
	TAXATION (44)
Terms and conditions (other than pay)	COLLECTIVE AGREEMENTS (5)
	CONTRACT OF EMPLOYMENT (7)
	DIRECTORS (8)
	EQUAL PAY (22)
	HOLIDAYS (27)
	PUBLIC SECTOR EMPLOYEES (35)
	RESTRAINT OF TRADE, CONFIDENTIALITY AND EMPLOYEE INTERVENTIONS (39)
	SERVICE LETTINGS (41)
	TRANSFER OF UNDERTAKINGS (50)
Safety and welfare	CHILDREN AND YOUNG PERSONS (3)
	EDUCATION AND TRAINING (13)
	HEALTH AND SAFETY AT WORK – I AND II (25, 26)
	MATERNITY AND PARENTAL RIGHTS (31)
	PAY – I (32)
	SICKNESS AND SICK PAY (42)
	TIME OFF WORK (47)
	VICARIOUS LIABILITY (54)
	WORKING TIME (55)
General management	ADVISORY, CONCILIATION AND ARBITRATION SERVICE (2)
	CODES OF PRACTICE (4)
	EMPLOYEE PARTICIPATION (15)
Trade unions	DISCLOSURE OF INFORMATION (9)

1.9 Introduction

	HEALTH AND SAFETY AT WORK – II (26)
	TRADE UNIONS – I AND II (48, 49)
Trade disputes	ADVISORY, CONCILIATION AND ARBITRATION SERVICE (2)
	CODES OF PRACTICE (4)
	STRIKES AND INDUSTRIAL ACTION (43)
Lay-offs	PAY – I (32)
	REDUNDANCY – I (36)
Discipline and breach of contract	TERMINATION OF EMPLOYMENT (46)
	UNFAIR DISMISSAL – II (52)
Termination of employment (generally)	TRADE UNIONS – I (48)
	MATERNITY AND PARENTAL RIGHTS (31)
	REFERENCES (38)
	RESTRAINT OF TRADE, CONFIDENTIALITY AND EMPLOYEE INTERVENTIONS (39)
	TERMINATION OF EMPLOYMENT (46)
	TRANSFER OF UNDERTAKINGS (50)
	UNFAIR DISMISSAL – I, II AND III (51, 52, 53)
	WRONGFUL DISMISSAL (56)
Redundancy	REDUNDANCY – I AND II (36, 37)
	UNFAIR DISMISSAL – II (52)
Retirement	RETIREMENT (40)
Claims against employer – Dismissals	EMPLOYMENT TRIBUNALS: I, II AND III (17, 18, 19)
	REDUNDANCY – I AND II (36, 37)
	UNFAIR DISMISSAL – I, II AND III (51, 52, 53)
	WRONGFUL DISMISSAL (56)
Insolvency of employer	INSOLVENCY OF EMPLOYER (29)

1.10 STANDARD SCALE OF FINES

At various points in the book, reference is made to the standard scale of maximum fines which may be imposed upon conviction of an adult of a summary offence (that is, one which falls to be tried by magistrates rather than by the Crown Court).

The standard scale of maximum fines is as follows.

Level on the scale	*Amount of maximum fine (£)*
1	200
2	500
3	1,000
4	2,500
5	5,000

(*Criminal Justice Act 1982, s 37(2)*, as substituted by *Criminal Justice Act 1991, s 17.*)

It should be noted that the *Legal Aid, Sentencing and Punishment of Offenders Act 2012* makes provision in *s 85* for the removal of the £5000 maximum on the standard scale of fines and, by *ss 86–87*, empowers the Secretary of State to increase the levels 1–4 of the standard scale fines to such sums considered appropriate. These provisions are, however, not yet in force.

Where the Crown Court tries an offence and imposes a fine following a conviction there is no maximum amount in the absence of some specific provision to the contrary (*Powers of Criminal Courts Act 1973, s 30*; *Criminal Law Act 1977, s 32(1)*).

Before a court (magistrates' court or Crown Court) fixes the amount of any fine, it must inquire into the financial circumstances of the offender. The amount must reflect the court's opinion of the seriousness of the offence, and the court must also take account of the circumstances of the case, including the financial circumstances of the offender. (*Criminal Justice Act 1991, s 18*, as substituted by *Criminal Justice Act 1993, s 65.*)

2 Advisory, Conciliation and Arbitration Service (ACAS)

2.1 The Advisory, Conciliation and Arbitration Service was established pursuant to powers conferred by the *Employment Protection Act 1975*. Its activities are now regulated by the *Trade Union and Labour Relations (Consolidation) Act 1992* (*'TULRCA 1992'*), as amended by the *Trade Union Reform and Employment Rights Act 1993* (*'TURERA 1993'*). ACAS continues in existence under *TULRCA 1992, s 247*. Its duties are to promote the improvement of industrial relations, in particular by exercising its functions in relation to the settlement of trade disputes (*TULRCA 1992, s 209* as amended by *TURERA 1993, s 43(1)*).

ACAS may charge fees for the exercise of its functions to persons who benefit from that exercise, and may be directed to do so by the Secretary of State (*TULRCA 1992, s 251A* as inserted by *TURERA 1993, s 44*). Fees are charged at present only for certain publications and seminars, and thus not for the key function of conciliation.

2.2 CONSTITUTION

The Secretary of State appoints the members of the Council of ACAS in accordance with the requirements laid down in *TULRCA 1992, s 248*. Those requirements ensure that both employers' organisations and workers' organisations are consulted before appointments are made and that a balance is maintained between employers' and workers' interests.

2.3 CONCILIATION

One function of ACAS is to conciliate in trade disputes. ACAS may appoint either an independent person or an officer of the Service to offer assistance to the parties to the dispute. During the course of conciliation the parties will be encouraged to use any existing agreed procedures to resolve the conflict (*TULRCA 1992, s 210*). Where ACAS exercises its functions under *s 210* with a view to bringing about a settlement of a recognition dispute, ACAS may be requested to hold a ballot of the workers involved in the dispute or ascertain the union membership of the workers involved in the dispute (*TULRCA 1992 s 210A(2)*). ACAS is not obliged to comply with such a request (*s 210A(9)*) but if a request is made under *s 210A(2)* and ACAS decides to act then it may require any party to the recognition dispute to supply ACAS with specified information concerning the workers involved in the dispute within a specified time (*s 210A(4)*). If there is non compliance ACAS will take no further steps to hold the ballot or ascertain the union membership of the workers involved in the dispute (*s 210A(8)*).

2.4 CONCILIATION IN EMPLOYMENT TRIBUNAL COMPLAINTS

ACAS appoints conciliation officers to conciliate on matters which are or could be the subject of proceedings before an employment tribunal (*TULRCA 1992 s 211*).

Conciliation officers may (and must if required to do so by a party to the complaint) take action to conciliate on most claims which can be brought before an employment tribunal, including claims of discrimination in employment, claims for equal pay and complaints against trade unions (*Employment Tribunals Act 1996* (*'ETA 1996'*), *s 18*). Either the person making the complaint or the person against whom the complaint or application is made may request the assistance of a conciliation officer. The power to conciliate also extends to redundancy payment cases (see **36.4** REDUNDANCY – I) and to issues relating to training (as introduced by the *Employment Relations Act 1999*; see *TULRCA 1992, s 70B*), detriment

2.4 Advisory, Conciliation and Arbitration Service (ACAS)

arising out of participation or involvement in a trade union recognition procedure pursuant to *TULRCA 1992, Sch A1 para 156* and complaints relating to failure to permit parental leave (see *ERA 1999, s 80*). A complete list of the employment tribunal jurisdictions to which the conciliation power applies is found in *subsections 18(1)(a)* to *18(1)(v)* of the *ETA 1996* (as amended).

Before a complaint is presented to an employment tribunal, the conciliation officer will only take action if requested to do so by either party to the potential complaint (*ETA 1996, s 18(3), (5)*, as amended with effect from 6 April 2009 by the *Employment Act 2008*). Upon receipt of such a request the conciliation officer may endeavour to promote a settlement between the parties without proceedings being instituted (*ETA 1996, s 18(3)*). Whilst conciliation may occur prior to issue of proceedings (see the figures for pre-claim conciliation above) and without such proceedings ultimately being issued, the requirement for action to have been taken in respect of which a complaint could be made will generally mean that ACAS will decline to become involved where a dismissal is contemplated but has not yet taken place.

Once a complaint has been presented to an employment tribunal, a conciliation officer must conciliate whether or not he is requested to do so if he considers that he could conciliate with a reasonable prospect of success or when he is requested to do so by both parties (*ETA 1996, s 18(1), (2)*).

Where the complaint is one of unfair dismissal, and the complainant has ceased to be employed by the employer against whom the complaint is made, the conciliation officer is required to seek the complainant's reinstatement or re-engagement. Where the complainant does not wish for either of these remedies, or where reinstatement or re-engagement is not practicable, the conciliation officer will attempt to obtain for him a sum by way of compensation (*ETA 1996, s 18(4)*). The same principles apply in relation to a potential complaint of unfair dismissal which has not been lodged in the employment tribunal at the time of conciliation (*ETA s 18(5)*). As a result of amendments made by the *Employment Act 2008* and the removal of the fixed periods for conciliation there is no limit upon the period during which a conciliation officer may seek to promote settlement by way of conciliation and this conciliation may in appropriate cases continue up to the point of an award of remedy by an employment tribunal.

Thus, if a complaint is presented to an employment tribunal, the respondent employer will often be contacted by a conciliation officer. The conciliation officer will usually outline the complainant's grievance and may convey the respondent's comments back to the complainant. If the respondent does not want his comments conveyed to the complainant he should make this clear to the conciliation officer. Nothing communicated to a conciliation officer in connection with the performance of his functions is admissible in evidence in any proceedings before an employment tribunal, except with the consent of the person who communicated it to the officer (*ETA 1996, s 18(7)*). It may also be of some comfort to those involved in the settlement of claims through ACAS to know that such communications attract absolute privilege for the purposes of any defamation proceedings as held in *Freer v Glover* [2005] EWHC 3341 (QB), [2006] IRLR 521 in which a solicitor acting for the employer involved in negotiations through ACAS was sued in defamation by the employee. Incidental publication of the alleged defamatory statement to ACAS staff was also protected by the privilege (*Lincoln v Daniels* [1962] 1 QB 237, [1961] 3 All ER 740, CA applied).

The important role of conciliation officers is emphasised by the fact that, subject to one important exception, an agreement to settle an employment tribunal complaint will only normally be binding on the parties if the agreement relates to a complaint or potential complaint where a conciliation officer has taken action in accordance with his statutory powers. The important exception concerns settlements reached after the employee has received advice from a relevant independent adviser (see EMPLOYMENT TRIBUNALS − I (17)).

In other cases, an agreement to settle a claim or a potential claim is unenforceable, leaving the complainant free to pursue his claim before an employment tribunal (*ERA 1996, s 203(1), (2)*; *SDA 1975, s 77(4)(a)*; *RRA 1976, s 72(4)(a)*). In *Moore v Duport Furniture Products Ltd* [1982] ICR 84, [1982] IRLR 31, HL, a conciliation officer was considered to have taken such action in circumstances where the parties had already reached a settlement. In that case, the officer ascertained that they had truly reached agreement, which he then recorded in writing on a form designed for the purpose (Form COT 3). Where a conciliation officer assisted the parties in reaching an oral agreement, that agreement was held to be binding, notwithstanding that it had not been recorded in writing (*Gilbert v Kembridge Fibres Ltd* [1984] ICR 188, [1984] IRLR 52, EAT; see also *Hennessy v Craigmyle & Co Ltd* [1986] ICR 461, [1986] IRLR 300, CA). A conciliation officer is not under a duty to advise an employee on the relevant legislation, but an agreement reached with his assistance may be set aside if he acts partially or adopts unfair methods (*Slack v Greenham (Plant Hire) Ltd* [1983] ICR 617, [1983] IRLR 271, EAT). Nor will a tribunal be bound by a sham COT 3 designed to mislead a government department (*Trafford Carpets Ltd v Barker* IDS 440, p 16).

An attack upon the binding nature of a COT3 agreement on the basis that the conciliation officer had not advised the employees properly as to their rights was rejected by the EAT in *Clark v Redcar and Cleveland Borough Council* [2006] ICR 897, [2006] IRLR 324, EAT. As part of an overall settlement negotiated in equal pay claims the employees signed COT3 agreements limiting the amount of back pay to be paid. Subsequently they sought to set them aside on the basis of ACAS failing to provide advice that they could achieve considerably more in compensation by proceeding with the claims. The EAT reaffirmed that the function of ACAS was to promote settlement and not to advise upon the merits of a party's case and to do so might compromise the role of the conciliation officer. While best practice might sometimes suggest that the conciliation officer should caution the employee to take further advice, failure to do so would not provide grounds to set aside the COT3 which would only be set aside in cases of bad faith or impropriety by the conciliation officer.

In order to ensure that an agreement to settle a complaint or potential complaint is enforceable, parties should normally seek the assistance of a conciliation officer to promote a settlement and have him record the agreement on the appropriate form (COT3). This is not however mandatory for a settlement to be effective. The extent to which the conciliation officer must "take action" for the purposes of ousting the jurisdiction of the employment tribunal under *s 203* of the *ERA 1996* has been recently considered by the EAT in *Alma Construction Ltd v Bonner* [2011] IRLR 204. The EAT held that the threshold for taking action was very low. The ACAS officer is not required to broker the settlement nor to record it, whether in a COT3 or otherwise. The duty is only to endeavour to promote settlement. So long as this has been done, the ACAS officer has taken action and, if a settlement was reached, it will be binding for the purposes of *s 203 ERA 1996* and the employment tribunal will have no jurisdiction subsequently to hear the claim. In that case the communication to the employer via the ACAS officer of the claimant's willingness to accept an offer of settlement was sufficient for the purposes of *s 203 ERA 1996*.

In *Livingstone v Hepworth Refractories Ltd* [1992] 3 CMLR 601, [1992] ICR 287, EAT, it was held that a COT 3 made where the conciliation officer was acting under the *Employment Protection Consolidation Act 1978* (now *ERA 1996*) was only effective to settle discrimination or equal pay claims if it was expressly stated to include such claims, whether brought under domestic or European law.

2.5   Conciliation in complaints to Central Arbitration Committee

ACAS will seek to promote a settlement of complaints by recognised trade unions of failure to disclose information (*TULRCA 1992, s 183(2)*; see TRADE UNIONS – I (48)).

2.5 Advisory, Conciliation and Arbitration Service (ACAS)

Proposals for compulsory early conciliation of employment disputes: Part II of The Enterprise and Regulatory Reform Bill 2012

Part II of the *Enterprise and Regulatory Reform Bill 2012* makes proposals to amend the *Employment Tribunals Act 1996* to include a new section (*s 18A*) which will oblige any prospective claimant to contact ACAS and to provide "prescribed information" about a potential claim before the institution of employment tribunal proceedings. A conciliation officer will then be obliged to "endeavour to promote a settlement between the persons who would be parties to the proceedings" during a prescribed period to be fixed by employment tribunal procedure regulations. If the conciliation officer forms the view that a conciliated settlement is not possible or the prescribed period expires without a settlement being reached, then it is proposed that the conciliation officer will issue a certificate to that effect to the prospective claimant. Subject to any exceptions to be provided for in the legislation, if the provisions are not complied with, and no certificate has been obtained by a prospective claimant, then the claimant will be prevented from instituting proceedings in the employment tribunal. It is proposed that the limitation periods for the presentation of claims will be amended to incorporate an extension for the prescribed conciliation period. House of Lords amendments of 23 March 2013 have further proposed a new *s 251B* to *TULRCA* which is intended, subject to defined exceptions, to prohibit ACAS from disclosing information which relates to a worker, an employer of a worker or a trade union and which is held by ACAS in connection with provision of a service by ACAS or its officers. It is proposed that a breach of the section will be an offence which is punishable on summary conviction to a fine not exceeding level 5 on the standard scale.

2.6 ARBITRATION

Where a trade dispute exists or is apprehended, ACAS may, with the consent of all parties to the dispute, refer the matters in dispute for the arbitration of:

(a)   an independent arbitrator or arbitrators, not being an employee of ACAS; or

(b)   the Central Arbitration Committee.

(TULRCA 1992, s 212(1).)

However, ACAS will first consider the likelihood of the dispute being settled by conciliation and, in the absence of special reasons, a matter will not be referred to arbitration until any agreed disputes procedure has been exhausted *(TULRCA 1992, s 212(2), (3))*.

An award by an arbitrator may be published if ACAS so decides and all the parties concerned consent *(TULRCA 1992, s 212(4)(b))*.

The *Arbitration Act 1950, Part I* does not apply to such an arbitration *(TULRCA 1992, s 212(5))*.

2.7 THE EMPLOYMENT RIGHTS (DISPUTE RESOLUTION) ACT 1998

By *s 212A* of *TULRCA* (introduced by *s 7* of the *Employment Rights (Dispute Resolution) Act 1998*, which came into force on 1 August 1998), ACAS was given the power to draw up a scheme for the voluntary (but binding) arbitration of unfair dismissal disputes subject to the approval of the Secretary of State. Following ACAS consultation on the scheme, which was expressed to be intended to be 'voluntary, speedy, informal, confidential and free from legal argument', the arbitration scheme came into effect in England and Wales on 21 May 2001. Guidance on the operation of the scheme is available on the ACAS website (www.acas.org.uk). The application of the scheme was, from 6 April 2004, extended to Scotland by the *ACAS Arbitration Scheme (Great Britain) Order 2004 (SI 2004/753)*. The scheme may be summarised (in brief outline) as follows (for further detail see EMPLOYMENT TRIBUNALS – I (17)).

First, it is important to note that the scheme is voluntary and is limited to unfair dismissal claims. If a claim for unfair dismissal is to be determined under the scheme, then any other claim (even if raised at the same time or on related facts) must go to the employment tribunal or be settled. If other related claims are to be heard in the employment tribunal, then the arbitration proceedings may be postponed pending the tribunal's determination. On submission of a claim to arbitration, both parties must waive in writing the right they would otherwise have in relation to an unfair dismissal claim. This includes waiver of the right to raise jurisdictional issues such as time limits, continuity of service and whether, in fact, the employee was dismissed.

The scheme provides for hearings to take place in private (unlike the normal tribunal procedure) and is intended to be speedy, non-legalistic and cost effective. The scheme is not intended for claims involving legal complexity or EC law; such claims, according to the Schedule, should remain the province of the employment tribunal. The arbitrators will be appointed by ACAS from the ACAS arbitration panel. In contrast to tribunal proceedings, the arbitration may take place anywhere, including the employee's place of work. There is no mechanism for compulsory attendance of witnesses or production of documents (although failure to produce/attend may be taken into account by the arbitrator in reaching his decision). Evidence will not be subject to the formality of tribunal procedure and will be given unsworn and without cross-examination. The arbitrator will, however, have the power to question witnesses or parties to determine the facts.

The arbitrator's decision will not take the form of detailed reasons. The arbitrator must, in reaching his decision, apply the recognised principles of fairness in the employment context (including ACAS Codes of Practice) and, additionally, must apply the *Human Rights Act 1998* and relevant EC law. The remedies available to a successful employee are the same as in the employment tribunal (reinstatement, re-engagement and compensation). The arbitrator's decision is final; there is no mechanism for appeal from the decision. The parties remain free to settle the matter at any time during the arbitration, however. To date the scheme has not proved to be very popular: the *ACAS Annual Report* 2006/07 revealed that in that year only three unfair dismissal cases were the subject of arbitration (down from 6 in 2005/06, 4 in 2004/05, 7 in 2003/04 and 23 in 2002/03). Data for subsequent years is not included in the relevant ACAS Reports.

The power of ACAS to arbitrate also extends to flexible working requests. See, on flexible working, *ERA 1996, ss 80F–80I* (as inserted by the *Employment Act 2002*). The ACAS flexible working arbitration scheme, introduced pursuant to *s 212A* of *TULRCA* (see the *ACAS (Flexible Working) Arbitration Scheme (England and Wales) Order 2003 (SI 2003/694)*) is similar in form and operation to the scheme relating to unfair dismissal. An arbitrator hears the claim and gives a final decision with limited rights of appeal or challenge available to the parties. If the parties have elected to go to arbitration, there is no right to go to the employment tribunal. The remedies and compensation which may be awarded by the arbitrator mirror those in the employment tribunal. As in the case of unfair dismissal arbitration, there is detailed guidance on the arbitration of flexible working disputes available on the ACAS website. Utilisation of this service is, however, infrequent. The *ACAS Annual Report* 2006–07 revealed that in that year no flexible working claims went to arbitration (the same as 2005/06; in 2004/05 one such claim went to arbitration). Data for subsequent years is not included in the relevant ACAS Reports.

2.8   ADVICE

ACAS is empowered, on request or on its own initiative, to give such advice as it thinks appropriate to employers, workers and their organisations on matters concerned with or affecting or likely to affect industrial relations. It may also publish general advice on matters

2.8 Advisory, Conciliation and Arbitration Service (ACAS)

connected with or affecting or likely to affect industrial relations (*TULRCA 1992, s 213* as substituted by *TURERA 1993, s 43(2)*). ACAS's helpline is extremely popular, with close to one million calls answered per year. The ACAS helpline telephone number is 08457 47 47 47.

ACAS publishes a number of guides in relation to various employment law issues with a series of advisory booklets, leaflets and handbooks, the latter directed particularly to small firms. In addition, ACAS has published a DVD guide to the Employment Tribunals giving advice on presentation and preparation for a claim and the hearing and has a series of e-learning packages available on its website. These publications are available from ACAS Public Enquiry Points and also from the ACAS website (www.acas.org.uk).

In addition, since July 2001, the Race Relations Employment Advisory Service ('RREAS') and Equality Direct (the telephone helpline for equality issues at work) form part of ACAS. The ACAS Equality Direct telephone number is 08456 00 34 44.

2.9 INQUIRY

ACAS may, if it thinks fit, inquire into any question relating to industrial relations generally or to industrial relations in any particular industry or in any particular undertaking or part of any undertaking (*TULRCA 1992, s 214(1)*).

The findings of such an inquiry, together with any advice given in connection with those findings, may be published by ACAS if it appears to it that publication is desirable for the improvement of industrial relations. Before deciding whether to publish, ACAS must send a draft of the findings to all the parties appearing to ACAS to be concerned, and take account of their views (*TULRCA 1992, s 214(2)*).

2.10 CODES OF PRACTICE

ACAS has a general power to issue new or revised Codes of Practice to give practical guidance for promoting the improvement of industrial relations (*TULRCA 1992, s 199*). It has issued three Codes of Practice so far:

No 1: Disciplinary and Grievance Procedures

No 2: Disclosure of Information

No 3: Time Off for Trade Union Duties

The Codes have not remained static since their first issue in 1985 and have been the subject of a number of revisions.

A wholly new Code of Practice No 1 was issued with effect from 6 April 2009 to reflect the repeal by the *Employment Act 2008* of the statutory dispute resolution procedures in relation to matters of discipline and grievance (which had been introduced by *Part 3* of the *Employment Act 2002* (with effect from 1 October 2004) and the *Employment Act 2002 (Dispute Resolution) Regulations 2004 (SI 2004/752)*. The old Code of Practice No 1, which provides guidance on the statutory dispute resolution procedures, has continuing limited relevance on a transitional basis in (probably few) remaining cases progressing through the employment tribunals and higher courts where the disciplinary or grievance process was commenced prior to 6 April 2009.

The Code of Practice No 2 on Disclosure of Information (third revision 2003) deals with disclosure of information to trade unions for the purposes of collective bargaining pursuant to the obligations contained in *ss 181* and *182* of *TULRCA 1992*.

The Code of Practice No 3 on Time Off for Trade Union Duties was revised with effect from 1 January 2010 by order of the Secretary of State (*Employment Protection Code of Practice (Time Off for Trade Union Duties and Activities) Order 2009 (SI 2009/3223)*).

For the legal effect of these Codes of Practice and the procedure to be followed in issuing them, see **4.3** CODES OF PRACTICE.

2.11   CONTACTING ACAS

ACAS headquarters are at Euston Tower, 286 Euston Road, London NW1 3JJ. Tel: 0207 396 0022. For information in relation to employment issues the ACAS Helpline (08457 47 47 47) should be used. The majority of ACAS publications and guides may be downloaded from its website (www.acas.org.uk).

ACAS main offices

East Midlands

Lancaster House,
10 Sherwood Rise,
Nottingham, NG7 6JE.
Tel: 0115 985 8253

East of England

Acas House,
Kempson Way,
Suffolk Business Park,
Bury St Edmunds,
Suffolk, IP32 7AR.
Tel: 01284 774 500

London

Euston Tower,
286 Euston Road,
London, NW1 3JJ.
Tel: 020 7396 0022

North East

Cross House,
Westgate Road,
Newcastle upon Tyne, NE1 4XX.
Tel: 0191 269 6000

North West

Commercial Union House,
2–10 Albert Square,
Manchester, M60 8AD.
Tel: 0161 833 8500

Pavilion 1,
The Matchworks,
Speke Road,
Speke,
Liverpool, L19 2PH.

2.11   Advisory, Conciliation and Arbitration Service (ACAS)

Tel: 0151 728 5600

South East

Suites 3–5,
Business Centre,
1–7 Commercial Road,
Paddock Wood,
Kent, TN12 6EN.
Tel: 01892 837 273

Cygnus House,
Ground Floor,
Waterfront Business Park,
Fleet,
Hampshire GU51 3QT.
Tel: 01252 816 650

South West

The Waterfront,
Welsh Back,
Bristol, BS1 4SB.
Tel: 0117 9065 200

West Midlands

Apex House,
3 Embassy Drive,
Calthorpe Road,
Edgbaston,
Birmingham, B15 1TR
Tel: 0121 345 1410

Yorkshire and Humber

The Cube,
123 Albion Street,
Leeds, LS2 8ER.
Tel: 0113 205 3800

Scotland

151 West George Street,
Glasgow, G2 2JJ.
Tel: 0141 248 1400

Wales

3 Purbeck House,
Lambourne Crescent,
Llanishen,
Cardiff, CF14 5GJ.
Tel: 029 2076 2636

3   Children and Young Persons

The employment of children and young persons is restricted by legislation, the most important of which is summarised below. In addition, a right for young persons in employment to take time off from work for study or training is outlined. Also summarised is the contractual capacity of children and young persons, insofar as it concerns contracts of employment.

Cross-reference. See EDUCATION AND TRAINING (13) for the 'New Deal' and other training schemes.

3.1   DEFINITIONS

Child. For the purposes of the statutory provisions relating to the employment of children, a child is a person not over compulsory school age (at present, 16 years – see *Education Act 1996, s 8*) (*Education Act 1996, s 558*).

Young person. A person who has ceased to be a child and who is under the age of 18 years (*Education Act 1996, s 579(1)*). (However, note that there is a different definition in the *Management of Health and Safety at Work Regulations 1999* – see **3.5** below.)

Minor. A person who is under the age of 18 years (ie a child or young person) (*Family Law Reform Act 1969, s 1*).

3.2   RESTRICTIONS ON EMPLOYMENT OF CHILDREN

The *Children (Protection at Work) Regulations 1998 (SI 1998/276)*, which came into force on 4 August 1998, amended the *Children and Young Persons Acts 1933* and *1963* in order to implement the provisions of the *EC Young Workers Directive on the Protection of Young People at Work (94/33)* relating to the employment of children. The *Children (Protection at Work) Regulations 2000 (SI 2000/1333)* and the *Children (Protection at Work) (No 2) Regulations 2000 (SI 2000/2548)*, which came into force on 7 June 2000 and 11 October 2000, respectively, made some additional minor amendments to the *Children and Young Persons Act 1933* so as to give further effect to the *EC Directive 94/33* referred to above.

The main provisions restricting the employment of children, as amended by the above-mentioned *Regulations*, are outlined below.

In general, no child may be employed whether paid or not:

(a)   if he is under the age of 14 years; or

(b)   to do any work other than light work; or

(c)   before the close of school hours on any day on which he is required to attend school; or

(d)   before seven o'clock in the morning or after seven o'clock in the evening on any day; or

(e)   for more than two hours on any day on which he is required to attend school; or

(f)   for more than 12 hours in any week in which he is required to attend school; or

(g)   for more than two hours on any Sunday; or

(h)   for more than eight hours or, if he is under the age of 15 years, for more than five hours on any day (other than Sunday) on which he is not required to attend school; or

3.2   Children and Young Persons

(i)   for more than 35 hours or, if he is under the age of 15 years, for more than 25 hours in any week in which he is not required to attend school; or

(j)   for more than four hours in any day without a rest break of at least one hour; or

(k)   at any time in a year unless at that time, he has had (or could still have), during a school holiday, at least two consecutive weeks without employment.

'Light work' is defined by reference to the *EC Directive 94/33* referred to above, and means work which (on account of the inherent nature of the tasks which are involved and the particular conditions under which they are performed) is not likely to be harmful to a child's safety, health, development, attendance at school or participation in work experience.

(*Children and Young Persons Act 1933, s 18(1), (2A)* as amended; see also **3.3** below.)

In *Ashby v Addison (t/a Brayton News)* [2003] ICR 667, [2003] IRLR 211, the EAT held that a 15-year-old paper boy was not a 'worker' within the meaning of the *Working Time Regulations 1998*, and was therefore not entitled to four weeks' paid annual leave in accordance with *reg 13* (see **27.2** HOLIDAYS). The definition of 'young person' in those regulations (ie a person who is over compulsory school age and under 18 — see **3.6** below) was not intended to include a child. Children are provided for by separate legislation, namely the *Children and Young Persons Act 1933, s 18(1)* which had been amended to give effect to the *EC Young Workers Directive* and which provided, in relation to holidays, that during a school holiday a child must have two consecutive weeks without employment (see (k) above).

In *Bebbington v Palmer (t/a Sturry News)* (UKEAT/0371/09/DM) [2010] All ER (D) 47 (Sep) the EAT held that the reference in the *Children and Young Persons Act 1933, s 18* to the 'employment' of children does not mean that children who work are necessarily employed under a contract of service. The term 'employment' in *section 18* also includes children 'who are are not employees in the strict sense of the word but are employed under contracts for services'. On the facts of that case, the claimant (a paper boy) was not an 'employee' and was therefore unable to claim unfair dismissal.

The *Education Act 1996, s 560* (replacing the *Education (Work Experience) Act 1973, s 1*) provides that, with certain exceptions, the enactments relating to the prohibition or regulation of the employment of a child in his last two years of compulsory schooling shall not apply where the employment is in pursuance of arrangements made or approved by the local authority, or by the governing body of a school on behalf of such an authority, with a view to providing him with work experience as a part of his education. However, the enactments regulating the employment of young persons apply to a child on a work experience programme (*Education Act 1996, s 560(4), (5)*).

3.3   Local authority powers

Local authorities are empowered under the *Children and Young Persons Acts 1933–1969* (as amended) to pass bye-laws restricting the employment of children. Among other matters, any such bye-laws may authorise:

(a)   the employment on an occasional basis of children aged 13 years (notwithstanding anything in **3.2**(a) above) by their parents or guardians in light agricultural or horticultural work;

(b)   the employment of children aged 13 years (notwithstanding anything in **3.2**(a) above) in categories of light work specified in the bye-law; and

(c)   the employment of children for not more than one hour before the commencement of school hours on any day on which they are required to attend school (notwithstanding anything in **3.2**(c) above).

(*Children and Young Persons Act 1933, s 18(2), as amended.*)

The employer who breaches such a bye-law will be guilty of a criminal offence as will any person (other than the person employed) by whose act or default a contravention took place (*Children and Young Persons Act 1933, s 21*).

In *Portsea Island Mutual Co-operative Society Ltd v Leyland* (1978) 77 LGR 164, [1978] ICR 1195, the Divisional Court quashed the convictions recorded against the company under *s 21, CYPA 1933*. A milk roundsman, exceeding his authority and contrary to the company's instructions, had engaged a boy of 10 years of age to deliver milk on a Sunday before 9 am, contrary to the local authority's bye-laws. Talbot J held ([1978] IRLR 556 at 558) that an employer can be liable for such a contravention only if either he employed the child or if an agent of his who is engaged to take persons into his employment (eg a personnel manager) did so.

If it appears to a local authority that a child is being employed in such a manner as to be prejudicial to his health, or otherwise to render him unfit to obtain the full benefit of the education provided for him, the authority may serve a notice in writing on the employer: (a) prohibiting him from employing the child, or (b) imposing such restrictions upon his employment of the child as appear to be expedient in the child's interests (*Education Act 1996, s 559(1)*). A local authority may serve a notice in writing on the parent or employer of a child requiring the parent or employer to provide the authority, within such period as may be specified in the notice, with such information as appears to be necessary for enabling them to ascertain whether the child is being employed in such a manner as to render him unfit to obtain the full benefit of the education provided for him (*Education Act 1996, s 559(2)*). A person who (i) employs a child in contravention of any prohibition or restriction imposed under *s 559(1)*, or (ii) fails to comply with the requirements of a notice served under *s 559(2)*, is guilty of an offence and liable on summary conviction to a fine or imprisonment or both (*Education Act 1996, s 559(3), (4)*).

3.4   Other provisions

The other provisions are:

(a)   No child may be employed in any industrial undertaking unless the undertaking is one in which only members of the same family are employed (*Employment of Women, Young Persons and Children Act 1920, ss 1(1), 3(2), Sch*).

(b)   No child may be employed in any sea-going United Kingdom ship (*Merchant Shipping Act 1995, s 55(1A)*, inserted by the *Merchant Shipping (Hours of Work) Regulations 2002 (SI 2002/2125)*).

(c)   Special provisions regulate the employment of children in entertainment (*Children and Young Persons Act 1933, ss 23–26* as amended by *EA 1989, Sch 3 Part III* and *SI 2000/1333; Children and Young Persons Act 1963, ss 37–42* as amended by *SI 1998/276* (see above)).

(d)   The *Management of Health and Safety at Work Regulations 1999 (SI 1999/3242)* also apply to the employment of children (see **3.5** below). In addition to his other obligations, every employer must, before employing a child, provide comprehensible and relevant information to the parents of (or those with parental responsibility for) the child on the outcome of the risk assessment, and on the control measures that the employer has introduced (*reg 10(2)*).

3.5 Children and Young Persons

3.5 EMPLOYMENT OF YOUNG PERSONS

Health and safety

In relation to the regulation of the employment of young persons, in recent years the emphasis has shifted from restrictions on employment itself to special provisions on health and safety of young persons in employment (and regulating rest periods, breaks and night work — see **3.6** below). Thus *EA 1989, s 10(1)* provided for the repeal of various enactments restricting the employment of young persons. In addition, the Secretary of State has power to repeal statutory provisions relating to the employment of persons or classes of persons who have not attained the age of 18 (or a specified lower age not less than 16); he may also amend such provisions so that they refer to school-leaving age rather than a specific age (*EA 1989, s 10(3)(b), (c)*). But the exercise of those powers may not affect provisions relating to the employment of persons under school-leaving age (*EA 1989, s 10(4)*). The powers given have so far been used to amend and revoke a number of statutory instruments (*Employment Act 1989 (Amendments and Revocations) Order 1989 (SI 1989/2311)*).

The *Health and Safety (Young Persons) Regulations 1997 (SI 1997/135)*, which came into force on 3 March 1997, implemented the health and safety provisions of the *EC Directive on the Protection of Young People at Work (94/33)*. They were based on proposals set out in a consultative document published by the Health and Safety Commission in March 1996. They extended the risk assessment and information requirements of the *Management of Health and Safety at Work Regulations 1992* by amending those *Regulations*, and they also removed various provisions relating to the health and safety of young persons which were regarded as outdated and unnecessary.

The *1992 Regulations* were revoked and replaced by the *Management of Health and Safety at Work Regulations 1999 (SI 1999/3242)* with effect from 29 December 1999; the *1999 Regulations* also revoked the *Health and Safety (Young Persons) Regulations 1997*, having incorporated the changes originally made by those Regulations. References below are to the *1999 Regulations*; note that in the *1999 Regulations* 'young person' means any person under 18, so that they also apply to the employment of children. The *1999 Regulations* do not apply to the master or crew of a ship (*reg 2*); for separate provisions governing the health and safety of young persons engaged as workers on United Kingdom ships, see the *Merchant Shipping and Fishing Vessels (Health and Safety at Work) (Employment of Young Persons) Regulations 1998 (SI 1998/2411)*. The last-named Regulations also prescribe rest periods for young persons so engaged: see **3.6** below.

Before young persons start work, the employer is required to assess the risks to their health and safety, taking particular account of:

(a)   their inexperience, their absence of awareness of existing or potential risks, and their immaturity;

(b)   the fitting-out and layout of the workplace and the workstation;

(c)   the nature, degree and duration of exposure to physical, biological and chemical agents;

(d)   the form, range and use of work equipment and the way in which it is handled;

(e)   the organisation of processes and activities;

(f)   the extent of the health and safety training provided or to be provided to young persons; and

(g)   risks from agents, processes and work listed in the Annex to *Directive 94/33* (referred to above).

(*Regulation 3(5).*)

In addition, every employer must ensure that young persons employed by him are protected at work from any risks to their health or safety which are a consequence of the factors referred to in (a) above (*reg 19(1)*). Furthermore, the employment of young persons is prohibited for work:

(i)   which is beyond their physical or psychological capacity;

(ii)   involving harmful exposure to agents which are toxic or carcinogenic, cause heritable genetic damage or harm to the unborn child, or which in any other way chronically affect human health;

(iii)   involving harmful exposure to radiation;

(iv)   involving the risk of accidents which it may reasonably be assumed cannot be recognised or avoided by young persons owing to their insufficient attention to safety or lack of experience or training; or

(v)   in which there is a risk to health from extreme cold or heat, noise or vibration.

In determining whether work will involve harm or risk for these purposes, the employer must have regard to the results of the assessment referred to above (*reg 19(2)*).

However, the prohibition in *reg 19(2)* does not apply in relation to young persons over school-leaving age where (1) the work is necessary for their training, (2) the young person will be supervised by a competent person, and (3) the risks are reduced to their lowest practicable level (*reg 19(3)*).

3.6   Rest periods, breaks and night work

Following the publication in February 1997 by the DTI of a consultation document to implement the provisions of *Directive 94/33* (see above) which cover night work, and entitlement to rest periods, for young persons, the DTI subsequently announced that it intended to implement those provisions by including them in the regulations for implementing the *EC Working Time Directive (93/104)*.

Both Directives were implemented by the *Working Time Regulations 1998 (SI 1998/1833)*, which came into force on 1 October 1998. With regard to young persons (referred to in those *Regulations* as 'young workers'), *Directive 94/33* sets a limit on working time of eight hours per day and 40 hours per week, and prohibits night work altogether. However, in the draft *Regulations* which were originally issued for consultation, the Government stated that it proposed to take advantage of the opt-outs available in the *Directive* which disapplied those limits, as it believed 'that the working time limits set out in the Working Time Directive provide sufficient protection for all workers'. Thus, the original wording of the *Working Time Regulations 1998* did not provide for separate limits on working time for young workers, and the adult limits were applicable to them. (For a summary of the adult limits, see **26.15** HEALTH AND SAFETY AT WORK – II.)

The opt-outs referred to above ceased to be available on 22 June 2000, and the Government issued a consultation document in December 2000 seeking views on how the remaining provisions of the *Directive* should be implemented. In June 2002, the Government issued a further consultation document (see webarchive.nationalarchives.gov.uk) to which draft amending *Regulations* were annexed. These amending *Regulations* were subsequently issued as the *Working Time (Amendment) Regulations 2002 (SI 2002/3128)* and came into force on 6 April 2003. From that date the *1998 Regulations* were amended so as to:

(a)   limit the working hours of young workers to no more than 40 hours per week, or eight hours in any one day – an employer must take all reasonable steps, in keeping with the need to protect the health and safety of workers, to ensure that these limits are complied with in respect of each young worker employed by him (*reg 5A*); and

3.6 Children and Young Persons

(b)   prohibit night working by young workers between 10pm to 6am (or 11pm to 7am) (*regs 2, 6A*).

These new provisions protecting young workers were added to the existing special entitlements in the *1998 Regulations* which apply to young workers, which are set out below:

(c)   a health and capacities assessment before being required to perform night work, and periodically thereafter (*reg 7(2)*);

(d)   a minimum daily continuous rest period of 12 hours (*reg 10(2)*);

(e)   two days off per week (*reg 11(3)*); and

(f)   a minimum 30-minute rest break where daily working time exceeds $4^{1}/_{2}$ hours (*reg 12(4)*).

Note that the protections and entitlements set out in (a) to (f) above are subject to the following exceptions.

Domestic servants. Regulations *5A, 6A,* and *7(2)* do not apply in relation to a young worker employed as a domestic servant in a private household (*reg 19*, as amended).

Armed forces. Regulations *5A, 6A, 10(2)* and *11(3)* do not apply in relation to a young worker serving as a member of the armed forces, although where such a young worker is accordingly required to work during the restricted period, or is not permitted the minimum rest period provided for in *reg 10(2)* or *11(3)*, he must be allowed an appropriate period of compensatory rest (*reg 25(2), (3)*, as amended).

Force majeure. Regulations *5A, 6A, 10(2)* and *12(4)* do not apply in relation to a young worker where his employer requires him to undertake work which no adult worker is available to perform and which:

(i)   is occasioned by either an occurrence due to unusual and unforeseeable circumstances, beyond the employer's control, or exceptional events, the consequences of which could not have been avoided despite the exercise of all due care by the employer;

(ii)   is of a temporary nature; and

(iii)   must be performed immediately.

Where the application of *regs 5A, 6A, 10(2)* or *12(4)* is excluded by virtue of (i) to (iii) above, and a young worker is accordingly required to work during a period which would otherwise be a rest period or rest break, his employer must allow him to take an equivalent period of compensatory rest within the following three weeks (*reg 27*, as amended).

Other restrictions applicable to young workers. Regulation *5A* does not apply in relation to a young worker:

(1)   where the young worker's employer requires him to undertake work which is necessary either to maintain continuity of service or production or to respond to a surge in demand for a service or product;

(2)   where no adult worker is available to perform the work; and

(3)   where performing the work would not adversely affect the young worker's education or training.

(*Regulation 27A(1)*, inserted by *SI 2002/3128*).

In addition, in the circumstances referred to in (1) to (3) above:

(a)   *reg 6A* does not apply in relation to a young worker employed—

  (i)   in a hospital or similar establishment; or

  (ii)   in connection with cultural, artistic, sporting or advertising activities; and

(b)   *reg 6A* does not apply, except in so far as it prohibits work between midnight and 4am, in relation to a young worker employed in—

  (i)   agriculture;

  (ii)   retail trading;

  (iii)   postal or newspaper deliveries;

  (iv)   a catering business;

  (v)   a hotel, public house, restaurant, bar or similar establishment; or

  (vi)   a bakery.

(*Regulation 27A(2)(3)*, inserted by *SI 2002/3128*.)

Where the application of *reg 6A* is excluded by para (*a*) or (*b*) above, and a young worker is accordingly required to work during a period which would otherwise be a rest period or rest break:

(i)   he must be supervised by an adult worker where such supervision is necessary for the young worker's protection; and

(ii)   he must be allowed an equivalent period of compensatory rest.

(*Regulation 27A(4)*, inserted by *SI 2002/3128*.)

Remedies. Regulation 30 (as amended) provides that a young worker may complain to an employment tribunal where his employer has refused to permit him to exercise any right he has:

(1)   under *reg 10(2)*, *11(3)*, or *12(4)*; or

(2)   to compensatory rest under *reg 25(3)*, *27A(4)(b)* or *27(2)*.

The time limit for the presentation of such a complaint is three months beginning with the day on which it is alleged that the exercise of the right should have been permitted (or in the case of a rest period or leave extending over more than one day, the date on which it should have been permitted to begin). If the tribunal is satisfied that it was not reasonably practicable for the complaint to be presented within the period of three months (see **17.7** EMPLOYMENT TRIBUNALS – I), then this time may be extended.

Where the tribunal finds the complaint well-founded, it must make a declaration to that effect, and may make an award of compensation to be paid by the employer to the worker. The amount of the compensation will be such as the tribunal considers just and equitable in all the circumstances having regard to:

(a)   the employer's default in refusing to permit the worker to exercise his right; and

(b)   any loss sustained by the worker which is attributable to the matters complained of.

(For separate provisions governing rest periods for young persons engaged as workers on United Kingdom ships, see the *Merchant Shipping and Fishing Vessels (Health and Safety at Work) (Employment of Young Persons) Regulations 1998 (SI 1998/2411), reg 6*.)

3.7 Children and Young Persons

3.7 WORK EXPERIENCE FOR YOUNG PERSONS AND OTHERS

The *Education Act 1996, s 560A* (as inserted by the *Apprenticeships, Skills, Children and Learning Act 2009, s 47*, with effect from 1 April 2010) provides that a local authority in England may secure the provision of work experience for persons in their area (a) who are over compulsory school age but under 19, or (b) who are aged 19 or over but under 25 and are subject to learning difficulty assessment. A local authority in England must (i) encourage participation in work experience by persons in their area who are within (a) or (b) above and (ii) encourage employers to participate in the provision of work experience for such persons (*Education Act 1996, s 560A(2)*).

3.8 TIME OFF FOR YOUNG PERSONS FOR STUDY OR TRAINING

A right for young persons in employment to take time off from work for study and training, by virtue of *ERA 1996, ss 63A–63C* (inserted by the *Teaching and Higher Education Act 1998, s 32*), came into effect on 1 September 1999 (see *SI 1999/987*). Note that when *Part I* of the *Education and Skills Act 2008* comes into force (expected to be between 2013 and 2015. see *s 173(10)*), *ERA 1996, ss 63A–63C* will apply only to young persons in Scotland and Wales. (*Part I* of the *2008 Act* will instead place a duty on all young persons in England to participate in education or training until the age of 18, with corresponding duties on employers and local education authorities to enable and support participation.)

An employee who:

(a)   is aged 16 or 17,

(b)   is not receiving full-time secondary or further education, and

(c)   has not attained the prescribed standard of achievement,

is entitled to be permitted by his employer to take time off during the employee's working hours in order to undertake study or training leading to a relevant qualification (*ERA 1996, s 63A(1)*). The study or training may be either on the premises of the employer (or principal – see below) or elsewhere (*ERA 1996, s 63A(7)*). For the 'prescribed standard of achievement', see the *Right to Time Off for Study or Training Regulations 2001 (SI 2001/2801)*, which revoked and replaced the *1999 Regulations (SI 1999/986)* with effect from 1 September 2001.

A 'relevant qualification' means an external qualification the attainment of which (i) would contribute to the attainment of the prescribed standard referred to in (c) above, or (ii) would be likely to enhance the employee's employment prospects, whether with his employer or otherwise (*ERA 1996, s 63A(2)(c)*). An 'external qualification' means an academic or vocational qualification awarded or authenticated by such person or body as may be specified in *Regulations* (as to which, see the *Schedule* to *SI 2001/2801* referred to above).

An employee who satisfies the requirements in (a) to (c) above, and is sub-contracted by his employer to another person ('the principal'), is entitled to be permitted by the principal to take time off for the purposes specified in *s 63A(1), ERA 1996* (*ERA 1996, s 63A(3)*). An 18-year-old employee who is undertaking study or training leading to a relevant qualification which he began before attaining that age has a similar right to time off (*ERA 1996, s 63A(4)*).

The amount of time off that an employee is to be permitted to take, and the occasions on which and the conditions under which time off is to be taken, are those that are reasonable in the circumstances having regard, in particular, to (a) the requirements of the employee's study or training, and (b) the circumstances of the business of the employer (or the principal) and the effect of the employee's time off on the running of that business (*ERA 1996, s 63A(5)*).

An employee who is allowed time off is entitled to be paid for the time taken off at the 'appropriate hourly rate', ie one week's pay divided by the number of normal working hours in a week for that employee when employed under the contract of employment in force on the day when the time off is taken (*ERA 1996, s 63B(1), (2)*). (For the calculation of the normal hourly rate where the number of normal working hours differs from week to week or over a longer period, see *ERA 1996, s 63B(3), (4)*.)

3.9   Remedy for refusal of, or remuneration for, time off

If the employer (or principal) has unreasonably refused the employee time off or has refused to pay him, the employee may present a complaint to an employment tribunal (*ERA 1996, s 63C(1)*). The time limit for the presentation of such a complaint is three months beginning with the day on which it is alleged the time off should have been allowed (or, as the case may be, on which the time off was taken). If the tribunal is satisfied that it was not reasonably practicable for the complaint to be presented within the period of three months (see **17.7** EMPLOYMENT TRIBUNALS – I), then this time may be extended (*ERA 1996, s 63C(2)*).

If the employment tribunal finds the complaint well-founded, it will make a declaration to that effect (*ERA 1996, s 63C(3)*). If the complaint is of an unreasonable refusal to permit the employee to take time off, the tribunal will also order the employer or principal to pay the employee remuneration for the period during which the time off should have been allowed (*ERA 1996, s 63C(4)*). If the complaint is of a refusal to pay the employee for the time off, the tribunal will also order the employer or principal to pay the employee the amount due to him (*ERA 1996, s 63C(5)*).

3.10   Right not to suffer detriment

By virtue of *ERA 1996, s 47A* (inserted by the *Teaching and Higher Education Act 1998, s 44*), an employee who is entitled to (i) time off under *ERA 1996, s 63A(1)* or *63A(3)*, and (ii) remuneration under *ERA 1996, s 63B(1)* for that time off (see **3.8** above), has the right not to be subjected to a detriment (ie an action short of dismissal) by his employer or principal on the ground that the employee exercised (or proposed to exercise) that right or received (or sought to receive) such remuneration.

If the employee suffers such a detriment, the remedy is to complain to an employment tribunal pursuant to *ERA 1996, s 48*. (For details, see **26.10** HEALTH AND SAFETY AT WORK – II.)

3.11   CONTRACTS OF EMPLOYMENT, AND MINORS

Contracts of employment form an important exception to the general principle that any contract made by a minor is unenforceable against him during his minority.

A contract of service or apprenticeship which enables a minor to earn a living is likely to be upheld as being for his benefit (*Doyle v White City Stadium Ltd* [1935] 1 KB 110, 104 LJKB 140, CA); this principle was followed by analogy in *Chaplin v Leslie Frewin (Publishers) Ltd* [1966] Ch 71, [1965] 3 All ER 764, CA, which concerned a contract for the publication of a book; see also *Mills v Inland Revenue Commissioners* [1972] 3 All ER 977. (*Doyle* and *Chaplin* were distinguished in *Proform Sports Management Ltd v Proactive Sports Management Ltd* [2006] EWHC 2812 (Ch), [2007] 1 All ER 542, which concerned a representation agreement with a professional footballer that had been entered into during his minority. Reference was also made to *Doyle* and *Chaplin* (albeit obiter) by Lady Hale in *Fisher v Brooker* [2009] UKHL 41, [2009] 4 All ER 789, in considering whether a minor can validly assign copyright by contract.) The effect of the entire contract must be considered; the contract will be upheld if on the whole it is for the minor's benefit (*Clements v London and*

3.11 Children and Young Persons

North Western Rly Co [1894] 2 QB 482, CA), but it will not be binding on the minor if it is not in his interests, or is clearly unreasonable or oppressive (*De Francesco v Barnum* (1890) 45 Ch D 430). Where a contract is, on the whole, for the minor's benefit, but it contains invalid covenants which are severable, such covenants may be struck out and the remainder of the contract upheld (see *Bromley v Smith* [1909] 2 KB 235, 78 LJKB 745).

The *Minors' Contracts Act 1987* made some limited amendments to the law relating to minors' contracts generally. In particular, it repealed the *Infants Relief Act 1874*, thereby enabling a minor, on or after reaching the age of majority, to ratify an otherwise unenforceable contract which he had entered into as a minor (*MCA 1987, s 1*).

4   Codes of Practice

Cross-references. See **9.4** DISCLOSURE OF INFORMATION for details of ACAS Code No 2 and **9.14** DISCLOSURE OF INFORMATION for the Codes of Practice in relation to Data Protection issued by the information Commissioner; **26.21** HEALTH AND SAFETY AT WORK – II for the HSC Code on Safety Representatives and Safety Committees; **47.2, 47.3** and **47.9** TIME OFF WORK for ACAS Code No 3 and the HSC Code on Time Off for Training of Safety Representatives.

4.1   The first Code of Practice (now revoked) was introduced under powers conferred by the *Industrial Relations Act 1971*. Since then a number of other Codes have been issued. Codes of Practice are written in clear terms for the layman in order to give practical guidance. Employers are advised to read the existing and any new Codes of Practice issued and to follow their provisions whenever applicable. Although following a Code of Practice does not guarantee success in any potential claim in an employment tribunal, the employer who can show that he has followed its provisions will be on firm ground.

In broad terms, these Codes of Practice cannot be enforced by law. Nor does breach of a Code *of itself* give rise to any liability. However, Codes may be taken into account in legal proceedings. This chapter considers the powers which exist enabling specified bodies or people to issue Codes and the particular legal effect of the different Codes.

4.2   **THE CODES OF PRACTICE ISSUED BY ACAS**

Power to issue the Codes

ACAS is given statutory power to issue Codes of Practice, subject to approval by both Houses of Parliament. That power is now contained in the *Trade Union and Labour Relations (Consolidation) Act 1992* ('*TULRCA*'), *s 199*. Three such Codes (as amended) have been issued.

ACAS Code of Practice No 1 on Discipline and Grievance Procedures. The newest version of this Code, which came into force on 6 April 2009, replaced the previous 2004 revision of Code No 1. The new code reflects the repeal of the statutory dispute resolution procedures by the *Employment Act 2008*. The Code, which comprises 45 paragraphs, sets out practical guidance to employers, employees and representatives and lays down principles for the handling of disciplinary and grievance issues in the workplace. It should be noted that the Code does not apply to dismissals on grounds of redundancy. The excessive formalism of the statutory dispute resolution procedures is removed. A failure to follow the Code does not, of itself, give rise to automatic liability in any proceedings nor does it remove jurisdiction to hear the complaint from the employment tribunals. The employment tribunals are, however, obliged to take the Code into account and are empowered to adjust any award by up to 25% for an unreasonable failure to comply with any provision of the Code (see further **4.3** below). The new Code applies in relation to matters of discipline or grievance arising after 6 April 2009. The effect of transitional provisions are that matters of discipline or grievance which commenced prior to 6 April 2009 continued to be governed by the statutory dispute resolution procedures of the *Employment Act 2002* and accordingly the 2004 version of ACAS Code of Practice No 1 on Discipline and Grievance Procedures (which was substantially revised in the light of the implementation, with effect from 1 October 2004, of the dispute resolution procedures in *Part 3* of the *Employment Act 2002*) continue to be of relevance and applicable to these remaining transitional cases. Where the disciplinary action or grievance matter commenced before 6 April 2009 the old regime applied subject to the application of certain cut off dates in July and October 2009. The result is that the old regime (and hence the old 2004 Code of Practice No 1) will, in a limited number of remaining cases now progressing through the employment tribunals and on appeal, continue to have relevance.

4.2 Codes of Practice

In addition to the Code of Practice, ACAS has also published guidance dealing with disciplinary and grievance situations titled 'Discipline and Grievances at Work: The ACAS Guide'. Unlike the Code, employment tribunals are not required to have regard to the ACAS guidance in reaching their decisions.

ACAS Code of Practice No 2 on Disclosure of Information to Trade Unions for Collective Bargaining Purposes. This Code of Practice is in its third revision (2003) and sets out relatively short guidance in relation to the obligations to disclose information to trade unions for collective bargaining purposes pursuant to the provisions of *ss 181* and *182* of *TULRCA*. Under *TULRCA* information must be disclosed in accordance with good industrial relations practice and, in considering what is good industrial relations practice, regard is to be had to any relevant provisions of the Code. The provisions of the code are to be taken into account in any proceedings before the Central Arbitration Committee (*TULRCA s 181(2)(b)*, *181(4)* and *207(1)* and *(2)*). Paragraphs 4–12 of the Code provide guidance on the types of information to be disclosed and non exhaustive examples of categories of information are set out in paragraph 11. Guidance on restrictions on the duty to disclose are provided in paragraphs 13–15 of the Code and the responsibilities of trade unions and employers are considered in paragraphs 16–21. Guidance on joint arrangements for disclosure of information are set out in paragraphs 22–23 of the Code.

ACAS Code of Practice No 3 on Time Off for Trade Union Duties and Activities. This Code of Practice has been revised with effect from 1 January 2010 by order of the Secretary of State (*Employment Protection Code of Practice (Time Off for Trade Union Duties and Activities) Order 2009 (SI 2009/3223)*). (See further TIME-OFF WORK (**47**)).

As each of the three Codes has during their history been the subject of substantial revision, in all cases the most up-to-date versions of the Codes should always be consulted, subject to the continued application of the 2004 version of Code of Practice No 1 in any cases still subject to the transitional provisions outlined above.

Each of the revised Codes is available for download in PDF format from the ACAS website (www.acas.org.uk).

Where ACAS proposes to issue a Code, or a revised Code, it must first publish a draft and consider any representations made to it. If ACAS decides to proceed, the draft (modified if need be) is transmitted to the Secretary of State, who may either approve it or publish his reasons for withholding approval. If the Secretary of State approves the draft, it is laid before Parliament (*TULRCA 1992, ss 200, 201*).

4.3 Legal effect

TULRCA 1992, s 207(1), *(2)* states that breach of the ACAS Codes does not render a person liable to proceedings. However, in any proceedings before an employment tribunal or the Central Arbitration Committee ('CAC'), any Code of Practice issued by ACAS is admissible in evidence and any provision of the Code which appears to the employment tribunal or the CAC to be relevant to any question arising in the proceedings must be taken into account in determining that question. It had long been established that non-compliance with a Code would not necessarily render a dismissal unfair, but 'a failure to follow a procedure prescribed in the Code may lead to the conclusion that a dismissal was unfair, which, if that procedure had been followed, would have been held to have been fair' (*W Devis & Sons Ltd v Atkins* [1977] AC 931 at 955). As a consequence of the amendments made by the *Employment Act 2008* (*s 3(1)*, *(2)*) and the repeal of the statutory dispute resolution procedures, a new *s 207A* has been added to *TULRCA 1992* with effect from 6 April 2009 whereby an employment tribunal is empowered in cases where it is satisfied that there was unreasonable failure to comply with the requirements of a relevant Code of Practice (that is to say Code of Practice No 1 as promulgated after 6 April 2009) to reduce or increase the award by up to 25% (*TULRCA 1992, s 207A(2)*, *(3)* and *(4)*).

4.4   CODES ISSUED BY THE THEN DEPARTMENT FOR TRADE AND INDUSTRY

Power to issue the Codes

TULRCA 1992, ss 203 and *204* empower the Secretary of State to issue Codes of Practice, after consultation with ACAS, to be approved by both Houses of Parliament. Such Codes are to contain practical guidance for the purpose of promoting the improvement of industrial relations or promoting desirable practices in relation to the conduct by trade unions of ballots and elections. The Codes currently applicable are The Code on Picketing (1992), the Code of Practice on Industrial Action Ballots and Notice to Employers (2005) and the Code of Practice on Access and Unfair Practices During Recognition Ballots (2005). The Code on Picketing is a reissued and revised version of the previous Code (see *Employment Code of Practice (Picketing) Order 1992 (SI 1992/476)*). The other two Codes were laid before Parliament on 18 July 2005 and came into force on 1 October 2005. The 2005 Codes incorporate changes made by the *Employment Relations Act 2004* (see TRADE UNIONS – I, II (48, 49)) as well as updating and revising the earlier Codes. Care should be taken to ensure that the 1 October 2005 versions of these Codes are consulted.

Copies of the revised Codes of Practice may be downloaded in PDF form from the Department for Business, Innovations and Skills ('BIS') website at www.bis.gov.uk/site/foi/publication-scheme/categories/employment-rights-codes-of-practice.

The Department of Trade and Industry Codes may supersede any part of or all of a Code issued by ACAS or a previous DTI or Department of Employment Code (*TULRCA 1992, s 208(2)*) (see above).

4.5   Legal effect

Although a failure to comply with the Codes issued by the Secretary of State does not itself render a person liable to proceedings, the Codes are stated to be admissible in evidence and to be taken into account, if relevant, in any proceedings not only before an employment tribunal or the CAC but also, in the case of a DTI or Department for Education and Employment Code, in any court (*TULRCA 1992, s 207(1), (3)*). Thus, in *Thomas v National Union of Mineworkers (South Wales Area)* [1986] Ch 20, [1985] ICR 886 at 920–921 Scott J granted an injunction, following violent picketing, to restrain the union from organising pickets in greater numbers than were suggested by the relevant Code.

4.6   CODES ISSUED BY THE BORDER AND IMMIGRATION AGENCY

The Border and Immigration Agency has issued two relevant Codes of Practice: the Border & Immigration Agency Code of Practice: Civil Penalties for Employers (2008) and the Border & Immigration Agency Code of Practice: Guidance for Employers for the Avoidance of Unlawful Discrimination in Employment Practice while Seeking to Prevent Illegal Working (2008). The Codes are made under the authority of *s 19* and *s 23* of the *Immigration, Asylum and Nationality Act 2006* and came into force on 29 February 2008.

The Civil Penalties Code gives guidance on the assessment of penalties in the event of employing illegal migrant workers and the factors taken into account in that assessment. The Code must be taken into account by the courts and may be used in legal proceedings.

The Guidance for Employers for the Avoidance of Unlawful Discrimination in Employment Practice while Seeking to Prevent Illegal Working Code provides guidance to employers on how to avoid a civil penalty for employing an illegal migrant worker in a way which does not result in unlawful race discrimination (paragraph 1). As a statutory code its provisions are admissible in evidence and must be taken into account in any relevant proceedings in the courts and in the employment tribunal. The Code seeks to summarise the relevant provisions prohibiting race discrimination and the responsibilities of an employer under *ss 15* and *21* of the *Immigration, Asylum and Nationality Act 2006* ("the *Act*") and provides short guidance in paragraphs **7.1–7.8** on avoiding race discrimination whilst complying with the responsibilities imposed by the Act.

4.7   THE POSITION PRIOR TO THE EQUALITY ACT 2010: (1) CODES RELATING TO RACIAL EQUALITY

History of the Codes

The *Race Relations Act 1976, s 47* empowered the Commission for Racial Equality to issue Codes of Practice containing practical guidance for either or both of the following purposes:

(a)   the elimination of discrimination in the field of employment; and

(b)   the promotion of equality of opportunity in that field between persons of different racial groups.

The first Code of Practice was issued in April 1984 by the Commission for Racial Equality ('CRE') and new Code of Practice on Racial Equality in Employment (2005) was issued in April 2006. This Code of Practice continues to apply to matters occurring before the coming into force of the relevant provisions of the *Equality Act 2010* on 1 October 2010.

The CRE had also published a Code of Practice on the Duty to Promote Racial Equality (in force from May 2002) as a consequence of the duty imposed by the *Race Relations (Amendment) Act 2000* on public bodies to promote racial equality (see DISCRIMINATION AND EQUAL OPPORTUNITIES – I, II, III (10, 11, 12)). This Code of Practice continues to apply to matters occurring before the coming into force of the relevant provisions of the *Equality Act 2010* on 1 October 2010.

4.8   Legal effect

The *Race Relations Act 1976, s 47(10)* (now repealed) provided that a failure to observe any provision in a Code of Practice shall not of itself render a person liable to proceedings. However, such Codes were admissible in evidence and, where relevant, were to be taken into account in any proceedings before an employment tribunal. See now, for matters occurring before 1 October 2010, *section 15(4)(b)* of the *Equality Act 2006* which maintains the admissibility of such Codes in evidence and provides that, where relevant, they be taken into account in determining any question arising in any such proceedings.

4.9   THE POSITION PRIOR TO THE EQUALITY ACT 2010: (2) CODES ISSUED BY THE EQUAL OPPORTUNITIES COMMISSION

History of the Codes relating to sex discrimination and equal pay

The *Sex Discrimination Act 1975, s 56A* empowered the Equal Opportunities Commission to issue Codes of Practice containing practical guidance for either or both of the following purposes:

(a)   the elimination of discrimination in the field of employment; and

(b)   the promotion of equality of opportunity in that field between men and women.

The Equal Opportunities Commission issued a Code of Practice which came into force on 30 April 1984. (See DISCRIMINATION AND EQUAL OPPORTUNITIES – I, II, III (10, 11, 12).)

A new Code of Practice on Equal Pay was introduced on 1 December 2003 by the *Code of Practice on Equal Pay Order 2003 (SI 2003/2865)*. This Code was admissible in evidence in any proceedings under the *SDA 1975* or the *Equal Pay Act 1970* (see **4.10** below) and included information on equal pay for pregnant women and those on maternity leave, the Equal Pay Questionnaire procedure and equal pay reviews and grievance procedures (see EQUAL PAY (22)). The Equal Opportunities Commission also issued the Gender Equality Duty Code of Practice (2007) in force from 6 April 2007 pursuant to *s 76E(1)* of the *SDA 1975*.

The Equal Opportunities Commission (along with the CRE and the Disability Rights Commission) was replaced with effect from 1 October 2007 by the Equality and Human Rights Commission established under the *Equality Act 2006*. The Codes of Practice relating to sex discrimination and equal pay continue to apply to matters occurring before the coming into force of the relevant provisions of the *Equality Act 2010* on 1 October 2010.

4.10   Legal effect

The *Sex Discrimination Act 1975, s 56A* (as amended by *TURERA 1993, Sch 7 para 15* and as modified by *SDA s 76E(3)*) provided that a failure to observe any provision in a Code of Practice shall not of itself render a person liable to proceedings. However, such Codes were admissible in evidence and, where relevant, were to be taken into account in any proceedings before an employment tribunal under that *Act* or the *Equal Pay Act 1970*. See now, for matters occurring before 1 October 2010, *section 15(4)(b)* of the *Equality Act 2006* which maintains the admissibility of such Codes in evidence and provides that, where relevant, they be taken into account in determining any question arising in any such proceedings.

THE POSITION PRIOR TO THE EQUALITY ACT 2010: CODES RELATING TO DISABILITY

4.11   History of the Disability Codes

The *Disability Discrimination Act 1995, s 53* empowered the Secretary of State to issue Codes of Practice containing such practical guidance as he considers appropriate with a view to:

(a)   eliminating discrimination in the field of employment against disabled persons and persons who have had a disability; and

(b)   encouraging good practice in relation to the employment of disabled persons and persons who have had a disability.

The Disability Rights Commission Code of Practice on Employment and Occupation was promulgated under powers conferred by *s 53A* of the *Disability Discrimination Act 1995*.

The Disability Rights Commission (along with the CRE and the Equal Opportunities Commission) was replaced with effect from 1 October 2007 by the Equality and Human Rights Commission established under the *Equality Act 2006*. The Codes of Practice relating to disability continue to apply to matters occurring before the coming into force of the relevant provisions of the *Equality Act 2010* on 1 October 2010.

4.12   Legal effect

A failure on the part of any person to observe any provision of a Code of Practice did not of itself make that person liable to any proceedings. However, such a Code was admissible in evidence in any proceedings under the *DDA 1995* before an employment tribunal, a

4.12 Codes of Practice

county court or a sheriff court and, where relevant, was to be taken into account in determining any question arising in any such proceedings (*DDA 1995, s 53A(8)* and *(8A)* (now repealed). For matters occurring before 1 October 2010, *s 15(4)(b)* of the *Equality Act 2006* applies, maintaining the admissibility of such Codes in evidence and provides that, where relevant, they be taken into account in determining any question arising in any such proceedings under the *DDA*.

4.13 GUIDANCE ON DISABILITY

In relation to the definition of disability, the Secretary of State, pursuant to *s 6(5)* of the *Equality Act 2010* and the *Equality Act 2010 (Guidance on the Definition of Disability) Appointed Day Order 2011 (SI 2011/1159)*, has produced "Guidance On Matters to be Taken Into Account In Determining Questions Relating to the Definition of Disability (2011)" which came into force on 1 May 2011. The guidance does not impose legal obligations in itself but by *Schedule 1, Paragraph 12* to the *Equality Act 2010* the guidance must be taken into account by an adjudicating body on the issue whether a person is disabled

4.14 THE EQUALITY ACT 2010: NEW CODES OF PRACTICE ON EMPLOYMENT AND EQUAL PAY

The *Equality Act 2010* received the Royal Assent (on 8 April 2010) and the major provisions relating to employment law have been brought into force with effect from 1 October 2010. The Equality and Human Rights Commission consulted during 2010 on draft Codes of Practice, the purpose of which are to offer statutory guidance on the *Equality Act's* employment and equal pay implications.

With effect from 6 April 2011 the Codes of Practice under the previous legislation, considered in outline above, have been revoked by *The Former Equality Commissions' Codes of Practice (Employment, Equal Pay, and Rights of Access for Disabled Persons) (Revocation) Order 2011 (SI 2011/776)* ("the *Revocation Order*"). By the *Revocation Order* each of the following Codes or Practice are revoked: the Code of Practice for the elimination of discrimination on the grounds of sex and marriage and the promotion of equality of opportunity in employment, issued by the former Equal Opportunities Commission under *section 56A* of the *Sex Discrimination Act 1975*, which came into effect on 30 April 1985 (*SI 1985/387*); the Code of Practice on Equal Pay, also issued by the former Equal Opportunities Commission under *section 56A* of the *Sex Discrimination Act 1975*, which came into effect on 1 December 2003 (*SI 2003/2865*); the Disability Discrimination Act 1995 Code of Practice on Employment and Occupation, issued by the former Disability Rights Commission under *section 53A* of the *Disability Discrimination Act 1995*, which came into effect on 1 October 2004 (*SI 2004/2302*); the revised Code of Practice on Racial Equality in Employment, issued by the former Commission for Racial Equality under *section 47* of the *Race Relations Act 1976*, which came into effect on 6 April 2006 (*SI 2006/630*); and the Disability Discrimination Act 1995 Code of Practice on Rights of Access: services to the public, public authority functions, private clubs and premises, issued by the former Disability Rights Commission under *section 53A* of the *Disability Discrimination Act 1995*, which came into effect on 4 December 2006 (*SI 2006/1967*).

The *Revocation Order* contains, in *art 3*, transitional provisions in relation to matters occurring, inter alia, prior to 1 October 2010. In any cases progressing through the employment tribunals relating to matters occurring prior to that date the previous various Codes of Practice considered above will remain relevant and applicable. In transitional cases the former Codes are to continue to have effect in relation to such proceedings for the purposes of *section 15(4)(b)* of the *Equality Act 2006*, which requires a court or tribunal to take a code into account in any case in which it appears to the court or tribunal to be relevant.

For matters occurring on or after 1 October 2010 the relevant Codes of Practice in the employment field will be the Equality Act 2010 Code of Practice on Employment and the Equality Act 2010 Code of Practice on Equal Pay. An additional new Code of Practice, the Equality Act 2010 Code of Practice on Services, Public Functions and Associations is outside the scope of this work. Each of the new codes are issued under *section 14(1)* of the *Equality Act 2006* (as amended by the *Equality Act 2010*) and are brought into force by the *Equality Act 2010 Codes of Practice (Services, Public Functions and Associations, Employment and Equal Pay) Order 2011 (SI 2011/857)*.

The Equality Act 2010 Code of Practice on Employment

The Code on Employment deals with all equalities issues in employment other than Equal Pay (see below). The Code is substantial, totalling 308 pages. As previously, by *section 15(4)(b)* of the *Equality Act 2006*, the courts and employment tribunals are obliged to take the new Code into account in any relevant case.

The Code is divided into two parts. The scheme of Part One of the Code, which is divided into Chapters 2–15, is to summarise the law relating to the various protected characteristics (Chapter 2), and then direct and indirect discrimination (Chapters 3 and 4). Disability discrimination has two separate chapters (Chapters 5 and 6) and harassment, pregnancy and victimisation are also considered separately (Chapters 7, 8 and 9 respectively). The summary of the obligations under the Act is set out in Chapter 10 and work relationships other than employment are considered in Chapter 11. Positive action is addressed in Chapter 12. Thereafter occupational requirements (Chapter 13), pay and benefits (Chapter 14) and enforcement (Chapter 15) are summarised.

Part Two of the Code (beginning at page 221) provides guidance on avoiding discrimination in recruitment (Chapter 16) and in employment (Chapter 17). Guidance on the content of equalities policies is found in Chapter 18 and Chapter 19 deals with guidance on termination of employment. The Code concludes (beginning at page 294) with three appendices on the Meaning of Disability (Appendix 1), Monitoring (Appendix 2) and Making Reasonable Adjustments to Work Premises – Legal Considerations (Appendix 3). The Code may be found at www.equalityhumanrights.com/legal-and-policy/equality -act/equality-act-codes-of-practice.

The Equality Act 2010 Code of Practice on Equal Pay

The Code of Practice on Equal Pay totals 62 pages. As previously the courts and employment tribunals are obliged to take the Code into account to the extent relevant in any equal pay case. (See paragraph 116 of the Code and *section 15(4)(b)* of the *Equality Act 2006*). The order of the Code is to, first, summarise the existing law relating to equal pay (paragraphs 22–91 of the Code). The provisions in relation to pregnancy, maternity and equal pay are summarised at paragraphs 92–101 with various examples. The new pay transparency provisions prohibiting secrecy are summarised at paragraphs 102–110. Thereafter the questionnaire procedure, burden of proof, employment tribunal procedure and awards are summarised (see paragraphs 111–157 of the Code). The second part of the Code (beginning at page 49) is a good practice guide headed "Good Equal Pay Practice" (see paragraphs 158–185 of the Code). The Code may be found at www.equalityhumanrights.com/legal-and-policy/equality-act/equality-act-codes-of -practice.

4.15   CODES ISSUED BY THE HEALTH AND SAFETY COMMISSION

Power to issue the Codes

Regulations made under the *Health and Safety at Work, etc Act 1974 ('HSWA 1974')* are sometimes supplemented by Codes of Practice approved and/or issued by the Health and Safety Commission (for details of which see **25.28** HEALTH AND SAFETY AT WORK – I) (*HSWA 1974, s 16*). A full consideration of these codes is beyond the scope of this book. Two such codes are directly relevant to employment law: the HSC Code of Practice on Safety Representatives and Safety Committees and the HSC Code of Practice on Time Off for Training Safety Representatives. They both supplement the *Safety Representatives and Safety Committees Regulations 1977 (SI 1977/500)* as amended by *SI 1992/2051*, made under *HSWA 1974*.

4.16   Legal effect

Non-compliance with a relevant HSC Code does not of itself render a person liable to any civil or criminal proceedings. However, where in any criminal proceedings a person is alleged to have committed an offence by contravening a provision for which a code of practice was in force, if breach of the Code is established, the offence is proved unless the court is satisfied that the requirement or prohibition was complied with otherwise than by observance of the Code (*HSWA 1974, s 17*).

4.17   CODES ISSUED BY THE INFORMATION COMMISSIONER

The Information Commissioner issued the Employment Practices Data Protection Code in four parts. Part 1: Recruitment and Selection: March 2002. Part 2: Employment Records: August 2002. Part 3: Monitoring at Work: June 2003. Part 4: Information about Workers Health: December 2004. The Code may be obtained from www.ico.gov.uk/upload/documents/library. The Code is issued pursuant to statutory authority conferred on the Information Commissioner by *s 51(3)(b)* of the *Data Protection Act 1998*. The Codes promulgated by the Information Commissioner do not have formal legal status or effect unlike the other codes of practice considered above. The Information Commissioner is, however, the enforcing authority for the purposes of the *Data Protection Act 1998* and the Code may reasonably be assumed to represents the views of the Information Commissioner in relation to the standards of practice to be expected of employers in relation to the subject matters covered by the Code. In addition to the Code the Information Commissioner has also published guidance in relation to the Code: 'Employment Practices Code: Supplementary Guidance'. This too may be downloaded from the Information Commissioner's website.

The Information Commissioner has been seeking consultation responses on a new Code of Practice concerning the right of individuals to make a subject access request under *s 7* of the *Data Protection Act 1998*. This is likely to be significant to employers who are frequently faced with subject access requests prior to or contemporaneous with the commencement of litigation by employees. In summary the draft Code provide some practical guidance including best practice recommendations on staff training, having a subject access request policy and responding to subject access requests on a centralised basis. It is noteworthy that the code does not require data controllers to suspend routine data destruction policies (even after a subject access request is made) and recognises that staff may legitimately hold personal data on personal devices or email accounts and staff are not required under the code to search such data sources unless there is good reason to believe relevant personal data is held. If archived sources are known to differ from current sources of data then they should be searched but there is no obligation to search archives if there is evidence that the material is the same. Furthermore, data controllers are not to be required to use complicated methods of recovering deleted data if the data has been deleted in accordance with normal data retention and deletion policies.

4.18   REVISION AND REVOCATION OF CODES

Provision has been made for the revision by the appropriate authority of those codes which are issued under *TULRCA 1992, s 203* (ie the Secretary of State and BIS for the DTI Codes; see **4.4** above) or which are issued under *TULRCA 1992, s 199* (ie the ACAS Codes; see **4.2** above). ACAS may revise its codes under *TULRCA 1992, s 201* and the Secretary of State may revise the DTI (now BIS) codes under *TULRCA 1992, s 205*. Similar procedural provisions apply as in the case of making new codes. The Secretary of State may, with Parliamentary approval, revoke either an ACAS or a DTI/BIS Employment Code (*TULRCA 1992, ss 202, 206*). In the case of an ACAS Code, he may do so only at the request of ACAS.

5   Collective Agreements

5.1   INTRODUCTION

The practice of collective bargaining, by which wage rates and terms and conditions of employment of workers are determined by negotiations between employers and trade unions, leading to collective agreements, is still relatively common in traditional heavy industries and most of the public sector, although its importance in the economy as a whole has declined as the incidence of union recognition has fallen over the last 30 years. National bargaining between trade unions and employer representatives is the norm in the public sector. Proposals to move to the fixing of rates of pay more locally were announced by the Chancellor in March 2012, but have made little progress in the face of strong union opposition.

In some industries in the private sector also, negotiations between representatives of associations of employers and the recognised trade unions at national level lead to collective agreements which in practice set norms for the industry or sector concerned, although there has not since the repeal of *Schedule 11* to the *Employment Protection Act 1975* been any statutory mechanism enabling workers within the sector to enforce the terms agreed collectively against a particular employer. This is in contrast to the practice which prevails widely in some other member states of the EU, and is reflected in the provisions found in EU Directives permitting the domestic implementation of obligations introduced by the Directive by way of collective agreement as an alternative to legislation.

Under the British system, collective agreements are generally not legally enforceable between the collective parties (employers and unions); however they may form the basis for the individual worker's contract of employment if it is agreed between the collective parties that they should do so. Whether a collective agreement, or a particular provision of the agreement, is in fact incorporated into the contract of a particular worker, however, is a matter of the construction and application of the express or implied terms of the contract between the worker and his or her employer, and not an automatic consequence of the stated intentions of the collective parties: see further **5.7** below.

5.2   DEFINITION

For the purposes of the *Trade Union and Labour Relations (Consolidation) Act 1992* (*'TULRCA 1992'*), a collective agreement is defined in *s 178* as 'any arrangement or agreement made by or on behalf of one or more trade unions and one or more employers or employers' associations' which relates to one or more of the following matters:

(*a*)   terms and conditions of employment, or the physical conditions in which any workers are required to work;

(*b*)   engagement or non-engagement, or termination or suspension of employment or the duties of employment, of one or more workers;

(*c*)   allocation of work or the duties of employment between workers or groups of workers;

(*d*)   matters of discipline;

(*e*)   a worker's membership or non-membership of a trade union;

(*f*)   facilities for officials of trade unions; and

(*g*)   facilities for negotiation or consultation, and other procedures, relating to any of the above matters, including the recognition by employers or employers' associations of the right of a trade union to represent workers in such negotiation or consultation or in the carrying out of such procedures.

5.2   Collective Agreements

This list of the possible subject matter for collective agreements does not mean that agreements must necessarily cover all of the listed areas. Employers are free (subject to the statutory procedure in *TULRCA 1992, Sch A1* for trade unions to obtain recognition) to agree to confer negotiating rights on a trade union to whatever more limited extent they may wish, as well as to define the categories of employees for whom the union is to be recognised, and similarly to make agreements covering only limited and specific aspects of the matters potentially within the scope of a collective agreement. This is a central feature of the voluntarist approach to the role of trade unions which has characterised British employment law for most of the post-war era.

5.3   LEGAL STATUS

It was established in the landmark case of *Ford Motor Co v AUEW* [1969] 2 QB 303 that collective agreements are not, at common law, generally legally enforceable between the parties to them. The basis for this conclusion was that it was not the intention of the parties to create legal relations, a necessary ingredient of any contractually binding agreement. This has remained the position since, save for the period during which the *Industrial Relations Act 1971* was in force; this reversed the presumption established in the *Ford* case, replacing it with a presumption that any collective agreement was intended by the parties thereto to be legally enforceable, unless the contrary was stated. During the period the *Act* was in force (1 December 1971 to 16 September 1974) the practice of collective parties in the vast majority of cases was to insert a clause in any agreement stating 'this is not a legally enforceable agreement' (known as a 'TINALEA' clause).

5.4   Following the repeal of the *Industrial Relations Act 1971*, the position at common law was restored by statute (the *Trade Union and Labour Relations Act 1974, s 18*, now consolidated in *TULRCA 1992, s 179(3)*). By virtue of *s 179(3)*, any collective agreement made before 1 December 1971, or after 16 September 1974, will be conclusively presumed not to have been intended by the parties to the agreement to be a legally enforceable contract unless the agreement:

(a)   is in writing, and

(b)   contains a provision which (however expressed) states that the parties intend that the agreement shall be a legally enforceable contract,

in which event it is conclusively presumed to be intended to be legally enforceable. Despite including the phrase "however expressed", condition (*b*) may not be satisfied by a mere statement in the agreement that the parties are to be bound by it (*National Coal Board v National Union of Mineworkers* [1986] ICR 736, [1986] IRLR 439). It is possible for an agreement to state that the parties intend a particular part of it to be legally enforceable, in which case the presumption against enforceability would apply to the rest. The position for any agreement made during the currency of the *1971 Act* remains that there is a presumption that the parties intended the agreement to be legally enforceable, unless (as is usually the case for such agreements made during that period as remain in force) the contrary is stated within the agreement.

However, where an employer is required to recognise a trade union in accordance with the provisions of *TULRCA 1992, Sch A1* (see TRADE UNIONS – I (48)), and the method of collective bargaining is specified by the Central Arbitration Committee under *paras 30* and *31* of *Sch A1*, any agreement reached through collective bargaining will have effect as a legally enforceable contract made between the parties; this will also be the case if the parties agree an alternative procedure for collective bargaining to that specified by the CAC. However, the only remedy for breach of any such agreement is an order for specific performance (*TULRCA 1992, Sch A1, para 31(6)*).

5.5   INCORPORATION INTO INDIVIDUAL CONTRACTS OF EMPLOYMENT

Although the great majority of collective agreements are not legally enforceable by the union against the employer or vice versa, they may, and in most cases in practice do, have legally binding consequences as between the employer and the individual employee. Their terms may be incorporated into individual contracts of employment either because the contract expressly provides for such incorporation, or because incorporation is an implied term of the contract deriving from custom and practice in the industry. In either case, the collective agreement will be incorporated, notwithstanding that the particular employee may not approve of what the union has negotiated, or may even have ceased to belong to the relevant union (see, eg *Tocher v General Motors Scotland Ltd* [1981] IRLR 55, EAT). On the other hand a collective agreement will not be incorporated into individual contracts of employment merely because the employer belongs to the association which negotiated that agreement (*Hamilton v Futura Floors Ltd* [1990] IRLR 478, OH). It does not matter that the agreement is as between the parties to it not legally enforceable, since it is the terms as incorporated into the individual employee's contract that fall to be enforced, and the contract of employment will very rarely not be legally enforceable. Thus, for example, in *Marley v Forward Trust Group Ltd* [1986] ICR 891, [1986] IRLR 369, the Court of Appeal held that an employee could enforce the terms of a collective agreement on redundancy which was incorporated into his contract, even though the agreement itself was expressed to be 'binding in honour only'.

5.6   The basis for the incorporation of terms of a collective agreement into an individual contract of employment is usually that the contract of employment expressly states that this is to be the case, often in terms covering not only agreements current at the time of the making of the contract, but also future agreements. Incorporation by implication as a matter of custom and practice is most likely to be established by evidence in those industries and sectors of the economy where traditions of collective bargaining are most strongly established and there is a long practice of the benefits of collective agreements being observed by the employer; it is a matter of evidence in each case whether the practice of applying collectively agreed terms is sufficiently 'reasonable, notorious and certain', to be regarded as custom and practice, or whether the term relied on has been sufficiently consistently applied by the employer to be incorporated by implication.

A further, but in practice less common, way for collectively negotiated terms to be contractually enforceable by individual employees is where the union acts as agent for the employees in negotiating the terms, typically for a specific group of employees who have engaged the union to negotiate on their behalf. An example of this process is *Edwards v Skyways Ltd* [1964] 1 WLR 349.

5.7   Even where there is an express incorporation of collective agreements into individual contracts of employment, it does not follow that all provisions of the agreements between the employer and the relevant union or unions will be incorporated. Whether a particular provision will be held by the courts to be incorporated depends on whether it is considered 'apt' for incorporation. Terms specifying rates of pay, hours of work or entitlements to benefits will readily be held to be apt for incorporation, but at the other end of the scale terms setting out a procedure for the resolution of disputes between the union and the employer will equally readily be treated as not apt for incorporation as contractual terms enforceable by an individual employee.

The leading case on the correct approach to what is apt for incorporation is *Alexander v Standard Telephones and Cables plc* [1991] IRLR 286. Hobhouse J summarised the position, in terms which have since been regularly cited as authoritative, thus:

'The principles to be applied can therefore be summarised. The relevant contract is that between the individual employee and his employer; it is the contractual intention of those two parties which must be ascertained. In so far as that intention is to be found in a written document, that document must be construed on ordinary contractual principles. Insofar as there is no such document or that document is not complete or conclusive, their contractual intention has to be ascertained by inference from the other available material including collective agreements. The fact that another document is not itself contractual does not prevent it from being incorporated into the contract if that intention is shown as between the employer and the individual employee. Where a document is expressly incorporated by general words it is still be necessary to consider, in conjunction with the words of incorporation, whether any particular part of that document is apt to be a term of the contract; if it is inapt, the correct construction of the contract may be that it is not incorporated. Where it is not a case of express incorporation, but a matter of inferring the contractual intent, the character of the document and the relevant part of it, and whether it is apt to form part of the individual contract is central to the decision whether or not the inference should be drawn.' (para 31)

Provisions dealing with, for example, relations between an employer and a union operate at a collective level and are inappropriate for incorporation as terms of individual contracts A number of cases illustrate the kind of provision which has been held not to be apt for incorporation into individual contracts. In *National Coal Board v National Union of Mineworkers* [1986] ICR 736, [1986] IRLR 439, the agreement set out the details of a conciliation scheme for the settlement of disputes. In the *Alexander* case itself, terms of a collective agreement specifying the procedure to be applied in a redundancy situation, and the criteria to be used for selection for redundancy, were held not to be apt for incorporation into the individual employees' contracts. Similarly in *Kaur v MG Rover Group Ltd* [2004] EWCA Civ 1507, [2005] IRLR 40 the Court of Appeal held that a provision in a collective agreement which stated that 'there will be no compulsory redundancy' did not have effect as a term of the individual contracts of employment between the employer and each employee.

In *Malone v British Airways plc* [2010] EWCA Civ 1225, [2011] IRLR 32, the Court of Appeal found that provisions of a collective agreement between the unions and the airline regarding minimum cabin crew complements for flights had not been incorporated into the contracts of employment. There was insufficient evidence of mutual intention to give the terms of the agreement enforceability by individual cabin crew members and the particular provisions were not apt for incorporation. The Court of Appeal focused in particular on what it saw as the disastrous consequences for the business if the provision were to be individually enforceable, such as flights having to be cancelled if not enough cabin crew members to fulfil the minimum manning levels were available, a consequence it concluded could not have been intended.

A further example of a finding that a term was not appropriate for incorporation is the Court of Appeal's decision in *George v Ministry of Justice* [2013] EWCA Civ 324 (16 April 2013, unreported), a case relating to an agreement for time off in lieu for prison officers who had worked more than 39 hours in a week.

5.8   The kinds of terms most likely to be found to be apt for incorporation are those conferring specific benefits or imposing specific obligations on employees, such as rates of pay, changes in working hours, or conditions to be observed for the taking of leave. What is apt may also be affected by the history of how agreements between the collective parties have been incorporated into employees' contracts. In *Henry v London General Transport Services Ltd* [2002] EWCA Civ 488, [2002] IRLR 472, the employers entered into negotiations with a union, the TGWU, in preparation for a management buy-out. There had been a history of negotiations with the TGWU but there was no express incorporation of terms collectively agreed. The TGWU and the employers agreed a framework agreement which contained new and less advantageous terms and conditions, including reduced pay. The tribunal held that the terms of the framework agreement were so fundamental that the past practice of negotiations leading to the incorporation of terms collectively agreed was not such as to enable these changes to be incorporated into individual contracts. The Court of Appeal disagreed. The matters which were the subject of the framework agreement were apt for incorporation into individual contracts. Further, if the appropriate custom and practice was established, it could be expected to cover all contractual terms. The tribunal had been wrong to draw a distinction between fundamental and other terms without identifying a basis for that distinction.

Guidance has been given by the High Court as to when a collectively agreed disciplinary procedure will be regarded as incorporated into individual contracts: see *Hussain v Surrey and Sussex Healthcare NHS Trust* [2011] EWHC 1670 (QB), para 168. Relevant factors include the importance of the procedure, the level of detail prescribed, the certainty of the terms of the procedure, whether the terms would if contractual be workable and whether the provisions appear in the context of other provisions having contractual effect.

In order for a term in a collective agreement to be incorporated into a contract of employment it may be necessary for an employee to have his attention drawn specifically to it. In *Worrall v Wilmott Dixon Partnerships Ltd* (UKEAT/0521/09) [2010] All ER (D) 107 (Jul), EAT, a council and its trade unions entered into a collective agreement regarding pay and redundancy and the terms were then inserted into a staff handbook. The handbook was generally available but not given to each employee. The EAT held that the term was not contractual as it had not been brought to the employee's attention and he could not therefore be said to have accepted the term. However this analysis is open to question, since it was the employee who sought to rely on the agreement, as it conferred a substantial benefit on him in connection with his redundancy. Further an express general incorporation of collective agreements into an individual's contract need not require that the individual has knowledge of each agreement; whether the incorporating provision does so require is a question of construction of the particular terms.

5.9   The principles applicable to the construction of collective agreements are the same as those which apply to other contracts: *Adams v British Airways plc* [1996] IRLR 574, CA. In particular, the Court of Appeal has confirmed that the principles for the construction of contracts set out by Lord Hoffmann in *Investors Compensation Scheme v West Bromwich Building Society* [1998] WLR 896 apply: see *Bull v Nottinghamshire and City of Nottingham Fire Authority* [2007] EWCA Civ 240, [2007] ICR 1631. Where the terms of a collective agreement are truly ambiguous, it is permissible to look at a clearly established practice, which continues both before and after an agreement is made, as evidence of what the parties meant by the agreement (*Dunlop Tyres Ltd v Blows* [2001] EWCA Civ 1032, [2001] IRLR .629; see also CONTRACT OF EMPLOYMENT (7)). In both the *Bull* case and in *Briggs v Nottingham University Hospitals NHS Trust* [2010] EWCA Civ 264, [2010] IRLR 504, the Court of Appeal looked at the context of the agreement and whether the surrounding circumstances, purpose of the agreement and background to the negotiations lent support to a particular construction.

The construction of a collective agreement for a three year pay deal was considered by the Court of Appeal in *Anderson v London Fire and Emergency Planning Authority* [2013] EWCA Civ 321, 11 April 2013. Reversing the EAT, the Court held that an agreement providing for two formulae for the third year's pay increase should be interpreted as requiring whichever formula produced the greater increase, since that gave effect to industrial common sense in the circumstances of the agreement. The court rejected the EAT's view (see [2012] IRLR 888) that the fact of two alternatives being stated gave the employer the right to choose which to implement as making no sense in the context of a negotiated pay agreement.

5.10   Like any contract, a collective agreement may have implied, as well as express, terms. The approach of the courts to whether a particular term should be implied into a collective agreement depends on the context as well as the term sought to be implied. In the case of *Ali v Christian Salvesen Food Services Ltd* [1997] 1 All ER 721, [1997] ICR 25, the Court of Appeal took a restrictive approach, acknowledging that such agreements are reached between the two sides of the industry and will inevitably involve compromises between their interests. The case concerned an 'annualised hours' contract, under which the employees were employed to work a notional 40-hour week but in fact were expected to work far more flexible hours based on an annual rota. There was no entitlement to overtime pay until the number of hours worked during a particular year exceeded a specified figure. The individual workers in the case had worked for more than 40 hours per week, but their contracts had been terminated before the number of hours worked in the year exceeded the specified figure. The question was whether they could claim overtime in respect of the number of hours which they had worked in excess of 40 per week. There was no express term which governed what should happen in this situation. The employees therefore based their case on an implied term. The Court of Appeal rejected the implication of a term to cover this situation. Waite LJ pointed out that this was one of several situations for which the collective agreement had not made provision. He refused to imply a term, stating that when a matter had not been covered in a collective agreement, the natural inference was that it had been intentionally omitted because it was either too controversial or too complicated to justify inclusion.

An example of a case where a term was held by the Court of Appeal to be implied into a collective agreement which was silent on the point is *Garratt v Mirror Group Newspapers Ltd* [2011] EWCA Civ 425, [2011] ICR 880. The case concerned a collective agreement between the employer and a newly recognised trade union for enhanced redundancy terms. The employer had in practice for many years made enhanced payments but had always required employees to enter into compromise agreements as a condition of payment. This was (as the Court found) very well known, and had never been disputed. The agreement itself, which had been expressly incorporated into Mr Garratt's contract, was silent on the point of compromise agreements, but the Court readily upheld a finding in the County Court that the requirement for a compromise agreement was to be implied on the basis of the mutual understanding of the parties.

5.11 CHANGES TO COLLECTIVE AGREEMENTS

Once the terms of a collective agreement are incorporated into individual contracts, the relevant contractual terms are, as a matter of general principle, unaffected by the termination of the collective agreement (*Robertson v British Gas Corpn* [1983] ICR 351, [1983] IRLR 302, CA; *Gibbons v Associated British Ports* [1985] IRLR 376; *Lee v GEC Plessey Telecommunications* [1993] IRLR 383). The question in each case is what the contract of employment provides, and the termination of a collective agreement is not determinative of that issue any more than its lack of legally binding status.

5.12 A related issue is the continuing effect of collective agreements following the transfer of employees under the *Transfer of Undertakings (Protection of Employment) Regulations 2006 (SI 2006/246) ('TUPE')* (see TRANSFER OF UNDERTAKINGS (50)). In *Whent v T Cartledge Ltd* [1997] IRLR 153, the employees had been employed by a local authority under contracts expressly incorporating collective agreements setting the rates of pay for local authority workers. They had transferred under *TUPE* to the respondent, which withdrew recognition from the trade union and pulled out of the collective agreement. The EAT nonetheless held that individuals retained the right under their individual contracts of employment to the benefits provided for by the collective agreement, including subsequent improvement in pay rates negotiated by the collective parties after the claimants' employment had transferred.

However, the Court of Appeal in *Alemo-Herron v Parkwood Leisure Ltd* [2010] EWCA Civ 24, [2010] IRLR 298 held, overruling *Whent*, that whilst the effect of *TUPE* was to preserve employees' contractual rights to the benefit of both current (at the time of the transfer) and later collective agreements and make them enforceable against the transferee, the judgment of the CJEU in *Werhof v Freeway Traffic Systems GmbH & Co KG*: C-499/04, [2005] ECR I-2397, [2006] IRLR 400 made clear that a static rather than dynamic interpretation of *Directive 2001/23/EC*, the parent Directive of *TUPE*, was required: the *Directive* did not require a transferee to be bound by a collective agreement other than the one in force at the time of the transfer. As *reg 4* of *TUPE* implemented *art 3(1)* of the *Directive*, a contractual term giving employees the right to pay increases negotiated from time to time by collective agreement was not protected on a transfer. The employees were not entitled to pay increases negotiated between the trade unions and local government employers after their transfer to a private sector employer.

Following a further appeal in *Alemo-Herron*, the Supreme Court held that the effect of *Werhof*, and in particular whether it required domestic legislation to go no further than the static approach adopted by the CJEU in *Werhof* itself, was unclear, and referred the case to the Court for clarification of this. The judgment of the ECJ is expected in the course of 2013; until this is given, the correctness of the Court of Appeal's judgment remains to be determined.

In any case, however, the Court of Appeal's decision in *Alemo-Herron* does not mean that the effect of subsequent statutory changes on collective agreements which have transferred under *TUPE* have to be ignored. Thus in *Worrall v Wilmott Dixon Partnerships Ltd* (UKEAT/0521/09/DM), [2010] All ER (D) 107 (Jul), an agreement to confer additional pensionable service on employees taking voluntary redundancy was held no longer to be effective following a change in legislation making it unlawful to confer this category of benefit on employees.

5.13 'NO STRIKE' CLAUSES

There are specific provisions restricting the incorporation into individual contracts of collective agreements which would restrict the right to take part in industrial action. Any provision of a collective agreement which prohibits or restricts the right of workers to engage in a strike or other industrial action, or has the effect of prohibiting or restricting that right, cannot be incorporated into the contract of employment of an individual worker unless the collective agreement:

(a)   is in writing; and

(b)   contains a provision stating that those terms shall or may be incorporated in such a contract; and

(c)   is reasonably accessible at his place of work to the worker to whom it applies and is available for him to consult during working hours; and

(d)   is one where each trade union which is a party to the agreement is an independent trade union (see **48.22** TRADE UNIONS – I); and

(e)   the individual contract with the worker expressly or impliedly incorporates those terms of the collective agreement relating to strikes.

(TULRCA 1992, s 180.)

Despite the fact that a collective agreement and an individual's contract of employment may comply with all the requirements of *s 180*, a court cannot order specific performance of a contract of employment or grant an injunction restraining a breach, or threatened breach, of such a contract which would have the effect of compelling the employee to do any work or attend at any place for the doing of any work (*TULRCA 1992, s 236*).

5.14 Collective Agreements

5.14 WORKFORCE AGREEMENTS

In a number of situations, statutory provisions giving effect in domestic law to EU Directives may be modified in their application by collective agreements. Examples are provisions in the *Working Time Regulations 1998* permitting the modification of some of the substantive rules in the *Regulations*, and the *Maternity and Parental Leave etc Regulations 1999* (allowing for the disapplication of the default rules for the taking of parental leave). Collective agreements may only be made where there is a recognised trade union with which the employer may negotiate. The disadvantages to employers and employees of the absence of any alternative facility for the modification of EU-derived statutory rights are met by provision in these *Regulations* for 'workforce agreements' negotiated between employers and elected representatives of the workforce. For details of the procedural requirements for a workforce agreement under the *Working Time Regulations* (other provisions for workforce agreements are in essentially identical terms) see **55.4 WORKING TIME**. Employee representatives elected to negotiate workforce agreements are afforded similar protection from retaliatory action to that afforded to trade union representatives.

5.15 DISCRIMINATORY AGREEMENTS

Under *section 145* of the *Equality Act 2010* terms in collective agreement, which discriminate against employees because of any protected characteristic are void. A qualifying person may apply to the Employment Tribunal for a declaration that the term is void (see *section 146*). A person qualifies under *section 146* if, but only if, he or she is, or seeks to be, an employee of the employer (or an employer) party to the collective agreement, and either is or may in the future be affected by the disputed term, or (if the term provides for particular treatment of individuals) may be subject in future to the treatment objected to. The remedy for a successful complainant is a declaration that the term is void.

Claims under *section 145* (as under the equivalent provisions in the various Acts and regulations replaced by the *Equality Act 2010*) are rare. An example of the use of the procedure (in an earlier formulation) is *Meade-Hill v British Council* [1995] IRLR 478, CA, where a mobility clause was challenged as indirectly discriminatory against female employees.

6   Continuous Employment

6.1   Many of the statutory employment protection rights such as the right to claim a redundancy payment and compensation for unfair dismissal are conferred only on those employees who have accrued sufficient continuous employment. Further, the calculation of a redundancy payment and of the basic award in unfair dismissal proceedings is based on the employee's length of continuous service. The length of an employee's period of continuous employment is calculated with a few exceptions according to provisions in *ERA 1996, ss 210–219*. The rules relating to continuous employment were previously contained in *EPCA 1978, s 151* and *Sch 13* as amended by *EA 1980, s 20* and *Sch 2*.

The provisions in *EPCA 1978, Sch 13*, as originally drafted, defined continuous employment in such a way as to exclude part-time workers from protection, or to make it more difficult for them to acquire the relevant rights. This result was achieved by incorporating, in the definition of continuous employment, a qualifying threshold of two years' continuous employment for at least 16 hours per week, or five years' continuous employment for between 8 and 16 hours per week. However, in *R v Secretary of State for Employment, ex p Equal Opportunities Commission* [1994] ICR 317, the House of Lords (reversing the Court of Appeal) held that those parts of *EPCA 1978, Sch 13* which differentiated between part-time and full-time workers contravened *art 141* (formerly *art 119*) of the EC Treaty.

As a result of the House of Lords' ruling, the Government introduced the *Employment Protection (Part-time Employees) Regulations 1995 (SI 1995/31)*. With effect from 6 February 1995, these *Regulations, inter alia,* deleted *paras 3* and *5–8* from *EPCA 1978, Sch 13* (together with a reference in *para 4* to the 16 hours' threshold), thereby providing that periods of part-time employment, irrespective of the number of hours worked per week, will count in the computation of continuous employment under *EPCA 1978*. Accordingly, there are no special rules relating to continuity for part-time employees in *ERA 1996*.

The more important provisions relating to continuity of employment are set out in this chapter.

6.2   **COMPUTATION OF PERIODS OF EMPLOYMENT**

Questions arising as to whether an employee's employment is of a kind which counts towards a period of continuous employment, or whether periods are to be treated as forming a single period of continuous employment, are to be determined week by week, but the length of an employee's period of employment is to be computed in *calendar months* and *years of twelve months* (*ERA 1996, s 210(1), (2), (3)*).

6.3   **Beginning and end of a period of continuous employment**

Subject to the provisions of *ERA 1996, s 211(2), (3)* an employee's period of continuous employment for the purpose of calculating his entitlement to any right under *ERA 1996* begins with the day on which he actually starts work and ends with the day by reference to which the length of his period of continuous employment falls to be ascertained for the purposes of the employment right in question (*ERA 1996, s 211(1)*). It is important to note that the day on which an employee actually started work must be included in the reckoning under *ERA 1996, s 211*, so that if, for example, an employee starts work on 2 April, and is dismissed on 1 April the following year, he will have one year's continuous employment (see *Pacitti Jones v O'Brien* [2005] IRLR 888). In *General of the Salvation Army v Dewsbury* [1984] ICR 498, the EAT held that 'starts work' in *EPCA 1978, s 151(3)* (the predecessor to *ERA 1996, s 211(1)*) was not intended to refer to the undertaking of the full-time duties of employment but was intended to refer to the beginning of the employee's employment under her contract of employment, which in that case was earlier than the former date.

6.4 EVENTS AFFECTING A PERIOD OF EMPLOYMENT

The rest of this chapter sets out the events which may affect the period of employment. The following matters are considered:

— weeks which count (see **6.6** below);

— change of employer (see **6.9** below);

— weeks, or part weeks, which do not count but which do not break continuity (see **6.10** below);

— events which break continuity (see **6.12** below).

6.5 PRELIMINARY POINTS

Presumption of continuity. A person's employment (by a particular employer) is presumed to have been continuous unless the contrary is shown (*ERA 1996, s 210(5)*). Except as provided in *ERA 1996, ss 215–217*, any week which does not count in computing a period of employment breaks the continuity of the period of employment (*ERA 1996, s 210(4)*).

Meaning of 'week'. For these purposes, a week runs from Sunday to Saturday (*ERA 1996, s 235*). So long as the employee is employed by the employer in two successive weeks, it does not matter that one job may have ended and another begun, nor how the first job ended (*Tipper v Roofdec Ltd* [1989] IRLR 419).

Statutory concept. The concept of continuity of employment is a statutory concept (see *Secretary of State for Employment v Globe Elastic Thread Co Ltd* [1979] ICR 706). This means that parties cannot destroy it by means of a contractual agreement (see *Collison v BBC* [1998] IRLR 238). (See **6.7** below.)

6.6 WEEKS WHICH COUNT

The following weeks count towards a period of continuous employment.

(a) Any week during the whole or part of which the employee's relations with his employer are governed by a contract of employment (*ERA 1996, s 212(1)*).

In *Roach v CSB (Moulds) Ltd* [1991] ICR 349, the EAT held that continuity had been broken where in two successive weeks the applicant had been employed first by the respondent, then by a third party, then by the respondent again in a different job. However, the EAT in Scotland held in *Sweeney v J & S Henderson (Concessions) Ltd* [1999] IRLR 306 that the long-criticised *Roach* decision was wrongly decided and that, so long as during the relevant weeks there is at least one day governed by a contract of employment with the relevant employer, it does not matter how the gap was created nor what the employee did during its currency (see also *Carrington v Harwich Dock Co Ltd* [1998] IRLR 567).

(b) Periods in which there is no contract of employment may count as periods of employment in certain circumstances. If in any week the employee is, for the whole or part of the week:

(i) incapable of work in consequence of illness or injury; or

(ii) absent from work on account of a temporary cessation of work; or

(iii) absent from work in circumstances such that, by arrangement or custom, he is regarded as continuing in the employment of his employer for all or any purposes, that week will count as a period of employment (*ERA 1996, s 212(3)*).

Not more than 26 weeks count under (b)(i) above between any periods of employment which themselves count for continuity purposes (*ERA 1996, s 212(4)*). The problems arising from these provisions are considered in more detail in **6.7** below.

(c)   An employee's contract of employment is deemed to continue during maternity leave with appropriate amendments so that there is no need for special provisions preserving continuity during the maternity period (*ss 71* and *73, ERA 1996* and *reg 9* of the *Maternity and Parental Leave Regulations 1999*). The same position applies in respect of continuity during any statutory adoption leave period (*ss 75A-B, ERA 1996* and *regs 19* and *21* of the *Paternity and Adoption Leave Regulations 2002 (SI 2002/2788)*); during parental leave (*ss 76* and *77, ERA 1996* and *reg 17* of the *Maternity and Parental Leave Regulations*); and during paternity leave (*s 80C(1), ERA 1996* and *reg 12* of the *Paternity and Adoption Leave Regulations*).

(d)   Intervals in employment where employment is deemed to continue by virtue of the provisions of *ERA 1996, ss 92(7), 97(2), 138(1)* and *145(5)* respectively also count. *Sections 92(7), 97(2)* and *145(5), ERA 1996* operate to treat an employee's employment as continuing until the expiry of the statutory minimum period of notice in circumstances where notice should have been given but was not, and the employee was thereby deprived of the minimum qualifying period of employment for claims for a written statement of reasons for dismissal, unfair dismissal and redundancy payments respectively. *Section 138(1), ERA 1996* operates to preserve continuity where an employee dismissed for redundancy has his contract renewed or is re-engaged after an interval of not more than four weeks. If a dismissed employee is reinstated or re-engaged in consequence of the presentation of a complaint of unfair dismissal, or as a result of action taken by a conciliation officer under the *Employment Tribunals Act 1996, s 18*, or as a result of a relevant compromise contract (see **18.29** EMPLOYMENT TRIBUNALS – II), the employee's continuity of employment is preserved and the weeks in any intervening period count. Further, if the employee has been paid a redundancy payment and it is a term of his reinstatement or re-engagement that he repay that sum, the continuity of his employment for redundancy payments purposes is not broken (*Employment Protection (Continuity of Employment) Regulations 1996 (SI 1996/3147); ERA 1996, s 219*).

6.7   Periods of 'no employment'

The true meaning of *ERA 1996, s 212(3)*, formerly *EPCA 1978, Sch 13 para 9* (see **6.6**(b) above) has given rise to various difficulties of interpretation.

Generally. Section 212(3) applies only where there is no contract of employment in existence and not where there is a contract of employment in existence, but the employee is not required to perform any work under that contract (*Ford v Warwickshire County Council* [1983] ICR 273; *Pearson v Kent County Council* [1993] IRLR 165). In *Pearson*, the Court of Appeal held that the critical question is why there is no contract during the week in question, and not why the previous contract of employment came to an end.

Illness and injury (s 212(3)(a)). This provision can apply so long as the employee is unfit for the work for which he was previously employed. Thus, continuity may be preserved even where the employee takes a temporary job with another employer until he is capable of returning to his former work (*Donnelly v Kelvin International Services* [1992] IRLR 496; see also *Pearson*, above).

Temporary cessation of work (s 212(3)(b)). In *Ford* the House of Lords held that the continuity of employment of a teacher whose contract came to an end at the end of every summer term but who was re-engaged in the autumn term was preserved during the

6.7   Continuous Employment

summer vacation by *EPCA 1978, Sch 13 para 9(1)(b)*, now *s 212(3)(b), ERA 1996*. Lord Diplock at 285 said that 'temporary' meant lasting only for a relatively short time, and that it was necessary to ask whether the interval between the two contracts was short in relation to their combined duration. This has become known as the 'mathematical' approach.

The test for "temporary cessation of work" under *s 212(3)(b)* does not require an examination of the expectation of parties of further work. What is required is to find the reason for the termination of the first contract of employment. If it has ended because of a temporary cessation of work, and the claimant is employed again, the case falls within *s 212(3)(b)*: *Hussain v Acorn Independent College* [2011] IRLR 463. So, in *Hussain*, a teacher who was employed as temporary cover in the summer term, and who was then employed permanently in the next college year when the teacher he was covering unexpectedly decided not to return to work, could aggregate both his temporary cover contract and his permanent contract for continuity purposes. It did not matter that he had no expectation of further work when his temporary cover contract expired.

In *Flack v Kodak Ltd* [1986] ICR 775 the Court of Appeal had to consider whether six workers in the photo finishing department of Kodak Ltd had sufficient continuous employment to pursue their employment protection rights. They had been employed intermittently over a number of years. Their period of employment depended on the extent of the department's work. The court decided that the correct approach in deciding whether a gap in an employee's employment, during which he is absent from work on account of a cessation of work, is a temporary cessation for the purposes of *EPCA 1978, Sch 13 para 9(1)(b)*, now *s 212(3)(b), ERA 1996*, is to take into account all the relevant circumstances and in particular to consider the length of the period of absence in the context of the period of employment as a whole. Thus, the court did not apply a strictly 'mathematical' approach and held that the periods of absence did not break the continuity of employment (see also *Berwick Salmon Fisheries Co Ltd v Rutherford* [1991] IRLR 203).

However, in *Sillars v Charringtons Fuels Ltd* [1989] ICR 475 the Court of Appeal held that it was still open to an employment tribunal, after considering the matter in the round, to conclude that the 'mathematical' approach should be applied in an appropriate case (for example, where there was a systematic pattern of events). That there was an intention to re-employ the applicant later did not necessarily mean that the cessation of work was temporary in the sense of being for a relatively short time.

The 'cessation of work' must involve a reduction in the employer's overall quantum of work, and not merely a decision to allocate work to some other employee (*Byrne v Birmingham City District Council* [1987] ICR 519). *Byrne* was followed in *Letheby & Christopher Ltd v Bond* [1988] ICR 480.

Regarded as continuing in employment (s 212(3)(c)). This provision might apply to, for example, a period of unpaid leave. However, it was held in *Letheby* (see above) that an employee employed under single separate contracts, who went on holiday at a time convenient to her employers, was not absent from work in circumstances such that by arrangement or custom she was regarded as continuing in employment, where there was no prior agreement between the parties that after each holiday period there was to be some continuation of her employment.

The Court of Appeal in *Curr v Marks & Spencer plc* [2002] EWCA Civ 1852, [2003] IRLR 74 stressed that *s 212(3)(c)* requires a mutual arrangement between employer and employee, and a 'meeting of minds' by the arrangement that both parties regard the ex-employee as continuing in employment for some purpose. The Court did not regard it as helpful to refer to the test of *s 212(3)(c)* as involving consideration of whether an employment relationship continues (regarded as the 'key question' by the EAT in *Letheby* and *Booth v United States of America* [1999] IRLR 16): this was not the statutory test. In *Curr*, an employee absent on a four-year maternity break scheme did not fall within *s 212(3)(c)*, although she was required to work for at least two weeks in each year of the break; was prohibited from accepting other paid employment without consulting her manager; and was in regular contact with the employer. This was because the other terms on which she took her maternity break clearly showed that employment was not regarded as continuing. On commencement of her break, she was required to resign, and was given her P45. At the end of the break, she had an option to be re-employed by the employer, but the scheme's emphasis on 're-employment' in fact showed that she was not regarded as continuing in employment during the break.

The EAT has reached conflicting decisions on whether an "arrangement" under *s 212(3)(c)* can be made retrospectively. In *Murphy v A Birrell & Sons* [1978] IRLR 458 and *Morris v Walsh Western UK Ltd* [1997] IRLR 562, it held that a retrospective agreement to treat the period of an employee's absence as continuous was insufficient to preserve continuity of employment under *s 212(3)(c)* (because continuity of employment is a statutory concept – see *Secretary of State for Employment v Globe Elastic Thread Co Ltd* [1979] ICR 706). On the other hand, in *Ingram v Foxon* [1984] ICR 685 and *London Probation Board v Kirkpatrick* [2005] IRLR 443, the EAT held that there is no temporal qualification to the term "arrangement" in *s 212(3)(c)*, and that arrangements can be made retrospectively. The conflict in the authorities has been resolved by the EAT's latest decision in *Welton v Deluxe Retail Ltd* [2013] IRLR 166. Langstaff P stated that an "arrangement" within *s 212(3)(c)* was not able to bridge a gap in continuity of employment unless it was in existence before, or arose contemporaneously with, the relevant weeks of absence from work during which there was no contract. He reviewed the authorities in detail, and stated that *Kirkpatrick* should no longer be followed.

6.8   Part-timers

As mentioned in **6.1** above, there is no difference in the provisions for calculating periods of continuous employment, in relation to their application to part-time employees as against full-time employees.

6.9   CHANGE OF EMPLOYER

Normally, to be continuous, employment must be with one employer. Separate companies must normally be treated as quite distinct entities. The 'corporate veil' may only be pierced if it is a mere facade concealing the true facts (*National Dock Labour Board v Pinn & Wheeler Ltd* [1989] BCLC 647). However, note the following points.

(a)   *Associated employers.* If an employee of an employer is taken into the employment of another employer who, at the time when the employee enters his employment is an 'associated' employer of the former employer, that change will not break the continuity of the employee's employment (*ERA 1996, s 218(6)*).

For the purposes of *ERA 1996*, any two employers are to be treated as associated if one is a company of which the other (directly or indirectly) has control, or if both are companies of which a third person (directly or indirectly) has control (*ERA 1996, s 231*). The definition of 'control' in *s 231* has been problematic over the years. The EAT held in *Hair Colour Consultants Ltd v Mena* [1984] ICR 671 that 'control' means voting control by a majority of shares (see also *South West Launderettes Ltd v Laidler* [1986] ICR 455). However, the Court of Appeal in *Payne v Secretary of State for Employment* [1989] IRLR 352 and in *Secretary of State for Employment v Chapman* [1989] ICR 771 held that whilst voting control is the usual and normal test for determining whether two employers are associated, that test is not conclusive. Further, the EAT held in *Tice v Cartwright* [1999] ICR 769 that the word 'control' in *s 231* dealt with practical rather than theoretical control so that two brothers in partnership controlled the company in which they each had a 50%

shareholding. (*Tice v Cartwright* has been applied by the EAT in *Da Silva Junior v Composite Mouldings & Design Ltd* [2009] ICR 416. See also, *Hartford v Swiftrim Ltd* [1987] ICR 439; and *Zarb v British Brazilian Produce Co (Sales) Ltd* [1978] IRLR 78 cf *Strudick v IBL* [1988] ICR 796; and *Russell v Elmdon Freight Terminal Ltd* [1989] ICR 629.)

The EAT has been willing to treat the term 'company' as including both a partnership of companies (*Pinkney v Sandpiper Drilling Ltd* [1989] IRLR 425) and a foreign entity equivalent to an English company (*Hancill v Marcon Engineering Ltd* [1990] ICR 103). However, not all bodies corporate (such as local authorities) are 'companies' within *ERA 1996, s 231* (*Gardiner v London Borough of Merton* [1980] IRLR 472). In *Hasley v Fair Employment Agency* [1989] IRLR 106, the Northern Ireland Court of Appeal pointed out that the section only requires the employer which is *controlled* to be a company; the *controlling* employer may be some other type of legal person.

(b)   *Transfers of a business.* If a trade or business or an undertaking is transferred from one person to another, the period of employment of an employee in the trade or business or undertaking at the time of the transfer counts as a period of employment with the transferee and is regarded as unbroken (*ERA 1996, s 218(2)*).

ERA 1996, s 218(2) will generally apply in cases where there has been a transfer of an undertaking for the purposes of the *Transfer of Undertakings (Protection of Employment) Regulations 2006* ("*TUPE*"), in which case continuity of employment is in any event preserved under *TUPE* (see *TUPE, reg 4(1)*). However, the operation of *ERA 1996, s 218(2)* is not restricted to cases in which there has been a transfer under *TUPE*, and if for one reason or another *TUPE* does not apply, continuity of employment may nevertheless be preserved under the statute. See for example *Oakland v Wellswood (Yorkshire) Ltd* [2010] ICR 902. In *Oakland*, the tribunal and EAT held that there had been no *TUPE* transfer, because the transferor was the subject of bankruptcy proceedings for the purposes of *reg 8(7)* of *TUPE*. Notwithstanding that, the Court of Appeal found that the employee's continuity of employment had been preserved by virtue of *ERA 1996, s 218(2)* (without needing to decide whether the tribunal's and EAT's conclusions on *reg 8(7)* of *TUPE* were correct). See further TRANSFER OF UNDERTAKINGS (50).

Case law on *ERA 1996, s 218(2)* has warned against artificial attempts to break continuity. In *Macer v Abafast Ltd* [1990] ICR 234 and *Gibson v Motortune Ltd* [1990] ICR 740, the EAT stated that the machinery of *EPCA, Sch 13 para 17(2)*, the predecessor to *ERA 1996, s 218(2)*, could operate even where the machinery of transfer led to a gap of more than one week between periods of employment. This approach was adopted by the Court of Appeal in *Clark & Tokeley Ltd v Oakes* [1998] IRLR 577, on the basis that there will often not be a precise time of transfer, which can take place over an extended period; and that what had to be examined when considering whether an employee was employed "at the time of transfer" was not the point when the legal formalities of transfer were completed, but the actual state of affairs as a matter of fact, which could cover a period of days or even weeks.

A similar result which preserves continuity may be obtained under *TUPE, reg 4(1)*, but on a different conceptual basis. Under *TUPE*, contrary to the position under *ERA 1996, s 218(2)*, a transfer does take place at a particular moment in time: see *Celtec Ltd v Astley* [2006] ICR 993, HL. However, *TUPE* operates so as to preserve the continuity of employment of employees automatically unfairly dismissed prior to the transfer for reasons related to the transfer: see *TUPE, reg 4(3)* and *reg 7(1)* and *Litster v Forth Dry Dock and Engineering Co Ltd* [1990] 1 AC 546; and see further TRANSFER OF UNDERTAKINGS (50).

(c) *Substitution of employer by statute.* If by or under an Act of Parliament, whether public or local, a contract of employment between any body corporate and an employee is modified and some other body corporate is substituted as the employer, the period of employment of the employee at the time when the modification takes effect counts as a period of employment with the second body corporate and is regarded as unbroken (*ERA 1996, s 218(3)*). For a case where, on the facts, the predecessor provision to *s 218(3)* was held not to apply, see *Gale v Northern General Hospital NHS Trust* [1994] IRLR 292.

(d) *Employment in schools/the National Health Service.* If an employee of the governing body of a maintained school is taken into the employment of the local authority responsible for the school, or vice versa, continuity of employment is preserved (*ERA 1996, s 218(7)*). Similarly, in certain circumstances, continuity of employment is preserved when an employee's employment switches from one health service employer to another, if he is undergoing professional training which involves successive employment by a number of different health service employers (*ERA 1996, ss 218(8)–218(10)* and *Employment Protection (National Health Service) Order 1996 (SI 1996/638)*).

(e) *Death of employer, partnerships, etc.* If, on the death of the employer, the employee passes into the employment of the personal representatives or trustees of the deceased, continuity is not broken. A change in partners, personal representatives or trustees does not break the continuity of an employee's employment (*ERA 1996, s 218(4), (5)*). The provision in *ERA 1996, s 218(5)* for preservation of continuity on a change in partners covers the situation where, after the change, there are no partners, but only a sole proprietor: see *Bower v Stevens* [2004] ICR 1582 and *Jeetle v Elster* [1985] ICR 389.

6.10 WEEKS WHICH DO NOT BREAK CONTINUITY

The following weeks do not count in the computation but do not break continuity. (This applies also where the events occur in only part of the week.)

(a) Any week during which the employee takes part in a strike (*ERA 1996, s 216(1), (2)*).

(b) Any week during which the employee is absent from work because of a lock-out (*ERA 1996, s 216(3)*).

(c) For the purpose of calculating the qualifying period for pursuing a claim to a redundancy payment and for the purpose of calculating the amount of the payment, any week during which the employee (i) was employed outside Great Britain (*ERA 1996, s 215(2)(a)*), and (ii) was not an employed earner for the purposes of the *Social Security Contributions and Benefits Act 1992* in respect of whom a secondary Class 1 contribution was payable under that Act (whether or not the contribution was in fact paid) (*ERA 1996, s 215(2)(b)*). For all other purposes, continuity continues during periods in which the employee is engaged in work wholly or mainly outside Great Britain (*ERA 1996, s 215(1)(a)*).

6.11 'Postponement' of start of employment

If an employee's period of continuous employment includes one or more periods which do not count in computing the length of the period but do not break continuity, the beginning of the period is treated as *postponed* by the number of days falling within that intervening period, or, as the case may be, by the aggregate number of days falling within those periods (*ERA 1996, s 211(3)*).

6.12   EVENTS WHICH BREAK CONTINUITY

Except as is otherwise specifically provided in *ERA 1996, ss 215–217*, any week which does not count in the computation breaks the continuity of a period of employment (*ERA 1996, s 210(4)*).

The receipt of a redundancy payment breaks continuity for redundancy qualification and payment purposes (*ERA 1996, s 214*). However, *s 214* does not apply where an employee, having received a redundancy payment (or equivalent payment), is reinstated or re-engaged by his employer on terms which include a requirement to repay the amount of that payment, and that requirement is complied with (*Employment Protection (Continuity of Employment) Regulations 1996 (SI 1996/3147)* – see also **6.6**(d) above). *Section 214* also does not apply where a 'redundancy payment' paid by the employer is not a payment which he is statutorily obliged to make (*Rowan v Machinery Installations (South Wales) Ltd* [1981] ICR 386; *Ross v Delrosa Caterers Ltd* [1981] ICR 393). Further, given that a 'redundancy payment' in this context means a statutory redundancy payment, and a right to such a payment depends on there having been a dismissal, it follows that where an employee's employment is transferred pursuant to *TUPE 1981*, there is no dismissal and therefore any payment received by the employee is not a statutory redundancy payment and will not break continuity under *s 214* (*Senior Heat Treatment v Bell* [1997] IRLR 614). However, this will not be the case where the Secretary of State has paid the equivalent of a statutory redundancy payment to an employee of an insolvent employer under *ERA 1996, s 167* (*Secretary of State for Trade and Industry v Lassman* [2000] IRLR 411).

6.13   TABLE OF QUALIFYING PERIODS FOR STATUTORY EMPLOYMENT PROTECTION RIGHTS

Employment right	Qualifying period
	NB Not all statutory employment protection rights require a qualifying period of continuous employment. For example, the general right to maternity leave does not depend upon 'continuous' employment as defined by *ERA 1996*.
Written statement of employment particulars	One month (see *ERA 1996, s 198*).
Guarantee payments/Payments during medical suspension	One month ending with the day before the period for which guarantee payment, etc is claimed (*ERA 1996, s 29(1)* and *s 65(1)*).
Minimum period of notice	One month (*ERA 1996, ss 86(1), 87(1)*).
	Any contract of a person who has been employed for three months which is a contract for a fixed term of one month or less is deemed for the purposes of *s 86* to have effect as if it were for an indefinite period and thus subject to the notice provisions (*ERA 1996, s 86(4)*).
Unfair dismissal Written reasons for dismissal	Two years (one year for employees whose continuous employment commenced before 6 April 2012). (*ERA 1996, s 108(1)* and *92(3)*).
	If an employee is dismissed by reason of a medical suspension requirement or recommendation under an enactment or a Code of Practice providing for health and safety at work, the qualifying period is one month (*ERA 1996, s 108(2)*).

		In certain other cases of unfair dismissal, no qualifying period is necessary. These are where the reason or principal reason for the dismissal:
	(*a*)	was a union-related reason (*TULRCA 1992, s 154*; and see **52.3**(a) U<small>NFAIR</small> D<small>ISMISSAL</small> – **II**);
	(*b*)	was the assertion of a statutory right (*ERA 1996, s 108(3)(g)*; and see **52.3**(c) U<small>NFAIR</small> D<small>ISMISSAL</small> – **II**);
	(*c*)	was a health and safety-related reason (*ERA 1996, s 108(3)(c)*; and see **52.3**(b) U<small>NFAIR</small> D<small>ISMISSAL</small> **II**);
	(*d*)	was a reason related to pregnancy, childbirth or maternity; maternity leave; adoption leave; parental leave; paternity leave; or time off for dependants under *ERA 1996, s 57* (*ERA 1996, s 108(3)(b)*; and see **31.6** M<small>ATERNITY AND</small> P<small>ARENTAL</small> R<small>IGHTS</small>);
	(*e*)	was a reason connected with the performance by an employee who is a pension scheme trustee of his functions as such a trustee (*ERA 1996, s 108(3)(e)*; see **52.3**(e) U<small>NFAIR</small> D<small>ISMISSAL</small> – **II**);
	(*f*)	was a reason connected with the performance by an employee representative (see **37.4** R<small>EDUNDANCY</small> – **II** and **50.18** T<small>RANSFER OF</small> U<small>NDERTAKINGS</small>), or a candidate in an election for such an employee representative, of his functions as such an employee representative or candidate (*ERA 1996, s 108(3)(f)*; see **52.3**(f) U<small>NFAIR</small> D<small>ISMISSAL</small> – **II**);
	(*g*)	was a reason connected with the refusal of Sunday work by a shop worker or betting worker (*ERA 1996, s 108(3)(d)*; see **52.3**(g) U<small>NFAIR</small> D<small>ISMISSAL</small> – **II**);
	(*h*)	was a reason related to working time (*ERA 1996, s 108(3)(dd)*; and see **52.3**(h) U<small>NFAIR</small> D<small>ISMISSAL</small> – **II**);
	(*I*)	was a reason connected with the assertion of rights under the *National Minimum Wage Act 1998* (*ERA 1996, s 108(3)(gg)*; see **52.3**(m) U<small>NFAIR</small> D<small>ISMISSAL</small> – **II**);
	(*j*)	was a reason connected with the making of a protected disclosure under *ERA 1996, ss 43A–43L* (*ERA 1996, s 108(3)(ff)* and *s 103A*; see **52.3**(n) U<small>NFAIR</small> D<small>ISMISSAL</small> – **II**);
	(*k*)	was a reason connected with the assertion of rights under the *Tax Credits Act 1999* (*ERA 1996, s 108(3)(gh)*; see **52.3**(t) U<small>NFAIR</small> D<small>ISMISSAL</small> – **II**);
	(*l*)	was a reason connected with the assertion of rights under the *Transnational Information and Consultation of Employees Regulations 1999* (*ERA 1996, s 108(3)(hh)*; see **52.3**(u) U<small>NFAIR</small> D<small>ISMISSAL</small> – **II**);

	(m)	was a reason connected with the assertion of rights under the *Part-time Workers (Prevention of Less Favourable Treatment) Regulations 2000 (SI 2000/1551) (ERA 1996, s 108(3)(i)*; see **52.3**(s) Unfair Dismissal – II);
	(n)	was a reason connected with the assertion of rights under the *Fixed-term Employees (Prevention of Less Favourable Treatment) Regulations 2002 (SI 2002/2034) (ERA 1996, s 108(3)(j)*; see **52.3**(v) Unfair Dismissal – II);
	(o)	was a reason connected with the assertion of flexible working rights under *ERA 1996, ss 80F–80G (ERA 1996, s 108(3)(gi)*; see **52.3** Unfair Dismissal – II);
	(p)	was a reason connected with trade union recognition or bargaining arrangements (*TULRCA 1992, Sch A1, paras 161–162* (see **52.3**(o) Unfair Dismissal – II);
	(q)	was that the employee exercised or sought to exercise the right, pursuant to *Employment Relations Act 1999, s 10*, to be accompanied to a disciplinary or grievance hearing or that the employee accompanied or sought to accompany another worker to such a hearing (*Employment Relations Act 1999, s 12(4)*. See **52.3**(p) Unfair Dismissal – II);
	(r)	was that the employee was dismissed for taking part in protected industrial action in the circumstances set out in *TULRCA 1992, s 238A*, introduced by the *Employment Relations Act 1999, s 16 and Sch 5*. (See **52.3**(q) Unfair Dismissal – II; or
	(s)	was a reason connected with the exercise of various negotiation or consultation rights within a "European Company" as defined in the *European Public Limited-Liability Company Regulations 2004 (SI 2004/2326)*. (See **52.3** Unfair Dismissal – II);
	(t)	was a reason connected with the exercise of various negotiation or consultation rights under the *Information and Consultation of Employees Regulations 2004 (SI 2004/3426)*. (See **52.3** Unfair Dismissal – II);
	(u)	was the fact that the employee has been summoned for jury service, or has been absent on jury service in the circumstances set out in *ERA 1996, s 98B*. (See **52.3** Unfair Dismissal – II (applying to dismissals from 6 April 2005));
	(v)	was a selection for redundancy for a reason which would have been automatically unfair if it had been the reason for dismissal (*ERA 1996, s 108(3)(h), s 105*);

	(w)	was the fact that the employee exercised or sought to exercise his right to be accompanied, or accompanied or sought to accompany another employee, at a meeting to discuss a statutory right to request not to retire: see the *Employment Equality (Age) Regulations 2006 (SI 2006/1031), Sch 6* and *ERA 1996, s 108(3)(n)*;
	(x)	was a reason connected with an employee's performance of various functions or exercise of various entitlements under the *European Cooperative Society (Involvement of Employees) Regulations 2006 (SI 2006/2059)*: see *reg 31* of *SI 2006/2059* and *ERA 1996, s 108(3)(o)*. The *2006 Regulations* relate to the formation of, and employees' participation in, European Cooperative Societies;
	(y)	was a reason connected with an employee's performance of various functions or exercise of various entitlements in respect of participation in a cross-border merger: see the *Companies (Cross-Border Mergers) Regulations 2007, regs 46–47* and *ERA 1996, s 108(3)(p)*;
	(z)	was for a reason relating to a "prohibited list" within *reg 3* of the *Employment Relations Act 1999 (Blacklists) Regulations 2010*. This applies essentially when an employee has been dismissed because his name has been included on a "blacklist" made or obtained by the employer, containing details of trade union membership or activities. See *ERA s 104F* and *s 108(gl)*;
	(za)	was that the employee made or proposed to make an application falling with *ERA 1996 s 63D* (statutory right to make request in relation to study or training); or exercised or proposed to exercise a right conferred on the employee under *ERA 1996 s 63F* (setting out the employer's duties in relation to an application under *ERA 1996 s 63D*); or brought proceedings against the employer under *ERA 1996 s 63I* (complaints to employment tribunals related to applications under *ERA 1996 s 63D*); or alleged the existence of any circumstance which would constitute a ground for bringing such proceedings. See *ERA s 104E* and *s 108(gk)*;
	(zb)	was a reason connected with an employee's performance or proposed performance of various functions or entitlements connected with negotiating rights in a European Public Limited-Liability Company. See *ERA, s 108(q)* and *reg 29(1)* of the *European Public Limited-Liability Company (Employee Involvement)(Great Britain) Regulations 2009 (SI 2009/2401)*;

55

	(zc)	was a reason specified in *reg 17(3)* of the *Agency Workers Regulations 2010 (SI 2010/93)*, where the employee is an agency worker. See *ERA s 108(r)* and *reg 17(1)* of the *Agency Workers Regulations 2010* (applying to dismissals from 1 October 2011).
		If the reason or principal reason for dismissal is the transfer of an undertaking or a reason connected with it, so that dismissal is automatically unfair by operation of *reg 8(1)* of the *Transfer of Undertakings (Protection of Employment) Regulations 1981*, the normal qualifying period applies (*Collective Redundancies and Transfer of Undertakings (Protection of Employment) (Amendment) Regulations 1995 (SI 1995/2587)*, effectively overruling *Milligan v Securicor Cleaning Ltd* [1995] IRLR 288 – see **6.1** above).
Redundancy payment		Two years (*ERA 1996, s 155*).
Consultation of appropriate representatives and notification of Secretary of State on redundancy		Three months, but only where the employment is under a fixed-term contract of three months or less or one made in contemplation of a specific task not expected to last for more than three months (*TULRCA 1992, s 282*).

7 Contract of Employment

(See also DTI booklet No 1 'Written statement of employment particulars' (PL 700).)

Cross-references. See CHILDREN AND YOUNG PERSONS (3) for statutory restrictions on their employment; RESTRAINT OF TRADE, CONFIDENTIALITY AND EMPLOYEE INTERVENTIONS (39); and COLLECTIVE AGREEMENTS (5) for their respective effects on individual contracts; 21.5 EQUAL PAY for the statutory equality clause; 32.6 PAY – I for illegal deductions from wages; 43.16 STRIKES AND INDUSTRIAL ACTION for the effect of industrial action on contracts; and 53.2–53.5 UNFAIR DISMISSAL – III for reinstatement and re-engagement orders. See TERMINATION OF EMPLOYMENT (46) and WRONGFUL DISMISSAL (56) for termination of contract rules. For restrictions on contracting out of statutory provisions, see 21.15 EQUAL PAY, 36.14 REDUNDANCY – I and 51.19 UNFAIR DISMISSAL – I.

7.1 The contract of employment is dealt with in this chapter under the following heads:

(a) Formation of the contract;

(b) The statutory requirement for written particulars of contract;

(c) Terms of the contract, including implied terms and unenforceable terms;

(d) Changes to contractual terms;

(e) Remedies for breach of the employment contract, and

(f) Contracts of employment and Sunday trading.

This chapter does not deal with the question of whether a particular agreement under which a person works is a 'contract of *employment*' for the purposes of *ERA 1996 s 230(1)*. That question is considered in EMPLOYEE, SELF-EMPLOYED OR WORKER? (14).

7.2 FORMATION

Requirements

The usual requirements of contract law apply: offer, acceptance, consideration, intention to create legal relations and certainty. For examples of the application of these principles, see: *Moore v President of the Methodist Conference* [2011] EWCA Civ 1581, [2012] ICR 432, [2012] IRLR 229 and *Anar v Dresdner Kleinwort Ltd* [2011] EWCA Civ 229, [2011] All ER (D) 88 (Mar). The parties' agreement is to be construed objectively in the factual context prevailing at the time of the agreement. On the importance of certainty, see *Judge v Crown Leisure Ltd* [2005] EWCA Civ 571, [2005] IRLR 823, where it was held that statements made at a Christmas party and in vague terms (such as "in due course" and "eventually") did not amount to a contractually binding agreement to increase the employee's pay. Contrast this with *Anar*, where neither the informal nature of the employer's assurances nor the imprecise scope of those assurances automatically precluded their enforceability.

A contract of employment may also be implied from the parties' conduct: *Franks v Reuters Ltd* [2003] EWCA Civ 417, [2003] IRLR 423, *Dacas v Brook Street Bureau (UK) Ltd* [2004] EWCA Civ 217, [2004] ICR 1437, [2004] IRLR 358 and *Cable & Wireless plc v Muscat* [2006] EWCA Civ 220, [2006] ICR 975, [2006] IRLR 354. The existence of a "factual substratum" suggestive of a contract of employment will not suffice to establish an implied contract (*Beattie v Leicester City Council* (UKEAT0386/09/SM) (20 January 2010, unreported)). Questions as to implied contracts of employment frequently arise in connection 'tripartite' relationships involving agency workers (see EMPLOYEE, SELF-EMPLOYED OR WORKER? (14)).

57

7.2 Contract of Employment

The fact that a contract of employment is void does not automatically mean that no "employment relationship" exists. For example, where a public authority's employment of an individual was *ultra vires*, there may nonetheless be a *de facto* employment relationship on the basis of which the individual may be treated as an employee for the purposes of *ERA* s. *230(1)* (*Eastbourne Borough Council v Foster* [2001] EWCA Civ 1091, [2001] LGR 529, [2002] ICR 234; *Lairikyengbam v Shrewsbury and Telford Hospital NHS Trust* [2010] ICR 66, [2009] All ER (D) 271 (Oct), EAT).

7.3 Form of the contract

A contract of employment may be either written or oral, or a mixture of the two. This means that – subject to the contractual principles summarised above – its form may range from a document drawn up by solicitors and signed by both parties, to a chat over a cup of tea in the canteen. One of the issues in *Cheltenham Borough Council v Laird* [2009] EWHC 1253 (QB), [2009] IRLR 621 (upheld on appeal: [2010] EWCA Civ 847) was whether the employment contract had been concluded by an oral agreement which predated the employee's completion of a medical questionnaire or by the consequent letter of appointment which postdated that questionnaire. The court found the latter to be the case, observing that it would be reasonably expected practice for appointments at this senior managerial level to be concluded in writing.

As the court in *Laird* suggested, senior executives will usually be employed pursuant to written agreements drafted by solicitors. These agreements are often for a fixed term. A director's contract of employment whose guaranteed term is longer than two years must be approved by a resolution of the members of the company. A guaranteed period is the period for which the director's employment may continue other than at the instance of the company and within which the company may not terminate the employment (see **8.3 DIRECTORS** and *Companies Act 2006, s 188*). In the event that the contract is not approved by the members, its provisions as to duration are void and there is instead substituted a term that the employment is terminable on reasonable notice (*s 189*). Such agreements frequently contain provisions dealing with the tenure by the employee of a directorship of the employing company. They may also contain restrictive covenants (see **RESTRAINT OF TRADE, CONFIDENTIALITY AND EMPLOYEE INTERVENTIONS (39)**).

Less senior employees may be asked to sign a standard form contract of employment. Alternatively, the contract may be contained in an exchange of letters, or terms may be agreed orally at an interview. Provided that the parties are in agreement over the essential terms of the contract, such as hours and wages, there will be a valid contract of employment enforceable by either party. However, an employer is under a duty to give his employees particulars in writing of certain important terms of their contracts (see **7.6** below).

7.4 Parties to the contract

Despite the rule that unincorporated associations can neither sue nor be sued in their own name, an employee can bring employment tribunal proceedings against the management committee of an unincorporated association: *Asim v Nazir* [2010] ICR 1225.

Occasionally, a question arises as to the identity of the employer where it is unclear which of a number of companies or other legal persons is the employer under the contract. In such cases, the employer is likely to be the person who has power to control the employee's activities (see *Clifford v Union of Democratic Mineworkers* [1991] IRLR 518; *Andrews v King (Inspector of Taxes)* [1991] STC 481, [1991] ICR 846). The question is resolved by considering all the circumstances (and documents) of the case (see for example the unreported Scottish case of *McVeigh v Livingstone* (UKEATS/0027/08/BI) (16 June 2009, unreported), where the tribunal scrutinised the claimant's wage slips, P60s and written particulars in resolving the question of whether the employer was the company or the individuals in control of that company).

See 23.8 FOREIGN EMPLOYEES for the rules as to which country's system of law governs the contract of employment.

7.5   An employer may engage or refuse to engage any person who has legal capacity, subject only to the statutory provisions relating to CHILDREN AND YOUNG PERSONS (3), discrimination on grounds of race or sex or disability or age or religion or belief or sexual orientation or trade union membership or non-membership (see DISCRIMINATION AND EQUAL OPPORTUNITIES – I (10), II (11), and III (12), 48.2 TRADE UNIONS – I) and the provisions relating to the employment of foreign nationals (see FOREIGN EMPLOYEES (23)).

7.6   WRITTEN PARTICULARS OF CONTRACT

Although the law does not require the contract itself to be in writing, employers are required to give each employee a written statement of particulars of certain important terms of the contract (see *ERA 1996, s 1* and CONTINUOUS EMPLOYMENT (6)). This statement is not itself the contract of employment, but it offers persuasive (though not conclusive) evidence of the terms of the contract (*Robertson v British Gas Corpn* [1983] ICR 351, [1983] IRLR 302, CA; *System Floors (UK) Ltd v Daniel* [1982] ICR 54, [1981] IRLR 475).

This written statement of particulars must be given to the employee not later than two months after the beginning of the employment. If, during that period, the employee is to begin work outside the UK for more than a month, the statement must be given to him not later than the time he leaves the UK to begin work (*ERA 1996, s 2(5)*).

The statement may be given in instalments during the two-month period (*ERA 1996, s 1(1)*). However, certain of the particulars must be included in a single document. These are the names of the parties, the dates when employment and continuous employment began, the particulars of remuneration, hours and holidays, the job title or description, and the place of work (*ERA 1996, s 2(4)*).

If employment ends within the two-month period, a statement must still be given (*ERA 1996, s 2(6)*), unless the employment continued for less than one month (*ERA 1996, s 198*).

Amendments to the *ERA 1996* introduced by the *Employment Act 2002* permit the use of documents as an alternative to a statement of particulars. If the employer gives the employee a contract of employment or an engagement letter which contains the information required by *ERA 1996, s 1* at the time when employment commences (*ERA 1996, s 7B*) or afterwards (*ERA 1996, s 7A(1)(c)*) that is sufficient to meet the obligations under *s 1*. If the document contains the material required by *s 3* (disciplinary procedure, etc) that is sufficient to comply with that section.

7.7   Particulars which must be given

The written statement must:

(a)   name the employer and the employee;

(b)   specify the date when the employment began; and

(c)   specify the date on which the employee's period of *continuous* employment began (taking into account any employment with a previous employer which counts towards that period).

(*ERA 1996, s 1(3)*.)

(For the day on which employment 'begins', see 6.3 CONTINUOUS EMPLOYMENT.)

It must also give the following particulars of terms of employment which are applicable as at a specified date not more than seven days before the date on which the statement is given:

(d)   the scale or rate of remuneration, or the method of calculating remuneration;

(e)   the intervals at which remuneration is paid (that is whether weekly, or monthly or at other specified intervals);

(f)   any terms and conditions relating to hours of work (including any terms and conditions relating to normal working hours);

(g)   any terms and conditions relating to:

   (i)   entitlement to holidays, including public holidays and holiday pay (the particulars being sufficient to enable the employee's entitlement, including any entitlement to accrued holiday pay on the termination of employment, to be precisely calculated);

   (ii)   incapacity for work due to sickness or injury, including any provisions for sick pay; and

   (iii)   pensions and pension schemes (unless the employee's pension rights depend on the terms of a pension scheme established under statute, and he is employed by a body or authority required under statute to give information concerning pension rights to new employees);

(h)   the length of notice which the employee is obliged to give and entitled to receive to terminate his contract of employment;

(i)   the title of the job which the employee is employed to do or a brief description of the work for which the employee is employed;

(j)   where the employment is not intended to be permanent, the period for which it is expected to continue or, if it is for a fixed term, the date when it is to end;

(k)   either the place of work or, where the employee is required or permitted to work at various places, an indication of that and of the employer's address;

(l)   any collective agreements which directly affect the terms and conditions of the employment, including the persons by whom they were made where the employer is not a party; and

(m)   where the employee is required to work outside the UK for more than a month, certain further particulars concerning that period, the currency of remuneration, any additional remuneration and benefits, and any terms and conditions relating to return.

(ERA 1996, s 1(4), (5).)

The Secretary of State may add to the list of particulars to be given *(ERA 1996, s 7)*.

Disciplinary and complaints procedures. The *ERA 1996* (as amended by *s 35, Employment Act 2002*) further requires that every statement given to an employee shall contain a note:

(A)   specifying any disciplinary rules applicable to the employee or referring to a document which is reasonably accessible to the employee and which specifies such rules. The employer must also specify any procedure applicable to the taking of disciplinary actions relating to the employee, or to a decision to dismiss the employee, or refer the employee to the provisions of another document which specifies such a procedure; and

(B)   specifying, by description or otherwise:

   (i)   a person to whom the employee can apply if he is dissatisfied with any disciplinary decision relating to him or any decision to dismiss him; and

    (ii)   a person to whom the employee can apply for the purpose of seeking redress of any grievance relating to his employment and the manner in which any such application should be made,

and where there are further steps to be taken in any such application, explaining those steps or referring to a document which is reasonably accessible to the employee and which explains them (*ERA 1996, s 3(1)*).

The requirement to give a note of disciplinary and complaints procedures does not apply to rules, disciplinary decisions, decisions to dismiss, grievances or procedures relating to HEALTH AND SAFETY AT WORK – **II (26)** (*ERA 1996, s 3(2)*).

Contracting-out certificate. The written particulars must include a note stating whether a contracting-out certificate is in force for the particular employment concerned (*ERA 1996, s 3(5)*). Such a certificate is issued where there is in place an occupational pension scheme which satisfies certain conditions.

Previously, employers who (together with any associated employer) employed less than 20 persons were exempted from the obligations in respect of informing employees of disciplinary procedures. That exemption is abolished by *s 36, Employment Act 2002*.

ERA 1996 does not require there to be provisions in the contract on all these matters (see *Morley v Heritage plc* [1993] IRLR 400). It simply requires notice of such provisions that do exist to be given to the employee. Where there are no provisions relating to any of the matters listed above, that fact must be stated, eg where no contractual sick pay is provided (*ERA 1996, s 2(1)*).

Certain classes of employee are also entitled to a statement setting out their right to refuse to work on Sundays under the provisions formerly in the *Sunday Trading Act 1994* and the *Betting, Gaming and Lotteries Act 1963* which have now been consolidated in the *ERA 1996* (see **7.48** below).

7.8   **Alternatives to inclusion of particulars in written statement**

ERA 1996, s 2(2), (3) provides that the written statement of particulars:

    (a)   may refer the employee to the provisions of some other document which he has reasonable opportunities of reading in the course of his employment, or which is made reasonably accessible to him in some other way, for particulars of any of the matters specified in *ERA 1996, s 1(4)(d)(ii)* and *(iii)* (sickness, sick pay and pensions); and

    (b)   may refer the employee to the law or to a collective agreement which directly affects his terms and conditions for particulars of the matters specified in *s 1(4)(e), ERA 1996* (length of notice), provided that any such collective agreement is one which he has reasonable opportunities of reading in the course of his employment or which is made reasonably accessible to him in some other way.

7.9   **Written particulars and changes in contract terms**

Any changes in the contractual terms or in other matters of which written particulars must be given must be the subject of a written statement given to the employee at the earliest opportunity and in any event not later than one month after the change (or the time of leaving the UK to work for more than one month, if that is the cause of the change) (*ERA 1996, s 4(1), (3)*). Similar provisions concerning the documents in which particulars may be set out again apply.

7.9 Contract of Employment

A mere change of the employer's name, or a mere change in employer which does not break CONTINUOUS EMPLOYMENT (6), does not require a complete new statement under *ERA 1996, s 1*, but does require a statement of change under *s 4 (ERA 1996, s 4(6), (8))*.

7.10 Exceptions

The requirement to give written particulars applies to all employees except:

(a)   seamen of various kinds (*ERA 1996, s 199, s 5(1)*); and

(b)   a person whose employment continues for less than one month (*ERA 1996, s 198*).

7.11 Employees' remedies for failure to give particulars

An employee who has not been provided with the necessary particulars may make a complaint relating to the failure to an employment tribunal (*ERA 1996, s 11(1)*). Claims under *s 11* are a relatively speedy way of having contractual employment rights determined.

An application may be made by either the employer or the employee if a statement of particulars has purportedly been given, but a question arises as to the particulars which ought to have been included or referred to in it (*ERA 1996, s 11(2)*). Where no *express* term has been agreed, it may be that the tribunal is able to *imply* a term after considering all the facts and circumstances of the relationship between the employer and the employee concerned (*Mears v Safecar Security Ltd* [1982] ICR 626). However, if there has been no express or implied agreement upon a particular term, the tribunal has no power to invent a term for the parties (*Eagland v British Telecommunications plc* [1993] ICR 644; and see **7.14** below). Nor is *s 11* to be used as a means of clarifying or interpreting an ambiguous term (*Construction Industry Training Board v Leighton* [1978] IRLR 60). This was confirmed by the Court of Appeal in *Southern Cross Healthcare Co Ltd v Perkins* [2010] EWCA Civ 1442, [2011] ICR 285, [2011] IRLR 247, where Maurice Kay LJ held at 29 that "the reference in *section 11(1)* of the *1996 Act* to a determination of 'what particulars ought to have been included', is not an invitation to judicial creativity, even under the rubric of "construction".

An employer's failure to include a term in the statement of particulars does not mean that the employer is unable to enforce that term: *Lange v Georg Schüneman GmbH* [2001] IRLR 244, ECJ.

The tribunal will, if it finds such a complaint under *s 11* well-founded, state the particulars which should have been given and the employer will be deemed to have given a statement including those particulars (*ERA 1996, s 12(1), (2)*). If the employer has been in breach of any of those terms, the employee may bring an action against him in the county court or the High Court or, if the breach involves a deduction from pay, in the tribunal under *ERA 1996, ss 13–27* (the former *Wages Act 1986* provisions) (see **32.6 PAY – I**). The right to present a complaint for failure to provide written particulars may be exercised by an employee who has been employed for more than two months. If the employment has ceased, the application to the tribunal must be made before the end of the period of three months beginning with the date on which the employment ceased or within such further period as the tribunal considers reasonable where it was not reasonably practicable for the application to be made within three months (*ERA 1996, s 11(4)*). (See **17.18 EMPLOYMENT TRIBUNALS**.)

There is no right to claim damages for a breach of the statutory duty to give written particulars, although in certain special circumstances an employer may be under a contractual duty to take reasonable steps to publicise a term (*Scally v Southern Health and Social Services Board* [1991] ICR 771, HL).

In the event that an employee brings a claim of a type specified in *Sch 5* to the *Employment Act 2002* (a wide range of claims including, but not limited to, unfair dismissal, discrimination and breach of contract cases) against an employer which is resolved in favour of the employee and, at the time when the proceedings were commenced, the employer was in breach either of his duty to provide a statement of particulars under *ERA 1996, s 1* or to a statement of changes under *ERA 1996, s 4*, then the tribunal must award the employee two weeks' pay (and may award four weeks' pay) even if it makes no other award (*EA 2002, s 38*). If the tribunal does make an award in favour of the employee, it must increase that award by two weeks' pay (and may increase it by four weeks' pay). However, if there are exceptional circumstances that would make the award or the increase to the award unjust or inequitable, then the tribunal does not have to order the additional award.

7.12   TERMS OF THE CONTRACT

Freedom to agree

Agreement remains the pivotal issue in construing employment contracts. As the Supreme Court has confirmed in *Autoclenz Ltd v Belcher* [2011] UKSC 41 (in the context of whether or not individuals were 'workers'), the fundamental question is "what was the agreement between the parties?" If the evidence showed that the written contractual terms did not reflect the parties' true agreement, then it can to that extent be disregarded.

The parties are free to agree any terms they wish, subject to certain limitations set out below. In determining the terms of a contract, a tribunal will have to consider the provisions of a written contract (if any). However, even in the case where there is a written contract, it will not be correct to consider only its terms unless it is established that the parties intended that the document should contain all the terms of the contract. It is open to the parties to agree some terms in writing and others orally (see the discussion in *Carmichael v National Power plc* [1999] 4 All ER 897, [1999] 1 WLR 2042, para 19). If an employment tribunal is called upon to interpret the terms of a contract, it must apply the same principles as an ordinary court. This means, for example, the words used must be interpreted in the context which existed and was known to both parties at the time when the contract was made (*Investors Compensation Scheme Ltd v West Bromwich Building Society* [1998] 1 All ER 98, HL) but that the parties' subsequent conduct is not admissible in construing their original written agreement (*Hooper v British Railways Board* [1988] IRLR 517). Where the terms of a written contract are truly ambiguous, it may be permissible to construe what the parties meant by using evidence of a clearly established practice, which continued both before and after the contract was made (*Dunlop Tyres Ltd v Blows* [2001] IRLR 629, CA; see also COLLECTIVE AGREEMENTS (5)). This latter principle should, however, be approached with caution: courts and tribunals will be reluctant to draw inferences from later conduct (*Choudhry v Triesman* [2003] EWHC 1203 (Ch)). The Tribunal may also consider whether a purported provision of a contract (or, indeed, the very basis of hiring an 'employee') is a 'sham' where neither party intended to create the legal rights and obligations which they set out (*Redrow Homes (Yorkshire) Ltd v Buckborough & Sewell* [2009] IRLR 34, EAT; *Protectacoat Firthglow Ltd v Szilagyi* [2009] EWCA Civ 98, [2009] ICR 835, [2009] IRLR 365; *Autoclenz*; see also EMPLOYEE, SELF-EMPLOYED OR WORKER? (14)).

7.13   Employer handbooks and policies

Employees will often be provided with a substantial volume of documentation on starting work. These documents may be presented under a variety of titles, such as employer policies and company handbooks. In practice, they are often more voluminous than the statement of written particulars or any document which is according to its own terms a contractual document. In many cases, it may be a matter of considerable practical importance to know whether or not these documents have contractual effect. This question may arise, for example, when the employer seeks to vary the provisions of a policy or of the company handbook. If the policy or handbook is contractual, it may not be unilaterally varied. The question may also arise when an employer is seeking to dismiss an employee. Where the handbook provides, for example, for a particular disciplinary procedure, and the employer proposes to dismiss in breach of that procedure, the employee may seek an injunction to restrain dismissal (see **7.42** below). Such an injunction can only be granted where the procedure relied upon has contractual effect. If the procedure does not have contractual force, there is no legal foundation for such an injunction.

There is no single test for determining whether documents such as disciplinary procedures have contractual effect: factors to consider include the certainty, level of detail and workability of the relevant provision, its importance to the working relationship and its context (*Hussain v Surrey and Sussex Healthcare NHS Trust* [2011] EWHC 1670 (QB)).

A code or policy is only to be regarded as having contractual effect when it may be regarded as conferring rights on employees. If it only lays down standards of good practice which an employer would be expected to follow, it does not have contractual effect (*Wandsworth London Borough Council v D'Silva* [1998] IRLR 193, CA). In *D'Silva* the employer sought unilaterally to alter the terms of a sickness policy. The employee alleged that this would be in breach of contract. The Court of Appeal held that since the policy was not intended to confer rights but was only a statement of good practice, the employer could alter the terms without securing the agreement of the employees.

In contrast, in *Attrill & Other v Dresdner Kleinwort Limited & Anor* [2013] EWCA Civ 394, the Court of Appeal held that the employer's announcement of a bonus pool (specifically aimed at retaining employees) during a 'Town Hall' meeting broadcast online was an offer capable of acceptance and of incorporation into the employees' contracts.

In *Keeley v Fosroc International Ltd* [2006] EWCA Civ 1277, [2006] IRLR 961, the Court of Appeal held that even where a handbook was expressly incorporated, that did not mean that the entire content of the handbook had contractual effect. It was particularly relevant to consider the importance of the provision for the employee. If it was clearly worded as conferring an entitlement on the employee, it was likely to have contractual effect. It was not determinative that the passage in the handbook was described as a policy.

Even where the policy is contractual, its effect will depend on the construction of the contract as a whole. Thus, the House of Lords held in *Taylor v Secretary of State for Scotland* [2000] IRLR 502 that the inclusion in the contract of an equal opportunities policy which undertook that there should be no discrimination on the grounds of age did not prevent the employer from dismissing an employee on the grounds that he had reached the minimum retirement age (see Retirement (**40**). See also *Bateman v Asda Stores Ltd* [2010] IRLR 370, [2010] All ER (D) 277 (Feb) where the handbook empowered the employer 'to review, revise, amend or replace' the contents of the handbook, including contractual matters such as pay. See also *Attrill* case (above).

7.14   Express or implied terms

The terms of the contract may be express or implied or incorporated.

Express terms are those that the parties specifically by reference agree upon. The express terms of the contract may be found in a document described as the contract of employment or in an offer letter or in oral exchanges between the parties or in other documents. The provisions set out in a statement of written particulars will be evidence of the express terms, albeit that the statement of written particulars is not the contract itself. The parties may agree upon certain points by reference to a document such as a collective agreement which thereby becomes incorporated into the agreement between the parties (see **5.2** Collective Agreements). See however, *Malone v British Airways* [2010] EWCA Civ 1225, [2011] ICR 125, [2011] IRLR 32, where the Court of Appeal upheld findings that provisions concerning staffing levels, set out in staff agreements and manuals, were not apt to be enforced by individual employees.

The core of a contract of employment is a contract whereby an employee agrees to work for an employer in return for pay. In the event that a contract of employment exists, this is the irreducible minimum. However, as set out below there are many other aspects to a contract of employment.

In *R v Hull University Visitor, ex p Page* [1992] ICR 67 at 80D–80F, Staughton LJ was of the view that a job advertisement should be read together with a letter of appointment (the case later went to the House of Lords: [1993] ICR 114). Implied and incorporated terms are dealt with below.

7.15 Common implied terms

Frequently, many terms of the contract will not be specifically set out or stated. There may be many rights and obligations on either side which are left unexpressed and unspecified. The general rule is that a term will be implied into a contract if it is so obvious that both parties would have regarded it as a term even though they had not expressly stated it as a term or if it is *necessary* to imply the term in order to give the contract business efficacy (*Liverpool City Council v Irwin* [1977] AC 239; *Scally v Southern Health and Social Services Board* [1991] ICR 771 at 781). Terms also may be implied if they are customary in the particular trade or calling, or form the usual practice of the particular employer, if it is sufficiently well known. Such a custom or practice must be 'reasonable, certain and notorious' (*Bond v CAV Ltd* [1983] IRLR 360; *Henry v London General Transport Services Ltd* [2002] ICR 910, [2002] IRLR 472). In order to become an implied term, a custom must be followed with regularity such that it becomes legitimate to infer that the parties follow the practice because they regard it as a legal obligation rather than that the practice is followed as a matter of policy: *Solectron Scotland Ltd v Roper* [2004] IRLR 4. For an important recent application of these principles, see *Garratt v Mirror Group Newspapers Ltd* [2011] EWCA Civ 425, where the Court of Appeal upheld an implied term that enhanced redundancy payments were available only to employees who signed compromise agreements.

Terms commonly implied are the *employee's* duties of:

(a)   fidelity;

(b)   obedience;

(c)   working with due diligence and care;

(d)   not using or disclosing the employer's trade secrets or confidential information;

and the *employer's* duties:

(e)   to take care for the employee's health and safety;

(f)   to provide redress for grievances;

(g)   (in some cases) not merely to pay but to provide work;

and the duties of *both parties:*

(h)   not to destroy the relationship of trust and confidence (see below for more detail);

(i)   to give a reasonable period of notice of termination, when no specific notice period has been agreed.

The above list is not exhaustive: other duties can arise in various circumstances. Some of them are dealt with below.

7.16 Contract of Employment

7.16 *Employee's duties*

Duty of fidelity

An employee has a duty to serve his employer faithfully and not to act against the interests of the employer's business. Thus, it would be in breach of an implied term of the contract of employment for the employee to set up a rival business to that of his employer during the period of his employment, unless he had been expressly permitted to do so, or to take more than preparatory steps towards doing so: *Balston Ltd v Headline Filters Ltd* [1990] FSR 385. However, mere preparations to set up a competing business after the termination of the employment are not necessarily a breach of contract (*Ixora Trading Inc v Jones* [1990] FSR 251).

The line between legitimate and illegitimate steps towards competing is difficult to draw. It has been held that it is not decisive to consider whether the employee's acts are described as preparatory: *Helmet Integrated Systems Ltd v Tunnard* [2006] EWCA Civ 1735, [2007] IRLR 126. It is a question for decision in each case whether the employee's conduct in seeking to set up a new business is legitimate or illegitimate. In the *Tunnard* case it was held that an employee did not act in breach of contract when he designed a product intended to compete with his employer's. The Court reached this view partly on the basis that the contract of employment did not sufficiently restrict his ability to prepare for future competition. That analysis does not sit happily with the existence of the implied duty of fidelity. The Court also noted that he was a salesman and not a technical designer. In principle, an employee crosses the line and acts unlawfully when his acts are inconsistent with his duty of fidelity (see *Shepherds Investments Ltd v Walters* [2006] EWHC 836 (Ch), [2007] IRLR 110, a case concerned primarily with directors; see also *Cobbetts LLP v Hodge* [2009] EWHC 786 (Ch), a case concerned with a solicitor negotiating for himself an equity share in a client company without obtaining the informed consent of his employer) and *Samsung Semiconductor Europe Ltd v Docherty* [2011] CSOH 32 (where the Court of Session stated that an employee's liability did not depend on his consciously assuming fiduciary duties). Another example (albeit that this was a case about a director's fiduciary duty) is *Foster Bryant Surveying Ltd v Bryant* [2007] EWCA Civ 200, [2007] IRLR 425. It is also a breach of contract for an employee to tender for future business from a customer of the employer in competition with the employer (*Adamson v B & L Cleaning Services Ltd* [1995] IRLR 193). For the implied obligation not to use or disclose the employer's trade secrets or confidential information, see **39.13 RESTRAINT OF TRADE, CONFIDENTIALITY AND EMPLOYEE INTERVENTIONS**.

7.17 *Duty to Obey Reasonable Employer Instructions*

The employee is also obliged by the implied terms of his contract of employment to obey the reasonable instructions of his employer and to carry out his work conscientiously and honestly. In *Sybron Corpn v Rochem Ltd* [1984] Ch 112, it was held that the terms and nature of a particular employment might be such that there was a contractual duty to disclose the misconduct of other employees (see also *Item Software (UK) Ltd v Fassihi* [2004] EWCA Civ 1244, [2005] ICR 450).

A work to rule or withdrawal of goodwill may amount to a breach of the implied obligation to serve the employer faithfully (*Secretary of State for Employment v Associated Society of Locomotive Engineers and Firemen (No 2)* [1972] 2 QB 455, [1972] ICR 19, CA; *British Telecommunications plc v Ticehurst* [1992] ICR 383).

The duties of obedience and fidelity are also owed to an employer to whom the employee is seconded (*Macmillan Inc v Bishopsgate Investment Trust plc* [1993] IRLR 393).

A distinction must be drawn between the duty to serve the employer in good faith, which is owed by all employees, and fiduciary duties, which are not an incident of every employment relationship. When a person is a fiduciary (such as a trustee or a company director), he is obliged to pursue another's interests at the expense of his own. In the case of an employee, his obligation is to comply with the express and implied terms of his contract (for a discussion of the distinction, see *Nottingham University v Fishel* [2000] IRLR 471). By way of further example of the difference, an employee is not under an implied obligation to reveal his own misconduct, but a fiduciary is under such an obligation (*Tesco Stores Ltd v Pook* [2004] IRLR 618); *Item Software (UK) Ltd v Fassihi* [2004] EWCA Civ 1244, [2005] ICR 450, *GHLM Trading Ltd v Maroo* [2012] EWHC 61 (Ch)). Senior employees may owe fiduciary obligations by reason of their seniority even if they are not directors: *Shepherds Investments Ltd v Walters* [2006] EWHC 836 (Ch), [2007] IRLR 110.

In *Cresswell v Inland Revenue Board* [1984] 2 All ER 713, [1984] ICR 508, it was held that an employee was expected to adapt to new methods and techniques in performing his duties, provided the employer arranged for him to receive the necessary training in the new skills and the nature of the work did not alter so radically that it was outside the contractual duties of the employee. If the employer has an express power to transfer the employee to other duties, he is not subject to an implied requirement to exercise that power reasonably, provided that he has some proper grounds for the exercise of the express power and he does not exercise it in such a way as to destroy trust and confidence between himself and the employee (*White v Reflecting Roadstuds Ltd* [1991] ICR 733). Similarly, an express right in the employer to require a particular number of hours per week to be worked must be construed as being subject to the employer's duty to safeguard the employee's health and safety (*Johnstone v Bloomsbury Health Authority* [1991] ICR 269).

7.18 *Duty to take due care in performance of duties*

An employee owes a contractual duty of care to his employer, breach of which can support a claim for damages (*Janata Bank v Ahmed* [1981] ICR 791, [1981] IRLR 457 applying *Lister v Romford Ice and Cold Storage Co Ltd* [1957] AC 555).

7.19 *Employer's duties*

Health and safety

It is an implied term of the contract of employment that the employer will take reasonable steps to ensure the employee's safety (see comments in *Dutton & Clark Ltd v Daly* [1985] IRLR 363, *Johnstone v Bloomsbury Health Authority* [1991] ICR 269 and HEALTH AND SAFETY AT WORK – I (25)). This includes providing a safe system of work. The duty to provide a safe system of work should not be limited to preventing physical injury. Employers also owe a duty to take reasonable care not to cause psychiatric harm to an employee by reason of the volume or character of work imposed on the employee. The standard of care depends on what is reasonable conduct for a person in the employer's position. What is reasonable depends on the nature of the relationship, the magnitude of the risk of injury that was reasonably foreseeable, the seriousness of the consequences for the employee if that injury should occur, and the cost and practicability of preventing the risk (*Walker v Northumberland County Council* [1995] IRLR 35).

In *Waltons & Morse v Dorrington* [1997] IRLR 488, it was held that a term was to be implied into every contract of employment that 'the employer will provide and monitor for employees, so far as is reasonably practicable, a working environment which is reasonably suitable for the performance by them of their contractual duties'. In that case, the employer acted in breach of the term by requiring a non-smoking secretary to work in a smoke-filled environment.

7.20 *Redress for grievances*

In *W A Goold (Pearmak) Ltd v McConnell* [1995] IRLR 516, the EAT held that it was an implied term that the employer would 'reasonably and promptly afford a reasonable opportunity to their employees to obtain redress of any grievance they may have' (see also

Contract of Employment

Ministry of Defence v Guellard [2009] All ER (D) 50 (Dec)).The basis for the implication of this term was the statutory obligation to include in the written statement of terms, a note specifying to whom and in what manner an employee might apply for the purpose of seeking redress of any grievance relating to employment (see 7.7 above).

7.21 *Duty to provide work*

In some cases, it may be argued that the employer's only obligation is to pay and that there is no duty upon an employer to provide work. In other words, so long as the employee is fully remunerated, the employer can ask him to stay at home without being in breach of contract. A contract of employment may, however, be subject to an implied obligation to provide work where earnings vary according to the work done, where an individual such as an actor is dependent upon publicity, or where the employee has skills that may atrophy through lack of use: *Langston v Amalgamated Union of Engineering Workers* [1974] 1 All ER 980, [1974] ICR 180 and 510, CA; *Breach v Epsylon Industries Ltd* [1976] ICR 316; *Spencer v Marchington* [1988] IRLR 392; and cf *Warren v Mendy* [1989] ICR 525. See also *Christie v Carmichael* [2010] IRLR 1016, where the Scottish EAT found that the employer was entitled to place an employee on garden leave, notwithstanding the lack of an express contractual provision to that effect, partly on the basis that the employee's skills would not atrophy. The range of cases in which the court will imply an obligation to provide work has widened following the decision of the Court of Appeal in *William Hill Organisation Ltd v Tucker* [1999] ICR 291, [1998] IRLR 313. There it was held that the question of whether there was an obligation to provide work depended on the facts of each case. The question was whether the consideration moving from the employer extended to an obligation to permit the employee to do the work or whether it was confined to a duty to pay the agreed remuneration. See also *SG&R Valuation Service Co LLC v Boudrais* [2008] EWHC 1340 (QB), [2008] IRLR 770, where it was held that even where the employee's contract does confer on him a right to work, that right would be foregone if the employee demonstrated in a serious way that he was not ready or willing to work. This was approved in *Standard Life Health Care Ltd v Gorman* [2009] EWCA Civ 1292, [2010] IRLR 233.

7.22 *Suspension only on reasonable grounds*

In *McClory v Post Office* [1992] ICR 758, the court was prepared to imply a term that the employer's express right to suspend the employee must only be exercised on reasonable grounds, although not to imply any term that the employer should when exercising that power observe the principles of natural justice. The case also contains a useful discussion of the circumstances in which an employee may have a contractual right to work overtime.

McClory was approved in *Watson v Durham University* [2008] EWCA Civ 1266, in the context of the employer making weak allegations of racism and then seeking to suspend the employee on that basis much later.

In *Marshall (Cambridge) Ltd v Hamblin* [1994] IRLR 260, the EAT held by a majority that an employee who has resigned has no right to work out his notice period (in the absence, of course, of any express term or custom and practice to the contrary). The employee's only right was to pay in lieu of notice, even though the majority of the employee's income was based on commission.

7.22a *Employee's economic well-being*

In *Scally v Southern Health and Social Services Board* [1991] ICR 771, the House of Lords held that the employer was under an implied duty to take reasonable steps to bring to the employee's attention a right which he had (in that case, to purchase extra years' service for superannuation purposes) that would be lost unless he took certain action, given that the employee could not reasonably have been expected to be aware of the relevant contractual term without it being drawn to his attention.

However, there is no implied term that the employer will take reasonable care of his employees' economic well-being: *Crossley v Faithful & Gould Holdings* [2004] EWCA Civ 293, [2004] IRLR 377.

7.22b *Continuation of employment and ill health payments*

Where a contract of employment contains terms entitling the employee to benefits during a period of ill health and the continued receipt of such benefits is dependent on the individual remaining in the employer's employment, a term will be implied that the employer will not dismiss the employee while he remains incapacitated so as to deprive him of the continued receipt of those benefits (*Aspden v Webbs Poultry & Meat Group (Holdings) Ltd* [1996] IRLR 521). A similar approach was taken in Scotland in *Adin v Sedco Forex International Resources Ltd* [1997] IRLR 280 (and see *Brompton v AOC International Ltd* [1997] IRLR 639, para 38, CA).

The extent to which an employer may dismiss an employee who is in receipt of sick pay and/or who anticipates that, if his contract of employment continues in force, he will in due course be entitled to early retirement or to some other benefit was the issue in the Court of Session case of *Hill v General Accident Fire and Life Assurance Corpn plc* [1998] IRLR 641. The employee in that case was in receipt of sick pay. If he had remained employed and in receipt of sick pay for a further four months, he would have been entitled to an ill-health retirement pension or to sickness and accident benefit. The employer terminated his contract by reason of redundancy. Mr Hill sued alleging that the termination of his employment was in breach of the implied duty of trust and confidence and that, whilst he was absent sick and in receipt of sick pay or with an anticipation of early retirement or other benefits, his employment could be terminated only by reason of his own repudiatory breach of contract. The court held that a person in Mr Hill's position could not be dismissed by reason of his absence, or for a specious reason, or for no reason at all. The power to dismiss included, but was not limited to, the case where the employee acted in repudiatory breach of contract. Accordingly, a dismissal by reason of redundancy was not in breach of the implied term of trust and confidence. In *Villella v MFI Furniture Centres Ltd* [1999] IRLR 468, a case concerning Permanent Health Insurance, the High Court formulated an implied term that the employer would not terminate the contract of employment, save for cause other than ill health, in circumstances which would deprive the employee of his continuing entitlement to benefit.

It has also been held that where an employer provides a benefit such as PHI and the insurer fails to pay, there is an implied obligation on the employer to pursue the insurer for payment, including, if need be, by litigation: *Marlow v East Thames Housing Group Ltd* [2002] IRLR 798. The extent of the obligation would of course depend on the merits of the employee's argument.

The *Aspden* line of cases has been applied by analogy to the case where an employer proposes to dismiss for redundancy and employees have the benefit of a contractual redundancy package. In *Jenvey v Australian Broadcasting Corpn* [2002] EWHC 927 (QB), [2003] ICR 79 it was held that where the employer had proposed to dismiss for redundancy with the consequence that the employee would enjoy a contractual payment, it was an implied term that the employer would not then dismiss for any other reason (apart from cause) if to do so would defeat those contractual rights.

7.22c *Discretionary payments and benefits*

Contracts of employment often contain provision for benefits which are dependent upon the exercise of discretion by the employer. By way of example, contracts providing an entitlement to bonus often confer a discretion on the employer in relation to the amount of the bonus. It is an implied term that such a discretion will be exercised rationally and lawfully: *Horkulak v Cantor Fitzgerald International* [2004] IRLR 942, approving *Clark v*

Contract of Employment

Nomura International Plc [2000] IRLR 766. In *Horkulak*, damages for breach of contract by not making a bonus payment were assessed on the basis of what the employer would have paid had it exercised the discretion genuinely and rationally. The court stood in the shoes of the employer and decided what sums would have been awarded once it was established that the sum awarded by the employer was in breach of contract. See also *Small v Boots Co Plc* [2009] IRLR 328.

However, the Court of Appeal has more recently stressed the limited role of the Court in such claims. It is no part of the Court's function to decide what bonus should have been awarded. The Court is concerned only to ensure that the employer complies with its legal obligation to exercise its discretion in good faith and rationally: see *Humphreys v Norilsk Nickel International (UK) Ltd* [2010] IRLR 976. The employer has a wide discretion and the burden of establishing that a bonus paid was irrational is 'a very high one': *Keen v Commerzbank AG* [2007] ICR 623, sub nom *Commerzbank AG v Keen* [2007] IRLR 132.

7.22d *Trust and confidence*

It is now well established that employment contracts contain an implied of mutual trust and confidence. This term is framed as follows: the parties to the contract will not, without reasonable and proper cause, conduct themselves in a manner calculated or likely to destroy or seriously damage the relationship of confidence and trust which should exist between employer and employee. This is a mutual duty, albeit that the overwhelming majority of the cases deal with breach of the term by the employer. This implied term has been approved by the House of Lords in the landmark decision of *Malik v BCCI SA (in liq)* [1998] AC 20, [1997] ICR 606. Although in *Malik* Lord Steyn said the term applied to conduct calculated **and** likely to have the requisite effects, the EAT has since confirmed that it is 'calculated **or** likely': *Baldwin v Brighton and Hove City Council* [2007] ICR 680, [2007] IRLR 232.

It has also been held that the test for determining whether the employer has acted in breach of this term is a severe one: the conduct of the employer must be such as to destroy or seriously damage the relationship (*Claridge v Daler Rowney Ltd* [2008] ICR 1267), and there must have been no reasonable and proper cause for the conduct (*Gogay v Hertford-shire County Council* [2000] IRLR 703, CA, paras 53–55; *Devon and Somerset Fire and Rescue Service v Tilke* (UKEAT/0303/09/RN) (25 January 2010, unreported)). This term is fundamental to the employment relationship and any breach of it is likely to be repudiatory: *Morrow v Safeway Stores plc* [2002] IRLR 9, EAT. However, it is important to bear in mind that both limbs of the term are important: conduct which destroys trust and confidence is not in breach of contract if there is a reasonable cause (*Hilton v Shiner Ltd Builders Merchants* [2001] IRLR 727*)*. The Court of Appeal has deprecated the use of loose language in some cases which may appear to extend the scope of the implied term (into, for example, an obligation of 'fair dealing'). The proper approach is to apply the language of the House of Lords in *Malik*: see *O'Brien v Transco plc (formerly BG plc)* [2002] EWCA Civ 379, [2002] ICR 721. Recent guidance comes from *Tullett Prebon Plc v BGC Brokers LP* [2011] IRLR 420: the question is whether, looking at all the circumstances objectively, the party's intention was to refuse performance of the contract.

The implied term that the employer will not act in a manner calculated or likely to destroy or seriously to damage the relationship of trust and confidence is capable of being relevant in a very wide range of circumstances. Breaches of this implied term are often cited in constructive dismissal cases and a number of examples are given in that context (see **51.7 Unfair Dismissal – I**).

It has been held that an employer's failure to adhere to statutory obligations may give rise to a breach of the implied term. Thus in *Nottinghamshire County Council v Meikle* [2004] IRLR 703 it was held that an employer's continuing failure to make the reasonable adjustments which were required to be made in order to accommodate the employee's disability was a breach of contract. (See also *Greenhof v Barnsley Metropolitan Borough Council* [2006] IRLR 98.) This reasoning should not be pushed too far. It is wrong to suggest that every breach by an employer of his statutory obligations involves a breach of contract: *Doherty v British Midland Airways Ltd* [2006] IRLR 90.

In *Hill v General Accident Fire and Life Assurance Corpn plc* [1998] IRLR 641, 1999 SLT 1157, the Court of Session specifically rejected a submission that, as a result of *Malik*, a new approach had to be taken to the interpretation of contracts of employment and that they had to be construed in a way which furthered mutual trust. The English courts have shown similar restraint. In *University of Nottingham v Eyett* [1999] IRLR 87, it was held that there had been no breach of the implied term by an employer who failed to advise the employee that if he delayed his retirement by a short time, he would be paid a higher pension than that which he actually received.

In considering the scope of the implied term of trust and confidence, it is important to bear in mind that the obligation in question relates to the maintenance of the trust and confidence which should exist in an employment relationship. There is no implied obligation on the employer to act reasonably: see *Post Office v Roberts* [1980] IRLR 347. The Privy Council placed an important limit on the scope of the implied term. Where there is an untrammelled express power in a contract (for example, to dismiss without cause or to require an employee to move location) the implied term cannot operate to limit the scope of that power: *Reda v Flag Ltd* [2002] IRLR 747. Implied terms in contracts must give way to and may not contradict express terms.

There is a further important limitation on the efficacy of the implied term of trust and confidence. It is inoperative in connection with decisions to terminate employment: *Johnson v Unisys Ltd* [2001] ICR 480. This reasoning is informed by policy considerations. Since Parliament has enacted the right not to be unfairly dismissed, it would be an abuse of the judicial function to develop or apply an implied contractual term that in effect displaced, or usurped, the statutory provisions in regulating the manner of dismissal. It would be wrong, for example, for the common law to develop a right which overlapped with the right not to be unfairly dismissed but which was not subject to the same limitations, in respect of, for example, continuity of employment and time limits for the presentation of claims, which Parliament has decided should apply to unfair dismissal claims.

Thus, an employee cannot complain that his dismissal was in breach of the implied term of trust and confidence. It is, however, possible to formulate a claim for breach of the implied term of trust and confidence in respect of things done by the employer to the employee before dismissal. A line is drawn between unfairness in respect of the dismissal itself, which can only be the subject of a statutory claim of unfair dismissal and unfairness before the dismissal which gives rise to a separate cause of action in contract. Usually, it is the employer's decision to dismiss, rather than any earlier act, which gives rise to loss. However, there may be exceptional cases where this is not so. Examples might include cases of unjustified suspension (as in *Gogay v Hertfordshire County Council* [2000] IRLR 703) or cases where an employee suffers psychiatric illness as a result of pre-dismissal unfairness. Examples of the latter are *Eastwood v Magnox Electric plc* and [2004] IRLR 733. In both cases employees alleged that they had suffered psychiatric illness as a result of the ways in which the employers had conducted investigations and disciplinary proceedings. The claims were originally struck out as having no basis in law in the light of *Johnson* but the House of Lords held that the claims, being based on allegations about pre-dismissal conduct, did disclose a cause of action and could proceed to trial.

In some cases, where a breach of the duty is alleged the question may arise whether the employer is liable for the act said to constitute the breach. Thus, in *Moores v Bude Stratton Town Council* [2001] ICR 271, [2000] IRLR 676 an individual councillor verbally abused an employee. When the employee resigned and claimed constructive dismissal, the issue arose whether the council was liable for the acts of the individual back-bench councillor. A majority of the EAT (Lindsay J dissenting) held that the council was liable. For the parameters of an employer's liability, see VICARIOUS LIABILITY (54). Even if the employer is not vicariously liable for the acts complained of, he may be directly liable for failing to supervise or prevent those acts: see *Waters v Metropolitan Police Comr* [2000] IRLR 720. In *Waters*, the House of Lords held that an employer might be liable to his employee in negligence if he knew of or foresaw acts being done by other employees which might cause physical or mental harm to the employee but did nothing to prevent or supervise such acts when it was in his power to do so. The argument in *Waters* was concerned with the tort of negligence. However, in that case there was no contract between the police officer and the commissioner. One can see how, in a case where there was a contract of employment, the implied term of trust and confidence would impose a similar duty in contract on the employer.

7.22e *Place of work*

There must be a contractual term, express or implied, dealing with the place where the employee may be required to work. If there is no express term, that term will be implied which the parties would have agreed if they had directed their minds to the problem. All the circumstances of the case will be considered, including the nature of the business, the nature of the employee's duties and his status, what the employee was told when engaged and whether he has in fact been moved from time to time, and whether there is any provision for the payment of expenses for working away from home. The term implied may be that the employee can be required to work anywhere within reasonable daily travelling distance of his home (*O'Brien v Associated Fire Alarms Ltd* [1969] 1 All ER 93; *Jones v Associated Tunnelling Co Ltd* [1981] IRLR 477; *Courtaulds Northern Spinning Ltd v Sibson* [1988] ICR 451). See also *Little v Charterhouse Magna Assurance Co Ltd* [1980] IRLR 19 and *Rank Xerox Ltd v Churchill* [1988] IRLR 280. However, such a 'mobility clause' (whether express or implied) may be coupled with implied obligations to give reasonable notice of any move (see *United Bank Ltd v Akhtar* [1989] IRLR 507; *Prestwick Circuits Ltd v McAndrew* [1990] IRLR 191; and cf *White*, above). Although there must be a term which identifies where the employee is to work, it is not necessary in every case to imply a mobility clause. Whether or not it is necessary to imply such a clause will depend on the nature of the work and the other facts of the case (*Aparau v Iceland Frozen Foods plc* [1996] IRLR 119). It appears that an employer may only effectively rely upon a mobility clause if he makes it clear that he is doing so (*Curling v Securicor Ltd* [1992] IRLR 549).

In *Bass Leisure Ltd v Thomas* [1994] IRLR 104, the EAT held that the place where an employee works is a question of fact to be determined by considering where the employee in fact works rather than where she can be required to work (see **35.7** REDUNDANCY – I). This approach was approved by the Court of Appeal in *High Tables Ltd v Horst* [1997] IRLR 513. (Compare *Gale v Northern General Hospital NHS Trust* [1994] IRLR 292, which was concerned specifically with the construction of the *National Health Service and Community Care Act 1990, s 6(1)*.)

7.22f *Termination of the contract*

In the absence of any express term governing the notice required to be given to terminate the contract, it is an implied term that reasonable notice of termination will be given. Reasonable notice will not be implied if to do so would contradict an express term, eg a term giving a party the right to terminate at any time without cause. The implication of the term is necessary in order to provide a means by which a contract of otherwise indefinite duration may be terminated. If the express terms make provision, there is no need to imply a term: *Reda v Flag Ltd* [2002] UKPC 38, [2002] IRLR 747. What is reasonable will depend on all the facts of the case (see **46.6** TERMINATION OF EMPLOYMENT).

7.22g   Incorporated terms

These are terms which are incorporated into the contract rather than being agreed individually between the parties. The principal source of incorporated terms is collective agreements (see COLLECTIVE AGREEMENTS (5)). The *Equal Pay Act 1970* incorporates into every contract of employment an 'equality clause'.

7.23   Unenforceable terms

Certain terms, while not being unlawful in the sense of rendering an employer liable to criminal prosecution or a civil action, may be unenforceable, as set out in **7.24–7.30** below.

7.24   *Terms which are unlawful or contrary to public policy*

A contract the terms of which are unlawful (eg to do an unlawful act) or which are contrary to public policy (eg a contract for an immoral purpose) is unenforceable. The same may be true where the contract, although capable of being performed lawfully, has in fact been performed illegally. Further, relief will not be granted to a party if to do so would 'affront the public conscience'. The general law as to illegality was summarised by the Court of Appeal in *Euro-Diam Ltd v Bathurst* [1990] 1 QB 1, [1988] 2 All ER 23. In *Colen v Cebrian (UK) Ltd* [2003] EWCA Civ 1676, [2004] ICR 568, the Court of Appeal gave the following guidance. In order for a contract to become unenforceable by reason of illegality, it must be shown either that the contract was entered into with the object of committing an illegal act or that it was performed with that objective. If the contract was lawful when entered into and was intended to be performed lawfully, an illegal act in the course of performance does not in every case make the entire contract unenforceable. It is necessary to consider the intentions of the parties to the contract. The court will not assist a party who has to rely on his own illegal act for the purposes of his claim. If he does not have to pray in aid the unlawful act, it is a question of fact in each case whether the method of performance of the contract or the degree of participation in the illegal act means that the contact is unenforceable by reason of illegality. The burden of establishing that the contract is illegal rests on the person making that allegation.

In *Payne v Enfield Technical Services Ltd* [2008] EWCA Civ 393, [2008] ICR 1423 and at [2008] IRLR 500, the Court of Appeal upheld the EAT's ruling that to defeat an unfair dismissal claim on the grounds that a contract of employment is illegal and unenforceable 'there must be some form of misrepresentation, some attempt to conceal the true facts of the relationship, before the contract is rendered illegal for the purposes of a doctrine rooted in public policy'.

In the employment context, illegality may arise in the context of defrauding the revenue. In that context (although the observation is of general application), the Court of Appeal has held that a party will only be prevented from relying on a contract by reason of illegality where the parties have knowingly entered arrangements which have to their knowledge represented the facts of the employment relationship as other than that they really were (cf *Enfield Technical Services* above, para 25). Thus, for example, it is not sufficient to prevent a person relying on a contract of employment that he has previously indicated to the Revenue that he was self-employed unless there was also some attempt to conceal the true facts – ie to claim to be self-employed when the parties know that the person is an employee. On similar facts, see also *Connolly v Whitestone Solicitors* (UKEAT/0445/10/ZT) (24 June 2011, unreported).

In another context, a foreign employee knowingly working illegally without a work permit will not be able to complain of unfair dismissal (*Sharma v Hindu Temple*, IDS Brief 464, p 5; for work permits, see **23.4**, FOREIGN EMPLOYEES). Similarly, the contract of employment of an employee taking employment in breach of the terms on which he has been permitted entry to the UK is likely to be unlawful (*Vakante v Governing Body of Addey and Stanhope*

School [2005] ICR 231, CA and *Zarkasi v Anindita* (UKEAT/0400/11/JOJ) (18 January 2012, unreported)), but working for less money than is stated on the employee's work permit application is not necessarily unlawful (*San Ling Chinese Medicine Centre v Lian Wei Ji* (UKEAT/0370/09) (25 January 2010, unreported).

If the unlawful element of the contract can be severed, a court may in certain circumstances allow the employee to pursue a claim based on the lawful elements of the contract (*Blue Chip Trading Ltd v Helbawi* [2009] IRLR 128). Further, if the employee was not aware of the fact that the contract was being performed unlawfully by the employer (by, for example, not deducting tax from remuneration) the employee may rely on the contract for the purposes of claiming employment protection rights (*Newland v Simons and Willer (Hairdressers) Ltd* [1981] ICR 521). However, ignorance of the law as opposed to the facts is no excuse (*Miller v Karlinski* (1945) 62 TLR 85). Nor is the fact that the parties did not intend to break the law relevant (*Salvesen v Simon* [1994] ICR 409). The mere fact that in the course of performing an otherwise lawful contract, the employee has committed an unlawful or immoral act does not bar him from bringing a claim for unfair dismissal (*Coral Leisure Group Ltd v Barnett* [1981] ICR 503; *Hewcastle Catering Ltd v Ahmed and Elkamah* [1992] ICR 626, [1991] IRLR 473, CA). Thus, the fact that an employee did not pay tax on occasional payments received outside his contract of employment did not have the effect of rendering the contract of employment illegal in *Annandale Engineering v Samson* [1994] IRLR 59. Further, the claim may be brought if the employer's conduct in participating in an illegal contract is so reprehensible in comparison with that of the employee that it would be wrong to allow the employer to rely on the illegality (cf *Euro-Diam*, above).

The distinction between unlawful tax evasion and lawful tax avoidance must be borne in mind. The fact that an employee lawfully arranges matters so as to minimise liability to tax does not render the contract of employment illegal (*Lightfoot v D & J Sporting Ltd* [1996] IRLR 64).

The fact that a contract is unenforceable by reason of illegality does not preclude a person employed under such a contract from bringing claims of sex or race (or presumably disability or religion or age or belief or sexual orientation) discrimination. The reason for this is that such actions do not seek to enforce the unenforceable contract (*Leighton v (1) Michael and (2) Charalambous* [1996] IRLR 67) unless the claim arises out of or is inextricably bound up with the conduct which causes the contract to be illegal (see *Hall v Woolston Hall Leisure Ltd* [2000] IRLR 578, CA, in which *Leighton* was approved; see also *Hougna v Allen* (UKEAT/0326/10/LA) [2011] All ER (D) 250 (Apr), for an example in the context of race discrimination).

7.25   *Terms automatically varied by statute*

Terms which, although they are agreed between the parties, are in breach of certain statutory provisions take effect as if varied to comply with those provisions. For example:

(a)   terms which are less advantageous than those which apply to a member of the opposite sex doing the same or like work, or work of equal value (see **21.8 EQUAL PAY**), or which infringe the law on sex discrimination; or

(b)   terms providing for the employment of directors for a guaranteed period of more than two years (see **8.3 DIRECTORS**).

7.26   *Restrictions upon contracting out of certain statutory provisions*

With some exceptions, for instance where a conciliation officer (see **2.3 ADVISORY, CONCILIATION AND ARBITRATION SERVICE**) has exercised his statutory powers in the settlement of certain claims or where there has been a valid compromise agreement (see **17.32 EMPLOYMENT TRIBUNALS**), an employer or employee may not contract out of the following Acts. Any attempt to do so will be ineffective.

Equality Act 2010 (see *s 144*)

Equal Pay Act 1970 (see *SDA 1975, s 77*)

ERA 1996, Part II (see *s 203(1), (2)*)

Trade Union and Labour Relations (Consolidation) Act 1992 (see *s 288*)

Working Time Regulations 1998 (save insofar as the *Regulations* permit the parties to agree that the operation of the *Regulations* is to be excluded or limited)

7.27   *Discriminatory terms*

Terms in contracts which are contrary to the provisions of the discrimination legislation are void and unenforceable against the person discriminated against: see *Equality Act 2010, s 143*. Similarly, any term in a collective agreement which discriminates on grounds of sex, sexual orientation or religion or belief is void and unenforceable against the party discriminated against: see *Equality Act 2010, s 145*.

7.28   *Terms in restraint of trade*

Sometimes, a contract will contain a term restricting the employee's freedom to work after he leaves his employment. Such terms will be regarded as 'in restraint of trade' and therefore unenforceable if their main purpose is simply to restrain competition. However, if the main purpose is to protect something in which the employer has a legitimate interest, such as trade secrets or confidential information, or to protect the employer's goodwill or *'customer connection'* (as it is called in this context), then such a term may be enforceable. These questions are discussed in more detail in RESTRAINT OF TRADE, CONFIDENTIALITY AND EMPLOYEE INTERVENTIONS **(39)**.

7.29   *Restrictions on industrial action*

Provisions in collective agreements which purport to restrict the right to take industrial action cannot form part of the individual contract of employment unless certain conditions are satisfied (see **5.5** COLLECTIVE AGREEMENTS).

7.30   *Unfair Contract Terms Act 1977*

The effect of the *Unfair Contract Terms Act 1977* (*'UCTA 1977'*) is to render certain types of contractual term unenforceable, and others unenforceable unless they satisfy a test of reasonableness laid down in *UCTA 1977, s 11* (namely, that the term was a fair and reasonable one to be included having regard to the circumstances which were, or ought reasonably to have been, known to or in the contemplation of the parties when the contract was made; in applying this test the court is directed to have regard to certain specific considerations).

Despite earlier indications to the contrary, it has now been held that *UCTA* does not apply to contracts of employment. The reason for this is that *UCTA* applies only to those who either 'deal as a consumer' or deal 'on the other [party's] written standard terms of business'. In *Keen v Commerzbank AG* [2006] EWCA Civ 1536, [2007] ICR 623, *sub nom Commerzbank AG v Keen* [2007] IRLR 132, the Court of Appeal held that an employee neither dealt as a consumer nor on his employer's standard terms of business. Employers do not deal with their employees as consumers; the business of an employer is not employing its staff.

In the light of this judgment, no further consideration is given to *UCTA* in this work.

7.31   CHANGES TO CONTRACTUAL TERMS

The general principle is that no change in the terms of an employee's contract may be made without his consent. Consent can come either from an employee's (express or implied) agreement to the proposed change, or from a pre-existing contractual provision allowing the employer unilaterally to effect variations. Where neither of these forms of consent is in place, a change in terms is likely to amount to a breach of contract.

If the proposed change is of great importance to the employer, the only course of action open to him in circumstances in which the employee does not consent, is to give notice to terminate the original contract and offer new terms. Great care must be taken to adhere to a fair procedure when doing this so as to avoid a successful claim for unfair dismissal (see UNFAIR DISMISSAL – II (52)).

A particular question which has caused difficulty is whether a change in terms and conditions mutually agreed between the parties can be enforced in the context of the transfer of an undertaking under the *Transfer of Undertakings (Protection of Employment) Regulations 1981 (SI 1981/1794)* ('*TUPE 1981*'), which have now been replaced by the *Transfer of Undertakings (Protection of Employment) Regulations 2006 (SI 2006/246)* ('*TUPE 2006*'). This subject is considered fully in TRANSFER OF UNDERTAKINGS (50).

7.32 Agreement

Consent may be express, by the employee agreeing to the change orally or, preferably, in writing (see *Judge v Crown Leisure Ltd* [2005] EWCA Civ 571, [2005] IRLR 823 on the importance, in discussions about contractual variation, of an intention to create legal relations). On the question of consideration for agreed variations, see *Lee v GEC Plessey Telecommunications* [1993] IRLR 383, where the High Court held that there was good consideration for any pay rise which followed pay negotiations, so that the employer was legally bound by the increased rate of pay.

Alternatively, consent may be *implied*, by the employee continuing to work for the employer without protest for a significant period of time whilst being aware of a change imposed by his employer. Where a change is imposed by the employer and the employee continues to work without objection, it may be that the employee will be held impliedly to have consented to the change. Where the change is one which has an immediate effect on the employee, continuing to work without protest may very well indicate consent. However, where the change is one which does not have an immediate practical effect, the court should exercise caution before inferring consent (*Jones v Associated Tunnelling Co Ltd* [1981] IRLR 477, *Aparau v Iceland Frozen Foods plc* [1996] IRLR 119, *Solectron Scotland Ltd v Roper* [2004] IRLR 4, *Cumbria County Council v Dow (No 2)* [2008] IRLR 109, EAT). In addition, the actual change in the employee's working conditions must be more than "trivial" under those changed conditions is to be regarded as implied consent: see the Court of Appeal decision in *Khatri v Co-operative Centrale Raiffeisen-Boerenleenbank BA* [2010] IRLR 715 applying *Solectron Scotland* (above).

A further example of a variation is *Attrill & Other v Dresdner Kleinwort Limited & Anor* [2012] EWCA Civ 394, where the variation was effected by the employees' implicit acceptance of an offer (concerning the bonus pool to be made available to employees) made during a 'Town Hall' meeting broadcast over the internet. This was an offer to vary the terms of the employees' contract and, in the circumstances, the employer had waived any requirement for the employees to communicate acceptance (although, if this requirement had not been waived, such communication of acceptance could not be inferred from the employees' remaining in employment). There was consideration for this variation. *Attrill* should also be noted for its discussion of implied acceptance of variations.

Where an employee protests but then continues to work for a considerable time, he may bear an evidential burden of showing that he did not impliedly agree to the new term (see *Henry v London General Transport Services Ltd* [2002] ICR 910, [2002] IRLR 472, where the employee continued to work for two years).

7.33 Variation clauses

In some contracts, the employer will expressly reserve a power to vary the terms. Such variation clauses are sometimes drafted in wide terms, purporting for example to allow the employer to make such changes as it sees fit from time to time. The answer to the question of whether or not such clauses are effective is a "qualified yes" (*Malone v British Airways* [2010] EWCA Civ 1225, [2011] ICR 125, [2011] IRLR 32; *Wandsworth London Borough Council v D'Silva* [1998] IRLR 193). These qualifications include the following. Courts take a strict approach to the interpretation of such clauses, and will construe them *contra proferentem*. Clear words are required to create a power unilaterally to alter the terms of the contract. Variation clauses specifying the terms which the employer is empowered to vary (as opposed to arrogating a general power to vary any term) are more likely to find favour with courts. The court is unlikely to favour an interpretation which does more than vary the contractual provisions with which the employer is required to comply. A court is unlikely to allow an interpretation which goes further and which may affect the rights of the employee under the contract. Thus, the extent to which an employer will be permitted to rely on an express provision entitling him to vary the terms of a contract, and so to evade the general rule that changes to contracts must be mutually agreed, is likely to be limited.

7.34   Variation, breach and termination

Any change in terms to which the employee does not consent is *prima facie* a breach of contract. If the change is a significant one, the employee may be entitled to resign and allege that he has been constructively dismissed (see **46.19** TERMINATION OF EMPLOYMENT). However, where an employer unilaterally imposes radically different terms of employment, it may be that the correct interpretation is that the employer has terminated the original contract and replaced it with another. Accordingly, there would be a dismissal by the employer (and immediate re-employment) which entitled the employee to bring unfair dismissal proceedings (*Hogg v Dover College* [1990] ICR 39; *Alcan Extrusions v Yates* [1996] IRLR 327; and see UNFAIR DISMISSAL– I (51)). For guidance on the question of whether the situation is one of dismissal and reengagement or mere variation of terms, see *Cumbria County Council v Dow (No 2)* [2008] IRLR 109, EAT and *Potter v North Cumbria Acute Hospitals NHS Trust* [2009] IRLR 900: where the parties have not (expressly or impliedly) agreed to terminate the old contract, their intention is to be ascertained from all the circumstances, including the "elasticity" of the original contract and the cumulative effect of any minor variations.

7.35   EMPLOYEE'S REMEDIES FOR BREACH OF CONTRACT OF EMPLOYMENT

If an employer is in breach of contract, his employee may bring proceedings in the High Court or the county court for sums due under the contract and for damages. The employee can bring such an action while remaining in employment. However, if the employer's breach of contract is sufficiently serious, the employee may treat himself as dismissed, leave, and bring proceedings for his prospective loss (see WRONGFUL DISMISSAL (56)) as well as for any sums outstanding at the date of dismissal. The courts are also able to grant declaratory relief. If the breach of contract involves a deduction from pay, the employee may present a complaint to the employment tribunal under *Part II* of the *ERA 1996* (which contains provisions formerly found in the *Wages Act 1986*) (see **32.6** PAY I). Employment tribunals now also have jurisdiction in relation to certain claims for contractual damages arising on the termination of an employee's employment (see below).

7.36   Damages

Extent of damages which can be claimed

Where an employee is dismissed summarily in breach of contract, the *prima facie* measure of damages is the sum which the employer would have had to pay in order to bring the contract to an end lawfully – that is to say, the sum payable in respect of the notice period. However, it will often be a term of the contract that the employer must follow a prescribed disciplinary or other procedure prior to dismissal. In such cases, if the employee can show that the conduct of the disciplinary procedure would take time and, therefore, extend the period of employment, he may be able to claim as damages lost wages for the time which the disciplinary or other procedure would have taken, in addition to pay for the notice period (see *Boyo v Lambeth London Borough Council* [1994] ICR 727, [1995] IRLR 50, CA and *Focsa Services (UK) Ltd v Birkett* [1996] IRLR 325). However, in assessing compensation, the tribunal must work on the basis that the outcome of the pursuit of the disciplinary or other procedure would have been the same (*Janciuk v Winerite* [1998] IRLR 63). This means that an employee cannot be compensated in a breach of contract claim on the basis that, had a contractual disciplinary procedure been pursued, he would not have been dismissed. The limit of compensation is the time which would have been taken to complete the procedure.

Damages payable will include damages for loss of pension rights that would have accrued had the employee not been dismissed summarily in breach of contract: *Silvey v Pendragon plc* [2001] IRLR 685.

On the question of whether payment in lieu of notice should include bonus payments, see *Locke v Candy and Candy Ltd* [2010] EWCA Civ 1350, where the Court of Appeal held by a majority (based on the particular contractual terms in issue) that an employee who was summarily dismissed shortly before the payment date of a discretionary bonus was not entitled to the bonus as part of his payment in lieu of notice, because the bonus clause stated that employees had to be employed in order to receive the bonus. However, where there is no express term making the payment of a bonus conditional upon being employed at that time, one cannot simply be implied: *Rutherford v Seymour Pierce Ltd* [2010] EWHC 375 (QB), [2010] IRLR 606. The court found that such a term was not necessary for the contract to operate satisfactorily, was manifestly unreasonable, and was not customary in that area of business.

Of course, an employee need not actually have commenced duties in order to be able to bring a claim. So, for example, where an offer of employment is made and accepted, there is a valid contract of employment even if the start date is postponed. If the contract is terminated before the actual start date, the employee will have a claim for wrongful dismissal. He may also have other claims such as discrimination (see *Sarker v South Tees Acute Hospitals NHS Trust* [1997] IRLR 328 and **20.5 ENGAGEMENT OF EMPLOYEES**).

7.37   *No damages for loss of the chance to claim unfair dismissal*

Sometimes, employers dismiss employees summarily in order to prevent the employee from accruing a sufficient period of qualifying employment to bring a claim for unfair dismissal. Thus, for example, a person with a month's notice period might be summarily dismissed two weeks before accruing one year's continuous employment. However, it has been held that a claim for damages for breach of contract cannot include damages for the loss of a chance to bring an unfair dismissal claim: *Harper v Virgin Net Ltd* [2004] EWCA Civ 271, [2004] IRLR 390, CA.

7.38   *Damages for loss of reputation*

In *Malik v BCCI SA* [1997] IRLR 462, the House of Lords accepted that it might be possible to recover damages for loss of reputation caused by a breach of contract, provided that a relevant breach of contract could be established and that requirements of causation, remoteness and mitigation are satisfied. It was not necessary that the conduct relied upon be directed at the employees. In that case, the individual employees alleged that their employer had run a corrupt and dishonest business and that, as a result, the employees were tainted by their involvement with their former employer and were at a disadvantage in the job market. These facts were assumed to be true for the purposes of the argument, although no findings were made in respect of them. The House of Lords held that it would be a breach of the implied term of trust and confidence to operate a dishonest business and that the employees were entitled to argue that they could recover damages for any consequent loss as a result of damage inflicted on their employment prospects. The correct measure of damages where the breach affects employment prospects is to ask: but for the breach by the employer, what would prospective employers considering the claimant's application have done and what would have been the outcome for the employee? (*BCCI SA v Ali (No 3)* [2002] EWCA Civ 82, [2002] IRLR 460).

7.39 *Pecuniary loss only*

The *Malik* case does not alter the principle that damages are not recoverable for the manner of a dismissal, according to the House of Lords in *Johnson v Unisys Ltd* [2003] 1 AC 518. By a majority of four to one, their Lordships held that there was no right at common law to recover damages for injury to feeling (even in the case where that injury manifested itself as a psychological injury) caused by dismissal. Their Lordships held that it would be wrong to develop by judicial invention a right to compensation in circumstances where Parliament had already intervened by creating the right not to be unfairly dismissed. The courts therefore ought not to allow persons to side-step the limits on that right which Parliament had put in place by the creation of an inconsistent common law right. Lord Hoffmann expressed the view (obiter) that damages for unfair dismissal should extend beyond pecuniary loss to include 'in an appropriate case . . . compensation for distress, humiliation, damage to reputation in the community or to family life'. However, the House of Lords subsequently declined to follow Lord Hoffmann's *obiter* comment and has re-affirmed that damages for unfair dismissal are limited to financial losses: *Dunnachie v Kingston upon Hull City Council* [2004] UKHL 36, [2004] IRLR 727.

A number of cases in which employees alleged that they had suffered psychiatric injury as a consequence of the investigative or disciplinary process followed by their employer, rather than their dismissal, were struck out at first instance on the ground that they were barred by *Johnson*. However, the House of Lords subsequently held that the effect of *Johnson* is only to preclude common law claims where the employee seeks to recover damages consequent on dismissal: *Eastwood v Magnox Electric plc* and *McCabe v Cornwall County Council* [2004] IRLR 733. Where it is possible to claim that loss or injury has flowed not from dismissal but from pre-dismissal steps (such as suspension or the anterior conduct of disciplinary procedures), then *Johnson* does not prevent claims being brought: see for example *Gogay v Hertfordshire County Council* [2000] IRLR 703, CA (compensation awarded for psychological injury as a consequence of the manner in which an allegation of misconduct was investigated). The Supreme Court has confirmed the position: in the conjoined appeals of *Edwards v Chesterfield Royal Hospital NHS Foundation Trust* and *Botham v Ministry of Defence* [2011] UKSC 58, [2012] 2 WLR 55, [2012] 2 All ER 278, [2012] ICR 201, [2012] IRLR 129, it was held (by a majority of 5-2) that the effect of *Johnson* was to preclude damages for loss attributable to the unfair manner of a dismissal in breach of the terms of the employment contract. Where provisions of the employer's disciplinary code are incorporated into the contract, they are nonetheless not ordinary contractual terms, with breaches falling to be dealt with under the *ERA 1996* rather than as free-standing claims for breach of contract.

7.40 *'Stigma' damages*

The employee is under a duty to mitigate his pecuniary loss, for example (where he has been dismissed) by seeking alternative employment. In *Chagger v Abbey National plc* [2010] ICR 397, [2010] IRLR 47, the claimant (who had been employed as a risk analyst) contended that he had been stigmatised by prospective employers, who were unwilling to employ him because he had brought successful claims against his former employer for unfair dismissal, discrimination and breach of contract. He therefore retrained to work as a teacher on a substantially lower salary. His former employer argued that the claimant's damages should not include the ongoing financial consequences of stigmatisation by third parties, since that was too remote from the former employer's unlawful act. The Court of Appeal found for the claimant on this point: an employee has to be compensated for the full loss flowing from the unlawful act of his former employer, and the involvement of third party prospective employers did not sever the causal chain. Damages may now therefore in principle extend to such 'stigma' effects. To date however, there are no reported cases of stigma damages being awarded: even in *Chagger* (upon remission to the Tribunal following the Court of Appeal decision referred to above) no such award was made.

7.41   *Express terms regarding damages*

In some contracts, most usually those of senior executives, there is a term which provides for prescribed sums to be payable by the employer on breach. A question may arise whether such terms are liquidated damages clauses, which are valid; or penalties, which are unenforceable. A clause is a liquidated damages clause where it represents a genuine pre-estimate of a party's loss in the event of breach. Where the amount to be paid appears designed to deter or punish the wrong-doer rather than to compensate the innocent party, the clause is a penalty. In *Murray v Leisureplay plc* [2005] IRLR 946 a clause entitling an executive to three years' pay on termination without the obligation to mitigate was held not to be a penalty. The Court held that a useful test was whether the sum to be paid was extravagant and unconscionable. See also *Tullett Prebon Group Ltd v El-Hajjali* [2008] IRLR 760 for an example of a liquidated damages clause, and *CMC Group Plc v Zhang* [2006] EWCA Civ 408 for an example of a penalty clause.

7.42   Injunctions

Circumstances in which injunctions may be granted

In certain circumstances, the courts will grant an employee an injunction to restrain the employer from taking action in breach of contract. This may be done to restrain the implementation of a dismissal where a contractual disciplinary or disputes procedure has not been exhausted (see, eg, *Irani v Southampton and South-West Hampshire Health Authority* [1985] ICR 590 and observations in *R v BBC, ex p Lavelle* [1983] ICR 99). In *Barros D'Sa v University Hospital and Warwickshire NHS Trust* [2001] IRLR 691, there was a two-stage disciplinary procedure. The first stage involved an investigation by an inquiry panel. The second stage involved a disciplinary hearing at which decisions would be taken as to the appropriate course of action depending upon the circumstances and the inquiry panel's recommendations. At the second stage, the employer sought to introduce new material and new allegations against the employee which had not been considered at the inquiry panel stage. The Court of Appeal granted an injunction to prevent the new material and allegation being considered. An employer was not entitled to depart from a contractual disciplinary procedure on the ground that he considered that the relationship of trust and confidence had broken down.

In *Mezey v South West London and St George's Mental Health NHS Trust* [2007] IRLR 237, 244, the Court of Appeal upheld the grant of an injunction to restrain a suspension on full pay on the basis that the decision to suspend, even if permitted by the express terms of the contract, could involve a breach of the implied term of trust and confidence. A further development in that case saw the Court of Appeal uphold the grant of a further injunction against the employer taking capability proceedings against an employee who had already been cleared by an investigatory panel ([2010] EWCA Civ 293).

An injunction has also been granted to restrain the enforcement of an instruction the employer was not contractually entitled to give (see *Hughes v Southwark London Borough Council* [1988] IRLR 55) and to prevent a dismissal which would be in breach of a contractual redundancy selection procedure (*Anderson v Pringle of Scotland Ltd* [1998] IRLR 64, 1998 SLT 754, OH). However, an injunction will only be granted in the exceptional case where the employer still has full confidence in the employee's continuing ability and other necessary attributes (*Powell v Brent London Borough Council* [1988] ICR 176; *Alexander v Standard Telephones & Cables plc* [1990] ICR 291). In *Robb v Hammersmith and Fulham London Borough Council* [1991] ICR 514, it was suggested that this might not be necessary where the employee will merely be remaining at home under suspension pending a disciplinary hearing. The better view is that no injunction should be granted unless trust and confidence remain between the employer and the employee. To grant an injunction in circumstances where trust and confidence did not remain would be inconsistent with the general rule that there cannot be specific performance of a contract of service. However, within modern contracts of employment, there are often a number of provisions which may be enforced by an injunction without compelling the parties to a contract of employment to perform their obligations to employ and/or to work. Where the parties are in agreement that the contract of employment subsists, albeit in a qualified form (such as where the employee is suspended), then the court may enforce by order parts of the contract which do not compel the parties to co-operate any more than they would be prepared to do in any event. Thus if, for example, the parties agree that the contract subsists albeit that the employee is suspended, then the court may enforce contractual provisions relating to, for example, discipline. Enforcement of such provisions in those circumstances does not require a reluctant employer to employ or a reluctant employee to work (see *Peace v City of Edinburgh Council* [1999] IRLR 417).

The injunction may, if necessary, be made conditional upon the employee undertaking to work in accordance with instructions (*Wadcock v London Borough of Brent* [1990] IRLR 223). Similarly, if new working practices are introduced in breach of contract, an injunction will not be granted where, for practical purposes, the old system cannot be restored (*MacPherson v Lambeth London Borough Council* [1988] IRLR 470). See also *Dietman v Brent London Borough Council* [1988] ICR 842, *Ali v Southwark London Borough Council* [1988] ICR 567, [1988] IRLR 100 and *Wishart v National Association of Citizens Advice Bureaux Ltd* [1990] ICR 794.

7.43   *Interlocutory injunctions*

The court will usually first be asked to grant an *interlocutory* injunction, ie one which seeks to restrain the alleged breach of contract pending trial (which may not happen for several months or even longer). At the interlocutory stage, the judge does not hear oral evidence and will not have time to determine complex questions that may arise. The correct approach is therefore to decide, first, whether there is a serious question to be tried and, second, whether any injustice caused by granting or refusing to grant the injunction could be properly compensated by an award of damages later. A 'serious question to be tried' means that there is an arguable case that the claimant is entitled to the relief sought. There must be evidence which supports each of the constituent parts of the claimant's claim. The judge will not determine whether the claimant's evidence is true. He will, however, have to see that there is at that stage a sufficient basis in fact and law to mean that the claim has some merit. If there is a serious question and damages would not be an adequate remedy, the court may grant an injunction, and the decision whether to do so will depend upon the 'balance of convenience'. This will often lead it to preserve the *status quo* (see *American Cyanamid Co v Ethicon Ltd* [1975] AC 396). For an example of an interlocutory injunction against dismissal, see *Lauffer v Barking, Havering and Redbridge University Hospitals NHS Trust* [2009] EWHC 2360 (QB), [2010] Med LR 68, where the employer's failure to apply its disciplinary procedure deprived the employee of the opportunity to clear his name and avoid dismissal. See also *Mezey v South West London and St George's Mental Health NHS Trust* [2010] IRLR 512, where the Court of Appeal upheld the granting of an injunction to restrain an NHS Trust from taking capability proceedings in breach of its disciplinary procedures.

Somewhat different considerations may apply where the decision at the interlocutory stage will effectively determine the dispute in favour of one party or the other. In those circumstances, the court will do its best to form a view as to which party has the stronger case (see *Lansing Linde Ltd v Kerr* [1991] ICR 428). Also, where the dispute turns upon a question of law or the construction of a document, the court has power to make a final determination of that question at an interlocutory stage (*Civil Procedure Rules, part 24*). For an example of this course being taken in an employment dispute, see *Jones v Gwent County Council* [1992] IRLR 521.

7.43 Contract of Employment

The courts will not generally make mandatory interlocutory orders for the continued payment of wages where these are sought as an indirect means of obtaining an injunction (see *Alexander*, above; *Jakeman v South West Thames Regional Health Authority and London Ambulance Service* [1990] IRLR 62).

7.44 Jurisdiction

Employment tribunals have jurisdiction to hear claims for breach of contracts of employment or contracts 'connected with employment' other than personal injury claims (*Employment Tribunals Extension of Jurisdiction (England and Wales) Order 1994 (SI 1994/1623)*).

The claim must be one which 'arises or is outstanding on the termination of the employee's employment' (*art 3(c)*). This means that the employee must have an enforceable but unsatisfied claim at the date of termination. The formulation does not enable tribunals to determine claims which, at the termination of employment, are contingent: *Peninsula Business Services Ltd v Sweeney* [2004] IRLR 49, EAT. *Article 5* specifically excludes a claim relating to:

(a) a term requiring the employer to provide living accommodation for the employee;

(b) a term imposing an obligation on the employer or the employee in connection with living accommodation;

(c) a term relating to intellectual property;

(d) a term imposing an obligation of confidence; and

(e) a term which is in restraint of trade.

Article 7 provides that an employee must present a contract claim:

(i) within three months of the effective date of termination of the contract giving rise to the claim (see **51.13 Unfair Dismissal – I**);

(ii) where there is no effective date of termination, within three months of the date when the employee last worked in the employment which has been terminated; or

(iii) within such further period as the tribunal considers reasonable, where it was not reasonably practicable for the employee to present a claim in time (see **18.25 Employment Tribunals – I**).

The tribunal has jurisdiction only in respect of contracts of employment or those connected with employment (*ERA 1996, s 3(2)*). Thus, an agreement compromising a wrongful dismissal claim effected during employment falls within the tribunal's jurisdiction: *Rock-it Cargo Ltd v Green* [1997] IRLR 581.

The provisions as to the time when a claim must be made mean that the employment tribunal does not have jurisdiction to consider a claim made during the currency of employment. Its jurisdiction is limited to claims submitted after the termination of the employment: see *Capek v Lincolnshire County Council* [2000] ICR 878, CA. Further, the claim must arise or be outstanding on the termination of employment. This means that the tribunal does not have jurisdiction to entertain claims that only arise for the first time after the employment has terminated, eg a settlement of a dismissal claim made after the employment has ended: *Miller Bros and F P Butler v Johnston* [2002] IRLR 386.

Employers are entitled to counterclaim (*arts 4, 8*). Counterclaims must be made at a time when a contract claim by an employee is already before the tribunal and has not been settled or withdrawn. The counterclaim must arise out of a contract with the employee who has made the contract claim.

The time limit for presenting counterclaims is six weeks from the date when the employer (or other respondent to the employee's contract claim) received a copy of the originating application in respect of that employee's contract claim. This period is subject to extension where it was not reasonably practicable for the employer's counterclaim to be presented in time (see **18.25** EMPLOYMENT TRIBUNALS – I).

The Order contains specific provisions relating to death and bankruptcy.

7.45 The maximum award which a tribunal may make in respect of a contract claim, or a number of contract claims relating to the same contract, is £25,000 *(art 10)*. In many cases, the potential value of a contractual claim may exceed £25,000. The question may arise whether a successful employee in the tribunal who recovers the maximum award may then bring fresh proceedings in the High Court for the remainder of the value of the contractual claim. In *Fraser v HLMAD Ltd* [2006] IRLR 687, [2006] ICR 1395, the Court of Appeal held that no further claim may be brought in the civil courts once a tribunal has ruled on a wrongful dismissal claim. The key point is that, once the court has decided a matter, a claimant may not ask another court to deal with that same matter again. The reason for this is that the employee no longer has a cause of action which he is able to litigate. The cause of action – breach of contract – has been replaced by, or 'merged in' the judgment of the tribunal. The concept of a cause of action merging in a judgment, so precluding a further action being brought in respect of the same cause of action, is well established in law (see *Halsbury's Laws*, Vol 26, paras 550–551). Further, there are several cases in which a party who has succeeded in one forum which has a limited power to award damages has been precluded from seeking to institute fresh proceedings in respect of the same matter in another forum in order to recover the shortfall. In *Hills v Co-operative Wholesale Society Ltd* [1940] 2 KB 435, an employee brought an action in the High Court and in the county court against his employer in respect of the same complaint. A defence of common employment was available to the employer in the High Court but not in the county court. The employer paid into the county court the maximum sum which the employee could recover in that forum and the employee accepted that sum. The Court of Appeal held that the employee could not continue with the High Court proceedings. His cause of action had been completely satisfied when he accepted the payment made in respect of the county court proceedings, notwithstanding that there was a limit on the sum that the county court could award. See also *Wright v London General Omnibus Co* (1877) 2 QBD 271; *Clarke v Yorke* (1882) 52 LJ Ch 32.

It is suggested that a person should not be entitled to bring the same cause of action simultaneously in the tribunal and in the county court or the High Court. Rather, he should be put to his election. An analogy is to be found in *Australian Commercial Research and Development Ltd v ANZ McCaughan Merchant Bank Ltd* [1989] 3 All ER 65 where a claimant who had commenced proceedings based on the same cause of action in both England and Queensland was put to his election. It is important that a person chooses carefully in which forum to begin, since cause of action estoppel may be created where an application to the tribunal is dismissed upon withdrawal by the applicant (*Barber v Staffordshire County Council* [1996] ICR 379, followed in *Osborne v Valve (Engineering) Services Ltd* (24 November 2000, unreported), EAT). In *Osborne* the court held that: (1) the principles of *res judicata* bar an employee from bringing High Court wrongful dismissal proceedings after the same cause of action has been determined by the tribunal; and (2) a 'determination' by the tribunal includes a dismissal by the tribunal following withdrawal of the claim. Therefore, the safest course to adopt in a case where an applicant wishes to pursue High Court wrongful dismissal proceedings after having already commenced tribunal proceedings is to invite the tribunal to stay the case before it. A stay does not determine the proceedings. It simply prevents further steps being taken until the stay is lifted.

However, a number of cases have suggested a more flexible approach to those who commence proceedings in the tribunal and withdraw in order to sue in the civil courts; the cases are not wholly easy to reconcile. In *Sajid v Sussex Muslim Society* [2002] IRLR 113, an applicant presented a breach of contract claim to a tribunal and later withdrew it. His express reason for withdrawing was in order to present the claim in a court whose jurisdiction to award damages was not limited to £25,000. The Court of Appeal held that his claim was entitled to proceed. The second proceedings did not offend the principle of *res judicata*, which was finality in litigation. Since it was clear that the purpose of withdrawal of the tribunal claim was so as to bring county court proceedings, the principle behind *res judicata* was not engaged. Unlike the applicant in *Barber*, Mr Sajid had not intended by withdrawing his claim to abandon his cause of action.

A different analysis prevailed in *Lennon v Birmingham City Council* [2001] EWCA Civ 435, [2001] IRLR 826, decided by the Court of Appeal before *Sajid* but not referred to in the latter case. In *Lennon*, the applicant brought and subsequently withdrew a complaint in which she alleged that she had been harassed and bullied by her employer. This was regarded by the employer as a complaint of sex discrimination. A tribunal dismissed the claim on withdrawal. Later she brought a claim in the county court in which she relied on the same allegations which had provided the foundation for her tribunal claim. The Court of Appeal held that the claim was rightly struck out under the doctrine of issue estoppel. The court expressly rejected the argument that the reason for the withdrawal of the complaint could be relevant: all that mattered was the simple fact of the dismissal of the claim by the tribunal on withdrawal.

The Court of Appeal has sought to reconcile the apparent tension between *Sajid* and *Lennon* in *Ako v Rothschild Asset Management Ltd* [2002] EWCA Civ 236, [2002] ICR 899 (applied in *Khan v Heywood and Middleton Primary Care Trust* [2007] ICR 24, *[2006] IRLR 793*). In *Ako*, the applicant lodged a complaint of discrimination, which was subsequently dismissed on withdrawal. A week after the dismissal of the first complaint, she lodged a second complaint containing the same allegations against the same respondent but also added a new respondent. It was found that her intention had not been to cease the litigation against Rothschild, but only to add in the additional respondent. The Court of Appeal held that, as a matter of general legal principle, a court could review the matrix of fact surrounding a legal act in order to understand its effect. Therefore, there could be cases where the circumstances surrounding the withdrawal of a claim meant that the cause of action was not exhausted. The court drew attention to procedural rules in the common law courts, which enabled proceedings that had been discontinued to be revived with permission. There was no such rule in the tribunal. Its omission meant that the strict application of the rules of estoppel could work an injustice.

However, the findings of an employment tribunal can create an issue estoppel in subsequent proceedings in the High Court, even where the issues were presented differently or supported by fresh arguments: *Green v Hampshire County Council* [1979] ICR 861; *Smith v Chelsea Football Club plc* [2010] EWHC 1168 (QB).

On the other hand, there will be no abuse of process where the issues being litigated in one forum (for example, a breach of contract claim in the High Court) were fundamentally different from those already being litigated in the other (for example, an unfair dismissal or victimisation claim in the Tribunal): *University of London v Tariquez-Zaman* [2010] EWHC 908 (QB).

7.46 **Disclosure**

This section is principally concerned with the remedies of the employee against the employer when the latter has acted in breach of contract. However, the situation may also arise when the employer has become mixed up in alleged wrongdoing by third parties. In *A v Company B Ltd* [1997] IRLR 405, an employee was dismissed by his employer after allegations of gross misconduct had been made to the employer by a third party. The employer did not identify the complainant or specify the nature of the complaints that had been made. The employee took the view that false allegations had been made about him and wished to institute an action against the third party alleging defamation. In order that the employee could prosecute that action, the High Court ordered that the employer disclose details of the allegations which had been made about him by the third party, following the principles laid down in *Norwich Pharmacal Co v Customs and Excise Comrs* [1974] AC 133.

7.47   EMPLOYER'S REMEDIES FOR BREACH OF CONTRACT OF EMPLOYMENT

Withholding or deduction of wages

If an employee does not perform any of his contractual duties, he is not entitled to his contractual wage. Thus, an employee is not entitled to be paid for days when he is on strike.

If the employee refuses to perform the full range of his contractual duties, particularly if this refusal is in pursuance of industrial action, the purpose of which is to disrupt the employer's business, the employee will not be entitled to his full contractual wage (see *Miles v Wakefield Metropolitan District Council* [1987] ICR 368). In *Wiluszynski v Tower Hamlets London Borough Council* [1989] IRLR 259, the Court of Appeal held that the Council was entitled to withhold the whole of the employee's wages when the employee refused to perform a substantial part of his duties and it was clear that the employer was not accepting the work which was performed as substantial performance of the contract. In *British Telecommunications plc v Ticehurst* [1992] ICR 383, it was held that a manager who intended to continue participating in a withdrawal of goodwill could be sent home without pay.

Alternatively, the employer may be able to deduct from the employee's wages a sum representing the financial loss suffered by him as a result of the employee's breach of contract (see *Sim v Rotherham Metropolitan Borough Council* [1986] ICR 897).

In *Cooper v Isle of Wight College* [2007] EWHC 2831 (QB), [2008] IRLR 124, it was held that the appropriate sum which an employer was entitled to deduct in respect of a one day strike was $1/260^{th}$ of a year's pay on the basis that there are 260 working days in the year.

In the case where the employee engages in action short of a strike, it is open to the employer to decline to make any payment on the basis that he is only prepared to accept full performance of the employee's obligations (*Miles* above). An employee who carries out only part of his duties does so at risk. There is no right to claim a quantum meruit. In *Spackman v London Metropolitan University* [2007] IRLR 744, the employee refused to perform some tasks and the employer deducted 30% of the employee's pay. Having held that the employer could lawfully have paid nothing, the court held that there was no breach of contract by deducting 30% of the employee's pay.

The employer's right to withhold pay may arise in many situations where the employee refuses to work. In *Luke v Stoke-on-Trent Council* [2007] EWCA Civ 761, [2007] ICR 1678, [2007] IRLR 777, the Court of Appeal held that an employer was entitled not to pay an employee who felt unable to attend her place of work after a breakdown in her relationship with her employer. The employer had reasonably required her to return to work. Since she had failed to do so, there was no entitlement to pay.

(See also **32.14 Pay – I.**)

7.47a   Acceptance of fundamental breach

If the employee is in fundamental breach of his contractual obligations, the employer can accept the breach and bring the contract to an end. Such a fundamental breach will generally consist of gross misconduct, extreme incompetence, or a major failure to carry out the work required of the employee. To go on strike will generally amount to a fundamental breach of contract. See also **43.2 Strikes and Industrial Action** and **56.6, 56.7 Wrongful Dismissal**.

7.47b   Contract of Employment

7.47b Damages

An employer may bring proceedings against an employee for damages for breach of contract (see, eg, *Janata Bank v Ahmed* [1981] ICR 791). Situations which may give rise to such proceedings are a breach of the employee's duty of fidelity, breach of his duty of care and failure to give the notice of termination he is contractually obliged to give. In practice, such claims are rare (but see *Cheltenham Borough Council v Laird* [2009] EWHC 1253 (QB), [2009] IRLR 621, an unsuccessful claim by a local authority against a former employee for the costs it would not have incurred if it had employed someone else). What is more common is an application for an injunction to restrain disclosure of confidential information or to enforce a restrictive covenant (see RESTRAINT OF TRADE, CONFIDENTIALITY AND EMPLOYEE INTERVENTIONS (39)).

Parties to contracts are entitled to make their own provision for compensation in the event of breach by one party. The law distinguishes between liquidated damages clauses (those containing genuine pre-estimates of loss and designed to compensate the innocent party) and penalty clauses (those designed to deter or punish a wrongdoer) – the former are unforceable, the latter are not. A payment to an employee on dismissal is likely to be regarded as a penalty if it is extravagant and unconscionable: *Murray v Leisureplay plc* [2005] EWCA Civ 963, [2005] IRLR 946. These clauses are relatively uncommon in employment contracts. In *Giraud UK Ltd v Smith* [2000] IRLR 763, however, the contract provided that in the event that the employee failed to give and work the notice period stipulated by the contract, there would be a deduction from his final payment 'equivalent to the number of days short'. The employee left without notice. The employer refused to make any final payment to the employee. The employer argued that it was entitled to a payment from the employee of four weeks' pay. The EAT confirmed that employment contracts may contain liquidated damages clauses, but found that in this case the clause was a penalty because there was no limit of liability to the employer's actual loss. See also *Tullett Prebon Group Ltd v El-Hajjali* [2008] EWHC 1924 (QB), [2008] IRLR 760 for an example of a liquidated damages clause successfully relied upon by an employer.

7.47c Injunction or specific performance

In no circumstances may the employee be compelled to work by injunction or by an order of specific performance. That was the common law and the principle is enacted in *TULRCA 1992, s 236*. That applies also if such compulsion will be the practical result of granting an injunction against a third party, eg the only alternative employer (*Warren v Mendy* [1989] ICR 525); the court will not make an order which would prevent the employee from earning his living. However, the Court of Appeal held in *Evening Standard Co Ltd v Henderson* [1987] ICR 588 that it may be possible to restrain an employee who does not give proper notice (see **46.17** TERMINATION OF EMPLOYMENT) from working elsewhere during his notice period so long as the employer will provide him with all his contractual benefits without actually requiring him to work. The *Henderson* principle was approved in *Provident Financial Group plc and Whitegates Estate Agency Ltd v Hayward* [1989] ICR 160, where an express contractual prohibition was relied upon. However, the Court of Appeal indicated that no injunction would be granted if the plaintiff's business had nothing to do with that of the new employer. It also recognised that an employee might need to work and exercise his skills (the employer in *Hayward* had put the employee on 'garden leave' during his notice period, whereas in *Henderson* work was available if the employee wanted it), and refused to grant an injunction after considering the non-competitive nature of the job the employee wished to take up, and the length of the unexpired notice period (see also *Warren*).

In *William Hill Organisation Ltd v Tucker* [1998] IRLR 313, the Court of Appeal appeared to impose further limitations on the availability of the 'garden leave injunction' remedy. The court held that it was necessary to consider in each case whether the consideration moving from the employer obliged the employer to permit the employee to do work, or whether the full extent of the obligation is to pay the employee. If the employer was obliged to permit the employee to carry out work, then the court would be unlikely to grant a garden leave injunction in the absence of an express provision which entitled the employer not to provide work and/or required the employee to agree not to attend work during the notice period. It was unlikely that such a provision would be implied. However, even where an express term was present, the court would not grant relief to any greater extent than would be granted in respect of a justifiable covenant in restraint of trade (see **39.6 RESTRAINT OF TRADE, CONFIDENTIALITY AND EMPLOYEE INTERVENTIONS**).

A garden leave injunction was granted in *SG&R Valuation Service Co LLC v Boudrais* [2008] IRLR 770 notwithstanding the absence of any express provision for garden leave in the employees' contracts. Although the employees had a right to work during their notice periods, this right was vitiated because the employees had, during their notice periods, committed wrongdoing by which they would or might profit. By those breaches of their contracts, they had "demonstrated in a serious way that they were not ready or willing to work, or that they had not rendered it impossible or reasonably impracticable for the employer to provide work". This principle – expressly described as a qualification to the right to work rather than an implied term of the employees' contracts – was approved by the Court of Appeal in *Standard Life Health Care Ltd v Gorman* [2009] EWCA Civ 1292, [2010] IRLR 233.

The same general principles relating to the grant of interlocutory injunctions apply as are discussed under 'Employee's remedies', above (see also **RESTRAINT OF TRADE, CONFIDENTIALITY AND EMPLOYEE INTERVENTIONS (39)**).

In *Associated Foreign Exchange Ltd v International Foreign Exchange (UK) Ltd* [2010] EWHC 1178 (Ch), [2010] IRLR 964, the court refused to grant an interlocutory injunction to restrain a former employee from breaching a 12-month non-solicitation covenant, because the market changed at such a pace that such protection was unnecessary and because this covenant was unlikely to be enforceable.

7.47d Account of profits

In some cases, the appropriate remedy for a breach of contract may be the restitutionary remedy of an account of profits. An account was ordered by the House of Lords in *A-G v Blake* [2001] IRLR 36. Such a remedy will only be available in exceptional circumstances where the normal remedies of damages, specific performance and injunction do not provide an adequate remedy. The case of *Blake*, a spy who had published a book in breach of his contractual duties to the Crown, was such an exceptional case.

7.48 CONTRACTS OF EMPLOYMENT AND SUNDAY TRADING

The *Sunday Trading Act 1994* relaxed the previously restrictive rules relating to Sunday trading. *Section 4* and *Sch 4* of the *Sunday Trading Act* introduced provisions relating to contracts of employment. Similar provisions relating to those who work in the betting industry were introduced into the *Betting, Gaming and Lotteries Act 1963* (new *Sch 5A*) by *s 20* of the *Deregulation and Contracting Out Act 1994*. These provisions have now been consolidated in the *ERA 1996*.

The relevant provisions apply to two types of worker: shop workers and betting workers. These terms are defined in *ERA 1996, s 232(1)* and *ERA 1996, s 233(1)*, respectively. A shop worker is someone who, under his contract of employment, is or may be required to do 'shop work'. That term is defined to mean work in or about a 'shop', and a 'shop' is defined to include any premises where any retail trade or business is carried on (*ERA 1996, s 232(3)*). 'Retail trade or business' includes barbers and hairdressers, the hiring of goods otherwise than for use in the course of a trade or business and retail sales by auction but it excludes catering business or the sale at theatres and places of amusement of programmes, catalogues and similar items (*ERA 1996, s 232(6)*).

A betting worker is a person who, under his contract of employment, is or may be required to do betting work. 'Betting work' means work at a track in England or Wales for a bookmaker on a day when the bookmaker acts as such at the track and which consists of or includes dealing with betting transactions, and work in a licensed betting office (*ERA 1996, s 233(2)*). A bookmaker is a person who receives or negotiates bets or conducts pool-betting operations or holds himself out as doing so.

The *Act* provides protection to two types of shop workers and betting workers. The first is the 'protected shop workers and betting workers'. This is a shop worker or betting worker who either:

(a)   was employed as a shop worker on 25 August 1994 or as a betting worker on 2 January 1995 (ie the day before the relevant provisions came into force) but was not on that day employed solely to work Sundays. He must also remain employed as a shop worker or betting worker at the 'appropriate date' and have been continuously employed between those two dates. In relation to cases of dismissal or the subjection of the employee to another detriment, the appropriate date is the effective date of termination or the date when the detrimental act or omission occurs, respectively; or

(b)   is a shop worker or betting worker who does not work Sundays and could not be required so to work.

(*ERA 1996, s 36.*)

The second type of protected shop worker or betting worker is an 'opted-out shop worker or betting worker'. This is a shop worker or betting worker who:

(i)   is or may be required to work on Sunday, but is not employed solely to work on Sundays; and

(ii)   has given a written 'opting-out notice', signed and dated by the employee, registering his objection to working on Sundays.

(*ERA 1996, s 41.*)

An opting-out notice takes effect three months after it has been given (*ERA 1996, s 41(3)*). A worker who has given an opting-out notice is then an opted-out worker for as long as he remains continuously employed under a contract of employment as a shop worker or a betting worker between the date of giving the notice and the appropriate date (*ERA 1996, s 41*).

A shop worker or betting worker ceases to be protected if:

(i)   he gives his employer a written 'opting-in notice', signed and dated by the employee, in which he expressly states that he wishes to work on Sundays or that he has no objection to being required so to work; and

(ii)   subsequently expressly agrees with his employer to do shop work or betting work on Sundays or on a particular Sunday.

(*ERA 1996, s 41(2).*)

A shop worker or betting worker is entitled not to be dismissed (*ERA 1996, s 101(1)–(3)*) or to be subjected to any other detriment (*ERA 1996, s 45(1)–(8)*) by reason of his refusal to work Sundays, whether as a protected shop worker or betting worker or as an opted-out shop worker or betting worker. The right not to be dismissed includes a right not to be selected for redundancy where the reason or the principal reason for selection is the employee's refusal to work Sundays (*ERA 1996, s 105(1), (4)*) (see UNFAIR DISMISSAL – II (52)). Dismissal of a shop worker or a betting worker for asserting the statutory rights created for the protection of such workers would be automatically unfair (*ERA 1996, s 104(4)*) (see UNFAIR DISMISSAL – II (52)).

It is not a detriment to refuse to pay the employee in respect of Sundays which he does not work, nor is it a detriment to pay those employees who do work Sundays a higher rate of pay or to offer them enhanced benefits (*ERA 1996, s 45(5), (6)*). Thus, employers are free to offer economic incentives to employees to work Sundays.

The qualifying periods and upper age limits which generally apply to unfair dismissal claims do not apply to the right not to be dismissed by reason of a refusal to work Sundays (*ERA 1996, ss 108(3), 109(2)*) (see UNFAIR DISMISSAL – I (51)).

Employers are required to give those shop workers and betting workers who are or may be required to work Sundays (but not those employed only to work on Sundays) a written statement setting out their right to opt out of working Sundays and not to be dismissed or subjected to any other detriment as a result of doing so. This requirement also applies to those employees who have given opting-in notices. The terms in which the statement must be given are prescribed by the *Act*. The statement must be given within two months of the date when the employee became a shop worker or a betting worker. If the employer fails to comply with this time limit and in the interim a shop worker or a betting worker serves an opting-out notice, that notice takes effect after only one month, rather than the three-month period laid down by *ERA 1996, s 41(3)* (*ERA 1996, s 42(2)*).

After the commencement date, any term in a contract of employment of a shop worker or betting worker who is not employed only to work on a Sunday which requires that worker to work Sundays is unenforceable. Similarly, any agreement by such a shop worker or betting worker that he will work Sundays is unenforceable. Where an employee has given an opting-in notice, the contract of employment is taken to be varied to the extent necessary to give effect to that notice (*ERA 1996, s 37*).

After a shop worker or a betting worker has given an opting-out notice, any term in his contract of employment requiring him to work Sundays after the elapse of the three-month notice period is unenforceable. Any other agreement between an employer and an opted-out shop worker or a betting worker to the effect that the worker is required to work Sundays is likewise unenforceable (*ERA 1996, s 43*).

Where a shop worker or a betting worker has worked a fixed number of hours each week (including Sundays) and the effect of ceasing to work on Sundays is to reduce the total hours which he works, there is no obligation on the employer to increase the hours the employee is required to work on weekdays to compensate for that reduction. Further, where an employee who has previously worked Sundays ceases to do so after the commencement of the *Schedule*, and it is not clear from the contract of employment what the employee's pay was in respect of working Sundays, an employer is entitled to reduce the employee's pay proportionately to take account of the fact that the employee no longer works on Sundays (*ERA 1996, ss 38, 39*).

A protected or opted-out shop worker may complain to an employment tribunal in respect of any detriment he suffers by reason of his refusal to work Sundays (*ERA 1996, s 48*). Complaints must be brought within three months of the act or failure to act complained of, subject to an extension of time where it was not reasonably practicable to present the claim in time.

Any agreement purporting to contract out of the rights created for shop workers and betting workers is void unless either a conciliation officer has intervened or the parties have entered an agreement which satisfies the requirements of *ERA 1996, s 203*. (See **51.20** UNFAIR DISMISSAL – I and **18.28** EMPLOYMENT TRIBUNALS – I.)

8   Directors

8.1   INTRODUCTION

Directors of companies are office-holders. They are not necessarily employees. However, directors often enter into service agreements, thereby becoming employees in addition to holding office. The appointment of a director is nevertheless independent of any contract of employment between a director and a company, although the contract of employment may contain provisions which have application to the office.

The provisions regulating the appointment to, and removal from, the office of a director are set out in the *Companies Act 2006* (*'CA 2006'*). The *Companies (Model Articles) Regulations 2008 (SI 2008/3229)* (*'MA Regulations'*) set out 'default' articles of association for different kinds of companies (with amendments taking effect from 27 April 2013). The *MA Regulations* apply to all companies incorporated under *CA 2006* on or after 1 October 2009. A company may adopt for its articles the whole or any part of those default articles. Accordingly, it is necessary to look at the precise terms of the articles of a company in order to determine the position in any particular case.

The old 'default' articles in *Table A* of the *Companies (Tables A to F) Regulations 1985 (SI 1985/805)* remain valid for any company incorporated under the Companies Act 1985 in the form they existed at the time of that company's incorporation.

CA 2006 also codified the rules governing the duties directors owe to their companies.

This chapter concerns the position of directors as employees. It does not set out the numerous responsibilities of directors under company law, nor address the power of the courts to control delinquent directors.

8.2   APPOINTMENT

A director may be employed by the other directors of a company under the authority of one of the articles of association. Such a director is often referred to as an executive director. The relevant provisions of the model articles provides that:

(1)   Directors may undertake any services for the company that the directors decide;

(2)   Directors are entitled to such remuneration as the directors determine:

  (a)   for their services to the company as directors, and

  (b)   for any other service which they undertake for the company.

(For private companies limited by shares: *para 19* of *Sch 1* to the *MA Regulations*; for private companies limited by guarantee: *para 19, Sch 2, MA Regulations*; for public companies, it is *para 23* of *Sch 3*.)

The relevant provision in *Table A* was *art 84*. As explained above, *Table A* remains valid for companies incorporated prior to 1 October 2009. It provides:

'Subject to the provisions of the Act, the directors may appoint one or more of their number to the office of managing director or to any other executive office under the company and may enter into an agreement or arrangement with any director for his employment by the company or for provision by him of any services outside the scope of the ordinary duties of a director. Any such appointment, agreement or arrangement may be made upon such terms as the directors determine and they may remunerate any such director for his services as they think fit. Any appointment of a director to an executive office shall terminate if he ceases to be a director but without prejudice to any claim to damages for breach of the contract of service between the director and the company. A managing director and a director holding any executive office shall not be subject to retirement by rotation.'

As explained above, the model articles of association may or may not be incorporated into the articles of a particular company. Even where they are not incorporated into the articles, executive directors are not usually subject to retirement by rotation. However, where a company is listed, the Governance Code (see **8.15** below) recommends that all directors should be submitted for re-election at regular intervals, at the first annual general meeting after their appointment ,and at least every three years thereafter (B.7.1). For financial years beginning on or after 29 June 2010, this increased to annually for directors of FTSE 350 companies.

Usually, the terms of the director's appointment will be recorded in a letter written under the authority of the board of directors, or in a service agreement which the board has approved. Where a board resolution contains the terms of the appointment, this may be sufficient evidence of the terms of the contract between the director and the company.

8.3 Relationship between articles and contracts of employment

Where the articles do not confer the directors with a power to employ one of their number, or if that power is not properly exercised, the employment contract between the employed director and the company will be void for want of authority. An example of this situation is *Guinness plc v Saunders* [1990] 2 AC 663. In *Guinness v Saunders*, a committee of the board purported to grant a director special remuneration pursuant to an alleged oral contract. The House of Lords held that this alleged contract was void. This was because the board had no power under the articles to delegate this power to the committee. Since there was no binding contract, their Lordships refused to permit the director to claim payment for actual services which he had performed (on a *quantum meruit* basis). He also could not claim an equitable allowance because it would be inequitable to permit the director to take advantage of his directorship in order to claim remuneration in such circumstances. This was in accordance with the general equitable principle that a director may not profit from the holding of his office. (This principle is often modified by the articles of association.)

The articles and board resolutions are deemed to be known by each director. Accordingly, a director cannot rely on ostensible authority, implied authority or assume that another director, the committee or the board have powers which they do not have: *Guinness v Saunders*, above, at 658, per Lord Templeman. When considering the position of an employed director, it is necessary to examine carefully the relationship between the articles and terms of any service agreement. In order to avoid any doubt, service agreements should expressly provide for the circumstances in which they can be terminated. They must be drafted having regard to the articles which are then in force. (It should also be noted that the employers of directors are obliged to provide a written statement of the particulars of employment, see further below at 8.6.)

In *Read v Astoria Garage (Streatham) Ltd* [1952] Ch 637, a managing director was appointed by a board resolution. This resolution contained no terms as to how the post might be terminated. A resolution of the board, later approved by the company in general meeting, removed the managing director from post. The relevant article provided that the appointment:

'shall be subject to determination *ipso facto* if he ceases for any cause to be a director or if the Company in general meeting resolves that the tenure of office as managing director . . . be determined.'

In the absence of an express term in the original resolution, the director was taken to have contracted on the terms of the articles. He therefore had no claim for wrongful dismissal since the employment had been terminated in accordance with the articles. By contrast, the director in *Nelson v James Nelson & Sons Ltd* [1914] 2 KB 770, CA was appointed in accordance with an article which enabled the board to make an appointment 'for such period as they think fit, and may revoke such appointment'. The duration of the agreement by which the director was appointed was for an indefinite period. It was held that the board had an unfettered power to appoint for such period as it deemed fit. However, the right to revoke only existed if the contract so provided. Since the contract did not contain a power to revoke, the director was entitled to damages for wrongful dismissal when his appointment was terminated.

The position must be judged by considering the articles as they are at the date of entering into the contract of service with the director. In *Southern Foundries (1926) Ltd v Shirlaw* [1940] AC 701, the company, subsequent to the appointment of a director, had adopted new articles which were less favourable to an employed director. It was held that the adoption of these new articles could not worsen the contractual position of an employed director. Accordingly, a dismissal taking place under the new articles was wrongful.

Service agreements may also contain implied terms. For example, in *Shindler v Northern Raincoat Co Ltd* [1960] 1 WLR 1038, a director sold his shares in the company to a different company under a contract of sale which provided that he would be appointed managing director for a period of ten years. This second company was subsequently resold to a third company. The third company did not wish to retain the director's services. In the director's successful claim for wrongful dismissal, it was held that it had become an implied term of his contract of service that the company would not do anything of its own motion to cause him to be removed as managing director in breach of the contract of sale. Diplock J distinguished *Read v Astoria Garage* (above) on the basis that, in *Shindler* and unlike in *Read*, there was evidence of a contract between the company and the director which was inconsistent with the articles. On the basis of the reasoning in *Southern Foundries v Shirlaw*, the director had been wrongfully dismissed in breach of that contract.

8.4   Employed or not?

Articles, such as the model articles, usually give the directors a very broad discretion as to the terms of appointment of one of their number. In particular, articles often provide a power to employ a director pursuant to a contract of employment or, instead, to enter into an agreement for the provision of services. A director may, in respect of additional services, be engaged as either an employee or as an independent contractor. The question of whether the director is an employee or an independent contractor may be of great importance. Many statutory employment rights, such as the right to claim unfair dismissal, are only conferred on employees.

It should also be noted that whether or not an individual is 'employed' may depend on the context in which the question is asked. This is because the definition of an 'employee' varies.

This matter is addressed in detail in Employee, Self-Employed or Worker? (14)). However, the questions pertaining to directors are to some degree distinct and merit separate attention.

Where there is no formal agreement, evidence as to the employment status of a director may be gleaned from board resolutions or minutes, correspondence between the parties and the manner in which the individual is paid and taxed. The courts have tended to consider directors who work full-time for a company and are paid a salary to be employees: *Trussed Steel Concrete Co Ltd v Green* [1946] Ch 115. An example is *Folami v Nigerline (UK) Ltd* [1978] ICR 277, where an accountant from a holding company was appointed managing director of the company's subsidiary and it was held that, having been paid by the subsidiary, the managing director was an employee for the purposes of statutory employment rights. A director who was remunerated by way of director's fees and had not been treated as an employee for the purposes of national insurance was held not to be an employee for the purpose of exercising statutory employment rights in *Parsons v Albert J Parsons & Sons Ltd* [1979] IRLR 117.

A person who is a controlling shareholder can also be an employee of that company. In *Secretary of State for Business, Enterprise and Regulatory Reform v Neufeld (Richard)* [2009] EWCA Civ 280, [2009] IRLR 475, the Court of Appeal considered the relevant authorities and confirmed that it is a question of fact whether or not such a shareholder/director is an employee. An employee's shareholding and/or degree of control of the company is not ordinarily relevant to the inquiry of whether a contract is one of employment, unless it gives rise to questions of whether the contract was genuine. For an application of *Neufeld*, see *Ashby v Monterry Designs Ltd* (UKEAT/0226/08/CEA) (18 December 2009, unreported).

With regard to directors, the 'control test' (see further **15.3**) is not particularly appropriate for determining whether a director is employed. This is because a director may be largely in control of the day-to-day running of the company or part of it (albeit that the 'control' in such a case is exercisable theoretically by the company: see *Secretary of State for Business, Enterprise and Regulatory Reform v Neufeld*, above). Indeed, a controlling share-holder, such as in *Neufeld*, can even ultimately decide whether or not he is dismissed. The 'organisation test', also known as the 'integration test' may be more appropriate. This test was set out by Denning LJ in *Stevenson (or Stephenson) Jordan and Harrison Ltd v MacDonald and Evans* (1952) 69 RPC 10, [1952] 1 TLR 101, CA as follows:

> 'Under a contract of service, a man is employed as part of the business and his work is done as an integral part of the business; whereas, under a contract for services, his work, although done for the business, is not integrated into it but is an accessory to it'.

Accordingly, a director who provides consultancy or advisory services to the company is likely to be an independent contractor, whereas an executive director who is engaged for the purposes of managing the business (or a part of it), and whose work forms an integral part of the business is likely to be an employee.

Clear written agreements may assist in clarifying the issues. However, courts are likely to look to the substance of the agreement rather than simply its form. In *Clark v Clark Construction Initiatives* [2008] ICR 635, [2008] IRLR 364, Elias J set out three circumstances in which a court would not give effect to a purported contract of employment: sham, ulterior purpose and where the parties do not conduct themselves in accordance with the contract. See also *Secretary of State for Business, Enterprise and Regulatory Reform v Neufeld*, above.

8.5   Scope of employment

The scope of a director's employment will be determined by the terms of any service agreement, and any board resolutions which are in force from time to time which grant him or her authority. The powers and duties of a director may be subject to variation by the board. Directors may be appointed to an executive function such as finance director of the company or group. Subject to the terms of the service agreement, the scope of the employment is capable of being completely changed, expanded or narrowed. Even the executive function may be subject to change in some circumstances.

It *Harold Holdsworth & Co (Wakefield) Ltd v Caddies* [1955] 1 WLR 352, it was held that the board could confine the responsibilities of a managing director to the affairs of a subsidiary where the contract provided that he was:

> 'appointed a managing director of the Company and as such managing director he shall perform the duties and exercise the powers in relation to the business of the

company and the business.. of its existing subsidiary company . . . .which may from time to time be assigned to or vested in him by the board of directors.'
(The court noted that Mr Caddies had been appointed 'a' rather than 'the' managing director.)

8.6 Written particulars

The employer of a director, like that of other employees, is obliged to provide a written statement of the particulars of the employment. The provisions of *ss 1 to 6* of the *Employment Rights Act 1996* apply to the employment of directors (see CONTRACT OF EMPLOYMENT (7)).

8.7 DIRECTORS' SERVICE CONTRACTS

A director's 'service contract' is defined, for the purposes of the relevant parts of *CA 2006*, in *s 227* as a contract under which:

(a)   a director of the company undertakes personally to perform services (as director or otherwise) for the company, or for a subsidiary; or

(b)   services (as director or otherwise) that a director of the company undertakes personally to perform are made available by a third party to the company, or to a subsidiary.

They are expressly stated not to be restricted to contracts for the performance of services outside the scope of the ordinary duties of a director.

8.8 Inspection

Under s *228* of *CA 2006*, a company must keep available for inspection a copy of every director's service contract with the company (or a subsidiary), or, if this is not in writing, a written memorandum setting out the terms of the contract. These documents must be kept available for inspection at the company's registered office or at a place specified by regulations. If they are kept at a place other than the registered office, the company must give notice to the registrar of where they are kept: *s 228(4)*. The documents must be retained and kept available for at least one year from the date of termination or expiry of the contract: *s 228(3)*.

The provisions apply to a variation in a director's service contract as well as to the original contract.

Section 228 does not specify the terms which are to be included in any memorandum setting out the terms of a service agreement where this is not in writing. Nevertheless, a memorandum should specify the main terms of the employment pertaining to salary, benefits and duration. It could also contain all the written particulars required by *s 1* of the *Employment Rights Act 1996*.

There is no longer any exception for service contracts with a short expiry date or for those who work wholly or mainly outside the United Kingdom.

All copies and memoranda which are required to be kept must be open to inspection to any member of the company without charge (*CA 2006, s 229(1)*).

If a company fails to comply with any of the above provisions, the company and every officer who is in default is liable to a fine and, for continued contravention to a daily default fine (*CA 2006, s 228(5), (6)*). If inspection of a copy or memorandum is refused, the court may order an immediate inspection or direct that a copy be sent to the person requiring it (*CA 2006, s 229(5)*).

8.9 Directors

8.9 Contracts with sole members who are also directors

Where, outside the ordinary course of the company's business, a limited company with only one member enters into a contract with that sole member who is a director, then unless the contract is in writing, the terms must be set out in a written memorandum or recorded in the minutes of the first meeting of the directors following the making of the contract. A failure to comply is an offence punishable by a fine not exceeding level 5 on the standard scale: see *s 231* of *CA 2006*.

8.10 Listing Rule requirements

The Financial Conduct Authority ('FCA') is the United Kingdom's Listing Authority ('UKLA'). (Prior to April 2013, the FCA was known as the Financial Services Authority or FSA). The FCA makes rules governing the admission and continuing obligations of listed companies. These are known as the *Listing Rules*. They can be found on the FCA's website at www.fca.org.uk. These generally include provisions as to directors' service contracts. Companies would be well advised to check the up-to-date provisions as they change from time to time.

In particular, according to the current version of the rules, a listed company must notify a Regulatory Information Service (RIS) of any change including:

(a)   the appointment of a new director stating the appointee's name and whether the position is executive, non-executive or chairman and the nature of any specific function or responsibility of the position;

(b)   the resignation, removal or retirement of a director (unless the director retires by rotation and is re-appointed at a general meeting of the shareholders);

(c)   important changes to the role, functions or responsibilities of a director; and

(d)   the effective date of the change if it is not with immediate effect (LR 9.6.11).

This notification must take place as soon as possible and in any event by the end of the business day following the decision or receipt of notice about the change by the company.

If the effective date of the change is not known, the notification should state this fact and the company should notify a RIS as soon as the date has been decided. (LR 9.6.12)

A listed company must also notify a RIS of the following information in respect of any new director appointed to the board:

(a)   details of all directorships held by the director in any other publicly quoted company at any time in the previous five years, indicating whether or not he is still a director;

(b)   any unspent convictions in relation to indictable offences;

(c)   details of any receiverships, compulsory liquidations, creditors voluntary liquidations, administrations, company voluntary arrangements or any composition or arrangement with its creditors generally or any class of its creditors of any company where the director was an executive director at the time of, or within the 12 months preceding, such events;

(d)   details of any compulsory liquidations, administrations or partnership voluntary arrangements of any partnerships where the director was a partner at the time of, or within the 12 months preceding, such events;

(e)   details of receiverships of any asset of such person or of a partnership of which the director was a partner at the time of, or within the 12 months preceding, such event; and

(f)   details of any public criticisms of the director by statutory or regulatory authorities (including designated professional bodies) and whether the director has ever been disqualified by a court from acting as a director of a company or from acting in the management or conduct of the affairs of any company (LR 9.6.13).

This notification must be given as soon as possible following the decision to appoint the director and in any event within five business days of the decision.

If there is no such information that is required to be disclosed about a director, then this should be notified to the RIS (LR 9.6.15).

Any changes in such information with respect to a current director should also be disclosed (LR 9.6.14).

8.11   Take-over Code

During the course of an offer, or even before the date of the offer if the board of an offeree company has reason to believe that a *bona fide* offer might be made imminently, *rule 21* of the *City Code on Take-overs and Mergers* will apply. Where *rule 21* applies, the board must not enter into contracts other than in the ordinary course of business without the approval of the shareholders of the company in general meeting (or in pursuant of a contract entered into earlier).

Note 5 of the notes to *Rule 21* indicates that the Panel on Take-Overs and Mergers will regard amending or entering into a service contract with, or creating or varying the terms of employment of, a director as entering into a contract 'otherwise than in the ordinary course of business' for the purpose of *Rule 21* if the new or amended contract or terms constitute an abnormal increase in the director's emoluments or a significant improvement in the terms of service. Accordingly, during an offer period, extending the duration of a service agreement or increasing a director's salary should not be effected without the prior agreement of the Panel.

The notes go on to state that this will not prevent any such increase or improvement which results from a genuine promotion or new appointment. However, the Panel must be consulted in advance in such cases.

8.12   Disclosure

Directors have obligations to disclose their interests in some circumstances. *Section 177(1)* of *CA 2006* provides that 'if a director of a company is in any way, directly or indirectly, interested in a proposed transaction or arrangement with the company, he must declare the nature and extent of that interest to the other directors'. Such a declaration may (but need not be) made at a meeting of directors or by notice in accordance with specified procedures (see *ss 184* and *185* of *CA 2006*). Any declaration must be made before the company enters into the relevant transaction or arrangement: *s 177(4)*, *CA 2006*. Furthermore, where a director has an interest in an existing transaction or arrangement entered into by the company and has not declared the interest under *s 177*, he must do so (*s 182*, *CA 2006*). The rules as to the nature of the declaration are the same as in *s 177*.

In relation to the disclosure obligation in *s 317* of *CA 1985*, the now repealed provision that *s 177* replaced, the obligation to disclose applied even where it was plain and obvious that the director had an interest such as in the case of service agreement: see *Runciman v Walter Runciman plc* [1992] BCLC 1084. However, *s 177(6)* of *CA 2006* now provides that a director need not declare an interest if, or to the extent that, the other directors are already aware of it or ought reasonably to be aware of it. The failure of a director to declare his interest renders a contract voidable at the instance of the company: see *Hely-Hutchinson v Brayhead Ltd* [1968] 1 QB 549, CA at 589, 594.

97

8.13 Directors

8.13 Duration of director's service agreement

The duration of a service agreement will largely be a matter of contract between the company and the director concerned. This may be subject, however, to any restrictions in the articles of association as well as to *s 188* of *CA 2006*, discussed further below.

8.14 *Section 188*

Pursuant to *s 188* of *CA* 2006, shareholder approval is required for any provision under which the guaranteed term of a director's employment with the company of which he is a director or, where he is the director of a holding company, within that group is, or may be, more than two years. (The previous provisions, contained in *s 319* of *CA 1985* only applied where the agreement could last for more than five years.)

The provision applies wherever the employment is to continue, or may be continued, otherwise than at the instance of the company, for a period of more than two years during which the employment cannot be terminated by the company by notice, or can be terminated but only in specified circumstances (*CA 2006, s 188(3)*). The section therefore applies to contracts terminable by notice, and to contracts with a minimum duration but which are intended to continue thereafter upon notice, as well as to fixed-term contracts. Specified circumstances would include, for example, the right to terminate for gross misconduct or incapacity. Therefore, any right to terminate on these grounds would not avoid the need for shareholder approval of the term of the contract.

Section 188(3) sets out a situation in which serial contracts are, to some degree, aggregated in determining the duration of the agreement. Where, more than six months before the end of the guaranteed term of a director's employment, the company enters into a further service contract, then *s 188* applies as if the unexpired period of the guaranteed term of the original contract were added to the guaranteed term of the new contract. The aim of this provision appears to be to catch the situation whereby a company attempts to circumvent *s 188* by employing a director on a series of short term contracts.

Where *s 188* requires a term to be approved, it must be approved by a resolution of the members of the company (or, where the director is or is to be employed by the holding company, by a resolution of the holding company) (*CA 2006, s 188(2)*). Before a resolution is passed, a written memorandum setting out the proposed agreement incorporating the term must be made available to members. In the case of a written resolution, this is done by sending or submitting the provision to every eligible member at or before the time at which the proposed resolution is sent or submitted. In the case of a resolution at a meeting, this is done by making the provision available for inspection both at the company's registered office for not less than 15 days ending with the date of the meeting, and at the meeting itself (*CA 2006, s 188(5)*).

If a term is incorporated into an agreement in contravention of *s 188*, it is void, and is, in certain circumstances, replaced by a term entitling the company to terminate the employment at any time by giving reasonable notice (*CA 2006, s 189*). This provision incorporates the common law concept of reasonable notice which is discussed in WRONGFUL DISMISSAL (56).

8.15 *Recommendations*

Currently, there are no other statutory restrictions on the duration of a director's service agreement.

However, the UK Corporate Governance Code ("Governance Code", formerly the "Combined Code on Corporate Governance") recommends that companies should set notice periods at one year or less.

The Governance Code sets out standards of good practice in relation to companies as well as more specific provisions. It was first issued (under its previous name) in 1998 and has been updated at regular intervals ever since. The current edition of the Code was published in September 2012 and applies to financial years beginning on or after 1 October 2012. Listed companies must, in order to comply with the *Listing Rules*, report on how they have applied the Main Principles of the Governance Code. They must also either confirm that they have complied with all the provisions of the Governance Code, or, alternatively, state that they have not, setting out which provisions they have has not complied with, the periods within which they did not comply and the reasons for non-compliance (*LR 9.8.6(5)* and *(6)* of the *Listing Rules*). This is often described as 'comply or explain'.

The Governance Code recommends that notice or contract periods should be set at one year or less (para D.1.5 of the Governance Code). If it is necessary to offer longer notice or contract periods to new directors recruited from outside a company, such period should reduce to one year or less after the initial period.

Since a company is only required to 'comply or explain', departures may be made from these provisions in certain circumstances. A departure from the provisions may be justified, for example, where a new recruit is only prepared to contract with the company on terms other than those recommended. If a company decides to set a longer notice or contract period than the recommendation, an explanation for this must be given in the company's disclosure statement.

8.16 DIRECTORS' DUTIES

Whether or not a director is employed by the company, he or she owes it duties. The nature and extent of the duties will depend on the circumstances of an individual case. He or she will owe the general duties owed by all directors to their companies as well as any additional or specific duties imposed by reason of the articles of association or any relevant board resolution. There will also be relevant express and implied duties under the contract of employment or other service agreement.

CA 2006 codified the existing law in this area with effect from October 2008.

8.17 The Companies Act 2006

The background to *CA 2006* was a number of major reports which indicated the need for a statutory codification of directors' duties. This is the first time that the duties owed by directors to their company have been set out in statute. The hope was apparently to make the rules clearer and more accessible.

Sections 170 to *177* of *CA 2006* set out the general duties that are owed by a director to the company. It is expressly stated that these duties are based on certain common law rules and equitable principles and have effect in place of those rules and principles (*CA 2006, s 170(3)*).

There has been some discussion in the case law about whether the codification changed the scope or content of the common law and equitable duties upon which the statutory duties were based. In *Towers v Premier Waste* [2011] EWCA Civ 923, Mummery LJ stated of the statutory rules that they "extract and express the essence of the rules and principles which they have replaced".

These general duties are to be interpreted and applied in the same way as common law rules or equitable principles and the courts will have regard to the corresponding rules and principles when interpreting and applying the general duties (*CA 2006, s 170(4)*). Where the duties have not been reformulated, the case law will assist in determining how these duties should be applied in individual cases. However, if there is any conflict, the new statutory provisions will clearly take precedence.

The consequences of a breach or threatened breach of *ss 170* to *177* are the same as would apply if the corresponding common law rule or equitable principle applied. They are enforceable in the same way as any other fiduciary duty owed to a company (*CA 2006, s 178*).

8.17 Directors

The precise duties owed by an employed director will depend on the articles of association, memorandum, and relevant board minutes as well as the express and implied terms of the service agreement as well as *CA 2006*.

8.18 Duty to act within powers

A director of a company must act in accordance with the company's constitution, and only exercise powers for the purposes for which they are conferred (*CA 2006, s 171*). This duty replaces similar pre-existing duties.

8.19 Duty to promote the success of the company

A director of a company is required to act in the way he considers, in good faith, would be most likely to promote the success of the company for the benefit of its members as a whole. In doing this, he must have regard to:

(a)   the likely consequences of any decision in the long term,

(b)   the interests of the company's employees,

(c)   the need to foster the company's business relationships with suppliers, customers and others,

(d)   the impact of the company's operations on the community and the environment,

(e)   the desirability of the company maintaining a reputation for high standards of business conduct, and

(f)   the need to act fairly as between members of the company.

(*CA 2006, s 172(1)*.)

This duty replaces the common law duty to act in good faith in the company's interests. The duty also overlaps with the duty to avoid conflicts of interest, see below at **8.22**.

'Success' is not defined in *CA 2006*. The DTI guidance notes suggest that it should be taken to mean 'long-term increases in value'.

It is not clear how much the pre-existing case law will assist in interpreting the new provisions. Despite the new language, it may be that courts will continue to apply the principles in a similar way.

Section 172 raises but does not answer a number of questions. It is not clear whether the company maintains its own interests separate from the interests of its current members at any time. This may be relevant, for example, to the question of whether a director can recommend the lower of two competing bids if it is considered that this is in the long term interests of the company albeit not in the interests of its existing members.

Another issue may arise if the factors to which the directors must have regard conflict. However, all that is required is that a director 'have regard to' the factors set out in *s 172*. Accordingly, so long as the factors are considered, it will not matter if some of the considerations point in different directions. It would be good practice for board minutes to refer to the factors in *s 172* when documenting the decision making process.

While the interests of a company are normally identified with those of its members, the interests of creditors as a class may be relevant if the company is in financial difficulties: *GHLM Trading Ltd v Maroo* [2012] EWHC 61 (Ch) at [164].

For an employed director, the duty of good faith arises both in his or her capacity as an employee, and as a director by which he or she owes various fiduciary duties to the company. It is necessary to distinguish between a director's fiduciary duties and an employee's obligation of fidelity.

100

An executive director must act in good faith in the interests of the company, and must not engage in competition with it or make secret profits. Such a duty may be more extensive than the parallel duty of a director who is not employed. For example, in *London and Mashonaland Exploration Co Ltd v New Mashonaland Exploration Co Ltd* [1891] WN 165, a decision decided well before *CA 2006* came into force, it was held that a director (albeit a dummy director who did not attend board meetings) did not commit any breach of duty by being appointed a director of a competing company. By contrast, if a full time employee works for a competing company part-time without the consent of his full-time employer, this has been held to amount to a serious breach of his contract: see *Hivac Ltd v Park Royal Scientific Instruments Ltd* [1946] Ch 169. This principle also applies to employed directors. For example, in *Thomas Marshall (Exports) Ltd v Guinle* [1979] Ch 227, [1978] ICR 905, a managing director traded on his own account on behalf of two other companies which he had set up in competition with the company. His service agreement had expressly provided that, while employed as a managing director, he would not engage in any other business without the company's consent. He was held to be in breach of his obligation of fidelity and good faith as an employee and in breach of his fiduciary duty as a director.

There is no free-standing duty requiring an employed director to disclose his own wrongdoing (albeit that there is a duty to disclose their own interests in some circumstances, see **8.12**, above). However, the fundamental common law duty to act in good faith in the interests of the company may require an employed director to disclose his own wrongdoing in certain circumstances, particularly where the wrongdoing constitutes a breach of fiduciary duties. For example, in *Item Software (UK) Ltd v Fassihi* [2004] EWCA Civ 1244, [2005] ICR 450, [2004] IRLR 928, the Court of Appeal held that an employed director was under a duty to disclose his own misconduct in seeking to divert a contract from the company to another company which he himself owned. In these circumstances, the company could recover damages for loss caused by the breach of duty. (Such a duty may also apply to senior employees, see *Tesco Stores Ltd v Pook* [2003] EWHC 823 (Ch), [2004] IRLR 618 and *Helmet Integrated Systems Ltd v Tunnard* [2006] EWCA Civ 1735, [2007] IRLR 126.) Although *Fassihi* was described as a "controversial" decision in *Brandeaux Advisers (UK) Ltd v Chadwick* [2010] EWHC 3241 (QB) at [47], it has been followed and was relied upon by the Court of Appeal in *Customer Services Plc v Ranson* [2012] EWCA Civ 841, [2012] IRLR 769. See also *GHLM Trading Ltd v Maroo* [2012] EWHC 61 (Ch) for a case in which the claimants failed to establish breach.

Directors (and senior employees) may be under a duty not to prepare to compete with their existing employers and, if they do so, to disclose their wrongdoing to their employer. Whether or not such a duty exists and whether or not a director will be found to be in breach of the duty depends very much upon the circumstances of an individual case. For contrasting recent examples, see *Tunnard* (where the employee was not in breach), *Shepherds Investments Ltd v Walters* [2006] EWHC 836 (Ch), [2007] IRLR 110 (where the director was in breach) and *Crowson Fabrics Ltd v Rider* [2007] EWHC 2942 (Ch), [2008] IRLR 288. In *Attwood Holdings Ltd v Woodward* [2009] EWHC 1083 (Ch), an employed director was held to be in breach of duty by failing to alert a company to an impending threat of competition from him and a colleague, by taking preparatory steps including approaches to customers and by retaining confidential information. In *Customer Services Plc v Ranson* [2011] EWHC 3304 (QB), Sir Raymond Jack held that an employee had owed fiduciary duties but had been entitled to discuss plans for his future with third parties, and to set up a potential contracting company without advising the company. However, he was in breach by obtaining contracting work and by transferring his business contacts from his company mobile phone for his own purposes. The Court of Appeal ([2012] EWCA Civ 841, [2012] IRLR 769 overturned that decision, holding that the employee was not a fiduciary at all.

Directors are likely to be under a duty to disclose the wrongdoing of their colleagues, whether subordinate or superior (for an example, see *Walters*, above). This duty applies regardless of whether this would inevitably involve the disclosure of the director's own misconduct (*Sybron Corpn v Rochem Ltd* [1984] Ch 112, [1983] 2 All ER 707).

A breach of any duty to disclose may lead to a subsequent agreement for payment to a director being avoided on grounds of mistake. This could include, for example, a termination payment. The Court of Appeal accepted in *Horcal Ltd v Gatland* [1984] IRLR 288 that a director was not under a duty to disclose his own *intended* wrongdoing. Accordingly, the company was not entitled to recover a termination payment in a situation where the director had not committed any wrongful act at the date of the termination agreement. A company may even be liable to the director for any unpaid salary earned by the director from the time of a breach of duty until termination, even where the breach could have justified summary dismissal had the company been aware of it (*Healey v Francaise Rubastic SA* [1917] 1 KB 946).

In *Re Allied Business and Financial Consultants Ltd: O'Donnell v Shanahan* [2009] EWCA Civ 75, [2009] BCC 822, a case concerning facts prior to the coming into force of the statutory duties, the Court of Appeal held that a director who takes personal advantage of information or an opportunity which comes to him in his capacity as a director will be liable even if the information or opportunity regards a matter outside the scope of the company's business.

In *QBE Management Services (UK) Ltd v Dymoke* [2012] EWHC 80 (QB), [2012] IRLR 458, Haddon-Cave J held that directors were under a positive duty to inform the company in a timely manner of any activity, actual or threatened, which might damage the company's interest.

In *Foster Bryant Surveying Ltd v Bryant* [2007] EWCA Civ 200, [2007] IRLR 425, the Court of Appeal reviewed the law relating to a director's fiduciary duties during a period of notice after he had resigned but before he had left office. In general terms, the director must act towards his company with honesty, good faith and loyalty, and must avoid any conflict of interest. On the facts of *Bryant*, a director who had resigned in innocent circumstances was not in breach of fiduciary duty when he agreed to be retained by a company's main client after his resignation became effective.

8.20   Duty to exercise independent judgment

A company director is required to exercise 'independent judgment'. However, this duty is not infringed by acting in accordance with agreements entered into by the company or as authorised by the company's constitution (*CA 2006, s 173*).

This is to some extent a new duty and there is no exactly equivalent duty at common law. The government stated in debate that this duty will not prevent directors from relying on the judgment of others in areas in which they are not expert and/or to delegate matters to committees. The duty is likely, however, to require individual directors to exercise independent judgment in deciding whether or not to accept advice or judgment from others even in such circumstances.

8.21   Duty to exercise reasonable care, skill and diligence

A director of a company must exercise 'reasonable care, skill and diligence' (*CA 2006, s 174(1)*). This is defined to mean the care, skill and diligence that would be exercised by a reasonably diligent person with the general knowledge, skill and experience that may reasonably be expected of a person carrying out the functions carried out by the director in relation to the company, and the general knowledge, skill and experience that the individual director has (*CA 2006, s 174(2)*). These provisions mean that the standard of care and skill required of a director will not be the same for all directors. It will depend not only on the nature of the company but also on the individual circumstances of the director in question.

Prior to the coming into force of *CA 2006*, the classic exposition of the general (implied) duties of a director was stated by Romer J in *Re City Equitable Fire Insurance Co Ltd* [1925] Ch 407:

'In order therefore to ascertain the duties that a person appointed to the board of an established company undertakes to perform, it is necessary to consider not only the nature of the company's business but also the manner in which the work of the company is in fact distributed between the directors and other officials of the company, provided also that this distribution is a reasonable one in the circumstances and not inconsistent with any express provisions in the articles of association. In discharging the duties of his position thus ascertained, a director must, of course, act honestly; he must also exercise some degree of both skill and diligence. To the question of what is the particular degree of skill and diligence required of him, the authorities do not I think give any clear answers. It has been laid down that so long as a director acts honestly he cannot be made responsible in damages unless guilty of gross or culpable negligence in a business sense'.

Romer J went on to set out the following specific principles:

'(1)   A director need not exhibit in the performance of his duties a greater degree of skill than may reasonably be expected from a person of his knowledge and experience. A director of a life insurance company, for instance, does not guarantee that he has the skill of an actuary or physician . . .

(2)   A director is not bound to give continuous attention to the affairs of his company. His duties are of an intermittent nature to be performed at periodical board meetings, and at meetings of any committee of the board upon which he happens to be placed . . .

(3)   In respect of all duties that, having regard to the exigencies of the business, and the articles of association, may properly be left to some other official, a director is, in the absence of grounds for suspicion, justified in trusting that official to perform such duties honestly.'

However, where a director is also an employee, the legal position is different. This is because an employee impliedly undertakes that he possesses, and will exercise, reasonable skill and competence in the work which he undertakes (*Harmer v Cornelius* (1858) 5 CBNS 236 and *Lister v Romford Ice and Cold Storage Co Ltd* [1957] AC 555). He owes an implied duty to his employer to take such reasonable care and skill in his work. (For other implied duties of employees see CONTRACT OF EMPLOYMENT (7)). These duties go beyond those set out in *Re City Equitable* and in CA 2006. These higher duties would apply to a director who is also an employee. Any breach of these implied duties may constitute a repudiatory breach of the contract, and therefore justify a company in terminating the employment contract without notice. If the contract is terminated, the director will usually be under a contractual obligation to resign his office with the company.

8.22   Duty to avoid conflicts of interest

Section 175 of *CA 2006* imposes a duty on directors to avoid conflicts of interest. These are situations in which the director has or could have a direct or indirect interest that conflicts, or possibly may conflict with, the interests of the company. The duty is expressed to apply particularly to the exploitation of any property, information or opportunity. It is immaterial whether the company could itself take advantage of any of these (*CA 2006, s 175(2)*). The duty does not apply to a conflict arising in relation to a transaction or arrangement with the company.

There are two exceptions to the duty. First, it is not infringed if the situation cannot reasonably be regarded as likely to give rise to a conflict of interest. Secondly, there is no breach where the matter has been authorised (*s 175(4)* and see *Bristol and West Building Society v Mothew* [1998] Ch 1 at 18 for the pre-existing law). For a private company, authorisation may be given by the matter being proposed to and authorised by the directors (unless this is invalidated by something in the company's constitution) (*s 175(5)(a)*). For a public company, where the constitution enables directors to authorise the matter, authorisation may be given by the matter being proposed and authorised in accordance with the constitution (s 175(5)(b)). (Public companies may wish to ensure that their articles of association allow for this.) Authorisation is only effective if any quorum requirement is met without including the potentially interested director and the matter was agreed without (or not counting) the vote of the interested director (s 175(6)).

The recent *Towers* case, above, did not engage the new statutory duties. However, Mummery LJ emphasised the strictness of the no-conflict duty in that it does not depend on proof of fault on behalf of the director or of loss on behalf of the company. A director is in breach regardless of whether he acted in good faith or whether the company could not itself have exploited the opportunity.

8.23   Duty not to accept benefits from third parties

A company director must not accept a benefit from a third party which is conferred by reason of his being a director or his doing (or refraining from doing) anything as director (*CA 2006, s 176*). A third party is any person other than the company, an associated body corporate or a person acting on one of their behalves. Benefits received by a director from a person by whom his services are provided to the company are not regarded as conferred by a third party (s 176(3)). The duty is not infringed if the acceptance of the benefit cannot reasonably be regarded as likely to give rise to a conflict of interest (s 176(4)).

8.24   Continuing obligations

A person who ceases to be director continues to be subject to the duty to avoid conflicts of interest (s 175) as regards the exploitation of any property, information or opportunity of which he became aware at a time when he was a director (s 170(2)(a)). Such a person will also continue to be subject to the duty not to accept benefits from third parties (s 176) as regards things done or not done by him before he ceased to be a director (s 170(2)(b)).

In *Thermasacan v Norman* [2009] EWCA 3694 (Civ), [2011] BCC 535, the Court of Appeal held that *s 175* could not be relied upon to extend the pre-existing law so as to support a blanket prohibition on canvassing or soliciting the business of any client of the company. The Court of Appeal analysed previous authority (*CMS Dolphin Ltd v Simonet* [2002] BCC 600, *Hunter Kane Ltd v Watkins* [2003] EWHC 186 (Ch) and *Foster Bryant Surveying Ltd v Bryant* [2007] EWCA Civ 200) and summarised its effects as follows:

(a)   A director is precluded from taking any property or business advantage, especially where he was a participant in the negotiations, even after his resignation, if the resignation was prompted or influenced by a desire to acquire for himself any maturing business opportunity.

(b)   However, a director is entitled to resign and is then entitled to use his general fund of skill and knowledge acquired while a director. This may even include business contacts and personal connections.

8.25   Indemnity

An employee is entitled to be indemnified by his employer in respect of expenses, costs and claims incurred by him on behalf of his employer during the proper performance of his duties as an employee. An employed director is similarly entitled to such an indemnity. This entitlement may be expressly set out under the articles. For example, under the Model Articles for Private Companies Limited by Shares (*para 20 of Sch 1* to the *MA Regulations*), the company may pay any reasonable expenses which the directors properly incur in connection with their attendance at meetings of directors or committees of directors, general meetings, or separate meetings of the holders of any class of shares or of debentures of the company, or otherwise in connection with the exercise of their powers and the discharge of their responsibilities in relation to the company. (For private companies limited by shares, see *para 20 of Sch 2* and for public companies, see *para 24 of Sch 3*.) In respect of companies incorporated before 1 October 2009, see *art 83 of Table A*.

However, there is a statutory limit on the scope of indemnities that may be afforded to a director (whether or not he is employed). Any provision that purports to exempt a director from any liability in connection with any negligence, default, breach of duty or breach of trust in relation to the company is void unless at least one of the following three exceptions applies. The first exception is that a company may purchase and maintain insurance (*CA 2006, s 232 (2)(a), s 233*). The second exception is a 'qualifying third party indemnity provision'. A 'qualifying third party indemnity provision' is provision for indemnity against liability incurred by the director to a person other than the company (or an associated company) where the following two conditions are satisfied.

(1)   The indemnity is not against any liability to pay a fine imposed in criminal proceedings or a sum payable to a regulatory body by way of penalty in respect of non-compliance with any requirement of a regulatory nature.

(2)   The indemnity is not against any liability incurred by the director in defending any criminal proceedings in which he is convicted (and the conviction has become final) or in defending any civil proceedings brought by the company or an associated company in which judgment is given against him, or in connection with any application under any specified provisions in which the court refuses to grant him relief. These provisions are *s 661(3)* or *(4)* (acquisition of shares by innocent nominee) or *s 1157* of *CA 2006* (general power to grant relief in case of honest and reasonable conduct). (With regard to *s 1157* see further **8.26** below.)

(*CA 2006, s 234*.)

The third exception is a 'qualifying pension scheme indemnity provision'. A 'qualifying pension scheme indemnity' is a provision indemnifying a director who is a trustee of an occupational pension scheme against liability incurred in connection with the company's activities as trustee of the scheme which meets the following conditions.

(1)   The indemnity is not against any liability of the director to pay a fine imposed in criminal proceedings or a sum payable to a regulatory body by way of penalty in respect of non-compliance with any requirement of a regulatory nature.

(2)   The provision does not provide any indemnity against any liability incurred by the director in defending criminal proceedings in which he is convicted (and the conviction has become final).

(*CA 2006, s 235*.)

Qualifying third party indemnity provision and qualifying pension scheme indemnity provision must be disclosed in the directors' report. The rules governing this disclosure are set out at *s 236* of *CA 2006*. Copies of any qualifying indemnity provision must be kept available for inspection (*CA 2006, s 237*) and must be open to inspection by any member of the company without charge (*CA 2006, s 238*).

8.26   Relief from liability

Section 1157 of *CA 2006* applies where a director is facing proceedings for negligence, default, breach of duty or breach of trust. In such circumstances, if it appears to the court hearing the case that the director has acted honestly and reasonably and, in all the circumstances (including those connected with his appointment) he ought fairly to be excused, that court may relieve him either wholly or partly from his liability on such terms as it thinks fit. Where such a director is tried by a judge with a jury, the judge may withdraw the case in whole or in part from the jury if satisfied that relief should be granted, and direct that judgment be entered for the defendant on such terms as are considered appropriate (*CA 2006, s 1157(3)*).

If a director has reason to believe that any such proceedings will or might be brought against him, he may apply to the court for relief and the court has the same power of relief as set out above (*CA 2006, s 1157(2)*).

See *Towers v Premier Waste* [2011] EWCA Civ 923 for a recent case where the court refused to relieve a director from liability pursuant to *section 1157*.

8.27 REMUNERATION

There is nothing in *CA 2006* to restrict or determine the amount of remuneration which may be paid to a director. The model articles set out in the *Schedules* to the *MA Regulations* provide that directors are entitled to such remunerations as the directors determine (a) for their services to the company as directors, and (b) for any other service which they undertake for the company (see *para 19* of *Sch 1*, *para 19* of *Sch 2* and *para 23* of *Sch 3*, as appropriate).

Article 82 of *Table A*, for companies incorporated before 1 October 2009, provides in relation to non-executive directors that:

> "The director shall be entitled to such remuneration as the company may by ordinary resolution determine and, unless the resolution provides otherwise, the remuneration shall be deemed to accrue from day to day."

With regard to executive directors appointed in accordance with the model articles (see **8.2** above), the amount of remuneration is a matter for the board. So long as the board exercises its power in good faith in accordance with the relevant provisions of the model code (or *art 84*, as appropriate), the company will be unable to avoid the terms agreed for remuneration. However, if remuneration is set at an excessive level, this might provide evidence of a failure to exercise the power in good faith.

8.28 Guidance: the Governance Code

A brief explanation of the operation of the Governance Code is set out at para **8.15** above. With regard to directors' remuneration, the Governance Code recommends that the board of directors establish a remuneration committee with delegated responsibility for setting remuneration levels for all executive directors and the chairman. This should include pension rights and any compensation payments. In relation to the level and make-up of remuneration for executive directors, the Governance Code recommends as follows.

The Main Principles include the following four broad principles.

(a) Levels of remuneration should be sufficient to attract, retain and motivate directors of the quality required to run the company successfully, but a company should avoid paying more than necessary for this purpose (Main Principles, Section D).

(b) A significant proportion of executive directors' remuneration should be structured so as to link rewards to corporate and individual performance (Main Principles, Section D).

(c) There should be a formal and transparent procedure for developing policy on executive remuneration and for fixing the remuneration packages of individual directors (Main Principles, Section D).

(d)   No director should be involved in deciding his or her own remuneration (Main Principles, Section D).

The detailed provisions contain the following recommendations.

(a)   Remuneration should be stretching and designed to promote the long-term success of the company (D.1).

(b)   The board should establish a remuneration committee of at least three, or in the case of smaller companies two, independent non-executive directors. In addition the company chairman may also be a member of, but not chair, the committee if he or she was considered independent on appointment as chairman. The remuneration committee should make available its terms of reference, explaining its role and the authority delegated to it by the board. Where remuneration consultants are appointed, they should be identified in the annual report a statement should be made available of whether they have any other connection with the company (D.2.1).

(c)   The remuneration committee should have delegated responsibility for setting remuneration for all executive directors and the chairman, including pension rights and any compensation payments. The committee should also recommend and monitor the level and structure of remuneration for senior management, as defined (D.2.2).

(d)   The remuneration committee should judge where to position the company relative to other companies. But they should use such comparisons with caution in view of the risk of an upward ratchet of remuneration levels with no corresponding improvement in performance (D.1).

(e)   Remuneration committees should be sensitive to pay and employment conditions elsewhere in the group, especially when determining annual salary increases (D.1).

(f)   In designing schemes of performance-related remuneration for executive directors, the remuneration committee should follow the provisions set out in Schedule A to the Code (D.1.1).

(g)   The remuneration committee should consider whether the directors should be eligible for annual bonuses. If so, performance conditions should be relevant, stretching and designed to promote the long-term success of the company. Upper limits should be set and disclosed. There may be a case for part payment in shares to be held for a significant period (Schedule A).

(h)   The remuneration committee should consider whether the directors should be eligible for benefits under long-term incentive schemes. Traditional share option schemes should be weighed against other kinds of long-term incentive scheme. Executive share options should not be offered at a discount save as permitted by the relevant provisions of the Listing Rules (Schedule A).

(i)   In normal circumstances, shares granted or other forms of deferred remuneration should not vest, and options should not be exercisable, in less than three years. Directors should be encouraged to hold their shares for a further period after vesting or exercise, subject to the need to finance any costs of acquisition and associated tax liabilities (Schedule A).

(j)   Any new long-term incentive schemes which are proposed should be approved by shareholders and should preferably replace any existing schemes, or at least form part of a well considered overall plan incorporating existing schemes. The total potentially available rewards should not be excessive (Schedule A).

(k)   Layouts or grants under all incentive schemes, including new grants under existing share option schemes, should be subject to challenging performance criteria reflecting the company's objectives, including non-financial performance metrics where appropriate. Remuneration incentives should be compatible with risk policies and systems (Schedule A).

(l)   Grants under executive share options and other long-term incentive schemes should normally be phased rather than awarded in one large block (Schedule A).

(m)   Consideration should be given to the use of provisions that permit the company to reclaim variable components in exceptional circumstances of misstatement or misconduct (Schedule A).

(n)   In general, only basic salary should be pensionable. The remuneration committee should consider the pension consequences and associated costs to the company of basic salary increases and any other changes in pensionable remuneration, especially for directors close to retirement (Schedule A).

(o)   The remuneration committee should carefully consider what compensation commitments (including pension contributions and all other elements) their directors' terms of appointment would entail in the event of early termination. The aim should be to avoid rewarding poor performance. They should take a robust line on reducing compensation to reflect departing directors' obligations to mitigate loss (D.1.4).

(p)   The remuneration committee should consult the chairman and/or chief executive about their proposals relating to the remuneration of other executive directors. The remuneration committee should also be responsible for appointing any consultants in respect of executive director remuneration. Where executive directors or senior management are involved in advising or supporting the remuneration committee, care should be taken to recognise and avoid conflicts of interest (D.2).

(q)   Where a company releases an executive director to serve as a non-executive director elsewhere, the remuneration report should include a statement as to whether or not the director will retain such earnings and, if so, what the remuneration is (D.1.2).

(r)   The chairman of the board should ensure that the company maintains contact as required with its principal shareholders about remuneration (D.2).

(s)   Shareholders should be invited specifically to approve all new long-term incentive schemes (as defined in the Listing Rules LR 9.4) and significant changes to existing schemes, save in the circumstances permitted by the Listing Rules (D.2.4).

Of course, many of these recommendations raise legal issues. For example, compliance with paragraph (m), above may give rise to penalty clauses.

8.29   Guidance: the Stewardship Code

The UK Stewardship Code, published in September 2012 sets out the Financial Reporting Council's ("FRC") principles of effective stewardship by investors. The Stewardship Code is directred to institutional investors, ie asset owners and asset managers with equity holdings in UK listed companies. It states that the FRC expects signatories of the Code to publish on their website or in another accessible form a statement that describes how the signatory has applied each of the seven principles of the Code or explains why an element of the Code has not been complied with. This is the same "comply or explain" basis as that which applies in relation to the Governance Code.

The third principle is that institutional investors should monitor their investee companies. This includes seeking to satisfy themselves that the company's board and committees adhere to the spirit of the UK Corporate Governance Code. This will include satisfying themselves that the company has complied with the provisions described in paragraph [8.28] above in relation to directors' remuneration.

The fourth principle is that institutional investors should establish clear guidelines on when and how they will escalate their stewardship activities. The Code advises that instances when institutional investors may want to intervene include when they have concerns about the company's remuneration.

8.30 The Remuneration Code

It should also be noted that an executive director of any organisation which is authorised by the Financial Conduct Authority ("FCA") will hold a controlled function under the FCA Handbook and will (except in extraordinary circumstances) be treated as a member of that organisation's "Code Staff" for the purposes of the FCA's Remuneration Code ("Remuneration Code"). As a member of Code Staff, the provisions of the Remuneration Code will apply to the assessment, method and timing of payment of that director's variable remuneration. The provisions of the Code are set out in SYSC19. A (Senior Management Arrangements, Systems and Controls) of the FCA Handbook.

In determining whether a particular organisation has complied with the Remuneration Code, the FCA applies a principle of 'proportionality'. In brief this means that each relevant organisation is expected to comply with the Remuneration Code to the extent and in a way that is appropriate to its size, internal organisation and the nature, the scope and the complexity of its activities. The detail of the Remuneration Code is outside the scope of this work but can be found at www.fca. org.uk.

8.31 Disclosure of directors' remuneration

The law on the disclosure of directors' remuneration will shortly be changing. The following two sections describe the law as currently in force. Please see paragraph [8.33] below for the position from 1 October 2013.

Section 412 of *CA 2006* empowered the Secretary of State to make regulations requiring certain information to be given in notes to a company's annual accounts about directors' remuneration.

The relevant regulations are the *Large and Medium-sized Companies and Groups (Accounts and Reports) Regulations 2008 (SI 2008/410)* ('*2008 Regulations*'). They apply to all companies other than those subject to the small companies regime. Small companies are addressed separately below at **8.31**.

Companies are required to provide information about directors' remuneration in notes to the company's accounts (*reg 8* and *Sch 5, 2008 Regulations*). Some of the provisions apply to both quoted and unquoted companies. However, quoted companies are exempted from some of the provisions.

Both quoted and unquoted companies must provide information as to:

(a)   the aggregate amount of remuneration paid to or receivable by directors;

(b)   the aggregate of the amount of gains made by directors on the exercise of share options;

(c)   the aggregate of the amount of money paid to or receivable by directors, and the net value of assets (other than money and share options) received or receivable by directors under long term incentive schemes; and

(d)   the aggregate value of any company contributions paid (or treated as paid) to a pension scheme in respect of directors and by reference to which the rate or amount of any money purchase benefits that may become payable will be calculated.

(*Sch 5, para 1(1)*.)

They must also provide information as to the number of directors (if any) to whom retirement benefits are accruing under money purchase schemes and under defined benefit schemes.

(*Sch 5, para 2(1)*.)

(The rules are slightly different for companies which are unquoted and whose equity share capital is not listed on AIM: see *para 1(3)*.)

Unquoted (but not quoted) companies must provide additional information in notes to the accounts as to details of the highest paid directors' emoluments (where the aggregates in (a), (b) and (c) above total £200,000 or more) (*para 2*). They are also required to provide information as to retirement benefits (*para 3*), compensation for loss of office (*para 4*), and sums paid to third parties in respect of directors' services (*para 5*).

Quoted companies are required to prepare a directors' remuneration report (see *s 420* of *CA 2006*). *Schedule 8* to the *2008 Regulations* sets out the information that must be contained in the report and requirements as to how it should be set out.

A director, or anyone who has been a director in the last five years, is obliged to give notice to the company of those matters relating to himself that may be necessary for these purposes (*CA 2006, s 412(5)*). Any default is an offence which is punishable by a fine not exceeding level 3 on the standard scale (*CA 2006, s 412(6)*).

(For the application of *s 412*, with modifications, to unregistered companies, see the *Unregistered Companies Regulations 2009, SI 2009/2436*.)

8.32   *Special provisions for small companies*

The rules are different for companies which fall under the 'small companies regime'. This regime applies to a company in respect of which, in its first financial year or, in any subsequent year and the preceding year, at least two of the following conditions are satisfied:

(a)   The turnover is not more than £6.5 million;

(b)   The balance sheet total is not more than £3.26 million;

(c)   The company has not more than 50 employees.

(*CA 2006, s 382*, as amended.)

Detailed rules as to how these are calculated are found in *s 382* of *CA 2006*.

A parent company only qualifies as small if the group headed by it qualifies as a small group (*s 383(1)*). A group only qualifies as small if the following conditions are satisfied:

(a)   The aggregate turnover is not more than £6.5 million net (or £7.8 million gross);

(b)   The balance sheet total is not more than £3.26 million net (or £3.9 million gross);

(c)   The group has not more than 50 employees.

Again, there are detailed rules about how these should be calculated. They are found in *s 383* of *CA 2006*.

Some companies are ineligible to be small companies. The small companies regime does not apply to a company that is, or was at any time within the relevant financial year:

(a)   a public company;

(b)   a company which is an authorised insurance company, a banking company, an e-money issuer, a MiFID investment firm or a UCITS management company;

(c)   a company that carries on insurance market activity; or

(d)   a member of an ineligible group.

(CA 2006, s 384(1), as amended.)

A group is ineligible if any of its members is:

(a)   a public company;

(b)   a body corporate (other than a company) whose shares are admitted to trading on a regulated market in an EEA State;

(c)   a person (other than a small company) who has permission under *Part 4A* of the *Financial Services and Markets Act 2000* to carry on a regulated activity;

(d)   a small company which is an authorised insurance company, a banking company, an e-money issuer, a MiFID investment firm or a UCITS management company; or

(e)   a person who carries out insurance market activity.

(CA 2006, s 384(2), as amended.)

Companies which fall within the definition of small companies are only required to give the following information:

(a)   the total (rather than the aggregates individually) of the amount of remuneration paid to or receivable by directors;

(b)   the amount of money paid to or receivable by directors, and the net value of assets (other than money, share options or shares) received or receivable by directors, under long term incentive schemes;

(c)   the value of any company contributions paid to a pension scheme and by reference to which the rate or amount of any money purchase benefits will be calculated;

(d)   the number of directors to whom retirement benefits are accruing under money purchase and defined benefit schemes;

(e)   the aggregate amount of any payments made to directors for loss of office; and

(f)   the aggregate amount of any consideration paid to or receivable by third parties for making available the services of a director.

(Schedule 3 to the *Small Companies and Groups (Accounts and Directors' Report) Regulations (SI 2008/409).)*

8.33   *Proposed developments*

Significant changes are expected to the regime for directors' remuneration in quoted companies.

The reforms are being implemented through a combination of primary legislation as part of the Enterprise and Regulatory and Reform Bill, the introduction of a new *Chapter 4A* of the *Companies Act 2006* and through secondary legislation which Department for Business

8.33 Directors

Innovation and Skills has published in draft (the *Large and Medium-sized Companies and Groups (Accounts and Reports) (Amendment) Regulations 2013*). The government's intention is that the reforms will come into force on 1 October 2013 and will take effect from the first Annual General Meeting of a company held in the company's financial year after that date. Payments required to be made under existing contracts and legal agreements entered into, and obligations arising, before the legislation introducing these reforms was published on 27 June 2012. However, all payments made under agreements entered into, amended or renewed on or after 27 June 2012 will be caught by the new rules.

Since the legislation has not at the time of writing been approved by Parliament, it is still subject to change. The following is therefore a brief description of the main changes.

The reforms will affect quoted companies, as defined by the *Companies Act 2006*. This means it applies to companies registered in the UK and with equity listed on the main market but not to AIM listed companies.

From the time the legislation comes into force, the directors' remuneration report will need to contain:

(a)   a statement by the chair of the remuneration committee;

(b)   the company's policy on directors' remuneration (the "remuneration policy"); and

(c)   information on how the remuneration policy was implemented in the financial year being reported upon (the "implementation report").

The remuneration policy will set out how the company proposes to pay directors including all forms of remuneration and explain how that proposal supports the company's long-term strategy and performance. The remuneration policy will also include details of the company's proposed approach to payments relating to recruitment and loss of office.

Shareholders will have a binding vote on a resolution to approve the remuneration policy. Companies will be required to put their remuneration policy to a shareholder resolution at the first AGM and thereafter at least every three years. If a company wishes to make changes to the remuneration policy, it will have to put a new policy to shareholders for approval at a general meeting.

Once a remuneration policy has been approved, a company will only be able to make remuneration and loss of office payments which are permitted within the limits of the policy, unless separately approved by shareholder resolution.

Companies will also have to produce an implementation report annually. That report will show how the approved pay policy has been implemented, and set out a single figure for the total pay directors received that year. The aim is to allow shareholders to make year on year comparisons.

Shareholders will have an annual advisory vote on a resolution to approve the implementation report. If a company fails to pass this resolution in a year in which the remuneration policy was not put to a shareholder resolution, this will trigger the need for the company to put the remuneration policy to shareholders the following year.

Further, from 1 October 2013, whenever a director leaves office, the company will be required to publish a statement setting out what payments the director has received or may receive in future. That statement will need to be published as soon reasonably practicable.

8.34 *Listing Rules requirements*

Listed companies must make a disclosure statement stating whether they have complied with the Governance Code and, if not, set out those provisions with which they have not complied, the period of non-compliance and the reasons for it (see further above at **8.15**).

Further, *rule 9.8.6* of the *Listing Rules* requires a company to include with its annual reports and accounts a report to the shareholders of the board containing a statement setting out all the interests of each director of the listed company (including the interests of all "connected persons", as defined), including all changes in interests that have occurred between the end of the period under review and one month prior to the date of the notice of the annual general meeting; or a statement that there have been no such changes.

Rule 9.8.8 requires the report to the shareholders of the Board to contain a statement of the company's policy on executive directors' remuneration and information in tabular form, unless inappropriate, together with explanatory notes on:

(a)   the amount of each element in the remuneration package of each director by name, including but not restricted to, basic salary and fees, the estimated money value of benefits in kind, annual bonuses, deferred bonuses, compensation for loss of office and payments for breach of contract or other termination payments;

(b)   the total remuneration for each director for the period under review and the corresponding prior period;

(c)   any significant payments made to former directors; and

(d)   any share options, including 'Save as you earn' options for each director by name.

The report must also contain:

(a)   details of any long-term incentive schemes, other than share options, including the interests of each director by name, in the long-term incentive schemes;

(b)   details of any entitlements or awards granted and commitments made under any long-term incentive schemes, showing which crystallize either in the same year or in subsequent years;

(c)   details of the monetary value and number of shares, cash payments or other benefits received by each director under any long-term incentive schemes;

(d)   details of the interests of each director in the long-term incentive scheme at the end of the period;

(e)   an explanation and justification of any element of a director's remuneration, other than basic salary, which is pensionable;

(f)   details of any director's service contract with a notice period in excess of one year or with provisions for pre-determined compensation on termination which exceeds one year's salary and benefits in kind, giving the reasons for such notice period;

(g)   details of the unexpired term of any service contract of a director proposed for election or re-election and, if any such director does not have a directors' service contract ,a statement to that effect;

(h)   a statement of the company's policy on the granting of options or awards under its employees' share scheme or other long term investment scheme, explaining and justifying any departure and any change in policy from the previous year;

(i)   for money purchase schemes, details of the contribution or allowance payable or made by the listed company in respect of each director;

(j)   for defined benefits schemes, details of the amount of increase during the period under review and of the accumulated total amount at the end of the period in respect of the accrued benefit to which each director would be entitled on leaving service or is entitled having left service; and either the transfer value of the relevant increase in accrued benefit or so much of the specified information as is necessary to make a reasonable assessment of the transfer value.

These requirements are additional to the information required by statute.

8.35 Pensions

Usually, the making of pension arrangements will be regulated by the company's articles of association. The model articles for companies incorporated on or after 1 October 2009 provide that a director's remuneration may take any form and include "any arrangements in connection with the payment of a pension, allowance or gratuity, or any death, sickness or disability benefits, to or in respect of that director" (*para 19, Sch 1, MA Regulations, para 19 of Sch 2, MA Regulations* or, *para 23, Sch 3, MA Regulations*, depending on the type of company).

The making of pension arrangements for directors was expressly authorised by *Article 87* of *Table A. Article 87* of *Table A*, which applies to companies incorporated before 1 October 2009, provides:

'The directors may provide benefits, whether by the payment of gratuities or pensions or by insurance or otherwise, for any director who has held but no longer holds any executive office or employment with the company or with any body corporate which is or has been a subsidiary of the company or a predecessor in business of the company or of any such subsidiary, and for any member of his family (including a spouse and a former spouse) or any person who is or was dependent on him, and may (as well before as after he ceases to hold such office or employment) contribute to any fund and pay premiums for the purchase or provision of any such benefit'.

For unquoted companies, the notes of accounts must show the excess retirement benefits paid to or receivable by directors or past directors (*para 3 of Sch 5* to the *Large and Medium-sized Companies and Groups (Accounts and Reports) Regulations 2008* (*SI 2008/410*) ('*2008 Regulations*')). The notes must disclose the aggregate of:

(a)   the amount of retirement benefits paid to or receivable by directors under pension schemes; and

(b)   the amount of retirement benefits paid to or receivable by past directors under such schemes,

as, in each case, is in excess of the retirement benefits to which they were each entitled on the date the benefits first became payable or 31 March 1997, whichever is the later.

The aggregate need not include excess amounts if:

(i)   the funding of the scheme was such that the amounts were or could have been paid without recourse to additional contributions; and

(ii)   the amounts were paid to or receivable by all pensioner members of the scheme on the same basis.

Companies which are subject to the 'small companies regime' (see **8.32** above) are not obliged to disclose this information.

For quoted companies, detailed provisions as to the disclosure of retirement benefits in respect of the directors' remuneration report are contained in *para 13 of Sch 8* to the *2008 Regulations* and for the disclosure of excess retirement benefits in *para 14 of Sch 8* to the *2008 Regulations*.

Following the coming into force of the new rules, with effect from 1 October 2013, the implementation report for listed companies (see above at 8.33) will be need to include a statement of all pension related benefits.

8.36   TERMINATION OF DIRECTORS' OFFICE

A company may, by ordinary resolution at a meeting, remove a director from office under *section 168* of *CA 2006*. This power applies regardless of any contrary provisions in the articles of association or in any service agreement. However, the section does not deprive a person removed under it of compensation or damages payable to him in respect of the termination of his appointment, or as circumscribing from any other power to remove a director (*CA 2006, s 168(5)*. Such a power may, for example, derive its authority under the articles.

The ordinary resolution may only be proposed if special notice of it has been given (pursuant to *CA 2006, s 168(2)*). A director has specified rights to protest against a proposal to remove him from office (see *CA 2006, s 169*).

Any service agreement will usually be terminated by the removal of a director from office. However, this is not invariably so. The outcome will depend on the terms of the service agreement. A person cannot, for example, continue as managing director if he or she is not a director. By contrast, there may be situations in which the office of director is wholly separate from the employment relationship. This might be the case where a manager has no right under his employment contract to be appointed or remain as a director. Such a person may continue in his employment as a manager despite the termination of his directorship. If the companies intend that the employment should end if the employee ceases to be a director, the service agreement should include a clause stating this. The converse position may also occur where the employment of an executive director may terminate whilst he or she remains in office. Usually, the board is responsible for terminating the executive appointment of a director, by a majority. Again, if it is intended that the executive appointment should be co-terminous with the appointment as a director, the service agreement should so provide. Service agreements often provide that the executive is required to resign from office as a director (and all other offices held by him in the company) in the event that the employment terminates. Service agreements may also contain power of attorney clauses to effect a resignation if a director fails to resign when he is obliged to do so.

8.37   Termination payments

It is not lawful for a company to make to a director any payment by way of compensation for loss of office, or as consideration for or in connection with his retirement from office, without particulars of the proposed payment (including the amount) being disclosed to members of the company and the proposal being approved by the company. This restriction is by virtue of *s 217* of *CA 2006*. It does not, however, prevent any payment made in good faith in discharge of an existing legal obligation, by way of damages for breach of an obligation, by way of settlement or compromise of any claim arising in connection with the termination or by way of pension in respect of past services (*CA 2006, s 220(1)*). Approval is not required where the amount concerned does not exceed £200 (*s 221*).

In *Taupo Totara Timber Co Ltd v Rowe* [1978] AC 537, a director was given the right, under the terms of his service agreement, to resign his office following a takeover. Further, he would then be entitled to a payment equivalent to five times his annual salary to be paid tax free. Following a takeover, the director sought to enforce this provision by giving notice. The Privy Council held that the payment did not require shareholder approval since it had been contractually agreed by the company. In that case, there was no suggestion that this was a liquidated damages clause which might amount to an unenforceable penalty clause.

8.37 Directors

The Privy Council approved the decision in *Taupo Totara Timber Co Ltd v Rowe* in the Australian case of *Lincoln Mills (Australia) Ltd v Gough* [1964] VR 193 in which it was held that the similar (but non-identical) provision in Victorian companies legislation applied only to payment to a director for loss of office and not in respect of loss of the employment.

In *Murray v Leisureplay plc* [2005] EWCA Civ 963, [2005] IRLR 946, the Court of Appeal considered an argument that a clause in a chief executive director's contract providing for the payment of one year's gross salary in the event of termination was unenforceable as a penalty. The Court of Appeal held that a clause will only be held to be a penalty if the party seeking to avoid it can demonstrate that the sum payable on breach is extravagant or unconscionable.

In respect of unquoted companies, details of compensation paid to directors for loss of office must be shown in notes to the accounts (under *Sch 5* to the *2008 Regulations*). There must be shown the aggregate amount of any compensation to director or past directors including compensation receivable for:

(a)   loss of office as a director of the company; or

(b)   loss, while a director of the company or on or in connection with his ceasing to be a director of it, of any other office in connection with the management of the company's affairs, or any office as director or otherwise in connection with the management of the affairs of any subsidiary undertaking of the company.

References to compensation include benefits otherwise than in cash and in relation to such compensation, references to its amount are to the estimated money value of the benefit. The nature of any such compensation must be disclosed. References to compensation for loss of office include:

(i)   compensation in consideration for, or in connection with, a person's retirement from office;

(ii)   where that retirement is as a result of a breach of the person's contract with the company or with a subsidiary undertaking, payments by way of damages or settlement in respect of the breach.

With regard to quoted companies, the directors' remuneration report must contain details of any 'significant award' made to any person who was not a director at the time but had previously been a director including compensation in respect of loss of office: *para 15 of Sch 8* to the *2008 Regulations*.

If a payment is made in contravention of *s 217*, it is held by the recipient on trust for the company making the payment and any director who authorised the payment is jointly and severally liable to indemnify the company that made the payment for any loss resulting from it.

Following the coming into force of the reforms described above at **8.33** with effect from 1 October 2013, any payments made to directors for loss of office will need to be consistent with the approved remuneration policy or separately approved by a shareholder resolution (unless payments are required to be made as part of a legal obligation entered into before 27 June 2012 and not amended or renewed since).

8.38 *Recommendations*

Paragraph D.1.4 of the Governance Code recommends that remuneration committees consider what compensation commitments, including pension contributions, their directors' terms of appointment would entail in the event of early termination. The aim should be to avoid rewarding poor performance. It is recommended that committees take a robust line on reducing compensation to reflect the departing directors' obligations to mitigate loss.

8.39 *Listing Rules*

The *Listing Rules* require listed companies to disclose in their report to shareholders any compensation paid to directors for loss of office and any significant payments made to former directors (rule 9.8.8 2(a) and (c)).

8.40 Company approval for property transfer

Payments to a director by way of compensation for loss of office, or as consideration for or in connection with retirement from office, where made in connection with the transfer of the whole or any part of the undertaking or property of a company, must have shareholder approval (*CA 2006, s 218*). Shareholder approval is not required, however, where payment is made of *bona fide* damages for breach of contract or by way of pension for past services (*s 220*). If approval is required but not obtained, the amount received is deemed to be held by the director in trust for the company (*s 222(2)*). Approval is not required where the amount concerned does not exceed £200 (*s 221*).

8.41 Payments on takeover

Payments to a director by way of compensation for loss of office, or as consideration for or in connection with a transfer of shares in the company resulting from a takeover bid, must also have the approval of the relevant shareholders (*CA 2006, s 219*). Again, there is an exception for *bona fide* damages for breach of contract or by way of pension for past services (*s 220*). If approval is required but not obtained, the amount received is deemed to be held by the director in trust for persons who have sold their shares as a result of the offer made. The director is also required to bear the expenses incurred in distributing that sum (*s 222(3)*).

8.42 TRANSFER OF UNDERTAKING

If an undertaking is sold or otherwise transferred or if there is a "service provision change" (see Transfer of Undertaking), the employment of all those employed in the undertaking automatically transfers from the transferor company to the transferee under the *Transfer of Undertakings (Protection of Employment) Regulations 2006 (SI 2006/246) ('TUPE')*. For the purposes of *TUPE*, a contract of employment is defined as any agreement between an employee and his or her employer which determines the conditions of employment. An 'employee' is any individual who works for another person whether under a contract of service or apprenticeship or otherwise but does not include anyone who provides services under a contract for services. Accordingly, an employed director will be an employee for the purposes of *TUPE*. Therefore, if the undertaking or part of undertaking in which the director is employed is transferred, the directors' employment contract will transfer to the transferee.

If the director is entitled under the contract of employment to be appointed director of the company which employs him or her, then failure to appoint him as a director of the transferee will amount to a repudiatory breach of contract, entitling the director to resign and claim constructive dismissal. The director will also be required to resign as a director of the transferor company or otherwise be removed from office.

Service agreements often contain provisions dealing with reconstructions. A typical agreement will exclude any claim brought by a director if he or she is offered employment with the successor company on no less favourable terms and conditions. In any event, *TUPE* would be likely to apply in these circumstances to the same effect.

(*TUPE* is addressed in detail in TRANSFER OF UNDERTAKINGS (50).)

9 Disclosure of Information

9.1   An employer is under a duty to disclose certain information to his employees and their representatives, by virtue of the *Trade Union and Labour Relations (Consolidation) Act 1992* (*'TULRCA 1992'*) (see **9.2–9.5** below), the *Transfer of Undertakings (Protection of Employment) Regulations 2006 (SI 2006/246)* replacing the previous *1981 Regulations (SI 1981/1794)* (see **9.6** below) and the *Health and Safety at Work, etc Act 1974* (see **9.7–9.8** below). Information may also have to be disclosed for the purposes of consultation about forthcoming redundancies (see **37.2 REDUNDANCY – II**). The trustees of occupational pension schemes are put under certain duties of disclosure by virtue of the *Occupational Pension Schemes (Disclosure of Information) Regulations 1996 (SI 1996/1655)* (see **9.9** below). Duties to afford access to certain records (as well as other obligations) arise from the *Data Protection Act 1988* (see **9.12** below), and the *Access to Medical Reports Act 1988* and *Access to Health Records Act 1990* (see **9.14** below).

Further, the employer is under a duty *not* to disclose certain types of information about his employees to third parties (see **9.17** below).

For the obligations of applicants to disclose information on matters of nationality and the like, see the *Asylum and Immigration Act 1996* and the *Immigration, Asylum and Nationality Act 2006* and see FOREIGN EMPLOYEES (**23**).

For the obligation to disclose information in relation to criminal convictions see EMPLOYEE'S PAST CRIMINAL CONVICTIONS (**16**).

As to disclosures of information made by employees concerning their employer or its business, the law of breach of confidence is relevant. (See RESTRAINT OF TRADE, CONFIDENTIALITY AND EMPLOYEE INTERVENTIONS (**39**).) Specific protection is also afforded in certain circumstances to employees who disclose information to third parties relating to wrongdoing by the *Public Interest Disclosure Act 1998*. This Act is considered in outline at the end of this chapter (see **9.17** below).

9.2   INFORMATION FOR COLLECTIVE BARGAINING

TULRCA 1992, Part IV Chapter I imposes an obligation on an employer to disclose information necessary for collective bargaining. He can no longer be in the advantageous position of withholding information about such matters as profits and wages when negotiating. The right to enforce such an obligation is given to trade unions recognised for the particular group of employees in whose interests the information is sought (for recognition, see **48.11** TRADE UNIONS – I). The sanctions for non-disclosure are wide: if the information required for negotiation is not disclosed, the Central Arbitration Committee ('CAC') may order that the terms and conditions under negotiation become part of the individual employee's contract of employment. The CAC may order these terms to take effect as claimed or in a modified form. If the employer refuses to implement these terms the employees affected may bring an action for breach of contract in the county court or High Court.

9.3   Duty to disclose

If, at any stage of collective bargaining, a representative of a trade union which is recognised by the employer requests, either orally or, if required by the employer, in writing, information which is both:

(a)   information without which the trade union representative would be, to a material extent, impeded in carrying on with the employer such collective bargaining; and

9.3 Disclosure of Information

(b)   information which it would be in accordance with good industrial relations practice that the employer should disclose for the purposes of collective bargaining,

the employer must (in writing, if requested by the representative) disclose such information, unless it falls within one of the exceptions below (*TULRCA 1992, s 181*).

Exceptions. The employer need not disclose the information where:

(i)   it would be against the interests of national security;

(ii) it is information which he could not disclose without contravening a prohibition imposed by or under an enactment;

(iii) it is information which has been communicated to the employer in confidence or which the employer has otherwise obtained in consequence of the confidence reposed in him by another person;

(iv) it is information relating specifically to an individual and he has not consented to its being disclosed;

(v)   it is information the disclosure of which would cause substantial injury to the employer's undertaking for reasons other than its effect on collective bargaining; or

(vi) it is information obtained by the employer for the purpose of bringing, prosecuting or defending any legal proceedings.

(*TULRCA 1992, s 182(1)*.)

In the performance of his duty under *TULRCA 1992, s 181*, an employer will not be required:

(A)   to produce, or allow inspection of, any document (other than a document prepared for the purpose of conveying or confirming the information) or to make a copy of, or extracts from, any document; or

(B)   to compile or assemble any information where the compilation or assembly would involve an amount of work or expenditure out of reasonable proportion to the value of the information in the conduct of collective bargaining.

(*TULRCA 1992, s 182(2)*.)

A union only has the right to information concerning matters which are relevant to collective bargaining for which it is recognised. Thus, although a union may have the right to represent a certain class of employee, unless it has a right to represent them *for the purpose of collective bargaining* it does not enjoy the statutory right to information (*R v Central Arbitration Committee, ex p BTP Tioxide Ltd* [1981] ICR 843).

Furthermore, information which would not assist collective bargaining need not be disclosed. Thus, the High Court refused to order the disclosure of figures obtained by the Ministry of Defence showing detailed tenders submitted by contract labour cleaners (*Civil Service Union v Central Arbitration Committee* [1980] IRLR 274).

9.4   Code of Practice

ACAS issued its Code of Practice No 2, on 'Disclosure of Information', in 1977 (and subsequently revised in 1998 and 2003. The Code does not provide a complete list of items which should be disclosed, as these will vary according to the circumstances, but merely provides some examples of information which should be considered for disclosure (see also CODES OF PRACTICE (4)). Some of the categories of negotiations for which information may have to be disclosed are set out below.

(a)   Negotiations over pay and benefits.

(b)   Negotiations on conditions of service.

(c)   Negotiations over manpower.

(d)   Negotiations over performance.

(e)   Financial negotiations.

The extent of the duty, and the exceptions, will be matters for interpretation in individual cases. A common sense view of what information is necessary in all the circumstances will be taken.

9.5   Consequences of failure to comply with a request for information

Initial failure to give information. If an employer fails to comply with a request for information from an independent trade union, the union may present a complaint to the CAC. If conciliation seems a possibility, the CAC will refer the matter to ACAS. If ACAS fails in its attempt at conciliation, or if the complaint is not considered initially suitable for conciliation, the CAC will proceed to hear and determine the complaint. The trade union and employer concerned are entitled to be heard, as is any person whom the CAC considers to have a proper interest in the complaint (*TULRCA 1992, s 183(1)–(4)*).

If the CAC finds the complaint wholly or partly well-founded, it will make a declaration specifying the following:

(a)   the nature of the information which it considers should originally have been provided;

(b)   the date (or, if more than one, the earliest date) on which the employer refused or failed to disclose that information or to confirm it in writing; and

(c)   a period (not being less than one week from the date of the declaration) within which the employer must disclose the information or confirm it in writing.

(*TULRCA 1992, s 183(5)*.)

Continued failure to give information. If the employer persists in failing to disclose the information specified in the CAC's declaration within the specified time limit, the trade union may present a further complaint to the CAC who will hear and determine the further complaint. The trade union and employer concerned are again entitled to be heard, as is any person whom the CAC considers has a proper interest in the complaint. If it finds the complaint well-founded, the CAC will issue a declaration specifying the information in respect of which it so finds (*TULRCA 1992, s 184*).

On or after presenting such a further complaint, the trade union may also present a claim relating to the terms and conditions of employment of employees of a description specified in the original claim for information (*TULRCA 1992, s 185(1)*). If the CAC finds or has found the further complaint well-founded, it may make an award that there be incorporated into those employees' contracts of employment:

(i)   the terms and conditions specified in the claim; or

(ii)   other terms and conditions which it considers appropriate.

The award may be back-dated to the date on which the CAC declared that the employer refused or failed to disclose (or confirm in writing) the information (see (b) above) (*TULRCA 1992, s 185(3)*). It may only be made in respect of a description of employees and shall comprise only terms and conditions relating to matters in respect of which the trade union making the claim is recognised by the employer (*TULRCA 1992, s 185(4)*).

9.5 Disclosure of Information

However, if at any time after a trade union has presented a claim under *TULRCA 1992, s 185(1)* to the CAC, and before the CAC has made its award, the employer gives the union the required information, the claim is treated as withdrawn *(TULRCA 1992, s 185(2))*.

Terms incorporated by an award remain in force until they are superseded or varied:

(a)   by a subsequent award under this procedure;

(b)   by a collective agreement between the employer and the union; or

(c)   by express or implied agreement between the employees and the employer as far as it improves any terms and conditions awarded under this procedure.

(TULRCA 1992, s 185(5)).

9.6   TRANSFER OF UNDERTAKINGS REGULATIONS

The *Transfer of Undertakings (Protection of Employment) Regulations 2006 (SI 2006/246)* (which apply to relevant transfers of an undertaking or a service provision change taking place after 6 April 2006) impose obligations upon transferors to disclose to transferees 'employee liability information' *(reg 11)*. Failure to make such disclosure is actionable in the employment tribunal by the transferee *(reg 12)*. Transferor and transferee employers must also consult in relation to employees affected by a relevant transfer and disclose information to recognised trade unions or elected representatives when there is a transfer to which the *Regulations* apply. Both the transferor and transferee vendor must inform representatives of recognised trade unions, or elected representatives, of certain specified matters which arise on the transfer *(regs 13–16)*. A failure to do so is actionable in the Employment Tribunal. See *Royal Mail Group Ltd v Communication Workers Union* [2009] IRLR 1046. (See further, TRANSFER OF UNDERTAKINGS **(50)**).

It should be noted that the recent government consultation on Proposed Changes to the Regulations has, in addition to the proposal to abolish completely the concept of "service provision change", proposed repealing the specific requirements regarding the notification of Employee Liability Information, but making it clear that the transferor should disclose information to the transferee where it is necessary for the transferee and transferor to perform their duties regarding information and consultation.

9.7   INFORMATION NECESSARY FOR HEALTH AND SAFETY PURPOSES

Employers are obliged by the *Health and Safety at Work, etc Act 1974 ('HSWA 1974')* to provide their employees with information necessary to ensure, so far as is possible, their health and safety at work *(HSWA 1974, s 2(2)(c))*. An employer must prepare and, when appropriate, revise a written statement of his general policy with respect to the health and safety at work of his employees and the organisation and arrangements for the time being in force for carrying out that policy, and bring the statement and any revision of it to the notice of all his employees *(HSWA 1974, s 2(3)*; see also **25.18** HEALTH AND SAFETY AT WORK – I). Failure to provide such written information is an offence which carries a maximum fine of £20,000 on conviction in a magistrates' court, and an unlimited fine on conviction in the Crown Court *(HSWA 1974, s 33(1), (1A), (3)*; *Magistrates' Courts Act 1980, s 32(2)*; and see **1.10** INTRODUCTION).

9.8   Safety representatives, and representatives of employee safety

Under *s 2(6)* of the *HSWA 1974* employers are required to consult with safety representatives from the workforce on health and safety matters. Safety representatives, appointed by a recognised trade union (see also **26.21** HEALTH AND SAFETY AT WORK – II), were given statutory powers to obtain certain information by the *Safety Representatives and Safety Committees Regulations 1977 (SI 1977/500), reg 7.* They are entitled, after giving the employer reasonable notice, to inspect and take copies of any document which the employer is legally obliged to keep, except a document consisting of or relating to any health record of an identifiable individual *(reg 7(1))*. In addition, an employer is obliged to make available to safety representatives any information within his knowledge relating to health, safety or welfare, which is necessary to enable them to fulfil their functions, *except*:

(a)   any information the disclosure of which would be against the interests of national security;

(b)   any information which he could not disclose without contravening a prohibition imposed by or under an enactment;

(c)   any information relating specifically to an individual, unless he has consented to its being disclosed;

(d)   any information the disclosure of which would, for reasons other than its effect on health, safety or welfare at work, cause substantial injury to the employer's undertaking or, where the information was supplied to him by some other person, to the undertaking of that other person; or

(e)   any information obtained by the employer for the purpose of bringing, prosecuting or defending any legal proceedings.

(Regulation 7(2), (3).)

Employees who are not covered by trade union-appointed safety representatives are entitled to be consulted by their employer on health and safety matters, by virtue of the *Health and Safety (Consultation with Employees) Regulations 1996 (SI 1996/1513)*. The consultation may be either with the employees directly or with representatives elected by the relevant employees (referred to in the *Regulations* as 'representatives of employee safety'). The employer must provide the necessary information to enable the employees or representatives to participate fully and effectively in the consultation. In the case of representatives, the information must also be sufficient to enable them to carry out their functions under the *Regulations*. Information within the categories (a) to (e) above need not be provided. (See also **26.22** HEALTH AND SAFETY AT WORK – **II.**)

9.9   OCCUPATIONAL PENSION SCHEMES

Under the *Occupational Pension Schemes (Disclosure of Information) Regulations 1996 (SI 1996/1655)* the trustees of such schemes must make available to members and prospective members and (in most instances) to their spouses and to beneficiaries and independent recognised trade unions, various categories of information. These include the constitution of the scheme *(reg 3)*, basic information about the scheme *(reg 4* and *Sch 1)*, information about entitlements *(reg 5* and *Sch 2)* and audited accounts and annual reports *(reg 6* and *Sch 3)*. Each of these regulations details the categories of persons and (where applicable) trade unions to whom the information is to be furnished.

9.10   THE INFORMATION AND CONSULTATION OF EMPLOYEES REGULATIONS 2004 (SI 2004/3426)

On 11 June 2001, the EU Social Policy Council agreed a draft Directive on informing and consulting employees. In March 2002 *Directive 2002/14/EC* ('the *Information and Consultation Directive*') was adopted by the member states. The *Directive* gives employees a right to be informed about the undertaking's economic situation and employment prospects, and

9.10   Disclosure of Information

be informed and consulted with a view to reaching agreement about decisions likely to lead to substantial changes in work organisation or contractual relations. The *Directive* was implemented in the UK by the *Information and Consultation of Employees Regulations 2004, SI 2004/3426* ('the *Regulations*').

The *Regulations* came into force on 6 April 2005 in relation to undertakings with 150 or more employees and 6 April 2007 for undertakings with 100 or more employees. In the case of undertakings with 50 or more employees, the commencement date was 6 April 2008. The *Regulations* do not apply to undertakings employing fewer than 50 employees. It is particularly important to identify whether there is an undertaking employing the requisite number of employees for the provisions of the *Regulations* to apply. The definition of undertaking in the *Regulations* (taken from the *Directive*) is 'a public or private undertaking carrying out an economic activity whether or not operating for gain'. As to calculating the number of employees engaged in the undertaking, this is averaged over a 12 month period. Further, only 'employees' are to be counted and accordingly subcontractors and temporary workers may be excluded from the calculation insofar as they are not 'employees'. The *Regulations* provide two ways in which information and consultation procedures may be established: first, by employee request and second, by the employer deciding to commence negotiations. If there is no existing mechanism for information and consultation in the undertaking then, for an employees' request to initiate the procedure, there must be a written request to the employer (or to the Central Arbitration Committee (CAC)) by not less than 10% of the employees employed in the undertaking. In cases where there is a pre-existing agreement, if a 10% request is made the employer must either enter into negotiations or ballot the employees on the issue of the continuance of the existing agreement. If 40% of the workforce (or a majority of those voting in the ballot) vote in favour of the request then the employer must enter into negotiations for a new agreement. Also, in the case of pre-existing agreements relating to information and consultation, it must in any event be determined if that agreement satisfies the requirements of the *Regulations* (*reg 8(1)*). To be valid the agreement must be in writing, cover all the employees in the undertaking, have been approved by the employees and set out how the employer is to give information to the employees or their representatives and how their views will be sought on the information provided. The EAT in *Stewart (J) v Moray Council* [2006] ICR 1253, [2006] IRLR 592 for the first time considered the *Regulations* in determining whether pre-existing agreements which had been negotiated with trade unions satisfied the requirements of the *Regulations*. On the facts the trade union representatives had agreed and approved the agreements but the agreements had not been specifically put to non-union employees for approval. The CAC rejected an argument that in these circumstances employee approval had not been obtained. It was held that the approval of the representatives was sufficient to satisfy the requirements of the *Regulations*. On the facts, however, one of the agreements failed the statutory requirement of setting out adequately how the employer would give information to the employees and consult with them. The CAC's decision was upheld by the EAT which went on to give guidance on the issue of union involvement and the issue of coverage under *reg 8(1)(b)*. The EAT also found that the requirement of approval by the employees (*reg 8(1)(c)*) could be met by collective approval by trade unions so long as the *majority* of employees were union members. In *Amicus v Macmillan Publishers Ltd* [2007] IRLR 378 the CAC upheld a complaint that the employer was in breach of the *Regulations* by failing to hold a ballot rejecting the employer's arguments that it was entitled to rely on pre-existing information and consultation agreements or that there was a negotiated agreement in place. The decision of the CAC entitled the union to apply for a penalty notice.

If there is no valid pre-existing agreement or no agreement at all and there has been an appropriate request and ballot, then the employer must enter into negotiations for an agreement with employees' representatives. Negotiations may last for up to six months (extendable by agreement).

For a negotiated agreement to be valid it must cover all the employees in the undertaking, be in writing and dated and signed by the employer, set out the circumstances in which the employer will inform and consult the employees and provide for the appointment or election of information and consultation representatives or for information and consultation directly with the employees (*reg 16(1)*). To be valid a negotiated agreement must also be approved by the employees by being signed by all or a majority of the negotiating representatives *and* by at least 50% of the employees in the undertaking *or* approved by 50% of the employees who vote in a ballot (*reg 16(2)*).

If the employer and representatives fail to reach a negotiated agreement (or if the employer fails to enter into negotiations following a 10% request) then the *Regulations* impose standard information and consultation procedures by default. In cases of a negotiated agreement, or where the standard procedures are imposed, the *Regulations* provide specific provisions in order to protect confidential information. By *reg 25* it will be a breach of statutory duty for an individual to disclosure confidential information subject to a right of challenge to the confidentiality in issue which will be heard by the CAC. In certain cases where the effect of disclosure would be potentially seriously prejudicial to the undertaking, the employer may be justified in withholding the information from employee representatives (*reg 26*). As to individual rights, the *Regulations* extend the standard rights to time off and protection against dismissal or detriment on the grounds of taking part in the activities of an information and consultation representative to the employees' representatives. The right to time off, however, does not apply to representatives who are exercising their functions pursuant to a pre-existing agreement. The enforcement of the *Regulations* on a collective level rests with the CAC which will be empowered to adjudicate on the issue of what is an 'undertaking', the number of employees employed in an undertaking, the employer's provision of data, validity of balloting and appointment or election of representatives and whether an employer has complied with obligations under a negotiated agreement or standard arrangement (as the case may be). The *Regulations* provide for substantial penalties for employers who default on their obligations: in cases of complaint of failure to comply with the terms of an agreement (which has been upheld by the CAC), there will be a right for employee representatives to apply to the Employment Appeal Tribunal for a penalty notice (of up to £75,000) to be issued against the employer. The time limit for such an application is three months from the date of the CAC's determination.

The consequences of failure to comply with the *Regulations* are likely to be substantial. In *Amicus v Macmillan Publishers Ltd* [2007] IRLR 378 the CAC upheld a complaint that the employer was in breach of the *Regulations* by failing to hold a ballot rejecting the employer's arguments that it was entitled to rely on pre-existing information and consultation agreements or that there was a negotiated agreement in place. The decision of the CAC entitled the union to apply to the EAT for a penalty notice and the EAT, issuing its first penalty notice in *Amicus v Macmillan Publishers Ltd* [2007] IRLR 885 fined the employer £55,000 commenting (Elias P.) that such a sum should 'deter others from adopting [a] . . . cavalier attitude to the obligations' imposed by the *Regulations*. See also *Darnton v Bournemouth University* [2010] ICR 524, [2010] IRLR 294 in which the EAT observed that previous cases on penalty would be likely to be of little assistance on the fixing of a penalty in another case. Following *Darnton*, some guidance on the approach to fixing a penalty in failure to ballot cases (see *regs 7* and *18*) was provided by *Brown v G4 Security (Cheltenham)* (UKEAT/0526/09/RN) [2010] All ER (D) 84 (Aug). When determining the penalty for a failure to ballot for employee representatives, as well as the non-exhaustive factors relevant to penalty set out in *reg 23(3)* (which comprise gravity of failure, period of time over which failure occurs, reasons for failure, number of employees affected and total number of employees employed) it is appropriate to take into account all additional relevant factors which should be weighted depending on the facts of the case. The proportion of employees affected is relevant as is the extent of any corrective measures taken by the employer following the CAC's determination of breach.

9.10 Disclosure of Information

Guidance on the operation of the *Regulations* is available from the Department for Business Innovation and Skills (BIS) website at www.bis.gov.uk/files/file25934.pdf (see, further, on the provisions of the *Directive* and *Regulations*: 15.4 EMPLOYEE PARTICIPATION). It should be borne in mind that the guidance is merely an interpretation of the law and not definitive. See *Darnton v Bournemouth University* [2009] IRLR 4 (CAC) in which the CAC concluded that the government guidance on the operation of *reg 14* of the *Regulations* was incorrect. The Employment Appeal Tribunal agreed with the CAC's interpretation, explaining that the guidance "has no special status" and that, in relation to *reg 14*, the guidance was wrong. See *Darnton v Bournemouth University* [2010] ICR 524, [2010] IRLR 294, EAT. Specifically in relation to disclosure of information, the Guidance at paragraphs 53–55 provides guidance on the information required to be provided under the *Regulations*. One matter which will often be of substantial concern to employers is disclosure of information which is also considered to be commercially confidential; whether the *Regulations* require the disclosure of such information and, if so, what protections are available to the employer to maintain confidence in the information. The Guidance explains (paragraph 76) that employers may: (1) restrict any information or document they provide to I&C representatives or others, so that it may not be passed on to anyone else (see *regulation 25*). The employer may do this where it is in the legitimate interest of the undertaking. This will include information that is share price sensitive; (2) withhold information or documents altogether that they would otherwise be required to give I&C representatives (see *regulation 26*). They may do this where disclosing it to them would seriously harm the functioning of the undertaking, or be prejudicial to it. In the event of a dispute in relation to confidential information the matter is to be resolved by the CAC. The guidance at paragraph 77 provides further information in relation to confidential information and the imposition of requirements of confidentiality upon the recipients.

9.11 DATA PROTECTION: THE BACKGROUND

The obligations in relation to the storage of personal data on a computer were originally governed by the *Data Protection Act 1984*, passed in response to the Council of Europe's Convention for the Protection of Individuals with regard to Automatic Processing of Personal Data. The *1984 Act* required those processing personal data to register with the Data Protection Registrar (*DPA 1984, s 5(1)*) and restrictions were imposed upon the use or disclosure of data (*DPA 1984, s 5(2)*). Those processing data in relation to employees were obliged to adhere to the 'data protection principles', which provided that the employee should be informed that he is the subject of personal data and be allowed access to such data, and that the data should be corrected or erased where appropriate (*DPA 1984, Sch 1 Part I, para 7*). In addition there were obligations to inform employees whether personal data was kept on them, and to supply a copy of the relevant information (*DPA 1984, s 21*). Finally, an employer could be required to pay compensation where damage was caused by reason of the inaccuracy, loss or unauthorised disclosure of data (*DPA 1984, ss 22, 23*). The current, and considerably more extensive and onerous, data protection obligations required by the *EU Data Protection Directive (95/46)* are now contained in the *Data Protection Act 1998*.

9.12 DATA PROTECTION ACT 1998

On 15 January 1998, the Government published a Data Protection Bill which was designed to implement the *EU Data Protection Directive (95/46)*. On 16 July 1998, the *Data Protection Act 1998* received Royal Assent. The *Data Protection Act 1998* repealed and replaced the *Data Protection Act 1984*. The *Directive* was required to be implemented by 24 October 1998 and, accordingly, it was expected that the *Act* would come into force by this date. However, it actually came into force on 1 March 2000 subject to extensive transitional provisions in relation to paper-based records (see *DPA 1998, Sch 8*). The final provisions of the *Data Protection Act* came into force on 24 October 2007. A full consideration of the law of data protection is beyond the scope of this work. There follows a short summary of the key features of the *Data Protection Act 1998*.

9.13   Data Protection Act 1998: an overview

Most significantly, the law of data protection is extended to cover paper files as well as information stored on computer (*DPA 1998, s 1(1)*). Information contained in a 'relevant filing system' is brought within the compass of the *Act*'s protection. A relevant filing system is defined as non-automated information relating to individuals which is 'structured either by reference to individuals or by reference to criteria relating to individuals, in such a way that specific information relating to a particular individual is readily accessible'. Personal data includes any expression of opinion about a person and indications of intention by the employer or any other person in relation to that individual (*DPA 1998, s 1(1)*). It follows that paper-based personnel records will clearly come within the data protection regime.

Schedule 1 to the *DPA 1998* sets out eight principles relating to the *processing* of personal data. 'Processing' includes collection, storage, organisation, retrieval, alternation, disclosure or destruction of data. The principles may be summarised as follows:

(a)   personal data shall be processed fairly and lawfully;

(b)   personal data shall be obtained only for specified and lawful purposes and shall not be processed in any manner incompatible with those purposes;

(c)   personal data shall be adequate, relevant and not excessive in relation to the purposes for which it is processed;

(d)   personal data shall be accurate and, where necessary, kept up to date;

(e)   personal data shall be kept for no longer than is necessary for the purposes for which it is processed;

(f)   personal data shall be processed in accordance with the rights of data subjects under the *Act*;

(g)   personal data shall be subject to appropriate technical and organisational measures to protect against unauthorised or unlawful processing and accidental loss, destruction or damage; and

(h)   personal data shall not be transferred to a country or territory outside the European Economic Area unless that country or territory ensures an adequate level of data protection.

In *Durant v Financial Services Authority* [2003] EWCA Civ 1746, [2004] FSR 573 the Court of Appeal gave guidance on the meaning of 'personal data' and on a 'relevant filing system'. The Court of Appeal concluded that 'personal data' did not include every piece of information relating to an individual but must have a 'continuum of relevance or proximity to the data subject'. The issue of whether the information was biographical and focused on the individual would assist in identifying personal data. As to 'relevant filing system', the Court of Appeal held that, in relation to manual records, the definition would only apply if the system was of sufficient sophistication to provide similar accessibly to that afforded by a computer system, but would exclude material only accessible by a manual search of files. Under *Part II* of the *Act* employees (as 'data subjects') have the right (by written request and upon payment of a fee) to be told by the employer whether personal data about them is being processed, to be given descriptions of the data and its recipients and to have the data supplied in an intelligible form (*DPA 1998, s 7*). The employer must comply with the request within 40 days. Put simply, employees are entitled in relation to paper records to receive a copy of their personnel file. Confidential references, however, given by the employer for the purposes of education, training or employment are excluded from the right under *s 7*. References given by third parties and held in a file by the current employer are not so excluded.

127

9.13　Disclosure of Information

An employee is given a right under *s 14* of the *DPA 1998* to apply to the High Court or the county court on the ground that personal data relating to him is inaccurate. The court may order the employer to rectify, destroy or erase, as the case may be, data containing expressions of opinion based on inaccurate information. Where the inaccurate data is disclosed to third parties, the court may order the employer to notify those persons that the inaccurate data has been corrected. By *DPA 1998, s 10*, an employee may issue written notice requiring an employer not to process personal data where it is likely to cause substantial and unwarranted damage and distress. By *DPA 1998, s 13*, data subjects may recover compensation not only for loss and damage as a result of inaccurate data processing or unauthorised disclosure but also, in certain cases, for distress caused thereby. *DPA 1998, s 12* limits the use of computers exclusively in certain forms of decision-making and employees may issue notices requiring that employers do not take a decision that significantly affects the employee *solely* on the automatic processing of personal data. The Information Commissioner has extensive powers of enforcement in relation to the *Act*.

Finally, it is significant to note that new restrictions are introduced in relation to the processing of 'sensitive personal data'. Such data is broadly defined as including ethnic or racial origins, political opinions, religious beliefs or other beliefs of a similar nature, trade union membership, physical or mental health and data relating to the commission or alleged commission of any offence or the sentence in relation to any such offence. The House of Lords has given guidance on the meaning of personal and sensitive data in *Common Services Agency v Scottish Information Comr* [2008] UKHL 47, [2008] 4 All ER 851, [2008] 1 WLR 1550. Information which has been manipulated to conceal the identity of living individuals will still be personal data where the individuals can be identified by the data controller. Their Lordships held that 'sensitive data' is a subset of 'personal data' and, as the information related to issues of health (the incidence of childhood leukaemia), it followed that, if the information was personal data, it would also be sensitive personal data. In relation to sensitive personal data, in addition to the *Sch 1* data protection principles, at least one of the conditions found in *Sch 3* to the *DPA 1998* must be satisfied. These conditions include the express consent of the employee for the following:

(i)　　that the processing is necessary for performing or exercising a right or obligation imposed by or in connection with employment;

(ii)　　that the processing is necessary in connection with legal proceedings or for the purposes of obtaining legal advice;

(iii)　　that the processing is necessary for the administration of justice or statutory duty; or

(iv)　　the processing of racial or ethnic origin information is necessary for the purposes of monitoring equality of opportunity or treatment.

Following recent changes to the sanctions applicable to breach of data protection obligations substantial financial penalties may be imposed. Under *sections 55A* and *55B* of the *Data Protection Act 1998*, introduced by the *Criminal Justice and Immigration Act 2008*, the Information Commissioner may, in certain circumstances, serve a monetary penalty notice on a data controller. The amount of the monetary penalty is determined by the Information Commissioner up to a maximum of £500,000. The Commissioner may impose a monetary penalty notice if a data controller has seriously contravened the data protection principles and the contravention was of a kind likely to cause substantial damage or substantial distress. In addition the contravention must either have been deliberate or the data controller must have known or ought to have known that there was a risk that a contravention would occur and failed to take reasonable steps to prevent it.

The Information Commissioner has published the Employment Practices Data Protection Code. The purpose of this Code is to ensure that, in relation to data obtained by employers on their employees, the storage and use of that data complies with the obligations imposed by the *Data Protection Act 1998* and also the *Human Rights Act 1998* (see HUMAN RIGHTS (28)). The Code is in four parts, all of which have now been published by the Information Commissioner. The first part deals with the recruitment and selection of employees and the second part concerns records management. The third part deals with monitoring at work and covers issues such as recording workers' activities by CCTV cameras, automated checking software and recording of workers' telephone calls. The final part of the Code relates to medical information and is titled 'Information about workers' health'. Much of this part of the Code deals with processing of sensitive personal data and covers the following areas: general considerations, occupational health schemes, medical examination and testing, drug and alcohol testing and genetic testing. The text of the Code, together with supplementary guidance, can be found on the Information Commissioner's website at www.ico.gov.uk. See also the ICO's "Data Protection Good Practice Note Subject Access and Employment References" which clarifies how the *Data Protection Act 1998* applies to employment references. The recommendations also apply to other types of reference, such as those provided for educational purposes.

9.14   ACCESS TO MEDICAL REPORTS

Medical reports obtained by an employer should obviously not be disclosed to third parties without the employee's consent.

The *Access to Medical Reports Act 1988* ('*AMRA 1988*') gives individuals a right of access to medical reports relating to them which are supplied by medical practitioners for employment purposes (*AMRA 1998, s 1*). An employer may not apply to a medical practitioner for such a report without the employee's consent (*AMRA 1998, s 3(1)*). The ACAS handbook 'Discipline at Work' includes a model letter of enquiry to an employee's doctor. The employee is entitled to see the report *before* it is supplied (*AMRA 1998, s 4*) and to withhold consent to the report being supplied (*AMRA 1998, s 5(1)*). There is also provision for the correction of errors (*AMRA 1998, s 5(2)*). If there is a failure to comply with the *Act*, an application may be made to the court (*AMRA 1998, s 8*).

The statutory definition of 'medical report' refers to a medical practitioner who is or has been responsible for the clinical care of the individual. Therefore, a report obtained from a company doctor after an examination carried out for a particular purpose is unlikely to be subject to the *Act*. Nor does an employer request a medical report within the meaning of the *Act* where he merely seeks confirmation of information already received (*McIntosh v John Brown Engineering Ltd*, IDS Brief No 441, p 3).

The *Access to Health Records Act 1990* came into force on 1 November 1991 and, in general, applies only to information recorded after that date. It applies to health records, other than those falling within the scope of the *Data Protection Act 1984* (see **9.12** above). Individuals have a right to apply for access to records relating to them to the health professional who holds those records (*AHRA 1990, s 3*). There is also a right to apply for inaccurate records to be corrected (*AHRA 1990, s 6*). The right of access is subject to certain exclusions (*AHRA 1990, ss 4, 5*). A 'health professional' as defined by *AHRA 1990, s 2* includes any registered medical practitioner, so that the *Act* may be expected to apply to company doctors. An application may be made to the court if the holder of a health record fails to comply with the *Act* (*AHRA 1990, s 8*).

9.15   CONFIDENTIAL INFORMATION RELATING TO EMPLOYEES

Apart from the specific statutory obligations referred to above, the employer will normally be under a common law duty not to disclose to third parties confidential information which he holds concerning his employees. In *Dalgleish v Lothian and Borders Police Board* [1991] IRLR 422, there was held to be a *prima facie* case that employees' names and addresses were confidential.

However, it may well be that in a competitive tendering situation in which it is expected that there will be a transfer of an undertaking to the successful contractor (see further on this issue TRANSFER OF UNDERTAKINGS (50)), there is little option but to disclose details of the workforce to potential tenderers. In such a case, it will be preferable to disclose the information, so far as possible, in such a way as not to identify individual employees.

9.16 DISCLOSURE OF INFORMATION BY EMPLOYEES: THE PUBLIC INTEREST DISCLOSURE ACT 1998

The *Public Interest Disclosure Act 1998 ('PIDA 1998')* received the Royal Assent on 2 July 1998 and came into force on 2 July 1999. This somewhat complicated piece of legislation introduces specific rights into the *ERA 1996* for those who disclose information about alleged wrongdoings, including the right not to suffer detriment in employment (*PIDA 1998, s 2*, inserting *ERA 1996, s 47B*) and the right not to be unfairly dismissed for making such disclosures (*PIDA 1998, ss 5, 7*). Such a dismissal will be automatically unfair and there is no qualifying period of employment, nor upper age limit. (See UNFAIR DISMISSAL – I (51).) The provisions of *PIDA 1998* do not apply to employment in the Security Service, the Secret Intelligence Service or the Government Communications Headquarters (*PIDA 1998, s 11*) nor to police officers nor persons employed under a contract of employment in the police service (*PIDA 1998, s 13*).

9.17 Protected disclosures by workers

In order for the protection afforded by the *Act* to apply, the disclosure must be made by 'a worker'. This is broadly defined in *s 43K, ERA 1996* (as inserted by *PIDA 1998, s 1*) and includes contractors acting under the control of the employer, persons on training courses and doctors, dentists, opticians and pharmacists providing services under statutory schemes. The protection is not without limits however. In *Bates van Winkelhof v Clyde & Co LLP* [2012] IRLR 992 the Court of Appeal held that a member of an LLP was not a "worker" for the purposes of *s 230* of the *ERA* and accordingly could not bring claims relating to protected disclosures in the employment tribunal. Leave to appeal to the Supreme Court has been sought.

Second, the disclosure must be a 'qualifying disclosure' as defined in a new *ERA 1996, s 43B* (*PIDA 1998, s 1*). A qualifying disclosure is information which, in the reasonable belief of the disclosing worker, shows one or more of the following six categories of wrongdoing:

(a)   that a criminal offence has been committed, is being committed or is likely to be committed;

(b)   that a person has failed, is failing or is likely to fail to comply with any legal obligation to which he is subject;

(c)   that a miscarriage of justice has occurred, is occurring or is likely to occur;

(d)   that the health or safety of any individual has been, is being or is likely to be endangered;

(e)   that the environment has been, is being or is likely to be damaged; or

(f)   that information tending to show any matter falling within any one of the preceding paragraphs has been, is being or is likely to be deliberately concealed.

In *Geduld v Cavendish Munro Professional Risks Management Ltd* [2010] ICR 325, [2010] IRLR 38 the EAT considered what was required for a disclosure of "information". At issue was whether the contents of a solicitors' letter was a qualifying disclosure. The EAT held that there was a distinction between communicating "information" (which is protected) and making an "allegation" which does not convey facts (and which is not protected. The distinction is well illustrated by an example given in Mrs Justice Slade's judgment in relation to the state of a hospital. To say "health and safety requirements are not being complied with" is an unprotected allegation. To say "the wards of the hospital have not been cleaned for two weeks and sharps were left lying around" is conveying "information" and is protected. On the facts the solicitor's letter contained only an allegation and was not a protected disclosure. See also *Goode v Marks & Spencer plc* (UKEAT/0442/09/DM) [2010] All ER (D) 63 (Sep) and *Smith v London Metropolitan University* [2011] IRLR 884, EAT in which *Cavendish Munro Professional Risks Management Ltd v Geduld* was applied on the "information" point. In *Goode* the EAT observed that the principle was applicable to circumstances where an employee expressed an adverse opinion of what the employer was doing or proposed to do (in that case a redundancy exercise).

The geographical location of the wrongdoing (ie whether inside or outside the United Kingdom) is irrelevant (*ERA 1996, s 43B(2)* inserted by *PIDA 1998, s 1*). A disclosure is not a qualifying disclosure, however, if a person making the disclosure commits a criminal offence in so doing, or if the disclosure is made in breach of legal professional privilege (*ERA 1996, s 43B(3), (4)* inserted by *PIDA 1998, s 1*). The Court of Appeal has held that the requirements under *s 43B* are (i) that the employee believes that the information disclosed meets the requirements of the section (ii) that the employee's belief is objectively reasonable and (iii) that the disclosure is made in good faith (*Babula v Waltham Forest College* [2007] EWCA Civ 174, [2007] IRLR 346). There is no absolute requirement that the legal obligation *in fact* exists, the objective reasonableness of the employee's belief is what is in issue (*Kraus v Penna plc* [2004] IRLR 260 disapproved). In *Korashi v Abertawe Bro Morgannwg University Local Health Board* [2012] IRLR 4, the EAT has given guidance on "reasonable belief". Although the test is objective this has to be considered taking into account the personal circumstances of the discloser. The question is whether it was reasonable for him to believe. Further, where an employee relies upon multiple alleged protected disclosures (as is very common), reasonable belief must be made out in relation to each of the disclosures and a general belief in the broad gist of the content of the disclosures is not enough.

Third, in order to be a 'protected disclosure', a qualifying disclosure must be made only to the category of persons contemplated in the *Act* and not to other persons (*ERA 1996, ss 43C–43H* inserted by *PIDA 1998, s 1*). There are six ways contemplated in which a worker may make a 'protected disclosure', the first four of which are as follows:

(i)   to the worker's employer or (in cases where the information relates to the conduct of another person or to matters for which a person other than the employer has legal responsibility) that other person (*ERA 1996, s 43C*);

(ii)   to a legal adviser in the course of obtaining legal advice (*ERA 1996, s 43D*);

(iii)   to a Minister of the Crown where the worker's employer is (a) an individual appointed under any enactment by a Minister of the Crown or (b) a body whose members are appointed by a Minister of the Crown (*ERA 1996, s 43E*);

(iv)   to a person prescribed by order made by the Secretary of State for the purposes of receiving qualifying disclosure information of relevant categories (*ERA 1996, s 43F*). The details of those persons and the relevant matters in respect of which they are prescribed are set out at length in the *Public Interest Disclosure (Prescribed Persons) Order 1999 (SI 1999/1549)* (as amended). A full list of all regulatory authorities which are prescribed persons to whom protected disclosures may be made is published by the Department of Business Innovation and Skills (BIS) together with a definition of the area of responsibility of each one and contact details. The list can be found at www.direct.gov.uk/en/Employment. Further, from 6 April 2010 the Employment Tribunal Service was empowered by the *Employment Tribunals (Constitution and Rules of Procedure) (Amendment) Regulations 2010 (SI 2010/131)* to provide a copy of the whole or part of any ET1 in which it is alleged a protected disclosure has been made to the relevant regulator. The consent of the claimant is required and the online form ET1 has been amended to provide for the claimant to indicate consent to disclosure.

The fifth category of protected disclosure will permit disclosures to be made to persons other than those contemplated in categories (i) to (iv) above but only if the worker makes the disclosure in good faith, reasonably believes the information to be substantially true, does not make the disclosure for the purposes of personal gain, one of a number of stringent conditions is satisfied, and in all the circumstances it is reasonable to make the disclosure (*ERA 1996, s 43G*). A disclosure is not made in good faith if an ulterior motive is the predominant purpose for making the disclosure even if the worker making the disclosure reasonably believed it was true (*Street v Derbyshire Unemployed Workers' Centre* [2004] EWCA Civ 964, [2004] 4 All ER 839). The burden of proving bad faith in relation to an employee's disclosure rests on the employer (*Bachnak v Emerging Markets Partnership (Europe) Ltd* (0288/05) (2006) 150 Sol Jo LB 435, EAT.

The conditions contemplated by this section are:

(A)   that the worker reasonably believes, at the time of making the disclosure, that he will be subjected to a detriment by the employer if the disclosure is made to the employer or a prescribed person (*ERA 1996, s 43G(2)(a)*); or

(B)   that, in cases where there is no prescribed person in relation to the relevant qualifying disclosure, the worker reasonably believes that evidence relating to the wrongdoing will be concealed or destroyed if a disclosure is made to the employer (*ERA 1996, s 43G(2)(b)*); or

(C)   that the worker has previously made a disclosure of substantially the same information to the employer or to a prescribed person (*ERA 1996, s 43G(2)(c)*).

Finally, in determining whether it was reasonable for the worker to make the disclosure under *s 43G, ERA 1996*, regard must be had to the identity of the person to whom the disclosure is made, the seriousness of the relevant failure, whether the relevant failure is continuing or likely to occur in the future, whether the disclosure is made in breach of a duty of confidence owed by the employer to another person, the action which the employer or person to whom a previous disclosure was made might reasonably have been expected to take as a result of the previous disclosure, and whether the worker complied with any procedure whose use by him was authorised by the employer (*ERA 1996, s 43G(3)–(4)*).

The final category of protected disclosure relates to disclosure of 'exceptionally serious failures' (*ERA 1996, s 43H*). In this situation the worker must make the disclosure in good faith, believing the information to be substantially true, not for personal gain in circumstances when the relevant failure is of an exceptionally serious nature and where in all the circumstances it was reasonable to make the disclosure. For an example of a disclosure to the local press being a protected disclosure see *Collins v National Trust* (2507255/05) (17 January 2006, unreported), EAT.

In determining reasonableness of the disclosure, particular regard shall be had to the identity of the person to whom the disclosure is made.

By *ERA 1996, s 43J* (inserted by *PIDA 1998, s 1*) a provision in an agreement (including a contract of employment) which purports to preclude a worker from making protected disclosures is rendered void.

In cases where an employee/worker has made a protected disclosure as defined in the *Act* and is subjected to a detriment or dismissal as a result by the employer, the remedy will be by way of complaint to an employment tribunal (*ERA 1996, ss 47B, 103A* inserted by *PIDA*

1998, ss 2, 5). It has been held by the EAT that an employee/worker could pursue a detriment claim under *s 47B* against his employer where the protected disclosure relied upon was made whilst employed by a previous employer (*BP Plc v Elstone and Petrotechnics Ltd* [2010] IRLR 558, EAT).

Under *ERA 1996, s 48(2)* it is "for the employer to show the ground on which any act, or deliberate failure to act, was done". In *NHS Manchester v Fecitt* [2012] IRLR 64, reversing the EAT, the Court of Appeal has held that the test in discrimination law of "in no sense whatsoever" derived from *Wong v Igen Ltd* [2005] 3 All ER 812 was not to be imported into the statutory test for whistleblowing. The correct test is whether 'the protected disclosure materially influences (in the sense of being more than a trivial influence) the employer's treatment of the whistleblower'.

Dismissal on grounds of having made a protected disclosure is automatically unfair and there is no qualifying period of employment or upper age limit. For the application of the burden of proof in such cases see *Kuzel v Roche Products Ltd* [2008] EWCA Civ 380, [2008] IRLR 530. As enacted, *PIDA 1998* contemplated that the compensation for unfair dismissal by reason of making a protected disclosure would be on the same basis as that applying to other categories of unfair dismissal. *Section 8, PIDA 1998* kept open the possibility of introducing a different basis for assessment of compensation by way of regulations to be introduced by the Secretary of State prescribing the manner of calculation of compensation in such cases (see *ERA 1996, s 127B*, inserted by *PIDA 1998, s 8(4)*). The relevant *Regulations (Public Interest Disclosure (Compensation) Regulations 1999 (SI 1999/1548))* remove the limit on an unfair dismissal compensatory award in relation to this category of dismissal (see *ERA 1996, s 124(1A)* and *s 103A*). Awards for injury to feelings as a result of subjection to a detriment (but not dismissal) will be calculated on the same basis as in discrimination cases (ie applying the guidance in *Vento v Chief Constable of West Yorkshire Police (No 2)* [2002] EWCA Civ 1871, [2003] IRLR 102). See *Virgo Fidelis Senior School v Boyle* [2004] IRLR 268, EAT. Following a detailed review of the authorities, the EAT in *Commissioner of Police for the Metropolis v Shaw* [2012] IRLR 291 has held that, when making an award of aggravated damages in a whistleblowing claim, such damages are an aspect of injury to feelings as they refer to increasing the injury to feelings by some act in addition to the wrong itself. Tribunals are advised to express the award by identifying the ordinary injury to feelings element and the aggravated element as subheadings of the overall injury to feelings award. In the case of a dismissal which is automatically unfair by reason of making a protected disclosure, as in other areas of unfair dismissal, no award can be made for injury to feelings (cf *Dunnachie v Kingston upon Hull City Council* [2004] IRLR 727, HL).

Interim relief is available in appropriate protected disclosure cases where the claimant is "likely" to succeed in the claim. See the *Employment Rights Act 1996, ss 128* and *129*. In *Dandpat v University of Bath* (UKEAT/408/09) (10 November 2009, unreported) and *Raja v Secretary of State for Justice* (UKEAT/0364/09/CEA) [2010] All ER (D) 134 (Mar) the EAT held that a claimant must show "a pretty good chance of success" (*Taplin v C Shippam Ltd* [1978] IRLR 450 (EAT) – a case under *TULR(C)A, s 163* – applied). More recently in *Ministry of Justice v Sarfraz* [2011] EAT 562, the EAT clarified that, in making an order for interim relief under *ss 128* and *129* of the *1996 Act*, the employment judge in a whistleblowing case must find that it was "likely" that the employment tribunal at the final hearing would find five things: (i) that the claimant had made a disclosure to his employer; (ii) that he believed that that disclosure tended to show one or more of the things itemised at (a)–(f) under *s 43B(1)* of the *1996 Act*; (iii) that that belief was reasonable; (iv) that the disclosure was made in good faith; and (v) that the disclosure was the principal reason for his dismissal. In that regard, the word "likely" does not mean "more likely than not" (that is at least 51% probability) but connotes a significantly higher degree of likelihood.

9.17 Disclosure of Information

In a careful and detailed judgment the Court of Appeal decided that the principles outlined in *Relaxion Group plc v Rhys-Harper* [2003] UKHL 33, [2003] 4 All ER 1113 in relation to acts of victimisation occurring after the termination of the employment contract do apply to detriments suffered after the termination of the employment relationship, for example an unfavourable reference provided by reason of having made a protected disclosure (see *Woodward v Abbey National plc* [2006] EWCA Civ 822, [2006] 4 All ER 1209, [2006] ICR 1436). *Fadipe v Reed Nursing Personnel* [2001] EWCA Civ 1885, [2005] ICR 1760 (Note) which had held that post-employment victimisation under *s 44* of the *ERA* (health and safety cases) was not protected should not now be followed after *Woodward*. In *Onyango v Berkley (t/a Berkley Solicitors)* [2013] UKEAT/0407/12/ZT, the issue was whether the protection against detriment could apply to the situation where the protected disclosure relied upon for the purposes of *s 43B, ERA* occurred after the termination of the employment. The EAT, applying *Woodwood*, concluded that, as a post termination detriment was actionable, there was no reason to exclude the situation where the protected disclosure relied upon also occurred post termination.

The breadth of application of the protection afforded by the concept of a protected disclosure is further illustrated by two cases involving dismissal occurring *after PIDA 1998* came into force but in relation to disclosures of information made *before PIDA 1998* came into force. In circumstances where the dismissal or other detriment imposed by the employer by reason of the disclosure occurred after 2 July 1999 an Employment Tribunal had jurisdiction to hear a complaint (see *Stolt Offshore Ltd v Miklaszewicz* [2002] IRLR 344 and *Meteorological Office v Edgar* [2002] ICR 149). In *Pinnington v City and Council of Swansea* [2005] EWCA Civ 135, [2005] ICR 685, however, the Court of Appeal held that a suspension from work which had commenced prior to the coming into force of *PIDA 1998* but which continued for two days during which the *Act* was in force did not amount to a detriment under *ERA, s 47B* in relation to the final two days as there was no distinct act or omission by the employer on those two days on the grounds of the employee having made a protected disclosure.

The wide ambit of 'protected disclosure' is further illustrated by *Parkins v Sodexho Ltd* [2002] IRLR 109 in which case the EAT held that a complaint by an employee to his employer of a breach of the contract of employment could be a protected disclosure in relation to 'any legal obligation'. It followed that a dismissal by reason of making the complaint could be automatically unfair under the provisions of the *PIDA* 1998 as contained in *ERA 1996*. In *Hibbins v Hesters Way Neighbourhood Project* [2009] ICR 319, [2009] IRLR 198 the EAT held that the protection afforded to whistleblowers is not limited to cases where the wrongdoing relates to wrongdoing or failure by the employer but extends to a disclosure relating to the default of any legal person.

The protection against detriment is not, however, without limits and does not extend to employees deciding to conduct an 'investigation' into possible misconduct by the employer by hacking into the employer's computer system or searching files for 'evidence'. Such activity does not amount to a 'disclosure'. See *Evans v Bolton School* [2006] EWCA Civ 1653, [2007] ICR 641, sub nom *Bolton School v Evans* [2007] IRLR 140 in which a disciplinary warning given to a teacher for hacking into a computer was held to be legitimate and not a detriment imposed by reason of a protected disclosure. It was held in *Waite v South East Coast Ambulance Service NHS Trust* [2009] All ER (D) 43 (Jan) that before a claimant may lodge a whistleblowing detriment claim under *s 48* of the *ERA* a written grievance must be submitted pursuant to the statutory grievance procedures. This no longer applies after 6 April 2009 with the repeal of the statutory grievance procedure provisions of the *Employment Act 2002* by the *Employment Act 2008 (Commencement No 1, Transitional and Savings) Order 2008 (SI 2008/3232)*.

In *NHS Manchester v Fecitt* [2012] IRLR 64 (above) the Court of Appeal held, applying *Majrowski v Guy's and St Thomas' NHS Trust* [2007] 1 AC 224, that the employer cannot be vicariously liable for the acts of employees which are not themselves unlawful. Thus acts of victimisation on grounds of having made a protected disclosure were not in themselves unlawful and there was, accordingly, no basis for vicarious liability. The decision of the EAT in *Carlisle-Morgan v Cumbria County Council* [2007] IRLR 314, [2007] All ER (D) 248 (Jan) (EAT) to the contrary was wrongly decided.

9.18   PROPOSALS FOR REFORM

The government's *Enterprise and Regulatory Reform Bill* proposed amendment to *s 43B* of the *ERA* to the effect that the disclosure would only be protected if, in the reasonable belief of the worker, the disclosure was made in the public interest. The current version of the Bill, following House of Lords amendments promulgated on 23 February 2013, further proposes removal of the requirement of "good faith" in relation to disclosures qualifying for protection, but with a power in the employment tribunal to reduce compensation in any cases where good faith is not found by up to 25%. In addition a new clause was proposed affording protection to workers who suffer detriment imposed by fellow workers or agents of the employer by reason of making protected disclosures, thus addressing the lacuna in protection identified in *NHS Manchester v Fecitt* [2012] IRLR 64 (above). In addition there are proposals in relation to extending the definition of a "worker" qualifying for protection.

10 Discrimination and Equal Opportunities – I

10.1 THE SCOPE AND APPROACH OF THIS CHAPTER

Scope

Over the course of the last half-century, UK employment law has seen the ongoing and often vigorous development of a body of equal opportunities law. The underlying concept is a straightforward one: people should not be subject to disadvantage in the job market or in the workplace for reasons that have nothing to do with the skills they have to offer or their performance of their duties. There has been a steady incrementing of characteristics of the employee upon which it is no longer accepted that an employer may base employment-related decisions. As the law stands they are: sex; marital or civil partnership status; race; disability; gender reassignment; religion or belief; sexual orientation; pregnancy or maternity leave; and age. These grounds are referred to below as the 'protected characteristics'.

On 8 April 2010, the *Equality Act 2010* ("*EA 2010*") received Royal Assent. Many of its most important provisions came into force on 1 October 2010. The principal purpose of the Act was to consolidate the numerous individual pieces of legislation that had previously made up the patchwork of the earlier law. This edition of the Handbook does not set out the old law. It does, however, retain material relating to caselaw decided under the former regime insofar as it remains relevant to the interpretation of *EA 2010*.

Discrimination on grounds of sex in respect of contractual terms and conditions, which is known more familiarly as "Equal Pay" or, to use the language of the *EA 2010*, "Equality of Terms", is treated separately (see EQUAL PAY (21)).

Approach

The approach taken below is first to explain the relevant general principle and immediately thereafter to indicate where particular issues arise in the context of its application to one or more of the protected characteristics.

10.2 LEGAL SOURCES AND GUIDANCE MATERIAL

Each protection against discrimination has been introduced by a legislative instrument. Sometimes the Domestic law implements an obligation originally to be found in a European legislative measure. However, even those measures, such as protection against discrimination on grounds of sex or race, which have domestic origins have since been shaped by European Law.

On 6 April 2011, the Employment and Human Rights Commission issued a Code of Practice on Employment (the "*EHRC* Code") which can be downloaded from the EHRC's website at the following address: www.equalityhumanrights.com/legal-and-policy/equality-act/equality-act-codes-of-practice. Tribunals and courts must take into account any part of the Code that appears to them relevant to any questions arising in proceedings.

The Home Office produced a series of guides providing short, clear explanations of the impact of *EA 2010* on different sectors. They may be found online at: www.homeoffice.gov.uk/publications/equalities/equality-act-publications/equality-act-guidance.

10.2 Discrimination and Equal Opportunities – I

In the light of the European Court of Justice's decision in *Eweida v United Kingdom*, the EHRC has issued further guidance on dealing with religious discrimination issues in the workplace. It can be downloaded from: www.equalityhumanrights.com/advice-and -guidance/your-rights/religion-and-belief/.

BASIC DISCRIMINATION CONCEPTS

Set out immediately below is a summary of the legislative framework applicable to each of the prohibited grounds:

10.3 Sex

Sex discrimination in employment is prohibited by the *EA 2010*. Sex is identified as a protected characteristic at *EA 2010, s 4*. Both men and women are protected (*EA 2010, s 11*).

Men cannot complain of sex discrimination where a woman has received "special treatment . . . in connection with pregnancy or childbirth" (*EA 2010, s 3(6)(b)*). However, in *Eversheds Legal Services Ltd v De Belin* [2011] IRLR 448, [2011] ICR 1137, EAT (a case brought under *SDA 1975*), it was held that where the "special treatment" was disproportionate, in the sense of being more favourable treatment than was reasonably necessary to compensate the woman for the disadvantages occasioned by her pregnancy, a claim could be brought by a man using the woman as a comparator.

Equal treatment between the sexes in employment is within the scope of competence of the European Union. The *Equal Treatment Directive (2006/54/EC)* ('*ETD 2006/54/EC*') is vertically directly effective which means that public sector workers are able to rely directly on its provisions. *EA 2010* is interpreted, so far as possible, so as to be consistent with the requirements of the *Directive*.

On 1 May 1999, the *Amsterdam Treaty* came into force. It amended *art 119* of the *Treaty of Rome* (now *art 157* of the *Treaty on the Functioning of the European Union*) incorporating a principle of equal treatment into the *Treaty* itself. This, in turn, has opened up the possibility of a horizontally directly effective right to equal treatment conferred on both public and private sector employees.

10.4 Marital or civil partnership status

"Marriage and civil partnership status" is identified as a protected characteristic at *EA 2010, s 4*. Only those who are married or who have a civil partner are protected (*EA 2010, s 8(2)*). The *Act* does not protect those who are discriminated against on grounds of being single.

A protection against discrimination on grounds of marital or family status was included in *ETD 76/207/EEC* but is absent from the *ETD 2006/54/EC* which superseded it. It is unclear whether or not the intention was to push marital status outside the range of protected characteristics for the purposes of European Law (see *Dunn v Institute of Cemetery and Crematorium Management* [2012] All ER (D) 173 (Feb)).

10.5 Race

Race is identified as a protected characteristic by *EA 2010, s 4*. For the definition of "race" see **10.20** below.

Article 19 of the *Treaty on the Functioning of The European Union* (formerly *art 13* of the *Treaty of Rome*) confers a power on the European Union to legislate to combat discrimination on a variety of grounds including 'racial or ethnic origin'. On 29 June 2000, the European Council issued the *Race Discrimination Framework Directive (Council Directive 2000/43/EC)*. The scope of the *Directive* is not identical to that of *EA 2010*. For instance, the *Directive* does not apply to discrimination on grounds of nationality (*art 3, para 2*).

10.6   Gender reassignment

Gender reassignment is identified as a protected characteristic at *EA 2010, s 4*. For the definition of "gender reassignment" see **10.21** below.

10.7   Religion or belief

Adherence to a particular religion or holding a particular religious or philosophical belief is identified as a protected characteristic at *EA 2010, s 4*. For the definition of "religion", "religious belief" and "philosophical belief" see **10.22** below. Lacking a particular religion or religious or philosophical belief is also a protected characteristic (*EA 2010, s 10*).

The protection has its origins in *art 19(1)* of the *Treaty on the Functioning of the European Union* which provides that 'the Council . . . may take appropriate action to combat discrimination based on . . . religion or belief . . . '. On 27 November 2000, the Council issued *Directive 2000/78/EC* establishing a general framework for equal treatment in employment and occupation ('the *Framework Directive 2000/78/EC*'). The directive included a prohibition of religious discrimination.

10.8   Sexual orientation

Sexual orientation is identified as a protected characteristic at *EA 2010, s 4*. For the definition of "sexual orientation" see **10.23** below.

The origin of the protection is, once again, *art 19* of the *Treaty on the Functioning of the European Union* and the *Framework Directive 2000/78/EC*.

10.9   Pregnancy or maternity leave

Pregnancy and Maternity are identified as protected characteristics at *EA 2010, s 4*. For the definitions of "pregnancy" and "maternity" see **10.24** below.

10.10   Age

Age is identified as a protected characteristic at *EA 2010, s 4*. For the definitions of "age" and "age group" see **10.25** below.

The *Act* is the present implementation of the age-related provisions of the *Framework Directive 2000/78/EC* which required member states to enact legislation prohibiting age discrimination in employment.

Following the case of *Mangold v Helm* [2006] IRLR 143 in the European Court of Justice, there is some question as to whether the *Directive* made it unlawful to discriminate on the grounds of age even prior to 1 October 2006 (that being the date on which the *Employment Equality (Age) Regulations 2006 (SI 2006/1031)* first implemented the *Directive*). This is a matter of some controversy and is not addressed in detail here. For a discussion by the Advocate General of the European Court of Justice which is somewhat critical of the judgment in *Mangold*, see *Félix Palacios* at paras 79 to 100. In *Bartsch v Bosch und Siemens Hausgeräte (BSH) Altersfürsorge GmbH*: C-427/06 [2009] All ER (EC) 113, [2009] 1 CMLR 163, the ECJ held that the prohibition on age discrimination was not mandatory in a case where the allegedly discriminatory measure was not intended to implement the *Directive* at a time before the time limit for transposing the *Directive* had expired. However, in the case of *Seda Kucukdeveci v Swedex GmbH & Co KG*: C-555/07 [2010] IRLR 346, the ECJ reiterated that the principle of non-discrimination on the ground of age should be regarded as a general principle of European Law and held that the European provisions may be relied upon to challenge legislation which was enacted prior to the coming into force of the directive.

10.11 Disability

Disability is identified as a protected characteristic at *EA 2010, s 4*. For the definition of "disability" see **10.26** below.

The *Act* is the present implementation in UK law of the prohibition against discrimination on grounds of disability to be found in the *Framework Directive 2000/78/EC*. In *HK Danmark*, acting on behalf of *Ring v Dansk Almennyttigt Boligselskab*: C-335/11 [2013] IRLR 571, the CJEU held that the *Framework Directive* had to be read, so far as possible, so as to be compatible with the *United Nations Convention on the Rights of Persons with Disabilities*.

10.12 MEANING OF DISCRIMINATION

There are four principal ways in which a person may discriminate against another:

(i)   by *directly* discriminating against them (**10.13** below);

(ii)   by *indirectly* discriminating against them (**10.34** below);

(iii)   by *victimising* them (**10.38** below); or

(iv)   by *harassing* them (**10.39** below).

In addition there are two forms of discrimination which are specific to disability discrimination:

(v)   failure to make reasonable adjustments (a close cousin of indirect discrimination) (**10.37** below); and

(vi)   discrimination arising from disability (**10.33** below).

There is also a discrete form of direct discrimination which prohibits unfavourable treatment of because of pregnancy or maternity leave (see **10.30**ff below).

10.13 DIRECT DISCRIMINATION

Direct discrimination is defined at *EA 2010, s 13(1)*:

"A person (A) discriminates against another (B) if, because of a protected characteristic, A treats B less favourably than A treats or would treat others."

The basic definition is modified insofar as it relates to age discrimination. If the protected characteristic is age, A does not discriminate against B if A can show A's treatment of B to be a "proportionate means of achieving a legitimate aim" (see further below at **10.34**).

The definition differs from that which applied under the pre-existing law in that rather than the less favourable treatment having to be "on grounds of" the relevant protected characteristic, the treatment has to be "because of it". The explanatory notes accompanying the Act suggest that the change in language is intended to make the legislation easier to understand but not to bring about any material change in the law (*EA 2010, EN Para 61*).

The account set out immediately below breaks the legislative tests into two elements: less favourable treatment and the reason for that treatment. Whilst that division reflects the manner in which a tribunal will usually approach the issue, in *Shamoon v Chief Constable of the Royal Ulster Constabulary* [2003] UKHL 11, [2003] 2 All ER 26, [2003] ICR 337 a number of their Lordships took the view that it may sometimes be appropriate to ask the latter question first. For an account of when it will be appropriate to do so, see **10.15** below.

Less favourable treatment

10.14 *Unfavourable and less favourable treatment distinguished*

Most people asked to state what the aim of anti-discrimination legislation might be would likely begin by suggesting that people should not be treated badly because of their protected characteristic. However, the test for direct discrimination is not whether a person treats another "unfavourably" because of their protected characteristic. Instead, the test requires that it be shown that someone has been treated "less favourably" than another. The reason why the legislation takes this approach is that rather than trying to ensure that people are treated well, it is aimed at ensuring that people are treated equally. So, for instance, few would argue against the proposition that a pay rise is a good thing. However, if an employer gives his ethnic minority employees smaller pay rises than he gives white employees because of their race he commits an act of unlawful discrimination. The ethnic minority employees have been favourably treated (their pay has increased) but they have been less favourably treated. The flipside is that an employer who treats all of his employees equally badly will not normally be found to have discriminated. It is the equality rather than the quality of the treatment that matters. For that reason, the House of Lords has suggested that the conduct of a hypothetical reasonable employer is irrelevant to the question whether he has unlawfully discriminated:

> 'The fact that, for the purposes of the law of unfair dismissal, an employer has acted unreasonably casts no light whatsoever on the question whether he has treated an employee less favourably for the purposes of the [*EA 2010*]'.

(*Glasgow City Council v Zafar* [1998] 2 All ER 953, [1997] 1 WLR 1659, [1998] ICR 120. See also *Martins v Marks & Spencer plc* [1998] IRLR 326.) Despite the House of Lords' robust rejection of the relevance of merely unreasonable treatment, other authorities have been prepared to recognise a limited and indirect relevance. Thus in *Law Society v Bahl* [2003] IRLR 640, EAT, the Employment Appeal Tribunal took the view that the more unreasonable the treatment the more the credibility of any non-discriminatory explanation proffered may be called into question. The question was considered more closely by the Court of Appeal (*Bahl v Law Society* [2004] EWCA 1070; [2004] IRLR 799). The Court of Appeal reiterated that unreasonable behaviour cannot found an inference of discrimination. An employer is not obliged, therefore, to lead evidence that others have been treated equally unreasonably. However, if there is no explanation for the unreasonable treatment the absence of an explanation (as opposed to the unreasonableness of the treatment) might found an inference. The Court of Appeal returned to the issue in a later case in which no explanation was provided and held that whilst a tribunal should not be 'too ready' to infer unlawful discrimination from unreasonable conduct in the absence of evidence of other discriminatory behaviour, it was 'not wrong in law' to do so (*Wong v Igen Ltd* [2005] EWCA Civ 142, [2005] 3 All ER 812, [2005] ICR 931). *Nelson v Newry and Mourne District Council* [2009] IRLR 548 approached the question from the opposite direction, appearing to suggest that the reasonableness of the employer's position pointed away from a conclusion of discrimination. In *Eagle Place Services Ltd v Rudd* [2010] IRLR 486, the EAT took yet another approach to the question of the relevance of the reasonableness of the employer's behaviour. The employer dismissed a disabled employee unreasonably. The employer said that the appropriate comparator would be someone towards whom they would have behaved equally unreasonably but who was not disabled. The EAT disagreed with the employer's analysis, holding that it was not open to the employer to say that they would have behaved unreasonably towards the comparator.

Even in cases where employees have plainly been treated differently, it may still be difficult immediately to determine whether there has been less favourable treatment. Thus, where male and female employees are subject to different but comparably restrictive dress requirements there is no less favourable treatment on grounds of sex (*Schmidt v Austicks Bookshops Ltd* [1977] IRLR 360, EAT; and see *Smith v Safeway plc* [1996] ICR 868, CA and *Department for Work and Pensions v Thompson* [2004] IRLR 348, EAT).

The test of what amounts to less favourable treatment is an objective one (*Burrett v West Birmingham Health Authority* [1994] IRLR 7, EAT). However, there may be a limited role for the subjective preferences of the complainant. Thus, where a local education authority provided more places for boys than for girls in selective schools, the House of Lords held that it was not necessary for the complainant to demonstrate that selective education was, objectively, 'better' than non-selective education. It was enough that, by denying the girls the same opportunity as the boys, the council was depriving them of a choice which was valued by them (or at least by their parents) and which was a choice obviously valued, on reasonable grounds, by many others (*Birmingham City Council v Equal Opportunities Commission* [1989] AC 1155, [1989] 2 WLR 520, HL).

It is the treatment itself rather than its consequences which must be different and less favourable (*Balgobin v Tower Hamlets London Borough Council* [1987] ICR 829, EAT).

Segregating a person from others on racial grounds is deemed to be less favourable treatment (*EA 2010. s 13(5)*). Thus, it is not open to an employer to argue that the provision of segregated facilities for his black employees is not discriminatory even though the facilities provided for black workers are equal to, if not better than, those provided for his white employees.

In the case of a pre-operative transsexual, avoiding less favourable treatment does not necessarily require that the complainant be treated as if their gender had already been changed. What is required in any case will depend on the particular circumstances (*Croft v Royal Mail Group plc* [2003] EWCA Civ 1045, [2003] IRLR 592: pre-operative male to female transsexual not treated less favourably when not allowed to use female toilets).

10.15 *Comparators*

As will be apparent from the examples given above, identifying direct discrimination involves the making of a comparison. It is open to an employee either to demonstrate that another specific individual employee has been more favourably treated (in which case that other employee is known as the 'comparator') or to establish that, absent any concrete examples, the tribunal may nevertheless still be sure that the employer would have treated another employee more favourably. In the latter case, the Tribunal considers what is known as a 'hypothetical comparator'. In either case it is the employee that has the burden of proof at this stage.

Identifying a suitable comparator

(a) General Requirement that there should be no material difference between the complainant and the comparator

The *EA 2010* requires that the circumstances of the comparator should not be materially different:

> "On a comparison of cases for the purposes of section 13 [direct discrimination] . . . there must be no material difference between the circumstances relating to each case." (*EA 2010, s 23(1)*)

The question whether a comparator is appropriate is one of "fact and degree" – the circumstances of the complainant and the comparator need not be identical (*Hewage v Grampian Health Board* [2012] UKSC 37, [2012] ICR 1054).

For guidance on the question of when circumstances will be materially different see *Dhatt v McDonalds Hamburgers Ltd* [1991] 3 All ER 692, [1991] 1 WLR 527, [1991] ICR 238: it was not discriminatory to treat potential employees differently according to whether they were or were not free to work in the United Kingdom without permission and, hence, it was legitimate to require evidence of such permission only from those who were not British or EU citizens. (See also *Wakeman v Quick Corpn* [1999] IRLR 424, CA: UK employees of a Japanese company could not complain about higher rates of pay enjoyed by colleagues seconded from Japan. The fact that they were seconded meant that their circumstances were materially different to those of the UK employees; but see *Spicer v Government of Spain* [2004] EWCA Civ 1046, [2005] ICR 213; *Bullock v Alice Ottley School* [1993] ICR 138: The comparator selected in a sex discrimination case concerned with a disparity in retirement ages was inappropriate because he performed a different job to that performed by the complainant; *Shomer v B & R Residential Lettings Ltd* [1992] IRLR 317, *Leeds Private Hospital Ltd v Parkin* [1992] ICR 571 and *Brook v Haringey London Borough Council* [1992] IRLR 478.) In *Lockwood v DWP* [2013] EqLR 206, EAT, a younger employee complained that those older than 35 had voluntary redundancy payments calculated on a more generous basis. The EAT determined that as the financial circumstances of those older than 35 tended to be different and they tended to find new work harder to come by, they were in materially different circumstances. Where a female prison officer complained about being made to search male prisoners the appropriate comparator was a man required to search female prisoners and not a man required to search men (*Saunders v Home Office* [2006] ICR 318, EAT). In a case where a Muslim school support worker was suspended for refusing to remove her veil when interacting with pupils the appropriate comparator was a woman who was not a Muslim who also covered her face: *Azmi v Kirklees MBC* [2007] ICR 1154.

When dealing with hypothetical comparators it might be possible to construe the legislation so as to require the tribunal to construct a comparator who is 'in effect, a clone of the applicant in every respect (including personality and personal characteristics)' save that they are, for instance, of a different race. However, that approach was rejected in *Madden v Preferred Technical Group CHA Ltd* [2004] EWCA Civ 1178, [2005] IRLR 46 (per Wall LJ at paragraph 87). The effect of such an approach would be to run together the two relevant questions, namely whether the complainant was less favourably treated and whether they were less favourably treated on the prohibited ground. The reasoning would be that if the complainant and comparator are identical in all respects save, for instance, for their race any less favourable treatment must, logically, be on racial grounds. In practice it can be very difficult to keep the two issues distinct. There are signs that this difficulty is being embraced by the appeal courts. In *Stockton on Tees Borough Council v Aylott* [2010] EWCA Civ 910, [2011] ICR 1279, the Court of Appeal invokes the decision of the House of Lords in *Shamoon v Chief Constable of the Royal Ulster Constabulary* [2003] UKHL 11, [2003] 2 All ER 26, [2003] ICR 337 and suggests that it will often be appropriate to start by identifying the reason for the treatment the employee complains of. If the answer is that the reason is a protected characteristic, the finding of less favourable treatment will likely follow as a matter of inevitability. Since the hypothetical comparator is designed to allow a tribunal to decide whether there has been less favourable treatment and that finding is, in turn, intended to be a signpost pointing to a prohibited and discriminatory reason for the employer's actions, the *Shamoon* approach effectively starts the journey at the point which had originally been identified as the destination. Adopting that approach will often make it unnecessary to identify a hypothetical comparator at all, as Mummery LJ himself makes clear in *Stockton* (see also *JP Morgan Europe Ltd v Chweidan* [2011] EWCA Civ 648, [2012] ICR 268). Where a tribunal determines, nevertheless, to identify one it should determine which circumstances are relevant by reasoning backwards from the reason for the treatment accorded to the complainant. As Mummery LJ puts it in *Stockton*:

'The relevant circumstances and attributes of an appropriate comparator should reflect the circumstances and attributes relevant to the reason for the action or decision which is complained of.'

The selection of the comparator is the responsibility of the complainant. However, in some circumstances, a tribunal that determines that the complainant's chosen comparator is inappropriate may be required to go on to make the comparison with a hypothetical comparator (see *Balamoody v UK Central Council for Nursing, Midwifery and Health Visiting* [2001] EWCA Civ 2097, [2002] IRLR 288: the complainant was unrepresented. The Court of Appeal appears to have felt that the tribunal had a rather better grasp of the nature of the complainant's case than he did himself).

(b) Comparators in cases of direct disability discrimination

Where the protected characteristic is disability *EA 2010, s 23(2)*, requires that the "circumstances" that must not materially differ between complainant and comparator specifically include a person's abilities. In other words, the complainant and comparator must have the same abilities. This may mean that the appropriate comparator is also a disabled person. At first glance this might appear illogical. However, the rationale is that direct disability discrimination is not intended to protect against less favourable treatment received because the employee lacks certain abilities but rather against less favourable treatment because they have a "particular disability". An example would be an employee who is dismissed because they are HIV+. Their abilities may be indistinguishable from those of any other employee but the employer is not prepared to employ people with that particular disability. Discrimination on the grounds that an employee lacks a particular ability is the subject of a separate protection dealt with at **10.39** below. It is known as "discrimination arising from disability" and differs to direct discrimination in that it is engaged where the employee is treated unfavourably (rather than *less* favourably) and a defence of justification is potentially available.

Watts v High Quality Lifestyles Ltd [2006] IRLR 850, [2006] All ER (D) 216 (Apr), EAT was the first appellate decision to consider direct disability discrimination. The claimant was a support worker who had suffered a number of injuries including cuts and bites in the course of his work with persons with learning difficulties. Upon revealing to management that he was HIV+, he was suspended and later dismissed on the grounds that his position was untenable after a risk assessment concluded that injuries involving broken skin were commonplace. The employment tribunal found that such treatment was on the grounds of disability and upheld his claim. However, the EAT found that the employment tribunal had failed to consider whether he had in fact been less favourably treated than a hypothetical comparator would have been. The EAT also found that in identifying the appropriate comparator, the Employment Tribunal should have found that the comparator had 'some attribute, whether caused by medical condition or otherwise, which is not HIV+ . . . [which] must carry the same risk of causing to others illness or injury of the same gravity, here serious and possibly fatal'. It is thought that this approach to identifying comparators might be to construe 'relevant circumstances' too narrowly. A comparator with an attribute carrying precisely the same risk of causing illness or injury to others would almost always be likely to be treated the same as the claimant, in which case the claim of direct discrimination would fail. The EAT's approach to comparator in this case, which requires that the comparator is effectively someone who is HIV+ by another name, could also let discrimination based on the stigma of being HIV+ slip through the net. In *Aylott v Stockton-on-Tees Borough Council* [2010] EWCA Civ 910, [2011] ICR 1278, the Court of Appeal considered that an employment tribunal had been entitled to exclude from the characteristics of its hypothetical comparator certain unsatisfactory aspects of the complainant's behaviour and performance on the basis that they stemmed from his particular disability. The tribunal had been entitled to exclude the particular disability itself from the comparison, but it seemed they could also exclude certain effects of the disability. The *Stockton* approach would appear, therefore, to take a more employee-friendly approach than

Watts, though the latter authority was cited by the Court of Appeal with approval (see *Aitken v Commissioner of Police of the Metropolis* [2011] EWCA Civ 582, [2012] ICR 78 where *Aylott* was distinguished on its facts. The ET in *Aitken* considered threatening behaviour should be part of the circumstances applicable to a hypothetical comparator and the complainant did not suggest at that stage that the behaviour arose from his disability).

How the costs of supporting someone with a disability should be factored into the necessary comparison for direct discrimination purposes was at issue in *Cordell v Foreign and Commonwealth Office* [2012] ICR 280, EAT. The complainant was profoundly deaf. She was not appointed to a diplomatic post in Kazakhstan because of the cost and difficulty maintaining continuity of the services of a lip-speaker. Her case was the cost should be compared to cost of paying for diplomats posted overseas having their children educated in boarding school. The circumstances of those with children needing education was said to be materially different. A comparison that allowed the complainant to be compared with parents was too general to be useful. The EAT preferred to taken the *Shamoon* approach (see **10.15** (a) above) and to ask the reason why the complainant was not appointed. The answer was not her disability but the costs of dealing with it, which meant that any less favourable treatment was not because of her disability and the claim for direct discrimination failed.

(c) Comparators in sexual orientation cases

Specific provision is made in relation to sexual orientation:

> "If the protected characteristic is sexual orientation, the fact that one person (whether or not the person referred to as B) is a civil partner while another is married is not a material difference between the circumstances relating to each case. (*EA 2010, s 23(3)*)."

(d) Comparators in Gender reassignment cases: absence due to undergoing a gender reassignment

EA 2010, s 16 makes specific provision protecting transsexuals who are absent from work because of a gender reassignment. A person's absence is treated as being because of gender reassignment "if it is because the person is proposing to undergo, is undergoing or has undergone [a] process (or part of [a] process)" for the purpose of reassigning the person's sex by changing physiological or other attributes of sex (*EA 2010, ss 7(1)* and *16(3)*). For the purposes of determining whether or not the employee has been treated less favourably because of their protected characteristic, *EA 2010, s 16* provides that the employee should be their own comparator. The Tribunal asks whether they would have been treated more favourably if they had been absent because of sickness or injury (*EA 2010, s 16(2)(a)*) or absent for some other reason where the Tribunal is satisfied that "it is not reasonable for [the employee] to be treated less favourably" (*EA 2010, s 16(2)(b)*).

(e) Comparators in pregnancy and maternity leave cases

There is a specific prohibition on treating a person unfavourably (as opposed to less favourably) to be found at *EA 2010, s 18*. Because what is prohibited is unfavourable treatment there is no need for a comparator. This reflects long-standing European authority to the effect that because only women may fall pregnant there is no appropriate male comparator. There is, in other words, no equivalent man whose circumstances could be said not to be materially different (see *Dekker v Stichting Vormingscentrum voor Jong Volwassenen (VJV - Centrum) Plus*: C-177/88 [1990] ECR I-3941, [1992] ICR 325 and *Webb v EMO Air Cargo (UK) Ltd* [1994] ICR 770, ECJ. For UK authority confirming the absence of a need for a comparator in pregnancy discrimination cases see *McGuigan v TG Boynes & Sons* [1999] 633 IDS Brief 6, EAT; *Smith v Gardner Merchant Ltd* [1998] IRLR 510 per Ward LJ obiter and *Fletcher v NHS Pensions Agency* [2005] ICR 1458, EAT). The *s 18* protection against unfavourable treatment on grounds of pregnancy is dealt with at **10.30** below.

However, *EA 2010, ss 4* and *13* appear to have the effect that pregnancy and maternity are also amongst the protected characteristics which are prohibited from being the reason for less favourable treatment. Perhaps surprisingly, it seems to be open to an employee who can make out a claim under *EA 2010, s 18* also to bring a claim under *s 13. EA 2010, s 18(7)* expressly precludes an employee bringing both a *s 18* pregnancy claim and a *s 13* sex discrimination claim. However, it does not preclude a *s 13* pregnancy discrimination claim. Why would a complainant ever want to bring a *s 13* pregnancy discrimination claim given the express protection conferred by *s 18*? The answer may be that there are cases of pregnancy discrimination that would not fall within *s 18*. The *s 18* protection is only available to a complainant during the so-called "protected period" (broadly from conception to the end of maternity leave – see *EA 2010, s 18(6)*). Thus, an employee who is discriminated against because she announces that she intends to become pregnant; because her employer discovers that she has miscarried; or because her employer mistakenly believes that she is pregnant cannot bring a *s 18* claim and will have to rely on *s 13*.

The uncertainty that remains is whether a complainant bring a *s 13* pregnancy discrimination claim has to identify a comparator. The need to establish less favourable treatment suggests that she does but since only women can announce an intention to get pregnant, miscarry or be mistakenly assumed to be pregnant, how can the apparent requirement for a comparator be reconciled with the European authorities identified above? The legislation provides no answer and the matter awaits appellate consideration.

(f) Comparators in sex discrimination cases: is a comparison necessary where the conduct complained of is 'gender-specific'?

The short answer is 'yes'. At one point the courts and tribunals had come to accept that a comparative approach might not always be possible or appropriate in sex discrimination cases. As explained above, it has long since been accepted that a woman treated unfavourably on grounds of pregnancy has no valid male comparator. Attempts have been made to extend the principle to other instances of so-called "gender-specific" treatment, typically in cases of harassment where the female victim of harassment was treated in a way that a male victim would not have been.

The House of Lords in *Macdonald v Advocate General for Scotland* [2003] UKHL 34, [2004] 1 All ER 339, [2003] ICR 937 (see also *Smith v Gardner Merchant Ltd* [1998] 3 All ER 852, [1998] IRLR 510) specifically reaffirmed the need for a comparator even where the alleged discriminatory behaviour could be said to be gender-specific.

(g) Irrelevance of whether the alleged discriminator shares the protected characteristic with the complainant.

EA 2010, s 24(1) makes express provision to the effect that it is irrelevant whether the alleged discriminator (referred to as "A") has the relevant protected characteristic:

> "For the purpose of establishing a contravention of this Act by virtue of Section 13(1), it does not matter whether A has the protected characteristic".

Performing the comparison

In most cases involving an actual comparator the comparison will be relatively straightforward. For instance, a complainant who has not been appointed to a particular post may seek to compare themselves to the person who was and evidence will centre on the selection process. Similarly, an employee who is made redundant may seek to compare themselves to someone who was retained in employment.

Matters are more complex when dealing with hypothetical comparators because the Tribunal will be asked to infer that the complainant has been less favourably treated. By definition one is dealing with a situation where there may be little direct evidence. In *Chief Constable of West Yorkshire v Vento* [2001] IRLR 124, the EAT suggested that a tribunal might look to see how 'unidentical but not wholly dissimilar cases' had been dealt with. Thus, someone whose circumstances differ sufficiently from those of the complainant to make them an inappropriate comparator may nevertheless have relevance in the context of the consideration of how a hypothetical comparator would have been treated.

In other cases a complainant may wish to lead evidence of, for instance, sexist comments made by the respondent on the basis that they tend to suggest a discriminatory attitude and thus that a male employee would have been treated differently. In such a case evidence principally relevant to the question whether less favourable treatment was on a prohibited ground may assist in establishing that the complainant would have been less favourably treated. Support for this approach may be found in *Shamoon v Chief Constable of the Royal Ulster Constabulary* [2003] UKHL 11, [2003] 2 All ER 26, [2003] ICR 337, in which a number of members of the House of Lords suggested that the constituent elements of the test could be approached in a different order to that described above where it was appropriate to do so. The decision in *Shamoon* was concerned with the law as it was before the enactment of *SDA 1975, s 63A*. That section formally reversed the burden of proof in sex discrimination cases. The reverse burden of proof, which now applies to all of the protected characteristics (see **10.3**) is to be found at *EA 2010, s 136*. As the burden only shifts where a prima facie case of discrimination has been established an exploration of the employer's reasons for actions as a first step would seem to jump the gun. However, the EAT has stressed the particular suitability of the *Shamoon* guidance when dealing with cases involving hypothetical comparators (see *Laing v Manchester City Council* [2006] ICR 1519, EAT). The Court of Appeal has sought to allow tribunals the greatest flexibility, holding both that whilst it is generally good practice to follow the two stage test, there is no necessary error of law if a tribunal does not do so (*Brown v Croydon London Borough Council* [2007] EWCA Civ 32, [2007] IRLR 259) and that it cannot be said to be an error of law in cases involving hypothetical comparators to deal first with the question of less favourable treatment (see *Madarassy v Nomura International plc* [2007] EWCA Civ 33, [2007] ICR 867 and *JP Morgan Europe Ltd v Chweidan* [2011] EWCA Civ 648, [2012] ICR 268).

10.16 *Positive discrimination*

There is only a very limited role in UK law for so-called 'positive discrimination'. It involves treating one group of employees more favourably (and thus their colleagues less favourably) on a prohibited ground but for well-intentioned reasons. As explained below (see **10.17**), the UK law largely disregards such intentions and motives. Well-intentioned discrimination is still unlawful. However, the law does allow a limited scope for positive discrimination. The essence of exception is that, in certain defined circumstances, positive discrimination may be lawful where the purpose is to redress the effect of pre-existing discriminatory disadvantage. A full consideration of positive discrimination may be found at **11.10** Discrimination and Equal Opportunities – II.

'Because of' the protected characteristic

10.17 *General principles*

EA 2010, s 13 prohibits less favourable treatment "because of a protected characteristic". The use of the formula "because of" in preference to that used in the earlier legislation, (ie "on grounds of") is not intended materially to alter the law. The explanatory notes accompanying the Act suggest that the intention is simply to make the meaning of the legislation more readily accessible (*EA 2010, EN, Para 61*).

The requirement that the less favourable treatment be "because of" the protected characteristic means that it is not sufficient for a tribunal to be satisfied that a complainant has been less favourably treated than their chosen actual or hypothetical comparator. The tribunal will also want to consider *why* the complainant was less favourably treated. It is only if the reason for the less favourable treatment was a protected characteristic that liability will be established. Broadly, once less favourable treatment has been shown, it is for the employer to show that it was not because of the relevant protected characteristic.

The issue is one of causation. The question of causation is generally resolved in other areas of the law by reference to the so-called 'but for' test. One might ask, for instance, 'but for the complainant's sex would she have been less favourably treated?' If the answer is 'no', causation could then be said to have been made out. The 'but for' approach was adopted in *James v Eastleigh Borough Council* [1990] 2 AC 751, [1990] 2 All ER 607. In that case pensioners were entitled to use a swimming pool for free. As the state pension age was higher for men than for women, men were disadvantaged. The complainant was able to say that 'but for' his sex he would have had a lower pension age and have been able to use the swimming pool for free.

The advantage of the 'but for' test in *James* was that it meant that the complainant did not have to show any discriminatory intention or motive. However, in other cases appeal courts have preferred an approach which concentrates on what might be called 'reasons for action'. In *Martin v Lancehawk Ltd (trading as European Telecom Solutions)* [2004] All ER (D) 400 (Mar), EAT, the Appeal Tribunal considered a case where an employer dismissed a female employee when their affair concluded. It was argued that as the employer would not have slept with a man, it could be said that 'but for' the complainant's sex she would not have been dismissed. The EAT found that there had been no discrimination. They felt that the 'reason why' the complainant was dismissed was the end of the affair and not her sex. Her sex was causally relevant but not causally determinative. The Appeal Tribunal also considered that the appropriate comparator was a homosexual lover and that such a lover would have been treated no differently. On that analysis the 'but for' test would not have been made out. However, the Appeal Tribunal went on, in any event, to reject the 'but for' test formulating instead a test based on 'the reason why' the employer has acted as he had, relying on dicta in *Chief Constable of West Yorkshire Police v Khan* [2001] UKHL 48, [2001] 1 WLR 1947, [2001] ICR 1065 and *Shamoon* (above). In *B v A* [2007] IRLR 576, EAT, the tribunal was said to have erred by applying the 'but for' test when, had they asked whether the claimant had been dismissed 'by reason' of her sex they would have concluded that she had not been – rather she had been dismissed because her employer, who was also her lover, had been motivated by sexual jealousy on seeing her in the company of another man.

The best guidance is first to apply the 'but for' test and then to ask whether it can nevertheless be said that 'the reason why' the complainant was less favourably treated was a reason other than the protected characteristic, always bearing in mind that it is not necessary to take the still further step of showing a discriminatory 'motive' underpinning the discriminatory reason for action. This last point is dealt with immediately below.

Provided that the causal question points to unlawful discrimination, the Tribunal is not required to go on to investigate the employer's motives or intention. Thus, unintentional direct discrimination is unlawful as are acts of direct discrimination performed for entirely non-discriminatory motives (see *R (on the application of E) v Governing Body of JFS (Secretary of State for Children, School and Families, interested parties) (United Synagogue intervening)* [2009] UKSC 15, [2010] IRLR 136 and *Ahmed v Amnesty International* [2009] ICR 1450, [2009] NLJR 1400, EAT). See also *Martin v Devonshires Solicitors* (UKEAT/86/10) [2011] ICR 352 which considers both *JFS* and *Ahmed* and proposes a distinction between "motive" which is irrelevant, and "motivation" which is not. On the other hand, the presence of a discriminatory motive or intention will plainly be compelling evidence pointing to a finding of unlawful discrimination *Nagarajan v London Regional Transport* [2000] 1 AC 501 at 519).

Discrimination will be treated as being because of the protected characteristic if the substantial or effective, although not necessarily the sole or intended, reason for the discriminatory treatment was the characteristic (see *R v Commission for Racial Equality, ex p Westminster City Council* [1984] ICR 770; affd in part [1985] ICR 827 – a race case). In *Barton v Investec Henderson Crosthwaite Securities Ltd* [2003] ICR 1205, EAT, the Employment Appeal Tribunal went further in the context of sex discrimination holding that sex should not be 'any part of the reasons for the treatment in question' (approved by the Court of Appeal in *Igen v Wong* (above). Even so, it must be a significant factor in the sense of being more than trivial. See also *Villalba v Merrill Lynch & Co Inc* [2007] ICR 469, EAT).

10.18 *Meaning of 'because of sex'*

EA 2010, s 11 provides:

> "In relation to the protected characteristic of sex –
>
> (a)   a reference to a person who has a particular protected characteristic is a reference to a man or to a woman; and
>
> (b)   a reference to persons who share a protected characteristic is a reference to persons of the same sex."

'Sex' is not defined in *EA 2010*. 'Woman' and 'man' are defined as being a female and male respectively of any age (*EA 2010, s 212*).

Before the UK enacted specific protection for transsexuals, the European Court of Justice decided that discrimination against transsexuals was a form of sex discrimination. In *P v S*: C–13/94 [1996] All ER (EC) 397, [1996] ECR I–2143, the European Court adopted a broad test which rendered unlawful any discrimination based 'essentially if not exclusively on the sex of the person concerned'.

10.19 *Meaning of 'because of marital or civil partnership status'*

EA 2010, s 8 provides:

> "(1)   A person has the protected characteristic of marriage and civil partnership if the person is married or a civil partner;
>
> (2)   In relation to the protected characteristic of marriage and civil partnership –
>
> (a)   a reference to a person who has a particular protected characteristic is a reference to a person who is married or a civil partner;
>
> (b)   a reference to persons who share a protected characteristic is a reference to persons who are married or are civil partners."

"Marriage" is not defined in the Act. The *EHRC Code* does provide some further guidance, however. It says of "marriage" that it will cover any formal union of a man and woman which is legally recognised in the UK as a marriage. In *Bick v Royal West of England Residential School for the Deaf* [1976] IRLR 326, a tribunal decided (with very considerable reluctance) that the predecessor provisions in the *SDA 1975* did not protect employees who were merely engaged. That decision was not followed in *Turner v Turner* (ET/2401702/04) which concluded that the right to marry enshrined in *Art 12* of the *European Convention on Human Rights*, meant that the provision had to be interpreted so as to require those dismissed because they are planning to marry are protected.

Equally, civil partnership is not defined in *EA 2010*, however a civil partner is someone who has been registered as the civil partner of a person of the same sex (see *Civil Partnership Act 2004, s 1*). The *EHRC Code* makes it clear that it also encompasses those whose civil partnerships have been registered abroad (Para 2.33).

For an example of direct discrimination on grounds of marital status see *Chief Constable of the Bedfordshire Constabulary v Graham* [2002] IRLR 239, EAT. In *Hawkins v Atex Group Ltd and Others* [2012] All ER (D) 71 (Apr), [2012] ICR 1315, the EAT indicated that the appropriate comparator will usually be somebody who is in a relationship akin to (but falling short of) marriage. That comparator ensures that the focus is on the significance of the married status itself and not, for instance, on the question of which particular individual the employee is married to.

10.20 Discrimination and Equal Opportunities – I

10.20 *Meaning of 'because of race'*

"Race" is defined by *EA 2010, s 9(1)* to include: "colour", "nationality" and "ethnic or national origins". A "racial group" is "a group of persons defined by reference to race" (*EA 2010, s 9(3)*).

In relation to the protected characteristic of race:

> "a reference to a person who has a particular protected characteristic is a reference to a person of a particular racial group" (*EA 2010, s 9(2)(a)*)

A racial group can comprise two or more distinct racial groups (*EA 2010, s 9(4)*). Thus, a French national will be a member of the racial group consisting of French people and of a racial group consisting of all foreign nationals.

EA 2010, s 9(5) conferred a power on a Minister of the Crown to amend *s 9* by order to provide for caste to be an aspect of race. *Section 65* of the *Employment Rights and Regulatory Reform Act 2013* ("*ERRRA 2013*") amends *EA 2010, s 9* by adding caste to the definition of race. The amendment is to take effect at a date that had not yet been appointed at the date of going to press.

A distinction is drawn between racial origin and citizenship: *Ealing London Borough Council v Race Relations Board* [1972] AC 342; *Tejani v Superintendent Registrar for the District of Peterborough* [1986] IRLR 502.

The House of Lords in *Mandla v Dowell Lee* [1983] 2 AC 548, [1983] 1 All ER 1062 held that 'ethnic . . . origins' in the definition of 'racial group' meant a group which was a segment of the population distinguished from others by a sufficient combination of shared customs, beliefs, traditions and characteristics derived from a common or presumed common past, even if not drawn from what in biological terms was a common racial stock (see also *Para 2.39* of the *EHRC Code*). On that basis, it held that Sikhs were a racial group entitled to the protection of the *RRA 1976*. In *R (on the application of E) v Governing Body of JFS (Secretary of State for Children, School and Families, interested parties) (United Synagogue intervening)* [2009] UKSC 15, [2010] IRLR 136, SC, the Supreme Court, by a majority, determined that there was a discrete and "narrower sense" of discrimination on grounds of ethnic origin which applied to less favourable treatment on the ground of "lineage" or "descent". In the particular case a Jewish faith school applied an admission criterion that required that each pupil's mother should either be Jewish by birth or else have converted to Judaism under the auspices of an Orthodox synagogue. The application of the criterion was held to be an act of direct discrimination on grounds of ethnic origin.

Where 'racial group', is defined by 'colour' the group may comprise people of more than one ethnic origin (*Lambeth London Borough Council v Commission for Racial Equality* [1990] ICR 768).

'National origins' means more than the legal nationality acquired at birth (*BBC Scotland v Souster* above). One may 'acquire' national origins by adherence.

Jews are members of a racial group (see, for example, *Seide v Gillette Industries* [1980] IRLR 427). So are gypsies in the sense of those who belong to the Romany race, although mere habitual wanderers are not (*Commission for Racial Equality v Dutton* [1989] QB 783, [1989] 1 All ER 306). Rastafarians are not an ethnic group (*Crown Suppliers (Property Services Agency) v Dawkins* [1993] ICR 517, CA). The Scots and the English are separate racial groups (*Northern Joint Police Board v Power* [1997] IRLR 610, EAT and *BBC Scotland v Souster* [2001] IRLR 150, Ct Sess).

In *Bradford Hospitals NHS Trust v Al-Shabib* [2003] IRLR 4, EAT, the tribunal decided that a grievance panel had treated the complainant less favourably on racial grounds when they formed an adverse impression of him as a result of his being 'difficult to control' and 'emotive'. The tribunal found that the respondent had erred by failing to take into account that, as an Iraqi, the complainant could not be expected to behave in a 'conventional Anglo–Saxon way'. However, the EAT found that it was not open to the tribunal to assume, in the absence of evidence, that there was a material difference in the manner in which 'Anglo–Saxons' and Iraqis might behave.

In *Simon v Brimham Associates* [1987] ICR 596, the Court of Appeal reached the somewhat surprising conclusion that an employment tribunal was entitled to find that a Jew who had withdrawn a job application when he learned that to be Jewish might preclude his selection was not discriminated against in circumstances in which the interviewer had merely asked him the same question about his religion as he would have asked any candidate, not knowing whether or not he was Jewish.

Where an employee was dismissed for fighting, he was not dismissed on racial grounds merely because his employer applied a policy of not taking into account acts of provocation and thus ignored the fact that he had been provoked by acts of racial abuse and violence. The policy was applied consistently to employees of all races: *Sidhu v Aerospace Composite Technology Ltd* [2001] ICR 167, CA.

The relevant race need not be the race of the employee that is the victim of the discrimination. For instance, in *Showboat Entertainment Centre v Owens* [1984] 1 All ER 836, [1984] 1 WLR 384, EAT a white employee was dismissed for refusing to carry out a discriminatory instruction. See the account of Associative Discrimination below at **10.27**.

In *Redfearn v Serco Ltd* [2006] EWCA Civ 659, [2006] ICR 1367, the Court of Appeal refused to extend the approach taken in *Showboat* to a case in which a white bus driver whose passengers and colleagues were mainly Asian was dismissed, in essence, for being a member of the British National Party. It was a condition of membership of that party that one should be white. The employee contended that the race of his passengers and colleagues had substantially contributed to the decision to dismiss him. The Court of Appeal distinguished *Showboat* on the basis that whilst it was within the policy of *RRA 1976* that those affected by an employer's racist policies should be protected, it did not follow that racists should be protected from the anti–discriminatory policies of their employers. The Court of Appeal in *English v Thomas Sanderson Blinds Ltd* [2008] EWCA Civ 1421; [2009] ICR 543, [2009] IRLR 206 expressed doubts about whether *Redfearn* had been correctly decided but accepted that they were bound by it. Mr Redfearn subsequently brought proceedings in the European Court of Human Rights ([2013] IRLR 51). The Court did not focus on the question whether the dismissal had constituted an act of race discrimination. Instead it found that there had been a breach of his *Art 11* right to Freedom of Association. The Court considered that he should have had access to an unfair dismissal remedy without the need to serve a period of qualifying employment. At April 2013, the Government proposed to deal with the ECtHR decision by amending *ERA 1996, s 108* to provide that a claim for unfair dismissal may be brought without the need for a qualifying period of service where the reason for dismissal "is or relates to the employee's political affiliation".

10.21   *Meaning of 'because of gender reassignment'*

A transsexual person is defined by *EA 2010, s 7(2)* to mean "a person who has the protected characteristic of gender reassignment". A person has the protected characteristic of gender reassignment if:

> "the person is proposing to undergo, is undergoing or has undergone a process (or part of a process) for the purpose of reassigning the person's sex by changing physiological or other attributes of sex" (EA 2010, s 7(1))

The *EHRC Code* emphasises that it is not necessary for an employee to have undergone any medical treatment before the protection is attracted (*Para 2.24*) – a proposal is sufficient. That is so, suggests the Code, even if the proposal is revoked (*Para 2.25*). Cross-dressing is covered only where "as part of the process of reassigning their sex, someone is driven by their gender identity to cross-dress" (*Para 2.26*).

In *Ashton v Chief Constable of West Mercia Constabulary* [2001] ICR 67, EAT considered a case concerning a transsexual undergoing a gender reassignment. As part of her treatment she received medication, which caused her to be depressed. Her depression affected her ability to work and she was dismissed on grounds of incapability. The EAT upheld the tribunal's finding that the fact that the incapability was a result of the side-effects of her medication did not establish a *causal* link between the dismissal and her sex and thus that she had not been unlawfully discriminated against.

In *A v Chief Constable of the West Yorkshire Police* [2002] EWCA Civ 1584, [2003] ICR 161, the Court of Appeal considered that, for the purposes of employment law, post-operative transsexuals fall to be treated for all purposes as having their re-assigned sex. Thus a post-operative male to female transsexual is to be treated as a woman rather than as a transsexual. Their Lordships reasoning was as follows: Post-operative male to female transsexuals are to be treated as women for the purposes of the European Convention on Human Rights (see *Goodwin v United Kingdom* (2002) 35 EHRR 447). The *ETD 76/207/EEC* (since repealed and replaced by the *ETD 2006/54/EC*) had to be interpreted, so far as possible, as being compatible with the *ECHR*. *SDA 1975* (the predecessor of the *EA 2010*), in turn, had to be interpreted, where possible, as being consistent with the *ETD 76/207/EEC*. However, the *Goodwin* case recognised that a departure from the normal rule may be required where 'significant factors of public interest . . . weigh against the interests of the individual applicant in obtaining legal recognition of her gender reassignment'. The decision was affirmed by the House of Lords ([2004] UKHL 21, [2004] ICR 806). The *Gender Recognition Act 2004* created a system of "gender recognition certificates". Anyone who holds a certificate must be treated according to their acquired gender.

The *EHRC Code* suggests that where a person has been diagnosed as having "Gender Dysphoria" or "Gender Identity Disorder" that may be an impairment within the meaning of the disability discrimination provisions of the *EA 2010* (*Para 2.28*).

10.22 *Meaning of because of religion or belief*

Meaning of 'belief'

"Belief" means any religious or philosophical belief and a reference to a belief includes a reference to a lack of belief (*EA 2010, s 10(2)*).

A reference to a person who has a particular characteristic is a reference to a person of a particular religion or belief and a reference to persons who share a protected characteristic is a reference to persons who are of the same religion or belief (*EA 2010, s 10(3)*).

Meaning of 'religion'

EA 2010, s 10(1) defines "religion", with some circularity, to mean "any religion". It also provides that any reference to religion includes a reference to a lack of religion with the effect that an employer is no more free to discriminate against atheists than he is against Christians. No more detailed definition is given. This represents, it would appear, a deliberate decision on the part of the Government taken when the protection was first introduced by the *Employment Equality (Religion or Belief) Regulations 2003, SI 2003/1660* (*"RBR 2003"*). The Government assumed that controversy about the scope of the definition will be rare and that in controversial cases it is best left to the courts and the tribunals to resolve the matter without further guidance.

It is tempting to suppose that it is the difficulty of defining 'religion' rather than the ease of doing so which has led the Government to avoid offering a more specific definition. The *EHRC Code* does not take matters very much further. It emphasises that a religion need not be "mainstream or well known". It does, however, have to have "a clear structure and belief system". Denominations or sects may be considered religions in their own right for the purposes of the *Act* (*EHRC Code, Para 2.54*)

Although not a matter which the *EHRC Code* touches upon, it is suggested that a religion will be concerned with the supernatural and, in particular, is likely to be theistic, ie it will be a belief about a god or gods.

The present context is not the only one in which this difficult definitional question has been faced and some assistance can be gained from consideration of those other contexts.

One context in which the issue has arisen is the law pertaining to charities. The advancement of religion is recognised as a charitable purpose (see *Income Tax Special Purposes Comr v Pemsel* [1891] AC 531). In their decision of 17 November 1999 in relation to an application for charitable status made by the Church of Scientology, the Charity Commissioners reviewed the existing case law on the definition of religion and derived the following characteristics:

(i)   a belief in a god, deity or supreme being (*R v Registrar General, ex p Sergedal* [1970] 2 QB 697 – though Buddhism qualified as a religion despite there being some doubt as to whether it required a belief in a supreme being);

(ii)   reverence and recognition of the dominant power and control of any entity or being outside their own body and life (*Sergedal* above); and

(iii)   faith and worship: faith in a god and worship of that god (*South Place Ethical Society* [1980] 1 WLR 1565).

The Commissioners identified a further significant factor, absent from the express words of the *EA 2010*; whilst the court will not consider the truth of the tenets of the relevant religion it will not treat as a religion everything which calls itself a religion. In practice the tribunal has adopted a similar approach. Because Charity Law is concerned with the 'advancement of religion', if the court is satisfied that the tenets of a particular sect 'inculcate doctrines adverse to very foundations of all religion and/or subversive of all morality' it will not be treated as 'advancing religion'. On its face the *EA 2010* covers all religions whether or not they espouse morally repellent precepts. This is likely to lead to problems in which religious precepts conflict with the interests of other protected groups. As we shall see below, the tribunals have adapted Human Rights law to create a requirement that the belief at issue be "worthy of respect in a democratic society".

Another context in which the definition of religion arises as an issue is the *European Convention on Human Rights*. This second context has a more direct relevance because the *EA 2010* implements a European Directive and European legislation has to be interpreted, wherever possible, so as to be compatible with the *European Convention on Human Rights*. ECHR, art 9(1) provides that 'everyone has the right to freedom of thought, conscience and religion'. The right also includes 'freedom to change . . . religion or belief . . . and freedom, either alone or in community with others and in public or in private, to manifest [one's] religion or belief, in worship, teaching, practice and observance'. However, whilst it might be hoped that a developed body of authority of the European Court of Justice would be available to assist in interpreting the scope of the words 'religion or belief', in fact there is remarkably little helpful case law. The Commission has assumed that Scientology is a religion (*X and Church of Scientology v Sweden* (1979) 16 DR 68) whereas the UK courts have consistently declined to confer that status upon them (though they would probably amount to a 'philosophical belief'). The court decided that 'Wicca' was not a religion on the ground that it had no clear structure or belief systems (*X v United Kingdom* (1977) 11 DR 55) (but note Wicca appeared as an example of a religion in the *ACAS Code* issued to assist with the interpretation of the *RBR 2003*).

10.22　Discrimination and Equal Opportunities – I

The *EHRC Code* lists (at *Para 2.53*) a number of what it describes as "commonly recognised religions": the Baha'i faith, Buddhism, Christianity, Hinduism, Islam, Jainism, Judaism, Rastafarianism, Sikhism and Zoroastrianism. However, the *EHRC Code* also stresses that a religion does not have to be "mainstream" or "well-known" and that "sects" and "denominations" may also be affected (*Para 2.54*).

Meaning of 'religious belief'

Religious belief is defined as follows:

> 'any religious　.　.　.　belief and a reference to belief includes a reference to a lack of belief

(*EA 2010, s 10(2)*)

The Act distinguishes, therefore, between religion and religious belief. The distinction arises from the fact that religious beliefs are not exclusively about a god or gods. Most religions profoundly affect what might be described as one's 'world view'. In other words, religious adherence affects what one believes about the world as well as what one believes about the supernatural (but see *R (on the application of Williamson) v Secretary of State for Education and Employment* [2001] EWHC 860 (Admin), [2002] 1 FLR 493 where Elias J opined that a religious belief, for the purposes of the *ECHR* was not simply a belief which is 'in accordance with the religious faith' but which 'embod(ied) or define(d)' the belief or conviction itself). When *Williamson* came before the House of Lords, their Lordships felt it unnecessary to explore the definitional question as the *ECHR*, like *EA 2010*, protects both religious and non-religious beliefs: [2005] 2 AC 246).

In *Eweida v British Airways* [2009] ICR 303, [2009] IRLR 78 (affd without considering this issue in [2010] EWCA Civ 80, [2010] ICR 890), the EAT decided that a belief could qualify as a religious belief even if it was unique to the employee (i.e no-one else shared the same belief) and without it being a mandatory requirement of an established religion.

In *Eweida*, the belief at issue was the visible wearing of a crucifix. In *Azmi v Kirklees MBC* [2007] ICR 1154, the belief was that of certain Muslims that Muslim women should only be in the presence of unrelated males when they are veiled. These are both examples of religious beliefs that deal not with whether there is a deity but how an adherent is expected to behave. A difficult question can arise as to whether the conduct that the employer is seeking to prevent should be treated as a religious belief or a "manifestation" of that belief. The latter concept is to be found in the *European Convention on Human Rights* (at *Art 9(2)*) and is dealt with separately below.

In refusing permission to appeal in the case of *Macfarlane v Relate Avon*, Lord Justice Laws touched upon a further distinction. The law, he said, protects "the right to hold and express a belief" but does not protect "that belief's substance" ([2010] EWCA Civ B1, [2010] IRLR 872). A similar position was adopted by the EAT in *Eweida* (above).

Meaning of 'philosophical belief'

Philosophical belief is defined as follows:

> 'any　.　.　.　philosophical belief and a reference to belief includes a reference to a lack of belief'

(*EA 2010, s 10(2)*)

As originally enacted *RBR 2003* protected those who held philosophical beliefs which could be said to be 'similar' to religious beliefs. The question how one identified a 'philosophical belief' which was sufficiently 'similar' to a religious belief as to fall within the scope of the legislation was harder to answer the more closely it was considered. Perhaps the defining characteristic of a religious belief is its theistic nature; it is a belief in a god or gods. If the belief is theistic it is a religious belief. If it is not it is difficult to see how it could be said to be in any way 'similar' because the defining characteristic is absent.

An alternative approach was to assume that the similarity with which the legislation was concerned arose not from the essence of the belief but rather its ancillary characteristics. This would seem to be the approach adopted in the *ACAS Code* which stressed the likely importance of there being a 'clear belief system' and the belief being one which is 'profound' and which affects the adherent's 'way of life or view of the world'. The *ACAS Code* offered Humanism as an example of the sort of belief that might qualify. Other examples would include Confucianism and some commentators have even suggested that Vegetarianism might qualify.

With effect from 30 April 2007, *RBR 2003, reg 2(1)* was amended. The requirement that the philosophical belief be 'similar' to a religious belief was removed. Under *EA 2010* simply holding a particular philosophical belief (or equally, not holding it) will suffice. The logical consequence of the present formulation must be that holding a belief that is philosophical but not similar to religious beliefs will qualify for protection.

In *McClintock v Department of Constitutional Affairs* [2008] IRLR 29, the EAT gave the following guidance:

> 'The test for determining whether views can properly be considered to fall into the category of a philosophical belief is whether they have sufficient cogency, seriousness, cohesion and importance and are worthy of respect in a democratic society: see *Campbell & Cosans v United Kingdom* [1982] 4 EHRR 293.'

McClintock was applied by the Employment Appeal Tribunal in *Nicholson v Grainger plc* [2010] ICR 360, EAT, which upheld a finding by the Employment Tribunal that a belief in man-made climate change was capable of amounting to a philosophical belief for the purposes of the regulations. In addition to the matters specifically identified as relevant in the quotation from *McClintock* above, the Appeal Tribunal emphasised that the belief must be genuinely held and that it must not (as was the case in *McClintock*) be merely an opinion or viewpoint based on the present state of information available. The Appeal Tribunal rejected 4 proposed limitations on the types of beliefs that would qualify for protection, finding: (1) The belief does not need to be shared by anyone else; (2) It need not form part of a "fully-fledged system of thought"; (3) It may be a political belief so long as it otherwise qualifies and (4) A philosophical belief based upon science may qualify.

In *Hashman v Orchard Park Garden Centre* [2011] EqLR 426 the Tribunal concluded that a belief in the sanctity of life and, more specifically, beliefs that fox-hunting and hare-coursing were incompatible with the sanctity of life were each beliefs qualifying for protection. The EAT dismissed an appeal on the basis that it had no reasonable prospect of success.

As an example of a belief that would not qualify the *EHRC Code* suggests a belief in a philosophy of racial superiority for a particular racial group. Such a belief would, it is suggested, be incompatible with human dignity and conflicts with the fundamental rights of others.

Manifesting a Religious Belief

The European Convention on Human Rights protects the manifestation of one's religion or beliefs at *Art 9(2)*:

> "Freedom to manifest one's religion or beliefs shall be subject only to such limitations as are prescribed by law and are necessary in a democratic society in the interests of public safety, for the protection of public order, health or morals, or for the protection of the rights and freedoms of others."

The *EA 2010* does not provide express protection for manifestation. The distinction between holding a belief and manifesting it has, however, arisen in the Domestic Law. It is a distinction which is expressly spelt out in the EHRC Code (at Paras 2.60 and 2.61). In *McConkey v Simon Community Northern Ireland* [2009] UKHL 24, [2009] ICR 787, Lord Simon said in relation to the *Fair Employment and Treatment (Northern Ireland) Order 1998, (SI 1998/3162)*:

> ' . . . [T]he Order is concerned with discrimination against someone on the basis of the religious belief or political opinion that he holds. It is not concerned with discrimination on the ground of actions that the person may take in support of that religious belief or political opinion'

Insofar as *McConkey* might be thought to mean that manifestation of belief falls outside the scope of *EA 2010*, that cannot be right in the light of the ECHR's decision in four joined cases: *Eweida and others v United Kingdom* 48420/10, 59842/10, 51671/10 and 36516/10. In two of the cases (*Eweida* and *Chaplin*), the complainants were challenging policies that precluded them from wearing crucifixes over their work clothes. In Eweida the reason for the policy (which was later abolished) was the employer's corporate image. The European Court of Human Rights concluded that wearing a religious symbol was a manifestation of religious belief. Departing from the trend of earlier authority, the Court decided that the freedom was not protected merely by the fact that the complainant could obtain work with another employer with a less restrictive policy (though that was a factor that could be taken into account in determining whether the restriction to which she objected was a proportionate interference with her right). The Court took the view that concern about corporate image was an inadequate basis for restricting Ms Eweida's rights and found that the UK had failed to provide proper protection for them. This led to inaccurate press comment to the effect that there was now a "right" to wear a cross to work. In *Chaplin* however, the complainant's case was rejected. Her employer forbade the wearing of a cross on a necklace because it created health and safety concerns. The Court felt that that provided a defensible basis for restricting her right. The other two cases concerned employees whose religious beliefs meant that they did not wish to provide services to same sex couples. In Ladele a registrar of births deaths and marriages did not wish to perform civil partnership ceremonies. In *Macfarlane* a Relate counsellor's employer concluded that he was not genuinely prepared to provide psychosexual counselling to same sex couples. In each case colleagues objected to the complainant's apparent unwillingness to comply with the employer's equality policies. Both complainants were unsuccessful in the Domestic courts. The European Court of Human Rights recognised that the situation gave rise to a necessary balancing of interests and concluded that the United Kingdom had been within the margin of appreciation available to it in fixing the balance in the manner in which it had.

10.23 *Meaning of 'because of sexual orientation'*

EA 2010, s 12(1) provides that sexual orientation means a person's sexual orientation towards:

(a)   "persons of the same sex" (ie gay men or lesbians);

(b)   "persons of the opposite sex" (ie heterosexuals); or

(c)   "persons of either sex" (ie bisexual persons).

No definition is given of 'sexual orientation' *per se*. The *Oxford English Dictionary* defines 'orientation' as 'the state of being oriented', 'a person's attitude or adjustment in relation to circumstances'. It follows that there is no requirement that a person be sexually active in order to be regarded as being of a particular sexual orientation. The *EHRC Code* says that "sexual orientation relates to how people feel as well as their actions". (*Para 2.65*).

The *EA 2010* does not cover asexuals or sexual orientation towards anything other than persons (eg bestiality), nor do they cover (regardless of orientation) sexual conduct or particular sexual preferences (eg sadomasochism, paedophilia, etc) or the absence of such (eg celibacy).

Before the enactment of a specific protection, there were a number of attempts made to establish that sexual orientation discrimination was a species of sex discrimination. However, the House of Lords ultimately determined that it is not an act of sex discrimination to treat an employee less favourably on grounds of their sexual orientation (*MacDonald v Advocate General for Scotland* [2003] UKHL 34, [2004] 1 All ER 339, [2003] ICR 937).

However, if an employer were to treat gay men less favourably than lesbian women (or vice versa), that would constitute sex discrimination on ordinary principles.

A reference to a person who has a particular protected characteristic is a reference to a person who is of a particular sexual orientation and a reference to persons who share a protected characteristic is a reference to persons who are of the same sexual orientation (*EA 2010, s 12(2)*). Nevertheless, where an employee who was known to be heterosexual was subjected to innuendo that he was gay, he was harassed 'on the grounds of sexual orientation' (see *English v Thomas Sanderson Blinds Ltd* [2008] EWCA Civ 1421; [2009] ICR 543, [2009] IRLR 206).

10.24   *Meaning of 'because of pregnancy or maternity leave'*

For the purposes of *EA 2010*, the protected characteristics are "pregnancy" and "maternity". Curiously, the Act omits to include a more detailed definition of the protected characteristic even though it has done so in respect of each of the others. In *Sahota v Home Office and another* [2010] ICR 772, the EAT opined that IVF treatment should be treated as equivalent to pregnancy only between the points in time at which follicular puncture and transfer of the embryo occurred.

EA 2010, s 18(2)(b) ensures that a woman is protected against unfavourable treatment because of a pregnancy-related illness. It is unclear whether less favourable treatment because of a pregnancy-related illness would fall within *EA 2010, s 13* as well and thus provide the basis for an allegation of direct discrimination. In the absence of clarification, the safest course would be to assume that it does.

The absence of more detailed definition of "maternity" is troubling as, on its face, "maternity" discrimination might be thought to have a broader scope than "maternity leave" discrimination (which is what was prohibited under the poredecessor provisions in the *SDA 1975*). However, *EA 2010, s 18*, though headed "Pregnancy and Maternity Discrimination: Work Cases", only prohibits discrimination because of compulsory maternity leave or because the employee exercises, has exercised or seeks to exercise her right to take ordinary or additional maternity leave. Whilst this may indicate that the protection against direct discrimination on grounds of maternity conferred by *EA 2010, s 13* is intended to have a similarly limited scope, the question remains an open one until it has been considered by the courts.

10.25   *Meaning of 'because of age'*

For the purposes of *EA 2010*, the protected characteristic is "age", a reference to a person having a particular protected characteristic is a reference to a person of a particular "age group" and an "age group" is defined as a "group of persons defined by reference to age, whether by reference to a particular age or to a range of ages" (*EA 2010, s 5*).

In *Wooster v Mayor and Burgesses of the London Borough of Tower Hamlets* [2009] IRLR 980, the EAT upheld a tribunal finding that a local authority treated a 48-year-old employee less favourably on the grounds of his age by refusing to redeploy him where the consequence of doing so would have been to avoid having to pay him an early retirement pension to which he would become entitled once he reached the age of 50. (Such treatment may be justified in certain circumstances: see *Woodcock v Cumbria Primary Care Trust* [2012] EWCA Civ 330 and Discrimination and Equal Opportunities – II (11).)

10.26 *Meaning of 'because of disability'*

EA 2010 s 6(1) provides:

"A person (P) has a disability if–

(a)   P has a physical or mental impairment, and

(b)   the impairment has a substantial and long-term adverse effect on P's ability to carry out normal day-to-day-activities,"

The elements of the test are then further defined by *EA 2010, Sch 1 Part 1*. That schedule substantially reproduces the former *DDA 1995, Sch 1* save that the former *paragraph 4(1)* is not reproduced so that the complainant does not have to show that one of the attributes formerly listed in that paragraph (i.e. mobility, manual dexterity, physical co-ordination, continence, the ability to lift, carry or otherwise move everyday objects; speech hearing or eyesight; memory or ability to concentrate, learn or understand; or perception of the risk of physical danger) is adversely affected. The exclusion of *paragraph 4(1)* makes the test a little less complicated to apply and arguably effects a modest broadening of its scope.

Guidance has been issued by the Secretary of State which applies to any case based upon a discriminatory act occurring (or, in the case of a continuing act, commencing) on or after 1 May 2011 (*Equality Act (Guidance on the Definition of Disability) Appointed Day Order 2011 SI 2011/1159*). The tribunal must take the guidance into account (*EA 2010, Sch 1, Part 1, Para 12*).

The EAT in *Goodwin v Patent Office* [1999] IRLR 4 laid down detailed guidance as to the approach to be taken by employment tribunals in determining whether or not a claimant is disabled. Readers should refer to this case for the full details of the EAT's guidance. In summary, the EAT held that in determining whether or not a claimant is disabled, the tribunal should look carefully at what the parties have said in the pleadings and clarify the issues, in most cases after standard directions to this effect or at a directions hearing; they should take a purposive approach to the construction of the legislative protections; they should refer expressly to any relevant provisions of the Guidance which have been taken into account (see below); in determining whether or not an impairment has an adverse effect on a person's ability to carry out activities, they should bear in mind that the fact that a person can, with difficulty or great effort, carry out these activities does not mean that his ability to carry them out has not been impaired; they should bear in mind that disabled persons are likely to play down the effect that a disability has on their activities; in determining what is a day-to-day activity, the tribunal's inquiry should not focus only on a particular or a special set of circumstances such as activities carried on in the home; in determining whether an adverse effect is substantial the tribunal may, where the claimant still claims to be suffering from the same degree of impairment as at the time of the events complained of, take into account how the claimant appears to the tribunal to 'manage' his condition; where a claimant is or had been on medication, the tribunal should, in determining whether there is an adverse effect, examine how the claimant's abilities were affected whilst on medication and how those activities would have been affected without the medication; and when addressing each of the conditions under *EA 2010, s 6(1)*, namely the 'impairment' condition, the 'adverse effect' condition, the 'substantial' condition and the 'long-term' condition, the tribunal should be careful not to lose sight of the overall picture.

The definition of disability used in *EA 2010* must, of course, be read, so far as possible, as to be compatible with the *Framework Directive 2000/78/EC*. The Directive does not specifically define "disability". However, in *HK Danmark*, acting on behalf of *Ring v Dansk*

Almennyttigt Boligselskab: C-335/11 [2013] IRLR 571, the CJEU held that the *Framework Directive* had to be read, so far as possible, as to be compatible with the *United Nations Convention on the Rights of Persons with Disabilities*. The *Convention* contains the following definition at *Art 1*:

> "Persons with disabilities include those who have long-term physical, mental, intellectual or sensory impairments which in interaction with various barriers may hinder their full and effective participation in society on an equal basis with others".

Impairments

The *Guidance* deals with the definition of impairment at *Paras 43–48*. It suggests that the terms should be given their "ordinary meanings". An impairment does not have to be the result of an illness, nor does the cause of an impairment have to be established, provided the tribunal is satisfied that it exists. According to the guidance (at *Para A7*), there is no need to consider the cause even if the likely cause is a condition which is excluded from the protective scope of the *Act*. So, for example, addiction to alcohol is deemed not to be an impairment (see below) but illnesses caused by alcohol addiction may cause other impairments which do fall within the scope of the protected characteristic. The Guidance provides that rather than focussing on the cause of the impairment, the focus should instead be on the effects of impairment on the person's ability to carry out normal day to day activities (*Para A4*).

In *College of Ripon and York St John v Hobbs* [2002] IRLR 185, the EAT held that the task of ascertaining whether there is a physical impairment did not involve drawing any rigid distinctions between an underlying fault or defect in the body on the one hand, and evidence of the manifestations or effects of that fault or defect on the other. Thus, an impairment can be something that consists simply of the effects of an illness as opposed to the illness itself. In that case, there was clear evidence that there was something physically wrong with the claimant's body. However, there was no conclusive medical evidence as to the precise cause. Notwithstanding this lacuna in the evidence, the EAT held that it was open to the tribunal to find that there was a physical impairment simply on the basis of the evidence that there was something wrong with the claimant physically (see also *Rugamer v Sony Music Entertainment UK Ltd* [2002] ICR 381, [2001] IRLR 644 and *Ministry of Defence v Hay* [2008] ICR 1247). This rather relaxed approach to ascertaining a physical impairment is to be contrasted with the more rigid approach recommended in cases of mental impairment. In *Morgan v Staffordshire University* [2002] IRLR 190, the EAT held (no doubt to the relief of employers faced with a barrage of medical certificates merely citing 'stress' or 'anxiety' as the reason for absence) that the occasional use of terms such as 'anxiety', 'stress' or 'depression' even by GPs will not amount to proof of a mental impairment (See also *J v DLA Piper UK LLP* [2010] IRLR 936, EAT). In particular, it was held that the occasional mention in medical notes or reference in the World Health Organisation's International Classification of Diseases of or to such terms would not be sufficient in the absence of informed medical evidence that said more. The EAT in that case also provided some detailed guidance for those seeking to establish a mental impairment. Readers are referred to the report of the *Morgan* case for the full details. In essence, however, the guidance reiterates the importance of expert medical evidence in this area. Both the *College of Ripon* and *Morgan* cases were noted with approval by the Court of Appeal in *McNicol* (see above). (See also *De Keyser Ltd v Wilson* [2001] IRLR 324.) However, readers should also refer to the decision of *Dunham v Ashford Windows* [2005] ICR 1584, [2005] IRLR 608, in which the EAT held that a person might have a mental impairment (such as learning difficulties) which did not amount to a mental illness. The Guidance supports this distinction between a mental impairment and mental illness (*Para A5*). Where there is dispute between the parties as to whether or not the employee has an impairment, or as to the nature of that impairment, the employer is entitled to adduce expert evidence to disprove the existence of such an impairment: *Hospice of St Mary of Furness v Howard* [2007] IRLR 944.

It may not always be possible, nor is it necessary, to categorise a condition as either a physical or mental impairment (*Guidance Para A6* and see also *McNicol v Balfour Beatty Rail Maintenance Ltd* [2002] EWCA Civ 1074, [2002] ICR 1498).

There was formerly a requirement that a mental illness had to be a "clinically well-recognised illness" before it could be a mental impairment but that requirement was repealed as from 5 December 2005 (*DDA 2005, s 18(2)*).

Certain things are deemed by the *Equality Act 2010 (Disability) Regulations 2010 (SI 2010/2128)* not to amount to impairments:

(a) Addiction to alcohol, nicotine or any other substance (*Reg 3(1)*) unless the addiction was originally the result of administration of medically prescribed drugs or other medical treatment (*Reg 3(2)*);

(b) A tendency to: set fires; steal; physical or sexual abuse of other persons; exhibitionis; and voyeurism (*Reg 4(1)*);

(c) Seasonal allergic rhinitis (or "hayfever") unless it aggravates the effect of any other condition (*Reg 4(2)* and *(3)*).

An employee may have a condition (eg a depressive illness) that does amount to a disability in its own right but which was caused by an excluded condition, (eg addiction to alcohol). The EAT has confirmed that an employee in these circumstances would be disabled notwithstanding the link with the excluded condition because it is not relevant to consider the cause of a particular disability (*Power v Panasonic (UK) Ltd* [2003] IRLR 151). Conversely, a person might have an excluded condition that is caused by or is a manifestation of an impairment that falls within the scope of *EA 2010* (See *Edmund Nuttall Ltd v Butterfield* [2005] IRLR 751, where the excluded condition – in that case, exhibitionism – was caused by depression).

Adverse effect

Under the old law, an impairment was *only* to be taken to affect the ability to carry out normal day-to-day activities if it affected one of the following:

(a) mobility;

(b) manual dexterity;

(c) physical co-ordination;

(d) continence;

(e) the ability to lift, carry or otherwise move everyday objects;

(f) speech, hearing or eyesight;

(g) memory or ability to concentrate, learn or understand; or

(h) perception of the risk of physical danger.

(*DDA 1995, Sch 1 para 4(1)*.)

The list set out above was not reproduced in the *EA 2010*. The nearest one comes to such a list is to be found in the *Appendix* to the *Guidance*. There one finds two lists. The first is entitled "An illustrative and non-exhaustive list of factors which, if they are experienced by a person, it would be reasonable to regard as having a substantial adverse effect on normal day to day activities". There is a second list, equally extravagantly entitled, which focuses on factors that it would not be reasonable to regard as having the necessary substantial adverse effect. The examples are too numerous to list here. The first example included in the first list is "difficulty in getting dressed, for example, because of physical restrictions, a lack of understanding of the concept, or low motivation". The first example included in the second list is "Inability to move heavy objects without assistance or mechanical aid, such as moving a large suitcase or heavy piece of furniture without a trolley". The *Guidance* stresses that the examples are indicators and not tests.

Substantial Adverse effects

An effect is substantial if it is more than minor or trivial (*EA 2010, s 212(1)* and *Guidance, Para B1*). Unless a matter can be classified as falling within the heading "trivial" or "insubstantial", it must be treated as substantial (*Aderemi v London and South Eastern Railway Ltd* [2013] EqLR 198, EAT).

In assessing the effect, the Guidance suggests that the following should be looked at: the time taken to carry out an activity, the way it is carried out; and the cumulative effects of the impairment (*Guidance, Paras B2–B5*). The tribunal should also consider the extent to which a person could reasonably be expected to modify his or her behaviour by, for example, use of a coping or avoidance strategy (*Guidance, Para B7*).

Para B11 of the *Guidance* stresses the importance of keeping in mind the fact that environmental conditions may exacerbate or lessen the effect of an impairment.

The EAT in the case of *Leonard v Southern Derbyshire Chamber of Commerce* [2001] IRLR 19 emphasised that when considering whether an impairment had a substantial adverse effect on the ability to carry out normal day-to-day activities, the tribunal must concentrate on what the claimant cannot do or can only do with difficulty. An approach that looks mainly to what the applicant can do may lead to the erroneous conclusion that because the claimant can still do many things, the adverse effect cannot be substantial. This approach was supported by the EAT in *Paterson v Metropolitan Police Comr* [2007] ICR 1522 where it held that, when assessing whether the effect of an impairment is 'substantial', the comparison to be made is between the way in which the individual in fact carried out the activity in question and the way he would have carried it out if not impaired. The mere fact that an employee can perform the duties of his job does not necessarily mean that he is not disabled. (See *Law Hospital NHS Trust v Rush* [2001] IRLR 611 and *Ekpe v Metropolitan Police Comr* [2001] IRLR 605.) In *Cruickshank v VAW Motorcast Ltd* [2002] IRLR 24, the EAT considered the position of an employee whose impairment (an asthmatic complaint) was such that he only appeared to suffer substantial adverse effects whilst present at the workplace. The employment tribunal had held that the employee was not a disabled person because it could not be said that there was an adverse effect on his normal day-to-day activities. The EAT disagreed and held that the tribunal had been wrong to confine its analysis of the claimant's ability to carry out normal day-to-day activities to his activities outside of the work environment. (See *Chief Constable of Dumfries & Galloway Constabulary v Adams* [2009] ICR 1034, [2009] IRLR 612, where the EAT confirmed that an activity undertaken in the course of employment would be a normal day-to-day activity if it was common to different types of employment.) In general terms, the principle that normal day-to-day activities are not to be determined only on the basis of a particular environment must be correct. However, where there is evidence that an employee only suffers substantial adverse effects when in a particular work environment (in the form, say, of a severe allergic reaction to the carpets in a particular office) and nowhere else, it might still be possible to argue that there was no substantial adverse effect on normal day-to-day activities or that the effects were not long term. The better approach in these circumstances (as suggested by the EAT in *Cruickshank*) would be to consider whether any reasonable adjustments could be made rather than attempting to argue that there is no disability.

Where two impairments are relied upon, neither of which on its own would satisfy the substantial adverse effect requirement under *DDA*, account should be taken of whether the impairments together have a substantial overall effect on the person's ability to carry out normal day-to-day activities. (See *Ginn v Tesco Stores Ltd* [2005] All ER (D) 259 (Oct), applied in *Patel v Oldham Metropolitan Borough Council* [2010] IRLR 280, which addressed the question whether an impairment that had developed from an initial impairment could be aggregated with the original to determine whether the longevity requirement was satisfied).

Long-term effects

By EA 2010, Sch 1, para 2:

"(1) The effect of an impairment is long-term if –

(a)   it has lasted for at least 12 months,

(b)   it is likely to last for at least 12 months, or

(c)   it is likely to last for the rest of the life of the person affected."

Even if an impairment ceases to have substantial adverse effect on the employee's ability to carry out normal day-to-day activities, it is treated as continuing to have that effect if it is likely to recur (*EA 2010, Sch 1, para 2(2)*). The cumulative effect of related impairments should be taken into account (*Guidance, Para C2*). In assessing whether an effect is "likely" to last for the periods identified in *EA 2010, Sch 1, para 2(1)(b)* and *(c)* above the tribunal should ask whether it "could well happen" (see *Guidance, Para C3* and *Boyle v SCA Packaging Ltd* above).

Normal day-to-day activities

The *Guidance* addresses "normal day-to day activities" in *section D*. General guidance is given at *Para D3*:

"In general, day-to-day activities are things people do on a regular or daily basis, and examples include shopping, reading and writing, having a conversation or using the telephone, watching television, getting washed and dressed, preparing and eating food, carrying out and taking part in social activities. Normal day-to-day activities can include general work-related activities, and study and education-related activities, such as interacting with colleagues, following instructions, using a computer, driving, carrying out interviews, preparing written documents, and keeping to a timetable or a shift pattern."

The term is not intended to include activities which are normal only for a particular person or a small group of people (*Para D4*). However, a normal day-to-day activity does not have to be something that the majority of people do (*Para D5*). Specialised activities such as watch-making or playing an instrument to a high standard are not included (*Paras D8* and *D9*).

In *Ekpe v Metropolitan Police Comr* [2001] IRLR 605, the EAT held that it was an error of law to conclude that an activity only done by women was not a normal day-to-day activity. However, a refusal to allow a person to progress in her professional life is not an adverse effect on normal day-to-day activities (see *Chief Constable of Lothian and Borders Police v Cumming* [2010] IRLR 109).

In *Leonard v Southern Derbyshire Chamber of Commerce*, the employment tribunal had considered the examples given in earlier guidance in determining whether or not the applicant's condition had a substantial adverse effect on her day-to-day activities. In deciding that the applicant was not disabled, the employment tribunal had balanced those examples in the Guidance that the claimant could do (such as being able to eat and drink) against those which the claimant could not do (such as negotiate pavement edges properly). The EAT held that this balancing exercise was inappropriate, 'since her ability to catch a ball did not diminish her inability to negotiate pavement edges safely'. As stated above, the correct approach involves considering all matters, but paying particular attention to those activities that the applicant cannot do.

Severe Disfigurement

Severe disfigurement is deemed to have the necessary substantial adverse effect (*EA 2010, Sch, para 3*). The Guidance gives the following examples of what might qualify to be protected under this provision: "scars, birthmarks, limb or postural deformation or diseases of the skin" (*Para B25*).

Tattoos and piercings are addressed at *Reg 5* of the *Equality Act 2010 (Disability) Regulations 2010, SI 2010/2128*. It is provided that they should not count as disfigurements having a substantial adverse effect on the ability of a person to carry out normal day-to-day activities.

Effect of medical treatment

It may be that the substantial adverse effects of an impairment may be avoided by medical treatment. That does not have the effect, however, of removing the employee from the protective scope of the Act. *EA 2010, Sch 1, para 5* provides:

"(1) An impairment is to be treated as having a substantial adverse effect on the ability of the person concerned to carry out normal day-to-day activities if:

(a)   measures are being taken to treat or correct it, and

(b)   but for that, it would be likely to have that effect.

(2) "Measures" includes, in particular, medical treatment and the use of a prosthesis or other aid

(3) Sub-paragraph (1) does not apply –

(a)   in relation to the impairment of a person's sight, to the extent that the impairment is, in the person's case, correctable by spectacle or contact lenses or in such other ways as may be prescribed

..."

The EAT in *Vicary v British Telecommunications plc* [1999] IRLR 680, commented (*obiter*) that the words 'or other aid' (*EA 2010, Sch 1, para 5(2)*) are probably intended to refer to aids such as Zimmer frames or sticks or wheelchairs and not to labour-saving household devices such as electric can-openers. An 'aid' in this context can also include surgically inserted plates and pins. (*Carden v Pickerings Europe Ltd* [2005] IRLR 720). The EAT in *Kapadia v Lambeth London Borough Council* [2000] IRLR 14 found that counselling sessions conducted by a consultant psychologist amounted to 'medical treatment', notwithstanding the fact that the counselling only comprised 'talking' to the claimant and the fact that no drugs were administered.

Medical treatment may, broadly, have one of three types of effect. First, it may temporarily alleviate the adverse effect. That is the set of circumstances with which the provision set out above is intended to deal. So, for instance, an asthmatic employee would probably be regarded as disabled within the meaning of the *Act* if his condition was such that if it were not controlled through the use of inhalers and medication, it would have a substantial adverse effect on his normal day-to-day activities. Similarly, an employee with a disabling depression, still has a disability even if the effects of the depression are controlled with anti-depressants. Since the medical treatment means the adverse effect is prevented, the tribunal has to deduce what would happen if the medical treatment ceased. Where a deduced effect is alleged, the employee is required to prove the disability with some particularity and clear medical evidence will usually be necessary. A mere assertion by the employee as to what would happen if the treatment ceased will probably not be sufficient (*Woodrup v Southwark London Borough Council* [2003] IRLR 111, CA). When assessing what would happen if treatment or a corrective measure ceased to be taken, the tribunal must ask itself whether it is "likely" that the substantial adverse effect would resume. That outcome is sufficiently likely if the tribunal is able to say that it "could well happen" (*SCA Packaging Ltd v Boyle* [2009] UKHL 37, [2009] NI 317).

The second type of effect that the measures might have is producing a permanent improvement such that it is unlikely that the substantial adverse effect will recur. In *Abadeh v British Telecommunications plc* [2001] ICR 156, the EAT decided that where continuing treatment has produced a permanent improvement, that improvement must be taken into account. Put another way, the tribunal should ask would happen if treatment stopped now and not what would happen if the claimant had never received treatment. The EAT further clarified that a "deduced effect" argument was only available at all if the medical treatment was continuing. *EA 2010, Sch 1, para 5* does not apply where the treatment has ceased (see also *Carden v Pickerings Europe Ltd* [2005] IRLR 720).

The third type of effect that measures might have is curing the underlying impairment itself. Again, the claimant cannot argue that they are a disabled person on the basis that they would have been had they not been cured.

However, where a measure brings about a permanent improvement or a cure such that a claimant cannot argue they are still disabled that does not mean that the employee will not have the protected characteristic of disability, that is because less favourable treatment of those who disabilities in the past is also prohibited (see below and *Guidance, Para 17*)

Deemed Disabilities

EA 2010, Sch 1, para 6 deems Cancer, HIV infection and multiple sclerosis to be disabilities.

Para 7 confers a power to prescribe that other conditions should also be deemed to be disabilities. On 1 October 2010 the *Equality Act 2010 (Disability) Regulations 2010, SI 2010/2128* came into force. *Reg 3* deems that addiction to alcohol, nicotine or any other substance is to be treated as not amounting to an impairment unless the addiction is the result of the administration of medically prescribed drugs or other medical treatment. *Reg 4* deems certain other conditions not to amount to impairments: a tendency to set fires, to steal or to physical or sexual abuse of other persons; exhibitionism or voyeurism.

Seasonal allergic rhinitis ("hay fever") cannot amount to an impairment in its own right but can be taken into account if it aggravates another condition.

Reg 6 deals with babies and young children. Although, of course, neither are likely to be employees, whether or not a child is disabled may affect whether an associative discrimination claim will succeed. Where a child under 6 has an impairment which does not have a substantial long term adverse effect on the ability of the child to carry out normal day to day activities, the impairment is deemed to have that effect if it would have it on a child who was older than 6.

Reg 7 deems to be disabled any person certified by a consultant ophthalmologist to be blind, severely sight impaired or partially-sighted.

For matters which are deemed by the Regulations not to amount to impairments, see the section on impairments above.

Progressive conditions

EA 2010, Sch 1, para 8 deals with progressive conditions. The effect of the provision is that even if the employee's condition creates an impairment which has an adverse effect which is not yet sufficiently "substantial" to qualify as a disability, it is treated as doing so if "the condition is likely to result in [them] suffering such an impairment".

Mere diagnosis of a progressive condition (other than one of the conditions giving rise to a deemed disability) would not be sufficient in itself. In *Mowat-Brown v University of Surrey* [2002] IRLR 235, the EAT held that it is not even enough simply for an applicant to establish that he has a progressive condition and that it has or has had an effect on his ability to carry out normal day-to-day activities. A claimant with a progressive condition must go on to show that it is more likely than not that at some stage in the future there will be a substantial adverse effect on his ability to carry out normal day-to-day activities. The *Guidance* (at *Para B19*) provides that in such cases, medical prognosis of the likely impact of the condition will be the normal route to establishing protection under the progressive conditions provisions. A person may be taken as having a disability even where the substantial adverse effect is as a result of the treatment for a progressive condition (eg an operation for prostate cancer that results in urinary incontinence) rather than the progressive condition itself (see *Kirton v Tetrosyl Ltd* [2003] EWCA Civ 619, [2003] ICR 1237, [2003] IRLR 353).

Para B32 of the *Guidance* suggests the protection will not apply where the progressive condition is successfully treated so as to remove any adverse effect.

Past Disabilities

EA 2010, s 6(4) provides that reference (however expressed) to a person who has a disability includes reference to a person who has had the disability. The *Guidance, Para B17* states that if medical treatment cures a condition, the employee may still be protected on the basis that they have had a disability in the past.

Disability "at the relevant time"

EA 2010, Sch1, para 9 provides:

> "(1) A question as to whether a person has a disability at a particular time ("the relevant time") is to be determined, for the purposes of section 6, as if the provisions of, or made under, this Act were in force when the act complained of was done had been in force at the relevant time.
>
> (2) The relevant time may be a time before the coming into force of the provisions of this Act to which the question relates."

The *Guidance* provides that the protection would cover those who continue to experience debilitating effects as a result of treatment for a past disability (*Para A16*).

The EAT in *Cruickshank v VAW Motorcast Ltd* [2002] IRLR 24 confirmed that in determining whether a person is disabled, the court should apply the appropriate test to the claimant's condition at the date of the alleged discriminatory act and not at the date of the hearing. This approach could present difficulties particularly where the effects of a particular condition tend to fluctuate or last for uncertain periods. The fact that by the date of the hearing, an adverse effect had in fact lasted for 12 months is not necessarily conclusive of it having been likely to have lasted that long as at the date of the discriminatory act. However, now that it has been confirmed that 'likely' in this context means 'could well happen', such difficulties will probably arise only rarely (see *SCA Packaging Ltd v Boyle* [2009] UKHL 37, [2009] NI 317, overruling *Latchman v Reed Business Information Ltd* [2002] ICR 1453). The guidance providing that an event is 'likely' to occur if it is more probable than not that it will happen has also been disapproved. 'Likely' is to be construed as meaning 'could well happen', and the cases referred to in this paragraph should be considered in that light. In *Swift v Chief Constable of Wiltshire Constabulary* [2004] IRLR 540, the EAT had held that in determining whether at a particular point in time a substantial adverse effect was likely to recur, the Tribunal was entitled to take account of evidence of what had happened since that time. However, the effect of *Swift* was doubted by the Court of Appeal in *McDougall v Richmond Adult Community College* [2008] EWCA Civ 4, [2008] ICR 431 (at paragraph 17). Rather, in *McDougall*, Pill LJ emphasised that a prediction as to the likelihood of recurrence must be made on the basis of the evidence available at the time of the act complained of. The central purpose of the legislation is to prevent discriminatory decisions and to provide sanctions if such decisions are made. Whether an employer has committed such a wrong is to be judged, therefore, on the basis of the evidence available at the time of the decision complained of. (See *Ministry of Defence v Hay* [2008] ICR 1247, where *McDougall* was distinguished on the basis that it did not apply where the decision as to whether someone was disabled did not turn upon any predictive element to be established on the facts known at the time of the alleged act of discrimination. In *Hay*, the question was not one of recurrence of a condition but of whether the claimant was suffering from an impairment or impairments which had a substantial adverse effect upon his normal day-to-day activities.)

10.27 Associative Discrimination - Cases where the member of the protected category is a third party

In most cases, a person who alleges that they have been discriminated against will be complaining that the have been treated less favourably because of their protected characteristic (i.e. because of their race, sex, sexual orientation, etc.) however, where, for instance, a white employee is dismissed for refusing to comply with an instruction not to deal with black customers, it is the customers' protected characteristic that is in issue rather than that of the employee. Discrimination which is based upon a third person's protected characteristic is known as "associative discrimination".

The coming into force of the *EA 2010* represented a substantial expansion of the scope of associative discrimination. Whereas under the pre-existing law, associative discrimination claims could only be brought in respect of certain protected characteristics, *EA 2010, s 13* extends the scope of protection to all of the protected characteristics save one. The exception is "marriage and civil partnership". A claim may only be brought where it is the person less favourably treated that is married or a civil partner (*EA 2010, s 13(4)*).

10.28 Perceived Discrimination – Cases where the complainant is assumed, incorrectly, to have the protected characteristic

The Government believes that the formulation of direct discrimination adopted in *EA 2010, s 13* has the effect that perceived discrimination is prohibited in relation to each of the protected characteristics. It remains to be seen how, in relation to perceived disability discrimination, the difficulties identified by the EAT in the *J v DLA Piper UK LLP* case ([2010] IRLR 936) will be overcome. The EAT found that *DDA 1995* (the predecessor legislation) did not protect an employee against dismissal because he was perceived to be disabled. The rationale was that the definition of a protected disability is so specific and requires so many factors to be considered that it will be, in practice, extremely difficult to determine whether the employer believed the employee was disabled as opposed, for instance, to merely being ill. In other words, protection against perceived disability discrimination was unworkable in practice. It is to be assumed that, however unworkable, it is a protection *EA 2010* is intended to introduce.

10.29 Combined Discrimination

Combined discrimination was a new form of discrimination that was to be introduced by *EA 2010*. It would have occurred where an employee was treated less favourably because of two protected characteristics. For instance, if a driving school were to decide that the job of driving instructor was not a suitable one for an older woman and refused to appoint a woman in her sixties to a position, their reason would not be the candidate's sex or her age but the combination of her sex and age. On 23 March 2011, the Government Equalities Unit announced that it no longer intended to proceed with its proposals to bring *EA 2010, s 14* into force. It is that provision which would otherwise have prohibited such discrimination.

10.30 Discrimination on the ground of pregnancy

EA 2010 provides two discrete protections for women who are discriminated against because of their pregnancy. First, pregnancy is identified as a "protected characteristic" at *EA 2010, s 4*. As a result, it would seem that it is possible for a woman to complain of direct discrimination where she is treated "less favourably" by relying on *EA 2010, s 13(1)*. This is dealt with at **10.24** above.

The second protection which *EA 2010*, provides is an express prohibition on employers treating employees unfavourably (as opposed to less favourably) because of their pregnancy (*EA 2010, s 18(2)(a)*):

'A person (A) discriminates against a woman if, in the protected period in relation to a pregnancy of hers, A treats her unfavourably –

(a) because of the pregnancy;   . . . '

This formulation differs from that found in the earlier law in that, although it was clear that a pregnant employee was not required to identify a comparator, she was still required to show that she had been "less favourably treated" which unhelpfully implied a residual need for comparison. Now the *Act* simply prohibits "unfavourable" treatment. Otherwise, the provisions are materially the same. In *Madarassy v Nomura International Plc* [2007] EWCA Civ 33, [2007] ICR 867, (a case decided under the old law but after the requirement for a comparator had been abolished) the Court of Appeal indicated that even in pregnancy cases a comparator might still be of use. Their Lordships had in mind a case where there is real doubt as to whether pregnancy was the reason for the treatment. Thus, where a pregnant employee is dismissed for dishonesty and claims that the employer only took the step of dismissing her (rather than disciplining her) because she was pregnant, it might be relevant to ask what had happened to male employees who had behaved in the same way. Where, however, the reason is a matter directly connected with the pregnancy (such as absence) it will not be appropriate to ask how a man with a similar absence record would have been treated.

The protection is specifically restricted to a "protected period" which begins when the pregnancy begins and ends, in cases where the employee is entitled to ordinary and additional maternity leave ("OML" and "AML"), either at the end of the additional maternity leave period or when she returns to work (if that is earlier) and in any other case at the end of the period of 2 weeks beginning with the end of pregnancy (*EA 2010, s 18(6)*). Thus an employer who dismisses an employee who informs him that she intends to try for a child does not act in breach of *s 18* as the protected period has not begun. In such a case the complainant would have two options: (1) bringing a *s 13* pregnancy discrimination case; or (2) bringing a *s 13* sex discrimination case. The approach of treating pregnancy-related discrimination falling outside the period as sex discrimination was taken by the ECJ in *Mayr v Backerei und Konditorei Gerhard Flockner OHG*: C-506/06 [2008] IRLR 387. A woman undergoing IVF treatment was dismissed between the removal of ova from her follicles and the replacement of a fertilised ovum in her uterus. The ECJ determined that she was not a pregnant worker for the purposes of *PWD 92/85* but could rely, instead on *ETD 76/207/EEC* (now the *ETD 2006/54/EC*).

On the other hand, once a protected period has begun, *EA 2010, s 18(7)* specifically requires that any pregnancy discrimination claim be brought under *s 18* rather than as a sex discrimination claim under *s 13*. If, during the protected period, the employee is treated less favourably because of her sex but not because of her pregnancy a claim under *EA 2010, s 13* would still be available.

An employee may complain about the implementation of a decision taken during the protected period even if the implementation itself does not occur until after the period has come to an end (*EA 2010, s 18(5)*). This, again, reflects the ECJ's approach: In *Paquay v*

Societe d'architectes Hoet + Minne SPRL: C-460/06 [2008] ICR 420, ECJ, the protection against dismissal afforded during the 'protected period' provided for by *PWD 92/85* was held to apply where an employer advertised the employee's job during the protected period but gave notice only once the protected period had finished. The *PWD* was interpreted as requiring that steps preparatory to a decision to dismiss should also be unlawful.

As it is a form of direct discrimination, pregnancy discrimination cannot be justified, The strictness of the principle is well illustrated by the case of *Mahlburg v Land Mecklenburg-Vorpommern*: C-207/98 [2000] ECR I-549, [2001] 3 CMLR 887. The ECJ considered the case of a pregnant woman who applied for and was refused a job intended to last for an indefinite period on the basis that, at the time at which she would otherwise have started the job, domestic law precluded her from working. Did the fact that the *ETD 76/207/EEC* (since repealed and replaced by *ETD 2006/54/EC*) was expressed to be without prejudice to such protective legislation mean that a refusal to appoint the claimant had not been discriminatory? The court decided that there had been an act of direct discrimination. The result pursued by the *ETD 76/207/EEC* was 'substantive, not formal, equality'. As a result, 'the application of provisions concerning the protection of pregnant women cannot result in unfavourable treatment regarding their access to employment'.

Cases in which the reason for the employee being unfavourably treated is the pregnancy per se will be rare. More commonly, the employer points to a reason connected with the pregnancy. In *Dekker* (above), the complainant applied for a job as a teacher. Although suitable she was not appointed because the respondent would have had to pay her a maternity allowance, which, because she would have been pregnant when appointed, the respondent would have been unable to recover under their insurance policy. The reason for the refusal to appoint was thus not the pregnancy per se but the substantial irrecoverable costs of the appointment. However, the ECJ approached the case on the basis that the refusal to appoint was on ground of pregnancy. The domestic courts have adopted a similar approach. In *O'Neill v Governors of St Thomas More RCVA Upper School* [1997] ICR 33, EAT, the Employment Appeal Tribunal considered a case where a Roman Catholic school dismissed a religious education teacher who was pregnant by a priest. The school argued that it was not the pregnancy itself but the circumstances of the pregnancy that provided the dominant motive for the decision to dismiss. The EAT held that the dismissal had been discriminatory and rejected the concept of dismissal for "pregnancy per se" as misleading. Instead the tribunal should simply ask itself whether, on an objective basis, the dismissal was on the ground of pregnancy. Pregnancy did not need, in the EAT's opinion, to be the sole or even the main ground for the decision to dismiss.

A common complaint made by employers is that an employee has 'deceived' them by not declaring that they are pregnant at a point at which an important decision is made. For example, in *Busch v Klinikum Neustadt GmbH & Co Betriebs-KG*: C-320/01 [2003] IRLR 625, ECJ, an employee absent on parental leave applied to return early. Having been allowed to do so, she declared she was pregnant and sought to take maternity leave which would have been unavailable to her during a period of parental leave. The employers tried to rescind their consent to her return from parental leave. The Court decided that the employee was not obliged to declare her pregnancy and, in any event, the employer would not have been entitled to take her pregnancy into account even if she had told them about it. That being so, they had discriminated against her.

In *Ministry of Defence v Pope* [1997] ICR 296, EAT, the Employment Appeal Tribunal held that where an employee terminated her pregnancy in order to avoid being dismissed for pregnancy, she could bring a claim against her employer for damages for injury to feelings. In its decision in *Webb* the ECJ had expressly referred to the need to prevent women feeling pressured into terminations as one of the policies underlying the maternity leave period.

In *New Southern Railways Ltd v Quinn* [2006] IRLR 266, EAT, an employer was found to have discriminated where it removed a pregnant employee from a trial position and returned her to her less senior and lower-paid position. The Tribunal was not prepared to treat the case as one of medical suspension.

A failure to comply with the obligation imposed by the *Management of Health and Safety Regulations 1999 (SI 1999/3242)* to carry out a risk assessment in respect of a pregnant employee may amount to an act of unlawful sex discrimination (see *Hardman v Mealon (t/a Orchard Lodge Nursing Home)* [2002] IRLR 516). However, there is no general obligation to carry out a risk assessment and there is only an obligation to do so where: (1) the employee notifies her employer in writing that she is pregnant; (2) the work is of a kind which could involve a risk of harm or danger to the health and safety of a new expectant mother or to the health and safety of her baby; and (3) the risk arises from either processes or working conditions or physical, biological or chemical agents in the workplace at the time specified in the non-exhaustive list at *Annexes I* and *II* of *Directive 92/85/EEC* (*O'Neill v Buckinghamshire County Council* [2010] IRLR 384, EAT).

Where an employee is prevented, by reason of her pregnancy, from performing her usual job tasks, a failure to consider alternative employment may be discriminatory on the basis that the employer has treated the employee less favourably in relation to access to opportunities for transfer within *EA 2010, s 39(2)(b)* (*Iske v P&O European Ferries (Dover) Ltd* [1997] IRLR 401, EAT).

There is a limit to how remote the reason can be from the pregnancy. Thus in *Walter v Secretary of State for Social Security* [2001] EWCA Civ 1913, [2002] ICR 540, the *Jobseeker's Allowance Regulations 1996 (SI 1996/207)* did not offend against the *Social Security Directive 79/7/EEC* (which prohibited sex discrimination in access to social security entitlements; see **22.5 European Union Law**) where a student breaking her studies to have a child was precluded from claiming the allowance. Those taking breaks from studies are treated under the Regulations as retaining their status as a student, a status which disqualifies them from making a claim. The Court of Appeal decided that the complainant's ineligibility to claim derived from her student status and not from her pregnancy.

10.31 Discrimination on ground of maternity leave

EA 2010, s 4 identifies "maternity" as a protected characteristic. *Part 2, Chapter 1* of the *Act* does not define what is meant by "maternity". The explanatory notes, equally, do not provide a definition. The significance of the lack of a definition is that "maternity" is a broader term than "maternity leave" and the earlier law only prohibited discrimination on the latter, narrower, ground. However, it is probable that *EA 2010* intends to do no more than reproduce the existing maternity leave-related protection. That view is reinforced by *EA 2010, s 18* which is headed "Pregnancy and maternity discrimination: work cases". Section 18 deals only with pregnancy discrimination (*EA 2010, s 18(2)*) and maternity leave discrimination (*EA 2010, ss 18(3) and (4)*). Despite the heading, there is no protection of maternity more generally.

EA 2010, s 18(3) prohibits a person from discriminating against a woman by treating her unfavourably because she is on compulsory maternity leave. Compulsory maternity leave is the two week period provided for by *ERA 1996, s 72(1)* (*EA 2010, s 213(3)*) (see **Maternity and Parental Leave 31.27**).

Unfavourable treatment because an employee "is exercising or seeking to exercise, or has exercised or sought to exercise [her] right to ordinary or additional maternity leave" is prohibited by *EA 2010, s 18(4)*. Ordinary maternity leave ("OML") is the right conferred by *ERA 1996, s 71(1)* (*EA 2010, s 213(4)* see **Maternity and Parental Leave 31.21**). Additional maternity leave ("AML") is the right conferred by *ERA 1996, s 73(1)* (*EA 2010, s 313(7)* see **Maternity and Parental Leave 31.28**).

Discrimination for a maternity-related reason was, prior to October 2005, treated as a form of sex discrimination. In order to preclude overlapping claims *EA 2010, s 18(7)(b)* disapplies *EA 2010, s 13* (the prohibition on direct sex discrimination) where the unfavourable treatment is for a reason falling within *EA 2010, s 18(3) or (4)*. However, since maternity is a protected characteristic in its own right (*EA 2010, s 4*), it would seem that a *s 13* action would potentially still be available on that discrete basis. *Section 13* requires, however, that there should be "less favourable treatment" which would seem, on its face, to require a comparator to be identified which means that in most cases occurring during the protected period, there would be little point bringing a *s 13* claim rather than a *s 18* claim.

The scope of the protection is broad and the courts and tribunals have interpreted the provision purposively. For instance, early cases concerning maternity leave considered attempts by employers to narrow the protective scope of the provision by drawing a distinction between the taking of the leave and the consequences for the employer's business of the employee's absence. The ECJ rejected the distinction in *Dekker v Stichting Vormingscentrum voor Jong Volwassenen (VJV - Centrum) Plus*: C-177/88 [1990] ECR I 3941, [1992] ICR 325 where an employer argued, unsuccessfully, that it did not discriminate against a pregnant applicant for employment by refusing to employ her since the real reason for not employing her was the adverse economic consequence of its inability to insure itself to recover the cost of the payments it would have to make to her during her maternity leave. Domestic authorities have taken the same line and establish, in general terms, that an employer may not use a maternity leave-related absence as either a reason for or (it would appear from the *Rees* and *Lewis Woolf* cases below) the occasion of treating a pregnant employee unfavourably.

However broad an interpretative approach is taken of the European and domestic provisions, there will still be some cases where *EA 2010, s 18* is not engaged and a claimant will have to rely upon the sex discrimination provisions. An example might be where an employer discriminates against an employee because he believes that she wishes to start a family and anticipates that she may wish to take maternity leave in the future. His act is not, on the face of it, rendered unlawful by *EA 2010, s 18*. It is likely, however, that his act will nevertheless amount to an act of unlawful sex discrimination falling within *EA 2010, s 13*. The same would likely be true of discrimination on ground of taking contractual maternity leave which is also not covered by *s 18*.

Cases decided under the previous legal regime remain useful in helping to assess when liability will be incurred. Set out below, therefore, is an account of ECJ and domestic case law relating to discrimination on ground of sex in so far as the acts complained of were motivated by or occurred against a background of maternity absence.

One line of cases deals with women who are penalised for maternity absence in ways falling short of dismissal. In *Caisse Nationale D'Assurance Viellesse Des Travailleurs Salaries v Thibault*: C-136/95 [1999] ICR 160, ECJ employees who had been present at work for at least six months in a particular year were entitled to a performance appraisal. A satisfactory appraisal would lead to a pay increase. Where the reason that an employee did not qualify for an appraisal was that she had been absent on maternity leave, it was an act of discrimination not to allow her an appraisal in any event. Contrast, however, *Hoyland v Asda Stores* [2005] ICR 1235, EAT; the claimant was not entitled to receive a bonus which had been earned by male colleagues during the period of her absence on maternity leave.

In *Land Brandenburg v Sass*:C-284/02 [2005] IRLR 147, the ECJ considered a different aspect of the effect of absence on benefits. Some benefits will be conditional on length of service. Should time spent absent on maternity leave count as service for those purposes? The ECJ held that the claimant should have been given credit for length of service for any period during which she had been on 'statutory maternity leave intended to protect women who have given birth'.

In *Blundell v Governing Body St Andrews Catholic Primary School* [2007] ICR 1451, an employer acted unlawfully when it failed to consult with a teacher who was absent on maternity leave as to the class she wished to teach the following year – something that it would have done had she been at work.

In *Herrero (Sarkatzis) v Instituto Madrileno de la Salud (Imsalud)*: C-294/04 [2006] IRLR 296, the ECJ determined that an employer acts unlawfully where it counts continuous service only from the day on which an employee takes up her duties rather than on the date of her appointment where the reason for the delay was the taking of maternity leave.

A second line of cases deals with claimants who are either not recruited or who are dismissed for reasons relating to maternity leave absences. *Webb* was itself a case concerned with absence. It is significant that both the ECJ and the House of Lords placed considerable emphasis on the fact that Ms Webb had been employed for an indefinite period. The implication is that the case might have been decided differently had the contract of employment been for a fixed term over the whole or major part of which Ms Webb would have been unavailable. The distinction was refined in *Caruana v Manchester Airport plc* [1996] IRLR 378, EAT where it was decided that a further distinction had to be drawn between cases where a woman is employed for a single 'one-off' fixed period, and cases where she is employed on a series of fixed-term contracts. The latter type of case should be treated in the same way as employment for an indefinite period. In previous editions, we have opined that even in cases where the engagement is to be for a single fixed term, it would nevertheless be an act of discrimination not to appoint a pregnant candidate by reason of her pregnancy. The basis of our view has been that it is not open to an employer to justify an act of direct discrimination. In *Tele Danmark A/S v Handels-og Kontorfunktion-aerernes Forbund i Danmark (HK)*: C-109/00 [2001] ECR I-6993, [2001] All ER (EC) 941, a woman was given a contract with a fixed maximum term of six months. The first two months of the contract would be spent being trained. The complainant was pregnant when she was offered the job. She did not tell the respondent. Her pregnancy had the effect that she was precluded from working for a substantial part of the fixed term. She was dismissed on the ground that she had failed to tell the respondent of her condition when applying for the job. The ECJ decided that the dismissal was contrary to *art 5(1)* of the *ETD 76/207/EEC* (since repealed by *Directive 2002/73/EC*). The non-discrimination principle it encapsulated is now to be found in *ETD 2006/54/EC*) and *art 10* of the *Pregnant Worker's Directive 92/85/EC*. The former provision is a general prohibition of less favourable treatment on grounds of sex. The latter is a specific prohibition on dismissal of pregnant workers during the period from conception to the end of maternity leave, 'save in exceptional cases not connected with their condition, which are permitted under national legislation and/or practice'. The court held:

> 'Since the dismissal of a worker on account of pregnancy constitutes direct discrimination on grounds of sex whatever the nature and extent of the economic loss incurred by the employer as a result of her absence because of the pregnancy, whether the contract of employment was concluded for a fixed or an indefinite period has no bearing on the discriminatory character of the dismissal. In either case, the employee's inability to perform her contract of employment is due to pregnancy.'

The court pointed out that neither directive distinguishes between those employed on fixed terms and those employed pursuant to contracts of indefinite duration. The European Court of Justice gave further consideration to the *Pregnant Worker's Directive* in *Jimenez Melgar v Ayuntamiento de Los Barrios*: C-438/99 [2001] ECR I-6915, [2003] 3 CMLR 67. The court determined that:

(i)   the Directive has direct effect;

(ii)   where a member state wishes to enact legislation permitting dismissals in exceptional circumstances, it need not specify the particular grounds on which such workers may be dismissed; and

(iii)   a refusal to renew a fixed-term contract is not a dismissal. However, such a refusal may breach the provisions of the *ETD 76/207/EEC* (now the *ETD 2006/54/EC*).

Where an employer refused to allow an employee to return after her maternity leave because he thought her temporary replacement was better at the job, the EAT considered that the employee's dismissal was discriminatory. The 'effective cause' had been the pregnancy as, had the employee not been absent as a result of her pregnancy, the replacement would never have been employed (*Rees v Apollo Watch Repairs plc* [1996] ICR 466, EAT. See also *Abbey National plc v Formoso* [1999] IRLR 222, EAT; an employee was dismissed for gross misconduct whilst absent on maternity leave. The lack of an opportunity to explain herself at a disciplinary hearing meant that the dismissal was discriminatory as her absence on maternity leave was the reason that she did not get a hearing).

The EAT seems to have gone further still in *Lewis Woolf Griptight Ltd v Corfield* [1997] IRLR 432, EAT. In the *Lewis* case, the tribunal found that the effective cause of the decision to dismiss was a breakdown in the relationship between the complainant and the respondent's Chief Executive. That reason was, of course, entirely gender-neutral. However, the respondent used an alleged failure by the complainant properly to exercise her right to return following maternity leave as a 'pretext' for the termination of her contract of employment. As this pretext was only available where the employee was a woman, the EAT reasoned, the dismissal was discriminatory.

10.32 Unfavourable treatment for reasons relating to a maternity-related illness

Under the earlier law, unfavourable treatment on grounds of a pregnancy-related illness was deemed to be discrimination on grounds of pregnancy (*SDA 1975, s 3A(3)(b)*). EA 2010, *s 18(2)* adopts a slightly different approach making unfavourable treatment on grounds of a pregnancy-related illness a specifically prohibited form of discrimination:

"A person (A) discriminates against a woman if, in the protected period in relation to a pregnancy of hers, A treats her unfavourably–

. . .

(b) because of illness suffered by her as a result of it."

In order to prevent overlapping heads of claim, *EA 2010, s. 18(7)(a)* disapplies the protection against direct sex discrimination where the unfavourable treatment complained falls within *EA 2010, s 18(2)(b)*.

For an explanation of the "protected period" see **10.30** above.

European case law provides helpful interpretative guidance: in *Brown v Rentokil Ltd*: C-394/96 [1998] All ER (EC) 791, [1998] ECR I-4185, the following principles were established.

(a)   An employee may not be dismissed by reason of absence arising from a maternity-related illness at any point between conception and the end of her maternity leave period ('the protected period').

(b)   Where the maternity-related illness occurs after the end of the protected period, a dismissal will not be discriminatory if a man would have been dismissed had he been absent, because of illness, for a comparable period.

(c)   Where the illness arises during the protected period but persists thereafter, only days of absence which occur after the end of the protected period may be relied upon by an employer in deciding to dismiss (*William B Morrison & Son Ltd* (1999) 648 IDS Brief, EAT).

In a case decided before the ECJ's decision in *Brown* (and, thus, against the context of the former domestic protective regime), the EAT went further still and held that a dismissal effected after the end of the protected period was contrary to *SDA 1975* if it was for a maternity-related illness that arose during the employee's period of maternity leave (*Caledonia Bureau Investment and Property v Caffrey* [1998] ICR 603).

10.33 Discrimination Arising from Disability

EA 2010 has introduced a new form of discrimination: "Discrimination arising from disability". The explicit aim of the new provision was to reverse the principal effect of the decision of the House of Lords in *London Borough of Lewisham v Malcolm* [2008] UKHL 43, [2008] IRLR 700. That decision had concerned a predecessor tort defined in the *Disability Discrimination Act 1995*: "disability-related discrimination". In *Clark v Novacold* [1999] ICR 951, (a case decided on the old law) the Court of Appeal considered a case in which an employee was dismissed for sickness absence. The absence stemmed from his disability. The reason for dismissal; absence, was, the Court reasoned, a reason which related, therefore, to his disability. The appropriate comparator was someone in respect of whom that reason was not available. This meant essentially asking whether the employer would have dismissed for absence someone who had not been absent. The apparent absurdity of the test was mitigated by the fact that disability-related discrimination was capable of being justified. In *Malcolm* the House of Lords concluded that liability should be made out only when a tribunal could be satisfied that the disability itself was part of the reason for termination. The appropriate comparator was someone who had been absent but not for a reason relating to their disability. This was widely considered to have neutered the protection and the new tort is intended, in effect to reinstate *Clark v Novacold*.

EA 2010, s 15 provides:

"(1) A person (A) discriminates against a disabled person (B) if –

(a)   A treats B unfavourably because of something arising in consequence of B's disability, and

(b)   A cannot show that the treatment is a proportionate means of achieving a legitimate aim.

(2) Subsection (1) does not apply if A shows that A did not know, and could not reasonably have been expected to know, that B had the disability."

If an employee has a disability that causes him to be frequently absent from work, dismissing him for that absence record will amount to a breach of *s 15(1)* unless it can be justified. That is the same outcome that applying the former provisions of the *DDA 1995* would have produced had *Malcolm* (above) not overturned *Clark* (above)

For a detailed treatment of the justification defence see **11.9**.

10.34 Indirect discrimination

The concept of indirect discrimination has always been easier to define than to apply in practice. In essence, it is concerned with cases where employers treat all of their employees in the same way but there is a disparity in the effect of that treatment. For instance, to insist that all of one's employees are at least 6 foot tall will exclude more women than men from employment. Similarly, to require one's employees to work Saturday shifts will have a different effect on Christian employees to the effect that it would have on Jewish employees.

The dividing line between direct and indirect discrimination is not always an easy one to draw but the two forms of discrimination are distinct statutory torts and the distinction makes a material difference, particularly because a defence of justification is available in cases of indirect but not all cases of direct discrimination (*R v Secretary of State for Defence* [2006] EWCA Civ 1293, [2006] 1 WLR 3213, [2006] IRLR 934; For an account of the justification defence see **11.9 DISCRIMINATION AND EQUAL OPPORTUNITIES – II**). To have a rule which requires that job applicants be white would plainly fall into the former category. An apparently neutral requirement, such as insisting that job applicants be graduates, may have an indirectly discriminatory effect because members of particular ethnic minorities are under-represented in tertiary education. It may be that the same broad set of facts may give rise both to a claim for direct and indirect discrimination. Thus, if a set of job requirements is indirectly discriminatory and, in addition, the interviewer favours members of one race over another, both claims may lie. However, in such a case the complainant will rely on different facts to make out each claim. A particular set of facts should normally (although not invariably) found one or other, but not both, sorts of claim (see *Jaffrey v Department of Environment Transport and the Regions* [2002] IRLR 688, EAT).

Before 2010, there were a number of subtly different statutory formulations of the test for indirect discrimination in operation. Since the coming into force of the *EA 2010* there is, a single, unified test. *EA 2010, s 19(1)*, provides:

> "A person (A) discriminates against another (B) if A applies to B a provision, criterion or practice which is discriminatory in relation to a relevant protected characteristic of B's".

The relevant protected characteristics are all of those listed in *EA 2010, s 4* with the single exception of "pregnancy and maternity" (*EA 2010, s 19(3)*). This represents an extension of the protection afforded to those whose relevant characteristic is disability or gender re-assignment as neither were protected against indirect discrimination under the previous regime.

A provision, criterion or practice is discriminatory in relation to a relevant protected characteristic of B's if:

(a)   A applies, or would apply, it to persons with whom B does not share the characteristic,

(b)   it puts, or would put, persons with whom B shares the characteristic at a particular disadvantage when compared with persons with whom B does not share it,

(c)   it puts, or would put, B at that disadvantage, and

(d)   A cannot show it to be a proportionate means of achieving a legitimate aim."

There is no definition of "provision", "criterion" or "practice" in the Act itself. The *EHRC Code* states:

> "[the terms] should be construed widely so as to include, for example, any formal or informal policies, rules practices, arrangements, criteria, conditions, prerequisites, qualifications or provisions. A provision, criterion or practice may also include decisions to do something in the future – such as a policy or criterion that has not yet been applied – as well as a 'one-off' or discretionary scheme." (Para 4.5)

The term 'provision' would be apt to include both contractual provisions and the provisions of non-contractual policies. It should be borne in mind that in cases of sex discrimination, unlawful discrimination in relation to contractual terms is combated by means of a separate legislative regime known, misleadingly, as 'Equal Pay' (see EQUAL PAY (21)). The term 'equal pay' is misleading because all discriminatory differences in contractual terms fall within the scope of that protective regime whether or not they are, strictly speaking, to do with pay. A provision may consist of a 'one-off decision' (*Starmer v British Airways plc* [2005] IRLR 862, EAT: decision not to allow an employee to reduce her work to 50% of normal hours constituted the application of a 'provision').

'Criterion' is self-explanatory and significant as many cases involving discrimination will be concerned with selection decisions whether for appointment, promotion or dismissal. There is no requirement (as there had been under the old sex and racial discrimination tests) for the discriminatory criterion to be an absolute bar to the member of the protected class. Thus a criterion that an applicant for a post should have English as a first language will be struck down if it disadvantages an employee of a particular race even if it appears on a list of desirable rather than required characteristics.

'Practice' naturally bears the widest of meanings. It enables the Tribunal to look past an employer's Human Resources policies and to look at the day to day experience of the employees.

A claim may be based on more than one provision, criterion or practice (or "PCP") and relate to the impact the combined PCPs have on more than one protected characteristic. Thus, in *Ministry of Defence v DeBique* [2010] IRLR 471, EAT, a soldier who was unable to obtain the necessary visa to allow her sister to move from St Vincent to assist her with childcare was adversely affected by a PCP that required her to be available for duty twenty four hours a day and seven days a week (which indirectly discriminated against women as they are more likely to have childcare responsibilities) and a PCP which precluded members of family living overseas from coming to the UK so as to assist with childcare (which indirectly discriminated against foreign nationals).

In some cases, the relevant PCP may be expressly defined by the employer. In other cases, the tribunal may need to formulate a PCP by analysing the employer's practice or behaviour. There may be a number of different formulations which are consistent with the underlying circumstances of the case. If a complainant can 'realistically identify a [PCP] capable of supporting [their] case . . . it is nothing to the point that [their] employer can with equal cogency derive from the facts a different and unobjectionable requirement or condition' (*Allonby v Accrington and Rossendale College* [2001] EWCA Civ 529, [2001] IRLR 364, CA).

Disparity of effect

At the heart of indirect discrimination is the notion that a single measure taken by an employer may affect different groups of employees very differently. In *Eweida v British Airways Plc* [2010] EWCA Civ 80, [2010] ICR 890, [2010] IRLR 322, [2010] 09 LS Gaz R 19 Lord Justice Sedley defined the purpose of indirect discrimination protection as not to "deal with the problem of group discrimination" but rather to "deal with the discriminatory impact of facially neutral requirements". That task is approached by asking whether "an identifiable group is adversely affected, whether actually or potentially, by some ostensibly neutral requirement". The practical consequence is that a complainant has to show more than just that they have been disadvantaged by the relevant requirement. They have to show that others who share their protected characteristic would also be adversely affected. In *Eweida* itself, the complainant's indirect discrimination claim failed because she was unable to show that any other employee shared her religious belief that she should wear a crucifix visibly. Ms Eweida took her case to Strasbourg. The European Court of Human Rights upheld her claim that the UK had failed to take adequate steps to protect her right to manifest her religion. The Court's analysis focused, however, on justification arguments. This leaves something of an uncertainty since Ms Eweida's failure before the UK courts was because she did not meet the statutory test for indirect discrimination. That suggests that the domestic test may need to be read down so as to ensure consistency with the ECtHR's decision.

In *Homer v Chief Constable of West Yorkshire* [2010] EWCA Civ 419, [2010] ICR 987, there is a suggestion that there must be a connection between the disadvantage and the protected characteristic. In the particular case, a legal adviser employed by a police authority complained that changes to the job grading structure used by his employer meant that to achieve the top grade he would have to obtain a law degree and that as he was in his sixties there was no time for him to obtain one. The Court of Appeal concluded that the particular disadvantage to which those in the 60–65 age group were subject did not result from the application of the requirement for a law degree but rather from the fact that members of the group would cease work before any benefit could be obtained from the degree if they acquired it. The decision was overturned by the Supreme Court ([2012] UKSC 15, [2012] IRLR 601) but on the ground that if the reason that the employee suffered the disadvantage was proximity to retirement, that was a matter that was indistinguishable from his age. Retirement could not be equated with voluntarily leaving employment at an earlier age precisely because retirement was not voluntary.

PCPs that distinguish between employees on the basis of length of service are often considered to adversely affect younger employees. Cases involving such PCPs have given rise to some complex law on the justification defence. Not all such provisions will have the necessary disparity of effect, one example is *Tyrolean Airways Tiroler Luftfahrt Gesellschaft mbH v Betriebsrat Bord der Tyrolean Airways Tiroler Luftfahrt Gesellschaft mbH*: C-132/11 [2012] IRLR 781. A provision in a collective agreement which required flight and cabin crew to have three years' employment with the airline before achieving a particular grade was not sufficiently linked (either directly or indirectly) to age for it to be discriminatory. The rule excluded experience gained with other airlines it was not an age-related provision.

In cases of indirect discrimination the complainant must show that the PCP, puts persons who share the same protected characteristic as the complainant at a 'particular disadvantage'. This term is not defined. It is unclear whether the use of the word 'particular' is intended to convey something more than mere disadvantage. It is thought likely that it is intended to indicate a requirement for a disadvantage which is substantial and not merely trivial or theoretical.

Assessing disparity of effect is a comparative process. Whereas, in a case of direct discrimination, one compares the treatment received by an individual with that received or which would have been received by another, indirect discrimination cases require comparisons between groups of employees. Taking, by way of example, a case of indirect sex discrimination, the Tribunal looks at the impact of the relevant PCP on the men and women affected by it. The first task of the Tribunal is to determine which group or groups of employees it is going to look at in order to perform the comparison. This is known as selecting the 'pool' for comparison. The task of identifying the relevant pool can be difficult and is often, in practice, determinative of the case (See, for example, *Chaudhury v British Medical Association* [2007] EWCA Civ 788, [2007] IRLR 800: In a case under the old test, the claimant complained that the BMA operated a policy (amounting to a requirement or condition) of refusing to support members in race discrimination claims against regulatory authorities. The Court of Appeal determined that had such a requirement or condition been applied the appropriate pool for assessing the disparity of its effect was not BMA members generally but those members who wished to bring such claims. Since all such members were equally disadvantaged, regardless of their race, no disparity of effect could be established).

EA 2010, s 23(2) requires that on a comparison of cases for the purposes of *s 19* "there must be no material difference between the circumstances relating to each case".

Because it may be possible in a particular case, to identify more than one potentially appropriate pool, the selection of the pool is, in the first instance, a matter for the claimant. However, the tribunal is not necessarily bound to adopt the pool suggested by the claimant and it may reject the claimant's pool where it considers that it is an artificial or arbitrary one (*Abbott v Cheshire and Wirral Partnership NHS Trust* [2006] EWCA Civ 523, [2006] ICR 1267). If the Tribunal decides to reject the claimant's proposed pool, it should explain its reasons for doing so in its decision (*Secretary of State for Trade and Industry v Rutherford (No 2)* at the EAT, reported at [2005] ICR 119 at 160). Once the Tribunal has resolved to determine the pool for itself, it does not have a broad discretion as to how the pool is identified. In most cases, the Court of Appeal suggested in *Allonby* ([2001] IRLR 364, CA), it should be a matter of logical deduction from the measure (ie the relevant provision, criterion or practice). In *Ministry of Defence v DeBique* [2010] IRLR 471, the EAT suggested that the tribunal should select from the range of pools available to them the one that will "realistically and effectively test the particular allegation before them". The starting point should be the whole of the group to which the provision, criterion or practice is applied, and the tribunal will be wary of any further sub-division (cf *London Underground Ltd v Edwards* [1995] IRLR 355, *Jones v University of Manchester* [1993] ICR 474, CA and *Rutherford v Secretary of State for Trade and Industry* [2006] UKHL 19, [2006] ICR 785 – provisions precluding claims for redundancy payments and unfair dismissal by those over 65 applied to the whole working population and not just those older employees for whom the 'retirement had some meaning'). *Rutherford* was not authority, the Court of Appeal concluded, for the 'routine selection of the widest pool'. Sedley LJ instead preferred to allow the tribunal a discretion as to the pool considered:

> 'In discrimination claims the key determinant . . . is the issue which the claimant has elected to pose and which the tribunal is therefore required to evaluate by finding a pool in which the specificity of the allegation can be realistically tested. Provided it tests the allegation in a suitable pool, the tribunal cannot be said to have erred in law even if a different pool, with a different outcome, could equally legitimately have been chosen.'

Equally, an expansion of the pool to include those who were not even potentially subject to the provision, criterion or practice, would be inappropriate (cf *Briggs v North Eastern Education and Library Board* [1990] IRLR 181). However, where the provision, criterion or practice relates to recruitment criteria the relevant pool might be very large and in *Greater Manchester Police Authority v Lea* [1990] IRLR 372, the EAT held that the employment tribunal had not erred in accepting that the economically active population was an appropriate pool for the purpose of determining the proportion of men and women who could comply with a condition of not being in receipt of an occupational pension. In *Lord Chancellor v Coker* [2001] IRLR 116, the EAT considered a case where the Lord Chancellor had decided to appoint a particular individual to be his special adviser. The appointment was challenged by two complainants who alleged that the failure publicly to advertise the position had resulted in their having been the subjects of acts of indirect sex and race discrimination, respectively. As the criterion was, in effect, that the candidate should be the relevant specific individual, the EAT concluded that no pool could sensibly be identified. The EAT's decision was upheld by the Court of Appeal ([2001] EWCA Civ 1756, [2002] ICR 321). The relevant criterion was identified before their Lordships as being a friend of the Lord Chancellor. The Court of Appeal concluded that the necessary disparity of impact could not be established. Looking at the pool of those qualified to perform the role, the criterion excluded almost the entirety of its members. The criterion could only be said to have a disproportionate effect where a significant proportion of the pool were able to satisfy it. That was not the case on the facts. Lord Phillips went on to opine that:

> 'Making an appointment from within a circle of family, friends and personal acquaintances is seldom likely to constitute indirect discrimination.'

Under the old law, the Claimant had to establish that a "considerably smaller proportion" of those who shared their protected characteristic could comply with the PCP. *EA 2010* requires, instead, that the claimant establish that those in the pool who share the claimant's protected characteristic should be at a "particular disadvantage". The old test was explicitly concerned with numbers and the case law set out below, decided under the old provisions, understandably focus on figures. The new test is not expressly concerned with numbers but it seems from the EHRC Code that statistics will still be important. In defining "disadvantage", *EHRC Code, Para 4.12* says:

'Statistics can provide an insight into the link between the provision, criterion or practice and the disadvantage that it causes.''

However, the *EHRC Code* recognises that the numbers of people involved may be too small or the evidence available too unreliable to allow for a statistical analysis. In such circumstances, the *EHRC Code* suggests (at *Para 4.13*), it would be neither practicable nor appropriate for a statistical approach to be taken and the tribunal may wish, instead, to rely upon expert evidence. Experts may also be appropriate where the tribunal requires some assistance in properly understanding the impact of a PCP on those with a particular protected characteristic (see *Para 4.14* which gives as an example expert evidence about the principles of a particular religious belief).

When the *EHRC Code* turns to providing guidance on carrying out the comparative exercise it turns again to numbers. The tribunal should ask (says *Para 4.21*) how many workers in the pool are (or would be) disadvantaged by the PCP despite not sharing the protected characteristic with the claimant. That number should be expressed as a proportion, which the guidance labels as "x". The same exercise is then repeated in relation to pool members who do share the protected characteristic. That proportion is labelled "y". The tribunal then compares "x" with "y" in order to determine whether the necessary particular disadvantage exists. *Para 4.22* advises:

'Whether a difference is significant will depend on the context, such as the size of the pool and the numbers behind the proportions. It is not necessary to show that the majority of those within the pool who share the protected characteristic are placed at a disadvantage.'

Turning to the case law on the old formulation, there was little guidance on how one determines whether a particular disparate impact is sufficient. The issue was referred to the European Court of Justice in *R v Secretary of State for Employment, ex p Seymour-Smith* [1999] ICR 447. The guidance provided by the ECJ was disappointingly vague. The ECJ decision echoed the language of the *SDA 1975* as it was prior to 1 October 2005 in requiring that a 'considerably smaller percentage' of women than men were able to satisfy the relevant condition. A mere statistically significant disparity was insufficient. However, the ECJ went on to hold that a 'lesser but persistent and relatively constant disparity over a long period' might suffice. It was hoped that the House of Lords might feel able to put a little meat on these bones when the matter came back for their further consideration in the light of the reference ([2000] ICR 244). The issue in *Seymour-Smith* was whether the requirement, introduced in 1985, that employees should have two years' continuous service before qualifying for protection against unfair dismissal indirectly discriminated against women. In 1985, 77.4% of men could comply with that requirement whereas only 68.9% of women could do so. In 1991, the year which their Lordships identified as being the critical one for the purposes of the particular case, the relevant percentages were 74.5% and 67.4%. None of their Lordships thought that those figures, on their own, suggested that a 'considerably smaller percentage' of women could comply. However, the majority felt that the disparity (which narrowed slowly to about 4.3% by 1993) fell into the category of the sort of 'persistent and relatively consistent' disparity that the ECJ had indicated might suffice. They determined, therefore, that the requirement was indirectly discriminatory although they went on to find that it was justified.

In practice, the tribunals are given a considerable margin of discretion in deciding when the percentages should be taken to indicate a sufficiently significant disparity. The courts had consistently rejected the adoption of a rule of thumb (see *McCausland v Dungannon District Council* [1993] IRLR 583 which was concerned with the construction of the *Fair Employment (Northern Ireland) Act 1976* which applies the same test of disparate impact to religious discrimination). In *Harvest Town Circle Ltd v Rutherford* [2002] ICR 123, EAT, the EAT expressed the pious (if rather faint) hope that 'as more cases of indirect discrimination are heard a more soundly based assessment of what is or is not properly regarded as a considerable or substantial disparity will develop'. In *London Underground Ltd v Edwards (No 2)* [1999] ICR 494, there was only one person in the pool of comparison who could not comply with the relevant requirement. 100% of the 2,023 men to whom the provision applied could comply. Of the 21 women affected, only the complainant could not comply. This meant that the proportion of women that could comply was 95.2%. Nevertheless, the Court of Appeal upheld the tribunal's decision that the proportion of women that could comply was considerably smaller.

The approach adopted in *Edwards* illustrates another general principle applicable to the assessment of disparate impact; one should not focus on the absolute numbers underlying the relevant proportions but on the percentages themselves. The principle was specifically endorsed by the ECJ in *Seymour-Smith* (but see *Harvest Town Circle Ltd* above, in which the EAT interpret *Seymour-Smith* as allowing a domestic court to look at either absolute numbers or relative proportions of those who could comply).

In many cases, the tribunal will look at the relevant proportions and simply subtract one from the other. In the *Edwards* case, for instance, one might say that 4.8% more men can comply than women. *McCausland* suggests taking a further mathematical step. Rather than subtracting the smaller percentage from the larger, one should calculate a ratio. In the *McCausland* case itself, 2.9% of Protestants could comply with the relevant requirement as compared with only 1.5% of Catholics. Simply subtracting one percentage from the other produces an unimpressive difference of only 1.4%. However, when one looks at the ratio of the two percentages one finds that the group of Catholics that could comply was only 71% of the size of the group of Protestants that could do so. A further variation was suggested by Lord Nicholls in *Barry v Midland Bank plc* [1999] ICR 859 at page 869. He suggested that having calculated what proportion of men and women fell within the advantaged and disadvantaged groups respectively one should then calculate a ratio of the proportions of those falling within the disadvantaged group. His approach is thus akin to the *McCausland* approach save that it focuses on those who cannot comply rather than those who can. However, in *Secretary of State for Trade and Industry v Rutherford* above, the Court of Appeal indicated that it would be wrong to focus only on the disadvantaged group. When *Rutherford* came before the House of Lords, Lord Walker of Gestingthorpe took the view that, save where special circumstances justify it, attention should be focused on the 'advantaged' group (*Rutherford v Secretary of State for Trade and Industry* [2006] UKHL 19, [2006] ICR 785). However, in *Grundy v British Airways plc* [2007] EWCA Civ 1020, [2008] IRLR 74, an equal pay case, the Court of Appeal held that an employment tribunal had been entitled to focus on the disadvantaged group. the position remains, therefore, somewhat unclear.

The EAT has sought to rely on *Seymour-Smith* as a basis for taking a much less mechanistic approach to the assessment of the sufficiency of disparity. In *Chief Constable of Avon and Somerset Constabulary v Chew* [2001] All ER (D) 101 (Sep), EAT, the EAT indicated that a 'flexible approach' could be adopted to assessing the sufficiency of any disparity. It was not always necessary to rely on statistics. Further, the tribunal was entitled to consider whether the objectionable provision was inherently more likely to produce a detrimental effect, which disparately affected a particular sex. Thus in *Chew*, a shift rota would likely be harder for those with childcare responsibilities to comply with, and women are more likely to have childcare responsibilities.

Personal disadvantage

The third element of the test is personal disadvantage. It does not matter if, for instance, persons of a particular religion or sex are disproportionately disadvantaged by a provision, criterion or practice, if the complainant is not. Thus a female employee cannot complain that she has been indirectly discriminated against as a result of an employer imposing a minimum height requirement if she is taller than the minimum requirement. Under the old test, inability to comply with the requirement or condition was not its own detriment (*Lord*

Chancellor v Coker [2001] IRLR 116, EAT). It is thought that a similar principle applies under the new test. The disadvantage must be the consequence of the application of the provision, criterion or practice and not the imposition of the measure itself.

Indirect discrimination: particular cases

10.35 *Sex discrimination and full-time work*

Provisions, criteria or practices which result in the less favourable treatment of part-time employees are frequently found indirectly to discriminate against women (cf *Bilka-Kaufhaus GmbH v Weber von Hartz*: 170/84 [1986] ECR 1607, [1986] 2 CMLR 701; *Clarke v Eley (IMI) Kynoch Ltd* [1983] ICR 165, EAT; *R v Secretary of State for Employment, ex p Equal Opportunities Commission* [1994] ICR 317), although it cannot be assumed that such a condition would have a discriminatory effect (see, for example, *Sinclair, Roche & Temperley v Heard* [2004] IRLR 763, EAT). Each case turns on its own facts and claimants have to be prepared to lead evidence which establishes a disparate impact (*Kidd v DRG (UK) Ltd* [1985] ICR 405).

Because the effects of a requirement to work full time are often complex, it is by no means always immediately obvious that the complainant had been less favourably treated. See, for instance, *Kachelmann v Bankhaus Hermann Lampe KG*: C-322/98 [2000] ECR I-7505, [2002] 1 CMLR 155, ECJ, in which the ECJ wrestled with the question of whether a bank's decision, following the deletion of a part-time post, to limit the selection pool for redundancy to part-time workers amounted to less favourable treatment or (as it ultimately decided) that to have included full-timers would be to have conferred an advantage on part-timers by effectively entitling them to be offered a full-time post if a full-timer were selected for redundancy.

Historically, the predominance of women in the part-time sector has been assumed to be related to the fact that they have traditionally been expected to be the providers of homecare to young children. This assumption underpins the reasoning of the EAT in the case of *Price v Civil Service Commission (No 2)* [1978] IRLR 3 which held that imposing a maximum age limit of 28 for appointment as an Executive Officer in the Civil Service was, in practice, to the disadvantage of women as they were more likely to have had career breaks in order to start a family. Similarly, in *Meade-Hill and National Union of Civil and Public Servants v British Council* [1996] 1 All ER 79, [1995] ICR 847, [1995] IRLR 478, the Court of Appeal was persuaded that the exercise of a contractual mobility clause might be discriminatory as women were more likely than their partners to be the 'second earner' and thus less able to re-locate. Whilst it appears that the tribunals and courts are frequently comfortable making such assumptions, in practice it is dangerous for an employer to do so. In *Skyrail Oceanic Ltd v Coleman* [1981] ICR 864, it was held that selection of a woman for redundancy on the assumption that men are more likely than women to be the primary supporters of their spouses and children could itself amount to unlawful discrimination.

The same issue arises in circumstances where a woman wishes to make changes to her work patterns following the birth of her child. In *Clymo v Wandsworth London Borough Council* [1989] ICR 250, an employer declined to allow an employee to change to a job-sharing (ie part-time) arrangement. The EAT held that the employer, having merely declined to provide an advantage not proffered to any employees in that grade, had not 'subjected' the employee to anything, and that there was no detriment. By contrast, in *Robinson v Oddbins Ltd* [1996] 27 DCLD 1 an employment tribunal held that the employee's request to job-share had not been properly considered and the company's reliance on a contractual clause requiring employees, when asked, to work hours over and above the standard working week had indirectly discriminated against women who were more likely to have childcare responsibilities (cf also *Puttick v Eastbourne Borough Council* (unreported, 1995, COIT 3106/2)). In another case, the EAT held that a refusal to allow a woman to job-share was not directly discriminatory in the absence of evidence that a man making a similar request would have had it granted; however, it did not consider the issue of indirect discrimination (*British Telecommunications plc v Roberts* [1996] IRLR 601). In practice, employers will need to be able to establish that there is a sensible justification for requiring that employees work full-time if they are to be safe from claims. In *Lockwood v Crawley Warren Group Ltd* [2001] 680 IDS Brief 9, EAT, this approach was extended still further. A female employee encountered difficulties with her childcare arrangements. She offered to work full-time from home or else to take up to six months' unpaid leave with a view to resolving the difficulties. She was offered two weeks of leave instead and resigned. The EAT decided that the refusal to allow her either to work from home or to take the leave she had asked for, amounted to the application of a condition or requirement. For an example of the circumstances in which a refusal to allow an employee to work flexibly was justified, see *Georgiou v Colman Coyle* [2002] 705 IDS Brief 12, EAT: the office was small; there was a need for two full-time solicitors; commercial clients expected a prompt and efficient service; the need to consult files and to be supervised meant that the complainant had to attend the respondent's premises; and reduced fee income would adversely affect the respondent's profitability.

10.36 *Sexual orientation*

It is lawful to offer access to benefits, facilities or services to married persons and civil partners to the exclusion of all other persons. *EA 2010, Sch 9, Part 3, Para 18(2)* specifically provides that that does not amount to an act of sexual orientation discrimination (but see *Maruko v Versorgungsanstalt der Deutschen Buhnen*: C-267/06 [2008] IRLR 450).

Many employers offered access to benefits, facilities or services exclusively to married persons which had the effect of excluding homosexual employees. *EA 2010, Sch 9, Part 3, Para 18(1)* provides that no claim for sexual orientation discrimination lies in relation to any such practice in so far as the relevant right had accrued before 5 December 2005 (on which date civil partnerships came into being) or is a right to a benefit which is payable in respect of periods of service before that date.

To bring a claim of indirect discrimination, it will be necessary for a complainant to identify himself as being of a particular sexual orientation, something that is not necessary for a complaint of direct discrimination, victimisation or harassment.

10.37 Disability: Duty to Make Reasonable Adjustments

Under the *DDA 1995*, there was no prohibition of indirect disability discrimination, instead there was a new creature: a duty to make reasonable adjustments where a disabled employee is placed a "substantial disadvantage" as the result of a provision, criterion or practice, physical feature of the employer's premises or the absence of an auxiliary aid. The principal difference between the ordinary duty not indirectly to discriminate and the duty to make reasonable adjustments is that the former is simply a path to compensation whereas the latter imposes a positive duty upon an employer to remove barriers to the effective participation in its workforce of those with disabilities.

When does the duty arise?

The duty is set out at *EA 2010, s 20* and is supplemented by a detailed schedule: *EA 2010, Sch 8*.

EA 2010, s 20 imposes a "requirement" on an employer:

(1)   whose provisions, criteria or practices puts a disabled person at a "substantial disadvantage" in relation to a relevant matter in comparison with persons who are not disabled (*s 20(3)*);

(2)   whose premises have a physical feature which puts a disabled person at a substantial disadvantage (*s 20(4)*); or

(3)   whose disabled employee will be put at a substantial disadvantage if they are not provided with an auxiliary aid (*s 20(5)*);

to "take such steps as it is reasonable to have to take to avoid the disadvantage" or to provide the auxiliary aid (as appropriate). A failure to comply with any of the requirements spelt out above is treated as a failure to comply with a duty to make reasonable adjustments (*EA 2010, s 21(1)*) which, in turn, amounts to an act of discrimination (*EA 2010, s 21(2)*).

The Act does not further define the phrase "provisions, criteria or practices". *EHRC Code* suggests that the terms should be construed widely and would include: "any formal or informal policies, rules, practices, arrangements or qualifications including one-off decision and actions" (*Para 6.10*). "Physical feature" is defined at *s 20(10)* so as to include "a feature arising from the design or construction of a building; a feature of an approach to, exit from or access to a building; a fixture or fitting, or furniture, furnishings, materials, equipment or other chattels, in or on the premises; or any other physical element or quality". References to auxiliary aids include references to auxiliary services (*s 20(11)*). It would appear that a 'provision, criterion or practice' could include an implied condition that a person is fit for the job they are employed to do. If it transpires that a person through disability can no longer fulfil that condition (i.e. the person is no longer capable of doing the job for which they were employed) then there may be a duty to consider any adjustments that could be made to remove the disadvantage caused by that implied condition (see *Archibald v Fife Council* [2004] UKHL 32, [2004] ICR 954, HL).

The Act further defines what may be expected by way of adjustments:

(1)   Where the relevant provision, criterion or practice or auxiliary aid relates to the provision of information the steps that it is reasonable for an employer to take include steps for ensuring that the information is provided in accessible format (*s 20(6)*); and

(2)   Where the disadvantage arises from a physical feature, avoiding the disadvantage may include: "removing the physical feature in question; altering it; or providing a reasonable means of avoiding it" (*s 20(9)*).

EA 2010, Sch 8 fleshes out the *s 20* test. In relation to employers two things are identified as "relevant matters": Deciding to whom to offer employment and employment itself (*EA 2010, Sch 8, Part 2, para (1)*).

In order for the duty to arise the employee must be subjected to a "substantial" disadvantage in comparison with persons who are not disabled. "Substantial" is defined at *EA 2010, s 212(1)* to mean "more than minor or trivial". The threshold is set deliberately low. The *EHRC Code* emphasises that the purpose of the comparison is to determine whether the disadvantage arises because of the disability and emphasises that, in contrast to the position with cases of direct and indirect discrimination, there is "no requirement to identify a comparator or comparator group whose circumstances are the same or nearly the same as the disabled person's" (*Para 6.16*).

No duty where Employer lacks knowledge of disability or disadvantage

Limitations on the duty are set out *EA 2010, Sch 8, Part 3*. An employer is not subject to a duty to make reasonable adjustments if he does not know and could not reasonably be expected to know:

(1)   In the case of an applicant or potential applicant for employment that the disabled person may be an applicant for the work in question;

(2)   In any other case, that an interested disabled person has a disability and is likely to be placed at the relevant substantial disadvantage.

In *Wilcox v Birmingham CAB Services Ltd* [2011] EqLR 810, the EAT departed from earlier authority (*Eastern and Coastal Kent PCT v Grey* [2009] IRLR 429) which had suggested that an employer could only rely on the exception if he could show that he lacked the actual or constructive knowledge referred to in both limbs of (2) above. That interpretation seemed to mean that an employer might be subject to the duty even where he was unaware (and could not reasonably have been expected to be aware) of the disability provided he could foresee that the employee might be subject to a disadvantage. In *Wilcox* the EAT took the view that unless the employer had actual or constructive knowledge of the disability, the question of substantial disadvantage did not arise.

Where an employer had no actual knowledge of a disability but is fixed with constructive knowledge (on the basis that he ought to have known) it is open to him to argue that he has nevertheless complied with the duty on the basis either that no reasonable adjustments were possible or else that he had in fact taken steps that resulted in him unwittingly discharging the duty (see *British Gas Services Ltd v McCaull* [2001] IRLR 60). The test is an objective one. It is the steps taken or not taken that are to be tested and not the employer's state of mind in taking or not taking such steps.

The Content of the Duty

The employer must take such steps as it is reasonable to have to take either to avoid the disadvantage or, in auxiliary aid cases, to provide the aid (*EA 2010, s 20(3) to (5)*). The employer cannot require the employee to pay its costs of complying with the duty (*EA 2010, s 20(7)*).

EA 2010, s 22 allows for regulations to further define the duty including defining what would and would not be reasonable in particular circumstances. No regulations have yet been issued that apply in employment cases.

The *DDA 1995* had, at *s 18B* guidance as to what sorts of measures might be required and what factors might be taken into account in determining reasonableness. The factors that were identified included:

(1)   the extent to which taking the step would prevent the effect in relation to which the duty is imposed;

(2)   the extent to which it is practicable for [the employer] to take the step;

(3)   the financial and other costs which would be incurred by [the employer] in taking the step and the extent to which it would disrupt any of his activities;

(4)   the extent of [the employer's] financial and other resources;

(5)   the availability to [the employer] of financial or other assistance with respect to taking the step; and

(6)   the nature of [the employer's] activities and the size of his undertaking.

The steps that might be taken included making adjustments to premises; allocating some of the disabled person's duties to another person; transferring him to an existing vacancy and altering his hours of work and training. The reasonableness factors and example adjustments do not appear to have been carried across to the *EA 2010*. However, there is no doubt that they remain relevant and they have been substantially reproduced at Chapter 6 of the *EHRC Code*. Guidance is set out at *Para 6.23* ff of the *EHRC Code*.

Employers should also be careful to identify what arrangement or what provision, criterion or practice is actually placing the disabled employee at a disadvantage in order that the appropriate adjustments can be considered. In *Paul v National Probation Service* [2004] IRLR 190, a tribunal rejected the claim of an claimant who had been refused a job after failing an occupational health assessment. The tribunal concluded that the claimant had not been placed at a disadvantage compared to others since all job applicants had to undergo an assessment. The EAT held that the tribunal had wrongly regarded the relevant arrangement as being the requirement to undergo an assessment. It was not the fact of the assessment that had placed the claimant at a disadvantage but the health adviser's assessment that the claimant's depressive illness rendered him unsuitable for the job. By focusing on the wrong 'arrangement' the tribunal omitted to consider whether there were any reasonable adjustments that the employer could have made (eg by obtaining specialist advice from the claimant's consultant on his fitness for the job). (See also *Smith v Churchills Stairlifts plc* [2005] EWCA Civ 1220, [2006] IRLR 41, where the Court of Appeal confirmed that the comparator for these purposes is readily identified by reference to the disadvantage caused by the relevant arrangements.)

The EAT has held that whether or not any adjustments were reasonable in the circumstances will be determined by the employment tribunal objectively (see *Morse v Wiltshire County Council* [1998] IRLR 352 and *HM Land Registry v Wakefield* [2009] All ER (D) 205 (Feb), EAT). Thus, it may not be sufficient for an employer simply to assert that adjustments were considered and thought to be unreasonable if the tribunal finds that there were other reasonable adjustments which could have been made by the employer (see also *Ridout v TC Group* [1998] IRLR 628). The employment tribunal will not be entitled, however, to rely upon a failure to make a reasonable adjustment where the particular adjustment in question was not raised as an issue and the parties have not had an opportunity to make submissions in relation to that adjustment (*Tarbuck v Sainsbury's Supermarkets Ltd* [2006] IRLR 664). Recognising that tribunals often fall into error when they fail to identify and address each of the separate elements of the 'failure to make reasonable adjustments' cause of action, the EAT has laid down useful guidance on the step-by-step process to be followed in such cases: *Environment Agency v Rowan* [2008] IRLR 20.

Clark v Novacold [1999] IRLR 318, EWCA was authority for the proposition that the duty to make reasonable adjustments did not apply to a dismissal. Following *Aylott v Stockton on Tees BC* [2010] EWCA Civ 910, that would seem no longer to be the cases. In an admittedly obiter consideration of the issue, Mummery LJ was inclined to accept that the effect of *Framework Directive 2000/78/EC, Art 3(1)(c)* was to require dismissals to fall within the scope of the duty. There would appear to be no duty to offer part-time employment as an alternative to dismissal in circumstances where the claimant had not asked to work part-time and where he was not fit for any form of work at the relevant time (*Callagan v Glasgow City Council* [2001] IRLR 724). Avoiding dismissal may involve offering the employee an alternative job at a higher grade which she is capable of doing without requiring her to undergo a competitive interview cf *Archibald v Fife Council* [2004] UKHL 32, [2004] ICR 954 and in certain circumstances (eg where there is an on-going reorganisation) it could even involve the creation of an entirely new job (*Southampton City College v Randall* [2006] IRLR 18). However, there is no obligation on an employer to create a post specifically, which is not otherwise necessary, merely to create a job for a disabled person (*Tarbuck v Sainsbury's Supermarkets Ltd* [2006] IRLR 664 but see *Chief Constable of South Yorkshire Police v Jelic* [2010] IRLR 744 where in the context of a "disciplined service" the EAT held that employer should have considered a job swap, ie creating a vacancy by forcing the incumbent to transfer to another role).

An employer is not required to modify its policies or procedures, for example in relation to sick pay, where it would not be reasonable to do so (*O'Hanlon v Revenue and Customs Comrs* [2007] EWCA Civ 283, [2007] ICR 1359, CA).

In *Gomez v Glaxosmithkline Services Unlimited* [2011] EqLR 804, the EAT considered the case of a claimant who suffered from severe depression and panic attacks. The claimant was found to have been leaving the site at which he worked without authorisation and using a colleague's security pass. He was dismissed for gross misconduct. He argued that the penalty should have been "adjusted" and that he should have been given a warning instead. The EAT concluded that the employer could not be reasonably required to take such a step as it risked the employer appearing to condone the practice. *Burke v College of Law and another* [2011] EqLR 454, EAT is a further example of an employer determining that a proposed adjustment would not have been reasonable. It is a case concerning a "qualification body" – one of the categories of non–employers covered by the Act. The claimant, who has MS, was re-sitting LPC exams. A series of adjustments were made including allowing them more time. However, the claimant had asked for still further time and the opportunity to take the exams at home. Those adjustments were declined. The EAT concluded that the examination's purpose was to "assess the ability of the candidate to demonstrate their competence and capability in the subject matter under time pressure." The time restriction was, therefore, a competence standard. See also: *Lowe v Cabinet Office* [2011] EqLR 803: The claimant had Asperger's Syndrome. She applied for admission to the Civil Service Fast Stream. The selection exercise involved application of a criterion that required a high standard of communication skills and assessment by group exercise. The tribunal accepted that no adjustment was reasonably required. The exercise was to find high quality applicants and the proposed adjustments would have destroyed the essence of the exercise).

In *Clark v Newsquest Media* [2011] EqLR 932 an employer required a diabetic employee to test her blood and inject herself in private. The tribunal concluded that employer was acting in breach of the duty.

The following have all been held by employment tribunals to be reasonable adjustments:

(i)   provision of subtitled training videos for Channel 5 Television re-tuners (*Williams v Channel 5 Engineering Services Ltd*, IDS Brief 609, p 13);

(ii)   discounting of disability-related absences in assessing absence record (*Cox v Post Office*, IDS Brief 609, p 14 but see *O'Hanlon v Revenue and Customs Comrs* [2007] IRLR 404 and below); and

(iii)   provision of a special 'Grahl' chair costing £1,000 for an employee with a club foot (*Tarling v Wisdom Toothbrushes Ltd*, 24 June 1997, COIT 1500148/97).

The employer's duty to make reasonable adjustments is confined to those which are 'job related' (see *Kenny v Hampshire Constabulary* [1999] IRLR 76). A disabled person may be in a position to obtain employment if he was provided with transport to get to the place of employment. However, the employer's duty in relation to that person, whilst extending to the making of adjustments to enable access to the employer's premises, would not extend to the provision of transport to get there from home. In *Kenny*, the job applicant had cerebral palsy and required assistance in carrying out his toilet functions. The EAT held that whilst there may be a duty to consider physical adjustments to enable access to the toilets, the employer was not under a duty to provide a personal carer to assist the claimant with his toilet needs. Such provision would address the claimant's personal needs but would not be job-related.

The extent to which tribunals should take into account the actual or assumed knowledge of an employer in the context of the duty to make reasonable adjustments has been considered by the EAT in *Ridout v TC Group* [1998] IRLR 628. In that case, a job applicant had disclosed in her application that she was disabled and had photosensitive epilepsy controlled by a daily dose of Epilim. She was shortlisted for an interview. Upon entering the room in which the interview was to be held, the claimant, who was wearing sunglasses around her neck, commented that she might be disadvantaged by the fluorescent lighting in the room. However, the claimant did not use the sunglasses during her interview nor did she say that she felt in any way disadvantaged. The claimant complained to the tribunal that the employer had failed in its duty to make reasonable adjustments in respect of the physical arrangements for the interview. The tribunal dismissed the complaint. The EAT held that the tribunal was correct to find that the employer was not in breach of its duty to make reasonable adjustments notwithstanding that it knew of the claimant's condition. The EAT added that the provisions of *DDA 1995, s 6* (the predecessor provisions) required the tribunal to measure the extent of the duty, if any, against the actual or assumed knowledge of the employer both as to the disability and its likelihood of causing the individual a substantial disadvantage in comparison with persons who are not disabled. In this case, no reasonable employer could be expected to know, without being told in terms by the claimant, that the arrangements which were made for her interview might disadvantage her. Thus, it would appear that the extent of the duty to make reasonable adjustments will depend partly on the amount of information volunteered by the disabled person as to any disadvantages being suffered. However, this does not mean that the employer can simply wait to be told of such disadvantages before a duty will arise. On the facts in *Ridout*, it may have been reasonable for the employer itself not to make further inquiries as to any disadvantage. Whether or not this will be so in other cases will be a question of fact for the tribunal. In *Mid-Staffordshire General Hospitals NHS Trust v Cambridge* [2003] IRLR 566, the EAT went so far as to hold that 'A proper assessment of what is required to eliminate the disabled person's disadvantage is . . .   a necessary part of the duty imposed by s 6(1) since that duty cannot be complied with unless the employer makes a proper assessment of what needs to be done.' However, this decision (which was followed by the EAT in *Southampton City College v Randall* [2006] IRLR 18) was held by the EAT in *Tarbuck v Sainsbury's Supermarkets Ltd* [2006] IRLR 664 to have been incorrectly decided. Elias J concluded in Tarbuck that ' . . . there is no separate and distinct duty' to consult employees and that the single question under section 3A(1) was whether the employer had complied with his obligations there set out (see *Hay v Surrey County Council* [2007] EWCA Civ 93, [2007] All ER (D) 199 (Feb) in which the EAT's reasoning in Tarbuck was approved and it was held that there is, similarly, no separate duty to undertake a risk assessment, although an employer who had failed to conduct such an assessment could not use ignorance by reason of that failure to excuse non compliance). The effect of these decisions is that consultation and/or risk assessments clearly remain prudent practice in any case where an employer is made aware of a disability, although the failure to take such steps would not of itself amount to a breach of the duty (see *Code of Practice, paras 5.12* and *7.29*). Indeed, the Court of Appeal has stated that a failure to conduct adequate investigations or assessments into the adjustments that can be made can amount to unjustified treatment of an employee. (See *Williams v J Walter Thompson Group Ltd* [2005] EWCA Civ 133, [2005] IRLR 376, which was not referred to in Hay v Surrey County Council). The EAT has stated that there was almost bound to be a breach of the implied term of trust and confidence where the employer had over a period of time seriously breached its obligation to make reasonable adjustments (*Greenhof v Barnsley Metropolitan Borough Council* [2006] IRLR 98).

The fact that a proposed adjustment would not prevent the disadvantage does not necessarily mean it was not one an employer could reasonably have been expected to have made. In *Noor v Foreign and Commonwealth Office* [2010] UK/EAT/470/10, [2011] ICR 695, the EAT overturned a tribunal decision to the effect that since any proposed adjustment to an interviewing process would still not have resulted in the complainant having been appointed, there was no breach of the duty.

10.38   Victimisation

In the United States, this form of discrimination is sometimes known as 'retaliation', a word which perhaps more accurately captures its essence than our own term 'victimisation'. There is little point conferring equal opportunity rights upon employees if their employers are free to punish them whenever they assert those rights. Thus the *EA 2010* protects those who rely on its provisions from being subjected to a detriment.

The coming into force of *EA 2010* marked a significant change to the law of victimisation. Under the previous law victimisation was treated as a form of discrimination, that is to say claimant needed to establish that there had been "less favourable treatment" on a prohibited ground. However, rather than the prohibited ground being a protected characteristic the previous law focused instead on the complainant having performed a protected act. *EA 2010, s 27* adopts a different model – that of subjection to a detriment. As a result a complainant now needs only to show that he has been treated badly, not that others have been treated better.

EA 2010, s 27(1) provides:

"A person (A) victimises another person (B) if A subjects B to a detriment because –

(a)   B does a protected act, or
(b)   A believes that B has done, or may do, a protected act.'"

"Protected act" is defined at *EA 2010, s 27(2)*:

"Each of the following is a protected act –

(a)   bringing proceedings under this Act;
(b)   giving evidence or information in connection with proceedings under this Act;
(c)   doing any other thing for the purposes of or in connection with this Act;
(d)   making an allegation (whether or not express) that A or another person has contravened this Act"

The reference in (d) above to contravening the Act includes committing a breach of an equality clause or rule (*EA 2010, s 27(5)*).

If what is alleged would not be unlawful under the relevant legislation there is no protected act. For example, in *Waters v Metropolitan Police Comr* [1997] IRLR 589 (a case on the old law) a police officer, who was harassed by a colleague whilst both were off-duty, complained. She was later less favourably treated by her employer and alleged victimisation. As her harasser had been off duty, the employer was not vicariously liable for his actions. For that reason, the harassment was not unlawful. In those circumstances, the later act of less favourable treatment could not amount to victimisation.

Bringing an internal complaint does not constitute bringing proceedings (*British Telecommunications plc v Grant* (1994) 518 IDS Brief, EAT) although it may, nevertheless, involve alleging a breach of the Act on the part of the employer and qualify for protection on that basis instead.

An employee performs a 'protected act' by giving evidence even where the evidence given is not in support of the complaint (*Kirby v National Probation Service for England and Wales (Cumbria Area)* [2006] IRLR 508, [2006] All ER (D) 111 (Mar), EAT obiter). Nor need the evidence be given orally; providing a witness statement would be sufficient (*National Probation Service* above, again obiter).

Participating in an investigation into allegations of discrimination made by a third party would qualify as having done something by reference to the relevant anti-discrimination legislation (see *National Probation Service* above).

Giving false evidence or information, or making a false allegation, is not a protected act if the evidence or information is given, or the allegation is made, in bad faith (*EA 2010, s 27(3)*). In *HM Prison Service v Ibimidun* [2008] IRLR 940, the EAT considered a case where an employee had brought a series of discrimination claims, some of which were upheld, others dismissed. One claim, the tribunal found, had been brought for the purpose of harassing the employer. The employer dismissed the employee for bringing that claim.

The EAT accepted that, properly analysed, the reason for the employee's dismissal was the harassment that resulted from the bringing of the claim. It would have been open to the EAT to conclude that the claim was both false and brought in bad faith. The EAT considered whether the claim was false, asking itself whether it could be said to be 'not in accordance with the truth or facts'. However, that consideration was *obiter* as the EAT decided that the claim should fail, instead, for want of causation: the reason for the dismissal was not the claim but the fact that it had been brought to harass the employer. This approach appears to sidestep the requirements of *s 27(3)*; it means that claims not brought in good faith (but which may not be false) fail on causation grounds. In *Martin v Devonshires Solicitors* [2011] ICR 352, the EAT expressed the opinion that where an employee raises groundless complaints as result of a mental illness, the case would not fall within the bad faith exception. However, where the employee was dismissed for, amongst other factors, her inability to accept that her claims were groundless the dismissal would not be on grounds of her having performed protected act.

Only individuals are entitled to be protected against detriment (*EA 2010, s 27(4)*).

It is important to note that the person doing the victimising need not be the person who was the subject of the original complaint of discrimination. Thus if a prospective employer decides not to appoint a candidate because he had brought or given evidence in proceedings against his former employer, that will amount to an act of victimisation.

The employer must subject the employee to a detriment "because" the latter has performed a protected act. The language used in *EA 2010, s 27* matches that in the definition of direct discrimination at *s 13*. It would seem to follow, therefore, that, the protected act has to be an effective and substantial cause of employer's detrimental actions but does not have to be the principal cause. Predecessor provisions required that the complainant should have been treated less favourably "by reason that" they had performed a protected act. Those words were closely analysed in *Chief Constable of West Yorkshire Police v Khan* [2001] IRLR 830, HL. It was decided that the provision did not "raise a question of causation as that expression is usually understood". One had to look at subjectively what was in the alleged discriminator's mind. Lord Scott observed that the words "by reason that" suggested that one was looking for "the real reason, the core reason . . . " Some caution needs to be exercised in relying on older authorities, therefore, since Lord Scott's comments would be difficult to reconcile with the proper approach to the test in direct discrimination cases and that is the approach which is now used in victimisation cases.

The sort of case in which the question of precisely why an employer subjected an employee to a detriment is likely to be most important is where there has been a protected act but the employer is contending that another related, but discrete, reason is their real reason for action. In *Aziz v Trinity Street Taxis Ltd* [1989] QB 463, [1988] 2 All ER 860, the Court of Appeal dealt with a number of points arising out of the construction of a predecessor provision in the *RRA 1976: s 2(1)*, and held in particular that it was necessary for a complainant to show that it was the very fact that his act had been done under, or by reference to, the race relations legislation that had influenced the unfavourable treatment. On the facts, the respondent association would have expelled any member who covertly recorded conversations, irrespective of whether that was done to support an allegation of racial discrimination and, therefore, the complaint of victimisation failed. It remains to be seen whether the courts will take a similarly narrow view of the new test.

There is no victimisation where the reason for the unfavourable treatment is the disruptive way in which complaints are made rather than the complaints as such (*Re York Truck Equipment Ltd*, IDS Brief 439, p 10). See also, *Martin v Devonshire Solicitors* [2011] ICR 352: An employee suffering from a mental illness repeatedly raised groundless complaints and was unable to accept that they were not well-founded. The employee was dismissed. The EAT upheld a finding that the reason for her dismissal was not the protected acts but a combination of "genuinely separable" factors including the risk to future management caused by her mental illness and her inability to accept that her complaints were groundless.

In *Woods v Pasab Ltd* [2012] EWCA Civ 1578, [2013] IRLR 305 an employee alleged that the pharmacy in which she worked was "a little Sikh Club" and was dismissed. The tribunal concluded that the comment amounted to a protected act but the Court of Appeal determined that the reason for the dismissal was her employer's belief that the comment was itself racist.

A line of authority on the old law addressed the question of whether respondents could be liable for steps taken in the context of defending legal proceedings. In *Khan* above, the House of Lords held that it was open to an employer faced with discrimination proceedings (and thus a protected act) to take honest and reasonable steps to protect its position in the relevant litigation even if that led to less favourable treatment. Thus, in *Khan* itself an employer could decline to issue a reference until the outcome of proceedings were known where the reference might otherwise have had to deal with matters that were in dispute. There are, however, limits. In *Derbyshire v St Helens Metropolitan Borough Council* [2007] UKHL 16, [2007] 3 All ER 81, it was stressed that the question whether the employer has acted in an honest and reasonable manner must be assessed from the perspective of the employee. On the facts, it was not open to an employer to write to claimants who had brought equal pay claims and to seek to persuade them to settle their claim by pointing out the possible negative consequences that the success of their claim might have for colleagues. In *South London & Maudsley NHS Trust v Dathi* [2008] IRLR 350, the EAT distinguished both *Khan* and *St Helens* and applied the principle of 'absolute immunity' to two letters written by representatives during the course of litigation. In one letter the representative refused certain disclosure, in the other the representative set out the grounds upon which it intended to resist a costs application. It was alleged that both letters amount to acts of discrimination and/or victimisation. *Khan* was distinguished on the basis that the reference had been sent against the background of proceedings but could not be said to have 'come into existence for the purposes of the proceedings' themselves. *St Helens* is distinguished on the basis that the letter sent in that case had 'gone too far' and amounted to an exercise in intimidation rather than an appropriate step in litigation.

10.39 Harassment

Harassment Relating to a Relevant Protected Characteristic

EA 2010, s 26(1) provides that:

> "A person (A) harasses another (B) if –
>
> (a)   A engages in unwanted conduct related to a relevant protected characteristic, and
>
> (b)   the conduct has the purpose or effect of –
>
> (i)   violating B's dignity, or
>
> (ii) creating an intimidating, hostile, degrading, humiliating or offensive environment for B."

The definition of harassment has a wide scope in that it covers harassment which "relates" to the relevant protected ground and not merely harassment which is "because of" the characteristic.

In determining whether conduct has the effect of violating B's dignity or creating the relevant environment for the purposes of *EA 2010, s 26(1)(b)* the Tribunal must take into account: B's perception; the other circumstances of the case; and whether it is reasonable for the conduct to have that effect (*EA 2010, s 26(4)*). In *Land Registry v Grant* [2011] EWCA Civ 769, [2011] ICR 1390, Elias LJ focussed on the words "intimidating, hostile, degrading, humiliating or offensive" and observed that:

> 'Tribunals must not cheapen the significance of these words. They are an important control to prevent trivial acts causing minor upsets being caught by the concept of harassment.'

The scope of the protection is limited in that not all of the protected characteristics defined at *EA 2010, s 4* are included. Specifically, harassment relating to "marriage and civil partnership" and "pregnancy and maternity" are not covered. Does that mean that it is lawful to harass someone on those grounds? The answer is probably not. Before there was any specific protection against harassment in the *SDA 1975* and the *RRA 1976* an employee wishing to complain that they had been harassed was obliged to take an indirect route. If they could show that they had been harassed "on grounds of" their race or sex they would bring a claim for direct discrimination. Harassing someone was treated as subjecting them to a detriment which was, in turn, a form of less favourable treatment. *EA 2010, s 212(1)* defines "detriment" so as specifically to exclude "conduct which amounts to harassment". The purpose is to ensure that someone who has been harassed is obliged to bring a *s 26* harassment claim rather than a *s 13* direct discrimination claim. However, the definition of "detriment" is said to be subject to *s 212(5)* which provides:

> "Where this Act disapplies a prohibition on harassment in relation to a specified protected characteristic, the disapplication does not prevent conduct relating to that characteristic from amounting to a detriment for the purposes of discrimination within section 13 because of that characteristic".

The effect of these rather roundabout provisions is that a complainant who has been harassed on grounds of marriage, civil partnership, pregnancy or maternity may be able to bring a direct discrimination claim under *EA 2010, s 13* but only if they can show that the harassment was "because of" the relevant protected characteristic and, further, that they were less favourably treated than a comparator. These additional requirements are unnecessary where a claim is based directly upon *s 26*.

An employee was harassed on grounds of sexual orientation when he was subjected to homophobic abuse by colleagues who knew that he was not a homosexual *English v Thomas Sanderson Blinds Ltd* [2008] EWCA Civ 1421, [2009] ICR 543. "Outing" a lesbian or gay employee may itself amount to harassment: *HM Land Registry v Grant* (above).

The test as to whether conduct has the relevant effect is not subjective. Conduct is not to be treated, for instance, as violating a complainant's dignity merely because he thinks it does. It must be conduct which could reasonably be considered as having that effect. However, the tribunal is obliged to take the complainant's perception into account in making that assessment. The intention of the alleged harasser may be relevant to determining whether the conduct could reasonably be considered to violate a complainant's dignity (*Richmond Pharmacology Ltd v Dhaliwal* [2009] IRLR 336, EAT). However, it is not necessary that the alleged harasser should have known that his behaviour would be unwanted (*Reed and Bull Information Systems Limited v Stedman* [1999] IRLR 299, EAT), Where an employer's action or inaction results in the an intimidating, hostile, degrading or offensive environment becoming worse he may be said to have in part "created" the resulting environment: *Conteh* above.

An employee who is harassed because of the religion of a colleague (where, for instance, he refuses to assist his employer in justifying the colleague's discriminatory dismissal) is himself unlawfully harassed (*Saini v All Saints Haque Centre* [2009] IRLR 74, EAT).

An employer will be liable for acts of harassment committed by its employees against other employees (see below). A complainant will sometimes wish to take a further step and allege that there should be a discrete liability for the employer's failure to protect the employee from the harassment they suffered or properly to investigate the matter once it was raised with them. If the reason for the employer's failure to take steps to protect the employee was the employee's protected characteristic, the employer would be liable for an act of direct discrimination on ordinary principles. Thus, if employers allows both male and female employees to be subject to harassment by colleagues (or indeed by third parties), they do not discriminate. However, if they take steps to protect men but not women a liability will arise.

A mere failure to investigate a complaint of harassment will not in and of itself involve any unlawful action on the part of an employer. Again, the question is whether the reason for the employer's inaction was a protected characteristic (*Home Office v Coyne* [2000] ICR 1443, EWCA). Where a manager failed to take action following a complaint of racial abuse his inaction was capable of amounting to "unwanted conduct" but, on the facts, his decision not to investigate was not taken on the grounds of race and, for that reason, did not amount to harassment: *Conteh v Parking Partners Ltd* (UKEAT/0288/10) [2011] ICR 341.

Harassment of a Sexual Nature

EA 2010, s 26(2) provides that A harasses B if A engages in unwanted conduct of a sexual nature which has the effect of violating B's dignity or creating an intimidating, hostile, degrading, humiliating or offensive environment for B. The Act does not define what is meant by conduct being "of a sexual nature".

As with the general form of harassment, the Tribunal must take into account B's perception, the other circumstances of the case and whether it is reasonable for conduct to have the alleged effect when assessing whether the conduct complained of had the effect of violating B's dignity or creating the relevant hostile atmosphere (*EA 2010, s 26(4)*).

Less favourable treatment of those who reject or submit to harassment

EA 2010, s 26(3) defines a third form of protection. It deals with an employee's reaction to certain forms of harassment and how, in turn, the employer treats the employee. Where an employee is subjected either to harassment of a sexual nature or harassment relating to gender reassignment or sex and either rejects or submits to that conduct any less favourable treatment that results because of that rejection or submission is unlawful.

The fact that the protection against "less favourable treatment" makes it a form of discrimination although the essence of the problem being dealt with seems more closely related to victimisation and might, therefore, have been expected to follow the "subjection to a detriment" model.

Employer's liability for harassment by third parties

EA 2010, s 40(2) makes employers potentially liable for harassment by third parties:

> "The circumstances in which A is to be treated as harassing B . . . include those where –
>
> (a)   a third party harasses B in the course of B's employment, and
> (b)   A failed to take such steps as would have been reasonably practicable to prevent the third party from doing so."

A third party is someone who is not A and is not an employee of A's (*EA 2010, s 40(4)*). There is an important limitation to liability: A is not liable unless he knows that B has been harassed in the course of his employment "on at least two other occasions by a third party". It does not, however, have to be the same third party on each occasion (*EA 2010, s 40(3)*).

In *Sheffield City Council v Norouzi* [2011] IRLR 897, EAT the respondent council was liable for racial harassment committed by a child in its care. The EAT acknowledged that some workplaces (prisons; care homes and perhaps some schools) may inevitably expose employees to a risk of harassment that cannot be easily prevented or eradicated. The Tribunal should not be too ready to find an employer liable in such circumstances.

Section 66 of the Enterprise and Regulatory Reform Act 2013 ("ERRA 2013") repeals EA 2010, s 40(2) to (4) inclusive from a date to be appointed..

Harassment that is not specifically related to a Protected Characteristic

10.39   Discrimination and Equal Opportunities – I

The *Criminal Justice and Public Order Act 1994* created an offence of 'intentional harassment'. It is committed where a person 'with intent to cause a person harassment, alarm or distress' uses threatening, abusive or insulting language or behaviour, or disorderly behaviour, or displays any writing, sign or other visible representation which is threatening, abusive or insulting, so that another person feels harassment, alarm or distress. The maximum penalties for the offence are six months in prison or a fine of £5,000. A further offence was created by the *Protection from Harassment Act 1997* (which came into force on 16 June 1997 (*SI 1997/1418*)). In addition to providing for harassers to be subject potentially to a fine or up to six months in prison, the Act creates a number of civil remedies, including damages and restraining orders backed by powers of arrest.

10.40   DISCRIMINATION IN EMPLOYMENT

Discrimination alone will not found liability. It is only certain forms of discrimination which are unlawful; principally discrimination in employment.

Discrimination and harassment is prohibited at every stage of employment: advertising vacancies; engagement of employees; promotion and other opportunities; and dismissal. For discrimination against non-employees, such as contract workers, office holders, etc, see **11.24** ff DISCRIMINATION AND EQUAL OPPORTUNITIES – **II**.

10.41   The meaning of 'employment'

EA 2010 protects "employees" but defines "employment" broadly so as to include not just those employed under a contract of employment or apprenticeship but also those engaged pursuant to contracts "personally to do work" (*EA 2010, s 83(2)*).

In *Mirror Group Newspapers Ltd v Gunning* [1986] ICR 145, a case about the predecessor provision in the *SDA 1975*, the Court of Appeal held that the provision referred to a contract, the dominant purpose of which was the execution of personal work or services. *EA 2010, s 83* would fall to be interpreted in the same way.

A sub-postmaster who was responsible for seeing that the work of the Post Office was carried out but was not obliged to carry out the work himself was also held not to be an employee even within the extended meaning of the *Act* (*Tanna v Post Office* [1981] ICR 374). A taxi driver was not employed under 'a contract personally to execute any work or labour' where there was no mutual obligation between himself and the cab firm to offer or to accept any work (*Mingeley v Pennock & Ivory* [2004] EWCA Civ 328, [2004] ICR 727).

An unpaid volunteer working at a Citizens' Advice Bureau was not an employee (*X v Citizens Advice Bureau (Equality and Human Rights Commission intervening)* ([2013] IRLR 146, [2013] ICR 249). Nor was the complainant a "worker" or someone pursuing an "occupation" for the purposes of the *Framework Directive 2007/78/EC*.

A person working under the Youth Opportunities Programme was also held not to be employed within the meaning of *RRA 1976, s 78* (another predecessor provision. See *Daley v Allied Suppliers Ltd* [1983] ICR 90).

Wippel v Peek and Cloppenburg GmbH & Co KG: C-313/02 [2005] ICR 1604, ECJ – the *ETD 76/207/EEC* protects workers who are engaged on an 'on demand' basis and who are not obliged to take on work offered. *EA 2010* must, of course, be interpreted, wherever possible, to be consistent with the directive.)

An associate minister in the Church of Scotland was employed under 'a contract personally to execute . . . work' despite being an office holder. The House of Lords concluded that she was both an office holder and an employee (*Percy v Board of National Mission of the*

Church of Scotland [2005] UKHL 73, [2006] ICR 134, HL(S)). The question (arising in a different context) as to whether part-time judges are workers has been determined by the CJEU: *O'Brien v Ministry of Justice* [2012] ICR 955.

The definition of employment is broad enough to cover the personal provision of services by a professional and even the retention of a firm of solicitors, instructions to a firm being, in reality, a contract entered into with each partner (*Loughran and Kelly v Northern Ireland Housing Executive* [1999] 1 AC 428, [1998] 3 WLR 735, [1998] ICR 828, HL(NI), distinguished in *Patterson v Legal Services Commission* [2003] EWCA Civ 1558, [2004] ICR 312 where there was no obligation on the complainant to carry out the work personally). Discrimination in appointing an arbitrator falls outside the scope of *RBR 2003* (and thus the *EA 2010*) – the arbitrator is engaged pursuant to a contract personally to provide services but is not subject to the necessary "control" of the parties to the arbitration (*Hashwani v Jivraj* [2011] UKSC 40, [2011] ICR 1004).

A person discriminated against by being dismissed does not have to have been employed for a qualifying period before being entitled to bring a claim.

The Act applies to members of the armed forces "as it applies to employment by a private person" (*EA 2010, s 83(3)*) save that references in the legislation to "associated employers" are "to be ignored". Also included within the scope of "employment" as defined are those in Crown employment (*EA 2010, s 83(2)(b)*), certain members of the House of Commons and House of Lords staff (*EA 2010, s 83(2)(c)* and *(d)* and police officers and cadets (*EA 2010, s 42*)).

A person without employees can still be an employer provided they are "seeking to employ one or more persons" (*EA 2010, s 83(4)*).

10.42   Territorial Jurisdiction

Whereas the previous law contained an express territorial restriction (for which see above), the *EA 2010* does not. *EA 2010, EN Para 15* states:

> "As far as territorial application is concerned, in relation to Part 5 (work) and following the precedent of the Employment Rights Act 1996, the Act leaves it to tribunals to determine whether the law applies, depending for example on the connection between the employment relationship and Great Britain."

It seems, therefore, that the tribunals are intended to have regard to the guidance given by the House of Lords in *Lawson v Serco* [2006] IRLR 289, HL (see UNFAIR DISMISSAL I, para **51.15**). In *Bates Van Winkelhof v Clyde & Co LLP* [2012] EWCA Civ 1207, [2012] IRLR 992 the Court of Appeal suggested that expatriate employees may not need to meet the requirement identified in *Lawson* that the claim should have connections with Great Britain and with British Employment Law that were as strong as those with the country in which they worked if they could show that they lived and/or worked part of the time in Great Britain. All that is needed in such a case are connections to Great Britain that are sufficiently strong to enable it to be thought that Parliament would have regarded it as appropriate for the tribunal to deal with the claim.

Even where an employee works entirely outside Great Britain, they may still be able to bring a claim in the tribunal where their employment falls within certain European rules on jurisdiction and judgment. These were considered in the context of discrimination cases by the EAT in *Simpson v Intralinks* [2012] ICR 1343. The complainant lived and worked in Germany for a company registered in the UK. Her contract provided for German Law to be applicable and for disputes to be resolved in Germany. Nevertheless, the EAT concluded that the tribunal had jurisdiction to hear claims of sex discrimination and equal pay. The analysis was as follows: *EC Council Regulation 44/2001* ("the *Brussels Regulation*") makes provision for jurisdiction in civil matters including employment disputes. *Art 19* permits an employer to be sued either in the state in which they are domiciled (in this case, in the UK) or in the state where the employee "habitually carries out [their] work" (in this case, Germany). The choice is the employee's and not that of the court. The choice of forum clause did not preclude UK proceedings because *Art 21* only allows departure from jurisdiction by agreement where the agreement was entered into after he dispute has arisen (which was not the case here). The EAT then turned to the question of the applicable law. That was to be determined by reference to the *Rome Convention* (since superseded by *Rome II*). *Art 3* of the *Rome Convention* provides that a contract should be governed by the law chosen by the parties (i.e. in this case German Law). However, there is provision for certain mandatory employment protection provisions to be given effect. *Art 7(1)* provides:

> "When applying under this Convention the law of a country, effect may be given to mandatory rules of the law of another country with which the situation has a close connection, if and insofar as, under the law of the other country, those rules must be applied whatever the law of applicable to the contract . . . "

The EAT was satisfied that the statutory provisions dealing with sex discrimination and equal pay were "mandatory provisions" as the underlying legislation provides that they may not be derogated from by agreement. If the *Brussels* rules pointed to Great Britain as having jurisdiction but the *Rome* rules point to foreign law being the applicable law, the EAT was prepared to countenance the tribunal having jurisdiction and applying foreign law save to the extent that mandatory provisions of domestic law took precedence.

EA 2010, s 81 provides that the protections to be found in *Part 5* of the Act only apply to work on ships or hovercraft and to seafarers in "such circumstances as are prescribed". No circumstances have yet been prescribed. *Section 82* allows for "specified provisions" of *Part 5* to be applied to "offshore work". "Offshore work" is defined to mean:

> "work for the purposes of:
>
> (a)   activities in the territorial sea adjacent to the United Kingdom,
> (b)   activities such as are mentioned in subsection (2) of section 11 of the Petroleum Act 1998 in waters within which subsection 8(b) or (c) of that section, or
> (c)   activities mentioned in paragraphs (a) and (b) of section 87(1) of the Energy Act 2004 in waters to which that section applies.

The *Equality Act 2010 (Offshore Work) Order 2010, SI 2010/1835* provides that *Part 5* of *EA 2010* applies to offshore work as if it were taking place in Great Britain unless it takes place in the Northern Irish Area (as defined by the *Civil Jurisdiction (Offshore Activities) Order 1987*) or is in connection with a ship which is in the course of navigation or a ship which is engaged in dredging or fishing (*Reg 2(1)*). Dredging is defined so as not to include excavation of the sea-bed or its subsoil in the course of pipe laying (*Reg 2(2)*). Jurisdiction is conferred on the English and Welsh Tribunals where the offshore work is being done in the "English Area" as defined in the *Civil Jurisdiction (Offshore Activities) Order 1987* and the offshore work consists of work falling within sub-paragraphs (a) or (b) of the definition set out above above. If the work falls within sub-paragraph (c) the jurisdiction is conferred on the High Court.

10.43 Advertisements

There is no specific prohibition on discriminatory advertising in *EA 2010*. However, the explanatory notes suggest that this is because the issue is dealt with elsewhere in the Act without, unhelpfully, identifying where else it is supposedly dealt with (*EA 2010*, EN Para 1024). It is likely that discriminatory advertisements will be actionable by individuals as a form of direct discrimination contrary to *EA 2010, s 13* consistent with the analysis of the ECJ in *Centruum voor Gelijkheid van kansen en voor racismebestrijding v Firma Feryn NV*: C-54/07, [2008] ICR 1390.

10.44 Engagement

EA 2010, s 39 provides that:

"An employer (A) must not discriminate against a person (B) –

(a)   in the arrangements A makes for deciding to whom to offer employment,

(b)   as to the terms on which A offers B employment,

(c)   by not offering B employment."

Thus, if an employer offers a woman three weeks' holiday, whereas a man doing the same job is entitled to five weeks, he is guilty of discrimination. Also, the woman's contract will be modified by the equality of terms provisions of the Act to give her the same holiday entitlement as that of the man (see EQUAL PAY (21)).

In *Saunders v Richmond-upon-Thames London Borough Council* [1978] ICR 75, it was assumed that questions asked at an interview constituted 'arrangements' within the meaning of (1) above. Whether or not the questions were unlawful was held to be a question of fact to be determined in each case. In *Brennan v JH Dewhurst Ltd* [1984] ICR 52, the arrangements made for interviewing applicants were operated so as to discriminate against women, and were therefore unlawful.

A refusal to re-instate a former employee following a dismissal does not constitute 'refusing to offer employment' (*Post Office v Adekeye* [1997] ICR 110, CA).

EA 2010, s 60(1) prohibits employers from asking about the health of an applicant for employment before offering them work (either conditionally or unconditionally – see *EA 2010, s 60(10)*) or, if the relevant person acting on behalf of the employer is shortlisting applicants, before including the applicant in the pool from which the employer intends to select the appointee. Breach can only be challenged by the EHRC (*EA 2010, s 60(2)*). Offering work includes making a conditional offer (*EA 2010, s 10*).

Merely asking the prohibited question does not in and of itself involve any disability discrimination, but it may be used as evidence to establish such discrimination (*EA 2010, s 60(3)*).

EA 2010, s. 60(6) disapplies the prohibition in a surprisingly broad range of circumstances. In each case asking the question must be necessary for the specified purpose. Those purposes are:

(1)   Establishing whether the applicant will be able to comply with a requirement to undergo an assessment or establishing whether a duty to make reasonable adjustments is or will be imposed on the employer in relation to the applicant in connection with the requirement to undergo assessment. For this purpose, an assessment is an "interview or other process designed to give an indication of a person's suitability for the work concerned" (*EA 2010, s 60(12)*);

(2)   Establishing whether the applicant will be able to carry out a function that is intrinsic to the work concerned. The exception is only available if the employer is satisfied that the function would still be intrinsic if the job were adjusted in accordance with the duty to make reasonable adjustments (*EA 2010, s 60(7)*);

(3)   Monitoring diversity in the range of people applying to the Employer for work;

(4)   Taking action to which *section 158* (ie the Positive Action provisions) would apply if references to persons who share (or do not share) a protected characteristic were references to disabled persons (or persons who are not disabled) and the reference to the characteristic were a reference to disability; or

(5)   If the Employer applies in relation to the work a requirement to have a particular disability, establishing that the applicant has that disability. The requirement has to be an occupational requirement and its application has to be a proportionate means of achieving a legitimate aim (*EA 2010, s 60(8)*).

The provision does not affect anything done for the purposes of national security vetting (*EA 2010, s 60(14)*).

Is an unsuccessful candidate who meets the criteria for selection entitled to information from the employer about whether someone has been appointed and, if so, on what criteria? UK Law had, until recently, a questionnaire procedure (for which see below). In *Meister v Speech Design Carrier Systems*: C-415/60 [2012] ICR 1066, the CJEU decided that as a matter of European Law, a candidate was not entitled to such information but a refusal to provide it might be something that could be taken into account in deciding whether or not the complainant had been the victim of discrimination.

10.45 *Racial discrimination: engagement and asylum and immigration*

The *Immigration, Asylum and Nationality Act 2006, s 15* makes it an offence for an employer to employ those whose immigration status precludes them from working in the UK. The *schedule* to the *Immigration (Restrictions on Employment) Order 2007 (SI 2007/3290)* specifies a number of documents ('statutory documents') which, if produced prior to engagement, the employer may rely upon as establishing that the job applicant is entitled to work in the UK. Provided the employer has complied with the requirements of *reg 6* which included taking all reasonable steps to check the validity of the document, it has a defence to any prosecution under the *Act*. There is a danger that in seeking to avoid liability under the *Act*, employers may treat job applicants from ethnic minorities differently. This in turn creates the risk of discrimination claims. The Home Office has produced a code of practice which includes guidance on avoiding discrimination (www.ukba.homeoffice.gov.uk/).

A failure to comply with the provisions of the code may be taken into account by an employment tribunal considering a claim of race discrimination.

The EAT has suggested that a foreign national complaining of discriminatory treatment may only be able to compare herself with other foreign nationals rather than with British citizens (*Sheiky v Argos Distributions Ltd* (1997) 597 IDS Brief 16).

An employer that declined to consider applicants from outside the EEA on grounds that they would be unlikely to be able to obtain work permits committed an act of indirect discrimination (*Osborne Clarke Services v Purohit* [2009] IRLR 341, EAT).

10.46 *Sex discrimination: terms offered – special provisions for those on maternity leave*

EA 2010, Sch 9, Part 3, Para 17 substantially reproduces the pre-existing law. *Para 17(1)* provides that a person does not contravene *EA 2010, ss 39(1)(b)* (discrimination as to the terms on which employment is offered) or *(2)* (discrimination as to the terms of employment, access to opportunities for promotion transfer or training or receiving any other benefit, facility or service, discriminatory dismissal or subjection to any detriment) by depriving a woman who is on maternity leave of any benefit from the terms of her employment relating to pay. However, "terms of employment" does not mean "contract of employment", *EA 2010. Sch 9, Part 3, Para 17(4)* provides:

"A reference to terms of her employment is a reference to terms of her employment that are not in her contract of employment, her contract of apprenticeship or her contract to do work personally".

The Act then creates an exception to the exception by providing that the reference to "benefit" from the terms of the woman's employment does not include a reference to –

(a) maternity-related pay (including maternity-related pay that is increase-related),

(b) pay (including increase-related pay) in respect of times when she is not on maternity leave, or

(c) pay by way of bonus in respect of times when she is on compulsory maternity leave.

(*EA 2010, Sch 9, Part 3, Para 17(2)*) with the effect that that there may be breaches of *EA 2010, s 39(1)(b) and (2)* in relation to those matters.

Pay means benefits: (a) that consist of the payment of money to an employee by way of wages or salary; and (b) that are not benefits whose provision is regulated by the employee's contract of employment or apprenticeship or her contract personally to do work.

"Maternity-related pay" is pay to which the employee is entitled: (a) as a result of being pregnant; or (b) in respect of times when she is on maternity leave (*EA 2010, Sch 9, Part 3, Para 17(6)*).

Pay is "increase-related" in so far as it is "to be calculated by reference to increases in pay that the woman would have received had she not been on maternity leave" (*EA 2010, Sch 9, Part 3, Para 17(3)*).

10.47 Opportunities in employment

There is an express prohibition on discrimination "in the way A affords B access to opportunities for promotion, transfer or training or for receiving any other benefit, facility or service (*EA 2010, s 39(2)(b)*).

In the case of receipt of a benefit, facility or service there is an exception to liability in the case of services which the employer offers to the public. The essence of the idea is that someone, for instance, who works for an airline, cannot bring a claim as an employee if she is treated less favourably when flying as a passenger on one of her employer's aircraft. She would be left to whatever remedies members the public would have, *EA 2010, Sch 9, Part 3, Para 19(1)* provides that:

"A person does not contravene [*EA 2010, s 39(2)(b)*] in relation to the provision of a benefit, facility or service to B if A is concerned with the provision (for payment or not) of a benefit, facility or service of the same description to the public"

A reference to the public includes a section of the public which includes B (*EA 2010, Sch 9, Part 3, Para 19(6)*).

There are exceptions to the general exclusion of liability in respect of benefits, facilities or services provided to the public. They, broadly, cover circumstances in which the fact that the complainant is an employee means that they are not sensibly to be treated as if they were simply another member of the public. The exceptions are set out at *EA 2010, Sch 9. Part 3, Para 19(3)*:

"Sub-paragraph (1) does not apply if –

(a) the provision by A to the public differs in a material respect from the provision by A to [other employees

(b) the provision to B is regulated by B's terms, or

(c) the benefit, facility or service relates to training."

The reference in (c) to "B's terms" means "the terms of B's employment" (*EA 2010, Sch 9, Part 3, Para 19(5)*. Similar provision is made in relation to contract workers, partners and office holders).

10.48 *Sex discrimination: opportunities afforded – special provisions for those on maternity leave*

There is a specific exception to liability under *EA 2010, s 39(2)* in respect of the terms of employment of women on maternity which relate to pay (*EA 2010, Sch 9, Part 3, Para 17(1)*). For a more detailed account of the exception see "Sex discrimination: terms offered – special provisions for those on maternity leave" above.

10.49 Dismissal

An express prohibition on discriminatory dismissal is to be found at *EA 2010, s 39(2)(c)*. Dismissal is defined by *EA 2010, s 39(7)* so as to include the termination of employment: (a) by the expiry of a period (including a period expiring by reference to an event or circumstance); and (b) by an act of B's (including giving notice) in circumstances such that B is entitled, because of A's conduct, to terminate the employment without notice. Termination by expiry of a period will not constitute dismissal if, immediately after the termination, the employment is renewed on the same terms (*EA 2010, s 39(8)*).

An employer's breach of its duties under the anti-discrimination legislation may amount to a breach of the implied duty of trust and confidence so as to repudiate the contract of employment and entitle the victim to treat themselves as having been constructively dismissed (*Shaw v CCL Ltd* [2008] IRLR 284, EAT).

10.50 Subjection to other detriment

EA 2010, s 39(2)(d) contains a "catch all" obligation not to subject employees to a detriment. This reproduces the pre-existing law.

A complainant seeking to establish that he has been subjected to a 'detriment' need not demonstrate that he has suffered a physical or economic consequence. It is sufficient to show that a reasonable employee would or might take the view that they had been disadvantaged in the circumstances in which they had to work (*Shamoon v Chief Constable of the Royal Ulster Constabulary (Northern Ireland)* [2003] UKHL 11, [2003] 2 All ER 26, [2003] ICR 337 and see *Ministry of Defence v Jeremiah* [1980] QB 87, [1979] 3 All ER 83 in which it was held that requiring only male supervisors to carry out dirty work was an unlawful detriment; see also *BL Cars Ltd v Brown* [1983] ICR 143; *Jiad v Byford* [2003] EWCA Civ 135, [2003] IRLR 232).

In *De Souza v Automobile Association* [1986] ICR 514, the Court of Appeal held that the Employment Appeal Tribunal had correctly concluded that Mrs De Souza had not been subjected to a 'detriment' as a result of overhearing a manager say to another manager, about her, to get his typing done by 'the wog'. The EAT in *Barclays Bank plc v Kapur* [1989] ICR 142 (appeal allowed, [1989] ICR 753) suggested, in a passage which was not a necessary part of its decision, that the words 'any other detriment' related to acts in connection with dismissal or disciplinary proceedings and were not wholly general in their scope. The correctness of this construction is, with respect, doubted. It is also open to argument whether *De Souza* was correctly decided, bearing in mind more recent cases dealing with harassment

Failure, after the termination of the employment contract, to confer a non-contractual benefit on a former employee will only exceptionally constitute a 'detriment' (*Relaxion Group plc v Rhys-Harper* [2003] UKHL 33, [2003] 4 All ER 1113).

10.51 *Harassment on grounds of marriage, civil partnership, pregnancy or maternity as a detriment*

EA 2010 provides (somewhat obliquely) that harassing an employee on grounds of marriage, civil partnership, pregnancy or maternity is deemed to be direct discrimination. The method by which this result is achieved is not straightforward and is explained immediately below.

Before there was a specific prohibition of harassment, victims would bring claims instead for direct discrimination. To be harassed was to be subjected to a detriment (see *Porcelli v Strathclyde Regional Council* [1986] ICR 564). That indirect protection was abandoned in favour of introducing a direct protection against harassment which is described at **10.39** above. However, the *EA 2010*, specifically excludes two protected characteristics from the scope of its express prohibition of harassment: marriage and civil partnership and pregnancy and maternity (see *EA 2010, s 26(5)*). It seems, however, that the intention is not to allow employees to be harassed on those grounds. The definition of "detriment" at *EA 2010, s 212* excludes harassment save that there is provision made at *s 212(5)* in the following terms:

"Where this Act disapplies a prohibition on harassment in relation to a specified protected characteristic, the disapplication does not prevent conduct relating to that characteristic from amounting to a detriment for the purposes of discrimination within section 13 because of that characteristic."

Therefore, harassing a woman because she is pregnant would amount to direct discrimination within *s 13*. The same would be true in the case of harassment because of marriage, civil partnership or maternity.

It should be noted that this indirect route does not entirely replicate the protection provided by the express prohibition on harassment. In particular, the employee will have to show that they have been "less favourably treated". This allows the employer to continue to run what has become known as the "bastard defence", ie because he is equally unpleasant to all employees an employee, though harassed, cannot establish that they have been less favourably treated.

Further it is unclear whether *EA 2010, s 40* (which makes employers liable, in certain defined circumstances (for which see **10.39** above) for harassment of their employees by third parties) is intended to apply to harassment relating to a protected characteristic in respect of which, to use the language of *EA 2010, s 212* the Act has "disapplie[d] a prohibition on harassment". However, as the Government intends imminently to repeal *section 40(2)* the point is perhaps academic.

Authorities which predate the introduction of the specific prohibition on harassment will be relevant to claims brought as direct discrimination claims. In *Reed and Bull Information Systems Ltd v Stedman* [1999] IRLR 299, the EAT gave guidance to tribunals dealing with three troublesome questions which commonly arise in harassment cases. The particular case was concerned was sexual harassment and the principles have been adapted below and expressed as matters of general principle:

(a)   *If an employee regards as harassment words or conduct to which many would not take exception or regard as harassment, has their claim been made out?*

The question is whether the behaviour has to be objectively offensive or whether it is sufficient that it should be offensive in the subjective opinion of the employee. The EAT steered a middle course. The fact that, objectively, the behaviour is not offensive does not dispose of the issue. If a particularly sensitive employee has made it clear that the conduct is unwelcome, any repetition may amount to harassment. Other forms of conduct are objectively hostile or offensive, and these do not require the employee to indicate that they are unwelcome before they may constitute harassment. This approach is consistent with that taken by *EA 2010, s 26* in relation to the specific prohibition of harassment.

(b)   *If the alleged harasser does not appreciate that their words or conduct are unwelcome, has the claim been proved?*

The EAT restated the general principle that, as with all cases of direct discrimination, the fact that the alleged discriminator lacks a discriminatory motive or intention will not prevent a finding of direct discrimination. If the alleged harasser should have known that conduct is unwelcome either because that risk was obvious or else because the victim has made it clear to him, he will be liable even if he did not intend to harass.

(c)   *Is a 'one-off act' sufficient to constitute harassment?*

A one-off act may be sufficient. The clearer it is that objectively the conduct was hostile or offensive, the more likely it is that a one-off act will suffice to establish harassment (see also *Insitu Cleaning Co Ltd v Heads* [1995] IRLR 4).

Further guidance was given in *Driskel v Peninsula Business Services Ltd* [2000] IRLR 151, EAT. First, where there are a number of alleged incidents, the tribunal should be careful to focus on their cumulative effect rather than concentrating upon whether individual incidents are trivial in nature. Second, simply because a male superior engages in vulgar behaviour with male colleagues does not mean that a woman is not treated less favourably when she is subjected to such behaviour. Behaviour of that kind directed at a woman is more likely to be intimidatory and to undermine her dignity than similar behaviour directed at a male colleague. (On the question of the objective nature of the test, the Administrative Court expressed a preference for the guidance given in *Driskel* over that given in *Reed*; *EOC v Secretary of State for Trade and Industry* [2007] EWHC 483 (Admin), [2007] ICR 1234 at para 33).

10.52 Post-employment discrimination

EA 2010 reproduces the pre-existing application of post-termination protections against discrimination.

EA 2010, s. 108(1) provides: provides:

"A person (A) must not discriminate against another (B) if –

(a)   the discrimination arises out of and is closely connected to a relationship which used to exist between them,

(b)   conduct of a description constituting the discrimination would, if it occurred during the relationship, contravene the Act."

A similar provision is made in relation to harassment at *EA 2010, s 108(2)*:

"A person (A) must not harass another (B) if –

(a)   the harassment arises out of and is closely connected to a relationship which used to exist between them, and

(b)   conduct of a description constituting the harassment would, if it occurred during the relationship, contravene the Act."

Since the Act is intended to be a consolidating measure, it does not matter whether the relationship ends before or after the commencement of *s 108* (*EA 2010, s 108(3)*).

Conduct is not treated as breaching *s 108* "in so far as it also amounts to victimisation" (*EA 2010, s 108(7)*). This provision was found in *Rowstock Ltd and another v Jessemey and the EHRC* [2013] IRLR 439, EAT to have the effect of precluding a complaint of post-employment victimisation altogether. It is, however, generally accepted that that cannot have been Parliament's intention. In *Onu v Akwiwu* [2013] IRLR 523 the President of the EAT reached the conclusion that *section 108(7)* did not preclude post-dismissal discrimination claims.

Where a tribunal makes a reinstatement order as a remedy for unfair dismissal, a discriminatory failure to comply with the order was not 'discrimination in employment' for the purposes of the predecessor provision in *RRA 1976* (*D'Souza v Lambeth London Borough Council* [2003] UKHL 33, [2003] 4 All ER 1113).

Other unlawful acts

10.53 *Instructions or pressure to commit unlawful acts*

EA 2010, s 111 prohibits employers from instructing, causing or inducing (whether directly or indirectly) an employee to commit an unlawful act of discrimination (or from attempting to do so).

EA 2010, s 111(1) creates a concept known as a "basic contravention" which involves the employee contravening any of the following in relation to a third party:

(a)   Part 3 of the Act (Services and Public Functions);

(b)   Part 4 of the Act (Premises);

(c)   Part 5 of the Act (Work);

(d)   Part 6 of the Act (Education);

(e)   Part 7 of the Act (Associations);

(f)   Section 108(1) (Post-employment discrimination);

(g)   Section 108(2) (Post-employment harassment); or

(h)   Section 112(1) (Knowingly helping another to commit a basic contravention).

EA 2010, s 111(1) prohibits an employer from instructing an employee to commit a basic contravention. *EA 2010, ss 111(2)* and *(3)* do the same thing in relation to causing or inducing a contravention respectively. Inducement may be either direct or indirect (*EA 2010, s 111(4)*).

Proceedings can be brought by the employee if they are subjected to detriment by their employer's conduct or by the third party that was the target of the employer's conduct. Proceedings may also be brought by the Commission (*EA 2010, s 111(5)*). A claim may be pursued even if the basic contravention never occurs and whether or not other proceedings have been (or could be) brought in relation to the employer's conduct (*EA 2010, s 111(6)*).

In *Weathersfield Ltd v Sargent (t/a Van and Truck Rentals) v Sargent* [1999] ICR 425, CA, the receptionist at a truck rental company was instructed to tell black or Asian enquirers that no vehicles were available. As a result, she found her position intolerable and resigned. The respondent argued that as any employee would have been given the same instruction, the complainant could not establish that she had been less favourably treated. The EAT concluded that the instruction affected employees 'differentially' in that some, but not all, would regard themselves as 'victims of mistreatment'. The appropriate comparator, therefore, was somebody who was prepared to go along with the employer's unlawful instruction. The EAT's decision was affirmed by the Court of Appeal.

An attempt to instruct, cause or induce an employee to commit a basic contravention is also actionable (*EA 2010, s 111(8)*).

In *Commission for Racial Equality v Imperial Society of Teachers of Dancing* [1983] ICR 473, the Employment Appeal Tribunal held that a prospective employer acted unlawfully by telling the head of careers at a school that he would prefer that the school did not put forward any coloured applicants.

10.54 *Liability for unlawful act of employee*

EA 2010, s 109 substantially reproduces the former regime of vicarious liability. *EA 2010, s 109(1)* provides:

"Anything done by a person (A) in the course of A's employment must be treated as also done by the employer".

10.54   Discrimination and Equal Opportunities – I

A broad interpretation is given to the concept of "in the course of . . . employment" (*Jones v Tower Boot Co Ltd* [1997] ICR 254, CA). In effect, it is open to a tribunal to find that an employer is liable for acts of discrimination where they are committed 'at work' instead of merely where they are committed 'as work'. The common law test has now 'caught up' (see *Lister v Helsey Hall Ltd* [2001] UKHL 22, [2002] 1 AC 215, HL at 46.7). Acts committed by colleagues away from the workplace are less likely to fall within the scope of the discrimination legislation (eg cf *Waters v Metropolitan Police Comr* [1997] IRLR 589, CA: sexual assault by one off-duty police officer on another in a police section house. Cf also *Sidhu v Aerospace Composite Technology Ltd* [2000] IRLR 602, CA: acts committed during the course of a 'family day' organised by an employer and held at an amusement park were not in the course of employment; and *HM Prison Service v Davis* (2000) 666 IDS Brief 14, EAT: harassment not in course of employment where employee visited colleague at her home, even though employer had power to discipline employees for misconduct committed away from the workplace) although that will not always be so. In *Chief Constable of Lincolnshire Police v Stubbs* [1999] ICR 547, EAT, the EAT upheld a finding that drinks after work and an organised leaving party were sufficiently work-related to be treated as 'extensions of work'.

A police officer will not, for most purposes, be treated as an employee. However police officers and police cadets are deemed, for the purposes of *Part 5* of the *Equality Act 2010*, to be employed by their chief officer (*s 42(1)*).

It does not matter whether the thing is done with the employer's knowledge or approval (*EA 2010 s 109(3)*). Vicarious liability does not extend to cover the offences created under *EA 2010* (with the exception offences under *Part 12* (disabled persons: transport)) (*EA 2010, s 109(5)*).

The employee who commits the discriminatory act is fixed with liability by *EA 2010, s 110(1)*:

> "A person (A) contravenes this section if –
>
> (a)   A is an employee   . . .
> (b)   A does something which by virtue of section 109(1)   . . . , is treated as having been done by A's employer   . . . , and
> (c)   the doing of that thing by A amounts to a contravention of this Act by the employer   . . . "

If the employer manages to establish the reasonable steps defence (for which see below), the employee may still be liable (*EA 2010, s 110(2)*). Even under the former regime, it was possible to bring a claim of victimisation against an individual employee even where the employer was not sued (*Barlow v Stone* [2012] IRLR 898).

The employee has a defence where he reasonably relies on a statement by the employer that the doing the act in question would not involve a contravention of the Act (*EA 2010, s. 110(3)*). If the employer makes such a statement which is false or misleading in a material respect and does so knowingly or recklessly, he commits an offence liable to a fine not exceeding level 5 on the standard scale (*EA 2010, s 110(5)*).

10.55 *Defence to vicarious liability*

EA 2010, s 109(4) provides:

> "In proceedings against A's employer (B) in respect of anything alleged to have been done by A in the course of his employment it is a defence for B to show that B took all reasonable steps to prevent A –
>
> (a)   from doing that thing, or
> (b)   from doing anything of that description."

See *Balgobin v Tower Hamlets London Borough Council* [1987] ICR 829). In determining whether the defence is made out, the tribunal should focus on what the employer has done prior to the occurrence of the act and not how he reacts once it has occurred (*Haringey London Borough Council (Haringey Design Partnership Directorate of Technical and Environmental Services) v Al-Azzawi* (2002) 703 IDS Brief 7, EAT). An employment tribunal may have regard to such matters as whether the employer has issued a written policy to employees on equal opportunities, whether it has given its managers training in such matters and whether it has taken steps to discipline employees if they have been guilty of unlawful discrimination. Where there were steps which it would have been reasonably practicable to take, it seems that the respondent must take them if he is to escape liability even if it cannot be shown that those steps would have prevented the discriminatory acts from occurring (*Canniffe v East Riding of Yorkshire Council* [2000] IRLR 555, EAT).

Where an employee's discriminatory behaviour occurs outside the course of his employment, an employer may have a primary, as opposed to a vicarious, liability if he has a sufficient control over the circumstances in which the behaviour occurred to have prevented it from happening and the reason for not exercising that control is a prohibited ground.

10.56 *Liability for unlawful act of agent*

EA 2010, s 109(3) treats the principal as having done anything that an agent has done with the principal's authority (*EA 2010, s 109(2)*). That does not mean that the act must have been done with the principal's knowledge or approval (*EA 2010, s 109(3)*).

In contrast to the position with employers there is no "reasonable steps" defence available to a principal.

EA 2010, s 110(1) fixes the agent with liability where:

"A person (A) contravenes this section if –

(a)   A is an   agent
(b)   A does something which by virtue of section 109(2) . . . , is treated as having been done by A's . . . , principal . . . and
(c)   the doing of that thing by A amounts to a contravention of this Act by the . . . principal"

It is no answer for the principal to say that it did not give the agent authority to discriminate. It will be enough if the agent has authority to do an act which may be carried out in a lawful or a discriminatory manner (*Lana v Positive Action Training in Housing (London) Ltd* [2001] IRLR 501, EAT).

The agent has a defence where he reasonably relies on a statement by the principal that the doing the act in question would not involve a contravention of the Act (*EA 2010, s 110(3)*). If the principal makes such a statement which is false or misleading in a material respect and does so knowingly or recklessly, he commits an offence liable to a fine not exceeding level 5 on the standard scale (*EA 2010, s 110(5)*).

10.57 *Liability for act of other third party*

The *EA 2010* creates a broad liability for failure to protect employees from harassment by third parties. The liability is established by *EA 2010, s 40* and is dealt with in detail at Para **10.39** above.

10.58 *Aiding unlawful acts*

EA 2010, s 112 makes it unlawful for a person knowingly to help another to commit what it calls a "basic contravention". A basic contravention is a breach of *Parts 3 to 7* of the *Act* inclusive (*Part 5* is the part that deals with work), *ss 108(1)* or *(2)* (post-termination discrimination and harassment) or *s 111* (instructing, causing or inducing contraventions).

The act must be unlawful in the sense that it must be possible to sue the person who committed the *Act*. In *May & Baker Ltd (t/a Sanofi-Aventis Pharma) v Okerago* [2010] IRLR 394, EAT an employee was harassed by an agency worker that her employer had hired. The agency worker's act was not capable of founding liability since she did not employ the complainant. That being so, there was no unlawful act for the employer to aid.

Although the new language talks of "helping" rather than "aiding" an unlawful act, there is no reason to believe that the change in language is intended to bring about a different result. The guidance given by case law on the predecessor provisions is likely to remain authoritative.

Guidance on the circumstances in which a person might be said to 'aiding' a discriminator was given by the House of Lords in *Anyanwu v South Bank Student's Union* [2001] UKHL 14, [2001] 2 All ER 353, HL. Two paid student executives of a student union were dismissed by the union after an investigation into their activities had resulted in the University expelling them. The complainants alleged that their dismissals had been discriminatory and that, as their expulsion had meant that dismissal was inevitable, the University should be treated as having aided the discriminatory dismissals. The House of Lords upheld the claim and offered, in the course of Lord Bingham's judgment, the following guidance: First, the word 'aids' in the statutory provision should be given its ordinary meaning. Second, a person may knowingly aid another to do an unlawful act without inducing the wrongdoer to act unlawfully or procuring the act of discrimination. Third, provided that the assistance given is not so insignificant as to be negligible, it does not matter whether the help is substantive or productive.

The case of *Hallam v Avery* [2001] UKHL 15, [2001] 1 WLR 655, HL, draws an important distinction that limits the circumstances in which a person may be said to have aided another to discriminate. On the particular facts, a local authority had agreed to hire out rooms to a gypsy couple for their wedding reception. The police warned the local authority that they had experienced problems with gypsy weddings in the past. The local authority sought to impose further conditions on the hiring of the room, which, it was found, amounted to an act of discrimination. The House of Lords considered that the judge at first instance had been entitled to find that the police had not aided the local authority in its act of discrimination. Since it was the Police's warning that seemed to have prompted the discriminatory act one might, at first glance, conclude that the warning and the discrimination were sufficiently entangled to allow a finding that the Police had knowingly aided the local authority to discriminate. It was important, however, in the view of Lord Millet, to focus on what the discriminatory act actually was. In this case it was deciding to impose conditions. The Council had made the decision on its own and had neither 'needed or obtained the aid of the police' in doing so. Aiding someone to commit a discriminatory act required 'a much closer involvement in the actual act of the principal than . . . encouraging or inducing on the one hand or causing or procuring on the other'. What was required was actual participation in the decision-making. It would seem from later cases (see immediately below) that even advising the local authority to impose conditions might not have been sufficient. The question whether a solicitor might be said to be aiding an act of discrimination in giving advice or in acting on instructions was considered in *Bird v Sylvester* [2007] EWCA Civ 1052, [2008] ICR 208. An employee unsuccessfully sued her employer for race discrimination. The employer's solicitor advised his client to take disciplinary proceedings against the employee in part because of the claim. On instruction, the solicitor wrote to the employee informing her that disciplinary action would be taken against her. The employee claimed that she had been unlawfully victimised and that the solicitor had knowingly aided the employer to discriminate. The Court of Appeal decided that the solicitor was not liable. The decision to discipline the employee had been the employer's alone. The solicitor had advised the employer to perform the discriminatory act, but that was insufficient. Turning to the letter sent to the employee in which the threat of disciplinary action was made, the Court of Appeal considered that it was 'very difficult to see how a solicitor who confines himself to giving objective legal advice in good faith as to the proper protection of his client's interests, and acts strictly upon his client's instructions, could be at risk of an adverse finding'. Their Lordships were not prepared to go so far as to hold that a solicitor might never be liable. Liability might arise where 'the solicitor himself actively promotes, perhaps for a malign motive, oppressive actions, and actively carries them along'.

A person does not 'aid' discrimination merely by creating an environment in which discrimination could occur. Fostering and encouraging a discriminatory culture may, however, suffice (*Gilbank v Miles* [2006] EWCA Civ 543, [2006] ICR 1297).

A person cannot "aid" another to commit an act which the latter had already committed at the point at which the employer first becomes involved. Thus, a failure to investigate an allegation of harassment does not mean that the employer should be taken to have aided the harasser (*May & Baker Ltd v Okerago* [2010] IRLR 394, EAT).

When might someone be said to be knowingly aiding a discriminator?

Hallam (above) had been decided on a different basis by the Court of Appeal ([2000] ICR 583, CA). Whilst the imposition of further conditions was an act of discrimination, it was decided that there was insufficient evidence that the police had been aware that, as a result of their advice, the local authority would treat the couple less favourably on grounds of their race. That being so, they could not be said knowingly to have aided an act of discrimination. Recklessness was insufficient; the police had to know that they were aiding a discriminator. See also *Sinclair, Roche & Temperley v Heard* [2004] IRLR 763, EAT.

In *Shepherd v North Yorkshire County Council* [2006] IRLR 190, EAT a council was accused of knowingly aiding a trade union to delay the implementation of a collective agreement. The agreement had the effect of prolonging a disparity in pay between male and female employees. The EAT decided that even if the Council had been aware that the union was discriminating, they could not be said to have knowingly aided the discrimination. There was a material difference between taking advantage of a failure by another and aiding that party to discrimination. The Council had had its own interests to protect in any collective negotiation. Further, the union had not needed the employer's assistance to discriminate. Where, during the course of his employment, an employee commits an act of discrimination, his employer may be liable for it (see above). The employee may also be liable in a personal capacity.

Guidance on when the employee may be said to have knowingly aided that his employer is given in *Allaway v Reilly* [2007] IRLR 864:

> 'If a fellow employee does an act in the course of employment which has the effect of discriminating against the claimant employee on grounds of sex and that is a result which can be concluded to have been within his knowledge at the time he carried out the act in question, the requirements of the subsection are met. Discrimination does not have to be what he intended nor does it have to have been his motive. It is enough that, on the evidence, the conclusion can be drawn that discrimination as the probable outcome was within the scope of his knowledge at the time. It would not need to be in the forefront of his mind nor would he need to have specifically addressed his mind to it. It must be enough if, in all the circumstances, it can properly be concluded that it was within the knowledge that was possessed by the alleged discriminator.'

The employee may be liable on this basis even in circumstances where the employer has succeeded in establishing the employer's defence (*Crofton v Yeboah* [2002] EWCA Civ 794, [2002] IRLR 634).

If a person found liable under the provision is an individual acting in the course of his employment, it may be proper for any award of compensation to be made only against the employer, who will generally be liable on the principles set out above (*Deane v Ealing London Borough Council* [1993] ICR 329).

10.58 Discrimination and Equal Opportunities – I

There is a defence to liability where A reasonably relies upon a statement by B that the act for which help is given does not contravene the Act (*EA 2010, s 112(2)*). If B makes such a statement, it is false or misleading in a material respect and B either knew or was reckless as to its falsity, B commits an offence punishable to a fine of up to level 5 on the standard scale (*EA 2010, s 112(3)* and *(4)*).

11 Discrimination and Equal Opportunities – II: Exceptions, Defences and Non-Employers covered by the Employment Rules

11.1   The *Equality Act 2010* ('*EA 2010*') came into force, for the most part, on 1 October 2010. It applies to all acts of discrimination occurring after 1 October 2010 or, in the case of 'acts extending over a period' (see **12.6** Discrimination And Equal Opportunities – III), to all acts that continue after 1 October 2010 even if they began before: see *art 7* of the *Equality Act 2010 (Commencement No 4, Savings, Consequential, Transitional, Transitory and Incidental Provisions and Revocation) Order 2010 (SI 2010/2317)*. The scope and application of the *EA 2010* and the predecessor legislation, the *Sex Discrimination Act 1975* ('SDA 1975'), the *Race Relations Act 1976* ('RRA 1976'), *Employment Equality (Religion or Belief) Regulations 2003* ('RBR 2003'), the *Employment Equality (Sexual Orientation) Regulations 2003* ('SOR 2003'), the *Disability Discrimination Act 1995* ('DDA 1995') and the *Employment Equality (Age) Regulations 2006* ('AR 2006') is described in Discrimination And Equal Opportunities – I **(10)**.

This chapter deals with the exceptions to the scope, and defences to the application of, that legislation ('the equality legislation'). In summary, an employer (or non-employer covered by the rules) may have a defence to claims of both direct and indirect discrimination where he can show that being of a particular race, religion or belief, sex or sexual orientation is a genuine requirement or qualification for a particular job (see below **11.2** ff). A defence of justification is also available to certain forms of discrimination (see below **11.9**) and a defence of lack of knowledge of disability to claims of discrimination arising from disability (see below **11.9A**). It also covers the application of the equality legislation to non-employers covered by the employment rules, such as trade organisations, vocational training providers, partnerships, barristers, police officers, the Crown etc. (see below **11.24** ff). Finally, the chapter deals briefly with the equality duties imposed on public authorities by the *EA 2010* and the predecessor legislation (below **11.37**).

There are also a number of general exceptions (or limits) to the scope of the equality legislation. Broadly speaking, the legislation does not prohibit discrimination where the employee is employed outside Great Britain (below **11.18**), or works under an illegal contract (below **11.19**), or where the discrimination relates to benefits that the employer also provides to the public (below **11.20**), is authorised by another enactment (below **11.21**), is necessary for the purposes of national security (below **11.22**) or where the employer qualifies for immunity under the *State Immunity Act 1978* (below **11.23**). In addition, there are a number of exceptions that are specific to each of the different grounds of discrimination, such as where communal accommodation is provided, or where the employment is for the purposes of an organised religion, or where a particular benefit is dependent on the employee having marital or civil partnership status (see below **11.11–11.16**).

There are also circumstances in which a respondent is permitted to discriminate positively in favour of persons of a particular race, sex, etc (see below **11.10** ff) and certain exemptions that apply only to charities, which in some instances permit positive discrimination in relation to certain groups or (at least) enable charities to continue to pursue their charitable objectives without incurring liability for discrimination (**11.10A**).

For the so-called 'reasonable steps' defence, which enables employers to avoid vicarious liability where they are able to show that they took all reasonable steps to prevent an employee from committing a particular act of discrimination see **10.54**, Discrimination And Equal Opportunities – I.

For enforcement of the equality legislation and remedies, see Discrimination And Equal Opportunities – III **(12)**.

11.1 Discrimination and Equal Opportunities – II

Note that because of its distinct legislative regime, discrimination on grounds of sex in respect of contractual terms and conditions is dealt with in a separate chapter (see EQUAL PAY (21).

The equality legislation implements in domestic law a number of European Directives, specifically the *Equal Treatment Directive (2006/54/EC)* ("ETD 2006") (on sex discrimination), the *Race Discrimination Framework Directive (2000/43/EC)* ("the Race Directive") and the *Framework Directive (2000/78/EC)* (which covers discrimination on grounds of religion or belief, disability, sexual orientation and age) ("the Framework Directive"). In accordance with usual principles of EU law, the relevant provisions of the domestic equality legislation are to be interpreted in conformity with the governing European Directives. Where there are irreconcilable differences between the domestic legislation and the European Directives, public sector workers will be able to rely on the Directives themselves under the principle of direct effect. See generally EUROPEAN UNION LAW (22).

11.2 GENUINE OCCUPATIONAL REQUIREMENT OR QUALIFICATION

Broadly speaking, where being of a particular race, religion or belief, sex, sexual orientation, age or disability can be shown to be a genuine requirement or qualification for a particular job, a respondent may have a defence to certain forms of both direct and indirect discrimination. The defence is not, however, a licence to discriminate. Thus, in general, and except where otherwise indicated below, the existence of a genuine occupational requirement or qualification is *not* a defence to a claim of discrimination in the terms of employment offered or afforded to the complainant, or discrimination taking the form of subjecting a complainant to a detriment other than dismissal, or to a claim of harassment.

Under the predecessor legislation to the *EA 2010*, there were (save in relation to disability) a large number of specific genuine occupational requirement exceptions. These are detailed below. However, most of those are not available under the *EA 2010*. Instead, the *EA 2010* contains a general exception for occupational requirement in *paragraph 1* of *Schedule 9*. It applies only to discrimination taking the particular forms set out in *paragraph 1(2)*, ie discrimination in determining how and to whom to offer employment, in the way that persons are afforded access to opportunities for promotion, transfer or training or for receiving any other benefit, facility or service and to discrimination in relation to dismissal. It does not apply to discrimination in the terms of someone's employment (or offer of employment), or to discrimination in the form of subjecting someone to a detriment other than dismissal, or to a claim of harassment. Under *paragraph 1* of *Schedule 9* a person will not contravene the *Act* by discriminating in one of the aforementioned ways if he applies in relation to work a requirement to have a particular protected characteristic and if he shows that, having regard to the nature or context of the work, it is: (a) an occupational requirement; (b) the application of the requirement is a proportionate means of achieving a legitimate aim; and, (c) the person to whom the requirement is applied does not meet it (or, for all protected characteristics except sex, the employer has reasonable grounds for not being satisfied that the person meets it).

In addition to this general exception, a handful of specific genuine occupational requirements or qualifications remain under the *EA 2010*. These are set out at the appropriate points below.

It is likely that the various specific exceptions that were available under the predecessor legislation but are not available under the *EA 2010* should now be regarded as examples of the sort of situation in which the new general genuine occupational requirement exception in the *EA 2010* is likely to apply.

Note that the *DDA 1995* contained no genuine occupational requirement/qualification exceptions. This exception is available for disability discrimination for the first time under the *EA 2010*.

11.3   Sex: genuine occupational qualification

In addition to the general exception set out above at **11.2**, the following genuine occupational requirement exceptions relating to sex are available under the *EA 2010*:

(a)   An exception for employment for the purposes of an organised religion where the application of the requirement engages 'the compliance or non-conflict principle' and the person to whom the requirement applies does not meet it (*para 2(1)* of *Sch 9*). The 'compliance principle' is engaged if the requirement is applied so as to comply with the doctrines of the religion (*para 2(5)*). The 'non-conflict principle' is engaged if, because of the nature or context of the employment, the requirement is applied so as to avoid conflicting with the strongly held religious convictions of a significant number of the religion's followers (*para 2(6)*).

(b)   An exception for service in the armed forces if it can be shown that a requirement for someone to be a man is a proportionate means of ensuring the combat effectiveness of the armed forces (*para 4, Sch 9*).

(c)   An exception for sporting events, specifically for acts done in relation to the participation of people as competitors in a 'gender-affected activity' (*s 195(1)*). A 'gender-affected activity' is a sport, game or other activity of a competitive nature where the physical strength, stamina or physique of average persons of one sex would put them at a disadvantage compared to average persons of the other sex as competitors in events involving the activity (*s 195(3)*).

Note also that the exception set out at (a) immediately above also applies to requirements that a person not be married or a civil partner, that they not be married to, or the civil partner of, a person who has a living former spouse or civil partner, or to requirements relating to circumstances in which a marriage or civil partnership came to an end (*para 2(4)(c)–(e)*).

These exceptions reflect some of those that are available under the *SDA 1975*, although there are a much wider range of specific genuine occupational requirement exceptions relating to sex available under the *SDA 1975*.

The *SDA 1975* provides that where being a man (or, as appropriate, being a woman) is a genuine occupational qualification ('a GOQ') for a job, a respondent may have a defence to a complaint of discrimination in relation to determining who to offer employment, in refusing employment or in access to opportunities for promotion, transfer or training. The defence is not available where the complainant's complaint is that he has been dismissed or subjected to any other detriment.

Being a man is only capable of being a GOQ for a job in certain defined circumstances, namely:

(a)   Where the essential nature of the job calls for a man for reasons of physiology (excluding physical strength or stamina) or, in dramatic performances or other entertainment, for reasons of authenticity, such that the essential nature of the job would be materially different if carried out by a woman.

Thus a woman may not be discriminated against simply because a job is perceived to require the physical strength and stamina of a man, provided that she is actually capable of performing the duties (ie provided the essential nature of the job would not be materially different if carried out by her). However, employers may discriminate for other physiological reasons, in particular where seeking male models or actors.

(b)   Where the job needs to be held by a man to preserve decency or privacy because:

(i)   it is likely to involve physical contact with men in circumstances where they might reasonably object to its being carried out by a woman; or

(ii)   the holder of the job is likely to do his work in circumstances where men might reasonably object to the presence of a woman because they are in a state of undress or are using sanitary facilities.

If an employer required his employees to work stripped to the waist, then in order to establish that he was justified in refusing to offer employment to women, a court hearing a complaint against him would, it is thought, decide whether that requirement was necessary for the performance of the task, or a mere whim on the part of the employer.

(c)   Where the job is likely to involve the holder of the job doing his work, or living, in a private home and needs to be held by a man because objection might reasonably be taken to allowing a woman –

(i)   the degree of physical or social contact with a person living in the home; or

(ii)   the knowledge of intimate details of such a person's life which is likely, because of the nature or circumstances of the job or of the home, to be allowed to, or available to, the holder of the job.

(d)   Where the nature or location of the establishment makes it impracticable for the holder of the job to live elsewhere than in premises provided by the respondent and:

(i)   the only such premises which are available for persons holding that kind of job are lived in, or normally lived in, by men and are not equipped with separate sleeping accommodation for women and sanitary facilities which could be used by women in privacy from men; and

(ii)   it is not reasonable to expect the respondent either to equip these premises with such accommodation and facilities, or to provide other premises for women.

(See, eg, *Sisley v Britannia Security Systems Ltd* [1983] ICR 628.)

(e)   Where the nature of the establishment, or the part of it within which the work is done, requires the job to be held by a man because:

(i)   it is, or is part of, a hospital, prison or other establishment for persons requiring special care, supervision or attention; and

(ii)   those persons are all men (disregarding any woman whose presence is exceptional); and

(iii)   it is reasonable, having regard to the essential character of the establishment or that part, that the job should not be held by a woman.

(f)   Where the holder of the job provides individuals with personal services promoting their welfare or education or similar personal services, and those services can most effectively be provided by a man.

(g)   Where the job needs to be held by a man because it is likely to involve the performance of duties outside the United Kingdom in a country whose laws or customs are such that the duties could not, or could not effectively, be performed by a woman.

(h)   Where the job is one of two to be held by a married couple or (with effect from 5 December 2005) civil partners: see *s 7, SDA 1975*, as amended by *s 251* of the *Civil Partnership Act 2004*. (See also below **11.14** for further discussion of civil partnership.)

(*SDA 1975, s 7(2)*, as amended by the *Sex Discrimination Act 1986, s 1(2)* and the *Employment Act 1989, s 3(2)*.)

These exceptions apply even where only some of the duties of the job fall within the above provisions, as well as where all of them do (*SDA 1975, s 7(3)*). However, where an employer already has female employees who are capable of carrying out the duties of a vacant post, and whom it would be reasonable to employ on those duties and whose numbers are sufficient to meet his likely requirements in respect of those duties without undue inconvenience, then he may not discriminate by filling the vacancy with another man, even if the vacancy falls within (*a*) to (*g*) above (*SDA 1975, s 7(4)*). (See, eg, *Etam plc v Rowan* [1989] IRLR 150 and also *Lasertop Ltd v Webster* [1997] IRLR 498, EAT.) It is existing employees that count. It is not open to a tribunal to find that the defence is defeated on the basis that it was open to the respondent to appoint new female employees capable of performing the relevant duties.

For the exception under the *SDA 1975* for ministers of religion see below 11.11(g).

11.4   Race: genuine occupational requirement or qualification

There are no specific exceptions for race under the *EA 2010*. Only the general genuine occupational requirement exception set out at 11.2 above is available.

The *RRA 1976*, as amended by the *Race Relations Act (Amendment) Regulations 2003 (SI 2003/1626)* ('*Race Relations Amendment Regulations*'), provides for two different genuine occupational exceptions. The first, the exception for genuine occupational requirement (*RRA 1976, s 4A*: 'the GOR exception'), applies with effect from 19 July 2003 in relation to discrimination on grounds of race or ethnic or national origins. Note that these grounds are a subset of the definition of 'racial grounds' used in the *Act* (see 10.20 DISCRIMINATION AND EQUAL OPPORTUNITIES – I). The second, the exception for genuine occupational qualification (*RRA 1976, s 5*: 'the GOQ exception'), applies where the first does not, ie in relation to discrimination on grounds of colour or nationality and to all racial discrimination occurring before 19 July 2003.

The GOR exception is available only where the discrimination relates to a determination as to who to offer employment, a refusal to offer employment or dismissal. The exception is not available for discrimination in the way in which the complainant is afforded access to opportunities for promotion, transfer or training. Unlike the exception under the *SDA 1975*, however, it *is* available as a defence to a dismissal complaint.

The first exception (the GOR exception) applies where it is shown that:

'having regard to the nature of the employment or the context in which it is carried out:

(a)   being of a particular race or of particular ethnic or national origins is a genuine and determining occupational requirement;

(b)   it is proportionate to apply that requirement in the particular case; and

(c)   either –

(i)   the person to whom that requirement is applied does not meet it; or

(ii)   the respondent is satisfied, and in all the circumstances it is reasonable for him not to be satisfied, that the person meets it.'
(*RRA 1976, s 4A(2)*).

It was suggested by the Department of Trade and Industry at the time of the introduction of the *SOR 2003* and *RBR 2003* that, in relation to the equivalent provision in those regulations (as to which see below 11.7 and 11.6) that, in order to ensure compatibility with the governing European Directive (*Directive 2000/78/EC*), the word 'genuine' in *s 4A(2)(a)* should be interpreted in its primary sense of 'actual, true', rather than its secondary sense of 'honestly held belief'.

The second exception (the GOQ exception) is only available where the discrimination takes the forms of discrimination in the arrangements made for the purpose of determining who should be offered employment; refusal or deliberate omission to offer employment; and discrimination in the way in which the complainant is afforded access to opportunities for promotion transfer or training. It is not available where the complainant's complaint is that he has been dismissed. In contrast to the general 'nature and context' principle that forms the basis of the GOR exception, the GOQ exception applies only in certain defined circumstances, namely where:

(a)   the job involves participation in a dramatic performance or other entertainment in a capacity for which a person of that racial group is required for reasons of authenticity; or

(b)   the job involves participation as an artist's or photographic model in the production of a work of art, visual image or sequence of visual images for which a person of that racial group is required for reason of authenticity; or

(c)   the job involves working in a place where food or drink is (for payment or not) provided to, and consumed by, members of the public or a section of the public in a particular setting for which, in that job, a person of that racial group is required for reasons of authenticity (thus, a respondent may lawfully discriminate in selecting waiters for an Indian or Chinese restaurant); or

(d)   the holder of the job provides persons of that racial group with personal services promoting their welfare, and those services can most effectively be provided by a person of that racial group (*RRA 1976, s 5(2)*).

The scope of the GOQ exception was discussed in *Tottenham Green Under-Fives' Centre v Marshall* [1989] ICR 214 and in *Lambeth London Borough Council v Commission for Racial Equality* [1990] ICR 768. In *Lambeth*, the Court of Appeal held that the use of the word 'personal' in *s 5(2)(d)* indicates that the identity of the giver and the recipient of the services is important. The Court of Appeal agreed with the Employment Appeal Tribunal that the *RRA 1976* appears to contemplate direct contact between the giver and the recipient – mainly face-to-face or where there would be susceptibility to personal, physical contact.

The GOQ exception applies where some of the duties fall within (*a*) to (*d*) above as well as where all of them do (*RRA 1976, s 5(3)*), and also where those duties are merely ones which it is desirable that the post-holder should carry out and are not fundamental to the post. However, it does not apply where the duties are too trivial to be taken into account or where they have been deliberately put into the job description as a sham or smokescreen (*Tottenham Green Under Fives' Centre v Marshall (No 2)* [1991] ICR 320).

It also does not apply where a respondent already has employees of a particular racial group who are capable of carrying out the duties of a vacant post and whom it would be reasonable to employ on those duties and whose numbers are sufficient to meet his likely requirements in respect of those duties without undue inconvenience, regardless of whether the vacancy falls within *s 5(2)* (*RRA 1976, s 5(4)*). As with cases of sex discrimination (see above **11.3**), it will be existing employees who count.

11.5   Gender reassignment: genuine occupational qualification

In addition to the general exception set out at **11.2** above, the *EA 2010* includes the following two specific exceptions for requirements that a person not be a transsexual person:

(a)   An exception for employment for the purposes of an organised religion where the application of the requirement engages 'the compliance or non-conflict principle' and the person to whom the requirement applies does not meet it (*para 2(1) of Sch 9*). The 'compliance principle' is engaged if the requirement is applied so as to comply with the doctrines of the religion (*para 2(5)*). The 'non-conflict principle' is engaged if, because of the nature or context of the employment, the requirement is applied so as to avoid conflicting with the strongly held religious convictions of a significant number of the religion's followers (*para 2(6)*).

(b)   An exception for service in the armed forces if it can be shown that a requirement is a proportionate means of ensuring the combat effectiveness of the armed forces (*para 4, Sch 9*).

These exceptions reflect some of the specific exceptions that are available under the predecessor legislation to the EA 2010. Those exceptions are as follows.

Following the insertion of *ss 7A* and *7B* into the *SDA 1975* by the *Sex Discrimination (Gender Reassignment) Regulations 1999 (SI 1999/1102)* ('*Gender Reassignment Regulations*') with effect from 1 May 1999 a genuine occupational qualification ('GOQ') defence is available in appropriate circumstances to allegations of sex discrimination brought by persons intending to undergo, undergoing or who have undergone gender reassignment ('transsexuals'). (See generally **10.21** Discrimination and Equal Opportunities – I.)

Broadly speaking, there are two circumstances where the GOQ defence may arise in relation to complaints by transsexuals. First, a gender reassignment may mean that the employee falls foul of a GOQ that the complainant be a man or, as appropriate, a woman. Second, there may be circumstances where the requirement is, in effect, not that the complainant should be a particular sex but that they should not be a transsexual.

(1)   *Where the requirement is that a complainant be a man or a woman*

Turning first to consider cases where the requirement is for a complainant of a specific sex, one finds that, for the most part, *SDA 1975, s 7A* simply extends the GOQ exception for sex discrimination (see above **11.3**) to cases involving transsexuals. However, there are three differences between the scope of the defence in cases involving transsexuals and its scope in other cases of sex discrimination. First, there is a defence available to a respondent even in cases where a respondent discriminates:

(a)   in the terms in which he offers employment; or

(b)   by dismissing the complainant, or by subjecting him to any other detriment (*SDA 1975, s 7A(1)*).

Second, the defence is subject to an overarching requirement that treatment meted out to the complainant is reasonable in view of the circumstances giving rise to the GOQ (*SDA 1975, s 7A(1)(b)*).

Third, the limitation on the GOQ defence to a claim of sex discrimination imposed by *s 7(4)* (ie that a GOQ defence cannot be used where a respondent already has female employees who are capable of carrying out the duties of a vacant post whom it would be reasonable to employ on those duties) applies to the dismissal of transsexuals as it does to the filling of vacant posts (*SDA 1975, s 7A(3)*).

Note, however, that the defence is not available where the complainant's sex has become the acquired gender under the *Gender Recognition Act 2004* ('*GRA 2004*'): *SDA 1975, s 7A(4)*, as inserted by *GRA 2004, s 14* with effect from 4 April 2005. The *GRA 2004* provides for the application by transsexuals for "gender recognition certificates". Where a gender recognition certificate has been issued to a person, this particular GOQ exception does not apply at all since the person becomes 'for all purposes' the acquired gender (*GRA 2004, s 9*).

(2)   *Where the requirement is that the complainant not be a transsexual*

SDA 1975, s 7B sets out the variation of the defence which deals with circumstances where it is thought that not being a transsexual is a GOQ. Those circumstances are in addition to those described above in relation to sex discrimination and are referred to as 'supplementary general occupational qualifications' ('supplementary GOQs'). The supplementary GOQs are as follows:

(a)   the job involves the holder of the job being liable to be called upon to perform intimate physical searches pursuant to statutory powers;

(b)   the job is likely to involve the holder of the job doing his work, or living, in a private home and needs to be held otherwise than by a person who is undergoing or has undergone gender reassignment, because objection might reasonably be taken to allowing such a person:

   (i)   the degree of physical or social contact with a person living in the home; or

   (ii)   the knowledge of intimate details of such person's life, which is likely, because of the nature or circumstances of the job or of the home, to be allowed to, or available to, the holder of the job;

(c)   the nature or location of the establishment makes it impracticable for the holder of the job to live elsewhere than in premises provided by the respondent, and:

   (i)   the only such premises which are available for persons holding that kind of job are such that reasonable objection could be taken, for the purpose of preserving decency and privacy, to the holder of the job sharing accommodation and facilities with either sex whilst undergoing gender reassignment; and

   (ii)   it is not reasonable to expect the respondent either to equip those premises with suitable accommodation or to make alternative arrangements; or

(d)   the holder of the job provides vulnerable individuals with personal services promoting their welfare, or similar personal services, and in the reasonable view of the respondent those services cannot be effectively provided by a person undergoing gender reassignment.

The supplementary GOQs set out in paras (c) and (d) above only apply where an employee intends to undergo or is undergoing a gender reassignment. They are not available where the employee has already undergone the reassignment (*SDA 1975, s 7B(3)*). Further, the supplementary GOQs may not be relied upon as a defence to discriminating against the employee:

(i)   in the terms on which they are offered employment (*SDA 1975, s 7B(1)(a)*);

(ii)   in the way in which the employee is afforded access to opportunities for promotion, transfer or training, other than where there is a deliberate refusal or a deliberate omission to afford such access to a job; or

(iii)   by subjecting him to any other detriment.

The case of *A v Chief Constable of West Yorkshire Police (No 2)* [2004] UKHL 21, [2004] ICR 806, HL was a case that concerned, in effect, a requirement that a police officer not be a transsexual. It was decided on the basis of the *SDA 1975* as it stood prior to the coming into force of the *Gender Reassignment Regulations* on 1 May 1999. However, the decision is relevant to the GOQ defence under the *SDA 1975*. *A* was a male-to-female transsexual who applied for a position as a police constable. Her birth certificate recorded her sex as 'male', but she had undergone gender reassignment surgery and was also in outward appearance female. The Chief Constable refused her application because he considered that in order to be a police officer it was necessary to be either a man or a woman, both in appearance and by birth. The Chief Constable relied for the genuineness of that requirement on *s 54(9)* of the *Police and Criminal Evidence Act 1984* ('*PACE*'), which stipulates that intimate searches must be carried out by a police officer of the same sex as the person searched. The House of Lords held that the jurisprudence of the European Court of Human Rights and the Court of Justice of the European Union required transsexuals to be recognised in their reassigned gender. Accordingly, *s 54(9)* had to be interpreted as applying to a transsexual's reassigned gender, thereby depriving the Chief Constable of his GOQ defence.

Note, however, that since the coming into force of the *GRA 2004* on 1 July 2004, transsexuals may apply for a gender recognition certificate. Where a gender recognition certificate has been issued to a person, that person becomes 'for all purposes' the acquired gender (*GRA 2004, s 9*). Where a person has not applied for a gender recognition certificate, it will be a matter for argument as to whether the reasoning of the House of Lords in *A* should apply to any provisions similar to *PACE, s 54(9)*. On the one hand, if the decision in *A* is viewed as being driven by the CJEU's interpretation of the *Equal Treatment Directive*, it should make no difference where Parliament has chosen to draw the line on recognition, since EU law is supreme. On the other hand, if the decision in *A* is viewed as being driven by the jurisprudence of the European Court of Human Rights, it could be argued that, Parliament having now enacted the *GRA 2004* and determined the precise circumstances in which gender recognition should be accorded to transsexuals, that determination is to be respected as a matter that falls within the 'margin of appreciation' accorded to sovereign states.

Finally, it should be noted that, with effect from 1 October 2005, a further *caveat* to the supplementary GOQs is inserted into *SDA 1975, s 7B* by the *Employment Equality (Sex Discrimination) Regulations 2005 (SI 2005/2467)* ("the 2005 Sex Discrimination Regulations"). That *caveat* is similar to provisions applying in respect of race (see above **11.4**) and sex (see above **11.3**): the supplementary GOQs do not apply where the employer:

(i)   already has transsexual employees who either have not undergone gender reassignment (and are not undergoing or intending to undergo gender reassignment) or (having already undergone reassignment) have become the acquired gender under *GRA 2004*; and,

(ii)   those employees are capable of carrying out the duties in question, are sufficient in number to meet the employer's likely requirements in respect of those duties without undue inconvenience and whom it would be reasonable to employ on those duties.

11.6   Religion or belief: genuine occupational requirement

In addition to the general exception set out at **11.2** above, under the *EA 2010* the exception available under the predecessor legislation (see below) for organisations with an ethos based on religion or belief is preserved in *paragraph 3* of *Schedule 9* to the Act. It applies where, having regard to the nature or context of the work, it is shown that a requirement to be of a particular religion or belief is: (a) an occupational requirement; (b) the application of the requirement is a proportionate means of achieving a legitimate aim; and, (c) the person to whom the requirement is applied does not meet (or the employer has reasonable grounds for not being satisfied that the person meets the requirement).

Under the predecessor legislation, the *RBR 2003*, a genuine occupational requirement ('GOR') is available in two sorts of cases. The exception only applies where the discrimination relates to the arrangements for determining who to offer employment, a refusal of employment, access to opportunities for promotion, transfer or training and dismissal.

The first type of case is like the GOR exception under the *RRA 1976* (see above **11.4**). In the first type of case the exception applies where, having regard to the nature of the employment or the context in which it is carried out, being of a particular religion or belief is 'a genuine and determining occupational requirement' (*reg 7(2)*).

11.6 Discrimination and Equal Opportunities – II

The second type of case is where the respondent has an ethos based on a religion or belief and, having regard to that ethos as well as to the nature of the employment, or the context in which it is carried out, being of a particular religion or belief is a GOR (*reg 7(3)*).

In both types of case, the mere existence of a GOR does not take the complainant outside the protective scope of the *Regulations*. First, it must also be shown that the complainant does not meet the requirement. Where it is not immediately clear whether the complainant meets the requirement, it is sufficient that the respondent is not satisfied, on reasonable grounds, that the complainant meets the requirement (*reg 7(2)(c)* and *(3)(c)*). Second, it must be proportionate to apply the requirement in the particular case (*reg 7(2)(b)* and *(3)(b)*).

Note that in *Glasgow City Council v McNab* [2007] IRLR 476 it was held a local education authority ('LEA') could not defend a discrimination claim in relation to a Catholic School for which it was responsible on the basis that it was an organisation with an ethos based on a religion or belief. Although the School had such an ethos, the employer and respondent to the claim was the LEA and it could not have a specific religious ethos.

11.7 Sexual orientation: genuine occupational requirement

In addition to the general exception set out at **11.2** above, the *EA 2010* contains an exception for employment for the purposes of an organised religion where the application of the requirement engages 'the compliance or non-conflict principle' and the person to whom the requirement applies does not meet it (*para 2(1)* of *Sch 9*). The 'compliance principle' is engaged if the requirement is applied so as to comply with the doctrines of the religion (*para 2(5)*). The 'non-conflict principle' is engaged if, because of the nature or context of the employment, the requirement is applied so as to avoid conflicting with the strongly held religious convictions of a significant number of the religion's followers (*para 2(6)*). This exception reflects specific exceptions available under the predecessor legislation.

The *SOR 2003* provide for two types of cases in which a respondent may rely on the genuine occupational requirement ('GOR') exception in defence to a claim of discrimination on grounds of sexual orientation. In both types of case the defence is only available where the discrimination relates to the arrangements for determining who to offer employment, a refusal of employment, access to opportunities for promotion, transfer or training and dismissal.

The first type of case is like the first type of case under the *RBR 2003* (see above **11.6**), ie the exception applies where, having regard to the nature of the employment or the context in which it is carried out, being of a particular sexual orientation is a 'genuine and determining occupational requirement'. The respondent must show that it was proportionate to apply the requirement in that particular case and that either the complainant did not meet the requirement as to sexual orientation or that it was reasonable, in all the circumstances, for the respondent to be satisfied that the complainant did not (*reg 7(2)*). In the absence of an express admission by the complainant, this will involve the tribunal determining whether the respondent's conclusion or assumption about the complainant's sexual orientation was a reasonable one.

The second type of case is where the employment is for the purposes of an organised religion and the respondent applies 'a requirement related to sexual orientation' in order:

(a)   to comply with the doctrines of that religion, or

(b)   owing to the nature or context of that employment, to avoid conflicting with the strongly held religious convictions of a significant number of the religion's followers (*reg 7(3)(a)* and *(b)*).

As with the first type of case, the respondent must also show that either the person to whom the requirement was applied did not meet that requirement or that it was reasonable for the respondent to have been satisfied that he did not (*reg 7(3)(c)*).

It was argued in *R (Amicus-MSF) v Secretary of State for Trade and Industry* [2004] EWHC 860 (Admin), [2004] IRLR 430 that *regs 7(2)* and *(3)* were incompatible with the governing European Directive (*Directive 2000/78/EC*). However, the High Court held that the *Regulations* were compatible. With regard to *reg 7(2)* (the first type of case), Richards J noted that, although the exception applied not only where the complainant did not in fact meet the requirement as to sexual orientation, but also where it was 'reasonable' for the respondent 'not to be satisfied' that the complainant met that requirement, the need for the respondent's decision to be 'reasonable' ensured that the decision could not be based on mere assumptions or social stereotyping. With regard to *reg 7(3)* (the second type of case), Richards J noted that the exception, as a derogation from the principle of equal treatment, had to be construed strictly. He noted that 'for the purposes of an organised religion' was a narrower expression than 'for the purposes of a religious organisation' or 'an ethos based on religion or belief', as used in the *RBR 2003*. Thus, employment as a teacher in a faith school was, he considered, likely to fall outside the exception as being 'for the purposes of a religious organisation' rather than 'for the purposes of an organised religion'. Further, he observed that the condition that the employer apply the requirement 'so as to comply with the doctrines of the religion' was an objective test and very narrow in scope. Similarly, the alternative condition that the exception be applied where required 'to avoid conflicting with the strongly held religious convictions of a significant number of the religion's followers' was also an objective test that would be difficult to satisfy in practice. He also noted that, although the phrase used in *reg 7(3)* 'a requirement related to sexual orientation' was linguistically wider in scope than the phrase 'being of a particular sexual orientation' used in *reg 7(2)*, it was difficult to see a practical difference between the two since 'being of a particular sexual orientation' necessarily encompassed matters relating to sexual behaviour, etc.

Compare the exception for employment for purposes of an organised religion with the exception for ministers of religion in the *SDA 1975*: see below 11.11(g).

11.8   Age: genuine occupational requirement

There are no specific exceptions for age under the *EA 2010*. Only the general genuine occupational requirement exception set out at **11.2** above is available.

AR 2006 recognised that there may be circumstances in which being of a particular age group may be a genuine requirement of the job. However, the existence of a genuine occupational requirement is no defence to discrimination taking one of the following forms under *AR 2006*:

(a)   discrimination on the terms on which employment is offered;

(b)   discrimination in the terms of employment afforded to an employee;

(c)   subjecting the employee to a detriment other than dismissal; and

(d)   harassing the employee.

The defence is *potentially* available where the discrimination takes one or more of the following forms:

(a)   discrimination in the arrangements made for determining to whom employment should be offered;

(b)   discrimination by refusing to offer, or deliberately not offering, employment;

(c)   discrimination in the opportunities offered an employee for promotion, transfer, or training;

(d)   discrimination by refusing to afford, or deliberately not offering, an opportunity; and

(e)   discrimination by dismissal.

AR 2006 do not list the circumstances in which such a principle might apply. Instead, they describe a general principle. Where, having regard to the nature of the employment, or the context in which the employment is carried out, possessing a characteristic related to age is a genuine and determining occupational requirement, a genuine occupational requirement might exist. However, the existence of the requirement is not in itself sufficient. It must also be proportionate to apply that requirement in the particular case (*reg 8(2)*).

As an exception to the law against discrimination, it is expected that tribunals and courts will take a strict interpretation of this provision. It is only where an employer can show that the requirement really is genuine and determining that discrimination would be found to be lawful. However, and perhaps surprisingly, in *Wolf v Stadt Frankfurt Am Main* [2010] IRLR 244, the CJEU found that legislation imposing an upper age limit of 30 for recruitment for frontline fire-fighting duties was justified as a genuine occupational requirement in accordance with the equivalent provision of the *Directive*, *Article 4(1)*. The genuine occupational requirement was physical fitness. The legislation was justified by the aim of preserving the operational capacity of the fire service and did not go beyond what was necessary to achieve that objective having regard to the number of years remaining following training during which officers could carry out physically demanding tasks.

11.9 JUSTIFICATION

A defence of justification is (and has always) been available to the following forms of discrimination:

*   *Indirect discrimination* on grounds of all the protected characteristics;

*   *Discrimination arising from disability* under the *s 15* of the *EA 2010*;

*   *Direct discrimination* on grounds of age only.

Under the *EA 2010* a single formula applies for indirect discrimination in relation to all the protected characteristics. A provision, criterion or practice that is applied to all, but which puts (or would put) persons of a particular protected characteristic at a particular disadvantage when compared with others (and which puts the complainant at that disadvantage) will nonetheless be justified if the employer can show it 'to be a proportionate means of achieving a legitimate aim' (*s 19(2)*). The same test applies on the face of the legislation for direct age discrimination (*s 13(2)*) and discrimination arising from a disability (*s 15(1)(b)*). However, so far as direct age discrimination is concerned, it is now established that a slightly different test applies in *Directive 2000/78/EC* and that accordingly *s 13(2)* of the *EA 2010* must be 'read down' accordingly. Whereas there is no limitation on the aims that may be regarded as legitimate for the purposes of justifying indirect discrimination, direct age discrimination can only be justified if the aim of the measure in question relates to "employment policy, the labour market or vocational training" and not "purely individual reasons particular to the employer's situation, such as cost reduction or improving competitiveness": see *art 6(1)* of *Directive 2000/78/EC* and *Seldon v Clarkson, Wright & Jakes* [2012] UKSC 16, [2012] ICR 716 (see further below). Moreover, the SC in *Seldon* accepted that although normally it will suffice if the employer succeeded in showing that the provision, criterion or practice was a proportionate means of achieving a legitimate aim in general, it could not be ruled out that it might be necessary in certain cases for the employer to demonstrate that the application of the provision, criterion or practice to the particular employee was justified in that particular case.

Under the predecessor legislation, the test for whether a provision, criterion or practice, was justified differed until recently depending on whether the complaint fell under the *SDA 1975*, related to discrimination on grounds of race or ethnic or national origins under the *RRA 1976*, or discrimination on grounds of colour or nationality under that *Act*, or fell under the *RBR 2003* or the *SOR 2003*, or the *DDA 1995*.

With the exception of discrimination on grounds of colour and nationality under the *RRA 1976*, the test had become the same in each of the Acts and Regulations as it is under the *EA 2010*, ie a 'proportionate means of achieving a legitimate aim' (*SDA 1975, s 1(2)*, as amended by the *Sex Discrimination Regulations 2005, reg 3*; *RRA 1976, s 1(1A)(c)*, as inserted by the *Race Relations Amendment Regulations* with effect from 19 July 2003; *RBR 2003, reg 3(1)(b)(iii)*; *SOR 2003, reg 3(1)(b)(iii)*).

This contrasts with the 'old' test, which required respondents only to show that the application of the relevant provision, criterion or practice was 'justifiable irrespective' of the sex/race etc. of the person to whom it was applied. The 'old' test still applies to indirect race discrimination on grounds of colour and nationality under the *RRA 1976* (*RRA 1976, s 1(1)(b)(ii)*), indirect race discrimination on any ground occurring prior to 19 July 2003 (*RRA 1976, s 1(1)(b)(ii)*) and indirect sex discrimination occurring prior to 1 October 2005 (*SDA 1975, s 1(2)(b)(ii)*).

The reason for the change in the test was so that the domestic legislation conformed with the governing European Directives (*Directive 76/207/EEC, art 2, para 2*, as amended by *Directive 2002/73*; *Directive 2000/43/EC, art 2, para 2(b)* and *Directive 2000/78/EC, art 2, para 2(b)*). It will be noted that the governing European Directives each provide that a respondent must demonstrate that the relevant provision, criterion or practice is 'objectively justified by a legitimate aim *and* the means of achieving that aim are appropriate and necessary'. Although the domestic legislation makes no mention of the requirements that the measure be 'appropriate and necessary', in line with the general principles for the application and interpretation of EC law (see **22.2 EUROPEAN UNION LAW**) tribunals no longer accept that a measure is proportionate unless a respondent has shown that it is both appropriate and necessary.

Although the test for justification has changed, the case law on the 'old' test has continued to be regarded as relevant by tribunals. Care should be taken, however, to ensure that the specific requirements of the 'new' test are always met.

A defence of justification is also available in principle to claims of disability-related discrimination under the *DDA 1995* (see **DISCRIMINATION AND EQUAL OPPORTUNITIES – I (10)**). However, the position following *Lewisham London Borough Council v Malcolm* [2008] UKHL 43, [2008] 1 AC 1399, is that most such claims will in fact be complaints of direct discrimination. As such, the circumstances in which a justification defence to disability-related discrimination will be available to employers must now be considered as being very limited indeed. Where the justification of disability-related discrimination is in issue, different considerations apply to those that are generally applicable to the defence of justification available to the types of discrimination set out in the bullet points above. In particular, first, the test for justification is whether the reason for the difference in treatment is both 'material to the circumstances of the particular case and substantial' (*DDA 1995, s 3A(5)*). In *Jones v Post Office* [2001] EWCA Civ 558, [2001] ICR 805 Arden LJ explained that for a reason to be 'material', there must be a 'reasonably strong connection between that reason and the circumstances of the individual case', and for it to be 'substantial', it 'must carry real weight and thus be of substance' although it need not necessarily be the best possible conclusion that could be reached in the light of all known medical science. Unlike for other justification defences (see below), the 'range of reasonable responses' test (familiar to those dealing with unfair dismissals) applies to the question of justification in disability-related discrimination. The second main difference is that in the case of an employer who has not complied with his duty to make adjustments (see Discrimination And Equal Opportunities – I (10)), the defence of justification is only available if the treatment in question would have been justified even if the duty had been complied with (*DDA 1995, s 3A(6)*). Thus, where an employee using a wheelchair is not promoted solely because the workstation for the more senior post is inaccessible to wheelchairs, the refusal to promote would not be justified if the furniture could be rearranged to make the workstation accessible. For cases on justification of disability-related discrimination see *Jones v Post Office* [2001] EWCA Civ 558, [2001] ICR 805; *Williams v J Walter Thompson Group Ltd* [2005] EWCA Civ 133, [2005] IRLR 376 and *O'Hanlon v Revenue and Customs Comrs* [2007] EWCA Civ 283, [2007] IRLR 404).

The general test for justification

The classic test for establishing whether or not discrimination may be justified is found in *Bilka-Kaufhaus GmbH v Weber Von Hartz (Case 170/84)* [1986] IRLR 317. There the Court of Justice of the European Union said that the national court (or tribunal) must be satisfied that the measures having a disparate impact 'correspond to a real need . . . are appropriate with a view to achieving the objectives pursued and are necessary to that end' (para 36). In more recent cases (see especially *R v Secretary of State for Employment, ex p Seymour-Smith and Perez* [1999] IRLR 253 and also *Kutz-Bauer v Freie und Hansestadt Hamburg*: C-187/00 [2003] IRLR 368) the CJEU has expanded on this, ruling that is for the national court (or tribunal) to ascertain:

(1)   whether the measure in question has a legitimate aim, unrelated to any discrimination based on any prohibited ground;

(2)   whether the measure is capable of achieving that aim; and

(3)   whether in the light of all the relevant factors, and taking into account the possibility of achieving by other means the aims pursued by the provisions in question, the measure is proportionate.

It is important for Tribunals to be clear about the three elements of the test. "Appropriate", "necessary" and "proportionate" are not interchangeable: see *Homer v Chief Constable of West Yorkshire* [2012] UKSC 15, [2012] ICR 704. To be proportionate, a measure has to be both an appropriate means of achieving the legitimate aim and a (reasonably) necessary means of doing so.

(1) Legitimate aim

To be legitimate, an aim must correspond to a "real need" on the part of the employer's business: *Bilka-Kaufhaus* (ibid), *R (Elias) v Secretary of State for Defence* [2006] 1 WLR 3213. This is not to be confused with a test of necessity: see *HM Land Registry v Benson* [2012] ICR 627 at paragraph 37.

Direct age discrimination

In relation to direct age discrimination only there is a limitation on the aims that may be regarded as legitimate. Direct age discrimination can only be justified if the aim of the measure in question relates to "employment policy, the labour market or vocational training" and not "purely individual reasons particular to the employer's situation, such as cost reduction or improving competitiveness": see *art 6(1) of Directive 2000/78/EC* and *Seldon v Clarkson, Wright & Jakes* [2012] UKSC 16, [2012] ICR 716. So far as direct age discrimination is concerned, therefore, *s 13(2)* of the *EA 2010* must be 'read down' accordingly.

The *Directive* gives examples of the sort of age discriminatory measures that might be permitted in pursuit of such aims, including (a) the setting of special conditions on access to employment and vocational training, employment and occupation, dismissal and remuneration conditions, for young people, older workers and persons with caring responsibilities in order to promote their vocational integration or ensure their protection; (b) the fixing of minimum conditions of age, professional experience or seniority in service for access to employment or to certain advantages linked to employment; (c) the fixing of a maximum age for recruitment which is based on the training requirements of the post in question or the need for a reasonable period of employment before retirement. These examples are not to be regarded as exhaustive: *Rosenbladt (Gisela) v Oellerking Gebau-dereinigungsges mbH*: C-45/09 [2011] 1 CMLR 1011, [2011] IRLR 51.

Aims that have been accepted as legitimate for the purposes of direct age discrimination include:

•   encouraging better access to employment and better distribution of work between the generations (*Félix Palacios de la Villa v Cortefiel Servicios SA*: C-411/05 [2008] All ER (EC) 249, [2007] IRLR 989, *Petersen v Berufungsausschuss für Zahnärzte für den Bezirk Westfalen-Lippe* [2010] IRLR 254 and *Hörnfeldt v Posten Meddelande AB*: C-141/11 [2012] IRLR 785), including encouraging the reasonable flow of new applicants for judicial posts (*Hampton v Lord Chancellor* [2008] IRLR 258, ET) and ensuring promotion opportunities for associate solicitors (*Seldon* ibid);

•   the efficient planning of the departure and recruitment of staff (*Fuchs and another v Land Hessen*, Joined Cases C-159/10 and C-160/10: [2011] IRLR 1043; *Seldon* and *Hörnfeldt*);

•   encouraging the recruitment of older persons (*Mangold v Helm* [2006] IRLR 143); and

•   running an organisation in a collegiate way and avoiding the indignity of disciplining staff for underperformance (*Rosenbladt, Seldon* and *Hörnfeldt*) or the possibility of disputes about an employee's fitness for work after a certain age (*Fuchs*).

In the light of the SC's decision in *Seldon* some earlier decisions may fall to be re-evaluated. Thus in *MacCulloch v Imperial Chemical Industries plc* [2008] ICR 1334, [2008] IRLR 846 the CA accepted that 'rewarding loyalty' and 'encouraging turnover' could be legitimate aims of measures that were directly discriminatory on grounds of age. It is difficult to see how aims thus expressed could be legitimate post *Seldon* for direct age discrimination.

For other cases on the justification of direct age discrimination see: *Lockwood v Department of Work and Pensions* [2013] Eq LR 206 (redundancy payments varying based on age were justified).

Indirect discrimination

So far as indirect discrimination of all forms is concerned, however, there is no restriction on the possible motivations that can in principle constitute legitimate aims. What constitutes a legitimate aim is a question of fact for the tribunal: see *Ladele v Islington London Borough Council* [2009] EWCA Civ 1357, [2010] ICR 532 at [45]. It will therefore be open to employers to demonstrate that any aim they seek to pursue is legitimate. This is consistent with the fact that justification must be applied on a case-by-case basis and that it is very difficult to anticipate all possible justifications.

In addition to the aims identified above as legitimate for the purposes of direct age discrimination claims, examples of aims that have been accepted as legitimate aims for the purposes of justifying indirect discrimination include:

•   facilitating the recruitment and retention of staff of appropriate calibre (*Homer v Chief Constable of West Yorkshire* [2012] UKSC 15, [2012] ICR 704);

•   recognising the legitimate expectations of employees who were already in receipt of a benefit (*Pulham v Barking and Dagenham London Borough Council* [2010] ICR 333, EAT);

11.9   Discrimination and Equal Opportunities – II

- preventing a windfall or receipt of excessive compensation (*Loxley v BAE Systems Land Systems (Munitions & Ordnance) Ltd* [2008] ICR 1348, [2008] IRLR 853, EAT and *Kraft Foods Ltd v Hastie* (UKEAT/0024/10/ZT) [2010] ICR 1355);

- achieving a stable workforce in the context of a fair process of redundancy selection (*Rolls Royce Plc v Unite the Union* [2010] ICR 1, CA);

- achieving a coherent pay structure, avoiding privatisations, job losses, cuts in hours, and employees receiving lower pay (*Allen v GMB* [2008] IRLR 690);

- rewarding employees for specific work performed, e.g. night work (*Blackburn v Chief Constable of West Midlands Police* [2008] EWCA Civ 1208, [2009] IRLR 135);

- ensuring a teacher is able to communicate effectively with her pupils (a requirement not to wear a veil while teaching: *Azmi v Kirklees Metropolitan Borough Council* [2007] IRLR 484); and,

- ensuring the employer is able to fulfil its contractual requirements to a third party (eg by requiring a security guard to work on a Friday lunchtime and not attend Muslim prayers: *Cherfi v G4S Security Services Ltd* [2011] EqLR 825).

In addition, the legitimate aims accepted in *MacCulloch* (above) of 'rewarding loyalty' and 'encouraging turnover' are plainly capable of constituting legitimate aims for the purposes of indirect discrimination even if there is now some doubt about their legitimacy in the context of direct age discrimination.

One type of legitimate aim has proved particularly controversial – cost-related aims. Given the limitation on legitimate aims for the purposes of justifying direct age discrimination, cost reduction will plainly not be a legitimate aim in the context of direct age discrimination: see *Seldon*. There is nothing express in the governing European legislation, or the domestic legislation, that imposes any such limitation on reliance on cost reduction as a legitimate aim when justifying indirect discrimination. Nonetheless, there is a long line of cases in which it has been held that cost may be relied on as justification provided it is combined with other factors: *Cross v British Airways plc* [2005] IRLR 423, EAT; *R (Elias) v Secretary of State for Defence* [2006] EWCA Civ 1293, [2006] IRLR 934. In *Woodcock v Cumbria Primary Care Trust* [2011] IRLR 119 the EAT expressed the view (*obiter*) that, as a matter of principle and of common sense, there should be no rule that considerations of cost could never be sufficient on their own to justify indirect discrimination. On appeal, however, the Court of Appeal ([2012] EWCA Civ 330) confirmed what was then generally understood to be the orthodox position that justification by reference to costs alone was impermissible. The CA referred to the line of cases establishing this principle, including *Schönheit v Stadt Frankfurt*: C-4/02 and C-5/02 [2004] IRLR 983, CJEU and *Kutz-Bauer v Freie und Hansestadt Hamburg*: C-187/00 [2003] IRLR 368, CJEU, *British Airways plc v Grundy*, *Cross v British Airways Plc* [2005] IRLR 423 and *Redcar and Cleveland BC v Bainbridge* [2008] ICR 249. See also *Osborne Clarke Services v Purohit* [2009] IRLR 341. However, in *Ministry of Justice v O'Brien* [2013] UKSC 6, [2013] 1 WLR 522 the Supreme Court reviewed the relevant authorities in the context of a claim under the *Part-time Workers (Prevention of Less Favourable Treatment) Regulations 2000* and reached the conclusion (at paragraph 69) that cost could not be relied on in order to justify discrimination (i.e. even in combination with other factors). That said, the Court did not consider it needed to decide whether *Woodcock v Cumbria Primary Care Trust* had been wrongly decided.

Although the Supreme Court has now held that cost cannot justify indirect discrimination, there are in fact a number of cases where the Tribunals and Courts have reached conclusions that could be characterized as being findings that costs alone can justify discrimination and which may continue to be followed despite the Supreme Court's ruling. Thus the courts appear to have had little difficulty with the notion that measures intended to avoid a 'windfall' or 'excessive compensation' to the employee – measures which the employer will inevitably have introduced to save itself money – have been held to be justified: see *Loxley v BAE Systems (Munitions & Ordnance) Ltd* [2008] ICR 1348, [2008] IRLR 853 and *Kraft Foods UK Ltd v Hastie* [2010] ICR 1355. That said, it should be noted that in those cases, the payments in question were held to serve some other legitimate purpose and so the courts were able to regard the quantum of the payment as being an aspect of the proportionality of the means of meeting the legitimate aim of (for eg in the case of severance pay) paying a reasonable sum of money on termination of employment to allow the employees time to find a new job. *HM Land Registry v S M Benson and ors* [2012] ICR 627 is another apparently anomalous case. Here, the EAT found that the Tribunal had wrongly found an employer's use of a 'cheapness criterion' in a redundancy situation to be unjustified indirect age discrimination. The EAT held that the 'cheapness criterion' fulfilled a legitimate aim of saving the employer money, and that it was justified because there was no practicable alternative means of achieving the same aim and the measure was not disproportionate. It is notable, however, that the case seems to have been decided by the EAT without reference to the authorities for the general principle that costs alone cannot justify discrimination.

Given these anomalous cases, and given that so far as disability discrimination is concerned costs can effectively justify indirect discrimination because it can be a reason why it is not reasonable to make an adjustment for a disabled person (see eg *Cordell v Foreign & Commonwealth Office* [2012] ICR 280 and **10.43 DISCRIMINATION AND EQUAL OPPORTUNITIES – I**), prior to *O'Brien* (ibid) the time appeared to be ripe for the CJEU to consider again whether or not costs alone can be relied on as justifying indirect discrimination. However, following *O'Brien* there is little prospect of any reference on that point being made from the UK in the near future.

In past cases where cost was relied on as a justification, it was not necessary precisely to quantify the costs, it was usually sufficient for there to be evidence as to the 'broad scale' of costs: see *Pulham and ors v London Borough of Barking & Dagenham* [2010] ICR 333. In that case the EAT also observed that, although it is open to an employer to rely on the fact that the particular budget to which the cost in question has been allocated is exhausted, this should never be regarded as a determinative factor since the allocation of cost centres to particular budgets is a matter that it is within the employer's power to vary if necessary.

While, notwithstanding the Supreme Court's decision in *O'Brien*, doubts remain about costs-related justifications, what is clear is that an aim that is itself discriminatory, or is 'inextricably linked to' the forbidden ground of discrimination, will not be legitimate and it will not be possible for justification to be established: see *Orphanos v Queen Mary College* [1985] IRLR 349, HL, applied in *R (Elias) v Secretary of State for Defence and Commission for Racial Equality* [2006] EWCA Civ 1293, [2006] IRLR 934. The latter case concerned the requirement in a non-statutory compensation scheme for persons interned by the Japanese during the Second World War that, in order to qualify for compensation, internees had to have been born in the UK or have a parent or grandparent born in the UK. The Court of Appeal held that although the Government's desire to limit the scheme to those with a close connection with Britain was a legitimate aim, and cost factors could potentially justify such a limitation, the actual criteria imposed by the Government were so closely connected with the unlawful ground of discrimination (national origins) that their use could not be justified. See also *Ministry of Justice v O'Brien* [2013] UKSC 6, [2013] 1 WLR 522 (aims intended to reward the greater contribution of full-time judges and encourage better candidates to apply for full-time judicial appointment were held not to justify discrimination against part-timers in relation to pensions because, in effect, the aims were themselves discriminatory).

For similar reasons, if an employer has recognised that a particular practice or policy may be discriminatory, it will not be possible for the employer to justify continuing that practice or policy even on a transitional or phasing-out basis: see *Pulham and ors v London Borough of Barking & Dagenham* [2010] ICR 333. However, the EAT also held in that case that if transitional arrangements have already been put in place which preserve features of a scheme that is subsequently held to be discriminatory, then it may be possible for the employer to justify the continuation of the transitional arrangements. Other examples of cases where the aim has been found to be itself discriminatory and therefore illegitimate include *Allonby v Accrington and Rossendale College* [2001] EWCA Civ 529, [2001] IRLR 364 (purpose of imposing the condition was to enable the employer to avoid a statutory protection against discrimination). Compare in this context *Osborne Clarke Services v Purohit* [2009] IRLR 341. That case concerned a firm of solicitors' practice of not offering training contracts to persons who required work permits. They sought to justify this indirect nationality discrimination on the grounds that: (i) they did not feel they could legitimately sign the work permit application form because that required the employer to certify that it was unable to fill the post with a national worker and in fact they were significantly over-subscribed with applicants for training contracts; and (ii) applications for work permits would increase the cost of the process of appointing trainees. The tribunal rejected the cost argument as being an 'unattractive way of justifying indirect discrimination'. As to the argument about the work permit criteria, the EAT ruled that in order to avoid unlawful discrimination, issues of requirement for work permits should only be considered once it had been decided on merit who should be awarded a training contract. Application should then be made to the British Immigration Authority ('BIA') and employers should leave it to the BIA to determine whether the work permit criteria were satisfied.

(2) Whether the measure is capable of achieving the aim

It is not sufficient for an employer to convince a tribunal that the treatment (in the case of age) or provision, criteria or practice (in indirect discrimination) had a legitimate aim. He also needs to show that it was appropriate and reasonably necessary in order to achieve that aim. As noted above, the requirement that the treatment or measure be appropriate means that it must actually contribute to the pursuit of the legitimate aim. There must not be a mismatch between the aim and the means. There are few examples of cases where it has been held that means employed are not at least capable of achieving the aim in question. However, one example which could be viewed as such is *Petersen*, where the CJEU held that a maximum age limit of 68 for panel dentists was not justified as being necessary for the protection of health where there was an exception for those practising outside the panel system. This was because it could not be regarded as essential for the protection of health in the light of the broad exception. (In this respect, *Petersen* concerned an exemption in *Article 2(5)* of the *Framework Directive* for measures which are necessary for the protection of health rather than justification under *Article 6*. It therefore did not address the question of whether it was permissible to assume based only on "general experience" that the performance of dentists declined after a certain age.) A better example is *Homer v Chief Constable of West Yorkshire* [2012] UKSC 15, [2012] ICR 704 in which the SC accepted that a requirement to have a law degree in order to enter a higher pay band may facilitate the recruitment and retention of staff of appropriate calibre. However, the SC considered that where the member of staff in question had been recruited much earlier and under a different system where a law degree was not required, the requirement to have one before being allowed to cross a pay threshold was unlikely to fulfil the aim of retaining valued staff. Indeed, in this author's view, the position is likely to be quite the contrary. See also *Hennigs v Eisenbahn-Bundesamt; Land Berlin v Mai*, joined Cases C-297/10 and C-298/10: [2012] IRLR 83, CJEU (the aim of rewarding experience is not achieved by age-related pay scales which apply irrespective of experience) and *Kücükdeveci v Swedex GmbH & Co KG*: C-555/07 [2011] 2 CMLR 703 (the aim of making it easier to recruit young people is not achieved by a measure which applies long after the employees have ceased to be young).

(3) Proportionality

The requirement that a measure be proportionate means that tribunals must seek to balance the discriminatory effect of the requirement or condition against the legitimate aim in question (see *Ojutiku v Manpower Services Commission* [1982] ICR 661; *Hampson v Department of Education and Science* [1989] ICR 179, overturned by the House of Lords ([1990] ICR 511) on grounds other than justification, which was not argued before their Lordships). The tribunal must consider both the quantitative and the qualitative effects of the discrimination, ie how many women or people of a particular racial group will suffer in consequence of it, and how seriously they will suffer (cf *Jones v University of Manchester* [1993] ICR 474 and also *EC Commission v Belgium* [1991] IRLR 393). Where the discriminatory effect is particularly acute, the measure is more likely to be disproportionate. Thus in *Seda Kucukdeveci v Swedex GmbH & Co KG*: C-555/07 [2010] IRLR 346, the CJEU ruled that a German law was unlawful which provided that periods of employment completed by an employee before reaching the age of 25 were not taken into account in calculating the notice period for dismissal. The discrimination was significant and the link to the legitimate aim tenuous.

Measures that apply to all without taking sufficient account of the different circumstances of particular groups will generally be disproportionate. Thus in *Ingeniorforeningen i Danmark, acting on behalf of Ole Andersen v Region Syddanmark*: C-499/08 [2011] 1 CMLR 1140 the CJEU considered a measure providing severance payments for all long-serving employees but not those over 65 was disproportionate because it applied to all employees over 65 regardless of whether they were actually drawing a pension. In *Mangold*, a measure aimed to encourage the recruitment of older persons was held to be disproportionate as it applied to all old people, regardless of whether they had been out of employment. The CJEU took a more lenient approach in the case of *Félix Palacios*. It held that the enforcement of a compulsory retirement age under a collective agreement was justified as being proportionate. The CJEU noted that the national authorities had a broad discretion in social and employment matters and it was for them to strike the appropriate balance. In *R (on the application of Unison) v First Secretary of State* [2006] EWHC 2373 (Admin), [2006] IRLR 926, the Secretary of State had changed the Local Government Pension Scheme, considering this to be necessary in order to comply with the *Directive* and the *Regulations*. The Secretary of State considered that the scheme would not be justified by the aim of rewarding loyalty as it treated those who remained in service in the same way as those who had left. The Court held that this position was not irrational.

When determining whether or not a measure is proportionate, it will be relevant to consider whether or not any lesser form of the measure would nevertheless serve the employer's legitimate aim. Thus, in *Azmi v Kirklees Metropolitan Borough Council* [2007] IRLR 484 (in which the Muslim claimant complained that she had been unlawfully discriminated against on grounds of her religious belief because she was not allowed to wear the veil while teaching at a primary school), the EAT held that the tribunal was right to have taken into account, in finding the requirement imposed by the school to be proportionate, the facts that (i) the respondent school had, before insisting on the claimant not wearing a veil, observed her teaching both with and without the veil and taken the view that she was much more effective without the veil, and (ii) the school had permitted her to wear the veil when moving around the school premises and had only required her not to wear the veil while teaching. Contrast, in the education field, *R (on the application of Watkins-Singh) v Governing Body of Aberdare Girls' High School* [2008] EWHC 1865 (Admin), [2008] ELR 561 where the High Court found that a school's policy forbidding jewellery was not justified because it prevented Sikhs from wearing Kara bangles which were of great importance to them and yet so small and unostentatious that the discriminatory effect of the policy was disproportionate and *G v St Gregory's Catholic Science College Governors* [2011] EWHC 1452 (Admin), [2011] EqLR 859 where the High Court found that a prohibition on pupils wearing hair in corn-rows was indirectly discriminatory on racial grounds and not justified as it was disproportionate. See also *Cherfi v G4S Security Services Ltd* [2011] EqLR 825 in which the EAT upheld a Tribunal's decision that a requirement for a security guard to work Friday lunchtimes was proportionate even though it prevented him (as a Muslim) from attending Friday prayers. The EAT held that the Tribunal had properly considered both the effect on the employee and the effect on the employer's business and had lawfully concluded that the requirement was a proportionate means of achieving the legitimate aim of meeting the employer's business need (which involved fulfilling contractual obligations to a third party). See further, to similar effect, *Mba v Merton LBC* [2013] ICR 658 (requirement to work on Sundays justified indirect discrimination against Christian employee).

There is one possible exception to the requirement to consider the proportionality of a particular aim. This is where the aim is itself the protection of fundamental rights. The argument made in the cases in which this has been suggested appears to be that the aim is sufficiently legitimate to justify the use of any means to achieve it. See in this regard *Islington London Borough Council v Ladele* [2010] IRLR 211. That case concerned the Council's requirement that its services be provided on a non-discriminatory basis. It had accordingly disciplined a registrar who, owing to her religious beliefs, refused to carry out civil partnership ceremonies. The Tribunal found that the Council's aim of providing non-discriminatory services was legitimate but considered that the use of disciplinary measures to achieve this aim was disproportionate. The EAT (whose decision was approved by the CA) overturned this decision, holding that since the Council's aim was legitimate and could not be achieved other than by imposing disciplinary sanctions on employees who sought to pick and choose the duties that they would perform, the Council's actions had not been unlawful. The CA confirmed that in those circumstances it was not necessary to go on to consider the proportionality of the means: since the legitimate aim was itself the protection of fundamental rights, to ask whether a particular means to achieving that aim was disproportionate "might well be characterised as invoking the tail to wag the dog" (Lord Neuberger, [51]): see also *McFarlane v Relate Avon Ltd* [2010] EWCA Civ 880, [2010] IRLR 872. It should further be noted that the EAT in *Ladele* considered that, if the Council had wished to accommodate the claimant's religious beliefs, it would have been lawful for it to do so, but the fact that this could have been done did not mean that the policy the Council had in fact adopted was unlawful. However, the CA held (*obiter*) that where a registrar had been designated as a civil partnership registrar it would be unlawful under the *Equality Act (Sexual Orientation) Regulations 2007* for her to refuse to provide registration services to homosexual couples (for which unlawful act the Council would be liable).

Mrs Ladele, Mr McFarlane and two other claimants, Ms Eweida (whose complaint was that British Airways had refused to allow her to wear a cross at work, cf *Eweida v British Airways Plc* [2010] EWCA Civ 80, [2010] ICR 890) and Ms Chaplin (a nurse who was refused permission to wear a necklace with a cross on it at work) took their cases to the ECrtHR, complaining that the UK had unlawfully interfered with their rights under *Art 9* of the *ECHR* to manifest their religious belief and/or had unlawfully discriminated against them contrary to *Art 14* of the *ECHR*. In conjoined proceedings (*Eweida and ors v United Kingdom*, App nos 48420/10, 59842/10, 51671/10 and 36516/10, [2013] IRLR 231) the ECrtHR upheld Ms Eweida's complaint, but rejected the others. In each case the ECrtHR considered that the applicant had established an interference with their rights under *Art 9* and/or *Art 14* and went on to consider whether that interference was justified. The test applied by the ECrtHR when considering justification is indistinguishable from that which applies in domestic law under the *EA 2010*. In each case the ECrtHR sought to balance the importance to the applicant of right to manifest his or her religious belief against the business need / aim of the applicant's employer. The ECrtHR did not take the view that just because an employer's aim was the protection of fundamental rights, there was no need to consider proportionality. Rather, in both the *Ladele* and *McFarlane* cases the fact that this was the employer's aim was merely treated as a factor that weighed heavily in the balance in favour of the interference being justified. The ECrtHR also held that although it is relevant to the assessment of justification in the employment context that an employee can avoid the interference by resigning his or her job, this fact on its own could never justify discrimination or interference with an employee's fundamental rights. In *Ladele, McFarlane* and *Chaplin* the ECrtHR considered that the UK had struck the right balance in holding the employer's action to be lawful. In *Eweida*, however, the ECrtHR considered that although the employer's aim of projecting a uniform corporate image was a legitimate one, it was not weighty one (and not as weighty as the health and safety reasons for not allowing Ms Chaplin to wear a cross, for example) and the fact that the employer had subsequently amended the policy made clear that it clear that it had not been vital to have the policy in the first place. The interference with Ms Eweida's rights had therefore been dispropor-tionate.

General principles

The question of whether discrimination is justified is one of fact for the employment tribunal (*Singh v British Rail Engineering* [1986] ICR 22).

The burden of proof is on the respondent to satisfy the tribunal that the measure applied was objectively justified for economic, administrative or other reasons (*Rainey v Greater Glasgow Health Board* [1987] ICR 129, an equal pay case in which the House of Lords held that the same principles are applicable to the *SDA 1975* as to the *Equal Pay Act 1970*; see 21.12 EQUAL PAY). (cf DISCRIMINATION AND EQUAL OPPORTUNITIES – III (12) for general discussion of the burden of proof.)

The test to be applied by the tribunal is an objective one: while the tribunal should take into account the reasonable needs of the respondent's business, the tribunal has to make its own judgment as to whether the provision, criterion or practice applied by the respondent is reasonably necessary: there is no scope for 'margin of discretion' or 'range of reasonable responses' approach when considering whether an indirectly discriminatory provision, criterion or practice is justified: *Hardys & Hansons plc v Lax* [2005] EWCA Civ 846, [2005] IRLR 726.

The tribunal must demonstrate that it has critically evaluated any defence of justification: its reasons for finding that a measure is a 'proportionate means of achieving a legitimate aim' must be apparent from the decision: *Redfearn v Serco Ltd*, above. In that case, the EAT held that the tribunal had not given sufficient reasons for finding that a requirement that no employee be a member of the British National Party was justified as a proportionate means of achieving the legitimate aim of protecting the health and safety of Asian passengers using the Respondent's services. See also *MacCulloch v Imperial Chemical Industries plc* [2008] ICR 1334, [2008] IRLR 846.

Although it has occasionally been suggested that some forms of indirect discrimination (most notably age discrimination) require a lesser degree of justification than others, the Court of Appeal has confirmed that such suggestions have no juridical basis and the same degree of justification is required for all grounds of discrimination: *R (on the application of the British Gurkha Welfare Society) v Ministry of Defence* [2010] EWCA Civ 1098, [2010] 1 WLR 1067 at [11]. Nonetheless, there is at least one category of case in which it is established that a slightly different approach should be taken, and that is in cases concerning treatment, provisions, criteria or practices based on length of service. These are dealt with at the end of this section.

What is clear is that the overall discriminatory effect of the measure will necessarily be greater in cases of direct discrimination and this will be a material factor when applying the proportionality test: see *MacCulloch v Imperial Chemical Industries plc* [2008] ICR 1334, [2008] IRLR 846 and *Incorporated Trustees of the National Council on Ageing (Age Concern England) v Secretary of State for Business, Enterprise and Regulatory Reform*: C-388/07 [2009] All ER (EC) 619, [2009] ICR 1080, CJEU. See also further above under 'proportionality'. The case law on justification of retirement and related measures is dealt with in a separate section below and in **(40)** RETIREMENT.

11.9   Discrimination and Equal Opportunities – II

It is not necessary as a matter of law for the alleged discriminator to have analysed the proportionality question at the time of adopting a rule or policy: see *Ministry of Justice v O'Brien* [2013] UKSC 6, [2013] 1 WLR 522, *Cadman v Health and Safety Executive* [2004] EWCA Civ 1317, [2004] IRLR 97 and the *Elias* case (above). It is always open to the alleged discriminator to justify the rule or policy by factors not expressly taken into account at the time of adopting the rule or policy: see *Schönheit v Stadt Frankfurt* conjoined cases C-4/02 and C-5/02 [2004] IRLR 983 and *Seldon v Clarkson Wright & Jakes* [2010] EWCA Civ 899, [2011] ICR 60 (affd on this point [2012] UKSC 16, [2012] ICR 716). However, where the alleged discriminator has not even considered questions of proportionality at the time of adopting a rule or policy, it may be more difficult for him to establish justification (cf *Ministry of Justice v O'Brien* ibid, *Hockenjos v Secretary of State for Social Security* [2004] EWCA Civ 1749, [2005] IRLR 471 and the *Elias* and *Seldon* cases, above).

Under the 'old' test, it was held that a measure may be justified even though the respondent has not produced detailed evidence to show that there was no other way of achieving his or her object (cf *Cobb* above). Under the 'new' test, it is much more likely that a failure to adduce cogent evidence of justification will result in a finding that justification is not made out: see *Starmer v British Airways plc* [2005] IRLR 862, EAT and also the Court of Appeal's decision in *Hockenjos v Secretary of State for Social Security* [2004] EWCA Civ 1749, [2005] IRLR 471 (below). In *Hampton v Lord Chancellor* [2008] IRLR 258, the employment tribunal held that the government's decision to set the retirement age for part-time recorders at 65 was not proportionate as it considered that the government's evidence was insufficiently conclusive. However, see *Pulham and ors v London Borough of Barking & Dagenham* [2010] ICR 333, in which the EAT held that an employer was not precluded from advancing a defence of justification in respect of pay protection arrangements merely because the arrangements had not been "carefully costed and crafted" at the time of implementation.

Nonetheless, in every case respondents need to take care to ensure that evidence adduced is aimed at the right issue. In *Whiffen v Milham Ford Girls' School* [2001] EWCA Civ 385, [2001] IRLR 468, the respondent attempted to justify a policy of responding to a redundancy situation by first allowing the contracts of temporary staff to lapse without renewal. The respondent argued that it needed to make redundancies and that the policy was gender-neutral. The Court of Appeal pointed out that all indirect discrimination cases concerned provisions which were gender-neutral on their face and that, where it had been found that an apparently gender-neutral provision had a disparate effect on a particular group (here, women), it was no justification that the policy might have operated non-discriminatorily in another situation. What required justification was that redundancies were first visited on temporary employees. See also *Garcia-Bello v Aviance UK Ltd* [2007] All ER (D) 318 (Dec): where there was no clear evidence that flexible shift patterns could not have been introduced, and therefore the Tribunal and EAT found that there was no justification for the disparate impact of the new shift patterns on those with childcare responsibilities (who were all female).

In particular, care must be taken in properly identifying and distinguishing the aim of the measure from the means used to achieve it. The fact that different measures with different aims could be introduced by an employer is not relevant in determining whether a particular measure with a legitimate aim is justified, what matters is whether there are more proportionate ways of achieving the aim of the measure in question: see *Blackburn and anor v Chief Constable of West Midlands Police* [2008] EWCA Civ 1208, [2009] IRLR 135 (aim of rewarding those who did night work was legitimate and therefore it was proportionate to pay those persons more – it did not matter that other police forces had decided not to reward night workers). See also *Allen v GMB* [2008] IRLR 690. In that case the CA considered the situation of a union which had decided, in negotiating with an employer in relation to various pay issues, to adopt a policy whereby employees' interests in relation to future pay deals were prioritised over claims to back pay under the *Equal Pay Act 1970*. The result was that those employees who had equal pay claims (a predominantly female group) received less by way of settlement than they might otherwise have done. The Tribunal held that the union's objective (which it identified as being to achieve single status, avoiding privatisations, job losses, cuts in hours, and members receiving lower pay under the new system) was legitimate, but that the means used to achieve that aim amounted to 'manipulation' and were unjustified. One factor in the Tribunal's conclusion was that it was considered that the amount accepted by the Union in settlement of the equal pay claims was bordering on negligent. The EAT found that the Tribunal had taken the wrong approach to the question of objective justification. The EAT considered that, once it had been accepted that an aim was legitimate then if the means adopted to achieve that aim were the only means available then the policy would be justified. The CA disagreed and upheld the Tribunal's decision The CA considered that the EAT had taken too narrow an approach to the concept of 'means'. The 'means' was not the balance struck by the union in the deal with the Council, but the methods used to persuade members to accept that deal. The Tribunal had been entitled to find that those methods had been manipulative and disproportionate to the legitimate aims pursued.

The fact that a discriminatory measure has been negotiated with the trade union or other workforce representatives will usually be a relevant factor in assessing whether or not the measure is justified. (This is consistent with the fact that achieving a stable workforce may be a legitimate aim, see *Rolls Royce Plc v Unite the Union* [2010] ICR 1, CA.) The fact that a rule has been agreed in the process of collective bargaining will not render an otherwise unlawful scheme lawful, but nonetheless weight will be given to the fact that the parties have agreed to a scheme that they (presumably) consider to be fair: *Loxley v BAE Land Systems* [2008] IRLR 853. See also *Rosenbladt v Oellerking Gebaudereinigungsgesellschaft mbH*: C-45/09 [2011] 1 CMLR 32, [2011] IRLR 51. Similarly, the fact that the terms in question have been agreed by the members of a partnership (*Seldon*) will be a relevant factor. However, employers and tribunals cannot through negotiation and agreement with workforce representatives abdicate their responsibility to assess for themselves whether a measure is proportionate: see *Pulham and ors v London Borough of Barking & Dagenham* [2010] ICR 333.

Treatment, provisions, criteria or practices based on length of service

Although generally speaking the same principles apply when considering justification of prima facie discriminatory measures regardless of the ground of discrimination relied on, it appears from the case law on equal pay that a slightly different approach is to be taken to cases involving disproportionate impact arising from the use of the criterion of length of service. There seems to be no reason why the same principles should not apply to indirect discrimination in relation to matters other than pay arising through use of a length of service criterion. It will sometimes be the case that use of the criterion of length of service will have a disproportionate impact on women because women tend to have more career breaks or shorter working lives than men. (It is also likely to be indirectly on the grounds of age.) However, the CJEU in *Danfoss* [1989] IRLR 532 held that, although the use of the criterion of length of service may involve some discrimination against women, the employer did not have to provide 'special justification' for that because, in essence it could be assumed that length of service brings with it greater experience and improved job performance. In *Cadman v Health and Safety Executive*: C-17/05 [2006] ICR 1623, [2006] IRLR 969 the CJEU retreated slightly from this, saying 'where recourse to the criterion of length of service . . . leads to disparities . . . between the men and women to be included in the comparison, (i) since, as a general rule, recourse to the criterion of length of service is appropriate to attain the legitimate objective of rewarding experience acquired which enables the worker to perform his duties better, the employer does not have to establish specifically that recourse to that criterion is appropriate to attain that objective as regards a particular job, unless the worker provides evidence capable of raising serious doubts in that regard; (ii) where a job classification system based on an evaluation of the work to be carried out is used in determining pay, there is no need to show that an individual worker has acquired experience during the relevant period which has enabled him to perform his duties better'.

The CA in *Wilson v Health and Safety Executive* [2009] EWCA Civ 1074, [2010] ICR 302 has now clarified the approach that should be taken to domestic cases involving a length of service criterion in the light of the CJEU decision in *Cadman*. The CA ruled that, so far as domestic law is concerned, the "serious doubts" test put forward by the CJEU in *Cadman* is only of relevance before trial (presumably as a ground for 'strike out'). The CA said that what a claimant needs to show, pre-trial, is that there is evidence from which, if established at trial, it can properly be found that the general rule in *Danfoss* and *Cadman* (that seniority and length of service are generally material differences other than sex) does not apply. The CA confirmed, however, that a claim involving a length of service criterion is to be approached in essentially the same way as any other claim involving indirect discrimination. The burden is on the claimant to show disparate impact and, if that is established, the burden shifts to the employer to justify the difference as necessary. The CA noted (at 52) that the Tribunal had allowed the employer a 'margin of appreciation' in relation to objective justification in this case. The CA indicated that there was no error of law in that approach.

Retirement and related provisions

Until 6 April 2011 there was a specific exception in *reg 30* of the *AR 2006* (preserved by the *EA 2010*) for retirement (see below **11.15** and also generally **RETIREMENT (40)**). Since 6 April 2011 the *Employment Equality (Repeal of Retirement Age Provisions) Regulations 2011 (SI 2011/1069)* have phased out the designated retirement age in reg 30 of the AR 2006 so that (at the latest from October 2012) there is no longer any self-justifying retirement age for employees and whether retirements and related provisions are justified falls to be considered in accordance with the standard principles for justifying indirect discrimination in relation to other protected characteristics (see above). There are, however, two important differences between the justification test as it applies to direct age discrimination and that which applies in relation to indirect discrimination. First, direct age discrimination can only be justified if the aim of the measure in question relates to "employment policy, the labour market or vocational training" and not "purely individual reasons particular to the employer's situation, such as cost reduction or improving competitiveness": see *art 6(1)* of Directive 2000/78/EC and *Seldon v Clarkson, Wright & Jakes* [2012] UKSC 16, [2012] ICR 716 (see above). (In *Seldon* the Tribunal had not appreciated this distinction between direct age discrimination and indirect discrimination. Accordingly, the matter was remitted for the Tribunal to consider whether a compulsory retirement age of 65 for solicitors in a partnership was justified or not.) Secondly, although normally it will suffice if the employer succeeds in showing that the provision, criterion or practice was a proportionate means of achieving a legitimate aim in general, it might be necessary in certain cases for the employer to demonstrate that the application of the provision, criterion or practice to the particular employee was justified in that particular case: see *Seldon*, ibid.

For further discussion of the case law on the justifications for retirements and related provisions see **RETIREMENT (40)**.

Other specific cases

For cases concerning justification of indirectly discriminatory requirements in relation to working practices in the armed forces, see *Macmillan v Ministry of Defence* (11 November 2003, unreported), EAT and *Boote v Ministry of Defence* (3 March 2004, unreported), ChD.

For justification of requirements or conditions that Sikhs who wear turbans should wear safety helmets on construction sites (a *prima facie* indirectly discriminatory provision) see below **11.12**.

For a consideration of the justification for a requirement to work on Sundays (which was indirectly discriminatory under the *RBR 2003*), cf *Williams-Drabble v Pathway Care Solutions Ltd* (ET, 10 January 2005, IDS Brief 776, p 8 and *Mba v Merton LBC* [2013] ICR 658). See, in like vein, *Cherfi v G4S Security Services Ltd* [2011] EqLR 825) (requirement to work on Friday lunchtimes justified despite disadvantage to Muslims wishing to attend Friday prayers).

Challenging domestic legislation

Where a complainant seeks to have a provision of domestic legislation disapplied on the basis that it has an indirectly discriminatory effect and is thus contrary to Community Law, it is open to the member state to seek to justify the provision. In *R v Secretary of State for Employment, ex p Seymour-Smith* [1995] ICR 889 the House of Lords, following a reference to the CJEU, laid down a three-part test for assessing whether or not a discriminatory legislative provision was justified:

(i)   Did the measure reflect a legitimate aim of social policy;

(ii)   Was the aim unrelated to any discrimination based on sex; and

(iii)   Could the Government reasonably consider that the means chosen were suitable for attaining the aim?

The CJEU further considered the issue in *Jørgensen v Foreningen af Speciallaeger and Sygesikringens Forhandlingsudvalg*: C-226/98 [2000] IRLR 726 and held that in deciding whether a member state had succeeded in demonstrating that a provision was justified, reliance on mere budgetary constraints would not be sufficient (see also *Kutz-Bauer v Freie Und Hansestadt Hamburg*: C-187/00 [2003] IRLR 368, CJEU).

The burden of proof for establishing justification is on the state: *Hockenjos v Secretary of State for Social Security* [2004] EWCA Civ 1749, [2005] IRLR 471. In *Hockenjos* the Court of Appeal considered a provision of the *Jobseeker's Allowance Regulations 1996* which had a clear disproportionate impact on men. The Court, applying the *Seymour-Smith* three-stage test, stressed that it was not necessary, in order for the claimant to succeed, for him to show that there was an obviously better way of achieving the legitimate aim. On the contrary, the burden was on the Secretary of State and his failure to apply his mind to the question of whether or not there was an alternative to the discriminatory provision meant that the burden of establishing justification had not been discharged. Note, however, that it is not necessary as a matter of law for the alleged discriminator to have analysed the proportionality question at the time of adopting a rule or policy: see *R (Elias) v Secretary of State for Defence and Commission for Racial Equality* [2006] EWCA Civ 1293, [2006] IRLR 934 (a case on a non-statutory scheme).

The *Seymour-Smith* test was also applied by the EAT in *Rutherford v Secretary of State for Trade and Industry* [2003] IRLR 858. That case concerned the statutory age limit on the right not to be unfairly dismissed (*ERA 1996, s 109*) and to receive redundancy pay (*ERA 1996, s 156*). The EAT held that the tribunal had erred in finding that the statutory age limit had a disparate impact on men and that, even if it did, the policy arguments advanced (that it enabled employers to create opportunities for younger employees without having to justify the dismissal of older employees) were legitimate aims, unrelated to sex, which the government was entitled to pursue. The EAT's decision on disparate impact was affirmed by the Court of Appeal ([2004] EWCA Civ 1186, [2005] ICR 119) and by the House of Lords ([2006] UKHL 19, [2006] ICR 785). However, both the Court of Appeal and the House of Lords found it unnecessary, in the light of that decision, to decide the question of justification. In the Court of Appeal, however, Mummery LJ observed that the EAT had adopted the correct approach in law, but that it was, properly speaking, a question of fact for the tribunal as to whether justification was made out in any particular case.

11.9 Discrimination and Equal Opportunities – II

Compare also *R (on the application of Age UK) v Secretary of State for Business, Innovation & Skills* [2010] ICR 260, on the question of whether the retirement provisions in the *AR 2006* are justified.

11.9A LACK OF KNOWLEDGE OF DISABILITY

A special defence is available to claims of discrimination arising from a disability under *s 15* of the *EA 2010* and to claims of failure to comply with the duty make reasonable adjustments under *s 20* of the *EA 2010* (see generally DISCRIMINATION AND EQUAL OPPORTUNITIES – I (10)). There will be no unlawful discrimination arising from a disability if the employer shows that he did not know, and could not reasonably have been expected to know, that the employee had the disability (*s 15(2)*). There will be no duty to make reasonable adjustments if the employer: (a) did not know, and could not reasonably have been expected to know, that the employee had the disability; and (b) was likely to be placed at a disadvantage by the arrangements in question (*Sch 8, para 20(1)(b)*). In relation to claims made by applicants for employment (or partnership, or candidates for a contract position, etc), the defence also applies where the employer did not know and could not reasonably have been expected to know that an interested disabled person is or may be an applicant for the work in question.

A similar defence was available to a claim of a failure to make reasonable adjustments under the *DDA 1995, s 4A(3)* and it is likely that courts and tribunals will take the same approach to the defences available under the *EA 2010*. In *Eastern and Coastal Kent Primary Care Trust v Grey* [2009] IRLR 429, the EAT held that the defence under the *DDA 1995, s 4A(3)* applies where the employer:

(i)   does not know that the disabled person has a disability;

(ii)   does not know that the disabled person is likely to be at a substantial disadvantage compared with persons who are not disabled;

(iii)   could not reasonably be expected to know that the disabled person had a disability; and

(iv)   could not reasonably be expected to know that the disabled person is likely to be placed at a substantial disadvantage in comparison with persons who are not disabled.

In *Secretary of State for Work and Pensions v Alam* [2010] ICR 665 and *Wilcox v Birmingham Cab Services Ltd* [2011] EqLR 810 the EAT emphasised again that it is necessary (for the purposes of the defence to a claim of failure to make reasonable adjustments) for the employer to show both that it did not know (actually or constructively) that the employee was disabled and that he did not know (actually or constructively) that the employee was placed at the relevant disadvantage by the disability. The EAT in *Wilcox* further confirmed that there was no conflict in this respect between *Grey* and *Alam* as some commentators appeared to have thought.

It is important to remember, though, that the same is not true of the defence to a claim of discrimination arising from disability under *s 15(2)*. To succeed on that defence it is only necessary to show that the employer did not know (actually or constructively) that the employee was disabled. If the employer does have actual or constructive knowledge of the disability then it does not matter whether or not the employer is aware that its reason for treating the employee as it does is something that arises in consequence of the disability or not.

Although generally speaking employers cannot rely on the lack of formal confirmation by an employee (or, even, his treating medical practitioners) that he is disabled in order to avoid a finding that they have discriminated, the *Wilcox* case was one in which the EAT held that the Tribunal had been entitled to find that it was inappropriate to impute constructive knowledge to the employer prior to receipt of a formal medical report. In that case the employee suffered from an unusual mental impairment and the EAT held that it had been open to the Tribunal to conclude that the employer could not reasonably have known both of that impairment and that its effects would be substantial and long term (so as to bring it within the definition of disability in *s 6* of the *EA 2010*) prior to receipt of medical evidence to that effect.

Generally speaking, however, employers must be aware of the potential discriminatory impact of their decisions whenever less favourable treatment is meted out. As suggested by the EAT in *H J Heinz Co Ltd v Kenrick* [2000] IRLR 144 (in a passage cited with apparent approval by Baroness Hale in the non-dissenting part of her opinion in *Lewisham London Borough Council v Malcolm* [2008] UKHL 43, [2008] 1 AC 1399), an employer is required to pause before dismissing an employee or treating an employee in a less favourable way in order to consider whether the reason for the dismissal or treatment might relate to disability and, if it might, to reflect on the *DDA 1995* and the *Code of Practice* before dismissing or treating the employee in that way.

11.10 POSITIVE DISCRIMINATION

Domestic law

Broadly speaking, positive discrimination is not permitted under the predecessor domestic equality legislation because discriminating in favour of one group of people generally involves unlawful discrimination against another group who are treated less favourably in comparison (*Lambeth London Borough Council v Commission for Racial Equality* [1990] ICR 768; though compare *Arnold v Barnfield College* [2004] All ER (D) 63 (Jul), EAT: mere existence of a policy of attracting more ethnic minority candidates not sufficient to indicate that there had been unlawful discrimination). Disability discrimination has always been an exception to this, discrimination against non-disabled persons, on grounds of disability, not being in and of itself unlawful. The *EA 2010* expressly provides that it is not an instance of unlawful discrimination for a disabled person to be treated more favourably than a non-disabled person is or would be treated: *EA 2010, s 13(3)*. Moreover, the duty to make reasonable adjustments (see DISCRIMINATION AND EQUAL OPPORTUNITIES – I (10)) can also be regarded as a form of positive discrimination.

The position under EC law has also always been less straightforward (see below).

Under the *EA 2010* there is now a generally applicable exception under *s 158* for 'positive action' and a specific exception under *s 159* for 'positive action' in relation to recruitment and promotion. The two exceptions are mutually exclusive (*s 158(4)(a)*), but they apply to any act done by anyone (ie by an employer or a trade union or an agency) that would otherwise be unlawful under the Act. The exception under *s 158* came into force on 1 October 2010 at the same time as the major part of the Act. The exception under *s 159* came into force on 6 April 2011 (*art 3, SI 2011/96*).

The general exception under *s 158* applies where a person reasonably thinks that: (a) persons who share a protected characteristic suffer a disadvantage connected to the characteristic; or (b) persons who share a protected characteristic have needs that are different from the needs of persons who do not share it; or (c) participation in an activity by persons who share a protected characteristic is disproportionately low (*s 158(1)*). In such circumstances the *EA 2010* does not prohibit a person from taking any action which is a proportionate means of achieving the aim of: (a) enabling or encouraging persons who share the protected characteristic to overcome or minimise that disadvantage; or (b) meeting those needs; or (c) enabling or encouraging persons who share the protected characteristic to participate in that activity (*s 158(2)*).

The specific exception for recruitment and promotion under *s 159* applies where a person reasonably thinks that: (a) persons who share a protected characteristic suffer a disadvantage connected to the characteristic; or (b) participation in an activity by persons who share a protected characteristic is disproportionately low (*s 159(1)*). In such circumstances the *EA 2010* will not prohibit a person from treating a particular candidate more favourably in connection with recruitment or promotion because they have a particular protected characteristic where that treatment is done with the aim of enabling or encouraging persons who share the protected characteristic to: (a) overcome or minimise that disadvantage; or (b) to participate in that activity (*s 159(2)*). However, the section only applies if 'all else is equal', specifically if those who are being considered for recruitment or promotion are as qualified as each other, and if the employer does not have a general policy of preferring candidates of a particular protected characteristic for recruitment or promotion (*s 159(4)(a), (b)*). Further, in all cases the positive discrimination must be a proportionate means of achieving the statutory aims set out above (*s 159(4)(c)*).

In addition, there are exceptions under the *EA 2010* for those providing supported employment for the disabled (*s 133(3)*) and for those providing training to non-EEA nationals who will not remain in the UK on completion of training (*para 4, Sch 23*).

See also **11.37** below for discussion of the equality duties imposed on all public authorities which, while not specifically authorising positive discrimination, do authorise and oblige public authorities to take positive action to eliminate unlawful discrimination.

Under the predecessor legislation there were a number of more specific exceptions for positive discrimination as follows.

(a)   *Access to training*

There is no specific exception for access to training under the *EA 2010*.

Under the predecessor legislation employers may discriminate positively in favour of a particular racial group or in favour of female or male employees in order to afford that group access to training and to encourage the members of that group to take advantage of opportunities for doing particular work, provided that, at any time within the 12 months immediately preceding the positive discrimination:

(i)   there were no persons of that group among those doing that work at that establishment; or

(ii)   the proportion of persons of that group among those doing that work at that establishment is comparatively small (*RRA 1976, s 38(1), (2)*; *SDA 1975, s 48(1), (2)*).

The *RRA 1976* specifies that the proportion of persons of that group must be 'small in comparison to':

(i)   all those employed by the respondent at that establishment; or

(ii)   the population of the area from which that respondent normally recruits persons for work in his employment at that establishment.

Other persons concerned with the provision of vocational training may also discriminate in favour of racial groups, men or women (as appropriate) where it reasonably appears to that person that there are no, or a comparatively small number, of members of that particular race, sex, etc doing that work in Great Britain (*RRA 1976, s 37*; *SDA 1975, s 47*). This particular exception specifically does not apply to discrimination by employers (*RRA 1976, s 37(3)* and *SDA 1975, s 47(4)*).

Similar provision is also made for positive discrimination in favour of persons of a particular religion or belief or sexual orientation where it reasonably appears to the person discriminating that it will prevent or compensate for disadvantages, linked to religion, belief, sexual orientation or age (or age group), respectively, suffered by persons of that religion or belief or sexual orientation or age (or age group) (as appropriate) (*RBR 2003, reg 25(1)*; *SOR 2003, reg 26(1)*; *AR 2006, reg 29(1)*). The ACAS Guidance on the *SOR 2003* and *RBR 2003* suggests that the exception would allow advertisements encouraging applications from people of a particular sexual orientation, religion or belief, provided it is made clear that selection will be on merit without reference to sexual orientation, religion or belief. The *Regulations* do not permit quota systems.

In addition, the *Employment Act 1989, s 8* provides that the Secretary of State may by order make special provision for vocational training for lone parents. Where such an order is made, discrimination in favour of lone parents in accordance with the order will not be regarded as unlawful under the *SDA 1975, s 3* (discrimination against married persons).

(b)   *Membership, etc of trade organisations*

There is no specific exception for membership, etc of trade organisations under the *EA 2010*.

Positive discrimination is permitted under the *SDA 1975* and the *RRA 1976* to encourage both membership of and post-holding in trade organisations (including discrimination in affording access to training for holding such posts) where, at any time during the previous 12 months, there were no or proportionally few postholders or members of the relevant racial group or sex in that organisation (*RRA 1976, s 38(3), (4), (5); SDA 1975, s 48(2), (3)*).

Similar provision is made by the RBR 2003 and the SOR 2003 to allow positive discrimination by trade organisations where it reasonably appears to the organisation that the act prevents or compensates for disadvantages linked to religion, belief, sexual orientation or age suffered by those of that religion, belief, sexual orientation or age (or age group) who are members of the organisation, or are eligible to become members, or hold, or are likely to hold, posts within that organisation (*RBR 2003, reg 25(2); SOR 2003, reg 26(2); AR 2006, reg 29(2)*). The exception extends to "encouraging" only people of a particular sexual orientation, religion or belief to become members of the organisation where it reasonably appears to the organisation that doing so would prevent or compensate for disadvantages suffered by people of that sexual orientation, religion or belief (*RBR 2003, reg 25(3); SOR 2003, reg 26(3); AR 2006, reg 29(3)*).

Under the *SDA 1975* (but not under the *RRA 1976, SOR 2003, RBR 2003* or *AR 2006*), trade organisations are also permitted to discriminate positively by setting quotas reserving a certain number of elected seats to men only or women only where in the opinion of the organisation the quotas are in the circumstances needed to secure a reasonable lower limit to the number of members of that sex serving on the body (*SDA 1975, s 49(1)*). However, discrimination in the arrangements for determining who is entitled to vote in an election of members of the body or in any arrangements concerning membership of the union or organisation itself is *not* permitted: *SDA 1975, s 49(2)*.

Note that although a set of barristers chambers is a 'trade organisation' within the meaning of the equivalent provisions of the *DDA 1995*, a pupil is not a 'member' of that organisation (*Higham v Meurig Lestyn Horton* [2004] EWCA Civ 941, [2005] ICR 292). (However, see **11.27** below for the general provisions relating to barristers.)

(c)   *Special treatment in connection with pregnancy or childbirth*

Special treatment afforded to women in connection with pregnancy or childbirth is permitted, and may not be taken account of when considering a claim of sex discrimination brought by a man: *SDA 1975, s 2(2)*. This rule is preserved under the *EA 2010* by *s 13(6)(b)*. However, in *Eversheds Legal Services Ltd v De Belin* [2011] IRLR 448, the EAT made clear that the exception is limited to such treatment as is necessary as a proportionate means of achieving the legitimate aim of compensating women for the disadvantages occasioned by their pregnancy or maternity leave. Thus, Eversheds had unlawfully discriminated against Mr De Belin when, in operating a redundancy selection procedure, they awarded his female colleague absent on maternity leave full marks for performance on the ground that she was not present at work to be assessed. The EAT held that Eversheds could have compensated the female colleague for the disadvantage she was under as a result of her maternity leave by assessing her performance during the period she was last at work. Since this would have been a fairer way of achieving the same aim, it followed that Eversheds had acted disproportionately and therefore unlawfully.

(d) *Special treatment of Sikhs in relation to the wearing of helmets on construction sites*

See below **11.13**.

(e) *Acts done to meet education, training or welfare needs of particular racial groups*

There is no specific exception in the *EA 2010* for such acts. However, the *RRA 1976* contains a further general exception for acts done for the purposes of protecting a particular racial group or groups. *Section 35* of the *RRA 1976* provides that nothing done by any body will be unlawful if it is done in order to afford persons of a particular racial group ('the protected group') access to facilities or services to meet the special needs of persons of that group in regard to their education, training or welfare, or any ancillary benefits. While this may appear to be a broad provision permitting positive discrimination, it is submitted that *s 35* will not render lawful an act of (negative) discrimination against a particular person or racial group unless that act is specifically done in order to provide services for the protected group. For example, it is unlikely that a trade organisation would be able to rely on this provision in order to justify having a membership consisting of only one racial group (or excluding a particular racial group) since a refusal of membership would not be directly related to the provision of services to the protected persons (though, where funds were limited, it ought to justify a refusal to provide legal services to members of the organisation if that was a 'special need' of the protected persons). This is particularly so given the specific express (and limited) provision as to positive discrimination by trade organisations (see above).

Positive action under EC law

Broadly speaking, the position in relation to positive action under EC law is, as one would expect, parallel to that under domestic law. However, the CJEU has held that *art 2(4)* of the version of *Council Directive 76/207/EEC* that was in force until 5 October 2005 (ie before the amendments made by *Council Directive 2002/73/EC*) permitted certain positively discriminatory measures. Measures permitted are those to the effect that where 'all else is equal' a female should be preferred for an appointment or promotion, provided that the measure is qualified by a requirement that consideration is given to the individual circumstances of each applicant: *Marschall v Land Nordrhein-Westfalen*: C-409/95 [2001] ICR 45, CJEU. However, where a national measure is not so qualified (*Kalanke v Freie Hansestadt Bremen*:C-450/93 [1996] ICR 314, CJEU), or that qualification is too vague to prevent appointments being made on the basis of sex alone (*Abrahamsson v Fogelqvist*:C-407/98 [2002] ICR 932, CJEU), the CJEU has held it to be incompatible with the *Directive* (cf also *EFTA Surveillance Authority v Norway*: E-1/02 [2003] IRLR 318, CJEU).

The wording of the old *art 2(4)* is wider than that of *art 2(8)*, which replaced it as from 5 October 2005 (compare 'measures to promote equal opportunity for men and women, in particular by removing existing inequalities' with the new version to be found in *art 2(8)* and *art 157(4)* of the Treaty: 'the principle of equal treatment shall not prevent any Member State from maintaining or adopting measures providing for specific advantages in order to make it easier for the under-represented sex to pursue a vocational activity or to prevent or compensate for disadvantages in professional careers'). However, it is likely that the type of positive discrimination permitted by *art 2(4)* will continue to be held by the CJEU to be permissible under the new wording of the *Treaty* and the *Directive*. Similarly, it is likely to be acceptable in relation to the other grounds of discrimination, as to which EC legislation currently provides that 'the principle of equal treatment shall not prevent any Member State from maintaining or adopting specific measures to prevent or compensate for disadvantages linked to' race, sexual orientation, etc (*Council Directive 2000/43/EC, art 5; Council Directive 2000/78/EC, art 7*). Further, with positive action now enshrined in *art 157(4)* of the *Treaty*, it is likely to be permissible for both private and public sector organisations positively to discriminate in this manner. Indeed, Parliament has assumed this to be the case by enacting *ss 158* and *159* of the *EA 2010*.

11.10A CHARITIES

Section 193 of the *EA 2010* sets out a number of exceptions to the Act for charities. By *s 193(1)* and *(2)*, a person is deemed not to contravene the *Act* if he restricts the provision of benefits to persons who share a protected characteristic if he does so pursuant to a charitable instrument and the provision of the benefits is (a) a proportionate means of achieving a legitimate aim or (b) for the purpose of preventing or compensating for a disadvantage linked to the protected characteristic. However, save for the protected characteristic of disability, this exception does not apply where the benefit in question is vocational training: *s 193(9)* and *(10)*.

Further, there are special rules about charitable instruments that refer to the provision of benefits by reference to 'colour'. By *s 193(4)* if a charitable instrument enables the provision of benefits to persons of a class defined solely by reference to colour, then henceforth the instrument has effect as if that reference were deleted and the instrument applied to persons generally. Where a charitable instrument refers to characteristics other than colour, it has effect as if the reference to colour were ignored. Further, the Charities Commission (or other charity regulator) does not contravene the *Act* only by exercising a function in relation to a charity in a manner which the regulator thinks is expedient in the interests of the charity, having regard to the charitable instrument.

By *s 193(3)* it is not a contravention of the *EA 2010* for a person who provides supported employment to treat persons who have the same disability (or a disability of a prescribed description) more favourably than those who do not have that disability (or a disability of such a description).

By *s 193(5)* it is not a contravention of the *EA 2010* for a charity that as of 18 May 2005 required members, or persons wishing to become members, to make a statement which asserts or implies membership or acceptance of a religion or belief to continue to do so. For this purpose, restricting the access by members to a benefit, facility or service to those who make such a statement is to be treated as imposing such a requirement. No new charity can impose such a requirement, however. Nor can a charity that formerly had such a requirement, but ceased to impose it for any period.

By *s 193(7)* it is not a contravention of the *Act* for a service provider, in relation to an activity which is carried on for the purpose of promoting or supporting a charity, to restrict participation in the activity to persons of one sex.

11.11 EXCEPTIONS SPECIFIC TO THE DIFFERENT GROUNDS OF DISCRIMINATION

Exceptions for sex discrimination

(a) *Where communal accommodation is provided*

The *EA 2010* provides an exception for any act of sex discrimination or gender reassignment discrimination done in relation to the admission of persons to communal accommodation, or the provision of a benefit, facility or service linked to the accommodation (*para 3(1)* of *Sch 23*). 'Communal accommodation' is defined as 'residential accommodation which includes dormitories or other shared sleeping accommodation which for reasons of privacy should be used only be persons of the same sex (*para 3(5)*). It can also include residential accommodation all or part of which should be used only by persons of the same sex because of the nature of the sanitary facilities serving the accommodation (*para 3(6)(c)*). A benefit, facility or service is linked to communal accommodation if it cannot properly and effectively be provided except for those using the accommodation (*para 3(7)(a)*).

For the exception to apply, the accommodation must be managed in a way which is as fair as possible to both men and women (*para 3(2)* and *3(7)(b)*). In determining whether the exception applies, account must be taken of whether and how far it is reasonable to expect that the accommodation should be altered or extended or that further accommodation should be provided, and of the frequency of the demand or need for use of the accommodation by persons of one sex as compared with those of the other (*para 3(3)*). Where the discrimination is on grounds of gender reassignment, account must also be taken of whether and how far the conduct in question is a proportionate means of achieving a legitimate aim (*para 3(4)*).

The provision in the *EA 2010* is substantially the same as that which applies under ss *46(3)–(5)* of the *SDA 1975*.

The exception means that if, for example, a company provided a holiday home for its employees but the sleeping arrangements were only suitable for men, then provided that it was only used occasionally and it was impractical to modify it for the use of the women or to build additional accommodation for them, such discrimination may be lawful.

Similarly, if a firm ran a residential training course in northern Scotland and accommodation could only be provided for men and it was fair so to do, failure to make the course available to women would not be unlawful discrimination because the benefit (the residential training course) is linked to the communal accommodation and cannot be properly and effectively provided without it.

Arrangements to compensate for detriment

It should be noted that sex discrimination is only permitted in the above circumstances where such arrangements as are reasonably practicable have been made to compensate for any detriment caused by the discrimination (*EA 2010, para 3(8)* of *Sch 23*; *SDA 1975, s 46(6)*). For example, training courses run by the ABC Company for a few days in the north of Scotland are not available to women employees because of the unsuitability of the accommodation: the company will *not* have a defence against a claim alleging discrimination unless it can show either that an alternative course had been provided or that, having been considered carefully, it was thought with good reason not to be practicable to provide it.

(b) *Pay*

For all grounds of discrimination other than sex, differences in pay fall to be considered under the general provisions on discrimination. Under the *SDA 1975, s 6(5) and (6)*, however, offering or paying a woman less remuneration than a man is not an act of unlawful discrimination. Instead, it will, if certain conditions are satisfied, be unlawful under the *Equal Pay Act 1970* ('*EqPA 1970*'). Thus, if a woman is engaged on like work or on work rated as equivalent to that of a man or on work of equal value to that of a man, a woman's contract will be modified by the *EqPA 1970* (through the mechanism of a statutorily-implied equality clause) so that she can claim pay equal to that which the man receives (see EQUAL PAY **(21)**). Less favourable treatment in relation to pay will still be an act of unlawful discrimination under the *SDA 1975* if the victim is a transsexual (*SDA 1975, s 6(8)*).

The same exclusionary rule applies under the *EA 2010*. Differences in pay that relate to terms in a woman's contract are covered by *ss 64–69 of the EA 2010* (which effectively re-enact the provisions of the *EqPA 1970*). However, by virtue of *s 70* the 'ordinary' sex discrimination provisions are disapplied in circumstances where the claim relates to a term of the woman's contract that falls to be modified by the statutory equality clause. They are also disapplied where the claim relates to contractual pay, but the statutory equality clause has no effect, unless the difference in pay constitutes direct discrimination under *ss 13* or *14* of the *Act* (*s 71*).

A similar exclusionary rule operates in respect of the new maternity equality clause created by the *EA 2010*: see *ss 72–76* of the Act.

(c) *Retirement, death and related benefits*

Sex discrimination in relation to death and retirement benefits is partially excluded from the scope of the *SDA 1975* by *s 6(4)*. Instead, such discrimination is dealt with primarily by the *Pensions Act 1995*. Sections 62 and 64 of the *Pensions Act 1995* imply into the rules of every occupational pension scheme an 'equal treatment rule' which operates in the same way as the more familiar 'equality clause' in the *Equal Pay Act 1970* (cf **21.5** EQUAL PAY). The partial exclusion under *s 6(4)* applies to discrimination taking the following forms:

(i)   Discrimination in the terms on which the woman is offered employment;

(ii)   Discrimination in the way the woman is afforded access to benefits etc.;

(iii)   Discriminatory dismissals; and

(iv)   Discriminatory subjection to any other detriment.

Where a person discriminates against a woman in one of those respects in relation to her membership of, or rights under, an occupational pension scheme, that discrimination will not be unlawful where, if provision had been made for that discrimination in the terms of the scheme, that term would have been compliant with the equal treatment rule in the *Pensions Act 1995*.

Note that it is unlawful to apply different compulsory retirement ages to men and women and that the *SDA 1975* still applies in relation to death and retirement benefits where the victim of the discrimination is a transsexual (*SDA 1975, s 6(8)*).

Similar provision is made for occupational pension schemes under *EA 2010*: see *ss 61–63* and *66–68*.

A fuller account of the equal opportunities issues relating to death or retirement benefits is set out in **21.16** EQUAL PAY and see also RETIREMENT **(40)**.

(d) *Members of the armed forces*

Broadly speaking, since 1 October 1997, the equality legislation applies to service in the armed forces as it does to other employment: cf the *Sex Discrimination (Complaints to Employment Tribunals) (Armed Forces) Regulations 1997 (SI 1997/2163)*, the *Race Relations (Complaints to Employment Tribunals) (Armed Forces) Regulations 1997 (SI 1997/2161)*; *RBR 2003, reg 36*; *SOR 2003, reg 36*; and see below **11.36**.

11.11 Discrimination and Equal Opportunities – II

Under the *EA 2010* there is a single exception for discrimination against women and transsexuals for service in the armed forces. The exception applies if it can be shown that the discrimination is a proportionate means of ensuring the combat effectiveness of the armed forces (*para 4, Sch 9*).

A similar exception for any act done 'for the purpose of ensuring the combat effectiveness of the armed forces' applies under the *SDA 1975, s 85(4)*. This was inserted into the *SDA 1975* by the *Sex Discrimination Act 1975 (Application to Armed Forces, etc) Regulations 1994 (SI 1994/3276)*. Its introduction raised a question as to whether the provisions of the *SDA 1975* complied with the *Equal Treatment Directive (Directive 76/207/EEC)*. The exemption was relied upon by the Army Board in *Sirdar v Army Board*: C-273/97 [2000] ICR 130. A woman who had applied to work as a chef in the Royal Marines was refused a transfer on the grounds that chefs were expected, where necessary, to be capable of fighting as a member of a commando unit. The complainant argued that *SDA 1975, s 85(4)* was contrary to the *Directive 76/207/EEC*. The matter was referred to the European court, which decided that whilst it was true that there was no Treaty right to derogate from equality legislation on grounds of national security, *art 2(2)* of the *ETD* nevertheless allowed the Army Board to refuse the complainant her transfer. *Article 2(2)* provides that *Directive 76/207/EEC* is 'without prejudice to the right of Member States to exclude from [the Directive's] field of application those occupational activities and, where appropriate, the training leading thereto, for which, by reason of their nature or the context in which they are carried out, the sex of the worker constitutes a determining factor'. In effect, the CJEU seems to have decided that being male is a genuine occupational requirement for a Royal Marine.

Prior to 1 October 2005, there was another exception available under the *SDA 1975* for sex discrimination in admission to the Army Cadet Force, Air Training Corps, Sea Cadet Corps, Combined Cadet Force, or any other cadet training corps for the time being administered by the Ministry of Defence was not unlawful (*SDA 1975, s 85(5)*). However, this was deleted by *reg 34* of the *Sex Discrimination Regulations 2005*.

(e) *Police officers*

Discrimination in height requirements and uniform or uniform allowances, which would otherwise constitute sex discrimination, is lawful in the employment of police constables (*SDA 1975, s 17(2), (3)*).

This exception is not included in the *EA 2010*. Such discrimination will only be lawful if it falls within the general exception for occupational requirements: see above **11.2**.

(f) *Prison officers*

Discrimination is lawful between male and female prison officers as to requirements relating to height (*SDA 1975, s 18(1)*). Men may be governors of women's prisons (*SDA 1975, s 18(2)*).

This exception is not included in the *EA 2010*. Such discrimination will only be lawful if it falls within the general exception for occupational requirements: see above **11.2**.

(g) *Ministers of religion*

Generally speaking, ministers of religion will be regarded as employees under employment legislation: see *Percy v Board of National Mission of the Church of Scotland* [2005] UKHL 73, [2006] ICR 134, although cf *New Testament Church of God v Stewart* [2007] EWCA Civ 1004, [2008] ICR 282 and *Moore v President of the Methodist Conference* [2013] UKSC 29, [2013] 2 WLR 1350. However, prior to 1 October 2005, there was an exception under the *SDA 1975* for employment for the purposes of an organised religion where a particular post-holder was required to be either male or female (or required not to be a transsexual) in order to comply with the doctrines of the religion or to avoid offending the religious susceptibilities of a significant number of its followers (*SDA 1975, s 19(1), (3), (4)*). That exemption was preserved, but with some changes, by *reg 20* of the *Sex Discrimination Regulations 2005* (which amended *SDA 1975, s 19* with effect from 1 October 2005). The amended version of *s 19* provided an exemption for employment for purposes of an organised religion where a requirement is applied that:

(a)   the employee be of a particular sex;

(b)   the employee not be undergoing or have undergone gender reassignment;

(c)   the employee not be married, or not be a civil partner;

(d)   the employee not have a living former spouse or civil partner (or that the employee's spouse or civil partner not have a living former spouse or civil partner); or

(e)   as to how the person, or the person's spouse or civil partner as at any time ceased to be married or ceased to be a civil partner.

The exemption only applied if the requirement in question was applied either so as to comply with the doctrines of the religion or because of the nature of the employment and context in which it is carried out, so as to avoid conflicting with the strongly-held religious convictions of a significant number of the religion's followers.

This exception is not included in the *EA 2010*. Such discrimination is only lawful if it falls within the general exception for occupational requirements: see above **11.2**, **11.3** and **11.7**.

(h) *Sports and competitions*

Section 44 of the *SDA 1975* excludes from the scope of the *SDA 1975* any act that relates to participation as a competitor in a sport, game or other competitive activity, provided that the activity has been confined to competitors of one sex because the physical strength, stamina or physique of the average woman puts her at a disadvantage to the average man in carrying out that activity.

A similar exception applies under *s 195* of the *EA 2010*: see above **11.3**.

11.12   Exceptions for race discrimination

(a) *Skills to be exercised outside Great Britain*

The predecessor legislation applies to training a person in skills intended to be exercised wholly outside Great Britain as it does to training for skills to be exercised in Great Britain, with one exception: discrimination on grounds of colour and nationality in the provision of such training falls outside the scope of the legislation: *RRA 1976, s 6*, as amended by the *Race Relations Act 1976 (Amendment) Regulations 2003 (SI 2003/1626)*).

This exception does not apply under the *EA 2010*. There is, however, an exception (in *para 4* of *Sch 23* to the *EA 2010*) for nationality discrimination in the provision of training to non-EEA residents where the trainer thinks that the non-resident does not intend to exercise in Great Britain skills obtained as a result.

(b) *Private household*

The predecessor legislation applies to employment for the purposes of a private household as it does to businesses, with one exception: discrimination on grounds of colour and nationality in relation to employment for the purposes of a private household is excluded from the scope of the *RRA 1976* by *s 4(3)*. The question is whether the employment is for the purposes of a private household 'to a substantial degree'. Thus, an applicant for a job as a chauffeur whose primary task was to drive a car for a company chairman could bring a complaint of racial discrimination (*Heron Corpn Ltd v Commis* [1980] ICR 713).

11.12 Discrimination and Equal Opportunities – II

This exception is not available under the *EA 2010*.

(c) *Seamen recruited abroad*

Under the predecessor legislation, seamen (whether employees or contract workers) recruited abroad to work on any ship may lawfully be discriminated against on grounds of their nationality unless their work is concerned with exploration of the sea bed or subsoil (or the exploitation of their natural resources) on the continental shelf, save for those parts of the continental shelf to which the law of Northern Ireland applies (*RRA 1976, s 9(1), (3)*). If the ground for the discrimination is any of the other 'racial grounds' (for which see **10.20** DISCRIMINATION AND EQUAL OPPORTUNITIES – I) they may lawfully be discriminated against in relation to their pay but not otherwise. 'Pay' includes retirement or death benefits (*RRA 1976, s 9(5)*, as amended by the *Race Relations Act 1976 (Amendment) Regulations 2003 (SI 2003/1626)*). There are no equivalent provisions in relation to sex discrimination or discrimination on grounds of religion, belief or sexual orientation.

This exception is not available under the *EA 2010*.

(d) *Sports and competitions*

Discrimination on the basis of a person's nationality, place of birth, or length of time for which he has been resident in a particular area will not be unlawful if it is done in selecting a person to represent a country, place or area, or any related association, in any sport or game (*RRA 1976, s 39*).

This exception is preserved in the *EA 2010* by *ss 195(5)* and *(6)*.

11.13 Exception for protection of Sikhs from discrimination in connection with requirements as to wearing of safety helmets

Properly speaking, this is not an exception, but a limitation on the availability of the defence of justification. Thus, where:

(a)   any person applies to a Sikh any provision, criterion or practice relating to the wearing by him of a safety helmet while he is on a construction site; and

(b)   at the time when he so applies the provision, criterion or practice that person has no reasonable grounds for believing that the Sikh would not wear a turban at all times when on such a site,

the provision, criterion or practice is taken to be one which cannot be shown to be a proportionate means of achieving a legitimate aim. It follows that the act of indirect discrimination will not be justified (see **11.9** above) (*reg 26(1)*).

Any special treatment afforded to a Sikh in consequence of *s 11(1)* or *11(2)* of the *Employment Act 1989* (exemption of Sikhs from requirements as to wearing of safety helmets on construction sites) is not to be regarded as giving rise, in relation to any other person, to any direct or indirect discrimination (*reg 26(2)*).

For the purposes of *reg 26* 'construction site' means any place in Great Britain where any building operations or works of engineering construction are being undertaken, but does not include any site within the territorial sea adjacent to Great Britain unless there are being undertaken on that site such operations or works as are activities falling within *art 8(1)(a)* of the *Health and Safety at Work etc Act 1974 (Application outside Great Britain) Order 2001*. 'Safety helmet' means 'any form of protective headgear'. 'Sikh' means 'a follower of the Sikh religion' and any reference to a Sikh being on a construction site is a reference 'to his being there whether while at work or otherwise' (*reg 26(3)* and *(4)*).

Since the coming into force of the *EA 2010*, this exception is preserved by dint of amendments to *s 12* of the *Employment Act 1989* by virtue of which discrimination in relation to the wearing of safety helmets by Sikhs is deemed to be lawful for the purposes of the *EA 2010*: see *para 5* of *Sch 27* to the *EA 2010*.

11.14 Exception for sexual orientation discrimination: benefits dependent on marital or civil partnership status

Any benefit to which access is dependent on marital status is likely to be indirectly discriminatory against homosexuals as homosexuals are not currently permitted to marry under national law, but only to become civil partners under the *Civil Partnership Act 2004*. Prior to 5 December 2005, *reg 25* of the *SOR 2003* nevertheless provided expressly that nothing in the *SOR 2003* should make it unlawful for an employer to prevent or restrict access to a benefit by reference to marital status. It was argued in *R (Amicus-MSF) v Secretary of State for Trade and Industry* [2004] EWHC 860 (Admin), [2004] IRLR 430 that *reg 25* was incompatible with the governing European *Directive 2000/78/EC*). Richards J held that *reg 25* was compatible because it reflected the limitation in *Recital 2* of the *Directive* which says that 'this *Directive* is without prejudice to national laws on marital status and the benefits dependent thereon'.

The provision was nevertheless amended with effect from 5 December 2005. It provided for a complete exclusion from the *SOR 2003* 'for anything which prevents or restricts access to a benefit by reference to marital status where the right to the benefit accrued or the benefit is payable in respect of periods of service prior to the coming into force of the *Civil Partnership Act 2004*' (ie prior to 5 December 2005). Where the right to the benefit accrues, or the benefit is payable, after that date, however, an employer is no longer permitted to make any distinction between married persons and civil partners. An employer may still, however, make a particular benefit available to, say, married persons and civil partners, but withhold the benefit from other employees, including those in long-term heterosexual or homosexual relationships. Under the *EA 2010* the exception in *reg 25* of the *SOR 2003* was preserved by *para 18* of *Sch 9* to the *EA 2010*.

The decision of the CJEU in *Maruko v Versorgungsanstalt der deutschen Bühnen*: C-267/06 [2008] IRLR 450 the CJEU showed that the amendment to the *SOR 2003* effected on 5 December 2005 was in fact required under EC law in any event. (In *Maruko* the CJEU held that it was unlawful for Germany to withhold a widower's pension from the widower of a civil partner, where it would have been payable to a married partner.) The *Maruko* judgment, and the subsequent judgment in *Jurgen Romer v Freie und Hansestadt Hamburg*: C-147/08 (10 May 2011), provided an indication, however, that under EU law it may not be permissible for UK legislation to limit the retrospective effect of the amendment made on 5 December 2005. In *Walker v Innospec Ltd* [2013] Pens LR 21 a Manchester Employment Tribunal determined that a provision of a pension scheme that prevented the civil partner of a member from being entitled to the same benefit as the married partner of a member breached the non-discrimination rule *ab initio*. The claimant was therefore entitled to benefit on the same terms as a married partner both in respect of benefits accrued before and after 4 December 2005. The Employment Tribunal considered that the point was sufficiently clear following *Maruko* and *Romer* that it was unnecessary to make a reference to the CJEU. It does not appear that the judgment is to be subject to appeal either. In principle, therefore, the point is still an 'open' one as a decision of the Employment Tribunal will not be binding on any other court or tribunal.

Employers should note that 'civil partnership' is defined in detail in the *Civil Partnership Act 2004* ('*CPA 2004*'). It includes not only those couples who have registered their partnership in the UK since the coming into force of that *Act*, but also those couples who have registered their partnership overseas whether before or after the coming into force of the *CPA 2004*. A large number of partnerships registered overseas are automatically to be recognised as 'civil partnerships' under the *CPA 2004*. These are listed in *Sch 20* to the *Act*. Other partnerships may be recognised if the conditions in *ss 212* to *218* of the *CPA 2004* (readers are referred to the text of the *Act*). Where a 'civil partnership' is recognised under the *CPA 2004*, it must also be recognised by employers for the purposes of *reg 25* of the *SOR 2003*.

11.15   Exceptions for age discrimination

(a) Retirement

Prior to 6 April 2011 there was an exception for retirement in the *AR 2006* as set out below. Under the *EA 2010*, the exception for retirement dismissals was preserved until 6 April 2011 so that at or over the age of 65 if retirement is the reason for the dismissal the dismissal was not unlawful by virtue of *Part 10* of the *Employment Rights Act 1996* (*para 8, Part 2, Sch 9*). Further, it was not unlawful for an employer to discriminate against employees who are close to retirement in certain respects. In particular, under *para 9* of *Part 2* of *Sch 9* to *EA 2010*, it was not unlawful for an employer to refuse to offer employment to an employee who is, or will be before the end of six months beginning with the date on which the application for employment had to be made, aged over 65, or, where this is higher, the normal retirement age for the employment concerned. These exceptions no longer apply. Since 6 April 2011 the *Employment Equality (Repeal of Retirement Age Provisions) Regulations 2011 (SI 2011/1069)* have phased out the designated retirement age in *reg 30* of the *AR 2006* so that (at the latest from October 2012) these exceptions are no longer available and whether or not retirements and related provisions are justified falls to be considered in accordance with the standard principles for justifying direct age discrimination. See also **11.9** above for discussion of justification of retirement and related provisions under the general discrimination principles. See **40.4** Retirement for the current law on retirement.

Prior to 6 April 2011, *reg 30(2)* of *AR 2006* provided that nothing in *Parts 2* or *3* of *AR 2006* 'shall render unlawful the dismissal of a person to whom this regulation applies at or over the age of 65 where the reason for the dismissal is retirement'. This exception, often dubbed the 'National Default Retirement Age' or 'NDRA', only applied to the dismissal of employees in the narrower sense of those employed on a contract of employment. There was no maximum age exemption for enforced retirement in other cases. An important example is that of partners, office holders and workers who are not employees. In such cases, any enforced retirement is unlawful unless the action can be justified. This can be illustrated by two recent decisions. In *Seldon v Clarkson Wright & Jakes* [2012] UKSC 16, [2012] ICR 716, the claimant was an equity partner in a solicitors' firm. As he was not an employee, the respondent's only defence to a compulsory retirement age of 65 was objective justification. This defence succeeded before the Tribunal, but the EAT held that retirement at 65 was not justified by the assumption that performance would decline around that age – an older age could have been chosen. The CA upheld the EAT's decision, but observed that once it was accepted (as it was) that retirement had a legitimate aim, it was difficult to see how selection of the age of 65 was not justified, particularly as that was still at that stage the national default retirement age for employees. The SC, however, held that the Tribunal had taken the wrong approach to considering whether or not a retirement age of 65 was justified and accordingly remitted the matter. See further above **11.9** for the approach to be taken to considering whether or not direct age discrimination (including the application of retirement ages) is justified. For further examples of when retirement ages may or may not be justified see **11.9** above.

Whether or not the reason for dismissal is retirement depends on the application of specific criteria set out in detailed provisions of *AR 2006*. See **40.3** Retirement.

'Heyday', part of Age Concern, brought judicial review proceedings challenging the legality of *AR 2006* on the ground that the blanket exception for retirement over 65 did not properly transpose the *Equality Directive*. The Administrative Court referred the matter to the Court of Justice of the European Union for a preliminary ruling. The CJEU held that *reg 30* was not necessarily unlawful but that it would be for the national court to determine whether the blanket exception for those dismissed at or over the age of 65 was justified. On its return to the Administrative Court (*R (on the application of Age UK) v Secretary of State for Business, Innovation & Skills* [2010] ICR 260), Blake J held that the NDRA was based upon a social policy aim of certainty, clarity and maintaining confidence in the labour market and that it was proportionate for there to be such a blanket exception. The judge further held that the choice of age of 65 was within the margin of appreciation when it was adopted in 2006 but that the conclusion might have been different had there been no suggestion of an upcoming government review. Blake J also indicated that he did not presently see how 65 could remain as the appropriate age after that review.

See **40.4** RETIREMENT for the current law on retirement.

(b) National minimum wage

The National Minimum Wage ('NMW') legislation allows for lower sums to be paid to younger workers. *Regulation 31* of *EA 2006* allowed employers to retain different pay between the bands but only if the younger workers are being paid less than the adult NMW. Surprisingly, if the employer pays the younger workers more than the adult NMW, but less than older employees, this will require objective justification.

The equivalent provision in *EA 2010* is *para 11* of *Part 2* of *Schedule 9*. See also *para 12* of *Part 2* in relation to apprentices.

(c) Certain benefits based on length of service

Regulation 32 of *AR 2006* makes some provision for employers to provide benefits to employees by reference to the length of their service.

The exception applies where a person ('A'), in relation to the award of any benefit by him, puts a worker ('B') at a disadvantage when compared to another worker ('C') if and to the extent that the disadvantage suffered by B is because B's length of service is less than that of C (*reg 32(1)*).

Where B's length of service is longer than five years, it must reasonably appear to A that the way in which the criterion of length of service is used fulfils a business need. Examples are given of encouraging loyalty or motivation, or rewarding experience (*reg 32(2)*).

'Benefit' does not include any benefit awarded to a worker by virtue of his ceasing to work for A (*reg 32(7)*).

In *Rolls Royce Plc v Unite the Union* [2009] EWCA Civ 387, [2010] 1 WLR 318, [2010] ICR 1, the Court of Appeal held that length of service criterion was capable of constituting 'the award of any benefit'. A majority also held that a length of service criterion of more than five years would reasonably fulfil the employer's need for a loyal and stable workforce and that, despite the wording of *reg 32(2)*, it was not necessary for the employer to itself believe that a business need was served.

There is some complication about the identification of the relevant five-year period. The employer can decide whether to determine this by reference to the total length of time the worker has been working for the employer, or the length of time the worker has been working for him doing work which he reasonably considers to be at or above a particular level (*reg 32(3)*).

In calculating the length of time a worker has been working for him, a person must calculate the length of time in terms of the number of weeks during the whole or part of which the worker was working for him (*reg 32(4)(a)*). The employer may discount any period during which the worker was absent from work (unless in all the circumstances, including the way in which other workers' similar absences have been treated, it is not reasonable to do so) (*reg 32(4)(b)*). The employer may also discount any period during which the worker was present at work where that preceded a period of absence and, in all the circumstances including the length of the absence, the reason for the absence, its effect on the worker's ability to discharge his duties, and the way in which other workers are treated, it is reasonable for the period to be discounted (*reg 32(4)(c)*).

Further, a worker is treated as having worked for A during any period during which he worked for another, if required to do so by *s 218 ERA 1996* (see CONTINUOUS EMPLOYMENT (6)).

The broadly equivalent provision in *EA 2010* to *reg 32* is *para 10* of *Part 2* of *Schedule 9*. *Paragraph 10* refers not only to benefits but also to facilities and services. It also expressly rules out those provided only by virtue of a person's ceasing to work (*para 10(7)*). Sub-paragraphs *10(3)* to *10(6)* explain how the length of service may be calculated.

(d) Enhanced redundancy benefits

Regulation 33 of *EA 2006* makes provision for employers to provide 'qualifying employees' with enhanced redundancy payments.

A 'qualifying employee' is an employee who is entitled to a redundancy payment by virtue of *s 135* of the *ERA 1996*, or who would be so entitled but does not have the two year qualifying period, or to an employee who agrees to the termination of his employment in circumstances where, had he been dismissed, he would have fallen into one of the former two categories.

Regulation 33 allows employers to give enhanced redundancy payments only to those who are entitled to a redundancy payment by virtue of *s 135 ERA 1996*, or those who agree to termination when, had they been dismissed, they would have been so entitled.

Employers may also give qualifying employees an enhanced redundancy payment which is less than that given to another such employee, so long as they are both 'calculated in the same way' (*reg 33(1)(a)*).

There are rules as to how the amounts must be calculated. The amount must be calculated as in the relevant provisions of the *ERA 1996* (*ss 162(1)–(3)*). However, in making the calculation, the employer may treat a week's pay as not being subject to a maximum amount, and/or multiply the appropriate amount allowed for each year of employment by a figure of more than one (*reg 33(4)(a)* and *(b)*). Having made the calculation, the employer may also increase the amount calculated by multiplying it by a figure of more than one (*reg 33(4)(c)*).

Where an enhanced redundancy scheme does not fall within this exception, it is potentially discriminatory and will fall to be justified in the usual way. For examples of this, see *MacCulloch* and *Loxley* above.

Similar provision is made in *para 13* of *Part 2* of *Schedule 9* of *EA 2010*.

(e) Provision of life assurance cover to retired workers

Regulation 34 of *EA 2006* provided an exception for the provision of life assurance to retired workers. Where an employer arranged for workers to be provided with life assurance after their early retirement on grounds of ill health, it was not unlawful to arrange for such cover to cease when the workers reached a normal retirement age, if one existed, or age 65, where there was no retirement age (*reg 34(1)*).

'Normal retirement age' means the age at which workers in the undertaking who held the same kind of position as the worker held at the time of his retirement were normally required to retire (*reg 34(2)*).

Similar provision was made in *para 14* of *Part 2* of *Schedule 9* of *EA 2010*. However, this was repealed by the *Employment Equality (Repeal of Retirement Age Provisions) Regulations 2011 (SI 2011/1069), reg 2(3)* with effect from 6 April 2011.

(f) Child care

Paragraph 15 of *Part 2* of *Schedule 9* to *EA 2010* provides that it is not unlawful age discrimination in a number of respects for a person to make arrangements for or to facilitate the provision of care for children of a particular age group. (Otherwise, this might give rise to a claim for "associative discrimination", ie where a person is discriminated against because of someone else's age: see DISCRIMINATION AND EQUAL OPPORTUNITIES – I at 10.25.) Facilitating the provision of care for a child includes paying for some or all of the cost of the provision, helping a parent to find a suitable person to provide care for the child, and enabling a parent to spend more time providing care or otherwise assisting the parent with respect to the care that they provide (*para 15(3)*). A 'child' is defined to be a person who has not attained the age of 17 (*para 15(3)* and care includes supervision (*para 15(4)*).

There was no similar provision in *EA 2006*.

(g) Contributions to personal pension schemes

A Minister of the Crown may by order (following consultation) provide that it is not an age contravention for an employer to use certain specified practices in relation to contributions to personal pension schemes (*para 16* of *Part 2* of *Schedule 9* to *EA 2010*).

11.16 Exceptions for disability discrimination

(a) Armed forces

Under the previous law, those serving in the naval, military or air forces of the Crown (*DDA 1995 s 61(7)*) were specifically excluded from the scope of the *DDA 1995*.

Paragraph 4(3) of *Schedule 9* to *EA 2010* applies the exemption in respect of "service in the armed forces".

(b) Facilities provided to the public

Where an employer is concerned with the provision (whether or not for payment) of benefits (including facilities and services) of any description to the public or to a section of the public which includes the employee in question, the sections of the *DDA 1995* relating to discrimination against a disabled employee in respect of the provision of benefits (*DDA 1995, s 4(2a); EA 2010, s 39(2)*) do not apply unless:

(i)   that provision differs in a material respect from the provision of benefits by the employer to his employees; or

(ii)   the provision of benefits to the employee in question is regulated by his contract of employment; or

(iii)   the benefits relate to training.

(*DDA 1995, s 4(3), (4); EA 2010, Sch 9, para 19*)

(c) Exemption for small businesses

As of 1 October 2004, there is no exemption for small employers from the provisions of *DDA 1995 (Amendment Regulations), reg 6*). No such exemption is included in the *EA 2010* either.

(d) Charities

Any act done by a charity pursuant to any charitable purpose connected with categories of persons determined by reference to any physical or mental capacity will not be unlawful under the employment provisions of the *DDA 1995* (*DDA 1995, s 18C*). See *EA 2010, s 193* for the current provisions relating to charities.

(e) Statutory office holders, police and prison officers, members of fire brigades

Whereas these and other categories of worker were excluded from the employment provisions of the *DDA 1995* prior to 1 October 2004, those provisions now apply to all employers in respect of people they employ to work wholly or partly at an establishment in Great Britain. The sole exception is in relation to the armed forces (*DDA 1995, ss 4(6), 64(7)*). See now **11.25** below for office holders generally and **11.26** below for police officers.

11.17 GENERAL EXCEPTIONS TO THE EQUALITY LEGISLATION

A number of other exceptions or defences are available to claims of both direct and indirect discrimination. As a matter of principle, these exceptions ought to be narrowly or strictly construed: *Lambeth London Borough Council v Commission for Racial Equality* [1989] IRLR 379; upheld on appeal ([1990] ICR 768) (although the principle of construction was not referred to in the judgments of the Court of Appeal).

11.18 Employment out of the territorial jurisdiction

In the *EA 2010* there are specific provisions applying the *Act* to employment on ships, hovercraft and other offshore work: see *ss 81–83*. However, otherwise the *EA 2010* does not include any specific provisions as to its territorial extent. It follows that whether or not a particular employment or act of discrimination falls under the jurisdiction of the *EA 2010* will have to be determined according to generally applicable principles on the conflict of laws: see generally FOREIGN EMPLOYEES, **23.9**. The courts and tribunals are likely to apply the principles that have been developed in relation to claims of unfair dismissal brought under the *Employment Rights Act 1996* ('*ERA 1996*') as that statute too contains no specific provision about territorial extent.

The case law as it has developed in relation to claims under the *ERA 1996* may be summarised as follows. The House of Lords in *Lawson v Serco Ltd* [2006] IRLR 289 held that an employment tribunal would have jurisdiction to consider a claim of unfair dismissal by an employee if he was 'employed in Great Britain'. Lord Hoffmann identified three potential categories of employee who would be regarded as 'employed in Great Britain' (ibid at paras 25-40):

The 'standard' case: an employee 'working in Great Britain' at the time of his dismissal (otherwise than on a casual visit);

The 'peripatetic' employee (such as an airline pilot): an employee based in Great Britain at the time of his dismissal;

The 'expatriate' case (ie an employee living, working and based abroad): normally such employment would be outside the territorial jurisdiction of the UK, unless the employee had 'strong connections' with Great Britain and British employment law.

Lord Hoffmann gave two examples of expatriate employees who would fall within the territorial jurisdiction of the *ERA 1996*: those posted abroad by a British employer for the purposes of a business carried on in Great Britain (such as a foreign correspondent on the staff of a British newspaper) and those expatriate employees of a British employer operating within what is in practice a British enclave in a foreign country (such as a British military base).

In *Ravat v Halliburton Manufacturing & Services Ltd* [2012] IRLR 315, the Supreme Court emphasised that Lord Hoffmann's three categories are merely examples of the application of the general principle that, in order for the Tribunal to have jurisdiction, the employee's employment must have much stronger connections with both Great Britain and with British employment law than with any other system of law. Their Lordships held that although the three categories were helpful, it was important to remember that there was no requirement of 'exceptionality' for expatriate employees. If they had strong connections with Great Britain and British employment law, then the Tribunal would have jurisdiction. This particular case concerned an employee who lived in Preston, Lancashire, but who was employed by a British subsidiary of an American multinational corporation to provide services to that corporation's German company and as a result spent half his time living and working in Libya and half of it living and working in the UK. The employment tribunal held that the claimant had a sufficiently strong connection with the UK to fall within the jurisdiction of the *ERA 1996*. The Scottish EAT reversed that decision, but the Court of Session restored the decision of the Tribunal and the Supreme Court upheld the Court of Session's decision. Their Lordships considered it to be important that the employer's business was in truth based in Great Britain, and that the employee had been treated as a 'commuter', being given assurances that his posting to Libya would not affect the benefits to which he would have been entitled as a UK-based employee and that the law of his contract would remain that of Britain. In practice his employment had continued to be managed from the employer's human resources department in Aberdeen, and the employee had maintained his home in Great Britain. See also *Ministry of Defence v Wallis* [2010] IRLR 1035.

In *Bates van Winkelhof v Clyde & Co LLP* [2012] EWCA Civ 1207, [2012] IRLR 992 the Court of Appeal had to consider whether or not UK employment tribunals had jurisdiction over discrimination claims brought by a solicitor who was a member of a UK LLP, but seconded to, and employed under, a contract with, a Tanzanian law firm. The employer argued that the Supreme Court in *Ravat* had held that in such cases it was necessary for a comparative exercise to be carried out by the Tribunal in order to ascertain whether the employee's connections with Great Britain were stronger than those with the territory in which he or she works. The Court of Appeal in Bates, however, clarified that such a comparative exercise is not required unless the employee is employed wholly abroad. In this case, where the claimant worked for at least part of her time in Great Britain, the only question was whether the connection with Great Britain was (to use Lord Hope's words in *Ravat*) "sufficiently strong to enable it to be said that Parliament would have regarded it as appropriate for the tribunal to deal with the claim".

The approach to be applied where the employee is not working at the date of dismissal was considered in *YKK Europe Ltd v Heneghan* [2010] IRLR 563. The EAT held that in these cases a broader factual inquiry will be required. The Tribunal will need to consider (among other things):   why the employee was absent from work, the length of his absence before dismissal, where he was working or based (and for how long) before his absence from work began, where the employee would have been working at the time of dismissal if he had not been absent from work, whether there was an active employment relationship between the date of his absence from work and the date of dismissal, from where the contract was being operated at dismissal, and whether the tribunal would have had territorial jurisdiction as at the date on which the claimant became absent from work. No factor is determinative and the weight to be given to the factors is for the tribunal. The EAT remitted the matter to the Tribunal to determine the question of jurisdiction.

The EAT in *Pervez v Macquarie Bank Ltd* [2011] IRLR 284 has recently confirmed that the principles discussed above are not 'cut down' in any way by *reg 19(1)* of the *Employment Tribunals (Constitution and Rules of Procedure) Regulations 2004* ("*the 2004 Regulations*"), which provides that an employment tribunal in England or Wales 'shall only have jurisdiction to deal with proceedings . . . where . . . one of the respondents resides or carries on business in England and Wales'. The EAT held that a respondent should be regarded as carrying on a business in England or Wales if it has (for eg) a peripatetic employee who is based here.

The above contrasts with the situation under the predecessor legislation, where specific provision is made as to the territorial extent of the Acts and Regulations. Broadly speaking, the predecessor equality legislation applies where a complainant does his work wholly or partly in Great Britain and does not apply where the complainant works wholly outside Great Britain (*RRA 1976, ss 4, 8(1), (1A); SDA 1975, ss 6(1), 10(1)*, both as amended; *RBR 2003, reg 9(1); SOR 2003, reg 9(1); AR 2006, reg 10(10)*. The question is whether, viewing the complainant's employment as a whole, he does his work wholly outside Great Britain (*Saggar v Ministry of Defence* [2005] EWCA Civ 413, [2005] ICR 1073). In setting out this test, the Court of Appeal in *Saggar* expressly disapproved the approach of the tribunal and the EAT, which had been to consider where the employee worked during the period in which the discrimination was alleged to have occurred. The tribunal and EAT had understood this to be the approach dictated by the Court of Appeal in *Carver (nee Mascarenhas) v Saudi Arabian Airlines* [1999] ICR 991. However, in *Saggar*, the Court of Appeal considered that the Court of Appeal in *Carver* had not laid down such a test. The EAT in *Saggar* ([2004] ICR 1708) suggested that a one-day working visit to Great Britain would not be sufficient to bring an employee within the tribunal's jurisdiction. This is probably still correct, notwithstanding the Court of Appeal's decision in that case. Where a discrimination complaint relates to a series of acts done over a period of time where the employee was initially working 'wholly outside' Great Britain, but then moved to work for the same employer in Great Britain, the fact that the series of acts amounts to a 'continuing act' or an 'act extending over a period' (cf *Hendricks v Metropolitan Police Comr* [2002] EWCA Civ 1686, [2003] ICR 530, [2003] IRLR 96) does not mean that the UK employment tribunals have jurisdiction over that part of the 'continuing act' which was done outside of Great Britain. The Tribunal only has jurisdiction over that part of the 'continuing act' which took place while the employee was employed in Great Britain. See *Tradition Securities and Futures SA v X and Y* [2009] ICR 88, [2008] IRLR 934. Where discrimination occurs during recruitment, the tribunal must consider whether it was within the contemplation of the parties that the employee's duties would be performed wholly outside Great Britain (*Deria v General Council of British Shipping* [1986] ICR 172; cf also *Saggar* in the EAT). For a case where employees were held to work 'partly' in Great Britain and therefore to fall within the jurisdiction of the UK tribunals see *British Airways plc v Mak* [2011] EWCA Civ 184, [2011] All ER (D) 256 (Feb) (duties on board the aircraft and overnight stays in the UK were sufficient to constitute work 'partly' in Great Britain). In *Mak* the CA also took the opportunity to clarify that where an employee works wholly or partly in Great Britain, it matters not whether the employee works at an establishment in Great Britain.

However, there were exceptions or qualifications to the rule that the equality legislation does not apply where a complainant works wholly outside Great Britain:

(1)   The tribunal's jurisdiction will not be excluded where the employment is at an establishment in another European Union member state and applying the exclusion would involve a breach of *art 48* of the *Treaty* (which provides for the free movement of workers within the European Union): *Bossa v Nordstress Ltd* [1998] IRLR 284. (Note that where a worker is 'posted' temporarily to another Member State, national legislation relating to equality of treatment will apply by virtue of the *Posted Workers Directive (Dir EC/96/71)*: see **23.3** FOREIGN EMPLOYEES.)

(2)   Where discrimination is on grounds of race or ethnic or national origins, sexual orientation, religion or belief or (with effect from 1 October 2005) sex (but not colour or nationality), the equality legislation will still apply if:

(i)   the respondent has a place of business at an establishment in Great Britain;

(ii)   the work performed by the complainant is for the purposes of the business carried on at that establishment; and

(iii)   the complainant is ordinarily resident in Great Britain either at the time when he applies for, or is offered, the employment, or at any time during the course of the employment (*SDA 1975, s 10(1)*, as amended by the *Sex Discrimination Regulations 2005, reg 11; RRA 1976, s 8(1A); RBR 2003, reg 9(2); SOR 2003, reg 9(2); EA 2006, reg 10(2)*). (See *Neary v Service Children's Education and ors* [2010] IRLR 1030: 'ordinarily resident' has the same meaning as that given to it by case law on income tax legislation. It refers to a person's abode in a particular place or country which he has adopted voluntarily and for settled purposes as part of the regular order of his life, whether of short or long duration. The only difference is that in discrimination cases, the focus must be on the particular situation prevailing at the time of the alleged discrimination. A person may be 'ordinarily resident' in two countries at once. However, Mr Neary, who was a teacher who had worked abroad since January 1991, and who lived and worked in Germany between April 2007 and November 2008, was to be regarded as 'ordinarily resident' in Germany in March 2008 despite (i) retaining a house in the UK (that was rented out); (ii) his German teaching contract being due to expire in November 2008; and (iii) retaining his car and his UK driving licence.)

(3)   The legislation applies to employment on board ships registered in Great Britain, except where the employee does his work wholly outside Great Britain. The ship is deemed to be the establishment at which the employee works for the purposes of the legislation (*RRA 1976, s 8(3); SDA 1975, s 10(2)(a), (3); RBR 2003, reg 9(3)(a); SOR 2003, reg 9(3)(a); DDA 1995, s 68(2); AR 2006, reg 10(3)*).

(4)   The *SDA 1975*, the *DDA 1995*, the *RBR 2003*, the *SOR 2003* and the *AR 2006* (but not the *RRA 1976*) apply to employment on aircraft or hovercraft registered in Great Britain and operated by a person who has his principal place of business, or is ordinarily resident, in Great Britain, except where the employee does his work wholly outside Great Britain. The aircraft or hovercraft is deemed to be the establishment at which the employee works for the purposes of the legislation (*SDA 1975, s 10(2)(b); DDA 1995, s 68(2), RBR 2003, reg 9(3)(b); SOR 2003, reg 9(3)(b); EA 2006, reg 10(3)(b)*).

Note also that there were specific provisions relating to employment concerned with exploration or exploitation of the sea bed or subsoil, employment on the Frigg gas field and other parts of the Continental Shelf: *RRA 1976, s 8(5); SDA 1975, s 10(5); RBR 2003, reg 9(4), (5); SOR 2003, reg 9(4), (5); DDA 1995, s 68(4A); EA 2006, reg 10(4), (5)*. The *Race Relations (Offshore Employment) Order 1987*, (*SI 1987/929*) and the *Sex Discrimination and Equal Pay (Offshore Employment) Order 1987*, (*SI 1987/930*) have been made pursuant to the powers in those provisions of the *SDA 1975* and *RRA 1975*. See now the *Equality Act 2010 (Offshore Work) Order 2010 (SI 2010/1835)* made under *s 82* of the *EA 2010*.

See also **10.42** DISCRIMINATION AND EQUAL OPPORTUNITIES – I.

11.19   Employment under an illegal contract

The test for excluding a tribunal's jurisdiction on grounds of illegality in relation to discrimination claims is not as strict as that used in cases of breach of contract. In breach of contract cases, a court or tribunal will not enforce a claim where the employment is pursuant to an illegal contract, or if there was an intention at the time of the formation of the contract to perform it illegally, or if the complainant has to rely on his or her illegal conduct in order to found his claim (*Colen v Cebrian (UK) Ltd* [2003] EWCA Civ 1676, [2004] ICR 568; though note that the court may in certain circumstances be prepared to

11.19 Discrimination and Equal Opportunities – II

'sever' the legal and illegal parts of a contract: *Blue Chip Trading Ltd v Helbawi* [2009] IRLR 128 and see generally **7.24 CONTRACT OF EMPLOYMENT**). By contrast, in discrimination cases, the fact that a contract is illegal or tainted by illegality will not exclude the tribunal's jurisdiction, unless the complainant's claim is so closely connected or inextricably bound up or linked with the complainant's illegal conduct that to allow the complainant to recover compensation would be to appear to condone that conduct (*Hall v Woolston Hall Leisure Ltd* [2001] ICR 99, CA, approving *Leighton v Michael* [1995] ICR 1091, EAT). In *Hall v Woolston Hall Leisure*, the CA held that where the complaint is concerned with a dismissal only, the fact of dismissal may not be sufficiently closely connected with the illegality as to preclude a claim. However, a claim in respect of discrimination relating to access to opportunities for promotion, transfer or training or any other benefits, facilities or services may be precluded: see *Governing Body of Addey and Stanhope School v Vakante* [2003] ICR 290, EAT, Further, the tribunal at the remitted hearing in that case decided that the dismissal as well as the manner in which the employer gave the employee access to training and other benefits were so inextricably linked with the employee's illegal conduct – obtaining employment in breach of immigration rules – that both claims were precluded. This decision was upheld on appeal: see [2004] EWCA Civ 1065, [2005] ICR 231. See also *Allen v Hounga* [2012] EWCA Civ 609, [2012] IRLR 685 where the Court of Appeal held that Ms Hounga's claim for discriminatory dismissal, as well as her claims for unfair dismissal, breach of contract, unpaid wages and holiday pay, were precluded on public policy grounds where she and her employer had conspired equally in arranging her unlawful entry into the country, on a false basis in breach of immigration rules, for the purpose of taking up the employment.

The burden of proof is on the party alleging illegality (*Colen v Cebrian (UK) Ltd*, above).

The Court of Appeal in *Woolston Hall Leisure* left undecided a question whether the limited grounds for derogation from the right not to suffer less favourable treatment conferred by *Directive 76/207/EEC* meant that illegality could not be used as a ground for refusing an employee a remedy. The point was also raised in *Vakante v Governing Body of Addey and Stanhope School (No 2)* [2004] ICR 279, EAT (in relation to the equivalent provision of the *Race Directive 2000/43/EC*). However, the Court of Appeal held that, since *Directive 2000/43* only came into force after the claimant's cause of action arose and, since it was clearly not intended to have retrospective effect, it could not assist the claimant ([2004] EWCA Civ 1065, [2005] ICR 231). This point was not revisited in *Allen v Hounga* (ibid).

11.20 Benefits provided to the public

The provisions relating to discrimination with regard to access to benefits of any description (including facilities and services) do not apply if the respondent is concerned with the provision (for payment or not) of benefits of that description to the public, or to a section of the public comprising the complainant in question, unless:

(i)   that provision differs in a material respect from the provision of the benefits to his employees (or non-employees covered by the employment rules: see below **11.24** ff); or

(ii)   the provision of the benefits to the complainant in question is regulated by his contract of employment (or equivalent for non-employees covered by the employment rules); or

(iii)   the benefits relate to training.

Para 19 of Sch 9 to the EA 2010.

The same exception applied under the predecessor legislation: see *RRA 1976, s 4(2)(b) and 4(4); SDA 1975, s 6(2)(a) and 6(7); RBR 2003, reg 6(2)(b) and 6(4); SOR 2003, reg 6(2)(b) and 6(4); AR 2006 7(6); DDA 1995, s 4(4).*

Thus, for example, a bank which provides loans to members of the public and to most employees on the same terms may not be taken to an employment tribunal by an employee who is denied a loan on grounds of race, sex, religion or belief, gender reassignment, disability, age or sexual orientation if the employee is not entitled to the loan under his contract of employment. However, it will be liable to an action by that employee in the county court under the provisions relating to discrimination in the provision of goods, facilities or services: *Part 3* of the *EA 2010*.

11.21 Discrimination in compliance with the law

In certain circumstances, it is a defence to a claim of discrimination that the act complained of was carried out in order to comply with, or pursuant to, a legal requirement. No such defence is available to claims of discrimination on grounds of religion or belief or sexual orientation.

Under the *EA 2010* regime, a person does not contravene certain provisions in relation to age, disability, religion or belief, sex or sexual orientation where the act must be done by virtue of a statutory requirement. These are set out below, together with the previous law.

There is also a general exception for discrimination on grounds of nationality and/or indirect discrimination on the basis of a person's place of ordinary residence or the length of time a person has been present or resident in the UK or an area within it that is authorised by another enactment or statutory instrument: see *para 1* of *Sch 23* to the *EA 2010*.

Racial discrimination

Prior to the amendments introduced with effect from 19 July 2003 by the *Race Relations Amendment Regulations*, there was a general defence available where the relevant act of discrimination was carried out pursuant to any enactment, Order in Council or statutory instrument, or in order to comply with a ministerial condition or requirement imposed pursuant to statute (*RRA 1976, s 41(1)*).

The scope of that provision was considered by the House of Lords in *Hampson v Department of Education and Science* [1990] ICR 511. Their Lordships held that the application of the defence was restricted to acts done in the necessary performance of an express obligation contained in an instrument, and did not extend to discretionary acts carried out by the Secretary of State, even in circumstances where he had a positive public duty to exercise his discretion. (See also *Dhatt v McDonalds Hamburgers Ltd* [1991] ICR 238.)

From 19 July 2003, the position was as follows:

(a) Where discrimination is on grounds of race, ethnic or national origins, no defence is available (*RRA 1976, s 41(1A)*);

(b) Otherwise, discriminatory acts are not unlawful if performed:

    (i) in pursuance of any enactment or Order in Council;

    (ii) in pursuance of any instrument made under any enactment by a Minister of the Crown; or

    (iii) in order to comply with any condition or requirement imposed by a Minister of the Crown by virtue of any enactment (*RRA 1976, s 41(1)* as amended);

(c) Where discrimination is on grounds of the complainant's nationality, place of ordinary residence or the length of time for which he has been present or resident in or outside the UK, the defence is available in the three circumstances set out in (b) immediately above but also:

(i)   in pursuance of any arrangements made by or with the approval of, or for the time being approved by, a Minister of the Crown; or

(ii)   in order to comply with any condition imposed by a Minister of the Crown (*RRA 1976, s 41(2)(d)* and *(e)*).

For the application of the exemption in *s 41(2)(d)* for acts done pursuant to arrangements made by or with the approval of a Minister of the Crown, see *R (on the application of Mohammed) v Secretary of State for Defence* [2007] EWCA Civ 1023, [2007] All ER (D) 09 (May).

This exception is preserved under the *EA 2010*: see *para 1* of *Sch 23* to the *EA 2010*.

Sex discrimination

A respondent is not guilty of an unlawful act if he discriminates in order to comply with a statute passed before the *SDA 1975*, or a statutory instrument made or approved (whether before or after the passing of the *SDA*) by or under an act passed before the *SDA*, if such provision is one concerning the protection of women (*SDA 1975, s 51*, as substituted by *EA 1989, s 3(3)*). Thus, discrimination in order to comply with college statutes enacted under a statute prior to *SDA 1975* was considered lawful in *Hugh-Jones v St John's College, Cambridge* [1979] ICR 848. Many such statutory requirements were removed as a result of *EA 1989*.

Discriminatory action taken by an employer to ensure the health and safety of his employees will not be considered unlawful if it is taken in compliance with his statutory obligations and in order to protect the complainant (or class of women to which the complainant belongs): *SDA 1975, s 51(1)(c)(ii)* and see *Page v Freight Hire (Tank Haulage) Ltd* [1981] ICR 299.

These exceptions are not preserved under the *EA 2010* in relation to discrimination in the employment sphere. The exceptions on the grounds of statutory authority which relate to the protected characteristic of sex relate only to services and education.

Religion or belief

Under the previous law, it was no defence to a claim for discrimination on the grounds of religious belief that the alleged discriminator was acting on statutory authority.

However, *Schedule 22* to *EA 2010* provides that a person does not unlawfully discriminate on the grounds of religion or belief by doing anything that he or she must do pursuant to a requirement of an enactment or a requirement or condition imposed by virtue of an enactment.

Sexual orientation

Similarly, in relation to sexual orientation, it was no defence to a claim for discrimination that the alleged discriminator was acting on statutory authority.

Now, although an exception is provided in *Schedule 22* to *EA 2010* in relation to statutory authority, it should be noted that this does not apply to discrimination in the employment sphere.

Disability

The *DDA 1995* does not render unlawful any act done pursuant to any enactment or statutory instrument or in order to comply with a ministerial condition or requirement imposed pursuant to statute (see *EA 2010, s 191* and *Sch 22* for similar provisions).

In the employment context the *DDA 1995* does not render unlawful any act done for the purpose of safeguarding national security if the doing of that act was justified by that purpose (*DDA 1995, s 59(1), (2A), (3); EA 2010, s 192*).

Age

In relation to age, under the previous law, a discriminatory act was not unlawful if it was done in order to comply with a requirement of any statutory provision (see *reg 27* of *AR 2006*). A statutory provision means any provision of an Act or an Act of the Scottish Parliament, an instrument made by a Minister of the Crown under an Act; and an instrument made under an Act or an act of the Scottish Parliament by the Scottish Ministers of a member of the Scottish Executive. This would include, for example, the minimum age requirement to become a licensee of a public house.

In *EA 2010*, there remains an exception if a person does anything that he or she must do pursuant to a requirement of an enactment (*para 1, Sch 22*). Reference to an enactment includes a reference to a Measure of the General Synod of the Church of England as well as an enactment passed or made on or after the date on which *EA 2010* was passed (see *para 1(3)*).

11.22 National security

Under the *EA 2010* there is a single general exception to the *Act* for anything done for the purpose of safeguarding national security, provided it is proportionate to that purpose. National security may also justify an exception to the rules on making enquiries about health and disability when vetting for employment: see *s 60(14)* of the *EA 2010*.

A similar exception applies under the predecessor legislation. Discrimination on grounds of sexual orientation, religion or belief, disability or age is not unlawful if it is done for the purpose of safeguarding national security, and the discriminatory act is justified by that purpose (*RBR 2003, reg 24*; *SOR 2003, reg 24*; *DDA 1995, s 59(2A)*; *EA 2006, reg 27*). An act of sex discrimination done for the purpose of safeguarding national security is also permitted by the *SDA 1975, s 52(1)*. However, it should be noted that no such derogation is available for sex discrimination in Community law, though cf *Sirdar v Army Board*: C-273/97 [2000] ICR 130, CJEU and above **11.11**(d). The *RRA 1976* permitted race discrimination where the act in question was done for the purpose of safeguarding national security and was justified by that purpose: *RRA 1976, s 42*.

Note also that, before the passing of the *Sex Discrimination (Amendment) Order 1988 (SI 1988/249)*, a certificate signed by, or on behalf of, a Minister of the Crown and certifying that an act specified in the certificate was done for the purpose of safeguarding national security was conclusive evidence that it was done for that purpose (*SDA 1975, s 52(2)*). However, following the amendments made by *SI 1988/249*, the defence no longer applies to discrimination in employment and related areas. This followed the decision of the Court of Justice of the European Union in *Johnston v Chief Constable of the Royal Ulster Constabulary* (Case 222/84) [1987] ICR 83, CJEU whereby a provision in a Northern Ireland Order, similar to the unamended *SDA 1975, s 52(2)*, was held to be contrary to *art 6* of *Directive 76/207/EEC* (see **22.6** EUROPEAN UNION LAW).

See also **11.11**(d) above for the exceptions relating to sex discrimination in the armed forces.

11.23 Employees working for those with State immunity

The immunity conferred by the *State Immunity Act 1978, s 16(1)(a)* extends to claims of discrimination. The provision does not infringe *art 6(1)* of the *European Convention on Human Rights*: *Fogarty v United Kingdom* [2002] IRLR 148, ECtHR. However, note that the Tribunal will scrutinise whether or not the employment in question in fact falls within the scope of the immunity. A restrictive approach will be taken. The question is whether the employment is part of the function of the diplomat in his mission. In *Abusabib v Taddese* [2013] ICR 603 the EAT held that a domestic servant employed solely in the diplomat's home was not part of the function of the mission and therefore he could not hide behind state immunity to avoid a discrimination claim. See also *Wokuri v Kassam* [2012] EWHC 105 (Ch), [2013] Ch 80.

11.24 NON-EMPLOYEES AND NON-EMPLOYERS COVERED BY THE EMPLOYMENT RULES

Contract workers

In recent times there has been a marked trend towards the use of contract workers. Contract workers are parties to a tri-partite arrangement. The first party is the person who has work which needs doing. He is known as the 'principal'. The principal enters into a contract with a second party who is obliged to supply employees to perform the work. The employees are known as 'contract workers' in relation to the principal.

Under the *EA 2010*, contract workers are covered by *s 41*. *Sections 41(1)* and *(3)* prohibit discrimination and victimisation of contract workers by 'principals':

(i)   as to the terms on which the principal allows the worker to do the work;

(ii)   by not allowing him to do it or continue to do it;

(iii)   in the way he affords him access to any benefits or by refusing or deliberately not affording him access to them; or

(iv)   by subjecting him to any other detriment.

There is also a specific prohibition on harassment of contract workers by 'principals' (*s 41(2)*). A 'principal' is defined as 'a person who makes work available for an individual who is (a) employed by another person and (b) supplied by that other person in furtherance of a contract to which the principal is a party (whether or not that other person is a party to it) (*s 41(5)*). A 'contract worker' is an individual supplied to a principal in furtherance of such a contract.

Contract workers and reasonable adjustments. The duty to make reasonable adjustments applies to the hirer of contract labour as it does to an employer. However, it might not be reasonable for a hirer of contract labour to make certain adjustments if the period for which the contract worker works for the hirer of contract labour is short (*Code of Practice, para 9.8*). The provider of contract labour may also have a duty to make a reasonable adjustment where a similar substantial disadvantage is likely to affect a contract worker as a result of the arrangements or premises of all or most of the hirers of contract labour to whom he might be supplied In such circumstances, the provider of contract labour would have to make any reasonable adjustment within his power which would overcome the disadvantage wherever it might arise. Thus, in a case of a blind word-processor operator working for an employment agency, it would be reasonable for the agency to provide her with a specially adapted computer to take with her to any temporary engagement to which she is sent because otherwise she would be suffering the same substantial disadvantage at all or most such engagements (*Code of Practice, para 9.10*).

In *Abbey Life Assurance Co Ltd v Tansell* [2000] IRLR 387, the applicant had set up his own company and was employed by it. That company supplied the applicant's services as a computer consultant to third parties under a contract with an employment agency, MHC. Abbey Life had an agreement with MHC to supply computer personnel. Abbey Life rejected the applicant's services and a complaint of disability discrimination was made to an employment tribunal. The tribunal held that the applicant was a contract worker for MHC within the meaning of what is now *s 4B*, *DDA 1995* and not Abbey Life. MHC appealed successfully to the EAT (see *MHC Consulting Services Ltd v Tansell* [1999] IRLR 677). The Court of Appeal dismissed Abbey Life's appeal against that decision, holding that Abbey Life was the 'principal' or the hirer of contract labour for the purposes of *DDA 1995*. The fact that Abbey Life's contract was with MHC and not the applicant's employer did not preclude the application of *s 4B*, *DDA 1995* as there was a chain of unbroken contracts between the applicant and the 'end user', namely, Abbey Life.

The genuine occupational requirement exception (above para **11.2**) applies to contract workers in relation to not allowing them to do, or to continue doing, particular work: see *para 1(2)(b)* of *Sch 9* to the *EA 2010*.

Similar provision was made in the predecessor legislation: see *SDA 1975, s 9(2), (2A)*, as amended; *RRA 1976, s 7(1), (3A)*, as amended; *RBR 2003, reg 8(1), (2); SOR 2003, reg 8(1), (2)*; and *EA 2006, reg 9(1), (2)*.

The provisions relating to the meaning of 'at an establishment in Great Britain' (above **11.18**) apply to principals as they do to employers under the predecessor legislation. So, too, do the genuine occupational requirement exceptions (*SDA 1975, s 9(3), (3A) and (3B); RRA 1976, s 7(3); RBR 2003, reg 8(3); SOR 2003, reg 8(3); AR 2006, reg 9(3)*; see above **11.2** ff) and the exceptions for benefits provided to the public (*SDA 1975, s 9(4); RRA 1976, s 7(5); RBR 2003, reg 8(4); SOR 2003, reg 8(4); AR 2006, reg 9(4)*; see above **11.2**).

The provisions relating to contract workers are designed to prevent an employer from escaping its responsibilities under the equality legislation by bringing in workers on sub-contract and should therefore be given a broad construction so as to provide statutory protection to a wide range of workers (*Jones v Friends Provident Life Office* [2004] IRLR 783, NICA). In that case, Carswell LCJ held (para 17) that, in order to fall within the relevant provisions, it is necessary to show that: (i) the contract between the employer and the principal is one under which it is contemplated that employees will be supplied by the former to the latter; and, (ii) the principal is in a position to influence or control the conditions under which the employee worked. However, in *Leeds City Council v Woodhouse* [2010] EWCA Civ 410, [2010] IRLR 625 the Court of Appeal ruled that the second of those conditions was not necessary. What matters is that the worker works 'for' the principal. Influence and control does not have to be shown in all cases.

The notion of a 'contract worker' extends to cover a case where the complainant works for a company operating a 'concession' within a department store. Thus, where a department store withdrew, on racial grounds, the necessary permission for the complainant to work in the store, the latter was entitled to bring proceedings against the former under *RRA 1976, s 7* (*Harrods Ltd v Remick* [1998] ICR 156, CA). However, it should be noted that the Northern Ireland Court of Appeal in *Jones v Friends Provident* considered that *Harrods Ltd v Remick* represented, possibly, too wide an interpretation of the relevant provisions. In particular, the Court in *Jones v Friends Provident* considered that it is unlikely to be sufficient for a complainant to establish merely that the principal benefited from the work done by them in order to bring that principal within the scope of the relevant provisions. Nevertheless, more complex contractual arrangements are probably covered by the provisions: see *MHC Consulting Services Ltd v Tansell* [2000] ICR 789, CA, a case under the *DDA 1995*. In that case the complainant contracted with a company that he had set up which company then contracted with a service provider, which in turn contracted with the ultimate beneficiary of the services. The beneficiary was a principal for the purposes of the *DDA 1995* notwithstanding the inclusion of an additional link in the contractual chain. In all cases, however, there must in fact be a *contractual* relationship: where arrangements take effect under statute (as, for example, the obligations placed on general practitioners and local health authorities under the *National Health Service (General Medical Services) Regulations 1992*) there may be no contractual relationship at all: *David-John v North Essex Health Authority* [2004] ICR 112, EAT. See also *Vidal-Hall v Hawley* (UKEAT/0462/07/DA) (21 February 2008, unreported) where the claim failed for lack of a contract between principal and the supplier of the worker.

A contract worker is not limited to comparing the treatment he has received with the manner in which the principal treats contract workers of different sexual orientation, racial group etc; he may also compare himself to employees of the principal (*Allonby v Accrington and Rossendale College* [2001] EWCA Civ 529, [2001] IRLR 364). Thus, a company which refused to allow an agency worker to return to work for it after she had been on maternity leave discriminated against her on the grounds of her sex, contrary to *SDA 1975, s 9* (*BP Chemicals Ltd v Gillick* [1995] IRLR 128, EAT). Similarly, where a local authority appointed a permanent worker in place of a contract worker who had left to take maternity leave, it was argued on behalf of the principal that the contract worker could not rely upon the provisions of the equivalent Northern Irish legislation. The principal had not refused to allow her to continue to do the work (she had merely left to start maternity leave) and by the time that she wanted to return there was no work for a contract worker to do, a permanent worker having been appointed. Nevertheless, the NICA held that the principal was liable to the contract worker who had been subjected to 'other detriment' (*Patefield v Belfast City Council* [2000] IRLR 664, NICA).

11.25 Office holders

In addition to the general provisions applying the equality legislation to the Crown, etc (see below **11.36**), specific provision is also made in relation to discrimination against office holders. Overwhelmingly, office holders are public sector appointees, often those with specific statutory powers or responsibilities. They have historically been considered not to be employed in a post but, rather, as holding an office which exists independently of the terms of their appointment. An example would be Registrars of Births, Deaths and Marriages. Following the decisions of the CJEU and Supreme Court in *O'Brien v Ministry of Justice* (respectively, C-393/10, [2012] ICR 955 and [2013] UKSC 6, [2013] 1 WLR 522) establishing that judges are 'workers' under European law, it is likely that many office holders will now also fall within the definition of 'employee' in *s 83* of the *EA 2010* and thus be covered by the standard rules on employees. However, the provisions in relation to office holders are likely still to remain relevant to such people, and also to those who are genuinely office holders and not employees or workers in European law.

Under the *EA 2010* office holders are covered by *ss 49–51*. *Section 49* makes provision in respect of appointments to personal offices (ie what are referred to below as 'general office holders'). *Section 50* makes provision in respect of 'public offices', prohibiting discrimination, victimisation and harassment in relation to appointments and dismissals. *Section 51* makes provision prohibiting discrimination, victimisation and harassment in relation to recommendations for appointment to public offices. An office or post which is both a personal office and public office is to be treated for the purposes of the *EA 2010* as being a public office only (*s 52(4)*). As under the predecessor legislation (see below), posts to which persons are elected rather than appointed are not covered (*s 52(5)*). There are also further excluded offices listed in *Schedule 6*. These include any office that would be covered by any of the other employment provisions (eg contract work, partnerships, etc) (see *para 1* of *Sch 6*), political offices (*para 2*) and honourable offices (eg life peerages or other dignities) (para 3). The genuine occupational requirement exception applies to office holders in the same way as to employees: see *para 1(2)(e)–(g)* of *Sch 9* to the *EA 2010* and generally **11.2** above.

Scope of the provisions relating to office holders

Each of the predecessor discrimination statutes and statutory instruments has slightly different provisions relating to the protection of office holders. Essentially, two different types of office holder are covered by the legislation.

First, office holders appointed by a Minister of the Crown and government departments ('public office holders'). Prior to 1 October 2005 both the *SDA 1975* and the *RRA 1976* made provision in relation to such appointments (*SDA 1975, s 86*; *RRA 1976, s 76*). Section 86 of the *SDA 1975* is repealed, with effect from 1 October 2005, by the *Employment Equality (Sex Discrimination) Regulations 2005, reg 13*. Section 76 of the *RRA 1976* remains in force. With effect from 1 October 2005, the *SDA 1975* now contains a broader provision, in the same terms as those in the *RBR 2003, SOR 2003, DDA 1995* and *AR 2006*, covering offices and posts to which appointments are made by (or on the recommendation of or subject to the approval of) a Minister of the Crown, a government department, the National Assembly for Wales or any part of the Scottish Administration (*SDA 1975, s 10B(1)*; *RBR 2003, reg 10(8)(b)*; *SOR 2003, reg 10(8)(b)*; *AR 2006, reg 12(8)(b)*; *DDA 1995, s 4C(3)(b)*).

Second, office holders generally. The *RRA 1976*, the *RBR 2003*, the *SOR 2003*, the *AR 2006*, the *DDA 1995* and (with effect from 1 October 2005) the *SDA 1975* define such offices as any office or post to which persons are appointed to discharge functions personally under the direction of another person, and in respect of which they are entitled to remuneration: (*SDA 1975, s 10A(1)*, as amended by the *Sex Discrimination Regulations 2005, reg 13*; *RRA 1976, s 76ZA(7)(b)* and *(c)*; *RBR 2003, reg 10(8)(a)*; *SOR 2003, reg 10(8)(a)*, *AR 2006, reg 12(8)(b)*; *DDA 1995, s 4C(3)(a)*). The holder of an office or post is to be regarded as discharging his functions under the direction of another person if that other person is entitled to direct him as to when and where he discharges those functions. He is not to be regarded as entitled to remuneration merely because he is entitled to payments:

(i)   in respect of expenses incurred by him in carrying out the functions of the office or post; or

(ii)   by way of compensation for the loss of income or benefits he would or might have received from any person had he not been carrying out the functions of the office or post (*SDA 1975, s 10A(4)*; *RRA 1976, s 76ZA(8)*; *RBR 2003, reg 10(9)*; *SOR 2003, reg 10(9)*; *AR 2006, reg 12(9)*; *DDA 1995, s 4C(4)(b)*).

Broadly speaking, political offices and posts are excluded from the scope of the legislation, and a list of specifically excluded posts is included in each of the *Acts* and *Regulations*, though there are differences between the *Acts* and *Regulations* as to how this exclusion is effected and the reader is referred to the provisions themselves: *SDA 1975, s 10A(3)*; *RRA 1976, s 76ZA(7)* and *(9)(b)*; *RBR 2003, reg 10(8)* and *(10)(b)*; *SOR 2003, reg 10(8)* and *(10)(b)*; *AR 2006, reg 12(8)* and *12(10)(b)*; *DDA 1995, s 4C(5)*. Note also that each of the *Acts* and *Regulations* expressly excludes election to an office or post from the definition of 'appointment' to an office or post: *SDA 1975, s 10A(5)*; *RRA 1976, s 76ZA(9)(a)*; *RBR 2003, reg 10(10)(a)*; *SOR 2003, reg 10(10)(a)*; *AR 2006, reg 12(10)(a)*; *DDA 1995, s 4F(1)*.

The provisions relating to both types of office holders are default provisions, applying only if the provisions relating to employees, contract workers, partnerships, etc., do not (*SDA 1975, s 86(1)* or, with effect from 1 October 2005, *s 10A(2)*; *RRA 1976, s 7(2)(a)*; *RBR 2003, reg 10(8)*; *SOR 2003, reg 10(8)*; *AR 2006, reg 12(8)*; *DDA 1995, s 4C(1)(a)*).

Note that, prior to 1 October 2005, the *SDA 1975* made no provision for the second type of office holder and none of the detailed provisions discussed below applied in relation to sex discrimination. Thus, appointments to a non-public office did not fall within the scope of the *SDA 1975*. However, it was a very rare case where an appointment was not caught by one of the other provisions relating to employees, contract workers, police officers, etc. Following the amendments to the *SDA 1975* by the *Sex Discrimination Regulations 2005*, the scope of the *SDA 1975* is now broadly in line with that of the *RRA 1976* and the *Regulations* and the detailed provisions discussed below apply also in relation to sex discrimination.

Unlawful discrimination against applicants for an appointment

In relation to appointment to public office, the *RRA 1976* and the *SDA 1975* (prior to 1 October 2005) provide that it is unlawful for the relevant Minister or government department to do any act that would be unlawful if the appointment was a position of employment covered by the provisions relating to discrimination in employment: *RRA 1976, s 76(2)*; *SDA 1975, s 86(2)*. With effect from 1 October 2005, *section 86* of the *SDA 1975* has been repealed, but equivalent provisions have been inserted into the *Act* by *reg 13* of the *Sex Discrimination Regulations 2005*. Like the *RRA 1976, RBR 2003, SOR 2003, DDA 1995* and *AR 2006*, the *SDA 1975* now provides in relation to appointment both to public office and to offices generally, that it is unlawful for a 'relevant person', in relation to an appointment to an office or post to discriminate against a person:

(a)   in the arrangements which he makes for the purpose of determining to whom the appointment should be offered;

(b)   in the terms on which he offers him the appointment; or

(c)   by refusing to offer him the appointment (*SDA 1975, s 10B(1)*, as amended with effect from 1 October 2005; *RRA 1976, s 76ZA(1)*; *RBR 2003, reg 10(1)*; *SOR 2003, reg 10(1)*; *AR 2006, reg 12(1)*; *DDA 1995, s 4D(1)*).

The relevant person in relation to an office or post, means:

(i)   any person with power to make or terminate appointments to the office or post, or to determine the terms of appointment;

(ii)   any person with power to determine the working conditions of a person appointed to the office or post in relation to opportunities for promotion, a transfer, training or for receiving any other benefit; and

(iii)   any person or body on whose recommendation or subject to whose approval appointments are made to the office or post (*SDA 1975, s 10B(9)*, as amended with effect from 1 October 2005; *RRA 1976, s 76ZA(8)(c)*; *RBR 2003, reg 10(10)(c)*; *SOR 2003, reg 10(10)(c)*; *AR 2006, reg 12(10)(c)*; *DDA 1995, s 4F(2)*).

Unlawful discrimination in relation to recommendations for appointment

It is unlawful, in relation to an appointment to public office, for a relevant person on whose recommendation (or subject to whose approval) appointments to the office or post are made, to discriminate against a person:

(a)   in the arrangements which he makes for the purpose of determining who should be recommended or approved in relation to the appointment; or

(b)   in making or refusing to make a recommendation, or giving or refusing to give an approval, in relation to the appointment (*SDA 1975, s 10B(2)*, as amended with effect from 1 October 2005; *RRA 1976, s 76(3), (5)*; *RBR 2003, reg 10(2)*; *SOR 2003, reg 10(2)*; *AR 2006, reg 12(2)*); *DDA 1995, s 4D(2)*).

In the *RRA 1976* this is extended to include recommendations and approvals in relation to a conferment by the Crown of a dignity or honour: *RRA 1976, s 76(4)*.

The same, or virtually the same, provisions apply to negative recommendations: see *SDA 1975, s 10B(11)*, as amended with effect from 1 October 2005; *RRA 1976, s 76(6)–(9)*; *RBR 2003, reg 10(10)(d)*; *SOR 2003, reg 10(10)(d)*; *AR 2006, reg 12(10)(d)*; *DDA 1995, s 4D(7)*.

Unlawful discrimination against holders of an appointment

It is unlawful for a relevant person, in relation to a person who has been appointed to an office or post to which this regulation applies, to discriminate against him:

(a)   in the terms of the appointment;

(b)   in the opportunities which he affords him for promotion, a transfer, training or receiving any other benefit, or by refusing to afford him any such opportunity;

(c)   by terminating the appointment; or

(d)   by subjecting him to any other detriment in relation to the appointment (*SDA 1975, s 10B(3)*, as amended with effect from 1 October 2005; *RRA 1976, s 76ZA(2)*; *RBR 2003, reg 10(3)*; *SOR 2003, reg 10(3)*; *AR 2006, reg 12(3)*; *DDA 1995, s 4D(3)*.)

Note that 'termination of the appointment' is deemed to refer additionally:

(a)   to the termination of the appointment by the expiration of any period (including a period expiring by reference to an event or circumstance), not being a termination immediately after which the appointment is renewed on the same terms and conditions; and

(b)   to the termination of the appointment by any act of the person appointed (including the giving of notice) in circumstances such that he is entitled to terminate the appointment without notice by reason of the conduct of the relevant person (*SDA 1975, s 10B(8)*, as amended with effect from 1 October 2005; *RRA 1976, s 76ZA(6)*; *RBR 2003, reg 10(7)*; *SOR 2003, reg 10(7)*; *AR 2006, reg 12(7)*; *DDA 1995, s 4D(3)(c)*).

Unlawful harassment of applicants for appointment or holders of an appointment

It is unlawful for a relevant person, in relation to an office or post to which this regulation applies, to subject to harassment a person:

(a)   who has been appointed to the office or post;

(b)   who is seeking or being considered for appointment to the office or post; or

(c)   who is seeking or being considered for a recommendation or approval in relation to an appointment to an office or post (*SDA 1975, s 10B(4)*, as amended with effect from 1 October 2005; *RRA 1976, s 76ZA(3)*; *RBR 2003, reg 10(4)*; *SOR 2003, reg 10(4)*; *AR 2006, reg 12(4)*; *DDA 1995, s 4D(4)*.)

Exceptions

The exceptions relating to genuine occupational requirements (*SDA 1975, 10B(5) and (6)*, as amended with effect from 1 October 2005; *RRA 1976, s 76ZA(4)*; *RBR 2003, reg 10(5)*; *SOR 2003, reg 10(5)*; *AR 2006, reg 12(5)*: see above **11.2** ff) and benefits provided to the public (*SDA 1975, s 10B(7)*, as amended with effect from 1 October 2005; *RRA 1976, s 76ZA(5)*, *RBR 2003, reg 10(6)*; *SOR 2003, reg 10(6)*; *AR 2006, reg 12(6)*: see above **11.20**) apply to complaints of discrimination by office holders as they do to employees. Note also that the provisions of the *RRA 1976* relating to office holders apply only to discrimination on grounds of race, ethnic or national origins and not to discrimination on grounds of colour or nationality.

11.26 Police

Police officers are office holders and not employees. However, *s 42(1)* of the *EA 2010* deems holding the office of constable to be treated as employment by the chief officer (in respect of any act done by the chief officer in relation to a constable or appointment to the office of constable) and by the responsible authority (in respect of any act done by the authority in relation to a constable or appointment to the office of constable). The 'chief officer' is:

(a)   in relation to an appointment under a relevant Act, the chief officer of police for the police force to which the appointment relates;

(b)   in relation to any other appointment, the person under whose direction and control the body of constables or other persons to which the appointment relates is;

(c)   in relation to a constable or other person under the direction and control of a chief officer of police, that chief officer of police;

(d)   in relation to any other constable or any other person, the person under whose direction and control the constable or other person is.

The 'responsible authority' is:

(a)   in relation to an appointment under a relevant Act (ie the *Metropolitan Police Act 1829*, the *City of London Police Act 1839*, the *Police (Scotland) Act 1967*, the *Police Act 1996*), the police authority that maintains the police force to which the appointment relates;

(b)   in relation to any other appointment, the person by whom a person would (if appointed) be paid;

(c)   in relation to a constable or other person under the direction and control of a chief officer of police, the police authority that maintains the police force for which that chief officer is the chief officer of police;

(d)   in relation to any other constable or any other person, the person by whom the constable or other person is paid.

Similarly, the predecessor equality legislation deems the relevant chief officer of police or police authority to be the employer of the complainant police officer as respects any act done by him or them in relation to that officer: *SDA 1975, s 17(1)*; *RRA 1976, s 76A(2)*; *RBR 2003, reg 11(1), (2)*; *SOR 2003, reg 11(1), (2)*; *AR 2006, reg 13(1), (2)*; *DDA 1995, s 64A(1), (2)*. The requirement that the act should be done by the chief officer (or, similarly, by the police authority) is not to be interpreted literally and will include acts performed by those to whom the chief officer has delegated authority (see *Chief Constable of Cumbria v McGlennon* [2002] ICR 1156, EAT).

If the chief officer of police or police authority for the force to which the complainant police officer belongs does not in fact have direction and control of the force, then the relevant respondent will be the chief officer or authority which *does* have direction and control of the complainant police officer's force: *SDA 1975, s 17(9)*; *RRA 1976, s 76B(3)*; *RBR 2003, reg 11(8)*; *SOR 2003, reg 11(8)*; *AR 2006, reg 13(8)*; *DDA 1995, s 64A(8)*.

Any proceedings which would lie against a chief officer of police should be brought against whoever holds the post of chief officer of police for the time being. If the post is vacant, proceedings should be brought against the person for the time being performing the functions of that office (*SDA 1975, s 17(5)*; *RRA 1976, s 76A(5)*; *RBR 2003, reg 11(4)*; *SOR 2003, reg 11(4)*; *AR 2006, reg 13(4)*; *DDA 1995, s 64A(4)*).

The relevant chief officer of police is vicariously liable for the actions of those police officers for whom he is responsible and he is treated as the respondent for that purpose (see VICARIOUS LIABILITY **(54)**). The legislation specifies that anything done by a police officer in the performance, or purported performance, of his functions shall be treated as done in the course of his employment (*SDA 1975, s 17(1A)(b)*; *RRA 1976, s 76A(3)(b)*; *RBR 2003, reg 11(2)*; *SOR 2003, reg 11(2)*; *AR 2006, reg 13(2)*; *DDA 1995, s 64A(2)*). Note that *s 76A* of the *RRA 1976* was inserted by the *Race Relations (Amendment) Act 2000* in response to the Court of Appeal's decision in *Chief Constable of Bedfordshire Police v Liversidge* [2002] ICR 1135. In that case, the Court of Appeal held that the Chief Officer did not fall to be treated as an employer for the purposes of *RRA 1976, s 32(1)* (ie the general provision relating to vicarious liability: see **10.54** DISCRIMINATION AND EQUAL OPPORTUNITIES – I). *Section 76A* reverses that decision.

Where proceedings are brought against a chief officer of police, any compensation, costs or expenses ordered against the chief officer are payable from the police fund. The chief officer can also recover the costs of successfully contesting proceedings from the fund in so far as they are not recovered from the complainant or other party. Finally, he can recover the cost of compromising proceedings brought against him, subject to his having obtained the approval of the relevant police authority for the settlement (*SDA 1975, s 17(4); RRA 1976, s 76A(4); RBR 2003, reg 11(3); SOR 2003, reg 11(3); AR 2006, reg 13(3); DDA 1995, s 64A(3)*).

Similarly, a police authority may, in such cases and to such extent as appear to it to be appropriate, pay out of the police fund any compensation, costs or expenses awarded by a court or tribunal against a person under the direction and control of the chief officer of police. It may also pay out of the police fund any costs or expenses incurred and not recovered by such a person, as well as any sum required in connection with the settlement of a claim that has or might have given rise to discrimination proceedings (*RRA 1976, s 76A(6); SDA 1975, s 17(5A); RBR 2003, reg 11(5); SOR 2003, reg 11(5); AR 2006, reg 13(5); DDA 1995, s 64A(5)*).

Further detailed provisions apply the legislation to cadets, employees and office holders of the Serious Organised Crime Agency and other police bodies (*EA 2010, ss 42(2)–(6) and 43(4)–(7); SDA 1975, s 17(6), (7), (9); RRA 1976, s 76B; RBR 2003, reg 11(6), (7), 11A; SOR 2003, reg 11(6), (7), 11A; AR 2006, regs 13(6), (7), (14); DDA 1995, s 64A(6), (7)* and *s* 56 of the *Serious Organised Crime and Police Act 2005*).

For circumstances in which police constables may lawfully be discriminated against see above **11.11**(e).

11.27 Barristers and advocates

Unlawful discrimination against applicants for pupillage or tenancy

It is unlawful for a barrister or barrister's clerk, in relation to any offer of a pupillage or tenancy, to discriminate against a person on any of the unlawful grounds:

(a)   in the arrangements which are made for the purpose of determining to whom the pupillage or tenancy should be offered;

(b)   in respect of any terms on which it is offered; or

(c)   by refusing, or deliberately not offering, it to him (*EA 2010, s 47(1); SDA 1975, s 35A(1); RRA 1976, s 26A(1); RBR 2003, reg 12(1); SOR 2003, reg 12(1); AR 2006, reg 15(1); DDA 1995, s 7A(1)*).

Unlawful discrimination against pupils or tenants

It is unlawful for a barrister or barrister's clerk, in relation to a pupil or tenant in the set of chambers in question, to discriminate against him:

(a)   in respect of any terms applicable to him as a pupil or tenant;

(b)   in the opportunities for training or gaining experience, which are afforded or denied to him;

(c)   in the benefits which are afforded or denied to him; or

(d)   by terminating his pupillage, or by subjecting him to any pressure to leave the chambers or other detriment (*EA 2010, s 47(2); SDA 1975, s 35A(2); RRA 1976, s 26A(2); RBR 2003, reg 12(2); SOR 2003, reg 12(2); AR, reg 15(2); DDA 1995, s 7A(2)*).

Unlawful harassment of pupils, tenants or applicants for pupillage or tenancy

It is unlawful for a barrister or barrister's clerk, in relation to a pupillage or tenancy in the set of chambers in question, to subject to harassment a person who is, or has applied to be, a pupil or tenant (*EA 2010, s 47(3); SDA 1975, s 35A(2A)*, as amended with effect from 1 October 2005; *RRA 1976, s 26A(3A); RBR 2003, reg 12(3); SOR 2003, reg 12(3); DDA 1995, s 7A(3)*).

Unlawful victimisation of pupils, tenants or applicants for pupillage or tenancy

It is unlawful for a barrister or barrister's clerk, in relation to a pupillage or tenancy in the set of chambers in question, to victimise a person who is, or has applied to be, a pupil or tenant (*EA 2010, s 47(4) and (5)*).

Unlawful discrimination by those instructing barristers

It is unlawful for any person, in relation to the giving, withholding or acceptance of instructions to a barrister, to discriminate against any person by subjecting him to a detriment, or to subject him to harassment (*EA 2010, s 47(6); SDA 1975, s 35A(3); RRA 1976, s 26A(3); RBR 2003, reg 12(4); SOR 2003, reg 12(4); AR 2006, reg 15(4); DDA 1995, s 7A(4)*).

'Barrister's clerk' includes any person carrying out any of the functions of a barrister's clerk. 'Pupil', 'pupillage', 'set of chambers', 'tenancy' and 'tenant' have the meanings commonly associated with their use in the context of barristers practising in independent practice, but 'tenancy' and 'tenant' also include reference to any barrister permitted to work in a set of chambers who is not a tenant (ie a 'squatter') (*EA 2010, ss 47(8) and (9); SDA 1975, s 35A(4); RRA 1976, s 26A(4); RBR 2003, reg 12(5); SOR 2003, reg 12(5); AR 2006, reg 15(5); DDA 1995, s 7A(5)*).

The exceptions for genuine occupational requirements (above **11.2** ff) and benefits provided to the public (above **11.20**) do not apply to barristers.

The provisions in respect of barristers extend to England and Wales only. Similar provision is made for advocates and their pupils in Scotland (*EA 2010, s 48; SDA 1975, s35B; RRA 1976, s 26B; RBR 2003, reg 13; SOR 2003, reg 13; AR 2006, reg 16; DDA 1995, s 7C*).

11.28 Partnerships

Unlawful discrimination against partners and candidates for partnership

Partners in firms, including limited liability partnerships, are not employees or workers (see *Bates van Winkelhof v Clyde & Co LLP* [2012] EWCA Civ 1207, [2012] IRLR 992) and so specific provision is made in the legislation prohibiting discrimination against partners and candidates for partnership. It is unlawful for a firm (or persons proposing to form a firm), in relation to a position as partner in the firm, to discriminate against a person on any of the unlawful grounds:

(a)   in the arrangements they make for the purpose of determining to whom they should offer that position;

(b)   in the terms on which they offer him that position;

(c)   by refusing to offer, or deliberately not offering, him that position; or

(d)   in a case where the person already holds that position:

    (i)   in the way they afford him access to any benefits or by refusing to afford, or deliberately not affording, him access to them, or

    (ii)   by expelling him from that position, or

(iii)   subjecting him to any other detriment (*SDA 1975, s 11(1), (2); RRA 1976, s 10(1), (2); RBR 2003, reg 14(1), (3); SOR 2003, reg 14(1), (3); AR 2006, reg 17(1); DDA 1995, s 6A(1)*).

Under EA 2010, it is also unlawful to discriminate against a person who is already a partner as to the terms on which the person is a partner: *s 44*.

'Expulsion' of a person from a position as partner is (in the *EA 2010, RRA 1976, RBR 2003, SOR 2003, DDA 1995* and *AR 2006*) defined additionally to refer to the termination of that person's position as partner by:

(a)   the expiration of any period (including a period expiring by reference to an event or circumstance), not being a termination immediately after which the partnership is renewed on the same terms; and

(b)   any act of his (including the giving of notice) in circumstances such that he is entitled to terminate it without notice by reason of the conduct of the other partners (*EA 2010, s 1(6); RRA 1976, s 10(6); DDA 1995, s 6A(4); RBR 2003, reg 14(8); SOR 2003, reg 14(8); AR 2006, reg 17(8)*).

Note that where one partner dissolves a two-person partnership the other partner is 'expelled' for the purposes of the provisions on partnerships and may sue the remaining partner (*Dave v Robinska* [2003] ICR 1248).

The legislation applies to limited partnerships and limited liability partnerships as it does to partnerships (with appropriate amendments of terminology) (*EA 2010, s 44(8), s 45; SDA 1975, s 11(5), (6); RRA 1976, s 10(4), (5); RBR 2003, reg 14(5), (6); SOR 2003, reg 14(5), (6); AR 2006, reg 17(6); DDA 1995, s 6C(2)*). Note, however, that for discrimination on grounds of colour or nationality, the RRA 1976 only applied to firms with six or more partners: *RRA 1976, s 10(1A)*.

Genuine occupational requirement

Genuine occupational requirement defences (see above **11.2** ff) are available to partnerships under the *EA 2010*: see *para 1(2)(c)* and *(d)* of *Sch 9*.

Under the *RBR 2003, SOR 2003* and *AR 2006*, an act falling into one of the categories set out above will not be unlawful if, had the complainant been an employee or applicant for employment, a genuine occupational requirement defence would have been available (*RBR 2003, reg 14(4); SOR 2003, reg 14(4); AR 2006, reg 17(4)*). Under the *RRA 1976* and the *SDA 1975* a genuine occupational requirement defence is only available where the discrimination takes the form of discrimination in the arrangements made for the purpose of determining who to offer a position as partner or a refusal to offer a position as partner: *SDA 1975, s 11(3), (3A); RRA 1976, s 10(3)*.

Special provision is made for a genuine occupational requirement defence to discrimination on grounds of gender reassignment (ie discrimination falling within *SDA 1975, s 2A*: see above **11.5**). A partnership will have a defence to any form of discrimination on grounds of gender reassignment where, if it were employment, being a man (or being a woman) would be a genuine occupational qualification for the job and the firm can show that the treatment is reasonable in view of the circumstances (*SDA 1975, s 11(3A), (3B)*). Where the discrimination takes the form of discrimination in the arrangements made for the purposes of determining who should be offered a position as partner, refusing to offer a position as partner or expelling a partner, it is not necessary for the firm to show that the treatment was reasonable in the circumstances, provided that it is able to show that there would be a supplementary genuine occupational qualification for the position in question: see above **11.5** for supplementary genuine occupational qualifications.

11.28 Discrimination and Equal Opportunities – II

Other exceptions

Prior to 1 October 2005 it was not unlawful to discriminate on grounds of sex against a partner (or potential partner) in relation to provision made for death and retirement. The exception applied to discrimination:

(a)   in the terms on which partnership is offered;

(b)   in a case where the person is already a partner:

  (i)   in the way he is afforded access to any benefits, etc; or

  (ii)   by expelling him from that position, or subjecting him to any other detriment.

However, it did not apply to provision for expulsion (and the act of expulsion) in relation to retirement: discrimination in such matters remained unlawful except where a genuine occupational requirement applies (*SDA 1975, s 11(4)*).

The exception in relation to provision made for death and retirement in *s 11(4)* is repealed, with effect from 1 October 2005, by the *Sex Discrimination Regulations 2005, reg 9(3)*.

See **11.11**(c) above for further discussion of the equality provisions relating to death and retirement benefits.

There is no exception for the retirement of partners.

Unlawful harassment of partners and candidates for partnership

It is unlawful for a firm, in relation to a position as partner in the firm, to subject to harassment a person who holds or has applied for that position (*EA 2010, s 44(3), (4); SDA 1975, 11(2A)*, as inserted with effect from 1 October 2005 by the *Sex Discrimination Regulations 2005; RRA 1976, s 10(1B); RBR 2003, reg 14(2); SOR 2003, reg 14(2); AR 2006, reg 17(2); DDA 1995, s 6A(2)*).

The *EA 2010* applies to partnerships in the same way as the predecessor legislation: *s 44* (partnerships), *s 45* (limited liability partnerships) and *s 46* of the *EA 2010*. The genuine occupational requirement exception (above para **11.2**) will apply to partnerships in the same way as to employees: see *para 1(2)(c)* and *(d)* of *Sch 9* to the *EA 2010*.

Unlawful victimisation of partners and candidates for partnership

It is unlawful for a firm, in relation to a position as partner in the firm, to victimise a person who holds or has applied for that position (*EA 2010, s 44(5) and (6)*). Under the predecessor legislation victimisation was merely a form of discrimination and no separate provision was made for it.

11.29 Trade organisations

A 'trade organisation' is defined in the discrimination legislation as:

(i)   an organisation of workers,

(ii)   an organisation of employers, or

(iii)   any other organisation whose members carry on a particular profession or trade for the purposes of which the organisation exists.

(*EA 2010, s 57(7); SDA 1975, 12(1); RRA 1976, s 11(1); RBR 2003, reg 15(4); SOR 2003, reg 15(4); AR 2006, reg 18(4); DDA 1995, s 13(4)*).

'Profession' is defined in the predecessor legislation so as to include 'any vocation or occupation', and 'trade' to include 'any business': (*SDA 1975, s 82(1); RRA 1976, s 78(1); RBR 2003, reg 15(4); SOR 2003, reg 15(4); AR 2006, reg 18(4)*).

The EAT has held that the National Federation of Self-Employed and Small Businesses Ltd is an 'employers' organisation': *National Federation of Self-Employed and Small Businesses Ltd v Philpott* [1997] IRLR 340. In *Medical Protection Society v Sadek* [2004] EWCA Civ 865, [2004] ICR 1263, the Court of Appeal considered the status of the Medical Protection Society, a membership organisation which had provided the claimant with advice and representation in relation to a claim he had brought against his employer, an NHS Trust. The Court held that the Society was 'an organisation of workers' within the first category of the definition of 'trade organisation' in s 11(1) of the RRA 1976, because medical and dental practitioners were properly classified as 'workers' even though they were 'members [of] a profession' within the third category of the definition of 'trade organisation' and even though some of them may be employees and others independent contractors. The Court considered that the EAT had been wrong to conclude that the Society fell within *both* the first and third categories of the definition: the third category was only a residual one.

Unlawful discrimination against applicants for membership of the organisation

Under the predecessor legislation, it is unlawful for a trade organisation to discriminate against a person:

(a)   in the terms on which it is prepared to admit him to membership of the organisation; or

(b)   by refusing to accept, or deliberately not accepting, his application for membership; (*SDA 1975, s 12(2); RRA 1976, s 11(2); RBR 2003, reg 15(1); SOR 2003, reg 15(1); AR 2006, reg 18(1); DDA 1995, s 13(1)*).

Pursuant to *s 57(1)* of *EA 2010*, it is additionally unlawful for a trade organisation to discriminate in the arrangements made for deciding to whom to offer membership of the organisation; or

Unlawful discrimination against members

It is unlawful for a trade organisation, in relation to a member of the organisation, to discriminate against him:

(a)   in the way it affords him access to any benefits or by refusing or deliberately omitting to afford him access to them;

(b)   by depriving him of membership, or varying the terms on which he is a member; or

(c)   by subjecting him to any other detriment (*EA 2010, s 57(2); SDA 1975, s 12(3); RRA 1976, s 11(3); RBR 2003, reg 15(2); SOR 2003, reg 15(2); AR 2006, reg 18(2); DDA 1995, s 13(2)*).

Note that, prior to 1 October 2005, *s 12* of the *SDA 1975* did not apply to provision made in relation to the death or retirement from work of a member (*s 12(4)*). This exception is repealed, with effect from 1 October 2005, by *reg 15(3)* of the *Sex Discrimination Regulations 2005*. (See **11.11**(c) above for discussion of the equality provisions relating to death and retirement benefits.)

Unlawful harassment of members and applicants for membership

It is unlawful for a trade organisation, in relation to a person's membership or application for membership of that organisation, to subject that person to harassment (*EA 2010, s 57(3); SDA 1975, s 12(3A)*, as inserted with effect from 1 October 2005 by the *Sex Discrimination Regulations 2005; RRA 1976, s 11(4); RBR 2003, reg 15(3); SOR 2003, reg 15(3); AR 2006, reg 18(3); DDA 1995, s 13(3)*).

In *Fire Brigades Union v Fraser* [1998] IRLR 697 (Court of Session, Inner House), the union provided support and assistance for the alleged victim of the harassment, but refused to provide assistance to the alleged harasser. The Court of Session overturned a decision of the employment tribunal that the alleged harasser had been the victim of an act of discrimination on the part of the union. Whilst it was true that the union treated the alleged victims of harassment more favourably, the tribunal was making the wrong comparison in comparing harasser and harassee. The proper question was whether a female alleged harasser would have been treated differently.

The genuine occupational requirement exception (above para **11.2**) does not apply to trade organisations.

11.30 Qualifications bodies

A qualifications body is an authority or body which can confer professional or trade qualifications: *EA 2010, s 54(2)*. A 'professional or trade qualification' is an authorisation, recognition, enrolment, approval or certification, which is needed for, or facilitates, engagement in a particular profession or trade. 'Confer' is defined to include the renewal or extension of a qualification (see *EA 2010, s 54(3); SDA 1975, s 13(1), (3); RRA 1976, s 12(1), (2); RBR 2003, reg 16(3); SOR 2003, reg 16(4); AR 2006, reg 19(3); DDA 1995, s 14A(5)*). Establishments of further and higher education and schools are excluded from the definition: EA 2010, 54(4). (Separate provision in relation to discrimination in education is made by both the *Acts* and the *Regulations*. Consideration of this is, however, outside the scope of this book.)

Under the predecessor legislation, it is unlawful for a qualifications body to discriminate against a person:

(a)   in the terms on which it is prepared to confer a professional or trade qualification on him;

(b)   by refusing or deliberately not granting any application by him for such a qualification; or

(c)   by withdrawing such a qualification from him or varying the terms on which he holds it

(SDA 1975, s 13(1); RRA 1976, s 12(1); RBR 2003, reg 16(1); SOR 2003, reg 16(1); AR 2006, reg 19(1); DDA 1995, s 14A(1))

Under *EA 2010*, it is additionally unlawful for a qualifications body to discriminate against a person:

(a)   in the arrangements made for deciding upon whom to confer a relevant qualification; and

(b)   by subjecting him to any other detriment

(EA 2010, s 53(1), (2))

It is unlawful for a qualifications body, in relation to a professional or trade qualification conferred by it, to subject to harassment a person who holds or applies for such a qualification (*EA 2010, s 53(3); SDA 1975, s 13(1A)*, as inserted with effect from 1 October 2005 by the *Sex Discrimination Regulations 2005; RRA 1976, s 12(1A); RBR 2003, reg 16(2); SOR 2003, reg 16(2); EA 2006, reg 19(2)*).

The *EA 2010* also specifically prohibits victimisation by qualifications bodies: *s 53(4)* and *(5)*.

A number of cases have considered the definition of 'qualifications body' for the purpose of these provisions. In *British Judo Association v Petty* [1981] ICR 660, it was held that *SDA 1975, s 13* was to be widely construed so as to render unlawful a discriminatory restriction in a judo referee's certificate, since the certificate would in fact facilitate the holder's trade or profession. In *Patterson v Legal Services Commission* [2003] EWCA Civ 1558, [2004] ICR 312 the Court of Appeal held that the conferral of a franchise by the Legal Services Commission enabling the applicant's firm to receive public funds for the provisions of services in certain categories of legal work was an 'authorisation' that 'facilitates engagement in' the profession of solicitor for the purposes of *RRA 1976, s 12*. The authorisation was conferred on both the applicant's firm and the applicant personally. However, the provisions relating to qualifications bodies are not to be so widely construed as to extend to the mere awarding of a contract, even by a body or authority which has a *de facto* monopoly in the particular trade (*Malik v Post Office Counters Ltd* [1993] ICR 93). The provisions are aimed at discrimination by professional bodies and not individual businesses. Thus, where a private medical health insurer would only make payments in respect of treatment given by practitioners holding certain recognised qualifications, a plastic surgeon could not bring a claim where the insurer refused to recognise her Greek medical qualifications (*Tattari v Private Patients Plan Ltd* [1997] IRLR 586, CA; see also *Loughran and anr v Northern Ireland Housing Executive* [1998] IRLR 593). Being a Justice of the Peace is not 'engagement in a particular profession' (*Arthur v A-G* [1999] ICR 631). However, appointment as a Justice of the Peace would now be covered by the provisions relating to office holders (see above **11.25**).

A number of cases have considered the position of political parties. In *McDonagh and Triesman v Ali* [2002] EWCA Civ 93, [2002] ICR 1026 the CA held (disapproving the EAT's decision in *Sawyer v Ahsan* [1999] IRLR 609) that the Labour Party is not a 'qualifications body' within the definition, at least in relation to the selection or nomination of candidates for elections. Although being an MP is a 'profession', the selection or nomination of candidates is not an 'authorisation' or 'qualification' for that profession. *Triesman* has now been approved by the House of Lords in *Watt (formerly Carter) v Ahsan* [2007] UKHL 51, [2008] 2 WLR 17. In that case, however, the House of Lords did confirm that although not a 'qualifications body', the Labour Party was an 'association' within the meaning of *s 25* of the *RRA 1976* (which applies to any association of persons of 25 or more members, regulated by a constitution, that does not fall within *s 11* of the *RRA 1976*. *Section 25* falls within *Part III* of the *RRA 1976*, is outside the jurisdiction of the employment tribunal and the scope of this work).

More recently, in *Kulkarni v NHS Education Scotland* [2013] Eq LR 34 the EAT (Scotland) held that NHS Education Scotland was not a 'qualifications body' or, at least, was not covered by *s 53* of the *EA 2010* in respect of its function of allocating trainees. Although having a trainee would facilitate a consultant surgeon's engagement in his profession, the EAT(S) was satisfied that the allocation of a trainee was not the conferral of 'an authorisation, qualification, recognition, registration, enrolment, approval or certification'.

Note that it is not possible to complain to an employment tribunal under this provision if the act complained of is one in respect of which an appeal, or proceedings in the nature of an appeal, may be brought under any enactment. In the predecessor legislation this exception was to be found in *SDA 1975, s 63(2); RRA 1976, s 54(2); RBR 2003, reg 28(2); SOR 2003, reg 28(2); AR 2006, reg 36(2); DDA 1995, s 17A(1A)*. The exception is now in *s 120(7)* of the *EA 2010*. The scope and effect of this provision were considered in *R v Department of Health, ex p Gandhi* [1991] ICR 805, *Khan v General Medical Council* [1996] ICR 1032, CA, *Tariquez-Zaman v GMC* (UKEAT/0292/06), *Chaudhary v Specialist Training Authority Appeal Panel and ors* [2005] ICR 1086, *Depner v GMC* (UKEAT/0457/11/KN) and, most recently, *Jooste v General Medical Council* [2012] Eq LR

1049, EAT (4 July 2012). These cases confirm that the exception applies where a person may bring a claim for judicial review of the decision of the qualifications body under *s 31* of the *Senior Courts Act 1981* as well as where a person has a statutory right of appeal to a specialist tribunal.

The genuine occupational requirement exception (above para **11.2**) does not apply to qualifications bodies.

Sex discrimination

Uniquely, the *SDA 1975* provides that, if the qualifications body has to consider an applicant's character, if there is evidence to show that an applicant has practised unlawful discrimination in connection with the carrying on of any profession or trade, that must be taken into account by the body (*SDA 1975, s 13(2)*). No such provision appears in the *EA 2010*.

Disability discrimination

Under the *DDA 1995* qualifications bodies benefit from an exception to the duty to make reasonable adjustments for disabled people. If the provision, criterion or practice in question is a 'competence standard' then the duty to make reasonable adjustments does not arise: *DDA 1995, s 14B(1)*. A 'competence standard' is "An academic, medical or other standard applied by or on behalf of a qualifications body for the purpose of determining whether or not a person has a particular level of competence or ability" (*DDA 1995, s 14A(5)*). Further, insofar as a qualifying body applies a competence standard to those seeking qualification and seeks to justify any disability-related discrimination against a disabled person, the application of the competence standard will only be justified if the same standard was applied to persons that did not have the particular disability and its application is a proportionate means of achieving a legitimate aim (*DDA 1995, s 14A(3)*).

In *Burke v The College of Law* UKEAT/0301/10/SM, the EAT considered the College of Law's requirement that Legal Practice Course exams be completed under timed conditions in an examination hall. The College of Law had already granted Mr Burke, who suffered from multiple sclerosis, 60% additional time. However, he contended that a reasonable adjustment would be that he be able to complete the exams over a number of days at home. The Tribunal (and the EAT) held that the requirement that the exam be completed under timed conditions was a competence standard. While the EAT recognised that there was a distinction to be made between an academic standard and the process by which it was assessed, and that in many cases the latter would be subject to the duty to make reasonable adjustments, the EAT accepted that, in the context of a professional examination which seeks to mimic (to some extent) conditions of practice, the time requirement was a competence standard. This was so even though the College of Law had already voluntarily made 'reasonable adjustments' to the time requirement: the fact that they had made the adjustment voluntarily did not mean they had been under a duty to so. Moreover, there was a qualitative difference between an extension of timed exam conditions and the home examination conditions proposed by the claimant. On appeal, the CA ([2012] EWCA Civ 37, [2012] EqLR 279) held that it was not necessary to decide whether or not the time requirement was a competence standard, the fact was that the Tribunal had looked at all the adjustments made by the College and had rightly concluded that reasonable adjustments had been made (including to the time requirement).

This exception for disability discrimination does not apply under the *EA 2010*. Instead, provision is made in *s 96(7)–(9)* for the relevant regulators of qualifications bodies to specify certain provisions, criteria or practices in relation to which qualifications bodies are not to be subject to the duty to make reasonable adjustments in relation to specified qualifications. The identity of the relevant regulators, the specified qualifications and the means by which the regulators must publish their specified provisions, criteria or practices (principally on their websites) are prescribed for by regulations for England (*SI 2010/2245*), Scotland (*SI 2010/315*) and Wales (*SI 2010/2217*).

Sexual orientation discrimination

The *SOR 2003* provides an exception equivalent to the genuine occupational requirement exception for discrimination in employment (see above **11.7**). *SOR 2003, reg 16(3)* provides that the provisions relating to discrimination by qualifications bodies do not apply to 'professional or trade qualifications conferred for the purposes of an organised religion where a requirement related to sexual orientation is applied to the qualification so as to comply with the doctrines of the religion or to avoid conflicting with the strongly held religious convictions of a significant number of the religion's followers'. No equivalent exception is available under the *EA 2010, SDA 1975, RRA 1976* or *RBR 2003*.

11.31 Providers of vocational training

The predecessor legislation contains specific provisions relating to providers of vocational training. The *EA 2010* covers such persons by way of the provisions for employment service-providers (see below).

Under the predecessor legislation, a 'training provider' is any person who provides, or makes arrangements for the provision of, training or facilities for training which would help fit another person for any employment: *SDA 1975, s 14(1); RRA 1976, s 13(1); RBR 2003, reg 17(4); SOR 2003, reg 17(4); AR 2006, reg 20(4)*. *DDA 1995* prohibits discrimination in the provision of "work placements" (*s 14C*) and "employment services" (*s 21A*, read with *ss 19* and *20*). "Vocational training" and "vocational guidance" are included within the scope of "employment services" (*DDA 1995, s 21A(1)(a), (b)*).

The *RBR 2003, SOR 2003* and *AR 2006* make clear that 'training' includes practical work experience provided by an employer to a person whom he does not employ; this is undoubtedly also within the meaning of 'training' in the *SDA 1975* (see especially *s 14(1B)*) and *RRA 1976* (training being defined under *s 78* of the *RRA 1976* as including '*any form of education or instruction*'). This point was confirmed by the EAT in *Chenge v Treasury Solicitor's Department* [2007] IRLR 386, in which the Department had sought to argue that the Government Legal Service vacation placement scheme (where successful applicants gain work experience placements for which they are paid only expenses) was not 'training' within the meaning of *s 13(1), RRA 1976*. The EAT held that the phrase '*any form of education*' could include education by watching as well as education by doing and that was no need to analyse in detail the syllabus of a scheme in order to decide whether it was a training scheme or a work placement scheme. There was no principled reason why *RRA 1976* should not apply to work experience or work placement. Nor did it matter how long a course took, though the EAT did note that if it was '*merely an educational visit*' that might fall in a different category. Previously, the EAT held in *Fletcher v NHS Pensions Agency* [2005] ICR 1458, that the NHS Pensions Agency, which provides bursaries to trainee midwives combining academic study at universities with practical training through clinical placements in the community and hospitals, is a 'training provider' within the meaning of *SDA 1975, s 14(1)* since the bursaries are a 'facility' for training.

However, where someone is appointed purely as a volunteer (even if they hope through that appointment to secure paid employment with the organisation), that is not 'vocational training'. Voluntary employment is outside the scope of the discrimination legislation: *X v Mid Sussex Citizens Advice Bureau* [2012] UKSC 59, [2013] IRLR 146.

The definition of 'training provider' excludes employers in relation to training for their own employees and also education establishments: *SDA 1975, s 14(2); RRA 1976, s 13(2); RBR 2003, reg 17(4); SOR 2003, reg 17(4); AR 2006, reg 20(4)*. This is because separate provision in relation to discrimination in education is made by both the *Acts* and the *Regulations*. Claims in relation to discrimination in education are excluded from the jurisdiction of the employment tribunals and are therefore outside the scope of this book. Note, however, that the mere fact that a provider of vocational training is acting as agent of an educational establishment does not mean that a claim against that provider is excluded from the jurisdiction of the employment tribunals, provided of course that the respondent otherwise falls within the definition of 'training provider' in the legislation: *Moyling v Homerton University Hospitals NHS Trust* (25 August 2005, unreported), EAT.

Unlawful discrimination against anyone undergoing or seeking to undergo vocational training

It is unlawful, in relation to a person seeking or undergoing training which would help fit him for any employment for any training provider to discriminate against him:

(a)   in the terms on which the training provider affords him access to any training (or any facilities concerned with such training);

(b)   by refusing or deliberately not affording him such access;

(c)   by terminating his training; or

(d)   by subjecting him to any other detriment during his training (*SDA 1975, s 14(1)*; *RRA 1976, s 13(1)*; *RBR 2003, reg 17(1)*; *SOR 2003, reg 17(1)*; *AR 2006, reg 20(1)*; see also *DDA 1995, ss 19(1)* and *21A*).

RBR 2003, SOR 2003, AR 2006 and, with effect from 1 October 2005, the *SDA 1975* also applies expressly to 'arrangements' made 'for the purpose of selecting people to receive vocational training' (*SDA 1975, s 14(1)(a)*, as amended by the *Sex Discrimination Regulations 2005*; *RBR 2003, reg 17(1)(aa)*; *SOR 2003, reg 17(1)(aa)*; *AR 2006, reg 20(1)(a)*).

In *Fletcher* the bursaries were stopped during the trainees' maternity leave: since the bursaries were 'facilities concerned with training', which were stopped because the claimants were pregnant, this was unlawful sex discrimination. The EAT ruled that the tribunal had been wrong to conclude that there was no unlawful discrimination because employees absent for other reasons were treated the same way.

All the exceptions that apply to discrimination by employers apply in relation to discrimination by providers of vocational training. The *RBR 2003, SOR 2003* and *AR 2006* provide that the training provider will have a defence where the alleged discrimination only concerns training for employment which, by virtue of the fact that the exception for genuine occupational requirement applies, the respondent could lawfully refuse to offer the person seeking training (*RBR 2003, reg 17(3)*; *SOR 2003, reg 17(3)*; *AR 2006, reg 20(3)*). The exceptions in the *RBR 2003, SOR 2003* and *AR 2006* for national security, positive action and the protection of Sikhs from discrimination in relation to the wearing of safety helmets apply generally to Parts II and III of both sets of *Regulations* and therefore apply to training providers as they do to employers. The *SDA 1975* and *RRA 1976* provide, simply, that all the exceptions that apply in relation to discrimination by employers apply also to training providers (*SDA 1975, s 14(2)*; *RRA 1976, s 13(2)*). (For exceptions see above **11.3, 11.10, 11.11, 11.12** and **11.17** ff.)

Unlawful harassment of persons undergoing or seeking to undergo training

It is unlawful for a training provider, in relation to a person seeking or undergoing training which would help fit him for any employment, to subject him to harassment (*SDA 1975, s 14(1A)*, as inserted with effect from 1 October 2005 by the *Sex Discrimination Regulations 2005*; *RRA 1976, s 13(3)*; *RBR 2003, reg 17(2)*; *SOR 2003, reg 17(2)*; *AR 2006, reg 20(2)*; *DDA 1995, s 21A(2)*).

11.32 Employment agencies, careers guidance, etc

The provisions relating to employment agencies apply in the predecessor legislation. The *EA 2010* covers such person by way of the provisions for employment service-providers (see below). Employment agencies are covered.

The *RBR 2003*, *SOR 2003* and *AR 2006* define an employment agency as 'a person who, for profit or not, provides services for the purpose of finding employment for workers or supplying respondents with workers'.

Under *DDA 1995*, employment agencies are covered as providers of "employment services", defined to include "services to assist a person to obtain or retain employment, or to establish himself as self-employed" (*s 21A(1)(c)*).

No definition is given in the *SDA 1975* or the *RRA 1976*, though both those *Acts*, like the *RBR 2003* and *SOR 2003*, state that references to the services of an employment agency include 'guidance on careers and any other services related to employment' (*SDA 1975, s 15(3), RRA 1976, s 11(3); RBR 2003, reg 18(6); SOR 2003, reg 18(6); AR 2006, reg 21(6)*). Education establishments are excluded from the definition of employment agencies (impliedly in the *SDA 1975* and the *RRA 1976*, expressly in the *RBR 2003* and *SOR 2003*: *reg 18(6)* and in *AR 2006, reg 21(6)*). (Separate provision in relation to discrimination in education is made by both the *Acts* and the *Regulations*. Consideration of this is, however, outside the scope of this book.)

Note that users of employment agencies may also be able to bring claims against the employer to whom they are supplied, either under the provisions relating to contract workers (see above **11.24**) or, in certain circumstances, as employees (see generally EMPLOYEE, SELF-EMPLOYED OR WORKER? **(14)**).

Unlawful discrimination against users and potential users of an employment agency

It is unlawful for an employment agency to discriminate against a person:

(a)   in the terms on which the agency offers to provide any of its services;

(b)   by refusing or deliberately not providing any of its services; or

(c)   in the way it provides any of its services (*SDA 1975, s 15(1); RRA 1976, s 14(1); RBR 2003, reg 18(1); SOR 2003, reg 18(1); AR 2006, reg 21(1)*).

All the exceptions that apply to discrimination by employers apply in relation to discrimination by employment agencies. The *RBR 2003*, *SOR 2003* and *AR 2006* provide that the agency will have a defence where the alleged discrimination 'only concerns employment which, by virtue of . . . (the) exception for genuine occupational requirement . . . the employer could lawfully refuse to offer the person in question' (*RBR 2003, reg 18(3); SOR 2003, reg 18(3); AR 2006, reg 20(3)*). The exceptions in the *RBR 2003, SOR 2003* and *AR 2006* for national security, positive action and the protection of Sikhs from discrimination in relation to the wearing of safety helmets apply generally to *Parts II* and *III* of both sets of *Regulations* and therefore apply to employment agencies as to employers. The *SDA 1975* and *RRA 1976* provide, simply, that the agency will have a defence where the alleged discrimination 'only concerns employment which an employer could lawfully refuse to offer the' person concerned (*SDA 1975, s 15(4); RRA 1976, s 14(4)*). (For circumstances in which an employer could lawfully refuse to offer employment see above **11.3, 11.10, 11.11, 11.12** and **11.17** ff.)

A further defence is available that is peculiar to employment agencies. An employment agency will not be liable for unlawful discrimination where it proves that 'it acted in reliance on a statement made to it by the employer to the effect that, by reason of (the existence of a genuine occupational requirement) its action would not be unlawful', provided that it also proves that it was reasonable for it to rely on the statement (*SDA 1975, s 15(5); RRA 1976, s 14(5); RBR 2003, reg 18(4); SOR 2003, reg 18(4); AR 2006, reg 21(4)*). Thus, if, for example, an employment agency relied on the statement of an employer who had been guilty of discrimination in the past, to the knowledge of the employment agency, it may be difficult for that agency to establish that it had acted reasonably in relying upon that statement.

If an employer knowingly or recklessly makes a statement to that effect which 'in a material respect is false or misleading', they thereby commit an offence punishable by a fine not exceeding level 5 on the standard scale (*SDA 1975, s 15(6)*; *RRA 1976, s 14(6)*; *RBR 2003, reg 18(5)*; *SOR 2003, reg 18(5)*; *AR 2006, reg 21(5)* see also **1.10** INTRODUCTION).

Unlawful harassment of users of an employment agency

It is unlawful for an employment agency, in relation to the provision of its services, to subject to harassment a person to whom it provides such services, or who has requested the provision of such services: *SDA 1975, s 15(1A)*, as inserted with effect from 1 October 2005 by the *Sex Discrimination Regulations 2005, reg 18*; *RRA 1976, s 14(1A)*; *RBR 2003, reg 18(2)*; *SOR 2003, reg 18(2)*; *AR 2006, reg 21(2)*; *DDA 1995, s 21A(2)*.

11.33   State provision of employment-related services

The provisions relating to state provision of employment-related services apply in the predecessor legislation. The *EA 2010* covers such person by way of the provisions for employment service-providers (see below).

Under the predecessor legislation, the prohibitions on discrimination and harassment also apply to the provision of facilities or services by the Secretary of State under the *Employment and Training Act 1973, s 2* (arrangements for assisting persons to obtain employment) and by the Scottish Enterprise or Highlands and Islands Enterprise under the *Enterprise and New Towns (Scotland) Act 1990, s 2(3)* (the equivalent provision for Scotland) (*SDA 1975, s 16(1), (1A)*; *RRA 1976, s 15(1), (1A)*; *RBR 2003, reg 19(1), (2)*; *SOR 2003, reg 19(1), (2)*; *AR 2006, reg 22(1), (2)*).

Similarly, the prohibitions on racial and sex discrimination and harassment apply where a local authority provides services under the *Employment and Training Act 1973, s 10* (*SDA 1975, s 15(2)*; *RRA 1976, s 14(2)*).

The provisions relating to the provision of facilities or services under the *Employment and Training Act 1973, s 2* are default provisions, applying only where the Secretary of State would not be covered by the provisions relating to employment agencies (see above **11.32**) or providers of vocational training generally (see above **11.31**): *SDA 1975, 16(2)*; *RRA 1976, s 15(2)*; *RBR 2003, reg 19(3)*; *SOR 2003, reg 19(3)*; *AR 2006, reg 20(3)*).

11.34   Employment service-providers

The *EA 2010* contains specific provision in relation to employment service-providers. This replaces the provision in the predecessor legislation on providers of vocational training, employment agencies and state provision of employment-related services, although case law on those types of provider (see above) will in the main continue to be relevant when construing the provision in the *EA 2010* on employment service-providers.

A non-exhaustive definition of employment service provision is given at *s 56(2)*. It includes the provision of vocational training, the provision of vocational guidance, the provision of a service for finding employment for persons, the supply of persons for work to employers, careers services and various other statutory services.

'Vocational training' is defined for the purposes of the section as 'training for employment' or 'work experience (including work experience the duration of which is not agreed until after it begins') (*s 56(6)*) and 'training' includes facilities for training (*s 56(8)*).

Section 55 makes it unlawful for any 'employment service-provider' to discriminate against, or victimise, persons:

(a)   in the arrangements they make for selecting persons to whom to provide, or to whom they offer to provide, their services;

(b)   as to the terms on which the service is provided;

(c)   by not providing, or not offering to provide, the service;

(d)   by terminating the provision of the service; or

(e)   by subjecting the individual to any other detriment (*EA 2010, s 55(1). (2), (4), (5)*).

There is also a specific prohibition on harassment by the employment service-providers: *EA 2010, s 55(3)*.

The employment services provision is a residual one that applies only where the other provisions relating to employment do not apply (*s 56(3)*). Training that is covered by the parts of the *Act* relating to schools and higher education is also excluded: *s 56(4)* and *(5)*.

The genuine occupational requirement exceptions (above para **11.2** ff) are applied indirectly to employment service-providers. They may refuse to provide employment services to persons where the services relate to employment of a type the offer of which could lawfully be refused to that person by virtue of a genuine occupational requirement: see *para 5 of Sch 9* to the *EA 2010*. An employment services provider will have a defence to any claim if he relies reasonably on a statement made by the person with the power to offer the work that a genuine occupational requirement would apply: *para 5(3)*. It is an offence for a person with the power to offer such work to knowingly or recklessly make a statement about a genuine occupational requirement that is false or misleading: *para 5(4)*. A person guilty of that offence is liable on summary conviction to a fine not exceeding level 5 on the standard scale: *para 5(5)*.

11.35 Trustees and managers of occupational pension schemes

EA 2010

The *EA 2010* makes specific provision in relation to occupational pension schemes. *Section 61(1)* provides that an occupational pension scheme must be taken to include a non-discrimination rule. A non-discrimination rule is a provision by which a 'responsible person' (A):

(a)   must not discriminate against another person (B) in carrying out any of his functions in relation to the scheme;

(b)   must not, in relation to the scheme, harass B;

(c)   must not, in relation to the scheme, victimise B (*s 61(2)*).

'Responsible persons' are the trustees or managers of the scheme, and employer whose employees are (or may be) members of the scheme and a person exercising an 'appointing function' in relation to an office the holder of which is, or may be, a member of the scheme (*s 61(4)*). An 'appointing function' includes the functions of appointing a person, terminating a person's appointment, recommending a person for appointment and approving an appointment (*s 61(6)*).

The non-discrimination rule does not operate in relation to a person who is already a pension credit member of the scheme, ie whose rights under the scheme have accrued: *s 61(5)*.

Section 62 makes specific provision to enable trustees and managers to make alterations to the scheme by resolution to conform with the non-discrimination rule, even if they do not have the power under the scheme to do so, or if the procedure for doing so would be liable to be unduly complex or protracted or involves obtaining consents which cannot be obtained or which can be obtained only with undue delay or difficulty.

There are a number of exceptions to these provisions for age discrimination under the *Equality Act (Age Exceptions for Pension Schemes) Order 2010 (SI 2010/2133)*. In summary, that Order excludes from the scope of the non-discrimination rule any rules, practices actions or decisions as they relate to rights accrued, or benefits payable, in respect of periods of pensionable service prior to 1 December 2006. It also excludes from the scope of the non-discrimination rule most rules, practices etc that use a person's age as determinative of contribution rates and benefits payable. *Reg 6* of the *2010 Order* also excludes rules, practices etc based on employee's length of service. Broadly speaking, trustees and managers will not discriminate by requiring contributions or making benefits available by reference to an employee's length of service, providing the employer has certified that he reasonably believes the rule in question serves a legitimate business need of its undertaking. Readers are referred to the text of the *Regulations* for further details.

Pre-*EA 2010*

The provisions in relation to occupational pension schemes in the predecessor legislation were similar.

The *RBR 2003* and *SOR 2003* (as amended with effect from 2 December 2003 by *The Employment Equality (Religion or Belief) (Amendment) Regulations 2003 (SI 2003/2828)* and *The Employment Equality (Sexual Orientation) (Amendment) Regulations 2003 (SI 2003/2827)* respectively) apply to trustees and managers of occupational pension schemes, as does the *DDA 1995* (as amended). *AR 2006* also apply to trustees and managers of pension schemes. However, there are detailed exceptions in relation to age set out in *Schedule 2* to *AR 2006*.

'Occupational pension scheme' has the same meaning as in the *Pensions Act 1995* (*RBR 2003, Sch 1A, para 1*; *SOR 2003, Sch 1A, para 1*; *AR 2006, Sch 2, para 1*).

Unlawful discrimination against members and prospective members of occupational pension schemes

Except in relation to rights accrued or benefits payable in respect of periods of service prior to 2 December 2003, it is unlawful for the trustees or managers of an occupational pension scheme to discriminate against 'a member or a prospective member of the scheme in carrying out any of their functions in relation to it (including in particular their functions relating to the admission of members to the scheme and the treatment of members of it)' (*RBR 2003, reg 9A(1)*; *SOR 2003, reg 9A(1)*; *AR 2006, reg 11(1)*).

Disability discrimination

It is unlawful for the trustees or managers of the scheme to discriminate against a disabled person contrary to the requirements of the non-discrimination rule. This provision which came into force on 1 October 2004 strengthens the position of disabled persons *vis-à-vis* their rights in relation to such schemes since it applies to any of the functions of the trustees or managers. However, this non-discrimination rule does not apply in relation to rights accrued, or benefits payable, in respect of periods of service before 1 October 2004. Readers should refer to the earlier incarnation of the non-discrimination rule for rights accruing before that date (*DDA 1995, s 4G*). Previously, regulations prescribed that less favourable treatment of a disabled person being considered for admission to a scheme is taken to be justified where, by reason of the disabled person's disability, the cost of providing any benefit under a scheme is likely to be substantially greater than it would be for a comparable person without that disability (*Disability Regulations, reg 4*). However, this has now been revoked (*Leasehold Premises Regulations, reg 3*). In addition, there is now a duty on the trustees and managers of such schemes to make reasonable adjustments where any provision, criterion or practice applied in respect of a scheme or any physical features of premises occupied by the trustees or managers places a disabled person at a substantial disadvantage in comparison to non-disabled persons. One such adjustment is the alteration of the scheme's rules (*DDA 1995, s 4H*). Claims in relation to such schemes can be brought in the tribunal although the tribunal does not have the power to award compensation in relation to arrears of benefits or otherwise (although a sum can be awarded for injury to feelings) except where the trustees or managers fail to comply with any recommendations made by the tribunal (*DDA 1995, ss 4J(4), 17A(5)*).

Unlawful harassment of members and prospective members of occupational pension schemes

It is also unlawful for trustees or managers in relation to the scheme, to subject a member or prospective member to harassment (*RBR 2003, reg 9A(2)*; *SOR 2003, reg 9A(2)*; *AR 2006, reg 11(2)*; *DDA 1995, s 4G(1)(b)*).

Inclusion of a 'non-discrimination rule' in the terms of the scheme

Sch 1A, para 2 of the *RBR 2003* and *SOR 2003, Sch 2, para 2* of *AR 2006* and *s 4G(1) DDA 1995* provide that every occupational pension scheme should be treated as including a 'non-discrimination rule' (compare the provisions relating to sex discrimination, above **11.11**(c)). The rule requires trustees or managers to refrain from 'doing any act which is unlawful by virtue of *reg 9A*' (or *reg 11*, in respect of age). All other provisions of the relevant pension scheme have effect subject to the non-discrimination rule (*RBR 2003, Sch 1A, para 3; SOR 2003, Sch 1A, para 3; AR 2006, Sch 2, para 2(2); DDA 1995, s 4G(2)*). The trustees or managers are given a power to alter the scheme by resolution so as to secure conformity with the non-discrimination rule where they either do not have an alteration power or else it is complex or dependent on the obtaining of consents which they are unable to obtain (*RBR 2003, Sch 1A, para 4; SOR 2003, Sch 1A, para 4; AR 2006, Sch 2, para 2(3); DDA 1995, s 4G(5)*). Resolutions may have a retrospective effect but cannot have effect in relation to any period prior to 2 December 2003 in relation to religion or belief, sexual orientation and disability (*RBR 2003, Sch 1A, para 5; SOR 2003, Sch 1A, para 5; DDA 1995, s 4G(4)*) and prior to 1 December 2006 in relation to age (*AR 2006, sch 2, para 2(4)*).

Note, however, that benefits dependent on marital or civil partnership status are excluded from the scope of the *SOR 2003*: see above **11.14**.

For remedies for breaches of the requirements in relation to occupational pension schemes, see **12.22** Discrimination and Equal Opportunities – III.

For the rules relating to sex discrimination by trustees and managers of pension schemes see above **11.11**(c).

There are no equivalent provisions relating to racial discrimination by trustees and managers of pension schemes.

The *EA 2010* applies to occupational pension schemes in the same way as the present legislation does: see *ss 61–63* of the *EA 2010*.

Detailed exceptions in relation to age

There are a number of detailed exceptions to the prohibition on discrimination by trustees and managers of pensions schemes on the grounds of age.

It should be noted that, although there is no sign of a challenge, these exemptions would themselves need to be justified in European Union Law. The *2006 Regulations* themselves state that the inclusion of a practice in the list of exemptions does not mean that it would otherwise be unlawful.

The following are, in summary, the practices which are exempted by *Sch 2* and so are lawful on the face of *AR 2006* in the case of occupational pensions:

    (a)   provisions which treat members or potential members of a scheme differently on the grounds of their length of service with an employer so long as that length of service is less than five years (*para 3A, Sch 2*);

(b)   length of service criteria of greater than five years, if it reasonably appears to the employer that this meets a business need (with regard to action by trustees or managers, they may rely on a confirmation by the employer) (*para 3A(2), Sch 2*);

(c)   setting minimum or maximum ages for admission, including different ages for different groups or categories of worker (*para 7(a), Part 2, Sch 2*);

(d)   setting a minimum level of pensionable pay for admission (provided this is not above one and a half times the lower earnings limit in *s 5(1)* of the *Social Security Contributions and Benefits Act 1992*, does not exceed an amount calculated by reference to the lower earnings limit where the aim is more or less to reflect the amount of the basic state retirement pension; or an amount calculated more or less to reflect the amount of the basic state retirement pension plus the additional state retirement pension) (*para 7(b), Part 2, Sch 2*);

(e)   the use of age criteria in actuarial calculations (para 8) (for a case in which this exemption was held to apply so as to preclude the claim see *Hulfield v Health & Safety Executive* UKEATS/0013/10/BI);

(f)   differences in contributions attributable to differences in pensionable pay (*para 9*);

(g)   under money purchase arrangements, different rates of contributions according to age where the aim is to equalise, or make more nearly equal, the amount of benefit to which members of different ages who are otherwise in comparable situations will become entitled (*para 10(a)*);

(h)   under money purchase arrangements, equal rates of contributions irrespective of age (*para 10(b)*);

(i)   under money purchase arrangements, any limitation on any employer contributions in respect of a member or member contributions by reference to a maximum level of pensionable pay (*para 10(c)*);

(j)   under defined benefits arrangements, different rates of contributions according to age to the extent that each year of pensionable service entitles members in a comparable situation to accrue the right to defined benefits based on the same fraction of pensionable pay, and the aim of setting the different rates is to reflect the increasing cost of providing the defined benefits in respect of members as they get older (*para 11*);

(k)   under defined benefit arrangements, any limitation on employer contributions in respect of a member or member contributions by reference to a maximum level of pensionable pay (*para 11A*);

(l)   a minimum age for entitlement to or payment of any age-related benefit to a member, provided that, in the case of any age-related benefit paid under a defined benefits arrangement before any early retirement pivot age, this benefit is subject to actuarial reduction for early receipt, and the member is not credited with additional periods of pensionable service (except where certain other exemptions for minimum ages for entitlement apply) (*para 12*);

(m)   a minimum age for entitlement to or payment of any age-related benefits under a defined scheme where it is not made subject to actuarial reduction for early receipt and/or it results from crediting the member with additional period of pensionable service, where a worker is an active or prospective member of the scheme as at 1 December 2006, the benefit may be paid at a minimum age with or without consent and the age-related benefit is enhanced in a specified manner (*para 13*);

(n)   a minimum age for payment or entitlement to a particular age-related benefit on grounds of redundancy where it is enhanced in a specified manner and paid either with or without consent (*para 13B*);

(o)   an early retirement or late retirement pivot age, including different ages for different groups or categories and any early retirement pivot age or later retirement pivot age for deferred members which is different than for active members (*para 14*);

(p)   a minimum age for any member of a scheme for payment or entitlement to a particular age-related benefit on grounds of ill health where the age-related benefit is enhanced in a specified manner and paid with or without consent (*para 15*);

(q)   the calculation of any death benefit payable in respect of a member by reference to some or all of the years of prospective pensionable service a member would have completed if he had remained in service until normal pension age or by reference to a fixed number of years of prospective pensionable service, death benefits calculated by reference to the period remaining in a pension guarantee period and any difference between death benefits between those who die before, on or after normal pension age in respect of deferred members (*para 15A*);

(r)   reducing a rate of pension to which a pensioner member is entitled at any time between age 60 and 65 by an amount not exceeding the relevant state retirement pension rate or the rate of the pension on payment where the relevant state retirement pension is greater (*para 16(1)*);

(s)   entitling a member, from the date he is entitled to present payment of a pension from a scheme, to an additional amount of pension which does not exceed the amount of the basic state retirement pension plus the additional state retirement pension that would be payable at state pension age (*para 16(1)*);

(t)   disentitling a member on reaching state pension age from being able to receive an additional amount of pension which does not exceed the amount of the basic state retirement pension plus the additional state retirement pension that would be payable at state pension age (*para 16(1)*);

(u)   the actuarial reduction of any pension payable from a scheme in consequence of a member's death to any dependent of the member where the dependent is more than a specified number of years younger than the member (*para 17*);

(v)   discontinuing life assurance to pensioner members who have retired from the scheme on ill health grounds once they reach the normal retirement age or, if none, at the age of 65 (*para 18*);

(w)   differences in the amount of any age-related benefit or death benefit attributable to differing lengths of service, so long as members in a comparable situation are entitled to accrue rights based upon the same fraction of pensionable pay (*para 19*);

(x)   certain differences in the fraction of pensionable pay at which any age-related benefit accrues, or the amount of death benefit, or age-related benefits, where the aim is to give members in a comparable situation the right to the same fraction proportion or multiple of pensionable pay without regard to pensionable service, and provided that each continues in pensionable service until normal pension age (*para 19A*);

(y)   where the aim is as in (s) above, setting a maximum amount of age-related benefits or death benefit equal to a fraction, proportion or multiple of the member's pensionable pay, or a minimum period of pensionable service (*para 19A(1) and (4)*);

(z)   where the aim is as in (s) above, setting different rates of member or employer contributions according to the age of the members where, for each year of pensionable service, members in comparable situations accrue different fractions of pensionable pay (*para 19B*);

(aa)   differences in the amount of age-related benefits or death benefits payable so far as this is attributable to differences in pensionable pay (*para 20*);

(bb)   limiting the amount of a benefit where this results from imposing a maximum number of years of service by reference to which the benefit is calculated and/or where it arises from imposing a maximum amount on the age-related benefit or death benefit equal to a fraction, proportion or multiple of pensionable pay (*para 21*);

(cc)   limiting age-related benefits or death benefits to those entitled to short service benefit (*para 22*);

(dd)   excluding from a calculation of pensionable pay an amount which does not exceed one and a half times the lower earning limit, aimed to reflect the basic state retirement pension, or calculated to reflect the basic state retirement pension plus the additional state retirement pension (*para 23*);

(ee)   differences in age-related or death benefits attributable to accrual of age-related benefit at a higher fraction for pensionable pay over the upper limit to reflect the additional state retirement pension (*para 23A*);

(ff)   limiting the amount of a benefit where this relates to all members joining or eligible to join on, after or before a particular date and which results from imposing a maximum level of pensionable pay by reference to which such benefit is calculated (*para 24*);

(gg)   closing a scheme, or a section of a scheme to workers who have not already joined it (*paras 25* and *25A*);

(hh)   increases of pensions in payment which are made only to members over 55 (*para 26*);

(ii)   different rates of increase of pensions for members of different ages (or of members who have contributed for different period) to maintain the relative value of members' pensions (*paras 27* and *28*);

(jj)   applying an age limit for transfer of the value of accrued rights, provided that this is not more than one year before the normal pension age (*para 29*); and

(kk)   where necessary to secure any tax relief or exemption available under *Part 4* of the *Finance Act 2004* or to prevent any charge to tax arising.

Part 3 of *Sch 2* sets out exceptions relating to contributions by employers to personal pension schemes. In particular, it is lawful for employers to pay different rates of contributions according to the age of the workers in respect of whom contributions are made where this is done to equalise, or make more nearly equal, the amount of benefit to which workers of different ages who are otherwise in a comparable situation will become entitled. It is also lawful to make different rates of contribution in respect of different workers to the extent that this is attributable to differences in remuneration payable to the workers.

Equality Act 2010

Unlike the *2006 Regulations*, *EA 2010* does not contain exemptions specifically for age. However, there will be a power for a Minister of the Crown to make exceptions in relation to rules, practices, actions or decisions relating to age (see *s 197*).

11.35A Local authority members

Section 58 of the *EA 2010* contains specific provision prohibiting local authorities from discriminating against a member of the authority in relation to the member's carrying out of 'official business' by not affording him access to training or other facilities or subjecting him to a detriment. By *s 59(4)*, 'official business' is anything the member does as a member of the authority, as a member of a body to which the member is appointed by the authority, or as a member of any other public body. A local authority must also not harass the member (*s 58(2)*) or victimise him (*s 58(3)*). However, *s 58(4)* provides that a member will not be subjected to a 'detriment' for these purposes only because the member is (a) not appointed or elected to an office of the authority, (b) not appointed or elected to, or to an office of, a committee or sub-committee of the authority, or (c) not appointed or nominated in exercise of an appointment power of the authority. By s 58(6) a duty to make reasonable adjustments also applies to a local authority (see also *paragraph 18* of *Schedule 8*). The genuine occupational requirement exception (above **11.2**) does not apply to qualifications bodies.

11.36   The Crown

In the *EA 2010* there are no specific provisions applying the *Act* to the Crown. It is to be supposed that it is considered that no specific provision is necessary because Crown employees will either be covered by the provisions for 'normal' employees, or by the provisions for office holders (above **11.25**).

Under the predecessor legislation, there are detailed provisions concerning the application of the legislation to:

(a)   the Crown, government departments, service in the armed forces, etc (*SDA 1975, s 85; RRA 1976, s 75; RBR 2003, reg 36; SOR 2003, reg 36; AR 2006, reg 44; DDA 1995, s 64*);

(b)   House of Commons staff (*SDA 1975, 85A; RRA 1976, s 75A; RBR 2003, reg 37; SOR 2003, reg 37; AR 2006, reg 45; DDA 1995, s 65*); and

(c)   House of Lords staff (*SDA 1975, s 85B; RRA 1976, s 75B; RBR 2003, reg 38; SOR 2003, reg 38; AR 2006, reg 46; DDA 1995, s 65*).

The effect of those provisions, broadly speaking, is that the equality legislation applies to the Crown, etc 'as it does to an act done by a private person'. To achieve this, references in the legislation to a contract of employment are deemed to include references to the terms of service of Crown servants (*SDA 1975, s 85(2); RRA 1976, s 75(2); RBR 2003, reg 36(2); SOR 2003, reg 36(2); AR 2006, reg 44(1)*; see also *DDA 1995, s 64(2)*) and aircraft or hovercraft 'belonging to or possessed by Her Majesty in right of the Government of the United Kingdom' are deemed to be 'establishments' for the purposes of determining whether a person is employed at an establishment in Great Britain (*SDA 1975, s 85(7); RRA 1976, s 75(4); RBR 2003, reg 36(4); SOR 2003, reg 36(4); DDA 1995, s 68(2); AR 2006, reg 44(5)* and see above **11.18**).

There are peculiarities specific to the different *Acts* and *Regulations*:

(a)   'Nothing' in the *SDA 1975* renders unlawful (i) an act done 'for the purpose of ensuring the combat effectiveness of the armed forces' (*SDA 1975, s 85(1)*) or (ii) discrimination in admission to the Army Cadet Force, Air Training Corps, Sea Cadet Corps, Combined Cadet Force, or any other cadet training corps for the time being administered by the Ministry of Defence.

(b)   'Nothing' in the *RRA 1976* invalidates 'any rules' (whether made before or after the passing of that *Act*) 'restricting employment in the service of the Crown or by any [prescribed] public body to persons of particular birth, nationality, descent or residence'; nor does it render unlawful 'the publication, display or implementation of any such rules, or the publication of advertisements stating the gist of any such rules' (*RRA 1976, s 75(5)*).

(c)   In the *RBR 2003*, the *SOR 2003* and *AR 2006*, the provisions relating to Crown employment etc have effect subject to the provisions which relate to the application of the *Regulations* to the police (see above **11.26**).

Special provision is made in relation to the enforcement of complaints by members of the armed forces (*SDA 1975, s 85(9A)–(9E); RRA 1976, s 75(8)–(9B)*; and regulations made under each of those provisions; *RBR 2003, reg 36(7)–(10); SOR 2003, reg 36(7)–(10)*).

Broadly speaking, the effect of those provisions is that a member of the armed forces may only present a complaint to the employment tribunal if he has made a complaint in respect of the same matter to an officer under the service redress procedures and that complaint has not been withdrawn. A complaint will be treated as having been withdrawn if, having made the complaint to an officer, the complainant subsequently fails to submit that complaint to the Defence Council. However, presenting a complaint to the employment tribunal does not prevent the continuation of the service redress procedures. (See generally **12.2** DISCRIMINATION AND EQUAL OPPORTUNITIES – III.)

By contrast, *AR 2006* and *DDA 1995* do not apply to the armed forces.

Detailed provisions also set out how the *Crown Proceedings Act 1947* applies to proceedings under the *SDA 1975* and the *RRA 1976*: *SDA 1975, s 85(8), (9)*; *RRA 1976, s 75(6), (7)*.

11.37 GENERAL EQUALITY DUTIES ON PUBLIC AUTHORITIES

Section 71 RRA 1976 has, since its amendment by the *Race Relations (Amendment) Act 2000* with effect from 2 April 2001, imposed a general duty on public authorities, when carrying out any of their functions, to have due regard to the need (a) 'to eliminate unlawful racial discrimination' and (b) 'to promote equality of opportunity and good relations between persons of different racial groups'. This new duty replaced an earlier, more limited, duty on public authorities contained in that section.

A similar duty has now been inserted into the *SDA 1975* by the *Equality Act 2006*. With effect from 6 April 2007, a new Gender Equality Duty ('GED') is imposed on all public authorities. By *s 76A(1) SDA 1975*, all public authorities are required, when carrying out their functions, to have due regard (a) 'to the need to eliminate unlawful discrimination and harassment', and (b) 'to promote equality of opportunity between men and women'.

DDA 1995, s 49A also imposes a general duty on public authorities in carrying out their functions to have due regard to the need to eliminate unlawful disability discrimination, the need to eliminate harassment, the need to promote equality of opportunity, the need to take steps to take account of disabled persons' disabilities (even where that involves treating disabled persons more favourably than other persons), the need to promote positive attitudes towards disabled persons and the need to encourage participation by disabled persons in public life (*DDA 2005, s 3*). A full analysis of these provisions is outside the scope of this book. Similar provisions in respect of the 'public sector equality duty' are at *Part 11* of *EA 2010*.

'Public authority' is defined for the purposes of the *SDA 1975* and *DDA 1995* in the same way as a 'public authority' under the *Human Rights Act 1998* as 'any person who has functions of a public nature'. Under the *RRA 1976* a list of public authorities covered by the general duty is given in *Sch 1A* to the *Act*. However, broadly speaking both the *RRA 1976*, the *DDA 1995* and the *SDA 1975* cover all bodies who have functions of a public nature, apart from certain specific exceptions, which include the House of Commons, House of Lords, the Scottish Parliament, judicial functions and the government intelligence services.

The duties in the *SDA 1975*, the *DDA 1995* and those in the *RRA 1976* apply to all the functions of a public authority including their employment and procurement functions. They therefore have an impact on the employment field because public authorities are required to comply with the general equality duties in relation to their own employees (and applicants for employment). In addition, private companies who wish to win contracts to perform services for public authorities in turn have to demonstrate that they are taking steps to promote gender equality in order to be selected by the public authority.

The general duties are stated to be 'without prejudice' to other provisions of the *SDA 1975*, the *DDA 1995* and the *RRA 1976* (*SDA 1975, s 76A(5); DDA 1995, s 49A(2)* and *RRA 1976, s 71(7)*). The accompanying Codes of Practice, issued under *SDA 1975, s 76E* and

RRA 1976, s 71C, explain that what is meant by this is that positive discrimination will be allowed (indeed, is required) insofar as it is designed to achieve equality of opportunity by, for example, targeting only men or only women when advertising a particular job or training opportunity. However, in relation to the actual appointment itself, positive discrimination remains prohibited. The GED duty applies in relation to all discrimination rendered unlawful by the *SDA 1975* or the *EqPA 1970*, ie it applies not only to unlawful discrimination as between men and women, but also in relation to unlawful discrimination against transsexual persons and unlawful discrimination on grounds of maternity. The general duty under the *RRA 1976* applies in relation to all discrimination rendered unlawful by the *RRA 1976* (ie to discrimination on grounds of race, nationality, ethnic group, etc).

In addition to the general duties under the *RRA 1976* and the *SDA 1975*, certain specific duties are introduced by dint of subsidiary legislation made under *SDA 1975, s 76B* and *RRA 1976, s 71A*. These specific duties include obligations on the public authority:

(a)   to prepare and publish gender and racial equality schemes, showing how it will meet its general and specific duties under the Acts and setting out its gender equality objectives;

(b)   in formulating its overall objectives, to consider the need to include objectives to address the causes of any gender pay gap;

(c)   to gather and use information on how the public authority's policies and practices affect gender and racial equality in the workforce and in the delivery of services;

(d)   to consult stakeholders (ie employees, service users and others, including trade unions) and take account of relevant information in order to determine its gender and racial equality objectives;

(e)   to assess the impact of its current and proposed policies and practices on gender and racial equality;

(f)   to implement the actions set out in its scheme within three years, unless it is unreasonable or impracticable to do so; and,

(g)   to report against the scheme every year and review the scheme at least every three years.

The GEDs are preserved under the *EA 2010* by *ss 149–157* of that Act, which came fully into force on 6 April 2011. *Section 149(1)* creates a new, truly general public sector equality duty ("PSED") (in the sense that it applies to all protected characteristics apart from marital/civil partnership status: see *s 159(7)*), which requires public authorities and others exercising public functions (*s 149(2)*), in the exercise of their functions, to have 'due regard to the need to':

(a)   eliminate discrimination, harassment, victimisation and any other conduct that is prohibited by or under the *EA 2010*;

(b)   advance equality of opportunity between persons who share a relevant protected characteristic and persons who do not share it;

(c)   foster good relations between persons who share a relevant protected characteristic and persons who do not share it.

Section 149(3) makes clear that the 'due regard' duty includes in particular a duty to have due regard to the need to remove or minimise disadvantages suffered by persons who share a relevant protected characteristic that are connected to that characteristic, to take steps to meet the needs of persons who share a relevant protected characteristic that are different from the needs of persons who do not share it, and to encourage persons who share a relevant protected characteristic to participate in public life or in any other activity in which participation by such persons is disproportionately low. *Section 149(5)* further stipulates that having due regard to the need to foster good relations between persons includes having due regard to the need to tackle prejudice and promote understanding. The section recognises that compliance with the PSED may involve treating some persons more favourably than others, but makes clear that this is not to be taken as permitting conduct that would otherwise be prohibited under the Act (*s 149(6)* and see **11.10** above for the exceptions for positive discrimination).

Note that the duty does not sanction treating some people more favourably than others where this would be conduct otherwise prohibited under the *EA 2010* (see *s 149(6)*).

In addition to the PSED, the *EA 2010* also imposed certain specific duties on public authorities for the purpose of enabling the better performance by the authority of its PSED: see *s 153*. Those specific duties are set out in the *Equality Act 2010 (Specific Duties) Regulations 2011*. They require public authorities to publish information to demonstrate their compliance with the PSED and to set (and publish) specific equality objectives.

For decisions on the general duties, see *Pieretti v Enfield LBC* [2010] EWCA Civ 1104; *R (Harris) v Haringey London Borough Council (Equality and Human Rights Commission intervening)* [2010] EWCA Civ 703, [2010] EqLR 98; *R (Domb) v Hammersmith and Fulham London Borough Council* [2009] EWCA Civ 941, [2009] LGR 843; *McCarthy v Basildon District Council (Equality and Human Rights Commission intervening)* [2009] EWCA Civ 13, [2009] BLGR 1013; *R (on the application of Baker) v Secretary of State for Communities and Local Government* [2008] EWCA Civ 141, [2008] LGR 239; *R (Brown) v Secretary of State for Work and Pensions and ors* [2008] EWHC 3158 (Admin); *R (Greenwich Community Law Centre) v Greenwich LBC* [2012] EWCA Civ 496; and *R (Bailey) v Brent LBC* [2011] EWCA Civ 1586, [2012] EqLR 168.

11.38 Enforcement

Enforcement of the general duties under all the Acts is the responsibility of the Equality and Human Rights Commission (*ss 31* and *32* of the *Equality Act 2006*). *Section 76A(6)* of *SDA 1975* and *s 156* of the *EA 2010* further make it clear that there is no 'cause of action at private law' in relation to an alleged breach of the GEDs or PSED. This leaves open the possibility of a judicial review claim by a private individual in relation to alleged breaches of these general duties, and many such claims have been brought (see **11.37** above). Permission to apply for judicial review may, however, be refused in such cases if the court considers that the option of complaint to the EHRC constitutes an adequate alternative remedy for the individual.

12   Discrimination and Equal Opportunities – III: Enforcement

12.1   The *Equality Act 2010* (*'EA 2010'*) makes provision in relation to nine 'protected characteristics' defined in *s 4*, namely: age, disability, gender reassignment, marriage and civil partnership, pregnancy and maternity, race, religion or belief, sex, and sexual orientation (see further DISCRIMINATION AND EQUAL OPPORTUNITIES – I (10) above). The vast majority of the provisions of the *EA 2010* in relation to employment and all those relevant to this chapter came into force on 1 October 2010. The *EA 2010* therefore now provides a unified code covering all anti-discrimination law. Insofar as the contents of this chapter are concerned, the *EA 2010* very largely replicates (and consolidates and simplifies) the provisions of the previous Acts and Regulations, namely the *Sex Discrimination Act 1975* (*'SDA 1975'*), the *Race Relations Act 1976* (*'RRA 1976'*), the *Employment Equality (Sexual Orientation) Regulations 2003 (SI 2003/1661)* (*'SOR 2003'*), the *Employment Equality (Religion or Belief) Regulations 2003 (SI 2003/1660)* (*'RBR 2003'*), the *Disability Discrimination Act 1995* (*'DDA 1995'*) and the *Employment Equality (Age) Regulations 2006 (SI 2006/1031)* (*'AR 2006'*). With effect from 1 October 2010 the *EA 2010* repealed (so far as is relevant for this chapter) those Acts and Regulations. However this chapter continues to make extensive reference to those Acts and Regulations for two reasons. First, there remain a number of cases working their way through the tribunal system under the old legislation. Secondly, as the *EA 2010* largely replicates the old legislation the vast majority of cases under the old legislation remains relevant to the interpretation of the equivalent provisions of the *EA 2010* and the understanding of those cases is assisted by citation of the old legislation.

No civil or criminal proceedings may be taken against any person for a breach of any provision of the *EA 2010* (and previously the *SDA 1975, RRA 1976, SOR 2003, RBR 2003, DDA 1995* or *AR 2006*), except where such an action is expressly provided for by the *EA 2010* (and previously by those Acts or Regulations) (*EA 2010, s 113(1)*; and previously *SDA 1975, s 62(1); RRA 1976, s 53(1); SOR 2003, reg 27(1); RBR 2003, reg 27(1); DDA 1995, Sch 3, para 2(1)*; and *AR 2006, reg 35(1)*). This does not restrict the making of quashing, mandatory or prohibiting orders (which are remedies obtained against public bodies upon an application for judicial review) or a complaint to the Pensions Ombudsman (*EA 2010, s 113(3)*; and previously the *SDA 1975, s 62(2); RRA 1976, s 53(2); SOR 2003, reg 27(2); RBR 2003, reg 27(2); DDA 1995, Sch 3, para 2(2)*; and *AR 2006, reg 35(2)*). One difference is that employment tribunals now have jurisdiction in relation to certain complaints relating to occupational pension schemes under the *EA 2010, s 120(2)–(5)*. The only means of direct enforcement open to an individual for discrimination, in relation to employment, is generally by application to an employment tribunal (see **12.2** below).

Since 1 October 2007 the Commission for Equality and Human Rights (also now known as the Equality and Human Rights Commission ('EHRC')), established under the *Equality Act 2006* (*'EA 2006'*) (see **12.23** – **12.24** below) has had additional powers to hold investigations (see **12.25** – **12.27** below), issue unlawful act notices (see **12.28** below) and may apply for an injunction in certain cases (see **12.29** – **12.30** below). Previously, in the case of sex, race and disability discrimination only, the Equal Opportunities Commission ('EOC'), the Commission for Racial Equality ('CRE') and Disability Rights Commission ('DRC') respectively exercised similar powers.

Where the *EA 2010* (or previously the *SDA 1975, RRA 1976, SOR 2003, RBR 2003, DDA 1995* or *AR 2006*) does not confer the rights granted by EU directives, such as the *EEC Directive 76/207* ('the *Equal Treatment Directive*') or the *Framework Directive 2000/78/EC*, individuals may rely upon these Directives in claims against state authorities (see further **35.8** PUBLIC SECTOR EMPLOYEES and **10.2** DISCRIMINATION AND EQUAL OPPORTUNITIES – I).

Discrimination and Equal Opportunities – III: Enforcement

The provisions under the *SDA 1975, RRA 1976, SOR 2003, RBR 2003, DDA 1995* and *AR 2006* were very similar and when referring to the previous legislation this chapter addresses the issue of enforcement in these six areas together, highlighting any relevant differences. The *EA 2010* (principally *Pts 9* and *10*) largely replicates those provisions.

Reference can also be made to *Harvey on Industrial Relations and Employment Law* (Harveys – L (Equal Opportunities) and PI (Practice and Procedure)).

12.2 APPLICATIONS TO AN EMPLOYMENT TRIBUNAL

Under the *EA 2010, s 120* an employment tribunal has jurisdiction to determine a complaint relating to (a) a contravention of *Pt 5* (work) and (b) a contravention of *ss 108* (relationship that has come to an end), *111* (instructing, causing and inducing contraventions) or *112* (aiding contraventions) that relates to *Pt 5*. An employment tribunal also has jurisdiction to determine various applications and questions in relation to occupational pension schemes which are outside the scope of this chapter (*EA 2010, ss 120(2)–(5)*).

At present there are conflicting EAT decisions on whether a claim can be brought for victimisation (as opposed to discrimination or harassment) occurring after the employment relationship has ended: see *Rowstock Ltd v Jessemey* [2013] IRLR 439 and *Onu v Akwiwu* (EAT 1/5/2013).

No claim can be brought by a person who is a volunteer rather than an employee or other "worker" (*X v Mid-Sussex CAB and another* [2012] UKSC 59, [2013] ICR 249).

Previously a person ('the complainant') could present a complaint to an employment tribunal that another person had committed an act of discrimination or harassment against them which was unlawful by virtue of any of the provisions relating to employment (*SDA 1975, s 63(1); RRA 1976, s 54(1); SOR 2003, reg 28(1); RBR 2003, reg 28(1); DDA 1995, s 17A;* and *AR 2006, reg 36(1)*).

The employer of a discriminator is also liable for the discrimination under the *EA 2010, s 109* (previously *SDA 1975, ss 41, 42; RRA 1976, ss 32, 33; SOR 2003, reg 22, 23; RBR 2003, reg 22, 23; DDA 1995, ss 57, 58;* and *AR 2006, reg 25, 26*).

A complainant is entitled to include an individual respondent (eg a fellow employee) in his claim to see that that person is called to account as it is not correct to say that the primary liability for discrimination rests with the employer (see *Barlow v Stone* [2012] IRLR 898), but the complainant will need to plead a case that could prove that the individual respondent satisfies the requirements for liability under these provisions (see *Allaway v Reilly* [2007] IRLR 864, EAT). Where a claimant brings a claim against an unincorporated association it is permissible to do so either in the name of the association or in the name of a representative respondent, provided that the members of the board or management committee are actually aware of the proceedings and that where allegations are made against specific members those are joined as respondents (see *Nazir v Asim* [2010] ICR 1225, EAT). A tribunal may not exercise the power of joinder under *rule 10(2)(k)* of the *Employment Tribunals (Constitution and rules of procedure) Regulations 2004 (SI 2004/1861), Sch 1*, to join a fellow employee as respondent at the request of the respondent employer where the claimant has disavowed any intention to pursue a claim against the fellow employee (see *Beresford v Sovereign House Estates* [2012] ICR D9, EAT).

In the case of sex and race discrimination members of the armed forces have also been able to bring claims in the employment tribunal since 1 October 1997 (previously pursuant to the (now repealed) *Sex Discrimination (Complaints to Employment Tribunals) (Armed Forces) Regulations 1997 (SI 1997/2163)* (as amended by the *Armed Forces Act 2006 (Consequential Amendments) Order 2009 (SI 2009/2054), art 2* and *Sch 1*) and the (now repealed) *Race Relations (Complaints to Employment Tribunals)(Armed Forces) Regulations 1997 (SI*

1997/2161) (as amended by the *Armed Forces Act 2006 (Consequential Amendments) Order 2009 (SI 2009/2054), art 2* and *Sch 1)*). Prior to October 1997 members of the armed forces had been subject to a separate statutory regime. Similar provisions were also contained in *SOR 2003, reg 36* and *RBR 2003, reg 36*, but not in *DDA 1995* and *AR 2006*, both of which expressly provided that they did not apply to service in any of the naval, military or air forces *(DDA 1995, s 64(7)*; *AR 2006, reg 44(4))*.

The *EA 2010, s 121* now makes similar provision to those previously in relation to race, sex, sexual orientation and religion or belief in relation to complaints by members of the armed forces and does now include complaints of age discrimination. Where a member of the armed forces has the right to bring a claim, he may only present a complaint to the employment tribunal if he has made a complaint in respect of the same matter to an officer under the service complaints procedures prescribed by regulations made under the *Armed Forces Act 2006, s 334*, and that complaint has not been withdrawn. A complaint will be treated as having been withdrawn if, having made the complaint to an officer neither that officer nor a superior officer has decided to refer the complaint to the Defence Council, and the complainant fails to apply for such a reference to be made. Presenting a complaint to the employment tribunal does not prevent the continuation of the service redress procedures. An employment tribunal will not have jurisdiction to hear a claim from a member of the armed forces if a 'service complaint' has not been accepted as valid by the prescribed officer under the services complaints procedure (eg because it was made out of time) and this requirement does not breach EU law (see *Molaundi v Ministry of Defence* [2011] ICR D19, (2011) 939 IDS Brief 21, EAT).

An exception to the jurisdiction of the employment tribunals for employment-related claims exists for acts committed (or treated as committed) by qualifications bodies. It is not possible to complain to the employment tribunal if the act complained of is one in respect of which an appeal, or proceedings in the nature of an appeal, may be brought under any enactment (the *EA 2010, s 120(8)*; and previously *SDA 1975, s 63(2)*; *RRA 1976, s 54(2)*; *SOR 2003, reg 28(2)(a)*; *RBR 2003, reg 28(2)(a)*; *DDA 1995, s 17A(1A)*; and *AR 2006, reg 36(2)(a)*). The scope and effect of these provisions under the *RRA 1976* were considered in *R v Department of Health, ex p Gandhi* [1991] ICR 805; *Khan v General Medical Council* [1994] IRLR 646, CA; and *Chaudhary v Specialist Training Authority Appeal Panel (No 2)* [2005] EWCA Civ 282, [2005] ICR 1086). In *Watt (formerly Carter) v Ahsan* [2007] UKHL 51, [2008] 1 AC 696, [2008] ICR 82, the House of Lords held that an employment tribunal had been a court of competent jurisdiction to decide that the Labour Party was a body conferring a qualification or authorisation needed for engagement in a profession or trade for the purposes of the *RRA 1976, s 12*, notwithstanding that a subsequent decision of the Court of Appeal had shown that decision to be wrong (and hence the claim should have been brought in the county court).

Tribunals also lack jurisdiction to hear complaints about discriminatory conduct in the course of judicial or quasi-judicial proceedings, and a police disciplinary board has been held to be a judicial body (*Heath v Metropolitan Police Comr* [2004] EWCA Civ 943, [2005] ICR 329). That immunity from suit does not extend to the decision to commence disciplinary proceedings nor to a chief constable's decision to dismiss (*Lake v British Transport Police* [2007] ICR 47, EAT). Moreover, a police disciplinary board's immunity from suit is not impeached so as to oust the employment tribunal's jurisdiction where the claimant merely seeks to advance before the employment tribunal a case that had been rejected by the board (*Lake v British Transport Police* [2007] EWCA Civ 424, [2007] ICR 1293, reversing the EAT's decision on this issue). In *South London & Maudsley NHS Trust v Dathi* [2008] IRLR 350, EAT, a claim for victimisation based on the respondent's letters in response to a costs application and an application for disclosure in the course of previous discrimination proceedings should have been struck out by the tribunal as the letters attracted absolute immunity as they had come into existence for the purpose of those proceedings. In *Parmar v East Leicester Medical Practice* [2011] IRLR 641, EAT, Underhill

P confirmed that the absolute privilege identified in *Heath* applies also to a witness who prepares a witness statement, even if a trial never takes place, and applies also to claims of alleged victimisation as well as other forms of discrimination.

Discrimination claims do not lapse on the death of the complainant. The deceased's estate may commence or continue proceedings (*Lewisham and Guys Mental Health NHS Trust v Andrews* [2000] ICR 707, CA). A discrimination claim is a 'hybrid' claim and a bankrupt has standing to bring such a claim provided that he limits the remedy sought to a declaration or compensation for injury to feelings (*Khan v Trident Safeguards Ltd* [2004] EWCA Civ 624, [2004] IRLR 961). Where a claimant employed as a member of a diplomatic mission by a foreign state claims for personal injury in a discrimination claim the employment tribunal does have jurisdiction to hear such a claim as it falls within the exception from state immunity for claims in respect of personal injury under the *State Immunity Act 1978, s 5* (see *Federal Republic of Nigeria v Ogbonna* [2012] ICR 32, EAT).

Where, following the transfer of business under the *Transfer of Undertakings (Protection of Employment) Regulations 1981 (SI 1981/1794)* (now the *Transfer of Undertakings (Protection of Employment) Regulations 2006 (SI 2006/2405)*), a complainant complained that the refusal of a reference by the transferor after the TUPE transfer was victimisation under the *RRA 1976, s 2*, any liability was that of the transferor and did not pass to the transferee (*Coutinho v Vision Information Services Ltd* (2008) 849 IDS Brief 12, EAT). In proceedings related to the latter case the Court of Appeal has held that an employment tribunal was wrong to strike out for want of jurisdiction a claim brought by the claimant in which he argued that the failure by the TUPE transferee to honour an award of compensation was itself victimisation for the purposes of the *RRA 1976, s 2* (see *Rank Nemo (DMS) Ltd v Coutinho* [2009] EWCA Civ 454, [2009] ICR 1296, [2009] IRLR 672).

The *EA 2010, s 140* now gives courts and employment tribunals the power to transfer between each other proceedings in certain circumstances. Where conduct has given rise to two or more separate proceedings under the *Act*, with at least one being for a contravention of *s 111* (instructing, causing or inducing contraventions), a court may transfer proceedings to an employment tribunal or an employment tribunal may transfer proceedings to a court (*EA 2010, s 140(1), (2), (3)*). A court or employment tribunal is to be taken for the purposes of *Pt 9* of the *EA 2010* to have jurisdiction to determine a claim or complaint transferred to it under the section (*EA 2010, s 140(4)*). A court or employment tribunal may not make a decision that is inconsistent with an earlier decision in proceedings arising out of the conduct (*EA 2010, s 140(5)*).

Final findings in previous relevant proceedings are treated as conclusive in proceedings under the *EA 2010* (*EA 2010, s 137(1)*). The 'relevant proceedings' are those under the *Race Relations Act 1968, ss 19* or *20*, the *EqPA 1970*, the *SDA 1975*, the *RRA 1976*, the *Sex Discrimination Act 1986, s 6(4A)*, the *DDA 1995, Pt 2* of the *EA 2006*, the *SOR 2003*, the *RBR 2003, AR 2006*, and the *Equality Act (Sexual Orientation) Regulations 2007 (SI 2007/1263)* (*EA 2010, s 137(2)*).

12.3   Burden of proof

The burden of proof has been an area that has generated much case law over previous years, particularly following the introduction of a 'reverse' burden of proof. The *EA 2010, s 136(2), (3)* provides for a 'reverse' burden of proof but in slightly different (and simpler) terms than under the previous *Acts* and *Regulations*:

(a)   If there are facts from which the court could decide, in the absence of any other explanation, that a person (A) contravened the provision concerned, the court must hold that the contravention occurred (*s 136(2)*).

(b)   This does not apply if A shows that A did not contravene the provision (*s 136(3)*).

This burden of proof applies to all the protected characteristics and proceedings for any type of contravention of the *Act* (*s 136(1)*). So the complications in relation to the potentially different treatment of race victimisation and colour and nationality claims discussed below is removed.

It is however important to understand the development of the burden of proof because much of the recent case law on burden of proof will remain relevant and because of the historic legacy of existing cases decided under the previous legislation.

But it is also important not to exaggerate the importance of the reversed burden of proof. Where the tribunal is in a position to make clear findings of fact in relation to allegedly discriminatory conduct, the reversed burden of proof has no effect, and the discussion below should be read with this fact in mind. See *Hewage v Grampian Health Board* [2012] UKSC 37, [2012] ICR 1054 per Lord Hope, paragraph 32.

SDA 1975 and *RRA 1976* both originally had the effect that the complainant had the burden of showing both that they had been less favourably treated and also that the less favourable treatment had been on grounds of sex or race. In practice, the burden proved difficult to discharge. Discrimination was very rarely overtly sexist or racist and the complainant had instead to persuade the tribunal to draw an inference. Complainants were assisted by case law (most famously *King v Great Britain-China Centre* [1992] ICR 516, CA) in which the following approach was advocated. First, the complainant had to establish a difference in sex or race and that they had been less favourably treated. Once this prima facie case had been established the tribunal was entitled to turn to the employer and seek an explanation for this disparity in treatment. If the employer's explanation was unsatisfactory the tribunal was entitled but not obliged (see *Glasgow City Council v Zafar* [1998] ICR 120, HL) to draw an inference that the less favourable treatment was on the relevant prohibited ground. The advantage of the guidance allowing rather than compelling the drawing of an inference is that it made allowance for the fact that humans are capable of acting inconsistently and unreasonably and yet not discriminatorily.

Over the last decade by way of a series of amendments to the Acts and in the new *SOR 2003*, *RBR 2003* and *AR 2006* a new split burden of proof was introduced in discrimination cases. Except for race victimisation claims and possibly race discrimination claims on grounds of colour or nationality, the new burden of proof was applicable to all other discrimination and harassment claims under the *SDA 1975, RRA 1976, SOR 2003, RBR 2003, DDA 1995* and *AR 2006*, including claims where the respondent was vicariously liable or knowingly aided a prohibited act. The relevant provisions were:

Sex	*SDA 1975, s 63A*
Marital status	*SDA 1975, s 63A*
Pregnancy or maternity leave	*SDA 1975, s 63A*
Gender reassignment	*SDA 1975, s 63A*
Race	*RRA 1976, s 54A*
Sexual orientation	*SOR 2003, reg 29*
Religion or belief	*RBR 2003, reg 29*
Age	*AR 2006, reg 37(2)*
Disability	*DDA 1995, s 17A(1C)*

Where, on the hearing of the complaint, the complainant proved facts from which the tribunal could conclude in the absence of an adequate explanation that the respondent:

(a)   had committed an unlawful act against the complainant falling within the jurisdiction of the employment tribunal; or

(b)   was either vicariously liable for such an act or had knowingly aided the commission of such an act;

the tribunal had to uphold the complaint unless the respondent proved that he did not commit, or as the case may be, was not to be treated as having committed, the act.

There was some conflict at the EAT level as to whether the old test continued to apply in cases of racial discrimination on grounds of colour or nationality. In *Okonu v G4S Services (UK) Ltd* [2008] ICR 598, EAT, the EAT held that it did and that it was therefore essential that a tribunal identified at an early stage which grounds were relied upon. However that approach was not taken in *Chagger v Abbey National plc* [2009] ICR 624, [2009] IRLR 86, EAT, where a different division of the EAT held that the *RRA 1976, s 54A* did apply in the case of discrimination on the grounds of colour. The EAT also noted that there was considerable overlap between the grounds for discrimination and a claimant complaining of discrimination on the grounds of colour would inevitably also be complaining on grounds of race or ethnic origin as well. The *Chagger* approach was followed in *Edozie v Group 4 Securicor plc* (2010) 894 IDS Brief 7, EAT. Whether *Okonu* or *Chagger* was correct, the reality was likely to be that it would be a rare case indeed where the point actually had practical import.

The EAT also held that the new reversed burden of proof under the *RRA 1976, s 54A* did not apply to victimisation claims under the *RRA 1976, s 2* (*Oyarce v Cheshire County Council* [2007] ICR 1693, EAT; affd by [2008] EWCA Civ 434, [2008] ICR 1179, [2008] IRLR 653). However the reverse burden of proof provisions under the *SDA 1975, s 63A* were held to apply to victimisation claims under the *SDA 1975, s 4* as *s 63A* was worded differently from the *RRA 1976, s 54A* (*Pothecary Witham Weld v Bullimore* [2010] IRLR 572, [2010] ICR 1008, EAT). These complexities will now be a thing of the past under the *EA 2010*.

Seminal general guidance on the application of the reverse burden of proof test was provided by the EAT in *Barton v Investec Henderson Crosthwaite Securities Ltd* [2003] ICR 1205, EAT at 1218F and by the Court of Appeal in *Wong v Igen Ltd* [2005] EWCA Civ 142, [2005] ICR 931. The guidance is set out below in full under the heading 'the revised *Barton* Guidance'. Although couched by reference to the *SDA 1975, s 63A*, it applied equally to the *RRA 1976, SOR 2003, RBR 2003, DDA 1995* and *AR 2006*, and is likely to be highly relevant to the approach to be adopted under the *EA 2010, s 136*.

The revised statutory test was similar to the approach adopted in *King* in that the burden was initially on the complainant to make out what might be described as the '*prima facie* case'. The respondent had then to give an explanation. However, the revised test was stricter because once a *prima facie* case was established the respondent then had the burden of proving that he did not act unlawfully. If he failed to discharge the burden, the tribunal had to find in favour of the complainant.

As indicated above, under the old test the tribunal would decide, once a *prima facie* case had been made out, whether the case was in truth one of discrimination on a prohibited ground or whether it was perhaps unreasonable or inconsistent but nevertheless non-discriminatory treatment. Because discretion is replaced with compulsion, it becomes particularly important to determine when the *prima facie* case has been made out. Case law indicates that it is now harder for the complainant to make out a *prima facie* case than it was under the old *King* test.

In order to establish a *prima facie* case at stage one there must be something that raises a suggestion that a prohibited factor may have been at work. In *Igen v Wong* above, their Lordships addressed the issue in the context of the analysis of the *RRA 1976*:

'The relevant act is, in a race discrimination case . . . that (a) in circumstances relevant for the purposes of any provision of the 1976 Act (for example in relation to employment in the circumstances specified in section 4 of the Act), (b) the alleged discriminator treats another person less favourably and (c) does so on racial grounds. All those facts are facts which the complainant, in our judgment, needs to prove on the balance of probabilities.'

The Court of Appeal confirmed in *Madarassy v Nomura International plc* [2007] EWCA Civ 33, [2007] ICR 867, [2007] IRLR 246, that a claimant must establish more than a difference in status (eg. sex) and a difference in treatment before a tribunal will be in a position where it 'could conclude' that an act of discrimination had been committed. See also *Adebayo v Dresdner Kleinwort Wasserstein Ltd* [2005] IRLR 514, [2005] All ER (D) 371 (Mar), EAT; *University of Huddersfield v Wolff* [2004] IRLR 534, EAT; *Fernandez v Office of the Parliamentary Commissioner* [2006] All ER (D) 460 (Jul), EAT; *Griffiths-Henry v Network Rail Infrastructure Ltd* [2006] IRLR 865, [2006] All ER (D) 15 (Jul), EAT; *Fox v Rangecroft* [2006] EWCA Civ 1112; and *Islington London Borough Council v Ladele* [2009] ICR 387, [2009] IRLR 154, EAT (affd [2009] EWCA Civ 1357, [2010] IRLR 211, CA). However there does not have to be positive evidence that any difference in treatment was on a prohibited ground in order to establish a *prima facie* case (*Network Rail Infrastructure Ltd* above). Even if the tribunal believes that the respondent's conduct requires explanation, before the burden can shift there must be something to suggest that the treatment was due to the claimant's possessing a protected characteristic (see *B and C v A* [2010] IRLR 400, EAT). It is not sufficient to shift the burden of proof that the conduct is simply unfair or unreasonable if it is unconnected to a protected characteristic (see *Comr of Police of the Metropolis v Osinaike* (2010) 907 IDS Brief 15, EAT; *St Christopher's Fellowship v Walters-Ellis* [2010] EWCA Civ 921).

Whilst tribunals must be alert to the existence of, for example, racial or sexual stereotypes, the burden will only shift if there is sufficient reason to believe that the respondent could have been motivated by such a stereotype (see *B and C*, above). In *Canadian Imperial Bank of Commerce v Beck* (2010) 912 IDS Brief 10, EAT, an employment tribunal was held to have been entitled to regard the use of the word "younger" in a job specification as, in the circumstances, sufficient to shift the burden of proof onto the respondent in an age discrimination case relating to redundancy selection. Conversely, an employment tribunal had erred by not concluding that a manager's asking whether the claimant's age might be a reason why he could not work to the respondent's expectations had caused the burden of proof to shift (see *James v Gina Shoes Ltd* [2012] EqLR 314, EAT).

In deciding whether or not a *prima facie* case has been made out, the tribunal should ignore any explanation proffered by the employer for the treatment, turning to it only once the burden has shifted (*Igen* above). However this does not mean that at the first stage the tribunal should consider only evidence adduced by the claimant and ignore the respondent's evidence. The tribunal should have regard to all the facts at the first stage to determine what inferences can properly be drawn (*Laing v Manchester City Council* [2006] ICR 1519, [2006] IRLR 748, EAT; approved by the Court of Appeal in *Madarassy* and *Appiah v Bishop Douglass Roman Catholic High School* [2007] EWCA Civ 10, [2007] ICR 897, [2007] IRLR 264; see also *Nelson v Newry and Mourne District Council* [2009] NICA 24, [2009] IRLR 548; *Asim v Nazir* [2010] ICR 1225, EAT; and *Mohmed v West Coast Trains Ltd* (2006) 814 IDS Brief 7, EAT). At this stage the tribunal will need to look at evidence that the act complained of occurred at all, evidence as to the actual comparator relied upon by the claimant, evidence as to whether the comparisons being made by the claimant were like with like, and available evidence as to the reasons for the differential treatment (*Madarassy* above). In *Madarassy* the Court of Appeal held that at the first stage the respondent may adduce evidence which: showed that the alleged acts did not occur; that, if they did occur, there was not less favourable treatment of the claimant; that the comparators chosen by the claimant or the situations chosen by the claimant were not like the claimant or the situations with which comparison was sought to be made; and that even if there was less favourable treatment it was not on prohibited grounds. It is submitted that there may be some difficulty for tribunals in distinguishing this last category of evidence which the Court of Appeal has held that they are entitled to consider and accept at the first stage and any putative explanation from the respondent that would be considered at the second stage.

The complainant must establish on the balance of probabilities that the employer has committed the potentially discriminatory act. It would not be appropriate to require an explanation from the employer for something that the employer *may* have done. Thus where an act may have been committed by the employer or by a third party a *prima facie* case will not have been established (*Igen* above).

Logically the employer may offer one of a number of sorts of explanations at the second stage, if he offers one at all; those that confirm discrimination, those that explain the disparity in a manner which makes it clear that there was no unlawful discrimination but which, to use the words of the EAT in *Sinclair, Roche & Temperley v Heard* [2004] IRLR 763, EAT 'redound to the employer's discredit', and those which explain away discrimination and are themselves worthy reasons. It is not sufficient to establish discrimination that the tribunal considers that the explanation given is not one that is objectively justified or reasonable as unfairness is not sufficient to establish discrimination (see *Network Rail Infrastructure Ltd* above). However, whilst a respondent may argue that it did not discriminate because it also treated a comparator unreasonably, it is not open to the respondent to argue that it did not discriminate because it would have treated a hypothetical comparator in an unreasonable way when it had no good reason to do so (see *Eagle Place Services Ltd v Rudd* [2010] IRLR 486, EAT).

The explanation cannot simply be asserted, it must be proven. As the facts supporting the explanation will be in the respondent's knowledge cogent evidence is expected in support of any explanation proffered (see *Barton* above). The Court of Appeal has emphasised in *EB v BA* [2006] EWCA Civ 132, [2006] IRLR 471 that where the burden of proof has shifted the respondent must be required to adduce the evidence necessary to discharge that burden, otherwise the protection afforded to a claimant by (in that case) the *SDA 1975, s 63A* is negated. The weight of the burden imposed on the respondent at the second stage will depend on the strength of the *prima facie* case established by the claimant at the first stage (see *Network Rail Infrastructure Ltd* and *Ladele* above; *Khan & King v The Home Office* [2008] EWCA Civ 578, (2008) 858 IDS Brief 16, CA; *Virdi v Metropolitan Police Comr* [2009] EWCA Civ 477, [2009] All ER (D) 62 (Jun)). Once the burden of proof has shifted the tribunal is not required expressly to reject the respondent's explanation in order to make a finding of discrimination; it can merely not accept the explanation, though it is preferable if it does make positive findings one way or the other (see *Pothecary Witham Weld*, and *Beck*, above).

In 'reasonable adjustments' cases under the *DDA 1995*, Elias J has suggested (see *Project Management Institute v Latif* [2007] IRLR 579, EAT) that the claimant is required, at the first stage: (a) to establish the provision, criterion or practice relied upon; and (b) to demonstrate substantial disadvantage. The burden then shifts to the respondent to show that no adjustment or further adjustment should be made.

Before the new test many authorities emphasised the importance of making clear findings of fact and explaining why inferences were (or were not) being drawn (see *Anya v University of Oxford* [2001] ICR 847, CA). The more recent authorities make the same point. There must be clear findings of fact in relation to less favourable treatment; a clear finding as to whether the burden has reversed (see *Wolff* above); clear findings of fact in relation to the explanation; and a clear finding as to whether the explanation offered has discharged the burden and, if not, why not (see *Sinclair, Roche & Temperley* above; *Bahl* below; and *Chatwal v Wandsworth Borough Council* [2011] EqLR 942, EAT).

Where an employer advances an obviously non-discriminatory explanation, the tribunal's decision should show that it has recognised that an explanation has been provided and, if it still wishes to conclude that the act was unlawfully discriminatory, explain expressly why it is rejecting the explanation (*Bahl v Law Society* [2003] IRLR 640, EAT).

In a case where it is alleged that an act was on grounds of sex and/or on racial grounds and the evidence does not satisfy the tribunal that either ground, considered independently, is made out, it is not open to the tribunal to decide that 'taken together' the treatment was unlawful on both grounds (*Bahl* above) (and the same would hold true for any other attempt to combine other prohibited grounds). However in *Ministry of Defence v DeBique* [2010] IRLR 471, EAT, it was held that an employment tribunal had been entitled, in a case of alleged indirect race and sex discrimination, to consider the combined effect of two PCPs (provision, criterion or practice). In that case a female single parent soldier from St Vincent and the Grenadines complained of indirect sex discrimination in relation to a requirement that she be available for duty 24 hours a day seven days a week, which the tribunal considered placed female soldiers at a particular disadvantage, and the effect of the immigration rules which meant that, unlike a UK soldier, she could not have a relative with her to assist with childcare.

EA 2010, *s 14* was to introduce the concept of combined discrimination where a claimant suffered less favourable treatment because of the combination of two (and only two) relevant protected characteristics (but not marriage and civil partnership or pregnancy and maternity). This was only to be available in relation to direct discrimination (not, as in *DeBique*, indirect discrimination). However, the Government has decided not to bring *s 14* into force.

The Court of Appeal has confirmed that it is not always necessary for a tribunal expressly to go through the two-stage test in sequence and instead can focus on the respondent's reasons for the treatment, for example where the comparator is hypothetical and the facts are not fundamentally in dispute (*Brown v Croydon London Borough Council* [2007] EWCA Civ 32, [2007] ICR 909, [2007] IRLR 259; *Secretary of State for Work and Pensions v McCarthy* (2010) 908 IDS Brief 11, EAT; see also *Laing, Khan and Ladele* above). Although it is generally good practice to go through the two-stage test there are cases where the claimant is not prejudiced by the tribunal omitting the first stage and going straight to the second stage and concluding that the respondent has discharged the burden of proving that the treatment was not on a prohibited ground (but see *Country Style Foods Ltd v Bouzir* [2011] EWCA Civ 1519, [2012] EqLR 163, for a case where an employment tribunal did err by failing to consider whether the burden of proof had shifted).

The revised Barton Guidance

(1)   Pursuant to *SDA 1975, s 63A*, it is for the claimant who complains of sex discrimination to prove on the balance of probabilities facts from which the tribunal could conclude, in the absence of an adequate explanation, that the employer has committed an act of discrimination against the claimant which is unlawful by virtue of *Part 2* or which, by virtue of *s 41* or *s 42* of *SDA 1975*, is to be treated as having been committed against the claimant. These are referred to below as 'such facts'.

(2)   If the claimant does not prove such facts he or she will fail.

(3)   It is important to bear in mind in deciding whether the claimant has proved such facts that it is unusual to find direct evidence of sex discrimination. Few employers would be prepared to admit such discrimination, even to themselves. In some cases the discrimination will not be an intention but merely based on the assumption that 'he or she would not have fitted in'.

(4)   In deciding whether the claimant has proved such facts, it is important to remember that the outcome at this stage of the analysis by the tribunal will therefore usually depend on what inferences it is proper to draw from the primary facts found by the tribunal.

(5)   It is important to note the word 'could' in the *SDA 1975*, s 63A(2). At this stage the tribunal does not have to reach a definitive determination that such facts would lead it to the conclusion that there was an act of unlawful discrimination. At this stage a tribunal is looking at the primary facts before it to see what inferences of secondary fact could be drawn from them.

293

(6)   In considering what inferences or conclusions can be drawn from the primary facts, the tribunal must assume that there is no adequate explanation for those facts.

(7)   These inferences can include, in appropriate cases, any inferences that it is just and equitable to draw in accordance with *SDA 1975, s 74(2)(b)* from an evasive or equivocal reply to a questionnaire or any other questions that fall within *SDA 1975, s 74(2)* (see *Dattani v Chief Constable of West Mercia Police* [2005] IRLR 327, EAT – *RRA 1976, s 65* (the equivalent provision to *SDA 1975, s 74(2)*) also covers evasive or equivocal pleading in a response to a claim).

(8)   Likewise, the tribunal must decide whether any provision of any relevant code of practice is relevant and, if so, take it into account in determining such facts pursuant to *SDA 1975, s 56A(10)* (now the *EA 2006, s 15(4)*). This means that inferences may also be drawn from any failure to comply with any relevant code of practice.

(9)   Where the claimant has proved facts from which conclusions could be drawn that the employer has treated the claimant less favourably on the ground of sex, then the burden of proof moves to the employer.

(10)   It is then for the employer to prove that he did not commit, or as the case may be, is not to be treated as having committed, that act.

(11)   To discharge that burden it is necessary for the employer to prove, on the balance of probabilities, that the treatment was in no sense whatsoever on the grounds of sex, since 'no discrimination whatsoever' is compatible with the Burden of Proof Directive.

(12)   That requires a tribunal to assess not merely whether the employer has proved an explanation for the facts from which such inferences can be drawn, but further that it is adequate to discharge the burden of proof on the balance of probabilities that sex was not a ground for the treatment in question.

(13)   Since the facts necessary to prove an explanation would normally be in the possession of the respondent, a tribunal would normally expect cogent evidence to discharge that burden of proof. In particular, the tribunal will need to examine carefully explanations for failure to deal with the questionnaire procedure and/or a code of practice.

See also HARVEYS – Division L.5.D.

12.4 Time limit

A complaint must be presented to a tribunal before the end of the period of three months beginning when the act complained of was done (*EA 2010, s 123(1)(a)*; and previously *SDA 1975, s 76(1); RRA 1976, s 68(1); SOR 2003, reg 34(1), (1A); RBR 2003, reg 34(1), (1A); DDA 1995, Sch 3, para 3(1)*; and *AR 2006, reg 42(1)*). Where the claim concerns, in whole or in part, a cross-border dispute to which *art 8(1)* of *Directive 2008/52/EC* ("the *Mediation Directive*") applies and a mediation (within the meaning of *art 3(a)* of the *Mediation Directive*) has started before the time limit expires but the time limit will expire before the mediation ends or less than four weeks after the mediation ends, the time limit under the *EA 2010, s 123(1)(a)* is extended until four weeks after the mediation ends (*EA 2010, s 140A(1), (5), (6)*). Where a tribunal has power to extend a time limit under the *EA 2010, s 123(1)(b)* that power is exercisable in relation to the limitation period as extended by *s 140A* (*EA 2010, s 140A(13)*). Insofar as it is still in force pursuant to transitional and saving provisions, the time limit under the *SDA 1976, s 76(1)* is now subject to similar extension provisions in relation to disputes to which *art 8(1)* of the *Mediation Directive* applies. Those provisions are contained in the *SDA 1976, s 76ZA*.

A six month time limit applies to complaints by members of the armed forces. From 1 October 2004 the three month time limit could be extended by the 'extended period' under the *Employment Act 2002 (Dispute Resolution) Regulations 2004 (SI 2004/752)*, reg 15. However, following the repeal of the *EA 2002, ss 29 to 33* and *Schedules 2 to 4* by the *Employment Act 2008, ss 1* and *20*, and subject to the transitional provisions under the *Employment Act 2008 (Commencement No 1, Transitional Provisions and Savings) Order 2008 (SI 2008/3232), art 3* and *Schedule*, such an extension is no longer available after 6 April 2009. The old rules on the statutory extension of time still remain relevant as cases work their way through the tribunal system. Under the old *EA 2002* regime, where the complaint was that the complainant was expressly dismissed on discriminatory grounds in breach of the *SDA 1975, RRA 1976, SOR 2003, RBR 2003, DDA 1995* or *AR 2006* the statutory dismissal and disciplinary procedures under the *EA 2002, Sch 2, part 1*, would apply rather than the statutory grievance procedures under the *EA 2002, Sch 2, part 2 (Lawrence v HM Prison Service* [2007] IRLR 468, EAT). Whether a claim in relation to benefits is properly characterised as concerning equal pay or sex discrimination will have significant consequences for the applicable time limit (see, for example, *Hosso v European Credit Management Ltd* [2011] EWCA Civ 1589, [2012] ICR 547, [2012] IRLR 235). See also HARVEYS – Divisions **L.5.E, PI.1.E.**

For the purposes of deciding when an act was done, in calculating the time limit:

(a)   where the inclusion of any term in any contract renders the making of the contract an unlawful act, that act shall be treated as extending throughout the duration of the contract;

(b)   any act extending over a period shall be treated as done at the end of that period (for an example, see *Calder v James Finlay Corpn Ltd* [1989] ICR 157n);

(c)   a deliberate omission shall be treated as done when the person in question decided upon it; and

(d)   in the absence of evidence establishing the contrary, if the cause for complaint is an omission rather than an act, the omission will be treated as having been decided upon when a person does something inconsistent with the omitted act or when the period within which he would reasonably be expected to have done the act has expired (*Cyprien v Bradford Grammar School* (EAT 15/03/2013)).

(*EA 2010, s 123(3), (4)*; and previously *SDA 1975, s 76(6); RRA 1976, s 68(7); SOR 2003, reg 34(4); RBR 2003, reg 34(4); AR 2006, reg 42(4)*; and *DDA 1995, Sch 3, para 3(3),(4)*.)

Whether a claim form contains a complaint of a particular act (which may affect the time limit by being the last in a series of connected acts) is a question of construction of the document, and therefore an error by the tribunal in this regard can found an appeal to the EAT (*Gregory Charles v Tesco Stores Ltd* [2013] Eq LR 260, CA).

12.5   *Omissions*

A difficulty of interpretation arose in cases where there was a delay between the point at which the discriminator decided upon a deliberate omission and the point at which he omitted to act. In *Swithland Motors plc v Clarke* [1994] ICR 231, EAT, the appellant decided, whilst negotiating the purchase of a car sales business from receivers, that in the event that its bid was successful it would follow its usual practice of employing only female sales staff. It would omit, therefore, to offer the existing male staff the opportunity to continue in employment. The purchase was completed more than three months after the decision to apply the policy had been taken. On its face *SDA 1975, s 76(6)(c)* appeared to suggest that the male employees were out of time to complain before they even knew that there was something to complain about. The EAT decided that the section had to be read as meaning 'decides at a time and in circumstances when he is in a position to implement that decision'. Time ran, therefore, from the date on which the business was purchased.

12.6 Discrimination and Equal Opportunities – III: Enforcement

12.6 *Acts extending over a period*

Applications in discrimination cases will often make reference to a number of alleged instances of discrimination stretching back over a period, only part of which is within three months of the date of submission of the claim. The tribunal must then assess whether the individual allegations together constitute an 'act extending over a period' or else are to be treated as a series of discrete events.

In *Barclays Bank plc v Kapur* [1991] ICR 208, the House of Lords held that the bank's stipulation that service in Africa would not count for pension purposes, although originally made years before the complaints were brought, subjected the applicant employees to a continuing disadvantage which by virtue of *RRA 1976, s 68(7)(b)* was to be treated as an act done when the employees retired. It was necessary to distinguish a continuing rule such as this from an act which merely had continuing consequences. In *Sougrin v Haringey Health Authority* [1992] ICR 650, a pay re-grading was held to fall into the latter category, but in *Littlewoods Organisation plc v Traynor* [1993] IRLR 154 the failure to take the remedial measures promised after an earlier act of discrimination was held to be a continuing act (see also *Matuszowicz v Kingston-Upon-Hull City Council* [2009] EWCA Civ 22, [2009] ICR 1170, [2009] IRLR 28, CA). However, in *Okoro v Taylor Wood Construction Ltd* [2013] ICR 580, CA, a construction company's decision to ban some contract workers from one of its sites was held to be a one-off act.

A number of apparently discrete acts may provide evidence of a policy, rule or practice. The existence of such a policy or practice may itself constitute a 'continuing act' (*Owusu v London Fire and Civil Defence Authority* [1995] IRLR 574). In *Cast v Croydon College* [1998] ICR 500, CA, an employee who was about to commence maternity leave asked to be allowed to return on a part-time basis. Her request was refused. She took her maternity leave, returned to work and repeated her request. When it was again refused she resigned, alleging that she was unable to comply with the requirement that she work full-time. She commenced proceedings in the tribunal. Only the second refusal was 'in time'. It was held that each refusal constituted a separate act of discrimination, because on each occasion the employer considered the matter afresh. Had it merely restated its earlier decision, the position might have been different. Further, the tribunal decided that the second refusal was merely a confirmation of the first and that the claim was out of time. However, the Court of Appeal determined, first, that the two refusals were discrete decisions and that the claim in relation to the second refusal was within time and, further, that the two refusals should have been treated as evidence of the existence of a 'policy' on the employer's part, the fact that the same decision was reached on each occasion was evidence of the existence of a discriminatory policy. The operation of such a discriminatory policy constituted an act 'extending over a period' within the meaning of *SDA 1975, s 76*. In contrast, in another case, the Court of Appeal has held that the time limit begins to run again on each occasion on which the policy is applied. Thus, where a complainant was refused the same request on a number of occasions, each refusal caused the three-month time limit to start afresh (*Rovenska v General Medical Council* [1998] ICR 85, CA). The EAT has held that an employment tribunal was entitled to conclude that a refusal by an employer to revoke a dismissal was entirely separate from the dismissal itself and not part of a continuing act (*Baynton v South West Trains Ltd* [2005] ICR 1730).

Other authorities have used terms such as 'rule', 'scheme', 'regime' or 'practice' as well as 'policy'. However, the Court of Appeal has stressed that such terms are merely examples of acts which may extend over a period. Their Lordships have adopted a broader description of what the tribunal should look for: an 'ongoing situation' or a 'continuing state of affairs' which may be contrasted with 'a succession of unconnected or isolated specific acts' (*Hendricks v Metropolitan Police Comr* [2002] EWCA Civ 1686, [2003] ICR 530, CA). Leave to appeal to the House of Lords was refused ([2003] ICR 999). It will be a relevant, but not conclusive, factor whether the same or different individuals were involved in the alleged incidents of discrimination over the period and where there is a break in contact of several

296

months a tribunal may be entitled to conclude that continuity is not preserved (see *Aziz v FDA* [2010] EWCA Civ 304 (unreported, 5 March 2010, CA)). The Court of Appeal has confirmed the *Hendricks* approach in *Lyfar v Brighton and Sussex University Hospitals Trust* [2006] EWCA Civ 1548, [2006] All ER (D) 182 (Nov), emphasising the need to focus on the substance of the complaints when assessing whether they form a continuous act. However, in order to establish the existence of a policy or practice, the complainant must establish some degree of 'co-ordination' (*Metropolitan Police Comr v Hendricks* (2002) 707 IDS Brief 8, EAT). In *Moxam v Visible Changes Ltd* [2012] Eq LR 202, EAT, the employment tribunal had erred by not applying a broad approach to 'racial grounds' to recognise that earlier instances of the use of racist language revealed that a manager had the same mindset as he had in relation to later, in-time incidents and therefore time should have been extended to include the earlier incidents. Following the House of Lords' decision in *Relaxion Group plc v Rhys-Harper* [2003] UKHL 33, [2003] ICR 867, the EAT has held that a serious of acts constituting an act extending over time can include an act taking place after the complainant has ceased to be an employee of the respondent (*BHS Ltd v Walker* (2005) 787 IDS Brief 11).

It will generally be an error of law for a tribunal to seek to determine whether there is an act extending over a period on the basis of legal argument alone without hearing any evidence and making findings of fact (see the 'public interest disclosure' case of *Arthur v London Eastern Rly Ltd (t/a One Stansted Express)* [2006] EWCA Civ 1358, [2007] IRLR 58). However, it is not enough for a claimant simply to assert that there is a continuing act or that there is an ongoing state of affairs, rather he or she must have an arguable basis for the contention that the complaints are so linked as to be a continuing act or an ongoing state of affairs (*Ma v Merck Sharp & Dohme Ltd* [2008] EWCA Civ 1426, [2008] All ER (D) 158 (Dec)). Conversely, a claimant is not required expressly to state in his claim form that there is a 'continuing act' if it is sufficiently clear to the respondent that such an argument would be raised in response to a limitation defence (see *Khetab v AGA Medical Ltd* (2011) 922 IDS Brief 9, EAT). In *Kerr v Ernst & Young Services Ltd* [2011] ICR D13, EAT, an employment judge was held to have erred in giving directions at a case management discussion that precluded a claimant from relying on complaints of discrimination against three individuals (on the grounds inter alia that too much time had elapsed) as she had no power at a case management discussion effectively to strike out parts of his claim. Further, even if she had had the power to do so, she had erred in not giving the opportunity for representations before making such an order.

In *Tyagi v BBC World Service* [2001] EWCA Civ 549, [2001] IRLR 465, the complainant sought to allege that he had been discriminated against in relation to an application for promotion. His claim was lodged 15 months after he had failed to obtain the promotion and a year after he had ceased to be employed by the respondent. He contended that the respondent operated a discriminatory recruitment policy which was still in place at the date of his application. That being so, he argued, his application was not out of time. The Court of Appeal found against him drawing a distinction between those who remained in employment at the time of complaint and those who did not. The former group was entitled to complain about discriminatory policies which affected the way in which their employer afforded them 'access to opportunities for promotion'. They could, therefore, complain about the existence of the policy itself. The latter were only able to complain about the arrangements made for the purpose of determining who should be offered a particular job and, thus, could not complain about the policy. See also *Ruhaza v Alexander Hancock Recruitment Ltd* [2012] EqLR 9, EAT.

In the case of a single act, time starts to run when the course of action is complete, that is when a complaint to a tribunal could first be made (*Clarke v Hampshire Electro-Plating Co Ltd* [1992] ICR 312; see also *Adekeye v Post Office* [1993] ICR 464). Where the alleged act of discrimination was the dismissal of an internal appeal relating to an unsuccessful promotion application time ran from the date of that decision, not the date that the claimant was notified of the decision (*Virdi v Metropolitan Police Comr* [2007] IRLR 24, EAT). In the case of a constructive dismissal which is alleged to be discriminatory, time runs from the complainant's resignation, not from the employer's repudiatory breach (*Meikle v Nottinghamshire County Council* [2004] EWCA Civ 859, [2005] ICR 1).

See also *Dimtsu v Westminster City Council* [1991] IRLR 450.

12.7 *Extension of time*

A tribunal may nevertheless consider a complaint or application which is out of time if, in all the circumstances of the case, it considers that it is just and equitable to do so (*EA 2010, s 123(1)(b)*; and previously *SDA 1975, s 76(5); RRA 1976, s 68(6); SOR 2003, reg 34(3); RBR 2003, reg 34(3); DDA 1995, Sch 3, para 3(2)*; and *AR 2006, reg 42(3)*).

One possible ground for doing so is that the complainant was unaware of his or her rights, another that she has received incorrect advice from her lawyer (*Hawkins v Ball and Barclays Bank plc* [1996] IRLR 258; *Chohan v Derby Law Centre* [2004] IRLR 685, EAT; *Virdi v Metropolitan Police Comr*, above; cf also *British Coal Corpn v Keeble* [1997] IRLR 336; *Dahous*, below, or where a complainant has delayed because she was awaiting the outcome of an internal appeal or grievance procedure (*Aniagwu v Hackney London Borough Council* [1999] IRLR 303, EAT). However exhausting internal procedures will not always justify a delay (*Robinson v Post Office* [2000] IRLR 804), and the Court of Appeal has since decided that *Aniagwu* is limited to its own facts (*Apelogun-Gabriels v Lambeth London Borough Council* [2001] EWCA Civ 1853, [2002] ICR 713). A tribunal is not required to accept a doctor's evidence that a claimant was unable due to psychiatric illness to present his claim in time where there was evidence that he had been fit enough to seek legal advice and had written coherent letters on unrelated matters within the limitation period (see *Chouafi v London United Busways Ltd* [2006] EWCA Civ 689, [2006] All ER (D) 33 (May)). In *Department of Constitutional Affairs v Jones* [2007] EWCA Civ 894, [2008] IRLR 128 (a case under the *DDA 1995*), the Court of Appeal held that a tribunal had been entitled to consider that the claimant's own inability to admit to himself that he was mentally ill and a disabled person for the purposes of the *DDA 1995* was a factor justifying delay in presenting a claim.

The tribunal may be assisted by considering the factors that the court is obliged to consider when extending time in personal injury cases (for which see the *Limitation Act 1980, s 33(3)* or *CPR rule 3.9(1)*). However it is not obliged to do so. Its obligation is simply to ensure that no significant circumstance is left out of account (*Afolabi v Southwark London Borough Council* [2003] EWCA Civ 15, [2003] ICR 800). One of the most significant factors which the tribunal should consider is whether a fair trial of the issue is still possible (*DPP v Marshall* [1998] ICR 518). Whilst the fact that a fair trial is impossible will most likely preclude extension of time, it does not follow that merely because a fair trial is still possible time should be extended (*Simms v Transco plc* [2001] All ER (D) 245 (Jan), EAT). If a respondent wishes to establish that a fair trial is no longer possible, he should consider leading evidence to establish the point (*Southwark London Borough Council*, above). An employment tribunal will err if it fails to take account of the prejudice to the employer of allowing a claim out of time (*Abegaze v South East Essex College* [2006] ICR 468, EAT).Conversely, an employment tribunal will err if it fails to recognise the absence of any real prejudice to an employer when refusing to exercise its discretion to extend time (*Baynton v South West Trains Ltd* [2005] ICR 1730, EAT). It was an error of law for a tribunal not to take account of the merits of the case when considering the balance of prejudice where the claimant had a good claim and there was no prejudice to the respondent (*Bahous v Pizza Express Restaurant Ltd* (2012) 945 IDS Brief 17, [2012] EqLR 4, EAT). The Inner House of the Court of Session held in *Malcolm v Dundee City Council* [2012] CSIH 13, [2012] EqLR 363 that an employment tribunal had taken an overly strict approach in refusing to extend time *after* it had held a 21 day hearing and concluded that allegations of harassment were well-founded on their merits. In considering applications for extension, the correct approach for the tribunal to take is to bear in mind that employment tribunal time limits are generally enforced strictly and to ask whether a sufficient case has been made out to exercise its discretion in favour of extension. It is not a question of extending time unless a good reason can be shown for not doing so (*Robertson v Bexley Community Centre (t/a Leisure Link)* [2003] EWCA Civ 576, [2003] IRLR 434). The discretion to extend time is not at large and the time limit will operate to exclude otherwise valid claims unless the claimant can displace it, although this does not mean that the discretion has to be used sparingly (see *Chief Constable of Lincolnshire Police v Caston* [2009] EWCA Civ 1298, [2010] IRLR 327, CA). Where time is extended an employee cannot rely on legislation that was not in force at the time of the act complained of if the act would not have been unlawful at the time that it was committed (see *Abegaze*, above).

In *Stevens v Bexley Health Authority* [1989] ICR 224, the EAT appeared to consider that the statutory time limits were not applicable to claims brought directly under European law, but more recent decisions have shown that view to be incorrect (see **21.18–21.19** EQUAL PAY, and **22.2** EUROPEAN UNION LAW).

See also HARVEYS – Divisions **L.5.E**(4), (5), **PI.1.F**(1), (3).

12.8   Formulating the complaint

Care must be taken in drafting the complaint. In *Chapman v Simon* [1994] IRLR 124, the Court of Appeal held that an employment tribunal is limited to considering those matters complained of in the originating application (see also, *Akinmolasire v Camden and Islington Mental Health & Social Care Trust* [2004] EWCA Civ 1351, [2004] All ER (D) 59 (Oct)). However where general accusations of sex discrimination were made in relation to a redundancy dismissal, an employee was entitled to receive from the tribunal a finding on whether or not a failure to offer alternative employment was discriminatory even though she had not specifically relied on the point (*Prowse-Piper v Anglian Windows Ltd* [2010] EWCA Civ 428 (12 March 2010, unreported, CA)). In the light of the Court of Appeal's decision in *Chapman* it is also advisable, when specifying the detriments to which it is alleged that the complainant was subjected, specifically to recite that employees who do not share the complainant's protected characteristic have not or would not be subjected to such detriments. In relation to racial discrimination, the EAT has held that the employment tribunal either at or before the substantive hearing needs to identity which categories of racial discrimination (ie colour, race, nationality or ethnic or national origin) are relied upon so that the correct comparator can be identified, although a claimant who is not sure may plead all or most of them (see *Okonu*, above; and also *Chagger*, above). The EAT held in *Baker v Metropolitan Police Comr* (2010) 899 IDS Brief 9, EAT, that it is not sufficient merely to tick the box on the ET1 form for the particular type of discrimination complained of (in that case disability) without pleading any details (although the EAT also held that the tribunal erred in not considering the claimant's application to amend the claim). An employment tribunal had been entitled to refuse to allow an amendment to a claim to plead associative disability discrimination where the tribunal had already made findings of fact which meant that the amended claim could not have succeeded (see *Brill v Interactive Business Communications Ltd* [2010] EWCA Civ 1604). Where default judgment has been entered against a respondent for failure to file a response in time, in assessing compensation at a remedies a tribunal may not make findings inconsistent with the case on liability pleaded in the claim form (see *Eaton v Spencer* [2012] ICR D7, EAT).

The Court of Appeal has determined that direct and indirect discrimination are separate claims which must be separately identified in a claim form (*Ali v Office of National Statistics* [2004] EWCA Civ 1363, [2005] IRLR 201). The EAT had previously held, in *Quarcoopome v Sock Shop Holdings Ltd* [1995] IRLR 353, that where an originating application stated that the claim was one of 'race discrimination', it incorporated any claim of discrimination whether direct, indirect or by way of victimisation. The decision in *Quarcoopome* was in some doubt after the Court of Appeal's decision in *Housing Corpn v Bryant* [1999] ICR 123, in which it was held that the originating application must set out the 'causative link' on which a claim is based. Thus an application alleging unfair dismissal could not be read as including a claim for victimisation where there was no hint of this. *Quarcoopome* had been strongly criticised by the EAT in *Smith v Zeneca (Agrochemicals) Ltd* [2000] ICR 800, which held that a direct discrimination claim is different from, and does not include, either a claim for victimisation or indirect discrimination. It is therefore now essential fully to plead the facts on which different types of allegation of discrimination are based. Where a complainant believes that his dismissal was both discriminatory and unfair, it is essential that both are pleaded. If he first pursues a claim for unfair dismissal, he will not be entitled later to bring a fresh discrimination claim (*Divine-Bortey v Brent London Borough Council* [1998] IRLR 525, CA, applying *Henderson v Henderson* (1843) 3 Hare 100).

Where a complainant relies on more than one alleged act of discrimination, it is up to the complainant to ensure that each of them is pursued at the hearing itself. The tribunal is not obliged to make a finding in relation to everything raised in pleadings, only in relation to those matters which the complainant pursues at the hearing (*Mensah v East Hertfordshire NHS Trust* [1998] IRLR 531, CA). Where more than one incident is complained about, it is important for a tribunal to be clear which complaints are relied upon as distinct justiciable causes of action (and if necessary consider whether time should be extended in relation to those matters) and those complaints that are merely relied on as evidence (see *Aylott v Stockton-on-Tees Borough Council* [2009] IRLR 533, EAT).

A claim cannot be amended to include a complaint in relation to an act or omission that would not have been unlawful at the time that it took place (see *Standard Life Bank Ltd v Wilson* (2008) 851 IDS Brief 5, EAT – a decision concerning age discrimination).

Where a claimant relies on an actual comparator in addition to a hypothetical comparator, this is an important detail of the claim and it should be set out in the claim form (if necessary by amendment) (see *Woodward v Santander UK plc* [2010] IRLR 834, EAT).

Although discrimination claims should only be struck out rarely and generally a full examination of the facts will be required, the EAT did uphold an employment tribunal's decision to strike out a set of race discrimination claims where undisputed documents and a failure to articulate an arguable basis for the claims warranted this (*Shestak v Royal College of Nursing* (2008) 152 Sol Jo (no 37) 30, [2008] All ER (D) 193 (Oct), (2009) 873 IDS Brief 12, EAT; although see, in contrast, *A v B* [2010] EWCA Civ 1378, [2011] ICR D9, in which the Court of Appeal held that the EAT had correctly overturned a decision to strike out a sex discrimination victimisation claim where there was held to be a more than fanciful prospect that the respondent would fail to discharge the reverse burden of proof; see also *Community Law Clinic Solicitors v Methuen* [2012] EWCA Civ 571).

Discrimination claims often create problems for case management because, as noted above, a claimant seeks to rely on a series of alleged incidents of discrimination, even if only as background material from which inference can be drawn. Whilst the basic rule is that evidence is admissible if it is relevant and inadmissible if it is irrelevant, evidence may be logically or theoretically relevant but too marginal and unlikely to assist the tribunal to justify its admission (see *HSBC Asia Holdings BV v Gillespie* [2011] IRLR 209, [2011] ICR 192, EAT). In *Gillespie* the EAT held that an employment judge had erred in not excluding evidence which allegedly went to the background of discriminatory acts where the evidence was not sufficiently relevant to justify the burden that would be placed on the respondent in addressing it. Underhill P held that, while in many cases, the best approach is to address the question of admissibility during the course of the substantive hearing, in some cases, particularly discrimination cases, this may not be practicable or fair and it may be appropriate to decide questions of admissibility in advance of the hearing, for example when the issue affects the hearing length, disclosure or the need for witness orders. Underhill P also suggested (obiter) that where a claimant raises complaints in relation to a large number of incidents of alleged discrimination, and it cannot be agreed that the claimant proceed with a sample only of his allegations, it may be possible instead to deal with his allegations in tranches rather than at a single hearing. However, whilst an employment judge may direct a claimant to set out clearly in a schedule the acts and omissions he or she complains of, there is no power to require a claimant to 'self select' which complaints he or she will pursue at the final hearing (see *McKinson v Hackney Community College* (2012) 942 IDS Brief 16, [2011] EqLR 1114, EAT).

12.9   Questionnaire and disclosure

The principal difficulty encountered by complainants is obtaining the information necessary to assess the strength of their case and to conduct it successfully once they are satisfied of its merits. To assist a person who considers that they may have been unlawfully discriminated against or subjected to harassment to decide whether to institute proceedings and, if they do so, to formulate and present the case in the most effective manner, such a person (whether an applicant or potential applicant) may serve, on the person against whom he or she has a complaint, a questionnaire in the form prescribed (*EA 2010, s 138*; and previously under respectively, *SDA 1975, s 74; RRA 1976, s 65; SOR 2003, reg 33; RBR 2003, reg 33; DDA 1995, s 56;* and *AR 2006, reg 41*) to gather information about their complaint. The questionnaire and the replies to it should be in the prescribed form (under previously, respectively, the *Sex Discrimination (Questions and Replies) Order 1975 (SI 1975/2048), Sch 1*; the *Race Relations (Questions and Replies) Order 1977 (SI 1977/842), Sch 1; SOR 2003, Sch 2* and *Sch 3; RBR 2003, Sch 2* and *Sch 3; Disability Discrimination (Questions and Replies) Order 2004 (SI 2004/1168)*; and *AR 2006, Sch 3* and *Sch 4*), or in a similar form adapted to the circumstances of the case.

The *EA 2010, s 138* makes provision for the questionnaire procedure in the new regime. P is someone who thinks that a contravention of *EA 2010* has occurred in relation to him. R is the person P believes has contravened the *EA 2010 (s 138(1))*. A question by P or an answer by R is admissible in evidence in proceedings (*s 138(2)*). *EA 2010* leaves it to a Minister of the Crown by Order to prescribe forms for the questions and answers to them. However, the questions and answers will be admissible whether or not any forms are used. The prescribed form of questionnaires and replies is now set out in the *Equality Act 2010 (Obtaining Information) Order 2010 (SI 2010/2194)*, which broadly follows the approach under the previous legislation (see below). It is permissible for a tribunal (or court) to draw an inference from a failure by R to answer a question before the end of the period of eight weeks beginning with the day on which the question was served or from an evasive or equivocal answer (*s 138(4)*). However, this is not the case where (*s 138(5)*):

(a)   R reasonably asserts that to have answered differently or at all might have prejudiced a criminal matter;

(b)   R reasonably asserts that to have answered differently or at all would have revealed the reason for not commencing or not continuing criminal proceedings;

(c)   R's answer is of a kind specified by an order of a Minister of the Crown;

(d)   R's answer is given in circumstances specified by an order of a Minister of the Crown;

(e)   R's failure to answer occurs in circumstances specified by an order of a Minister of the Crown.

Under the *EA 2010, s 138(7)* a Minister may prescribe the period within which a questionnaire must be served in order to be admissible under the *EA 2010, s 138(3)*.

Previously a similar regime applied to questionnaires. A questionnaire and the replies to it were only admissible in evidence before an employment tribunal if it was served on the person (or company) questioned within the following time limits:

(a) where it had been served before a complaint had been presented to a tribunal, within the period of three months beginning when the act complained of was done, or (subject to the repeal with effect from 6 April 2009 of the *EA 2002, ss 29 to 33 and Schedules 2 to 4* by the *Employment Act 2008, ss 1* and *20*, and subject to the transitional provisions under the *Employment Act 2008 (Commencement No 1, Transitional Provisions and Savings) Order 2008 (SI 2008/3232), art 3* and *Schedule*) within the 'extended period' under (the now revoked subject to transitional provisions) *SI 2004/752, reg 15*); or

(b) where it was served when a complaint has been presented to a tribunal, either within the period of 21 days beginning with the day on which the complaint was presented or later with the leave of the tribunal and within a period specified by a direction of the tribunal.

(*SDA 1975, s 74(2)(a)*, and *SI 1975/2048, art 5; RRA 1976, s 65(2)(a)*, and *SI 1977/842, art 5; SOR 2003, reg 33(4); RBR 2003, reg 33(4); SI 2004/1168, art 4; AR 2006, reg 41(4)*.) If the questionnaire was not served within the relevant time limit, it was not admissible as evidence before the tribunal.

The form for the reply was previously set out in *SI 1975/2048, Sch 2, SI 1977/842, Sch 2, SOR 2003, Sch 3, RBR 2003, Sch 3, SI 2004/1168, Sch 2*; or *AR 2006, Sch 4*. If it appeared to the tribunal that the respondent deliberately, and without reasonable excuse, omitted to reply within a reasonable period or that his reply was evasive or equivocal, the tribunal could draw any inference from that fact that it considered just and equitable to draw, including an inference that he committed an unlawful act (*SDA 1975, s 74(2)(b); RRA 1976, s 65(2)(b); DDA 1995, s 56(3)(b)*). In the case of sex discrimination or racial discrimination on grounds of race or ethnic or national origins or discrimination under the *DDA 1995, SOR 2003, RBR 2003* and *AR 2006* an omission to reply within eight weeks of service, could give rise to such an inference (*SDA 1975, s 74(2), (2A)* as amended by the *Employment Equality (Sex Discrimination) Regulations 2005 (SI 2005/2467); RRA 1976, s 65(2)(b)* as amended by the *Race Relations Act 1976 (Amendment) Regulations 2003 (SI 2003/1626); SOR 2003, reg 33(2); RBR 2003, reg 33(3); AR 2006, reg 41(2)*.)

The EAT has held in *Dattani v Chief Constable of West Mercia Police* [2005] IRLR 327, EAT, that failure to answer, or evasive or late answers to, any question raised of the respondent by a complainant can justify the drawing of inferences. This might include information contained in the respondent's response to the claim or in further and better particulars. However a failure to answer a question in a questionnaire or otherwise to provide information or documents does not automatically raise a presumption of discrimination. A tribunal must consider in the particular circumstances of the case whether the failure in question is capable of constituting evidence supporting the inference that the employer acted discriminatorily in the manner alleged and, if so, whether in the light of any explanation supplied by the employer it does in fact justify the inference (*D'Silva v NATFHE* [2008] IRLR 412, EAT). In *Meister v Speech Design Carrier Systems GmbH*: C-415/10 [2012] ICR 1006, the CJEU held that, whilst EU law did not entitle a worker who had a plausible claim that he met the requirements of a job to have access to information on whether an employer had employed another applicant and the criteria upon which the appointment had been made, it was for the national court to determine whether the refusal of an employer to disclose such information was liable to compromise the objectives of EU law. The Court went on to state that it could not be ruled out that the refusal to allow access to such information could be one of the factors to take into account in establishing facts from which it might be presumed that discrimination had occurred.

A questionnaire may be obtained from the offices of the EHRC.

The EAT has suggested that, where a complainant wishes to obtain further information, an application for leave to serve a further questionnaire should be made to the tribunal (*Carrington v Helix Lighting Ltd* [1990] ICR 125).

The EAT confirmed that, by virtue of the (now revoked subject to transitional provisions) *Employment Act 2002 (Dispute Resolution) Regulations 2004 (SI 2004/752), reg 14*, the submission of a questionnaire did not constitute the submission of a grievance for the purposes of the (now repealed subject to transitional provisions) *EA 2002, s 32, Sch 2* (*Holc-Gale v Makers UK Ltd* [2006] IRLR 178, [2006] ICR 462).

An employer may be asked by which criteria he chose an employee for a particular post, but he is not obliged to answer an unreasonable question such as the name and address of a successful applicant for a post (*Oxford v Department of Health and Social Security* [1977] ICR 884). He may also be asked, for example, for the numbers of men and women in particular posts and in the workforce as a whole and, if the case is one of failure to select for appointment or promotion, the breakdown by, for example, sex of applicants at the various stages of the selection process.

In pursuing a claim before an employment tribunal, an applicant may ask for the disclosure of documents by his employer or prospective employer. For the power of an employment tribunal to order the disclosure of documents which are relevant to the proceedings, see **18.11–18.13 EMPLOYMENT TRIBUNALS – II**. However, in *Science Research Council v Nassé* [1979] ICR 921, the House of Lords held that tribunals should not order the disclosure of reports or references given and received in confidence, except when it is necessary for disposing fairly of the proceedings that the confidence should be overridden. In *Canadian Imperial Bank of Commerce v Beck* [2009] EWCA Civ 619, [2010] IRLR 740 the Court of Appeal summarised the position as being that an order for disclosure should be made if it was "necessary for fairly disposing of the proceedings" and that while relevance was a factor it was not sufficient on its own to warrant the granting of an order and conversely confidentiality does not, of itself, warrant refusal of an order.

In *West Midlands Passenger Transport Executive v Singh* [1988] ICR 614, the Court of Appeal upheld an employment tribunal's order for discovery of a schedule of statistics showing the ethnic origins of candidates for promotion and those actually promoted during the period preceding the alleged discrimination. The decision also gives guidance as to when discovery should be refused because, although relevant, it would be oppressive. The Court of Appeal further held that it might be possible, first, to infer from statistics that there had been discrimination against members of a racial group in general, and then to infer (in the absence of a satisfactory explanation in the particular case) that the applicant as a member of that group was discriminated against.

However, an employment tribunal does not have the power to require a schedule of statistics to be produced where the necessary information is not already in existence. In such circumstances, the questionnaire procedure should be used (*Carrington* above).

The Court of Appeal has held that, where a respondent claimed to be prohibited by law from disclosing the reasons why a claimant failed a security vetting, or indeed from disclosing the legal basis for that prohibition, a tribunal erred in law by ordering the respondent to disclose the reason why the claimant was not appointed to a post (*Barracks v Coles* [2006] EWCA Civ 1041, [2007] ICR 60, [2006] IRLR 73).

The EAT has held that evidence about a 'without prejudice' discussion with a complainant about bringing her employment to an end could be adduced as there was no dispute at the time attracting privilege and, in any event, the public interest in having discrimination allegations properly determined meant that it would be an abuse to apply the 'without prejudice' rule in that case (*BNP Paribas v Mezzotero* [2004] IRLR 508). However in *Woodward v Santander UK plc* [2010] IRLR 834, the EAT sought to emphasise that *Mezzotero* did not create a new exception to the without prejudice rule and that the policy reasons behind the rule that parties be able to negotiate freely applied with particular force where parties were seeking to settle discrimination claims. The EAT held that the exception to the without prejudice rule for unambiguous impropriety applied only in the clearest cases, and was not engaged in the present case.

12.9 Discrimination and Equal Opportunities – III: Enforcement

In *Vaseghi v Brunel University* (2006) 818 IDS Brief 10, EAT, the EAT held that discussions with two employees about settlement of their discrimination claims took place in circumstances where the without prejudice privilege was waived and that the importance of establishing the truth in discrimination cases may tip the scales of justice against maintaining the privilege where the claimants' case would be severely prejudiced by not being able to refer to the discussions. The Court of Appeal affirmed the EAT's judgment holding that in the particular and unusual circumstances of the case where the grievance procedure had in effect been a trial of the victimisation issue before an independent panel at which both parties gave evidence of the previous negotiations there was a waiver (*Brunel University v Vaseghi* [2007] EWCA Civ 482, [2007] IRLR 592). The Court of Appeal also held that by pleading its response in the way it did and attaching a copy of the grievance report the university had confirmed its intention to waive privilege and it was too late to amend the response to withdraw that waiver.

In disability discrimination cases there will often be a need for the claimant to be examined by a single jointly instructed medical expert to assist the employment tribunal to determine the question of whether the claimant is disabled. Persistent failure by a claimant to cooperate with a joint medical expert may justify the striking out of the claim (see *Chambers-Mills v Allied Bakers* [2011] EWCA Civ 277).

See also HARVEYS – Divisions **L.5.C, PI.1.N.**

12.10 Conciliation

When a complaint has been presented to an employment tribunal, the conciliation officer must endeavour to promote a settlement of the complaint if:

(a)   he is requested to do so both by the complainant and the respondent; or

(b)   in the absence of requests by the complainant and the respondent, he considers that he could act with a reasonable prospect of success.

(*Employment Tribunals Act 1996* ('*ETA 1996*'), *s 18(1), (2)*). His services may also be sought by a prospective party before the presentation of a complaint (*ETA 1996, s 18(3)*).

Information given to the conciliation officer in the performance of his duties is not admissible in evidence before the tribunal except with the consent of the giver of the information (*ETA 1996, s 18(7)*). Thus, frequently a conciliation officer will contact the employer to investigate the possibility of the removal of the cause of complaint. An employer is not obliged to give the conciliation officer information.

An ACAS conciliation officer has no responsibility to see that the terms of a settlement are fair to the employee and, indeed, a conciliation officer should not advise the parties on the merits of the case (see *Clarke v Redcar & Cleveland Borough Council* [2006] ICR 897, [2006] IRLR 324, EAT, for guidance on the role of a conciliation officer). The ACAS conciliation officer does not have to broker a settlement or record it in order for an agreement reached effectively to oust the employment tribunal's jurisdiction pursuant to the *ETA, s 18(2)*, he merely needs to endeavour to promote settlement (*Allma Construction Ltd v Bonner* [2011] IRLR 204, EAT). Where one party makes an offer to another that is sufficiently definite to indicate an intention to be bound, covering the essentials of the contract in question, and it is accepted, then a contract is concluded which, if an ACAS conciliation officer has been involved, will be sufficient to oust the employment tribunal's jurisdiction. It does not matter if there are additional matters that could have been included in the agreement and what are the "essentials" of the agreement will vary from case to case (see *Bonner* above).

See also **2.4 ADVISORY, CONCILIATION AND ARBITRATION SERVICE (ACAS)**. For the validity of settlements, see **12.33** below.

See also HARVEYS – Divisions PI.3, PI.1.T.

12.11 Restriction of publicity

The *ETA 1996, s 11* empowered the Secretary of State to make regulations allowing for the restriction of publicity in cases where the commission of a sexual offence, or sexual misconduct, is alleged. Regulations were subsequently made which give powers to restrict publicity to both the employment tribunals and the Employment Appeal Tribunal. There are, broadly, two powers. The first is a power to ensure that the tribunal's own documents do not identify the parties concerned. The second power enables the tribunal to restrict others from reporting the identity of the parties or matters which might lead to them being identified. These powers are likely to be most relevant in some cases of sex discrimination, and now sexual orientation discrimination. Similar powers to make restricted reporting orders exist in relation to proceedings under the *DDA 1995*, or now under the *EA 2010, s 120* where the complaint relates to disability, on the application of the complainant or of its own motion where evidence of a personal nature is likely to be heard by the employment tribunal hearing the complaint (*ETA 1996, s 12(1), (2)*). Evidence of a personal nature would be evidence of a medical, or other intimate nature, which might reasonably be assumed to be likely to cause significant embarrassment to the complainant if reported (*ETA 1996, s 12(7)*).

Where a case appears to involve allegations of the commission of a sexual offence, the tribunal is required to omit or delete from the register, and any judgment, document or record of proceedings which will otherwise be available to the public, any 'identifying matter which is likely to lead members of the public to identify any person affected by or making such an allegation' (*Employment Tribunals (Constitution and Rules of Procedure) Regulations 2004 (SI 2004/1861), Sch 1, rule 49*). The EAT is similarly required by the *Employment Appeal Tribunal Rules 1993 (SI 1993/2854), rule 23(2)*. A sexual offence means an offence of rape and related offences, and certain other offences including indecent assault, under-age intercourse and incest (*ETA 1996, s 11(6)*). A case will 'involve' such allegations even if they are not the basis of the claim or central to the decision-making; it is enough that they will fall to be considered (*X v Metropolitan Police Comr* [2003] ICR 1031, EAT). The employment tribunal and EAT has the power to order that their judgments be anonymised in the case of an alleged sexual offence as the *ECHR Article 8* right to privacy of the victim of such an offence is 'well-recognised' (see *B and C v A* [2010] IRLR 400, EAT). The EAT has held that (in the absence of an express power to do so) it has a duty to protect a party's rights under the *ECHR Article 8* by interpreting its powers under the *ETA 1996, s 30(3)* to regulate its own procedure so as to anonymise its judgment and delete from its public records any matter likely to lead to the identification of a party (*A v B* [2010] IRLR 844, [2010] ICR 849, EAT). In that case the claimant brought unfair dismissal proceedings following his dismissal stemming from unproven allegations of child sex abuse. The EAT held that his right to reputation under *ECHR Article 8* had to be weighed against the protection of freedom of expression under *ECHR Article 10* and that the balance, in the circumstances of the case, clearly favoured maintaining the claimant's anonymity.

Where a case appears to involve allegations of sexual misconduct the employment judge may make a temporary restricted reporting order on application by one of the parties or of the tribunal's own motion (*SI 2004/1861, Sch 1, rule 50(1), (2), (3)*). The parties may apply to have the temporary restricted reporting order revoked or converted into a full restricted reporting order within 14 days of the temporary order being made, otherwise the order lapses after 14 days (*rule 50(4), (5)*). A full restricted reporting order can only be made if the parties are given the opportunity to advance oral argument at a pre-hearing review or a hearing as to whether the order should be made (*rule 50(6)*). A full restricted reporting order remains in force until the tribunal's judgment on liability and remedy is sent to the parties, unless revoked earlier (*rule 50(9), (11)*). If the claim is withdrawn before judgment is issued (pursuant to rule 25(3)) with the order still in place, then the tribunal has no jurisdiction to consider the revocation of the order after the withdrawal with the effect that it continues in perpetuity (*Davidson v Dallas McMillan* [2009] CSIH 70, [2010] IRLR 439, Ct of Session). The tribunal has a discretion to allow non-parties (such as journalists) to make submissions as to the revocation or variation of a restricted reporting order (see *Davidson*, above). Sexual misconduct is defined in *ETA 1996, s 11(6)* to mean the commission of a sexual offence, sexual harassment, or other adverse conduct related to sex (whether in its character or in its having reference to the sex or sexual orientation of the person at whom it is directed).

A restricted reporting order is one prohibiting the publication in Great Britain, in a written publication available to the public, of matter likely to lead members of the public to identify a person as one who is affected by or is the person making the allegation, or the inclusion of such matter in programs for reception in Great Britain. A corporate body is not a person for these purposes (*Leicester University v A* [1999] ICR 701). Contravention of a restricted reporting order is a criminal offence carrying a fine not exceeding level 5 on the standard scale (see **1.10** INTRODUCTION). The EAT has decided that the European Union law requirement that domestic procedural rules should not make enforcement of, *inter alia*, the directly effective right to equal treatment conferred on public sector workers by the *Equal Treatment Directive*, 'virtually impossible' or 'excessively difficult' (see **22.2** EUROPEAN UNION LAW) allows tribunals to make restricted reporting orders in cases other than where sexual misconduct is alleged. In that particular case, the EAT was satisfied that, without a restricted reporting order, the particular complainant would have been deterred from bringing her claim of discrimination on grounds of her transsexuality (*Chief Constable of the West Yorkshire Police v A* [2001] ICR 128, EAT).

The order should be no broader than is necessary to achieve the purpose of the legislation, which is to protect the identity of the alleged victim and perpetrator, and of any witness whose anonymity is essential to the proper conduct of the litigation. A restricted reporting order should not, therefore, conceal the identity of the complainant in circumstances where she does not wish to be anonymous (*R v London (North) Industrial Tribunal, ex p Associated Newspapers Ltd* [1998] IRLR 569; see also *X v Metropolitan Police Comr*, above, for application of the same reasoning in the case of a claim brought by a transsexual). An employment tribunal had been entitled to consider that a change of mind by two claimants whose identity was previously covered by an order and the addition of six new media organisations seeking to revoke or vary the order was sufficient grounds to justify reconsidering the order (*Tradition Securities and Futures SA v Times Newspapers Ltd* [2009] IRLR 354, EAT). In that case the EAT also held that there was much to be said for orders being as specific as possible, although in that case it was not useful to specify what kind of material was or was not likely to lead to the named individual alleged perpetrators being identified.

In *F v G* [2012] ICR 246, EAT, Underhill P held that an employment tribunal has wide powers unconstrained by the particular wording of *rules 49* or *50* to make anonymity orders or restricted reporting orders to the extent necessary to protect the *ECHR, article 8* rights of third parties (in that case of disabled students at the college where the claimant had worked) even where there was no allegation of a sexual offence or sexual misconduct. The President also observed that there was no reason why a decision on anonymity had to be made once and for all at the start of proceedings but instead a tribunal could make an interim decision on anonymity and then a final decision when judgment was delivered, at which time the tribunal would be best placed to assess all the relevant factors.

The EAT is similarly empowered to make restricted reporting orders by *SI 1993/2854, rule 23(3), (5), (5A)* (as amended by the *Employment Appeal Tribunal (Amendment) Rules 2004 (SI 2004/2526), rule 15*).

For a more detailed consideration of restricted reporting orders, see **18.18–18.19** EMPLOYMENT TRIBUNALS – **II**, and also HARVEYS – Divisions **PI.1.W**(5), (6), **PI.2.H**(1), (2).

12.12 Remedies

Where an employment tribunal finds that a complaint presented to it is well-founded, it must make such of the following orders as it considers just and equitable:

(a)   An order declaring the rights of the complainant and the respondent in relation to the act to which the complaint relates (*EA 2010, s 124(1)(a)*; and previously *SDA 1975, s 65(1)(a); RRA 1976, s 56(1)(a); SOR 2003, reg 30(1)(a); RBR 2003, reg 30(1)(a); DDA 1995, 17A(2)(a)*; and *AR 2006, reg 38(1)(a)*). Such a declaration may state, for example, that the complainant is entitled to certain training facilities or should be considered for a certain position.

(b)   An order requiring the respondent to pay to the complainant compensation of an amount corresponding to any damages he could have been ordered by a county court to pay to the complainant if the complaint had fallen to be dealt with under the jurisdiction of the county court (*EA 2010, s 124(1)(b)*; and previously *SDA 1975, s 65(1)(b); RRA 1976, s 56(1)(b); SOR 2003, reg 30(1)(b); RBR 2003, reg 30(1)(b); DDA 1995, s 17A(2)(b)*; and *AR 2006, reg 38(1)(b)*. Once a tribunal has decided to award compensation the amount must be computed on the basis of what damages would be recoverable in a county court, and not on the basis of what the tribunal thinks is just and equitable (the *EA 2010, s 124(6)*; *Hurley v Mustoe (No 2)* [1983] ICR 422). If the complainant was barred from applying for a particular benefit, the tribunal must, in assessing compensation, consider the percentage chance that the application would have succeeded (*Calder v James Finlay Corpn Ltd* [1989] ICR 157n).

(c)   An "appropriate recommendation" pursuant to *EA 2010, s 124(1)(c)*, namely a recommendation that within a specified period the respondent takes specified steps for the purpose of obviating or reducing the adverse effect of any matter to which the proceedings relate (a) on the claimant or (b) on any other person (*EA 2010, s 124(3)*) Previously a tribunal could make a recommendation that the respondent take, within a specified period, action appearing to the tribunal to be practicable for the purpose of obviating or reducing the adverse effect on the complainant only of any act of discrimination to which the complaint relates (*SDA 1975, s 65(1)(c); RRA 1976, s 56(1)(c); SOR 2003, reg 30(1)(c); RBR 2003, reg 30(1)(c); DDA 1995, s 17A(2)(c)*; and *AR 2006, reg 38(1)(c)*).

See also HARVEYS – Divisions **L.6, L.7.**

12.13 Compensation: general principles

Until the mid-1990s, awards of compensation in cases of sex or race discrimination were subject to a statutory maximum for compensatory awards for unfair dismissals. However, following the decision of the ECJ in *Marshall v Southampton and South West Hampshire Regional Health Authority (No 2)* [1993] IRLR 445, that capping compensation meant victims of discrimination did not have an 'effective remedy', the upper ceiling on the size of awards was removed by the *Sex Discrimination and Equal Pay (Remedies) Regulations 1993 (SI 1993/2798)* (subsequently the *Employment Tribunals (Interest on Awards in Discrimination Cases) Regulations 1996 (SI 1996/2803)* – see below). Prior to 3 July 1994, compensation for employment-related acts of race discrimination was also subject to the same statutory maximum (by the former *RRA 1976, s 56(2)*). The *Race Relations (Remedies) Act 1994*, removed the limit.

Where an employer is found to be vicariously liable for its employees' discriminatory acts, it will normally be required to make a payment in compensation. However, it does not follow that the individual discriminators should escape the consequences of liability. Where they have been named as individual respondents, it is open to the tribunal to make an order that they, too, should make a payment in compensation (see *Gbaja-Biamila v DHL International (UK) Ltd* [2000] ICR 730, EAT). Tribunals are entitled to order that liability be on a joint and several basis. However, in *London Borough of Hackney v Sivanandan* [2013] IRLR 408 the Court of Appeal held that where the same, "indivisible", damage is done to a claimant by concurrent tortfeasors – ie either tortfeasors who are liable for the same act (joint tortfeasors) or tortfeasors who separately contribute to the same damage – each is liable for the whole of that damage. As between any particular tortfeasor and the claimant no question of apportionment arises. As between joint tortfeasors the position is determined under the *Civil Liability (Contribution) Act 1978* but this has no impact on the liability of any of them to the claimant. As the Court said in *Sivanandan* it is not clear whether the ET has jurisdiction to decide the position as between joint tortfeasors or whether this requires separate proceedings in the County Court.

Exemplary damages may now be available in discrimination cases as a result of the decision of the House of Lords in *Kuddus v Chief Constable of Leicestershire Constabulary* [2001] UKHL 29, [2002] 2 AC 122.

The Court of Appeal overturned an employment tribunal's decision to strike out a successful claimant's claim as to remedy on the grounds that there had been a failure actively to pursue the claim and a fair hearing was no longer possible after a number of years had passed following the liability decision (see *Abegaze*, CA above).

For decisions relating to the assessment of compensation see *Alexander v Home Office* [1988] ICR 685, *North West Thames Regional Health Authority v Noone* [1988] ICR 813, *Sharifi v Strathclyde Regional Council* [1992] IRLR 259, and the cases summarised below. See also HARVEYS – Divisions **L.6.C, L.7.**

12.14 Compensation: Indirect discrimination

In cases of indirect discrimination a tribunal's power to award compensation is more limited. Where the tribunal is satisfied that the respondent intended the discriminatory consequences of the provision, criterion or practice compensation can be ordered. Such an intention may be inferred where it is established that the employer was aware that discriminatory consequences would flow from its actions (*JH Walker Ltd v Hussain* [1996] ICR 291; and see *London Underground Ltd v Edwards* [1995] ICR 574 for the circumstances in which indirect discrimination may be said to have been intentional). If the respondent is able to prove that he had no intention of treating the complainant unfavourably on discriminatory grounds compensation may not be available. Before awarding compensation for unintentional indirect discrimination the tribunal is required first to consider whether, if it had no power to order compensation it would make a declaration and/or recommendation. If it decides that it would not do so, it can move on to consider compensation. If it decides that it would do so, it should first make the declaration or recommendation and then ask itself whether it is just and equitable to make an award of compensation as well (*EA 2010, s 124(4), (5)*). Previously there was no power to award compensation for unintentional indirect discrimination until the *Sex Discrimination and Equal Pay (Miscellaneous Amendments) Regulations 1996 (SI 1996/438)*, which inserted a new *s 65(1B)* into the *SDA 1975*, gave tribunals, for the first time, a power to make awards of compensation in cases of unintentional indirect sex discrimination on the same basis that now exists under the *EA 2010*. The *SOR 2003, reg 30, RBR 2003, reg 30, DDA 1995, s 17A* and *AR 2006, reg 38* contained similar provisions. In the case of race discrimination there was no such mechanism for awarding compensation for unintentional indirect discrimination (*RRA 1976, s 57(3)*).

12.15 Compensation: pecuniary loss

The measure of loss is tortious. In other words, a complainant must be put, so far as possible, into the position that he would have been in had the act of discrimination not occurred (*Ministry of Defence v Cannock* [1994] ICR 918, EAT). Thus, the tribunal must ask itself, 'If there had been no unlawful discrimination, what would have happened?'.

Where the act complained of is a discriminatory dismissal, the tribunal will have to decide whether the complainant would have been dismissed in any event if there had been no discrimination (see *O'Donoghue v Redcar and Cleveland Borough Council* [2001] EWCA Civ 701, [2001] IRLR 615, CA; *Abbey National plc v Chagger* [2009] ICR 624, [2009] IRLR 86, EAT; affd *sub nom Chagger v Abbey National plc* [2009] EWCA Civ 1202, [2010] ICR 397, [2010] IRLR 47). The tribunal often carries out a similar exercise when calculating compensation for unfair dismissal. However, in the context of discrimination proceedings, there is a significant difference of approach. In unfair dismissal cases, one asks whether a reasonable employer would have dismissed in any event. In discrimination cases, however, one asks whether the actual respondent would have dismissed (*Abbey National plc v Formoso* [1999] IRLR 222). As the unlawful act is the discrimination, not the dismissal itself, the question is whether (and when) the dismissal would have occurred on non-discriminatory grounds (or whether and when the employee would have left the respondent's employment of his own choice) (*Chagger*, above, and *Wardle*, below). In cases where the complainant alleges that her dismissal was both unfair and discriminatory, this difference may significantly complicate the process of calculation. However, a reduction of compensation to reflect the chance that the employee might have left under a compromise agreement, based on evidence of pre-hearing negotiations but without any evidence of waiver of privilege, is unfair (*Gallop v Newport City Council* [2013] IRLR 23). In *Chagger*, above, the EAT stated that although there were conceptual differences between discriminatory and unfair dismissals it would be unsatisfactory if a radically different approach from the approach in *Polkey v A E Dayton Services Ltd* [1988] AC 344, [1988] ICR 142, [1987] IRLR 503, HL, were to be adopted in discrimination cases. While the starting point in analysing future loss may be the period during which the claimant would have remained employed with the respondent had there been no dismissal, a tribunal has to recognise that a discriminatory dismissal means that the dismissed employee enters the labour market not at a time or in circumstances of his or her choosing, thereby potentially altering the claimant's career path. The proper assessment of loss is determined by asking when the claimant might be expected to obtain another job with equivalent salary (*Chagger v Abbey National plc* [2009] EWCA Civ 1202, [2010] ICR 397, [2010] IRLR 47, reversing the EAT on this point).

The mere fact that there is an element of speculation involved in assessing whether a claimant would have been dismissed anyway is not a reason for an employment tribunal to refuse to engage with the assessment exercise if evidence is advanced by the employer that he might have been dismissed (see *Eversheds Legal Services Ltd v De Belin* [2011] ICR 1137, [2011] IRLR 448, EAT). Determining what would have happened in the absence of discrimination may involve the tribunal in assessing percentage chances. For instance, in cases of pregnancy dismissal, the tribunal will usually have to assess the chance that the complainant would, but for the dismissal, have returned to work. It is not necessarily perverse for the tribunal to conclude that there is a 100% chance that the relevant event would have occurred (*Ministry of Defence v Hunt* [1996] ICR 544, EAT). A tribunal is not required to take account of contingencies that it regards as too remote or which are unlikely to arise during the period for which it considers that the claimant should be compensated (see *Wooster v Mayor and Burgesses of the London Borough of Tower Hamlets* [2009] IRLR 980, EAT). Where there are a number of contingent possibilities, the proper approach is to cumulate the percentages (eg where there is a 75% chance that a woman would have returned to work following the birth of her child had she not been dismissed and a 50% chance of her having received a pay rise thereafter, her loss should be assessed on the basis of the chance of her having earned at the higher rate, that is 50% × 75% – see *Hunt* above).

12.15 Discrimination and Equal Opportunities – III: Enforcement

In *Wardle v Credit Agricole Corporate and Investment Bank* [2011] EWCA Civ 545, [2011] ICR 1290, [2011] IRLR 604 the Court of Appeal held that it is wrong for a tribunal to approach compensation for career loss by awarding damages until the point where it can be sure that the claimant will find an equivalent job, rather, in the normal case, if a tribunal assesses that a claimant is likely (ie it is more probable than not) to get an equivalent job by a specific date that is the date up to which loss is fairly to be assessed. Exceptionally a tribunal may be entitled to conclude on the evidence before it that there is no real prospect of the claimant ever securing an equivalent job, in which the tribunal has to assess loss as continuing for the rest of the claimant's working life. (The Court of Appeal also delivered a supplemental decision in this case on the effect of an adjustment in the overall level of compensation awarded consequent upon an appeal on the level of statutory uplift under the *EA 2002, s 31(3)* – [2011] EWCA Civ 770, [2011] IRLR 819).

Where an employer has made an *ex gratia* payment on dismissal or any other payment which falls to be deducted from the award, the proper approach is to make the deduction before applying the percentage chance (*Hunt* above; *Ministry of Defence v Wheeler* [1998] ICR 242; cf *Digital Equipment Co Ltd v Clements (No 2)* [1998] IRLR 134, CA).

In assessing percentage prospects of particular events occurring, the tribunal is encouraged to rely upon statistical evidence. However, such evidence is simply one factor to take into account. Thus in *Vento v Chief Constable of West Yorkshire Police (No 2)* [2002] EWCA Civ 1871, [2003] ICR 318, the tribunal had been entitled to conclude that there was a 75% chance that the complainant would have remained in the police force until retirement (a period of 21 years of service) despite statistics suggesting that only 9% of female officers leaving the respondent's service had served for longer than 18 years. The fact that a claimant is in receipt of incapacity benefit does not, in itself, mean that he or she is incapable of working during the same period and therefore not eligible for compensation for loss of earnings during that period, rather an employment tribunal needs to consider all the evidence as to whether the claimant can work (*Sheffield Forgemasters International Ltd v Fox* [2009] ICR 333, [2009] IRLR 192, EAT). In *Brash-Hall v Getty Images Ltd* [2006] EWCA Civ 531, (2006) 811 IDS Brief 5, the Court of Appeal held that, where an employee had been dismissed constructively and in a discriminatory manner and the tribunal had decided that she would have been made redundant anyway, her compensation could only include the amount she would have received in contractual severance payment if she proved that she would have signed a severance agreement.

In *Bullimore v Pothecary Witham Weld (No 2)* [2011] IRLR 18, EAT, Underhill P emphasised that questions of causation and remoteness are addressed according to different principles. Causation is a factual issue of whether the damage would have occurred 'but for' the wrongful act, whereas questions of remoteness involve a value judgment as to what was 'direct' or 'natural' or 'foreseeable' as a consequence. Where an employer for an illegitimate reason (in that case to victimise the claimant) gave an adverse reference leading to a prospective employer not offering a job or withdrawing an offer it was hard to see why that was too remote to attract compensation. The EAT held that there was no rule that a subsequent tortious act (eg the prospective employer itself unlawfully victimising the claimant) breaks the 'chain of causation'. In that case the employment tribunal had erred in not awarding compensation for loss of earnings stemming from victimisation by way of a damaging reference.

It is well established that a discriminator's motives are not relevant when it comes to deciding whether or not an act is discriminatory. However, a majority of the EAT (consisting of the two lay members) has decided that motives may be relevant when it comes to assessing compensation (*Chief Constable of Greater Manchester Police v Hope* [1999] ICR 338). Upholding the tribunal's decision that the complainant had been the victim of an act of direct race and sex discrimination, it nevertheless went on to decide that, in the absence of discriminatory intent, the tribunal should have made a nil award of compensation.

Normal principles of mitigation apply. In *Cannock* (above), the EAT gave a strong indication that a woman dismissed by reason of pregnancy ought not to recover compensation relating to a period more than six months after the date of the birth of her child unless she is actively engaged in looking for work at that date. However, the tribunal is entitled to bear in mind the difficulties which a woman with a small child may face in obtaining work (*Hunt* above). Her personal characteristics and the state of the labour market at the relevant time would also be relevant considerations. In *DeBique v Ministry of Defence (No 2)* (2012) 941 IDS Brief 7, EAT, an employment tribunal had been entitled to award no compensation for loss of earnings where the claimant was found to have unreasonably refused an offer of redeployment to a post where her child care obligations could be reconciled with her duties. In that case the EAT emphasised that the assessment of the reasonableness of a claimant's efforts to mitigate her loss were very much a matter of fact for the tribunal. As with unfair dismissal an employee can mitigate their loss by setting up in business, in which case the tribunal should consider when calculating compensation both lost remuneration and the costs incurred in setting up the business (if reasonably incurred) (*Dove v Aon Training Ltd* [2005] EWCA Civ 411, [2005] IRLR 891).

In *Chagger*, above, the EAT held that the risk that future potential employers might decline to employ the claimant because of his discrimination claim (so-called 'stigma loss') was too remote to be reflected in compensation payable by the respondent former employer. However the Court of Appeal reversed the EAT on this point holding that there was no reason why a respondent should not be liable for so-called stigma losses resulting from the refusal of third party potential employers to employ the claimant, even if those refusals are unlawful. The Court held that a tribunal should take a sensible and robust approach and not simply rely on the assertion of stigma or speculation, but where there was very extensive evidence of attempted mitigation failing to result in a job the tribunal would be entitled to conclude that the claimant was unlikely to obtain future employment in the industry. The Court also considered that there could be exceptional cases where stigma loss was the only head of damage, for example where the respondent would have dismissed even had there been no discrimination, however the onus would be on the claimant to prove such loss.

Where a complainant receives a sum in respect of future loss, a discount should be made for accelerated receipt unless the sums concerned are so small as to make it an unnecessary complication (*Bentwood Bros (Manchester) Ltd v Shepherd* [2003] EWCA Civ 380, [2003] ICR 1000). In *Chagger*, above, the EAT has suggested that if the Ogden Tables are used in complex calculations of future loss, tribunals should do so only with a proper understanding of their limitations and give proper consideration to the contingencies not reflected in the tables.

Compensation should be calculated on the basis of net rather than gross loss of earnings (*Visa International Service Association v Paul* [2004] IRLR 42, EAT). In *Chan v Hackney London Borough Council* [1997] ICR 1014, the EAT decided that an employment tribunal had been right to deduct sums received by way of invalidity benefit from the compensatory award.

See also HARVEYS – Division L.6.C.

12.16   Compensation: injury to feelings

The amount of compensation awarded may include a sum for injury to feelings resulting from an act of discrimination (*EA 2010, ss 124(5)* read with *119(4)*; and previously *SDA 1975, s 66(4); RRA 1976, s 57(4); DDA 1995, s 17A(4)*; and *AR 2006, reg 38(1)(b)* read with *reg 39(3)*).

For a sum to be awarded for injury to feelings it is not necessary for the claimant to be aware that the employer's reason for the treatment was discriminatory, although such knowledge might well serve to increase the hurt and therefore the award (see *Taylor v XLN Telecom Ltd*

[2010] ICR 656, [2010] IRLR 499, EAT, explaining that this was not contrary to the Court of Appeal's judgment in *Skyrail Oceanic Ltd v Coleman* [1981] ICR 864). See also *Wileman v Minilec Engineering Ltd* [1988] ICR 318; *Murray v Powertech (Scotland) Ltd* [1992] IRLR 257. It follows that in a case concerned with a discriminatory dismissal, the fact that the complainant would have been dismissed at a later date in any event is not a ground for reducing the award for injury to feelings. The purpose of the award is to compensate the complainant for the 'anger, upset and humiliation' caused by the fact that he knows that he has been discriminated against. That upset is not displaced by the prospect that he might have been dismissed lawfully at a later date (*O'Donoghue v Redcar and Cleveland Borough Council* [2001] IRLR 615, EAT). Although evidence will be required of injury to feelings, a tribunal will readily conclude that some injury to feelings has arisen from a discriminatory act (see *Abegaze v Shrewsbury College of Arts & Technology* [2009] EWCA Civ 96, [2010] IRLR 238, CA). A tribunal erred in law in making no award at all for injury to feelings where it found that the claimant was merely angry and frustrated as a result of discrimination (*Assoukou v Select Services Partners Ltd* [2006] EWCA Civ 1442, [2006] All ER (D) 122 (Oct).

In *Munchkins Restaurant Ltd v Karmazyn* (2010) 907 IDS Brief 7, EAT, the EAT slightly uneasily accepted that an employment tribunal had not erred in awarding the same amount of compensation for injury to feelings to four claimants for sex discrimination despite their differing lengths of service. An increasing 'tariff' of compensation for injury to feelings for subsequent, repeat acts of discrimination is not automatically appropriate (*London Borough of Hackney v Sivanandan* [2011] ICR 1374, [2011] IRLR 740, EAT.

The assessment of the appropriate sum to award in any case is a difficult one. General guidance on assessing compensation for injury to feelings where an act of harassment results in psychiatric or physical injury was given in *HM Prison Service v Johnson* [1997] ICR 275. Compensation for injury to feelings should be compensatory and not punitive, although it should not be set at so low a level as to 'diminish respect for the policy of the anti-discriminatory legislation'. It should also 'bear some similarity to the range of awards in personal injury cases and in exercising their discretion tribunals should remind themselves of the value in everyday life of the sum they had in mind' (*Johnson*, above). Subjecting the complainant to a disciplinary investigation, moving him to a different location and allowing a grievance procedure to drag on for 14 months were all factors a tribunal could take into account in awarding damages for injury to feelings (*British Telecommunications plc v Reid* [2003] EWCA Civ 1675, [2004] IRLR 327). The test of relevance was whether the matters arose from the act of discrimination and were consequential on it.

The Court of Appeal has identified three broad bands of compensation to assist the tribunals (*Vento v Chief Constable of West Yorkshire Police (No 2)* [2002] EWCA Civ 1871, [2003] ICR 318). The lowest band of awards originally ran from £500 to £5,000. The band is said to be appropriate for 'less serious' cases where the act of discrimination is an 'isolated' or 'one-off' incident. The middle band was £5,000 to £15,000 and should be used for 'serious cases which do not merit an award in the highest band'. Awards in the highest band fell between £15,000 and £25,000. The highest band is designed for use in the 'most serious' cases, eg where there has been a 'lengthy campaign of discriminatory harassment on the ground of sex or race'. Awards of less than £500 should be 'avoided altogether'. Awards of more than £25,000 should be made in only the 'most exceptional' cases. The upper limits of the bands were revised by the EAT in *Da'Bell v NSPCC* [2010] IRLR 19 to take account of inflation: £6,000 for the lower band, £18,000 for the middle band and £30,000 for the upper band. It will not, however, be an error of law for an employment tribunal not expressly to engage in an uprating exercise or refer to *Da'Bell* provided it assesses the quantum of compensation in 'today's money' (see *Bullimore v Pothecary Witham Weld (No 2)* [2011] IRLR 18, EAT).

In *Simmons v Castle* [2013] 1 All ER 334, [2013] 1 WLR 1239 the Court of Appeal declared that, with effect from 1 April 2013, the proper level of general damages in "all civil claims for (i) pain and suffering; (ii) loss of amenity; (iii) physical inconvenience and discomfort; (iv) social discredit; (v) mental distress; or (vi) loss of society of relatives", would be 10 per cent higher than previously (save in certain cases where a claimant had previously entered into a conditional fee agreement). On the face of it, this increase may be applicable to the *Vento* bands as uprated in *Da'Bell* but the point has not yet been tested.

In the *Johnson* case, the EAT had made reference to the Judicial Studies Board's guidelines on compensation for post-traumatic stress disorder as a useful source of guidance. The guidelines adopt a four-band classification of cases as 'minor', 'moderate', 'moderately severe' and 'severe'. In *Zaiwalla & Co v Walia* [2002] IRLR 697, EAT, the EAT found that the tribunal had erred by treating the injury to feelings suffered by the particular complainant as analogous to a 'moderately severe' stress disorder. The complainant had been belittled, bullied and harassed over a three-month period, and was left feeling despair and suffering from panic attacks and prolonged tearfulness. Nevertheless, a moderately severe disorder is one which promises 'some recovery with professional help' but with a 'significant disability' being experienced for the 'foreseeable future'. The EAT considered the case was more closely analogous to the 'moderate category' (the victim will have 'largely recovered and any continuing effects will not be grossly disabling'). The effect of this analogy being drawn was to decrease the award from £15,000 to £10,000.

The Court of Appeal in *Vento (No 2)* (above) itself made reference to the JSB guidelines suggesting that they continue to provide a useful source of assistance to a tribunal. As the JSB's four bands do not map precisely onto the Court of Appeal's three bands, reading them together may allow a more finely-tuned approach.

Reference to awards made in defamation proceedings as a guideline for assessing the appropriate award for injury to feelings has been deprecated by the EAT (*Vento v Chief Constable of West Yorkshire Police (No 2)* [2002] IRLR 177, EAT).

A question arises as to how a tribunal is to assess injury to feeling where there are a number of different discriminatory acts, possibly in relation to different grounds of discrimination. Generally a broad brush approach should be adopted as an artificial attempt to assess injury to feelings in relation to each act would be a wholly unreal task. However there may be cases that require a more nuanced approach where the tribunal does need separately to consider the level of injury to feelings caused by different individual acts whilst having overall regard to the magnitude of the global sum to be awarded (*Al Jumard v Clwyd Leisure Ltd* [2008] IRLR 345, EAT).

For the purpose of setting the size of the award, the tribunal should ignore the fact that the complainant will receive interest on the sums awarded (*Ministry of Defence v Cannock*, above). In *Orlando v Didcot Power Station Sports and Social Club* [1996] IRLR 262, the EAT considered statistics which indicated that the removal of the statutory cap on compensation had not resulted in a significant increase in the average size of awards made for injury to feelings.

In *Ministry of Defence v Anderson* [1996] IRLR 139, the EAT overturned an award of £250 on the grounds that it was perversely low, and stated that £500 was 'at or near the minimum' level of award which would ordinarily be appropriate. The EAT in *Moonsar v Fiveways Express Transport Ltd* [2005] IRLR 9 has found that an award of £1,000 was not too low in a case where the female complainant's colleagues had viewed pornography on the internet in her presence. In another case, where the discrimination was not directed at the complainant personally, there was no slur on his reputation or character and he was only marginally inconvenienced an award of £750 was appropriate (*Moyhing v Barts and London NHS Trust* [2006] IRLR 860, EAT). The EAT in *Glasgow City Council v McNab* [2007] IRLR 476 held that an award of £2,000 for injury to a feelings was at the upper end of the appropriate range of awards, but did not fall outside that range, in a case of religious discrimination where a teacher was not appointed to a temporary promotion because he was not a Roman Catholic. In *Ministry of Defence v O'Hare (No 2)* [1997] ICR 306, the EAT considered two pregnancy discrimination cases where employees had been faced with a choice of losing their job or aborting their pregnancies. £2,000 was suggested as a guideline figure for cases where an employee was required to make such a choice. Where the employee actually opted to abort, matters were more difficult, but a bracket of £1,500 to £3,000 was suggested for cases where the injury to feelings was 'relatively transient' with a further bracket of £3,000 to £7,500 where the injury was 'more durable'. In *Vento (No 2)* above, the EAT overturned an award of £50,000 on the basis that it was 'manifestly excessive', substituting an award of £25,000. The complainant had suffered a 'moderate' psychiatric injury as a result of the discriminatory treatment received. The psychiatric injury had been compensated by an award of £9,000.

For guidance on avoiding double recovery in cases where complainants suffer both injury to feelings and a psychiatric injury, see 'Compensation: personal injury' immediately below. In *Voith Turbo Ltd v Stowe* [2005] IRLR 228, EAT, the EAT observed, *obiter*, that a dismissal on grounds of race discrimination was always very serious and could not be regarded as one-off and suitable for a lower band award. In *Miles v Gilbank* [2006] ICR 12, the EAT upheld an award of £25,000 for injury to feelings resulting from the bullying and harassment of a pregnant employee repeatedly and consciously inflicted with total disregard for the welfare of the employee or her unborn child. This was affirmed by the Court of Appeal ([2006] EWCA Civ 543, [2006] ICR 1297, [2006] IRLR 538), which held that if the discrimination involved the well-being of the claimant's unborn child, this increased the seriousness.

For guidance on the circumstances in which the appeal tribunal will be prepared to interfere with the amount of an award under this heading, see *ICTS (UK) Ltd v Tchoula* [2000] IRLR 643, EAT. An appellate court will only interfere if the award is so much out of line that it amounts to an error of law through a misdirection in principle or is for some other reason, such as an erroneous evaluation of the facts, plainly wrong (*R (Elias) v Secretary of State for Defence* [2006] EWCA Civ 1293, [2006] IRLR 934). The EAT has demonstrated that it will overturn awards even if 'correctly categorised' so that its powers are not limited to correcting mis-categorisations (see *Doshoki v Draeger Ltd* [2002] IRLR 340, EAT). An example of this is *Massey v UNIFI* [2007] EWCA Civ 800, [2008] ICR 62, [2007] IRLR 902, a case of unjustified union discipline where the Court of Appeal raised the award for injury to feelings to £12,500 where it considered that an award of £7,500 was too far down the middle *Vento* category as the injury to feelings was intense and prolonged.

The tax treatment of awards for injury to feelings differs from that in relation to the treatment of compensation for pecuniary loss arising from discrimination - the former not being taxable, the latter generally being taxable. There is no need for a tribunal to award compensation for injury to feelings on a grossed up basis as there is no authority that tax is payable on such an award (*Orthet Ltd v Vince-Cain* [2005] ICR 374, EAT). A compensation payment for discrimination made under a compromise agreement will only be taxable if discrimination is the cause of the termination of employment and will only be taxable to the extent that it meets the financial loss caused by the termination of the employment (see *Oti-Obihara v Revenue and Customs Comrs* [2010] UKFTT 568 (TC), [2011] IRLR 386, First-tier Tribunal (Tax Chamber)). Compensation for the violation of the right not to be discriminated against will not be taxable and where a compromise agreement does not distinguish these elements it is necessary first to establish what amount relates to compensation for financial loss arising from the termination of the employment (including future loss of earnings). The *Oti-Obihara* case was an appeal in relation to the Revenue's determination of the incidence of tax. In *Norman v Yellow Pages Sales Ltd* [2010] EWCA Civ 1395 the Court of Appeal rejected the claimant's argument that the respondent was in breach of a compromise agreement brokered via ACAS because it had failed to apportion the settlement sum between non-taxable injury to feelings compensation and taxable compensation for loss of income. The Court held that in the absence of an express provision in the compromise agreement as to such apportionment, there was no room to read in an obligation to apportion.

See also HARVEYS – Division L.7.B.

12.17 Compensation: personal injury

Where the injury to feelings is such that it results in the onset of psychiatric illness, the complainant may recover compensation for personal injury in the tribunal (*Sheriff v Klyne Tugs (Lowestoft) Ltd* [1999] ICR 1170). It is thought that the same principle would apply where an employee is physically injured in the course of harassment. It may not always be easy to distinguish where injury to feelings stops and injury to mental health begins and there is consequently a danger of double recovery. In *HM Prison Service v Salmon* [2001] IRLR 425, the EAT suggested that in such cases it was open to a tribunal to make a single award for injury to feelings and to include an element for psychiatric harm. Tribunals should make it clear what they are doing.

Damages for personal injury are recoverable for any harm caused by the discriminatory act and not simply harm which was reasonably foreseeable (*Essa v Laing Ltd* [2003] ICR 1110, EAT). Although this decision was upheld on appeal by a majority of the Court of Appeal, there was some suggestion that the simple causation test may only apply to cases of racial abuse and not discrimination more widely ([2004] EWCA Civ 02, [2004] ICR 746). It will not avail a discriminator that the harm was related to a pre-existing condition if the unlawful act caused the harm, although where there is evidence that the harm was likely to have occurred at some point in the future a discount for acceleration will be necessary (see *Massey v UNIFI*, above). However when more than one event contributes to the harm suffered by a claimant the extent of the respondent's liability is limited to the contribution to the harm made by its discriminatory conduct (see *Thaine v London School of Economics* [2010] ICR 1422, EAT – in that case only 40%). The Court of Appeal remitted a case for rehearing when new evidence was obtained which might have materially affected the employment tribunal's assessment of the extent of the depressive illness that the tribunal had found had been exacerbated by the respondent's discriminatory conduct (see *Blundell v Governing Body of St Andrew's Catholic Primary School* [2011] EWCA Civ 427, [2012] ICR 295).

See also HARVEYS – Division L.7.C.

12.18 Compensation: aggravated and exemplary damages

Aggravated damages may be awarded in discrimination cases where the complainant is able to establish a causal link between 'exceptional or contumelious conduct or motive' on the employer's part and her injury to feelings. Such damages may be appropriate, for instance, where an employer has failed properly to investigate the applicant's complaint of discrimination (*Johnson* above). The promotion of the alleged discriminator while he was still subject to disciplinary proceedings for his alleged discrimination was a matter a tribunal could take into account in awarding aggravated damages (see *British Telecommunications*, above). There has been some uncertainty over whether any sum awarded under this head should be incorporated into the award for injury to feelings. This approach was approved, *obiter*, by the EAT in *Gbaja-Biamila v DHL International (UK) Ltd* [2000] ICR 730, EAT (adopting the approach of the Northern Ireland Court of Appeal in *McConnell v Police Authority for Northern Ireland* [1997] IRLR 625, NICA). However, in *ICTS (UK) Ltd v Tchoula* [2000] IRLR 643, EAT, the EAT declined to find that the tribunal had erred by making a separate award of aggravated damages. The Court of Appeal has now confirmed the approach in *ICTS* and overruled *McConnell* by holding that aggravated damages should not be aggregated with damages for injury to feelings (*Scott v IRC* [2004] EWCA Civ 400,

[2004] IRLR 713). In *Commissioner of Police for the Metropolis v Shaw* [2012] ICR 464, [2012] IRLR 291, EAT, Underhill P stated that aggravated damages are an aspect of injury to feelings reflecting the making more serious of the injury to feelings by some additional element which would fall into one of three categories: (a) the manner in which the wrong was committed, (b) motive (but only if the claimant was aware of the motive), or (c) subsequent conduct (eg by the employer not taking the complaint seriously, failure to apologise or conduct at trial). The ultimate question would always be what additional distress was caused to a particular claimant in the particular circumstances of the case and tribunals should be cautious about focusing on the respondent's conduct. However, a tribunal should ask itself whether the conduct, objectively viewed, was capable of having that aggravating effect: *HM Land Registry v McGlue* (EAT 6/2/2013). Aggravated damages have been awarded where the respondents made a malicious and unfounded complaint to the police about the claimants after dismissal which the employment tribunal considered to be linked to the earlier discriminatory behaviour (see *Bungay v Saini* (2011) 938 IDS Brief 13, [2011] EqLR 1130, EAT).

A tribunal awarding aggravated damages should seek to avoid double recovery by having regard to the overlap between the heads of damage (see *Ministry of Defence v Fletcher* [2010] IRLR 25, EAT). The tribunal should look at whether the overall award is proportionate to the totality of the claimant's suffering and generally the large majority of awards would be in the range £5,000 to £7,500 (see *Shaw*, above). In *Shaw*, above, Underhill P confirmed that the only purpose of aggravated damages is compensatory and they should not be awarded in order to punish a respondent (in the process thereby doubting observations to the contrary in *Fletcher*).

Exceptionally, an award of aggravated damages may be appropriate where the manner in which a respondent has conducted proceedings has aggravated the harm caused by the original act of discrimination (*Zaiwalla & Co* and *Fletcher* above).

The position regarding the availability of exemplary damages is less clear. The law had been that exemplary damages were not available in discrimination cases because these are statutory torts that did not exist at the time of the House of Lords decision in *Rookes v Barnard* [1964] AC 1129 (see *AB v South West Water Services Ltd* [1993] QB 507; *Deane v Ealing London Borough Council* [1993] ICR 329; *Ministry of Defence v Meredith* [1995] IRLR 539). However in *Kuddus v Chief Constable of Leicestershire Constabulary* [2001] UKHL 29, [2002] 2 AC 122 (a case of alleged misfeasance in public office) the House of Lords confirmed that the availability of exemplary damages depends on the nature of the tortious behaviour rather than whether or not the precise cause of action relied upon was recognised prior to 1964. There are two categories of case where exemplary damages may be awarded: (1) where there is oppressive, arbitrary or unconstitutional action by servants of the Government; or (2) where the tortfeasor's conduct was calculated to make a profit for himself that may exceed any compensation payable to the claimant (see *Rookes v Barnard*, above). The award of exemplary damages in discrimination cases will be rare and will occur only where the conduct falls into one of the two categories identified in *Rookes v Barnard* and the award of compensatory damages (including aggravated damages) will not sufficiently punish the respondent's conduct (*Bradford City Metropolitan Council v Arora* [1991] IRLR 165, CA). Where the first limb of the *Rookes v Barnard* test is in issue careful consideration will need to be given to whether the respondent can be said to have acted as agent or servant of the Government, even at a local level. In *Virgo Fidelis Senior School v Boyle* [2004] IRLR 268 the EAT held that the management of a voluntary-aided school were not agents or servants of the Government. In contrast, in *Arora* the Court of Appeal rejected the argument that the selection committee for a senior position in a college for which the respondent council had authority were exercising a private function of the council and could not be liable for exemplary damages. The principles governing the award of exemplary damages were considered by the EAT in *Fletcher*, above. While 'ordinary' employment law functions performed under statute by an official of a public body with sufficient seniority might, in principle, attract an award of exemplary damages the conduct must be conscious and contumelious and the award in that case was set aside where there was no finding by the tribunal that the failure to operate effective redress procedures was conscious. The EAT emphasised that such damages are punitive, not compensatory, and that double recovery must be avoided. In *R (Elias) v Secretary of State for Defence*, above, the Court of Appeal held that on the facts the discrimination in that case was not of such a nature as to make aggravated or exemplary damages appropriate.

Exemplary damages will not be available in cases under the *EqPA 1970* as such claims are contractual, rather than tortious (see *Allan v Newcastle-upon-Tyne City Council* [2005] IRLR 504, EAT). This principle presumably still applies to the 'equality of terms' provisions under the *EA 2010, Pt 5 Chapter 3*, which replace the *EqPA 1970*, as these are still framed by reference to the terms of a claimant's contract of employment.

See also HARVEYS – Division **L.7.D**.

12.19 Compensation: discrimination and unfair dismissal

Where a complainant has been the victim of a dismissal which is both discriminatory and unfair (ie contrary to the right not to be unfairly dismissed conferred on certain employees by the *ERA 1996*), the tribunal has a choice of two compensatory regimes. As compensation for unfair dismissal is subject to a statutory maximum, whilst awards made under the anti-discrimination legislation are unlimited, the tribunal will almost invariably use the latter regime. However, the one clear advantage of the unfair dismissal regime is that it allows the tribunal to order the respondent to reinstate, or to re-engage, the complainant. If the respondent does not comply with such a re-employment order, the matter is re-listed for a compensation hearing. A penal 'additional award' may be made (see **53.14** UNFAIR DISMISSAL – III). Although the statutory language states that where the matter returns for compensation issues to be considered, compensation should be awarded in accordance with the provisions of the *ERA 1996* the EAT has made it clear that the statute should not be taken to preclude the tribunal from using the *RRA 1976* regime (or that under the other discrimination regimes and now the *EA 2010* regime) (*D'Souza v Lambeth London Borough Council* [1997] IRLR 677). Making a re-employment order does not take away a complainant's right to unlimited compensation for the act of discrimination. However, if a tribunal orders re-employment and awards compensation for injury to feelings at the first remedies hearing, there is a risk that it will be taken to have made a final order in relation to compensation for discrimination, thereby precluding it from making a further award for loss arising from the discrimination where the re-employment order is not complied with. If the tribunal wishes to keep open the possibility of further compensation under the anti-discrimination regime, it should say so expressly (*Lambeth London Borough Council v D'Souza* [1999] IRLR 240, CA).

That case also provided guidance in relation to the calculation of pension loss. Understandably reluctant to have to hear detailed and contested evidence from actuaries, tribunals more usually adopt the less precise but less complicated approach of awarding the complainant a sum equivalent to the contributions that the respondent would have made into the pension scheme had the employee not been dismissed. In *D'Souza* a complication arose from the fact that the respondent was at that time enjoying a contributions holiday. The EAT makes it clear that the contributions holiday should not result in the complainant's compensation being reduced. Compensation should be calculated on the basis of contributions at what would have been the ordinary rate. The complainant is not being compensated for the loss of contributions but for the loss of a pension. The contributions method is a way of approximating the loss and should not be followed slavishly if it is plainly not going to compensate the complainant for the loss of his pension. The EAT in *Clancy v Cannock Chase Technical College* [2001] IRLR 331 has again stressed the need for accurate assessment of pension loss to ensure that complainants are fully compensated. In the light of this the Third Edition of the guidelines on pension loss for employment tribunals, *Compensation for*

12.19 Discrimination and Equal Opportunities – III: Enforcement

Loss of Pension Rights – Employment Tribunals ('the Booklet'), now sets out a 'substantial loss approach' better suited to the calculation of significant pension loss. This method will often be more appropriate in serious discrimination cases and should be adopted in cases where the loss is expected to last more than two years (*Orthet Ltd v Vince-Cain* [2005] ICR 374, EAT). In *Greenhoff v Barnsley Metropolitan Borough Council* [2006] ICR 1514 the EAT held that a tribunal should set out why it adopted a particular approach to pension loss and why other approaches, particularly those set out in the Booklet, were rejected. The EAT also gave guidance about the steps that tribunals should go through in considering pension loss. See also *Chief Constable of West Midlands Police v Gardner* [2012] EqLR 20, EAT, in which the need for a tribunal to explain why it was departing from the approach in the Booklet or the Ogden Tables was again emphasised. The EAT in that case also noted that Ogden multipliers may be better suited to current economic conditions than those specified for the 'substantial approach' in the Booklet.

The outcome of an unfair dismissal claim is not automatically determined by the outcome of a successful discrimination claim in relation to dismissal (see *Eversheds Legal Services Ltd v De Belin* [2011] ICR 1137, [2011] IRLR 448, EAT). Where a dismissal is fair, even though also an act of victimisation, the complainant will only be entitled to compensation for injury to feelings (*Lisk-Carew v Birmingham City Council* [2004] EWCA Civ 565, [2004] 20 LS Gaz R 35). Conversely, a respondent cannot rely upon a subsequent unfair dismissal to break the chain of causation in relation to a complainant's continuing losses (*HM Prison Service v Beart (No 2)* [2005] EWCA Civ 467, [2005] ICR 1206, upholding the EAT in *HM Prison Service v Beart (No 2)* [2005] IRLR 171).

12.20 Compensation: awards of interest

The *EA 2010, s 139(1)* provides for regulations to be made enabling employment tribunals to include interest on an amount awarded in proceedings under the Act. Interest is payable on any sums awarded currently pursuant to the *Employment Tribunals (Interest on Awards in Discrimination Cases) Regulations 1996 (SI 1996/2803)* (now having effect under *EA 2010, s 139* by virtue of the *Equality Act 2010 (Commencement No.4, Savings, Consequential, Transitional, Transitory and Incidental Provisions and Revocations) Order 2010 (SI 2010/2317), art 21(1), Sch 7*). Interest should be awarded on the complainant's net and not gross loss (*Bentwood Bros (Manchester) Ltd v Shepherd* [2003] EWCA Civ 380, [2003] ICR 1000).

Where the tribunal is concerned with a sum other than an award for injury to feelings, it is required to identify a 'mid-point date'. This date is the halfway point between the date on which the act of discrimination complained of occurred and the date on which the interest is being calculated (*SI 1996/2803, reg 4*). Interest is then awarded in respect of the period from the mid-point date to the date of calculation (*reg 6(1)(b)*). A different rule applies to the calculation of interest on awards for injury to feelings. By *reg 6(1)(a)*, interest is awarded for the whole period from the date of the act of discrimination through to the date of calculation.

Interest is simple interest and accrues from day to day (*reg 3(1)*). By *reg 3(2)*, the rate to be applied in England and Wales is that prescribed for the Special Investment Account by *rule 27(1)* of the *Court Funds Rules 1987 (SI 1987/821)* (although the Court Funds Rules 1987 have now been revoked and replaced by the *Court Funds Rules 2011 (SI 2011/1734)*). In Scotland, the relevant rate is that fixed for the time being by the *Act of Sederunt (Interest in Sheriff Court Decrees or Extracts) 1975 (SI 1975/948)*. Where the rate has varied over the relevant period the tribunal may, in the interests of simplicity, apply a median or average of the rates (*reg 3(3)*).

If a respondent has made a payment to the complainant prior to the date of calculation, the date of payment is treated as if it were the date of calculation for the purposes of calculating the interest to be awarded (*reg 6(2)*).

The tribunal is given a discretion to calculate interest by reference to periods other than those set out above, or even to use different periods for different elements of the award. The discretion may be exercised only where the tribunal is of the opinion that:

(a)   there are exceptional circumstances, whether relating to the claim as a whole or to a particular element of the award; and

(b)   those circumstances have the effect that serious injustice would be caused if interest were to be awarded by reference to the period or periods specified in *reg 6(1)(a)* or *(b)* or *6(2)*.

See also HARVEYS – Division L.6.C(10).

12.21 Recommendations

The *EA 2010, s 124(1)(c)* empowers tribunals to make an appropriate recommendation. An appropriate recommendation is a recommendation that within a specified period the respondent takes specified steps for the purpose of obviating or reducing the adverse effect of any matter to which the proceedings relate (a) on the claimant or (b) on any other person (*s 124(3)*). This can therefore extend the scope of recommendations to benefit persons other than the claimant (for example fellow employees or future job applicants), which may be particularly relevant if the claimant is no longer employed by the respondent. Previously a tribunal was empowered to make a recommendation that the respondent take, within a specified period, action appearing to the tribunal to be practicable for the purpose of obviating or reducing the adverse effect on the complainant of any act of discrimination to which the complaint related. This was held not to give the tribunal power to recommend that an applicant for promotion who was discriminated against be promoted to the next open post (*British Gas plc v Sharma* [1991] ICR 19). Where statutory rules govern an appointment, a tribunal cannot recommend an applicant's appointment. It can merely recommend that the appointing body be made aware of the need to comply with the anti-discrimination legislation and of other relevant matters (*North West Thames Regional Health Authority v Noone* [1988] ICR 813).

A tribunal should only make recommendations that are practicable but the exercise of that discretion will only be interfered with on appeal if exercised wholly wrongly, taking account of irrelevant considerations or failing to take account of relevant ones (*Lycée Charles de Gaulle v Delambre* [2011] EqLR 948, EAT). In *Vento (No 2)* (see above), the respondent was held vicariously liable for the actions of certain of the complainant's colleagues. The colleagues were not themselves parties. The tribunal recommended that the respondent should meet with the colleagues and raise with them the adverse findings made by the tribunal's decision. This recommendation was endorsed by the EAT. However, the EAT, whilst acknowledging the very broad discretion conferred upon the tribunal, overturned a further recommendation that the respondent should suggest to the colleagues that they should make an apology in writing to the complainant. The EAT considered the recommendation was inappropriate because:

(1)   the complainant had already had an apology from her 'employer';

(2)   the colleagues were not parties and had not been given an opportunity to put their side of the case to the tribunal;

(3)   the recommendation could not be enforced and if the colleagues refused to apologise, that would aggravate the situation; and

(4)   an ordered apology would have little worth as it would not appear sincere.

Recommendations cannot be specifically enforced. However, if, without reasonable justification, the respondent to a complaint fails to comply with a recommendation made by an employment tribunal that he take certain action and it thinks it just and equitable to do so:

(i)   the tribunal may increase the amount of compensation required to be paid to the complainant in respect of the complaint by a compensation order; or

(ii)   if an order for compensation could have been made, but was not, the tribunal may make such an order.

(*EA 2010, s 124(7)*; and previously *SDA 1975, s 65(3)(a), (b); RRA 1976, s 56(4)(a), (b); SOR 2003, reg 30(3); RBR 2003, reg 30(3); DDA 1995, s 17A(5)*; and *AR 2006, reg 38(3)*.)

See also Harveys – Divisions **L.6.D, L.7.F.**

12.22 Remedies in cases involving pension schemes

The *EA 2010, s 126* makes similar provision for remedies in relation to complaints of discrimination involving pension schemes with respect to all protected characteristics as existed under the previous Acts and Regulations. An employment tribunal may grant remedies if it finds that there has been a contravention of a provision referred to in *EA 2010, s 120(1)* in relation to either (a) the terms on which persons become members of an occupational pension scheme, or (b) the terms on which members of an occupational pension scheme are treated. In those circumstances, in addition to the remedies available under *s 124(1)*, the tribunal may also by order declare:

(a)   if the complaint relates to the terms on which persons become members of a scheme, that the complainant has a right to be admitted to the scheme; and

(b)   if the complaint relates to the terms on which members of the scheme are treated, that the complainant has a right to membership of the scheme without discrimination (*s 126(2)*).

An order under the *EA 2010, s 126(2)* may make provision as to the terms on which or the capacity in which the claimant is to enjoy the admission or membership and may have effect in relation to a period before the order is made (*s 126(4)*).

A tribunal may only make an order for compensation in relation to an occupational pension scheme under the *EA 2010, s 124(2)(b)* for compensation for injury to feelings or (by virtue of *s 124(7)*) for failure to comply with a recommendation (*s 126(3)*). The Court of Appeal has confirmed that there was no incompatibility with EU law in a tribunal not granting a declaration of entitlement where part-time female employees who were indirectly discriminated against in accessing a pension scheme would in fact have opted out of membership of the scheme (see *Copple v Littlewoods plc* [2011] EWCA Civ 1281, [2012] 2 All ER 97, [2012] IRLR 121). The Court considered that the question was whether on the balance of probabilities the women would have joined the scheme during the closed period.

Previously the *SOR 2003, RBR 2003, DDA 1995* and *AR 2006* contained specific provisions relating to discrimination or harassment involving pension schemes. The numbering of the relevant provisions was identical under the *SOR 2003* and the *RBR 2003*. The provisions in *AR 2006* and *DDA 1995* were differently numbered. Claims against managers or trustees of pension schemes brought under *reg 9A* of *SOR 2003* or *RBR 2003*, under *ss 4G, 4H* of *DDA 1995*, or *reg 11* of *AR 2006* had (subject to the availability of a complaint to the Pensions Ombudsman and any right, where appropriate, to commence judicial review proceedings (see *reg 27(2)* of *SOR 2003* and *RBR 2003; DDA 1995, Sch 3, para 2*; or *reg 35(2)* of *AR 2006*) to be brought in the employment tribunal. This included cases where the claim was based on relationships which have come to an end (*SOR 2003, reg 21; RBR*

2003, reg 21; DDA 1995, s 16A; and *AR 2006, reg 24*), was a claim alleging vicarious liability, or was a claim alleging that a person had knowingly aided an unlawful act. The relevant employer was required to be a party to the proceedings (*SOR 2003, Sch 1A, para 6; RBR 2003, Sch 1A, para 6; DDA 1995, s 41(1)*; and *AR 2006, Sch 2, Part 1, para 5*).

'Pensioner members' (for whom see *Pensions Act 1995, s 124(1)*) were not entitled to a remedy from the tribunal (*SOR 2003, Sch 1A, para 7(1)(b); RBR 2003, Sch 1A, para 7(1)(b); DDA 1995, s 47(1)(c)*; and *AR 2006, Sch 2, Part 1, para 6(1)(b)*).

Otherwise, where the tribunal concluded that a claim was well-founded, it had the following remedy options:

(1)   In cases concerned with admission to membership, the tribunal could make an order declaring that the complainant be admitted to the scheme. The tribunal could make such provision as it considered appropriate as to the terms on or the capacity in which the complainant was to be admitted.

(2)   In cases concerned with the terms on which members are treated, the tribunal could make an order declaring that the complainant should be entitled to membership without discrimination. Again, the order could not have a retrospective effect and could make such provision as it considered appropriate as to the terms on or the capacity in which the complainant could enjoy membership.

(3)   The tribunal could make an order compensating the complainant for injury to feelings but not otherwise compensate the complainant, whether in relation to arrears of benefits or otherwise, unless the respondent refused to comply with a recommendation (though there was no specific power set out to make a recommendation).

The right to seek an investigation or determination by the Pensions Ombudsman was specifically preserved (*reg 9A(1)* of the *SOR 2003* and *RBR 2003* added by amendment in, respectively, the *Employment Equality (Sexual Orientation) (Amendment) Regulations 2003 (SI 2003/2827)*, the *Employment Equality (Religion or Belief) (Amendment) Regulations 2003 (SI 2003/2828)*, *DDA 1995, Sch 3, para 2(2)*, and *AR 2006, reg 35(2)*).

ENFORCEMENT BY THE EHRC

12.23 Commission for Equality and Human Rights

Until the creation of the Commission for Equality and Human Rights or EHRC, there had been three commissions created by statute to promote equality and eliminate discrimination: the EOC, the CRE and the DRC. There were no corresponding bodies for sexual orientation, religious or age discrimination. However Part I of the *EA 2006* created the single EHRC. The EHRC took over the functions of the DRC, EOC and CRE also has responsibility for fighting discrimination on the grounds of sexual orientation, religion or belief, and age. The EHRC is also tasked with promoting human rights. The provisions of *Part I* of the *EA 2006* came fully into force on 1 October 2007 under the *Equality Act 2006 (Commencement No 3 and Savings) Order 2007 (SI 2007/2603), art 2*. The DRC, CRE and EOC were dissolved from the same date under the *Equality Act 2006 (Dissolution of Commissions and Consequential and Transitional Provisions) Order 2007 (SI 2007/2602), art 3* (made under the *EA 2006, ss 36–38*). *SI 2007/2603, art 3* and *SI 2007/2602, art 5* make saving and transitional provisions respectively. The *SDA 1975, ss 53–61, 67–73* and *Sch 3*, the *RRA 1976, ss 43–52* and *58–64* and *Disability Rights Commission Act 1999*, which set up and gave powers to the EOC, CRE and DRC respectively, now stand repealed (*EA 2006, s 40* and *Sch 3*). Readers who need to consider the transitional arrangements are referred to those orders and to the discussion of the functions of the EOC, CRE and DRC in previous editions of this work.

12.23 Discrimination and Equal Opportunities – III: Enforcement

The responsibilities of the EHRC are wide-ranging and, to a considerable extent, fall outside the scope of this work, so the discussion below focuses on those aspects of the EHRC's enforcement powers that are relevant to discrimination in the employment field. The functions of the EHRC, so far as they concern discrimination in employment, are broadly similar to those of the former EOC, CRE and DRC, although wider in scope. Below the functions of the EHRC alone are considered. However, due to the similarity between the functions of the EHRC and those of the EOC, CRE and DRC, where relevant, previous case law concerning the EOC, CRE or DRC is referred to.

On the EHRC see also HARVEYS – Division L.1.E.

12.24 The *EA 2006* received Royal Assent on 16 February 2006. Part 1 of the Act established the EHRC (*EA 2006, ss 1, 2, Sch 1*). The EHRC has a general duty to encourage and support the development of a society in which:

(a)   people's ability to achieve their potential is not limited by prejudice or discrimination,

(b)   there is respect for and protection of each individual's human rights,

(c)   there is respect for the dignity and worth of each individual,

(d)   each individual has an equal opportunity to participate in society, and

(e)   there is mutual respect between groups based on understanding and valuing of diversity and on shared respect for equality and human rights.

(*EA 2006, s 3*).

The EHRC has a duty to prepare, and regularly review, a strategic plan of the activities that it will pursue in the exercise of its functions after it has consulted various parties (*EA 2006, ss 4, 5*).

The EHRC is required in exercising its powers to:

(a)   promote understanding of the importance of equality and diversity;

(b)   encourage good practice in relation to equality and diversity;

(c)   promote equality of opportunity;

(d)   promote awareness and understanding of rights under the *EA 2010* (previously the equality enactments);

(e)   enforce the *EA 2010* (previously the equality enactments));

(f)   work towards the elimination of unlawful discrimination; and

(g)   work towards the elimination of unlawful harassment.

(*EA 2006, s 8(1)*).

'Unlawful' is defined as contrary to the *EA 2010* (previously the equality enactments) (*EA 2006, s 34* as amended). The equality enactments were (until they were repealed and replaced by the *EqA 2010*) the *EPA 1970*, the *SDA 1975*, the *RRA 1976*, the *DDA 1995*, Part 2 of the *EA 2006*, regulations made under *Part 3* of the *EA 2006*, the *SOR 2003*, the *RBR 2003* and the *AR 2006* (*EA 2006, s 33(1)*, which was repealed when the *EA 2010* comes into force). In fulfilling its duties under *s 8* the EHRC must take account of any relevant human rights (*EA 2006, s 9(4)*). The EHRC is required to monitor the effectiveness of the equality and human rights enactments and give advice and make recommendations to central government on changes to the law (*EA 2006, s 11*). The equality and human rights enactments are the *Human Rights Act 1998*, the *EA 2006* and the *EA 2010* (*EA 2006*, s 11(3)(c) as amended). The EHRC is required to monitor progress towards achieving its aims under the *EA 2006, s 3*, and issue a report on this progress every three years (*EA 2006*, s 12). The EHRC is also required to issue an annual report on its performance (*EA 2006*, Sch 1, para 32).

The EHRC may issue a code of practice in connection with a matter addressed by the *EA 2010* (and previously the *EqPA 1970*, *SDA 1975*, *Pts 2–4*, *s 76A* and orders under *ss 76B*, 76C, the *RRA 1976*, *Pts 2–4* and *s 71*, *DDA 1995*, *Pts 2–4* and *5A*, *EqA 2006*, *Pt 2* and regulations made under *Pt 3*, *SOR 2003*, *Pts 2, 3*, *RBR 2003*, *Pts 2, 3*, and *AR 2006*, arts 2, 3 (*EA 2006*, s 14(1) as amended). Before issuing a code the EHRC must publish its proposals, consult such persons as it thinks appropriate and submit a draft to the Secretary of State for approval (*EA 2006*, ss 14(6), (7)). A failure to comply with a code of practice does not make a person liable to criminal or civil proceedings but a code is admissible in evidence in such proceedings and shall be taken into account by a court or tribunal if it appears relevant (*EA 2006*, s 15(4)). The EHRC has published a new Code of Practice on Employment, which is available on the EHRC website, and which reflects the new anti-discrimination law set out in the *EA 2010*.

The EHRC has the power to institute or intervene in legal proceedings (including judicial review) if it appears to the Commission that the proceedings relate to a matter in connection with which it has a function (*EA 2006*, s 30). This makes explicit on the face of the statute a power that the EOC, CRE and DRC were held to have. In *R v Secretary of State for Employment, ex p Equal Opportunities Commission* [1994] 1 All ER 910, [1994] ICR 317, the House of Lords considered that the EOC had *locus standi* to challenge by judicial review proceedings a refusal by the Secretary of State to accept that English law was sexually discriminatory in certain respects, and their Lordships also held (by a majority) that the Divisional Court was a proper forum for the challenge in question. The EHRC has already exercised this power to intervene in an number of discrimination cases in the employment field (see, for example, *Oyarce v Cheshire County Council* [2008] EWCA Civ 434, [2008] ICR 1179, [2008] IRLR 653; *Slack v Cumbria County Council* [2009] EWCA Civ 293, [2009] IRLR 463; *Bainbridge v Redcar and Cleveland Borough Council* [2008] EWCA Civ 885, [2009] ICR 133, [2008] IRLR 776; and *Seldon v Clarkson Wright & Jakes* [2012] UKSC 16, [2012] ICR 716) and *Rowstock Ltd v Jessemey* [2013] IRLR 439 (see 12.2 above). In *R (on the application of McCarthy) v Basildon District Council* [2008] EWHC 987 (Admin), [2008] All ER (D) 118 (May) (a planning case) the Court of Appeal rejected an application by the local authority to prevent the EHRC intervening by way of written submissions because its intervention would be profitable as it could give guidance to the Court.

The EHRC has a website, www.equalityhumanrights.com. Its offices are at: Arndale House, The Arndale Centre, Manchester, M4 3AQ (telephone 0161 829 8100, fax 0161 829 8110, and email info@equalityhumanrights.com; 3 More London, Riverside Tooley Street, London, SE1 2RG (telephone 020 3117 0235, fax 0203 117 0237, and email info @equalityhumanrights.com); 3rd floor, 3 Callaghan Square, Cardiff, CF10 5BT (telephone 02920 447710, fax 02920 447713, and email wales@equalityhumanrights.com); and The Optima Building, 58 Robertson Street, Glasgow, G2 8DU (telephone 0141 228 5910, fax 0141 228 5912, and email scotland@equalityhumanrights.com).

12.25 Formal inquiries and investigations

The EHRC has an express power to conduct inquiries into any matter relating to its duties under the *EA 2006, ss 8, 9* and *10* (*EA 2006, s 16(1)*). If, during an inquiry the EHRC begins to suspect that a person has committed an unlawful act it must: (a) in continuing the inquiry, so far as possible, avoid further consideration of whether the person has committed an unlawful act, (b) commence an investigation, (c) may use information acquired during the inquiry in the investigation, and (d) ensure that any aspect of the inquiry which concerns the person investigated is not pursued while the investigation is in progress (*EA 2006, s 16(2)*).

The EHRC has the power to investigate whether a person has committed an unlawful act or has not complied with an unlawful act notice issued under *s 21* or an undertaking made in an agreement made under *s 23*, but may only investigate whether a person has committed an unlawful act if it suspects the person to have done so (such suspicion may, but need not, arise as a result of an inquiry under *s 16*) (*EA 2006, ss 20(1), (2), (3)*). In relation to the EOC, CRE and DRC it had been held that if they did not have a suspicion that the subject of an investigation had committed an unlawful act of discrimination, the investigation and any non-discrimination notice based upon it might be challenged (*Prestige Group plc, Re, Commission for Racial Equality v Prestige Group plc* [1984] 1 WLR 335, [1984] ICR 473, HL; *Hillingdon London Borough Council v Commission for Racial Equality* [1982] AC 779).

Before settling the report of an investigation recording a finding that a person has committed an unlawful act or has failed to comply with an unlawful act notice or an undertaking, the EHRC is required to send a draft to the person and specify a period of at least 28 days in which the person may make written representations, which the EHRC must consider (*EA 2006, s 20(4)*). Schedule 2 to the *EA 2006* sets out supplemental provisions concerning investigations (*EA 2006, s 20(5)*).

Where the EHRC conducts an inquiry it is required to publish the terms of reference in a manner that it considers likely to bring the inquiry to the attention of persons whom it concerns or who might be interested in it, and in particular to the attention of any person specified in the terms of reference (*EA 2006, Sch 2, para 2*). Before holding an investigation the EHRC is required to prepare terms of reference specifying the person to be investigated and the nature of the alleged unlawful act, give the person the notice, give that person the opportunity to make representations about the terms of reference, and having considered such representations publish the terms of reference once settled (*EA 2006, Sch 2, para 3*). The EHRC is required to make arrangements for persons to make representations (which may, but need not, include oral representations) in relation to inquiries, investigations and assessments and must give any person specified in the terms of reference the opportunity to make representations (*EA 2006, Sch 2, paras 6, 7*). The EHRC must consider any representations made but need not do so, if it considers it appropriate, where the representations are not made by a person specified in the terms of reference or by a 'relevant lawyer' (i.e. either (a) an advocate or solicitor in Scotland, or (b) a person who, for the purposes of the *Legal Services Act 2007*, is an authorised person in relation to an activity which constitutes the exercise of a right of audience or the conduct of litigation (within the meaning of that *Act*)) (*EA 2006, Sch 2, para 8*, as amended). In relation to formal investigations by the EOC, CRE or DRC it has been held that the persons concerned were not entitled to cross-examine witnesses (*R v Commission for Racial Equality, ex p Cottrell and Rothon* [1980] 1 WLR 1580).

12.26 *Information.* The EHRC has powers to require persons to provide information by issuing a notice in the course of an inquiry, investigation or assessment (*EA 2006, Sch 2, para 9*). Such a notice may require a person to provide information in his possession, produce documents in his possession, or give oral evidence, and may specify the form of information, documents or evidence and the timing, but a notice may not require a person to provide information that he is prohibited from disclosing by an enactment, do anything that he could not be compelled to do in proceedings in the High Court or Court of Session, or require a person to attend at a place unless the EHRC undertakes to pay the expenses of his journey (*EA 2006, Sch 2, para 10*). A recipient of a notice may apply to a county court (in England and Wales) or a sheriff (in Scotland) to have the notice cancelled on the grounds that the requirement imposed by it is unnecessary having regard to the purpose of the inquiry, investigation or assessment, or is unreasonable (*EA 2006, Sch 2, para 11*). Where the EHRC believes that a person has failed, or is likely to fail, without reasonable excuse to comply with a notice it may apply to a county court (in England and Wales) or a sheriff (in Scotland) for an order requiring the person to take such steps as are specified in the order (*EA 2006, Sch 2, para 12*). A person commits an offence if he fails to comply with a notice under *para 9* or an order under *para 12(2)*, falsifies any document provided in accordance with such a notice or order, or makes a false statement in giving oral evidence in accordance with a notice under *para 9*, and such an offence is punishable on summary conviction by a fine not exceeding level 5 on the standard scale (*EA 2006, Sch 2, para 13*, and see **1.10** INTRODUCTION).

12.27   *The Commission's report*. The EHRC is required to publish a report of its findings following an inquiry, investigation or assessment and may make recommendations as part of the report or in respect of a matter arising in the course of the inquiry, investigation or assessment, which may be addressed to any class of persons (*EA 2006, Sch 2, paras 15, 16*). A tribunal or court may have regard to the findings of a report but shall not treat it as conclusive, and a person to whom a recommendation is addressed shall have regard to it (*EA 2006, Sch 2, paras 18, 19*).

It is an offence for a Commissioner, Investigating Commissioner or employee of the EHRC to disclose any information acquired by the EHRC by way of representations made in relation to, or in the course of, an inquiry under the *EA 2006, s 16*, an investigation under *s 20*, an assessment under *s 31* or a notice under *s 32*, or from a person with whom the EHRC enters into, or considers entering into, an agreement under *s 23* (*EA 2006, ss 6(1), (2)*). Disclosure of such information is permitted only if the disclosure is:

(a)   for the purposes of a function of the EHRC under the *EA 2006, ss 16, 20, 21, 24, 25, 31, or 32*;

(b)   in a report of an inquiry, investigation or assessment published by the EHRC;

(c)   in pursuance of an order of a court or tribunal;

(d)   with the consent of the person to whom the disclosed information relates;

(e)   in a manner that ensures that no person to whom the disclosed information relates can be identified;

(f)   for the purposes of civil or criminal proceedings to which the EHRC is a party; or

(g)   if the information was acquired by the EHRC more than 70 years before the date of the disclosure.

(*EA 2006, s 6(3)*).

Contravention of these rules is made an offence punishable on summary conviction with a fine not exceeding level 5 on the standard scale *(EA 2006, s 6(6)*; and see **1.10** INTRODUCTION).

12.28 Unlawful act notices and other remedies

Remedies available to the EHRC. The EHRC has a wider range of remedies available to it than the EOC, CRE and DRC. Where, following investigation, the EHRC is satisfied that a person has committed an unlawful act it has the power to issue a notice specifying the unlawful act and the provision of the *EA 2010* (or previously the equality enactments) that has been infringed – an 'unlawful act notice' – and the notice may require the person to prepare an action plan to avoid repetition or continuation of the unlawful act or recommend action to be taken for that purpose (*EA 2006, s 21(1), (2)* (as amended), *(4)*). A person in receipt of a notice may within six weeks beginning with the date on which the notice was given appeal to an employment tribunal or county court (depending on which of these would have jurisdiction to consider a claim in respect of the alleged unlawful act) on the grounds that either (a) the person did not commit the unlawful act specified in the notice or (b) the requirement to prepare an action plan was unreasonable (*EA 2006, ss 21 (5), (7)*). On such an appeal the court or tribunal may affirm, annul or vary the notice, affirm, annul or vary the requirement, or make an order for costs or expenses (*EA 2006, s 21(6)*). The *Employment Tribunals (Constitution and Rules of Procedure) Regulations 2004 (SI 2004/1861), Sch 5* (as amended) regulates the procedure to be adopted upon the hearing of appeals against unlawful act notices. For further procedural guidance from the EAT under the pre-1 October 2004 regime for appeals against non-discrimination notices set out in the *Employment Tribunals (Constitution and Rules of Procedure) Regulations 1993 (SI 1993/2687), Sch 6*, see *Commission for Racial Equality v Amari Plastics Ltd* [1982] QB 265, [1981] 3 WLR 511, [1981] ICR 767, approved by the Court of Appeal at [1982] ICR 304. In appropriate cases a non-discrimination notice issued by the EOC, CRE or DRC could also be challenged by way of an application for judicial review using the procedure under *Part 54* of the *CPR* (formerly *Order 53* of the *Rules of the Supreme Court* (*Hillingdon London Borough Council v Commission for Racial Equality* [1982] AC 779; *R v Commission for Racial Equality, ex p Westminster City Council* [1984] ICR 770; affd [1985] ICR 827, CA).

Where the EHRC issues a notice under *s 21* requiring a person to prepare an action plan the notice must specify the time within which the person must give the EHRC a first draft plan (*EA 2006, s 22(2)*). On the receipt of the first draft plan the EHRC may approve it or give the person notice that it is inadequate and require the person to submit a revised draft by a specified time, possibly with recommendations as to the content of the revised draft (*EA 2006, s 22 (3), (4)*). The EHRC is empowered to apply to a county court (in England and Wales) or (in Scotland) a sheriff for an order requiring a person to produce a first draft plan by a specified time, or a revised draft plan by a specified time and in accordance with any directions as to its contents (*EA 2006, s 22(6)*). Where, within six weeks of the person giving the draft plan to the EHRC, it has not issued a notice that the draft plan is inadequate or applied for an order under *s 22(6)(b)*, or where such an order is refused, the action plan will come into effect (*EA 2006, s 22(5)*). The EHRC may agree with the person who prepared it to vary an action plan (*EA 2006, s 22(7)*).

The EHRC is empowered to seek an order from the county court or sheriff within five years of an action plan coming into force requiring a person to act in accordance with the plan or to take specified action for a similar purpose (*EA 2006, s 22(6)(c)*). It is a criminal offence punishable on summary conviction by a fine not exceeding level 5 on the standard scale to fail to comply with an order under *s 22(6)* without reasonable excuse (*EA 2006, s 22(9); and see **1.10** INTRODUCTION*).

The EHRC has another new remedy for potential unlawful acts contrary to the *EA 2010* (or previously the equality enactments). Under the *EA 2006, s 23*, the EHRC may enter into an agreement with a person under which the person undertakes not to commit an unlawful act of a specified kind or to take, or refrain from taking, other specified action, and the EHRC agrees not to proceed against the person under *ss 20* or *21* in respect of any act of that specified kind (*EA 2006, s 23(1)*). The EHRC will only be able to enter into an agreement if it believes that the person has committed an unlawful act but a person will not be taken to have admitted to the commission of an unlawful act only by virtue of entering into an agreement (*EA 2006, ss 22(2), (3)*).

INJUNCTIONS

12.29 Persistent discrimination

The EHRC is empowered, where it thinks that a person is likely to continue to commit an unlawful act, to apply (in England and Wales) to a county court for an injunction or (in Scotland) to the sheriff for an interdict to prevent the person from committing the act (*EA

2006, s 24(1)). The EHRC is also able, if a person subject to an agreement under the *EA 2006, s 23* has failed, or is likely to fail, to comply with an undertaking, to apply to a county court or sheriff for an order requiring the person to comply with the undertaking or such other order as the court or sheriff may specify (*EA 2006, s 24(2), (3)*).

12.30 Advertisements and instructions or pressure to discriminate

Prior to the *EA 2010* coming into force on 1 October 2010 only the EHRC had power to bring proceedings in relation to discriminatory advertising or instructions or pressure to discriminate contrary to the *SDA 1975, ss 38–40, the RRA 1976, ss 29–31*, the *DDA 1995, ss 16B* and *16C*, and the *EA 2006, ss 54, 55* (religious discrimination: advertising and instructions or pressure to discriminate) (*EA 2006, s 25(1), (2)*; and see *Ruhaza v Alexander Hancock Recruitment Ltd* [2012] EqLR 9, EAT). Where the EHRC believed that a person had committed an act to which *s 25* applied it could present a complaint to an employment tribunal where the alleged act was unlawful by reference to the *SDA 1975, Pt 2*, the *RRA 1976, Pt 2*, the *DDA 1995, Pt 3*, or the *EA 2006, Pts 2*, and *3* (in so far as it related to employment services), or otherwise in the county court (in England and Wales) or to a sheriff (in Scotland) (*EA 2006, s 25(3)*). Such a complaint or application was to be made within the six month period beginning with the date (or last date) on which the alleged unlawful act occurred, or with the permission of the tribunal, court or sheriff (*EA 2006, s 26(1)*). On an application under *s 25(3)* the court, sheriff or tribunal could determine whether the allegation was correct (*EA 2006, s 25(4)*).

The EHRC was also empowered to apply to a county court (in England and Wales) for an injunction or to a sheriff (in Scotland) for an interdict where a tribunal, court or sheriff had determined under *s 25(4)* that a person has done an act to which the section applied or the EHRC considered that a person has done such an act, and the EHRC believed that if unrestrained the person was likely to do another such act (*EA 2006, s 25(5), (6)*). A court or sheriff could not rely upon a determination under *s 25(4)* while an appeal against that determination was pending or might be brought (disregarding the possibility of an appeal out of time with permission) (*EA 2006, s 26(2)*). Any application under the *EA 2006, s 25(5), (6)* had to be brought within five years of the unlawful act occurring or with the permission of the court or sheriff (*EA 2006, s 26(3)*).

The *EA 2010* repeals *EA 2006, ss 25* and *26* (*EA 2010, s 211, Sch 26, paras 6, 14* and *15, Sch 27, Pt 1*).

A new *EA 2006, s 24A* now makes provision in relation to:

(a)   an act which is unlawful because, by virtue of any of *EA 2010, ss 13* to *18*, it amounts to a contravention of any of *Pts 3, 4, 5, 6* or *7* of that *Act,*

(b)   an act which is unlawful because it amounts to a contravention of the *EA 2010, s 60(1)* (or to a contravention of *ss 111* or *112* of that *Act* that relates to a contravention of *s 60(1)* of that *Act*) (enquiries about disability and health),

(c)   an act which is unlawful because it amounts to a contravention of the *EA 2010, s 106* (information about diversity in range of election candidates etc),

(d)   an act which is unlawful because, by virtue of the *EA 2010, s 108(1)*, it amounts to a contravention of any of *Pts 3, 4, 5, 6* or *7* of that *Act*, or

(e)   the application of a provision, criterion or practice which, by virtue of the *EA 2010, s 19*, amounts to a contravention of that *Act*.

For the purposes of the *EA 2006, ss 20* to *24*, it is immaterial whether the EHRC knows or suspects that a person has been or may be affected by the unlawful act or application (*EA 2006, s 24A(2)*). An unlawful act includes making arrangements to act in a particular way which would, if applied to an individual, amount to a contravention mentioned in the *EA 2006, s 24A(1)(a)* (*EA 2006, s 24A(3)*). Nothing in the *EA 2006* affects the entitlement of a person to bring proceedings under the *EA 2010* in respect of a contravention mentioned in the *EA 2006, s 24A(1)* (*EA 2006, s 24A(4)*).

12.31   ASSISTANCE FOR PERSONS DISCRIMINATED AGAINST

The EHRC is able to make grants to another person in pursuance of its duties under the *EA 2006, ss 8, 9* and *10*, which may be subject to conditions (*EA 2006, s 17*). The EHRC may assist an individual who is, or may become, a party to legal proceedings where the proceedings relate to the *EA 2010* (and previously the equality enactments) and the individual alleges that he has been the victim of behaviour contrary to that Act (or those enactments)) (*EA 2006, s 28(1)*, as amended). This assistance may take the form of legal advice, legal representation, facilities for settlement of a dispute, or any other form of assistance (*EA 2006, s 28(4)*). Where the proceedings partly relate to matters other than the *EA 2010* (or previously the equality enactments) the assistance may be given in relation to any aspect of the proceedings but must cease if the proceedings cease to relate to the *EA 2010* (or previously the equality enactments) (*EA 2006, s 28(6)*). The Lord Chancellor may by order disapply this restriction in specified kinds of cases (*EA 2006, s 28(7)*). For these purposes the section is taken to apply to any provisions of EU law that confer rights on individuals and relate to discrimination on the grounds of sex (including gender reassignment), racial origin, ethnic origin, religion, belief, disability, age or sexual orientation (*EA 2006, s 28(12), (13)*). Where an individual receives assistance from the EHRC under *s 28* and the individual becomes entitled to costs either as a result of settlement or an award by the court or tribunal the EHRC's expenses in providing assistance will be charged on any sum paid to the individual by way of costs (*EA 2006, s 29*).

12.32   EFFECT ON CONTRACTS

A term of a contract is unenforceable against a person in so far as it constitutes, promotes or provides for treatment of that or another person that is of a description prohibited by the *EA 2010* (*EA 2010, s 142(1)*). A relevant non-contractual term is unenforceable against a person in so far as it constitutes, promotes or provides for treatment of that or another person that is of a description prohibited by the Act, in so far as the Act relates to disability (*EA 2010, s 142(2)*). A relevant non-contractual term is defined as a term which (a) is a term of an agreement that is not a contract, and (b) relates to the provision of an employment service within *ss 56(2)(a)* to *(e)* or to the provision under a group insurance arrangement of facilities by way of insurance (*EA 2010, s 142(3)*).

Previously a term of a contract was void where:

(a)   its inclusion rendered the making of the contract unlawful by virtue of the *Acts* or *Regulations*;

(b)   it was included in furtherance of an act rendered unlawful by the *Acts* or *Regulations*; or

(c)   it provided for the doing of an act which would be rendered unlawful by the *Acts* or *Regulations*.

(*SDA 1975, s 77(1)*; *RRA 1976, s 72(1)*; *SOR 2003, reg 35 and Sch 4, part 1, para 1(1)*; *RBR 2003, reg 35 and Sch 4, part 1, para 1(1)*; *DDA 1995, s 17C and Sch 3A, part 1, para 1(1)*; and *AR 2006, reg 43 and Sch 5, part 1, para 1(1)*.)

Thus, a term in a contract for the provision of a discriminatory training programme would be rendered void by those provisions. A term in a contract for an advertisement which provided for the inclusion of a discriminatory expression would similarly be void. In *Jivraj v Hashwani* [2010] EWCA Civ 712, [2010] IRLR 797, [2010] ICR 1435, the Court of Appeal held that a provision in an arbitration clause that the appointed arbitrator had to be a member of the Ismaili community was void as it involved discrimination on the grounds of religion or belief contrary to the *RBR 2003, regs 2* and *6*, and as a result the whole arbitration clause was void because removal of the offending provision rendered the agreement substantially different from that originally intended (this decision was reversed by the Supreme Court on the basis that an arbitrator was not employed under a contract personally to do work such as to fall within the *RBR 2003* and, in any event, the requirement in question was a genuine occupational requirement – [2011] UKSC 40, [2011] ICR 1004, [2012] IRLR 827).

Also previously a term which constituted (or was in furtherance of or provided for) unlawful discrimination against a party to a contract was not made void, but was unenforceable against that party (*SDA 1975, s 77(3); RRA 1976, s 72(3); SOR 2003, reg 35* and *Sch 4, part 1, para 1(2); RBR 2003, reg 35* and *Sch 4, part 1, para 1(2); DDA 1995, s 17C* and *Sch 3A, part 1, para 1(2);* and *AR 2006, reg 43* and *Sch 5, part 1, para 1(2)*). For example, a term in a contract with a woman which states that she cannot use a smoking room normally reserved for men was not enforceable in a court of law.

A party to the contract may apply to a county court in England and Wales or a sheriff court in Scotland which may remove or modify the discriminatory term, provided that all persons affected have been notified of the application (*EA 2010, s 143(1), (2)*; and previously *SDA 1975, s 77(5); RRA 1976, s 72(5); SOR 2003, reg 35* and *Sch 4, part 1, para 3(1); RBR 2003, reg 35* and *Sch 4, part 1, para 3(1); DDA 1995, s 17C* and *Sch 3A, part 1, para 3(1);* and *AR 2006, reg 43* and *Sch 5, part 1, para 3(1)*).

The *EA 2010, s 145* provides that a term of a collective agreement is void in so far as it constitutes, promotes or provides for treatment of a description prohibited by the *Act*, and a rule of an undertaking is unenforceable against a person in so far as it constitutes, promotes or provides for treatment of the person that is of a description prohibited by the *Act*. A qualifying person (as defined by the *EA 2010, s 146(5), (6)*) may make a complaint to an employment tribunal that a term is void, or that a rule is unenforceable, as a result of *s 145* (*s 146(1)*). A person will only be able to make such an application if either the term or rule may in the future have effect in relation to him, and where the complaint alleges that the term or rule provides for treatment of a description prohibited by the *Act*, he may in the future be subjected to treatment that would (if he were subjected to it in present circumstances) be of that description (*EA 2010, s 146(2)*). If the tribunal finds that the complaint is well-founded, it must make an order declaring that the term is void or the rule is unenforceable (*EA 2010, s 146(3)*).

This is similar to the position that obtained previously. By the *Sex Discrimination Act 1986, s 6* (as amended), *SDA 1975, s 77* was made to apply to any term of a collective agreement (see COLLECTIVE AGREEMENTS (5)) (even if not intended to be legally enforceable) or to any rule made by an employer for application to his employees or to applicants for employment. Similar provisions are contained in *RRA 1976, s 72A, SOR 2003, reg 35* and *Sch 4, part 2, RBR 2003, reg 35* and *Sch 4, part 2, DDA 1995, s 17C* and *Sch 3A, part 2*, and *AR 2006, reg 43* and *Sch 5, part 2*. These provisions also applied to any rule made by an organisation of workers, an organisation of employers, or an organisation whose members carry on a particular profession or trade for whose purposes it exists, for application to its members and prospective members. They also applied to any rule made by an authority or body which can confer an authorisation or qualification needed for, or facilitating, engagement in a particular profession or trade, for application to those who have received or seek to receive such authorisation or qualification. Persons who are (as the case may be) employees, members or the recipients of authorisations or qualifications, or who are genuinely and actively seeking to become such, and who have reason to believe that the offending term or rule may at some future time have effect in relation to them could complain to an employment tribunal. If the tribunal found the complaint well-founded, it would declare the term or rule void. In the context of multiple equal pay claims, the EAT has held that there was no alternative, consistent with the EU law obligation to provide an effective remedy, to the employment tribunal considering granting declarations under *SDA 1975, s 77* that a collective agreement was contrary to the principles of equal pay at the same time as considering the equal pay claims themselves, notwithstanding that the claimants could test the disputed terms in the context of the equal pay claims (*UNISON v Brennan* [2008] ICR 955, [2008] IRLR 492, EAT).

See also EQUAL PAY (21).

Local authorities used to be prohibited from inserting clauses into their contracts obliging the other party to comply with the discrimination legislation, because these are 'non-commercial matters' (*Local Government Act 1988, s 17*; and see *R v Islington London Borough Council, ex p Building Employers Confederation* [1989] IRLR 382). However the *EA 2010* amends the *Local Government Act 1988, s 17* so that the section does not prevent a public authority to which it applies from exercising any function regulated by the section with reference to a non-commercial matter to the extent that the authority considers it necessary or expedient to do so to enable or facilitate compliance with (a) the duty imposed on it by the *EA 2010, s 149* (public sector equality duty), or (b) any duty imposed on it by regulations under the *EA 2010, ss 153* or *154* (powers to impose specific duties) (the *Local Government Act 1988, s 17(10)*, inserted by the *EA 2010, s 211(1), Sch 26, paras 1, 2(b)*).

See also HARVEYS – Division **L.5.B**.

12.33 SETTLEMENT OF A CLAIM

A term of a contract is unenforceable by a person in whose favour it would operate in so far as it purports to exclude or limit a provision of or made under the *EA 2010* (*EA 2010, s 144(1)*). A clause in a members' agreement in a firm of solicitors which purported to require any disputes between members to be referred for alternative dispute resolution and thence for final resolution through arbitration was held to be unenforceable by virtue of the *EA 2010, s 144* in *Clyde & Co LLP v Bates van Winkelhof* [2011] EWHC 668 (QB), [2011] IRLR 467. Slade J held that the *EA 2010, s 144(1)* was not just concerned with agreements to exclude the right not to be discriminated against but also agreements to exclude the enforcement of those rights in proceedings. The effect of the clause in the agreement was to preclude the continuation of sex discrimination proceedings in the employment tribunal and was therefore void and unenforceable.

There is one exception to the rule against contracting out of the anti-discrimination legislation. Contracts or agreements settling or compromising a complaint relating to discrimination in employment (and previously complaints relating to the *Equal Pay Act 1970, s 2* (see **21.22** EQUAL PAY)) are enforceable against the complainant only where the contract is made with the assistance of a conciliation officer (see **2.4** ADVISORY, CONCILIATION AND ARBITRATION SERVICE (ACAS)), or where the contract is a compromise contract meeting certain statutory conditions (see **18.29–18.37** EMPLOYMENT TRIBUNALS – II) (*EA 2010, s144(4)*; and previously *SDA 1975, s 77(4)(aa)* as inserted by *TURERA 1993, Sch 6, para 1*, and *Employment Rights (Dispute Resolution) Act 1998, s 9; RRA 1976, s 72(4)* as amended by *TURERA 1993, Sch 6, para 2(4A)* and *Employment Rights (Dispute Resolution) Act 1998, s 9; SOR 2003, reg 35* and *Sch 4, part 1, para 2; RBR 2003, reg 35* and *Sch 4, part 1, para 2; DDA 1995, s 17C* and *Sch 3A, Part 1, para 2*; and *AR 2006, reg 43* and *Sch 5, Part 1, para 2*;).

It is most important to comply with these provisions when settling such a complaint, otherwise, despite a sum to settle the complaint having been paid, a complainant may still pursue his application to an employment tribunal. However, the EAT has held that there is nothing in law that requires a tribunal to ensure that a compromise agreement is binding within the *SDA 1975* or *RRA 1976* before it permits a claim to be dismissed where the parties have reached what is otherwise a contractual agreement (*Mayo-Deman v University of Greenwich* [2005] IRLR 845). An employment tribunal does have jurisdiction to consider whether a compromise agreement is a valid agreement (eg is not induced by a misrepresentation) (see *Industrious Ltd v Horizon Recruitment Ltd v Vincent* [2010] ICR 491, [2010] IRLR 327, EAT).

The requisite conditions for 'a qualifying compromise contract' under the *EA 2010, s 147(3)* (and also previously for a valid compromise agreement under the Acts and Regulations) are the following:

(a)   the contract must be in writing;

(b)   the contract must relate to the particular complaint;

(c)   the complainant must have received advice from an independent advisor (previously 'a relevant independent adviser') as to the terms and effect of the proposed contract and in particular its effect on his ability to pursue a complaint before an employment tribunal;

(d)   there must be in force, when the adviser gives the advice, a contract of insurance, or an indemnity provided for members of a profession or professional body, covering the risk of a claim by the complainant in respect of loss arising in consequence of the advice;

(e)   the contract must identify the adviser; and

(f)   the contract must state that the conditions (*c*) and (*d*) are satisfied.

Item (*f*) must not be ignored as the failure to include all the conditions in the relevant statutes in a compromise agreement will invalidate the agreement even if the substance of the requirements is met (*Lunt v Merseyside TEC Ltd* [1999] ICR 17, CA; *Palihakkara v British Telecommunications plc* (2007) 823 IDS Brief 18, EAT). An employee was not precluded from bringing an equal pay claim despite signing a compromise agreement purporting to settle all claims that she 'believed' that she had which referred expressly to the *EqPA 1970*, where the employee was not aware that she had an equal pay claim when she signed the compromise agreement (*Hilton UK Hotels Ltd v McNaughton* [2006] All ER (D) 327 (May), EAT). A claimant is not required to have presented a claim or articulated a grievance for a compromise agreement to relate to a 'particular complaint' (*McWilliam v Glasgow City Council* [2011] IRLR 568, EAT). An agreement that referred only to claims arising out of the termination of a claimant's employment did not cover discrimination claims arising prior to termination (*Palihakkara*, above). In *Bainbridge v Redcar and Cleveland Borough Council; Williams v Redcar and Cleveland Borough Council* [2007] IRLR 494, EAT, a COT3 which covered 'all claims . . . in connection with the terms of [the claimants'] contracts of employment' was held to be unambiguous and enforceable (see *Clarke v Redcar and Cleveland Borough Council*, above). The requirement for the claimant to receive advice on 'the terms and effect' of the agreement does not mean that the independent adviser is required to offer a view on whether the deal is a good one for the claimant (*McWilliam*, above).

A person was a 'relevant independent adviser' in relation to the previous Acts and regulations for the purposes of paragraph (*c*) immediately above if:

(a)   he is a qualified lawyer;

(b)   he is an officer, official, employee or member of an independent trade union who has been certified in writing by the trade union as competent to give advice and as authorised to do so on behalf of the trade union; or

(c)   he works at an advice centre (whether as an employee or a volunteer) and has been certified in writing by the centre as competent to give advice and as authorised to do so on behalf of the centre.

The *EA 2010, s 147(4)* now adopts this definition for 'an independent adviser' and adds (d) 'a person of such description as may be specified by order'.

A person is not an 'independent adviser' to the complainant if he is (*s 147(5)* as amended):

(a)   a person (other than the complainant) who is a party to the contract or the complaint;

(b)   a person who is connected to a person within paragraph (*a*);

(c)   a person who is employed by a person within paragraph (*a*) or (*b*);

(d)   a person who is acting for a person within paragraph (*a*) or (*b*) in relation to the contract or the complaint;

(e)   a person within subsection (4)(*b*) or (*c*), if the trade union or advice centre is a person within paragraph (*a*) or (*b*);

(f)   a person within subsection (4)(*c*) to whom the complainant makes a payment for the advice.

Any two persons are to be treated as connected if one is a company of which the other (directly or indirectly) has control, or else if both are companies of which a third person (directly or indirectly) has control (*EA 2010, s 147(8)*).

The words 'to the complainant' and '(other than the complainant)' were inserted into the *EA 2010, s 147(5)* with effect from 6th April 2012 by the *Equality Act 2010 (Amendment) Order 2012 (SI 2012/334)*. The original drafting of the *EA 2010, s 147* caused a certain amount of debate because on a literal interpretation a solicitor acting for a claimant might be said to be acting for a party (ie the claimant) in relation to the complaint and therefore could not qualify as an independent adviser. The cautious view was that a claimant had to instruct a fresh solicitor to advise on a compromise contract (and even then might not escape from the problem) or else that only a settlement through ACAS could be effective. The alternative view was that the literal interpretation created an absurd result that Parliament plainly did not intend and that the reference to 'a party' in *s 147(5)(a)* must mean a party other than the claimant (this interpretation was preferred by the Government's Equality Office).

'Qualified lawyer' means (as respects England and Wales) a person who, for the purposes of the *Legal Services Act 2007*, is an authorised person in relation to an activity which constitutes the exercise of a right of audience or the conduct of litigation (within the meaning of that *Act*), and (as respects Scotland) an advocate (whether in practice as such or employed to give legal advice), or a solicitor who holds a practising certificate (*EA 2010, s 147(6)*).

The definition of a 'qualified lawyer' has been extended, with effect from 1 October 2004, to include a Fellow of the Institute of Legal Executives practicing in a solicitors' practice (see: *Equality Act 2010 (Qualifying Compromise Contract Specified Person) Order 2010 (SI 2010/2192)*; and previously for the purposes of the *SDA 1975* and *RRA 1976*, the *Compromise Agreements (Description of Person) Order 2004 (SI 2004/754)*, as amended by the *Compromise Agreements (Description of Person) Order 2004 (Amendment) Order 2004 (SI 2004/2515)*; for the purposes of the *SOR 2003*, the *Employment Equality (Sexual Orientation) Regulations 2003 (Amendment) Regulations 2004 (SI 2004/2519)*); for the purposes of the *DDA 1995*, the *Compromise Agreements (Description of Person) Order 2005*

(SI 2005/2364); and, for the purposes of the *RBR 2003*, the *Employment Equality (Religion or Belief) Regulations 2003 (Amendment) (No 2) Regulations 2004 (SI 2004/2520)*; all of which had been amended by the *Legal Services Act 2007 (Consequential Amendments) Order 2009 (SI 2009/3348), art 2)*.

'Independent trade union' has the same meaning as in the *Trade Union and Labour Relations (Consolidation) Act 1992* (see **48.22** TRADE UNIONS – I).

See also HARVEYS – Division **PI.1.U**.

13   Education and Training

13.1   An employer has no obligation at common law to provide facilities for the education and training of his employees unless they are engaged under a contract of apprenticeship or their contract of employment provides otherwise. Similarly he does not have to allow employees time off for day-release or sandwich courses. However, with effect from 1 September 1999, young persons in employment have the right to take time off from work in order to undertake study or training leading to a 'relevant qualification' (see 3.8 CHILDREN AND YOUNG PERSONS). It should also be noted that when Part I of the Education and Skills Act 2008 comes into force (expected to be between 2013 and 2015: see s 173(10)), it will place a duty on all young persons in England to participate in education or training until the age of 18, with corresponding duties on employers and local education authorities to enable and support participation.

In addition, an employer should not ask his employee to carry out a task requiring a special skill unless he has ensured that the employee possesses those skills or unless the employer has undertaken to train the employee. (If he does so and an accident occurs he may be liable, see 25.5–25.7 HEALTH AND SAFETY AT WORK – I.) For the income tax treatment of training costs, see the Income Tax (Earnings and Pensions) Act 2003, s 311.

Various bodies and schemes have been created by the Government to encourage the education and training of employees and those seeking employment. At governmental level, the responsibility for higher and further education, employment, and skills is currently vested in the Department of Business, Innovation and Skills (BIS). The BIS's main office is at 1 Victoria Street, London SW1H 0ET, and its enquiry unit can be contacted on 020 7215 5000. Further information can be obtained from the BIS's website at www.gov.uk/government/organisations/department-for-business-innovation-skills, where a facility is available for sending an e-mail to the BIS in respect of a specific query.

Until recently, the body responsible for funding the delivery of training in England was the Learning and Skills Council, but with effect from 1 April 2010 this body has been dissolved and replaced by the new Skills Funding Agency (by virtue of the Apprenticeships, Skills, Children and Learning Act 2009 — see below), which houses the National Apprenticeships Service. There are different arrangements in Wales and Scotland (see 13.8 below).

As mentioned above, the Apprenticeships, Skills, Children and Learning Act 2009 has made important changes in relation to the delivery of training in England. Amongst other matters, the Act has also made provision about apprenticeships in England and Wales, and has introduced a right for a 'qualifying employee' to apply to his or her employer to undertake study and/or training. Some of these changes took effect in April 2010, certain other changes took effect in 2011, and others are not yet in force; these provisions are dealt with in 13.9 onwards below.

As a result of the formation of the Conservative/Liberal Democrat Coalition Government following the general election in May 2010, there have been further changes in this area. In this connection, in November 2010 the government published its skills strategy, entitled Skills for Sustainable Growth; see www.bis.gov.uk//assets/biscore/further-education -skills/docs/s/10-1274-skills-for-sustainable-growth-strategy.pdf. In December 2011 the Government published New Challenges, New Chances, its reform plan building on Skills for Sustainable Growth, together with the Skills Investment Statement 2011–2014. For further details, see www.gov.uk/government/publications/skills-investment-statement-for -2011-to-2014-new-challenges-new-chances. The 'New Deal', set up by the previous Labour government in 1998, has been replaced by the Work Programme (see 13.6 below).

13.2   APPRENTICESHIPS

Apprenticeships offer what must be the oldest form of training in skilled trades for young people.

The apprenticeship is normally for a fixed term of years or until a set qualification is achieved, the apprentice, his parent or guardian (if he is a minor), and the employer entering into a written agreement. The agreement will usually be in a form common to all apprenticeships for the trade concerned. In general the apprentice will have time off to attend college and take examinations.

A contract for apprenticeship may not be terminable for misconduct in the same way as an ordinary contract of employment; and in the event of wrongful termination, different principles apply to the assessment of damages (*Dunk v George Waller & Son Ltd* [1970] 2 QB 163).

In *Wallace v C A Roofing Services Ltd* [1996] IRLR 435, Sedley J in the High Court held that a contract of apprenticeship (unlike a contract of employment or training contract) cannot be terminated on the grounds of redundancy, falling short of closure or a fundamental change in the character of the employers' enterprise. He stated that a contract of apprenticeship remains a distinct entity at common law; its first purpose is training, and the execution of work for the employer is secondary. Thus, the ordinary law as to dismissal does not apply. The contract is for a fixed term and is not terminable at will, unlike a contract of employment at common law.

Wallace was applied in *Whitely v Marton Electrical Ltd* [2003] IRLR 197, in which the EAT held that a 'modern apprenticeship agreement', under which an employer agrees to employ an apprentice 'for the duration of the training plan', is different from an ordinary contract of employment and is not terminable on notice. The provision in the agreement requiring the apprentice to comply with the employer's terms and conditions of employment did not mean that the employer's terms as to notice of termination applied to the apprentice. Where any provision of the employer's terms and conditions were inconsistent with those of the agreement, the agreement must prevail because it was plainly the agreement which the parties intended should govern their relationship. However, in *Thorpe v Dul* [2003] ICR 1556, the EAT remitted the case for the employment tribunal to decide, as a question of fact, the legal status of the modern apprenticeship agreement in that case.

The cases referred to above were reviewed by the Court of Appeal in *Flett v Matheson* [2006] EWCA Civ 53, [2006] IRLR 277. Some eight months after commencing employment at the age of 16, the employee entered into a tripartite individual learning plan (ILP) with the employer and a training provider, which was stated to be carried out under advanced modern apprenticeship arrangements (see also **13.7** below). The employee was subsequently dismissed without notice, and claimed unfair dismissal and/or breach of contract of employment. The EAT held that the employee was employed under a contract of employment but not under a contract of apprenticeship; the employee appealed against the latter finding.

Allowing the appeal, the Court of Appeal held that a modern tripartite apprenticeship arrangement can constitute a common law contract of apprenticeship. In its view, the important issue is the nature and duration of the employer's obligations under the agreement. The fact that part of the training is provided by a third party is not crucial to the analysis of those obligations. In the present case, the ILP had the essential features of an apprenticeship. The contract of employment was varied or overlaid by the ILP, and that variation gave rise to additional obligations on the employer. The individual learning plan was called an 'apprenticeship' and provided for a combination of off and on the job training for a lengthy period. What occurred at the workplace was part of the training. While the employer did not provide the more academic part of the training, he was required to give the apprentice time off to obtain it and to fund the cost of attendance at classes. It was not open to the employer to dismiss on reasonable notice, subject to making reasonable efforts to find another employer willing and able to continue the training. If attempts to find another employer failed, the obligations on the employer remained and, save in certain specified circumstances, the apprentice could not be dismissed within the period of training.

If they satisfy the necessary qualifying conditions, apprentices enjoy the statutory employment protection rights (*Employment Rights Act 1996, s 230(2); Equality Act 2010, s 83(2)*). Note that an 'apprenticeship agreement' under *section 32* of the *Apprenticeships, Skills, Children and Learning Act 2009* (see **13.7** and **13.11** below) will not be treated as being a contract of apprenticeship, but will be treated as being a contract of service (*Apprenticeships, Skills, Children and Learning Act 2009, s 35*).

The Employment Appeal Tribunal, on the basis of the evidence before it that the Law Society recommended the operation of a dual system whereby a clerk was articled to an individual partner in a firm of solicitors under a deed of articles but was employed by the firm under a contract of employment, held that an articled clerk was engaged under such a system (*Oliver v J P Malnick & Co* [1983] 3 All ER 795, [1983] ICR 708).

In *Edmonds v Lawson* [2000] QB 501, [2000] 2 WLR 1091, [2000] ICR 567, the Court of Appeal (allowing an appeal from Sullivan J: [2000] IRLR 18) held that, although a pupil barrister was employed under a contract by the set of barristers' chambers where she was taken on as a pupil, the contract was not a contract of apprenticeship or an equivalent contract. The pupil was, therefore, not a 'worker' for the purposes of the *National Minimum Wage Act 1998*, and was not entitled to be paid the national minimum wage ('NMW'). (For the NMW for apprentices, see **13.7** below; and see generally **32.9** Pay – I.)

Flett v Matheson was followed (and *Edmonds v Lawson* was considered) in *Lee v Chassis & Cab Specialists Ltd* (UKEAT/0268/10/JOJ) [2011] All ER (D) 178 (Feb), (Transcript) where the EAT, in allowing an appeal from the employment tribunal, held that on the evidence the claimant in that case was an apprentice and not an employee. He was therefore excluded from the NMW by virtue of *SI 1999/584, reg 12(2)*, referred to above.

(See also **13.9** to **13.11** below.)

13.3   RECOVERY OF TRAINING COSTS

Problems are sometimes encountered in practice where an employer expends significant sums of money on training an employee, for example, by sending him on outside courses, and the employee then leaves his job shortly afterwards, in some instances without giving proper notice.

The wasted training costs will not usually be recoverable in the absence of an express agreement to that effect. That is so even if the employee leaves without giving proper notice, because the costs would have been incurred whether or not that breach of contract had occurred.

An agreement for the repayment of training costs in the event of an early departure will have to be very carefully drafted in order to be enforceable. If it applies where there is a breach of contract by the employee, it may be struck down as a 'penalty clause' unless it can be said to represent a genuine pre-estimate of loss suffered by the employer (*Giraud UK Ltd v Smith* [2000] IRLR 763; *Sands-Ellison v One Call Insurance* [2003] All ER (D) 389 (Mar); *Tullett Prebon Group Ltd v El-Hajjali* [2008] All ER (D) 427 (Jul); *Imam-Sadeque v Bluebay Asset Management (Services) Ltd* [2013] IRLR 244). This will usually mean, for example, that the proportion of the costs to be repaid must depend upon how long the employee remains after being trained (a clause meeting that requirement was upheld in *Neil v Strathclyde Regional Council* [1984] IRLR 14). Another possible argument against an agreement to repay training costs is that it is in restraint of trade, although the contention in *Neil* that the clause in that case was also illegal and unenforceable as an unlawful

13.3   Education and Training

restrictive covenant or, alternatively, as being contrary to public policy because it was an undue restraint on the employee's liberty, was rejected at first instance (*Strathclyde Regional Council v Neil* [1984] IRLR 11; the point was not pursued on appeal). The reasoning in *Neil* was upheld in *Transocean Maritime Agencies SA Monegasque v Pettit* 1997 SCLR 534.

13.4   INDUSTRIAL TRAINING BOARDS

Industrial Training Boards were established by the Secretary of State for Employment under the *Industrial Training Act 1982* ('*ITA 1982*'), as amended (most recently by *EA 1989*), which repealed and replaced the *Industrial Training Act 1964*, as amended. The Boards' role is to ensure that the quantity and quality of training are adequate to meet the needs of the industries for which they are established, and they may:

(a)   provide or secure the provision of such courses and other facilities (which may include residential accommodation) for the training of those persons as the Board considers adequate, having regard to any alternative courses or facilities available;

(b)   approve alternative courses and facilities;

(c)   publish recommendations regarding the length and nature of courses and standards to be attained in training;

(d)   make tests for ascertaining the standards recommended and award certificates of the attainment of those standards;

(e)   assist persons in finding facilities for being trained for employment in the industry;

(f)   carry out, or assist others to carry out, research into any matter relating to training for employment in the industry; and

(g)   provide advice about training connected with the industry.

(*ITA 1982, s 5(1)*.)

An Industrial Training Board may enter into contracts of service or apprenticeship with persons who intend to be employed in the industry and to attend courses or avail themselves of other facilities provided or approved by the Board (*ITA 1982, s 5(2)*).

Industrial Training Boards may provide advice on training. They may also:

(i)   pay maintenance and travelling allowances to persons attending courses provided or approved by the Board;

(ii)   make grants or loans to persons providing courses or other facilities approved by the Board, to persons who make studies for the purpose of providing such courses or facilities, and to persons who maintain arrangements to provide such courses or facilities which are not for the time being in use;

(iii) pay fees to persons providing post-school education in respect of persons who receive it in association with their training in courses provided or approved by the Board; and

(iv)   make payments to persons in connection with arrangements under which they or employees of theirs make use of courses or other facilities provided or approved by the Board.

(*ITA 1982, s 5(4)*.)

Forms are available from the relevant Industrial Training Board for the employer to provide the information enabling him to claim such a payment as is mentioned under (iv) above.

An Industrial Training Board, with the approval of the Secretary of State, may require employers in the industry to furnish returns and other information, to keep certain records and to produce them for examination by the Board (*ITA 1982, s 6(1)*). Penalties may be imposed for the infringement of any of these provisions. Penalties also exist for knowingly or recklessly furnishing false records or information.

Two statutory Boards remain: the Construction Industry Training Board ('CITB') and the Engineering Construction Industry Training Board ('ECITB').

Provision is made for the imposition of a levy from time to time on employers in the industry, for the purpose of raising money towards meeting the expenses of each Board (*ITA 1982, s 11*). A levy is imposed by means of a 'levy order' made by the Secretary of State. The most recent levy orders took effect on 28 March 2012 (*Industrial Training Levy (Construction Industry Training Board) Order 2012 (SI 2012/958)* and *Industrial Training Levy (Engineering Construction Industry Training Board) Order 2012 (SI 2012/959)*).

Where ITBs have been abolished, their place has been taken by independent employer-led Industry Training Organisations ('ITOs'). ITOs are now having to meet searching new criteria, which will result in a smaller number of more effective and strategic bodies. Those who meet the criteria will be known as National Training Organisations.

13.5   SERVICES FOR SCHOOL-LEAVERS

The *Trade Union Reform and Employment Rights Act 1993* substituted new *ss 8–10A* in the *Employment and Training Act 1973* so as to place a duty on the Secretary of State to secure the provision of careers guidance and placing services ('relevant services') for people attending schools and colleges. The Secretary of State is also given power to arrange for the provision of relevant services for other people, and may direct local authorities to provide (or arrange for the provision of) relevant services. The *1973 Act* requires the providers of relevant services to provide them in accordance with the directions given by the Secretary of State. The Chief Inspector of Education, Children's Services and Skills in England must inspect and report on the provision of services in England in pursuance of *s 8* or *s 9* by any person or institution, when requested to do so by the Secretary of State; he may also undertake other inspections of the provision of those services as he thinks fit. However, any such inspection may not relate to services provided for persons who are over 20 years old. (*ETA 1973, s 10B*, inserted by the *Learning and Skills Act 2000* and amended by the *Education Act 2005* and the *Education and Inspections Act 2006*).

13.6   WORK PROGRAMME

As mentioned in **13.1** above, the New Deal has been replaced by the Work Programme. The Work Programme is designed to help people prepare for, find and stay in employment. It is delivered for Jobcentre Plus by specialist organisations, called 'providers'.

Further details are available at www.dwp.gov.uk/youth-contract/key-initiatives/wage -incentives/local-work-programme-providers/.

13.7   WORK-BASED TRAINING

Work-based training opportunities are currently provided through various types of apprenticeships (currently known as Intermediate Level Apprenticeships, Advanced Level Apprenticeships and Higher Apprenticeships), and other training initiatives, all types of apprenticeship involve working and training with an employer, and studying for other qualifications (usually with a training provider). In the past, apprenticeships were aimed primarily at people aged between 16 and 24, but apprenticeship opportunities for people aged 25 or over were introduced in August 2007. Apprenticeships are designed by the Sector Skills Councils (as to which, see www.ukces.org.uk/ourwork/sector-skills-councils), while the National Apprenticeships Service helps to fund the training.

A national minimum wage (NMW) for apprentices was introduced on 1 October 2010 (*National Minimum Wage Regulations 1999 (SI 1999/584), reg 13* (as substituted by *SI 2010/1901*)). The wage applies to all apprentices aged under 19 (including those working under an 'apprenticeship agreement' within the meaning of *section 32* of the *Apprenticeships, Skills, Children and Learning Act 2009* (see **13.11** below)), and apprentices aged 19 or over in the first year of their apprenticeship. (Apprentices aged 19 or over who have already spent a year on their apprenticeship must be paid at least the full NMW rate appropriate to their age.) The apprentice minimum wage is currently £2.65 per hour and applies to time working, plus time spent training that is part of the apprenticeship. If an apprentice is on a higher wage, the employer must continue to pay that amount for the remainder of the training or until the apprentice becomes eligible for the full NMW. (See **32.9 PAY – I.**)

For further information regarding apprenticeships, see www.apprenticeships.org.uk. Note that for all apprenticeships that commenced on or after 6 April 2012, the requirement to be employed under an 'apprenticeship agreement' (see above) is a condition for completion of an apprenticeship (see the *Apprenticeships (Form of Apprenticeship Agreement) Regulations 2012 (SI 2012/844)*). Without it, an 'apprenticeship certificate' (see **13.11** below) cannot be issued. The only circumstances whereby an apprenticeship can be completed without an apprenticeship agreement being in place are covered by the specific occupations in a limited number of frameworks covered by the 'alternative completion conditions' (see the *Apprenticeships (Alternative English Completion Conditions) Regulations 2012 (SI 2012/1199)*). Apprentice redundancy is also covered under the alternative completion conditions.

For the purposes of health and safety legislation, trainees are treated as the employees of the person whose undertaking is providing training (*Health and Safety (Training for Employment) Regulations 1990 (SI 1990/1380)*). For the application of discrimination laws see DISCRIMINATION AND EQUAL OPPORTUNITIES – I, II, III (10, 11, 12); an 'Equal Opportunities Toolkit' has also been produced for use in conjunction with training for young people.

13.8   SKILLS TRAINING

Since 1 April 2010, the Skills Funding Agency has been responsible for funding and regulating adult skills training in England; for further information, see skillsfundingagency.bis.gov.uk/. As previously mentioned, the Skills Funding Agency also houses the National Apprenticeships Service, which is working to develop relationships with employers. In Wales, the regulation and funding of adult skills training is the responsibility of the Welsh Assembly Government; for further information, see wales.gov.uk/topics/educationandskills. In Scotland, since 2008 these functions are the responsibility of Skills Development Scotland; for further details, see www.skillsdevelopmentscotland.co.uk/our-services/services-for-individuals.aspx.

Another relevant service is *learndirect*, which is a Government-sponsored initiative in flexible learning that provides courses (mainly on-line) and information through its network of learning centres; for further information, see www.learndirect.co.uk. See also the new Government website, which provides information and advice to adults who wish to earn new skills, gain new qualifications, or retrain; further information can be found on www.gov.uk/browse/working/finding-job.

13.9   APPRENTICESHIPS, SKILLS, CHILDREN AND LEARNING ACT 2009

As mentioned in **13.1** above, the *Apprenticeships, Skills, Children and Learning Act 2009* (referred to below as 'the *Act*') has now been enacted. This follows the publication of a White Paper by the Government in March 2008, and subsequently a draft Bill in July 2008.

The provisions of the *Act* that are of relevance to this chapter are the changes to the structure for funding education and training (dealt with briefly in **13.10** below), and also the provisions set out in *Part 1* of the *Act*, which is headed 'Apprenticeships, Study and Training'. Part 1 is in turn divided into two chapters: chapter 1 ('Apprenticeships', *sections 1* to *39*) and chapter 2 ('Study and Training', *section 40*). Chapter 1 is dealt with briefly in **13.11** below, and chapter 2 (which sets out a new statutory right for an employee to request his employer to allow him to undertake study or training) is dealt with in greater detail in **13.12** onwards below.

13.10   Structural changes

The *Act* dissolved the Learning and Skills Council (LSC). The LSC's responsibility for funding education and training for young people in England over compulsory school age but under 19 was transferred to local education authorities (initially supported by a new Young People's Learning Agency, although this was abolished by the *Education Act 2011* with effect from 1 April 2012; see *SI 2012/924*). In addition, the *Act* creates the office of Chief Executive of Skills Funding. The Chief Executive, with his staff, constitutes the Skills Funding Agency and has taken on the LSC's responsibility for funding post-19 education and training in England. These provisions (in *Part 4* of the *Act*) came into force on 1 April 2010 (see the *Apprenticeships, Skills, Children and Learning Act 2009 (Commencement No 2 and Transitional and Saving Provisions) Order 2010 (SI 2010/303)*). *Part 4* of the *Act* was subsequently amended by the *Education Act 2011* so as to impose a duty on the Chief Executive to fund apprenticeship training, by securing the provision of proper facilities for every young person in certain specified groups who has secured an apprenticeship opportunity. The effect of this section is to give higher funding priority for apprenticeship training for these young persons. This duty is known as 'the apprenticeship offer'. (*Apprenticeships, Skills, Children and Learning Act 2009, ss 83A, 83B*, in force 1 September 2012 (see *SI 2012/1087*)); *Apprenticeships (the Apprenticeship Offer) (Prescribed Persons) Regulations 2013 (SI 2013/560)*, in force 6 April 2013).

13.11   Apprenticeships

Sections 1 to *39* of the *Act* make provision about apprenticeships in England and Wales, including provisions about the issuing of 'apprenticeship certificates'. Normally, to receive such a certificate, an applicant will need to have been a party to an 'apprenticeship agreement' which, at the date on which it was entered into, related to a recognised 'apprenticeship framework'. The conditions will also require the applicant, while working under the agreement, to have completed a course of training for the principal qualification identified by the framework in question, and to have met all the other requirements specified for the award of a certificate. (These are known as the 'standard completion conditions', although there are 'alternative completion conditions' that apply in prescribed circumstances: see further **13.7** above.) Note that at the time of writing, certain provisions of *chapter 1* of *Part 1* of the *Act* are in force from the following dates:

(a)   30 September 2010 — *ss 23* to *27* (see also *Apprenticeships (Specification of Apprenticeship Standards for England) Order 2011 (SI 2011/219)*, in force 1 March 2011; *Apprenticeships (Modifications to the Specification of Apprenticeship Standards for England) Order 2013 (SI 2013/575)*, in force 6 April 2013) (*Apprenticeships, Skills, Children and Learning Act 2009 (Commencement No 4) Order 2010 (SI 2010/2374)*);

(b)   1 March 2011 — *ss 12, 13, 15, 16* (see also *Apprenticeships (Transitional Provision for Existing Vocational Specifications) (England) Order 2011 (SI 2011/901)*, in force 13 April 2011), *s 38* (see also *Apprenticeship Sectors (Specification) Order 2011 (SI 2011/220) (Apprenticeships, Skills, Children and Learning Act 2009 (Commencement No 5) Order 2011 (SI 2011/200)*);

(c)   6 April 2011 — *s 1* (see also *Apprenticeships (Alternative English Completion Conditions) Regulations 2012 (SI 2012/1199)*, in force 1 May 2012); *ss 3 to 6* (see also *Apprenticeships (Issue of Apprenticeship Certificates) (England) Regulations 2011 (SI 2011/900)*); *ss 11* (England only), *17, 32 to 36* (England only), (see also *Apprenticeships (Form of Apprenticeship Agreement) Regulations 2012 (SI 2012/844)*, in force 6 April 2012), *37, 39* (England only) *(SI 2011/200)*);

(d)   1 August 2011 — *ss 32 to 36* (Wales) (see also *Apprenticeships (Form of Apprenticeship Agreement) Regulations 2012 (SI 2012/844)*, in force 6 April 2012) *(SI 2011/200)*).

13.12 Study and training

Section 40 of the *Act* inserts new *sections 63D to 63K (Part VIA)* into the *ERA 1996*. These provisions came into force on 6 April 2010 (except in relation to small employers and their employees). (See *SI 2010/303, Sch 3*.) A 'small employer' means an employer who employs fewer than 250 employees (for the detailed definition, see *SI 2010/303, Sch 3, col 2*). Originally, *SI 2010/303* stated that these provisions would come into force on 6 April 2011 in relation to small employers and their employees, but this was revoked by the *Apprenticeships, Skills, Children and Learning Act 2009 (Commencement No 2 and Transitional and Saving Provisions) Order 2010 (Amendment) Order 2011 (SI 2011/682)*.

13.13 *Statutory right to make request in relation to study or training*

A 'qualifying employee' (ie an employee who is not excluded by *section 63D(7)* (see below), and who has been continuously employed for a period of not less than 26 weeks: *Employee Study and Training (Qualifying Period of Employment) Regulations 2010 (SI 2010/800)*) may make an application under *section 63D* to his or her employer (*ERA 1996, s 63D(1)*). The application must state that it is an application under *section 63D* (*ERA 1996, s 63D(5)*), and must be made for the purpose of enabling the employee to undertake study or training (or both) within *section 63D(4)*, ie where its purpose is to improve:

(a)   the employee's effectiveness in the employer's business; and

(b)   the performance of the employer's business.

The following persons are excluded by *section 63D(7)*:

(i)   a person of compulsory school age (or, in Scotland, school age);

(ii)   a person to whom *Part 1* of the *Education and Skills Act 2008* (duty to participate in education or training for 16 and 17 year olds) applies;

(iii)   a person who, by virtue of *section 29* of that *Act*, is treated as a person to whom that *Part* applies for the purposes specified in that section (extension for person reaching 18);

(iv)   a person to whom *section 63A* of the *ERA 1996* (right to time off for young person for study or training — see 3.7 CHILDREN AND YOUNG PERSONS) applies;

(v)   an agency worker; or

(vi)   a person of a description specified by the Secretary of State in regulations.

Nothing in *ERA 1996, Part VIA* prevents an employee and an employer from making any other arrangements in relation to study or training (*ERA 1996, s 63D(8)*).

13.14 *Section 63D application: supplementary provisions*

A *section 63D* application may (a) be made in relation to study or training of any description (subject to what is stated below); (b) relate to more than one description of study or training (*ERA 1996, s 63E(1)*).

In particular, the study or training need not be intended to lead to the award of a qualification to the employee (*ERA 1996, s 63E(3)*), and may be such that it would:

(i)   be undertaken on the employer's premises or elsewhere (including at the employee's home);

(ii)   be undertaken by the employee while performing the duties of the employee's employment or separately;

(iii)   be provided or supervised by the employer or by someone else;

(iv)   be undertaken without supervision;

(v)   be undertaken within or outside the United Kingdom.

(*ERA 1996, s 63E(2)*).

A *section 63D* application must give the following details of the proposed study or training (*ERA 1996, s 63E(4)(a)*):

(A)   its subject matter;

(B)   where and when it would take place;

(C)   who would provide or supervise it;

(D)   what qualification (if any) it would lead to.

The application must also explain how the employee thinks the proposed study or training would improve (i) the employee's effectiveness in the employer's business, and (ii) the performance of the employer's business (*ERA 1996, s 63E(4)(b)*).

For detailed requirements as to the form of the application, and the information it must contain, see the *Employee Study and Training (Eligibility, Complaints and Remedies) Regulations 2010 (SI 2010/156)*.

13.15 *Employer's duties in relation to section 63D application*

Where an employer receives a *section 63D* application from an employee, and the employer has not received such an application from the employee within the previous 12 months, he must deal with the application in accordance with regulations made by the Secretary of State (*ERA 1996, s 63F(4)*). The employer may refuse the application (or, as the case may be, part of the application) only if he thinks that one or more of the permissible grounds for refusal applies in relation to the application (or, as the case may be, that part) (*ERA 1996, s 63F(1), (5), (6)*). The permissible grounds for refusal are:

(a)   that the proposed study or training to which the application, or the part in question, relates would not improve (i) the employee's effectiveness in the employer's business, or (ii) the performance of the employer's business;

(b)   the burden of additional costs;

(c)   detrimental effect on ability to meet customer demand;

(d)   inability to re-organise work among existing staff;

(e)   inability to recruit additional staff;

(f)   detrimental impact on quality;

(g)   detrimental impact on performance;

(h)   insufficiency of work during the periods the employee proposes to work;

(i)   planned structural changes;

(j)   any other grounds specified by the Secretary of State in regulations.

(ERA 1996, s 63F(7)).

For the detailed requirements imposed on the employer on receiving a *section 63D* application (including a requirement to hold a meeting with the employee within 28 days of receiving the application), see the *Employee Study and Training (Procedural Requirements) Regulations 2010 (SI 2010/155)*.

13.16 *Employee's duties in relation to agreed study or training*

Where an employer has agreed to a *section 63D* application (or part of one) made by an employee in relation to particular study or training, the employee must inform the employer if he (a) fails to start or complete the agreed study or training, or (b) undertakes, or proposes to undertake, study or training that differs from the agreed study or training in any respect (including those specified in *section 63E(4)(a)* — see **13.14** above) *(ERA 1996, s 63H)*. For the requirements as to the way in which the employee is to comply with this duty, see the *Employee Study and Training (Procedural Requirements) Regulations 2010 (SI 2010/155), reg 20*.

13.17 *Complaint to employment tribunal*

An employee who makes a *section 63D* application may present a complaint to an employment tribunal that:

(a)   the employer has failed to comply with *section 63F(4), (5)* or *(6)* (see **13.15** above), or

(b)   the employer's decision to refuse the application, or part of it, is based on incorrect facts.

(ERA 1996, s 63I(1)).

No such complaint may be made in respect of an application which has been disposed of by agreement or withdrawn *(ERA 1996, s 63I(2))*. Where an application that has not been disposed of by agreement or withdrawn, a complaint under *section 63I* may only be made if the employer:

(i)   notifies the employee of a decision to refuse the application (or part of it) on appeal; or

(ii)   commits a breach of certain requirements set out in *SI 2010/155*, namely the failure to hold a meeting or a failure to notify a decision *(ERA 1996, s 63I(3)*; *Employee Study and Training (Eligibility, Complaints and Remedies) Regulations 2010 (SI 2010/156), reg 5)*.

An employee also has a right to complain to an employment tribunal that the employer has failed, or threatened to fail, to comply with *reg 16(2), (3)*, or *(5)* of *SI 2010/155* (right of employee to be accompanied by companion at meeting to consider *s 63D* application; right of companion to address meeting or confer with employee; right of employee to have meeting postponed if companion unavailable) (*Employee Study and Training (Procedural Requirements) Regulations 2010 (SI 2010/155), reg 17*).

An employment tribunal may not consider a complaint under *s 63I* unless the complaint is presented:

(A)   before the end of the period of three months beginning with the relevant date; or

(B)   within any further period that the tribunal considers reasonable, if the tribunal is satisfied that it was not reasonably practicable for the complaint to be presented before the end of that period of three months.

(*ERA 1996, s 63I(5)*).

The relevant date is the date on which the employee is notified of the decision on the appeal or (as the case may be) the date on which the breach was committed (*ERA 1996, s 63I(6)*).

13.18 *Remedies*

If an employment tribunal finds a complaint under *s 63I* well-founded it must make a declaration to that effect and may (a) make an order for reconsideration of the *s 63D* application; (b) make an award of compensation to be paid by the employer to the employee (*ERA 1996, s 63J(1)*).

The amount of any compensation must be the amount the tribunal considers just and equitable in all the circumstances, but must not exceed the permitted maximum of 8 weeks' pay (*ERA 1996, s 63J(2), (3); Employee Study and Training (Eligibility, Complaints and Remedies) Regulations 2010 (SI 2010/156), reg 6*).

If an employment tribunal makes an order for reconsideration of the *s 63D* application, *s 63F* (see **13.15** above) and regulations under that section (ie. *SI 2010/155*) apply as if the application had been received on the date of the order (instead of on the date it was actually received) (*ERA 1996, s 63J(4)*).

13.19 *Right not to suffer detriment, and right not to be unfairly dismissed*

Detriment. An employee has the right not to be subjected to any detriment (ie an action short of dismissal) by any act, or any deliberate failure to act, by the employee's employer done on the ground that the employee:

(a)   made (or proposed to make) a *s 63D* application;

(b)   exercised (or proposed to exercise) a right conferred on the employee under *section 63F*;

(c)   brought proceedings against the employer under *s 63I*; or

(d)   alleged the existence of any circumstance which would constitute a ground for bringing such proceedings.

(*ERA 1996, s 47F(1)*, inserted by the *Apprenticeships, Skills, Children and Learning Act 2009, s 40(1), (3)*).

Unfair dismissal. An employee who is dismissed is to be regarded for the purposes of *Part X* of the *ERA 1996* as unfairly dismissed if the reason (or, if more than one, the principal reason) for the dismissal is that the employee took (or proposed to take) any of the actions specified in (a) to (d) under *Detriment* above.

(*ERA 1996, s 104E*, inserted by the *Apprenticeships, Skills, Children and Learning Act 2009, s 40(1), (4)*).

14   Employee, Self-Employed or Worker?

Cross-reference. See also CONTRACT OF EMPLOYMENT (7), TEMPORARY AND SEASONAL EMPLOYEES 45.2, PUBLIC SECTOR EMPLOYEES (35).

14.1   This chapter examines the distinction between who is an employee and who is self-employed. This was described in *Johnson Underwood Ltd v Montgomery* [2001] EWCA Civ 318, [2001] ICR 819, [2001] IRLR 269, para 1 as a 'troublesome question'. It is important for many purposes to determine whether a person is an employee. The legal rights enjoyed by employees differ in many ways from the rights enjoyed by those who are not employees. For example, an employee will enjoy many of the statutory employment protection rights discussed elsewhere in this book if he meets the necessary qualifying requirements. In particular, it is only employees who are entitled to bring claims of unfair dismissal or to recover redundancy payments.

Different treatment by the tax authorities is another important distinction. An employee's earnings are liable to tax under *Schedule E* to the *Income and Corporation Taxes Act 1988*, and tax is deducted under the PAYE system, whereas a self-employed person is liable to tax under *Schedule D*. HMRC publishes a leaflet ES/FS1 'Employed or self-employed for tax and National Insurance contributions'.

The question of whether a person is an employee or self-employed is determined by reference to the contract under which he works – is it a contract of employment or a contract 'for services'?

However, it is not necessary to be an employee in the legal sense discussed below in order to enjoy all statutory rights. Many statutory provisions, in particular those enacted in more recent years, either use a statutory definition of employment which is wider than merely being employed under a contract of service, or they confer protection on a class of person called 'workers'.

The *Equality Act 2010* defines employment in *section 83(2)(a)* as meaning "employment under a contract of employment, a contract of apprenticeship or a contract personally to do work"

The provisions of the *Employment Rights Act 1996* ('*ERA*') prohibiting unlawful deductions from wages applies to 'workers', who are defined in *section 230* to include those employed under a contract of service but also any contract:

> 'whereby the individual undertakes to do or perform personally any work or services for another party to the contracts whose status is not by virtue of the contract that of a client or customer of any profession or business undertaking carried on by the individual'.

The provisions of *ERA* dealing with protected disclosures apply to 'workers' as so defined. There is also an extended definition of worker in *section 43K*.

Other legislation which applies to workers as defined above includes the *National Minimum Wage Act 1998* and the *Working Time Regulations 1998*.

There are therefore many occasions when it will be necessary to decide whether a person is a worker, even if not an employee.

This chapter will first consider the legal definition of employee before dealing with the concept of a 'worker'.

14.2   CONTRACT OF SERVICE AND CONTRACT OF EMPLOYMENT

The terms 'contract of service' and 'contract of employment' are identical in meaning. The former is the more archaic term which was used when the parties to the contract were known as 'master' and 'servant'. The term 'contract of employment' for the purposes of *ERA* includes a contract of apprenticeship (*ERA, section 230(2)*).

14.3   DISTINGUISHING A CONTRACT OF EMPLOYMENT FROM A CONTRACT FOR SERVICES

The question of who is an employee is not straightforward. It is necessary to determine which workers are employees for a number of reasons. For example, certain employment protection rights apply only to those employed under a contract of employment. Also, principals are vicariously liable for the acts of their employees but not for the acts of independent contractors hired by them.

Thus, the issue in law is how to distinguish between a *contract of employment* (also known as a *contract of service*) on the one hand, and a *contract for services* on the other. Some elements of the nature of the distinction between the two types of contract emerge from their names. Under a contract *of* service, a person agrees to serve another. Under a contract *for* services, a person agrees to provide certain services to another.

The starting point is to establish whether there is a contract at all between the alleged employer and alleged employee. There are contexts in which the analysis of the contracts will require some thought. For example, when a person works for another through an employment agency, there will usually be two contracts: (i)between the agency and the worker on the one hand; and (ii) between the agency and the agency's client (the business for which the worker actually carries out his work) on the other. There will not ordinarily be an express contract between the worker and the client. In the absence of a contract between worker and client, the worker cannot be an employee of the client: *Hewlett Packard Ltd v O'Murphy* [2002] IRLR 4. The effect of this is that the worker has no employment protection rights as against the client business for which he or she works. This has been recognised in a number of cases to be unsatisfactory. However, it has also been held that even if there is no express contract between the worker and the client of the agency, in certain circumstances it may be possible to imply a contract between those persons through their conduct. Thus if in fact the same person consistently works for and under the direction of the client of an employment agency, it may be possible to imply a contract between the worker and the end client. A contract can only be implied between the worker and the client where it is *necessary* to do so: *James v Greenwich London Borough Council* [2008] EWCA Civ 35, [2008] ICR 545, [2008] IRLR 302. Mere length of work is insufficient to justify the implication of such a contract. It will usually be necessary to identify some words or conduct which permit the conclusion that the agency relationship which originally existed no longer accurately reflects how the work is being performed (see paras 53–61 of the EAT's judgment in *James* [2007] IRLR 168, approved by the Court of Appeal). (See also *Franks v Reuters Ltd* [2003] EWCA Civ 417, [2003] ICR 1166; *Dacas v Brook Street Bureau (UK) Ltd* [2004] EWCA Civ 217, [2004] IRLR 358; *Cable & Wireless plc v Muscat* [2006] EWCA Civ 220, [2006] IRLR 354. A significant degree of integration of the agency worker into an organisation is not sufficient to imply a contract. Further, where the inference is that the parties would have acted in exactly the same way if there had been no contract, this will be fatal to the implication of a contract (see *Tilson v Alstom Transport* [2010] EWCA Civ 1308, [2011] IRLR 169)

However, the need to imply a contract has been mitigated to some extent by the *Agency Workers Regulations 2010 (SI 2010/93)* which came into force on 1 October 2011.

Once the existence of a contract is established, the next question is whether the contract is a contract of employment or of some other sort. There are three essential elements which must be present in every contract of employment. These form the irreducible core of the contract of employment, without which a contract cannot be regarded as a contract of service:

(a)   the contract must impose an obligation on a person to provide work personally;

(b)   there must be mutuality of obligation between employer and employee; and

(c)   the worker must expressly or impliedly agree to be subject to the control of the person for whom he works to a 'sufficient' degree.

If any of these three elements is not present, the contract is not a contract of employment. If each element is present, the contract may be a contract of employment. Whether or not it is will depend on an assessment of all the other circumstances.

Dealing with those elements which must be present in order for a contract to be a contract of employment, the first – that the person must be obliged to provide work personally – was made clear in *Express and Echo Publications Ltd v Tanton* [1999] IRLR 367. In that case, the contract provided that if the worker was unable or unwilling to do the work personally, he had to provide a substitute. The Court of Appeal held that the power to send a substitute meant that this could not be a contract of employment. The irreducible minimum of a contract of employment was an obligation on the worker to provide his services personally. The obligation to undertake work personally does not cease to exist where there is a power to send a substitute only where the worker is *unable* to do the work: *James v Redcats (Brands) Ltd* [2007] IRLR 296. The point about *Tanton* was that the worker could send a substitute if he did not want to do the work as well as if he could not. Where the employee must do the work personally if he is able, then the requirement of personal obligation is satisfied.

However, where a contract contains a limited power to delegate, such power does not lead inescapably to the conclusion that the contract is not a contract of employment: *MacFarlane v Glasgow City Council* [2001] IRLR 7. According to the EAT in *MacFarlane*, the clause in *Tanton* allowing the worker to send a replacement was 'extreme'. The worker in *Tanton* was not under any personal obligation ever to attend work. He was always entitled to send a substitute. In *Macfarlane*, the worker was entitled to send a replacement only in the event that he was unable to attend work. Therefore, the clause was of far more limited effect, and was not sufficient of itself to justify the conclusion that the contract was not a contract of employment (see also *Community Dental Centres Ltd v Sultan-Darmon* [2010] IRLR 1024).

In *Staffordshire Sentinel Newspapers Ltd v Potter* [2004] IRLR 752, the EAT provided guidance on the application of *Tanton* and *MacFarlane*. If there is a clear express contractual term that does not impose personal obligations on the individual, effect must be given to that term unless it is a sham or there has, on the facts, been a variation of the contract. In that case what happened in practice is not relevant. Where there is no clear express term, it is necessary to consider both the written terms of the contract and what happened in practice in order to determine what was the true agreement between the parties.

In considering 'delegation' and 'obligations' clauses in contracts of employment alleged to be a sham the Court of Appeal in *Consistent Group Ltd v Kalwak* [2008] EWCA Civ 430, [2008] IRLR 505 held that a decision that the contract is in part a sham required a finding that both parties intended to paint a false picture as to the true nature of their respective obligations. However, the EAT held in *Redrow Homes (Yorkshire) Ltd v Buckborough & Sewell* [2009] IRLR 34 that a contractual term may be considered a sham not only where the parties intend to deceive a third party but also where the parties simply do not intend for the term to apply. The Court of Appeal looked at sham obligations again in *Protectacoat*

14.3 Employee, Self-Employed or Worker?

Firthglow Ltd v Szilagyi [2009] EWCA Civ 98, [2009] IRLR 365 and decided that, in order for a court or tribunal to find that an agreement is a sham, there is no need for it to find that the parties intended to deceive a third party. If it is asserted that the document does not describe the true relationship between the parties, it is for the court or tribunal to decide what the true relationship is. Smith LJ held that when determining the true legal relationship of the parties the preferable approach is to ask whether or not the words of the written contract represent the true intentions or expectations of the parties, not only at the inception of the contract but, if appropriate, as time goes by.

In *Autoclenz Ltd v Belcher* [2011] UKSC 41, [2011] ICR 1157, [2011] IRLR 820, the Supreme Court confirmed that in the employment context the Court will look to the reality of the arrangements between the parties, as opposed to concentrating on the written terms of any agreement, in determining the true nature of the relationship. In *Autoclenz*, this meant that a written term purporting to permit the use of a substitute did not preclude the conclusion that a contract of employment existed when in practice the right was not exercised.

The second requirement   that there be a mutuality of obligations – means that for the entire duration of the contract under consideration, both the employer and the employee must be under legal obligations to one another. Of course, without the presence of an obligation towards another party, there would not be a contract at all. Thus the requirement for mutual obligations is relevant to the question whether there is a contract at all: *Stephenson v Delphi Diesel Systems Ltd* [2003] ICR 471; *Cotswold Developments Construction Ltd v Williams* [2006] IRLR 181. In the ordinary case, the obligations in question will be an obligation on the employee to work and an obligation on the employer to pay for that work. It may not be necessary in every case for there to be obligations to work and to provide work. It may be sufficient if there is an obligation on the employee to accept and do such work as is offered to him and on the employer to pay the employee for the work which is done and, if there are periods when there is no work for the employee to do, to pay a retainer. In the absence of such a retainer in periods where there is no work to be done, there will be no contract of employment between the parties. The clearest exposition of this principle is to be found in *Clark v Oxfordshire Health Authority* [1998] IRLR 125. However, see also *O'Kelly v Trusthouse Forte* [1984] QB 90, [1983] 3 All ER 456, [1983] ICR 728, *Nethermere (St Neots) v Gardiner* [1984] ICR 612 and *Hellyer Bros Ltd v McLeod* [1987] 1 WLR 728, [1987] ICR 526, CA. In *St Ives Plymouth Ltd v Haggerty* [2008] All ER (D) 317 (May) (Elias P) the EAT accepted, following *Nethermere* and *Airfix Footwear Ltd v Cope* [1978] ICR 1210, that there may exceptionally be circumstances where the pattern of work is such that it may be possible to infer an obligation to work simply from the continual repetition of work being offered and accepted.

In *Quashie v Stringfellow Restaurants Limited* [2012] EWCA Civ 1735, [2013] IRLR 99, the Court of Appeal affirmed that in the absence of any obligation on the employer to pay the worker for services provided there was no contract of employment. The claimant lap dancer was remunerated by the fees paid for visitors to the club and was therefore not an employee of the club.

The House of Lords has reiterated that the existence of mutual obligations between the parties is the irreducible minimum of a contract of employment (*Carmichael v National Power plc* [2000] IRLR 43). Hence, in a case where workers were engaged as power station guides on a 'casual as required' basis, there was no contract of employment. There was no obligation on the workers to work. Indeed, they had failed to attend on a number of occasions and had not been disciplined. Further, there was no obligation on the company to provide work.

Where the terms of a contract expressly negate mutuality of obligations, there cannot be a contract of employment: *Stevedoring and Haulage Services Ltd v Fuller* [2001] EWCA Civ 651, [2001] IRLR 627. In that case, the worker worked under a series of individual contracts, each of which recorded that there was no obligation to offer or accept any further contract. In those circumstances, it was impermissible to imply an over-arching or umbrella contract of employment pursuant to which each individual contract was issued.

The third element – that the employer must have a sufficient degree of control over the employee – does not mean that work must necessarily be carried out under the employer's actual supervision or control. In a more general sense, it requires that ultimate authority over the employee in the performance of his work resides in the employer, so that the employee is subject to the latter's orders and directions.

The necessity of control derives from the judgment of McKenna J in *Ready Mixed Concrete (South East) Ltd v Minister of Pensions and National Insurance* [1968] 2 QB 497 at 514. McKenna J's remarks on control have been cited with approval in the majority of subsequent important cases dealing with the essential ingredients of an employment contract. The Court of Appeal has re-affirmed that in the absence of sufficient control, there cannot be a contract of employment. What constitutes sufficient control – and whether that means the imposition of a framework within which a person works or direct supervision of the performance of a person's functions – will vary from case to case. But control is a necessary condition of a contract of employment: *Johnson Underwood Ltd v Montgomery* [2001] EWCA Civ 318, [2001] IRLR 269. Once there is mutuality of obligation such that there is a contract, control is relevant for deciding whether the contract is a contract of employment: *Stephenson v Delphi Systems Ltd* [2003] ICR 471.

If the contract does not impose an obligation to provide services personally or if there is no mutuality of obligation throughout the period under consideration, or if there is no control present, then the contract in question cannot be a contract of employment. If all these elements are present, the contract may be one of employment. It will then be necessary to consider the surrounding circumstances to determine the nature of the relationship.

In order to determine, once the irreducible minimum requirements are present, whether the contract is a contract of employment, it is necessary to paint a picture from the accumulation of relevant details. This means not only looking at specific matters, but also standing back and considering the overall picture. This approach derives from *Hall (Inspector of Taxes) v Lorimer* [1994] 1 All ER 250, [1994] 1 WLR 209, [1994] STC 23, 66 TC 349, [1994] ICR 218. Matters which are relevant are too numerous to list in full. However, they might include payment by wages or salary; whether the worker provides his own equipment; whether he is subject to the employer's disciplinary and grievance procedures; receipt of sick pay or contractual holiday pay; provision of benefits traditionally associated with employment such as a pension scheme, health care or other benefits; whether the worker is a part of the employer's business; whether there are restrictions on working for others.

Some cases have focused on factors which distinguish an employee from a person in business on his own account. The sorts of details which may be relevant include whether:

(a)   he is employed as part of the business of the employer and his work is done as an integral part of that business;

(b)   he provides his own equipment;

(c)   he hires his own helpers;

(d)   he takes a degree of financial risk;

(e)   he has responsibility for investment and management; and

(f)   how far he has the opportunity of profiting from sound management in performing his task.

14.3 Employee, Self-Employed or Worker?

This list is derived from *Market Investigations Ltd v Minister of Social Security* [1969] 2 QB 173, *per* Cooke J at 185. In *Lee Ting Sang v Chung Chi-Keung* [1990] 2 AC 374, [1990] ICR 409, the Privy Council said that the best expression of the test was that stated in the *Market Investigations* case: is the person concerned in business on his own account? This test was again applied in *Andrews v King (Inspector of Taxes)* [1991] STC 481, [1991] ICR 846, where the Vice-Chancellor went on to say that the essence of business was that it was carried on with a view to profit (whereas it was not open to the employee there to make an increased profit from the way in which he carried out his tasks). The importance of this criterion has recently been emphasised by the Court of Appeal in *Stringefellow Restaurants Limited*. However, it is not a matter of running through these indicia as if they were an all-purpose checklist. Part of the function of painting the picture is to determine what are the significant details in the instant case and to look at the whole arrangement. Thus, in *Hall v Lorimer*, a vision mixer who supplied no tools, equipment or money to his business and did not hire staff was still self-employed. The key factor was that he was a professional person who worked for a variety of people for short periods and was not dependent on any one paymaster.

However, more recently it has been observed that one cannot safely rely on a simple dichotomy between the employed and those on business on their own account. There are categories of person who are not in business on their own account but who are not, for that reason alone, necessarily to be regarded as employees. In particular, many statutory provisions either contain a wider definition of employee than that which is used in the common law (for example, the discrimination legislation) or extend protection to a category of persons called 'workers' who are not employed but not in business on their own account either: see *James v Redcats (Brands) Ltd* [2007] IRLR 296.

As a general rule, the greater the degree of personal responsibility an individual undertakes in any of the matters set out above, the more likely he is to be considered an independent contractor rather than an employee.

The way in which a person is treated for tax may be relevant but is not decisive. The tax and employment regimes are separate and do not necessarily have to give the same answer as to a person's status.

In assessing all of these factors, it is legitimate in a case where the contract is said to be based partly on oral exchanges and on conduct to consider evidence of the way in which the parties understood their relationship and the way in which they conducted themselves in practice (see *Carmichael v National Power plc* [1999] 4 All ER 897, [1999] 1 WLR 2042, [1999] ICR 1226, [2000] IRLR 43 and also now *Autoclenz*). However, the conduct of the parties cannot be relied upon for the purpose of implying a term which flatly contradicts an express term: *Stevedoring and Haulage Services Ltd v Fuller* [2001] EWCA Civ 651, [2001] IRLR 627. In *Stevedoring and Haulage Services*, workers were engaged on terms that specifically negated mutuality of obligation in that they made it clear that there was no obligation to offer or accept employment beyond the individual engagement which was the subject of the contract. The conduct of the parties (which remained the same throughout several renewals of the contract) could not override those express written terms by creating mutual obligations to offer and to accept work outside the individual engagement.

Where the nature of the relationship between the parties is in doubt or is ambiguous, it is open to the parties, by agreement, to stipulate what the legal situation between them is to be (*Massey v Crown Life Insurance Co Ltd* [1978] 2 All ER 576, [1978] 1 WLR 676, [1978] ICR 590). However, all the circumstances of the relationship must be considered, and the courts will look behind the parties' intentions, and labels, to ascertain the true nature of the agreement (*Young & Woods Ltd v West* [1980] IRLR 201). Where a person worked for an employment agency and the tribunal found that there were mutual obligations and considerable control, it was incorrect to decide that there was no contract of employment on the basis that this is what the parties had originally intended. The label applied by the parties would only be decisive where all the other factors were evenly balanced: *Dacas v Brook Street Bureau (UK) Ltd* [2003] IRLR 190 (on appeal [2004] EWCA Civ 217, [2004] IRLR 358).

It is wrong to say that a person is an employee simply because he is not self-employed. There may also be intermediate categories of worker (*Dacas v Brook Street* [2004] IRLR 358). But to enjoy the statutory rights which apply only to employees (e.g. to claim unfair dismissal), the person must be an employee.

Note also that a full-time working director of his family firm (who drew fees rather than being paid a salary) was held to be self employed (*Parsons v Albert J Parsons & Sons Ltd* [1979] ICR 271), as were musicians with a London orchestra (*Winfield v London Philharmonic Orchestra Ltd* [1979] ICR 726) and a sub-postmaster (*Hitchcock v Post Office* [1980] ICR 100, *Wolstenholme v Post Office Ltd* [2003] ICR 546). A police cadet was held not to be an employee or an apprentice (*Wiltshire Police Authority v Wynn* [1981] QB 95, [1980] 3 WLR 445, 79 LGR 591, [1980] ICR 649). A Presbyterian minister was held not to be an employee, as was a Sikh priest (*Davies v Presbyterian Church of Wales* [1986] 1 All ER 705, [1986] 1 WLR 323, [1986] ICR 280; *Singh v Guru Nanak Gurdwara* [1990] ICR 309, CA). But in *Percy v Board of National Mission of the Church of Scotland* [2005] UKHL 73, [2006] 2 WLR 353, [2006] ICR 134 a minister of the Church of Scotland was held to be employed within the wider definition of that term in the *Sex Discrimination Act* (see also *New Testament Church of God v Stewart* [2008] IRLR 134). There is no rule of law that a person who provides services via a company cannot be an employee (*Catamaran Cruisers Ltd v Williams* [1994] IRLR 386). It has been held that a volunteer is not an employee because of the absence of consideration moving from the recipient of the volunteer's services. There is no obligation on that party to make payment and, in the absence of payment, there is no consideration and no contract: *Melhuish v Redbridge Citizens' Advice Bureau* [2005] IRLR 419, EAT. It is necessary to consider the purpose of a contract in order to decide whether it is a contract of employment. Thus an arrangement by which a prisoner undertook work as part of his rehabilitation was not a contract of employment because that was not its purpose: *M&P Steelcraft Ltd v Ellis* [2008] ICR 578.

The Court of Appeal considered the status of a modern apprenticeship agreement between a trainee, an employer and a Training and Enterprise Council or some other educational establishment in *Flett v Matheson* [2006] EWCA Civ 53, [2006] ICR 673. The Court of Appeal overturned the EAT's decision that such an arrangement created a contract of employment between the individual and the employer. The Court held that the purpose of the arrangement was to provide practical aspects of training. The apprentice was to be released from work to attend academic training. The Court approved the distinction which had been drawn between an employment contract and a contract for apprenticeship in *Whitely v Marton Electrical Ltd* [2003] ICR 495. In the event, the Court in *Flett* remitted the matter for the Tribunal to make further findings of fact.

A general practitioner is not employed by a health authority. GPs are under obligations in relation to the nature of the work they undertake. But since these obligations are imposed by statutory instrument and not by contract, those obligations do not make the GP an employee of the health authority: *David-John v North Essex Health Authority* [2004] ICR 112, EAT.

Equity partners are generally not employees. However, there are many different forms of partnership arrangements where individuals are not traditional equity partners. The *Partnership Act 1890, section 2(3)* provides that receiving a share of the profits is prima facie evidence of a partnership. But, there is old authority that suggests where an individual receives a salary as well as a share in the profits, there is strong evidence that he is an employee, not a partner (*Ross v Parkyns* (1875) LR 20 Eq 331). It is necessary to consider all the circumstances to determine whether or not an individual is an employee. In *Stekel v*

14.3 Employee, Self-Employed or Worker?

Ellice [1973] 1 WLR 191 Megarry J considered that under a partnership agreement a salaried partner on a fixed salary, not dependent on profits, could still be a true partner at least if he was entitled to a share in the profits on a winding-up. There is no requirement for an individual to have a minimum share of profits or involvement in management decisions before they can be regarded as a partner. The fact that an individual has the rights and duties of a partner and an entitlement to a residue of the firm if wound up can be sufficient (see *Tiffin v Lester Aldridge LLP* [2011] IRLR 105). In *Kovats v TFO Management LLP* [2009] ICR 1140 the EAT examined *section 4(4)* of the *Limited Liability Partnerships Act 2000* which provides that a member of a limited liability partnership shall not be regarded for any purpose as employed by the limited liability partnership unless, if he and the other members were partners in a partnership, he would be regarded for that purpose as employed by the partnership. Judge Birtles held that "any purpose" includes *section 230* of *ERA* and therefore the same test applied for partners in an LLP as in the case of traditional partnerships. In *Bates van Winklehof v Clyde & Co LLP* [2012] EWCA Civ 1207, [2012] IRLR 992, the Court of Appeal held that a member of a limited liability partnership who would have been a partner in an *1890 Act* partnership had it not been registered as a limited liability partnership could be neither an employee under nor a worker and therefore could not pursue a claim in respect of an alleged protected disclosure.

There may be contracts which are neither contracts of employment nor contracts for services but which fall into an intermediate category (*Construction Industry Training Board v Labour Force Ltd* [1970] 3 All ER 220; *Ironmonger v Movefield Ltd (t/a Deering Appointments)* [1988] IRLR 461, EAT). It is thought that a person who works under such a contract will, for most purposes, be in the same position as one who is self-employed. However, such persons may also be regarded as 'workers' for other statutory purposes such as the Working Time Regulations and the provisions in relation to unlawful deductions of wages.

In *O'Kelly v Trusthouse Forte plc* [1984] QB 90, [1983] 3 All ER 456, [1983] 3 WLR 605, [1983] ICR 728, the majority of the Court of Appeal held that an appellate court could only interfere with a decision of an employment tribunal on the question of whether an individual was an employee if it could be shown that the employment tribunal had erred in law or reached a perverse conclusion. See also *Lee Ting Sang v Chung Chi-Keung* [1990] 2 AC 374, [1990] 2 WLR 1173, [1990] ICR 409, [1990] IRLR 236; *Hall v Lorimer* [1994] ICR 218. However, when the issue whether a person is an employee or self-employed depends on the construction of a written document, this will involve questions of law (*Davies v Presbyterian Church of Wales*) but only to the extent that it appears that the parties intended all the express terms of their contract to be contained in the document (*Ministry of Defence HQ Defence Dental Service v Kettle* (UKEAT/0308/06/LA) [2007] All ER (D) 301 (Jan)). Whether or not that was their intention is a question of fact (*Carmichael v National Power plc* [2000] IRLR 43).

Can a controlling shareholder be an employee? A question sometimes arises as to whether a person who controls the shareholding in the employing enterprise can also be employed by that enterprise. This arises often in cases where a company has become insolvent and a majority shareholder or director claims to be an employee and therefore entitled to payments from the Secretary of State under *section 182* of *ERA*. The most recent guidelines on the issue were given in *Secretary of State for Business, Enterprise and Regulatory Reform v Neufeld (Richard) (2) Howe (Keith)* [2009] EWCA Civ 280, [2009] IRLR 475. There is no reason in principle why a controlling shareholder should not be an employee. The mere fact that a person is a shareholder or profits from the success of a business does not mean that he cannot be an employee. It is no answer to argue that the extent of the individual's control of the company meant that the control condition of a contract of employment could not be satisfied. There are three cases in which it would be legitimate not to give effect to a contract of employment between a controlling shareholder and his company. First where the contract is itself a sham. Second where the contract was entered into for an ulterior purpose (such as to obtain payment from the Secretary of State upon the company's insolvency). Third where the parties do not conduct themselves in accordance with the contract – either because they never intended to or because the relationship ceases to reflect the terms of the contract. Where a contract is in place, the onus is on the party seeking to deny it to show that it is not what it appears to be. If the parties conduct themselves in accordance with the terms of the contract, that is a strong indicator of a contract of employment. By contrast if their conduct is inconsistent, it may be held that there is no such contract.

Specific engagements. When one asks whether a person was employed or self-employed, the question usually concerns the general relationship between the parties to the contract. The question – although rarely framed in these terms – is whether the 'general engagement' between the parties was a contract of employment or a contract for services. Often it will be necessary to consider whether, over a period, a person was an employee. This will be the case, for example, when one is concerned to determine whether a person has sufficient continuity of service to bring an unfair dismissal claim. However, in some cases it may be relevant to enquire whether a particular or specific engagement was a contract of employment or a contract for services. Thus, for example, in the case of a regular casual worker who is paid only when work is available but who is not paid in times when there is no work, it may be that the general engagement is not a contract of employment because of a lack of mutual obligations. However, it may be that, when the worker does actually work, the relationship is one of employment. Thus, it would be said that the worker was employed for each 'specific engagement' (for an example where the distinction was drawn, see *Clark v Oxfordshire Health Authority* [1998] IRLR 125). The process for analysing whether a specific engagement is a contract of employment is the same as that set out above. However, the focus is on each particular assignment when the worker does actually work and not on the general relationship.

There may be several reasons why it is necessary to determine whether there was a contract of employment for each specific engagement. For example, the regular casual worker may wish to claim unfair dismissal. Because there is no mutuality of obligations, he cannot establish sufficient continuity of employment by relying on the general relationship. However, if each specific engagement was a contract of employment then it may be that he could establish sufficient continuity by relying on the statutory provisions which allow for gaps in employment to be bridged (see CONTINUOUS EMPLOYMENT (6)). This was the case in *Prater v Cornwall County Council* [2006] EWCA Civ 102, [2006] 2 All ER 1013, [2006] ICR 731 where a teacher was employed on a number of assignments. There was no overarching contract of employment because there were no mutual obligations between assignments. But the Court of Appeal held that this was irrelevant to determining the person's status when she was performing an assignment. If the conditions of employment were satisfied for each assignment, then the worker was an employee whilst undertaking them. The question then was whether gaps when there was no contract could be bridged. *James v Redcats (Brands) Ltd* [2007] IRLR 296 also supports the point that a person's status between engagements is irrelevant to that person's status when an assignment is being performed.

An example in the case law where the court focused on the specific engagement is *McMeechan v Secretary of State for Employment* [1997] IRLR 353. The case concerned a person who worked via an employment agency for a number of different companies. The last company for which he worked went into insolvent liquidation without having paid him for his assignment. He made a claim against the Secretary of State in respect of those payments under *ERA 1996, section 182 et seq.* The question before the Court of Appeal was whether the worker could be regarded as an employee of the agency for the purposes of the *specific* engagement in respect of which he was not paid regardless of his status for the purpose of his *general* engagement by the agency. The Court of Appeal held that a person may be an employee for the purposes of specific engagements even though the general relationship between the parties is not one of employer and employee. It is then a question of assessing the person's status when he does in fact turn up for work regardless of the fact that there may be no general obligation on him to do so.

14.3 Employee, Self-Employed or Worker?

Employment agencies. Where a person is found work by an employment agency, there will be a contract between the worker and the agency (which may or may not be a contract of employment) and a separate contract between the agency and the person to whom the services are provided. But absent a further contract between the worker and the recipient of the services, the worker will not be an employee of that person (see *Costain Building and Civil Engineering Ltd v Smith* [2000] ICR 215, EAT). However, it may be possible to infer a contract between the worker and the recipient of services from the conduct of both those parties: *James v London Borough of Greenwich* [2008] IRLR 302; *Cable & Wireless plc v Muscat* [2006] IRLR 354. It is also possible that the contract with the agency may in truth be a contract of employment. In *Royal National Lifeboat Institution v Bushaway* [2005] IRLR 674, the EAT held that a tribunal had been entitled to ignore an entire agreement clause in finding that a person was employed by the client of an agency. (See also **45.2 TEMPORARY AND SEASONAL EMPLOYEES**).

The complexity of this area of the law is demonstrated by *Evans v Parasol Ltd* (UKEAT/0536/08/RN upheld by the Court of Appeal [2010] EWCA Civ 866, [2011] ICR 37) in which the EAT noted it would be a bold employment judge who was willing to strike out a claim by an agency worker against a possible employer when an individual worked under agency type arrangements.

In *Motorola Ltd v (1) Davidson and (2) Melville Craig* [2001] IRLR 4, the EAT was concerned to consider whether a person taken on by a recruitment agency, Melville Craig, to work for Motorola, was to be regarded as employed by Motorola for the purposes of a complaint of unfair dismissal. The EAT upheld the decision of the tribunal that there was sufficient control by Motorola over Mr Davidson in fact to mean that the relationship was one of employer-employee even though Motorola had no direct legal control over Mr Davidson. It was sufficient that Motorola had indirect control over Mr Davidson in that it could give directions to Melville Craig, including a direction no longer to send Mr Davidson to work for Motorola. Further, at the site, there was a sufficient degree of control in fact. The appeal was unusual in that the only issue argued was that of control. Hence, the case does not lay down any wider propositions about persons engaged by employment agencies becoming employees of the agency's clients. The importance of the case is in the stress which it lays on 'practical aspects of control that fall short of direct legal rights' and the recognition that an employment relationship may be created by a combination of practical control and indirect legal control.

The Court of Appeal has reiterated in *Johnson Underwood Ltd v Montgomery* [2001] EWCA Civ 318, [2001] ICR 819, [2001] IRLR 269 that the essential test to apply in judging whether a person is employed by a recruitment agency (or, indeed, by a hirer) is the existence of irreducible minima of mutual obligation and control. To the extent that Waite LJ in *McMeechan* appeared to reduce mutual obligation and control to mere factors to be taken into account, the absence of which would not necessarily be decisive, Buckley J indicated that he was wrong to do so.

In *Montgomery*, the courts below had already determined that the applicant was not an employee of the hirer (a finding which the applicant did not challenge). The result of the Court of Appeal's finding was that the applicant was held not to be an employee of the respondent agency either, since the agency had little or no control over her. The court indicated its unhappiness with this state of affairs, which left the applicant without a remedy and in a state of legal limbo. However, it stated that the solution to her dilemma lay with Parliament. The government issued regulations governing the relationships between recruitment bureaux, work-seekers and hirers, *The Conduct of Employment Agencies and Employment Businesses Regulations 2003 (SI 2003/3319)*. The regulations require that recruitment businesses should be required to clarify whether their relation to work-seekers is one of an employment business or an agency (*reg 14*). (The distinction between agencies and employment businesses in the *Regulations* is derived from the *Employment Agencies Act 1973*. Under *section 13* of the *Act*, agencies find workers employment with employers;

employment businesses supply persons to act for, or under the control of, other persons.) The Regulations also require that employment businesses must state in any agreement with work-seekers whether the work-seeker is engaged by them under a contract of service or contract for services (*reg 15*).

In *Bunce v Postworth Ltd (t/a Skyblue)* [2005] EWCA Civ 490, [2005] IRLR 557, the Court of Appeal held that an agency worker was not an employee of the agency either because of the general relationship between the parties or when the worker was engaged on a specific assignment. There were no mutual obligations as between agency and worker for the purposes of individual assignments nor was there sufficient control

In *Dacas v Brook Street Bureau* [[2004] EWCA Civ 217, [2004] IRLR 358, the Court of Appeal analysed the circumstances in which a person provided to another by an agency could be employed by the end user. The analysis was approved in *Cable & Wireless v Muscat* [2006] IRLR 354, [2006] ICR 975. However, the Court of Appeal added the important qualification that a contract could only be implied between the worker and the end user when it was 'necessary' to do so in order to give the relationship business reality. The question of necessity was considered in *Beck v Camden London Borough Council* (UKEAT/0121/08/ZT) [2008] All ER (D) 09 (Sep) and in *Sridhar v East Living Ltd* (UKEAT/0476/07/RN) [2008] All ER (D) 290 (Nov). It is only where express contractual arrangements do not adequately explain the legal relationship between the parties that the question of whether there is an implied contract between an agency worker and an end user might arise. The tribunal must specifically consider whether it is necessary to imply a contract rather than looking solely at whether the conduct of the parties was consistent with an employment relationship.

Later cases have indicated that it will be difficult to show that it is necessary to imply such a contract. In *James v Greenwich London Borough Council* [2008] IRLR 302, the Court of Appeal repeated the necessity test. The Court also approved observations in the EAT that in the usual agency relationship there were no mutual obligations between the worker and the end user: the end user was not obliged to pay the worker. The end user was also not able to insist on a particular worker being provided. It was the agency which was obliged to pay, but it did not control the worker. It would only be in exceptional circumstances that it was necessary to imply a contract. The express terms of the contract described the relationship and it would not be necessary to imply a contract. It might be possible to infer a contract from the parties' conduct if that departed from the express terms of the contracts. But the mere fact that an agency worker worked for an end user for a long time could not justify the implication of a contract. The judgment of the Supreme Court in *Autoclenz* does not refer to 'necessity' as a separate test to be applied when analysing the nature of the contractual relationship between the parties, and it may suggest that this requirement has been over-stated in *James* and other cases.

In *Cairns v Visteon UK Ltd* [2007] IRLR 175, [2007] ICR 616, the EAT toyed with the idea that there could be two contracts of employment – one with the agency and one with the end user. However, this could not resolve the problem that it would only be possible to imply a contract where it was necessary to do so. Also, there would be enormous practical problems – would both employers have to follow the dismissal procedures in the event of a dismissal?

The present state of the law is thus that it will only be in exceptional circumstances that an agency worker will be held to have a contract of employment with the end user.

The problems faced by agency workers have to some extent been ameliorated by the *Agency Workers Regulations 2010*. Workers supplied by a temporary work agency to work "temporarily for and under the supervision and direction of a hirer" are covered by the *Regulations*. The definitions exclude the genuinely self-employed, those working through their own limited liability company (provided they are genuinely self employed) and those working on "managed service contracts". Upon completion of a 12 week qualifying period,

14.3   Employee, Self-Employed or Worker?

an agency worker is entitled to the same pay, holidays and other basic conditions as if he or she had been recruited directly by the hirer on day one of the assignment, whether as an employee or a worker. In identifying the "same basic working and employment conditions terms", agency workers may compare their terms with direct recruits of the hirer working in "the same" or "broadly similar" role, not necessarily in the same office or establishment. The *Regulations* reduce the need to infer a contract of employment between the worker and the recipient of services. Although in order to qualify for certain employment protection rights such as the right not to be unfairly dismissed agency workers will still need to demonstrate they are employees.

14.4   SOME LEGAL CONSEQUENCES OF THE DISTINCTION
(The lists set out below are not exhaustive.)

For the employee
Rights
An employee enjoys (subject to satisfaction of the qualifying conditions) the following rights:

(1)   Unfair dismissal protection

(2)   Redundancy payment entitlement

(3)   Written particulars of terms of employment

(4)   Statutory minimum period of notice

(5)   Guarantee payment

(6)   Medical suspension payment

(7)   Protection from discrimination on grounds of race, sex, marital status, disability, gender reassignment, religion or belief or sexual orientation.

(8)   Equal pay

(9)   Maternity rights

(10)   Time off for trade union activities, duties, etc

(11)   Not to be refused employment because of membership or non-membership of a trade union

(12)   To be employed for the agreed period or be given the agreed length of notice

(13)   To be provided with a safe place of work and to have reasonable care taken of his safety

(14)   To be paid statutory sick pay

(15)   To be paid his wages free of any deductions not properly authorised

(16)   In the case of those employed as shop workers or betting workers, the right to object to working on Sundays

(17)   To limits on working time and the right to paid holidays under the *Working Time Regulations 1998*

Obligations

(1)   To obey the employer's lawful orders

(2)   To work faithfully and with due diligence

(3)   To give the contractually agreed or statutory minimum period of notice to terminate the employment

(4)   To pay income tax by way of deductions under the PAYE scheme

(5)   To pay employee's National Insurance contributions

14.5   For the employer

Rights

These are:

(1)   To benefit from the employee's obligations set out above

Obligations

(1)   To observe the employee's rights set out above

(2)   To deduct tax under the PAYE scheme

(3)   To keep the necessary statutory sick pay records

(4)   To make the appropriate National Insurance contributions

14.6   Self-employed – the self-employed person

Rights

These are:

(1)   To benefit from all his contractual entitlements

(2)   Not to be discriminated against on grounds of race, sex, marital status, disability, gender reassignment, religion or belief or sexual orientation and to the right to claim equal pay with a comparator of the opposite sex

(3)   Where applicable, to be provided with a safe place and safe system of work

(4)   To be paid his wages free of any deductions not properly authorised

(5)   To limits on working time and to the benefit of annual leave in accordance with the *Working Time Regulations 1998*

Obligations

(1)   To fulfil his contractual obligations

(2)   To work with due skill and diligence

(3)   To pay income tax under *Schedule D*

(4)   To pay self-employed person's National Insurance contributions

14.7   Self-employed – the person who engages a self-employed person

Rights

These are:

(1)   To benefit from the self-employed person's contractual obligations

Obligations

(1)   To observe the self-employed person's rights set out above

14.8 Employee, Self-Employed or Worker?

14.8 Employees and office-holders

Another distinction may be identified between employees who are employed under a contract of employment and 'office-holders' who may not be employees or have the rights of employees (such as the right to complain of unfair dismissal). In *Johnson v Ryan* [2000] ICR 236, the worker was a local authority rent officer appointed pursuant to the *Rent Act 1977*. It was argued that, as an office-holder, the worker was not entitled to present a claim of unfair dismissal. The EAT identified three categories of 'office-holder'. First, those whose rights and duties are defined by the office they hold and not by any contract. An example is police officers. Second, persons who are called office-holders but who in reality are employed under contracts of service. Third, those who are both employees and office-holders. An example is company directors. In determining whether a worker who is described as an office-holder is an employee, the factual situation must be considered. Relevant matters include whether the worker receives a salary, whether the salary was fixed and whether the worker's duties were subject to close control by the employer or whether the worker worked independently. The EAT held that a rent officer was an employee. In doing so, it noted that the recent approach of the appellate courts had been to take an inclusive approach to employee protection (see generally PUBLIC SECTOR EMPLOYEES (35)).

In *Percy v Board of National Mission of the Church of Scotland* [2005] UKHL 73, [2006] 2 WLR 353, [2006] ICR 134, the House of Lords held that a minister of the Church of Scotland was employed within the broader meaning of that term in the Sex Discrimination Act. Holding an office and being an employee were not mutually exclusive. The legal question is whether there was an intention to create legal relations. The Court of Appeal adopted the same approach in *New Testament Church of God v Stewart* [2008] IRLR 134, but added that in deciding whether there was the necessary intention, one had to have regard to the religious principles of the church in question. If those principles precluded a legally binding relationship between the church and the minister, it could mean that no contract of employment would be found.

O'Brien v Ministry of Justice [2013] UKSC 6, [2013] ICR 499, [2013] IRLR 315 considers the position of part-time fee paid recorders. The Supreme Court has confirmed that part-time fee paid recorders are engaged in an employment relationship by the Ministry of Justice and are 'workers'. The court also held that there was no objective justification for not providing part-time fee paid record with *pro rata temporis* pension rights.

14.9 Workers

It has already been indicated that many of the provisions of employment legislation providing protection to individuals are not confined to those who are to be regarded in law as employees. Much protection is accorded to those who satisfy the definition of 'worker'.

That definition (found, for example, in *section 230* of *ERA* and in similar form in the *Working Time Regulations* and elsewhere) is wider than the definition of employee because it includes those who undertake to 'do or perform personally any work or services for another party to the contracts whose status is not by virtue of the contract that of a client or customer of any profession or business undertaking carried on by the individual'.

This wider definition applies to a number of employment rights which are referred to in the start of this chapter. Reference should be made to each individual chapter for an explanation of the classes of person who benefit from the right. However, because there are now so many provisions which protect 'workers', this chapter seeks to provide an introduction to that concept.

The definition can be seen as comprising two elements. First the individual must be under an obligation personally to do work. Second, the person for whom the work is done must not be a client or customer of a business being run by the individual. The second limb is obviously necessary because otherwise the truly self-employed would be caught by a definition which required only that the person do work personally.

Several cases have considered what is meant by the definition of worker. The cases are decided under different provisions, but because the definition is the same, no distinction needs to be drawn based on the legal context of the decision. It is legitimate to consider decisions under the discrimination legislation and under other provisions which use the term worker, such as the *National Minimum Wage Act* and the *Working Time Regulations*.

In *James v Redcats (Brands) Ltd* [2007] IRLR 296, the EAT held that one had to draw a careful distinction between employees, workers and those engaged in their own business. When a right extended to workers, it was only the last category that was excluded. The EAT referred to cases such as *Lee v Chung* (cited above) and said that the dichotomy suggested in those cases between employees and the self-employed could be too simple. It was necessary also to draw a further distinction between those in business on their own account and workers. The EAT suggested that it was useful to consider a 'dominant purpose' test, derived from discrimination cases. If the dominant feature of the arrangement was that the person was to provide personal service then, even if the prerequisites of employment were missing, the person was likely to be a worker. Where a genuine right to substitution exists there is no personal service and there cannot be worker status. It is not sufficient that the individual might be obliged to personally find a substitute if unable to work (see *Community Dental Centres Ltd v Sultan-Darmon* [2010] IRLR 1024).

The leading case is now *Jivraj v Haswani* [2011] UKSC 40, [2011] ICR 1004, [2011] IRLR 827, in which the Supreme Court held that the correct test is whether the contract provides for services to be rendered by an independent contractor or whether the service provider consents to work under the control of another, and is therefore a worker. The Court concluded that an arbitrator was outside this definition due to a lack of control or subordination.

Byrne Bros (Formworks) Ltd v Baird [2002] IRLR 96 was a case under the *Working Time Regulations*. The EAT concluded that labour-only sub-contractors had been correctly identified as workers notwithstanding that they had a limited power to send a substitute, the individuals were still under a personal obligation. Referring to the second part of the definition, the EAT said that the aim was to extend protection to an intermediate class of person between employees and those who are carrying on business on their own account. Such people, although not employees, are subordinate to the person for whom they work and hence in need of protection. The EAT said that a consideration of who was a worker would involve the same sorts of factors as are considered in deciding who is an employee 'but with the boundary pushed further in the putative worker's favour'. In *Wright v Redrow Homes (Yorkshire) Ltd* [2004] EWCA Civ 469, [2004] 3 All ER 98, [2004] ICR 1126, [2004] IRLR 720 the Court of Appeal held that the question whether there was an obligation to undertake work personally depended on the terms of the contract and not what happened in practice. Pill LJ cautioned against relying too heavily on policy reasons when deciding who was a worker.

In dealing with the second part of the definition (that the person for whom the work is done is not a client or customer of a business undertaken by an individual), the EAT in *Cotswold Developments Construction Ltd v Williams* [2006] IRLR 181 suggested that the paradigm case of a person who did work for clients was a professional such as a solicitor or barrister. The paradigm case of a person who did work for customers was the owner of a shop or a tradesman such as a domestic plumber. The EAT suggested that a helpful test would be to consider whether the individual marketed his services to the public generally (in which case he would not be a worker) or whether he was integrated into the business of his principal (in which case he would be a worker).

The cases thus distinguish between those who are running their own business and those who, although not employed, are providing services as a part of another's business. In *Bacica v Muir* [2006] IRLR 35, the EAT suggested that factors such as working on the basis of a CIS certificate (in the construction industry), having accounts prepared for submission to

14.9 Employee, Self-Employed or Worker?

the Inland Revenue, being free to work for others and in fact doing so, being paid a rate which included an overhead allowance and not being paid when not working were all factors indicating that a person was undertaking his own business.

The Supreme Court has confirmed that unpaid volunteers are not workers: *X v Mid Sussex Citizens Advice Bureau* [2013] All ER 1038.

15   Employee Participation

15.1   OVERVIEW

There was, until fairly recently, little statutory provision in the UK for employees to participate or become involved in the affairs of the organisations in which they work. Some legislation in the 1970s (the *Health and Safety at Work Act 1974* and the *Employment Protection Act 1975*) compelled employers with recognised trade unions to consult with their employees on such matters as health and safety, disclosure of information and on redundancies. European Community obligations led to further legislation, widening consultation requirements in the case of redundancies, transfers of undertakings, and health and safety. Further legislation was introduced by the Labour Government. For example, the *ERA 1999* requires employers to recognise trade unions where this is desired by a majority of the relevant workforce (see TRADE UNIONS – I (48)). Separately, workforce consultation was incorporated into the bidding process of the Private Finance Initiative.

The statutory landscape has now changed dramatically, however, as a result of legislation originating at EU level. The *Social Protocol* to the *Maastricht Treaty on European Union* gave the EU the power, *inter alia*, to adopt directives concerning the information and consultation of workers. The *Treaty* came into force on 1 November 1993. At the time, the United Kingdom 'opted out' of the *Social Protocol*. However, the Labour Government which came to power in 1997 ended the opt-out. On 1 May 1999 the Treaty of Amsterdam came into effect, incorporating the *Social Protocol* into the *EC Treaty* (see further EUROPEAN UNION LAW (22)). One effect of this has been to give increased emphasis to securing framework agreements on social legislation through negotiation between European-level trade union and employer bodies (the 'social partners'). One such agreement resulted in the *Directive on Parental Leave (96/34)* (see generally MATERNITY AND PARENTAL RIGHTS (31)).

There are now five separate EU measures relating to informing and consulting employees and employee participation:

(1)   The *European Works Council Directive (94/45)*, adopted in September 1994, was the first employment measure adopted under the *Social Protocol*. This places obligations on companies with more than 1,000 employees, including at least 150 employees in a second European member state, and was implemented in national legislation by the *Transnational Information and Consultation of Employees Regulations 1999 (SI 1999/3323)*. A recast *European Works Council Directive* was agreed in May 2009 and came into force, in the main, in June 2011. The *1999 Regulations* were amended with effect, in the main, from 5 June 2011 to reflect this (see below **15.22**).

(2)   The original *European Works Council Directive* was followed by *Directive 2002/14/EC* 'establishing a general framework for informing and consulting employees in the European Community'. This places obligations on smaller, national companies and was implemented into domestic law by the *Information and Consultation of Employees Regulations 2004 (SI 2004/3426)*, as amended by *SI 2006/514* (see below **15.4**).

(3)   The *European Company Statute* (consisting of *EU Council Regulation 2157/2001* and *Directive 2001/86/EC*) enables companies operating in more than one member state to be established as a single company under EC law. This was originally implemented domestically by the *European Public Limited-Liability Company Regulations 2004 (SI 2004/2326)* and is now implemented, in Great Britain, by the *European Public Limited-Liability Company (Employee Involvement) (Great Britain) Regulations 2009 (SI 2009/2401)* (see below **15.30**).

15.1 Employee Participation

(4)   Similar provisions apply to European Cooperative Societies under *Regulation 1435/03* and *Directive 2003/72/EC*, implemented domestically by the *European Cooperative Society Regulations 2006 (SI 2006/2059)*.

(5)   Finally, EC rules in relation to employee participation following cross-border mergers between companies, contained in *Directive 2005/56/EC*, have been implemented domestically by the *Companies (Cross-Border Mergers) Regulations 2007 (SI 2007/2974)*.

Amendments have been made to the various sets of regulations to give effect to the *Agency Workers Regulations 2010 (SI 2010/93)*.

These various sets of regulations are detailed and complex, running cumulatively to many hundreds of pages. This chapter provides an overview of the main provisions. However, regard should be had to the regulations in their entirety. Practitioners advising on issues under any of the regulations will also, of course, be well advised to consider authorities decided under each set of regulations in relation to the comparable provisions of the other EU and domestic measures.

Decisions of the Central Arbitration Committee ('CAC') (and other information and consultation legislation) are available at: www.cac.gov.uk/index.aspx?articleid=2389.

15.2   OBLIGATIONS OF COMPANY DIRECTORS

Directors to have regard for interests of employees

By the *Companies Act 2006 ('CA 2006')*, *s 172*, a director of a company must act in the way he considers, in good faith, would be most likely to promote the success of the company for the benefits of its members as a whole. In doing so, he must have regard to six mandatory considerations, including the interests of the company's employees (*CA 2006, s 172(1)*). This duty is owed to the company alone (not to individual employees): *CA 2006, s 170*. However, shareholders (including employee shareholders) may enforce the *s 172* duty with the court's permission, by means of a derivative action on behalf of the company under *CA 2006, s 260*.

15.3   Directors' reports

By the *Large and Medium-sized Companies and Groups (Accounts and Reports) Regulations 2008 (SI 2008/410) ('the Reports Regulations')*, *reg 10* and *Sch 7, para 11* (together with the *CA 2006, ss 415* and *416*), the directors' report for any company which employs over 250 persons on average in each week during the relevant financial year must contain a statement describing the action that has been taken during that financial year to introduce, maintain or develop arrangements aimed at:

(a)   providing employees systematically with information on matters of concern to them as employees;

(b)   consulting employees or their representatives on a regular basis so that the views of employees can be taken into account in making decisions which are likely to affect their interests;

(c)   encouraging the involvement of employees in the company's performance through an employees' share scheme or by some other means;

(d)   achieving a common awareness on the part of all employees of the financial and economic factors affecting the performance of the company.

15.4   THE INFORMATION AND CONSULTATION OF EMPLOYEES REGULATIONS 2004

In February 2002, EC member states adopted *Directive 2002/14/EC* 'establishing a general framework for informing and consulting employees in the European Community'. The *Directive* provides for undertakings with at least 50 employees in any one member state to provide their employees with information and to consult with them over a wide range of issues concerning the operation of the organisation. As the ECJ noted in *Holst v Dansk Arbejdsgiverforening*: C-405/08 [2010] 2 CMLR 49, the *Directive* envisages that Member States may allow management and the workforce to play a leading role in its implementation, although it remains the responsibility of Member States to ensure that all workers are afforded the full protection for which the *Directive* provides.

The *Directive* has been implemented into domestic law by the *Information and Consultation of Employees Regulations 2004 (SI 2004/3426)*, as amended (the '*ICE Regulations*').

- The *ICE Regulations* were made under *s 42* of the *Employment Relations Act 2004*. Their purpose, as explained by the EAT in *Darnton v Bournemouth University* [2010] ICR 524 at [2], is "*to provide for the establishment of arrangements under which employees can be informed and consulted by their employers about matters of mutual concern*".

- Guidance on the *ICE Regulations* is available on the BIS website: www.bis.gov.uk/policies/employment-matters/rights/info-con. This includes the detailed guidance issued by the DTI (as was) in January 2006: www.bis.gov.uk/files/file25934.pdf. However, this guidance "has no special status": see the EAT in *Darnton v Bournemouth University* [2010] ICR 524 at [18] and the CAC in *Coombs & Holder v GE Aviation Systems Ltd* IC/43/(2012) at §55.

15.5

Employees in undertakings with 50 or more employees in the United Kingdom have a right to be informed and consulted on a regular basis about issues in the organisation for which they work: see *reg 3* and *sch 1* to the *ICE Regulations*. (The *ICE Regulations* applied originally only to undertakings with 150 or more employees, but this threshold has gradually been reduced.)

The number of employees in an undertaking is calculated by taking the average number of employees employed by the employer over the preceding 12-month period (*reg 4(1), (2)*). Employees who work for less than 75 hours in each month may count as 'half' an employee for this purpose (*reg 4(3)*).

From 1 October 2011, by virtue of the *Agency Workers Regulations 2011 (SI 2010/93)*, an agency worker who has a contract with a temporary work agency shall be treated as an employee of that agency for these purposes for the duration of his or her assignment (*reg 3A*).

15.6   Undertakings

The *ICE Regulations* apply to 'undertakings' whose registered office, head office or principal place of business is situated in Great Britain (*reg 3*). Where the registered office is in Great Britain, and the head office or principal place of business is in Northern Ireland, or vice versa, the *ICE Regulations* only apply where the majority of employees are employed to work in Great Britain.

An undertaking is defined as a 'public or private undertaking carrying out an economic activity, whether or not operating for gain' (*reg 2*). This will cover almost all employers. However, there is uncertainty about whether particular parts of the public sector are carrying out economic activities: see eg *Henke v Gemeinde Schierke and Verwaltungsgemein-schaft Brocken*: C-298/94 [1996] ECR I-4989, [1997] ICR 746, ECJ, *Mayeur v Association Promotion de l'Information Messine (APIM)*: C-175/99 [2002] ICR 1316, ECJ and *Collino v Telecom Italia SpA*: C-343/98 [2000] ECR I-6659, [2002] ICR 38, ECJ; cf. the definition of 'undertaking' in the *Transfer of Undertakings (Protection of Employment Regulations 1981 (SI 1981/1794)* and the authorities in relation thereto (**50.3** TRANSFER OF UNDERTAKINGS).

The DTI Guidance suggests (in paragraph 5) that, in the case of a company, the definition of an undertaking in the *ICE Regulations* covers separately incorporated legal entities, rather than organisational entities such as an establishment, division or business unit. The CAC reached the same conclusion in *Coombs & Holder v GE Aviation Systems Ltd* IC/43/(2012) by reference to the language of the *ICE Regulations*, holding – without any enthusiasm – that an undertaking meant a single legal entity capable of being an employer, and that a group of legal entities was not itself an undertaking.

15.7   Employee requests for data

Employees or their representatives have the right to make a written request for their employer to supply them with data for the purpose of ascertaining the number of people employed by the employer in the UK (and therefore whether or not the *ICE Regulations* apply) (*reg 5*).

A complaint that an employer has failed to provide the data, referred to in *reg 5(3)*, or that the data is false or incomplete in a material particular, may be presented to the CAC up to one month after the date of the request (*reg 6*). Where the CAC finds the complaint to be well-founded, it will order the employer to disclose the data to the complainant (*reg 6(2)*).

15.8   Initiation of obligations under the ICE Regulations

The obligations under the *ICE Regulations* to inform and consult do not apply automatically, even where the employer has sufficient employees for the *ICE Regulations* to apply in principle. Instead, the obligations must be initiated by either the employer or the employees.

15.9   *Initiation by the Employer*

Employers may initiate negotiations under the *ICE Regulations* by giving notice in writing in accordance with *reg 11(1)*. Notice must be published in such a manner as to bring it to the attention of all the employees of the undertaking, so far as is reasonably practicable (*reg 11(2)*).

15.10   *Employee Requests*

In addition, an employer must generally initiate negotiations for an agreement in respect of information and consultation where it receives a valid employee request (*reg 7(1)*). To be valid, an employee request must be made by at least 10% of the employees in the undertaking (subject to a minimum of 15 and a maximum of 2,500 employees), either as a single request or a number of separate requests over a six-month period (*reg 7(1)–(3)*). Requests must be in writing and sent to the registered office, head office or principal place of business of the employer, or to the CAC (*reg 7(4)*). A request must specify the names of the employee(s) making it and the date on which it is sent (*reg 7(4)*). Where the request is sent to the CAC, the CAC is then required to notify the employer of the request, request from the employer such information as it needs to verify the number and names of the employees who have made the request, and inform the employer and the employees who have made the request how many employees have made the request (*reg 7(5)–(6)*).

General Considerations

15.11   As a general rule, no employee may request negotiation (or renegotiation) of any agreement, and no employer may give notice of an intention to negotiate (or renegotiate) any agreement within three years of:

(a)   the date of the conclusion of any negotiated agreement under the *ICE Regulations* (see below **15.14**); or

(b)   the date when the standard information and consultation provisions began to apply (see below **15.15**, but note the provision in *reg 18(2)* for the renegotiation of the standard provisions 'at any time'); or

(c)   the date of the employee request, where the employer has held a ballot following an employee request which has resulted in endorsement of a pre-existing agreement (see below **15.17** (*reg 12(1)*)).

There is an exception to the general rule where there are material changes in the undertaking during the three-year period having the result that an agreement in force no longer covers all the employees of the undertaking, or, if it is a pre-existing agreement (as to which see below **15.17**) can no longer be said to have been approved by all the employees of the undertaking (*reg 12(2)*).

If the employer considers that there was no valid employee request, or an employee (or employee's representative) considers that an employer notification was not valid, a complaint may be presented to the CAC (*reg 13(1), (2)*). Complaints must be presented to the CAC within one month of the date of the employee request or the date of the employer notification (*reg 13(3)*). If the CAC finds the complaint made out, it may make a declaration to that effect (*reg 13(1)–(2)*).

Note that in order to initiate negotiations for an agreement in relation to employees in more than one undertaking, it is necessary for there to be a valid employee request or employer notification in relation to each undertaking (*reg 14(6)*).

15.12 Negotiated agreements

Where a valid employee request has been made or employer notice has been given (see above **15.8–15.11**), the employer is obliged to initiate negotiations by taking the steps set out in *reg 14*. The employer must, as soon as reasonably practicable:

(a)   make arrangements satisfying the requirements of *reg 14(2)* for the employees of the undertaking to elect or appoint negotiating representatives;

(b)   inform the employees in writing of the identity of the negotiating representatives; and

(c)   invite the negotiating representatives to enter into negotiations to reach a negotiated agreement (*reg 14(1), (2)*).

Reg 14(1) requires an employer to take these steps as soon as reasonably practicable. In *Darnton v Bournemouth University* [2010] ICR 524, the EAT rejected an argument that there is any implied requirement in *reg 14* for an employer to do so in any event within three months of the employee request. Whilst this appears to be what the DTI Guidance issued in 2006 envisaged, and whilst the EAT recognised that it would be unusual for it not to be reasonably practicable to complete these steps within three months of the employee request, the statutory requirement is simply as stated in *reg 14(1)*: "as soon as reasonably practicable".

As to the election or appointment of negotiating representatives, there are only two requirements in *reg 14(2)*: (i) the election or appointment must be arranged in such a way that all employees of the undertaking are represented by one or more representatives; and (ii) all employees of the undertaking must be entitled to take part in the election or appointment of the representatives and, if there is a ballot, all employees must be entitled to vote in the ballot.

15.13   Employee Participation

15.13 Complaints about the election or appointment of negotiating representatives

Complaints about the election or appointment of negotiating representatives may be made to the CAC within 21 days of the election or appointment (*reg 15(1)*). If the CAC finds the complaint well-founded it must make an order requiring the employer to arrange for the process of election or appointment to take place again (*reg 15(2)*).

15.14 Negotiated agreements

Once negotiating representatives have been appointed, the *ICE Regulations* are designed to encourage employers, employees and their representatives to agree information and consultation arrangements which suit their particular circumstances. Thus, the *ICE Regulations* specifically require employer and employee representatives to work in a spirit of co-operation (*reg 21*).

The *ICE Regulations* are notably non-prescriptive with respect to the substance of the arrangements for information and consultation, for example as to the subjects, method, timing or frequency of any information provision or consultation. Guidance as to the possible content of an agreement may be gained from the standard information and consultation provisions, which will apply in default if the parties fail to reach a negotiated agreement (see below **15.15**).

There are, however, some express requirements with which any negotiated agreement must comply (*reg 16(1)*). Any agreement must:

(a)   Cover all employees of the undertaking (either in a single agreement or in different parts);

(b)   Set out the circumstances in which the employer must inform and consult the employees to which it relates;

(c)   Be in writing;

(d)   Be dated;

(e)   Be approved by the employees in accordance with the *ICE Regulations* (see below);

(f)   Be signed by or on behalf of the employer;

(g)   Either:

    (i)   provide for the appointment or election of information and consultation representatives to whom the employer must provide the information and whom the employer must consult; or

    (ii)   provide that the employer must provide information directly to the employees to which it relates and consult those employees directly; and

(h)   Provide that where an employer is to provide information about the employment situation under any part of that agreement, that information shall include suitable information relating to the use of agency workers in that undertaking.

In addition, to be valid, a negotiated agreement must have been signed by all the negotiating representatives, or, if it is only signed by a majority of the negotiating representatives, it must have been approved by at least 50% of the employees in the undertaking either: (i) in writing, or (ii) in a ballot (*reg 16(3), (4)*).

If a ballot is held:

(a)   The employer must make such arrangements as are reasonably practicable to ensure that the ballot is fair, all employees must be entitled to vote, and the ballot must be conducted so as to secure that those voting do so in secret (again so far as is reasonably practicable) and the votes given in the ballot are accurately counted (*reg 16(5)*).

(b)   The employer must inform all employees entitled to vote of the result of the ballot as soon as is reasonably practicable (*reg 16(6)*).

(c)   A complaint may be presented to the CAC in circumstances where an employee representative considers that the ballot for approval of a negotiated agreement has not complied with the *ICE Regulations* (*reg 17(1)*). Complaints may only be made by a negotiating representative (and not by an employee). They must be made within 21 days of the date of the ballot. If the CAC finds the complaint well-founded it must order the employer to re-run the ballot (*reg 17(2)*).

A time limit is set on negotiations: they may last (in the first instance) for no more than six months commencing at the end of the period of three months beginning with the date on which the valid employee request was made or the valid employer notification was issued (*reg 14(3)*). However, time spent holding a ballot to determine whether or not to use a pre-existing agreement rather than negotiate a new one (see below **15.17**) or on making an application to the CAC is ignored when calculating the six-month negotiating period (see *reg 14(3), (4)* for the detailed provisions on the calculation of time). If the employer and a majority of the negotiating representatives agree, before the end of the six-month period to extend the period for negotiation, it may be extended by such further period(s) as the parties agree (*reg 14(5)*). In its decision in *Darnton v Bournemouth University* (IC/22/2009) (20 May 2009, unreported) the CAC held in paragraph 62 that it was crucial, to satisfy the requirements of the *ICE Regulations* that any agreement to extend the negotiation period was reached prior to the expiry of the time-limit, that the agreement to extend was itself explicit and that the period covered by the extension was made clear.

15.15   Standard information and consultation provisions

Where no arrangements are agreed, standard provisions on information and consultation will apply automatically from six months after the date on which negotiations should have started (if they did not start) or on which the negotiating period ended (if agreement was not reached): *reg 18(1)*. The standard provisions are set out in *reg 20*. In summary, they require the employer:

(a)   to provide information and consultation representatives (as to the election and appointment of which, see below) with information on:

    (i)   the recent and probable development of the undertaking's activities and economic situation;

    (ii)   the situation, structure and probable development of employment within the undertaking and on any anticipatory measures envisaged, in particular, where there is a threat to employment within the undertaking (and from 1 October 2011 such information must include suitable information relating to the use of agency workers (if any) in that undertaking); and

    (iii)   decisions likely to lead to substantial changes in work organisation or in contractual relations, including those referred to in *ss 188–192* of the *Trade Union and Labour Relations (Consolidation) Act 1992* (see generally REDUNDANCY – **II**: PRACTICE AND PROCEDURE (**37**)) and *regs 13–16* of the *Transfer of Undertakings (Protection of Employment) Regulations 2006* (see **50.18** TRANSFER OF UNDERTAKINGS) (*reg 20(1)*);

(b)   to consult the information and consultation representatives as to developments, threats and changes to employment within the undertaking (*reg 20(3)*); and

(c)   to ensure that the timing, method and content of the consultation are appropriate, that it takes place with the appropriate level of management and that a reasoned response is given by the employer to any opinion expressed by the representatives (*reg 20(4)*).

The information in *(a)* above must be given at a time, in a fashion and with such content as are appropriate to enable the information and consultation representatives to conduct an adequate study and, where necessary, to prepare for consultation (*reg 20(2)*).

Note that although there is an obligation to inform and consult on developments, threats and changes to employment within the undertaking, the obligation under the *ICE Regulations* ceases once the duties in *s 188* of *TULR(C)A 1992* or *reg 13* of *TUPE* or *regs 11–13* of the *Pension Scheme Regulations* apply, provided that the employer gives notification in accordance with *reg 20(5)*.

15.16   Whenever the standard provisions are going to apply, there is an obligation on the employer to arrange for the holding of a ballot of its employees to elect information and consultation representatives (*reg 19(1)*). There must be one representative for every 50 employees (or part thereof), provided that there are always at least two and not more than 25 representatives (*reg 19(3)*). The requirements for the holding of ballots under *reg 19* are set out in *Sch 2*.

Complaints in relation to the conduct of a ballot for the election of information and consultation representatives may be made to the CAC by any employee or employees' representative (*reg 19(4)*). Where the CAC finds the complaint well-founded, it must order the employer to arrange, or re-arrange and hold the ballot (*reg 19(5)*). If such an order is made, the complainant employee or employee's representative may also make an application to the Employment Appeal Tribunal, within three months of the CAC's decision, for a penalty notice to be issued against the employer (*reg 19(6)*). See **15.20** below for the issue of penalties.

15.17 Pre-existing agreements

If a valid employee request to negotiate an agreement under the *ICE Regulations* is made by fewer than 40% of employees employed in the undertaking (see above **15.9**), but there is a pre-existing agreement which:

(a)   is in writing;

(b)   sets out how the employer is to give information to the employees or their representatives and seek their views on such information;

(c)   covers all the employees of the undertaking; and

(d)   has been approved by the employees,

the employer may, instead of initiating negotiations (see above **15.12**), hold a ballot to seek the endorsement of the employees for the employee request (*reg 8(1), (2)*). However, the option is only open to the employer where the employee request has been made by fewer than 40% of the employees employed in the undertaking (*reg 8(1)*).

Where the pre-existing agreement covers more than one undertaking, the employer may hold a combined ballot for all the undertakings so covered if the employee request either alone or aggregated with any requests made by employees in the other undertakings is made by fewer than 40% of the employees in all the undertakings (*reg 9(1), (2)*). However, even if the pre-existing agreement covers more than one undertaking, it is still open to the original undertaking to ballot only its own employees (*reg 9(3)*).

If the employer wishes to hold a ballot, he must inform the employees in writing within one month of the date of the employee request and arrange for the ballot to be held as soon as reasonably practicable thereafter (but no fewer than 21 days after the employer has informed the employees of its intention to hold a ballot): *reg 8(3)*. The requirements for the ballot are the same as for the ballot for employee approval of a negotiated agreement where only a majority of the negotiating representatives have signed the agreement (see above **15.14**), save that the employees are only to be regarded as having endorsed the employee request if at least 40% of the employees employed in the undertaking and the majority of the employees who vote in the ballot have voted in favour of endorsing the request (*reg 8(4), (6)*).

If the employees endorse the employee request, the employer is under a duty to initiate negotiations as described in **15.12** above (*reg 8(5)(b)*). If the employees do not endorse the employee request, the employer is not under such an obligation (*reg 8(5)(c)*) and the pre-existing agreement will continue to govern information and consultation within the undertaking.

An employee or employees' representative who believes that the employer has not complied with the requirements of the *ICE Regulations* in relation to the holding of a ballot to endorse an employee request may complain to the CAC (*regs 8(7)–(8)* and *10*). There is a time limit of 21 days for the bringing of complaints, which runs from the date the employer informed the employees of its intention to hold a ballot (if it is the employer's entitlement to hold a ballot that is disputed) or from the date of the ballot (if it is alleged that the employer has failed to comply with a ballot requirement): *reg 10(1), (2)*. There is no time limit for complaints that an employer has failed to inform employees that it intends to hold a ballot, or (having announced that it intends to hold a ballot) fails to hold it within the requisite time period (*reg 8(7), (8)*). Where the CAC finds the complaint well-founded, it shall or may (as appropriate) order the employer to hold the ballot (*regs 8(9)* and *10(3)(c)*) or commence negotiations in accordance with the procedure described at **15.12** above: *reg 10(3)(a), (b)* and *(c)(i)*.

From 1 October 2011, where information about the employment situation is to be provided by an employer under a pre-existing agreement, such information must include suitable information relating to the use of agency workers (if any) in that undertaking (*reg 8A*).

15.18 In *Stewart (J) v Moray Council* [2006] ICR 1253, [2006] IRLR 592 the EAT concluded that, where an undertaking had in place multiple agreements relating to the provision of information to its employees, the requirement under *reg 8(1)(b)* of the *ICE Regulations* that a pre-existing agreement should cover all the employees of that undertaking was met by all the agreements read together. However, each of the other requirements under *reg 8(1)* had to be met by each individual agreement so that the provisions relating to the holding of a ballot could apply. The EAT also held that employees are covered by the terms of a collective agreement within the meaning of *reg 8(1)(b)* if that agreement is intended to regulate their terms and conditions (whether or not they are union members) or if they fall within a category of employees intended to be regulated by that agreement. Further, *reg 8(1)(c)* does not prescribe any particular way in which employee approval needs to be demonstrated (eg by ballot or by written support): this is a matter of fact for the CAC. The EAT considered that it would usually (but not always) be legitimate to infer approval if, at the time the agreement was made, the majority of the employees covered by the agreement were members of the union or unions which are parties to that agreement.

15.19 Confidential information

An employer is not required to disclose any information or document for the purposes of the *ICE Regulations* where the nature of the information or document is such that, according to objective criteria, its disclosure would seriously harm the functioning of, or would be prejudicial to, the undertaking (*reg 26(1)*). Any dispute between an employer and information and consultation or employee representatives in relation to the nature of information or a document that an employer has refused to disclose may be referred to the CAC (*reg 26(2)*). The CAC has power to order the disclosure of the information or document where it considers that disclosure would not be seriously harmful or prejudicial, and has power to prescribe the terms on which it should be disclosed (*reg 26(3), (4)*).

If an employer discloses any information or document, pursuant to its obligations under the *ICE Regulations*, and requires that information or document to be held in confidence and not to be disclosed to others except, where terms permit him to do so, in accordance with those terms, then any disclosure by the recipient in breach of those terms will be actionable by the employer as a breach of statutory duty (*reg 25(1)–(3)*). This is in addition to any right which any person might have in relation to that disclosure otherwise than under the *ICE Regulations* (*reg 25(4)*). The employer will not, however, have any right of action for breach of statutory duty under the *ICE Regulations* if the recipient reasonably believed the disclosure to be a 'protected disclosure' within the meaning of *s 43A* of the *Employment Rights Act 1996* (*reg 25(5)*) and see **9.17–9.18 DISCLOSURE OF INFORMATION.**

There is a right for a recipient to apply to the CAC for a declaration that it was unreasonable for the employer to require him to hold the information or document in confidence (*reg 25(6)*). If the CAC considers that disclosure of the information or document by the recipient would not, or would not be likely to, harm the legitimate interests of the undertaking, it must make a declaration to that effect (*reg 25(7)*). Where it does so, the information or document shall not be regarded as having been entrusted to any recipient on terms requiring it to be held in confidence (*reg 25(8)*).

15.20   Complaints

In addition to the various rights to bring complaints to the CAC mentioned above, a complaint may be presented to the CAC where an employee representative considers that an employer is not acting in accordance with an agreement negotiated under the *ICE Regulations* or with the standard arrangements. The time limit for presenting complaints is three months from the date of the alleged failure. If the complaint is upheld, the CAC may make a declaration and order the employer to take such steps as are reasonable for it to take in order to comply with the terms of the negotiated agreement or the standard arrangements (see *reg 22(1)–(5)*).

If the CAC makes such a declaration (whether with or without such an order) an application may be made to the Employment Appeal Tribunal for a penalty notice to be issued, under which the employer may be required to pay up to £75,000 (*regs 22(6), (7)* and *23*). The time limit for such applications is three months from the date of the CAC's declaration (*reg 22(6)*).

In *Darnton v Bournemouth University (No 2)* (UKEAT/0391/09/RN) (4 March 2010, unreported) the EAT rejected an argument that the University had reasonable excuse for its failure to comply with the *ICE Regulations* within the meaning of *reg 22(7)*, such that no penalty notice should be issued. It held that simply taking a wrong view about a material matter was not, without more, sufficient to constitute a reasonable excuse (paragraph 9). It was not necessary for the EAT to determine whether reliance on mistake expert advice would constitute reasonable excuse as there was no sufficient evidence before it that the University had in fact relied on such advice.

Matters to be taken into account by the EAT when setting the amount of the penalty include: the gravity of the failure; the period of time over which the failure occurred; the reason for the failure; the number of employees affected by the failure; and the number of employees employed by the undertaking or, where a negotiated agreement covers employees in more than one undertaking, the number of employees employed by both or all of the undertakings (*reg 23(3)*). In *Darnton (No 2)*, paragraph 12, the EAT indicated that *"the assessment of the right level of penalty is in the nature of a broad evaluation, and a nice analysis of the weight to be given to individual components is unrealistic"*. It considered that it should have regard to all relevant considerations, which may cover a wide range and are not necessarily limited to those specific in *reg 23*. Moreover, assistance from other decided cases was not likely to be useful, including cases under the other jurisdictions. Similarly, in *Brown v G4 Security (Cheltenham)*, (UKEAT/0526/09/RN) [2010] All ER (D) 84 (Aug) the EAT reiterated that each case is fact-specific, that there is a need to take into account the matters listed in *reg 23* but that *reg 23* is not an exhaustive list: "Depending on the circumstances of the particular case additional factors may be taken into account and the weight of each of them will depend on the facts of the case under consideration." The EAT added, in *G4 Security*, that in its view, the number of employees in the undertaking was not particularly relevant in determining the gravity of the breach, as breach of obligations under the *ICE Regulations* affecting all employees in a small workforce may be almost as significant as a breach affecting a small proportion of a much larger workforce.

In *Amicus v Macmillan Publishers Ltd* [2007] IRLR 885, the EAT issued a penalty notice against Macmillan requiring it to pay £55,000. The penalty notice was issued in circumstances where the EAT found that Macmillan had adopted a 'wholly cavalier attitude' to its obligations under the *ICE Regulations* (see also the CAC decision reported at [2007] IRLR 378). In contrast, in *Darnton (No 2)*, the EAT imposed a penalty of £10,000. It held that the fact that the breach complained of was not deliberate and did not result from any deliberate disregard of the University's obligations under the *ICE Regulations* or even an attitude of carelessness or insouciance towards those obligations, was an important mitigating factor, In addition, on the facts, 'shadow' information and consultation procedures had been in place for a considerable period. Nevertheless, the EAT was concerned to ensure that any penalty was more than negligible. It held that the scheme of the *ICE Regulations* required unexcused errors by the University to be marked by a real penalty. In *Brown v G4 Security (Cheltenham)*, UKEAT/0526/09/RN (27 April 2010), a penalty of £20,000 was imposed.

15.21 Employment protection

Employee representatives have the right to reasonable paid time off during working hours for the purpose of performing their functions as representatives (*regs 27, 28*). A complaint that an employer has unreasonably refused to permit the employee representative a reasonable amount of paid time off, or has failed to pay the whole or part of any amount to which the employee is entitled, may be presented to an employment tribunal (*reg 29(1)*). The time limit for bringing a complaint is 'three months beginning with the day on which the time off was taken or on which it is alleged the time off should have been permitted' (*reg 29(1)(2)(a)*). If the tribunal is satisfied that it was not reasonably practicable for the complaint to be presented before the end of the period of three months, then it may extend time for such further period as it considers reasonable (*reg 29(2)*). Where a tribunal finds a complaint well-founded, it must make a declaration and order the employer to pay the employee an amount equivalent to the amount of time off it should have allowed the employee, or the amount it should have paid the employee (as appropriate): *reg 29(3)–(5)*.

In relation to the right to time off work, see generally TIME OFF WORK (47).

An employee who is an employees' representative, negotiating representative, information and consultation representative or a candidate in an election to be any such representative, and who is dismissed is to be regarded as unfairly dismissed if the reason or (if more than one) the principal reason for dismissal is that the employee:

(a)   performed or proposed to perform any functions or activities as such a representative or candidate;

(b)   exercised or proposed to exercise an entitlement under *regs 27* or *28* to reasonable paid time off for performing any of those functions;

(c)   made or proposed to make a request to exercise such an entitlement (or did so through a person acting on his behalf).

(Reg 30.)

Such an employee is also protected from detriment on these grounds (*reg 32*).

In addition, an employee who is dismissed is to be regarded as unfairly dismissed if the reason or (if more than one) the principal reason for dismissal is that the employee:

(d)   exercised, or proposed to exercise, (in good faith) any entitlement to complain (or appeal) to an employment tribunal, the CAC or the EAT in connection with any rights conferred by the *ICE Regulations*;

(e)   requested, or proposed to request data in accordance with *reg 5* (above **15.7**);

(f)   acted with a view to securing that an agreement was or was not negotiated or that the standard information and consultation provisions did or did not become applicable;

(g)   indicated that he supported or did not support the coming into existence of a negotiated agreement or the application of the standard information and consultation provisions;

(h)   stood as a candidate in an election in which any person elected would, on being elected, be a negotiating representative or an information and consultation representative;

(i)   influenced or sought to influence by lawful means the way in which votes were to be cast by other employees in a ballot arranged under the *ICE Regulations*;

(j)   voted in such a ballot;

(k)   expressed doubts as to whether such a ballot had been properly conducted; or

(l)   proposed to do, failed to do, or proposed to decline to do, any of the things mentioned in sub-paragraphs (f) to (j) above.

(Reg 30 and ss 105(7H) and *108(3), ERA 1996.)*

Such an employee is also protected from detriment on these grounds (*reg 32*).

There is an exception where an employee has, in the performance of any of his functions or activities as a representative or candidate disclosed any confidential information in breach of the provisions of the *ICE Regulations* (*reg 30(4)* and see **15.19**). Such dismissals will be potentially fair, unless the employee reasonably believed the disclosure to be a 'protected disclosure' within the meaning of *s 43A* of the *Employment Rights Act 1996* (see **9.17–9.18** DISCLOSURE OF INFORMATION). See also generally **52.3** UNFAIR DISMISSAL- II: THE FAIRNESS OF THE DISMISSAL.

An employee also has the right not to be subjected to a detriment for any of the above actions (or inactions): *reg 32*. This is subject to an identical exception for protected disclosures (*reg 32(4)*). A complaint that an employee has been subjected to a detriment in contravention of *reg 32* may be presented to an employment tribunal in the same manner as complaints under the *Employment Rights Act 1996* for subjection to a detriment on other grounds (*reg 33*). Compare **48.37** TRADE UNIONS – I: NATURE AND LIABILITIES.

These requirements reflect *art 7* of the *Directive*, by which Member States are required to ensure that employees' representatives, when carrying out their functions, enjoy adequate protection and guarantees to enable them to perform properly the duties which have been assigned to them. In *Holst v Dansk Arbejdsgiverforening*: C-405/08 [2010] 2 CMLR 49 the ECJ indicated that the *Directive* does not require that any more extensive protection against dismissal be granted to employees' representatives. However, any measure adopted to transpose the *Directive*, whether provided for by legislation or by collective agreement, must comply with the minimum protection threshold laid down in *art 7*.

15.22 EUROPEAN WORKS COUNCILS

The original *European Works Council (EWC) Directive (94/45)* applied in EEA states except the UK from 22 September 1996, and was subsequently extended to the UK by *Directive 9//74*. A recast *EWC Directive 2009/38/EC* (the '*New Works Council Directive*'), which was agreed on 6 May 2009 and came into force, in the main, on 6 June 2011, has made a number of substantive changes to the original.

The purpose of the *Directives* is to improve the right to information and to consultation of employees in Community-scale undertakings and Community-scale groups of undertakings.

They require the establishment of an European-level information and consultation procedure or a European Works Council ('EWC') in all undertakings (or groups of undertakings) employing:

(a)   at least 1,000 workers in the EEA, with

(b)   at least 150 workers in each of at least two member states.

(The EEA comprises the EU member states, Norway, Iceland and Liechtenstein.)

15.23 The *Directives* have been implemented in national legislation by the *Transnational Information and Consultation of Employees Regulations 1999 (SI 1999/3323)* (as amended) (the '*TICE Regulations*').

The original *TICE Regulations*, as previously amended, were further amended to give effect to the *New Works Council Directive* by the *Transnational Information and Consultation of Employees (Amendment) Regulations 2010 (SI 2010/1088)*, made under *s 2(2)* of the *European Communities Act 1972*. These amendments came into force, in the main, on 5 June 2011. This chapter refers to the amended form of the *TICE Regulations*, save where otherwise stated.

BIS issued detailed guidance on the Amendment Regulations in April 2010, which is available   online: www.berr.gov.uk/assets/biscore/employment-matters/docs/10-888-transnational-information-consultation-regulations-2010-guidance.pdf.

There are significant differences between the *TICE Regulations* as they stand now and as they stood before 5 June 2011. Practitioners need to consider carefully whether the issue before them falls under the *TICE Regulations* in their pre-amendment or amended form. In outline terms, the amended *TICE Regulations* will apply to all EWCs save to the extent specified in *Part IX* and especially amended *regs 44–45A* (which exempt from most of the new provisions agreements establishing an EWC or information and consultation procedure which were signed between 5 June 2009 and 4 June 2011 or signed between 15 December 1999 and 4 June 2009 and then revised between 5 June 2009 and 4 June 2011, and certain forms of agreement in force prior to specified dates in the 1990s).

Note that the *TICE Regulations* do not apply to Community-scale undertakings which had pre-existing voluntary agreements in force before 23 September 1996 under the original *Directive* which cover the entire workforce, or to voluntary agreements made prior to 16 December 1999 by undertakings which are subject to the 15 January 2000 implementation date (*regs 44, 45*).

15.24 Number of employees

In order to determine whether an undertaking (or group of undertakings) has the necessary number of employees to qualify as a Community-scale undertaking (or group of undertakings) for the purposes of the *Directive* and *TICE Regulations*, an average is taken of the two years preceding the relevant date (*reg 6*). For UK employees this means adding together the number of UK employees in each month in the two year period preceding the relevant date (as defined in *reg 6(4)*) and dividing the total by 24 (see *reg 6(2)–(3)*). For this purpose, employees who are contracted to work 75 hours or less in a normal month without overtime may be counted as half an employee for that month if the UK management so decides (*reg 6(3)*). For employees elsewhere, calculations are to be made according to the law and practice of the member state concerned (*reg 6(1)(b)*).

When an employee or employees' representative seeks information to establish whether the organisation is part of a Community-scale undertaking (or group of undertakings), management must provide details of the average numbers of employees employed in the UK and in each of the other member states in the past two years (*reg 7*). As amended, *reg 7* also now requires management to obtain and provide information relating to the structure of the undertaking (or group of undertakings) and its workforce in the UK and in each of the other member states in the past two years, and to provide suitable information relating to the use of agency workers.

The CAC may order disclosure where the employer has failed to comply (*reg 8*).

In *Betriebsrat der Bofrost Josef H Boquoi Deutschland West GmbH & Co KG v Bofrost Josef H Boquoi Deutschland West GmbH & Co KG*: C-62/99 [2001] ECR I-2579, [2004] 2 CMLR 53, [2001] IRLR 403, the ECJ stated, in relation to *Directive 97/74*, that an undertaking which is part of a group is required to supply information on number of employees, etc to workers' representatives, even where it has not yet been established that the management to which the request for information is addressed is the management of a controlling undertaking within the group (see also *Betriebsrat der Firma ADS Anker GmbH v ADS Anker GmbH*: C-349/01 [2004] ECR I-6803, [2004] 3 CMLR 14, (2004) 763 IDS Brief 11 ('*ADS Anker*')). Workers are entitled to have access to information enabling them to ascertain whether they have the right to request that negotiations on an EWC be opened with central management. The sorts of information that the group may be obliged to supply includes information on the average total number of employees, their distribution across the member states, the establishments of the undertaking and the group undertakings, and on the structure of the undertaking and of the undertakings in the group, as well as the names and addresses of the employee representatives which might participate in the setting-up of an EWC (*Gesamtbetriebsrat der Kühne & Nagel AG & CoKG v Kühne & Nagel AG & Co KG*: C-440/00 [2004] ECR I-787, [2004] 2 CMLR 54, [2004] IRLR 332). The group's obligation to supply information extends only to such information as is 'essential' (*Kühne & Nagel*, paragraphs 64 and 69) to the opening of negotiations for establishing an EWC. In *ADS Anker* (above), the ECJ ruled that it was for the national court to determine what information was 'essential'.

Where the central management of a Community-scale group of undertakings is not located in an EU member state, then the management ('the deemed management') required to provide information to employees and employees' representatives is the management of the undertaking employing the greatest number of employees in any member state: *art 4(2)* of the *New Works Council Directive* and see *Kühne & Nagel*. In order to fulfil its obligations under the *New Works Council Directive*, the deemed management must request the information from other undertakings in the group and the other undertakings must supply that information to the deemed management.

15.25 Requests for an EWC

Central management situated in the UK is required to initiate negotiations for the establishment of a European Works Council ('an EWC') or an information and consultation procedure if it receives either:

(a)   a valid request from 100 employees or from employees' representatives who represent at least that number in at least two undertakings or establishments in at least two different member states; or

(b)   separate requests by employees or employees' representatives which, taken together, mean that 100 employees or employees' representatives representing that number have made requests in at least two undertakings or establishments in at least two different member states.

(Regulation 9(1), (2).)

All such requests must be in writing, dated (with the date of sending) and sent to central or local management (*reg 9(3)*). Alternatively, central management may initiate negotiations on its own initiative (*reg 9(5)*).

Such requests must be in writing, dated and sent to central or local management (*reg 9(3)*). Central management may initiate negotiations on its own initiative (*reg 9(5)*). Disputes over the validity of requests to set up an EWC are to be referred to the CAC within three months, and undertakings which consider that they have a valid voluntary agreement but which receive a request to establish an EWC may also apply to the CAC to decide the point (*reg 10*).

These requirements also apply where the central management is not situated in a member state and the representative agent of central management is located in the UK and, in other cases, where a UK-based establishment or group has more employees than other establishments or groups in member states (*reg 5(1)*).

15.26 Special negotiating body

A 'special negotiating body' ('SNB') is to be established to represent employees in their negotiations with management on the setting up of an EWC or arrangements for implementing an information and consultation procedure (*reg 11*). It consists of representatives of employees from all Member States in which employees are employed to work (*reg 12*). For SNBs constituted on or after 5 June 2011, employees in each Member State shall elect or appoint one SNB member for each 10% (or fraction of 10%) of the total number of employees in all Member States which those employees represent (*reg 12(2)*). (Under the old *TICE Regulations*, the number of representatives for each member state had been decided by a formula set by the state in which the central management (or representative agent if the central management is outside the EEA) was located.) The SNB is then required to inform central management and local managements and the European social partner organisations of its composition and of the date on which it proposes to start negotiations: *Regulation 12(4)*.

UK members of the SNB are to be elected by a ballot of UK employees. Requirements for the ballot are set out in *regs 13* and *14*. There is no need for a ballot where there already exists a consultative committee carrying out an information and consultation function whose members were elected by a ballot of UK employees (*reg 15*). In these circumstances the committee may nominate from its number UK representatives for the SNB as set out in *reg 15*.

Central management and the SNB must negotiate in a spirit of cooperation, with a view to reaching written agreement on the detailed arrangements for informing and consulting employees (*reg 17(1)*).

15.26   Employee Participation

In order to reach an EWC agreement, central management must convene a meeting with the SNB, informing local managements accordingly. SNBs are to take decisions by majority vote except that two-thirds of the votes are needed on a decision not to open, or to terminate, negotiations. The SNB may be assisted in these negotiations by experts, including representatives of European trade organisations (*reg 16(2)–(3)*). Any expert appointed by the SNB may, at the SNB's request, attend any meeting with central management under *reg 16(1)* in an advisory capacity.

SNB members are entitled to meet within a reasonable time both before and after any meeting with central management, without the central management or its representatives being present, using any means necessary for communication at those meetings (*reg 16(1A)*). Reasonable expenses relating to the negotiations necessary to enable the SNB to carry out its functions in an appropriate manner are to be borne by central management, including the expenses of one expert where applicable (*reg 16*).

15.27   Setting up an EWC

Where the SNB and central management agree to establish an EWC, the agreement must specify:

(a)   the undertakings or establishments covered;

(b)   the composition of the EWC, number of members, allocation of seats (taking into account, so far as reasonably practicable, the need for balanced representation of employees by role, gender and sector) and term of office of the members;

(c)   the functions and procedure for information and consultation of the EWC and arrangements to link this with information and consultation of national employee representation bodies;

(d)   the venue, frequency and duration of meetings;

(e)   where the parties decide that it is necessary to establish a select committee, the composition of the select committee, the procedure for appointing its members, the functions and the procedural rules;

(f)   the financial and material resources allocated to the EWC;

(g)   the date of entry into force of the agreement and its duration, the arrangements for amending or terminating the agreement, the circumstances in which the agreement is to be renegotiated including where the structure of the Community-scale undertaking or Community-scale group of undertakings changes and the procedure for renegotiation of the agreement.

(*Regulation 17(4)*.)

Central management and the SNB may decide in writing to establish an information and consultation procedure instead of an EWC (*reg 17(3)*). However, such agreement must specify a method by which the representatives can meet to discuss the information conveyed to them (*reg 17(5)*).

In addition, where information disclosed under an EWC agreement or an information and consultation procedure includes information as to the employment situation in the Community-scale undertaking or, as the case may be, the Community-scale group of undertakings, this must include suitable information relating to the use of agency workers (*reg 17(9)*).

A statutory EWC, governed by the *Schedule* to the *TICE Regulations* (as opposed to an EWC as described in *reg 17(4)* and *(6)*), is to be set up if:

(a)   the parties agree;

(b)   central management refuses to start negotiations within six months of the date on which a valid request was made; or

(c)   no agreement has been concluded within three years of the request being made, provided the SNB has not taken a decision to terminate (or not to start) negotiations.

(*Regulation 18.*)

The *Schedule* contains a 'statutory model' comprising a standard set of rules for the constitution of a statutory EWC governing its competence, composition, meetings and procedures. In particular, it lists topics about which the EWC is to be informed and consulted (see the *Schedule* at *para 7(3)–(4)*).

Central management and the EWC or information/consultation representatives are under a duty to work in a spirit of co-operation with due regard to their reciprocal rights and obligations (*reg 19*).

The amended *TICE Regulations* contain more detailed requirements as to the information to be provided by management to EWC members or to information and consultation representatives and as to consultation with such members or representatives than previously: see eg. the new *reg 18A*. From 1 October 2011, however, they limit information and consultation to transnational matters: *reg 18A*. They also introduce requirements to link information and consultation of EWCs with information and consultation of national employee representation bodies: see *reg 19E*. At the same time, the amended *TICE Regulations* require EWCs to inform employees' representatives or, if there are no such representatives, employees themselves, of the content and outcome of the information and consultation procedure (with a right of complaint to the CAC if they fail to do so): see *regs 19C–19D*.

The amended *Regulations* also contain a new focus on the 'means' required by an EWC. Thus they require central management to provide EWC members with the means to fulfil their duty to represent collectively the interests of the employees of the undertaking or group of undertakings concerned: see *reg 19A*. They also require central management to provide EWC members and SNB members with the means required to undertake any necessary training: see *regs 19B* and *25*.

Finally, the amended *Regulations* contain provision on 'adaptation' where there are significant changes in the structure of the Community-scale undertaking or group of undertakings: *reg 19F*.

The CAC will rule on disputes about the operation of an EWC or the failure to establish an EWC. If a complaint is well-founded, the CAC must make a decision to that effect and may make an order requiring central management to take appropriate steps by a specified date. In addition, on an application by a relevant applicant within three months of a CAC decision, the EAT will issue a penalty notice requiring central management to pay an amount to the Secretary of State (*regs 20, 21*). The maximum penalty to be imposed is £100,000 (*reg 22(2)*). The EAT also hears appeals on points of law from the CAC (*reg 38(8)*). Both the EAT and CAC may refer cases to ACAS if they believe that a dispute is reasonably likely to be settled by conciliation (*reg 39(1)*).

15.28 Confidential information

Present and former members of SNBs, EWCs, information/consultation representatives and relevant experts assisting them must not disclose information which central management requires to be kept confidential (*reg 23(1)*). Civil action may be taken by management for breach of this statutory duty of confidence except where the individual reasonably believed disclosure to be a protected disclosure within the meaning of *s 43A* of the *Employment Rights Act 1996*, as inserted by the *Public Interest Disclosure Act 1998* (*reg 23(1)–(5)*). Members or representatives can appeal to the CAC for a declaration if they believe UK central management is imposing confidentiality requirements unreasonably. A declaration will be made if the CAC considers that disclosure would not, or would not be likely to, 'prejudice or cause serious harm to the undertaking' (*reg 23(6)–(7)*).

Management may withhold any information which, according to objective criteria, would seriously harm the functioning of, or be prejudicial to, the undertaking. The CAC will rule on disputes over whether a document or information should be disclosed and will order disclosure where it considers, on objective criteria, that no serious harm or prejudice would result (*reg 24*).

15.29 Employment protection

Members of SNBs, EWCs, information/consultation representatives and candidates for election as such members are entitled to take reasonable time off work, with pay, to carry out their functions (*regs 25–27*). See TIME OFF WORK (**47**).

Such employees also have the right not to be subjected to a detriment by the employer on the ground that they performed their functions or activities or made a request for statutory time off or payment for time off or proposed to do so (*reg 31*). Additional rights not to be victimised apply to any employee whether or not he or she falls within the above categories. It is unlawful (by *reg 31(5), (6)*) to subject an employee to a detriment on the grounds that the employee:

(a) took proceedings in tribunal to enforce a right or entitlement under the *TICE Regulations* (provided any claim is made in good faith);

(b) exercised any entitlement to apply or complain to the EAT or CAC;

(c) requested information under *reg 7*;

(d) acted with a view to securing (or not securing) the setting up of an SNB, an EWC or information/consultation procedure;

(e) indicated that he supported (or did not support) the setting up of an SNB, an EWC or information/consultation procedure;

(f) stood as a candidate for election to be an SNB or EWC member or information/consultation representative, influenced or sought to influence how votes are cast in a ballot under the *TICE Regulations*, voted in such a ballot or questioned the conduct of the ballot; or

(g) proposed to do any of the above, or failed to do or proposed to decline to do, any of (d) to (f) above.

It is also automatically unfair under *reg 28* to dismiss an employee for such a reason (or for such a principal reason, where there is more than one reason) (see UNFAIR DISMISSAL – II (**52**)).

Complaints of detrimental treatment may be made to an employment tribunal within three months of the act or failure to act or, if that is not reasonably practicable, within such further period as the tribunal considers reasonable (*reg 32*). Compensation may be awarded if the complaint is well-founded, see *ERA 1996, s 49*. Complaints may be settled by ACAS conciliation or by valid compromise agreements (*reg 41*).

15.30 EUROPEAN COMPANIES (SES)

Longstanding proposals for a European Company Statute ('ECS'), which would allow European Companies or 'Societas Europaea' ('SEs') to be formed under European law, came to fruition on 8 October 2001 with the adoption by the EU Council of Ministers of *Regulation 2157/2001.*

The ECS gives companies operating in more than one member state, with a share capital of more than 120,000 Euro, the option of being established as a single company under EU law, able to operate throughout the EU with one set of rules and a unified reporting system. The *Regulation* is accompanied by a *Directive* on worker involvement (*Directive 2001/86/EC*).

15.31 The *Directive* and *Regulation* were originally implemented domestically by the *European Public Limited-Liability Company Regulations 2004 (SI 2004/2326)* (the '*EPLC Regulations*'). Under the *EPLC Regulations*, before an SE can be registered, the various companies or establishments involved in its creation must have complied with the requirements of *Regulation 2157/2001* in relation to the information, consultation and participation of employees (*reg 12*).

However, the *EPLC Regulations* were amended by *SI 2008/948* and, much more extensively, by *SI 2009/2400*, subject to transitional provisions in *SI 2009/2400 reg 2* and *Sch 2*. In particular, *SI 2009/2400* extended the reach of the *EPLC Regulations* to the entirety of the UK, and not just Great Britain. Most significantly for present purposes, *SI 2009/2400* revoked *Part 3* of the *EPLC Regulations* dealing with employee involvement.

Part 3 of the *EPLC Regulations* has been replaced since 1 October 2009 by the combination of:

(a)   The *European Public Limited-Liability Company (Employee Involvement) (Great Britain) Regulations 2009 (SI 2009/2401)*, applicable to SEs with a registered office in Great Britain (the 'GB Regulations'); and

(b)   The *European Public Limited-Liability Company (Employee Involvement) (Northern Ireland) Regulations (SI 2009/2402)*, applicable to SEs with a registered office in Northern Ireland.

This chapter addresses the *GB Regulations* only.

The Explanatory Memorandum states that there are no substantive differences between the *GB Regulations* and the prior provisions of *Part 3* of the *EPLC Regulations*.

The requirements of the *GB Regulations* apply whenever a company intends to establish an SE whose registered office is to be in Great Britain, or an SE has its registered office in Great Britain (*reg 4(1)*). In relation to the election or appointment of members of the 'special negotiating body' (below **15.33**) or employee representatives, the requirements apply whenever there are employees of the relevant company in Great Britain (*reg 4(2)*). In relation to matters of enforcement and employee protection, the GB Regulations also apply where any subsidiary or establishment of a relevant company or SE, or an employee or employees' representative, is registered or situated in Great Britain (*reg 4(3)*).

15.32 Employer's duty to provide information

Regulation 5 places a duty on the participating company (or companies) to provide information to employee representatives (or, if there are no such representatives, the employees themselves) whenever they decide to form an SE. The company must, as soon as possible after publishing the terms of any draft merger, or creating a holding company, or agreeing a plan to form a subsidiary or to transform into an SE, provide information to employees which, at least (by *reg 5(1), (2)*):

15.32   Employee Participation

(a)   identifies the participating companies, concerned subsidiaries and establishments;

(b)   gives the number of employees employed by each participating company and concerned subsidiary and at each concerned establishment; and

(c)   gives the number of employees employed to work in each EEA State; and

(d)   provides specified information in relation to agency workers (from 1 October 2011).

Complaints that a company has failed to provide information, or has provided information that is false or incomplete in a material particular may be presented to the CAC by an employee's representative or (if there is no such representative) an employee (*reg 6(1)*). If the CAC finds the complaint well-founded, it must order the disclosure of the information in question (*reg 6(2)*).

There is a continuing obligation on the company to provide information as to progress in establishing an SE (*reg 5(3)*). The obligation is to provide that information to the 'special negotiating body' (see below **15.33**).

15.33   The special negotiating body

The company or companies proposing to form an SE are obliged to set up a 'special negotiating body' ('SNB') (*reg 8(1)*). The function of the SNB is to reach an 'employee involvement agreement' with the participating companies (see below **15.34**). The SNB consists of employee representatives elected from the employees in each member state. The employees from each member state have the right to elect one representative for each 10% or fraction of 10% which those employees represent (and so on, *reg 8(2)*). Where more than one company is involved there must be at least one representative from each company (*reg 8(3)*). Employees must be informed of the identity of the members of the SNB as soon as practicable and in any event within one month of the election (*reg 8(5)*). There is provision for appointing additional members and for changing members in certain circumstances (*reg 8(4), (6)*).

Complaints in relation to the establishment of (or failure to establish) an SNB may be presented to the CAC by a person elected or appointed to the SNB, an employees' representative (or, if there is no such representative, the employee) or a participating company or concerned subsidiary (*reg 9(1)–(2)*). Complaints must be made within one month of the last date on which the participating companies complied or should have complied with the obligation to inform employees of the identity of members of the SNB (*reg 9(3)*). Where the CAC finds an application well-founded it must make a declaration to that effect and the participating companies will continue to be under an obligation to comply with their duties under the *GB Regulations* (*reg 9(4)*).

The requirements of the ballot for the election of representatives are set out in *regs 10* and *11*. Any UK employee or UK employees' representative who believes that the arrangements for the ballot of the UK employees do not comply with the requirements of the *GB Regulations* may present a complaint to the CAC (*reg 10(4)*). Complaints must be presented within a period of 21 days beginning on the date on which the management published the final arrangements for the ballot (*reg 10(4)*). Where the CAC finds the complaint well-founded it must make a declaration to that effect and may make an order requiring the management to modify the arrangements it has made for the ballot of UK employees so as to comply with the requirements of the *GB Regulations* (*reg 10(5)*).

Where there is already a 'consultative committee' within the organisation concerned, the company is relieved of the obligation to arrange a ballot and instead the 'consultative committee' is permitted to appoint one or more of its own members to the SNB (*regs 12(1)* and *(3)*). A 'consultative committee' is defined as a body of persons which represents all the employees of the participating company, consists wholly of persons who are employees of the participating company or its concerned subsidiaries, whose normal functions include carrying out 'an information and consultation function', and which is able to carry out its functions without interference from the management of the participating company (*reg 12(4)*). 'Information and consultation function' is defined in *reg 12(5)* as 'receiving, on behalf of all the employees of the participating company, information which may significantly affect the interests of the employees of that company, but excluding information which is relevant only to a specific aspect of the interests of the employees, such as health and safety or collective redundancies; and being consulted by the management of the participating company on that information'. Most trade unions will be 'consultative committees' within the *GB Regulations*.

Where such a consultative committee exists, it is entitled to appoint so many of its number (or, with the permission of the management of the participating company, a trade union representative who is not an employee of the company) to the SNB as that company would be entitled to elect under a ballot (*reg 12(2)*). The consultative committee must then publish the names of those it has appointed to the SNB in such a manner as to bring them to the attention of the management of the participating company and, so far as reasonably practicable, the employees and employees' representatives (and those of its concerned subsidiaries) (*reg 12(5)–(6)*).

Where the management of a participating company, an employee or an employee's representative believes that a 'consultative committee' does not fulfil the requirements of *reg 12*, or that the representative appointed by that committee is not entitled to be appointed, they may complain to the CAC (provided they do so within 21 days of the publication of the names of the representatives purportedly appointed by the consultative committee) (*reg 12(7)–(9)*). If the CAC finds the complaint well-founded, it must make a declaration (*reg 12(8)*). Any appointment made by the consultative committee will then be of no effect and appointment of representatives must thereafter be by ballot (*reg 12(9)*).

15.34   Negotiated employee involvement agreement

The task of the SNB is to reach an employee involvement agreement with the (proposed) SE (*reg 7*).

The parties are under a duty to negotiate in a spirit of co-operation (*reg 14(2)*). An initial six-month time limit is set within which to reach agreement, but with provision for extension for up to 12 months from the date the original time-limit began running by agreement between the parties (*reg 14(3)*).

There are no specific requirements as to the substance of the agreement to be reached on employee involvement, save that the elements of employee involvement at all levels must be at least as favourable as those which exist in the company to be transformed into an SE (*reg 15(4)*).

However, to be valid, the agreement must be in writing and must specify the agreement reached on certain key points (*by reg 15*):

(a)   the scope of the agreement;

(b)   the composition, number of members and allocation of seats on the representative body;

(c)   the functions and the procedure for the information and consultation of the representative body;

(d)   the frequency of meetings of the representative body;

(e)   the financial and material resources to be allocated to the representative body;

(f)   if, during negotiations, the parties have decided to establish one or more information and consultation procedures instead of a representative body, the agreement must specify the arrangements for implementing those procedures;

(g)   if, during negotiations, the parties have decided to establish arrangements for participation, the agreement must record the substance of those arrangements including (if applicable) the number of members in the SE's administrative or supervisory body which the employees will be entitled to elect, appoint, recommend or oppose, the procedures as to how these members may be elected, appointed, recommended or opposed by the employees, and their rights; and

(h)   in all cases, the date of entry into force of the agreement and its duration, the circumstances, if any, in which the agreement is required to be re-negotiated and the procedure for its re-negotiation.

In addition, from 1 October 2011, where under the employee involvement agreement the SE's competent organ is to provide information on the employment situation in that company, such information must include suitable information relating to the use of agency workers (*reg 15(3A)*).

There are specific rules as to how decisions must be taken by the SNB, and what level of majority is required for each sort of decision (an absolute majority generally, but two thirds where a decision would result in a reduction of participation rights) (*reg 16(1)–(3)*).

For the purpose of negotiations, the SNB may be assisted by experts of its choice (*reg 16(5)*). The participating company or companies must pay for any reasonable expenses of the SNB, though the company is not required to pay for the expenses of more than one expert (*reg 16(6)*).

The details of any decision taken by the SNB must be published to the employees represented on the body as soon as reasonably practicable and, in any event no later than 14 days after the decision has been taken (*reg 16(4)*).

Complaints in relation to decisions of the SNB may be presented to the CAC by a member of the SNB, an employees' representative, or where there is no such representative in respect of an employee, that employee (*reg 18(1)*). Complaints may only be presented on the grounds that (a) the decision was not taken by the requisite majority, or (b) that the SNB failed to publish a decision as required by the *GB Regulations*. The time limit for presentation of complaints is 21 days from the date the SNB did or should have published their decision. Where the CAC finds the complaint well-founded it must make a declaration that the decision was not taken properly and that it is to have no effect (*reg 18(2)*).

15.35 Standard rules on employee involvement

Where no employee involvement agreement has been reached within the six-month (or twelve-month extended) time limit in r*eg 14(3)*, or the parties have so agreed, the 'standard rules on employee involvement' will apply (*reg 19*). These are detailed and complex and are set out in the *Schedule* to the *GB Regulations*. In summary, however, the standard rules provide as follows:

(a)   The management of the SE must arrange for the establishment of a 'representative body';

(b)   The representative body must be composed of employees of the SE and its subsidiaries and establishments (one member for each 10% or fraction thereof of employees of the SE, its subsidiaries and establishments employed for the time being in each member state). Its members must be elected or appointed by the EEA of the SNB, by whatever method the SNB decides;

(c)   Once the representative body has been established for four years, it must decide whether to open negotiations with the management of the SE to reach an employee involvement agreement or whether the standard rules should continue to apply. If a decision is taken to open negotiations the procedure described at **15.34** above will apply, save that references to the SNB should be read as being references to the representative body;

(d)   For the purpose of informing and consulting on questions which concern the SE and any of its subsidiaries or establishments in another EEA state and questions which exceed the powers of the decision-making organ in a single EEA state, the management is obliged to:

    (i)   prepare and provide to the representative body regular reports on the progress of the business of the SE and the SE's prospects;

    (ii)   provide the representative body with the agenda for meetings of its administrative, management or supervisory committees and copies of all documents submitted to any general meeting of the SE's shareholders.

    (iii)   Inform the representative body when there are exceptional circumstances affecting the employees' interests to a considerable extent, particularly in the event of relocations, transfers, the closure of establishments or undertakings or collective redundancies;

(e)   If the representative body so desires, the management must meet with it at least once a year to discuss the reports on the progress of the business. Such meetings should relate, in particular, to the structure, economic and financial situation, the probable development of business and of production and sales, the situation and probable trend of employment, investments and substantial changes concerning organisation, introduction of new working methods or production processes, transfers of production, mergers, cut-backs or closures of undertakings, establishments or important parts thereof and collective redundancies;

(f)   Where there are exceptional circumstances affecting the employees' interests, the representative body (or, if it so decides, a select committee constituted in accordance with *paragraph 2* of the *Schedule* to the *GB Regulations*) must be permitted to meet with the most appropriate level of management and, if the SE does not act in accordance with the representative body's opinion as to what should be done in the circumstances, the representative body may request a further meeting to seek agreement;

(g)   The members of the representative body must inform the employees' representatives or, if no such representatives exist, the employees of the SE and its subsidiaries and establishments, of the content and outcome of the information and consultation procedures;

(h)   The representative body and the select committee of the representative body may be assisted by experts of its choice;

(i)   The costs of the representative body must be borne by the SE, which must also provide the members of that body with financial and material resources needed to enable them to perform their duties in an appropriate manner, including (unless agreed otherwise) the cost of organising meetings, providing interpretation facilities and accommodation and travelling expenses. However, again, where the representative body or the select committee is assisted by more than one expert the SE is not required to pay the expenses of more than one of them.

15.35 Employee Participation

Again, from 1 October 2011, where under the standard employee involvement agreement the SE's competent organ is to provide information on the employment situation in that company, such information must include suitable information relating to the use of agency workers (*Schedule, para 8A*).

15.36 Alternative arrangements

The members of the SNB may 'opt out' of any sort of employee involvement, in which case the usual national rules on employee involvement will apply, and the obligations to agree employee involvement procedures under the *GB Regulations* will fall away (*reg 17(3)*). The 'opt out' may be exercised by the SNB deciding, by a two thirds majority vote, not to open negotiations for an employee involvement agreement or to terminate any such negotiations (*reg 17(1)*). The SNB cannot, however, 'opt out' if the SE is to be formed by way of transformation of an existing company, and the existing company is one in which any of the employees have the right to participate in the board of that company (*reg 17(2)*). Procedures for agreeing employee involvement under the *GB Regulations* may, provided at least two years have passed since the decision to 'opt out' be 'reactivated' by an employee request that is:

(a)   in writing; and

(b)   made by at least 10% of the employees of, or by employees' representatives representing at least 10% of the total number of employees employed by the participating companies and its concerned subsidiaries, or (where the SE has been registered) the SE and its subsidiaries (*reg 17(4)*).

Where the SE has been registered, the SE may agree to the SNB being reconvened earlier than the specified two years.

15.37 Disputes and complaints

Disputes about the operation of an employee involvement agreement or the standard rules on employee involvement may be referred to the CAC by a member of the representative body or (where no representative body has been elected or appointed) an information and consultation representative or employee of the SE (*reg 20(1)*). There is a three-month time limit, running from the date on which the defaulting party allegedly failed to comply with the agreed procedure (*reg 20(2)*). If the CAC finds a complaint well-founded it may make a declaration and an order requiring the defaulting party to take requisite steps to remedy the default (*reg 20(4)–(5)*).

In the event of the CAC making such a declaration, the aggrieved party has three months in which to apply to the Employment Appeal Tribunal for a penalty notice to be awarded against the defaulting party (*reg 20(6)*). Matters to be taken into account by the EAT when setting the amount of the penalty include: the gravity of the failure; the period of time over which the failure occurred; the reason for the failure; the number of employees affected; and the number of employees employed by the undertaking (*reg 21(3)*).

15.38 Employment protection

Similar provisions apply in relation to rights to reasonable paid time off (*regs 26–28*), protection from dismissal (*regs 29–30*) and protection from other detriment (*regs 31–32*) as apply under the *ICE Regulations* (see above **15.21**).

15.39 EUROPEAN CO-OPERATIVE SOCIETIES (SCES)

Directive 2003/72/EC, accompanying *Regulation 1435/03* on the establishment of European Co-operative Societies (or 'Societas Cooperativa Europaea') (SCEs), prescribed requirements as to employee involvement in SCEs, with effect from 18 August 2006. Together, these measures are known as the *Statute for a European Cooperative Society.*

In *Validity of Regulation 1435/2003, Re: European Parliament v EU Council*: C-436/03 [2006] ECR I-3733, [2006] 3 CMLR 3, the ECJ held that the *Regulation* was correctly adopted under *art 308 EC,* as it has as its purpose the creation of a new form of co-operative society in addition to national forms, and leaves unchanged the different national laws already in existence (see [44]-[46]).

15.40 The *Directive* has been implemented domestically by the *European Cooperative Society (Involvement of Employees) Regulations 2006 (SI 2006/2059)* (the '*SCE Regulations*'). These were implemented under *s 2(2)* of the *European Communities Act 1972* (unlike the *ICE Regulations,* which were made under *s 42* of the *Employment Relations Act 2004*).

An SCE is an organisation which has as its principal object the satisfaction of its members' needs and/or the development of their economic and social activities, in particular through the conclusion of agreements with them to supply goods or services or to execute particular work or commissions: *reg 3* read with *EC Regulation 1435/03, art 1(3).*

The *SCE Regulations* apply to an actual or proposed SCE which will have its registered office in the UK, except where, at the relevant time:

(a)   the total workforce is less than 50;

(b)   the total workforce comprises employees employed to work in only one EEA state; and either—

(c)   if a participating individual (a natural person directly participating in the establishing of an SCE: *reg 3*) intends to form an SCE, all or all but one of the other parties to its formation are participating individuals, or

(d)   if a participating legal entity (as defined in *art 2* of the *Directive*) intends to form an SCE, all of the other parties to its formation are participating individuals.

(*Regs 4(2)* and *5(1)–(2)*.)

The *SCE Regulations* do not apply where an SCE has been registered and, at the relevant time, paragraphs (*a*) to (*c*) above applied: *reg 5(3)*. However, the *SCE Regulations* will apply in modified form if a formerly exempt SCE sees its total workforce increase to 50 or more employees, including employees employed to work in at least two different EEA states (even if that does not continue to be so), or if a valid employee request is made to that effect (*reg 6*). Regard should be had to the detailed provisions as to exemption in *regs 5* and *6*.

Note that particular provisions of the *SCE Regulations* apply to SCEs which have UK employees or other connections to the UK, but which do not fall within *reg 4(2)*, see *regs 4(3)–(4)*. Where the registered office of an SCE governed by participation transfers to the UK from another EEA state, at least the same level of employee participation rights must continue post-transfer (*reg 5(4)*).

Nothing in the *SCE Regulations* shall prejudice the rights of employees of an SCE, its subsidiaries or establishments to involvement (cf participation) as provided for by law or practice in the EEA state in which they were employed immediately prior to the SCE's registration (*reg 43*).

15.41 Duty to provide information

Reg 7 places a duty on the participating individual or the competent organ of a participating legal entity to provide information to employee representatives (or, if there are no such representatives, the employees themselves) as soon as possible after publishing draft terms of merger or conversion or agreeing a plan to form an SCE. The relevant employee representatives and employees are those of the participating individual or legal entity, any concerned subsidiaries and concerned establishments (*reg 7(1)*). The information must, as a minimum (*reg 7(2)*):

(a)   identify the participating individuals, legal entities, subsidiaries and establishments, and any concerned subsidiaries or establishments;

(b)   give the number of employees employed by each participating individual, legal entity, subsidiary and at each establishment (and, from 1 October 2011, provide specified information in relation to agency workers); and

(c)   give the number of employees employed to work in each EEA State.

Where there is a 'special negotiating body' (see below **15.42**), there is a continuing obligation on each participating individual and the competent organs of each participating legal entity to provide information to as to progress in establishing the SCE (*reg 7(3)*).

Complaints as to a failure to provide information, or provision of information that is false or incomplete in a material particular may be presented to the CAC by an employee's representative or (if there is no such representative) an employee (*reg 8(1)*). If the CAC finds the complaint well-founded, it must order the disclosure of the information in question (*reg 8(2)*).

15.42 The special negotiating body

The individuals or legal entities proposing to form an SCE are obliged to set up a 'special negotiating body' ('SNB') (*reg 10(1)*). The function of the SNB is to reach an 'employee involvement agreement' with the participating individuals and entities (*reg 9*).

The constitution of the SNB is complex, and is governed by *reg 10*. Employees must be informed of the identity of the members of the SNB as soon as reasonably practicable and in any event within one month of the election (*reg 10(5)*). The method used to elect or appoint representatives should seek to promote gender balance (*reg 10(1)*).

Complaints in relation to the establishment of (or failure to establish) an SNB may be presented to the CAC by a person elected or appointed to the SNB, an employees' representative (or, if there is no such representative, the employee) or a participating individual, legal entity or concerned subsidiary (*reg 11(1)–(2)*). Complaints must be made within one month of the last date on which the participating individuals and participating legal entities complied or should have complied with the obligation to inform employees of the identity of members of the SNB (*reg 11(3)*). Where the CAC finds an application well-founded it must make a declaration to that effect and the participating individuals and legal entities will continue to be under an obligation to comply with their duty under *reg 10(1)* to set up an SNB (*reg 11(4)*).

The requirements for ballots of UK employees to elect the UK members of the SNB are set out in *regs 12* and *13*. Any UK employee or UK employees' representative who believes that the arrangements for the ballot of the UK employees do not comply with the requirements of the *SCE Regulations* may present a complaint to the CAC (*reg 12(4)*). Complaints must be presented within 21 days from the date on which the relevant employers published the final arrangements for the ballot. Where the CAC finds the complaint well-founded it must make a declaration to that effect and may make an order requiring the relevant employers to modify their arrangements for the ballot of UK employees so as to comply with the requirements of the *SCE Regulations* (*reg 23(5)*).

However, the participating individual or participating legal entity is not obliged to arrange a ballot where it already has a relevant consultative committee (*regs 14(1)–(2)*). Instead, the committee is entitled to appoint the UK member or members of the SNB who would otherwise have been elected, having regard to the fact that the method used should seek to promote gender balance (*reg 14(2)(a)*). The committee can appoint either one of its number or, with the permission of the relevant participating individual or participating legal entity, a trade union representative who is not an employee of that individual or entity (*reg 14(2)(b)*). The consultative committee must then publish the names of those it has appointed to the SNB in such a manner as to bring them to the attention of the participating individual or legal entity and, so far as reasonably practicable, employees and employees' representatives (and those of concerned subsidiaries) (*reg 14(5)*).

Where the participating individual or legal entity, or an employee or an employee's representative believes that a consultative committee does not fulfil the requirements of *reg 14(3)*, or that the representative appointed is not entitled to be appointed, they may complain to the CAC within 21 days of the publication of the names of the purported representatives (*reg 14(6)*). If the CAC finds the complaint well-founded, it must make a declaration to that effect (*reg 14(7)*). Any appointment made by the consultative committee will then be of no effect and a ballot is required (*reg 14(8)*).

15.43 Negotiated employee involvement agreement

The task of the SNB is to reach an employee involvement agreement with the participating individuals and competent organs of the participating legal entities (*reg 16*). The parties must negotiate in a spirit of co-operation (*reg 16(2)*). There is an initial six-month time limit for agreement, but this can be extended for up to 12 months from the day on which the original time limit began running by agreement between the parties (*reg 16(3)*).

There are few specific requirements as to the substance of the agreement to be reached on employee involvement. To be valid, the agreement must be in writing and must specify the agreement reached on certain key points. These are broadly the same as those which apply in relation to SEs (see above, **15.34**) with, in addition, specification of the substance of any agreed arrangements for employees or their representatives to participate in and vote in the general meeting or any section or sectorial meetings of the SCE (*reg 17*). The standard rules on employee involvement (see below, **15.44**) will only apply if there is express provision to that effect (*reg 17(3)*). Note also that in relation to an SCE to be formed by conversion, the employee involvement agreement must preserve elements of employee involvement which are at least as favourable as those which exist in the cooperative to be converted into an SCE (*reg 17(4)*). From 1 October 2011, where under the employee involvement agreement information is to be provided on the employment situation in the SCE, such information must include suitable information relating to the use of agency workers (*reg 17(6)*).

There are specific rules as to how decisions must be taken by the SNB, what level of majority is required for each sort of decision, and the assistance of experts (*regs 18–19*). These are broadly similar to those which apply to SNBs established in relation to SEs (see above, **15.34**).

Members of the SNB, employees' representatives (or where there is no such relevant representative, employees) may complain to the CAC that an SNB decision was not taken by the requisite majority, or that the SNB failed to publish a decision as required by the *SCE Regulations*. The time limit for presentation of complaints is 21 days from the date the SNB did or should have published their decision (*reg 20(1)*). Where the CAC finds the complaint well-founded it must make a declaration that the decision was not taken properly and that it is to have no effect (*reg 20(2)*).

15.44 Standard rules on employee involvement

Detailed and complex 'standard rules on employee involvement' are set out in *reg 21* and *Sch 2* to the *SCE Regulations*. In general, these will apply where (*reg 21*):

389

15.44 Employee Participation

(a)   the parties so agree; or

(b)   no employee involvement agreement has been reached within the six-month (or twelve-month extended) time limit in *reg 16(3)* and where: (i) the participating individual and legal entities agree that they should apply, and so continue with the registration of the SCE, and (ii) the SNB has not taken any decision under *reg 19(1)* to 'opt out' of negotiations.

Note that there are further detailed provisions in *reg 21(3)* and *(5)* as to when the standard rules on participation in *Pt 3* of *Sch 2* will apply. Where the standard rules on participation apply and more than one form of employee participation exists in the participating legal entities, the SNB shall decide which of the existing forms of participation are to exist in the SCE (*reg 21(4)*).

15.45 Alternative arrangements

The members of the SNB may 'opt out' of any sort of employee involvement, in which case the usual national rules on employee involvement will apply, and the obligations to agree employee involvement procedures under the *SCE Regulations* will fall away (*reg 19(3)*). The 'opt out' may be exercised by the SNB deciding, by a two thirds majority vote, not to open negotiations for an employee involvement agreement or to terminate any such negotiations (*reg 19(1)*). The SNB cannot, however, 'opt out' if the SCE is to be formed by way of conversion if any employees of the cooperative to be converted have participation (*reg 19(2)*). Procedures for agreeing employee involvement under the *SCE Regulations* may be 'reactivated' by an employee request in similar circumstances as applied in relation to SEs (*reg 19(4)* and see above, **15.36**).

15.46 Disputes and complaints

Complaints that a participating individual or the competent organ of a participating legal entity or of the SCE has failed to comply with the employee involvement agreement or the standard rules on employee involvement may be referred to the CAC by a member of a representative body, or (in the absence of such a body) an information and consultation representative or an employee (*reg 22(1)*). There is a three-month time limit, running from the date of the alleged failure (*reg 22(2)*). If the CAC finds a complaint well-founded it must make a declaration and may make an order requiring the defaulting party to take requisite steps to remedy the default (*reg 22(4)–(5)*).

In addition, if an employees' representative (or, in the absence of such representative, the employees) believes that a participating individual, legal entity or SCE is misusing or intending to misuse the SCE or powers in the *SCE Regulations* for the purposes of depriving employees of their right to employee involvement, or withholding rights to employee involvement, he may present a complaint to the CAC (*reg 24(1)–(2)*). Where such a complaint is made either prior to registration or within a period of 12 months of the registration of the SCE, the CAC must uphold the complaint unless the respondent proves that it did not misuse or intend to misuse the SCE or the powers in the *SCE Regulations* (*reg 24(2)*). If the CAC finds the complaint to be well-founded, it shall make a declaration to that effect and may make an order requiring the participating individual, legal entity or SCE to take remedial action (*reg 24(3)*).

In the event of the CAC making either such declaration, the applicant has three months in which to apply to the Employment Appeal Tribunal for a penalty notice against the defaulting party (*reg 22(6)* and *reg 24(3)(b)*). Broadly similar provisions govern such applications as in relation to SEs: see *regs 22(6)–(9), 23* and *24(3)(b)* and above, **15.37**.

15.47 **Confidential information**

Similar provisions apply in relation to confidential information (*reg 26*), and the withholding of information or documents which would seriously harm the functioning of or be prejudicial to the SCE or the participating legal entity or individual, or any subsidiary or establishment thereof (*reg 27*) as apply under the *ICE Regulations* (see above **15.19**).

15.48 **Employment protection**

Broadly similar provisions apply in relation to rights to reasonable paid time off (*regs 28* to *30*), protection from dismissal (*regs 31* and *32*) and protection from other detriment (*regs 33* and *34*) as apply under the *ICE Regulations* (see above, **15.21**)

15.49 **CROSS-BORDER MERGERS**

The *Companies (Cross-Border Mergers) Regulations 2007 SI 2007/2974* (the '*Merger Regulations*'), as amended, which came into force on 15 December 2007, implement *Directive 2005/56/EC* on cross-border mergers between limited liability companies.

The *Merger Regulations* contain detailed requirements applicable to cross-border mergers involving at least one company formed and registered in the UK and at least one company formed and registered in another EEA state or involving the formation of a new company which is to be a UK company (*regs 2, 3*). They apply to unregistered companies, as well as registered companies (*reg 5*). They also prescribe minimum requirements as to the information to be provided to employees and their representatives prior to any merger, and to employee participation following such a merger.

The requirements of the *Merger Regulations*, and in particular the provisions under which the UK courts may order meetings of members or creditors, have been considered by David Richards J in *Re Oceanrose Investments Ltd* [2008] EWHC 3475 (Ch), [2009] Bus LR 947, by Rose J in *Re Wood DIY Ltd* [2012] BCC 67, [2012] BCC 67, by Sales J in *Diamond Resorts (Europe) Ltd, Re* [2012] EWHC 3576 (Ch), and by Henderson J in *In the Matter of Itau BBA International Limited* [2013] Bus LR 490.

15.50 A 'cross-border merger' means:

(a)   a merger by absorption, as defined in *reg 2(2)*;

(b)   a merger by absorption of a wholly-owned subsidiary, as defined in *reg 2(3)*; or

(c)   a merger by formation of a new company, as defined in *reg 2(4)*.

15.51

In the most part, the employee participation requirements contained in the *Merger Regulations* apply only when the *transferee company* is a UK company (as defined in *reg 3*). The entirety of *Part 4* ('employee participation') applies where the transferee company is a UK company and where:

(a)   in the six months before the publication of draft terms of merger, a merging company has over 500 employees on average, and has a system of employee participation (specific provision is made in *reg 22(1A)* as to the treatment of agency workers); or

(b)   a UK merging company has a proportion of employee representatives amongst its directors; or

(c)   a merging company has employee representatives amongst members of the administrative or supervisory organ or their committees or of the management group which covers the profit units of the company: *reg 22(1)*.

Employee Participation

However, chapter 4 (election of UK members of the special negotiating board) and chapters 6–9 (confidential information, employee protection, complaints and enforcement) of *Part 4* of the *Merger Regulations* apply to a UK merging company, its employees or their representatives, regardless of whether the transferee company is a UK company (*reg 22(2)*).

The *Merger Regulations* apply in Northern Ireland in modified form (*reg 22(3)*).

15.52 Employee participation is defined for the purposes of the *Merger Regulations* as the influence of the employees and/or employee representatives in the transferee company or a merging company by way of a right to elect or appoint some of the members of the company's supervisory or administrative organ (or recommend or oppose the appointment of some or all such members) (*reg 3(1)*).

An employee, for these purposes, is someone who has entered into or works under a contract of employment and includes, where the employment has ceased, an individual who worked under a contract of employment (*reg 3(1)*). Employee representatives are trade union representatives (if the employer recognises an independent trade union is recognised by their employer for the purpose of collective bargaining in respect of the relevant employees), or other employees who have been elected or appointed to positions in which they are expected to receive particular types of information (*reg 3(1)*). See further the definitions in *reg 3*.

15.53 The pre-merger process

Parts 2 and *3* of the *Merger Regulations* set out requirements in relation to the pre-merger process. In short, the *Merger Regulations* require certain information to be provided to employee representatives or employees of UK merging companies as part of the pre-merger process in cross-border mergers, and require the merging companies to consider any report by employee representatives: see, in particular, *regs 8* and *10*. In addition, the draft terms of merger (which must be certified by a court) must contain information on the procedures by which any employee participation rights are to be determined in accordance with *Part 4* of the *Merger Regulations* (see above **15.51**) (*reg 7(2)(j)*). Each UK company involved in a cross-border merger can apply for a court order certifying that the pre-merger requirements in *regs 7–10* and *12–15* have been complied with (*reg 6* and note also *reg 16*).

15.54 Duty on merging company to provide information

As soon as possible after adopting draft terms of merger under *reg 7*, each merging company must provide certain minimum information to its employee representatives (or, if no such representatives exist, the employees themselves) (*reg 23(1)*). That information must as a minimum, by *reg 23(2)*:

(a)   identify the merging companies;

(b)   notify any decision taken by the merging companies pursuant to *reg 36* (ie a decision to apply statutory standard rules of employee participation); and

(c)   give the number of employees employed by each merging company.

From 1 October 2011 such information must include suitable information in relation to the use of agency workers (*reg 23(3)*).

Each merging company is also subject to a continuing obligation to provide information such as is necessary to keep the 'special negotiating body' (see below **15.55**) informed of the plan and progress of establishing the UK transferee company, up until the date upon which the consequences of the cross-border merger take effect (on which see *reg 17*) (*reg 23(3)*).

An employee representative (or, where no such representative exists, an employee) may complain to the CAC that a merging company has failed to provide information as required by *reg 23*, or that the information is false or incomplete in a material particular (*reg 24(1)*). If the CAC finds the complaint well-founded it must order the company to disclose information (*reg 24(2)*).

15.55   The special negotiating body

Unless the merging companies decide, pursuant to *reg 36*, that the statutory standard rules of employee participation applicable in cross-border mergers set out in *reg 38* are to apply to a UK transferee company, each merging company must make arrangements to establish a 'special negotiating body' ('SNB') (*reg 25(1)*). The task of the SNB will then be to reach an 'employee participation agreement' with the merging companies: *reg 25(2)* and see below **15.56**.

The composition (and election) of an SNB is prescribed by *reg 26*, the requirements in relation to a ballot to elect the UK members of an SNB are set out in *regs 33* and *34* and the representative role of each SNB member is defined by *reg 35*. Employees must be informed of the identity of the members of the SNB as soon as reasonably practicable and in any event within one month of the election (*reg 26(4)*). There is provision for appointing additional members and for changing members in certain circumstances (*reg 26(5)*).

Complaints in relation to the establishment of (or failure to establish) an SNB may be presented to the CAC (*reg 27(1)*). Where it is alleged that the failure is attributable to the conduct of the merging company, an application may be presented by a person elected to the SNB or by an employee representative (or, if there is no such representative, an employee) (*reg 27(2)*). Where it is alleged that the failure is attributable to the conduct of the employees or the employee representatives, an application may be presented by the merging company (*reg 27(3)*).

Complaints must be made within one month of the last date on which the merging companies complied or should have complied with the obligation to inform employees of the outcome of elections for membership of the SNB (*reg 27(4)*). Where the CAC finds an application under *reg 27(2)* well-founded it must make a declaration to that effect. If the complaint was made by an SNB representative, employee representative or employee, the merging companies will continue to be under an obligation to comply with their duty under *reg 25* (*reg 27(5)*). If it was made by a merging company, the companies no longer continue to be under that obligation (*reg 27(6)*).

15.56   Negotiated employee participation agreement

The merging companies and the SNB are to negotiate in a spirit of cooperation with a view to reaching an employee participation agreement (*reg 28(2)*).

There are no specific requirements as to the substance of the agreement to be reached. However, to be valid, the employee participation agreement must be in writing and must specify the agreement reached on certain key points:

(a)   the scope of the agreement;

(b)   the substance of any arrangements for employee participation (if, during negotiations, the parties decide to establish such arrangements), including (if applicable) the number of directors of the UK transferee company which the employees will be entitled to elect, appoint, recommend or oppose, the procedures as to how these directors may be elected, appointed, recommended or opposed by the employees, and their rights; and

(c)   the date on which the agreement enters into force, its duration and the circumstances of (and procedure for) any re-negotiation.

15.56 Employee Participation

(*Reg 29(1)–(2)*.)

From 1 October 2011, where under the employee participation agreement the transferee company is to provide information on the employment situation in that company, such information must include suitable information relating to the use of agency workers (if any) in that company (*reg 29(2A)*).

The employee participation agreement will only be subject to the statutory standard rules of employee participation set out in *reg 38* if it contains a provision to that effect (*reg 29(3)*).

There is an initial six-month time limit within which they are to reach agreement (beginning one month after the last date on which SNB members were elected or appointed), but with provision for extension for up to 12 months from the date from which the original six-month time limit ran by agreement between the parties (*reg 28(3)*).

There are specific rules as to how decisions must be taken by the SNB, and what level of majority is required for each sort of decision (an absolute majority generally, but two thirds in certain circumstances where a decision would result in a reduction of participation rights) (*reg 30(1)–(4)*). The SNB may decide not to open negotiations to reach an employee participation agreement or to terminate negotiations already opened (in which case the duty of the parties to negotiate will cease) (*reg 31*). Such a decision must be taken by a 'particular prescribed' form of two thirds majority (*reg 31(1)*).

The details of any decision taken by the SNB must be published in such a manner as to bring the decision, so far as reasonably practicable, to the attention of the represented employees, as soon as reasonably practicable and within 14 days after the decision has been taken (*reg 30(5)*).

For the purpose of negotiations, the SNB may be assisted by experts of its choice (*reg 30(6)*). The merging companies must pay for any reasonable expenses of the SNB, though the company is not required to pay for the expenses of more than one expert (*reg 30(7)*).

Complaints in relation to decisions of the SNB may be presented to the CAC by a member of the SNB, an employee representative, or where there is no such representative in respect of an employee, that employee (*reg 32(1)*). Complaints may only be presented on the grounds that: (*a*) the decision was not taken by the requisite majority, or (*b*) that the SNB failed to publish a decision as required by the *Merger Regulations* (*reg 32(1)*). The time limit for presentation of complaints is 21 days from the date the SNB did or should have published their decision (*reg 32(2)*). Where the CAC finds the complaint well-founded it must make a declaration that the decision was not taken properly and that it is to have no effect (*reg 32(3)*).

15.57 Standard rules of employee participation in a UK transferee company

The *Merger Regulations* contain 'standard rules' on employee participation, in *reg 38*.

The merging companies may opt for these rules to apply to a UK transferee company from the date upon which the consequences of the cross-border merger take effect (on which see *reg 17*), without negotiating with the SNB, the employee representatives or the employees (*reg 36*).

In addition, these 'standard rules' apply to a UK transferee company where:

(a)   the parties agree that they should; or

(b)   the period specified in *reg 28(3)* has expired without the parties reaching an employee participation agreement and:

(i)   the merging companies agree that they should; and

(ii)   the SNB has not taken any decision either not to open or to terminate the negotiations under *reg 31* (*reg 37(1)*);

and provided that:

(c)   before registration of the UK transferee company, one or more forms of employee participation existed in at least one of the merging companies and either:

(i)   that participation applied to at least one third of the total number of employees of the merging companies, or

(ii)   that participation applied to less than one third of the total number of employees of the merging companies but the SNB has decided that the standard rules of employee participation should apply (*reg 37(2)*).

(*Reg 37*).

From 1 October 2011, for these purposes, agency workers whose contract within *reg 3(1)(b)* of the *Agency Workers Regulations 2010* was not a contract of employment with one or more temporary work agencies that were merging companies at the relevant time, are to be treated as having been employed by such an agency or agencies for the duration of their assignment with a hirer (*reg 37(2A)*).

Where the standard rules of employee participation apply and more than one form of employee participation existed in the merging companies, ordinarily the SNB shall decide (and inform the merging companies) which of those forms shall apply in the UK transferee company (*reg 37(3)*). However, if the SNB fails to make such a decision, the merging companies become responsible for determining the form of employee participation in the UK transferee company (*reg 37(4)*). In addition, the merging companies will also be so responsible where one or more forms of employee participation existed within them but they chose, without any prior negotiation, to be directly subject to the standard rules (*reg 37(4)*).

The standard rules of employee participation are set out in *reg 38*. They include that:

(a)   the employee representatives of the UK transferee company (or if there are no such representatives, the employees) have the right to elect, appoint, recommend or oppose the appointment of a number of directors of the transferee company, such number to be equal to the number in the merging company which had the highest proportion of directors (or their EEA equivalent) so elected or appointed (subject to *reg 39*, see below);

(b)   subject to (*c*) below, the employee representatives (or if there are no such representatives, the employees) shall decide, taking into account the proportion of employees of the transferee company formerly employed in each merging company, on the allocation of directorships, or on the means by which the transferee's employees may recommend or oppose the appointment of directors;

(c)   in making the decision in (*b*) above, if the employees of one or more merging companies are not covered by the proportional criterion set out in (*b*), the employee representatives (or if there are no such representatives, the employees) shall appoint a member from one of those merging companies including one from the UK, if appropriate; and

(d)   every director of the transferee company who was elected, appointed or recommended by the employee representatives or employees is a full director with the same rights and obligations (including the right to vote) as the directors representing shareholders.

15.57 Employee Participation

From 1 October 2011, where under the standard rules of employee participation the transferee company is to provide information on the employment situation in that company, it must include suitable information relating to the use of agency workers (if any) in that company (*reg 38(5)*).

Note that where the 'standard rules' apply following prior negotiation, the UK transferee company may choose to limit the proportion of directors elected, appointed, recommended or opposed through employee participation to a level which is the lesser of the highest proportion in force in the merging companies prior to registration, or one third of the directors (*reg 39*).

Specific protective provision is made in relation to subsequent domestic mergers (*reg 40*).

15.58 Disputes and complaints

Disputes about whether the transferee company has failed to comply with the terms of an employee participation agreement or the standard rules on employee participation may be referred to the CAC by an SNB, or (where no SNB has been elected or appointed, or an SNB has been dissolved) an employee representative or employee (*reg 53(1)–(3)*). There is a three-month time limit, running from the date of the alleged failure to comply with the agreed procedure (*reg 53(2)*). If the CAC finds a complaint well-founded it must make a declaration to that effect and may make an order requiring the transferee company to remedy the default (*reg 53(4)–(5)*).

In addition, if an employee representative (or where there is no such representative in relation to an employee, an employee) believes that a transferee or merging company is misusing or intending to misuse the transferee company or the powers in the *Merger Regulations* for the purpose of depriving the employees of that merging or transferee company of their rights to employee participation or withholding such rights, he may complain to the CAC (*reg 54(1)*). Such complaint must be made within 12 months from the date upon which the consequences of the merger take effect (on which, see *reg 17*) (*reg 54(2)*). The CAC must uphold the complaint unless the respondent proves that it did not misuse or intend to so misuse the transferee company or the powers in the *Merger Regulations* (*reg 54(3)*). If the CAC finds the complaint to be well-founded it must make a declaration to that effect and may make an order requiring the transferee company or merging company to take specified remedial action (*reg 54(4)*).

In the event of the CAC making either such declaration, the applicant has three months in which to apply to the Employment Appeal Tribunal for a penalty notice against the relevant company (*regs 53(6) and 54(5)*). The EAT must issue a penalty notice unless satisfied that the failure resulted from a reason beyond the relevant company's control or that it has some other reasonable excuse for its failure (*regs 53(7) and 54(6)*). When setting the amount of the penalty, up to a maximum of £75,000, the EAT must take into account: the gravity of the failure; the period of time over which it occurred; the reason for the failure; the number of employees affected by the failure; and the number of employees employed by the undertaking (*reg 55*).

Note that no order of the CAC under *regs 53 or 54* can suspend or alter the effect of any act done or of any agreement made by the transferee company or merging company (*regs 53(9) and 54(7)*).

15.59 Confidential information

Similar provisions apply in relation to confidential information (*reg 41*), and the withholding of information or documents which would seriously harm the functioning of or be prejudicial to a transferring or merging entity (*reg 42*) as apply under the *TICE Regulations* (see above **15.28**).

15.60 Employment protection

The *Merger Regulations* also contain rights to reasonable paid time off for SNB members, directors of transferee companies or candidates as such (*regs 43* to *45*), protection from dismissal (*regs 46* and *47*) and protection from other detriment (*regs 49* to *51*).

15.61 OTHER CONSULTATION RIGHTS

In addition to the specific legislative provisions discussed above, the influence of the European Community may be seen in the recent development of other legislation on employee consultation. For example, employers must consult with trade union representatives in certain cases where a large number of redundancies are planned (see eg. *section 188* of the *TULR(C)A* and REDUNDANCY – II (37)) and in relation to transfers of businesses (see eg the *Transfer of Undertakings (Protection of Employment) Regulations 2006 (SI 2006/246)*, *reg 13* and **50.18** TRANSFER OF UNDERTAKINGS). For recognition of trade unions, see **48.19**ff TRADE UNIONS– I: NATURE AND LIABILITIES. Employers in both unionised and non-unionised workplaces are obliged to consult over certain health and safety issues (see eg the *Safety Representatives and Safety Committees Regulations 1977 (SI 1977/500)*, the *Health and Safety (Consultation with Employees) Regulations 1996 (SI 1996/1513)* and see HEALTH AND SAFETY AT WORK – II (26)).

15.62 In addition, for further details as to employers' duties to disclose certain information to employees and their representatives, such as in relation to collective bargaining and occupational pension schemes, see DISCLOSURE OF INFORMATION (9).

15.63 *TULR(C)A, s 70A* and *Schedule A1*, which came into effect on 6 June 2000, contain statutory procedures for the recognition of a trade union for collective bargaining purposes where the union has achieved a specified level of support and the union and employer are unable to reach agreement voluntarily. (For further details, see TRADE UNIONS – I (48).)

Under the statutory procedure the employer is not obliged to bargain on training matters but has a duty to consult in relation to such matters (*TULR(C)A 1992, s 70B*). Representatives of the union must be invited to a meeting at least every six months for the purpose of:

(a)   consulting on the employer's policy on training for workers within the bargaining unit;

(b)   consulting on the employer's plans for training those workers in the following six months; and

(c)   reporting about training provided for those workers since the previous meeting.

The employer must provide relevant information to the trade union at least two weeks before the meeting (*TULR(C)A 1992, s 70B(4)* and *(4A)*). Enforcement is through the employment tribunals.

15.64 The *Employment Relations Act 1999, s 30* authorises the Secretary of State to provide money for the purpose of encouraging and helping employers (or their representatives) and employees (or their representatives) to improve the way in which they work together. Money may be provided as grants or otherwise, on such terms as the Secretary of State thinks fit. The Partnership at Work Fund was created in 1999, in order to encourage the development of industrial relations by encouraging employers and employees to work together effectively, but was closed following a review in 2004.

16   Employee's Past Criminal Convictions

16.1   SPENT CONVICTIONS

The *Rehabilitation of Offenders Act 1974* ('*ROA 1974*') provides that, after a period of time, people who have been convicted of criminal offences and who have served their sentences are, with some exceptions (see **16.4** below), not obliged to disclose those convictions. The length of time which must elapse before a person's conviction becomes 'spent' in this way depends upon the nature of the sentence imposed and runs from the date of sentence. Certain sentences, such as imprisonment or custody for life, sentences of imprisonment, youth custody or detention in a young offender institution, or corrective training for a term exceeding 30 months, and detention during Her Majesty's pleasure, can never become spent (*ROA 1974, s 5(1)*; as amended by *Criminal Justice Act 1982, ss 77, 78, Sch 14 para 36, Sch 16*). An offender whose conviction has become spent is known as a 'rehabilitated person' (*ROA 1974, s 1(1)*).

16.2   Non-disclosure of spent convictions

Subject to certain exceptions, a rehabilitated person is to be treated for all purposes in law as a person who has not committed or been charged with or convicted of the offence in question. Evidence of such matters may not be adduced in judicial proceedings and questions should not be asked in such proceedings which cannot be answered without revealing such matters; if asked, they need not be answered (*ROA 1974, s 4(1)*). This also applies to employment tribunal proceedings (*ROA 1974, s 4(6)*).

Further, if questions about past convictions and related matters are put in other circumstances (such as at a job interview or on an application form), they may be answered on the basis that they do not refer to spent convictions, and the person questioned shall not be subjected to any liability or otherwise prejudiced in law by failing to acknowledge or disclose his spent convictions (*ROA 1974, s 4(2)*). Any obligation imposed on a person, by a rule of law or an agreement or arrangement (which would include a contract of employment), to disclose any matters does not require the disclosure of spent convictions or ancillary matters (*ROA 1974, s 4(3)(a)*).

A person who reveals another's spent criminal convictions may raise the defence of justification (ie truth) in any subsequent action for libel or slander, provided that the revelation was not made with malice (*ROA 1974, s 8(3), (5)*).

16.3   Spent convictions and dismissal

A spent conviction or a failure to disclose such a conviction are not proper grounds for dismissing or excluding a person from any office, profession, occupation or employment or for prejudicing him in any way in any occupation or employment (*ROA 1974, s 4(3)(b)*). Thus, an employer may not dismiss an employee merely because he discovers that the employee has a conviction which has become spent. In *Hendry v Scottish Liberal Club* [1977] IRLR 5, a Scottish employment tribunal held that a spent conviction for possession of cannabis had to some extent influenced the club's decision to dismiss the employee. Therefore, the reason for the dismissal could not fall within the range of permitted reasons and the dismissal was unfair (see **52.2** UNFAIR DISMISSAL – II). A security officer is not an occupation excluded from the benefit of the *ROA 1974* (see **16.4** below) and, consequently, an employer who dismissed two security officers for failing to disclose a spent conviction was held to have dismissed them unfairly (*Property Guards Ltd v Taylor and Kershaw* [1982] IRLR 175).

16.3 Employee's Past Criminal Convictions

Furthermore, the fact that a person has a spent conviction is not a proper ground for an employer to refuse to engage that person, unless the person falls within a category to which the *Exceptions Order* applies (see below) (*ROA 1974, s 4(3)(b)*). However, it is not clear what remedy there would be for such a refusal: possibly it would be an action for breach of statutory duty.

16.4 EXCEPTIONS

The *Rehabilitation of Offenders Act 1974 (Exceptions) Order 1975 (SI 1975/1023)* (as variously amended) provides that people following certain occupations and professions are obliged (despite the provisions of *ROA 1974, s 4(2)*) to disclose any spent convictions and may be dismissed or excluded from employment because of such a conviction (despite the provisions of *ROA 1974, s 4(3)*). Those professions and occupations include: doctors, nurses, midwives, dentists, barristers, solicitors, accountants, teachers, police officers and (by virtue of *SI 1986/2268*, which amends the *(Exceptions) Order 1975*) directors or other officers of building societies. The *Rehabilitation of Offenders Act 1974 (Exceptions) (Amendment) Order 1986 (SI 1986/1249)* also amends the *(Exceptions) Order 1975* by substituting, for a number of specific excepted occupational groups, a general exception covering any office or employment which is concerned with the provision of accommodation, care, leisure and recreational facilities, schooling, social services, supervision or training to persons under 18 years, where the holder of the office or employment would have access to such minors in the normal course of his duties or if the duties are carried out wholly or partly on the premises where such provision takes place. Further amendments to the *(Exceptions) Order 1975* are made by the *Osteopaths Act 1993, s 39(2), (4)*, by the *Chiropractors Act 1994, s 40(2), (4)*, and by the *Insurance Companies (Third Insurance Directives) Regulations 1994 (SI 1994/1696)*. The application of the *(Exceptions) Order 1975* to work 'in connection with the provision of social services' was considered by the EAT in *Wood v Coverage Care Ltd* [1996] IRLR 264.

By virtue of the *1975 Order*, as amended, an applicant for, or candidate for admission to, any profession or occupation specified in the *Order*, or which falls within the general exception referred to above, is not statutorily excused from the obligation to disclose spent convictions where a question is asked in order to assess his suitability for any profession, occupation, office or employment in the circumstances described, if the question relates to the applicant for such a post or (where applicable) if it relates to a person who lives in the same household as the applicant, and the provision of the services mentioned would normally take place in that household.

The *Rehabilitation of Offenders Act 1974 (Exceptions) Order 1975* was further amended by the *Rehabilitation of Offenders Act 1974 (Exceptions) (Amendment) Order 2002 (SI 2002/441)*, which came into force on 29 February 2002. The professions to which the rehabilitative provisions of the *ROA 1974* do not apply are extended to include chartered psychologists, actuaries, registered foreign lawyers, legal executives and receivers appointed by the Court of Protection. Further employments subject to exemption from some of the provisions of the *ROA 1974* will now include the Crown Prosecution Service, Customs and Excise, the National Crime Squad, the National Criminal Intelligence Service, those working with vulnerable adults and certain employments in the RSPCA. Further exceptions relate to National Lottery Commission personnel, air traffic workers, and to the licensing of taxi drivers and National Lottery licences. Most recently, by the *Rehabilitation of Offenders Act 1974 (Exceptions) (Amendment) (England and Wales) Order 2008 (SI 2008/3259)*, which came into force on 18 December 2008, the *Exceptions Order* extends the definition of a conviction to include a caution and makes further extensions and modifications to the category of persons to whom the exemption provisions apply. Thus in relation to the broad categories of persons to whom the exceptions to the Act apply, cautions as well as convictions will not become spent and will always be disclosable.

A further exception to the *Act* is set out in the *Financial Services Act 1986, s 189*, which provides that convictions for offences involving fraud or dishonesty, or for offences under legislation relating to companies (including insider dealing), various financial institutions, insolvency, consumer credit and consumer protection, shall not be regarded as spent for the purposes of certain proceedings, questions and actions specified in *FSA 1986, Sch 14*.

With the introduction of major provisions of the *Safeguarding of Vulnerable Groups Act 2006* (see further **16.8** below) the *Rehabilitation of Offenders Act 1974 (Exceptions) Order* has been further amended to confer the right to ask questions regarding spent convictions and spent cautions where a person seeks to work in controlled activity with children or vulnerable adults within the meaning of the *Safeguarding of Vulnerable Groups Act 2006*. The right is, however, limited to circumstances where the person seeking such work is barred from regulated activity relating to children or vulnerable adults. See the *Rehabilitation of Offenders Act 1974 (Exceptions) (Amendment) (England and Wales) Order 2008 (SI 2010/1153)* which came into force on 31 March 2010.

16.5   EFFECT OF PROVISIONS FOR REHABILITATION

If, for example, at an interview, an applicant is asked whether he has any criminal convictions, a negative answer may mean:

(i)   that he has no previous convictions;

(ii)   that he has convictions but they are spent; or

(iii) that he has convictions which are not spent and he is not telling the truth.

If the employer subsequently discovers, after engaging the applicant, that he has previous convictions:

(a)   if these are not spent, he may consider the applicant for dismissal if such a dismissal would be fair in all the circumstances (see **52.4** UNFAIR DISMISSAL – **II**); or

(b)   if these are spent, he may not take any action, unless there are other reasons which justify him in doing so.

If the applicant reveals at an interview that he has previous convictions:

(A)   if the convictions are spent, they do not form a good reason for refusing the applicant the job; or

(B)   if they are not spent, they may form good grounds for refusing the applicant the job (and there will be no legal redress if the applicant is refused the job on such grounds).

Any agreement or arrangement that an applicant must reveal past convictions is ineffective so far as spent convictions are concerned (see **16.2** above).

Applicants for any position in a profession or occupation excluded from the protection of the *Act* (see **16.4** above) must answer questions relating to previous convictions and may be refused or dismissed from such employment for a conviction or for failing to disclose such a conviction.

16.6   REHABILITATION PERIODS

The period of rehabilitation is related to the length of the sentence which was passed on the offender. The main rehabilitation periods presently applicable are set out below.

16.6　Employee's Past Criminal Convictions

Sentence	Rehabilitation period
Imprisonment, custody, or detention for life, or detention at Her Majesty's pleasure.	Not applicable
Imprisonment, youth custody, detention in a young offender institution for a term exceeding 30 months.	Not applicable
Imprisonment, youth custody, detention in a young offender institution or corrective training for between 6 and 30 months.	10 years
Imprisonment, youth custody or detention in a young offender institution for 6 months or less.	7 years
Fine, or (in the case of adults) probation.	5 years
Detention under the Children and Young Persons Act 1933, s 53 for between 6 and 30 months.	5 years
Detention under above Act for 6 months or less.	3 years
Probation (in the case of minors).	2½ years from conviction, or (if later) when the probation order ceases to have effect
Conditional discharge, binding over, care or supervision order.	1 year or the duration of the order, if longer
Disqualification from driving.	Period of disqualification
Absolute discharge.	6 months

(*ROA 1974, s 5* as amended. Note that for those placed on probation prior to 3 February 1995, the rehabilitation period is one year (*Criminal Justice and Public Order Act 1994, Sch 9 para 11(2)*; *Criminal Justice and Public Order Act 1994 (Commencement No 5 and Transitional Provisions) Order 1995 (SI 1995/127)*).)

It is important to note that *Chapter 8* of *Part 3* of the *Legal Aid, Sentencing and Punishment of Offenders Act 2012* (*ss 139–149*) when in force will amend *section 5* of the *Rehabilitation of Offenders Act 1974* to introduce new rehabilitation periods in place of those set out above. See also on disclosure of old convictions and compatibility with *art 8* of the *ECHR T (and others) v Chief Constable of Greater Manchester and others* [2013] EWCA Civ 25, considered at the end of **16.7** below.

16.7　REFORM OF ACCESS TO PAST CRIMINAL CONVICTIONS: PART V OF THE POLICE ACT 1997

Part V of the *Police Act 1997* ('*PA 1997*'), which received Royal Assent on 27 March 1997, contains a number of provisions for access to the records of employees' past convictions. The *Act* provides for the issue of a number of certificates which may be sought by the employee or provided to an employer in order to satisfy a prospective employer of the accuracy of the employee's disclosure of criminal convictions (*PA 1997, ss 112–127*).

An applicant may apply, upon payment of a fee, for a 'criminal conviction certificate' ('CCC') which records all convictions of the applicant (as defined in the *Rehabilitation of Offenders Act 1974* but excluding spent convictions) or states that there are no such convictions, as the case may be (*PA 1997, s 112*). This provision is not yet in force in England and Wales but is in Scotland and is available from Disclosure Scotland.

An application may be made for a 'criminal record certificate' ('CRC') in cases where *s 4(2)(a)* or *(b)* of the *Rehabilitation of Offenders Act 1974* have been excluded by order of the Secretary of State. The application must be countersigned by a 'registered person' within the meaning of the *Act* (*PA 1997, s 120*) who confirms that the information is sought in relation to a matter which is exempt from the provisions of the *Rehabilitation of Offenders Act 1974* (*PA 1997, s 113(2)*). The CRC is broader than the CCC in that it includes details of *all* convictions (including spent convictions) and also details of all cautions administered, or confirms the absence of any convictions or cautions, as the case may be (*PA 1997, s 113(3), (5)*). The certificate will be sent to the registered person and copied to the applicant (*PA 1997, s 113(4)*). Similarly, in the case of application for Crown employment, a CRC may be issued in cases of exempted questions concerning an applicant's suitability for Crown appointment (*PA 1997, s 114*).

An 'enhanced criminal record certificate' ('ECRC') may be obtained in relation to applications for certain sensitive employments (*PA 1997, s 115*). The application must be countersigned by a registered person who confirms that the certificate is sought in relation to considering the applicant's suitability for employment in a number of positions defined in the *Act* or for the purpose of considering the applicant for a number of licences as defined (*PA 1997, s 115(2)*). The positions covered are:

(a)   training, caring, supervising or being in sole charge of persons under 18 (*PA 1997, s 115(3)*); and

(b)   training, caring supervising or being in sole charge of persons over 18 if the position is one specified in regulations made by the Secretary of State (*PA 1997, s 115(4)*).

The other matters in relation to which an ECRC may be sought are gaming and gaming licences (*PA 1998, s 115(5)(a), (b)*), lottery management and promotion (*PA 1998, s 115(5)(c), (d)*), child minding (*PA 1998, s 115(5)(e)*) and foster placement and the approval of persons as foster carers (*PA 1998, s 115(5)(f), (g)*).

The ECRC (as in the case of the CRC) gives details of all convictions and cautions (or their absence) but, in addition, the Secretary of State will request the Chief Officer of every relevant police force to provide any information which the Chief Officer considers relevant to the issue of the applicant's suitability for such a position; this information will be included in the certificate (*PA 1997, s 115(7)*). The application, meaning and effect of *s 115(7)* has been considered authoritatively in *R (X) v Chief Constable of the West Midlands Police* [2004] EWCA Civ 1068, [2005] 1 All ER 610, [2005] 1 WLR 65. It was held that the Chief Constable was under a duty to disclose if the information might be relevant, unless there was some good reason for not making such a disclosure, and that he was not required to afford the subject of the information a right to make representations. Further *s 115* has been held to engage *Art 8* of the *European Convention for the Protection of Human Rights and Fundamental Freedoms* but has been held to be compliant with that *Article* (see *R(X) v Chief Constable of the West Midlands Police* (above). See also *R (L) v Metropolitan Police Comr* [2006] EWHC 482 (Admin), [2006] All ER (D) 262 (Mar), *R v Local Authority and Police Authority in the Midlands, ex p LM* [2000] 1 FLR 612), *R (on the application of Pinnington) v Chief Constable of Thames Valley Police* [2008] EWHC 1870 (Admin), [2008] All ER (D) 405 (Jul).

Additionally, the Chief Officer may provide further information which ought not to be included in the certificate on the grounds that its disclosure may hamper detection or prevention of crime but which may be disclosed directly to the registered person signing the application (*PA 1997, s 115(8), (9)*). The discretion afforded is broad and extends to any information which may, in the opinion of the Chief Officer, be relevant. It has been explained judicially that 'any' means just what it says and is not limited in its scope to information relating to criminal conduct: see *R (L) v Metropolitan Police Comr* [2006] EWHC 482 (Admin) [2006] All ER (D) 262 (Mar). By *s 116*, the issuing of ECRCs are extended to Crown employment.

16.7 Employee's Past Criminal Convictions

In *Desmond v Chief Constable of Nottinghamshire Police* [2011] EWCA Civ 3 the Court of Appeal held that the police are not obliged in tort to take reasonable care when providing information under the *PA 1997* about a job applicant for the purposes of the ERRC certificate. The Court of Appeal held that statute does not confer a common law cause of action for breach of statutory duty in the information provided by the police or by refraining from providing information. The Court observed that the procedure's purpose of protecting vulnerable young people would be jeopardised if the police owed a tortious duty of care towards the person the subject of the check. The Court further observed that an aggrieved individual was not without alternative avenues of redress including the statutory remedy of correcting an inaccurate certificate contained in *s 117* of the *PA 1997*, a judicial review application and/or a claim under the *Human Rights Act 1998* for breach of *art 8*, breach of the *Data Protection Act 1998* or claims for misfeasance in public office and/or maladministration. The *Protection of Freedoms Act 2012* introduces a new *s 117A* to the *PA 1997* which provides for an independent monitor to whom application may be made to determine if information is not relevant or ought not to be included in a certificate.

In the case of each certificate outlined above, the Secretary of State may refuse to issue a certificate unless satisfied of the applicant's identity, which may involve the provision of fingerprints to confirm identity (*PA 1997, s 118*). If the applicant believes that any of the information contained in any certificate is inaccurate, he may apply in writing to the Secretary of State for a new certificate (*PA 1997, s 117*). On the utilisation of *s 117* see *R(B) v Secretary of State for Home Department and Metropolitan Police Comr* [2006] EWHC 579 (Admin), [2006] All ER (D) 370 (Mar). It is an offence to falsify or alter certificates or use certificates belonging to another (*PA 1997, s 123*). It is also an offence for employees of registered bodies or recipients of CRC or ECRC information to disclose the information contained in the certificates otherwise than in the course of their duties (*PA 1997, s 124*). The Secretary of State issued in April 2009 a revised Code of Practice in relation to the provision of information under the *Act* (*PA 1997, s 122(1), (2)*). The Code, titled 'Code of Practice and Explanatory Guide for Registered Persons and other recipients of Disclosure Information', is available from www.official-documents.gov.uk/document/other.

The *Protection of Freedoms Act 2012* makes certain minor amendments to the provisions of *Part V* of the *PA 1997* and criminal record certificates are now obtained from the newly created Disclosure and Barring Service ("DBS").

The government announced in March 2013 that new legislation will be enacted to filter out certain convictions from disclosure on a criminal record certificate. The filtering rules which are now before parliament for consideration are as follows:

An adult conviction will be removed from a criminal record certificate if:

(i)   11 years have elapsed since the date of conviction

(ii)   it is the person's only offence and

(iii)   it did not result in a custodial sentence.

Even then, it will only be removed if it does not appear on the list of specified offences. If a person has more than one offence, then details of all their convictions will always be included. An adult caution will be removed after 6 years have elapsed since the date of the caution – and if it does not appear on the list of specified offences.

For those under 18 at the time of the offence:

(i)   a conviction received as a young person would become eligible for filtering after 5.5 years – unless it is on the list of specified offences, a custodial sentence was received or the individual has more than one conviction

(ii)   a caution administered to a young person will not be disclosed if 2 years have elapsed since the date of issue – but only if it does not appear on the list of specified offences.

These proposed changes are made in response to the Court of Appeal's decision in *R (T and others) v Chief Constable of Greater Manchester and others* [2013] EWCA Civ 25, in which the Court of Appeal held that the disclosure of all cautions and convictions, however old or minor, on a DBS Certificate was incompatible with Article 8 of the Convention for Human Rights. In that case the claimants contended that, in certain respects, the provisions of the *Police Act 1997*, the *Rehabilitation of Offenders Act 1974* and the *Rehabilitation of Offenders Act 1974 (Exceptions) Order* were incompatible with article 8 of the European Convention on Human Rights. The Court of Appeal held that the provisions of the *PA 1997*, requiring disclosure of all convictions, were incompatible with art 8 rights as the disclosure of all convictions and cautions relating to recordable offences was disproportionate to the legitimate aim of protection of the public.

16.8   THE SAFEGUARDING OF VULNERABLE GROUPS ACT 2006

The *Safeguarding Vulnerable Groups Act 2006* ("the *Act*") received Royal Assent on 8 November 2006 and significant provisions came into force on 12 October 2009. The Act provides that it is an offence to employ a person to work with children or vulnerable adults unless they were registered with the then Independent Safeguarding Authority ("ISA"). A main function of the ISA was the maintaining of two lists of persons barred from carrying out regulated activity in relation to children and, separately, vulnerable adults. From 12 October 2009 it was an offence for a barred individual to seek or undertake regulated activity with children and vulnerable adults and it was an offence for a Regulated Activity Provider (as defined in the *Act*) to knowingly employ a barred person in relation to regulated activity (*Safeguarding Vulnerable Groups Act 2006 (Commencement No 6, Transitional Provisions and Savings) Order 2009 (SI 2009/2611)*). A "Regulated Activity" was any activity which involves contact with children or vulnerable adults, eg fostering and childcare, specified activities involving contact with children or vulnerable adults in specified places or at specified times or overnight and activities involving workers in defined positions of responsibility. A "Controlled Activity" included support work in the health or further education field, support work in adult social care and work for specified organisations which would involve frequent access to sensitive records relating to children and/or vulnerable adults. Other provisions relating to registration under a vetting and barring scheme, which were due to commence in July 2010, were not brought into force and new legislation in the *Protection of Freedoms Act 2012* creates a new scheme considered in outline below.

In *R (Royal College of Nursing) v Secretary of State for the Home Department* [2010] EWHC 2761 (Admin), [2011] Fam Law 231, provisions of the *Act* providing for a person to be automatically placed on a barred list in the event of a caution or conviction were held to breach *art 6* of the *ECHR* and were incompatible with the *Human Rights Act* because the provisions did not permit representations to be made prior to being placed on the list. In other respects, in relation to appeal and minimum barring period, the Act was however found to be compliant with the *ECHR* and *HRA*.

16.9   THE PROTECTION OF FREEDOMS ACT 2012

The *Protection of Freedoms Act 2012* ("the *Act*") amends the *Safeguarding Vulnerable Groups Act 2006* and creates a new corporate body, the Disclosure and Barring Service ("DBS"). The relevant amending provisions are found in *Part V* of the *Act*.

Sections 64–76 of the *Act* make amendments to the definition of regulated activity and the definition of vulnerable adults under the *Safeguarding Vulnerable Groups Act 2006* (see *ss 64–66*) and abolish the concept of controlled activity and monitoring (*ss 68–69*). Changes are made to the test for barring decisions (*s 67*) and the information required in order to

16.9 Employee's Past Criminal Convictions

make a barring decision is addressed in s 70. A power of review of barring decisions by the DBS of its own motion is provided for in *s 71* of the *Act*. By *s 72* an affected person may apply for information relating to a barring decision.

Section 73 of the *Act* introduces a new *s 34ZA* into the *Safeguarding Vulnerable Groups Act 2006* which requires a regulated activity provider to check that any relevant person is not barred prior to engaging that person. The duty also extends to suppliers of personnel.

Section 87 of the *Act* creates the DBS and by *s 87* the ISA is dissolved and its functions transferred to the DBS. *Schedule 8* of the *Act* provides further detail in relation to the constitution and operation of the DBS. Information in relation to the DBS may be obtained from its website www.gov.uk/government/organisations/disclosure-and-barring-service.

16.10 RECORDING EMPLOYEES' CRIMINAL CONVICTIONS

The *Data Protection Act 1998* limits the right of an employer to process data on employees' criminal convictions without the express consent of the employee, save for limited purposes specified in the *Act* (*DPA 1998, Sch 3*). (See further **9.12** Disclosure of Information.)

17   Employment Tribunals – I

17.1   HISTORY

Employment tribunals (known until 1998 as 'industrial tribunals') are the principal forum for adjudicating disputes between employees (and prospective or former employees, and in some cases other workers) and employers. The tribunals, which were originally created in 1964 to decide disputes about liability to pay Industrial Training Levy, have over the years been given significant additional jurisdiction, increasingly so in recent years.

The workload of the employment tribunals has, unsurprisingly, fluctuated over the 49 years of their operation. In more recent years the number of cases rose from a low of 29,304 applications registered in 1988–89, to 236,100 in 2009–10. The figures have been affected in recent years in particular by significant numbers of multiple claims, mostly for equal pay, which have led to considerable variations in the total number of claims from year to year, and recently large numbers of claims for holiday pay by air crew, reissued every three months. The underlying trend of single claims has been gradually rising in recent years, reaching a high point of over 70,000 such claims in 2009–10, but both the total number of claims (218,100) and the number of individuals bringing separate claims fell back in 2010–11 and again in 2011–12 (186,300).

Statistics of numbers of cases do not give the full picture of the volume and complexity of the tribunals' case load in recent years. The number of individual claims under separate jurisdictions raised in each case has been steadily rising and now averages approx. 1.7 per case. The trend to more complex cases and lengthier hearings has been reinforced by the extension of the tribunals' jurisdiction to cover discrimination on grounds of religion or belief, sexual orientation and age and claims by agency workers as well as the dramatic increase in the numbers of multiple equal pay claims.

The increase in workload since the 1990s, which has not been matched by increases in resources, has put a considerable strain on the tribunal system. This has led to a number of measures intended to improve efficiency and effectiveness. Various changes to procedures were made by the *Trade Union Reform and Employment Rights Act 1993 ('TURERA 1993')* and new rules of procedure were made the same year; further reforms were enacted by the *Employment Rights (Dispute Resolution) Act 1998 ('ERDRA 1998')*. Since 2000, several further initiatives have been taken.

(a)   New Rules of Procedure were introduced as from July 2001 (the *Employment Tribunals (Constitution and Rules of Procedure) Regulations 2001 (SI 2001/1171)* and their Scottish counterpart *(SI 2001/1170)*). Those new rules embodied a number of changes, of which the most significant were:

   (i)   The introduction of an Overriding Objective for tribunals, which must be taken into account in interpreting the rules of procedure and in deciding issues affecting the conduct of the proceedings. The Overriding Objective is 'to deal with cases justly', which includes so far as practicable ensuring that the parties are on an equal footing, saving expense, dealing with cases in ways proportionate to their complexity, and ensuring that they are dealt with expeditiously and fairly. The parties are required to assist in the achievement of this objective.

   (ii)   Tribunals were given powers to order a claim (or defence) to be struck out on the ground that it was 'misconceived', a term defined as including having 'no reasonable prospects of success'.

407

(iii)   The power to award costs was extended to cases where the bringing or conducting of proceedings was 'misconceived' (defined as above), and the amount that could be awarded on a summary assessment by the tribunal was raised from £500 to £10,000. In addition the deposit that could be ordered at a pre-hearing review was increased to a maximum of £500; previously it had been £150.

These changes were retained and built on in further reforms of the rules in 2004, 2009 and 2012 (see below). During 2012, a comprehensive review of the rules was undertaken under the chairmanship of Underhill J (as he then was) and new rules contained in the *Employment Tribunals (Constitution and Rules of Procedure) Regulations 2013, SI 2013/1237* ('the *2013 Regulations*') will come into force on 29 July 2013. This new rules will be covered in depth in a future edition of this work.

(b)   Following the recommendations of a Government Task Force which had been appointed to reassess the workings of the employment tribunal system as a whole, which recommended a greater emphasis on the early resolution of disputes, major changes in the procedure for making claims to employment tribunals were introduced by the *Employment Act 2002* and accompanying *Dispute Resolution Regulations*. The details of these procedures, which are now largely of historical interest following the repeal of the relevant provisions of the *2002 Act* by the *Employment Act 2008*, are briefly noted at **17.2** below. At the same time, various changes in tribunal procedure were made by Rules of Procedure which came into force on 1 October 2004 (the *Employment Tribunals (Constitution and Rules of Procedure) Regulations 2004, SI 2004/1861* ('the *2004 Regulations*'; the *Rules* themselves are in *Schedule 1* to the *Regulations* ('*the ET Rules*')). The *Regulations* and *Rules* apply equally to England and Wales and to Scotland, with some minor differences of terminology (in practice there are rather greater differences between the two jurisdictions). The *ET Rules* have been retained, with relatively minor further amendments, following the repeal of the principal provisions of *Part 2* of the *Employment Act 2002*. As indicated above, new rules of procedure set out in the *2013 Regulations* will come into force on 29 July 2013.

(c)   A major review of the tribunal system generally, under Sir Andrew Leggatt, a former Lord Justice of Appeal (*Tribunals for Users*, TSO August 2000) led to the creation by the *Tribunals, Courts and Enforcement Act 2007*, of a unified tribunal system, with a transfer of responsibility for employment tribunals from the DTI to the Ministry of Justice, but with the employment tribunals retaining their separate identity, and the existing tripartite structure of membership.

The *2007 Act* expressly preserves the separate identity of employment tribunals and the EAT, but not their administrative independence from the rest of the new tribunal system. The Tribunals Service was given the responsibility for the administration of employment tribunals and the Employment Appeal Tribunal, with BIS (as successor to the DTI) retaining responsibility for the Rules of Procedure. Subsequently the Tribunals Service has been merged with HM Courts Service to form HM Courts and Tribunals Service, which came into being on 1 April 2011. In Scotland, a Scottish Tribunals Service does not presently have responsibility for employment tribunals. A consultation in 2012 considered whether the employment tribunals and EAT in Scotland should transfer to that service; ultimately, however, no such proposals were contained in the *Tribunals (Scotland) Bill*, part of the Programme for Government 2012–13.

One change of detail made by the *2007 Act* (*Sch 8 para 36*, inserting a new *s 3A* into the *ETA 1996*) is the re-naming of employment tribunal chairmen (as they had been designated since 1964) as Employment Judges; Regional Chairmen became Regional Employment Judges. The change took effect on 1 November 2007.

(d)   There have been a number of other developments aimed at promoting the early resolution of employment disputes. A scheme for voluntary arbitration through ACAS in unfair dismissal cases, foreshadowed by the *ERDRA 1998*, came into operation in 2001 for England and Wales and early 2004 in Scotland. It has subsequently been extended to cover disputes about the right to request flexible working arrangements. However, the scheme has had a very limited impact, with less than 100 cases referred to it since its inception. See further **18.37** below. Despite the limited impact of the voluntary arbitration service, there has been increasing interest in alternative dispute resolution schemes for employment disputes, and initiatives in this area include the development of mediation services by ACAS (which received 150 cases in 2006–7, rising each year to 241 in 2009–10 but falling back to 223 cases in 2010–11) and in January 2009 the introduction of a facility for judicial mediation within the employment tribunals themselves (see **18.31** below for details).

A further initiative introduced by ACAS in 2009, with significant initial success, has been a facility for Pre-claim Conciliation, before a claim is presented to an employment tribunal. Nearly 10,000 cases were referred to this scheme in its first year, and over 17,000 in the second year, 2010–11; of these 47.7% were recorded as successfully resolved, whilst 74% were not followed by tribunal claims (a more generous measure of success).

Building on these schemes, by *section 7* of the *Enterprise and Regulatory Reform Act 2013*, a new requirement will be introduced during 2013, requiring prospective claimants under certain jurisdictions of the tribunal to provide information to ACAS prior to presenting their claim to the tribunal. This requirement is to remedy the fact that only around one fifth of claimants contacted ACAS for advice before submitting their claims. Provision is made for a certificate of compliance to be issued by an ACAS conciliation officer, and for consequential adjustments to the time limits for presenting the claims (see **18.29** below for details).

17.2

The changes affecting the powers and procedure of employment tribunals introduced via the *Employment Act 2002* and the *Employment Act 2002 (Dispute Resolution) Regulations 2004*, with effect from 1 October 2004, were largely reversed by the repeal of the relevant parts of that *Act* by the *Employment Act 2008*, with effect from 6 April 2009 and the consequential lapse of the *Regulations*. However partly because of transitional provisions affecting claims brought before then, and some claims brought thereafter, the provisions have continued to generate considerable case law, and for this reason a brief summary of the features of the legislation is given below.

(a)   A requirement for claimants to go through workplace grievance procedures where relevant, before a claim can be made to a tribunal, with power to reduce compensation if the claimant does not do so (and increase it if the employer does not provide a procedure, or dismisses or takes disciplinary action without following the applicable statutory procedure) (*2002 Act, s 31*);

(b)   Changes in the time limits for commencing tribunal claims to allow time for internal procedures to be concluded without the necessity to present a claim to preserve the employee's rights; the employee is not permitted to present his or her claim to the tribunal in certain cases until after the employer has been given the opportunity to resolve it under the grievance procedure, and in certain circumstances the time limit for claiming is automatically extended by three months (*ss 32, 33*);

(c)   Provision for a limited conciliation period for ACAS to attempt to secure a settlement; if the case was not settled within that period (or any extension of it), ACAS ceased to be under a duty to offer its assistance in any further attempts at settlement (s 24: this provision was repealed, and the implementing provisions in the *ET Rules* were revoked, with immediate effect both for new cases and those already before the tribunals, on 6 April 2009).

The changes introduced by the *2002 Act* proved to be widely disliked, and the approach of the courts to their interpretation has generally been based in the importance of preserving rights of access to justice rather than literal application of the legislation. In March 2007 the DTI instituted a consultation exercise on whether the procedures introduced by the *2002 Act* should be scrapped, as recommended by a Review commissioned by the Department. The consultation exercise confirmed the Government in its view that the procedures should be repealed, and the legislation to repeal the statutory dispute resolution procedures and associated procedural requirements, received the Royal Assent as the *Employment Act 2008* in November 2008.

The relevant provisions of the *2008 Act* were brought into force on 6 April 2009, but subject to significant exceptions, contained in the *Employment Act 2008 (Commencement No 1, Transitional Provisions and Savings) Order 2008, SI 2008/3232*. This Order preserves the old law in cases where either of the statutory dismissal and disciplinary procedures applied, if the employer dismissed the employee, or initiated the statutory procedure, on or before 5 April 2009. The old law also applies in cases where either of the statutory grievance procedures applied, if the matter the subject of the claim occurred on or before 5 April 2009, or, if it extended over a period spanning that date, if the employee either presented a claim or submitted a written grievance before 5 July 2009 (or in certain cases 5 October 2009). For those cases where the old law applies, not only was the acceptance of a claim still subject to the preconditions in *s 32* of the *Employment Act 2002* (where applicable) but also the provisions of *s 31* giving tribunals powers to increase or decrease compensation by up to 50% where there has been a failure to comply with the applicable statutory procedure, continue to apply.

Other changes introduced at the same time as the repeal of the *2002 Act* included simplified tribunal claim and response forms. However the procedure for screening claims prior to acceptance for compliance with procedural requirements such as using the prescribed claim form and providing the mandatory information on it, has also been retained, albeit the requirements of the new claim form are less prescriptive. New forms and new procedures for screening claims upon presentation are introduced by the Rules within the *2013 Regulations*.

One feature of the 2002 reforms that has been retained in modified form is the power given to tribunals to increase or decrease compensation in certain circumstances; the tribunal may increase or decrease the sum awarded by up to 25% if satisfied that the employer or employee, as the case may be, has unreasonably failed to comply with a provision of a relevant ACAS Code of Practice (*Trade Union and Labour Relations (Consolidation) Act 1992, s 207A*, inserted by the *Employment Act 2008, s 2*). The relevant ACAS Code is that on disciplinary and grievance procedures, which was reissued in a simplified and shortened form to accompany the legislative changes. One consequence of these provisions is that cases on uplifts to compensation under *s 31* of the *Employment Act 2002* may be relevant to the equivalent provisions introduced by the *2008 Act*. Two such cases are *Wardle v Credit Agricole Corporate and Investment Bank* [2011] IRLR 604 and *Abbey National v Chagger* [2010] ICR 397. The Court of Appeal held that it was incumbent when setting the percentage increase or decrease to have regard to the size of the award; it also considered that the maximum uplift should be reserved for the most exceptional and serious cases; there must be proportionality. The spirit of the ACAS Code of Practice should be followed even if the case is not one of misconduct: see *Lund v St Edmunds School, Canterbury* (UKEAT/0514/12) – a 'some other substantial reason' dismissal. Uplifts cannot be made in favour of workers as opposed to employees: see *Local Government Yorkshire and Humber v Shah* (UKEAT/0587/11).

17.3   There have been three further developments affecting the operation and procedure of employment tribunals since the repeal of the *2002 Act*.

(a)   In January 2011, the Department for Business, Innovation and Skills (BIS, the successor to the DTI) launched a further round of consultation on proposals to reform the employment tribunal system to remove what the consultation document stated were regarded as unjustifiable burdens the working of the existing system places on business (*Resolving Workplace Disputes*). In addition to a change in substantive employment rights (the extension of the qualifying period of service for unfair dismissal claims to two years, since implemented for employees whose employment commences on or after 6 April 2012) the consultation paper proposed a requirement to submit all claims initially to ACAS, to be passed on to the tribunal only if not successfully conciliated within a set period, likely to be a month (see **18.29** below); greater powers for tribunals to dispose of weak claims by striking out, including powers to do so on paper without a hearing; an increase in the maximum deposit that can be required (to £1,000) and the limit on costs orders (to £20,000); abolishing payments of expenses to witnesses; delegating to Legal Officers some of the interlocutory work now undertaken by employment judges; taking written witness statements as read at hearings; extending the provision for cases to be heard by a judge sitting alone to cover unfair dismissal; introducing penalties for employers found liable by a tribunal; and reducing the use of lay members in the EAT.

The outcome of this consultation was announced in November 2011; broadly, this was that it is the Government's intention to proceed with all of the proposals summarised, and some, which can be implemented by secondary legislation, were brought into effect on 6 April 2012 by the *Employment Tribunals (Constitution and Rules of Procedure) (Amendment) Regulations 2012, SI 2012/468*. These changes are the addition of unfair dismissal claims to the categories of cases where an employment judge can sit alone (with a discretion to order a full panel under the *Employment Tribunals Act 1996, s 4(5)*: see the *Employment Tribunals Act 1996 (Tribunal Composition) Order 2012, SI 2012/988*); an increase in the maximum sum that can be ordered as a deposit to £1,000 and the maximum sum that can be awarded for costs to £20,000; ending the payment of travel expenses for witnesses, with a new power for the tribunal to order a party to pay these expenses; and a new rule providing that witness statements, where used, are to be taken as read unless the tribunal directs otherwise (this does not affect the position in Scotland that witness statements are generally not used). Although all these changes came into effect on 6 April 2012, all but the first only apply to cases presented on or after that date (see *Reg 3* of the *2012 Regulations*).

Most of the other changes required legislation. The *Enterprise and Regulatory Reform Act 2013, Part 2* was enacted on 25 April 2013. Some provisions are already in force; others have commencement dates appointed throughout 2013 (see *s 103*). The Act makes provision for conciliation through ACAS prior to instituting proceedings (*s 7, s 8, s 9*); the prohibition on disclosure of information held by ACAS (*s 10*); the extension of decision making to legal officers (*s 11*); changes to the composition of the Employment Appeal Tribunal so that, by default, appeals are heard by a judge sitting alone but with power to direct that lay members sit on the case (*s 12*); no qualifying period of employment for dismissals for political opinions (*s 13*); confidentiality of negotiations before termination of employment (*s 14*); the Secretary of State to have power to order the increase or decrease in the limit of the compensatory award in unfair dismissal cases(*s 15*); the power of the Tribunal to award financial penalties payable to the Secretary of State of between £100 and £5,000 where the Tribunal concludes the employer has breached any of the worker's rights to which the claim relates and there are one or more aggravating features (*s 16*); various changes to the law on protected disclosures (*ss 17–21*); and renaming compromise agreements (*s 23*).

(b)   In a separate but parallel development, in December 2011 the Ministry of Justice published consultation proposals for the introduction of fees for employment tribunal claims. Proposals were then based on a Government decision, announced in October 2012, that fees would be introduced, the consultation being limited to the levels of fees, when and how they would be payable, remission for those of limited means, and other issues arising. The Government aimed to save £10 million a year from the cost of the employment tribunals (just over £80 million in 2010–11) by levying fees, but questions were raised by consultees about whether the level of exemptions and administrative cost of determining disputes about fees will affect this figure.

The consultation on fees closed in March 2012. There was a generally hostile response from professional bodies representing employment practitioners.

On 29 July 2013, the *Employment Tribunals and the Employment Appeal Tribunal Fees Order 2013* will come into force. That order will provides for the payment of fees for (i) issuing a claim, (ii) the listing of a final hearing (iii) the making of certain specified applications by a respondent (the applications being: reconsidering a default judgment, reconsidering a judgment after a final hearing, dismissing a claim upon withdrawal, bringing an employer's contract claim), or (iv) by a Respondent upon a listing for judicial mediation.

The level of fees are specified in the draft order. Issue fees of either £160 or £250 and hearing fees of either £230 or £950 (in each case dependant on the type of claim, claims being divided for this purpose into 'type A' and 'type B' claims) are payable by the Claimant. The lower level of fee will apply to straightforward claims such as unauthorised deductions and claims for statutory redundancy payments; the higher level will apply for most claims (e.g. unfair dismissal, discrimination, whistleblowing etc). Different level of fee apply for grouped claims (but will not exceed the sum that would have been due had the claims been presented individually). Fees for the specified Respondent applications vary from £60 to £350 depending on the application and type of claim. The fee for judicial mediation is set at £600. Schedule 3 of the Order sets out the proposed scheme for granting full and part remission in respect of the fees that would otherwise be payable. Full details of the fee arrangements will be included in the next edition of this work.

(c)   An additional announcement made by BIS on the occasion of the publication of the Government's response to the January 2011 consultation was the creation of a small group, chaired by Underhill J (as he then was), the immediate past President of the EAT, to conduct a 'root and branch' review of the *ET Rules*, with a view to the simplification both of the *Rules* and their operation. The group reported in July 2012. A further consultation on those proposed rules was launched in September 2012 and the Government's response to that exercise published in March 2013. As a result of the review, on 28 May 2013, the *Employment Tribunals (Constitution and Rules of Procedure) Regulations 2013, SI 2013 No 1237* ('the *2013 Regulations*') were made. The *2013 Regulations* contain the new Rules in *Schedule 1*. The new rules will come into force on 29 July 2013 and will be comprehensively considered in a future edition of this work.

17.4   Rules of Procedure

The *2004 Regulations* contain provisions for the appointment and tenure of office of the Presidents of the Tribunals (one for England and Wales and one for Scotland), the Vice-President (for Scotland only), Regional Employment Judges (in England and Wales only) and Employment Judges and members. The *Regulations* also cover the composition of tribunals for particular cases, special rules for cases involving issues of national security, and a number of ancillary provisions which are referred to at relevant points in the text below. *Schedule 1* contains the rules of procedure applicable to most claims, and is referred to as the *Employment Tribunals Rules of Procedure 2004* ('the *ET Rules*'). The other Schedules now cover the following:

(a)	*Schedule 2:*	Complementary rules for National Security cases;
(b)	*Schedule 3:*	Training levy appeals;
(c)	*Schedule 4:*	Appeals against improvement and prohibition notices issued under the *Health and Safety at Work, etc Act 1974*;
(d)	*Schedule 5:*	Appeals against non-discrimination notices issued by the Equality and Human Rights Commission.
(e)	*Schedule 6:*	Complementary rules for Equal Value cases (added by *SI 2004/2351*).

The *2004 Regulations* and *ET Rules* made considerable changes in the substance of the procedure to be applied by tribunals. The *Rules* were written in what is intended to be simpler language more readily understandable by litigants without legal training; there have however been judicial criticisms of the quality of drafting of the *Rules* and this was a key driver behind the development of the forthcoming rules contained within the *2013 Regulations*. As part of the simplification, a number of changes in terminology were introduced by the *2004 Regulations*:

(i)   Those applying to a tribunal are referred to as 'claimants' rather than 'applicants'; however there is no change to the term 'respondent'.

(ii)   The document by which an application is made to the tribunal is called a 'Claim Form' instead of an 'originating application'.

(iii)   The response by a respondent is called a 'Response Form' rather than a 'notice of appearance'.

(iv)   What were known as either directions hearings or interlocutory hearings became Case Management Discussions ('CMDs'), and preliminary hearings became Pre-hearing Reviews ('PHRs').

(v)   What was formerly called a Decision became a Judgment.

The *2008 Regulations* added a further category of hearing, known as interim hearings, which are for determining applications for interim relief in certain categories of unfair dismissal claims. The procedure for such hearings is now specified in *Rule 18A*.

17.5   Alongside the changes of terminology are changes of substance. Below is a brief summary of the principal changes of substance effected by the *2004 ET Rules*. These changes are not affected by the further amendments to the *ET Rules* by the *2008 Regulations*, or by the repeal of the *Employment Act 2002*, except where indicated.

(a)   Differently designed Claim Forms (known as Form ET1) and Response Forms (Form ET3) were introduced, together with electronic equivalents available on the tribunals' website (now accessed via www.justice.gov.uk/tribunals/employment). Use of the paper or electronic version of the prescribed forms is mandatory. Separately, the information required to be given on the Claim Form is prescribed in more detail. The forms were simplified somewhat following the repeal of the *2002 Act*, but the requirements to use the prescribed form and provide the information indicated on the form as mandatory were retained.

(b)   A screening process applies by which the tribunal secretariat weed out claims not containing the required information, or otherwise appearing to be outside the tribunal 's jurisdiction. Such cases are referred to a Judge for decision whether to refuse to accept and register the claim. (Such refusals are open to review, or appeal.) Claims not submitted on the prescribed form are returned to the claimant by the secretariat with a copy of the form for completion and resubmission.

(c)   Response Forms must be received by the tribunal within 28 days following the date that the Claim Form was sent to the respondent (not, as previously, 21 days from the date of *receipt*). Unless an extension of time has been requested before the period for responding has elapsed, and subsequently granted, if no Response Form has been received in due time, a Judge may issue a default judgment in favour of the claimant; the respondent may apply to have the default judgment reviewed, but this application will only be granted if the Judge hearing the review application is satisfied that there are reasonable prospects of successfully defending the claim, and may still be refused if there were no good reasons for failing to submit the Response Form in time. Late or incomplete responses may simply be rejected by a Judge, in which case the respondent will be treated as not having responded, and if the prescribed form has not been used, the Response will be rejected by the secretariat and returned to the respondent. Changes to the *ET Rules* from 5 April 2009 include a requirement, rather than a discretion, to issue default judgments, unless one or more of a limited number of exceptions applies.

(d)   The types of hearing of a case that can be held were rationalised. The possible categories are:

    (i)   Case Management Discussions (CMDs), conducted by an Employment Judge sitting alone, and in private, and which cannot deal with substantive issues in the claim, or applications to strike out a claim or response. CMDs are used to make any of a large range of possible case management orders and directions to prepare the case for a full hearing.

    (ii)   Pre-hearing Reviews (PHRs), which are held in public, normally by a Judge sitting alone (but a party may request a full tribunal). PHRs can deal with preliminary issues such as whether the claim was presented in time or whether the Claimant had sufficient service to complain of unfair dismissal and applications to strike out all or part of a claim or response, in addition to the former function, retained under the *ET Rules*, of considering whether a claim or response has reasonable prospects of success and, if not, giving a costs warning and ordering a deposit as a condition of continuing to pursue it. Evidence can be given at a PHR (except, probably, where the only issue is whether a deposit should be ordered: the position in such cases is not entirely clear; the relevant Rule is *Rule 18(2)(c)*).

    (iii)   Interim hearings, a new category added by the *2008 Regulations*, inserting a new *ET rule 18A*, to hear applications for interim relief in certain categories of unfair dismissal claims.

    (iv)   Hearings, which may be of the entire case or a preliminary issue (if not dealt with at a PHR) or just on liability or remedy. A Hearing (capitalised in the *Rules* to distinguish it from other types of hearings) must normally be in public and before a full tribunal, unless the claim is one which under *s 4* of the *Employment Tribunals Act 1996* can be determined by a Judge sitting alone (in such cases there is, as previously, a discretion to refer the matter to a full tribunal).

(v)   Review hearings, which will be before a Judge alone if the review is of a refusal to accept a Claim Form or Response Form, but otherwise normally before the tribunal or Judge, as the case may be, whose decision is the subject of an application for a review.

(e)   Decisions of tribunals which represent the final determination (subject to any appeal or review) either of the whole of a case or a specific issue (such as jurisdiction), have been renamed Judgments; tribunals may also issue 'orders' (formerly referred to as 'directions') in relation to any requirements imposed the parties at an interim stage in the proceedings or dealing with other case management issues. All Judgments must be made or confirmed in writing and signed by the Judge. Reasons (the former distinction between summary and extended reasons has been discontinued) may be given orally or in writing, and if given orally will not automatically be followed by written reasons unless this is requested by a party within 14 days of the issuing of the Judgment. Reasons for orders will be given if requested at the time, but not necessarily in writing.

(f)   Further powers to award costs (the Scottish term is 'expenses') were introduced for cases presented on or after 1 October 2004. These enable a tribunal to make an award in favour of a party who is not legally represented, to cover the costs of his or her time in preparing for the hearing (a 'preparation time order'), covering such hours as the tribunal assesses as reasonable at a fixed hourly rate. This was initially set at £25 an hour, but with an automatic increase of £1 an hour each year from 6 April 2005, so that from 6 April 2013 the rate is £33 an hour. Preparation time orders cannot be made if a costs order is also made (or vice versa) and can only be made under the same conditions as a costs order. The second new type of order, a wasted costs order, can be made against a representative, provided the representative is acting for profit, and is either an order to pay costs to the other party, or an order disallowing the representative's charges to his or her client in whole or in part. Tribunals may have regard to the means of the paying party in deciding whether, and if so how much, to award by way of costs.

(g)   A number of other changes of detail were made, including the procedure for making restricted reporting orders, and wider powers to conduct hearings by telephone or video link. New powers were given to Judges to order a non-party to produce documents in his or her possession relevant to the issues in the case, and to join as a party any person the Judge considers has an interest in the outcome of the case.

(h)   The public register of applications was closed on 1 October 2004. The register of decisions (now a register of judgments) has been retained, and judgments and written reasons remain available for public inspection, but proposals to post all judgments and written reasons on line have not yet been implemented. Following a ruling by the Information Commissioner under the *Freedom of Information Act 2000* (Case FS 50080369, 2 October 2008; the decision can be accessed at www.ico.gov.uk) information about the identity of respondents to proceedings must now be disclosed to interested parties.

The *Regulations* also confer power on the Presidents to issue Practice Directions regulating the procedure of tribunals and the manner of exercise of the powers conferred on tribunals and Employment Judges by the *Regulations* and *Rules*. The first Practice Directions issued under this power, which apply in Scotland only, were issued in December 2006; they cover lists of documents, sists (the Scots Law term for stays) for mediation and the procedure for counterclaims in contract cases. Other Practice Directions are issued from time to time by both Presidents to give directions for particular categories of cases, such as staying (sisting in Scotland) claims affected by a pending reference to the Court of Justice of the European Union (CJEU), or transferring all cases against a particular respondent to the same tribunal office.

Further changes made by the *2008 Regulations* introduced a requirement (rather than, as previously, a discretion), in certain cases brought after 5 April 2009, for an Employment Judge to issue a default judgment where a respondent has not submitted a response or it has not been accepted. The *Regulations* have also introduced new procedures for hearing applications for interim relief (as noted at (*d*(iv)) above), and for the automatic dismissal of claims where there has been an ACAS-conciliated settlement.

A further change in procedure, applicable for claims presented on or after 6 April 2010 and where a claim has been made under the provisions of the *ERA 1996* introduced by the *Public Interest Disclosure Act 1998*, allows for the claimant's underlying 'whistleblowing' disclosure to be forwarded by the tribunal secretariat to the relevant Regulator for investigation, if the claimant has signified a wish for this to be done. This does not affect the procedure for hearing the claim itself.

As from 6 April 2012 a number of the changes proposed in Resolving Workplace Disputes in 2011 have been implemented as from 6 April 2012, but in most cases only in relation to claims presented on or after that date. Further changes as a result of the *Enterprise and Regulatory Reform Act 2013* come into force during the course of 2013. The details of these changes are summarised at **17.3(a)** above.

Finally, as noted above, the *2013 Regulations* containing new Rules of Procedure will come into force on 29 July 2013, along with the provisions for the payment of fees. See at **17.3(b)** and (c) above.

17.6 ADMINISTRATION

The employment tribunals are constituted under the *Employment Tribunals Act 1996 ('ETA 1996')* (a consolidating Act replacing equivalent earlier legislation) and the *Regulations* and *Rules of Procedure* made under the powers conferred by the *ETA 1996*. (The changes effected by the *Employment Acts 2002* and *2008* were made by way of amendments to the enabling provisions of the *1996 Act*.) The overall responsibility for the running of the employment tribunals in England and Wales is vested in the President of the Employment Tribunals, a judicial officer appointed by the Lord Chancellor (*2004 Regulations, reg 4*). The tribunal system is divided into 12 regions, each with a Regional Employment Judge also appointed by the Lord Chancellor (*2004 Regulations, reg 6*). There is a separate President of the Employment Tribunals for Scotland, and a Vice-President, both appointed by the Lord President of the Court of Session (*2004 Regulations, regs 4, 7*). Tribunals sit at all the regional centres and at a various other permanent centres and an increasing number of *ad hoc* centres.

The administration of tribunals (and of the EAT) is now the responsibility of HM Courts and Tribunals Service ('HMCTS'), which came into existence on 1 April 2011, merging the former Tribunals Service with HM Courts Service. The Tribunals Service itself came into existence in 2006 as an executive agency of the then Department for Constitutional Affairs, now the Ministry of Justice, and was given a statutory basis by the *Tribunals, Courts and Enforcement Act 2007*. The merger of the two services does not affect the office of Senior President of Tribunals created by the *2007 Act*. The Senior President (currently Lord Justice Sullivan) has overall responsibility for all tribunals. HMCTS is responsible for the administration of some twenty separate statutory tribunals, including the provision of premises, staff and facilities such as computing.

The various tribunals within the remit of the Tribunals Service (and now HMCTS) have been brought together into a unified structure, with an Upper Tribunal replacing the various appellate tribunals and most of the first instance tribunals grouped into a number of Chambers reflecting their areas of jurisdiction. Employment tribunals and the Employment Appeal Tribunal have however retained their separate status, identity, judiciary and rules of procedure, although increasingly not their separate premises.

At present HMCTS is responsible for tribunals in Scotland as well as England and Wales; a recent consultation has not resulted in legislative proposals for the employment tribunals in Scotland to become part of that Service.

There is a Central Office of Employment Tribunals (COET) at Bury St Edmunds, which maintains the public Register of Judgments. Originally, all applications had to be sent to the Central Office but, since 1996, Claims have been required to be lodged at local offices. The relevant office is determined by the postcode of the claimant's place of work or former place of work, and claims presented electronically are automatically routed to the appropriate office based on the postcode given by the claimant for his or her (former) workplace. There is a separate Central Office of Tribunals for Scotland, in Glasgow (to which all Scottish claims are sent, and which houses the Register of Scottish Judgments), and there are separate offices for the Presidents of the Tribunals in England and Wales and Scotland (in London and Glasgow, respectively).

17.7   COMPOSITION

Tribunals are drawn from three panels (*2004 Regulations, reg 8*):

(a)   Employment Judges, who are appointed by the Lord Chancellor on the recommendation of the Judicial Appointments Commission (a body established by the *Constitutional Reform Act 2005*), or in Scotland by the Lord President of the Court of Session (there is a Scottish Judicial Appointments Board, but its responsibilities do not extend to recommending appointments to the employment tribunals judiciary), and must have a five-year legal qualification (this was reduced from seven years in 2008). Appointments are both full-time and part-time.

(b)   Persons appointed by the Secretary of State for Business, Innovation and Skills after consulting organisations representative of employees.

(c)   Persons so appointed after consultation with organisations representative of employers.

The members drawn from panels (*b*) and (*c*) (variously referred to as 'lay members', 'wing members' and 'the industrial jury') all serve part-time. The Presidents are required to maintain separate panels of Judges, and of each of the two categories of lay members, who are considered suitable to hear cases involving issues of national security, and the tribunal assigned to such a case will be composed of a member of each special panel (*2004 Regulations, regs 10, 11*). There is also a power to establish panels of Judges and members with specialist knowledge to hear particular categories of proceedings for which such knowledge would be beneficial (*reg 8(5)*). This power has been used to create specialist panels to hear equal pay cases, but there are no plans at present for other specialist panels.

The Department of Trade and Industry (now BIS) has in recent years attempted with some success to recruit more women, members of ethnic minorities, and younger people to the panels of lay members. Recruitment is now undertaken by advertising vacancies and selection by interviews. Lay members are paid a daily fee for sitting.

The composition, and methods of appointment and reappointment to membership, of the employment tribunals have in the past given rise to a potential difficulty under the *Human Rights Act 1998 ('HRA 1998')*. Article 6 of the *European Convention on Human Rights*, which the *HRA 1998* incorporates into UK law, confers the right to a determination of issues relating to civil rights (which includes most if not all issues brought before employment tribunals) at a fair and public hearing before an independent and impartial tribunal. The issue was raised whether employment tribunals could satisfy this requirement in cases where the Secretary of State for Trade and Industry was a party to the proceedings, as where claims were made against the Secretary of State because the employer was insolvent. Changes in the method of appointment of Judges and lay members in 2000 largely removed the potential conflicts of interest, and the creation of the Tribunals Service, together with the transfer of responsibility for recommending the appointment of Judges to the Judicial Appointments Commission (and appointments in Scotland being made by the Lord President), is thought to have resolved the problem, but this must remain open to possible judicial determination.

17.8   A full tribunal consists of one member from each panel. Decisions may be by majority. A tribunal may sit with only one lay member if both or all parties agree (*2004 Regulations, reg 9(3)*); in that event the Judge has a casting vote. If one party is neither present nor represented at a hearing, the tribunal cannot proceed to sit with only two members. This anomaly was intended to be rectified by *s 4* of *ERDRA 1998*; however, as of April 2013 this provision has still not been brought into force. If agreement is sought to the tribunal sitting with only one lay member, the parties must be informed as to whether the lay member is from the employers' or employees' panel: *Rabahallah v British Telecommunications plc* [2005] ICR 440 (following *De Haney v Brent Mind* [2003] EWCA Civ 1637, [2004] IRLR 348, a case about the equivalent situation in the EAT). In *Rabahallah*, the EAT recommended that the parties be asked to sign a standard form to confirm that informed consent has been given to the tribunal sitting or continuing with only one lay member. A tribunal with two lay members drawn from the same panel is not a properly constituted tribunal and any decision by such a panel would be a nullity.

Tribunals normally sit in public; the circumstances in which they may sit in private or reporting of proceedings may be restricted are explained below (see **17.18–17.19** below). The importance of a public hearing was reiterated in *Storer v British Gas plc* [2000] 2 All ER 440, [2000] 1 WLR 1237, [2000] ICR 603, [2000] IRLR 495, where the Court of Appeal set aside a decision on a preliminary issue reached at a hearing held in the private office of the Regional Employment Judge because no tribunal room was available. The court dismissed as irrelevant the argument that no members of the public had been prevented from attending the hearing.

17.9 Judges sitting alone

A full tribunal is required for the Hearing of most claims: however, certain categories of proceedings must be heard by a tribunal consisting of a Judge sitting alone, unless a Judge (not necessarily the same person who hears the case) directs to the contrary (*ETA 1996, s 4*). An important change to the categories of cases which can be heard by a judge sitting alone was made by the *Employment Tribunals Act 1996 (Tribunal Composition) Order 2012, SI 2012/988*, adding unfair dismissal claims to the list with effect from 6 April 2012. The principal categories of case covered by these provisions are now:

(a)   applications for interim relief in relation to dismissal in health and safety and public interest disclosure cases (*ERA 1996, ss 128–132*) or for trade union reasons (*TULRCA 1992, ss 161, 165* and *166*);

(b)   applications against the Secretary of State under *ERA 1996, ss 170* and *188* or *Pension Schemes Act 1993, s 126* (where the former employer is insolvent);

(c)   applications under the *ERA 1996, s 23* or *TULRCA 1992, s 68A* (unlawful deductions from wages, etc);

(d)   applications under the following provisions of *ERA 1996: s 11* (particulars of employment terms and itemised pay statements), *s 34* (guarantee payments), *s 70* (remuneration during suspension on medical grounds), *s 111* (unfair dismissal), *s 163* (redundancy payments), and *s 206(4)* (appointment of 'appropriate person' in proceedings, following the death of an employee);

(e)   applications under *TULRCA 1992, s 192* or *reg 11(5)* of the *Transfer of Undertakings (Protection of Employment) Regulations 2006 (SI 2006/246)* (failure to pay a protective award);

(f)   claims for breach of contract under the *Employment Tribunals Extension of Jurisdiction (England and Wales) Order 1994 (SI 1994/1623)* or the equivalent Scottish order;

(g)   Claims under the *Working Time Regulations 1998, reg 30* (and equivalent provisions applying to certain categories of worker not covered by the *1998 Regulations*) for holiday pay or pay in lieu of holiday not taken prior to the termination of employment, but not other claims under the *1998 Regulations* (this category of cases was added as from 6 April 2009);

(h)   Stage 1 hearings of equal value claims under the *Equal Pay Act 1970* (by an amendment to *Sch 6* to the *2004 Regulations*, made by the *2008 Regulations* and effective from 6 April 2009);

(i)   proceedings where both or all parties have given their written consent to a hearing before a Judge alone (whether or not consent has been subsequently withdrawn);

(j)   proceedings where the claimant has given written notice withdrawing the claim; and

(k)   proceedings where the respondent (or all respondents if more than one) does not contest the claim, or no longer does so.

(ETA 1996, s 4(2).)

For claims in categories not listed above, there is no power for a judge sitting alone to hear the case (as distinct from conducting a CMD or PHR in the case) and any decision made following such a hearing would be a nullity: *Nascimento v British Bakeries Ltd* [2005] All ER (D) 20 (Sep), EAT; *Insaidoo v Metropolitan Resources North West Ltd* [2011] All ER (D) 04 (May). In this connection it may be noted that whilst claims under *TULRCA 1992, s 192* for payment of a protective award already made under *s 189* can be heard by a judge sitting alone (as stated in (e) above), claims for a protective award to be made under *s 189* require a full panel, so a judgment upholding or refusing such a claim by a judge sitting alone is a nullity: *Weedon v Pinnacle Entertainment Ltd* (UKEAT/0217/11). It should be stressed that if any of the claims in a case where more than one claim has been made fall outside the list above, the case must be heard by a full panel (unless the claim requiring a full panel has been withdrawn or struck out before the hearing). As an example in claims for unfair dismissal and for failure to provide written reasons for dismissal: the latter claim must be heard by a full tribunal, and the addition of such a claim will normally necessitate that the unfair dismissal claim is also heard by a full panel.

The provision at (k) above was given greater significance by the decision of the EAT in *Parfett v John Lamb Partnership Ltd* (UKEAT/0111/08) [2008] All ER (D) 22 (Jul), holding that it covers cases where the Respondent either has not submitted a response or has not had the response accepted, with the result that he is debarred from defending the case. In such cases a default judgment may be issued without any hearing, but if a hearing is judged necessary, either on the merits of the claim or (more commonly) to determine remedy, it may be before a Judge sitting alone.

In addition, CMDs are always heard before a Judge sitting alone, regardless of the type or complexity of the claim, and this is generally the case for PHRs. In the latter case there is a discretion to order a hearing before a full tribunal, but only if this has been requested at least 10 days in advance by one of the parties, and the Judge considering the request considers that there will be one or more substantive issues of fact to be determined at the PHR, and that it is desirable that the matter be heard by a full tribunal (*ET Rules, rule 18(3))*. The requirement for Judges to sit alone for a PHR unless a party has requested a full tribunal may result in cases which would before the role of PHRs was expanded by the *2004 ET Rules* have been regarded as suitable for a full tribunal being finally determined without the participation of lay members (as to this see the comments of the EAT in *Sutcliffe v Big C's Marine Ltd* [1998] ICR 913), and this has resulted in a significant reduction in the proportion of cases in which lay members participate. The Judge who orders a PHR has no direct power to stipulate a full tribunal, and can at most only encourage the parties to ask for one. This makes it particularly important that a party whose case has been referred to a PHR should consider whether to ask for a full tribunal, and to make any application in good time.

Until 2009, an important omission from the list of claims which could be heard by a Judge sitting alone was claims for holiday pay under the *Working Time Regulations 1998 ('WTR')*, *reg 30*. Following the ruling of the Court of Appeal in *IRC v Ainsworth* [2005] EWCA Civ 441, [2005] IRLR 465 that claims for unpaid holiday pay under the *WTR* could only be brought under *reg 30*, and not as a complaint of unlawful deductions under *Part II* of the *ERA 1996*, it became necessary for any claim for arrears of pay which included a statutory holiday pay claim to be heard by a full tribunal. As a result, the *ETA 1996, s 4(2)* was amended with effect from 6 April 2009 by the *Employment Tribunals Act 1996 (Tribunal Composition) Order 2009, SI 2009/789*, by adding holiday pay claims under the *WTR* to the list of categories of claim which may be heard by a judge sitting alone. However the amendment does not extend to other claims under the *WTR*; claims in relation to rest breaks, rest periods and compensatory rest remain subject to the general requirement that a Hearing must be before a full tribunal. The *2009 Order* also made equivalent amendments to the regulations conferring rights to paid holiday for sea fishermen, aircrew in civil aviation, and workers on inland waterways. However, the addition of claims for holiday pay under the *WTR 1998* has since largely lost its importance, following the decision of the House of Lords (under the name of *Revenue and Customs Comrs v Stringer* [2009] UKHL 31, [2009] ICR 985, [2009] IRLR 677), overruling the Court of Appeal's decision in *IRC v Ainsworth* and holding that such claims may be brought under *Part II* of the *ERA 1996*. This may afford advantages in terms of time limits, and claims under *Part II* may also be heard by a judge sitting alone (see paragraph *(c)* above).

An order can be made, in any case falling within *ETA 1996, s 4(2)*, for the Hearing to be before a full panel. The power to make such orders has become much more significant with the addition of unfair dismissal to the categories of cases which can be heard by a judge sitting alone, a controversial change opposed by the majority of consultees in the consultation which preceded it. In an unfair dismissal case in which the members outvoted the judge, Lady Smith in *McCafferty v Royal Mail Group Plc* (UKEATS/0002/12) that that tribunals should give "careful consideration" to the parties' canvassed views.

Factors which must be considered in deciding whether to direct a full panel include whether there is a likelihood of a dispute of fact making this desirable (a point likely to be raised very commonly for unfair dismissal cases); whether there is a likelihood of a point of law arising making a Hearing before a Judge alone desirable; the views of the parties; and the existence of any concurrent proceedings which have to be heard by a full tribunal (*ETA 1996, s 4(5)*).

There have been conflicting authorities in the past on the extent of the obligation to consider ordering a hearing before a full panel in cases within *s 4(2)*. The EAT has revisited its previous decisions, and the position, based on *Gladwell v Secretary of State for Trade and Industry* [2007] ICR 264, [2006] All ER (D) 154 (Nov) and *Sterling Developments (London) Ltd v Pagano* [2007] IRLR 471, [2007] All ER (D) 01 (May), is currently as follows:

(a)   Listing, including a decision whether to list a case before a Judge sitting alone or a full tribunal, is a judicial function, but it is permissible for a Regional Employment Judge to lay down a general policy on listing, subject to the consideration of individual cases.

(b)   There is a discretion to refer a case that may be heard by a Judge alone to a full panel, and the exercise or non-exercise of this discretion is open to challenge by an appeal. In the event of an appeal, if the Judge has not given reasons for the way the discretion was exercised, the EAT may ask for reasons. The implication of this is that the point must be considered, and a decision made, for each case.

(c)   The parties should be told of their right to request a full panel, either at a CMD, if one is held, or in the Notice of Hearing; any request for a full panel should be judicially considered.

(d)   The Employment Judge responsible for the Hearing should consider whether a full panel is needed, having regard to any developments in the case (such as that it has become clear that there are significant disputes of fact), but also having regard to the desirability of not creating delay or expense.

(e)   It may be necessary to canvass the views of the parties on whether the Hearing should go ahead before the Judge alone, but it is not an error of law to fail to do so or to fail to give reasons for declining to order a full tribunal, and the Judge is not bound to accede to the wishes of the parties.

(f)   It may be necessary to at least consider ordering a full panel even if neither party asks for one, since unrepresented litigants may not appreciate the possibility of a full panel or why that would be desirable in the particular case.

The EAT in *Gladwell* declined to decide whether (as had been held in the earlier case of *Sogbetun v Hackney London Borough Council* [1998] ICR 1264, [1998] IRLR 676), a failure to exercise the discretion given by *s 4(5)* made the subsequent proceedings a nullity. It is this point in particular on which earlier cases differ, but in the light of the more recent guidelines the question has become largely academic, as a failure to follow the points indicated is likely to provide the basis for a successful appeal by the aggrieved party.

17.10   There is provision in the *ETA 1996, ss 4(6A)* and *7(3A)* (added respectively by the *ERDRA 1998, s 2* and the *Employment Act 2002, s 26*) for certain proceedings to be disposed of by an Employment Judge without a hearing. These powers have been partly implemented by the *2004 ET Rules*, which permit (and in some circumstances require) a Judge to issue a default judgment in favour of a claimant, either on liability only or including awarding the remedy claimed, if the respondent has failed to submit a Response Form within the time limit (*ET Rules, rule 8*).

The *Employment Act 2008, s 4*, made a further amendment to the *ETA 1996, s 7*, the effect of which is that *ET Rules* may provide for monetary claims to be decided by a Judge on the papers, and without a hearing, in the absence of objection by either party; the need for active consent to the matter being decided without a hearing would thus be removed. However the amendments to the *ET Rules* needed to implement this new provision had not, as at April 2013, been made. The use of the powers to widen the scope for decisions to be taken without hearings is one of the areas covered by the new rules contained in the *2013 Regulations*. No steps have been taken to implement proposals for dispensing further with hearings pending the coming into force of the new Rules.

A Judgment can also be issued without a hearing if all parties have agreed in writing as to its terms (*rule 28(2)*), and a Judgment dismissing the claim can be issued without the need for a hearing if it has been withdrawn by the claimant and the respondent requests such an order within 28 days of the notice of the withdrawal being sent to him or her (*rule 25(4)*, replacing the former practice that a claim would be dismissed automatically on the applicant notifying the tribunal that the claim was withdrawn). A new *rule 25A*, added by the *2008 Regulations*, provides for the automatic dismissal of claims where this course has been agreed to by the parties as part of a settlement achieved by ACAS conciliation and duly recorded in writing, and the claim is then withdrawn in accordance with the terms of settlement.

In certain circumstances also, a claim may be struck out for non-compliance by the claimant with an order of the tribunal without the right to a further hearing: see *Sodexho Ltd v Gibbons* [2005] ICR 1647, [2005] IRLR 836, EAT (striking out for non-payment of a deposit ordered at a PHR), but such a step is a judicial act and therefore a Judgment within the meaning of *rule 28*, and therefore open to review in certain circumstances: see further **18.15–18.16** and **18.75–18.76**.

In addition, there is provision for a case to be heard in the absence of a party who fails to attend (and is not represented) at the Hearing (*ET Rules, rule 27(5)*) or in the absence of a respondent who has been excluded from participating in the proceedings by virtue of *rule 9* for failure to submit a valid Response Form in time.

17.11 JURISDICTION

It is important to appreciate at the outset that employment tribunals are creatures of statute, and therefore have only such powers and jurisdiction as have been conferred on them by statutory provision. Jurisdiction cannot be conferred, or enlarged, by agreement between the parties to a case, or by the acquiescence or silence of a party. This does not mean that the tribunal cannot resolve a dispute about whether it has jurisdiction. Such disputes arise relatively frequently, and must be determined when they do arise; but if the tribunal erroneously holds that it has jurisdiction and proceeds to exercise it, the assertion of jurisdiction is open to challenge on appeal. Similarly, jurisdiction cannot be conferred simply by agreement, or a concession by one party which the party subsequently withdraws before there is a binding determination of the case: *Radakovits v Abbey National plc* [2009] EWCA Civ 1346, [2009] IRLR 307 (employer initially conceding claim in time, but later withdrawing concession; tribunal held bound to determine whether it had jurisdiction once the point was in dispute). (But, as was noted by Sedley LJ in *Clark v Clark Construction Initiatives Ltd* [2008] EWCA Civ 1466, [2009] ICR 718, at para 14, if the question determining jurisdiction is one of fact, there may be no practical grounds for appealing against an erroneous determination of the facts necessary to confer jurisdiction; and see *Kudjodji v Lidl Ltd* (UKEAT/0054/11): once tribunal has decided it has jurisdiction, and subject to any appeal, a different tribunal hearing the case at a later stage cannot reopen that decision.)

Tribunals have jurisdiction both under English and Scots law, and under EU law. The jurisdiction under English and Scots law is entirely statutory; jurisdiction under EU law derives from principles of EU law itself. The total number of separate jurisdictions is now in excess of 70, albeit many of these arise extremely infrequently in practice. The principal statutory provisions, which all apply equally to Scotland, are:

(a)   *Employment Rights Act 1996* ('*ERA 1996*'), as amended (unfair dismissal, redundancy payments, disputes over written particulars of employment and itemised pay statements, unlawful deductions from wages or requirements to make payments to employers (formerly under the *Wages Act 1986*), breaches of the *National Minimum Wage Act 1998*, guarantee payments, rights to time off for public duties, protection from detriment in certain health and safety (and other) cases and as a result of a protected disclosure under the *Public Interest Disclosure Act 1998*, time off for family emergencies, maternity, paternity, adoption and parental leave issues, failure to pay during medical suspension, issues over requests for flexible working arrangements, written reasons for dismissal, claims (other than pension claims) against the Secretary of State in insolvency cases, interim relief in certain unfair dismissal cases and a number of minor and ancillary matters);

(b)   *TULRCA 1992* (unfair dismissal or action short of dismissal for trade union reasons or for participation in industrial action; offering inducements not to join a union or to opt out of collective agreements; blacklisting complaints; time off for union and other duties; failure to consult recognised unions or employee representatives over proposed redundancies; claims for payment of protective awards made for such failures to consult; failure to consult recognised unions over training; and disputes over union membership, disciplinary action against members and expulsions);

(c)   *Equality Act 2010, ss 120* (claims under *Part 5* of the *Act* (work)) and *127* (claims of breach of an equality clause or rule under the equality of terms provisions of the *Act*) and *ss 122* and *128* (cases referred to the tribunal by a court);

(d)   *Employment Tribunals Extension of Jurisdiction (England and Wales) Order 1994* and the equivalent Scottish Order (claims in contract and employers' counterclaims, subject to a maximum jurisdiction of £25,000);

(e)   *Working Time Regulations 1998 (SI 1998/1833), regs 30–32* (complaints of dismissal or subjection to detriment for insisting on entitlements to breaks or rest periods, or refusing to agree to work hours in excess of the maximum, and of refusal to permit the exercise of rights to annual leave, rest breaks or rest periods conferred on workers by the *Regulations* or to provide compensatory rest, or to pay for annual leave or in lieu of accrued leave rights on termination of employment; also complaints of detrimental treatment or dismissal of those elected as representatives to negotiate workforce agreements, or standing as candidates for election);

(f)   *National Minimum Wage Act 1998, ss 22, 24* (appeals against penalty notices issued by compliance officers, and complaints of detriment by workers; complaints of underpayment are made under the *ERA 1996, Part II*);

(g)   *Employment Relations Act 1999 ('ERA 1999'), s 11* (failure to permit workers to be accompanied at grievance or disciplinary hearing or to postpone hearing for that purpose);

(h)   *Part time Workers (Prevention of Less Favourable Treatment) Regulations 2000 (SI 2000/ 1551), reg 8* (infringement of right not to be less favourably treated; subjection to detriment for assertion of rights);

(i)   *Fixed-term Employees (Prevention of Less Favourable Treatment) Regulations 2002 (SI 2002/2034), reg 7* (infringement of right not to be less favourably treated; subjection to detriment for assertion of rights) and *reg 9(5)* (application for declaration of status as permanent employee);

(j)   *Transfer of Undertakings (Protection of Employment) Regulations 2006 (SI 2006/246), regs 12* (failure to notify employee liability information to transferee) and *15* (failure to inform or consult with trade unions or employee representatives, and associated claims for non-payment of protective awards);

(k)   *Equality Act 2006, ss 21, 25* (appeals against unlawful act notices issued by the Commission for Equality and Human Rights, and applications by the Commission to restrain certain unlawful acts under the discrimination legislation);

(l)   *Agency Workers Regulations 2010 (SI 2010/93), reg 18* (with effect from 1 October 2011, complaints of infringements of the rights conferred by the *Regulations*, including equality of treatment with directly employed staff);

(m)   *Employment Relations Act 1999 (Blacklists) Regulations 2010 (SI 2010/493), regs 5, 6, 9* (refusal to employ or provide agency services to, or subjecting to detriment, workers, by reference to blacklists);

(n)   miscellaneous legislation (including claims arising from failure to consult recognised union over application to contract out of occupational pension scheme and certain other claims under the *Pension Schemes Act 1993*; appeals against industrial training levies; appeals against improvement and prohibition notices; disputes over time off for safety representatives and union learning representatives and other employee representatives given statutory rights to paid or unpaid time off; proceedings against employment agencies under the *Deregulation and Contracting Out Act 1994*).

The jurisdictions under the *Equality Act 2010* replace several heads of jurisdiction under the various statutes and regulations it replaces, principally the *Equal Pay Act 1970, Sex Discrimination Act 1975, Race Relations Act 1976* and *Disability Discrimination Act 1995*, and the regulations on discrimination on grounds of sexual orientation, religion or belief and age. Part of the latter, the *Employment Equality (Age) Regulations 2006, SI 2006/1031*, providing for the procedure for requests to remain in employment after a notice to retire was issued remained in force after the revocation of the main regulations, but was revoked as from 6 April 2011 (see the *Employment Equality (Repeal of Retirement Age Provisions) Regulations 2011, SI 2011/1069*) but subject to transitional provisions which may result in claims arising after that date.

The EAT has held in relation to complaints of unlawful deduction from wages under *ERA 1996, Part II* that tribunals have no jurisdiction to hear complaints of non-payment or under-payment of Statutory Sick Pay, where the employer disputes liability to pay, as such disputes are reserved to the Inland Revenue (now HM Revenue and Customs): *Taylor Gordon & Co Ltd (t/a Plan Personnel) v Timmons* [2004] IRLR 180. The reasoning applies equally to disputes about entitlement to Statutory Maternity Pay, Statutory Paternity Pay and Statutory Adoption Pay. The tribunal also has no jurisdiction to determine the amount of an unquantified bonus claimed to be due in order to determine whether a failure to pay the bonus was an unlawful deduction from wages, since only a claim for non payment of a specific sum said to be owed to the claimant can be made under *Part II*: *Coors Brewers Ltd v Adcock* [2007] EWCA Civ 19, [2007] IRLR 440; see also *Kingston upon Hull City Council v Schofield & Others* [2012] UKEAT 0616/11. The definition of 'wages' in the *ERA 1996* provides further parameters to the Tribunal's jurisdiction to determine claims of this type. Notable exceptions from the definition are payments in respect of expenses: see *London Borough of Southwark v O'Brien* [1996] IRLR 420 and *Qantas Cabin Crew (UK) Ltd v Lopez and Hooper* [2013] IRLR 4.

A further limitation on the jurisdiction of tribunals is that they cannot interpret the contractual terms of employees in proceedings for a determination of whether a statement of the particulars of terms of employment given to the claimant were correct: *Southern Cross Healthcare Co Ltd v Perkins* [2010] EWCA Civ 1442, [2011] IRLR 247 (a case concerning a dispute over the amount of holiday entitlement the claimants' contracts conferred).

It should be noted that tribunals in England and Wales, and in Scotland respectively, only have jurisdiction over cases with the required territorial connection with the respective part of Great Britain. If a claim over which only the tribunals in Scotland have jurisdiction is presented in England or Wales, or vice versa, the claim is ineffective and the receiving tribunal has no jurisdiction to deal with it (or even to transfer the papers to the correct country): *McFadyen v PB Recovery Ltd* (UKEATS/0072/08) (31 July 2009, unreported).

The initial requirements for jurisdiction are set out in the *2004 Regulations, reg 19*; this confers jurisdiction where the respondent resides or carries on business in England and Wales, or Scotland, as the case may be. (This may allow for a claim to be brought in either jurisdiction if the respondent carries on business in both.) A broad approach to the question whether the respondent carries on business within the jurisdiction was adopted in *Pervez v Macquarie Bank Ltd (London Branch)* [2011] ICR 266, [2011] IRLR 284, EAT, where it was held that the respondent (an Australian company) carried on business in England through the presence, working on secondment in London, of the claimant (who had been based in Hong Kong), although the respondent had no other presence in the jurisdiction. In addition, for England and Wales, there is jurisdiction if the County Court would have had jurisdiction had the remedy been by way of an action in that court. For contractual claims this will be the case if the contract is governed by English law or provides for the jurisdiction of the English courts, or if the cause of action arises within the jurisdiction. In Scotland there is jurisdiction if the place of execution or performance of the contract of employment concerned was in Scotland; the second limb of this test will only be satisfied if the place of performance is wholly or substantially in Scotland (*Prescription Pricing Authority v Ferguson* [2005] IRLR 464). The *ET Rules, rule 57,* give powers to transfer cases between jurisdictions, provided that the tribunal receiving the claim has jurisdiction, and otherwise by reference to the balance of convenience in the proceedings (this provision is sometimes used to transfer cases so that all related claims against a particular employer can be dealt with together by the same tribunal).

It should be noted that all of these points are separate from the jurisdictional issues which arise in relation to whether legislation conferring a substantive employment right applies to the particular circumstances of employment with an extra-territorial element; these issues are discussed elsewhere in this book in the context of the particular rights concerned.

17.12 Jurisdiction over EU law

Tribunals' jurisdiction is statutory, but there is no statutory provision giving the tribunal power to determine claims under EU law. The basis for tribunals hearing such claims has therefore been a source of legal difficulty.

There is clear authority recognising tribunals' jurisdiction where a claimant relies on *art 157* of the *Treaty on the functioning of the EU* (formerly *art 141* of the *Treaty of Rome* (equal pay claims)): *Pickstone v Freemans plc* [1989] AC 66, [1987] 3 All ER 756, [1987] 3 WLR 811, [1987] 2 CMLR 572, [1987] ICR 867. Claims relying on the *Equal Treatment Directive 76/207* (now replaced by the consolidating *Directive 2006/54*) against state authorities have been acknowledged to be within the jurisdiction of tribunals since the principle of direct effect was established by the European Court of Justice in *Marshall v Southampton and South West Hampshire Area Health Authority (Teaching)*: C-152/84 [1986] QB 401, [1986] ICR 335 and are now relatively common. The position in relation to other *Directives* depends on whether the particular provision concerned is sufficiently 'clear, precise and unconditional' to have direct effect, a question of EU law and thus ultimately for the CJEU.

Rulings of the Court of Appeal to the effect that tribunals have no jurisdiction to hear 'freestanding' claims under EU law, and that any such claims must be made under the relevant statute with the offending provision disapplied (*Biggs v Somerset County Council* [1996] 2 All ER 734, [1996] 2 CMLR 292, [1996] ICR 364; *Staffordshire County Council v Barber* [1996] ICR 379) have since been overtaken by developments in the case law of the CJEU, in particular *Mangold v Helm*: C-144/04 [2006] IRLR 143, *Impact v Minister for Agriculture and Food*: C-268/06 [2008] IRLR 552, *Kücükdeveci v Swedex GmbH*: C-555/07 [2010] IRLR 346, and *Dominguez v Centre Informatique du Centre Ouest Atlantique*: C-282/10 [2012] IRLR 321. The effect of these and other decisions is that a claim may be made in a domestic forum to give effect to a right conferred by EU law, whether or not fully and correctly transposed into domestic law by the member state, once the date for transposition has passed; such enforcement may in some circumstances be against private sector respondents as well as public bodies. The basis for the employment tribunal being an appropriate forum for such claims can be derived from the *Impact* case, where the CJEU ruled that a specialist tribunal with power to determine claims under national legislation implementing a *Directive* must also have power to decide claims made directly under the *Directive*, if alternative means of pursuing the claim would involve sufficiently serious procedural disadvantages.

17.12   Employment Tribunals – I

In addition, whether or not it is possible to maintain a claim in an employment tribunal directly under EU law, the EAT has held that the tribunal has power, even in proceedings against a non-state entity, to disapply, or read words into, a statutory provision, if this is necessary to give effect to a right conferred by EU law, and the rewriting of the statutory provision 'goes with the grain' of the domestic legislation: *Coleman v EBR Attridge Law LLP* [2010] 1 CMLR 846, [2010] ICR 242.

The Court of Appeal's decisions referred to above have two main effects (neither of which would appear to be affected by the *Impact* decision):

(a)   Procedural provisions, particularly those relating to time limits for making claims, contained in the relevant national legislation apply equally where that legislation is used as a basis for a claim relying on EU law. (The same principle applies to other procedural rules; for an example, see *Livingstone v Hepworth Refractories Ltd* [1992] ICR 287.)

(b)   Claims against the Government for damages for failure to implement EU Directives cannot be brought in the tribunal; the claim must be made in the High Court against the Attorney-General, or in Scotland the Lord Advocate (*Secretary of State for Employment v Mann* [1997] ICR 209, CA; for an example of such a claim, see *R v A-G for Northern Ireland, ex p Burns* [1999] IRLR 315).

However, there are still considerations of EU law which may affect how any discretion under the national legislation has to be exercised (eg to extend time), whether time limits run against the claimant and whether restrictions on remedies available under the national statute are compatible with EU law (*Marshall v Southampton and South West Hampshire Area Health Authority (No 2)*: C-271/91 [1994] QB 126, [1993] ICR 893 and *Levez v T H Jennings (Harlow Pools) Ltd*: C-326/96 [1999] IRLR 36, [1999] ICR 521 (both decisions of the CJEU)). For an interesting example see *Chief Constable of West Yorkshire Police v A* [2000] IRLR 465 (tribunal has power under EU law to make restricted reporting order protecting identity of transsexual claimant; see further **17.18** below).

The CJEU has endorsed the principle of the application of national time limits to cases reliant on EU law, provided that the time limits are no less favourable than for those for similar claims in domestic law and do not render the exercise of rights under EU law impossible in practice: *Fisscher v Voorhuis Hengelo BV*: C-128/93 [1994] IRLR 662, [1995] ICR 635. For a case where a limit was held to infringe this principle, see *Magorrian v Eastern Health and Social Services Board*: C-246/96 [1998] ICR 979, [1998] IRLR 86.

17.13   Human Rights Act 1998

Proceedings under the *HRA 1998, s 7* can only be brought in those courts or tribunals designated as 'appropriate'. As no designation has been made for employment tribunals, it follows that no 'freestanding' claims can be brought in the tribunal under that *Act*. (See on this *Whittaker v Watson (P & D) (t/a P & M Watson Haulage)* [2002] ICR 1244, confirming that the EAT is in the same position, and cannot therefore issue a declaration that a statutory provision is incompatible with the *HRA 1998*.) However, tribunals are 'public authorities' within *s 6* of the *Act*, and thus are required not to act in a way which is incompatible with rights secured by the *European Convention on Human Rights* unless compelled to do so by legislation. This means that issues of alleged infringement of a party's human rights may be raised in the course of tribunal proceedings, and the tribunal may find it necessary to take the *Convention* into account in the course of deciding substantive or procedural issues in the case. To that extent the position is similar to that under EU law, but the power to overrule primary legislation incompatible with a directly applicable EU obligation does not have a direct parallel. For guidance on how the *Convention* affects the application of the general law of unfair dismissal see *X v Y* [2004] EWCA Civ 662, [2004] IRLR 625, CA and *Turner v East Midlands Trains Ltd* [2013] ICR 525.

As a separate point, the right under *art 6* of the *Convention* to a fair trial in the determination of one's civil rights imposes obligations on tribunals as the forum in which that right is afforded in most employment cases. In addition to the obligations of independence and impartiality, discussed at **17.7** above, tribunals are required to afford a determination 'within a reasonable time' in order to satisfy *art 6*. Even the relatively generous timescale applied by the European Court of Human Rights in its jurisprudence under *art 6* was held to have been exceeded in *Somjee v United Kingdom* [2002] IRLR 886, where a series of applications to the tribunal and appeals to the EAT, with lengthy delays at a number of stages, had led to a nine year delay between the initial application and its final determination. However delay is not in itself a ground of appeal: rather the question in any appeal where there has been serious delay, whether in issuing the tribunal's judgment or more generally, is whether there is a real risk that the party appealing has in substance been deprived of the right to a fair trial in accordance with *Art 6*: *Bangs v Connex South Eastern Ltd* [2005] EWCA Civ 14, [2005] 2 All ER 316, [2005] IRLR 389, where the Court of Appeal laid down guidance on the correct approach to such appeals. The earlier decision of the EAT in *Kwamin v Abbey National plc* [2004] ICR 841, in which a broader approach was taken, was disapproved by the Court. In more mundane situations, compliance with the timeliness requirement of *Art 6* is a relevant factor for a tribunal in deciding whether to grant an adjournment, if the effect of doing so would be to create any significant delay or further delay in the proceedings.

Issues in relation to *Art 6* are frequently raised in employment tribunals (particularly by litigants in person) but in practice rarely add to the general principles of fairness embodied in the Overriding Objective (see **17.14** below for this), and given effect in more detail by the *ET Rules*. Two examples may be given. The Supreme Court has held, in *Home Office v Tariq* [2011] UKSC 35, [2011] IRLR 843, that the special procedure for National Security cases laid down by *Sch 2* to the *2004 Regulations*, under which a Special Advocate is appointed to advance the claimant's case and the claimant is denied access to sensitive evidence heard in private, does not breach the requirements of *Art 6*. In *Power v Greater Manchester Police Authority* (UKEAT/0087/10), the EAT held that there was no incompatibility with *Art 6* in a case where the claimant was denied the opportunity of cross-examining the person alleged to have discriminated against him (because the employer chose not to call her as a witness); the right under *Art 6* to cross-examine witnesses applies to criminal, not civil, proceedings. It is also worth noting the approach taken to *Art 6* in internal proceedings before the employer, recently clarified by the Supreme Court in *R (G) v Governors of X School* [2012] 1 AC 167 and the Court of Appeal in *Mattu v University Hospitals Coventry and Warwickshire NHS Trust* [2013] ICR 270.

In addition, *Art 6* is often cited in appeals based on the inadequacy of an employment tribunal's reasons; but in practice the higher courts' interpretation and application of the obligation to give reasons under *ET Rule 30(6)* and general principles of common law fully meets the requirements derived from *Art 6*. See further **18.63**.

Issues of the right to privacy under *Art 8* of the *Convention* may arise in the context of what evidence a tribunal should admit, where it is asserted that the obtaining or use of the evidence involved or would involve an impermissible interference with that right. An example of this argument being deployed (albeit unsuccessfully on the facts) is *Chairman and Governors of Amwell View School v Dogherty* [2007] IRLR 198 (admissibility of covert tape recording of Governors' private deliberations following disciplinary hearing). On the same topic, see now *Vaughan v Lewisham Borough Council* [2013] All ER (D) 80.

In *Woodrup v Southwark London Borough Council* [2002] EWCA Civ 1716, [2003] IRLR 111, the Court of Appeal considered an argument that employment tribunals are engaged in the provision of services to the public within *Part III* of the *Disability Discrimination Act 1995*, which would entail a duty to make reasonable adjustments in favour of disabled parties in the conduct of the proceedings. Without formally ruling on the point, both members of the Court (Simon Brown and Clarke LJJ) expressed strong doubts as to the suggestion that there is such a legal duty on tribunals. This view is now reflected in the express exclusion of judicial acts, including things done on the instructions a person exercising judicial authority, from the general duty of public bodies not to discriminate against disabled persons in the exercise of any of their functions: *Equality Act 2010, Sch 3, para 3*, replacing equivalent provisions in the *Disability Discrimination Act 1995, ss 21B(1), 21C(1)*. Such acts may well attract judicial immunity from any claim that might be brought: for a recent example, see *Engel v PATROL* (UKEAT/520/12). In practice tribunals do their best to accommodate to the needs of disabled litigants, provided the tribunal staff are made aware of the particular disability.

17.14   THE OVERRIDING OBJECTIVE

Regulation 3 of the *2004 Regulations* provides that the Overriding Objective of the *Regulations* and the *ET Rules* is to enable tribunals and Judges to deal with cases justly. This objective is spelt out as including, so far as practicable, ensuring that the parties are on an equal footing; dealing with cases in ways that are proportionate to the complexity or importance of the issues (there is no reference to the amounts at stake, but this may be reflected in the importance of the issues), ensuring that the case is dealt with expeditiously and fairly; and saving expense. The Overriding Objective differs slightly from that set out in the *Civil Procedure Rules 1998* (as amended). The *Civil Procedure Rules 1998* also includes specific reference to allotting an appropriate share of the Court's resources to a case, enforcing compliance with rules, practice direction and orders, and to dealing with cases in a way proportionate to the amount of money involved and the financial position of each party.

It is the duty of tribunals and Judges to seek to give effect to the Overriding Objective when exercising any power under the *Regulations* or the *Rules* and in interpreting any provision of them, and the duty of the parties to assist the tribunal to further the objective.

The extent to which the conduct of tribunal proceedings will be influenced by these overarching provisions will vary according to the circumstances, but it can generally be said that it would not be consistent with the Overriding Objective, or the parties' duty of co-operation, for a party who is legally represented or otherwise well resourced to seek to exploit technical or procedural points against an unrepresented litigant, or to drive up costs by excessive applications for additional disclosure or information. Deliberate delaying tactics, the concealment until the last minute of relevant evidence, or attempting to overload the tribunal with excessive and marginally relevant documentation are examples of behaviour that would be judged unreasonable by reference to the Objective, and which could result in an award of costs against the offending party.

Case law on the provisions of pre-2001 rules equivalent to the *ET Rules* should now be read subject to the effect of the Overriding Objective (which was introduced in 2001). An example of the impact of the Objective on previous interpretations of comparable provisions in previous versions of the *ET Rules* is *Williams v Ferrosan Ltd* [2004] IRLR 607, where the EAT held that the power of a tribunal to review its decisions 'in the interests of justice' (now contained, in the same terms, in *rule 34(3)* of the *2004 ET Rules*) should not be restricted to cases where new facts had arisen subsequently or there had been a procedural mishap, but should be applied more widely to give effect to the Objective, effectively overruling the earlier and narrower approach taken by the EAT in *Trimble v Supertravel Ltd* [1982] ICR 440. This approach has been strongly endorsed in a case under the *2004 ET Rules*: *Sodexho Ltd v Gibbons* [2005] ICR 1647, [2005] IRLR 836, EAT.

17.15   COMMENCING PROCEEDINGS

A person who wishes to bring a claim ('the claimant') commences proceedings by presenting a Claim Form to the appropriate tribunal office. The information accompanying the official Claim Form gives details of how to identify the correct office (depending on the postcode of the claimant's (former) place of work). The claim is presented when it is received rather than when it is sent. For further details see **17.21** below. Applications may be presented by personal delivery, by post or fax, or electronically.

In conjunction with the introduction of the *2004 Regulations*, a Claim Form, Form ET1, was prescribed by the Secretary of State under the powers conferred by *reg 14*; there is a separate page (Form ET1a) on which the names and addresses of additional claimants must be listed. The use of this form (which is obtainable from Jobcentres and CABx as well as tribunal offices and online via www.justice.gov.uk or www.direct.gov.uk) is mandatory. Following the repeal of the relevant provisions of the *EA 2002* on 6 April 2009, an updated version of the Claim Form (identified as 'ET1 v 3') was introduced and the form used for claims covered by the *2004 Regulations* has been withdrawn. The electronic version of the form can either be completed and submitted online, or downloaded for separate completion and submission by fax, post or in person.

In addition to using the prescribed form, the following information must be given by the claimant:

(a)   the name and address of the claimant, or of each claimant if more than one person is making a claim on the same form;

(b)   the names and addresses of each respondent;

(c)   details of the claim.

(Rule 1(4).)

Where two or more claimants claim using the same form (which is specifically permitted by *rule 1(7)* where the claims arise out of the same facts) the required information must be given for each claimant, and if there is more than one respondent it must be given in relation to each respondent.

17.16   If the prescribed form is not used, the tribunal secretariat will return the claim to the claimant and not register it. A standard letter explaining the need to use the prescribed form is sent, with a blank form enclosed (*ET Rules, rule 3(1)*). It will then be open to the claimant to resubmit the claim in the correct form, but it will only be recorded as presented when this is done. If that is outside the time limit for the claim, the tribunal will have no jurisdiction to consider the claim unless it can be persuaded to extend time (for the law on extension of time see **17.25–17.33**). This procedure is unaffected by the change in the prescribed form.

The position is more complex if a claimant presents a claim using the prescribed Claim Form but does not give all the required information. The power to prescribe includes the power to stipulate which sections of the form must be completed (*ET Regulations 2004, reg 14(1)(c)*). However the administrative power to refuse to register the form only applies where the prescribed Claim Form has not been used, not where it has been used but not all the mandatory sections have been completed (*ET Rules, rules 1(3), 2(1)*). A separate power to refuse to accept the form if it is incomplete, or the tribunal does not have the power to consider the particular complaint, is given by *rule 2(2)*; but under this provision the matter must be referred to an Employment Judge for determination.

The purpose of the provisions stipulating what information must be provided is to ensure that the claim is made in the proper manner, and that the time of the tribunal is not wasted in obtaining adequate information from the claimant. However concerns that strict application of the requirements could lead to a claimant being deprived of the right to have his or her case heard, especially if the incomplete form was submitted at the very end of the applicable limitation period, led the EAT to interpret these provisions (as they then stood) broadly in favour of claimants. In *Grimmer v KLM Cityhopper UK Ltd* [2005] IRLR 596, the claimant appealed against the rejection of a Claim Form in which she had given as the details of her complaint the phrase 'Flexible working', with a sentence setting out why she believed the employer had rejected her request to work flexibly. The EAT held that sufficient information had been given; the correct test was:

> 'Whether it can be discerned from the claim as presented that the claimant is complaining of an alleged breach of an employment right which falls within the jurisdiction of the employment tribunal.'

A similarly benevolent approach was taken by the EAT in *Richardson v U Mole Ltd* [2005] IRLR 668, where the employee had not ticked the box to indicate that he was an employee of the respondent (one of the items of information then required), but it was apparent from other material on the completed form that he did so claim (and the point was in any event not in dispute). Burton P held the refusal to accept this Claim Form to be perverse, and indicated that in general, minor or immaterial omissions should not be penalised in this way. This case is no longer directly relevant following the removal of the requirement to give this information in claims subject to the post-2008 legislation, but the principle will continue to be relevant to a failure to give information still required to be given when using the new form. The EAT has since held that there is no power to reject a claim form simply because it is difficult to read; unless the mandatory information is illegible (in that it cannot be read without resort to a magnifying glass), the correct response is to accept the form but direct the Claimant to provide the particulars in a legible format: *May v Greenwich Council* [2010] All ER (D) 105 (May).

In two further decisions, the EAT has held that there is a right of appeal against the refusal of the secretariat to register the claim and that a claim should not be rejected because of an immaterial irregularity or omission (*Grant v In 2 Focus Sales Development Services Ltd*, [2007] All ER (D) 281 (Jan); *Hamling v Coxlease School Ltd* [2007] IRLR 8); in *Grant* the irregularity was that the claim form had been submitted by fax, and as received and printed out it was smaller than the size of the prescribed form; in *Hamling* it was that the Claimant's address had been omitted, her solicitors' address having been given instead as the address for correspondence. In *Grant* the President of the EAT, Elias J, commented that it would be 'a constitutional outrage' if a public official could take a decision with the effect of blocking a citizen's recourse to law, without any means of challenge to the decision, and endorsed the point made in *Grimmer* that the rules of procedure were, and should be applied as, subordinate to the statutory rights the tribunals are empowered to enforce. See also *Police Comr v Rixon* (UKEAT/0126/10/SM) [2010] All ER (D) 75 (May), where the claimant's address was initially withheld for security reasons, and *UNISON v National Probation Service South Yorkshire* (UKEAT/0339/09/SM) [2010] IRLR 930, where the claim was presented with the separate page (ET1a) used to list additional claimants omitted. In both cases the EAT held that the claims should have been accepted (in the second case it was the claim of the second claimant, Unison, whose name and address should have been included on the form ET1a, which had initially been overlooked, and when the point was raised, had been rejected, but it was clear from the particulars of the claim that it was intended that Unison should be a claimant in the case).

These cases are helpful to unrepresented parties. Their effect is that in practice, the Judge considering a claim (or response: *Butlins Skyline Ltd v Beynon* [2007] ICR 121 shows a similar approach to administrative rejection of responses) which does not strictly comply with the requirements to provide information is likely to direct that it should be accepted, but the claimant (or respondent) directed to supply the missing (or illegible) particulars; but it would be unwise for a claimant to assume that this will happen. In any event, there are potentially serious consequences if inadequate details of the claim are given; see **17.17** below.

17.17 It is also important for other reasons than the risk of rejection at the initial stage of presentation for claimants to complete the Claim Form carefully, and as completely and accurately as possible. If the Claim Form does not specify each of the particular claims being asserted, difficulties may arise if the claimant subsequently seeks to rely on a further claim, depending in part on whether the new claim arises out of the same factual allegations already set out in the Claim Form, and/or on whether the time limit for bringing the new claim has expired by the time the further claim is first raised with the tribunal. Whilst claimants acting without legal representation are accorded more leeway by tribunals, it is important to ensure that all claims the claimant is able to advance are properly identified in the Claim Form. In particular, in discrimination cases the tribunal has no power to determine specific allegations of acts alleged to be discrimination which are not made in the Claim Form (or added by amendment with the permission of the tribunal): *Chapman v Simon* [1994] IRLR 124; *Nagarajan v London Regional Transport* [1998] IRLR 73, CA. The Court of Appeal has held that a complaint of direct race discrimination does not, as such, encompass a complaint of *indirect* discrimination; this must be separately pleaded, or added by amendment: *Ali v Office of National Statistics* [2004] EWCA Civ 1363, [2005] IRLR 201. See further **18.10** below. In addition to possible difficulties over amendment, if the grounds are not sufficiently particularised, an order to provide further information may be made. Moreover, if a claimant gives evidence which differs from the narrative in the Claim Form, he or she may be challenged to explain the inconsistency.

TIME LIMITS FOR CLAIMS

17.18 General

All applications to employment tribunals must be presented within a certain time limit, which varies according to the particular statutory provision relied on. The statutory provisions as to time limits are relatively complex, as they differ according to the particular statutory provisions relied on. It is important to appreciate a number of basic points about time limits.

(a)   Time limits go to the jurisdiction of the tribunal. A claim presented after the time limit has expired cannot be considered at all on its merits, however strong these may be, unless the tribunal can be persuaded to extend time under the limited discretionary powers to do so conferred by the relevant statute. There is power to extend time in relation to almost all the statutory jurisdictions of the tribunals, but the criteria vary according to the particular type of claim; full details are given in **17.25–17.33** below.

(b)   Time limits do not only lay down the latest date for bringing a claim. In relation to some (though not all) jurisdictions, the tribunal is precluded from hearing a claim because it was brought prematurely, *before* the relevant time period began to run. In addition, under the *Employment Act 2002*, some claims could not be presented until 28 days had elapsed after a written grievance had been submitted to the employer; for details of this the 23rd edition of this *Handbook* should be consulted.

(c)   Time limits apply to the *presentation* of a claim, that is, its delivery (physically or electronically) to the relevant office of the tribunal (see (*e*) below for further details on how the date of presentation is calculated in marginal situations).

(d)   Time runs from a particular event, the nature of which varies depending on the particular jurisdiction. It may be both important and difficult to determine what is the relevant date in a particular case – notoriously so where it is the 'effective date of termination' that is in issue, as in an unfair dismissal claim. Normally it is the date of the event which starts the clock running, not the date (if later) on which the individual becomes aware of the event (eg an unlawful deduction from wages which the employee does not spot on first receiving the relevant payslip). However some events, such as termination of employment, may require communication to the employee to be effective (cf *Gisda Cyf v Barratt* [2010] UKSC 41, [2010] IRLR

1073]). See further **17.22** below. (This point may be important not just in determining when time starts to run for presenting a claim, but also whether there is a claim at all, as where legislation comes into force after the first point in time at which the right to complain arises: see for a good example *Coutts & Co plc v Cure* [2005] ICR 1098.)

(e)   The usual formulation of the time limit in employment legislation is that the complaint must be presented within a period (usually of three months) beginning with the date of the relevant event, such as the dismissal. This means that that date is the first day of the three-month period, which therefore ends one day earlier in the third following month. The correct way of calculating the three-month period is to take the day of the month of the day immediately prior to the date (eg of dismissal) and go forward three months. Thus if the employee is dismissed on 1 June, the last date for presentation is 31 August, but if the date of dismissal was 30 April, the correct last date is 29 July; some anomalies may arise from months of different lengths. See further *Pruden v Cunard Ellerman Lines Ltd* [1993] IRLR 317 and *University of Cambridge v Murray* [1993] ICR 460.

(f)   The principal exceptions to the three-month time limit are claims for a statutory redundancy payment (six months from the 'relevant date', usually the date of dismissal) and equal pay (during, or within six months following the termination of, the relevant employment). One category of claims, for interim relief in certain categories of unfair dismissal claim (see *ERA, ss 128–132; TULRCA 1992, ss 161–163*), has a time limit of only seven days from the effective date of termination.

(g)   It is not necessarily possible to circumvent time limits for a particular claim by presenting an application under one jurisdiction and then applying to add further claims. The rules on amendment of claims (see **18.30** below) require tribunals balance the prejudice or hardship that would be suffered by each party if the amendment is, or is not, allowed, taking into account, if it be the case, that the new claim has been raised for the first time after the time limit has expired. This may result in the application to amend being refused, particularly if made at the last minute before the Hearing (see further on amendments generally **18.10**).

(h)   Since time points are a matter going to the jurisdiction of the tribunal, they may be raised at any time in the proceedings. The point may be (and quite frequently in practice is) raised by the tribunal itself, and in such cases it must be considered and decided on although the respondent is content to have the matter adjudicated on its merits. It is even possible (as an exception to the normal practice) for the issue of time to be raised for the first time in the course of an appeal: for an example see *Landon v Lill* (EAT/1486/00) (9 October 2002, unreported).

(i)   The time point is often considered as a preliminary issue separately from the substantive hearing; as it may raise questions of fact, evidence can be called by either or both parties. Under the *2004 ET Rules*, the time point can be dealt with at a PHR (*Rule 18(2)*). Sometimes it is inappropriate to determine the issue of jurisdiction separately, for example where it involves the same factual issues as have to be determined on the merits of the case: see *Ironsides Ray & Vials v Lindsay* [1994] ICR 384, [1994] IRLR 318. The general approach of the EAT before the introduction of the *2004 ET Rules* was to discourage the separation of preliminary points unless they were clearly distinct from other issues arising in the case: see eg *Wellcome Foundation v Darby* [1996] IRLR 538 and *Sutcliffe v Big C's Marine Ltd* [1998] ICR 913. The *2004 Rules* have given more weight to the PHR procedure, and the practice of ordering PHRs to determine time issues has again become more common, at least in unfair dismissal cases; however in discrimination cases, where evidence of alleged discrimination over a relatively extended period may be admissible even if the claims founded on that evidence are held to be out of time, and where arguments about whether acts continue over a period are frequent, tribunals are markedly more reluctant to deal separately with time points (see the Court of Appeal's judgment in *Hendricks v Commissioner of Police for the Metropolis* [2003] IRLR 96.

(j)   Special provisions apply to the presentation of claims by members or former members of the armed forces; see **28.4** for details.

17.19 Changes following the Employment Act 2002

Subject to some complex transitional provisions, which in almost all cases do not apply to claims presented after 5 October 2009, the points made in this section in previous editions of this Handbook no longer apply following the repeal of *ss 29–33* of the *Employment Act 2002* and the associated *Schedules* with effect from 6 April 2009. For that reason and in the interests of space, the detailed discussion of the effects of the *2002 Act* on time limits and the presentation of claims were omitted from the 24th and 25th edition and are similarly omitted here.

17.20 In this section in previous editions of the Handbook, the circumstances in which the *2002 Act* and the *Regulations* made under it could lead to an extension of the time for presenting a claim were explained. For the reasons given above, this material too has been omitted from this edition. Reference may be made to the 23rd edition for details.

17.21 PRESENTATION OF A CLAIM

A claim is presented by sending a completed Claim Form to the Secretary of the Employment Tribunals at the appropriate local office for the claimant's (former) place of work. Which office is the correct one is determined by the postcode of the relevant workplace. Technically, the Claim Form can be sent to any office in England and Wales (for a case arising in either country) or Scotland (where the claimant is or was employed in that country) (*ET Rules, rule 1(1), (2)*; see **17.11** above as to the limits on the jurisdiction of tribunals in England and Wales and Scotland respectively and the transfer of cases between the two).

If a Claim Form is sent to the wrong office it will simply be forwarded to the correct office; the date of presentation will be the date it reaches the first office. However the jurisdictions north and south of the border are separate, and if the Claim Form is presented in England and Wales when the correct venue for the claim is Scotland, or vice versa, the claim will not be regarded as having been presented within the correct jurisdiction; it cannot simply be transferred, and the claimant is at risk of being out of time if he or she subsequently presents a fresh Claim Form in the correct jurisdiction. This was confirmed by the EAT in Scotland in *McFadyen v PB Recovery Ltd* (UKEATS/0072/08), where a claim had been completed online giving the postal address of the employer as Bristol, but not including the address in Glasgow where the claimant had worked; this had led to the claim being automatically routed to the Bristol tribunal. Following the rejection of that claim, the claimant presented a fresh claim in Scotland giving the correct details, but out of time, and the dismissal of that claim was upheld by the EAT.

If the Claim Form arrives at a tribunal office before midnight on the last day of the three-month limitation period, it is presented in time (*Post Office v Moore* [1981] ICR 623; see further below for the very different position if it is received even a few seconds after midnight). Claims sent by fax are accepted, if received in time. Claimants submitting claims by fax are discouraged from sending a second copy by post. For the position if a faxed claim form is not completely received, see *Hutchinson 3G UK Ltd v Francois* [2009] EWCA Civ 405, [2009] ICR 1323. The Court of Appeal has given general guidance about presentation by post: *Sealy v Consignia plc* [2002] EWCA Civ 878, [2002] 3 All ER 801, [2002] IRLR 624, and this has in part been applied by analogy to presentation by e-mail. The guidance is set out at **17.25**(vi) below. As to the presentation of claims electronically, see further below.

Since a Claim Form is presented if it is placed through a letter-box or dealt with in some way held out by a Tribunal Office as a means whereby it will accept communications, when the limitation period ends on a non-working day the time limit is not automatically extended to the next working day (*Swainston v Hetton Victory Club Ltd* [1983] 1 All ER 1179, [1983] ICR 341; *Sealy v Consignia plc, above*). It was formerly the position that where there was no letter-box or other authorised means by which a complaint could have been presented on a day when the tribunal office was closed, the time for presenting the complaint would be extended to the next working day (*Ford v Stakis Hotels and Inns Ltd* [1987] ICR 943). However widespread availability of fax facilities, and since November 2002 the facility to present a Claim Form electronically, make it difficult to see how there is room for this possibility in the great majority of cases. Brooke LJ in *Sealy v Consignia plc* considered that this was not a ground for extending the time limit to the next working day, but rather a situation where a tribunal would need to consider whether the absence of a means of physical delivery of a hard copy of the claim had rendered it not reasonably practicable to present the claim in time.

It is the claimant's responsibility to ensure that the Claim Form is in fact received by the tribunal. Generally, acknowledgements of receipt of applications are sent out on the same day as the claim is received, or the following working day, and if an acknowledgement is not received it is important to check the position with the tribunal office as soon as practicable, if necessary by telephoning the tribunal office to confirm receipt. See further **17.25**(vi) below.

The EAT has had to consider what constitutes presentation when a claim is submitted by e-mail. In one case, *Mossman v Bray Management Ltd* [2005] All ER (D) 06 (Apr), EAT, it was held that where the claimant had clicked the 'submit' button for the completed form, but it had not been received on the tribunal website, it had not been presented. However in *Tyne and Wear Autistic Society v Smith* [2005] IRLR 336, the opposite conclusion was reached on the basis of only slightly different facts, and additional information. The claimant in that case had received an acknowledgement of receipt, and the Claim Form had reached the server of the company hosting the tribunals' website, but had not reached the tribunal office, for unknown reasons.

The *Tyne and Wear* case has since been applied by analogy to presentation by fax (see below) and it is submitted that it is to be preferred to *Mossman*. This view is reinforced by the decision of the EAT in *Patel v South Tyneside Council* (UKEATPA/0917/11) that an appeal to the EAT was duly presented when sent by email to the correct address, followed by a notification of 'successful delivery' by the host server, Daemon, but did not (again for an unknown reason) reach the EAT's Inbox. The reasoning applies equally to the process of submitting a claim by email.

If transmission to an employment tribunal office is successful, an e-mail receipt is generated, and unless such a receipt is received, the claimant should contact the tribunal office to check whether the Claim Form has in fact been received, and if necessary resubmit it. The website contains a warning that receipt cannot be guaranteed, and it is prudent to take the warning at face value. For the position on extension of time if a claim submitted electronically is not received, see **17.25**(vi) below.

Subsequently the EAT has had to determine what constitutes presentation of a claim sent by fax. In *Yellow Pages Sales Ltd v Davie* (UKEATS/0017/11) the claim had been faxed and a transmission report was generated indicating it had been received by the tribunal's fax machine, but no trace of the form could be found when the matter was subsequently raised with the tribunal. The EAT held that the tribunal was right to find that the claim had been presented in time, applying by analogy the *Tyne and Wear* case.

A claim submitted electronically is treated as having been presented when it is *received* on the server used to receive claims and responses for the Tribunals Service. That may be a few seconds later than the time of *sending*. This may be important; in two cases the Court of

Appeal and the EAT respectively upheld the dismissal of claims as out of time which were presented electronically, but received respectively 88 seconds and 8 seconds after midnight of the last day for presentation: *Beasley v National Grid* [2008] EWCA Civ 742, [2007] All ER (D) 110 (Aug), EAT and *Miller v Community Links Trust* [2007] All ER (D) 196 (Nov), EAT. In the first case the delay was the result of incorrectly typing in the tribunal e-mail address; in the second, the claim had been submitted at one second before midnight but took nine seconds to arrive. The same points would apply to receipt of a claim submitted by fax, in the event of any discrepancy between the time of transmission and the time of receipt. By parity of reasoning with the EAT's decision in *Woodward v Abbey National plc* [2005] IRLR 782, a fax is not 'presented' until all of the pages have been received.

17.22 EXTENSION OF TIME

Different statutes have provided different criteria for the extension of time. It is important to appreciate that the tribunal cannot extend time unless the relevant condition is satisfied; in addition, in relation to the first category of criteria noted below, even if it is satisfied, the tribunal must decide the further question whether the length of extension sought to validate the claim is reasonable. The principal categories of criteria, and the jurisdictions to which each applies, are as follows:

(i) that it was not reasonably practicable to present the Claim Form within time: unfair dismissal; unlawful deduction from wages; subjection to a detriment for a reason within *ERA 1996* and *TULRCA 1992*; most other claims within *ERA 1996* and *TULRCA 1992*; claims under the *Working Time Regulations 1998*; claims for breach of contract;

(ii) that it would be just and equitable to extend time: unlawful discrimination under the *Equality Act 2010, s 120*; less favourable treatment or subjection to detriment under the *Part-time Workers (Prevention of Less Favourable Treatment) Regulations 2000, reg 8* or the *Fixed-term Workers (Prevention of Less Favourable Treatment) Regulations 2002, reg 7*; redundancy payments (subject to a maximum extension of six months: *ERA 1996, s 164*); claims under the *Agency Workers Regulations 2010, reg 17*;

(iii) no provision for extension (except in cases of concealment of the information on which the claim is based): equal pay claims (see the *Equality Act 2010, s 127*). See further **17.27** below.

The tests to be applied by the tribunals in relation to each of the first two criteria are considered below, at **17.25–17.26** and **17.29–17.30** respectively.

It should be noted that if there is a disputed issue as to whether a claim was presented in time, and/or whether, if not, time should be extended, it will be necessary, where the relevant facts are in dispute, that evidence is adduced at the hearing, whether this is the substantive hearing or a PHR: cf *Sodexo Health Care Services Ltd v Harmer* (UKEATS/0079/08).

17.23 Establishing when time starts to run in dismissal cases: the 'effective date of termination'

In claims alleging unfair dismissal, time starts to run from and including the 'effective date of termination' ('EDT': see *ERA 1996, s 97*). The EDT has been described judicially as a 'statutory construct' and normal contractual principles do not necessarily determine when the EDT falls. The (now relatively extensive) case law has established the following points.

(a)   If an employee is summarily dismissed, either orally or by notice in writing given to him or her at the time of dismissal, and whether or not the employer also makes a payment in lieu of the notice not given, the EDT is the date on which he or she is dismissed or ceases to work (*ERA 1996, s 97(1)*; *Dedman v British Building and Engineering Appliances Ltd* [1974] 1 All ER 520, [1974] 1 WLR 171, [1974] ICR 53).

(b)   However, if the employer gives notice to terminate a contract of employment and either requires or does not require the employee to work during the notice period, the EDT is not the date on which the employee ceases work but the date on which the notice expires. This situation is to be contrasted with where the employer dismisses and exercises a payment in lieu of notice clause so as to bring the contract to an end either immediately or on short notice accompanied by a payment instead of giving full notice. There, as described in (a) above, the EDT will be when the contract actually comes to an end. In *Societe Generale, London Branch v Geys* [2012] UKSC 63, [2013] IRLR 122, the Supreme Court held that to exercise the PILON clause in question it was not sufficient for the employee to receive their payment in lieu, but that they also receive notification form the employer in clear an unambiguous terms, that such a payment has been made and was made in the exercise of the contractual right to terminate the employment with immediate effect. If some notice of termination is given, and the parties subsequently agree to bring forward the date of termination (as may happen if the employee has another job to go to), the earlier date will be the EDT: an example in the redundancy context is *Palfrey v Transco Plc* [2004] IRLR 916.

(c)   If the employer dismisses summarily but communicates the decision by letter, the EDT is the date on which the employee receives and reads the letter, not the date on which the employer takes the decision to dismiss, or the date on which the letter is sent, or even received (if, for instance, the employee is away from home and does not see the letter until a few days later: *McMaster v Manchester Airport plc* [1998] IRLR 112). This conclusion was applied by the Supreme Court in a case with similar facts, *Gisda Cyf v Barratt* [2010] UKSC 41, [2010] IRLR 1073, with the caution that a claimant could not postpone the EDT by deliberately avoiding opening or reading a letter of dismissal.

(d)   If the employee resigns without notice (as in a constructive dismissal case), or by giving notice, and does so directly to the employer, the EDT will be the date on which the notice is given, or on the expiry of the period of notice given.

(e)   If the employee resigns without notice and communicates his or her resignation by letter to the employer, the EDT is the date on which the letter is received by the employer, and (probably) seen and read at least by someone in the employer's organisation, not necessarily the actual addressee: *Horwood v Lincolnshire County Council*, (UKEAT/0462/11), following a decision to the same effect in *Potter v R J Temple (in Liquidation)* (UKEAT/0478,03), where the employee had resigned by fax, and *George v Luton Borough Council* (UKEAT/0311/03). If the employee gives, say, a week's notice, the week will run from the date of receipt of the notice, not (if later) the date on which the notice was seen and read by the relevant manager. (See further **17.24** below as to how the period of notice is calculated.)

(f)   If the employee is dismissed (or resigns) on notice, and during the currency of the notice the employer summarily dismisses the employee, the (earlier) date on which the summary dismissal occurs becomes the EDT in substitution for the (later) date on which the original notice would have expired: *Parker Rhodes Hickmott Solicitors v Harvey* (UKEAT/0455/11); if the result of the second dismissal is that the employee has less than the minimum period of service required to make a claim of unfair dismissal, that is the effect of the second dismissal and the employee cannot claim unfair dismissal (unless for a reason to which the qualifying service requirement does not apply): *M-Choice Ltd v Aalders* (UKEAT/0227/11), applying *Patel v Nagesan* [1995] IRLR 370.

The determination of the EDT is a question of fact which should be decided in a practical and common sense manner having regard to what the parties understood at the time: *Newman v Polytechnic of Wales Students Union* [1995] IRLR 72. However, the applicable date is a matter of law, and a date other than that derived from a correct application of legal principles to the facts cannot simply be agreed by the parties: *Fitzgerald v University of Kent at Canterbury* [2004] EWCA Civ 143, [2004] IRLR 300. Similarly the EDT cannot be changed by the unilateral action of the employer in treating the date of the employee's resignation as later than it in fact was and paying her accordingly: *Horwood v Lincolnshire County Council* (above). Whilst the parties cannot themselves, unilaterally or by agreement, change what in fact is the EDT, they can of course set the EDT at a particular date by their actions, as where the parties agree to bring forward the date of termination so that the employee can leave to get another job, or the employee resigns without notice during the currency of notice of dismissal by the employer.

If the employee invokes an internal appeal procedure to appeal against his dismissal, time normally starts to run from the date of the original dismissal, *not* the date of the dismissal of the appeal, unless the contract provides for the employment to continue until the appeal is determined (*J Sainsbury Ltd v Savage* [1981] ICR 1); for an example of a situation where the EDT was held to be the date of dismissal of the appeal, see *Drage v Governors of Greenford High School* [2000] IRLR 314, CA. This was also found to be the case in *Hawes & Curtis Ltd v Arfan, Mirza* (UKEAT/0229/12), where the EAT found that the parties had agreed after the employees appealed that their contracts would be kept open and in existence until the appeal hearing. For a case where the EDT was held to be affected by a decision to reinstate the employee following an appeal, which in turn was overruled by more senior management, see *London Probation Board v Kirkpatrick* [2005] IRLR 443; see also Unfair Dismissal – I (51). See also as to the potential complexities of identifying the EDT where the employer removes the employee from the payroll *Kirklees Metropolitan Borough Council v Radecki* [2009] EWCA Civ 298, [2009] ICR 1244 and compare *Societe Generale, London Branch v Geys*, above. .

17.24   If notice of dismissal is given, the employee is not 'dismissed' until the notice expires: see *H W Smith (Cabinets) Ltd v Brindle* [1973] ICR 12, CA. Thus under ordinary principles a claim of unfair dismissal could not be presented during the notice period, and this was confirmed to be the case by the NIRC in *Penrose v Fairey Surveys Ltd* [1973] ICR 26. This led to a change in the law to allow applications in respect of dismissal with notice to be presented during the period the notice is running (the provision giving effect to this is now *ERA 1996, s 111(3)*). This facility has been held to apply equally in a case of a claim of constructive dismissal where the employee resigns with notice: *Presley v Llanelli Borough Council* [1979] ICR 419. However, notice of dismissal must be unequivocal, and specify a date for the dismissal, in order to be effective; so an ultimatum to an employee who was absent from work that if he did not return by a stated deadline, his employment would be treated as terminated, was held by the EAT not to be a sufficiently unequivocal notice of dismissal to be effective as such, so that a complaint presented before the deadline had expired was premature and outwith the tribunal's jurisdiction: *Rai v Somerfield Stores Ltd* [2004] IRLR 124, [2004] ICR 656. On the other hand a notice of dismissal which is to take effect on a stated date unless the employee appeals, and in that event on the date that the appeal is rejected, is sufficiently unconditional to constitute such a notice, and a complaint of unfair dismissal before the determination of the appeal is not premature: *Governing Body of Wishmorecross School v Balado* (UKEAT/0199/11). For the position relating to claims under the *Equality Act 2010* where the complaint is of dismissal, see **17.29** below.

A further complication is that it may be unclear when a notice of dismissal or resignation starts to run. Subject to any express statement to the contrary in the notice, the period of notice runs from the start of the day following the day on which the notice was communicated to the employee; this applies equally to written (including by email or text message) and oral notice and the position is not affected by the employer failing to pay the employee for the full period of notice: *Wang v University of Keele* [2011] IRLR 542. There is no equivalent authority on when notice of resignation starts to run, but it is submitted that the same approach should be adopted, by parity of reasoning.

If there is any ambiguity in a notice of dismissal as to when it is to take effect, this should be resolved against the employer, as the party giving the notice: *Chapman v Letheby and Christopher Ltd* [1981] IRLR 440, EAT, *Teva (UK) Ltd v Heslip* [2009] All ER (D) 277 (Jul); *Wang* (above).

For some purposes, the EDT is extended by a period equivalent to the employee's statutory notice entitlement, if the dismissal is summary; however, this does not apply for the purposes of computing the time limit for presenting a claim.

Different issues as to when time starts to run may arise in non-dismissal cases, particularly in relation to complaints about a continuing state of affairs or omissions. This point is addressed at **17.29** below.

17.25 'Not reasonably practicable' to present in time

An extension of time may be granted by the tribunal to validate a late complaint of unfair dismissal if, but only if, it is satisfied (the onus of proof being on the claimant) that it was 'not reasonably practicable for the complaint to be presented before the end' of the three-month period: *ERA 1996, s 111(2)*. The complaint must nevertheless have been presented 'within such further period as the tribunal considers reasonable' in order for an extension to be granted. The wording quoted is repeated in virtually identical terms in several other statutory provisions conferring jurisdiction on the tribunal: see **17.22** above. The EAT has confirmed that the principles and case law in relation to unfair dismissal claims apply equally to such other categories of claim: *GMB v Hamm* [2000] All ER (D) 1830 (claim for protective award); *Wandsworth London Borough Council v Covent Garden Market Authority* [2011] EWHC 1245 (QB) (appeal against health and safety Improvement Order). The comments which follow in this section accordingly apply equally to such claims.

It is a question of fact in each case whether it was reasonably practicable to present a claim in time. This question has generated extensive reported authority, but the Court of Appeal and EAT have repeatedly stressed that particular decisions should not be taken as laying down hard and fast rules (particularly as to the effect of the employee receiving advice). Following a review of the authorities, the Court of Appeal in *Palmer v Southend-on-Sea Borough Council* [1984] 1 All ER 945, [1984] 1 WLR 1129, [1984] ICR 372 was able to offer no more specific test than that the tribunal should ask whether it was 'reasonably feasible' to present the claim in time – a test which May LJ acknowledged was easier to state than to apply. The general approach to be adopted was stated by the Court of Appeal in *Marks & Spencer plc v Williams-Ryan* [2005] EWCA Civ 470, [2005] IRLR 562 to be that the statute should be given a liberal interpretation in favour of the employee. In a subsequent case, *Theobald v The Royal Bank of Scotland plc* [2007] All ER (D) 04 (Jan), the EAT suggested that this is against the weight of other authority; however the predominant view is that the liberal approach still applies: see *Northamptonshire County Council v Entwhistle* [2010] IRLR 740; *El-Kholy v Rentokil Initial Facilities Services (UK) Ltd* (UKEAT/0472/12).

Some examples of the application of the test of whether it was reasonably practicable for the applicant to present his or her complaint in time are set out below. These should be treated as indicative rather than decisive. A full summary of the most important points and authorities can be found in para 5 of the judgment of Underhill J in *Northampton-shire County Council v Entwhistle*, above.

(i)   It is not reasonably practicable for an employee to bring a complaint of unfair dismissal until he or she has (or could reasonably be expected to have acquired) knowledge of the facts giving him or her grounds to apply to the tribunal (*Machine Tool Industry Research Association v Simpson* [1988] ICR 558; *Marley (UK) Ltd v Anderson* [1996] IRLR 163; *Cambridge and Peterborough Foundation NHS Trust v Crouchman* [2009] All ER (D) 96 (May)); *Cullinane v Balfour Beatty Engineering Services Ltd* (UKEAT/0537/10)). An extreme example of the point is *Howlett Marine Services Ltd v Bowlam* [2001] IRLR 201, where the three-month time limit for claiming payment under a protective award had expired before the award was actually made by the tribunal.

(ii)   With the passage of time since unfair dismissal legislation was introduced and the publicity given to unfair dismissal cases, a claimant is unlikely to be able to show that it was not reasonably practicable for him or her to present a complaint because of ignorance of the right to claim for unfair dismissal. If the claimant ought reasonably to have known of his or her right to claim, then it will probably be held that it was reasonably practicable to present a complaint within the time limit, whether he or she in fact knew of the right or not (see *Porter v Bandridge Ltd* [1978] 1 WLR 1145, [1978] ICR 943). However it is always necessary for the tribunal to consider what the claimant knew, and whether his or her lack of relevant knowledge was reasonable.

(iii)   Where an employee has knowledge of his or her rights to claim unfair dismissal, there is an obligation upon him or her to seek information or advice about the enforcement of those rights (*Trevelyans (Birmingham) Ltd v Norton* [1991] ICR 488), and accordingly ignorance of time limits may well be held not to be reasonable if the claimant was aware of the right to claim but made no further enquiries about how or when to do so: *Reed in Partnership Ltd v Fraine* (UKEAT/0520/10). In *Norton*, the EAT also held that a decision to await the outcome of related criminal proceedings did not render the presentation of a complaint within the three-month time limit not reasonably practicable. Similarly in *Wandsworth London Borough Council v Covent Garden Market Authority* [2011] EWHC 1245 (QB), a decision to wait for a scheduled interview with the police to see if further relevant material emerged was held not to be a factor making it not reasonably practicable to comply with the time limit (for a health and safety appeal to which the same time limit applies).

(iv)   The fact that the employee has been re-employed as a consultant by the employer and is reluctant to jeopardise this arrangement by making a claim does not necessarily render it not reasonably practicable to claim in time (*Birmingham Optical Group plc v Johnson* [1995] ICR 459). Similarly, in *London Underground Ltd v Noel* [2000] ICR 109, the fact that the employer had offered the dismissed employee another job but then withdrew the offer did not affect the question whether it was reasonably practicable for the employee to present her claim in time, since from the outset she had knowledge of the facts giving rise to a claim for unfair dismissal.

(v)   Before the introduction of the statutory dispute resolution procedures, it was well established, following *Palmer v Southend-on-Sea Borough Council*, above, that the fact that an internal appeal was pending did not render it not reasonably practicable to present the complaint before the final resolution of the appeal. This view was adopted by the EAT in *Bodhu v Hampshire Area Health Authority* [1982] ICR 200, and later confirmed by the Court of Appeal in *Palmer*. Following the coming into force of the *Dispute Resolution Regulations* and the related provisions of the *2002 Act*, this was called into question, and in *Ashcroft v Haberdashers' Aske's Boys' School* [2008] IRLR 375 (a case where the outcome of his appeal against dismissal had been notified to the claimant only five hours before the expiry of the three month time limit), the EAT held that the new law, and in particular *reg 15* of the *Dispute Resolution Regulations*, had to be taken as overruling this line of authority. However, despite the policy attractions of this approach, it is submitted that following the repeal of the *2002 Act* and associated Regulations, *Palmer* again applies as binding authority; this view was expressed, *obiter*, by Underhill P in *John Lewis Partnership v Charman* (UKEAT/0079/11). However, if a claimant reasonably believes that he or she is not permitted to bring a claim whilst an appeal is still pending, and the appeal is not decided until the time limit has expired, it is open to the tribunal to hold that it was not reasonably practicable to claim in time: *Charman*, above. Whether such a belief is reasonable will be a question of fact in each case.

It should also be appreciated that even if it only becomes practicable to present the claim within the dying days of the three month period, it may well be held to have been reasonably practicable to do so; claimants are expected to move quickly if they are aware that the time limit is nearly upon them (and hence it was an error of law for a tribunal not to consider whether it was reasonably practicable for the claimant to present her claim in the three days between being informed that police investigations (the existence of which she believed to be a bar to claiming) had ended and the expiry of the three months: *Kauser v Asda Stores Ltd*, [2007] All ER (D) 195 (Oct), EAT).

(vi)   The principles applicable where an application is posted immediately before the deadline were fully reviewed by the Court of Appeal in *Sealy v Consignia plc* [2002] EWCA Civ 878, [2002] 3 All ER 801, [2002] IRLR 624. Brooke LJ, with the concurrence of the other members of the court, set out guidance which can be summarised as follows:

(1)   A complaint is 'presented' when it arrives at the tribunal office.

(2)   If it is proved that it was impossible to present the complaint in time, for example because the office was locked and did not have a letter-box, it is possible to argue that it was not reasonably practicable for the complaint to be presented in time.

(3)   If the complaint is presented by post, it will be assumed, unless the contrary is proved, to have been received at the time that a letter would have been delivered in the ordinary course of post.

(4)   If the letter was sent by first-class post it is legitimate to assume that this would be the second day after it was posted (excluding Sundays, Bank Holidays, Christmas Day and Good Friday: see on this point *Coldridge v HM Prison Service* (UKEAT/0728/04); the presumption is also now embodied in the *ET Rules, rule 61(2)(a)* that a document duly posted will arrive in the ordinary course of post).

(5)   If the letter does not arrive at the expected time, but is delayed in the post, a tribunal may conclude that it was not reasonably practicable to present it in time.

(6)   If a form is date-stamped on a Monday by a tribunal office but the time limit expired on the preceding Saturday or Sunday, and it is found by the tribunal that it was posted by first-class post not later than the Thursday, it will be open to the tribunal to find as a fact that it arrived on the Saturday (and thus was in time), or alternatively to extend time as a matter of discretion.

(7)   There is no room for any unusual subjective expectation by the claimant that a letter may arrive earlier than the second working day after it is posted. The test is objective.

(8)   If despite being posted the day before the final day, the application arrives on the final day of the relevant period, it is in time.

If the application of the points set out above results in a finding that the claim would but for some unusual or unforeseen event have been received by the tribunal office in time, it does not matter that the claimant could have avoided the problem by sending the claim in earlier: see per Hart J at para 19. However, the risk of additional delay and cost being incurred in securing an extension of time for a claim that is delayed in the course of post makes it prudent to present claims earlier if possible. For an example of a case where delay in the post was accepted as justifying an extension of time, see *Lancaster v DEK Printing Machines Ltd* (EAT/623/99) (application sent by Royal Mail special delivery).

In relation to appeals to the EAT, there is express provision in the *EAT Rules 1993* that where time for the service expires on a non-working day, time is extended to the next working day (*rule 37(2)*), but there is no equivalent provision in the ET Rules, with the consequence that if the last day for presenting a claim is a Sunday, and it is posted on Friday, the presumed date of receipt will be too late to assist a claimant if the Claim Form is not in fact delivered until the Monday: *Coldridge v HM Prison Service* (UKEAT/0728/04). Burton P suggested in that case an amendment to the *ET Rules* to extend the time limit automatically to the next working day, but this has not been implemented.

The guidelines at (4) and (5) above were applied by analogy to presentation by e-mail in *Initial Electronic Security Systems Ltd v Avdic* [2005] IRLR 671, where the Claim Form had been submitted by e-mail at 2.30 pm on the last day, but had not been received. The EAT held that there was a presumption that an e-mail will be received in the ordinary course of transmission within 30–60 minutes of being sent, and if it is not, the sender can argue that it was thereby not reasonably practicable to present the claim in time. (It would still be necessary in such a case to show that he or she had acted promptly in following up the matter when no acknowledgement was received, and had resubmitted the claim expeditiously.)

(vii)   Where the employee is prevented by serious illness from claiming in time, it will normally be held not to have been reasonably practicable to present the claim in time. In *Schultz v Esso Petroleum Ltd* [1999] 3 All ER 338, [1999] ICR 1202, [1999] IRLR 488, the employee became ill some six weeks before the time limit expired and was unable to instruct solicitors. The Court of Appeal rejected an argument that an extension of time should be refused since he could have claimed before he fell ill: the Court held that although the whole period of three months is relevant, it is necessary to focus particularly on the latter part of the period of three months. This decision was applied by the EAT in *Agrico UK Ltd v Ireland* (EATS/0042/05), in support of a finding that it had been perverse of a tribunal to hold that it had not been reasonably practicable to present the claim in time where the Claim Form had been left by the claimant's solicitor for his secretary to complete and send in on the last day for presentation, but she fell ill and was absent that day, and the matter was not attended to until she returned to work the following day. The tribunal's error was to focus exclusively on the end of the three months, and not consider the practicability of the claim having been presented earlier. It is difficult to reconcile this approach and that in the *Avdic* case, above, and it would be helpful to have further clarification from the Court of Appeal of the position where an intention to submit at the last moment goes wrong for unforeseen reasons.

(viii)   If the claimant instructs solicitors or advisers to act on his or her behalf and through their default the Claim Form is not presented in time, the tribunal will consider that it was reasonably practicable for the claim to be presented in time, and will not entertain the claim. As Lord Denning MR said in *Dedman v British Building and Engineering Appliances Ltd* [1974] 1 All ER 520, [1974] 1 WLR 171, [1974] ICR 53:

> 'I would suggest that in every case the tribunal should inquire into the circumstances and ask themselves whether the man or his advisers were at fault in allowing [the time limit] to pass by without presenting the complaint. If he was not at fault, nor his advisers – so that he had just cause or excuse for not presenting his complaint within [the time limit] – then it was "not practicable" for him to present it within that time.'

See also *Walls Meat Co Ltd v Khan* [1979] ICR 52, [1978] IRLR 499, CA, *Riley v Tesco Stores Ltd* [1980] ICR 323, *Croydon Health Authority v Jaufurally* [1986] ICR 4, and *El-Kholy v Rentokil Initial Facilities Services (UK) Ltd* (UKEAT/0472/12). The point is not limited to lawyers; if the claimant has placed his case in the hands of his trade union, he may be fixed with the consequences of delay on the union's part, as in *Cullinane v Balfour Beatty Engineering Services Ltd* (UKEAT/0537/10). However, in *Harvey's Household Linens Ltd v Benson* [1974] ICR 306 it was held that Department of Employment officials were not 'advisers' for this purpose, so their error ought not to be attributed to a claimant who followed their advice; this was followed in *Dixon Stores Group v Arnold* (EAT/772/93). The same applies to advice given by tribunal employees (*Rybak v Jean Sorelle Ltd* [1991] ICR 127; and see *London International College v Sen* [1993] IRLR 333). In *Alexanders Holdings Ltd v Methven* (EAT/782/93), the EAT upheld a finding in the case of a claimant who believed, as a result of ambiguous advice from the Department of Social Security, that he was not permitted to present his claim for three months following dismissal, that it was not reasonably practicable for him to do so in time.

The question whether a claimant is fixed by the error of his or her adviser is sometimes said to turn on whether the adviser concerned was a 'skilled adviser'. That is a question of fact, depending on the particular circumstances of the case: *Theobald v Royal Bank of Scotland plc* [2007] All ER (D) 04 (Jan). The EAT in this case also makes the distinction between instructing an adviser to act on the employee's behalf, in which case it will usually be held to have been reasonably practicable to present the claim in time, and taking advice from an adviser but retaining control over the submission of the claim, where the fault of the adviser in giving erroneous advice will not count against the claimant; however this distinction was rejected by the EAT in the subsequent case of *T Mobile (UK) Ltd v Singleton* [2011] All ER (D) 12 (May), where it was held that the mere taking of advice from a solicitor was sufficient to fix the claimant with the solicitor's negligence in failing to alert him to the correct time limit. In the same case it was held that the employer is under no duty to take active steps to correct a misunderstanding by the employee of the correct time limit.

In *Marks & Spencer plc v Williams-Ryan* [2005] EWCA Civ 470, [2005] IRLR 562, however, the Court of Appeal upheld a finding that it was not reasonably practicable for the claimant to claim in time where she had been led by misleading information provided by the employer to understand that she could not present a tribunal claim until her internal appeal against dismissal had been concluded (and that process was in turn delayed beyond the three month limit). The important distinction here is between inaction and actively (or unintentionally) misleading. See also *Aryeetey v*

Tuntum Housing Association, [2007] All ER (D) 174 (Oct) (not reasonably practicable to present claim when claimant advised by Employment Judge during related proceedings that a further claim was not necessary).

(ix)   A rather stricter view of ignorance of rights may be taken where the rights are based on principles of European law overriding restrictions in domestic law. Thus, in *Biggs v Somerset County Council* [1996] 2 All ER 734, [1996] 2 CMLR 292 [1996] ICR 364, the Court of Appeal held as a matter of law that it was reasonably practicable for Ms Biggs to present a claim for unfair dismissal at a time when (as a part-time employee) she was expressly debarred by statute from the right to complain and the statute was only held to infringe EU law many years later.

17.26

If it is not reasonably practicable to present a claim in time, the tribunal may allow an extension of time of such further period as it considers reasonable. There is no fixed limit, and each case must be considered on its facts in the light of the employee's explanation for the delay: *Marley (UK) Ltd v Anderson* [1996] ICR 728, CA. The EAT has commented that the tribunal has an unfettered discretion as to how long an extension of time to allow in the light of all the circumstances, albeit the discretion must be exercised judicially: *Howlett Marine Services Ltd v Bowlam* [2001] IRLR 201. In practice, however the starting point is that there is an obligation on claimants to act expeditiously in asserting their rights in the tribunal, so that even a relatively short delay beyond the point when it became reasonably practicable to present the claim may be more than is reasonable in the absence of an explanation for the further delay; in *Theobald v The Royal Bank of Scotland plc* (EAT/0444/06) [2007] All ER (D) 04 (Jan), a delay of 13 days was held on the facts to be too long, and in *Nolan v Balfour Beatty Engineering Services Ltd* (UKEAT/0109/11) a decision allowing an extension of 11 weeks from when the claimant became aware of the facts entitling him to claim was held to be perverse.

For the practical application of the process of assessing a reasonable time, see *James W Cook & Co (Wivenhoe) Ltd (in liq) v Tipper* [1990] ICR 716, at 724–725, CA, as explained in *Marley (UK) Ltd v Anderson* (above). It has been suggested that the tribunal should consider the same questions as in applying the 'reasonable practicability' test, particularly as regards the claimant's state of mind and state of knowledge, but focusing on what was reasonable rather than what was practicable: *Thompson v Northumberland County Council*, [2007] All ER (D) 95 (Sep). More recently, the EAT has twice held that the same approach should be used to whether the extension sought is reasonable as to whether it was not reasonably practicable to present the claim in time: *Nolan*, above, and *Cullinane v Balfour Beatty Engineering Services Ltd* (UKEAT/0537/10), both claims under the trade union blacklisting legislation.

A claimant who loses the opportunity to have his or her case heard by the tribunal because of the negligence of professional advisers is able to sue them in the ordinary courts. The claim is for the loss of a chance of making a successful claim, so that an assessment of the prospects of success in the tribunal would have to be made when calculating damages.

If a claimant wishes to pursue his or her claim in another forum (eg in proceedings for wrongful dismissal (see WRONGFUL DISMISSAL (56)) but also wishes to preserve the right to proceed in the tribunal, he or she should submit a Claim Form, using the 'Further Information' section to explain the position, and seek to have the tribunal proceedings stayed (*Warnock v Scarborough Football Club* [1989] ICR 489; and see **18.22** below).

17.27 Redundancy payments

A time limit of six months applies. This period runs from the 'relevant date', which is defined in *ERA 1996, s 145* and is in most cases (where there has not been a trial period in alternative employment) the same as the EDT (see for details of this **17.23** and **17.24** above).

17.27   Employment Tribunals – I

The EAT in *Watts v Rubery Owen Conveyancer Ltd* [1977] 2 All ER 1 held that a claim for a redundancy payment may not be presented until the dismissal has taken effect (unless the claim is based on the special procedure for claim in redundancy payments where the employee has been laid off or placed on short time working). However the Court of Appeal in *Bon Groundwork Ltd v Foster* [2012] EWCA Civ 252, [2012] IRLR 517 acknowledged that the decision in *Watt* has since been heavily criticised, and declined to rule on whether it is still good law. In order to preserve the right to institute tribunal proceedings, it is sufficient that within the six-month period following the 'relevant date' the employee has made a claim by notice in writing to the employer; or referred the claim to a tribunal; or presented a claim of unfair dismissal to the tribunal; or that a payment (not necessarily the full entitlement) has been agreed and paid. The effect of any of these actions is to preserve the right to claim indefinitely (*ERA 1996, s 164(1)*). The six-month time limit may be extended by up to a further six months if the tribunal is persuaded that it is just and equitable to do so (*ERA 1996, s 164(2), (3)*). See **17.30** below for the principles applicable to a 'just and equitable' extension of time. There is no jurisdiction to extend time beyond the further period of six months: *Crawford v Secretary of State for Employment* [1995] IRLR 523.

17.28 Equal pay

The standard time limit laid down by *s 129* of the *Equality Act 2010* is six months from the date the employee ceased to be employed by the respondent employer (*ss 129(3), 130*). A claim may, of course, be made whilst the applicant is still employed. The time limit provisions are modified in cases about pension rights. All of these points applied equally to claims under the predecessor legislation, the *Equal Pay Act 1970*. The validity of the six-month time limit was challenged as contrary to EU law in *Preston v Wolverhampton Healthcare NHS Trust* [2001] UKHL 5, [2001] ICR 217, but was upheld, subject to qualifications (see below) by the House of Lords.

Following amendments made by the *Equal Pay Act 1970 (Amendment) Regulations 2003 (SI 2003/1656)*, there are three categories of case in which the time limit may be extended. First, whilst normally the limit applies to each contract where an employee is employed under a number of contracts, even if the contracts are immediately consecutive, where there is a succession of contracts at regular intervals forming part of a stable employment relationship (a 'stable employment case'), time only runs from the end of the last such contract (*Equality Act 2010, ss 129(3), 130(3)*). Second, where the employer deliberately concealed from the claimant a fact relevant to his or her claim and without knowledge of which he or she could not reasonably have been expected to institute the proceedings, and the claimant did not discover and could not with reasonable diligence have discovered the fact until after the end of the period of employment (a 'concealment case') time is extended to six months from the day on which the claimant discovered, or could with reasonable diligence have discovered, the fact (*ss 129(3), 130(4)*). Third, if at the date of the ending of his or her employment (or any later date from which time would otherwise run by virtue of either of the other exceptions) the claimant is under a disability, ie is a minor (or under 16 in Scotland) or is of unsound mind (a 'disability case'), time runs from the date that he or she ceases to be under such a disability (*ss 129(3), 130(7)*).

Subject to these exceptions, the tribunal has no jurisdiction to extend time. However, provided that a claim is presented in time, ie (usually) within six months following the termination of the employment, an equal pay claim relating to a job in which the employee had ceased to be employed some time previously may be pursued: *Young v National Power plc* [2001] 2 All ER 339, [2001] ICR 328, CA: see further on this *Allan v Newcastle-upon-Tyne City Council* [2005] ICR 1170, [2005] IRLR 504, EAT.

The Court of Appeal has given guidance in *Slack v Cumbria County Council (Equality and Human Rights Commission intervening)* [2009] EWCA Civ 293, [2009] ICR 1217 on the position where a claimant was employed for a continuous period by the same employer but, because of changes in such matters as hours of work, new contracts were issued during that period. The Court's conclusion was that time would not start to run against the employee in relation to the prior period of employment simply because she signed a new contract, since the situation would normally fall within the scope of the 'stable employment relationship' exception in what is now *Equality Act 2010 ss 129(3), 130(3)*. In the light of that conclusion, the Court went on to hold that the time limits (then laid down by the *Equal Pay Act 1970*) were compatible with the requirements of European law.

The House of Lords has ruled that where an employee's employment has been transferred under the *Transfer of Undertakings (Protection of Employment) Regulations 1981*, time for making a claim in respect of employment with the previous employer runs from the date of the transfer, not the eventual end of the employment with the transferee employer: *Powerhouse Retail Ltd v Burroughs* [2006] UKHL 13, [2006] IRLR 381. The same principle would apply to a transfer under the replacement *2006 Regulations*. This limitation does not however apply where the claim is against the current employer, based on a term derived from the application of an equality clause during the previous employment but which then transferred with the claimant under the Regulations to her new employer: *Gutridge v Sodexo Ltd* [2009] EWCA Civ 729, [2009] ICR 1486.

It should be noted that claims for equal pay under the *Equality Act 2010* can also be brought in the High Court or County Court, based on the contractual equality clause implied into all employment contracts by the equality of terms provisions of the *2010 Act*. Like any contractual claim in the ordinary courts, such claims may be brought at any time within six years of the breach (the time limit in Scotland is five years). The Court has power to strike a claim out if it could 'more conveniently' be brought in the employment tribunal. In *Abdulla v Birmingham City Council* [2012] ICR 1419, the Supreme Court confirmed this position. The Court indicated that prior to the expiry of time to bring a claim in the tribunal, in most cases it would be more convenient to dispose of the case in the Tribunal. However, after that time period has expired, and the claim is time-barred in the tribunal, a Court could not conclude the claim would more conveniently be disposed of in the tribunal. Parliament had allowed the claims to be brought in the civil courts as well as in the tribunal.

17.29 Unlawful discrimination

A claim must be presented to the tribunal 'not after the end' of the period of three months 'beginning when the act complained of was done': *Equality Act 2010, s 123(1)*. There are specific provisions to deal with discrimination by omission, which is to be treated as occurring when the person in question decided upon it; and an act extending over a period is to be treated as done at the end of that period: see *s 123(3)*. The latter provision covers the maintenance of a continuing policy or state of affairs, as well as a continuing course of discriminatory conduct such as harassment: see *Barclays Bank plc v Kapur* [1991] 2 AC 355, [1991] 1 All ER 646, [1991] ICR 208, [1991] IRLR 136; and *Okoro v Taylor Woodrow Construction Ltd* [2013] ICR 580. The same provisions as to time limits and extensions of time apply to each of the *Part-time Workers (Prevention of Less Favourable Treatment) Regulations 2000*, the *Fixed-term Employees (Prevention of Less Favourable Treatment) Regulations 2002* and the *Agency Workers Regulations 2010*. See further **17.33** below.

The line between a continuing policy or course of conduct and a single act with continuing consequences is illustrated by cases on each side of the line in *Owusu v London Fire and Civil Defence Authority* [1995] IRLR 574. The leading case on what it is necessary to show to establish an act continuing over a period is now *Hendricks v Metropolitan Police Comr* [2002] EWCA Civ 1686, [2003] 1 All ER 654, [2003] ICR 530. In this case the Court of Appeal emphasised that whilst a policy or practice of discrimination will normally provide a basis for a claim that there was a discriminatory act continuing over a period, it is not a necessary precondition, as earlier cases had appeared to indicate. The correct test is whether the acts complained of are linked, and are evidence of a continuing discriminatory state of affairs. In *Lyfar v Brighton and Sussex University Hospitals Trust* [2006] EWCA Civ 1548, [2006] All ER (D) 182 (Nov), the Court of Appeal confirmed that its decision in *Hendricks* was to be followed, in preference to *Robertson v Bexley Community Centre* [2003] EWCA Civ 576, [2003] IRLR 434, a case decided after *Hendricks* but which does not refer to it, and applies the requirement of a policy or practice. A relevant factor in whether or not a series of acts is to be regarded as an act continuing over a period is whether the same person or persons is or are responsible for each of the acts: *Aziz v FDA* [2010] EWCA Civ 304, 154 Sol Jo (no 14) 29. As to the relevance of such matters as evidence that later events were acts of discrimination, see *HSBC Asia Holdings BV v Gillespie [2011] ICR 192*. If the issue whether a number of incidents amounted to an act continuing over a period is being considered at a PHR (as may be the case when some but not all or the incidents would be out of time if treated separately) the test is whether the claimant has made out a prima facie case for the incidents being treated collectively as an act continuing over a period: *Lyfar v Brighton and Sussex University Hospitals NHS Trust* [2006] EWCA Civ 1548, *Aziz v First Division Association* [2010] EWCA Civ 304.

The fact that it has not been specifically pleaded in the claim that the various acts of alleged discrimination alleged form part of an act continuing over a period does not preclude the tribunal from treating them as such for the purpose of the running of time, at least if the respondent had been sufficiently alerted to the point: *Khetab v Aga Medical Ltd* (UKEAT/0313/10).

Where a discriminatory policy is operated by a respondent, time begins to run afresh each time the policy is operated to the detriment of the claimant: *Rovenska v General Medical Council* [1998] ICR 85. If the complainant is an employee, the continued existence of the policy or practice, or state of affairs evidenced by the specific acts, postpones the running of time until the policy is discontinued or rescinded or (if earlier) the employment ends: *Cast v Croydon College* [1998] ICR 500. This is not necessarily the case, however, where a claimant complains of repeated rejections of job applications: cf *Tyagi v BBC World Service* [2001] EWCA Civ 549, [2001] IRLR 465; each rejection is likely to be treated as a separate cause of action, with time running accordingly. Time does not start to run in respect of an act of discrimination until the discriminator is in a position to put into effect his or her discriminatory intention: *Swithland Motors plc v Clarke* [1994] IRLR 275 (as to the position in dismissal cases, see below).

The *Equality Act 2010* and the *Part-time Workers, Fixed-term Employees Regulations* and *Agency Workers Regulations* also make specific provision for when time runs where what is complained of is a deliberate omission (such as a refusal to make adjustments to the working arrangements for a disabled employee). In such cases the principle is that time runs from the date on which the employer decided not to act, rather than from the date of the employee becoming aware of this fact. As there will often be no direct evidence of the relevant date, there are further provisions treating the employer as having decided not to act when he does an act inconsistent with doing the act omitted, or at the end of a reasonable period within which he could be expected to have acted. These provisions were considered by the Court of Appeal in *Matuszowicz v Kingston-Upon-Hull City Council* [2009] EWCA Civ 22, [2009] 3 All ER 685, [2009] IRLR 288. The Court held that the statutory provisions must be taken to apply equally to a non-deliberate omission – as where the employer simply failed to make the required adjustment in a disability case (as this case was). Recognising the difficulty that employees may have in appreciating when time starts to run in these circumstances, the Court urged tribunals to allow some latitude to employees to take account of their difficulty in judging when a reasonable time had passed for the employer to act.

Another difficult issue in relation to when time starts to run is where the complaint is of discrimination by way of, or leading to, dismissal. It is now clearly established (after earlier conflicting case law) that time runs from the date of the dismissal (rather than (if earlier) the date on which notice was given): see the cases cited in *British Gas Services Ltd v McCaull* [2001] IRLR 60 at para 25. In *Derby Specialist Fabrication Ltd v Burton* [2001] 2 All ER 840, [2001] ICR 833 this principle was followed in a race discrimination case where the claim was for constructive dismissal. The EAT held that this constituted a 'dismissal' within *s 4(2)* of the *RRA 1976* and it was not therefore necessary to rely on the discriminatory acts which had led to the employee's resignation as 'detriments' (in which case the claim would have been out of time). The same conclusion has now also been reached by the Court of Appeal in relation to the *DDA 1995*: *Meikle v Nottinghamshire County Council* [2004] EWCA Civ 859, [2004] 4 All ER 97, [2005] ICR 1, [2004] IRLR 703, following *Catherall v Michelin Tyres plc* [2003] ICR 28, EAT, and disapproving the earlier contrary view expressed by a different division of the EAT in *Metropolitan Police Comr v Harley* [2001] ICR 927.

A point not directly arising in these cases, and on which there is no direct authority, is whether a claim alleging discrimination by way of dismissal may be presented before the claimant has been dismissed, in the sense applied in the cases cited above. There is nothing obvious in the wording of the statutory provisions on time limits to prevent this, as a claim is merely required not to be presented after the end of the period specified. Under the legislation on discrimination prior to the *Equality Act 2010*, the complaint to be presented was that the respondent 'has committed' an act of unlawful discrimination (see eg the *Sex Discrimination Act 1975, s 63(1)* wording which did preclude a complaint of dismissal being presented before the dismissal took effect, and there was (and is) no equivalent in the discrimination legislation of *ERA 1996 s 111(3)*, which specifically allows the presentation of a complaint of unfair dismissal during the notice period: see **17.24** above. However the position is less clearly expressed in the *Equality Act 2010, ss 120(1)* and *123(1)*; the former provision refers to complaints 'relating to' a contravention of relevant parts of the *Act*, and 'not after the end' of a period does not necessarily mean also 'not before the beginning'. The prudent course, in the circumstances, is not to present a claim before the dismissal has taken effect.

17.30 'Just and equitable' extension of time

A tribunal has discretion to extend time where it would be 'just and equitable' to do so: *Equality Act 2010, s 123(3)*; *Part-time Workers (Prevention of Less Favourable Treatment) Regulations 2000, reg 8, Fixed-term Employees (Prevention of Less Favourable Treatment) Regulations 2002, reg 8*; *Agency Workers Regulations 2010, reg 18*. This is a broader discretion than the 'not reasonably practicable' test and the EAT has (albeit with limited success) discouraged the development of authorities on the application of the test: see *Hutchinson v Westward Television Ltd* [1977] ICR 279, [1977] IRLR 69.

The Court of Appeal has emphasised that there is no presumption in favour of the extension of time. The onus is on the claimant to convince the tribunal that it is just and equitable to extend time, in the context that time limits in employment cases are intended to apply strictly: *Robertson v Bexley Community Centre* [2003] EWCA Civ 576, [2003] IRLR 434. However, in *Chief Constable of Lincolnshire Police v Caston* [2009] EWCA Civ 1298, [2010] IRLR 327, the Court of Appeal emphasised that the comments in *Robertson* merely indicated that there was a broad discretion, the question being one of fact and judgment rather than policy; 'there is no principle of law which indicates how generously or sparingly the power to enlarge time is to be exercised' (per Sedley LJ). Because of the breadth of the discretion, the appellate courts are reluctant to interfere with the exercise of the discretion if the issue is appealed.

The fact that the onus is on the claimant to make out a case for an extension of time means that it is often necessary, or at least helpful, for the claimant to give evidence in support of the claim for an extension. However, the EAT has confirmed that evidence from the claimant is not a precondition for an extension; other material before the tribunal, such as documents, may be sufficient to establish the balance in favour of the claimant: *Accurist Watches Ltd v Wadher* [2009] All ER (D) 189 (Apr).

If there are circumstances which otherwise render it just and equitable to extend time, the length of the extension required is not of itself a limiting factor, unless the delay would prejudice the possibility of a fair trial: *Afolabi v Southwark London Borough Council* [2003] EWCA Civ 15, [2003] ICR 800, where the Court of Appeal upheld an extension of time of nearly nine years where the claimant had without fault on his part been unaware of the facts relied on to support his claim, and had acted reasonably promptly when those facts came to his knowledge. However it will be exceptional that a delay of or approaching that order would not render a fair trial impossible, especially where facts are disputed and there is no clear contemporaneous documentation.

Other factors which a tribunal should take into account in the exercise of its discretion will depend on the facts of each case, and cannot be exhaustively listed. They will however include the reason for the delay, whether the claimant was aware of his or her rights to claim, and/or of the time limit, the conduct of the employer, the length of the extension sought, and the prejudice that would be suffered by the employer if the claim were permitted to proceed (necessarily balanced against the prejudice to the claimant if he or she is refused an extension of time). Tribunals are encouraged to consider by analogy the checklist of factors listed in the *Limitation Act 1980, s 33* (which confers discretion to extend time for personal injury claims in the courts), but the EAT has stated that this process is not mandatory (*Chohan v Derby Law Centre* [2004] IRLR 685). There is authority for the proposition that the most important factor in whether to extend time is whether the delay has affected the ability of the tribunal to conduct a fair trial of the issues: *DPP v Marshall* [1998] ICR 518. However it is suggested that this should not be relied on as a reason not to attach weight to other factors such as serious and avoidable delay by the claimant in claiming, or in obtaining advice about a possible claim.

An example of a specific factor being taken into account in favour of a claimant is *Department of Constitutional Affairs v Jones* [2007] EWCA Civ 894, [2008] IRLR 128, where the Court of Appeal accepted as a valid reason for extending time the claimant's inability or unwillingness to admit to himself or others that he was disabled (by clinical depression).

The EAT has held that where delay in presenting a claim is attributable to incorrect legal advice from the claimant's solicitor, this should not be visited on the claimant by refusing an extension of time, notwithstanding that the claimant may have a valid claim in negligence against the solicitor, since this would confer a windfall on the respondent: *Chohan v Derby Law Centre*, above. This does not mean that time *should* be extended in all such cases, but that all other factors must also be considered. See also *Hawkins v Ball* [1996] IRLR 258 for a more cautious approach to this point, and *Wright v Wolverhampton City Council* (UKEAT/0117/08) [2009] All ER (D) 179 (Feb), applying the principles to poor advice given by a trade union representative. By contrast, where the delay in presentation is down entirely to the claimant, a tribunal is more likely to refuse an application for a just and equitable extension of time: see *De Souza v Manpower UK Ltd* [2013] All ER (D) 199 (Feb), where the application was one day out of time.

Case law prior to the implementation of the *Dispute Resolution Regulations* had established that a decision by the employee to delay presenting a claim whilst an internal grievance procedure or appeal was being pursued would not necessarily be a sufficient reason to extend time under the 'just and equitable' principle, even if the delay had not prejudiced the employer. It was only one of the relevant factors to be taken into account, and the weight to be attached to it was a matter for the tribunal in the light of the facts of each case: *Apelogun-Gabriels v Lambeth London Borough Council* [2001] EWCA Civ 1853, [2002] ICR 713, [2002] IRLR 116 overruling *Aniagwu v Hackney London Borough Council* [1999] IRLR 303 and affirming *Robinson v Post Office* [2000] IRLR 804. It is probable that following the repeal of the dispute resolution legislation, the position as stated in *Apelogun-Gabriels* again applies.

The principle established in relation to unfair dismissal claims by the Court of Appeal in *Biggs v Somerset County Council* [1996] ICR 364, that a failure to appreciate that European law confers a right to claim apparently excluded by the UK statute does not make it 'not reasonably practicable' to claim in time, does not apply to discrimination claims. The 'just and equitable' test is wider, and an understandable misapprehension as to the state of the law is a relevant factor in deciding whether to extend time: *British Coal Corpn v Keeble* [1997] IRLR 336. Not all misunderstandings of the law will be accepted as excuses however; see *University of Westminster v Bailey* [2009] All ER (D) 47 (Nov), where the EAT held that it was not an acceptable reason for a 19 month delay that the claimant, a senior lecturer in HR, did not realise that the *Sex Discrimination Act 1975* applied equally to men. It has been suggested that a change in the law could render it just and equitable to extend time to allow a claim which could not have been brought as the law had previously been understood to be: *Foster v South Glamorgan Health Authority* [1988] ICR 526.

Whilst it is open to a tribunal to consider as a preliminary point whether a discrimination claim is out of time, and if so whether it is just and equitable to extend time, in most cases tribunals will not accede to applications for a PHR, unless there is a clear point which would potentially dispose of the entire case. Discrimination cases are usually 'fact-sensitive', and it is therefore preferable to hear all the evidence before deciding issues as to the ambit of the tribunal's jurisdiction, particularly where at least part of the complaint is clearly in time. Matters which in themselves may be out of time may still be evidentially relevant, and the tribunal will in such cases have to hear evidence about the earlier matters, at least as background, in any event. In such cases there is little potential to save time or cost by holding a preliminary hearing, and indeed there may be a duplication of evidence over two hearings. The House of Lords in *SCA Packaging Ltd v Boyle* [2009] UKHL 37, [2009] IRLR 746 approved, in obiter comments, views expressed in earlier EAT cases to the effect that preliminary hearings should only be ordered sparingly, such as where 'there is a succinct, knockout point which is capable of being decided after only a relatively short hearing'. This is unlikely to be the case where at least some of the allegations made are in time. If the question whether to extend time is decided at the hearing of the substantive claim, and the tribunal finds the allegations concerned well-founded, it will require very significant reasons to refuse an extension of time, since the prejudicial effect of refusing an extension would be to deny the claimant a remedy for a proven wrong: see *Bahous v Pizza Express Restaurant Ltd* (UKEAT/0029/11).

17.31 **Unlawful deductions from wages and claims arising from a failure to pay holiday pay or the National Minimum Wage**

A complaint of unlawful deduction from wages must be presented within the period of three months beginning with the date of the deduction or enforced payment complained of, or such further period as the tribunal considers reasonable if it is satisfied that it was not reasonably practicable to present the claim within the three-month period: *ERA 1996, s 23(4)*. See **17.25** and **17.26** above for the application of the 'not reasonably practicable' test.

For the purpose of calculating the time limit, a failure to pay is not treated as an unlawful deduction until the last date on which the employer was contractually permitted to make the payment concerned, even if part payment was made earlier: *Group 4 Nightspeed Ltd v Gilbert* [1997] IRLR 398. It follows that a claim presented *before* the last date for payment may be outside the jurisdiction of the tribunal because it is premature: *Hyde v Lehman Brothers Ltd* [2004] All ER (D) 40 (Aug), EAT. Where the complaint is of a series of deductions or payments, time runs from the last such deduction or payment (*ERA 1996, s 23(3)*) and the tribunal can order repayment in respect of the entire series: see *Reid v Camphill Engravers* [1990] ICR 435. Note, however, that payments that would fall due after those complained in the claim form do not form part of the series for these purposes: *Qantas Cabin Crew (UK) Ltd v Lopez and Hooper* [2013] IRLR 4 (where instalment 2 of a relocation payment due 2 years after the first instalment had not fallen due and was not complained about in the claim; the EAT held the complaint was about a single payment, instalment 1, and was out of time – see para 64). A separate issue is whether a Tribunal can order repayment in respect of deductions in a series that were made after the claim was presented but up to the date of the hearing. In *Arthur H Wilton Ltd v Peebles* (EAT/835/93), the EAT appears to have indicated that this would be possible, but the point was not argued and it is submitted the better view is that the Tribunal only has jurisdiction to order those deductions made to the date of presentation. There is no direct authority on the question whether claims can extend back for longer than the contractual limitation period of six years (five in Scotland) but it is submitted that the limitation period would apply. Guidance as to the application of the time limits both to single deductions and to a series of deductions was given by the EAT in *Taylorplan Services Ltd v Jackson* [1996] IRLR 184.

Complaints by workers of a failure by their employer to pay the National Minimum Wage must be brought as claims for unlawful deductions from wages under *Part II* of the *ERA 1996* by virtue of the *National Minimum Wage Act 1998, ss 17, 18*, and the foregoing comments therefore apply equally to such claims. The Court of Appeal ruled in *Ainsworth v IRC* [2005] EWCA Civ 441, [2005] IRLR 465 that claims for holiday pay or payment in lieu for accrued but untaken holidays under the *Working Time Regulations 1998* could only be brought by way of a complaint under *reg 30* of the *1998 Regulations*, but this was reversed by the House of Lords when the case eventually reached it on appeal (sub nom *Revenue and Customs Comrs v Stringer* [2009] UKHL 31, [2009] ICR 985, [2009] IRLR 677). The difference between the two routes to the tribunal is that whilst essentially the same time limit provisions apply under *reg 30* as for a complaint of unlawful deductions, there is no equivalent in *reg 30* of the 'series of deductions' provision in *ERA 1996, s 23(3)*. Claims in respect of other provisions of the *1998 Regulations* which may be the subject of complaint to the tribunal are also subject to a three-month time limit, with any extension dependent on the 'not reasonably practicable' criterion.

17.32 Contract claims

Claims in contract brought under the *Employment Tribunals Extension of Jurisdiction (England and Wales) Order 1994 (SI 1994/1623)* or the equivalent Scottish Order may only be made if the claim arises out of, or is outstanding at the date of termination of, the employment concerned. The time limit for presentation is the same as in unfair dismissal cases and subject to the same 'not reasonably practicable' extension.

Time runs from the EDT where the employee has been dismissed, and in other cases from the employee's last day of work in the employment concerned (*art 7*). There is no provision equivalent to that for unfair dismissal cases permitting the claim to be presented during the notice period (*ERA 1996, s 111(3)*), and a breach of contract claim presented before the EDT is premature, with the result that the tribunal has no jurisdiction to determine it (*Capek v Lincolnshire County Council* [2000] IRLR 590, CA). The EAT has held (in *Miller Bros and F P Butler Ltd v Johnston* [2002] ICR 744) that the tribunal has no jurisdiction to consider a claim for breach of contract where the contract was only concluded after the employment had terminated (in that case a compromise agreement which the employer had failed to implement).

Contract claims are the only class of claim in respect of which an employer may counterclaim. A counterclaim may only be brought if presented at a time when the employee's claim is before the tribunal (ie it has been presented and not withdrawn) and is subject to a time limit of six weeks beginning with the day the employer received from the tribunal a copy of the employee's Claim Form (*Employment Tribunals Extension of Jurisdiction (England and Wales) Order 1994, art 8*). The same 'not reasonably practicable' test applies to any application for an extension of time. The validity of the counterclaim is not, however, affected by whether the claim itself was brought in time: all that is relevant is that a claim has been brought and a counterclaim is presented within the time limit running from the date of presentation of the claim (*Patel v RCMS Ltd* [1999] IRLR 161).

The counterclaim must contain the information specified in *rule 7* of the *ET Rules*, ie the respondent's name and address, the name and address of each claimant against whom a counterclaim is made, and details of the counterclaim. There is no prescribed form for counterclaims (and no specific section on the Response Form for making one), and the *ET Rules* do not specify any requirements as to the claimant's response to the counterclaim. These are therefore matters which have to be dealt with in each case by Case Management Orders (see **18.2** below). A Practice Direction issued by the President of the employment tribunals in Scotland (No 3 of December 2006) requires that respondents making a counterclaim should if reasonably practicable state in the counterclaim the amount being claimed, and that claimants must, if they intend to resist the counterclaim, notify the tribunal office of this within 28 days of receiving it, and give their reasons for so doing. This Practice Direction does not apply in England and Wales but its requirements are likely to be reflected in case management orders.

17.33 Other claims

For details of time limits for other classes of claim, and provisions as to extension of time, the relevant statutory provisions should be consulted. Three points of importance merit mention here:

(a)   Claims under the *Part-time Workers (Prevention of Less Favourable Treatment) Regulations 2000*, the *Fixed-term Employees (Prevention of Less Favourable Treatment) Regulations 2002*, and the *Agency Workers Regulations 2010*, alleging either less favourable treatment or subjection to a detriment by way of victimisation, are subject to provisions as to the applicable time limit, when time runs and extensions of time which are substantially the same as those in the anti-discrimination statutes: see **17.29** and **17.30** above. This contrasts with claims of subjection to detriment under *Part IVA* of the *ERA 1996*, where the 'not reasonably practicable' test applies: *ERA 1996, s 48(3)(b)*. An application under *reg 9* of the *Fixed-term Employees (Prevention of Less Favourable Treatment) Regulations 2002* for a declaration that the employee is a permanent employee may be made at any time provided that the employee has requested a statement to that effect from the employer, and that he or she is still employed by the employer when the tribunal application is made: *reg 9(6)*.

(b)   Complaints by trade unions or employee representatives, or in certain circumstances individual employees, under the *Transfer of Undertakings (Protection of Employment) Regulations 2006* ('*TUPE*'), *reg 15*, of a failure to inform or consult over a relevant transfer, are subject to a three-month time limit, time running from the date of the transfer, and any extension is subject to the 'not reasonably practicable' criteria. However the EAT has held that a complaint may also be presented before the transfer has occurred, where it is alleged that there has been a material breach of the duty to inform or to consult: *South Durham Health Authority v UNISON* [1995] ICR 495. A similar position arises in relation to complaints of failure to consult recognised trade unions or employee representatives about proposed redundancies (*TULRCA, s 188*): a complaint must be presented either before the last of the dismissals the subject of the complaint takes effect or within the period of three months beginning with that date (*s 189(5)*) but there is no restriction on earlier presentation, provided that the employer is subject to an obligation to consult (ie the employer proposes redundancies) and it is alleged that there has been a breach of the obligation.

(c)   Complaints of failure to pay sums due under a protective award made under either of the two above provisions are subject to separate time limits. In a case under *TUPE*, the time limit is three months beginning with the date of the order for a protective award (with the possibility of an extension if presentation in time was not reasonably practicable: *reg 15(12)*). If the award is made, or varied, by the EAT following an appeal, the time for claiming runs from the date of the EAT's order: *Dillon v Todd*

(UKEATS/0010/11). In redundancy cases, the period of three months runs from the last day in respect of which the protective award was made, again with the possibility of extension. However, it is possible that the protective award is not made (or confirmed on appeal) until after the time limit has expired. In such a case the claimant must rely on the 'not reasonably practicable' extension, and should therefore not delay in presenting his or her claim: *Howlett Marine Services Ltd v Bowlam* [2001] IRLR 201.

17.34 ACTION FOLLOWING PRESENTATION

Upon receipt of a Claim Form, the Secretary of the Tribunals is required to determine whether the claim or part of it should be accepted. The circumstances in which a claim may be rejected are set out in *ET Rules, rule 3*, and are as follows:

(a)   If the claim is not on the prescribed Claim Form, the Secretary is required to refuse to accept it, and it will simply be returned to the claimant with a letter explaining the need to use the correct form and a copy of the form. If the claimant then submits the prescribed form, the date of presentation will be the date of resubmission.

(b)   Additionally, the Secretary will not accept a claim or part thereof if the Claim Form does not include all the required information (as to which, see **17.15** above), or if he or she considers that the tribunal does not have the power to consider the claim. This procedure may be used to weed out at the outset claims where there is a clear jurisdictional bar to an otherwise permissible claim (eg the claimant lacks the service required to make an unfair dismissal claim, but not where the claim is out of time, since this might be overcome by a successful application for an extension of time).

The most significant of the reasons for not accepting a claim in practice was the claimant not having complied with the *Employment Act 2002, s 32*. The repeal of this provision has therefore significantly reduced the proportion of cases subjected to pre-acceptance screening out, but it remains in place and all claims received are routinely scrutinised to identify any grounds for non-acceptance.

The Judge's decision to reject a Claim Form, or any part of it, must be recorded in writing, together with the reasons for the decision, and sent to the claimant as soon as reasonably practicable, together with information as to how the decision may be reviewed (*ET Rules, rule 3(5)*). Unless the claimant successfully applies for a review of the decision, it is treated as not having been received. The same applies to a part of the Claim Form which has been rejected.

An application for a review must be made in writing within 14 days of the date the decision not to accept the claim was sent to the Claimant, and must set out the grounds of the application (*rule 35(1), (2)*). The time limit may be extended by an Employment Judge if he or she considers it just and equitable to do so. The permissible grounds for a review are that the decision was wrongly made as a result of an administrative error, or that the interests of justice require such a review (*rule 34(3), (4)*).

If the claimant applies for a review, this will be referred to a Judge (not necessarily the Judge who took the decision, to determine whether a review should be granted, or refused on the ground that it has no reasonable prospects of success (*ET Rules, rule 34(3)*). The *ET Rules* are silent as to whether, if the application is not summarily rejected, there must be a formal hearing, but it appears to be implicit that this is the case (by the combined effect of *rules 14* and *36*). The possible outcomes of a review are that the original decision is confirmed, varied or revoked, in which case it must be taken again, by an Employment Judge and without a (further) hearing (*rule 36(3)*). The EAT has held that 'administrative error' includes an error by a party (*Sodexho Ltd v Gibbons* [2005] IRLR 836), and this would be sufficient to cover accidental omission of the prescribed information, or putting the wrong dates of employment on the form so as to make it appear that the claimant lacked the required service to claim. The same case holds that the 'interests of justice' ground of review is to be interpreted to give effect to the Overriding Objective.

There is no power to review a refusal by the secretariat to accept a claim because it was not submitted on the prescribed form. However the EAT has held that such a decision is open to appeal: *Grant v In 2 Focus Sales Development Services Ltd*, [2007] All ER (D) 281 (Jan) (a case where the claim had been submitted by fax, causing it to be received in a slightly reduced format, and it had been rejected for that reason, wrongly, as the EAT held). Similarly, where a Claim Form is rejected by an Employment Judge, the prospective claimant may appeal to the EAT as an alternative to, or in addition to, an application for a review: *Richardson v U Mole Ltd* [2005] IRLR 668. However the grounds for an appeal would usually be limited to perversity (as in that case), and in the light of the broad approach to powers of review taken by the *Sodexho* case, an application for a review is the preferable recourse for a disappointed claimant who is too late simply to put in a correctly completed Claim Form.

There have been a number of cases illustrating the limits on the power of an employment judge to refuse to accept a claim form. An early example of a successful appeal is *Hamling v Coxlease School Ltd* [2007] IRLR 8, where the claim form did not give the claimant's address, but did give the address of the solicitors acting for her (see also *Police Comr v Rixon* [2010] All ER (D) 75 (May), where the claimant's address was withheld for security reasons). In *Young v Hexion Speciality Chemicals UK Ltd* (UKEATS/0023/09/BI), it was held not to be a reason to refuse to register a claim that the claimant had not given a start date for his employment, so that it was not possible to know whether he had a year's service at the date of his dismissal; it would have been permissible to refuse to accept the claim if he had given that information and it was clear that he lacked the required service for a claim of unfair dismissal, and that was his claim. In *May v Greenwich Council* [2010] All ER (D) 105 (May), it was held to be impermissible to reject a claim form simply because parts of it were difficult or even impossible to read, if the required information (see **17.15** above for this) was at least legible. In both of the latter cases, the simple remedy would be to accept the claim and write to the claimant asking for either the missing information or a legible transcript of the illegible parts of the form.

One reason for refusing to register a claim is that the claim form does not disclose a claim within the jurisdiction of the tribunal. Refusal on these grounds requires the decision of an employment judge; an example is *Kulikaoskas v Macduff Shellfish Ltd* [2011] ICR 48, EAT, a claim for 'associative' pregnancy discrimination. (The question whether such a claim can be made has subsequently been referred to the CJEU.)

If the Secretary or a Judge decides to accept a claim, a copy must be sent to each respondent, together with a blank response form and information about how to respond, the time limit for doing so and the consequences of not responding within the time limit. Information must also be given about any applicable provision for conciliation. Information is also required to be given about which parts of the claim have been accepted and which rejected, in any case where the claim has been accepted only in part. (*ET Rules, rule 2(2)*). The parties are also notified of the case number and address for correspondence. The papers are also copied at this point to the relevant ACAS office if (as in almost all cases) there is provision for conciliation in the relevant legislation.

The tribunal has no power under *rule 34* to review the decision to accept the claim, as this is expressly limited to reviewing decisions not to accept a claim or part. If the respondent wishes to assert that the claim should not have been accepted, it is necessary to appeal (by analogy with the claimant's appeal in *Richardson v U Mole Ltd*, above), or, more practically, to apply for a PHR to determine the jurisdictional issue on which the acceptance is challenged.

Prior to the introduction of the *2004 Regulations*, all originating applications were entered into a public register. This register was discontinued and closed on 1 October 2004, principally in response to concerns that it was being abused by largely unregulated organisations which used the information about parties contained in it to cold call the parties offering representation in the proceedings. There is now no public record of claims, or claimants or respondents, other than the register of judgments. However see further **17.5(h)** for the Information Commissioner's ruling requiring disclosure of names and addresses of respondents to tribunal claims under the *Freedom of Information Act 2000*.

17.35   RESPONSE BY THE RESPONDENT

If a respondent wishes to defend a claim, he or she must complete and return a written response within 28 days of the date that the Claim Form was sent to him or her (*ET Rules, rule 4(1)*). Time runs from the date the Claim Form was sent to the respondent not the date it was received (this point was expressly confirmed by the EAT in *Bone v Fabcon Projects Ltd* [2007] 1 All ER 1071, [2006] ICR 1421, [2006] IRLR 908) and the response must be received by the tribunal office, not merely sent, by the end of the 28th day following the sending out of the Claim Form. It should be noted that the claim form will not be regarded as having been 'sent' to a respondent if there are material inaccuracies in the name and address to which it was addressed by the tribunal, and as a consequence it is not in fact received by the respondent: *Chowles (t/a Granary Pine) v West* (UKEAT/0473/08) (claim sent to a Mr Charles instead of Chowles, and to address with incomplete postcode). However, the EAT has since held (see *Jarretts Motors Ltd v Wells* [2009] All ER (D) 350 (Jul)) that material errors in the name and/or address given for the respondent do not affect the position if the notice of the claim is in fact received by the respondent within the time for responding; the fact that it is delayed may provide grounds for an extension of time, but nothing more.

A respondent may submit the response to two or more claimants' claims on the same Response Form, provided that the claims each arise out of the same set of facts, and either the grounds for resisting the claims are the same in each case, or the respondent does not resist the claims. Similarly, two or more respondents to the same claim may respond using the same Response Form, provided that the grounds of resistance are the same for each respondent or the claim is not resisted (*ET Rules, rules 4(2), 6(1)*). There is no apparent sanction against a joint response being submitted in a case where the respondents' grounds of resistance differ, provided that the prescribed form is used and all required information given, and respondents commonly respond in this way in practice. A blank Response Form is sent to respondents with the notification of the claim; the electronic version may be used if the respondent wishes (it is accessed via HM Courts and Tribunals Service website, www.justice.gov.uk). There is a separate version of the form for use in responding to multiple claims.

The respondent should set out with some care the grounds upon which he or she wishes to resist the claim, because if he or she omits a ground and wishes to raise it at any subsequent tribunal hearing, the claimant may successfully resist an application to amend the response or apply for an adjournment, possibly at the respondent's expense, to consider the additional matter (see also *Hotson v Wisbech Conservative Club* [1984] IRLR 422). In *Panama v London Borough of Hackney* [2003] IRLR 278, the Court of Appeal emphasised that serious allegations such as those of dishonesty must be put with sufficient formality at an early enough stage to provide a full opportunity for answer. Also, as with the claimant's Claim Form, any statement made by a respondent in the response may be challenged at the hearing.

The degree of detail is a matter of judgment, but it needs to be remembered that the claimant may apply for an order for further particulars of the grounds set out by the respondent; further information may also be required by order of the tribunal of its own motion.

If the claim, or one of the claims, is for breach of contract, or for a sum due under a contract, the respondent may in addition to responding to the claim make a counterclaim. It is only in cases where the claim is made under the *Employment Tribunals Extension of Jurisdiction (England and Wales) Order 1994* or its Scottish equivalent that such a step is possible. The counterclaim may, but need not necessarily, be included with the response. For further details see **17.32** above.

17.36 Failure to respond in time and extensions of time

If the response is not presented in time, in general the respondent is not entitled to take any further part in the proceedings, and a default judgment will usually be issued in favour of the claimant (see **17.38** below). He or she may, however, apply to the tribunal for an extension of time for submitting the response. An application for an extension of time may only be granted if it is just and equitable to do so. Such an application must be made *before* the expiry of the 28 day limit for submitting the response, in writing, and must explain why the time limit cannot be complied with. If the respondent is legally represented, there is an additional requirement to notify all other parties to the proceedings of the application and the reasons for it, and to inform them of their right to object to the application within seven days of receiving the copy, and confirm to the tribunal that this has been done. (This was originally the effect of *ET Rules, rules 4(4)* and *11*; the *2008 Regulations* have recast the provisions in the *rules 4(4A)–(4E)*, but without changing the substance of the requirements of notification.) If the respondent does not notify the claimant of the application, the tribunal will do so (thereby somewhat delaying consideration of the application, although the tribunal may require an immediate reply if the matter is urgent).

Although the rules do not say so in terms, it appears to follow from the notification requirements that in practice an application for an extension of time needs to be made well before the time limit for presenting the reply will expire, since otherwise the tribunal cannot decide the application, having given the other party or parties time to submit objections, and notify the respondent of the decision, before the deadline has passed. Whilst there is nothing to prevent an extension of time from being granted retrospectively (provided it was applied for within the time limit for responding), the respondent takes a grave risk if he or she relies on such an extension being granted and fails to present a response within the time limit.

There is as yet no direct judicial guidance on when it will be just and equitable to grant an extension of time for a response. Since the consequence of refusal of an extension may be to prevent the respondent from defending the claim at all, there is a strong argument for the exercise of discretion in the respondent's favour, at least in any case where there is no objection from the claimant, or no prejudice to the claimant is likely to be occasioned if the requested extension is granted. In other cases, the reasons for the respondent's inability to submit a response are likely to be scrutinised with care, but the granting of extensions is by no means uncommon.

One obvious situation in which extensions will be sought is where the respondent did not receive the Claim Form until some time after it was sent (either because of postal delays, or the respondent's absence, or because the claimant had given an incorrect address). If genuine, these reasons are likely to be compelling factors in favour of an extension of time: compare *Bone v Fabcon Projects Ltd*, above, para **17.35**, where the claim was not received from the tribunal until, having heard of the claim through ACAS, the employer contacted the tribunal office and had it re-sent. However, as an alternative to applying for an extension, the respondent may be in a position to submit a response with the bare minimum of reasons for resisting the claim, and an offer to provide full particulars as soon as the necessary information can be obtained. This approach may also need to be adopted if there is insufficient information about the subject matter of the complaint in the Claim Form; however in most cases this will not necessarily be regarded as a compelling reason for an extension of time, since in most cases the respondent will be fully aware of the point in dispute because it will have been considered as a grievance or have been the subject of disciplinary proceedings.

If the respondent did not receive the form because it was incorrectly addressed, he or she may be able to argue that it was not 'sent'. In these circumstances if the respondent becomes aware of the claim soon enough, it may be possible to tell the tribunal the claim has not been received and ask for it to be re-served. The tribunal will not automatically accede to such a request, and if a default judgment has already been issued by the time the respondent contacts the tribunal, the only practical remedy for the respondent is to apply for a review of that judgment under *rule 33*: see *Chowles (t/a Granary Pine) v West*, above, para **17.35**, for an example.

17.37   In addition to the requirement to use the prescribed Response Form, if a response does not contain all the required information, or is received by the tribunal after the time limit (plus any extension) has expired, it will be referred to an Employment Judge to decide whether to accept or reject it (*ET Rules, rules 6(2), (3)*). There appears to be no discretion under the literal terms of the rule to accept a response at this stage if it is late or incomplete, but it is clear from the cases referred to below that the rule is to be interpreted as permitting a discretion not to reject a response for trivial or immaterial omissions of required information, or where there is good reason for lateness. The same conclusion follows by parity of reasoning from the cases on the acceptance of claims despite immaterial errors or omissions (see **17.16** and **17.34** above).

The respondent will be notified of any decision to reject a response, and the reasons for it, in writing, and is entitled to apply for a review of the rejection of the response in accordance with *rule 34*, but only on the grounds of an administrative error or that a review is in the interests of justice; see however *Butlins Skyline Ltd v Beynon* [2007] ICR 121, which holds that an administrative decision to reject a response is also open to appeal. Failing a successful review or appeal, the respondent cannot take any part in the proceedings other than by way of appearing as a witness or applying for a review of a default judgment (see **17.38** below); the respondent has the very limited comfort that he or she will be sent a copy of any judgment in the proceedings, and may request written reasons for the judgment (*ET Rules, rule 9*). In *D&H Travel v Foster* [2006] ICR 1537, Elias P held that were it not for the availability of a review, there would be a real question as to the compatibility of *rule 9* with *Art 6* of the ECHR.

The scope for review of the non-acceptance of a response has been clarified by the EAT in *Moroak (t/a Blake Envelopes) v Cromie* [2005] IRLR 535 and *Pendragon plc v Copus* [2005] ICR 1671. The EAT in *Moroak* rejected the argument that there could be no power to review non-acceptance because there was no right under *rule 4(4)* to apply for an extension of time to present the response once the 28 day limit had expired. Non-acceptance was itself a decision open to review, and if it was in the interests of justice to extend time and admit a late response, the tribunal should do so. The test to be applied was that set out (in relation to previous *Rules of Procedure*) by the EAT in *Kwik Save Stores Ltd v Swain* [1997] ICR 49, which requires the tribunal to balance all relevant factors, with particular weight being given to whether the respondent would suffer greater prejudice by being denied relief than the claimant would suffer if relief were granted to the respondent. The merits of the defence, so far as readily ascertainable at this stage in the proceedings, may also be relevant. (The *Moroak* case concerned a response sent in 44 minutes late following a malfunction of the respondent's representative's computer, which the EAT unsurprisingly regarded as causing no prejudice to the claimant.) In *Pendragon*, the EAT makes it clear that the absence of a good reason for the failure by the respondent to submit a response in time, whilst clearly an important consideration, is not on its own a bar to granting relief from the consequences: see also to this effect *Thornton v Jones* (UKEAT/0068/11). A failure on the part of a tribunal to consider an application for review of the non-acceptance of a response was found to be an error of law in *South East Leisure Group Ltd v Vachoumis* (UKEAT/0270/10).

Review on the ground of administrative error is wide enough to include an error by the respondent, such as in omitting necessary information from the response, or (possibly) sending it to the wrong address: see *Sodexho Ltd v Gibbons* [2005] IRLR 836. When applying for a review of non-acceptance the EAT has held that the tribunal may overlook an erroneous label put on an application for review: *Jarretts Motors Limited v Wells* [2009] All ER (D) 350 (Jul). Underhill P emphasised that tribunals were obliged to adopt as flexible an approach as possible in order to mitigate the injustice than can be caused by what he described as "complex and rigid rules" (para 9).

As a general point, the latitude towards respondents shown in these decisions is clearly much greater than that shown towards claimants whose claims are presented out of time and seek an extension of time under the 'not reasonably practicable' dispensation, and, to a lesser extent, to those seeking an extension on just and equitable grounds. The simple explanation for the apparent discrepancy is that it is the claimant who seeks to invoke the powers of the tribunal, and can therefore be expected to do so promptly, whereas the respondent has not initiated, and probably does not want to be party to, the litigation; and these differences of context lead to different expectations as to compliance with the requirements of the tribunal. Once proceedings have been fully initiated, there is less evidence of a difference of approach to the parties' conduct, and in particular to failure to comply with directions.

In the alternative, non-acceptance of a response is a decision open to appeal, although as the grounds for review are significantly less rigorous, that is the more appropriate route. A further reason for review being the more appropriate alternative is that the respondent is entitled to apply for written reasons for the rejection of the response if this is done for the purposes of a review application, but not (because of an apparent defect in the drafting of the *Rules*) for the purposes of an appeal: *Leefe v NSM Music Ltd* [2006] ICR 450; *VMI (Blackburn) Ltd v Camm* (UKEAT/0011/11). It is possible both to apply for a review of the non-acceptance of the response, and, if the review is unsuccessful, to appeal the review decision. The *VMI* case clearly demonstrates the risks of failure to pursue each of these options; the respondent was excluded from a remedy hearing and unable to challenge the sum awarded either at time or in its subsequent appeal.

EPEM Ltd v Huggins (UKEAT/0019/12) is an example of a case where a response was originally accepted but then was struck out for non-compliance with an unless order. In such circumstances, the EAT construed rule 9 to apply. The correct mechanism for the respondent's application in that case was *rule 10(4)* which provides for the review of unless orders.

17.38 DEFAULT JUDGMENTS

The *2008 Regulations* have tightened up the procedure for issuing default judgments. Formerly, under the *ET Rules*, a default judgment in favour of the claimant could be issued at any time after the date for presenting a response (as extended, if applicable) has passed without a response having been accepted (*rule 8(1)*), but there was no *obligation* to do so. The position now is that a default judgment must be issued, unless the Judge considering the papers is not satisfied that he or she has sufficient information to do so. In that event, an order for the provision of whatever additional information the Judge considers appropriate must be made (*rule 8(1A)*). Rather surprisingly, if the information ordered is not provided, the Judge is required to issue a default judgment notwithstanding the lack of information (*rule 8(1B)*).

There are certain circumstances in which a default judgment either must not or need not be issued. If the case has been settled, a default judgment must not be issued; a judgment issued in such circumstances (eg in ignorance of the settlement) has no effect: *rule 8(6)*. A judgment need not be issued if the Judge is not satisfied that the tribunal has jurisdiction to determine the claim, or has sufficient evidence that the claim form has not been received by the respondent (*rule 8(2A)*).

A default judgment may deal solely with liability, or also with remedy. In practice it is common that such judgments are limited to liability; a default judgment on remedy would only be appropriate where it is clear from the papers what the claimant is claiming, and this is unlikely except in claims for unlawful deductions or redundancy payments (and it may not be clear in many such cases what amount is being claimed). The provision requiring Judges to order the provision of additional information where this is required for making a default judgment are intended to enable more such judgments to deal also with remedy. In any case, a claimant who wishes to have a default judgment covering remedy made is free to submit additional information without waiting for an Order to that effect, preferably by way of a Schedule of Loss; the Judge can necessarily only determine what remedy is appropriate in the light of the information available to him or her at the time of deciding (*rule 8(3)*).

If the default judgment is for liability only, there is no provision in the rules for a second default judgment dealing with remedy. A Hearing will therefore be necessary for this purpose. However, the respondent will not normally be permitted to participate in that Hearing unless he or she has successfully challenged the non-acceptance of the Response Form by way of review or appeal. The limits to this approach are shown by *D&H Travel Ltd v Foster* [2006] ICR 1537, where the respondent failed to serve a response in time, and a default judgment on liability was issued. The respondent attended at the remedy hearing, but the tribunal declined to hear it; the EAT held that this was an error. The respondent's attendance was an implied application to review the rejection of its late response, and it would have been proportionate as between the parties to have allowed the review and permitted the respondent to take part in the remedy hearing. It should be noted that even if a respondent is permitted to take part in a remedy hearing following a default judgment on liability, the tribunal cannot reopen any issues determined by the default judgment, and issues relevant to remedy must therefore be decided on the basis of the claimant's claims as upheld in the default judgment: *Eaton v Spencer and others t/a/ Wiggles Experience* (UKEAT/0177/11).

If a default judgment is issued, it will be sent to the parties and entered in the register of judgments (*rule 8(4)*). There is no requirement that reasons for the judgment be given. Either party may apply for a review of the judgment in accordance with *rule 33*. In the case of the claimant, this is likely to arise only in relation to remedy, if the tribunal has awarded less than he or she considers should have been awarded. Application must be made within 14 days of the date on which the default judgment was sent to the parties; the time limit can be extended by the Judge if it is just and equitable to do so (*rule 8(1)*); an example would be where the respondent only became aware of the proceedings, or the judgment, after the time limit for review had expired, because an incorrect address had been given by the claimant: see *Chowles (t/a Granary Pine) v West* (UKEAT/0473/08). The application must state the reasons for seeking the review. If it is the respondent who is applying, the application must also attach the proposed response to the claim, and include an application for an extension of time for the response to be accepted, and an explanation for the failure to present it in time and/or with all the required information (*rule 33(2)*). Failure to apply for an extension of time is however a technicality which should not be used to refuse an application for a review where there are good grounds for the review: *Bournemouth Borough Council v Leadbeater* (UKEAT/0010/11) (respondent had not received claim).

A review is conducted in public by an Employment Judge sitting alone (not necessarily the same Judge who issued the default judgment) unless all parties have agreed that the review can take place without a hearing. The Judge may reject the application for a review, or grant it but affirm the default judgment, or the default judgment may be varied or revoked in whole or in part (*rule 33(2), (3)*). If it is the respondent who has applied for the review, the effect of a successful application is likely to be that the response will be accepted, and the respondent will be able to defend the claim in the normal way, but this is not automatic (*rule 33(7)*).

There are few criteria in the *ET Rules* as to when an application by a claimant should be granted; this will therefore be a simple question of whether there are good grounds for varying the original award. The Judge may vary or revoke the judgment if, but only if, the respondent can show that there are reasonable prospects of successfully defending the claim (or, as the case may be, successfully disputing the amount of compensation, or any other remedy, awarded). In addition the Judge is required to have regard to whether there was good reason for the respondent not having presented his or her response in time (*rule 33(5), (6)*). Thus a failure to submit a complete and timely response may lead to even a meritorious defence being excluded from consideration. However the EAT has held that the absence of good reason for failing to submit a valid response in time is not as such a bar to review of the default judgment. *Pendragon plc v Copus* [2005] ICR 1671; and see *Pestle and Mortar v Turner* (UKEAT/0652/05), and *Thornton v Jones* (UKEAT/0068/11), where the default judgment was revoked despite a finding that there was no good reason for the respondent's failure to present its response on time. The general approach adopted in the earlier cases was also reiterated by the EAT in *Jarretts Motors Ltd v Wells* [2009] All ER (D) 350 (Jul).

The position in relation to applications by a respondent for a review is made more complex by the fact that different rules apply for a review of a refusal to accept a response, and review of a default judgment; a respondent who has had a late response rejected but by the time he or she seeks a review has become the subject of a default judgment may need to invoke both procedures, under *rules 34* and *33* respectively (and see *Jarretts Motors Ltd v Wells*, above, where a flexible approach by tribunals to applications for a review citing the wrong rule was advocated by the EAT).

The existence of two separate procedures for review raises the question whether different criteria apply to a review under *rule 34* (where a default judgment has not been issued), as against the criteria under *rule 33* (where one has). *Rule 33* requires the tribunal to consider the respondent's prospects of successfully defending the claim; this is not expressed in terms as a consideration relevant to the general power of review under *rule 34* in the interests of justice, but if it is not required to be taken into account, the position of the respondent will differ for no obviously relevant reason. The adoption by the EAT in both *Moroak* and *Pendragon* of the approach mandated in the *Kwik Save* case may remove the substance of this point.

A point not addressed by the EAT in *Moroak* or *Pendragon* is what test has to be applied in determining whether the respondent has reasonable prospects of successfully defending the claim (or part of it). There is as yet no appellate authority on this point. A subsidiary point is whether it is enough that the respondent has reasonable prospects of disputing the amount of compensation claimed or likely to be claimed, even if there is no reasonable prospect of defending on the issue of liability. It would not make sense to deny a respondent the right to contest remedy where there are real issues in dispute, merely because liability will probably be established.

A further question, subsequently answered by the EAT, is whether the respondent has the right to be heard at any review of a default judgment initiated by the claimant; on the face of the *Rules*, the respondent is not entitled to appear, unless the tribunal has in the meantime accepted the response, since *rule 9*, which specifies the extent to which such a respondent may participate in the case, only provides for him or her to *apply* for a review. However the EAT has accepted that the exclusion of the respondent from participating in a hearing convened at his or her request would be absurd, and that the rules should be interpreted so as to permit the respondent to be heard: *Terry Ballard & Co (a firm) v Stonestreet* [2007] All ER (D) 176 (Mar); *Jarretts Motors Ltd v Wells*, above.

As an alternative to a review application, a party may appeal against a default judgment. However, in practice it is difficult to envisage circumstances in which it would be preferable to appeal rather than apply for a review. Since permissible grounds of appeal are limited to points of law, it would be much more likely in the majority of cases that grounds for a review could be identified.

18   Employment Tribunals – II

18.1   THE OVERRIDING OBJECTIVE AND CASE MANAGEMENT

The traditional approach to litigation in Britain was that it was for the parties to prepare and present their respective cases, with relatively little management of the proceedings by the court. That approach, which was to a considerable extent followed in the early years of the operation of employment tribunals, was superseded in the civil courts in England and Wales by the requirements of the *Civil Procedure Rules 1998* for the active management of cases to ensure that the principles embodied in the Overriding Objective are achieved in practice. The move towards much more active management of cases was followed in employment tribunals, both in England and Wales and Scotland, with the introduction by the *2001 Regulations* of the Overriding Objective of dealing with cases justly. The revision of the *Regulations* in 2004 developed the process further. The *2004 Rules* (unlike previous *Rules*) apply equally to England and Wales and Scotland, but there are still significant differences of procedure and terminology, reflecting differences in the practice of the civil courts in the two jurisdictions.

It is important to appreciate that the various powers of case management given to the tribunal, as described below, are required to be interpreted and exercised so as to give effect to the Overriding Objective, which is now set out in *reg 3* of the *2004 Regulations*. This requires that the tribunal should, so far as practicable, ensure that the parties are on an equal footing, deal with issues in a way that is proportionate to the complexity and importance of the issue and expeditiously and fairly, and save expense. The parties to tribunal proceedings are required by *reg 3* to assist the tribunal to further the Overriding Objective.

It is to be noted that the Overriding Objective in *reg 3* of the *2004 Regulations* differs slightly from that set out in the Civil Procedure Rules 1998 (as amended). The latter includes within the concept of dealing with a case justly specific reference to allotting an appropriate share of the Court's resources to a case, enforcing compliance with rules, practice direction and orders, and to dealing with cases in a way proportionate to the amount of money involved and the financial position of each party.

18.2   CASE MANAGEMENT POWERS OF THE TRIBUNAL

The case management powers of the tribunal are primarily exercised by the making of orders (the term the *ET Rules* use to cover what were formerly either directions or orders). Orders may be issued by an Employment Judge on his or her own initiative, having reviewed the case file, or on the application of one of the parties without a hearing, or at a hearing. Hearings intended solely to deal with case management issues are called Case Management Discussions ('CMDs'), and are held in private with an Employment Judge sitting alone (*ET Rules, rule 17(1)* as amended by *SI 2005/1865*); such hearings may be conducted by telephone, or, by prior arrangement, by video link if facilities are available. However, case management orders may be made at any type of hearing, and certain orders may not be made at a CMD.

The principal types of case management orders which may be made at a CMD are set out in the *ET Rules, rule 10(2)*. The list is not intended to be exhaustive, but no order which determines the civil rights or obligations of a party may be made at a CMD, since this would not be a determination at a public hearing for the purposes of *art 6* of the *European Convention on Human Rights* (see the *ET Rules, rule 17(2)* requiring CMDs to be held in private). Thus it is not possible for a claim or part of a claim to be struck out at a CMD (see *Kerr v Ernst & Young Services Ltd* (UKEAT/0567/10): an order that allegations be treated as background only could not be made at CMD, as it amounted to striking the allegations out as substantive claims), or (probably) for an order to be made requiring a party to pay costs; see further **18.5** below. It should be noted that the term 'order' in this context has a wider meaning than in the definition given in *rule 28* ('which may be issued in relation to interim matters and . . . will require a person to do or not to do something'): see *Hart v English Heritage* [2006] IRLR 915, paras 29, 30; but for present purposes the difference has no obvious practical consequences.

The types of order listed in *rule 10(2)* are as follows:

(a) General orders as to how the proceedings are to be conducted, including orders laying down time limits;

(b) Orders that a party provide further information;

(c) Orders requiring the attendance of any person in Great Britain to give evidence, or to produce documents or information ('witness orders'),

(d) Orders (against any person in Great Britain, not just a party to the proceedings) requiring that person to give disclosure of documents to a party and to allow the party to inspect the documents, provided that such an order could be made by the County Court (or in Scotland by a Sheriff); if such an order is sought against a non-party to the proceedings it can only be made if the disclosure sought is necessary in order to dispose fairly of the claim or to save expense (*rule 10(5)*);

(e) Orders extending a time limit, whether or not it has already expired, but subject to a number of limitations made by the rules applicable to the particular time limits which specify either that the time limit can only be extended if the Judge considers it just and equitable to do so, or specify the required manner and timing of an application to extend time;

(f) Orders requiring the provision of written answers to questions put by the tribunal;

(h) Orders staying (or in Scotland sisting) the proceedings or part thereof;

(i) Orders that part of the proceedings (eg the issue of liability, or one of the claims) be dealt with separately;

(j) Orders that different claims be heard together (whether or not the same parties are involved in each claim), often referred to as orders for consolidation, although that term is not used in the *Rules*; such orders may only be made if all affected parties have had the opportunity to make oral or written representations as to whether the order should be made: *ET Rules, rule 10(7)*;

(k) Orders joining as a respondent any person who the Judge considers may be liable for the remedy claimed in the proceedings;

(l) Orders dismissing the claim against a respondent who is no longer directly interested in the claim (eg because the part of the claim affecting that respondent has been struck out or withdrawn);

(m) Orders postponing or adjourning any hearing;

(n) Orders varying or revoking other orders;

(o) Orders giving notice to the parties of a Pre-hearing Review or Hearing;

(p) Orders giving notice under *rule 19* (requiring a party to show cause at a later hearing why that party's case or part thereof should not be struck out on one or more of the grounds given in *rule 18(7)* (below));

(q) Orders giving permission to amend a claim or response;

(r) Orders permitting the joining as a party of any person the Judge or tribunal considers has an interest in the outcome of the proceedings;

(s)   Orders for the preparation and/or exchange of witness statements (these are now standard practice in England and Wales, but witness statements are used only exceptionally in Scotland);

(t)   Orders regarding the use of expert witnesses in the proceedings.

(The lettering in this list corresponds to that in *rule 10(2)*; there is no paragraph (g) because *rule 10(2)(g)*, which provided for orders relating to fixed conciliation periods, was revoked in 2009 following the abolition of fixed conciliation periods.)

The scope and use of the principal categories of orders listed above is discussed further below at **18.7–18.14**. It is important to emphasise that the list is illustrative not exhaustive. The types of order listed above may, if required, be made at any stage in the proceedings, and either at a CMD or other hearing, or on the written application of a party or on the Judge's own initiative. There are, however, a number of provisions as to the status and effect of different types of order, and as to the procedure for applying for such orders.

18.3   Applying for orders

A party can apply at any stage of the proceedings for an order (in the wider sense of any order, decision or ruling under *rule 10*), and can ask that the application be dealt with on paper, or at a CMD or other type of hearing. The appropriate forum for considering the application will depend on when it is made and how far the case has progressed. As a general rule, the earlier in the proceedings an application is made, the more likely it is to be granted.

The requirements for applications for orders are contained in *ET Rules, rule 11*. This provides that any application for an order, unless it is made during the course of a hearing, must be made in writing, and contain an explanation of how the order sought would help the tribunal to deal with the proceedings efficiently and fairly.

In addition, if the party applying is legally represented, the representative must send details of the application to all other parties, and advise them that they may object to the application, in writing, within seven days of receiving the notification, or (if earlier) before the date of the hearing. The notice must also explain that if a party does object, he or she must send a copy of the objection to all other parties as well as to the tribunal itself. The party applying must confirm to the tribunal that the required notifications have been sent (*rule 11(4)*). Compliance with this requirement is important since if the applicant for an order omits to confirm that the other party has been notified, the tribunal will require this to be done before the application is considered.

There is no equivalent obligation of notification imposed on parties who are not legally represented, and if the party making the application has not done so, the tribunal will itself inform all other parties of the application and their right to object. However, since this may delay consideration of the application, it is advisable for a party who is not legally represented to follow the procedure in *rule 11(4)*. A judge may shorten the time for a response to an application if he or she considers that this is in the interests of justice (*rule 11(4A)*), and this is often done when applications are made shortly before a hearing is due to take place.

An application which is to be considered at a hearing must be made, in writing, at least 10 days before the hearing is due to take place, if a hearing has been listed, unless this is not reasonably practicable, or the Judge permits a shorter notice period in the interests of justice (*ET Rules, rule 11(2), (4A)*). (This does not prevent applications being made during a hearing, as commonly happens, for instance, when a point arises for the first time as a result of evidence given in the course of the hearing.)

There is one exception to the requirement to notify all parties of an application, which is where the application is for a witness order (*rule 11(5)*). This is because it may be inappropriate for the other party or parties to be aware that a witness order has been sought or granted in certain cases.

18.3 Employment Tribunals – II

The outcome of an application for an order will be notified to all the parties in writing if the matter is not dealt with at a CMD or other hearing. (In the case of a witness order or an order against a non party for disclosure, the normal practice is for the tribunal to leave it to the party in whose favour the order was made to notify the person subject to the order. Other parties are not notified of the making of witness orders, but if an order for disclosure is made, the other parties are notified of the order by the tribunal.) Any order made, whether at a hearing or not, must be recorded in writing and signed by the Employment Judge (*rule 10(8)*). There is no requirement for reasons for the order to be given. If a case management order is made at a hearing, and reasons are requested at the time, they must be given, either orally or subsequently in writing; if the order is made on the Judge's initiative or following a written application, reasons may be given, and will usually be provided if this is requested by a party, but there is no obligation on the Judge to give reasons unless requested to do so by the EAT (see *rule 30(1)–(3)*).

If an order is made against a party who has not had an opportunity to make representations before the order is made (as when the order is made on the Judge's own initiative, or is an order against a non-party), the order is subject to the right of the person subject to the order to apply to the tribunal to revoke or vary it. Any such application must be made in writing, before the date for compliance with the order, and giving reasons for objecting to the order. The provisions above as to informing all other parties apply to such applications if made by a party, but would appear not to apply to applications to set aside made by a non-party. In practice it can be expected that the tribunal will notify all parties of an application by a non-party to set aside an order against him or her (unless it is a witness order, in which case only the party requesting it would be advised of the application to set it aside). An application to set aside an order may be considered on the papers or at a hearing ordered for the purpose (*ET Rules, rule 12(2), (3)*; and see *Reddington v Straker & Sons Ltd* [1994] ICR 172).

In addition to applications to set aside orders made without notice to the party concerned, it is possible to apply for an order to be varied or revoked. The availability of the general power to vary or revoke orders made under *rule 10* has been confirmed by the EAT: see *Onwuka v Spherion Technology UK Ltd* [2005] ICR 567 and *Hart v English Heritage* [2006] IRLR 915. This is distinct from the power of review, which these cases also confirm is not available for orders. However it is important to note that as a matter of practice a tribunal or Judge will not vary or revoke an order unless there has been a material change of circumstances: *Goldman Sachs Services Ltd v Montali* [2002] ICR 1251, a decision affirmed in relation to the *2004 ET Rules* in *Hart v English Heritage* (above); see further **18.7** below.

Correspondence between a party or representative and the tribunal, such as an application for an order or a response objecting to the application, is afforded absolute immunity from claims based on it, in the same way as the claim and response are immune from being used as the basis of a further claim: *Dathi v South London and Maudsley NHS Trust* [2008] IRLR 350. Accordingly a letter from the respondent to the tribunal opposing an application for costs (and also a further letter to the claimant's representative declining to give voluntary disclosure) was immune from suit as an act of alleged victimisation.

18.4 Sanctions for non-compliance with Orders

Any person (whether a party to the proceedings or not) who without reasonable cause fails to comply with a witness order or an order for disclosure commits a criminal offence punishable on summary conviction with a fine not exceeding £1,000 (*ET Act 1996, s 7(4)*). This fact must be conveyed by a penal notice attached to any such order made under *ET Rules, rule 10(2)(c)* or *(d)* (para (c) or (d) in **18.2** above). In practice the sanction of prosecution is not used (although it may be threatened for a recalcitrant recipient of an order for disclosure or to attend as a witness); this has given added weight to the sanctions available to the tribunal itself (as distinct from being dependent on other agencies for enforcement), but these are of necessity only available where the default is that of a party to the proceedings.

The sanctions (other than referring the case to the relevant authority for possible prosecution, if applicable) available to the tribunal if a party fails to comply (or is late in complying) with an order, or with any requirement laid down by a Practice Direction, are that the tribunal may make an order for costs, or a preparation time order, against the offending party, or, in more serious cases, order that the party's claim or part thereof be struck out, or that a response or part thereof be struck out and/or that the respondent be debarred from defending the claim (*ET Rules, rule 13(1)*). The potentially drastic consequences for a party of the powers to strike out a claim or response necessitate that such powers are used sparingly and only for extreme cases of disregard of orders or cases where the consequences for the possibility of a fair trial are significant. See further **18.16** below.

Rule 13(2) introduces an intermediate option, long available to the courts, of the making of an 'unless' order: unless the party complies with an order by a stated date, his or her case is to be struck out on the date for compliance without further consideration or notice (*Rule 13(2)*). Such an order amounts to a conditional judgment which takes effect, striking out the claim or response, in the event of non- (or even partial) compliance with the requirement of the unless order: see *Scottish Ambulance Service v Laing* (UKEATS/0038/12) and *Royal Bank of Scotland v Abraham* (UKEAT/0305/09). In practice such an order will only normally be made after there has been a failure to comply with an earlier order, and the general power to review the consequential striking out of the claim or, in the case of a response, to vary or revoke orders, can be used to relieve the party concerned of the consequences of an 'unless' order if it is shown that the party would otherwise suffer serious injustice. See further **18.6** and **18.16** below.

18.5   Orders which cannot be made at a Case Management Discussion

In addition to the general provision that no order may be made at a CMD which determines the civil rights or liabilities of a party (*rule 17(2)*), the *ET Rules* provide that certain specific categories of order cannot be made at a CMD. These are:

(a)   An order determining the entitlement of any person to bring or contest particular proceedings;

(b)   An order striking out all or part of a claim or response, or part thereof, on any of the grounds on which such an order may be made at a PHR or substantive Hearing;

(c)   A restricted reporting order (other than a temporary order under *rule 50* pending a decision whether to make a full order; the latter must be dealt with at a PHR or Hearing);

(d)   An order that a party must pay a deposit as a condition of continuing to pursue or defend a claim.

The first three are specifically excluded by the terms of *rule 17(2)* (and see *Way v Powercraft (Retail) Ltd* [2008] All ER (D) 151 (Aug): no general power to strike out claim at a CMD, and *Kerr v Ernst & Young Services Ltd* (UKEAT/0567/10) applying the principle to an order that particular claims within a discrimination case could only be treated as background, not substantive claims); the fourth is an order which by *Rule 18* may only be made at a PHR. In addition, the effect of the general prohibition on orders determining a person's civil rights or obligations is probably wide enough to exclude the making of an order for costs or a preparation time order at a CMD, although there is as yet no direct authority on this point. A tribunal may, by consent, convert a CMD to a PHR at the hearing (thereby giving short notice by agreement under *Rule 14(4)*) in order to assume the power to make orders determining a person's civil rights.

18.6   Pre-hearing Reviews and interim hearings

Changes made to the *ET Rules* in 2004 have conferred a much more significant role in the case management process on Pre-hearing Reviews (PHRs). Formerly, such a hearing could only be used for a consideration, on the papers and with the benefit of the parties' submissions but without hearing any evidence, of whether a claim or response, or some particular part of either, had little reasonable prospect of success, in which case the tribunal could order the payment of a deposit of up to £500 as a condition for that party being permitted to continue to pursue or (as the case might be) defend the point. In practice it was almost always the claim that was subjected to this scrutiny, in the relatively small proportion of cases that were referred to a PHR.

This procedure remains available through a PHR, and is discussed further below (see **18.15**; the maximum deposit that may be ordered was increased to £1,000 in cases presented on or after 6 April 2012). However the *2004 ET Rules* have significantly enlarged the role of PHRs, with the consequence that the making of a deposit order is now a much less important feature of these hearings. PHRs may now be used to determine any preliminary issue in a case, even if this results in the effective determination of the whole proceedings (eg because the claim is dismissed for lack of jurisdiction: *rule 18(5)*). Preliminary issues may include such matters as whether a claim was presented in time (and if not, whether time should be extended); whether the claimant is or was an employee or a worker, where the status of the claimant is in dispute; whether he or she had sufficient service to qualify for the right claimed; whether the claimant is or has been disabled; or whether a transfer amounted to a relevant transfer for the purposes of the *Transfer of Undertakings (Protection of Employment) Regulations 2006*. PHRs may also be used to decide whether to make a Restricted Reporting Order ('RRO': see **18.18**).

The House of Lords has however indicated strongly, albeit in *obiter* comments, that it is in many cases not appropriate to hold a PHR, particularly to determine issues that are not completely separate from the issues that will remain to be decided at any full Hearing: *SCA Packaging Ltd v Boyle* [2009] UKHL 37, [2009] IRLR 746, per Lord Hope at paras 9–10, Lord Rodger at para 45 and Lord Neuberger at para 82. Their Lordships cautioned against the holding of a PHR unless there is 'a succinct knockout point' to be decided. In particular, as in the *SCA* case, the issue whether a claimant is disabled is not necessarily sufficiently separable from the other issues in a claim of disability discrimination to justify it being made the subject of a separate hearing; nor are time points in discrimination cases where part at least of the claim is in time, since evidence of earlier incidents is likely to be admissible even if those incidents are as such out of time, as supporting evidence in relation to the matters which are in time; thus it is unlikely that any time would be saved by having a separate preliminary hearing. See also *Rossetti Marketing Limited v Diamond Sofa Company Limited* [2012] EWCA Civ 1021 in which Lord Neuberger MR warned that "while often attractive prospectively, the siren song of agreeing or ordering preliminary issues should normally be resisted" (para 1) and *English v Thomas Sanderson Limited* [2009] ICR 543 in which the Court of Appeal held that a Tribunal should approach the use of a preliminary issue procedure with circumspection in any case where the result may be influenced by the details or nuance of the facts (paras 35, 36, 43). On the other hand in cases where it is arguable that the entire claim is out of time, a tribunal is likely to agree to that issue being addressed at a PHR because of the potential 'knockout' point involved.

PHRs are conducted in public (unless the provisions of *rule 16* permitting a hearing in private apply – see **18.51**), and are conducted by an Employment Judge sitting alone, unless a hearing before a full panel is ordered. However this can *only* be done if a party applies in writing for a full panel at least 10 days before the hearing, and the Judge considering the application considers that it would be desirable to have a full panel because of the substantive issues of fact to be determined at the PHR. There is no power for the Judge on the day to convert the hearing to one before a full panel, and any application for an adjournment to enable a party to make the necessary application is likely to be viewed with disfavour and may result in an application for the costs thrown away (*ET Rules, rule 18(1), (3)*). It is therefore essential for a party wishing to have any preliminary issue decided by a full tribunal to apply promptly for an order to that effect. The fact that normally a PHR will be heard by an Employment Judge sitting alone is not generally regarded by tribunals as a good reason not to order the determination of factually complex preliminary points in this way.

The hearing of a PHR may be conducted by telephone or video link, provided that suitable arrangements are in place for members of the public to hear or see the proceedings: *rule 15;* however in practice this facility is very rarely used (as distinct from the practice of telephone CMDs, which is relatively common).

In addition to the determination of preliminary issues, PHRs are used to decide applications to strike out a claim or response, or part thereof. The power to strike out may be exercised on any of the following grounds:

(a)   That the claim or response, or part to be struck out, is scandalous or vexatious, or has no reasonable prospect of success;

(b)   That the manner in which the proceedings have been conducted by or on behalf of the party whose case is to be struck out has been scandalous, unreasonable or vexatious;

(c)   That there has been non-compliance by the party whose case is to be struck out with an order or practice direction;

(d)   That the claim has not been actively pursued (this applies only to claims, not responses);

(e)   That it is no longer possible to have a fair hearing of the claim (this also applies only to a claim).

(*ET Rules, rule 18(7)(b)–(f), (8)*).

Applications to strike out can in most cases only be considered if a notice has been sent by the tribunal to the party concerned informing him or her of the order being sought or proposed, and giving him or her the opportunity to give reasons why such an order should not be made; the party affected may then request that the matter be decided at a hearing, and if such a request is made, the order can only be made at a PHR or full hearing; if no request is made, the matter may be dealt with without any hearing (*ET Rules, rules 18(6), 19(1)*).

Prior notice is not required if the party has been given an opportunity to 'show cause' orally (*rule 19(1)*). This makes it possible to deal with an application to strike out a claim or response, for instance because of conduct in the face of the tribunal, without having to adjourn to a separate hearing in order to enable the notice to be sent.

However the normal practice is for written notice to be given to the parties of the fact that a strike-out order is to be considered. A similar procedure for prior notification to the parties applies to the making of a restricted reporting order at a PHR.

Where the reason for striking out is failure to comply with an 'unless' order made under *rule 13*, notice is not required at all, and is not normally given; if the Judge reviewing the papers is satisfied that there has been non-compliance, the order is made without further inquiry. However, an order striking out a claim or response technically (and somewhat confusingly) converts the original 'unless' order into a judgment within the definition of that term in *rule 28*, and thus (at least on the current state of the authorities) open to review, as well as appeal, at the instance of the aggrieved party (see *Sodexho Ltd v Gibbons* [2005] IRLR 836, and see further **18.16**).

For more detailed consideration of the powers to make orders at PHRs and the grounds on which they may be made, see **18.15–18.18** below.

A new category of hearing, called interim hearings, has been introduced by the *2008 Regulations*, adding a new *ET Rule 18A*, for the sole purpose of deciding applications for interim relief in those categories of unfair dismissal claim where this relief is available (interim relief involves either immediate reinstatement pending a full hearing, or if the employer will not reinstate, an order that the claimant be paid his or her normal pay until the hearing). Formerly applications for interim relief were dealt with as preliminary issues at a PHR, and *Rule 18A* provides that hearings of applications for interim relief are to be conducted on the same basis as PHRs; this means that the hearing of an interim relief application will be held before a judge sitting alone unless the procedure for applying for a full tribunal is complied with and the application granted. *Rule 18A* does not specify how the hearing is to be conducted beyond referring to the procedure for PHRs. It appears to follow that it is open to the parties to adduce evidence, either documentary or by calling witnesses, but the practice as to whether the tribunal will agree to hearing witnesses varies as between tribunals. The exclusion of witness evidence may be regarded as a permissible exercise of case management powers in the interests of the expedition, which is given the highest priority in interim relief cases, but in an extreme case refusal to permit the calling of witnesses could be challenged on appeal as a procedural irregularity. The EAT has held that the tribunal is bound to hear and determine interim relief applications, however complex the underlying facts, if a timely application under one of the relevant jurisdictions has been presented: *Raja v Secretary of State for Justice* (UKEAT/0364/09); see also *London City Airport Ltd v Chacko* (UKEAT/0013/13).

Rule 14 of the *ET Rules* makes general provisions about hearings which apply equally to PHRs and interim hearings. The provisions of *rule 14(2)* and *(3)*, which deal with the way in which hearings are to be conducted, are considered below at **18.52**. In addition it should be noted that there is a general requirement, which applies equally to PHRs, that notice of any hearing (other than a CMD, which may be called on 'reasonable' notice, which may be very short if necessary, and an interim hearing, for which only seven days' notice is required under the primary legislation concerned: see the *ERA 1996 s 128(4)*, *TULRCA 1992, s 162(2)*), must be sent to the parties at least 14 days before the date of the hearing, unless the parties all agree to shorter notice (*rule 14(4)*). 'Sent' refers to the date of despatch, not receipt, so the notice may be received less than 14 days before the hearing date. The notice of the PHR must say that the parties have the right to submit written representations (which must be received by the tribunal at least 7 days before the hearing, unless the Judge agrees to consider representations received nearer to the hearing: *rule 14(5)*), and to advance oral argument at the hearing. Although the notice is not required to draw attention to this, evidence can be called at a PHR in the same way as at a Hearing, except when the PHR is only for the purpose of considering whether to make a deposit order (see further **18.15**) or the order for the holding of the PHR specifies that there is to be no witness evidence.

18.7   CASE MANAGEMENT POWERS IN PRACTICE

In the following paragraphs under this heading, consideration is given to the scope of the more important case management powers of the tribunal, and the criteria for their exercise. The following paragraphs should be read subject to the caution that some of the cases referred to were decided before the introduction of the Overriding Objective by the *2001 Rules*. In a number of cases the Overriding Objective has led to a change in practice, as indicated below.

A consequence of the greater emphasis on case management by the tribunal is the greater use of CMDs, particularly in the more complex kinds of cases. The Court of Appeal had previously stressed the desirability of a directions hearing (the predecessor of the CMD) in discrimination cases to enable the tribunal to deal with preliminary matters, identify the issues in dispute and establish a realistic time estimate for the hearing so that the case could be listed for long enough to avoid adjournments and delays in the substantive hearing: *Martins v Marks and Spencer plc* [1998] IRLR 326. Its comments were reiterated, specifically in relation to claims based on the *Public Interest Disclosure Act 1998*, in *ALM Medical Services Ltd v Bladen* [2002] EWCA Civ 1085, [2002] ICR 1444. Despite this, there is no uniform practice on the ordering of CMDs, and it is often left to the parties to identify the need for a CMD, even in discrimination cases and some relatively complex claims; however it is increasingly the practice to list CMDs as a matter of course in discrimination cases and other potentially complex cases identified by an employment judge in the initial screening now given to all cases on receipt of the response.

CMDs may be, and often are, ordered to deal with particular points arising in the course of a case, such as a disputed application for an order for disclosure of documents. Such instances apart, the practice increasingly is to have a standard agenda for CMDs (although the content of this may differ between regions) and standard questionnaires which parties are asked to complete and exchange in advance of the hearing. The information thus made available to the Judge conducting the CMD considerably increases the opportunity for active case management of the proceedings; it may have the incidental effect of requiring the parties to focus on the preparations needed for their case to be ready for hearing at an earlier stage than may have been common in the past.

Often at CMDs, the Tribunal will set out to identify the issues arising in the case with the parties. The parties are expected to attend with sufficient knowledge about the case to allow for this rigorous exercise to take place. Cost consequences might follow if the CMD cannot achieve its objectives (for an example, see *Wilsons Solicitors v Johnson* [2011] ICR D21). At many CMDs, the issues will be reduced to writing and form an agreed list of issues. As the Court of Appeal explained in *Parekh v The London Borough of Brent* [2012] EWCA Civ 1630 (para 31), a list of issues is a useful case management tool developed by the tribunal to bring some semblance of order, structure and clarity to proceedings. If the list of issues is agreed, then that will, as a general rule, limit the issues at the substantive hearing to those in the list (on which see also *Land Rover v Short* (UKEAT/0496/10). However, the tribunal that hears the case is not required to stick slavishly to the list of issues where to do so would impair the discharge of the core duty to hear and determine the case in accordance with the law and the evidence (on which see also *Price v Surrey County Council* (UKEAT/0450/10; *Wilcox v Birmingham CAB Services Ltd* (UKEAT/0293/10)). After the CMD, the tribunal will send to the parties a copy of the orders made and a note of the discussion, which will include any list of issues. The Court in *Parekh* considered that where the issues were agreed, it would be difficult to see how the content of the list could ever be the proper subject of an appeal on a question of law. Alternatively, if the list was not agreed and it is contended that it is an incorrect record of the discussions, or there has been a material change in circumstances, the proper procedure is not to appeal, but to apply to the tribunal to reconsider the matter in the interests of justice (para 32).

Orders for the preparation of chronologies, agreed facts, skeleton arguments etc are becoming increasingly common at CMDs and parties should consider ahead of a CMD whether they would be appropriate to the circumstances of the individual case.

One aspect of case management which is increasingly likely to be encountered, particularly in complex discrimination cases where numerous incidents have been raised by the claimant, is the application of the requirement in the Overriding Objective of proportionality: that the case be conducted in a manner proportionate to the importance and complexity of the issues in dispute. Employment Judges cannot arbitrarily limit the scope of the issues to be tried

18.7 Employment Tribunals – II

(see *McKinson v Hackney Community College* (UKEAT/0237/11) where an order limiting the number of incidents the claimant was permitted to rely on to six was set aside on appeal), but directions may be given limiting the number of documents to be put before the tribunal, or the time to be allowed for particular witnesses or for the Hearing as a whole; or requiring a claimant to identify and put forward at the Hearing only the most important incidents forming part of his or her case, with the other incidents stayed to a later hearing (in the hope that a decision on the selected issues will enable the parties to resolve their differences on the outstanding matters): see *HSBC Asia Holdings BV v Gillespie* [2011] ICR 192. This approach is considered consistent with the restrictions on the powers of the tribunal in CMDs that prevent the striking out of even parts of a claim (see **18.5** above).

The tribunal has power to vary orders made under *rule 10;* this power is given by *rule 10(2)(n)* (see also *Onwuka v Spherion Technology UK Ltd* [2005] ICR 567, *Hart v English Heritage* [2006] ICR 655, [2006] IRLR 915 and *North Tyneside Primary Care Trust v Aynsley* [2009] All ER (D) 125 (May)). However the EAT has held that the power to vary an order (unless it was originally made without the party affected having had an opportunity to make representations before the order was made) should not be exercised unless there has been a material change in circumstances (*Goldman Sachs Services Ltd v Montali* [2002] ICR 1251, where a preliminary hearing had been ordered on the issue of whether some of the claimant's complaints were out of time, but the tribunal appointed to hear the preliminary point instead directed that the issue should be determined at the substantive hearing; this decision was set aside by the EAT; see further *Sodexho Ltd v Gibbons* [2005] IRLR 836 and *Hart*, above, where the comment was made that there are stronger objections to reopening a decision taken after argument on the point than where the basis of the application is a point which had not been considered when the order was first made).

18.8 Further information about parties' cases

Additional information about a claim or response may be required because it fails to give sufficient details to enable the other party to know the case he or she has to meet; or the grounds stated may be ambiguous as to the facts or the basis in law of the claim. Orders to give additional information (previously referred to as 'further particulars') are designed primarily to spell out or clarify the party's case. The criterion which the applicant for an order for additional information is required to address in making the application is how the provision of that information will assist *the tribunal* in dealing with the proceedings efficiently and fairly (*ET Rules, rule 11(3)*). However this is wide enough to embrace the need for the applicant for the order to know the case he or she has to meet, since if that is not achieved it is difficult for the tribunal to deal with the proceedings fairly. A tribunal will not normally order the provision of additional information unless a written request has been made and either refused or ignored; the main exception is where an Employment Judge on reviewing the file considers that particulars or clarification are needed for the tribunal's own benefit as well as the parties'. Occasionally, but increasingly frequently, orders for further information are made against claimants before the response has been served, where the Judge reviewing the claim form considers that there is insufficient information to identify clearly the claims made or the issues raised by the claimant.

The EAT in *Byrne v Financial Times Ltd* [1991] IRLR 417 set out general principles governing the ordering of further particulars, which it is thought remain applicable to orders to provide additional information. These include the principle that the parties should not be taken by surprise at the last minute; that particulars should only be ordered when necessary to do justice in the case or to prevent adjournment; that the order should not be oppressive; that particulars are for the purposes of identifying the issues not for the production of evidence; and that complicated pleadings battles should not be encouraged.

Particulars of generalised allegations of discrimination may be ordered more readily than in other categories of case because of the potential seriousness of such allegations and the need for the tribunal to be able to identify clearly the allegations it is required to determine. In

Secretary of State for Work and Pensions (Jobcentre Plus) v Constable [2010] All ER (D) 190 (Nov), where the claim was of automatically unfair dismissal for having made a protected disclosure under *ERA 1996 s 103A*, the EAT expressed the view that the respondent was entitled to know what the claimant claimed the disclosure was, when, how and to whom it had been made, and how it was alleged to have led to the dismissal, and ordered particulars to that effect to be provided. However the EAT has also held in an equal pay case that it was not appropriate for a tribunal to order the respondent to provide particulars of its material factor defence before the claimants had identified whom they intended to rely on as comparators: *Amey Services Ltd v Cardigan* [2008] IRLR 279.

Additional information may be ordered not only in relation to the claim or response as served, but in relation to any other matter relevant to the proceedings – for instance the claimant's losses or attempts to find alternative work, or, in equal pay or discrimination cases, the kind of information that is commonly sought by way of statutory questionnaires (see below). In particular, the practice of ordering claimants to provide a Schedule of Loss has now become relatively standard practice in all tribunal regions.

18.9   Questionnaires

An alternative procedure for obtaining information from the respondent, or from a prospective respondent before proceedings are started, applies in discrimination cases. The claimant or prospective claimant can serve a statutory questionnaire on the respondent in accordance with regulations made under the *Equality Act 2010, s 138*. A questionnaire must normally be served within 21 days following presentation of the Claim Form, or before proceedings have been started but within three months following the alleged discrimination: see the *Equality Act (Obtaining Information) Order 2010 (SI 2010/2194)*; the order also enables the tribunal to give permission for a further questionnaire to be served in the course of the proceedings, or extend time for the service of an initial questionnaire. The *2010 Order* also prescribes a form of questionnaire for use in equal pay cases. It should be noted that the Questionnaire procedure is to be removed by the repeal of *s 138* by the *Enterprise and Regulatory Reform Act 2013*, but no date has been given for the implementation of this provision of the *2013 Act*.

There is no obligation on respondents to reply to such questionnaires, and the tribunal has no power to order answers. Its only direct power is to grant an extension of the time limit laid down in each case for serving a questionnaire or to grant leave to serve a further questionnaire. The sanction for not answering within a reasonable time (this is set as eight weeks) or answering inadequately or evasively, is that in certain circumstances the tribunal hearing the case may draw adverse inferences against the respondent: *Equality Act 2010, s 138(4)*. The EAT has held that the same power to draw adverse inferences from equivocal or evasive responses, or failure to respond, applies equally in discrimination cases in relation to questions outside the statutory questionnaire procedure; this would therefore cover replies to requests for information framed as questions (*Dattani v Chief Constable of West Mercia Police* [2005] IRLR 327) and this is now specifically provided for in the *Equality Act 2010*: see *s 138(4)*. A tribunal is not however obliged to infer discrimination from a deficient response to a questionnaire, and the EAT has repeatedly warned tribunals that inferences should only be drawn from failure to answer questionnaires, or the nature of the replies, if this is justified in the particular circumstances, not simply because of the respondent's default: see for further guidance on this *D'Silva v NATFHE* [2008] IRLR 412 and *Deer v Walford* (UKEAT/0283/10).

Similar procedures have been provided for part-time workers by the *Part-time Workers (Prevention of Less Favourable Treatment) Regulations 2000, reg 6*, and for fixed-term employees under the *Fixed-term Employees (Prevention of Less Favourable Treatment) Regulations 2002, reg 5*, to enable workers or employees respectively to ask their employers to explain the reasons for apparently less favourable treatment than that given to comparable full-time or, as the case may be, permanent workers. The consequences of failing to reply or deficient replies are also as under the *Equality Act 2010*. *Regulation 16* of the *Agency Workers Regulations 2010* makes similar provision for questions to be raised by agency workers of the agency or hirer, as appropriate, with similar consequences for failure to respond.

18.10 Amendments and adding new claims

It is open to any party to apply for permission to amend his or her claim or, as the case may be, response. Amendments may be necessary to correct or clarify details of the particulars already given, or to add information about a claim; sometimes amendments seek to go further, and to add to the claim, or put forward a new or different reason for resisting the claim. In practice it is also not uncommon that 'additional information' provided by a party, voluntarily or in response to a request, raises new allegations or heads of claim: in such cases the principles applicable to amendments apply. The same principles apply, with any necessary modifications, to applications by respondents to amend their response, for instance by adding a new ground of resistance to the claim or taking a point as to the tribunal's jurisdiction.

The principles applicable to amendments are summarised below. The leading case on the principles applicable is *Selkent Bus Co Ltd v Moore* [1996] ICR 836. In this case Mummery J set out general principles both as to the procedure to be followed in relation to amendments and the criteria governing the tribunal's exercise of discretion whether to allow the amendment. Points of procedure are covered below. In relation to discretion, Mummery J emphasised that the tribunal:

> 'should take into account all the circumstances and should balance the injustice and hardship of allowing the amendment against the injustice and hardship of refusing it.'

The relevant circumstances are likely at least to include the nature of the amendment, the applicability of time limits (as to which see (f) and (g) below) and the timing and manner of application. The relevant circumstances are likely at least to include the nature of the amendment, the applicability of time limits (as to which see (f) and (g) below) and the timing and manner of application; they should not generally be denied punitively where no real prejudice will be done by them being granted: *Sefton NBC v Hincks* [2011] ICR 1357. When considering an amendment, a tribunal should consider the all the circumstances and carry out the balancing exercise identified in *Selkent* or risk making an error of law (see eg *Thomas v Samurai Incentives & Promotions Ltd* (UKEAT/0006/13).

Further points relevant to the procedure for applying, and the criteria for the exercise of the tribunal's discretion, are set out below.

(a)   A party may only amend his or her claim or response with the permission of the tribunal. If permission is given on a written application without the other party having an opportunity to oppose the application, or without the amendment having been directly considered by the tribunal (as where permission to amend is given in general terms) the permission is provisional and the other party may apply to have it set aside: *Reddington v Straker & Sons Ltd* [1994] ICR 172, EAT. This is expressly confirmed by *rule12(2)* in relation to orders made without any opportunity for the opposing party to make representations; it is implicit that this also applies to a general permission to amend, where the opposing party has not had the opportunity to object to the particular amendment. Guidance as to when an application to amend should be dealt with at a CMD or PHR, and not simply on paper, is given in *Selkent* (above). Normally an application to amend should not be *refused* without affording the party applying the opportunity for an oral hearing of the application, but this is subject to any exceptional factors that may make it unnecessary to permit a hearing: *Mouteng v Select Services Partner Ltd* [2008] All ER (D) 25 (Jun).

(b)   It is important, particularly in discrimination cases, to appreciate that the tribunal only has jurisdiction to adjudicate on the acts complained of, so that it is necessary to amend the Claim Form to refer specifically to any further complaints (and to obtain permission to do so) if they are to be relied on: see *Smith v Zeneca (Agrochemicals) Ltd* [2000] ICR 800 and generally *Chapman v Simon* [1994] IRLR 124.

(c)   The tribunal has no power to amend a claim or response on behalf of a party; it can only grant or refuse permission on application being duly made: see *Margarot Forrest Care Management v Kennedy* (UKEATS/0023/10). Any application to amend should set out the precise wording of the amendment proposed, so that the other party can know the claim he or she has to meet: *Ladbrokes Racing v Traynor* (UKEATS/0067/06). Guidance as to the procedure to be adopted when an application to amend is made during the hearing is given in the *Ladbrokes* case, where the issue was the introduction of unpleaded allegations of procedural unfairness of the claimant's dismissal. Amongst other points, the decision in *Ladbrokes* emphasises the importance of any amendment being precisely formulated before a decision can be taken on whether to permit it, and, where an application to amend made during a hearing is disputed, of the tribunal giving reasons for its decision on the point.

(d)   A distinction is made between amendments which add a new or different claim, and those which merely amend the factual or legal basis of an existing claim, for instance by adding further facts in support of a claim that a dismissal was unfair. Both can be made by way of amendment: the EAT in *Prakash v Wolverhapmton City Council* [2006] All ER (D) 71 (Nov) held that a new claim can be "presented" by an application to amend an existing claim as well as by the issue of a separate originating application. Applications to amend the factual or legal basis of an existing claim are admissible whenever application is made, subject to the discretion of the tribunal, which is exercised in accordance with the principles laid down in the *Selkent* case. The timing of the amendment as well as its nature is likely to be of importance, but it is possible (and not uncommon in practice) for amendments to be allowed up to or even during the hearing, where no prejudice is caused to the other party; it is likely to be relevant to establish whether there was good reason for any delay in applying to amend. The same principles apply to an application by a respondent to amend the response: *Chadwick v Bayer plc* [2002] All ER (D) 88 (Jun) (a case involving an application to withdraw an admission of liability).

(e)   There is a fine line between a new claim and a claim implicit in the facts already pleaded, but not expressly identified as a claim. Examples of what is a new claim can be found in *Housing Corpn v Bryant* [1999] ICR 123, CA (victimisation in addition to a claim of direct sex discrimination); *Harvey v Port of Tilbury (London) Ltd* [1999] ICR 1030 (applicant alleging unfair dismissal seeking amendment to add claim that dismissal was disability discrimination); *Ali v Office of National Statistics* [2004] EWCA Civ 1363, [2005] IRLR 201 (complaint of direct racial discrimination does not cover indirect discrimination); and *Potter v North Cumbria Acute Hospitals NHS Trust* [2008] ICR 910, [2009] IRLR 22 (addition of new comparators for equal pay claim). A case on the other side of the line is *Eltek (UK) Ltd v Thomson* [2000] ICR 689, where an amendment to a claim of pregnancy-related discrimination against an employee was permitted to base the claim on her status as a contract worker; the distinction was based on the same pleaded facts and was still an allegation of sex discrimination. However, this decision is difficult to reconcile with the decisions cited above, and should be regarded as confined to its own facts. The earlier EAT decision of *Quarcoopome v Sock Shop Holdings Ltd* [1995] IRLR 353, that an allegation of discrimination encompassed both direct and indirect discrimination and victimisation has effectively been overruled by *Ali* (above).

(f)   Before the introduction of the *2004 ET Rules*, it was generally understood that an amendment to add a new claim could not be made outside the applicable time limit for the claim (subject to the tribunal's discretion to extend time in accordance with the relevant statutory criteria for the particular new claim). More recent cases have established that provided that the original claim was presented within the time limit for the claim to be added (or that time limit plus any extension the tribunal finds would have been justified on the facts of the case), the decision whether to amend is to be determined as a matter of discretion, applying the *Selkent* principles, but giving particular weight to the fact that at the time of the application for permission to amend, a fresh claim would be rejected as out of time. The principal relevant cases are *Lehman Brothers Ltd v Smith* [2005] All ER (D) 177 (Oct), EAT, *Transport and General Workers Union v Safeway Stores Ltd* [2007] All ER (D) 14 (Jun), EAT and *Evershed v New Star Asset Management* (UKEAT/0249/09). The position has now been made clear by the Court of Appeal, which dismissed an appeal against the last of these EAT decisions, upholding the reasoning of the EAT: *New Star Asset Management Holdings Ltd v Evershed* [2010] EWCA Civ 870. However the weight given to the competing considerations in each case will usually make it more difficult to persuade a tribunal to permit an amendment to be made after the time limit for a new claim has expired, if it would add a new claim, not least because in a case where the time limit has not yet expired, it is open to the claimant simply to present a second claim.

(g)   Where however the original claim was presented after the claim sought to be added would have been time-barred, there is no general jurisdiction to permit the time limit to be circumvented by adding the claim by amendment. This may only be done if the tribunal is persuaded that time would have been extended had the claim sought to be added been brought as part of the original claim, and then only if the balance of factors to be considered under *Selkent* favours giving permission.

(h)   The general view of practitioners was until recently that only matters which could have been the subject of a claim at the time of presentation of the originating application could be added by an amendment to the original claim: allegations of matters occurring *after* the claim was presented could not be added (since they could not have been included at the time), and a fresh application would be needed to pursue such matters as substantive claims. This view now appears to be incorrect in the light of the EAT's decision in *Prakash v Wolverhampton City Council* [2006] All ER (D) 71 (Nov), that an amendment could be made to a claim of unfair dismissal to add a complaint of dismissal occurring after the original claim had been presented. It was also suggested by the EAT that this reflected the practice in discrimination cases. Independently of this decision, in discrimination cases subsequent events may, if relevant, be relied on as *evidence* supporting the inference of discrimination sought to be made in relation to the substantive allegations, and an amendment to this effect may be permitted.

(i)   It has been somewhat controversial whether the tribunal can take into account the underlying merits when an amendment is proposed. It is often said that this is an appropriate consideration for the tribunal under 'all the circumstances' when considering an amendment which would add a new claim. In *Woodhouse v Hampshire Hospitals NHS Trust* (UKEAT/0132/12), the EAT held that the balance of hardship and prejudice may in all the circumstances include an examination of the merits: "there is no point in allowing an amendment to add an utterly hopeless case" (para 15). However, otherwise it should be assumed that the case is arguable. There, the EAT held the tribunal had impermissibly taken into account the strength of the evidence relating to the proposed claims when at that stage there had been no disclosure given in relation to those claims. As to considering the merits of proposed claims, see also *Cooper v Chief Constable of West Yorkshire Police* (UKEAT/0035/06) at para 17.

(j)   One other category of amendment requiring mention is an amendment to add a party or alter the name of a party. The discretion of the tribunal in dealing with such amendments is governed by similar principles to those set out above, summarised in *Cocking v Sandhurst (Stationers) Ltd* [1974] ICR 650; and see *Drinkwater Sabey Ltd v Burnett* [1995] ICR 328 and *Birch v Walsall Metropolitan Borough Council* (UKEAT/0376/10). A party may be added or substituted even at the hearing in an appropriate case, eg where a manager rather than the employing company had been identified as the employer in an unfair dismissal case: *Linbourne v Constable* [1993] ICR 698. One point raised, but not decided, in the *Walsall* case is whether the effect of an amendment to add a respondent operates as from the time of permission to amend, or from when the claim was originally brought (as had generally been understood to be the position before this case). The point is of relevance to how far back claims for back pay can be made in equal pay cases (which *Walsall* was), as well as affecting whether a point on time limits can be taken by the party added by amendment.

(k)   All of the cases referred to in paragraph (i) are about the addition or substitution of a respondent. It might be thought that different principles apply to the addition of a claimant, since this amounts, for the new claimant, to the bringing of a claim for the first time, and if the applicable limitation period has expired, it should therefore only be possible to add the claimant if the circumstances justifying an extension of time are made out. However the EAT has held that a more liberal approach, effectively applying *Selkent* criteria as explained above, is appropriate: *Enterprise Liverpool Ltd v Jonas* (UKEAT/0112/09) (a case where a trade union applied to be substituted for the individual claimant in a claim of failure to consult over a proposed transfer of an undertaking).

18.11 Disclosure of documents

Disclosure (formerly known as discovery) is the process in civil litigation where each party discloses to the other all documents relevant to the proceedings and not protected from disclosure. The tribunal's power to order disclosure is the same as that of the civil courts under *Part 31* of the *Civil Procedure Rules 1998 ('CPR')*, or in Scotland that of the Sheriff Court (*ET Rules, rule 10(2)(d)*). An important consequence of this is that the scope of disclosure should be consistent with the Overriding Objective of civil litigation (see 18.1 above).

There is no automatic disclosure in tribunals – unless given voluntarily or ordered by the tribunal it must be specifically asked for. However it has increasingly become the practice of tribunals in England and Wales, although not in Scotland, to order mutual disclosure at an early stage of the proceedings. In Scotland a Practice Direction issued in December 2006 requires the mutual notification by the parties of the documents each intends to rely on at least 14 days before the Hearing (these are referred to as Productions, and the list of documents as an Inventory).

The formal process of disclosure involves supplying a list of all the documents in a party's possession and allowing the other party to inspect and take copies. In practice the parties may agree simply to supply copies of all the documents concerned.

An increasingly important element in disclosure of documents is the retrieval of e-mails. These are equally documents, and are disclosable not only if paper copies have been put on a file, but also if retained electronically within the party's computer system (this extends to deleted or archived e-mails, if they can still be accessed).

18.11 Employment Tribunals – II

Disclosure may be either general (ie covering the case as a whole) or specific (ie covering identified documents or classes of documents). Parties ordered to disclose documents need only undertake a reasonable search for relevant documents. A party giving voluntary disclosure need not disclose all documents; however, a document cannot properly be kept back if its non-disclosure would render a disclosed document misleading: *Birds Eye Walls Ltd v Harrison* [1985] ICR 278, where the claimant was permitted to amend his claim to add new grounds part way through the hearing after coming into possession of a relevant document in the possession of the employer that had not been included in its earlier disclosure. The same point probably applies to documents the concealment of which would render oral evidence misleading. Failure to disclose a relevant document can lead to very serious consequences, as shown by *Aslam v Barclays Capital Ltd* (UKEAT/0405/10), where the subsequent production by the respondent of a crucial document not disclosed before the hearing led to an order by the EAT for the re-hearing of the entire case.

The obligation to disclose documents is a continuing one, so that if further documents come to light, or come into existence, during the course of the proceedings, they must be disclosed if they are relevant to material already disclosed, or within the terms of an order for disclosure. This principle was applied by the Court of Appeal in *Scott v IRC* [2004] EWCA Civ 400, [2004] IRLR 713 in relation to a new policy on permitting employees to continue to work beyond the normal retirement age, which was adopted whilst the claim was proceeding and which affected the basis on which the claimant's claim for compensation for future loss of earnings would fall to be calculated.

The normal and recommended practice, where either disclosure has not been ordered by the tribunal at an early stage in the proceedings or the disclosure given appears to be incomplete, is for disclosure, or additional specific disclosure, to be requested by correspondence in the first instance. If this request is refused, ignored or not fully complied with, an application should be made to the tribunal for an order.

18.12 The test for whether disclosure of a particular document or class of documents should be ordered is whether disclosure is necessary for disposing fairly of the proceedings. This involves more than just relevance; an application for disclosure of a large quantity of documents of marginal relevance is likely to be refused on the ground of excessive burden on the other party, in accordance with the Overriding Objective, which includes the requirement to act proportionately to the importance and complexity of the case. A good example of a refusal of excessive disclosure is *British Aerospace plc v Green* [1995] ICR 1006, CA, where, in a case arising from a substantial redundancy selection exercise, disclosure of assessment records of several hundred employees was refused. See also *King v Eaton Ltd* [1996] IRLR 199.

The ambit of disclosure is likely to be widest in discrimination cases, because of the need to show evidence from which inferences can be drawn (*West Midlands Passenger Transport Executive v Singh* [1988] 1 WLR 730, [1988] ICR 614). However, even in discrimination cases a test of relevance still applies; further guidance is given in *Ministry of Defence v Meredith* [1995] IRLR 539 and *Canadian Imperial Bank of Commerce v Beck* [2009] EWCA Civ 619.

Confidentiality is not as such a reason for refusing disclosure. In a doubtful case the tribunal may inspect the documents before deciding whether they are sufficiently relevant to overcome the need to respect confidentiality (see *Science Research Council v Nasse* [1980] AC 1028, [1979] 3 All ER 673, [1979] 3 WLR 762, [1979] IRLR 465, [1979] ICR 921). However if disclosure is ordered, it must be disclosure to the other party or parties; the tribunal cannot order disclosure to itself alone: *Knight v Department of Social Security* [2002] IRLR 249. If necessary in order to preserve confidentiality, the tribunal can order disclosure subject to anonymising the document and/or deleting passages which would or might reveal the identity of the author or source of a statement, a procedure known as redaction: *Asda Stores Ltd v Thompson* [2002] IRLR 245 (a case concerning disclosure of witness statements taken under terms of confidentiality in an investigation of alleged drug dealing). Further guidance as to the procedure to be followed where a party wishes to disclose documents subject to redaction is given in *Asda Stores Ltd v Thompson (No 2)* [2004] IRLR 598. The tribunal also has power to restrict disclosure to the party him or herself and his or her representative, and to limit the purpose for which disclosure is given to the conduct of the particular case (see the *Knight* case, above; this is in any event an implied condition of any non-voluntary disclosure of documents that are not subsequently put into the public domain by being referred to in the course of a public hearing). One class of documents the disclosure of which is commonly made subject to restrictions is the claimant's medical records, and medical reports on the claimant; the tribunal may limit disclosure to the legal representatives and medical advisers of the respondent to protect the confidentiality of the claimant's medical history.

If, exceptionally, a party cannot disclose a document without acting unlawfully, it is wrong in principle to order disclosure: *Barracks v Coles* [2006] EWCA Civ 1041, [2007] ICR 60, a case about a police officer refused security clearance for reasons the police force was unable lawfully to disclose.

Disclosure can only be ordered of existing documents; it cannot be used to require the creation of a document (eg by compiling statistics): *Carrington v Helix Lighting Ltd* [1990] ICR 125. The restricting effect of this point is considerably eased by the tribunal's general power to order a party to provide additional information, which can include in an appropriate case a table, chart or schedule containing relevant information (including a Schedule of Loss, or a table giving numbers of staff classified by grade and ethnic origin – the issue in the *Carrington* case), and by the availability of the questionnaire procedure in discrimination cases: see **18.9** above.

18.13   Documents privileged from disclosure

Certain documents are immune from disclosure. These include those subject to legal professional privilege and (with qualifications) public interest immunity. Legal professional privilege covers both legal advice privilege and litigation privilege. The former applies only to communications with and from professional legal advisers, not, for instance, an accountant, a trade union official, or lay adviser (including a professional but not legally qualified consultant): as recently confirmed by the Supreme Court in *R (on the application of Prudential Plc) v Special Commissioner of Income Tax* [2013] 2 All ER 247; see also *New Victoria Hospital v Ryan* [1993] ICR 201; *Howes v Hinckley and Bosworth Borough Council* [2008] All ER (D) 112 (Aug). Litigation privilege has wider application, covering communications with advisers who are not lawyers (see *Scotthorne v Four Seasons Conservatories (UK) Ltd* (UKEAT/0178/10)) but only in relation to communications the primary purpose of which is in relation to pursuing, defending or avoiding actual or anticipated litigation; for further details, specialist works on the subject should be consulted. Legal professional privilege can be waived; guidance was given by the EAT in *Brennan v Sunderland City Council* [2009] ICR 479 as to how to assess whether privilege has been waived. Public interest immunity is also a specialised area of law outside the scope of this work; the leading recent cases relevant to its application in tribunal proceedings are *Balfour v Foreign and Commonwealth Office* [1994] ICR 277 and *R v Chief Constable of West Midlands, ex p Wiley* [1995] 1 AC 274 (overruling *Halford v Sharples* [1992] 3 All ER 624, [1992] 1 WLR 736, [1992] ICR 583).

'Without prejudice' communications between the parties are in a slightly different category, as they are in their nature already known to both parties. They are, however, not admissible as evidence before the tribunal unless both parties agree, or to prove the contents of an agreement subsequently reached, or, exceptionally, where non-disclosure of the document would lead to the concealment of 'unambiguous impropriety' on the part of the party seeking to exclude the document, or where, if the content of the without prejudice communication was excluded, something akin to a dishonest case would be put before the tribunal (the authority for the last point is *Independent Research Services Ltd v Catterall* [1993] ICR 1, EAT). For an example where the exception was held not to be made out, and disclosure was refused, see *Brodie v Ward (t/a First Steps Nursery)* [2008] All ER (D) 115 (Feb). The same principle applies to evidence of oral communications conducted without prejudice.

However, the privilege against disclosure to the tribunal only applies to genuinely 'without prejudice' communications, ie those generated as or forming part of an attempt to settle a dispute. There must be a dispute, such that the parties must have contemplated that if not resolved, the matter might proceed to litigation, although it is not necessary that either party has actually threatened litigation. The dividing line has been described by the Court of Appeal as not always clear and highly dependent on the particular circumstances of each case: *Framlington Group Ltd v Barnetson* [2007] EWCA Civ 502, [2007] ICR 1439, [2007] IRLR 598.

By contrast, a meeting called by an employer to put proposals to the employee for a severance package was held by the EAT in *BNP Paribas v Mezzotero* [2004] IRLR 508 not to be within the privilege (with the result that the employee could rely on what was said at the meeting to support a complaint of sex discrimination), despite the fact that she was pursuing a grievance at the time, both because there was no dispute to which the proposals were directed, and also because it would be wrong to allow the employer to rely on the privilege when the status of the meeting was first raised unilaterally after it had begun, and had not been agreed in advance. However a subsequent analysis of the law by the EAT in *Woodward v Santander plc* (UKEAT/0250/09) led it to the conclusion that *Mezzotero* does not lay down any new exception to the 'without prejudice' rule, but is better understood as an application of the 'unambiguous impropriety' exception, the impropriety being the act of discrimination committed in the course of the allegedly without prejudice meeting. In *Woodward* itself, the EAT upheld the exclusion by the tribunal of evidence that in the course of without prejudice negotiations the respondent's solicitors had said that the respondent would not provide a reference for the employee, a point she wished to use in evidence to support her claim of victimisation by the giving of poor references.

In addition, the privilege attached to without prejudice discussions may be waived by the conduct of a party (in a case where the other party also seeks to rely on the discussions): see *Brunel University v Vaseghi* [2007] EWCA Civ 482, [2007] IRLR 592 (privilege waived by making reference to discussions during grievance hearing before independent panel, and by referring to them in response form) and *National Centre for Young People with Epilepsy v Boateng* (UKEAT/0440/10) (dispute about validity of agreement reached at mediation based on allegations against party's own solicitor constituted waiver of privilege by that party). In *Gallop v Newport City Council* [2013] IRLR 23, the EAT considered a case in which, during evidence on remedy, one of the wing-members of the tribunal asked about negotiations over a proposed compromise agreement. The EAT held that the tribunal had erred: it was wrong in principle to have admitted evidence as to compromise negotiations absent a clear waiver by the parties. The Judge should have immediately intervened to cut off the wholly impermissible line of enquiry.

A separate but related statutory provision excludes disclosure of any communication made (orally or in writing) to an ACAS conciliation officer to a tribunal without the consent of the party who made the communication: *ETA 1996, s 18(7)*. In addition, parties engaging in mediation will almost always agree that if the mediation is unsuccessful, any documents produced for the purpose of the mediation, as well as anything said during it, is confidential; this confidentiality will not be overridden by an order for disclosure in the absence of the most compelling reasons. The obligation of confidentiality is applied as a matter of course to any judicial mediation conducted in the employment tribunal.

It is possible to restrict the 'without prejudice' nature of communications by adding the qualification 'save as to costs', to the effect that such communications may be relied on in any issue as to costs, after the tribunal has determined the claim itself. See further **18.36** below.

In addition to the above, and relevant to unfair dismissal complaints, the *Enterprise and Regulatory Reform Act 2013, s 14* will insert a new *section 111A* into the ERA which makes evidence of "pre termination negotiations" inadmissible in proceedings on a complaint under s 111 (unfair dismissal). "Pre-termination negotiations" are defined to mean "any offer made or discussions held, before the termination of the employment in question, with a view to it being terminated on terms agreed between the employer and employee". This definition includes negotiations and offers whether made by the employer or employee. It is designed to catch a wider range of discussions than those caught by the common law without prejudice rule set out above. The Explanatory Notes to the *Act* state (para 82): "The purpose of *section 14* is to provide a means for employers and employees to discuss settlement before any dispute has actually arisen, with certainty that the offer and any discussions about it cannot be used as evidence against them in a subsequent unfair dismissal claim."

There are three exceptions: (i) the rule does not apply where, on the complainant's case, the circumstances are such that a provision of an Act of Parliament requires the complainant to be regarded as unfairly dismissed; (ii) where the tribunal considers anything said or done was "improper, or was connected with improper behaviour", then the rule only applies to the extent that the tribunal considers just; and (iii) the rule does not affect the admissibility on the question of costs or expenses of evidence of an offer made on the basis that the right to refer to it on the question of costs or expenses is reserved.

One issue not covered by *s 14* is the issue of waiver: arguably this doctrine has no place in respect of discussions caught by *s 111A* because the statute mandates that such discussions are inadmissible in the circumstances specified. *Section 14* will come into force on a date yet to be appointed by the Secretary of State: see *s 103(3)* of the *2013 Act*.

18.14 Witness orders

An order for the attendance of a witness can be sought if the witness is believed to have relevant knowledge or information to give and the party seeking the order believes he or she may not attend voluntarily. A witness order is in practice often needed where an employer would otherwise not be cooperative in releasing the witness. Orders are almost invariably required to secure the attendance of police officers. As indicated above (**18.3**) an ordered witness may apply before the hearing to set aside the order; however, there is no minimum period of notice of the order that has to be given to the witness. It is normally for the party obtaining the order to ensure it is served on the intended witness, although some tribunal offices undertake the service of witness orders.

The granting of witness orders is a matter of discretion; the tribunal must consider whether the witness is likely to be able to give relevant evidence and whether the giving of that evidence is necessary, and may refuse unjustified requests as a part of the general power to control and manage the proceedings and in the interests of proportionality to the issues in dispute. In particular, the tribunal may properly limit the number of witnesses who are to be heard on a particular issue of fact, especially where the issue is not central to case: *Noorani v Merseyside TEC Ltd* [1999] IRLR 184. In *McBride v Standards Board for England* (UKEAT/0092/09), the EAT held that it is open to the tribunal as part of its general case management powers to impose restrictions in advance on the number or identity of witnesses to be called at the Hearing, not just as part of the process of managing the proceedings in the course of the Hearing itself.

Evidence is admissible only if relevant to an issue in the proceedings, and is generally relevant only if it relates to issues which are *in dispute* between the parties, and where issues of fact are agreed (for instance a note of a meeting is agreed by both parties) it is not necessary to call a witness to 'prove' that which is not in dispute. This may apply equally to issues of character: claimants often assume, for instance, that evidence of their good character is an important part of their case, but it would only be relevant in practice if good character is an issue in the case, and then only if it is disputed by the employer.

The use of genuinely reluctant witnesses is a matter requiring considerable care. The party calling the witness cannot normally prompt him or her, dispute what he or she says or cross-examine him or her, and so may be faced with an unsympathetic witness giving unhelpful or damaging evidence that cannot effectively be challenged. There is no guarantee that the tribunal will intervene to probe the witness to rectify this, and the concept of a witness being formally treated as a 'hostile witness' is all but unknown in employment tribunal litigation. It may also be difficult to establish in advance what evidence a reluctant witness is in a position to give. For these reasons an application by a claimant for witness orders in respect of managers of the employer is nearly always inadvisable, and likely to be refused.

One way around this difficulty is for the tribunal to be asked to call the witness concerned itself; the witness can then be offered for cross-examination by both parties. The EAT has confirmed that tribunals have this power: *Clapson v British Airways plc* [2001] IRLR 184, a case where the claimant himself was called by the tribunal after his representative indicated that he would not be called. However, the power is used very sparingly, and in general it remains the responsibility of the parties to put evidence before the tribunal and call any witnesses they rely on.

The use of expert witnesses in tribunal proceedings is still relatively rare, but has become somewhat more common, especially in cases where a claim that the applicant is disabled is disputed, or there is a claim for compensation for personal injury in a discrimination claim. In unfair dismissal cases there may be technical issues affecting the computation of compensation, the calculation of pension loss in particular, which may on occasion require an expert witness. (In such cases it is advisable to apply to the tribunal for an order for issues of remedy to be heard separately, to avoid unnecessary costs being incurred on experts' fees.) Separate procedures apply in equal value cases, where the tribunal may be required to appoint an independent expert; details of the applicable rules are in *Sch 6* to the *2004 Regulations.*

The EAT has given detailed guidance on the procedures to be adopted when expert evidence is required: *de Keyser Ltd v Wilson* [2001] IRLR 324. The main points are that there is no presumption that expert evidence will be allowed merely because one party wishes to call an expert; where appropriate the parties should use a joint expert, or at least if one party is calling an expert the other party should have an opportunity to agree to the terms of the instructions to the expert; and where there are experts on both sides, the tribunal should give directions setting out a timetable for the experts to meet to attempt to agree, or at least define, the issues in dispute. Guidance as to when a party may call its own expert to contradict the evidence of the joint expert was given by the EAT in *Hospice of St Mary of Furness v Howard* [2007] IRLR 944 (a case concerning medical evidence of the claimant's disability): the question for the tribunal is the same as that under *CPR 1998, Part 35* as explained in *Daniels v Walker* [2000] 1 WLR 1382.

An expert witness, even if instructed by one party and not jointly, has an overriding duty to the tribunal, which takes precedence over his or her duty to the party instructing him or her. There are also strict rules which govern how parties should interact with a joint expert: see *Peet v Mid-Kent Healthcare Trust: Practice Note* [2002] 1 WLR 210.

In practice, the use of joint experts may be inhibited by difficulties in agreeing who pays for the expert. As the EAT stated in *de Keyser*, the tribunal has no power, beyond its general powers to award costs, to order the parties to share the cost, or for one party to bear the cost, of an expert witness. However the tribunal itself has limited powers to pay for an expert where a joint appointment has been ordered; any party seeking the appointment of an expert should make enquiries as to the availability of funds for this purpose.

It would be a serious matter, quite possibly amounting to contempt of court, for an employer to seek to prevent one of his or her employees from being called to give evidence or to influence his or her evidence (*Peach Grey & Co v Sommers* [1995] 2 All ER 513, [1995] ICR 549, [1995] IRLR 363). Any such attempt could also be regarded as scandalous or unreasonable conduct, entitling the tribunal to strike out the response in a sufficiently clear case. The employer may, however, seek to obtain a statement from such a witness as part of the preparation for the case; as a general principle, which applies to both parties, there is no 'property' in a witness.

The use of witness statements is discussed at **18.46** below.

18.15 DEPOSIT ORDERS AND STRIKING OUT

Deposit orders

One of the case management powers available to the tribunal is the making of a deposit order, which is an order (in principle against either party, but in practice it is used most often against claimants) that the party will not be permitted to continue to take part in the proceedings unless that party pays a deposit of an amount ordered by the tribunal, and subject to a warning that if the party persists in maintaining the relevant claim or contention, the tribunal may make an order for costs against him or her. The criterion for issuing a costs warning and making a deposit order is that the party's case, or a particular contention put forward by the party 'has little reasonable prospect of success'.

The question whether to make a deposit order must be dealt with at a PHR. This may be on the application of the other party or as a result of an order made by the tribunal of its own initiative, and the issue of a deposit order may be referred for hearing at a PHR together with any other issues in the case which are judged appropriate for determination at a PHR, or as the sole issue for determination. All parties to the proceedings may submit written representations and/or appear and present oral argument, but evidence may not be adduced (*rule 18(2(c))*). The tribunal (comprising an Employment Judge sitting alone unless there has been a successful application for a full tribunal – see **18.6**) considers the Claim Form and Response, the representations (which may include relevant documents) and argument. A deposit order may also be made after hearing evidence at a PHR ordered to consider striking out a claim or response, where the tribunal refuses to strike out the case, but considers that the lesser sanction is appropriate.

If it determines that a party's case (or part thereof) has little reasonable prospect of success, the tribunal may make an order against that party requiring him or her to deposit a sum not exceeding £500 as a condition of being permitted to continue to take part in the proceedings (*ET Rules, rule 20(1)*). The maximum sum has been increased to £1,000 by the *Employment Tribunals (Constitution and Rules of Procedure) (Amendment) Regulations 2012, reg 2(2)*, but only for cases presented on or after 6 April 2012 (see *reg 3*); for cases already before the tribunal at that date, the lower limit therefore still applies. The tribunal must have regard to the party's means in fixing the sum, so far as they are reasonably ascertainable (*rule 20(2)*); the *rule* does not make clear how the tribunal may ascertain the party's means, but in practice this does not appear to cause difficulty. In *Oni v NHS Leicester City* (UKEAT/0144/12) the EAT recommended the completion of the County Court means form EX140 by the party whose means are to be taken into account. A party's means may include a student loan: *Simpson v Chief Constable, Strathclyde Police* (UKEATS/0030/11).

If a deposit is ordered it must be paid within 21 days from the date the order was sent to the party (this period is extendable, on cause shown, by up to 14 days). If it is not so paid, the claim or, as the case may be, response is struck out (*ET Rules, rule 20(4)*). *Regulation 15(6)* of the *2004 Regulations* makes it clear that 'sent' refers to despatch not receipt, overruling case law to the contrary on the previous *Regulations*. The deposit paid by a party is refundable unless at the main hearing an order for costs is made against that party (*rule 20(5)*). As to the effect of an order for a deposit under *rule 20* in relation to orders for costs, see **18.71**.

The value of the deposit order procedure for respondents is that many claimants who are warned that they are at risk of a costs order do not pursue their claim. Such applications can also be considered as a lesser alternative to the striking out of a claim or response as misconceived, if the order for the holding of a PHR provides for this. The number of deposit orders made in recent years has averaged 400, ranging from 491 in 2007 to 335 in 2010; the average deposit ordered was about £250, and just over 10% of orders made were against respondents (these figures are taken from the Impact Assessment published by BIS alongside *Resolving Employment Disputes* in November 2011).

Guidance as to the correct approach to whether a claim or response 'has little reasonable prospect of success' is given (in relation to the similarly worded test in *Part 24* of the *CPR 1998*) by the Court of Appeal decision in *Swain v Hillman* [2001] 1 All ER 91. The utility of the deposit order procedure in weeding out unmeritorious claims and responses is in practice limited by the fact that no evidence can be given. If there are serious conflicts of fact on the pleadings, a tribunal may not be able to judge what the prospects are, but the EAT has held that in deciding what prospects of success a claim or response may have, the tribunal can take into account the credibility of the facts asserted, and the likelihood that they can be established at a hearing: *Jansen van Rensburg v Royal Borough of Kingston-upon-Thames* (UKEAT/0096/07). This case was not cited in the later case of *Sharma v New College Nottingham* (UKEAT/0287/11), and the EAT's conclusion in that case that the same test should be applied for a deposit order as for the striking out of a claim as having no reasonable prospects of success is considered to be wrong, as it fails to give weight to the difference in wording between 'no' and 'little' reasonable prospect of success, and undermines the objectives of the deposit order procedure. The distinction between a deposit order and striking out was also highlighted in *H M Prison Service v Dolby* [2003] IRLR 694, where the EAT described the two sanctions respectively as 'the Yellow card' and 'the Red card'.

There is no power to review a deposit order under *rule 34*, but there is power to vary or revoke the order under *rule 10(2)(n)*. In *Sodexho Ltd v Gibbons* [2005] IRLR 836, the EAT upheld the use of this power to restart the time for payment of the deposit where it had transpired that the claimant had not received the order, having put an incorrect address for his solicitor on the Claim Form. The same case holds that the striking out of a claim or response if the deposit is not paid is technically a judgment, and therefore can be reviewed under *rule 34* (and was reviewable for 'administrative error' on the facts referred to). An appeal, either against the deposit order or the striking out of a claim or response for failure to pay the deposit ordered, is also possible, but less likely to be appropriate given the much more limited grounds of appeal. In principle it is possible for a party to make a second application for a deposit order if the first is unsuccessful, but this is only likely to be entertained if the material circumstances have changed significantly.

18.16   Striking out

The tribunal has power to strike out the claim or response, or a part or parts of either, or order that a respondent be debarred from defending a claim altogether, as a sanction for failure to comply with an order made under any of the tribunal's case management powers (*ET Rules, rule 13(1)(b)*).

The power to strike out is subject to the important safeguard that the tribunal must first send a notice in writing to the party concerned giving him or her the opportunity to show cause why the tribunal should not do so (unless the party has already been given an opportunity to show cause orally): *rule 19(1)*. In practice any decision to strike out for non-compliance with an order is likely to be taken at a PHR (although the issue may also arise at the Hearing; it cannot be taken at a CMD: *rule 17(2)* and *Way v Powercraft Retail Ltd* [2008] All ER (D) 151 (Aug)).

The significant exception to the requirement to give an opportunity to show cause is where an 'unless' order has been made under *rule 13(2)* and not complied with. The operation of 'unless' orders has been considered recently in a number of cases in the EAT and one decision of the Court of Appeal which have highlighted the difficulties surrounding the working of the *ET Rules* in this area. The relevant rules have indeed been described by the then President of the EAT, Underhill J, as a 'pig's breakfast': *North Tyneside Primary Care Trust v Aynsley* [2009] All ER (D) 125 (May). The effect of the decisions in *Uyanwa-Odu v Schools Office Services Ltd* (UKEAT/0294/05), *Neary v Governing Body of St Albans Girls' School* [2009] All ER (D) 30 (Jan), *EPI Coaches Ltd v Lafferty* [2009] All ER (D) 81 (Apr), *North Tyneside* case and *Scottish Ambulance Service v Laing* (UKEATS/0038/12) is that if the order is not complied with by the due date (even if the non-compliance is partial), the claim, or as the case may be response, is struck out automatically, without the need for further judicial intervention. As Lady Smith remarked in *Laing*, if the parties wish confirmation of their position in relation to an unless order, the onus is on them to communicate with the tribunal, but that ought not to be treated by the tribunal as an opportunity to revisit the question of whether the unless order should have been issued.

However the effect of the automatic strike-out of a claim, although not of a response, is that the original unless order is converted into a judgment, which may therefore be reviewed under *rule 34*: *Uyanwa-Odu*, *Neary*, (which reviews fully the relevant cases). *Neary* was the subject of a further appeal to the Court of Appeal, which reversed the decision of the EAT on the merits, but without disagreeing with the analysis of the effects of non-compliance with an 'unless' order (*Neary v Governing Body of St Albans Girls School* [2009] EWCA Civ 1190, [2010] ICR 473).Note that Smith LJ in *Neary* considered that the EAT's finding that the remedy of review was available in the case of a strike out taking effect for non-compliance with an unless order was not "wholly free from difficulty" (para 5). In *Thind v Salvesen Logistics Ltd* (UKEAT/0487/09), the EAT applied the decision in *Neary*, but reached the opposite result, overturning the striking out of the claim, where the breach of an 'unless' order had resulted from a combination of delay by a medical expert in providing a report and inadvertence by the claimant's solicitors.

So far as the response is concerned, because striking it out does not bring the proceedings to an end the position is technically different, in that the strike-out order is not a 'judgment' and there is therefore no power of review of the order under *rule 34*; but the same result can be achieved by reconsidering the order under the power given by *rule 10(2)(n)* (*North Tyneside*, applying *Hart v English Heritage* [2006] IRLR 915; this point was not addressed in the *EPI Coaches* case).

As to the criteria to be applied when reviewing or reconsidering the original order in the light of its consequences, the Court of Appeal in *Neary* rejected the view expressed by the EAT that the tribunal must consider each of the factors listed in the pre April 2013 formulation of *CPR rule 3.9*, which set out the factors to be considered in the High Court where there is an application from relief from sanctions. The Court concluded that the decision whether to grant relief is simply a matter of discretion. As to what factors are likely to be relevant to the exercise of that discretion in particular cases, the fact that there has been a breach of the order will always be relevant, but not necessarily decisive. The principles in the *Blockbuster* case (see below) are relevant; in particular it will be important for the tribunal to determine whether a fair trial of the case is still possible; thus if (as in the *North Tyneside* case) the defaulting party has since complied with the 'unless' order, it may be disproportionate to deny that party a hearing, whether as claimant or respondent. However where there has been a persistent and unexplained failure to comply with orders, the tribunal is entitled to say 'enough is enough' (as the Court of Appeal held was the case in *Neary*).

A further complicating factor in many cases where there has been an 'unless' order and it is asserted by the other party that there has been a failure to comply with it is that that point may itself be in dispute (for instance there may be a dispute about whether the party has complied fully with an order to give particulars or disclose documents). In such cases the issue can only be fairly resolved by a hearing, leading to a judgment on the disputed issue of non-compliance, which may in turn be open to appeal. These procedural complications may remove much of the value of 'unless' orders as orders of last resort.

The requirement to give the offending party an opportunity to show cause (in cases where there has not been an 'unless' order) has been held by the EAT to be mandatory, so that a 'show cause' notice sent before the deadline for compliance was ineffective and invalid: *Beacard Property Management and Construction Ltd v Day* [1984] ICR 837. This case involved a much earlier version of the *ET Rules*, but is thought that this remains the position under the 2004 *ET Rules*.

The striking out of a claim or response for non-compliance with an order short of an 'unless' order has been described by the Court of Appeal as a 'draconic power', not to be too readily exercised: *James v Blockbuster Entertainment Ltd* [2006] EWCA Civ 684, [2006] IRLR 630. The Court of Appeal has twice ruled that striking out as a sanction should only be applied where it is proportionate to the offence: *Bennett v Southwark London Borough Council* [2002] EWCA Civ 223, [2002] IRLR 407, where the issue was a party's conduct during the Hearing; and *Blockbuster*, where it was failure to comply with orders.

The guiding principle in deciding whether or not to strike out a party's case for non-compliance with an order is the requirements of the Overriding Objective. These require the tribunal to consider all relevant factors, including in particular what prejudice the other party has suffered, the issue of proportionality of the sanction, whether a lesser sanction could cure the prejudice, and as an overriding consideration, whether a fair trial remains possible. These points were articulated by the EAT in *Armitage v Weir Valves & Controls (UK) Ltd* [2004] ICR 371, where the employers successfully appealed against the striking out of their notice of appearance because they had been 10 days late in complying with a direction to exchange witness statements. (See also *Hazelwood v Eagle* [2009] All ER (D) 55 (May), where the EAT set aside a strike-out made because the claimant was in persistent breach of an order to supply medical evidence of a claimed disability. A case going the other way on similar facts is *Bennett v London Probation Service* (UKEAT/0194/09); however in that case the claimant had indicated that she would never disclose the reports.) In *GCHQ v Bacchus* (UKEAT/0373/12) the EAT imposed an unless order rather than taking the draconian step of striking out where the claimant had refused to comply with an order requiring him to attend an appointment with a psychiatrist for the purpose of the respondent obtaining its own expert report, without which it would have been significantly disadvantaged in the litigation.

In *Maresca v Motor Insurance Repair Research Centre* [2004] 4 All ER 254, [2005] ICR 197, a case concerning the striking out of a claim for failure to comply with a case management order for mutual disclosure of documents, the EAT held that in considering whether to strike out a party's case, the tribunal should have regard to the factors listed in the pre-April 2013 version of *CPR 1998, rule 3.9*. (These include whether the application for relief was made promptly, whether the default was intentional, and whether the expected hearing date can still be met if the original order is now complied with.) The relevance of these considerations has been reiterated in several subsequent cases, but with the important proviso that it will not be an error of law for a tribunal to fail to refer to or consider each of the factors in the old *CPR rule 3.9* if the factors not considered are not relevant to the particular case. However, the more recent decision of the Court of Appeal in *Neary*, above, that it was not necessary to consider each of the factors in the old *CPR rule 3.9* where there had been a failure to comply with an 'unless' order is an indication that such an exercise is now rather less likely to be regarded as essential in other cases where the sanction for non-compliance with orders is under consideration. This position is further reinforced by the amendment of *CPR rule 3.9* post April 2013: the list of factors has been replaced by a requirement that the Court considers all the circumstances of the case, including the need for litigation to be conducted efficiently and at proportionate cost, and the need to enforce compliance with rules, practice directions and orders.

In *Blockbuster*, the Court of Appeal held that striking out could only be justified if *either* the offending party has been guilty of deliberate and persistent disregard of required procedural steps, *or* the unreasonable conduct of the case by that party (not necessarily deliberately so) has made a fair trial impossible. These are gateways to the exercise of the power; they do not necessitate the exercise of the power. Thus in *Osborne v Premium Care Homes Ltd* [2006] All ER (D) 272 (Oct), the sanction of debarring the respondent from defending the case on liability but permitting it to defend itself at the remedy stage was held to be a proper and proportionate response to breaches of orders that had made a fair trial on liability impossible (compare the similar sanction applied by the EAT where a response had not been submitted in time in *Foster v D & H Travel Ltd* [2006] ICR 1537).

The incorporation of *art 6* of the *European Convention on Human Rights*, through the *Human Rights Act 1998*, provides a possible basis for challenges to striking-out decisions on the ground that the party (particularly a claimant) is deprived of the right to a determination of his or her civil rights by way of a fair and public hearing. However the case law of the European Court of Human Rights (which guides the decision-making of UK courts and tribunals) indicates that the proper judicial use of powers to control litigants, including striking out, does not in principle offend the *Convention*. (See also *Soteriou v Ultrachem Ltd* [2004] EWHC 983 (QB), [2004] IRLR 870 (striking out where contract of employment tainted by illegality not contrary to *art 6*).)

18.17 There are a number of other grounds on which a party's case may be struck out, in whole or in part. The tribunal may make such an order, if it thinks fit:

(a) on the grounds that the offending case or part is scandalous or vexatious, or has no reasonable prospect of success;

(b) on the grounds that the manner in which the proceedings have been conducted by the offending party has been scandalous, unreasonable or vexatious;

(c) in relation to a claim, if it has not been actively pursued;

(d) also in relation to a claim, if the Judge or tribunal considers that it is no longer possible to have a fair hearing of the claim.

(*Rule 18(7)(b), (c), (d) and (f)* respectively.)

In relation to each of these powers, the requirement to send a 'show cause' notice to the party affected referred to above applies, unless the party has had the opportunity to make oral submissions against the order. Striking out orders under any of these headings can only be made at a PHR or a Hearing. The various grounds are considered below in the order set out above. The Government consultation paper of January 2011 included a proposal to permit the striking out of very weak claims on the papers without a hearing. In Mr Justice Underhill's draft new rules of procedure, every case would be subject to initial consideration of the claim form and the response by an Employment Judge who would assess the prospects of success of the claim or response (or part thereof) as pleaded and make an order dismissing such claim/response or part thereof on a date specified in the order. There would be the right of the affected litigant to challenge that view at a hearing. The operation of the new rules as enacted (which may not follow precisely the formulation proposed by the Underhill review) will be considered in a forthcoming edition of this work.

The power to strike out a party's case as having no reasonable prospect of success was introduced by the *2001 Regulations*. The power mirrors the power of the High Court under *Part 24* of the *CPR 1998* to give summary judgment where a case has no reasonable prospect of success, as to which there is helpful guidance in *Swain v Hillman* [2001] 1 All ER 91, CA. A tribunal is usually unlikely to entertain an application to strike out the claim or response at a PHR in factually contentious cases, since tribunals are reluctant to deny a party the opportunity to put his or her case to the tribunal except on the strongest grounds. The drastic nature of the power justifies caution in its exercise; the tribunal has a discretion to strike out, and is not required automatically to do so merely because it determines that the claim (or defence) has no reasonable prospects of success.

The importance of not striking out discrimination cases in particular in any but the clearest of cases has been reinforced by *dicta* in the House of Lords: *Anyanwu v South Bank Students' Union* [2001] UKHL 14, [2001] IRLR 305 (see Lord Steyn at para 24, Lord Hope at para 39). See also *Balamoody v UK Central Council for Nursing, Midwifery and Health Visiting* [2001] EWCA Civ 2097, [2002] ICR 646, paras 31–50 and *HM Prison Service v Dolby* [2003] IRLR 694 and, for a similar approach to whistleblowing cases, *Boulding v Land Securities Trillium Ltd*, [2006] All ER (D) 158 (Nov), EAT, and *Ezsias v North Glamorgan NHS Trust* [2007] EWCA Civ 330, [2007] 4 All ER 940, [2007] ICR 1126, [2007] IRLR 603. The Court of Appeal in *Ezsias*, which has come to be regarded as the leading case on striking out claims as misconceived, emphasised that it would only be in exceptional cases that it would be appropriate to strike out a claim where the central facts were in dispute and the evidence relating to them had not been heard; an example of an exceptional situation might be where the facts asserted by one party were clearly and directly contradicted by contemporaneous documentation.

The approach applied in *Ezsias* was affirmed by the Court of Appeal in *A v B and C* [2010] EWCA Civ 1378, where the court refused to strike the claim out despite evident weaknesses in it, because there were significant factual issues which could only be resolved by evidence. In *Timbo v Grenwich Council for Racial Equality* (UKEAT/0160/12) the EAT overturned a decision to strike out in a discrimination claim as misconceived even though the application was made at the end of the Claimant's evidence at the final hearing and after the Respondent's statements had been read by the tribunal. The tribunal ought to have evaluated the core factual dispute in light of all the evidence. As the EAT said: "It is one thing to reach, at the half time stage, a provisional view that a witness's evidence is unsatisfactory and that it is unlikely to be accepted if there is evidence to the contrary. It is another thing altogether to reach a concluded view that a witness's evidence must inevitably be rejected in its entirety even if there is no evidence to contradict it" (para 48).

An example of the striking out of a discrimination claim where the factual basis for inferring discrimination was considered to be simply too weak to establish an arguable case is *ABN AMRO Management Services Ltd v Hogben* (UKEAT/0266/09), where a claim of age discrimination (in selecting employees for alternative posts in a redundancy situation) relied on comparators both younger and older than the claimant. Where the claim as pleaded is legally misconceived, striking out is fully justified; good recent examples are *Hadfield v Health and Safety Executive* (UKEATS/0013/10) and *Hawkins v Atex Group Ltd* [2012] IRLR 807.

A possible solution to the problem in cases involving factual disputes is exemplified by *Eastman v Tesco Stores Ltd* [2012] All ER (D) 264. There, the tribunal heard evidence on the core area of factual dispute at the PHR dealing with the strike out application (the core issue was whether there had been express agreement to employment continuing through a four year career break). Having heard that evidence, and resolved it against the claimant, the tribunal struck out the complaint for having no reasonable prospects of success. The EAT endorsed that approach and distinguished the case from those where no evidence is heard at the PHR and the factual disputes remain unresolved at the PHR.

The Court of Appeal has held that where the central issue is the construction of a written contract, one must be careful not to take the suggestion that the case should be determined at trial with fuller investigation into the facts too far. Whilst the factual matrix is key to understanding what the parties must have intended by the words they used, it far from follows that the need to know what that matrix was requires a full trial with discovery, evidence and cross examination: see Jacob LJ at paras 4–5 in *Khatri v Cooperateive Centrale RaifeisenBoerenleenbank BA* [2010] IRLR 715 (a case involving summary judgment under the *CPR 1998*).

One consequence of changes introduced by the *2004 Regulations* is that, as noted above, the questions whether a deposit should be ordered or an order made to strike out all or part of a claim or response can both be dealt with at a PHR. As striking out is a more drastic remedy – what has been described as showing the 'Red card' (as compared to the 'Yellow card' of a deposit order and costs warning: see *HM Prison Service v Dolby* [2003] IRLR 694) – tribunals can be expected to consider the merits of the case more rigorously when considering that sanction. One important difference between the two powers is that evidence can be called in support of or in opposition to a strike-out application under *rule 18* but not where the only issue is whether to make a deposit order and give a costs warning. It is open to a party (and advisable in practice) to apply for both orders in the alternative.

The conduct of a representative, as well as a party, may be grounds for striking out the party's case under *(b)* above, and it is not open to the party to 'disown' the representative: *Harmony Healthcare plc v Drewery* (EAT/866/00) (respondent's representative assaulting claimant's representative in waiting room). However, the tribunal should only use the drastic sanction of striking out a claim or defence if this is a proportionate response to the offence: *Bennett v Southwark London Borough Council* [2002] EWCA Civ 223, [2002] IRLR 407, a case with helpful guidance on what constitutes 'scandalous' conduct. See also *Bolch v Chipman* [2004] IRLR 140, where guidance was given by the EAT both as to the procedure to be followed and the basis for making a strike-out order, in a case where the unreasonable conduct alleged was a threat of violence. The EAT stressed that the ground for striking out is not simply unreasonable *behaviour* but *conducting the proceedings* in an unreasonable manner.

Even where there has been unreasonable conduct on the part of a party or representative, the tribunal must still consider whether striking out the claim or response would be a proportionate sanction, and in particular whether a fair trial is still possible (in which case striking out would rarely be proportionate). The Court of Appeal has commented that it will only be in a very unusual case that it would be justified to strike out on procedural grounds a claim which has reached the point of trial: *James v Blockbuster Entertainment Ltd* [2006] EWCA Civ 684, [2006] IRLR 630. An example of a case where striking out was held to be justified because a fair trial was no longer possible (because of intimidation of the claimant by a director of the respondent outside the tribunal) is *Force One Utilities Ltd v Hatfield* [2009] IRLR 45, EAT.

The question what amounts to unreasonable or vexatious conduct may arise in relation to the claimant's persistence in a claim when the respondent is prepared to concede all or part of the claim. In this connection it is important to remember that the remedies available to the claimant may include a declaration (that he or she has been unlawfully discriminated against, or unfairly dismissed) as well as compensation. Thus it has been held not to be vexatious for a claimant to pursue his or her claim for unfair dismissal even after the respondent has offered to pay the maximum sum which the tribunal could award, so long as the respondent has not admitted that the dismissal was unfair (*Telephone Information Services Ltd v Wilkinson* [1991] IRLR 148). In *Nicolson Highlandwear v Nicolson* [2010]

IRLR 859, the EAT held in awarding expenses to the respondent that it was unreasonable of a claimant to pursue a claim of unfair dismissal leading to a finding that the dismissal was procedurally unfair but with a nil award of compensation, but the *Wilkinson* case was not cited and the authority of *Nicholson* on this point is therefore doubtful. On the other hand, a claimant who decides at the last moment to withdraw a claim, thereby causing the respondent unnecessary work and expense in preparing for the case, may well be held to have acted unreasonably in delaying the withdrawal: *McPherson v BNP Paribas (London Branch)* [2004] EWCA Civ 569, [2004] 3 All ER 266, [2004] IRLR 558 (a case on liability for costs in such circumstances).

Where *res judicata* or issue estoppel (see **18.26** below) does not apply, the party seeking an order to strike out the other party's case must show that there is a special reason why relitigation of the issue would be an abuse of process and therefore vexatious (*Department of Education and Science v Taylor* [1992] IRLR 308; and see *Blaik v Post Office* [1994] IRLR 280 and *Staffordshire County Council v Barber* [1996] ICR 379 on the principles applicable where a claimant who has failed in, or withdrawn, a claim under domestic law attempts to pursue the same point by way of a claim based on EU law).

The last two grounds for striking out apply only to a claim, and are closely related. The fourth ground, that a fair trial is no longer possible, was introduced by the *2004 Regulations*. The occasions when it would be appropriate to strike out a claim on either ground will be very rare. An example of when a fair trial is no longer possible would be where a case has been adjourned on several occasions, over such a period that witnesses are either no longer available or liable to have no recollection of relevant events. To this extent it overlaps with the power to strike out a claim which has not been actively pursued: it is unlikely that such a claim would be struck out whilst the possibility of a fair trial remains, unless the claimant has clearly indicated that he or she no longer intends to pursue the claim.

The leading authority on the test to be applied where it is asserted that the claim has not been actively pursued is *Evans v Metropolitan Police Comr* [1993] ICR 151, [1992] IRLR 570 which held that *Birkett v James* [1978] AC 297, in turn the leading case on the equivalent rule in civil cases, applied to employment tribunals. *Birkett v James* holds that claims should not be struck out unless there has either been intentional or contumelious default by the claimant, or inordinate and inexcusable delay leading to a substantial risk that a fair trial will not be possible, or to substantial prejudice to the respondent.

Four cases in which applications to strike the claim out because it had not been actively pursued are *Peixoto v British Telecommunications plc* [2008] All ER (D) 240 (May), where the hearing had been delayed for three years by the claimant's illness and there was no prognosis as to when she would be fit to give evidence; the EAT upheld the order striking out the claim made by the tribunal; *Rolls Royce plc v Riddle* [2008] IRLR 873, where the claimant failed to attend a hearing and was unable to support his claim to have been too ill to attend with medical evidence; in this case the EAT overruled the tribunal's decision not to strike out the claim; *Abegaze v Shrewsbury College of Arts and Technology* [2009] EWCA Civ 96, [2010] IRLR 238, where the claim had been struck out (both for this reason and because a fair trial was no longer possible) after a seven year delay, following a finding for the claimant on liability, caused in part by the claimant failing to take the steps necessary for the holding of a remedy hearing, but the Court of Appeal, reversing the EAT, held that the claim should not be struck out because rigorous case management orders could still achieve a fair hearing on remedy, and striking the claim out after liability had been established was therefore a disproportionate sanction; and *Balls v Downham Market High School & College* [2011] IRLR 217, where the EAT held that the tribunal had been in error in striking out a claim which had been combined with a claim by the claimant's wife, also employed by the same respondent; the wife's claim had been struck out after she was imprisoned for theft from the respondent, but the EAT accepted that the claimant's case was separate from his wife's, and that he had been trying unsuccessfully to reactivate it after being exonerated in relation to the theft.

The Court of Appeal's view in *Abegaze* was significantly influenced by the fact that the claimant had already secured a finding in his favour on liability, and would therefore be deprived of his remedy if the claim was struck out. Nevertheless the contrast between the extreme delay in *Abegaze* and the facts of *Rolls Royce*, above, suggests that the decision of the EAT in the latter case is out of line with the later Court of Appeal decision and should not now be regarded as authoritative.

18.18 RESTRICTED REPORTING ORDERS

Some employment tribunal cases involving allegations of sexual misconduct attract considerable publicity in the media, all too often prurient and embarrassing to those involved. In order to diminish the adverse effect on the parties of such publicity, the *ET* and *EAT Rules* contain powers for tribunals and the EAT respectively to restrict publication of material identifying those involved in such cases. These were first given by the *1993 ET Regulations* and *EAT Rules*, which introduced the power to make restricted reporting orders and register deletion orders. Equivalent powers were introduced by the *Disability Discrimination Act 1995* for cases where evidence of a personal nature is to be given (see now the *ETA 1996, ss 12* and *32*). The provisions relating to restricted reporting orders are now contained in *rules 50* and *51* of the *ET Rules*, and *rules 23* and *23A* of the *EAT Rules*. See **18.19** below for details of register deletion orders.

A restricted reporting order may be made by the tribunal of its own motion or on the application of a party. The precondition is that the case involves allegations of sexual misconduct. This is not limited to claims of discrimination by sexual harassment; it may include cases where the applicant's dismissal was for an alleged sexual offence (see eg *Securicor Guarding Ltd v R* [1994] IRLR 633) or any other proceedings in which allegations of sexual misconduct are expected to form part of the evidence, and regardless of whether or not the allegations can be substantiated: *X v Stevens* [2003] IRLR 411. 'Sexual misconduct' means a sexual offence, sexual harassment or other adverse conduct, of whatever nature, related to sex: *ETA 1996, s 11(6)*. The criterion in disability discrimination cases is whether 'evidence of a personal nature' is likely to be given (*ET Rules, rule 50(1)(b)*).

The primary purpose of a restricted reporting order is to protect parties, and sometimes witnesses, from being placed under inappropriate pressure when giving evidence by the fear of the publicity that may be given to their evidence.

It prohibits, subject to criminal penalty, the publication in Great Britain of any matter likely to lead members of the public to identify a person as the person making, or a person affected by, the allegations of misconduct or, in a disability case, to identify the complainant or any other person named in the order (*ETA 1996, ss 11(2), 12(3)*). The scope of the power to make orders enables protection to be given not only to the alleged victim and miscreant in a sexual misconduct case, but also the employer, and individual employee respondents to the claim, if not directly covered otherwise. However, the EAT has ruled (departing from a previous decision) that a body corporate cannot be the subject of a restricted reporting order (*Leicester University v A* [1999] IRLR 352, following *R v London (North) Industrial Tribunal, ex p Associated Newspapers Ltd* [1998] ICR 1212 in preference to *M v Vincent* [1998] ICR 73). The tribunal must specify the persons who must not be identified (*ET Rules, rule 50(8)(a)*). It is open to the tribunal to specify in the order that particular persons must not be named, not in order to protect their identity but because identifying them would lead to the identification of those for whose protection the order is made: *Tradition Securities & Futures SA v Times Newspapers Ltd* [2009] IRLR 354.

A restricted reporting order (other than a temporary order, for which see below) may only be made either at a PHR or at a Hearing, after the parties have been given an opportunity to make oral submissions as to whether an order should be made and as to the terms of any order; it is one of the categories of order that may not be made at a Case Management Discussion (CMD) (*ET Rules, rules 17(2), 18(7)(g), 50(2), (6)*). Because of the wider public interest in justice being dispensed publicly, tribunals should not automatically order a restriction on publication simply – indeed especially – because both parties seek it: *X v Z Ltd* [1998] ICR 43, CA. The point was followed in *R v London (North) Industrial Tribunal, ex p Associated Newspapers Ltd* (above), in which Keene J stated that the words 'a person affected by the allegations of misconduct' should be interpreted narrowly, having regard to the principle of the freedom of the press to report court and tribunal proceedings fully and contemporaneously. In *Vatish v Crown Prosecution Service* (UKEAT/0164/11) the EAT set aside an order made to protect a witness who had not asked for protection and whose evidence had already been given by the time the order was made.

The wider interest in public justice is reflected in a new provision in the *2004 ET Rules* giving interested parties (in practice this will almost always be media representatives) the right to make representations at the hearing at which the decision is made whether to impose an order *(rule 50(7))*. The *rules* do not contain any equivalent provision allowing interested parties to apply for the revocation of an order, but the Court of Session, overruling the EAT, has held that tribunals can entertain applications from the press for an order to be revoked: *Davidson v Dallas McMillan* [2009] CSIH 70, [2010] IRLR 439. In addition, as the EAT noted in *Dallas McMillan*, it is open to press organisations to apply to be joined as parties to the proceedings for the purpose of making such an application; this was done in *Tradition Securities*, above.

A new power was introduced by the 2004 *ET Rules* enabling a Judge to make a temporary restricted reporting order, either on application by a party or of his or her own motion, and either without any hearing, or at a CMD. The parties must be notified of a temporary order and informed of their right to apply for the continuance of the order; if no party applies within 14 days, the order lapses, but if an application to continue it is made, the order remains in force until the question whether it should be continued can be determined, either at a PHR or at the full Hearing (*ET Rules, rule 50(2)–(5)*). This is a useful provision to deal with the situation where a party anticipates media interest in the case and seeks emergency protection from publicity.

A restricted reporting order remains in force until the promulgation of the final judgment in the case, unless revoked earlier. The EAT in the *Tradition Securities* case, above, held that an application to revoke, or vary the terms of, an order should only be entertained if there has been a change in the relevant circumstances since the order was made; but such changes may include the fact that a representative of the press, having become aware of the order, seeks to have the order revoked or varied, or that a party for whose benefit the order was made now no longer wishes to have the protection afforded.

Once a final judgment has been given, the restriction on reporting the identities of those covered by the order falls away. This underlines the point that the purpose of the order is not to provide indefinite or permanent anonymity for the individuals covered by the order, but rather to ensure that they are not unduly pressured by the fear of publicity in giving their evidence. Where the judgment is given separately on liability and the tribunal will need to hold a further hearing to decide on remedy, the order remains in force until the final remedy judgment is issued: *ET Rules, rule 50(8)(b)*, confirming the effect of *Chief Constable of West Yorkshire Police v A* [2001] ICR 128. The tribunal has no power to entertain an application for the revocation of an order once the proceedings are at an end: see *Davidson v Dallas McMillan*, above, where the point was expressly confirmed by the Court of Session. This has the consequence that if the claim is settled after liability has been determined but before a remedy hearing is concluded, or is withdrawn, the order will remain in force indefinitely.

A notice drawing attention to the existence of the order must be placed on the tribunal door (*ET Rules, rule 50(8)(c)*). Guidance as to the scope and dissemination of orders has also been given by the High Court in *R v Southampton Industrial Tribunal, ex p INS News Group Ltd* [1995] IRLR 247.

The relatively narrow category of cases in which orders can be made, and the limited duration of the protection conferred by an order, may result in individuals who would be embarrassed, or might be subjected to harassment, if their identity was publicised, being deterred from bringing claims by the lack of protection available. Considerations of this kind led the tribunal in the *West Yorkshire* case, above, to hold that there is a further power to order restrictions on reporting tribunal proceedings in any case where this is necessary to ensure that a claimant seeking to assert enforceable rights under EU law (in this case a remedy for refusal to engage the claimant as a police officer because she was a transsexual) is not deterred from doing so by fear of publicity. The basis for this decision was the requirement of *art 6* of the *Equal Treatment Directive 1976* for member states to afford access to effective remedies for victims of unlawful sex discrimination. This point was expressly left open by the EAT in the *West Yorkshire* case, but in *X v Stevens*, above, it held that both the EAT under its inherent jurisdiction, and tribunals using their powers under *ET Rules 2001, rule 15(1)* (now *ET Rules, rules 14(3)* and *60(1)*) to regulate their own procedure, could make restricted reporting orders where this was necessary in order to prevent a claimant from being deterred from pursuing a claim, and regardless of whether the statutory conditions for a restricted reporting order or register deletion order were met and whether the respondent was or was not a state authority.

Whilst the basis for this power was initially stated to be the effective enforcement of rights under EU law, an alternative, and wider power may be derived from the obligation of a tribunal (and the EAT) as a public body to give effect so far as it can to the rights safeguarded by the *European Convention on Human Rights*: this is required by the *Human Rights Act 1998, s 6*. The rights protected include those to privacy under *Art 8*; in an appropriate case the conferring of anonymity on a party or witness may be justified as a means of safeguarding that person's *Art 8* rights. The EAT in *A v B* [2010] IRLR 844 (supplementary judgment at p 856) has applied this principle to justify the making of a permanent anonymity order in relation to an appeal where the claimant had been the subject of unsubstantiated allegations of paedophile activities, and the approach taken in that case could, it is suggested, apply equally in a case in the employment tribunal where the safeguarding of the anonymity of a party is considered to be required to secure the protection of his or her *Art 8* rights but the *ET Rules* do not cater for the circumstances. A similar conclusion was reached in *B and C v A* [2010] IRLR 400, where the EAT considered a permanent anonymity order to be justified to protect a complainant of sexual violence (not the claimant in the case).

The reliance in these cases on *Art 8* of the *Convention* provides a basis also for orders to be made protecting the identity of those who are not parties, or even witnesses, in the proceedings, where identification would be a sufficiently serious and unjustified interference with their privacy. This point was confirmed by the EAT in *F v G* [2012] ICR 246, where a permanent order was made to protect the identity of severely disabled students at the respondent college in circumstances where evidence about their sexual lives would be given in the course of the proceedings. The judgment of Underhill P in this case contains a full and helpful discussion of the range of orders that may be made and the basis for each.

In practice it is relatively common that privacy is afforded to individuals who feature in the evidence in a case, such as children or medical patients, by a direction that they are not to be identified by name in the course of evidence, and avoiding identification in the judgment.

For discussion of the equivalent provisions governing appeals to the EAT, see **18.26** below.

18.19 Where allegations of a sexual offence are involved, there was prior to 2004 a separate power to make a 'register deletion order'. This had the effect of requiring that the public register of judgments and any other public documents generated in the proceedings were modified so as to prevent identification of persons making or affected by the allegation (*ETA 1996, s 11(1)(a)*). Under the *2004 Regulations* (*ET Rules, rule 49*), it is no longer necessary to have an order of the tribunal; the rule simply imposes a requirement on the Judge, and the Secretary in preparing judgments and reasons for placing on the register, to delete any matter likely to identify persons making or affected by the allegations in any case where it appears that there are allegations of a sexual offence. This provision applies indefinitely, and is mandatory. In practice, in any doubtful case the matter is likely to be referred to the Judge who heard the case for a ruling. Following the abolition of the register of applications in October 2004, the principal importance of *rule 49* is that the identity of affected parties remains concealed after the promulgation of the final judgment in the case. However, as was stressed by the EAT in *F v G*, above, this provision only applies where there is an allegation of a sexual offence; the broader powers established in *A v B* and *F v G* must therefore be used in any other case where there is a sufficiently pressing need for the protection of any individual's *Art 8* rights.

18.20 MISCELLANEOUS POWERS OF THE TRIBUNAL

In addition to the general power of the tribunal to issue orders, and to regulate its own procedure (as to which see respectively *ET Rules, rules10(1), 14(3)* and *60(1)*)), there are a number of specific powers given to the tribunal, which can be exercised in most cases by an Employment Judge rather than a full tribunal (see *rule 10(1)*)).

18.21 Extension of time

An Employment Judge may extend the time appointed by or under the *ET Rules* for doing any act, whether or not the time has expired (*rule 10(2)(e)*). However this is subject to the qualification that time may only be extended for certain purposes if the Judge considers that it is just and equitable to do so; this qualification applies to the extension of time for submitting a response, for applying for a review or a costs or preparation time order, and for applying for written reasons for a judgment where reasons were given orally. In addition, time may only be extended for the purpose of submitting a response to the claim if an application has been made before the time limit expired: *rule 4(4)*; see however *Moroak (t/a Blake Envelopes) v Cromie* [2005] IRLR 535, holding that there is a power to review the non-acceptance of a late response, which may effectively circumvent this provision where the interests of justice so require.

There is no general provision in the *ET Rules* giving the converse power, to abridge time, but in limited circumstances a judge may abridge time, for instance when a party is given the opportunity to comment on an application made in accordance with *rule 11(4)* and a decision on the application is required urgently.

18.22 Stay of proceedings

The power to order a stay (or sist in Scotland) of proceedings is conferred by *ET Rules, rule 10(2)(h)*. A stay operates to suspend the proceedings, not to end them. Applications to stay tribunal proceedings are often made, and frequently granted, where there are concurrent proceedings in the High Court (or Court of Session) and the employment tribunal arising out of the same employment. Tribunal proceedings may also be stayed pending the outcome of foreign litigation (*JMCC Holdings Ltd v Conroy* [1990] ICR 179). Conversely, the tribunal might be seen as the more appropriate venue to determine the complaints before it ahead of proceedings elsewhere (see eg *BUQ v HRE* [2012] EWHC 2827 where the tribunal was acknowledged to be better placed than High Court to determine the truth or otherwise of disputed claims of sexual harassment). The EAT should only interfere with the tribunal's decision to postpone or continue with the proceedings before it if that decision resulted from an error of law or if it was perverse (*Carter v Credit Change Ltd* [1980] 1 All ER 252, [1979] ICR 908; *Automatic Switching Ltd v Brunet* [1986] ICR 542).

An example of a case where the EAT was persuaded to overturn the refusal of a stay is *GFI Holdings Ltd v Camm* [2008] All ER (D) 74 (Sep), where the claimant was pursuing a claim in the High Court for unpaid bonuses the determination of which would involve deciding issues that would also arise in his tribunal claim (for unfair dismissal). For further discussion of the factors to be taken into consideration, see *First Castle Electronics Ltd v West* [1989] ICR 72, *Bowater plc v Charlwood* [1991] ICR 798 and *Chorion plc v Lane* [1999] All ER (D) 194 (where the High Court proceedings had been brought by the former employer). The position has been restated by the EAT in *Mindimaxnox LLP v Gover* (UKEAT/0225/10) and *Paymentshield Group Holdings Ltd v Halstead* [2012] ICR D5, both cases where a stay was ordered by the EAT on the basis that there was a significant overlap between the issues to be decided in the tribunal and High Court proceedings (and, in the first case, with court proceedings in Cyprus). Other factors which may affect whether or not a stay of the tribunal proceedings should be granted are the delay that this may cause, the degree of complexity of the issues (complexity being a factor favouring giving priority to the High Court proceedings), the nature of the issues (see *BUQ* above), and the different costs regimes in the two jurisdictions, as well the relative importance of each set of proceedings and the stage each has reached. In *Paymentshield*, the fact that the High Court action had not been commenced (only a formal letter before action had been served) was held not to be a sufficient reason to displace the other factors favouring giving priority to the Court proceedings.

It may sometimes be appropriate for proceedings to be stayed pending the outcome of an appeal, or a reference to the CJEU, the result of which is likely to determine, or at least influence, the outcome of the particular case. In *Johns v Solent SD Ltd* [2008] IRLR 88, the EAT ordered a stay of a claim for unfair dismissal and age discrimination where the claimant alleged that she had been forced to retire, because the issue of the validity of the relevant provisions of the *Employment Equality (Age) Regulations 2006* had been referred to the CJEU in another case, and the EAT's decision was followed by a Practice Direction by the President of Tribunals that all similar cases should be stayed pending the CJEU's ruling.

A different reason for seeking a stay of the proceedings is that the parties wish to attempt to settle their dispute by alternative means, such as through mediation (see further **18.31**). Tribunals encourage the use of such alternatives to litigation. In Scotland this encouragement has been formalised into a Practice Direction on the sisting of cases for mediation, issued in December 2006.

One reason for staying tribunal proceedings where related proceedings between the parties are anticipated is that the doctrine of *res judicata* (ie that issues decided in one set of proceedings cannot be relitigated) may apply so as to bind the High Court later. This will only be true if precisely the same issue arises in both sets of proceedings (see *Munir v Jang Publications Ltd* [1989] ICR 1; *Crown Estate Comrs v Dorset County Council* [1990] Ch 297; *Soteriou v Ultrachem Ltd* [2004] EWHC 983 (QB), [2004] IRLR 870) and the decision of the tribunal on the particular point was necessary to the determination of the issues before it, and within its jurisdiction (see for both points *Bon Groundwork Ltd v Foster* [2012] IRLR 517, and for a discussion of the principles of *res judicata* see **18.26** and **18.27** below). A stay can necessarily only be granted once the proceedings to be stayed have been commenced, and there is no equivalent procedure to suspend the running of time limits for the bringing of tribunal proceedings. A claimant who wishes to bring both High Court (or county court) and tribunal proceedings, and to pursue the former first, should therefore present his or her claim to the tribunal within the statutory time limit and immediately apply for a stay pending the outcome of the other proceedings, explaining that the tribunal claim has been made at that time to ensure the claim is not time-barred (*Warnock v Scarborough Football Club* [1989] ICR 489).

Where the proceedings are for unfair dismissal of participants in industrial action, there is specific power for the tribunal to adjourn the proceedings where certain civil proceedings have been brought in relation to the industrial action (effectively a claim for an injunction or interdict) until those proceedings, including any appeal, have been determined (*ET Rules, rule 55*).

18.23 Joining additional parties and dismissing a party

It is sometimes necessary for a claimant to apply to join one or more additional respondents to the claim. This may arise, for instance, where the respondent originally named disputes that it is or was the employer, or an issue arises as to whether the claimant's employment was transferred to a third party following a transfer of the former employer's undertaking. The addition or substitution of parties by amendment is discussed further at **18.10**(i) and (j) above; and see generally *Birch v Walsall Metropolitan Borough Council* (UKEAT/0376/10) and *Enterprise Liverpool Ltd v Jonas* [2009] All ER (D) 115 (Aug).

A tribunal may at any time, on the application of any person or of its own motion, order that any person the Judge or tribunal considers may be liable for the remedy claimed be joined as a party to the proceedings (*Rule 10(2)(k)*). Joinder may be ordered by a Judge alone or by a full tribunal. An important limitation on the power of joinder, before it was removed as part of the revision of the *ET Rules* in 2004, was that a party could not be joined unless relief was sought against him or her by another party. In practice this was the claimant, since there was (and still is), except in the special cases referred to in the following paragraph, no power for the tribunal to make orders for contribution between respondents, and orders for disclosure of documents or further particulars are not 'relief'. The 2004 *ET Rules* meet this difficulty by giving the Judge power to join any person he or she considers has an interest in the outcome of the proceedings. The new power (contained in *Rule 10(2)(r)*) is also wide enough to permit an interested third party such as a trade union to be joined where a claim is in the nature of a test case with implications for its members generally, or for press organisations to be joined in order to apply for the revocation of a restricted reporting order (see **18.18** above). However the EAT has held that a party may only be joined on an application by an existing party to the proceedings who wishes to make a claim against the party to be joined, or on application by the person seeking to be joined; a Judge cannot join a third party on his or her own initiative: *Beresford v Sovereign House Estates Ltd* [2012] ICR D9. The rule does not in terms state that joinder is as a respondent but that is the practice: there is no category of 'interested party' (as there is in some High Court proceedings) and it would be inappropriate to join a party under *rule 10(2)(r)* as a claimant. (The position is different if a claim has been brought by the wrong claimant and there is an application to substitute the correct claimant: an example is *Enterprise Liverpool Ltd v Jonas* [2009] All ER (D) 115 (Aug), where the correct claimant for compensation for failure to consult employees affected by the transfer of an undertaking was the union, not the individual employee who had brought the initial claim: see further **18.10**(j).)

When either the employer or the complainant claims that dismissal was due to union pressure (see UNFAIR DISMISSAL – III (53)) a tribunal must grant an application to join the union as a party to proceedings if it is made before the hearing of the complaint, and may do so if the application is made after the commencement of the hearing but before an award is made (*TULRCA 1992, s 160(1), (2)*); the tribunal then has the power to order that the party joined pay some or all of any compensation awarded. A similar procedure operates under the *Transfer of Undertakings (Protection of Employment) Regulations 2006, reg 15(5)*), where a transferor facing a complaint of failure to inform employee representatives of measures envisaged by the transferee, who intends to allege that this was due to the default of the transferee in breach of *reg 13(4))*, must notify the transferee of this intention; in this case, notification automatically makes the transferee a party and no order of the tribunal is necessary (but the tribunal must be advised of the joinder so that the transferee can be informed of the hearing, etc).

Analogous issues can arise in discrimination cases, where a claim is brought against more than one respondent (typically the employer or former employer, and one or more individual managers said to have committed the acts of discrimination for which the employer is vicariously liable); the tribunal may in appropriate cases make an award against the respondents jointly and severally (see *Gilbank v Miles* [2006] EWCA Civ 543, [2006] IRLR 538 and *London Borough of Hackney v Sivanandan* [2013] IRLR 408, CA (see also the EAT's judgment at [2011] IRLR 740); the latter case establishes that unless the respondents are each responsible for clearly separate loss or damage suffered by the claimant, liability for compensation will always be joint and several). A joint and several award may be enforced in full against any of the respondents against whom it is made, a point of particular importance where (as in the cases cited) the employer has become insolvent. It is open to a respondent, as well as the claimant, to apply to have a further respondent joined, as was done in *Finlay v Cyron* (UKEAT/0121/11) (employer applying to join former manager alleged to have been the person responsible for the discrimination alleged by claimant).

A point which has posed difficulty is whether tribunals have power to make orders under the *Civil Liability (Contribution) Act 1978* for contribution between respondents who have been held jointly liable for an award of compensation. Although not the same as making a contribution order between respondents, a practice developed over time where tribunals did apportion liability between employer and employee respondents in discrimination claims so that each was separately liable to the claimant for that part of the compensation. In *Way v Crouch* [2005] IRLR 603, the EAT endorsed such apportionments as doing practical justice; however in *Sivanandan* (above), another division of the EAT disagreed, concluding that the tribunal had no power to make an apportionment (para 24). Way was ultimately overruled by the Court of Appeal in *Sivanandan* on this point (paras 82, 84). Following these decisions, the specific issue of contribution orders arose in *Brennan v Sunderland City Council* [2012] ICR 1183. The EAT held emphatically that the tribunal had no jurisdiction to entertain a claim under the *1978 Act* (para 19); such a claim should be made in the civil courts.

It is therefore important for a claimant alleging discrimination to consider whether to claim against individuals in addition to the employer. An application to add an individual respondent after the proceedings have been started is subject to the considerations referred to in **18.10** above.

There is a corresponding power to dismiss from the proceedings a respondent who is no longer directly interested in the proceedings: *rule 10(2)(l)*. Usually, the powers to join and dismiss parties will be exercised by a Judge on the papers or at a CMD, but they may if necessary be exercised by the full tribunal at a Hearing, or by the Judge at a PHR. Any dispute about the right of a party joined by the tribunal to contest the claim can be decided at a PHR (*rule 18(7)(a)*).

18.24 Powers in relation to multiple claims

Representative claimants or respondents. Where many people have the same interest in defending a claim, one or more of them may be cited as the person or persons against whom relief is sought, or may be authorised by the tribunal, before or at the hearing, to defend on behalf of all the persons so interested. This was formerly expressly provided for by the *ET Rules* (*ET Rules 2001, rule 19(3)*). There is no equivalent express provision in the 2004 *Rules*, but the general case management powers of the tribunal are sufficiently wide to cover the point (and see *Affleck v Newcastle Mind* [1999] IRLR 405 (claim against one member of a committee of unincorporated association on behalf of all the members of the committee)).

Consolidation. A tribunal may order that two or more applications be heard together, often, but technically incorrectly, referred to as consolidation of the proceedings. The relevant power is not subject to express restrictions on the circumstances of its use (see *rule10(2)(j)*). In practice an order is likely to be made if the same question of law or fact arises in each case, or if the remedy claimed in them arises out of the same set of facts, such as if several workers claim redundancy payments on the closure of a business, or if for some other reason it is desirable to hear the claims together; consolidation will also normally be appropriate if a claimant has brought more than one claim against the same respondent. The parties must have an opportunity to make representations before such an order is made (*rule 10(7)*).

Test cases. If there are a large number of claims raising the same question, some may be selected as lead, or test, cases, and attempts to reopen the issues thus determined in later cases may be struck out as an abuse of process (*Ashmore v British Coal Corpn* [1990] ICR 485; contrast *Department of Education and Science v Taylor* [1992] IRLR 308). The power to order test cases is not contained in a specific rule, but is part of the tribunal's general powers to regulate its own proceedings and to give directions. The large numbers of multiple claims for equal pay currently being brought against local authorities and NHS Trusts usually require the selection of test cases, and a high level of active case management, to keep the issues to be heard by the tribunal within manageable limits.

18.25 Transfer of proceedings

Where a claim is pending before an employment tribunal in England or Wales which could be determined by a tribunal in Scotland, and it is more convenient to do so, the claim can be transferred to Scotland, and vice versa (*rule 21*). However this facility is only available if proceedings have been commenced in a tribunal which has jurisdiction to determine the claim; transfer to the other jurisdiction after the relevant time limit has expired does not operate retrospectively to bring the claim within time: see *McFadyen v PB Recovery Ltd* (UKEATS/0072/08), and the discussion at **17.21** above.

18.26 Estoppel and prevention of abuse of process

One important aspect of preventing abuse of the tribunal's process is the prevention of the relitigation of issues previously decided, or which could have been decided by the tribunal in earlier proceedings between the parties. This requires consideration of the legal doctrine of estoppel. There are a number of relevant forms of estoppel which may be relied on in tribunal proceedings: these are cause of action estoppel, which prevents the relitigation of a *claim* which has already been decided between the parties; issue estoppel, which may prevent a party from seeking to pursue a claim dependent on *facts* which are the subject of a prior and contrary finding in proceedings between the same parties; and a wider form of issue estoppel (sometimes referred to as the rule in *Henderson v Henderson* (1843) 3 Hare 100) which lays down that parties to litigation must bring forward their whole case and, except in special circumstances, will not be permitted to bring fresh proceedings in a matter which could and should have been litigated in earlier proceedings, but was omitted through negligence, inadvertence or accident. The first two forms of estoppel (often referred to collectively as *res judicata*) are considered further in **18.27** and **18.28** below.

For an example of the operation of the rule in *Henderson v Henderson*, in the context of an employment tribunal claim, see *Sheriff v Klyne Tugs (Lowestoft) Ltd* [1999] IRLR 481 (action for personal injury allegedly caused by racial harassment struck out by the Court of Appeal, as this claim could and should have been pursued as part of the claimant's tribunal claim of racial discrimination against the same employers, which had been settled).

The principle to be applied in deciding whether it is an abuse of process to pursue a claim which could have been raised in prior proceedings was reviewed and restated by the House of Lords in *Johnson v Gore Wood* [2002] 2 AC 1, where Lord Bingham summarised the principles (at p 31) as being that the court or tribunal must consider whether in all the circumstances the bringing of proceedings is an abuse of process; the circumstances will include whether the proceedings are brought against the same defendant or respondent, why the claimant failed to include the issues now pursued in the earlier proceedings and whether the later action involves unjust harassment or oppression of the party sued. The EAT has confirmed that it is these principles that should be applied, not a narrower approach based on an earlier decision of the Court of Appeal, *Divine-Bortey v Brent London Borough Council* [1998] ICR 886: see *Parker v Northumberland Water* [2011] IRLR 652. The onus is on the respondent to establish abuse of process. See also *Thomas v Devon County Council* [2008] All ER (D) 236 (Feb), EAT (where after withdrawing one claim, the claimant was permitted to proceed with a second claim in the absence of any prejudice to the respondent).

A related but equally venerable doctrine, of the merger of causes of action, arose in *Fraser v HLMAD Ltd* [2006] EWCA Civ 738, [2006] IRLR 687, where it was held that a successful claim under the tribunal's contractual jurisdiction precluded the claimant from then bringing High Court proceedings to recover the balance of the damages for wrongful dismissal. His claim had been valued by the tribunal at some £80,000, but its power to make an award under the *Extension of Jurisdiction Order 1994* was (and is) limited to £25,000, and the merger of his claim prevented him from pursuing the balance through separate proceedings.

18.27   The doctrines of cause of action and issue estoppel both apply to employment tribunals. The principle is that a decision on a specific claim or issue which has either not been appealed, or has been affirmed on appeal, is binding in any future litigation between the same parties, even if the decision was wrong in fact or law. Thus in *Watt (formerly Carter) v Ahsan* [2007] UKHL 51, [2008] 2 WLR 17, [2008] ICR 82, the House of Lords held that a tribunal was bound to follow a previous decision in earlier proceedings between the parties although in the meantime the Court of Appeal had held in unrelated proceedings that the interpretation of the relevant law which the tribunal had applied in the first case was wrong; in the result the tribunal was bound in law to apply an incorrect interpretation of the law in the second proceedings.

The doctrine of cause of action estoppel applies equally to a judicial decision by an Employment Judge to dismiss a claim; this prevents the relitigation of the claim between the same parties where it has already been the subject of a binding determination dismissing the claim, even though that may have been as a consequence of withdrawal by the claimant, and not a considered conclusion reached after the hearing of the case. This kind of estoppel has been the subject of three decisions of the Court of Appeal, which are not easily reconciled.

(1)   In *Lennon v Birmingham City Council* [2001] IRLR 826, the claimant had brought tribunal proceedings alleging sex discrimination resulting in a stress-related illness. She withdrew the proceedings before the hearing, and they were dismissed by the tribunal at her request. She then commenced county court proceedings in respect of stress-related ill health based on the same allegations (of offensive and intimidatory behaviour by fellow employees). The Court of Appeal, following *Barber v Staffordshire County Council* [1996] 2 All ER 748, [1996] IRLR 209, held that the county court claim was rightly struck out as an attempt to relitigate matters which had been judicially determined by the tribunal's decision dismissing her earlier claim.

(2)   However in *Sajid v Sussex Muslim Society* [2001] EWCA Civ 1684, [2002] IRLR 113, a contrary conclusion was reached where the claimant had initially brought a breach of contract claim in the tribunal which he quantified well in excess of the maximum the tribunal could award, and then withdrew that claim specifically in order that he could pursue it in the High Court. *Barber* was distinguished because the withdrawal and subsequent dismissal of the claim was done with a view to pursuing the dispute elsewhere and not intended to determine the dispute.

(3)   Finally in *Ako v Rothschild Asset Management Ltd* [2002] EWCA Civ 236, [2002] 2 All ER 693, [2002] ICR 899, on facts materially indistinguishable from *Lennon*, the court nevertheless held that it was necessary and permissible to look at the surrounding circumstances; tribunals, unlike courts, did not have a procedure for discontinuance of proceedings (which does not trigger an estoppel), and if in substance the withdrawal was a discontinuance it should not bar fresh proceedings based on the same facts.

The gap in the *ET Rules* identified in *Ako* has since been rectified by a new provision in the *2004 ET Rules*, allowing for withdrawal without dismissal of the proceedings necessarily following: see **18.28** below for details. The EAT has held that these changes remove the basis for the exception to the general principles of cause of action estoppel created by *Ako*: see *Cokayne v British Association of Shooting and Conservation* [2008] ICR 185, discussed below. In any case where rights of future action may need to be preserved it is important for a claimant to make clear to the respondent and the tribunal why he or she is withdrawing his or her claim. Mummery LJ in *Ako* also recommends that tribunals ask claimants to state the reason for withdrawal before making an order dismissing the claim. This approach was further endorsed by the EAT in *Verdin v Harrods Ltd* [2006] IRLR 339 when discussing how the tribunals should approach cases where consent for an order dismissal a claim on withdrawal is not given (see para. 39).

Issue estoppel is a narrower principle: where a court or tribunal of competent jurisdiction has decided an issue of fact in proceedings between parties, those parties are then bound by that finding in any subsequent proceedings between them. The principle applies to decisions of employment tribunals which either have been upheld on appeal or not appealed, but only if the determination of the particular issue was within the jurisdiction of the tribunal and necessary to its decision. A case where neither of these conditions was satisfied is *Bon Groundwork v Foster* [2012] IRLR 517, where the tribunal in earlier proceedings between the parties had held that the claimant had not been dismissed for redundancy in circumstances where it had no jurisdiction to decide the point because the claimant had not been dismissed at all at the time of his claim.

The related Scots law doctrine of *lis alibi pendens*, under which a claim will be barred if it is the same as a claim already raised in litigation pending between the same parties, does not as such apply to employment tribunal proceedings: *Lynch v East Dunbartonshire Council* [2010] ICR 1094. However the fact of a second claim being brought in these circumstances may provide grounds for the striking out of the second claim under *rule 18(7)* as vexatious, a point which would apply equally in English proceedings. The case itself did not justify this characterisation, as the second proceedings had been brought to protect the claimants' position after the respondents had challenged the competency of the first proceedings on the question whether the claimants had complied with the statutory grievance procedure, as then required by the *Employment Act 2002, s 32*. For an example of the application of the principles of *res judicata* in Scots Law, and an explanation of the principles, see *Holmes v Greater Glasgow Health Board* (UKEATS/0045/11) (claim for sick pay struck out where previous claim in respect of an earlier period of the same absence had been dismissed).

In *Christou v London Borough of Haringey* [2013] EWCA Civ 178, the Court of Appeal held that a decision taken by an employer on an internal disciplinary complaint did not constitute a determination of an issue which establishes the existence of a legal right. Accordingly, the doctrine of res judicata is not applicable to such decisions.

18.28 Withdrawal and dismissal of claims

The claimant may withdraw his or her claim at any stage in the proceedings. This may be done because a settlement has been reached, or because the claimant does not want to proceed with the claim, or wishes to pursue the issue through other proceedings. Prior to the coming into force of the 2004 *ET Rules*, the practice if a claimant withdrew the claim was for the tribunal to issue a formal order dismissing it. Some of the potential difficulties that this could cause are set out at **18.27** above. The *ET Rules* introduced a new procedure (*Rule 25*), but this rule was drafted in terms described by the Court of Appeal as 'lamentable' (*Khan v Heywood & Middleton Primary Care Trust* [2006] IRLR 793). The claimant must notify the tribunal in writing of his or her wish to withdraw the claim or a particular part of it, and as against which respondent or respondents (if there are more than one) it is withdrawn. Alternatively, a claim or part thereof may be withdrawn orally at a hearing. A withdrawal takes effect immediately and (to the extent of the withdrawal) brings proceedings to an end without any further action by the Tribunal (see *Khan*).The withdrawal is then notified by the tribunal to the other parties. (As to withdrawal of part of a claim, see *Verdin v Harrods Ltd*, below.)

The fact that a claimant absents him or herself from a hearing does not necessarily amount to the withdrawal of the claim: *Smith v Greenwich Council* [2011] ICR 277, EAT. In that case the claimant had asked for an adjournment to give him time to work on the case; when this was (as he believed) refused, he indicated his intention to appeal and left the hearing. The EAT held that this was not withdrawal by conduct, not least because the statement that he intended to appeal was inconsistent with withdrawing the claim. The tribunal should only have treated the claim as withdrawn if the claimant had said expressly that he was withdrawing his claim. Tribunals have also been advised by the EAT not to treat a claimant as having withdrawn or abandoned part of his or her claim, or a particular contention, without making sure that that is the claimant's intention, and that he or she understands the consequences of doing so: *Segor v Goodrich Actuation Systems Ltd* (UKEAT/0145/11).

Once notice of withdrawal of the claim has been given, it cannot be revoked by the claimant: *Khan* (above). However the claim will only be *dismissed* if the respondent applies for an order to that effect. The application must be made within 28 days of the notice of withdrawal being sent to the respondent; the time limit can be extended if a Judge considers it just and equitable to do so (*ET Rules, rule 25(3), (4), (5)*).

The effect of withdrawal of a claim has been explained by the EAT in *Verdin v Harrods Ltd* [2006] IRLR 339. The consequence of withdrawal, without more, is that the proceedings automatically come to an end, but the claimant is not precluded from pursuing the claim in other proceedings (including further proceedings in the tribunal, subject to the applicable time limits); if the tribunal claim has been dismissed, however, the bringing of further proceedings (in the tribunal or elsewhere) is likely to be regarded as an abuse of process. The last point has now been made clear by an amendment to *rule 25(4)* made by the *2008 Regulations* which makes it explicit that once a claim has been dismissed, the claimant cannot commence a further claim against the respondent for the same, or substantially the same, cause of action unless the decision to dismiss the first claim is successfully reviewed or appealed.

Because of the consequences for a claimant of dismissal of the claim, there is no automatic right to an order dismissing the claim; indeed the claimant has the right to apply for a review of such an order, or to appeal against it (*rule 25(4)*). In this way, the potential difficulties of withdrawal for claimants discussed in **18.27** above should be avoided. However, in order to avoid the possibility of an order for dismissal of the claim being made in such circumstances, a claimant should explain to the tribunal when withdrawing the claim the basis on which it is being withdrawn, and whether there is any reason not to dismiss the claim. In *Cokayne v British Association for Shooting and Conservation* [2008] ICR 185, the claimant withdrew a constructive dismissal claim he had presented before the grievance procedure had been completed, and failed to explain that this was in order to re-present the claim after his grievance appeal was rejected. The first claim was dismissed and the EAT held that that presented a bar to the second claim, because the complaint of constructive dismissal was made *res judicata* by the dismissal of the first claim. It did not matter that the claimant had made clear to the respondent his intention to bring the second claim, or that the second claim was not in the general sense an abuse of process, since there are no exceptions to the operation of *res judicata* in this context. This clearly presents a trap for unwary claimants: the only solution in the particular case was for the claimant to apply for a review of the dismissal of the withdrawn claim, a step encouraged by the EAT. Consistently, in *Verdin* (above), the EAT identified the following two questions as being relevant to whether a dismissal order should be made. Is the withdrawing party intending to abandon the claim? If the withdrawing party is intending to resurrect the claim in fresh proceedings, would it be an abuse of process to allow that to occur? (see para 39).

Where a claim is withdrawn but not dismissed, the file will be closed and retained for a year before being destroyed; however it is open to any party to make an application for costs or a preparation time order. A subsequent claim based on the same facts as such a claim might nonetheless amount to an abuse of process under *rule 18(7)(b)* and therefore be dismissed: see eg *Mills v London Borough of Brent* (UKEAT/0545/11).

The *2008 Regulations* have introduced a new procedure, in *rule 25A*, for the automatic dismissal of cases where there has been an ACAS-conciliated settlement, recorded in writing, and the parties have confirmed as part of their agreement that the claim should be dismissed following withdrawal by the claimant. Once the claimant then notifies the tribunal that the claim is withdrawn, and the tribunal has received written evidence of the agreement for dismissal of the claim, it must be dismissed, with the same consequences as under *rule 25(4)*.

18.29 CONCILIATION AND SETTLEMENT OF CLAIMS

The majority of tribunal claims are either withdrawn (often after a private settlement between the parties) or settled through the auspices of an ACAS conciliation officer. Almost all employment disputes within the jurisdiction of the tribunal are within the scope of ACAS conciliation, including breach of contract claims and claims for statutory redundancy payments (*ETA 1996, s 18(1)*). The role of ACAS in relation to tribunal claims was significantly restricted by changes introduced by the *2004 ET Regulations*. These introduced fixed conciliation periods for most categories of cases (excluding discrimination claims), either a standard period of 13 weeks (from the date of presentation of the claim) or a short period of seven weeks. Once that period ended, ACAS ceased to have a duty to conciliate, and in practice would decline to do so. However these provisions did not find general favour, and the relevant *ET Rules* were revoked as from 6 April 2009, with no transitional provisions; meanwhile in anticipation of the change in the rules, ACAS had changed its policy in April 2008, and since then has been prepared to offer the services of a conciliation officer at any stage in the proceedings.

The position now is that once a claim has been presented, and until it is finally disposed of, ACAS has a duty to attempt to conciliate if so requested. Prior to the presentation of a claim, ACAS merely has the power to provide conciliation services: *ETA 1996, s 18(2), (3)*, as substituted by the *Employment Act 2008, s 5*. However, as a contribution to promoting the resolution of employment disputes without resort to litigation, in April 2009 ACAS instituted a new Pre-Claim Conciliation Service, which in October 2009 was extended to cover all cases in which it has conciliation powers. Parties may access the service by telephoning the ACAS Helpline (08457 474747). The initial take up of the scheme was significant, with nearly 10,000 referrals in the first year of the service. ACAS has recorded the settlement of nearly half of all matters referred under this scheme, and estimates that 70% of cases referred do not go on to become tribunal claims. It should be noted that using this service does not affect the running of time limits for claims, so that in some cases it will be necessary to present a claim to protect the claimant's position; in that event the conciliation services of ACAS remain available.

In January 2013, BIS consulted on proposals for expanding the role of ACAS in attempting to settle disputes before proceedings are issued (Early Conciliation: A consultation on proposals for implementation, January 2013). A new requirement will be introduced by the *Enterprise and Regulatory Reform Act 2013*, s 7, which in turn adds *sections 18A* and *18B* to the *ETA*. This change will come into force on a date to be appointed by the Secretary of State: see *s 103(3)* of the *2013 Act*; BIS has announced that this is scheduled for early 2014. The background concern (see para 58 of the 2013 Act's Explanatory Notes) was that less than one fifth of claimants contacted ACAS for advice before submitting their claims. Subject to exceptions, the new *s 18A*, *ETA* requires prospective claimants under certain jurisdictions of the tribunal (referred to as "relevant proceedings" and defined in *s 18*, *ETA*) to provide information to ACAS prior to presenting their claim to the tribunal. ACAS in turn sends that information to a conciliation officer who is under a duty by *section 18A(3)* to promote a settlement between the parties during the prescribed period. If the conciliation officer concludes settlement is not possible, or if the prescribed period expires without settlement having been reached, the conciliation officer must issue a certificate to the prospective claimant to that effect, but may continue to promote a settlement even after the prescribed period. A prospective claimant who is obliged to comply with this procedure is prevented from presenting an application without the certificate from the conciliation officer. Exceptions are provided for cases where (i) the requirement is complied with by another person instituting relevant proceedings relating to the same matter, (ii) where proceedings that are not relevant proceedings are instituted at the same time as relevant proceedings, (iii) and where ACAS has been contacted by a person against whom relevant proceedings are being instated and *section 18B* applies. The matters to be prescribed, will be so prescribed in future employment tribunal procedure regulations.

Section 8 of the *2013 Act* will make corresponding changes to limitation periods to allow for conciliation. The details are set out in *Schedule 2* to the *Act* but in general:

(i)   the time period beginning with the day after the day on which the prospective claimant complies with the requirement to provide information to ACAS ("Day A") and ending with the day on which the complainant receives or is treated as having received the conciliation officer's certificate ("Day B") is not to be counted when working out time limits; and

(ii)   if a time limit would otherwise have expired during the period beginning with Day A and ending one month after Day B, the time limit expires instead at the end of that period; and

(iii)   any power to extend time is exercisable in relation to a time limit as extended by these rules.

The date on which a complainant is to be treated as having received a conciliation officer's certificate is yet to be prescribed by regulations.

The functions of conciliation officers are discussed in some detail in *Clarke v Redcar & Cleveland Borough Council* [2006] IRLR 324. It is not the conciliation officer's responsibility to ensure that the terms of any settlement are fair to the employee (or employer), and the conciliation officer should never advise a party as to the merits of the case, or advise the employee whether he or she could expect to get more compensation from the tribunal. The primary function is to promote a settlement by whatever legitimate means the officer thinks appropriate in the circumstances. These limitations are considered important to protect the impartiality of the conciliation service. In practice, some conciliation officers are more ready to express views on the value of claims or draw claimants' attention to typical levels of awards or the maximum that can be awarded for the claims being raised.

Anything said to a conciliation officer is confidential and cannot be disclosed to the tribunal without the consent of the communicator (*ETA 1996, s 18(7)*). If a settlement is reached with the aid of the conciliation officer it is recorded on a Form COT3. It is the policy of ACAS not to be involved in settlements where it has no conciliation role, ie the conciliation officer is merely asked to record a settlement reached privately.

18.30 An alternative to ACAS conciliation or private negotiations is mediation. This method of dispute resolution, which is increasingly favoured by the courts, and increasingly commonly used in civil litigation, has not yet become common in employment tribunal cases (but see **18.31** below for details of the judicial mediation scheme now operated within the tribunal system). However it is becoming less unusual, particularly in relatively high value claims, and cases where there is the prospect of related civil litigation. Mediation is a method of structured negotiations led by an independent mediator, who meets with both parties in the course of the mediation and attempts to guide each to common ground and to make concessions to facilitate settlement. Unlike an arbitrator, a mediator cannot impose a decision on the parties; the extent to which mediators are prepared to express views on what would be suitable terms for settlement varies considerably. A number of organisations now offer the services of trained mediators, and mediation has a relatively high rate of success. It also has advantages of privacy, and often of speed. A further advantage is that, if the parties so agree, terms of settlement can be included which could not be obtained from the tribunal, such as an apology or a reference.

Generally, mediations are set up as private arrangements between the parties and the mediator. The major disadvantage of this is that the parties must bear the cost of engaging the mediator, as well as their own costs of preparing for and attendance at the mediation, and this usually makes the option less attractive, and may make it impracticable, in claims for modest compensation, or where the employee is not in a position to meet his or her share of the mediation cost and the employer is not willing to meet the whole cost. One way of meeting this problem is to make use of one of the free mediation services now offered in employment cases.

The first of the free services to be introduced is operated by ACAS. The parties can agree, typically as part of a conciliated agreement, to have the claim referred to a mediator nominated by ACAS. This service, although relatively little known, has become well established, with 150 cases in 2006–7 rising to 241 in 2009–10 and falling only slightly to 223 in 2010–11; details are published in *ACAS Annual Reports*. Some two thirds of cases referred for ACAS mediation are either settled or partially settled in the course of mediation, and in a total of over 90%, ACAS considers that some progress towards settlement is made.

18.31 A more recent innovation is the introduction of a facility for judicial mediation within the employment tribunals. A pilot scheme offering the (free) services of an Employment Judge to mediate between the parties if they so wish was run in 2006–7, which was assessed as successful (but it should be noted that when the results of a research project based on the pilot scheme were finally published by the Ministry of Justice in early 2010, the report indicated that the success rate for mediations was no higher than the settlement rate for cases not referred to mediation, raising doubts about the cost effectiveness at least of the pilot).

Provision was made, by an amendment to the *ETA 1996* by the *Tribunals, Courts and Enforcement Act 2007*, for judicial mediation to be given more formal status, and a national scheme was introduced in January 2009. This facility is currently provided free to the parties (a fee of £600, payable by the respondent, is specified in the draft *Employment Tribunals and the Employment Appeal Tribunal Fees Order 2013*), and uses Employment Judges trained in mediation skills; the Judge is excluded from any future involvement in the proceedings should the mediation not be successful. The parties must bear any costs incurred in preparing for the mediation, attendance of representatives etc, but subject to the point that reimbursement of such costs by the other party may form part of the terms of settlement. Because of resource considerations, mediation is only offered in a limited range of cases, generally those discrimination claims which are considered likely to involve a hearing of at least three days, and with priority given to cases where the claimant is still employed.

Both parties must agree to a reference to mediation. There is no guarantee that mediation will be offered even if the parties' views are canvassed (this is done at a CMD) and both agree, because of the limited numbers of Judges who have been trained to undertake mediations. If it is agreed that there will be a mediation, it will normally be scheduled for a full day, at the tribunal offices, and appropriate directions given to the parties about any documents etc. An order for the preparation and exchange of mediation position statements is becoming increasingly common. One point which is emphasised in the information given to parties invited to consider mediation is that it is essential that a person with the authority to agree terms of settlement is available to attend the mediation.

A further important point is that the proceedings are in private, and anything said in the course of the mediation is strictly confidential and will not be admissible in any tribunal proceedings that may follow in the event that the mediation does not achieve a settlement. If the mediation is successful, the agreed terms will be incorporated into a formal order of the tribunal.

The practice is that judicial mediators adopt a purely facilitative approach, and do not offer opinions on the merits of claims or what might be appropriate terms for settlement. This has led to criticism from some users of the scheme, but there is also concern that too interventionist an approach might be felt by some parties as undue pressure to settle on terms with which they are unhappy. The usual procedure is for the judicial mediation to be held at a tribunal office, for the parties to have separate rooms and for the mediator to liaise between them. Often joint sessions are held in a tribunal room at the start of the day and, if the mediation is successful, at the end.

No statistics have been published for the numbers and outcomes of judicial mediations, but anecdotal evidence indicates that there is a relatively high success rate, and that demand for mediations fully meets, if not exceeds, the availability of appropriately trained employment judges. However the future of the facility has been put in doubt by the plans for a fee (of £600, payable by the respondent) to be charged for judicial mediation; this has been one of the more strongly criticised aspects of the fees proposals.

18.32 Conciliated settlements

Normally, an agreement not to pursue a claim in the tribunal is void and unenforceable as an attempt to contract out of statutory rights (*ERA 1996, s 203(1)*, *Equality Act 2010*, *s 144(1)*, and equivalent provisions in other statutes). The breadth of this provision is shown by the decision of the High Court in *Clyde & Co LLP v Bates van Winkelhof* [2011] IRLR 467, where a provision in a partnership agreement in a firm of solicitors providing for binding arbitration of disputes between partners was held ineffective to prevent an equity partner from bringing whistleblowing and sex discrimination claims. An exception to the general principle is claims for breach of contract; but see further on this **18.35** below. For the position where the parties agree a settlement subject to a consent judgment by the tribunal, and the tribunal subsequently issues the judgment, see *Carter v Reiner Moritz Associates Ltd* [1997] ICR 881, and *Mayo-Deman v University of Greenwich* [2005] IRLR 845.

An agreement reached where a conciliation officer has taken action under one of the relevant statutes is a statutory exception to *s 203(1)*: the agreement will, subject to its terms, be binding on the parties. Endorsing an agreement on a Form COT3 is sufficient 'action': *Moore v Duport Furniture Products Ltd* [1982] ICR 84. Provided that a conciliation officer has taken action there is no more formality required for a binding agreement that for any other contract; thus settlement can be reached orally (see *Duru v Granada Retail Catering Ltd* [2001] All ER (D) 97 (Jul) and *Allma Construction Ltd v Bonner* [2011] IRLR 204) but it is strongly advisable to reduce the terms of the agreement to writing as soon as possible, to avoid later disputes about the terms of the agreement (as occurred in *Duru*) or even whether an agreement was reached at all (as was in dispute in the *Allma* case). It is also important that any written record of the agreement made is properly worded to compromise all claims intended to be covered by it.

Issues may also arise subsequently as to the meaning, scope or application of a COT3 agreement. The ordinary principles of law for the interpretation of contracts apply to such agreements. Unlike compromise agreements (see below) a settlement reached through ACAS conciliation may in principle cover any disputes between the parties, including disputes that have not arisen at the time of the settlement. However, as a matter of construction, a court or tribunal will expect very clear words to convey the parties' intention to compromise future disputes: *Royal National Orthopaedic Hospital Trust v Howard* [2002] IRLR 849; *McLean v TLC Marketing* (UKEAT/0429/08). In an extreme case a conciliated settlement agreement may be set aside, eg if the conciliation officer acted in bad faith or adopted unfair methods to procure a settlement, but it would not be enough to justify setting aside the agreement that the conciliation officer had not adopted best practice, provided that he or she had acted in good faith: *Clarke v Redcar & Cleveland Borough Council* [2006] IRLR 324 (an unsuccessful attempt to set aside agreements to settle a large number of equal pay claims).

A party will normally be bound by a settlement signed by his or her authorised representative, even if not a lawyer: *Freeman v Sovereign Chicken Ltd* [1991] ICR 853. However this is only so if the party has held out the representative as being his or her representative (as by including details of the representative on the Claim Form or Response Form). If a representative merely holds him or herself out as having the requisite authority, an agreement reached by the opposing party with the representative will not bind the 'client': *Gloystarne & Co Ltd v Martin* [2001] IRLR 15.

Where the agreement reached through ACAS conciliation so provides, and the claim that has been settled is withdrawn, the claim will be automatically dismissed by the tribunal: *ET Rules, rule 25A*; see **18.28** above.

18.33 Compromise agreements

In the absence of ACAS conciliation, before 1993 the only option to secure an effective compromise of a tribunal claim, in practice, was to include a term in the agreement that the claimant would apply to the tribunal to have his or her claim dismissed on withdrawal; or if the parties were at the tribunal when a settlement was reached, an application could be made to the tribunal for an appropriate order. The former procedure has the disadvantage that the claimant can change his or her mind before making the application; the practice therefore is to make any payment conditional on the application to withdraw being made. (It is important that the respondent also applies to have the claim dismissed, not merely withdrawn or stayed, since in the latter case – in the absence of a binding agreement to the contrary – the case can subsequently be reopened: see **18.28** above.)

Both of the procedures referred to above are still available, but TURERA 1993 added a further and potentially more effective avenue of binding settlement, namely, a compromise agreement. The scope for compromise agreements was extended by ERDRA 1998. The principal relevant statutory provisions are now in *ERA 1996, s 203, Equality Act 2010, s 147, TULRCA 1992, s 288, Working Time Regulations 1998, reg 35*, and *National Minimum Wage Act 1998, s 49*. The *Part-time Workers (Prevention of Less Favourable Treatment) Regulations 2000, reg 9* provides that *ERA 1996, s 203* applies as if the *Regulations* were contained in that *Act*, and there are similar provisions in the *Fixed-term Employees (Prevention of Less*

Favourable Treatment) Regulations 2002, reg 8 and in the *Transfer of Undertakings (Protection of Employment) Regulations 2006, reg 18* (rectifying the anomaly that there was no equivalent provision in the predecessor *1981 Regulations*). The *Equality Act 2010, s 147* refers to compromise contracts rather than compromise agreements, but is otherwise (following an amendment to correct an alleged drafting defect: **18.34** below) materially identical; references below to compromise agreements include compromise contracts as appropriate.

It is to be noted that some common claims cannot be settled by a compromise agreement, for example claims for the failure to inform and consult under *TUPE 2006*, claims for failure to consult in collective redundancy cases under *TULCRA 1992, s 188* and claims for the right to statutory maternity, paternity and adoption pay. A COT3 can be used to settle such claims. Under the *Enterprise and Regulatory Reform Act 2013*, compromise agreements are to be renamed "settlement agreements".

18.34   A compromise agreement is an agreement to refrain from issuing or continuing proceedings under one of the statutes or regulations listed in **18.33**. In order for a compromise agreement to be binding, the following conditions must now be satisfied:

(a)   The agreement must be in writing;

(b)   It must relate to the particular complaint or proceedings (see further below);

(c)   The claimant must have received advice from a relevant independent adviser as to the terms and effect of the proposed agreement and in particular its effect on his or her ability to pursue his or her rights before an employment tribunal;

(d)   There must be in force, when the adviser gives the advice, a contract of insurance, or an indemnity provided for members of a profession or professional body, covering the risk of a claim by the claimant in respect of loss arising in consequence of the advice;

(e)   The agreement must identify the adviser; and

(f)   The agreement must state that the conditions regulating compromise agreements under the relevant Act or Regulations are satisfied.

A provision in the Bill which became the *Employment Act 2002* removing the requirement at (*b*) above was withdrawn during the Bill's passage through Parliament because of fears that it could facilitate the misuse of the compromise agreement procedure by requiring prospective employees to sign such agreements as a condition of being offered employment. As a consequence it is not possible to compromise all and any potential future disputes or claims under this procedure.

The requirements at (*e*) and (*f*) are applied strictly. It is not sufficient that there *is* an independent adviser and that the statutory requirements *have* been satisfied; it is essential that this be stated. In *Lunt v Merseyside TEC Ltd* [1999] ICR 17, the EAT upheld a decision that a compromise agreement which did not contain the statement required at (*f*) above was therefore void; this must apply equally to (*e*). In *Palihakkara v British Telecommunications plc* [2007] All ER (D) 131 (Jan), EAT, the EAT went further and held that a statement that the conditions under *ERA 1996, s 203* were satisfied was not effective to validate the agreement so far as it related to complaints of sex and race discrimination, although the requirements for such complaints were the same as those set out in *s 203* for complaints under *ERA 1996*. It is therefore necessary to state that the requirements for compromise agreements under the particular statute or statutes applicable for *each claim* intended to be compromised are satisfied; it is not completely clear following this decision whether it would be enough to say that the conditions under *s 203* 'and all similar statutory provisions' are satisfied, although it would be very surprising if this were not so.

The following are the categories of 'relevant independent advisers' who may act in compromise agreements:

(i)   Qualified lawyers;

(ii)   Fellows of the Institute of Legal Executives;

(iii)   Officers, officials, employees or members of an independent trade union; or

(iv)   Employees or volunteer workers at advice centres,

in each of the last two categories subject to the individual being certified in writing by the union or advice centre as competent and authorised to give advice. A 'qualified lawyer', means a barrister or advocate in practice as such or employed to give legal advice, or a solicitor holding a practising certificate.

In addition:

(A)   The adviser must not be, or be employed by, or be acting in the matter for, the employer or an associated employer;

(B)   In the case of a trade union or advice centre, that organisation must not be the employer or an associated employer; and

(C)   Advice from an advice centre worker must be free (but a union may apparently charge for its services).

Following widespread concern that there might be a drafting error in the provisions of the *Equality Act 2010* replacing the equivalents in the former discrimination statutes (which led to conflicting advice from Leading Counsel being obtained by the Law Society) with the result that a lawyer who had acted for or advised a party during a dispute could not then act as the independent adviser required as a condition of the validity of a compromise contract under *s 147*, the Government, whilst maintaining that the section was fully effective, made an amendment to *s 147* to remove the perceived doubts, with effect from 6 April 2012 (see the *Equality Act 2010 (Amendment) Order 2012, SI 2012/334*), and it is now clear that a lawyer who has advised the employee can act as the independent adviser for the purposes of a compromise agreement settling claims under the *2010 Act*.

A compromise agreement may be used to compromise more than one complaint, provided it clearly identifies each of the complaints being compromised and the relevant statutory provisions: *Lunt v Merseyside TEC Ltd* [1999] ICR 17. This case also confirms that claims can be validly compromised without the need to commence tribunal proceedings; but there must be an actual complaint: as noted above, a compromise agreement cannot settle potential disputes which have not yet arisen. This last point is a significant restriction on the utility of compromise agreements where the parties wish to ensure a 'clean break'. Moreover, compromise agreements are likely to be strictly construed, and any ambiguity resolved against the employer, as in *Palihakkara v British Telecommunications plc*, above, where an agreement to compromise all claims arising out of the termination of the employment was held not to cover claims of discrimination against the claimant whilst she had been employed.

The effective scope of compromise agreements was clarified and restricted by the Court of Appeal in *Hinton v University of East London* [2005] EWCA Civ 532, [2005] IRLR 552, and advice on the framing of agreements was also offered. The agreement must specifically identify the 'particular proceedings' (or the complaints which could lead to proceedings) being compromised. This entails for tribunal proceedings that the actual case be identified, and the agreement should identify complaints by a brief description of the complaint and a reference to the statutory provision under which the claim is asserted. A bare reference to the relevant statute is unlikely to be sufficient, especially if the statute is the *ERA 1996* or the *Equality Act 2010*, since these each cover a wide range of separate types of complaint.

Mummery LJ added the advice that it is good practice to include a summary of the factual and legal basis of the complaint or proceedings to identify the subject matter of the compromise more clearly. It is also generally unwise to rely on standard form compromise agreements or simply include a list of all the statutory provisions in relation to which compromise agreements may be required under the statute. The policy underpinning these points is that compromise agreements are a device to protect employees when agreeing to relinquish their statutory rights, and the statutory provisions should be construed to give effect to that policy.

The role of the independent adviser in the settlement of large multiple claims was considered by the EAT in *McWilliam v Glasgow Cty Council* [2011] IRLR 568. In this case there were several thousand potential or actual claimants for equal pay, and a general settlement had been negotiated with the relevant trade unions. A panel of firms of solicitors was set up by the Council, with arrangements put in place to ensure that they were independent of any influence from the council; group presentations were arranged, followed by individual meetings, and the individual claimants were given the opportunity to take away their agreements rather than signing on the spot. Advice given was limited to the binding effect of the agreements in preventing the employees from pursuing claims; no advice was given on the merits of their claims. The EAT held that these arrangements met the requirements for compromise agreements. In particular, advice as to the merits of a claim is not required by the statutes.

A further restriction on the scope of compromise agreements was shown by the EAT's decision in *Hilton UK Hotels Ltd v McNaughton* [2006] All ER (D) 327 (May). This case decides that a compromise agreement will not be interpreted as compromising a claim referred to in the agreement if at the time of the agreement the claimant did not appreciate that she had a possible claim, even though the independent adviser should have advised on the possibility. (The case concerned a part-time pension claim, and the adviser had not appreciated that the claimant had previously worked part-time.)

It should also be remembered that compromise agreements are a particular kind of contract, and are subject to the general law of contract in relation to everything except the particular statutory framework under which they may override the general restriction on contracting out of statutory rights. So, for instance, a compromise agreement procured by a misrepresentation by the employee may be set aside under ordinary contractual principles: see *Crystal Palace FC (2000) Ltd v Dowie* [2007] EWHC 1392 (QB), [2007] IRLR 682 (where however the Court held that it was not possible in that particular case to set the agreement aside because it was no longer possible to restore the position to that prevailing before the agreement was made; the employer's remedy would therefore have to be in damages).

If a claimant brings a claim in the employment tribunal and the respondent disputes the tribunal's jurisdiction on the ground that there is a valid compromise agreement, and the claimant in turn disputes the validity of the agreement, the tribunal has jurisdiction to determine whether the agreement is valid or not: *Horizon Recruitment Ltd v Vincent* [2010] ICR 491, EAT, a case where the claimant sought to argue that the agreement was tainted by misrepresentation.

18.35   An agreement to refrain from instituting or continuing proceedings in a contract claim brought in the tribunal will be binding without the need for any special requirements to be satisfied. The position where an agreement compromises both statutory and contractual claims is more complex. If it meets the requirements for a statutory compromise agreement it is clearly valid, and equally so for the claims which do not require the formality of a compromise agreement to be settled, but the position if the agreement does not satisfy the statutory requirements is the subject of conflicting authorities in the EAT: *Sutherland v Network Appliance Ltd* [2001] IRLR 12 holds that the contractual claim is validly compromised but *Hoeffler v Kwik Save Stores Ltd* (EAT/803/97) holds the opposite (in a case where one of the issues settled by the agreement was the parties' respective rights of appeal to the EAT, which it was held are outside *ERA 1996, s 203*).

A compromise agreement settling a prospective unfair dismissal claim, under which the employer agrees to make a payment to the employee, is a 'contract connected with employment' for the purposes of the tribunal's contract jurisdiction, so that the employee can bring a claim in the tribunal (subject to the relevant time limits) for money due under the agreement: *Rock-It Cargo Ltd v Green* [1997] IRLR 581. However, if the compromise agreement is not made until after the employment has terminated, the tribunal's contractual jurisdiction is not available to enforce it, since the claim is not outstanding on the termination and does not arise on termination: *Miller Bros and FP Butler Ltd v Johnston* [2002] IRLR 386. The same is presumably so if the complaint is of a breach of the agreement occurring after the employment has terminated.

18.36 'Calderbank' offers

Attempts to settle tribunal claims by negotiation are not always successful, and parties are sometimes inhibited from entering into negotiations by the fear that if the case is not settled, disclosure of offers made will weaken their case at the tribunal. However, such negotiations, conducted on a 'without prejudice' basis, are not normally admissible in the tribunal without the consent of both parties. This is so even if the term 'without prejudice' was not used, if it is clear that the parties intended the negotiations to be confidential.

A limited exception to this is that the party making an offer may reserve the right to rely on the offer in support of an application for costs (or expenses in Scotland), if he or she is successful at the tribunal. Correspondence conducted 'without prejudice save as to costs' (known as 'Calderbank' correspondence after the case in which its use was first sanctioned by the Court of Appeal) is admissible in support of an application for costs after the tribunal has made its substantive decision. There is, however, considerable doubt as to how far such offers may be taken into account by the tribunal. The point was expressly left open by the Court of Appeal in *Kovacs v Queen Mary and Westfield College* [2002] EWCA Civ 352, [2002] ICR 919. The EAT has since held that although the mere fact that the employer made an offer to settle for more than the tribunal awarded (or the claimant offered to accept less than he or she subsequently secured from the tribunal) is not a reason to award costs, the fact of rejecting a reasonable offer to settle *may* amount to unreasonable conduct, for which costs can be awarded, and Calderbank letters are admissible to establish that offers were made but not accepted in support of the claim of unreasonable conduct: *Kopel v Safeway Stores plc* [2003] IRLR 753. See further **18.71** as to the circumstances in which a costs order may be made.

18.37 ACAS ARBITRATION SCHEMES

Section 7 of the *ERDRA 1998* provides for the making of a scheme by ACAS, subject to the approval of the Secretary of State, for the determination of unfair dismissal claims by private arbitration. The process of establishing a scheme proved unexpectedly protracted, but it was finally brought into effect, for England and Wales only, in May 2001. It was extended to Scotland in 2004. The *ACAS Annual Reports* have consistently recorded a disappointingly small take-up of the scheme, with only 61 cases registered in the six years to 31 March 2009, of which only four were registered in the years 2007–8 and 2008–9 together (*ACAS Annual Reports, 2007–8* and *2008–9*). Figures for the period from April 2009 have not been published by ACAS.

The Scheme is now contained in a Schedule to the *ACAS Arbitration Scheme (Great Britain) Order 2004 (SI 2004/753)*, and is given effect by *TULRCA 1992, s 212A*, as inserted by *ERDRA 1998, s 7*. The Scheme is lengthy (running to 227 paragraphs, including some containing separate provisions for England and Wales and for Scotland) and is supported by a separate Guide published by ACAS, which should be consulted by any party considering the submission of a dispute to arbitration under the Scheme. The Arbitration Scheme is entirely voluntary, in the sense that it requires the agreement of both parties, and it is available only for unfair dismissal claims.

The *Employment Act 2002* amended *s 212A* to provide for a similar arbitration scheme in relation to disputes over requests for flexible working arrangements raised under the provisions of the *ERA 1996* (as added by the *2002 Act*) conferring the right to make such requests. A Scheme (for England and Wales only) was made by the *ACAS (Flexible Working) Arbitration Scheme (England and Wales) Order 2003 (SI 2003/694)*. This was extended to Scotland by the *ACAS (Flexible Working) Arbitration Scheme (Great Britain) Order 2004, SI 2004/2333*.

18.38 PREPARING FOR THE HEARING

The length of time from presentation of a claim to a Hearing varies considerably. HM Courts and Tribunals Service and its predecessors, the Tribunals Service, and before it the ETS, have for many years set performance targets for tribunals, one of which is that 75% of single cases will receive a first hearing within 26 weeks of receipt of the Claim Form, but success in achieving this figure has been variable, both over time and in different regions, and is currently thought to be declining. For relatively simple cases many tribunal regions are now able to list a hearing date within a few weeks of the deadline for a response, but it is not unusual for there to be a delay of several months if a case needs to be listed for more than one day.

The tribunal must give the parties at least 14 days' notice of the date of the Hearing, or of any other hearing apart from a CMD, unless shorter notice is agreed (*ET Rules, rule 14(4))*). The 14 day period is calculated from the date the notice is sent out, not the date it is received (see *reg 15(5)*). In practice, longer notice is usually (but not always) given. The usual practice for simple cases is to issue a notice of hearing without first checking with the parties whether the date is suitable (but in Scotland it is the practice to consult the parties before listing). In cases involving only claims for unlawful deductions, unpaid holiday pay and/or breach of contract (known as 'short track' cases), most tribunal regions issue a notice of hearing at the same time that the Claim Form is sent to the respondent, with a hearing date as early as possible after the short fixed conciliation period has expired. Some tribunals now hold evening sittings for short track cases.

If a date is given which causes problems, an application can and should be made as soon as possible, and if possible within 14 days, to change the date. Such applications are matters of discretion for the tribunal but are much more likely to be granted if made promptly giving clear reasons. The standard notice of a Hearing date indicates that applications for postponement made more than 14 days after notification of the hearing date will be allowed only in exceptional cases. There is no automatic right to postponement of a hearing even if *both* parties request a postponement, and it is difficult on appeal to dispute a refusal to postpone (*Employment Service v Nathan* (EAT/1316/95), IDS Brief 568; *London Fire and Civil Defence Authority v Samuels* (EAT/450/00), IDS Brief 669); it is therefore important to apply as early as possible and with full reasons for the request. For an example of a successful appeal against the refusal of a postponement agreed by both parties, see *Chancerygate (Business Centre) Ltd v Jenkins* (UKEAT/0212/10).

Sometimes a listed hearing can be adjourned by the tribunal, often at short notice, for reasons of resource allocation (such as no judge being available to take the case). In *University of East Anglia v Amaik Wu* (UKEAT/0361/12), the tribunal had listed a multiple day hearing which had to be adjourned on the working day before it was due to start because of a lack of judges to hear it. The tribunal then relisted the hearing without reference to the parties' available dates. This impacted upon one of the respondent's witnesses who was due to attend a wedding abroad. The respondent therefore applied for a relisting which was refused by the tribunal judge. The EAT found the judge erred by taking into account irrelevant circumstances and failing to take into account the fact that the tribunal had not sought dates to avoid. The EAT recorded that "in general the understanding is that a prompt response [to a listing] asking for another date based on witness availability is dealt with sympathetically" (para 14). Deciding the point *de novo*, the EAT granted the adjournment; central were the facts that: the witness was crucial, the application prompt, the tribunal did not seek dates to avoid, the witness had a significant role at the wedding.

18.39   Listing arrangements

Cases are usually listed in the first instance for one day, and if a case is likely to take longer than a day it is important to apply at an early stage for a longer listing; otherwise the tribunal will have to reconvene, possibly months later, if the case is not completed within the allotted day (it is very rare indeed that the case would be continued the following day in those circumstances). The same considerations apply to 'short track' cases, which are normally listed in the first instance for a one-hour hearing. For apparently complex cases, particularly those to be listed for more than a day, most regions write to the parties advising them of the intention to list the case and requiring notification to the tribunal if a party considers the proposed time allocation to be inappropriate. It is important to respond to such an invitation, since the tribunal may hold the parties to a time allocation even if at the hearing they suggest that the time allowed is insufficient, and this is also an opportunity to give the tribunal dates to be avoided because eg a witness will not be available. In Scotland parties are asked to identify the witnesses they intend to call and how long the evidence of each will take to be heard, and the time allocated to the case is based on the parties' responses.

The basis on which cases are listed, unless otherwise indicated, is that sufficient time should be allowed not only to hear the evidence and submissions of the parties, but also for the tribunal to reach and announce its decision, and to deal if appropriate with remedies. Anecdotally, a figure often mentioned by judges as the time required for deliberations is around 25% of the time required to hear the evidence. Parties are now generally warned of this approach, and are advised also of the tribunal's power to set a timetable to ensure that the case is completed within the time available.

Hearings are normally scheduled to take place at the Regional Office or other office of the tribunal at which the case has been presented (or to which the file has been transferred), but there are also a number of hearing centres at which cases are heard but which do not have a permanent staff presence. Increasingly, hearing centres shared with other tribunals are used, on the basis either of availability of tribunal rooms or of geographical convenience for the parties (the latter in particular in more rural areas); if travel to the tribunal office administering the case is likely to be difficult or expensive for a party, enquiries should be made of the tribunal as to whether it will be possible to list the case for hearing at a more convenient location. In Scotland, local Sheriff Courts are used for hearings in more remote locations.

Special priority is given to interim hearings of applications for interim relief (see **53.18** Unfair Dismissal – III). Only seven days' notice of the claim and of the hearing is required, and postponements will only be granted in exceptional cases (the statutory provisions stipulating this are *ERA 1996, s 128(4), (5)* and *TULRCA 1992, s 162(2), (4)*; because of an apparent drafting error however, the period of notice of the hearing required by *rule 14* is a minimum of 14 days). Interim relief applications are dealt with at interim hearings (for details see *rule 18A*). Where a CMD is held prior to the substantive Hearing, the 14-day notice provision does not apply to the CMD (*rule 14(4)*), and much shorter notice is sometimes given to deal with urgent applications. Where a CMD is held it is usual to deal with the listing of the main Hearing at that time, and parties or representatives are expected to have with them the dates of availability of witnesses to facilitate this.

There are several steps a party should take prior to the hearing – preferably earlier rather than later. These are addressed in the following sections.

18.40   A decision should be taken whether a legal or other representative is to be engaged; if so, this should be done in good time to enable the representative to prepare for the hearing and take any necessary interlocutory steps. There is no restriction on who may represent a party in the tribunal (see *Bache v Essex County Council* [2000] 2 All ER 847, [2000] IRLR 251). In general no legal aid is now available. The legal assistance for the preparation of the case used to be available to claimants of limited means, but (apart from in limited circumstances in Scotland) this ceased to be so on the coming into force on 1 April 2013 of the *Legal Aid, Sentencing and Punishment of Offenders Act 2012*. There are now only very limited circumstances in which legal aid assistance is available in England and Wales. It is limited to telephone advice in discrimination cases (contact the Civil Legal Advice information line for details: 0845 345 4345 or claonlineadvice.justice.gov.uk).

Employers are often represented by an appropriate manager or a trade association official, employees by a union officer or a Citizens' Advice Bureau (CABx) or advice centre worker The fact that no representative is given on the Claim Form or Response Form by no means necessarily indicates that the party concerned will not be represented. Whoever is to represent a party, it is desirable that the representative be consulted in good time before the hearing. It is also important that the tribunal is notified promptly of the appointment of a representative, with contact details, and of any change in arrangements for representation, to avoid the all too common situation that correspondence from the tribunal, including notice of hearings, does not reach the party or his or her current representative.

A number of organisations offer their services as representatives in tribunal proceedings, either as consultants offering a package of advice and representation to employers, or on a no win no fee basis for claimants. Concerns about the quality of representation offered by some of these organisations, and the lack of any professional or statutory regulation of their conduct, led to the introduction of a requirement, under the *Compensation Act 2006, Part 2*, for claims management services (including those providing representation in employment tribunals for reward) to be regulated. It is a criminal offence for a person or organisation who, or which, is not registered with the regulator (the Secretary of State for Justice) to provide representation for claimants (but not respondents) in employment tribunal proceedings for reward (including on a no win, no fee basis). In *Miller v Community Links Trust* [2007] All ER (D) 196 (Nov), the EAT referred an unregulated representative to the Regulator for possible action. A number of categories of representatives are exempt from regulation under the *Compensation Act 2006*, including lawyers, trade unions and the CABx; for full details see the *Compensation (Exemptions) Order 2007 (SI 2007/209)*. The *Compensation Act 2006* only applies to England and Wales, and there is no equivalent statutory regulation of representatives acting for reward in Scotland.

Before engaging a representative on a no win no fee basis, a prospective claimant needs to appreciate that the representative will normally have to be paid out of whatever compensation is awarded if the claim succeeds, since costs are not usually awarded, but compensation is assessed without regard to this liability. By way of further regulation of 'no win no fee' agreements, the *Damages-Based Agreements Regulations 2013 (SI 2013/609)*, which came into force on 1 April 2013, prohibit agreements in employment cases which provide for payment of more than 35% (including VAT) of the compensation recovered, whether by way of settlement or as an award of the tribunal: *reg 7*. This mirrored the provisions in the preceding *Damages-Based Agreements Regulations 2010*, which remain in force for agreements made before 1 April 2013. Neither set of Regulations extends to Scotland.

In an extreme case the conduct of a representative may lead to sanctions being imposed by the tribunal on the party represented, including striking out that party's case (see *Bennett v Southwark London Borough Council* [2002] EWCA Civ 223, [2002] IRLR 407). The tribunal also has the power to make a wasted costs order against a representative acting for profit (including under a no win, no fee agreement), ie an order that the representative must pay the other party's costs, or debarring the representative from recovering costs incurred from his or her client. See further **18.73** below.

For those, particularly claimants, who cannot afford to pay for legal representation, free representation may be available through one or other of a number of organisations including the Citizens' Advice Bureaux (CABx) and the Free Representation Unit (6th Floor, 289–293 High Holborn, London WC1V 7HZ, tel. 020 7611 9555), and in discrimination cases application may be made for legal assistance to the Equality and Human Rights Commission, although the Commission's budget for legal assistance is limited, and funding is concentrated on cases with wider implications or meeting priority criteria.

Most trade unions provide a free representation service for members, either through union officials or union-appointed solicitors, and usually subject to being satisfied that the claim has some merit. An increasing number of claimants are represented by lawyers paid for under legal expenses insurance (often provided as an optional addition to household insurance) and it is important that a claimant should check at as early a stage as possible whether this facility may be available. Further advice on possible sources of free professional representation can be obtained through CABx.

18.41 Consideration should be given to whether an application for any case management orders, or a CMD, is needed. Orders may be any of those listed in **18.2** above or other orders, such as for a PHR (see **18.15** above) or the joinder of parties (see **18.23** above) or for a restricted reporting order (see **18.18** above). A CMD may be listed by the tribunal of its own motion. Most commonly this happens in discrimination cases; where the issues appear complex; or where a party's application for an order has been opposed. It may also be necessary to apply to the tribunal for a PHR to determine a particular preliminary point (such as whether it has jurisdiction over the claim).

A party may wish to apply for permission to amend the claim or response. An application which is likely to be contested should not be granted by the tribunal without the opposing party being given an opportunity to resist the application (in writing or, if the tribunal so orders, at a CMD) and if an amendment is allowed *ex parte*, without such an opportunity, the opposing party may apply to the tribunal to have the order set aside (see *Reddington v S Straker & Sons Ltd* [1994] ICR 172, and *ET Rules, rule 12(3)*). A tribunal should not normally decide an application to amend a Claim Form which raises an issue of substance, without giving the parties an opportunity to make representations at a CMD (*Smith v Gwent District Health Authority* [1996] ICR 1044). The practice in relation to applications to amend was restated by the EAT in *Selkent Bus Co Ltd v Moore* [1996] ICR 836. For more details, see **18.10** above.

18.42 It is sometimes necessary for a party to apply for a postponement of the hearing, either because a witness becomes unavailable or for a variety of other reasons. Any such application should if possible be made with the agreement of the other party. However even agreed applications are not necessarily granted by the tribunal. It is important to give full reasons for the application, especially if it is opposed. The earlier the application is made, the more likely it is to be granted. If the application is made on grounds of ill-health, medical evidence will be required by the tribunal. In deciding applications, tribunals are entitled to have regard to the public interest in cases being heard as promptly as reasonably practicable, now reinforced by the incorporation into domestic law of the right under *art 6* of the *European Convention on Human Rights* to have a dispute decided within a reasonable time. In practice an application for a postponement of the hearing is made in quite a high proportion of cases, often very shortly before the hearing; although there are no statistics as to the percentage of applications granted and refused, experience suggests that the majority are refused. If a hearing was listed at a CMD, it is particularly difficult to persuade the tribunal to change the listing because a witness is not available: *London Fire and Civil Defence Authority v Samuels* (EAT/450/00). For the position where an application is made on the morning of the hearing or immediately before the hearing date, see **18.54**.

18.43 The relevant documentary evidence should be identified. Documentation likely to be relevant will include the contract of employment or letter of engagement, statutory statement of particulars of employment, relevant parts of any staff handbook (such as a disciplinary procedure), any written warnings, records of performance or attendance (if these are relevant issues), the letter of dismissal and any correspondence notifying the employee of the disciplinary investigation or hearing, notes or minutes of any relevant meetings, appeal documents if applicable, documents demonstrating the need for a redundancy, and documents relevant to quantification of the claim, such as payments made to the employee and pension documentation. The employee may need to produce documentation showing his or her attempts to mitigate his or her loss and any earnings since dismissal, as well as evidence of pay and benefits prior to dismissal, and social security benefits received after termination. In cases where a grievance has been raised, the documentation relating to the grievance, grievance hearings and any appeal will be required.

The parties will be expected, particularly if both have professional representation, to agree a bundle of documents including those to be relied on by both sides; it is now standard practice for the tribunal to make an order to this effect. Such a bundle may be referred to as an 'agreed' bundle; this means that the authenticity of the documents is not disputed, but not that their relevance or accuracy is necessarily conceded. The bundle should be paginated (ie each page should be consecutively numbered) and, if substantial, indexed. Six copies will be needed for the hearing (three for the tribunal, or one if an Employment Judge is sitting alone, and one each for each party and for the witnesses).

Some tribunal regions in England have adopted a practice of limiting the number of pages of documentation parties may include, but practice on this varies, and is subject to consideration of any reasoned case a party may make to put in more than the maximum number of pages.

In Scotland, documents produced to the tribunal are referred to as 'productions'. Parties with legal representation are required by a Practice Direction to notify each other of what productions each party intends to rely on, and provide copies, 14 days before the hearing; in straightforward cases it is unusual for any specific orders to be made for disclosure or exchange of productions, but it is nevertheless important to prepare sufficient copies of the documents, numbered and indexed (this is referred to as an 'inventory of productions'), as failure to do so will inevitably extend the length of the hearing; if possible there should be a joint bundle of productions. The usual practice is to number each document (which may be more than one page) separately.

As the rules of evidence do not apply fully in tribunals, it is not necessary formally to prove the documents in the tribunal bundle, unless the genuineness or accuracy of a document is disputed (eg in the latter case, minutes of a meeting). If there is a dispute, a witness who can confirm the accuracy of the document from personal knowledge should be called. Where there may be issues of authenticity, originals of any documents should wherever possible be available at the hearing.

There are no formal rules as to who should produce the sets of documents needed for the hearing. The usual practice is for the party advancing a case to take this responsibility (ie the claimant in discrimination or breach of contract cases, but the employer in unfair dismissal cases where the dismissal is admitted). However, it has in recent years become increasingly common for the respondent to accept the burden of preparing the bundles, and the requirement of the Overriding Objective that the parties should so far as possible be put on an equal footing has led to it becoming part of the common practice of tribunals, at least in cases with substantial documentation, to require respondents to undertake this task. Often the tribunal will encourage agreement on the question of the cost of preparing and duplicating the bundle, but its powers to award costs are limited to those in the rules - see 18.69 and onwards below.

18.44 One category of documents is not normally admissible before a tribunal; this is 'without prejudice' correspondence. This means correspondence conducted in an attempt to reach a settlement of a dispute; it is only admissible either to prove an agreement reached as a result or if *both* parties agree. For further details of the limits of the 'without prejudice' privilege see **18.13** above. Correspondence is sometimes conducted under the heading 'Without prejudice save as to costs'. This preserves the right of the party putting forward proposals to refer to the correspondence after the substantive issues have been decided by the tribunal, solely in support of an application for costs – see further **18.36** above. In unfair dismissal cases the effect of the new *s 111A, ERA* should also be considered: pre-termination negotiations will, pursuant to that section (when in force) become inadmissible in proceedings, subject to three exceptions. See further **18.13** above.

18.45 The relevant witnesses should be identified and their statements taken. An employer in an unfair dismissal case will usually need to call at least the manager who took the decision to dismiss the employee and, if applicable, the manager who decided the appeal. In a redundancy case, evidence of the redundancy situation, of the reasons for the decision to select the claimant, of consultation with the claimant and any recognised union, and of attempts to redeploy, may all be required. Where there has been a disciplinary hearing and the reason for the dismissal was that the manager decided on the evidence that the employee was guilty of misconduct, it is not the tribunal's function to re-try the case or decide for itself as to the employee's guilt; it should not therefore normally be necessary to call all those persons who were involved in the disciplinary hearing (apart from the manager conducting the hearing) or any earlier investigation. It may, however, be necessary to call the manager conducting any separate investigation prior to the disciplinary hearing, particularly so if there is any dispute as to the sufficiency or fairness of the investigation. In some cases it might be justifiable to call witnesses to the underlying allegations of misconduct as although this evidence does not go to liability for unfair dismissal, it can go to questions of contributory fault and liability for wrongful dismissal: see *London Ambulance Service v Small* [2009] IRLR 563, CA. As to the employee, whether any additional witness is to be called depends on the availability (and sometimes willingness) of those who have knowledge of relevant events.

In most cases issues about the admissibility of particular evidence will be decided by the tribunal hearing the case in the course of the hearing. However it is open to the tribunal in the exercise of its case management powers to rule in advance of the hearing on the admissibility of particular evidence which a party proposes to call. This may be done where there is a dispute about admissibility based on legal arguments, such as whether the evidence is covered by legal professional privilege, but exceptionally a ruling may be based on proportionality. Thus in *HSBC Asia Holdings BV v Gillespie* [2011] ICR 192, [2011] IRLR 209, the EAT ruled that the tribunal should have excluded in advance evidence the claimant in a discrimination case intended to introduce at the hearing as background, in order to show a discriminatory culture within the respondent bank, covering a period of 10 years going back 18 years from the date of the claim, and involving departments of the bank, and individuals, who were not affected at all by the substantive allegations of harassment. Underhill P pointed out that whilst evidence that is irrelevant is inadmissible, relevance alone is not necessarily sufficient to justify admission; where the evidence is of marginal relevance, it may be disproportionate to admit it, as in this case where admission of the evidence would necessitate the calling of much additional evidence by the respondent to seek to rebut the allegations made, which were not the substantive complaints for which a remedy could be granted. In Vaughan v Lewisham Borough Council [2013] All ER (D) 80, in a discrimination claim the claimant had sought permission to rely on some 39 hours of covert recordings she had made of her conversations with managers and colleagues which she asserted went to the pleaded issues. The claimant did not supply any transcripts to the tribunal. The EAT held that the judge had been correct to refuse to admit the recordings: it was not possible to form any view on the relevance or proportionality of the proposed evidence on the material that the claimant had produced. It was not enough to assert their centrality to pleaded allegations. The claimant was at liberty to make a fresh focused application to the tribunal, producing the transcripts and tapes which she wanted to rely on.

The EAT went on to confirm that although the practice of making secret recordings is "to put it no higher, very distasteful", recordings are not inadmissible simply because of the way in which they were taken; see also *Dogherty v Chairman and Governors of Amwell View School* (UKEAT/0243/06).

18.46 For hearings in England and Wales, witnesses will need to be asked to prepare written statements of their evidence (legal representatives will normally prepare drafts themselves following an interview with each witness). These should be typed or legibly written, using short, numbered paragraphs. It is important that all relevant matters of which the witness has knowledge are covered. Whilst the practice as to timing is not consistent between tribunal regions, the almost universal practice is that the tribunal will direct the parties to prepare witness statements, and to exchange them prior to the hearing. Sometimes the tribunal will also direct that the witness statements will be taken as the evidence-in-chief of the witness. This means that the party calling the witness will not be able to ask him or her additional questions without the permission of the tribunal. If there is good reason why a statement cannot be produced for a particular witness, it is advisable to apply to the tribunal for an order exempting that witness from the general requirement for statements to be exchanged in advance.

The practice as to how witness statements are used at the hearing was in the past that in most cases the tribunal would invite the witnesses to give their evidence by reading the statement; sometimes (usually where the facts did not appear to be substantially in dispute, or in more lengthy cases) the tribunal would pre-read the statements and simply ask the witnesses to confirm the truth of their contents. The practice has now been changed, but formally only for claims presented on or after 6 April 2012, by the *Employment Tribunals (Constitution and Rules of Procedure) (Amendment) Regulations 2012 (SI 2012/468); reg 2(2)* adds a new *rule 27(2)* to the *ET Rules*, which provides that if there is a witness statement, it stands as the witness's evidence-in-chief unless the tribunal directs otherwise. This means that the standard practice is that the witness will not have to read out the statement, but it will be read by the tribunal; and the witness will only be able to give additional evidence in chief if the tribunal agrees. The change reflects guidance given by the EAT in *Mehta v Child Support Agency* [2011] IRLR 305. In summary, Underhill P's guidance (which is likely to influence tribunals in deciding whether all or part of a statement should be read out) is that it is not a requirement of fairness that every witness statement is read out in full to the tribunal, but there may be cases where this is desirable, particularly if a party is unrepresented; it is not necessary for all statements to be treated in the same way: a witness may for instance be asked to read the key parts of his or her statement, the rest being read privately by the tribunal; and wherever possible, the tribunal should proceed with the agreement of the parties, taking care to ensure that any unrepresented party fully understands what is proposed, and agrees to the course proposed. In practice it will often be necessary for the tribunal to ask questions of the witness (or the representative of the party calling the witness) to clarify points in the statement, and to identify clearly documents referred to and the parts of documents the witness is referring to in the statement, so that these too can be read.

If it will not be possible to call a witness, evidence can be given by way of a signed statement, which should contain a statement confirming that the witness believes the facts stated in the statement to be true (a 'statement of truth'). Such evidence should be sent to the tribunal and the other party at least seven days before the hearing; it is then admissible as of right as a written representation (see *ET Rules, rule 14(5)* and **18.47** below). If tendered late, the tribunal may decline to consider it. In any case, however, the weight to be attached to evidence in this form is affected by the unavailability of the witness (for however cogent a reason) for cross-examination. Accordingly, unless the evidence is not in dispute, great caution should be used in relying on written evidence instead of a live witness.

The practice in Scotland is still that witness statements are not normally used as a means of giving evidence, or exchanged before the hearing. Instead, at least where there is legal representation, witnesses are usually interviewed before the hearing by the representative (a procedure known as 'precognosing' the witness), and a proof of evidence prepared, which can serve as a script for the advocate calling the witness. If there are particular reasons why it would be desirable for the evidence (or evidence of specific witnesses) to be given by way of written statements, early application should be made to the tribunal for directions on the point. Where witness statements are used, the new rules will apply equally.

18.47   It is open to any party to submit representations in writing to the tribunal; they must be submitted (and sent to each other party) at least seven days before the hearing date, unless the tribunal consents to a shorter period (*ET Rules, rule 14(5), (6)*). Written representations may be made by a party attending the hearing, or in lieu of attendance. However, the latter course is extremely hazardous, since the absent party cannot deal with questions from the tribunal, points that arise unexpectedly or assertions made in evidence by the other party. In all but the simplest cases, attendance in person or by a representative is essential. The provision of written representations under the *ET Rules* outlined above is not to be confused with the practice of submitting a written skeleton argument; sometimes the tribunal will make an order for such skeletons to be exchanged and filed by a particular time, but otherwise, the parties are free to present them to the tribunal at the time of the hearing.

18.48   The current practice of tribunals in straightforward cases is to deal with all questions including, if appropriate, remedy, at one hearing. Accordingly, and unless the tribunal has directed that remedy will be dealt with subsequently, parties should come to the hearing prepared to deal with evidence relevant to remedy. This means that the claimant should include in his or her statement details of the earnings lost, any income received from new employment or state benefits, and information relevant to any claim that he or she has failed to take reasonable steps to mitigate his or her loss. In most regions the standard orders issued in unfair dismissal and discrimination cases include a requirement for the claimant to serve a Schedule of Loss detailing the amounts claimed, benefits received etc. The respondent should have the necessary information to put before the tribunal to establish take home pay (if disputed) and the value of any employment benefits. If there is likely to be a dispute about this, relevant documentation should be in the bundle. (It does not follow that the tribunal will have the time to deal with remedy, and it may agree to give the parties time to attempt to agree the remedy; however cases are listed on the basis that time is allowed for the tribunal to hear the case, reach and deliver its decision, and then deal with remedy if necessary.) If it is anticipated that additional evidence will need to be called in relation to remedy, particularly if expert evidence (eg on pension loss) will be needed, it may be advisable to apply well before the hearing for a direction that remedy will be dealt with separately at a second hearing. In Scotland the practice is that all issues including remedy will be dealt with together, before the decision on liability is given, if at all possible, although split hearings are becoming less uncommon, especially if expert evidence is required on the issue of remedy.

18.49   THE HEARING

Tribunal hearings are usually conducted in modern rooms with the three members of the tribunal sitting at a table on a slightly raised dais and the claimant and respondent sitting at tables facing the tribunal. There is a table at which the witness sits to give evidence. A full tribunal is composed of a legally qualified Employment Judge, one member with management experience and one member with trade union experience; as to cases where the Judge may sit alone or with just one other member, see **17.8** and **17.9** above. The proceedings are public (although in practice members of the public not connected with the proceedings attend relatively infrequently). For the power of the tribunal to sit in private, see **18.51** below. Hearings may be held by telephone or video link, so that it is possible, for instance, for evidence from a witness who is abroad to be heard by video link. In practice this happens infrequently, as most hearing centres are not equipped for video conferencing, and special arrangements therefore need to be made in advance; but if there are good reasons for such arrangements, an early application for a direction should be made to the tribunal.

The Judge and members should be addressed as 'Sir' or 'Madam'. Proceedings are formal but considerably less so than in an ordinary court. Witnesses (including a party if giving evidence) are required to give their evidence on oath or under affirmation (rule 27(3); the clerk will check on the preference of each witness in this respect). In Scotland, witnesses are excluded from the tribunal room until called to give their evidence (this does not apply to a party who is also a witness).

Before the hearing starts, the clerk will speak to both parties and make a list of names of representatives and witnesses, and will collect copies of documents each party intends to rely on to give to members of the tribunal.

18.50 Bias or conflict of interest

The judgment of a tribunal will be open to appeal if the circumstances give rise to a perception of bias on the part of the judge or a lay member of the tribunal. The test is an objective one: would a reasonable independent observer, in full possession of the facts, consider that there was a real possibility of bias, arising either from the relationship between the judge or member and a party or witness, or the conduct of the hearing. The former aspect is considered in this section; as to allegations of bias in relation to the conduct of the hearing see **19.23–19.24** below.

If any tribunal member has any connection with either of the parties, or the events in issue in the case, that fact should be made known to all concerned at the outset, and the case relisted before a fresh tribunal if necessary (*University College of Swansea v Cornelius* [1988] ICR 735). If a party raises an objection to the composition of the tribunal before the hearing commences, then unless that objection is irresponsible or frivolous it is preferable to reconstitute the tribunal if possible (*Halford v Sharples* [1992] ICR 146 at 171, EAT, a point not considered further when the case reached the Court of Appeal). See further on the circumstances in which participation by a particular Tribunal Judge or member in a hearing may be regarded as creating an appearance of bias *Locabail (UK) Ltd v Bayfield Properties Ltd* [2000] QB 451, [2000] 1 All ER 65, [2000] 2 WLR 870, [2000] IRLR 96, *Jones v DAS Legal Expenses Insurance Co Ltd* [2003] EWCA Civ 1071, [2004] IRLR 218, *Hamilton v GMB*, [2007] IRLR 391 and *Honey v Swansea City Council* [2008] All ER (D) 311 (Nov) (where failure by one of the lay members of the tribunal to disclose that he was, in his capacity as a trade union official, involved in a current dispute with the respondent local authority led to the judgment of the tribunal being set aside). The tests applied by the EAT in cases of alleged bias are discussed further at **19.23–19.24** below.

A finding of an appearance of bias was made in *Peninsula Business Services Ltd v Rees* (UKEAT/0335/08) where the (part-time) judge was in practice as a solicitor, and her firm had advertised its services as superior to those offered by consultants, of whom the appellant was one of the best known; by implication it could be thought her firm, and hence she, had an interest adverse to that of the appellant firm. It was also held that this point no longer applied in a second case involving the same judge and appellant heard after she had taken up a full-time appointment, as the conflict of interest could no longer apply.

Whilst a connection between the judge (or a lay member) and a party or witness is likely, unless the parties consent to the judge or member sitting, to provide grounds for appeal, this is much less likely to be so where the connection is with a representative of one of the parties; see for instance *Williams v Cater Link Ltd* (UKEAT/0393/08): no perception of bias where (full-time) judge had whilst still in practice instructed counsel subsequently appearing for one of the parties in the case. A fundamental point is that the judge must not have any kind of financial interest in the proceedings. Technically, this would extend to minor interests such as holding a small shareholding in a large corporation that is the respondent to the proceedings; in practice parties would be unlikely to object to the judge sitting in these circumstances, but the interest should be disclosed. Interests held in common with large sections of the population, such as being a resident and Council Tax payer in the area of a local authority that is a respondent, or a user of the services of a utility or transport company, need not be declared.

The *Jones* case (above) makes the important point that if the Judge discloses an interest and invites the parties to indicate whether they agree to the case proceeding before him or her, and a party makes no objection, then provided that sufficient disclosure of the potential conflict of interest has been given, the party will be taken to have waived any right to challenge the fairness of the hearing on appeal by reference to the Judge's declared interest. The Court of Appeal also stressed the importance of giving the parties, particularly if unrepresented, a full explanation of the options available to them and time to consider their position, and of taking a full note of what the parties are told. These principles were applied by the EAT in *Adamson v Swansea University* (UKEAT/0486/09), where it was held that the claimant had given informed consent to the case being heard by an employment judge who had disclosed a personal acquaintance with a witness in the case. For a recent example, see *Bhardwaj v FDA* [2013] All ER (D) 31.

The fact that an accusation of bias has previously been made against a Judge by one of the parties, or that the Judge has in previous proceedings made adverse comments about a party or witness, is not of itself a reason for the Judge to withdraw from hearing a case (in technical language, to recuse him or herself): *Ansar v Lloyds TSB Bank plc* [2006] EWCA Civ 1462, [2007] IRLR 211, a case in which the Court of Appeal set out detailed guidance on the relevant principles to be applied. *WestLB AG London Branch v Pan* (UKEAT/0308/11) is an example of the application of *Ansar* by the EAT to overturn a decision by the employment judge to recuse herself after an objection by the claimant, taken without giving the other party a chance to be heard, and despite the judge considering that the objection was not justified. As to the circumstances in which a tribunal should recuse itself where an allegation of bias in the conduct of the case is made by a party or his or her representative, see *Bennett v Southwark London Borough Council* [2002] EWCA Civ 223, [2002] IRLR 407.

In sex discrimination cases, both sexes will normally be represented on the tribunal, and in race discrimination cases at least one member should have special knowledge of race relations; however, these are not mandatory requirements.

18.51   When hearing may be in private

Tribunal hearings are generally conducted in public and may be reported in the media. The requirement to sit in public applies to a Hearing and to a PHR, and the hearing of an application for interim relief, but not to a CMD, which must be held in private (*ET Rules, rules 17(1), 18(1), 26(3)*). The tribunal has power under *rule 16(1)* to direct that evidence or representations be heard in private if in the opinion of the tribunal it would be likely to consist of information which could not be disclosed without a breach of a statutory prohibition or which had been communicated to or obtained by the person concerned in confidence, or which if publicly disclosed could cause substantial damage to that person's undertaking or the undertaking in which he or she works, for reasons other than the effect of disclosure on collective bargaining. The reference to information obtained in confidence may allow for medical evidence to be given in private. There is power to make an order in advance of the Hearing for particular evidence to be heard in private: *McBride v Standards Board for England* (UKEAT/0092/09).

The EAT has held that the relevant statutory provisions referred to in *rule 16* include the tribunal's duty under *s 6* of the *Human Rights Act 1998* not to act in such a way as to infringe protected human rights, so that there may be a duty to sit in private for the reception of evidence if the public reception of the evidence would be an impermissible violation of the right of privacy of an individual under *Art 8* of the *Human Rights Convention* (*XXX v YYY* [2004] IRLR 137 (reversed by the Court of Appeal on other grounds [2004] IRLR 471), a case involving a video recording containing pictures of a young child). A less drastic way of protecting rights of privacy may be the giving of a direction that particular individuals (such as children or patients) are not to be identified by name in the course of the proceedings. The EAT has also held that where the tribunal has to determine whether particular evidence relied on by one of the parties is privileged as a without prejudice communication, the test for whether the tribunal should sit in private to hear this aspect of the case will depend on whether it is likely that evidence will be given which is covered by the confidentiality attaching to without prejudice communications; if so, that factor has to be balanced against the general public interest in open justice: *Eversheds LLP v Gray* (UKEAT/0585/11). If the tribunal decides to hold a hearing or part thereof in private, it must give reasons for doing so (*ET Rules, rule 16(2)*); a decision to sit in private, or not to do so, is open to appeal, as occurred in the *Eversheds* case.

In addition, the tribunal may sit in private if directed to do so by a Minister of the Crown for reasons of national security. (*ET Rules, rule 54(1)(a)*; and see *AB v Ministry of Defence*, UKEAT/0101/09.) *Rule 54* also contains more general powers to control the conduct of tribunal proceedings in national security cases. An example of such an order under equivalent provisions in previous *ET Rules* is *Fry v Foreign and Commonwealth Office* [1997] ICR 512 (order did not extend to excluding claimant's husband who was assisting the presentation of her case). The EAT has suggested that there may be good reasons for 'closed evidence' (ie evidence heard in private session) to be heard before open evidence in cases involving Crown employment and/or national security: *Farooq v Commissioner of Police of the Metropolis* [2008] All ER (D) 187 (Jun). This point was endorsed by the Court of Appeal in *Home Office v Tariq* [2010] EWCA Civ 462, a case in which the Court held that the procedure laid down for cases involving national security (*Sch 2* to the *ET Regulations 2004*), involving the exclusion of the claimant from part of the proceedings with a Special Advocate appointed to represent his interests during that part of the hearing, was not incompatible with *art 6* of the *European Convention on Human Rights*. The Court's decision in *Tariq* has subsequently been upheld by the Supreme Court: *Home Office v Tariq* [2011] UKSC 35, [2011] IRLR 843.

Subject to the provisions permitting a hearing in private, failure to hold the hearing at a place made accessible to the public renders any resulting judgment a nullity, even if no members of the public wished to attend the hearing: *Storer v British Gas plc* [2000] IRLR 495. There is no general power to exclude the press or public from a hearing where the power to sit in private does not apply but the evidence is of a sensitive or salacious nature: *R v Southampton Industrial Tribunal, ex p INS News Group Ltd* [1995] IRLR 247; and see as to the importance attached to tribunal hearings being conducted in public *R v London (North) Industrial Tribunal, ex p Associated Newspapers Ltd* [1998] ICR 1212.

The reporting of proceedings in cases involving allegations of sexual misconduct or evidence of a personal nature in disability discrimination cases is subject to special procedures for the restriction of reports identifying the parties concerned: see **18.18** above.

18.52 Conduct of the hearing

The general principle is that the tribunal is free to regulate its own procedure within the framework of the *Rules of Procedure* (*ET Rules, rule 60(1)*). This is subject to general legal principles designed to ensure fairness to the parties, and to the specific rules of procedure, including the Overriding Objective. The *Rules* place a general obligation on the Employment Judge or tribunal 'so far as it appears appropriate to do so, [to] seek to avoid formality in his or its proceedings' (*rule 14(2)*). The tribunal is not bound by the rules of evidence which apply in a court of law and is enjoined by *rule 14(3)* to 'make such inquiries of persons appearing before him or it and witnesses as he or it considers appropriate', and to conduct the hearing:

> 'in such manner as he or it considers most appropriate for the clarification of the issues and generally for the just handling of the proceedings.'

This broad discretion results in considerable variation in the extent to which particular tribunals conduct cases in an inquisitorial way or leave it to the parties to present their case as they think best; much depends on the style of individual Judges. See further as to the tribunal's powers to manage the proceedings **18.56** below. The EAT has, however, stressed that a degree of formality and structure is necessary; informality can be counter-productive and tribunals should normally adhere to the generally recognised rules of procedure (*Aberdeen Steak Houses Group plc v Ibrahim* [1988] ICR 550). Although this case pre-dates the revisions of the *Rules* in 2001 and 2004, it is still relevant. In particular, tribunals are required to observe such basic rules of fair conduct or natural justice as the rules against bias on the part of a Judge (*Laher v London Borough of Hammersmith and Fulham* (EAT/215/91), IDS Brief 531; for a more recent example of a case where there was found to be an appearance of bias on the part of the Judge see *Diem v Crystal Services plc* [2006] All ER (D) 84 (Feb), EAT (comment on colour of claimant's skin)). See also *Gill v Humanware Europe* (UKEAT/0312/08), where the EAT held that there was an appearance of bias when the judge (as it was alleged) had had a private conversation with counsel for the respondent in the course of the hearing.

It is a general principle that decisions which require to be taken in the course of the hearing on points of case management (such as whether to grant a party's application for an adjournment) should not be taken by the judge without consulting the lay members, if there are lay members sitting: *Jones v Corbin* (UKEAT/0504/10).

The Judge should alert the parties before taking a point on which they have not addressed the tribunal (*Laurie v Holloway* [1994] ICR 32); and see *Launahurst Ltd v Larner* [2010] EWCA Civ 334 (error of law to base decision on point not raised by or with the parties during the hearing). It has also been held that the tribunal should not rely on cases discovered through its own researches without giving the parties an opportunity to make submissions on them: *Albion Hotel (Freshwater) Ltd v Maia e Silva* [2002] IRLR 200; but see also *Sheridan v Stanley Cole (Wainfleet) Ltd* [2003] EWCA Civ 1046, [2003] IRLR 885, adopting a less strict view on this point, and *Clark v Clark Construction Initiatives Ltd* [2008] EWCA Civ 1446, [2009] ICR 718, where it was held that the citation of cases was not in the circumstances material to the decision.

The Judge and members must also, unsurprisingly, remain attentive throughout the hearing: thus the Court of Appeal in *Stansbury v Datapulse plc* [2003] EWCA Civ 1951, [2004] IRLR 466 set aside the judgment of a tribunal reached after a hearing during which one of the lay members had fallen asleep after allegedly drinking alcohol during the lunch break.

The Court of Appeal has emphasised that despite the relative informality accorded to tribunal proceedings, employment tribunals are not inquisitorial bodies, so that where the burden of proof rests on a particular party, the onus is on that party to put evidence before the tribunal enabling that burden to be discharged: *McNicol v Balfour Beatty Rail Maintenance Ltd* [2002] EWCA Civ 1074, [2002] ICR 1498, a case where the claimant's status as a disabled person was in dispute. However, the Court indicated that the tribunal should use its case management powers to ensure that a claimant appreciated the kind of medical evidence that might be needed to establish disability. More generally, tribunals are not under a duty to ensure that every allegation in a Claim Form is dealt with, regardless of whether the claimant puts forward evidence or argument in support of it (*Mensah v East Hertfordshire NHS Trust* [1998] IRLR 531, CA; and see *Hyde-Walsh v Ashby*

[2008] All ER (D) 225 (Feb), EAT: tribunal has discretion whether to draw attention to a head of claim apparently overlooked by the claimant). This point is particularly important because of the general rule that arguments and points not taken at the tribunal hearing cannot be raised for the first time by way of appeal: see **19.15** below.

The EAT has held that the tribunal has discretion whether to permit a respondent to withdraw an admission: *Nowicka-Price v Chief Constable of Gwent Constabulary* (UKEAT/0268/09). The factors that should be taken into account in considering whether to exercise the discretion (and presumably also where it is the claimant who seeks to withdraw an admission or concession) are those listed for civil cases in *CPR Part 14*.

18.53 Order of presenting the parties' evidence

In preparing for the hearing, a representative needs to consider whether he or she, or the other party's representative, will be required to open the case. The party bearing the burden of proof normally opens: in an unfair dismissal case this is the employer if dismissal is admitted, as he or she must show the reason; if dismissal is disputed (as often happens in constructive dismissal claims) the employee normally opens. The employee also normally opens in discrimination cases and claims for breach of contract or unlawful deduction of wages. Where there are claims which involve an initial burden of proof on each party, the tribunal will decide who should go first having regard to the wishes of the parties and any other factors appearing relevant (this may include in particular which party's evidence is more likely to assist the tribunal's initial understanding of the dispute). Tribunals do not normally permit the party who starts to make an opening statement, and if one is permitted it should be a reasonably brief introduction to the parties, the facts, the issues in dispute, the key documents and the principal contentions on any points of law that arise. Opening statements are not permitted at all in Scotland.

18.54 Non-attendance of parties and applications to adjourn

If a party fails to attend a Hearing, the tribunal has power under *rule 27(5)* to dismiss the claim (if it is the claimant who has failed to attend) or dispose of it in the absence of the non-attending party, or adjourn the proceedings to another date. However the tribunal must, before proceeding to dismiss or dispose of the proceedings consider any information which has been made available by the parties (*rule 27(6)*)

There are a wide range of circumstances in which this discretion may fall to be exercised. One which arises relatively frequently is the failure of a party (in practice nearly always the claimant) to attend coupled with an application for an adjournment of the hearing on the grounds of the absent party's ill-health. Guidance has been given by the Court of Appeal in two cases – *Teinaz v Wandsworth London Borough Council* [2002] EWCA Civ 1040, [2002] IRLR 721 and *Andreou v Lord Chancellor's Department* [2002] EWCA Civ 1192, [2002] IRLR 728 – as to how a tribunal should apply the conflicting considerations of justice when such an application is made on or immediately before the date of the hearing. The tribunal is entitled to require clear medical evidence to satisfy it that the impediment to attendance is genuine, the burden being on the party making the application. If there is clear and uncontradicted evidence that a party is medically unfit to attend the hearing, it will often be an error of law to proceed with the hearing in the absence of a party, even if this causes considerable inconvenience or delay to the proceedings, since the absent party is in effect denied a fair hearing of his or her case: see *Chang-Tave v Haydon School* (UKEAT/0153/10). The *Teinaz* case itself also relied expressly on *Art 6, ECHR* as demanding nothing less than an adjournment in those circumstances (see e.g. para 21). That said, in Transport for *London v O'Cathail* [2013] IRLR 310, the Court of Appeal held that it can be legitimate for a tribunal to take the exceptional step of rejecting an application for an adjournment on medical grounds, even in the face of unchallenged medical evidence supporting an adjournment. The Court emphasised that whilst the position of the potentially absent claimant is highly relevant, it is not determinative of every case. Overall fairness to both parties must be considered in the round and not pre-determined by the situation of one of the parties. *Art 6, ECHR* does not compel the tribunal to the conclusion that it is always unfair to refuse an application for an adjournment on medical grounds, if it would mean that the hearing would take place in the party's absence: the tribunal must balance the adverse consequences of procceding with the hearing in the absence of one party against the right of the other party to have a trial within reasonable time and the public interest in prompt and efficient adjudication of cases.

Where the evidence is unclear as to the applicant's fitness to attend or continue with the hearing, *Teinaz* emphasised that the tribunal has a power to give a direction to enable doubts to be resolved, e.g. by allowing for a short adjournment for further enquiries to be made. In *Iqbal v Metropolitan Police Authority* (UKEAT/0186/12), the EAT held that where an application for an adjournment on health grounds is made during the hearing, the tribunal should have regard to medical evidence including that in the bundle (eg expert and occupational health reports). Further, HHJ Richardson held when making further enquiries, a tribunal was entitled to entitled to ask the litigant to take with him a short letter drafted by the Tribunal explaining the assistance that the Tribunal can give to litigants in person and explaining what assistance and opinion it is that is required from the medical practitioner (para 20).

Further guidance on the factors to be weighed up in determining last minute applications to adjourn was given in *D'Silva v Manchester Metropolitan University* (UKEAT/0336/09/LA) [2011] All ER (D) 05 (May), where the EAT upheld a decision to refuse an adjournment sought on the ground that the claimant claimed to be unfit to appear (but without supporting medical evidence) and sought an adjournment to arrange for representation, having lost his legal representation just before the hearing; the EAT held that the claimant was an educated and intelligent man with a full grasp of his claim and was therefore not sufficiently disadvantaged by the lack of representation to justify the cost and inconvenience to the respondent of an adjournment.

It is also not uncommon in practice that one party or the other does not attend without prior warning or explanation. The Court of Appeal has ruled that if the claimant fails to attend the hearing, the tribunal has a very wide discretion in the light of the available evidence whether to dismiss the claim, proceed in the claimant's absence or adjourn to another date: *Roberts v Skelmersdale College* [2003] EWCA Civ 954, [2003] ICR 1127. The usual procedure in such a case, whether it is the claimant or respondent who has failed to attend, is for a member of the tribunal staff to telephone the party concerned to seek an explanation for their absence. This practice was endorsed by the EAT in *Cooke v Glenrose Fish Co* [2004] ICR 1188, and the EAT has since held that a failure to attempt to contact the missing party would provide grounds for a review of any decision taken in that party's absence: *Euro Hotels (Thornton Heath) Ltd v Alam* (UKEAT/0006/09). The same approach was adopted by the EAT in a case where the parties had been ordered to lodge written submissions, the claimant's had not been received, and the tribunal proceeded to reach its decision without any attempt to contact him to find out what had happened: *Quashie v Methodist Homes Housing Association* (UKEAT/0422/11). The EAT held that the tribunal was not entitled to assume that the claimant had decided not to make submissions, and its failure to investigate the matter deprived her of a fair hearing.

An option often adopted in practice when the claimant fails to attend, if the claim is of unfair dismissal, where the respondent has the initial burden of proof, is for the tribunal to hear the respondent's evidence and submissions before deciding the case on its merits, in the absence of the claimant. If the claimant does not attend for claimed medical reasons but without providing sufficient evidence of incapacity, the tribunal may refer the case to a PHR to consider striking the claim out as not being actively pursued; see *Rolls Royce Ltd v Riddle* [2008] IRLR 873; but see also *Abegaze v Shrewsbury College of Arts and Technology* [2009] EWCA Civ 96, [2009] All ER (D) 209 (Feb) and **18.17** above.

In the case of non-attendance of a respondent, if when contacted by the tribunal an excuse or explanation for non-attendance is offered, the respondent should be told of the right to apply for an adjournment, and any such application must be considered before the tribunal decides how to proceed: *Beswick Paper Ltd v Britton* (UKEAT/0104/09); this would presumably equally be so if it is the claimant who fails to attend but proffers an explanation. See also *Southwark London Borough Council v Bartholomew* [2004] ICR 358, EAT. If the respondent fails to appear without good reason having been given, the tribunal will usually agree to hear the claimant's case and give a decision in the respondent's absence.

If a representative for the party attends, the representative is entitled to be heard even though the party has not attended (see *Astles v A G Stanley Ltd* (UKEAT/1275/95), IDS Brief 588).

It is also not uncommon that both parties attend the hearing but an application is made for an adjournment because of a last minute development affecting the conduct of the case, most commonly the sudden illness of an important witness. In such a case, the tribunal will consider the matter in the light of the views of both parties, and balancing the interests of justice as between the parties. An example can be found in *North Bristol NHS Trust v Harrold* (UKEAT/0548/11), where the EAT endorsed a tribunal's decision to refuse a respondent's application to adjourn a hearing on the final day of a three day hearing in order to allow the respondent to call further witnesses; the EAT held a tribunal should not accede automatically to the wishes of one of the litigants, but rather balance the interests of both parties.

In *Firouzian v Metroline Travel Ltd* (UKEAT/0233/12), the EAT held the tribunal was entitled to refuse to adjourn a PHR on the question of disability until after the claimant's criminal trial. That trial was in respect of causing death by dangerous driving arising out of his employment as a bus driver. The claims of disability and race discrimination arose from how the claimant was allegedly dealt with under internal proceedings as a result of the same driving incident. The EAT held there was no risk of prejudicing the criminal trial because of the lack of overlap between the issues on the PHR and that trial. The tribunal had been entitled to refuse to postpone the PHR.

If the case is determined in the absence of a party and it later transpires that that party had not received notification of the hearing date, the tribunal may review its decision: see 18.74–18.75 below. An application for a review may also be made, and would need to be considered on its merits, if there is any other reason for the absence of the party which had not been known to the tribunal when a decision to proceed with the hearing had been taken. The issue for the tribunal will in each case be what is the balance of the interests of justice as between the decision reached standing or being set aside and the case being referred for a hearing, or re-hearing. It may be relevant to the determination of this point that the expense and inconvenience to the attending party of a re-hearing can be compensated by an order for costs; but it is generally a factor of little weight against ordering a re-hearing that the party whose representative failed to attend the hearing may recover any losses from the representative: see *Euro Hotels (Thornton Heath) Ltd v Alam*, above.

18.55 Rights of representation

The right of a party to be represented at a hearing by whoever he or she chooses (whether or not professionally qualified) is expressly given by *s 6, ETA 1996*. In *Bache v Essex County Council* [2000] IRLR 251, the Court of Appeal ruled that the tribunal therefore has no power to 'sack' a party's representative under its general power to control the proceedings. If it does so, this is a ground of appeal notwithstanding the acquiescence of the party at the time. However, denial of representation by the chosen person did not render the hearing a nullity, and on the facts the decision was upheld.

The EAT has applied the principle in *Bache* in a case where the employers unsuccessfully sought an order forbidding the claimant from using a particular firm of solicitors to represent him at the hearing because of a claimed conflict of interest: *Dispatch Management Services (UK) Ltd v Douglas* [2002] IRLR 389. However, if the party's chosen representative behaves inappropriately, the tribunal's powers to act in response to the misbehaviour of a party (in an extreme case extending to the striking out of the claim or defence, provided that this is a proportionate response: see *Bennett v Southwark London Borough Council* [2002] EWCA Civ 223, [2002] IRLR 407) are equally available in respect of conduct of the representative acting on behalf of the party: *rule 18(7)*. If the representative is acting for profit, the further sanction of a wasted costs order (see **18.73** for this) is available to the tribunal.

The tribunal has no power to impose a representative on an unrepresented party. This point was confirmed in *Johnson v Edwardian International Hotels Ltd* [2008] All ER (D) 23 (May), where the tribunal had sought to have the Official Solicitor appointed as the claimant's litigation friend, after he had made claims that he was the victim of a conspiracy involving the Prime Minister and the Jehovah's Witnesses to procure his dismissal. The EAT held that the tribunal's only recourse was to use its case management powers, including the power to strike out the claim on the ground that it had no reasonable prospects of success.

A person who is representing him or herself in a tribunal is known as a 'litigant in person'; this phrase is now to be preferred to 'self-represented litigant': see *Practice Guidance: Terminology for Litigants in Person* (issued by Lord Dyson MR, March 2013). The equivalent expression in Scotland is 'party litigant'.

18.56   Tribunal's powers to control the procedure

The tribunal has a considerable discretion as to the management of the proceedings before it. A party does not have the right to cross-examine come what may. The tribunal has a duty to keep the inquiry before it within reasonable bounds, and it does not have to allow lengthy and detailed cross-examination on matters that do not appear to it to be of assistance. These points were emphasised by the EAT in *Zurich Insurance Co v Gulson* [1998] IRLR 118.

It is for the parties to determine what evidence they wish to put before the tribunal, but whilst the *ET Rules* provide that the parties are entitled to give evidence, call witnesses, ask questions and address the tribunal (see *rule 27(2)*), this is subject to the general power of the tribunal conferred by *rule 14(3)*. The EAT has confirmed that this gives the tribunal a discretion to exclude even relevant evidence, where for instance the evidence is unnecessarily repetitive or of only marginal relevance: *Digby v East Cambridgeshire District Council* [2007] IRLR 585 (and see for the power of the tribunal to exclude irrelevant and marginally relevant evidence in advance of the hearing *HSBC Asia Holdings BV v Gillespie* [2011] ICR 192, EAT, above at **18.45**). This discretion must be exercised consistently with the parties' rights under *Art 6* of the *European Convention on Human Rights*, to a fair hearing of their respective cases. However *Art 6* does not give unlimited protection to whatever a party may want. It has been confirmed, for instance, in *Power v Greater Manchester Police Authority* (UKEAT/0087/10), that there is no general right for a claimant to cross-examine the person alleged to have discriminated against him or her under *Art 6*, so that it was not a ground of appeal that the respondent had not called the decision-taker concerned as a witness, thereby preventing the claimant from cross-examining her. See also *Khan v Vignette Europe Ltd* (UKEAT/0134/09), where the EAT upheld a tribunal's refusal of a request by the claimant for an adjournment part-way through a hearing to enable him to undertake religious observances for Ramadan.

The tribunal may also, in the interests of devoting a proportionate amount of time to issues within the case, curtail unnecessarily lengthy evidence or cross-examination. However, that discretion must be exercised judicially and is open to challenge on appeal if exercised by reference to irrelevant considerations or perversely, as in the *Digby* case. It is an increasingly common practice for tribunals to set time limits on stages in the proceedings, such as cross-examination of a particular witness or the making of a closing submission, usually as part of a timetable set at the start of the hearing to ensure that it is concluded within the time available. Such restrictions should not be so restrictive as to deny a party the opportunity to put his or her case.

In his judgment in *Bache*, Mummery LJ made the following statement of the principles governing the conduct of tribunal hearings:

'(1)   At the hearing the tribunal must follow a procedure which is fair to both sides. It must normally allow each party to call relevant evidence, to ask relevant questions of the other side's witnesses and to make relevant submissions on the evidence and the law.

(2)   The tribunal is responsible for the fair conduct of the hearing. It is in control. Neither the parties nor their representatives are in control of the hearing.

(3)   Procedural fairness applies to the conduct of all those involved in the hearing. Just as the tribunal is under a duty to behave fairly, so are the parties and their representatives. The tribunal is accordingly entitled to require the parties and their representatives to act in a fair and reasonable way in the presentation of their evidence, in challenging the other side's evidence and in making submissions. The rulings of the tribunal on what is and is not relevant and on what is the fair and appropriate procedure ought to be respected even by a party and his representative who do not agree with a ruling. If the party and his representative disagree with a ruling, an appeal lies against it if the tribunal has made an error of law.'

The Court of Appeal has expressed the view that it is always desirable that any irregularity in procedure, such as the Judge or a member falling asleep, or the making of inappropriate comments, should be raised at the time, but failure to do so (particularly if the party subsequently complaining was not represented at the time) is not necessarily a bar to raising the point on appeal: *Stansbury v Datapulse plc* [2003] EWCA Civ 1951, [2004] IRLR 466, para 23. Peter Gibson LJ acknowledged the difficulty that even a legal representative may have in raising such a point, since if the objection is unsuccessful the person complained about will continue to sit in the case.

The procedure in practice is that the Judge (who, along with the lay members, will have read the Claim Form and Response Form) may first seek to clarify what issues are, or remain, in dispute between the parties. A list of issues might have been agreed or set as a result of a CMD (see discussion at 18.7). If there is an agreed list of issues, that will, as a general rule, limit the issues at the substantive hearing to that list: see *Land Rover v Short* (UKEAT/0496/10) as approved in *Parekh v London Borough of Brent* [2012] EWCA Civ 1630. However, both the Court of Appeal in *Parekh* and the EAT in *Price v Surrey County Council* (UKEAT/0450/10), a judgment given, unusually, by the Senior President of Tribunals, Carnwath LJ, sitting as an EAT judge, have emphasised the importance of the tribunal that hears the case satisfying itself as to precisely what issues do require to be decided, and not simply accepting what the parties may have agreed as the issues or sticking slavishly to a list of issues. This is particularly the case, as in *Price*, where the list agreed between the parties was not a helpful framework for deciding the case. The list in *Price* was attached to the judgment as an illustration of how not to prepare a list of issues not least because it failed to distinguish clearly between the central issues and the detailed factual allegations. Having said that, the tribunal hearing the case does not have carte blanche to decide new points: it is confined to deciding the pleaded issues and cannot when considering the evidence adjudicate upon additional allegations or complaints: see *Chapman v Simon* [1994] IRLR 124, *Foster v Bon Groundwork* [2012] IRLR 517. To do otherwise will deny the party affected a fair hearing: *British Gas Services Ltd v McCaull* [2001] IRLR 60. Further, where the issues have been properly identified and formulated, the hearing will focuse upon and only upon the issues as so identified: see *Tucker v Partnership in Care Ltd* (UKEAT/0455/09).

The judge will also deal at the start of the hearing with any preliminary points such as correcting the name of the respondent, considering any applications to amend the Claim Form or Response Form and ruling on any disputes about disclosure of documents or attendance of witnesses either party wishes to raise. It should be noted that a substantive change in the name or identity of the respondent will necessitate an adjournment of the proceedings to enable the newly identified respondent to attend the hearing: *Johanson t/a Kaleidascope Child Care* (UKEAT/0541/10), where the claim was against a limited company, but (in its absence) the tribunal agreed to change the name of the respondent to that of an individual trading in the name of the company.

The usual procedure after any of the foregoing points that may arise have been addressed is as follows:

(a)   the party upon whom the burden of proof rests normally opens (the claimant in a discrimination case, the employer in an unfair dismissal claim where dismissal is conceded; if there are issues on which there is a burden of proof on both parties in turn, the tribunal is likely to hear submissions from the parties before deciding who should go first: see **18.53**);

(b)   the party called upon to open:

    (i)   may occasionally be permitted to make an opening statement giving an outline of the case (but this is increasingly rare except in the most substantial and complex cases and is not permitted in Scotland: see **18.53** above); and

    (ii)   calls his or her evidence, each witness giving evidence on oath or under affirmation (with the witness's statement normally being taken as his or her evidence-in-chief, and being read by the tribunal before the witness is called)and being open to cross-examination by the other party, and questions by the members of the tribunal;

(c)   the other party:

    (i)   calls his or her evidence; and

    (ii)   makes a closing speech (usually called submissions); and

(d)   the party who opened the case then makes submissions (in Scotland the order of making submissions is reversed).

See further as to the content of submissions, and the use of written submissions, **18.58** below.

Procedural issues arising during the hearing will be ruled on by the judge, but should be decided by all members of the tribunal if it is a full tribunal, not the judge alone. If a party withdraws or abandons a claim or part of a claim, the tribunal should satisfy itself that the party (particularly if not professionally represented) understands the consequences of doing so, and does intend to withdraw or abandon the claim or contention: *Segor v Goodrich Actuation Systems Ltd* (UKEAT/0145/11).

18.57 Witnesses

Witnesses are examined on oath or affirmation. They give their evidence seated at a table and should address the Judge as 'Sir' or 'Madam'. If, as is almost always required in England and Wales, a written witness statement has been prepared, the tribunal will normally have pre-read the statement themselves (for guidance as to the reading of witness statements see *Mehta v Child Support Agency* [2011] IRLR 305, above at **18.46**). Additional questions may then be asked if necessary, with the permission of the tribunal. Where a claimant is unrepresented, the Judge may ask more questions to elicit relevant matters. In Scotland, evidence-in-chief is given by way of answers to questions from the party's representative, or if the party has no representative, by way of narrative or in answer to questions from the tribunal.

Documents should be introduced in the witness statements in chronological or other systematic order by the witness who can best deal with them. It is desirable, if possible, to cross-refer in the written witness statements to the page numbers of any relevant documents, and to invite the tribunal to read the documents or relevant parts together with the witness statement.

When the representative of one party cross-examines a witness of the other party, he or she should put questions to the witness and not make comments or statements. It must be remembered that there is a dual purpose to cross-examination. One is to test the truthfulness and reliability of the witness; the other is to put the questioner's version of the facts to the witness so far as it concerns him or her, so that he or she has an opportunity of commenting on it. A failure to do this may prejudice the cross-examiner's case. It is a general principle that a party or representative may not cross-examine his or her own witness; the concept of a 'hostile witness' is in practice almost unknown.

Parties acting in person, and non-legally qualified representatives, often have difficulty in cross-examining witnesses, through inexperience or unfamiliarity with what is required. In these circumstances the Judge may assist in giving guidance as to what questions can be asked and how they may be put, but should not take over the cross-examination of the witness, as this may lead to an appearance of bias in favour of the party being assisted. How far a Judge will be prepared to go in assisting a party in these circumstances is very much a matter of personal style, and therefore dependent on the particular Judge.

Witnesses will not normally be permitted to refer to notes whilst giving evidence, unless these are agreed documents or a note taken by the witness at the time of an event or very soon thereafter; the witness may refer to such notes to refresh his or her memory of the event.

The *ET Rules* give a general power to the tribunal to exclude a person who is to appear as a witness from the Hearing until that person gives evidence, if it considers it to be in the interest of justice to do so (*rule 27(4)*). In Scotland it is the practice to require witnesses to wait outside the tribunal room until they are called to give their evidence; however, this is very infrequently done in English or Welsh proceedings.

The powers of the tribunal extend to a power to call witnesses of its own initiative (or at the request of a party who is for some good reason unable or unwilling to call the witness): *Clapson v British Airways plc* [2001] IRLR 184.

The evidence given by a witness in tribunal proceedings carries absolute privilege in the law of defamation, and is also within the principle of judicial immunity from suit which applies generally to judicial proceedings. Thus in *Parmar v East Leicester Medical Practice* [2011] IRLR 641 it was held that statements in a witness statement prepared for tribunal proceedings could not be used to found a claim of victimisation. However the principle of judicial proceedings immunity is not wide enough to cover intimidating behaviour directed by a respondent at the claimant outside the tribunal room: *Nicholls v Corin Tech Ltd* (UKEAT/0290/07).

The practice in the past has been that witnesses attending a hearing have been entitled to reclaim their travelling and subsistence expenses from the administration. However the repayment of witness expenses was discontinued from 6 April 2012, for cases presented on or after that date; instead the tribunal has power to order a party to pay the witness's expenses (the paying party may either be the party calling the witness or the opposing party): *ET Rules, Rule38(1)(c)*.

18.58 Other points of procedure

The Judge is required to keep a full note of the evidence given; this is normally done in longhand, or occasionally on a laptop computer; the taking of notes sometimes results in a speed of proceedings which many observers not used to tribunal proceedings find rather slow. The notes are important not only to assist the tribunal in reaching its judgment (especially if the hearing is adjourned part-heard, or judgment is reserved) but also for the benefit of the EAT, if necessary, on any subsequent appeal.

Submissions, or closing speeches, are the opportunity to put to the tribunal the points the party considers should lead the tribunal to find in that party's favour, on each of the issues remaining in dispute. This may involve putting forward propositions as to what the relevant legal principles to be applied are, if necessary with the citation of relevant cases, as well as highlighting points of evidence, and reasons why it is submitted that the evidence of particular witnesses on disputed issues should be preferred. If cases are relied on, copies of the cases should be available to hand to the tribunal, and any particular passages in judgments that are relied on highlighted or drawn to the tribunal's attention. It is open to any party or representative to prepare written submissions or skeleton arguments and invite the tribunal to read them, and this is commonly done by legal representatives, particularly so in longer cases and cases where there are disputed points of law. Occasionally, the provision of written submissions may be directed in advance by the tribunal as part of its case management function, but this is rarely done except in lengthy cases. Written submissions are rarer in Scotland.

In addition, tribunals sometimes ask the parties to make their final submissions in writing, when there is not enough time to complete the case without an adjournment. The parties' representatives may sometimes suggest this. The EAT has given guidance to tribunals as to the procedure to be followed if written submissions are to be provided in place of, rather than in support of, oral submissions: *Barking and Dagenham London Borough Council v Oguoko* [2000] IRLR 179. The procedure should only be implemented with the consent of both parties, and each party must be served a copy of the other's submissions and given time to comment on them (comments being limited to correction of factual errors and responses to any new points of law not previously raised) before the tribunal proceeds to reach its decision. These points were reiterated by the EAT in *Blitz v Equant Integration Services Ltd (t/a Orange Business Services)* [2008] All ER (D) 203 (Jan), EAT, where the point was made that it is particularly important that each party should have the opportunity to comment, preferably orally, on the written submissions of the other. The EAT has held that where a tribunal ordered written submissions and those from the respondent were received in time, but the claimant's submissions were not (having gone astray) it was incumbent on the tribunal to make at least a telephone enquiry of the claimant before proceeding to reach a decision without her submissions: *Quashie v Methodist Homes Housing Association* (UKEAT/0422/11).

In a lengthy or legally complex case, the tribunal may ask for written submissions in addition to oral submissions. In such cases, adequate time must be allowed for the other party's representative, and the tribunal, to read and digest the written submissions before the oral submissions are made: *Sinclair Roche & Temperley v Heard* [2004] IRLR 763.

18.59   It is open to a party to submit at the conclusion of the other party's evidence that there is no case to answer. This should be done without prejudice to the right to call evidence if the submission is rejected. However, the making of such submissions has increasingly been discouraged by the higher courts, especially in discrimination cases where it is necessary to weigh the circumstantial evidence of discrimination with the employer's explanation in assessing whether the evidence justifies an inference of discrimination: see *British Gas plc v Sharma* [1991] ICR 19, where it was described as 'exceptional' for such a submission to be appropriate in a discrimination case. The principles were restated in *Clarke v Watford Borough Council* (EAT/43/99), in terms expressly approved by the Court of Appeal in *Logan v Customs and Excise Comrs* [2003] EWCA Civ 1068, [2004] IRLR 63, as follows:

'(1)   There is no inflexible rule of law and practice that a tribunal must always hear both sides, although that should normally be done.

(2)   The power to stop a case at "half-time" must be exercised with caution.

(3)   It may be a complete waste of time to call on the other party to give evidence in a hopeless case.

(4)   Even where the onus of proof lies on the [claimant], as in discrimination cases, it will only be in exceptional or frivolous cases that it would be right to take such a course.

(5)   Where there is no burden of proof, as under *s 98(4)* of the *Employment Rights Act*, it will be difficult to envisage arguable cases where it is appropriate to terminate the proceedings at the end of the first party's case.'

It should be noted that the reference above to the burden of proof in discrimination cases pre-dates changes in the burden introduced from 2001 onwards; however the point made at (4) above is if anything stronger where only an initial burden is placed on the claimant.

18.60 For the sake of certainty, it is best to obtain a clear indication from the employment tribunal at the commencement of the hearing of whether it will consider liability and remedy separately, and if so, when it will consider evidence and argument on contributory fault and/or on whether a *Polkey* reduction in compensation should be made if a dismissal is found to be procedurally unfair. The EAT has held that it is an error of law for the tribunal to deal with the *Polkey* point without giving the parties an opportunity to make submissions on it: *Market Force (UK) Ltd v Hunt* [2002] IRLR 863; *Grace v BF Components Ltd* (UKEAT/0006/05). By analogy this would apply equally to the issue of contribution, or the amount of any uplift or reduction in compensation under *s 207A, TULRCA 1992*. The point is an illustration of the more general point that it would be an error of law for the tribunal to decide a case on a point the parties have not raised or had an opportunity to deal with; see *Launahurst Ltd v Larner* [2010] EWCA Civ 334 for an example of a case where this was held to have occurred.

The usual practice, in the absence of a direction to the contrary, is that the tribunal will proceed to deal with remedy, if time permits, immediately following its decision on liability (and assuming that that decision is in the claimant's favour). However, it is unusual (at least in England and Wales) for a tribunal to hear evidence relating solely to compensation before it has reached a decision on liability. In *Iggesund Converters Ltd v Lewis* [1984] ICR 544, the EAT suggested ways in which employment tribunals could deal with evidence and argument on the reduction of an award for contributory fault, and in *Ferguson v Gateway Training Centre Ltd* [1991] ICR 658 it suggested that the Judge should restate which issues are being considered prior to final submissions. The EAT has also emphasised that it is important that the tribunal gives the parties a chance to be heard on any issue of remedy before deciding the point: *Duffy v Yeomans & Partners Ltd* [1993] ICR 862.

The EAT has held that in unfair dismissal cases, the tribunal *must* consider the issue of contributory fault if it appears to arise on the evidence: *Swallow Security Services Ltd v Millicent* [2009] All ER (D) 299 (Mar). If the point is to be considered, the tribunal would have to alert the parties to this, to enable them to make submissions on the point.

The practice in Scotland is that unless there has been a prior direction that issues of remedy be dealt with separately, the tribunal will hear evidence on all issues together, and will give a single judgment covering both liability and remedy; the usual practice in all but the most straightforward cases is for the judgment to be reserved and delivered in writing. If there is good reason for keeping the issue of remedy separate (such as that there will be insufficient time within the period listed for the hearing to deal with all issues, or expert evidence will be needed in relation to issues of remedy) an early application should be made for a direction for the hearing to deal in the first instance with liability only.

18.61 Sometimes in the course of the hearing the Judge will give an indication to the parties of the tribunal's provisional view as to the merits of the case, or more commonly a particular issue in the case. This may be done for a number of reasons: to encourage the parties to settle, or give them assistance to settle by giving an indication as to the likely outcome on a particular point or the case as a whole; to identify which issues should be focused on in evidence or cross-examination; or to identify the issues on which submissions are particularly sought. Caution is needed in giving any kind of preliminary indication of the tribunal's view, since this may be interpreted as indicating that the decision has already been reached, or provide a basis for a later appeal on grounds of apparent bias. However the Court of Appeal has confirmed that, provided that it is made quite clear that any views expressed are provisional, there is no objection in principle to the Judge expressing a view in the course of the case: *Jiminez v Southwark London Borough Council* [2003] EWCA Civ 502, [2003] IRLR 477. By contrast, in *Gee v Shell UK Ltd* [2002] EWCA Civ 1479, [2003] IRLR 82, the Court of Appeal held that there had been procedural unfairness where the Judge had warned the claimant (who was acting in person) that she was at risk of an award of costs against her, in circumstances where there was no real basis for an award of costs, and she felt obliged to withdraw her claim to avoid the costs sanction.

18.62 THE JUDGMENT AND REASONS

The *2004 Regulations* made significant changes to the way in which the final determination of the tribunal after a Hearing (or a PHR to determine a preliminary point) is conveyed to the parties. What was formerly called a decision is now termed a judgment, and the former distinction between summary and extended reasons was abolished.

The position now, by virtue of *rule 30*, is that a judgment may either be given orally at the conclusion of the Hearing or PHR, in which case it must subsequently be reduced to writing and signed by the Judge, and is then sent to the parties; or it may be reserved, in which case the written, signed, judgment will be sent to the parties in due course. As noted above, in Scotland the usual practice for all but the most straightforward cases is for the judgment to be reserved. If the judgment is reserved, reasons in writing will be sent at the same time as the judgment itself. However if the judgment is pronounced at the hearing, and reasons are given orally at the time, written reasons are no longer given unless a party specifically requests that they be supplied, at the time the judgment is sent out in written form or within 14 days thereafter (this period is extendable if the Judge considers it just and equitable to do so: *rule 30(5)*). In addition, the Judge may be required to provide written reasons if the EAT so requests for the purpose of an appeal. The written reasons will normally be required as a prerequisite to an appeal against a judgment. A proposal published in the December 2011 consultation for the introduction of a fee payable if reasons in writing are requested has been dropped.

The provisions of *rule 30* governing written reasons have the somewhat surprising consequence that if the judgment is not reserved, and neither party chooses to ask for reasons in writing, there will be no formal record of the reasons available to the press or other interested parties. Even in a case raising issues of wider public interest, there appears not only to be no duty, but even no *power* to give the reasons in writing, provided they have been given orally and none of the parties makes a request for written reasons and the matter is not appealed. This is particularly significant since judgments, and the written reasons for them, are matters of public record.

The Judge or tribunal must also give reasons for orders made under case management powers if so requested before or at the hearing (which can be a CMD or PHR as well as a Hearing) at which the order is made: *ET Rules, rule 30(1)(b)*. The reasons may be given orally or in writing, and there is no right for a party to require that the reasons be given in writing; in practice if such a request is made, it would be unusual for the Judge to refuse it, not least because the request may be a prelude to an appeal, and if the order is appealed without the benefit of written reasons, these are likely to be requested by the EAT. The *Rules* make no provision as to reasons for orders that are made on paper; this means that it is a matter for the Judge making the order to decide whether to provide reasons, but the giving of reasons cannot be compelled, except possibly by way of an appeal.

The tribunal may reach a unanimous or majority judgment (*rule 28(4)*). In the rare cases in which the tribunal is composed only of two members (eg because of the illness of a member part-way through the proceedings) the Judge has a casting vote. *Rule 31* makes provision for judgments, orders or written reasons to be signed on behalf of a Judge who is unavailable through death, incapacity or absence, either by the President, Vice President or Regional Employment Judge, if the judgment etc was of an Employment Judge alone, or by the other members of the tribunal.

The Court of Appeal in *Anglian Home Improvements Ltd v Kelly* [2004] EWCA Civ 901, [2005] ICR 242, [2004] IRLR 793 has given guidance that a tribunal should if at all possible avoid a majority decision, if necessary reserving its decision to give the members time to reflect and the Judge an opportunity to prepare reasons which accurately reflect the majority view (especially if he or she is in the minority).

HM Courts and Tribunals Service sets a target for the promulgation of written judgments and reasons, which is currently that they must be promulgated within four weeks of the conclusion of the Hearing in 85% of cases; this target has been met consistently in recent years, although some tribunal offices have in some years fallen below the target. However occasionally there have been instances of serious delays in issuing the judgment in cases where the judgment was reserved at the end of the hearing. In one such case, *Bangs v Connex South Eastern Ltd* [2005] EWCA Civ 14, [2005] IRLR 389, the Court of Appeal, in the course of refusing to overturn the tribunal's decision, gave guidance as to how such delay is to be considered in the context of an appeal. Delay in issuing a judgment is not of itself an error of law and therefore not as such a ground of appeal. The key question, the Court held, is whether due to the delay there was a real risk that a party had been denied or deprived of the right to a fair trial.

In the related case of *Kwamin v Abbey National plc* [2004] IRLR 516, the EAT had taken a broader approach, which was disapproved by the Court of Appeal; it had also given strong guidance, which was implicitly approved by the Court of Appeal, as to the need to avoid lengthy delays in reaching and issuing reserved judgments. Three-and-a-half months is the longest acceptable time for the delivery of judgment following the conclusion of the Hearing (or the delivery of written submissions, if later), and except in the most complex cases, longer delay without proper explanation (such as illness) would be regarded as culpable; it does not however follow that such delay justifies an appeal. An extreme example of delay occurred in *Carpenter v City of Edinburgh Council* (UKEATS/0038/07), where the judgment was issued over three years after the hearing had concluded; the EAT overturned the decision, not because of the delay itself, but because of a number of points on which it appeared from the terms of the reasons that the tribunal had forgotten relevant evidence.

18.63   Adequacy of reasons

The *2004 Rules* set out for the first time in detail what matters must be covered in the reasons given for a judgment (but not an order): *rule 30(6)* lists the required information as:

(a)   The issues identified as relevant to the claim;

(b)   If some of the issues were not determined, which, and why not;

(c)   The findings of fact relevant to the issues determined;

(d)   A concise statement of the applicable law;

(e)   How the relevant findings of fact and the applicable law have been applied;

(f)   An explanation of how any compensation awarded has been calculated (which may be by way of a table).

There is an additional and specific duty to give an explanation of any award of interest, and reasons for any decision not to award interest, in discrimination and equal pay cases (*Employment Tribunals (Interest on Awards in Discrimination Cases) Regulations 1996 (SI 1996/2803), reg 7*); where the *Employment Protection (Recoupment of Jobseeker's Allowance and Income Support) Regulations 1996* apply, there is a requirement for the tribunal to state that they apply, and to specify the 'prescribed amount' (the part of the compensation covering the period during which benefits were received, which is then available for the DWP to recover the benefits before the balance is payable to the successful claimant).

The EAT has held that it is an error of law on the part of the tribunal not to give reasons meeting the requirements of *rule 30(6)*: *Greenwood v NWF Retail Ltd* [2011] ICR 896. However in the same case the EAT quoted with approval comments of Buxton LJ in *Balfour Beatty Power Networks Ltd v Wilcox* [2007] IRLR 63, at para 25, that:

> ' . . . the rule is surely intended to be a guide and not a straitjacket. Provided it can be reasonably spelled out from the determination of the employment tribunal that what rule 30(6) requires has been provided by that tribunal, then no error of law will have been committed.'

The statutory requirements reflect and to some extent consolidate requirements increasingly emphasised by the appellate courts as a necessary part of the judicial process: see in particular *English v Emery Reimbold & Strick Ltd* [2002] EWCA Civ 605, [2003] IRLR 710. However in *Greenwood* the EAT said that the more relevant authority on sufficiency of reasons in employment tribunals is *Meek v City of Birmingham District Council* [1987] IRLR 250, CA.

The following statement by Bingham LJ in *Meek* is generally regarded as the leading statement of principle on inadequacy of reasons as a ground of appeal, and is regularly referred to for this purpose:

> 'It has on a number of occasions been made plain that the decision of an [Employment] Tribunal is not required to be an elaborate formalistic product of refined legal draftsmanship, but it must contain an outline of the story which has given rise to the complaint and a summary of the Tribunal's basic factual conclusions and a statement of the reasons which have led them to reach the conclusion which they do on those basic facts. The parties are entitled to be told why they have won or lost. There should be sufficient account of the facts and of the reasoning to enable the EAT . . . to see whether any question of law arises; and it is highly desirable that the decision of an [Employment] Tribunal should give guidance both to employers and trade unions as to practices which should or should not be adopted.'

Whilst the tribunal must reach a conclusion on all the issues required by the statute concerned to be decided, and at least consider all the relevant facts, its decision need only refer to the important and/or controversial points: *High Table Ltd v Horst* [1997] IRLR 513. It is, however, important that the tribunal properly identifies the legal rules and tests it has applied in reaching its decision: *Conlin v United Distillers* [1994] IRLR 169, para 6.

Further guidance on the adequacy of reasons was given by the Court of Appeal in *Tran v Greenwich Vietnam Community Project* [2002] EWCA Civ 553, [2002] IRLR 735. Reasons need not be lengthy, but should be sufficient to explain to the parties how the tribunal got from its findings of fact to its conclusions. In addition, whilst the reasons are primarily addressed to those already familiar with the context of the case, it is desirable that the reasoning can be ascertained from the face of the decision; in any case it is necessary that the decision is sufficiently reasoned to enable an appellate court or tribunal to ascertain what the tribunal's findings of fact and reasons for its conclusions were. The decision of the Court of Appeal in *Anya v University of Oxford* [2001] EWCA Civ 405, [2001] IRLR 377 contains important comments on the need for tribunals in discrimination cases to set out the findings reached on the issues of primary fact, and an explanation why the tribunal does or does not draw inferences of discrimination from the facts as found.

A number of cases have highlighted the need for tribunals to give reasons for specific elements in their judgments; these include the exercise of the discretionary power to increase or reduce compensation under *Employment Act 2002, s 31* (the same point presumably applies to the replacement power under *TULRCA 1992, s 207A*), and decisions on contributory fault (in relation to which the Court of Appeal has suggested that the tribunal should make findings of fact separate from those made in relation to the fairness of the dismissal: *London Ambulance Service v Small* [2009] EWCA Civ 220, [2009] IRLR 563).

The alleged inadequacy of the tribunal's reasons (often put as a complaint that the judgment was not '*Meek*-compliant') is one of the most frequent grounds of appeal. However, the EAT is in practice rarely prepared to overturn a tribunal's judgment simply on the grounds that the reasons given are inadequate. The Court of Appeal in the *English* case stressed that it is not a good ground of appeal that the reasons for a judgment are inadequate if it is clear from reading the judgment with knowledge of the evidence given and submissions made why the point in question was decided as it was. However a rather stricter approach was taken by the Court of Appeal in *Bahl v Law Society* [2004] IRLR 799 (a discrimination case), emphasising that only in a limited class of cases will it be possible to make good in that way inadequate reasons given by the tribunal.

The EAT has adopted a practice, in many but not all of the cases where an appeal is brought on the ground of inadequate reasons, to remit the case to the tribunal for it to clarify or amplify its reasons, prior to the hearing of the substantive appeal. The legality of the practice (which had been in doubt because of conflicting decisions of the Court of Appeal on the EAT's powers) was initially confirmed by the EAT in *Burns v Consignia plc (No 2)* [2004] IRLR 425, and subsequently (but on a different basis) by the Court of Appeal itself in *Barke v SEETEC Business Technology Centre Ltd* [2005] EWCA Civ 578, [2005] IRLR 633, and the procedure is often referred to as a '*Burns/Barke* reference' accordingly. The power is to be found in the *ET Rules, rule 30(3)(b)*, which requires the tribunal to provide reasons for any order or judgment if requested by the EAT. This power can equally be used where reasons were either not given at all (in the case of an order) or only given orally (for either an order or a judgment). The EAT also has the necessary power under a general provision giving it the power to regulate its own procedure (*ETA 1996, s 30(1)*). The Court added that the procedure should not be used in cases where the reasons were fundamentally deficient, or there is an allegation of bias, or a danger that the tribunal will tailor its response to shoring up the original decision rather than give its true reasons (a point taken up again by the Court in *Woodhouse School v Webster* [2009] EWCA Civ 91, [2009] IRLR 568, where it was stressed that the judge should not in responding go beyond clarification of reasons to advocacy for the original decision). See further on the use of the *Burns/Barke* procedure *Korashi v Abertawe Bro Morgannwg University Local Health Board* [2011] EWCA Civ 187, [2011] All ER (D) 09 (Mar).

18.64 Changing and correcting the decision

A judgment given orally at the end of the hearing is a final decision. The powers of a tribunal to change its judgment subsequently, prior to promulgation in writing (eg where there is a subsequent change in the relevant case law), are very limited. In *Lamont v Fry's Metals Ltd*

[1985] ICR 566 the Court of Appeal assumed, without deciding the point, that a tribunal can recall its judgment before it is entered in the Register. However, it should then give both parties an opportunity of addressing further argument to the tribunal (see also *Arthur Guinness Son & Co (Great Britain) Ltd v Green* [1989] ICR 241, EAT; *Gutzmore v J Wardley (Holdings) Ltd* [1993] ICR 581). More recent EAT decisions have emphasised the limits on the power of recall, and suggest that there is no power on recall to change the substantive judgment (*Spring Grove Services Group plc v Hickinbottom* [1990] ICR 111; *Casella London Ltd v Banai* [1990] ICR 215). However in *CK Heating Ltd v Doro* [2010] ICR 1449, the EAT held that a tribunal was entitled to recall for further consideration a decision, announced orally at the end of the hearing but which had not been issued as a written judgment, that the claimant's compensation would be reduced by 30% for contributory fault. Although in general the parties are entitled to regard an oral statement of the result of a hearing as final, until the written judgment is issued it is open to the tribunal, if it considers it to be in the interest of justice to do so, to recall its decision. There is less objection to a decision being recalled in these circumstances if there will not be any requirement for reconsideration of the primary facts, or further evidence.

There is a power to correct clerical errors in a judgment by a certificate signed by the Judge, or the Regional Judge, President or Vice President (*ET Rules, rule 37(1)*). This power is however limited; thus in *Bone v Newham London Borough Council* [2008] EWCA Civ 435, [2008] IRLR 546 the Court of Appeal held that the tribunal did not have the power to 'correct' its judgment by inserting a finding that the dismissal of the claimant was an act of sex discrimination, having recorded the opposite in its original written judgment.

It has been held by the EAT that if the form of a certificate issued under *rule 37(1)* is the substitution of a complete corrected version of the judgment and reasons for the original version, time for appealing starts to run from the date of the certificate of correction: *Kennaugh v Lloyd-Jones (t/a Cheshire Tree Surgeons)* [2006] All ER (D) 363 (Nov). The better practice is therefore only to identify the words or passage corrected; this will not affect the running of time.

The issue of deviation in the written reasons for a judgment (as opposed to the judgment itself) from the oral reasons was considered by the EAT in *The Partners of Haxby Practice v Collen* [2013] All ER (D) 11 (Feb). Whilst the EAT accepted that normally written reasons supplied pursuant to rule 30(3) will correspond closely to the oral reasons given at the conclusion of the hearing, it was acknowledged there will almost always be some degree of editing. Underhill J held that this editing process may, depending on the circumstances and temperament of the judge, be more or less substantial; every now and then there will be cases where the process of revision is so extensive that the reasoning in support of a conclusion differs in substance from the oral reasoning. The EAT held there was "no shame in this" and a departure from initially expressed reasoning does not involve any error of law. The written reasons, where supplied, are the sole authoritative statement of the tribunal's reasons and the oral reasons are superseded. The oral reasons might, however, still remain relevant to allegations of apparent bias or where they might elucidate some ambiguity in the written reasons.

The power of review is considered at **18.74–18.75** below.

18.65   Register of judgments

There is a public register of tribunal judgments and written reasons. All such judgments and reasons are entered in it and available for public (and press) scrutiny, except in cases of national security or where the tribunal has sat in private and it so orders (*ET Regulations, reg 17, ET Rules, rule 31(1) and (2)*). In a case appearing to involve allegations of a sexual offence, material identifying individuals making or affected by the allegations is deleted from the public copy (*rule 49*)). Necessarily only written reasons can be included in the Register, a factor which parties should consider before deciding whether to ask for written reasons where the reasons have been given orally.

18.66 REMEDIES AND ENFORCEMENT

The remedies available in the tribunal depend on the particular jurisdiction covering the case, and are discussed together with the substantive law elsewhere in this book. A number of additional points require mention.

A judgment ordering the payment of money made by a tribunal is enforceable as if it was a judgment of the County Court (or in Scotland the Sheriff Court). The fact that an appeal is pending does not itself suspend the remedy awarded, but if an application to enforce it is made to the County Court, the other party will usually be granted a stay of execution pending the appeal.

Tribunals have no power to enforce their own non-monetary judgments except by awards of compensation; the best examples are an additional award for failure to comply with an order for re-employment in an unfair dismissal case (*ERA 1996, s 117(3)–(5)*), and power to increase compensation if the employer has failed without reasonable justification to comply with a recommendation in a discrimination case (*Equality Act 2010, s 124(7)*).

The absence of any enforcement machinery other than the County Court has led in a significant number of cases to real difficulties in the successful claimant recovering the compensation awarded, even disregarding cases where the employer is insolvent (in which case there may be a claim against the Secretary of State: see INSOLVENCY OF EMPLOYER (29)). Research commissioned by the Ministry of Justice (*Research into the enforcement of employment tribunal awards in England and Wales*, Ministry of Justice Research Series 9/09, May 2009) found that only 61% of those claimants interviewed who had received a tribunal award had received any payment; only 53% had been paid in full. Reasons for non-payment included 29% of non-paying employers simply refusing to pay, whilst 39% no longer existed or had gone bankrupt. The National Association of Citizens' Advice Bureaux had earlier proposed that awards of compensation should be paid by the state, with the right to recover the money from the employer passing to the Government (*Hollow Victories*, March 2005). This proposal was not accepted by the Government, but the *Tribunals, Courts and Enforcement Act 2007 s 142* (adding a new *s 19A* to the *ETA 1996*) has introduced some improvement in the position. The position now is that once the judgment has been formally registered with the County Court, any of the various means of enforcement of County Court judgments can be initiated without the need first to apply for the Court to order the respondent to pay the sum awarded and then to allow time for payment. A similar but simpler procedure applies in Scotland, where the enforcement of a payment ordered by a judgment is undertaken by the Sheriff Court on the authority of the judgment of the tribunal.

The Court of Appeal has held that failure to pay compensation awarded to a claimant in a discrimination case may be made the subject of a claim of victimisation: *Rank Nemo (DMS) Ltd v Coutinho* [2009] EWCA Civ 454, [2009] IRLR 672.

Where the tribunal has given judgment in favour of the claimant on liability but adjourned the question of remedy, it is open to the parties to reach a private agreement as to the remedy, subject to a formal consent judgment being made by the tribunal. Such an agreement, provided that it is embodied in a judgment, is binding without the need to comply with the requirements for a compromise agreement (as to which, see **18.33–18.35** above): *Carter v Reiner Moritz Associates Ltd* [1997] ICR 881. Alternatively, if the parties wish to keep the terms of the agreement confidential, the tribunal may be asked to make a consent order staying (or in Scotland sisting) the proceedings for a period to allow for payment of the agreed sum (the amount of which need not be set out in the order), with provision for the case to be dismissed if no application is made to restore it within a stated period.

18.67   Interest on awards

Interest is payable on any compensation ordered by a tribunal which has not been paid within 42 days of the issue of the written decision. Interest starts to run at the end of the 42-day period and is payable at the rate fixed from time to time under the *Judgments Act 1838* applicable at the date it starts to accrue. The current rate is 8% (this had not been changed as at date of going to press, despite the general collapse in interest rates in 2008–9). If compensation is subsequently increased or decreased on appeal, the new amount is subject to interest from the original date (*Employment Tribunals (Interest) Order 1990 (SI 1990/479)*).

Normally, tribunals cannot award interest as a remedy in its own right, however long the delay since the matters giving rise to the remedy. The principal exception to this is in discrimination and equal pay cases. The relevant regulations (which originate from regulations in sex discrimination and equal pay cases introduced in 1993 to give effect to a decision of the ECJ (*Marshall v Southampton and SW Hampshire Health Authority (No 2)* [1993] ICR 893)) are currently the *Employment Tribunals (Interest on Awards in Discrimination Cases) Regulations 1996 (SI 1996/2803)* (the '*1996 Interest Regulations*'). There is no automatic right to interest under the *1996 Interest Regulations*, but the tribunal is required to consider the question even if not asked to do so (*reg 2(1)(b)*). In practice, in any case where there is a significant time lag between the discrimination and the decision, a tribunal may be expected to award interest unless there are special reasons for not doing so.

The rate of interest is that laid down from time to time under *rule 27(1)* of the *Court Funds Rules 1987 (SI 1987/821)* as the rate of interest for the Special Investment Account (*reg 3(2)*); this is currently (and since 1 July 2009) 0.5%, having been reduced in stages in 2009 from the former rate of 6%. Where the calculation period covers periods of varying rates of interest, an average rate can be taken (*reg 3(3)*). There are detailed rules as to the period in respect of which interest should be awarded (*reg 6*) and the normal rules as to interest on the total sum (including interest) awarded by the tribunal are varied, so that interest on the sum awarded (at the higher *Judgment Act* rate) runs from the day after the day on which the decision on remedy is issued, unless the respondent pays in full within 14 days (*reg 8*).

In an attempt to remedy the injustice to claimants that may arise from the lack of any power to award interest in, for instance, unfair dismissal cases, the Court of Appeal in *Melia v Magna Kansei Ltd* [2006] IRLR 117 held that compensation may be increased to reflect delay in receipt, by analogy with the reduction that may be made in calculating future loss to reflect accelerated payment. The latter is usually set at 2.5% a year, and the Court ruled that compensation could be increased at that rate for the delay between the date of dismissal and the date of the award. This principle applies primarily where there is also a discount for accelerated payment for future loss, but it is submitted that it is not limited to such cases, and thus amounts to a limited general power to award interest, at least where there has been significant delay between the dismissal and the decision on remedy.

18.68   Recoupment of benefits received

Where an employee has received Jobseeker's Allowance, Income Support or Income-related Employment and Support Allowance between the date of dismissal and the date of the award of compensation for unfair dismissal (and certain other forms of compensation such as a protective award in redundancy consultation cases, but not compensation for loss of earnings in discrimination cases), there is a procedure for the Department for Work and Pensions to recover whatever amount of these benefits has been paid to the claimant during that period. This is known as 'recoupment', and is regulated by the *Employment Protection (Recoupment of Jobseeker's Allowance and Income Support) Regulations 1996 (SI 1996/2349)* (the title of the *Regulations* has not been amended to reflect the addition of Income-related

Employment and Support Allowance from November 2010). Recoupment only applies to the benefits listed above; other social security benefits are not affected. For details of how Employment and Support Allowance and other social security benefits may be taken into account in assessing compensation see 53.6 Unfair Dismissal – III.

The system of recoupment is that the tribunal identifies the proportion of its award that relates to loss of income between dismissal and the date of the award; this is known as 'the prescribed element', and must be separately identified in the judgment and reasons. The employer should withhold this amount from any payment to the employee until notified by the Department for Work and Pensions how much it wishes to recoup from the award; notification must be given within 21 days, and the amount recoupable will be the amount of benefits paid, up to the maximum of the prescribed element. The employer must then pay the amount recouped to the DWP instead of the employee. If an award is made by the tribunal for future loss, the employee may lose relevant benefits during the period covered by the award, but this does not affect the amount or payment of the actual award.

The recoupment system applies only to an award by the tribunal. Whilst it ensures that neither the employer nor the employee benefits from the social security benefits paid to the employee, it may reduce quite considerably the value in the employee's hands of the tribunal's award. This does not apply to a payment agreed by the parties – a significant incentive to settle the amount of any compensation. Since recoupment does not apply to awards in discrimination cases, Jobseeker's Allowance, Income Support and Income-related Employment and Support Allowance do have to be taken into account (subject to rather complex rules affecting particular benefits) in calculating the employee's net losses in such cases.

18.69 COSTS

Costs (referred to in Scotland as 'expenses') are awarded to a successful party only in relatively limited circumstances. However the range of circumstances was somewhat broadened by changes in the relevant provisions of the *ET Regulations* made in 2001. Further changes in the powers of the tribunal to award costs came into effect on 1 October 2004, under the *2004 Regulations*, although these only apply in cases where the claim was presented on or after that date (*reg 20(2)–(5)*). The maximum amount that may be awarded by a tribunal without referring the assessment of the costs to the County Court or Sheriff Court was increased by the *Employment Tribunals (Constitution and Rules of Procedure) (Amendment) Regulations 2012* ('the 2012 Regulations') from £10,000 to £20,000, but only for cases first presented on or after 6 April 2012.

18.70   The powers available to a tribunal under the *ET Rules* are to award costs or expenses to be paid by one party to the other (or in limited circumstances to the Secretary of State: a 'costs order' or 'expenses order'), to order the payment of a sum to compensate for time spent preparing the case (a 'preparation time order') and make a wasted costs order against a party's representative. The *2012 Regulations* have added a power to order a party to pay the expenses incurred by a witness attending the hearing, but only in cases presented on or after 6 April 2012. The party against whom an order is made is referred to as the 'paying party', and the party in whose favour the order is made as the 'receiving party' (*rule 38(1)(a)*). A number of general points need to be made about these powers:

(a)   Orders may be made against or in favour of a respondent who has not had his or her response accepted, in relation to any part the respondent has taken in the proceedings (eg applying for a review of a default judgment). However if the respondent has not participated in the proceedings because it was prevented from doing so, having failed to have a response accepted, no costs can be awarded against it: *Sutton v The Ranch Ltd* [2006] ICR 1170; this is so even though the claimant may have incurred costs, eg in proving losses at a remedies hearing.

(b)   A costs or expenses order can only be made in favour of a receiving party who was legally represented (ie by a barrister, advocate or solicitor with a current practising certificate) at the Hearing, or if the proceedings are determined without a Hearing, is legally represented at the time the proceedings are determined (*rule 38(2), (5)*).

(c)   It is not possible to make both a costs or expenses order and a preparation time order in the same proceedings and in favour of the same party (*rule 46(1)*). Thus a party represented initially by a non-practising solicitor, but by Counsel for the Hearing, could only recover its costs of Counsel, and could not obtain a separate preparation time order for the cost of retaining the non-practising solicitor: *Ramsay v Bowercross Construction Ltd* (UKEAT/0534/07). This point may also cause difficulties if a party obtains orders on more than one occasion during the proceedings, and either becomes or ceases to be legally represented between the making of the orders. To meet this potential difficulty, *rule 46(2)* gives the tribunal power to make an order part way through the proceedings but to defer until the conclusion of the proceedings determining which category of order it should be. This will necessitate also deferring the decision as to the amount of the award; and it cannot meet the problem highlighted in *Ramsay*.

(d)   It is thought that a costs order cannot be made at a CMD, since it is an order determining the paying party's civil rights or obligations: see *rule 17(2)*. In practice, apart from a provisional order made under *rule 46(2)*, the requirement referred to in (*b*) above is likely to prevent the making of a costs order before at least the hearing on liability has been concluded, or the case has come to an end without a full merits hearing.

(e)   It is probable that a costs order cannot be made in respect of costs incurred before the claim or (in favour of the respondent) the response was presented. This was the view of the EAT in *Health Development Agency v Parish* [2004] IRLR 550. See further (f) below, and also *Sutton v The Ranch Ltd*, above.

(f)   Costs awards are intended to be compensatory, not punitive (a point confirmed by the Court of Appeal in *Lodwick v Southwark London Borough Council* [2004] EWCA Civ 306, [2004] IRLR 554). The EAT has held that this means that where costs are claimed because a party has acted unreasonably in conducting a case, the costs awarded should be no more than is proportionate to the loss caused to the receiving party by the unreasonable conduct: *Barnsley Metropolitan Borough Council v Yerrakalva* [2011] EWCA Civ 1255, [2012] IRLR 78.

The award of costs is still relatively unusual. Following the broadening of the grounds on which costs could be awarded under the *2001 Regulations*, the frequency and amount of orders increased somewhat. The total number of awards (excluding orders for wasted costs, and preparation time orders) has historically averaged a little over 400 a year, with about three quarters of awards being made in favour of respondents. However, in 2011–12, there were a total of 1,411 awards (116 to claimants and 1,295 to respondents). These figures were skewed by one multiple-claimant case in which all 800 claimants have been made liable for a total award of £4,000 attributed in the system as £5.00 each. The maximum award was £36,466 (upon detailed assessment by the county court), median award (unsurprisingly) £5.00 and the average award £1,292. Excluding the 800 claimant case, the median would have been £1,730 and the average £2,973.

The sections below set out the provisions as to each of the four categories of orders available to the tribunal. For simplicity, references to costs and costs orders are intended to encompass expenses and expenses orders in Scottish proceedings.

18.71 Costs orders

The relevant provisions of the *ET Rules* governing the power to make, and the making and terms of, costs orders are briefly as follows:

(a) If the paying party has, in the opinion of the tribunal, acted vexatiously, abusively, disruptively or otherwise unreasonably in bringing or conducting proceedings, or his or her representative has so acted in conducting them, or if the bringing or conducting of the proceedings by that party has in the tribunal's opinion been 'misconceived', the tribunal may make an order. 'Conducting' proceedings applies equally to a respondent as to a claimant. 'Misconceived' is defined by *reg 2(2)* as including 'having no reasonable prospect of success'. For the meaning of 'vexatiously', see **18.72** below. Note that technically the tribunal is *required* to consider the award of costs, even if no application is made; but it has a discretion whether actually to *make* the award, and as to the amount (*rule 40(2), (3)*). It would be unusual for a tribunal to exercise its discretion in favour of making a costs order in any case where the receiving party did not apply for costs, and it is suggested that the authorities mentioned in **18.72** below which appear to hold that in some categories of case there is an obligation to award costs should be read subject to this qualification.

(b) Costs may be awarded against a party if a hearing has to be postponed or adjourned through that party's fault (*rule 40(1)*). In respect of certain complaints of unfair dismissal, costs *must* also be awarded where the claimant has expressed a wish to be reinstated or re-engaged which has been communicated to the respondent at least seven days before the hearing of the complaint, and a postponement or adjournment of the hearing has been caused by the respondent's failure, without good reason, to adduce reasonable evidence as to the availability of the job from which the claimant was dismissed, or of comparable or suitable employment (*rule 39*). These points are subject to the receiving party being eligible for a costs order under *rule 38(2)*, by virtue of being legally represented; if this condition is not met, a preparation time order either may or must, as the case may be, be made instead.

(c) A costs order may require the paying party to pay the whole or part of the other party's costs or expenses as assessed (by a County Court Costs Judge under the *CPR 1998*) if not otherwise agreed, or be for an agreed amount, or for a stated sum (not exceeding £20,000) fixed by the tribunal (*ET Rules, rule 41(1)*). The limit on fixed costs was introduced by the *2001 Rules* and was retained in the *2004 Rules*; it does not apply to costs agreed between the parties or assessed by the County Court. The maximum that can be awarded without a reference to assessment was increased from £10,000 to £20,000 by the *Employment Tribunals (Constitution and Rules of Procedure) (Amendment) Regulations 2012 (SI 2012/468)*, but the increase only applies if the claim was presented on or after 6 April 2012; for cases already in progress on that date, the limit of £10,000 will continue to apply. In assessing costs summarily, the tribunal is likely to refer to the guidelines used in summary assessments of costs in the High Court and County Court as to what are reasonable hourly rates for solicitors to claim in different parts of the country (these rates, which are published annually in the Supreme Court Practice, apply only to England and Wales). Similar criteria for the taxation of expenses in the Sheriff Court apply in Scottish proceedings.

(d) If the conditions in (a) or (b) above are satisfied, the paying party may also (or as an alternative) be ordered to pay to the Secretary of State the whole or a part of witness allowances paid by the Secretary of State to witnesses for their attendance at the tribunal (*rule 38(1)(b)*). This power is very rarely used; for instance there were only three such orders in 2010–11. Following the discontinuance for cases presented on or after 6 April 2012 of the payment of witnesses expenses by the Secretary of State, a new power was conferred on tribunals by the *Employment Tribunals (Constitution and Rules of Procedure) (Amendment) Regulations 2012* to order a party to pay some or all of the expenses incurred in attending the tribunal by a witness. This new power, in the form of a new *ET Rule 38(1)(c)*, appears to be wide enough to cover witnesses attending voluntarily a well as those subject to a witness order, and the party ordered to pay may be the winning as well as the losing party, and the witness need not have been called for that party. The power is discretionary, and there is no restriction specified in the *Rule* as to when an order may be made, but it is most likely that orders will be made against parties calling a witness, where the attendance of the witness was ordered, or was found to be unnecessary. Other circumstances justifying an order are likely to emerge from cases in due course when awards are subject to an appeal.

(e)   In deciding whether to make an order for costs, and if so in determining the amount to be awarded, the tribunal is permitted but not required to have regard to the means of the party against whom the order is made (*rule 41(3)*, reversing the decision of the Court of Appeal in *Kovacs v Queen Mary and Westfield College* [2002] EWCA Civ 352, [2002] IRLR 414 that there was no power to take means into account under the previous *Rules*). It was observed by Simon Brown LJ in *Kovacs* that logically, the discretion to have regard to the paying party's means would require the tribunal also to consider the means of the receiving party (para 10), and by Chadwick LJ that if means are a relevant factor, it would not be reasonable for a tribunal to make an award that it was satisfied the paying party could not meet (para 32). This in turn highlights the point that the tribunal has no specific powers to inquire into the means of a party for this purpose. Neither of the points raised in *Kovacs* is reflected in the *ET Rules*, and it is therefore unclear how far they can be taken as surviving the reversal of the substantive decision in *Kovacs*. Two further points were made by the EAT in *Jilley v Birmingham and Solihull Mental Health NHS Trust*, [2008] All ER (D) 35 (Feb), EAT. First, the tribunal should state clearly whether or not it has taken the paying party's means into account in making its order as to costs. Secondly, if payment of all the receiving party's costs would be beyond the claimant's means, it may order payment of a specified proportion of the costs; this might presumably permit an order for costs to be assessed, subject to a maximum liability of a stated amount. In a subsequent decision the EAT has held that even if the claimant does not raise the issue of means, it should be raised by the tribunal, particularly before a very large order is made: *Doyle v North West London Hospitals NHS Trust* (UKEAT/0271/11), a case where an order to pay all the respondent's costs, estimated at £95,000, had been made. Contrast *Osonnaya v Queen Mary University of London* (UKEAT/0225/11) in which the EAT held that the tribunal is required, if the matter is raised, to consider ability to pay, but if the matter is not raised, there is no authority imposing a legal duty on the Judge to raise the question, even with a litigant in person. It is not necessary to take the claimant's means into account if she was voluntarily absent from the proceedings when the point arose (*Mirikwe v Wilson & Co Solicitors* (UKEAT/0025/11), or if the evidence of means given by the claimant is contradictory or unreliable (*Shields Automotive Ltd v Greig* (UKEATS/0024/10)). The last mentioned case is also authority for the point that 'means' can include equity in a home, even if not readily realisable. In *Oni v NHS Leicester City* (UKEAT/0144/12) the EAT held that there should be a proper consideration of means where the claimant asserted limited means and where the costs claimed were anticipated to be large. The EAT recommended the completion of the County Court means form EX140 by the party whose means are to be taken into account.

(f)   It is not completely clear how far the power to take into account the paying party's means extends to taking the means of an organisation, such as a trade union, representing him or her into account. In a case decided before the *ET Rules* were amended to allow the conduct of a representative to be taken into account in deciding whether to make a costs order, the EAT held that the conduct of the case by a trade union representative did not entitle the tribunal to take the union's means into account in deciding the issue of a costs order against the claimant: *Omar v Worldwide News Inc* [1998] IRLR 291. This approach was however later doubted in *Beynon v Scadden* [1999] IRLR 700; it may in any case no longer be applicable following the change in the *ET Rules* permitting the award of costs on account of the unreasonable conduct of the proceedings by a party's representative. However any costs order would only be enforceable against the party against whom it is made, and it does not necessarily follow that a union would accept liability to reimburse its members in such a situation; this may make a tribunal reluctant to disregard the limited means of the claimant, even if permitted to do so.

(g)   If there has been a PHR, and a party was ordered to pay a deposit, and that party loses, the tribunal must consider whether to make a costs order on the ground of the losing party's unreasonable conduct in persisting in having the matter determined. However the tribunal is not *required* to make such an order solely on this ground unless, having considered the reasons given for the making of the deposit order, it considers that the reasons given were substantially the same as the reasons for finding against the party at the Hearing. If costs are awarded, the deposit is used to pay, or in part payment of, the costs; if not, or if the costs awarded are less than the deposit, the deposit or balance is refunded to the party concerned (*rule 47*). An example of the application of this power to award costs is *Deer v Walford* (UKEAT/0283/10).

(h)   An application for costs may be made at any time, either at a CMD or PHR, or at the conclusion of a Hearing, or subsequently in writing, but cannot be finally determined at a CMD; see further **18.70**(c) and (d) above as to the difficulties involved in making an order before the proceedings have been concluded. If an application for costs is made after judgment is given finally determining the claim, it must be received by the tribunal no later than 28 days from the issuing of the judgment, unless a Judge can be persuaded to grant an extension of time because he or she considers it to be in the interests of justice to do so. Note that for the purposes of time running for an application for costs, the date of issue of the judgment is the date on which it is given orally, in the case of an unreserved judgment, not the date on which the written judgment is subsequently sent to the parties (*rule 38(7), (8)*).

(i)   If an application for costs is made at the hearing, the other party will be given an opportunity to oppose the application orally. In any other case, an order cannot be made unless the intended paying party has been given an opportunity to give reasons why the order should not be made. This may be by way of a further hearing, or on paper, as the Judge may direct (*rule 38(9)*). The party claiming costs should, if the sum claimed is more than nominal, prepare a schedule showing the costs incurred and the amount claimed.

(j)   If within 14 days of the date of the order either party requests written reasons for a costs order, reasons must be given in writing (*rule 38(10)*). This codifies the Court of Appeal's comments in *Lodwick v Southwark London Borough Council* [2004] EWCA Civ 306, [2004] IRLR 554 as to the importance of a tribunal giving sufficient reasons for both the fact and the amount of an award of costs.

(k)   There is in principle a power under *rule 13(1)* for the tribunal to make an 'unless' order for the payment of costs (*Criddle v Epcot Leisure Ltd*, [2005] All ER (D) 89 (Aug)). The effect of this would be that if the costs are not paid by the date required, the party's case would automatically be struck out; for a claimant this means that the proceedings would be at an end, whilst a respondent in that position would be debarred from further participation in the case. In practice however it is difficult to see how this power could ever be exercised, since no order can be made (except on the provisional basis permitted by *rule 46(2)*, which precludes the fixing of the amount awarded), until it is known whether the receiving party was legally represented at the Hearing, or the proceedings have ended.

18.72

There have been several decisions on the scope of the power to award costs, when and how the discretion to do so should be exercised, and what costs should be awarded if an order is made. The leading cases are now *Barnsley Metropolitan Borough Council v Yerrakalva* [2011] EWCA Civ 1255, [2012] IRLR 78 and *Arrowsmith v Nottingham Trent University* [2011] EWCA Civ 797. A number of points can usefully be drawn from these and other relevant cases.

It is important to bear in mind that costs orders are relatively rare, but a tribunal is not obliged to refer to that fact in its reasoning, provided that it follows the statutory, two-stage procedure of first determining whether there has been unreasonable conduct etc, and then exercising a discretion whether to make an award, and if so of what amount or proportion of costs incurred: *Power v Panasonic (UK) Ltd*, [2005] All ER (D) 130 (Jul), EAT, following *Salinas v Bear Stearns International Holdings Inc* [2005] ICR 1117. On the other hand, the mere fact that the tribunal makes an award of aggravated damages against the respondent does not justify making an order for costs: *Saiger v North Cumbria Acute Hospitals NHS Trust* (UKEAT/0325/10).

The bringing or maintaining of a claim which has no reasonable prospect of success (and is therefore in the terms of the ET Rules 'misconceived') is a sufficient reason for the tribunal to conclude that the party should be made liable for costs; this is equally so for a respondent which has presented, or maintained through the proceedings, a defence which had no reasonable prospect of success. It is a factor relevant to the exercise of the tribunal's discretion whether to award costs on this ground that the tribunal has warned the party concerned that he or she is at risk of a costs order, but such a warning is not a prerequisite to the making of an order; nor is it a prerequisite that the receiving party has put the paying party on notice that there may be an application for costs. (See for an example *Deer v Walford* (UKEAT/0283/10), where the respondent was awarded its full costs, following a four-day hearing, on the grounds both that the claim had been misconceived from the outset and that a deposit had been ordered on substantially the grounds that the claim failed; the award was upheld by the EAT.)

The conduct of a party's representative, as well as that of the party him or herself, can provide the basis for an award of costs; the party is in effect fixed with the consequences of his or her choice of representative. However, not all conduct of tribunal proceedings by a representative which causes additional cost to the other party is necessarily unreasonable; thus it was held by the EAT in *Francois v Castle Rock Properties Ltd* (UKEAT/0260/10) that the incompetent presentation of the claimant's case by her representative, an inexperienced solicitor, which had unnecessarily prolonged the hearing, was nevertheless on the facts not unreasonable conduct of the case, and there was therefore no justification for an award of costs.

Where a party's unreasonable conduct, such as by failing to comply with orders for disclosure, exchange of witness statements or other case management orders, leads to a case having to be adjourned, the tribunal may award the other party its costs thrown away because of the 'lost' hearing. These are in effect wasted costs, but an order for costs thrown away is not the same as an order for 'wasted costs' under *rule 48*, which is an award against a representative; see **18.74**. Guidance as to the computation of costs thrown away has been given by the EAT in *Carruthers v London School of Economics Student Union* (UKEAT/0183/10). A good example of a finding of unreasonable conduct (by the respondent) leading to an unnecessary hearing is *Godfrey Morgan Solicitors Ltd v Marzon* (UKEAT/0465/11).

It has been accepted by the Court of Appeal that deliberately delaying notification of a decision to withdraw a claim can constitute unreasonable behaviour (*McPherson v BNP Paribas (London Branch)* [2004] IRLR 558); the same would be true of unjustifiable delay in conceding liability, or an issue in the claim such as whether the claimant is disabled. This should not be relied on to penalise a party who, perhaps in the light of disclosure of documents or seeing the other party's witness statements, or the failure of settlement negotiations, takes a pragmatic decision to abandon a claim or defence. The unreasonable behaviour lies in then failing to inform the other party and the tribunal of the decision promptly, thereby allowing the other party to incur further costs (and possibly preventing the tribunal from listing another case for the date listed for the hearing).

A party may also be found to have acted unreasonably if he or she has rejected an offer to settle the proceedings, either made openly or 'without prejudice save as to costs', but it is not unreasonable behaviour to reject an offer simply because the tribunal's decision is more favourable to the party making the offer (eg the claimant is awarded less than the respondent had offered, or even nothing at all): *Kopel v Safeway Stores plc* [2003] IRLR 753. This decision has the effect that the tribunal may take into account offers made without prejudice save as to costs (often referred to as 'Calderbank' offers; see **18.36** above), but costs do not automatically follow in the way that would be the case in equivalent situations in the High Court. See also *Power v Panasonic (UK) Ltd*, above, where a costs order was upheld on appeal in circumstances where the claimant was found by the tribunal to have put an unrealistically high value on her claims, rejected offers substantially in excess of what she was eventually awarded, and acted intransigently in negotiations; and see *G4S Security Services (UK) v Rondeau* (UKEAT/0207/09), where costs were awarded by the EAT on the basis of an appellant having unreasonably rejected offers to settle an appeal until he accepted the same offer on the morning of the hearing.

In a case involving a claim of discrimination, one of the remedies is a declaration by the tribunal that the claimant was discriminated against. It will not necessarily be unreasonable conduct for a claimant to refuse a reasonable monetary offer where he or she is seeking such a declaration and the respondent is not prepared as part of the terms of settlement to admit liability. This principle was applied to unfair dismissal in *Telephone Information Services Ltd v Wilkinson* [1991] IRLR 148, EAT, but the opposite view was taken by the EAT in the later case of *Nicolson Highlandwear Ltd v Nicolson* [2010] IRLR 859, EAT, where the claimant had succeeded in obtaining a finding of unfair dismissal but the EAT considered that he had had no reasonable basis for pursuing the claim, since it was inevitable on the facts that he would not be awarded any compensation (he had admitted to defrauding his employers, and the tribunal had made a nil award). However *Wilkinson* was not cited, and the case cannot therefore be regarded as excluding the argument in other cases that it may be reasonable to pursue a claim of unfair dismissal purely to establish a finding to that effect.

Awards of costs on the basis that the paying party has acted vexatiously in the bringing or conduct of the proceedings are rare, since it is not necessary to show such extreme conduct in order to make a case for an award of costs. However a tribunal would be much more likely to exercise its discretion in favour of such an order if it found vexatious conduct. The essential difference between vexatious and merely unreasonable conduct is that the party concerned need not be aware that his or her claim has no reasonable prospect of success in order for it to be misconceived (and therefore the bringing of it to be unreasonable), but if a party pursues a claim knowing it has no reasonable prospect of success, or depends on false evidence, or pursues the claim out of malice towards the other party or for some other ulterior reason, his or her conduct may be found to be vexatious. See further *E T Marler Ltd v Robertson* [1974] ICR 72. For a party's conduct in bringing or pursuing a case to be labelled as 'vexatious', or even 'misconceived', it will normally be necessary, at least where the factual issues are disputed, for the tribunal to have heard and determined the dispute, and accordingly a tribunal should not award costs on this basis where the claim has been struck out on jurisdictional grounds: *Dean & Dean (a Firm) v Dionissiou-Moussaoui* [2011]

EWCA Civ 1332. Further helpful guidance on what constitutes vexatious conduct of litigation can be found in the judgment of Lord Bingham CJ in *A-G v Barker* [2000] 2 FCR 1, [2000] 1 FLR 759, at 763–4, and in *A-G v Roberts* [2005] All ER (D) 138 (Jul).

The EAT has also held that where a tribunal finds on the evidence that a party has deliberately lied in evidence to the tribunal, that is necessarily at least unreasonable conduct, and should usually result in a costs order: *Daleside Nursing Home Ltd v Mathew* (UKEAT/0519/08) (a case where the tribunal had found that the racially abusive words alleged by the claimant had not in fact been used) and *Dunedin Canmore Housing Association Ltd v Donaldson* (UKEATS/0014/09). These cases were followed and applied in *Nicolson*, above, where the claimant had in evidence admitted what amounted to fraudulent conduct against his employer; the EAT held that it was an error of law for the tribunal not to award expenses. These cases must however now be read in the light of a number of subsequent decisions most notably, *Barnsley Metropolitan Borough Council v Yerrakalva* [2011] EWCA Civ 1255, [2012] IRLR 78 and *Arrowsmith v Nottingham Trent University* [2011] EWCA Civ 797, [2012] ICR 159.

In *Yerrakalva*, the tribunal had awarded the respondent council all of its costs after the claimant withdrew her claim part-way through the Proceedings. It found that she had lied, in particular in exaggerating her claimed disability, but also criticised the council for the way it had defended the case. The Court of Appeal held that the tribunal was entitled to find the claimant's conduct was unreasonable, but not to award 100% of the council's costs, and reduced the award to 50%. Mummery LJ said (at para 41):

> 'The vital point in exercising the discretion to order costs is to look at the whole picture of what happened in the case and to ask whether there has been unreasonable conduct by the claimant in bringing and conducting it, and in doing so, to identify the conduct, what was unreasonable about it and what effects it had.'

The costs awarded need not be precisely calculated to reflect the additional cost to the respondent caused by the claimant's unreasonable conduct, but should broadly reflect what had been caused by the erring party (the same points would apply equally to an unreasonable respondent). Mummery LJ also clarified that his Lordship's comments in *Macpherson v BNP Paribas (London Branch)* [2004] IRLR 558, which had been widely taken as indicating that a causal link need not be established, were not intended to have that effect but only to indicate that a precise correlation need not be established.

In *Arrowsmith*, the tribunal had applied the *Daleside* case on the basis that the fact that (as it had found) the claimant had told untruths as part of her case was evidence that she had conducted the case unreasonably. The Court of Appeal, in upholding a costs order against the claimant, emphasised that *Daleside* does not create a rule, and each case depends on its own facts; on the facts of this case, it was fully open to the tribunal to find her conduct to be unreasonable and award costs against her. In both of the Court of Appeal judgments the Court emphasises that it is a question of fact whether conduct is unreasonable, and therefore provided the tribunal correctly directs itself as to the law, its decision on that point, and equally on whether to exercise its discretion to award costs, will rarely be open to challenge on appeal.

It is also right to note that the EAT rejected the proposition that there was a general principle from the above cases that an award of costs must follow when a party fails to establish a central allegation in their case: *HCA International Ltd v May-Bheemul* [2009] All ER (D) 154 (Jun). That division of the EAT held that findings of perversity in the earlier cases arose because of their special facts.

Since then, in *Topic v Hollyland Pitta Bakery* (UKEAT/0523/11), the EAT has confirmed that a claim can be found to be misconceived, and costs awarded, even in the absence of lying. There the claimant had genuinely believed she suffered discrimination, although her beliefs had no basis in reality. The genuineness of her beliefs was not relevant to whether the claim was misconceived but was relevant to the exercise of discretion whether or not to award costs, and if so, how much. The award of costs against the claimant was upheld on the facts.

18.73 Preparation time orders

Preparation time orders are intended to compensate a party who is not legally represented at the Hearing (or the conclusion of proceedings which do not reach a Hearing) for time spent preparing the case. This covers time spent by the receiving party personally, or (where applicable) by his or her employees, by a representative who is not a practising lawyer, or by a legal representative who was engaged at an earlier stage in the proceedings. Paragraphs (a), (b) and (e) to (k) in **18.71**, and the points in **18.72** about when a costs order should be made, apply equally, with appropriate modifications in terminology, to preparation time orders (see *rules 42–44*). The paying party may also be ordered to make a payment to the Secretary of State as referred to in **18.71(d)**.

The amount to be awarded by way of a preparation time order is assessed by the tribunal by applying an hourly rate to a notional number of hours allowed as preparation time. The hourly rate is fixed by *rule 45(2)* and *(4)*. The rate was initially fixed at £25 an hour, but subject to an automatic increase of £1 an hour each year. From 6 April 2013 the rate is £33 an hour. (The *Rule* does not make it clear whether the annual increase applies to awards *made* after the relevant date, or only to *work done* after the date of the increase.) The same hourly rate applies regardless of whose time is being compensated; it will thus be the same for a claimant who had been dismissed from a job paid at the National Minimum Wage as for a solicitor engaged to prepare the case for hearing but not used to conduct the case at the Hearing.

The time allowed is what the tribunal assesses to be a reasonable and proportionate amount of time to spend on preparation having regard to such matters as the complexity of the case, the number of witnesses and the amount of documentation involved. Only time spent in preparation for the hearing will be compensated, not time spent attending the hearing itself. *Andrew v Eden College* (UKEAT/0438/10), applying *rule 42(3)*. Awards for preparation time were limited to a maximum of £10,000 (*rule 45(2)*); this sum was increased in line with the increase in the maximum award of costs for cases presented on or after 6 April 2012, to £20,000.

The principle referred to at **18.71(e)**, that the tribunal may have regard to the paying party's means in deciding whether to make an order and if so the amount, applies equally to preparation time orders (*rule 45(3)*); however it is not clear how this principle is to be applied in determining the amount – in particular whether the tribunal can reduce the hourly rate, or make an award for fewer hours' preparation time, or both. The points made at **18.71(e)** as to the uncertainty surrounding certain observations in *Kovacs* apply equally here.

18.74 Wasted costs orders

The power to make wasted costs orders was entirely new within the tribunal system when it was introduced in 2004. However the equivalent provisions have existed for many years in the civil courts, where experience has been that they are rarely made, no doubt in considerable part because of the necessary procedural safeguards for representatives potentially subject to such orders. A wasted costs order is an order against a party's representative, which may be either that the representative pay to the receiving party the whole or part of any wasted costs, or repay to his or her client any costs already paid to the representative by the client, or disallowing the representative from recovering such costs not yet paid, or any combination of these (*rule 48(1), (2)*). In addition or alternatively, the representative may be ordered to meet personally any allowances paid by the Secretary of State for the attendance of any person at the hearing (*rule 48(2)(b)*). There is as yet no provision for wasted costs to be awarded in favour of a witness who has incurred the cost of attending the tribunal, but any expenses paid to such a witness by a party are 'costs' for the purposes of an award of wasted costs in favour of that party (*rule 38(3)*).

The term 'representative' is defined to exclude any representative who is not acting for profit, such as a trade union official or CAB adviser, or a representative who is employed by the party, such as a manager of the employing company. However the term is not limited to legal representatives, and is expressly applied to a representative acting under a conditional fee agreement (*rule 48(4), (5)*). 'Wasted costs' are defined as costs incurred by a party (who may be the representative's own client, or may not be represented at all) as a result of any improper, unreasonable or negligent act or omission on the part of the representative, or, where there has been improper, negligent or unreasonable conduct after the costs were incurred, costs that are such that the tribunal considers it unreasonable for the party who incurred those costs to have to pay (*rule 48(3)*).

There is a requirement that the tribunal must give the representative a reasonable opportunity to make oral or written representations before making a wasted costs order. In addition the tribunal may (but is not obliged to) take into account the representative's ability to pay (*rule 48(6)*); it is submitted that where the representative is a company or firm, it is the means of that entity, not the individual representative, that is to be considered, and it is the company or firm against which any order should be made, but these points are not made clear by the *Rules*. As with costs orders, reasons must be given if requested within 14 days of the order; unusually, *rule 48(9)*, which contains this requirement, expressly prohibits any extension of time for requesting written reasons.

There are a number of potential practical difficulties in this procedure. The first and most basic is that there may be a conflict of interest between a representative and his or her client. In these circumstances (eg where the tribunal is considering disallowing the representative's fees), the client will have to be advised to consider obtaining separate representation, and the representative will have to be given the opportunity to engage his or her own advocate; this will almost inevitably necessitate an adjournment of the hearing. Second, the question whether a representative was negligent may turn on what instructions were given by the client, and/or what advice was given by the representative. In the case of legal representatives, such matters are covered by legal professional privilege, which can only be waived by the client. (Non-lawyer representatives may also be subject to litigation privilege preventing them from disclosing their client's instructions without the consent of the client: *Scotthorne v Four Seasons Conservatories (UK) Ltd* (UKEAT/0178/10).) The client will be deemed to have waived privilege if he or she claims wasted costs against the representative, but not in other cases, such as where the other party has made the application. The tribunal will not be able to draw inferences against the representative from the refusal of the client to waive privilege.

The leading case on wasted costs in the civil courts is *Ridehalgh v Horsefield* [1994] Ch 205, [1994] 3 All ER 848. The EAT in *Mitchells Solicitors v Funkwerk Information Technologies York Ltd*, [2008] PNLR 717, [2008] All ER (D) 99 (Apr) held that the guidelines laid down in *Ridehalgh* should equally be applied by a tribunal in considering whether the make a wasted costs order. The principles to be followed are:

(a)   The wasted costs jurisdiction should only be exercised with great caution and as a last resort.

(b)   An order should only be made if the tribunal is satisfied that the representative's conduct was improper, unreasonable or negligent. (For an example of what constitutes such conduct see *Wilsons Solicitors v Johnson* [2011] ICR D21 (failure of claimant's solicitors to produce coherent particulars of his claims justified an order.)

(c)   A legal representative should not be held to have so acted simply because of having acted for a party who has pursued a hopeless case; an order can only be made on this basis if it is shown that the representative presented a case he or she regarded as bound to fail, and in doing so has failed in his or her duty to the court, and the proceedings amounted to an abuse of process.

(d)   The tribunal must take into account that unless the representative's client has waived privilege, the representative will be likely not to be able to explain why the case has been conducted in the manner it was.

(e)   It must be shown that the representative's conduct caused the person applying for costs to incur unnecessary costs.

The tribunal must exercise a discretion at two stages: it must first decide whether the circumstances render the application justified and proportionate, in which case (but only if so) it can proceed to hear the application. Having done so, there is a further discretion to be exercised whether to make an order (and in what terms).

The judgment in *Mitchells Solicitors* contains a helpful and detailed analysis of both substantive and procedural issues likely to arise on a wasted costs application. The necessity to consider first whether the application should be entertained at all was emphasised by the Court of Appeal in *Gill v Humanware Europe Ltd* [2010] EWCA Civ 799, [2010] IRLR 877, where the Court concluded that the application (which had resulted in an award of only £750) should not have been entertained at all on grounds of proportionality of the time and cost involved in determining the application. The decision is also authority for the points that normally there should be a hearing unless the parties agree to the matter being decided on the papers, particularly so where there are contested issues of fact; and that costs should only be awarded to compensate for additional costs incurred by the receiving party, not for costs that would have been incurred in any case (the costs in issue being of an appeal to the EAT). Further helpful guidance on the procedure to be followed is given in *Godfrey Morgan Solicitors Ltd v Cobalt Systems Ltd* [2012] ICR 305.

In contrast to an ordinary costs order, there is no express provision for the employment tribunal to refer the assessment of a wasted costs order made under rule 48 to the County Court. The tribunal itself must therefore deal with the assessment and make an order for a specified sum. So held the EAT in *Casqueiro v Barclays Bank* [2012] ICR D37, in which Slade J also observed that this may reflect a drafting oversight in the rules.

18.75 REVIEW

The powers of a tribunal to review a judgment have been enlarged by the *2004 Regulations*. Powers to review a decision to refuse to accept a Claim Form or Response, or a default judgment, are considered at **17.34**, **17.37** and **17.38** respectively, and are not considered further here.

Those provisions apart, a tribunal only has power to review a judgment, or an order for costs, expenses, preparation time or wasted costs (*ET Rules, rule 34(1)(b)*). A judgment for these purposes is defined to include any decision, including a determination of a preliminary point, which finally disposes of a particular issue, as well as a judgment on liability or remedy, or both (*rule 28(1)(a)*). This has been held to include the striking out of a claim when a deposit ordered at a PHR was not paid (*Sodexho Ltd v Gibbons* [2005] IRLR 836), and would also include striking out a claim for other reasons such as unreasonable conduct (*rule 18*) or non-compliance with an 'unless' order made under *rule 13* (see *Tisson v Telewest Communications Group Ltd*, [2008] All ER (D) 42 (May), EAT and *Neary v Governing Body of St Albans Girls' School* [2009] EWCA Civ 1190, [2010] ICR 473, EAT; strictly, the effect of the striking out is to convert the conditional 'unless' order into a judgment, which may then be reviewed) and the formal dismissal of a case on the application of a respondent following withdrawal by the claimant (*rule 25*), but not the automatic striking out of a response, as opposed to a claim (see above) for non-compliance with an unless order (*North Tyneside Primary Care Trust v Aynsley* [2009] ICR 1333, EAT).

There is no power to review any other order; in particular case management orders are not open to review. This will not normally present a problem, since there is a general power to vary or revoke such orders, which can be exercised without the formality of a review; but the tribunal will not normally vary an order unless there has been a change of circumstances or new facts have become available: *Onwuka v Spherion Technology UK Ltd* [2005] ICR 567; *Hart v English Heritage* [2006] IRLR 915; *North Tyneside*, above. This power also provides a route for the tribunal to vary an unless order against a respondent by extending time, to relieve it of the sanction of the automatic striking out of the response (as in the *North Tyneside* case, above).

A judgment can be reviewed on any of the following grounds:

(a)   the decision was wrongly made as a result of an administrative error; it should be noted that this is not limited (as under the previous *Rules*) to errors on the part of the tribunal staff – an error on the part of a party, including the party seeking a review, will suffice in an appropriate case: *Sodexho Ltd v Gibbons* [2005] IRLR 836;

(b)   a party did not receive notice of the proceedings leading to the decision;

(c)   the decision was made in the absence of a party;

(d)   new evidence has become available since the conclusion of the hearing which could not have been reasonably known of or foreseen; or

(e)   the interests of justice require such a review.

(*Rule 34(3)*.)

An application for a review must be made to the Secretary of Tribunals in writing within 14 days from the date the judgment or order was sent to the parties, unless it has been made orally at the hearing; time may be extended by a Judge if he or she considers it just and equitable to do so (*rule 35(1), (2)*). If made in writing, the application must identify the grounds for review in accordance with the list above.

An application for a review must be considered (without a hearing being required, although it would appear that a hearing *may* be ordered for the purpose) by the Judge who, or the Judge presiding over the tribunal which, issued the judgment, or if that is not practicable, by a Regional Employment Judge or the Vice President or a Judge nominated by one of those office holders, or (exceptionally) by the President. The application must be rejected if in the opinion of the Judge or other office holder considering it, there is no reasonable prospect of the judgment or order being varied or revoked (*rule 35(3)*).

There is a separate power for the Judge or tribunal who or which issued the judgment concerned to review it of his or her or their own initiative. This power can only be exercised on one or more of the grounds listed above, and only on the condition that a notice is sent to the parties informing them of the intention to review the judgment or order, and explaining in summary form the grounds for the proposed review, within 14 days of the date on which the original judgment or order was sent to the parties. The EAT has confirmed that the tribunal has no power to initiate a review of a judgment unless these formalities are complied with: *CK Heating Ltd v Doro* [2010] ICR 1449. The notice must also offer the parties an opportunity to give reasons why there should not be a review *rules 34(5), 36(2)*). However the rules are silent as to how any reasons given in opposition to the proposal to review are to be considered, and it appears that they will in practice be considered within the review hearing rather than as a separate and prior process.

It is also possible for a review to be instituted following an appeal to the EAT. The EAT has developed a practice in some cases of staying appeals to give the appellant an opportunity to apply for a review of the decision sought to be appealed. There is no obligation on the Judge who then receives a review application to grant a review, and each application will be considered on its merits; but in these circumstances, if the would-be appellant applies promptly for a review, it would be unlikely that the application would be refused solely on the ground that it is made out of time.

If an application by a party for a review is not refused under *rule 35(3)*, the review will be conducted either by the Judge or tribunal who or which decided the case or, if that is not practicable, by a different Judge or tribunal appointed either by a Regional Employment Judge, the Vice President or the President. If the review has been directed on the Judge's or tribunal's own initiative, it may *only* be heard by the Judge who issued the judgment, or by the tribunal as originally constituted.

A review is a formal oral hearing at which if necessary evidence can be called. If the application is granted, the tribunal will either vary the decision or revoke it and order a re-hearing (*rule 36(3)*). If, on the review, the tribunal concludes that the original decision was wrong, the power to vary is wide enough to allow variation by substitution of the opposite result, eg unfair rather than fair dismissal: *Stonehill Furniture Ltd v Phillippo* [1983] ICR 556. On the other hand, if the previous judgment is revoked, the matter must be re-decided, either without a hearing, if the judgment was originally issued without a hearing having been held, or at a fresh hearing (*rule 36(3)*).

18.76 The criteria for a review were previously relatively narrow, but have been widened by recent judicial authority. The test for whether fresh evidence should be admitted on a review is that laid down by the EAT in *Wileman v Minilec Engineering Ltd* [1988] ICR 318; see **19.16** below. The interests of justice include justice to the party which was successful at the hearing, and the public interest in the finality of litigation.

The review procedure enables errors which occur in the course of the proceedings to be corrected regardless of whether the error is major or minor (*Trimble v Supertravel Ltd* [1982] ICR 440), but until recently it was considered that it ought not to be invoked when an error of law was alleged after the parties have had a fair opportunity to present their case without procedural mishap. In a decision prior to the introduction of the Overriding Objective into the *ET Rules*, the EAT held that the incompetence of a party's representative is not a sufficient reason for a review of the decision: *Ironsides, Ray and Vials v Lindsay* [1994] ICR 384 (failure to argue that it was just and equitable to extend time in a discrimination case). The EAT has however held in several recent decisions that the introduction into the *ET Rules* of the Overriding Objective justifies a significantly less strict approach.

Where there is an obvious advantage in a mistake being addressed through a review rather than requiring a party to appeal, it is in the interests of justice to permit a review: *Williams v Ferrosan Ltd* [2004] IRLR 607 (a case where compensation had been awarded on a mistaken view on the part of both parties' representatives, and the Judge, as to whether it would be taxable); and see also *Sodexho Ltd v Gibbons* [2005] IRLR 836, in which *Williams* was strongly endorsed, and *Maresca v Motor Industry Repair Research Centre* [2005] ICR 197. A broad and non-technical approach to the power to review a judgment in the interests of justice was also shown in the case of *Southwark London Borough Council v Bartholomew* [2004] ICR 358.

In *Council of the City of Newcastle upon Tyne v Marsden* [2010] ICR 743 the President of the EAT, Underhill J, reviewed the case law and concluded that *rule 34(3)(e)* confers a broad general discretion which should not be encrusted with too much case law, and that whilst the interests of finality in litigation remained important, this was not a conclusive argument. The President concluded that the principles underlying such decisions as *Trimble* and *Lindsay* remained valid as drawing attention to the underlying principles, which it would be wrong to ignore; but a liberal approach to the exercise of the discretion conferred by *rule 34(3)(e)* was nevertheless permissible. The position now is therefore that it is open to the tribunal to review its decision if it considers that the interests of justice, broadly applied, justify such action.

Where a party wishes to rely on fresh evidence, the EAT has given very clear guidance to the effect that the most appropriate way to do so is by way of an application for a review of the tribunal's decision, rather than an appeal to the EAT, since the tribunal is better placed to decide whether the evidence would if available at the original hearing have made any difference to its conclusions: *Adegbuji v Meteor Parking Ltd* (UKEATPA/1570/09); *Korashi v Abertawe Bro Morgannwg University Local Health Board* [2012] IRLR 4. The President of the EAT, Langstaff J, has reinforced this point by a Practice Statement dated 17 April 2012 (available on the EAT website) which states that if an application to adduce fresh evidence is raised in an appeal to the EAT, the appeal will normally be stayed to allow the appellant to apply to the tribunal to review its decision; if the tribunal refuses a review, that decision is of course open to appeal.

There is a separate power for the Judge to correct clerical errors or accidental slips (*rule 37*). This power is sometimes used to correct errors in the computation of compensation. It should not be used to make changes of substance to the judgment, such as the addition of a finding that the unfair dismissal of the claimant was also an act of unlawful discrimination: *Bone v Newham London Borough Council* [2008] EWCA Civ 435, [2008] ICR 923.

18.77 VEXATIOUS LITIGANTS

The EAT has power, upon an application by the Attorney General, to make a restriction of proceedings order against a person who has habitually and persistently and without any reasonable ground either instituted vexatious proceedings in an employment tribunal or before the EAT (whether against the same person or against different persons), or made vexatious applications in tribunal or EAT proceedings. The effect of such an order, which may be for a limited or an indefinite period, is that employment tribunal and EAT proceedings may not be commenced or continued, and applications in such proceedings may not be made, without the leave of the EAT. The EAT may not give leave unless satisfied that the proceedings or application are not an abuse of process and that there are reasonable grounds for them; there is no appeal from a refusal of leave (*ETA 1996, s 33*).

The first order made under s 33 was made in *A-G v Wheen* [2000] IRLR 461; the decision gives guidance as to the scope of the power and how the EAT should exercise the discretion conferred by it. The order was subsequently upheld by the Court of Appeal ([2001] IRLR 91); the court rejected an argument that an order was in breach of the litigant's rights under *art 6* of the *ECHR*. A useful review of the criteria for making a restriction of proceedings order can be found in the judgment in *A-G v Roberts* [2005] All ER (D) 138 (Jul).

The power of the High Court to make a civil restraint order under the *Civil Procedure Rules, r 3.11*, only gives the court power to make such an order in relation to proceedings in the High Court or County Court (despite a ruling to the contrary effect by an employment tribunal in *Vidler v UNISON* [1999] ICR 746 in relation to the predecessor power under the *Supreme Court Act 1981, s 42(1A)*), but in *Law Society v Otobo* (20 April 2011, unreported), Ch D, it was held that a civil restraint order prohibiting a person from instituting tribunal proceedings without the permission of the Court could be made under the inherent jurisdiction of the Court.

18.78 PROCEDURE IN CERTAIN SPECIALIST JURISDICTIONS

The procedures described above apply to proceedings covered by *Sch 1* to the *ET Regulations*. Other Schedules set out complementary rules of procedure in claims involving national security (*Sch 2*) and claims for equal pay for work of equal value (*Sch 6*; see EQUAL

PAY (21)), and certain specialist jurisdictions (see 17.4 above for details). These rules of procedure should be consulted if relevant; the jurisdictions concerned are either too specialised to justify a detailed discussion here, or are outside the scope of this book.

19   Employment Tribunals – III: Appeals

19.1   THE EMPLOYMENT APPEAL TRIBUNAL

Status and jurisdiction

An appeal from the decision of an employment tribunal is heard by the Employment Appeal Tribunal ('EAT'), save for appeals to the High Court or Court of Session in health and safety cases involving appeals against improvement and prohibition notices, and in certain special jurisdictions outside the scope of this book. An appeal can only be brought on a point of law (see further below).

The EAT is a tribunal created by statute, and its substantive jurisdiction is statutory: *ETA 1996, s 21*. It also has both statutory (by *s 30(3) ETA 1996*) and (limited) inherent jurisdiction to regulate proceedings before it, as a superior court of record (ie of equivalent status to the High Court): see in particular *X v Stevens* [2003] IRLR 411, discussed at **19.26** below.

In addition to its appellate functions the EAT has certain limited jurisdictions as a court of first instance, in relation to information and consultation of employees; these rarely arise in practice and are not considered in detail in this chapter.

The EAT is not a 'court' within the meaning of *s 4* of the *Human Rights Act 1998*, and it therefore does not have the power to make a declaration that a statutory provision is incompatible with a Convention right guaranteed by the *Human Rights Act 1998:* see *Whittaker v Watson (P & D) (t/a P & M Watson Haulage)* [2002] ICR 1244, where it was suggested that in a case where there was a serious issue of compatibility the EAT should dispose of the appeal on paper, giving permission to appeal to the Court of Appeal.

19.2   The status and effect of decisions of the EAT was the subject of a public statement by its then President, Morison J, on 3 April 1998 ([1998] IRLR 435). The EAT is a single appellate court which sits in divisions and may sit anywhere in Great Britain (in fact, it normally sits in London and Edinburgh, and once a year also in Cardiff). Both judicial and lay members may, and occasionally do, sit in both principal centres. In the past commentators have referred to apparent differences in approach of the EAT in Scotland on particular issues, and raised questions as to how far a decision given in Scotland binds English tribunals, and vice versa. The statement makes it clear that all tribunals are equally bound by decisions of any division of the EAT wherever given.

Despite the foregoing, the EAT sitting in England or Wales is not formally bound by decisions of the Court of Session on appeals from the EAT sitting in Scotland, and the EAT sitting in Scotland is not bound by decisions of the Court of Appeal on appeals from the EAT in England or Wales. The consequences of this were starkly demonstrated in *Marshalls Clay Products Ltd v Caulfield* [2003] IRLR 552, a case on 'rolled up' holiday pay under the *Working Time Regulations 1998*, where the EAT refused to follow a decision of the Court of Session (*MPB Structures Ltd v Munro* [2002] IRLR 601); the Court of Appeal ([2003] IRLR 350) held that it had been entitled to do so, and that its decision was right, thereby raising the prospect of a different interpretation of the same legislation binding tribunals north and south of the border. A further example of an apparent conflict is between the decisions of the EAT sitting in England (on the interpretation of the *Fixed-term Employees (Prevention of Less Favourable Treatment) Regulations 2002*) in *Sharma v Manchester City Council* [2008] IRLR 336 and *Carl v University of Sheffield* [2009] IRLR 616, and the earlier decision of the Inner House in *McMenemy v Capita Business Services plc* [2007] IRLR 400, reaching a different interpretation, which appears not to have been drawn to the attention of the EAT in *Sharma* but was in *Carl*. The only way to resolve such differences is by way of further appeal to the Supreme Court, a United Kingdom Court, whose decisions are binding in both jurisdictions, or, as happened in the *Marshalls Clay Products* case, by a reference to the CJEU (see *Robinson-Steele v RD Retail Services Ltd*: C-131/04 [2006] ECR I-2531, [2006] ICR 932).

Decisions of the EAT are not formally binding on the EAT itself. They are normally followed, even if in a later case the EAT has doubts about the correctness of the previous decision, unless the EAT is satisfied after argument that the first decision is clearly wrong. However on occasion the EAT has overruled a previous decision; good examples are *Woodward v Abbey National plc* [2005] IRLR 782, overruling *Clark v Midland Packaging Ltd* [2005] 2 All ER 266, on the question when a Notice of Appeal is taken as received by the EAT, and *OTG Ltd v Barke* [2011] IRLR 272, overruling *Oakland v Wellswood (Yorkshire) Ltd* [2009] IRLR 250, on whether the exception in *reg 8(7)* of the *Transfer of Undertakings (Protection of Employment) Regulations 2006* applied to a company in administration. (The *Barke* decision was subsequently held by the Court of Appeal to be correct: *Key2Law (Surrey) LLP v De'Antiquis* [2012] IRLR 212.)

In addition, the range of representation means that the EAT's attention is not always drawn to relevant reported decisions, resulting on occasion in mutually inconsistent decisions, which the EAT in a subsequent case must choose between; this problem has become greater since the unreported decisions of the EAT have become publicly available on its website (since 1 April 2011 housed within the Judicial website www.justice.gov.uk; in addition, all final judgments of the EAT issued since 1992 are now available on www.bailii.org).

19.3   The jurisdiction of the EAT to hear appeals from decisions of employment tribunals is conferred principally by *ETA 1996, s 21*. This provides that an appeal lies to the EAT on any question of law arising from any decision of, or arising in any proceedings before, an employment tribunal under any of a large number of statutory provisions listed in the section. The statutory nature of the EAT's jurisdiction, the itemisation of the statutory provisions in s 21, and the proliferation of statutes and regulations conferring additional jurisdictions on employment tribunals has led on occasions to errors of drafting being found to have failed to confer jurisdiction on the EAT over a particular class of appeal; most recently this was held to be so in relation to appeals concerning the statutory right of accompaniment under the *Employment Relations Act 1999, s 10* (*Refreshment Systems Ltd (t/a Northern Vending Services) v Wolstenholme* (UKEAT/608/03) (2004) Times, 2 March). This oversight was corrected by the *Employment Relations Act 2004, s 38*. However subject to this point (which has arisen only very infrequently) any decision of an employment tribunal or judge is in principle open to appeal, not just a formal judgment or decision given after a hearing. Even a failure to act, or delay in making a decision, may be the subject of an appeal: see *Paw v HM Revenue and Customs*, (UKEATPA/0703/11), where HHJ McMullen QC held that a letter written on the instructions of a judge stating that the tribunal could not give advice and stating the procedure for making a complaint could be the subject of an appeal if a point of law could be identified, as the letter arose in the course of proceedings before the tribunal.

19.4   Composition

The composition of the EAT has traditionally mirrored that of the employment tribunals. The judicial members are High Court or Circuit Judges, with one High Court Judge appointed as President for three years at a time. One Court of Session judge is also allocated to the EAT and presides over most Scottish appeals. The lay members are formally appointed by the Queen on the recommendation of the Lord Chancellor and the Secretary of State (*ETA 1996, s 22(1)(c)*), and are selected for their experience in employment matters. They are generally very senior and experienced in their respective fields. Since April 2006, the Judicial Appointments Commission has become responsible for selection of candidates for lay membership in England and Wales.

19.5   The EAT normally sits in divisions of three, although there is provision for a panel of five (one judicial member and two from each of the panels of lay members). Full appeals from decisions of employment tribunals constituted of an employment judge sitting with lay members must be heard by a judge sitting with lay members. Where the decision under appeal was taken by an employment judge sitting alone, the appeal will usually be heard by a judge alone; there is a discretion to constitute a full panel of three for such cases (*ETA 1996, s 28(4)*) but it is infrequently exercised. The Government in November 2011 announced a significant change in the composition of the EAT, as part of the package of reforms of the employment tribunal system which were the subject of consultations earlier that year. The change will remove the requirement for the EAT to be constituted with lay members altogether, replacing this with a discretion to convene a panel with lay members for specific cases. The implementation of this change is to be made by the Enterprise and Regulatory Reform Bill, which at the time of going to press was expected to receive Royal Assent at the end of April 2013; the provision restricting the use of lay members is expected to be brought into effect later in 2013.

The increased number of cases heard in the employment tribunals by an employment judge sitting alone has already resulted in a considerable increase in the proportion of appeals heard by a judge sitting alone, a trend accentuated by the change in the composition of employment tribunals introduced for hearings from 6 April 2012, whereby unfair dismissal cases are heard by an employment judge sitting alone, unless the discretion to order a full tribunal under *ETA 1996, s 4(5)* has been exercised or the claim includes another claim which requires to be heard by a full tribunal. In addition, issues arising in the EAT after a notice of appeal has been lodged but prior to the full hearing of an appeal are determined by a judicial member (often the President) sitting alone. Such matters include hearings for directions (when held) and appeals from decisions of the Registrar on preliminary points taken under *rule 20* (eg on extending time for a Notice of Appeal). References under *rule 3(10)* arising from a decision of the Registrar or a Judge that an appeal should not be admitted at the preliminary sift (see below for this) are also required to be heard by a Judge alone; such cases have become increasingly common following a tightening of the practice of rejecting apparently hopeless appeals at the sift stage.

Where an appeal is required to be heard by a panel of three, the hearing may proceed in the absence of one of the lay members, but only with the agreement of all parties to the appeal (*ETA 1996, s 28(3)*). The Court of Appeal has ruled that it is a prerequisite to proceeding under this rule that the parties are informed as to which of the panels (employer or employee) the missing member belongs to: *De Haney v Brent Mind* [2003] EWCA Civ 1637, [2004] ICR 348. There is no facility for the EAT to sit with only one member at a preliminary hearing, even with the consent of the appellant, unless the respondent also consents, but the respondent is usually not entitled to be heard, and will therefore usually not be present to give consent if a lay member is unexpectedly prevented from attending.

Legal aid has in the past been available to individuals for appeals from employment tribunals, subject to the normal conditions, although in practice it was very rarely granted. However with effect from 1 April 2013 the *Legal Aid, Sentencing and Punishment of Offenders Act 2012* removed this facility for cases in England and Wales. Legal aid is however still available for appeals in Scotland.

19.6   Practice and administration

The case load of the EAT grew significantly during the 1990s, although not at the same rate as the employment tribunals, but the number of appeals has declined somewhat in recent years. The number of potential appeals received has ranged in recent years between a peak of 2,084 in 2003–4, and a low of 1,728 in 2005–6. In recent years there has been a modest increase in the number of potential appeals received from 1,963 in 2009–10 to 2,048 in 2010–11 and 2,172 in 2011–12. A significant proportion of these potential appeals are screened out at the preliminary sift (see **19.17** for an explanation of this) and are never registered as full appeals; the number actually registered as appeals was 1,235 in 2003–4, but fell to 836 in 2005–6. In 2007–8 only 659 cases were registered as appeals permitted to proceed either to a full or a preliminary hearing. (The equivalent figures for later years have not been given in the published statistics, but the total numbers of cases dismissed as out of time, sifted out and withdrawn before registration in 2010–11 and 2011-12 were 1,415 and 1,502 respectively.) The number of hearings held in 2010-11 was 176 preliminary and 363 full hearings; in 2011–12 there were 155 preliminary and 506 full hearings.

Serious delays in the hearing of appeals in England and Wales (but not in Scotland) occurred in the early 1990s, and again in the early 2000s. However, following the appointment of Burton J as President in 2002, the number of courts sitting was increased, and various procedural reforms were adopted to ensure the more expeditious hearing of appeals. Improved administrative arrangements, increased judicial resources and a more rigorous screening of potential appeals have together brought the problems of delay under control.

19.7 The procedures of the EAT are regulated by *Rules* made under the *ETA 1996 s 30*; the current rules are the *Employment Appeal Tribunal Rules 1993 (SI 1993/2854)* (the '*EAT Rules*') as amended by the *Employment Appeal Tribunal (Amendment) Rules 2001 (SI 2001/1128)* and the *Employment Appeal Tribunal (Amendment) Rules 2004 (SI 2004/2526)* (the '*2004 Rules*'). A review of the *EAT Rules* was commissioned by the President of the EAT in 2012, but no formal proposals for amendment have yet been announced (as at 1 April 2013) and it is understood that any changes will be delayed until after the implementation of changes to the *ET Rules* in the summer of 2013.

As part of the process of regulating its own procedure, and also as a means to improve the appellate process, the EAT has from time to time issued Practice Directions. A significantly revised *Practice Direction* was issued on 9 December 2004 ([2005] IRLR 94). This in turn was reissued, with relatively minor updating and amendments, on 22 May 2008 ([2008] IRLR 621; referred to in this chapter as 'the *2008 Practice Direction*', or simply the *Practice Direction*). The text of the *Practice Direction* is available on the EAT website (now part of the Judicial website, www.justice.gov.uk), and it is strongly advised that this be read carefully by anyone involved as a party to an appeal or as a representative. It applies to all appeals, whenever instituted. The EAT has however held that it is not mandatory for the EAT to follow the Practice Direction, and in the event of any inconsistency between its provisions and those of the EAT Rules, it is the latter which prevail: *Zinda v Governing Body of Barn Hill Community High* [2011] ICR 174. The President of the EAT may also issue Practice Statements or the guidance of practitioners; most recently a Practice Statement issued by Langstaff P on 17 April 2012 gives guidance on applications to admit fresh evidence, and the citation of authorities. Practice statements are posted on the EAT's website. The 2012 statement included the announcement that copies of the most commonly cited authorities would be available for reference at all EAT hearings and copies need not therefore be provided by the parties; a list of these authorities is annexed to the President's statement on the EAT website.

The *Practice Directions* of 2002 and 2004 introduced significant changes in procedure, including the adoption of the Overriding Objective (see **19.14** and **18.1** above) and a duty for parties to co-operate with the EAT in achieving it, new obligations on the parties (rather than, as hitherto, the staff of the EAT) to prepare and submit the documentation to be considered at each appeal, and new 'tracks' to which different categories of appeal are allocated. All of these features are retained in the *2008 Practice Direction*. The Overriding Objective was formally incorporated into the *EAT Rules*, along with other amendments to bring the *Rules* into harmony with the *2004 ET Regulations*, and changes in the power to award costs, by the 2004 Rules referred to above.

19.8   Administratively the EAT falls within the responsibilities of HM Courts and Tribunals Service (an agency of the Ministry of Justice and the successor to the Tribunals Service) but it remains separate from those appellate tribunals which have been grouped together into Chambers of the Upper Tribunal, starting from November 2008, under the reforms to the tribunal system generally introduced by the *Tribunals, Courts and Enforcement Act 2007*. Ministerial responsibility for the EAT Rules lies, rather confusingly, with BIS. The position of the EAT in Scotland is also somewhat anomalous, as HMCTS is responsible principally for the Courts and tribunals in England and Wales, but also for tribunals with jurisdiction in non-devolved areas of the law, such as employment. Discussions were in progress, as at 1 April 2013, on the creation of a Scottish Tribunals Service and the possible transfer to it of responsibility for the EAT in Scotland.

19.9   APPEALS

The procedure for appeals to the EAT is governed by the *EAT Rules*, as amended, supplemented by the *2008 Practice Direction*. The *EAT Rules* also contain modifications to the procedure for appeals in the (very infrequent) cases where the modified procedure for national security cases in *Sch 2* to the *ET Regulations* applies. These modifications are too specialised to be covered in detail in this chapter.

As part of the consultation preceding the making of the *2004 Amendment Rules*, the DTI solicited views on whether a statutory requirement should be introduced that permission would be required to appeal to the EAT; however this proposal was widely opposed and was not pursued (and was not resurrected in the January 2011 consultation paper on tribunal reform issued by its successor, BIS). There has however been a further strengthening of the procedures for weeding out obviously hopeless appeals without a hearing, by means of the amended *EAT Rules* and associated changes first introduced by the *2004 Practice Direction*.

In July 2012, following a consultation exercise, the Ministry of Justice announced that a requirement to pay a fee to institute an appeal to the EAT would be introduced at the same time as fees for employment tribunal claims; subject to Parliamentary approval of regulations (to be made under the *Courts, Tribunals and Enforcement Act 2007, s 42*), it is expected that the requirement will apply to appeals on or after a date likely to be in July 2013. A fee of £400 will be payable for submitting an appeal, with a further fee of £1,200, payable by the appellant, if the case proceeds to a full hearing. Final details of the arrangements for charging and paying for fees, including full and partial remission of fees for appellants on modest incomes, had not been finally announced as at 1 April 2013; consultations on revised criteria for the remission of all categories of fees in civil proceedings were opened by the Ministry of Justice on 18 April 2013.

19.10   Who may appeal

Any party to the proceedings in an employment tribunal may appeal against an adverse decision (for the scope of what decisions may be the subject of an appeal see **19.3** above). Those who may appeal include a respondent to the original claim who has not presented a response, or whose response was not accepted by the tribunal (eg because it was out of time) and who has therefore not been permitted to take part in the proceedings: *Atos Origin IT Services UK Ltd v Haddock* [2005] ICR 277, [2005] IRLR 20, EAT; *Butlins Skyline Ltd v Beynon* [2007] ICR 121 (and see the *2008 Practice Direction, para 16*, for the procedural steps required of such an appellant); and a claimant whose Claim Form has been rejected, either by an Employment Judge or by the secretariat, and who wishes to appeal against its rejection: see respectively for appeals against rejection by an Employment Judge and by the secretariat *Richardson v U Mole Ltd* [2005] IRLR 668 and *Grant v In 2 Focus Sales Development Services Ltd* [2007] All ER (D) 281 (Jan), EAT. It is not yet clear whether there will be any possibility of appealing against the rejection of a claim by the employment tribunal because of non-payment of the required fee, once fees are introduced.

19.11   Institution and content of appeals

Appeals to the EAT must be instituted by presenting a Notice of Appeal on, or substantially in accordance with the prescribed form (Form 1) to the EAT within 42 days from the date on which the written reasons were sent to the parties or, in a case where the reasons for the judgment were not reserved and written reasons were not requested when the judgment and reasons were given orally or within 14 days thereafter, within 42 days of the judgment being sent to the parties. An appeal from an order or other decision not in the form of a judgment must be presented within 42 days of the date of the order etc (*rule 3(3)*). There is currently (as at 1 April 2013) no fee payable for submitting an appeal; but see as to this **19.9** above. Form 1, and a number of other forms for appeals and applications in relation to the more specialist jurisdictions of the EAT, are set out in the *Schedule* to the *EAT Rules*.

The requirement for presentation means that the Notice of Appeal must be received by the EAT within the prescribed time. *Rule 37(1A)* requires that any act required to be done on or before a particular day must be done before 4 pm on that day; this includes the lodging of a Notice of Appeal: *Woodward v Abbey National plc* [2005] IRLR 782. It was also held in that case that the whole of the documentation required as part of a Notice of Appeal must be received by the EAT office by the deadline; this means that an appeal submitted by fax is only in time if the whole of the fax has been received on the EAT machine by 4 pm on the final day. With this important proviso, service may be by fax as well as by post or personal delivery; there is as yet no formal provision in the *EAT Rules* permitting a Notice of Appeal (or other documents) to be served by e-mail, but the EAT website confirms that appeals may be lodged by email (with the required accompanying documents attached) and this method of service is now relatively commonly used. However appellants should be aware that the EAT has limited capacity to receive large scanned documents, and the alternative of sending an electronic link to the documents required to be lodged is not accepted: see further **19.14** below. In *Patel v South Tyneside Council* (UKEATPA/0917/11) the EAT ruled that an appeal submitted by email was validly presented when the appellant received a 'successful delivery' notification from Daemon, the host server for the EAT, although no trace of the Notice of Appeal could be found at the EAT itself.

The EAT Rules permit service of notices, including a Notice of Appeal, at any office of the EAT (there are only two, in London and Edinburgh), so technically, and in contrast to the position governing presentation of a claim, a Notice of Appeal would be validly lodged if received in time at the Scottish office in respect of an appeal from a tribunal in England, and vice versa. However it is not sufficient that the Notice of Appeal is sent in error to the tribunal whose decision is to be appealed, if it is not in fact received by the EAT within the applicable time limit, and such an error is unlikely to be considered a sufficient reason to extend time: *Pierre-Davis v North West London Hospitals NHS Trust* (UKEATPA/1496/08). In practice appeals should always be sent to the office in the country in which the decision under appeal was taken, and are then administered by that office. There is no separate office in Wales, although a limited number of appeals from tribunals sitting in Wales are heard in Cardiff; the appropriate EAT office for appeals from Wales is the London office. The address of the London Office is Fleetbank House, 2–6 Salisbury Square, London EC4Y 8JX; the Edinburgh Office is at 52 Melville Street, Edinburgh EH3 7HF. The email addresses are respectively londoneat@hmcts.gsi.gov.uk and edinburgheat@hmcts.gsi.gov.uk.

The date from which time for appealing starts to run is the day after the date on which the judgment or reasons is or are sent (ie despatched, not received) to the parties or, in the case of an order, the day following the date of the order; the applicable date is recorded on the document containing the judgment, reasons or order itself. The day on which a judgment or order is sent or made does not count in calculating the 42 days. 'Sent' means sent and not received: *Gdynia America Shipping Lines (London) Ltd v Chelminski* [2004] EWCA Civ 871, [2004] ICR 1523, a point reiterated by the *2008 Practice Direction (para 1.8.1)*. Any delay in the postal transmission of a decision may therefore reduce in practice the time available to prepare and submit an appeal, but this is only likely to justify an extension of time if the delay extends to all or almost the whole of the 42 day period (see the *Dodd* case referred to at **19.14** below). The period for lodging an appeal is automatically extended to the next working day if it expires on a day on which the offices of the EAT are closed; in practice this will only apply to public holidays, since it is not the practice of tribunals to make orders or send out judgments on a Saturday or Sunday.

19.12 Documentation to be submitted

In addition to the Notice of Appeal, on or substantially in accordance with Form 1, the appellant must submit (i) a copy of the judgment or order which is the subject of the appeal; (ii) a copy of the written reasons for that judgment or order, if any; (iii) in the case of an appeal against a judgment, if written reasons are not enclosed, an explanation of why not; and (iv) also in the case of an appeal against a judgment copies of the claim and response forms (ET1 and ET3) or an explanation of why they are not included (*EAT Rules, rule 3(1)*). Form 1 also specifies the additional documentation required where there has been an application to review the decision the subject of the Notice of Appeal (see below). If there are no written reasons for the judgment being appealed, the appellant must include in the Notice of Appeal an application for the EAT to exercise its discretion to hear the appeal without written reasons, or to request the tribunal to supply them (*Practice Direction, para 2.3*).

A *Practice Statement* issued by the President in February 2005 ([2005] IRLR 189) makes it clear that all the required documentation must be received by the EAT in order for an appeal to be treated as lodged; so, for instance, if the judgment under appeal and any written reasons are not submitted by the deadline, the Notice of Appeal will be treated as out of time. The requirement for all the documentation to be lodged within the time limit for appealing is very strictly applied: in *Woods v Suffolk Mental Health Partnership NHS Trust*, (UKEATPA/0360/06), an extension of time was refused where the Notice of Appeal was submitted on the last day with an incomplete copy of the claim form, and the missing pages were not received until after the time for appealing had expired; the refusal of an extension of time was subsequently upheld by the Court of Appeal ([2007] EWCA Civ 1180). Occasionally a more lenient view may be taken of failure to include all documents, as in *Singh-Rathour v Taylor* (UKEATPA/0879/10/SM) [2011] All ER (D) 64 (May), where a respondent appealing a costs order failed to include the response forms of other respondents to the original proceedings who had no interest in the appeal, and *Hine v Talbot* (UKEATPA/1783/10), where the documents had been scanned and emailed to the EAT but two pages of the judgment had been fed through the scanner together; see also *Desmond v Cheshire West and Chester Council*, at **19.14** below. However, it would be very unwise to rely on such an exercise of leniency occurring.

If there has been an application for a review, the application, and if available the judgment or order determining it, must be included with the Notice of Appeal (*Practice Direction, para 2.2*), but it appears from the wording of the *Practice Direction* that failure to do so will not lead to the appeal being treated as not validly lodged. It has been stated that the use of a document other than the prescribed form will be permitted only in exceptional cases

(*Martin v British Railways Board* [1989] ICR 24); however, in practice this requirement is not enforced, particularly not against unrepresented appellants, provided at least that the document contains the information required to complete Form 1 and is accompanied by the required documents.

19.13 It is important that the grounds for the appeal are fully and clearly set out. The *Practice Direction* makes it clear (*para 2.7*) that there is no automatic right to add to or amend grounds of appeal, and permission to pursue a ground of appeal may be refused if it has not been set out in the original Notice of Appeal; even if permission to amend is given, there may be adverse costs consequences for the appellant. Delay in applying to amend a Notice of Appeal is likely to lead to permission to amend being refused; for a detailed review of considerations affecting applications to amend see **19.27** below.

19.14 Time limits and extension of time

The time limit for instituting appeals is very strictly enforced (see eg *Mock v IRC* [1999] IRLR 785: last minute failure of computer of counsel preparing the Notice of Appeal not sufficient excuse for appeal being lodged one day late; *Woodward v Abbey National plc* [2005] IRLR 782: last page of faxed Notice not received until 4.06 pm on final day for appealing; extension only allowed because previous authority had suggested it was sufficient if the *first* page arrived in time). Every appeal lodged out of time must be accompanied by an application for an extension of time under *EAT Rules, rule 37* setting out the reasons for the delay. The time limit for an appeal applies even though there may be a pending application to the tribunal to review its decision (*Practice Direction, paras 3.4, 3.5*). Nor is the fact that an application for legal aid or other public funding is pending a reason for exceeding the time limit: *Marshall v Harland and Wolff Ltd (Practice Note)* [1972] ICR 97; *Practice Direction, para 3.8*.

The strict approach to the time limit adopted by the EAT has been upheld by the Court of Appeal, notwithstanding that a less rigorous approach applies to appeals to that court: *Aziz v Bethnal Green City Challenge Co Ltd* [2000] IRLR 111; *Jurkowska v Hlmad Ltd* [2008] EWCA Civ 231, [2008] IRLR 430 (where however a decision to grant an extension of time of 33 minutes in respect of a missing accompanying document was upheld on the particular facts: see further below for this).

General guidance as to the criteria for allowing appeals out of time has been given in *United Arab Emirates v Abdelghafar* [1995] ICR 65, a decision endorsed by the Court of Appeal in *Jurkowska* (and see *Practice Direction, para 3.7*). The principles have also been re-summarised by the EAT in *Muschett v Hounslow London Borough Council* [2009] ICR 424, and again more recently in *Hine v Talbot* (UKEATPA/1783/10).

In summary, the principles to be applied are that:

(a)   There is an interest in the finality of litigation, so stricter rules apply at the appeal stage than before a case has been heard.

(b)   The grant of an extension of time is an indulgence, and will only be granted in rare and exceptional cases (equally so where the appellant is a litigant in person).

(c)   The EAT must first be satisfied that it has been given a full, honest and acceptable explanation for the delay in submitting the appeal (or documents omitted).

(d)   The merits of the appeal are rarely relevant.

(e)   Lack of prejudice to the other party will not normally be a relevant factor in favour of extending time (but any prejudice to the proposed respondent *would* be a factor against an extension).

(f)   The foregoing points are guidelines, not intended to fetter the discretion of the Registrar and Judge in each case.

The EAT has rejected in terms an argument that these criteria for the application of the time limit for appeals are inconsistent with the Overriding Objective: *Waller v Bromsgrove District Council* (UKEATPA/0019/07).

The most recent decision of the Court of Appeal, *O'Cathail v Transport for London* [2012] EWCA Civ 1004, [2012] IRLR 1011, affirms the established approach, emphasising also that whilst the length of the extension of time sought is relevant, the primary focus is on whether there is a good excuse for the delay, that the strict requirement to lodge in time applies equally to the requirement to lodge all the specified accompanying documents as to the Notice of Appeal itself, and that the EAT must balance the interests of both parties. The Court in that case upheld the refusal by the EAT of a one day extension to validate the late submission of the judgment and reasons of the employment tribunal, despite the fact that the appellant, acting in person, was disabled and had suffered a panic attack on the final day for submission of the appeal.

For examples of exceptional circumstances held by the EAT to justify an extension of time, see *Dodd v Bank of Tokyo-Mitsubishi Ltd*, [2005] All ER (D) 74 (Dec) (tribunal judgment not received by appellant's solicitor until the 42nd day following its issue); *Jurkowska* (solicitors for appellant had not received judgment and mistakenly believed reasons, issued later, included the judgment; this decision was upheld by the Court of Appeal); *Hakim v Italia Conti Academy of Theatre Arts* (UKEATPA/1444/08) (application supported by medical evidence of claimant's dyslexia); and *Hancocks v Cambian Education Services Ltd* (UKEATPA/0824/10) [2011] All ER (D) 64 (May)(combination of appellant's ignorance of right of appeal and misleading information given by employment tribunal office). A further example of the exercise of discretion on exceptional facts is *Desmond v Cheshire West and Chester Council* (UKEATPA/0027/12), where the appellant had tried to submit his appeal electronically on day 41 but it had been rejected because the attached files were too large for the EAT server to accept, and he then resubmitted the appeal with an electronic link to the ET1 and judgment, unaware of the EAT policy of not accepting documents sent via links (albeit the policy is stated on the EAT website).

In *Peters v Sat Katar Co Ltd* [2003] IRLR 574, the Court of Appeal allowed an appeal against a refusal to extend time where a litigant in person had posted her Notice of Appeal 14 days before the deadline but it had been lost in the post. It was, in the Court's view, not reasonable to expect an unrepresented party to realise the need to check with the EAT that the Notice had been received. However, an appeal out of time will not necessarily be permitted merely because a decision of a higher court has changed what was generally understood to be the law in favour of the intending appellant: *Setiya v East Yorkshire Health Authority* [1995] ICR 799.

The Registrar of the EAT will determine any application for an extension of time to validate the Notice of Appeal or Respondent's Answer/cross-appeal (see below for these) on the basis of written representations from the parties (*Practice Direction, para 3.6*). Any party aggrieved by the Registrar's decision (including a respondent to the appeal, if the decision is to extend time) may appeal to a judge of the EAT within five days of the date the Registrar's decision is sent to the parties (*EAT Rules, rule 21; Practice Direction, para 4.3*). Appeals against decisions of the Registrar not to extend time are by way of a re-hearing, and evidence may be (and not uncommonly is) given, particularly where there is an issue as to the sufficiency of the explanation for the lateness of the appeal.

A more general power to extend time (used in relation to extending the time for compliance with later steps in the appeal process, including orders made on the sift) is given by *rule 37* of the *EAT Rules*; applications for extensions are considered in the first instance by the Registrar, with a right of appeal against a refusal. Time limits are not as strictly enforced at later stages of an appeal as in relation to the submission of the appeal, but are still applied relatively strictly, and failure to comply with a deadline without seeking an extension of time is highly risky, as the sanctions include the striking out of an appeal or debarring the respondent to the appeal from participating in the hearing; see further **19.15** below.

19.15   Responding to the Notice of Appeal

The procedure for responding to an appeal depends initially on how the appeal itself is treated by the EAT. All appeals are subject to a sift, as explained at **19.17** below, and only if the appeal is accepted at the sift, or subsequently on an appeal under *rule 3(10)* or after a preliminary hearing, is the respondent to the appeal required to respond formally. (There is an exception to this in some cases where a preliminary hearing has been ordered: the respondent may be directed to provide a concise statement giving reasons why the appeal should be rejected at the preliminary stage. However this is not the formal response to the appeal referred to below.)

If the appeal is allowed to proceed to a full hearing, a respondent to an appeal who wishes to resist the appeal must set out his or her grounds of resistance, and cross-appeal where applicable (see below), in or substantially in accordance with Form 3 (this is referred to as a 'Respondent's Answer') and deliver it to the EAT within the time specified by the Registrar (*EAT Rules, rule 6*; the form is set out in the *Schedule*, and the time limit for filing the response is usually set at 14 days). The respondent may rely on the reasons given by the tribunal, or (alternatively or additionally) other grounds put forward to the tribunal but not relied on by it in support of its findings. These should be set out fully at the outset; the same considerations as to amendments to the Notice of Appeal (as to which see **19.27** below) apply equally to any application to amend the Respondent's Answer.

If an appeal is registered, the respondent is given the opportunity to cross-appeal, that is, to appeal against any elements of the judgment or order under appeal that are adverse to him or her. Directions as to the time for filing the cross-appeal will be notified to the respondent at the same time that he or she is directed to file a Respondent's Answer. If there is a cross-appeal, the procedure applicable to appeals under *rule 3(7)* applies equally to the cross-appeal (*rule 6(12), (14)–(16)*); see **19.17** below for details. If the cross-appeal is accepted following scrutiny under *rule 3(7)*, it will be dealt with in accordance with directions given by a Judge or the Registrar; these can be expected to follow broadly the same procedures as for the appeal; further details are given in the *Practice Direction*. It has not yet been confirmed (as at 1 April 2013) whether the new fees regime for appeals will include a requirement to pay a separate fee for cross-appeals.

The time limit for submitting a Respondent's Answer is not as strictly enforced as that for submitting a Notice of Appeal, partly because the period for compliance is shorter, and partly because the debarring of a respondent to an appeal might lead to the appeal being allowed without the EAT being aware of the full picture, whereas striking out the appeal means that there is no decision on the merits of the appeal. However, the fact that there is a discretion to extend time does not mean that an extension will be granted readily; matters relevant to the exercise of the discretion include the length of and reasons for the delay, and the extent of any prejudice the other party would suffer if an extension is granted. If a response is not lodged in time and no extension is granted, the respondent will be debarred from taking any further part in the appeal. The prudent course is therefore always to comply with the deadline set, and if it is anticipated that that will not be possible, to apply as soon as possible for an extension of time. The principles are discussed in *Slingsby v Griffiths Smith Solicitors (a firm)* [2009] All ER (D) 150 (Feb); this case is also authority for the point that the principles applicable to extension of time for a Notice of Appeal apply equally stringently to any cross-appeal.

19.16   Grounds of appeal

The EAT's jurisdiction is limited to appeals on points of law. In practice, one of the three most common grounds of appeal is 'perversity' (the other two are bias and insufficiency of reasons, both discussed below). Perversity is recognised to be a separate head of appeal but is narrowly construed and rarely successful. See *Piggott Bros & Co Ltd v Jackson* [1992] ICR

85, *East Berkshire Health Authority v Matadeen* [1992] ICR 723 and *Yeboah v Crofton* [2002] EWCA Civ 794, [2002] IRLR 634, and the discussion of these cases at **19.35**. It is not acceptable for an appellant to contend that 'the decision was contrary to the evidence' or that 'there was no evidence to support the decision', or to advance similar contentions, unless full and sufficient particulars identifying the particular matters relied upon are set out in the Notice of Appeal (*Practice Direction, para 2.6*).

There are also specific requirements to be observed where a ground of appeal is bias or similar unfairness: see **19.23–19.25** for details. It is not a valid ground of appeal that the decision appealed against was a majority decision (even where the Employment Judge was the minority): *Chief Constable of Thames Valley Police v Kellaway* [2000] IRLR 170. However a serious procedural irregularity, leading to a hearing which was unfair to the appellant, may be the subject of an appeal on that ground, as may a failure to give adequate reasons for the tribunal's conclusions (see **19.36**).

The EAT will not normally entertain appeals which are, or have become, academic: for an example see *Evans v University of Oxford* (UKEATPA/1510/09) (appeal against refusal to adjourn hearing; by the time appeal due to be heard, hearing had been adjourned).

19.17 Preliminary sifting of appeals

All Notices of Appeal are subject to a preliminary paper sift by either the Registrar or a Judge, in accordance with *rule 3(7)*. In practice the sifting is now undertaken by a Judge in almost all cases. If it appears to the Judge reviewing the Notice that it discloses no reasonable grounds for bringing the appeal, or is an abuse of the EAT's process or otherwise likely to obstruct the just disposal of proceedings, the prospective appellant is notified that no further action will be taken on the appeal. When such a notice is served, the appellant may serve a fresh Notice of Appeal within the time limit remaining for serving a Notice of Appeal, or within 28 days from the date on which the notification was sent to him or her, whichever is the later (*EAT Rules, rule 3(8)*). Such a notice is treated as if it were the original Notice of Appeal and had been lodged in time (and is therefore open to rejection under the same procedure) (*EAT Rules, rule 3(9)*). Alternatively, the prospective appellant may challenge the rejection of the appeal under *rule 3(7)*; in such cases the Registrar will refer the matter for a hearing before a Judge sitting alone (*EAT Rules, rule 3(10)*).

It is open to an appellant both to follow the *rule 3(8)* procedure and thereafter, if the amended Notice of Appeal is again rejected, to appeal under *rule 3(10)*: *Haritaki v South East England Development Agency* [2008] IRLR 945 (a case which helpfully summarises the procedure under *rule 3*). However this case also clarifies that an appellant cannot both appeal against the rejection of the original notice of appeal and then, if that appeal is unsuccessful, submit a fresh notice of appeal and repeat the process: see also on this point *Plank v Atkins Ltd* (UKEATPA/0799/09), a case which also confirms that if the fresh Notice of Appeal is in substantially the same terms as the original Notice, that will be treated as an abuse of process. It is not permissible to circumvent the limits on challenging the rejection of an appeal under *rule 3(7)* by applying for a review of that decision: *Zinda v Governing Body of Barn Hill Community High* [2011] ICR 174.

The time limits for serving a fresh Notice of Appeal, and for appealing under *Rule 3(10)*, are enforced strictly, applying the same principles as for the time limit for the initial Notice of Appeal, a practice approved by the Court of Appeal in *Morrison v Hillcrest Care Ltd* [2005] EWCA Civ 1378. An example of a case where an extension of time for a *rule 3(10)* appeal was granted is *Mitchell v Barratt Homes (Leeds) Ltd* (UKEATPA/0903/08), where the delay was attributable to the appellant having erroneously appealed from the rejection of his appeal on the sift to the Court of Appeal, which had refused his appeal as premature.

As an indication of the prospects of a successful challenge to the refusal to allow an appeal to proceed under *rule 3(7)*, HHJ McMullen QC in the course of his judgment in *Haritaki* stated that in 2007–8, of a total of 917 appeals initially sifted out, there were applications under *rule 3(10)* in 210 cases, of which 29 were wholly or partly successful. An adverse decision of the Judge at a *rule 3(10)* hearing may be further appealed (with permission, either of the EAT or the Court of Appeal) to the Court of Appeal (in Scotland such an appeal would be to the Court of Session, also subject to obtaining permission to appeal). Applications for permission to appeal further are relatively frequent, but very rarely successful.

A hearing under *rule 3(10)* is effectively a re-hearing, and the judge will take a decision on the application on the basis of the material before him or her, not the more limited material that may have been available at the sift stage. It is open to the Judge hearing an application under *rule 3(10)* to permit only one, or some, of the grounds of appeal to proceed to a full or preliminary hearing, and this is in practice a common outcome of successful *rule 3(10)* hearings. In that event only the permitted ground or grounds will be entertained at the later hearing, and an appellant wishing to pursue further any of the grounds disallowed would have to seek permission to appeal to the Court of Appeal (or in Scotland to the Court of Session): see further **19.19** below. The judge may also permit the appellant to amend the Notice of Appeal at this stage. Any such permission is provisional, and subject to the right of the respondent to apply to have the permission to amend set aside: see *Readman v Devon Primary Care Trust* (UKEAT/0116/11) and **19.27** below.

The Registrar also deals with interim applications, which must be made by notice in writing (*EAT Rules, rules 19, 20*). She disposes of such applications herself or refers them to a Judge, who may him or herself refer them for hearing before the EAT. An appeal lies against a decision of the Registrar (*EAT Rules, rule 21*). There are separate procedures for applications for restricted reporting orders; see further below for these.

19.18 In 1997 the practice was introduced of referring all appeals (other than urgent interlocutory appeals) to *ex parte* preliminary hearings at which the appellant would be required to demonstrate that the appeal raised an arguable point of law, and any directions (eg for production of the Employment Judge's notes of evidence) would be dealt with. Normally, only the appellant would be required to attend a preliminary hearing, although a respondent might be invited to appear in exceptional cases, eg to deal with an application by the appellant for fresh evidence to be admitted, or where there was a cross-appeal. Experience showed, however, that this practice added to the EAT's workload, and in an increasing number of cases where it was clear from the papers that there was an arguable point of law in the appeal, the requirement of a preliminary hearing was dispensed with. The *2002 Practice Direction* adopted a new approach (retained in the *2004* and *2008 Practice Directions*) by which (except in Scotland) each appeal is allocated to one of four tracks:

(a)   action under *rule 3(7)* (ie that no action is taken on the appeal, subject to the further steps open to the prospective appellant explained above);

(b)   reference to an *ex parte* preliminary hearing (for cases where there is doubt whether the Notice of Appeal discloses an arguable point of law; occasionally permission is given to the prospective respondent to appear at the preliminary hearing);

(c)   reference to a full hearing;

(d)   reference to a fast track, used for cases of importance and urgency, where a decision will determine the outcome of other pending cases, for cases involving reinstatement or interim relief, and for interlocutory appeals.

(2008 Practice Direction, para 9.)

Directions are now as a consequence normally dealt with on paper, and a party seeking particular directions should therefore apply as soon as practicable by letter. It is open to the parties to make a reasoned application for an appeal to be allocated to the fast track, or for the hearing to be expedited. Directions made on paper are subject to the right of any party to the appeal to apply for a variation of the terms of the directions, an extension of time, or additional directions.

19.19 Preliminary hearings

Where a preliminary hearing is to be held, it is now the practice to order or invite the respondent to the appeal to make concise written submissions as to why the appeal should not be allowed to proceed to a full hearing (*Practice Direction, para 9.8*). The standard directions for preliminary hearings include a requirement for the respondent to lodge any cross-appeal, which will then also be considered at the preliminary hearing (with the consequence that both parties will have the opportunity to put their respective cases). In any case, the appellant will be required to submit a skeleton argument in support of the appeal in advance of the preliminary hearing. Standard directions for preliminary hearings also deal with such matters as applications to admit fresh evidence, or for notes of the evidence before the tribunal to be produced (see **19.21** below), and requiring an appellant alleging bias or a procedural defect to provide evidence on affidavit to support the allegation (see further **19.23–19.25** below). It is usual that the latter direction is expressed in terms that amount to an 'unless' order: if the appellant fails to comply within the time limit (typically 14 days from the date of the order) the relevant parts of the Notice of Appeal will be dismissed.

The outcome of a preliminary hearing may be that the appeal is dismissed, referred to a full hearing, or permitted to proceed but only on some of the grounds advanced in the Notice of Appeal. In the latter category of case, the EAT may not consider any other ground of appeal at the substantive hearing of the appeal, unless there are exceptional reasons to do so, but the appellant may seek permission to appeal to the Court of Appeal against what is effectively the dismissal of part of the appeal: *Miriki v General Council of the Bar* [2001] EWCA Civ 1973, [2002] ICR 505. Permission may also be given at this stage to amend the Notice of Appeal, but the respondent (unless present at the hearing and thus given an opportunity to object to the proposed amendment) will in such cases have the opportunity to apply to have the amendment set aside (see generally *Practice Direction, para 9.14*) and **19.33** below). In 2011–12, 100 out of 155 appeals heard at a preliminary hearing were permitted to proceed to a full hearing; the other 55 were dismissed.

Hearings for directions may also be held under *EAT Rules, rule 24*, and there is a general power to give directions under *EAT Rules, rule 25* and to waive compliance with the normal rules under *EAT Rules, rule 39*.

19.20 Where a separate hearing or PHR is held by the employment tribunal on a preliminary issue and the tribunal gives a judgment, it is open to the losing party to appeal, and time for appealing runs from the date the reasons for the judgment on the preliminary issue are sent to the parties (or the date the written judgment is sent, if reasons have not been given in writing). However, the EAT has stated that it is only in exceptional cases that such an appeal will be *heard* before the final determination of the case by the tribunal: *Sutcliffe v Big C's Marine Ltd* [1998] ICR 913. One reason for this approach is that there may be a second appeal from the final decision of the tribunal, and in that event it is a better use of judicial resources for both appeals to be heard together. Appeals against interlocutory case management orders, by contrast, often need to be, and are, heard very speedily.

Conversely, where a party applies to the employment tribunal for a review of a judgment, and the application is refused, time for appealing against the original decision is not suspended, but if the refusal to review, or the outcome of the review, is to be challenged a separate appeal must be lodged, with time for this running from the date of the refusal, or review judgment, as the case may be. Such double appeals are not uncommon, and are whenever practicable taken together at a single hearing.

19.21 Notes of evidence

An issue often arising on an appeal is what evidence the tribunal had heard on a particular point. Normally, the only admissible evidence of this is the Employment Judge's note of the evidence given. These notes are not produced automatically or on the direct request of a party to the tribunal but only if ordered by the EAT. Reasons must be given in support of any application for an order for the production of the notes. The *2008 Practice Direction, para 7*, sets out the procedure to be followed in, and the criteria applicable to, an application for production of the Employment Judge's notes. Applications must be made promptly, giving reasons in accordance with the criteria set out in the *Practice Direction*. Appellants should make their application together with the Notice of Appeal; if this is not done, and the case is referred to a preliminary hearing, the application for notes must be made at that hearing. In other cases, applications will be considered on paper by the Registrar or a Judge. The procedure is that the parties are expected if possible to agree a note of the evidence in question; normally they are given 21 days to do so, and (if this does not prove to be possible) any further application for the Employment Judge's notes must be accompanied by evidence of the steps taken to agree the evidence (such as relevant correspondence).

There is no automatic right to production of the Employment Judge's notes simply because the appellant alleges that the decision was perverse: *Hawkins v Ball and Barclays Bank plc* [1996] IRLR 258, EAT. 'Fishing expeditions' are specifically disapproved by the *Practice Direction* (see *para 7.7*), with a warning that unreasonable applications may lead to an order for costs against the offending party.

19.22 Reference back to tribunal for clarification of reasons

A relatively recent innovation in the EAT's procedure is the reference back of appeals which are based on the inadequacy of the tribunal's reasons, for amplification or clarification of the reasons under challenge. It had been thought that there was no power for the EAT to refer a case back to the tribunal, whether for reconsideration of its findings or to clarify or amplify its reasons, except as part of the disposition of the case after hearing and deciding the appeal; this view was based on obiter comments by the Court of Appeal in *Tran (Kien) v Greenwich Vietnam Community Project* [2002] EWCA Civ 553, [2002] IRLR 735 on the ambit of *ETA 1996, s 35(1)*. However a different view was expressed, in relation to civil appeals generally, in the later case of *English v Emery Reimbold & Strick Ltd* [2002] EWCA Civ 605, [2002] 3 All ER 385, [2002] 1 WLR 2409, [2003] IRLR 710, and following that decision, the EAT held in *Burns v Consignia (No 2)* [2004] IRLR 425 that there is such a power.

This view was subsequently endorsed by the Court of Appeal, but on different grounds, in *Barke v SEETEC Business Technology Centres Ltd* [2005] EWCA Civ 578, [2005] IRLR 633. The view expressed in *Tran* was held to be correct, but it was held that there is power to remit derived from the provision (newly introduced in 2004) in the *ET Rules, rule 30(3)(b)*, for tribunals to be required to provide reasons if requested by the EAT; alternatively, the inherent jurisdiction of the EAT allowed this course to be adopted. The procedure for referral back has become known by reference to the leading cases as a '*Burns/Barke*' order. The power may be exercised on a Judge's initiative or at a preliminary hearing; the appeal then proceeds on the reasons as clarified or amplified. The Court of Appeal has stated that a *Burns/Barke* reference should not be made where the reasons given by the tribunal are too deficient to be remedied by amplification, and also that the judge responding to a request for clarification or amplification of reasons should limit him or herself to doing that, and should not attempt to justify or argue in support of the original decision: *Woodhouse School v Webster* [2009] EWCA Civ 91, [2009] IRLR 568. For further guidance on the use of procedure see *Korashi v Abertawe Bro Morgannwg University Local Health Board* [2011] EWCA Civ 187, [2011] All ER (D) 09 (Mar).

if it was to be the subject of an appeal (see *Peter Simper & Co Ltd v Cooke* [1986] IRLR 19 and *Red Bank Manufacturing Co Ltd v Meadows* [1992] ICR 204). The Court of Appeal reviewed the position and gave general guidance in *Stansbury v Datapulse plc* [2003] EWCA Civ 1951, [2004] IRLR 466, a case where the original decision was set aside for procedural irregularity on evidence that one of the lay members had fallen asleep during the proceedings after having consumed alcohol during the lunch break. The test where the issue was not raised with the tribunal at the time is one of reasonableness, recognising in particular that while it is desirable that the matter should be raised at the time, so that if possible corrective action can be taken, it is difficult even for a legal representative, let alone an unrepresented party, to raise a complaint against a member of the tribunal who, if the complaint is not accepted, will proceed to adjudicate on the case.

Where it is claimed that there was procedural unfairness as a result of a ruling of the tribunal in the course of the hearing, the failure of the disadvantaged party to object at the time does not necessarily prevent the point from being taken on appeal, especially if the appellant had not been professionally represented: *Bache v Essex County Council* [2000] 2 All ER 847, [2000] IRLR 251.

19.26 Restricted Reporting and Anonymity Orders

Rule 23 of the *EAT Rules* contains provisions which closely follow those of *rules 49* and *50* of the *ET Rules* conferring powers on tribunals to make restricted reporting orders and for the exclusion from public documents of matter identifying affected parties in the case of allegations of a sexual offence. The latter is treated as an administrative responsibility of the Registrar, and does not require an application by a party (*rule 23(2)*). In other cases, a restricted reporting order may only be made either on a temporary basis or, on the application of a party or of the EAT's own motion, having given the parties an opportunity to be heard on the matter (*rule 23(3), (5)*). A temporary order lasts for 14 days unless a party applies for it to be extended, in which case the order continues in force until that application has been heard and determined (*rule 23(5A)–(5C)*).

There are however important differences in the scope of the powers. There is no equivalent provision in *rule 23* to the provision in *rule 50* of the *ET Rules* enabling interested third parties such as press representatives to be given an opportunity to make representations before an order is made. In addition, the power to make orders securing the permanent anonymity of a party is restricted by the express wording of the *ETA 1996, s 31* (which is the statutory authority for *rule 23*) to appeals against the making or refusal by a tribunal of restricted reporting orders and certain interlocutory appeals: appeals against final judgments of a tribunal are therefore not covered.

The last point has led to a series of cases in which the EAT has held that it nevertheless has power to order the anonymisation of public documents relating to the case, including judgments. In *Chief Constable of West Yorkshire Police v A* [2001] ICR 128 and *X v Stevens* [2003] IRLR 411 the reason for anonymity was that the claimant in each case would otherwise have been inhibited in pursuing a claim based on an EU right, and protection was thus considered necessary to ensure that that right could be given full effect. In the first case, the EAT under Lindsay P relied on the direct effect of the *EU Equal Treatment Directive*, while in the second, Burton P preferred to base the power on the inherent jurisdiction of the EAT as a superior court of record (see **19.1** above for this). In two further cases not involving any EU right, *B v A* [2010] IRLR 400 and *A v B* [2010] IRLR 844, the EAT, in both cases under Underhill P, held that where it was necessary to make an order in order to protect the rights of the party concerned to privacy under *art 8* of the *European Convention on Human Rights*, this could be done. The basis for doing so was clarified in a supplemental judgment in *A v B* [2010] IRLR 844 at 856) as the application of the EAT's general power to regulate its own procedure, conferred by *ETA 1996, s 30(3)*. The cases concerned claims of unfair dismissal; the dismissal in *A v B* had followed a report to the employer by the police of allegations that the claimant had been engaged in paedophile activities overseas and in *B v A* an allegation of rape made against the claimant by a fellow employee.

Whilst the point has not been directly addressed in any of the decisions to date, it is suggested that the reasoning in these cases would apply equally to justify the making of an order protecting the anonymity of a non-party, such as a witness, whose privacy rights would otherwise be compromised by public disclosure of his or her identity: the anonymity requiring protection in *B v A* was that of the victim of the alleged rape, who was not herself a party to the proceedings but whose rights under *art 8* were asserted by the employer, which was. See further *F v G* [2012] ICR 246 (anonymity order made by tribunal on privacy grounds for the protection of vulnerable students of the respondent college upheld on appeal). The general powers of the EAT as a superior court of record are considered to be wide enough to justify in an appropriate case the equivalent of a restricted reporting order in the employment tribunal, that is to say an order restricting what details of the submissions made at the appeal, which might identify persons entitled to protection from identification, may be reported publicly.

For further details of the scope of and case law relating to restricted reporting orders see **18.18–18.19**.

19.27   Amendments to the Notice of Appeal

Appellants frequently seek to amend their Notice of Appeal. This may be because they have advice that was not available before the Notice of Appeal was lodged, typically when an ELAAS representative (see **19.28** below) is made available to a previously unrepresented appellant at a preliminary or *rule 3(10)* hearing. Permission is required for any amendment, and the respondent to the appeal has the right to resist any application for permission. For this reason, if permission is given at a hearing at which the respondent is not present the permission is expressed as provisional, and is subject to the respondent's right within a set time (usually 14 days) to apply to have the permission set aside.

Permission to amend to add a ground of appeal will not be given unless the EAT is satisfied that the amendment raises a point of law which is at least arguable. There is also an important difference between amendments which clarify a ground of appeal already in the Notice of Appeal and amendments which raise entirely new points. The other factors the EAT will take into account in deciding whether to give permission to amend are set out in *Khudados v Leggate* [2005] ICR 1013, at para 86:

(a)   Whether the application for permission was made as soon as the need for amendment was known;

(b)   Whether a full, honest and acceptable explanation has been given for any delay in applying;

(c)   The extent to which permitting the amendment would delay the appeal;

(d)   Whether permitting the amendment will cause prejudice to the respondent (over and above the inevitable prejudice of having to deal with a ground of appeal that it would not otherwise have to meet), and conversely whether denying permission will cause prejudice to the appellant;

(e)   In some cases the merits of the proposed additional or amended ground will be relevant

(f)   The public interest in the expeditious conduct of the EAT's business and efficient use of its resources.

These factors are further considered in *Readman v Devon Primary Care Trust* (UKEAT/0116/11), where Underhill P makes the point that a less stringent approach to permission to amend is taken at *rule 3(10)* hearings, since they are often the first point at which the appellant has legal advice about the potential points of law that could be pursued in the appeal, and because there will be no prejudice to the respondent since it will not up to that point have been required to take any action on the appeal. A similar point is made in *King v Royal Bank of Canada* [2012] IRLR 280 in relation to appeals by litigants in person, who should be given more latitude in relation to a failure to identify all the potential grounds of appeal at the outset, particularly in the light of the difficulty many lay persons have in obtaining legal advice. *King* contains a full and helpful summary of the considerations relevant to whether permission to amend should be given: see paras 31–44.

19.28 CONDUCT OF THE APPEAL

Representation

As in employment tribunals, there is no restriction as to the persons who may represent a party to an appeal (*ETA 1996, s 29(1)*). In the nature of the proceedings, legal representation is more common than in the employment tribunals, but by no means universal. A scheme known as ELAAS has existed since 1996 for the provision of professional advice for, and, if desired, representation of, unrepresented appellants at preliminary hearings. This is operated with the active encouragement of the EAT by experienced barristers and solicitors who provide free representation on a rota basis. The Free Representation Unit and the Bar Pro Bono Unit also provide free representation in an increasing number of cases.

Concerns about the prevalence of organisations offering representation to parties in employment litigation, often on a no win no fee basis, but which were not subject to external scrutiny of their competence or professional standards, led to the introduction by the *Compensation Act 2006* of a scheme of regulation of claims management bodies, including those which provide representation in employment tribunals or the EAT for reward. It is a criminal offence for an unregulated person or body to undertake regulated claims management services for reward (including under conditional fee arrangements); those exempt from regulation include lawyers and trade unions, as well as those, such as the CAB, not acting for reward. The term 'regulated claims management services' covers the representation of claimants (but not respondents) in employment tribunal proceedings and any subsequent appeal to the EAT. The regulator is the Secretary of State for Justice. The *2006 Act* does not apply to Scotland, and there is currently no equivalent regulation of representatives who are not practising lawyers in Scotland.

19.29 Preparation for the hearing

The EAT will have before it at the substantive hearing the Notice of Appeal, the respondent's answer, the decision of the employment tribunal and any documents which were before the employment tribunal and which are relied on by the parties as relevant to the appeal. It is the responsibility of the appellant to lodge copies of a core bundle of documents (if possible this should be an agreed bundle, and it should be in the format set out in *para 6* of the *2008 Practice Direction* and contain the documents listed there, together with any other documents relevant to the appeal). Irrelevant documents should not be included. Permission is required for the submission of a bundle exceeding 100 pages. The Employment Judge's notes should be included in the appeal papers if their production was ordered.

A party seeking to show that no reasonable tribunal could have reached the conclusion it reached on the evidence will almost certainly require the notes of evidence, or a jointly agreed note supplied by the parties (*Piggott Bros & Co Ltd v Jackson* [1992] ICR 85 at 96).

(This view was qualified by the EAT in *Hawkins v Ball and Barclays Bank plc* [1996] IRLR 258, where the evidence was clearly recorded in the tribunal's decision and the issue was whether the conclusions reached from that evidence were perverse.) Any application for an order to produce all or part of the notes must be made in accordance with *para 7* of the *Practice Direction*; see **19.21** above.

19.30   Most cases are listed for a fixed date. It is the practice of the EAT that the listing office consults the parties, or as appropriate their representatives, over dates to avoid, and as a consequence once a hearing is listed, cogent reasons will be needed to secure a postponement. It is the duty of the parties to advise the EAT if for any reason the time estimate given for the hearing is likely to be inadequate or too long. Parties are also required to notify the EAT immediately of any settlement which results in the appeal being withdrawn; the Court of Appeal has stated that it is a strict professional duty of legal representatives to avoid waste of judicial time by notifying settlements of cases under appeal immediately, particularly if a settlement is achieved in the immediate run up to the hearing of the appeal: *Yell Ltd v Garton* [2004] EWCA Civ 87, (2004) Times, 26 February. Shorter, and urgent, appeals may be called on at short, sometimes very short, notice.

19.31 Skeleton arguments

In accordance with *para 13* of the *Practice Direction*, skeleton arguments are required to be lodged with the EAT and exchanged between the parties' representatives, normally 21 days in advance of the hearing (precise timing varies depending on the length of notice of the hearing and type of hearing); appellants may lodge a skeleton argument with the Notice of Appeal, and should prepare an agreed chronology of relevant events. Skeleton arguments are also required for preliminary hearings, and should be lodged 10 days in advance. The format and content of skeleton arguments are prescribed in some detail in *para 13* of the *2008 Practice Direction*. The requirements for skeleton arguments do not apply in Scotland unless specifically directed.

Parties intending to rely on authorities are expected to provide copies for the use of the judge and (if present) members. The President, Langstaff J, in a Practice Statement issued on 17 April 2012, indicated that authorities should be presented in a ring binder, in chronological order and separately tabbed, using the officially reported versions with headnotes wherever available, and with the relevant passages highlighted; and that only cases which are authority for a legal principle, rather than merely illustrative, should be relied on. Parties are expected whenever possible to co-operate in producing a single joint bundle of authorities. The EAT has available for reference its own copies of the most frequently cited cases, and it is not necessary to provide copies of any of the listed cases for the hearing. The full list of cases to which this practice applies is posted on the EAT website.

It is the practice of the EAT to read the papers, and skeleton arguments, in advance and representatives can expect to be asked questions arising from their and the other party's skeleton arguments as well as points arising in the course of their oral submissions.

19.32 The hearing

The hearing before the EAT consists of legal argument; it is not the practice to hear evidence again, and therefore witnesses who attended the tribunal do not need to attend the appeal. Exceptions to this, where witnesses may be required to give evidence, include where there is an appeal against a refusal by the registrar to extend time for a late notice of appeal: in such cases, evidence may be given to explain the delay in submitting the Notice of Appeal; and in relation to allegations of bias or improper conduct in the course of the hearing, where if the events in issue are disputed, the EAT may wish to hear live evidence from those present (other than the Employment Judge and members, who will never be required to give evidence). If fresh evidence is put forward this is done by way of affidavit, or a witness statement with a signed Statement of Truth.

19.33   Raising points not taken at the tribunal hearing

A party is not normally permitted to raise points of law which were conceded or abandoned, or never raised at all, before the employment tribunal, especially where such points would require further investigation of the facts. The law and practice on this issue was reviewed by the EAT in *Glennie v Independent Magazines (UK) Ltd* [1999] IRLR 719, following the decision of the Court of Appeal in *Jones v Governing Body of Burdett Coutts School* [1998] IRLR 521, which established that the EAT's discretion to allow a new point of law to be raised, or a conceded point to be reopened, should be exercised only in exceptional circumstances, for compelling reasons. This was especially so if the result would be to open up fresh issues of fact which, because the point was not in issue, were not sufficiently investigated before the employment tribunal. The facts that the point is of wider importance, or that the amount at stake in the claim is very significant, are not reasons to depart from the general practice: *UNISON v Leicestershire County Council* [2006] EWCA Civ 825, [2006] IRLR 810 (where the tribunal had made a protective award totalling several million pounds). An example of an exceptional case is *Lipscombe v Forestry Commission* [2007] EWCA Civ 428, [2007] All ER (D) 132 (May), where a litigant in person was permitted by the Court of Appeal to rely on a point not taken at the hearing, which involved undisputed facts and was decisive of whether the tribunal had jurisdiction.

The various authorities were again reviewed by the EAT, and the principles fully set out, in *Rance v Secretary of State for Health* [2007] IRLR 665. There is a discretion whether to allow the raising of new points or the reopening of conceded points, but it will be exercised only in exceptional cases, particularly so where the effect of taking the point would be that fresh issues of fact would have to be investigated; on the other hand the fact that the point goes to the tribunal's jurisdiction is not a trump card. Within these general principles, the earlier cases provide examples of the sort of case in which the discretion is, or is not, likely to be exercised in favour of the party seeking to raise the point.

19.34   Fresh evidence

Appellants not infrequently seek to put additional evidence before the EAT to undermine the basis for the decision under appeal. It is at least arguable that this is not a permissible ground of appeal, since the tribunal cannot be said to have erred in law in failing to take account of evidence which was not put before it; this point was noted, but not decided, by the EAT in *Adegbuji v Meteor Parking Ltd* (UKEATPA/1570/09). Irrespective of that point, the EAT has repeatedly urged that the usual way of seeking to have additional evidence considered is by applying to the tribunal itself for a review of the decision: see for example *Korashi v Abertawe Bro Morgannwg University Local Health Board* [2012] IRLR 4.

The matter has now been made the subject of a Practice Statement by the President, Langstaff J, issued on 17 April 2012, and accessible via the EAT website. The statement explains that there is a strong preference for fresh evidence applications to be pursued by way of review since this is quicker than an appeal, which if successful would result in the matter being referred back to the tribunal to consider the evidence, and more suitable since the tribunal which took the original decision is better placed to assess whether the proposed fresh evidence would have affected its decision. Accordingly it is likely that if an appeal includes an application to admit fresh evidence, the appeal will be stayed for the appellant to apply to the tribunal for a review of its original decision, based on the fresh evidence. This does not of course preclude a subsequent appeal on the ground that the tribunal erred in refusing to admit the evidence. Despite the general approach, it may still exceptionally be more appropriate for an application for the admission of fresh evidence to be considered by the EAT, for instance if this is one of a number of issues in the appeal and it would delay or unnecessarily complicate matters for the fresh evidence point to be referred back to the tribunal for a review.

Whether the point is dealt with by way of review or appeal, the principles of the admissibility of fresh evidence are essentially the same. A party will not be permitted to adduce factual matters before the EAT which it chose not to put before the employment tribunal (*Bingham v Hobourn Engineering Ltd* [1992] IRLR 298). The test for the admission of fresh evidence is as set out in *Wileman v Minilec Engineering Ltd* [1988] ICR 318, adopting the established formula applied in appeals from the civil courts to the Court of Appeal, as set out in *Ladd v Marshall* [1954] 1 WLR 1489. The three requirements, which are cumulative, are set out in the *2008 Practice Direction, para 8.2*, as follows

> '8.2.1   the evidence could not have been obtained with reasonable diligence for use at the Employment Tribunal hearing;
>
> 8.2.2   it is relevant and would probably have had an important influence on the hearing;
>
> 8.2.3   it is apparently credible.'

The application of these requirements is fully reviewed in the judgment of the EAT in *Korashi v Abertawe Bro Morgannwg University Local Health Board* (above).

The procedure if the issue is pursued before the EAT is that the evidence sought to be admitted should be submitted in the form of one or more sworn affidavits or witness statements with a signed Statement of Truth, or exhibited to an Affidavit or witness statement if the evidence is in documentary form. The evidence should normally be submitted together with the Notice of Appeal or Respondent's Answer (*Practice Direction, para 8*). If leave to admit the evidence is given, the case will usually be remitted for a rehearing, but the cogency of the evidence may occasionally be such that the original decision is simply reversed.

19.35 Errors of law and perversity

The EAT can only overturn the decision of an employment tribunal if the tribunal can be shown to have erred in law. Where an appeal succeeds, the point of law on which the tribunal erred should be identified in the EAT's decision (*British Gas plc v McCarrick* [1991] IRLR 305). The error of law may be an express misdirection or it may be inferred from the fact that the conclusion of the tribunal was one which no reasonable employment tribunal, properly directing itself as to the relevant legal principles, could have reached; in other words, that the decision of the tribunal was so inconsistent with the correct application of the law that it was either a perverse decision or reached applying incorrect legal principles.

Even if the EAT would have come to a different conclusion, it must not interfere with the decision of the employment tribunal unless an error of law is identified (*Retarded Children's Aid Society Ltd v Day* [1978] 1 WLR 763, [1978] ICR 437). Misunderstanding or misapplication of the facts does not of itself amount to an error of law unless the tribunal proceeds upon a basis contrary to the undisputed or indisputable facts (*British Telecommunications plc v Sheridan* [1990] IRLR 27).

Perversity is recognised as a separate ground of appeal, and is often relied on, but rarely successfully because of the high standard required to establish that a decision was perverse. Unless the employment tribunal has misdirected itself in law, its decision should not be disturbed on the ground of perversity unless the decision under appeal was not a permissible option (*Piggott Bros & Co Ltd v Jackson* [1992] ICR 85). In *Piggott*, the Court of Appeal held (at 92) that in concluding that the decision under appeal was not a permissible option, the EAT will almost always have to be able to identify a finding of fact which was unsupported by *any* evidence or a clear self-misdirection in law by the employment tribunal (see also *Hough v Leyland DAF Ltd* [1991] ICR 696, in which the EAT pointed out that a finding of fact was not perverse merely because the tribunal had reached it by way of inference and without any direct evidence). However, the EAT in *East Berkshire Health Authority v Matadeen* [1992] ICR 723 held that a conclusion drawn from unassailable facts could be attacked as perverse. The approach adopted in *Piggott* represented a departure from the test of whether one could say of a decision, 'My goodness, that was certainly wrong', formulated in *Neale v Hereford and Worcester County Council* [1986] ICR 471.

Subsequently, Mummery J has categorised perversity as including a decision that on the evidence before the tribunal is 'irrational', 'offends reason', 'must be wrong', 'is not a permissible option', or 'flies in the face of properly informed logic': *Stewart v Cleveland Guest (Engineering) Ltd* [1994] IRLR 440 at 443.

The Court of Appeal gave further guidance as to the correct approach to deciding perversity appeals in what has come to be regarded as the leading case on perversity appeals, *Yeboah v Crofton* [2002] EWCA Civ 794, [2002] IRLR 634:

> 'Such an appeal ought only to succeed where an overwhelming case is made out that the employment tribunal reached a decision which no reasonable tribunal, on a proper appreciation of the evidence and the law, would have reached.'

(Mummery LJ at para 93)

The court also warned of the danger of turning an appeal on a point of law into a rehearing of parts of the evidence.

19.36 Inadequacy of reasons

The alleged inadequacy of the reasons given by a tribunal is a frequently raised ground of appeal. A failure by an employment tribunal to give adequate (or any) reasons for a judgment or order, or a substantive finding in the proceedings, may amount to an error of law rendering the decision liable to be set aside on appeal. As to the adequacy of reasons, see the citation from *Meek v City of Birmingham District Council* [1987] IRLR 250, CA in **18.63** above and the cases cited there. It should be noted that the decision in *Meek* predates the introduction of a more prescriptive approach to the content of reasons for judgments by *rule 30* of the *ET Rules 2004*, and a somewhat less tolerant approach to inadequately expressed reasons is apparent in EAT decisions, particularly in cases involving allegations of discrimination, than was formerly the case. In *Greenwood v NWF Retail Ltd* [2011] ICR 896, the EAT held that failure to comply with *ET Rule 30(6)* was in itself an error of law. However the EAT went on to confirm that this does not require the tribunal to follow precisely or rigidly the format prescribed by *Rule 30(6)*, provided that each of the matters specified in the rule was addressed. The EAT noted with approval the comment of Buxton LJ in *Balfour Beatty Power Networks v Wilcox* [2006] EWCA Civ 1240, [2007] IRLR 63 that:

> 'the rule is surely intended to be a guide and not a straitjacket. Provided it can be reasonably spelt out from the determination of the employment tribunal that what rule 30(6) requires has been provided by that tribunal, then no error of law will have been committed.'

The EAT may also, if inadequacy of reasons is given as a ground of appeal, remit the case to the tribunal for it to clarify or amplify its reasons, prior to hearing the substantive appeal: see **19.22** above.

19.37 Procedural failures

A separate category of error of law is a failure by the tribunal to afford the parties a fair hearing, whether through some serious procedural failure or through bias, or where the circumstances have created a real danger, or a perception, of bias. Cases falling within this general categorisation would include, for instance, those where relevant evidence was unjustifiably excluded or a party was prevented from putting forward part of his or her case, or the tribunal failed to invite the parties to deal with a particular point before deciding it or relied on a point of law not canvassed at the hearing; the Employment Judge or a member sitting despite a potential conflict of interest; and inappropriate conduct by the Judge or a member in the course of the hearing (see generally as to these potential grounds **19.23–19.25** above). Excessive delay in delivering judgment following the hearing is not of itself an error of law, and will only provide grounds for appeal if in the circumstances there is a real risk that the appellant was deprived of the right to a fair trial: *Bangs v Connex South Eastern Ltd* [2005] EWCA Civ 14, [2005] 2 All ER 316, [2005] IRLR 389. Thus in *Grosvenor v Governing Body of Aylesford School* (UKEAT/0001/08) a delay of a year in promulgating the judgment was held not to provide a ground of appeal on the basis that the judgment, albeit excessively long, was adequately reasoned.

It may also be a ground of appeal that the tribunal has decided the case on a point not relied on by the parties and on which the losing party has not been given the opportunity to make submissions. An example is *Launahurst Ltd v Larner* [2010] EWCA Civ 334, where the tribunal held that the contract under which the claimant was held out to be self-employed was a sham, a point not advanced by him or raised with the respondent at the hearing. In addition, it may be a ground of appeal that the tribunal relied in reaching its decision on legal authorities not cited by the parties and on which they have not been given an opportunity to make submissions: *Clark v Clark Construction Initiatives Ltd* [2008] EWCA Civ 1446, [2009] ICR 718; however this does not prevent the citation of authority to support uncontentious or incidental points in the tribunal's judgment: *Stanley Cole (Wainfleet) Ltd v Sheridan* [2003] EWCA Civ 1046, [2003] ICR 1449.

19.38 Disposal of the appeal

There are essentially two possible outcomes if an appeal is successful. Either the matter may be remitted (to the original tribunal or a fresh tribunal), to be considered further in the light of the EAT's judgment or for a complete rehearing; or the EAT may substitute a decision in favour of the appellant, eg that the dismissal was fair, rather than unfair. In cases not involving a specific point of statutory construction, which may necessarily determine the result, the EAT is careful not to usurp the tribunal's role as arbiter of facts. It will therefore not substitute a decision unless there is only one decision that a tribunal correctly directing itself in law could have reached (*Morgan v Electrolux Ltd* [1991] ICR 369).

Where an error of law is identified, the EAT must allow the appeal unless the conclusion of the employment tribunal was plainly and unarguably right, notwithstanding the misdirection (*Dobie v Burns International Security Services (UK) Ltd* [1984] 3 All ER 333, [1985] 1 WLR 43, [1984] ICR 812). Equally, the position (at least until recently) is that unless the decision was plainly and arguably wrong, the EAT should not substitute a different decision but should remit the matter for rehearing. However, recent decisions of the Court of Appeal have shown a degree of division as to the desirability of the EAT deciding a point rather than remitting it to the tribunal to decide. *Buckland v Bournemouth University Education Corporation* [2010] ICR 908 supports the EAT taking the decision itself if no further evidence is required, but a more cautious approach was advocated in *Tilson v Alstom Transport* [2010] EWCA Civ 1308, [2011] IRLR 169, in which Elias LJ said:

> 'it is only where the employment tribunal, properly directing itself in law, could reach only one legitimate decision that the EAT can substitute that decision for the one improperly reached by the employment tribunal'.

Buckland was not cited to the Court in *Tilson*, and it is at least arguable that the former case should be followed (and Elias LJ in *Tilson* stated that 'there is much to be said for a relaxation of the established principles'). It is therefore likely that a more liberal use of the power to substitute its decision for that of the tribunal will be taken by the EAT (for an example see *Mindimaxnox LLP v Gover* (UKEAT/0225/10). For an example of a case where the tribunal's decision was considered sufficiently plainly wrong that the Court of Appeal overturned the decision of the EAT to remit it for re-hearing, and substituted a finding in favour of the appellant, see *Devon and Somerset Fire and Rescue Service v Tilke* [2010] EWCA Civ 1402.

The same principles apply to appeals from interlocutory orders or judgments as to appeals from final judgments (*Adams and Raynor v West Sussex County Council* [1990] ICR 546). A good example of a case where an interlocutory order, fixing a hearing, was overturned because the employment judge had taken into account an irrelevant factor, is *Gillingham Football Club v McCammon* (UKEAT/0625/11); as often occurs in urgent appeals, in that case the EAT, with the parties' agreement, proceeded to re-decide the issue on the material before it rather than remit it to the tribunal.

The EAT in *Sinclair Roche & Temperley v Heard* [2004] IRLR 763 gave guidance which is frequently cited as to the factors to be considered in determining whether a case should or should not be remitted to the same tribunal.

19.39 If a case is ordered by the EAT to be remitted (to the same or a fresh tribunal) following a successful appeal, the tribunal which hears the case on remission only has jurisdiction by reason of the remission. It cannot, therefore, even with the agreement of the parties, reopen or deal with issues other than those remitted for its consideration. This conclusion was reached by the Court of Appeal in *Aparau v Iceland Frozen Foods plc* [2000] 1 All ER 228, [2000] IRLR 196, where (in a constructive dismissal case) the issue remitted to the tribunal was whether a term had been incorporated in the contract of employment. This was then conceded, with the consequence that the constructive dismissal claim was made out, but the employers persuaded the tribunal to deal with the fairness of the dismissal, which had not been disputed at the original hearing. The Court of Appeal held that its decision on that point was a nullity. These principles would not, however, prevent the tribunal from dealing with a point affecting its jurisdiction to deal with the matters remitted.

19.40 Where both the parties to an application to an employment tribunal agree that the decision of the tribunal was in error and reach a proposed settlement, the parties may not themselves reverse that decision but must refer the matter to the EAT. The parties should draw up a formal order and request the EAT to accept it, ratify it and make it part of the order of the Appeal Tribunal. However, unless the consent order is part of an overall settlement of the proceedings (in which case the EAT will usually agree to the order without hearing full argument – see *British Publishing Co Ltd v Fraser* [1987] ICR 517) a consent order will not be granted unless the EAT is persuaded by argument at a hearing that the decision appealed against was wrong in law; and if the effect of the proposed order is to remit the case to the tribunal for further consideration, the EAT will give a reasoned judgment on the appeal: *J Sainsbury plc v Moger* [1994] ICR 800. (See also *2008 Practice Direction, para 15.3.*)

19.41 OTHER POWERS OF THE APPEAL TRIBUNAL

For the purpose of disposing of an appeal, the EAT may exercise any powers of the body or officer from whom the appeal was brought (*ETA 1996, s 35*). It also has the same general powers as the High Court in relation to production of documents, attendance of witnesses, contempt of court and other matters incidental to its jurisdiction (*ETA 1996, s 29(2)*). As to the EAT's powers to make restricted reporting orders, see **19.26** above.

The *2002 Practice Direction* introduced new procedures regarding the transcription of judgments of the EAT, and these have been retained in the 2004 and 2008 revisions. Unless the decision is reserved or the EAT so directs as part of its judgment given orally, or, in the case of a preliminary hearing, the judgment is given in the absence of the appellant, a transcript will only be drawn up if requested by one or both parties within 14 days (*2008 Practice Direction, para 18*). The *Practice Direction* gives more detailed information about the arrangements for handing down reserved judgments and any consequential applications (for permission to appeal, for costs etc). In Scotland the practice is that judgments are normally reserved. Judgments given following full hearings which are ordered to be transcribed, or are reserved and handed down, are posted on the EAT website (now housed on the Judicial website, www.justice.gov.uk) as are some judgments given in appeals under rule 3(10) which finally dispose of the proceedings: *Practice Direction, para 18.8*.

19.42   COSTS

The powers of the EAT to award costs (expenses in Scotland) were significantly recast by the *2004 Amendment Rules*. The provisions are now contained in *rules 34–34D*. The scheme of the new provisions follows that of the *ET Rules* in providing separately for the costs incurred by unrepresented parties, and in introducing wasted costs orders.

A party may apply for a costs order at any stage during the appeal, or within 14 days of the date the order finally disposing of the proceedings is sent to the parties *(rule 34(4))*. However, unless the paying party is given an opportunity at the hearing to make representations against the making of an order, it can only be made after an opportunity to make such representations has been afforded by notice to the party concerned *(rule 34(5))*. The representations will normally be dealt with on the papers, but if it is considered appropriate, they can be referred for a further hearing. Written reasons must be given for a costs order if a party so requests within 21 days of the date of the order *(rule 34(6))*.

The statistics published by the Ministry of Justice do not include details of the numbers and amounts of awards of costs or expenses; experience in practice is that awards are relatively uncommon but far from unknown.

19.43   Grounds for costs orders

The principal circumstances in which a costs order can be made against a party are that the paying party has brought proceedings that were unnecessary, improper, vexatious or misconceived, or that there has been unreasonable delay or other unreasonable conduct by the paying party. Without prejudice to the general application of those criteria, costs may be ordered in three specific cases, namely where the paying party has not complied with a direction of the EAT, or has amended a Notice of Appeal, Respondent's Answer or similar document, or has caused an adjournment of the proceedings *(rule 34A(1), (2))*. The most important of these conditions is the bringing of an appeal which is misconceived (ie has no reasonable prospect of success), and unreasonable conduct by a respondent, which may include resisting an appeal on misconceived grounds. In practice, however, there will rarely be grounds for an award of costs under either head, since misconceived appeals are likely to be screened out, at latest at the preliminary hearing, before the respondent to the appeal needs to incur significant costs in resisting it. It will also only very rarely be the case that it can be said that defending a decision of a tribunal against an appeal is as such unreasonable conduct (a view confirmed by the Court of Appeal in *Afolayan v MRCS Ltd* [2009] EWCA Civ 796). The *manner* in which an appeal is pursued or defended may however be unreasonable even though the party concerned has a case with some merit. An example of a case where expenses were awarded on the ground that the appeal was so lacking in merit as to be misconceived is *Morgan v Greater Glasgow Health Board* (UKEATS/0044/11). The EAT has no jurisdiction to make an order for costs incurred in the employment tribunal.

There are limits on the making of an order for costs against the respondent to an appeal who has not had an answer accepted by the EAT: in such a case *rule 34(3)* allows for a costs order (in favour of, as well as against, the respondent) in relation to his or her conduct of any part of the proceedings in which he or she has taken part; the necessary limitation implied by this is that if a respondent takes no part in the appeal, there is no power to award costs against that respondent (compare in relation to costs in the employment tribunal *Sutton v The Ranch Ltd* [2006] ICR 1170).

Further guidance on when the bringing or pursuit of an appeal can be categorised as unreasonable is given in *Iron and Steel Trades Confederation v ASW Ltd (in liquidation)* [2004] IRLR 926. In *G4S Security Services (UK) v Rondeau* (UKEAT/0207/09/DA), the EAT awarded costs against the respondent to the appeal, who had refused a reasonable offer of settlement by the appellant, only to accept it at the door of the court. An example of a case where costs were awarded against a successful appellant because the proceedings were 'unnecessary' is *Fowler v British School of Motoring* [2006] All ER (D) 93 (May), where the appellant employer had failed for no good reason to present its response to the original claim in time, and successfully appealed against the tribunal's refusal to review a decision that it should not be permitted to take part in the proceedings. The appeal was 'unnecessary' because the appellant could and should have submitted its response in good time.

The fact that the preconditions for an award of costs exist does not entitle the receiving party to an order. The EAT has a discretion whether to award costs (and its exercise of that discretion will rarely be disturbed on appeal: see *Afolayan*, above). If it decides to do so, it has a further discretion to take into account the means of the paying party *(rules 34A(3), 34B(2))*. The powers available subject to this discretion are to award a sum determined by the EAT itself by summary assessment, or an agreed sum, or to award costs subject to a detailed assessment by the High Court or taxation by the Auditor of the Court of Session *(rule 34B(1))*.

19.44 Amounts and means

There are separate rules as to the amount that may be awarded where the receiving party is a litigant in person (in Scotland a party litigant), equivalent to the powers of the tribunal to make a preparation time order. It should however be noted that, in contrast to the position in employment tribunals, the general power to award costs is not confined to an award to legally represented parties; any party who does not fall within the definition of a litigant in person or a party litigant is eligible for an award of costs in accordance with *rule 34B*. A litigant in person is defined to include a company or corporation which is acting without a legal representative, and a solicitor, barrister, advocate or other person qualified to conduct litigation who is appearing for him or herself *(rule 34D(7))*. This does not cover a company represented by an in-house lawyer, or an individual represented by a non-legal representative, including a relative or friend, or a professional consultant who is not a lawyer; the latter are therefore eligible for ordinary costs orders under *rule 34A*.

The conditions for an award of costs in favour of a litigant in person are the same as for any other party. The costs recoverable may not exceed two thirds of the costs that would be payable if the party had had legal representation (with an exception for any disbursements, such as a payment for legal advice, which may be recovered in full if a full award is made and the payment was of a reasonable amount) *(rule 34D(2))*. Within this overall restriction, the costs recoverable are payments for advice, and for expert assistance in assessing the claim for costs, and expenses incurred in the proceedings (eg for photocopying or travel to the hearing), and compensation for time spent preparing the case and attending the hearing *(rule 34D(3))*. In relation to this head, the rate of payment will either be the amount the party can prove he or she has lost (eg lost wages) or a flat rate of £33 an hour (from 6 April 2013; this will increase annually in the same way as the equivalent rate for preparation time orders: see **18.73** for further details) *(rule 34D(4), (5))*. The amount awarded will be subject to the EAT's assessment of what was a reasonable and proportionate amount of time to spend preparing for the hearing.

19.45 Wasted costs orders

The powers to make wasted costs orders and the procedures to be followed are set out in new *rule 34C*. This is for all practical purposes in exactly the same terms, with necessary modifications of terminology, as *rule 48* of the *ET Rules*, and reference should therefore be made to the discussion of that *Rule* at **19.73** above for details. Guidance on the procedure to be followed in the EAT when considering a wasted costs application (as distinct from the hearing of an appeal against an order made by a tribunal) was given by the Court of Appeal in *Gill v Humanware Europe Ltd* [2010] EWCA Civ 799, [2010] ICR 1343, [2010] IRLR 877.

19.46   REVIEW

The EAT may review any order made by it on the grounds that:

(a)   the order was wrongly made as the result of an error on the part of the EAT or its staff;

(b)   a party did not receive proper notice of the proceedings leading to the order; or

(c)   the interests of justice require such review.

(*EAT Rules, rule 33.*)

Orders which may be reviewed are not limited to final determinations of appeals, it may on occasion be appropriate for the EAT in the course of a hearing to review an order made earlier in the proceedings, such as an order specifying the grounds of appeal which may be considered (see *Khan v Vignette Europe Ltd* (UKEAT/0350/08)). The circumstances in which the review procedure can be invoked are rare (see *Stannard & Co (1969) Ltd v Wilson* [1983] ICR 86). In *Jenkins v P & O European Ferries (Dover) Ltd* [1991] ICR 652, the EAT on its own initiative was prepared to review its earlier decision on the ground that it recognised that there was a fundamental error of law in that decision, but in *Blockleys plc v Miller* [1992] ICR 749 it appeared to prefer a narrower approach. In *Digital Equipment Co Ltd v Clements (No 2)* [1997] ICR 237 the EAT reviewed, and reversed, its initial decision in circumstances where that decision had been given in ignorance of another decision on essentially the same point of law; the review thus enabled the EAT to resolve the law on a point on which there would otherwise have been conflicting authorities. There is as yet no reported decision of the EAT on whether its powers of review in the interests of justice have been enlarged by the addition to the *EAT Rules* of the Overriding Objective, but this would be consistent with the view taken by the EAT of the equivalent change in the *ET Rules* (see eg *Williams v Ferrosan Ltd* [2004] IRLR 607).

However there is no jurisdiction to review a decision not to register an appeal taken under *Rule 3(7)* on the sift; the appropriate course for an aggrieved appellant to take is either to submit a fresh notice of appeal under *Rule 3(8)* or apply for a hearing under *Rule 3(10)*: see *Zinda v Governing Body of Barn Hill Community High* [2011] ICR 174. The EAT in that case accepted, however, that it might exceptionally be appropriate to permit a review of a decision taken under one of the procedures in *Rule 3* on the basis of fresh evidence having become available, if the point first arose after any time limit for appealing had expired.

Where the EAT has not formally drawn up and issued the order embodying its decision, it has a wider power of review based on its inherent jurisdiction as a superior court of record, and need not confine itself to the *Blockleys* approach: *Bass Leisure Ltd v Thomas* [1994] IRLR 104 at 108–109. Exceptionally, the EAT may reach a provisional decision, notify the parties accordingly and invite further submissions before pronouncing final judgment; this was done in *Rubenstein and Roskin (t/a McGuffies Dispensing Chemists) v McGloughlin* [1997] ICR 318, [1996] IRLR 557.

19.47   FURTHER APPEALS

A further appeal may be taken to the Court of Appeal (or in Scotland, the Court of Session) on a point of law, but only with permission from the EAT or the Court of Appeal or Court of Session (*ETA 1996, s 37(1), (2)*). Permission should be sought initially from the EAT.

If the EAT refuses permission, an application may be made to the Court of Appeal (or the Court of Session, as the case may be). The principles to be applied upon such an application were considered by the Court of Session in *Campbell v Dunoon and Cowal Housing Association Ltd* [1992] IRLR 528. The restrictions on 'second appeals' to the Court of Appeal introduced by the *Access to Justice Act 1999, s 55* do not apply to appeals from the EAT, and the introduction of more restrictive criteria in relation to other areas does not appear significantly to have affected the Court of Appeal's practice in granting permission to appeal in employment cases. The Leggatt Report included a recommendation that the more restrictive test in *s 55* be applied to appeals from the EAT. This, if implemented, could result in a significant reduction in the number of appeals heard by the Court of Appeal in employment cases, and arguably greater uncertainty owing to conflicting reported decisions of the EAT, but no steps to implement it have yet been put forward. It should nevertheless be emphasised that compelling reasons are needed to persuade the Court to give permission to appeal.

In appeals from the EAT, the Court of Appeal is a second-tier appellate court and is concerned with whether the decision of the employment tribunal was right, not with whether the EAT was right (*Hennessy v Craigmyle & Co Ltd* [1986] ICR 461; *Campion v Hamworthy Engineering Ltd* [1987] ICR 966). However, the Court of Appeal itself has recently expressed serious reservations about the correctness of this approach (*Gover v Propertycare Ltd* [2006] EWCA Civ 286, [2006] All ER (D) 408 (Mar), per Buxton, Lloyd and Richards LJJ), and it may fairly be regarded as arguable in the light of these reservations. Where the EAT has allowed an appeal from the original decision of the tribunal, the focus of a further appeal to the Court of Appeal is inevitably directed more to whether there was sufficient basis for that decision.

The time limit for lodging an appeal to the Court of Appeal with the permission of the EAT is 14 days from the date on which the order or judgment of the EAT was drawn up, unless the EAT gives a longer period; if permission is refused, an appellant's notice must be served on the court, by way of application for permission to appeal, within the same 14-day period (*Civil Procedure Rules 1998, r 52.3*).

The normal practice of the Court of Appeal is that costs follow the event, so that a successful appellant is usually entitled to, and will be awarded, his or her costs. This is equally the case for appeals from the EAT despite the general principle that the employment tribunals and EAT are costs-free jurisdictions in which an award of costs requires specific justification. However recent developments have reduced the risks to litigants of more modest means of the usual costs regime of the Court. In *Governing Body of St Albans Girls' School v Neary (No 2)* [2009] EWCA Civ 1214, the Court of Appeal refused to award costs to the employers, who had successfully appealed against the refusal of the EAT to strike out the claimant's claim for breach of an unless order. The fact that the employee had been taken to the Court by his ex-employer, rather than the other way round, coupled with the employee's impecuniosity, was considered by the Court to be in the circumstances a reason to depart from the normal rule that costs follow the event.

An amendments to the *Civil Procedure Rules 1998*, applicable from 1 April 2013, gives the court power on an appeal from a jurisdiction where costs are not normally awarded to make an order in advance of the appeal limiting the costs recoverable by the successful party, having regard to the means of the parties, the circumstances of the case and the interests of justice (*CPR Rule 52.9A*). The use of this power was foreshadowed by the decision in *Manchester College v Hazel* [2013] EWCA Civ 281 that the employee respondents to an appeal by the employer should be protected from an award of costs against them if the appeal succeeded (the employees having agreed not to seek costs if the appeal was refused).

A further appeal lies to the Supreme Court if the Court of Appeal or Court of Session, or the Supreme Court itself, gives permission. A number of special rules govern Supreme Court appeals.

19.47   Employment Tribunals – III: Appeals

In Scotland, the appeal from the EAT is to the Inner House of the Court of Session, and thence to the Supreme Court. In Northern Ireland, appeals lie directly from the tribunal to the Northern Ireland Court of Appeal, and thence to the Supreme Court. Leave to appeal is required at each stage, except that appeals to the Northern Ireland Court of Appeal (which involve the stating of a case by the tribunal) are a matter of right.

19.48 ISSUES OF EU LAW

Where the outcome of an application or an appeal turns on a question of EU law, the answer to which is unclear, the tribunal or court may, or if it is a court of final appeal must, refer the question to the Court of Justice of the European Union (CJEU) under *art 234* of the *Treaty of Rome*. The parties to the application or appeal can request a reference in these circumstances. In *Enderby v Frenchay Health Authority and Secretary of State for Health* [1991] ICR 382, the EAT suggested that national appeals procedures ought normally to be exhausted before a reference was made, but the Court of Appeal ([1992] IRLR 15) decided to refer the case to the CJEU before making any order itself. A number of cases have been referred to the CJEU by employment tribunals, both before and after *Enderby*: see eg *Neath v Hugh Steeper Ltd*: C-152/91 [1994] 1 All ER 929, *Smith v Avdel Systems Ltd*: C-408/92 [1995] ICR 596, *P v S and Cornwall County Council*: C-13/94 [1996] IRLR 347, *Robinson-Steele v RD Retail Services Ltd*: C-131/04 [2006] ECR I-2531, [2006] ICR 932 and *Coleman v Atttridge Law*: C-303/06, [2008] IRLR 722.

The tribunal, and the EAT, should not refer a matter to the CJEU unless its ruling is 'necessary' for the determination of the case; if the case may turn on questions of fact, these should first be determined by the tribunal. However, in *Attridge Law v Coleman* [2007] IRLR 88, the EAT held, rejecting an appeal against an order of the tribunal referring an issue to the CJEU at a preliminary stage in the case, that a reference could be 'necessary' even if the point would not be determinative of the case, if the ruling sought was necessary to do justice. One important practical consequence of a reference to the CJEU being made by either the employment tribunal or the EAT, rather than a higher court, is that the costs of the proceedings before the CJEU are subject to the same rules as those applying to the referring court or tribunal, so that a party seeking a ruling from the CJEU is less at risk of an award of costs if the ruling is adverse if the reference is made before the case reaches the Court of Appeal or the Court of Session.

Where an employment tribunal has made a finding in relation to an incident, it is not necessarily unreasonable for the police to form their own view, unrestricted by the tribunal, and to disclose the incident to a prospective employer: *R (W) v Chief Constable of Warwickshire* [2012] EWHC 406 (Admin).

20.5   ENGAGEMENT

An employer should inform a new employee of the terms and conditions under which he is to work and his commencement date and time. This should be done by letter (if not by a formal signed agreement), although a purely verbal agreement may be sufficient to found an employment relationship (as in *Ferguson v John Dawson & Partners (Contractors) Ltd* [1976] 1 WLR 1213). He is obliged by law to give the employee written particulars of those terms and conditions within two months of the commencement of his employment (see **7.6** CONTRACT OF EMPLOYMENT). An offer may be made 'subject to satisfactory references' and in *Wishart v National Association of Citizens Advice Bureaux Ltd* [1990] ICR 794, [1990] IRLR 393 the Court of Appeal considered that this meant only satisfactory to the employer, subject to an obligation of good faith.

The *actual day* on which employment commences has importance under the rules for computing continuity of employment (see **6.3** CONTINUOUS EMPLOYMENT) irrespective of whether the employee actually performs any duties on that day (see *General of the Salvation Army v Dewsbury* [1984] ICR 498).

20.6   EMPLOYMENT AGENCIES

For the law regulating employment agencies, and the status of those recruited through such agencies, see **45.2** TEMPORARY AND SEASONAL EMPLOYEES.

20.7   Data Protection Act 1998

If information about an applicant is stored on a computer, the provisions of the *Data Protection Act 1998* must be complied with (see **9.13** *et seq* DISCLOSURE OF INFORMATION).

20.8   WITHDRAWAL OF OFFERS OF EMPLOYMENT

Once an offer of employment has been made and accepted, a valid contract exists even though the date when the employee is due to start work may be delayed. If in these circumstances the employer retracts the offer or terminates the contract prior to the actual commencement of work, the employee will not be without a remedy. There are three remedies which may potentially be available to the employee depending on the circumstances. First, there may be a claim for wrongful dismissal (see WRONGFUL DISMISSAL (56)). That claim may be brought before the employment tribunal or the county court. Second, if the reason for the dismissal is an inadmissible reason, there may be a claim of unfair dismissal. No period of qualifying employment is necessary when the reason for dismissal is an inadmissible reason (see **52.3** UNFAIR DISMISSAL – II). The authority for these propositions is *Sarker v South Tees Acute Hospitals NHS Trust* [1997] ICR 673. Third, it may be possible to bring a claim alleging that the dismissal was discriminatory on grounds of age or sex or race or disability or religion or belief or sexual orientation (see DISCRIMINATION AND EQUAL OPPORTUNITIES – **1, II, III (10, 11, 12)**). An example in the discrimination context is *Mamedu v Hatten Wyatt Solicitors* [2008] All ER (D) 76 (Apr), EAT. The Court of Appeal has confirmed that obligations of trust and confidence apply to both employer and employee from the outset of the contract where the agreement is one to take up employment at a future date (a so-called forward contract): *Tullett Prebon Plc v BGC Brokers LP* [2011] EWCA Civ 131, [2011] IRLR 420.

21 Equal Pay

Cross-reference. See Discrimination and Equal Opportunities – I (10) for the rules forbidding discrimination on grounds of sex in matters other than the terms and conditions of employment and also 11.3 Discrimination and Equal Opportunities – II.

21.1 Since the coming into force on 29 December 1975 of the *Equal Pay Act 1970* ('*EqPA 1970*'), women have been able to claim equal pay with men, and vice versa. The accession of Great Britain to the *Treaty of Rome* on 1 January 1973 also affected women's rights to equal pay since *art 157* (formerly *art 141*) provides that 'Each Member State shall during the first stage ensure and subsequently maintain the application of the principle that men and women should receive equal pay for equal work'. *Article 157* and *Directive No 75/117* ('the *Equal Pay Directive*') provide a European underpinning of the domestic rights to equal pay (see below **21.3**). The provisions which currently provide for equal pay between men and women are found in the *Equality Act 2010* ('*EA 2010*').

21.2 THE LEGISLATIVE FRAMEWORK

Domestic legislation

EA 2010 consolidates the provisions previously found in the *EqPA 1970* into a single anti-discrimination statute alongside other aspects of discrimination law. The key provisions are found in Chapter 3 of Part 5 EA 2010. The EA 2010 also contains a prohibition on pay confidentiality clauses which prevent employees from discussing their pay with colleagues (*EA 2010, s 77*) and a power to require employers with 250 or more employees to provide reports on the gender pay gap in their business (*EA 2010, s 78*), although the latter power has not yet been brought into force and the present Government has no plans to do so.

Prior to 1st October, 2010 the *EqPA 1970* provided the domestic legal framework for the elimination of discrimination between the sexes in the terms of their contracts of employment. Because a large number of equal pay cases (including local authority 'multiples') continue to be heard under the *EqPA 1970*, this chapter continues to include reference to the *EqPA 1970* as well as *EA 2010*.

Prior to it being superseded by the *EA 2010*, the *EqPA 1970* had been amended by a good deal of subsequent legislation including: the *Sex Discrimination Act 1975* ('*SDA 1975*'), the *Equal Pay (Amendment) Regulations 1983 (SI 1983/1794)* ('the *1983 EqP Regulations*'), the *Sex Discrimination Act 1986*, the *Pensions Act 1995* ('*PA 1995*'), the *Armed Forces Act 1996*, the *Employment Rights (Dispute Resolution) Act 1998*, the *Equal Pay Act 1970 (Amendment) Regulations 2003 (SI 2003/1656)* and the *Equal Pay (Questions and Replies) Order 2003 (SI 2003/722)*. Further provision relating to equal pay is made by the *Social Security Act 1989*, the *Sex Discrimination and Equal Pay (Remedies) Regulations 1993 (SI 1993/2798)*, the *Armed Forces Act 1996*, the *Sex Discrimination (Gender Reassignment) Regulations 1999 (SI 1999/1102)* ('the *Gender Reassignment Regulations*') and the *Employment Equality (Sex Discrimination) Regulations 2005*.

The *1983 EqP Regulations* were introduced in an attempt to bring the United Kingdom into conformity with EU requirements. They introduced for the first time the right to claim equal pay for work of equal value in circumstances in which the jobs of the claimant and the comparator had not been rated as equivalent under a job-evaluation scheme.

The *EqPA 1970* and the examples set out below are framed with reference to women but they are to be read as applying equally to men. The *EA 2010* is framed in gender neutral language.

21.2 Equal Pay

Part-time workers. Discrimination against part-time workers was for some time (and is still to a certain extent) dealt with by way of the protection against indirect sex discrimination in the *SDA 1975* and in *Chapter 1* of *Part 5 EA 2010* (see **10.34** DISCRIMINATION AND EQUAL OPPORTUNITIES – I). However, since 1 July 2000, part-time workers have been protected in relation to pay and other detriments by the *Part-time Workers (Prevention of Less Favourable Treatment) Regulations 2000 (SI 2000/1551)* ('*Part-time Workers Regulations*') (LESS FAVOURABLE TREATMENT OF PART-TIME WORKERS (30); see also **21.18** below).

Transsexuals. In 1996, the European Court of Justice, now the Court of Justice of the European Union (CJEU) decided that discrimination against transsexual employees constituted sex discrimination (*P v S and Cornwall County Council: C-13/94* [1996] IRLR 347). The *Sex Discrimination (Gender Reassignment) Regulations 1999 (SI 1999/1102)* inserted into the *SDA 1975* provisions relating to discrimination against those who intend to undergo, are undergoing or have undergone a gender reassignment (see, in particular *SDA 1975, ss 2A* and *4*). Matters relating to pay discrimination are ordinarily excluded from the scope of *SDA 1975* by *s 4(4)–(6)* (see **11.11** DISCRIMINATION AND EQUAL OPPORTUNITIES – II). However, those subsections are specifically disapplied in relation to transsexuals by *sub-s 4(8)*. It is important to note that although a right not to suffer pay discrimination is very closely related to a right to equal pay, there are significant differences. For instance, transsexuals do not rely upon an equality clause to underpin their right to receive the same pay as their comparators. The rules relating to claims by transsexuals are set out at **21.13** below. The *EA 2010* has made gender reassignment a protected characteristic: see *s 4* of that Act.

Code of Practice. Note that a code of practice prepared by the EOC came into force on 26 March 1997 and is admissible as evidence in *EqPA 1970* and *Sex Discrimination Act 1975* ('*SDA 1975*') proceedings: see the re-issued *Equal Opportunities Commission Code of Practice on Equal Pay (2003)*. A new *Equal Pay: Statutory Code of Practice* has now been issued by the Equalities and Human Rights Commission under the *EA 2010*.

21.3 EU Provisions

The foundation of the right to equal pay in EU law is contained in what is now *art 157* of the *Lisbon Treaty* (formerly *art 141* of the *Treaty of Rome*) (the '*Treaty*') which provides:

'Each Member State shall ensure that the principle of equal pay for male and female workers for equal work or work of equal value is applied.

For the purposes of this Article, "pay" means the ordinary basic or minimum wage or salary and any other consideration, whether in cash or in kind, which the worker receives, directly or indirectly, in respect of his employment from his employer.

Equal pay without discrimination based on sex means:

(a)   that pay for the same work at piece rates shall be calculated on the basis of the same unit of measurement;

(b)   that pay for work at time rates shall be the same for the same job.'

Article 157 and *Directive No 2006/54/EC* ('the *Recast Directive*' which replaced *Directive No 75/117* from 15th August, 2009) provide a European underpinning to domestic rights to equal pay. These provisions have been relied upon as an aid to construction of domestic law and, increasingly, as a basis for disapplying inconsistent provisions of domestic legislation (cf *Scullard v Knowles* [1996] IRLR 344 and below). However, it is not possible in all circumstances to enforce *art 157* claims directly before the domestic courts (see EUROPEAN UNION LAW (22)).

The Council of the EU has also adopted *Directive 86/378/EEC* on the progressive implementation of the principle of equal treatment for men and women in occupational social security schemes, including pension schemes. *Directive 96/96/EC* (which came into effect on 1 July 1997) amended *Directive 86/378/EC* to take account of the CJEU's decision in *Barber v Guardian Royal Exchange Assurance Group* [1990] ICR 616. *Directive 86/378/EEC* has also been repealed and replaced by the provisions of the Recast Directive from 15th August, 2009.

The *Recast Directive* provides at *Article 14* (which replaces *Article 5.1* of *Directive No 76/207* (the '*Equal Treatment Directive*')):

> "There shall be no direct or indirect discrimination on grounds of sex in the public or private sectors, including public bodies, in relation to:
>
> ...
>
> (c) employment and working conditions, including dismissals, as well as pay as provided for in Article 141 of the Treaty..."

See also **10.2** Discrimination and Equal Opportunities – I and generally European Union Law (**22**).

The meaning of 'work' in EU law

Article 157 enshrines the right to equal pay for equal work. The appropriate definition of 'work' for this purpose has proven to be wider than might initially be imagined. In *Davies v Neath Port Talbot County Borough Council* [1999] ICR 1132, EAT, the issue was whether attending a union-organised course for elected health and safety representatives constituted 'work' for the purposes of *art 157*. Relying on an analogy with the CJEU cases of *Botel*: C-360/90 [1992] ECR I-3589 and *Lewark*: C-457/93 [1996] ECR I-243, the EAT determined that:

> 'Attending a training course organised by a recognised trade union is still related to the employment relationship and is safeguarding staff interests which is ultimately beneficial to the employer.'

The effect of this finding was that the complainant, who ordinarily worked part-time, was able to claim full-time pay as she was attending the course on a full-time basis. Reliance on *art 157* enabled the EAT to avoid applying *TULRCA 1992, s 169* which would otherwise have required her to be paid her normal part-time pay. *Section 169* has had an indirectly discriminatory effect and was thus contrary to *art 157* and was not applied.

The meaning of 'pay' in EU law

It is now well established that 'pay' in *art 157* is to be given a broad meaning. In *Barber v Guardian Royal Exchange Assurance Group*: C-262/88 [1990] ICR 616, it was held that a benefit is in the nature of pay if the worker is entitled to receive it from his employer by reason of the existence of the employment relationship. Thus, it included benefits paid by the employer upon compulsory redundancy, even where they consisted of pension payments made after the termination of employment. It did not matter that the payment was received only indirectly from the employer (eg through the trustees of a pension scheme). The CJEU reached a similar decision in *Kuratorium Für Dialyse und Nierentransplantation eV v Lewark* [1996] IRLR 637, ruling that compensation paid pursuant to a German statute for loss of earnings whilst attending training sessions for participants in staff councils is pay. (Contrast, however, *Manor Bakeries Ltd v Nazir* [1996] IRLR 604, EAT: employee entitled to paid time off pursuant to a collective agreement to attend a trade union conference. The paid time-off was not 'pay' for the purposes of *art 157* as attending the conference was not 'work' and pay is remuneration for work.) In *Barber*, the CJEU also observed that pensions from both contributory and non-contributory schemes were 'pay' within *art 157*. (See also *Bilka-Kaufhaus GmbH v Weber von Hartz*: 170/84 [1987] ICR 110.) The CJEU, unusually, specifically limited the effect of its decision by stating that it could not be relied upon to claim entitlement to a pension prior to 17 May 1990 (the date of the decision). This matter is considered in greater detail at **21.15** *et seq* below.

21.3 Equal Pay

A long-standing controversy over whether compensation for unfair dismissal is pay for the purposes of *art 157* was resolved by the decision of the CJEU in *R v Secretary of State for Employment, ex p Seymour-Smith and Perez*: C-167/97 [1999] ICR 447. The CJEU decided that the basic and compensatory awards (for which see **53.7** and **53.10** UNFAIR DISMISSAL – III) are deferred pay to which the worker is entitled (ultimately) by reason of his employment. The fact that the compensation consisted of a judicial award did not invalidate that conclusion. However, neither an order for reinstatement nor for re-engagement (for which see **53.2** and **53.3** UNFAIR DISMISSAL – III) is 'pay'. The CJEU does not seem to have considered the status of the monetary award made in cases where re-employment is ordered.

Pay includes sums paid in lieu of notice and also covers payments made by the Secretary of State on the insolvency of an employer in respect of the employee's contractual entitlement to notice (*Clark v Secretary of State for Employment* [1997] ICR 64, CA).

Further, 'pay' within *art 157* includes a statutory redundancy payment or an *ex gratia* payment upon redundancy (see *McKechnie v UBM Building Supplies (Southern) Ltd* [1991] ICR 710 for entitlement to equal statutory and contractual redundancy payments).

In *Rinner-Kuhn v FWW Spezial-Gebaudereinigung GmbH & Co KG*: 1/1/88 [1989] IRLR 493, 'pay' was held to include the statutory sick pay which an employee was entitled to receive from her employer; see also *EC Commission v Belgium*: C-173/91 [1993] IRLR 404.

The CJEU has, in recent times, been expanding the definition of 'pay' to cover contractual terms which relate to the calculation of entitlements or to requirements imposed as prerequisites to the granting of entitlements. In *Hill v Revenue Comrs and Department of Finance*: C-243/95 [1999] ICR 48, CJEU, the CJEU considered the employment conditions of certain Irish civil servants. Salary was dependent on length of service. Employees who worked half-time earned half of the full-time rate. However, when they moved to full-time employment their pay did not double. Instead, they were placed on the full-time pay spine at a level that gave them credit for only half of the actual period that they had worked for their employer. In other words, their length of service was pro-rated to reflect their previous part-time status. The CJEU decided that the method adopted by the employer for converting part-timers to full-time status constituted 'pay' within *art 157* and that it was, in the particular circumstances, discriminatory and not justified. However, terms with a less direct connection to pay rates may be treated differently. In *Gerster v Freistaat Bayern*: C-1/95 [1998] ICR 327, Bavarian civil service regulations, which required that periods of part-time service should (depending on the number of hours worked) either be entirely or partly discounted when assessing eligibility for consideration for promotion, were held not to offend *art 157*. The CJEU distinguished *Nimz*: C-148/89 [1991] IRLR 222, in which a complainant had successfully challenged a similar rule which gave part-time workers only partial credit for their periods of service. In *Nimz* promotion was practically automatic on completion of the relevant period of service. As the provision in *Gerster* was only concerned with eligibility for promotion, the connection to pay was insufficiently direct to bring the case within the scope of *art 157* which was not concerned with inequalities relating to 'access to career advancement'. The CJEU opined, however, that the rule was potentially contrary to the *Equal Treatment Directive (EEC/76/207)*. It was left to the national court to decide whether or not the respondent's contention that the requirement was intended to ensure that employees had sufficient experience (and was therefore objectively justified) was made out.

The dividing line between what constitutes 'pay' and what is a 'working condition' that falls to be considered under the *Equal Treatment Directive* (and now, the *Recast Directive*) has been addressed by the CJEU in a number of cases. *Kording v Senator für Finanzen*: C-100/95 [1997] IRLR 710 concerned German legislation which exempted employees with sufficient length of service from having to take certain examinations. Part-time workers had to work a longer period which was pro-rated to the proportion of full-time hours that they worked. The CJEU considered that the provision was not 'pay', but that it was nevertheless indirectly discriminatory (though capable of objective justification). Similarly, the provision of subsidised nursery places to female staff only is to be regarded as a 'working condition' within the meaning of the *Equal Treatment Directive* rather than 'pay' within *art 157*: *Lommers v Minister van Landbouw Natuurbeheer en Visserij*: C-476/99 [2002] IRLR 430. The CJEU held that the fact that the fixing of certain working conditions may have pecuniary consequences is not sufficient to bring such conditions within the scope of *art 157*, which is a provision based on the close connection between the nature of the work done and the amount of pay. However, the CJEU went on to hold that measures giving a specific advantage to women with a view to eliminating inequality (such as providing nursery places for working mothers only) was not contrary to the *Equal Treatment Directive*, in particular, where male single parents were given places on the same conditions. (See also *Steinicke v Bundesanstalt für Arbeit*: C-77/02 [2003] IRLR 892. schemes of membership that may have pecuniary consequences not 'pay', though they were indirectly discriminatory contrary to the *Equal Treatment Directive*).

21.4 THE RIGHT TO EQUAL PAY IN THE EQUALITY ACT 2010 AND THE EQUAL PAY ACT 1970

The equal pay provisions in *Chapter 3* of *Part 5* of *EA 2010* apply by reason of *s 72 EA 2010* to persons who are employed or who hold "a personal or public office". Employment is defined by *s 83* of *EA 2010* as including "employment under a contract of employment, a contract of apprenticeship or a contract personally to do work" as well as Crown employment and employment as a "relevant member" of House of Commons or House of Lords staff. Service in the armed forces is deemed to be employment by *s 83(3)* of *EA 2010*.

The position under the *EqPA 1970* was that the right to equal pay applied:

(a)   to women employed in an establishment in Great Britain whether they were British or not and regardless of the law governing their contract of employment (*EqPA 1970, s 1(1), (11)*);

(b)   to men as well as women (*EqPA 1970, s 1(13)*).

'Employed' under *EqPA 1970* was defined as 'employed under a contract of service or of apprenticeship or a contract personally to execute any work or labour' (*EqPA 1970, s 1(6)(a)*). The definition therefore included contracts personally to perform services (cf **14.3 EMPLOYEE, SELF-EMPLOYED OR WORKER?**).

Office-holders. As set out above, the equal pay provisions in *Chapter 3* of *EA 2010, Part 5* apply to personal or public office holders. Personal office holders are defined by *EA 2010, s 49* as those holding an office or post to which to which a person is appointed to discharge a function personally under the direction of another person, and in respect of which an appointed person is entitled to remuneration. Public office holders are defined by *EA 2010, s 50(2)* as those holding an office or post appointment to which is made by a member of the executive, or subject to the approval of a member of the executive, or in relation to which appointment is made on the recommendation of, or subject to the approval of the House of Commons, the House of Lords, the National Assembly for Wales or the Scottish Parliament. Following the decisions of the CJEU and Supreme Court in *O'Brien v Ministry of Justice* (respectively, C-393/10, [2012] ICR 955 and [2013] UKSC 6, [2013] 1 WLR 522) establishing that judges are 'workers' under European law, it is likely that many office holders will now also fall within the definition of 'employee' in *s 83* of the *EA 2010* and thus be covered by the standard rules on employees. However, the provisions in relation to office holders are likely still to remain relevant to such people, and also to those who are genuinely office holders and not employees or workers in European law.

The position under *EqPA 1970* was that statutory office-holders were formerly excluded from the provisions of the *EqPA 1970*. However, with effect from 1 October 2005, office-holders (with the exception of holders of political office) were expressly brought

21.4 Equal Pay

within the scope of the *Act: EqPA 1970, s 1(6A)–(6C)* as amended by *reg 35* of the *Employment Equality (Sex Discrimination) Regulations 2005*. *Section 1(6A)* of the *Act* extended the right to equal pay to those holding an office or post to which persons were appointed to discharge functions personally under the direction of another person, and in respect of which they were entitled to remuneration, or any office or post to which appointments are made by (or on the recommendation of or subject to the approval of) a Minister of the Crown, a government department, the National Assembly for Wales or any part of the Scottish Administration. This amendment followed the decision of the Northern Ireland Court of Appeal in *Perceval-Price v Department of Economic Development* [2000] IRLR 380, holding that an identically worded provision in the *Equal Pay Act (Northern Ireland) 1970* was incompatible with *art 157* as the right to equal pay conferred by the *EC Treaty* extends to all 'workers' as defined by the CJEU in *Lawrie-Blum v Land Baden-Wurttemberg*: 66/85 [1986] ECR 2121 (a case about *art 48* of the *EC Treaty*). In *Lawrie-Blum*, the CJEU identified the 'essential feature' of an employment relationship as being that 'for a certain period of time a person performs services for and under the direction of another person in return for which he receives remuneration'. The NICA concluded that the tribunal chairmen fell within that definition despite their status as statutory office-holders, and disapplied the exclusion.

Employees posted abroad. Employment in an establishment in Great Britain formerly required that the employee should not work 'wholly or mainly outside Great Britain'. However, the *Equal Opportunities (Employment Legislation) (Territorial Limits) Regulations 1999 (SI 1999/3163)* removed the words 'or mainly' from the relevant provision. The effect is that the legislation now covers workers posted abroad. The *Regulations* came into effect on 16 December 1999. With effect from 1 October 2005, employment is regarded as being at an establishment in Great Britain if (a) the employee does her work wholly or partly in Great Britain, or (b) if she does her work wholly outside Great Britain but her employer has a place of business at an establishment in Great Britain, her work is for the purposes of the business carried on at that establishment, and she is ordinarily resident in Great Britain at the time when she applies for or is offered the employment, or at any time during the course of the employment: *SDA 1975, s 10* as amended by the *Employment Equality (Sex Discrimination) Regulations 2005, reg 11(2)*.

For the current law and provisions dealing with the territorial extent of the *EA 2010* see generally **11.18 DISCRIMINATION AND EQUAL OPPORTUNITIES – II**.

Women suspended on maternity grounds. Women whose pay is reduced when they are suspended on maternity grounds may not seek to challenge the reduction by bringing claims under the *EA 2010* or under the predecessor provisions in *EqPA 1970*. *ERA 1996, ss 66–70* represent a complete code governing the contractual entitlements of such women (*British Airways (European Operations at Gatwick) Ltd v Moore* [2000] IRLR 296, EAT) and see further **(31) MATERNITY AND PARENTAL RIGHTS**. This position is now reflected in *paragraph 2* of *Schedule 7* to the *EA 2010* which provides that the 'sex equality clause' will not apply in respect of special treatment of women in connection with pregnancy or childbirth. However, there are circumstances in which women absent on maternity leave may bring challenges in relation to pay and benefits paid to them while on maternity leave: see further below **21.14** and **21.21**. There are also separate provisions in *ss 73* and *74* providing for a maternity equality clause.

Members of the armed forces. Members of the armed forces were formerly expressly excluded from the scope of *EqPA 1970*. However, *EqPA 1970* was amended by the *Armed Forces Act 1996, s 24* to allow claims to be brought. This was brought into force on 1 October 1997 by the *Armed Forces Act 1996 (Commencement No 3 and Transitional Provisions) Order 1997 (SI 1997/2164)* and the *Equal Pay (Complaints to Employment Tribunals) (Armed Forces) Regulations 1997 (SI 1997/2162)*. The position under *EA 2010* is dealt with by a deeming provision, deeming members of the armed forces to be employees: see *EA 2010, s 83(3)*.

21.5   The equality clause

Neither the *EqPA 1970*, or the *EA 2010* straightforwardly prohibit direct and indirect discrimination in matters of contractual entitlement. Instead, the *EqPA 1970* adopted a rather oblique and artificial approach. By *s 1(2)* it implied an 'equality clause' into any contract of employment that does not already include one. The equality clause operated whenever a woman was doing like work, work of equal value or work rated as equivalent to that of a man (*s 2(1)*). The *EA 2010* adopts a similar approach. *Section 66(1)* creates an equality clause. The clause has the effect that:

(a)   any term of a person's contract which is less favourable than that of an appropriate comparator is modified so as to be not less favourable;

(b)   where a person's contract does not have a term which corresponds to a beneficial term in the contract of an appropriate comparator, the person's contract is modified so as to include such a term: *EA 2010, s 66(2)*;

(c)   where the employer does not seek to, or fails to, establish that the difference between the person's contract and the comparator's is genuinely due to a material factor which is not the difference of sex and which is not indirectly discriminatory and cannot be justified (*EA 2010, s 69*) (see **21.11** below).

Appropriate comparators are those doing "equal work" as defined in *EA 2010, s 65*, i.e. those doing:

(a)   *like work* (see below **21.6**); or

(b)   *work rated as equivalent* (see below **21.7**); or

(c)   work of *equal value* (see below **21.8**).

Thus, for example, if a man and a woman are engaged on like work and the man is paid £500 per week for that work, but the woman only £400, the equality clause will operate so as to entitle the woman to £500 per week. Also, if the man's contract contains a clause which entitles him to be paid during absence from work due to sickness, but the woman's contract contains no such clause, the woman's contract will be deemed by law to include such a clause. (For appropriate comparators see below **21.9**.)

The operation of the equality clause also allows male colleagues of female equal pay claimants to bring 'piggyback' contingent claims using the female claimants as comparators and to recover sums equivalent to those awarded to such comparators by way of arrears: *Llewellyn v Hartlepool Borough Council* [2009] ICR 1426, [2009] IRLR 796.

The equality clause applies to all terms and conditions of employment and not only to pay (eg *Sun Alliance and London Insurance Ltd v Dudman* [1978] ICR 551, relating to a contractual term granting a mortgage interest allowance). The provisions of the *SDA 1975* and the *EqPA 1970* were considered to contain an interlocking but mutually exclusive prohibition on discrimination on grounds of sex: *SDA 1975, s 6(6)* and *Peake v Automotive Products Ltd* [1977] ICR 480. The *EqPA 1970* applied where the contract regulated the provision of benefits in the form of money: *Grundy v British Airways plc* [2005] All ER (D) 94 (Aug), EAT; reversed on other grounds by the CA [2007] EWCA Civ 1020, [2008] IRLR 74). It was not necessary for the payment in question to be expressly provided for in the contract. Provided that the contract 'regulated' the payment it would fall under *EqPA 1970* and not under the *SDA 1975*: thus a so-called 'discretionary' bonus scheme would fall to have been considered under *EqPA 1970* if the discretionary element of it was in fact only as to the amount paid to all employees in any one year and not as to whether or not the employee is entitled to a bonus at all: *Hoyland v Asda Stores Ltd* [2006] IRLR 468. In that case the Court of Session expounded a 'but for' test in order to determine whether or not the payment fell to be considered under *EqPA 1970* or the *SDA 1975*, ruling that if the payment would not have been made 'but for' the existence of the contract of employment, then *EqPA 1970* applied. However, it is doubtful whether this is the correct approach since on that basis any benefit conferred on an employee qua employee would have to be regarded as covered by the *EqPA 1970*. The better approach is perhaps to be found in *Hosso v European Credit Management* [2012] ICR 547. In that case, Stanley Burnton LJ found that where the contract granted an employer a discretion as to whether and in what amount to confer a benefit, then the exercise of that discretion was not 'regulated' by the contract of employment and so any claim for discriminatory exercise of the discretion had to be pursued under the *SDA 1975* and not the *EqPA 1970*. Stanley Burton LJ considered that the difficulty with pursuing an equal pay claim where the term in question provided for a contractual discretion was that there was no difference in the terms of the complainant and the comparator's contracts of employment such that the equality clause could operate. Mummery LJ did not express a view on this reasoning preferring to confine his reasoning to the facts of *Hosso* which related to a share option scheme where the claimant and her comparator had the benefit of the same scheme (on the same terms). However, if Stanley Burnton LJ is correct, *Hayland v Asda Stores Limited* has been effectively confined to its facts.

Section 70 of the *EA 2010* preserves the mutual exclusion of 'ordinary' sex discrimination and equal pay claims currently set out in *s 6(6)* of the *EqPA 1970*. Where the 'sex equality clause' operates (or would operate but for the success of the employer's 'genuine material factor' defence: see below **21.10**), no claim for 'ordinary' sex discrimination may be made in relation to a contractual term relating to pay. However, where the 'sex equality clause' has no effect on a contractual term relating to pay (eg because no real comparator can be identified), then a direct (but not an indirect) discrimination claim may be brought in relation to that term: see *s 71*.

It is however clear that the equality clause cannot operate so as to give the complainant a more favourable term than that contained in her comparator's contract. Where, for instance, qualified female employees are paid at the same rate as male trainees, the employee cannot rely on the clause to secure a premium over the rate paid to a trainee selected as a comparator (see *Enderby v Frenchay Health Authority (No 2)* [2000] ICR 612, CA), but a sex discrimination claim could now be brought using the male trainees as evidence to help establish the position for a hypothetical comparator.

In *Hayward v Cammell Laird Shipbuilders Ltd* [1988] ICR 464, the House of Lords rejected the argument that the 'total remuneration package' must be taken into account when making the comparison between a woman's pay and a man's. What must be compared is each distinct provision of the contract dealing with pay and benefits in kind. The applicant was thus entitled to the same rate of basic pay and overtime pay as her male comparator even if she was more favourably treated in other respects, in this case paid meal breaks, additional holidays and better sickness benefits. However, it can be difficult to determine what constitutes a distinct provision or term of the contract. In *Degnan v Redcar & Cleveland Borough Council* [2005] EWCA Civ 726, [2005] IRLR 615, the Court of Appeal held that attendance allowances paid to male employees were all part of a single term of the contract together with their hourly rate and fixed bonuses for the purposes of the comparison of the terms in the woman's contracts. This approach was held to be consistent with *Hayward* in that it did not lump together different terms but instead looked at the reality of the situation by classifying all these payments which related to the same subject-matter as coming under the same contractual term, being 'provision for monetary payment for the performance of the contract by employees during normal working hours'. All monetary payments received by the men should be aggregated and divided by the number of hours in the working week to give an hourly rate which, if lower for women than men, should be increased for women to eliminate the difference. This approach, of treating different payments as different elements of a single contractual term, does sit uneasily with the prohibition on taking a 'swings and roundabouts' approach in *Hayward*. This approach is also difficult to reconcile with the CJEU's decision in *Elsner–Lakeberg v Land Nordrhein-Westfalen* [2005] IRLR 209 in which it held that, in order to determine whether the principle of equal pay is being complied with, genuine transparency permitting an effective review is assured only if that principle applies to each aspect of remuneration, excluding any general overall assessment of the consideration paid. In that case, the CJEU held that it was necessary for there to be separate comparison in respect of the pay for regular hours and the pay for additional hours. Following *St Helens & Knowsley Hospital NHS Trust v Brownbill* [2011] IRLR 815 the scope for applying the approach taking in the *Degnan* case has been further limited. In *Brownbill* the Court of Appeal, upholding a decision of the EAT, held that the tribunal should have carried out a comparison between the rates paid to the complainants and their comparators for unsocial hours work. Broadly speaking, the comparators received lower rates of pay, but higher rates for unsocial hours. Overall, most of the complainants were better paid than their comparators. The tribunal noted that if the claims succeeded the complainants would be even more highly paid than their comparators and held that the claims failed. The EAT and Court of Appeal disagreed, holding that the pay for unsocial hours was a distinct term for distinct work, present in both the contracts of the claimants and their comparators, and the proper approach was to compare the pay received by the complainants and comparators for unsocial hours work and determine whether there was a genuine material factor other than the difference in sex justifying the inequality (see **21.11** below). The matter was remitted to the tribunal. In so deciding Maurice Kay LJ held that *Degnan* was not an exception to the principles set out in *Hayward*. It was merely a particular application of Hayward by looking at the reality of the contractual provisions on the facts of the particular case.

Section 66(2) of EqPA 1970 appears to have accepted the analysis of the law as set out in *Hayward v Cammell Laird Shipbuilders Ltd* [1988] ICR 464 by requiring a comparison as between the term in a woman's contract and the "corresponding term" of the contract of the relevant comparator rather than by comparing the term in a woman's contract with "a term of a similar kind" as was required by *s 1* of *EqPA 1970*.

It was suggested in *Hayward* that the 'material factor' defence under *EqPA 1970, s 1(3)* and now found in *section 69 EA 2010* (see **21.10–21.12** below) might be available to an employer who could show that the unfavourable character of the term in the woman's contract was due to the more favourable character of the other terms. Broadly, the same approach is taken by the CJEU in relation to claims based upon *art 157* (see *Barber v Guardian Royal Exchange Assurance Group: C-262/88* [1990] ICR 616 and *Jämställdhetsombudsmannen v Örebro läns landsting: C-236/98* [2000] ECR I-2189, [2001] ICR 249, CJEU).

Note, however, that once it has been established that there is a 'genuine material factor' (see **21.10–21.12** below) that justifies a difference in pay the equality clause will not operate so as to 'correct' a particular term of an employee's contract simply because that employee is, by the date of the hearing, a member of a group of women who are being paid less than a group of men: see *Armstrong v Newcastle Upon Tyne NHS Hospital Trust* [2005] EWCA Civ 1608, [2006] IRLR 124.

For indirect discrimination under the *EqPA 1970* and *EA 2010*, see below **21.11**.

21.6 Like work

A woman is regarded as employed on like work with men if, but only if, her work and theirs is of the same or of a broadly similar nature and the differences (if any) between the things she does and the things they do are not of practical importance in relation to the performance of her contract of employment. 'Like work' has been defined by *s 65(2)* of *EA 2010* as meaning that "A's work and B's work are the same or broadly similar and such differences as there are between their work are not of practical importance in relation to the terms of their work". *Section 65(3)* of *EA 2010* states that in considering differences between the work of a claimant and her comparator, for the purposes of determining whether or not the two are engaged on 'like work' "it is necessary to have regard to the frequency with which differences between their work occur in practice and the nature and extent of the differences".

Thus, although the job descriptions of male and female employees or their written job specifications may be different, if the differences in their duties are of no practical importance, the women will be considered to be employed on like work with the men. The question of what is or is not a difference of practical importance will always be one of fact and degree depending upon the particular circumstances of the case. If, for example, male guillotine operators in a paper mill are required once in two weeks to lift reams of paper whereas women are not, the lifting is purely incidental to their main employment and is not of practical importance. Accordingly, it is not a difference which would prevent the women's right to equal pay.

The EAT has stated in *Capper Pass Ltd v Lawton* [1977] ICR 83, that 'in deciding whether the work done by a woman and the work done by a man is "like work" within the meaning of *s 1(4)* of the *EqPA 1970* the employment tribunal has to make a broad judgment. The intention is that the employment tribunal should not be required to undertake too minute an examination, or be constrained to find that work is not like work merely because of insubstantial differences. In order to be like work within the *Act*'s definition the work need not be of the same nature; it need only be broadly similar.' In that case, a cook in the directors' dining room was held to be engaged on like work with the assistant chefs of the company's factory canteen. The fact that women do their work at a different time of the day from men may not prevent them from claiming that they are engaged upon like work (*Dugdale v Kraft Foods Ltd* [1977] ICR 48; *National Coal Board v Sherwin* [1978] ICR 700; contrast with *Thomas v National Coal Board* [1987] ICR 757 in which the EAT held that a male canteen worker on permanent night-shift was not employed on like work with female day-shift canteen workers).

However, the duties actually performed are not the only considerations to be taken into account in deciding whether a woman is engaged on like work. In *Eaton Ltd v Nuttall* [1977] ICR 272, the EAT held that 'In considering whether there is like work, though the most important point is what the man does and what the woman does, the circumstances in which they do it should not be disregarded. One of the circumstances properly to be taken into account is the degree of responsibility involved in carrying out the job.'

Article 157 uses the term 'same work' rather than 'like work'. However, the case law on the European provision suggests that a tribunal should not simply confine its consideration to the duties actually performed. In *Angestelltenbetriebsrat der Wiener Gebeitskrankenkasse v Wiener Gebeitskrankenkasse* [1999] IRLR 804, the CJEU considered a case concerning psychotherapists. Whilst the psychotherapists were all engaged in 'seemingly identical activities', they could be divided into those who had had training in psychology to graduate level and those who had been trained as general practitioners. The graduate psychologists, the majority of whom were women, were paid less. The CJEU decided that training and qualifications could be matters which were relevant to the determination whether the work and/or job were the same and were not merely relevant to a possible material factor defence. It should be noted, however, that although the CJEU purported to proceed on the basis that the applicants and their comparators were engaged in the same activity, it also observed that the former general practitioners, who were better qualified, could be called on to perform 'different tasks or duties'. It is not a case, therefore, where it could be said that the applicants and their comparators necessarily performed identical tasks. The CJEU seems to have had a broader notion in mind when it referred to the 'activity' in which both groups were engaged. In *Brunnhofer v Bank der Osterreichischen Postsparkasse AG*: C-381/99 [2001]

IRLR 571, CJEU, the CJEU followed *Angestelltenbetriebsrat*, to draw the conclusion that the existence of an identical collective agreement governing the employment of two employees was not in itself sufficient to show that they performed the same work, or work of equal value.

If a woman's work is more onerous or more responsible than a man's, she may not be considered to be engaged on like work, even though less well paid (*Waddington v Leicester Council for Voluntary Service* [1977] ICR 266). However, she may now be able to obtain equal pay on the basis described in *Murphy v Bord Telecom Eireann* [1988] ICR 445 (see also **21.8** below).

21.7   Work rated as equivalent

A woman may claim equivalence with a man even though she is not engaged on like work, if a job-evaluation study has been carried out in respect of his work and hers, and her job has been rated as equivalent to the man's in terms of the demand made on a worker under various headings (ie effort, skill, decision), or would have been rated as equivalent but for the evaluation being made on a system setting different values for men and women on the same demand under any heading (*EqPA 1970, s 1(5)*).

This remains the case pursuant to *s 65(1)(b)* and *s 65(4)* and *(5)* of *EA 2010. Section 65(4)* and *(5) EA 2010* provide that work will be rated as equivalent where a job evaluation study *"gives an equal value"* to the jobs *"in terms of the demands made on a worker"* where it would give such an equal value were it not a *"sex-specific system"*. A system is sex-specific system *"if for the purposes of one or more of the demands made on a worker, it sets values for men different from those it sets for women"* (*s 65(2)*).

The principal methods of job evaluation are set out in ACAS Advisory Booklet No 1, 'Job evaluation'. These methods are known as job ranking, paired comparison, job classification, points assessment and factor comparison. See also the *Equal Pay: Statutory Code of Practice* available at www.equalityhumanrights.com. For the purposes of *s 1(5)*, the comparison of jobs must be done by reference to the same job-evaluation study (*Paterson (KD) v Islington London Borough* (23 April 2004, unreported), EAT). A job evaluation must be carried out on an objective basis. The principles were set out in *Eaton Ltd v Nuttall* (see above **21.6**). The job of each worker covered by the study must be valued in terms of the demand made on the worker under the various headings (eg effort, skill, responsibility) in the study (*Bromley v H & J Quick Ltd* [1988] ICR 623). Thus, it will not suffice simply to compare 'whole jobs'. The assessment should be qualitative, not quantitative – matters such as a difference in the number of hours worked go to the defence of material factor (see **21.10–21.12** below), not to evaluation of the job (*Leverton v Clwyd County Council* [1989] ICR 33). Whilst the study as a whole must be objective, it is permissible for it to contain certain subjective elements, so long as they are not themselves inadvertently discriminatory. It is for the employer to explain how any job-evaluation study worked and what was taken into account at each stage (see also *Rummler v Dato-Druck GmbH* [1987] ICR 774). The validity of a job evaluation study which is not impartial or which is not conducted on a scientific basis may be challenged if reliance is placed on such a study to claim or to resist a claim for equal pay.

In determining whether two jobs have been given an equal value by a job-evaluation study, it is necessary to look at the full results of the study, including the allocation to grade or scale at the end of the evaluation process. Thus, in *Springboard Sunderland Trust v Robson* [1992] ICR 554, the EAT held that the applicant and a male comparator were employed on work rated as equivalent because each of their scores resulted in an allocation of the same grade, albeit their scores in a job-evaluation study had been different.

If no job-evaluation study has been carried out, there is no legal requirement for an employer to conduct one. However, once a job-evaluation study has been undertaken and has resulted in a conclusion that the job of a woman is of equal value to that of a man, the

21.7 Equal Pay

woman may claim equal pay, despite the fact that the employers may not have implemented the scheme (*O'Brien v Sim-Chem Ltd* [1980] ICR 573). Where a valid job-evaluation study has been carried out and a woman's job has been rated as slightly lower than her male comparator, it is not permissible for a tribunal, by reliance on extraneous expert evidence, to find that the difference is insignificant: *Home Office v Bailey* [2005] IRLR 757. But, for work to be rated as equivalent there must be a *completed* job-evaluation study, and there is no complete job-evaluation study unless and until the parties who have agreed to the carrying out of the study have accepted its validity (*Arnold v Beecham Group Ltd* [1982] ICR 744).

21.8 Work of equal value

Where a woman is employed on work which is not like work or work which has been rated as equivalent to that of a male comparator, she may claim equal pay with a man if her work is of equal value to his, in terms of the demands made on her, eg under such headings as effort, skill and decision (*EA 2010, s 65(6)* and *EqPA 1970, s 1(2)(c)*). Relying upon EU law, she may also claim equal pay where she is doing work of *greater* value (*Murphy v Bord Telecom Eireann*: 157/86 [1988] ICR 445 and *Bainbridge v Redcar & Cleveland Borough Council (No. 2)* [2008] EWCA Civ 885, [2008] IRLR 776). Employees of one sex may use *EA 2010, s 65(1)(c)* to claim equal pay with those of the other sex doing a quite different job. Using this provision, a female cook employed as a canteen assistant succeeded in a claim for equal pay with male skilled tradesmen (see *Hayward v Cammell Laird Shipbuilders Ltd* [1988] ICR 464). The fact that one man is being paid the same as a woman for doing like work to hers is no longer a bar to the woman claiming equal pay with another man doing a different job of equal value to hers (see *Pickstone*). In that case, the House of Lords held that the construction of *EqPA 1970* which enabled them to achieve this result was consistent with EU law. (For the procedure to be adopted on claims based on work of equal value see **21.22** below.)

A woman will not be able to succeed in an equal value claim if a valid job-evaluation study has concluded that she and her male comparator do work which is *not* of equal value (*EA 2010, s 2A(2)* and *EqPA 1970, s 2A(2)*). It was suggested by the EAT in *Dibro Ltd v Hore* [1990] ICR 370 at 377 that a job-evaluation study carried out at the request of the employer after the institution of proceedings which evaluates the jobs of the applicants and the comparator may be relied upon for the purposes of *s 2A(2)* (see also *Avon County Council v Foxall* [1989] ICR 407). In *McAuley v Eastern Health and Social Services Board* [1991] IRLR 467, the Northern Ireland Court of Appeal held that an employment tribunal had correctly concluded that the work of the applicants and that of their comparator could not be regarded as having been given different values under a job-evaluation study so as to preclude their equal value claim, in circumstances in which the job-evaluation study was prepared in respect of health boards in Great Britain and its results applied in Northern Ireland only through a policy of maintaining parity of remuneration with Great Britain.

A claimant may use a new job-evaluation study which rates her as equivalent to a man as evidence in support of an equal value claim in relation to the period pre-implementation of the job-evaluation study but a tribunal cannot necessarily work back from the fact that two jobs are now rated as equivalent to assume that they had equal value prior to implementation; see *Redcar & Cleveland BC v Bainbridge (No 2)* [2008] EWCA Civ 885 [2008] IRLR 776. A JES is of evidential value only in an equal value claim and does not even raise a presumption of equal value for the employer to rebut: see *Hovell v Ashford and St Peter's Hospital NHS Trust* [2009] ICR 1545. However, it is not the case that an employment tribunal must always have the benefit of an independent expert report before finding equality where a woman's job has been marked lower than a comparator's job in a JES.

For guidance on how 'equal value' claims should be assessed where the woman's (or the man's) job has changed over time, see *Potter v North Cumbria Acute Hospitals NHS Trust* [2008] ICR 910, EAT.

21.9   Persons with whom an employee may claim equivalence

The man with whom a woman seeks to compare herself is known as the 'comparator'.

EqPA 1970, s 1(6) allowed a complainant to compare herself with others in the 'same employment' which is defined as follows:

' . . . men shall be treated as in the same employment with a woman if they are men employed by her employer or any associated employer at the same establishment or establishments in Great Britain which include that one and at which common terms and conditions of employment are observed either generally or for employees of the relevant classes.'

Similar provision is made in the *EA 2010*: the comparator must be employed by the same employer or an associated employer and (a) work at 'the same establishment' (*s 79(3)*); or (b) if not working at the same establishment, 'common terms' must apply at each establishment (*s 79(4)*). For office holders (including police officers), the same person must be responsible for paying the claimant and her comparator (*s 79(5)* and *(8)*). There are also specific provisions for members of the House of Commons (*s 79(6)*) and House of Lords (*s 79(7)*). The general principles about comparators developed in the case law under the *EqPA 1970* thus remain relevant under the *EA 2010*.

The following principles have developed in relation to comparators who are employed by the complainant's employer at the same establishment as her. The questions of (i) what constitutes the 'same establishment' and (ii) in what circumstances employees at different establishments are to be regarded as employed on 'common terms and conditions of employment' are more complicated and are returned to below.

General rules about comparators

In contrast to cases brought under *SDA 1975* (or under *Chapter 1 of Part 5 EA 2010*), the orthodox position prior to the coming into force of the *EA 2010* was that an employee could not use a 'hypothetical' comparator. In other words, she could not base a claim on an allegation that if a man were employed, for instance, on like work, he would be paid more (cf **10.15** DISCRIMINATION AND EQUAL OPPORTUNITIES – I). Nor could a woman absent on maternity leave rely on an actual male comparator to bring a claim under the equal pay provisions in the *EqPA 1970* since there is no appropriate comparator for a pregnant woman, although in *Alabaster v Barclays Bank plc and Secretary of State for Social Security* [2005] EWCA Civ 508, [2005] IRLR 576 the CA held that in a claim for a pay increase received before the beginning of maternity leave to be taken into consideration when calculating statutory maternity pay, it was appropriate to disapply those parts of *s 1* of the *EqPA 1970* which impose a requirement for a male comparator (see further below **21.14** for maternity leave and pay arrangements). However, under the *EA 2010* a woman may bring a claim where there is no 'actual' comparator as a direct (but not an indirect) sex discrimination claim: see *EA 2010, s 71*. The previous case law on comparators for the purposes of the *EqPA 1970* will nevertheless remain relevant to the identification of 'evidential' comparators, whose circumstances may be considered by Tribunals in determining (i) whether or not the woman is being paid less than a hypothetical male comparator; and, if so (ii) whether there is a genuine material factor justifying the difference in pay.

It should be noted that although the *EA 2010* on its face requires a woman to identify an actual comparator if she wishes to bring an indirect sex discrimination claim, there may be a class of cases where this requirement will need to be 'read down' in order to comply with EU law. Thus in *Allonby v Accrington and Rossendale College*: C-256/01 [2004] IRLR 224, the CJEU was asked to decide whether a male comparator with the right to join a pension scheme was necessary in a claim brought by part-time employees who had been dismissed and re-engaged as self-employed contractors to lecture at their former college. The complainant could not identify a male comparator who, like herself, was not an employee.

The question was whether the statutory requirement that, in order to join the pension scheme, a teacher be employed under a contract of employment, should, if found to have a differential impact on women, be set aside. The CJEU set out the orthodox position that a worker cannot rely on *art 157* in order to claim pay to which she could be entitled if she belonged to the other sex unless, now or in the past, there were workers in the undertaking concerned who perform or performed comparable work. However, where national legislation was the cause of the differential impact (the statutory requirement to be an employee in order to join the pension scheme being a provision of domestic law) there is no need to point to a comparator: it will be sufficient to show a statistical disadvantage. In the absence of objective justification for the national legislation, the requirement to be an employee should be set aside where it is shown that, among the teachers who are workers within *art 157* and fulfil all other conditions for membership of the pension scheme, a much lower percentage of women than men is able to fulfil that condition. In short, the CJEU held that where it is the national legislation that is the sole source of the different treatment, there is no need to identify a particular comparator, as the comparison can be done by examining the position nationally using statistics. As indicated, this decision sits uncomfortably with the *EA 2010*, which requires an 'actual' comparator for indirect discrimination claims.

Where a comparator is required under the *EqPA 1970* and for indirect discrimination claims under the *EA 2010*, selection of an appropriate comparator is a matter for the employee (*Ainsworth v Glass Tubes and Components Ltd* [1977] ICR 347). She may select more than one individual, although tribunals have been warned by the House of Lords to be alert to prevent abuse of the procedure by applicants who 'cast their net over too wide a spread of comparators' (*Leverton v Clwyd County Council* [1989] ICR 33). There is no requirement that the comparator should be in any way 'typical' of his class (although the Court of Appeal in *North Yorkshire County Council v Ratcliffe* [1994] IRLR 342 considered that such a requirement might be thought to be implicit in the *EqPA 1970*. The issue was not considered by the House of Lords when it heard the subsequent appeal.)

There is nothing to prevent a complainant from selecting as a comparator a male employee whom she believes is engaged in work of a lesser value than her own. However, if she is successful in her claim she will only receive the pay awarded to her comparator. A complainant cannot use the *EqPA 1970* to establish a salary differential in her favour (*Enderby v Frenchay Health Authority (No 2)* [2000] ICR 612, CA, CA), (although a sex discrimination claim could now be brought using the male employee as evidence to help establish the position for a hypothetical comparator).

In *Hartlepool Borough Council v Llewellyn* [2009] IRLR 796 the EAT found that male claimants could pursue contingent "piggyback" claims citing female comparators whose terms and conditions of employment had been modified by operation of *s 2(1)* of *EqPA 1970*. However, since the *EqPA 1970* required a real comparator, such claims could only be pursued in respect of periods where female comparators had actually received greater sums than the male claimants either by reason of terms found in the employment contract or alternatively by reason of a declaration of the employment tribunal.

Even under the *EqPA 1970* it was well-established that there is no requirement for contemporaneous employment between the complainant and her chosen comparator and express provision to this effect is made in *s 64(2) EA 2010*. Lindsay P, giving the judgment of the EAT in *Kells v Pilkington plc* [2002] IRLR 693, held that the effect of the CJEU's decision in *Macarthys Ltd v Smith* was that there was no requirement for contemporaneous employment and once the need for that has gone, there was, on the face of things, no specified period under the *EqPA 1970* within which comparisons can or cannot be made. This was confirmed by the Court of Appeal in *Gutridge v Sodexo* [2009] IRLR 721 where it was accepted that after a TUPE transfer, a transferring employee could continue to compare herself with a comparator whose employment did not transfer. The six-year period of limitation in *s 2(5), EqPA 1970* (see **21.19** below) is concerned with the period of default which can be compensated for, rather than the period during which comparison is acceptable.

Although considerable difficulties may arise in claims based on comparisons with predecessors from many years ago, these are difficulties of fact and evidence and not difficulties of law: see *Kells v Pilkington* at paras 8–15. However, this does not mean that a complainant can compare herself with a successor in her role: see *Walton Centre for Neurology and Neurosurgery NHS Trust v Bewley* [2008] ICR 1047, [2008] IRLR 588 in which the EAT held that an earlier decision of the EAT that had held that comparison with a successor was permissible (*Hallam Diocese Trustee v Connaughton* [1996] ICR 860) was wrongly decided. The comparison must involve a 'concrete appraisal' of the work actually performed and using a successor as a comparator would be akin to using a hypothetical comparator which is not permitted under Community law: *Bewley.*

The same establishment

As set out above, under *EqPA 1970, s 1(6)* and *EA 2010, s 79(3)* it is not sufficient for a complainant to be employed by the same employer as her comparator in order to claim equivalence. She must also either be employed at the 'same establishment' as her comparator or be able to show commonality of terms and conditions of employment (as to the latter see below). 'Establishment' is not defined in the *EqPA 1970*, or *EA 2010*, nor is it expressly used in *Art 157*. In *Defrenne v Sabena*: C-43/75 [1976] ICR 547 the CJEU stated that the then *Art 119* applied where men and women carried out 'in the same establishment or service'. In *South Ayrshire Council v Morton* [2002] IRLR 256 Lord Justice Clerk observed that it was apparent from this paragraph of *Defrenne* that 'the scope of the enquiry is not always confined to the claimant's own workplace or his own employer'. In *Edinburgh City Council v Wilkinson* [2012] IRLR 202 the Court of Session was of the view that whether or not a complainant and comparator worked at the same establishment was a question of fact requiring an evaluation of the relevant facts and circumstances. The term "establishment" was not intended to refer to a 'body' or an 'undertaking'. It was primarily directed to the place of work such as a particular complex or group of buildings and the organisational structure would also be a particularly important definitional element. The existence of a mobility clause in a contract of employment may suggest that the employer runs different establishments. On the facts of that case, where the complainants were local authority employees employed in schools, hostels and libraries and sought to compare themselves with male manual employees, the complainants and their comparators were employed in different physical locations and distinct entities. Those entities had a high degree of permanence and stability, different organisational structures and their own workforces which performed specific tasks. The employment tribunal was therefore entitled to conclude that the employees worked at different establishments.

Different establishments – common terms and conditions of employment

If the complainant and her comparator are employed at different establishments then in order to claim equivalence, the complainant must show that 'common terms and conditions of employment' are observed by the employer at the establishments in question 'either generally or for employees of the relevant classes' (*EqPA 1970, s 1(6); EA 2010, s 79(4)*). Note that this requirement is not to be confused with the requirement for the complainant to identify a like term in the comparator's contract with which to claim equality (as to which see above **21.5**). What is necessary is that the complainant show that employees doing the same job as the comparator are employed on common terms and conditions at the establishments in question. A difficulty arises, however, where there are no employees doing the same job as the comparator who work in the establishment in which the complainant is employed. In those circumstances, it is necessary to show that if the male comparator was employed in the same establishment as the complainant, he would be employed on 'broadly similar' terms and conditions as he is in his current employment: see *British Coal Corpn v Smith* [1996] IRLR 404 and *South Tyneside Metropolitan Borough Council v Anderson* [2007] EWCA Civ 654, [2007] IRLR 715 and *Beddoes v Birmingham City Council* [2011] EqLR 838, EAT (affd on other grounds [2012] EWCA Civ 585). It was at one stage held (see *Dumfries* *and Galloway Council v North* [2009] ICR 1363, EAT) that it was necessary for a complainant to show that there was a 'real possibility' of the comparator actually being employed at the same establishment as the claimant. However, the Scottish Court of Session ([2011] CSIH 2, [2011] IRLR 239) overturned the EAT's decision in that case holding that there is no 'real possibility' requirement. The CS referred with approval to the observations of the EAT in *City of Edinburgh Council v Wilkinson* [2010] IRLR 756 that ' . . . if it is shown that members of the comparator group are always employed on common terms and conditions, then it is legitimate to assume that they would be employed on those terms and conditions at the claimants' establishment and men and women would thus be shown to be in the same employment . . . '. The CS remitted the matter to the employment tribunal to decide whether the complainant school staff and their comparator refuse collectors, gardeners etc were employed in the 'same employment', emphasising that the issue is one of fact for the employment tribunal. This aspect of the EAT's decision in *Wilkinson* has been upheld by the Court of Session: see [2012] IRLR 202.

For the purpose of comparison where 'common terms and conditions' apply to the relevant class of employees, the relevant class is the class of employee which includes the comparator. It is not necessary that there should be common terms and conditions applied at both establishments to the complainant's class of employee (*North Yorkshire County Council v Ratcliffe* [1994] IRLR 342, CA). In order to establish that terms are 'common', the employee does not need to go so far as to show that they are identical (*British Coal Corpn* and *Anderson* ibid). Terms which are 'broadly similar' will suffice. In *Leverton v Clwyd County Council* [1989] ICR 33, the Court of Appeal suggested that a case where two establishments were covered by the same collective agreement would be a simple example of the sort of circumstances in which terms and conditions could be said to be 'common'. Whether or not there is a sufficient degree of similarity between the terms and conditions is a question of fact for the tribunal.

Associated employers

If two or more employers are associated (ie if one is a company of which the other directly or indirectly has control or if both are companies of which a third person directly or indirectly has control; see **6.9 CONTINUOUS EMPLOYMENT**) a woman working in a factory owned by Company A can claim equivalence with a man working in another factory owned by an associated company, Company B, provided that broadly similar terms and conditions of employment apply either generally or for employees of the class of which the comparator is a member (*EqPA 1970, s 1(6)(c)*; *EA 2010, s 79(3)(a)* and *79(4)(a)*). Because the statutory language requires one of the allegedly associated employers to be a 'company', it appeared to exclude the possibility of two public sector employers being associated. However, in *Scullard v Knowles* [1996] IRLR 344 the EAT held that such an exclusion would be contrary to *art 157* and should be treated as 'displaced' by the broader European approach. Similarly, in *Fox Cross Claimants v Glasgow City Council* UKEATS/0027/12/BI, the Scottish EAT held that the word "company" had to be construed so as to include a limited liability partnership and a community interest company.

The 'single source' test

Challenges made under European Union law to the validity of the requirement in *s 1(6)* of the *EqPA 1970* (and reproduced in material respects in the *EA 2010, ss 79(3)* and *(4)*) that comparators be in the 'same employment' have resulted in the development of an additional 'single source' test for equal pay comparisons: *Lawrence v Regent Office Care Ltd* [2003] ICR 1092. The CJEU held that although there was nothing in the wording of *art 157* to suggest that its application was limited to situations in which men and women worked for the same employer, where, as in *Lawrence*, the differences in pay of workers of different sex performing equal work or work of equal value could not be attributable to a single source, such as a collective agreement, there was no one body responsible for the inequality which could restore equal treatment. Such a situation did not come within the scope of *art 157* and the work and pay of the different sets of workers could not be compared on the basis of *art 157*. See also *South Ayrshire Council v Morton* [2001] IRLR 28. This approach has been confirmed by the CJEU in *Allonby v Accrington and Rossendale College*: C-256/01 [2004] IRLR 224, CJEU. In *Allonby*, the applicant worked as a lecturer in the respondent college, but was a self-employed worker, hired by the college through an agency holding a database of lecturers. She claimed comparison with a named, salaried teacher at the college. The issue was whether working in the same establishment or service, for the benefit of a single employer, but under different contracts with different employers, was nevertheless working in the same employment for the purposes of *art 157*. The Court of Appeal ([2001] EWCA Civ 529, [2001] IRLR 364) referred the issue to the CJEU. The CJEU reiterated that *art 157* did not require the applicant to be employed by the same employer as her comparator and that a 'single source' would suffice. However, the CJEU considered on the facts of that case that there was no 'single source'. The fact that her pay as an employee of the agency was influenced by the rates of pay paid by the College did not mean that her pay and her comparator's was set by a 'single source'. This was so even though she may provide the same services as the man and for the benefit of the man's employer.

The 'single source' test was also considered by the Court of Appeal in *Robertson v Department for Environment, Food and Rural Affairs* [2005] EWCA Civ 138, [2005] ICR 750. In that case, the complainant and her comparator were both civil servants in common employment (all employed by the Crown). The CA held this was neither a necessary nor sufficient basis for an equal pay comparison. The bare fact of common employment is not enough: it is necessary in all circumstances to consider whether the terms and conditions were traceable to one source. The relevant body is the one which is responsible for the inequality and which could restore equal treatment. This will often but not always be the same employer. As responsibility for negotiating civil servant pay had been delegated down to the individual departments, an inter-department comparison did not involve comparison of pay from a single source and was not permissible. See also *Armstrong v Newcastle upon Tyne NHS Hospital Trust* [2005] EWCA Civ 1608, [2006] IRLR 124: in that case, although both sets of employees were employed by the same NHS Trust, which had endeavoured to a certain extent to harmonise terms and conditions across the hospitals for which it was responsible, the Court of Appeal held that the tribunal was right to find that the Trust had not assumed responsibility for the setting of terms and conditions of employment across all its hospitals and that therefore female employees in one hospital could not compare themselves with male employees in another. It remains to be seen what approach will be taken to employers hiving off their pay negotiations for different departments to different decision-making bodies or companies in order to avoid a 'single source' for cross-departmental comparison.

In *Beddoes v Birmingham City Council* [2011] EqLR 838 the position of non-teaching staff was considered in community schools. The local authority employed those staff, but acting on the requirements of the governing body of the school. It was asserted, therefore, that there was no single source as between the complainants and their comparators, the terms and conditions of employment in relation to the comparators being set by the local authority. The EAT rejected the argument. First, the argument failed by reason of the decision in *North Cumbria Acute Hospitals NHS Trust v Potter* [2009] IRLR 176 where the EAT had held that it was not necessary to 'read down' *EqPA 1970, section 1(6)* so include the 'single source test'. Secondly, the argument failed on the facts (and on an application of the decision of the Court of Appeal in *South Tyneside MBC v Anderson* [2007] ICR 1581). Finally, the EAT considered that in most cases the requirement of a 'single source' was unlikely to be any different to the requirements of *EqPA 1970, section 1(6)* since in most cases, a complainant will be able to compare herself with the employer's other employees (subject to satisfying the establishment criterion) and there will be a 'single source' because the employer will have the power to determine the terms and conditions of each its own employees. This part of the EAT's decision was not appealed to the Court of Appeal ([2012] EWCA Civ 585), which upheld the EAT's decision on other grounds.

21.9 Equal Pay

In all cases where the question of 'single source' arises it is important to remember that the principle as enunciated in *Lawrence* requires both that a single body is responsible for the inequality and that it is capable of restoring equal treatment: *North Cumbria Acute Hospitals NHS Trust v Potter* [2009] IRLR 176 and *Fox Cross Claimants v Glasgow City Council* UKEATS/0027/12/BI.

21.10 Defence of 'genuine material factor' – general approach

Although a woman may establish that she is engaged on like work, work rated as equivalent to that of a man or work of equal value, she will not be able to claim equivalence with that man if the employer can show that the variation between the woman's contract and the man's contract is genuinely due to a material factor which is not the difference of sex (*EqPA 1970, s 1(3)*). In the case of equality claimed on the basis of *like work* or *work rated as equivalent*, that factor *must* be a material difference between the woman's case and the man's (*EqPA 1970, s 1(3)(a)*). In the case of equality claimed on the basis of *work of equal value*, that factor *may* be a material difference between the woman's case and the man's (*EqPA 1970, s 1(3)(b)*). Thus, in establishing a defence to a claim based on like work or work rated as equivalent, any difference in terms must be explained (and, in some cases, objectively justified: see below) by a difference between the woman's case and the man's case. In a claim based on work of equal value the defence includes but is not limited to such differences.

The defence of genuine material factor continues to apply under the equal pay provisions set out in the *EA 2010*. By *s 69* of *EA 2010* a 'sex equality clause' will not have any effect where the 'responsible person' is able to show that the difference is because of a material factor. (A 'responsible person' is defined at *s 80* of *EA 2010* as the employer of a person or alternatively the person responsible for paying remuneration to that person.) That material factor must not be a factor which is directly discriminatory (*s 69(1)(a)* of *EA 2010*), nor one which is indirectly discriminatory (*s 69(1)(b)* and *(2)* of *EA 2010*). An indirectly discriminatory factor is defined as being a factor which results in "persons of the same sex doing work equal to A's" being "put at a particular disadvantage when compared with persons of the opposite sex doing work equal to A's" and where that factor is not "a proportionate means of achieving a legitimate aim".

The question whether an employer may succeed in a 'material factor' defence by relying upon a factor which does not objectively justify the difference in pay between the employee and her comparator received considerable judicial attention prior to the coming into force of the *EA 2010*. The 'old law' on this issue is set out below. The *EA 2010* has clarified the position that all pay differentials do not have to be objectively justified by an employer. The employer will only be required to justify pay differentials where it relies, to explain such differentials, on a factor which is *prima facie* indirectly discriminatory as putting persons of one sex at a particular disadvantage as compared to those of another sex doing the work (*s 69(1)(b)* and *(2)*). "Particular disadvantage" will likely be established by reference to statistical information. It is probable, therefore, that the line of defence to an indirect discrimination claim identified in *Armstrong*, *Gibson* and *Hamilton* (see the '*Pre EA 2010 approach*' section below), namely that an employer can avoid the need to justify a pay differential if it is able to show that statistics which one their face establish a *prima facie* case of indirect sex discrimination are in fact wholly explained by factors unrelated to sex.

Pre EA 2010 approach

There was for some time a marked difference in the approach taken to the scope of the defence at European and domestic levels. The European approach was set out in *Enderby v Frenchay Health Authority* [1994] ICR 112: it requires that a difference in pay be objectively justified. Further, *Enderby* requires, subject to a de minimis principle, that the whole of the difference must be justified.

The approach taken by the UK courts has been, traditionally, less demanding. The domestic approach has been simply to require the employer to be able to account for the difference by reference to a factor which is material but is not the sex of the employee. Thus, in *Yorkshire Blood Transfusion Service v Plaskitt* [1994] ICR 74, the employer succeeded in establishing a defence in circumstances where the disparity in pay was due to a mistake. Whilst an error may explain an unlawful disparity, it clearly cannot be said to justify it. Nevertheless, if a factor provides no sensible basis for justifying the disparity, domestic tribunals have tended to conclude that the factor is not 'material'. In *Tyldesley v TML Plastics Ltd* [1996] ICR 356, the EAT made an ambitious attempt to reconcile the domestic and European approaches. The principle which the EAT developed may be summarised as follows: if the factor relied upon by the employer is one which may itself be tainted by sex discrimination, it must be shown that the factor objectively justifies the difference; however, if it is not tainted by sex discrimination, the factor need only explain the difference. The EAT decision in *Tyldesley* was approved by the House of Lords in *Strathclyde Regional Council v Wallace* [1998] ICR 205, HL and *Glasgow City Council v Marshall* [2000] ICR 196, HL) and applied by the EAT in *Parliamentary Comr for Administration v Fernandez* [2004] ICR 123; *King's College London v Clark* (2003) IDS Brief 747, p 11 (in which the EAT held that a mistake and a *TUPE* transfer adequately explained the difference in pay); and *Armstrong v Newcastle Upon Tyne NHS Hospital Trust* [2005] EWCA Civ 1608, [2006] IRLR 124. In *Armstrong* the Court of Appeal held that the need to provide objective justification does not arise in cases in which the bare Enderby statistics, taken in isolation, suggest *prima facie* discrimination but there are other factors which suggest that the statistics are not good evidence of such prima facie discrimination so that the pay differential can be said not to be the difference of sex. In *Sharp v Caledonia Group Services Ltd* [2006] IRLR 4, the EAT, having cited the author of this chapter's then view that the issue 'remains vexed', proceeded to eschew the *Glasgow CC v Marshall* approach in favour of the more stringent European approach in the *Enderby* and *Brunnhofer* cases, the latter of which the EAT considered 'provides clear guidelines in equal pay cases as to the need for objective justification in all cases'. However, in *Armstrong* Lord Justice Buxton warned that, 'once the House of Lords has determined the meaning of [European Union rules] it is not open to domestic courts to resort to the decisions of the Court of Justice on which the House of Lords based its analysis in order to find a different or wider meaning'. Although Lord Justice Buxton does not appear to have been referred to the Sharp case, this would appear to be a condemnation of the approach taken by the EAT in that case and a reaffirmation that *Glasgow CC v Marshall* should continue to be applied unless and until the issue is reconsidered by the House of Lords or the CJEU.

This the EAT did in *Villalba v Merrill Lynch & Co Inc* [2006] IRLR 437 and *Surtees v Middlesbrough Borough Council* [2007] IRLR 869, holding that once an employer has established that a difference in pay was owing to factors other than sex, the employer is not required to go further and objectively justify the difference in pay. In *Villalba*, which concerned bonus payments based on performance assessments, it held to be sufficient that the employer had shown that sex was not a factor in its decision-making. (Or, rather, that it was not a 'significant influence' on its decision-making, as per Lord Nicholls in *Nagarajan v London Regional Transport* [1999] IRLR 572, HL.) In *Surtees* Elias P referred to the formulation set out in Villalba and observed that if the argument that 'the mere fact that a woman is making a comparison with a man whose job is of equal value itself automatically requires that any difference in pay is objectively justified, even though the employer shows that the difference has nothing to do with sex' is correct, then 'equal pay has broken loose from its moorings in discrimination law'. In that case, Elias P ruled that, where the employer has succeeded in explaining the difference in pay by reference to a factor that is not tainted by sex discrimination, he does not need to go further and objectively justify the use of that factor. On appeal from Elias P's judgment, the Court of Appeal in *Bainbridge/Surtees* [2008] IRLR 776 considered arguments about the approach adopted by the Court of Appeal in *Armstrong* (supra) but held that it was not the right case to analyse that case. It did however express a tentative view that, in circumstances of apparent disparate impact, it was possible for an employer to satisfy a tribunal that a pay differential was not due to the difference of sex without having to show objective justification but only where the statistical evidence was not very strong or convincing.

In *Gibson v Sheffield City Council* [2010] EWCA Civ 63, [2010] IRLR 311, the CA examined the issue again. That case concerned bonus schemes which had been introduced in the 1960s for manual workers in the Council (street cleaners, refuse collectors, maintenance, etc.) and subsequently consolidated into salary. As a result, the manual workers were paid over 30% more basic salary than the claimants who worked as care workers and school meals supervisors. The manual workers were overwhelmingly male, the care workers and school meals supervisors overwhelmingly female. The Tribunal found that the bonus schemes had initially been introduced for genuine productivity reasons, but since consolidation into basic pay the additional money was being paid without reference to productivity. The Tribunal found that it would not have been possible, because of the nature of their work, for similar bonus schemes to have been introduced for the claimants' roles and, in any event, that their work ethic had always been good. The Tribunal held that the reason for the difference in pay was the need to provide payments for increased productivity, and that this was unrelated to gender. Accordingly the Tribunal held, following *Marshall* and *Armstrong*, that it was not necessary for it to go on to determine whether the difference in pay was objectively justifiable. Smith LJ and Kay LJ in the Court of Appeal (although not Pill LJ) expressed the view that Armstrong was correct in principle and that an employer can avoid the need for objective justification if it can show that, notwithstanding that statistics have been produced which show that the pay practice in question has an adverse impact on women, the adverse impact has arisen as a result of factors wholly unrelated to gender. On the facts of the particular case, however, the CA ruled that the Tribunal had been wrong to find that the schemes were not sex-tainted. The matter was remitted to the Tribunal to consider the question of objective justification.

The cases show just how difficult it is for a Tribunal to determine whether or not a particular pay practice is 'tainted by sex discrimination'. In the *Armstrong* case (above) the Trust's explanation for the difference in pay between catering and portering staff was that the catering staff bonuses had been removed in order for the workforce to be competitively tendered in the market. A decision had been taken not to 'contract out' the portering contracts because portering was not subject to Compulsory Competitive Tendering and any decision to do so might therefore attract more controversy. The tribunal found that these reasons were 'tainted by sex discrimination'. However, the tribunal relied on its own experience to the effect that male workforces were more likely to be unionised and to object to contracting out and on that basis held the employer's explanation to be 'tainted by sex discrimination'. The CA ruled that it had not been open to the tribunal so to hold in the light of its findings of fact as to the Trust's reasons. The Court distinguished the *Ratcliffe* case (above) on the basis that in that case the tribunal had made an express finding as to the Council's reason for its decision to contract-out the domestic ancillary services and it was that express reason (rather than a further reason inferred by the Tribunal from its own experience) that the tribunal found was tainted by sex discrimination. Buxton LJ further observed that in the Ratcliffe case the House of Lords appeared to have been satisfied that the employer had failed to show any material difference between the comparator groups other than the difference in sex. In *Armstrong*, however, there were a number of differences between the two groups. The CA remitted the case to the Tribunal to determine again, in the light of its judgment, whether the bonus arrangements had a disparate impact on female employees, whether the decision to put domestic services out to tender, or to discontinue the domestic services' bonus scheme, was an act of discrimination and (if so) whether a GMF defence had been established. On remission (cf [2010] ICR 674) the Tribunal found (and the EAT upheld the decision) that there was a disparate impact and that the decision to withdraw the female catering staff bonuses to bring their pay into line with a labour market for domestics which was itself sexually discriminatory such that the arrangements were 'tainted by sex'. Objective justification was therefore required, but the Trust had failed to establish it.

In the *Gibson* case, by contrast to the first appeal in *Armstrong*, the CA overturned the Tribunal's decision that there was no sex taint on the grounds that it was perverse: the CA considered that the statistics were overwhelming and there had been a history of 'stereotyping' so (even though no similar bonus scheme could have been devised for the women's jobs) the 'sex taint' was present.

In *Newcastle-upon-Tyne NHS Hospitals Trust v Armstrong* [2010] ICR 674 and *Bury Metropolitan Borough Council v Hamilton* [2011] IRLR 358, the EAT (Underhill P presiding) has now given the clearest guidance to date on the approach that should be taken by tribunals to the *GMF* defence and the question of objective justification. The 'structured approach', as the EAT has termed it, is as follows (*Bury v Hamilton*, para 14):

•   It is necessary first to identify the explanation for the differential complained of. The burden of proof is on the employer.

•   It is then necessary to consider whether that explanation is 'tainted with sex'. What that not altogether happy metaphor means is that the explanation relied on must not itself involve sex discrimination, whether direct or indirect.

•   In considering whether the explanation involves direct or indirect discrimination, the ordinary principles of the law of discrimination apply. That means that:

   –   If the differential is the result of direct discrimination the defence under *s 1(3)* will fail;

   –   If the differential involves indirect discrimination of either the PCP-type or the *Enderby*-type (as to this distinction, see **21.11** below) the defence will fail unless the employer proves that the differential is objectively justified as being a proportionate means of achieving a legitimate aim;

   –   If the employer's explanation involves neither direct nor indirect discrimination the defence will succeed, even if the factor relied on cannot be objectively justified.

•   In considering the employer's explanation, the ordinary principles governing the burden of proof in discrimination claims will apply. Thus if the claimant shows a prima facie case of discrimination (in the sense explained in *Madarassy v Nomura International plc* [2007] IRLR 246), the burden shifts to the employer to prove the absence of such discrimination. (See generally DISCRIMINATION AND EQUAL OPPORTUNITIES – III (12)).

The 'structured approach' advanced by the EAT must, in this author's view, be correct as a matter of legal principle. It is also clear and readily capable of application by employment tribunals. However, it arguably does not deal with one strand of the case law, approved twice at Court of Appeal level in the *Armstrong* and *Gibson* cases (supra) (and accepted by the EAT in *Bury v Hamilton* as binding upon it: see para 17), namely that there is an additional line of defence available to an employer in a case where a complainant has proved a *prima facie* case of indirect discrimination. In such cases, the Court of Appeal held that it was open to an employer at that stage to show that the apparent adverse impact on women is caused by factors other than sex so that there is then no need for the employer to go on to objectively justify the difference in pay.

21.10   Equal Pay

See also, in this regard, *Sunderland City Council v Brennan* [2012] EWCA Civ 413, [2012] IRLR 507 and *Cooksey (GMB Claimants) v Trafford BC* [2012] Eq LR 744 and note that, in the latter case, the EAT observed (at para 97) that this 'no sex taint' *Armstrong* defence to indirect discrimination is highly likely to be available in practice where the *prima facie* case of indirect discrimination arises as a result of the application of a PCP applied by the employer (the first type of indirect discrimination described at **21.11** below). Rather, it will be relevant only where the indirect discrimination is to be found in the *Enderby*-type indirect discrimination, i.e. where there is a *prima facie* case of indirect discrimination arising as a result of a state of affairs (the second type of indirect discrimination case described below).

21.11   'Prima facie' indirect discrimination and the 'material factor' defence

The model adopted by the *EqPA 1970*, in which an employee compares her terms and conditions with those of a specific comparator, works well enough in relation to cases of direct discrimination. Indeed, it favours the complainant in that, once she has established that her male colleague enjoys different and more favourable terms, the employer must then establish that the difference is due to a material factor which is not a difference in sex. In effect, to use the language of *SDA 1975*, the employee need only establish that she has been 'less favourably treated'. She need not show that the less favourable treatment is 'on the ground of her sex'; it is for the employer to show that the difference in sex is not the ground of the difference in treatment (see **21.10** above). However, the *EqPA 1970* is much less obviously suited to dealing with cases of indirect discrimination. (For the concept of indirect discrimination see **10.34** Discrimination And Equal Opportunities – I.) Nonetheless, the 'structured approach' to the 'material factor' defence that has been enunciated by the EAT in *Bury Metropolitan Borough Council v Hamilton* [2011] IRLR 358 (above, **21.10**) requires the tribunal, as a step in considering an employer's defence, to determine whether or not a 'prima facie' case of indirect discrimination has arisen. However, this issue has caused the courts and tribunals significant difficulties.

The *EA 2010* attempts to codify the law on indirect discrimination in equal pay claims. However, it does so through a circuitous route. First, a real comparator of the opposite sex must be identified by the complainant who is doing equal work (as defined by *s* 65), but being paid more: see *s* 66. The employer must then show both that the difference in treatment is not the difference in sex (*s 69(1)(a)*) and, if the factor that is causing the difference in pay puts persons of one sex at a particular disadvantage (s 69(2)), that the factor is a proportionate means of achieving a legitimate aim (*s 69(1)(b)*). See further above **21.10**.

Although there has been considerable doubt on the issue (cf, for eg, *Bailey v Home Office* [2005] EWCA Civ 327, [2005] IRLR 369) it is now generally recognised that there are two forms of indirect discrimination that arise in relation equal pay (see *Bury Metropolitan Borough Council v Hamilton and ors* [2011] IRLR 358, EAT):

- where the employer applies a provision, criterion or practice which puts or would put women at a particular disadvantage when compared with men (the 'PCP'-type of discrimination);

- where two groups of employees doing work of equal value receive different pay and there is a sufficiently substantial disparity in the gender break-down of the two groups (referred to as discrimination arising from a 'state of affairs', or *Enderby*-type discrimination, having first been recognised in the decision of the CJEU in *Enderby v Frenchay Health Authority* [1993] IRLR 591).

These two forms are not mutually exclusive: *Cooksey (GMB Claimants) v Trafford BC* [2012] Eq LR 744.

In cases of the first type of indirect discrimination, the employee's terms will often be identical to those of her male comparator. In such cases, the issue will centre instead on a benefit which, whilst theoretically available to the complainant, is contingent on her satisfying a provision, criterion or practice ('PCP') which fewer women than men are able to satisfy. For instance, the contracts of both employees may provide that they are entitled to join their employer's pension scheme only if they work full-time. It is difficult to apply the equality clause to such cases. What is needed in order to eliminate the discrimination is not the addition to the complainant's contract of a clause already present in her comparator's, but the replacement of the term common to both contracts with one which does not have a discriminatory effect. For this reason, there was initially some doubt as to whether or not *EqPA 1970* prohibited indirect discrimination at all although it has now long been established that indirect discrimination is contrary to both UK and European law (*Jenkins v Kingsgate (Clothing Productions) Ltd* [1981] ICR 715, EAT, *Bilka-Kaufhaus GmbH v Weber von Hartz*: C-170/84 [1987] ICR 110, CJEU).

Thus if pay criteria are adopted which apparently tend to favour men, it is for the employer to justify those criteria. Such criteria would include ones less favourable to part-time workers (see, eg *Arbeiterwohlfahrt der Stadt Berlin eV v Botel*: C-360/90 [1992] IRLR 423 and *Vroege v NCIV Institut voor Volkshuisvesting BV*: C-57/93 [1994] ECR I-4541, [1995] ICR 635, CJEU and generally **21.18** below).

In cases of the second type of indirect discrimination, it is not necessary for the complainant to follow the formal steps of identifying a provision, criterion or practice, choosing a pool for comparison and establishing a disparate impact. Thus in *Enderby v Frenchay Health Authority*: C-127/92 [1994] ICR 112, CJEU (the case in which the second type of discrimination was first recognised) the CJEU decided that the employer could be called upon objectively to justify a difference in pay once the complainant had demonstrated that 'significant statistics disclosed an appreciable difference in pay between two jobs of equal value, one of which was carried out almost exclusively by women and the other predominantly by men'. Whilst this approach focuses on disparities in pay, it plainly does not require the identification of any condition or requirement (now PCP). In *Ministry of Defence v Armstrong* [2004] IRLR 672, the EAT favoured the Enderby approach, holding that there is no need for a tribunal always to adopt the formulaic approach of the *SDA 1975* when considering whether there is a disparate impact for the purposes of *EqPA, s 1(3)*. Cox J stressed (para 46) that the question in all cases is 'whether there is a causative link between the applicant's sex and the fact that she is paid less than the true value of her job as reflected in the pay of her named comparator'. Tribunals should 'focus on substance, rather than form and on the result, rather than route taken to arrive at it'.

Nonetheless, this has caused confusion in practice and the distinction between the two types of indirect discrimination has been doubted. Thus in *Bailey v Home Office* [2005] EWCA Civ 327, [2005] IRLR 369 the Court of Appeal held that the tribunal's attempt to fashion a condition or requirement out of the circumstances of the case had led it into error. It rejected the EAT's attempt to distinguish between condition and requirement/PCP cases on the one hand and cases which did not have an obvious condition or requirement/PCP but which involved a disparity of pay between two groups on the other. In each case, the Court of Appeal ruled that the tribunal is concerned to determine whether what on its face is a gender-neutral practice may be disguising the fact that female employees are being disadvantaged as compared with male employees to an extent that signifies that the disparity is *prima facie* attributable to a difference of sex. The Court of Appeal held that the statistical approach in *Seymour-Smith* could be used in either case. A common approach to both types of cases has the merit of ensuring that the Act is applied consistently to all forms of indirect discrimination. On the facts of *Bailey*, the Court of Appeal held that the tribunal could sufficient disparate impact requiring justification where there was one group of employees which contained a significant number, even though not a clear majority, of female workers whose work is rated as equal to that of another group of employees who are predominantly male and who receive greater pay. The fact that the disadvantaged group contained a significant number of men was not a bar to a claim.

It is certainly the case that in relation to both types of indirect discrimination there will often be an issue as to whether there is a sufficiently substantial disparity in the gender make-up of the two groups to give rise to a *prima facie* case of indirect discrimination.

In particular, the 'almost exclusively by women' formula used by the CJEU in *Enderby* has given rise to a number of difficulties of interpretation. The Court of Appeal in *British Road Services Ltd v Loughran* [1997] IRLR 92, CA, having carefully considered *Enderby*, took the view that it would suffice if there were a 'significant proportion of women' in the claimant's group. Later cases have attempted to establish a more precise formula, though with little success.

When it made its reference to the CJEU in *R v Secretary of State for Employment, ex p Seymour-Smith and Perez* [1999] ICR 447, the House of Lords asked for guidance on the circumstances in which a court is entitled to conclude that a provision has an indirectly discriminatory effect. It is well settled that there must be a disparity in the impact of the provision as between men and women; but how does one judge whether the disparity is great enough to allow the court to conclude that there is a discriminatory effect? Will any statistically significant difference do, or is something more required? Characteristically, in giving guidance, the CJEU posed as many questions as it answered. The CJEU declined to give any precise guidance as to the assessment of disparate impact; it merely observed that the national court must be satisfied that the proportion of women that can comply must be 'considerably smaller' than the proportion of men who can do so. In that case, which was concerned with the upper age limit on the availability of the right to claim unfair dismissal, the particular period with which the court was concerned was 1985, the date on which the former requirement of one year's service was increased to two years. At that point, the proportion of men who could comply with the requirement was 77.4%, whereas the proportion of women who could comply was 68.9%. Since that time the gap has narrowed. The CJEU observed that these figures did not suggest a sufficient disparity of impact to result in a discriminatory effect. However, the Court also observed that a small but persistent difference may result in a finding of discrimination. No guidance was given as to how this new, alternative test will operate. The majority of the House of Lords found the relevant provision to be discriminatory on the basis of this 'alternative' test. They do not appear to have seen it as an alternative, however (see **10.34 DISCRIMINATION AND EQUAL OPPORTUNITIES − I**).

In assessing whether a statistically relevant difference in pay has been established, the CJEU in both *Enderby* (at para 17) and *Seymour-Smith* and *Perez* (at para 62) emphasised that it is for the national court to decide whether the pools of employees selected for comparison "cover enough individuals, whether they illustrate purely fortuitous or short-term phenomena and whether, in general, they appear to be significant". Further guidance on the proper test to be applied can be gleaned from *Barry v Midland Bank* [1999] ICR 859, HL. Lord Nicholls remarked at 869 that a comparison between the proportions of men and women disadvantaged by a particular provision could on its own be misleading, because those proportions would be affected by the comparative sizes of the disadvantaged and non-disadvantaged groups. (For an example of a case where the tribunal was so misled, see *Best v Tyne and Wear Passenger and Transport Executive (t/a Nexus)* [2007] ICR 523, EAT in which the EAT ruled that the tribunal had been wrong to find that a disparate impact had been established in circumstances where the disadvantaged group was mainly male, albeit that there were more women in the disadvantaged group than there were women in the advantaged group − in such circumstances there was no disparate impact on women generally.) In *Barry v Midland Bank*, Lord Nicholls suggested that the better guide would often be found by expressing the proportions of men and women in the disadvantaged groups as a ratio of each other. Moreover, the absolute size of numbers of those disadvantaged remains relevant, since a low ratio may be of little significance in a small company, but of considerable significance in a large company. Thus in *Audit Commission v Haq (S)* (UKEAT/0123/10/LA) (18 March 2011, unreported) the EAT held that the numbers involved were insufficient to give rise to a *prima facie* case of discrimination. In that case senior and junior administrative roles had been amalgamated and a pay protection policy implemented which meant that former senior administrators were paid more in the new role because they had previously been paid more. Two of the four former senior administrators were male (and both the senior administrators retained were male), whereas all nine former junior administrators were female. The tribunal found that there was unjustified indirect discrimination. The EAT overturned that decision, holding that the numbers involved were too small to give rise to a *prima facie* case of indirect discrimination on that ground alone. The CA ([2012] EWCA Civ 1621, [2013] IRLR 206) reversed the EAT on this point, upholding the Tribunal decision. The CA took the view that the numbers were sufficient. Post the amalgamation the numbers were sufficient to establish a prima facie case of discrimination. The employer could not rebut that case because, historically, the fact that all nine former junior administrators were female was itself evidence of a sex taint. In the absence of evidence of any other source of discrimination, the claims must fail. Cf also see *Armstrong v Newcastle Upon Tyne NHS Hospital Trust* [2005] EWCA Civ 1608, [2006] IRLR 124 where it was held that a failure by a tribunal to make a finding that the employer's arrangements have a 'considerable' impact on women prior to concluding that an arrangement is discriminatory will be an error of law: (although cf *Gibson v Sheffield City Council* [2010] EWCA Civ 63, [2010] IRLR 311).

Care must also be taken in selecting the appropriate pools for comparison. In *Abbott v Cheshire & Wirral Partnership NHS Trust* [2006] EWCA Civ 523, [2006] IRLR 546 the Court of Appeal ruled that, while it was for the claimant in the first instance to select a pool for comparison, it was open to the employer to dispute the appropriateness of that pool, and it was for the tribunal to determine the appropriate pool for comparison purposes. The CJEU has noted that it is not permissible for a claimant to create the appearance of a difference in pay between groups of male and female employees by arbitrarily identifying as 'pools' a number of male employees who are paid more, and a number of female employees who are paid less. There has to be some connection between the employees in each group that means their circumstances can meaningfully be considered collectively: *Specialarbe-jderforbundet i Danmark v Dansk Industri, acting for Royal Copenhagen A/S* C-400/93 [1995] IRLR 648, CJEU, paragraph 36.

The proper approach to selection of the pool and statistical evidence was considered in *Secretary of State for Trade and Industry v Rutherford (No 2)*. This concerned a challenge to the upper age limit of 65 for unfair dismissal claims in *ss 109* and *156 ERA 1996* on the basis that it had a disparate impact on men which could not be objectively justified. The tribunal selected a pool consisting of those employees for whom retirement at 65 had 'some real meaning', being those aged 55 to 74. The Court of Appeal ([2004] EWCA Civ 1186, [2005] ICR 119) held that the tribunal had erred in law in concentrating on the 'disadvantaged group'. The Court of Appeal considered that the tribunal should have based its assessment of adverse impact on the statistics for the entire workforce to which the requirement of being under 65 applied and then primarily compared the respective proportions of men and women who could satisfy that requirement. Adopting this approach, the statistics clearly established that the difference in the working population between the proportion of men aged under 65 who could comply and the proportion of women under 65 who could comply was very small indeed. Accordingly, the complainants had failed to establish that there was any indirect sex discrimination against men in the imposition of the upper age limit. The Court of Appeal rejected the submission that the *Burden of Proof Directive (97/80/EC)* (which provides that ' . . . indirect discrimination shall exist where an apparently neutral provision, criterion or practice disadvantages a substantially higher proportion of the members of one sex unless that provision, criterion or practice is appropriate and necessary and can be justified by objective factors unrelated to sex') altered the guidance given in *Seymour-Smith*. The Court observed that the definition of indirect sex discrimination in the *Burden of Proof Directive* describes when indirect discrimination exists and does not prescribe the methodology for assessing the statistical evidence in order to determine whether or not that state of affairs exists. It has been left to the courts and tribunals to work out from case to case a satisfactory method for assessing whether or not there is disparate adverse impact in any case. The Court of Appeal's approach to the issue of disparate impact had what might be termed an 'attractive simplicity'. On appeal, the House of Lords ([2006] UKHL 19, [2006] IRLR 551) disagreed with the Court of Appeal's approach, but the judgments of their Lordships are not models of clarity as to the approach that is to be preferred. A majority of their Lordships rejected the classification of the case as one of (even potential) indirect discrimination. They each considered that this was not a case where one could speak coherently of those who are 'able to satisfy' a rule or requirement and those who are not. Since the rule in question simply imposes a disadvantage on those who stay in employment after the age of 65, there was therefore no comparison to be made since all men and all women over the age of 65 were equally disadvantaged. Lord Nicholls and Lord Walker, however, took a statistical approach as the Court of Appeal had done. However, unlike the Court of Appeal, they focused on the disadvantaged group (ie on the percentage of the workforce over 65), but emphasised how small this group was in comparison to the workforce as a whole. They noted that the proportion of the entire workforce affected by the age limit was 1.2%. 1.4% of the male workforce was affected, and 1% of the female workforce. Lords Walker and Nicholls considered that those proportions were simply too small to indicate a 'substantial' disadvantage to the male workforce.

In *Grundy v British Airways Plc* [2007] EWCA Civ 1020, [2008] IRLR 815 the Court of Appeal considered *Rutherford* and emphasised that the issue of whether or not there was a disparate impact was a question of fact in each case to be determined by the Tribunal. The Court observed that there was no rule as to what pool would or would not be appropriate, though care should be taken that the pool was not so small as to be unrepresentative or so large that like was not being compared with like. Similarly, there was no rule that one must always look at the advantaged or the disadvantaged groups. The job for the Tribunal is to identify a cohort within which the genuine material factor defence can be objectively tested. That means that employees within each pool chosen must share relevant characteristics and not exclude employees who also share those characteristics: *Cooksey (GMB Claimants) v Trafford BC* [2012] Eq LR 744.

While the Tribunal enjoys some latitude in its selection of pools, a Tribunal can still err in law by selecting the 'wrong' pool. In *Abbott v Cheshire* (supra), claims were brought by hospital domestic workers (almost entirely female) whose terms and conditions did not include a right to a bonus. They sought to compare themselves to hospital porters (entirely male) whose terms and conditions included a right to a bonus. The employers had argued that the proper comparator pool was not just the porters, but the porters and the catering staff. The catering staff were predominantly female and had also received bonuses. The Court of Appeal ruled that the tribunal had been wrong to reject the employer's argument as to pool: the three groups were plainly comparable. However, the Court of Appeal considered that the right result had been reached in any event because the porters and catering staff together were still 65% male in comparison to the domestic staff who were almost exclusively female: that was sufficient to establish a prima facie case of discrimination. The Court of Appeal also rejected an argument (based on *Specialarbejderforbundet i Danmark v Dansk Industri, acting for Royal Copenhagen A/S*: C-400/93 [1995] IRLR 648, CJEU) that the comparator group (of 37) was too small in order to establish a valid statistical difference in the proportions of male and female workers. The Court of Appeal considered that it would be wrong to set minimum numerical requirements because that would mean that indirect discrimination could never be established for small employers.

In *Pike v Somerset County Council* [2010] ICR 46, the CA considered a claim by a retired teacher who had returned to teaching part-time. She was unable to rejoin the Teachers' Pension Scheme and her service from then on did not count towards her pensionable employment. However, if she had returned to teaching full-time, she would have been able to rejoin the scheme. The competing pools comprised: (a) retired teachers who had returned to work, and (b) all members (whether or not retired) of the pension scheme. The CA held that the correct pool included retired teachers only. The pool was to be defined as a group in which all the members wanted a particular benefit, but the benefit was denied to some members because of a criterion applicable to the benefit. The members of the claimant's proposed pool, namely teachers returning after retirement, all wanted the benefit of their service being pensionable, but that benefit was denied to part-timers. Those who were members of the pension scheme but had not retired were uninterested in the post-retirement rules. They derived no advantage from the post-retirement rule favouring full-timers; it simply did not apply to them.

The introduction of equal pay questionnaires under the *Equal Pay (Questions and Replies) Order 2003* (see **21.22** below) assisted complainants with gathering appropriate statistics to show disparate impact and to enable complainants to pierce the culture of secrecy. However, the questionnaire procedure is not available for claims commenced after 25 April 2013 as *s 138* of the *EA 2010* was repealed by *s 66* of the *Enterprise and Regulatory Reform Act 2013*. The importance of transparency is nonetheless emphasised in the Equal Pay: Statutory Code of Practice published by the Equality and Human Rights Commission. Complainants may in future also find assistance in the results of 'equal pay audits' (see further below).

Under *s 77* of the *EA 2010* individuals are also protected from retaliation or victimisation where they seek, or provide, disclosures about the terms of their work (including how much they are paid) (*ss 77(4)* and *(5)*. Contractual terms purporting to restrict such disclosures will be void (*ss 77(1)* and *(2)*). In addition, *s 78* of the *EA 2010* makes provision (not yet in force, and the coalition government does not intend to bring it into force) requiring employers with 250 or more employees (and other employers who may be specified in delegated legislation) to publish information relating to the pay of employees for the purpose of showing whether there are differences in the pay of male and female employees.

21.12 Specific considerations in relation to the 'material factor' defence

The House of Lords in *Rainey v Greater Glasgow Health Board* [1987] ICR 129 resolved earlier doubts upon the matters which may be taken into account in considering a defence of 'material factor' under *s 1(3)* in favour of holding that it is open to a tribunal to consider the merits of any factor advanced by an employer in support of such a defence. At 140, Lord Keith stated:

> "The difference must be "material", which I would construe as meaning "significant and relevant", and it must be between "her case and his". Consideration of a person's case must necessarily involve consideration of all circumstances of that case. These may well go beyond what is not very happily described as "the personal equation", ie the personal qualities by way of skill, experience or training which the individual brings to the job. Some circumstances may on examination prove to be not significant or not relevant, but others may do so, though not relating to the personal qualities of the employee. In particular, where there is no question of intentional sex discrimination whether direct or indirect (and there is none here) a difference which is connected with economic factors affecting the efficient carrying on of the employer's business or other activity may well be relevant."

He held that the defence available in *EqPA 1970, s 1(3)* is equivalent in scope to the defence of justification held by the European court in *Bilka-Kaufhaus Gmbh v Weber von Hartz* C-170/84: [1987] ICR 110 to be available under *art 157*. (Guidance is given in the *Danfoss* case (C-109/88, above) as to the factors which the CJEU has considered to be relevant to the objective justification of differences in pay under *art 157*.)

Although each case will therefore turn on its particular facts and circumstances, certain general points of principle have been considered in the cases as set out below.

Note that where, applying the 'structured approach' set out by the EAT in *Bury v Hamilton* (above, **21.10**) it is necessary for the tribunal to consider whether a particular indirectly discriminatory situation or PCP is objectively justified, the approach to the question of justification should be the same as for any other case of discrimination, i.e. the employer must show that there is a legitimate aim and that the means used to achieve that aim are proportionate: see Discrimination And Equal Opportunities – II (11).

Factors relevant to equal value as well as the 'material factor' defence

In *Davies v McCartneys* [1989] ICR 705, the EAT held that a defence was made out under s 1(3) despite the fact that some of the matters relied upon, such as circumstances in which the job was performed, were relevant to an assessment of whether the jobs were of equal value. In *Christie v John E Haith Ltd* [2003] IRLR 670, the EAT held that the mere fact that a particular factor may be relevant in the evaluation exercise to determine the question of equal value was not a ground for excluding it as part of a *s 1(3)* defence: the principle in *Davies v McCartneys* was not limited to cases where there had not actually been a determination of equal value taking into account the factors in question. Once an employee has shown that she is engaged on like work, work rated as equivalent to that of a man, or work of equal value to that of a man it is for the employer to prove that he has a defence under *s 1(3)* (*Financial Times Ltd v Byrne (No 2)* [1992] IRLR 163). See also *Kenny and ors v Minister for Justice, Equality and Law Reform* Case C 427/11 at §29 and *Angestellten-betriebsrat der Wiener Gebeitskrankenkasse v Wiener Gebeitskrankenkasse* [1999] IRLR 804 at §29, where the CJEU holds that the fact that one group of employees doing a job has professional training and the other does not can both be a factor pointing to a finding that the employees are not doing 'like work' and a factor justifying any differential in pay.

The 'genuine' requirement

The factor relied upon must in fact be genuine and not a sham; see *Hartlepool Borough Council v Dolphin* [2009] IRLR 168 in which the EAT held the tribunal was entitled to find that productivity bonuses paid to men were a sham. The employer's assertion that an explanation was all that needed to be shown could not be accepted. The tribunal's task had been to determine whether the schemes had been genuine, by deciding whether they were intended to achieve and in fact achieved productivity improvements; its approach, in holding that the monitoring measures were not enough to satisfy it that the schemes were genuinely intended to improve productivity, was correct. Note, however, that tribunals should guard against using the word 'sham' unless there has actually been dishonesty on the part of the employer. If it is the case, for example, that productivity bonuses were justified when first introduced but cease to be so, that does not mean they are a 'sham', but merely that they are no longer justified: see *Bury Metropolitan Borough Council v Hamilton* [2011] IRLR 358.

The 'genuine' requirement simply means that the factor relied on must truly be the reason for the difference in pay. Thus, for example, if there is evidence that women are systematically disadvantaged, it will not be acceptable to say simply that pay awards are based on the quality of work – it would be plain from the result that the system was being abusively applied (*Danfoss*).

The distinction between the legitimate aim and the means used to achieve it

In considering whether a prima facie indirectly discriminatory measure is objectively justified (see above **21.11**), care must be taken in properly identifying and distinguishing the aim of the measure from the means used to achieve it. The fact that different measures with different aims could be introduced by an employer is not relevant in determining whether a particular measure with a legitimate aim is justified, what matters is whether there are more proportionate ways of achieving the aim of the measure in question: see *Blackburn v Chief Constable of West Midlands Police* [2008] EWCA Civ 1208, [2009] IRLR 135 (aim of rewarding those who did night work was legitimate and therefore it was proportionate to pay those persons more – it did not matter that other police forces had decided not to reward night workers). See also *Allen v GMB* [2008] IRLR 690. In that case the CA considered the situation of a union which had decided, in negotiating with an employer in relation to various pay issues, to adopt a policy whereby employees' interests in relation to future pay deals were prioritised over claims to back pay under the *EqPA 1970*. The result was that those employees who had equal pay claims (a predominantly female group) received less by way of settlement than they might otherwise have done. The Tribunal held that the union's objective (which it identified as being to achieve single status, avoiding privatisations, job losses, cuts in hours, and members receiving lower pay under the new system) was legitimate, but that the means used to achieve that aim amounted to 'manipulation' and were unjustified. One factor in the Tribunal's conclusion was that it was considered that the amount accepted by the Union in settlement of the equal pay claims was bordering on negligent. The EAT found that the Tribunal had taken the wrong approach to the question of objective justification. The EAT considered that, once it had been accepted that an aim was legitimate then if the means adopted to achieve that aim were the only means available then the policy would be justified. The CA disagreed and upheld the Tribunal's decision. The CA considered that the EAT had taken too narrow an approach to the concept of 'means'. The 'means' was not the balance struck by the union in the deal with the Council, but the methods used to persuade members to accept that deal. The Tribunal had been entitled to find that those methods had been manipulative and disproportionate to the legitimate aims pursued.

Timing of the justification/explanation

The material difference or factor relied upon must be one which exists throughout the period during which there is a difference in pay. For example, where a woman was appointed at a lower rate of pay than existing male employees because of financial constraints, there was no defence to her equal pay claim after those constraints had ceased to exist (*Benveniste v University of Southampton* [1989] ICR 617). However, where employees are on appointment placed at different points on a pay scale as a result of having different qualifications or experience, a continuing difference in pay as the employees move up that payscale as a result of annual increments will be lawful, provided that the continuing difference is wholly explained by the operation of the payscale and there was no discrimination in the initial decision as to where the employee was placed on the payscale on appointment: *Secretary of State for Justice (sued as National Offenders Management Service) v Bowling* [2012] IRLR 382. In that case the EAT said that that would even be the case if the employees' subsequent experience in the job meant that the man's initial advantage as a result of his qualifications and experience had been entirely wiped out by the woman's personal development in the role.

An initial difference in pay between male and female employees performing the same work cannot be justified on the basis of factors, such as a difference in performance levels, which become known only after the employees concerned have taken up their duties and which can only be assessed during the employment relationship (*Brunnhofer v Bank der Osterreichischen Postsparkasse AG*: C-381/99 [2001] IRLR 571, CJEU). However, such factors will obviously be relevant when what is complained about is the level of an annual bonus which is based on an assessment of an employee's performance during the year: *Villalba v Merrill Lynch & Co* [2006] IRLR 437.

'Red-circling' of existing pension entitlements will not amount to a genuine material factor where, although justifying an initial difference in pension entitlement, it does not provide justification for maintaining the differential over twenty years: *Home Office v Bailey* [2005] IRLR 757. See also *Cumbria County Council v Dow (No 1)* [2008] IRLR 91, EAT (difference in pay which arose from a bonus scheme originally designed to improve productivity was not objectively justified where the scheme had ceased to be effective and the bonus payments had in practice become automatic additions to the pay of the male comparators).

After-the-event justification

The Court of Appeal in *Cadman v Health and Safety Executive* [2004] EWCA Civ 1317, [2005] ICR 1546 has reiterated that 'after the event' justification is permissible so that an employer may rely on matters which did not consciously and contemporaneously feature in its decision making at the time. The CJEU adopted the same approach in *Schönheit (Hilde) v Stadt Frankfurt am Main*: C-4/02 and C-5/02 [2003] ECR I-12575, [2004] IRLR 983. See also *Pulham v Barking and Dagenham London Borough Council* [2010] ICR 333 where the EAT held that an employer was not prevented from advancing a justification defence in respect of pay protection arrangements merely because they had not been "carefully costed and crafted" at the time of implementation.

Differences in hours worked

The House of Lords held in *Leverton v Clwyd County Council* [1989] ICR 33 that, if there was no significant difference between the hourly rates of pay of the applicant and her male comparator, it would be a legitimate, if not a necessary, inference that the difference between their total salaries was due to, and justified by, the difference in the number of hours worked. This approach was adopted by the CJEU in *Stadt Lengerich v Helmig* [1995] IRLR 216 which held that, prima facie, there is unequal treatment wherever the overall pay of full-time employees is higher than that of part-time employees for the same number of hours worked. The CJEU determined that there was no discrimination where part-time employees only received pay at overtime rates once they had worked the equivalent of a full-time worker's ordinary weekly hours rather than once they had completed the number of hours which they themselves ordinarily worked each week.

Qualifications / training

In *Angestelltenbetriebsrat der Wiener Gebeitskrankenkasse v Wiener Gebeitskrankenkasse* [1999] IRLR 804 and *Kenny and ors v Minister for Justice, Equality and Law Reform* Case C 427/11 the CJEU accepted that differences in levels of professional training between the two groups of employees could justify differing levels of pay.

The importance of transparency

The CJEU in *Danfoss* held that where an undertaking applies a system of pay which is totally lacking in transparency, it is for the employer to show that his practice concerning wages is not discriminatory. The Court of Appeal in *Calder v Rowntree Mackintosh Confectionery Ltd* [1993] IRLR 212 apparently accepted that the transparency principle applied in English law, but held that it did not require the employer to explain exactly how a figure for shift premium was achieved. By contrast, in an important decision on City bonus payments, *Barton v Investec Henderson Crosthwaite Securities Ltd* [2003] IRLR 332, the EAT held that the tribunal erred in appearing to condone the lack of transparency in the employer's bonus system on the basis of its 'industrial knowledge' that the City 'bonus culture' was one of secrecy. Although the bonus claim was brought under the *SDA*, the lack of transparency was also relevant to the material factor defence in the *EqPA* claim: see paras 30 and 37.

Note also that there have been obiter indications in UK authorities that, in cases where there is a challenge to a pay system which is alleged to be indirectly discriminatory, the clarity and simplicity of the system may amount to a material factor. Put another way, the material factor may consist of the 'administrative convenience' of operating a simple and straight-forward system, or equally, the administrative inconvenience of having to alter it (cf Dillon and Hirst LJJ in *R v Secretary of State for Employment, ex p Equal Opportunities Commission* [1993] 1 All ER 1022, [1993] ICR 251, CA, and *Barry v Midland Bank plc* [1999] ICR 319, CA; the Court of Appeal's decision in *Barry* was upheld by the House of Lords ([1999] ICR 859), but on a different basis: their Lordships looked at the 'primary object' of the redundancy scheme in considering whether it was discriminatory, rather than reserving such issues to a consideration of whether the scheme could, if it had a disparate impact, be justified.

'Productivity bonuses' and attendance allowances

A number of cases have involved so-called 'productivity bonuses' and/or attendance allowances paid to male manual workers. See, for eg, *Degnan v Redcar & Cleveland Borough Council* [2005] EWCA Civ 726, [2005] IRLR 615; *Armstrong v Newcastle Upon Tyne NHS Hospital Trust* [2005] EWCA Civ 1608, [2006] IRLR 124; *South Tyneside Metropolitan Borough Council v Anderson* [2007] EWCA Civ 654, [2007] IRLR 715; *Surtees v Middlesbrough Borough Council* [2007] IRLR 869, EAT; *Cumbria County Council v Dow and ors* [2008] IRLR 91; *Bury Metropolitan Borough Council v Hamilton* [2011] IRLR 358; and *Gibson v Sheffield City Council* [2010] EWCA Civ 63, [2010] IRLR 311; and *Sunderland City Council v Brennan* [2012] EWCA Civ 413, [2012] IRLR 507. Those cases show that in general employers have in practice found it difficult to justify bonuses that have applied to groups of (mainly) male workers but not to groups of (mainly) female workers. In such cases the tribunal will consider whether or not there was when the bonus was introduced, and whether there continues to be, a good reason for the payment of the bonus (e.g. performance improvement or maintaining productivity) or whether the bonus is in reality an 'attendance allowance' paid simply because the employee attends work (in which case it will not be justified). The tribunal will also consider whether or not a similar scheme could have been introduced for the female workers. However, even a finding that no similar scheme could have been introduced will not prevent the tribunal concluding that having the bonus for the male workers is not justified: see, eg, *Gibson v Sheffield City Council* [2010] EWCA Civ 63, [2010] IRLR 311 (although note that in that case the tribunal had found that what were originally productivity bonuses had effectively become mere attendance allowances).

Seniority and length of service as factors

The CJEU has held that differences in seniority and length of service are generally material differences (not requiring special justification), at least where the employer is distinguishing between full-time workers (*Handels-Og Kontorfunktionaerernes Forbund i Danmark v Dansk Arbejdsgiverforening ('Danfoss')* [1991] ICR 74). In two subsequent cases, however, the CJEU appeared to doubt the correctness of *Danfoss* or at least have second thoughts as to its general application: see *Nimz v Freie und Hansestadt Hamburg*: C-184/89 [1991] ECR 1-297 and *Gerster v Freistaat Bayern*: C-1/95 [1997] ECR I-5253, [1998] ICR 327. In *Cadman v Health and Safety Executive* the Court of Appeal therefore referred the issue to the CJEU again. The CJEU (Case C-17/05, [2006] IRLR 969) affirmed that, as a general rule, an employer may rely on seniority and length of service as being genuine material differences not requiring special justification or (at least where pay is based on a job evaluation system) evidence that the individual in question has indeed acquired experience during his or her years in service. However, the CJEU made clear that, if the complainant provides evidence capable of giving rise to 'serious doubts' as to whether the criterion of length of service is, in the circumstances, appropriate to attain the legitimate objective of rewarding experience which enables the worker to perform his duties better, then the burden will shift to the employer to justify in detail reliance on the criterion of length of service by proving, as regards the job in question, that length of service goes hand in hand with experience and that experience enables the worker to perform his duties better. The CA in *Wilson v Health and Safety Executive* [2009] EWCA Civ 1074, [2010] ICR 302 clarified the approach that should be taken to domestic cases involving a length of service criterion in the light of the CJEU decision in *Cadman*. The CA ruled that, so far as domestic law is concerned, the "serious doubts" test put forward by the CJEU in *Cadman* is only of relevance before trial (presumably as a ground for 'strike out'). The CA said that what a claimant needs to show, pre-trial, is that there is evidence from which, if established at trial, it can properly be found that the general rule in *Danfoss* and *Cadman* (that seniority and length of service are generally material differences other than sex) does not apply. The CA confirmed, however, that a claim involving a length of service criterion is to be approached in essentially the same way as any other equal pay claim involving indirect discrimination. The burden is on the claimant to show disparate impact and, if that is established, the burden shifts to the employer either to explain or justify the difference as necessary (see further the discussion at **21.10** above). The CA noted (at 52) that the Tribunal had allowed the employer a 'margin of appreciation' in relation to objective justification in this case. The CA indicated that there was no error of law in that approach.

In *Secretary of State for Justice v Bowling* [2012] IRLR 382 the EAT (Underhill P presiding) held that a salary point scale applied by the civil service amounted to a good GMF defence. The salary scale explained the difference in pay between the claimant and her comparator. It continued to explain the differential throughout the claimant's employment and there was no reason to suppose that there was any sex taint in the application of the salary scale. A similar approach was adopted in *Skills Development Scotland Co Limited v Buchanan and others* [2011] UKEATS/0042/10 in which the EAT (Lady Smith presiding) held that transferred terms and conditions of employment which required future increases in salary amounted to a genuine material factor which explained the difference in pay throughout the period and which were not sex-tainted.

Market forces

One 'extrinsic factor' which may, in certain circumstances, justify a difference in pay is the scarcity of suitably qualified employees to fill a particular post. In such circumstances, an employer may be able to justify a resultant difference in pay as consisting of a necessary premium paid to obtain the scarce skills which the more highly paid employee has to offer (*Enderby v Frenchay Health Authority* [1994] ICR 112). Note that it is for the employer to show that the market dictated the higher rate of pay and not for the Claimant to show that the pay was too high: see *Cumbria County Council v Dow and ors* [2008] IRLR 91, EAT. In *Ratcliffe v North Yorkshire County Council* (above) the women concerned, who were catering assistants, had been the subject of a job-evaluation exercise. Their job had been rated as equivalent to that of certain other employees engaged in very different jobs and they had received the same pay. Their function was subject to competitive tendering. A competing company had much lower overheads as it paid its (largely female) staff lower wages than those paid by the Council. In order properly to compete, the Council believed it needed to reduce the pay of its own catering assistants. The majority of the tribunal found that whilst there was a material difference between the circumstances of the women and their comparators, namely that the women were employed in functions which had to be subjected to the market, the market itself was not sexually neutral and therefore the material difference was 'due to [a] difference in sex'. The catering sector was regarded as 'women's work' and the pay of those employed by the competing company, was discriminatorily low. The Court of Appeal disagreed ([1994] IRLR 342). It found that the defence was made out on the controversial basis that even if the competing company's pay rates were discriminatory it did not follow that the Council discriminated if it lowered its own rates in order to compete. The decision of the House of Lords in *Ratcliffe* ([1995] IRLR 439) is not a model of clarity. What is clear is that their Lordships found that the tribunal was entitled to reach the view that the defence had not been made out. It does not appear, however, that the basis of the decision was that the pay reduction was tainted by the competing company's discrimination. Lord Slynn noted (ibid, at 442): 'The fact, if it be a fact, that [the competing company] discriminated against women in respect of pay and that the [Council] had to pay no more than [the competing company] in order to be competitive does not however conclude the issue'. Unfortunately, it is not clear, from what follows, what their Lordships considered to be the conclusive factor. 'The basic question is whether the [Council] paid women less than men for work rated as equivalent. The reason they did so is certainly that they had to compete . . . The fact, however, is that they did pay women less than men engaged on work rated as equivalent. The employment tribunal found and was entitled to find that the employers had not shown that this was genuinely due to a material difference other than a difference of sex.' The decision does not, in the view of the author, mean that the need to establish or maintain a difference in pay will never found a successful *s 1(3)* defence, merely that the employer had not discharged the burden in the particular case.

Pay protection arrangements

In some cases where an employer has identified that there is an 'equal pay issue' as between two groups of employees, the employer has sought to equalise pay over the course of a number of years, by gradually reducing the pay of the highest-paid group, but in the meantime offering 'pay protection' to existing employees within that group. In *s 69(3)* of *EA 2010* a statutory basis for the lawfulness of 'pay protection' policies is provided. *Section 69(3)* provides that "the long-term objective of reducing inequality between men's and women's terms of work is always to be regarded as a legitimate aim". However, it does not follow that an employer who has made use of a pay protection policy will be able to succeed in the material factor defence. Employment tribunals are likely to scrutinise carefully a pay protection policy, in order to determine whether or not it is proportionate as to achieving any legitimate aim, particularly where the employer has already recognised that differentials in pay are tainted by historic discrimination.

In *Bainbridge v Redcar and Cleveland Borough Council/Surtees v Middlesbrough Borough Council (Bainbridge/Surtees)* [2008] EWCA Civ 885, [2008] IRLR 776, CA, the Council sought to justify a four-year 'pay protection' scheme introduced in the aforementioned circumstances on grounds that may broadly be described as cost (ie because it would have been too expensive to pay the predominantly female group more) and employee relations (ie in relation to the predominantly male group). However, the CA (and EAT) approved the Tribunal's finding that the Council had failed to establish the genuine material factor defence because the 'pay protection' policy was irredeemably tainted by sex discrimination as it amounted to perpetuating the benefit of the past sex discrimination. The Council's argument was that there was nothing inherently discriminatory in providing a 'soft landing' to protect employees from a sudden and drastic drop in pay. The Court of Appeal rejected the claimants' argument that as a matter of law, giving pay protection to the beneficiaries of past pay discrimination was always a breach of the *EqPA 1970*. However, the Court of Appeal also rejected the Council's argument that there was no *prima facie* sex discrimination in respect of the pay protection and held that the tribunal was right to look at the underlying reason for the pay protection and to find that it was causally related to historic unlawful sex discrimination. The burden of proof then shifted to the Council to objectively justify this *prima facie* discrimination. The Court of Appeal's judgment is not wholly clear as to when and how this can be justified, holding both that: (a) justification will be difficult where the employer knew or strongly suspected that there was past pay discrimination (see paragraph 133 of *Bainbridge/Surtees*), and/or (b) where the employer knows it is perpetuating past discrimination this can be justified if it considers the matter carefully and there is a good reason for pay protection to be offered only to the losers (paragraphs 149, 156 and 173 of *Bainbridge/Surtees*). Although the Court of Appeal in *Bainbridge/Surtees* was keen to stress the point made in the EAT that its decision did not rule out all 'pay protection' policies, its decision has in practice left employers conducting a job evaluation scheme in a Catch 22 situation; the 'losers' will be unhappy if they do not receive 'pay protection' but the 'winners' will be unhappy at what they now see as historic pay discrimination.

21.12 Equal Pay

See now *Bury Metropolitan Borough Council v Hamilton* [2011] IRLR 358 in which the EAT has sought to clarify the approach that should be taken to pay protection cases. The EAT ruled that in any case where past direct discrimination has been 'recognised', the continuation for the future of such discrimination in the form of transitional or phasing-out arrangements cannot be justified. However, transitional arrangements that continue past indirect discrimination (as to which see below) will not be unlawful if they can be justified. In order to establish justification the employer will need in all cases to advance cogent and specific reasons for the pay protection arrangements. Where cost is relied on as a reason for justifying the arrangements, evidence of the costs themselves and the financial context must be adduced. Mere assertions of unaffordability will not suffice. The tribunal will need to apply the proportionality test. In doing so it will be relevant to consider the employer's state of knowledge about the discriminatory effect of his provisions and the extent to which he tries to minimise that effect. However, note the earlier, partly contradictory, EAT decision in *Pulham and ors v London Borough of Barking & Dagenham* [2010] ICR 333 (an age discrimination case), in which the EAT held that if an employer has recognised that a particular practice or policy may be discriminatory, it will not be possible for the employer to justify continuing that practice or policy even on a transitional or phasing-out basis. This case does, though, make the important point that the fact that the pay protection arrangements have been agreed with a trade union or workforce representatives will be relevant, but that fact does not relieve the employer and, in turn, the Tribunal from independently considering whether the arrangements are justified.

See *Audit Commission v Haq (S)* [2012] EWCA Civ 1621, [2013] IRLR 206 for a case in which pay protection arrangements were held to be pursuing a legitimate aim and to be justified. In that case, the EAT overturned the ET's decision on this point, and the EAT's judgment on this issue was upheld by the CA on appeal. The CA held that the ET had been wrong in law in rejecting the Commission's aims in this regard as illegitimate. The CA also considered that it was legitimate for an employer to take into account that without the pay protection arrangements the Commission might have been prejudiced as a result of losing the services of the employees in question.

Industrial relations

Good industrial relations may be taken into account as one factor among others in deciding whether a difference in pay is objectively justified by factors unrelated to any discrimination on grounds of sex: *Kenny and ors v Minister for Justice, Equality and Law Reform* Case C 427/11 at para 50. Good industrial relations cannot be used as a factor on its own justifying discrimination, however, because the interests of good relations are also subject to the observance of the principle of non-discrimination (*Kenny* ibid para 48). Further, collective agreements, like individual worker contracts, and legislative provisions, must not discriminate unlawfully between men and women: *Enderby v Frenchay Health Authority* ([1994] ICR 112 at para 21.

However, in equal value claims, differences in contractual entitlements sometimes arise from the complainant and her comparator having been represented by different negotiating bodies. The justificatory force of this factor was considered by the CJEU in *Enderby*. In *Enderby* a woman employed as a speech therapist sought to establish an inequality of pay by comparing herself with two men – a clinical psychologist and a pharmacist. It having been established that the woman was engaged in work of equal value to that of the comparators, the employer sought to justify the difference in pay by showing that the pay rates had resulted from different collective bargaining processes, each of which was free from any sex bias. The CJEU found, in effect, that whilst this explained the difference in pay it did not, where the complainant's job was 'carried out almost exclusively by women and the [comparator's] . . . predominantly by men', objectively justify it and in those circumstances the employer did not have a defence. This 'almost exclusively by women' formula has given rise to a number of difficulties of interpretation (see above **21.11**). In relation to the question of the significance of representation by different negotiating bodies, the Court of Appeal in *British Road Services Ltd v Loughran* [1997] IRLR 92, CA made it clear that the *Enderby* decision does not decide that the factor can never justify a difference in pay. They also rejected an argument that the mere fact of there being different bargaining structures would always justify a disparity in pay, provided that the group of employees engaged to perform the complainant's job is not comprised 'almost exclusively' of women. Instead, they decided that if there is a 'significant proportion of women' in the claimant's group, the tribunal is obliged to look carefully at the bargaining structures in order to satisfy itself that there was no discriminatory effect.

In *Bainbridge/Surtees* (supra), the Court of Appeal rejected an argument that the difference in pay (an attendance allowance paid to a predominantly male group of employees) was the result of separate collective bargaining which was a non-sex based reason for the difference. The Court of Appeal held that separate collective bargaining could be a GMF defence but that the tribunal had been entitled to infer that there was a sex-taint where there was a marked difference in the sex balance between the two groups and there was no other reason to explain the difference in pay so that the fact of separate collective bargaining would not, of itself, be likely to disprove the possibility of sex discrimination. See also *Grundy v British Airways plc* [2008] EWCA Civ 875, [2008] IRLR 815 where the Court of Appeal held that attention had to be paid by negotiators of collective agreements to the possibility that such differentials would have a disparate impact on employees of one gender. If that was overlooked, with a consequent breach of one group's equality clauses, the oversight could not logically be justified by reference to the collective agreement which resulted.

In *Coventry City Council v Nicholls* [2009] IRLR 345, Elias P rejected an argument that the pay differential was adequately explained by a 'supervening cause', namely the alleged intransigence of the trade unions to reaching an agreement on single status pay arrangements which would have equalised pay. The EAT held that 'union hostility to change is incapable of constituting a new explanation for the difference in pay such that it can be said that a pay differential whose roots lay firmly in sex discrimination, has at some indeterminate point ceased to have anything to do with sex . . . properly analysed, the union's stance may be said to explain why the discrimination was not removed earlier than it was, but it does not supersede, in the sense of replacing, the original discriminatory explanation for the difference in pay'. In any event, 'ultimately the ability to remedy unequal pay was always in the council's own hands . . . .'.

Cost

It was for a long time been established that budgetary factors alone cannot justify discrimination against one of the sexes (*Schonheit v Stadt Frankfurt Am Main* [2004] IRLR 983), although it was widely accepted that cost considerations could be prayed in aid where the difference in pay was objectively justified by some other factor (*Cross v British Airways plc* [2006] EWCA Civ 549, [2006] ICR 1239, *Redcar & Cleveland Borough Council v Bainbridge* [2007] IRLR 91, EAT and *Osborne Clarke Services v Purohit* [2009] IRLR 341). See also *Pulham and ors v London Borough of Barking and Dagenham* [2010] ICR 333 in which the EAT accepted that cost could form part of a defence of justification for pay protection arrangements and that in such cases it is not necessary for there to be precise evidence on costs: some indication of the 'broad scale' of costs will do. In that case the EAT also observed that, although it is open to an employer to rely on the fact that the particular budget to which the cost in question has been allocated is exhausted, this should never be regarded as a determinative factor since the allocation of cost centres to particular budgets is a matter that it is within the employer's power to vary if necessary. The EAT also observed that, although relevant, it is not sufficient for an employer to rely on the fact that a particular budget has been exhausted since the budget to which a particular cost is allocated is a matter for the employer. In *Woodcock v Cumbria Primary Care Trust* [2011] IRLR 119 the EAT expressed the view (*obiter*) that, as a matter of principle and of common sense, there should be no rule that considerations of cost could never be sufficient on their own to justify indirect discrimination. However, on appeal the Court of Appeal ([2012] EWCA Civ 330) reaffirmed the orthodox position justification by reference to costs alone is impermissible. Most recently, in *Ministry of Justice v O'Brien* [2013] UKSC 6, [2013] 1 WLR 522 the Supreme Court reviewed the relevant authorities in the context of a claim under the *Part-time Workers (Prevention of Less Favourable Treatment) Regulations 2000* and reached the conclusion (at paragraph 69) that cost could not be relied on in order to justify discrimination (i.e. even in combination with other factors). That said, the Court did not consider it needed to decide whether *Woodcock v Cumbria Primary Care Trust* had been wrongly decided.

Although the Supreme Court has now held that cost cannot justify indirect discrimination, there are in fact a number of cases where the Tribunals and Courts have reached conclusions that could be characterized as being findings that costs alone can justify discrimination and which may continue to be followed despite the Supreme Court's ruling. Thus the courts appear to have had little difficulty with the notion that measures intended to avoid a 'windfall' or 'excessive compensation' to the employee – measures which the employer will inevitably have introduced to save itself money – have been held to be justified: see *Loxley v BAE Systems (Munitions & Ordnance) Ltd* [2008] ICR 1348, [2008] IRLR 853 and *Kraft Foods UK Ltd v Hastle* [2010] ICR 1355. That said, it should be noted that in those cases, the payments in question were held to serve some other legitimate purpose and so the courts were able to regard the quantum of the payment as being an aspect of the proportionality of the means of meeting the legitimate aim of (for eg in the case of severance pay) paying a reasonable sum of money on termination of employment to allow the employees time to find a new job. *HM Land Registry v S M Benson and ors* [2012] ICR 627 is another apparently anomalous case. Here, the EAT found that the Tribunal had wrongly found an employer's use of a 'cheapness criterion' in a redundancy situation to be unjustified indirect age discrimination. The EAT held that the 'cheapness criterion' fulfilled a legitimate aim of saving the employer money, and that it was justified because there was no practicable alternative means of achieving the same aim and the measure was not disproportionate. It is notable, however, that the case seems to have been decided by the EAT without reference to the authorities for the general principle that costs alone cannot justify discrimination.

Given these anomalous cases, and given that so far as disability discrimination is concerned costs can effectively justify indirect discrimination because it can be a reason why it is not reasonable to make an adjustment for a disabled person (see eg *Cordell v Foreign & Commonwealth Office* [2012] ICR 280 and **10.43 DISCRIMINATION AND EQUAL OPPORTUNITIES – I**), prior to *O'Brien* (ibid) the time appeared to be ripe for the CJEU to consider again whether or not costs alone can be relied on as justifying indirect discrimination. However, following *O'Brien* there is little prospect of any reference on that point being made from the UK in the near future.

Mistake

In the absence of direct or prima facie indirect discrimination, a mistake may provide a good material factor defence: see **21.10** above. See *Yorkshire Blood Transfusion Service v Plaskitt* [1994] ICR 74, *Tyldesley v TML Plastics Ltd* [1996] ICR 356 (approved by the House of Lords in *Strathclyde Regional Council v Wallace* [1998] ICR 205, HL and *Glasgow City Council v Marshall* [2000] ICR 196, HL); *Parliamentary Comr for Administration v Fernandez* [2004] ICR 123; and *King's College London v Clark* (2003) IDS Brief 747, p 11 (in which the EAT held that a mistake and a TUPE transfer adequately explained the difference in pay).

21.13 TRANSSEXUALS

In order to take advantage of the right to equal pay conferred on transsexuals, a person must:

(a)   intend to undergo, be undergoing or have undergone a gender reassignment (*SDA 1975, s 2A*) (for the definition of gender reassignment see **10.21 DISCRIMINATION AND EQUAL OPPORTUNITIES – I**);

(b)   be engaged under a 'contract of service or of apprenticeship, or a contract personally to execute any work or labour' (*SDA 1975, s 82(1)*); and

(c)   not do their work wholly outside Great Britain (*SDA 1975, ss 6(1), 10(1)*) (for exceptions, see **11.5** DISCRIMINATION AND EQUAL OPPORTUNITIES – II).

Certain ministers of religion are also excluded (see **11.11(g)** DISCRIMINATION AND EQUAL OPPORTUNITIES – II).

An employer must not, in relation to matters of pay, discriminate directly against a transsexual (see **10.21** et seq DISCRIMINATION AND EQUAL OPPORTUNITIES – I). There is no prohibition on indirect discrimination against transsexuals. This limited the effectiveness of the protections for transsexuals prior to the coming into force of the *Gender Recognition Act 2004* ('*GRA 2004*') on 1 July 2004. Thus, where, for example, an occupational pension scheme provided for benefits payable to be dependent on marital status, that was indirectly discriminatory against transsexuals who could not marry in their reassigned gender. However, such discrimination was not unlawful under the *SDA 1975*. In *KB v National Health Service Pensions Agency: C-117/01* [2004] ICR 781, the CJEU considered whether this situation was contrary to *art 157* of the *Treaty*. It noted that a failure to recognise a transsexual's reassigned gender and to permit them to marry was a breach of the *European Convention on Human Rights* (*Goodwin v United Kingdom* (2002) 35 EHRR 447, ECtHR) and went on to rule that the situation was also incompatible with *art 157* of the *Treaty*. However, also in line with the ECtHR, the CJEU held that it was for the member states to determine the conditions under which legal recognition is given to a change of gender. Accordingly, the court ruled that it was for the national court to determine whether a transsexual was able to rely on *art 157* in order to gain recognition of her right to nominate her partner as the beneficiary of a survivor's pension. Under the *GRA 2004*, transsexuals are now able to apply for a gender recognition certificate, and may marry in their reassigned gender. The decision in *KB* will still be relevant for transsexuals who have not obtained such a certificate. (For claims relating to pension entitlements generally, see **21.16** below.)

The normal time limits for a sex discrimination claim apply to claims of discrimination by transsexuals. The claim must be lodged with the tribunal within three months of the date on which the last act of discrimination occurred (*SDA 1975, s 76(1)*). In this respect, the limitation is less generous than that applicable to claims brought under the *EqPA 1970* which allow claims to be made within six months of the termination of the complainant's employment (*EqPA 1970, s 2(4)*). However, the *SDA 1975* time limit may be disapplied where the tribunal considers it just and equitable that it should do so (*SDA 1975, s 76(5)*). The complainant is also spared the cumbersome tribunal procedure applicable to equal pay claims (for which see **21.21** below). Compensation may include an award for injury to feelings. Further, where an award of compensation is made, interest is payable pursuant to the *Employment Tribunals (Interest on Awards in Discrimination Cases) Regulations 1996 (SI 1996/2803)*. (See generally DISCRIMINATION AND EQUAL OPPORTUNITIES – III (12).)

The prohibition on discrimination against those who are proposing to undergo, are undergoing or have undergone a process of gender reassignment (including in respect of arrangements in relation to pay) is set out in *ss 4* and *7* as well as *Chapter 2* of *Part 2* of *EA 2010*.

21.14 MATERNITY PAY

(See generally MATERNITY AND PARENTAL RIGHTS (31).)

The *EqPA 1970* had been amended (with effect from 1 October 2005) to expressly provide for the equality clause to apply to maternity-related pay in certain circumstances: *reg 36* of the *Employment Equality (Sex Discrimination) Regulations 2005*. Section *1(2)* of the *EqPA*

1970 then provided for the equality clause to apply to pay increases and bonus in certain circumstances. The *EA 2010* was not intended to make substantive changes to the law. *Section 73* provides for a 'maternity equality clause' to be included in a contract of employment. Under *s 74* the maternity equality clause operates on a contract of employment in the same manner as *s 1(2)(d)* to *(f)* of *EqPA 1970* previously operated.

Section 1(2)(d) of the *EqPA 1970* provided for the calculation of maternity-related pay as follows, where:

(i)   any term of the woman's contract regulating maternity-related pay provides for any of her maternity-related pay to be calculated by reference to her pay at a particular time (now *EA 2010, s 74(1)*),

(ii)   after that time (but before the end of the statutory maternity leave period) her pay is increased, or would have increased had she not been on statutory maternity leave (now *EA 2010, s 74(2)*), and

(iii)   the maternity-related pay is neither what her pay would have been had she not been on statutory maternity leave nor the difference between what her pay would have been had she not been on statutory maternity leave and any statutory maternity pay to which she is entitled (now *EA 2010, s 74(3)*),

if (apart from the equality clause) the terms of the woman's contract do not provide for the increase to be taken into account for the purpose of calculating the maternity-related pay (now *EA 2010, s 74(4)*), the term mentioned in sub-paragraph (i) above shall be treated as so modified as to provide for the increase to be taken into account for that purpose.'

'Maternity-related pay' was defined in *s 5A* of the *EqPA 1970* as follows:

pay (including pay by way of bonus) to which she is entitled as a result of being pregnant or in respect of times when she is on statutory maternity leave, except that it does not include any statutory maternity pay to which she is entitled.

Statutory maternity leave included ordinary maternity leave, additional maternity leave and compulsory maternity leave: *s 5B* of the *EqPA 1970* (as amended). (See now *EA 2010, s 74(9)*.)

Pay increases following a return from statutory maternity leave were governed by *s 1(2)(f)* of the *EqPA 1970* (as amended) as follows:

if (apart from the equality clause) the terms of the woman's contract regulating her pay after returning to work following her having been on statutory maternity leave provide for any of that pay to be calculated without taking into account any amount by which her pay would have increased had she not been on statutory maternity leave, the woman's contract shall be treated as including a term providing for the increase to be taken into account in calculating that pay.

See now *EA 2010, s 74(8)*.

Again, with effect from 1 October 2005, *s 1(2)(e)* of the *EqPA 1970* (as amended) provided for contractual bonuses to be paid as follows:

if (apart from the equality clause) the terms of the woman's contract as to—

(i)   pay (including pay by way of bonus) in respect of times before she begins to be on statutory maternity leave,

(ii)   pay by way of bonus in respect of times when she is absent from work in consequence of the prohibition in section 72(1) of the Employment Rights Act 1996 (compulsory maternity leave), or

(iii)   pay by way of bonus in respect of times after she returns to work following her having been on statutory maternity leave, do not provide for such pay to be paid when it would be paid but for her having time off on statutory maternity leave, the woman's contract shall be treated as including a term providing for such pay to be paid when ordinarily it would be paid.

(See now *EA 2010, s 74(6)* and *(7)*.)

The CJEU held in *Gillespie v Northern Health and Social Services Board: C-342/93* [1996] IRLR 214, that women whose pay is reduced when they are suspended on maternity grounds may not seek to challenge the reduction by bringing claims under *EqPA 1970*. This position was compatible with *art 157*: a woman absent on maternity leave is not entitled to full pay. Women taking maternity leave are in a unique position which is not comparable with that of a man actually at work (see **10.9** DISCRIMINATION AND EQUAL OPPORTUNITIES   I). However, that does not mean that a woman is excluded from all equal pay rights while on maternity leave. The following case-law will remain relevant for pre-1 October 2005 cases and any cases not covered by the amendments to the *EqPA 1970* and/or the *EA 2010*.

Any increases in pay awarded during a woman's maternity leave must be taken into account when calculating the amount of maternity pay to which a woman is entitled, regardless of whether that increase is backdated to the reference period for calculating statutory maternity pay (as it was in *Gillespie*) or is awarded with only prospective effect at any time up until the end of the maternity leave (*Alabaster v Woolwich plc and Secretary of State for Social Security*: C-147/02 [2005] ICR 695 and *Alabaster v Barclays Bank (No 2)* [2005] EWCA Civ 508, [2005] IRLR 576). This principle was given statutory force in the amended *EqPA 1970* and now in the *EA 2010*.

In *Edwards v Derby City Council* [1999] ICR 114, the EAT considered an unusual case in which the male comparator was in receipt of full pay even though he was not at work. The complainant was a teacher absent on maternity leave and in receipt of half-pay. Her maternity leave overlapped with a half-term holiday. Had she not been absent on maternity leave, she would have received full pay without having to attend work. The EAT rejected her claim that she should have received full pay during the half-term period, relying on *Gillespie* as authority for the proposition that a woman absent on maternity leave was in a unique position which could not be compared with that of those working normally even if, in the particular circumstances, that might include periods in which no actual duties were performed. The decision was made, however, before the CJEU gave its ruling in *Boyle v Equal Opportunities Commission*: C-411/96 [1998] ECR I-6401, [1999] ICR 360, CJEU. In that case, EOC employees absent on maternity leave were entitled to three months' full pay and thereafter a period at a reduced rate. Those absent as a result of sickness were entitled to six months' full pay. In the fourth month of an absence, therefore, an employee absent through sickness would receive more than an employee absent on maternity leave. An employee fell sick during her maternity leave and wished to be put on sick leave. The EOC's contract of employment allowed the employee to move onto sick leave but only on the basis that the maternity leave was terminated. The CJEU decided that the provision was discriminatory. The employee had to be allowed to swap into a period of sick leave and then to swap back. *Boyle* is an example of a case where it has been decided, in effect, that though a pregnant woman is not comparable to a man with an illness, a pregnant woman with an illness may be treated as being comparable (see also *Handels-og Kontorfunktionaernes Forbund I Danmark, acting on behalf of Hoj Pederson v Faelesforeningen for Danmarks Brugsforninger, acting on behalf of Kvickly Skive*: C-66/760 [1999] IRLR 55: national legislation providing that men who are unfit to work through illness should receive full pay but women absent from work as a result of a pregnancy-related condition should not, is contrary to *art 157*; *Osterreichischer Gewerkschaftsbund v Wirtschaftskammer Osterreich* (2004) 760 IDS Brief, p 9: period of voluntary parental leave not comparable to compulsory military or civilian service; cf also *P & O European Ferries (Dover) Ltd v Iverson* (1999) IDS Brief 640, p 6).

21.14   Equal Pay

In *Abdoulaye v Regie National des Usines Renault SA*: C-218/98 [1999] IRLR 811, the CJEU had to consider a provision in a collective agreement which governed the terms and conditions of Renault employees. Female employees not only continued to receive their full salary whilst on maternity leave but also received a lump sum to compensate them for the 'occupational disadvantages' that arose from their absence. Male employees argued that new fathers should receive the same bonus. However, the court decided that men were not subject to the same disadvantages. Unlike the women, they did not lose the chance of promotion or the right to performance-related pay for the period of maternity leave, nor did they suffer the resulting loss in the length of service.

The CJEU considered yet another variation on the theme of payments due or refused to those on maternity leave in *Lewen v Denda*: C-333/97 [2000] IRLR 67. A firm paid Christmas bonuses to those in 'active' employment on 1 December each year. The complainant was absent on maternity leave on the relevant date. She was refused a bonus and claimed that her employers had breached *art 157*. The court felt that the result hinged upon the nature of the payment. A requirement that an employee should be in active employment was not discriminatory if the purpose of the payment was to encourage those at work to be loyal and to work hard in the following year. If, on the other hand, the purpose of the payment was to reward the employees for having worked hard in the previous year, it would be discriminatory to refuse to make any payment at all to those absent on parental leave. An employer could legitimately pro-rate the bonus to take account of the employee's absence from work, provided no account was taken of any period during which, by reason of her pregnancy, the employee was prohibited from attending work. For an example of a permissible proportionate reduction in bonus paid in recognition of work undertaken by the workforce during a period of ordinary maternity leave, see also, *Hoyland v Asda Stores Ltd* [2006] IRLR 468 (Court of Session).

Gruber v Silhouette International Schmeid GmbH & Co KG: C-249/97 [1999] ECR I-5295, p 8 was a case concerned with termination payments. In Austria, those who simply resign from employment receive no payment. However, those who resign for 'important reasons' and who have been employed for more than three years receive a payment. The European court determined that the 'important reasons' justifying payments had in common that they were all either concerned with poor working conditions or with misconduct on the part of the employer. Those who work for longer than five years and resign within a certain period after childbirth receive smaller payments. The complainant, who resigned after having had a child, argued that she should be entitled to compare herself with those who resigned for 'important reasons' and to pay her a reduced sum resulted in discrimination contrary to *art 157*. The court rejected her argument. Her situation was not analogous to that of someone who resigned because of poor working conditions or employer misconduct. That being so, her proposed comparison, and thus her claim, was ill-founded.

The suggestion in *Gillespie* that women absent on maternity leave are not entitled to receive pay is subject to an important qualification. The CJEU did suggest in *Gillespie* that 'the amount payable [to a woman absent on maternity leave] could not . . . be so low as to undermine the purpose of maternity leave, namely the protection of women before and after giving birth'. The *Pregnant Workers Directive EEC/92/85* requires member states to provide that women absent from work on maternity leave receive an 'adequate allowance' for 14 weeks (*arts 8(1)* and *11(2)(b)*). An allowance will be adequate provided that it is at least equivalent to what the employee would receive if she were absent through illness. In effect it requires that SMP should be at least as generous as SSP. A number of cases have since raised claims that sums received by the complainants during maternity leave did not amount to an 'adequate allowance'. In *Iske v P & O European Ferries (Dover) Ltd* [1997] IRLR 401, the EAT was asked to consider the adequacy of SMP. It declined to do so, although it suggested that it might have been prepared to consider the issue had the respondent been an emanation of the state. In *Gillespie v Northern Health and Social Services Board (No 2)* [1997] IRLR 410, the Northern Ireland Court of Appeal rejected a complaint that an

The statutory scheme under *PA 1995* had an unusual interrelation with the *EqPA 1970*. By *PA 1995, s 63(4)*, *s 62* of that *Act* should be construed 'as one' with *EqPA 1970, s 1*. The *PA 1995* did not introduce any new enforcement mechanism. Instead, it extended the existing *EqPA 1970* measures (*ss 2* and *2A*) to cover the enforcement of the equal treatment rule.

The provisions were supplemented by the *Occupational Pension Schemes (Equal Treatment) Regulations 1995 (SI 1995/3183) ('OPS(ET) Regulations 1995')*. The *Regulations* provided that, save in cases where a claim is made by a retired employee (*reg 7*), the tribunal had no power to make any award of compensation in relation to an alleged breach of an equal treatment rule (*reg 3*). Instead, the tribunal was given a power to declare that the equal treatment rule had been breached. Where the complaint related to access to membership of the scheme, the tribunal could make a declaration that the employee is or was entitled to membership of the scheme (*reg 5*). The declaration of entitlement to join has to specify a 'deemed entry date' which may not be more than two years before the institution of proceedings (*reg 5*). Declarations that the rule had been breached in relation to terms on which members are treated could not relate to any period of service prior to 17 May 1990 (*reg 6*). In any case in which it is declared that the equal treatment rule had been breached, the employer could be required to provide additional resources so as to give effect to the declaration or, in the case of pensioner members, to provide the necessary funds for an award of compensation. The additional resources must be provided without recourse to additional contributions either from the complainant herself or any other member of the scheme (*regs 5–7*). Perhaps for this reason the employer was entitled to appear and be heard in any case in which it is alleged that the equal treatment rule had been breached whether or not it is specified as a respondent by the employee (*reg 4*).

The second relevant statute was *SDA 1975* (as amended by *PA 1995*) which prohibited discrimination against a woman in relation to her membership of, or rights under, an occupational pension scheme:

(a)   in the arrangements which an employer makes for the purpose of determining who should be offered employment;

(b)   in the terms on which it offers her employment;

(c)   by refusing or deliberately omitting to offer her employment;

(d)   in the way it affords her access to opportunities for promotion, transfer or training, or any other benefits, facilities or services, or by refusing or deliberately omitting to afford her access to them; or

(e)   by dismissing her, or subjecting her to any other detriment.

Otherwise, pension-related matters are excluded from the scope of *SDA 1975* by *s 6(4)* and *(4A)* save in relation to acts of pension-related discrimination against transsexuals (see above **21.13**).

The final element in the statutory scheme was *EqPA 1970* (again, as amended by *PA 1995*). *Section 6(1B)* extended the operation of the equality clause to cover any term in the contract relating to a person's membership of, or rights under, an occupational pension scheme, unless the term was one in relation to which the equal treatment rule would be excluded. The clause and the rule, therefore, have co-extensive scopes of operation. *OPS(ET) Regulations 1995* established a new enforcement regime. The regime was substantially identical to that applicable to claims based on an alleged breach of the equal treatment rule (see above). Again, unless the complainant is already retired (*reg 12*) no award of compensation could be made (*reg 9*). The relief available was declaratory, but the declaration could have the effect of requiring the employer to allocate resources to the pension scheme in order to give effect to the declaration (*regs 10–12*).

21.16   Equal Pay

SSA 1989, Sch 5, paras 5 and *6* also made provision for the protection of rights of access to, and to benefits under, a pension scheme for employees absent on maternity or family leave.

Note that the Pensions Ombudsman's decision that a pension rule excluding those who earn less than the lower earnings limit was indirectly discriminatory and infringed *art 157* (*Shillcock v Uppingham School* [1997] Pens LR 207) has been overturned on appeal (*Trustees of Uppingham School Retirement Benefit Scheme for Non-Teaching Staff v Shillcock* [2002] EWHC 641 (Ch), [2002] IRLR 702) where it was held that: (1) there was no difference in treatment where the purpose of the rule was to achieve a broad integration between benefits under the scheme and the provision of the state pension; and (2) in any event, the rule could be objectively justified where its purpose was to achieve integration with the state scheme (see *Birds Eye Walls Ltd v Roberts* [1994] IRLR 29). (As to claims based on *art 157*, see **21.18**, **21.19** and **21.22** below.)

(For pension claims by transsexuals see also **21.13** above.)

21.17   Barber and claims based on art 157

The impetus for the statutory scheme described above came from Europe. *Directive 86/378/EEC* required member states to introduce measures providing for equal rights to membership of occupational pension schemes by 1 January 1993. The UK had drafted legislation which was set out at *Social Security Act 1989, Sch 5* but before it could be brought into force it was overtaken by events, specifically the decision of the CJEU in *Barber*. The CJEU decided that pensions from both contributory and non-contributory schemes were 'pay' within the meaning of *art 157*. The effect of the decision was that an obligation not to discriminate in relation to access to, or benefits under, a pension scheme was found already to exist without the need for implementing domestic legislation.

The potential consequences of the decision were so great that the CJEU took the unusual step of specifically limiting the effect of its decision by stating that it could not be relied upon to claim entitlement to a pension with effect from a date prior to 17 May 1990 (the date of the decision) unless the applicant had already commenced proceedings by that date. It was not initially clear whether the limitation excluded all claims relating to periods of service before the stipulated date or only those where the benefits arising out of such service were also payable prior to 17 May 1990. The precise scope of the limitation was later clarified in *Ten Oever v Stichting Bedrijfspensioenfonds voor het Glazenwassers- en Schoonmaakbedrijf*: C-109/91 [1995] ICR 74, in which the CJEU determined that *Barber* only applied to benefits payable in respect of periods of service after 17 May 1990 (but cf *Dietz v Stichting Thuiszord Rotterdam*: C-435/93 [1996] IRLR 692 below). This interpretation corresponds with the Protocol to the Maastricht Treaty on European Union which reads as follows:

> 'Benefits under occupational pension schemes shall not be considered as remuneration if and insofar as they are attributable to periods of employment prior to 17 May 1990.'

The *Barber Protocol* applies only to claims relating to the level of benefit provided and not to claims alleging denial of access to benefits. For instance, the formerly commonplace refusal of pension schemes to admit part-time workers was indirectly discriminatory on grounds of sex. Where a former part-time employee complains that she was refused access to membership, the *Protocol* does not apply and her claim may, subject to any other domestic limitations, go back as far as 8 April 1976, that being the date on which the CJEU gave its decision in *Defrenne* (*Deutsche Telekom AG v Schröder*: C-50/96 [2000] ECR I-743, [2002] 2 CMLR 583) (see also below **21.19**).

In *Quirk v Burton Hospitals NHS Trust* [2002] EWCA Civ 149, [2002] IRLR 353, the Court of Appeal had to consider the effect of a provision in the *National Health Service Pension Scheme Regulations 1995* (*SI 1995/300*). Formerly, female members of the NHS Pension scheme could, in certain circumstances, retire early at 55. Men could only take early retirement once they were 60. The *1995 Regulations* corrected this discriminatory situation by providing that both men and women could retire at 55. However, whereas a woman retiring at 55 received a pension calculated by reference to her whole period of service, a man doing the same would receive a pension calculated by reference only to his service since 17 May 1990. Unsurprisingly, the woman's pension would be greater than that of a man with a comparable length of service. A male complainant sought to argue that the *1995 Regulations* were incompatible with *art 157*. He contended that the provision had the effect of precluding him from access to benefits in respect of his pre-1990 service. The Court of Appeal decided that, properly analysed, the case was not an 'access to benefits' case at all. The complainant was a member of the scheme. The contentious provision simply resulted in his receiving less money. It was, therefore, a 'level of benefit' case and the *Barber Protocol* applied. Lord Justice Buxton opined that the 'access'/'level of benefit' dichotomy was an unhelpful basis for analysis. The tribunal should ask itself whether the alleged discrimination relates to an age condition which varies according to sex. If it does, it is a case to which the *Barber Protocol* applies.

Following the *Barber* decision, a number of cases were referred to the CJEU with the intention of clarifying the difficult issues left unresolved by the *Barber* decision itself. The following matters have now been settled. Benefits payable to survivors fall within *art 157* (*Ten Oever v Stichting Bedrijfspensioenfonds voor het Glazenwassers en Schoonmaakbedrijf*: C-109/91 [1995] ICR 74) as do benefits payable under non-contracted out supplementary schemes (*Moroni v Collo GmbH*: C-110/91 [1995] ICR 137). Benefits payable under schemes which have at all times been 'single sex' are not, nor are benefits payable as a result of contributions made by employees on a voluntary basis, covered (*Coloroll Pension Trustees Ltd v Russell*: C-200/91 [1995] ICR 179).

Where a member state provides for men and women to become entitled to a State pension at different ages (eg in the UK women become so entitled at 60 whereas men become entitled at 65, although the *Pensions Act 1995* provides for progressive implementation of a common age of entitlement of 65 over a period of 10 years beginning on 6 April 2010), occupational pension schemes sometimes provide for payment of a 'bridging pension', the purpose of which is to ensure that employees, of whichever sex, receive the same total sum by way of pension when their State entitlements are aggregated to their entitlements under the scheme. Between the ages of 60 and 65 in the UK male and female employees would, under such a scheme, receive the same total sum but the male employees would receive substantially more from their employers. It follows, therefore, that under a 'bridging pension' male employees will receive more 'pay' than their female colleagues over the period. However, the State pension is not 'pay' for the purposes of *art 157* (see further 21.3 above). In *Roberts v Birds Eye Walls Ltd*: C-132/92 [1994] ICR 338 the CJEU held that it is not contrary to *art 157* to take account of an employee's entitlement to a State pension when calculating benefits payable under a bridging pension; see also *Trustees of Uppingham School Retirement Benefit Scheme for Non-Teaching Staff v Shillcock* [2002] EWHC 641 (Ch), [2002] IRLR 702. Inequality of employer's contributions to a scheme (as opposed to the benefits payable to the employee under the scheme) which result from the use of different actuarial factors for men and women is not contrary to *art 157* (*Neath v Hugh Steeper Ltd*: C-152/91 [1995] ICR 158 and *Coloroll Pension Trustees Ltd v Russell*: C-200/91 [1995] ICR 179).

Claims made in relation to pension inequality may be made against the trustees of the scheme as well as against the employer (*Coloroll* above). Claims may, of course, be made in respect of exclusion from membership of the scheme as well as in relation to the benefits payable under it. Where the employee has been excluded from the scheme, the *Barber* temporal limitation does not apply to the claim. That is true both in relation to the straightforward exclusion claim and, surprisingly, to any ancillary claim for non-payment of benefits (*Dietz v Stichting Thuiszorg Rotterdam*: C-298/94 [1996] IRLR 692). A woman seeking a remedy in respect of such a denial of access to membership must pay the contributions which she would have paid had she been admitted to membership at the appropriate time if she is to be entitled to any benefits under the scheme in respect of the period of her exclusion (*Fisscher v Voorhuis Hengelo BV*: C-128/93 [1995] ICR 635).

The CJEU has also given guidance on how a scheme should approach the task of modifying its rules so as to provide for equality. No action need be taken in relation to benefits payable in respect of periods of service prior to 17 May 1990 by reason of the temporal limitation established in *Barber*. Benefits payable in respect of the period between 17 May 1990 and the date on which the scheme is amended to provide for equality should be rounded up to the higher of the differential rates. After entitlements have been equalised, however, the scheme may reduce benefits overall provided that it is done in a way which involves no discrimination and which is consistent with the obligations of the employer and/or trustees under national laws and the contract of employment or rules of the scheme. Equalisation must be done in one step, it is not lawful for the employer or trustee to equalise benefits progressively over a transitional period (*Smith v Advel Systems Ltd*: C- 409/92 [1995] ICR 596). Schemes which reduced male entitlements to match female entitlements between 17 May 1990 and the date on which the discriminatory scheme was actually amended ('the *Barber* window') will be unlawful for that period, and male employees will be entitled to claim the difference in pension benefits attributable to any difference in pension entitlement arising during the *Barber* window: *Harland and Wolff Pension Trustees Ltd v Aon Consulting Financial Services Ltd* [2006] EWHC 1778 (Ch), [2007] ICR 429.

The decision of the CJEU in *Bestuur van het Algemeen Burgerlijk Pensioenfonds v Beune*: C-7/93 [1995] IRLR 103 settled a long-running controversy over whether benefits payable under schemes established by statute and applicable to State employees are 'pay' for the purposes of *art 157*. There was domestic authority to the effect that they were not (*Griffin v London Pensions Fund Authority* [1993] ICR 564, which concerned a Local Government Superannuation Scheme). In *Beune* benefits payable under the statutory scheme applicable to the Dutch civil service were held to fall within *art 157* on the basis that they complied with what the CJEU termed the 'only possible decisive criterion', namely, whether the pension is paid to the worker by reason of the employment relationship between himself and his former employer. Whilst being 'decisive' the criterion is not, according to the court, 'exclusive'. Some consideration of the balance between the relative importance to the determination of the benefits payable of social policy on the one hand, and employment-related questions on the other may still be necessary. Employment-related questions will include whether the scheme applies to a particular category of worker only and whether the benefits are directly related to length of service.

On 1 July 1997, *Directive 96/96/EC* came into force. It amended *Directive 86/378* to take account of the *Barber* decision and a number of the subsequent authorities.

21.18   The part-time workers litigation

The *Preston* litigation concerned claims brought by many thousands of part-time workers before employment tribunals alleging that they have been indirectly discriminated against as a result of having been refused membership of their occupational pension scheme on the ground that they worked part-time. Until it was amended by *PA 1995*, the *EqPA 1970* only prohibited directly discriminatory exclusion from membership. In the circumstances, each applicant relies upon *art 157* and the *Barber* decision to found his or her claim.

The cases raised many questions about whether employees may enforce rights based on European legislation in the domestic courts and tribunals and, if so, as to the appropriate procedural rules which apply to such claims. Such questions are dealt with in greater detail at **21.17** above in the context of a more general consideration of the application of *art 157* in the UK. In the *Preston* litigation, two points have now been resolved: firstly, the claims are brought in the employment tribunal on the basis that the incompatible domestic legislation should be disapplied rather than as a 'free standing' *art 157* claim (see further **21.22** below); and, secondly, the claimant's remedy is limited to a declaration of entitlement to membership of the relevant scheme and to benefits whilst a member.

The first series of test cases was considered by the Birmingham Employment Tribunal, and appeals from those decisions were decided by the EAT (*Preston v Wolverhampton Healthcare NHS Trust* [1996] IRLR 484), the Court of Appeal ([1997] IRLR 233), the House of Lords ([1998] ICR 227), the CJEU on a referral from the House of Lords ([2000] IRLR 506) and the House of Lords on its return from the CJEU ([2001] IRLR 237).

The CJEU in *Preston* held that the two-year limitation period for arrears of pay contained in *EqPA 1970, s 2(5)* was incompatible with Community law. On return to the House of Lords, their Lordships concluded that due to this incompatibility, the respondent employers could not rely on that section to defeat a claim for periods prior to the two years to be taken into account, subject to the employee paying contributions owing in respect of the period for which membership was claimed retroactively. Future pension benefits therefore had to be calculated by reference to full and part-time periods of service subsequent to 8 April 1976 as the date when the CJEU held in *Defrenne v Sabena*: C-43/75 [1976] ICR 547 that *art 157* had direct effect. See now the *Equal Pay Act 1970 (Amendment) Regulations 2003*.

In respect of the six-month limitation period formerly contained in *EqPA 1970, s 2(4)*, the CJEU held that the requirement to bring proceedings within six months of the termination of employment was not incompatible so long as such limitation period was not less favourable for actions based on Community law than for those based on domestic law. The CJEU decided that an action alleging a breach of the *Act* was not a domestic action 'similar' to a claim for infringement of *art 157*. The House of Lords on return held that the claim in Community law was to establish the right of retroactive access to the pension schemes. That was not similar in form to a claim in contract for damages but in substance the eventual benefit to the employee was sufficiently similar for the purposes of testing equivalence. Although the limitation period for a claim in contract was six years, that period did not run from the termination of employment. Since a claim in contract could only go back six years, whereas a claim brought within six months of termination could go back to the beginning of employment or 1976, it could not be said that the provisions of *EqPA 1970, s 2(4)* were less favourable than those applying to a claim in contract despite the apparent difference in length of the limitation periods. Therefore the provisions of *s 2(4)* did not violate Community law as to effectiveness and equivalence.

In relation to employees on successive short-term contracts, the House of Lords held that it was clear from the CJEU's judgment that where there were intermittent contracts of service without a 'stable employment relationship' the period of six months ran from the end of each contract, but where such contracts were concluded at regular intervals in respect of the same employment in a stable employment relationship the period ran from the end of the last contract. Their Lordships referred the question of which applicants were in stable employment relationships back to the employment tribunal.

After the employment tribunal's decisions in the test cases, a second round of appeals reached the Court of Appeal (*Preston v Wolverhampton Healthcare NHS Trust (No 3)* [2005] ICR 222 (*'Preston (No 3)'*). Three issues on appeal to the EAT related to the circumstances in which there would be a breach of the equality clause. The EAT held:

(1)   The equality clause is breached where part-time employees are excluded from a pension scheme that is available to full-time employees, irrespective of whether the part-time employee would have joined the scheme if it had been made available to her. However, in such a case, although there will always be a breach of the equality

clause, where an employee would not in fact have joined the pension scheme had she had the option to do so, no remedy will be granted. This 'opt out' principle has since been held to be compliant with EU law: see *Copple and others v Littlewoods Plc* [2012] IRLR 121, CA. In that case, the CA also emphasised that the burden is on the employee to show that she would have joined the scheme if it had been made available to her. In this respect, the CA noted that a Tribunal would be entitled to infer from failure to join the scheme once eligible to do so that the employee would not have joined the scheme during an earlier period had she not been wrongly excluded in breach of the equality clause. (See also *Andrews v Kings College Hospital NHS Foundation Trust* [2012] EqLR 1032.)

(2)   However, there is no breach of the equality clause where membership of the scheme is obligatory for full-time employees but only optional for part-time employees.

(3)   Although it had been (rightly) accepted before the tribunal that the imposition of a qualifying hours threshold in relation to membership of occupational pension scheme was a breach of the equality clause, where an employer removed that threshold but failed to inform his employees that was not itself either a breach or a continuing breach of the equality clause. It may well, however, be a breach of an implied term of the employment contract (see *Scally v Southern Health and Social Services Board* [1991] ICR 771, *Andrews v Kings College Hospital and anor* [2012] Eq LR 1032 and **7.9, 7.13** CONTRACT OF EMPLOYMENT).

A fourth issue concerned the limitation period: the EAT held that a 'stable employment relationship' consisting of a succession of short term contracts (see further below **21.19**) ceased, and the six-month limitation period began to run, where one of the two essential features of the relationship was no longer present, i.e. the same employment or periodicity of employment. These features will not be present where there is no longer an intention to employ, or to work, on a regular basis.

A fifth issue concerned the point at which the time limit begins to run where an employee's employment has been transferred from one employer ('the transferor') to a new employer ('the transferee') under the *Transfer of Undertakings (Protection of Employment) Regulations 1981* ('*TUPE*'; see TRANSFER OF UNDERTAKINGS **(50)**). The EAT held that time begins to run against the transferor from the end of the employee's employment with the transferee, and not from the date of the transfer. Only this last issue was appealed to the Court of Appeal in *Powerhouse Retail Ltd v Burroughs* [2004] EWCA Civ 1281. The Court of Appeal (affd [2006] UKHL 13, [2006] IRLR 381) reversed the EAT's decision and held that time runs for the purposes of a pensions claim from the date of the transfer, pensions being the one element of the contract of employment that does not transfer under *TUPE*. The EAT in *Sodexo Ltd v Gutridge* [2009] ICR 70, [2008] IRLR 752 confirmed that time runs from the date of the transfer for the purposes of all equal pay claims involving a *TUPE* transfer and that a transferred employee can claim against the transferee in respect of a pay inequality which arose during employment with the transferor (and see also *Trimble v North Lanarkshire Council* UKEATS/0048/12/BI). The decision in *Sodexo* was applied in *Foley and ors v NHS Greater Glasgow & Clyde* [2013] ICR 342. However, in *Foley*, the appellant employees sought to argue for the first time on appeal that this rule breached the principle of "effectiveness" under EU law because it was excessively difficult or virtually impossible in practice for a claimant to comply with it. The EAT refused to entertain this argument because there had been insufficient findings of fact by the ET for it to be properly considered. The argument therefore remains open for another day.

A further limitation issue was determined by the tribunal, but not appealed to the EAT or Court of Appeal. The tribunal held that, where a series of employments are covered by an overarching pensions scheme, time starts to run from the end of each employment and not from the end of the series (unless, of course, they are *TUPE* transfers, in which case they count as a single employment).It should also be noted that it was conceded before the tribunal that a male part-time worker could bring a claim if he could identify a female comparator with the right to join the pension scheme by operation of her equality clause (for another example of such a case, see *Pepper v Lancashire County Council* [2008] All ER (D) 122 (Jan)). In such cases, the part-time worker is permitted to join the scheme for the period during which he or she was forbidden to join the pension scheme by dint of the operation of the then rules on part-time workers. Whether or not such employees are entitled to make claims in respect of the period *after* the rules preventing part-time workers from joining the scheme had been amended will depend on the worker's reason for not joining the scheme at the point: see *Pepper*, ibid.

One of the questions referred to the CJEU in *Allonby v Accrington and Rossendale College* [2004] IRLR 224 was whether or not the requirement for a comparator was incompatible with EU law. The CJEU limited its ruling to the facts of that particular case, which concerned access to the statutory Teachers' Superannuation Scheme. It ruled that, where state legislation (such as the Teachers' Superannuation Scheme) was at issue, there is no need for an employee to point to a comparator: it will be sufficient to show statistical disadvantage. It seems that a comparator will still be necessary where state legislation is not in issue.

Information Bulletins and up-to-date information on the case management of the part-time pension claims can be found on the part-time worker pension cases section of the tribunal service website (www.justice.gov.uk/tribunals/employment/part-time-workers/faqs).

21.18ATHE EQUALITY ACT 2010 AND PENSIONS

EA 2010 attempts to codify the large number of provisions relating to sex discrimination and occupational pension schemes in one statute. As such, the case law under the previous pensions regime (above **21.15** to **21.18**) will remain relevant to cases under the *EA 2010*. In summary, the key provisions of the *EA 2010* are:

(a)   s 61 of *EA 2010* which provides for a non-discrimination rule in relation to every pension scheme and which will prohibit discrimination, harassment and victimisation in respect of a member or a person who become a member of an occupational pension scheme;

(b)   s 67 of *EA 2010* which provides for the operation of a sex equality rule in relation to the terms of an occupational pension scheme and which regulates both access to the occupational pension scheme and the treatment of members of an occupational pension scheme. In accordance with the decisions of the CJEU in *Barber v Guardian Royal Exchange Assurance Group* (supra) and *Defrenne v Sabena* (supra) discriminatory terms in relation to access to the pension scheme do not operate in relation to pensionable service prior to 8 April, 1976 (*s 67(9)*) and discriminatory terms in relation to which members of the scheme are treated does not operate prior to 17 May, 1990 (*s 67(10)*). *Section 67* of *EA 2010* replaces *s 62* of *PA 1995*;

(c)   s 68 of *EA 2010* which permits trustees and managers of occupational pension schemes to alter the scheme rules so as to comply with the sex equality rule. This provision replaces *s 65* of *PA 1995*;

(d)   s 75 of *EA 2010* which replaces *paragraph 5* of *schedule 5* to the *SSA* and which requires that a woman who is on maternity leave is entitled to continuing membership of an occupational pension scheme throughout any period of maternity leave and that a woman who is paid during maternity leave is entitled to accrue rights as though she were paid her usual salary notwithstanding that the woman is only required to make contributions to the scheme based on the pay that the woman actually receives.

21.18A Equal Pay

The rather strange method by which contractual terms providing for discriminatory access to an occupational pension were governed (see *s 6* of *EqPA 1970* and *OPS(ET) Regulations 1995*) has been removed by *EA 2010* and claims in respect of discriminatory terms of contracts which regulate access to an occupational pension scheme will be pursued in the same manner as all complaints of equal pay.

Under the *EA 2010, s 127(4)* an employment tribunal has jurisdiction to determine an application by the trustees or managers of an occupational pension scheme for a declaration as to their rights and those of a member in relation to a dispute about the effect of an equality rule (see above **21.18A**). The County Courts and High Court jurisdiction in relation to breaches of contract is expressly preserved (*s 127(9)*).

The remedies permitted in a 'pensions case' are governed by *s 133* of *EA 2010* and remain limited to declaratory relief, in relation to entitlement to join the pension scheme for the period after 8 April, 1976 and in relation to treatment as a member of the pension scheme for the period after 17 May, 1990.

Where claims are pursued by 'pensioner members' of an occupational pension scheme, the applicable remedies are set out in *s 134* of *EA 2010*. In such cases, the court or tribunal may award compensation as well as making a declaration (*s 134(2)*). Compensation may be awarded in respect of the period six years prior to the date on which proceedings were instituted, although in a 'concealment' or 'incapacity' case (see below **21.19A**), the 'arrears date' is six years from the date of the breach (*s 134(5)*). If the court or tribunal makes an award under this section, then the employer must provide such resources to the scheme as are necessary to secure for the complainant (without contribution or further contribution by the complainant or other members) the amount of the award (*s 134(4)*).

REMEDIES FOR UNEQUAL PAY

21.19 Jurisdiction of the employment tribunals

Any claim brought by virtue of the *EqPA 1970* or the equal pay provisions in the *EA 2010*, whether for arrears of remuneration or damages, may be brought before an employment tribunal (*EqPA 1970, s 2(1)* and *EA 2010, s 127*).

A tribunal can hear a case in the following circumstances:

(a) Where the employee is complaining about the breach of an equality clause or rule (*EqPA 1970, s 2(1)*, now *EA 2010, s 127(1)*).

(b) An employer may apply to the tribunal for an order declaring his and the employee's rights in relation to an equality clause (*EqPA 1970, s 2(1A)*, now *EA 2010, s 127(3)*).

(c) Under the *EqPA 1970, s 2(2)* the Secretary of State could refer a question to the tribunal on behalf of an aggrieved employee where it is not reasonable to expect the parties to take steps to have the question determined. No similar power is contained in the *EA 2010*.

(d) Under the *EA 2010, s 127(4)* an employment tribunal also has jurisdiction to determine an application by the trustees or managers of an occupational pension scheme for a declaration as to their rights and those of a member in relation to a dispute about the effect of an equality rule (see above **21.18A**).

(e) Where an equal pay claim is proceeding in the civil courts (see below **21.19E**), a court may on application of any party or of its own motion refer a question to an employment tribunal and stay the proceedings meanwhile (*EqPA 1970, s 2(3)*; now, *EA 2010, s 128(2)*).

Note that it will not necessarily be an abuse of process (and nor will a claim necessarily be *res judicata* or otherwise precluded by the rule in *Henderson v Henderson*) where a claimant, having been successful in one claim under the *EqPA 1970*, subsequently brings a second claim identifying a different (and more highly paid) comparator in respect of the same period of employment: *Bainbridge v Redcar and Cleveland Borough Council* [2007] IRLR 494, [2007] All ER (D) 409 (Mar), EAT.

21.19A Time limits

Prior to 19 July 2003, no claim in respect of an equality clause could be referred to an employment tribunal otherwise than by virtue of (*e*) above, unless the woman had been employed in the employment within the six months preceding the date of the reference. The question of the compatibility of this limitation period was referred to the CJEU by the House of Lords in *Preston v Wolverhampton Healthcare NHS Trust* [1998] ICR 227. The CJEU decided ([2000] IRLR 506) that the limitation was not, in principle, contrary to Community law. However, that decision was qualified in two respects. First, the CJEU stated that the national court would have to be satisfied that the limitation was not less favourable than the limitations applied to comparable domestic law claims. Second, the CJEU addressed the application of this limitation period to circumstances where an employee has been employed pursuant to a series of discrete contracts of employment. In *Preston* the CJEU held that the limitation should not apply from the date of termination of each employment contract in a case where the employee is engaged pursuant to a series of such contracts so that it can be said that a 'stable employment relationship' existed across the period of time covered by the individual contracts. On return to the House of Lords ([2001] IRLR 237), the six-month limitation period was held to be compatible with Community law but the issue of what constitutes a 'stable employment relationship' was remitted back to the employment tribunal: see **21.18** above for the progress of the *Preston* part-time workers pensions litigation.

With effect from 19 July 2003, *EqPA 1970* was amended by the *Equal Pay Act 1970 (Amendment) Regulations 2003* so that no claim in respect of an equality clause may be referred to an employment tribunal otherwise than by virtue of (*e*) above unless the proceedings are instituted on or before the 'qualifying date' (*EqPA 1970, s 2(4)*). These provisions have been replicated in tabular form in *EA 2010, ss 129–130*. The 'qualifying date' before which a claim must be brought varies depending on which of the following five categories applies to the circumstances of the claim (*EqPA 1970, s 2ZA; EA 2010, s 129*):

A stable employment case

(a)   A 'stable employment case' means a case where the proceedings relate to a period during which a stable employment relationship subsists between the woman and the employer, notwithstanding that the period includes any time after the ending of a contract of employment when no further contract of employment is in force. In a stable employment case, the qualifying date is the date falling six months after the date on which the stable employment relationship ended. See *EA 2010, s 129* and *130(3)* and further *Degnan v Redcar and Cleveland Borough Council* [2005] IRLR 504, *Rance v Secretary of State for Health* [2007] IRLR 665 for consideration of what constitutes 'stable employment'.

A concealment case

(b)   A 'concealment case' is a case where the employer deliberately concealed from the woman any fact (referred to as a 'qualifying fact') which is relevant to the contravention to which the proceedings relate, and without knowledge of which the woman could not reasonably have been expected to institute the proceedings, and the woman did not discover the qualifying fact (or could not with reasonable diligence have discovered it) until after the last day on which she was employed in the employment, or the day on which the stable employment relationship between her and the employer ended (as the case may be). In a concealment case, the qualifying date is the date falling six months after the day on which the woman discovered the qualifying fact in question (or could with reasonable diligence have discovered it). See *EA 2010, s 129* and *130(4)–(6)*.

A disability case (referred to as an incapacity case under EA 2010)

(c)   A 'disability case' means a case where the woman was under a disability at any time during the six months after the last day on which she was employed in the employment, the day on which the stable employment relationship between her and the employer ended, or the day on which she discovered (or could with reasonable diligence have discovered) the qualifying fact deliberately concealed from her by the employer (if that day falls after the day(s) referred to above, as the case may be). In a disability case, the qualifying date is the date falling six months after the day on which the woman ceased to be under a disability. See *EA 2010, s 129* and *130(7)–(9)*.

A case which is both a concealment and a disability case

(d)   In such a case, the qualifying date is the later of the two dates which would otherwise apply if it were just disability or just a concealment case. See *EA 2010, s 129*.

A standard case

(e)   A 'standard case' is a case which is not a stable employment case, a concealment case, a disability case or a case which is both a concealment and a disability case: see *EA 2010, s 139(2)*. In a standard case, the qualifying date is the date falling six months after the last day on which the woman was 'employed in the employment'. The meaning of that phrase was determined by the House of Lords in *Preston v Wolverhampton NHS Trust (No.1)* [1998] IRLR 197. Lord Slynn, with whose judgment Lords Goff, Lloyd, Nolan and Hope agreed, approved the analysis of Otton LJ delivering judgment in the Court of Appeal in that case ([1997] IRLR 233, 241) who said that the time limit runs 'from the end of the contract of employment alleged to contain the equality clause in respect of which the claim is made'. In *Slack v Cumbria County Council (Equality and Human Rights Commission intervening)* [2009] EWCA Civ 293, [2009] IRLR 463, CA (under the name of *Cumbria County Council v Dow (No.2)* in the EAT [2008] IRLR 109), the Court of Appeal upheld the EAT's decision that where it was clear from the contractual documents that employer and employee had agreed to effect a change to the contract by means not of a variation but rather by means of a termination and re-engagement (in contrast to the decision of the EAT in *Potter v North Cumbria Acute Hospitals NHS Trust* [2009] IRLR 900 where a change to contractual documents was found to be a variation) then time will start to run in respect of the previous contract from the date of termination where this is in accordance with the mutual intention of the parties. The potential harshness of this approach was alleviated in the Court of Appeal by the (new) argument that these were stable employment cases as there were a series of uninterrupted contracts and the cases were remitted back to the tribunal on this: *Fox v North Cumbria University Hospitals NHS Trust* [2010] EWCA Civ 729, [2010] IRLR 804. See also *Winder v Aston University* [2007] All ER (D) 45 (Nov), EAT.

The tribunal has no discretion to extend time in a claim under *EqPA 1970* or under *EA 1010*. In this respect the time limit for sex discrimination claims is more generous as it allows for an extension of time where the tribunal considers it to be just and equitable: see **12.3 DISCRIMINATION AND EQUAL OPPORTUNITIES – III**. Nor can the time limit be waived or varied by agreement between the parties: *Secretary of State for Health v Rance* [2007] IRLR 665.

21.19B Compensation

Where a court (see **21.19E** below for the jurisdiction of the civil courts) or tribunal upholds a complaint relating to a breach of an equality clause or rule (other than a breach with respect to membership of or rights under an occupational pension scheme) it may (a) make a declaration to that effect; and/or (b) order the employer to pay compensation to the employee in the form of an award by way of arrears of pay or damages (*EA 2010, ss 132(1)* and *(2)*).

If the claim is successful, the amount awarded will be the difference in pay between that of the claimant and the 'equal' or 'equivalent' employee. In certain cases, such as those involving performance-related pay or bonuses, that may require the tribunal to engage in the speculative exercise of devising an equivalent performance-related bonus scheme to apply to the group of workers to which the claimant belongs in order to determine the appropriate level of award: see *South Tyneside Metropolitan Borough Council v Anderson* [2007] All ER (D) 410 (Mar) (not appealed on this point: [2007] EWCA Civ 654, [2007] IRLR 715).

Compensation for non-economic loss is not recoverable in a claim under the *EqPA 1970*: *Degnan v Redcar and Cleveland Borough Council* [2005] IRLR 504.

Note also, that the tribunal will not grant a declaration that there has been discrimination where in fact the employee has suffered no loss: see *Copple and others v Littlewoods Plc* [2012] IRLR 121. That case concerned a large number of part-time pensions claims. However, the EAT held that since most of the claimants would not actually have joined the scheme even if it had been open to them to do so, although there had been discrimination, no declaration would be granted since that would be to put the claimants in a better position than, say, a man who, despite having the option to join the scheme in his contract of employment, had not done so at the time.

The limitation provisions under the *EA 2010* now stipulate that a court or tribunal may not award compensation in respect of any time before the 'arrears day' (*s 132(3)*). The 'arrears day' in a 'standard case' (see above **21.19A**) is the day falling 6 years before the day on which proceedings were instituted. The 'arrears day' in a concealment or incapacity (formerly, disability) case is the day on which the breach first occurred (*s 132(4)*).

Formerly, the *EqPA 1970* contained a two-year limitation period. This was held by the CJEU in *Preston v Wolverhampton Healthcare NHS Trust* to be incompatible with Community law. On return to the House of Lords ([1998] ICR 227, HL), it was held that the respondent employers could not rely on this two-year limitation which must be disapplied. The respondent employers could not therefore defeat a claim for periods prior to the two years to be taken into account, subject to the employee paying contributions owing in respect of the period for which membership was claimed retroactively. Future pension benefits had to be calculated by reference to full and part-time periods of service subsequent to 8 April 1976 as the date when the CJEU held in *Defrenne v Sabena*: 43/75 [1976] ICR 547 that *art 157* had direct effect. See now the *Equal Pay Act 1970 (Amendment) Regulations 2003*.

Following the CJEU's declaration of incompatibility in *Preston*, with effect from 19 July 2003, *EqPA 1970, s 2ZB* provides that arrears of pay may be recovered up to six years back from the 'arrears date'. As noted above, these provisions have now been replicated in the *EA 2010*.

However, note that where the claim is based on the job having been rated as equivalent by the employer, there can be no claim for back pay: the employee will be entitled to equal wages only from the date that the job was rated as equivalent: *Bainbridge v Redcar and Cleveland Borough Council* [2007] IRLR 494.

The meaning of the words "proceedings were instituted" which set the relevant arrears date in a 'standard case' was considered by the EAT in *Prest and others v Mouchel Business services and another* [2011] ICR 1345. The issue in that case was that proceedings had been amended

so as to include new comparators. The tribunal found that the arrears date was the date on which the application to amend the ET1 had been made. The EAT disagreed holding that the original and amended claims were, in substance, the same claims as both of the comparators were in one of the two classes of comparators named in the original claim. Consequently, proceedings were instituted on the date that the ET1 was originally presented to the employment tribunal. However, the matter may have been different in circumstances where the work done by the new comparator had been different from the work done by the comparators originally named in the ET1.

The *Sex Discrimination and Equal Pay (Remedies) Regulations 1993 (SI 1993/2798)* (now replaced by the *Employment Tribunals (Interest on Awards in Discrimination Cases) Regulations 1996 ('SI 1996/2803'))* conferred on the employment tribunal a power to award interest on sums awarded under the *EqPA 1970*. The tribunal is required to identify a 'mid-point date'. This date is the halfway point between the date on which the act of discrimination complained of occurred and the date on which the interest is being calculated (*reg 4*). Interest is then awarded in respect of the period from the mid-point date to the date of calculation (*reg 6(1)(b)*), except that interest on any sum for injury to feelings is to be awarded for the whole of the period from the date of the act of discrimination to the date of calculation (*reg 6(1)(a)*). Interest is simple interest and accrues from day to day (*reg 3(1)*). By *reg 3(2)* the rate to be applied in England and Wales is that prescribed for the Special Investment Account by *rule 27(1)* of the *Court Funds Rules 1987 (SI 1987/821)*. In Scotland the relevant rate is that fixed for the time being by the *Act of Sederunt (Interest in Sheriff Court Decrees or Extracts) 1975 (SI 1975/948)*.

If a respondent has made a payment to the complainant prior to the date of calculation, the date of payment is treated as if it were the date of calculation for the purposes of calculating the interest to be awarded (*reg 6(2)*).

The tribunal is given a discretion to calculate interest by reference to periods other than those set out above, or even to use different periods for different elements of the award (*reg 6(3)*). The discretion may be exercised only where the tribunal is of the opinion that:

(a)   there are exceptional circumstances, whether relating to the claim as a whole or to a particular element of the award; and

(b)   those circumstances have the effect that serious injustice would be caused if interest were to be awarded by reference to the period or periods specified in *reg 6(1)(a)* or *(b)* or *6(2)*.

21.19C Equal Pay Audits

Section 132 of the *EA 2010*, which deals specifically with equal pay cases, contains no specific power to make a 'recommendation' such as is contained in *EA 2010, s 124(1)(c)* for other discrimination claims: see **12.21 DISCRIMINATION AND EQUAL OPPORTUNITIES – III**. However, it is arguable that equal pay cases also fall within the scope of *s 124(1)(c)* since that section applies to all contraventions of *Part 5* of the *Act*, which includes in principle contraventions of the equality clause: see *s 120(1)* and *124(1)*. Nonetheless, *s 98* of the *Enterprise and Regulatory Reform Act 2013* has now created a new power for employment tribunals to make a very specific type of 'recommendation' in an equal pay case. That *Act* inserts a new *s 139A* into the *EA 2010*. This is an enabling provision which permits regulations to be made (consultation on the contents of which opened on 23 May 2013) requiring employment tribunals to order a respondent to carry out an equal pay audit in any case where the tribunal finds that there has been a breach of the equality clauses in the *EA 2010* or a contravention of the sex discrimination provisions relating to pay. This power is additional to the power to award compensation to the individual claimant (above), and to the power to impose a financial penalty on an employer (below). The purpose of such audits is 'to identify

action to be taken to avoid equal pay breaches occurring or continuing' (s 139A(3)). The Act requires the regulations to provide for an equal pay audit not to be ordered where the tribunal considers that: (a) an audit completed by the respondent in the previous 3 years meets requirements prescribed for this purpose; (b) it is clear without an audit whether any action is required to avoid equal pay breaches occurring or continuing; (c) the breach the tribunal has found gives no reason to think that there may be other breaches; or (d) the disadvantages of an equal pay audit would outweigh its benefits (s 139A(5)). Otherwise, the Act allows for the regulations to make further provision as to the content of an audit, any circumstances in which an audit may be required to be published or disclosed to any person, the powers and duties of the tribunal for deciding whether an order has been complied with, and for the tribunal to have power, where a person fails to comply with an order to carry out an equal pay audit (s 138A(2), (6) and (8)). In the first regulations to be made under the section, the amount of such a penalty may not exceed £5,000 (s 139A(8)). That limit will not apply to subsequent regulations. Similarly, there will be power in the first regulations (but not in subsequent regulations) made under the section to provide for an exemption from the equal pay audit provisions for small and/or new businesses.

21.19D Financial penalties for employers

Section 16 of the *Enterprise and Regulatory Reform Act 2013* inserts a new *s 12A* into the *Employment Tribunals Act 1996* which will, when in force, permit a tribunal to order an employer to pay a penalty to the Secretary of State if it concludes that the employer has breached any of the worker's rights to which the claim relates, and is also of the opinion that the breach has one or more aggravating features (s 12A(1)). This power may be used in addition to, or as an alternative to, awarding compensation to the employee or ordering the employer to carry out an equal pay audit (see above). However, where a tribunal has already decided to order the employer to pay compensation to the employee, the amount of any penalty awarded must be 50% of the value of the compensation awarded, except that if the amount of the financial award is less than £200, the amount of the penalty shall be £100, and if the amount of the financial award is more than £10,000, the amount of the award shall be £5,000 (s 12A(5)). In cases where two or more workers' claims have been considered together and the employer is ordered to pay a penalty in respect of any of those claims, the amount of the penalties in total shall be at least £100, the amount of a penalty in respect of a particular claim shall be no more than £5000 or no more than 50% of the amount of any compensation awarded to the employee (whichever is the lesser). If the total of the financial compensation awarded on all the conjoined claims is less than £200, then the penalty is capped at £100 (ss 12A(6) and (7)). In all other cases, the penalty must be at least £100 and no more than £5000 (s 12A(3)). In deciding whether to make a penalty order, and in deciding the amount of such order, the tribunal must have regard to the employer's ability to pay (s 12A(2)). Once a penalty order is made, it cannot be reviewed simply because the tribunal is subsequently called on to award compensation for failure a failure by the employer to comply with an order of the tribunal (such as an order for a recommendation under s 124(7) of the EA 2010 or an order to carry out an equal pay audit) (s 12A(9)). This provision does not affect the Tribunal's general powers to review awards, however. Finally, it is to be noted that penalties awarded under these new provisions are to operate like parking tickets: an employer who pays within 21 days of the order will have the amount of the penalty reduced by 50%: s 12A(10).

21.19E Equal Pay Claims and the Civil Courts

Because the right to equal pay in the *EqPA 1970* and the *EA 2010* is given effect by way of the deemed inclusion of an equality clause in the worker's contract (see above **21.5**), it is possible for claims for equal pay to be brought in the civil courts by way of a claim for breach of contract. The *EA 2010* explicitly preserves the jurisdiction of the civil courts in respect

of equal pay (*s 127(9)* of *EA 2010*), subject to provisions permitting the striking out of claims where such claims could be more conveniently dealt with by an employment tribunal and for the transferring of issues to the employment tribunal: see *s 128* of *EA 2010*.

The *EqPA 1970* contained identical provision to *s 128(2)* of the *EA 2010* at *s 2(3)* as follows: "Where it appears to the court in which any proceedings are pending that a claim or counter-claim in respect of the operation of an [equality clause] could more conveniently be disposed of separately by an [employment tribunal], the court may direct that the claim or counter-claim shall be struck out; and (without prejudice to the foregoing) where in proceedings before any court a question arises as to the operation of an [equality clause], the court may on the application of any party to the proceedings or otherwise refer that question, or direct it to be referred by a party to the proceedings, to an [employment tribunal] for determination by the tribunal, and may stay or sist the proceedings in the meantime." This section of the *EqPA 1970* suggested that the civil courts have jurisdiction over equal pay claims but raised the question of whether or not an equal pay claim which would be out of time in the employment tribunal, could be pursued by making use of the longer limitation periods permitted in contract claims in the civil courts or whether such claims fall to be struck out, under *EqPA 1970, section 2(3)* on the basis that it would be more convenient to hear them in the employment tribunal (having regard to the expertise of the employment tribunals in equal pay cases and the specialist rules of procedure).

In *Abdulla v Birmingham City Council* [2010] EWHC 3303 (QB), [2011] IRLR 309 Colin Edelman QC (sitting as a deputy High Court Judge) declined to strike out an equal pay multiple under *EqPA 1970, s 2(3)*. He considered that a construction of *EqPA 1970, s 2(3)* which permitted claims to be struck out on the basis that they could be more conveniently disposed of in the employment tribunal, even though they could not be heard in the employment tribunal (by reason of the time bar) would amount to the imposition of the employment tribunal time limit on claims in the civil courts even though Parliament had chosen not to enact the same time limit in the different sets of proceedings. He also considered that the European principle of equivalence was engaged and required that equal pay proceedings in the civil courts should have equivalent time limits to contract claims in the civil courts. A rather different approach was suggested by Slade J in *Ashby v Birmingham City Council* [2011] EWHC 424 (QB), [2011] IRLR 473. Slade J drew on the jurisprudence which applied in the context of staying claims in this jurisdiction on an application of the *forum non conveniens* principles. She concluded that it was essential in applying *EqPA 1970, s 2(3)* to consider the reason why the claims had been pursued in the civil courts and why timely claims were not issued in the employment tribunal. Where the failure to issue a timely claim in the employment tribunal was reasonable, she opined that "the interests of justice are likely to be served by enabling claimants to continue litigating in a forum which has jurisdiction to hear their claims. Such considerations could affect the decision as to whether the claims could be more conveniently disposed of in the Employment Tribunal or, if a judge so concluded, whether discretion should be exercised to strike out the claims in the County Court." When the question came before the Court of Appeal in *Birmingham City Council v Abdulla* [2012] IRLR 116 the Court of Appeal preferred the approach of Colin Edelman QC to that of Slade J. Mummery LJ considered that the purpose of *section 2(3)* was to enable claims to be dealt with in the most appropriate forum and not to leave claimants without any remedy. Consequently, it would not be appropriate to strike out equal pay claims pursued in the civil courts exercising the section 2(3) power when the claims would be out of time such that the employment tribunal would have no jurisdiction to entertain them. The Court of Appeal did not therefore need to express an opinion upon the question of the European principle of equivalence. Mummery LJ did not find the comparison with the staying of claims on an application of the *forum non conveniens* principles, which had influenced the decision in *Ashby*, helpful. However, he did accept that the reasons why a claimant had allowed the time limit in the employment tribunal to expire, may be relevant in the exercise of judicial discretion given by *EqPA 1970, s 2(3)* albeit that he opined that it would be in exceptional case that it would be an abuse of process for

claimants to continue with claims in the civil courts where they could not be pursued in the employment tribunal. On appeal to the Supreme Court in *Abdulla* ([2012] UKSC 47, [2013] IRLR 38) a majority of the Supreme Court (Lords Wilson and Reed and Lady Hale) favoured the approach of Colin Edelman QC. The majority considered that although in most cases it will be more convenient for the tribunal to dispose of a claim in respect of the operation of an equality clause, if such a claim would be out of time in the employment tribunal, it would never be more convenient for it to be brought there and the civil court should not strike the claim out. Nor were the reasons why the claim had not been brought in time in the employment tribunal relevant to the question of whether it should be struck out by the High Court. However, in the view of the majority, those reasons might be relevant to the question of costs, since such claims should normally be dealt with in the employment tribunal, where each side would normally bear its own costs. The SC further noted that the power under *s 2(3)* of the *EqPA 1970* (now *EA 2010, s 128(2)*) for a civil court to refer any issue in an equal pay claim for determination by a tribunal is not subject to any time limit and should not be forgotten.

21.20   Agricultural Wages Orders

If such an order contains any discriminatory term, it may be referred by the Secretary of State to the Central Arbitration Committee ('CAC') for amendment. He may be requested to do so by employer or worker representatives on the Agricultural Wages Board, or may do so on his own motion. If the CAC decides that the amendments should be made, the Agricultural Wages Board must make an order giving effect to those amendments not later than five months from the date of the decision (*EqPA 1970, s 5*).

The *EA 2010* does not replicate *s 5* of *EqPA 1970*.

21.21   PROCEDURE IN EQUAL PAY CLAIMS

The *Employment Tribunals (Constitution and Rules of Procedure) Regulations 2004 (SI 2004/1861)* ('the *2004 Regulations*') governed the procedure relating to all claims before employment tribunals with effect from 1 October 2004 to 1 July 2013 (see EMPLOYMENT TRIBUNALS – I (17)). . With effect from 1 July 2013, employment tribunal procedure will be governed by the *Employment Tribunals (Constitution and Rules of Procedure) Regulations 2013 (SI 2013/1237)* ('the *2013 Regulations*').

Proceedings in equal pay claims are started in the same way as all proceedings before employment tribunals, by the filing of a Claim (*2004 Regulations, Sch 1, rule 8*). The respondent enters a Response (*2004 Regulations, Sch 1, rule 16*). The tribunal has power to order the discovery and inspection of documents, and the attendance of witnesses (*2004 Regulations, Sch 1, rules 31* and *32*).

The new rules also contain specific provisions relating to the making of claims by multiple claimants whose claims are based on the same set of facts (*rule 9*) and to responding to such claims (*rule 16(3)*). These will often be relevant in group equal pay claims. In addition, there is specific provision in the new *rule 36* for lead cases to be identified 'where a Tribunal considers that two or more claims give rise to common or related issues of fact or law'. In such cases, the other claims will be stayed while the lead case will go forward to a preliminary or substantive hearing. Any decision made in the lead case 'shall be binding' on each of the parties to the other cases stayed behind the lead case (*rule 36(2)*) unless, within 28 days of the Tribunal's decision any party successfully applies for an order that the decision does not apply to , and is not binding on the parties to, a particular related case. These provisions are likely to lead to more efficient handling of equal pay claims involving multiple claimants.

Note that the, now repealed, statutory grievance and disciplinary procedures in *Sch 2* to the *Employment Act 2002* continue to apply to claims under the *EqPA 1970* until 4 October 2009 in the case of an equal pay claim that relates to a period prior to 6 April 2009. Accordingly, for claims governed by these old procedures, an employee must have set out her complaint in writing and sent a copy of it to her employer at least 28 days prior to commencing proceedings in the employment tribunal. In *Hurst v Suffolk Mental Health Partnership NHS Trust* [2009] EWCA Civ 309, [2009] IRLR 452, the Court of Appeal confirmed that it is sufficient for the first step of an equal pay grievance to inform the employer that the claim was brought under the *1970 Act* and further detail is not required. As such, where comparators are named in a grievance and a subsequent claim seeks to rely on different comparators it is very likely that the claim will not be barred from proceeding by reason of *EA 2002, section 32*: see *Amery v Perth and Kinross Council* [2012] CSIH 11, *Sefton Metropolitan Borough Council v Hincks* [2011] ICR 1357 and *Abendshine v Sunderland City Council* [2012] ICR 1087.

The amendment of proceedings by the addition of new comparators in a claim under the *EqPA 1970* does add a new cause of action: *Bainbridge v Redcar and Cleveland Borough Council* [2008] EWCA Civ 885, [2009] ICR 133 and *Potter v North Cumbria Acute Hospitals NHS Trust* [2009] IRLR 900, EAT (which held further that the new cause of action was not necessarily out of time and that the complexities of litigation under the *EqPA 1970* should be taken into account when deciding whether to permit an amendment to add new comparators).

Like work or work rated as equivalent. If a claim for equal pay is brought asserting that the claimant is employed on like work or work rated as equivalent with a male comparator, the issues to be determined by the tribunal are whether the work is like work, or has been rated as equivalent under a valid job evaluation study. If it is raised, the tribunal will then decide whether the claimant has a genuine material factor defence under *EqPA 1970, s 1(3)* or *EA 2010, s 69*. These claims are determined under the ordinary rules of procedure in schedule 1 to the *2004 Regulations*.

Work of equal value. Under the predecessor to the 2004 *2004 Regulations*, equal pay claims in which it was alleged that the work done was work of equal value were the subject of complementary rules of procedure contained in *Sch 3* to the regulations. The 2004 *2004 Regulations*, as originally enacted, made no reference to equal value claims. This omission was rectified by *Employment Tribunals (Constitution and Rules of Procedure) (Amendment) Regulations 2004 (SI 2004/2351)* which inserts *Schedule 6* to the *2004 Regulations* to provide for a new procedure to be adopted in equal value claims which is intended to reduce the costs and delay in equal value claims. This *Schedule* has now largely been replicated in *Schedule 3* of the *2013 Regulations*.

By s 2A of the *EqPA 1970* as amended by *Equal Pay Act 1970 (Amendment) Regulations 2004 (SI 2004/2352)* with effect from 1 October 2004 and from 1 October 2010 by the *EA 2010, s 131(2)*, where a dispute arises as to whether any work is of equal value, the Tribunal may proceed to determine that question itself or appoint an independent expert on this basis. This amendment removes the defence that there are no reasonable grounds for determining that the work was of equal value so that the Tribunal is left with a straight choice between deciding the question for itself or appointing an expert.

In a case where there has already been a job evaluation study which has given different values to the work of the claimant and the comparator, the employment tribunal must determine that the work is not of equal value unless it has reasonable grounds for suspecting that the study discriminated on the grounds of sex, or there are other reasons why it is not suitable to be relied upon: *s 2A(2)* and *2A(2A)* of the *EqPA 1970* as amended and *EA 2010, s 131(5)* and *(6)*.

In response to widespread concerns about the costs and delay involved in the independent expert procedure, *Sch 6* to the *2004 Regulations* and *Sch 3* to the *2013 Regulations* and *Sch 3* to the *2013 Regulations* makes provision for a two-stage procedure with an 'indicative timetable'. In cases not involving an independent expert, the indicative timetable takes a total of 25 weeks and allows for a Stage 1 equal value hearing within 3 weeks of the Response with the merits hearing to follow within 18 weeks. In cases where an expert is appointed, the indicative timetable takes 37 weeks and provides for a Stage 1 equal value hearing within 3 weeks of the Response, a Stage 2 hearing within 10 weeks of Stage 1, the expert's report within 4 weeks of Stage 2, written questions to the expert 4 weeks after his or her report and the merits hearing within a further 8 weeks. However, the requirement to hold a Stage 1 or a Stage 2 equal value hearing does not preclude holding more than one of each of those types of hearing or other hearings from being held in accordance with the ordinary Tribunal rules of procedure in *Sch 1* to the *2004 Regulations: rule 13 (2)* of *Sch 6* to the *2004 Regulations* and *rule 12(2)* of *Sch 3* to the *2013 Regulations*.

The new procedure for equal value claims provides as follows.

In making all directions in relation to equal value claims, the Tribunal is required (see *rule 2(2)* of *Sch 3* to the *2013 Regulations*).

Stage 1 Equal Value Hearing. Where there is a dispute as to whether one person's work is of equal value to another's, the Tribunal shall conduct a hearing called a 'Stage 1 Equal Value Hearing. At the hearing the Tribunal shall (*rule 4* of *Sch 6* to the *2004 Regulations* and *rule 3* of *Sch 3* to the *2013 Regulations*):

(a)   strike out the claim if, by virtue of the claimant's and her comparator's work having been rated differently in a job evaluation study, their work is not of equal value;

(b)   determine whether or not the claimant and her comparator's work are of equal value, or alternatively require an independent expert to prepared a report on the question (and hear evidence and submissions for the purpose of deciding these issues);

(c)   if the Tribunal decides to require an independent expert to prepare a report on the question, the Tribunal must fix a date for a 'Stage 2 Equal Value Hearing';

(d)   if the Tribunal decides not to require an independent expert to prepare a report, then a date for a final hearing must be fixed.

Under the *2004 Regulations* there was also a specific power in *rule 4* to order disclosure to the expert of all documents and evidence relevant to the question of equal value disclosed between the parties. This specific power is now contained in *rule 2(1)(b)* of *Sch 3* to the *2013 Regulations. Rule 2* also gives the Tribunal specific power to limit the parties to facts that they have put in evidence and disclosed by a date set by the Tribunal (*rule 2(1)(a)*).

At the Stage 1 Equal Value Hearing, the tribunal shall also, unless it considers it inappropriate, make the following 'standard orders' (*rule 5* of *Sch 6* to the *2004 Regulations* and *rule 4* of *Sch 3* to the *2013 Regulations*):

(a)   before the end of the period of 14 days after the date of the Stage 1 hearing the claimant shall:

   (i)   disclose in writing to the respondent the name of any comparator, or, if the claimant is not able to name the comparator he shall instead disclose such information as enables the comparator to be identified by the respondent; and

   (ii)   identify to the respondent in writing the period in relation to which he considers that the claimant's work and that of the comparator are to be compared;

(b)   before the end of the period of 28 days after the date of the Stage 1 hearing:

(i)   where the claimant has not disclosed the name of the comparator to the respondent, if the respondent has been provided with sufficient detail to be able to identify the comparator, he shall disclose in writing the name of the comparator to the claimant;

(ii)   the parties shall provide each other with written job descriptions for the claimant and any comparator;

(iii)   the parties shall identify to each other in writing the facts which they consider to be relevant to the question;

(c)   the respondent is required to grant access to the claimant and his representative (if any) to his premises during a period specified by the tribunal or chairman in order for him or them to interview any comparator;

(d)   the parties shall before the end of the period of 56 days after the date of the stage 1 equal value hearing present to the tribunal a joint agreed statement in writing of the following matters:

(i)   job descriptions for the claimant and any comparator;

(ii)   facts which both parties consider are relevant to the question;

(iii)   facts on which the parties disagree (as to the fact or as to the relevance to the question) and a summary of their reasons for disagreeing;

(e)   the parties shall, at least 56 days prior to the hearing, disclose to each other, to any independent or other expert and to the tribunal written statements of any facts on which they intend to rely in evidence at the hearing; and

(f)   the parties shall, at least 28 days prior to the hearing, present to the tribunal a statement of facts and issues on which the parties are in agreement, a statement of facts and issues on which the parties disagree and a summary of their reasons for disagreeing.

Where the Tribunal has decided to appoint an independent expert to prepare a report on the question, the Tribunal or a Chairman may if it or he considers it appropriate (for example where a party is not legally represented etc) at any stage of the proceedings order an independent expert to assist the tribunal in establishing the facts on which the independent expert may rely in preparing his report: *rule 6 (2)* of *Sch 6* to the *2004 Regulations* and *rule 5* of *Sch 3* to the *2013 Regulations*. *Rule 2(1)(d)* of *Sch 3* to the *2013 Regulations* also makes specific provision in relation to joint reports being produced by experts where more than one expert is instructed in proceedings.

See generally the decision of the Scottish EAT in *Amey Services Ltd v Cardigan* [2008] IRLR 279 for discussion of the need for the Claimant to identify comparators before the Respondent is required to give details of any genuine material factor defence.

Stage 2 Equal Value Hearing. At the Stage 2 hearing the Tribunal shall make a determination of facts on which the parties cannot agree which relate to the question and shall require the independent expert to prepare his report on the basis of facts which have (at any stage of the proceedings) either been agreed between the parties or determined by the tribunal (referred to as 'the facts relating to the question'): *rule 7(3)* of *Sch 6* to the *2004 Regulations* and *rule 6(1)* of *Sch 3* to the *2013 Regulations*. The facts relating to the question shall be the only facts on which the tribunal shall rely at the hearing, subject to an application by the independent expert for some or all of the facts relating to the question to be amended, supplemented or omitted: *rule 7(5)* and *(6)* of *Sch 6* to the *2004 Regulations* and *rule 6(2)* and *(3)* of *Sch 3* to the *2013 Regulations*.

At the Stage 2 hearing the Tribunal shall, unless it considers it inappropriate to do so, make the following 'standard orders' having regard to the indicative timetable (*rule 7(4)* of *Sch 6* to the *2004 Regulations* and *rules 6(1)(b)* and *7* of *Sch 3* to the *2013 Regulations*):

(a)   make any orders which it considers appropriate;

(b)   fix a date for the hearing, having regard to the indicative timetable;

(c)   order, by a date specified by the Tribunal (with regard to the indicative timetable) the independent expert to prepare his report on the question and shall (subject to any special provision made in national security proceedings) have sent copies of it to the parties and to the tribunal; and

(d)   order the independent expert to prepare his report on the question on the basis of the facts relating to the question.

The merits hearing. In proceedings in relation to which an independent expert has prepared a report, unless the Tribunal determines that the report is not based on the facts relating to the question, the report of the independent expert shall be admitted in evidence in those proceedings: *rule 9(1)* of *Sch 6* to the *2004 Regulations* and *rule 8(1)* of *Sch 3* to the *2013 Regulations*. If the Tribunal does not admit the report of an independent expert, it may determine the question itself or require another independent expert to prepare a report on the question: *rule 9(2)* of *Sch 6* to the *2004 Regulations* and *rule 8(2)* of *Sch 3* to the *2013 Regulations*. The Tribunal may refuse to admit evidence of facts or hear argument as to issues which have not been disclosed to the other party as required by these rules or any order made under them, unless it was not reasonably practicable for the party to have so complied: *rule 9(3)* of *Sch 6* to the *2004 Regulations* and *rule 8(3)* of *Sch 3* to the *2013 Regulations*.

The role of the independent expert. When a Tribunal requires an independent expert to prepare a report with respect to the question or to assist in establishing the facts, it shall inform that independent expert of the duties and powers he has under this rule: *rule 10(1)* of *Sch 6* to the *2004 Regulations* and *rule 9(1)* of *Sch 3* to the *2013 Regulations*. The independent expert shall have a duty to the Tribunal to:

(a)   assist it in furthering the overriding objective in *reg 3* of the *2004 Regulations* and in *rule 2* of *Sch 1* to the *2013 Regulations*;

(b)   comply with the requirements of the rules and any orders made by the Tribunal in relation to the proceedings;

(c)   keep the Tribunal informed of any delay in complying with any order in the proceedings (with the exception of minor or insignificant delays in compliance);

(d)   comply with any timetable imposed by the Tribunal or chairman in so far as this is reasonably practicable;

(e)   inform the Tribunal or a chairman on request by it or him of progress in the preparation of the independent expert's report;

(f)   prepare a report on the question based on the facts relating to the question and (subject to the provisions for national security cases) send it to the Tribunal and the parties; and

(g)   attend hearings in the proceedings.

An expert is under a duty to assist the Tribunal on matters within his expertise and this duty overrides any obligation to the person from whom he has received instructions or by whom he is paid: *rule 11(2)* of *Sch 6* to the *2004 Regulations* and *rule 10(2)* of *Sch 3* to the *2013*

Regulations. The independent expert may make an application for any order or for a hearing to be held as if he were a party to the proceedings: *rule 10(3) of Sch 6 to the 2004 Regulations* and *rule 9(3) of Sch 3 to the 2013 Regulations.* An independent expert shall be given notice of all hearings, orders or judgments in those proceedings as if a party to those proceedings and when a party is required to provide information to another party, such information shall also be provided to the independent expert: *rule 10(6) of Sch 6 to the 2004 Regulations* and *rule 12(1) of Sch 3 to the 2013 Regulations.* At any stage of the proceedings the Tribunal may, after giving the independent expert the opportunity to make representations, withdraw the requirement on the independent expert to prepare a report. If it does so, the Tribunal may itself determine the question, or it may determine that a different independent expert should be required to prepare the report: *rule 10(4) of Sch 6 to the 2004 Regulations* and *rule 9(4) of Sch 3 to the 2013 Regulations.* When a Tribunal determines that an independent expert is no longer required, the expert shall provide the Tribunal with all documentation and work in progress relating to the proceedings by a date specified by the Tribunal in a form which the tribunal is able to use: *rule 10(5) of Sch 6 to the 2004 Regulations* and *rule 9(5) of Sch 3 to the 2013 Regulations.* Such documentation and work in progress may be used in relation to those proceedings by the Tribunal or by another independent expert.

When the claim alleges that the jobs changed over the period in which equal value is claimed, a tribunal may, in the exercise of its case management powers, commission an expert's report based on the claimants' and comparators' jobs as they stood on the date the claims were presented and defer consideration of changes in job content to a later stage in the proceedings: see *Potter v North Cumbria Acute Hospitals NHS Trust* [2008] ICR 910, EAT.

Use of expert evidence. Expert evidence shall be restricted to that which, in the opinion of the tribunal, is reasonably required to resolve the proceedings: *rule 11(1) of Sch 6 to the 2004 Regulations* and *rule 10(1) of Sch 3 to the 2013 Regulations.* No party may call an expert or put in evidence an expert's report without the permission of the Tribunal and no expert report shall be put in evidence unless it has been disclosed to all other parties and any independent expert at least 28 days prior to the hearing: *rule 11(3) of Sch 6 to the 2004 Regulations* and *rule 10(3) of Sch 3 to the 2013 Regulations.* (See generally *Baines v Blackpool Borough Council* [2008] All ER (D) 95 (Jan), EAT, on the use of expert evidence in an equal value case.) In proceedings in which an independent expert has been required to prepare a report on the question, the Tribunal shall not admit evidence of another expert on the question unless such evidence is based on the facts relating to the question: *rule 11(4) of Sch 6 to the 2004 Regulations* and *rule 10(4) of Sch 3 to the 2013 Regulations.* (See, in this regard, *Middlesbrough Borough Council v Surtees (No. 2)* [2007] IRLR 981, EAT: this rule gives the discretion to admit the expert evidence of a second party's expert, but the words 'unless such evidence is based on the facts' mean that what the expert can give evidence about must exclude the facts which are not challenged and which represent a sacrosanct position following findings or agreement at an earlier stage in the proceedings.) Unless the Tribunal considers it inappropriate to do so, any such expert report shall be disclosed to all parties and to the Tribunal on the same date on which the independent expert is required to send his report to the parties and to the Tribunal: *rule 11(4) of Sch 6 to the 2004 Regulations* and *rule 10(4) of Sch 3 to the 2013 Regulations.* If an expert (other than an independent expert) does not comply with these rules or an order made by the Tribunal or a chairman, the Tribunal may order that the evidence of that expert shall not be admitted: *rule 11(5) of Sch 6 to the 2004 Regulations* and *rule 10(5) of Sch 3 to the 2013 Regulations.* Where two or more parties wish to submit expert evidence on a particular issue, the Tribunal may order that the evidence on that issue is to be given by one joint expert only. When such an order has been made, if the parties wishing to instruct the joint expert cannot agree who should be the expert, the Tribunal may select the expert: *rule 11(6) of Sch 6 to the 2004 Regulations* and *rule 10(6) of Sch 3 to the 2013 Regulations.*

Written questions to experts. *Rule 12* of *Sch 6* of the 2004 Regulations and rule 11 of *Sch 3* to the 2013 Regulations makes provision for written questions to be put to experts (including an independent expert) on their report. The question must be: put once only; put within 28 days of the date on which the parties were sent the report; for the purpose only of clarifying the factual basis of the report; copied to all other parties and experts involved in the proceedings at the same time as they are sent to the expert who prepared the report; and answered within 28 days of receiving the question. An expert's answers to questions shall be treated as part of the expert's report: *rule 12(4)* of *Sch 6* and *rule 11(3)* of *Sch 3*. Where a party has put a written question to an expert instructed by another party and the expert does not answer that question, or does not do so within 28 days, the Tribunal may order that the party instructing the expert may not rely on the evidence of that expert: *rule 12(5)* of *Sch 6* and *rule 11(4)* of *Sch 3*.

Burden of proof

The same burden of proof provisions apply to equal pay claims as to other discrimination claims: see *EA 2010, s 136(1)–(4)*. The burden of proof is on the claimant. However, if there are facts from which the court could decide, in the absence of any other explanation, that the employer has contravened the provision concerned, the tribunal must hold that the contravention occurred, unless the employer shows that it has not contravened the provision. See further Discrimination and Equal Opportunities III, 12.3.

Help for complainants

With effect from 6 April 2003, claimants or potential claimants in equal pay claims were able to serve questionnaires in the same manner as under the other discrimination statutes. The *Equal Pay (Questions and Replies) Order 2003 (SI 2003/722),* provided for such questionnaires to be served before a claim was presented to a tribunal or within 21 days after such a claim or such longer period as the tribunal may on application allow. The tribunal could then draw adverse inferences, including an inference that the equality clause has been breached, where an employer deliberately and without reasonable cause failed to reply in the eight-week period specified by *reg 4* of the *Order* or where an employer's reply was evasive or equivocal: *EqPA 1970, s 7B*. Such questionnaires were particularly useful to complainants who bear the burden of establishing a disparate impact by reference to statistics: see *Nelson v Carillion Services Ltd* [2003] EWCA Civ 544, [2003] ICR 1256, CA.

These provisions were re-enacted in *s 138* of the *EA 2010*. However, the questionnaire procedure is not available for claims commenced after 25 April 2013 as *s 138* of the *EA 2010* was repealed by *s 66* of the *Enterprise and Regulatory Reform Act 2013*.

Note also that *s 78* of the *EA 2010* makes provision (not yet in force, and the coalition government does not intend to bring it into force) requiring employers with 250 or more employees (and other employers who may be specified in delegated legislation) to publish information relating to the pay of employees for the purpose of showing whether there are differences in the pay of male and female employees.

21.22   EFFECT ON CONTRACTS

A term in a contract which purports to exclude or limit any provision of the *EqPA 1970* is unenforceable by any person in whose favour the term would operate (*Sex Discrimination Act 1975, s 77(3)*; and see **12.32 Discrimination and Equal Opportunities – III**). These provisions have been replaced by *s 142* to *147* of *EA 2010* which make similar provision. However, a contract settling a complaint to an employment tribunal will be upheld if it was made with the assistance of a conciliation officer (*Sex Discrimination Act 1975, s 77(4)*; and see **2.3 Advisory, Conciliation and Arbitration Service**). It will also be upheld if it meets the statutory conditions for a compromise agreement entered into after the employee has had

21.22 Equal Pay

independent advice (*SDA, s 77(4)(aa), (4A)*; and see **17.25 EMPLOYMENT TRIBUNALS**). In other circumstances, an agreement by a woman that she will not bring a claim for equal pay will be void, and the payment of any sum to compromise such a claim will not prevent her from continuing with her complaint. In *Nimz v Freie und Hansestadt Hamburg* [1991] IRLR 222, the CJEU held that where there is indirect discrimination in a provision of a collective agreement, the national court is required to disapply that provision, without requesting or awaiting its prior removal by collective negotiation (see also *Kowalska v Freie und Hansestadt Hamburg*: C-33/89 [1992] ICR 29, CJEU).

21.23 Collective agreements

Prior to the coming into force of *SDA 1986* a collective agreement containing differing provisions for men and women could by *EqPA 1970, s 3* be referred (at the request of any party to the agreement or the Secretary of State) to the Central Arbitration Committee ('CAC') which had jurisdiction to modify contracts governed by the collective agreement. *EqPA 1970, s 3* is now repealed by *SDA 1986* which provides that collective agreements (whether they would otherwise be legally enforceable or not) are deemed automatically unenforceable and void insofar as they provide for the inclusion in a contract of employment of a provision which contravenes *EqPA 1970, s 1*. Discriminatory collective agreements which are contracts can be referred to a county court by a person interested in the agreement. The court may remove or modify any unenforceable term (*SDA 1975, s 77; SDA 1986, s 6*). A tribunal may grant a declaration of incompatibility in existing proceedings before it under the *EqPA 1970* without the need to issue separate proceedings; see *UNISON v Brennan* [2008] ICR 955. Actual or potential employees have certain rights to complain to employment tribunals about discriminatory collective agreements (*SDA, s 6(4A)*), as inserted by *TURERA 1993, s 32*; see **12.32 DISCRIMINATION AND EQUAL OPPORTUNITIES – III**). Declarations made by the CAC prior to the repeal of *EqPA 1970, s 3* continue in force (*SDA 1986, s 9*). In *Nimz v Freie und Hansestadt Hamburg*: C-184/89 [1991] IRLR 222, the CJEU held that where there is indirect discrimination in a provision of a collective agreement, the national court is required to disapply that provision, without requesting or awaiting its prior removal by collective negotiation (see also *Kowalska v Freie und Hansestadt Hamburg*: C-33/89 [1992] ICR 29, CJEU).

This provision has now been replaced by *s 145(1) EA 2010* which makes similar provision.

21.24 Protection for complainants

Under *s 77* of the *EA 2010* individuals are protected from retaliation or victimisation where they seek, or provide, disclosures about the terms of their work (including how much they are paid) (*ss 77(4)* and *(5)*). Contractual terms purporting to restrict such disclosures are void (*ss 77(1)* and *(2)*).

22   European Union Law

22.1   THE EUROPEAN UNION AND ITS LAW

European Union ('EU') law has applied to the United Kingdom since its accession to the European Communities on 1 January 1973. There are three basic sources of EU law:

(i)   the provisions of the *Treaty on the Functioning of the European Union ('TFEU')*, previously known as the *EC Treaty* or the *Treaty of Rome*;

(ii)   EU legislation; and

(iii)   decisions of the Court of Justice of the European Union ('ECJ').

Two treaties provide the constitutional underpinning of the EU: the *TFEU* and the *Treaty on European Union ('TEU')*.

Changes to key terminology were introduced by the *Treaty of Lisbon*, which came into force on 1 December 2009. The *Lisbon Treaty* is not autonomous. Instead, it amended both the *Treaty of Rome*, changing its name to the *TFEU*, and altering the numbering of the Articles contained in it; and the *Maastricht Treaty*, changing its name to the *TEU*. The *Lisbon Treaty* also abandoned the term 'the European Community' ('EC'), replacing it for all purposes with 'the European Union', which was part of a move to give the EU a single legal personality. Additionally, the *Lisbon Treaty* put the EU's *Charter of Fundamental Rights* on a legal basis for the first time (see *Art 6(1)* of the *TEU*). However, the Charter's effect in the UK is heavily restricted by an 'opt-out' secured by the UK government: *Art 1* of a protocol on the application of the *Charter* to the UK and Poland states that the *Charter* does not extend the ability of any EU or national court to find that the laws, regulations or administrative provisions, practices or action of Poland or the UK are inconsistent with the *Charter*.

The *Treaty of Rome* was made in 1957. It has been substantially amended since. The *Single European Act* of 1986, the *Maastricht Treaty* of 1991, the *Treaty of Amsterdam* of 1997, the *Treaty of Nice* of 2001 and the *Lisbon Treaty* have all introduced significant changes. The *Treaty of Amsterdam* resulted in a renumbering of the Articles of the *EC Treaty*; and the *Lisbon Treaty* resulted in a further renumbering. The new numbering is used below though, where applicable, the old numbering is included in square brackets for ease of reference, with the post-*Amsterdam* numbering appearing first, followed by the original numbering. The *TFEU* sets out the fundamental principles of the EU. The provisions that are particularly relevant to the EU's powers in the employment law field are *Arts 19 [13], 115 [94, 100], 114 [95, 100A], 151 [136, 117], 153 [137, 118], 154 [138, 118A], 155 [139, 118B], 156 [140, 118C], 157 [141, 119], 294 [251, 189B]* and *220 [302, 235]*.

EU legislation takes the form of regulations and directives. Regulations are the closest equivalent to an Act of Parliament (in that they are 'directly applicable', ie they do not need to be implemented by national legislation) whereas directives are instructions to member states to bring their national legislation into conformity with EU requirements.

The EU also promulgates 'recommendations'. Recommendations have no legal effect, but ought, as a matter of European law, to be taken into account when construing national legislation adopted in order to implement them or where they are designed to supplement binding EU measures (*Grimaldi v Fonds des Maladies Professionnelles*: 322/88 [1989] ECR 4407, [1991] 2 CMLR 265, ECJ). The EAT adopted this approach to the *Recommendation on the Dignity of Men and Women at Work* (see **22.6** below) in *Wadman v Carpenter Farrar Partnership* [1993] IRLR 374.

22.2   European Union Law

What if the state has failed to introduce legislation which properly and fully implements the European law by the date specified in the directive? In those circumstances the Commission is empowered by *Art 258 [226, 169]* to bring enforcement proceedings against the defaulting member state (see for example *EC Commission v United Kingdom*: C-382/92 [1994] ECR I-2435, [1994] ICR 664). *Article 259 [227, 170]* contains a related but rarely used power for other member states to bring similar proceedings. Within our own jurisdiction legislation purporting to implement EU law has been successfully challenged using judicial review (for instance *R v Secretary of State for Employment, ex p Equal Opportunities Commission* [1994] ICR 317, HL and *Equal Opportunities Commission v Secretary of State for Trade and Industry* [2007] ICR 1234). In addition, there are three mechanisms by which European legislation which has not yet been implemented (or properly implemented) may be given effect in British courts and tribunals: (1) a *Francovich* claim against the government for failure to implement; (2) reliance on the direct effect of the European legislation to bring a claim to enforce a European right; and (3) reliance on the direct effect of the European legislation to disapply an inconsistent domestic provision.

(1) *Francovich claims*

First, the landmark decision of *Francovich and Bonifaci v Italy*: C-6/90 and C-9/90 [1991] ECR I-5357, [1995] ICR 722, ECJ decided that an individual may have an EU law claim for damages against the state for failure properly to implement a directive. *Francovich* claims should be brought in the High Court; employment tribunals do not have jurisdiction to hear such claims (*Secretary of State for Employment v Mann* [1996] ICR 197, EAT, affirmed by the Court of Appeal [1997] ICR 209). The appropriate defendant is the Attorney General (*Mann; R v Secretary of State, ex p EOC* above). In order to bring a claim, the claimant will have to show that the unimplemented European provision is intended to confer rights on individuals. She must also establish that the breach is sufficiently serious and that the failure to implement the European provision is causally connected to the loss incurred (*Francovich* above). The ECJ's decision in *Brasserie du Pêcheur SA v Germany*: C-46/93 [1996] IRLR 267 provides useful guidance as to the scope of the substantive and procedural rights of an individual wishing to bring a *Francovich* claim. Where the relevant provision is enacted in an area of policy in relation to which a wide discretion is reserved to the member state the breach must be 'manifest' and 'grave'. Factors relevant to deciding whether a particular failure to implement is sufficiently serious include: the clarity and precision of the European provision, the breadth of the discretion reserved to the member state and the question whether the default was intentional. A breach will almost certainly be 'sufficiently serious' where a member state fails to implement a provision in circumstances where the ECJ has already ruled that there is an infringement or where it fails to take any steps to implement the directive before the date specified for implementation (*Dillenkofer v Germany*: C-178/94 [1997] IRLR 60, ECJ).

The member state cannot:

(a)   restrict the right to damages to cases where intentional or negligent default can be established;

(b)   adopt procedural rules governing the bringing of *Francovich* claims which are less favourable than those applying to analogous domestic claims or which have the effect of making it impossible or excessively difficult for individuals to obtain damages;

(c)   impose limits on the amount of damages recoverable which would have the effect that the compensation available was not commensurate with the loss suffered.

(2) *Claims to enforce a directly effective European right*

Secondly, the ECJ's doctrine of 'direct effect' means that, in some circumstances, an enforceable right may be conferred on an individual whether or not there has been any implementing legislation. There are three sources of directly effective rights: Articles of the

Treaty, EU regulations and EU directives. An example of the first is the right to equal pay conferred by *Art 157 [141, 119]*. The ECJ decided that this particular provision was directly effective in the case of *Defrenne v Sabena*: 43/75 [1976] ICR 547.

A directly effective provision may be either horizontally or vertically directly effective. A provision which has only vertical direct effect is one which creates rights which an individual may enforce against the state but not against other individuals. A provision which has horizontal direct effect creates a right which may be enforced against other individuals.

Some, though not all, directly effective Treaty provisions have horizontal direct effect. An example of the application of horizontal direct effect is the case of *Barber v Guardian Royal Exchange Assurance Group*: C-262/88 [1990] ICR 616. Existing domestic anti-discrimination legislation excluded, broadly speaking, matters relating to pensions. In *Barber* the ECJ decided that occupational pensions were 'pay' within the meaning of *Art 157 [141, 119]*. As a result, individuals were able to bring a claim if they suffered sex discrimination in relation to the benefits paid under a pension scheme. European law filled the gap left by the domestic legislation.

Where a member state fails properly to implement a directive by the due date, a directive may be the source of directly effective rights. However, these rights have only vertical direct effect (*Faccini Dori v Recreb Srl*: C-91/92 [1995] All ER (EC) 1; but cf *CIA Security International SA v Signalson*: C-194/94 [1996] ECR I-2201, [1996] All ER (EC) 557, ECJ in which a defendant to a counterclaim was entitled to have the domestic provision upon which the counterclaim was based disapplied on the basis that it had not been notified to the European Commission as required by *Directive 83/189/EEC*, thus arguably giving some limited horizontal effect to the directive). The rationale is that the state cannot rely on its own failure to implement the right to defend itself against those who might have been able to exercise the right against it. See also *R v Durham County Council, ex p Huddleston* [2000] 1 WLR 1484, [2000] 2 CMLR 229, CA.

Direct effect can arise only after expiry of the time allowed for implementation of a directive (*Suffritti v Istituto Nazionale della Previdenza Sociale (INPS)*: C-140/91, C-141/91, C-278/91 and C-279/91 [1992] ECR I-6337,[1993] IRLR 289), although it is immaterial that the factual situation relied upon by the individual arose before the implementation deadline (*Verholen v Sociale Verzekeringsbank Amsterdam* [1992] IRLR 38). But for this purpose the 'state' includes any body, whatever its legal form, which has been made responsible by the state for providing a public service under the control of the state, and which has special powers for that purpose (*Foster v British Gas plc* [1991] ICR 84 and 463 and see *National Union of Teachers v St Mary's Church of England (Aided) Junior School (Governing Body)* [1997] ICR 334, CA – a voluntary aided school is an emanation of the state; see further **35.7 PUBLIC SECTOR EMPLOYEES**). The individual seeking to rely upon the directive must be a citizen of an EU member state (*Bernstein v Immigration Appeal Tribunal* [1988] Imm AR 449), and must be a person of a kind within the scope of the directive (*Verholen*, above).

Not all treaty provisions or directives are directly effective. The precise requirements for direct effect to be established are complex, but the provision concerned must be clear, unconditional and precise.

A directly effective right may, in theory, operate in one of two main ways. The right may be used in order to disapply a bar to an existing domestic remedy, or it may create a 'free-standing' right to a remedy. In many cases both types of operation may be appropriate. For instance, in a case similar to *Barber* (above) a claimant may argue either that the EU right works to disapply the exclusion of pension-related discrimination from the existing domestic legislation or that there is a free-standing right to an equal pension under *Art 157 [141, 119]* which, being horizontally directly effective, may be enforced against other individuals. The distinction between the two affects the question of what court or tribunal may consider cases based on European law, and what time limits apply to them.

22.2 European Union Law

It was at one point simply assumed that the employment tribunal had jurisdiction to hear claims based directly upon *Art 157* (*Stevens v Bexley Health Authority* [1989] IRLR 240; *Secretary of State for Scotland and Greater Glasgow Health Board v Wright and Hannah* [1993] 2 CMLR 257, [1991] IRLR 187, EAT). The difficulty was that the employment tribunal has a statutory jurisdiction. In other words, it could only hear the cases which a statute had specifically conferred jurisdiction upon it to hear. No statute has ever conferred jurisdiction on the employment tribunal to hear cases which are directly based upon *Art 157*. In two cases (*Biggs v Somerset County Council* [1996] IRLR 203 and *Barber v Staffordshire County Council* [1996] ICR 364) the Court of Appeal stated very clearly that the tribunal does not have jurisdiction to hear 'free-standing' *Art 157* claims. However, the ECJ and EAT have since held that, in the context of enforcing rights based on a directive, a national specialist court which is granted jurisdiction in matters relating to transposing legislation must have jurisdiction to hear claims arising directly from the directive thereby transposed: *Impact v Minister for Agriculture and Food*: C-268/06 [2008] IRLR 552 and *UNISON v Brennan* [2008] ICR 955, EAT. This is so provided that it is established that the obligation on the claimant to bring, at the same time, a separate claim based directly on the directive before an ordinary court would involve procedural disadvantages liable to render excessively difficult the exercise of the rights conferred on him by Community law. This principle probably applies to claims based directly on *Art 157*, since employment tribunals' equal pay jurisdiction is derived from domestic equal pay legislation which aims to transpose *Art 157*.

The question of what time limits apply to claims based directly on *Art 157* is not straightforward. Broadly speaking, European law has left the question of time limits to the member state subject to the following general principles of equivalence and effectiveness:

(i)   the time limits applied to the enforcement of EU law rights should be no more restrictive than those which apply to analogous domestic claims (see *Preston v Wolverhampton Healthcare NHS Trust* [2000] IRLR 506, ECJ and [2001] UKHL 5, [2001] IRLR 237);

(ii)   the time limits should not make the enforcement of the rights impossible in practice (see *Rewe-Zentralfinanz GmbH v Landwirtschaftskammer für Saarland*: 33/76 [1977] 1 CMLR 533 and *Fisscher v Voorhuis Hengelo BV*: C-128/93 [1994] IRLR 662); and

(iii)   provisions which seek to limit the amount of compensation recoverable by restricting the extent to which a claim may be back-dated are less likely to be considered to make enforcement of rights impossible than more straightforward time limits (*Steenhorst-Neerings v Bestuur van de Bedrijfsvereniging voor Detailhandel, Ambachten en Huisvrouwen: C-338/91* [1993] ECR I-5475, [1994] IRLR 244; *Johnson v Chief Adjudication Officer (No 2): C-410/92* [1994] ECR I-5483, [1995] IRLR 157 and *Preston v Wolverhampton Healthcare NHS Trust* [2001] IRLR 237).

There was formerly thought to be a fourth principle, namely that where the right which the claimant seeks to enforce is a vertically directly effective right, time will not begin to run until the directive has been properly implemented (*Emmott v Minister for Social Welfare: C-208/90* [1993] ICR 8). But in *Fantask A/S v Industriministeriet (Erhvervsministeriet)*: C-188/95 [1997] ECR I-6783, [1998] All ER (EC) 1 the ECJ decided that *Emmott* was restricted to its own facts and applied the *Rewe* criteria. See also *Danske Slagterier v Bundesrepublik Deutschland*: C-445/06 [2009] 3 CMLR 311.

(3) *Reliance on directly effective European legislation to disapply a domestic bar to a claim*

The third mechanism by which unimplemented European legislation may be given effect in domestic courts and tribunals derives from the decision in *Biggs v Somerset County Council* [1995] ICR 811 (affirmed by the Court of Appeal at [1996] ICR 364) which concerned a woman who did not qualify for protection against unfair dismissal because she worked part-time. The claim was prompted by the decision of the House of Lords in the *EOC* case (above) that the hours thresholds contained in *Employment Protection (Consolidation) Act 1978* were indirectly discriminatory and could not be justified, contrary to the *Equal Treatment Directive*. The claim was submitted many years after the relevant dismissal. An issue arose, therefore, as to what the relevant time limit was. The claimant argued, inter alia, that her claim was for equal pay under *Art 157 [141, 119]*. The 'pay' in question was compensation for unfair dismissal. Though once a matter of considerable controversy, the ECJ has now decided that unfair dismissal compensation is pay for the purposes of *Art 157 [141, 119]* (*Seymour-Smith* [1999] ICR 447, ECJ). The applicant relied upon *Rankin v British Coal Corpn* [1993] IRLR 69 to support an argument that there was no time limit for EU rights other than a requirement that they be brought within a reasonable time. In her submission this meant within a reasonable time of the decision in *EOC* which was the point at which it first became clear that she might have a claim.

The decision of the EAT in *Biggs* was to the effect that the claim was not brought under *Art 157 [141, 119]* but rather under the domestic legislation. The significance of the EU right was that it operated to override and disapply what would otherwise have been a bar to the bringing of proceedings under the domestic law. As the claim was under domestic law the domestic time limit (three months from the date of dismissal) applied unless it was itself inconsistent with EU law which it was not. A radically 'free-standing' European right of the sort argued for by the claimant would not have been enforceable in the employment tribunal as its jurisdiction is strictly defined by statute. No statute has conferred on the industrial tribunal any jurisdiction to consider claims based solely on EU law, which are independent of the operation of any domestic legislation (cf also *McManus v Daylay Foods Ltd* (unreported) EAT/82/95 and *Preston v Wolverhampton Healthcare NHS Trust* [1997] IRLR 233, CA for the application of the same reasoning to claims for a redundancy payment and in relation to the indirectly discriminatory exclusion of part-timers from access to membership of occupational pension schemes respectively). The decision was expressly limited to a consideration of cases based upon *Art 157 [141, 119]*. The EAT accepted that as a result of *Emmott*, cases based on a directive might fall to be treated differently.

The obligation of English courts to determine questions of EU law in accordance with the decisions of, and the principles laid down by, the ECJ is to be found in the *European Communities Act 1972, s 2(1)*. The national court is entitled to take a point of EU law of its own motion (see also *Verholen*, above, where the Advocate General suggested that it was under a positive obligation to do so). *Article 267 [234, 177]* of the *Treaty of Rome* provides a mechanism whereby national courts may, and sometimes must, refer questions to the ECJ for a preliminary ruling. The jurisdiction of employment tribunals to determine whether a domestic provision is in fact incompatible with EU law was confirmed by the Court of Appeal in *R (on the application of Manson (Finian)) v Ministry of Defence* [2005] EWCA Civ 1678, [2006] ICR 355.

In *Mangold v Helm*: C-144/04 [2006] IRLR 143, the ECJ held that the domestic court was obliged to set aside provisions of national legislation which were incompatible with a directive even before the expiry date for implementation of the directive had passed. This conclusion was based in part on a controversial finding by the ECJ that non-discrimination on grounds of age is a 'general principle' of EU law, the source of which was held to be found in various international instruments and in the constitutional traditions common to the member states.

There was considerable doubt amongst commentators as to whether *Mangold* was correct. The soundness of this approach and the existence of a general principle of non-discrimination on grounds of age were doubted expressly by the Advocate General in *Palacios de la Villa v Cortefiel Servicios SA* [2007] IRLR 989. However, in *Seda Kucukdeveci v Swedex GmbH & Co KG*: C-555/07 [2010] IRLR 346, [2010] All ER (D) 126 (Feb) the ECJ followed *Mangold*. It held that the *Equal Treatment Framework Directive* is a specific application of a general principle of EU law which prohibits age discrimination; and that this principle was breached by a German law providing that employment before the age of 25 was to be disregarded when calculating service-related notice periods. On this basis, the ECJ held that the national court was required, even in a dispute between private individuals, to disapply the offending national law which was incapable of interpretation in line with the directive. In effect, and controversially, because of the conflict with established principles, this decision gave horizontal direct effect to a directive.

22.3 EU REQUIREMENTS AFFECTING EMPLOYMENT LAW

EU employment legislation has been enacted or proposed in relation to a wide variety of different areas, notably the following:

(a)   free movement of labour;

(b)   equal access to social security benefits;

(c)   equal pay and equal treatment;

(d)   information on terms of employment;

(e)   redundancy procedure;

(f)   rights on the transfer of an undertaking;

(g)   health and safety at work;

(h)   information and consultation;

(i)   agency workers;

(j)   posted workers;

(k)   employees of insolvent employers;

(l)   fixed-term workers;

(m)   capping bankers' bonuses.

These are examined briefly in the following paragraphs. More detailed expositions of these areas may be found elsewhere in this book: see the cross-references below.

22.4 FREE MOVEMENT OF LABOUR

Articles 45–48 [39–42, 48–51] of the *TFEU* require member states to permit the free movement of workers between member states. No discrimination based on nationality may be exercised against EU nationals in relation to employment, remuneration or other conditions of work and employment. Free access to employment is a fundamental right, and there must be a judicial remedy against decisions which refuse the benefit of that right to EU nationals (*Union Nationale des Entraîneurs et Cadres Techniques Professionnels du Football (UNECTEF) v Heylens*: C-222/86 [1987] ECR 4097, [1989] 1 CMLR 901, ECJ). Directives and regulations relating to these Articles have been passed. Great Britain has complied with these requirements so that EU nationals have a right to enter the country to take or seek work without the necessity of obtaining a work permit.

Article 45 [39, 48] of the *TFEU*, as a directly enforceable provision, was relied upon by the EAT in its decision in *Bossa v Nordstress Ltd* [1998] ICR 694 to disapply *ss 4* and *8(1)* of the *Race Relations Act 1976*. These sections had excluded those whose work was wholly or mainly outside Great Britain from bringing claims in the employment tribunal.

Directives regulate the mutual recognition of qualifications in member states for professions such as medicine and dentistry. *Directive 2005/36/EC* deals with mutual recognition of professional qualifications. EU nationals employed or seeking work here have the right to remain and to bring their families with them (see also FOREIGN EMPLOYEES (23)).

22.5 EQUAL ACCESS TO SOCIAL SECURITY BENEFITS

TFEU Art 48 [42, 51] provides for the passing by the Council and Parliament of the EU of such measures in the field of social security as are necessary to provide freedom of movement to workers. Such regulations, which provide for the aggregation of social security benefits which may have been paid in different member states, and for the payment of benefit in one member state where contributions have been made in another member state, have been passed (*Regulation 883/2004*; *Regulation 987/2009*). The regulations also ensure that the rules about liability to pay national insurance in the UK while working elsewhere in the EU are in line with the rules applied by the other Member States. Equal treatment between men and women in matters of social security, including occupational social security schemes, is largely dealt with by *Directive 79/7/EEC* and *Directive 2006/54/EC*; however, the ECJ has also held certain domestic social security provisions to be contrary to the *Equal Treatment Directive 76/207/EEC* (*Meyers v Adjudication Officer*: C-116/94 [1995] IRLR 498, a UK case about 'Family Credit'). A detailed account of this area is beyond the scope of this book.

22.6 EQUAL PAY AND EQUAL TREATMENT

Equality between men and women is an explicit objective of the EU (*Art 8 [3(2)]*). In all its activities, the EU must aim to eliminate inequalities, and to promote equality between men and women *(Art 8)*. *Art 157 [141, 119]* obliges each member state to ensure and maintain the principle that men and women should receive equal pay for equal work. Further, *Council Directive 76/207/EEC* required member states to take the measures necessary to implement the principle of equal treatment for men and women in relation to the following stages of employment: engagement, training, promotion, working conditions and dismissal; and *Directive 75/117/EEC* required member states to take measures necessary to achieve equal pay between the sexes. *Directives 76/207/EEC* and *75/117/EEC* were repealed and replaced by *Directive 2006/54/EC*.

The UK sought to comply with the requirements imposed by *Art 157* and *Council Directives 75/117/EEC* and *76/207/EEC*. However, in a number of cases, the ECJ held that the UK had failed to comply fully with its EU obligations and further legislation has had to be introduced. See eg *EC Commission v United Kingdom of Great Britain and Northern Ireland*: 61/81 [1982] ECR 2601, [1982] ICR 578, ECJ. The domestic courts have also proven to be willing to find, without a reference to the ECJ, that domestic legislation is incompatible with European provisions. See eg *Equal Opportunities Commission v Secretary of State for Trade and Industry* [2007] IRLR 327. Domestic law protection from sex discrimination is now contained in the *Equality Act 2010*. See also EQUAL PAY (21) and DISCRIMINATION AND EQUAL OPPORTUNITIES – I (10).

In October 1992 a *Directive on the Protection of Pregnant Women at Work* (*Directive 92/85/EEC*) was adopted, which has led to the inclusion of a number of new and improved maternity rights provisions in the *Employment Rights Act 1996*. See also MATERNITY AND PARENTAL RIGHTS (31). In 2008 the EU Commission proposed a new directive, to replace the current one. However, the EU has, to date, still not been able to agree on a replacement directive.

Parental leave. The government sought to implement the *Parental Leave Directive (Directive 96/34/EC*, now replaced by *Directive 2010/18/EC*) by bringing into force the *Maternity and Parental Leave Regulations 1999 (SI 1999/3312)*. The domestic provisions confer a right to leave only on parents of children born on or after 15 December 1999. The compatibility of this restriction with EU law was referred to the ECJ (*R v Secretary of State for Trade and Industry, ex p Trades Union Congress* [2000] IRLR 565). Consequent amendments were made to ensure compliance with the directive: see the *Maternity and Parental Leave (Amendment) Regulations 2001 (SI 2001/4010)*. The *Parental Leave (EU Directive) Regulations 2013* implemented *Directive 2010/18/EC* by amending provisions relating to parental leave in the *Employment Rights Act 1996* and the *Maternity and Parental Leave Regulations 1999*.

Part-timers. The *Part-time Workers (Prevention of Less Favourable Treatment) Regulations 2000 (SI 2000/1551)* implement the *EU Part-time Work Directive (97/81/EC)*.

In December 1991 the Commission adopted a *Recommendation on the Protection of the Dignity of Men and Women at Work (92/131/EEC)*, which is not legally binding, but will be taken into account by courts and tribunals (see **22.1** above). It may be especially relevant to complaints of sex discrimination founded upon incidents of sexual harassment (see DISCRIMINATION AND EQUAL OPPORTUNITIES   I (10)). A further *Recommendation on Child Care* was adopted in March 1992.

Discrimination on grounds other than sex. Article 19 [13] of the *TFEU* confers a power on the EU to legislate against discrimination on grounds of racial or ethnic origin, religion or belief, disability, age and sexual orientation. The European Council has adopted two directives which are intended to give effect to the broad anti-discrimination principles found in *Art 19* of the *TFEU*.

The first is *Council Directive 2000/43/EC* of 29 June 2000 implementing the principle of equal treatment between persons irrespective of racial or ethnic origin. The directive prohibits direct and (unless it is objectively justified) indirect discrimination on grounds of racial or ethnic origin in both the public and private sectors. It does not prohibit discrimination on grounds of nationality. Harassment is expressly to be treated as an act of direct discrimination. Victimisation is also prohibited. There is a genuine occupational requirement defence. The provisions of the directive are now implemented by the *Equality Act 2010*.

The second directive is *Council Directive 2000/78/EC* of 27 November 2000 establishing a general framework for equal treatment in employment and occupation. The directive prohibits direct and unjustified indirect discrimination on grounds of 'religion or belief, disability, age or sexual orientation'. Like the *Race Discrimination Framework Directive* described above, it applies to both public and private sectors, prohibits harassment and victimisation, and includes an 'occupational requirement' defence. *Article 5* of the directive introduces a duty to take proportionate and appropriate measures to enable disabled persons to have access to, participate in or advance in employment or to undergo training which is analogous to the obligation imposed to by the *Equality Act 2010, ss 20* and *39(5)* to make reasonable adjustments: see *Navas (Chacon) v Eurest Colectividades SA*: C-13/05 [2006] ECR I-6467, [2007] ICR 1, ECJ. *Article 6* creates a defence of objective justification in cases of direct age discrimination. The directive is now implemented in Great Britain by the *Equality Act 2010*.

In November 2012 the European Commission adopted a proposal for a directive on improving the gender balance among non–executive directors of companies listed on stock exchanges and related measures. The proposed directive sets an objective of a 40% presence of the under-represented gender among non–executive directors of companies listed on stock exchanges. The Commission's proposal falls under the ordinary legislative procedure, which means that the Council and the European Parliament will need to approve the final text of the directive as co-legislators.

22.7   INFORMATION ON TERMS OF EMPLOYMENT

Directive 91/533/EEC (the *Information on Conditions of Employment Directive*) was adopted in October 1991. As a result of this directive, the United Kingdom, by means of amending the *Employment Protection (Consolidation) Act 1978* (now the *Employment Rights Act 1996*), extended the rights which already existed for employees to receive written particulars of the terms of their employment (see **7.4** CONTRACT OF EMPLOYMENT).

22.8   REDUNDANCY PROCEDURE

Directive 98/59/EC contains requirements for the approximation of the laws of member states relating to collective redundancies. This was complied with by the enactment of provisions now to be found in *TULRCA 1992, ss 188–198*. See **37.2–37.6** REDUNDANCY – **II**.

The ECJ found that by restricting the obligation to consult prior to collective redundancies to circumstances where the employer recognises a trade union in respect of the class of employees affected, the UK had failed properly to implement the predecessor to *Directive 98/59/EC*, *Directive 75/129/EEC* (*EC Commission v United Kingdom*: C-383/92 [1994] ECR I-2479, [1994] ICR 664, ECJ). In order to remedy this, the *Collective Redundancies and Transfer of Undertakings (Protection of Employment) (Amendment) Regulations 1995 (SI 1995/2587)* were enacted (see also **22.9** below).

22.9   RIGHTS ON TRANSFER OF BUSINESS

The *Transfer of Undertakings (Protection of Employment) Regulations 1981 (SI 1981/1794) (*now repealed and replaced by the *Transfer of Undertakings (Protection of Employment) Regulations 2006 (SI 2006/246)* were intended to implement the requirements of *Directive 77/187/EEC* (the *Acquired Rights Directive*). In fact, the *1981 Regulations* proved to be defective in several respects, and various amendments were made by the *Trade Union Reform and Employment Rights Act 1993* in an attempt to bring them into line with the directive. However, subsequent to those amendments being made, a further failure properly to comply was identified in *EC Commission v United Kingdom*: C-382/92 [1994] ECR I-2435, [1994] ICR 664 when the ECJ found that by restricting the obligation to consult prior to a transfer to circumstances where the employer recognises a trade union in respect of the class of employees affected, the UK had failed properly to implement *Directive 77/187/EEC*. In order to remedy this, the *Regulations* mentioned in **22.8** above *(SI 1995/2587)* were enacted.

On 12 March 2001, a new *Transfers Directive (2001/23/EC)* came into force. It is intended to codify the *Acquired Rights Directive (77/187/EEC)* and the amendments thereto adopted in 1998 (which are described in the main text). The *Transfer of Undertakings (Protection of Employment) Regulations 2006 (SI 2006/246)* came into force with effect from 6 April 2006 and are intended to implement the *Transfers Directive.*

(See TRANSFER OF UNDERTAKINGS (**50**).)

22.10   HEALTH AND SAFETY

Between 1977 and 1986, the EU adopted directives on various aspects of health and safety, including safety signs, lead, asbestos and noise. A framework directive, *Directive 89/391/EEC* on the introduction of measures to encourage improvements in the safety and health of workers at work, was adopted in 1989. A number of statutory instruments have implemented the framework directive in national law (e.g. the *Management of Health and Safety at Work Regulations 1999 (SI 1999/3242)*, the *Health and Safety (Consultation with Employees) Regulations 1996 (SI 1996/1513)*, the *Control of Substances Hazardous to Health Regulations 2002 (SI 2002/2677)*).

22.10 European Union Law

The framework directive also provides for further directives, known as 'daughter' directives, to be made in particular areas (e.g. work equipment, personal protective equipment). A number of daughter directives have been made (e.g. *Directive 89/654/EEC* concerning the minimum safety and health requirements for the workplace, *Directive 2009/104/EC* concerning the minimum safety and health requirements for the use of work equipment by workers at work) and implemented in national law by health and safety regulations (e.g. the *Workplace (Health, Safety and Welfare) Regulations 1992 (SI 1992/3004)*).

(See 25.25 HEALTH AND SAFETY AT WORK – I.)

22.11 WORKING TIME

One directive which was adopted despite the objections of the UK is the *Working Time Directive 93/104/EC* (now repealed and replaced by *Directive 2003/88/EC*). It provided, with certain exceptions, for a maximum 48-hour week including overtime, averaged over four months. There was also provision for a minimum daily rest period of 11 consecutive hours, for a weekly break of not less than 35 consecutive hours, and for restrictions upon the length of night shifts. Finally there was provision for a minimum of four weeks' paid holiday per annum.

Whilst the directive was adopted under the provisions of the *TFEU* relating to Health and Safety at Work, the view of the UK government was that, in substance, it was an attempt to regulate conditions of employment, a matter which is outside the EU's competence. The UK brought a challenge to the directive in the European Court of Justice which was rejected by the Court (*United Kingdom v EU Council*: C-84/94 [1997] ICR 443).

In *Dominguez v Centre Informatique du Centre Ouest Atlantique* [2012] IRLR 321 the ECJ held that the right to four weeks' paid annual leave in *Art 7(1)* of the directive has vertical direct effect. Thus, the claimant was to be able to rely directly on *Art 7(1)*, but only if the referring court was satisfied that her employer, which dealt with social security, was an emanation of the state.

The *Working Time Regulations 1998 (SI 1998/1833)* came into force on 1 October 1998. The provisions of the *Regulations* relating to annual leave are summarised in HOLIDAYS (27); as to the provisions relating to hours of work and rest breaks, see 26.15 HEALTH AND SAFETY AT WORK – II. In *R (on the application of the Broadcasting, Entertainment, Cinematographic and Theatre Union) v Secretary of State for Trade and Industry*: C-173/99 [2001] ICR 1152 the ECJ held that *reg 13* of the *Regulations*, restricting entitlement to paid annual leave to workers continuously employed for 13 weeks by the same employer, constituted an impermissible restriction on the rights conferred by the *Working Time Directive*. Consequential alterations to the *Regulations* were made by the *Working Time (Amendment) Regulations 2002 (SI 2002/3128)* with effect from 6 April 2003: see HOLIDAYS (27). In *European Commission v United Kingdom*: C-484/04 [2006] ECR I-7471, [2007] ICR 592, the ECJ held that the UK had failed to fulfil its obligations under the *Working Time Directive* by issuing guidance on the *Regulations* which advised employers that they must make sure that workers can take their rest, but were not required to make sure they do take their rest.

The *Working Time Directive (93/104/EEC)* excluded employment in certain sectors from its scope. The sectors were: road, rail, air, inland waterway and lake transport, sea fishing, other work at sea, and doctors in training. *Directive 2000/34/EC* extended the application of the directive to non-mobile workers in the excluded sectors (with a special transitional period for its application to doctors in training). A consolidating *Directive 2003/88/EC* was adopted on 4 November 2003 and this is now the *Directive* governing this area (see WORKING TIME (55)). This has been implemented by the *Working Time (Amendment) Regulations 2003 (SI 2003/1684)*.

A specific directive covering the organisation of the working time of seafarers (*1999/63/EC*) was adopted on 21 June 1999. Domestic provision is made for sea fishermen and the inland water way sector by the *Fishing Vessels (Working Time: Sea Fishermen) Regulations 2004 (SI 2004/1713)* and the *Merchant Shipping (Working Time: Inland Waterways) Regulations 2003 (SI 2003/3049)*.

The *Working Time Directive 2003/88/EC* has recently been under review by the EU. However, in February 2013, the Commission announced that the European social partners had failed to come to an agreement on the review. As a result of this failure, it is expected that the Commission will draft a new legislative proposal.

22.12 INFORMATION AND CONSULTATION

The *European Works Councils Directive 94/45/EC* (now repealed and replaced by *Directive 2009/38/EC*) was adopted under the Social Protocol procedure. See EMPLOYEE PARTICIPATION (15). The original *Directive* was implemented with effect from 15 January 2000 by the *Transnational Information and Consultation of Employees Regulations 1999 (SI 1999/3323)*. *Directive 2009/38/EC* was implemented by way of amendment to the *1999 Regulations*: see the *Transnational Information and Consultation of Employees (Amendment) Regulations 2010 (SI 2010/1088)*.

The *Directive of the European Parliament and of the Council 2002/14/EC* establishing a general framework for informing and consulting employees in the EU has been implemented in the UK by the *Information and Consultation of Employees Regulations 2004 (SI 2004/3426)*.

22.13 AGENCY WORKERS

The *EC Temporary Workers Directive (Directive 2008/104/EC)* provides for, amongst other things:

* equal treatment between temporary agency workers and permanent workers from the commencement of their work in terms of basic working and employment conditions (including working time, overtime, breaks, rest periods, night work, holidays and pay);

* the ability for member states to derogate from this by way of collective agreements or through agreements between social partners at national level (which the UK has done by implementing a 12-week qualifying period for agency workers' rights to equal basic working and employment conditions, which has been agreed by the TUC and the CBI); and

* temporary agency workers to be informed about permanent employment opportunities with the hirer.

The UK implemented the directive through the *Agency Workers Regulations 2010 (SI 2010/93)* which came into force in October 2011.

See TEMPORARY AND SEASONAL EMPLOYEES (45).

22.14 POSTED WORKERS

The *Posted Workers Directive (Directive 96/71/EC)* aims to strike a balance between workers' rights on the one hand, and freedom of movement of services and freedom of establishment on the other. It aims to address lack of clarity about which law applies to workers who are posted from one undertaking within the EU to another; to avoid local terms and conditions being undermined by the use of "cheaper" foreign workers; and to avoid abuse of foreign workers. Broadly, it provides that temporarily posted workers should enjoy the same basic minimum employment rights as workers in the country to which they are posted. The rights covered by the directive include maximum work periods, minimum paid holidays, minimum rates of pay, health and safety and hygiene at work, and protective measures for pregnant women or those who have recently given birth. It does not cover all statutory employment rights; for example, the right not to be unfairly dismissed is outside the scope of the directive.

There are no UK Regulations which implement the directive. Rather, UK legislation relevant to the directive (e.g. the *Working Time Regulations 1998* and the *National Minimum Wage Act 1998*) applies to all workers, whether they are employed on a temporary or a permanent basis in the UK.

The EU Commission has proposed that *Directive 96/71* be supplemented by a further directive, which would establish a common framework of provisions, including measures to prevent circumvention or abuse of the existing rules. The Commission's proposed new directive, which was published in March 2012, is yet to be approved by the European Council and the European Parliament.

See FOREIGN EMPLOYEES (**24.3**).

22.15 EMPLOYEES OF INSOLVENT EMPLOYERS

Minimum rights for the employees of insolvent employers were specified by *Directive 80/987/EEC*, which has now been repealed and replaced by *Directive 2008/94/EC* (see **29.1** INSOLVENCY OF EMPLOYER).

22.16 FIXED-TERM WORKERS

On 28 June 1999, the Council adopted a directive transposing into European law a framework agreement on fixed-term work (*1999/70/EC*). The directive was implemented in the UK by the *Fixed-term Employees (Prevention of Less Favourable Treatment) Regulations 2002 (SI 2002/2034)*. It prohibits less favourable treatment of fixed-term workers on account of their fixed-term status, save where such treatment is objectively justified; and restricts successive renewals of fixed-term contracts (see **45.8** TEMPORARY AND SEASONAL EMPLOYEES).

22.17 CAPPING BANKERS' BONUSES

"*CRD IV*" is a major package of proposed reforms to the EU's capital requirements regime for credit institutions and investment firms. Most of the package lies outside the field of employment. However, included within the proposals is a "*cap*" on bankers' bonuses, which would require that the value of a individual's bonus should be no greater than the value of his or her basic salary; in other words, the ratio of bonus to basic salary should not exceed 1:1. However, the ratio could be raised to 1:2 with the express permission of the shareholders. The purpose of these proposals is to disincentivise excessively risky behaviour by bankers.

These measures were agreed by the EU Council in March 2013. The Council has proposed that they be included in the CRD IV Directive, which is likely to require implementing legislation in the UK by 1 January 2014.

23   Foreign Employees

23.1   ENTITLEMENT TO WORK IN THE UK

The first issue which arises in respect of employees who are not nationals of the UK is whether they are lawfully entitled to work in this country. The existing regime draws a broad distinction between nationals of Member States of the European Economic Area ('EEA'), which now comprises 27 Member-States, and others.

- *Migrant workers from within the EEA* — Employees who are nationals of countries within the EEA are generally entitled to work in the UK, see further the *Immigration (European Economic Area) Regulations 2006 (SI 2006/1003)* which came into force on 30 April 2006. An exception to this general rule was created by the *Accession (Immigration and Worker Registration) Regulations 2004 (SI 2004/1219)* (as amended by *SI 2006/1003*). Under the *2004 regulations*, individuals who are nationals of recently acceded Member-States (apart from Cyprus and Malta) and who wanted to work in the UK for more than one month were required to register with the home office 'Worker Registration Scheme' as soon as they found work. The Worker Registration Scheme closed on 30 April 2011. However, Bulgarian and Romanian nationals will, unless they are exempt, still need to apply for permission to work.

- *Migrant workers from outside the EEA* — With the exception of Swiss nationals and Bulgarian and Romanian nationals, individuals who are not nationals of a Member State of the EEA currently have their entitlement to work in the UK decided by the points-based system which came into force in the UK in November 2008. The points-based system largely replaced the long-standing work permits scheme. Swiss nationals are exempted from the points-based system and are accordingly free to work in the UK. Bulgarian and Romanian nationals will continue to need work permits. See further below the discussion of the important changes to the points-based system introduced with effect from 6 April 2011.

At present, responsibility for administering the points-based system and the more limited work permit scheme applicable to Bulgarian and Romanian nationals lies with the UK Border Agency. The Agency's website contains detailed information and guidance on the procedure governing the application of the system: www.ukba.homeoffice.gov.uk. Information for EEA nationals on working in another EEA country is available through the EURES network at europa.eu.

23.2   NATIONALS OF THE EUROPEAN ECONOMIC AREA

The principle of free movement of labour, which is now applicable to all members of the EEA, is derived principally from *art 39* (formerly *art 48*) of the Treaty of Rome as amended, and *Regulation 1612/68*. Other relevant pieces of legislation include *Directive 68/360, Regulation 1251/70*(repealed by *Regulation 635/2006*), *Directive 90/365* and *Directive 90/364*. On 30 April 2006, the *Immigration (European Economic Area) Regulations 2006 (SI 2006/1003)* came into force in the UK. These regulations govern the freedom of movement of citizens of EU states and their families (including civil partners). Although Turkey and certain other states have Association Agreements with the EU, these confer no general right of free movement upon individuals (*R v Secretary of State for the Home Department, ex p Narin* [1990] 2 CMLR 233; but see also *Sevince v Staatssecretaris van Justitie*: C-192/89 [1992] 2 CMLR 57).

23.2 Foreign Employees

The family of an EEA worker may also come to this country without any restriction on their right of entry. EEA nationals are entitled to the same treatment as UK nationals with regard to pay, working conditions, access to housing and property, training, social security and trade union rights. They are free, if unemployed but seeking work, to claim jobseeker's allowance for up to three months if they have been claiming benefit in their own country for at least four weeks. There is also a considerable body of EU legislation directed towards establishing equivalence of mutual recognition of professional qualifications by member states (see **22.4 EUROPEAN UNION LAW**). More restrictive rules however apply to the families of Bulgarian and Romanian nationals.

Pursuant to the *Immigration (European Economic Area) Regulations 2006*, EEA nationals (and Swiss nationals) may, along with their families, reside in the UK for an initial period of three months, provided that they have a valid passport or identity card and do not become an unreasonable burden on the domestic social security system. After the initial three month period has expired, the EEA/Swiss national may continue to reside in the UK along with their family for so long as they continue to be a 'qualified person'. A person will be a 'qualified person' for the purposes of the Regulations if he or she is: a job-seeker, a worker, a self-employed person, a self-sufficient person or a student. EEA and Swiss nationals will acquire a permanent right of residence if they have both resided and worked in the UK for more than five years.

Member states are entitled to except employment in the public service from the general requirement of free movement, and to reserve such employment for their own nationals (*EC Treaty, art 39(4)*); see also **PUBLIC SECTOR EMPLOYEES (35)**. These provisions have given rise to a substantial number of reported cases in national courts and in the ECJ, a detailed discussion of which is beyond the scope of this book.

Collective agreements must take account of comparable employment completed in the public service of another member state for the purposes of seniority and promotion (*Schöning-Kougebetopoulou v Freie und Hansestadt Hamburg*: C-15/96 [1998] All ER (EC) 97). A clause in a collective agreement which treats foreign nationals differently in this respect breaches *art 39* of the Treaty of Rome and *Regulation 1612/68* on freedom of movement. For an ECJ ruling concerning the relationship between *art 39* and national legislation denying termination payments to a worker who left employment in order to take up work in another member state, see *Graf v Filzmoser Maschinenbau GmbH*: C-190/98 [2000] All ER (EC) 170.

See also **EUROPEAN UNION LAW (22)**.

23.3 EUROPEAN UNION: POSTED WORKERS

Measures have been taken to implement in the UK the *Posting of Workers Directive (96/71)* which came into force on 16 December 1999. The *Directive* now applies to all EEA states. Broadly, it provides that minimum terms and conditions laid down by national laws, regulations or collective agreements should apply to workers posted temporarily by their employer to work in another State.

Article 1 provides that the *Directive* applies to undertakings which:

(a)   post workers to another member state on their account and under their direction under a contract concluded between the undertaking and a party in the other state for whom the services are intended;

(b)   make intra-company postings; or

(c)   are temporary employment undertakings or agencies which hire out workers to undertakings established or operating in an EU member state.

A further requirement in each case is that there must be an employment relationship between the undertaking making the posting and the worker during the period of posting. The terms and conditions of employment covered by the *Directive* are set out in *art 3*, as follows:

(i)   maximum work periods and minimum rest periods;

(ii)   minimum paid annual holidays;

(iii)   minimum rates of pay, including overtime rates (but not supplementary occupational pension schemes);

(iv)   conditions of hiring out workers, in particular the supply of workers by temporary employment undertakings;

(v)   health, safety and hygiene at work;

(vi)   measures to protect at work pregnant women, new mothers, children and young people; and

(vii)   equality of treatment between men and women and other provisions on non-discrimination.

Various flexibilities are permitted under the *Directive*, such as not applying the minimum rate of pay to postings of less than one month. However, the UK Government has decided not to take advantage of any of the exemptions.

Workers may enforce their rights under the *Directive* in the territory of the member state to which they were posted without prejudice to their rights in the country where they are normally employed (*art 6*).

In *Mazzoleni*: C-165/98 [2001] ECR I-2189, the ECJ ruled (15 March 2001) that the principle of freedom of movement did not preclude one member state from requiring an undertaking established in another state which provides services in the territory of the first state to pay its workers the minimum remuneration fixed by the national rules of that state. However, application of these rules might prove to be disproportionate where the workers operate in a frontier region and are required to carry out their work, on a part-time basis and for brief periods, in more than one member state. It is for the host member state to decide the extent to which the imposition of a minimum wage is necessary and proportionate to protect the workers in question. In a number of cases emanating from Germany, the ECJ has examined the compatibility of certain domestic laws governing posted workers with the principle of freedom of movement. These cases include: *Finalarte Sociedade de Construcao Civil Lda v Urlaubs- und Lohnausgleichskasse der Bauwirtschaft*: C-49/98 [2001] ECR I-7831; *European Commission v Germany*: C-341/02 [2005] ECR I-2733, ECJ; *Ruffert (Dirk) v Land Niedersachsen*: C-346/06 [2008] ECR I-1989, [2008] All ER (EC) 902, ECJ; and *Hudzinski v Agentur fur Arbeit Wesel - Familienkasse*: C-611/10 [2012] 3 CMLR 23. The Posting of Workers Directive was considered by the High Court in *R (on the application of Low) v Secretary of State for the Home Department* [2009] EWHC 35 (Admin), [2009] 2 CMLR 539. In that case, an Irish company had hired non-EU nationals to work in certain catering establishments in the UK. The Secretary of State refused to confirm that these workers had a right to work under EU law. The applicants applied to have that decision judicially reviewed. They sought to argue that they had a right to work in the UK on an application of *art 49* of the Nice Treaty and/or under the *Posting of Workers Directive*, particularly because the Irish company which employed them had a right to provide services in the UK. The High Court rejected the claim. It held that the arrangements constituted an unlawful attempt to circumvent enforceable UK immigration laws. The Court of Appeal upheld the High Court's judgment, [2010] EWCA Civ 4.

23.3 Foreign Employees

Most existing UK legislation relevant to the *Directive* applies to all workers, whether they are employed on a temporary or permanent basis in the UK (eg the *Working Time Regulations 1998*, the *National Minimum Wage Act 1998*, and health and safety legislation). For a discussion of the effect of the Directive on the application of the *Employment Rights Act 1996* see the Court of Appeal's judgment in *Lawson v Serco Ltd* [2004] EWCA Civ 12, [2004] ICR 204 and the opinion of Lord Hoffman in the House of Lords [2006] UKHL 3, [2006] ICR 250 at 256 para 13.

In March 2012, the European Commission proposed new rules designed to increase the protection of posted workers. The rules are aimed in particular at improving levels of monitoring and compliance with the requirements imposed by the Directive. This was debated in Council later in 2012. For further information on the proposals visit the Commission's website at: ec.europa.eu.

23.4 NON-EEA NATIONALS

Up until November 2008, nationals from outside the EEA and Switzerland who were subject to immigration control were generally obliged to obtain work permits in order to be able to take up employment in the UK. On 26 November 2008, the work permit system was largely abolished and replaced by tier 2 of the points-based system (although work permit arrangements continue for employers wishing to recruit Bulgarian and Romanian nationals). This system is operated by the UK Border Agency. Under the points-based system, migrant workers need to pass a points-based assessment before they are given permission to enter or remain in the United Kingdom. As originally constituted, the points-based system consisted of five tiers, with each tier having different points requirements. Points are awarded to reflect the migrant's ability, experience, age and, where appropriate, the level of need within the sector in which the migrant will be working.

(a) tier 1 was concerned with highly skilled workers, for example scientists and entrepreneurs (this tier was effectively abolished with effect from 6 April 2011, for which see below);

(b) tier 2 is concerned with skilled workers with a job offer, for example teachers and nurses;

(c) tier 3 (currently suspended) is concerned with low skilled workers filling temporary shortages, for example construction workers for a particular project;

(d) tier 4 is concerned with students; and

(e) tier 5 is concerned with youth mobility and temporary workers, for example musicians coming to play in a concert.

A number of significant changes to the points-based system were introduced with effect from 6 April 2011. The key changes include the following: tier 1 is effectively closed, save that 1000 visas will be made available per annum under a new 'exceptional talent' route; the issuing of visas in respect of tier 2 skilled workers is subject to an annual cap of 20,700; employers seeking to recruit tier 2 workers no longer have an annual allocation for the number of workers they can bring into the country but instead need to apply to the UK Border Agency for a certificate of sponsorship for each specific vacancy; the annual tier 2 cap does not apply in cases where the employer is seeking to fill a vacancy attracting a salary of £150,000 or more; tier 2 workers from outside the EU who want to come to the UK will need to have a graduate level job, speak an intermediate level of English, and meet specific salary and employment requirements. Guidance on the new approach to tier 2 visas along with other information about the points-based system can be found on the UK Border Agency's website: www.ukba.homeoffice.gov.uk. Organisations which apply to sponsor a migrant worker must agree to comply with a range of duties relating to the sponsoring arrangements, including duties relating to record-keeping, reporting (for example, where the sponsored worker fails to turn up to work) and allowing UK Border Agency staff to make announced and unannounced site visits. For further information on the obligations of sponsor organisations see the UK Border Agency website: www.ukba.homeoffice.gov.uk.

23.5 IMMIGRATION, ASYLUM AND NATIONALITY ACT 1996

Since 27 January 1997, it has been an offence to employ a person who is not entitled, under the Immigration Rules, to work in the UK. Originally, this offence was provided for under s 8 of the *Asylum and Immigration Act 1996* ('*AIA 1996*'). However, on 29 February 2008, s 8 AIA 1996 was repealed and replaced by provisions in the *Immigration Asylum and Nationality Act 2006* (IAN).

23.6 *Sections 15–26* of *IAN* in particular constitute a statutory scheme governing the treatment of employers who employ persons not lawfully entitled to work in the UK. Under *s 15*, the Secretary of State may issue a penalty notice to employers who employ persons: (a) who have no leave to enter or remain in the UK; or (b) whose leave is invalid, has ceased to have effect or does not entitle them to work in the UK. The penalty notice will require the employer to pay a specific amount subject to a statutory maximum. The employer will be excused from paying the penalty if he complied with certain 'prescribed requirements' relating to the employment, unless he knew at the time that the employment was unlawful despite his having complied with the requirements. The 'prescribed requirements' are provided for under the Immigration (Restrictions on Employment) Order 2007. The requirements imposed under the Order include that employers must scrutinise the passports and biometric immigration documents held by their potential employees and keep copies of those documents. Under *s 16*, the employer has a right to object to the notice by sending an objection to the Secretary of State. *Section 17* provides that the employer also has a right of appeal to the court against the penalty notice. The introduction of a penalty notice regime is one of the key novelties of the scheme introduced under *IAN*. Under *s 19*, the Secretary of State must issue a Code of Practice relating to the giving of penalties. Pursuant to s *21*, a person who employs someone who is subject to immigration control knowing that he or she is either in the UK unlawfully or is not lawfully entitled to work in the UK will be guilty of an offence and liable, on conviction, to imprisonment and/or a fine. *Section 22* provides that an employer (whether corporate or not) shall be treated as knowing a fact about an employee for the purposes of *s 21* if a person within the employing body has responsibility for an aspect of the employment and knows that fact. *Section 22(2)* makes provision for officers of the employer to be liable to conviction along with the employer itself in circumstances where the offence is committed with the consent or connivance of the officer. Under *s 23*, the Secretary of State is required to issue a code of practice to assist employers in avoiding racially discriminatory behaviour in the context of their complying with their obligations under *IAN*. The current version of the code can be found on the on the UK Border Agency website, along with general guidance for employers on the application of *IAN*.

In *Vakante v Governing Body of Addey & Stanhope School* [2004] EWCA Civ 1065, [2004] 4 All ER 1056, the Court of Appeal considered the question of whether a claimant could pursue complaints of race discrimination against the respondent employer in circumstances where, as a person who was subject to immigration control, he had entered into an employment with the respondent knowing that the employment was unlawful. The Court of Appeal found that the claims of race discrimination could not be pursued because they were inextricably bound up with the claimant's own illegal acts and any other conclusion would create the impression that the Tribunal was condoning the illegal conduct. Compare that judgment with the judgment of the Employment Appeal Tribunal in *Blue Chip Trading Ltd v Helbawi (A)* (UKEAT/0397/08/LA) [2009] IRLR 128. In *Helbawi*, a foreign student had breached the Immigration Rules by working more than 20 hours per week for his employer. The EAT held that the fact that some of the work done by the student was unlawful did not render the entire contract of employment illegal. Instead, the contract was severable from the unlawful arrangements so that the student could pursue a claim under the contract in respect of those times when he was working lawfully and in accordance with the Immigration Rules. See further the Court of Appeal's judgment in *Hounga v Adenike Allen & Anor* [2012] EWCA Civ 609: Nigerian national worked for the respondents as an au pair; the tribunal was barred from hearing her claim of race discrimination on the basis that she had illegally posed as a member of the respondents' family in order to obtain entry into the United Kingdom. The Supreme Court has now granted permission to appeal in *Hounga*.

APPLICABLE LAW V JURISDICTION

Where a particular employment relationship has a foreign element, questions may arise in the context of any *common law claim* brought by the employee as to what law governs the claim. Thus, for example, where an employee who is based in France seeks to sue his British-based employer for breach of contract, a question may arise as to whether the claim is to be decided under English or French law. Alternatively, where a British-based employee is injured whilst travelling for work abroad, a question may arise as to whether any tortious claim for personal injury brought by the employee is governed by English law or the law of the country where the accident took place.

Importantly, the question of what law governs a particular common law claim brought by an employee (the applicable law question) is entirely distinct from the question of whether the court has jurisdiction to hear the particular claim (the jurisdiction question). Thus, for example, a contract may be governed by the laws of Saudi Arabia. However, this is not in itself determinative of whether the English courts have jurisdiction to hear the claim. It is also important to be aware that, so far as *statutory employment claims* are concerned, the question which needs to be posed is not: 'what law governs the contract of employment?' but rather: 'Is this a claim which falls within the territorial scope of the particular legislation?'. If the claim falls within the territorial scope of the particular legislation, then, irrespective of what law governs the contract of employment, the employment tribunal will have jurisdiction to hear the claim. These issues are examined in further detail below.

23.7 APPLICABLE LAW – CONTRACT AND TORT

Where an employer and employee are both English, and the work is done in England, it will generally be clear that the contract of employment is governed by English law, and there will normally be no doubt as to the jurisdiction of the English courts to deal with any contractual disputes which may arise. However, where there is a foreign element of some kind, difficult questions may arise concerning the system of law which governs the contract, and as to where any proceedings may be brought in this country. This is an extremely complicated area of law, and what follows is intended only as a simplified outline guide.

The *Contracts (Applicable Law) Act 1990* was enacted to give force in the United Kingdom to the *Rome Convention on the Law Applicable to Contractual Obligations* of 1980. That was a treaty between the EC member states, and provision is made for the ECJ to be given jurisdiction to determine questions concerning its interpretation (see EUROPEAN UNION LAW (22)). However, the Act applies to all contracts, not merely to those with an EC connection. With effect from 17 December 2009, the *Convention* ceased to apply in the UK and was replaced by a new *Regulation EC No 593/2008*, known as *Rome I*.

Under the *Convention*, a contract was governed by the system of law chosen by the parties, such choice being either expressed or demonstrated with reasonable certainty by the terms of the contract or the circumstances of the case (*art 3(1)*). However, in the case of a contract of employment, a choice of law made by the parties could not deprive an employee of the protection afforded to him by the mandatory rules of the system of law which would apply if no such choice had been made (*art 6(1)*). Mandatory rules are those which cannot be derogated from by contract in the law of the country concerned (*art 3(3)*). Hence, for example, under the *Convention*, if an English employee worked in Great Britain for an English employer, it is not possible to deprive him of the right to claim unfair dismissal (51), (52), (53)by providing that the contract shall be governed by, say, Hong Kong law (see further *Base Metal Trading Ltd v Shamurin* [2003] EWHC 2419 (Comm), [2004] 1 All ER (Comm) 159). In addition to showing deference to mandatory rules of the forum, the *Convention* made clear that the application of a rule of law specified by the *Convention* may be refused if it is 'manifestly incompatible with the public policy (*ordre publique*) of the forum' (*art 16*). In *Duarte v Black and Decker Corpn* [2007] EWHC 2720 (QB), [2008] 1 All ER (Comm) 401, the High Court was called upon to consider whether English common law principles relating to the enforcement of restrictive covenants in a contract of employment effectively overrode the governing law of the contract, which was in that case the law of Maryland. The court held that English common law rules relating to the enforcement of restrictive covenants in employment contracts did not constitute mandatory rules of the English forum and, hence, *art 6.1* of the *Convention* was not engaged in respect of the covenants. However, the court also decided that those common law rules enshrined public policy principles which should be applied to the contract under *art 16* of the *Convention*. As it happens, the court found that the law of Maryland in any event operated so as to ensure that the covenants were too wide to be enforceable.

Under *art 7(1)* of the *Convention*, even if one system of law applies (e.g. English law), effect could be given to the mandatory rules of the law of another country with which the contract has a close connection (e.g. France), provided that those mandatory rules would be applied under French law whatever system of law governed the contract, and depending upon the nature and purpose of those rules and the consequences of their application or non-application. However, importantly *art 7(1)* did not have the force of law in the United Kingdom (*Contracts (Applicable Law) Act 1990 Act, s 2(2)*).

Under the *Convention*, if the parties to a contract of employment had not chosen the system of law which was to govern the contract, then it would be governed by:

(a)   the law of the country in which the employee habitually carries out his work in performance of the contract, even if he is temporarily employed in another country; or

(b)   if the employee does not habitually carry out his work in any one country, the law of the country in which the place of business through which he was engaged is situated,

unless it appears from the circumstances as a whole that the contract is more closely connected with another country, in which case the contract shall be governed by the law of that country (*art 6(2)*).

With effect from 17 December 2009, the *Convention* ceased to apply in the UK. The law governing any contract of employment is now to be determined by reference to *Regulation EC No 593/2008*, known as *Rome I*. So far as employment contracts are concerned, the provisions of *Rome I* broadly mirror those contained in the *Convention* (see in particular *art 8*).

The rules determining what law is to apply to claims in tort brought by an employee against an employer have evolved over time. Originally, non-statutory common law rules applied, see, eg *Sayers v International Drilling Co NV* [1971] 3 All ER 163 and *Johnson v Coventry Churchill International Ltd* [1992] 3 All ER 14. From 1 May 1996 until 11 January 2009, the common law rules were abolished and superseded by provisions contained in the *Private*

23.7   Foreign Employees

International Law (Miscellaneous Provisions) Act 1995 ('*PILMPA*'). Under *PILMPA*, the general rule was that the applicable law would be the law of the country in which the events constituting the tort in question occur (*s 11(1)*). That rule was displaced where, viewed overall, it appeared that the tort was more closely connected to a country other than that which would be appropriate if the general rule were applied (*s 12(1)*). See further *Harding v Wealands* [2006] UKHL 32, [2006] 3 WLR 83 where the House of Lords decided, in respect of an accident which took place in New South Wales, that the provisions of *PILMPA* did not operate to enable the capping provisions contained in New South Wales personal injury legislation to apply to quantification by the UK courts of personal injury damages. However, with effect from 11 January 2009, the provisions of PILMPA, insofar as they relate to torts in the employment context were superseded by *Regulation EC No 864/2007*, known as *Rome II*. Under *art 4* of *Rome II*, the general rule is that the law which applies to the tort is the law of the country where the damage occurred. However, this general rule may be displaced in circumstances where the parties are habitually resident in another country at the time the damage occurs (*art 4(2)*) or where it is clear from all the circumstances that the tort is manifestly more closely connected with another country (*art 4(3)*). Specific provision is made in *Rome II* for particular non-contractual obligations in *arts 5–13*. Those relevant to the employment context are *art 6* (unfair competition), *art 8* (intellectual property rights, for example database rights) and *art 9* (industrial action).

23.8   JURISDICTION

Common law claims

Where an employee brings a claim based on breach of the contract of employment or, alternatively, a claim in tort against his employer and the events about which the employee complains have a connection with more than one country, questions may arise as to whether the defendant can properly be served with proceedings and, further, whether the UK is the appropriate country in which the claims should be brought.

In the context of claims brought against foreign defendants in the ordinary courts, reference must be made to *Part 6* of the *CPR* which contains detailed provisions on the question of when a foreign defendant may be served with proceedings. Service out of the jurisdiction will require the permission of the courts, save where the requirements of *CPR 6.33* have been met. If permission is required, the court will only consider granting permission in circumstances where the requirements contained in *CPR PD 6B paragraph 3.1* have been met. The courts will not grant permission where the domestic courts are clearly not the most appropriate forum for the claim. For an example of a case in which the domestic courts were considering whether they were the proper forum for tortious claims brought by foreign employees see *Lubbe v Cape plc* [2000] 4 All ER 268.

Where a breach of contract claim is brought in the Employment Tribunal, *rule 61(4)(h)* of *Sch 1* to the *Employment Tribunals (Constitution and Rules of Procedure) Regulations 2004*, will apply. The proper application of *rule 61(4)(h)*, which does not on its face expressly mirror the requirements as to service contained in the *CPR*, has yet to be considered in any detail by the appellate courts or tribunals.

Where the defendant is domiciled in an EC member state, the *Civil Jurisdiction and Judgments Act 1982* ("*CJJA*") applies. *CJJA* originally gave effect to the *Brussels Convention*. More recently, it has given effect to *Regulation 44/2001* (the '*Brussels I Regulation*'), which came into force on 1 March 2002. (The regulation covers all member states except Denmark, in respect of which the *Brussels Convention* still applies. Changes to the existing law in the UK required by the *Brussels I Regulation* are contained in the *Civil Jurisdiction and Judgments Order 2001 (SI 2001/3929)*). The *CJJA* deals not only with jurisdiction, but also with the enforcement of judgments in other member states. Questions of interpretation arising under the *Convention* or the *Brussels I Regulation* may be referred to the ECJ (see EUROPEAN UNION LAW (**22**)). Similar provisions apply under the *Lugano Convention* where the defendant is domiciled in an EFTA member state (*Civil Jurisdiction and Judgments Act 1991*).

Under the *Brussels I Regulation,* the normal rule is that the defendant must be sued in the state in which he is domiciled (*art 2*). However, special rules apply to claims brought under contracts of employment. These rules are contained in *s 5* (*arts 18–21*) of the *Brussels I Regulation.* Under this section, an employer domiciled in a member state may be sued by his employee either: in the courts of the state where the employer is domiciled; or in the courts for the place where the employee habitually carries out his work or in the courts for the last place where he did so; or, if the employee does not or did not habitually carry out his work in any one country, in the courts for the place where the business which engaged the employee is or was situated (*art 19*) (In *Weber v Universal Ogden Services Ltd*: C-37/00 [2002] IRLR 365, the ECJ held that the relevant criterion for establishing the employee's habitual place of work was, having regard to the whole duration of employment, the place where he or she has worked the longest on the employer's business. See also: *Rutten v Cross Medical Ltd* [1997] IRLR 249, ECJ and *Mulox IBC Ltd v Geels*: C-125/92 [1994] IRLR 422, ECJ. In *Harada Ltd (t/a Chequepoint UK) v Turner* [2001] EWCA Civ 599, [2001] All ER (D) 82 (Apr), the Court of Appeal held that an employment tribunal had jurisdiction to hear a wrongful dismissal claim made by an English employee working in Spain for an Irish offshore company since the central management and control of the company was exercised in England). Thus, the *Regulation* is fairly generous when it comes to claims brought against the employer by the employee. The *Regulation* is rather less generous when it comes to claims brought against the employee by the employer. The employer may bring proceedings only in the courts of the Member State in which the employee is domiciled, although he may counter-claim in the courts of another Member State in response to a claim brought by the employee (*art 20*). The *Brussels I Regulation* makes clear that exclusive jurisdiction clauses can only be enforced against an employee when those clauses are entered into after the particular dispute has arisen (*art 21(1)*). Under *art 18(2)* of the *Brussels I Regulation* an employer will be 'deemed to be domiciled' in a member state if it has a branch, agency or other establishment in that member state and the dispute arises out of the operations of that branch, agency or establishment.

In *Samengo-Turner v J & H Marsh & McLennan (Services) Ltd* [2007] EWCA Civ 723, [2007] 2 All ER (Comm) 813, [2008] IRLR 237, the Court of Appeal was called upon to apply the provisions of *s 5* of the *Brussels I Regulation* in a case where the employees were claiming that they were entitled to an anti-suit injunction to restrain breach of contract claims brought against them in New York. The employees were both domiciled and employed to work in the UK. When they notified their UK-based employer that they were terminating their employment in order to go and work for a competitor, claims were brought against them in New York for repayment of bonuses which had been awarded to them under a bonus agreement. The employees argued that they were entitled to the anti-suit injunction because, although the companies who could sue under the bonus agreement included US-based companies other than their employer, the reality was that the bonus agreement formed part of their contract of employment with the UK employer and, accordingly, on an application of *arts 18* and *20*, claims under that agreement would have to be brought in the UK, where the employees were domiciled. The Court of Appeal agreed with these arguments, holding that the employees were entitled to anti-suit injunctions restraining the New York proceedings.

For a decision on jurisdiction concerning proceedings involving employers located in two different Member states see *Glaxosmithkline v Rouard*: C-462/06 [2008] ICR 1375. In that case, the claimant was employed in the first instance by a French domiciled employer. His employment was then transferred to a UK domiciled employer, albeit that his contract with the UK employer imported certain entitlements which the claimant had enjoyed under his contract with the French company, including entitlements as to continuity of service. When

23.8 Foreign Employees

the claimant was dismissed from his employment with the UK company, he sought to bring claims in France against both the French and the UK company. He asserted that he was entitled to proceed against the UK company on an application of *art 6(1)* of the *Brussels 1 Regulation* (*art 6(1)* entitles a claimant to sue a number of defendants in the place where any one of them is domiciled, provided that the claims are so closely connected that it is expedient to hear and determine them together to avoid the risk of irreconcilable judgments resulting from separate proceedings). The ECJ held that the claimant could not rely on *art 6(1)* to draw the UK company into the French proceedings for the simple reason that there was a comprehensive code to deal with claims brought in respect of employment contracts which was contained in *s 5* of the *Brussels I Regulation*; on an application of that code, no claim could be brought by the employee against the UK company in the French courts.

In matters relating to tort, the *Brussels I Regulation* provides that the employer may be sued either in the courts of the member state where he is domiciled (*art 2(1)*) or in the courts for the place where the harmful event occurred (*art 5(3)*).

Where proceedings involving the same cause of action and between the same parties are brought in the courts of different contracting states, a court other than the court 'first seised' is to stay proceedings and where the jurisdiction of the court first seised is established, other courts are to decline jurisdiction (*art 27* of the *Brussels I Regulation*). In the case of *Turner v Grovit*: C-159/02 [2004] All ER (EC) 485, the ECJ was called upon to decide whether it was possible under the *Brussels Convention* for the English courts to grant restraining orders in respect of proceedings in another Convention country on the ground of abuse of process. The ECJ concluded that the functioning of the Convention was underpinned by the necessity for the contracting state to place trust in the judicial systems and institutions of other states and that, accordingly, it did not permit the jurisdiction of a court to be reviewed by a court in another contracting state other than in the special cases enumerated in *art 28*. These principles apply with equal force to the provisions of the *Brussels I Regulation*.

The employment tribunals have no jurisdiction to hear common law tortious claims brought by employees, whether foreign or domestic. However, they do have jurisdiction to hear breach of contract claims brought in respect of particular contracts of employment under the *Employment Tribunals Extension of Jurisdiction (England and Wales) Order 1994*. Article 3 of that Order provides that the tribunal will have jurisdiction to hear the particular claim in circumstances where, had the claim been brought in the ordinary courts, the courts would have been jurisdiction to hear and determine the claim. The effect and scope of *art 3* in respect of foreign employment was considered by the Court of Appeal in *Crofts v Cathay Pacific Airways Ltd* [2005] EWCA Civ 599, [2005] ICR 1436.

It is important to note that *Employment Tribunal Regulations*, which came into force on 1 October 2004, contain specific regulations as to jurisdiction. In particular, *reg 19* provides that the tribunal will 'only have jurisdiction to deal with proceedings' where certain pre-conditions are met. Materially, under *reg 19*, if the cause of action did not arise in England or Wales, then the question of whether the tribunal has jurisdiction to hear the claim will turn on whether the respondent or one of the respondents resides or carries on business in England or Wales. This provision could arguably operate to exclude certain claims brought against foreign employers. It remains to be seen whether this regulation, which is contained in secondary legislation, can be effectively relied upon to ensure that employees who have rights under primary enactments are prevented from prosecuting those claims in the tribunal.

A common law claim which is brought by an employee in the ordinary courts will usually be subject to the doctrine of *forum non conveniens* with the result that claim will not be allowed to proceed before the domestic courts if there is another more appropriate (foreign) forum for the claim (see further *Spiliada Maritime Corpn v Cansulex Ltd* [1987] AC 460,

HL). It would seem that following a change in the Employment Tribunal Rules of Procedure wrought by the *Employment Tribunals (Constitution & Rules etc) Regulations 2004*, the doctrine can generally be applied equally by the Employment Tribunals in the context of breach of contract claims which are brought before them (see further *Crofts v Cathay Pacific* [2005] EWCA Civ 599, [2005] ICR 1436). However, following the judgment of the ECJ in *Owusu v Jackson* [2005] QB 801, it is strongly arguable that the forum non conveniens doctrine cannot be applied in a case where the English court automatically has jurisdiction to hear the claim under *s. 5* of the *Brussels I Regulation*.

23.9   Statutory claims

Discrimination Claims

Where an employment relationship incorporates a foreign element (e.g. the employee has worked for his employer abroad), a question will often arise as to whether, in view of that foreign element, the employee has the right to bring a discrimination claim against his employer in the domestic employment tribunal. This question is often referred to as the territorial jurisdiction or territorial application question. Up until recently, answering this question entailed applying the express territorial jurisdiction provisions contained in the relevant anti-discrimination enactments see further: *s 1* of the *Equal Pay Act 1970*; *ss 6* and *10* of the *Sex Discrimination Act 1975* (as amended by the *Employment Equality (Sex Discrimination) Regulations 2005 (SI 2005/2467)*; *ss 4* and *8* of the *Race Relations Act 1976*; *ss 4(6)* and *68* of the *Disability Discrimination Act 1995*; and *reg 9* of the *Employment Equality (Religion and Belief) Regulations 2003*, *Employment Equality (Sexual Orientation) Regulations 2003* and *reg 10* of the *Employment Equality (Age) Regulations 2006*. Whilst there were some differences in how these provisions were framed across the different enactments, in general the employee would enjoy the protection of British anti-discrimination legislation provided that he or she worked 'wholly or partly in Great Britain'. On 1 October 2010, the new *Equality Act 2010* came into force. A principal aim of that Act was to consolidate all the myriad discrimination enactments into a single piece of legislation. One effect of the introduction of the Equality Act is that the territorial application question now has to be considered afresh. Below, consideration is given both to the territorial jurisdiction principles which applied under the original anti-discrimination enactments and to the position which now obtains under new Equality Act.

The Pre-Equality Act Position

As was indicated above, in cases involving an employment relationship which incorporated a foreign element, the question whether the employee could bring discrimination claims in Great Britain against his or her employer generally turned on whether the employee had done his work either 'wholly or partly in Great Britain'. In the case of *Saggar v Ministry of Defence* [2005] EWCA Civ 413, [2005] IRLR 618, the Court of Appeal was obliged to determine the meaning of the expression 'does his work wholly or partly in Great Britain' in the context of a claim brought under the *Race Relations Act 1976*. The issue arose in the context of certain complaints of racial discrimination which had been brought by an MOD employee who had initially been based in the UK for 16 years but had then been permanently stationed abroad. The issue for the Court of Appeal was whether the fact that the employee had, in the early phase of his employment, been based in the UK was sufficient to establish that he had worked 'wholly or partly in Great Britain' for the purposes of the Act. The Court of Appeal held that the correct approach was to focus not on the employment relationship as a whole, from its beginning to end, rather than merely on the time when the discrimination was alleged to have occurred. More recently, in *Tradition Securities and Futures SA v X* [2009] ICR 88, [2008] IRLR 934, the Employment Appeal Tribunal considered the concept of 'doing work wholly or partly in Great Britain' in the context of an employee who worked initially in France but then transferred to work in the UK. The employee went on to bring claims of sex discrimination in the English employment tribunal in respect of the period when she worked in France. The issue for the EAT was whether the *Sex Discrimination Act 1975* applied to the French phase of the employee's employment. The EAT concluded that it did not. It arrived at this conclusion based on the following analysis: during the period the employee was employed in France there would have been no question of her bringing claims under the *Sex Discrimination Act 1975* in the English employment tribunal as she would have not have worked wholly or partly in Great Britain during any part of this period; it could not be accepted that the right to claim discrimination in respect of this earlier period could, in effect, be retrospectively created as a result of the employee latterly coming and working in Great Britain. In *British Airways Plc v Mak* (UKEAT/0055/09/SM), a question arose as to whether certain cabin crew members who were based in Hong Kong could pursue claims of age and race discrimination against British Airways in the English employment tribunal. It was not in dispute that, as part of their duties, the claimants flew in and out of London airports and, further, that, whilst they were in the UK they performed certain airport duties and also undertook training. The employment tribunal decided that the work done by the claimants in Great Britain was sufficient to establish that they worked 'partly in Great Britain' and, hence, they could pursue their age and race discrimination claims. British Airways appealed the tribunal's judgment on the basis that the work done in Great Britain was *de minimis* and, hence, was insufficient to found jurisdiction. The EAT, having considered the Court of Appeal's judgment in *Saggar v Ministry of Defence*, accepted that jurisdiction could not be established if the work done here was *de minimis*. However, it rejected British Airways' case on the basis that the tribunal had properly found as a fact that the work done by the claimants had not been *de minimis* in all the circumstances. The Court of Appeal rejected British Airways' appeal against the EAT's judgment, [2011] EWCA Civ 184. However, the Supreme Court has now granted permission to appeal.

Where employees have been working exclusively in another Member State of the European Union, a question may arise as to whether they may pursue discrimination claims in the domestic employment tribunals, notwithstanding that they have never actually done any work in the UK. This was an issue which arose in the case of *Ministry of Defence v Wallis & Grocott* [2011] EWCA Civ 231. In that case, two female claimants who had formerly been employed by the Ministry of Defence at NATO headquarters in Belgium brought claims of sex discrimination (and unfair dismissal) in the English employment tribunal. It was not in dispute before the tribunal that, whilst employed by the MOD, the claimants had worked exclusively in Belgium. The MOD argued that, in the circumstances and pursuant to the express provisions of the *Sex Discrimination Act 1975*, the tribunal had no jurisdiction to hear the claimant's sex discrimination claims as their employment with the MOD had not entailed them working 'wholly or partly in Great Britain'. The claimants, relying on a judgment of the EAT in *Bleuse v MBT Transport* (as to which see further below), argued that the tribunal did have jurisdiction to hear their discrimination claims, particularly because any other result would amount to an unlawful denial of the rights which they enjoyed under the directly effective *EU Equal Treatment Directive (No. 76/207)*. The tribunal accepted the claimants' arguments and held that it had jurisdiction to hear the discrimination claims (it also concluded that it had jurisdiction to hear the unfair dismissal claims – see further below). The tribunal's decision was upheld first by the EAT and then by the Court of Appeal. The Court of Appeal, agreeing with the EAT, held that the claimants enjoyed the protection of the directly effective rights afforded under the Directive and that, in order to give effect to those rights, the provisions of the SDA would have to be read down so as to afford the tribunal jurisdiction to hear the claims.

A related question faced the Supreme Court in *Duncombe v Department for Education & Skills* [2011] ICR 495. The Supreme Court considered the application of the *Fixed Term Employees (Prevention of Less Favourable Treatment) Regulations 2002* to employees of English employers, who had always worked in another EU country. Like the equality legislation explored above, the Regulations also enacted EU law. The Court found that it was unnecessary for it to reach a conclusion on whether the *Regulations* applied in this situation.

However, it commented that if it had had to do so, it would have needed to make a reference to the CJEU. It found that, intuitively, employees ought to be protected in other EU countries, but that this issue was not yet *acte clair*.

See also *Williams v University of Nottingham* [2007] IRLR 660, where the EAT concluded that principles derived from the House of Lords' judgment in *Lawson v Serco* (discussed further below) should inform the Tribunal's approach to the application of certain express territorial jurisdiction provisions in the *Disability Discrimination Act 1995*.

Territorial Jurisdiction under the Equality Act 2010

Whilst many practitioners may have expected the new *Equality Act 2010* to embody express territorial jurisdiction provisions similar to those contained in the original discrimination enactments, in fact the *Equality Act* contains no express territorial jurisdiction provisions at all. It is simply silent on the subject. The Explanatory Notes to the Act do not themselves shed much light on how the tribunals are to approach questions of territorial jurisdiction in respect of claims brought under the Act. They merely state that: 'the Act leaves it to tribunals to determine whether the law applies, depending for example on the connection between the employment relationship and Great Britain'. As matters currently stand, it is entirely unclear what kind of 'connection' is needed to found territorial jurisdiction. In a recent case, the Employment Appeal tribunal held that determining whether claims fell within the jurisdictional ambit of the *EA 2010* required the application of the test outlined by the House of Lords in *Lawson v Serco* (as to which see further below) – see *Bates Van Winklehoff v Clyde & Co LLP* (UKEAT/0169/12/RN). However, importantly the EAT reached this conclusion in circumstances where it was accepted by both parties that *Lawson v Serco* principles, which were devised in the context of a number of claims brought under the *Employment Rights Act 1996* ('ERA 1996'), applied equally under the *EA 2010* as they did under *ERA 1996*. This decision was appealed to the Court of Appeal ([2012] EWCA Civ 1207), but there was no challenge to the judgment on this point. It remains to be seen whether this approach will be challenged in future cases.

Other Statutory Claims

The question whether foreign employees enjoy the rights afforded under the *ERA 1996*, particularly the right to claim unfair dismissal, was addressed by the House of Lords in the joined cases of *Lawson v Serco Ltd, Botham v MOD and Crofts v Veta Ltd* [2006] UKHL 3, [2006] ICR 250 ('*Lawson v Serco*'). The following principles were enunciated by the House of Lords in *Lawson v Serco*:

(a)   the question whether a particular claim falls within the territorial ambit of the unfair dismissal provisions contained in the Employment Rights Act 1996 will depend on the nature of the particular employment arrangements in issue in the case;

(b)   in 'standard cases' (ie cases where the employee works in Great Britain), the employee will be able to pursue their claim of unfair dismissal if they were 'working in Great Britain at the time of the dismissal';

(c)   in cases involving 'peripatetic employees' (eg airline pilots and international travelling salespersons), the employee will be able to pursue their claim of unfair dismissal if they were 'based in Great Britain' during the employment (cf. *Hunt v United Airlines Inc* [2008] ICR 934, EAT);

(d)   in cases involving 'expatriate employees' (ie employees who work and live abroad), the employee will not be able to pursue their claim of unfair dismissal in the absence of 'exceptional circumstances'. Those exceptional circumstances could include, for example: where the employee was posted abroad by a British-based employer to work on behalf of or as a representative of that employer (such a situation might arise in the case of a foreign correspondent posted to a foreign country by a British newspaper); or where the employee is working abroad but within a 'political or social enclave' (for example a British military base).

In practice, the greatest difficulties in applying the *Lawson v Serco* principles tend to arise in the context of 'expatriate employee' cases.

The question of what will render an expatriate employee's case sufficiently exceptional such that it falls within the scope of *ERA 1996* was recently considered by the Supreme Court in *Ravat v Halliburton Manufacturing & Services Ltd* [2012] UKSC 1. In *Ravat*, an English national was employed by a subsidiary of a multinational corporation. The subsidiary was based in Scotland. However, the employee discharged his duties in Libya. The work done by Mr Ravat was done for the benefit of a German subsidiary of the multinational corporation. Mr Ravat continued to live in England during the period of his employment and commuted to his work in Libya, spending 28 days there followed by 28 days in England. Consistent with his commuter status, Mr Ravat's contract of employment afforded him the same benefits which he would have enjoyed had he been employed in England. Moreover, his employer had assured him that English law would govern the contract. Mr Ravat was dismissed from his employment by a manager employed by another British-based subsidiary who was based in Cairo. The Supreme Court concluded that the Scottish employment tribunal had been entitled to conclude that it had jurisdiction to hear Mr Ravat's claim for unfair dismissal. On the wider question of when an expatriate employee's case would be sufficiently exceptional to fall within the scope of *ERA 1996*, the Supreme Court took the view that, in order to amount to an exceptional case, the employment would have to have a stronger connection with Great Britain than with the place where the employee worked. The place where the employee discharged his duties was highly relevant to but not necessarily determinative of the application of this test. Other relevant factors would include: the nationality of the employee; the place of recruitment and the location of the employer. In every case, it would be a question of fact and degree whether an expatriate employee's case was sufficiently exceptional such that it fell outside the general rule. In cases where the employee was. in effect, only a quasi-expatriate employee (i.e. because they worked abroad but continued to live in Great Britain) the general rule should in any event be applied more loosely. In cases where the employment involved a number of subsidiary companies of a larger multinational, it was important to be aware of the foreign elements which any foreign subsidiaries introduced into the employment relationship. However, those elements should not be relied upon so as to ignore the reality of the employee's situation. In Mr Ravat's case, it was unrealistic to treat his employment as falling outside the scope of *ERA*. This was particularly in view of the facts that: Mr Ravat was British and had been recruited in Great Britain; the employer's business was based in Great Britain; the employer had chosen to treat Mr Ravat as a commuter and, accordingly, had preserved all his contractual entitlements as though he had been employed in Great Britain; the employer had given Mr Ravat assurances to the effect that he would continue to enjoy the protection of English law; and, further, Mr Ravat had continued to live in England throughout his employment.

The approach adopted by the Supreme Court in *Ravat* echoes the approach adopted in the earlier case of *Duncombe v Department for Education & Skills (No. 2)* [2011] UKSC 36, [2011] 4 All ER 1020. The issue which arose in *Duncombe* was whether teachers who were employed by the Department for Education and Skills to work in European schools throughout the European Union enjoyed the protection from unfair dismissal conferred by *ERA 1996*. The Supreme Court concluded that they did. The Supreme Court took the view that the test approved in *Lawson v Serco* was whether the employment had a closer connection with Great Britain than with the foreign jurisdiction. In *Duncombe*, whilst the teachers were classic expatriate employees in that they lived and worked abroad, the facts of their cases were sufficiently exceptional to bring them within the scope of the legislation.

Relevant factors here included that the teachers were employed to work in effect within international enclaves; they had no particular connection with the countries within which they were working and they did not pay local taxes.

What *Lawson*, *Ravat* and *Duncombe* all confirm is that, whilst in the majority of cases expatriate employees will not fall within the scope of *ERA 1996*, there will be exceptional cases where the general rule does not apply. In marginal cases, it will be particularly important to consider a whole range of factors affecting the location of the employment relationship including not least: the nature and location of the employer's business; the nationality of the employee; where the employee was recruited; where the employee worked; where the employee lived during the period of the employment; whether the employee commuted from Great Britain; where the employee was taxed; whether the contract was designed to afford the employee benefits which were peculiar to the foreign jurisdiction or to the domestic jurisdiction; whether the employee had any particular connection to the place where the duties were discharged and whether the employer gave assurances to the effect that the employee would be protected by domestic employment law.

Whilst the House of Lords in *Lawson v Serco* did not decide the point, it is generally accepted that the *Lawson v Serco* principles apply not merely to unfair dismissal provisions but also to all the other provisions of the *Employment Rights Act 1996* (see further *Bleuse v MBT Transport Ltd* [2008] IRLR 264 and, more recently, *Dhunna v Creditsights Ltd* (UKEAT/0246/12/LA), both of which concerned the application of provisions contained in the *Working Time Regulations 1998*. See also *Bates Van Winklehoff v Clyde & Co LLP* [2012] EWCA Civ 1207, in which the Court of Appeal accepted that the *Lawson v Serco* principles could apply to a whistleblowing case).

Additional Considerations

Where an employee works in another Member State of the European Union, a question may arise as to whether that employee can rely on directly effective EU rights in order to pursue claims in the domestic employment tribunals. This question has been considered in a number of recent cases. In *Bleuse v MBT Transport Ltd* [2008] IRLR 264, the EAT held that an expatriate employee who had worked in other Member States of the EU was entitled to bring claims under the *Working Time Regulations 1998* against his UK based employer. This was despite the fact that he had never worked in the UK. The EAT reached this conclusion on the basis that this was the result which was required by directly effective provisions of the *Working Time Directive 2003/88*. A similar conclusion was reached by the Court of Appeal in the context of a claim brought under the *Fixed-term Employees (Prevention of Less Favourable Treatment) Regulations 2002* ("the 2002 Regulations"): *Duncombe v Department for Education & Skills* [2009] EWCA Civ 1355, [2010] IRLR 331. However, the Court of Appeal's judgment in *Duncombe* was subsequently overturned by the Supreme Court, albeit on other grounds, *Duncombe v Department for Education & Skills* [2011] UKSC 14, [2011] 2 All ER 417. The Supreme Court found that it was unnecessary for it to reach a conclusion on whether the *Regulations* applied in this situation. However, it commented that, if it had had to do so, it would have needed to make a reference to the CJEU since this issue was not yet *acte clair*. In the circumstances, query whether the Court of Appeal's analysis in *Duncombe* can properly be relied upon. It should be noted that the *Duncombe* case subsequently came before the Supreme Court for a second time, *Duncombe v Department for Education and Skills (No. 2)* [2011] UKSC 36, [2011] 4 All ER 1020. On this second occasion, the claimant teachers succeeded in persuading the Supreme Court that their cases did fall within the scope of the *ERA 1996* on an application of *Lawson v Serco* principles (see above).

In *Holis Metal Industries Ltd v GMB and Newell Ltd* [2008] IRLR 187, the EAT concluded that the *Transfer of Undertakings (Protection of Employment) Regulations 2006* had the potential to apply to the transfer of undertakings which were situated in the UK prior to the transfer but were then transferred outside of the EU.

23.9 Foreign Employees

Following the judgment of the House of Lords in *Lawson v Serco*, it would seem that domestic employment tribunals cannot apply the common law doctrine of *forum non conveniens* in the context of statutory claims which come before it (see in particular per Lord Hoffmann at para 24). Thus, where the domestic employment tribunal has territorial jurisdiction to hear a particular statutory claim, it cannot then refuse to hear the claim on the basis that there is arguably some more appropriate forum within which the claim could be heard.

When bringing a claim against a foreign respondent in the Employment Tribunal, the rules of service provided for in *rule 61(4)(h)* of the Tribunal Rules (as set out in *Schedule 1* to the *Employment Tribunals (Constitution & Rules etc) Regulations 2004*) must be considered. No authoritative guidance as to how this rule should be applied in the case of a foreign respondent has yet been provided by the appellate courts or tribunals. However, in the case of *Pervez v Macquarie Bank Ltd (London Branch)* (UKEAT/0246/10/CEA) [2011] ICR 266, [2011] IRLR 284, the EAT held that *rule 19(1)* of the Tribunal Rules, which ostensibly purports to limit the tribunal's jurisdiction to hear claims, could not be relied upon to oust the tribunal's jurisdiction in circumstances where that jurisdiction was afforded under primary legislation. Thus, in *Pervez*, the fact that the claimant's employer was based in Hong Kong and, hence, could not apparently be sued in the tribunal pursuant to *rule 19(1)* of the Tribunal Rules, did not operate to prevent the tribunal hearing the claimant's claims of unfair dismissal and race and religious discrimination. The tribunal had jurisdiction to hear these claims under the relevant primary enactments and that jurisdiction could not be excluded through the application of a rule contained in secondary legislation.

24   Government Proposals

24.1   EMPLOYMENT LAW REVIEW

In May 2010, the Government embarked on a Parliament-long review of employment law with the aim of achieving a "flexible, effective and fair labour market" – Employment Law 2013: Progress on Reform, BIS ("Progress Update"). As at the time of writing the Government was half-way through the review in the course of which a number of consultation papers have been issued and responded to by the Government, some reforms have already been implemented (e.g. the increase in the qualification period for unfair dismissal claims), the *Enterprise and Regulatory Reform Bill* (which contains provisions concerning employment law) has continued its progress through Parliament, and further consultation and evidence gathering is planned in respect of other proposed reforms. The Progress Update contains a useful timeline of completed and proposed reforms up to the end of the current Parliamentary period in 2015. Information about the current state of the review can be obtained from the websites of the Department for Business Innovation and Skills ("BIS"): www.bis.gov.uk; and the Ministry of Justice: www.justice.gov.uk. Many of the proposed reforms are quite far-reaching and have the potential to affect fundamentally the way in which the tribunal system may be accessed. The purpose of this chapter is merely to provide a brief guide to some of the key aspects of the review and proposed reforms. As these proposals are subject to constant change until final implementation, readers are advised to consult government websites and publications for the most up-to-date and comprehensive position.

This Chapter sets out a brief history of the review process, some of the key proposals made by the Government and the planned consultations and evidence gathering exercises.

24.2   EMPLOYMENT LAW REVIEW – A BRIEF HISTORY

Believing that the employment tribunal system was "not working as originally planned", the Government committed to a review of employment law which was launched in May 2010. Whilst the UK labour market is recognised by the OECD as the third most lightly regulated amongst developed countries (after the USA and Canada), the Government considered that there was more that could be done to ensure that UK employment laws provide the framework needed to ensure economic growth, and that there was a need to address the perception that the employment relationship was "one-sided" in favour of the employee. In particular, the business community is said to have expressed concern that the fear of the employment tribunal system ultimately acts as a barrier to growth.

The Employment Law Review is extensive. Some of the key events in the review timeline are as follows:

On 27 January 2011, BIS and the Tribunals Service (now HM Courts and Tribunals Service) issued a consultation document entitled, 'Resolving Workplace Disputes' ("the RWD consultation"), which contained a number of proposals to change the current system.

The RWD consultation included proposals for:

(a)   mediation and dispute resolution without involving the tribunal (See **24.4** below);

(b)   an increased role for ACAS (See **24.4** below);

(c)   changes to the constitution, practice and procedure of employment tribunals. (See **24.3** below);

24.2   Government Proposals

(d)   the introduction of fees for using employment tribunals (although this was not a matter on which views were expressly sought in the RWD consultation). (See **24.5** below);

(e)   the extension of the qualifying period for unfair dismissal from one to two years. (See UNFAIR DISMISSAL); and

(f)   the introduction of a system of penalties for employers found to have breached an individual's rights. (See **24.4** below).

The RWD consultation closed on 20 April 2011 having received over 400 responses from individuals, the legal professional, business organisations, trade unions and others.

The Government response to the RWD consultation was published in November 2011. The response announced some firm changes which were to be brought into effect, announced that there would a fundamental review of procedural rules by Mr Justice Underhill ("the Underhill Review") and set out other reforms in respect of which further consultation and evidence gathering would take place. The Underhill Review was completed in July 2012 and the Government's response (following consultation) was published on 14 March 2013. It is envisaged that the new tribunal rules will come into force in Summer 2013. (See **24.3** and **24.4** below).

In January 2011, BIS produced an Employer's Charter with the aim of dispelling "many of the myths about what an employer can and cannot do in managing their staff reasonably, fairly   and   lawfully"   (www.bis.gov.uk/assets/biscore/employment -matters/docs/e/employerscharter). The Employer's Charter (which has since been updated) sets out a series of things which an employer can do as long as it acts fairly and reasonably. These include being able to contact a woman on maternity leave and ask when she plans to return, and being able to dismiss an employee for poor performance. Each point in the online version of the Charter links to more detailed information on other Government websites.

In February 2011, the Government commissioned a major report on the sickness absence system in order to help combat the 140 million days lost annually to sickness absence. The report   on   sickness   absence,   which   was   published   in   November   2011 (www.dwp.gov.uk/docs/health-at-work.pdf), made a number of recommendations aimed at helping people return to work from periods of sickness absence more quickly and allowing employers to manage such periods more effectively. The Government published its response to that report in January 2013 and accepted many of the recommendations. (www.dwp.gov.uk/policy/welfare-reform/sickness-absence-review/) A range of measures have been announced including the establishment of an independent health and work assessment advisory service providing a state-funded assessment by occupational health professionals for employees after four weeks' sick leave, the publication of revised "fit note" guidance for GPs, employers and individuals, and the abolition of statutory sick pay record keeping requirements.

In April 2011, the Government issued its Red Tape Challenge, which is said to have provided the Government with "an additional lens through which to view the obligations on businesses in employing people, by focusing on specific regulations":

In May 2011, BIS issued a consultation document on Modern Workplaces ("the MW consultation"), which included plans for "a culture of flexible, family-friendly employment practices". This involved plans for: a system of flexible parental leave; a universal right to request flexible working; changes to the *Working Time Regulations* affecting the interaction of annual leave with sick leave and family-friendly leave; and measures to encourage equal pay for equal work between men and women. The MW consultation closed on 8 August 2011 and the Government response was published in November 2012.Key proposals include an increase in entitlement to unpaid parental leave from 13 to 18 weeks (see **24.7** below) and the introduction of a right for fathers and partners of pregnant women to take time off to attend antenatal appointments.

In December 2011, the Ministry of Justice also issued a consultation document seeking views on two options for a system of fees for tribunals ("the Fees consultation"). The Fees consultation closed on 6 March 2012 and the Government's response was published on 13 July 2012 when it announced that a new tribunal fee structure based on Option 1 would be introduced in the latter half of 2013 (See **24.5** below)

In March 2012, the Government issued a call for evidence on dealing with dismissal and the proposal for compensated no fault dismissal ("NFD"). The Government published its response in September 2012 and, having considered the responses and the position in other countries, concluded that "there is insufficient support for or evidence that NFD would have a positive impact on the UK labour market". The earlier proposals for "protected conversations" in relation to terminating employment are also not being taken forward.

In April 2012, several of the proposed reforms (including the increase in the qualifying period for unfair dismissal) took effect.

On 23 May 2012, the *Enterprise and Regulatory Reform Bill* ("*ERRB*") had its first reading in Parliament. ERRB is currently at the report stage in House of Lords and is expected to come into force in Summer 2013. [See **24.4** below]

On 17 January 2013, the Government commenced consultation exercises in respect of proposed changes to *TUPE* (including in particular the removal of the service provision change provisions); early conciliation; and regulation of the recruitment sector. (See **24.6** below)

On 14 March 2013, the Government published the Progress Update, which summarises the changes implemented as a result of the Employment Law Review so far and the developments planned for the remainder of this Parliament.

24.3   UNDERHILL REVIEW

In 2011, the Government asked Mr Justice Underhill, former President of the EAT, to undertake a thorough review of employment tribunal rules and to develop and recommend a revised procedural code in line with specified Terms of Reference. The Terms of Reference include ensuring that proceedings can be handled quickly and efficiently with an emphasis on (a) helping proceedings to resolve themselves otherwise than through judicial determination at hearings and (b) dealing robustly and consistently with cases appearing to have little or no reasonable prospect of success with a view to fairness for all parties, the tribunal and its resources. Mr Justice Underhill's recommendations were presented to Ministers in July 2012. The Government launched a consultation exercised in September 2012 to ask some further questions on the way Tribunals operate. That consultation ended on 23 November 2012 and the Government's response was published on 14 March 2013. The full detail of the Underhill Review and the Government's response cannot be set out here but can be viewed at:

(www.gov.uk/government/uploads/system/uploads/attachment data/file/141906/ 13-696-government-response-to-employment-tribunal-rules-review-by-mr-justice -underhill.pdf)

In a press release issued by the Government on 14 March 2013, it was announced that the proposals which have been accepted include:

* new strike out powers to ensure that weak cases that should not proceed to full hearing are halted at the earliest possible opportunity;

* guidance from the Employment Tribunal Presidents to help ensure that judges deal with hearings in a consistent manner which ensures parties know what to expect;

24.3 Government Proposals

- making it easier to withdraw and dismiss claims by cutting the amount of paper work required; and

- a new procedure for preliminary hearings that combines separate pre-hearing reviews and case management discussions. This will reduce the overall number of hearings and lead to a quicker disposal of cases saving time and costs for all parties.

Some of the proposals arising out of the Underhill Review have been incorporated in the ERRB which is considered below (see **24.4**). The new tribunal rules are expected to come into force in Summer 2013.

24.4 ENTERPRISE & REGULATORY REFORM BILL

At the time of writing, ERRB was at the report stage in the House of Lords and is due to come into force in Summer 2013. ERRB includes a number of key provisions relating to employment and which have arisen out of the Government's Employment Law Review. The following references to the ERRB are to the version which was current as at 9 February 2013. (www.publications.parliament.uk/pa/bills/lbill/2012-2013/0083/2013083.i-vi.html):

Early Conciliation. Currently, *ETA, s 18(3)* provides a discretionary power for ACAS to provide pre-claim conciliation to parties in an employment dispute where either party requests it and where the conciliator believes that there is a reasonable prospect of a settlement being reached. Clause 7 of ERRB inserts new *ss 18A* and *18B* in the *ETA* making pre-claim conciliation mandatory:

(a)   Before presenting a complaint, prospective claimants will be required to submit prescribed information about their claim to ACAS (*ETA, s 18A(1)*). The requirement will not apply in respect of prescribed cases, e.g. in claims of interim relief where the statutory time limits would preclude it (*ETA, s 18A(7)*);

(b)   The ACAS officer shall during the prescribed period (one month) endeavour to promote a settlement that avoids proceedings being instituted. *ETA s 18A(3)* and *(8)*. If during the prescribed period, the ACAS officer concludes that a settlement is not possible or the prescribed period ends without a settlement having been reached, the officer shall issues a certificate to that effect to the prospective claimant, although the officer may continue to promote settlement after the expiry of the period (*ETA s 18A(4)* and *(5)*);

(c)   A prospective claimant subject to these requirements will not be entitled to present a complaint without a relevant certificate from the ACAS officer *ETA, s 18A(8)*);

(d)   Where the prospective claimant is no longer employed, the officer may (in respect of a claim of unfair dismissal) attempt to promote reinstatement or reengagement. (*ETA, s 18A(9)*)

Limitation periods will be extended to facilitate conciliation before the institution of proceedings (ERRB, cl 8). In January 2013, the Government launched a consultation exercise on proposals (including draft regulations) for the implementation of early conciliation including the contents of the relevant form and certificate, the steps to be taken to make contact with prospective claimants and respondents, and the jurisdictions to be excluded. The consultation closed on 15 February 2013.

Decisions by legal officer. ERRB, Clause 10 will insert a new *s 4(6D)* in *ETA* whereby a person appointed as a "legal officer" in accordance with regulations may determine proceedings of a specified description (likely to be more straightforward and low value tribunal claims) and where all parties consent in writing. Any such determination by a legal officer will be treated as if made by the tribunal.

EAT composition. ERRB, Clause 11 will amend *ETA, s 28* with the effect that judges will sit alone in the EAT unless they direct otherwise. In the event of such a direction, there shall be an equal number of employer-representative and worker-representative members.

Confidentiality of settlement negotiations in unfair dismissal cases. ERRB, Clause 12 will insert a new *s 111A* in *ERA* under which evidence of pre-termination settlement negotiations will be inadmissible as evidence in any claim brought under *ERA, s 111*, i.e. claims of ordinary unfair dismissal *(ERA, s 111A(1))*. However, *ERA, s 111A(1)* will not apply where the complainant is to be regarded for the purposes of that part of *ERA* as unfairly dismissed. Furthermore, in respect of anything said or done which in the tribunal's opinion was improper or was connected with improper behaviour, the rule on inadmissibility under *s 111A(1)* will only apply to the extent considered just by the tribunal *(ERA, s 111A(4))*. This latter provision is intended to mirror the test of "unambiguous impropriety" which is an established exception to the common law 'without prejudice' rule. There is to be a Code of Practice giving guidance on what amounts to improper behaviour in this context. (Government Response: Ending the Employment Relationship Consultation)

Cap on compensatory award for unfair dismissal. Clause 13 of the ERRB confers a power on the Secretary of State to amend *ERA, s 124* so as to vary the cap on compensatory awards for unfair dismissal. The effect of the amendment will be that the limit cannot be decreased to less than the lower of median annual earnings (defined in *ERA, s 124(9)*) and the individual's annual earnings. The Government intends to introduce a cap of one year's earnings on compensatory awards for unfair dismissal to sit alongside the maximum overall cap on compensation which is currently set at £74,200. (Government Response: Ending the Employment Relationship Consultation).

Financial penalties. Employment tribunals have the power to award various remedies to successful claimants including financial awards. However, tribunals currently do not have the power to penalise an employer for its breach of employment law. In order to encourage compliance, ERRB, Clause 14 will insert a new *section 12A* in *ETA* which will give tribunals the discretion to impose financial penalties on employers where the breach of employment rights has aggravating features such as malice. The award can be made irrespective of the nature of the remedy awarded to the claimant. Any such financial penalty, if imposed, must be at least £100 and cannot exceed £5,000. *(ETA, s 12A(2))*, and where the claimant is in receipt of a financial award, then any penalty must be set at 50% of that award subject to these limits. *(ETA, s 12A(3))*.

Whistleblowing. In response to the growing number of whistleblowing complaints arising out of disclosures with no public interest aspect, ERRB, cl 15(1) will amend *ERA, s 43B* by requiring that a qualifying disclosure must be one which is, in the reasonable belief of the worker making the disclosure, "made in the public interest". This amendment will mean that a disclosure will not be protected for the purposes of ERA if it concerns only personal interests, e.g. the employer's failure to comply with an obligation to provide the correct amount of the individual's holiday pay. However, on 21 February 2013, the Government announced that the protection for whistleblowers is to be extended by conferring protection from harassment by co-workers because of a disclosure. The provisions governing this added protection will mirror similar vicarious liability provisions under existing equalities legislation. (BIS Press Release: 21 February 2013).

Tribunal Procedure: Deposit Orders and costs. Some of the proposed amendments arising out of the Underhill Review are provided for in ERRB. ERRB, Clause 16 amends ETA in the following respects:

(a)   The existing power to make regulations regarding the payment of a deposit as a condition of continuing with a claim is amended so as to enable regulations to be made providing for deposit orders in respect of a specific allegation or argument in a claim. This will enable the Government to make tribunal regulations which will allow tribunals to take a more targeted approach in discouraging weaker aspects of a claim.

685

24.4   Government Proposals

(b)   *ETA, section 13A(3)* prevents employment tribunal regulations from allowing for costs orders and preparation time orders in favour of the same person in the same proceedings. This is considered to be unfair to unrepresented parties as it could prevent such persons from recovering witness expenses. The amendment will allow regulations that permit costs orders and preparation time orders to be made in respect of the same person.

Compromise Agreements. Compromise agreements are to be called "settlement agreements" on the basis that this more accurately describes their content and will also encourage the involvement of those who might not wish to be seen as 'compromising'. (ERRB, cl 18). Following consultation, the Government has asked ACAS to include non-compulsory template letters and a model settlement agreement in a Code of Practice together with appropriate guidance for their use. Although the Government has decided not to set guideline tariffs for settlement agreements, there is to be guidance as to the considerations that may be taken into account when negotiating and deciding the level of the financial settlement. It is expected that the Code of Practice and guidance will be place by Summer 2013. (Government Response. Ending the Employment Relationship Consultation).

Repeal of third party harassment provisions. ERRB, Clause 58 will repeal the requirement for employers to take reasonable steps to protect employees from third-party harassment pursuant to *EA, s 40(2)* and *40(4)*.

Abolition of Equality Act questionnaires. ERRB, Clause 59 will abolish the discrimination questionnaire procedure under *EA, s 138.*

24.5   FEES

One of the more controversial proposals of the Employment Law Review is concerned with a system of fees payable by claimants in order to proceed with employment tribunal claims

Currently, claimants do not have to pay any fee to issue a claim in the employment tribunal. The Lord Chancellor has a power to introduce fees for employment tribunals and the EAT. (See *Tribunals Courts and Enforcement Act 2007, s 42*). The Government announced its intention to introduce a system of fees for employment tribunals in the RWD consultation. The Fees consultation, which commenced in December 2011 and closed on 6 March 2012, was concerned with which of two options for the fee system should be introduced, rather than with whether there should be a fee system at all.

The Fees consultation set out two options, Option 1 (which, if implemented, would be introduced in 2013) and Option 2 (which, if adopted, would require further primary legislation). On 13 July 2012, the Government published its response to the Fees consultation and announced that Option 1 with some amendments will be pursued and not Option 2.

Fees – Option 1. Under Option 1, a Claimant will be charged two fees: The first fee would be charged at the stage of issuing the claim; and a second fee would be charged if the claim proceeds to a hearing. Under the initial proposal there were three levels of fee at each stage, Levels 1, 2 and 3, depending on the type of claim involved. There was also to be a charge for seeking written reasons.

In the Government's response to the consultation, it has been confirmed that Levels 2 and 3 would be merged, thus leaving just two levels, Level 1 and Level 2. Level 1 claims are generally for sums due on termination of employment e.g. unpaid wages, payment in lieu of notice and redundancy payments. Level 2 claims include those relating to unfair dismissal, discrimination, equal pay and whistleblowing claims.

Other changes to the initial proposals are that:

- There is to be no separate fee for seeking written reasons;
- A small number of claims will be reallocated to new fee levels; and
- There is to be a reduction in the number of bands for multiple claims from 5 to 3.

The response also made changes to the indicative fee levels for single claims to employment tribunals under Option 1. The final fee structure proposal for such claims is now as follows:

Fee	Level 1 Claims	Level 3 Claims
Issue fee	£160	£250
Hearing fee	£230	£950

For claims involving more than one claimant (multiple claims), the final fee structure is as follows:

Level 1 Claims	Number of Claimants in Multiple Claim		
	2–10 (2 x single fee)	11–200 (4 x single fee)	>200 (6 x single fee)
Issue Fee	£320	£640	£960
Hearing Fee	£460	£920	£1380
Total	£780	£1560	£2340

Level 1 Claims	Number of Claimants in Multiple Claim		
	2–10 (2 x single fee)	11–200 (4 x single fee)	>200 (6 x single fee)
Issue Fee	£500	£1000	£1500
Hearing Fee	£1900	£3800	£5700
Total	£2400	£4800	£7200

Other fees for certain specified applications that may be made after a claim has been accepted are as follows:

	Review Default Judgment	Application to dismiss following settlement	Mediation by the judiciary	Counter-claim	Application for review
Level 1	£100	£60	—	£160	£100
Level 1	£100	£60	£600	—	£350

There will also be a fee for appeals to the EAT as follows:

	Appeal Fee	Hearing Fee	Total
EAT fee	£400	£1200	£1600

The Government has decided to adopt the proposal to extend the current HMCTS civil courts remission system to protect access to justice in employment tribunals and the EAT for those cannot afford to pay the fees. A review of remissions will be undertaken as part of

24.5   Government Proposals

a wider review required for the introduction of Universal Credit. It is stated that the review will "aim to produce a single remissions system for courts and tribunals which is simpler to use, more cost efficient and better targeted to ensure that those who can afford to pay fees do so, while continuing to provide access to the courts and tribunal system to those who cannot." (Government Response: Charging Fees in Employment Tribunals and the EAT).

The employment tribunal will have the power to order that the unsuccessful party reimburses the fees paid by the successful party so that the cost is ultimately borne by the party who caused the system to be used.

24.6   RECENTLY LAUNCHED CONSULTATIONS

Three separate consultations were launched on 17 January 2013:

(a)   *TUPE*. This is a consultation on potentially far-reaching changes to TUPE ("Transfer of Undertakings (Protection of Employment) Regulations 2006: Consultation on Proposed Changes to the Regulations"). The proposed changes include the following:

- • repealing the provisions dealing with "service provision changes";

- • repealing the specific requirements regarding the notification of Employee Liability Information;

- • changing the wording of certain TUPE provisions so that they more closely reflect the wording of the Acquired Rights Directive and EU case law (e.g. relating to changes to contracts; protection against dismissal and substantial changes in working conditions to the material detriment of employees);

- • amending the meaning of "entailing changes in the workforce" so that it covers changes in the location of the workforce;

- • providing that a transferee can consult on collective redundancies with the transferring employees prior to the transfer; and

- • allowing micro businesses to inform and consult employees directly regarding transfers, rather than through representatives.

This TUPE consultation closes on 11 April 2013.

(b)   *Early Conciliation*: This consultation on proposals for the implementation of early conciliation processes is considered above under ERRB (See **24.4** above).

(c)   *Recruitment Sector*. This is a consultation on reforming the regulatory framework for employment agencies and employment businesses ("Recruitment sector legislation: Consultation on reforming the regulatory framework for employment agencies and employment businesses"). The Government wants to reform how the sector is regulated, removing costly and complex regulations where possible and simplifying the relevant regulations. The consultation closes on 11 April 2013.

24.7   OTHER PROPOSED DEVELOPMENTS

There are numerous other developments and proposals (many of which are summarised in the Progress Update), including the following:

(a)   *Employee Shareholder Status*. The Growth and Infrastructure Bill will insert a new *ERA, s 205A* under which the employer and employee may agree that, in consideration for a minimum of £2000 worth of shares, the employee will suffer the loss or diminution of the following employment rights:

- The right not to be unfairly dismissed. There will be an exception for health and safety cases, automatically unfair cases, or cases where the dismissal is discriminatory under EA;

- The right to a statutory redundancy payment;

- The right to request time off for study or training under *section 63D* of the *1996 Act*;

- The right to make a request for flexible working under *section 80F* of the *1996 Act*; and

- The period of notice for early return from statutory maternity, adoption or additional paternity leave is increased from 8 weeks to 16 weeks.

(b) *Children and Families Bill.* Clause 101 of this Bill will amend ERA, s 80F(1) by extending the right to flexible working to all employees.

(c) *The Parental Leave (EU Directive) Regulations 2013.* The Government has issued a draft of The Parental Leave (EU Directive) Regulations 2013 which implement the Parental Leave Directive into UK law. Regulation 3 will amend regulation 14 of the Maternity and Parental Leave etc Regulations 1999 to increase a qualifying employee's entitlement to parental leave from 13 weeks to 18 weeks.

(d) *Collective Redundancies.* Following a call for evidence in respect of the consultation periods for collective redundancies which concluded in early 2012, the Government launched on 21 June 2012 a 12-week consultation on a package of reforms, based around reducing the 90-day minimum period for large redundancies; issuing a new, non-statutory, Code of Practice to address a number of key issues affecting collective redundancy consultations; and improving guidance for employers and employees on the support on offer from government.

On 21 December 2012, the Government issued its response to the consultation. It concluded that:

- It would remove the 90-day minimum period and replace it with a 45-day minimum period for redundancies of 100 or more. There will be a review of the operation and impact of the shorter statutory period on the labour market once there has been time to see its full effect;

- There would be new non-statutory Guidance from ACAS on collective redundancy consultations. This will address the principles and behaviours behind a good quality consultation, with a particular focus on dealing effectively with the most contentious issues, such as providing guidance on what is an 'establishment'; and

- Legislation will be introduced to exclude fixed-term contracts which have reached their agreed termination point from collective redundancy consultation obligations, in line with the exemption allowed for in the Directive. However, a fixed-term contract would need to have a clear termination point in order for it to benefit from this exemption, and the exemption would not apply where the employer is considering early termination of the contract as a result of redundancy.

These changes are expected to come into force in 2013.

(e) There will be a review (intended to commence shortly) of the paperwork obligations arising out of the Agency Workers Regulations;

24.7 Government Proposals

(f)   The Government proposes to consolidate the current separate regulations on National Minimum Wage and publish a set of improved regulations by the end of April 2013; and

(g)   In relation to criminal records checks, the Home Office aims to introduce a portable Disclosure and Barring Service (DBS) Check by summer 2013, to reduce delays in recruitment by allowing employers to check online whether an individual's DBS check is up-to-date.

25   Health and Safety at Work – I: The Legal Framework

The law relating to health and safety is both long-established and rapidly developing. To that end, keeping track of it is difficult, like most other legal subject-matter. However, the Health and Safety Executive ('HSE') produces a wide range of free and priced information on health and safety in the workplace. See also www.hse.gov.uk.

Cross-reference. See HEALTH AND SAFETY AT WORK – II (26) for specific legislation and health and safety issues.

25.1   THE LEGISLATIVE FRAMEWORK

An employer is under a common law duty to have regard to the safety of his employees. He is also liable at common law for accidents caused by acts of his employees where the employees were acting in the course of their employment. The assessment of damages in personal injury actions is beyond the scope of this book. In addition to these common law duties, statutory obligations have been imposed upon employers in certain circumstances by such enactments as the *Occupiers' Liability Act 1957*, the *Occupiers Liability Act 1984* (see **25.12** below) and the *Health and Safety at Work, etc Act 1974* (see **25.16** below). An employer owes specific statutory duties to his own employees, members of the public who are affected by the activities of the employer, and other people's employees working on the employer's premises. A breach of an employer's statutory duties under the *Health and Safety at Work, etc Act 1974* ('*HSWA 1974*') imposes only criminal liability, although a breach of health and safety regulations made thereunder, insofar as damage is caused, will give rise to civil liability unless the regulations provide otherwise (see **25.43** below). The recently enacted *Enterprise and Regulatory Reform Act 2013*, by *section 69*, substantially amends *section 47* of the *1974 Act*. The consequence is that in cases where previously strict liability attached to an employer, it will become necessary for the claimant to show direct fault on the part of the employer. The mere occurrence of an accident without more will not sound in liability. The reform is not retrospective and will only apply to accidents after implementation, the date of which has yet to be revealed.

Under provisions in the *Employment Rights Act 1996*, employees are protected from dismissal or victimisation by the employer in health and safety cases (see **52.3** UNFAIR DISMISSAL – II and **26.8** HEALTH AND SAFETY AT WORK – II). In addition, an employer who fails to fulfil his legal duties may face a claim for constructive dismissal should an employee resign as a result of an alleged breach of the employer's duty of care. For example, in *British Aircraft Corpn v Austin* [1978] IRLR 332, an employer's obstinate and unjustified refusal to deal with a safety grievance was held to justify a complaint of constructive dismissal when the employee resigned (see **26.11** HEALTH AND SAFETY AT WORK – II).

25.2   THE COMMON LAW DUTY

An employer is obliged to take such steps as are reasonably necessary to ensure the safety of his employees. The definition of 'employee' is given a wide interpretation by the courts (*Lane v Shire Roofing Co (Oxford) Ltd* [1995] IRLR 493, [1995] PIQR P 417, CA). In *Autoklenz v Belcher* (2011) UKSC 41 the Supreme Court explained that the question of status was to be determined by having regard to the true nature of the arrangement between the parties rather than by slavishly accepting documentation which might not be accurate. The duty to ensure safety is not an absolute one and the mere occurrence of an accident does not of itself necessarily impose liability on the employer (see *McCook v Lobo* [2002] EWCA Civ 1760, [2003] ICR 89). All the circumstances of the accident will be investigated in deciding whether the employer acted reasonably or not. If an accident occurs as a result of the employer's failure to comply with his duty to his employees, he is liable for any resulting injury or damage.

25.2 Health and Safety at Work – I: The Legal Framework

Where a job has inherent risks to health and safety which are not commonly known but of which the employer is or ought to be aware, and if the employer cannot guard against those risks by taking precautionary measures, then he has a duty to inform prospective employees of the risks if knowledge of them would be likely to affect a sensible and level-headed person's decision on whether or not to accept the job (*White v Holbrook Precision Castings* [1985] IRLR 215). The employer must keep abreast of contemporary knowledge in the field of accident prevention (*Baxter v Harland and Wolff plc* [1990] IRLR 516; *Bowman v Harland and Wolff plc* [1992] IRLR 349). In *Williams v University of Birmingham* [2011] EWCA Civ 1242 the Court of Appeal emphasised that one must look to the knowledge of risk at the time of exposure , here to asbestos in the early 1970s , and must not make the error of applying hindsight .

The employer's compliance with his common law duty of care is usually tested under the following headings:

(a)   providing a safe place of work;

(b)   providing a safe means of access to the place of work;

(c)   providing a safe system of work;

(d)   providing safe plant and equipment;

(e)   employing competent fellow employees; and

(f)   protecting employees from unnecessary risk of injury.

However, these are simply specific aspects of the employer's overall general duty not to be negligent, and so should be viewed as examples of ways in which employers can take steps to ensure that their employees are reasonably safe at work.

25.3   Safe place of work

An employer is obliged to see that the place where his employees work is reasonably safe in all the circumstances. A place of work must be safely constructed and adequately maintained in a reasonable state of repair. An employer would be as guilty of failing to provide a safe place of work if, for example, a platform high above the ground on which men were required to stand was not adequately fenced as if one of the planks provided for the platform were rotten and liable to give way.

So far as construction of the workplace is concerned, it is not sufficient to show that the employer engaged a competent contractor to provide a safe place (*Paine v Colne Valley Electricity Supply Co Ltd and British Insulated Cables Ltd* [1938] 4 All ER 803, *per* Goddard LJ at 807). This reflects the general principle that the employer's duty of care to his employees is non-delegable. If, however, an employer maintains an adequate system of inspection of the workplace and despite inspection, a part of the workplace becomes inadequate or defective, the employer will probably not have been in breach of his common law duty. (He may nevertheless be in breach of a statutory provision which imposes a stricter duty.)

Temporary conditions affecting the workplace. A place of work which is intrinsically safe may become unsafe by the occurrence of certain events. Liquid may be spilt on a workshop floor making it slippery, a fence may be temporarily removed or an object placed in an unfamiliar position. All these events could cause accidents. The employer's liability will depend upon whether a reasonable employer would in the particular circumstances have taken measures to avoid the accident or different measures from those in fact taken. What is reasonable will vary according to the facts of the case. If a man slips on an oil slick at his workplace and thereby injures himself, his employer's potential liability may well vary according to how long the oil had been present (or according to the frequency with which such spillages occur, as in *Bell v Department of Health and Social Security* (1989) Times, 13 June). If the oil had been spilt just a few minutes before the accident there may well be no liability, whereas if it had been there for half a day, the position would be different. In *Thomas v Bristol Aeroplane Co Ltd* [1954] 2 All ER 1, an employer was held not to be in breach of the common law duty of care in failing to take steps to remove from the entrance to the factory frozen snow which had fallen about a quarter of an hour before the factory opened.

Employee working on other premises. An employer owes a general duty to his employee to provide him with a safe place of work whether he is employed on the employer's own premises or elsewhere; see the House of Lords judgment in *McDermid v Nash Dredging and Reclamation Co Ltd* [1987] AC 906, [1987] ICR 917. However, the extent of that duty when the employee is on other premises may well be less than when he is on his employer's premises. The test again is: did the employer in question act as a reasonable employer would have acted in the circumstances? Thus, if an employer sends a window-cleaner to premises he knows to be unsafe, he may well be held liable for any accident caused as a result of the state of the premises. If he does not know whether the premises are safe or not, then, depending on the convenience of inspection and the degree of risk involved, he may be held negligent in failing to inspect and, if necessary, make those premises safe (*General Cleaning Contractors Ltd v Christmas* [1953] AC 180).

The extent of an employer's duty in relation to employees working on other premises was considered by the Court of Appeal in *Square D Ltd v Cook* [1992] IRLR 34. An employer must take all reasonable steps to ensure the safety of his staff and this includes the premises where the staff are required to work (whether occupied by the employer or by a third party). This duty cannot be delegated. However, the duty is not an absolute one and considerations such as the place where the work is to be done, the nature of the building on the site concerned, the experience of the employee who is sent to work at such a site, the nature of the work he is required to do, the degree of control that the employer can reasonably be expected to exercise in the circumstances and the employer's own knowledge of the defective state of the premises are all factors to be taken into account. These considerations apply whether the third party's premises are in the UK or abroad. However, the court may take a different view of the employer's duty where staff are sent to work abroad for a considerable period of time. The Court of Appeal suggested that in such an instance, the employer may be expected to inspect the site personally and satisfy himself that the occupiers are conscious of their obligations concerning the safety of people working there.

25.4   Safe means of access

It is the duty of every employer to provide his employees with a safe means of access to their place of work. Thus, if access to a factory is by means of a footpath, that footpath should be kept in a reasonable state of repair.

Sometimes it is hard to distinguish the means of access to the place of work from the place of work itself. A painter may use a ladder to reach a position from where to carry on his decorating. The ladder may in certain circumstances be considered the means of access and in others the place of work. In any event the common law duty of care in relation to both is the same.

25.5   Safe system of work

A system of work is the method used for carrying out the work, the sequence of events followed. It includes such things as manning of operations, provision of equipment, and supervision. It may be that the system used by an employer is intrinsically unsafe or it may be that there is in existence a suitable system of work but that the system itself is applied unsatisfactorily. For example, an employer who provides insufficient workers to carry out a task may be held liable for any accident caused thereby.

25.5 Health and Safety at Work – I: The Legal Framework

One defect in an otherwise unimpeachable system may render the whole system unsafe. If, for example, the procedures for carrying out blasting in a quarry were adequate but the warning given to workers in the quarry to leave was too short, the whole system would thereby be rendered unsafe. Similarly, it would be considered an unsafe system to require men who had insufficient training or supervision to carry out a task which would otherwise be considered safe.

Where an operation is so inherently dangerous that it should not be performed at all, the employer must provide explicit instructions banning employees from carrying it out (*King v Smith* [1995] ICR 339).

Employers who require their workers to carry out manoeuvres which involve several actions should first check to see whether there are any relevant statutory requirements relating to the procedure. Before devising a system of working they should consult the employees who are to work the system or their representatives. Where the workforce is unionised, the employer has a duty to consult with union-appointed safety representatives. Non-unionised groups of workers or their representatives must also be consulted (see **26.20** HEALTH AND SAFETY AT WORK – II). If the procedure is at all complicated, employers should consult the Health and Safety Executive (see **25.26**).

Duty based on reasonable steps. The duty to provide a safe system of work is not an absolute one. The duty is to take reasonable steps to provide a system which will be reasonably safe, having regard to the dangers necessarily inherent in the operation. In deciding what is reasonable, long-established practice in the trade (although not necessarily conclusive) is generally regarded as strong evidence in support of reasonableness (*General Cleaning Contractors Ltd v Christmas* [1953] AC 180 *per* Lord Tucker at 195). Nevertheless, acceptable standards of safety change over the years and the courts will have regard to current best practice. In deciding the extent of the duty the courts will take into account: (i) the size of the danger; (ii) the likelihood of an accident occurring; (iii) the possible consequences of the occurrence of an accident; and (iv) the steps needed to eliminate all risk and the cost of doing so (*Edwards v National Coal Board* [1949] 1 KB 704).

Ensuring implementation of safety measures. It is not sufficient to provide a safe system of work. An employer should take such steps as are reasonably practicable to see that the system is implemented. If it is within his knowledge that a piece of safety equipment is persistently not used, he should take reasonable steps to encourage his workers to use it (*Bux v Slough Metals* [1974] 1 All ER 262). However, this duty is not so onerous as the duty to provide the safety equipment, etc in the first place. As Lord Radcliffe said in *Qualcast (Wolverhampton) Ltd v Haynes* [1959] AC 743 at 753: 'the courts should be circumspect in filling out that duty with the much vaguer obligation of encouraging, exhorting or instructing workmen or a particular workman to make regular use of what is provided'. In *Crouch v British Rail Engineering Ltd* [1988] IRLR 404 it was held to be insufficient on the facts merely to make safety goggles available for collection from a point about five minutes away. The failure to have them available where they were needed encouraged the taking of risks.

25.6 Safe equipment and materials

An employer is under a common law duty to provide equipment, materials and clothing to enable his workmen to carry out their duties in safety. As with the system of work, the duty is not an absolute one. It may be, for example, that goggles costing £300 per pair are marginally safer than those costing £50 per pair. In deciding whether an employer was in breach of his duty in failing to provide his employees with the more expensive goggles, the court would have regard to the difference in effectiveness between the cheaper and the more expensive goggles, the degree of risk involved, and the additional cost.

When an employer bought materials from a reputable supplier, and injury was caused by an undetected defect in those materials, his failure to examine the materials would not render him liable for the accident at common law. However, under the *Employers' Liability (Defective Equipment) Act 1969*, if an employee is injured by reason of a defect in the equipment, the injury is by statute deemed to be attributable to the fault of the employer. This does not affect the employer's right to allege that the accident was wholly or partly due to negligence on the part of the employee; nor does it affect any remedy the employer may have against his supplier. Thus, if an employee is injured by a piece of metal flying from a defective high-pressure hose, supplied to him by his employer, he could succeed in a claim against the employer for his injury. The employer could only seek to reduce the damages awarded against him by showing that the accident was caused or contributed to by the fault of the employee and/or by claiming against the supplier of the hose.

Under *s 1(3)* of the *Employers' Liability (Defective Equipment) Act 1969* 'equipment' includes any plant, machinery, vehicle, aircraft and clothing. A ship is 'equipment' for the purposes of *s 1(3)* (*Coltman v Bibby Tankers Ltd, The Derbyshire* [1988] ICR 67). 'Equipment provided by the employer' includes materials (in this case a flagstone) which an employee is given by the employer to do the job (*Knowles v Liverpool City Council* [1993] IRLR 588. The contention that 'equipment' was confined to the tools of the job was rejected; a nail, a brick and a piece of timber all amount to equipment.

25.7   Fellow workers

An employer is under a duty to provide competent fellow workers. Thus, if an employee of his is injured because of the known inadequacy of a fellow worker, the employer is liable to that employee in damages for the injury caused by the fellow worker. Even if the employee's action is untypical, the employer may nevertheless be held liable by reason of his VICARIOUS LIABILITY (54). This principle also applies to the employer's duty not to engage or continue to employ employees who are known to indulge in dangerous 'horseplay' (*Hudson v Ridge Manufacturing Co Ltd* [1957] 2 QB 348). Liability on the part of an employer when one employee assaults another in the workplace has been considered in the conjoined appeals of *Wallbank v Wallbank Fox Designs Ltd* and *Weddall v Barchester* [2012] EWCA Civ 25. Lord Phillips in *The Catholic Care Child Welfare Society and others v Various claimants and The Institute of Brothers of the Christian Schools* [2012] UKSC 56 [at 19] wisely observed that the law was on the move. The absence of a conventional contract of employment between a religious body and some members of it who abused children did not prevent a finding of vicarious liability. The relationship was akin to employment and so the body was liable. One can anticipate interesting arguments about liability arising for the acts of volunteers and others who do not fulfil conventional employment criteria and yet, arguably, come within the ambit of quasi-employment.

An employer may not contract out of his liability to his employees for the negligence of fellow workers. The *Law Reform (Personal Injuries) Act 1948, s 1(3)* renders void any agreement to that effect.

25.8   Protection from risk of injury

An employer is under a duty to take reasonable care to see that his employees are not subjected to any unnecessary risks of injury. In *Charlton v Forrest Printing Ink Co Ltd* [1980] IRLR 331, the Court of Appeal held that an employer has a duty to take steps to eliminate a risk which he knows or ought to know is a real risk and not a mere possibility which would never influence the mind of a reasonable man. The Court of Appeal in *Coxall v Goodyear Great Britain Ltd* [2002] EWCA Civ 1010, [2003] ICR 152, considering whether or not an employer was under a duty to prevent an employee from doing work which he was willing to do because of a risk to his health, depended largely on the actual nature and extent of the risk. Consequently, if on the facts the employer were negligent in failing to either move the employee from the job in question or dismiss him in order to protect him from the danger, the employer would become liable.

Where a risk is not obvious, the employee will succeed only if he can show that the state of knowledge in the relevant industry at the relevant time was such that the employer knew or ought to have known of that risk. But an employer must keep reasonably abreast of developing knowledge, and if he has greater than average knowledge of the risks, he may have to take greater than average precautions (*Stokes v Guest Keen & Nettlefold (Bolts and Nuts) Ltd* [1968] 1 WLR 1776).

An employer may also be liable in certain circumstances for psychiatric illness caused by work if it is reasonably foreseeable (see *Page v Smith* [1996] AC 155 for the principles involved, and *Walker v Northumberland County Council* [1995] IRLR 35 and *Cross v Highlands and Islands Enterprise* [2001] IRLR 336 at **26.24** HEALTH AND SAFETY AT WORK – **II**). The House of Lords in *White v Chief Constable of South Yorkshire Police* [1999] IRLR 110 overturned the ruling of the Court of Appeal in *Frost v Chief Constable of South Yorkshire Police* [1997] IRLR 173 relating to an employer's liability for work-related psychiatric illness. The case concerned police officers who sustained psychiatric damage as a result of tending to victims of the Hillsborough football stadium disaster which was caused by the employer's admitted negligence. Compensation for physical injury caused by negligence was recoverable if it was reasonably foreseeable that the conduct would cause such injury. Where this situation does not apply (ie the claimant is not within the range of foreseeable physical injury), individuals are 'secondary victims' and, in order to recover compensation for psychiatric injury, it was necessary that the conditions set out in *Alcock v Chief Constable of South Yorkshire Police* [1992] 1 AC 310 should be satisfied:

(a)   there must be a close tie of love and affection between the claimant and the victim;

(b)   the claimant must have been present at the accident or its immediate aftermath; and

(c)   the psychiatric injury must have been caused by direct perception of the accident or its immediate aftermath and not by hearing about it from someone else.

Since the officers did not have sufficiently close ties to the victims, their claim failed. The House of Lords concluded that the employment relationship did not put the officers in a special position in this regard. See also *Robertson and Rough v Forth Road Bridge Joint Board* [1995] IRLR 251, *Young v Charles Church (Southern) Ltd* (1997) 33 BMLR 101, CA and *Hunter v British Coal Corpn* [1999] QB 140, CA.

The House of Lords in *Corr (Administratrix of Corr dec'd) v IBC Vehicles Ltd* [2008] UKHL 13, [2008] ICR 372 held an employer liable for the suicide of their employee who had been badly injured in an accident at work six years before.Mr Corr had become severely depressed as a result of his injuries. His death was attributable to the accident for which the employer had been to blame. This is an example of the classic maxim that one must take the claimant as one finds him. Whilst extreme depression was not an inevitable consequence of injury it happened to have been so here and thus the defendant was liable.

In mainstream stress cases it had been the conventional approach to apportion liability where there were a combination of causes, some of which were non-tortious, that lead to injury. This would occur, for example, where it was accepted that the employer was culpable but the claimant had other non work related problems too. No more. In *Dickins v O2 Plc* [2009] IRLR 58 the Court of Appeal accepted, obiter, that stress was an injury incapable of division and so the claimant would be entitled to full compensation where the employer had made a material contribution to the injury.

In cases of industrial disease, it may often be difficult to determine whether the employee's illness was *caused* by the employer's breach of duty. The decision of the House of Lords in *Fairchild v Glenhaven Funeral Services Ltd* [2002] UKHL 22, [2003] 1 AC 32 contains a comprehensive review of the relevant authorities. The Supreme Court has now decided in *Sienkiewicz v Greif (UK) Ltd* [2011] UKSC 10, [2011] ICR 391 that the *Fairchild* principle can equally apply where there was only one relevant defendant and also that a claim may succeeed without the need to prove that guilty exposure doubled the risk of harm. Here,the evidence was that the employer negligently exposed the victim to 18% more asbestos than would be found in the general environment. Accordingly, the employer was liable. In cases of mesothelioma only, s 3 of the *Compensation Act 2006* enables a claimant to recover in full from any culpable employer even though the victim was exposed to asbestos in more than one job.

In *Chandler v Cape Industries Ltd* [2012] EWCA Civ 525 the Court of Appeal upheld a finding that a parent company was liable for the negligence of a subsidiary which was now defunct. The parent was liable because the respective businesses were similar (asbestos production), it had or ought to have had superior knowledge of health risks, it knew of an unsafe system of work at the subsidiary and it had intervened in the business of the subsidiary.

25.9   Vicarious liability for acts of employees

An employer is liable for the acts of his employee if they are committed in the course of the employee's employment. This is known as vicarious liability. The modern test is whether the incident was job related or job connected. An incident can be job related even if it forms no part of the employee's authorised work. In *Lister v Hesley Hall Ltd* [2001] 2 WLR 1311 it was found that a teacher who abused a pupil was acting in the course of employment even though what he did was criminal, unauthorised and something that no teacher should ever have done. Thus, if a van delivery driver drives negligently while in the normal course of his duties and causes an accident, his employer is held liable for the resulting damage or injury. Sexual abuse of a child by a priest was held to be the responsibility of the Archdiocese in *Maga v Roman Catholic Archdiocese of Birmingham* [2010] EWCA Civ 256. Likewise, the Court of Appeal held the employer liable when an employee stole silver bullion which was to be transported abroad from a secure compound which he was authorised to enter. This question is dealt with in more detail in VICARIOUS LIABILITY (54).

25.10   Employee working under direction of third party

The primary employer remains liable for the safety of an employee who is working under the direction of a third party. However, where the employee suffers an accident which is wholly due to the third party's negligence in breach of its duty of care, the primary employer may be able to recover full indemnity from the third party in accordance with the *Civil Liability (Contribution) Act 1978* (*Nelhams v Sandells Maintenance Ltd* (1995) Times, 15 June, CA).

25.11   Independent contractors

With the exception of the statutory occupier's liability (see **25.12** below), in general an employer is not liable for acts of an independent contractor engaged by him, provided that he exercised due diligence in selecting the contractor for the task. (For criminal liability in respect of the negligence of an independent contractor, see **25.19** below.)

25.12 OCCUPIERS' LIABILITY ACT 1957

Apart from the common law duties of an employer to provide his employees with a safe place of work, as an occupier of premises he owes his employees, and other visitors, the common duty of care imposed by the *Occupiers' Liability Act 1957* (*'OLA 1957'*). The extent of the duty which is owed to trespassers is defined by the *Occupiers' Liability Act 1984*. An outline is given below of the duties imposed on an employer, as the occupier of premises, to employees and other visitors by the *OLA 1957*.

25.13 Meaning of 'occupier'

An occupier of premises may be the owner, the lessor, or the licensee (a person who merely has permission to occupy). An occupier need not have exclusive control over premises in order to have a duty to persons who visit those premises; more than one person may owe a duty in respect of the same premises. For example, both an employer and an independent contractor may be held to be occupiers of premises where the employer has engaged the independent contractor to carry out work on the premises.

25.14 Duty of occupier

The extent of the duty of care is defined in *OLA 1957, s 2(2)* as:

> 'a duty to take such care as in all the circumstances of the case is reasonable to see that the visitor is reasonably safe in using the premises for the purposes for which he is invited or permitted by the occupier to be there.'

In defining the extent of the duty, the courts will take into account the *degree of control over the premises actually enjoyed* by the occupier and, if applicable, the division of duties between the two occupiers of the same premises. Thus, if a harbour authority leases a certain wharf to a shipping company and an employee of that company suffers an accident due to the state of repair of the wharf, the apportionment of blame will depend on the actual degree of control exercised by the harbour authority and the shipping company.

Children and persons pursuing a calling. OLA 1957, s 2(3) provides a little help in defining the extent of the duty of care to be exercised in relation to children and to persons on the premises in pursuance of a particular calling.

> 'The circumstances relevant for the present purpose include the degree of care, and of want of care, which would ordinarily be looked for in such a visitor, so that (for example) in proper cases:
>
> (a)   an occupier must be prepared for children to be less careful than adults; and
> (b)   an occupier may expect that a person, in the exercise of his calling, will appreciate and guard against any special risks ordinarily incident to it, so far as the occupier leaves him free to do so.'

The duty under *OLA 1957, s 2(2)* is to see that the visitor is reasonably safe in using the premises for the purpose for which he or she is there. This covers the static state of the premises and does not extend to dangers occurring to employees of contractors as a result of activities they are performing on the premises. The House of Lords, in its landmark ruling in *Fairchild v Glenhaven Funeral Services Ltd* [2002] UKHL 22, [2002] IRLR 533, overruled the Court of Appeal's decision ([2002] EWCA Civ 1881, [2002] IRLR 129) that claimants were not entitled to recover damages from their former employers in relation to mesothelioma, a form of cancer which develops as a result of negligent exposure to asbestos.

Unanimously, their Lordships held that the victim, on grounds of so-called 'justice', should not be deprived of a remedy because it cannot be established which of a series of different employers caused the alleged harm. As Lord Nicholls put it: '*Any other outcome would be deeply offensive to instinctive notions of what justice requires and fairness demands.*' Consequently, employers may now be held liable for damage which they did not cause. The House of Lords established a right to damages by departing from the orthodox test of causation where justice so requires, by establishing a notion of joint liability. For instance, on the facts of this case, it was sufficient that the employer's breach of duty materially increased the risk that the claimants would contract mesothelioma. Therefore, the *Fairchild* ruling presupposes negligence by all employers. Clearly, the impact of this historic ruling is that once a breach of duty can be established, then each employer becomes liable for the full damages.

25.15 Faulty work by independent contractor

If an accident occurs as a result of faulty work by an independent contractor employed at the premises which the employer occupies, *OLA 1957, s 2(4)(b)* provides that:

> 'the occupier is not to be treated without more ["without more" in the sense of "on those facts alone"] as answerable for the danger if in all the circumstances he had acted reasonably in entrusting the work to an independent contractor and had taken such steps (if any) as he reasonably ought in order to satisfy himself that the contractor was competent and that the work had been properly done.'

Thus, if injury is caused to a visitor to the premises by the fault of an independent contractor, the occupier will not be held liable for the injury or damage so caused if he can show that:

(a)   he acted reasonably in entrusting the work to the independent contractor (it may be held to be reasonable to employ an independent contractor where the work to be done is of a skilled or specialist nature and is beyond the capabilities of the employer);

(b)   he exercised a reasonable degree of care in selecting the independent contractor to see that he was competent to do the task entrusted to him; and

(c)   he checked so far as was possible to see that the work was properly carried out.

For example, an employer may need to have his factory rewired. He may have no electricians in his employ and, therefore, need to engage an outside firm. If he has reasonable grounds for regarding that firm as competent, he will not ordinarily be expected to supervise the firm's activities in order to ensure that a safe system of work is being used. But if he knows or has reason to suspect that the firm is using an unsafe system of work, it may well be reasonable for him to take steps to see that it is made safe. If he does not, he might be liable to one of his own or the firm's employees injured, eg by receiving an electric shock (*Ferguson v Welsh* [1988] IRLR 112, on different facts). He may also be liable to the employee for breach of other statutory provisions.

25.16 THE HEALTH AND SAFETY AT WORK, ETC ACT 1974

The *Health and Safety at Work, etc Act 1974* (*'HSWA 1974'*) lays down general principles to be followed by employers governing the health and safety at work of employees. It also establishes the Health and Safety Commission ('the Commission') and the Health and Safety Executive ('the Executive'); gives powers to inspectors to issue improvement notices and prohibition notices; and imposes certain civil and criminal liabilities upon employers. The Executive publishes many explanatory guides and booklets. In the autumn of 2010 the Government published and accepted the report of Lord Young who concluded that the law was unduly onerous and a more proportionate approach should be taken. It is highly probable that the law will be simplified with lower burdens being imposed upon those in low risk environments. Rescue workers should also be put beyond the risk of prosecution where they take heroic actions when striving to save life and limb.

25.17 Health, safety and welfare

The provisions of *HSWA 1974, Part I* (as expressed in s *1(1)*) are designed to have the effect of:

(a)   securing the health, safety and welfare of persons at work;

(b)   protecting persons other than persons at work against risks to health or safety arising out of, or in connection with, the activities of persons at work; and

(c)   controlling the keeping and use of explosive or highly flammable or otherwise dangerous substances, and generally preventing the unlawful acquisition, possession and use of such substances.

Regulations and codes of practice are issued under *HSWA 1974* to give effect to the general principles set out and also to enforce the provisions of a large body of health and safety legislation which is set out in *Sch 1* to the *Act*. Among the more important regulations made under *HSWA 1974* are the *Health and Safety (First-Aid) Regulations 1981 (SI 1981/917)*, the *Reporting of Injuries, Diseases and Dangerous Occurrences Regulations 1995 (SI 1995/3163)* and the *Electricity at Work Regulations 1989 (SI 1989/635)*. There are also many regulations dealing with specific problems such as asbestos at work. From 1 October 1989 a large number of outdated Statutory Instruments were replaced upon the coming into force of the *Control of Substances Hazardous to Health Regulations 1988* ('*COSHH*'). The *1988 Regulations* were subsequently amended and replaced by the *2002 Regulations (SI 2002/2675)* of the same name. *COSHH* has been described as 'the most far-reaching health and safety legislation since 1974'. Further important changes have taken place with the implementation of EC Directives on health and safety issues by regulations made under *HSWA 1974*. These regulations cover, *inter alia*, noise at work, management of health and safety, display screen equipment (VDUs), manual handling, work equipment, and workplace health, safety and welfare.

Further details of regulations made under *HSWA 1974* are contained in HEALTH AND SAFETY AT WORK – II (26) under specific subject headings.

As will be seen below, inspectors appointed under the *Act* have powers to enforce the legislation set out in *Sch 1* as well as the provisions of the *Act* itself, and health and safety regulations.

The protection of *HSWA 1974* is extended by *Health and Safety (Training for Employment) Regulations 1990 (SI 1990/1380)* to those receiving work experience provided pursuant to a training course or programme, or training for employment, or both, except if the training is received on a course run by an educational establishment.

25.18 Employer's obligations under HSWA 1974

HSWA 1974 contains provisions broadly equivalent to the common law duty of care of an employer to his employees (see **25.2** above) (*HSWA 1974, s 2(1), (2)*). Criminal liability under *HSWA 1974* can arise even where senior management has taken all reasonable steps to protect employees. A failure at local management level may be attributable to the employing organisation (*R v Gateway Foodmarkets Ltd* [1997] IRLR 189). A failure by an employer to comply with the requirements relating to the safety of his employees may also in certain circumstances constitute a fundamental breach of contract entitling the employee to resign and claim that he was constructively dismissed (*British Aircraft Corpn Ltd v Austin* [1978] IRLR 332).

Health and safety policy statement. Employers are obliged to prepare (and, if necessary, revise) a written statement of their general policy with respect to the health and safety at work of their employees and the organisation and arrangements for carrying out that policy.

In addition, employers must bring such information to the notice of all of their employees (*HSWA 1974, s 2(3)*). The length and complexity of the notice required will depend on the nature of the employer's undertaking. Such information should in all cases be placed on an easily accessible notice board. In addition, information relating to health, safety and welfare must be given to employees by means of posters and leaflets approved and published by the Health and Safety Executive. From 1 July 2000 employers are required to use a revised version of the poster; additional detail is provided on aspects of the *Management of Health and Safety at Work Regulations 1999 (SI 1999/3242)* and new sections have been incorporated for the insertion of the names and locations of safety representatives and competent persons together with their health and safety responsibilities. Copies of the form of approved poster or leaflet may be obtained from HSE Books (see the *Health and Safety Information for Employees Regulations 1989 (SI 1989/682)*). Alternative health and safety posters may be approved by the HSE provided certain criteria are met (the *Health and Safety Information for Employees (Modifications and Repeals) Regulations 1995 (SI 1995/2923)*).

Employers who carry on undertakings in which for the time being they employ fewer than five employees are exempted from the requirement of *s 2(3)* by the *Employers' Health and Safety Policy Statements (Exception) Regulations 1975 (SI 1975/1584)*.

25.19 Employers and the self-employed

Employers and self-employed people are obliged to conduct their undertakings, so far as is reasonably practicable, in a way which will ensure that persons who may be affected, not being their employees, are not exposed to risks to health or safety (*HSWA 1974, s 3(1), (2)*). The conduct of the undertaking extends to the manner in which equipment is made available for use by employees outside business hours (*R v Mara* [1987] ICR 165). The Court of Appeal has ruled that it is not necessary to prove actual danger to members of the public for criminal liability to arise. It is sufficient to show that there is a risk which might be run (*R v Science Museum (Board of Trustees)* [1994] IRLR 25, 158 JP 39).

Subject to reasonable practicability, s *3(1)* creates an absolute prohibition on exposing non–employees to risk. It is no defence to argue that the employer is not liable because senior management was not involved in the incident (*R v British Steel plc* [1995] IRLR 310). It may not be sufficient to show that the employer has issued a code of instructions on a safe system of work. In certain circumstances tangible technical equipment may be necessary to ensure safety (*R v Rhône-Poulenc Rorer Ltd* [1996] ICR 1054, CA).

Nevertheless, employers should not necessarily be held criminally liable under s *3(1)* for an isolated act of negligence by the employee performing the work (*R v Nelson Group Services (Maintenance) Ltd* [1999] IRLR 646). It is a sufficient obligation to require the employer to show that everything reasonably practicable was done to see that the person doing the work had the appropriate skill and training, was adequately supervised and provided with safe equipment, and that a safe system of work was laid down.

In February 1997 Port Ramsgate, together with others, was convicted of a breach of *s 3(1)* and heavily fined following the collapse of a ferry passenger walkway which caused the death of six people. The port had employed highly reputable contractors and designers and made arrangements for safety checks but, according to the judge, it had not ensured that proper quality assurance provisions were included in the contract or given detailed thought to its own responsibilities for the design, construction and installation of the walkway.

In *R v Associated Octel Co Ltd* [1997] IRLR 123 the House of Lords held that an employer was criminally liable under s *3(1)* for the negligence of an independent contractor in respect of injuries sustained by an employee of the contractor while undertaking maintenance and repair work for the employer. The conduct of the employer's undertaking could cover ancillary activities carried out by independent contractors, particularly when the activity was carried out on the employer's premises.

Regulations may be introduced compelling employers and self-employed people to give information relating to health and safety to people (not being their employees) who may be affected by the way in which they conduct their undertakings (*HSWA 1974, s 3(3)*).

25.20   Duties of occupiers

Obligations are imposed on occupiers of 'non-domestic' premises in respect of persons who are not their employees but who are working on their premises or using plant or substances provided for use on the premises (*HSWA 1974, s 4*). They must take such measures as are reasonable for persons in their position to ensure, so far as is reasonably practicable, that the premises, plant and machinery are safe and without risks to the health of the non-employees working there. These provisions would apply to protect workers who were sent by their employer, for example, to re-decorate a client's factory. The nature of the duties imposed by *HSWA 1974, s 4* was considered by the House of Lords in *Austin Rover group Ltd v HM Inspector of Factories* [1990] ICR 133.

Operators in control of an establishment or installation which involves the use of dangerous substances are required to take all measures necessary to prevent major accidents and to limit their consequences to people and the environment, under the *Control of Major Accident Hazards Regulations 1999 (SI 1999/743)*, which came into force on 1 April 1999. Known as '*COMAH*', the *1999 Regulations* (which primarily affect the chemical industry) revoke and replace the *Control of Industrial Major Accident Hazards Regulations 1984 (SI 1984/1902)*. Under the *1999 Regulations*, operators are obliged to notify the competent authority about their activities and prepare a major accident prevention policy.

25.21   Duties of manufacturers

Manufacturers, designers, importers and suppliers of articles or substances for use at work are placed under a duty to ensure so far as is reasonably practicable that the design of their product is safe, to carry out necessary tests for so ensuring and to provide adequate information about the use of the product and the conditions necessary for its safe use (*HSWA 1974, s 6*, as amended by the *Consumer Protection Act 1987, s 36* and *Sch 3*). The manufacturers, designers, importers or suppliers of articles for use at work are exempt from such duties if they obtain a written undertaking from their customers that the customer will take specified steps sufficient to ensure, so far as is reasonably practicable, that the article will be safe and without risk to health when properly used (*HSWA 1974, s 6(8)*). This exemption is qualified where the goods are imported (*HSWA 1974, s 6(8A)*).

25.22   Duties of employees

Every employee while at work has the duty:

(a)   to take reasonable care for the health and safety of himself and of other persons who may be affected by his acts or omissions at work; and

(b)   to co-operate with his employer, or any other person, in ensuring that requirements or duties imposed by the relevant statutory provisions (including those specified in *Sch 1*) are complied with.

(*HSWA 1974, s 7*.)

Thus, if an employer is required to provide his workers with goggles, supervisors should, if that task is delegated to them, ensure that adequate goggles are available. Also, the workers themselves are under an obligation to wear them.

25.23 Interference with safety measures

No person may intentionally or recklessly interfere with or misuse anything provided in the interests of health, safety or welfare in pursuance of any of the relevant statutory provisions (*HSWA 1974, s 8*). Thus, an employee who removes a safety guard provided by his employer, in breach of the regulations, is in breach of *s 8* and is guilty of an offence for which in a magistrates' court he may be fined up to level 5 on the standard scale and in the Crown Court there may be an unlimited fine (*HSWA 1974, s 33(1)(b), (3)(b)*; see **1.10** INTRODUCTION).

Such conduct may also justify dismissal, provided the employee was properly instructed about the safety measures and had been made aware that interference could lead to dismissal (*Martin v Yorkshire Imperial Metals Ltd* [1978] IRLR 440).

25.24 No charge for safety measures

An employer may not charge any employee of his for anything done or supplied in compliance with any specific requirement of the relevant statutory provisions (*HSWA 1974, s 9*). If, for example, an employer is required to provide an employee of his with a mask, he may not require that employee to contribute towards the cost of that mask.

25.25 EU LEGISLATION

The influence of European-derived legislation in the health and safety field is substantial. The original *Treaty of Rome*, as amended by the subsequent Treaties of Maastricht, Amsterdam and Nice (see **22.1** EUROPEAN UNION LAW), provides in *art 137* (formerly *art 118A*) for the adoption of Directives in connection with improvements to the working environment to protect workers' health and safety. Such Directives are subject to the co-decision procedure whereby the European Parliament jointly adopts proposals with the Council of Ministers. Health and safety directives are normally implemented in UK law by means of regulations made under *HSWA 1974*.

A surge in EU health and safety legislation occurred following the adoption of the so-called *Framework Directive (89/391)*, implemented on 1 January 1993. The *Directive* imposes a number of general obligations upon both employers and employees. Whereas much English legislation uses the standard of what is 'reasonably practicable', the EC approach is to set absolute standards and to permit a defence of *force majeure* for non-compliance (see *art 5(4)* of the *Directive*).

Five further Directives, laying down detailed requirements, were initially adopted pursuant to the Framework Directive. They relate to minimum requirements for safety and health in the workplace (*89/654*), the use of machines and equipment (*89/655*), the use of personal protective equipment (*89/656*), the use of visual display units (*90/270*) and the handling of heavy loads (*90/269*).

In addition, Directives have been adopted on, *inter alia*: carcinogens (*90/394, 97/42, 99/38*), biological agents (*90/679*), construction sites (*92/57*), health and safety signs (*92/58*), and protection of pregnant workers (*92/85*).

Regulations have been made by statutory instrument to implement the EC Directives referred to above. For further details of Regulations within the scope of this book, see HEALTH AND SAFETY AT WORK – II (26) under the specific subject heading.

25.26 THE HEALTH AND SAFETY COMMISSION AND EXECUTIVE

HSWA 1974, s 10 establishes the Health and Safety Commission and the Health and Safety Executive. The Commission is made up of both employer and employee representatives and the Executive is made up of three of the Commission's appointees approved by the

Secretary of State for the Environment, one of whom is first chosen as the director of the Executive and who is consulted as to the appointment of the other two members. The Commission's chief function is to advise, authorise research and make suggestions for the implementation of the provisions of the *HSWA 1974*. It may make suggestions for the passing of regulations. The Executive also has the duty of providing information and advice to any government minister who requests it.

The Commission may either direct the Executive or authorise any other person to investigate and make a special report on any accident, occurrence, situation or other matter that the Commission thinks is necessary or expedient to investigate, or (with the consent of the Secretary of State) direct an inquiry to be held into any such matter (*HWSA 1974, s 14(1)(2)*). The *Health and Safety Inquiries (Procedure) Regulations 1975*, as amended.

(SIs 1975/335; 1976/1246) lay down the procedure for the conduct of such inquiries. Since civil or criminal liability for an accident may depend on the outcome of such an inquiry, proper representation is essential.

25.27 Information

HSWA 1974, s 27 enables the Commission to obtain information necessary for the discharge of its functions, or for provision to an enforcing authority (eg the Executive or an inspector) of information necessary to discharge its duties.

25.28 Codes of Practice

The Commission is empowered by *HSWA 1974, s 16* to approve and issue Codes of Practice for the enforcement of *ss 2–7* or of health and safety regulations introduced under the *Act*, or any other existing statutory provisions. Approved Codes give guidance on methods of complying with regulations and on what is considered reasonably practicable.

25.29 ENFORCING AUTHORITIES AND INSPECTORS

The Health and Safety Executive and local authorities are responsible for the enforcement of the *Health and Safety at Work Act 1974*. From 1 April 1998 the *Health and Safety (Enforcing Authority) Regulations 1998 (SI 1998/494)* re-enact, with amendments, the *1989 Regulations* of the same name (*SI 1989/1903*) which are revoked. *Schedule 1* sets out the main activities which determine whether local authorities will be enforcing authorities.

The enforcement powers under *HSWA 1974* cover all the 'relevant statutory provisions', which comprise the provisions of *HSWA 1974, Part I*, all the enactments specified in *HSWA 1974, Sch 1* and regulations made under them, and any health and safety and agricultural health and safety regulations (*HSWA 1974, s 53(1)*).

In January 2002 the Health and Safety Commission published its revised enforcement policy statement which, for the first time, sets out specific criteria to enable enforcement officers to decide when to investigate health and safety incidents, and to prosecute breaches of the law. The statement may be viewed on the HSE's website at www.hse.gov.uk/pubns/. This policy provides clarity on offences and the penalties available, as well as the HSE's role in investigations and inquiries. Since 2001 the HSC has published a list of health and safety offenders convicted and a prosecutions database.

25.30 Powers of inspectors

Every enforcing authority has the power to appoint inspectors. An inspector has many powers to enforce the statutory provisions for which his enforcing authority has responsibility. He may enter premises, if necessary accompanied by a police constable, take measurements and photographs and make other records, and take samples of articles or substances found in any premises which he has power to enter and of the atmosphere in or near such premises. If he fears that an article or substance found on premises which he has power to enter has caused or is likely to cause danger to health or safety, he may have it dismantled or subjected to any process or test. He may not destroy it unless that action is necessary for the performance of his duties. The inspector may take possession of a dangerous or potentially dangerous article or substance to examine it, to ensure that it is not tampered with or to ensure that it is available for use as evidence in any proceedings under the *HSWA 1974*. When he takes possession of any article, the inspector must fix, in a conspicuous position, a notice giving particulars of the article or substance and stating that he has taken possession of it (*HSWA 1974, s 20(2)(a)–(i), (4)*).

An inspector may require persons to answer questions in the course of his investigations and to sign a declaration of the truth of their answers. He may require the production of books and documents and take copies of them. If he requires any facilities or assistance in the course of his investigations, he may require the person able to do so to provide him with such facilities (*HSWA 1974, s 20(2)(j)–(l)*). No answer given by a person to an inspector is admissible in evidence against that person or the husband or wife of that person (*HSWA 1974, s 20(7)*). The section does not compel a person to disclose a document which could be withheld on grounds of legal professional privilege in High Court proceedings (such as an opinion of counsel) (*HSWA 1974, s 20(8)*).

Where an inspector has reasonable cause to believe that an article or substance on premises he is empowered to enter is a cause of imminent danger of serious personal injury, he may seize it and cause it to be rendered harmless (*HSWA 1974, s 25(1)*).

25.31 IMPROVEMENT AND PROHIBITION NOTICES

Improvement notices

If an inspector is of the opinion that a person:

(a)   is contravening one or more of the relevant statutory provisions (see **25.29** above); or

(b)   has contravened one or more of those provisions in circumstances that make it likely that the contravention will continue or be repeated,

he may serve on that person a notice (referred to as 'an improvement notice') (*HSWA 1974, s 21*).

An improvement notice must: (i) state that he is of that opinion; (ii) specify the provisions which in his opinion are being or have been contravened; (iii) give particulars of the reasons for his opinion; and (iv) require that person to remedy the contravention within a specified period.

The specified period in (iv) above is not to be shorter than that allowed for an appeal to an employment tribunal (which is 21 days from the date of the service on the appellant of the notice appealed against; see *Employment Tribunals (Constitution and Rules of Procedure) Regulations 2001, Sch 5 (SI 2001/1171)*).

25.32 Prohibition notices

If an inspector regards any activities as involving or potentially involving *a risk of serious personal injury*, he may serve on the person in control of those activities a notice known as 'a prohibition notice' (*HSWA 1974, s 22*).

A prohibition notice must:

(a)   state the opinion of the inspector;

(b)   specify the matters which in his opinion give or, as the case may be, will give rise to the risks;

(c)   where in his opinion any of those matters involves or will involve a contravention of any of the relevant statutory provisions, state that he is of that opinion, specify the relevant provision or provisions, and give particulars of the reasons why he is of that opinion; and

(d)   direct that the activities to which the notice relates shall not be carried on by or under the control of the person on whom the notice is served unless the matters specified in the notice and any associated contraventions so specified have been remedied.

A direction given in pursuance of (d) above takes effect immediately if the inspector is of the opinion, and states it, that the risk of serious personal injury is or will be imminent. For example, in *BT Fleet Ltd v McKenna* [2005] EWHC 387 (Admin), (2005) Times, 5 April, QBD, Evans-Lombe J. held that an improvement notice served by a health and safety Inspector, pursuant to *HSWA 1974, s 21*, should be clear and easily understood for it to be operative.

Improvement and prohibition notices may make reference to any approved Code of Practice (see **25.28** above) (*HSWA 1974, s 23(2)(a)*).

25.33 Withdrawal of notices

Where an improvement notice or a prohibition notice which is not to take immediate effect has been served, the notice may be withdrawn by an inspector at any time before it takes effect and the period before it takes effect may be extended or further extended by an inspector at any time when an appeal against the notice is not pending (*HSWA 1974, s 23(5)*).

25.34 APPEALS AGAINST THE NOTICES

A person on whom an improvement or prohibition notice is served may, within 21 days, appeal to an employment tribunal (*Employment Tribunals (Constitution and Rules of Procedure) Regulations 2001 (SI 2001/1171), Sch 5, rule 2(1)*). A tribunal may extend the period for lodging an appeal (on an application made in writing to the Secretary of the Tribunals either before or after the expiration of the time limit) if it is satisfied that it is not or was not reasonably practicable for an appeal to be brought within that time (*rule 2(2)*).

One or more assessors may be appointed for the purposes of any such appeals brought before an employment tribunal (*HSWA 1974, s 24(4)*).

The tribunal may either cancel or affirm the notice and, if the tribunal affirms it, may do so either in its original form or with such modifications as the tribunal may in the circumstances think fit (*HSWA 1974, s 24(2)*).

25.35 Suspension of notices pending appeal hearing

Where an appeal is brought within the time limit allowed:

(a)   *Improvement notice*: the bringing of the appeal has the effect of suspending the operation of the notice until the appeal is finally disposed of or, if the appeal is withdrawn, until the withdrawal of the appeal (*HSWA 1974, s 24(3)(a)*); and

(b)   *Prohibition notice*: the bringing of the appeal will not affect the notice unless, on application by the appellant, the tribunal so directs, in which case the prohibition notice will be suspended from the time that the tribunal gives its direction (*HSWA 1974, s 24(3)(b)*).

25.36 Cost of remedy required

In deciding whether an improvement notice which required the cleaning and repainting of walls should be cancelled or not, an employment tribunal sitting at Shrewsbury held that the company's financial position was irrelevant and evidence relating to its financial position would not be admitted (*T C Harrison (Newcastle-under-Lyme) Ltd v Ramsey (K) (HM Inspector)* [1976] IRLR 135). It may therefore be no ground for appeal against such notices that the company cannot afford to remedy the defects.

25.37 CRIMINAL PROCEEDINGS

The HSE publishes an annual report naming companies and individuals convicted in the previous 12 months of flouting health and safety law. The names of those convicted are also listed on the HSE's website.

HSWA 1974, s 33 lists various offences including:

(a)   failure to discharge a duty under *ss 2–7* (see **25.18–25.22** above) (*HSWA 1974, s 33(1)(a)*);

(b)   contravention of any health and safety regulations or any requirement or prohibition imposed under such a regulation (*HSWA 1974, s 33(1)(c)*);

(c)   contravention of any requirement or prohibition imposed by an improvement notice or a prohibition notice (including any such notice as modified on appeal) (*HSWA 1974, s 33(1)(g)*);

(d)   intention to obstruct an inspector in the exercise or performance of his powers or duties (*HSWA 1974, s 33(1)(h)*).

Criminal offences are triable either summarily (ie in the magistrates' court) or on indictment (ie in the Crown Court) or 'either way' (ie where the defendant may normally elect the mode of trial). In respect of offences committed on or after 6 March 1992, *HSWA 1974, s 33(1A) and (2A)* (inserted by *Offshore Safety Act 1992, s 4*) empowers a magistrates' court to impose a fine of up to £20,000 for breaches of *HSWA 1974, ss 2–6* (see (*a*) above), failure to comply with an improvement or prohibition notice (see (*c*) above), and failure to comply with a court remedy order under *HSWA 1974, s 42* (see **25.39** below).

On indictment the penalty may be a fine unlimited in amount and/or, for certain offences, imprisonment for up to two years (*HSWA 1974, s 33(2)–(4)*; see **1.10** INTRODUCTION).

In two cases, the courts have emphasised that where a company is convicted of offences under the *HSWA 1974* the financial penalties imposed should reflect the seriousness of the case. In *R v F Howe & Son (Engineers) Ltd* [1999] IRLR 434, the Court of Appeal indicated that the general level of fine for health and safety offences was too low and outlined some of the factors which should be taken into account by the courts when setting the level of fines. These observations were subsequently given unqualified support by the Court of Appeal in *R v Rollco Screw and Rivet Co Ltd* [1999] IRLR 439.

In *R v Davies (David Janway)* [2003] ICR 586, an employer was convicted and fined for being in breach of *ss 3(1)* and *33(1)* of the *HSWA 1974*, having failed to discharge the duty to conduct his undertaking in such a way as to ensure that he did not expose his employees to risks to their health and safety. The Court of Appeal, dismissing the employer's appeal, ruled that the *HSWA 1974* was regulatory and designed to protect and that the defence of 'reasonably practicable' was not incompatible with the *Human Rights Act 1998*. Consequently, £15,000 fine and £22,544.32 costs were upheld.

Current maximum penalties for offences specified in the Health and Safety at Work etc Act 1974, section 33 (HSWA)

HSWA SECTION	HSW(O)B, Schedule 6A, Item	CURRENT MAXIMUM
33(1)(a) Sections 2, 3, 4 and 6 – the general duties on employers and others	1	**Summary** - a fine not exceeding £20,000 **Indictment** - an unlimited fine
33(1)(a) Section 7 – duty on employees	2	**Summary** - a fine not exceeding £5,000 **Indictment** - an unlimited fine
33(1)(b) Section 8 – duty not to interfere with or misuse things provided for health and safety	3	**Summary** - a fine not exceeding £5,000 **Indictment** - an unlimited fine
33(1)(b)	4	**Summary**

Section 9 – duty not to charge employees for things done to meet requirements of relevant statutory provisions		– a fine not exceeding £5,000 **Indictment** – an unlimited fine
33(1)(c) Contravening requirements of health and safety regulations, licences or authorisations	5	**Summary** – a fine not exceeding £5,000 **Indictment** – an unlimited fine
33(1)(d) Contravening requirements imposed specifically in relation to public inquiries or special investigations	6	**Summary only** – a fine not exceeding £5,000
33(1)(e) Contravening any requirement imposed by an inspector under section 20 (eg to give information for an investigation, or to leave premises undisturbed after an incident) or under section 25	7	**Summary** – a fine not exceeding £5,000 **Indictment (section 25 breaches only)** – an unlimited fine
33(1)(f) Preventing another person from appearing before an inspector, or from answering an inspector's question	7 (continued)	**Summary only** – a fine not exceeding £5,000

33(1)(g) Contravening an improvement or prohibition notice	7 (continued)	**Summary** - 6 months' imprisonment, or a fine not exceeding £20,000, or both **Indictment** - 2 years' imprisonment or an unlimited fine or both
33(1)(h) Obstructing an inspector	8	**Summary only** - a fine not exceeding £5,000
33(1)(i) Contravening any notice issued under section 27(1) (general powers of HSC/E to obtain information)	9	**Summary** - a fine not exceeding £5,000 **Indictment** - an unlimited fine
33(1)(j) Disclosing information in breach of HSWA section 27(4) or 28	10	**Summary** - a fine not exceeding £5,000 **Indictment** - 2 years' imprisonment, an unlimited fine, or both

33(1)(k), (l) and (m) Offences relating to deception	11	**Summary** - a fine not exceeding £5,000 **Indictment** - an unlimited fine
33(1)(n) Falsely to pretend to be an inspector	11	**Summary only** - a fine not exceeding £5,000
33(1)(o) Failure to comply with a court remedy order (section 42)	13	**Summary** - 6 months' imprisonment, or a fine not exceeding £20,000, or both **Indictment** - 2 years' imprisonment or an unlimited unlimited fine or both
33(3) (in so far as no other penalty is specified) Penalties for health and safety offences arising from 'existing statutory provisions' (pre-1974 enactments) set out in HSWA Schedule 1	14	**Summary** - a fine not exceeding £5,000 **Indictment** - an unlimited fine
33(4)(a), (b) and (c) Offences of	Covered under Bill	**Summary** - a fine not exceeding

breaching licensing	items	£5,000
or explosives	above	**Indictment**
requirements		- 2 years'
		imprisonment
		or an unlimited
		fine or both

Any explosive article or substance may be forfeited by order of the court and may be destroyed (*HSWA 1974, s 42(4)*).

Breaches of Codes of Practice approved by the Health and Safety Commission (see **25.28** above) are not in themselves criminal offences. However, if in a prosecution for a contravention of the *Act* or the Regulations, it is shown that there was a failure to observe any relevant Code, then that contravention will be considered proven unless the court is satisfied that the requirement or prohibition was complied with in an alternative, acceptable manner (*HSWA 1974, s 17(2)*).

25.38 Personal liability of directors and other company officers

Under *HSWA 1974, s 37*, personal liability is imposed on any director, manager, secretary or other similar officer of a company (or any person who was purporting to act in that capacity) if an offence is committed by the company under *HSWA 1974*, or any of the other health and safety legislation specified in *HSWA 1974, Sch 1*, with the consent or connivance, or due to the neglect, of any such person.

In practice, such prosecutions are rare. However, several successful prosecutions of directors and senior managers have resulted, for example, in *Armour v Skeen* [1977] IRLR 310 (the director of roads and bridges for a Scottish regional council) and *R v Mara* [1987] IRLR 154 (the director of a cleaning company).

Defining who is responsible. In *Tesco Supermarkets Ltd v Nattrass* [1972] AC 153, in a prosecution of a company for a breach of the *Trade Descriptions Act 1968*, Lord Reid observed that:

' . . . a board of directors can delegate part of their functions of management so as to make their delegate an embodiment of the company within the sphere of delegation.'

In that case, the company was held not to have delegated any of its functions, so that the acts or omissions of the store manager were not acts of the company itself; the House of Lords therefore quashed the company's conviction. However, the Court of Appeal decision in *R v British Steel plc* [1995] IRLR 310 has cast doubt on whether the approach of the House of Lords in a consumer protection case is sufficiently stringent for health and safety legislation.

In *R v Boal* [1992] IRLR 420, the Court of Appeal defined 'manager' in relation to personal liability under the *Fire Precautions Act 1971*. The court held that the relevant provision was intended:

' . . . to fix with criminal liability only those who are in a position of real authority, the decision-makers within the company who have both the power and responsibility to decide corporate policy and strategy. It is to catch those responsible for putting proper procedures in place; it is not meant to strike at underlings.'

Where directors have been convicted of offences under the *HSWA 1974*, the Court of Appeal has said that the penalties imposed should make it clear that directors had a personal responsibility which could not be shuffled off to the company (*R v Rollco Screw and*

Rivet Co Ltd [1999] IRLR 439). See also, *R v Transco* [2006] All ER (D) 416 (Mar), CA, where in assessing the level of fine, the Court takes account of the employer's knowledge regarding their responsibility for any breach of health and safety.

Company Directors Disqualification Act 1986. A director found guilty of an indictable offence under *HSWA 1974* (whether on indictment or summarily) may be disqualified from holding office as a director under the *Company Directors Disqualification Act 1986, s 2(1)*. The first such disqualification occurred in 1992 when a director was disqualified for two years after being found guilty of serious breaches of *HSWA 1974*. The director had been fined £5,000 for refusing to comply with a prohibition notice in relation to dangerous rock falls where men were working. In September 1998, the managing director of a recycling company was disqualified under the *Company Directors Disqualification Act 1986* following a breach of the *Provision and Use of Work Equipment Regulations 1992* (see **26.12** HEALTH AND SAFETY AT WORK – II) which had resulted in a serious injury to an employee operating an unguarded machine.

In July 2001 the HSC published guidance on health and safety responsibilities for company directors and board members (IND(G) 343, HSE) of public sector and voluntary organisations. In particular, the guidance specifies that Boards need to:

(a)   accept joint responsibility and leadership for their organisations' health and safety performance;

(b)   appoint one Board member as a health and safety director;

(c)   ensure that each Board member accepts his or her individual role in providing health and safety leadership;

(d)   ensure that all Board decisions reflect their health and safety intentions;

(e)   encourage the active participation of workers in improving health and safety; and

(f)   keep up-to-date with all health and safety issues affecting the organisation and review performance regularly.

25.39 Order to remedy default

If a person is convicted of an offence and it appears to the court that the matter is one which it is in his power to remedy, the court may, in addition to or instead of imposing any punishment, order him (within such time as may be fixed by the order) to take such steps as may be specified in the order to remedy the situation. The time fixed by such an order may be extended or further extended by order of the court on an application made before the end of the time originally fixed or as extended (*HSWA 1974, s 42(1), (2)*). Failure to comply with an order under *HSWA 1974, s 42* is an offence (*HSWA 1974, s 33(1)(o)*), which is punishable: (i) on summary conviction, by up to six months' imprisonment and/or a fine of up to £20,000; and (ii) on indictment, by up to two years' imprisonment and/or an unlimited fine (*HSWA 1974, s 33(2A)*, inserted by *Offshore Safety Act 1992, s 4*).

25.40 Time for bringing proceedings

Summary proceedings may be brought at any time within six months from the date on which there comes to the knowledge of an enforcing authority evidence to justify a prosecution (*HSWA 1974, s 34(3)*). A failure to do something required by the Act is treated as continuing until the requirement is complied with, so that the six-month period runs from the last day on which the requirement was not complied with (*HSWA 1974, s 34(2)*). The time limit is extended in cases where there is a special report under *s 14(2)(a)*, a report of an inquiry under *s 14(2)(b)*, a coroner's inquest, or a public inquiry (in Scotland) into a death, to three months from the making of the report or three months from the conclusion of the inquest or inquiry (*HSWA 1974, s 34(1)*).

25.41 Defence

Many of the statutory provisions contain the modification 'so far as is reasonably practicable', or 'practicable' or to use 'the best practicable means to do something'. In those cases the onus is on the accused to prove that it was not practicable or not reasonably practicable to do more than was in fact done to satisfy the duty or requirement, or that there was no better practicable means than was in fact used to satisfy the duty or requirement (*HSWA 1974, s 40*). However, where proceedings are brought under *HSWA 1974, s 33(1)(g)* for contravention of an improvement notice, the offence is established if there has been a non-compliance with a requirement of the notice irrespective of whether compliance was reasonably practicable (*Deary (HM Inspector of Factories) v Mansion Hide Upholstery Ltd* [1983] IRLR 195).

In addition, since 11 July 2001 the defence that UK health and safety provision did not apply in the part of the business outside the jurisdiction (ie not situated in the UK) was abolished by the *Health and Safety at Work etc Act 1974 (Application outside Great Britain) Order (SI 2001/2127)*.

25.42 Corporate killing

The successful prosecution for manslaughter following the death of 23 cocklers on Morecambe Bay in February 2004, and consequential sentencing on 21 counts of manslaughter, re-emphasised the need to tighten up existing laws on corporate manslaughter. Under the Common Law a conviction for corporate manslaughter is obtainable only where a senior individual in a company (the 'controlling mind') is shown to have been grossly negligent and thereby responsible for the fatal accident. This is difficult to prove where managerial responsibilities are divided as is typical in a large organisation. Tragic incidents involving major train crashes and the sinking of a cross-channel ferry failed to yield convictions.

The *Corporate Manslaughter and Corporate Homicide Act 2007*, implemented in April 2008, seeks to make it easier to secure convictions against organisations. The Act creates no new duties and nor does it render individuals liable to prosecution. Liability for the new offence depends on a finding of gross negligence in the way in which the activities of the organisation are run. In summary, the offence is committed where, in particular circumstances, an organisation owes a duty to take reasonable care for a person's safety and the way in which activities of the organisation have been managed or organised amounts to a gross breach of that duty and causes the person's death. How the activities were managed or organised by senior management must be a substantial element of the gross breach. The likely impact of the Act should not be exaggerated. The Government has estimated that there will be about one prosecution a month.

Section 1(1) defines the new offence, which will be called corporate manslaughter in England and Wales and Northern Ireland and corporate homicide in Scotland.

The elements of the new offence are:

(a)   The organisation must owe a 'relevant duty of care' to the victim. The relevant duties of care are set out in *section 2*.

(b)   The organisation must be in breach of that duty of care as a result of the way in which the activities of the organisation were managed or organised. This test is not linked to a particular level of management but considers how an activity was managed within the organisation as a whole. *Section 1(3)* stipulates that an organisation cannot be convicted of the offence unless a substantial element of the breach lies in the way the senior management of the organisation managed or organised its activities.

(c)   The way in which the organisation's activities were managed or organised must have caused the victim's death. This means that the management failure need not have been the sole cause of death; it need only be a cause.

(d)   The management failure must amount to a gross breach of the duty of care. *Section 1(4)(b)* sets out the test for whether a particular breach is 'gross'. The test asks whether the conduct that constitutes the breach falls far below what could reasonably have been expected. *Section 8* sets out a number of factors for the jury to take into account when considering this issue. There is no question of liability where the management of an activity includes reasonable safeguards and a death nonetheless occurs.

Since only an organisation can be guilty the penalty upon conviction is a fine without limit. The court can also order that remedial measures be taken and it may make a publicity order requiring the defendant to publicise the conviction. The Act is extensive in application; employers, suppliers, Government departments, transport providers and others face liability. Valuable guidance may be found on the HSE website and the Government guidance notes upon the Act are exemplary.

In the first conviction under the *Act* in February 2011 Cotswold Geotechnics (Holdings) ltd, a small company with 8 employees, was fined £385,000 after an employee was killed when a trench caved in. The company was allowed to pay the fine at the rate of £38,500 per annum as else it would have been forced out of business. This is a clear indication that massive penalties will be applied upon conviction.

25.43 CIVIL LIABILITY

Breaches of *HSWA 1974, ss 2–8* cannot form the basis of a civil action (*HSWA 1974, s 47(1)(a)*) but breach 'of a duty imposed by health and safety regulations   . . .   shall, so far as it causes damage, be actionable except in so far as the regulations provide otherwise' (*HSWA 1974, s 47(2)*). In other words, a civil action can be brought where a breach of the health and safety regulations causes damage, unless the regulations prevent such an action from being brought.

Any provision in any agreement to contract out of liability for such breaches is void unless the health and safety regulations provide otherwise (*HSWA 1974, s 47(5)*).

25.44 CONTRIBUTORY NEGLIGENCE

In any successful action against the employer for breach of duty at common law or under some enactment, the amount of damages may be reduced in proportion to the degree to which the employee failed to take reasonable steps for his own safety (*Law Reform (Contributory Negligence) Act 1945, s 1(1)*). The *Act* applies where both the employer and employee have contributed to the damage. For example, in *Bux v Slough Metals Ltd* [1974] 1 All ER 262 the employee's failure to use the goggles with which he was provided contributed to the extent of the injury he suffered and reduced his damages by 40%. It is for the employer to allege and establish contributory negligence. In *Dziennik v CTO Gesellschaft Fur Containertransport MBH* [2006] EWCA Civ 1456, [2006] All ER (D) 157 (Nov) the Court of Appeal held that since the employer had not pleaded the issue it was wrong of a Trial Judge to deduct 60%, of the compensation awarded even though there was overwhelming evidence to justify that decision. The Court of Appeal indicated in *Pitts v Hunt* [1991] 1 QB 24, [1990] 3 All ER 344 that there was no such thing as 100% contributory fault. The purpose of contribution was to apportion blame, not to put it all at the door of the claimant and the tenor of the *1945 Act* anticipated that, after deduction, the claimant would be left with something. This very point was recently reiterated by the same court in *Brumder v Motornet Services and Repairs Ltd* [2013] EWCA Civ 195.

25.45 CORONER'S INQUESTS

In some health and safety incidences, interaction with the coroner is necessary. A coroner enquires into reported deaths. It is the coroner's duty to find out the medical cause of the death, if it is not known, and to enquire about the cause of it if it was due to violence or otherwise appears to be unnatural. In most cases the deceased's own doctor, or a hospital doctor who has been treating him or her, is able to give a cause of death. However, there are a number of circumstances under which a death will be reported to the coroner. For example, when no doctor has treated the deceased during his or her last illness or when the death was sudden or unexpected or unnatural. Yet deaths are usually reported to the coroner by the police or by a doctor called to the death if it is sudden. A doctor will also report a patient's death if unexpected. In other cases, the local registrar of deaths may make the report. Whenever the death has been reported to the coroner the registrar must wait for the coroner to finish his or her enquiries before the death can be registered.

25.46 CORONER'S FINDINGS

The coroner may decide that death was natural and that there is a doctor who can sign a form saying so. In this case the coroner will advise the registrar. The coroner may ask a pathologist to examine the body. If so, the examination must be done as soon as possible. The coroner or his or her staff will, unless it is impracticable or cause undue delay, give notice of the arrangements to, amongst others, the usual doctor of the deceased and any relative who may have notified the coroner of his or her wish to be medically represented at the examination. If the examination shows the death to have been a natural one, there may be no need for an inquest and the coroner will send a form to the registrar of deaths so that the death can be registered by the relatives and a certificate of burial issued by the registrar. If the person is to be cremated, the certificate may be issued by the coroner.

25.47 INQUESTS

An inquest is not a trial. It is a limited inquiry into the facts surrounding a death. It is not the job of the coroner to blame anyone for the death, as a trial would do. The inquest is an inquiry to find out who has died, and how, when and where they died, together with information needed by the registrar of deaths so that the death can be registered. Most inquests are held without a jury. There are particular reasons when a jury will be called, including if the death occurred in prison or in police custody or if the death resulted from an incident at work. In every inquest which is held with a jury, it is the jury, and not the coroner, which makes the final decision. The High Court has decided in *Roach v Home Office* [2009] EWHC 312 (QB), [2009] NLJR 474 that in principle the costs of attending an inquest or indeed a Health and Safety prosecution may be recoverable in subsequent civil proceedings where a claim for damages is pursued.

25.48 'INTERESTED PERSONS'

An 'interested person' is someone who can question a witness at an inquest. They can be:

(a)   a parent, spouse, child and anyone acting for the deceased;

(b)   anyone who gains from a life insurance policy on the deceased;

(c)   any insurer having issued such a policy;

(d)   anyone whose actions the coroner believes may have contributed to the death, accidentally or otherwise;

(e)   the chief officer of police (who may only ask questions of witnesses through a lawyer);

(f)   any person appointed by a government department to attend the inquest;

(g)   anyone else who the coroner may decide also has a proper interest.

26 Health and Safety at Work – II: Specific Legislation and Health and Safety Issues

Cross-reference. See HEALTH AND SAFETY AT WORK – I (25) for safety duties at common law and the general legislative framework.

26.1 ACCIDENT REPORTING

Notification of accidents, diseases and dangerous occurrences. The current regulations governing the notification and recording of accidents are the *Reporting of Injuries, Diseases and Dangerous Occurrences Regulations 1995 (SI 1995/3163)*. The reporting rules have been amended with effect from 6th April 2012. Whereas before it was obligatory to report an occurrence , as defined below , where the individual was incapacitated for 3 days or more that period has been extended to only apply to incapacity for 7 days or more (excluding the day of the incident. The employer now has 15 days to report the incident from the date it occurred. Employers should anticipate more reforms as the Government has embraced the recommendations made by Lord Young in autumn 2010 that a lighter regulatory touch is needed. Note that an incident involving incapacity must still be recorded albeit not reported by the employer. The HSE has issued explicit guidance that an entry in a workplace accident book will satisfy this obligation.

An employer must notify the Health and Safety Executive ('HSE') or local authority, whichever is in the circumstances the enforcing authority (see **25.29** HEALTH AND SAFETY AT WORK – I), of:

(a)   an accident arising out of or in connection with work resulting in:

    (i)   the death of any person;

    (ii)   a 'major injury' (specified in *Sch 1*) to any person at work;

    (iii)   hospital treatment of a person not at work; or

    (iv)   major injury to a person not at work as a result of an accident in connection with work at a hospital;

(b)   a dangerous occurrence (specified in *Sch 2*);

(c)   an accident connected with work as a result of which a person at work is incapacitated for work for more than seven days;

(d)   the death of an employee within one year of being injured as the result of a notifiable accident or notifiable dangerous occurrence (this applies whether or not the accident was reported at the time it occurred);

(e)   any person suffering from one of the reportable work-related diseases specified in *Sch 3*;

(f)   any 'gas incident' as specified in *reg 6*.

(*Regulations 3–6.*)

In cases under (*a*) and (*b*) the enforcing authority must be notified by the fastest practicable means in the first instance, and a report on the prescribed form must be sent to that authority within 15 days (*reg 3*).

In cases under (*c*) a report must be sent on an approved form within 15 days of the accident. Category (*d*) requires notification in writing as soon as the employer becomes aware of the death. Under (*e*) a report on an approved form must be made forthwith and for cases falling within (*f*) notification is required immediately, followed by a report within 14 days. Accident reports must be made on Form F2508 and disease reports on Form F2508A. For notification to the HSE, a central reporting system for the whole of the UK is in operation. Users have the choice of contact by telephone, by emailing electronic copies of the report forms or via a website, or continuing to complete Form F2508 and sending them by normal post or fax. See www.riddor.gov.uk.

Road accidents are not covered by the *Regulations*, except where they result from exposure to a substance which is being transported, the loading or unloading of vehicles, specified roadworks or where a train is involved (*reg 10*). See *Road Safety Act 2005*.

The definition of 'accident' includes acts of non-consensual physical violence done to a person at work.

Examples of 'major injuries' are: amputations, fractures (other than to fingers or toes), certain dislocations, loss of sight, chemical or hot metal burns or penetrating injury to the eye and injuries requiring hospital attendance for more than 24 hours (*Sch 1*).

Records must be kept of all notifiable accidents, dangerous occurrences and reportable diseases, containing the necessary particulars set out in *Sch 4*. They must be kept at the place of work to which they relate, or at the usual place of business of the responsible person as defined in the *Regulations*, for a period of three years from the date the details were entered in the records (*reg 7*).

Accidents to self-employed persons are covered if they were working under the control of someone else, in which case the obligations attach to the person in control of the premises where the accident occurred.

Special rules within *RIDDOR 1995* are applied specifically to mines, quarries, railways and pipe-lines.

A consultation exercise was conducted in 2001 on the HSC's proposal to introduce a compulsory duty on companies and other organisations to investigate all reportable workplace accidents, ill health or incidents which could have resulted in serious injury.

Major accident hazards. Operators of premises liable to major accident hazards are, in addition, subject to a special regime under the *Control of Major Accident Hazards Regulations 1999 (SI 1999/743)* from 1 April 1999 (see **25.20** HEALTH AND SAFETY AT WORK – **I**).

Notification of industrial injuries. An employee who suffers an 'industrial injury' must report the accident to his employer. Notice of the accident may be given orally or in writing, and may be given by someone else on the employee's behalf. It is sufficient notice if the accident is recorded in the accident book (see below). The employer is required to take reasonable steps to investigate the accident and must, on request, provide all information uncovered to the Department for Work and Pensions. Failure by an employee to notify an accident may jeopardise his entitlement to industrial injury benefits.

Accident book. Every employer who normally employs 10 or more persons on or about the same premises in connection with a trade or business must keep an accident book (Form BI 510) in which specified particulars of accidents may be recorded, as must (however few employees they have) all employers who are owners or occupiers of a mine or quarry or of a 'factory' within the meaning of the *Factories Act 1961, s 175* (*Social Security (Claims and Payments) Regulations 1979 (SI 1979/628), reg 25*). *Part 3* of the *Data Protection Code of Practice (Employment)*, issued on 11 June 2003, sets out basic rules for employers to follow in relation to monitoring employee activities. Such activities may include accidents. Hence, accident books kept by employers will fall within these provisions.

The Government has promised to reduce the burden of regulation and it may well be that, in the near future, a number of the above measures will be deleted or diluted.

26.2   ALCOHOL AND DRUG MISUSE

Problems arising from consumption of alcohol and misuse of drugs are seen as an increasing problem in the workplace. Employers have a duty of care, both at common law and under *HSWA 1974, s 2*, to ensure, so far as reasonably practicable, the health, safety and welfare at work of their employees. In addition, they are required to assess risks to health and safety under the *Management of Health and Safety at Work Regulations 1992* (see **26.17**). An employer who allows a person under the influence of drink or drugs to continue working could be in breach of its duty of care by putting the employee or others at risk.

Under the *Transport and Works Act 1992* it is a criminal offence for certain transport workers in safety-sensitive posts, primarily in the railway industry, to be unfit through drink or drugs while working. Transport system operators are required to show all due diligence in order to prevent an offence being committed.

It is an offence for occupiers of premises (such as employers) knowingly to allow the production or supply of controlled drugs on their premises or to permit the smoking of cannabis (*Misuse of Drugs Act 1971, s 8*).

Dependency on alcohol or drugs is an illness. Where an employee's performance or misconduct is found to be a result of alcohol dependency this should normally be handled as a capability issue (see **52.6** UNFAIR DISMISSAL – II). ACAS advises that drug dependency should be treated in the same way. However, the fact that use of non-prescription drugs is illegal may justify disciplinary action depending on the circumstances. One-off incidents of excessive consumption of alcohol by employees who are not alcohol-dependent would normally be dealt with according to disciplinary procedures. Off-duty use of alcohol or drugs is not normally the legitimate concern of the employer unless it has a connection with the workplace, damages the reputation of the employer's business or undermines trust and confidence in the employee.

As part of an overall health and safety policy, employers are advised to have a written policy on alcohol and drug misuse. Once a policy is in place, it should be applied consistently (*Angus Council v Edgley* EAT/289/99).

26.3   Drug testing

Drug testing is a controversial and sensitive issue. The HSE warns that testing is only likely to be acceptable if it is part of an organisation's health policy and is clearly designed to prevent risks to the misuser and others. Testing programmes should be introduced only with the consent of existing employees. Otherwise this may be seen as a breach of the implied term of trust and confidence, leading to constructive dismissal (see **51.7** UNFAIR DISMISSAL – I). Pre-employment testing where applicants are asked to take a test voluntarily raises fewer legal problems. In all cases individuals need to be assured of the integrity of the screening process and medical confidentiality. Company policies should indicate the action which will be taken if testing yields a positive result.

Drug testing (except in highly safety-critical areas) is unlikely to be justified unless there is a reasonable suspicion of drug use that has an impact on safety. Employers should also bear in mind the effect on protection of privacy of the *1950 European Convention on Human Rights* and the *Human Rights Act 1998* (see **28.6** HUMAN RIGHTS).

26.4   CONSTRUCTION SITE MANAGEMENT

Some 2.2 million workers make up the UK's construction industry. The *Construction (Design and Management) Regulations 1994 (SI 1994/3140)* gave effect to the EC Directive on temporary or mobile construction sites (*92/57*). The *Regulations* impose detailed requirements with respect to design and management aspects of construction work, placing new obligations on all parties involved in construction projects. The *1994 Regulations* were amended by the *Construction (Design and Management) (Amendment) Regulations 2002 (SI 2002/2380)*. A revised Approved Code of Practice ('ACOP') and guidance on the *Construction (Design and Management) Regulations 1994 (SI 1994/3140)* have been published by the Health and Safety Commission and came into force on 1 February 2002. The revised ACOP is designed to clarify roles and responsibilities, placing emphasis on managing health and safety throughout the life of a project.

Further effect has been given to *Directive 92/57* by the *Construction (Health, Safety and Welfare) Regulations 1996 (SI 1996/1592* as amended by *SI 1999/3242)* which also incorporate three sets of existing Regulations which have been modernised and simplified.

Note that no statutory provision or rule of law is to be taken as imposing, upon a Sikh on a construction site, any requirement to wear a safety helmet at any time when he is wearing a turban (*EA 1989, s 11*). However, a Sikh who does not comply with a requirement that would otherwise have been imposed, and is injured, may recover damages in tort only to the extent that he would have suffered injury even if wearing a helmet (*EA 1989, s 11(5)*). A person who does require a Sikh to wear a safety helmet on a construction site will probably be guilty of indirect racial discrimination, and if he has no reasonable grounds to believe that the Sikh would not wear a turban at all times when on site, he will not be permitted to justify that requirement (*EA 1989, s 12(1)*). Nor will special treatment afforded to a Sikh in consequence of s *11* constitute racial discrimination against anyone else (*EA 1989, s 12(2)*). See *Construction (Head Protection) Regulations 1989 (SI 1989/2209)*.

26.5   DISPLAY SCREEN EQUIPMENT

The *Health and Safety (Display Screen Equipment) Regulations 1992 (SI 1992/2792)* give effect to the EU Directive relating to the use of display screen equipment (eg VDUs) (*90/270*). Broadly, the *Regulations* require every employer, after making a suitable and sufficient analysis of each workstation (ie display screen equipment, its accessories and the surrounding work environment) to ensure that it meets the detailed requirements set out in the *Schedule* to the *Regulations*. Users of display screen equipment must: (i) be provided with eye and eyesight tests on request, both initially and at regular intervals thereafter; (ii) be provided with adequate health and safety information relating to the equipment; and (iii) have their daily work routine planned in such a way that they have periodical interruptions from using the equipment. See also **26.29** on work-related upper limb disorders.

The ECJ has given a ruling on the application of *Directive 90/270* in *Dietrich v Westdeutscher Rundfunk*: C-11/99 [2000] ECR I-5589. *Article 2(a)* of the *Directive* and *reg 1(2)* of the *Health and Safety (Display Screen Equipment) Regulations 1992* provide that 'display screen equipment' means 'an alphanumeric or graphic display screen, regardless of the display process involved'. The court concluded that the term 'graphic display screen' had to be interpreted broadly and therefore included screens that display film recordings, whether in analogue or digital form. A film cutter in a television production studio was therefore entitled to the protection of the provisions of the Directive.

Regulation 3 of the *Health and Safety (Miscellaneous Amendments) Regulations 2002 (SI 2002/2174)*, by removing the limitation in relation to workstation users and operators, so as to widen the remit to all users, amends *reg 3* of the *DSE Regulations 1992*.

26.6   ELECTRICITY AT WORK

The *Electricity at Work Regulations 1989 (SI 1989/635)* place a duty on employers to assess all foreseeable risks associated with work activities involving electricity which might give rise to personal injury or danger. Electrical equipment covers everything from power lines to electric kettles.

Employers are required to install safe systems of working with well-maintained equipment (*reg 4*). Steps must be taken to avoid danger in the use of equipment where it is reasonably foreseeable that it will be exposed to adverse or hazardous environments (*reg 6*). Specific precautions are laid down with regard to the insulation and protection of conductors (*regs 7–9*).

Regulations 12 and *13* lay down requirements for cutting off the supply, isolation and for working on dead equipment. No person should be engaged in work near a live conductor except where it is reasonable in all the circumstances and suitable precautions are taken to prevent injury (*reg 14*). Special attention should be paid to adequate working space, means of access and lighting where work is to be done on electrical equipment (*reg 15*), and no person should work on electrical equipment unless he or she possesses appropriate technical knowledge or is adequately supervised (*reg 16*).

26.7 EMPLOYMENT PROTECTION

The *Employment Rights Act 1996* ('*ERA 1996*') provides that certain dismissals in health and safety cases are to be deemed automatically unfair (see **52.3** UNFAIR DISMISSAL – II below), and confers protection on employees in such cases from unfavourable treatment. Two recent EAT decisions are illuminating. In *Oudahar v Esporta Group Ltd* [2011] IRLR 730 an employee refused to mop behind a fridge because maintenance work had taken place and electrical wires were protruding from the wall. It was no answer to his legitimate and reasonable belief in a danger being present for the employer to show objectively that the perceived danger did not exist. His refusal should have been taken seriously. In *Jaoa v Jurys Hotel Management Ltd* (2011) UKEAT/210/11 an employee was found to have a reasonable belief that it was dangerous to his health to require him to work on 9 successive night shifts even though this was strictly lawful and within the provisions of the *Working Time Regulations*.

26.8 Detriment in health and safety cases

ERA 1996, s 44 confers on an employee the right not to be subjected to any detriment by any act (short of dismissal), or any deliberate failure to act, by his employer done on the ground that:

(a)   having been designated by the employer to carry out activities in connection with preventing or reducing risks to the health and safety of employees at work, he carried out, or proposed to carry out, any such activities;

(b)   being a health and safety representative or member of a safety committee, in accordance with any statutory arrangements or by reason of being acknowledged as such by the employer, he performed or proposed to perform any functions as such a representative or member;

(c)   he took part (or proposed to take part) in consultation with the employer in accordance with the *Health and Safety (Consultation with Employees) Regulations 1996 (SI 1996/1513)* or in an election for representatives of employee safety;

(d)   where there is no representative or it is not possible to raise the matter by this means, he brought to his employer's attention, by reasonable means, circumstances which he reasonably believed were harmful or potentially harmful to health and safety;

(e)   in circumstances of serious or imminent danger which he could not reasonably be expected to avert, he left, or proposed to leave, his place of work or any dangerous part of his place of work; or

(f)   in circumstances of serious or imminent danger, he took, or proposed to take, appropriate steps to protect himself or other persons from the danger. 'Other persons' includes members of the public (*Masiak v City Restaurants (UK) Ltd* [1999] IRLR 780).

26.8 Health and Safety at Work – II

'Circumstances of danger' is not confined to dangers arising out of the workplace itself. It can include dangers caused by the misbehaviour of fellow employees (*Harvest Press Ltd v McCaffrey* [1999] IRLR 778). For the purposes of (*f*) above, whether the steps which the employee took, or proposed to take, were appropriate will be judged by reference to all the circumstances including, in particular, his knowledge and the facilities and advice available to him at the time (*ERA 1996, s 44(2)*). An employee will not be regarded as having suffered any detriment on the ground specified in (*f*) above if the employer shows that it was, or would have been, so negligent for the employee to take the steps which he took, or proposed to take, that a reasonable employer might have treated him as the employer did (*ERA 1996, s 44(3)*).

Provided a safety representative acts in good faith when pursuing a genuine health or safety matter, there is no duty to act reasonably (*Shillito v Van Leer (UK) Ltd* [1997] IRLR 495). In *Goodwin v Cabletel UK Ltd* [1997] IRLR 665 the Employment Appeal Tribunal held that the manner in which designated employees carry out health and safety activities can fall within the statutory protection. Tribunals must consider whether the way in which such employees approach their concerns about safety takes them outside the scope of health and safety activities.

26.9 Whistleblowing on safety

The *Public Interest Disclosure Act 1998* ('*PIDA 1998*'), which came into force 2 July 1999, provides further protection against victimisation by employers in specified circumstances if workers who ordinarily work in Great Britain raise concerns about, *inter alia*, health and safety issues (*ERA 1996, s 47B*, inserted by *PIDA 1998, s 2*). The legislation protects not only direct employees but also most other workers including, specifically, agency workers, homeworkers, NHS practitioners and trainees on vocational or work experience schemes (*ERA 1996, s 43K* inserted by *PIDA 1998, s 1*). Provided certain conditions are met workers will be protected against detrimental treatment (or dismissal, see **52.3** UNFAIR DISMISSAL – II) if they reveal information about the workplace relating to: a criminal offence; failure to comply with a legal obligation; a miscarriage of justice; endangering health and safety; or damage to the environment. Information disclosed which tends to show that any of the above matters is being deliberately concealed would also qualify for protection (*ERA 1996, s 43B* inserted by *PIDA 1998, s 1*). Workers are required to raise their concerns initially with the employer or prescribed regulator. External disclosures are protected only if stringent conditions are met; an exception is made for 'exceptionally serious cases' (*ERA 1996, ss 43C–43H*, inserted by *PIDA 1998, s 1*). In *Goode v Marks And Spencer plc* (2010) UKEAT/442/09 the mere expression of disquiet by way of opinion about what an employer was proposing to do (change certain employment terms and conditions) was held not to be a protected disclosure at all.

'Detrimental treatment' under *PIDA 1998* covers the victimisation short of dismissal of workers, any deliberate failure to act and the termination of contract of non-employees. *See Pinnington v Swansea City Council* [2005] EWCA Civ 135, [2005] ICR 685 and *Street v Derbyshire Unemployed Workers' Centre* [2004] EWCA Civ 964, [2005] ICR 97.

26.10 The remedy

An employee has the right to complain to an employment tribunal for a declaration and compensation if he has suffered a detriment by an act, or failure to act, done on any of the grounds specified in (*a*) to (*f*) in **26.9** above. On such a complaint it is for the employer to show the ground on which any act, or deliberate failure to act, was done (*ERA 1996, s 48(1), (2)*). Workers who have suffered detrimental treatment for making a protected disclosure are able to make a complaint to an employment tribunal (*ERA 1996, s 48(1A)*, inserted by *PIDA 1998, s 3*).

The employee may make a complaint within three months of the act, or failure to act, complained of (or the last act or failure, where that act or failure is part of a series of similar acts or failures). Where the tribunal is satisfied that it was not reasonably practicable for the complaint to be presented within three months, it may be presented within such further period as the tribunal considers reasonable (*ERA 1996, s 48(3)*; as to the meaning of 'the date of the act' and 'a deliberate failure to act', see *ERA 1996, s 48(4)*).

If the tribunal finds the complaint well-founded it will make a declaration to that effect and order compensation to be paid to the employee. The compensation will be such amount as it considers just and equitable in the circumstances, having regard to the right infringed and any loss which is attributable to the act or failure which infringed his right (*ERA 1996, s 49*). In the case of workers penalised for making a protected disclosure the tribunal may award such compensation as it considers just and equitable.

26.11 Breach of safety regulations and unfair dismissal

A failure by an employer to have regard for the safety of his employees can be considered a fundamental breach of contract entitling the employee to resign and claim that he has been constructively dismissed. In *British Aircraft Corpn Ltd v Austin* [1978] IRLR 332, the Employment Appeal Tribunal held that the employer's failure to give consideration to the employee's request that she should be provided with protective goggles incorporating the prescription lenses of her spectacles amounted to conduct entitling the employee to resign and, when she did resign, to claim that she had been constructively dismissed under what is now *ERA 1996, s 95(1)(c)*.

Where employees refuse to work with materials which in the past have adversely affected their health, and as a consequence are dismissed, the dismissals will be held to be unfair if the employer has not taken adequate steps to remedy the danger (*Piggott Bros & Co Ltd v Jackson* [1991] IRLR 309).

An employer may fairly dismiss an employee for breach of safety regulations if he brought the regulations to the attention of the employee and made clear to him the fact that such a breach would lead to dismissal (*Martin v Yorkshire Imperial Metals* [1978] IRLR 440).

26.12 EQUIPMENT FOR WORK

Three main sets of EU-derived Regulations set minimum standards for the provision and use of equipment at work:

The *Provision and Use of Work Equipment Regulations 1998 (SI 1998/2306) (PUWER)* give effect to the EC Directive relating to the use of machines and equipment *(89/655)* and amending *Directive 95/63*. The *Regulations* came into force on 5 December 1998, replacing *1992 Regulations* of the same name *(SI 1992/2932)*. *Regulations 4–10* set out general requirements with which employers must comply, for example in relation to suitability, maintenance and inspection. The requirement contained in *reg 5(1)* of the *1998 Regulations* for work equipment to be maintained in an efficient state and working order and in good repair imposes an absolute duty on employers (*Stark v Post Office* [2000] ICR 1013, CA). The very purpose of the *Regulations* is to make the employer liable for the unexplained and indeed inexplicable incident held the Court of Appeal in *Ball v Street* [2005] EWCA Civ 76, [2005] All ER (D) 73 (Feb). There are limits to the ambit of the Regulations. In *Smith v Northamptonshire County Council* [2009] UKHL 27, [2009] 4 All ER 557 the claimant had to collect a patient from home. The NHS had installed a wooden wheelchair ramp at the property. The ramp collapsed injuring Mrs Smith who relied on *Regulation 5* in a claim against her local authority employer. Since the employer had not installed the ramp and had no control over it, it would be wrong to treat it as work equipment and so the claim failed.

More specific requirements, concerning, for example, specific hazards, extremes of temperature, lighting, maintenance operations and dangerous parts are set out in *regs 11–24* (see *Horton v Taplin Contracts Ltd* [2002] EWCA Civ 1604, [2003] ICR 179). In *Horton* the Court of Appeal emphasised that the target of achieving suitability of work equipment for its purpose was to be measured by reference to such hazards to anyone's health and safety as were reasonably foreseeable (Bodey J). In addition the *1998 Regulations* impose requirements relating to mobile work equipment and power presses. The provisions relating to mobile work equipment do not apply until 5 December 2002 to equipment provided for use in an undertaking before 5 December 1998. Since 14 April 1999, certain duties set out in the *Regulations* are modified by the *Police (Health and Safety) Regulations 1999 (SI 1999/860)*. The effect is to take account of the special circumstances in which police officers sometimes have to work. For provisions applying to UK ships and to others when in UK waters, see the *Merchant Shipping and Fishing Vessels (Personal Protective Equipment) Regulations 1999 (SI 1999/2205)*, in force since 25 October 1999.

Since 5 December 1998 the *Lifting Operations and Lifting Equipment Regulations 1998 (SI 1998/2307)* (LOLER) gather together requirements relating to lifting equipment formerly contained in industry-specific legislation, and implement certain provisions of EC *Directives 89/655* and *95/63*. *Directive 2001/45* of 27 June amends *Directive 89/655* concerning the minimum health and safety requirements for the use of work equipment, so that it covers worker safety when using equipment to carry out work at height.

The *Personal Protective Equipment at Work Regulations 1992 (SI 1992/2966) (PPE)* give effect to the EC Directive relating to the use of personal protective equipment *(89/656)*. Personal protective equipment is defined as all equipment (including clothing giving protection against the weather) which is intended to be worn or held by a person at work and which protects the employee against health and safety risks. Broadly, the *Regulations*, which came into force on 1 January 1993, require employers to ensure that suitable personal protective equipment is provided for their employees and impose various other require-ments, for example in relation to maintenance and storage of the equipment. Personal protective equipment supplied from 1 July 1995 must bear the 'CE' marking. Under *HSWA 1974, s 9* employers are barred from charging employees for equipment provided in accordance with a specific statutory requirement. Recently, the House of Lords clarified in *Fytche v Wincanton Logistics plc* [2004] UKHL 31, [2004] ICR 975, a majority (3:2) ruling (Lady Hale and Lord Hope dissenting), that *reg 4* of the *1992 Regulations* required employers to provide suitable equipment to protect employees against an identified risk. Such a duty was further maintained by repairs required under *reg 7(1)*. Yet the latter duty only extended to repairs for the purposes of ensuring that assessed risks under *reg 4* are met.

In *Threlfall v Hull City Council* [2011] ICR 209 the claimant employee suffered lacerations when clearing garden waste. The employer had supplied conventional gardening gloves whilst appreciating that stronger , but more expensive , ones were available. Smith LJ held that the duty to risk assess meant that the employer should have given positive thought to the hazards that might be encountered and the failure to actively consider alternatives put the employer in breach.

The Court of Appeal in *Hyde v The Steeplechase Company (Cheltenham) Ltd* [2013] EWCA Civ 545 reiterated that the thrust of these provisions is intended to be stringent and onerous upon an employer. The Judge at first instance had wrongly applied a common law approach in finding that , since the defendant had acted reasonably , it was not liable for an accident.

For further details, see www.hse.gov.uk/equipment/legilsation.htm

26.13 FIRE PRECAUTIONS

Fire safety requirements at work are governed by the *Fire Precautions Act 1971* (*'FPA 1971'*), as amended by the *HSWA 1974* and the *Fire Safety and Safety of Places of Sport Act 1987*, and by the *Fire Precautions (Workplace) Regulations 1997 (SI 1997/1840)* as amended from 1 December 1999 by the *Fire Precautions (Workplace) (Amendment) Regulations 1999 (SI 1999/1877)*.

It is an offence under the *FPA 1971* not to have a fire certificate in respect of work premises covered by the Act. Before granting a certificate the fire authority will inspect the premises to satisfy itself as to the means of escape, securing the means of escape, fire-fighting equipment and warning methods. Breaches of a fire certificate may result in prosecution of a body corporate and of 'any director, manager, secretary or other similar officer' if the offence was attributable to neglect on their part (*s 23*). In *R v Boal* [1992] IRLR 420 the Court of Appeal ruled that 'manager' in this context meant a person in a position of real authority, a decision-maker with the power and responsibility to decide corporate policy and strategy.

Under the *Fire Precautions (Workplace) Regulations 1997 (SI 1997/1840)*, in force from 1 December 1997, employers are required to comply with specific requirements in relation to: fire-fighting equipment; fire detectors and alarms; measures for fire-fighting; emergency routes, exits and evacuations; and maintenance of equipment and devices. Enforcement is the responsibility of the fire authorities. From 1 December 1999 the exemption from the *Regulations* for workplaces with a current fire certificate issued under the *1971* and *1987 Acts* is revoked. Updated guidance for employers on the Regulations was issued by the Stationery Office and the HSE in July 1999.

26.14 FIRST AID

First aid requirements are contained in the *Health and Safety (First Aid) Regulations 1981 (SI 1981/917)*, supplemented by an Approved Code of Practice (revised 1997). Employers are placed under a duty to make adequate and appropriate provision for first aid (*reg 3*). The *1997 Code of Practice* and accompanying notes stress the duty of the employer to make an assessment of first aid needs appropriate to the circumstances of each workplace. A checklist is included for evaluating first aid requirements and guidance given on criteria for deciding on the extent of first aid equipment, first aid boxes and facilities which are necessary and on the number of first aiders required. The guidance notes explain how first aid provision should be related to the level of risk. Employers must inform their employees of the arrangements that have been made in connection with the provision of first aid, including the location of equipment, facilities and personnel (*reg 4*). *Regulation 2* of the *Health and Safety (Miscellaneous Amendments) Regulations 2002 (SI 2002/2174)* amends *reg 2* of the existing *1981 Regulations* so as to require that a first-aid room must be easily accessible and sign-posted. This amendment gives effect to *Annex II* of *Directive 89/654/EEC* (OJ L393 30.12.1989).

26.15 HOURS OF WORK

The *Working Time Directive (93/104)*, as amended 2000/34, imposes requirements relating to hours of work, night work, breaks and holidays. Provisions restricting the working hours of children and young persons are contained in the *Young Workers' Directive (94/33)*. From 1 October 1998 the *Working Time Regulations 1998 (SI 1998/1833)* implement the *Working Time Directive* together with aspects of the *Young Workers' Directive* which relate to young persons (ie those who have reached minimum school leaving age but are under 18). For details of provisions relating to working hours, night work and breaks, see WORKING TIME (55). For statutory holiday provisions, see HOLIDAYS (27).

26.16 INSURANCE AGAINST LIABILITY

The *Employers' Liability (Compulsory Insurance) Act 1969*, as amended, obliges every employer carrying on a business in Great Britain to maintain insurance, under one or more approved policies with an authorised insurer, against liability for bodily injury or disease sustained by employees and arising out of and in the course of their employment in Great Britain. An employer is not obliged to insure members of his family (*s 2(2)(a)*). Insurance companies issue annual certificates which must be displayed at every place where the employer carries on business so that they may be easily seen and read by every person employed there. From 1 January 1999 the *Employers' Liability (Compulsory Insurance) Regulations 1998 (SI 1998/2573)* fix the limit of the sum to be insured at not less than £5m in respect of any one occurrence. The *Regulations* require employers to keep certificates for 40 years and give powers to inspectors to inspect past certificates.

There is generally no duty upon the employer to protect his employees from economic loss as opposed to physical injury. Hence it was not a breach of duty to fail to arrange or advise insurance for an employee sent to work in a country without compulsory motor insurance (*Reid v Rush & Tompkins Group plc* [1990] ICR 61).

26.17 MANAGEMENT OF HEALTH AND SAFETY AT WORK

The *Management of Health and Safety at Work Regulations 1999 (SI 1999/3242)* came into effect on 29 December 1999, re-enacting *1992 Regulations* of the same name, with modifications. The Regulations give effect to the EC 'Framework Directive' (*89/391*), the 'Temporary Workers' Directive' (*91/383*), and certain provisions of the 'Pregnant Workers' Directive' (*92/85*) and 'Young Workers' Directive' (*94/33*).

The *1999 Regulations* are accompanied by an Approved Code of Practice and guidance issued in March 2000.

The *Health and Safety (Miscellaneous Amendments) Regulations 2002 (SI 2002/2174)* which came into force on 17 September 2002 amended various long-established regulations, including the *1981 First Aid, 1992 Display Screen Equipment, 1992 Manual Handling Operations, 1992 Protective Personal Equipment, 1992 Workplace, 1998 Lifting Operations and Lifting Equipment*, and *1999 Quarries Regulations*. Whilst many of these amendments are minor, they seek to ensure full European compliance with their requisite Directives.

Every employer (and self-employed person) must make a risk assessment relating to his premises, so as to identify the measures he needs to take to comply with the health and safety and fire precautions requirements applicable to him; the assessment must be reviewed when necessary and (where there are more than five employees) recorded. Assessment of the risks to young people must be made before they start work, taking their immaturity and other specified factors into account (*reg 3*). When an employer implements any preventive and protective measures, it is to be done on the basis of the following principles:

(a)   avoiding risks;

(b)   evaluating the risks which cannot be avoided;

(c)   combating the risks at source;

(d)   adapting the work to the individual, especially as regards the design of workplaces, the choice of work equipment and the choice of working and production methods, with a view in particular to alleviating monotonous work and work at a predetermined work rate and to reducing their effect on health;

(e)   adapting to technical progress;

(f)   replacing the dangerous with the non-dangerous or the less dangerous;

(g)   developing a coherent overall prevention policy which covers technology, organisation of work, working conditions, social relationships and the influence of factors
relating to the working environment;

(h)   giving collective protective measures priority over individual protective measures;
and

(i)   giving appropriate instructions to employees.

(*Regulation 4, Sch 1.*)

Every employer must also make, and give effect to, adequate health and safety arrangements,
including the effective planning, organisation, control, monitoring and review of the
preventive and protective measures. Where there are five or more employees, these
arrangements must be recorded in writing (*reg 5*).

Every employer must ensure that his employees are provided with appropriate health
surveillance (*reg 6*), and must appoint one or more competent persons to assist him in
undertaking the preventive and protective measures. Where there is a 'competent person' in
the employer's employment then that person must be appointed as the competent person to
assist in undertaking health and safety measures, in preference to a competent person from
another source (*reg 7*).

Every employer must, *inter alia*:

(a)   establish (and where necessary, give effect to) procedures to be followed in the event
of serious and imminent danger to persons working in his undertaking; and

(b)   nominate a sufficient number of competent persons to implement such procedures
in relation to the evacuation of the premises.

The procedures referred to in (*a*) above must:

(i)   so far as is reasonably practicable, require persons at work who are exposed to serious
and imminent danger to be informed of the nature of the hazards and the steps to
be taken to protect them from it;

(ii)   enable the persons concerned to stop work and proceed to a place of safety in the
event of being exposed to serious, imminent and unavoidable danger; and

(iii)   require the persons concerned to be prevented from resuming work where there is
still a serious and imminent danger.

(*Regulation 8.*)

Employers are required to ensure that any necessary contacts with external services are
arranged, particularly as regards first aid, emergency medical care and rescue work (*reg 9*).

Employees must be provided with comprehensible and relevant health and safety information (*reg 10*), as must non-employees working in the employer's undertaking (*reg 12*) and
temporary workers (*reg 15*). When employing school-age children, employers must inform
their parents or guardians of the risks and control measures introduced (*reg 10*). Where two
or more employers share a workplace, they must co-operate as necessary to enable them to
comply with the applicable health and safety and fire precautions requirements, and
co-ordinate measures they are taking to comply with such requirements (*reg 11*).

Employers must take into account employees' capabilities as regards health and safety in
entrusting tasks to them. Employees must be provided with adequate health and safety
training within working hours, which must be repeated where appropriate (*reg 13*).

Employees must use all machinery and equipment in accordance with the training they have received. They must inform the employer of: (i) any work situation which represents an immediate danger to health and safety; and (ii) any shortcoming in the employer's protection arrangements for health and safety (*reg 14*).

An assessment must be made of workplace risks to new and expectant mothers, and measures must be taken to avoid any risk by altering working conditions or hours of work. Where it is not practicable to take these steps the woman should be suspended from work (subject to *ERA 1996, s 67*). Where it is necessary for her health and safety, a new or expectant mother must be removed from night work (*regs 16, 17*). (See also the *Suspension from Work (on Maternity Grounds) Order 1994 (SI 1994/2930)*.) In *Day v T Pickles Farms Ltd* [1999] IRLR 217, the EAT emphasised that employers must undertake an assessment of the workplace risks to pregnant women as soon as a woman of child-bearing age is employed. It is not sufficient to wait until an employee becomes pregnant.

Young persons must not be employed in certain dangerous or harmful work activities unless it is necessary for their training, the risks are reduced to the minimum, and they are competently supervised. Children must never be permitted to do such work (*reg 19*).

In criminal proceedings employers have no defence for a contravention of their health and safety obligations by reason of any act or default caused by an employee or by a person appointed to give competent advice (*reg 21*).

Since October 2003, the *Management of Health and Safety at Work Regulations 1999 (SI 1999/3242)* have been amended to allow employees to claim damages from their employer if they suffer illness or injury as a result of a breach of the *Regulations*. Amending *reg 22*, the lifting of the civil liability exclusion will ensure full compliance with the *Health and Safety Framework Directive 89/391*.

26.18   MANUAL HANDLING OF LOADS

The HSE estimates that some 12.3 million working days have been lost due to work-related musculoskeletal disorders. As a result, some 1.1 million people a year are affected, making manual handling the most common cause of occupational illness in the UK. According to HSE statistics, some 37% of reported accidents are related to manual handling incidents. The *EU Manual Handling Operations Regulations 1992 (SI 1992/2793)* as amended by *SI 2002/2174*, give effect to the EU Directive relating to the manual handling of loads (*90/269*). Broadly, the *Regulations* require each employer, so far as reasonably practicable, to avoid the need for his employees to undertake manual handling operations involving a risk of injury. That is a real risk, a foreseeable possibility of injury, not a probability (see *O'Neill v DSG Retail Ltd* [2002] EWCA Civ 1139, [2003] ICR 222). It is important to be able to show that consideration has been given to ways of avoiding such operations. Where it is not reasonably practicable, the employer is required to assess such operations and reduce the risk of injury arising from them to the lowest practicable level. For a case interpreting 'reasonably practicable' in this context, see *Hawkes v Southwark London Borough Council* (20 February 1998, unreported), CA. Emphasising the importance of providing, where practicable, information to employees on the weight of loads they are required to handle was noted in *Swain v Denso Marston Ltd* [2000] ICR 1079, CA.

Regulation 4 of the *Health and Safety (Miscellaneous Amendments) Regulations 2002 (SI 2002/2174)* amends the *1992 Regulations* by adding *reg 4(3)* by specifying factors to be taken account of, in determining whether operations involve risk, particularly of back injury to workers. The new regulation adds that particular regard should be given to: (a) the physical suitability of the employee to carry out the task; (b) the clothing and footwear the person is wearing; (c) the person's knowledge and training; and (d) the results of any relevant risk assessments. This amendment gives full effect to *Annex II* of *Directive 90/269/EEC* (OJ L156 25.6.90).

The *Regulations* also contain, in *Sch 1*, a list of the factors to which an employer must have regard (tasks, loads, working environment, individual capability and other factors) and the relevant questions which must be considered in each case when making an assessment of manual handling operations. Guidance on the *Regulations* has been published by the HSE (revised November 1998).

Since 31 December 1998, the *Merchant Shipping and Fishing Vessels (Manual Handling Operations) Regulations 1998 (SI 1998/2857)* give effect to *Directive 90/269* in respect of shipping activities in the UK. The *Regulations* apply to UK-registered ships and, in part, to ships registered outside the UK when they are in UK waters.

The HSE has developed an online manual handling chart tool (MAC Tool) to help identify high risk workplace manual handling activities.

26.19 NOISE AT WORK

According to the HSE, over 170,000 people in the UK suffer deafness, tinnitus or other ear conditions as a result of exposure to excessive noise at work. The *Control of Noise at Work Regulations 2005* (the *Noise Regulations*), in force since 6 April 2006 (except for the music and entertainment sectors where they come into force on 6 April 2008), replace the long-standing *Noise at Work Regulations 1989 (SI 1989/1790)* which came into force on 1 January 1990. The aim of these new *Noise Regulations* is to ensure that workers' hearing is protected from excessive noise at their place of work, which could cause them to lose their hearing and/or to suffer from tinnitus (permanent ringing in the ears). The 'Financial Times ' reported on may 19th 2012 that the number of industrial deafness claims rose by 25% in 2011 to approximately 35,000.

The level at which employers must provide hearing protection and hearing protection zones is now 85 decibels (daily or weekly average exposure) and the level at which employers must assess the risk to workers' health and provide them with information and training is now 80 decibels. There is also an exposure limit value of 87 decibels, taking account of any reduction in exposure provided by hearing protection, above which workers must not be exposed.

There is a general duty upon the employer to reduce the risk of damage to the hearing of his employees from exposure to noise to the lowest level reasonably practicable.

The Supreme Court has decided, by a bare 3–2 majority, that claimants exposed to noise levels of 85 decibels during the 1970s and 1980s could not recover damages for noise induced deafness since the employer was neither negligent nor in breach of the duty imposed by *section 29* of the *Factories Act 1961*. See *Baker v Quantum Clothing Group Ltd* [2011] UKSC 17.

In *Keefe v Isle of Man Steam Packet Co Ltd* [2010] EWCA Civ 683 the Court of Appeal declared that where an employer had failed to monitor noise levels, evidence of which would clearly determine whether exposure was unlawful, the evidence of the employer should be treated with some scepticism and that of the claimant should be treated benevolently.

The *Schedule* to the *Regulations* contains formulae for calculating an employee's 'daily personal noise exposure' and its weekly average. These are to be applied without taking into account the effect of ear protectors. If any employees are likely to be exposed to noise or sound pressure in excess of certain specified levels, the employer must ensure that a competent person makes a noise assessment identifying which employees are so exposed and providing such information with regard to the noise to which they may be exposed as will facilitate compliance with various duties imposed by the *Regulations*. Noise assessments must be reviewed if there is reason to suspect that they are no longer valid, or if there has been a significant change in the relevant work.

Where any employees are likely to be exposed to certain specified noise or sound pressure levels, their exposure to noise must so far as is reasonably practicable be reduced, other than by the provision of personal ear protection), and also so far as practicable be provided with suitable personal ear protectors to keep the risk of damage to below that arising from exposure to those levels. Employers must also, so far as reasonably practicable, identify by signs 'ear protection zones' where such exposure is likely and prevent employees from entering them without personal ear protectors.

At certain specified lower levels of noise, an employee must so far as practicable be provided with suitable and efficient personal ear protectors at his request.

There are also duties relating to ensuring the proper use and maintenance of equipment provided and to informing and training employees.

The HSE may grant exemptions from certain requirements where average weekly exposure does not exceed given levels.

Employees themselves are under a duty to use personal ear protectors and other protective measures and to report defects to the employer, and the self-employed are brought within the scope of the *Regulations*.

26.20   SAFETY REPRESENTATIVES

Employers are obliged to consult with employees over health and safety matters. Two different régimes operate: one for groups of workers in respect of which a union is recognised and the other where there is no union recognition.

As a result of responses to its discussion document on improving worker consultation on health and safety matters, the HSC has confirmed that it proposes to replace the *1977* and *1996 Regulations*, relating to the rights of safety representatives in unionised and non-unionised workplaces, with harmonised arrangements based on the principles of the *1977 Regulations*.

26.21   Union-appointed safety representatives

Employers must recognise, afford facilities and allow time off for the training of safety representatives appointed in accordance with the *Safety Representatives and Safety Committees Regulations 1977 (SI 1977/500 as amended by SI 1992/2051, SI 1996/1513, SI 1999/860)* made under the *HSWA 1974, s 2(4)*. Safety representatives are appointed by a trade union recognised by an employer from among the employees of a unionised workforce, with certain exceptions, eg members of the British Actors' Equity Association or of the Musicians' Union who need not be employees (*regs 3(1), 8(2)*). The representative should, if possible, either have been employed by his employer throughout the preceding two years or have had at least two years' experience in similar employment (*reg 3(4)*).

Safety representatives represent the employees in consultations with the employer over arrangements for their health and safety at work. Every employer is under a duty to consult safety representatives regarding such arrangements (*HSWA 1974, s 2(6)*); without prejudice to that general duty, employers are now required to consult safety representatives with regard to a number of specified health and safety matters, and to provide safety representatives with such facilities and assistance as they may reasonably require for the purposes of carrying out their functions under *HSWA 1974, s 2(4)* and the *Regulations (reg 4A*, inserted by the *Management of Health and Safety Regulations 1992 (SI 1992/2051))*. See also the Code of Practice and guidance notes, *Safety representatives and safety committees* (third edition 1996).

In addition, safety representatives have other functions, including the investigation of potential hazards and complaints about health, safety or welfare. They can make representations about such matters and attend meetings of safety committees (*reg 4(1)*). (See also **9.8**

DISCLOSURE OF INFORMATION.) Employers must allow safety representatives time off with pay to perform these functions (*reg 4(2)*). An employer must also permit safety representatives time off with pay to undergo training to fulfil these duties. (See **47.9–47.10 TIME OFF WORK** and the *Code of Practice on Time off for the Training of Safety Representatives*.) A safety committee must be established if two or more safety representatives request one in writing (*reg 9*). Safety representatives and others enjoy special protection from dismissal and action short of dismissal (see **26.9** above, **52.3 UNFAIR DISMISSAL – II**).

26.22 Non-unionised workers

From 1 October 1996 the obligation on employers to consult over health and safety matters was extended to employees who are not covered by trade union-appointed safety representatives (*Health and Safety (Consultation with Employees) Regulations 1996 (SI 1996/1513)*).

Employers may consult either with their employees directly or through elected representatives (*reg 4*). Employees will be entitled to receive such information as is necessary to participate fully and effectively in the consultation process (*reg 5*). The functions of elected representatives are to make representations to the employer on health and safety issues and to represent employees in consultations with inspectors (*reg 6*). Elected representatives are entitled to time off with pay for training and to carry out their duties, and are protected against dismissal and victimisation (*regs 7, 8*).

26.23 SMOKING AT WORK

The EAT, in *Waltons and Morse v Dorrington* [1997] IRLR 488, held that there is a term implied into employment contracts that 'the employer will provide and monitor for his employees, so far as is reasonably practicable, a working environment which is reasonably suitable for the performance by them of their contractual duties'. In this particular case, a non smoker was held to have been constructively dismissed when she was required, despite her protests, to work in a smoke-affected atmosphere.

The *Health Act 2006* prohibited smoking in the workplace from 2 April 2007 in Wales, from 30 April 2007 in Northern Ireland and from 1 July 2007 in England.

26.24 STRESS

Stress-related illness connected with work remains a controversial and topical issue for employers. According to the HSE, nearly 1 in 3 of workers across the EU (some 40 million people, estimated 5 million Britons) report that they are affected by stress at work (see www.hse.gov.uk), losing some 12.8 million working days lost in 2004–2005.

26.25 Common law liability

'Many, alas, suffer breakdowns and depressive illnesses and a significant proportion could doubtless ascribe some at least of their problems to the strains and stresses of their work situation: be it simply overworking, the tension of difficult relationships, career prospect worries, fears or feelings of discrimination or harassment, to take just some examples. Unless, however, there was a real risk of breakdown which the claimant's employers ought reasonably to have foreseen and they ought properly to have averted there can be no liability.' This statement from Simon Brown LJ in *Garrett v Camden London Borough Council* [2001] EWCA Civ 395, [2001] All ER (D) 202 (Mar) sets out the relevant legal test to be applied by the Court when considering a common law action in negligence.

In *Sutherland v Hatton* [2002] EWCA Civ 76, [2002] IRLR 263 the Court of Appeal has set out guidelines for determining employer liability for psychiatric injury caused by stress at work, summarised below.

The ordinary principles of employers' liability apply. First, the kind of harm to the particular employee must be reasonably foreseeable. Foreseeability depends on what the employer knows (or ought reasonably to know) about the individual. It may be harder to foresee mental conditions than physical injury, but may be easier in a known individual. Unless the employer knows of a particular problem or vulnerability, it is usually entitled to assume that the employee can withstand normal job pressures. No occupations should be regarded as intrinsically dangerous to mental health. The court listed a number of factors likely to be relevant in establishing foreseeability, such as the nature and extent of the work done by the employee. In general, an employer does not need to make detailed inquiries of the employee or his or her medical adviser.

To trigger the employer's duty to take steps, the indications of likely harm to the employee's health must be obvious enough for the reasonable employer to realise that something should be done. An employer will only be in breach of duty if it fails to take steps which are reasonable in the circumstances. Where an employer offers a confidential advice service with referral to counselling, it is unlikely to be in breach of its duty. It will not amount to a breach of duty to allow a willing employee to continue in a job if the only reasonable step involves dismissal or demotion.

The steps an employer could and should have taken need to be identified. For the employee, it must be shown that the breach of duty caused or materially contributed to the harm suffered. So long as the breach by the employer was material rather than merely negligible the employer will be liable in full for the injury sustained. See the discussion in *Bailey (by her father and litigation friend) v Ministry of Defence* [2008] EWCA Civ 883, [2009] 1 WLR 1052, 103 BMLR 13.

Where stress risks are a feature of a particular job, a risk assessment should be made under the *Management of Health and Safety at Work Regulations 1992* (see **25.17** above) in the same way as for the risk of physical injury. It is important that complaints of working conditions or workloads causing stress are dealt with quickly and thoroughly and efforts made to reduce the risk of future health problems.

In cases of bullying the claimant might be able to rely on the civil cause of action established by *s 3* of the *Protection from Harassment Act 1997* as was the case in *Green v DB Group Services (UK) Ltd* [2006] EWHC 1898 (QB), [2006] IRLR 764. A secretary bullied by fellow employees established both negligence and breach of duty under the *1997 Act*. A significant advantage of the Act is that it provides for a six year limitation period. The common law time limit to institute proceedings is three years. However, the Court of Appeal in *Conn v Sunderland City Council* [2007] EWCA Civ 1492, [2008] IRLR 324, [2007] All ER (D) 99 (Nov) has taken a restrictive approach to civil claims under the Act. Conduct must be criminal in nature to found a valid civil claim. The same court took a more lenient approach in *Ferguson v British Gas Trading Ltd* [2009] EWCA Civ 46, [2009] 8 LS Gaz R 18 and refused to strike out a claim made under the 1997 Act where the claimant alleged that she had been pursued aggressively by a utility company for payment of unjustified bills. In *Dowson v Chief Constable of Northumbria Police* [2010] EWHC 2612 (QB) a group of police officers failed in their claims. They alleged that a Detective Chief Inspector had constantly criticised and undermined them and subjected them to vulgar abuse. It was held that this was not sufficiently oppressive to cross the threshold on liability. Simon J did state, obiter, that unjustified and abusive arguments with an employee could be actionable. It is submitted that the court was influenced considerably by the notion that police officers are to be seen as robust and what might be acceptable here could well be unlawful in, say an office or hospital. In *Jones v Ruth* [2012] 1 All ER 490 the Court of Appeal awarded the claimant damages of £28,750 for harassment injury.

As well as claims for damages, it is also possible that employees whose complaints of excessive stress have gone unheeded could resign and claim constructive dismissal on the basis that the employer failed in the duty of care or breached the implied term to maintain the relationship of trust and confidence.

The High Court in *Sayers v Cambridgeshire County Council* [2006] EWHC 2029 (QB), [2007] IRLR 29 rejected a stress claim based upon a breach of the *Working Time Regulations*. The claimant established that she was working 55 hours a week and had never signed an individual opt –out agreement. Since a breach is a criminal matter the court decided that no civil remedy was intended by the legislature.

26.26 SUBSTANCES HAZARDOUS TO HEALTH

References in this section are to provisions of the *Control of Substances Hazardous to Health Regulations 2002 (SI 2002/2677)*, now in force, which replaced the *1999 Regulations* of the same name (except for *regs 4* and *20*, which are due in force in 2004). Employers' duties remain unaffected. The main change in the *1999 Regulations* is the removal of the *Schedule* listing maximum exposure limits ('MELs') from the *Regulations*. These appear instead in the HSE's publication *EH40* which is revised annually.

The definition of a substance hazardous to health is contained in *reg 2(1)*, and includes:

(a)   substances listed as dangerous for supply and whose specified nature of risk is very toxic, harmful, corrosive or an irritant;

(b)   substances for which the HSC has approved a maximum exposure limit or an occupational exposure standard;

(c)   a biological agent;

(d)   dust of any kind, when present at specified concentrations in air of total inhalable dust or respirable dust;

(e)   other substances which create a comparable hazard to the health of any person.

Employers owe duties under *COSHH Regulations 2002* to their employees and, so far as reasonably practicable and with certain exceptions, to other persons who may be affected by the work which they carry on (*reg 3*). The Executive has powers to grant exemption certificates (*reg 14*).

An employer may not carry on any work liable to expose any employees to any substance hazardous to health unless he has made a suitable and sufficient assessment of the risks to their health and of the steps necessary to meet the requirements of *COSHH* (*Dugmore v Swansea NHS Trust* [2002] EWCA Civ 1689, [2003] ICR 574). The assessment must be reviewed forthwith if there is reason to suspect that it is no longer valid or if there has been a significant change in the work to which it relates (*reg 6*).

The employer must ensure that the exposure of his employees to hazardous substances is either prevented or, where this is not reasonably practicable, adequately controlled (*reg 7(1)*). So far as reasonably practicable, that objective is to be secured by measures *other* than the provision of personal protective equipment, although that is also to be provided where necessary. Special measures apply to exposure to carcinogens (*reg 7(2), (3), (4)*).

Employers are under a duty to take all reasonable steps to ensure that control measures, protective equipment etc. are properly used or applied, and employees are under a duty to make full and proper use of such facilities, to return them after use and to report any defects to their employer (*reg 8(1), (2)*). The employer must maintain control measures and equipment in an efficient state, in efficient working order and in good repair, and keep records of tests carried out on them (*reg 9*).

In appropriate cases the employer must ensure that the exposure of employees to hazardous substances is monitored (*reg 10*) and/or that the relevant employees are under suitable health surveillance. In certain specified cases that must include medical surveillance, as a result of which the employer may be barred from engaging an employee for the work concerned (*reg 11*).

Employees whose work may expose them to hazardous substances are to be provided with suitable and sufficient information, instruction and training to enable them to know the risks of exposure and the precautions which should be taken (*reg 12*).

The Health and Safety Commission has approved a number of relevant Codes of Practice: 'Control of Substances Hazardous to Health', 'Control of Carcinogenic Substances' and 'Control of Biological Agents' are published in a single volume (revised 1999). Codes of Practice on the control of vinyl chloride at work, control of substances hazardous to health in pottery production, prevention or control of legionellosis and on the safe use of pesticides for non-agricultural purposes are also available. The Executive has published 'COSHH assessments: a step by step guide to assessment and the skills needed for it' and 'Health Surveillance under COSHH'. EH40, which lists the occupational exposure limits for use in complying with *COSHH*, is updated annually.

The *COSHH Regulations 2002* do not cover asbestos or lead which are subject to specific legislation, including the *Control of Asbestos at Work Regulations 1987 (SI 1987/2115)* and the *Control of Lead at Work Regulations 1998 (SI 1998/543)*, both revised in 2002.

The *COSHH Regulations* have been extended in Northern Ireland – see *COSHH (Amendment) Regulations (NI) 2005, SI 2005/165*.

Additional requirements are applied to particularly dangerous substances by the *Chemicals (Hazard Information and Packaging for Supply) Regulations 1994 (SI 1994/3247* as amended by *SI 1996/1092, SI 1997/1460, SI 1998/3106, SI 1999/197, SI 1999/3165; SI 2000/2381; SI 2000/2897)*, the *Dangerous Substances (Notification and Marking of Sites) Regulations 1990 (SI 1990/304)* and the *Notification of New Substances Regulations 1993 (SI 1993/3050)*.

Seven sets of Regulations on the carriage of dangerous goods by road and rail came into force on 1 September 1996. These are accompanied by six 'Approved Documents' and a Code of Practice. However, following the Cullen Inquiry, rail safety regulation has been overhauled, as previously noted, in the newly enacted (since 10 July 2003), *Railways and Transport Safety Act 2003*.

Rail safety has been enhanced under *Sch 3* to the *Railways Act 2005*, providing standards and regulations in relation to the transfer of safety functions connected with railways.

26.27   VIBRATION AT WORK

The new *Control of Vibration at Work Regulations 2005* came into force on 6 July 2005. These new regulations will help both employers and employees to take preventive action from vibration risks in the workplace. These Regulations comply with *European Physical Agents (Vibration) Directive (Directive 2002/44)* which seeks to deal with the control of diseases caused by vibration at work from equipment, vehicles and machines.

Hand Arm Vibration (HAV) is a major cause of occupational ill health and it is estimated around five million workers are exposed to HAV in the workplace. Two million of these workers are exposed to levels of vibration where there are clear risks of developing disease.

See www.hse.gov.uk/vibration/index.htm. Also, see the HAV Health Surveillance scheme and vibguide.

26.28   VIOLENCE AND BULLYING AT WORK

The employer's duty of care at common law and under *HSWA 1974, s 2* means that an employer needs to provide adequate security precautions where it is reasonably foreseeable that employees may suffer violence in the course of their work (which, given the escalation of violent incidents at work, probably covers every workplace). When making the risk assessment required under the *Management of Health and Safety at Work Regulations 1992*, as amended in 1999, (see **26.17** above) the possibility of violence to employees must be evaluated. When an employee has been the victim of an attack and the employer has taken inadequate safety measures, the employee may resign and claim constructive dismissal (*Dutton & Clark Ltd v Daly* [1985] IRLR 363), or claim damages for negligence.

The HSE leaflet *Violence at Work: a guide for employers* sets out a strategy for the effective management of violence.

Employees must also be safeguarded against bullying or harassment at work either by members of the public or fellow employees. Such behaviour, if not causing actual physical harm, may have a detrimental effect on an employee's morale and health. Where insufficient action is taken to stamp out the problem it is possible that the employer may be held liable for personal injury even if psychological damage only is caused. Intentional harassment is a criminal offence under the *Public Order Act 1986, s 4A* (as inserted by the *Criminal Justice and Public Order Act 1994*). From 16 June 1997, the *Protection from Harassment Act 1997* creates two new criminal offences of harassment and provides a civil remedy whereby an individual can apply for an injunction and damages against the harasser. Racially aggravated harassment constitutes a separate offence from 30 September 1998 (*Crime and Disorder Act 1998, ss 31, 32*).

It is imperative that all complaints from employees of violence, bullying or harassment are investigated fully and prompt action taken where necessary. The failure to do so could provoke a constructive dismissal claim before the Employment Tribunal. It could also found the basis of a claim in negligence as it did in *Green v DB Group Services (UK) Ltd* [2006] EWHC 1898 (QB), [2006] IRLR 764 where allegations of workplace bullying were not acted upon and the victim was awarded over £800,000 in damages.

The Court of Appeal delivered a confused and confusing judgment in *Weddall v Barchester Healthcare Ltd* [2012] EWCA Civ 25. The case was conjoined with *Wallbank v Wallbank Fox Designs Ltd*. Both claimants were the unfortunate victims of assault perpetrated by a fellow employee. In the former case the court held that the act of violence was gratuitous and unconnected with employment so the defendant was not liable. With respect, it would appear that the assault arose because the claimant had given a fellow employee a lawful instruction to come in and work so as to cover someone who was absent. In the latter case the claimant was attacked after giving an employee a direction to turn on an oven in the factory where they worked. This incident was held to be one for which the employer was liable, it being job related. The distinction is fine if not imperceptible.

26.29 WORKPLACE STANDARDS

The *Workplace (Health, Safety and Welfare) Regulations 1992 (SI 1992/3004)* give effect to the EC Directive concerning the minimum health and safety requirements for the workplace (*89/654*). The *Regulations* came into force on 1 January 1993 in respect of any new workplace, and apply to any modification, extension or conversion of an existing workplace on or after that date. In respect of any other existing workplace, the requirements came into effect on 1 January 1996. *Regulation 6* of the *Health and Safety (Miscellaneous Amendments) Regulations 2002 (SI 2002/2174)* amends the *1992 Regulations* to give complete or clearer effect to the technical definitions of its key terms, such as the meaning of 'workplace'. These requirements supersede provisions in the *Factories Act 1961 (ss 1–7, 18, 28, 29, 57–60* and *69), Offices, Shops and Railway Premises Act 1963 (ss 4–16),* and *Agriculture (Safety, Health and Welfare Provisions) Act 1956 (ss 3, 5, 25(3)* and *(6)).*

The requirements under the Regulations are imposed on employers, persons having control of a workplace, and any person who is deemed to be the occupier of a factory by virtue of s *175(5)* of the *Factories Act 1961 (reg 4)*. The requirements relate to the following matters:

(a)   maintenance of workplaces, and of equipment, devices and systems (*reg 5*);

(b)   ventilation of enclosed workplaces (*reg 6*);

(c)   temperature in indoor workplaces (including provision of thermometers) (*reg 7*);

(d)   lighting (*reg 8*);

(e)   cleanliness and waste materials (*reg 9*);

(f)   room dimensions and space (*reg 10*);

(g)   workstations and seating (*reg 11*);

(h)   conditions of floors and traffic routes, and organisation of traffic routes (*regs 12, 17*);

(i)   falls or falling objects (*reg 13*);

(j)   windows, doors, gates, walls, skylights and ventilators (*regs 14–16, 18*);

(k)   escalators and moving walkways (*reg 19*);

(l)   sanitary conveniences (*reg 20*);

(m)   washing facilities (*reg 21*);

(n)   drinking water (*reg 22*);

(o)   accommodation for clothing, and facilities for changing clothing (*regs 23, 24*); and

(p)   facilities to rest and to eat meals (*reg 25*).

Regulation 24 requires facilities to be provided for changing clothes when workers have to wear special clothing for work and, for reasons of health or propriety, cannot be expected to change in another room. 'Special clothing' in this context means any clothing which would not ordinarily be worn other than for work, such as a distinctive uniform (*Post Office v Footitt* [2000] IRLR 243).

26.30 Safety signs

The *Health and Safety (Safety Signs and Signals) Regulations 1996 (SI 1996/341)* implements the EC Directive on safety signs and signals *(92/58)*. All workplace safety signs are required to be of a type referred to within the Regulations.

26.31 WORK-RELATED UPPER LIMB DISORDERS ('WRULDS')

Work-related upper limb disorders or 'RSI' (repetitive strain injury) as they are commonly known, are becoming an increasingly worrying issue for employers, particularly in relation to keyboard users. Although there have only been a small number of claims successfully pursued through the courts, a number of employers have settled claims for large sums of money.

In 1996 a secretary who had developed 'writer's cramp' (a WRULD disorder) as a result of an excessive typing workload succeeded before the Court of Appeal in a claim that her employer had been negligent in allowing her to type for long periods on a word processor without breaks. The court held that it was reasonably foreseeable that a WRULD condition could occur with the amount of typing involved and that the company had negligently failed to warn the employee of the need to take breaks. This ruling was overturned by the House of Lords in *Pickford v Imperial Chemical Industries plc* [1998] IRLR 435, primarily because of inconclusive medical evidence. In addition the employer was held not to be in breach of the duty of care in failing to warn of the need to take breaks because, unlike a typist, a secretary could organise the workload to avoid continuous working on a word processor. (A statutory requirement to provide information to workers on health and safety risks associated with VDUs is now contained in the *Health and Safety (Display Screen Equipment) Regulations 1992 (SI 1992/2792)* (see **26.6** above).)

The possibility of contracting WRULDs can be minimised by paying attention to posture, ergonomics, job design and working methods and conditions.

26.31 MINERS KNEE

This osto-arthritic condition is not one for which the employer was liable, held the Court of Appeal in 2012. The claims have been abandoned.

27 Holidays

27.1 The right of an employee to a period of paid holiday is regulated by his contract (see **27.9** below) and, since 1 October 1998, by the *Working Time Regulations 1998 (SI 1998/1833)* (see **27.2–27.6** below). In addition, in certain fields of employment, separate statutory provision is made (see **27.7–27.8** below).

27.2 STATUTORY RULES

Working Time Regulations 1998

The *Working Time Regulations 1998 (SI 1998/1833)* came into force on 1 October 1998. They implemented the *Working Time Directive 93/104/EC* which has now been replaced by the *Working Time Directive 2003/88/EC*. The *Regulations* confer a right on workers to take paid annual leave (*reg 13(1)*). There is no continuous service requirement to qualify for paid annual leave. Initially, *reg 13(7)* did specify that only workers with 13 weeks' continuous service qualified. However, this limitation was ruled contrary to European law by the European Court of Justice ('ECJ') in *R (on the application of the Broadcasting, Entertainment, Cinematographic and Theatre Union) v Secretary of State for Trade and Industry ('BECTU')*: C-173/99 [2001] IRLR 559. As a consequence of this decision, *regs 13(7)* and *13(8)* were revoked with effect from 25 October 2001.

'Worker' is defined in the *Regulations* to include employees and those employed under a contract pursuant to which they undertake personally to provide services. However, those who are in business on their own account and whose 'employer' is in reality their customer or client are not workers (*reg 2(1)*). In *James v Redcats (Brands) Ltd* [2007] ICR 1006, [2007] IRLR 296 the EAT suggested (in a case under the National Minimum Wage Act 1998 which adopts the same definition of worker) that for a person to be a worker the obligation personally to provide services must be the dominant feature of the contract, an approach borrowed from the test for whether someone is 'employed' for the purposes of the discrimination statutes. There is a constant stream of case law on the definition of worker and a more detailed review can be found earlier in this book in EMPLOYEE, SELF-EMPLOYED OR WORKER **14.9**.

Children under the age for compulsory schooling are not workers and, therefore, are not entitled under the *Regulations* to paid holiday: *Ashby v Addison* [2003] ICR 667, [2003] IRLR 211, EAT.

In *Gibson v East Riding of Yorkshire Council* [2000] IRLR 598 the Court of Appeal, overturning the decision of the EAT, held that *art 7* of the *Working Time Directive*, which sets out a right to paid holiday, does not have direct effect. This meant that employees could not rely directly on *art 7* of the *Directive* before the domestic courts, but only on their rights under the *Regulations*. However in a recent decision, *Dominguez v Centre Informatique du Centre Ouest Atlantique*: C-282/10 [2012] IRLR 321, the ECJ suggested that *art 7* of the *Directive* did have direct effect and could be relied upon by workers where their employer was an emanation of the state. Subsequently, in *NHS Leeds v Larner* [2012] ICR 1389, [2012] IRLR 825, the Court of Appeal confirmed that *art 7* of the *Directive* was directly effective. As the employer in that case was an emanation of the state the Claimant was entitled to rely directly on *art 7* to support her claim.

For further discussion of the *Working Time Regulations* and *Directive* see WORKING TIME **(55)**, EUROPEAN UNION LAW **(22)** and HEALTH AND SAFETY AT WORK – II **(26)**.

27.3 Holidays

27.3 Period of leave

Annual entitlements under the *Regulations* are based upon the concept of a 'leave year'. A leave year commences on the date set out in a relevant agreement. A relevant agreement means a workforce agreement, a collective agreement which is incorporated into the contract of employment, or any other agreement in writing which is legally enforceable as between the worker and his employer (normally this will simply be the contract of employment). In the absence of such an agreement, the leave year commences on 1 October 1998 and on the anniversary of that date for those workers already in employment on that date, and, for workers who started work after 1 October 1998, on the date their employment commenced (*reg 13(3)*).

When the *Regulations* were introduced, they entitled a worker to four weeks' annual leave in each leave year (*reg 13(1)*). For a worker working a five day week this amounted to 20 days' annual holiday. Public holidays (of which there are normally eight each year) may count towards the worker's annual leave entitlement. The fact that an employer could count public holidays towards the four week entitlement was much criticised by workers and trade unions. The Department for Trade and Industry (as it then was) sought to address this criticism by introducing the concept of additional annual leave (*reg 13A*) with effect from 1 October 2007. Additional annual leave entitlements in *reg 13A* incrementally increased the total annual leave entitlement under the *Regulations* to 5.6 weeks. Until leave years which commenced on or after 1 April 2009, transitional provisions governed the exact entitlement to additional leave (readers should refer to *reg 13A(2)* to determine the exact entitlement to additional leave during the transitional period).

For all leave years which commenced on or after 1 April 2009, the total entitlement to annual leave (*reg 13*) and additional annual leave (*reg 13A*) is 5.6 weeks per year. For a person working five days a week, this increases the entitlement to 28 days' annual leave per year. *Reg 13A(3)* further provides that the aggregate entitlement to annual leave and additional annual leave is subject to a maximum of 28 days. So an employee working six days a week would only be entitled to a total of 28 days' annual leave. When considering the entitlement to leave under the *Regulations*, it should not be forgotten that the *Regulations* set only minimum requirements: more generous provisions relating to annual leave may be made in the contract of employment.

The distinction between annual leave and additional annual leave is also relevant to the treatment of leave at the end of the leave year. A worker may not carry forward from one leave year to the next any of the four weeks' annual leave (*reg 13(9)(a)*) (save in cases of sickness absence, or various types of maternity and parental leave – see **27.3A** below). Nor may an employer pay a worker in lieu of permitting him to take annual leave except on termination of his employment (*reg 13(9)(b)*). The prohibition of payment in lieu of annual leave is intended to remove any incentive for workers to accept additional payment rather than taking leave as this would undermine the health and safety objectives of the *Directive*: see *Federatie Nederlandse Vakbeweging v Netherlands State*: C-124/05 [2006] ECR I-3423, [2006] ICR 962, ECJ. The position with additional annual leave is different. A relevant agreement may provide for any additional annual leave to be carried forward into the immediately following leave year (ie leave carried over under this regulation should not then be carried over into a subsequent leave year)(*reg 13A(7)*). In addition, during the transitional period, an employer could pay a worker in lieu of the additional annual leave (*reg 13A(6)*). However, for leave years which commenced on or after 1 April 2009, an employer is not permitted to make a payment in lieu of additional annual leave.

Finally, to add to the complexity of the current statutory provisions, *reg 26A* provides that the entitlement to additional annual leave under *reg 13A* does not apply in certain situations where, as at 1 October 2007, a relevant agreement provided an annual leave entitlement which was at least the equivalent to the now extended statutory entitlement (ie 5.6 weeks or 28 days).

The leave entitlement is based on the entire leave year. However, save for workers in their first year of employment, the *Regulations* do not make provision for leave to be accrued incrementally on a month by month basis. So, for example, subject to agreement with the employer (which is discussed at **27.5** below), a worker would be entitled under the *Regulations* to take all his or her annual and additional annual leave at the very start of the leave year. By contrast, workers in their first year of employment accrue entitlement to leave at the rate of one-twelfth of their entitlement on the first day of each month and leave under the *Regulations* may only be taken after it has been accrued (*regs 13(5)* and *13A(5)*).

In *Zentralbetriebsrat der Landeskrankenhauser Tirols v Land Tirol* [2010] IRLR 631 the ECJ gave important guidance on dealing with accrued annual leave when a worker changes from full time to part time employment during the leave year. It held that the combined effect of the *Part Time Workers Directive* and the *Working Time Directive* was that a reduction of working hours when moving from full-time to part-time employment does not reduce the right to annual leave that the worker has accrued during the period of full-time employment if the worker did not have the opportunity to take that accrued leave. Again it is rather unclear how this ECJ decision would be applied under the *Regulations* and, in particular, what the ECJ meant by referring to a worker 'not having the opportunity to exercise the right' to take accrued leave. However, the sensible approach would be to allow annual leave accrued as a full time worker to be carried over into a period of part time employment (provided it is in the same leave year). So, for example, an employee working 5 days a week for 6 months of the leave year will accrue 2 weeks – or 10 days – paid annual leave under the *Regulations* (the leave accrued would be 14 days including additional annual leave; this example, however, refers only to on annual leave as the ECJ decision in *Land Tirol* would not technically apply to additional annual leave as additional leave reflects a domestic policy decision rather than the implementation of the *Directive*). If the worker then chose to take that accrued leave at a time when he or she had changed to working 3 days a week, he or she would still be entitled to 10 days' paid leave, rather than just 6 days' (which would be two weeks' leave based on the worker's part time hours). Of course, while working part time, that worker would only accrue leave based on the 3 day week. Based on the ECJ's decision it appears that if the worker then changed back to full time work, he or she would only be entitled to carry over the leave actually accrued (i.e. 3 days' leave per week).

The question of how entitlement to leave is accrued is particularly relevant to workers who do not work for the entire leave year. How is leave entitlement calculated in these cases? Three particular scenarios are commonly encountered in the workplace. First, as mentioned above, a worker may commence employment part-way through the leave year. Where this happens, in that leave year the worker is entitled to the proportion of the annual leave entitlement equal to the proportion of the leave year for which he is employed (*regs 13(5)* and *13A(5)*).

The second scenario is that the worker leaves the employment part way through the leave year. In this situation, *reg 14* provides a mechanism to compare the amount of leave taken by a worker in that part of the leave year which he worked with the amount of leave accrued. So, for example, if a worker left the employment exactly six months through the leave year, he would have accrued half his annual leave entitlement; this can be compared to the amount of leave actually taken. *Reg 14* then sets out procedures for dealing with any difference between leave accrued and leave taken. These procedures are discussed at **27.4**A below.

27.3A Annual Leave, Absence from Work and Illness

The third scenario occurs where, although the worker remains employed throughout the leave year, he is absent for part or all of the year due to, for example, illness. Neither the *Regulations* nor the *Directive* expressly address this situation or the relationship between illness and annual leave. Accordingly, it has been left to the courts to seek a solution, although the Government's Modern Workplaces consultation proposes that these issues will be addressed in amended *Regulations*.

Until clarification is provided in amended *Regulations*, employers, workers and Tribunals will need to find answers from an increasingly complex collection of decisions of both the ECJ and the domestic courts. A detailed review of those cases is beyond the scope of this chapter. However the points below seek to draw out the key principles of those cases – with the caveat that a number of new decisions are expected in 2013, which may change the position again.

The key points to be taken from the decisions of the ECJ are:

•   Paid annual leave "is a particularly important principle of Community social law from which there can be no derogations".

•   Entitlement to annual leave accrues during sickness absence.

•   Workers must be given the opportunity to take annual leave. Accordingly, workers should not lose their entitlement to annual leave simply because they are unable to take that annual leave as a result of sickness. This was initially decided by the ECJ's decisions in the joined cases of *HM Revenue and Customs v Stringer and Schultz-Hoff v Deutsche Rentenversicherung Bund* [2009] ICR 932, [2009] IRLR 214. The ECJ specifically noted that the aims of the *Directive* could be achieved in more than one way. For example, workers could be permitted to take annual leave while they are on sick leave. In addition or alternatively, where a worker has been unable to take annual leave because he is sick, he could be permitted to take that leave later, even if that meant carrying the untaken leave over into the next leave year.

•   In *Pereda v Madrid Movilidad SA* [2009] IRLR 959 the ECJ held that where a worker does not wish to take annual leave during a period of sick leave, the employer must grant him annual leave for a different period, if necessary, by permitting him to carry leave over to a new leave year. More recently in *Asociación Nacional de Grandes Empresas de Distribución (ANGED) v Federación de Asociaciones Sindicales (FASGA) and others*: C-78/11 [2012] ICR 1211, [2012] IRLR 779 the ECJ held that a worker who falls ill during a period of annual leave must be permitted to interrupt that annual leave and take the untaken annual leave at a later date (even if that resulted in the leave being carried over to a new leave year). In such a case the employer would clearly be entitled to require the worker to provide proof of illness during the holiday.

•   Although the decision in *Pereda* identified circumstances in which a worker must be allowed to carry leave over into a new leave year, in *KHS AG v Schulte*: C-214/10 [2012] IRLR 156 the ECJ held that national rules or relevant agreements could limit the period for which annual leave could be accrued during long term absence. In *Schulte* a provision of a German Collective Agreement provided that any entitlement to annual leave which accrued during sickness absence would lapse 15 months after the end of the leave year in which it was accrued. The ECJ gave guidance that any carry over period must be "substantially longer" than the leave year but accepted that the period of 15 months in the case before it was permissible. In a subsequent case, *Neidel v Stadt Frankfurt am Main*: C-337/10 [2012] ICR 1201; [2012] IRLR 607 the ECJ held that a 9 month carry over period was insufficient.

•   Entitlement to annual leave cannot be made conditional on a worker carrying out a minimum amount of work in the leave year. In *Dominguez v Centre Informatique du Centre Ouest Atlantique*: C-282/10 [2012] IRLR 321 the ECJ held that a French provision making entitlement to paid annual leave conditional upon an employee doing one month of actual work during the leave year was inconsistent with the *Directive*.

• Where a worker's employment terminates, he is entitled to be paid in lieu for annual leave which has accrued but which the worker was unable to take due to sickness (even where that is annual leave accrued over more than one leave year): see *HM Revenue and Customs v Stringer*.

• Issues also commonly arise in relation to carrying over annual leave while on maternity and parental leave. For example in *Zentralbetriebsrat der Landeskranken-hauser Tirols v Land Tirol* [2010] IRLR 631 the ECJ held that the effect of the *Working Time Directive* and the *Framework Agreement on Parental Leave* was that a worker who took parental leave could carry over, until after the parental leave, any annual leave accrued prior to the worker taking parental leave.

A major difficulty thrown up by the ECJ's decisions is the apparent inconsistency between the decision in *Pereda* (recognising that in certain cases workers must be permitted to carry leave over into the next leave year) and *reg 13(9)* of the *Regulations* which provides that leave cannot be carried over from one leave year to the next.

In *NHS Leeds v Larner* [2012] ICR 1389, [2012] IRLR 825, the Court of Appeal (Mummery LJ) suggested that *reg 13(9)* of the *Regulations* could be interpreted consistently with the ECJ decisions referred to above in the following way (the words in italics have been added by the Court of Appeal to ensure consistency with the *Directive*):

"Leave to which a worker is entitled under this regulation may be taken in instalments, but— (a) it may only be taken in the leave year in respect of which it is due, *save where the worker was unable or unwilling to take it because he was on sick leave and as a consequence did not exercise his right to annual leave* . . . ."

While the *Larner* case was decided by the direct application of *art 7* of the *Working Time Directive* (as the Claimant was employed by an emanation of the state) rather than under the *Regulations*, until the *Regulations* are amended following the Modern Workplaces' consultation, the approach in *Larner* is almost certain to be followed by Tribunals. Accordingly, employers should permit workers to carry over annual leave if they have not been able to, or have chosen not to, take it due to illness. In addition, following the guidance of the ECJ in *Schulte*, it would be prudent for employers to allow this leave to be carried over for more than a single leave year if that situation arises (although in most cases other than very long periods of sickness absence the worker ought to have an opportunity to take the carried over annual leave in the next leave year).

The ECJ decisions may set out the principles for the complex interaction between illness and annual leave. However further problems arise when trying to put those principles into practice.

Annual Leave and Giving Notice during Illness

As explained in **27.5** below, *reg 15* of the *Regulations* sets out a procedure for the employer and worker to agree or determine when annual leave is taken. Where a worker wishes to claim entitlement to be paid in respect of annual leave during a period of sickness absence, the worker would have to give notice to the employer and would then be entitled to receive paid annual leave. A worker on long term sick leave who has exhausted sick pay may well want, or need, to be paid in respect of annual leave while they remain ill, rather than carrying that annual leave over.

In other cases, as the ECJ noted in *Stringer*, a worker may simply wish to keep annual leave which she could not take because she was ill until after she has recovered (even if that means carrying it over into a new leave year). In that case, should the worker be required to give notice of the intention to carry that annual leave over to the next leave year? This issue was considered by the Court of Appeal in *NHS Leeds v Larner* [2012] ICR 1389, [2012] IRLR 825. As mentioned above, the Claimant in this appeal relied directly on *art 7* of the *Working Time Directive* (as she was employed by an emanation of the state). The Court of Appeal noted that *art 7* did not include the notice requirements contained in the *Regulations*. Accordingly, it held that the Claimant was not required by *art 7* to make a request during her sickness absence in order to carry over her annual leave. In addition the Court of Appeal (Mummery LJ) endorsed the argument that *reg 15(1)* of the *Regulations* had no application in cases where a worker had not returned from sickness absence during the leave year and had had no opportunity to take annual leave. Again, while these comments on *reg 15(1)* are *obiter* they are almost certain to be followed in subsequent cases.

Taking Annual Leave on Return to Work after Sick Leave

A further difficulty arises in cases where a worker is unable to take leave due to sickness but returns to work in the same leave year. In such a case, is the worker permitted to carry leave over, or is she required to take her leave in the current leave year? In *NHS Leeds v Larner* Mummery LJ hinted, by reference to the EAT decision in *Fraser v Southwest London St George's Mental Health Trust* [2012] ICR 403, that there would be no entitlement to carry over annual leave where the worker was able to take it in the current leave year. Accordingly, the focus in such cases is likely to be on whether the worker was reasonably able do so. This will be fact specific and will depend on the amount of accrued but untaken leave and the period between the worker returning to work from her sickness absence and the end of the leave year.

Annual Leave and Additional Annual Leave: Should they be treated in the same way?

As explained below, the government has proposed that annual leave under *reg 13* and additional annual leave under *reg 13A* should be treated differently when considering the right to carry over annual leave which cannot be taken due to illness. This reflects that the leave under *reg 13* is the leave required by the *Directive*, while leave under *reg 13A* goes beyond the *Directive* and is a national policy. Notwithstanding this point, in at least one first instance decision, *Adams and another v Harwich International Port Ltd* ET/1503084/10, a Tribunal held that the *Regulations* could be interpreted to allow sick workers to carry over their entire 5.6 weeks' statutory holiday entitlement to the next leave year. While this approach had the benefit of simplicity, the ECJ reached a different conclusion in *Neidel v Stadt Frankfurt am Main*: C-337/10, [2012] ICR 1201, [2012] IRLR 607, confirming that the *Directive* did not require national law to permit additional leave to be carried over in cases of illness. The ECJ made a similar point in *Dominguez v Centre Informatique du Centre Ouest Atlantique*: C-282/10 [2012] IRLR 321. In *Larner* the Court of Appeal refused to determine this point, but strongly hinted that it considered that Neidel had already provided the answer.

However, one further caveat must be borne in mind in relation to the treatment of annual leave and additional annual leave. Where other Directives are also in play such as those governing maternity leave, it would appear to be unlawful not to permit the carryover of additional annual leave. For example in *Gomez (Merino) v Continental Industrias del Caucho SA*: C-342/01 [2004] ECR I-2605, [2005] ICR 1040, the ECJ held that, in relation to maternity leave, where a Member State had provided for a longer entitlement to annual leave than the minimum prescribed by the *Working Time Directive*, the Pregnancy Directive 92/85 also applied to the entitlement to that additional annual leave. Accordingly that annual leave could not be operated in a way which undermined the taking of maternity leave (see further discussion of the *Merino Gomez* case at **27.5** below).

Proposed Amendments

As the above summary illustrates, the relationship between annual leave and sick pay is complex. Part of the difficulty has been that neither the *Directive* nor the *Regulations* provided any guidance on these issues. As a result the ECJ and domestic courts were left to provide solutions on a case by case basis – typically in response to cases with relatively unusual facts.

The amendments to the *Regulations* which are being considered as part of the Modern Workplaces consultation will hopefully resolve many of the issues considered above. At the time of writing the Government has not provided its response to the consultation process (perhaps due to the need to take into account the on-going stream of cases from the ECJ). However, in summary, the initial key proposals in the consultation document were:

- The 4 weeks' annual leave under *reg 13* and the 1.6 weeks' additional annual leave under *reg 13A* will continue to accrue during sickness absence.

- The *Regulations* will allow annual leave to be rescheduled where the worker has been unable to take annual leave due to illness (whether he fell ill before or during the leave). This will include a right to carry over untaken leave where there is no opportunity to reschedule that annual leave in the current leave year.

- However the right to reschedule and carry over will be limited to the 4 weeks' annual leave under *reg 13*. It will not apply to the 1.6 weeks' additional annual leave under *reg 13A* (or any further contractual leave to which a worker is entitled in excess of 5.6 weeks/28 days). This will require employers and workers to know under which provision each particular period of leave is being taken. The government has proposed that this could be determined by a local agreement, failing which the amended *Regulations* will specify the order in which leave is deemed to be taken (the suggestion is that *reg 13* leave would be deemed to be taken first followed by all other types of annual leave).

- The carry over rights will also apply where leave cannot be taken due to maternity, paternity, parental or adoption leave. However this right will extend to both annual leave under *reg 13* and additional annual leave under *reg 13A*.

Conclusion on Annual Leave and Illness

Until the *Regulations* are amended, to avoid costly legal disputes, it would be prudent for employers to give a worker, who is sick during a period of annual leave, the option of still taking annual leave during the period of sickness or taking annual leave at a later date, even if this means carrying the annual leave missed through sickness over to the next leave year, and beyond where the worker is absent for a very long time.

One source of comfort for employers and workers is that while complex issues do arise when considering sickness absence and annual leave, the reality is that these issues will only arise in exceptional cases: typically where workers are on long term sick leave, or they have left taking their annual leave until the end of the leave year and then fallen ill. In most cases, where workers fall sick during or shortly before a period of annual leave, and request that the period be treated as sick leave, they will be able to take the annual leave which they missed as a result of sickness later in the same leave year.

27.3B Annual Leave and Reasons for Absence other than Illness or Maternity etc

Workers may be absent from work for reasons other than illness, maternity leave, paternity leave, parental leave or adoption leave etc. For example, a worker may agree a period of unpaid leave or a sabbatical. Do they continue to accrue annual leave entitlement during such absences? Again the *Directive* and *Regulations* do not provide an answer. However, some guidance can be found in the ECJ decision in *Heimann and another v Kaiser GmbH*:

C-229/11 [2013] IRLR 48. In that case, the employer dismissed a number of employees due to financial difficulties. However it then agreed with its works council to extend the employment contracts of the dismissed workers for one year from the date of their dismissal on a zero hours short-time working basis. This suspended the workers' obligation to work and the employer's obligation to pay them a salary. The purpose of that extension was to give the workers the opportunity of receiving, for the year following their dismissal, a statutory allowance payable during periods of zero hours short-time working. The ECJ held that the *Working Time Directive* permitted national law or relevant agreements to provide that annual leave accrued in proportion to the time actually worked during the leave year (as it would for part time workers). Accordingly, such a law or agreement could provide that annual leave did not accrue during periods where no work was being performed. In reaching this conclusion the ECJ explained that the situation of a worker unable to work as a result of an illness, and that of a worker on short-time working, are fundamentally different. In particular, the ECJ noted, during the period of short-time working, the worker was free to rest or to devote himself to recreational and leisure activities, whereas a worker on sick leave would be subject to physical or psychological constraints caused by illness.

The reasoning of the ECJ in *Heimann* ought to apply equally to other absences not caused by illness, or maternity or paternity leave, such as unpaid leave and sabbaticals. However in such cases employers should be advised expressly to agree with the worker that he will not accrue annual leave during the period of absence (and to record that agreement in writing).

27.4 Payment for Annual Leave

A worker is entitled to be paid for any period of leave at the rate of a week's pay for each week of leave. In *British Airways plc v Noble* [2006] EWCA Civ 537, [2006] ICR 1227, [2006] IRLR 533 the Court of Appeal reiterated that pay while on holiday should be the same as pay while at work. The application of this simple principle to various employment situations is not, however, as straightforward as it sounds.

Calculating a Week's Pay

A week's pay under the *Regulations* is calculated in accordance with the rules in *ERA 1996, ss 221–224 (reg 16)*. These rules distinguish between workers who have normal working hours and those that do not. The provisions are complex and are discussed in more detail in REDUNDANCY – I (36) and PAY– I (32)). However, it is important to note that, in certain situations, pay as determined under *ERA 1996, ss 221–224* may not be the same as the actual pay earned by a worker in a typical working week. For example, where an employee has normal working hours, overtime only qualifies as part of a week's pay where the overtime is fixed under the contract of employment. The effect is that only contractual hours are included and, for example, non-contractual overtime hours are not. This can lead to situations where, although the employee regularly works substantial periods of overtime, pay while on holiday is based upon the lower number of contractual hours. For example, in *Bamsey v Albion Engineering and Manufacturing plc* [2004] EWCA Civ 359, [2004] ICR 1083, [2004] IRLR 457 the employee worked significant overtime. However as his contractual hours were only 39 this formed the basis of his entitlement to holiday pay. He argued that this was contrary to the *Working Time Directive* which required workers to be paid during holiday periods at the same or similar level to their normal income when actually at work and that the *Working Time Regulations, reg 16* should be interpreted purposively to ensure that this was achieved. The Court of Appeal rejected this argument and confirmed that non-contractual overtime did not form a part of a week's pay for workers. It also concluded that this interpretation was not contrary to the purpose of the *Directive* which did not require member states to guarantee more pay during a holiday period than a worker was contractually entitled to even if the worker regularly worked periods of non-contractual overtime.

Where, however, a worker does not have normal working hours a week's pay is calculated under *ERA 1996, s 224*, by averaging his pay over the last 12 weeks in which he worked. A further impact of the application of the rules in *ERA 1996, ss 221–224* is that commission payments are, in many cases, not taken into account when determining a week's pay: see *Evans v Malley Organisation Ltd* [2002] EWCA Civ 1834, [2003] ICR 432, [2003] IRLR 156.

The long standing approach to calculating holiday pay in accordance with *ERA 1996, ss 221–224* was, however, thrown into doubt by the ECJ's decision in *Williams v British Airways*: C-155/10 [2011] IRLR 948. In that case, the claimant pilots argued that while on holiday they should receive basic salary plus 2 supplements which they received while working. The first was a flying pay supplement (or 'FPS') which was an additional payment of around £10 per hour spent flying. The second was a time away from base allowance (or 'TAFB') which British Airways regard as a payment to cover expenses (but which the HMRC regard as overgenerous for this purpose and a portion of which is taxable as remuneration). The ECJ decided that pay during annual leave must be comparable or equivalent to pay normally received when working but that remuneration intended to cover expenses incurred while working need not be paid during annual leave.

The ECJ's decision has now been considered by the Supreme Court [2012] ICR 1375, [2012] IRLR 1014, which remitted the case to the Employment Tribunal to determine (i) the average value of the FPS over a representative period (as the FPS was clearly part of normal remuneration); and (ii) whether the TAFB was genuinely intended exclusively to cover expenses (in which case it would not be payable during annual leave).

Although *Williams* was brought under the *Civil Aviation (Working Time) Regulations 2004*, the ECJ's reasoning will apply equally to cases under the *Working Time Regulations* and *Directive*. As a result it seems likely that, in the near future, there will be a further challenge that calculation of holiday pay by reference to *ERA 1996, ss 221–224* may lead to results which are inconsistent with the *Working Time Directive*. If such a challenge succeeds (as seems almost certain following *Williams*) further amendment of the *Working Time Regulations* will be required.

Remuneration under the Working Time Regulations and the Contract of Employment

The right to annual paid holiday does not affect the right of a worker to remuneration under his contract. However, any contractual remuneration paid during a period of leave will be offset against leave payments due under the *Regulations*, and similarly any payment for a period of leave under the *Regulations* will be offset against a claim for contractual remuneration for the same period (*regs 16(4)* and *(5)*). In addition, as the EAT's decision in *Crossland v Corps of Commissionaires Management Ltd* (UKEAT/0014/10/LA) (18 August 2010, unreported) shows, the terms of the contract of employment may make provision for holiday pay to be calculated in a more favourable way than permitted by *ERA 1996, ss 221–224*. In such cases, a claim under the contract will be more valuable than a claim under the *Regulations*.

Holiday Pay must be Paid at the Time Holiday is Taken

For some time there was debate and dispute about whether an employer could 'roll up' holiday pay: ie whether the *Regulations* allowed the rate of pay while actually working to be enhanced to include an element referable to holiday pay so that no additional pay was due when the worker took leave. The ECJ decided in *Robinson-Steele v RD Retail Services Ltd* [2006] ICR 932, [2006] IRLR 386 that the *Directive* required that workers were paid for annual leave at the time they took it. Accordingly 'rolling up' holiday pay is contrary to the *Regulations* and *Directive*. The ECJ explained this decision on the basis that, although the *Directive* did not expressly lay down when payment for leave should be made, the purpose of the requirement of payment for annual leave is to put the worker, during annual leave, in a position which is, as regards remuneration, comparable to periods of work. Therefore, the entitlements to annual leave and to payment for that leave are two aspects of a single right. The rationale which underlies this conclusion is that workers may be discouraged from taking leave if they will receive no remuneration during that period of leave.

The ECJ's decision resolves the inconsistencies between the approaches in England and Scotland in favour of the approach of the Court of Session in Scotland which had concluded that rolled up holiday pay was unlawful: see *Munro v MPB Structures Ltd* [2003] IRLR 350. By contrast the Court of Appeal and the EAT in England had held that, subject to certain restrictions, rolling up holiday pay into pay for periods when the worker was actually working did comply with the *Regulations*: see, as background, *Marshalls Clay Products v Caulfield* [2004] ICR 1502, [2004] IRLR 564, CA and *Smith v AJ Morrisroes & Sons Ltd* [2005] ICR 596, [2005] IRLR 72, EAT.

Bearing in mind that, prior to the ECJ decision in *Robinson-Steele*, rolled up holiday pay was thought to be lawful (at least in England and Wales), it is unsurprising that the practice had been commonly adopted in a number of industries where working patterns are irregular and/or unpredictable (for, example, industries with certain shift patterns and recruitment businesses providing temporary staff). It is now clear that this will not comply with the *Regulations*. However this does not necessarily mean that any workers who have benefited from rolled up holiday pay can gain a windfall by claiming payment for leave at the time they take it notwithstanding that they have already been paid for that leave through rolled up holiday pay. In this regard, the ECJ held that the *Directive* did not preclude sums paid transparently and comprehensibly as rolled up holiday pay being set off against the payment due for specific leave which is actually taken by a worker. *Lyddon v Englefield Brickwork Ltd* [2008] IRLR 198 is an example of a case where the Employment Tribunal and EAT applied such a set off because the agreement between Mr Lyddon and his employer in relation to rolled up holiday pay, whilst contrary to the *Regulations*, was sufficiently clear and transparent.

27.4A Payment on termination of employment

Where a worker's employment is terminated and he has accrued but untaken leave to which he is entitled under the *Regulations*, the employer must pay him in lieu of that untaken leave (*reg 14*). The case law considered above in relation to the accrual of annual leave during sick leave is often relevant in cases under *reg 14*. In particular, this issue may arise where a worker is dismissed on the ground of capability after a prolonged period of absence due to ill-health. In such cases, the Court of Appeal held in *Larner* that the accrued annual leave should include annual leave from previous leave years which the worker could not take due to ill-health. In particular Mummery LJ proposed that, in order to ensure consistency with the *Working Time Directive* a new *reg 14(5)* could be read into the *Regulations* to provide that:

> "Where a worker's employment is terminated and on the termination date he remains entitled to leave in respect of any previous leave year which carried over under regulation 13(9)(a) because of sick leave, the employer shall make him a payment in lieu equal to the sum due under regulation 16 for the period of untaken leave."

While this comment was, again, arguably obiter as the case was decided by the direct application of *art 7* of the *Working Time Directive*, it is almost certain to be followed in practice by Tribunals.

The amount payable to the worker who has accrued but untaken leave may be specified in a relevant agreement. A relevant agreement may not, however, specify that no sum is to be paid: see *Witley and District Men's Club v Mackay* [2001] IRLR 595, EAT, in which an agreement that no sum was to be paid for accrued holiday where the worker was dismissed on grounds of dishonesty was void under *reg 35(1)(a)*.

In the absence of such an agreement, the amount payable is to be calculated by determining the amount the worker would have been paid under *reg 16* for the period of leave accrued but untaken (ie the period of leave which, in proportion to the leave year, he is entitled to take), less the period of leave he has in fact taken (*reg 14(3)*). Compensation for failure to pay for accrued but untaken holiday on termination of employment is not limited by principles of justice and equity under *reg 30(4)*; *reg 30(5)* requires a tribunal to make an award for the actual sum due: *Witley and District Men's Club v Mackay* (above). An employer may specify in a relevant agreement that, where a worker has at the date of his dismissal taken more than his accrued leave entitlement, he reimburse his employer, for example, by making a payment or undertaking additional work (*reg 14(4)*). In the absence of a relevant agreement, the employer will not be entitled to claw back payment for holidays taken but not accrued and no term can be implied which would allow such a claw back: see *Hill v Chapell* [2003] IRLR 19, EAT.

27.5   Notice requirements and when leave is taken

The procedures which must be complied with when a worker requests, or an employer refuses, annual leave, may be specified in a relevant agreement (*reg 15(5)*). In the absence of such an agreement, the provisions of *reg 15(1)–(4)* apply as follows. A worker must give notice of the dates he intends to take leave. The notice period must be equivalent to at least twice the period of leave he is proposing to take. An employer may refuse leave on the requested dates by serving a counter-notice on the worker at least as many days before the proposed leave commences as the number of days' leave refused. The employer may also require a worker to take all or part of his leave on certain dates by giving him notice of that requirement; the length of notice must be at least twice the period of leave he requires the worker to take.

It is important to recognise that the notice provisions set out in *reg 15* may be varied or excluded by a relevant agreement (*reg 15(5)*): see *Industrial and Commercial Maintenance Ltd v Briffa* [2008] All ER (D) 105 (Sep). In *Briffa* the contract of employment provided that, following notice of the termination of employment, the employee would be required to take any outstanding annual leave during the notice period. The employee's notice period was only a week, and he had accrued 4 days' leave (so proper notice of leave could not be in accordance with *reg 15* which requires the advance notice of leave to be given at least twice as long before the leave is to be taken as the length of the period of leave). However, the EAT held that the contract amounted to a relevant agreement which varied *reg 15*. Accordingly, the employer was entitled to require the employee to take all his outstanding annual leave during his notice period.

Sumsion v BBC (Scotland) [2007] IRLR 678 is an extreme example of how an employer might make use of the entitlement to require a worker to take leave on certain days. Mr Sumsion was contracted to work a six day week (Monday to Saturday) during a fixed term contract. He was entitled to six days leave during this time and he requested that the leave be taken in a block. The BBC refused this request and required that he take a day's leave every second Saturday. The Employment Tribunal and EAT concluded that this was lawful and Mr Sumsion was receiving the annual leave to which he was entitled. The EAT may have been influenced in this decision by the short term nature of the contract as it commented that in certain cases this approach may have been unlawful if it did not permit a worker to take 'real' leave.

A similar conclusion was reached by the *Supreme Court in Russell v Transocean International Resources Ltd* [2012] ICR 185, [2012] IRLR 149 which related to the annual leave entitlements of oil field workers who worked a shift pattern of two weeks offshore, two weeks onshore. They were not required to work during the onshore periods. The Supreme Court upheld the decisions of the Court of Session and EAT that: (i) onshore periods could be treated as annual leave and (ii) the workers had been given notice, in accordance with *reg 15*, that annual leave was to be taken during the onshore periods. Accordingly the workers' entitlement to annual leave was met during their 26 weeks onshore, and they could not claim a further 4 weeks' leave out of the periods they were scheduled to be on the rigs.

The decision in *Lyons v Mitie Security Ltd* [2010] IRLR 288 provides a further example of the operation of the notice requirements under the *Regulations*. Although the facts of the case were unusual, the EAT did have to decide an issue of more general importance, namely whether an employer was entitled, under the *Regulations*, to deny a worker's request for leave where this prevented the worker exercising his right to annual leave because, for example, the worker could not then take his or her remaining leave before the end of the leave year. This type of situation would commonly arise in cases where the worker requests annual leave towards the very end of the leave year. Will the employer be obliged either to grant the request to enable the worker to take their annual leave or to permit leave to be carried over? Or will the worker lose his or her entitlement at the end of the leave year? In *Lyons* the EAT held that, while an employer could not operate the notice requirements in an unreasonable, arbitrary or capricious way so as to deny any entitlement lawfully requested, there was no inalienable right to leave. Accordingly, a worker may lose their entitlement under the *Regulations* if he or she requests leave very late in the leave year and the employer genuinely cannot accommodate that request. Again, these issues are unlikely to arise that regularly in practice. Nonetheless, workers would be well advised to request holiday early. At the same time, as the EAT noted in *Lyons*, employers should consider whether any refusal of a request for leave may be unreasonable or lead to grievances and litigation.

The right of an employer to require leave to be taken at certain times may, however, be restricted in certain situations. For example, in *Gomez (Merino) v Continental Industrias del Caucho SA*: C-342/01 [2004] ECR I-2605, [2005] ICR 1040, the ECJ concluded that a worker returning from maternity leave had to be allowed to take her statutory leave entitlement even though it meant that she would take the leave outside the established periods for leave set out in a workforce agreement. See also, *Pereda and Landtirol*, considered at paragraph **27.3** above.

27.6   Remedies

A worker may complain to an employment tribunal that his employer has refused to allow him to take annual leave (*reg 30(1)(a)*) or has failed to pay him sums due in respect of leave which he has taken (*reg 30(1)(b)*). A complaint must be presented to the tribunal within three months of the date of the act complained of. The tribunal may also extend time where it considers it was not reasonably practicable for the worker to submit his claim within three months (*reg 30(2)*).

If the employment tribunal finds that a claim under *reg 30(1)(a)* (refusal to allow a worker to take annual leave) is well-founded, the tribunal must make a declaration to that effect and, in addition, may order payment of such compensation as it considers just and equitable in all the circumstances, having regard to the employer's default in refusing to permit the worker to exercise his right, and any loss sustained by the worker as a consequence of that refusal (*regs 30(3) and 30(4)*). If the complaint is made under *reg 30(1)(b)* (failure to make a payment for leave taken during employment or leave accrued but untaken on termination), and the tribunal finds that the complaint is well-founded it must order payment of the sum due for that period of leave (*reg 30(5)*).

In addition, in *Revenue and Customs v Stringer* [2009] UKHL 31, [2009] ICR 985, [2009] IRLR 677, the House of Lords confirmed that that a claim for holiday pay to which a worker was entitled under the *Regulations* could be brought as a claim for unlawful deductions of wages under *Part II, ERA 1996*. In reaching this conclusion the House of Lords overturned the decision of the Court of Appeal ([2005] ICR 1149, [2005] IRLR 465) who had held that *reg 30* was intended to provide a single and exclusive regime for the enforcement of the statutory rights in the *Regulations*. The House of Lords' decision will make a significant difference in some cases as *Part II, ERA* provides that the time limit for presenting a claim where there has been a series of deductions of pay is 3 months from the date of the last deduction in the series (see *s 23(3) ERA 1996*). Accordingly a worker could bring a claim for failures to permit paid holiday stretching back over a significant period of time (whereas under *reg 30*, which does not have a provision dealing with a series of failures to pay holiday pay, a separate claim would have to be brought within 3 months of each failure).

The House of Lords plainly envisaged that a worker could bring an unlawful deduction of wages claim if the worker had taken holiday but not been paid for it. However it is less clear whether such a claim should be available where the employer refuses to permit a worker to take paid holiday and the worker decides to work rather than take the holiday in order to avoid a loss of earnings. In such a case, as the worker has continued to attend work and be paid for doing so, he will earn the same as normal and there would appear to be no deduction from wages. Instead the loss suffered by the worker would be the loss of the health, relaxation and other benefits associated with taking a period of annual leave. The *Regulations* recognise the distinction between these two scenarios and in the latter a Tribunal is entitled to award just and equitable compensation (see *regs 30(1)(a)* and *30(4)* of the *Regulations*). Where, however, a worker is not paid for holiday which is actually taken, the *Regulations* provide that the compensation must be the amount of money which ought to have been paid to the worker during the period of leave (see *regs 30(1)(b)* and *30(5)*).

Despite this distinction, in *Canada Life Ltd v Gray* [2004] ICR 673 the EAT concluded that a worker could bring an unlawful deductions claim in respect of his or her annual leave entitlement regardless of whether or not the leave had actually been taken, and that the series of deductions could extend back into previous leave years. More recently in *Fraser v Southwest London St George's Mental Health Trust* [2012] ICR 403 the EAT took a different approach and suggested that a worker could not recover unpaid holiday as a deduction from wages where he or she had not actually taken the leave in question. It is suggested that the EATs conclusion on this issue was correct because, as explained above, in such cases there has been no actual deduction of pay but rather a loss of the benefits of taking annual leave.

Following the House of Lords decision in *Stringer*, Employment Tribunals are again being asked to determine deduction from wages claims for significant periods of unpaid annual leave. In *Rawlings v Direct Garage Door Co Ltd* ET 2800547/06 the Tribunal held that that an employee on long term sick leave could claim untaken holiday that had accrued over a 15 month period (i.e. for more than a single leave year).

However, as mentioned above, an unlawful deductions claim must be made within 3 months of the last in the series of deduction. This may limit the circumstances in which a worker can recover significant arrears in respect of holiday pay. The Employment Tribunal decision in *Khan v Martin McColl* (ET/1702926/09) (22 March 2010, unreported) illustrates the point. Mr Khan had been on long term sick leave. He resigned due to his illness in mid-2009 (at which point he had accrued but not taken leave from 2008 and 2009). The employer paid him in respect of his accrued but untaken leave for 2009. He brought a claim for payment of his untaken leave from 2008. The Tribunal held that Mr Khan's claim for unlawful deductions from wages in respect of the 2008 leave was out of time. As the employer had paid Mr Khan his 2009 holiday entitlement on termination of employment, the last of the series of deductions was prior to the start of 2009. This issue has not yet been tested on appeal. However it is suggested that the argument that the last deduction was made on 31 December 2008 is questionable, given that under the *Regulations* payment in lieu of annual leave may only be made on the termination of employment. On that basis, the date for the payment of Mr Khan's leave which he could not take in 2008 due to illness (and which therefore could have been carried over to 2009) was the date his employment ended, rather than 31 December 2008.

A further issue which may need to be considered in relation to claims for unpaid annual leave over an extended period is whether leave carried over due to illness may lapse if not taken within a certain time. The current *Regulations* provide in *reg 13A(7)* that additional

27.6 Holidays

annual leave may be carried over but must then be taken in the next leave year. However the *Regulations* do not deal with this issue for annual leave under *reg 13*. As mentioned above **27.3**A in *KHS AG v Schulte*: C-214/10 [2012] IRLR 156 the ECJ held that national rules or relevant agreements could limit the period over which annual leave could be accrued during long term absence provided any carry over period was "substantially longer" than the leave year. While the government's initial proposed amendments to the *Regulations* did not address this issue, the actual amendments will hopefully do so. If they do not, employers could include a provision in their contracts of employment or policies dealing with accrued leave lapsing. However caution is needed. It is not certain that a Tribunal would accept the validity of such a policy in the absence of a statutory provision. In addition, the carry over period would need to be substantially longer than a year. In *Schulte* 15 months was held to be sufficient. However there is no guarantee that a Tribunal would adopt that approach. Accordingly, a carry-over period of 18 months or 2 years would be safer.

In addition to claims based on entitlements to annual leave under the *Regulations*, a worker may also be entitled to bring a claim for unlawful deduction of wages or breach of contract on the basis that, under his contract of employment, he was entitled to holiday pay or payment in lieu of accrued but untaken holiday. This will depend on the interpretation of the contract of employment and is discussed at paragraph **27.9** below.

27.7 Agricultural workers

Under the *Agricultural Wages Act 1948*, *s 3*, as substituted by *EPA 1975*, *s 97(1)*, *Sch 9 Pt 1*, the Agricultural Wages Board may direct that holidays be allowed and that certain rates of pay be given for holidays. An agreement inconsistent with the order is void (*s 11*). Failure to allow holidays or give holiday pay specified in the order gives rise to a right to claim by the worker as well as liability for a criminal offence and a fine of level 3 on the standard scale (*s 4*). Special provisions are applicable to agricultural workers under the *Working Time Regulations 1998*, *Sch 2*. In this context, however, the Government has indicated that it intends to abolish the Agricultural Wages Board (by way of provisions in the *Enterprise and Regulatory Reform Bill*) and amend the *Working Time Regulations* so that agricultural workers fall within their scope.

27.8 Civil aviation workers

Statutory leave entitlements for crew members employed in civil aviation are governed by the *Civil Aviation (Working Time) Regulations 2004* which implement the *Aviation Working Time Directive (2000/79/EC)*.

Regulation 4 provides that 'a crew member is entitled to paid annual leave of at least four weeks, or a proportion of four weeks in respect of a period of employment of less than one year'. As with the *Working Time Regulations*, this leave may be taken in instalments and may not be replaced by a payment in lieu, except where the crew member's employment is terminated, and the right is enforceable through a claim to the Employment Tribunals.

However the *Civil Aviation (Working Time) Regulations 2004* do not contain any of the detailed mechanisms in the *Working Time Regulations* for determining when annual leave may be taken and the rate of pay during leave. They also have different provisions in relation to remedies.

These lacunae have been the source of a number of claims, most notably, *Williams v British Airways plc*: C-155/10 [2011] IRLR 948 (ECJ) and [2012] ICR 1375; [2012] IRLR 1014 (Supreme Court) (referred to in **27.4**A above) which concerned a claim by pilots who only received basic pay when they took annual leave despite the fact that when they were actually working they had a contractual entitlement to additional remuneration in the form of 2 supplements. The issue was what payment the pilots should receive during annual leave given that the *Civil Aviation (Working Time) Regulations 2004* did not make any provision for how pay should be calculated (unlike the *Working Time Regulations 1998* which expressly refer to *ERA 1996, ss 221–224*). The ECJ concluded that during annual leave workers must receive comparable or equivalent pay to what they receive when actually working, but that this did not include payments to cover expenses. As explained above, the Supreme Court has remitted 2 questions to the Employment Tribunal to determine whether the supplements were part of the pilots' normal remuneration.

A further consequence of the lack of detailed provisions for calculating pay in the *Civil Aviation (Working Time) Regulations 2004* is that there is no definition of the period over which average or normal pay should be calculated (under the *ERA 1996*, the reference period is 12 weeks). However the Supreme Court in *Williams* gave guidance that in cases under these *Regulations* the relevant reference period could be determined by the employer (and/or included a relevant agreement) provided that it was representative. Failing that, the Employment Tribunal should determine the length of the representative reference period so that the level of "normal" remuneration to be paid during annual leave could be calculated.

Specific regulations have also been made for certain other industries: see the *Fishing Vessels (Working Time: Sea-fishermen) Regulations 2004 (SI 2004/1713)*; the *Merchant Shipping (Working Time: Inland Waterways) Regulations 2003 (SI 2003/3049)*; and the *Merchant Shipping (Hours of Work) Regulations 2002 (SI 2002/2125)*.

27.9 CONTRACT

The *Working Time Regulations 1998* lay down a minimum paid annual holiday entitlement. The contract of employment may, however, make more generous provision than provided for by the *Regulations*. In such circumstances, the contract will determine the employee's rights in respect of that more generous provision. Authorities on the common law on employee's rights to holidays which were decided before the *Regulations* came into force must now be read subject to those *Regulations*.

Particulars of holiday entitlement are among those the employer is obliged by the *Employment Rights Act 1996, s 1(4)(d)(i)* to supply in writing to the employee (see 7.7(g) CONTRACT OF EMPLOYMENT). In the absence of express provisions, certain terms relating to holidays have been implied by the courts.

It is thought likely that in most industries, in the absence of express provision, it will be held to be an implied term of the contract of employment that bank holidays may be taken as paid holiday: see *Tucker v British Leyland Motor Corpn Ltd* [1978] IRLR 493 at 496, in which a County Court judge decided that ' . . . if no express contractual provision or regular usage to the contrary is established an hourly paid employee is entitled to a day's holiday on recognised public holidays without fear of dismissal as an absentee; and that if he is entitled to a guaranteed minimum weekly wage he is entitled to be paid for that day without having to work additional hours in that week.'

It was held in *Hurt v Sheffield Corpn* (1916) 85 LJKB 1684, that the right to a holiday accrued only at the end of the year in the absence of any express provision to the contrary. Although this does not accord with the normal modern practice, the Court of Appeal in *Morley v Heritage plc* [1993] IRLR 400 declined to disapprove the decision in *Hurt*.

In *Morley*, it was held that there was no implied term in the contract that the employee should be paid for accrued but untaken leave when he left part-way through the year. However, in an appropriate case it might be possible to imply such a term as a matter of custom and practice. The decision of the EAT in *Janes Solicitors v Lamb-Simpson* (1996) 541 IRLB 15 suggests that in the case of an oral contract where there is nothing in writing, there is a wide area over which terms could be implied on the basis of business

27.9   Holidays

efficacy, including one as to accrued holiday pay. In addition, in *Wang v Beijing Ton Ren Tang (UK) Ltd* (UKEAT/0024/09/DA) [2010] All ER (D) 84 (Jan), the EAT held that a provision in a worker's contract that, on the termination of her employment, the worker could recover pay in lieu of all untaken holiday (i.e. not just untaken holiday from the final leave year) was valid and not contrary to the *Regulations* (which, as explained above, prohibit in most cases the carrying over of leave from one year to the next), Accordingly, where a worker's contact includes such a term, and the worker has untaken leave from a number of leave years, he or she should claim under the contract rather than the *Regulations*. However, in the absence of any term on the payment of accrued but untaken leave, a claim could be brought under the *Regulations* in respect of untaken leave in the last leave year (see **27.4** above).

The contract may also provide that the employer is entitled, on the termination of employment, to claw back payment for holidays taken by the worker but not accrued. However in the absence of an express provision of the contract of employment, no term can be implied which would allow such a claw back: see *Hill v Chapell* [2003] IRLR 19, EAT. Not only would a deduction in the absence of express agreement be contrary to the *Regulations*, it could also be an unlawful deduction from wages under *section 13* of the *Employment Rights Act 1996*, and a breach of contract.

Where there is a contractual entitlement to pay due under the contract for accrued but untaken holiday the contract may also make express provision as to how that entitlement is calculated. In the absence of such provision, there is inconsistent EAT authority as to how the rate of a day's pay should be calculated where the worker is paid an annual salary. The two approaches adopted have been to divide annual salary by 365 or to divide it by the actual number of working days. Obviously the former calculation will mean that the worker is entitled to lower payment for each untaken day of accrued holiday. In *Thames Water Utilities v Reynolds* [1996] IRLR 186 the EAT concluded that the *Apportionment Act 1870* applied with the result that a day's pay was to be calculated by dividing annual salary by 365. In *Taylor v East Midlands Offender Employment Consortium* [2000] IRLR 760 the EAT accepted that the *Apportionment Act* did apply in calculating a day's pay. However on the facts of the case, the pay for the employee's 10 days accrued but untaken holiday were 'grossed up' to 14 days pay to take account of weekends necessarily included in the 10-day holiday period. Thus the EAT found a way to mitigate the apparent harshness of the decision in *Thames Water*.

Subsequently (at a preliminary hearing) in *Leisure Leagues UK Ltd v Maconnachie* [2002] IRLR 600 the EAT concluded that the approach in *Thames Water* was wrong for two reasons. First, the approach was at odds with the virtually universal practice in industry in respect of the calculation of holiday pay in respect of holiday entitlement which is by reference to a day's work rather than calendar days per year. Second, *Thames Water* predated the *Working Time Regulations*. The issue was resolved by *Yarrow v Edwards Chartered Accountants* [2007] All ER (D) 118 (Aug), in which HHJ Peter Clarke (who had also sat on *Thames Water*) declined to follow his own decision in *Thames Water* and, instead, applied *Maconnachie*. His reasons for doing so were that: (i) judicial comity required him to follow the more recent decision, and (ii) in any event the advent of the *Regulations* required a different approach than that which had been adopted in *Thames Water*.

28   Human Rights

28.1   INTRODUCTION

The employment relationship may give rise to issues involving human rights law. At the individual level, human rights law may give an employee important protection against acts of discrimination or protect the employee's privacy or right to a fair hearing. Similarly, in relation to collective labour relations, human rights law is relevant to the right of members of a trade union to associate, to join a trade union of their choice and to take part in industrial action.

From 2 October 2000, with the coming into force of the *Human Rights Act 1998*, the domestic courts have been required to interpret United Kingdom law in accordance with the provisions of the European Convention on Human Rights and Fundamental Freedoms ('the Convention'). Prior to the *Act* coming into force, the Convention did not form part of the domestic law of the UK but was an international obligation which could, in appropriate cases, be used as an aid to the interpretation of unclear UK statutory provisions. An aggrieved individual seeking to rely upon the Convention was required to seek to present a case to the European Court of Human Rights for the determination of that court. This process could be expensive and very slow. Whilst the right of petition to the European Court remains as the final source of determination and jurisprudence on Convention Rights, issues of Convention rights may now be determined directly in the UK domestic courts.

This chapter presents an overview of the Convention and the historical development of the rights most relevant to the employment relationship, identifying some of the key decisions of the European Court of Human Rights and instances where Convention principles have assisted the UK courts in interpreting statutory provisions. The chapter goes on to consider, in outline, the key provisions of the *Human Rights Act* and its application and recent UK decisions in the employment sphere raising issues under the *Act*.

28.2   THE CONVENTION

Effect of the Convention

The European Convention on Human Rights and Fundamental Freedoms is an international treaty which was drawn up in 1950 and came into force in 1953. The Convention sets out in broad terms a number of fundamental rights and freedoms. It also established the European Commission of Human Rights and the European Court of Human Rights, both based in Strasbourg. It should be emphasised that the Convention and its institutions are entirely separate from the law and institutions of the European Community. The subscribing states are the members of the Council of Europe. Also, unlike European Community Law, the provisions of the Convention are not part of domestic law; they only bind the Government. The main text of the Convention, which has been amended by several protocols, can be found in Command Paper *Cmd 8969* (1953), published by the Stationery Office.

If a state which is a party to the Convention interferes with or abrogates any of the rights or freedoms enshrined in the Convention, a complaint may be made by any other party state. More importantly, the Convention allows for a right of direct complaint by an *individual* affected by an alleged breach of the Convention (such an individual right of complaint is very rare in international law). The Government of the United Kingdom ratified the Convention in 1950. However, it was not until 1966 that the UK Government recognised the jurisdiction of the European Court of Human Rights and accepted the right of an individual in the UK to petition the court.

28.3   Procedure for petition by an individual

In outline the procedure is as follows. The aggrieved individual must pursue every remedy available under UK law. When he has exhausted these 'domestic' remedies, without having his complaint satisfactorily resolved, he may present his petition to the European Commission of Human Rights. The Commission investigates the complaint. If it decides that there is, or may be, a breach of the Convention and that the complaint is admissible, it will endeavour to obtain a settlement between the parties. If no settlement is reached, the Commission will refer the case, together with its report, to the European Court of Human Rights. The court will then proceed to decide on the complaint.

UK legal aid is not available for petition, but limited legal aid is available from the Council of Europe. ECHR cases are now also among the limited categories of litigation in which English lawyers are now permitted to work on a conditional fee basis.

28.4   KEY DECISIONS OF THE ECHR ON FREEDOM OF ASSOCIATION, THE RIGHT TO PRIVATE LIFE AND OTHER RELEVANT PROVISIONS

One of the most significant cases concerning UK collective employment law to reach the European Court of Human Rights was the British Rail closed shop case, *Young, James and Webster v United Kingdom* [1981] IRLR 408, [1983] IRLR 35.

Article 11 of the Convention provides:

'1.   Everyone has the right to . . . freedom of association with others, including the right to form and to join trade unions for the protection of his interests.
2.   No restrictions shall be placed on the exercise of these rights . . . [certain exceptions permitted].'

In the *Young, James and Webster* case, the court held that the requirement on the applicants to join one of the unions specified in the closed shop agreement between British Rail and the railway unions, in circumstances where there had been no such requirement at the time when they were engaged, amounted to a restriction on the freedom guaranteed by *art 11* because the alternative to their joining was that they would lose their jobs ([1981] IRLR 408 at 409). The court made substantial monetary awards to the applicants.

The decision left the general question of the consistency of closed shop agreements with *art 11* unclear. Now that the right of individuals not to join a specified trade union has been entrenched and the pre-entry closed shop has been outlawed (see TRADE UNIONS – I (48)), it has become less important to resolve that issue. However, in *Sibson v United Kingdom* (1993) 17 EHRR 193, the court held that there was no breach of *art 11* where the complainant had no objection based on conviction to being a member of the union concerned, and where non-membership would not lead to dismissal (but rather to a move to another depot at which he could be required to work under his contract); contrast *Sigurjonsson v Iceland* (1993) 16 EHRR 462.

In a further important decision of collective employment rights (*Wilson and NUJ v United Kingdom*; *Palmer, Wyeth and RMT v United Kingdom*; *Doolan v United Kingdom* [2002] IRLR 568) the ECHR ruled that the UK was in breach of the right of freedom of association under *art 11* by permitting employers to use financial incentives to persuade employees to surrender trade union rights (see *s 146(1)(a) TULRCA 1992*). This is the first case in which the ECHR has upheld a claim relating to trade union rights under *art 11*. (For example, in the past, a complaint by workers at GCHQ that they were not permitted to belong to trade unions was not referred to the court by the Commission, which accepted the Government's argument based upon national security.) The *Wilson* decision prompted the introduction of *s 29* of the *Employment Relations Act 2004* which introduced new sections into *TULRCA 1992* conferring a right upon workers not to have an offer made by the employer for the purpose of inducing the worker not to be a member of a union or to take part in the activities of the union.

The corollary of the right to associate is the right to disassociate, which arose for consideration in *Associated Society of Locomotive Engineers and Firemen v United Kingdom (Application No 11002/05)* [2007] IRLR 361, ECtHR. The case involved the expulsion of a trade union member who was a member of the BNP. The Court held that the issue was the balance between the individual's right to associate and the right of the union to disassociate. *Article 11* did not place an obligation on the union to admit anyone who wished to join, particularly as an individual's livelihood was not dependent upon membership of a union and collectively bargained benefits would apply to all employees whether union members or not. Accordingly, the expulsion did not breach the ECHR.

The substantive nature of the associative rights protected by *Art 11* has been significantly expanded by the recent decision of the ECHR in *Demir v Turkey* [2009] IRLR 766. Previous decisions, whilst upholding the right to join (or not join) trade unions, had not held that the associative right extended to a right to bargain collectively or enter into collective agreements. In *Demir* the ECHR held that such a substantive right must now be recognised as "the right to bargain collectively with the employer has, in principle, become one of the essential elements of the right to form and join trade unions". Moreover, the ECHR stated that there may in addition be "positive obligations" on the State to secure effective enjoyment of the right to collectively bargain. This is likely to be significant in the context of UK domestic legislation.

Another area of employment law to which the Convention might be relevant is picketing (see STRIKES AND INDUSTRIAL ACTION (43)), given that *arts 10* and *11* protect freedom of expression and assembly (see *Middlebrook Mushrooms Ltd v TGWU* [1993] IRLR 232 at para 25). In *Unison v United Kingdom* [2002] IRLR 497, the ECHR dismissed an application in relation to an alleged breach of *art 11* rights by the imposition of an injunction restraining a strike which fell outside the definition of a 'trade dispute' (see STRIKES AND INDUSTRIAL ACTION (43)). The ECHR concluded that a prohibition upon a strike was a restriction on the freedom of association right in *art 11(1)*. The restraint was, however, in compliance with *art 11(2)* as a proportionate measure necessary in a democratic society for the protection of others (in this case, the employer). The point of significance in the case is the recognition that restraint upon the right to strike may, in appropriate circumstances, be a breach of *art 11*.

In *Redfearn v United Kingdom* [2013] IRLR 15 the ECHR held that the dismissal of a bus driver, who was dismissed by his employer when he was elected as a local councillor representing the British National Party and in relation to whom there was no remedy in UK law for dismissal on grounds of political opinion or affiliation, was a contravention of *art 11* read in the light of *art 10*. In that case unfair dismissal would have provided a remedy but the claimant did not have the requisite period of qualifying service. The UK government's arguments on justification for the qualifying period failed as, in other areas requiring protection (for example whistleblowing), no qualifying period was required. Thus the exclusion of the claimant from the protection of unfair dismissal was not proportionate and, hence, an infringement of *art 11* rights.

Article 10 has also been invoked (unsuccessfully) as part of a challenge to the statutory restrictions upon the political activities of certain local government employees (*NALGO v Secretary of State for the Environment* (1992) 5 Admin LR 785 and see 35.2 PUBLIC SECTOR EMPLOYEES). However, in *Vogt v Germany* (1995) 21 EHRR 205, the court held that the dismissal of a teacher employed in a state school on the grounds of membership of the German Communist Party breached *arts 10* and *11* of the Convention. In *Heinisch v Germany* [2011] App No 28274/08, ECtHR the ECHR considered a dismissal following an instance of "whistleblowing". It was held that Article 10 was engaged and, accordingly, the employer had a legitimate interest in protecting its business reputation, and so the question became whether the sanction of dismissal used against the employee had been proportionate. The Court held on the facts that it was not. In *Szima v Hungary* [2013] IRLR 59 the ECHR held that the demotion and fining of a union official who posted articles critical of the police on a website was not a breach of *art 10* as the actions pursued the legitimate aim of preserving order in the police force and was necessary in a democratic society.

Article 14 provides that the rights conferred by the Convention are to be exercised without any discrimination on grounds of *inter alia* race or sex (see, eg *Schuler-Zgraggen v Switzerland* (1993) 16 EHRR 405).

In *Halford v United Kingdom* [1997] IRLR 471, *art 8* of the Convention which protects private and family life was successfully invoked by a United Kingdom employee before the European Court of Human Rights. The court held that the applicant, a former Police Assistant Chief Constable, had been subjected to telephone tapping by her employer in an attempt to gather material to be used against her in a sex discrimination claim she was pursuing against her employer. The court in an important judgment held that such recording, without the knowledge of the employee, was a breach of the right to private life and correspondence. The applicant was awarded £10,000 compensation for non-pecuniary loss. *Halford* was considered in *Copland v United Kingdom* [2007] 45 EHRR 37 where the ECtHR held that Article 8(1) was infringed when a public sector employer monitored, collected and stored personal information relating to an employee's telephone, e-mail and internet usage at work.

Further, in the important case of *Smith and Grady v United Kingdom* [1999] IRLR 734, the European Court of Human Rights has concluded that a ban on homosexuals in employment contravenes the right to respect for private life (*art 8*). As is well known, the UK armed forces did not permit homosexual men or women to serve. Persons known to be homosexual were the subject of an 'administrative discharge' from the armed services. The applicants brought test cases challenging their discharges by way of judicial review in the UK courts, alleging that the policy banning homosexuals was a breach of the *ECHR* and the *EC Equal Treatment Directive*. The domestic challenges were ultimately unsuccessful. Before the European Court of Human Rights, however, the applicants were successful, the court finding that the investigation into their homosexuality and their subsequent discharge from the armed forces violated *art 8*. The court concluded that such investigations were not 'necessary in a democratic society' (*art 8(2)*). The court further found that there was an infringement of *art 13* in that there was 'no effective remedy' before a national authority in relation to the violation of the right to respect for their private lives. A supplementary alleged violation of *art 3* ('degrading treatment or punishment') was not, however, made out on the facts. The court stated, nevertheless, that treatment on the basis of a bias against a homosexual minority could, in principle, fall within the scope of *art 3* but a minimum level of severity of treatment was required to bring such action within the scope of that article. The court held that it was not necessary to examine an alleged violation of *art 10* (right to freedom of expression) but commented that the silence imposed on the applicants in relation to their sexual orientation could not be ruled out as a potential interference with freedom of expression. In a further case, *Salgueiro da Silva Mouta v Portugal* [2001] 1 FCR 653, ECtHR, the ECHR found that denial of the right to visit the child by a male homosexual was a breach of *arts 8* and *14*. In *Goodwin v United Kingdom* [2002] IRLR 664, the ECHR held that the UK's failure to give legal recognition to gender reassignment was a breach of *arts 8* and *12* (the right to marry). The decision may have implications for employment in relation, say, to the provision of pensions and certain fringe benefits. *Goodwin* was considered by the House of Lords in *A v Chief Constable of West Yorkshire Police* [2004] UKHL 21, [2004] IRLR 573, a case involving discrimination by the police against a transsexual. The House of Lords held that such discrimination was contrary to the provisions of the *EC Equal Treatment Directive* and, accordingly, recourse was not needed to reliance upon human rights law.

More recently, in *Pay v United Kingdom* (Application 32792/05) [2009] IRLR 139, the ECHR considered *art 8* in the context of a United Kingdom dismissal case. The claimant, a probation officer working with sex offenders, had brought an unfair dismissal claim. His employers having discovered his involvement in the merchandising of bondage and sadomasochistic products and other matters took the view that these activities were incompatible with his position as a probation officer and in particular one working with sex offenders. The issue before the ECHR was whether this dismissal was an infringement of the claimant's right to respect for his private life. The ECHR concluded that notwithstanding the 'public' nature of the activities in question, *art 8* protection still applied but that the dismissal was proportionate to the legitimate aim pursued, namely protecting the reputation of the probation service. In the light of this decision it would seem that the ambit of what is private life will not be subject to a simple division between a private and public place but that, even when *art 8* is engaged, it is likely that dismissal will be justified on the reputational damage basis in many cases, although such a response must be a proportionate one in the circumstances.

Denial of access to the courts and the rights conferred by *art 6* have also arisen in the employment context before the ECHR. In *Fogarty v United Kingdom* [2002] IRLR 148 an employee of the US Embassy in London had successfully brought a sex discrimination claim. In relation to subsequent victimisation proceedings following non-appointment to other posts, the US claimed immunity under the *State Immunity Act 1978*. The complainant complained of a breach of *art 6(1)* on the grounds of denial of access to the courts. The ECHR held that the claim fell within *art 6(1)* but that sovereign immunity was an aspect of international law and within the margin of appreciation allowed to states to limit access to the courts. By contrast the ECHR ruled that there was a contravention of the *Article 6* right to a fair hearing in *Sabeh El Leil v France* [2011] IRLR 781 where a French court dismissed the unfair dismissal claim of an employee of the Kuwaiti embassy (a French national employed as an accountant) because Kuwait had State immunity against court actions in France. Exclusion from the jurisdiction had to be justified and here it was not. As such this decision may have implications for the UK and the general immunity conferred by the *State Immunity Act 1978*. In *Devlin v United Kingdom* [2002] IRLR 155 the ECHR held that, in the context of a discrimination claim, the issue by the Secretary of State of a national security certificate blocking proceedings in the tribunal was a disproportionate restriction on the applicant's right of access to the courts and, accordingly, a breach *of art 6(1)*. Damages of £10,000 were awarded. See also *Devenney v United Kingdom* (2002) Times, 11 April where a similar judgment was given by the ECHR and the same sum awarded by way of damages.

In *Somjee v United Kingdom* [2002] IRLR 886 the judicial process in the Employment Tribunal and the Employment Appeal Tribunal was found wanting. At the end of various hearings it had taken eight years for Ms Somjee's discrimination and unfair dismissal complaints to be fully dealt with and more than seven years in the case of her victimisation claim. The ECHR held that a significant proportion of the blame for the delay rested with the Employment Tribunal and the Employment Appeal Tribunal and that such delay constituted a violation of the right to a fair hearing 'within a reasonable time' under *art 6* of the Convention. Ms Somjee was awarded 5,000 euros plus costs.

28.5   **THE POSITION PRIOR TO THE HUMAN RIGHTS ACT 1998: THE CONVENTION AS AN AID TO INTERPRETATION**

Prior to the coming into force of the *Human Rights Act 1998*, as the Convention was not incorporated in UK law, it could not be relied upon directly in domestic courts and tribunals. However, it was, like other treaties, cited on the basis that Parliament is presumed to have intended to legislate consistently with the UK's international obligations unless the contrary intention appears. But there was no scope for such a presumption to operate where the statutory words were clear. The position was reviewed by the House of Lords in *R v Secretary of State for the Home Department, ex p Brind* [1991] 1 AC 696 and in *Derbyshire County Council v Times Newspapers Ltd* [1993] AC 534.

28.5   Human Rights

In a number of cases the UK courts showed a willingness to apply Convention principles as an aid to interpretation of domestic law. By way of example, in *Camelot Group plc v Centaur Communications Ltd* [1998] IRLR 80 the Court of Appeal upheld an order for the delivery up to the plaintiff of confidential information sent to a journalist (employed by the defendant) by an employee of Camelot. The purpose of Camelot seeking the order was to identify their disloyal employee. The Court of Appeal in applying *s 10* of the *Contempt of Court Act 1981* (which gives certain protections to journalists from disclosure of their sources of information) held that the domestic court would give the greatest weight to the judgments of the European Court of Human Rights in cases where the facts are similar to the case before the domestic court, and considered in detail the ECHR's decision in *Goodwin v United Kingdom* (1996) 22 EHRR 123. Under the *Human Rights Act 1998*, the courts are required to adopt such an approach where issues of Convention rights are raised (see **28.6** and **28.7** below).

It is also material to note that the jurisprudence of the European Court of Justice, applying EUROPEAN UNION LAW **(23)** (which *is* part of English law), is heavily influenced by the Convention (see eg *R v Kirk*: 63/83 [1984] 3 CMLR 522). See also *Grant v South-West Trains Ltd*: C-249/96 [1998] IRLR 206, ECJ, a case on discrimination against homosexual persons brought under *art 141* (formerly *art 119*) of the EC Treaty in which the ECJ considered some of the jurisprudence on, and relevant articles of, the European Convention on Human Rights.

28.6   HUMAN RIGHTS ACT 1998

The *Human Rights Act 1998* (which received the Royal Assent on 9 November 1998) came into force on 2 October 2000 and is a radical reform of the status of the Convention in domestic law. The *Act* requires that the courts interpret United Kingdom law in accordance with the Convention. *Section 1* of the *HRA 1998* lists those articles of the Convention to which the *Act* is to apply and those articles are set out as *Sch 1* to the *Act*. By *HRA 1998, s 2* a court or tribunal determining a question in connection with a Convention right must take into account relevant judgments, decisions, declarations and opinions made or given by the Commission and Court of Human Rights and the Committee of Ministers of the Council of Europe. Primary and subordinate legislation are to be read, wherever possible, as being compatible with Convention rights but are not rendered void if incompatible (*HRA 1998, s 3*). Certain courts will be given the power to make a declaration of incompatibility when satisfied that the provision of primary legislation is incompatible with a Convention right (*HRA 1998, s 4*). This power does not, however, extend to an employment tribunal or the EAT. Accordingly, a detailed consideration of the *Act* is beyond the scope of this work.

The effect of the *Act*, as more cases are brought in domestic law relying upon Convention rights, is likely to be considerable in many fields; not least employment law, where *art 6* (the right to a fair hearing), *art 8* (the right to respect for private and family life), and also *arts 10, 11* and *14* (considered in **25.4** above) are likely to be of the greatest importance. The *Act* makes it unlawful for a 'public authority' to act in contravention of the Convention (*HRA 1998, s 6*). Those aggrieved will be able to bring proceedings against the authority in question (*HRA 1998, s 7*). The definition of 'public authority' is broad and includes any body whose function is of a public nature (*HRA 1998, s 6(3)*) and includes, expressly, courts and tribunals. The definition would appear to be sufficiently broad to apply to, for example, privatised public utilities.

The *Act* provides for remedies including an award of damages analogous to the principles applied by the European Court of Human Rights in relation to compensation (*HRA 1998, s 8*). Ministers of the Crown are given the power to amend offending legislation following a declaration of incompatibility (*HRA 1998, s 10*). Finally, in relation to any new legislation, a Minister of the Crown is required in either House prior to the second reading of the Bill to make a statement that the provisions of the Bill are compatible with the Convention rights or to state that, despite incompatibility, the Government wishes the House to proceed with the Bill in any event (*HRA 1998, s 19*).

28.7   THE APPLICATION OF THE HUMAN RIGHTS ACT 1998 IN EMPLOYMENT CASES

A number of cases have arisen in employment law raising issues under the *Human Rights Act 1998* particularly in relation to the right to a fair hearing (*art 6*) and the right to private and family life (*art 8*). The paragraphs below provide illustrations. As a point of procedure, it is to be observed that the Court of Appeal has sought to discourage a perceived tendency for Employment Tribunals to treat EC and human rights issues as appropriate for determination as preliminary issues (see *Barracks v Coles (Secretary of State for the Home Department intervening)* [2006] EWCA Civ 1041, [2007] ICR 60). In the light of this, it is likely that such arguments will have to be raised as part of the full hearing of the claim rather than at a preliminary point.

(a) Article 6

Article 6 provides for "a fair and public hearing within a reasonable time by an independent and impartial tribunal". Its application has been considered in a variety of employment related contexts with the issue of its application to disciplinary proceedings in particular generating a substantial body of law. In summary the majority of internal disciplinary proceedings will not engage *art 6* if the employee has the right to bring proceedings in the employment tribunal in satisfaction of the requirements of *art 6*.

A-G v Wheen [2001] IRLR 91 concerned *s 33* of the *Employment Tribunals Act 1996* which permitted the Attorney General to make a restriction of proceedings order against a litigant barring him from bringing further proceedings without the leave of the EAT on the grounds of vexatious institution of proceedings. The Court of Appeal held that *s 33* did not conflict with the right to a fair hearing under *art 6(1)* of the *Convention*. The Court of Appeal stated that the right under *art 6(1)* was not an absolute right but was to be balanced between the rights of the citizen to use the courts and the rights of others (and the court) to avoid wholly unmeritorious claims. Further, the order made *did* provide for access to the Employment Tribunal system but required permission first. As access was not prohibited, but was provided on terms, there could be no breach of *art 6(1)*.

In *Tehrani v United Kingdom Central Council for Nursing, Midwifery and Health Visiting* [2001] IRLR 208, 2001 SLT 879, the issue was to what extent *art 6* of the *Convention* (namely, the entitlement 'to a fair and reasonable public hearing within a reasonable time by an independent and impartial tribunal established by law') applied to disciplinary proceedings other than in a court of law. Whilst *art 6* may not apply to purely internal disciplinary inquiries, it was held in *Tehrani* that, when disciplinary proceedings determine the right to practice a profession, *art 6* may apply, as the decision of the Council's Professional Conduct Committee fell within a 'determination' of 'civil rights and obligations' for the purposes of *art 6*. It followed that there was an entitlement to a hearing before an independent and impartial tribunal. However, the Court of Session held that a professional disciplinary tribunal was not required to meet all the requirements of an independent and impartial tribunal if the disciplinary procedures provided for a right of appeal to a court of law. The Court of Session, following a review of relevant authorities, concluded that the case law of the ECHR established that there was no breach of the Convention if the disciplinary tribunal is subject to the control of a court of full jurisdiction, which court complies with the requirements of *art 6(1)*. This case raises important questions in relation to professional disciplinary bodies which do not have a statutory right of appeal to a court. If the disciplinary body is not sufficiently independent or important to satisfy *art 6(1)*, it is not clear whether a right to present subsequent complaints in an Employment Tribunal will be sufficiently akin to a statutory right of appeal to satisfy the exception recognised in the jurisprudence of the ECHR.

In *Kulkarni v Milton Keynes Hospital NHS Trust* [2009] IRLR 829 the Court of Appeal held, in the context of a doctor facing serious disciplinary charges, that the doctor was entitled to be represented by a lawyer instructed by Medical Protection Society. The facts of the case were unusual in that there was an express contractual term permitting representation by various persons, including a legally qualified person who "will not be representing the practitioner formally in a legal capacity". Holding the words quoted above to be devoid of meaning the court of Appeal concluded that the doctor was entitled contractually to be represented by a lawyer instructed by the MPS. Of broader significance, it appeared, were Lady Justice Smith's (*obiter*) observations on *art 6*. Whilst *art 6* would not be engaged in ordinary disciplinary proceedings, where the effect of the disciplinary proceedings could deprive the employee of the right to practice his or her profession *art 6* could, in Smith LJ's view, be engaged conferring the right to legal representation. Thus where the outcome could be effectively barring from employment in the NHS the right would be engaged. This reasoning if correct would, *prima facie*, be applicable to a large number of occupations where a decision to dismiss by an employer would have the effect of freezing the employee out of employment in his chosen field. See, however, the discussion of *Mattu v University Hospitals of Coventry and Warwickshire NHS Trust* [2012] EWCA Civ 641 below.

The scope of application of *Kulkarni* was, in practice, very limited (and see, in *R (on the application of Kirk) v Middlesbrough Borough Council* [2010] IRLR 699, a case involving a disciplinary hearing in relation to a social worker, *art 6* was held not to be engaged).

Similarly, in *Hameed v Central Manchester University Hospital NHS Foundation Trust* [2010] EWHC 2009 (QB) the High Court held that *Kulkarni* (above) was exceptional and that each case must be considered on its own facts in the light of the gravity of the charge, the likelihood of dismissal and the individual's chance of practising their profession in the future if dismissed. On the facts this was not a case where the practising of the profession would be lost. Accordingly, there was no right to rely upon *art 6* in relation to the disciplinary process. Leave to appeal on the *art 6* point was, however, granted.

In an important decision, *R (on the application of G) v Governors of X School* [2011] IRLR 766, the Supreme Court effectively limited the expansion of the *Kulkarni* principle. The case involved disciplinary proceedings against a teacher accused of misconduct. If the charges were upheld there was an obligation to report the findings to the Independent Safeguarding Authority ("ISA") (see EMPLOYEE'S PAST CRIMINAL CONVICTIONS **16.8**) for consideration whether the teacher was to be included on the list of persons considered to be unsuitable to work with children. The decision was to be taken by the ISA but the outcome of the disciplinary process would have a significant influence or effect on the ISA's decision. On this basis the Court of Appeal concluded that *art 6* was engaged so as to entitle the teacher to legal representation. This was overturned by the Supreme Court which did not consider that there was a sufficient connection between the disciplinary proceedings and the ISA proceedings for *art 6* to apply at the disciplinary hearing concluding that the ISA would exercise its independent judgment on the issue of barring. Although the case appears restrictive of further development in this area it is important to note that the reasoning in *Kulkarni* was not expressly disapproved and was explained as involving circumstances where the employer's disciplinary process would be determinative of the employee's right to work in his chosen profession.

A number of further cases have considered the extent to which the composition of a disciplinary panel can be challenged relying upon art 6 and the right to an independent and impartial tribunal established by law. Applying the same principles as articulated in

Kulkarni, reliance on *art 6* on this basis has proved unsuccessful. See *R (on the application of Puri) v Bradford Teaching Hospitals NHS Foundation Trust* [2011] IRLR 582; *Hameed v Central Manchester University Hospital NHS Foundation Trust* [2010] EWHC 2009 (QB) (above).

The most recent example is *Mattu v University Hospitals of Coventry and Warwickshire NHS Trust* [2012] IRLR 661 in which the Court of Appeal concluded that an NHS trust's disciplinary decision to dismiss an employee under his contract of employment did not determine any civil right of his within the meaning of *Art 6*. The case is particularly significant in that the majority of the Court of Appeal expressly disapproved Smith LJ's *obiter dicta* in *Kulkarni* (above) that *art 6* could be engaged where the effect of upholding the disciplinary charges would, effectively or in practice, bar the practitioner from practising his chosen profession in the future. The Court of Appeal held that a contractual decision to dismiss did not determine civil rights and obligations (which could only be determined by public or professional bodies; compare *Tehrani* above) even if the practical effect of that contractual decision was to "freeze-out" the employee from his chosen employment. *Article 6* would only be engaged at the stage of determination of the question of whether the dismissal was in breach of contract or unfair (ie at the judicial determination stage). Leave to appeal to the Supreme Court in *Mattu* has been refused. Accordingly, it is now clear that the "*Kulkarni* principle" of the potential application of *art 6* in disciplinary decisions simply has no application to contractual disciplinary decisions by employers (which are, of course, the vast majority of cases).

In the context of disciplinary procedure, *R (on the application of Bonhoeffer) v General Medical Council* [2011] EWHC 1585 (Admin), High Court is significant in that the Court concluded, drawing upon *art 6* jurisprudence, that a professional conduct body erred in law in admitting hearsay evidence in relation to serious allegations of child abuse. The Court concluded that the more serious the allegation, the more important it was to ensure that the accused be afforded fair and proper procedural safeguards. This is a potentially important development and it remains to be seen how broadly it may be applied in other disciplinary proceedings involving serious allegations of wrongdoing.

As to the Employment Tribunal system itself and *art 6(1)*, it had been suggested in *Smith v Secretary of State for Trade and Industry* [2000] IRLR 6 that the Employment Tribunals may not be independent when determining matters on redundancy payments from the DTI as the DTI appointed lay members of the tribunals. The case was not appealed. In *Scanfuture UK Ltd v Secretary of State for Trade and Industry* [2001] IRLR 416, the EAT revisited the question of whether the mechanism of appointment of lay members to the Employment Tribunal breached *art 6(1)* of the *Convention*. It is significant to note that the procedures for the appointment of lay members have changed since the procedures which were in place in 1999 (the time of the Employment Tribunal decision in *Scanfuture*). The EAT found that the new procedures complied with the ECHR. As to the position in 1999, the EAT concluded that the procedures for the appointment of lay members breached *art 6(1)* of the *Convention*. The application of *art 6* has also led to successful appeals against decisions of the employment tribunal which have been issued after a lengthy period of delay. See also the consideration of *art 6* in the context of allegations of bias in relation to an employment tribunal in *Jones v DAS Legal Expenses Insurance Co Ltd* [2003] EWCA Civ 1071, [2004] IRLR 218. In *Kwamin v Abbey National plc* [2004] IRLR 516 the EAT emphasised that it is a fundamental principle of natural justice that a fair trial includes the absence of excessive or avoidable delay by the tribunal and that the same principle is enshrined in the right to a fair trial within a reasonable period in *art 6*. In *Kwamin* the decisions under appeal had been delivered 7.5, 12 and 14.5 months after the end of the hearings respectively. The EAT gave guidance that, whilst it remained for an appellant to show that the result was unfair as a consequence of delay, employment tribunal decisions must be delivered within 3.5 months (after which there would, in the view of the EAT be 'culpable delay'). The issue of whether *arts 6* and *8* may require certain tribunal hearings to be conducted in private (beyond the categories of cases for which statutory provision for the tribunal sitting in private is already made) has been raised in *XXX v YYY*. The EAT had held that *arts 6* and *8* required the tribunal to sit in private. On appeal (*XXX v YYY* [2004] EWCA Civ 231, [2004] IRLR 471) the Court of Appeal reached its decision on different grounds relating to relevance of the evidence in issue. Accordingly the *art 6* and *8* points on the need for a tribunal to sit in private (outside the existing categories of claims) remain undecided at Court of Appeal level.

In *Home Office v Tariq* [2011] UKSC 35 the Supreme Court considered whether the use of closed proceedings in an employment law context was compatible with *art 6*. The claimant, an immigration officer, brought claims of race and religious discrimination following his suspension because of national security concerns. The employment tribunal adopted the closed material procedure in the interests of national security under *rule 54(2)* of *Schedule 1* of the *ET Rules* and the claimant contended that the procedure was contrary to art 6. The Supreme Court concluded that he closed material procedure did not violate *art 6* and was necessary on grounds of national security. Further there was no absolute requirement that the claimant see the allegations against him in order to challenge them. *Art 6* did not prescribe a uniform approach to all cases and the character of the proceedings (eg a civil claim as opposed to criminal charges) and the circumstances of a particular case can justify derogating from the right to see the allegations in issue. *Rule 49* of the *Employment Tribunal Rules of Procedure* (permitting anonymity orders) was considered in *A v B* [2010] IRLR 844 and the EAT concluded that it also had the power to anonymise a judgment if the loss of a claimant's anonymity would involve a breach of his *art 8* rights. See also *B and C v A* [2010] IRLR 400.

In *R v Securities and Futures Authority, ex p Fleurose* [2002] IRLR 297 the Court of Appeal held, in relation to disciplinary proceedings of the SFA (which could result in a fine and/or suspension), that such proceedings were not a criminal charge or offence for the purposes of *art 6* of the Convention. Nevertheless, the SFA were required to prove the allegations, to permit the accused to prepare a defence in the knowledge of the 'charges' and to allow a proper opportunity to give evidence and call evidence and to question witnesses giving evidence in support of the allegations.

In *R (on the application of Wright) v Secretary of State for Health* [2009] UKHL 3, [2009] 2 All ER 129 a declaration of incompatibility with the HRA was issued in relation to *Part VII* of the *Care Standards Act 2000*. That Act, for the purposes of protection vulnerable persons, made provision for a list to be kept of persons considered unsuitable to work with vulnerable adults. The Act also provided for workers to be placed provisionally on the list where concerns arose about their conduct pending final determination in relation to their conduct. The Court held these provisions, for provisional listing without the right to be heard, to be incompatible with the workers' right to a fair hearing under *art 6* of the Convention and also the right to respect for private and family life under *art 8*. The House of Lords subsequently confirmed on appeal that these so called POVA and POCA lists were indeed incompatible with *art 6* (see *R (on the application of Wright) v Secretary of State for Health* [2009] UKHL 3, [2009] 2 All ER 129). The POCA and POVA lists are to be replaced by new provisions under the *Safeguarding Vulnerable Groups Act 2006* but their Lordships in *Wright* ventured no opinions as to whether the new system would be less vulnerable to challenge under *art 6* than the old.

In *Dispatch Management Services (UK) Ltd v Douglas* [2002] IRLR 389, the EAT considered the situation where an application was made to remove representatives in Employment Tribunal proceedings on the grounds of conflict of interest. The Court of Appeal in *Bache v Essex County Council* [2000] IRLR 251 had held that there was no power in an Employment Tribunal to interfere with a party's choice of representative. In *Douglas*, the EAT held that this principle of non-interference was not inconsistent with the right to a fair hearing under *art 6* of the Convention.

In *Whittaker v Watson (P & D) (t/a P & M Watson Haulage)* [2002] ICR 1244, 67 BMLR 28 the EAT confirmed that it was not a 'court' for the purposes of hearing a submission that domestic legislation was incompatible with Convention rights. Referring to the definition of 'court' in *s 4(5)* of the *Human Rights Act 1998*, the EAT held that the conclusion was clear but puzzling (not least when the EAT was composed of a High Court judge sitting with lay members) and was, perhaps, a result which had not been intended in the drafting of the legislation.

On the issue of adjournment of hearings, the Court of Appeal held in *Teinaz v Wandsworth London Borough Council* [2002] EWCA Civ 1040, [2002] IRLR 721 that, in order to comply with the right to a fair trial under *art 6*, a litigant whose presence is needed for the fair trial of a case and who is unable to attend through no fault of his own will usually have to be granted an adjournment regardless of the inconvenience of such adjournment to the court or other parties (see also *Andreou v Lord Chancellor's Department* [2002] EWCA Civ 1192, [2002] IRLR 728). The practice of part-time EAT judges appearing as counsel before lay members of the EAT with whom they had previously sat in a judicial capacity and the compatibility of that practice with *art 6* reached the House of Lords in *Lawal v Northern Spirit Ltd* [2003] UKHL 35, [2003] IRLR 538. Overturning the decision of the Court of Appeal (which had upheld the decision of the EAT), the House of Lords held that such a practice tended to undermine confidence in the judicial system and ought to be discontinued. In determining whether there is bias in terms of the right to a hearing before an impartial tribunal under *art 6(1)* or the common law test of bias, the principle to be applied was that stated by the House of Lords in *Porter v Magill* [2001] UKHL 67, [2002] 2 AC 357 namely whether a fair minded and informed observer, having considered the given facts, would conclude that there was a real possibility that the tribunal was biased. The key to this test is public perception of the possibility of unconscious bias. On apparent bias of tribunal members and *art 6* see *City and County of Swansea v Honey* UKEAT/0465/09.

The principle that illegal contracts will not be enforced by the Courts was the subject of an *art 6* challenge in *Soteriou v Ultrachem Ltd* [2004] EWHC 983 (QB), [2004] IRLR 870. A claim of wrongful dismissal was struck out by reason of illegality. The Claimant contended that this contravened the right to a fair hearing and also that the strike out was contrary to *art 1* of the *First Protocol* to the *Convention*. These arguments were rejected. The Court held that art 6 was not breached as the issue of illegality was part of the substantive law of contract and not a mere procedural bar and that, in any event, the strike out would have been legitimate under *art 6(2)*. As to the claim based upon the *First Protocol* right (in relation to 'possessions'), it was held that, although a claim of breach of contract could indeed be a 'possession', there was no deprivation of a possession here as the contract was unenforceable (on the grounds of illegality) and therefore conferred no 'possession' which the claimant could complain that he was deprived and that the claimant had had his case considered substantively as part of the strike out application.

(b) Article 8

In relation to the right to private life, in the context of employment litigation, this right must be balanced with the right of the parties to have a fair trial of the issues between them. In *De Keyser Ltd v Wilson* [2001] IRLR 324, the EAT considered the *art 8* right to respect for private and family life in the context of an unfair dismissal claim in which the applicant alleged she suffered from a depressive illness caused by stress at work. In the course of the proceedings, the applicant agreed to be seen by the employer's medical expert and a letter of instruction was drafted on behalf of the employer to the expert which letter included certain details of the applicant's private life. The employment tribunal struck out the employer's notice of appearance on the basis that the employer's conduct of the proceedings was scandalous and in breach of the applicant's Convention right to privacy. Allowing the employer's appeal, the EAT held that there was no breach of *art 8* and that in relation to the need, in the context of the case, for a medical examination, the right to privacy was qualified as far as necessary by the right of both parties to have a just trial of the issues between them. In judicial review proceedings, the provisions of the *Employment Equality (Sexual Orientation) Regulations 2003* were found to be compatible with the convention rights in *art 8* and *art 14* (see *R (on the application of Amicus – MSF section) v Secretary of State for Trade and Industry* [2004] EWHC 860 (Admin), [2004] IRLR 430).

In *Whitefield v General Medical Council* [2002] UKPC 62, [2003] IRLR 39 the Privy Council considered the extent to which *art 8* was engaged in circumstances where the respondent, the General Medical Council, made it a condition of the applicant's continued practice as a doctor that he 'abstain absolutely from the consumption of alcohol'. The Privy Council held that the condition was not a breach of *art 8(1)* and in any event would, in the circumstances, have been justified under *art 8(2)*.

The provisions of the Human Rights Act are only directly applicable against public authorities. However, in the context of proceedings before the employment tribunal, Convention rights (and in particular the rights contained in *art 8*) may nonetheless be relevant in proceedings before the employment tribunal even where the employer is in the private sector. This is illustrated by the decision of the Court of Appeal in *X v Y* [2004] EWCA Civ 662, [2004] IRLR 625. The case concerned a dismissal by the employer for the employee's failure to disclose a caution. The employee contended that the dismissal was unfair as breaching the Convention right to respect for family life. While the claim failed on the facts, the Court of Appeal accepted that, if a dismissal was on grounds of an employee's private conduct within *art 8*, and was an interference with the right to respect for private life, that fact would be relevant to the determination of a claim of unfair dismissal whether the employer was a public authority or not. This is because the employment tribunal must, under *s 3* of the *Human Rights Act* read and give effect to relevant legislation (in this case the general provisions as to fairness of dismissal in *s 98* of the *ERA*) in a way which is compatible with Convention Rights such as *art 8*. In such circumstances there is no basis to treat a public employer differently from a private employer. Accordingly, say the Court of Appeal, it would not normally be fair to dismiss an employee for a reason which was an unjustified interference with the employee's private life. For a consideration of the role of *art 8* in relation to the fairness of the dismissal of a employee employed by a public sector employer see *Pay v Lancashire Probation Service* [2004] IRLR 129, EAT where the EAT held that a tribunal should effect consideration of Convention rights in the context of the fairness or otherwise of a dismissal by interpreting the words 'reasonably or unreasonably' in *s 98(4)* of the *ERA* as including the words 'having regard to the applicant's Convention rights'. Accordingly, in assessing the fairness in all the circumstances, consideration must be given to whether there had been an interference with the applicant's Convention rights and also any matters advanced by the employer as justification for such an interference. On the facts of *Pay*, in the EAT the applicant was unsuccessful in establishing that the *art 8* right to private life was engaged and, in relation to the *art 10* right of freedom of expression, the interference in issue was found to be justified in the circumstances. Notwithstanding the outcomes on the facts of both *X v Y* and *Pay*, the cases provide important indications of the likely relevance of Convention rights to the issue of the substantive fairness of dismissals both in the private and public sector. See **28.4** above in relation to *Pay* in the ECHR.

On the (generally limited) relevance of *art 8* to the general enquiry as to fairness of dismissal under *s 98(4)*, *ERA* see *Turner v East Midlands Trains Ltd* [2012] EWCA Civ 1470 in which the Court of Appeal held that the application of *art 8* (where engaged) did not result in any higher standard of procedural fairness than that which was required under the range of reasonable responses test. See also *X v Y* [2004] IRLR 625 (CA) and *Leach v OFCOM* [2012] IRLR 839 (CA) which suggest that *art 8* arguments will add little to the application of the test under *s 98(4)*, *ERA*.

Issues of surveillance of employees arose in *McGowan v Scottish Water* [2005] IRLR 167, EAT. The employee, suspected of falsely claiming on time sheets, was put under surveillance by private investigators engaged by the employer. The employee was dismissed in the light of evidence obtained on the surveillance. In an unfair dismissal claim the employee alleged the surveillance was a breach of *art 8*. This was rejected by the Scottish EAT on the facts of the case. The EAT held that *art 8* was indeed engaged in circumstances of covert surveillance but the central issue was that of proportionality. In the circumstances of suspected serious fraud, the surveillance was undertaken for legitimate reasons and was held to be proportionate. The case is significant in illustrating that, where employers do engage in covert surveillance of employees by whatever means, *art 8* is engaged and a 'strong presumption' (per Lord Johnston) of invasion of the right to family life will arise. Accordingly, it will be of central importance for an employer to be able to show that the interference arising was for a legitimate purpose and also 'proportionate' in all the circumstances which will involve consideration of the seriousness or gravity of the issue which prompted the surveillance and the extent of the surveillance exercise undertaken. The admissibility of covert recordings of a disciplinary hearing was considered in *Chairman and Governors of Amwell View School v Dogherty* [2007] IRLR 198. On the facts the EAT held that an employment tribunal had not, in allowing some of the covert recordings to be admitted in evidence, breached the school's governors' *art 8* rights. Recording of the private deliberations of the panel were, however, excluded on public policy grounds.

Rule 49 of the Employment Tribunal Rules of Procedure (permitting anonymity orders) was considered in *A v B* [2010] IRLR 844 and the EAT concluded that it also had the power to anonymise a judgment if the loss of a claimant's anonymity would involve a breach of his *art 8* rights. See also *B and C v A* [2010] IRLR 400.

Closely related to the right to family and private life is the right to peaceful enjoyment of possessions. In *Nerva v United Kingdom* [2002] IRLR 815 the ECHR held that the decision of the UK High Court and the Court of Appeal that tips included in cheque and credit card payments were the property of the employer and could be used by them to discharge their statutory obligations to pay the applicant waiters a minimum level of remuneration did not amount to a breach of the applicants' rights under *art 1* of the *First Protocol to the Convention* to the peaceful enjoyment of their possessions (see **32.21** Pay – I). See also *Legal & General Assurance Ltd v Kirk* [2001] EWCA Civ 1803, [2002] IRLR 124 in which the Court of Appeal held that a right to seek a particular employment cannot constitute a possession for the purposes of *art 1* of the *First Protocol to the Convention*. Similarly, in *R (Malik) v Waltham Forest NHS Primary Care Trust (Secretary of State for Health, interested party)* [2007] EWCA Civ 265, [2007] 4 All ER 832, [2007] ICR 1101, the Court of Appeal (reversing the decision of the Administrative Court at [2006] IRLR 526) held, in essence, that the right to practice a profession cannot be regarded as a 'possession' for the purposes of *art 1* of the *First Protocol*. In that case a medical practitioner had been unlawfully suspended and contended that his inclusion on a NHS medical performers list was a possession (inclusion on the list being a requisite for practice akin to a licence) and the suspension had interfered with the peaceful enjoyment of that 'possession'. The Court of Appeal rejected the contention that inclusion on the list was a possession for the purposes of *art 1*. *Art 1*, the Court of Appeal held does not cover an anticipated future right to income and thus the decision represents a substantial limitation upon the applicability of *art 1* in employment claims.

(c) Other Convention rights in the employment context

Article 9 protects freedom of thought, conscience and religion and the right to manifest religion or belief in worship, teaching, practice and observance. Its application to the requirement of Sunday working was considered in *Copsey v WWB Devon Clays Ltd* [2005] EWCA Civ 932, [2005] IRLR 811. In that case a change in shift pattern giving rise to an obligation to work on a Sunday led to the dismissal of the claimant for whom Sunday working was incompatible with his religious beliefs. The claimant brought a claim for unfair dismissal and alleged a breach of *art 9*. His claim was dismissed by the employment tribunal. On appeal to the Court of Appeal the decision of the Tribunal was upheld. Mummery LJ held that *art 9* was not in any event engaged as the employee was not compelled to work on a Sunday – he could always leave and get alternative employment (*Stedman v United Kingdom* [1997] 23 EHHR CD 168 applied). Rix and Neuberger LJJ held that *art 9* might be engaged but, applying the test of reasonableness and *s 98(4)* of the *ERA*, reasonable steps had been taken to accommodate the employee and accordingly the employment tribunal had not erred in reaching the decision which it did. This approach to human rights issues being engaged at the level of the general fairness of a dismissal under *s 98(4)* of the *ERA* is consistent with the approach adopted in relation to *art 8* in *Pay v Lancashire Probation Service* [2004] IRLR 129 and in *X v Y* [2004] EWCA Civ 662, [2004] IRLR 625 (see **28.7**(b) above).

In *Eweida v British Airways plc* [2010] ICR 890 the Court of Appeal held that an employer's policy forbidding visible jewellery, which prevented displaying a cross on a necklace while at work, had not amounted to indirect discrimination under the *Employment Equality (Religion or Belief) Regulations 2003 SI 2003/1660*. The Court rejected the argument that *art 9* was relevant to the employee's case. Relying on *Kalac v Turkey* [1997] 27 EHRR 552, the Court held that *art 9* did not protect all acts motivated or inspired by religion or belief. If there are other ways in which an employee can practise or observe his or her religion then a breach of *art 9* is unlikely.

Art 9 has been relied on, so far without success, in cases of employees refusing to carry out certain aspects of their work on the ground that it conflicted with their religious beliefs and where that refusal conflicted with the rights of others and thus could not be accommodated. In *Ladele v London Borough of Islington* [2010] ICR 532, CA the claimant refused to conduct civil partnership services in relation to same-sex couples. The Court of Appeal held that the employer Council did not discriminate against the claimant on the ground of religion when it threatened her with dismissal for refusing to carry out the services. The claimant's *art 9* rights should not override the Council's need to ensure equality. A similar conclusion was reached in *McFarlane v Relate Avon Ltd* [2010] ICR 507 which raised very similar issues. In *McClintock v Department for Constitutional Affairs* [2008] IRLR 29 the EAT held that a Justice of the Peace, who resigned from the Family Panel when his request to be excused from cases that might lead to the adoption of a child by a same-sex couple was rejected, was not discriminated against on the ground of his religious belief and nor were his *art 9* rights infringed and/or any infringement would have been justified under *art 9(2)*.

In *Eweida v United Kingdom* [2013] IRLR 231 the ECHR has given judgment in relation to the claims in *Eweida*, *Ladele*, *McFarlane* and also in relation to *Chaplin* (a case involving a nurse who was prohibited from wearing a cross at work in accordance with hospital policy). In Ms Eweida's case the ECHR held that the prohibition in issue did breach her *art 9* rights. The wearing of the cross was a manifestation of religion and the interference was not justified or proportionate. Conversely in *Chaplin*, although interference with religious manifestation was made out, the prohibition in a nursing content of jewellery on health and safety grounds was justified. The claims in *Ladele* and *McFarlane* each failed before the ECHR, with the court concluding that the interference in issue was justified. The ECHR stressed that the aim of the employer was to secure the implementation of its policy of providing a service without discrimination to others. This was considered by the ECHR to be the most important factor in justifying the requirements in issue, given that the ECHR generally allows national authorities a wide margin of appreciation when striking the balance between competing Convention rights. Thus where the manifestation of religious belief will conflict with the rights of others (or where eg health and safety obligations are engaged) a prohibition on the manifestation is likely to be justified. Where, however, there is no such competing interest or right it is likely (as in Ms Eweida's case) to fail to be a justified interference with the *art 9* rights of the complainant.

Articles 10 and *11* on freedom of expression and association respectively were engaged in *Gate Gourmet London Ltd v Transport and General Workers Union* [2005] EWHC 1889 (QB), [2005] IRLR 881. This case involved applications for injunctions restraining picketing at Heathrow Airport. Fulford J held that in deciding whether to grant such an injunction appropriate weight must be given to the 'right to picket' (as a consequence of the *art 10* and *art 11* rights). On the facts of the case an order was granted limiting the number of pickets but the decision is significant in its express recognition in the domestic courts of effectively the right to picket in relation to an employment dispute (see also *Unison v United Kingdom* [2002] IRLR 497 above at **28.4**). *Redfearn v Serco Ltd (t/a) West Yorkshire Transport Service)* [2006] EWCA Civ 659, [2006] IRLR 623 involved the dismissal of an employee because of him standing as a candidate for the British National Party. The claim was brought under the *Race Relations Act 1976* (the claimant having insufficient continuous employment to bring an unfair dismissal claim) raising claims of direct and indirect discrimination which were both rejected. Issues of freedom of expression were raised under the *Human Rights Act* relying upon *art 10* but these were rejected by the domestic court on the basis of applying *art 17* of the Convention which provides that nothing in the Convention gives a right to engage in activities which themselves are aimed at destroying Convention rights and freedoms. See however *Redfearn v United Kingdom* (above) in which the ECHR has held the dismissal in *Redfearn* and the absence of effective remedy in UK law was a breach of *art 10* and *art 11* rights of the complainant.

In *Hill v Governing Body of Great Tey Primary School* [2013] IRLR 274 *art 10* was in issue in an unfair dismissal claim. In that case a school employee had contacted parents and the press in relation to a child being hurt in the playground. An employment tribunal found her subsequent dismissal unfair having regard to *art 10*. On appeal the EAT confirmed that *art 10* was engaged and an employment tribunal must adopt a structured approach to the issue including making a structured assessment of proportionality.

In *Ministry of Justice v Prison Officers Association* [2008] EWHC 239 (QB), [2008] ICR 702, [2008] IRLR 380 the issue of the 'right to strike' in the context of *art 11* was considered by a domestic court. The Prison Officers Association had been subject to an injunction restraining their strike action (in circumstances of a no strike agreement being in force). In seeking to discharge the injunction various arguments based on *art 11* were unsuccessful before the Court. The Court held that *art 11*, whilst protecting freedom of association, contains no express right to strike and, even if it did, *art 11(2)* gave considerable freedom to a member state to restrict such a right. Accordingly the injunction restraining strike action was maintained.

The question of whether the complex balloting and notice provisions contained in *Part V* of the *Trade Union and Labour Relations (Consolidation) Act 1992 (TULR(C)A)* infringe the right to freedom of association under *art 11* has been considered in *Metrobus Ltd v Unite the Union* [2010] ICR 173. The Court of Appeal rejected the Union's contention that the provisions of *TULR(C)A* presented obstacles so numerous and so complex that errors by unions were almost inevitable, and that for this reason the rights under *art 11* were so constrained as not to be effectively exercisable in respect of industrial action. A similar argument was rejected in *EDF Energy Powerlink Ltd v National Union of Rail, Maritime and Transport Workers* [2010] IRLR 114.

28.8 OTHER INTERNATIONAL OBLIGATIONS RELEVANT TO HUMAN RIGHTS

The Council of Europe has also promulgated, and the United Kingdom has ratified, the *European Social Charter*, which contains provisions relating to, for example, annual holidays and the right to strike. This should not be confused with the Social Charter and the Social Chapter to the Maastricht Treaty agreed by the EC (see **22.3** EUROPEAN UNION LAW). There is an Additional Protocol which has not been signed by the UK.

28.8   Human Rights

The International Labour Organisation ('ILO') is a specialist body of the United Nations. It has issued a number of conventions, some of which have been ratified by the United Kingdom. They deal with matters such as health and safety, freedom of association and racial discrimination. UK law has been held by the ILO to infringe these conventions in a number of respects. However, there is no remedy for any such breaches in English courts or tribunals.

29 Insolvency of Employer

29.1   In the event of insolvency, an employer is likely to have limited funds which are insufficient to pay all its debts. These debts may include sums due to employees, for example payment of wages. Some statutory protection is afforded to employees in this situation.

First, under the *Insolvency Act 1986*, employees' rights to payment of certain sums due to them from their employer take precedence over payment of debts to other creditors. Second, under the *ERA 1996* (which in part implements the *EC Directive on Insolvency Protection 2008/94/EC*), the Secretary of State offers a limited guarantee to pay certain sums due to employees from their employers, and to make up unpaid employer pension contributions, out of the National Insurance Fund. Third, statutory maternity, paternity, adoption and sick payments may be claimed from HM Revenue and Customs. Fourth, under the *Pensions Act 2004*, compensation for loss of pension entitlements following insolvency of an employer may be payable from the Pension Protection Fund. Finally, in certain circumstances, a receiver or administrative receiver of a company may take on personal liability under an employee's contract of employment.

A detailed analysis of the law of insolvency is beyond the scope of this book. See *Tolley's Company Law* for a detailed treatment of corporate insolvency. A brief outline of the provisions affecting employees is set out below.

29.2   CLAIMS GIVEN PRECEDENCE BY THE INSOLVENCY ACT 1986

Under the *Insolvency Act 1986*, s 386 and *Sch 6* any claim to remuneration payable to an employee, in respect of the four-month period immediately preceding the insolvency of the employer, is treated as a preferential debt and given precedence over other creditors' claims. 'Remuneration' is defined to include:

(a)   wages or salary (including commission);

(b)   a guarantee payment under *Part III, ERA 1996* (see Pay– I (32));

(c)   a payment for time off work under *ERA 1996, ss 53* (time off to look for work or training in the event of redundancy), and *56* (time off for ante-natal care) or *TULRCA 1992, s 169* (time off for trade union activities) (see generally Time Off Work (47));

(d)   a payment on medical suspension or on maternity grounds under *Part VII of ERA 1996* (see Maternity and Parental Rights (31) and Pay – I (32));

(e)   a protective award made under *s 189* of *TULR(C)A 1992* (see Redundancy – II (37));

(f)   accrued holiday pay (see Holidays (27)); and

(g)   remuneration payable in respect of a period of holiday or absence from work through sickness or good cause.

(*Insolvency Act 1986, Sch 6, paras 9–15.*)

The maximum total sum which may be treated as a preferential debt under *s 386* is £800 (save that remuneration for accrued holiday pay under *para 10* of *Sch 6* is not subject to this cap) (*Insolvency Proceedings (Monetary Limits) Order 1986 (SI 1986/1996), art 4*). If the employers' assets are insufficient to pay claims for remuneration, each individual claim ranks equally and is to be paid in equal proportions to other such claims.

The test whether an employee is an employee for the purposes of *s 386* and *Sch 6* falls to be determined by whether the employee has a contract for services or a contract of employment: see *Eaton v Robert Eaton Ltd* [1988] ICR 302 and Employee, Self-Employed or Worker? (14).

29.2 Insolvency of Employer

An employee may have other contractual or statutory claims against his employer which are not treated as preferential debts under *s 386* and *Sch 6* (including any claim for sums in excess of £800 which are owed as remuneration, etc). Such claims must be proved in the normal way under the *Insolvency Rules 1986 (SI 1986/1925)* as amended.

Recent cases of relevance include *Day v Haine* [2008] EWCA Civ 626, [2008] ICR 1102, [2008] IRLR 642, where it was found that protective awards granted to a number of employees after a company had gone into liquidation were provable debts of the company as they were liabilities to which the company might become subject after the date of the liquidation by reason of an obligation incurred before that date (see **29.5** below for payment of protective awards by the Secretary of State). Also see *Leeds United Association Football Club Ltd, Re* [2007] EWHC 1761 (Ch), [2007] ICR 1688, which clarified that there is no priority given to damages for wrongful dismissal when claimed by employees as creditors against their employer's insolvency.

29.3 PAYMENTS OUT OF THE NATIONAL INSURANCE FUND: EMPLOYMENT RIGHTS ACT 1996

Where their employer is insolvent employees may claim redundancy payments from the Secretary of State for Trade and Industry under *ERA 1996, Part XI* and certain other debts owed to employees under *ERA 1996, Part XII*. Payments are made by the Redundancy Payments Office from the National Insurance Fund on behalf of the Secretary of State. The statutory provisions, in part, implement the *Insolvency Protection Directive 2008/94/EC*. Under the *Directive* where an employer has its registered office in one member state but also employs workers in another member state, it is the guarantee institution of the member state in which the employee is employed which must pay out in the event of an insolvency (*Everson and Barrass v Secretary of State for Trade and Industry and Bell Lines Ltd*: C-198/98 [2000] IRLR 202, ECJ). *Article 8a* of the *Insolvency Protection Directive* provides 'when an undertaking with activities in the territories of at least two Member States is in a state of insolvency . . . the institution responsible for meeting employees' outstanding claims shall be that in the Member State in whose territory they work or habitually work'. In *Sweden v Holmqvist*: C-310/07 [2009] ICR 675, [2008] IRLR 970 the ECJ held that 'activities', for this purpose, means a stable economic presence in the latter State, featuring human resources which enable it to perform activities there.

Any debts which fall outside the scope of these statutory provisions (or any excess above the statutory maximum payable) may be claimed by the employee as a creditor against his employer's insolvency.

29.4 Redundancy payments

Where an employer is insolvent, and has failed to pay in whole or in part:

(a)   a statutory redundancy payment;

(b)   a payment under a formal compromise agreement made in respect of a claim to a statutory redundancy payment; or

(c)   a redundancy payment under a collective agreement approved under the collective contracting out provisions (*ERA 1996, s 157*),

to which an employee is entitled, the employee may apply to the Redundancy Payments Office for payment (*ERA 1996, ss 166–167*).

'Insolvency' for these purposes is defined in *ERA 1996, s 166(5)* to *(8)*. The mere fact of insolvency (in the sense of not being able to meet debts) is not enough (*Secretary of State for Employment v McGlone* [1997] BCC 101). *Section 166(6)* defines insolvency where the employer is an individual. Where the employer is a partnership, the test as to whether or not the employer is insolvent will only be satisfied if every partner has been adjudged bankrupt (*Secretary of State for Trade and Industry v Forde* [1997] ICR 231). Where the employer is a company, insolvency is defined in *ERA, s 166(7)*. It is not sufficient that a company has been struck off the register: *Secretary of State for Trade and Industry v Walden* [2000] IRLR 168. *Section 166(8)* applies where the employer is a limited liability partnership. In each case, the employee seeking payment out of the National Insurance Fund must show that the employer falls within the relevant definitions of insolvency. If he fails to do so, there is no discretion to make a payment and the employee will not be entitled to payment (*Secretary of State for Trade and Industry v Walden* [2000] IRLR 168). The employer (even if a foreign company) must have entered insolvency proceedings in Great Britain. The same definitions of insolvency are used to determine whether the Secretary of State is obliged to make a payment under *ERA 1996, Part XII*: see **29.5** below.

An individual who is a controlling shareholder (or director) of the company he works for may also be an employee of that company for the purposes of obtaining a redundancy payment from the Secretary of State: see *Secretary of State for Business, Enterprise and Regulatory Reform v Neufeld (Richard)* [2009] EWCA Civ 280, [2009] IRLR 475, CA. For the position of self-employed workers see *Alade v Secretary of State for Trade and Industry* [2007] All ER (D) 08 (May), EAT.

There is no express time limit for making an application to the Secretary of State for a redundancy payment, but if the employee is out of time to claim the payment from his employer (see *ERA 1996, s 164*), he may not claim it from the Secretary of State (*Crawford v Secretary of State for Employment* [1995] IRLR 523).

Where an employee applies for a payment under *s 166*, the amount payable is determined in accordance with *s 168*. This will normally be the amount of a statutory redundancy payment. However, where there is a compromise agreement or collective agreement under *s 157* in relation to the redundancy payment, the Secretary of State will pay out whichever is the less of a statutory redundancy payment or the amount payable under the compromise agreement/ collective agreement.

The Secretary of State, where an employee applies for a payment under s 166, has the power to request in writing that the employer provide information and documents to allow the Secretary of State to decide whether the application is well founded. Failure to comply with such a request without reasonable excuse is a criminal offence (*ERA 1996, s 169*). In addition, in cases where the Secretary of State makes a payment, he will assume the rights of the employee as against the employer, and any monies recovered from the employer pursuant to this right are paid into the National Insurance Fund (*ERA 1996, s 167(3)* and *(4)*).

Disputes relating to payments by the Redundancy Payments Office are to be referred to the employment tribunal under *ERA 1996, s 170*. The employee may refer a dispute to a tribunal without joining his employer as a party to the proceedings (*Jones v Secretary of State for Employment* [1982] ICR 389). However, the EAT has suggested that it may be proper on such occasions to join the company in liquidation for the purposes of discovery (*Bradley v Secretary of State for Employment* [1989] ICR 69).

29.5   Other guaranteed debts: arrears of pay, notice and holiday pay etc

If, on an application made to him in writing by an employee, the Secretary of State is satisfied:

(a)   that the employer of that employee has become insolvent;

(b)   that the employment of the employee has been terminated; and

(c)   that on the appropriate date the employee was entitled to be paid the whole or part of any debt set out in (i) to (v) below,

the Secretary of State must pay him his entitlement out of the National Insurance Fund (*ERA 1996, s 182*). 'Insolvency' for these purposes is defined in *ERA 1996, s 183* in the same terms as the definition in *s 166* relating to the Secretary of State's obligation to pay redundancy payments in the event of an employer's insolvency: see **29.4** above.

This right applies to the following debts:

(i)   any arrears of pay in respect of one or more (but not more than eight) weeks; arrears of pay are deemed to include the following statutory payments: a guarantee payment under *Part III, ERA 1996* (however, this will not include contractual guarantee payments in excess of the statutory scheme: *Benson v Secretary of State for Trade and Industry* [2003] ICR 1082, [2003] IRLR 748, EAT), any payment for time off for trade union duties, remuneration for suspension on medical or maternity grounds, and remuneration under a protective award (*ERA 1996, s 184(2)*);

(ii)   any amount which the employer is liable to pay the employee for the statutory minimum period of notice under *ERA 1996, s 86*, or for any failure of the employer to give the period of notice required;

(iii) any holiday pay due for a period or periods of holiday not exceeding six weeks in all, both for holidays already taken and holiday entitlement accrued but not taken, and to which the employee became entitled during the 12 months ending with the appropriate date;

(iv)   any basic award of compensation for unfair dismissal (see **53.7** U NFAIR D ISMISSAL – III);

(v)   any reasonable sum by way of reimbursement of the whole or any part of any fee or premiums paid by an apprentice or articled clerk.

(*ERA 1996, s 184(1)*.)

'Appropriate date' in relation to arrears of pay and holiday pay means the date on which the employer becomes insolvent. An employee may therefore only claim unpaid wages and holiday pay which accrued before the insolvency of his employer. In relation to a protective award and to a basic award of compensation for unfair dismissal, the appropriate date is the latest of:

(1)   the date on which the employer became insolvent;

(2)   the date of the termination of the employee's employment; and

(3)   the date on which the award was made.

In relation to any other debt, the appropriate date is the later of the dates mentioned in (1) and (2) above (*ERA 1996, s 185*).

The total amount payable to an employee in respect of any debt referred to above, where that debt is calculated according to a period of time, may not exceed £450 for any one week (or proportionately less for a period less than one week) (*ERA 1996, s 186* as amended by *SI 2012/3007* with effect from 1 February 2013). The House of Lords held, *obiter*, that the cap is not contrary to *EC Directive 80/987: Mann v Secretary of State for Employment* [1999] IRLR 566. Assessment of the amount due to the employee for arrears of pay and holiday should be made on the basis of salary net of tax and National Insurance contributions. When applying the statutory cap, tax and National Insurance contributions should be deducted from the sum payable *after* it has been capped, rather than deducting them from the total sum owing to the employee and then applying the cap (*Morris v Secretary of State for Employment* [1985] ICR 522, [1985] IRLR 297, EAT, followed in *Titchener v Secretary of State for Trade and Industry* [2002] ICR 225, [2002] IRLR 195, EAT).

The eight-week limit in respect of which an employee may claim arrears of pay under *s 184(1)(a)* is a permitted derogation to the *EC Directive* and, as a derogation, it must be interpreted restrictively, so as to afford maximum benefit to the employee. Accordingly, it must be construed as permitting an employee to choose the eight weeks in respect of which his claim is most valuable: see *Mann v Secretary of State for Employment* [1999] IRLR 566, HL and *AGR Regeling v Bestuur van der Bedrijfsvereniging voor de Metaallnijverheid*: C-125/97 [1998] ECR I-4493, [1999] ICR 605, ECJ (a case on the meaning of the *EC Directive* which *ERA 1996, s 182* partly implements). See further *Mau v Bundesanstalt fur Arbeit*: C-160/01 [2003] ECR I-4791, [2004] 1 CMLR 1113.

Where an employee claims notice pay under *s 184(1)*, the amount he may recover depends on whether he worked out his notice or was unlawfully dismissed without notice. In the former case, he may recover his arrears of pay from the Secretary of State as a liquidated sum. In the latter case, he is subject to the normal rules on mitigating his loss. Thus, the Secretary of State may in those circumstances, in assessing the amount he is liable to pay, take into account any earnings of the employee during the notice period, or, where the employee has failed to mitigate his loss properly, any earnings he should have received (*Secretary of State for Employment v Cooper* [1987] ICR 766, EAT; *Secretary of State for Employment v Stewart* [1996] IRLR 334, EAT). He may also deduct from the amount payable the amount of state benefits the employee has received during the notice period, which he would not have received but for his dismissal (see *Westwood v Secretary of State for Employment* [1985] ICR 209, HL).

The liability of the Secretary of State to make payments under *s 182* cannot exceed that of the insolvent employer. Thus, where the insolvent employer would be entitled to set-off against the debt owed by him to the employee sums owed by the employee to him, the Secretary of State is entitled to deduct from the amount he pays the employee the amount of the employer's set-off (see *Secretary of State for Employment v Wilson* [1997] ICR 408, [1996] IRLR 330, EAT).

Where an insolvency practitioner such as a trustee in bankruptcy, liquidator, administrator or receiver has been (or is required by law to be) appointed, the Secretary of State will not normally make any payment from the National Insurance Fund until the insolvency practitioner sends the Secretary of State a statement of what is due to the employee. The Secretary of State may, however, at his discretion, satisfy himself that the employee's claim is valid and that he does not need a statement before paying the claim (*ERA 1996, s 187*). Once payment has been made to the employee by the Secretary of State, the employee's rights to claim the debt against his employer are transferred to the Secretary of State. In addition, any sums payable as the result of a subsequent decision of an employment tribunal requiring an employer to pay the debt to the employee must be paid to the Secretary of State (*ERA 1996, s 189*). Following an application under *s 183*, the Secretary of State has the power to request in writing that the employer provide information and documents to allow the Secretary of State to decide whether the application is well founded. Failure to comply with such a request without reasonable excuse is a criminal offence (*ERA 1996, s 190*).

29.6   Remedy under ERA 1996 Part XII

A person who has applied for payment of other guaranteed debts may, within the period of three months beginning with the date on which the decision of the Secretary of State on that application was communicated to him (or if that is not reasonably practicable, within such further period as is considered reasonable), present a complaint to an employment tribunal that:

29.6 Insolvency of Employer

(a)   the Secretary of State has failed to make any such payment; or

(b)   any such payment by him is less than the amount which should have been paid.

(ERA 1996, s 188.)

If the employment tribunal finds the complaint well-founded, it will make a declaration to that effect and state the amount due from the Secretary of State. See *Secretary of State for Employment v Reeves* [1993] ICR 508 for the law relating to interest upon the tribunal's award in such a case (for interest generally, see 17.33 EMPLOYMENT TRIBUNALS – I).

29.7 Unpaid contributions to occupational pension schemes

The Secretary of State may make payments out of the National Insurance Fund into an occupational pension scheme if he is satisfied that an employer has become insolvent and that, at the time he became insolvent, there remained unpaid relevant contributions falling to be paid by him to the scheme. Application for payment is to be made by the person competent to act in respect of the pension scheme *(Pension Schemes Act 1993 ('PSA 1993'), s 124(1))*. 'Relevant contributions' are defined as contributions to be paid by the employer on his own behalf or on behalf of an employee from whose pay a deduction has been made for that purpose *(PSA 1993, s 124(2) and 124(6))*.

The amount payable in respect of contributions of an employer on his own behalf is the least of the following:

(a)   the balance of relevant contributions remaining unpaid on the date when the employer became insolvent and payable by the employer on his own account to the scheme in respect of the 12 months immediately preceding that date;

(b)   the amount certified by an actuary to be necessary for the purpose of meeting the liability of the scheme on dissolution to pay the benefits provided by the scheme to or in respect of the employees of the employer;

(c)   an amount equal to 10% of the total amount of remuneration paid or payable to those employees in respect of the 12 months immediately preceding the date on which the employer became insolvent.

Where the scheme is a money purchase scheme, the sum payable is the lesser of the amounts in *(a)* and *(c)* above.

(PSA 1993, ss 124(3) and (3A) (as inserted by the *Pensions Act 1995*).)

The sum payable in respect of unpaid contributions on behalf of an employee may not exceed the amount deducted from the pay of the employee in respect of the employee's contributions to the occupational pension scheme during the 12 months immediately preceding the date on which the employer became insolvent *(PSA 1993, s 124(5))*.

The liquidator, receiver or trustee in bankruptcy (or other 'relevant officer', as defined) must make a statement to the Secretary of State of the amounts so owing before any payment out of the National Insurance Fund may be made *(PSA 1993, s 125(3), (4))*. However, the Secretary of State may make a payment from the National Insurance Fund if he is satisfied that he does not require such a statement in order to determine the relevant amounts *(PSA 1993, s 125(5))*.

The rights and remedies of the persons competent to act in respect of the scheme will be transferred to the Secretary of State *(PSA 1993, s 127(1))*.

A person who has applied to the Secretary of State for payment of pension contributions may present a complaint to the Employment Tribunal that the Secretary of State has failed to make any such payment or that any such payment by him is less than the amount which should have been paid (*PSA 1993, s 126*). The provisions in relation to remedy are the same as those for claims for payment of guaranteed debts under Part XII *ERA 1996:* see **29.6** above.

Following the decision of the ECJ in *Robins and another v Secretary of State for Work and Pensions* C-278/05 [2007] 2 CMLR 269, [2007] IRLR 270, that UK legislation did not provide the minimum degree of protection of accrued occupational pension rights required by *Article 8* of *EC Directive 80/987*, the *Financial Assistance Scheme (Miscellaneous Amendments) Regulations 2007/3581* (and subsequent regulations made under *s 286* of the *Pensions Act 2004* (as amended by the *Pensions Acts 2007, 2008* and *2011*)) were enacted to determine the pension protection provided for qualifying employees upon an 'insolvency event' occurring in respect of their employer.

29.8   Pensions Act 2004

The *Pensions Act 2004* provides protection for employees of employers which become insolvent. The Act established a new body corporate, the Pensions Regulator, together with the Pension Protection Fund, the Board of the Pension Protection Fund and the Pension Protection Fund Ombudsman.

Chapter 3 of *Part 2* to the *Act (ss 126–181A)* provides for pension protection for 'eligible' pension schemes in the event that the employer suffers an 'insolvency event'. The complex details of the protection offered are set out in detail in the Act and also in the *Pension Protection Fund (Compensation) Regulations 2005 (SI 2005/670)*, the *Financial Assistance Scheme (Miscellaneous Amendments) Regulations (SI 2007/3581)* and subsequent regulations made under *s 286* of the *Pensions Act 2004* (as amended by the *Pensions Acts 2007, 2008* and *2011*). However, in summary the Board of the Pension Protection Fund will, in defined circumstances, be under a duty to assume responsibility for eligible schemes following an insolvency event. The Board may pay compensation to members of the pension scheme whose pensions are affected by the insolvency pursuant to the pension compensation provisions set out in Sch 7.

The *Pension Protection Fund and Occupational Pension Scheme (Levy Ceiling and Compensation Cap) Order 2013 (SI 2013/105)* caps the relevant compensation at £34,867.04, with effect from 1 April 2013.

29.9   Statutory maternity, paternity, adoption and sick pay

An employee who, due to the insolvency of his or her employer, is unable to obtain statutory maternity pay, paternity pay, adoption pay or sick pay may claim such payment from HM Revenue and Customs: see *Statutory Maternity Pay (General) Regulations 1986 (SI 1986/1960), regs 7* and *30, the Statutory Paternity Pay and Statutory Adoption Pay (General) Regulations 2002 (SI 2002/2822), reg 43* and *the Statutory Sick Pay (General) Regulations 1982 (SI 1982/894), reg 9B* respectively. See also MATERNITY AND PARENTAL RIGHTS (31) and SICKNESS AND SICK PAY (42).

29.10   OTHER CONSEQUENCES OF INSOLVENCY AND RELATED EVENTS

Insolvency frequently necessitates the dismissal of the employees formerly engaged by the insolvent business. Insolvency itself does not absolve employers from the duty to have consultation with the unions and employees before the dismissal notices are sent out (see the cases cited in **37.6** REDUNDANCY – II).

29.10   Insolvency of Employer

The *Transfer of Undertakings (Protection of Employment) Regulations 2006 (SI 2006/246)*, *regs 8 and 9* make special provision with regard to employee rights where at the time of a relevant transfer the transferor is subject to relevant insolvency proceedings. See **50.11** TRANSFER OF UNDERTAKINGS. The special provision for the (partial) disapplication of *TUPE* in insolvency situations applies only when the *TUPE* transfer occurs after insolvency proceedings have been formally 'instituted' and when the insolvency practitioner is acting in that capacity and has been appointed as such; see *Secretary of State for Trade and Industry v Slater and others* [2007] IRLR 928. The effect of TUPE is partially disapplied where the employer is in insolvency proceedings which are 'relevant insolvency proceedings' within *reg 8(6)* of *TUPE*. The effects of *TUPE* are disapplied almost in their entirety (NB but not in respect of the information and consultation obligations in *regs 11* and *13–16* of *TUPE*) if the insolvency proceedings fall within *reg 8(7)* of *TUPE*. Whether insolvency proceedings are 'relevant' insolvency proceedings within *reg 8(6)* or *(7)* of *TUPE* depends on whether they were instituted 'with a view to the liquidation of the assets' of the employer.

The EAT held that as the primary object of an administration is to rescue the company as a going concern that purpose is inconsistent with the liquidation of the assets of the company so that an administration can never fall within *reg 8(7)* of *TUPE*; *OTG Ltd v Barke* [2011] IRLR 272. The Court of Appeal in *Key2Law (Surrey) LLP v De'Antiquis* [2011] EWCA Civ 1567, [2012] IRLR 212 has confirmed that the "absolute" approach to administration proceedings applies and not the "fact-based" approach. Administration proceedings instituted pursuant to *Insolvency Act 1986, Sch B1* never fall within *TUPE*, *reg 8(7)*. *TUPE* applies to companies in administration and there is no scope for argument on the individual facts of each case.

Reg 8(7) does not apply to the purchase of a business or assets from a company in administration, including sales using pre-pack arrangements, so that in such a case the employees of the insolvent transferor will transfer to the purchaser. In *Pressure Coolers Ltd v Molloy* [2011] IRLR 630 the EAT considered the effect of *TUPE* on liability to pay compensation in a pre-pack administration, where the claimant, after having been dismissed by the transferee on redundancy grounds, had brought successful employment tribunal claims. Adopting a purposive approach to *TUPE*, *reg 8(3)*, the EAT concluded that liability lay with the transferee, not the Secretary of State, because the dismissal had occurred after the transfer date.

Subject to the application of the *Transfer of Undertakings (Protection of Employment) Regulations* (see TRANSFER OF UNDERTAKINGS (50)), the effect of a winding-up order made by the court is to terminate the contracts of employment made by the company (*Re General Rolling Stock Co* (1866) LR 1 Eq 346; *Measures Bros Ltd v Measures* [1910] 2 Ch 248). The same occurs where a receiver is appointed by the court (*Reid v Explosives Co Ltd* (1887) 19 QBD 264; *Midland Counties District Bank Ltd v Attwood* [1905] 1 Ch 357), and if employees continue to work for the business they will be deemed to have entered into new contracts of employment with the receiver.

However, a voluntary winding-up does not terminate contracts of employment, because the liquidator is an officer of the company and the personality of the employer does not change (*Midland Counties District Bank*, above). Nor does the appointment of a (contractual) receiver who is an agent of the company otherwise than by the court (eg under a loan security agreement) have that effect, at any rate unless the employees concerned are directors or managers who could not continue to perform their functions without a conflict with the exercise of the receiver's powers (*Re Foster Clark Ltd's Indenture Trusts* [1966] 1 WLR 125; *Re Mack Trucks (Britain) Ltd* [1967] 1 WLR 780; *Griffiths v Secretary of State for Social Services* [1974] QB 468; *Nicoll v Cutts* [1985] PCC 311; *Re Ferranti International plc* [1994] 4 All ER 300 (Ch D), [1995] 2 All ER 65 (HL)). See also *Deaway Trading Ltd v Calverley* [1973] 3 All ER 776; and *Pambakian v Brentford Nylons Ltd* [1978] ICR 665, 122 Sol Jo 177, EAT. The appointment of an administrator, as agent of the employer, does not automatically terminate contracts of employment.

The institution of insolvency proceedings gives rise to a statutory moratorium on commencing or pursuing proceedings against the insolvent employer without the consent of the insolvency practitioner or the court; *Insolvency Act 1986, Sch B1*. Exceptional circumstances will be required before the courts will only lift the moratorium to permit employees seeking to enforce money claims for protective awards, unfair dismissal etc; see *Unite the Union v Nortel Networks UK Ltd (in administration)* [2010] EWHC 826 (Ch), [2010] IRLR 1042.

29.11 Liability of administrative receivers and administrators

An administrative receiver is, essentially, a receiver or manager of substantially the whole of a company's property appointed on behalf of the holders of debentures secured by a floating charge (*Insolvency Act 1986, s 29(2)*). By contrast, a person may be appointed as the administrator of a company by an administration order of the court, by the holder of a floating charge or by the company or its directors (*Insolvency Act 1986, Sch B1 paras 10, 14 and 22* respectively). The administrative receiver or administrator will be treated as adopting the contract of employment of an employee if he continues the employment relationship for 14 days after appointment (*Insolvency Act 1986, s 44(2)* and *Sch B1, para 99(5)(a)*). An administrative receiver or administrator will not be able to avoid adoption of the contract simply by writing to employees expressly to state that he is not adopting the contracts. If he takes advantage of the services of existing employees without negotiating new contracts of employment for more than 14 days he will be regarded as having adopted their contracts (*Powdrill v Watson* [1995] 2 AC 394; see also *Re Antal International Ltd* [2003] EWHC 1339 (Ch), [2003] 2 BCLC 406).

An administrative receiver will be personally liable on any contract of employment adopted by him in carrying out his functions. Any such liability is limited to 'qualifying liabilities', essentially contractual liabilities for payment of a sum by way of wages or salary or contribution to an occupational pension scheme where that liability is incurred while the administrative receiver is in office and in respect of services rendered wholly or partly after the adoption of the employment contract. However, the administrative receiver is entitled to be indemnified out of the company's assets (*Insolvency Act 1986, s 44* as amended by *Insolvency Act 1994*). For the law prior to 15 March 1994, see *Powdrill v Watson* [1995] 2 AC 394.

An administrator does not undertake a personal liability. 'Qualifying liabilities' for wages, salary and pension contributions after the adoption of the contract are, however, given 'super priority' in that they are charged on the company's property in their custody or control in priority to most other charges and securities including the fees and expenses of the administration (*Insolvency Act 1986, Schedule B1, para 99*; see also *Re Allders Department Stores Ltd (in administration)* [2005] ICR 867). In *Krasner v McMath* [2005] EWCA Civ 1072, [2006] ICR 205 the Court of Appeal concluded that an administrator's liabilities to employees of a company in administration for protective awards and payments in lieu of notice were not payable in priority to the expenses of the administration (save that any payments in lieu of notice where an employer did not require an employee to work during his notice period and paid his wages attributable to that period in a lump sum would be payable in priority as such payments constitute wages as set out in *Delaney v Staples (RJ) (t/a De Montfort Recruitment)* [1992] 1 AC 687, [1992] ICR 483, HL).

In *Larsen v Henderson* [1990] IRLR 512 an important suggestion was made by the Scottish Court of Session that a receiver owes a duty of care to the employees of a company in receivership to adopt such method of achieving his desired end as will have the least adverse effect upon them. There is considerable doubt as to whether this suggestion is, in fact, correct.

30   Part-Time Workers

30.1   LEGAL SOURCES

Part-time workers are protected from discrimination under both European and domestic law.

- The European Council adopted *Directive 97/81/EC* on part-time work (containing '*the Framework Agreement*') on 15 December 1997. The *Framework Agreement* was concluded by the European Social Partners and is aimed at eliminating discrimination against part-time workers and contributing to the encouragement and development of part-time work. The *Directive* was given force in the United Kingdom by a second directive, *Directive 98/23/EC*.

- The European Courts have held that the prohibition on discrimination in cl 4 of the *Framework Agreement* is a specific expression of the principle of equality, which is a fundamental principle of EU law, and that cl 4 must be interpreted against that backdrop. See, for example: *Istituto Nazionale della Previdenza Sociale v Bruno*: C-395/08 & C-396/08, [2010] IRLR 890.

- The Directive has been implemented domestically by the *Part-Time Workers (Prevention of Less Favourable Treatment) Regulations 2000 (SI 2000/1551)* ('the Regulations'), as amended. Importantly, however, the Regulations were made under *s 19* of the *Employment Relations Act 1999* and not *s 2* of the *European Communities Act 1972* and, in some respects, the protections in the *Regulations* go beyond those mandated by the *Directive* (see further **30.20** below).

The *Regulations* provide a simpler, gender-neutral route than the anti-discrimination legislation for tackling discrimination against part-time workers. A part-time worker may still, however, have a claim in the alternative under the *Equality Act 2010* or *Equal Pay Act 1970*. In *Voss v Land Berlin*: C-300/06 [2007] ECR I-10573, [2008] 1 CMLR 49, for example, the ECJ held that a difference in treatment which is detrimental to part-time workers could be contrary to the principle of equal pay and therefore require objective justification. See also, for example, *Pike v Somerset County Council* [2009] EWCA Civ 808, [2010] ICR 46, [2009] IRLR 870 (in relation to a provision of the *Teachers' Superannuation (Consolidation) Regulations 1988* which disadvantaged part-time workers); *Meerts v Proost NV*: C-116/08 [2010] All ER (EC) 1085, ECJ (in relation to notice pay for workers who are taking part-time parental leave); and *Copple v Littlewoods plc* [2012] ICR 354 (in relation to occupational pension schemes). This chapter is concerned with the *Regulations* only.

As to the application of sex discrimination legislation to part-time workers, see DISCRIMINATION AND EQUAL OPPORTUNITIES I (10), II (11), and III (12)and EQUAL PAY (21).

30.2   Guidance Material

Sections 20 and *21* of the *Employment Relations Act 1999* allow the Secretary of State to issue a Code of Practice, broadly in relation to part-time work and the *Framework Agreement*. To date, no code has been issued. BERR (as it then was) issued Guidance Notes to accompany the *Regulations* which provide advice on how to comply with the law as well as on how employers can widen access to part-time work, although these do not appear to have been updated (www.bis.gov.uk/files/file23861.pdf). Some limited guidance is provided in the Explanatory Note to the *Regulations*.

30.3   Part-Time Workers

30.3   Direct effect

In *Zentralbetriebsrat der Landeskrankenhauser Tirols v Land Tirol*: C-486/08 [2010] IRLR 631, the ECJ held that *cl 4(1)–(2)* of the *Framework Agreement* (i.e. the non-discrimination provision) is unconditional and sufficiently precise for individuals to be able to rely upon it before a national court (see paragraphs 21–25). This is consistent with the approach taken by the domestic courts. In *R (on the application of Manson (Finian)) v Ministry of Defence* [2005] EWHC 427 (Admin), [2005] All ER (D) 270 (Feb), Moses J considered, *obiter*, that *cl 4* of the *Framework Agreement* has direct effect. In *Christie v Department for Constitutional Affairs and Department for Work and Pensions* [2007] ICR 1553, an appeal against a decision that there was no directly enforceable right did not get through the EAT 'sift'. The President refused leave for the point to be argued and did not express any opinion on it (see [23]).

30.4   WHO HAS THE RIGHT?

Workers

The majority of rights under the *Regulations* are granted to 'workers'. The definition of 'worker' in *reg 1(2)* is the same as that in *s 230(3)* of the *Employment Rights Act 1996*. It covers individuals who have entered into, work or worked under a contract of employment or any other contract, whether express or implied and (if it is express) whether oral or in writing, whereby the individual undertakes to do or perform personally any work or services for another party to the contract, whose status is not by virtue of the contract that of a client or customer of any profession or business undertaking carried on by the individual (see EMPLOYEE, SELF-EMPLOYED OR WORKER? (14)).

Applicants for employment are not within the scope of the *Regulations*. In addition, it is important to note that *reg 7(1)* (unfair dismissal) applies only to 'employees' (see **30.21**).

The *Regulations* apply to those in Crown employment and to House of Lords and House of Commons staff: *regs 12, 14* and *15*. They also apply to persons appointed as police cadets or holding the office of constable other than under a contract of employment, who are treated as employed under a contract of employment for these purposes: *reg 16*. Special provisions apply to constables who are seconded to the Serious Organised Crime Agency: *regs 16(1A)–(1B)*.

The *Framework Agreement* applies to 'workers who have an employment contract or employment relationship as defined by the law, collective agreement or practice in force in each Member State'. In *O'Brien v Ministry of Justice*: C-393/10 [2012] IRLR 412 the CJEU explained:

- None of the terms 'worker', 'employment contract' or 'employment relationship' are defined in the *Framework Agreement*. The *Directive* and the *Framework Agreement* do not aim at complete harmonisation of national laws in this area, but only to establish a general framework for eliminating discrimination against part-time workers. Member States are free to define those terms in accordance with national law and practice. It is for national law to determine whether a person in part-time work has a contract of employment or an employment relationship.

- However, Member States may not apply rules which are liable to jeopardise the achievement of the objective pursued by the *Framework Agreement* and deprive it of its effectiveness. In particular, a Member State cannot remove certain categories of people from the scope of the protection offered by the *Framework Agreement* at will, violating its effectiveness.

• The exclusion of fee-paid judges from the protection of the Regulations would be permitted only if the nature of the employment relationship concerned is "*substantially different*" from that between employers and their employees who are 'workers' under national law.

In *Ministry of Justice (formerly Department for Constitutional Affairs) v O'Brien* [2013] UKSC 6, [2013] 1 WLR 522, the Supreme Court held that fee-paid judges are 'workers' for the purposes of the *Regulations*. Recorders were not self-employed free agents who could make their own choices as to the work they would do, and where and when that work was to be done.

30.5 Casual workers and members of the armed forces

In *Wippel v Peek & Cloppenburg Gmbh & Co Kg*: C-313/02 [2004] ECR I-9483, [2005] ICR 1604, the ECJ considered the status of 'framework contracts of employment' or 'work on demand' contracts, which set out applicable rates of pay, but provide no fixed working hours, no guarantee of income, and that the worker can accept or refuse the job offered each week without having to give any reason for doing so. The ECJ considered that such contracts do fall within the scope of the *Directive*, provided that the following conditions are met: (a) that such workers have a contract or employment relationship recognised by law, collective agreement or practices in force in the member state; (b) that they work 'part-time', ie their normal working hours are less than those of a comparable full-time worker; and (c) that in regard to part-time workers working on a casual basis, the member state has not excluded them from the benefit of the terms of the *Framework Agreement*, pursuant to *cl 2(2)*.

Under UK law, a framework contract would lack the mutuality of obligation necessary to amount to a contract of employment (see EMPLOYEE, SELF-EMPLOYED OR WORKER? (14)). Depending on the precise terms of the framework contract, an individual may also fall outside the domestic definition of a 'worker' if he or she has not 'undertaken to perform any work or services', e.g. if the individual is not obliged to accept any work offered to her under the framework contract.

As to the armed forces:

• The *Regulations* apply to members of the armed forces, subject to specific exceptions: *reg 13(1)*. They apply to individuals employed by Reserve Associations established for the purposes of *Part XI* of the *Reserve Forces Act 1996* ('the 1996 Act'): *reg 13(1)*. However, they do not apply to service as a member of the reserve forces in so far as that service consists of undertaking training obligations under *ss 38, 40* or *41* of the *Reserve Forces Act 1980, s 22* of the *Reserve Forces Act 1996* ('the 1996 Act'), regulations made under *s 4* of the *1996 Act* or voluntary training or duties under *s 27* of the *1996 Act*: *reg 13(2)*.

• *Reg 7(1)* (unfair dismissal) does not apply to members of the armed forces: *reg 13(1)*. In addition, a complaint concerning the service of any person as a member of the armed forces may only be presented to an employment tribunal under *reg 8* of the *Regulations* if that person has already made a complaint in respect of the same matter to an officer under the service redress procedures, and that complaint has not been withdrawn: *reg 13(3)–(6)*.

Is the exclusion in respect of reservists in *reg 13(2)* compatible with the Directive? At first instance in *R (on the application of Manson (Finian)) v Ministry of Defence* [2005] EWHC 427 (Admin), [2005] All ER (D) 270 (Feb), Moses J expressed the obiter view that it is compatible. *Cl 2(2)* of the *Framework Agreement* permits member states to exclude part-time workers who work on a casual basis from the protections of the *Framework Agreement*, provided that they do so for objective reasons and after prescribed consultation.

30.5 Part-Time Workers

Moses J noted that 'casual worker' is not defined: it is a term left to member states to define pursuant to *recital 16* and to the *Framework Agreement* (although any definition must not diminish the class of part-time worker so as to deprive the *Directive* of any force).

30.6 Fee-paid holders of judicial office

The *Regulations* do not apply to any individual in his capacity as the holder of a judicial office if he is remunerated on a daily fee-paid basis: *reg 17*.

Both the Court of Appeal in *O'Brien (O'Brien v Department for Constitutional Affairs* [2008] EWCA Civ 1448, [2009] ICR 593, [2009] IRLR 294) and, earlier, the EAT in *Christie v (1) Department for Constitutional Affairs and (2) Department for Work and Pensions* [2007] ICR 1553, a case brought by a part-time chairman of various social security appeal tribunals, had concluded that the exclusion in *reg 17* was compatible with the Directive, being consistent with the discretion given by the *Directive* and the *Framework Agreement* to member states. The Supreme Court in *O'Brien* [2010] UKSC 34, [2010] IRLR 883 took a more cautious approach. It noted that it was common ground: (1) that there was no single definition of "worker" for all Community law purposes; (2) that in contrast to the position under other Directives (where references to workers have an autonomous European meaning), the effect of *cl 2(1)* of the *Framework Agreement* read with *recital 16* of the *Directive* was to make domestic law relevant to the interpretation of the expression 'worker'; but also (3) that domestic law must respect the underlying purposes of the EU legislation and must not oust or "trump" the principles underlying that legislation in such a way as to frustrate them. As to how those principles fell to be applied in relation to the exclusion in *reg 17*, a reference to the CJEU was necessary. The Court added that it was a cause for concern that the exclusion in *reg 17* "has some appearance of being a deliberate ad hoc exclusion of a particular category while their full-time or salaried part-time colleagues, doing the same or similar work, will be entitled to judicial pensions on retirement".

In March 2012 the CJEU gave judgment in *O'Brien*: C-393/10 [2012] IRLR 412, holding that:

• It is for each Member State to define the concept of 'workers who have an employment contract or an employment relationship' for the purposes of the *Framework Agreement*. However, Member States may not apply rules which are liable to jeopardise the achievement of the objective pursued by the *Framework Agreement* and deprive it of its effectiveness, by arbitrarily excluding a category of persons from the protection the *Framework Agreement* offers.

• The exclusion of fee-paid judges from the protection of the *Regulations* would be permitted only if the nature of the employment relationship concerned is "*substantially different*" from the hat between employers and their employees who are 'workers' under national law.

• The term "worker" is used in the definition of the scope of the *Framework Agreement* to draw a distinction from a self-employed person, and the national court would have to bear in mind that this distinction is part of the spirit of the *Framework Agreement*. It would be necessary for the national court to consider the rules for appointing and removing judges, and the way in which their work is organised. For example, judges are expected to work during defined times and periods, and are entitled to sick pay, maternity or paternity pay and other similar benefits. The CJEU also noted that the fact that judges are subject to terms of service and might be regarded as workers within the meaning of cl 2.1 of the *Framework Agreement* does not undermine the principle of the independence of the judiciary or the right of Member States to provide a particular status for the judiciary. It merely aims to extend to those judges the scope of the principle of equal treatment and to protect them against discrimination as compared with full-time workers.

- Full-time judges and recorders perform essentially the same activity. Accordingly, if fee-paid judges are workers for these purposes, the *Framework Agreement* precludes discrimination between full-time judges and fee-paid part-time judges for the purposes of access to the relevant retirement pension scheme, unless such a difference in treatment can be justified by objective reasons. Again, whether or not that is so would be a matter for the national court. However, the CJEU noted that "*budgetary considerations cannot justify discrimination*".

In *Ministry of Justice (formerly Department for Constitutional Affairs) v O'Brien* [2013] UKSC 6, [2013] 1 WLR 522, the Supreme Court held, in light of the CJEU's judgment, that fee-paid judges are 'workers' for the purposes of the *Regulations*. Recorders are not self-employed free agents who can make their own choices as to the work they do, and where and when they do that work. They are expected to observe the terms and conditions of their appointment, and may be disciplined if they fail to do so. The Court noted that the very fact that most recorders are self-employed barristers or solicitors merely serves to underline the different character of their commitment to the public service when they undertake the office of recorder. They are in an employment relationship within the meaning of cl 2.1 of the *Framework Agreement* and so must be treated as "workers" for the purposes of the *Regulations*.

30.7 QUALIFYING PERIOD

There is no qualifying period for entitlement to the rights conferred by the *Regulations*.

30.8 DISCRIMINATION

Less favourable treatment

A part-time worker has the right not to be treated by his employer less favourably than a comparable full-time worker: (a) as regards the terms of his contract; or (b) by being subjected to any other detriment by his employer: *reg 5(1)*. However, the right applies only if the treatment is on the ground that the worker is a part-time worker, and if it is not objectively justified: *reg 5(2)*.

A person is being treated less favourably 'as regards the terms of his contract' if those contractual terms are less favourable. He or she does not have to wait until that term is triggered to his detriment before beginning proceedings: see *Sharma v Manchester City Council* [2008] ICR 623, at [45].

It is likely that the same approach will be taken to 'detriment' as has been adopted in relation to other anti-discrimination provisions (see DISCRIMINATION AND EQUAL OPPORTUNITIES – I (10)). Pressuring an individual to work full time, issuing an ultimatum to that effect, or selecting him or her for redundancy are all examples of potential less favourable treatment. Requiring a part-time worker to work a higher proportion of 'standby' to rostered hours than a full-time worker can also constitute a detriment: *Gibson v Scottish Ambulance Service* (EATS/0052/04) (16 December 2004) at [13].

30.9 *The pro rata principle*

The *Regulations* require that the 'pro rata principle' be applied to determine whether a part-time worker has been treated less favourably than a comparable full-time worker unless it is inappropriate: *reg 5(3)*. That principle – which is defined in *reg 1(2)* – means that where a comparable full-time worker receives or is entitled to receive pay or some other benefit, a part-time worker is to receive or be entitled to receive not less than the proportion of that pay or other benefit that the number of his weekly hours bears to the number of weekly hours of the comparable full-time worker. 'Weekly hours' means, by *reg 1(3)*: (a) the number of hours a worker is required to work under his contract of employment in a week in which he has no absences from work and does not work any overtime; or (b) where the number of such hours varies according to a cycle, the average number of such hours.

The original source for the 'pro rata principle' is *cl 4(2)* of the *Framework Agreement*.

A tribunal considering *reg 5* should always consider whether it is 'appropriate' to apply the pro rata principle. It will usually be appropriate to do so where the claim is based on a difference in pay for hours worked in the ordinary course of events: *James v Great North Eastern Railway* [2005] All ER (D) 15 (Mar), EAT. However, in *Matthews v Kent and Medway Towns Fire Authority*, a tribunal held that it was inappropriate to apply the pro rata principle over the whole range of a financial package for fire fighters which included pension benefit, sick pay and pay for additional duties. This conclusion was not challenged on appeal (House of Lords decision reported at [2006] ICR 365).

The role of the pro rata principle was further considered by the EAT and then the Court of Session in *McMenemy v Capita Business Services Ltd* [2007] IRLR 400 (CS). Employees at a call centre which operated seven days a week were entitled to public holidays which 'fell on [their] normal working day'. The claimant worked part-time, Wednesday to Friday. He was not allowed time off in lieu when public holidays fell on a Monday, although full-time workers in his team who normally worked on Mondays were given the day off. He argued that he had a stand-alone right to pro rata treatment as regards holidays, and that he could demonstrate that he received less holiday than a comparable full-time worker. The tribunal, EAT and Court of Session dismissed his claim. The EAT held that the tribunal had been entitled to conclude that the reason that the claimant was receiving the treatment complained of was not because he was a part-time worker but because he did not work on a Monday. The tribunal did not err in failing to have regard to the pro rata principle because *reg 5(3)* is not an independent right, and is not something that a tribunal must have in mind when considering whether any less favourable treatment is on the ground that the employee is a part-time worker (see **30.16** below). The Court of Session agreed: the pro-rata principle relates only to the logically first question whether or not a part-time worker has been treated less favourably than a full-time worker.

30.10   *Overtime*

Where part-time workers only receive overtime rates once they have worked the equivalent of a full-time worker's weekly hours, not once they have completed the hours they themselves ordinarily work each week, there is no less favourable treatment: *reg 5(4)*. This reflects the orthodox position with regards to equal pay: see *Stadt Lengerich v Helmig* [1996] ICR 35, CJEU and **21.12 EQUAL PAY**. It does not affect the right of part-time workers to receive other payments such as unsocial hours payments, weekend payments or other forms of enhanced pay on comparable terms to full-time workers.

In *James v Great North Eastern Railways* [2005] All ER (D) 15 (Mar), the EAT held that the *reg 5(4)* exception did not apply to an 'additional hours payment' made to full-time workers. Full-time employees were contractually obliged to work a 40 hour week judged over the length of an 8-week roster cycle. Employees could also be required to work overtime. Pay for the first 35 hours was paid at basic rate; they then received an 'additional hours payment' for the next five hours, being 1¼ times basic pay, and any overtime over and above the 40 hours was paid at 1¼ times basic pay. Pay for the set hours for part-time workers was at the same basic rate as full-time equivalent posts, with pay for any overtime up to 35 hours being at the same basic rate. Pay for additional hours over 35 hours was at 1¼ times basic pay but part-time workers did not receive an 'additional hours payment'. The EAT held that the payment in question must amount to a 'true' overtime payment to fall within the *reg 5(4)* exception. The 'additional hours payment' made to full-time workers was pay for the contractual rostered hours that they worked and, accordingly, the *reg 5(4)* was not applicable.

30.11 *Paid annual leave*

In *Zentralbetriebsrat der Landeskrankenhauser Tirols v Land Tirol* C-486/08, [2010] IRLR 631 the CJEU held that the pro rata principle in *cl 4(2)* of the *Framework Agreement* could not be applied to reduce ex post facto annual leave which had been accumulated (but not yet taken) during a period of full-time work. EU law, and in particular *cl 4(2)*, precluded a national provision under which a worker who moved from full- to part-time either suffered a reduction in the paid annual leave which he had accumulated but not been able to exercise while working full-time, or was required to take that leave with a reduced level of pay. *Land Tirol* was endorsed by the CJEU in *Heimann v Kaiser GmbH*: C-229/11 [2013] IRLR 48.

30.12 *Occupational Pensions*

In *Istituto Nazionale della Previdenza Sociale v Bruno* C-395/08 & C-396/08, [2010] IRLR 890, the CJEU held that the *Framework Agreement* precluded national legislation under which part-time vertical-cyclical workers (i.e. workers working only during certain periods of the year) were treated less favourably than comparable full-time workers in relation to the qualifying period for accruing pension rights, unless that treatment could be objectively justified. The Court held, in particular, that the prohibition of discrimination in relation to "employment conditions" found in the *Framework Agreement* and *Directive* extended to occupational pensions dependent on an employment relationship (and the ECJ gave guidance as to when social-security type pensions would fall within that definition) and confirmed that that prohibition extended to the future effects of situations which arose prior to the *Framework Agreement* and *Directive* coming into force (e.g. periods of employment before the *Directive* came into force which were qualifying service requirements for future retirement pensions).

30.13 Comparators

The *Regulations* involve the making of a comparison between a part-time worker and a 'comparable' full-time worker, unless *regs 3* and *4* apply. Special provisions apply in relation to a full-time worker who drops down to part-time, or someone returning from less than 12 months' maternity leave.

30.14 *Actual comparator*

Do the *Regulations* require an 'actual' comparator (as is ordinarily the case under the *Equal Pay Act 1970*: see **21.9** EQUAL PAY), or will a hypothetical comparator suffice (as under the *Equality Act 2010*: see **10.15** DISCRIMNATION AND EQUAL OPPORTUNITIES – I)?

- The wording of the *Regulations* suggests that a narrow comparison is all that is envisaged, and that if there is no full-time comparator employed by the same employer, any claim will fail. However, the wording of the *Directive* is somewhat wider, stating that 'where there is no comparable full-time worker in the same establishment, the comparison shall be made by reference to the applicable collective agreement or, where there is no applicable collective agreement, in accordance with national law, collective agreements or practice'.

- In *Carl v University of Sheffield* [2009] ICR 1286, the EAT confirmed that a part-time worker must show that he or she has been treated less favourably than an *actual* full-time comparator. The definition of a comparable full-time worker in *reg 2(4)* does not include the "or would" formula found in *s 1(1)(a)* of the *Sex Discrimination Act 1975* or *s 1(1)(a)* of the *Race Relations Act 1976* (i.e. "*a person discriminates against a woman if … on the ground of her sex he treats her less favourably than he treats or would treat a man*"). The EAT noted that a hypothetical comparator is expressly permitted in certain circumstances under *regs 3* and *4* and that this suggests that these two exceptional categories are the only cases in which reliance on a hypothetical comparator is permissible. In addition, the EAT endorsed the dicta of Lady Smith in *McMenemy v Capita Business Services Ltd* [2006] IRLR 761 to the effect that a hypothetical comparator was probably 'not apposite' under the *Regulations* and that the *Framework Agreement* does not require any other conclusion. In *McMenemy*, Lady Smith had noted that the ECJ had held in *Wippel v Peek & Cloppenburg GmbH & Co KG* [2005] ICR 1604 that a particular part-time contract was not in breach of the *Directive* when there was no full-time worker in the establishment with the same type of contract or employment relationship to enable a comparison and had not gone on to construct a hypothetical comparator.

• The decision in *Carl* is consistent with the early observations of the EAT in *Tyson v Concurrent Systems Inc Ltd* [2003] All ER (D) 09 (Sep) and *Lynch v Royal Mail Group plc* [2003] All ER (D) 11 (Sep). The effect of this restriction is likely to be that the *Regulations* will not provide protection for the many part-time workers who do jobs only done by part-timers.

30.15 *Identifying 'part-time' and 'full-time' workers*

The first step is to identify 'full-time workers' and 'part-time workers'.

• A worker is a part-time worker if he is 'paid wholly or in part by reference to the time he works and, having regard to the custom and practice of the employer in relation to workers employed by the worker's employer under the same type of contract, is not identifiable as a full-time worker': *reg 2(2)*.

• By contrast, he is a full-time worker if he is 'paid wholly or in part by reference to the time he works and, having regard to the custom and practice of the employer in relation to workers employed by the worker's employer under the same type of contract, is identifiable as a full-time worker': *reg 2(1)*.

These definitions are structured by reference to workers employed under "*the same type of contract*". *Reg 2(3)* provides that each of the following groups shall be regarded as being employed under different types of contract, for the purposes both of determining whether a worker is full- or part-time in the first place and of comparing the treatment of full- and part-time workers: (a) employees employed under a contract that is not a contract of apprenticeship; (b) employees employed under a contract of apprenticeship; (c) workers who are not employees; and (d) any other description of worker that it is reasonable for the employer to treat differently from other workers on the ground that workers of that description have a different type of contract. As to the authorities on the meaning of "*the same type of contract*" in this context, see further **30.16** below.

The *Regulations* used to provide that those working under fixed term contracts were employed under different types of contract to those who worked under permanent contracts. However, the distinction between fixed-term and permanent contracts was removed by the *Part-Time Workers (Prevention of Less Favourable Treatment) Regulations 2000 (Amendment) Regulations 2002, SI 2002/2035* with effect from 1 October 2002 in order to give effect to the *Fixed-Term Employees (Prevention of Less Favourable Treatment) Regulations 2002, SI 2002/2034*, which prohibit discrimination between fixed term employees and comparable permanent employees.

In *Hudson v University of Oxford* [2007] EWCA Civ 336, [2007] All ER (D) 356 (Feb) the Court of Appeal allowed an appeal against a tribunal decision to strike out Mr Hudson's claim of less favourable treatment on the basis that it had no reasonable prospects of success. Mr Hudson was employed by the University under two part-time contracts. He claimed that, in reality, he had had one full-time job and that he had been less favourably treated when compared with other full-time employees. The Court of Appeal considered it arguable that (1) his contention that the reality was that he had a single full-time job did not necessarily preclude him from having been a part-time worker as defined in *reg 2(2)* of the *Regulations*; (2) to the extent that he was a part-time worker under one of his contracts, he was, on account of his job, treated less favourably than relevant full-time comparators; and

(3) he was so treated on the ground that he was contractually and within the terms of *reg 2* a part-time worker. He was therefore permitted to pursue his claims under the *Regulations*. The Court of Appeal left open the question whether the comparison should be between a part-time worker doing two jobs and a full-time worker doing both jobs together, or whether each part-time contract had to be looked at separately and compared with a full-time worker under separate contracts.

30.16 *Identifying a 'comparable full-time worker'*

The second step is to determine whether the part-time workers' full-time colleagues are 'comparable full-time workers' within the meaning of *reg 2(4)*.

A full-time worker will be a 'comparable full-time worker' in relation to a claimant part-time worker within the meaning of *reg 2(4)* where, at the time that the less favourable treatment occurs:

(a)   both workers are employed by the same employer under the same type of contract, and both are engaged in the same or broadly similar work (having regard, where relevant, to whether they have a similar level of qualification, skills and experience); and

(b)   the full-time worker works or is based at the same establishment as the part-time worker.

If there are no full-time workers who satisfy the requirements in (a) above, a full-time worker who satisfies those requirements but who works or is based at a different establishment may be considered: *reg 2(4)(b)*.

In *O'Brien v Ministry of Justice*: C-393/10 [2012] IRLR 412 the CJEU noted that 'comparable full-time worker' is defined in *cl 3* of the *Framework Agreement* as 'a full-time worker in the same establishment having the same type of employment contract or relationship, who is engaged in the same or a similar work/occupation, due regard being given to other considerations which may include seniority and qualification/skills' and that *"those criteria are based on the content of the activity of the persons concerned"*. Accordingly, the CJEU concluded that full-time judges and recorders were in a comparable situation, notwithstanding that they have different careers as recorders retain the opportunity to practise as barristers, because they perform essentially the same activity.

30.17 *'Same type of contract'*

What does the requirement that a comparable full-time worker be employed by the same employer as the part-time worker *"under the same type of contract"* actually mean?

Reg 2(3) provides that the following categories of workers are employed under different types of contract: (a) *"employees employed under a contract that is not a contract of apprenticeship"*; (b) *"employees employed under a contract of apprenticeship"*; (c) *"workers who are not employees"*; and (d) workers in a long-stop category - *"any other description of worker that it is reasonable for the employer to treat differently from other workers on the ground that workers of that description have a different type of contract"*.

The leading authority is *Matthews v Kent and Medway Towns Fire Authority* [2004] ICR 257 (in the EAT); [2005] ICR 84 (in the Court of Appeal) and [2006] ICR 365 (in the House of Lords). This was a test case brought by part-time ('retained') firefighters who claimed that they were treated less favourably than comparable full-time firefighters in that they were denied access to statutory pension arrangements, they were denied increased pay for additional responsibilities and their sick pay arrangements were calculated on a less favourable basis. The Courts decided as follows:

30.17   Part-Time Workers

(a)   The ET and the EAT considered that the retained firefighters were employed under a different type of contract from full-time firefighters, as it was reasonable for the employer to treat them differently within the meaning of *reg 2(3)(d)*. The ET had found many differences and special features in working patterns as between the two groups.

(b)   The Court of Appeal took a different approach. It held that both retained and full-time firefighters belonged to category (a) in *reg 2(3)*, being employees employed under a contract that was not a contract of apprenticeship.

(c)   A majority of the House of Lords (Lord Mance dissenting) upheld the approach of the Court of Appeal. They held that the requirement that the part-time worker and the full-time worker proposed as a comparator be employed under the same type of contract is directed to comparable types of employment relationship rather than comparable terms and conditions of employment. The categories set out in *reg 2(3)* are defined broadly in a way that allows for a wide variety of different terms and conditions within each category. The categories are mutually exclusive. Under *reg 2(3)(d)* the courts are asked to examine a type of worker who is different from any of those previously mentioned in *reg 2(3)(a)–(c)*. While it is difficult to think of a type of contract which is different to those mentioned in *reg 2(3)(a)–(c)*, a contract will only fall within *reg 2(3)(d)* if a worker does not fall into one of the other categories. It is a long-stop or residual category. It is not designed to allow employers to single out particular kinds of part-time working arrangements and treat them differently from the rest.

In *Wippel v Peek & Cloppenburg GmbG & Co KG* [2005] ICR 1604 (see **30.4**), the ECJ considered the position of part-time workers who worked according to need under 'framework contracts'. It held that as there was no full-time worker who worked according to need under a 'framework contract', there was no comparable full-time worker who worked under the same type of employment contract or relationship as the part-time worker within the meaning of the *Framework Agreement*. The employment relationship differed, as to subject matter and basis, between a full-time worker (working under a 'traditional' contract) and the claimant (working under a 'framework contract').

30.18 *'The same or broadly similar work'*

Matthews v Kent and Medway Towns Fire Authority (see **30.17**) also provided guidance on what is meant by "*the same or broadly similar work*". The tribunal had held that retained firefighters were not engaged in the same or broadly similar work as full-time firefighters. That finding was upheld by the EAT and the Court of Appeal, but then rejected by the House of Lords:

(a)   The EAT and Court of Appeal found that full-time firefighters carried out measurable additional job functions, such as educational, preventive and administrative tasks which were not carried out by retained firefighters. There were differences in entry standards, probationary standards and on-going training, which led to differences in the level of qualification and skills. They noted that differences in recruitment procedures and promotion prospects also served to illustrate the different work carried out by full-time firefighters compared to retained firefighters, as full-time firefighters are recruited to do a job with measurable additional functions and overwhelmingly constitute the recruitment pool for promotion to higher grades. In short, the EAT and Court of Appeal did not accept that firefighting was the central role of all operational fire fighters, such that retained and full-time firefighters must be engaged in broadly similar work.

(b)   The House of Lords disagreed. The majority (Lord Nicholls, Lord Hope and Baroness Hale) held that the tribunal had erred in concentrating on the differences in the work carried out by retained and full-time firefighters, rather than assessing the weight to be given to the similarities in such work. They emphasised that tribunals are conducting a different exercise from that required by *s 1(4)* of the *Equal Pay Act 1970* (in the context of a scheme which imposes an equality clause upon the contracts of employment of women who are employed on like work with men (see **21.6 EQUAL PAY**)). The test in the *Regulations* is a threshold condition which is the precursor to considering whether there has been less favourable treatment which cannot be objectively justified. The question is not whether the work is different, but whether it is the same or broadly similar. The *Regulations* are inviting a comparison between two types of workers whose work will almost inevitably be different to some extent. In carrying out the assessment, particular weight should be given to the extent to which the work of part-time and full-time workers is exactly the same. If a large component of the work is exactly the same, the question is whether any differences are of such importance as to prevent the work of the two groups being regarded overall as 'the same or broadly similar'. Where both full- and part-timers do the same work, but the full-timers have extra activities with which to fill their time, this does not mean that the work under consideration is not nevertheless the same or broadly similar overall. The importance of the work which the workers do to the work of the enterprise as a whole is also of great importance in this assessment. If full-timers do the more important work and part-timers are brought in to do the more peripheral tasks, it is unlikely that the work of the two groups is the same or broadly similar. However, where full-timers and part-timers spend much of their time on the core activity of the enterprise, the fact that full-timers may do some extra tasks will not prevent their work being the same or broadly similar to that of the part-timers.

The case was remitted to the tribunal for reconsideration of whether the retained and full-time firefighters are engaged in the same or broadly similar work, where the ET determined that the part-time firefighters were carrying out the same or broadly similar work to the full-time firefighters. There was a substantial body of work comprising the firefighter's 'central duties' that were the same for both roles, and the full-timers' additional skills and experience, while relevant, did not contribute 'something different to the work'.

30.19 *The scope of the comparison*

The EAT in *Matthews v Kent and Medway Towns Fire Authority* [2004] ICR 257, EAT (see **30.12** above) followed the approach of the House of Lords in *Hayward v Cammell Laird Shipbuilders Ltd* [1988] AC 894 and held that each specific term of the contract must be compared, rather than a 'broad brush' comparison. In the House of Lords in *Matthews*, Baroness Hale (with whom Lord Nicholls and Lord Hope agreed) did not rule out the possibility that a less favourable term might be so well balanced by a more favourable one that it could not be said that part-timers were treated less favourably overall. Nor did she rule out the possibility that more favourable treatment on one point might supply justification for less favourable treatment on another. On the facts, however, she found it difficult to see how a differently structured pay package for retained fire-fighters could justify total exclusion from the pension or sick pay schemes, unrelated to the hours actually worked.

30.20 *Specific circumstances where a comparator is not required*

There are two circumstances in which *Regulations* do not require a strict comparative approach.

First, if an individual becomes a part-time worker having previously worked in a job on a full-time basis, he can compare his part-time conditions with his previous full-time contract. *Reg 3* applies where the worker was a full-time worker within the meaning of *reg 2(1)* but, following a termination or variation of his contract, he continues to work under a new or varied contract, whether of the same type or not, that requires him to work for a lower number of weekly hours than the number he was required to work immediately before the termination or variation. The effect of *reg 3(2)* is that *reg 5* applies to such a worker as if he were a part-time worker and as if there were a comparable full-time worker employed under the terms that applied to him immediately before the termination or variation.

Secondly, if an individual who had previously worked in a job on a full-time basis returns to a part-time role after a period of absence of up to twelve months, such as maternity leave, he or she can compare their new part-time conditions with their previous full-time contract: *reg 4*.

- This regulation applies where the worker was a full-time worker within the meaning of *reg 2(1)* immediately before the period of absence (irrespective of whether the absence followed a termination of her contract), and where she returns to work for the same employer within 12 months of the date on which her absence started. The worker must return to the same job or a job at the same level under a contract in which she is required to work for a number of weekly hours that is lower than the number she was required to work immediately before the period of absence, regardless of whether the new contract is a different contract or a varied contract, or whether it is of the same type as the original contract or not: *reg 4(1)*.

- *Reg 5* applies to such a worker as if she were a part-time worker and as if there were a comparable full-time worker employed under: (a) the contract under which she was employed immediately before the period of absence; or (b) where it is shown that, had she continued to work under the original contract, a variation would have been made to its term during the period of absence, the original contract including that variation: *reg 4(2)*.

30.21 'On the ground that the worker is a part-time worker'

It is not sufficient for a tribunal to be satisfied that a claimant part-time worker has been less favourably treated than his or her full-time comparator. Liability will lie only if the less favourable treatment is *"on the ground that the worker is a part-time worker"*: *reg 5(2)(a)*.

Unfortunately, there is a division between English and Scottish authority as to the meaning of *"on the ground that"* in *reg 5* of the *Regulations*. In England and Wales, the EAT held in *Carl v University of Sheffield* [2009] ICR 1286 that 'on the ground that' means that part-time work must be the effective and predominant cause of the less favourable treatment complained of; it need not be the only cause. This had similarly been the conclusion of the EAT in *Sharma v Manchester City Council* [2008] ICR 623, but the EAT in *Sharma* had not had cited to them a contrary decision of the Court of Session, *McMenemy v Capita Business Services Ltd* [2007] IRLR 400. In Scotland, *McMenemy* remains authority for the proposition that the less favourable treatment of part-time workers will only be prohibited where it is for the sole reason that the workers work part-time (following an earlier decision of the Scottish EAT in *Gibson v Scottish Ambulance Service* (EATS/0052/04)). In *Carl*, the EAT noted that it was not bound by decisions of the Court of Session and declined to follow the approach taken in *McMenemy*. Judge Peter Clark noted that the expression "on the ground that" or "on the grounds of" appears frequently in domestic legislation and agreed with Elias J in *Sharma* that domestic legislation may go further than the protection contained in the *Framework Agreement*.

It is respectfully submitted that the approach in *Carl* and *Sharma* is to be preferred. It was conceded in *McMenemy* that the *Regulations* should be construed consistently with the *Framework Agreement* and that they did not go further than the *Framework Agreement*. The Court of Session referred to the wording of *cl 4(1)* of the *Framework Agreement* to the effect that 'part-time workers shall not be treated in a less favourable manner than comparable full-time workers solely because they work part-time . . . ' and held that 'solely' means that less favourable treatment must be for the reason that workers work part-time and for that reason alone. It is submitted that the EAT in *Carl* was right to doubt the correctness of the original concession. The *Regulations* were made under *s 19* of the *Employment Relations Act 1999* and not under *s 2* of the *European Communities Act 1972*. It was therefore open to Parliament to go further than the *Framework Agreement*. It is further submitted that the absence of the word 'solely' in the *Regulations* is crucial to the analysis and that, properly construed, the *Regulations* do go further than the *Directive* in this regard. The phrase 'on the grounds that' in the *Regulations* should be interpreted in the same way as the 'on the prohibited grounds' test in other discrimination legislation (see **10.3–10.11 DISCRIMINATION AND EQUAL OPPORTUNITIES – I** for application of the 'on the prohibited grounds' test in other contexts).

In *Komeng v Sandwell MBC* [2011] EqLR 1053 the EAT commented, at [45], that tribunals should take care before accepting an explanation that the reason for less favourable treatment lies merely in general poor administration, because of the risk that this masks discrimination on prohibited grounds.

30.22 Objective justification

Any less favourable treatment may be justified on objective grounds: *reg 5(2)(b)*.

The concept of objective justification is treated in the same way under the *Regulations* as in other anti-discrimination contexts (see **11.9 DISCRIMINATION AND EQUAL OPPORTUNITIES – II** and **21.11 EQUAL PAY**). Less favourable treatment will be objectively justified only if it can be shown that the treatment: (1) has a legitimate objective, such as a genuine business objective; (2) is necessary to achieve that objective; and (3) is an appropriate way of achieving that objective.

In *O'Brien v Ministry of Justice*: C-393/10 [2012] IRLR 412 the CJEU commented that the concept 'objective grounds' within the meaning of cl 4 of the *Framework Agreement* must be understood as not permitting a difference in treatment between part-time workers and full-time workers to be justified on the basis that the difference "*is provided for by a general, abstract norm*" and, on the contrary, that the unequal treatment must "*respond to a genuine need be appropriate for achieving the objective pursued and be necessary for that purpose*" (see paragraph 64). The CJEU added, in this context, that "*budgetary considerations cannot justify discrimination*" (see paragraph 66). When the case was remitted to the Supreme Court, the Court rejected the Ministry of Justice's attempts to justify a difference in treatment in pension provision for part-time and full-time judges, holding that they were not made out on the evidence. It adopted the guidance given by Advocate General Kokott [2012] ICR 955 to the effect that the unequal treatment at issue must be justified "*by the existence of precise, concrete factors, characterising the employment condition concerned in its specific context and on the basis of objective and transparent criteria for examining the question whether that unequal treatment responds to a genuine need and whether it is appropriate and necessary for achieving the objective pursued*". It concluded that the aims of giving a greater reward to those who are thought to need it most or to those who make the greatest contribution, or recruiting a high quality judiciary might all be legitimate aims – but that the Ministry of Justice had failed to make out the specific basis for such justification on the evidence. For example, an employer might devise a scheme which rewarded its workers according to need rather than to their contribution, but the criteria would have to be precise and transparent, but that was not the case in relation to the provision for part-time judges, some of whom would need occupational pension provision, others of whom would not. Equally, the proper approach to differential contributions is to make special payments for extra responsibilities – which was not the case here. There was (the Court found) blanket discrimination between part-time and full-time judges which had not been justified. *O'Brien* concerned only a recorder, but the Court noted in terms that it seemed unlikely that the ministry's argument could be put any higher than it has been in relation to any other holder of part-time judicial office.

30.23   RIGHT TO RECEIVE A WRITTEN STATEMENT OF REASONS FOR LESS FAVOURABLE TREATMENT

A worker who considers that his employer may have treated him in a manner which infringes a right conferred upon him by *reg 5* may request in writing from his employer a written statement giving particulars of the reasons for the treatment: *reg 6*. The employer must provide such a statement within 21 days of the worker's request and such written statements will be admissible as evidence in any proceedings under the *Regulations*. A tribunal may draw inferences from an employer's refusal to answer or provision of an evasive or equivocal response: *reg 6(3)*.

Reg 6 does not apply where the treatment in question consists of the dismissal of an employee, and that employee is entitled to a written statement of reasons for his dismissal under *s 92* of the *Employment Rights Act 1996* (see **46.14, 46.15** TERMINATION OF EMPLOYMENT).

30.24   PROTECTION FROM DETRIMENT

A worker has the right, by *regs 7(2)–(3)*, not to be subjected to any detriment by an act, or deliberate failure to act, by his employer done on the ground that:

(i)   he has brought proceedings against the employer under the *Regulations*;

(ii)   he has requested a written statement under *reg 6*;

(iii)   he has given evidence or information in connection with any proceedings under the *Regulations* brought by any worker;

(iv)   he has done anything under the *Regulations* relating to his employer or any other person;

(v)   he has alleged that his employer has infringed the *Regulations*;

(vi)   he has refused or proposed to refuse to forego any right under the *Regulations*; or

(vii)   the employer believes or suspects that he has done or intends to do any of these things.

However, neither *reg 7(1)* (unfair dismissal) nor *reg 7(2)* (protection from detriment) applies in relation to an allegation that the employer has infringed the *Regulations* (or that the employer believes or suspects that the worker has made or intends to make such an allegation) if the allegation made by the worker is false and not made in good faith: *reg 7(4)*.

30.25   RELATIONSHIP WITH UNFAIR DISMISSAL

Reg 7(1) provides that an employee who is dismissed is to be regarded as unfairly dismissed for the purposes of *Part X* of the *Employment Rights Act 1996* if the reason or principal reason for his dismissal is that:

(i)   he has brought proceedings against the employer under the *Regulations*;

(ii)   he has requested a written statement under *reg 6*;

(iii)   he has given evidence or information in connection with any proceedings under the *Regulations* brought by any worker;

(iv)   he has done anything under the *Regulations* relating to his employer or any other person;

(v)   he has alleged that his employer has infringed the *Regulations*;

(vi)   he has refused or proposed to refuse to forego any right under the *Regulations*; or

(vii)   the employer believes or suspects that he has done or intends to do any of these things.

Save as set out in *reg 7*, a breach of the *Regulations* does not make any dismissal automatically unfair: *Pipe v Hendrickson Europe Ltd* [2003] All ER (D) 280 (Apr), EAT. In such cases, a tribunal must ascertain the reason for the dismissal, and then determine whether the dismissal was unfair within the terms of *s 98(4)* of the *Employment Rights Act 1996* (see UNFAIR DISMISSAL – II (52)). The act of discrimination may be an important factor for the tribunal to take into account when carrying out this evaluation, but it does not automatically follow that the dismissal is unfair.

30.26 APPLICATIONS TO AN EMPLOYMENT TRIBUNAL

A worker may present a complaint to an employment tribunal that his employer has infringed a right conferred on him by *reg 5* (less favourable treatment) or *reg 7(2)* (victimisation): *reg 8(1)*. Where a worker presents a complaint to a tribunal under the *Regulations*, it is for the employer to identify the ground for the less favourable treatment or detriment: *reg 8(6)*. A claim for breach of the *Regulations* that includes an allegation that the *Regulations* themselves are incompatible with *Directive 97/81* cannot be brought by way of judicial review, and must be brought in the tribunal: *R (on the application of Manson) v Ministry of Defence* [2005] EWCA Civ 1678; [2006] ICR 355.

30.27 TIME LIMITS

A claim must be presented to a tribunal before the end of the period of three months beginning with the date of the less favourable treatment or detriment to which the complaint relates: *reg 8(2)*. A six month time limit applies to complaints by members of the armed forces: *reg 8(2)*.

Where an act or failure to act is part of a series of similar acts or failures comprising the less favourable treatment, the time runs from the last of those acts. For the purposes of calculating the date of the less favourable treatment or detriment, *reg 8(4)* and *8(5)* provides that:

(a)   where a term in the contract is less favourable, that treatment shall be treated, subject to (b) below, as taking place on each day of the period during which the term is less favourable;

(b)   where an application relies on *regs 3* or *4* the less favourable treatment shall be treated as occurring on, and only on, in the case of *reg 3*, the first day on which the applicant worked under the new or varied contract and, in the case of *reg 4*, the day on which the applicant returned; and

(c)   a deliberate failure to act contrary to *reg 5* or *7(2)* shall be treated as done when it was decided on. In the absence of evidence establishing the contrary, a person shall be taken to decide not to act when he does an act inconsistent with doing the failed act, or if he has done no such inconsistent act, when the period expires within which he might reasonably have been expected to have done the failed act if it was to be done.

A tribunal may consider a complaint which is out of time if, in all the circumstances of the case, it considers that it is just and equitable to do so: *reg 8(3)*.

30.28 REMEDIES

Where an employment tribunal finds that a complaint presented to it under *reg 8* is well-founded, it shall take such of the following steps as it considers just and equitable:

(a)   *Making a declaration as to the rights of the complainant and the employer in relation to the matters to which the complaint relates: reg 8(7)(a).*

(b)   *Ordering the employer to pay compensation to the complainant: reg 8(7)(b).*

Where a tribunal orders compensation, the amount of the compensation awarded shall be such as the tribunal considers just and equitable in all the circumstances having regard to (a) the infringement to which the complaint relates, and (b) any loss which is attributable to the infringement having regard, in the case of an infringement of the right conferred by *reg 5*, to the pro rata principle, except where it is inappropriate to do so: *reg 8(9)*. The loss shall be taken to include any expenses reasonably incurred by the complainant in consequence of the infringement and loss of any benefit which he might reasonably be expected to have had but for the infringement: *reg 8(10)*.

Compensation in respect of less favourable treatment on the grounds of part-time status (i.e. less favourable treatment contrary to *reg 5* of the *Regulations*) will *not* include compensation for injury to feelings: *reg 8(11)*.

In *Tyson v Concurrent Systems Inc Ltd* [2003] All ER (D) 09 (Sep), EAT, the appellant sought to argue that stigma damages and stigma compensation were not excluded by *reg 8(11)*. The EAT doubted whether stigma damages which did not include loss of earnings produced by the stigma could be brought within the provisions of *reg 8*.

Normal principles of mitigation apply: *reg 8(12)*. Where the tribunal finds that the act, or failure to act, to which the complaint relates was to any extent caused or contributed to by the action of the complainant, it shall reduce the amount of the compensation by such proportion as it considers just and equitable having regard to that finding: *reg 8(13)*.

(c)   *Recommending that the employer take, within a specified period, action appearing to the tribunal to be reasonable, in all the circumstances of the case, for the purpose of obviating or reducing the adverse effect on the complainant of any matter to which the complaint relates: reg 8(7)(c).*

If the employer fails, without reasonable justification, to comply with a recommendation made by an employment tribunal under *reg 8(7)(c)* the tribunal may, if it thinks it just and equitable to do so, increase the amount of compensation required to be paid to the complainant in respect of the complaint where an order for compensation has already been made, or may make such an order for the first time: *reg 8(14)*.

(For a more detailed discussion of these rules in relation to other anti-discrimination legislation, see DISCRIMINATION AND EQUAL OPPORTUNITIES – III (12).)

30.29 RESTRICTION ON CONTRACTING OUT

The restriction on contracting out of employment rights contained in *s 203* of the *Employment Rights Act 1996* applies in relation to the *Regulations* as if they were contained in the *1996 Act: reg 9* (see **51.19, 51.20** UNFAIR DISMISSAL – I).

(The requirements for a valid compromise agreement which satisfies the statutory conditions are addressed at **18.33–18.35** EMPLOYMENT TRIBUNALS – **II.**)

30.30 LIABILITY OF EMPLOYERS AND PRINCIPALS

As in other anti-discrimination legislation, anything done by a person in the course of his employment is treated for the purposes of the *Regulations* as also done by his employer, whether or not it was done with the employer's knowledge or approval: *reg 11(1)*. Anything done by a person as agent for the employer with the authority of the employer is treated as also done by the employer: *reg 11(2)*.

In proceedings under the *Regulations* against any person in respect of an act alleged to have been done by a worker of his, it shall be a defence for that person to prove that he took such steps as were reasonably practicable to prevent the worker from (a) doing that act, or (b) doing, in the course of his employment, acts of that description: *reg 11(3)*.

(See further **10.54** DISCRIMINATION AND EQUAL OPPORTUNITIES – **I.**)

31   Maternity and Parental Rights

Cross-references. See UNFAIR DISMISSAL – I **(51)** and II **(52)** for the general rules on unfair dismissal; EQUAL PAY **(21)** and DISCRIMINATION AND EQUAL OPPORTUNITIES – I **(10)** for the rules prohibiting discrimination against women.

31.1   There have been rapid changes in recent years in the statutory framework protecting pregnant women and parents with young children.

Historically, the *Employment Protection Act 1975* created statutory rights for female employees. These provisions were re-enacted in the *Employment Protection (Consolidation) Act 1978* (*'EPCA 1978'*). An additional right, the right to paid time off for ante-natal care, was conferred by the *Employment Act 1980*, which also amended the existing provisions, and statutory rights were further extended by the *Trade Union Reform and Employment Rights Act 1993* (*'TURERA 1993'*).

With the exception of the law relating to statutory maternity pay (which is contained in the *Social Security Contributions and Benefits Act 1992*), all the relevant legislation was consolidated into the *Employment Rights Act 1996* (*'ERA 1996'*). Most of the rights and principles set out in the *ERA 1996* which relate to maternity leave have found their way into the *Employment Relations Act 1999* (*'ERA 1999'*), or appear in the regulations made under the *ERA 1999*, principally the *Maternity and Parental Leave, etc Regulations 1999 (SI 1999/3312)*.

The *Employment Act 2002* (*'EA 2002'*) and accompanying regulations ushered in significant changes to the law on maternity and paternity rights, extending the period of ordinary maternity leave from 18 weeks to 26 weeks, and the period of additional maternity leave to 26 weeks from the date when ordinary maternity leave has ended. The *Work and Families Act 2006*, and accompanying regulations, have introduced further changes, including a right to additional paternity leave to enable parents, in effect, to share the right to additional leave to care for their child (see **31.47** below). The *Equality Act 2010* has since brought further protections in respect of maternity and pregnancy.

Female employees who can satisfy the relevant qualifying conditions enjoy the following statutory rights:

(a)   paid time off to receive ante-natal care;

(b)   26 weeks' ordinary maternity leave and 26 weeks' additional maternity leave;

(c)   protection from dismissal by reason of pregnancy or childbirth;

(d)   protection from detriment by reason of pregnancy, childbirth or maternity;

(e)   maternity pay;

(f)   return to work after ordinary maternity leave or additional maternity leave;

(g)   offer of alternative work before being suspended on maternity grounds;

(h)   remuneration on suspension on maternity grounds.

The *Social Security Act 1989, Sch 5 paras 2, 5, 6*, contains provisions which deal with unfair maternity and family leave provisions in employment-related benefits schemes. These provisions are intended to implement *Directive 86/378/EEC* (see **22.5** EUROPEAN UNION LAW) and were brought into force to a limited extent on 23 June 1994 (*Social Security Act 1989 (Commencement No 5) Order 1994 (SI 1994/1661)*).

31.2 Maternity and Parental Rights

31.2 The law as to sex discrimination (see DISCRIMINATION AND EQUAL OPPORTUNITIES – I (10), II (11), and III (12)) has also historically been extremely important in defining the extent of the protection which the law confers on women in connection with pregnancy or childbirth and, indeed, in connection with IVF treatment (on which see *Mayr v Backerei und Konditorei Gerhard Flockner OHG*: C-506/06 [2008] IRLR 387 and, recently, *Sahota v Home Office* [2010] ICR 772) (see **31.9** below). In *Kulikaoskas v MacDuff Shellfish* [2011] ICR 48 the Scottish EAT held in a claim brought by the partner of a pregnant woman that the *Sex Discrimination Act 1975* did not protect against associative sex discrimination. The EAT left open the question whether the same result would be reached under the *Equality Act 2010*. The Inner House of the Court of Session referred the matter to the CJEU on 11 January 2012.

As to the *Equality Act 2010* generally, which separates maternity and pregnancy discrimination from sex discrimination in most cases, see section **31.5** below.

31.3 The requirement to carry out risk assessments in respect of pregnant women is beyond the scope of this chapter. However, see *O'Neill v Buckinghamshire County Council* [2010] IRLR 384.

31.4 In 2008, the European Commission proposed a number of new rights in relation to maternity leave as part of proposed revisions to the *Pregnant Workers Directive EC 1992/85*. The Government consulted on those proposals during 2009 and published a response in 2010. In October 2010 the European Parliament adopted amendments to the *Directive* which went beyond even those proposed by the Commission, including a right to 20 weeks' paid maternity leave, two weeks' paid paternity leave and breastfeeding leave. These were politically controversial and were broadly rejected by the European Council in late 2010. It remains to be seen how the *Directive* will be taken forward as there is currently something of an impasse between the legislative organs of the EU.

In June 2010 the European Parliament agreed a new *Directive 2010/41/EU* to provide for increased protections for self-employed workers, including a right to maternity leave for self-employed women and their partners. The UK has taken the view that existing domestic legislation already provides sufficient compliance for the purposes of the new Directive. As to the right to maternity allowance in UK law, see **33.20** below.

31.4A CHILDREN AND FAMILIES BILL

On 4 February 2013 the Coalition Government introduced into the House of Commons the Children and Families Bill. As and when it is eventually passed and enacted it promises to make changes of considerable importance in relation to statutory rights to leave and pay (Part 6), time off work for ante-natal care (Part 7) and flexible working (Part 8). This chapter will not note the proposed changes laid out in Part 8 on flexible working, but ACAS have already commenced consultation on a new Code of Practice to take account of proposed new right of all employees to request flexible working and the abolition of the existing statutory process.

Given the early stage of the Bill's progress at the time of writing, the broad thrust of the draft changes in Parts 6 and 7 only will be set out here. Future editions of this work will require amendment to take account of the final form of the changes.

Part 6 will introduce a new right to shared parental leave and shared parental pay for eligible working parents. The right of the mother will remain unchanged, but if the mother chooses to bring their leave and pay or allowance to an early end, eligible working parents will be able to share up to the balance of the remaining leave and pay. Eligible adopters will be given equivalent rights, and adoption leave and pay will be extended to prospective parents in the fostering-to-adopt system, as it will to those in formal surrogacy arrangements. All of these matters will be subject to the jurisdiction of the Employment Tribunals.

Much of the detail of the shared parental leave scheme is to be set out in regulations. The Government is, at the time of writing, consulting on its proposals for shared parental leave. It is expressly presented as shared parental leave so as to differentiate it from EU-derived concepts of flexible leave. The consultation ends in May 2013 and will not be responded to before the summer of 2013.

Part 7 intends to create a new right for employees and certain agency workers who have a qualifying relationship with a pregnant woman or the expected child (i.e. the father, parent or intended parent, husband, civil partner, or partner) to take unpaid leave to attend up to 2 ante-natal appointments during the pregnancy. It will also create a new right for an adopter (including a prospective adopter in a fostering case) to take paid leave to attend up to 5 introductory meetings and for the other adopter in a joint adoption case to take unpaid leave to attend up to 2 introductory meetings before the child is placed. Breach of the new rights will be within the jurisdiction of the Employment Tribunals.

31.5   EQUALITY ACT 2010

Maternity and pregnancy are protected characteristics under the *Equality Act 2010*, (see *section 4* and, in relation to work, *section 18*).

Section 18 provides codified protections for women in relation to pregnancy (and pregnancy-related illnesses) and maternity leave at work. It provides that:

(a)   a person discriminates against a woman if, in the protected period in relation to a pregnancy of hers, he treats her "unfavourably" because of the pregnancy, or because of illness suffered by her as a result of it;

(b)   a person discriminates against a woman if he treats her unfavourably because she is exercising or seeking to exercise, or has exercised or sought to exercise, the right to ordinary or additional maternity leave.

The protected period begins when the pregnancy begins and ends (a) if she has the right to ordinary and additional maternity leave, at the end of the additional maternity leave period of (if earlier) when she returns to work after the pregnancy, or (b) if she does not have that right, at the end of the period of two weeks beginning with the end of the pregnancy (*section 18(6)*). This is supplemented by *section 18(5)* of the *Equality Act*, which provides that if the treatment of a woman is in implementation of a decision taken in the protected period, the treatment is to be regarded as occurring in that period (even if the implementation is not until after the end of that period).

Section 13 prohibits direct discrimination in relation to protected characteristics including maternity and pregnancy. However, by *section 18(7)*, *section 13* (so far as relating to sex discrimination) does not apply to treatment of a woman insofar as it is in the protected period in relation to her and is for a reason mentioned in sub-paragraph (a) above, or it is for a reason mentioned in sub-paragraph (b). In addition, interestingly *section 13* provides that in general less favourable treatment of a woman because of sex includes less treatment of her because she is breast-feeding but then excludes this in relation to *Part 5* of the *Act* – ie except in relation to work.

Maternity and pregnancy are excluded from the relevant protected characteristics for the prohibition of indirect discrimination in *section 19* of the *Act* and of harassment in *section 26* of the *Act* (although it is likely that pregnant women will nevertheless be protected by the prohibition on indirect sex discrimination and harassment because of sex). They will also be excluded from the relevant protected characteristics for the purposes of a combined discrimination (dual characteristics) claim under *section 14* of the *Equality Act*, although the Government has announced that it does not intend to bring the provision into force.

31.5 Maternity and Parental Rights

See also *ss 72–76* of the *Equality Act 2010* (akin to the provisions on equal pay) which introduce into women's contracts a new statutory "maternity equality clause" to regulate maternity related pay (ie contractual pay other than statutory maternity pay), bonus payments and pay increases.

As to the operation of the *Equality Act 2010*, and its definitions and scope, see in general DISCRIMINATION AND EQUAL OPPORTUNITIES – I (10), II (11), and III (12).

31.6 PAID TIME OFF FOR ANTE-NATAL CARE

An employee who is pregnant and who has, on the advice of a registered medical practitioner, registered midwife or registered nurse, made an appointment to attend at any place for the purpose of receiving ante-natal care, is entitled: (*a*) not to be unreasonably refused time off during her working hours to enable her to keep the appointment (*ERA 1996, s 55(1) and 57(1)*); and (*b*) to be paid for the period of absence at the appropriate hourly rate (*ERA 1996, s 56(1)*). (See also *art 9* of the *Pregnant Workers Directive EC 92/85*.)

31.7 Qualifying requirements

There is no minimum qualifying period of employment for the enjoyment of these rights. However, in respect of all save the first appointment for ante-natal care for which she seeks time off work, the employee must, if requested to do so by her employer, produce for his inspection:

(a)   a certificate from a registered medical practitioner, registered midwife or registered nurse stating that she is pregnant; and

(b)   an appointment card or some other document showing that the appointment has been made.

(ERA 1996, s 55(2)–(3) and s 55(5).)

If an employer could reasonably refuse to allow an employee time off to attend an ante-natal appointment – for example, if she was a part-time employee and could arrange to attend during her time off – yet he allows her time off, it is thought that he is not obliged to pay her during the period of her absence provided that he obtains her agreement and makes it clear that the time is not being given in satisfaction of a statutory obligation. This qualification is an important one: if an employee is entitled to take time off in accordance with the provisions of *ERA 1996, s 55(1)*, she is automatically entitled to be paid for the time taken (*ERA 1996, s 56(1)*). (See *Gregory v Tudsbury Ltd* [1982] IRLR 267.)

31.8 Right to remuneration

The employee is entitled to payment from her employer for the period of her absence, at the appropriate hourly rate. That rate is the amount of one week's pay divided by:

(a)   the number of normal working hours in a week for that employee when employed under the contract of employment in force on the day when the time off is taken;

(b)   where the number of such normal working hours differs from week to week or over a longer period, the average number of such hours, calculated by reference to the hours worked during the period of 12 weeks ending with the last complete week before the day on which the time off is taken; or

(c)   where the number of hours worked in a week differs, but the employee has not been employed long enough for the 12-week calculation to be made, a number which fairly represents the number of normal working hours in a week taking into account (as appropriate in all the circumstances) the average number of hours which the employee could expect under her contract and the average number of hours worked by other employees of the same employer in comparable employment.

(*ERA 1996, ss 56(2)–(6) and 225(3)*; and see PAY – I (32).)

31.9 Remedies

An employee may present a complaint to an employment tribunal to the effect that her employer has unreasonably refused her time off as required by *s 55(1)* of the *ERA* or has failed to pay her the whole or part of any amount to which she is entitled under *s 56(1)* (see *ERA 1996, s 57(1)*). Such a complaint must be presented within the period of three months beginning with the date of the appointment concerned, or within such further period as the tribunal considers reasonable in a case where it is satisfied that it was not reasonably practicable for the complaint to be presented within the period of three months (*ERA 1996, s 57(2)*; for reasonable practicability see **17.7** EMPLOYMENT TRIBUNALS – I). By analogy with the time limit in unfair dismissal cases, it is thought that it will not be considered to be reasonably practicable for an employee to present a claim until she is aware or ought reasonably to be aware of her rights (see *Nu-Swift International Ltd v Mallinson* [1979] ICR 157). Where an employment tribunal finds a complaint well-founded, it will make a declaration to that effect and make an order for payment of the amount of money due under the statutory provisions (*ERA 1996, s 57(3)–(5)*). The employee's statutory right to remuneration does not affect her contractual right, but any contractual remuneration will go to discharge her statutory entitlement, and vice versa (*ERA 1996, s 56(5)–(6)*).

31.10 Agency Workers

From 1 October 2011 agency workers who have worked for the qualifying period prescribed in *reg 7* of the *Agency Workers Regulations 2010 (SI 2010/93)* (ie working in the same role with the same hirer for 12 continuous calendar weeks), have comparable rights as against both their temporary work agency and their hirer (*ERA 1996, ss 57ZA–57ZD*).

31.11 SUSPENSION FROM WORK ON MATERNITY GROUNDS

An employee will be taken to be suspended from work on maternity grounds if her employer suspends her on the ground that she is pregnant, has recently given birth, or is breastfeeding a child, and he does so in consequence either of a relevant statutory requirement, or of a recommendation contained in a relevant provision of a Code of Practice issued or approved under *s 16* of the *Health and Safety at Work Act 1974* (see **26.17** HEALTH AND SAFETY AT WORK – II), which means a provision specified in an order made by the Secretary of State (*ERA 1996, s 66*). Suspension may only be invoked if removing the hazard to health or transferring to an alternative role is not available or would be insufficient to remedy the risk to health and safety: *Gassmayr v Bundesminister fur Wissenschaft und Forschung*: C-194/08 [2010] ECR I-6281.

The *Suspension from Work (on Maternity Grounds) Order 1994 (SI 1994/2930)* specified the following provisions for these purposes:

(a)   *reg 13A(3)* of the *Management of Health and Safety at Work Regulations 1992 (SI 1992/2051)* (suspension from work of new or expectant mother to avoid risk from any processes or working conditions, or physical, biological or chemical agents); this provision is now set out in *reg 16* of the *Management of Health and Safety at Work Regulations 1999 (SI 1999/3242) (the 'MHSW Regulations')*;

(b)   *reg 17* of the *MHSW Regulations* (certificate from a registered medical practitioner).

31.11 Maternity and Parental Rights

In addition, *regs 8(3)* and *9(2)* of the *Merchant Shipping and Fishing Vessels (Health and Safety at Work) Regulations 1997 (SI 1997/2962)* are specified for these purposes by the *Suspension from Work on Maternity Grounds (Merchant Shipping and Fishing Vessels) Order 1998 (SI 1998/587)*.

Other provisions as to suspension include those in the *Suspension from Work on Maternity Grounds (Merchant Shipping and Fishing Vessels) Order 1998 (SI 1998/587)*. For discussion of the concept of 'suspension' see *New Southern Railway Ltd v Quinn* [2006] ICR 761, EAT.

31.12 Right to alternative work

Before being suspended on maternity grounds, the employee must be offered suitable alternative work if the employer has it available. This means work which is of a kind both suitable in relation to her and appropriate for her to do in the circumstances, and to which terms and conditions not substantially less favourable than her own apply (*ERA 1996, s 67(1), (2)*).

If the employer fails to offer the employee such work which is available, she may complain to an employment tribunal, which has power, if it finds the complaint well-founded, to award such compensation as is just and equitable having regard to the infringement of the employee's right and to any loss which she has sustained because of it (*ERA 1996, s 70(4), (6), (7)*). The complaint must be presented before the end of the period of three months beginning with the first day of the suspension, or within such further period as the tribunal considers reasonable where it is satisfied that it was not reasonably practicable to present the complaint within three months (*ERA 1996, s 70(5)*; see **17.7 EMPLOYMENT TRIBUNALS – I**).

In *British Airways (European Operations At Gatwick) Ltd v Moore* [2000] ICR 678, the EAT upheld a finding that airline cabin crew who were employed on ground-based work only during their pregnancy had not been offered suitable alternative work while they were pregnant. The terms and conditions offered to them were substantially less favourable: they were given their basic pay only, not the flying allowances which they would normally have received had they been airborne.

31.13 Right to remuneration

If an employee is suspended from work on maternity grounds, she is entitled to remuneration at the rate of a week's pay for each week of suspension, unless she has been offered suitable alternative work which she has unreasonably refused (*ERA 1996, ss 68, 69(1)*; **36.12 REDUNDANCY – I**). This statutory right does not affect any contractual rights to remuneration during her suspension which the employee may have, and any contractual payments which are made go towards discharging the statutory obligation and vice versa (*ERA 1996, s 69(2), (3)*).

If the employer fails to pay the whole or part of the remuneration which is due under *ERA 1996, s 68*, the employee may complain to an employment tribunal. If it finds the complaint well-founded, the tribunal will order payment of the amount due (*ERA 1996, s 70(1), (3)*). The complaint must be presented before the end of the period of three months beginning with the unremunerated day to which it relates, or within such further period as the tribunal considers reasonable where it is satisfied that it was not reasonably practicable to present the complaint within three months (*ERA 1996, s 70(2)*; **17.7 EMPLOYMENT TRIBUNALS – I**).

31.14 Agency Workers

From 1 October 2011 agency workers who have worked for the qualifying period prescribed in *reg 7* of the *Agency Workers Regulations 2010 (SI 2010/93)* (ie working in the same role with the same hirer for 12 continuous calendar weeks), have comparable protections where the supply of that worker to a hirer is ended on maternity grounds pursuant to one of the measures in **31.11** above or *reg 20* of the *Conduct of Employment Agencies and Employment Businesses 2003* (*ERA 1996, ss 68A–68D, 69A* and *70A*).

31.15 Pregnant Workers Directive

In *Parviainen v Finnair Oyj*: C–471/08 [2011] ICR 99, the CJEU has held that where an employer transfers a pregnant employee to another job to avoid health risks during her pregnancy, *art 11* of the *Pregnant Workers Directive* requires that she receive her basic pay together with any compensation or allowances related to her status (eg related to her seniority, qualifications or length of service). *Gassmayr v Bundesminister fur Wissenschaft und Forschung*: C–194/08 [2010] ECR I-6281 held that *art 11* is directly enforceable in national courts.

31.16 PROTECTION FROM DISMISSAL BY REASON OF PREGNANCY

An employee will automatically be held to have been unfairly dismissed if the reason or principal reason for his or her dismissal is connected with any of the following:

(a)   her pregnancy;

(b)   the fact that she has given birth to a child, where her ordinary or additional maternity leave period is ended by the dismissal;

(c)   the application of a requirement or recommendation such as is referred to in *ERA 1996, s 66(2)* (suspension from work on maternity grounds; see **31.6** above);

(d)   the fact that she took, sought to take or availed herself of the benefits of ordinary or additional maternity leave;

(e)   the fact that he or she took or sought to take parental leave or time off under the *ERA 1996, s 57A* (time off to care for dependants);

(f)   the fact that she failed to return to work after a period of ordinary or additional maternity leave in circumstances where her employer did not notify her of the date on which the period in question would end, and she reasonably believed that the period had not ended, or he gave her less than 28 days' notice of the relevant end date, and it was not reasonably practicable for her to return on that date;

(g)   the fact that she undertook, considered undertaking or refused to undertake work during her statutory maternity leave period in accordance with *reg 12A* of the *MPL Regulations*;

(h)   the fact that he or she declined to sign a workforce agreement for the purposes of the *MPL Regulations*;

(i)   the fact that he or she performed (or proposed to perform) any functions or activities as a workforce representative or as a candidate to be such a representative;

(*Reg 20* of the *MPL Regulations*; *ERA 1996, s 99*.)

An employee will also be treated as having been unfairly dismissed if the reason for the dismissal is that he or she is redundant, but where the circumstances constituting the redundancy applied equally to one or more employees in the same undertaking who held similar positions and who have not been dismissed, and it is shown that the reason or the principal reason for which he or she was selected for dismissal is a reason connected with the above matters (*reg 20(2)*).

In addition, a woman will be treated as having been automatically unfairly dismissed even if there is a genuine redundancy situation if the employer fails to comply with the requirements set out in *reg 10* for dealing with redundancies during ordinary or additional maternity leave (*reg 20(1)(b)* and see *Simpson v Endsleigh Insurance Services Ltd* [2011] ICR 75). The dismissal for redundancy must, however, end the maternity leave period.

There is no longer a small employers' exemption for automatically unfair dismissal. However, there is an exemption in non-redundancy situations, if the employer can show that it is not reasonably practicable (for a reason other than redundancy) to permit the employee to return to a job which is both suitable for her and appropriate for her to do in the circumstances; and an associated employer offers her a job of that kind, and she accepts or unreasonably refuses that offer (*reg 20(7)*). It is for the employer to establish that he has satisfied this statutory defence (*reg 20(8)*).

Even though the dismissal may not be treated as automatically unfair, however, it may still be unfair according to ordinary principles of the law of unfair dismissal. If the employee is dismissed because another employee has been engaged in her position, that will not be an acceptable reason for her dismissal (*McFadden v Greater Glasgow Passenger Transport Executive* [1977] IRLR 327).

Under the previous legislation, it was held that the words 'or any other reason connected with her pregnancy' were to be interpreted broadly (*Clayton v Vigers* [1989] ICR 713). This included a pregnancy-related illness, such as post-natal depression arising in the period of maternity leave following childbirth (*Caledonia Bureau Investment and Property v Caffrey* [1998] ICR 603, [1998] IRLR 110, EAT). The same broad interpretation is likely to apply under the present legislation, but see also *Atkins v Coyle Personnel plc* [2008] IRLR 420, EAT in relation to paternity leave (see below, **31.47**).

In *Ramdoolar v Bycity Ltd* [2005] ICR 368, the EAT held that for a dismissal to be automatically unfair for a reason connected with pregnancy, the employer must know, or believe in the existence, of the pregnancy. It is not sufficient that symptoms of pregnancy existed which the employer ought to have realised meant that the employee was pregnant. The EAT left open the possibility, however, that a dismissal may be automatically unfair if an employer, detecting the symptoms of pregnancy and fearing the consequences, dismisses the employee before his suspicion could be proved right.

A dismissal in connection with pregnancy and the taking of maternity leave may also amount to sex discrimination (see *The Employment Equality (Sex Discrimination) Regulations 2005 (SI 2005/2467)* and, for an example, *Eversheds Legal Services Ltd v De Belin* [2011] ICR 1137 where a man succeeded in a sex discrimination claim in respect of preferential treatment given to a woman on maternity leave in redundancy selection scoring which went beyond what was reasonably necessary to compensate a woman for the disadvantages occasioned by her pregnancy/maternity leave).

31.17   Qualifying period

There is no qualifying period for a complaint of unfair dismissal where the dismissal is for any of the reasons set out in *ERA 1996, s 99* (see above, **31.9**), nor (although less common!) is there any upper age limit (*ERA 1996, ss 108(3)*). See also **46.14** TERMINATION OF EMPLOYMENT for the obligation to give reasons for dismissal of pregnant employees.

31.18   PROTECTION FROM DETRIMENT BY REASON OF PREGNANCY

Reg 19 of the *MPL Regulations* (and the *ERA 1996, s 47C*) confers a statutory right protecting a woman from being subject to any detriment (other than dismissal) by any act, or any deliberate failure to act, by her employer if it is done for the reason that:

(a)   she is pregnant;

(b)   she has given birth to a child, if the act or failure to act takes place during the employee's ordinary or additional maternity leave period;

(c)   she is the subject of a relevant requirement, or a relevant recommendation, as defined by s *66(2)* of the *ERA 1996*;

(d)   she took, sought to take or availed herself of the benefits of, ordinary or additional maternity leave; or

(e)   she took or sought to take parental leave or time off under the *ERA 1996, s 57A*;

(f)   she failed to return to work after a period of ordinary or additional maternity leave in circumstances where her employer did not notify her of the date on which the period in question would end, and she reasonably believed that the period had not ended, or he gave her less than 28 days' notice of the relevant end date, and it was not reasonably practicable for her to return on that date;

(g)   she undertook, considered undertaking or refused to undertake work during her statutory maternity leave period;

(h)   the fact that she declined to sign a workforce agreement for the purposes of the *MPL Regulations*;

(i)   the fact that she performed (or proposed to perform) any functions or activities as a workforce representative or as a candidate to be such a representative.

A woman is treated as availing herself of the benefits of ordinary or additional maternity leave if, during her ordinary or additional maternity leave period, she avails herself of the benefit of any of the terms and conditions of her employment preserved by *s 71* or *s 73* of *ERA 1996*: *reg 19(3)–(3A)*.

The failure of an employer to pay a woman on maternity leave wages, salary or a bonus which she would have earned had she been at work cannot be a 'detriment' within the meaning of *reg 19*: see *Hoyland v Asda Stores Ltd* [2005] ICR 1235.

31.19 Remedies

Where an employee has suffered such a detriment, she may claim to an employment tribunal pursuant to *ERA 1996, s 48*. On such a complaint, it is for the employer to show the ground on which any act, or deliberate failure to act, was done. The complaint must be presented within the period of three months beginning with the date of the act or failure to act, or the last of the series of similar such acts. Time for presenting a complaint can be extended where (as in the case for unfair dismissal) the employment tribunal is satisfied that it was not reasonably practicable for the complaint to be presented within the period of three months.

If the complaint is well-founded, the employment tribunal shall make a declaration to that effect, and may make an award of compensation. The amount of compensation shall be such as the tribunal considers to be just and equitable in all the circumstances, having regard to the infringement to which the complaint relates, and any loss attributable to the act in question (*ERA 1996, s 49*).

31.20 MATERNITY LEAVE

Pt VIII, ERA 1996 (ss 71–75), and the *MPL Regulations* made thereunder, provide for a statutory right to maternity leave. It is necessary to distinguish between three types of maternity leave: (*a*) ordinary maternity leave; (*b*) compulsory maternity leave; and (*c*) additional maternity leave.

31.20　Maternity and Parental Rights

Church of England clergy now have the right to maternity, paternity, parental and adoption leave in accordance with directions given by the Archbishops' Council: see the *Ecclesiastical Offices (Terms of Service) Regulations 2009 (SI 2009/2108), reg 23* and the *Ecclesiastical Offices (Terms of Service) Directions 2010 (SI 2010/1923)*.

31.21　Right to ordinary maternity leave

An employee who is absent from work at any time during her ordinary maternity leave period is entitled to the benefit of the terms and conditions of employment which would otherwise have been applicable to her, such as holiday entitlement, even if they do not arise under her contract of employment, although this does not confer any entitlement to remuneration (*ERA 1996, s 71* and *reg 9*). The *MPL Regulations* define 'remuneration' as wages or salary only (*reg 9(3)*).

The employee is also bound during this period by any obligations arising under these same terms and conditions (*ERA 1996, s 71* and *reg 9*).

In *Gomez (Merino) v Continental Industrias del Caucho S.A: C-342/01 [2004] ECR I-2605; [2005] ICR 1040*, the ECJ held that a worker must be able to take the paid annual leave to which she is entitled under the *Working Time Directive* during a period other than the period of her maternity leave.

31.22　In order to enjoy the right to ordinary maternity leave ('OML'), the employee must generally:

(a)　　notify her employer of:

(i)　　her pregnancy;

(ii)　　the expected week of childbirth ('EWC'); and

(iii)　　the date on which she intends her OML period to start;

no later than the 15th week before her EWC or, if that is not reasonably practicable, as soon as is reasonably practicable; and

(b)　　if requested to do so by her employer, produce for his inspection a certificate from a registered medical practitioner or a registered midwife stating the EWC (*reg 4(1)*).

The notification of the date on which the employee intends her OML period to start must be in writing, if the employer so requests (*reg 4(2)*). Note that OML cannot start any earlier than the beginning of the 11th week before the EWC (*reg 4(2)*). As to these notification provisions, and for an example of a case in which it was found to have been not reasonably practicable for the employee to comply with *reg 4*, see the decision of the EAT in *St Alphonsus RC Primary School v Blenkinsop* (UKEAT/0082/09, 18 May 2009).

However:

(a)　　where the period of OML commences the day following the first day after the beginning of the 4th week before the EWC on which she is absent from work wholly or partly because of pregnancy, by *reg 6(1)(b)*, the employee must notify her employer as soon as is reasonably practicable that she is absent wholly or partly because of pregnancy and of the date on which her absence on that account began (*reg 4(3)*); and

(b)　　where childbirth occurs before the notified leave date or before the employee has notified such a date (see *reg 6(2)*), the employee must notify her employer that she has given birth (and on which date) as soon as is reasonably practicable after the birth (*reg 4(4)*).

810

Such notice must be given in writing if the employer so requests (*reg 4*).

The date upon which the employee commences OML may be varied if she gives 28 days' notice before the date that is being varied, or 28 days' notice before the new date, whichever is earlier (or if those dates cannot be complied with, she gives notice as soon as it is reasonably practicable to do so) (*reg 4(1A)*). Such notice must be in writing if the employer so requests.

31.23 The OML period commences with the date which the employee notifies as the date on which she intends her absence to commence (see above **31.15**), or if earlier, the first day on which she is absent from work wholly or partly because of pregnancy or childbirth after the beginning of the 4th week before the EWC (*reg 6(1)–(2)*). If childbirth occurs before the relevant date, OML commences on the day after the day of the birth (*reg 6(2)*). Note that 'childbirth' means the birth of a living child *or* the birth of a child whether living or dead after 24 weeks of pregnancy (*reg 2(1)*).

31.24 The OML period continues for 26 weeks or until the latest of the end of the compulsory maternity leave period, the expiry of any period during which there is any statutory prohibition on the employee working by reason of her recently having given birth, or upon her dismissal (*reg 7*).

31.25 Apart from in a redundancy situation (see **31.27** below), an employee returning after an isolated period of OML is ordinarily entitled to return to the job in which she was employed before her absence (*reg 18*). 'Job' means the nature of the work that she is employed to do in accordance with her contract, and the capacity and place in which she is so employed (*reg 2(1)*).

The purpose of this provision is to put the returning employee back into a situation as near as possible to that which she left: see *Blundell v Governing Body of St Andrews Catholic Primary School* [2007] ICR 1451, EAT. In that case, it did not mean that the returning teacher had to be offered the job of teaching the particular class that she had taught before her maternity leave. The work that she was employed to do was that of a teacher, her capacity was viewed as a class teacher rather than the teacher of a particular reception class, and her place of work was the school and not a particular classroom. Note that the right to return to the job carries with it the right to return on terms and conditions no less favourable than those that the employee would have enjoyed had she not been absent, and with her seniority, pension and similar rights as they would have been had she not been absent (*reg 18A*).

31.26 An employee who has a contractual or other right to maternity leave may not exercise both that and the statutory right separately, but may take advantage of whichever right is in any particular respect more favourable. The provisions of *ERA 1996* and of the *Regulations* then apply, modified as necessary, to the exercise of the composite right (*reg 21*).

31.27 Compulsory maternity leave

An employee entitled to OML in accordance with *ERA 1996* shall not be permitted by her employer to work for a period of two weeks commencing with the day on which childbirth occurs. (This is described as 'compulsory maternity leave' (*ERA 1996, s 72*, and the *MPL Regulations, reg 8*). Failure to comply with this prohibition renders the employer liable on summary conviction to a fine (*ERA 1996, s 72(5)*).

Note that an occupier of a factory will be subject to a fine if he knowingly allows a woman to be employed therein within four weeks after she has given birth: *Public Health Act 1936, s 205*.

31.28 **Additional maternity leave**

An employee who qualifies for OML now qualifies automatically for additional maternity leave ('AML') as well (*reg 4*). (There is no longer any qualifying period of employment for this right.) She will continue to have the benefit of her terms and conditions of employment during AML (and is bound by any obligations), in the same way as during OML (*reg 9* and see above **31.14**). Note that the position in relation to women whose EWC was before 5 October 2008 is governed by the *MPL Regulations* as they stood prior to amendment by the *Maternity and Parental Leave* and the *Paternity and Adoption Leave (Amendment) Regulations 2008 (SI 2008/1966)*.

The right to AML continues until the end of the period of 26 weeks from the date upon which it commences, unless the employee is dismissed before that date (*reg 7(4)*).

The AML period commences on the day after the last day of the employee's OML period (*reg 6(3)*). Importantly, where the employee notifies her employer under reg 4 of the date on which her OML period will commence or has commenced, the employer shall notify her of the date on which her AML period shall end either 28 days of the date on which he received the notification (where the notification is under *reg 4(1)(a)(iii), (3)(b)* or *(4)(b)*) or within 28 days on which the employee's OML period commenced (where the notification is under *reg 4(1A)*) (*reg 7(6),(7)*).

31.29 An employee who is entitled to AML might be able to return to work before the end of the AML period. To do so, she has to give her employer not less than 8 weeks' notice of the date on which she intends to return (*reg 11(1)*). If she does give this notice, then it would appear that her employer cannot seek to postpone her return date.

Where an employee does not give eight weeks' notice of her intended return date and attempts to return to work earlier than the end of her AML period, then her employer is entitled to postpone her return to such a date as will mean that he has eight weeks' notice of her return (*reg 11(2)*). The only exception to this is that the postponement cannot extend beyond the date of the end of the AML period (*reg 11(3)*). During the period of postponement, the employer is under no contractual obligation to pay any remuneration until the date to which the employee's return was postponed, save where he has failed to notify her of when the AML period was due to end (*reg 11(4)–(5)*).

An employee is now entitled to change her mind as to when to return to work during the additional maternity leave period, if she has already given notice of return before the end of that period or if the employer has (in line with the procedure above) postponed her return date (*reg 11(2A)–(2B)*). If the employee wishes to return to work later than the original return date, she must give her employer not less than 8 weeks' notice ending with the original return date. If she wishes to return earlier than the original return date, she must give at least 8 weeks' notice of the new return date.

Unlike the situation under the earlier legislative provisions, the employee does not need to inform her employer that she intends to exercise her right to return at the end of the AML period unless she is specifically requested to do so by her employer. In addition, an employer is no longer entitled to request confirmation that the employee will be returning to work at the end of the AML period (the former *reg 12* has been revoked).

31.30 The right on redundancy is the same as for employees seeking to return after OML (see **31.27** above).

31.31 The returning employee has the right to return to the job in which she was employed before her absence or, if it is not reasonably practicable for the employer to permit her to return to that job, to another job which is both suitable for her and appropriate for her to do in the circumstances (*reg 18(2)*). The definition of 'job' is the same as for returnees from OML: see *Blundell v Governing Body of St Andrews Catholic Primary School* [2007] ICR 1451 and see above 31.18. The right is also to return on terms and conditions no less favourable than would have applied if the employee had not been absent. She is entitled to the same seniority, pension rights and similar rights as she would have enjoyed if she had not taken any additional maternity leave (*reg 18A*). There is no right as such to return to work on a part-time basis, or on terms preferable to the returning employee: see *British Telecommunications plc v Roberts* [1996] ICR 625, EAT. Nevertheless, an employer's refusal to permit an employee to job share or return part-time might constitute indirect sex discrimination (*Hardys & Hansons plc v Lax* [2005] ICR 1565, CA).

31.32   The legislation has nothing to say about the vexed question of women who fail to return to work on the return date. It may well be that the law under the previous legislation will prevail. It may be useful therefore to consider the decision of the House of Lords in *Halfpenny v IGE Medical Systems Ltd* [2001] ICR 73, construing the former legislation.

The facts of *Halfpenny* are relatively straightforward. The employee failed to return to work on the notified return date for reasons of ill-health, supported by a medical certificate. As she had not exhausted her contractual entitlement to sick leave and had a good reason for her absence, her employer was found to have dismissed her wrongfully by refusing to extend her period of leave. In addition, the employer was found to have discriminated against the employee on grounds of her sex as it would have allowed a male employee to continue sick leave with pay.

In the Court of Appeal ([1999] IRLR 177), it was held (confirming the earlier decision of *Crees v Royal London Mutual Insurance Society Ltd* [1998] IRLR 245) that to avail herself of the right not to be unfairly dismissed following maternity leave, an employee need not physically return to work on the notified day of return. An employee was held to have exercised the right to return to work following maternity leave (and also preserved her continuity of employment) merely by giving the appropriate notice of return before the notified date of return.

This aspect of the decision was overturned by the House of Lords, where it was held that an employee did not avail herself of the 'return to work' merely by giving the appropriate notice of return if she did not actually return to work on the notified day. Rather, the employee had to give the appropriate notice and also demonstrate that, on the notified date for return, she had done something consistent with the due performance by her of her revived contract of employment. Normally, this would mean that she actually returned to work physically. If, however, under the contract she would not be bound to return on that day (eg as a result of an accident, a strike, or poor weather conditions) she merely had to have done something to demonstrate that she would have returned to work otherwise. If she were ill, she would have to provide the necessary certificates that would be required of her under the contract.

The House of Lords went on to decide that where the employee had demonstrated the appropriate conduct for a 'return to work', she would be treated as having been 'dismissed' by her employer if he refused to let her return, for the purposes of the law of unfair dismissal only. She had no right, however, to claim that she had been wrongfully dismissed as the contract of employment would be treated as having been suspended until her actual return. This aspect of the decision may have been overtaken by the fact that the period of AML during which the contract continues ends pursuant to the legislation.

31.33   An employee who has both a statutory and a contractual right to return to work may not exercise the two rights separately, but may take advantage of whichever right is the more favourable in any particular respect (*reg 21*).

31.34   Redundancy during maternity leave

If, during the OML or AML period, redundancy makes it impracticable to continue to employ an employee under her existing contract, she is entitled to be offered alternative employment with her employer, his successor (as defined by *ERA 1996, s 235(1)*) or an associated employer (see **6.9(a)** Continuous Employment) if a suitable available vacancy exists. The offer must be made before the old employment ends, and the new employment must commence immediately the old employment ends. It must involve work of a kind suitable in relation to the employee and appropriate for her to do in the circumstances, and the terms and conditions as to capacity, place of employment and otherwise must not be substantially less favourable than under the old contract (*reg 10*).

These provisions have been considered by the EAT in *Simpson v Endsleigh Insurance Services Ltd* [2011] ICR 75. Amongst other things, the EAT indicated that: (i) the requirement of suitability in *reg 10(2)* can only sensibly be tested by the requirement that it is coupled with a new contract of employment which complies with *reg 10(3)* – the provisions should not be looked at in isolation; (ii) there is no requirement on the employee to engage in this process and it is up to the employers, knowing what they do about the employee, to decide whether or not a vacancy is suitable; and (iii) the EAT was "by no means satisfied" that an employer could choose to test suitability by assessment and interview, contrary to the suggestion in the IDS Handbook on Redundancy.

More favourable treatment of a woman for a reason related to her pregnancy can be less favourable treatment of a man for sex-related reasons and unlawful discrimination: *Eversheds Legal Services v De Belin* [2011] ICR 1137. In that case the EAT considered that the protection of special treatment afforded to women in connection with pregnancy or childbirth under *paragraph 2* of *Schedule 7* to the *2010 Act* must be proportionate, and in *De Belin* the employer could have compared periods for the purposes of redundancy scoring where both employees had been at work.

31.35 Dismissal of replacement

Where an employer engages an employee to take the place of one who is absent due to pregnancy, the subsequent dismissal of that employee upon the resumption of work by the original employee will be considered to be a dismissal for a substantial reason (see **52.14** Unfair Dismissal – II) only if the employer informs the employee in writing, on engaging her, that her employment will be terminated on the resumption of work by another employee who is, or will be, absent wholly or partly because of pregnancy or childbirth or adoption or additional paternity leave, or the end of a period of suspension from work on maternity grounds, and if the employee is dismissed in order to make it possible to give work to the returning employee (*ERA 1996, s 106*). The language used in the written information must be clear and unambiguous: see *Victoria and Albert Museum v Durrant* [2011] IRLR 290.

However, this fact does not, in itself, make the dismissal fair. The employment tribunal will consider whether the dismissal was fair in all the circumstances (see further **52.4** Unfair Dismissal – II). The EAT in *Victoria and Albert Museum v Durrant* also indicated, *obiter*, that *s 106* does not operate in all cases to deem the reason for dismissal to be some other substantial reason. In some cases the reason for dismissal might be eg redundancy. Notwithstanding that *s 106* is engaged.

31.36 Right to written statement of reasons for dismissal

An employee is entitled to a written statement giving particulars of the reason for her dismissal (without having to request it, and irrespective of how long she has been employed), if she is dismissed whilst pregnant or after childbirth in circumstances in which her OML or AML period ends by reason of the dismissal: *ERA 1996, s 92(4)*.

31.37 Work during statutory maternity leave

An employee may carry out up to 10 days' work for her employer during her statutory maternity leave period without bringing her maternity leave to an end (*reg 12A(1)*). Work means any work done under the contract of employment and may include training or any activity undertaken for the purposes of keeping in touch with the workplace (*reg 12A(3)*). Such work does not extend the total duration of the statutory maternity leave period (*reg 12A(7)*).

Any work carried out on any date constitutes a day's work for these purposes (*reg 12A(2)*). However, reasonable contact from time to time between an employee and her employer (eg to discuss her return to work) does not bring the maternity leave period to an end (*reg 12A(4)*). There is no right for an employer to require that an employee work during the statutory maternity leave period, and no right for an employee to work during this period (*reg 12A(6)*). The employee does not lose her entitlement to SMP during the 10 keeping in touch days but any additional payment for the work done is a matter of contract between her and the employer.

31.38 STATUTORY MATERNITY PAY

The statutory provisions relating to the system of statutory maternity pay ('SMP'), first introduced by the *Social Security Act 1989*, have been consolidated into the *Social Security Contributions and Benefits Act 1992* ('*SSCBA 1992*'). The relevant provisions have been the subject of significant amendments to reflect the *Pregnant Workers Directive* (*Directive 92/85/EEC*).

The legislative scheme governing payment of SMP and, in particular, the rules on when the SMP period commences have now been considered by the Upper Tribunal in *Wade v North Yorkshire Police Authority* [2011] IRLR 393, UT (TCC).

There may also be a contractual right to maternity pay under a woman's contract of employment. If the employee fails to return to work and contractual maternity pay becomes repayable to the employer pursuant to a term of the contract, either the employer or the employee may be able to recover the National Insurance contributions on such pay from the Secretary of State.

31.39 Qualifying requirements

An employee must normally satisfy the following conditions before she can qualify for SMP:

(a)   she must have been continuously employed by her employer for at least 26 weeks ending with the week immediately preceding the 14th week before the EWC, but have ceased to work for him (see CONTINUOUS EMPLOYMENT (6));

(b)   her normal weekly earnings, for the period of 8 weeks ending with the week immediately preceding the 14th week before the EWC, must be not less than the lower limit for the payment of National Insurance contributions (currently £109),

(c)   she must have become pregnant and reached, or been confined before reaching, the start of the 11th week before the expected week of confinement.

(*SSCBA 1992, s 164(1), (2)*.)

'Confinement' is defined as labour resulting in the issue of a living child, or labour after 24 weeks of pregnancy resulting in the issue of a child whether alive or dead (*SSCBA 1992, s 171(1)*). 'Employee' is defined as meaning a woman who is gainfully employed in Great Britain either under a contract of service or in an office (including elective office) with general earnings (*SSCBA 1992, s 171(1)*). (Note that this definition is subject to various other statutory provisions, including those in *s 171(1)* itself and in *reg 17* of the *Statutory Maternity Pay (General) Regulations 1986 (SI 1986/1960)* (the '*SMP Regulations*').)

There are certain exceptions to the above requirement of continuous employment. Thus, the employer remains liable to pay SMP if the period of continuous employment was not less than eight weeks and he brought the contract of employment to an end solely or mainly for the purpose of avoiding his liability for SMP (*reg 3* of the *SMP Regulations*). In addition, the right to SMP survives if the woman is confined more than 14 weeks before the expected date of confinement, and would, but for her confinement, otherwise have qualified (*reg 4* of the *SMP Regulations* as amended by *SI 1994/1367, reg 3*).

For the purpose of calculating continuity of employment, it is the existence of the contract of employment which is crucial, and not whether the employee is in fact working. In *Secretary of State for Employment v Doulton Sanitaryware Ltd* [1981] ICR 477, EAT (decided under the previous law relating to maternity pay), it was held on the facts that the parties intended the contract to continue even though the employee had stopped working (she had been put on a list of 'prolonged absentees').

It is clearly intended that the right to SMP should not be conditional upon an intention to return to work after the confinement.

There is no entitlement to SMP in respect of any week in which the employee is in legal custody or sentenced to a term of imprisonment, other than a suspended sentence, or in respect of any subsequent week within the maternity pay period (*reg 9* of the *SMP Regulations*).

Members of Her Majesty's forces are excluded from the right to SMP (*SSCBA 1992, s 161(2)*). The right extends to persons working for the Crown (*s 161*), within the EC, to employees who are absent from Great Britain on holiday or for business purposes at any time during the maternity pay period, as well as to certain mariners (see the *Statutory Maternity Pay (Persons Abroad and Mariners) Regulations 1987 (SI 1987/418)*, as amended by *Social Security Contributions, Statutory Maternity Pay and Statutory Sick Pay (Miscellaneous Amendments) Regulations 1996 (SI 1996/777), reg 4*).

SSCBA 1992, s 164(6) provides that any agreement is void in so far as it purports to exclude or limit the right to SMP.

31.40 Procedure for making a claim

The employee must give her employer (or the person liable to make payments of SMP) 28 days' prior notice of the date from which she expects his liability to pay SMP to begin, or if that is not reasonably practicable, such notice as is reasonably practicable (*s 164(4)* and *reg 23* of the *SMP Regulations*). That notice must be in writing if the liable person so requests (*SSCBA, s 164(5)*).

The employee must also provide the liable person with a maternity certificate signed by a doctor or midwife as evidence of her pregnancy and of the expected date of confinement and there is a prescribed form for such certificates (*reg 22 of the SMP Regulations; Social Security Administration Act 1992, s 15; Statutory Maternity Pay (Medical Evidence) Regulations 1987 (SI 1987/235)*).

31.41 Period of entitlement

SMP is payable in respect of each week during the 'maternity pay period'. The maternity pay period will be a period of 39 consecutive weeks (*reg 2(2)* of the *SMP Regulations*). In general, when it starts depends upon when the employee gives notice and stops work *(reg 2(1)* of the *SMP Regulations).* However, ordinarily the first day of the period will not be earlier than the 11th week before the expected week of confinement, nor later than the day immediately following the day of confinement. Note that *reg 2* of the *SMP Regulations* contains other specific rules on the start of the maternity pay period. The *SMP Regulations* do not permit payment to cease upon dismissal.

These rules were considered by the Upper Tribunal in *Wade v North Yorkshire Police Authority* [2011] IRLR 393, UT (TCC). The UT provided detailed guidance the start date for SMP and observed that a woman could nominate a date from which she wished to claim statutory maternity pay and would be ceasing to work "in conformity with [a] notice" for the purposes of *reg 2(1)* even if she has previously ceased to work on some other basis (in a way analogous to her right to claim statutory maternity leave from a date of her choosing, even if she had previously been away from work for e.g. annual leave or sick leave).

SMP is not ordinarily payable by an employer in respect of a week during any part of which the woman works under a contract of service with him *(SSCBA, s 165(4)).*

31.42   Amount of payments

SSCBA 1992, s 166 provides for two rates of payment. (Note: the application of *s 166* is modified by *SI 1986/1960, reg 4(3)* (as amended by *SI 1994/1367, reg 3*) where the employee is confined more than 14 weeks before the expected date of confinement, and would, but for her confinement, otherwise have qualified; see **31.32** above.)

For the first six weeks of the maternity pay period, the rate is calculated as being 90% of the employee's normal weekly earnings for the period of 8 weeks immediately preceding the 14th week before the EWC (there is no minimum rate of payment) *(SSCBA, s 166(2)).* The calculation is done by reference to actual earnings, regardless of any abnormal amounts in those 8 weeks. After the first six weeks, the payment for the remaining 33 weeks is set at the lesser of £136.78 per week or the rate payable during the first six weeks *(SCCBA, s 166(1)(b); reg 6* of the *SMP Regulations).* The rate of SMP is amended annually.

In any case where a woman is awarded a pay increase (or would have been awarded such an increase had she not then been absent on statutory maternity leave) and the pay increase applies to the whole or any part of the period between the beginning of the relevant period and the end of her period of SML, her normal weekly earnings should be calculated as if such sum was paid in that period: *reg 21(7)* of the *Statutory Maternity Pay (General) Regulations 1986 SI 1986/1960.* This regulation was amended in order to give effect to the decision of the ECJ in *Gillespie v Northern Health and Social Services Board: C-342/93* [1996] ICR 498. Thus the EAT had held in *Alabaster v Woolwich plc* [2000] ICR 1037 that in calculating maternity pay, a woman was entitled to the benefit of all increases in her basic salary which took effect between the start of the 'relevant period' (the period of 8 weeks immediately preceding the 14th week before the EWC) and the end of her maternity leave, and not just backdated pay increases. The EAT also held that the proper remedy for failure to make appropriate payments of maternity pay was an action for unlawful deduction of wages. The matter was referred to the ECJ, which held ([2005] ICR 695) that a woman who receives a pay increase before the start of her maternity leave is entitled to have the increase taken into consideration even though the pay rise was not backdated to the relevant reference period for the purposes of the *1996 Amendment Regulations.*

SMP should be paid in the like manner and at the same time as the employee would normally be paid, or if there is no agreement as to a pay day, or no normal pay day, on the last day of a calendar month *(regs 27, 29* of the *SMP Regulations).* It does not exclude any contractual benefits to which the employee may be entitled, but the employer is entitled to set off SMP against contractual remuneration in respect of the same period and vice versa *(SSCBA, Sch 13 para 3).* In other words, the employer has to meet the more onerous of the contractual and statutory burdens, but not both of them. Similarly, tax, National Insurance contributions and any other regular deductions fall to be deducted from SMP.

HMRC Guidance entitled 'SMP – Salary-Sacrifice and Non-cash Benefits' (August 2008), explains that all pay elements count as pay, including car allowances, shift allowances, bonuses and commission payments. Attempts by employers to cease to provide cash or non-cash benefits, whether discretionary or under contract, are likely to result in discrimination claims.

31.43 Remedy for non-payment

If the employer fails to make payments of SMP to which the employee believes herself to be entitled, the employee may first of all require the employer within a reasonable time to supply her with a written statement of the position which he is adopting (*Social Security Administration Act 1992, s 15(2)*). Where an employer decides that he has no liability to pay SMP or further SMP, he must also furnish her with the details of and reasons for his decision, and with other information, in connection with the making of a claim by her for a maternity allowance or incapacity benefit or employment and support allowance (*reg 25A* of the *SMP Regulations* (inserted by *SI 1990/622*)). If the dispute is not resolved, either the employee or the DWP may refer the matter to an HMRC officer (*Statutory Sick Pay and Statutory Maternity Pay (Decisions) Regulations 1999 (SI 1999/776)*: *Taylor Gordon & Co Ltd v Timmons* [2004] IRLR 180 (on SSP); *Hair Division Ltd v Macmillan*, EAT (12 October 2012, unreported). An employer's continued refusal to pay after an adverse determination is an offence.

If the employee is unable to obtain her entitlement from the employer (which may be because he has become insolvent), she is entitled to look to the Secretary of State for payment (*regs 7, 30* of the *SMP Regulations*).

However, if her employer does not dispute the entitlement to SMP, and the complaint is that the payment has not been paid (or not paid in the correct amount), this may be brought as a wages claim because SMP is within the definition of wages in *ERA, section 27: Hair Division*.

31.44 Recoupment by employer

The system whereby the employer recoups payments of SMP made by him is similar to that which are used to apply to statutory sick pay (see SICKNESS AND SICK PAY (**42**)). In short, the relevant moneys are deducted by the employer from National Insurance contributions which would otherwise fall to be remitted by him. Apart from 'small employers' (broadly, those whose contributions payments for the qualifying tax year do not exceed £45,000, and who are entitled to recover 103% of each payment), employers will be able to recover only 92% of each payment of SMP. Small employers are entitled to recover an 'additional payment', equal to 4.5% of each payment of SMP, which is intended to recoup the National Insurance contributions payable on such payments.

The system of recoupment is governed by regulations made under *SSCBA 1992, s 167* (substituted by *EA 2002, s 21(1)*). These are the *Statutory Maternity Pay (Compensation of Employers) and Miscellaneous Amendment Regulations 1994 (SI 1994/1882)*, as amended.

Employers can, in certain circumstances, obtain advance recovery of SMP from HMRC (*EA 2002, s 21(2); Statutory Maternity Pay (Compensation of Employers) and Miscellaneous Amendment Regulations 1994 (SI 1994/1882), reg 5* (as amended by *SI 2003/672*)).

31.45 Maternity allowance

Women who do not qualify for SMP may be entitled to receive Maternity Allowance instead: see the *SSCBA, s 35(1)*.

31.46 PARENTAL LEAVE

The *MPL Regulations* give effect to provisions contained in the *EU Parental Leave Directive (96/34)*. They create a right to unpaid parental leave in respect of children born or adopted on or after 15 December 1999. Amendments have been made to the *MPL Regulations* to ensure compliance with the *Directive*: see the *Maternity and Parental Leave (Amendment) Regulations 2001 (SI 2001/4010);* the *Maternity and Parental Leave (Amendment) Regulations 2002 (SI 2002/2789)*; the *Maternity and Parental Leave etc.* and the *Paternity and Adoption Leave (Amendment) Regulations 2006 (SI 2006/2014)*; the *Maternity and Parental Leave etc.* and the *Paternity and Adoption Leave (Amendment) Regulations 2008 (SI 2002/1966)*; and the *Parental Leave (EU Directive) Regulations 2013 (SI 2013/283)*.

There are two further developments which remain afoot in relation to parental leave.

(1)   First, in March 2010 the EU Council adopted a further Directive extending the period of parental leave to four months: the *Parental Leave Directive 2010/18/EU*. This was implemented by the *Parental Leave (EU Directive) Regulations 2013 (SI 2013/283)* with effect from 8 March 2013.

(2)   Secondly, at the date of writing the Government has carried out a consultation on a proposed new system of shared parental leave ('the Modern Workplace consultation'), but has indicated that it does not intend to enact any proposals to be effective before April 2015.

31.47

Any employee with one year's continuous service who has, or expects to have, responsibility for a child is entitled to be absent from work on parental leave for the purpose of caring for that child: *reg 13(1)*. 'Responsibility' means 'parental responsibility' or registration as the child's father: *reg 13(2)*.

Parental leave is unpaid.

Enforcement of this right is by complaint to an employment tribunal (*ERA 1996, s 80(1)*).

The period of parental leave is now set at 18 weeks for each child (*reg 14(1)*); parents of disabled children (i.e. children entitled to disability living allowance) may take up to 18 weeks' leave (*reg 14(1A)*). Ordinarily, this entitlement must be exercised before the child's 5th birthday or, where the child was adopted, whichever is the sooner of the 5th anniversary of the adoption or the child's 18th birthday (*reg 15(1)(a)*). Parents of disabled children can take parental leave until the child's 18th birthday (*reg 15(3)*). Where a child was born before 15 December 1999, and his fifth birthday was on or after that date, parental leave could only be taken up until 31 March 2005: see *reg 15(2)*.

The *MPL Regulations* envisage that parental leave arrangements will be governed by contract in most workplaces. Where there is no such agreement, default provisions apply: *reg 16* and *Sch 2*.

Under the default provisions, leave can only be taken in blocks of one week at a time (except in a case where the child in question is entitled to a disability living allowance): *Sch 2, para 7*. A week's leave is defined in *reg 14*. It is not open to an employee to take one day's parental leave (unless this is agreed to by his employer as part of a *Workforce Agreement*): see *New Southern Railways Ltd (formerly South Central Trains Ltd) v Rodway* [2005] EWCA Civ 443, [2005] ICR 1162, CA. The maximum that can be taken is four weeks' leave in respect of any individual child during a particular year: *Sch 2, paras 8* and *9*. The default provisions also contain 'conditions of entitlement' for the taking of parental leave. These include the provision of evidence of responsibility if required, notice to the employer of the leave dates, and the ability of the employer to postpone leave in certain circumstances (see *Sch 2, paras 1 to 5*).

31.48   Maternity and Parental Rights

31.48 The *Regulations* provide protection against victimisation. An employee is protected against detriment by reason of taking or seeking to take parental leave, declining to sign a workforce agreement or performing any function or activity as a workforce representative or candidate (or proposing to do so): *reg 19(2)* and *ERA 1996, s 47C*. He or she will have been automatically unfairly dismissed if dismissed for such a reason: *reg 20(3)* and *ERA 1996, s 99*. There are also further protections in relation to asserting a statutory right in the *ERA 1996, s 104*.

In *New Southern Railways Ltd* (above), an employee sought to take one day's leave to look after his son. This was refused by the employer. The employee took the day off anyway, and was subsequently issued with a disciplinary warning for being absent without permission. The EAT and Court of Appeal overturned the decision of an employment tribunal that he had been victimised because the disagreement as to whether or not he was entitled to take one day's parental leave was for 'a reason related to parental leave'. The Court of Appeal held that victimisation by the employer must be 'done for a prescribed reason', which is one prescribed by the *MPL Regulations*. As the employee could not lawfully take one day of parental leave under the 'Default Provisions', the disciplinary action was not for a prescribed reason, and was therefore lawful.

31.49 Certain contractual provisions continue to apply during the parental leave period, including the implied obligations of trust and confidence and good faith (*reg 17*).

31.50 There is also a right to return to work after parental leave. An employee who takes parental leave for a period of four weeks or less, which was an isolated period of leave or the last of two or more consecutive periods of statutory leave which did not include any period of AML or additional adoption leave, or a period of parental leave of more than four weeks, is entitled to return from leave to the job in which he or she was employed before the absence: *regulation 18(1)*. Otherwise, or where an employee takes parental leave for a period of more than four weeks, the employee is entitled to return from leave to the job in which he or she was employed before her absence or, if it is not reasonably practicable for the employer to permit her to return to that job, to another job which is both suitable and appropriate for her to do in the circumstances: *reg 18(2)*. The returning parent has a right to return with the seniority, pension rights and similar rights as if they had not been absent, and on terms and conditions not less favourable than those which would have applied if they had not been absent: *reg 18A(1)*. The provisions are analogous to those for mothers returning after maternity leave (see **31.18** above).

31.51 In *Meerts v Proost NV*: C 116/08 [2009] ECR I-10063 the CJEU held, by reference to clauses 2.6 and 2.7 of the *Framework Agreement on Parental Leave*, that an employer who dismisses a full-time employee without giving statutory notice or having 'urgent cause' whilst that employee is taking part-time parental leave is obliged to pay compensation on the basis of that employee's full-time salary (not the reduced salary paid during his parental leave). The CJEU accepted the Advocate General's view that national legislation which entailed a reduction in employment rights in the event of parental leave could discourage workers from taking such leave and could encourage employers to dismiss workers who are on parental leave rather than other workers. This would run directly counter to the aim of the *Framework Agreement*, one of the objectives of which is to make it easier to reconcile working and family life.

There remains a real question whether UK law properly implements the Framework Agreement, in light of the decision in *Meerts*. By *reg 17* of the *MPL Regulations*, an employee who takes parental leave is entitled, during that leave, to the benefit of her terms and conditions of employment relating to notice of termination given by her employer. However, under the enabling provision for the *MPL Regulations* in *section 77* of the *ERA*, 'terms and conditions' for these purposes do not include terms and conditions as to remuneration. At least arguably therefore, an employee dismissed whilst taking parental leave is entitled only to statutory notice pay, not contractual.

In *Zentralbetriebsrat der Landeskrankenhauser Tirols v Land Tirol*: C-486/08 [2010] IRLR 631 the CJEU ruled that *clause 2.6* of the *Framework Agreement* on Parental Leave precludes a national provision whereby workers on parental leave lose their right to paid annual leave accumulated during the year preceding the birth of their child. *Clause 2.6* requires that rights acquired or in the process of being acquired by the worker on the date on which parental leave starts are to be maintained as they stand until the end of parental leave and apply after that leave. It covers all the rights and benefits, whether in cash or in kind, derived directly or indirectly from the employment relationship, which the worker is entitled to claim from the employer at the date on which parental leave starts, including the right to paid annual leave.

In *Chatzi v Ipourgos Ikonomikon*: C-149/10 (16 September 2010, unreported), the CJEU confirmed that the right to leave is that of the parent rather than the child, so that multiple births do not entitle an additional period of leave, albeit that national law should permit flexibility to take account of the needs of having, for example, twins.

In addition, in *Pedro Manuel Roca Alvarez v Sesa Start Espana ETT SA*: C-104/09, [2011] All ER (EC) 253, the CJEU held that the principle of equal treatment in *Directive 76/207/EEC* precluded a Spanish law which allowed mothers to take "breastfeeding leave" in the first nine months following the birth of their child irrespective of the employment status of the child's father, but only allowed fathers to take such leave if the child's mother was also in employment (the appellant's wife was self-employed).

There is scope to argue, in light of the judgment in *Roca Alvarez*, that the full extent of the differential between rights afforded to fathers under UK parental leave and paternity leave legislation and those afforded to mothers under maternity leave legislation is not objectively justified.

31.52 Paternity leave

The law in relation to 'paternity leave' has changed dramatically in recent years:

(a)   The *Employment Act 2002* introduced an entitlement to a short period of 'paternity leave'. This is described in this chapter as 'ordinary' paternity leave. The details are set out in the *Paternity and Adoption Leave Regulations 2002 (SI 2002/2788)* (the 'PAL Regulations').

(b)   There is also now a right to 'additional' paternity leave under the *Additional Paternity Leave Regulations 2010 (SI 2010/1055)* (the 'Additional PL Regulations'), which came into force on 6 April 2010 (in relation to children whose expected week of birth begins on or after 3 April 2011). The *Additional PL Regulations* implement powers in the *Work and Families Act 2006*. In effect they allow parents to share additional leave between them.

This expansion of paternity rights is timely, in light of the decision of the CJEU in *Pedro Manuel Roca Alvarez v Sesa Start Espana ETT SA*: C-104/09 [2011] All ER (EC) 253 (see **31.51** above).

31.53 *Entitlement to 'ordinary' paternity leave*

An employee is entitled to paternity leave under *reg 4* of the *PAL Regulations* (i.e. to be absent from work for the purpose of caring for a child or supporting the child's mother) if:

(a)   he has been continuously employed for a period of not less than 26 weeks ending with the week immediately preceding the 14th week before the expected week of the child's birth (note the provisions in *reg 4(3), (5)* where the child is born early or is stillborn);

(b)   he is either the child's father or is married to or is the civil partner or partner of the child's mother (note that this definition may include a female civil partner or partner of the child's mother);

(c)   he has or expects to have responsibility for bringing up the child (main responsibility, if he is not the child's father); and

(d)   he has complied with the requirements to give notice (and, in certain cases, provide evidence) set out in *reg 6* of the *PAL Regulations*.

31.54 *'Ordinary' paternity leave*

The employee may take either one week's leave, or two consecutive weeks' leave: *reg 5(1)*. This leave may only be taken during the period commencing with the child's birth or the date on which the child is placed with the adopter and ending either 56 days' later or, if the child is born before the first day of the expected week of its birth, 56 days after that date: *reg 5(2)*.

Before taking 'ordinary' paternity leave, the employee must notify his employer that he intends to do so, specifying the expected week of childbirth, the length of leave that he has chosen to take (see *reg 5(1)*), and the date on which he has chosen to take such leave (see *reg 5(3)–(4)*): *reg 6(1)*. Such notice must be given in or before the 15th week before the expected week of the child's birth or as soon as reasonably practicable if notice could not have been given sooner: *reg 6(2)*. In addition, if requested by the employer, the employee must sign a declaration that he is taking leave for the purpose of caring for the child or supporting the child's mother (per *reg 4(1)*) and that he satisfies the eligibility requirements in *reg 4(2)(b)–(c)*: *reg 6(3)*.

There is a mechanism in the *PAL Regulations* to vary the date on which 'ordinary' paternity leave will begin, including where the birth is late: *reg 6(4)–(8)*.

31.55 *Benefits during 'ordinary' paternity leave*

During the course of paternity leave, an employee is entitled to the benefit of all the terms and conditions that would have applied if he or she had not been absent (save for those in relation to remuneration, ie. wages or salary), and remains bound by the obligations that arise out of those terms and conditions: *reg 12*.

An employee is entitled to return to the same job at the end of an isolated period of paternity leave or the last of two or more consecutive periods of statutory leave which did not include any period of AML, or additional adoption leave or a period of parental leave of more than four weeks (*reg 13(1)*). In all other cases, he or she is entitled to return to the same job or, if this is not reasonably practicable, to another job which is suitable and appropriate for him or her to do in the circumstances (*reg 13(2)*). The employee's return to work broadly carries with it the same seniority, pension and similar rights and the right to no less favourable terms and conditions than he would have enjoyed had he not taken leave (*reg 14*).

31.56 *Entitlement to additional paternity leave*

Additional paternity leave is available for the purpose of caring for a child whose expected week of birth falls on or after 3 April 2011 (*regs 3* and *4* of the *Additional PL Regulations*). This is in contrast to the short period of ordinary paternity leave under the *PAL Regulations*, which extends in addition to absence for the purpose of caring for the child's mother (*reg 4* of the *PAL Regulations*).

By *reg 4* of the *Additional PL Regulations*, an employee is entitled to additional paternity leave if:

(a)   he has been continuously employed for a period of not less than 26 weeks ending with the week immediately preceding the 14th week before the child's expected week of birth (note the provisions in relation to early births in *reg 4(4)*);

(b)   he remains in continuous employment with that employer until the week before the first week of his additional paternity leave;

(c)   he is either the child's father or, if he is not the child's father, he is married to or is the partner or civil partner of the child's mother (again, this definition could include the female partner or civil partner of the child's mother);

(d)   he has, or expects to have, the main responsibility for the child's upbringing (apart from any responsibility that the mother may have);

(e)   he has complied with the applicable notification and evidence requirements in *regs 6* and *7* of the *Additional PL Regulations*;

(f)   the child's mother is entitled, because of becoming pregnant with the child, to maternity leave, statutory maternity pay or maternity allowance and has returned to work (or is treated as having returned to work) as defined in *reg 25* of the *Additional PL Regulations*; and

(g)   the child's mother has signed the mother declaration referred to in *reg 6* of the *Additional PL Regulations*.

Separate provision is made for additional paternity leave in the event of the mother's death: see *regs 10–13* of the *Additional PL Regulations*.

31.57   *Additional paternity leave*

A person may take a continuous period of additional paternity leave of any multiple of complete weeks between two and 26 weeks, and may take that leave at any time within the period beginning 20 weeks after the child's birthdate and ending on the child's first birthday (*reg 5*). In addition, *regs 7* and *9* of the *Additional PL Regulations* govern the commencement, variation or cancellation of additional paternity leave, *reg 29* governs the termination of additional paternity leave where the person is dismissed during that period, *reg 30* contains provisions for the early return from a period of additional paternity leave and *reg 24* applies where the child in question dies.

Additional paternity leave cannot begin until eight weeks after the date the person gave leave notice to his employer under *reg 6* of the *Additional PL Regulations* (*reg 5(4)*). Reg 6 requires that, not less than eight weeks before his chosen start date for additional paternity leave, the person give his employer:

(a)   "leave notice" (a written notice specifying the child's expected week of childbirth, the child's date of birth, and the dates the person has chosen under *reg 5* as the start and end dates of his additional paternity leave);

(b)   an "employee declaration" (a signed written declaration stating that the purpose of the period of leave will be to care for the child, and that the person satisfies the eligibility conditions in *reg 4(2)(c)–(d)* of the *Additional PL Regulations*); and

(c)   a "mother declaration" (a written declaration by the mother giving the information specified in *reg 6(2)(c)* of the *Additional PL Regulations*).

The person must provide a copy of the child's birth certificate and the name and address of the employer of the child's mother (or, if the mother is self-employed, her business address) within 28 days of any request to that effect from his or her employer, provided that the request is made within 28 days of receipt of the "leave notice": see *reg 6(3)*.

An employer who receives leave notice from an employee under *reg 6(1)* or a subsequent notice under *reg 7(1)* must confirm the relevant dates to the employee in writing within 28 days: *reg 8(1)*. The employer must also give such confirmation in certain circumstances under *reg 8(2)*.

In addition, the person must give his employer written "withdrawal notice" under *reg 6(4)* as soon as reasonably practicable if he no longer satisfies the conditions in *reg 4(2)(c) or (d)* or if the child's mother no longer satisfies the conditions in *reg 4(5)* of the *Additional PL Regulations*. An employer has a number of rights when an employee gives such "withdrawal notice": see *reg 6*.

31.58 *Benefits during additional paternity leave*

During the course of additional paternity leave, a person is entitled to the benefit of all the terms and conditions that would have applied if he had not been absent (save for those in relation to remuneration, ie. wages or salary), and remains bound by the obligations that arise out of those terms and conditions: see *reg 27* of the *Additional PL Regulations*. He will gain special protection where, during his additional paternity leave period, it is not practicable by reason of redundancy for the employer to continue to employ him under his existing contract: see *reg 28*.

In addition:

(a)   A person taking additional paternity leave of no more than 26 weeks will be entitled to return to the same job at the end of an isolated period of paternity leave or the last of two or more consecutive periods of statutory leave which did not include any period of AML, or additional adoption leave or a period of parental leave of more than four weeks (*reg 31(1)*). Otherwise, the person is entitled to return to the same job or, if this is not reasonably practicable, to another job which is suitable and appropriate for him to do in the circumstances (*reg 31(2)*). The employee's return to work broadly carries with it the same seniority, pension and similar rights and the right to no less favourable terms and conditions than he would have enjoyed had he not taken leave (*reg 32*).

(b)   A person who has the benefit of both a statutory right to additional paternity leave and a corresponding contractual right may not exercise both separately but may take advantage of whichever right is, in any particular respect, the more favourable (and the relevant statutory provisions shall apply, modified as necessary to give effect to more favourable contractual terms, to the exercise of such a composite right: *reg 35*).

In addition, a person may carry out up to ten days' work for his employer during an additional paternity leave period without bringing that period to an end, but his employer cannot require that he do so (and he cannot demand to do so): see *reg 26* of the *Additional PL Regulations*.

Following *Pedro Manuel Roca Alvarez v Sesa Start Espana ETT SA*: C-104/09, [2011] All ER (EC) 253, in which the CJEU held that the principle of equal treatment in *Directive 76/207/EEC* precluded a Spanish law which allowed mothers to take "breast-feeding leave" in the first nine months following the birth of their child irrespective of the employment status of the child's father, but only allowed fathers to take such leave if the child's mother was also in employment (the appellant's wife was self-employed), there may be scope to argue that the full extent of the differential between rights afforded to fathers under UK parental leave and paternity leave legislation and those afforded to mothers under maternity leave legislation is not objectively justified. The position can be usefully reviewed following any enactment of the changes under the Children and Families Bill (see **31.4A** above).

31.59 ADOPTION LEAVE AND PATERNITY LEAVE IN RELATION TO ADOPTED CHILDREN

Entitlement to adoption leave has been introduced:

(a)   under the *PAL Regulations*, both as adoption leave per se (see especially *regs 8–14*) and as a form of paternity leave in relation to an adopted child (see especially *regs 15–27* where the employee has 26 weeks' qualifying service (*reg 15*);

(b)   under the *Additional PL Regulations*, as a form of additional paternity leave in relation to adopted children who are matched to a person who is notified of having been matched on or after 3 April 2011 (see especially *reg 3* and *regs 14–23*); and

(c)   under the *Additional Paternity Leave (Adoptions from Overseas) Regulations 2010 (SI 2010/1059)* (the '*Overseas Adoptions Additional PL Regulations*') and the *Employment Rights Act 1996 (Application of Section 80BB to Adoptions from Overseas) Regulations 2010 (SI 2010/1058)*, as additional paternity leave in relation to employees married to or the civil partner or partner of an adopter whose child enters Great Britain on or after 3 April 2011.

The detailed rules applicable to adoption leave per se are broadly similar to those applicable to the comparable provisions for ordinary and additional maternity leave. Those applicable to paternity leave in relation to adopted children are broadly similar to those applicable to ordinary and additional paternity leave. Those considering or advising on issues relating to adoption leave (both per se and as a form of paternity leave) must have regard to the commencement dates for the differing provisions of the 2010 regulations (including protections from detriment / dismissal).

31.60 PROTECTION AGAINST DETRIMENT IN RELATION TO PATERNITY OR ADOPTION LEAVE

As with employees taking maternity leave, employees are protected against suffering detriment in certain circumstances in relation to paternity or adoption leave: *reg 28* of the *PAL Regulations*, *reg 33* of the *Additional PL Regulations*, *reg 23* of the *Overseas Adoptions Additional PL Regulations* and *ERA 1996, s 47C*. Dismissal of an employee for a reason connected with the fact that he took, or sought to take, paternity or adoption leave, or for a series of other specified related reasons, will be an automatically unfair dismissal, save in prescribed circumstances, as will the dismissal of a person on additional paternity leave for the reason that he is redundant where *reg 28* of the *Additional PL Regulations* or *reg 18* of the *Overseas Adoptions Additional PL Regulations* as appropriate have not been complied with: *reg 29* of the *PAL Regulations*, *reg 34* of the *Additional PL Regulations*, *reg 24* of the *Overseas Adoptions Additional PL Regulations* and *ERA 1996, s 99*.

However, note that the protections in relation to additional paternity leave in the *Additional PL Regulations* only come into effect on 6 April 2010: the protection from detriment provisions have effect only in relation to an act or failure to act which takes place on or after that date, and the protection from unfair dismissal applies only where the effective date of termination within the meaning of *section 97* of the *Employment Rights Act 1996* falls on or after that date (*reg 3*).

Similarly, the protections in the *Overseas Adoptions Additional PL Regulations* only come into effect on 9 April 2010 and the same applies to the protection from detriment/dismissal provisions therein.

In *Atkins v Coyle Personnel plc* [2008] IRLR 420, the EAT observed that there had to be a causal connection between the dismissal and the taking of paternity leave in a claim under *reg 29* of the *PAL Regulations*, rather than some vague, less stringent connection. The mere fact that a dispute between employee and manager originated in an incident when the employee was on paternity leave will not be sufficient by itself to establish the causal connection.

31.61 STATUTORY PATERNITY AND ADOPTION PAY

Employees who satisfy certain qualifying conditions are entitled to statutory paternity pay or statutory adoption pay for up to two weeks in the sum of the lesser of £136.78 per week or 90% of his normal weekly earnings (determined in accordance with the *Statutory Paternity Pay and Adoption Pay (General) Regulations 2002 (SI 2002/2822)*): *Statutory Paternity Pay and Statutory Adoption Pay (Weekly Rates) Regulations 2002 (SI 2002/2818)*, as regularly amended.

In addition, employees who satisfy the relevant qualifying conditions are entitled to additional statutory paternity pay in accordance with the detailed requirements of the *Additional Statutory Paternity Pay (General) Regulations 2010 (SI 2010/1056)* or the *Additional Statutory Paternity Pay (Adoptions from Overseas) Regulations 2010 (SI 2010/1057)* and the *Additional Statutory Paternity Pay (Weekly Rates) Regulations 2010 (SI 2010/1060)*. See also variously the *Additional Statutory Paternity Pay (Birth, Adoption and Adoptions from Overseas) (Administration) Regulations 2010 (SI 2010/154)*, the *Statutory Paternity Pay (Adoption), Additional Statutory Paternity Pay (Adoption) and Statutory Adoption Pay (Adoptions from Overseas) (Persons Abroad and Mariners) Regulations 2010 (SI 2010/150)* and the *Additional Statutory Paternity Pay (National Health Service Employees) Regulations 2010 (SI 2010/152)*.

32   Pay – I: Payments, Pay Statements and Miscellaneous Statutory Pay Rights

Cross-references. See PAY – II (33) for statutory deductions from pay; EQUAL PAY (21) for the rules against sex discrimination in pay; TRADE UNIONS – II (49) for deduction of trade union subscriptions.

32.1   INTRODUCTION

An employee's right to payment for his services is, of course, fundamental to the employment relationship and is principally governed by the particular terms of the contract of employment between the individual employee and employer. For example, the rate of pay and the intervals at which payment is made are governed by the individual employee's contract of employment, which also provides for any bonuses, commission, overtime, holiday pay or sick pay which may be payable. Such matters must be included in the written particulars of the contract of employment given by the employer to the employee (see **7.4** CONTRACT OF EMPLOYMENT). There is, however, a substantial overlay of statutory rights and protection afforded to employees in relation to payment for their services in the form of the right not to suffer unauthorised deductions from wages, the right to a National Minimum Wage and the right to itemised pay statements. These important rights are considered below.

Various other statutory rights to payment, such as statutory sick pay (see SICKNESS AND SICK PAY (42)) and statutory maternity pay (see MATERNITY AND PARENTAL RIGHTS (31)) are considered in other chapters in this work. Certain miscellaneous statutory rights to payment, namely, guarantee payments and medical suspension payments are outlined towards the end of this chapter. In addition there is an overview of the principles applicable to the calculation of 'a week's pay' – a statutory concept relevant to calculation of the sums payable under a number of the statutory employment rights such as the right to a redundancy payment and the payment of a basic award in a claim for unfair dismissal.

32.2   PAYMENT OF WAGES AND DEDUCTIONS FROM WAGES

Deductions from employees' pay were originally regulated by the *Wages Act 1986 ('WA 1986')*. The *WA 1986* had replaced the *Truck Acts*, which had formerly restricted payment of wages other than in cash (but see **32.3** below). The *WA 1986* made special provision for employees in retail employment affording them greater protection against deductions from their wages. The provisions of the *WA 1986* are all consolidated in *Part II* of the *Employment Rights Act 1996*. In this section of this chapter, references below are to the *Employment Rights Act 1996 ('ERA')* unless otherwise stated. In very rare cases, involving contracts of employment predating 1987, it may be necessary to have regard to the previous law as set out in **32.3** and **32.4** below. In the vast majority of cases the position will be governed exclusively by the provisions of *Part II* of the *ERA* as discussed in **32.6** *et seq* below.

32.3   PAYMENT OF WAGES

WA 1986, s 11 (now repealed) removed restrictions on the way in which payment of wages to manual and other workers may be made. The method of payment is now to be determined solely by the terms of the contract. It will be either the subject of express agreement or determined by an implied term. If no express agreement is reached it is likely that the method of payment impliedly agreed will be that which is customary in the industry.

The provisions of *WA 1986* replaced the old restrictions on the payment of wages contained in the *Truck Acts* and the *Payment of Wages Act 1960*. *Section 11* came into force on 1 January 1987 (*The Wages Act 1986 (Commencement) Order 1986 (SI 1986/1998)*). However, because *s 1* of the *Truck Act 1831* operated by implying into the contract of employment a term that wages were payable in coin and not otherwise, it would appear that the contractual terms thus created survived the repeal of the *Act*. In other words, where the worker was employed pursuant to an unamended contract of employment created before 1 January 1987, it may be necessary on rare occasions to refer to the provisions set out in **32.4** and **32.5** below, but the requirement of pay in coin is now contractual rather than statutory and may be varied by consent. Such consensual variation will be implied if payment has in fact been other than in coin for a lengthy period.

32.4   PAYMENT OF WAGES: PRE-1987 POSITION

Until 1 January 1987, all wages payable to a manual labourer for work done by him, with certain exceptions, had to be paid to him in current coin of the realm or, if he so requested, by payment into a bank account or by cheque, postal order or money order (*Truck Act 1831, s 3; Payment of Wages Act 1960, s 1*). Any agreement to the contrary was illegal, null and void. If an employer acted in breach of the *Truck Acts*, for example, by payment in kind by the delivery of goods, or by payment by cheque against the employee's wishes:

(a)   the employee could sue for the wages due, no allowance being made for the value of the goods supplied; and

(b)   the employer was guilty of an offence.

(*Truck Act 1831, s 9.*)

A foreman did not fall within the protection of the *Truck Acts* (*Brooker v Charrington Fuel Oils Ltd* [1981] IRLR 147).

32.5   Exceptions

These are:

(i)   The provision of medicine or medical attendance, fuel materials, tools and accommodation could form part of the consideration for the employee's services (*Truck Act 1831, s 23*).

(ii)   Payments to domestic servants did not need to comply with the requirements as to payment in coin (*Truck Act 1831, s 20*).

(iii)   Contracts for the provision for agricultural workers of food, non-intoxicating drink, a cottage or other similar allowances or privileges were not illegal if money wages were paid in addition to these benefits (*Truck Amendment Act 1887, s 4*).

32.6   DEDUCTIONS FROM WAGES: THE CURRENT PROVISIONS

No deduction from a worker's wages may be made unless either:

(a)   it is required or permitted by a statutory or contractual provision; or

(b)   the worker has given his prior written consent to the deduction.

(*ERA 1996, ss 13(1), 15(1).*)

It is extremely important that deductions are not made in breach of this provision. Not only may sums wrongfully deducted be ordered to be repaid, but the employer may lose the right to recover the sums which he was seeking to deduct by any means at all (see **32.8** below).

If the deduction is made pursuant to a contractual provision, the terms of the contract must have been shown to the worker or, if not in writing, its effect notified in writing to the worker before the deduction is made (*ERA 1996, ss 13(2), 15(2)* and see *Kerr v Sweater Shop (Scotland) Ltd; Sweater Shop (Scotland) Ltd v Park* [1996] IRLR 424, EAT). In *Mennell v Newell & Wright (Transport Contractors) Ltd* [1997] IRLR 519 the Court of Appeal held that an employment tribunal had no jurisdiction to deal with *threatened* deductions from wages as the *Act* stated that a tribunal could only hear complaints where an employer had actually made a deduction. Accordingly, a threat of dismissal in order to impose a variation of the contract of employment so as to enable an employer to make deductions from wages did not amount to a breach of the relevant wages provisions of the *ERA 1996*. In *Discount Tobacco and Confectionery Ltd v Williamson* [1993] ICR 371, it was held that for there to be prior written consent, the consent must precede not only the deduction itself, but also the event or conduct giving rise to the deduction. What has to appear in writing in either case is not merely provision for repayment of the sum concerned but for it to be deducted *from wages* (*Potter v Hunt Contracts Ltd* [1992] ICR 337).

The above provisions do not apply to deductions:

(i)   made in order to reimburse the employer for any overpayment of wages or expenses made for any reason;

(ii)   made pursuant to any statutory disciplinary proceedings;

(iii)   which are statutory payments due to a public authority. In *Patel v Marquette Partners (UK) Ltd* [2009] IRLR 425, [2009] ICR 569, EAT, the (unsurprising) application of this exclusion to a deduction in the form of a taxation decision in relation to a bonus was considered. The policy underlying the exclusion of such matters from the general provision of *s 13* of the *ERA* is that challenges to a statutory authority's decision that money is owing must be made under the specific legislation empowering the deduction (e.g. the tax legislation) and thus the exclusion in *s 14(3)* was to be generally construed in an non technical way;

(iv)   payable to third parties, for example, trade union dues, made either pursuant to a contractual term to the inclusion of which the worker has agreed in writing, or otherwise with his prior written agreement or consent (but as to union dues, see **47.1** TRADE UNIONS – **II** for restrictions on the deduction of union dues);

(v)   made from a worker's wages for taking part in a strike or other industrial action; or

(vi)   made, with the worker's prior written agreement or consent, for the purpose of satisfying an order of a court or tribunal for the payment of an amount by the worker to the employer.

(*ERA 1996, ss 14, 15.*)

It is irrelevant whether deductions made for a purpose falling within these exceptions are in fact lawful and justified. Such issues are outside the jurisdiction of the tribunal under the *ERA 1996* in any event (*Sunderland Polytechnic v Evans* [1993] ICR 392, in which the EAT disapproved its own earlier reasoning in *Home Office v Ayres* [1992] ICR 175; see also *SIP (Industrial Products) Ltd v Swinn* [1994] ICR 473). In an important clarification, however, in *Gill v Ford Motor Co Ltd; Wong v BAE Systems Operations Ltd* [2004] IRLR 840, the EAT held that where an exception provided by *s 14* is relied upon by an employer, the employment tribunal must make findings of fact as to whether the *s 14* ground is actually engaged on the facts of the case. This does not, however, oblige the tribunal to make findings as to whether, as a matter of contract, such deductions are lawful as the enquiry is limited to whether the factual basis for reliance upon a *s 14* exception is made out.

Equivalent restrictions apply to the receipt of payments by an employer, from a worker employed by him, in his capacity as the worker's employer (*ERA 1996, s 15(1), (5)*).

The scope of the wages provisions of the *ERA 1996* is dependent upon the meaning given to the crucial terms 'wages', 'deduction' and 'worker'.

Wages. Wages are defined by *ERA 1996, s 27(1)* to mean any sums payable to the worker by his employer in connection with his employment, including:

(A)   any fee, bonus, commission, holiday pay or other emolument referable to his employment (or unpaid commission; see *Robertson v Blackstone Franks Investment Management Ltd* [1998] IRLR 376, CA below);

(B)   sums payable pursuant to orders for reinstatement or re-engagement (see UNFAIR DISMISSAL – III (53));

(C)   sums payable pursuant to interim orders for the continuation of a contract of employment (see **53.21** UNFAIR DISMISSAL – III);

(D)   PAY – I (32), guarantee payments, medical suspension payments (see further below), remuneration on suspension on maternity grounds (see MATERNITY AND PARENTAL RIGHTS (31)), certain payments for TIME OFF WORK (47) and remuneration under protective awards (see **37.6** REDUNDANCY – II),

(E)   statutory sick pay (see SICKNESS AND SICK PAY (42)); and

(F)   statutory maternity pay, paternity pay and adoption pay (see MATERNITY AND PARENTAL RIGHTS (31)).

A non-contractual bonus also counts as wages when payment is made (*ERA 1996, s 27(3)*). The EAT in *Kent Management Services Ltd v Butterfield* [1992] ICR 272 appeared to suggest that the *WA 1986* extended to any sums of the relevant kinds which would normally be expected to be paid, even if there was no strict contractual entitlement to receive them (see also *Farrell Matthews & Weir v Hansen* [2005] IRLR 160 below). Further, an employment tribunal has no jurisdiction, in relation to a claim of unlawful deduction from wages, to determine an applicant's *entitlement* to statutory sick pay where that entitlement was disputed by the employer. In relation to statutory sick pay, the exclusive jurisdiction for the determination of disputes as to entitlement rests with the Inland Revenue and, on appeal, the Inland Revenue Commissioners. The employment tribunal only has jurisdiction in relation to statutory sick pay where the employer admitted entitlement to statutory sick pay but had withheld all or part of that pay. The same limitation will apply in relation to statutory maternity, paternity or adoption pay. See *Taylor Gordon & Co Ltd v Timmons* [2004] IRLR 180, EAT.

However, the following payments are excluded from the definition of wages by *s 27(2)*:

(I)   advances under loan agreements or by way of an advance of wages;

(II)   payments in respect of expenses incurred in carrying out the employment (for example a car mileage allowance; see *Southwark London Borough v O'Brien* [1996] IRLR 420 EAT but compare *Mears v Salt* UKEAT/0522/11 EAT where it was held on the facts that a longstanding "travel allowance" was in fact the payment of an emolument and not caught by the exclusion for expenses);

(III)   payments by way of pension, allowance or gratuity in connection with the worker's retirement or as compensation for loss of office;

(IV)   any payment referable to the worker's redundancy; and

(V)   any payment otherwise than in his capacity as a worker.

Benefits in kind are not treated as wages unless they are vouchers, stamps or similar documents of a fixed monetary value capable of being exchanged for money, goods or services (*ERA 1996, s 27(5)*). This would embrace, for example, luncheon vouchers.

Particular doubts arose as to whether a payment in lieu of notice amounts to wages. However, the House of Lords in *Delaney v Staples* [1992] ICR 483 held that it did not. Wages were payments in respect of the rendering of services during the employment, so all payments in respect of the termination of the contract are excluded, save to the extent that they are expressly caught by *s 27(1)*.

In *Robertson v Blackstone Franks Investment Management Ltd* [1998] IRLR 376, the Court of Appeal, upholding the decision of the EAT, held that commission payments which become payable after the termination of employment are 'wages' within the definition of *ERA 1996, s 27* and, accordingly, are protected against unauthorised deductions made by the employer. The statutory requirement was that the sum was payable 'in connection with the employee's employment' but it did not require the sum to be payable *during* the currency of the employee's contract. The Court of Appeal further held that the employer was entitled to set off sums paid as an advance against future commission in assessing the amount payable. To hold to the contrary would contravene *ERA 1996, s 25(3)* which obliges a tribunal to take into account sums 'already paid or repaid' by the employer to the worker. In *New Century Cleaning Co Ltd v Church* [2000] IRLR 27, the Court of Appeal held that the employer did not breach the provisions of *Part II* of the *ERA 1996* in reducing the amount of money paid to teams of employees for each job done by the team. On the facts of the case, which concerned a window-cleaning business, there was no express or implied contractual term for identifying the amount of money which each team would be paid nor any such term relating to the distribution of the money among the team. Accordingly, there was no breach of *ERA 1996, s 13(3)* which relates to the amount of wages 'properly payable' to each employee. The amount payable to each member of the team was not sufficiently certain to allow the wages to be ascertained prior to allocation of the money to each individual.

In *Farrell Matthews & Weir v Hansen* [2005] IRLR 160 the issue of discretionary bonuses as 'wages' was further considered. In that case a solicitor was paid an annual discretionary bonus in instalments. The claimant left her employer in circumstances where £9,000 of the bonus was still outstanding. The EAT held that a deductions from wages claim under s 13 had been rightly allowed. The employer's argument relying upon *ERA s 27(3)* that non-contractual bonus could only become wages when actually paid was rejected by the EAT which held that once the bonus payable had been declared by the employer the sum became payable and amounted to wages within the meaning of *ERA s 27(1)*. Similarly, in *Tradition Securities and Futures SA v Mouradian* [2009] EWCA Civ 60, [2009] All ER (D) 100 (Feb) it was held by the Court of Appeal that claims for deductions from bonus payments could be brought under the unlawful deductions jurisdiction, even where there is a dispute over alleged variations to the bonus scheme, provided the employer has fully exercised its discretion to make a payment under the scheme and the amount claimed is quantified, and payment is due.

The issue of quantification of the sum in issue is crucially relevant to whether a claim may be brought under the deduction from wages provisions of the *ERA*. In *Adcock v Coors Brewers Ltd* [2007] EWCA Civ 19, [2007] All ER (D) 190 (Jan), sub nom Coors Brewers Ltd v Adcock, the Court of Appeal considered whether a claim in relation to an *unquantified* discretionary bonus could be advanced under the provisions of *Part II* of the *ERA*. While such claims could be brought under the Employment Tribunal's *contractual* jurisdiction after termination of employment (by analogy with the discretionary bonus cases such as *Clark v Nomura plc* [2000] IRLR 766 which had been brought as a contractual claim in the High Court) that jurisdiction is limited to £25,000 whilst the jurisdiction under the provisions of *Part II* of the *ERA* is unlimited. The Court of Appeal held (applying *Delaney v Staples* [1992] ICR 483, HL) that the jurisdiction under *Part II* of the *ERA* is limited to claims brought on the premise that a *specific amount of money* by way of wages is owing. Accordingly, the jurisdiction does not extend to an unquantified claim in relation to an unidentified sum (such as a claim to a discretionary bonus). Such claims will remain limited to the contractual jurisdiction and, in relation to claims with a potential value of in excess of £25,000, or whether the employee remains in the employer's employment, will still have to be brought in the Courts rather than the employment tribunal. See also, applying the principle of the requirement of quantifiability as a precondition to a claim under s 13 of the *ERA*, *Mouradian v Tradition Securities and Futures SA* [2009] EWCA Civ 60, *Allsop v Christiani and Neilsen Ltd* (UKEAT/0241/11) and *Kingston-upon-Hull CC v Schofield* UKEAT/0616/11 (6 November 2012).

Deductions. A broad definition of deductions is contained in *ERA 1996, s 13(3), (4)*. Where the total amount of any wages that are paid on any occasion by an employer to any worker employed by him is less than the total amount of the wages properly payable on that occasion (after deductions), the amount of the deficiency counts as a deduction, unless it is attributable to an error of computation as defined by *s 13(4)*. A conscious decision not to pay a particular sum which is caused by the employer's mistaken interpretation of the contract of employment is not such an error of computation (*Yemm v British Steel plc* [1994] IRLR 117; *Morgan v West Glamorgan County Council* [1995] IRLR 68).

It is clear that the tribunal may have to resolve disputes about the facts and about the construction and application to the facts of the worker's contract in order to determine what sums are in fact properly payable on a particular occasion (*Greg May (Carpet Fitters and Contractors) Ltd v Dring* [1990] ICR 188), and what deductions are in fact authorised (*Fairfield Ltd v Skinner* [1992] ICR 836). Again, there were originally doubts as to whether *s 13(3), ERA 1996* applies only to cases where there is some amount due as wages and the employer has sought to recover some *other* sum allegedly due to him by setting it off against those wages, or whether it also extends to the case where the employer has simply refused to pay the wages allegedly due or some part of them (usually because he denies that they are due at all). In *Delaney v Staples* [1991] ICR 331, the Court of Appeal held that a total non-payment *was* a deduction. The House of Lords ([1992] ICR 483) did not have to consider this point on appeal. In *Francis v Elizabeth Claire Care Management Ltd* [2005] IRLR 858 the EAT held that 'deduction' had a wide meaning and can include a case of failure to pay wages on time (rejecting robustly the employer's argument that there was no right to be paid on time). In that case, the employee was dismissed for complaining about the late payment. Unsurprisingly, that dismissal was held to be automatically unfair as a dismissal for asserting a statutory right (ie the right not to suffer deductions from wages. See also *s 104* of the *Employment Rights Act 1996* and **52.3(d)** Unfair Dismissal – II.). In *Lucy v British Airways plc* [2009] All ER (D) 58 (Jan) the distinction between a claim to a deduction from wages and a breach of contract claim was helpfully illustrated. The issue was whether a claim for loss of a flying pay supplement was an unlawful deduction from wages or a breach of contract claim which should be pursued in the civil courts. The claimant had previously been paid a supplement when carrying out flying duties. Following closure of the base at which the claimants worked, they continued to be paid basic pay but not flight supplements (as they were not flying). The EAT held that for the claims to fall within *Part II* of the *ERA* they must be quantifiable and held that the claims could be quantified. The claimants failed, however, on the issue whether the sums in question were wages. The EAT held they were not as they were only payable when the claimants were actually undertaking flying duties. Accordingly, there could be no claim to a deduction from wages but there might be a claim for contractual loss based upon breach of contract arising from the withdrawal of a contractual scheme.

In *Bruce v Wiggins Teape (Stationery) Ltd* [1994] IRLR 536, the *WA 1986* (as it then was) was held to cover a situation in which the employer, in breach of contract, reduced the employee's wages. In *Morgan* (above), the wages provisions of the *ERA 1996* were similarly applied where the employer had demoted the employee without having power to do so. In *Hussman Manufacturing Ltd v Weir* [1998] IRLR 288, the employer had a contractual right to change the employee's working hours. After the employee was moved from night shift he was worse off as a result of loss of unsocial hours pay. The EAT held that a reduction in income which is the result of a lawful act by the employer is not a deduction. The EAT acknowledged, however, that in exceptional cases the unilateral exercise of such a contractual right by the employer might breach the implied term of mutual trust and confidence. In a situation where there is no contractual right to change the hours of work, a unilateral change by the employer, without the consent of the workers, to short-time working and, consequently, a reduction in remuneration, will amount to an unlawful deduction from wages: *International Packaging Corpn (UK) Ltd v Balfour* [2003] IRLR 11. In *Beveridge v KLM UK Ltd* [2000] IRLR 765, the EAT considered whether it was an unlawful deduction from wages to fail to pay any salary to an employee (who, following a period of sickness absence, claimed to be fit and willing to return to work) during a six-week period when the employer wished to satisfy itself that the employee was in fact fit to return. The EAT held that, in the absence of express provision to the contrary, an employee who offers his services is entitled to be paid wages. Accordingly there was an unlawful deduction for wages for the purposes of *Part II* of *ERA 1996* (see **51.7** UNFAIR DISMISSAL – I.).

An illustration of the sometimes complicated exercise of contractual construction in relation to determining entitlement to payment for the purposes of *s 13* of the *ERA 1996* is the Court of Appeal decision in *Dunlop Tyres Ltd v Blows* [2001] EWCA Civ 1032, [2001] IRLR 629 which involved the construction of ambiguous contractual terms in a collective agreement as to rates of pay. The Court of Appeal concluded that, on the proper construction of the agreement, the employees were entitled to triple pay for public holidays and, accordingly, the claim for unlawful deduction of wages was well founded. See also *Henry v London General Transport Services Ltd* [2002] EWCA Civ 488, [2002] IRLR 472. An example of the requirement of employee consent to variations to the rate of remuneration is provided by *Davies v MJ Wyatt (Decorators) Ltd* [2000] IRLR 759. In that case, the employer, in an attempt to meet its obligations to provide paid holiday under the *Working Time Regulations*, unilaterally reduced the employees' hourly pay in order to fund the holiday payment. Unsurprisingly, this amounted to an unlawful deduction from wages. In relation to holiday pay to which an employee is entitled under the *Working Time Regulations*, there may be an overlap between the right to recover these sums (in the event of non payment) under the *Working Time Regulations* and under the *ERA 1996, s 13*. In *List Design Group Ltd v Douglas* [2003] IRLR 14 it was held that even though the claim to holiday pay was out of time under the relevant provisions of the *Working Time Regulations*, it was recoverable pursuant to the *ERA 1996* as an unauthorised deduction from wages. This conclusion was upheld by the House of Lords in *HM Revenue and Customs v Stringer* [2009] IRLR 667 which confirms that failure to pay holiday pay under the WTR can constitute an unauthorised deduction from wages under the *ERA 1996*.

In *Mears v Salt* UKAT/0522/11 the EAT confirmed that, in determining whether there had been an unlawful deduction from wages, as the employment tribunal was required by *s 13(3)* of the *ERA* to determine the "total amount of wages properly payable" this required the tribunal to construe and interpret the relevant contract including identifying any applicable implied terms. The argument, by analogy with the provisions in *Part I* of the *ERA* (to the effect that, in relation to statements of terms and conditions, the tribunal may only declare the terms and conditions but not interpret them) was accordingly rejected.

Finally, the fact that the government declares a public holiday does not necessarily give rise to a right to additional payment for that day. In *Campbell and Smith Construction Group Ltd v Greenwood* [2001] IRLR 588, the EAT held that the failure by an employer to pay an additional day's pay for the Millennium public holiday (which, on the facts, the employees were already contractually entitled to take as holiday) was not an unlawful deduction from wages. The EAT stated that a government declaration of an additional so-called public holiday does not, of itself, entitle employees to an additional day's paid holiday.

Worker. By *s 230(3), ERA 1996* those entitled to the protection from deductions from wages include persons working under contracts of apprenticeship and contracts for services as well as contracts of employment (see EMPLOYEE, SELF-EMPLOYED OR WORKER? **(14)**). The contract for services must be one whereby the individual undertakes to do or perform personally any work or services for another party to the contract whose status is not, by virtue of the contract, that of a client or customer of any profession or business undertaking carried on by the individual.

32.7   Deductions from wages of, and receipt of payments from, workers in retail employment

Special provisions apply to deductions from the wages of workers in retail employment and to payments by such workers, on account of cash shortages or stock deficiencies. Retail employment is defined as employment involving the carrying out by workers of retail transactions – the sale or supply of goods, or the supply of services (including financial services) – directly with members of the public (*ERA 1996, s 17(1)–(3)*).

The employer of a worker in retail employment may not deduct for cash shortages or stock deficiencies more than one-tenth of gross wages payable to the worker on a particular pay day (*ERA 1996, s 18(1)*). The employer must make such a deduction not more than 12 months after the date when he discovered or ought reasonably to have discovered the shortage or deficiency (*ERA 1996, s 18(2), (3)*).

If such a worker's pay is calculated by reference to cash shortages or stock deficiencies, the difference between the payment made when there are shortages and when there are not is treated as a deduction and the difference may not be more than one-tenth on any pay day (*ERA 1996, s 19(1)*).

In addition, the employer of a worker in retail employment may not receive from the worker any payment on account of a cash shortage or stock deficiency, unless certain requirements are met. The employer must:

(a)   notify the worker in writing of his total liability to him in respect of that shortage or deficiency; and

(b)   make a demand for payment which is:

   (i)   in writing; and

   (ii)   on a pay day.

(*ERA 1996, s 20(1), (2)*.)

The demand must be made not earlier than the first pay day on or after the date of the written notification and not later than 12 months after the date when the employer discovered or ought reasonably to have discovered the shortage or deficiency (*ERA 1996, s 20(3)*).

The amount demanded on a particular pay day must not exceed one-tenth of the gross wages payable to the worker on that day, or the balance of that one-tenth remaining after any deductions on account of cash shortages or stock deficiencies (*ERA 1996, s 21(1)*).

The restriction of deductions and payments to one-tenth of gross wages (and the requirements referred to in (*a*) and (*b*) above) do not apply to deductions or payments made from the final payment of wages. Nor do *ss 20* and *21* apply to payments made after the final payment of wages (*ERA 1996, ss 20(5), 21(3), 22(1)–(4)*). However, after the 12-month time limit referred to above has expired, the employer may neither receive payments (even after the final payment of wages), nor bring legal proceedings for recovery unless he has made a demand in accordance with *ss 20* or *21* within that time limit (*ERA 1996, ss 21(3), 22(4)*).

Even if legal proceedings are taken against a worker still in retail employment, a court which finds him liable to pay sums in respect of a shortage or deficiency must make provision so that the rate of payment does not exceed that which the employer could recover under *s 20* or *s 21* (*ERA 1996, ss 21(3), 22(4)*).

32.8   Remedies

The worker's exclusive remedy for breach by his employer of the statutory provisions outlined above is to present a complaint to an employment tribunal (*ERA 1996, s 23(1)*). The remedy of a worker for any contravention of *ss 13(1)*, *15(1)*, *18(1)* or *21(1)* is by way of a complaint to an employment tribunal under *s 23(1)* and not otherwise (*ERA 1996, s 205(2)*). However, the Court of Appeal has held in *Rickard v PB Glass Supplies Ltd* [1990] ICR 150 that what is now *s 205(2)* was not intended to prevent an employee from pursuing a claim in contract before the county court or High Court for moneys due to him where the non-payment is alleged by the employer to be due to the fact that no payment is due at all. Such a claim may now also be brought in the employment tribunal, within certain limits (see **7.23** CONTRACT OF EMPLOYMENT).

A complaint may be made that:

(a)   an unauthorised deduction has been made contrary to *s 13(1)* or *s 15(1)*;

(b)   an unauthorised payment has been received by the employer contrary to *ss 15(1)* or *20(1)*;

(c)   deductions exceeding the limit set by *s 18(1)* have been made; or

(d)   the employer has received more than the limit set by *s 21(1)*.

(*ERA 1996, s 23(1)*.)

The time limit for presenting a complaint to an employment tribunal under these provisions is three months beginning with the date of the deduction or the receipt of which complaint is made. The tribunal has jurisdiction to extend the time limit where it is satisfied that it was not reasonably practicable for the complaint to be presented within the relevant period of three months (see **17.8** EMPLOYMENT TRIBUNALS – I). Guidance on dealing with limitation points arising under those provisions was given by the EAT in *Taylorplan Services Ltd v Jackson* [1996] IRLR 184. It is to be noted that the right to make a complaint relates only to 'unauthorised' deductions. Deductions made by an employer in accordance with a direction given by a public authority pursuant to statute are authorised deductions, therefore the right not to suffer unlawful deductions does not apply, and a tribunal has no jurisdiction to hear a claim in respect of them (*Patel v Marquette Partners (UK) Ltd* [2009] ICR 569).

Where a series of deductions or payments are made, in certain circumstances, the time limit runs from the date of the last payment (*ERA 1996, s 23(3)*). A complaint may then be made about the entire unlawful series (*Reid v Camphill Engravers* [1990] IRLR 268). See also *Group 4 Nightspeed Ltd v Gilbert* [1997] IRLR 398, EAT. In *Arora v Rockwell Automation Ltd* [2006] All ER (D) 112 (May), EAT the EAT held (applying *Group 4 Nightspeed Ltd v Gilbert*) that, in relation to an unlawful deductions claim, time starts to run, not from the date of termination of the contract, but from the date of the payment of wages containing the shortfall.

Where an employment tribunal finds that a complaint under *s 23(1)* is well-founded, it will make a declaration to that effect and, where an unlawful deduction or payment has been made, will order the employer to pay (or, as the case may be, repay) to the worker the amount of the deduction or payment (*ERA 1996, s 24*).

If the wages provisions of the *ERA 1996* have been satisfied in respect of an amount less than the deduction, the employer will be ordered to pay the worker the difference between the amount actually deducted and that which could lawfully have been deducted (*ERA 1996, s 25(1), (2)*).

In making the order, the tribunal will take into account payments or repayments already made to the worker (*ERA 1996, s 25(3)*). *Section 25(3)* applies to any payment made by an employer in respect of a deduction at any time prior to the date on which the tribunal makes its order and is not limited to amounts paid *before* the deduction (see *Robertson v Blackstone Franks Investment Management Ltd* [1998] IRLR 376).

Where a tribunal has ordered an employer to pay or repay a worker any amount (the relevant amount), the amount which the employer is entitled to recover by whatever means in respect of the matter which gave rise to the deduction or payment (including cash shortages or stock deficiencies) is reduced by the relevant amount (*ERA 1996, s 25(4), (5)*). In other words, sums wrongfully deducted cannot later be recovered at all, even if they were properly owing to the employer. The correctness of this far-reaching proposition was confirmed by the EAT in *Potter v Hunt Contracts Ltd* [1992] ICR 337.

Where an order is made under *ERA 1996, s 11* and *ss 23–25* (see **32.20** below) the aggregate of the amount ordered to be paid by the employer to the worker will not exceed the amount of the deduction (*ERA 1996, s 26*).

Parties cannot, by agreement, exclude or limit the operation of *ERA 1996, ss 23–25* except where agreement has been reached to refrain from presenting or continuing with a complaint where a conciliation officer has taken action in accordance with *s 18(2)* or *(3)* of *ERA 1996* or where the employee has entered into a compromise agreement which meets certain conditions, principally that legal advice has been taken (*ERA 1996, s 203(1), (2)*; for compromise agreements, see **17.32** EMPLOYMENT TRIBUNALS – I).

These provisions do not apply to employment where under his contract the person employed ordinarily works outside Great Britain (*ERA 1996, s 196(2), (3)*; and see **51.15** UNFAIR DISMISSAL – I).

32.9   THE NATIONAL MINIMUM WAGE ACT 1998

The *National Minimum Wage Act 1998* ('*NMWA 1998*') received the Royal Assent on 31 July 1998 and came fully into force on 1 April 1999. Many of the detailed provisions as to the operation of the National Minimum Wage ('NMW') are contained in the *Regulations*. The *National Minimum Wage Regulations 1999 (SI 1999/584)* were issued in March 1999 and also came into force on 1 April 1999. (See also *Tolley's National Minimum Wage: A Practical Guide* (ISBN: 075450 226–0).)

All 'workers' (see *NMWA 1998, s 54* and below) are to be paid at a rate which is not less than the NMW. As to the level of the NMW, the main points as now enacted in the *Regulations* are as follows:

(a)   with effect from 1 October 2012 the NMW for workers aged 21 (previously 22) has been raised to £6.19 (previously £6.08) (*reg 11* as amended by the *National Minimum Wage (Amendment) Regulations 2012 (SI 2012/2397)*).

(b)   with effect from 1 October 2012 the NMW for workers aged 18–20 remains at the rate of £4.98 per hour (*reg 13(1)* as amended by the *National Minimum Wage Regulations 1999 (Amendment) Regulations 2010 (SI 2011/2345)*).

(c)   workers under 18 continue to be entitled to £3.68 per hour with effect from 1 October 2012 (*reg 13(2)* as amended by the *National Minimum Wage Regulations 1999 (Amendment) Regulations 2010 (SI 2011/2345)*).

(d)   workers aged under 19 engaged on a contract of apprenticeship or workers aged over 19 but employed on the first 12 months of a contract of apprenticeship are now entitled from 1 October 2012 to the new rate of £2.65 (up from £2.60) (*reg 13(3)* as amended by the *National Minimum Wage (Amendment) Regulations 2012*).

Certain categories of workers are expressly excluded by *reg 12* (as amended) from entitlement to the NMW at any of the rates set out above. In summary, the excluded categories are as follows:

(i)   workers engaged on certain "Government arrangements" (such as "Programme Led Apprenticeships") and schemes designed to provide training, work experience or temporary work (such as "Apprenticeships or Advanced Apprenticeships"). See *reg 12(4A)–12(7)*;

(ii)   workers engaged in work experience of less than one year pursuant to a course of higher education are excluded from the NMW by *reg 12(8), (9)* and *(9A)*;

(iii)   workers who were homeless persons working in return for shelter an benefits pursuant to a not for profit scheme are not entitled to the NMW provided all of the conditions of *reg 12(10),(11)* and *(12)* are satisfied; and

(iv)   workers participating in the European Community Leonardo da Vinci programme or the European Community Youth in Action Programme or the European Community Erasmus Programme or Comenius Programme are not entitled to the NMW (*reg 12(13)–(16)*).

Guidance and up to date information on the NMW may be found from links on the BIS website at www.bis.gov.uk/policies/employment-matters/rights/nmw.

Detailed provisions are contained in the *Regulations* for the purpose of calculating whether a worker has been paid the NMW. Thus, the individual's hourly rate of pay must be determined by reference to total remuneration over a 'relevant pay reference period' and the hours worked during that period. The pay reference period is one month or a shorter period if the worker is paid by reference to such shorter period (eg a week) (see *reg 10*). Regulations exist for allocation of pay to relevant periods (*reg 30*). As to determining the actual remuneration received in the relevant period, *regs 30–37* set out in detail the treatment of various types of payment. Gross pay must be determined and the following payments will be included for the purpose of calculation:

(i)   incentive payments including commission; and

(ii)   bonuses.

It is important to note that since 1 October 2009 tips, service charges, gratuities and cover charges cannot be used to make up National Minimum Wage pay by amendments made to the *NMW Regulations* by the *National Minimum Wage Regulations 1999 (Amendment) Regulations 2009 (SI 2009/1902)*. Previously it had been held that tips and gratuities paid through the payroll system could be used in discharge of the *NMWA 1998* remuneration obligations (see *Nerva v United Kingdom* [2002] IRLR 815, ECtHR, (see **28.7 HUMAN RIGHTS**) but that tips distributed through a "tronc" system (and not directly through the employer's payroll) did not count towards the national minimum wage (*Annabels (Berkeley Square) Ltd v Revenue and Customs Comrs* [2009] EWCA Civ 361). The position has now been simplified (and helpfully clarified) so that eligible workers will receive at least the National Minimum Wage in base pay with any tips being paid in addition. In addition a voluntary code of best practice on service charges, tips, gratuities and cover charges has been introduced with the aim to improve the information provided to customers and workers. The code is intended to provide practical guidance to businesses on how to operate in a fair and transparent way and aims to ensure that businesses are able to provide their customers with sufficient information to make an informed choice before they leave a tip or gratuity or pay a service charge. The relevant guidance and code of practice may be accessed from www.bis.gov.uk/policies/employment-matters/rights/nmw.

A worker's basic pay, from which enhancements such as time and a half payments are calculated, must comply with the NMW and the enhanced rate of pay is not the relevant hourly rate of pay for the purposes of the Regulations. This remains that case even if the worker never receives only the basic pay, but is always paid at the enhanced rate, for example where the worker always works night shifts which are remunerated at the enhanced rate (*Hillier v Hamilton House Medical Ltd* (2009) EAT Appeal No. UKEAT/0246/09), [2009] All ER (D) 319 (Nov)

Certain deductions are ignored for the purpose of calculating the remuneration in the relevant period (eg tax and National Insurance deductions, deductions in respect of the worker's conduct in relation to which he is contractually liable, deductions in respect of loans or overpayment, deductions in relation to accidental overpayment and deductions in relation to the purchase of shares, options or other securities (*reg 33*)). The general principle is that benefits in kind are not to be included for the purpose of calculating the remuneration (*reg 9*). The exception to this is living accommodation provided by the employer. The 'value' of the accommodation is set by *reg 36* (as amended by the *National Minimum Wage (Amendment) Regulations 2012 (SI 2012/2397)* and cannot exceed, with effect from 1 October 2012, £4.82 for each day the accommodation is provided, giving a maximum of £33.74 per week. Travel expenses to a temporary workplace and related subsistence costs paid by an employer and eligible for tax relief are also excluded from the calculation of payments for the purposes of the NMW with effect from 1 January 2011 by amendments made to *reg 31* by the *National Minimum Wage (Amendment) (No. 2) Regulations 2010 (SI 2010/3001)*.

Regulations 31 and *36* in relation to accommodation and deductions have been considered by the Court of Appeal in *Leisure Employment Services Ltd v Revenue and Customs Comrs* [2007] EWCA Civ 92, [2007] IRLR 450. Upholding the decision of the EAT, the Court of Appeal held that, in relation to holiday resort workers living on site in accommodation provided by the employer, it was not permissible to count a £6 sum per fortnight which they had agreed to pay for gas and electricity as counting towards the minimum wage as the total permitted by *reg 36* in relation to accommodation had already been exhausted by their rent payments. Accordingly, the employer was in breach of the NMW. Conversely, a "sleep-in payment" paid to a care worker was held not to amount to an allowance within the meaning of *reg 31 (1)(d)* of the *Regulations* and could therefore be taken into account when calculating whether the worker had received the minimum wage (*Smith v Oxfordshire Learning Disability NHS Trust* (2009) EAT Appeal No. UKEAT/0176/09), [2009] ICR 1395, [2009] All ER (D) 170 (Aug)

The provisions for the calculation of the number of hours worked by the worker in the relevant pay reference period are similarly complicated. There are four types of work which can be carried out:

(A)   time work (*reg 3*) which is paid by reference to the time which a worker works;

(B)   salaried hours work (*reg 4*) which deals with the situation where a worker is paid under the contract for a fixed number of hours a year and is paid an annual salary in instalments;

(C)   output work (*reg 5*) which covers piece-work and commission-related working (as amended by the *National Minimum Wage Regulations 1999 (Amendment) Regulations 2004 (SI 2004/1161)* with effect from 1 October 2004 with further amendments coming into force on 6 April 2005); and

(D)   unmeasured work (*reg 6*) which provides a residual category.

The hours worked must be calculated in accordance with the *Regulations*. A detailed consideration of these provisions is beyond the scope of this work. For the detail of the provisions and the methods of calculation the reader is referred to *Tolley's National Minimum Wage: A Practical Guide* (ISBN: 075450 226-0).

32.10 Coverage of the Act

Section 54(3) defines 'worker' for the purpose of the *NMWA 1998* as 'an individual who has entered into or works under (or where employment has ceased worked under):

(a)   a contract of employment;

(b)   or any other contract, whether express or implied and (if it is express) whether oral or in writing, whereby the individual undertakes to do or perform personally any work or services for another party to the contract whose status is not by virtue of the contract that of client or customer of any profession or business undertaking carried on by the individual.'

Regulation 12 of the *National Minimum Wage Regulations 1999 (SI 1999/584)* and *s 54* (the definition of Worker) of the *National Minimum Wage Act 1998* were considered by the Court of Appeal in the context of a pupil barrister in *Edmonds v Lawson* [2000] IRLR 391. The claimant was a pupil in the defendant's chambers and was over the age of 31. Accordingly, she did not fall within *reg 12(2)* which, at that time, excluded only workers under the age of 26 on the first 12 months of a contract of apprenticeship from the NMW. At first instance Sullivan J held that the applicant was entitled to the NMW on the basis that during her pupillage there was a contract of apprenticeship between the applicant and the barristers' chambers (see [2000] IRLR 18). On appeal, the Court of Appeal held that the pupillage arrangement between the applicant and the chambers had the essential characteristics of an intention to create legal relations and, accordingly, there was a legally binding contract between the applicant and the chambers. The Court of Appeal held, however, allowing the appeal, that the contract was not a contract of apprenticeship and did not fall within the definition of a contract of employment within *s 54(3)* of the *NMWA 1998*. In relation to *s 54(3)(b)* (which relates to any other contract whereby the individual undertakes to do or perform personally any work or services for another party) the Court of Appeal held that the pupil did not undertake to perform work or services for the members of the chambers and in the event that the pupil did any work for which she was paid, the person for whom the work was done was the pupil's professional client. Accordingly, the pupil was not entitled to the benefit of the National Minimum Wage. In *Lee v Chassis & Cab Specialists Ltd* (UKEAT/0268/10/JOJ) [2011] All ER (D) 178 (Feb) the EAT held that apprentice status at common law (not a case where the specific exceptions for government arrangements in *reg 12* applied) was not negated by the involvement of a third party in the provision of training and, accordingly, the claimant worker was properly subject to the (then) exception excluding apprentices from the coverage of the NMW. See also *Flett v Matheson* [2006] IRLR 277.

Prisoners, share fisherman and voluntary workers working for no remuneration are expressly not covered (*NMWA 1998, ss 43–45*). Persons who are covered by the Act include Crown employment (*NMWA 1998, s 36*), most work on board ships registered in the United Kingdom (*NMWA 1998, s 40*), work in the armed services (*NMWA 1998, s 37*) and in the House of Commons and House of Lords (*NMWA 1998, ss 38, 39*). Additionally (and importantly), home workers are expressly included in the coverage of the *Act* (*s 35*) as are agency workers (*NMWA 1998, s 34*). The definition of 'home worker', in *s 35* of the *NMWA 1998*, is intended to cover persons whose place of work is not materially under the control of the person for whom the work is being done: *IRC v Post Office* [2003] IRLR 199.

The coverage of the *NMWA* was further considered in *James v Redcats (Brands) Ltd* [2007] IRLR 296 in which the EAT had to determine if a parcel courier was a 'worker' or a 'home worker' or not covered by the *NMW* at all (as had been held by the employment tribunal). The decision of the EAT provides important and helpful guidance on the issue of 'worker' generally, the requirement of mutuality of obligation, and emphasises that in marginal cases a person is *presumed* to qualify for the *NMW* unless the contrary is established (*NMWA s 28*). As to the issue of 'homeworker', a submission that to qualify a person must have some identified 'place' from which they work (albeit not necessarily their own home) was rejected in the light of the general policy of the *NMWA*. Thus a person engaged in delivery or distribution of items could nevertheless be a 'homeworker' for the purposes of the *NMWA*.

By *Reg 2(2)* of the *National Minimum Wage Regulations* an employer is exempt from the obligation to pay the NMW where the worker lives with the family and is treated as a family member "in particular as regards to the provision of accommodation and meals and the sharing of tasks and leisure activities", so long as there is no deduction from wages for food or accommodation. The provision was intended to apply to eg au pairs, nannies and companions. In *Julio v Jose* [2012] IRLR 180, the EAT considered this exemption for live-in domestic workers. The claimants were foreign domestic workers employed in the respondents' households. The EAT held that the exemption must be narrowly interpreted and it must be shown that the relevant individual was genuinely being treated as a family member. On the facts *reg 2(2)* applied in respect of all the claimants and accordingly they were not entitled to the NMW. In *Nambalat v Taher* [2012] IRLR 1004 (Court of Appeal), on appeal from the decision of the EAT in *Julio v Jose* [2012] IRLR 180, the Court of Appeal upheld the decision of the EAT that the claimants fell within the exclusion in *reg 2(2)*, Pill LJ confirmed that the exception should be carefully and narrowly construed and cautioned that employment tribunals must be astute to ensure that the exception was not used as a device for obtaining cheap domestic labour.

The Secretary of State is afforded an additional power to make regulations applying the minimum wage to persons not otherwise covered (*NMWA 1998, ss 41* and *42*). By the *National Minimum Wage (Offshore Employment) Order 1999 (SI 1999/1128)* the operation of the *NMWA 1998* has been extended to workers in offshore employment, defined as employment in United Kingdom territorial waters, exploring or exploiting natural resources in the UK sector of the continental shelf or (in a foreign sector) a cross boundary petroleum field. *Section 22* of the *Employment Relations Act 1999* inserts a new *s 44A* into the *NMWA 1998*. By this section the exclusion from the entitlement to the NMW (see *ss 43–45*) is extended to cover residential members of religious communities. Accordingly, it would appear that nuns and monks will be excluded from entitlement to the NMW. The relevant provisions came into force on 25 October 1999.

The power to set the rate is conferred by *NMWA 1998, s 2* (for the current rates, see above). *NMWA 1998, s 3* gives the power to the Secretary of State to exclude persons under 26 from the operation of the National Minimum Wage or to apply a different hourly rate to such persons. The statutory role of the LPC and the obligations of the Secretary of State to refer matters to the LPC are set out in *ss 5–8* and *Sch 1*.

32.11 Written records and pay statements

In addition to the fixing of the minimum wage, the *Act* casts further obligations upon employers of maintaining records in relation to hours worked and payments made to workers in a manner to be prescribed by the regulations (*NMWA 1998, s 9*). By *reg 38(1)* the employer is obliged to keep records 'sufficient to establish that [the worker] is remunerated at a rate at least equal to the national minimum wage'. The records must be kept in such a way that the information about a worker in respect of a pay reference period may be produced in a single document (*reg 38(2)*). Workers may require the employer to produce the records and the worker may take a copy in order to determine if the worker is in fact being paid the minimum wage (*NMWA 1998, s 10*). Failure to comply with such a request may lead to a complaint being made to an employment tribunal (*NMWA 1998, s 11*). If the tribunal upholds the complaint it shall make a declaration to that effect and order that the employer pay the worker a sum equivalent to 80 times the relevant National Minimum Wage (*NMWA 1998, s 11(2)*). The Act in *s 12* provides a power for regulations to be made to provide workers with a National Minimum Wage statement which would be similar to the right an itemised statement under the provision of *ERA 1996* (see below). Following widespread opposition to this proposal the *Regulations* in their present form contain no obligation to provide a National Minimum Wage statement.

32.12 Failure to pay the National Minimum Wage: individual remedies

A failure to pay to an employee the National Minimum Wage entitles the employee to commence proceedings in the employment tribunal or the county court to recover the difference between what has been paid and what ought to have been paid under the National Minimum Wage. By amendments to *s 17* of the *NMWA* (introduced by the *Employment Act 2008, s 8*), where a worker has been paid at a rate less than the national minimum wage he can claim the difference based upon the rate of the national minimum wage applying at the time of the arrears being determined as if it had been at that rate throughout the periods the employer was in default. This new method of calculating arrears has retrospective effect and thus applies even if the arrears period predated the coming into force of the new provisions. The claim may be brought either as a breach of *Part II* of the *ERA 1996* as an unlawful deduction from wages or as a breach of contract claim. In relation to workers (as defined in *NMWA 1998, s 54(3)*) who are not covered by the provisions of *Part II* of the *ERA 1996* (see above) because they do not satisfy the particular definition of worker in *s 230(3)*, *ERA 1996*, they are deemed to be covered by the provisions by *s 18* of the *National Minimum Wage Act 1998*. An employee has a right not to suffer a detriment (*NMWA 1998, s 23*) nor to be dismissed by reason of bringing proceedings relating to the enforcement of the National Minimum Wage (*NMWA 1998, s 25* which inserts *ERA 1996, s 104A*). (See also **52.3 UNFAIR DISMISSAL – II.**) As to proceedings in the employment tribunal, claims relating to non-payment of the NMW, may be heard by an employment tribunal chairman sitting alone (*NMWA 1998, s 27* amending *ETA 1996, s 4*). The burden of proof in such cases will be unusual: it will be presumed that the employee is paid less than the minimum wage unless the employer establishes the contrary (*NMWA 1998, s 28*). This principle applies whether the proceedings are brought in the employment tribunal under *Part II* of the *ERA 1996* or for breach of contract claims whether in the county court or in the employment tribunal. Accordingly, this will be an added incentive for employers to keep proper records as required in order to be able to establish that a worker has in fact been paid, at least, the National Minimum Wage. The worker's right to present a complaint that he has been subjected to a detriment in contravention of *s 23* is contained in *s 24* which extends the powers in *ss 48* and *49* of the *ERA 1996* to detriment cases arising in relation to the National Minimum Wage. On a related point, the EAT held in *Paggetti v Cobb* [2002] IRLR 861 that, in assessing a compensatory or basic award for unfair dismissal, calculations pursuant to *ss 221–229* of the *ERA 1996* were automatically subject to the NMW. This principle applies even if the claimant has not made a specific NMW claim as it is sufficient if, prior to the dismissal, he was remunerated at a rate less than the NMW. On the facts of the instant case, the applicant was only paid £120 for a 63-hour week. Compensation was, accordingly, to be assessed based upon the NMW rate. In *Blue Chip Trading Ltd v Helbawi* [2009] IRLR 128 a student subject to immigration restrictions on working was only permitted to work up to 20 hours per week during term time but could work without restriction during vacations. He knowingly worked more than the 20 hours he was permitted to work during term time. He claimed that he had not been paid the NMW. The EAT held that it would be contrary to public policy to allow the claimant to recover for any work done during the period he was knowingly in breach of the working limits. However, he could recover the NMW in relation to those periods when he was not subject to limitations on periods of work (such as the vacations) as in that case the unlawful elements of his performance could be severed.

Devices adopted by employers to attempt to meet the minimum wage obligation without additional expenditure are unlikely to succeed in practice. In *Laird v AK Stoddart Ltd* [2001] IRLR 591, the EAT considered whether there was a breach of the *NMWA 1998* or an unlawful deduction from wages contrary to *s 13(1)* of *ERA 1996* in circumstances where the employer consolidated part of an employee's attendance allowance into the basic hourly rate for the job in order to comply with the NMW requirement (at that time £3.60 per hour). By *reg 31* of the *National Minimum Wage Regulations 1999 (Amendment) Regulations 2000 (SI 2000/1989)*, certain payments are not to be taken into account in calculating the total remuneration. This exclusion includes an attendance allowance. Accordingly, the employer sought to reduce the attendance allowance and increase the basic pay to comply with the NMW. The employees were not consulted. The EAT held that there was no breach of the *NMWA 1998*. The EAT went on, however, to hold that the reduction in the attendance allowance was an unlawful deduction from wages for the purposes of *s 13* of the *ERA 1996* as there was no consent to the change and *s 27* of the *ERA 1996* required attendance allowances to be taken into account in determining whether there was any unlawful deduction from wages. Moreover, an employer cannot minimise his obligations by attempting to exclude certain work time from the calculation of hours worked. By way of example, in *British Nursing Association v Inland Revenue (National Minimum Wage Compliance Team)* [2002] IRLR 480, the Court of Appeal upheld the decision of the EAT ([2002] EWCA Civ 494, [2001] IRLR 659) that nurses providing a night service by telephone from home were working throughout the shift period for the purposes of the *NMWA 1998*, although free to do whatever they wanted between telephone calls. The fact that there was an obligation to be ready to answer the call throughout the night shift meant that the nurses were working throughout the shift and were engaged on 'time work' within the meaning of the *NMWA 1998* (see **32.9** above). It is also worthy of note that this case was an appeal from an enforcement notice served by the Inland Revenue – an example of a State as opposed to individual remedy in relation to the *NMWA 1998* (see below). The *British Nursing Association* case was followed by the Court of Session in *Scottbridge Construction Ltd v Wright* [2003] IRLR 21. That case concerned a nightwatchman, who was permitted by his employer to sleep on the employer's premises whilst at work. It was held that he was engaged on 'time work' for the purposes of the *NMWA 1998* and, accordingly, was entitled to the NMW for all the hours he was required to be on the premises, including time asleep as, even if asleep, he could respond to an alarm when he awoke and was thus liable to perform functions at every stage during the night. Conversely, in *Walton v Independent Living Organisation Ltd* [2003] IRLR 469 the Court of Appeal held that a live-in carer, required to be on the client's premises for a consecutive period of 72 hours each week, was only entitled, under the *NMWA 1998*, to payment in respect of the time that she was actually carrying out her duties as her work was properly characterised as 'unmeasured work' (with a daily average agreement falling within *reg 28*) and not 'time work' and, accordingly, *British Nursing Association* and *Scottbridge Construction* (above) were distinguished (see **32.9** above). In *McCartney v Oversley House Management* [2006] ICR 510 (EAT) *British Nursing Association* was applied in relation to 'on-call' work holding that a manager at a residential home with 'on call' obligations was engaged on 'salaried hours work' with the result that it was found that the employee was remunerated at a rate below that permitted by the *NMW*. In *Burrow Down Support Services Ltd v Rossiter* [2008] ICR 1172, the EAT applied the *British Nursing Association* decision and *Scottbridge Construction Ltd v Wright* to conclude that notwithstanding changes introduced to *reg 15* of the *NMW Regulations* the previous cases remained good law so that a night sleeper at a care home who was permitted to sleep but had to be available throughout the night shifts to deal with emergencies was entitled to the NMW for each hour of the shift. The issue of time asleep was further considered in *South Manchester Abbeyfield Society Ltd v Hopkins* (UKEAT/0079/10/ZT) [2011] ICR 254, [2011] IRLR 300. The Claimants were employed in housekeeping roles with "on call" periods overnight. The EAT held that such periods when the employee was sleeping did not qualify for the NMW (although the same periods might count for the purposes of the working time regulations). The provision of *regs 15(1A)* and *16(1A)* would only apply to the periods that the worker was "awake for the purposes of working". In *City of Edinburgh Council v Lauder UK* EATS/0048/11 the EAT held that "on-call" time of a sheltered housing residential warden provided with accommodation was not time which qualified for the NMW, applying *British Nursing Association*, *Scottbridge Construction Ltd v Wright* and *South Manchester Abbeyfield Society Ltd v Hopkins* (above).

32.13 Failure to pay the National Minimum Wage: state remedies

The *Act* also provides a system whereby the right to minimum wage may be enforced by state officials rather than individuals. The enforcement mechanisms were substantially modified by the *Employment Act 2008* which introduced new *s 19–19H* into the *NMWA* replacing the old *ss 19–22F* with a new regime of enforcement notices with effect from 6 April 2009.The relevant officers are HM Revenue & Customs and in the agricultural sector, the agricultural wages inspectors (see *NMWA 1998, s 13*). Officers may require an employer to produce records, allow access to premises and provide information in order to determine an issue under the *Act* (*NMWA 1998, s 14*). Officers may take copies of records produced. Information which is so obtained may be used only for the purposes of the *Act* or for criminal or civil proceedings relating to the *Act* if authorised by the Secretary of State (*NMWA 1998, s 15*). By a further amendment contained in the *Employment Act 2008* the information may, however, be supplied to officers acting for the purposes of the *Employment Agencies Act 1973* and may thereafter be used for the purposes of that Act. Similarly, the information may be disclosed to a relevant worker or agency worker for the purpose of assisting the officer in the enforcement of the obligations under the *Act*.

In cases where it appears that an employer is paying less than the National Minimum Wage the new *s 19* of the *NMWA* provides with effect from 6 April 2009 for the issue of a 'notice of underpayment' requiring the employer to pay to the worker, within a 28-day period, sums due in accordance with the provision for calculation of arrears of the NMW under *s 17* of the *Act*.

By *s 19A*, the employer may also, from 6 April 2009, be required to pay a financial penalty because of the failure to pay the NMW within 28 days. The amount of the penalty is 50 per cent of the arrears of the NMW as calculated subject to a minimum of £100 and a maximum of £5000 (*s 19(6), (7)*). Payment of the penalty may be suspended pending determination of any criminal charges under *s 31* (*s 19B*). A policy document titled *"Policy on HM Revenue & Customs Enforcement, Prosecutions And Naming Employers Who Flout National Minimum Wage Law"* has been promulgated with effect from January 2011 by BIS in relation to the operation of the regime introduced by the *Employment Act 2008* and can be found at www.bis.gov.uk/assets/biscore/employment-matters/docs/n/11-529-national-minimum-wage-enforcement-prosecutions.pdf. The Policy is intended to identify when employers who have breached the NMW will be publicly named and is intended to raise awareness of the NMW enforcement mechanisms and to deter employers who may seek to breach the NMW obligations. The policy in sections 5.2 and 5.3 sets out the general criteria to be applied for naming employers (eg knowing breach, failure to keep NMW records, obstruction of compliance officers or previous failure to pay arrears). Provision is made for employers to make representations before they are named (section 5.5). In addition, on 4 September 2012 the government announced that it would adopt a policy of publicising enforcement action taken in the courts and employers would be named in a press release in the hope that bad publicity is an effective way to deter breach of the NMW obligations.

A right of appeal against a notice of underpayment lies to the employment tribunal (*s 19C*). In the event of non-compliance with a notice of underpayment, an officer may present a complaint for unlawful deduction of wages on behalf of relevant workers (*s 19D*). Non-compliance with a notice to pay a penalty may be enforced in the county court by the relevant officer (*s 19E*). Provision is also made for withdrawal and replacement of notices of underpayment (*ss 19F, 19G*).

In *IRC v Bebb Travel plc* [2002] IRLR 783 the EAT had held that, on a proper construction of the legislation, compliance officers were not entitled, pursuant to *s 19* of the *NMWA 1998*, to serve an enforcement notice on the respondent employer requiring it to pay arrears of wages in respect of employees who had ceased employment before the notice was issued. This unsatisfactory result was reversed by the passage of the *National Minimum Wage (Enforcement Notices) Act 2003* which came into force on 8 July 2003. The new *Act* amended *s 19* of the *NMWA 1998* to ensure that an enforcement notice may be served on an employer who has not paid an employee a rate of pay at least equal to the NMW whether or not the worker is still employed. The further revisions introduced by the *Employment Act 2008* maintain this position. See *s 19(1)* which provides that a notice of underpayment may relate to any period for which the worker at any time qualified for the NMW.

Finally, if the preceding enforcement measures are to no avail, there is a criminal offence created for employers who wilfully breach their obligations to workers under the Act. It is an offence:

(i)   to fail to refuse or wilfully neglect to pay the minimum wage (*NMWA 1998, s 31(1)*);

(ii)   to fail to keep records as required by *s 9* (*NMWA 1998, s 31(2)*);

(iii)   to falsify *s 9* records (*NMWA 1998, s 31(3)*);

(iv)   to knowingly provide false information to an officer (*NMWA 1998, s 31(4)*); or

(v)   to obstruct or delay an officer or to refuse to answer questions or furnish information (*NMWA 1998, s 31(5)*).

Each offence under *s 31* was originally only punishable on summary conviction with a fine not exceeding level 5 on the Standard Scale (see **1.10** INTRODUCTION) (*NMWA 1998, s 31(9)*). In the case of a body corporate, if an offence is committed with the consent, connivance or by the neglect of an officer of the company, that officer, as well as the body corporate, is guilty of the offence (*NMWA 1998, s 32*). Proceedings for offences under the *Act* were limited to the Magistrates Court but with amendments introduced by the *Employment Act 2008*, the potential for greater penalties is introduced as the offence, in serious cases, may be tried on indictment as well as summarily.

The ability to effectively police whether employers are abiding by their obligations to pay the NMW is enhanced by the provisions of *s 39* of the *Employment Relations Act 1999* which permits revenue officials to disclose information which comes into their possession in the course of carrying out the function of Commissioners of the Inland Revenue to other agencies for the purposes of the *National Minimum Wage Act 1998*. The information may be disclosed to the Secretary of State for any purpose relating to the *National Minimum Wage Act 1998*. That information may be supplied by the Secretary of State for any purpose relating to the *National Minimum Wage Act 1998*. That information may be supplied by the Secretary of State to any person acting under *s 13(1)(b)* of the *NMWA 1998* or to the agricultural wages inspectors. The provisions of *s 39* came into force on 25 October 1999.

32.14 OTHER DEDUCTIONS FROM WAGES

In *Sim v Rotherham Metropolitan Borough Council* [1986] ICR 897, it was held that the principle of equitable set-off applied to contracts of employment. In other words, where an employee's breach of contract has caused the employer loss, the employer is in principle entitled to retain for himself sums representing the amount of that loss when he pays the employee's wages. This saves the employer from paying the full wage and suing for damages for breach of contract. However, the court retains a discretion to disallow the set-off. Further, if there is no contractual provision or written consent permitting a deduction by way of set-off, for the employer to make such a deduction may contravene the wages provisions of the *ERA 1996* (see **32.6** above; this will not be an obstacle where the deduction is made for taking part in industrial action).

The leading authority on the employer's right to pay less than the full contractual wage where the employee refuses to carry out all his contractual duties is the decision of the House of Lords in *Miles v Wakefield Metropolitan District Council* [1987] ICR 368. A superintendent registrar with a normal working week of 37 hours, including three hours on Saturday mornings, took industrial action and refused to conduct weddings on Saturdays. He worked normally during the rest of the week. It was held that the council was entitled to deduct 3/37ths from his normal salary, even though the registrar would have been willing to perform duties other than the conduct of weddings on Saturdays (in fact, the council instructed him to work normally or not at all).

Lord Brightman and Lord Templeman took the view that a worker not performing the full range of his contractual duties was not entitled to his full wages but to a *quantum meruit* payment based upon the value of the work actually done. The other law Lords in *Miles* did not, however, express a view on the *quantum meruit* point. An employer placed in such a position by a partially performing employee must make it clear to the employee that he is not waiving that employee's breach of contract in failing to perform the full range of his contractual duties. He should state that, whilst the breach continues, he will make a specified adjustment to the employee's wages.

However, an employer cannot be *compelled* to accept and pay for something significantly less than the efficient performance of all the employee's contractual duties (*MacPherson v Lambeth London Borough Council* [1988] IRLR 470). In *Wiluszynski v Tower Hamlets London Borough Council* [1989] IRLR 259 the Court of Appeal, dealing with a council employee who had refused to perform a material part of his duties, held that the council was entitled to withhold the whole of his pay. This decision was arrived at only because the council had clearly informed the employee that if he attempted to undertake limited work, he would not be paid for it. See also *British Telecommunications plc v Ticehurst* [1992] ICR 383. Recently, in *Spackman v London Metropolitan University* [2007] IRLR 744 (Co Ct) a test case relating to claimant lecturers some of the issues raised by *Sim*, *Miles* and *Wiluszynski* arose again for consideration. In *Spackman* recovery was sought of deductions made by the university in respect of days in which the lecturers participated in industrial action short of strike and thus provided partial performance. Rejecting the claim to full pay on the basis that an employer is not obliged to accept partial performance, the judge went on to hold that employees participating in collective industrial action have no right to remuneration at all by way of *quantum meruit* and if they present for work and undertake some duties or even the substantial majority of those duties they run the risk of being paid nothing by the employer. The fact that the university had paid anything at all was more than the employees wee legally entitled to expect. In *Luke v Stoke-on-Trent City Council* [2007] EWCA Civ 761, [2007] ICR 1678, [2007] IRLR 777 an employee refused to return to their job unless conditions were met and refused a temporary transfer to a different location, following an investigation into the employees allegations of bullying. The employers decision to stop wages was upheld by the court of Appeal on the application of the principle, recognised in *Miles* (above) of 'no work, no pay'.

Where an employee is actually required to work only on, say, 245 days in the year, and that employee participates in a one-day strike, the question frequently arises as to whether the employer is entitled to deduct 1/245 or only 1/365 of the annual salary in respect of that day. It is thought that this may depend upon the precise terms of the contract of employment, and upon the nature of the work done (eg does it require extensive preparation outside actual working hours?). In *Smith v Bexley London Borough Council*, IDS Brief 448, p 5, a county court judge took the approach more favourable to the employer. However, in *Re Bank of Credit and Commerce International SA* [1994] IRLR 282, Evans-Lombe J, although approving this approach where the question was what a lost day had cost the employer, held that, when considering what part of a monthly salary had accrued by the date of a dismissal, the total number of days in that month had to be taken into account, and not merely working days; this point was not considered on appeal. (See also *Thames Water Utilities v Reynolds* [1996] IRLR 186, EAT applying *Re Bank of Credit and Commerce International SA*.) In *Leisure Leagues UK Ltd v Maconnachie* [2002] IRLR 600, however, in the context of holiday pay, the EAT held that the correct denominator was the number of working days in the year (in this case, 233 days) and the *Thames Water* decision was distinguished on the basis it predated the *Working Time Regulations*. Clearly, this is an area which would benefit from a clear and exhaustive judicial statement of the principles to be applied. The issue of holidays working days and deductions recently arose for determination in *Cooper v Isle of Wight College* [2007] EWHC 2831 (QB), [2008] IRLR 124 in the context of apportioning annual salary in order to calculate a day's pay for the purpose of deductions to be made for participation in days of industrial action. The employer contended that the employees only provided actual services on 228 days of the year (deducting 32 days of statutory and contractual holiday) and that this should be used for calculating the value of a day's pay. Rejecting this argument it was held that the paid holidays had to be brought into account for the apportionment exercise so that the wage payable for any one day was 1/260th of the annual wage and not 1/228th as the employer had contended. Thus the correct approach to apportionment in the context of calculating appropriate deductions for participation in industrial action is, it appears:

(i)   calculate a day's salary based upon working days (and not days of the year (*Smith v Bexley* above and *Cooper* above): and

(ii)   working days include contractual and statutory holidays for this purpose (*Cooper* (above).

The court will not normally make mandatory interlocutory orders for the payment of wages; in clear cases, the employee's remedy is to apply for summary judgment (*Jakeman v South West Thames Regional Health Authority and London Ambulance Service* [1990] IRLR 62).

32.15 OVERPAYMENT

Payments made under a mistake of law or fact are, in principle, recoverable by the party who made the payment. This would extend to a mistaken overpayment of wages. However, if the employee in good faith changes his position by incurring expenditure which he would not otherwise have incurred, he may have a defence in whole or part to any subsequent claim to recover the overpayment (*Lipkin Gorman (a firm) v Karpnale Ltd* [1991] 2 AC 548; see also *Avon County Council v Howlett* [1983] 1 All ER 1073, [1983] 1 WLR 605).

32.16 ITEMISED PAY STATEMENTS

An employer must give any employee of his, at or before the time at which any payment of wages or salary is made to him, a pay statement in writing containing the following particulars:

(a)   the gross amount of the wages or salary;

(b)   the amounts of any variable and any fixed deductions from that gross amount and the purposes for which they are made, unless a statement of fixed deductions has been given to the employee (see **32.17** below);

(c)   the net amount of wages or salary payable; and

(d)   where different parts of the net amount are paid in different ways, the amount and method of payment of each part payment.

(*ERA 1996, s 8.*)

Tips paid by customers to a waiter in a restaurant were held not to be wages within the meaning of *EPCA, s 8* (now *ERA 1996, s 8*), and his employers were therefore not required to give particulars of such tips or of payments from them to the manager of the restaurant (*Cofone v Spaghetti House Ltd* [1980] ICR 155).

32.17 Statement of fixed deductions

Provided that the employer has given in writing a standing statement of fixed deductions, there is no need to itemise fixed deductions on an employee's pay statement, but simply to state the total amount of the deductions. This standing statement should give the following information:

(a)   the amount of each deduction;

(b)   the intervals at which the deduction is to be made; and

(c)   the purpose for which it is made.

(ERA 1996, s 9(1)–(3).)

A statement of fixed deductions may be amended, whether by the addition of a new deduction or by a change in the particulars or cancellation of an existing deduction, by notice in writing containing particulars of the amendment given by the employer to the employee *(ERA 1996, s 9(3))*.

It must be remembered that a standing statement of fixed deductions only remains effective for 12 months from the date on which it is given to the employee. Before the expiry of the 12-month period, the employer must re-issue the statement, together with any amendments, in consolidated form *(ERA 1996, s 9(4))*.

32.18 Exclusions

The requirement for an employer to provide an employee with a pay statement does not apply:

(a)   to persons engaged in police service *(ERA 1996, s 200(1))*;

(b)   to employment as a merchant seaman, or as a master or member of the crew of a fishing vessel where the employee is remunerated only by a share in the profits or gross earnings of the vessel *(ERA 1996, s 199(2)(4))*.

32.19 Application to an employment tribunal

If an employer does not give any employee of his a pay statement, the employee may refer the matter to an employment tribunal to determine what particulars ought to have been included in a statement so as to comply with the requirements in **32.11** above *(ERA 1996, s 11(1))*. An employee may also apply to a tribunal, as may an employer, to determine provisions which should have been included in a pay statement or a standing statement of fixed deductions, but which have been omitted *(ERA 1996, s 11(2))*.

Any application concerning a pay statement must be brought while the employee is still employed by the relevant employer, or within three months of the date on which the employment ceased *(ERA 1996, s 11(4))* or within such further period as the tribunal consider treasonable where satisfied that it was not reasonably practicable for the application to be made before the end of the period of three months *(ERA s 11(4)(b))*.

32.20 Tribunal order

Where, on a reference under these provisions, an employment tribunal finds that an employer has failed to give an employee a pay statement or that a pay statement or standing statement of fixed deductions does not, in relation to a deduction, contain the particulars required to be included in that statement, the tribunal will make a declaration to that effect.

Where the tribunal further finds that any unnotified deductions have been made from the pay of the employee during the period of 13 weeks immediately preceding the date of the application (whether or not such deductions were made in breach of the contract of employment), the tribunal may order the employer to pay the employee a sum not exceeding the aggregate of the unnotified deductions so made (*ERA 1996, s 12(3)–(5)*; see **32.8** above for the relationship between *ERA 1996, s 11* and *ss 23–25*).

For example, an employee may be required by his contract of employment to pay subscriptions to a sports club of £1 per week. If the employer does not notify the employee of this deduction, either in a note with his pay packet or in a statement of fixed deductions, then, on an application to an employment tribunal, the tribunal may order the employer to repay the employee a sum of up to £13, which is equivalent to the employee's subscriptions for the previous 13 weeks.

In *Milsom v Leicestershire County Council* [1978] IRLR 433, an employment tribunal held that an employer was in breach of the requirement to give an itemised pay statement. A sum had been deducted from the employee's wages, the only explanation being that it was a 'miscellaneous deduction/payment'. The tribunal ordered the employer to pay £25 to the employee for the failure to give a proper statement, despite the fact that the employee was well aware of the reason for the deduction and that the employer was entitled under the contract between the parties to make such a deduction.

However, in *Scott v Creager* [1979] ICR 403, the EAT held that where an employer had made unnotified deductions, an employment tribunal had not erred in awarding a sum to the employee equal to the amount by which the pay she actually received fell short of the net pay she should have received.

32.21 GRATUITIES AND TRONCS

The authorities relating to a system whereby customers' gratuities are pooled in a 'tronc' and distributed among employees (typically, restaurant staff) were reviewed by the Court of Appeal in *Nerva v RL & G Ltd* [1996] IRLR 461. This was a case dealing with whether payments out of a tronc counted towards the minimum remuneration required under a Wages Council order; it establishes that a gratuity left by a customer as a cash tip is normally held on trust for the benefit of the restaurant's employees, whereas payments received by those employees in respect of such a gratuity added to a customer's cheque or credit-card payment are not held on trust, but instead form part of their remuneration. The case, under the name *Nerva v United Kingdom* (Application 42295/98) [2002] IRLR 815, went to the European Court of Human Rights (see **28.7** HUMAN RIGHTS). The ECHR upheld the decision of the Court of Appeal concluding that an employer could use such payments in discharge of remuneration obligations to the waiter employees and that such a practice did not amount to a breach of the applicants' rights (under Article 1 of Protocol No 1 to the European Convention on Human Rights) to peaceful enjoyment of their possessions. On the exclusion with effect from 1 October 2009 of such payments from the calculation of whether there has been compliance with the NMW and for the government's code of practice on such payments. See **32.9** above.

32.22 PAY ON TERMINATION OF EMPLOYMENT

Upon termination of employment, an employer should pay to the former employee any of the following sums which may be due, depending upon the circumstances: wages in lieu of notice (see **46.9** TERMINATION OF EMPLOYMENT); accrued holiday pay (see **27.4A** HOLIDAYS); reimbursement of expenses; other contractual payments; and redundancy pay (see REDUNDANCY – I (36)).

If the employee is paid weekly or monthly and the employment has terminated part-way through the week or month, he will be taken to have earned a rateable proportion of his wages or salary for that period. This is the result of applying the *Apportionment Act 1870*, which provides by *s 2* that (*inter alia*) all annuities and other periodical payments in the nature of income shall be considered as accruing from day to day, and shall be apportionable in respect of time accordingly. 'Annuities' are defined by *s 5* to include salaries and pensions. It is possible to exclude apportionment by an express stipulation to the contrary (*Apportionment Act 1870, s 7*). The *Act* is also capable of being applied to a payment such as an annual bonus when the employee leaves part-way through the year (see, on the application of the *Apportionment Act 1870, Thames Water Utilities v Reynolds* [1996] IRLR 186, EAT and *Re Bank of Credit and Commerce International SA* [1994] IRLR 282) and compare *Leisure Leagues UK Ltd v Maconnachie* [2002] IRLR 600 at **32.14** above. See also *Item Software (UK) Ltd v Fassihi* [2004] EWCA Civ 1244, [2004] IRLR 928.

32.23   GUARANTEE PAYMENTS FOR WORKLESS DAYS

The *Employment Protection Act 1975* created certain rights to payment when no work is done owing to circumstances beyond the control of the employee. These provisions are now contained in the *Employment Rights Act 1996 ('ERA 1996')*. These are of benefit, chiefly, to hourly paid employees and to workers on piece rates.

32.24   RIGHT TO GUARANTEE PAYMENT

Workless day

Where any employee, throughout a day during any part of which he would normally be required to work in accordance with his contract of employment, is not provided with work by his employer by reason of:

(a)   a diminution in the requirements of the employer's business for work of the kind which the employee is employed to do; or

(b)   any other occurrence affecting the normal working of the employer's business in relation to work of the kind which the employee is employed to do,

he is, subject to certain exceptions, entitled to a guarantee payment (*ERA 1996, s 28(1)–(3)*).

A threatened power cut is such an occurrence (*Miller v Harry Thornton (Lollies) Ltd* [1978] IRLR 430).

If a worker can turn down work given to her she is not normally 'required to work' within the meaning of the section and is not entitled to a guarantee payment when not provided with any work (*Mailway (Southern) Ltd v Willsher* [1978] ICR 511; *York and Reynolds v Colledge Hosiery Co Ltd* [1978] IRLR 53). It was held at employment tribunal level that variations to the contract to reduce the days worked may mean that the employee would no longer normally be required to work on the workless days. See *Clemens v Peter Richards Ltd (t/a John Bryan)* [1977] IRLR 332 and *Daley v Strathclyde Regional Council* [1977] IRLR 414. In *Abercrombie v Aga Rangemaster Ltd* [2013] IRLR 13 this issue was considered by the EAT which held that a formal agreed variation to the employees' contracts of employment, albeit for a fixed temporal period (in that case a 6 month period in which Fridays were not to be worked with an equivalent reduction in pay), had the effect that Friday ceased to be a day on which the employees would be normally be required to work for the purposes of *ss 28(1)* and *30(1)*, *ERA*. The EAT held that there was no requirement in s 28(1) of the ERA for any variation of the employees' contract to be permanent in order to change the employees' normal working hours and thus disentitle the employees to guarantee payments. An appeal to the Court of Appeal is due to be heard in July 2013.

If an employer provides some although not the usual amount of work during a day, that is not considered a 'workless day' for which an employee is entitled to a guarantee payment. Examples of situations which may cause a day to be 'workless' are a lack of orders, under (*a*), or any other occurrence such as a power cut affecting the normal working of the employer's business in relation to work of the kind which the employee is employed to do, under (*b*).

Where employment begins before midnight and extends into the next day, the period of employment for the purpose of deciding which is the workless day is defined as follows:

(i)   if the employment before midnight is, or would normally be, of longer duration than that after midnight, that period of employment is treated as falling wholly on the first day; and

(ii)   in any other case, that period of employment is treated as falling wholly on the second day.

(*ERA 1996, s 28(4), (5).*)

32.25 Qualifying period

In order to qualify for the entitlement, an employee must have been continuously employed for one month ending with the day before the workless day (*ERA 1996, s 29(1)*). (See CONTINUOUS EMPLOYMENT (6).)

An employee who is employed:

(a)   under a contract for a fixed term of three months or less; or

(b)   under a contract made in contemplation of the performance of a specific task which is not expected to last for more than three months,

is not entitled to a guarantee payment unless he has been continuously employed for a period of more than three months ending with the day before that in respect of which the guarantee payment is claimed (*ERA 1996, s 29(2)*).

32.26 Exclusions

Trade disputes. An employee is not entitled to a guarantee payment in respect of a workless day if the failure to provide him with work occurs in consequence of a strike, lock-out or other industrial action involving any employee of his employer or of an associated employer (*ERA 1996, s 29(3)*; for 'associated employer' see **6.9**(a) CONTINUOUS EMPLOYMENT). Thus, a dispute with his employer involving members of another union at his workplace or of employees of his employer at a factory in another part of the country, which causes a halt in production, disentitles an employee from receiving a guarantee payment.

Offer of suitable alternative work. An employee is not entitled to a guarantee payment in respect of a workless day if:

(a)   his employer has offered to provide alternative work for that day which is suitable in all the circumstances (whether or not it is work which the employee is employed to perform under his contract) and the employee has unreasonably refused that offer; or

(b)   he does not comply with reasonable requirements imposed by his employer with a view to ensuring that his services are available.

(*ERA 1996, s 29(4), (5).*)

Both objective and subjective tests are involved in deciding what is 'suitable' and 'reasonable' within the meaning of (*a*) above. No general rules can be laid down, but what tribunals will have in mind are pay, hours, geographical location and skill required. So far as (*b*) is concerned, clearly, if an employer asked an employee to telephone to find out whether work was available, that would be considered a reasonable requirement. It has been held that a wide variety of alternative work may be suitable if it is only temporary. See *Purdy v Willowbrook International Ltd* [1977] IRLR 388, IT; *Meadows v Faithful Overalls Ltd* [1977] IRLR 330, IT.

32.27 Amount of payment

The amount of the guarantee payment payable in respect of any day is the sum produced by multiplying the *number of normal working hours* in that day by the *guaranteed hourly rate* (*ERA 1996, s 30(1)*).

The 'guaranteed hourly rate' is the amount of one week's pay (see below **32.34**) divided by the number of normal working hours in that week. In calculating 'normal working hours' where the number of working hours in a week fluctuate, one takes the average number of working hours over the 12 weeks ending with the last complete week before the day in respect of which the guarantee payment is payable. If the employee has not been employed for 12 weeks, a calculation is made having regard to:

(a)   the average number of normal working hours in a week which the employee could expect in accordance with the terms of his contract; and

(b)   the average number of such hours of other employees engaged in relevant comparable employment with the same employer.

(*ERA 1996, s 30(2)–(4)*.)

If any employee's contract has been varied or a new contract has been entered into for short-time working, the calculation is made by reference to the last day that the original contract was in force (*ERA 1996, s 30(5)*).

The amount of a guarantee payment payable to an employee in respect of any day will not exceed £24.20 (with effect from 1 February 2013: *Employment Rights (Increase of Limits) Order 2012 (SI 2012/3007)*). The previous maximum was £23.50. Further, such payments cannot exceed five days in any period of three months. The present maximum annual liability is therefore £484 (*ERA 1996, s 31*). Any contractual remuneration paid to an employee in respect of a workless day goes towards discharging any statutory liability of the employer to pay a guarantee payment in respect of that day and, conversely, any guarantee payment paid in respect of a day goes towards discharging any liability of the employer to pay contractual remuneration in respect of that day (*ERA 1996, s 32*). Thus, if any employee is paid on a weekly or monthly basis, irrespective of the work actually done, these payments will go towards discharging any statutory liability. Contractual payments made in respect of any workless days are to be taken into account when calculating the maximum number of days within the three-month period for which the employee is entitled to a payment (*Cartwright v G Clancey Ltd* [1983] ICR 552).

The Secretary of State may by order exempt certain industries from these provisions where there is in force a collective agreement or an agricultural wages order which complies with certain conditions (*ERA 1996, s 35*).

32.28 Remedy for failure to make payment

An employee may present a complaint to an employment tribunal that his employer has failed to pay the whole or any part of a guarantee payment to which he is entitled. The tribunal, if it finds the complaint well-founded, will order the employer to pay the complainant the amount of guarantee payment which it finds due to him (*ERA 1996, s 34(1), (3)*). Such a complaint must be presented to a tribunal before the end of the period of *three months* beginning with the workless day (or within such further period as the tribunal considers reasonable, when it is satisfied that it was not reasonably practicable for the complaint to be presented within the period of three months; see **17.25** EMPLOYMENT TRIBUNALS – I) (*ERA 1996, s 34(2)*).

32.29   MEDICAL SUSPENSION PAYMENTS

Statutes and regulations safeguard workpeople from exposure to health hazards. They may provide, for example, that a factory be closed when the atmosphere in it becomes contaminated. At common law, if a factory closed down in compliance with regulations relating to the health of the factory workers, the workers were not entitled to be paid for the time lost unless their contracts provided otherwise. However, now where an employee is suspended from work by his employer on medical grounds in compliance with any law or regulation concerning the health and safety of workers, he may be entitled to be paid remuneration by his employer while he is so suspended for a period not exceeding 26 weeks. The provision which leads to him being suspended must be one of those for the time being specified in *ERA 1996, s 64(3)*. At present only the *Control of Lead at Work Regulations 1980 (SI 1980/1248)*, *reg 16*, the *Ionising Radiations Regulations 1985 (SI 1985/1333)*, *reg 16* and the *Control of Substances Hazardous to Health Regulations 1988 (SI 1988/1657)*, *reg 11*, are so specified. (See also **31.31** MATERNITY AND PARENTAL RIGHTS for an employee's right to remuneration when suspended on maternity grounds.)

32.30   Qualifying conditions

An employee will be regarded as suspended from work only if, and so long as, he continues to be employed by his employer but is not provided with work or does not perform the work he normally performed before the suspension (*ERA 1996, s 64(5)*).

In order to be entitled to claim a medical suspension payment, the employee must have been continuously employed for a period of one month ending with the day before that on which the suspension begins (*ERA 1996, s 65(1)*).

An employee who is employed:

(a)   under a contract for a fixed term of three months or less; or

(b)   under a contract made in contemplation of the performance of a specific task which is not expected to last for more than three months,

is not entitled to a medical suspension payment unless he has been continuously employed for a period of more than three months ending with the day before that on which the suspension begins (*ERA 1996, s 65(2)*).

For continuity of employment, see CONTINUOUS EMPLOYMENT (6).

32.31   Exclusions from right to payment

These are:

(a)   An employee will not be entitled to a medical suspension payment in respect of any period during which he is incapable of work by reason of disease or bodily or mental disablement (*ERA 1996, s 65(3)*).

(b)   An employee is not entitled to a medical suspension payment in respect of any period during which:

(i)   his employer offered to provide him with suitable alternative work, whether or not it was work the employee was engaged to perform; and

(ii)   the employee unreasonably refused to perform that work.

(*ERA 1996, s 65(4)(a)*.)

If, for example, a man is engaged as a machine operator in the toolroom of a factory and the toolroom has to be closed for medical reasons for a few weeks, it may be considered unreasonable for the operative to refuse to work on a similar type of machine in a different part of the factory, provided he is offered the same rate of pay as that which he had previously received.

(c)   An employee is not entitled to a medical suspension payment in respect of any period during which he did not comply with reasonable requirements imposed by his employer with a view to ensuring that his services were available (*ERA 1996, s 65(4)(b)*).

Therefore, if an employer sent a man home because his workplace was medically unsafe but asked him to telephone each day to find out whether his services were required, and the employee failed to do so, he may be deprived of his right to a medical suspension payment.

32.32 Amount of payment

The employee is entitled to a week's pay in respect of every week of suspension (with proportionate reduction for part of a week) (*ERA 1996, s 69(1)*). A week's pay is calculated in accordance with *ERA 1996, ss 220–229* (see below **32.34**). If an employee is entitled to payment during suspension on medical grounds by a term of his contract, he will only be able to claim from the employer the additional amount by which his statutory entitlement exceeds the contractual entitlement. Any payment under a contract goes to discharge the statutory liability and vice versa (*ERA 1996, s 69(2), (3)*). Thus, if an employee's week's pay is £450 (the same as the statutory week's pay; see the *Employment Rights (Increase of Limits) Order 2012 (SI 2012/3007)*) and on suspension from work on medical grounds he is contractually entitled to £300, he can claim £150 as a statutory medical suspension payment. If, however, the week's pay is £500 and the contractual entitlement £300, the statutory medical suspension payment will still be capped at £150.

32.33 Remedy for failure to make payment

If an employer fails to make a medical suspension payment, an employee may present a complaint to an employment tribunal in respect of that payment (*ERA 1996, s 70(1)*).

The complaint must be presented to the tribunal within three months beginning with the day in respect of which the claim is made (or within such further period as the tribunal considers reasonable, in a case where it is satisfied that it was not reasonably practicable for the complaint to be presented within the period of three months) (*ERA 1996, s 70(2)*; for reasonable practicability, see **17.25** EMPLOYMENT TRIBUNALS – I).

Where an employment tribunal finds a complaint well founded, it will order the employer to pay the complainant the amount of remuneration which it finds is due to him (*ERA 1996, s 70(3)*).

32.34 'A WEEK'S PAY'

The amount of money payable under several of the statutory employment protection rights depends upon a calculation based on the week's pay of the employee concerned. For example, a week's pay is the basis for the calculation of a redundancy payment and of the basic award in a claim for unfair dismissal.

32.34 Pay – I

The calculation of a week's pay differs according to whether the employee is in employment for which there are normal working hours or whether he is in employment for which there are no normal working hours.

The statutory rules governing 'a week's pay' are set out in *ERA 1996, ss 221–229*, formerly *EPCA 1978, Sch 14*.

32.35 EMPLOYMENT FOR WHICH THERE ARE NORMAL WORKING HOURS

If the employee's normal working hours are the same every week and his remuneration for employment in normal working hours does not vary with the amount of work done in the period, the amount of a week's pay is the amount which is payable by the employer under the contract of employment in force on the calculation date if the employee works throughout his normal working hours in a week (*ERA 1996, s 221(2)*). One possible complication is illustrated by *Agard v Westminster Kingsway College* (UKEATPA/0767/10/SM) (14 December 2010, unreported). Here the employee worked 20 hours per week for 40 weeks of the year but could not take holiday during this (term-time) 40 week period. The holiday was 5.39 weeks. The EAT held that in such circumstances the calculation of a week's pay should add in the holiday weeks giving 45.39 working weeks by which the annual salary would be divided. See also *Gilbert v Barnsley Metropolitan Borough Council* (UKEAT/674/00) [2002] All ER (D) 45 (Apr).

Where the amount of the remuneration varies with the amount of work done but the number of normal working hours does not vary, the amount of a week's pay is the amount of remuneration for the number of normal working hours in a week calculated at the *average* hourly rate of remuneration payable by the employer to the employee in respect of the period of 12 weeks:

(a)   where the calculation date is the last day of a week, ending with that week;

(b)   in any other case, ending with the last complete week before the calculation date.

(*ERA 1996, s 221(3)*.)

This is the provision which must be applied even where the variation may be attributable to the amount of work done by other employees (*Keywest Club Ltd (t/a Veeraswamys Restaurant) v Choudhury* [1988] IRLR 51, EAT).

Where the employee is required under his contract to work during normal working hours on days of the week or at times of the day which differ from week to week or over a longer period so that the remuneration payable for or apportionable to any week varies, the amount of a week's pay is based upon the average remuneration paid and the average number of hours worked in the last 12 weeks before the calculation date (*ERA 1996, s 222*).

For the purposes of these calculations, weeks in which the employee was not paid because he was not working are excluded, and a previous working week is brought into account (*ERA 1996, s 223(1), (2)*).

32.36 Overtime

In a case where remuneration for employment in normal working hours is unaffected by any variable element in the pay structure, overtime hours and payment for them only fall within the calculation if the employer is obliged to provide, and the employee is obliged to work, the overtime (*Tarmac Roadstone Holdings Ltd v Peacock* [1973] 2 All ER 485, [1973] 1 WLR 594, [1973] ICR 273; *Gascol Conversions Ltd v Mercer* [1974] ICR 420). Thus, where overtime is voluntary and there is no such variable element, a week's pay is simply the contractual amount payable for the normal working hours in a full week, excluding overtime

(ERA 1996, ss 221(2), 234(1), (2)). The same definition of a week's pay applies where a minimum number of hours of overtime is fixed by the contract of employment except that, in such a case, 'normal working hours' include that minimum number of hours of compulsory overtime *(ERA 1996, s 234(3))*.

However, where there is a variable element in the employee's remuneration dependent on results, eg piece rates, productivity bonus, or commission, the amount of a week's pay is to be calculated in accordance with *ERA 1996, s 221(3)* and *223(3)*. *Section 223(3)* provides as follows:

> 'Where, in arriving at the (average) . . . hourly rate of remuneration, account has to be taken of remuneration payable for, or apportionable to, work done in hours other than normal working hours, and the amount of that remuneration was greater than it would have been if the work had been done in normal working hours (or, in a case within *s 234(3)* falling within the number of hours without overtime), account shall be taken of that remuneration as if –
>
> (*a*)   the work had been done in normal working hours, falling within the number of hours without overtime in a case within *s 234(3)*; and
>
> (*b*)   the amount of that remuneration had been reduced accordingly.'

In *British Coal Corpn v Cheesbrough* [1990] 2 AC 256, [1990] 1 All ER 641, [1990] 2 WLR 407, [1990] ICR 317, the House of Lords had to consider the situation where there was a variable element, namely, a weekly bonus paid to the employee for work done during normal working hours. The employee also regularly worked voluntary overtime, which was paid at time and a half, but no additional bonus was paid in respect of overtime. In such a case, the effect of *ERA 1996, s 223(3)* was that the total hours worked in the relevant weeks (including overtime) had to be taken into account, but the overtime premium was to be disregarded, and the overtime was to be treated as having been worked in normal working hours. The House of Lords held that the overtime was to be treated as having been paid at the basic hourly rate, without the addition of an amount to reflect the employee's weekly bonus. On the particular facts, this worked against the employee because his bonus had to be spread over more hours, thereby reducing his average rate of remuneration and the amount of his 'week's pay'.

32.37 EMPLOYMENTS FOR WHICH THERE ARE NO NORMAL WORKING HOURS

The amount of a week's pay is the amount of the employee's average weekly remuneration in the period of 12 weeks:

(a)   where the calculation date is the last day of a week, ending with that week;

(b)   in any other case, ending with the last complete week before the calculation date.

In arriving at the average weekly rate of remuneration no account shall be taken of a week in which no remuneration was payable by the employer to the employee, and remuneration in earlier weeks is brought in so as to bring the number of weeks of which account is taken up to 12 *(ERA 1996, s 224)*.

32.38 THE CALCULATION DATE

In ascertaining the 'calculation date' for the purpose of the calculations described above, it is necessary to look to *ERA 1996, ss 225, 231*. Different calculation dates apply for the various purposes for which it may be necessary to ascertain the amount of a week's pay.

32.39 THE AMOUNT OF A WEEK'S PAY

For the purposes of calculating the amount of a week's pay, remuneration includes wages, salaries and expenses insofar as they represent profit in the employee's hands (*S & U Stores Ltd v Wilkes* [1974] 3 All ER 401). It also includes an incentive bonus, irrespective of whether the bonus is identifiably related to the particular employee's efforts (*British Coal Corpn v Cheesbrough* [1990] 2 AC 256, [1990] 1 All ER 641, [1990] 2 WLR 407, [1990] ICR 317). The amount of remuneration without deduction of tax is taken into account for the purposes of calculating a basic award and a redundancy payment (*Secretary of State for Employment v John Woodrow & Sons (Builders) Ltd* [1983] ICR 582). In *W A Armstrong & Sons v Borril* [2000] ICR 367, the EAT held that a week's pay for the purpose of a redundancy payment payable to an agricultural worker was the amount specified in the *Agricultural Wages Order* without deduction of board and lodging.

The amount of a week's pay for certain calculations is subject to statutory maxima. The present limit on the amount of a week's pay for the purpose of calculating a basic award of compensation for unfair dismissal and for calculating a redundancy payment is, with effect from 1 February 2013, £450 (*Employment Rights (Increase of Limits) Order 2012 (SI 2012/3007)*). The previous limit, for matters arising prior to 1 February 2013, was £430.

33   Pay – II: Attachment of Earnings

33.1   An *attachment of earnings order* is a means of enforcing a court order that a person must pay a sum of money. The order is made by the court and operates as an instruction to that person's employer to deduct sums from his earnings and pay them directly to the court office. The employer must also notify the court of certain matters. The *Attachment of Earnings Act 1971* ('*AtEA 1971*'), as amended, sets out the obligations of employers and the methods of calculating the deductions. Similar systems for attachment of earnings have been introduced in order to assist with the enforcement of the council tax (see 33.10 below) and of child support maintenance under the *Child Support Act 1991* or the *Child Support, Pensions and Social Security Act 2000* ('*CSPSSA 2000*') as the case may be (see **33.11** below).

An attachment of earnings order may be made by a court if it appears to it that a person has failed, or is likely to fail, to pay in a satisfactory way sums due from him. Orders may be made for the payment of:

(a)   **maintenance:**

    (i)   if under a High Court maintenance order, an attachment of earnings order may be made in the High Court or the county court;

    (ii)   if under a county court maintenance order, an order may be made in the county court;

    (iii) if under a magistrates' court maintenance order, an order may be made in a magistrates' court;

(b)   **payments under an administration order** (dealing with a number of debts owed by the same person) – county court;

(c)   **payment under a legal aid contribution order** pursuant to section 17(2) of the *Access to Justice Act 1999* and Regulations under that Act. – magistrates' court.

(*AtEA 1971, s 1(1)–(3)* as amended.)

Where a county court makes an administration order in respect of a debtor's estate, it may also make an attachment of earnings order to secure the payments required by the administration order (*AtEA 1971, s 5(1)*).

The person who is obliged to make the deduction is the employer. No obligation rests on someone who as servant or agent makes payments to the employee (*AtEA 1971, s 6(2)*).

33.2   EARNINGS FROM WHICH THE DEDUCTIONS ARE MADE

Earnings, for the purposes of attachment of earnings, include wages or salary together with bonuses, commission, overtime pay and other emoluments payable under a contract of employment in addition to wages or salary. Pensions, annuities and compensation for loss of office are also included as is statutory sick pay (*AtEA 1971, s 24(1)* as amended by, *inter alia, Social Security Act 1985, s 21, Sch 4 para 1; Social Security Act 1986, Sch 10 para 102; Pension Schemes Act 1993, s 190, Sch 8 para 4*).

The following payments are not treated as earnings:

(a)   sums payable by any public department of the Government of Northern Ireland or a territory outside the United Kingdom;

(b)   income or allowances payable to the debtor as a member of Her Majesty's forces other than pay or allowances payable by his employer to him as a special member of a reserve force (see the *Reserve Forces Act 1996*);

(c)   pensions, allowances or benefits payable under any social security enactment (including, in particular, statutory maternity pay);

(d)   pensions or allowances payable in respect of disablement or disability;

(e)   except in relation to a maintenance order, wages payable to a person as a seaman, other than wages payable to him as a seaman of a fishing boat;

(f)   guaranteed minimum pension within the meaning of the *Pensions Schemes Act 1993*;

(g)   a tax credit within the meaning of the *Tax Credits Act 2002*.

(*AtEA 1971, s 24(2)* as amended by, inter alia, *Social Security Pensions Act 1975, s 65; Merchant Shipping Act 1979, s 39; Merchant Shipping Act 1995, s 314(2), Sch 13 para 46; Pension Schemes Act 1993, s 190, Sch 8 para 4; Tax Credits Act 2002, s 47, Sch 3, para 1*).

In order to determine whether payments made by him are earnings, an employer may apply to the court which made the order (*AtEA 1971, s 16(1), (2)*). While such an application, or an appeal from the finding on such an application, is pending, an employer will not incur any liability for non-compliance with the order to which the application relates (*AtEA 1971, s 16(3)*).

33.3   DEDUCTIONS FROM PAY

Where an employer receives an attachment of earnings order which relates to one of his employees, he must make such deductions from his employee's pay as are specified in the order (*AtEA 1971, s 6 as amended by Courts and Legal Services Act 1990, Sch 17 para 5; Access to Justice Act 1999, s 90, Sch 13 paras 64, 66, Tribunals, Courts and Enforcement Act 2007; Collection of Fines (Final Scheme) Order 2006 (SI 2006/1737)*).

The court may use the following terms.

(a)   '*Attachable earnings*': that part of the employee's earnings to which an attachment of earnings order applies (usually income after statutory deduction).

(b)   '*Normal deductions*': the sum to be deducted from the employee's income on each pay day.

(c)   '*Protected earnings*': the earnings below which no deduction may be made.

33.4   Calculating the deduction

If an attachment of earnings order is made, then the employer must, on pay day:

(a)   if the attachable earnings are greater than the protected earnings:

    (i)   deduct the lesser of the normal deduction and the amount of the excess; and

    (ii)   in the case of orders *not* made to secure the payment of a judgment debt or payments under an administration order, deduct any *arrears* still outstanding, insofar as the excess allows;

(b)   if the attachable earnings are equal to or less than the protected earnings, take no action (but the arrears are increased by the amount due).

(*AtEA 1971, Sch 3 Pt I; ERA 1996, s 240, Sch 1 para 3.*)

Example. A part-time employee earns, on average, £90 per week after tax, National Insurance, etc but because the employee is on piece-work his weekly earnings may vary. The court has ordered the employee to pay £300 at a *normal deduction rate* of £15 per week, and has decided that his *protected earnings rate* is to be £60 (ie, the employee will always be allowed to take home £60, provided that he earns that much). The order does not relate to a judgment debt or an administration order.

The following table shows his pay, and the deductions over a five-week period.

Week no.	Attachable earnings	Deductions under the order	Take home	Comments
	£	£	£	
1	90	15	75	Normal deduction
2	95	15	80	Normal deduction
3	70	10	60	Only £10 deducted, Jones takes home his protected earnings
4	95	20	75	Normal deduction plus £5 of arrears
5	100	15	85	Normal deduction

See also *Pepper v Pepper* [1960] 1 WLR 131.

33.5 Priority of orders

Where there are two or more orders in existence, which are not to secure either the payment of judgment debts or payments under an administration order, then the employer must deal first with the first in time and apply the residue of the debtor's earnings over and above his protected earnings to subsequent orders, dealing with them in date order. Where there are several types of orders in existence, those to satisfy judgment debts or administration orders must be dealt with after the rest (*AtEA 1971, Sch 3 Pt II paras 7, 8*).

33.6 Time limits

It should be noted that the following notices should be complied with, within seven days:

(a)   an attachment of earnings order (*AtEA 1971, s 7(1)*);

(b)   a variation (*AtEA 1971, s 9(2)*);

(c)   a notice of cessation or discharge (*AtEA 1971, s 12(3)*).

33.7 EMPLOYER'S OBLIGATIONS TO NOTIFY COURT

An employer must notify the relevant court as follows.

(a)   Where a person is served with an attachment of earnings order directed to him and the debtor is not in his employment, *or* subsequently ceases to be in his employment, he must within 10 days give notice of that fact to the court (*AtEA 1971, s 7(2)*). In relation to a deductions from earnings order (see 33.11 below) there is a similar obligation to notify the Secretary of State (*SI 1992/1989 Reg 16(1), (2)*).

(b)   If the court orders him to do so, the employer must give the court, within a specified period, a statement signed by him or on his behalf of the debtor's earnings and anticipated earnings (*AtEA 1971, s 14(1)(b)*). In relation to a deductions from earnings order (see 33.11 below) similar requirements are imposed by the *Child Support Information, Evidence and Disclosure Regulations 1992 (SI 1992/1812)*

(c)   If he becomes the debtor's employer and knows that the order is in force and by what court it was made, he must within seven days of his becoming the debtor's employer or acquiring that knowledge (whichever is the later) notify that court in writing that he is the debtor's employer and include in his notification a statement of the debtor's earnings and anticipated earnings (*AtEA 1971, s 15(c)*). In relation to a deductions from earnings order (see **33.11** below) similar obligations are imposed (*SI 1992/1989 Reg 16(3)*).

33.8   PENALTIES FOR NON-COMPLIANCE

If an employer, required to comply with any of the above provisions relating to deductions or notice, fails to do so, he may be liable on conviction in a magistrates' court to a fine of not more than level 2 on the Standard Scale (see **1.10** INTRODUCTION) or he may be fined up to £250 by a judge of the High Court or the county court (*AtEA 1971, s 23*, as amended). Furthermore, if he gives a notice or makes any statement on these matters which he knows to be false in a material particular then, in addition to being fined, he may be imprisoned for not more than 14 days. It should be noted that the *Legal Aid, Sentencing and Punishment of Offenders Act 2012* makes provision in *ss 86–87* for the Secretary of State to increase the levels 1–4 of the standard scale fines to such sums considered appropriate. These provisions are, however, not yet in force (see **1.10** INTRODUCTION).

It will be a defence for an employer to prove:

(a)   that he took all reasonable steps to comply with the attachment of earnings order; or

(b)   that he did not know and could not reasonably be expected to know that the debtor was not in his employment, or had ceased to be so, and that he gave the required notice as soon as reasonably practicable after that fact came to his knowledge.

(*AtEA 1971, s 23(5)*.)

33.9   OTHER MATTERS

Clerical costs. When an employer makes a deduction in compliance with an order from an employee's earnings, he is entitled to deduct £1 (or such sum as is currently applicable) for clerical and administration costs (*AtEA 1971, s 7(4)(a); Attachment of Earnings (Employer's Deduction) Order 1991 (SI 1991/356), art 2*). The employer must give the employee a statement in writing of the deduction (*AtEA 1971, s 7(4)(b)*).

Pay statements. The employee must be given a pay statement showing, among other things, deductions from his pay. An employer need not, on each occasion upon which a payment of wages is made, give separate particulars of a fixed deduction. It is sufficient if he supplies a statement of the aggregate amount of fixed deductions having supplied a standing statement in writing of each fixed deduction stating:

(a)   the amount of the deduction; and

(b)   the intervals at which the deduction is to be made; and

(c)   the purpose for which it is made.

Any such standing statement is valid for 12 months. It may be amended (by adding a new deduction or altering or cancelling an existing one) by a written notice to the employee, detailing the amendment. If the employer wishes to continue to rely on the statement, it must be reissued in a consolidated form, incorporating any amendments previously notified to the employee, at intervals not exceeding 12 months.

(*ERA 1996, ss 8, 9*.) (See further **32.17** PAY – I.)

If an employer requires advice or information concerning an attachment of earnings order or subsequent procedures he should contact the court where the order was made.

33.10   COUNCIL TAX

Attachment of earnings for failure to pay the council tax is provided for by the *Council Tax (Administration and Enforcement) Regulations 1992 (SI 1992/613)*, as amended (by, inter alia, the *Local Government Changes for England (Community Charge and Council Tax, Administration and Enforcement) Regulations 1995 (SI 1995/247)*, the *Local Authorities (Contracting Out of Tax Billing, Collection and Enforcement Functions) Order 1996 (SI 1996/1880)*, the *Community Charge and Council Tax (Administration and Enforcement) (Amendment) (Jobseeker's Allowance) Regulations 1996 (SI 1996/2405)*, the *Council Tax (Administration and Enforcement) (Amendment) Regulations 1998 (1998/295)* and the *Council Tax (Administration and Enforcement) (Amendment) (England) Regulations 2004 (SI 2004/927)*. There must first be an outstanding sum in respect of which the relevant billing authority (in general, a district or borough council) has obtained a liability order from magistrates pursuant to *reg 34*. The authority is then itself empowered by *reg 37(1)* to make an attachment of earnings order to secure the payment of any outstanding sum covered by the liability order.

The attachment order is directed to the debtor's employer, and is in a prescribed form (*reg 37(2)*). A duty to comply with an order served upon him is imposed on the employer by *reg 37(3)*. Non-compliance is an offence unless the employer proves that he took all reasonable steps to comply with the order, and is punishable by a fine not exceeding level 3 on the Standard Scale (*reg 56(2)*; and see **1.10** INTRODUCTION).

The amount to be deducted under the order is regulated by *reg 38* and *Sch 4*. An amount is specified for any given level of net earnings. 'Earnings' has the same meaning as in the *AtEA 1971* (see **32.2** above and see *reg 32(1)*), and the net earnings are arrived at by the deduction of income tax, primary class 1 contributions under the *Social Security Act 1975* and certain amounts deductible for the purposes of a superannuation scheme (*reg 32(1)*).

The employer must notify the debtor in writing of the total sum deducted up to the date of each notification (*reg 39(2)*). The notice should be provided at the same time as a pay statement (*reg 39(3)*) The employer may deduct the sum of £1 towards administrative costs for each deduction made (*reg 39(1)*).

While such an order is in force, the debtor is under a duty to notify the authority of changes in his employment pursuant to *reg 40*. The ex-employer is under a similar duty (*reg 39(4)*), as is the new employer if he knows of the order (*reg 39(6)*).

If two or more orders are made under these provisions (or such an order is made following the making of an order under the *AtEA 1971*), the priority between them is governed by *reg 42*.

33.11   CHILD SUPPORT MAINTENANCE

A similar system to that under the *AtEA 1971* operates in relation to the enforcement of the payment of child support maintenance by an absent parent, under the *Child Support Act 1991* ('*CSA 1991*') and under the *Child Support, Pensions and Social Security Act 2000* ('*CSPSSA 2000*'). Orders under the *CSA 1991* or *CSPSSA 2000* (which apples to orders made after 3 March 2003) are referred to as 'deduction from earnings orders', and the procedure is set out in the *Child Support (Collection and Enforcement) Regulations 1992 (SI 1992/1989)*, as amended by, inter alia, the *Child Support (Collection and Enforcement and Miscellaneous Amendments) Regulations 2001 (SI 2001/162)* and the *Child Support*

33.11   Pay – II: Attachment of Earnings

(Miscellaneous Amendments) (No. 2) Regulations 2008 (SI 2008/2544). The regime is similar to that under the *AtEA 1971* and is therefore not dealt with separately in this chapter. Priority between deduction from earnings orders, and between one or more such orders and one or more attachment of earnings orders, is governed by *reg 24* of the *Child Support (Collection and Enforcement) Regulations 1992.* See also **33.7** ante.

34   Probationary Employees

34.1   LEGAL STATUS

Many employers when engaging new employees state that they will initially be employed for a 'probationary' period. An employee may have reduced contractual rights (for example, a shorter contractual notice period) during their probationary period, but their status as a probationer has no effect on their statutory rights. For example, unless their employment continues for less than a month, a probationer will have to be given written particulars of the main terms of their employment (see **7.4** CONTRACT OF EMPLOYMENT). During the probation period, it is an implied contractual term that the employer will take reasonable steps to maintain an appraisal, giving guidance by advice or warning where necessary: *White v London Transport Executive* [1981] IRLR 261.

34.2   DISMISSING A PROBATIONER

It is a commonly held but mistaken belief that giving a new employee the status of probationer enables the employer to dispense with that employee's services, if he is found to be unsatisfactory, without the normal hazards of dismissal, such as a claim for unfair dismissal. The labelling of an employee as a 'probationer' has virtually no effect on the employer/employee relationship. If a probationer with the necessary length of service is dismissed, he may bring a claim for unfair dismissal as may any other employee in a similar situation. The fact that he only had probationer status will not automatically make the dismissal fair. It is merely a circumstance which the tribunal will take into account in deciding whether the dismissal was fair or unfair.

In *Post Office v Mughal* [1977] ICR 763 at 768, the Employment Appeal Tribunal laid down guidelines for employment tribunals considering the fairness of the dismissal of an employee during a probationary or trial period. They considered that the following question should be asked: 'Have the employers shown that they took reasonable steps to maintain appraisal of the probationer throughout the period of probation, giving guidance by advice or warning when such is likely to be useful or fair; and that an appropriate officer made an honest effort to determine whether the probationer came up to the required standard, having informed himself of the appraisals made by supervising officers and any other facts recorded about the probationer?'. In *Anandarajah v Lord Chancellor's Department* [1984] IRLR 131, the EAT cautioned against reliance on previous authority – in that case Mughal – in assessing the fairness of a dismissal. The preferred approach was to apply the statutory test now set out in *Employment Rights Act 1996, s 98(4), (6)* to the circumstances of each case. However, in *British Heart Condition v Harrison* EAT/1354/96 the EAT found the *Mughal* guidelines useful. In particular, in *Harrison* the EAT noted that a probationer must be taken to know that they are on trial and that they can expect to be judged strictly against a reasonable standard. Where a probationer has been unfairly dismissed, there may be particular Polkey issues for the Employment Tribunal to consider when assessing the compensatory award. For example, would the probationer have passed the probation period if they had not been unfairly dismissed and, if so, what difference would that have made to their employment prospects if they had subsequently resigned: *Davidson-Hogg v Davis Gregory Solicitors and Howarth* (UKEAT/0512/09/ZT) (15 November 2010, unreported).

The above considerations apply where a probationer has the qualifying length of service to bring an unfair dismissal claim. Note that in the case of dismissals for certain impermissible reasons (including trade union activities, union membership or non-membership, health and safety activities, pregnancy or childbirth, refusal of a protected shop worker or betting

34.2 Probationary Employees

worker or opted-out shop worker or betting worker to do shop work on a Sunday, the assertion of a statutory right) there is no qualifying period (see Unfair Dismissal – I (51)). Further, employees who claim that their dismissal was discriminatory, can bring claims under the *Equality Act 2010* without establishing any qualifying period of employment.

34.3 EXTENDING A PROBATION PERIOD

If the end of the contractual probation period is approaching and an employer is not yet sure whether to dismiss the employee or not, the probation period can be extended if the contract includes an express right for the employer to do so or if the employee agrees to an extension. If the employer fails to exercise any such right before the end of the probation period, then the employee automatically passes the probation period; an employer does not have an implied right to extend an employee's probationary period for a reasonable time in order to assess their suitability (*Przybylska v Modus Telecom Ltd* (UKEAT/0566/06/CEA) [2007] All ER (D) 06 (May)). If an employee is placed on garden leave before the end of their probation period and subsequently dismissed without having been formally confirmed in post, they have nevertheless passed their probation period: *Cornell ('Lynne) v Revenue and Customs Comrs* (TC00108) [2009] UKFTT 140 (TC), [2009] STI 2199.

Note that as a probationer often has different terms and conditions, status and benefits, the extension of an employee's probationary period of employment is generally a detriment: *N v Lewisham London Borough Council* (UKEAT/156/09) [2009] ICR 1538.

35   Public Sector Employees

35.1   Many people are employed in the public sector, for example in the Civil Service, the police, as teachers or by local authorities. Much of the law described in other chapters of this book applies equally to such people. However, there may sometimes be special factors to bear in mind when dealing with or advising upon public sector employment.

In many cases, there are specific statutory provisions which affect employment in particular areas of the public sector. The provisions set out below are among the most important, but it will be important to look carefully at all the relevant statutes and Statutory Instruments when dealing with an individual case.

35.2   CROWN SERVANTS

The civil service is made up of all permanent but non-political offices and employments (except for those in the armed forces) held under the Crown. Crown servants have a special status in the eyes of the law, albeit that the common law position has been much changed by statute. At common law, the Crown servant is employed at the pleasure of the Crown. That is, he can be dismissed at will – without notice and without the need to show cause or to follow any particular procedure (see *Dunn v R* [1896] 1 QB 116; *Council of Civil Service Unions v Minister for the Civil Service* [1985] AC 374).

There has for many years been a controversy as to whether Crown servants in fact have a CONTRACT OF EMPLOYMENT (7) at all. The question was considered by the Divisional Court in *R v Civil Service Appeal Board, ex p Bruce* [1988] 3 All ER 686, [1988] ICR 649 (the Court of Appeal did not express an opinion when it considered the case). It was suggested that there was nothing unconstitutional in a Crown servant having a contract of employment: the question was whether that was the intention of the Crown when the employment began. In *Bruce*, it was said that the evidence suggested no such intention in relation to civil servants prior to 1985 (which was the case in question), but a likelihood that future civil service appointments *would* be on the basis of contract. However, in *R v Lord Chancellor's Department, ex p Nangle* [1992] 1 All ER 897, [1991] ICR 743, the Divisional Court upon similar facts concluded that *Bruce* was wrong and that a contract *did* exist for current civil servants. This decision has recently been applied by the High Court to civil servants appointed by the Postmaster General: in *British Telecommunications Plc v Royal Mail Group Ltd* [2010] EWHC 8 (QB), [2010] All ER (D) 10 (Jan). See also *McClaren v Home Office* [1990] ICR 824.

The employment statutes avoid the question of whether there is an employment contract, by deeming that there is such a contract for specific purposes or by explicitly including or excluding civil servants. An example of the former approach is *TULRCA 1992, s 245*, which deems Crown servants to have a contract of employment for the purpose of liability for torts involving the inducement or threatened inducement of a breach of contract (see **43.2 STRIKES AND INDUSTRIAL ACTION**), and of certain provisions of *TULRCA 1992*.

Civil servants enjoy most of the normal statutory rights by virtue of *ERA 1996, s 191*. This provision applies many of the sections of *ERA 1996* to individuals employed under or for the purposes of a government department or any officer or body exercising on behalf of the Crown functions conferred by a statutory provision (see *Adult Learning Inspectorate v Beloff* (UKEAT/0238/07/RN) [2008] All ER (D) 254 (Jan) for the wide scope of this expression), including the right to pursue a claim for UNFAIR DISMISSAL – I (51). The main exceptions are the right to a minimum notice period (because of the doctrine that employment by the Crown is terminable at will) and the right to a statutory redundancy payment (although redundancy payments are in fact made to civil servants when appropriate: see *R (Public and Commercial Services Union) v Minister for the Civil Service* [2010] EWHC 1027 (Admin),

[2010] ICR 1198; and a civil servant's right under a scheme to a redundancy payment can constitute a possession for the purposes of the ECHR: *R (Public and Commercial Services Union) v Minister for the Civil Service* [2011] EWHC 2041 (Admin), [2012] 1 All ER 985, [2011] IRLR 903). Not only does *ERA 1996, s 191* fail to apply the statutory redundancy payment rights to such employees, any employee whose employment is treated for the purposes of pensions and other superannuation benefits as being in the civil service of the state, is explicitly prevented from claiming a statutory redundancy payment by *ERA 1996, s 159*. For continuity of employment see *ERA 1996, s 191*.

Similarly to the approach regarding rights under *ERA 1996*, civil servants have rights by virtue of *TULRCA 1992, s 273*, with the exception of the collective redundancy procedures in *Chapter 2* of *Part IV* of that Act.

The *Transfer of Undertakings (Protection of Employment) Regulations 2006 (SI 2006/246)* (*TUPE*) apply to transfers of undertakings from the public sector to the private sector, but not to the administrative reorganisation of public administrative authorities or to the transfer of administrative functions between public administrative authorities (*reg 3(5)*). However, the Cabinet Office's non statutory Statement of Practice 'Staff Transfers in the Public Sector' in effect guarantees 'TUPE-equivalent' treatment for public sector employees who are transferred within the public sector. In addition, from 2005 until 13 December 2010, the Code of Practice on Workforce Matters in Public Sector Service Contracts required private sector employers to provide the same terms and conditions for new employees as for employees who had transferred from the public sector. This Code has been replaced by six voluntary Principles of Good Employment Practice. Further, the *Employment Relations Act 1999, s 38* enables the Secretary of State to make regulations extending the TUPE protections to other staff and this power has been exercised in relation to the creation of OFCOM, the Greater London Authority, the Rent Officer Service and the Research Councils UK Shared Services Centre to date.

The *Equality Act 2010, s 83(2)* provides that "employment" includes Crown employment for the purposes of *Part 5, Work*. The *Equality Act 2010, s 83(5)* provides that in the case of a person in Crown employment a reference to the person's dismissal is a reference to the termination of the person's employment. *Paragraph 5* of *Schedule 22* to the *Equality Act 2010* makes various exceptions to the prohibitions on discrimination for rules restricting Crown Employment to persons of particular birth, nationality, descent or residence. The applicable rules are the *Race Relations (Prescribed Public Bodies) (No. 2) Regulations 1994 (SI 1994/1986)*.

In relation to industrial action in the public sector, there is an extension to the statutory immunity from claims in tort for action taken in contemplation or furtherance of a trade dispute (see **43.3 STRIKES AND INDUSTRIAL ACTION**). Whereas the dispute must normally be between the workers concerned and their employer in order to attract the immunity, a dispute between a Minister of the Crown and any workers is treated as a dispute between those workers and their employer if the dispute relates to matters which:

(a)   have been referred for consideration by a joint body on which statutory provision is made for the Minister to be represented, or

(b)   cannot be settled without the Minister exercising a statutory power.

(*TULRCA 1992, s 244(2)*.)

35.3 ARMED FORCES

The armed forces are not part of the civil service and, to date, the statutory protections have not been applied to them so extensively. The main statutory provisions specific to service in the armed forces include the *Armed Forces Acts 1991, 1996, 2001, 2006* (the repeal of the

2006 Act is due to come into effect in November 2013) and *2011*, the *Armed Forces Redundancy Scheme Order 2006 (SI 2006/55)* (as amended by *SI 2011/208* and *2011/3013*) and the *Armed Forces (Redundancy, Resettlement and Gratuity Earnings Schemes) (No. 2) Order 2010 (SI 2010/832)*.

Members of the armed forces have the protection of the equality legislation by virtue of the *Equality Act 2010, s 83(3)*, which provides that *Part 5, Work* applies to service in the armed forces as it applies to employment by a private person. *Paragraph 4 of Schedule 9* to the *Equality Act 2010* provides for various exceptions relating to the armed forces. In particular, the armed forces are not prohibited from discriminating in specified respects in relation to service in armed forces if they can show that requiring the employee to be male or not transsexual is a proportionate means of ensuring the combat effectiveness of the armed forces. *Part 5* of the *Equality Act 2010* does not apply to service in the armed forces at all in relation to age or disability. *Part 5* of the *Equality Act 2010* does not apply to work experience in the armed forces in relation to disability.

Members of the armed forces have the right to make a complaint about any matter relating to their service (*Armed Forces (Redress of Individual Grievances) Regulations 2007 (SI 2007/3353)*). The High Court has recently considered the scope of this right, including human rights issues: *Crosbie v Secretary of State for Defence* [2011] EWHC 879 (Admin).

If and when *ERA 1996, s 192* comes into force, on a date to be fixed by regulations (*ERA 1996, Sch 2, para 16*), most of the rights enjoyed by other Crown servants, eg unfair dismissal, will be extended to members of the armed forces, although not any rights associated with trade union membership.

35.4   POLICE

Police officers are officers of the peace and, as such, are not Crown servants. The main statutes are the *Police Act 1996* (a consolidating statute), the *Police Reform Act 2002*, the *Police Reform and Social Responsibility Act 2011* and the *Police (Complaints and Conduct) Act 2012*. The *Police Act 1996* includes provisions barring membership of trade unions other than the Police Federation (*s 64*) and making it a criminal offence to induce or attempt to induce breaches of discipline, which would include the taking of industrial action (*s 91*). Police officers are generally excluded from the benefit of various statutory rights, including the right to complain of UNFAIR DISMISSAL – I, II, III (51, 52, 53) and the right to complain of an unlawful deduction of wages (see *Metropolitan Police Comr v Lowrey-Nesbitt* [1999] ICR 401), by *ERA 1996, s 200(1)*. They may, however, claim in relation to detriment on the ground that, or dismissal by reason that, they made a protected disclosure: *ERA 1996,s 43KA* (and see *Lake v British Transport Police* [2007] EWCA Civ 424, [2007] ICR 1293).

Police officers also have the protection of the discrimination legislation by virtue of the *Equality Act 2010, s 42* which provides that holding the office of constable and appointment as police cadet (with some exceptions) are treated as employment by the chief officer or relevant authority for the purposes of *Part 5, Work*.

35.5   LOCAL GOVERNMENT

Local government employees generally have a contract of employment (with the exception of some officers such as coroners) and therefore have the normal employment rights (except where the statute provides otherwise). However, it should be remembered that the local authority is a creature of statute, which limits its powers to those provided by statute. Local authorities have the power to appoint such staff as are necessary for the proper discharge of their statutory functions on such reasonable terms and conditions as the local authority thinks fit, under the *Local Government Act 1972, s 112*. This power is subject to the *Localism*

Act 2011, s 41 which requires local authorities to comply with its pay policy statement. Terms and conditions are agreed at a national level (with some scope for local variations) with the National Joint Council, incorporated in the collective agreement known as the Green Book. Also see the *Local Authorities (Standing Orders) (England) Regulations 2001 (SI 2001/3384)*.

Local authorities face some restrictions on who they can appoint. By *s 116* of the *Local Government Act 1972*, members of an authority may not be appointed to any paid office with that authority. Further restrictions are contained in the *Local Government and Housing Act 1989*: certain posts are 'politically restricted', which means that their holders may not be members of *any* local authority without express exemption (*ss 1–3*); with certain exceptions, all appointments must be made on merit (*s 7*); and authorities must ensure so far as practicable that they are not represented in negotiations about terms and conditions of employment by members of the authority who are also in local authority employment or who are officials or employees of trade unions whose members include local authority employees (*s 12*). The *Local Government Officers (Political Restrictions) Regulations 1990 (SI 1990/851)* have been held not to contravene the European Convention on Human Rights (*Ahmed v United Kingdom* (Application 22954/93) (1998) 29 EHRR 1, [1999] IRLR 188, European Court of Human Rights).

There are further rules in relation to specific posts (chief officers), including the local authority's Head of the Paid Service and monitoring officer. All employees of a local authority are also officers, but an officer (including a chief officer) does not have to be an employee: *Pinfold North Ltd v Humberside Fire Authority* [2010] EWHC 2944 (QB). The *Local Authorities (Standing Orders) Regulations 1993 (SI 1993/202)* require local authorities to incorporate in standing orders provision relating to their staff. These must include provision for the appointment of chief officers and for investigation by a designated independent person (known as a DIP) in case of alleged misconduct by a chief officer.

The *Transfer of Undertakings (Protection of Employment) Regulations 2006 (SI 2006/246)* do not apply to the administrative reorganisation of public administrative authorities or to the transfer of administrative functions between public administrative authorities (*reg 3(5)*). Note that the Code of Practice on Workforce Matters in Local Authority Service Contracts was abolished on 23 March 2011. See **50.9 TRANSFER OF UNDERTAKINGS**.

The position is more complicated in respect of school staff. School teachers' pay and conditions of employment are subject to control by the Secretary of State for Education and Employment by virtue of the *Education Act 2002, ss 119–130*; and compensation for redundancy is subject to regulations made under the *Superannuation Act 1972*, now the *Teachers (Compensation for Redundancy and Premature Retirement) Regulations 1997 (SI 1997/311)*. The identity of the employer (in practice) depends on which of the following two categories the school falls within: (*a*) community, voluntary controlled, community special and maintained schools; or (*b*) foundation, voluntary aided and foundation special schools. The former category have delegated budgets and, by virtue of the *Education (Modification of Enactments Relating to Employment) (England) Order 2003 (SI 2003/1964)*, the *ERA 1996* generally applies as if the governing body were the employer. The complicated interrelationship of the employment responsibilities of the local education authority and the governing body was considered by the Court of Appeal in *Murphy v Slough Borough Council* [2005] EWCA Civ 122, [2005] ICR 721 and (in relation to comparators under the *EqPA*) by the CA in *South Tyneside Metropolitan Borough Council v Anderson* [2007] EWCA Civ 654, [2007] ICR 1581 (considered by the Inner House of the Court of Session, Scotland, in *North v Dumfries and Galloway Council* [2011] CSIH 2). *Murphy* was recently considered by the Employment Appeal Tribunal in *Butt v Bradford Metropolitan District Council* (UKEAT/0210/10/ZT) [2010] All ER (D) 92 (Oct) and *Birmingham City Council v Akhtar* [2011] 3 CMLR 42, [2011] Eq LR 838.

35.6   AVAILABILITY OF JUDICIAL REVIEW

Generally, an employment tribunal will be the appropriate forum for an employee to bring a claim against a public sector employer. However, those who work in the public sector may sometimes seek to assert their rights, not simply in an employment tribunal or in an action for tort or breach of contract in the ordinary courts, but by way of an application for judicial review. This is a means of challenging the unlawful actions and decisions of public authorities and bodies exercising statutory power. The possible grounds for such challenge include procedural unfairness, acting outside the statutory powers and irrationality. Applications are heard in the Administrative Court and the procedure is governed by the *Civil Procedure Rules, Part 54* (note also the *Practice Direction* and the *Pre-Action Protocol*). Its features include a need to obtain permission to proceed from the court and a strict time limit (applications must be brought promptly, and *in any event* within three months of the action challenged).

Historically there has been much academic debate about the circumstances in which a claim must (or cannot) be brought by way of judicial review (see eg *O'Reilly v Mackman* [1983] 2 AC 237 and *Roy v Kensington and Chelsea and Westminster Family Practitioner Committee* [1992] 1 AC 624, [1992] 1 All ER 705, [1992] 2 WLR 239, [1992] IRLR 233). Whilst in recent years (and particularly since the introduction of the *Civil Procedure Rules*), the categorisation of claims has become less important, it remains the case that only claims involving a public law element can proceed by way of judicial review.

A helpful statement of the position in the employment context is to be found in the judgment of Woolf LJ in *McClaren v Home Office* [1990] ICR 824. He concluded that judicial review was generally an unnecessary and inappropriate remedy for public sector employees, but that there were two types of case where it might be available. One was where the decision impugned was that of a tribunal or other body (such as the Civil Service Appeal Board) which had a sufficient public law element and was not wholly domestic or informal. The other was where the employee was adversely affected by a decision of *general* application which was alleged to be flawed (the decision to bar trade union membership at GCHQ was an example of this).

This decision was applied in *R (Davies) v Pennine Acute Hospitals* [2010] EWHC 2887 (Admin) and *R (Kirk) v Middlesbrough Borough Council* [2010] EWHC 1035 (Admin), [2010] IRLR 699 and in both cases the High Court found that judicial review was not available because the issues were essentially private law matters. However, see the Court of Appeal's important decision in *R (Shoesmith) v Ofsted* [2011] EWCA Civ 642, [2011] PTSR D13, 154 Sol Jo (no 17) 27 which related to the dismissal of the Director of Children's Services, Haringey Council. The Claimant issued a claim for judicial review challenging an Ofsted report, the action of the Secretary of State in removing the Claimant from her statutory office based upon that report and the actions of Haringey in subsequently dismissing her from its employment. In this case, the Court of Appeal found that the issues were amenable to judicial review because the position of Director of Children's Services had been created, required and defined by statute. More recently, in *R (Lock) v Leicester City Council* [2012] EWHC 2058 (Admin), the High Court distinguished *Shoesmith*. The claimant applied for judicial review of the defendant local authority's decision to dismiss her from her post as chief executive. The Court found that it could consider the decision to terminate her statutory role as designated head of paid service. However, it could not consider the termination of her contractual role as chief executive. The decision is currently subject to appeal.

An application for judicial review was also considered in *Crosbie v Secretary of State for Defence* [2011] EWHC 879 (Admin), where the claimant was an army chaplain whose fixed term contract had not been renewed and who (unsuccessfully) alleged various breaches of public law principles and *Article 6, ECHR*.

35.6   Public Sector Employees

It should also be remembered that the court hearing an application for judicial review has an overriding discretion as to whether any relief should be granted. One possible reason for refusing to consider a claim or to grant relief is that some alternative remedy was available and should have been pursued. Thus in *Bruce* the Divisional Court accepted that there was a sufficient public law element for an unsuccessful appeal against dismissal to the Civil Service Appeal Board to be judicially reviewable, but held that only in exceptional cases would it be right not to confine the applicant to his remedy in an industrial tribunal. The Court of Appeal upheld the refusal of relief on the facts without expressing a view on the general proposition. In *R v Hammersmith and Fulham London Borough Council, ex p NALGO* [1991] IRLR 249, it was held that a local authority's redundancy selection policy should be tested by way of cases brought in the tribunal alleging unfair dismissal or discrimination, and not by way of judicial review. In *R (Shoesmith) v Ofsted* [2011] EWCA Civ 642, the Court of Appeal confirmed that in the great majority of cases proceedings in the employment tribunal will be the better, if not the only, remedy where a local authority employee has been dismissed. It suggested that the exceptions would be cases where the remedy available in the employment tribunal was inadequate because of the statutory cap on compensation or where the case raised significant issues falling out with the scope of an employment tribunal's inquiry. On the facts of this case, the Court of Appeal found that there was a benefit in the Claimant being able to bring all her claims (against Ofsted, the Secretary of State and her local authority employer) in one set of proceedings and that success in judicial review proceedings would be more valuable in financial and reputational terms, due to the cap on compensation in the employment tribunal. For these reasons, the right to bring an unfair dismissal claim in the employment tribunal was not an equally convenient and effective alternative remedy for the Claimant.

If available, judicial review can provide a powerful remedy to the employee, as it did in *R v Civil Service Appeal Board, ex p Cunningham* [1991] 4 All ER 310, [1992] ICR 816, where a decision of the Board was struck down because of the Board's failure to give adequate reasons. In the case of *R (Shoesmith) v Ofsted* [2011] EWCA Civ 642, the Court of Appeal declared that the Claimant's dismissal had been unlawful and ordered the local authority to pay compensation (the amount of which had not been determined at the time of writing).

35.7   LITIGATING AGAINST PUBLIC AUTHORITIES

A local authority has an express power under the *LGA 1972, s 222* to prosecute, defend or appear in legal proceedings, and an implied power to compromise litigation. However, a public body can lawfully compromise a dispute with an employee (or ex employee) only in circumstances where it is acting within the scope of its statutory powers in doing so. One application of the *ultra vires* doctrine is that any sum paid to settle a claim must not be excessively generous. See *Gibb v Maidstone and Tunbridge Wells NHS Trust* [2009] EWHC 862 (QB), [2009] All ER (D) 209 (Apr) where an NHS Trust paid its Chief Executive £100,000 in excess of what she could have been awarded by an employment tribunal in return for her leaving its employment. The High Court found that this was excessive generosity, which led to a finding that the payment was irrational and therefore the compromise agreement was void. However, this decision was overturned by the Court of Appeal, which found that the sum was not excessively generous because the NHS Trust was entitled to take into account the employee's length of service and chances of re-employment: [2010] EWCA Civ 678.

In litigation against public authorities, in particular government departments, attempts to obtain documents by way of an order for disclosure may sometimes be met by a claim that those documents should not be disclosed because they are subject to public interest immunity. This means that the interest in preventing the disclosure of such documents outweighs the interest in the court or tribunal having all the relevant evidence. The court may itself examine the documents in order to decide whether they ought to be disclosed. See in particular *Conway v Rimmer* [1968] AC 910, *Air Canada v Secretary of State for Trade* [1983] 2 AC 394, *R v Chief Constable of West Midlands Police, ex p Wiley* [1995] 1 AC 274, *R (Corner House Research) v Director of the Serious Fraud Office (BAE Systems plc, interested party)* [2008] UKHL 60, [2009] AC 756 and *R (Mohamed) v Secretary of State for Foreign and Commonwealth Affairs* [2010] EWCA Civ 65, [2010] 4 All ER 91.

Occasionally employment disputes will also raise questions of national security (see, eg *Council of Civil Service Unions v Minister for the Civil Service* [1985] AC 374). Provision is made for requiring or enabling tribunals and the EAT to sit in private in cases involving national security or confidential information (*ETA 1996, ss 10* and *10A* respectively). See also *Employment Tribunals (Constitution and Rules of Procedure) Regulations 2004 (SI 2004/1861), regs 11* and *12* and *para 54* of *Sch 1*, and *Employment Appeal Tribunal Rules 1993 (SI 1993/2854), rule 30A*. The Supreme Court held that the former were not intrinsically unlawful, provided that sufficient safeguards were in place and the procedure was used flexibly in the context of the case, as it progressed: *Home Office v Tariq* [2012] 1 AC 452. In *Rahman v Commissioner of Police of the Metropolis* (UKEATPA/0076/09/RN), the EAT held that the tribunal could and should routinely direct that the appointed special advocate may communicate freely with the excluded person and his representatives at any time before he sees the closed material. In *AB v Ministry of Defence* [2010] ICR 54, [2009] All ER (D) 135 (Sep), the Employment Appeal Tribunal gave guidance on the correct approach when an application is made for a closed hearing before the EAT on national security grounds.

Where in the opinion of any Minister of the Crown the disclosure of any information would be contrary to the interests of national security, disclosure of that information will not be required by certain provisions of *ERA 1996*, and no person may disclose that information in any court or tribunal proceedings relating to any of those provisions (*ERA 1996, s 202*). The rights generally available to employees who have made a protected disclosure do not apply in relation to employment in the Security Service, the Secret Intelligence Service, or the Government Communications Headquarters. (*ERA 1996, s 193*).

35.8   EUROPEAN UNION LAW

All employment relationships are now affected by EUROPEAN UNION LAW **(22)**. However, public sector employees may find themselves in a special position because of the way in which the doctrine of 'direct effect' is applied.

Some categories of EC legislation (the Treaties themselves, and regulations) become applicable once promulgated without any need for further action by member states. In the case of *Directives*, however, the intention is that member states should, within a given time, take such steps as they consider appropriate to implement the *Directive* in their territory. The European Court of Justice has frequently held that, if a member state fails to comply with its obligation (either because it does nothing or because what it does is held not to achieve all that the *Directive* requires) then, although that *Directive* cannot be relied upon in proceedings against private persons, provided that the *Directive* is clear and unconditional, it may be relied upon against that State. The State may not take advantage of its own wrong in failing to introduce measures to implement the *Directive*. In order for a person to be able to rely on a *Directive* against the State, the terms of the *Directive* must be clear and it must be unconditional, ie it must require no further implementing measures or time before it is intended to have effect.

It was this doctrine which enabled the applicant in *Marshall v Southampton and South West Hampshire Area Health Authority (Teaching)* [1986] ICR 335 to succeed in her claim of unlawful sex discrimination based on discriminatory retiring ages at a time before the *Sex Discrimination Act 1986* was passed. The health authority which employed her was agreed to be an organ of the state, so that she could rely directly upon *Directive 76/207/EEC*, unlike private sector employees (see **22.6** EUROPEAN UNION LAW).

35.8 Public Sector Employees

The question of whether a nationalised industry (since privatised) is the state for these purposes fell to be considered in *Foster v British Gas plc*. The House of Lords referred the question to the European Court of Justice, which held ([1991] ICR 84) that the doctrine applies to 'a body, whatever its legal form, which has been made responsible, pursuant to a measure adopted by the state, for providing a public service under the control of the state and has for that purpose special powers beyond those which result from the normal rules applicable in relations between individuals'. The House of Lords ([1991] ICR 463) went on to hold that British Gas before privatisation fell within this definition. However, mere control by the state is not enough, and so the doctrine did not apply to a manufacturing company which was wholly owned by the state but which did not provide a public service and possessed no special powers (*Rolls-Royce plc v Doughty* [1992] ICR 538). The doctrine did apply to a water company privatised under the *Water Act 1989* and *Water Industry Act 1991* (*Griffin v South West Water Services Ltd* [1995] IRLR 15), and to the governing body of a voluntary aided school (*National Union of Teachers v St Mary's Church of England Aided Junior School (Governing Body)* [1997] ICR 334, [1997] IRLR 242, CA). In *Hillman v London General Transport Services Ltd* (14 April 1999, unreported), the EAT held that the respondent company was simply a commercial concern and was not an emanation of the state, applying *Foster v British Gas plc*.

36   Redundancy – I: The Right to a Redundancy Payment

Cross-references. TRANSFER OF UNDERTAKINGS **(50)**. See **52.11** UNFAIR DISMISSAL – **II** for dismissal on grounds of redundancy, and PAY – **I (32)** for details of the calculation of the employee's weekly pay. See CONTRACT OF EMPLOYMENT **(7)** for principles applicable to enhanced redundancy payments claimed under the contract of employment.

36.1   The *Redundancy Payments Act 1965* (*'RPA 1965'*) introduced the right of employees who lost their jobs in certain circumstances to a payment from their employers irrespective of whether they had another job to go to. The *RPA 1965* was amended by the *Employment Protection Act 1975* (*'EPA 1975'*) and the provisions, as amended, were re-enacted in the *Employment Protection (Consolidation) Act 1978* (*'EPCA 1978'*). The provisions are now contained in the *Employment Rights Act 1996* (*'ERA 1996'*).

36.2   PRE-CONDITIONS FOR PAYMENT

The conditions which must be fulfilled for a person to be entitled to a redundancy payment are:

(a)   that he was an employee;

(b)   that he had been continuously employed for the requisite period;

(c)   that he was dismissed (as defined); and

(d)   that the dismissal was by reason of redundancy.

(*ERA 1996, ss 135, 155.*)

Certain employees are excluded from the right to a redundancy payment (see **36.10** below).

36.3   APPLICANT MUST HAVE BEEN AN EMPLOYEE

Only 'employees' are entitled to claim a redundancy payment. Thus, those engaged under a contract for services are not entitled to make such a claim. 'Employee' is defined as:

'   . . .   an individual who has entered into or works under (or, where the employment has ceased, worked under) a contract of employment.'

(*ERA 1996, s 230(1)*)

See EMPLOYEE, SELF-EMPLOYED OR WORKER? **(14)**.

If the respondent to an application for a redundancy payment (ie the employer) disputes the fact that the applicant was an employee, it is for the applicant to prove that he was.

36.4   Continuous employment for the requisite period

In order to be entitled to a redundancy payment, an applicant must have been *continuously employed for a period of two years ending with the relevant date* (see below for 'relevant date') (*ERA 1996, s 155*).

The rules for computing continuous employment are dealt with in detail in CONTINUOUS EMPLOYMENT **(6)**.

The relevant date. The relevant date in relation to the dismissal of an employee:

36.4 Redundancy – I: The Right to a Redundancy Payment

(a)   where his contract of employment is terminated by notice, whether given by his employer or by the employee, means the date on which that notice expires;

(b)   where his contract of employment is terminated without notice, means the date on which the termination takes effect; and

(c)   where he is employed under a limited-term contract which terminates by virtue of the limiting event without being renewed under the same contract, means the date on which the termination takes effect.

(*ERA 1996, s 145.*)

This provision corresponds to the definition of the 'effective date of termination' for the purposes of unfair dismissal contained in *ERA 1996, s 97(1)*; for a discussion of its application see **51.13 UNFAIR DISMISSAL – I**.

If an employee is dismissed with no notice or less than the statutory minimum period of notice, for the purposes, *inter alia*, of calculating the qualifying period of employment, the relevant date will be the date upon which the statutory minimum period of notice would have expired had it been given (*ERA 1996, s 145(5)*). (See **46.7 TERMINATION OF EMPLOYMENT.**) However, this provision does not affect the employer's right to dismiss without notice for an employee's gross misconduct (*ERA 1996, s 86(6)*). In the event of such a dismissal, the statutory minimum period of notice will not be added on for the purpose of computing the length of continuous employment.

36.5 Changes in the ownership of the business

The *Transfer of Undertakings (Protection of Employment) Regulations 2006 (SI 2006/246)* are discussed fully in **TRANSFER OF UNDERTAKINGS (50)**. By virtue of the *Regulations*, on a 'relevant transfer' of an undertaking, the existing employees' contracts of employment are not terminated. On completion of such a transfer all the transferor's rights, powers, duties and liabilities under or in connection with any such contract are transferred to the transferee (*Transfer of Undertakings Regulations, reg 4(2)(a)*). Therefore, such an employee will be deemed not to have been dismissed by the transferor and the continuity of his employment will be preserved.

36.6 The employee must have been 'dismissed'

There is no presumption of dismissal and, if the employer disputes the fact, it is for the employee to prove it. For redundancy payments purposes, dismissal has a statutory meaning instead of merely meaning termination of the contract by the employer. Sub-paragraph (*a*) below reflects the common law position (see **46.5 TERMINATION OF EMPLOYMENT**), and occurs most frequently in practice, while (*b*) would not be a dismissal at common law. In addition, certain forms of termination of the contract at common law are disregarded for redundancy payments purposes (see below).

An employee will be taken to be dismissed by his employer if, but only if:

(a)   the contract under which he is employed by the employer is terminated by the employer, whether it is terminated by notice or without notice;

(b)   where under that contract he is employed for a limited term, the contract terminates by virtue of the limiting event without being renewed under the same contract; or

(c)   the employee terminates that contract with or without notice in circumstances such that he is entitled so to terminate it without notice by reason of the employer's conduct (not being termination by reason of a lock-out).

(*ERA 1996, s 136(1), (2)*.)

The statutory definition of dismissal for redundancy payments purposes is the same as for the purposes of unfair dismissal (see UNFAIR DISMISSAL – I (51)).

Where in accordance with any enactment or rule of law any act on the part of an employer, or any event affecting an employer, operates so as to terminate a contract of employment, that is treated for redundancy payments purposes as a termination by the employer, even if it would not otherwise amount to such a termination (*ERA 1996, s 136(5)*; and see *Pickwell v Lincolnshire County Council* [1993] ICR 87).

Situations where no dismissal occurs. An employee is deemed not to have been dismissed in certain circumstances where a dismissal by reason of redundancy has in fact taken place. Two examples are given below.

(i)   *Renewal or re-engagement.* If an employee's contract is renewed or he is re-engaged under a new contract of employment and:

   (A)   the offer, whether in writing or not, is made before the ending of the existing contract; and

   (B)   it is to take effect either immediately on the ending of the original employment or within a period of not more than four weeks thereafter (if the contract ends on Friday, Saturday or Sunday, the new employment must take effect four weeks from the following Monday),

   no dismissal will be deemed to have taken place in respect of the termination of the original contract (*ERA 1996, s 138(1)*).

   If the terms and conditions of the new employment differ wholly or in part from the original contract, the employee has a trial period of four weeks from the ending of the original employment, or such longer period as may be agreed in writing, within which to decide whether to accept or reject the offer (see **36.12** below). If he rejects the offer or if the employer terminates or gives notice to terminate the contract for a reason connected with the change in contractual terms, within that period, the employee will be taken to have been dismissed on the date of termination of the original contract for the reason that contract was terminated (*ERA 1996, s 138(2)–(6)*).

(ii)   *Offers of employment by associated companies.* It should be noted that where the employer is a company, any reference to re-engagement by the employer is construed as including a reference to re-engagement by *that company or by an associated company*, and any reference to an offer made by the employer is construed as including a reference to an offer made by an associated company (*ERA 1996, s 146(1)*). For the meaning of 'associated company', see **6.9**(a) CONTINUOUS EMPLOYMENT.

Employee who leaves prematurely. An employee who leaves his employment before his employer's notice of dismissal expires may lose his right to a redundancy payment. If the employee gives written notice to terminate his employment on a date earlier than that given by his employer, he will not lose his right to a redundancy payment if the employer does not object to his premature departure. If, however, the employer does object and serves on the employee a written request to withdraw his notice, warning him that if he does not do so the employer will contest any liability to make a redundancy payment, he may lose the right to such a payment. If the employer withholds the redundancy payment, the employee may apply to an employment tribunal which will decide whether the employee is entitled to the full payment, or no payment, or part of the payment. The tribunal will consider whether the employee's action in leaving prematurely was reasonable or unreasonable in the circum-

36.6   Redundancy – I: The Right to a Redundancy Payment

stances (*ERA 1996, ss 136(3), 142(1), (2)*). If, however, the parties agree by mutual consent to substitute some other date of termination for the date specified by the employer, no such question arises (*CPS Recruitment Ltd v Bowen and Secretary of State for Employment* [1982] IRLR 54).

36.7   Redundancy must be the reason for dismissal

In order to be entitled to a redundancy payment, the employee must be dismissed by reason of redundancy. An employee who has been dismissed by his employer is, unless the contrary is proved, presumed to have been dismissed by reason of redundancy for the purposes of any claim for a redundancy payment (*ERA 1996, s 163(2)*). There is, however, no formal burden of proof upon the employer. The tribunal must decide whether the presumption has been rebutted on the basis of all the evidence before them: see *Greater Glasgow Health Board v Lamont* UKEATS/0019/12.

'Redundancy' is defined as follows:

'For the purposes of this Act an employee who is dismissed shall be taken to be dismissed by reason of redundancy if the dismissal is wholly or mainly attributable to –

(*a*)   the fact that his employer has ceased or intends to cease:

(i)   to carry on the business for the purposes of which the employee was employed by him, or

(ii)   to carry on that business in the place where the employee was so employed, or

(*b*)   the fact that the requirements of that business:

(i)   for employees to carry out work of a particular kind, or

(ii)   for employees to carry out work of a particular kind in the place where the employee was employed by the employer,

have ceased or diminished or are expected to cease or diminish.'

(*ERA 1996, s 139(1)*; note that a different definition applies for the purposes of the redundancy consultation provisions of *TULCRA 1992* (see **37.3** REDUNDANCY – **II**).)

Sub-paragraph (*a*) covers the closure of the employer's business as a whole, or, alternatively, just at the place where the employee is employed. The test for determining 'the place where the employee was employed' is primarily a factual one, although the employee's contractual terms may provide evidence of the place of work where the employee did go from place to place (see *High Table Ltd v Horst* [1998] ICR 409, CA). Thus, if an employee had as a matter of fact worked in only one location, then the existence of a contractual mobility clause (entitling the employer to transfer him) will not widen the definition of the place where the employee was employed under *ERA 1996, s 139(1)* (see also *Bass Leisure Ltd v Thomas* [1994] IRLR 104).

Under sub-para (*b*) it must be considered whether the business requires so many employees to carry out certain work. In deciding whether there has been a cessation or diminution in the requirements of the business for employees to carry out 'work of a particular kind', it was uncertain whether the work is defined by what is required under an employee's contract of employment ('the contract test'), or by what an employee is actually doing ('the function test'), or by a blend of the two. Until 1997, it was assumed that the Court of Appeal in *Cowen v Haden Ltd* [1983] ICR 1 had established that the proper test was the contract test. However, the EAT in *Safeway Stores plc v Burrell* [1997] ICR 523 disagreed with this interpretation of *Cowen v Haden* and stated that the terms of an employee's contract of employment were irrelevant when determining whether there was a redundancy situation within the meaning of *ERA 1996, s 139(1)*. The House of Lords confirmed in the case of *Murray v Foyle Meats Ltd* [2000] 1 AC 51, [1999] 3 All ER 769, [1999] 3 WLR 356, [1999]

876

ICR 827 that both the 'contract test' and the 'function test' are an unnecessary gloss on the plain wording of the statute. Further, the Court of Appeal held in *Shawkat v Nottingham City Hospital NHS Trust (No 2)* [2001] EWCA Civ 954, [2001] IRLR 555 that whether there was less need for employees to carry out work of a particular kind was always a question of fact for a tribunal to decide.

The House of Lords in *Murray* approved the reasoning of the EAT in *Safeway Stores v Burrell* (see above), one of whose conclusions was that 'bumped employees' will be dismissed by reason of redundancy. A 'bumping' situation will exist where Smith, whose job is no longer required, is put by his employer into Brown's position, so that Brown is dismissed instead of Smith. The reasoning in *Safeway Stores v Burrell* would mean that Brown was redundant, because the employer's requirement for work of a particular kind had diminished, and because Brown was dismissed as a result. It is not necessary that any reduction in the employer's requirements for work of a particular kind should be a reduction in the type of work that Brown himself carried out. *Safeway Stores v Burrell* follows earlier authority (see *W Gimber & Sons Ltd v Spurrett* (1967) 2 ITR 308; applied by the EAT in *Elliott Turbomachinery Ltd v Bates* [1981] ICR 218) in reaching this conclusion. The EAT decision in *Church v West Lancashire NHS Trust* [1998] ICR 423 initially created some uncertainty as to whether *Safeway Stores* was correct, but those doubts were dispelled by *Murray*, and more recently, by the EAT in *Stankovic v City of Westminster* [2001] All ER (D) 340 (Oct), EAT. Indeed, the EAT specifically stated in *Stankovic* that *Church* was no longer good authority on the point.

A redundancy situation within the meaning of ERA 1996, s 139(1)(b) will also exist where the amount of work available for the same number of employees has reduced. So, for example, where an employer offers employees reduced working hours following a downturn in business, and an employee is dismissed for refusing to accept reduced working hours, the dismissal is for redundancy: see *Packman v Fauchon* [2012] ICR 1362. (In *Packman*, Langstaff P considered in detail the EAT's decision to the opposite effect in *Aylward v Glamorgan Holiday Homes Ltd* UKEAT/167/02, and declined to follow it.)

Where an employee is employed on a succession of fixed-term contracts this can, in principle, give rise to a dismissal by reason of redundancy on the expiration of each fixed-term contract (*Pfaffinger v City of Liverpool Community College* [1997] ICR 142).

36.8   Redundancy payments for lay-off and short time

Special provisions relating to redundancy claims by piece-workers who are laid off or put on short time are contained in *ERA 1996*. An employee is considered to be *laid off* during a particular week if under his contract he gets no pay of any kind from his employer for that week because there is no work for him to do although he is available for work (*ERA 1996, s 147*). An employee is considered to be on short time for a week if during that week he gets less than half a week's pay (*ERA 1996, s 147(2)*).

A redundancy payment may only be claimed by a worker laid off or on short time if he gives notice in writing to his employer of his intention to claim and the claim is submitted within four weeks of:

(a)   the end of a continuous period of lay-off or short time of four or more weeks' duration; or

(b)   the end of a period of six weeks' lay-off or short time out of 13 weeks (where not more than three weeks were consecutive).

(*ERA 1996, s 148.*)

He must then terminate his contract of employment by giving the contractual period of notice or one week's notice, whichever is the greater (*ERA 1996, s 150(1)*).

The notice to terminate must be given within the following time limits:

(a)   if the employer does not give a counter-notice (see **36.9** below) within seven days after the service of the notice of intention to claim, that period is three weeks after the end of those seven days;

(b)   if the employer gives a counter-notice within those seven days, but withdraws it by a subsequent notice in writing, that period is three weeks after the service of the notice of withdrawal; and

(c)   if the employer gives a counter-notice within those seven days and does not so withdraw it, and a question as to the right of the employee to a redundancy payment in pursuance of the notice of intention to claim is referred to a tribunal, that period is three weeks after the tribunal has notified to the employee its decision on that reference.

(ERA 1996, s 150(3).)

Even if an employee fails to comply with these statutory requirements, he may claim that he has been constructively dismissed for redundancy if he is laid off in fundamental breach of his contract of employment (*A Dakri & Co Ltd v Tiffen* [1981] ICR 256; cf *Kenneth McRae & Co Ltd v Dawson* [1984] IRLR 5).

36.9   Counter-notice

An employee who gives a notice of intention to claim pursuant to *ERA 1996, s 148* will not be entitled to a redundancy payment if, on the date of service of that notice, it was reasonably to be expected that he would (if he continued to be employed by the same employer), not later than four weeks after that date, enter upon a period of employment of not less than 13 weeks during which he would not be laid off or kept on short time (*ERA 1996, s 152(1)*).

However, an employer cannot take advantage of this rule unless, within seven days after service of the notice of intention to claim, he gives the employee notice in writing that he will contest liability to make a redundancy payment (*ERA 1996, s 152(1)(b)*). If the employee wishes to pursue his claim after the service of a counter-notice, an employment tribunal must be asked to determine whether he is entitled to a redundancy payment (*ERA 1996, s 149*).

36.10   Exclusions from right to payment

The following are excluded from the right to a redundancy payment.

(a)   Masters or crew of a fishing vessel who are not remunerated otherwise than by a share of the profits or gross earnings of the vessel (*ERA 1996, s 199(2)* (see *Goodeve v Gilsons (a firm)* [1985] ICR 401)).

(b)   Civil servants and other public employees (*ERA 1996, s 159*).

(c)   Persons employed in any capacity under the Government of any territory or country outside the United Kingdom (*ERA 1996, s 160*).

(d)   Domestic servants in a private household where the employer is the parent (or step-parent), grandparent, child (or step-child), grandchild or brother or sister (or half-brother or half-sister) of the employee. References to step-parent or step-child include relationships arising through civil partnership: see the *Civil Partnership Act 2004, ss 246, 247, Sch 21* (*ERA 1996, s 161*).

(e)   Employees who have been offered employment on the same terms and conditions as their original employment or offered *suitable alternative employment* and in either case have *unreasonably refused the offer* (see **36.12** below) (*ERA 1996, s 141(1)–(3)*).

(f)   Employees who have been offered suitable alternative employment, and have unreasonably terminated their contracts during the statutory trial period (see **36.12** below) (*ERA 1996, s 141(4)*).

(g)   Employees who are dismissed for misconduct. If notice is given for this reason it must be accompanied by a statement in writing that the employer would, because of the employee's conduct, be entitled to terminate the contract without notice. If the employee is dismissed without notice, there is no need to give any statement in writing that dismissal was on the ground of misconduct (*ERA 1996, s 140(1)*). The employer is entitled to terminate when the employee has been in fundamental breach of his contract of employment (*Bonner v H Gilbert Ltd* [1989] IRLR 475). This provision does not apply where the dismissal is for taking part in a strike (*ERA 1996, s 140(2)*). The tribunal, in any event, has a discretion to award the whole or part of a redundancy payment to the dismissed employee where it is just and equitable to do so (*ERA 1996, s 140(3)*).

(h)   Employees who are dismissed if an *exemption order* is in force (*ERA 1996, s 157*). An exemption order is an order made by the Secretary of State for Business, Innovation and Skills exempting an employer or a group of employers from liability to make redundancy payments under the *Act* where they have similar or more advantageous agreements with their employees for making payments on redundancy.

36.11 Time limit for claims

Employees are not entitled to a redundancy payment unless, before the end of the period of six months beginning with the relevant date:

(a)   the payment has been agreed and paid;

(b)   the employee has made a claim for the payment by notice in writing given to the employer;

(c)   a question as to the right of the employee to the payment, or as to the amount of the payment, has been referred to an employment tribunal; or

(d)   a complaint of unfair dismissal has been presented by the employee to a tribunal.

(*ERA 1996, s 164(1)*.) (For the meaning of 'relevant date', see **36.4** above.)

If, however, within the *next* six months, the employee takes the action in (*b*), (*c*) or (*d*), a tribunal may award a redundancy payment if it considers it just and equitable to do so having regard to the reason for the delay (*ERA 1996, s 164(2)*).

An application for a redundancy payment is 'referred' to an employment tribunal when it is received by the tribunal office and not when it is sent by the employee (*Secretary of State for Employment v Banks* [1983] ICR 48).

See also **36.14** below.

36.12 UNREASONABLE REFUSAL OF SUITABLE ALTERNATIVE EMPLOYMENT

An employee who is dismissed by reason of redundancy loses his right to a redundancy payment if he unreasonably refuses an offer of suitable alternative employment. The offer of alternative employment:

36.12   Redundancy – I: The Right to a Redundancy Payment

(a)   must be made by his original employer or an associated employer (*ERA 1996, s 141(1)*; and see **6.9**(a) CONTINUOUS EMPLOYMENT);

(b)   must be made before the ending of his employment under his previous contract (*ERA 1996, s 141(1)*);

(c)   may be oral or in writing;

(d)   must take effect either immediately on the ending of the employment under the previous contract or after an interval of not more than four weeks thereafter (*ERA 1996, s 141(1)*). The alternative employment will be treated as taking effect immediately on the ending of the employment under the previous contract if that employment ends on a Friday, Saturday or Sunday, and the alternative employment is to commence on or before the next Monday. The interval of four weeks is calculated accordingly (*ERA 1996, s 146(2)*). An offer which is not ongoing and which would take effect prior to the dismissal will not satisfy *ERA 1996, s 141(1)* (*McHugh v Hempsall Bulk Transport Ltd*, IDS Brief 480, p 6); and

(e)   must be either.

    (i)   on the same terms and conditions as the previous contract; or

    (ii)   suitable employment in relation to the employee.

(*ERA, s 141(3)*.)

If the terms and conditions of the renewed or new contract of employment differ (wholly or in part) from the corresponding provisions of his previous contract, the employee has a statutory trial period of four weeks, beginning with the ending of his previous employment, in which to decide whether the alternative employment is suitable for him. The four-week trial period means four calendar weeks. Thus, 11 days when the factory was closed over Christmas had to be taken into account (*Benton v Sanderson Keyser Ltd* [1989] ICR 136). This four-week period may be extended by agreement, for the purpose of retraining the employee for employment under the new or renewed contract. Such an agreement must:

(i)   be made before the employee starts work under the renewed or new contract;

(ii)   be in writing;

(iii)   specify the date of the end of the trial period; and

(iv)   specify the terms and conditions of employment which will apply in the employee's case after the end of that period.

(*ERA 1996, s 138(6)*.)

Although the employer is no longer required, in making the offer, to give the employee details of the changes in terms and conditions in writing, where applicable, employers may still find it useful to do so. The employer, however, remains obliged to give written particulars of the main terms of an employee's employment within one month of the change (*ERA 1996, s 4(1)*). (See **7.7** CONTRACT OF EMPLOYMENT.)

An employee whose contract was repudiated by his employers is entitled, in accordance with the common law, to a reasonable period in which to decide whether to enter into a new contract or to treat himself as dismissed (see TERMINATION OF EMPLOYMENT (**46**)). So an employee whose contract is repudiated, and who is given alternative employment which does not fall within the terms of *ERA 1996 s 138(1)*, has a reasonable period within which to decide whether to accept the repudiation and claim a redundancy payment: see *Turvey v C W Cheney & Son Ltd* [1979] ICR 341. However, the *Turvey* case should not be seen as authority for the proposition that the common law can operate to extend the statutory four-week period under *ERA 1996, s 136*. If alternative employment is offered within the terms of *ERA 1996 s 138(1)*, the four-week period cannot be extended save under *s 138(6)*: see *Optical Express Ltd v Williams* [2008] ICR 1.

If the employee accepts the alternative employment, which was offered before the termination of his original employment and which takes effect not more than four weeks thereafter, he is deemed not to have been dismissed on the termination of the original employment for the purposes of determining any liability of the employer for redundancy payments (*ERA 1996, s 138(1)*; see *Jones v Governing Body of Burdett Coutts School* [1997] ICR 390, EAT, cf *Ebac Ltd v Wymer* [1995] ICR 466). If, during the trial period, the employee terminates the contract or gives notice to terminate it, or if the employer, for a reason connected with or arising out of any difference between the renewed or new contract and the previous contract, terminates the contract or gives notice to terminate it, the employee is treated as having been dismissed on the date on which his original contract came to an end (*ERA 1996, s 138(2), (4)*).

If, during the trial period, the employer dismisses the employee for a reason unconnected with or not arising out of the change, the employee can bring an unfair dismissal claim on the basis of the fairness of the dismissal in the trial period (*Hempell v W H Smith & Sons Ltd* [1986] ICR 365).

If the terms of the new contract are suitable and the employee unreasonably terminates the contract during the trial period, he will not be entitled to a redundancy payment by reason of his dismissal under the original contract (*ERA 1996, s 141(4)*).

The question of the suitability of an offer of alternative employment is an objective matter, whereas the reasonableness of the employee's refusal depends on factors personal to him and is a subjective matter to be considered from the employee's point of view (meaning that the importation of a "reasonable band of responses" test analogous to that used in unfair dismissal is not appropriate: see *Readman v Devon Primary Care Trust* (CA, 6 February 2013). So, for example, the offer to a butcher's shop manager of a job as a supermarket butchery department manager may be suitable alternative employment, but his perceived loss of status may make it reasonable for him to refuse it (*Cambridge & District Co-operative Society v Ruse* [1993] IRLR 156). The Court of Appeal in *Spencer and Griffin v Gloucestershire County Council* [1985] IRLR 393 has said that in evaluating the separate questions of suitability of employment and reasonableness of refusal, the employment tribunal is entitled to look at factors which may prove, on analysis, to be common to both. In that case, the Court of Appeal, in upholding a decision of an employment tribunal, considered that a refusal by an employee to do work of a lower standard than the employee considered reasonable, may be a reason for holding that the work offered is not suitable or has been reasonably refused.

36.13   AMOUNT OF THE PAYMENT

The amount of the redundancy payment is based upon the employee's age, length of continuous employment and gross average wage.

The calculation of continuity is made in accordance with rules set out in *ERA 1996, ss 210 to 219*, formerly *EPCA 1978, Sch 13*; see **36.4** above and CONTINUOUS EMPLOYMENT (6).

Contractual agreements relating to continuity of employment cannot affect an employer's statutory liability to make a redundancy payment (*Secretary of State for Employment v Globe Elastic Thread Co Ltd* [1980] AC 506, [1979] 2 All ER 1077, [1979] 3 WLR 143, [1979] ICR 706). Therefore, if an employer agrees to preserve an employee's continuity of employment where there is no continuity in accordance with the statutory provisions, he will be contractually liable to make a redundancy payment calculated in accordance with his agreement, but not liable to make any payment under statute.

36.13 Redundancy – I: The Right to a Redundancy Payment

The amount of the redundancy payment is calculated by reference to the period, ending with the relevant date, during which the employee has been continuously employed. (For the meaning of 'relevant date' see **36.4** above.) There is then allowed:

(a)   one and a half week's pay for each such year of employment which consists wholly of weeks in which the employee was not below the age of 41;

(b)   one week's pay for each such year of employment (not falling within (*a*) above) which consists wholly of weeks in which the employee was not below the age of 22; and

(c)   half a week's pay for each such year of employment not falling within either of the preceding sub-paragraphs.

(*ERA 1996, s 162(1), (2).*) The maximum number of years to be taken into account in calculating a redundancy payment is 20 (*ERA 1996, s 162(3)*). A previous redundancy payment breaks continuity for this purpose (*ERA 1996, s 214(2)*).

A week's pay is calculated in accordance with *ERA 1996, ss 221–229*, formerly *EPCA 1978, Sch 14*. The calculation is based on average wages without deduction of tax, not taking into account overtime, unless the employer is contractually bound to provide and the employee to work such overtime. Where an employee is on short-time working on the calculation date, "a week's pay" should be that provided for by the original contract of employment, notwithstanding the short-time working: see *Dutton v Jones* UKEAT/0236/12. (See Pay – I (32) for full details.)

With effect from 1 February 2013, the maximum amount of a week's pay allowed in computing a statutory redundancy payment is £450 (*ERA 1996, s 227* and the *Employment Rights (Increase of Limits) Order 2012 (SI 2012/3007)*). Thus, the current maximum redundancy payment is £13,500.

36.14 REFERENCES TO EMPLOYMENT TRIBUNAL AND RESTRICTION ON CONTRACTING OUT

Any question arising as to the right of an employee to a redundancy payment, or as to the amount of a redundancy payment, is to be referred to and determined by an employment tribunal (*ERA 1996, s 163(1)*).

Any provision in any agreement (whether a contract of employment or not) is *prima facie* void insofar as it purports to exclude or limit any provisions relating to redundancy, or to preclude any person from bringing any proceedings in respect of a redundancy payment before an employment tribunal (*ERA 1996, s 203(1)*).

However, an employee will be bound by a settlement agreement reached following action by a conciliation officer, or by a compromise contract which satisfies the statutory conditions, including that the employee should have had independent advice (*ERA 1996, s 203(2)*; and see **2.4** Advisory, Conciliation and Arbitration Service and **17.25** Employment Tribunals – I).

36.15 Ready Reckoner for Redundancy Payments

To use the Table — Read off employee's age and number of complete years' service. The Table will then show how many weeks' pay the employee is entitled to. It should be noted that although the Table runs only between the ages of 20 and 64, service before and after these ages does count for redundancy purposes, and there is no age below or above which redundancy payments cannot be claimed.

The Table may also be used to calculate the basic award for unfair dismissal, although in such a case the service required (save where dismissal is for one of the reasons set out in chapter 51.11 UNFAIR DISMISSAL – I – in respect of which no qualifying period is necessary) is one year rather than two (unless the employee's employment commenced on or after 6 April 2012, in which case the service required is two years).

AGE (years)	SERVICE (years)																		
	2	3	4	5	6	7	8	9	10	11	12	13	14	15	16	17	18	19	20
20	1	1½	2	2½	—														
21	1	1½	2	2½	3	—													
22	1	1½	2	2½	3	3½	—												
23	1½	2	2½	3	3½	4	4½	—											
24	2	2½	3	3½	4	4½	5	5½	—										
25	2	3	3½	4	4½	5	5½	6	6½	—									
26	2	3	4	4½	5	5½	6	6½	7	7½	—								
27	2	3	4	5	5½	6	6½	7	7½	8	8½	—							
28	2	3	4	5	6	6½	7	7½	8	8½	9	9½	—						
29	2	3	4	5	6	7	7½	8	8½	9	9½	10	10½	—					
30	2	3	4	5	6	7	8	8½	9	9½	10	10½	11	11½	—				
31	2	3	4	5	6	7	8	9	9½	10	10½	11	11½	12	12½	—			
32	2	3	4	5	6	7	8	9	10	10½	11	11½	12	12½	13	13½	—		
33	2	3	4	5	6	7	8	9	10	11	11½	12	12½	13	13½	14	14½	—	
34	2	3	4	5	6	7	8	9	10	11	12	12½	13	13½	14	14½	15	15½	—
35	2	3	4	5	6	7	8	9	10	11	12	13	13½	14	14½	15	15½	16	16½
36	2	3	4	5	6	7	8	9	10	11	12	13	14	14½	15	15½	16	16½	17
37	2	3	4	5	6	7	8	9	10	11	12	13	14	15	15½	16	16½	17	17½
38	2	3	4	5	6	7	8	9	10	11	12	13	14	15	16	16½	17	17½	18

Age	2	3	4	5	6	7	8	9	10	11	12	13	14	15	16	17	17½	18	18½
39	2	3	4	5	6	7	8	9	10	11	12	13	14	15	16	17	17½	18	18½
40	2	3	4	5	6	7	8	9	10	11	12	13	14	15	16	17	18	18½	19
41	2	3	4	5	6	7	8	9	10	11	12	13	14	15	16	17	18	19	19½
42	2½	3½	4½	5½	6½	7½	8½	9½	10½	11½	12½	13½	14½	15½	16½	17½	18½	19½	20½
43	3	4	5	6	7	8	9	10	11	12	13	14	15	16	17	18	19	20	21
44	3	4½	5½	6½	7½	8½	9½	10½	11½	12½	13½	14½	15½	16½	17½	18½	19½	20½	21½
45	3	4½	6	7	8	9	10	11	12	13	14	15	16	17	18	19	20	21	22
46	3	4½	6	7½	8½	9½	10½	11½	12½	13½	14½	15½	16½	17½	18½	19½	20½	21½	22½
47	3	4½	6	7½	9	10	11	12	13	14	15	16	17	18	19	20	21	22	23
48	3	4½	6	7½	9	10½	11½	12½	13½	14½	15½	16½	17½	18½	19½	20½	21½	22½	23½
49	3	4½	6	7½	9	10½	12	13	14	15	16	17	18	19	20	21	22	23	24
50	3	4½	6	7½	9	10½	12	13½	14½	15½	16½	17½	18½	19½	20½	21½	22½	23½	24½
51	3	4½	6	7½	9	10½	12	13½	15	16	17	18	19	20	21	22	23	24	25
52	3	4½	6	7½	9	10½	12	13½	15	16½	17½	18½	19½	20½	21½	22½	23½	24½	25½
53	3	4½	6	7½	9	10½	12	13½	15	16½	18	19	20	21	22	23	24	25	26
54	3	4½	6	7½	9	10½	12	13½	15	16½	18	19½	20½	21½	22½	23½	24½	25½	26½
55	3	4½	6	7½	9	10½	12	13½	15	16½	18	19½	21	22	23	24	25	26	27
56	3	4½	6	7½	9	10½	12	13½	15	16½	18	19½	21	22½	23½	24½	25½	26½	27½
57	3	4½	6	7½	9	10½	12	13½	15	16½	18	19½	21	22½	24	25	26	27	28
58	3	4½	6	7½	9	10½	12	13½	15	16½	18	19½	21	22½	24	25½	26½	27½	28½
59	3	4½	6	7½	9	10½	12	13½	15	16½	18	19½	21	22½	24	25½	27	28	29
60	3	4½	6	7½	9	10½	12	13½	15	16½	18	19½	21	22½	24	25½	27	28½	29½
61	3	4½	6	7½	9	10½	12	13½	15	16½	18	19½	21	22½	24	25½	27	28½	30
62	3	4½	6	7½	9	10½	12	13½	15	16½	18	19½	21	22½	24	25½	27	28½	30
63	3	4½	6	7½	9	10½	12	13½	15	16½	18	19½	21	22½	24	25½	27	28½	30
64	3	4½	6	7½	9	10½	12	13½	15	16½	18	19½	21	22½	24	25½	27	28½	30

37   Redundancy – II: Practice and Procedure

(See BIS guidance "Redundancy Consultation and Notification" from 2006, and ACAS advisory booklet "How to manage collective redundancies" (published April 2013).

Cross-reference. See REDUNDANCY – I (36) for the right to a redundancy payment.

37.1   If an employer dismisses an employee by reason of redundancy, he has a number of statutory obligations in addition to that of making the employee a redundancy payment.

He may be liable in a claim of unfair dismissal unless he acts fairly. He must allow the employee reasonable time off work to look for alternative employment. If the proposed dismissal is of 20 or more employees at one establishment within 90 days, the employer must consult 'appropriate representatives' of the employees concerned. For the meaning of 'appropriate representatives' in this context, see **37.4** below.

This chapter considers the following.

(a)   The requirements for consultation before making an employee redundant (see **37.2–37.6** below).

(b)   The basic 'fair dismissal' considerations relating to proposed redundancies (see **37.8** below).

The chapter ends with a checklist of redundancy dismissal procedure.

37.2   CONSULTATION AND NOTIFICATION REQUIREMENTS

The Trade Union and Labour Relations (Consolidation) Act 1992 ('TULRCA 1992'), as amended by the Trade Union Reform and Employment Rights Act 1993 ('TURERA 1993') and relevant regulations, impose far-reaching obligations on employers to notify and consult appropriate employee representatives about proposed redundancies. TULRCA 1992, s 193 also imposes obligations on employers to notify the Secretary of State for Employment about proposed redundancies. The statutory provisions give effect to the EC Collective Redundancies Directive 98/59/EC, amending Directive 75/129/EEC and Directive 92/56/EEC (see **22.8** EUROPEAN UNION LAW). For the use of the Directive as an aid to construction of the statute, see *Hough v Leyland DAF Ltd* [1991] ICR 696; but cf *Re Hartlebury Printers Ltd* [1993] 1 All ER 470, [1992] ICR 559.

37.3   Meaning of 'redundancy'

In *TULRCA 1992, Part IV Chapter II*, which contains the statutory consultation and notification requirements, references to 'dismissal as redundant' are references to dismissal for a reason not related to the individual concerned or for a number of reasons all of which are not so related (*TULRCA 1992, s 195(1)* as substituted by *TURERA 1993, s 34(5)*). This is a substantially different definition from that which applies for redundancy payments purposes (see **36.7** REDUNDANCY – I). For the purposes of any proceedings under *TULRCA 1992*, where an employee is or is proposed to be dismissed, it shall be presumed that he is or is proposed to be dismissed as redundant unless the contrary is proved (*TULRCA 1992, s 195(2)* as substituted by *TURERA 1993, s 34(5)*). It follows from the definition of 'dismissal as redundant' in *TULRCA 1992, s 195(1)* that the collective consultation and notification provisions in *TULRCA 1992* can apply to proposed dismissals, notwithstanding the fact that there is no intention to lose jobs or workers. Thus, where an employer seeks to change the terms and conditions of employment of a part or group of the workforce by giving notice of termination to the employees concerned and offering them re-engagement on new terms, the employer may be under a duty to consult in accordance with *TULRCA 1992, s 188* (*GMB v MAN Truck & Bus UK Ltd* [2000] IRLR 636).

The provisions of *TULRCA 1992, Part IV, Chapter II* do not apply to employment under a contract for a fixed term, unless the employer proposes to dismiss an employee on a fixed-term contract before the term has expired: see *TULRCA 1992, s 282* as amended with effect from 6 April 2013.

37.4   Notification to appropriate representatives

Where an employer is proposing to dismiss as redundant at least 20 employees at an establishment within a period of 90 days or less, he must consult about the dismissals 'appropriate representatives' of the affected employees (*TULRCA 1992, s 188(1)* as amended by the *Collective Redundancies and Transfer of Undertakings (Protection of Employment) (Amendment) Regulations 1999 (SI 1999/1925)*). The class of 'affected employees' includes not only those who may be dismissed, but also any employee affected by the proposed dismissals or who may be affected by measures taken in connection with those dismissals (*TULRCA 1992, s 188(1)* as amended by *SI 1999/1925*) An employer has to include employees whom it is hoped to redeploy in calculating the number it proposes to dismiss as redundant, if what is proposed amounts to a termination of the employee's existing contract of employment (*Hardy v Tourism South East* [2005] IRLR 242, EAT). This is because the applicable definition of dismissal for the purposes of *TULRCA s 188* (that in *ERA 1996, s 95*) refers to the termination of an employee's contract, with or without notice. Employees who volunteer for redundancy pursuant to an invitation from the employer should be included in the numbers of those the employer proposes to dismiss as redundant: see *Optare Group v Transport and General Workers' Union* [2007] IRLR 931.

The 'appropriate representatives' of any affected employees are:

(a)   if the employees are of a description in respect of which an independent trade union is recognised, representatives of the trade union; or

(b)   in any other case, either:

    (i)   employee representatives appointed or elected by the affected employees for other purposes but who have authority to receive information and to be consulted about the proposed dismissals on their behalf; or

    (ii)   employee representatives elected by the affected employees for the purposes of *TULRCA 1992, s 188* and in accordance with the statutory procedure set out in *TULRCA 1992, s 188A*.

(*TULRCA 1992, s 188(1B)* as amended by *SI 1999/1925*.)

'Representatives of a trade union' are officials or other persons authorised by the union to carry on collective bargaining with the employer (*TULRCA 1992, s 196(2)* as substituted by the *Collective Redundancies and Transfer of Undertakings (Protections of Employment) (Amendment) Regulations (SI 1995/2587)*). 'Recognition', in relation to a trade union, is defined by *TULRCA 1992, s 178(3)* as meaning the recognition of the union by an employer, or two or more associated employers, to any extent, for the purpose of collective bargaining (as defined by *TULRCA 1992, s 178(1)*). In *National Union of Gold, Silver and Allied Trades v Albury Bros Ltd* [1979] ICR 84, the Court of Appeal held that recognition should not be held to be established unless there was clear and unequivocal evidence of an express agreement, or conduct from which recognition should be inferred which involved not a mere willingness to discuss but a positive decision to negotiate on one or more of the issues specified in what is now *TULRCA 1992, s 178(2)*.

It has long been understood that, in order to comply with the requirements of *TULRCA 1992, s 188*, the employer must begin consultations before giving individual notices of dismissal (*National Union of Teachers v Avon County Council* [1978] IRLR 55). However, in *Junk v Kühnel*: C-188/03 [2005] IRLR 310, the CJEU ruled that, for the purposes of *Directive 98/59/EC*, consultation must in fact already have been completed before employees are given notice of dismissal. This is because a 'redundancy' for the purposes of the Directive means the declaration of an employer of its intention to terminate the contract of employment (ie the giving of notice), rather than actual dismissal on the expiry of notice

Consultation must not be a sham exercise; there must be time for the representatives, who are consulted, to consider properly the proposals that are being put to them (*Transport and General Workers' Union v Ledbury Preserves (1928) Ltd* [1985] IRLR 412). Fair consultation involves giving the body consulted a fair and proper opportunity to understand fully the matters about which it is being consulted, and to express its views on those subjects, with the consulting employer thereafter considering those views properly and genuinely. The process of consultation is not one in which the employer is obliged to adopt any or all of the views expressed by the person or body whom he is consulting (*R v British Coal Corpn and Secretary of State for Trade and Industry, ex p Price* [1994] IRLR 72). Further, the consultation envisaged by *s 188* cannot begin until the information required by the section, as set out below, has been given (*E Green & Son (Castings) Ltd v Association of Scientific, Technical and Managerial Staffs* [1984] ICR 352; see also *GEC Ferranti Defence Systems Ltd v MSF* [1993] IRLR 101 and [1994] IRLR 104).

The employer does not 'propose' to dismiss until he has reached the stage of having formulated a specific proposal (*Hough v Leyland DAF Ltd* [1991] ICR 696). Thus, the word 'propose' connotes an intention in the mind of the employer (*Scotch Premier Meat Ltd v Burns* [2000] IRLR 639). Significantly, the EAT held in the *Burns* case that where an employer had determined a plan of action which had two alternative scenarios only one of which necessarily included redundancies then this was capable of amounting to the employer 'proposing to dismiss' employees. It was, however, emphasised that this was essentially a question of fact for the employment tribunal to determine. In addition, a 'proposal' to dismiss does not necessarily have to be made by the person with power to carry out the dismissal (*Dewhirst Group v GMB Trade Union* [2003] All ER (D) 175 (Dec), EAT). For further consideration of what is meant by a 'proposed' dismissal, and for the application of *TULRCA 1992, s 188* where administrators have been appointed, see *Re Hartlebury Printers Ltd* [1993] 1 All ER 470, [1992] ICR 559, *R v British Coal Corpn, ex p Vardy* [1993] ICR 720 and *MSF v Refuge Assurance plc* [2002] IRLR 324. In *MSF* the EAT held that *s 188* did not have the same meaning as *Directive 75/129* (now, *Directive 98/59*), which requires consultation when collective redundancies are first 'contemplated'. 'Contemplation' means 'having a view', and refers to a relatively early stage in the decision-making process, whereas 'proposes' relates to a state of mind which is much more certain (see also *Scotch Premier Meat Ltd v Burns* [2000] IRLR 639 and *R v British Coal Corpn, ex p Vardy* [1993] ICR 720). More recently the EAT in *Unison v Leicestershire County Council* [2005] IRLR 920 approved the tribunal's finding that a 'proposal' meant 'something less than a decision that dismissals are to be made and more than a possibility that they might occur'. While not inconsistent with *Vardy* or *MSF*, this ruling suggests that an employer may "propose" to dismiss employees at an earlier stage of the decision-making process than previously understood. Of course, insofar as there is any difference between the requirements of the *Directive* and that of *TULRCA 1992*, employees of 'the State' may be able to rely directly on the *Directive* (cf *Griffin v South West Water Services Ltd* [1995] IRLR 15) (see **22.2** EUROPEAN UNION LAW; **35.7** PUBLIC SECTOR EMPLOYEES).

In circumstances where decisions on collective redundancies are taken within a group of companies with a parent company and subsidiaries, the obligation to consult always lies with the subsidiary company which employs the workers, and never with the parent, irrespective of whether the decision in connection with collective redundancies is made by the parent or the subsidiary. Where the parent company makes decisions on redundancy across the group, consultation obligations are only triggered once the subsidiary in which collective redundancies would be made has been identified: see *Akavan Erityisalojen Keskusliitto AEK ry v Fujitsu Siemens Computers Oy*: C-44/08 [2010] ICR 444, CJEU.

Where a consultation is required, it must begin 'in good time', and in addition:

(a)   if an employer is proposing to dismiss *at least 100* employees at any one establishment within a period of 90 days or less, the consultation must begin at least *45* days before the first of the dismissals takes effect; and

(b)   in any other case in which consultation is required, consultation must begin at least 30 days before the first of the dismissals takes effect.

(*TULRCA 1992, s 188(1A)*, as substituted by *SI 1995/2587*, and as amended by *SI 2013/763* with effect from 6 April 2013)

The Government intends to reduce the period of consultation required in cases where there is a proposal to dismiss at least 100 employees from 90 days to 45 days with effect from 6 April 2013, and has drafted legislation to that effect (the proposed *Trade Union and Labour Relations (Consolidation) Act 1992 (Amendment) Order 2013*). The draft legislation, which amends *TULRCA 1992, s 188(1)*, would apply where a relevant "proposal" was made on or after 6 April 2013.

The phrase 'before the first of the dismissals takes effect' obviously refers to the proposed date of the first dismissal, not the actual date, otherwise the provisions would be unworkable (see *E Green & Son (Castings) Ltd v ASTMS* [1984] IRLR 135, following *GKN Sankey Ltd v National Society of Motor Mechanics* [1980] IRLR 8). On the basis of *Junk v Kühnel*: C-188/03 [2005] IRLR 310, consultation for the purposes of *Directive 98/59/EC* must be completed before notice of dismissal is given (see above). The EAT in *Unison v Leicestershire* [2005] IRLR 920 held that it was possible to read *TULRCA 1992 s 188(1)* consistently with EC law by construing the phrase "proposing to dismiss" as meaning "proposing to give notice of dismissal". The effect of this construction is that the full consultation must be completed before notices of dismissal are issued. Whether consultation has begun 'in good time' is a matter of fact and degree for the employment tribunal: see *UNISON v Leicestershire County Council* [2006] EWCA Civ 825, [2006] IRLR 810, CA.

The CJEU held in *Rockfon A/S v Specialarbejderforbundet i Danmark*: C-449/93 [1996] ICR 673 that the word 'establishment' under *Directive 75/129* referred to the local employment unit, that is the unit to which the workers made redundant are assigned to carry out their duties. Thus, for example, the fact that a contract contains a mobility clause allowing the worker to be moved elsewhere is not relevant: see *Renfrewshire Council v Educational Institute of Scotland* [2013] ICR 172. Although the term 'establishment' connotes a distinct entity assigned to perform particular tasks, an 'establishment' need not have any legal, economic, or administrative autonomy, nor have a management that can independently effect collective redundancies, nor be geographically separate from other units of the undertaking in question: see *Athinaiki Chartopoiia AE v Panagiotidis*: C-270/05 [2007] IRLR 284, interpreting *Directive 98/59* (the successor to *Directive 75/129*). The question as to what constitutes 'one establishment' is essentially a question of fact for the employment tribunal (*Bulwick v Mills & Allen Ltd* (8 June 2000, unreported), EAT.

The meaning of "establishment" for the purposes of *TULRCA 1992, s 188* is a matter of controversy. The purpose behind the decision in *Rockfon* was to promote workers' rights by providing for consultation in the widest range of situations. However, the means of implementing *Directive 98/59* adopted in *TULRCA 1992, s 188* means that a literal application of *Rockfon* to the meaning of "establishment" in domestic law has precisely the opposite effect, as pointed out by the EAT in *Renfrewshire Council v Educational Institute of*

Scotland [2013] ICR 172. (Nevertheless, the EAT in *Renfrewshire* did not feel able to depart from the established and literal approach to *Rockfon* taken in domestic cases such as *MSF v Refuge Assurance plc* [2002] ICR 1365). The meaning of "establishment" is a matter on which the Government has specifically asked ACAS to provide advice in new guidance on collective redundancy consultations, intended for issue on 6 April 2013.

For the purposes of the consultation, the employer must disclose in writing to the appropriate representatives:

(i)   the reasons for his proposals;

(ii)   the number and descriptions of employees whom it is proposed to dismiss as redundant;

(iii)   the total number of employees of any such description employed by the employer at the establishment in question;

(iv)   the proposed method of selecting the employees who may be dismissed;

(v)   the proposed method of carrying out the dismissals with due regard to any agreed procedure, including the period over which the dismissals are to take effect;

(vi)   the proposed method of calculating the amount of any redundancy payments otherwise than in compliance with a statutory obligation;

(vii)   the number of agency workers working temporarily for and under the supervision and direction of the employer,

(viii) the parts of the employer's undertaking in which those agency workers are working, and

(ix)   the type of work those agency workers are carrying out.

(*TULRCA 1992, s 188(4)* as amended by *TURERA 1993, s 34(2)(a)*, *SI 1995/2587.*, and *SI 2010/93*.)

Where the employer has invited affected employees to elect representatives, but the affected employees fail to do so within a reasonable time, then the employer must give the requisite information to each affected employee individually (*TULRCA 1992, s 188(7B)* as inserted by *SI 1999/1925*).

The information must be provided in proper form: it will not do to say that it may be gleaned from the surrounding circumstances and from a number of documents (*Sovereign Distribution Services Ltd v TGWU* [1990] ICR 31).

The consultation must include consultation about ways of avoiding the dismissals, reducing the number of employees to be dismissed and mitigating the consequences of the dismissals, and must be undertaken by the employer with a view to reaching agreement with the appropriate representatives (*TULRCA 1992, s 188(2)* as substituted by *SI 1995/2587*). The fact that consultation must be undertaken with a view to reaching agreement means that it is tantamount to negotiation (*Junk v Kühnel*: C-188/03 [2005] IRLR 310). An employer must consult on all the matters set out in *s 188(2)*, *TULRCA 1992*, which are to be viewed disjunctively. Furthermore, it is not open to an employer to argue that consultation would, in the circumstances, be futile or useless (*Middlesbrough Borough Council v TGWU* [2002] IRLR 332).

Until recently, the domestic courts held that *TULRCA s 188* did not require consultation about the reasons for the redundancy, including whether or not a plant should close (see *Vardy*, and two cases following *Vardy*: *Middlesbrough v TGWU* and *Securicor Omega Express Ltd v GMB* [2004] IRLR 9). However, the EAT has more recently taken a different approach in *UK Coal Mining Ltd v National Union of Mineworkers (Northumberland Area)* [2008] ICR 163, [2008] IRLR 4. In the *UK Coal Mining* case, the Employment Appeal Tribunal observed that at the time *Vardy* was decided, *TULRCA s 188* required consultation only 'about the dismissal'. After amendments made in 1995, *TULRCA s 188* now required consultation over 'ways of avoiding dismissals'. This inevitably involved engaging with the reasons for dismissals. So, where dismissals were inextricably linked with the closure of a plant, a duty to consult over the closure would arise. The EAT in *UK Coal Mining* followed *Vardy* and *MSF* in holding that the wording 'proposing to dismiss' in *TULRCA s 188* connoted a more certain state of mind than the wording 'contemplating dismissals' in Directive 98/59. Nevertheless, the EAT indicated that this would not prevent the consultation obligation from extending to the closure of a plant: in a closure context where it is recognised that dismissals will inevitably, or almost inevitably, result from the closure, dismissals will be proposed at the point when closure itself is proposed.

The question whether the *Vardy* or *UK Coal* approach should be preferred is at present unclear. In *United States of America v Nolan (Christine)* [2011] IRLR 40, the Court of Appeal referred to the CJEU the issue whether *Directive 98/59* gives rise to consultation obligations when the employer is proposing, but has not yet made, a strategic business decision that will inevitably lead to redundancies; or whether it gives rise to consultation obligations only when such a strategic decision has actually been made, and the employer then proposes consequential redundancies. The Court of Appeal stated that it was referring the question because it was unclear from the CJEU's judgment in *Akavan Erityisalojen Keskusliitto Alek RY and others v Fujitsu Siemens Computers OY* C-44/08 [2009] IRLR 944 which approach was to be preferred. The Court also stated that *TULRCA, s 188* was not intended to impose a wider consultation obligation than that contained in *Directive 98/59* (so that the proper approach to *TULRCA, s 188* would be determined by the meaning of the *Directive*). The CJEU, however, declined to rule on the reference on the basis that *Directive 98/59* did not apply to workers employed by public administrative bodies or by establishments governed by public law, and this included civilian staff at a military base: *United States of America v Nolan* C-583/10 [2013] ICR 193.

Specified employers may also be obliged to inform and consult appropriate representatives about economic decisions likely to lead to changes in work organisation or contractual relations under the *Information and Consultation of Employees Regulations 2004, SI 2004/3426*.

Failure to consult with the appropriate representatives, or to do so within the stipulated time when it was reasonably practicable to do so, may lead to the employer being held liable to pay each redundant employee a protective award (see 37.6 below). Such a failure is also likely to render the dismissals unfair (*Kelly v Upholstery and Cabinet Works (Amesbury) Ltd* [1977] IRLR 91; *North East Midlands Co-operative Society Ltd v Allen* [1977] IRLR 212; *Polkey v A E Dauton (or Dayton) Services Ltd* [1988] AC 344, [1988] ICR 142, HL; but cf *Hough*, above).

37.5 Election of employee representatives

If elections are held for employee representatives they must be held in accordance with the provisions of *TULRCA 1992, s 188A* (as inserted by *SI 1999/1925*). This provides that:

(a)   the employer shall make such arrangements as are reasonably practical to ensure that the election is fair;

(b)   the employer shall determine the number of representatives to be elected so that there are sufficient representatives to represent the interests of all the affected employees having regard to the number and classes of those employees;

(c)   the employer shall determine whether the affected employees should be represented either by representatives of all the affected employees or by representatives of particular classes of those employees;

(d)   before the election the employer shall determine the term of office as employee representatives so that it is of sufficient length to enable information to be given and consultations under this section to be completed;

(e)   the candidates for election as employee representatives are affected employees on the date of the election;

(f)   no affected employee is unreasonably excluded from standing for election;

(g)   all affected employees on the date of the election are entitled to vote for employee representatives;

(h)   the employees entitled to vote may vote for as many candidates as there are representatives to be elected to represent them or, if there are to be representatives for particular classes of employees, may vote for as many candidates as there are representatives to be elected to represent their particular class of employee; and

(i)   the election is conducted so as to secure that:

    (i)   so far as is reasonably practicable, those voting do so in secret; and

    (ii)   the votes given at the election are accurately counted.

(TULRCA 1992, s 188A(1).)

Further, if after an election held in accordance with this procedure, an elected representative ceases to act as a representative so that employees are no longer represented then they shall elect another representative by an election held in accordance with the requirements at (*a*), (*e*), (*f*) and (*i*) above *(TULRCA 1992, s 188A(2))*.

An employer is not necessarily obliged to hold a formal election if it simply accepts all candidates as appropriate representatives: *Phillips v Xtera Communications Ltd* [2012] ICR 171. An "election" for the purposes of *s 188A(1)* occurs when, pursuant to fair arrangements, the number of candidates matches the number of representatives to be elected, and no further candidates are proposed. In such circumstances, there is no need for a ballot or vote.

37.6 Protective award

If an employer fails to comply with any of the statutory requirements for consultation or fails to do so within the appropriate time, a complaint may be made to an employment tribunal by the trade union where the failure relates to trade union representatives, or by any of the affected employees or by any of the employees who have been dismissed as redundant where the failure relates to the election of employee representatives, or in the case of any other failure relating to employee representatives, by any of the employee representatives to whom the failure related and, in any other case, by any of the affected employees or by any of the employees who have been dismissed as redundant (*TULRCA 1992, s 189* as amended by *SI 1999/1925*).

A protective award is an award in respect of employees in respect of whose dismissal or proposed dismissal the employer has failed to comply with a requirement of *s 188*: *TULRCA 1992, s 189(3)*. So, for instance, it cannot cover employees whom the employer originally proposed to dismiss, but subsequently decided to keep on (whether as a result of consultation or otherwise). They may be employees whom it was originally proposed to dismiss, but they are not employees whom it "is proposed" to dismiss: see *Securicor Omega Express v GMB* [2004] IRLR 9.

A protective award can only be made in favour of those in respect of whom a complaint of breach has been proved by themselves or their representative. So, where a claim is made by a trade union, the protective award will benefit only those employees within the bargaining unit in respect of which the union is recognised: *TGWU v Brauer Coley Ltd (in administration)* [2007] IRLR 207. Similarly, where a claim is made by an individual employee, the employment tribunal can only make an award in the individual claimant's favour, and cannot make an award that benefits other redundant employees: *Independent Insurance Company Ltd v Aspinall* [2011] IRLR 716. Note also that an individual employee who is not an employee representative cannot bring a claim in respect of a failure relating to employee representatives (other than a failure relating to the election of representatives): see *Northgate HR Ltd v Mercy* [2007] EWCA Civ 1304, [2008] ICR 410, [2008] IRLR 222.

If a question is raised on any such complaint as to whether or not any employee representative was an appropriate representative for the purposes of *s 188*, the burden of proof will be on the employer to show that the employee representative had the authority to represent the affected employees (*TULRCA 1992, s 189(1A)* as inserted by *SI 1999/1925*). Also, where the alleged failure relates to the election of employee representatives, the burden will be on the employer to show that the statutory election procedure in *s 188A* has been complied with.

The complaint must be presented before the date on which the last of the dismissals to which the complaint relates takes effect, or during the period of three months beginning with that date, or within such further period as the tribunal considers reasonable in a case where it is satisfied that it was not reasonably practicable for the complaint to be presented during the period of three months (*TULRCA 1992, s 189(5)* as amended by *SI 1995/2587*; and see **17.25 EMPLOYMENT TRIBUNALS – I**).

It is a defence to such an application for an employer to show that there were special circumstances which rendered it not reasonably practicable for him to comply with the requirements, and that he took all such steps as were reasonably practicable in those circumstances (*TULRCA 1992, s 188(7)* as amended by *TURERA 1993, s 34(2)(c)*). For example, an unforeseen financial crisis may make it necessary to close down a plant at short notice so that consultations can only take place during a shorter period than that prescribed by law.

In *Clarks of Hove Ltd v Bakers' Union* [1979] 1 All ER 152, [1978] 1 WLR 1207, [1978] ICR 1076, the Court of Appeal held that insolvency is not on its own a special circumstance and that it depends entirely on the course of the insolvency whether the circumstances can be described as special or not. (See also *Angus Jowett & Co Ltd v National Union of Tailors and Garment Workers* [1985] ICR 646, [1985] IRLR 326, EAT; *Re Hartlebury Printers Ltd* [1993] 1 All ER 470, [1992] ICR 559.) The employer may not neglect his duty under *TULRCA 1992, s 188* merely because he considers that consultation will achieve nothing (*Sovereign Distribution Services Ltd v TGWU* [1990] ICR 31).

Section 188(7) precludes the employer from relying upon a failure to provide information by the person whose decision led to the proposed dismissals if that person directly or indirectly controls the employer. The meaning of this provision was considered in *GMB and Amicus v Beloit Walmsley Ltd* [2004] IRLR 18. The EAT determined that: (i) the mischief at which this provision is aimed is a controlling entity's delay in providing the employer with information. Any period of delay in providing information must therefore count against the employer, for the purposes of determining whether or not the duty under *TULRCA 1992, s 188* could have been complied with; (ii) there must be a causal link between the decision, and the proposed dismissals. However, it is not necessary that the person making the decision contemplates any particular number of dismissals, at any particular establishment; (iii) the 'information', required to be provided by *TULRCA s 188(7)*, is not confined to the 'information' required to be disclosed by *TULRCA s 188(4)*. It includes information necessary to begin the process of consultation.

An employer would appear to escape its information and consultation obligations under *s 188* if he invites any affected employees to elect representatives and has given enough time to allow for an election but such election is not organised (*TULRCA 1992, s 188(7A)*; and see *R v Secretary of State for Trade and Industry, ex p UNISON* [1996] IRLR 438).

Where a tribunal finds the complaint well-founded it makes a declaration to that effect and may also make a protective award (*TULRCA 1992, s 189(2)*). A protective award is an order that an employer make payments for the protected period in respect of specified employees who have been dismissed, or whom it is proposed to dismiss, as redundant without complying with the statutory requirements for consultation. The length of the period will be what is considered to be just and equitable by the tribunal in the circumstances having regard to the seriousness of the employer's default and will be up to 90 days, beginning on the date on which the first of the dismissals to which the complaint relates was proposed to take effect, or the date of the award, whichever is the earlier (*TULRCA 1992, s 189(4)*, as amended by *SI 1999/1925*). See *Transport and General Workers' Union v Ledbury Preserves (1928) Ltd* [1986] ICR 855; *E Green & Son (Castings) Ltd v Association of Scientific, Technical and Managerial Staffs* [1984] ICR 352. The purpose of the award is to provide a sanction for breach by the employer of the obligations in *TULRCA s 188*, not to compensate employees for any loss suffered: hence the futility of consultation is not relevant to the making of a protective award (*GMB v Susie Radin Ltd* [2004] EWCA Civ 180, [2004] 2 All ER 279, [2004] ICR 893, reversing *Spillers-French (Holdings) Ltd v USDAW* [1980] 1 All ER 231, [1980] ICR 31, [1979] IRLR 339). Nor is the employer's insolvency relevant to the size of any protective award: the employment tribunal should focus simply upon the seriousness of the employer's default in failing to comply with its statutory duty (*Smith v Cherry Lewis Ltd* [2005] IRLR 86). In the *Susie Radin* case, the Court of Appeal stated that how the length of the protected period is assessed is a matter for the tribunal, but a proper approach in a case where there has been no consultation is to start with the maximum period and reduce it only if there are mitigating circumstances justifying a reduction. Mitigating circumstances may, however, include any steps taken by the employer before proposals have crystallised in relation to keeping employees informed or consulted, even if there has been no consultation under *TULRCA s 188* itself (*AMICUS v GBS Tooling Ltd (in administration)* [2005] IRLR 683). A union's obstructive approach to statutory consultation may also be taken into account when assessing the correct level of a protective award: see *GMB v Lambeth Service Team; TGWU v Lambeth Service Team* [2005] All ER (D) 153 (Jul), EAT. Furthermore, when assessing the seriousness of the default, it is relevant to consider both the culpability of the employer and the harm or potential for harm of the default: see *Shanahan Engineering Ltd v Unite the Union* UKEAT/0411/09. There is no connection between the length of the statutory consultation period, and the length of the protective award. Even if the employer proposed to dismiss fewer than 100 employees, so that the minimum consultation period was 30 days, rather than 90 days, before the first dismissal took effect, the proper protective award for a complete failure to consult is 90 days: see *Hutchins v Permacell Finesse Ltd (In Administration)* [2008] All ER (D) 112 (Jan).

Where a tribunal has made a protective award, every employee to whom it relates is entitled to be paid remuneration by the employer for the protected period at the rate of a week's pay (see PAY – I (32)) for each week of the period (*TULRCA 1992, s 190(1), (2), (5)*). There is no upper limit on the amount of a week's pay for this purpose.

If an employee, specified in the award, receives payments under his contract of employment during the protected period, those payments no longer go to discharge his employer's liability under the protective award, nor vice versa (*TURERA 1993, s 34(3)*, which repealed *TULRCA 1992, s 190(3)*; see also *Cranswick Country Foods plc v Beall* [2007] ICR 691.

37.6   Redundancy – II: Practice and Procedure

Liability for protective awards will transfer as a result of a transfer of an undertaking under the *Transfer of Undertakings (Protection of Employment) Regulations 1981 (SI 1981/1794)* (*Alamo Group (Europe) Ltd v Tucker* [2003] ICR 829, following *Kerry Foods Ltd v Creber* [2000] ICR 556 and not following *TGWU v McKinnon* [2001] ICR 1281 – see also Transfer of Undertakings (50)).

Disallowance of payment under award. If an employee remains employed during a protected period and:

(i)   he is fairly dismissed by his employer for a reason other than redundancy;

(ii)   he unreasonably terminates the contract of employment; or

(iii)   he unreasonably refuses an offer of suitable alternative employment made to take effect before or during the protected period,

he will not be entitled to payment under the protective award in respect of any period during which he would have been employed but for the dismissal, termination or refusal of employment (*TULRCA 1992, s 191(1)–(3)*). If the offer of alternative employment embodies terms which differ from those under which he previously worked, the employee has a trial period of four weeks beginning with the commencement date of the new contract (or by agreement in writing, a longer period) (*TULRCA 1992, s 191(4)–(6)*; see also **36.6** Redundancy – I). If during the trial period, the employment is terminated by the employer for a reason connected with the change to the new or renewed employment, or by the employee, the employee remains entitled to his protective award unless he acted unreasonably in terminating or giving notice to terminate the contract (*TULRCA 1992, s 191(7)*).

Remedy for non-payment of award. If an employer fails to pay a protective award, the employee concerned may present a complaint to an employment tribunal which will order the employer to make the payment (*TULRCA 1992, s 192(1), (3)*). The time limit for the presentation of a complaint by an individual employee for failure to pay a protective award is three months from the day or last day of the failure to make the payment, or such further period as the tribunal considers reasonable in a case where it is satisfied that it was not reasonably practicable for the complaint to be presented within the period of three months (*TULRCA 1992, s 192(2)*; and see **17.25** Employment Tribunals – I).

The Employment Appeal Tribunal held in *Howlett Marine Services Ltd v Bowlam* [2001] IRLR 201 that the three months' time limit for bringing a complaint in respect of non-payment of a protective award under *TULRCA 1992, s 192(2)* runs from the last day of the protected period. Moreover, this remains the case even when the protective award was made by a tribunal well after the expiry of the protective period. However, the EAT held in *Howlett* that in these circumstances it would obviously not have been 'reasonably practicable' to present a complaint within the three months' time limit so that the tribunal would still have jurisdiction to hear it provided that it was presented in such further period of time as was reasonable.

37.7   NOTIFICATIONS TO THE DEPARTMENT FOR BUSINESS, INNOVATION AND SKILLS

An employer must send written notification of certain redundancies to the Department for Business, Innovation and Skills ('BIS'). If he proposes to make 100 or more employees redundant at one establishment within a period of 90 days or less, the employer must notify the Secretary of State in writing at least 45 days before giving notice to terminate an employee's contract in respect of any of those dismissals (*TULRCA 1992, s 193(1)*, as amended by *SI 2006/2387* and *SI 2013/763*). If he proposes to make 20 or more employees redundant at one establishment within a period of 90 days or less, the employer must give at least 30 days' notice (*TULRCA 1992, s 193(2)*, as amended by *SI 1995/2587* and *SI 2006/2387*).

Redundancy – II: Practice and Procedure 37.9

The notice must be in a prescribed form and sent to the specified office. Forms are available from the local BIS office. If consultation with appropriate representatives is required, the representatives concerned must be identified and the date when consultations began must be stated (*TULRCA 1992, s 193(4)*, as amended by *SI 1995/2587*). Where consultation with appropriate representatives is required, he must give a copy of the notice to those representatives (*TULRCA 1992, s 193(6)*, as amended by *SI 1995/2587*). If there are special circumstances which make it impossible for the employer to comply with any of the requirements of notifying BIS or the representatives concerned, he must take such steps to comply as are reasonably practicable in the circumstances (*TULRCA 1992, s 193(7)* as amended by *TURERA 1993, s 34(4)*). Ignorance of the statutory obligation to notify BIS cannot constitute such special circumstances (*Secretary of State for Employment v Helitron Ltd* [1980] ICR 523); see also **37.5** above.

In *Vauxhall Motors Ltd v TGWU* [2006] IRLR 674, the employer sent written notification of proposed redundancies twice in respect of a single redundancy exercise, because the length over which redundancy proposals were considered (approximately two years) meant that the first notification had expired. The union argued that following the second notification, fresh consultation should have occurred under *TULRCA 1992, s 188*. The EAT disagreed, stating that the lodging of notification was immaterial to the question of whether the employers were in breach of *TULRCA 1992*.

Failure to notify BIS may lead to a conviction and fine of up to level 5 on the Standard Scale in a magistrates' court (*TULRCA 1992, s 194(1);* and see **1.10** INTRODUCTION).

(Fines currently capped at level 5 are made fines of an unlimited amount by *Legal Aid, Sentencing and Punishment of Offenders Act 2012, s 85*: but that section is not yet in force.)

37.8 FAIRNESS OF THE DISMISSAL

Where redundancy is the reason for a dismissal the employer will be liable in a claim for unfair dismissal in addition to the redundancy payment if he fails to act fairly. The principles governing the fairness of dismissals for redundancy are set out in full in UNFAIR DISMISSAL – II (52), and in particular in **52.11**. The main points to bear in mind are that the dismissal may either be automatically unfair, or unfair because the employer has failed to act reasonably in all the circumstances.

Automatic unfairness arises, subject to certain exceptions, where an employee is selected for an inadmissible reason. Circumstances where the employer may be held to have acted unreasonably include where he has failed to consult the trade unions or individuals involved (his obligations in this respect may go beyond the express statutory obligations dealt with in **37.4** above), where selection criteria are inadequate or have been improperly applied, or where inadequate efforts have been made to find alternative employment for those whose jobs have disappeared.

37.9 CHECKLIST OF REDUNDANCY DISMISSAL PROCEDURE

In practical terms, the first step in the redundancy dismissal procedure is the business decision on the necessity of making one or more employees redundant. Thereafter the following actions should be considered and undertaken as necessary.

(a)   *Preliminary procedure* (not necessarily in chronological order)

      (i)   Where the proposal is to issue notices of dismissal for redundancy to at least 20 employees within 90 days or less, consult with the appropriate representatives of the employees concerned within the appropriate time limits on the measures to be taken which are set out below. Provide them with all necessary information. (Provide each affected employee with the necessary information where the affected employees fail to elect representatives within a reasonable time.)

    (ii)   Decide on the number of employees to be made redundant.

    (iii)   Invite volunteers for redundancy.

    (iv)   Consider whether alternative jobs are available within the organisation or group. If it should be necessary to retrain employees for those jobs, consider the practicability of doing this.

    (v)   Select employees to be made redundant in accordance with any customary arrangement or agreed procedure. If no such arrangement or procedure exists, establish, if possible with the agreement of the relevant unions or employee representatives, objective criteria for selection, and apply them.

    (vi)   Consult with individuals affected before a final decision is taken.

    (vii)   Inform those employees as soon as possible of their impending redundancies.

    (viii)   Allow them time off to look for other employment.

    (ix)   Notify BIS of impending redundancies within the appropriate time limits.

(b)   *Dismissal notices* (taking due note of the time limits – see below)

NB Consultations must be completed before notices of dismissal are sent out.

Time limits. The date on which the dismissal is to take effect should be fixed having regard to the obligations of the employer as regards notice (see TERMINATION OF EMPLOYMENT (46)) and with an eye on the following time limits.

For step (*a*)(i):

(A)	'in good time'	in all cases in which consultation is required and in any event:
(B)	45 days before first notice of dismissal (note however the government's proposed reduction to 45 days – see 37.4 above)	100+ employees in one establishment to be dismissed within 90 days
(C)	30 days before first notice of dismissal	20–99 employees in one establishment to be dismissed within 90 days

For step (*a*)(ix), as (B) and (C) for step *(a)*(i) above.

38 References

38.1 An employer may be requested to provide a general reference or specific details about an employee or ex-employee. The request may come from the employee, a prospective employer or any other person interested in obtaining such information. (For example, the employee may need a reference in order to obtain a mortgage or a lease of residential premises.) The request may be for a reference to be given over the telephone, but more usually it will be for a written document.

38.2 THE EMPLOYER'S OBLIGATION

An employer is not obliged to provide such a reference, regardless of whether the employee was dismissed: see for example *Ros and Angel v Fanstone* [2007] UKEAT/0372/07 (unreported). As one of the terms of settlement of a claim or a potential claim before an employment tribunal, an employer may agree to provide a reference, and he will then be bound to do so, assuming the agreement to be enforceable (see **38.8** below).

38.3 CONTENTS

If the enquiry for a reference poses certain questions, then clearly those issues should be dealt with. If, however, the request is a general one, for example, from a prospective employer, the following matters will commonly be dealt with.

(a)   Length of service.

(b)   Positions held.

(c)   Competence in the job.

(d)   Honesty.

(e)   Time-keeping.

(f)   Reason for leaving.

(g)   Any other particular remarks about the employee, such as long periods of absence due to sickness.

(h)   Any relevant remarks of a more personal nature about the employee.

For references relating to a certain level of employee, some employers complete a form dealing with these matters. However, for a more senior employee such a form may give an inadequate picture and a full letter may be more appropriate.

38.4 EMPLOYER'S LIABILITIES

To the employee

References given by one employer to a prospective employer may not be made the grounds for a libel action by the employee even if the information given proves to be inaccurate, provided that the employer believes the information to be correct and gives it without malice. This is because the employer (or ex-employer) and the prospective employer have a common interest in the statement made about the employee, and the statement is protected

38.4   References

by what is known as 'qualified privilege'. As Lord Ellenborough CJ said in 1818: 'In the case of master and servant, the convenience of mankind required that what is said in fair communication between man and man, upon the subject of character, should be privileged, if made *bona fide* and without malice. If, however, the party giving the character knows what he says to be untrue, that may deprive him of the protection which the law throws around such communications' (*Hodgson v Scarlett* (1818) 1 B & Ald 232; see also *Sutherland v British Telecommunications plc* (1989) Times, 30 January). The defence of qualified privilege may, however, be lost if the statement is not merely passed between people having a mutuality of interest in the subject matter but falls into the hands of a third person. Thus, all references should be carefully marked 'private and confidential'.

In *Spring v Guardian Assurance plc* [1994] ICR 596, the House of Lords (Lord Keith dissenting) held that an employer owes a duty of care to an employee about whom he writes a reference. The employer's duty is to take reasonable care in the preparation of the reference, and he will be liable to the employee in negligence if he fails to do so and the employee thereby suffers damage.

The obligation on the employer is to provide a true, accurate and fair reference. The reference must not give a misleading impression. However, as long as the reference is accurate and does not tend to mislead, there is no obligation on the employer to set great detail or to be comprehensive. In *Bartholomew v London Borough of Hackney* [1999] IRLR 246, the employer stated that the employee had been suspended and was subject to disciplinary action, which action ceased upon an agreed termination of the employee's employment. The employee complained that a reference was negligent because it failed to say that he strongly disputed the charges. The reference was held not to be negligent. It was accurate and fair and did not cease to be so simply because it did not recite chapter and verse.

In *Kidd v Axa Equity and Law Life Assurance Society plc* [2000] IRLR 301, the High Court held that the duty of care on an employer did not require the employer to provide a reference which was fair, full and comprehensive. The duty is to take reasonable care. That means not giving misleading information whether by selective provision of information or by the inclusion of information in a manner that would lead a reasonable recipient to draw a false or mistaken inference. However, there is no duty to give a full or comprehensive reference, nor to refer to all material facts. See also *Byrnell v British Telecommunications Plc* [2009] EWHC 727 (QB), where the High Court rejected an argument that a purely factual reference (referring only to dates of employment and the former employee's role) was so inadequate as to constitute no "reference" at all.

Subsequent to *Bartholomew*, the Court of Appeal has further considered the requirements of accuracy and fairness in a reference for an employee who has resigned while under investigation, so that the investigation was never completed: *Cox v Sun Alliance Life Ltd* [2001] EWCA Civ 649, [2001] IRLR 448. In *Cox*, the employer provided an inaccurate and unfair reference, suggesting that it would have had a reasonable basis for dismissing the employee on the grounds of dishonesty amounting to corruption. Mummery LJ drew an analogy between the principle to be applied and the proper approach of a tribunal to dismissal for misconduct, as set out in *British Home Stores Ltd v Burchell* [1978] IRLR 379. If an employee is to be fairly dismissed for misconduct, the employer must genuinely believe in the employee's guilt, must have reasonable grounds for that belief, and must have carried out a reasonable investigation. The same principles will render negligent a reference that alludes to an employee's misconduct, when the employer has not carried out an investigation, and does not have reasonable grounds for believing in his misconduct.

On this latter issue, see *Jackson v Liverpool* [2011] EWCA Civ 1068. The ex-employer had provided a partial reference, in that it had not answered two of the questions posed by the prospective new employer. The ex-employer had a telephone conversation with the prospective new employer in which he explained that there were certain unresolved allegations concerning discrepancies in the ex-employee's record-keeping, but had made it clear that these were only allegations. Contrary to the finding of the first-instance judge, the Court of Appeal held that the ex-employer had not behaved unfairly or otherwise negligently.

In order to succeed in an action based on an allegedly negligent reference, a claimant will have to show first that the information contained in the reference is misleading, second, that it would be likely to have a material effect on a reasonable recipient and, third, that the defendant was negligent in compiling the reference. In *Bullimore v Pothecary Witham Weld Solicitors* (UKEAT/0189/10/JOJ) [2011] IRLR 18, an employer gave a former employee an unfairly adverse reference which led to the withdrawal of a subsequent offer of employment. The EAT held that the employee's loss was not too remote from the employer's actions, and the employee could recover for loss of earnings and injury to feelings. Compare this with *Brown v Baxter (T/A Careham Hall)* UKEAT/0354/09/SM (7 July 2010, unreported), where it was found that the employer would have given an unfavourable reference even if it had not dismissed the employee. The unfavourable reference therefore was not "a consequence" of the dismissal, and should not have been reflected in the damages awarded to the employee. The employee sought to rely on the "stigma damages" principle arising from *Chagger v Abbey National plc* [2009] EWCA Civ 1202, [2010] ICR 397, [2010] IRLR 47 (see CONTRACTS OF EMPLOYMENT (7)), but this was dismissed as irrelevant: the usual principles of causation applied.

The EAT has held that the implied term of trust and confidence in a contract of employment requires the employer to provide a reference that is 'fair and reasonable'. If the employer fails to do so, the employee may resign and claim constructive dismissal (see *TSB Bank plc v Harris* [2000] IRLR 157). However, that case was decided prior to *Kidd*, and *Bartholomew* was not referred to.

A former employee who is refused a reference or given a bad reference because he or she had made a complaint of discrimination or done some other protected act under the *Equality Act 2010* would be entitled to sue for victimisation provided that the claim arose out of the incidents of the employment relationship or was sufficiently proximate to the employment or that there was a substantive connection between the complaint and the employment. This entitlement was first recognised in the context of sex discrimination law by the decision of the European Court of Justice in *Coote v Granada Hospitality Ltd: C-185/97* [1999] ICR 100. It was there held that an employer who refused to provide a reference to an ex-employee on the grounds that the employee had brought legal proceedings to enforce the right to equal treatment of men and women would be liable for victimisation. At the time of this decision the position under domestic law was that the discrimination legislation only applied to events occurring during employment and not afterwards: *Adekeye v Post Office (No 2)* [1997] IRLR 105. The EAT has held that the *Sex Discrimination Act 1975* ('*SDA 1975*') can be construed consistently with this decision (*Coote v Granada Hospitality Ltd (No 2)* [1999] IRLR 452). More recently the House of Lords has overturned *Adekeye* and held that the protection afforded to employees by the discrimination legislation is not coterminous with the existence of a contractual relationship. Therefore claims may be brought by former employees so long as there is a substantive connection between the discriminatory conduct alleged and the employment relationship, whenever the discriminatory conduct arises: *Relaxion Group plc v Rhys-Harper* [2003] UKHL 33, [2003] 4 All ER 1113. See also *Metropolitan Police Service v Shoebridge* UKEAT/0234/03.

An employee who was refused a reference after employment had ended or who was provided with a poor reference because he had made a protected disclosure under *Part IVA* of the Employment Rights Act 1996 (see DISCLOSURE OF INFORMATION (9)) would be able to allege that that the failure to provide the reference to or the content of it involved the employee being subjected to a detriment on the ground that the employee had made a protected disclosure, contrary to *s 47B*: *Woodward v Abbey National plc* [2006] IRLR 677, CA.

38.4 References

McKie v Swindon College [2011] EWHC 469 (QB), [2011] IRLR 575 involved circumstances more unusual than standard reference scenarios. The ex-employer sent an email to the new employer, during the ex-employee's probation period with the latter, stating that it had concerns about the ex-employee (who had an unblemished personnel record) in terms of the safeguarding of children. The new employer dismissed the employee as a result. This email stemmed from concerns which had been raised by one of the ex-employee's former colleagues, but the email to the new employer appeared to go beyond what that colleague had alleged. The Court found the ex-employer to be liable for negligent misstatement: its email was fallacious, and it had behaved unfairly in the process it had followed in sending the email. It owed its ex-employee a duty of care, and the economic loss suffered was foreseeable. By application of *Caparo Industries Plc v Dickman* [1990] 2 AC 605, the ex-employer was liable in negligence.

38.5 To the recipient

The recipient of a negligent reference may also be able to sue the person giving the reference for any loss suffered. It is reasonably foreseeable that the recipient of a reference will act on its contents and if he relies on a reference which is inaccurate because it was carelessly drawn up and thereby suffers loss, the giver of the reference may be held liable to pay the recipient damages on account of his negligence (cf *Hedley Byrne & Co Ltd v Heller & Partners Ltd* [1964] AC 465).

There is no sure way of avoiding the possibility of liability for negligent mis-statements in references since the *Unfair Contract Terms Act 1977* ('*UCTA 1977*'). Disclaimers such as 'The above information is given in confidence and in good faith. No responsibility, however, can be accepted for any errors, omissions or inaccuracies in the information or for any loss or damage that may result from reliance being placed upon it' may have been effective to exclude liability before the *UCTA 1977* came into force, but now such a disclaimer will only be effective insofar as it 'satisfies the requirement of reasonableness' (*UCTA 1977, s 2(2)*). The 'explanatory provisions' of the *Act* state that such a notice of disclaimer will satisfy this requirement of reasonableness where it is 'fair and reasonable to allow reliance upon it, having regard to all the circumstances obtaining when the liability arose or (but for the notice) would have arisen' (*UCTA 1977, s 11(3)*). If the reference purports to give facts which are ordinarily within the knowledge of an employer, it is thought that liability cannot now be excluded for negligent mis-statement of those facts. If, however, it contains an opinion as to the employee's suitability for a certain post which he has not filled in the past, it may be considered reasonable to insert a disclaimer for such a statement of opinion.

38.6 Data Protection Act 1998

If information about an employee is stored on a computer, the provisions of the *Data Protection Act 1998* must be complied with (see **9.13** *et seq* DISCLOSURE OF INFORMATION).

38.7 LIABILITY OF PERSONS OTHER THAN THE EMPLOYER

It is frequently the case that employment will be dependent on a satisfactory medical report being presented to the prospective employer. In *Kapfunde v Abbey National plc and Daniel* [1998] IRLR 583, the claimant was refused employment on the basis of a medical report. She sought to sue the author of the report alleging that it was negligent. The Court of Appeal dismissed the claim holding that a medical practitioner who compiles a report about a prospective employee does not owe a duty of care to the prospective employee. There is insufficient proximity between the author of the report and the prospective employee. It may well be, however, that the medical practitioner owes a duty of care to the prospective employer.

38.8   REFERENCES AND EMPLOYMENT PROTECTION RIGHTS

Although employees do not have a statutory right to a reference, references may affect proceedings in employment tribunals. A good reference may be powerful evidence against an employer who tries to justify the dismissal of an employee on grounds of misconduct or incompetence. Similarly, a reference which is inconsistent with written reasons for a dismissal supplied to an employee may be persuasive in enabling the employee to show that those written reasons were inadequate or untrue, thus entitling him to an award under *ERA 1996, s 93* (see **46.15** TERMINATION OF EMPLOYMENT).

A reference may sometimes be used to compromise a claim for unfair dismissal. If a reference is given in such circumstances, care should be taken to ensure that the reference is accurate and complete and the compromise reached with the assistance of a conciliation officer (see **2.4** ADVISORY, CONCILIATION AND ARBITRATION SERVICE).

38.9   EMPLOYMENT CONDITIONAL UPON REFERENCES

Sometimes, a contract of employment may be offered 'subject to satisfactory references'. In *Wishart v National Association of Citizens' Advice Bureaux Ltd* [1990] ICR 794, the Court of Appeal was strongly of the opinion that such a provision was satisfied only if the references supplied were subjectively satisfactory to that particular employer. However, it recognised that it was arguable that the requirement was an objective one.

39 Restraint of Trade and Confidential Information

39.1 INTRODUCTION

Considerations of restraint of trade operate in employment law in two distinct ways: first, there is the common law doctrine of restraint of trade comprising a body of rules under which certain contractual restraints must be justified before the court will enforce them. Secondly, a court will have regard to the impact of restraints on trade in any form in situations where the common law doctrine does not apply, or cannot be applied in accordance with its rules, as a factor influencing its discretion to grant or withhold the remedy of an injunction and in framing the terms of any injunction granted. The latter operation of what may be called 'considerations' of restraint of trade is seen most clearly in so-called 'garden leave' and 'springboard' injunction cases. Confusion between restraint of trade as a narrow doctrine of the law of contract and as a factor in the exercise of judicial discretion as to whether or not to grant an injunction, has led to considerable confusion in the law and, on occasion, to judicial error: see *J A Mont (UK) Ltd v Mills* [1993] IRLR 172.

Obligations of confidentiality that arise in the employment situation are also apt to cause confusion and, again, a clear distinction must be drawn between those obligations which underpin, in part, the doctrine of restraint of trade and those which give rise to relief and remedies which lie outside that doctrine altogether.

It is impossible in a work of this nature to do more than briefly sketch the main principles of these large and partially interlocking fields of law which apply specifically to the employment relationship. Hence we do not deal in this chapter with restraint of trade principles as they apply to business sale agreements, shareholder agreements or partnerships, etc, even where there may be partial overlaps of principle. It should, however, be noted that the statutory regulation of competition in the United Kingdom has recently undergone major changes to bring it into line with European models: see *Competition Act 1998* and *Enterprise Act 2002*. These reforms affect the common law doctrine of restraint of trade and, in certain circumstances, displace it altogether: see *Days Medical Aids Ltd v Pihsiang Machinery Manufacturing Co Ltd* [2004] EWHC 44 (Comm), [2004] 1 All ER (Comm) 991. The domestic statutory controls, over restraints ancillary to mergers and acquisitions of businesses, however, apply to individuals only if they may be treated as 'undertakings', i.e. if they have a controlling interest in the business merged or acquired. The vast majority of employees will not, therefore, fall within the provisions of *Part I* of the *Competition Act 1998* or *Art 101* of the *Lisbon Treaty*. For this reason, we do not attempt a review of competition law in this chapter. However, although the principles of competition law do not apply directly to most employees, they may have an indirect impact in shaping public policy, from which the common law doctrine itself springs (see further below **39.5**).

Proceedings in relation to the enforcement or breach of covenants in restraint of trade must in almost all cases be brought in the ordinary courts, and not in the employment tribunals. This is because most disputes in relation to the enforcement or breach of such covenants will fall outside the jurisdiction of the employment tribunals, since any claim in respect of such a covenant will not (as a general rule) be one that 'arises or is outstanding' on the termination of the employee's employment so as to bring it within the scope of the *Employment Tribunals Extension of Jurisdiction (England and Wales) Order 1994*. (This Order extended the jurisdiction of the employment tribunals so as to encompass, for the first time, breach of contract claims by employees and, where the employee has brought such a claim, counterclaims for breach of contract by the employer: see *Peninsula Business Services Ltd v Sweeney* [2004] IRLR 49 and generally **7.22c** and **7.22d** CONTRACT OF EMPLOYMENT). Further, the employment tribunals' contractual jurisdiction (as set out in the *Extension of Jurisdiction Order*) only extends to the power to award damages for breach of contract: the employment tribunals have no power to issue injunctions, which is the usual remedy sought by the claimant in restraint of trade cases (see below **39.16**).

There have been a handful of cases in which the question of the enforceability of covenants in restraint of trade has been raised as part of a claim falling within the jurisdiction of the employment tribunals, for example where an employee's refusal to sign up to covenants in restraint of trade is relied on by an employer as a reason for dismissing an employee, or where sums deducted pursuant to a covenant in restraint of trade are claimed as an unlawful deduction from wages. However, the Court of Appeal has now confirmed that, in both those situations, the employment tribunal need not determine whether or not the covenant in question is reasonable and enforceable. Thus in *Willow Oak Developments Ltd (t/a Windsor Recruitment) v Silverwood* [2006] EWCA Civ 660, [2006] IRLR 607 the Court of Appeal confirmed previous authority to the effect that a refusal on the part of an employee to sign up to new terms and conditions of employment that included covenants in restraint of trade was capable (whether or not the restraints were reasonable) of being a potentially fair reason for dismissing an employee. However, the Court of Appeal observed that the reasonableness (or otherwise) of the restraints was a (non-determinative) factor which the employment tribunal could take into account when determining whether or not it was in fact fair to dismiss the employee for that reason under *ERA 1996, s 98(4)* (see generally **52.14** UNFAIR DISMISSAL – **II**). The Court of Appeal disapproved the earlier decision of the EAT in *Forshaw v Archcraft Ltd* [2006] ICR 60 in which it was held that, if the new term sought to be imposed by the employer was in fact an unreasonable restraint of trade, then an employee dismissed for failing to sign up to that term had been unfairly dismissed. As to unlawful deductions from wages claims under *s 23* of the *Employment Rights Act 1996*, the EAT in *Peninsula Business Services* (above) confirmed that deductions pursuant to clauses in restraint of trade are to be treated in the same way as deductions pursuant to any other clause in the employee's contract: provided the covenant is set out in writing, and the employee has agreed to it in writing, the employer will have a defence to any such claim in the employment tribunal. The employee's remedy in such circumstances lies in a claim for breach of contract in the ordinary courts: see generally PAY – I: PAYMENTS, PAY STATEMENTS AND MISCELLANEOUS STATUTORY PAY RIGHTS (32).

We propose to review first the law in relation to the common law doctrine of restraint of trade (below **39.2**), then to review confidential information (below **39.13**) and to consider restraint of trade as a discretionary element in granting injunctive relief outside of the narrow common-law doctrine of restraint of trade (including so-called 'garden leave' and 'springboard' injunctions) (below **39.14**, **39.15**). Finally, we consider procedural issues and remedies (below **39.16**).

39.2   THE COMMON LAW DOCTRINE OF RESTRAINT OF TRADE

Although of ancient origin the doctrine in its modern form may be traced to the speech of Lord McNaghten in *Nordenfelt v Maxim Nordenfelt Guns and Ammunition Co Ltd* [1894] AC 535, 565:

> 'All interference with individual liberty of action in trading, and all restraints of trade of themselves, if there is nothing more, are contrary to public policy, and therefore void. That is the general rule. But there are exceptions: restraints of trade and interference with individual liberty of action may be justified by the special circumstances of a particular case. It is a sufficient justification, and indeed it is the only justification, if the restriction is reasonable – reasonable, that is, in reference to the interests of the parties concerned and reasonable in reference to the interests of the public, so framed and so guarded as to afford adequate protection to the party in whose favour it is imposed, while at the same time it is in no way injurious to the public.'

It follows that in applying the common law doctrine of restraint of trade it is necessary to consider the following fundamental issues:

(1)   what restraints of trade are covered by the doctrine?

(2)   what are the legitimate interests of the parties?

(3)   is the restraint injurious to the public interest?

39.3   What restraints are covered?

A very large number of contracts or contractual provisions will impose some limits on a person's freedom to trade (for example, a contract to sell specific goods or a lease of a property prohibiting the use of the premises for business purposes). Such contracts or provisions are not subject to the restraint of trade doctrine: see *Esso Petroleum Co Ltd v Harper's Garage* [1968] AC 269.

Various tests have been propounded to identify restraints which do, or do not, fall within the doctrine. The best of these tests, it is submitted, is contained in the speech of Lord Pearce in the *Esso* case:

> 'The doctrine does not apply to ordinary commercial contracts for the regulation and promotion of trade during the existence of the contract, provided that any prevention of work outside the contract, viewed as a whole, is directed towards the absorption of the parties' services and not their sterilisation. Sole agencies are a normal and necessary incident of commerce and those who desire the benefits of a sole agency must deny themselves the opportunities of other agencies. So, too, in the case of a film star who may tie herself to a company in order to obtain from them the benefits of stardom   . . .   parties habitually fetter themselves to one another.
>
> When a contract only ties the parties during the continuance of the contract and the negative ties are only those which are incidental and normal to the positive commercial arrangements at which the contract aims, even though those ties exclude all dealing with others, there is no restraint of trade within the meaning of the doctrine and no question of reasonableness arises. If, however, the contract ties the trading activities of either party after its determination, it is a restraint of trade and the question of reasonableness arises. So, too, if *during* the contract one of the parties is too unilaterally fettered so that the contract loses its character of a contract for the regulation and promotion of trade and acquires the predominant character of a contract in restraint of trade. In that case   . . .   the question whether it is reasonable arises.'

Applying this to a contract of employment, it is clear that the doctrine will apply to restraints imposed on the employee's working activities or fields of work after the original contract has ended. It is also clear from that test, however, that the doctrine can apply to some employment contracts, or provisions within those contracts, intended to operate during the currency of the employment relationship. Thus extravagantly oppressive and one-sided employment contracts may be held unenforceable during their lifetime: see *Young v Timmins* (1831) 1 Cr & J 331. The doctrine may also apply where, for example, other contractual provisions may be imposed which have the substantive effect of restraining the freedom of the employee to move jobs (for example, provisions clawing back bonuses if an employee goes to work for a rival or depriving an employee of commission which he has earned during the currency of his employment if he leaves to work for a rival). Some cases have considered such clauses solely by reference to the common law penalty doctrine (eg *Imam-Sadeque v BlueBay Asset Management (Services) Ltd* [2012] EWHC 3511 (QB)). Where the restraint of trade doctrine has been relied upon, the courts have not been consistent in their treatment of these kinds of provisions. In *Sadler v Imperial Life*

Assurance Co of Canada Ltd [1988] IRLR 388, HC the doctrine was held to apply to a covenant depriving an employee of commission payable post termination of his employment if he went to work for a rival. The provision in question was held unenforceable and severed from the agreement, thereby entitling the employee to recover the commission payments (see also *Marshall v NM Financial Management Ltd* [1997] 1 WLR 1527, [1997] IRLR 449, CA). However, in *Peninsula Business Services Ltd v Sweeney* [2004] IRLR 49 the EAT held that a provision in an employee's contract denying him post-termination commission was not a restraint of trade since it did not impose any restraint on him as to whom he might work for or what he might do: it was merely an 'economic disincentive' to discourage the employee from leaving his employment. The EAT's decision in *Peninsula* seems far too restrictive in its refusal to apply the doctrine of restraint of trade to the provision in question. The doctrine is not based upon the form of the contractual restraint, but upon its substantive effect: 'whether a particular provision operates in restraint of trade is to be determined not by the form the stipulation wears but . . . by its effect in practice. . . . The clause in question here contains no direct covenant to abstain from any kind of competition or business, but the question to be answered is whether, in effect, it is likely to cause the employee to refuse business which otherwise he would take or, looking at it in another way, whether the existence of this provision would diminish his prospects of employment' (*per* Lord Wilberforce, *Stenhouse Australia Ltd v Phillips* [1974] AC 391, PC at 402F-H). In the *Stenhouse* case the clause held to be unenforceable as an unreasonable restraint of trade was a profit-sharing clause imposed on an employee of an insurance broker as part of a settlement agreement entered into on the termination of his employment. The clause provided that, in the event that any client of the employer within a period of five years from the date of termination of the employment placed any insurance business (of the type transacted by the employer) with the departing employee, the departing employee would be entitled to a one-half share of the commission received in respect of such transaction. See also **20:20** *London Ltd v Reilly* [2012] EWHC 1912 (Ch) where the judge refused to follow *Peninsula v Sweeney* (ibid).

It is of crucial importance to distinguish between post-termination restraints and garden leave provisions. An exclusive services provision in an employment contract operating during the currency of the employment relationship will not have the doctrine applied to it. Nonetheless, if, during the currency of the employment contract, the employer puts the employee on garden leave and seeks an injunction to prevent the employee, during that notice period, from working for a competitor, the court will pay heed to the restrictive effect of the exclusive services provision in determining whether to grant such an injunction and, if so, for what period. This is not the application of the doctrine of restraint of trade but the application of considerations of restraint of trade in the exercise of a judicial discretion: see *Symbian Ltd v Christensen* [2001] IRLR 77, *Provident Financial Group plc and Whitegates Estate Agency Ltd v Hayward* [1989] 3 All ER 298, [1989] ICR 160, CA and *Mont v Mills* (supra).

It is a cardinal principle of the application of the common law doctrine of restraint of trade that the court must determine the enforceability of the contract or contractual provision concerned as at the date the contract was entered into, not at the date when it comes to be enforced (see *Gledhow Autoparts Ltd v Delaney* [1965] 1 WLR 1366, *Home Counties Dairies Ltd v Skilton* [1970] 1 WLR 526, *Commercial Plastics Ltd v Vincent* [1965] 1 QB 623, *Allan Janes LLP v Balraj Johal* [2006] EWHC 286 (Ch), [2006] ICR 742 and *Patsystems Holdings Ltd v Neilly* [2012] EWHC 2609 (QB)). Thus if a restrictive covenant is adjudged to be invalid at the date it was entered into, it cannot be saved by a subsequent renegotiated contract of employment referring to an agreement or general acknowledgment by an employee that his previous terms 'remain unchanged' (*Patsystems*, ibid). It is accordingly apparent that the restraint of trade doctrine in its pure form may be readily applied to an employee's post-termination restraints, but cannot in its 'pure' form be applied to disputes which arise in relation to garden leave injunctions. In the case of exclusive service provisions in contracts of employment their reasonableness at the date the contract is entered into is obvious: they are there to provide the employer with the means of ensuring that the employee's skills and endeavours are fully absorbed. Thus they satisfy Lord Pearce's test at that stage. It is only when they are deployed during notice periods as the basis for seeking injunctive relief to enforce garden leave that they cease to have the character of a provision to absorb skills and endeavours and take on the character of a provision aimed at sterilising the employee.

It also follows from the aforementioned cardinal principle that in judging the reasonableness of contractual restraints the court cannot consider events occurring after the contract containing the restraints is entered into. However, when judging whether a covenant has been breached the court will, of course, look at the circumstances at the date of the alleged breach. A good illustration of the distinction between judging whether a covenant is valid and judging whether it is breached is furnished by *Phoenix Partners Group LLP v Asoyag (Maurice)* [2010] EWHC 846 (QB), [2010] IRLR 594. In that case (an interim injunction application) the judge held that it was likely that the restrictive covenants would, at trial, be held enforceable. However, those restrictive covenants prohibited the covenantor from joining a business "which competes with" the business of the covenantee and from soliciting or dealing with clients "in competition with" the business of the covenantee. At the date of the alleged breach, as the judge held, the covenantee had discontinued doing business of the particular kind covered by the covenants and, accordingly, the judge held that there was no breach of the covenant.

There is one area of potential difficulty in applying this rule as to the date when the court must consider the reasonableness of any covenant in restraint of trade, namely that caused by the effect of the *Transfer of Undertakings (Protection of Employment) Regulations 2006* ('the *2006 TUPE Regulations*', which replace the *1983 TUPE Regulations* with effect from 6 April 2006: see generally Transfer of Undertakings (50)). The effect of those *Regulations* is that, where there is a 'relevant transfer' of an undertaking or part of one, employees whose contracts would otherwise be terminated by that transfer are instead subject to a statutory novation of their existing employment contract so that the transferee company is substituted for the transferor company. *Regulation 4(1)* of the *TUPE Regulations* provides that, following a transfer, an employee's contract of employment 'shall have effect after the transfer as if originally made between the person so employed and the transferee'. If *reg 4(1)* were to be applied literally then it would have the effect of rendering certain restrictive covenants (which prohibit dealing with customers of a specified business) imposed by the specified business (the transferor) upon its employees nugatory if the transfer that takes place had the result of substituting in every respect (and at all material times) the transferee for the transferor. In *Morris Angel & Son Ltd v Hollande* [1993] IRLR 169 the court considered the effect of *reg 5(1)* of the *1983 TUPE Regulations* (now *reg 4(1)* of the *2006 TUPE Regulations*) on a restrictive covenant in the employee's contract of employment which prohibited him, for a period of one year after the contract came to an end, from seeking 'to procure orders from or do business with any person, firm or company who has, at any time during the one year immediately preceding the cesser done business with [Group Y]'. The business of Group Y was sold to X Ltd and on the date of sale the employee's contract of employment with Group Y was terminated. The employee sought to contend that the effect of the transfer was to substitute in the restrictive covenant for clients of Group Y the clients of X Ltd. Accordingly, the employee contended that he could not be in breach of the covenant by canvassing or soliciting persons who had been clients of group Y during the period one year prior to the termination of his contract because the effect of the old *reg 5(1)* was to alter the wording of the covenant 'clients of X Ltd' which, as a matter of fact, he had not solicited or dealt with after the termination of his employment. At first instance, it was held that the old *reg 5(1)* applied so that, although the transferee company could enforce the covenant, the customers with whom he was prohibited from doing business after termination were those of the transferee X Ltd. It followed that there was no breach of the covenant in question. On appeal, the Court of Appeal preferred a construction of the rules under which the transferee company was deemed to have been the owner of the transferor's business during the relevant 12-month period (i.e. the 12 months prior to the termination of the employment contract). Thus, the customers with whom the employee was prohibited from dealing under the covenants were those of the part of the business transferred (ie those of Group Y prior to the transfer). It followed that the employee was in breach and an interim injunction was ordered.

Any attempt to impose a new restrictive covenant upon employees following a TUPE transfer was, prior to 6 April 2006, almost bound to fail. Such variations to an employee's contract of employment were unenforceable under *reg 5(1)* of the *1983 TUPE Regulations* even if they formed part of a 'package' which was to the overall benefit of the employee (see *Credit Suisse First Boston (Europe) Ltd v Lister* [1998] IRLR 700). However, under the *2006 TUPE Regulations* variations to an employee's contract that are implemented for 'economic, technical or organisational' reasons entailing changes in the workforce will be valid even if the reason for the variation is connected to the transfer. So if in a particular case the reason for seeking to change the restrictive covenants is an 'ETO' reason, then such a variation will be valid. Under the *2006 TUPE Regulations* employees should be informed of the identity of the transferee employer prior to the transfer. If they are not, then their entitlement to object under *reg 4(7)* may be exercised after the transfer so that the transferee cannot enforce post-termination restrictive covenants in their contracts of employment (see *New ISG Ltd v Vernon* [2007] EWHC 2665 (Ch), [2008] ICR 319). See also Transfer of Undertakings (50).

39.4 The interests of the parties

In order to justify a contract or provision in restraint of trade it must be proved that it is reasonable in the interests of the parties. This does not mean that the provision in question must support the interests of both parties equally. Rather, it means: 'For a restraint to be reasonable in the interests of the parties it must afford *no more than* adequate protection of the party in whose favour it is imposed . . . though in one sense no doubt it is contrary to the interests of the covenantor to subject himself to any restraint, still it may be for his advantage to be able so to subject himself in cases where, if he could not do so, he would lose other advantages, such as . . . the possibility of obtaining employment or training under competent employers' (*Herbert Morris Ltd v Saxelby* [1916] 1 AC 688, 707 *per* Lord Parker). It is now firmly established that the burden of proof in relation to this first step in the justification process is on the party seeking to enforce that covenant: see *Mason v Provident Clothing and Supply Co Ltd* [1913] AC 724 *per* Viscount Haldane, LC at 733 and Lord Shaw at 741 and *Herbert Morris*, above, at 700, 707 and 715. This will normally, but not invariably, be the employer (see, for example, *Wyatt v Kreglinger and Fernau* [1933] 1 KB 793, where it was the employee who sought to enforce the covenant in question because that covenant was the sole consideration supporting the employee's pension entitlement).

The courts will not enforce any provision against mere competition (such covenants are generally referred to as 'covenants in gross'). It is of the essence that an employer demonstrates that he has a legitimate interest to protect. Preventing competition *per se* is not a legitimate interest. Covenants in restraint of trade are upheld not on the ground that the employee 'would, by reason of his employment or training, obtain the skill and knowledge necessary to equip him as a possible competitor in the trade, but that he might obtain such personal knowledge of and influence over the customers of his employer or such an acquaintance with his employer's trade secrets as would enable him, if competition were allowed, to take advantage of his employer's trade connection or utilise information confidentially obtained' (*per* Lord Parker in *Herbert Morris*, above, 709). This quotation from Lord Parker demonstrates that, historically, the courts had recognised two legitimate interests of the employer justifying the imposition of a reasonable restraint: (a) trade secrets (and confidential information); and, (b) customer connection.

The categories of legitimate interest that may be protected by an employer are not, however, confined to the two interests mentioned by Lord Parker. The modern approach to the identification of interests justifying provisions in restraint of trade is not based on a narrow categorisation: ' . . .   the employer's claim for protection must be based upon the identification of some advantage or asset inherent in the business which can properly be regarded as, in a general sense, his property and which it would be unjust to allow the employee to appropriate for his own purposes, even though he, the employee, may have contributed to its creation. For while it may be true that an employee is entitled and is to be encouraged to build up his own qualities of skill and experience, it is equally his duty to develop and improve his employer's business for the benefit of his employer. These two obligations interlock during his employment: after its termination they diverge and mark the boundary between what the employee may take with him and what he may legitimately be asked to leave behind to his employers' (per Lord Wilberforce *Stenhouse Australia Ltd v Phillips*, ibid at p 400). Thus, in recent years new interests of an employer have been identified by the courts as justifying the protection of provisions in restraint of trade. In *Office Angels Ltd v Rainer-Thomas* [1991] IRLR 214, CA the court recognised as a legitimate interest of an employment agency the pool of workers on the agency's books. In *Dawnay, Day & Co Ltd v de Braconier d'Alphen* [1997] IRLR 285, affd [1998] ICR 1068, CA the court recognised as a legitimate interest the stability of an employer's workforce, holding that a covenant imposed on an employee prohibiting him from soliciting his former colleagues to leave their employment was a reasonable restraint. Nevertheless, some caution needs to be exercised in framing contractual provisions in restraint of trade. Client connection is an important aspect of the goodwill of any business, but it is not the exclusive component of that goodwill. A competent and hard-working employee who does not have any dealings with clients may enhance the reputation of his employer's business, and the reputation of the business is part of its goodwill, but an employer cannot prohibit an employee from going to work for a competitor upon termination of his employment merely to protect the enhanced reputation of his business to which the employee has contributed. the employee is entitled to take with him his own skills and knowledge, even where those skills and knowledge have contributed to the reputation enjoyed by the employer (see *Countrywide Assured Financial Services Ltd v Smart* [2004] EWHC 1214 (Ch)).

Another interest that in practice one frequently sees employers seeking to protect are their suppliers. Thus one sees covenants aimed at prohibiting a former employee from dealing with suppliers of his former employer or, in extreme cases, from seeking to solicit or entice the supplier to cease to be a supplier of the former employer. The latter kind of covenant was considered in *Landmark Brickwork Ltd v Sutcliffe and ors* [2011] IRLR 976. In that case Slade J granted an interim injunction to enforce it, without giving reasons. However, while an employer is of course entitled to restrain an employee from inducing a supplier to break an existing contract with the employer (since that is in any event a tort to induce or procure the breach of a contract), it is hard to see what legitimate interest an employer has in preventing its employees from dealing with its suppliers generally. Such a covenant merely inhibits the suppliers' ability to trade and has no impact on the employer's business. The only situation in which an employer might have a legitimate interest in protecting its suppliers would be if the supplies in question were scarce so that if an employee took supplies from the supplier there would be insufficient to supply the employer. Even a covenant such as that considered in the *Landmark* case (ie prohibiting the employee from seeking to dissuade a supplier from continuing to supply the employer) might not be protecting a legitimate business interest if the supplies were readily obtainable elsewhere and the employee was not (in approaching the supplier) misusing the employer's confidential information.

Having identified a legitimate interest to protect, the contract or contractual provision in question must be no more than adequate to protect that interest. Clearly the reasonableness of the ambit or duration of any restraint is tied to the nature of the interest in question. If it is sought by an employer to protect his customer connection, that may be achieved by post-termination restraints which prohibit for a reasonable period of time the ex employee from soliciting or dealing with those customers with whom the employee had contact during the course of his employment. *Prima facie* there would be no justification for imposing on that employee a post-termination restraint which prohibited him from entering into employment with a competitor. However, if an employer wishes to protect trade secrets or confidential information he may be justified in imposing a post-termination restraint prohibiting the employee from joining a competitor for a reasonable period of time. It is dangerous for an employer to seek too wide a protection for a limited interest because a court is entitled to look at the nature of the restraints imposed with a view to determining whether a lesser restraint would have been adequate to protect the employer's interest: see *Office Angels*, above. We return to the various forms of restraint and issues of reasonableness in more detail below.

Difficulties can arise in relation to corporate groups. Sometimes the employer company within the group will be a mere holding company which does not itself conduct any business. In such an instance, provided that the group is vertically aligned, the court will readily hold that the holding company has a legitimate interest to protect arising from the business conducted by its subsidiaries and can therefore enforce the covenant if valid (see *Stenhouse v Phillips*, ibid and *Beckett Investment Management Group Ltd v Hall* [2007] EWCA Civ 613, [2007] ICR 1539). In such cases the parent or holding company is treated as conducting its business through the agency of its subsidiaries. However, in relation to horizontally organised groups, such an analysis is not possible (see *Henry Leetham & Sons Ltd v Johnstone-White* [1907] 1 Ch 322). In light of the fact that many persons employed within corporate groups are employed by a service company, close attention should be paid to the drafting of any restrictive covenants in employment contracts entered into by the service company to ensure that they properly embrace the legitimate interests of the subsidiaries for whom the employees will in fact be working.

Another case on restructuring of a business arose in *Towry EJ Ltd v Barry William Prosser Bennett and ors* [2012] EWHC 224 (QB). In that case Company A purchased shares of Company B. A number of employees then left. Company B was restructured and ceased to have any employees. It then commenced proceedings against the departed employees seeking to enforce post-termination restrictive covenants, both for the period whilst it was still in business and also for a period after that. Counsel for the employees submitted that there is a free-standing principle that a covenantee cannot enforce a covenant if he no longer has a legitimate business interest to protect. There is some force in that submission since the doctrine of restraint of trade is one founded in public policy (see above **39.2**) and it is hard to see why as a matter of public policy a covenant in restraint of trade should be enforceable in the absence of a protectable legitimate interest. At least, where an employer is no longer trading it should be the case that neither interim nor final injunctions will be granted since if the employer is not trading it can be suffering no more than nominal damage. However, in *Towry* Cox J held that the covenant was enforceable and that there was no free-standing principle that a restrictive covenant only remained enforceable for as long as the employer continued to have a legitimate business interest to protect. However, that case concerned only claims for breach of contract and inducement (which failed on the facts) and there was no claim for an injunction. (Cf *Phoenix Partners Group LLP v Asoyag* [2010] IRLR 594 for a case in which a post-termination covenant was not enforceable where an employer had ceased to do business because it was framed in terms preventing the employee from competing; since the employer had ceased to do business, the employee was not competing; see also *BFCA Ltd v Butt* (8 February 2013, unreported), QBD.

It is important to note that an interest of an employer in his customer connection can be protected even if the employee is not moving to a competitor business. Recent cases such as *Caterpillar Logistics Services (UK) Ltd v Paul Huesca de Crean* [2012] EWCA Civ 156, *[2012] ICR 981* and *Generics (UK) Ltd v Yeda Research and Development Co Ltd and anor* [2012] EWCA Civ 726, [2012] CP Rep 39 support, in principle, the protection of customer connection by prohibiting employees on reasonable terms from going to work with a customer. Such covenants are important in the area of service industries where employees are seconded to, or spend substantial periods of time, working for, or within the premises of, clients and can therefore establish strong relationships with those clients who may choose to poach those employees to save themselves the costs of paying the employer's fees for providing services through those employees. It may also be that these kind of 'customer' covenants can be justified on the basis of confidential information (although it must be recognised that there will be a substantial overlap, or sharing, of information between the customer and employer in these kinds of cases).

39.5   The public interest

Much confusion has arisen about the second step in the justification process enunciated by Lord McNaghten in the *Nordenfelt* case (see above, **39.2**). Problems arise for two reasons: first, the doctrine of restraint of trade is a creation of public policy which collides head on with another public policy, namely the sanctity of contract; secondly, in some cases (particularly those decided in the early part of the 20th century) judges tend to use the expressions 'public policy' and 'public interest' interchangeably (see for example Cozens-Hardy MR in *Sir WC Leng & Co Ltd v Andrews* [1909] 1 Ch 763). This confusion has led in more recent times to judicial debate about whether the doctrine of restraint of trade has been properly applied in the past in distinguishing between the private interest of the parties and public policy in the sense of public interest (see, for example, *per* Lord Reid in the *Esso Petroleum* case (above, at p 300E)). It is submitted that the true analysis of the doctrine is as follows:

(a)   It is contrary to public policy for parties to a contract to enter into restraints which go beyond the reasonable protection of legitimate private interests (the first limb of Lord McNaghten's test).

(b)   It is also contrary to public policy for parties to a contract to enter into restraints which are no more than adequate to protect a private legitimate interest recognised by the law, if those restraints are contrary to the public interest (the second limb of Lord McNaghten's test).

(c)   It follows that, in theory at least, a covenant which satisfies public policy to the extent that it is no more than adequate to protect a private legitimate interest may fail to satisfy public policy because it is not in the public interest.

Unfortunately, it is not possible to identify any cases in the employment field which clearly illustrate proposition (c). In a number of cases, eg *Sir WC Leng* (above), *Herbert Morris v Saxelby* (above), *Strange (SW) Ltd v Mann* [1965] 1 WLR 629, *Countrywide Assured Financial Services Ltd v Smart* (above) and *Commercial Plastics Ltd v Vincent* [1965] 1 QB 623, the courts have held covenants to be against 'public policy' (and sometimes against the 'public interest') where, it is submitted, the real basis for the decisions in those cases is that there is no legitimate interest of the covenantee to protect or, alternatively, that the restraints go beyond what is reasonable to protect that interest. This is against public policy in the sense set out in (a) above, but is not illustrative of the principle in (c) above. (The only exception in these cases would appear to be the, (perhaps) *obiter*, statement of Farwell LJ in the *Sir WC Leng* case above at p 334.)

In a number of cases the public interest (as distinct from public policy) has been raised as a discrete ground of attack on contractual restrictions, but with a marked lack of success. Although Lord Denning MR in *Oswald Hickson Collier & Co v Carter-Ruck* [1984] AC 720n appeared to hold that it was contrary to 'public policy' that a fiduciary (a solicitor) should be precluded by a restrictive covenant from acting for a client who wanted him to act, that decision was swiftly departed from: see *Edwards v Worboys* [1984] AC 724n; *Bridge v Deacons* [1984] AC 705 and *Allan Janes LLP v Balraj Johal* [2006] EWHC 286 (Ch), [2006] ICR 742. See also, in relation to the medical profession, *Kerr v Morris* [1987] Ch 90, [1986] 3 All ER 217.

Probably the real reason why issues of public interest do not generally arise for decision, at least in employment cases, is because restraints which customarily appear in employment contracts normally have no impact on the public at large and hence the public interest. Moreover the onus of proving that a restraint is injurious to the public interest is upon the person (normally the employee) who is making that allegation. The burden is a heavy one: *A-G Commonwealth of Australia v Adelaide Steamship Co Ltd* [1913] AC 781 at 797 *per* Lord Parker. It is, however, submitted that one area in which the issue of public interest is of great significance in the employment field is where an employee challenges an indirect restraint upon his freedom. These kind of restraints arise where the employee has no direct restraint imposed upon him in his contract of employment but nonetheless is fettered by contractual restraints which his employer has entered into with other parties. In these cases the private interests of the parties are not in issue because the parties are not challenging the enforceability of the restraints: a third party (the employee) is challenging the restraints in so far as they affect him and not the parties to the contract. (See *Eastham v Newcastle United Football Club Ltd* [1964] Ch 413 and *Greig v Insole* [1978] 3 All ER 449 and compare *Kores Manufacturing Co Ltd v Kolok Manufacturing Co Ltd* [1957] 3 All ER 158 which involved an agreement between two employers not to employ each other's employees for a period of five years after their leaving the employment of the respective parties. In fact, however, in that case, the challenge to the agreement was not made by an employee but by one of the parties. Nonetheless, the Court of Appeal opined, *obiter*, that such an agreement could not be justified under the restraint of trade doctrine because of its indirect effect upon employees.)

It was suggested by Lord Hodson in the *Esso* case that issues of the burden of proof in relation to the interests of the parties and the public interest will seldom arise because, once the agreement is before the court, it is open to the scrutiny of the court in all its surrounding circumstances 'as a question of law': *Esso*, above, 319. It is submitted that this is not right. In the employment situation the employer must (if he seeks to enforce a restraint) establish that the covenant is in the interests of the parties in the narrow sense required by the doctrine. If the employee wishes to challenge the restraint on the ground that it is injurious to the public interest he cannot rely on the employer to furnish the court with the evidence required to prove injury to the public: the onus is on him to do that. The evidence which would require the court to consider the impact of a restraint upon a particular market is likely to be voluminous and to require expert opinion. Most employees would lack the financial means to undertake the provision to the court of that kind of evidence themselves. It is therefore extremely improbable that a court will have furnished to it in an employment case all the evidence that is required to deal properly with the issue of the public interest. It may be, however, that restraint of trade law is entering into a new era where issues of public interest will become more prominent. In the case of *Dranez Anstalt v Hayek (Zamir)* [2002] EWCA Civ 1729, [2003] 1 BCLC 278 restrictive covenants entered into by the inventor of a new ventilator for use in hospitals were held to constitute unreasonable restraints of trade by the Court of Appeal amongst other grounds on the basis that they offended against the public interest in restricting the inventor from making further developments which would be of great benefit to the public. There are, too, the developments in competition law to which reference has already been made (see above **39.1**). Competition law will not normally have any relevance to employees as they are not 'undertakings' for the purposes of competition law. However, the European Commission has issued guidance in Commission Notice [2005] OJ C-56/24 as to its position in relation to ancillary restraints taken upon the merger or acquisition of a business as follows: "*Non-competition clauses are justified for periods of up to three years, when the transfer of the undertaking includes the transfer of customer loyalty in the form of both goodwill and know-how. When only goodwill is included, they are justified for up to two years.*" This Guidance was adopted by the OFT in its previous Mergers Assessment Guidance, but the most recent joint OFT

/ Competition Commission guidance does not refer to this. Nonetheless, it is possible that these periods may be taken as a 'benchmark' for public policy in cases involving the common law of restraint of trade.

39.6 Judging the reasonableness of restraints

Construction of covenants in restraint of trade

The principles which a court should apply to the construction of covenants in restraint of trade do not materially differ from the principles applicable to the construction of any other written terms. Those principles are derived from the speech of Lord Hoffmann in *Investors Compensation Scheme v West Bromwich Building Society* [1998] 1 WLR 896 at 912H–913E (see *Beckett Investment Management Group Ltd v Hall*, ibid). The approach of the Court is exemplified in the case of *Clarke v Newland* [1991] 1 All ER 397. In that case, the Court concluded that the following approach should be adopted. First, the court should consider the construction of the term in question without having regard to the issue of validity or invalidity of the covenant, ie the court must decide what the contractual provision means before it decides whether the provision is reasonable or not. Second, the court must have regard to the object of such restraints, namely the protection of one of the parties against trade rivalry. Finally, the court must construe the provision in context, that is to say, having regard to the factual matrix at the date when the contract was made. By following this approach, a court ought to avoid the worst excesses of an over-literal construction or of an over-purposive approach. The vice inherent in the over-literal construction of a covenant in restraint of trade is that the court ignores the intent of the parties and construes the covenant so that it extends to situations not contemplated by the parties:

> 'Another matter which requires attention is whether a restriction on trade must be treated as wholly void because it is so worded as to cover cases which may possibly arise, and to which it cannot be reasonably applied . . . Agreements in restraint of trade, like other agreements, must be construed with reference to the object sought to be obtained by them. In cases such as the one before us, the object is the protection of one of the parties against rivalry in trade. Such agreements cannot be properly held to apply to cases which, although covered by the words of the agreement, cannot reasonably be supposed ever to have been contemplated by the parties, and which on a rational view of the agreement are excluded from its operation by falling, in truth, outside and not within its real scope.'

Haynes v Doman [1899] 2 Ch 13, CA, *per* Lindley LJ at 24–25.

In this respect much criticism has been levelled at the decision in *Commercial Plastics v Vincent* [1965] 1 QB 623. A purposive approach to construction is well illustrated by the following cases. In *Moenich v Fenestre* (1882) 67 LT 602 the expression 'any trade or business' in a restrictive covenant was held to mean, contextually, 'any trade or business as commission merchant'. In *G W Plowman & Son Ltd v Ash* [1964] 1 WLR 568 a covenant requiring an employee after termination of the employment 'not [to] canvass or solicit for himself or any other person . . . any farmer or market gardener who shall . . . have been a customer of the employers' was construed by the court as meaning, in the context of the employment agreement read as a whole, 'not to canvass or solicit with respect to the goods which the employee dealt with during his employment'. In *Home Counties Dairies Ltd v Skilton* [1970] 1 WLR 526 the words 'dairy produce' were construed by the court as being limited to only that sort of dairy produce with which the employee had been concerned whilst in employment. (See also *Hollis & Co v Stocks* [2000] IRLR 712.) In *TFS Derivatives Ltd v Morgan* [2004] EWHC 3181 (QB), [2005] IRLR 246 'business' was held to refer to a particular business activity of the investment company in question, and not to the whole of the 'business entity' that was the company: see also *Dyson Technology Ltd v Strutt* [2005] EWHC 2814 (Ch), [2005] All ER (D) 355 (Nov), but compare the approach taken in *Wiggle Ltd v Burge* which appears to be out of line with these authorities (9 May 2012, QB, unreported).

However, the Court can be guilty of, in effect, re-writing a covenant by an over-purposive approach (see *Littlewoods Organisation Ltd v Harris* [1977] 1 WLR 1472, CA). The court ought not to be over indulgent when faced with ill-drafted and ambiguous provisions in restraint of trade. In *J A Mont (UK) Ltd v Mills* [1993] IRLR 172, CA a sales and marketing director of a paper mill entered into a severance agreement with his employer to terminate his employment. Under this agreement the employee received one year's remuneration although he was not required to work for the employer during that period. The severance agreement contained the following restraint: 'This total payment is made on condition that you do not join another company in the tissue industry within one year of leaving our employment'. The Court of Appeal held that the wording of the covenant was too wide because it operated worldwide and restrained the defendant from working in any capacity whatsoever in any sector of the tissue industry. The employer argued that the court should apply a purposive construction to the covenant to cut down its ambit. The Court of Appeal refused to do so, holding that it was clear that the employer had made no attempt whatever 'to formulate the covenant so as to focus upon the particular restraint necessary to guard against [the employee's] possible misuse of confidential information, the only legitimate target for imposing any restraint on his future employment'. The Court of Appeal relied heavily on the consideration that if covenants, *ex facie* too wide, could always be 'rescued' by the court implying restrictions to the restraint in order to render it enforceable then employees would be trapped into accepting excessive restraints or facing expensive litigation. This vice has long been recognised by the courts:

> 'It would in my opinion be *pessimi exempli* if, when an employer had exacted a covenant deliberately framed in unreasonably wide terms, the courts were to come to his assistance and, by applying their ingenuity and knowledge of the law, carve out of this void covenant the maximum of what he might validly have required. It must be remembered that the real sanction at the back of these covenants is the terror and expense of litigation, in which the servant is usually at a great disadvantage, in view of the longer purse of his master. It is sad to think that in this present case this appellant, whose employment is a comparatively humble one, should have had to go through four courts before he could free himself from such unreasonable restraints as this covenant imposes, and the hardship imposed by the exaction of unreasonable covenants by employers would be greatly increased if they could continue the practice with the expectation that, having exposed the servant to the anxiety and expense of litigation, the Court would in the end enable them to obtain everything which they could have obtained by acting reasonably.'

(*Mason v Provident Clothing and Supply Co Ltd* [1913] AC 724, *per* Lord Moulton at 745.)

Accordingly, in construing provisions in restraint of trade the courts must establish a balance between extreme literalism and extreme liberalism. However, the approach to construction enunciated in *Clark v Newland* leads to one difficulty. It is a principle of contractual construction that in resolving ambiguities a court must strive to render the contractual term in question legal rather than illegal. Faced with an ambiguity which on one construction would render it too wide to be enforceable under the restraint of trade doctrine (thereby rendering the contractual provision 'illegal') and an alternative construction which would render the provision of narrower impact (and therefore legal), the court must choose the latter. It is not clear how, if the court is not permitted to have regard to the consequences of its construction exercise, it is able at the same time to comply with this principle (see *Mills v Dunham* [1891] 1 Ch 576). This principle has been confirmed in more recent cases where the courts have accepted that if, having examined the restrictive covenant in the context of the relevant factual matrix, there remains an element of ambiguity, the court should adopt the construction that would render the covenant lawful under the restraint of trade doctrine: see *Turner v Commonwealth and British Minerals Ltd* [2000] IRLR 114 at para 14 *per* Waller LJ and *TFS Derivatives Ltd v Morgan* [2004] EWHC 3181 (QB), [2005] IRLR 246 at para 43 *per* Cox J.

39.7 *Severance*

An English court is not permitted to uphold a covenant in restraint of trade by reducing its ambit or duration for that is to impose a new bargain upon the parties: see *J A Mont (UK) Ltd v Mills* (supra) and *Provident Financial Group plc and Whitegates Estate Agency Ltd v Hayward* (supra). (In many foreign jurisdictions courts do have this power.) Under English law, the covenant either satisfies the test of reasonableness as drawn and properly construed or it does not. Any provision in a contract (and one frequently sees them) stating that the covenants in question 'if held to be unenforceable, but would be enforceable if the ambit or duration of them were reduced, may be reduced accordingly' are of no effect and probably constitute an unlawful attempt to oust the jurisdiction of the court (see *Living Design (Home Improvements) Ltd v Davidson* [1994] IRLR 69). Moreover, a covenant imposing restraints of trade: 'so far as the law would allow' will be held too vague to be enforceable (see *Davies v Davies* (1887) 36 Ch D 359, CA. In the recent case of *Tullett Prebon plc v BGC Brokers LP* [2010] EWHC 484 (QB), [2010] IRLR 648 the learned judge at trial (point not considered on appeal: [2011] EWCA Civ 131, [2011] IRLR 420) appeared to overlook this fundamental principle and we deal further with this error below at **39.14**.

Nonetheless, the English court does have the power of severance. That is to say, to sever the whole or parts of contractual provisions too wide to be enforceable leaving in place those parts which the court considers reasonable. A contractual provision imposing a restraint of trade may be in simple or compound form. Very frequently seen in employment contracts are covenants which proscribe a number of separate activities thus: '[the employee] shall not, for a period of twelve months after termination of this contract, solicit, or canvas, or entice away, or deal with any client of the employer' (or words to that effect). A court may take the view that in the circumstances of any particular case it would be reasonable for an employer to protect himself against solicitation of his clients, but that, for example, it is unreasonable for the employer to require protection against the employee dealing with his clients. The common law, as part of the exercise of construction of a provision in restraint of trade, permits the court to uphold part of the restrictions imposed whilst holding invalid other restrictions in such composite clauses. The process by which the court does this is colloquially referred to as 'blue-pencilling' in respect of those parts of a covenant struck out as unreasonable. The fundamental condition which must be satisfied in order for the court to be able to blue-pencil any part of a provision which it considers to be an unreasonable restraint is that, as a matter of construction, the severed part is independent of the other parts of the provision in question. It is not enough that a provision or part of a provision can be severed without injury to the language or sense of the remainder: see *Attwood v Lamont* [1920] 3 KB 571 *per* Younger LJ at 593: 'The doctrine of severance has not, I think, gone further than to make it permissible in a case where the covenant is not really a single covenant but is in effect a combination of several distinct covenants. In that case, and where the severance can be carried out without the addition or alteration of a word, it is permissible. But in that case only.' [emphasis added]. See also *per* Lord Sterndale MR at 577. In this respect *Atwood* remains good law, but one feature of that decision, namely that in employment cases the court retained a discretion, where the conditions of severance were otherwise met, whether in fact to sever a covenant or part thereof has been overruled (see *T Lucas & Co v Mitchell* [1974] Ch 129, CA). Moreover, in *Mason v Provident Clothing and Supply Co Ltd* [1913] AC 724 at 745 Lord Moulton opined that in employment cases severance was possible only if covenants or parts thereof, which were to be severed, were trivial or merely technical. That qualification similarly did not survive the *Lucas* decision.

In *Sadler v Imperial Life Assurance Co. of Canada Ltd* [1988] IRLR 388 the judge adopted a three-fold test for the severance of restrictive covenants in employment contracts:

(a)   the court must be able to excise one or more of these independent restraints without having to add words to the agreement, or modify the wording of what remains;

(b)   there must remain adequate consideration to support that or those part(s) of the covenant which remain after the blue-pencilling of the unreasonable parts;

(c)   the removal of the unenforceable provision does not so change the character of the contract that it becomes 'not the sort of contract that the parties entered into at all'.

Since the *Sadler* decision, at least one judge in *Marshall v NM Financial Management Ltd* [1997] 1 WLR 1527, [1995] ICR 1042 appears to have taken the *Sadler* test as abrogating the need to embark upon the first and fundamental step of determining whether a covenant is a single covenant or a combination of several distinct covenants. The Court of Appeal reviewed the principles of severance in *Beckett Investment Management Group Ltd v Hall* (ibid). There, Kay LJ (with whom the other members of the court agreed) held the *Sadler* threefold test to be 'a useful way of approaching these cases and should be adopted' (ibid, para 43). It is clear, however, from the rest of his judgment that he was not in any way intending to remove the necessity for the first fundamental step identified in *Attwood* (above). However, in *Advantage Business Systems Ltd v Hopley (James)* [2007] EWHC 1783 (QB), [2007] All ER (D) 399 (Jul) the judge concluded that Kay LJ *was* abandoning the first step identified in *Attwood*. It is respectfully submitted that the correct approach towards the application of the three-fold test is exemplified in the judgment of Field J in *Duarte v Black and Decker Corpn* [2007] EWHC 2720 (QB), [2008] 1 All ER (Comm) 401. Having reviewed the authorities set out above, Field J concluded (at para 114): 'In my judgment, the non-compete covenant is not in effect a combination of several distinct covenants but is really a single covenant. To remove any or some of the corporate groups listed in Schedule A [to the covenant in question] would be to change the character of the contract so it becomes not the sort of contract that the parties entered into at all. Accordingly, it is not permissible to sever out any of the Schedule A corporate groups, particularly to the extent of just leaving [one nominated competitor].' In short, it is submitted the fundamental first step required by the *Attwood* decision remains part of the three-fold test advanced in *Sadler* and approved by the Court of Appeal in the *Beckett* decision. This was the approach taken by the Court in *Francotype-Postalia Ltd v Whitehead* [2011] EWHC 367 (Ch).

It follows from this approach to severance that if the entire consideration to support a covenant (for example, to pay to a retiring employee a pension) is constituted by an unenforceable obligation in restraint of trade then the obligation to pay the pension is likewise unenforceable. The blue-pencilling of the one obligation not to compete with the employer results in the disappearance of the obligation to pay the pension: see *Wyatt v Kreglinger* [1933] 1 KB 793 and *cf Marshall v N M Financial Management Ltd* (above). (In the latter case the Court of Appeal held that the obligation to pay monies was sufficiently supported by other consideration to enable to the court to strike out the offending obligation in restraint of trade whilst preserving the obligation to pay the employee the monies in question.) The draughtsman of restrictive covenants must exercise some caution. The mere insertion of the word 'or' may not be sufficient to render one part of the covenant in restraint of trade disjunctive or 'independent' of another part: see, for example, *British Reinforced Concrete Engineering Co Ltd v Schelff* [1921] 2 Ch 563, Ch D (though note that *British Reinforced Concrete* was a case of a business sale agreement restraint) and *Scully UK Ltd v Lee* [1998] IRLR 259, CA. In the *Marshall* case (ibid), the judge added to the threefold test a fourth test: namely that the severance exercise 'should be in accordance with public policy'. What this is intended to mean, far less add, is obscure. This fourth test does not seem to have been applied in any other case.

39.8   *Testing reasonableness*

General approach

The court's approach to enforcement of restraints in employment contracts is far less sympathetic than its approach to restraints arising in commercial transactions such as business sale agreements, agency agreements, distribution agreements and agreements between equity partners (see *Herbert Morris Ltd v Saxelby* [1916] 1 AC 688, *Systems Reliability Holdings plc v Smith* [1990] IRLR 377 and *Allied Dunbar (Frank Weisinger) Ltd v Weisinger* [1988] IRLR 60). It is frequently suggested that the reason for the closer scrutiny paid by English courts to employment contracts than to other forms of commercial bargain is because employees are by and large not in a strong bargaining position when compared to employers. Whereas this may no doubt have some veracity, it is not a full explanation of the rigour with which the court approaches covenants in restraint of trade in employment contracts. Indeed, the courts recognise that not all employees are in an unequal bargaining position: 'Managing directors can look after themselves' (see *M and S Drapers (a firm) v Reynolds* [1957] 1 WLR 9, CA; see also *Hanover Insurance Brokers Ltd v Schapiro* [1994] IRLR 82 and *TFS Derivatives*, above). The principal reason why courts are more generous towards restraints between equity partners, for example, is because those restraints are <u>mutual</u> and because a partnership resembles (to some extent, at least) a 'business' sale agreement: see *Bridge v Deacons* [1984] AC 705, PC. A business sale agreement creates intrinsically different interests for protection than those that exist between employer and employee (see *Herbert Morris v Saxelby*). In addition, the vendor of the business will receive an enhanced consideration if he is prepared to undertake not to compete with the business he sells. In employment contracts there is no mutuality of obligation: an employer does not undertake not to compete with the employee if the employee were to set up a rival business on the termination of his employment. Neither is there any enhancement, necessarily, of the remuneration that an employee receives during the currency of the employment contract because he assumes obligations under a restrictive covenant operative only post termination of his employment. In this latter respect, an employer who pays a sum of money to an employee in consideration of the employee accepting provisions in restraint of trade as part of a settlement for the termination of his contract of employment, is not absolved from having to justify the restraints imposed on the employee under the ordinary principles of the restraint of trade doctrine (see *J A Mont (UK) Ltd v Mills* [1993] IRLR 172 and *Turner v Commonwealth and British Minerals Ltd* [2000] IRLR 114). In *Turner* the Court stated that regard may be had to the additional payment made to the employee on settlement as one factor in considering reasonableness. (See also *Thurstan Hoskin & Partners v Jewill Hill & Bennett* [2002] EWCA Civ 249, [2002] All ER (D) 62 (Feb).) It is submitted that if this means that the more money that is paid to an employee the greater the restraint that may be imposed, then this is wrong in principle. Restraints of trade cannot be purchased outright (see *J A Mont (UK) Ltd v Mills*, ibid).

Having ascertained what the proper meaning of the provisions imposing restraints may be (see above **39.6**) the court must next determine whether on that proper construction the covenants are reasonable in the sense of being no more than adequate to protect that legitimate interest.

Covenants may be unreasonable in the following respects:

(a)   the nature of the restraint;

(b)   the ambit of the restraint;

(c)   the duration of the restraint.

Nature of the restraint

The approach of the court is first to identify the legitimate interest or interests which the employer is seeking to protect by the restraints in question. Restraints can take a wide variety of forms, but broadly fall into two categories:

39.8 Restraint of Trade and Confidential Information

(a)   Restraints against conducting or being engaged or interested in a competing business (whether specifically identified or not in the covenant) for a period of time; and

(b)   Restraints which prohibit a limited kind of competitive activity, such as soliciting or dealing with customers.

The former category of restraint (a non-compete restraint) may be in a wide form prohibiting an employee from joining a competitor's business regardless of the field of that business in which he is proposing to work, or it may be limited to prohibiting him working for a competitor in the particular field in which the employee has been engaged by the former employer imposing the covenant. The more limited form of non-compete provision is now more frequently encountered in modern contracts of employment, but the wider form of restraint is sometimes still upheld by the courts: see *Norbrook Laboratories (GB) Ltd v Adair* [2008] EWHC 978 (QB), [2008] IRLR 878.

The court, having identified an interest of the employer justifying protection, is entitled to look at the nature of the restraint deployed to determine whether the legitimate interest could have been protected by a narrower restraint than, for example, either a wide or narrow non-compete provision (see *Office Angels Ltd v Rainer-Thomas* [1991] IRLR 214, CA). In identifying the legitimate interest to be protected the court is entitled to look at any express words in the contract which may identify that interest (*Office Angels*). If the employer has categorically identified the interest he seeks to protect (for example, client connection) he cannot, when the covenant comes to be tested in court, claim that the restraint in fact is aimed at protecting a different interest (for example, confidential information: see *Office Angels*). This, however, is a matter of construction: see *Patsystems Holdings Ltd v Neilly* [2012] EWHC 2609 (QB). Again, if the interest to be protected is, for example, client connection or the stability of the employer's workforce a covenant in the nature of a non-compete provision risks being held to be disproportionate for such interests may be protected by a covenant directed at the prohibition of specific competitive acts, such as the soliciting or dealing with customers, or the soliciting or enticing away of staff. It follows that the nature of the interest to be protected will dictate the nature of the restraint which should be employed by the employer to protect the interest. Non-compete provisions are generally only justifiable if the nature of the interest to be protected is trade secrets and confidential information: see *per* Simon Brown LJ in *J A Mont (UK) Ltd v Mills* [1993] IRLR 172. This is because it is notoriously difficult to police covenants which merely restrain the disclosure or use of confidential information. Moreover, it is notoriously difficult for a covenantee to know what information is truly confidential and which he cannot use or disclose and what information is merely part of his stock of accumulated knowledge and experience which he is entitled to disclose or use. Accordingly an employer may protect his trade secrets and confidential information by imposing on an employee a covenant restraining that employee for a reasonable period of time from joining a competitor, at least in the same field of activity in which he was engaged for the former employer (see *Littlewoods Organisation Ltd v Harris* [1977] 1 WLR 1472, CA; *Printers & Finishers Ltd v Holloway* [1964] 3 All ER 54n, [1965] RPC 239; and *David (Lawrence) Ltd v Ashton* [1991] 1 All ER 385, [1989] ICR 123, CA). Nevertheless, caution must be exercised in drafting non-compete restraints so as to ensure that the definition of 'competitor' is not too widely drawn, thereby rendering the covenant unenforceable: see *Norbrook Laboratories*, ibid.

In some cases the court has upheld non-compete provisions where the interest to be protected is client connection. The basis for this is that in some instances it may be impossible, or, at least, very difficult for the employer to 'police' a more limited covenant restraining soliciting or dealing with clients (see *Scorer v Seymour-Johns* [1966] 1 WLR 1419, *per* Salmon LJ, p 1427C-E, *Turner v Commonwealth and British Minerals Ltd* [2000] IRLR 114, *per* Waller LJ at para 18 and *TFS Derivatives Ltd v Morgan* [2004] EWHC 3181 (QB), [2005] IRLR 246).

It is, however, submitted that the courts should be suspicious of assertions that it is difficult to police non-solicitation and non-dealing covenants. If it is difficult to do so, it is likely to be because there is no firm connection between the client and the employer in the first place, and the justification sometimes advanced for area non-compete restraints (namely that they are intended to protect what is in effect passing trade) is surely, for that reason, wrong in principle. If trade is passing it is difficult to see how the employee can gain any material knowledge of, or influence over, such clientele. In the *TFS Derivatives* case the court appeared to assume that it would be difficult to police non-solicitation and non-dealing covenants in circumstances in which the only evidence proffered by the employer to support this assertion was their experience of losing clients when an employee had previously left their employment. However, the employer did not at the same time suggest that that other employee had surreptitiously breached his non-solicitation and non-dealing covenants. If clients leave an employer in circumstances in which the employer is not asserting that their departure is consequent upon breaches of restrictive covenants by a former employee, it is difficult to see how the conclusion may be drawn that the covenants in question cannot be effectively policed. It is equally, if not more, plausible that the covenants were simply ineffective to achieve their purpose.

In a recent decision (*Thomas v Farr Plc* [2007] EWCA Civ 118, [2007] IRLR 419) the Court of Appeal held that a covenant prohibiting the solicitation of clients would not be sufficient to protect confidential information relating to those clients because such a covenant could not be policed. This was because the covenantor did not, in his work for the competitor company which he had joined, actually deal with clients himself. Prohibiting him from soliciting clients would not in any way inhibit his ability to pass on confidential information about those clients learnt whilst working for the covenantee to those members of staff in the competing company who *were* actually dealing with clients. Whereas it is extremely difficult to police covenants merely restraining the disclosure or use of confidential information, it is submitted that it is very far from self-evident that non-solicitation or non-dealing covenants taken to protect customer connection cannot be policed and no such assumption ought to be made without evidence of some sort to that effect. The fact is that breaches (or alleged breaches) of non-solicitation/-dealing covenants are regularly uncovered by covenantees: see for example *Allan Janes LLP v Johal (Balraj)*, above, and *Advantage Business Systems Ltd v Hopley (James)* [2007] EWHC 1783 (QB), [2007] All ER (D) 399 (Jul).

The court also held in the *TFS Derivatives* case that a non-compete provision was justified to protect confidential information. However, the court does not appear to have fully analysed the restraint in question to determine whether its duration was in fact commensurate with the length of time in which such information may have been of continuing use to a competitor. Compare *Duarte v Black and Decker Corpn*, ibid, where the judge, in determining that a two-year restraint on joining a competitor to protect confidential information would be unlawful under English law, considered the likely 'shelf-life' of the confidential information in question (cf *Norbrook Laboratories*, ibid).

The ambit of the restraint

The ambit of a restraint will comprise the following elements:

(a)   the geographical area within which the restraint is to operate;

(b)   the proscribed actions (eg non-solicitation or non-dealing with clients and the class of client not to be solicited or dealt with).

Geography

Restraints may be worldwide (and will be so construed) if they contain no express or, perhaps, implied geographical limitation (see *Commercial Plastics Ltd v Vincent*, above). Worldwide non-compete restraints may be justifiable on the basis that they are necessary to

39.8 Restraint of Trade and Confidential Information

protect trade secrets or confidential information: see *Scully UK Ltd v Lee*, above. Conversely, a restraint against soliciting or dealing with clients will not require an express geographical limitation (see *G W Plowman & Son Ltd v Ash* [1964] 1 WLR 568), even if clients may be located throughout the world, because the restraint is limited by the class of proscribed person. In many employment contracts radial or other area restraints are frequently employed. These are extremely clumsy instruments and appear to be a hang-over from the old common-law 18th and 19th-century rules about 'general' and 'partial' restraints. Area restraints must have a functional correspondence with the legitimate interest to be protected (see *Office Angels* and *Landmark Brickwork Ltd v Sutcliffe and Ors* [2011] IRLR 976). Thus, a local business whose customers are drawn exclusively or substantially from a radius of, say, five miles from the place of that business cannot justify a radial restraint of ten miles. Equally, the area in which a restraint is to operate will be considered carefully by the court. Thus, a radial restraint of five miles, for example, may be justifiable in rural or lightly populated areas, but could not be justified in a major conurbation where it may cover populations of a million or more: see *Fellowes & Son v Fisher* [1976] QB 122 and *Spencer v Marchington* [1988] IRLR 392. The real difficulty with radial or area restraints is that they are unnecessary if the protection is sought for the purposes of, say, customer connection because a non-solicit or non-compete covenant will suffice. It is difficult to see how they can be justified on the basis that they are necessary to protect confidential information or trade secrets since such interests are not confined to territorial boundaries (see *Scully UK Ltd v Lee*, above). Neither can radial restraints be justified on the basis of an interest in the stability of the workforce because solicitation of employees can readily be conducted from outside the radius imposed and, again, a more focused form of protection is afforded by a non-solicitation/non-enticement of staff covenant. The only practical effect of an area restraint, over and above that of a more limited non-solicitation or non-dealing covenant, is that it will prevent an ex employee from competing with his ex employer for new customers, ie customers who have not dealt with the former employer before (see *Allan Janes LLP v Balraj Johal*, above). Accordingly, radial restraints of the non-compete provision variety extend the protection afforded to an employer beyond that element of good will, namely existing client connection which he is entitled to protect. In business sale agreements it may be legitimate for the purchaser to protect himself against the vendor acquiring future business which ought otherwise to go to the business sold (see *Allied Dunbar (Frank Weisinger) Ltd v Weisinger* [1988] IRLR 60). The acquisition of new clients by reason of recommendation of existing clients is, however, based on the reputation of the business which, although it forms part of the goodwill on a business sale, forms no part of a legitimate interest to protect in the case of employer/employee covenants (see *Countrywide Assured Financial Services Ltd v Smart* [2004] EWHC 1214 (Ch)).

The proscribed actions

If the proscription is against conducting, or joining, or being employed in (or being otherwise interested in) another business then the covenant will be too wide if the proscribed business is described as 'a similar business' to that of the employer. An employer may be entitled to protect himself from unfair competition by the employee, but he is not permitted to prohibit the ex employee from joining or setting up a business which is merely 'similar' and not competitive (see *Scully v Lee* [1998] IRLR 259, CA, but cf *Spafax Ltd v Harrison* [1980] IRLR 442, CA, where the court reached the opposite conclusion). It is sometimes held by the courts that it is not legitimate to bar an employee from working in a competitive business in an area of work in which he has not been engaged in the employer's business (see, for example, *Commercial Plastics v Vincent*, above) or in a part of a competitor's business which does not compete with the former employer. Given, however, that a non-compete covenant may generally only be justified on the basis that it protects trade secrets or confidential information, it is difficult to see the logic behind such decisions: a former employee may impart confidential information of his former employer to a competing business after he leaves his employment and joins that competing business, regardless of the capacity in which he is working with the competitor or the department in which he may be engaged: see *Symbian Ltd v Christensen* [2001] IRLR 77 and *Norbrook Laboratories* ibid at para 81.

Lesser forms of restraint, such as non-solicitation or dealing with customers, may be too wide if the class of customer with which the ex employee may not deal is drawn too widely. For example, covenants which prohibit soliciting or dealing with any client of the employer will be too wide if the employer has many hundreds or thousands of customers and the employee covenantor has dealt with only a limited number of them whilst employed: see *Marley Tile Co Ltd v Johnson* [1982] IRLR 75 and *Office Angels*, above. However, courts have upheld covenants that are not limited to dealings with clients which the employee has dealt with whilst employed: see *Gilford Motor Co. Ltd v Horne* [1933] Ch 935, CA, *Plowman v Ash* (above), *Business Seating (Renovations) Ltd v Broad* [1989] ICR 729, *Allan Janes LLP v Balraj Johal*, above, *Thurstan Hoskin & Partners v Jewill Hill & Bennett* [2002] EWCA Civ 249, [2002] All ER (D) 62 (Feb) and *Safetynet Security Ltd v Coppage* 2BM40032 (15 August 2012, unreported). The better view is, however, that proscribed classes of customers should be limited to those that the employee has dealt with or, at least, may have knowledge about because the employee in question has overseen the work of other employees dealing with them (see *Spafax v Harrison*, above). Similarly, the class of customer ought to be limited to those persons who were clients of the employer for a defined period of time prior to the termination of the employee's contract of employment. In this way the covenant will not embrace persons who may have been clients prior to the employment of the employee, but were not clients of the employer at any time during the period of the employee's employment. However, in *Plowman v Ash* (above) the Court of Appeal held that an employer is entitled to protect by a non-dealing covenant customers who have ceased to deal with that employer during the currency of the employment contract in which that restraint appeared. This seems contrary to principle. It is of the essence of a reasonable restraint that it should protect the employer only against unfair competition by the employee, which means the exploitation by the employee of his knowledge about, and influence over customers that he has acquired during his employment (see *per* Lord Parker in *Herbert Morris v Saxelby*, above). A covenant will be too wide in its ambit if it purports to prohibit the ex employee from soliciting or dealing with persons who only become customers of the employer after the employee has left his employment (see *Konski v Peet* [1915] 1 Ch 530). There is a limited exception to this, namely prospective customers. An employer is entitled to protect himself against solicitation or dealing with prospective customers, at least where those prospective customers have been in negotiation with the employer prior to the employee leaving his employment and the employee has had contact with that prospective customer in the course of the negotiations (see *International Consulting Services (UK) Ltd v Hart* [2000] IRLR 227 and *Advantage Business Systems Ltd v Hopley* ibid, but compare *Associated Foreign Exchange Ltd v International Foreign Exchange UK Ltd* [2010] EWHC 1178 (Ch), [2010] IRLR 964).

The problem posed by the existence of contradictory authorities on whether the class of clients not to be solicited or dealt with ought to be closed by reference to clients actually dealt with by the employee remains to be resolved, the Court of Appeal having failed to grapple with the issue in *Dentmaster (UK) Ltd v Kent* [1997] IRLR 636.

Difficulty can arise even with limited restraints on dealing with customers where the market may be small and the customers therefore limited in number. This difficulty may be exacerbated by the use of ambiguous phraseology (see *Austin Knight (UK) Ltd v Hinds* [1994] FSR 52). The courts regard a non-solicitation covenant as being the least form of restraint and therefore more readily justifiable (see *Stenhouse Australia Ltd v Phillips*, above, *Scully v Lee*, above and also *Premier Model Management Ltd v Bruce* [2012] EWHC 3509 (QB)).

39.8 Restraint of Trade and Confidential Information

There is remarkably little authority on what constitutes 'solicitation'. In *Wessex Dairies Ltd v Smith* [1935] 2 KB 80 a milkman, prior to the termination of his employment contract, informed his customers, that he was leaving his existing employment, but would be available to do business with them again after a specified date in the future. The Court of Appeal held that this constituted solicitation of his employer's customers. In *Taylor Stuart & Co v Croft (Timothy)* (1998) 606 IRLB 15 an employee subject to a non-solicitation restraint despatched a letter to clients on the headed notepaper of a new firm he was proposing to establish as follows:

> 'Dear X,
>
> This is to inform you that I left the Partnership of Taylor Stuart & Co on 18 November 1994. With effect from 1 December 1994 I shall be establishing my own professional practice and can be contacted as above.'

The court held that it was of the essence of solicitation that the client should be requested to transfer his custom. Accordingly, the letter would have been unobjectionable if it had been limited to its first sentence, but constituted a solicitation because of the second, which invited the addressees to contact him. Other forms of solicitation less direct than that involve advertising. In *Trego v Hunt* [1896] AC 7 it was held that an advertisement not directed specifically to the clients of the business concerned, but more generally, did not constitute 'solicitation'. In *Towry EJ Ltd v Bennett and ors* [2012] EWHC 224 (QB) the learned judge held, as must be right, that solicitation can occur even though a client or customer makes the first approach to the employee. It is of the essence of a solicitation that the employee engages in requesting, persuading or encouraging a person to place business with them or on behalf of their employer. It is plain that a customer who makes a first approach to the employee along the lines of 'what are you doing now, having left your former employer?' can be solicited with the response 'I'm in the same line of business as before. Have you got any work that my new employer could do for you?' In that situation who makes the first approach is irrelevant, it is the substance of the conversation that matters. See also the discussion of the meaning of 'solicitation' in *QBE Management Services (UK) Ltd v Dymoke* [2012] IRLR 458 at paragraphs 184 to 185. There must be a 'direct and specific' appeal, whether by advertisement or otherwise.

Further difficulties arise where, in addition to a prohibition on 'solicitation', a draughtsman of a restrictive covenant adds other expressions such as: 'enticing away' or 'interfering with' the clients or customers of the employer. The word 'canvas' is synonymous with soliciting (see *QBE Management Services ibid* and *Customer Systems Plc v Ranson* [2012] EWCA Civ 841, [2012] IRLR 769). In other such cases, it is difficult for the court to know whether the covenant merely prohibits solicitation in the sense of making the first approach or whether acts beyond making the first approach are also prohibited such as to render the covenant a prohibition against dealing with customers even if those customers make the first approach to the employee: see *Austin Knight (UK) Ltd v Hinds* [1994] FSR 52 and *Hanover Insurance Brokers v Schapiro*, above, *per* Dillon LJ, but *cf* Nolan LJ. In *Hydra plc v Anastasi* [2005] EWHC 1559 (QB), [2005] All ER (D) 276 (Jul) Royce J held in respect of a covenant 'not to solicit or entice away any employee of the employer for a period of twelve months following the termination of the covenantor's employment' that the word 'entice' meant 'tempt, lure, persuade and inveigle'. In that case the facts established were that the covenantee employer company was a small business with few employees and it was therefore entitled to protect the entirety of its employees from poaching by a former employee and, further, on the facts the employee who had left to join the covenantee's rival business had himself approached the covenantor and sought to persuade him to let him join the new venture. In those circumstances, there was no breach of the covenant not to entice away an employee. It seems therefore that, even in the extended meaning of the word 'entice' given by Royce J, the essential ingredient of that term is making the first approach.

It is to be observed that the views of the client cannot affect or influence the court in determining whether to enforce a non-solicitation or non-dealing covenant. In *John Michael Design plc v Cooke* [1987] ICR 445 a client intervened in an application by a claimant employer for interim injunctive relief against former employees to restrain them from dealing with former clients of the employer. The client protested that the interim injunction should not extend to prohibit the former employees from dealing with the intervenor because the intervenor had no intention whatsoever of doing any further business with the claimant. At first instance, the judge acceded to the intervenor's argument. The Court of Appeal, however, held that there should be no qualification of the interim injunction to enforce the restrictive covenants in question so as to exclude from its ambit an individual client. Rather, the Court of Appeal held that the restrictive covenant was most necessary to the claimant in the cases of clients refusing to do future business because, manifestly, if a client proposed to remain loyal to the claimant employer there was no need for the protection of the restrictive covenant.

Until the case of *Dawnay, Day & Co Ltd v de Braconier d'Alphen* [1998] ICR 1068 there was conflicting authority at Court of Appeal level as to whether an employer could justify a restraint on soliciting his employees to leave his employment. In the *Dawnay, Day* case it was held that an employer had a legitimate interest in the stability of his workforce, at least so far as senior employees were concerned. However, in *Dawnay, Day* there were two restraints relating to the protection of the workforce in the employment contracts in question. The first restraint prohibited soliciting senior employees to leave their employment. The second restraint prohibited the covenantor employing the covenantee's senior employees. The claimants sought relief only in respect of the first of these covenants which the judge held to be reasonable. The judge, however, opined *obiter* that the second form of restraint would be too wide to be enforceable. The objection to any form of restraint prohibiting an ex employee from employing in his business, or in a business that he has joined, a colleague of his at his former employers is that it amounts to a restraint on that colleague from seeking or obtaining work with whom he pleases. In *Kores Manufacturing Co Ltd v Kolok Manufacturing Co Ltd* (above) two employers in the same industry entered into an agreement that they would not employ members of each other's staff for a period of time after those employees had left their respective employment. The Court of Appeal held that this provision was unenforceable because it was not limited to senior employees who might carry away trade secrets or confidential information to the competitor. However, the Court of Appeal also opined, *obiter*, that the covenant was against public policy because it would prevent employees of each of the parties from seeking employment with the other in circumstances in which those individual employees did not have in their employment contracts any restraint prohibiting them from joining a competitor. The effect of the covenant in *Kores Manufacturing Co Ltd v Kolok Manufacturing Co Ltd* was to enable the two employers to achieve through the back door what they had failed to achieve through the front.

However, in *TFS Derivatives* (above) one of the restrictive covenants in the employee's contract was as follows: '[you will not] for six months employ, engage or work with an employee for the purpose of the supply of relevant services or a business which competes, or which plans to compete with, or is similar to a relevant business'. The learned judge held that this covenant went 'no further than is reasonably necessary in all the circumstances to protect [a legitimate interest] of the employer'. The judge did not, however, grant an injunction to enforce this restraint on the grounds that there was no evidence of breach. However, the judge's attention does not appear to have been drawn to the decision in *Dawnay, Day* (above) or to *Kores Manufacturing Co Ltd v Kolok Manufacturing Co Ltd* (above). Employers seeking to impose restrictions on the solicitation of their staff should be cautious about distinguishing for the purposes of such protection those staff occupying positions of importance to the covenantor's business or have training or business or technical knowledge and experience from those members of staff who do not: see *TSC Europe (UK) Ltd v Massey* [1999] IRLR 22. In small organisations, however, it may be that all the staff will have the necessary qualities or importance to justify protection against solicitation by an ex employee.

Duration

Whether the length of any restraint renders it unreasonable is a matter of impression for the judge. In *Stenhouse Australia Ltd v Phillips* [1974] AC 391 (above) Lord Wilberforce stated that the question of a reasonable duration for a covenant in restraint of trade could not 'advantageously form the subject of direct evidence. It is for the judge, after informing himself as fully as he can of the facts and circumstances relating to the employer's business, the nature of the employer's interest to be protected, and the likely effect on this of solicitation, to decide whether the contractual period is reasonable or not. An opinion as to the reasonableness of elements of it, particularly of the time during which it is to run, can seldom be precise, and can only be formed on a broad and commonsense view' (*Stenhouse*, 402). The question that the court must ask itself is: 'what is a reasonable time during which the employer is entitled to protection against solicitation of clients with whom the employee had contact and influence during employment and who were not bound to the employer by contract or by stability of association' (ibid). Thus even limited restraints, such as non-solicitation of client covenants, will be subject to close scrutiny to determine whether their duration is too long given the circumstances of the covenantee's business and the covenantor's role in that business: see *Associated Foreign Exchange Ltd v International Foreign Exchange UK Ltd* [2010] EWHC 1178 (Ch), [2010] IRLR 964. So far as the protection of confidential information is concerned acute problems are likely to arise in relation to fixing a reasonable duration for a post-termination covenant restraining an employee from engaging in competition with the employer. Logically, if the covenant is designed to protect trade secrets or equivalent confidential information in the sense of information that would never be disclosed by the employer and could not be 'reverse engineered' by a rival then it would be reasonable to impose a lifetime prohibition on the employee working for a competitor. Yet the courts constantly refer to the necessity, even when protecting trade secrets and equivalent confidential information, of keeping the non-compete provision to a reasonable duration: see, for example, *per* Cross J in *Printers and Finishers Ltd v Holloway (No 2)* [1965] 1 WLR 1. Where a covenant over a limited geographical area is taken to protect confidential information, the courts have, in the past, accepted a non-compete provision of unlimited duration: *Haynes v Doman* [1899] 2 Ch 13, CA. But, as the Court of Appeal has recently observed in *Scully v Lee* (above), confidential information knows no territorial boundaries and, accordingly, the imposition of an area blanket restraint to protect confidential information is, in itself, illogical. All that can be said about the duration of covenants to protect confidential information is that it must be an issue of fact in every case as to the reasonableness of the duration of the covenant and it is submitted that the covenant's duration must necessarily be a function of how long the information to be protected is likely to remain confidential, or, at least, useful to a competitor (see *Norbrook Laboratories v Hopley* ibid and *Duarte v Black and Decker Corpn* ibid). Thus, if the confidential information to be protected is information relating to a proposed business strategy the covenant cannot endure for longer than the period during which the strategy is to remain confidential before being implemented (in effect, made public) by the employer. This, however, does not resolve the essential problem presented by extremely confidential technical information (for example, the secret of the recipe for the manufacture of Coca-Cola – anecdotally the most treasured and most protected trade secret in the world). Would it be permissible for that company to impose a lifetime ban on an employee who knew what the recipe was from joining a competitor like Pepsi-Cola? The law has yet to grapple with this problem. It is, however, clear that a judge is <u>not</u> bound by precedent to uphold as reasonable a restraint of the same duration and in the same field as a previous judge: see *Dairy Crest Ltd v Pigott* [1989] ICR 92, CA. It is equally clear that the more limited the ambit of the restraint, the greater the period of duration that will be upheld: see *Stenhouse v Phillips*, above, and *Fitch v Dewes* [1921] 2 AC 158. However, it must be doubtful that the latter case would, on the same facts, nowadays be followed (see, for example, *Allan Janes LLP v Balraj Johal*, above).

(Subject always to the caveat that judges should not slavishly follow precedent in restraint of trade cases, but rather examine the reasonableness of covenants in the light of the facts of each case, for a convenient compendium of cases where covenants have been upheld, or not, see *Restrictive Covenants Under Common and Competition Law* (4th edn, Sweet & Maxwell), Kamerling & Osman, p 381ff.)

39.9   *What is the consequence of a finding of unreasonableness?*

Many judges (see, for example, Lord McNaghten in *Nordenfelt*, above, and Cox J in *TFS Derivates*, above) have erroneously described a covenant in restraint of trade which is not justifiable as being 'void'. This is not correct. A covenant in unreasonable restraint of trade is merely unenforceable. The significance of this distinction is that a covenant in restraint of trade is not illegal in the sense of it being a criminal offence to enter into or perform the obligations so imposed: *Apple Corpn Ltd v Apple Computer Inc* [1992] FSR 431, Ch D. Accordingly, covenants in restraint of trade, the proper law of which is English law will be enforced by an English court by, for example, a worldwide injunction even if the restraint may be invalid under the law of other jurisdictions. Equally, whole contracts may be found to be in restraint of trade (see, for example, *A Schroeder Music Publishing Co Ltd v Macaulay* [1974] 1 WLR 1308).

39.10 Other elements

Consideration

There is considerable debate as to whether a court is permitted to look at the adequacy of the consideration which supports any contract or provision in restraint of trade as part of the court's investigation into the reasonableness of the covenant. Authorities against the court considering adequacy of consideration include: *M and S Drapers (a firm) v Reynolds* [1957] 1 WLR 9, CA *per* Hodson LJ and *Allied Dunbar (Frank Weisinger) Ltd v Weisinger* [1988] IRLR 60, paras 30–32 *per* Millett J. Contradicting these authorities are: Lord McNaghten in *Nordenfelt* (above) at 565, Lord Hodson (apparently dissenting from his own earlier judgment in *M and S Drapers*) in *Esso Petroleum v Harper's Garage* (above) at 318D-F and Lord Pearce in the same case at 323E-F. The better view, it is submitted, is that the court cannot look to the adequacy of the consideration in the sense of determining whether the value of the bargain to the party restrained is the same as the value imparted to the covenantee. The court does not ask 'whether the consideration is equal in value to that which the party gives up or loses by the restraint under which he has placed himself . . . it is impossible for the court . . . to say whether, in any particular case, the party restrained has made an improvident bargain or not'. Rather the test is whether 'the restraint of a party from carrying on a trade is larger and wider than the protection of the party with whom the contract is made can possibly require': (*per* Tindale CJ, *Hitchcock v Coker* (1837) 6 Ad & El 959). It is therefore submitted that the issue of consideration has become confused because in many cases the courts have elided the issue of consideration in the technical sense of the contractual rule that there must be adequate consideration to support a bargain enforceable by the courts with consideration in the sense of a balance of benefit between the parties bestowed under a contract. The latter form of consideration may be considered only to the extent that the covenantee does not under the bargain struck extract more protection from the covenantor than is reasonable to protect the covenantee's legitimate interests. If it were legitimate to consider the adequacy of consideration, then it would follow that covenants in restraint of trade could be purchased outright, which is clearly not the law (see *Mont v Mills* ibid). The more money paid to the covenantor, either specifically as consideration to support a restrictive covenant, or by way of salary or other emoluments of employment, the longer the restraint that could be imposed upon him. This cannot be right because the nature, ambit and duration of a covenant can never be greater than is merely adequate to protect a legitimate interest. The legitimate interest does not change as a function of the amount of money paid to a covenantor. Equally, taking into account the adequacy of consideration would mean that low-paid employees could never have valid restrictions imposed upon them, even although the employer might have legitimate interests to protect. The court has rejected in a recent case the notion that low pay vitiates a restrictive covenant: see *Norbrook Laboratories* ibid. Extreme cases do, however, arise in which the courts will indulge in balancing the benefit and burden as between the two parties: see *Schroeder v Macaulay* (above) and *M and S Drapers (a firm) v Reynolds* [1957] 1 WLR 9, CA. There must be some consideration to support the restraint and it should be noted that in this respect a deed will not be sufficient if it is a seal alone: see *Hutton v Parker* (1839) 7 Dowl. 739. Equally, restrictive covenants cannot be supported where the only consideration for them is a promise to perform an existing contract: see *WRN Ltd v Ayris* [2008] EWHC 1080 (QB), [2008] IRLR 889.

39.11 *Repudiatory breach*

An employer in repudiatory breach of an employment contract, where that breach is accepted as terminating the same by the employee, cannot enforce any post-termination restraints: *General Billposting Co Ltd v Atkinson* [1909] AC 118. However, the fact that a restrictive covenant purports to apply upon termination of the contract of employment, 'howsoever caused, whether lawfully or unlawfully', does not itself render the covenant too wide and unenforceable: cf *Rock Refrigeration v Jones and Seward Refrigeration Ltd* [1997] 1 All ER 1, [1996] IRLR 675. There was a period when this proposition was doubted by the courts and it was held that restrictive covenants purporting to apply upon termination of the contract of employment 'howsoever caused, whether or lawfully or unlawfully' were held to be too wide. However, in the *Rock Refrigeration* case this argument was resolved in favour of upholding covenants expressed to apply even to a termination of the employment contract occasioned by a repudiatory breach by the employer. The Court of Appeal held that the doctrine of restraint of trade does not become engaged unless and until the contract of employment containing the restraints is lawfully terminated. Thus, if the employer repudiates the contract, which is then terminated by the acceptance of that repudiation by the employee, the restrictive covenant does not fall to be considered at all under the restraint of trade doctrine because both parties to the contract which has been repudiated are discharged from future performance of their express contractual obligations: see *Photo Production Ltd v Securicor Transport Ltd* [1980] AC 827. The principle of *Securicor* is that upon acceptance of repudiatory breach express future obligations upon both parties (the innocent and the guilty) to a contract are discharged, whereupon implied secondary obligations (such as the obligation to pay damages for breach) come into force. However, despite the (minority) views expressed by Phillips LJ in *Rock Refrigeration* (above), it is submitted that the court cannot at this stage imply obligations in restraint of trade because they are, *prima facie*, contrary to public policy and unenforceable (see *Wallace Bogan & Co v Cove* [1997] IRLR 453). (To this principle there are the very narrow exceptions of an implied obligation in business sale agreements on the part of the vendor not to solicit customers of the business sold (see *Trego v Hunt*, above) and an implied obligation on the part of employees not to make use of or disclose trade secrets or equivalent confidential information of their employers after the termination of the employment contract (see *Faccenda Chicken v Fowler*, above).) It is inconceivable beyond these two implied obligations that a court will impose by implication any other provisions in restraint of trade because it is contrary to public policy in the broad sense to do so. The decision in *Rock Refrigeration* does, however, reveal a real danger for employers (identified by Phillips LJ). If an employer accepts a repudiatory breach by an employee as terminating the contract of employment he will (under the principle in the *Securicor* case) be in danger of losing the protection of any post-termination restraints in the contract of employment. It should be noted, however, that the majority of the court in *Rock Refrigeration* considered that a repudiatory breach did not discharge an employee from his obligations of confidentiality (see also *Campbell v Frisbee* [2002] EWHC 328 (Ch), [2002] EMLR 656). It is for this reason that it is crucial for employers to provide expressly in any contract of employment for a right to terminate the contract (ie in accordance with its terms) in the event of any conduct of the employee which would constitute a repudiatory breach (for example, gross misconduct). If the contract of employment is terminated in accordance with an express term of that kind then the rules relating to repudiatory breach do not apply because the employer will have terminated the contract in accordance with its express terms and will not have to rely on any implied obligation arising under common law but can rely instead on the obligations expressed in the contract of employment as applying post-termination of the same.

The recent decision in *RDF Media Group Plc v Clements* [2007] EWHC 2892 (QB), [2008] IRLR 207, which relates to repudiatory breach and its impact on covenants in restraint of trade, is likely to cause very serious difficulties if followed. In this case, the judge held that an employee against whom the employer had committed a breach of the implied duty of trust and confidence was not entitled to treat the contract as repudiated because that employee had committed a prior breach of that same implied duty which was not known to the employer at the date on which the employer breached that duty. Because the employee could not treat the contract as repudiated, covenants he had entered into in a shareholders agreement continued to operate. Not only does this decision fly in the face of long-established principles of repudiatory breach of employment contracts (see *Healey v Francaise Rubastic SA* [1917] 1 KB 946, which was upheld in the House of Lords in *Ramsden v David Sharratt & Sons Ltd* (1930) 35 Com Cas 314, HL, and *Howard v Pickford Tool Co Ltd* [1951] 1 KB 417), but it is based upon an authority relating to commercial arbitrations (*Bremer Vulkan Schiffbau und Maschinenfabrik v South India Shipping Corpn Ltd* [1981] AC 909, HL) which although a decision of the House of Lords was much criticised at the time and has subsequently been superceded in any event by statutory reforms of arbitration. In *Food Corpn of India v Antclizo Shipping Corpn, The Antclizo* [1988] 2 All ER 513, [1988] 1 WLR 603, HL Lord Goff commented on the *Bremer* case as follows: 'It is not understating the position to record that the effect of this decision and, indeed, the reasoning upon which it is based, has provoked serious disquiet among the whole commercial community. In particular, it has been suggested that the mutual obligation resting upon both parties to proceed with their reference to arbitration, as expressed by Lord Diplock, bears no relation to commercial reality . . . '. In *Tullett Prebon plc v BGC Brokers LP* [2010] EWHC 484 (QB), [2010] IRLR 648 the judge refused to follow the *RDF* case (decision affd on appeal [2011] EWCA Civ 131; [2011] IRLR 420). The same judge (Jack J) again refused to follow the RDF case in a more recent decision: *Brandeaux Advisers (UK) Ltd v Chadwick* [2010] EWHC 3241 (QB), [2011] IRLR 224 holding that an unaccepted repudiation was a "thing writ in water" (see the *Howard* case supra).

In *Lonmar Global Risks Ltd v West* [2011] IRLR 138 an employee was subject to 12 months post termination non-solicitation and dealing covenants set out in clause 14A of his employment contract. Clause 14B stated: "Clause 14A shall apply in the event of termination of the . . . employment in all circumstances except unlawful termination by [the employer]". It was argued on behalf of the employee that an unfair dismissal by the employer would fall within the expression "unlawful termination". At trial the judge ruled that "unlawful termination" meant unlawful termination at common law ie a wrongful dismissal not a mere unfair dismissal. The judge went on to hold the covenants enforceable.

39.12 Conflict of laws

Because the law of restraint of trade arises as a matter of public policy, foreign law, even if it is the proper law of the contract, cannot dictate the validity or invalidity of a provision in restraint of trade. Contracts of employment the proper law of which is a foreign law will not be enforced by an English court if the restraints in question are unenforceable under the public policy of England and Wales: see *Rousillon v Rousillon* (1880) 14 Ch D 351. A distinction must be made between principles relating to mandatory rules of English law and English public policy. The restraint of trade doctrine is not a mandatory rule for the purposes of Article 6(1) of the Rome Convention. Rather, it falls under Article 16 of that Convention: see *Duarte v Black and Decker Corpn* [2007] EWHC 2720 (QB), [2008] 1 All ER (Comm) 401 and *BGC Capital Markets (Switzerland) LLC v Rees* [2011] EWHC 2009 (QB). Accordingly, where covenants in restraint of trade are expressed to be governed by a proper law other than the law of England, and would be enforceable under that proper law, but not under the English doctrine of restraint of trade, then the result of the application of the specified foreign law would be 'manifestly incompatible with English public policy': *Duarte*, ibid. It follows that the approach that should be taken to covenants expressed to be governed by foreign law is for the English court first to determine whether those covenants would be valid under that foreign law. If not, then there is no need to apply the doctrine of restraint of trade to them. If however, the court decides that the covenants would be valid under the chosen foreign law, then the English court must go on to apply its own doctrine of restraint of trade to those covenants. If invalid under the English doctrine of restraint of trade, then the English law 'trumps' the chosen foreign law.

39.13   TRADE SECRETS AND CONFIDENTIAL INFORMATION

The courts have long recognised that trade secrets are a legitimate interest which an employer may protect by imposing a covenant limiting the field of activity in which an ex employee may engage after leaving his employment (see, for example, Lord Parker in *Herbert Morris v Saxelby*, above, and *Printers and Finishers Ltd v Holloway* [1964] 3 All ER 54, [1965] RPC 239). In this respect, therefore, obligations of confidentiality that an employee owes his employer have an important role to play in the doctrine of restraint of trade. However, obligations of confidentiality, if breached by an employee either during or after the employment contract has ended, may give rise to claims for relief which lie outside any claim for breach of restrictive covenants in employment contracts, specifically the so-called 'springboard injunction'. In recent years, decisions of the court have led to much confusion in these areas, such that discussions of the principles of the law of confidentiality now resemble medieval theological debates about how many angels can dance on pinheads.

It is necessary, therefore, to identify certain basic principles relating to the obligations of confidence owed by employees to their employers. The obligation of good faith and fidelity (now transmuted into an obligation of trust and confidence: see generally **7.13** CONTRACT OF EMPLOYMENT) implied into all contracts of employment has as an incident of that larger duty a specific obligation that the employee shall not make use of, or disclose, for the benefit of a competing business information acquired by the employee about his employer's business in the course of his employment (see *Robb v Green* [1895] 2 QB 1). In that case an employee during his contract of employment made a list of the names and addresses of his employer's clients and, following the termination of his employment, used that list to canvas the clients of the former employer for a rival business established by the employee. The employee was held to have breached the implied duty of good faith and fidelity in so acting and was ordered by injunction to hand over the list he had made to his former employer and to pay damages. The decision was affirmed on appeal ([1895] 2 QB 315). It is of the greatest significance to observe that the defendant contended that the information contained on the list which he had made was information that could be obtained from sources within the public domain. The trial judge (Hawkins J) did not accept that all the information could have been so sourced, but added (p 18) that even were that true the employee had nonetheless acted in breach of his duty in creating a convenient compilation of material for the purpose of assisting an intended competitor. (For a more recent case on the scope of the employee's obligations of good faith and fidelity while in employment, see *Helmet Integrated Systems Ltd v Tunnard* [2006] EWCA Civ 1735, [2007] IRLR 126, in which the Court of Appeal accepted that the employee had not breached his obligations to his employer by taking, during his employment and unbeknownst to his employer, steps preparatory to competing with his employer; see also *Khan v Landskerr Childcare Ltd* UKEAT/0036/12/DM, *Imam-Sadeque v BlueBay Asset Management (Services) Ltd* [2012] EWHC 3511 (QB) and **7.16 CONTRACT OF EMPLOYMENT.** Note, however, that the position is otherwise for company directors and very senior employees: see *Crowson Fabrics Ltd v Rider and ors* [2007] EWHC 2942 (Ch), [2008] IRLR 288 and **8.16 DIRECTORS.**)

Some ninety years after *Robb v Green* [1895] 2 QB 1 the Court of Appeal embarked on an analysis of the duties of confidentiality owed by an employee: see *Faccenda Chicken Ltd v Fowler* [1986] ICR 297, CA. At first instance in that case, Goulding J had analysed the position thus ([1984] ICR 589 at 598–599):

> 'Let me now deal with the alleged abuse of confidential information. I must make it clear that anything I say about the law is intended to apply only to cases of master and servant. In my view information acquired by an employee in the course of his service, and not the subject of any relevant express agreement, may fall as regards confidence into any of three classes. First, there is information which, because of its trivial character or its easy accessibility from public sources of information, cannot be regarded by reasonable persons or by the law as confidential at all. The servant is at liberty to impart it during his service or afterwards to anyone he pleases, even his master's competitor. An example might be a published patent specification well known to people in the industry concerned . . .   Secondly, there is information which the servant must treat as confidential (either because he is expressly told it is confidential, or because from its character it obviously is so) but which once learned necessarily remains in the servant's head and becomes part of his own skill and knowledge applied in the course of his master's business. So long as the employment continues, he cannot otherwise use or disclose such information without infidelity and therefore breach of contract. But when he is no longer in the same service, the law allows him to use his full skill and knowledge for his own benefit in competition with his former master; and . . .   there seems to be no established distinction between the use of such information where its possessor trades as a principal, and where he enters the employment of a new master, even though the latter case involves disclosure and not mere personal use of the information. If an employer wants to protect information of this kind, he can do so by an express stipulation restraining the servant from competing with him (within reasonable limits of time and space after the termination of his employment). Thirdly, however, there are, to my mind, specific trade secrets so confidential that, even though they may necessarily have been learned by heart and even though the servant may have left the service, they cannot lawfully be used for anyone's benefit but the master's. An example is the secret process which was the subject matter of *Amber Size & Chemical Co Ltd v Menzel* [1913] 2 Ch 239.'

Goulding J went on to hold that the information that had been used by the defendants upon leaving the plaintiff company's employment and setting up a rival business fell into the second of the three categories and, accordingly, there was no breach of duty involved in its use by the defendants. This was not a case in which there were any post-termination restraints in the defendants' contract of employment with Faccenda limiting their business activities in any way. Goulding J, however, opined (above, 599E) that an employer can protect the use of information in the second category, even though it does not include any information in the third category (ie a trade secret or its equivalent) by means of a restrictive covenant. The Court of Appeal held:

(1)   That in contracts of employment confidentiality obligations of the employee are to be determined by that contract.

(2)   Absent any express term relating to confidential information in an employment contract, the obligations of the employee in respect of the use and disclosure of information are the subject of implied terms.

(3)   During the currency of the employment relationship the obligations in relation to
        the use and disclosure of information are included in the implied term imposing a
        duty of good faith and fidelity (or trust and confidence) on the employee. The Court
        of Appeal declined to consider the precise limits of the confidentiality obligation
        arising out of that implied term during the currency of the employment contract,
        but observed:

    (a)   that the extent of the duty of good faith will vary according to the nature of
            the contract; and

    (b)   that that duty would be broken if an employee makes a list of customers, or
            memorises such a list, for use after his employment ends, even though there
            is no legal impediment on the employee soliciting or doing business with
            those customers after he leaves his employment. For this proposition
            the Court of Appeal returned to and relied on *Robb v Green* (above).

(4)   The implied term imposing an obligation on the employee not to use or disclose
        information learnt during his employment after the determination of the same is
        more restricted in its scope than the obligation during the currency of the
        employment contract and arising from the general duty of good faith and fidelity.
        Specifically, the implied post-termination obligation does not extend to all informa-
        tion given to, or acquired by, the employee while in his employment, and may not
        cover information which is only 'confidential' in the sense that it falls within the
        broader category of information that is protected during the currency of the
        employment contract as an incident of the obligation of good faith and fidelity. For
        this proposition the Court of Appeal relied upon the judgment of Cross J in *Printers
        and Finishers Ltd v Holloway* [1965] RPC 239 at 253:

> 'In this connection one must bear in mind that not all information which is
> given to a servant in confidence and which it would be a breach of his duty for
> him to disclose to another person during his employment is a trade secret
> which he can be prevented from using for his own advantage after the
> employment is over, even though he has entered into no express covenant with
> regard to the matter in hand. For example, the printing instructions were
> handed to Holloway to be used by him during his employment exclusively for
> the plaintiffs' benefit. It would have been a breach of duty on his part to divulge
> any of the contents to a stranger while he was employed, but many of these
> instructions are not really 'trade secrets' at all. Holloway was not, indeed,
> entitled to take a copy of the instructions away with him; but in so far as the
> instructions cannot be called 'trade secrets' and he carried them in his head, he
> is entitled to use them for his own benefit or the benefit of any future employer.'

(See also *E Worsley & Co Ltd v Cooper* [1939] 1 All ER 290.)

Accordingly, the Court of Appeal (*obiter*) disagreed with Goulding J's judgment
where he stated that an employer can protect 'category 2' information (not also
falling within 'category 3') by means of an express post-termination restraint.
The Court said:

> 'In our view the circumstances in which a restrictive covenant would be
> appropriate and could be successfully invoked emerge very clearly from the
> words used by Cross J in *Printers & Finishers Ltd v Holloway* [ibid] . . . If
> the managing director is right in thinking that there are features in the
> plaintiffs' process which can fairly be regarded as trade secrets and which their
> employees will inevitably carry away with them in their heads, then the proper
> way for the plaintiffs to protect themselves would be by exacting covenants
> from their employees restricting their field of activity after they have left their

employment, not by asking the court to extend the general equitable doctrine to prevent breaking confidence beyond all reasonable bounds.'

On this analysis, as the Court of Appeal pointed out, it is impossible to provide a comprehensive list of those things which constitute trade secrets, or equivalent confidential information, that will be protected by the implied obligation of confidence operating post-termination and which would therefore form a legitimate interest justifying an express post-termination restraint limiting the fields of activity in which the ex employee may work for a period of time. Secret processes of manufacture are an obvious example of such information but 'innumerable other pieces of information are capable of being trade secrets, though the secrecy of some information may be only short lived . . . the fact that the circulation of certain information is restricted to a limited number of individuals may throw light on the status of the information and its degree of confidentiality'.

(5)   The Court of Appeal went on to hold that in order to determine whether any particular item of information falls to be protected under the implied obligation of confidentiality operative after the termination of the employment contract a court must consider all the circumstances of the case, including the following matters:-

(a)   the nature of the employment (ie was the employee engaged in a capacity where confidential material was habitually handled by him and he might, accordingly, be expected to realise its sensitivity);

(b)   the nature of the information itself (ie only information which is a 'trade secret' or the equivalent of a trade secret is protected by the post-termination implied obligation);

(c)   whether the employer impressed on the employee the confidentiality of the information;

(d)   whether the relevant information can be easily isolated from other information which the employee is free to use or disclose.

The decision by the Court of Appeal in *Faccenda Chicken* has been criticised by some judges and by some textbook writers. In *Balston Ltd v Headline Filters Ltd* [1987] FSR 330 Scott J doubted the Court of Appeal's opinion that information falling within Goulding J's second category which did not also fall within his third category (termed by some textbook writers as 'mere confidential information') could not be protected by an express post-termination restraint. Similarly, in *Systems Reliability Holdings plc v Smith* [1990] IRLR 377, Harman J refused to follow this part of the Court of Appeal's judgment in *Faccenda*. See also *Lancashire Fire Ltd v SA Lyons & Co Ltd* [1997] IRLR 113, CA, per Bingham LJ, para 16 and *A T Poeton (Gloucester Plating) Ltd v Horton* [2001] FSR 169, [2000] ICR 1208, CA.

It is respectfully submitted that these doubts are erroneous. First, it is unquestionably a matter of principle that it is against public policy to restrain the use by an ex employee of knowledge and skills that he has acquired in the course of his employment: see *Herbert Morris v Saxelby*, above, per Lord Parker and *Commercial Plastics Ltd v Vincent* [1965] 1 QB 623. If the employer is to have a legitimate interest to protect in confidential information that information must fall into a special category of sensitivity beyond the mass of more mundane information that an employee will necessarily accumulate during his employment. Second, the Court of Appeal's decision in *Faccenda* does not warrant the criticism that has been levelled against it that it constitutes an excessively narrow view of the obligations of confidentiality in employment contracts or the class of information that may legitimately be protected by an express post-termination restraint or by the implied obligation of confidence operating after the contract of employment has come to an end. As the Court of Appeal pointed out, innumerable other pieces of information besides secret processes of manufacturing may constitute trade secrets, or their equivalent, and thus fall within the protection of express or implied post-termination obligations. Thus in one industry the identity of clients or customers may constitute the equivalent of a trade secret, as will information about the prices charged to those customers by the employer. In other businesses (as in *Faccenda* itself) the same kind of information will constitute only information protectable during the currency of the employment contract, but not afterwards. To an extent, confusion that has arisen since *Faccenda* is the product of quibbles about vocabulary: the expression 'trade secrets' is no doubt more apt to describe information relating to secret processes of manufacture than it is to describe information such as the identity of customers, but there is no sensible reason why one should not describe the latter information as 'information the equivalent of a trade secret' where it is treated as so equivalent in certain industries or businesses. It would, perhaps, be better if the use of the expression 'trade secrets' was abandoned altogether and replaced with the expression 'protectable confidential information'. It was certainly the view of Staughton LJ in *Lansing Linde Ltd v Kerr* [1991] 1 WLR 251, 260B that the problem was one of vocabulary: 'It appears to me that the problem is one of definition: what are trade secrets, and how do they differ (if at all) from confidential information? [It has been] suggested that a trade secret is information which, if disclosed to a competitor, would be liable to cause real (or significant) harm to the owner of the secret. I would add, first, that it must be information used in a trade or business and, secondly, that the owner must limit the dissemination of it or at least not encourage or permit widespread publication.'

There are reasons to doubt the test there propounded by Staughton LJ for identifying protectable confidential information, not least because it appears to place too much emphasis on the subjective view of the employer as to the status of information as distinct from the correct test which must needs be based upon the objective view of the court, but Staughton LJ, nonetheless, correctly identified the confusion that can arise from the terminology that abounds in these cases.

A second area of confusion arises from the difference between the implied obligation of confidentiality which survives after the employment contract has come to an end and the protection that may be afforded by an express post-termination restraint. The implied obligation is limited to an obligation not to disclose or make use of 'protectable confidential information'. This obligation should not be extended to prohibit an employee who possesses such information from going to work for a competitor of his former employer: see *Caterpillar Logistics Services (UK) Ltd v Paula Huesca de Crean* [2012] EWCA Civ 156, [2012] ICR 981 and *Generics (UK) Ltd v Yeda Research and Development Co Ltd* [2012] EWCA Civ 726, [2012] C.P. Rep. 39. It merely restrains him, when working for that competitor, from disclosing or using, the protectable confidential information. (Note that the position is different for self-employed professionals such as lawyers, accountants and patent attorneys who may be made the subject of so-called 'barring-out' orders preventing them from acting in litigation against a former client where it is necessary in order to avoid a significant risk of disclosure of 'protectable confidential information': see *Bolkiah v KPMG* [1999] 2 AC 222 and note the view of Sir Robin Jacobs in *Generics (UK)* ibid that the same principle might apply to in-house lawyers.)

As has been pointed out above (39.8), an obligation not to disclose or make use of confidential information in the course of new employment is virtually impossible to police. Accordingly, employers frequently resort to an express post-termination restraint limiting the fields of activity in which the former employee may be involved for a period following the termination of the employment (ie a non-compete provision or, at least, an obligation not to join that part of a competitor's business which competes with the former employer). It is respectfully submitted that Scott J's reservations in *Balston* about the Court of Appeal's decision in *Faccenda* were based on confusion between the scope of the implied obligation of confidentiality and the more practical protection that can be afforded by post-termination non-compete restraints. Equally, in the *Systems Reliability* case, it should be observed that the learned judge had characterised the restraints that he was dealing with as having arisen with respect to a business sale agreement, and not an employment contract. As has also been pointed out above (**39.8**), the court's approach to business sale agreements and the restraint of trade doctrine is very different to the approach adopted to restraints in employment contracts.

In a recent decision the Court of Appeal has re-stated the *Faccenda* principle and held that only information the equivalent of a trade secret can be protected by a post-termination non-compete restraint: see *Thomas v Farr plc* [2007] EWCA Civ 118, [2007] IRLR 419.

In conclusion, it is submitted that the law on an employee's obligations of confidentiality may be stated as follows:

(a)   During the currency of the employment contract the employee is bound as an incident of his implied obligation of trust and confidence not to disclose or make use of the mass of information he acquires about his employer's business. The information covered by that obligation is limited so as to exclude only information which is trivial or in the public domain. However, it should be noted that if the employee sources and removes lists of customers or other information from the records of his employer for use in a rival business it does not matter that that information may be available in the public domain or that that information was originally compiled by the employee in the service of the employer. That information belongs to the employer and the employee cannot use it without breaching the implied obligation of confidentiality that existed during the life of his employment contract: see *Crowson Fabrics Ltd v Rider* [2008] IRLR 288 and *Pennwell Publishing (UK) Ltd v Ornstien* [2007] EWHC 1570 (QB), [2007] IRLR 700. NB many compilations of information contained within an employer's computer systems will independently attract protection as databases under the *Copyright, Designs and Patents Act 1988 (as amended)*, but this lies outside the scope of this chapter.

(b)   After the contract of employment comes to an end the employee is subject to an implied obligation not to disclose to, or make use for the benefit of, a competitor information which constitutes protectable confidential information, ie information which has the status of a trade secret or its equivalent. It is an issue of fact, in every case, depending on all the circumstances and applying the various guidelines, whether or not information falls into this category. Certain information, such as the identity of clients or customers is capable of falling into this category, but not necessarily in all businesses. The same is true of price information and many other kinds of information. No comprehensive list can therefore be drawn up of this kind of information. It is, however, clear that technical information regarding manufacturing processes and high level strategic business plans (for example, whether and, if so, when old models are to be replaced by new) will be likely to fall into this third category of protectable confidential information regardless of the nature of the business concerned.

(c)   The protection afforded by the implied confidentiality obligation operating after the employment contract has come to an end is limited to disclosing or making use of the information concerned. This implied obligation is therefore of limited practical use to an employer because it does not prevent the employee from going to work for a rival and, once within a rival's business, it is impossible for the employer to monitor whether or not the employee is disclosing or making use of the concerned information.

(d)   Accordingly, an employer who rightly considers that an employee may in the course of his employment acquire information falling within the class of protectable confidential information (ie a trade secret or equivalent confidential information) has a legitimate interest to protect under the doctrine of restraint of trade and may justify imposing a covenant restricting the field of activity of that employee when he leaves his employment. The covenant must, however, be reasonable as to its ambit and duration. Although 'category 3' confidential information can, in certain circumstances, justify worldwide restraints because confidentiality knows no territorial limitations (see *Scully v Lee*, above), in other cases, the evidence may show that a worldwide restraint will be held to be too wide to be enforceable (see *Lansing Linde Ltd v Kerr*, above and *Commercial Plastics Ltd v Vincent*, above). It may also be the case that a non-compete provision, ie one prohibiting an employee who possesses confidential information in the third category from working in any capacity for a competitor will also be held to be too wide in its ambit: see *Commercial Plastics v Vincent*. The contrary argument, however, is that it is legitimate to restrain an employee with 'category 3' confidential information from working in any capacity for a competitor because he is still in a position, at the very least, to reveal that information to the competitor that he joins even where he may be employed by that competitor in the part of its business which does not compete with the former employer or he joins it in a capacity in which he does not need to make use of or disclose that information in order to perform his new duties. These are difficult considerations which the court must weigh in considering the reasonableness of any post-termination restraint taken to protect 'category 3' confidential information.

(e)   An express restrictive covenant in an employment contract not to make use of the employer's confidential information during or after the employment will be construed so as to apply to 'Faccenda Category 2' information during the contract but only 'Faccenda Category 3' information after the contract has ended: see *SBJ Stephenson Ltd v Mandy* [2000] IRLR 233.

(f)   The duration of an express restrictive covenant is frequently unlimited in time, but this is not fatal to the validity of such an express covenant: *SBJ Stephenson v Mandy* (ibid) and *Caterpillar Logistics Services (UK) Ltd v Huesca de Crean* [2012] EWCA Civ 156, [2012] ICR 981.

In *Brandeaux Advisers (UK) Ltd v Chadwick* [2010] EWHC 3241 (QB), [2011] IRLR 224, the defendant employee transferred by email from her work computer to her personal computer vast quantities of confidential materials concerning the Claimants' investment funds. It appears that the employee was "storing" the materials for the purposes of using them in the event that litigation ensued between her and her employer and/or in case there was a dispute with Regulators (she had been chief compliance officer for the Claimants' Group).

The Claimant bought proceedings against the defendant for breach of express confidentiality terms in her contract and for breach of the implied duty of fidelity. The defendant contended that there were implied terms in her contract of employment which entitled her to use her employer's confidential information or disclose it to third parties where such use or disclosure was "fairly required for her legitimate interests or to protect her legal rights or to defend herself" and that she was so entitled where the use or disclosure was in the public interest including use or disclosure in relation to financial regulators.

The judge held that this was not a case involving legitimate whistleblowing (and even if it had been he doubted whether using confidential information in reporting matters to a regulator could ever justify the wholesale transfer of an employer's information onto an employee's personal computer). Moreover the judge doubted that the possibility of future litigation could ever justify an employee so transferring confidential information of their employer. An employee should, in the event of a dispute, rely upon the court's disclosure process to provide relevant documents. In the event, on the facts, the judge held that the employee was not entitled to transfer the information and in so doing was in repudiatory breach of her contract of employment.

39.14 RESTRAINT OF TRADE AS A DISCRETIONARY ELEMENT IN GRANTING INJUNCTIVE RELIEF

Garden leave injunctions

It is now clear (see *Symbian v Christensen*, above) that considerations of restraint of trade play an important part in influencing the court's discretion to grant injunctive relief to enforce express or implied negative obligations of employees during notice periods. This is not the application of the 'classic' doctrine of restraint of trade. It differs in the following fundamental respects from the classic doctrine:-

(a)   the court is enforcing contractual rights which at the time the contract is made would not be subject to the restraint of trade doctrine in its classic form because those rights of the employer (namely the right to exclusive service by the employee) would not, under the classic doctrine, be considered a restraint of trade;

(b)   the court looks to the position as at the date when garden leave is imposed rather than the position when the contract was first entered into;

(c)   the court is able to temper the relief granted, both as to the ambit of any injunction and as to its duration; the court is not obliged to impose injunctive relief which exactly mirrors the contractual provisions in question (see *GFI Group Inc v Eaglestone* [1994] IRLR 119);

(d)   it would seem that the court can take into account interests of the employer which go beyond the legitimate interests that the court would uphold in enforcing post-termination restraints under the restraint of trade doctrine. In *Provident Financial* Dillon LJ considered it legitimate, in principle, to grant garden leave injunctions not only when there was a risk to the employer's confidential information or client connection from the departing employee, but also where the employee would merely enhance a competitor's business if he joined it during his notice period. This appears to come perilously close to supporting covenants in gross (ie covenants against mere competition).

Thus, the court can impose injunctions restraining an employee on garden leave from joining or assisting a competitor of the employer for a period less than the notice period stipulated in the contract of employment (*GFI v Eaglestone*, above). Equally, the court may limit the injunctive relief granted – and will so limit it – to restrain the employee only from working for a competitor during the whole or part of the notice period, but will not restrain an employee during his notice period from working for a new employer not in competition with the existing employer: see *Provident Financial Group plc v Hayward* [1999] ICR 160. There is no principle which requires a court to refuse to enforce a covenant in restraint of trade operating post termination of a contract of employment where a court has, during the notice period of the employee under that contract, granted a 'garden leave' injunction: see *Credit Suisse Asset Management Ltd v Armstrong* [1996] ICR 882, CA. However, the Court of Appeal in that case opined that the position might be different, and the post-termination restraint not enforced, in circumstances where it was preceded by a very lengthy period of garden leave, ie of a year or more. It should also be observed that the decision in *Armstrong* does not prevent a court, when judging the reasonableness of a covenant operating post-termination, from taking into account a period of garden leave. Thus, if an employee is subject to a post-termination restraint prohibiting him from joining a competitor after termination of his employment and that employee is also subject to a garden leave provision during his notice period the court may conclude (looking at the contract from the date it was entered into) that the combination of the garden leave period and the non-compete period would involve too lengthy a 'sterilisation' of the employee in question. This is particularly so where the employee is subject to other post-termination restraints such as a non-solicitation or non-dealing covenant. The court may strike down the non-competition covenant but uphold the non-solicitation and non-dealing provisions: see *Credit Suisse First Boston (Europe) Ltd v Padiachy* [1999] ICR 569, [1998] IRLR 504. Nevertheless, it should not be supposed that a period of garden leave is to be regarded as a desirable alternative to post-termination restraints: in *TFS Derivatives Ltd v Morgan* [2004] EWHC 3181 (QB), [2005] IRLR 246, counsel for the employee sought to argue that a three-month non-compete clause was unlawful because the interest to be protected (client connection) could more appropriately and reasonably have been protected by a 'garden leave' clause of six months. He invited Cox J to make general observations as to the reasonableness and greater attraction of garden leave clauses generally. Cox J declined, observing that a six-month garden leave clause could legitimately be regarded as more onerous for the employee than a three-month non-compete because it prevented the employee from working at all. She also noted that the employer may understandably not wish to pay the employee for six months of no work and, further, that such a clause may not, in any case, be adequate to protect the employer's interests because it would not operate on summary termination of the contract by either party.

In *Tullett Prebon plc v BGC Brokers LP* [2010] EWHC 484 (QB), [2010] IRLR 648 Jack J held that as a matter of discretion in imposing injunctive relief he could enforce fully by injunction for the full term of notice garden leave provisions and then enforce, but for a duration shorter than the contractual term, post-termination restraints. This is impermissible because it amounts to re-writing the post-termination restraints by reducing the duration thereof by means of an injunction. In so doing, he clearly overlooked *Mont v Mills* (supra) and *Provident Financial v Hayward* (supra). This point was not considered on appeal in *Tullett*: [2011] EWCA Civ 131, [2011] IRLR 420. However, in *QBE Management Services (UK) Ltd v Dymoke and ors* [2012] EWHC 80 (QB), [2012] IRLR 458 Haddon-Cave J confirmed the orthodox position.

39.15   Restraint of trade and springboard relief

Employees who commit breaches of duty to their employer whilst employees by copying or removing customer lists or other confidential information for use in a rival business either during or after the termination of their employment contracts may be restrained by 'springboard injunction' from dealing with the customers whose details they have filched from their employer (see *Roger Bullivant Ltd v Ellis* [1987] ICR 464 and *PSM International plc v Whitehouse* [1992] IRLR 279, CA).

Recently the court has also shown itself to be willing to grant springboard relief to counteract the effect of breaches of duty other than the duty of confidentiality. Thus in *Midas IT Services Ltd v Opus Portfolios Ltd* (21 December 1999, unreported), Ch D, springboard relief injuncting a company which it was alleged had procured breaches of the duty of trust and confidence by a senior employee of the claimant for a period of six months from acquiring a licence to distribute software was granted. The breaches of duty allegedly induced by the enjoined company were not breaches of the obligations of confidentiality. This authority was followed in *UBS Wealth Management (UK) Ltd v Vestra Wealth LLP* [2008] EWHC 1974 (QB), [2008] IRLR 965, the court holding explicitly that springboard relief was not limited merely to breach of confidence cases. Where there has been mass poaching by illicit means of employees and/or clients, springboard injunctions may issue to restrain the poacher from employing employees illicitly poached or from dealing with clients illicitly solicited. The ambit and duration of such springboard injunctions are necessarily fact sensitive and it is not possible to formulate guidelines.

However, in all cases the ambit and duration of springboard injunctions will be influenced by considerations of restraint of trade. A springboard injunction necessarily interferes with the enjoined parties' right to do certain kinds of business with certain people and judges appreciate that the effect of imposing such injunction will be to impose restraints of trade in circumstances in which an employee may not have any express post-termination restraints in his contract of employment:

'I am acutely conscious of the fact that competition should be encouraged and I am acutely conscious of the fact that it must be quite wrong to impose a restraint which is effectively only going to operate to stop a man using his acquired skills rather than to stop him using confidential information which he ought never to have taken into use at all.'

Fisher-Karpark Industries Ltd v Nichols [1982] FSR 351.

Nonetheless, the judge granted the springboard injunction in that case against employees who it was alleged had misused confidential information of their employer in a rival business.

'Interim injunctions can be granted to prevent defendants . . . from obtaining an unjust headstart in, or a springboard for, activities detrimental to the person who provided them with confidential information. . . . However, in relation to that type of information, as distinct from that concerning real trade secrets, the court should be concerned that it does not, in granting such an injunction, give the injured party more protection than he realistically needs and, in particular, discourage or prohibit what in the course of time becomes legitimate competition.'

per May LJ in *Bullivant v Ellis*, above, at 481G-H.

'The [springboard] injunction is directed to fairness of competition. Because the policy of the law is to encourage and certainly not to restrain fair competition the injunction is limited in duration to that period in which, in the court's estimation, the person injuncted could reasonably be expected to have assembled the confidential information using lawful means if earlier the assembled information comes as such into the public domain'

per Blackburn J in *Midas IT Services Ltd v Opus Portfolios Ltd* (unreported, Ch D, 21 December 1999, pp 13–14)

In one springboard case at least (*Bullivant v Ellis*, above), the Court of Appeal considered that the appropriate duration of springboard relief in respect of an employee who had removed a card index of clients from his employer prior to the termination of his contract which he afterwards used in a rival business ought to be limited to the same period of a post-termination restraint in his contract of employment prohibiting dealing with his former employer's customers. It is submitted, however, that this direct correlation between springboard relief and the period of any post-termination restraint will not be invariably be adopted by the courts. Some forms of activity by employees in breach of their duties of trust and confidence whilst employed either in respect of the removal or misuse of confidential information or in respect of other wrongdoings, such as the canvassing or soliciting of the employer's customers during their employment for a rival business will cause serious harm requiring periods of restraint by springboard injunction of a longer duration than any post-termination restraint in the employment contract. After all, post-termination restraints are framed at the outset of a contract to protect a limited class of interests and in the expectation that the employee will abide by his contractual duties during his employment. The employer cannot, in framing covenants which are no more than adequate to protect his interests, anticipate and build into such covenants protection against any possible breach of trust and confidence which might be committed by the employee during his contract of employment.

In *Tullett Prebon plc v BGC Brokers LP* [2010] EWHC 484 (QB), [2010] IRLR 648 the court was invited to grant springboard relief against the defendant restraining it from recruiting any of the claimants' staff for a period of 18 months from the first grant of interim injunctive relief in the proceedings. The judge determined that an appropriate period for such form of relief would be approximately 12, not 18, months and that the basis on which it should be granted was not springboard relief, but as a *quia timet* injunction. The judge held that the recruitment of the claimant's staff had been achieved by illicit means and that the claimant was entitled to fear that such means might be deployed again. Since those means were difficult to detect it was necessary to injunct the defendants from any recruitment of the Claimant's staff. The difficulty with this approach is that the logic of it points not to a limited period of relief but, rather, to a permanent injunction. Moreover, there seems no principled basis upon which this form of *quia timet* relief can be subject to a limited duration. The judge appears to have held that he could limit the period of this form of relief to 14 days from the delivery of his judgment in this case. He stated "There is no justification for any further substantial extension of the relief. The court must assume that the exposure of BGC's conduct as set out in the judgment will curb unlawful recruitment in the future. BGC is a substantial and ostensibly responsible company. The relief against BGC will be continued for 14 days from the delivery of the judgment so the judgment may be absorbed. It will then end." The learned judge did not explain upon what basis it could be assumed that the defendant would, by reason of having absorbed his judgment, cease to pursue its illicit poaching operations. It is respectfully submitted that springboard relief is to be preferred in these kinds of case because it is relief which is intrinsically subject to limitations of duration. This point was not considered on appeal in *Tullett*: [2011] EWCA Civ 131; [2011] IRLR 420. However, *QBE Management Services (UK) Ltd v Dymoke and ors* [2012] EWHC 80 (QB), [2012] IRLR 458 restores what it is submitted are the proper principles of springboard relief in this area, in particular, that the length of springboard relief must be a function of how long it would have taken the defendants to achieve the springboard advantage had they employed lawful means to do so.

39.16 PROCEDURAL MATTERS

Pleading

Because the common law doctrine of restraint of trade requires contractual provisions falling within it to be justified before they are enforceable, employers seeking to enforce such provisions ought to plead in their particulars of claim the grounds justifying the restraint. Equally, a defendant who wishes to attack a covenant as unenforceable should raise in his defence the grounds upon which he claims the covenant is unenforceable. It would appear that a court cannot of its own motion raise issues of unenforceability of covenants under the restraint of trade doctrine: see *Petrofina (Great Britain) Ltd v Martin* [1966] Ch 146. Accordingly, the parties must raise these issues themselves. It is to be observed, however, that there have been instances in which a court has, of its own volition, taken the point that a covenant is in unlawful restraint of trade: see *Marion White Ltd v Francis* [1972] 1 WLR 1423.

In cases which raise issues of confidential information (whether as justifying a covenant in restraint of trade or otherwise) the information claimed to be confidential must be properly and fully particularised in any statement of case and as early as possible (see *Ocular Sciences Ltd v Aspect Vision Care Ltd* [1997] RPC 289). In particular, where injunctions restraining disclosure or use of confidential information are sought the confidential information to be protected must be fully particularised: see *Caterpillar Logistics Services (UK) Ltd v Huesca de Crean* [2012] EWCA Civ 156, [2012] ICR 981. In order to protect highly confidential information from public disclosure in the course of proceedings orders should be sought from the court at the earliest possible stage that particulars of confidential information contained in any statement of case should not be available on the court file for public inspection. The best practice is to plead the details of any confidential information at issue between the parties in a confidential annexure to the statement of case.

39.17 Injunctions

It has long been recognised by the courts that the proof of loss and damage arising from a breach of a post-termination restraint in an employment contract is a difficult, if not impossible, matter. Accordingly, in the vast majority of cases, the covenantee will seek to enforce restraints by way of injunction. However, it must be remembered that an injunction is a discretionary remedy and, even where a court holds a restraint to be valid, it will retain a residual discretion as to whether to enforce that contractual restraint by injunction or not. Thus, if an employer delays before seeking an injunction, such that a substantial part of the period of the restraint sought to be enforced has elapsed before injunctive relief is sought, then the court may not grant an injunction at all: see *Wincanton Ltd v Cranny* [2000] IRLR 716, CA. The personal circumstances of the defendant in injunction cases may also be relevant in that the court will weigh any hardship that might be occasioned by the imposition of an injunction (see *Corporate Express Ltd v Day* [2004] EWHC 2943 (QB), [2004] All ER (D) 290 (Dec)). It is, however, submitted that injunctions should not be refused merely because the defendant is likely to be impoverished by them for that would create a licence to breach contractual duties based upon a means test. Some special or exceptional hardship would need to be shown for an injunction to be refused by a court: see *Norbrook Laboratories*, ibid.

For the purposes of interim injunction, there is no special rule applicable to restrictive covenants in employment contracts. The principles in *American Cyanamid Co v Ethicon Ltd* [1975] AC 396 will apply and if the covenantee raises serious issues to be tried as to the enforceability of that covenant an interim injunction will almost invariably be granted: see *Lawrence David Ltd v Ashton* [1991] 1 All ER 385, [1989] ICR 123. The court will, if requested by the defendant against whom an interim injunction has been granted, generally order a 'speedy trial'. In the event that a 'speedy trial' is not possible before the period of the restraint in question elapses, however, a different approach will be taken by the court to the grant of an interim injunction. In such a case, the court must go beyond deciding whether there is a serious issue to be tried and attempt some assessment of the claimant's prospect of success at trial: see *Lansing Linde Ltd v Kerr* [1991] 1 WLR 251, *per* Staughton LJ at 258. The court should not, however, allow the hearing of an application for interim injunctions in these circumstances to degenerate into a prolonged battle based upon evidence which cannot be tested at that stage by cross-examination. It is to be noted that issues as to the proper construction of a restrictive covenant (see above **39.6**) should normally be resolved at the interlocutory stage, unless the construction of the covenant depends on disputed facts that cannot properly be resolved without a trial: see *Arbuthnot Fund Managers Ltd v Rawlings* [2003] EWCA Civ 518, [2003] All ER (D) 181 (Mar). The recent decision in *Landmark Brickwork Ltd v Sutcliffe and ors* [2011] IRLR 976 seems to be a departure from the *Arbuthnot* guidance. It is respectfully submitted that construction issues must be resolved by the Court on an interim application, unless (and this will be a rare case) there is a dispute as to the factual matrix from which the contract arose. It cannot be right for a Court to impose an injunction based on a contract in restraint of trade without the Court determining what the true ambit of the restraint may be. The approach in *Landmark*, it is respectfully submitted, cannot be correct.

For the procedure on obtaining interim injunctions see *Parts 23* and *25* of the *Civil Procedure Rules*. Injunctions can also be sought as final relief at trial.

When considering whether to make, and making, an application for an interim injunction without notice or on short notice, it is vital to take note of the guidance given by Silber J in *CEF Holdings Ltd v Mundey* [2012] EWHC 1524 (QB), [2012] IRLR 912. That case well illustrates the dangers of short notice and without notice applications. It should never be forgotten by practitioners that an action to restrain by injunction employees or former employees may have the effect of destroying a nascent business or otherwise seriously damaging a person's ability to earn a living in the manner of their choosing. To take such a step without affording the employee an opportunity properly to be represented and resist such an application should really only be contemplated in extreme cases, for example where there is clear evidence that a former employee has obtained and is misusing or proposing to misuse confidential information of his former employer or where there is clear evidence that former employees are engaged in surreptitious efforts to suborn the loyalty of other employees or surreptitious efforts illicitly to capture or divert work from former employer's customers. In any event, in all cases where an application for injunctive relief is made without notice or on short notice the applicant must have carried out as full an investigation as possible into the circumstances of alleged misconduct and relayed to the Court those circumstances together with any other factual or legal defence that may be available to the defendant to the Court asked to grant an injunction. Fundamental to the obligation to make full and frank legal disclosures as well as factual disclosures is the obligation to alert the Court to any matters which may go to whether or not the Court has a jurisdiction to grant the injunctive orders sought or any of them, as well as to alert the Court if the interim injunction may effectively dispose of the injunction part of the case such that the Court should apply the principles in *Lansing Linde Ltd v Kerr* rather than the 'standard' *American Cyanamid* test

39.18   Declaration

It is, of course, open to a covenantor (employee) to challenge the enforceability of a covenant in restraint of trade by initiating legal proceedings seeking a declaration that the covenant in question is unenforceable. It is not clear, and must be open to doubt, whether a defendant could obtain an interim declaration to this effect pending trial, even a speedy trial. Alternatively, where a court refuses a claimant an injunction on the basis that there is only a very short period left for the restraint to run, it may nonetheless grant the claimant a declaration that the covenant in question is reasonable and enforceable (see *Corporate Express Ltd v Day* [2004] EWHC 2943 (QB), [2004] All ER (D) 290 (Dec)).

39.19   Damages where confidential information or trade secrets are involved

As for damages, there is a dearth of reported cases upon how damages for breach of a post-termination restraint are to be calculated. On ordinary principles, however, an employer can only recover for loss of any profit that he might have made had the covenant not been breached rather than his loss of revenue. In the event that customers have been filched by an ex employee in breach of a restraint against soliciting or dealing with them, the court may be able to assess at trial the loss of profits incurred by the employer up to the date of trial, but will be faced with the difficult task of assessing future loss which must be based on the employer's chance of retaining those customers: see *SBJ Stephenson Ltd v Mandy* [2000] IRLR 233.

39.20   Accounts of profits

Where an employee has breached a post-termination restraint prohibiting him from joining a competitor and it can be demonstrated that he has revealed to that competitor confidential information or trade secrets of the employer, an account of profits may be ordered by the court. This will, however, be an account of profits for breach of confidence rather than for breach of the negative covenant not to join a competitor. Despite the House of Lords' decision in *A-G v Blake* [2001] 1 AC 268 that accounts of profits can, in certain circumstances, be ordered against an employee for breach of a negative restraint, it is submitted that this principle cannot and should not be applied in the case of ordinary employees outside government security services. The award of an account of profits for breaches of confidence is a discretionary one. Unlike in cases of breach of fiduciary duty, the claimant does not have an automatic entitlement to an account of profits for such breaches: *Walsh v Shanahan, Leonard and SLH Properties Ltd* [2013] EWCA Civ 411.

40 Retirement

40.1 RETIREMENT AGE

The age at which an employee must retire was once a matter solely to be determined by the contract of employment. In the past, employers and employees were free to agree a contractual retirement age, in which case employment would terminate without the need for further action by the parties at the date the employee reaches the relevant age.

However, following the coming into force of the *Employment Equality (Age) Regulations 2006* ('*2006 Regulations*') on 1 October 2006, any retirement age lower than 65 has been unlawful unless it could be objectively justified. This remained the case following the coming into force of the *Equality Act 2010* in October 2010.

The next development was that the "national default retirement age" of 65 was revoked by the *Employment Equality (Repeal of Retirement Age Provisions) Regulations 2011 (SI 2011/1069)* ('*Repeal Regulations*'). This means that <u>any</u> "retirement" dismissal is now unlawful unless it can be objectively justified.

The state pension age is not of itself a contractual retiring age. Indeed it would be unlawful sex discrimination for an employer to require employees to retire at state pension age, since this disadvantages women whilst pension age differs according to sex. Under the *Pensions Act 1995*, the state pension age is being equalised at age 65. This was being phased in over a 10 year period which commenced on 6 April 2010. The *Pensions Act 2011* amended the timetable and state pension age will now be equalised at 65 by November 2018. The state pension age will then increase to 66 for both men and women from December 2018 to October 2020. The government has also announced its intention to introduce further rises to 67 (between 2034 and 2036) and to 68 (between 2044 and 2046). However, the government has announced plans to revise the legislation so that the rise to 67 will occur between 2026 and 2028 and to introduce a regular and structured method to consider future changes taking into account life expectancy.

Pensionable age under an occupational pension scheme is distinct from both the contractual retirement age and the state pension age (although each may be the same). It is unlawful to provide different pensionable ages for men and women in an occupational pension scheme following the decision of the ECJ in *Barber v Guardian Royal Exchange Assurance Group*: C-262/88 [1991] 1 QB 344 that pension benefits were 'pay' within *art 141* of the *Treaty of Rome* (formerly *art 119*): see further EQUAL PAY (21) for the UK legislation giving effect to this decision; note that this does not affect pensions earned by service prior to 17 May 1990 (the date of the *Barber* decision). It follows that, so long as pensionable age under the statutory provisions is different according to sex, (ie 60 for women and 65 for men), an employer cannot simply use the state pension age for an occupational pension scheme (see, for example, the ECJ's decision in *Kleist v Pensionsversicherungsanstalt*: C-356/09 [2010] All ER (D) 37 (Dec)). The courts have on occasion allowed rectification of pension schemes to equalise the retirement age for men and women where the trustees have intended but failed to amend the relevant scheme (see, for example, *Pioneer GB Ltd v Webb* [2011] EWHC 2683 (Ch) and *Industrial Accoustics Ltd v Crowhurst*, Ch (15 May 2011, unreported)).

The question as to whether an individual has retired (eg for the purposes of a pension scheme) is usually one of fact and degree; thus the House of Lords has held that a managing director who withdrew from active involvement in the running of a company but remained in office as an unpaid non-executive director had retired: *Venables v Hornby* [2003] UKHL 65, [2004] ICR 42. The Court of Appeal has held that a provision in a pension scheme conferring enhanced benefits on employees who 'retire at the request of' the employer applies to those employees who take voluntary redundancy or early retirement, but not those who are made compulsorily redundant: *AGCO Ltd v Massey Ferguson Works Pension Trust Ltd* [2003] EWCA Civ 1044, [2004] ICR 15.

40.2   EMPLOYMENT PROTECTION AND RETIRING AGE

The enforced retirement of an employee is often a source of resentment, and may provoke a claim for unfair dismissal and for age discrimination. (If there is no provision in the contract for retirement and contractual notice is not given, there could also be a claim for wrongful dismissal.)

Until October 2006, most employees were unable to bring claims for unfair dismissal if, on or before the effective date of termination, they had attained the 'normal retiring age' or, if none, the age of 65. A body of case law considered the meaning of 'normal retiring age' and there were exceptions for most 'automatically unfair' dismissals. In *Rutherford v Secretary of State for Trade and Industry* [2006] UKHL 19, [2006] ICR 785, [2006] IRLR 551 the House of Lords rejected a claim that the age ceiling on claims of unfair dismissal amounted to indirect sex discrimination against men. (Similar considerations might also have applied in relation to the now repealed 'National Default Retirement Age' of 65, introduced by the 2006 Regulations.)

The *2006 Regulations* removed the age ceiling on the right to complain of unfair dismissal as of 1 October 2006. They added 'retirement' as a potentially fair reason for dismissal in certain circumstances and set out the circumstances in which a dismissal was deemed to be by reason of retirement and when such a dismissal was fair.

Similarly, the *2006 Regulations* revoked a provision which previously restricted the right to a redundancy payment to those who had attained the 'normal retiring age' or, where there was no such age, the age of 65.

There was also an exception from the prohibition on age discrimination for dismissals by reason of retirement at or above the age of 65 (the 'National Default Retirement Age').

The above was unaffected by the coming into force of the *Equality Act 2010*. However, the *Repeal Regulations* changed the situation entirely. "Retirement" is no longer listed as a potentially fair reason for dismissal. Further, the National Default Retirement Age was also repealed. This means that, unless the employer can prove that the retirement is "some other substantial reason" for the dismissal, the dismissal will be unfair within the meaning of *s 98* of the *Employment Rights Act 1996*. Also, unless the employer can objectively justify the dismissal, the dismissal will additionally constitute discrimination on the grounds of age.

An employee required to retire in breach (or in the absence) of a contractual retirement age will be able to make a claim for breach of contract. However, if the employer gives the notice required under the contract, the fact that the reason for giving notice is to enforce retirement will not render an otherwise lawful dismissal a breach of contract. This is so even where the employer has an equal opportunity policy which includes provisions excluding age discrimination: *Taylor v Secretary of State for Scotland* [2000] ICR 595.

40.3   The Old Law – Employment Equality (Age) Regulations 2006

The separate chapters on discrimination (DISCRIMINATION AND EQUAL OPPORTUNITIES I (10), II (11), and III (12)) set out further detail of the provisions of the *2006 Regulations* and the *Equality Act 2010*. In particular, those chapters address questions relating to matters such as objective justification.

The following section summarises the key provisions of the *2006 Regulations* in so far as they relate to retirement. The coming into force of the *Equality Act 2010* in October 2010 did not have any significant effect on the relevant law and some key provisions remained in force.

However, the *Repeal Regulations* brought substantial changes which are discussed below at **40.4**. They came into force, subject to complicated transitional provisions, on 6 April 2011.

The scheme under the *2006 Regulations* continues to apply in some cases which are still being considered by the courts and tribunals. The analysis is therefore retained in this edition.

The *2006 Regulations* came into force on 1 October 2006 and the relevant provisions of the *Equality Act 2010* on 1 October 2010. The key principles under that now-repealed regime are, in summary, as follows:

(a) Dismissing an employee by reason of retirement was a potentially discriminatory act, unless the employee was at or over the age of 65 (subject to the matters discussed further below). Retirement of an employee below the age of 65 amounted to age discrimination, unless the retirement was a proportionate means of achieving a legitimate aim (*reg 30(2)* read with *reg 3(1)*, *2006 Regulations*; *s 4*, *s 13*, *Equality Act 2010*). (The question of when a dismissal was 'by reason of retirement' is discussed further below.)

(b) If the reason for the dismissal was retirement, it was not unlawful to dismiss an employee who was at or over the age of 65 (*reg 30(1)* of the *2006 Regulations*; or *para 8(1)* of *Sch 9* to the *Equality Act 2010*). The age of 65 was therefore described as the "National Default Retirement Age" or "NDRA". Although a legal challenge to the compatibility of the NDRA with European Community Law was unsuccessful, the judge held that this was only in the light of an upcoming government review: see (*R (on the application of Age UK) v Secretary of State for Business, Innovation & Skills* [2010] ICR 260) (As explained below, the NDRA has subsequently been repealed).

(c) Employers were obliged to give employees written notice of the date upon which it was intended that they would retire. This notice had to be given not more than one year and not less than six months before dismissal: *para 2(1)*, *Sch 6*, *2006 Regulations*. Employers were also required to notify employees of the right to make a request not to retire on that date. The essential information had to be given within the notification itself without the need to refer to extraneous documents: *Howard v Campbell's Caravans Ltd* (UKEAT/0609/10/LA) (unreported). In *R & R Plant Hire (Peterborough) Ltd v Bailey* [2012] EWCA Civ 410, [2012] IRLR 503, the Court of Appeal held that, in so doing, the employer had also specifically to state that any request be made pursuant to *para 5* of *Sch 6* to the *2006 Regulations*. If an employer failed to give such notice, an employment tribunal could make an award of compensation of up to 8 weeks' pay subject to the limit on a week's pay set out in *s 227(1)(b)* of the *Employment Rights Act 1996* (*para 11* of *Sch 6*).

(d) An employer who had failed to give notice was under a continuing duty to do so until the 14th day before dismissal (*para 4* of *Sch 6*).

(e) Employees had a statutory right to make a request to their employers not to retire on the intended retirement date. A request had to be in writing and had to be stated to be such a request. In any request, the employee had to propose that his employment should continue indefinitely, for a stated period, or until a stated date. An employee was only able to make one request. The request had to be made within time limits. If the employer had given notice in accordance with (c) above, the employee had to make the request more than three months but not more than six months before the intended date of retirement. If the employer had not complied with (c), then the employee could make a request not more than six months before the intended date of retirement (*para 5* of *Sch 6*).

(f)   Employers were under a duty to consider any such request (*para 6 of Sch 6*). In *Compass Group Plc v Adoyele* [2011] IRLR 802, the EAT held that the employer was obliged to consider the matter in good faith, in the sense that he must genuinely have considered whether it should be accepted. Employers were entitled to have a policy of refusing requests but this could not be an inflexible rule: see [7]. The employer was required to hold a meeting to discuss the request with the employee within a reasonable period after receiving it. Both the employer and the employee were required to take all reasonable steps to attend the meeting. The duty to hold a meeting did not apply if the employer and the employee agreed that the employment would continue indefinitely, or for an agreed period, and the employer had given notice of this to the employee. If it was not practicable to hold a meeting within a reasonable period, the employer could consider the request without holding a meeting provided that he considered any representations made by the employee. The employer was then required to give the employee written and dated notice of the decision. If the employer decided to refuse the request, the notice was required to confirm that the employer wished to retire the employee, the date on which the dismissal would take effect and how the decision might be appealed (*para 7 of Sch 6*).

(g)   Employees were entitled to appeal in writing against a refusal to a request. If an employee appealed, the employer was required to hold a meeting with the employee to discuss the appeal (unless the appeal was upheld or this was not reasonably practicable). The employer was then required to notify the employee in writing of the decision on the appeal. There were fairly strict time limits for each of these stages (*para 8 of Sch 6*).

The *2006 Regulations* removed the age limit on the right to complain of unfair dismissal. Instead, retirement became a potentially fair reason for dismissal (see *s 98(2)(ba), ERA 1996*). In order for a 'retirement' dismissal to have been fair, the employer had to show that retirement was the reason for the dismissal and also that the dismissal was fair. These were not questions of fact which a tribunal might determine in all the circumstances. Instead, there were specific provisions determining when these conditions are met.

Although the *Equality Act 2010* largely repealed the *2006 Regulations*, the provisions described above in *Schedule 6* of the *Regulations* were unaffected and remained in force until their repeal by the *Repeal Regulations*.

Was retirement the reason for the dismissal under the 2006 Regulations regime?

Again, it must be stressed that the following only applies to dismissals which were unaffected by the *Repeal Regulations* which came into force on 5 April 2011.

It was only when specified criteria were met that retirement was taken to be the reason for a dismissal. The specification relied on the concept of 'normal retirement age'. This was defined to mean the age at which employees in the employer's undertaking who hold, or have held, the same kind of position as the employee were normally required to retire (*ERA, s 98ZH*). A body of case law had built up around the meaning of the slightly different phrase 'normal retiring age'. These authorities might have been helpful in the context of the normal retirement age, although unlikely to be binding. For a helpful restatement of the principles concerned in determining the 'normal retiring age' by the Court of Appeal, see *Barclays Bank plc v O'Brien* [1994] IRLR 580.

Retirement was taken to be the reason for a dismissal in the following circumstances:

(a)   the employee had no 'normal retirement age', the date of termination fell after the employee's 65th birthday, the employer had properly notified the employee of the intended retirement in accordance with *para 2 of Sch 6* to the *2006 Regulations*, and the employment contract terminated on the intended date;

(b)   there was a 'normal retirement age', that age was 65 or higher, the date of
       termination fell after the employee reached the normal retirement age, the employer
       had properly notified the employee and the employment contract terminated on the
       intended date; or

(c)   there was a 'normal retirement age' of under 65, this retirement age was justified, the
       date of termination was on or after the date when the employee reached this age, the
       employer had properly notified the employee, and the employment terminated on
       the intended date.

(See *ERA 1996, ss 98ZA to 98ZE* as inserted, since repealed.)

Retirement was not the reason for the dismissal if:

(a)   the employee had no 'normal retirement age' and the date of termination fell before
       the date when the employee reached the age of 65;

(b)   the contract of employment terminated before the intended date of retirement
       (regardless of whether or not there was a 'normal retirement age', what that age was,
       whether or not the employee was over 65 or over the 'normal retirement age' and
       whether the employer had properly notified the employee.);

(c)   there was a 'normal retirement age', and the date of termination fell before the date
       on which the employee reached that age; or

(d)   there was a 'normal retirement age' of under 65 and it constituted unlawful
       discrimination under the *2006 Regulations* for the employee to have that normal
       retirement age (ie it cannot be justified).

(See *ERA 1996, ss 98ZA to 98ZE*, since repealed.)

It should be noted that, on the face of these provisions, if there was an unjustified normal
retirement age of under 65, then an employer could *never* retire an employee, even when that
employee had reached the age of 65.

In other cases, the Tribunal (or court) was required to consider whether or not retirement
was the reason for the dismissal more generally. In so doing, the Tribunal was required to
have particular regard to:

(a)   whether the employer informed the employee of the intended retirement more than
       14 days before the intended date of retirement;

(b)   how long before the notified retirement date the notification was given; and

(c)   whether or not the employer followed the procedures relating to the duty to consider
       a request to work beyond retirement

(*s 98ZF of ERA 1996* as inserted, since repealed).

Was the dismissal fair under the 2006 Regulations regime?

If the reason or principal reason for a dismissal was retirement, the employee was regarded
as unfairly dismissed if and only if there had been a failure on the part of the employer to
comply with one or more of the following provisions of *Sch 6* to the *2006 Regulations*:

(a)   the continuing duty to notify the employee of the retirement until 14 days before the
       intended date of retirement (*para 4*, if not already given under *para 2*);

(b)   the duty to consider the employee's request not to be retired (*para 6 and 7*); and

(c)   the duty to consider an appeal against the decision to refuse a request not to be
       retired (*para 8*).

40.3   Retirement

In all other circumstances, a retirement dismissal was fair.

As will be clear from these provisions, employers under the *2006 Regulations* regime were obliged to follow a precise and fairly rigorous procedure before retiring an employee. However, so long as the employer properly followed the procedure, it was unlikely that a retired employee would be able to bring a successful claim for unfair dismissal (or age discrimination). However, this did not mean that an employer could never be liable for loss following a properly notified retirement dismissal. If, for example, an employee resigned claiming constructive dismissal on the basis that his employer was making him retire by reason of a protected disclosure, the employee's loss did not cease at the date that the retirement dismissal was to take place: *Freeman v Ultra Green Group Ltd (in creditors voluntary liquidation)* (UKEAT/0239/11/CEA). In assessing compensation for an unfair dismissal, the tribunal must consider whether or not, if a fair procedure had been followed, the employee would have been dismissed at the same time or shortly thereafter in any event: *Rowstock Ltd v Jessemy*, EAT (26 September 2012, unreported).

These provisions remained in force following the coming into force of the *Equality Act 2010* in October 2010.

40.4   The Existing Law following the Employment Equality (Repeal Of Retirement Age) Regulations 2011

The *Repeal Regulations* made significant changes to the statutory framework in relation to retirement. Subject to the transitional provisions which are set out further below, they came into force on 6 April 2011.

The important effects are as follows:

(a)   Retirement at or above the age of 65 is not an exception to the protection against age discrimination (*reg 2(2)* of the *Repeal Regulations* repealed *para 8* of *Sch 9* to the *Equality Act 2010* so as to remove the retirement exception). Accordingly, a dismissal at any age constitutes a potentially age discriminatory act unless it can be objectively justified by showing that the decision is a proportionate means of achieving a legitimate aim.

(b)   A decision not to recruit someone because at the time of their application they are aged 65 (or, if greater, the normal retirement age) or over or will be within six months also potentially constitutes age discrimination (*reg 2(3)* of the *Repeal Regulations* repealed *para 9* of *Sch 9* to the *Equality Act 2010*).

(c)   Retirement is no longer listed as a potentially fair reason for dismissal (*s 98(2)(ba)* of the *Employment Rights Act 1996* has been removed). The provisions set out in *s 98ZA–98ZH* for determining whether or not a dismissal was by reason of retirement and for judging the fairness of that dismissal have therefore also been repealed. An employer now has to show that the dismissal was for "some other substantial reason" and fairness will be determined in accordance with the usual principles under *s 98(4)* (see UNFAIR DISMISSAL (51)).

(d)   *Schedule 6* of the *2006 Regulations* has been repealed, thus repealing the right of employees to request to continue working following retirement and the duty on employers to consider any such request.

The transitional provisions are as follows.

The old regime applied if notification of retirement was given under *para 2* or *4* of *Sch 6* to the *2006 Regulations* prior to 6 April 2011 if the employer reached age 65 (or the normal retirement age if this is higher) before 1 October 2011 (*reg 5(1)* of the *Repeal Regulations*). However, even in relation to an employment where this applied:

(a)   an employer could not issue a notification on or after 6 April 2011 in relation to such an employee; and

(b)   an employee could not make a request to continue working on or after 5 January 2012.

(see *reg 5(4)* of the *Repeal Regulations*)

From 6 April 2011, the old regime did not apply in any case where the normal retirement age was below 65 (see *reg 5(6)*, *Repeal Regulations*).

40.5   JUSTIFYING RETIREMENT DISMISSALS

Employers can no longer rely simply on compulsory contractual retirement ages as a defence to claims for age discrimination or unfair dismissal. Since 1 October 2011, employers have been required objectively to justify any and all retirement dismissals. If a retirement dismissal cannot be justified, it will constitute discrimination on the grounds of age and would also be likely to be unfair.

Since the retirement exception never applied to contract-workers, office-holders, barristers, advocates and partners, there has always been a requirement to justify any "retirement" of those non-employees. There have therefore been a few domestic authorities which have addressed whether such retirements can be justified. In *Hampton v Ministry of Justice* [2008] IRLR 258, an employment tribunal held that the compulsory retirement of a part-time Recorder at the age of 65 could not be objectively justified.

In *Seldon v Clarkson Wright & Jakes* [2012] UKSC 16, [2012] IRLR 590 a firm of solicitors sought to justify the compulsory retirement of a partner at the age of 65. The tribunal at first instance accepted that the retirement was a proportionate means of achieving the legitimate aims of ensuring that associates were given a reasonable opportunity to become partners, facilitating the planning of the partnership and limiting the need to expel under performing partners. The EAT held that, although the tribunal was entitled to find that having a compulsory retirement age was justified, there was no evidence to support the justification of fixing the retirement age at 65. The Court of Appeal disagreed. The Supreme Court dismissed a further appeal. In doing so, the following useful guidance was given as to how the courts will assess the justification of retirement dismissals (see paragraphs [50] to [58] per Lady Hale):

(1)   The justification of direct age discrimination is different from the justification of indirect discrimination. Only certain kinds of aim are capable of justifying direct age discrimination. The aims must be social policy objectives of a public interest nature rather than purely individual reasons particular to the employer's situation such as cost reduction or improving competitiveness.

(2)   A certain amount of flexibility is permitted to employers in the pursuit of legitimate social policy aims.

(3)   The ECJ has identified a number of different legitimate aims in the context of justifying direct age discrimination. The following are those most likely to be relevant in the context of justifying a retirement dismissal:

•   promoting access to employment for younger people,

•   the efficient planning of the departure and recruitment of staff,

•   sharing out employment opportunities fairly between the generations,

•   ensuring a mix of generations of staff so as to promote the exchange of experience and new ides,

- rewarding experience,

- facilitating the participation of older workers in the workforce,

- avoiding the need to dismiss employees on the ground that they are no longer capable of doing the job which may be humiliating to the employee concerned, and

- avoiding disputes about the employee's fitness for work over a certain age.

(4)   These legitimate aims form two broad groups: inter-generational fairness and dignity.

(5)   It is necessary to ask whether an aim is legitimate in the particular circumstances of the employment concerned;

(6)   Even if there is a legitimate aim, it is still necessary to enquire whether that aim was in fact being pursued, although the aim need not have been articulated or even realised at the time when the measure was first adopted.

(7)   The means chosen must also be both appropriate and necessary to achieve the end.

(8)   The gravity of the effect upon the employees discriminated against has to be weighed against the importance of the legitimate aims in assessing the necessity of the particular measure.

(9)   Where a general rule was justified, the existence of that rule would usually justify the treatment which resulted from it.

(10)   In the context of intergenerational fairness, it is relevant that at an earlier stage of life, a partner or employee might have benefited from the rule.

On the facts of Seldon, the Supreme Court held that:

(1)   staff retention and workforce planning were both directly related to the legitimate social policy aim of sharing out professional employment opportunities fairly between generations;

(2)   limiting the need to expel partners by way of performance management was directly related to dignity aims;

(3)   the matter would be remitted to the employment tribunal because it was possible that the tribunal would have regarded the choice of a mandatory retirement age of 65 as a proportionate means of achieving the first two aims.

The Irish Equality Court ("IEC") has considered the justification of compulsory retirement in two recent cases. In *Doyle v ESB International Ltd* [2013] 1 CMLR 48, the IEC held that the compulsory retirement of a graphic designer shortly after his 65th birthday was lawful. That Court held that the dismissal was justified by reason of the aims of avoiding the embarrassment of compulsory medical examinations, offering career pathways to new employees and having a consistent rule across the workplace. By contrast, in *Sweeny v Aer Lingus TEO* [2013] 1 CMLR 51, the IEC held that a compulsory retirement at aged 65 was not justified. The only justification put forward by the employer was that it would be perverse for the complainant to receive a pension while still working. The IEC held that it was well established that receipt of a pension entitlement did not necessitate retirement and so no legitimate aim had been put forward.

The Court of Justice of the European Communities has also considered the justification of retirement dismissals in a number of cases.

In *Fuchs v Land Hessen* [2011] IRLR 1043, the CJEU held that a law providing for a compulsory retirement age was not precluded by the *Equal Treatment Directive* and that legitimate aims would include establishing an age structure that balances younger and older employees, encouraging the recruitment and promotion of young people and preventing disputes about employees' fitness to work beyond a certain age. By contrast, in *Prigge v Deutsche Lufthansa AG* [2011] IRLR 1052, the ECJ held that a compulsory retirement age of 60 for pilots set out in a collective agreement was unlawful. It was not "necessary for the protection of health" within the meaning of *Article 2(5)* and nor was it justified under *Article 6(1)* as an aim such as air traffic safety does not fall within the aims as it was not a "social policy objective". The CJEU has recognised that the automatic retirement of employees at an age when they are entitled to draw a pension has, for a long time, been a feature of employment law in many Member States and that it is widely used in employment relationships (see especially *Rosenbladt v Oellerking Gebaudereinigungsgesellschaft mbH*: C-45/09 [2011] 1 CMLR 32, [2011] IRLR 51; *Félix Palacios de la Villa v Cortefiel Servicios SA*: C-411/05 [2008] All ER (EC) 249, [2007] IRLR 989, and *Petersen v Berufungsausschuss für Zahnärzte für den Bezirk Westfalen-Lippe* [2010] IRLR 254). The CJEU has noted in these cases that retirement raises issues as to the balance to be struck between political, economic, social, demographic and/or budgetary considerations and the choice to be made between prolonging people's working lives or, conversely, providing for early retirement. It has repeatedly accepted that in such social policy matters the national authorities enjoy a wide margin of discretion (see also *Mangold v Helm*: C-144/04 [2005] ECR I-9981, [2006] 1 CMLR 43). The CJEU has in these cases accepted that the aim of sharing employment between the generations, with its associated benefits, should, in principle, be regarded as objectively and reasonably justifying differences in treatment on grounds of age such. However, what will be scrutinized carefully in each case is the proportionality of the retirement or measure in question, in particular whether it actually serves that legitimate aim, or whether the aim could be achieved in another way or without 'catching' the particular employee or employee group in issue.

In *Hörnfeldt v Posten Meddelande AB*: C-141/11 [2012] 3 CMLR 37, [2012] IRLR 785, [2012] Eq LR 892, the CJEU held that a Swedish law, under which compulsory retirement below 67 was prohibited while an employer could terminate an employment contract at 67 was not precluded, despite not taking into account the amount of an employee's retirement pension, The CJEU reiterated its *Rosenbladt* position as to balance, and considered that promoting access of young people to a profession is a legitimate aim. The Court held that the measure was appropriate and necessary as it reduced obstacles for those who wished to work beyond 65, made it easier for young people to enter and/or remain in the labour market and made it possible to avoid situation in which elderly workers are terminated in humiliating circumstances. It was necessary, despite not taking into account the amount of retirement pension an individual would receive as it conferred an unconditional right to work until 67, did not provide a mandatory scheme of automatic retirement in that the contracting parties could agree to a fixed term contract beyond the age of 67 and takes into account the availability (if not the amount) of a retirement pension.

On references to the CJEU, the CJEU has in some cases ruled that the question of proportionality is one that must be addressed by the national Court. Thus it was in the 'Heyday' challenge [2009] ICR 1080, CJEU. On its return to the Administrative Court (*R (on the application of Age UK) v Secretary of State for Business, Innovation & Skills* [2010] ICR 260), Blake J held that the national default retirement age was based upon a social policy aim of certainty, clarity and maintaining confidence in the labour market and that it was proportionate for there to be such a blanket exception. The judge further held that the choice of age of 65 was within the margin of appreciation when it was adopted in 2006 but that the conclusion might have been different had there been no suggestion of an upcoming government review. Blake J also indicated that he did not presently see how 65 could remain as the appropriate age after that review. It was this decision that led to the removal of the *reg 30* exception to the *AR 2006* and the end of the national default retirement age.

40.5 Retirement

In *Palacios* (above), however, the CJEU went so far as to find the measure in question actually justified and did not leave the matter to the national court. The significant difference between 'Heyday' and *Palacios* was that in *Palacios* the default retirement provision was contained in a collective agreement. The CJEU considered it important that it had specifically been considered and agreed by the social partners that a default retirement age (corresponding to the age at which individuals become entitled to a state pension) was appropriate and necessary in the context of the particular labour market at issue. In *Rosenbladt* (above), too, the CJEU held the compulsory retirement provision to be justified and did not leave the matter to the national court. Again, the provision in question was in a collective agreement which the CJEU considered enabled specific account to be taken of the nature of the labour market in question (cleaning in this case). The CJEU also considered it to be important that although there was a provision for automatic retirement at 65, German law also prohibited anyone over the age of 65 from being refused employment on grounds of age. This was thought important since it struck an appropriate balance between the aim of maintaining access to the labour market for younger people, whilst also permitting those who wished to work beyond 65 to do so. Similarly, in *Fuchs v Land Hessen*, Joined Cases C 159/10 and C-160/10; [2011] IRLR 1043 the CJEU found provisions of regional German law which required state prosecutors to retire at age 65 unless it was in the interests of the service for their employment to be extended by periods of up to one year, up to a maximum retirement age of 68, was justified. The factors that the CJEU held to be particularly important were: (i) that this was a profession in which the number of posts available was limited and accordingly there was a particular need to have a compulsory retirement age in order to allow the recruitment of younger workers; (ii) that the workers would not suffer financial hardship as they could continue working as independent legal advisers with no age limit, or they could draw a pension upon retirement; (iii) although budgetary considerations could not themselves provide justification, they could support the decision made about the age at which to draw the line; (iv) political considerations could also be taken into account; (v) the fact that the measure in question related only to one region of Germany was not significant; (vi) nor was the fact that there was (temporarily) a slight mismatch between the measure and the national retirement age (which had risen to 67 for workers other than civil servants). The CJEU emphasized the importance of the national authority adducing specific evidence of justification and not relying on assertions, as the CJEU considered had happened in the *Age UK* case (above).

Cases where compulsory retirement ages have been held not to be justified include:

Prigge v Deutsche Lufthansa AG: C-447/09 [2011] IRLR 1052 where the CJEU found that German legislation requiring pilots to retire at 60 was not justified in the interests of safety because, although the physical capabilities required of pilots did tend to become impaired in older age, there was no evidence that pilots ceased to possess the necessary physical capabilities at 60.

In *European Commission v Hungary*: C-286/12 [2013] CMLR 44, the CJEU held that a Hungarian law which created an abrupt change from a retirement age of 70 to one of 62 for judges, notaries and prosecutors was not justified and went beyond what was necessary. Although the aims (standardising age limits and facilitating access for young lawyers) were legitimate, the measure was not appropriate and necessary as there was no evidence that more lenient provisions could not have achieved the same ends.

Certain retirement-related measures have also been approached by the courts in the same way as retirement. See, eg *Georgiev v Tehnicheski universitet – Sofia, filial Plovdiv*: C-250/09 and C-268/09 [2011] 2 CMLR 179 (provision for university professors to have 12-month contracts only after 65 and to be compulsorily retired at 68 held by CJEU to be capable of justification, although it was for the national court to decide whether it was a proportionate means of pursuing the legitimate aim pursued), *Kraft Foods UK Ltd v Hastie* [2010] ICR 1355 (provisions capping redundancy pay at the level that would have been received had employment ceased at 65 proportionate and justified) and compare

Ingeniorforeningen i Danmark v Region Syddanmark: C-499/08 [2011] 1 CMLR 35 (measure providing severance payments for all long-serving employees but not those over 65 was disproportionate because it applied to all employees over 65 regardless of whether they were actually drawing a pension).

For a detailed analysis of the law on objective justification outside the retirement context, see further DISCRIMINATION AND EQUAL OPPORTUNITIES II (11) at 11.9.

40.6 EARLY RETIREMENT

There is no legal impediment to employees voluntarily retiring early, subject only to the giving of any notice required under the contract of employment. Where there is a pension scheme, of which the employee is a member, the scheme may provide for the drawing of a pension on early retirement, generally with the consent of the employer. Occupational pension schemes which meet the requirements for Inland Revenue approval (the vast majority do, since this is a condition for favourable tax treatment) are precluded from paying a pension earlier than age 55 except where retirement is on grounds of ill-health. For employees over 55, early retirement may be used as an inducement to accept redundancy, and pension scheme rules typically offer one or more of the following benefits:

(a)   immediate payment of the pension that would have been payable at pensionable age, without reduction for early payment;

(b)   commutation of part of the pension to a lump sum;

(c)   conferment of additional years of service in computing the pension; and

(d)   permitting the employee to divert all or part of a severance payment into the pension scheme to purchase added years.

The position of individuals depends on the detail of usually complex scheme rules, operating within limits defined by Inland Revenue requirements. The European Court of Justice has ruled (*Beckmann v Dynamco Whicheloe Macfarlane Ltd*: C-164/00 [2002] All ER (EC) 865) that benefits by way of payment of an immediate and/or augmented pension on termination of employment for redundancy are not 'old age, invalidity or survivors' benefits' within the meaning of the *Acquired Rights Directive 1977*, and accordingly the right to such benefits is preserved when an employee is transferred to a new employer as a result of a relevant transfer of the former employer's undertaking, or part thereof. The ECJ has reiterated these conclusions, in relation to voluntary early retirement, and confirmed their application to public sector pension schemes regulated by statutory provisions: *Martin v South Bank University*: C-4/01 [2004] 1 CMLR 472. See also *reg 10* of the *Transfer of Undertakings (Protection of Employees) Regulations 2006* (see TRANSFER OF UNDERTAKINGS (50)). This has particular practical significance where employees transfer from public sector employers such as the NHS as a result of the contracting out of services, since the responsibility for funding often very expensive early retirement or redundancy terms will fall on the transferee employer. However, in *Procter & Gamble Co v Svenska Cellulosa Aktiebolaget SCA* [2012] EWHC 1257 (Ch), it was held that benefits first triggered as early retirement benefits became "old age benefits" at normal retirement age. Accordingly, the transferee was liable to meet the cost of early retirement up to normal retirement age but not afterwards.

Where an employer offered employees the opportunity to take early retirement and received too many applicants, it is sometimes permissible to apply a "cheapness criteria" to select those whose applications would be successful, despite any indirect age discrimination: *HM Land Registry v Benson* [2012] IRLR 373.

Ill-health retirement is frequently provided for in pension scheme rules. There is no standard set of criteria or procedures. Rules typically require medical evidence sufficient to satisfy the employer, the trustees or both that the employee is incapacitated from either performing any work or from his usual occupation. The requirement may be that the incapacity is expected or likely to be permanent, and rules may provide for the suspension of the payment of a pension (during the period until the employee reaches pensionable age) on evidence that he or she is again capable of work. For guidance as to the interpretation and application of criteria in scheme rules determining eligibility for ill-health retirement, see *Derby Daily Telegraph Ltd v Pensions Ombudsman* [1999] IRLR 476.

The benefits provided under the rules of pension schemes also vary considerably, but typically include immediate payment of an unreduced pension, sometimes with added years. The statutory pension schemes for police officers and firefighters provide for enhanced benefits, known as 'injury awards', where members retire on ill-health grounds as a result of an injury sustained in the course of duty. There are defined procedures for assessing the degree of incapacity (beyond incapacity for active police or fire service) and elaborate rights of appeal under each set of regulations.

Despite the pension advantages of ill-health retirement, if the employee objects to retiring, and if he or she is disabled within the meaning of the *Equality Act 2010* (or, previously, the *Disability Discrimination Act 1995*), the possibility that enforced retirement constitutes disability discrimination needs to be considered (particularly following the overturning of the House of Lords decision in *Lewisham London Borough Council v Malcolm* [2008] UKHL 43, [2008] 1 AC 1399 by the *Equality Act 2010*). See further DISCRIMINATION AND EQUAL OPPORTUNITIES II (11) at 11.9. Ill-health retirement may also constitute age discrimination, see further DISCRIMINATION AND EQUAL OPPORTUNITIES I (10) at 10.40.

Decisions whether to grant or refuse an ill-health pension are subject to limited control by the courts; good examples are *Harris v Shuttleworth (Lord)* [1994] ICR 991, CA on the correct interpretation of the definition of incapacity and *Mihlenstedt v Barclays Bank International Ltd* [1989] IRLR 522 on the employer's duty to act in good faith in assessing medical evidence of incapacity (discussed further at **40.12** below) and the *Derby Daily Telegraph* case (above) on the duty to construe the rules in a purposive and practical way.

40.7   CHANGING THE RETIREMENT AGE

Where the contract provides for a particular retirement age, the legal principles governing changes in terms of the contract of employment apply equally to any attempt to change the retirement age. In the absence of consent by the employees, or incorporation of an agreement reached through collective bargaining, a change cannot be unilaterally imposed through the contract. The failure of an employee to object to a change notified to him, as by a new statement of particulars of terms, does not amount to acceptance of the change by silence. This is most clearly so where the change has no immediate practical effect on the employee: *Aparau v Iceland Frozen Foods plc* [1996] IRLR 119.

This may have no practical consequences where the employer seeks to increase the retirement (as distinct from pension) age, since this would be no more than a promise to defer enforced retirement. Nor would a lowering of the age by unilateral notification, not accepted by the employee, prevent the employer from retiring an employee at the lower age by giving the contractual notice of termination (as a matter of contract). However, such a dismissal would in all probability be open to challenge as unfair and, might also amount to unlawful age discrimination (see above).

A variation to a contractual retirement age agreed between an employee and the transferee following a TUPE transfer is enforceable by the employee against the transferee. However, the employee would also be able to hold the transferee to the pre-transfer contractual position. In effect, such an employee can choose which he prefers: *Regent Security Services Ltd v Power* [2007] EWCA Civ 1188, [2008] 2 All ER 977, [2008] IRLR 66.

A term of a contract is unenforceable against a person in so far as it constitutes, promotes, or provides for treatment of that or another person that constitutes discrimination contrary to the *Equality Act 2010*, including age discrimination (*s 142*). (The broadly equivalent provision in the *2006 Regulations* was para *1, Sch 5*.)

Different considerations apply to changes in pensionable age under an occupational pension scheme. In relation to past service, such changes may be precluded by the rules of the scheme unless they are in all respects advantageous to the members affected. Changes designed to equalise pension ages between men and women following the ECJ's decision in *Barber v Guardian Royal Exchange Assurance Group:* C-262/88 [1991] 1 QB 344 are, in addition, subject to restrictions arising from principles of EU law: *Smith v Avdel Systems Ltd*: C-408/92 [1995] All ER (EC) 132; see further EQUAL PAY (22). Whilst these requirements do not prohibit a change that would have the effect, as regards future service, of 'levelling down' rights as a matter of European law, this is subject to the requirements of national law as to the validity of any change. The consent of individual employees would be required for a change in the pensionable age, even for benefits derived from future service, where that age is expressly or impliedly a term of the contract.

40.8   BENEFITS AFTER RETIREMENT

Employers may provide certain benefits to employees which continue beyond retirement. Even if the benefits are expressly provided to be discretionary they will nevertheless almost certainly be 'pay' in EU law: *Garland v British Rail Engineering Ltd* [1983] 2 AC 751, ECJ (concessionary travel facilities for families of retired employees); such benefits must therefore be provided without discrimination on grounds of sex.

If a benefit is contractual it must be provided, even if it becomes unduly expensive to continue its provision: *Baynham v Philips Electronics (UK) Ltd* (1995) IDS Brief 551 (private medical insurance during retirement). As there is no basis for compelling a former employee, who cannot be dismissed, to agree to abandon a continuing contractual right, the employer has no option but to 'buy out' the benefit or continue to provide it. The inclusion of such provisions in the contract of employment is therefore a matter requiring great caution.

40.9   PENSIONS

The law of pensions is outside the scope of this book. It is a large and complex area which it would not be practicable fully to summarise here. Pensions law rests mainly on the principles of the law of trusts (most pension schemes are administered, and the funds held, by trustees) and increasingly detailed statutory regulation. The principal legislation governing pension schemes is the *Pension Schemes Act 1993*, a consolidating Act, together with the *Pensions Act 1995*, the *Pensions Act 2004* and, most recently, the *Pensions Act 2011*. In addition, stakeholder pension schemes, are the subject of *Part I* of the *Welfare Reform and Pensions Act 1999* and supporting Regulations: see **40.10** below for brief details.

The *Pensions Act 2004* was a major piece of new legislation. Among other things, it established a new Pensions Regulator (replacing the Occupational Pensions Regulatory Authority) with a remit including the prevention of fraud and ensuring the proper funding of pension schemes as well as a Board of the Pension Protection Fund. The Board is responsible for administering a compensation scheme for employees in private sector pension schemes, who risk losing accrued pension rights if their employer becomes insolvent and the pension scheme is insufficiently funded. Other provisions include a requirement for the transferee employer following a transfer within the *Transfer of Undertakings (Protection of Employment) Regulations 2006* to provide those employees who have transferred with pension benefits for future service broadly comparable with those previously enjoyed.

Reform to the state pension was introduced in the *Pensions Act 2007* and to the private pension system in the *Pensions Act 2008*. The latter was aimed at enabling and encouraging more people to build up a private pension income to supplement the basic state pension.

40.9 Retirement

The *Pensions Act 2008* was followed by the *Workplace Pensions Reform Regulations 2010*. These reforms focused on the introduction of "automatic-enrolment" into workplace pensions schemes, from which an individual would need actively to opt-out, combined with a minimum employer contribution and the creation of a pension scheme, now known as the National Employment Savings Trust ("NEST") that could be used by any employer.

The *Pensions Act 2011*, which gained Royal Assent on 3 November 2011, made a number of changes including:

(a)   increasing the state pension age to 66 between 2018 and 2020, to be applied to both men and women; and

(b)   an expansion of the requirement for automatic enrolment.

In January 2013, the government published a new draft Pensions Bill. The draft Bill contains provisions to introduce a single-tier pension which would, for future pensioners, replace the current two-component State Pension with a single component flat-rate pension. It also includes provisions which would provide for a review of the State Pension age every five years, with the first review taking place in the next Parliament. Such a review would be based around the principle that people should expect to spend a certain proportion of their adult life in retirement and would be informed by actuarial reports. The draft Bill also sets out a number of provisions relating to private pensions.

The government has sought comments on the report and has stated that the Select Committee will publish a report, which the government will consider before introducing a Pensions Bill at the earliest opportunity.

Areas of particular relevance to employment are dealt with below: stakeholder pensions; discrimination and pension rights and benefits; the rights of members to elect trustees under the *Pensions Act 1995* and the legal protection of employee trustees; employers' duties in respect of pension schemes; and the machinery available to resolve employees' disputes and grievances about pension rights. Brief notes about some of the principal features of pension schemes, and pension terminology are given first. A helpful summary of the various types of state and occupational pensions is given in the booklet '*Compensation for Loss of Pension Rights*' (D Sneath, C Sara, C Daykin and A Gallop, 3rd edn, TSO 2003).

Pension schemes may be described as occupational or personal. *Personal pension schemes* are money purchase funds invested by the pension provider on behalf of the individual and used to purchase an annuity at retirement. Within statutory limits employee contributions are tax deductible. Employers may agree to make contributions, but are under no obligation to match contributions they would have made on the employee's behalf to the *occupational pension scheme*.

Occupational pension schemes may be *statutory* (the major public sector schemes covering a quarter of the employed workforce, principally the civil service and armed forces, local government and NHS workers, teachers and the police and fire service, under the *Superannuation Act 1972* and specific statutory regulations) or established by trust deed, to which the scheme rules are usually appended. They may be either *defined benefit*, also referred to as *final salary*, schemes, or *money purchase* schemes. The former provide benefits based on pensionable salary and years of service, normally either 1/60 or 1/80 of pensionable salary for each year of pensionable service. A lump sum retirement benefit may be provided, in addition to pension based on 1/80 of salary, or by commuting the capital value of part of the pension in 1/60 schemes (subject to limits imposed by the Inland Revenue). All the principal statutory public sector schemes are final salary schemes.

All major public sector schemes and most private sector schemes also provide for a (usually reduced) pension to be payable to a surviving spouse, often referred to as *survivor's benefit*. Some schemes extend the coverage of survivors' benefits to unmarried partners. In such cases, it would be unlawful to limit the benefit to partners of the opposite sex to the member concerned; but the restriction of benefits to the deceased member's spouse where the right to the benefit accrued or the benefit is payable in respect of periods of service prior to the coming into force of the *Civil Partnership Act 2004* is lawful, as is the conferring of a benefit on married persons and civil partners to the exclusion of other persons: see *Equality Act 2010, para 18* of Part 3 of Sch 9; or, prior to 1 October 2010, *reg 25* of the *2003 Regulations*. In *R (ota Cockburn) v Secretary of State for Health* [2011] EWHC 2095 (Admin), Supperstone J held that disregarding the period of pensionable service prior to a certain date when calculating widower's but not a widow's pension was lawful having regard to the cost of retrospective equalisation.

Money purchase schemes (also referred to as *defined contribution* schemes) have fixed rates of contribution, and benefits are purchased according to market conditions from the investment yield of the contributions. Following *Bridge Trustees Ltd v Yates* [2011] UKSC 42, [2011] 1 WLR 1912, [2011] ICR 1069, (in which the Supreme Court held that an equilibrium of assets and liabilities was not a requirement of a money purchase scheme), the government introduced a new clearer definition of a money purchase scheme (see *ss 181, 181A* and *181B* of the *Pension Schemes Act 1993* as amended/inserted by the *Pensions Act 2011*). The government then introduced provisions in the *Pensions Act 2011*, clarifying the relevant definitions.

Defined benefit schemes are funded by employer and employee contributions. Employees contribute a fixed percentage of salary and other pensionable earnings. Some schemes are non-contributory. The employer contributes the balance required to fund the scheme sufficiently, in accordance with an actuarial review of the liabilities of the scheme conducted at regular intervals. If the scheme is in surplus, the employer's contributions may be temporarily suspended (a 'pensions holiday'). There are complex rules, largely outside the scope of this book, as to the permissible uses of pension fund surpluses; see **40.16** for the most important cases on this.

Pensionable salary is the reference point for the calculation both of benefits under a defined benefit scheme and employee contributions. What earnings fall to be treated as pensionable is primarily a matter for the rules of the particular scheme; normally this will cover basic salary, but the position may be more complex where total pay is made up of a number of additional components such as shift allowances, production bonuses and other allowances. In *Newham London Borough Council v Skingle* [2003] EWCA Civ 280, [2003] 2 All ER 761, the Court of Appeal held that pensionable salary for the purpose of the *Local Government Pension Scheme Regulations 1997* included overtime payments, but only where, as in the instant case, the overtime was in effect obligatory on the employee, a school caretaker, who had been required to perform duties out of normal working hours by the nature of his job.

Schemes generally provide for employees to purchase additional years of pensionable service, up to the scheme maximum, by making *additional voluntary contributions* ('AVCs') up to an overall permitted maximum of 15% of pensionable earnings. (These are distinct from *free-standing additional voluntary contributions* ('FSAVCs') which are either single payment or periodic contribution personal pension schemes marketed by pension companies and purchased direct by employees, using the balance of tax relief available to the employee and not used up by contributions to the employer's occupational scheme.)

Pension schemes may provide additional benefits, including (as well as survivors' benefits as described above) pensions for surviving children or other dependants. Death in service benefit, in effect life insurance, of up to a maximum of four times pensionable salary, is commonly provided. The availability of these benefits, and of increases in benefits provided, is a matter primarily for the rules of the particular scheme, but increasingly the statutory framework of approved pension schemes lays down not only maximum benefits permitted within the framework of a favourable tax regime, but minimum standards that must be met.

40.9 Retirement

Contributions to personal pension schemes attract tax relief up to limits. For the tax years 2011/2012, 2012/2013, and 2013/2014 the limit on tax relief is £50,000. From tax year 2014/2015 onwards, the annual allowance will go down to £40,000.

Prior to 6 April 2011, the annual allowance was higher and different rules applied. Please see previous editions of this work for a brief description of the old rules.

The value of pension funds is necessarily dependent on the underlying value of investments in which the funds are held, and the amount of pension that can be bought from a fund of a given value depends on current annuity rates, which are lower for women than for men owing to differences in life expectancy. In a case relating to the *Goods and Services Directive*, the ECJ recently held, in *Association belge des Consommateurs Test-Achats ASBL v Conseil des ministres*: C-236/09 [2011] NLJR 363, [2011] Pens LR 145, that the use of gender based insurance premiums was contrary to the principle of equal treatment. In its decision, the ECJ did not refer to the *Equal Treatment Directive* (which prohibits occupational pension schemes from discriminating on the grounds of sex) or to its own previous case law such as *Coloroll Pension Trustees Ltd v Russell*: C-200/91 [1995] All ER (EC) 23, in which it held that the use of gender based actuarial factors does not contravene *art 157* of the *Treaty on the Functioning of the EU* (formerly *art 141* and, prior to that, *art 119* of the *Treaty of Rome*). The effect of *Test-Achats* remains to be seen. However, it would seem that it is difficult to see why the use of gender-based actuarial factors would be contrary to the principle of equal treatment in relation to insurance premiums but not in relation to pensions.

Sharp falls in the values of equities, following a steady decline in the rate of annuities which can be purchased on the realisation of pension fund investments, led many major employers to conclude that the provision of defined benefit pension schemes had become too expensive. Accordingly employers have, in significant numbers, adopted policies of closing their defined benefit schemes to new entrants, offering instead to contribute to new defined contribution schemes. Less commonly but more controversially, some employers have sought the closure of their defined benefit schemes in relation to future service of current members. The legality of such a step may be open to challenge, but whether it is challengeable in any particular case will depend on the precise terms of the employees' contracts, and of the pension scheme rules. A further distinction is that the rights earned by past service are likely to be protected by the rules of the Scheme from any retrospective adverse change, whereas rights to be accrued by future service are likely only to be protected (if at all) as a matter of contract. There is a general consensus that the benefits available under a defined benefit scheme are of greater value to employees than the alternative of money purchase scheme membership.

In *R (ota Staff Side of the Police Negotiating Board) v Secretary of State for Work and Pensions* [2011] EWHC 3175 (Admin), a judicial review of the Government's decision to alter the basis upon which public service pensions were adjusted to take account of inflation was unsuccessful. This change was likely to reduce the value of benefits to pension scheme members over time. In *R (ota Public and Commercial Services Union) v Minister for the Civil Service* [2011] EWHC 2041 (Admin), [2011] IRLR 903, McCombe J held that the rights of civil servants under the Civil Service Compensation Scheme which included redundancy and early retirement benefits, constituted possessions within the meaning of *Article 1* of the *First Protocol of the European Convention on Human Rights 1950*. However, the introduction of a new Scheme that reduced those benefits was a lawful proportionate interference with those rights.

A different but related matter of concern has arisen in a number of cases where a pension scheme has been wound up following the insolvency of the employer. The rules of each scheme determine the order in which claims on the scheme must be met in such circumstances; typically these require that the claims of those already in receipt of a pension must be met first. If the scheme is in deficit (which is possible up to a permitted margin, and more likely at a time of declining share prices) this may leave a serious shortfall for employees who were active (ie contributing) members of the scheme at the date of its closure, whose pensions may be dramatically reduced as a result. The *Pensions Act 2004* addressed this problem in two ways, by changing the priorities required to be followed in distributing the scheme assets, and by creating a compensation scheme for employees who lose accrued pension rights.

The *members* of a pension scheme are those employees who, being eligible, have elected to join the scheme, retired employees in receipt of a pension, and those former employees who have retained the right to a deferred pension payable at pensionable age. Employees who leave the service of the employer may withdraw their contributions, but only if pensionable service is under two years, or transfer the value to another employer's scheme or a personal pension. In either case the employee ceases to be a member of the first scheme. *Transfer values* are calculated by reference to actuarial valuations, but actual criteria depend on the rules of each scheme. A lump-sum payment is made to the new scheme which gives credit for years of service depending on its own advisers' computations of the cost of purchasing service. *Transfer values* may not therefore fully reflect accrued service. Further, the actuarial factors used include mortality tables reflecting the different life expectancy of, and therefore different cost of providing pensions for, each sex, so that transfer values may differ according to sex. The ECJ has held that this does not contravene *art 157* (formerly *art 141* and before that *art 119*) of the *Treaty of Rome* (*Coloroll Pension Trustees Ltd v Russell*: C-200/91 [1995] All ER (EC) 23). This exception is preserved by the UK legislation giving effect to EU law (see **21.17** EQUAL PAY for details) (but see above concerning the uncertain effect of the *Test-Achats* case). The same consequences, and legal exceptions, apply to the value attributed, in terms of additional years of service, to AVCs.

The *State Earnings Related Pension Scheme* ('SERPS'), established in 1975, was designed as a fallback for employees who do not benefit from occupational pensions. Pension schemes which met prescribed minimum standards could apply to be *contracted out* of SERPS. *Contracting out* was the norm for larger schemes, not least because both employer and employee paid lower rates of National Insurance if the employee was in a contracted-out scheme. In place of the SERPS pension the scheme was required to assure a *Guaranteed Minimum Pension*, protected by more stringent rules as to indexation and preservation where benefits are transferred or commuted. SERPS was replaced in April 2002, but for future earnings only, by the *State Second Pension*. Because the change is not retrospective, rights under SERPS will exist, in preserved form, for very many years. The State Second Pension accrues at different rates on banded earnings between the National Insurance lower earnings limit and the National Insurance upper earnings limit. Additionally, there are some credits for earnings for people with a long-term illness or disability.

The *Pensions Act 2007* provided for the abolition of contracting out on a money-purchase basis. Since 6 April 2012, it is no longer possible to contract out of the State Second Pension through a money-purchase scheme or a personal pension or stakeholder pension scheme. Those who already contract out will be able to continue to make their own contributions and benefit from any employer contributions but will not be able to benefit from any rebate of National Insurance contributions. It is, however, possible to contract out in a final salary or career average scheme.

The Pensions Bill 2013 contains provisions which would replace the two-component state pension with a single component flat-rate pension that would be set above the basic level of means-tested report.

40.10 Stakeholder pensions

The legislation for this form of pension is *Part I* of the *Welfare Reform and Pensions Act 1999* (which is largely enabling) and the *Stakeholder Pensions Scheme Regulations 2000 (SI 2000/1403)* as amended. The intention behind these pensions was to encourage individuals, particularly those with modest earnings, and who are not members of occupational pension schemes, to make provision for their retirement. Stakeholder pensions are private sector schemes but subject to registration, minimum standards of performance and approved schemes of governance. Schemes are required to be flexible, so that contributions can be suspended or varied, and any individual who is not contributing to a contracted out occupational pension scheme, including minors and those not in employment, can contribute up to a fixed amount per year. Contributions are made net of standard rate income tax, which is made up by the State, even if the individual is not a taxpayer. If earnings are sufficient, contributions in excess of the fixed amount a year gross can be made, with corresponding tax relief.

In the past, employers could, but could not be obliged to, contribute to individual employees' pensions. However, with the coming into force of the *Pensions Act 2008*, for the first time employers are being required to enrol eligible workers into a qualifying workplace pension arrangement, see further below for details.

Prior to the coming into force of the Pensions Act 2008, the situation was as follows. Employers with five or more employees who do not have a contracted-out occupational pension scheme for which all employees (with very limited exceptions) are eligible must designate a stakeholder scheme as, effectively, the preferred scheme: *s 3, Welfare Reform and Pensions Act 1999*, as amended. The obligations on employers in relation to a designated scheme (which must be one available to all the employer's employees) include:

(a)   consulting the employees or their representatives as to the choice of scheme;

(b)   supplying all employees with information about the scheme;

(c)   affording representatives of the scheme reasonable access to employees to provide information about the scheme; and

(d)   agreeing on request to collect employees' contributions from pay and remit them to the scheme.

There are limited exemptions, principally for employers with fewer than five employees, and in respect of some short-term employment. Contravention of any of these obligations renders the employer liable to civil penalties under *s 10* of the *Pensions Act 1995* of up to £5,000 in relation to an individual or £50,000 in other cases: such penalties are imposed by the Pensions Regulator (see **40.15** below).

Employers designating a particular stakeholder scheme are exempted from any duty to investigate or assess the performance of the scheme (*s 3(8) Welfare Reform and Pensions Act 1999*).

The above provisions are being replaced when the relevant provisions of the *Pensions Act 2008* comes into force.

40.11 Automatic enrolment under the Pensions Act 2008

The *Pensions Act 2008* ("*2008 Act*") puts into law reforms to the private pension system set out in the White Paper "Personal Accounts: a new way to save" published in December 2006. It contains a number of measures aimed at encouraging greater private pension saving.

The regime requires employers to enrol "eligible jobholders" automatically into an "automatic enrolment scheme" with effect from the date upon which such jobholders become eligible. Once an "eligible jobholder" is enrolled, the employer will be under an obligation either to make minimum contributions (if it is a defined contribution scheme) or to offer a minimum level of benefits (if it is a defined benefit scheme). Employers will also be under an obligation to provide certain information to eligible jobholders including information about automatic enrolment, what it means and their right to opt out.

The key duties to be imposed are contained in *sections 2* to *8* of the *Pensions Act 2008*, as amended ("*2008 Act*"). They will be imposed month by month over a multiple year "staging period" depending on the size of the employer. Employers with the most employees will be required to comply with the duties first. It is currently anticipated that employees with less than 50 employees will have until 2015 to comply with the duties. The relevant date in relation to each employer is called the "staging date".

The first task is to identify who is an "eligible jobholder". A "jobholder" is defined in *section 1* of the *2008 Act* as a worker:

(a)   who is working or ordinarily works in Great Britain under the worker's contract;

(b)   who is aged at least 16 and under 75; and

(c)   to whom "qualifying earnings" are payable in the relevant pay reference period.

"Worker" is defined in *s 88(3)* as an individual who has entered into or works under a contract of employment or any other contract by which the individual undertakes to do work or perform services personally for another party to the contract. "Contract of employment" is defined as a contract of service or apprenticeship, whether express or implied and (if it is express) whether oral or in writing (*s 88(1)*). These definitions are very similar to those set out in *s 230* of the *Employment Rights Act*. EMPLOYEE OR NOT [See Employee or Not insert parar ref] However, contracts of a client or customer of a profession or business undertaking are excluded (*s 88(4)*).

In relation to agency workers, in the absence of a workers' contract between the worker and either the agent or the principal, then the regime applies as if there was a workers' contract and whichever of the agent or the principal is responsible for paying the agency worker in respect of the work (or which of them does actually pay (*s 89*). Further, that person is treated as the employer for the purposes of automatic enrolment.

"Qualifying earnings" are defined in *s 13(1)* as the part, if any, of the gross earnings payable to that person in that period that is more than £5,564 but not more than £42,475 in a pay reference period of 12 months from 15 June 2012 until 5 April 2013 or more than £5,668 but not more than £41,450 for periods from 6 April 2013 (figures amended by *art 2(2)* of the *Automatic Enrolment (Earnings Trigger and Qualifying Earnings Band) Regulations 2013, SI 2013/667*). "Earnings" is defined to mean:

(a)   salary, wages, commission, bonuses and overtime;

(b)   statutory sick pay;

(c)   statutory maternity pay;

(d)   ordinary statutory paternity pay or additional statutory paternity pay;

(e)   statutory adoption pay; and

(f)   sums prescribed for the purposes of the section.

        (*s 13, 2008 Act*)

Where the pay reference period is less than 12 months, the figures are adjusted proportionately (*s 13(2)*).

Workers who receive gross earnings of more than the maximum figure will still qualify as jobholders. However, contributions will only be payable on the qualifying earnings.

A "jobholder" is "eligible":

(a)   who is aged at least 22,

(b)   who has not reached pensionable age, and

(c)   to whom earnings of more than £8,105 from 15 June 2012 until 5 April 2013 or
        £9,440 from 6 April 2013 onwards are payable by the employer in the relevant pay
        reference period.

(s 3, 2008 Act, as amended)

Further guidance has been published by the Pensions Regulator, see the Pensions
Regulator's Guidance Note No. 1 "Employer duties and defining the workforce" as to who
will count as a worker. The guidance states, for example, that office-holders such as
non-executive directors, company secretaries, board members and trustees are not workers
but that casual or zero hours workers are likely to be if the other conditions are satisfied.

Section 3 of the *Pensions Act* is the provision imposing the automatic enrolment duty.
Employers must enrol eligible jobholders in an automatic enrolment scheme with effect
from the "automatic enrolment date" (*s 3(2)*). This is defined as the first day on which the
section 3 duty applies to the jobholder (*s 3(7)*). This means either the staging date for the
employer or, if later, the date upon which the individual becomes an eligible jobholder
There are, however, provisions for deferral for up to three months upon written notice in
accordance with detailed rules set out in *section 4*.

Employers will only be required to comply with the key duties from the applicable staging
date. The Pensions Regulator has published an anticipated staging date deadline for all
employers. The first staging date was 1 October 2012 for those employers employing 120,000
people or more in their largest PAYE scheme as of 1 April 2012. For other employers, the
staging dates are as follows:

•   1 November 2012 for employers with a PAYE scheme of 50,000 to 119,999;

•   1 January 2013 for employers with a PAYE scheme of 30,000 to 49,999;

•   1 February 2013 for employers with a PAYE scheme of 20,000 to 29,999;.

•   1 March 2013 for employers with a PAYE scheme of 10,000 to 19,999;

•   1 April 2013 for employers with a PAYE scheme of 6,000 to 9,999;

•   1 May 2013 for employers with a PAYE scheme of 4,100 to 5,999;

•   1 June 2013 for employers with a PAYE scheme of 4,000 to 4,099; and

•   1 July 2013 for employers with a PAYE scheme of 3,000 to 3,999.

On 28 November 2011, Steve Webb, the Minister for Pensions, announced that the
timetable for small businesses employing less than 50 employees was delayed. The currently
proposed staging dates for small employers can be found on the Department of Work and
Pensions website.

The Pensions Regulator's Guidance Note No. 2 "Getting Ready" states that an employer's staging date will not be affected if the number of people in an employer's PAYE scheme
subsequently changes after 1 April 2012 even if that change is significant. This and further
guidance   notes   can   be   found   on   the   Pensions   Regulator's   website   at
www.thepensionsregulator.gov.uk.

In order to be an "qualifying automatic enrolment scheme", a pension scheme must be an
"automatic enrolment scheme" which "qualifies" by meeting certain quality requirements.
To be an "automatic enrolment scheme":

•   it must **not** prevent the employer from making the requirements for a jobholder
        automatically to become an active member of the scheme; or

- require the jobholder to express a choice in relation to any matter or to provide any information, in order to remain an active member.

(*section 17*)

In order to be a "qualifying scheme" it must:

- be an occupational pension scheme or a personal pension scheme;

- be registered under *Chapter 2* of *Part 4* of the *Finance Act 2004* (ie be registered for tax purposes); and

- satisfy the minimum "quality requirement" in relation to that a particular jobholder whilst that jobholder is an active member.

(*section 16*)

The "quality requirement" is defined differently for different pension scheme types (money purchase, defined contribution etc) and for UK and non-UK schemes. The detailed provisions are set out in *sections 20* to *28* of the *2008 Act* with further guidance in the Pensions Regulator's detailed guidance Note No. 4 "Pension Schemes".

If an employer does not wish to use an existing pension scheme or set up a new pension scheme, then it may use the National Employment Savings Trust ("NEST"). NEST is a central pension scheme established by a corporation set up by the Government. NEST is an occupational direct contribution scheme. Employers who use it must meet the minimum contribution requirements for such schemes to satisfy the minimum "quality requirement". This requires the employer to make contributions of at least 3% of the jobholder's qualifying earnings and require that the total contributions paid by the jobholder and the employer are at least 8%.

The duty to employers will not apply if, at the relevant date, the jobholder is already an active member of a qualifying scheme.

In addition to the requirement of automatic enrolment, employers are also obliged not to take any action by which a jobholder would cease to be an active member of a qualifying scheme or by which the scheme would cease to be a qualifying scheme (*section 2(1)*, *2008 Act*). Employers are not in breach of the section if the jobholder remains an active member of another qualifying scheme or if he or she requests to leave the scheme (*section 2(2)*). Nor are they in breach if an eligible jobholder ceases to be a member of a scheme for a prescribed period before joining another scheme.

Employers are also required automatically to re-enrol jobholders who were but are no longer members of the scheme for particular reasons. For details, see *section 5* of the *2008 Act* and *Parts 2* and *3* of the *Occupational and Personal Pension Schemes (Automatic Enrolment) Regulations 2010, SI 2010/772* ("*2010 Regulations*").

Finally, employers are required to provide employees with prescribed information in relation to their rights under *sections 2* to *8* of the *2008 Act* (see *section 10* of the *2008 Act*). The details are clearly set out in the Pension Regulator's detailed guidance Note No. 5 "Automatic Enrolment".

Opting out

Eligible jobholders are entitled to opt out of the scheme under *section 8* of the *2008 Act*. However, this is only possible during an "opt-out" period. This is a one month period following the later of the date on which the jobholder first became an active member of the pension scheme and the date upon which he or she was provided with written enrolment information (see *regulation 9* of the *2010 Regulations*). The notice must also be in a specified form set out in the schedule to those Regulations.

40.11   Retirement

Jobholders who have opted out can choose to opt back in but they may only do so once in the 12 month period from when they first choose to opt back in (*section 7*).

There are also detailed obligations to keep records.

"Non-eligible jobholders" and "entitled workers"

Non-eligible jobholders have the right to opt in to an automatic enrolment scheme (although their employer has no duty automatically to enrol them) (*s 7, 2008 Act*). They would then also have the right to opt out, if they so chose. Employers are also under obligations to inform these jobholders them about:

• their right to opt in;

• the fact that the opt-in notice must be in writing and signed or, if given by means of electronic communication, must include a statement that the worker personally submitted the notice;

• where they can find further information about pensions and saving for retirement.

This information must be provided within one month of the employee first satisfying the conditions of a non-eligible jobholder.

(*Regulation 17* of the *2010 Regulations*)

There is a final category of workers who have some rights in the new regime, "entitled workers". These are individuals aged between 16 and 75 who work (or ordinarily work) in the UK and have earnings below "qualifying earnings". These workers have the right to join a registered pension scheme (which need not be an automatic enrolment scheme or even a qualifying scheme. They must also be provided with information similar to that which must be provided to non-eligible jobholders.

Enforcement

Employers who wilfully fail to comply with the automatic enrolment duty, the automatic re-enrolment duty or the duty to allow jobholders to opt in will commit a criminal offence. The officers of a body corporate which commits such an offence may be liable to a fine or prison term of up to two years if the offence has been committed with the consent or connivance of an officer or is attributable to any neglect on the part of the officer (see *sections 45* to *47* of the *2008 Act*).

Employers will be prohibited from making any statement or asking any question directly or by an agent for the purposes of recruitment which indicates (expressly or impliedly) that an application for employment may be determined by reference to whether or not an applicant might opt out of automatic enrolment (*s 50(1), 2008 Act*).

Pursuant to *section 55*, employees have a right not to be subjected to any detriment by an act, or a deliberate failure to act, by the worker's employer, done on the ground that

(a)   any action was taken, or was proposed to be taken, with a view to enforcing in favour of a worker one of the specified employers' duties,

(b)   the employer was prosecuted under *s 45* as a result of action taken for the purpose of enforcing in favour of the worker one of the specified employers' duties, or

(c)   any of the specified employers' duties apply or will or might apply to the worker.

It is immaterial whether or not the requirement does apply or whether or not it has in fact been contravened but any claim that the requirement applies or has been contravened must be made in good faith (*s 55(2)*).

A dismissal cannot be a detriment within the meaning of *s 55*. However, a new *section 104D* has been inserted into the *Employment Rights Act 1996* which provides that an employee is unfairly dismissed if the reason or principal reason for the dismissal is that:

(a)   any action was taken, or was proposed to be taken, with a view to enforcing in favour of a worker one of the specified employers' duties,

(b)   the employer was prosecuted under s 45 as a result of action taken for the purpose of enforcing in favour of the worker one of the specified employers' duties, or

(c)   any of the specified employers' duties apply or will or might apply to the worker.

Again, it is immaterial whether or not the requirement does apply or whether or not it has in fact been contravened but any claim that the requirement applies or has been contravened must be made in good faith (*s 55(2)*).

A worker may present a complaint to an employment tribunal that he or she has been subjected to a detriment in contravention of *section 55*. Where the complaint is in relation to the termination of a contract which is not a contract of employment, the limits on compensation which apply to unfair dismissal compensation apply (see *ss 56(3)* and *(4)*).

There are restrictions on agreements to limit the operation of the scheme (*section 58, 2008 Act*) which are similar to those familiar from the *Equality Act 2010*.

40.12   Discrimination and occupational pension schemes

The *Equality Act 2010 EA 2010"*) contains provisions which prohibit discrimination in relation to pensions. Occupational pension schemes are deemed to include a "non-discrimination rule" (*s 61(1)*). A "non-discrimination rule" is a provision by virtue of which a responsible person (A) must not discriminate against another person (B) in carrying out any of A's functions in relation to the scheme, and must not, in relation to the scheme, harass or victimise B (*s 61(2)*).

The provisions of an occupational pension scheme have effect subject to the non-discrimination rule. A "responsible person" is a trustee or manager of the scheme, an employer whose employers are, or may be, members of the scheme and a person responsible for appointing a person to an office, where the office holder is or may be a member of the scheme (*s 61(4)*).

A discriminates against B for the purposes of *EA 2010* if A treats B less favourably than A treats or would treat others "because of a protected characteristic" (*s 13*). Disability, sex and age are among the protected characteristics. A discriminates against B indirectly by applying a provision, criterion or practice which A applies or would apply to others with whom B does not share the characteristic, but puts those sharing the characteristic at a particular disadvantage, puts B to that disadvantage and which A cannot show to be a proportionate means of achieving a legitimate aim (*s 19*). A also discriminates against a disabled person, B, if A treats B unfavourably because of something arising in consequence of B's disability, and A cannot show that the treatment is a proportional means of achieving a legitimate aim (*s 15*). Harassment and victimisation are defined in *ss 26* and *27* respectively.

A duty to make reasonable adjustments also applies to a responsible person (*s 20*).

Section 62 provides trustees and managers of occupational pension schemes the power, by resolution, to alter their scheme's rules to conform to the non-discrimination rule.

Where there is a breach of a non-discrimination rule, it is possible to bring proceedings under *Part 9* of *EA 2010* in the employment tribunal. (This does not prevent the investigation or determination of any matter by the Pensions Ombudsman.) The tribunal, if it finds a complaint well-founded, may make an order declaring that the complainant has a right to be admitted to the scheme or to membership of the scheme without discrimination (*para 6 of Sch 2*). In such cases, the tribunal may not make an order for compensation for age discrimination except for injury to feelings or where a respondent fails to comply with a recommendation (*para 6(4), Sch 2*).

The particular position in relation to each of sex and age discrimination is addressed further below.

40.13 *Sex discrimination and pension benefits*

There are further important restrictions on discrimination in the provision of benefits and terms of membership. In addition to the application of rules of sex equality and equal pay between the sexes, the *Social Security Act 1989 ('SSA 1989'), Sch 5*, gives protection to women who take paid maternity leave, and members of both sexes who take paid parental leave. Periods of paid maternity leave since 23 June 1994 must count as pensionable service. 'Paid' includes receipt of flat-rate Statutory Maternity Pay. However, contributions by employees may not be required to exceed the relevant percentage of pensionable salary applicable to employees generally, assessed on actual pay. The Pensions Act 2004 extended the provisions of *SSA 1989* to periods of statutory paid paternity and adoption leave. The *SSA 1989* does not provide for employer contributions; in a defined benefit scheme the employer is likely to pay the applicable percentage of actual pay, but a significant additional pension burden would affect the overall requirements certified by the actuary on a scheme valuation. In a money purchase scheme the position appears to be that the employer must make up any shortfall.

See generally DISCRIMINATION AND EQUAL OPPORTUNITIES – I (10) and EQUAL PAY (21).

The *SSA 1989* does not require unpaid maternity or parental leave to count as pensionable service. It is therefore a matter for the scheme rules as to whether any such periods are counted, and if so how they are funded. The effect of the decision of the ECJ in *Gillespie v Northern Health and Social Services Board: C-342/93* [1996] All ER (EC) 284 is that exclusion of unpaid leave from service does not contravene either *art 157* or the EU *Equal Pay* or *Equal Treatment Directives*.

However, the ECJ has ruled in *Boyle v Equal Opportunities Commission: C-411/96* [1998] All ER (EC) 879 that it is a breach of the *Pregnant Workers Directive (92/85)* to exclude from pensionable service any part of the core 14 weeks' maternity leave conferred by the *Directive*, whether it is paid or unpaid. The statutory framework for ordinary maternity leave, which is (since April 2003) a maximum of 26 weeks, requires the continuation of all contractual terms and conditions except those concerning remuneration (*ERA 1996, s 71(4),(5)*); 'remuneration' is defined by the *Maternity and Parental Leave, etc Regulations 1999 (SI 1999/3312), reg 9(3)* as limited to sums payable by way of wages or salary, and therefore not including contributions by the employer to the pension fund. This achieves the implementation of the *Boyle* decision, but for a longer period of maternity leave. All periods of statutory paid paternity and adoption leave which began on or after 6 April 2005 are treated in the same way as maternity leave (*paras 5A and 5B of Sch 5* to the *Social Security Act 1989* as inserted by the *Pensions Act 2004*).

The ECJ has also ruled that a reduction in the pension of civil servants who have worked part time contravened *art 157* since it affected a considerably higher proportion of women than men, if the reduction in the pension was greater than the proportion of the reduction of working hours: *Schönheit (Hilde) v Stadt Frankfurt am Main: C-4/02* and *C-5/02* [2003] ECR I-12575.

However, where it is established that the denial of access to an employer's pension scheme indirectly discriminated against part-time workers on the grounds of sex, the part-time employees are not entitled to a declaration of entitlement if they would have opted out of the scheme even if they had been eligible to join: *Copple v Littlewoods Plc* [2011] EWCA Civ 1281, [2012] ICR 254.

40.14 *Age discrimination and pension benefits*

EA 2010 does not contain exemptions specifically for age. However, there is a power for a Minister of the Crown to make exceptions in relation to rules, practices, actions or decisions relating to age. The relevant Order is the *Equality Act (Age Exceptions for Pension Schemes) Order 2010 (SI 2010/2133)*. That Order provides that it is not a breach of the non-discrimination rule:

(a)   for the employer, or trustees or managers of a scheme to maintain or use in relation to the scheme the rules, practices, actions or decisions:

  (i)   which are set out in *Schedule 1* to the *Order* (see the *Order* itself for the detail); or

  (ii)   as they relate to rights accrued or benefits payable in respect of periods of pensionable service prior to 1 December 2006;

(b)   for the employer to maintain or use practices, actions or decisions set out in *Schedule 2* to the *Order* in relation to the payment of contributions (see the *Order* itself for the detail);

(c)   for the trustees or managers to follow certain rules, practices, actions or decisions in relation to length of service (see *art 6*, as inserted by *SI 2010/2285* for the detail).

40.15 Employee pension trustees

Most pension schemes provide for the appointment by the employer of the trustees of the scheme. Many schemes provide for the appointment of a trustee company as sole trustee; its directors are in such cases usually nominated by the employer. Despite the stringent legal obligations of trustees to the members of the scheme, concern that in practice trustees are often vulnerable to pressure from the employer to take decisions in the employer's interest led to a significant change in the law.

Sections 241–242 of the *Pensions Act 2004* require at least one third of the trustees of a pension scheme established under a trust to be member-nominated, and the same minimum proportion of member-nominated directors where a trust company is the sole trustee. Further, the Secretary of State now has the power (by order) to increase the proportion to a half.

The *Occupational Pension Schemes (Member-nominated Trustees and Directors) Regulations 2006 (SI 2006/714)* set out detailed exceptions to the requirement for member-nominated trustees and member-nominated directors of corporate trustees for certain schemes, including small schemes and those that have few members.

The *Pensions Act 2004* also contains provisions requiring all individual trustees and corporate trustees to have knowledge and understanding of certain specified documents and legal principles.

Member-nominated trustees need not all be employees, but in practice most will be. Those who are employees have the right to be permitted to take reasonable time off for training in their duties and for the performance of those duties, and to be paid for such time off (*ERA 1996, ss 58–60*, consolidating provisions introduced by the *Pensions Act 1995*). They may bring a claim to the employment tribunal if the employer does not permit them to take the time off or pay them for it: *s 60, ERA 1996*. There is no equivalent right for candidates for election. Employee trustees are also protected from suffering detriment short of dismissal by reason of their performance or proposed performance of their functions as such (*ERA 1996, s 46*) and from dismissal for that reason (*ERA 1996, s 102*). The ambit of these provisions is similar to, but not identical to, the statutory rights and protection given to officials of an independent trade union and to statutory safety representatives and representatives of employee safety; see **47.2** and **47.9** TIME OFF WORK.

40.15 Retirement

Member-nominated trustees have the same duties in law to the beneficiaries of the trust funds as other trustees. Where (as will often be the case in practice) the nominated trustees have been put forward as candidates by trade unions there is a potential for conflict between their obligations as trustees and advocacy of union policy on such matters as ethical investment of funds or non-investment in competitor industries: see for a good practical example *Cowan v Scargill* [1985] Ch 270 (resolving the conflict in favour of the trustee obligations).

40.16 Employers' duties in respect of pension schemes

The obligations of pension trustees in relation to the management of funds, the alteration of rules and decisions as to individual cases are outside the scope of this book. A helpful judicial discussion of the position is to be found in *Stannard v Fisons Pension Trust Ltd* [1992] IRLR 27 (and see *Hillsdown Holdings plc v Pensions Ombudsman* [1997] 1 All ER 862, where the employer was ordered to return to the pension fund a surplus improperly paid out by the trustees). Further, it was recently held in *Power v Trustees of the Open Text (UK) Ltd Group Life Assurance Scheme* [2009] EWHC 3064 (Ch), [2010] SWTI 567 that the obligation of pension trustees does not extend to proposing benefit improvements.

There have also been a number of important decisions dealing with the rights and obligations of employers as opposed to trustees.

In *Mihlenstedt v Barclays Bank International Ltd* [1989] IRLR 522, the Court of Appeal held that, where a contract of employment provides for membership of a pension scheme, there is an implied obligation upon the employer to discharge his functions under the scheme in good faith and, so far as lies within his power, to procure the scheme's benefits for the employee. However, as recently emphasised in *Prudential Staff Pensions Ltd v The Prudential Staff Assurance Co* [2011] EWHC 960 (Ch), this implied duty does not go so far as to require an employer to arrive at a decision which is substantially fair or reasonable, see discussion below.

In *Mettoy Pension Trustees Ltd v Evans* [1991] 2 All ER 513, it was held that, where an employer was given a discretion under the rules of the scheme as to how certain surplus funds were to be applied, that was to be treated as a fiduciary power: the employer was under a duty to the objects of the power (the beneficiaries under the scheme) to consider whether and how to exercise it, and (presumably) to do so fairly and in good faith. Similarly, it was held in *Imperial Group Pension Trust Ltd v Imperial Tobacco Ltd* [1991] 2 All ER 597 that an employer's power under the rules of the scheme to give or withhold consent to an amendment of the rules had to be exercised in good faith, and the employer could only have regard to his own financial interests to the extent that to do so was consistent with that obligation of good faith. Thus the employer's rights had to be exercised with a view to the efficient running of the scheme, and not for the collateral purpose of forcing its members to give up their accrued rights. The Vice-Chancellor based this conclusion upon the employer's implied obligation to maintain the trust and confidence of its employees (see **7.15** CONTRACT OF EMPLOYMENT). However, in *British Coal Corpn v British Coal Staff Superannuation Scheme Trustees Ltd* [1995] 1 All ER 912, Vinelott J held that whilst the duty to act in good faith in relation to amendments was related to the duty applicable in cases of distribution of a surplus, it was not a fiduciary duty in the full sense. He found that it could not be said that *any* exercise of the relevant power of amendment had to be invalid if and insofar as the amendment might benefit the employer directly or indirectly. Further, in *Prudential Staff Pension Scheme, Re* [2011] EWHC 960 (Ch), [2011] Pens LR 239, Newey J reiterated that the obligation of good faith was not to be taken as requiring an employer to arrive at a decision which was "fair" when exercising a power given to him in apparently unfettered terms by the scheme rules. In deciding to award pension increases on a less generous basis than previously, the employer's power was to fiduciary and he was entitled to have regard to his own interests.

The question of recovery by the employer of surplus pension funds was considered in *National Grid Co plc v Mayes* [2001] UKHL 20, [2001] 2 All ER 417, upholding the right of the employer to appropriate a substantial surplus in the pension fund to meet debts owed by it to the fund. This case turned principally on the construction of the particular rules, and does not lay down any new general principles.

Where the pension scheme rules afford a benefit to employee members which is only available subject to the employee making an application or taking steps which necessitate being aware of the availability of and conditions for the benefit, the employer is under an applied contractual duty to draw to employees' attention the benefit and the necessity to take action to obtain or preserve it: *Scally v Southern Health and Social Services Board* [1992] 1 AC 294. An extension of this approach was shown in *Aspden v Webbs Poultry and Meat Group (Holdings) Ltd* [1996] IRLR 521, where the High Court held that an express term permitting dismissal on notice was subject to an implied term that it would not be used so as to defeat the employee's claim to disability benefits also provided for by the contract. This reasoning would apply equally to ill-health pension benefits. The implied term applied in *Aspden* received support, *obiter*, in the Court of Appeal in *Brompton v AOC International Ltd* [1997] IRLR 639 at 643, but was given a more limited construction in *Hill v General Accident Fire and Life Assurance Corpn plc* [1998] IRLR 641. See also *Villella v MFI Furniture Centres Ltd* [1999] IRLR 468.

The limits to the principle established by *Scally* are shown in *University of Nottingham v Eyett* [1999] 2 All ER 437: where an employee is aware of his entitlement to a benefit and is taking a decision as to how to maximise it, the employer is not under a positive duty to warn him that he has not chosen the most advantageous way. *Eyett* was approved and applied in the Court of Appeal in *Outram v Academy Plastics* [2000] IRLR 499, where a claim that employers owed a duty of care to an employee who had resigned after 20 years' service and later re-joined the employer, to advise him to re-join the employer's pension scheme, was struck out as having no prospect of success. Two points were emphasised: the established law that trustees of a pension scheme do not owe a duty of care to advise scheme members faced with choices about pension matters; and the principle (confirmed in *Scally*) that there cannot be any wider duty owed by an employer to an employee in tort than that owed in contract.

An employer answering queries from pension scheme trustees about a former employee's work record owes no duty of care to that employee which could make him liable for damages in negligence (*Petch v Customs and Excise Comrs* [1993] ICR 789; but cf *Spring v Guardian Assurance plc* [1995] 2 AC 296, referred to in **38.4 REFERENCES**).

40.17 Claims and disputes over pension rights

Some employees' claims in relation to pension rights may be taken to an employment tribunal. These include claims in respect of membership or benefits made under the *Equality Act*. Such claims may be made in appropriate cases against the trustees as well as (or instead of) the employer.

In addition, employees' rights against employers in relation to pensions are in their nature contractual, and the Court of Appeal has held this to be so in principle also for the member's relationship to the trustees (*Harris v Shuttleworth (Lord)* [1994] ICR 991, CA). Accordingly, pension disputes may be taken to an employment tribunal by an aggrieved employee, if they arise on or are outstanding at the termination of his employment, under the *Employment Tribunals Extension of Jurisdiction (England and Wales) Order 1994 (SI 1994/1623)* or the parallel Scottish Order. Claims against the trustees based on the contract of membership are permissible because the Order applies to claims under contracts connected with employment, and does not limit claims to those against the former employer. (This jurisdiction may not apply where the scheme is a statutory public sector scheme with the right to membership conferred, and benefits prescribed, by statute.)

However, there are important limitations to the tribunal's contractual jurisdiction. The only remedy it can award is damages, with a statutory maximum of £25,000. Claims can also be brought only following termination of employment, and within a three-month time limit. Claims must arise out of, or be outstanding on, the termination of the employment. In pension claims remedies such as a declaration of rights or a direction to the employer or trustees to determine a claim in accordance with law are often of importance, and claims may have a value considerably in excess of £25,000 where a pension payable for the rest of the claimant's life is in issue. Such claims must be brought in the ordinary courts and are in consequence rare.

However, there are other avenues to pursue claims and disputes, of increasing practical importance. The *Pensions Act 1995, s 50* created a statutory requirement for all occupational pension schemes (except those with only one member or where all the members are trustees) to establish a procedure for the internal resolution of all disputes raised by or on behalf of members or their dependents or prospective members. (This requirement applies equally to stakeholder pension schemes.) *Sections 50 to 50B of the Pensions Act 1995*, inserted by the *Pensions Act 2004*, set out requirements which these procedures must meet. Secondary legislation made under *s 50* sets out further detailed provisions.

A remedy of growing importance is a complaint to the Pensions Ombudsman (11 Belgrave Road, London SW1V 1RB, tel: 020 7630 2200; www.pensions-ombudsman.org.uk). The Pensions Ombudsman is a statutory body constituted under *ss 145–151* of the *Pension Schemes Act 1993* (as amended by the *Pensions Act 1995*), and his decisions are enforceable in law, subject to a right of any aggrieved party to appeal on a point of law to the High Court. For an example of a case exploring the extent of the right to appeal, see *Dolland v Trustees of BTG Pension Fund* [2011] All ER (D) 247 (Apr). The Pensions Ombudsman may determine any question of fact or law, or claim of maladministration raised by or on behalf of a scheme member, against either the employer or the scheme trustees, or the managers or administrators of a pension scheme. There are limited exceptions to this jurisdiction in relation to public sector schemes and he cannot normally act where the complainant has instituted court or tribunal proceedings (but the fact that such proceedings could be brought has no bearing on his jurisdiction). The High Court has held that the sanctions available to him include the award of compensation for distress and inconvenience, but the Court of Appeal expressly left this point open: *Westminster City Council v Haywood* [1998] Ch 377. Subsequent cases such as *Maclaine v Prudential Assurance Co Ltd* [2006] EWHC 2037 (Ch) have awarded compensation for this.

There is a time limit of three years for lodging complaints (extendable at his discretion in limited circumstances): *reg 5* of the *Personal and Occupational Pension Schemes (Pensions Ombudsman) Regulations 1996 (SI 1996/2475)*. Complaints should first be referred to the Pensions Advisory Service (TPAS) for possible informal resolution, and this step needs to have been completed, so that the complaint can be lodged before the expiry of the three-year time limit. TPAS can be contacted at 11 Belgrave Road, London SW1V 1RB, tel 0845 601 2923; further information is available on its website (www.opas.org.uk). There is a right of appeal to the High Court against final, but not preliminary, decisions of the Pensions Ombudsman. (However, in cases where there is no right of appeal an application for judicial review may be possible: see on both these points *Legal & General Assurance Society Ltd v Pensions Ombudsman* [2000] 2 All ER 577.) The Pensions Ombudsman is not automatically a party to an appeal, but may apply to appear in the appeal; in that event, if his decision is not upheld, the successful party may obtain an order for the Ombudsman to pay its costs on the appeal (*Moores (Wallisdown) Ltd v Pensions Ombudsman (Costs)* [2002] 1 All ER 737).

The Pensions Ombudsman has issued a number of determinations of far-reaching significance, particularly in relation to the use by employers of surpluses in pension funds; this has been accompanied by an increase in the number of appeals against his determinations, which have highlighted restrictions in the powers conferred on him by the *1993 Act*:

see, eg *Westminster City Council v Haywood* (above) and *Edge v Pensions Ombudsman* [2000] Ch 602, [1999] 4 All ER 546, holding that the Pensions Ombudsman cannot entertain complaints which could only be remedied by steps which would adversely affect the interests of third parties not party to the determination. (See also on this point *Marsh & McLennan Companies UK Ltd v Pensions Ombudsman* [2001] IRLR 505.)

The Pensions Regulator is the principal regulatory body controlling the activities of pension funds and trustees. It was established under the *Pensions Act 2004*, replacing the Occupational Pensions Regulatory Authority. Individual complaints continue to be dealt with by the Pensions Advisory Service.

41 Service Lettings

41.1 Some employers provide residential accommodation for their employees. They may do so because the nature of the work is such that the job can be done more efficiently if the employee is close at hand. Another reason may be that the work is in a part of the country in which there is a shortage of accommodation, and the only way in which the employer can attract workers is to provide them with somewhere to live.

The provision of such accommodation poses a dilemma for both employee and employer when the employment relationship comes to an end. The interest of the employee in retaining security of tenure in his home conflicts with the interest of the employer in regaining the accommodation so that he can use it for the employee's replacement. Another question is the extent to which rent controls apply.

It is not possible to give more than a broad outline of this area of law in a book on employment law, and those wishing to find more detailed discussion should consult such works as *Woodfall's Landlord and Tenant* or *Hill and Redman's Law of Landlord and Tenant*. That is particularly true of some of the complex transitional provisions associated with the change from the regime of the *Rent Act 1977* ('*RA 1977*') to that of the *Housing Act 1988* ('*HA 1988*'). Nor have we sought to deal here with matters such as the scope of the landlord's and the tenant's respective repairing obligations. A summary of the law as it affects employees is set out below. It has been assumed that situations such as that of a resident landlord are unlikely to arise in the employment context.

41.2 NATURE OF THE OCCUPANCY

It is of the greatest importance to distinguish between a *service tenancy* and a *service licence*. The grounds on which possession may be recovered from a tenant as opposed to a licensee are limited by statute (see below).

The test for distinguishing between a tenancy and a licence has been re-stated by Lord Templeman, giving the decision of the House of Lords in *Street v Mountford* [1985] AC 809 (see also *Bruton v London and Quadrant Housing Trust* [2000] 1 AC 406, HL). In *Street v Mountford*, Lord Templeman also gave guidance about the position of service occupiers.

> 'To constitute a tenancy the occupier must be granted exclusive possession for a fixed or periodic term certain in consideration of a premium or periodical payments' (p 818E).

> 'A service occupier is a servant who occupies his master's premises in order to perform his duties as a servant. In those circumstances the possession and occupation of the servant is treated as the possession and occupation of the master and the relationship of landlord and tenant is not created; see *Mayhew v Suttle* (1854) 4 E & B 347. The test is whether the servant requires the premises he occupies in order the better to perform his duties as a servant:

"Where the occupation is necessary for the performance of services, and the occupier is required to reside in the house in order to perform those services, the occupation being strictly ancillary to the performance of the duties which the occupier has to perform, the occupation is that of a servant";

> per Mellor J in *Smith v Seghill Overseers* (1875) LR 10 QB 422, 428'. (p 818G–H).

A requirement that the employee live in certain accommodation for the better performance of his duties (so that he is a licensee and not a tenant) may be expressed in his contract of employment or may be implied. A chauffeur who is given a flat above the garage, or a

41.2   Service Lettings

housekeeper who is given accommodation in the premises she is charged with looking after, would, save in exceptional circumstances, be considered to be occupying that accommodation for the better performance of his or her duties. Employers may consider it wise to state expressly in any contract of employment or letter of offer of employment (where it is the case) that the employee will be required to occupy certain premises for the better performance of his duties and that his occupation is to cease upon the termination of the employment. But such a statement will not avail the employer if it does not accurately reflect the reality of the situation: cf *Aslan v Murphy* [1989] 3 All ER 130. An employee will be a licensee rather than a tenant where he exclusively occupies an employer's residential accommodation in anticipation that, at a reasonable time in the future, the employment will benefit from that occupation; this applies notwithstanding that at the time when the employee entered into occupation, the occupation was irrelevant to his existing duties (*Norris v Checksfield* [1991] 4 All ER 327).

If the employee is not a service licensee in this sense, he may still be a lodger and not a tenant if the employer provides attendance or services which require him or his servants to exercise unrestricted access to, and use of, the premises. Otherwise, however, the agreement to grant exclusive possession for a term at a rent points to the creation of a tenancy. Indeed, in *Ashburn Anstalt v Arnold* [1989] Ch 1, the Court of Appeal held that even a rent was not an essential constituent of a lease (although this case was overruled by the House of Lords in *Prudential Assurance Co Ltd v London Residuary Body* [1992] 2 AC 386; and cf *Bostock v Bryant* (1990) 61 P & CR 23). Two cases illustrate the application of these principles in employment cases.

In *Postcastle Properties Ltd v Perridge* [1985] 2 EGLR 107, the plaintiffs brought a possession action for an estate cottage. The occupant, a man of 80 years, had been employed by the plaintiffs' predecessor in title. He remained in occupation, and continued to work for and to pay £1.50 per week rent to the plaintiffs after they purchased the premises. He was held to have a tenancy. Strong evidence was needed to rebut the presumption of tenancy, which was not forthcoming in that case.

In *Royal Philanthropic Society v County* [1985] 2 EGLR 109, the defendant was employed as a houseparent at the plaintiff's school. Initially he was provided with furnished accommodation in the school building. He was a licensee of the room. On marrying, he was provided with a house some miles from the school. Approximately one year later his employment came to an end, whereupon a notice to quit was served. Possession was successfully claimed in the county court. This was overturned on appeal, the Court of Appeal holding that the defendant was a tenant. Fox LJ said:

> 'The overall effect of *Street v Mountford* as we understand it is that an occupier of residential accommodation at a rent for a term is either a lodger or a tenant . . . ' (p 1071).

> 'The employment, it seems to us, is material only if there is a true service occupancy, ie where the servant requires the premises for the better performance of his duties as a servant . . . ' (p 1072).

Referring to a variety of factors put forward by counsel for the plaintiffs in his attempt to show that no tenancy was created, such as the informality of the paperwork, the relationship of the parties, and the fact that the previous occupancy was that of lodger, Fox LJ said:

> ' . . . it seems to us that they amount really to an attempt to go back to the approach, disapproved by the House of Lords in *Street v Mountford*, of examining the circumstances with a view to ascertaining the intention of the parties. The only intention that is relevant under the law as it now stands "is the intention demonstrated by the agreement to grant exclusive possession for a term at a rent" (*Street v Mountford* at p 891).' (p 1072)

These decisions serve to demonstrate that, although the employment relationship continues as before, the nature of the employee's occupancy of premises may change.

Somewhat different considerations may apply in cases of joint occupation (see, eg *Mikeover Ltd v Brady* [1989] 3 All ER 618; *Stribling v Wickham* [1989] 2 EGLR 35).

41.3   RECOVERY OF POSSESSION

In order to recover possession from an occupying employee or ex-employee, the employer/landlord will first have to ensure that the employee's *contractual* right to occupy, whether under a licence or a tenancy, is brought to an end. If the employee does not leave voluntarily, it will then be necessary to obtain an order for possession, generally in the county court. In the case of a tenancy, the court's powers to make such an order are restricted by statute.

It is important that the employer does not seek to regain possession, whether by forcible eviction or by harassment without recourse to court proceedings. Such a course of action will contravene the *Protection from Eviction Act 1977* ('*PFEA 1977*').

Where premises are let as a dwelling under a tenancy or licence, even under a tenancy which is not statutorily protected, it is not lawful for the owner to exercise a right of re-entry or forfeiture under the lease, or to enforce his right to recover possession, otherwise than by court proceedings (*PFEA 1977, ss 2, 3(1), (2B)*). 'Let as a dwelling' means 'let wholly or partly as a dwelling', so *PFEA 1977, s 2* applies to premises which were let for mixed residential and business purposes (*Patel v Pirabakaran* [2006] EWCA Civ 685, [2006] 4 All ER 506). However, premises let for such mixed purposes are not 'let as a separate dwelling' within *Rent Act 1977, s 1* (*Tan v Sitkowski* [2007] EWCA Civ 30, [2007] All ER (D) 16 (Feb)). In a recent case, it has been held that *article 6* of the *European Convention on Human Rights* (ie. the right to a fair hearing before an independent and impartial tribunal for the determination of civil rights) was satisfied where *PFEA 1977, s 3* was invoked by a local authority (*Coombes v Waltham Forest London Borough Council* [2010] 2 All ER 940).

There is a deemed tenancy for these purposes whenever a person has exclusive possession of any premises under the terms of his employment (*PFEA 1977, s 8(2)*).

It is a criminal offence unlawfully to deprive the employee of his occupation (*PFEA 1977, s 1(2)*). It is also an offence if a person, with the intention of causing the residential occupier to give up occupation or to refrain from exercising any rights or pursuing any remedy open to him, does acts which are likely to interfere with the peace and comfort of the occupier, or his family, or persistently withdraws or withholds services normally required for the occupation of the premises as a residence (*PFEA 1977, s 1(3)*, as amended by *HA 1988, s 29*). Where that intent cannot be shown, an offence is nonetheless committed if the employer or his agent, without reasonable grounds, does acts likely to interfere with the peace or comfort of the residential occupier or members of his household or persistently withdraws or withholds services reasonably required for the occupation of the premises as a residence, knowing or having reasonable cause to believe that that conduct is likely to cause the occupier to give up occupation or to refrain from exercising a right or remedy (*PFEA 1977, s 1(3A), (3B)*, as inserted by *HA 1988, s 29*). The offence of harassment under *PFEA 1977, s 1(3)* may be committed even if the actions complained of do not otherwise amount to a civil wrong (*R v Burke* [1991] 1 AC 135). As to whether occupiers are 'residential occupiers' for the purposes of *PFEA 1977, s 1(3A)*, see *Prosecution Appeal (No 28 of 2007); R v Harris* [2008] All ER (D) 190 (Feb).

Further, a right to damages for unlawful eviction (in addition to any existing rights to claim in tort or for breach of contract) is created by *HA 1988, s 27* (see *Tagro v Cafane* [1991] 2 All ER 235, *Sampson v Wilson* [1996] Ch 39, *Osei-Bonsu v Wandsworth London*

41.3   Service Lettings

Borough Council [1999] 1 All ER 265 and *Loveridge v Lambeth London Borough Council* [2013] All ER (D) 110 (May)). Where a landlord obtained an order for possession from the court and applied for a warrant for possession against a tenant, the tenant remained protected under *PFEA 1977, s 3(1)* (see above) until the warrant had been executed and was therefore entitled to damages for unlawful eviction under *HA 1988, s 27* when the landlord forcibly evicted the tenant before such execution (*Haniff v Robinson* [1993] QB 419, [1993] 1 All ER 185).

Once the licence or tenancy has been brought to an end and the employer is seeking to recover possession, the employer ought not to accept further payments of rent (at least without making clear in writing the basis on which he does so), because the acceptance of such payments may lead to the creation of a fresh tenancy. If the employee continues to occupy the premises after he should have left, compensation will eventually be recoverable by order of the court (called 'mesne profits'). As to the liability of a former secure tenant (who had become a 'tolerated trespasser') for mesne profits, see *Jones v Merton London Borough Council* [2008] EWCA Civ 660, [2008] 4 All ER 287. (However, note that provisions in *Schedule 11* to the *Housing and Regeneration Act 2008* (which, with some exceptions, came into force on 20 May 2009) will in effect prevent the creation of 'tolerated trespassers' in future, by amending the *Housing Acts 1985, 1988* and *1996* so as to provide that a possession order made against (inter alia) a secure or assured tenant will not end the tenancy until the tenant is evicted.)

41.4   Service licence

A true *service licence* can be determined on termination of the relevant employment contract, with the notice period provided for in the contract. If the contract is silent on this point, then reasonable notice should be given. It is unlikely that a period of less than four weeks would be reasonable. If the licence is a *periodic licence* (ie one which continues from week to week or month to month, rather than for a fixed term), a minimum of four weeks' notice to terminate it must be given in the prescribed form (*PFEA 1977, s 5(1A)* as inserted by *HA 1988, s 32*; *Notices to Quit, etc (Prescribed Information) Regulations 1988 (SI 1988/2201)*). The termination of a licence which is expressed to come to an end with the termination of the employee's employment need not comply with the requirements of *PFEA 1977, s 5(1A)* as to notice, because such a licence is not a 'periodic licence' for the purposes of that provision (*Norris v Checksfield* [1991] 4 All ER 327).

On the termination of a *service licence* the employer can take proceedings for possession. He will have to show:

(a)   that the premises were occupied by the employee for the duration of his employment (or for some agreed lesser period), and for the better performance of his duties;

(b)   that the employment (or the lesser period) has ended, or that proper notice to determine the licence has been given;

(c)   that either the agreed notice has been given or the former employee has been given an adequate period in which to vacate the premises;

(d)   that no new arrangement has been created since the contract ended (therefore it is unwise to accept further payments of rent without specifying the basis on which this is done).

In *Whitbread West Pennines Ltd v Reedy* [1988] ICR 807, the former employee sought to argue that possession should not be ordered against him because there was pending an unfair dismissal claim in which he sought reinstatement (see **53.2 UNFAIR DISMISSAL – III**). The argument failed. The Court of Appeal held that for the replacement employee to move into the accommodation would not make reinstatement any less practicable, and that in any event the employer could elect not to reinstate but to pay enhanced compensation instead. In a case where the licence to occupy terminates along with the employment, it does so notwithstanding that the dismissal is wrongful (*Ivory v Palmer* [1975] ICR 340) or contractually lawful but statutorily unfair (*Carroll v Manek*, (1999) 79 P & CR 173).

41.5   Service tenancy

Tenancies in existence prior to 15 January 1989 continue to be governed by *RA 1977* or *Housing Act 1980* ('*HA 1980*'). Tenancies entered into on or after that date, however, are governed by *HA 1988*. Tenancies entered into on or after 28 February 1997 are affected by amendments made to *HA 1988* by the *Housing Act 1996* ('*HA 1996*'). Various kinds of tenancy therefore fall to be considered.

(i)   *Protected tenancies under RA 1977.* These are automatically converted into *statutory tenancies* when the original, contractual tenancy expires through effluxion of time or a notice to quit is served.

(ii)   *Protected shorthold tenancies under HA 1980.* These arose where, before the grant of the tenancy, the landlord served a prescribed notice indicating that this was the nature of the tenancy. The term must have been between one and five years, with the landlord having no right to end it sooner whilst the tenant complied with his obligations (*HA 1980, s 52*).

(iii)   *Assured tenancies under HA 1988.* This will now be the normal basic type of tenancy (but see (v) below). The tenant must be an individual who occupies the dwelling as his only or principal home, and the letting must not be one which is specifically excluded from protection (*HA 1988, s 1*). As to the meaning of 'dwelling' in *HA 1988, s 1*, see *Uratemp Ventures Ltd v Collins* [2001] UKHL 43, [2002] 1 AC 301.

(iv)   *Assured shorthold tenancies under HA 1988 (pre-HA 1996 tenancies).* These are similar in concept to the old protected shorthold tenancies, but their scope is less restricted. They must be for a fixed term of not less than six months, contain no landlord's right to terminate during the first six months if the tenant complies with his obligations, and the grant must be preceded by service of a notice in the prescribed form (*HA 1988, s 20*). The notice may be served on the tenant's authorised agent (*Yenula Properties Ltd v Naidu* [2002] EWCA Civ 719, [2003] HLR 229). A notice not in the prescribed form nor 'substantially to the same effect' is invalid (*Manel v Memon* (2000) 33 HLR 235 — applied in *Kahlon v Isherwood* [2011] EWCA Civ 602, [2011] All ER (D) 205 (May), a case on *HA 1988, s 19A* and *Sch 2A* (see (v) below)). Also invalid is a notice which fails to state correctly the landlord's name (*Gill v Cremadez* [2000] CLY 3876); see also *Ravenseft Properties v Hall* [2001] EWCA Civ 2034, [2002] HLR 624 and *Osborn & Co Ltd v Dior* [2003] EWCA Civ 281, [2003] HLR 649.

(v)   *Assured shorthold tenancies under HA 1988 (post-HA 1996 tenancies).* Any assured tenancy which is entered into on or after 28 February 1997 (otherwise than pursuant to a contract entered into before that date) will be an assured shorthold tenancy, unless it falls within one of the exceptions set out in *HA 1988, Sch 2A* (as to which, see *Andrews v Cunningham* [2007] All ER (D) 343 (Jul)) (*HA 1988, s 19A*, inserted by *HA 1996, s 96*). Unlike pre-*HA 1996* assured shorthold tenancies, no notice need be served by the landlord on the tenant prior to the grant, and the tenancy need not be for a fixed term. However, if requested to do so in writing, a landlord under a post-*HA 1996* assured shorthold tenancy has a duty to provide a tenant with a written statement of the principal terms of the tenancy where these are not evidenced in writing (*HA 1988, s 20A*, inserted by *HA 1996, s 97*).

41.5　Service Lettings

In order to recover possession from a service tenant, the contractual tenancy must be terminated. This will occur if (in the case of a fixed-term tenancy) the term of the tenancy expires without being renewed, if the landlord claims to forfeit the lease where the lease makes provision for forfeiture for breach of certain terms in it, or (in the case of a periodic tenancy) if the landlord serves a notice to quit.

Expiry of term. If the tenancy is for a fixed term of, for example, two years, the contractual tenancy will automatically terminate on the expiry of the two-year period and it is not necessary for a notice to quit to be served.

Forfeiture for breach of a term of the lease. Except in the case of forfeiture for the non-payment of rent, the landlord must serve a notice under the *Law of Property Act 1925, s 146* on the tenant, specifying the breaches complained of and requesting him to remedy the same within a reasonable period of time and to pay reasonable compensation.

Notice to quit. A notice to quit should be in writing and some acknowledgement of receipt should be asked for. If sent by post, it should be sent by recorded delivery. To be valid the notice to quit must expire on the proper day. The notice to quit must expire at the end of the period of the tenancy. Because specifying a wrong date is fatal to a notice to quit, landlords should add the following saving clause in the notice to quit after the specified date: 'or at the expiration of the (week/month) of your tenancy which shall expire next after the expiration of four weeks from the service upon you of this notice'. The notice to quit must be served not less than four weeks before the date on which it is to take effect (*Protection from Eviction Act 1977, s 5*). Information prescribed by the *Notices to Quit, etc (Prescribed Information) Regulations 1988 (SI 1988/2201)* must be included in the notice to quit; otherwise it will be invalid.

No rent must be accepted after discovery of a breach of a term in the lease which gives the landlord the right to forfeit, such as unlawful sub-letting. Accepting rent may be construed as waiving the breaches complained of or creating a new tenancy.

41.6　Situations in which possession may be claimed from tenant

Where a *protected shorthold tenancy* or an *assured shorthold tenancy* comes to an end, the court *must* grant the landlord possession if the proper procedure is followed. In the case of an assured shorthold tenancy, this involves giving the tenant not less than two months' notice in writing that possession is required. The notice must specify a date that is the last date of a period of the tenancy (*Fernandez v McDonald* [2003] EWCA Civ 1219, [2003] 4 All ER 1033; see also *Notting Hill Housing Trust v Roomus* [2006] EWCA Civ 407, [2006] 1 WLR 1375). In the case of a post-*HA 1996* assured shorthold tenancy (see category (v) in **41.5** above), a possession order may not be made so as to take effect earlier than six months after the beginning of the tenancy (where the tenancy is a replacement tenancy, the six-month period runs from the beginning of the *original* tenancy) (*HA 1988, s 21*, as amended by *HA 1996, ss 98, 99*). The procedural requirements in relation to the old protected shorthold tenancy were somewhat more complex: see *HA 1980, s 55; RA 1977, s 98(2), Sch 15 Case 19*. Possession of properties let on shorthold tenancies can also be recovered on the same grounds as are available in the case of ordinary tenancies.

In the case of a *protected tenancy* under *RA 1977*, the landlord must bring himself within one of a number of specified 'Cases' set out in *Sch 15*. Those Cases in *Sch 15 Part I* are 'discretionary' grounds, in that they require the court to be satisfied also that it is reasonable to grant possession; they include grounds such as arrears of rent or the causing of a nuisance. Those Cases in *Sch 15 Part II* constitute mandatory grounds for possession. In addition, the court may make an order, if it is reasonable to do so, where suitable alternative accommodation is or will be available for the tenant. See generally *RA 1977, s 98*.

The ground particularly relevant to pre-1989 service lettings is *Case 8* (a discretionary ground): this arises if the landlord requires the premises for a whole-time employee, the existing tenant was granted a tenancy in consequence of his employment, and he has ceased to be in that employment.

A similar approach governs recovery of possession under *assured tenancies* under *HA 1988*. Again, there are both mandatory and discretionary grounds, and where one of the latter is established the court will have to be persuaded that it is reasonable to order possession (*HA 1988, s 7, Sch 2*). *Ground 16* is a discretionary ground which applies where the dwelling-house was let to the tenant in consequence of his employment by the landlord or a previous landlord, and the tenant has ceased to be in that employment. It will be seen that this is less stringent, from the landlord's point of view, than *Case 8* under *RA 1977* (see above), because it is not necessary to show that the accommodation is required for another employee. However, to do so would obviously assist the argument that it was reasonable to order possession. The availability of suitable alternative accommodation is another discretionary ground (*Ground 9*).

As in the case of RA 1977 (see s 100), the court has a wide discretion under HA 1988, s 9 to adjourn possession proceedings and to suspend the execution of orders; see generally *White v Knowsley Housing Trust* [2008] UKHL 70, [2008] All ER (D) 115 (Dec).

41.7   Tenants of public authorities

Under *HA 1985*, security of tenure was conferred upon tenants of local authorities and of certain other public bodies. However, various categories are excluded from security of tenure. Those which are pertinent to employment include:

(a)   Cases where the tenant is an employee of the landlord; or of:

    (i)   a local authority,

    (ii)   a new town corporation,

    (iii)   the governors of an aided school;

    (iv)   an urban development corporation;

    (v)   a housing action trust;

and his contract of employment requires him to reside in the dwelling for the better performance of his duties.

In *Surrey County Council v Lamond* [1999] 1 EGLR 32 (see also [1999] 2 CLY 3736), the Court of Appeal held that in deciding whether for this reason a tenancy was not a secure tenancy, the court needed to ascertain what duties the employee was to perform and then determine whether it was genuinely practicable for the employee to perform them if he did not occupy the dwelling concerned; see also *Hughes v Greenwich London Borough Council* [1994] 1 AC 170, HL, *Elvidge v Coventry City Council* [1994] QB 241, [1993] 4 All ER 903 and *Brent London Borough Council v Charles* (1997) 29 HLR 876, CA. In *Wragg v Surrey County Council* [2008] EWCA Civ 19, [2008] All ER (D) 09 (Feb), the Court of Appeal construed this provision as laying down two distinct conditions: (i) that 'his contract of employment requires him to occupy the dwelling-house'; (ii) that the requirement was 'for the better performance of his duties'. Condition (i) looked only to the terms of the contract: did the contract contain such a requirement or not? However, condition (ii) raised an issue of fact outside the contract: 'the question was not whether the contract stated that the requirement was for the better performance of his duties, but whether the requirement was in fact for the better performance of his duties'.

41.7 Service Lettings

(b)   Where the tenant is a member of the police force, and the dwelling is provided rent-free by regulations made under the *Police Act 1996*. (See *Holmes v South Yorkshire Police Authority* [2008] EWCA Civ 51, [2008] HLR 532.)

(c)   Where the tenant is employed by a fire and rescue authority; and

(i)   he is contractually bound to live close to a particular fire station; and

(ii)   the dwelling-house was let to him by the authority so that he could comply with the condition.

(d)   Cases where temporary accommodation is granted in order to assist employees who are new to an area to find permanent accommodation there, provided that it is linked to an offer of employment to a person who was not resident in the district immediately before the grant, that it does not exceed one year and that the tenant is informed, in writing, of the circumstances in which the exception applies and that the landlord is of the opinion that it falls within that exception.

(*Housing Act 1985, Sch 1 paras 2(1), (2), (3), 5(1)*, as amended.)

41.8 RENT CONTROL

Occupation under a *licence* is not subject to rent control.

Where the employee went into occupation under a *RA 1977 protected tenancy* or a *protected shorthold tenancy*, he could apply under *Part IV* of that *Act* for a fair rent to be registered, and the landlord was not then entitled to charge a greater rent (*RA 1977, s 44*). Now that new protected tenancies cannot be created, that provision will be of diminishing importance, although the possibility of such an application remains.

A tenant under an *assured tenancy* under *HA 1988* has no right to challenge the contractual rent which he has agreed to pay, whether the rent demanded of him is that originally agreed upon, or has subsequently been varied pursuant to a rent review clause. However, if the contractual tenancy comes to an end and the landlord wishes to increase the rent, he must serve notice of the proposed increase upon the tenant in a prescribed form (*HA 1988, s 13*). The tenant may then go before a Rent Assessment Committee and seek a determination that the proposed new rent exceeds that which might reasonably be expected to be obtained in the open market, by a willing landlord, on the same terms of letting (*HA 1988, s 14*). There are strict time limits within which any reference by the tenant to the Rent Assessment Committee must be made.

A tenant under an *assured shorthold tenancy* may refer the rent charged to the Rent Assessment Committee, during the initial fixed term of the tenancy (in the case of a pre-*HA 1996* assured shorthold tenancy) or during the first six months of the tenancy (in the case of a post-*HA 1996* assured shorthold tenancy). However, the Committee may reduce the rent only if:

(i)   there is a sufficient number of similar dwelling-houses in the locality let on assured tenancies (whether shorthold or not) for a proper determination to be possible; and

(ii)   the rent charged is *significantly* higher than the rent which the landlord might reasonably be expected to obtain having regard to the rents payable under other assured tenancies in the locality.

(*HA 1988, s 22*, as amended by *HA 1996, s 100*.)

978

41.9 AGRICULTURAL TIED HOUSES

Where the employee is or was engaged in agriculture or forestry, special rules may apply. A discussion of these rules is beyond the scope of this book. They are to be found in the *Rent (Agriculture) Act 1976* as amended by *HA 1988*, and in *HA 1988, ss 24, 25* (as amended by *HA 1996, s 103*).

42   Sickness and Sick Pay

Cross-references. See TERMINATION OF EMPLOYMENT (46) for sickness and frustration of contract of employment; for sickness and unfair dismissal, see 52.8 UNFAIR DISMISSAL – II.

42.1   In relation to pay for periods of sickness, the following may apply:

(a)   contractual provisions for sick pay (see 42.2 below);

(b)   the statutory right to a specified level of sick pay ('statutory sick pay', see 42.3–42.8 below).

As in many areas of employment law, statutory payments are offset against contractual payments and vice versa. This 'offsetting' of payments during sickness is considered in 42.9–42.11 below.

Employers may now opt out of the statutory sick pay scheme, so long as they provide the same minimum level of remuneration as an employee would be entitled to as a matter of statute. (See 42.3 below.)

Persistent illness may constitute such incapacity for work as to warrant dismissal (see 52.8 UNFAIR DISMISSAL – II).

In rare circumstances, sickness may render performance of the contract so radically different from that contemplated by the parties as to amount to a frustration of the contract (see 46.3 TERMINATION OF EMPLOYMENT).

42.2   CONTRACTUAL PROVISIONS FOR SICK PAY

An employer may agree to pay his employees while they are absent due to ill-health. Such payments commonly run for a specified period of time and are subject to conditions.

The written particulars given to an employee setting out the terms and conditions of his employment must state whether or not the employer makes payments for periods of absence due to sickness and, if so, upon what terms (see 7.4 CONTRACT OF EMPLOYMENT). In *Mears v Safecar Security Ltd* [1983] QB 54, [1982] 2 All ER 865, [1982] 3 WLR 366, [1982] ICR 626, the Court of Appeal held that where such a term is not specified or agreed, the tribunal must consider all the facts and circumstances to ascertain the term to be implied. There is no presumption of a contractual right to sick pay. An employment tribunal must look to all the facts and circumstances, and to the conduct of the parties since the contract began.

Where there is a contractual right to sick pay, but no provision as to its duration, the court will imply a reasonable term (*Howman & Son v Blyth* [1983] ICR 416).

For the failure to comply with the statutory duty to specify in the written particulars of terms of employment what provisions for sick pay apply, see 7.7 CONTRACT OF EMPLOYMENT.

42.3   STATUTORY SICK PAY

(For further details see HMRC's booklet 'Employer Handbook for Statutory Sick Pay' (E14) (2011)).

Since 1983, all employees, subject to certain specified exceptions (see 42.4 below), have been entitled to receive statutory sick pay ('SSP') from their employers, who until recently were able to recover the greater part of it from National Insurance contributions (see 42.6 below).

42.3   Sickness and Sick Pay

The entitlement limit is, generally, 28 weeks in a three-year period. The basic provisions are now consolidated into the *Social Security Contributions and Benefits Act 1992* ('*SSCBA 1992*'). The main set of regulations is the *Statutory Sick Pay (General) Regulations 1982 (SI 1982/894)* as amended, principally by the *Statutory Sick Pay (General) Amendment Regulations 1986 (SI 1986/477)*, the *Statutory Sick Pay (General) Amendment (No 2) Regulations 1987 (SI 1987/868)* and the *Social Security Contributions, Statutory Maternity Pay and Statutory Sick Pay (Miscellaneous Amendments) Regulations 1996 (SI 1996/777)*.

The essential requirements for qualification are that an employee must:

(a)   have four or more consecutive days of sickness (including Sundays and holidays) during which he is too ill to be capable of doing his work (see further **42.5** below); and

(b)   notify his absence to his employer, subject to certain statutory requirements and any agreement between them; and

(c)   supply evidence of incapacity – this is also a matter for the employer: a common example of an employer's requirement would be:

(i)   a 'self-certificate' for periods of four to seven days;

(ii)   a doctor's certificate or other evidence of sickness for periods after the first seven days.

(*SSCBA 1992, ss 151, 152, 156; Statutory Sick Pay (General) Regulations 1982, reg 7.*) The medical evidence that can be required of an employee is prescribed by the *Statutory Sick Pay (Medical Evidence) Regulations 1985*, as amended in 2010 (*SI 2010/137*).

Employers cannot require employees to contribute towards payments (*SSCBA 1992, s 151(2)*).

Employees may still be entitled to SSP even if they are absent from Great Britain on holiday or for business purposes at any time during the incapacity (*SI 1996/777, reg 3*).

An employer may choose to opt out of the statutory sick pay scheme, provided that he continues to pay contractual remuneration to his employees at or above the SSP rate and does not make his employees contribute to the cost of their sick pay up to that rate. Such employers still have to comply with certain documentary and record keeping requirements (see **42.7** below).

42.4   Excluded employees

The following categories of employee are not entitled to receive SSP. These are an employee:

(a)   having average weekly earnings less than the weekly lower earnings limit for National Insurance ('NI') contribution liability (currently £109 per week);

(b)   going sick within 57 days of having previously been entitled to incapacity benefit;

(c)   going sick within 85 days of having previously been entitled to an employment and support allowance;

(d)   who has done no work for his employer under the contract of service;

(e)   going sick during a stoppage of work at his place of employment due to a trade dispute, unless he proves that at no time has he had a direct interest in that dispute;

(f)   who is pregnant and goes off sick during the maternity pay period (see **31.11** MATERNITY AND PARENTAL RIGHTS);

(g)   who has already been due 28 weeks' SSP from his employer in any one 'period of incapacity for work' (or any two or more 'linked' periods) (see **42.5** below);

(h)   who, subject to certain provisions, has already been due 28 weeks' SSP from his former employer, and the gap between the first day of incapacity with the new employer and the last day on which SSP was paid by the former employer is eight weeks or less;

(i)   who is in legal custody at any time on the first day of incapacity.

(*SSCBA 1992, Sch 11*, as amended by the *Statutory Sick Pay Act 1994, s 1; Social Security Act 1985, s 18(2)(d); Statutory Sick Pay (General) Regulations 1982 (SI 1982/894); Statutory Sick Pay (General) Amendment Regulations 1986 (SI 1986/477)*.)

Where the employer is notified that an excluded employee has been absent for four consecutive days or more, he is legally bound to send a form to the employee not later than seven days after being so notified (or, where this is impracticable, not later than the first pay day in the following tax month). This form provides the explanation to the employee and the DWP of why SSP is not being paid, and allows the employee to claim state sickness benefit instead (*Statutory Sick Pay (General) Regulations 1982 (SI 1982/894), reg 15*, as amended).

It should also be noted that agency workers on assignments of less than three months are not entitled to SSP. The repeal of the previous exclusion from SSP for those whose 'contract of service was entered into for a specified period of not more than three months' did not apply to agency workers: see *Revenue and Customs Comrs v Thorn Baker Ltd* [2007] EWCA Civ 626, [2008] ICR 46.

42.5   The payment period

The period of four or more days of sickness (see **42.3** above) is called a 'period of incapacity for work' ('PIW'). Two or more PIWs which are separated by eight weeks or less are said to be 'linked' and are counted as one PIW (*SSCBA, s 152; Statutory Sick Pay (General) Amendment Regulations 1986 (SI 1986/477)*).

During a PIW, SSP is payable *only*:

(a)   while there is a 'period of entitlement', as defined (eg payment will cease, in the normal case, if the employment ends); *and*

(b)   for days within the PIW which are 'qualifying days'.

The intention behind the idea of 'qualifying days' was that they would be the days on which the employee would normally be required to work, but it is open to employers in all cases to specify the pattern of qualifying days by agreement with the employees concerned. Each week must have at least one qualifying day, and qualifying days must not be defined by reference to the days of sickness (*Statutory Sick Pay (General) Regulations 1982 (SI 1982/894); Statutory Sick Pay (General) Amendment Regulations 1985 (SI 1985/126)*).

SSP is not payable for the first three qualifying days in a PIW (*SSCBA 1992, s 155(1)*). It is paid for the fourth qualifying day onwards until either the employee becomes well again or the maximum payment period is reached (*SSCBA 1992, s 155(2)*).

The maximum entitlement to SSP is now 28 weeks in any period of entitlement. A period of entitlement, as between an employee and his employer, is a period beginning with the commencement of a period of incapacity for work and ending with the earliest of:

(i)   the termination of that period of incapacity for work;

(ii)   the day on which the employee reaches, as against the employer concerned, his maximum entitlement to statutory sick pay;

42.5   Sickness and Sick Pay

(iii)   the day on which the employee's contract of service with the employer concerned expires or is brought to an end;

(iv)   in the case of an employee who is, or has been, pregnant, the day immediately preceding the beginning of the disqualifying period (as defined by *SSCBA 1992, s 153(12)*) (*SSCBA 1992, s 153(2)*).

A period of entitlement ends after three years if it has not otherwise ended (*Statutory Sick Pay (General) Regulations 1982 (SI 1982/894), reg 3(3)*, inserted by *SI 1986/477*).

Employees who are still sick when their entitlement to SSP terminates may be entitled to state benefits. Employers of such employees must inform them in a prescribed form of the reason for the termination of SSP (*Social Security Administration Act 1992, s 130; Statutory Sick Pay (General) Regulations 1982 (SI 1982/894), reg 15*, as amended by *Statutory Sick Pay (General) Amendment Regulations 1986 (SI 1986/477)*, and by *Statutory Sick Pay (General)(Amendment) Regulations 2008 (SI 2008/1735)*). *SSCBA 1992, Sch 12* deals with the relationship between statutory sick pay and other benefits and payments.

42.6   The amounts payable and recoverable

Employees who earn less than the lower weekly earnings limit for NI liability (£109) are excluded from SSP (*SSCBA 1992, Sch 11 para 2(c)*). In all other cases, the amount of SSP payable is £86.70. Thus, the maximum amount payable over 28 weeks is £2,427.60 (*SSCBA 1992, s 157(1)*, as amended by the *Social Security (Incapacity for Work) Act 1994, s 8(1)*).

SSP is considered as earnings for PAYE, income tax and NI contribution purposes (*SSCBA 1992, s 4(1); Income and Corporation Taxes Act 1988, s 150*).

Right of recovery. The right of employers to recover from their NI contributions amounts paid by way of SSP was abolished by the *Statutory Sick Pay Act 1994*. Small employers are no longer granted relief on payments of SSP above a certain threshold. Instead, any employer may recover an amount paid out as SSP if, and to the extent that, it exceeds 13% of his liability to pay NI contributions in the income tax month in question (*Statutory Sick Pay Percentage Threshold Order 1995 (SI 1995/512)*, which revoked the *Statutory Sick Pay (Small Employers' Relief) Regulations 1991 (SI 1991/428)* with effect from 6 April 1995). The same principles apply to employers who opt out of the SSP scheme if and to the extent that the amount which he would have paid out in SSP exceeds the percentage threshold.

42.7   Records

Employers are obliged to keep records for SSP purposes. In particular, the following *minimum* information must be recorded by the employer and retained for at least three years.

(a)   Dates of each employee's PIWs.

(b)   Any payment of SSP made in respect of any day within a PIW, except where the payment is by way of contractual remuneration which equals or exceeds the SSP payable in respect of that day.

(*Statutory Sick Pay (General) Regulations 1982 (SI 1982/894), reg 13; Statutory Sick Pay (General) Amendment Regulations 1986 (SI 1986/477), reg 5; Social Security Contributions, Statutory Maternity Pay and Statutory Sick Pay (Miscellaneous Amendments) Regulations 1996 (SI 1996/777), reg 2; Statutory Sick Pay (General) Amendment Regulations 1996 (SI 1996/3042), reg 2.*)

The statutory records must be retained for at least three years, and must be stored in such a way that inspectors can have access to them.

In addition, accounting records must be kept showing, *inter alia*, details of all SSP payments made, along with those of pay, NIC and PAYE income tax. Revenue records must be retained for seven years.

Employers may find it useful to keep fuller records, eg self-certification forms, medical certificates, dates of all absences and the reasons for them. Such records can be used for the purposes of audit, and may also help to identify personnel problems.

Where employers opt out of the SSP scheme, they will still need to keep basic records of sickness absence and amounts paid so that the NI inspector can check that the employees are receiving their full entitlement. The employer will need to record the following details:

(i)   the first day for which SSP liability arises;

(ii)   the last day for which SSP liability arises;

(iii)   the number of weeks and days of SSP entitlement; and

(iv)   the number of SSP qualifying days (see **42.5** above).

42.8   Disputes

If an employer does not pay an employee SSP, the employee may ask him to give written reasons for the decision, and the employer must comply within a reasonable time (*Social Security Administration Act 1992, s 14(3)*).

If the employee wishes to challenge the employer's decision, he may ask for a determination of the issue by Her Majesty's Revenue and Customs (*Statutory Sick Pay and Statutory Maternity Pay (Decisions) Regulations 1999 (SI 1999/776)*). A challenge to HMRC's decision can be made to the First-Tier Tax Tribunal (Tax). For a recent example of a dispute as to whether an employee was entitled to sick pay, see *Mitre Plastics v Revenue and Customs Comrs* (TC00720) [2010] UKFTT 455 (TC). An employment tribunal does not have jurisdiction to determine whether an employee is entitled to statutory sick pay, although it would have jurisdiction to determine a claim of unlawful deduction from wages if the employer admitted entitlement but withheld payment of SSP: *Taylor Gordon & Co Ltd (t/a Plan Personnel) v Timmons* [2004] IRLR 180, EAT; *Sarti (Sauchiehall St) Ltd v Polito* [2008] ICR 1279.

As far as evidence of incapacity is concerned, the employer cannot require the employee to produce a medical certificate from a doctor for the first seven days of sickness. With that qualification, he can request the employee to provide reasonable evidence of incapacity, such as a self-certificate for absences of up to seven days (*Social Security Administration Act 1992, s 14; Statutory Sick Pay (Medical Evidence) Regulations 1985 (SI 1985/1604)*).

42.9   OFFSETTING PAYMENTS MADE DURING SICKNESS AGAINST SSP

Any contractual remuneration paid to an employee for a day of sickness is to be offset against the SSP due for the *same day* (*SSCBA 1992, Sch 12 para 2*). An employer can never pay the employee an amount in total which is *less* than the SSP due.

In personal injury actions, any special damages claimed will be subject to a deduction for SSP paid (*Palfrey v Greater London Council* [1985] ICR 437). The same principle was applied to payments under a non-contributory permanent health insurance scheme in *Hussain v New Taplow Paper Mills Ltd* [1987] 1 All ER 417, [1987] 1 WLR 336, [1987] ICR 28.

42.10   Sickness and Sick Pay

42.10   Contributory sickness schemes

An employee must not contribute to his own SSP. Thus, in the case of a jointly funded, ie 'contributory', sickness scheme, the amount of sick pay which will be offset against SSP must be in the proportion that the employer's contribution bears to the joint contributions to the scheme.

42.11   Contributory pension schemes

In the case of contributory pension schemes, offsetting will depend on how the pension scheme defines salary for calculation purposes: if salary is defined as 'earnings subject to PAYE income tax', then any SSP paid should be included in earnings for pension purposes. In that case the employee's pension contribution would be deducted from his full gross sick pay, ie including the SSP element. (See, in particular, the *Occupational Pensions Board Announcement No 2 (March 1983)*.)

42.12   PERMANENT HEALTH AND SALARY CONTINUANCE BENEFITS

It is increasingly common for employers to provide their employees with permanent health or salary continuance benefits during periods of long-term sickness or incapacity, lasting usually more than six or twelve months. Employers will normally provide these benefits by taking out insurance coverage for the benefit of their employees.

The right of an employee to receive permanent health or salary continuance benefits will usually depend on the terms of the insurance policy entered into by the employer, as the contract of employment will probably state that the benefits payable to the employee in the event of long-term incapacity are 'subject to' or 'governed by' the rules of the insurance policy. However, where the employer makes no reference to its insurance policy in documents provided to an employee, then the employer cannot rely upon the terms of the policy as against the employee. The employer will be bound by the words of its own contractual documentation with the employee: see *Jowitt v Pioneer Technology (UK) Ltd* [2003] EWCA Civ 411, [2003] ICR 1120. Also, where the insurance policy provides for significant exemptions to the payment of benefits (eg disentitling employees to benefits on leaving service), the employer will not be able to rely on these exemptions as against the employee if the employee was not shown the policy itself or was not told that he should read it (*Villella v MFI Furniture Centres Ltd* [1999] IRLR 468).

In *Briscoe v Lubrizol Ltd* [2002] EWCA Civ 508, [2002] IRLR 607, the Court of Appeal held that the claimant's entitlement to disability benefit depended upon his satisfying the definition of 'disablement' contained in the employer's insurance policy ('totally unable . . . to perform his normal occupation'), rather than the definition set out in the company information handbook ('unable to follow any occupation'). The court referred to the decision in *Villella*, and held that 'the court looks unfavourably upon an employer who seeks to restrict his contractual obligation as described in a handbook in reliance upon a policy which he has not brought to the attention of his employee; but that does not mean, by way of corollary, that where the handbook expressly or by implication refers to such a policy and purports to summarise its effect upon the employee's rights in a manner which is disadvantageous to the employee, the court will similarly regard the handbook as definitive of those rights'. The court looked at all the facts and determined that it was the clear contractual intention of the parties to bestow upon the employee the benefits provided for in the insurance policy, rather than the handbook.

As the employee will not be a party to the insurance policy, he will ordinarily not be entitled to enforce his rights to receive these benefits directly against the insurer. Rather, he will have to enforce those rights against the employer, who in turn will probably seek to join the insurer as a third party (*Rutherford v Radio Rentals Ltd* 1993 SLT 221). Where, under the contract of employment, the employer is obliged to pay over to the employee such sums as it receives from the insurer, then the employer will be under a duty to take all reasonable steps to secure that the insurance benefits are paid. This may include the pursuit of litigation against the insurer if necessary (*Marlow v East Thames Housing Group Ltd* [2002] IRLR 798).

An employee is not automatically deprived of his entitlement to receive salary continuance benefits from his employer merely because the employer ceases to pay his insurance premiums or terminates the policy (*Bainbridge v Circuit Foil UK Ltd* [1997] IRLR 305).

42.13 Effect on the right to terminate the contract of employment

The existence of these benefits may restrict the employer's ability to terminate the contract of employment. In circumstances where the insurance policy provides that benefits will only be paid in respect of employees who continue to be employed by the policy-holder (ie the employer), the courts may imply a term into the contract of employment to the effect that the employer cannot bring the contract to an end solely with a view to terminate those benefits, or for a specious or arbitrary reason or for no reason at all, while the employee was incapacitated for work (see *Hill v General Accident Fire and Life Assurance Corpn plc* [1998] IRLR 641; compare *Aspden v Webbs Poultry and Meat Group (Holdings) Ltd* [1996] IRLR 521 and see *Lloyd v BCQ Ltd* [2012] UKEAT 0148/12/1211) (see **7.22B** CONTRACT OF EMPLOYMENT). In *Lloyd*, the EAT held that such a term would not be implied where the contract of employment made no reference to permanent health insurance benefits, and the contract expressly permitted termination for long-term absence. Relying on *Reda v Flag Ltd* [2002] UKPC 38, the EAT held that an *Aspden*-type term could not be implied.

In *Briscoe v Lubrizol Ltd* [2002] EWCA Civ 508, [2002] IRLR 607, the Court of Appeal had to determine whether the employer was justified in terminating a contract of employment, the effect of which would be to deprive the employee of his entitlement to disability benefit. The Court of Appeal reviewed the case law and held that 'the employer ought not to terminate the employment as a means to remove the employee's entitlement to benefit but the employer can dismiss for good cause whether that be on the ground of gross misconduct or, more generally, for some repudiatory breach by the employee'. On the facts, the Court of Appeal held that the employer was entitled to treat the contract as having come to an end: the employee, who had been off work for a prolonged period of time, had disobeyed the employer's lawful instruction to attend so as to discuss his long-term absence; he was in breach of an instruction to return the employer's calls to re-arrange that appointment; and his continued absence from work was unexplained by any current medical report. In the circumstances, he was held to have been in breach of the duty of trust and confidence, which justified the employer in treating the contract of employment as having been terminated.

42.14 Effect of permanent health benefits on the calculation of damages

Payments made by an employer under a permanent health insurance plan are not treated as remuneration or earnings from employment within the meaning of the *Administration of Justice Act 1982, s 10(i)*. Rather, they are to be regarded as a 'contractual' pension or benefit and are therefore not taken into account so as to reduce damages to an employee suing in respect of injuries sustained as a result of an accident at work (*Lewicki v Brown and Root Wimpey Highland Fabricators Ltd* [1996] STC 145, [1996] IRLR 565).

42.15 'Unable to follow any occupation'

Permanent health insurance schemes often require the employee to show that he is unable to follow his own occupation for a period of time and thereafter that he is 'unable to follow any occupation' if he is to obtain long-term benefits. In *Walton v Airtours plc* [2002] EWCA Civ 1659, [2003] IRLR 161, the Court of Appeal held that the words 'unable to follow any occupation' had to be read in a common sense practical way and any inability must be assessed realistically. It was held that the phrase connoted being engaged in regular work for a substantial or indefinite period. It was enough that an employee could work on a temporary basis, or was able to start a new job for a few days but not continue thereafter to earn income. See also *Jowitt v Pioneer Technology (UK) Ltd* [2003] EWCA Civ 411, [2003] ICR 1120, [2003] IRLR 356.

43 Strikes and Industrial Action

Cross-references. See TRADE UNIONS – I (48) for the liability of unions for industrial action and HUMAN RIGHTS (28).

43.1 LIABILITY FOR INDUSTRIAL ACTION – BACKGROUND

The right to take industrial action takes the form, in this country, of statutory *immunity* for action which would otherwise attract legal liability at common law. The statutory immunity first appeared in something like its present form in the *Trade Disputes Act 1906, s 3*, and its scope has varied frequently since then.

This area of the law has been and is likely to continue to be influenced by the right to freedom of association embodied in *art 11* of the *ECHR*, which was incorporated into domestic law by the *Human Rights Act 1998*. In *Demir v Turkey* (App no 34503/97) (2008) 48 EHRR 1272, [2009] IRLR 766, the European Court of Human Rights held for the first time that the right to bargain collectively should in general form part of the right to freedom of association. In addition, the requirements of European law may impact on the ability of workers to take industrial action. In *International Transport Workers' Federation v Viking Line ABP*: C-438/05 [2008] All ER (EC) 127, [2008] ICR 741 the European Court of Justice held that the right to freedom of establishment embodied in Article 43 of the EC Treaty could in principle be unlawfully restricted by industrial action aimed at preventing a ferry operator from registering one of its vessels in a different country in order to lower its labour costs. However, it was also held that such a restriction might be justified by an overriding public interest (such as the protection of workers) provided that it was proportionate to the objective in question. The ECJ adopted a similar approach to the potential impact of industrial action on the right of freedom to provide services under Article 49 of the EC Treaty in *Laval un Partneri Ltd v Svenska Byggnadsarbetareforbundet*: C 341/05 [2008] All ER (EC) 166, [2008] IRLR 160.

The current basic immunity and the qualifications upon it are contained in the *Trade Union and Labour Relations (Consolidation) Act 1992* ('*TULRCA 1992*') as amended. In *Metrobus Ltd v Unite the Union* [2009] EWCA Civ 829, [2010] ICR 173 the Court of Appeal rejected the argument that the notification provisions contained in TULRCA 1992 were so difficult or onerous as to give rise to a breach of *art 11* of the *ECHR*.

In deciding whether legal proceedings can be taken against individuals (or unions) carrying on industrial action, it first must be ascertained whether a tort is being committed, for example, inducing a breach of contract (see **43.2** below). Then it must be ascertained whether the act amounting to the commission of that tort attracts the immunity conferred by *TULRCA 1992*.

This will involve consideration of whether the act was done in contemplation or furtherance of a trade dispute, whether the industrial action has the support of a ballot, whether the industrial action has been properly initiated, and whether the immunity has been lost because the action is unlawful secondary action or for some other reason.

The law relating to trade disputes is extremely complex. What appears below is an outline of the principles involved.

43.2 LIABILITY AT COMMON LAW

The law relating to the so-called 'economic torts' has developed gradually over the years; it is a difficult area which in many respects is still unclear. The most frequently encountered of the torts relate, broadly, to interference with contractual relations (note that *TULRCA 1992, s 245* deems Crown servants to have contracts of employment for these purposes). They include:

43.2   Strikes and Industrial Action

(a)   direct inducement of a breach of contract. A union which calls a strike will almost always induce the relevant employees to breach their contracts of employment;

(b)   the indirect inducement or procurement of a breach of contract by unlawful means. For example, A may be able to sue the union if his contract to obtain goods from B is breached by B when the union induces B's employees to go on strike in breach of their contracts of employment;

(c)   interference with business by unlawful means. This may include the case where the performance of contracts is impeded but there is no actual breach;

(d)   intimidation. This is designed to deal with the situation where the harm results, directly or indirectly, not from the actual using of unlawful means, but from the threat of such use;

(e)   conspiracy, ie an agreement either to do an unlawful act or to do a lawful act by unlawful means. The effect of the second limb is that an act done by two or more people may be unlawful even though it would have been lawful if done by one person acting alone.

Apart from the usual requirements of causation and foreseeability, it will usually be necessary to show that the defendant knows of the relevant contract and intends to procure its breach or the interference with its performance. Conspiracy is made out only where the agreement is to do an unlawful act, or where the defendant's predominant purpose is to injure the plaintiff, and not to further his own legitimate interests (see most recently *Lonrho plc v Fayed* [1992] 1 AC 448).

Some of the most important of the many authorities on the economic torts are *D C Thomson & Co Ltd v Deakin* [1952] Ch 646, *J T Stratford & Son Ltd v Lindley* [1965] AC 269, *Torquay Hotel Co Ltd v Cousins* [1969] 2 Ch 106, *Merkur Island Shipping Corpn v Laughton* [1983] ICR 490, *News Group Newspapers Ltd v SOGAT '82 (No 2)* [1987] ICR 181, *Middlebrook Mushrooms Ltd v TGWU* [1993] ICR 612; *Timeplan Education Group Ltd v National Union of Teachers* [1997] IRLR 457; *OBG Ltd v Allan* [2008] 1 AC 1; and *Total Network SL v Revenue & Customs Comrs* [2008] UKHL 19, [2008] 1 AC 1174, [2008] 2 All ER 413.

Although it is usually a breach of contract which is ultimately at the root of liability, that is by no means necessarily the case. See, eg *Lonrho plc v Fayed*, above (allegation of intentional infliction of harm by unlawful means based upon fraudulent misrepresentation made to, but not causing loss to, third party). Doubt surrounds the extent to which breach of a statutory duty or a penal statute may be relied upon as unlawful means if the breach is not itself actionable. See *Lonrho Ltd v Shell Petroleum Co Ltd (No 2)* [1982] AC 173; *Barretts & Baird (Wholesale) Ltd v Institution of Professional Civil Servants* [1987] IRLR 3; *Associated British Ports v TGWU* [1989] 1 WLR 939 (point not argued in the House of Lords); and *OBG Ltd v Allan* [2008] 1 AC 1.

Any successful picket will almost certainly involve the *prima facie* commission of the tort of inducing a breach of contract or of interference with contract by unlawful means (see *Union Traffic Ltd v TGWU* [1989] ICR 98). Picketing may also involve the torts of nuisance and intimidation (especially if it is mass picketing), or of trespass (see *Mersey Dock and Harbour Co v Verrinder* [1982] IRLR 152, *Thomas v National Union of Mineworkers (South Wales Area)* [1985] ICR 886, *News Group Newspapers Ltd v SOGAT (1982)* [1987] ICR 181) (see **43.9** below).

43.3   THE IMMUNITY FOR LIABILITY

TULRCA 1992, s 219 provides as follows:

'(1)   An act done by a person in contemplation or furtherance of a trade dispute shall not be actionable in tort on the ground only:

   (a)   that it induces another person to break a contract or interferes or induces any other person to interfere with its performance; or

   (b)   that it consists in his threatening that a contract (whether one to which he is a party or not) will be broken or its performance interfered with, or that he will induce another person to break a contract or to interfere with its performance.

(2)   An agreement or combination by two or more persons to do or procure the doing of any act in contemplation or furtherance of a trade dispute shall not be actionable in tort if the act is one which, if done without any such agreement or combination, would not be actionable in tort.'

This formula provides immunity from actions based upon the most common of the economic torts. However, it is possible to formulate a cause of action which falls outside *s 219* (see, eg *Prudential Assurance Co Ltd v Lorenz* (1971) 11 KIR 78 (inducing breach of fiduciary duty); *Associated British Ports v TGWU* [1989] 1 WLR 939 (inducing breach of statutory duty; the point was not argued in the House of Lords)). In such cases it is probably irrelevant that the act complained of may also constitute an inducement to breach of contract which does fall within the immunity.

The statutory immunity does not protect employees from actions by their employers for breach of contract. However, in practice it is unlikely to be worthwhile for an employer to sue individual employees for losses arising from industrial action (see **43.16(d)** below).

43.4   'A TRADE DISPUTE'

'Trade dispute' is given a statutory definition for this purpose by *TULRCA 1992, s 244(1)*, namely:

   '. . . a dispute between workers and their employer which relates wholly or mainly to one or more of the following, that is to say:

   (a)   terms and conditions of employment, or the physical conditions in which any workers are required to work;

   (b)   engagement or non-engagement, or termination or suspension of employment or the duties of employment, of one or more workers;

   (c)   allocation of work or the duties of employment as between workers or groups of workers;

   (d)   matters of discipline;

   (e)   a worker's membership or non-membership of a trade union;

   (f)   facilities for officials of trade unions; and

   (g)   machinery for negotiation or consultation, and other procedures, relating to any of the above matters, including the recognition by employers or employers' associations of the right of a trade union to represent workers in any such negotiation or consultation or in the carrying out of such procedures.'

In *s 244* 'employment' includes any relationship whereby one person personally does work or performs services for another (*TULRCA 1992, s 244(5)*).

'Worker', in relation to a dispute with an employer, means:

(a)   a worker employed by that employer; or

(b)   a person who has ceased to be employed by that employer where:

   (i)   his employment was terminated in connection with the dispute; or

991

(ii)   the termination of his employment was one of the circumstances giving rise to the dispute.

(*TULRCA 1992, s 244(5)*.)

The test of whether there is a trade dispute is an *objective* test (*NWL Ltd v Woods* [1979] ICR 867). A dispute for political reasons which is unconnected with terms and conditions of employment is not considered to be a trade dispute. One such case involved a refusal by broadcasting technicians to make a broadcast to South Africa during the apartheid era (*BBC v Hearn* [1977] IRLR 273). Similarly, a proposed strike intended as a protest against Government policies was held not to be in contemplation or furtherance of a trade dispute (*Express Newspapers v Keys* [1980] IRLR 247). In *Mercury Communications Ltd v Scott-Garner* [1984] ICR 74, an injunction was granted to restrain industrial action since the court held that the risk to jobs did not appear to be the major factor in the dispute. However, if the union genuinely wishes to achieve its demands relating to terms and conditions of employment (or any other matter falling within *TULRCA 1992, s 244(1)*, it is not relevant to establish whether those demands are realistic (*Associated British Ports v TGWU* [1989] 1 WLR 939, a point not argued on appeal). See also *Newham London Borough Council v NALGO* [1993] ICR 189.

If workers take industrial action in this country in order to further a trade dispute abroad, then, provided that the outcome of the dispute relating to matters occurring outside the UK is likely to affect them in one or more of the aspects specified in *s 244(1)*, it will be considered to be a trade dispute for the purpose of the immunity conferred by *s 219* (*TULRCA 1992, s 244(3)*).

Although the dispute must be between workers (not merely the union) and their employer, it will be sufficient to show that it results from the breakdown of negotiations in which the union was acting on behalf of those workers; and in any event a 'Yes' vote in the strike ballot will amount to an adoption of the dispute by the workers (*Associated British Ports v TGWU* [1989] I WLR 939, a point not argued on appeal).

Where a dispute relates to terms and conditions, a strike will be treated as 'in furtherance of a trade dispute' even if some of those balloted and who may be called out are not themselves affected by the terms and conditions in dispute: see *British Telcommunications plc v Communications Workers Union* [2003] EWHC 937 (QB), [2004] IRLR 58. However, in *University College London Hospitals NHS Trust v Unison* [1999] ICR 204, the Court of Appeal upheld an injunction granted against the defendant union following a dispute relating to the future terms and conditions of the employees of a number of private companies which it was proposed should take over the activities of the claimant hospital trust. It was held that a dispute about the terms and conditions of employees of third party employers, who had never been employed by the subject of the proposed strike action, was not a trade dispute within the meaning of *TULRCA 1992, s 244(1)*. Nor was a dispute that was mainly concerned with the terms and conditions of existing employees with an unidentified future employer a trade dispute within the meaning of the section. This approach was held by the European Court of Human Rights to be in accordance with the right to freedom of association contained in *art 11(1)* of the European Convention of Human Rights in *Unison v United Kingdom* [2002] IRLR 497. Interestingly, however, the European court accepted for the first time that the prohibition on the right to strike was an interference with the *art 11(1)* right which required justification under *art 11(2)*, albeit the restriction was justified in that case.

In contrast with the approach in the *University College London Hospitals NHS Trust* case, in *Westminster City Council v Unison* [2001] EWCA Civ 443, [2001] ICR 1046, the Court of Appeal held that a dispute which was predominantly about the change in the identity of the employer consequent on the transfer of employees from a local authority to a private company did fall within the definition of trade dispute.

In *P (a minor) v National Association of School Masters/Union of Women Teachers* [2003] UKHL 8, [2003] ICR 386, the House of Lords held that a dispute as to the reasonableness of an order by the head teacher of a school that the staff should teach an excluded pupil, who had subsequently been reinstated, did amount to a trade dispute as to the teachers' terms and conditions of employment. The dispute related to the teachers' terms and conditions in the sense that it concerned the nature and extent of their contractual obligation to teach the pupil.

Thus, subject to the limits outlined above and to the further restrictions considered below, a person or a trade union may take part in industrial action so long as it is in contemplation or furtherance of a trade dispute as defined.

43.5 'In contemplation or furtherance . . . '

If there is a trade dispute, the question whether a particular act is in contemplation or furtherance of it is to be judged *subjectively*. In *Express Newspapers Ltd v McShane* [1980] ICR 42, the House of Lords held that 'If the party who does the act honestly thinks at the time he does it that it may help one of the parties to the trade dispute to achieve their objectives and does it for that reason, he is protected by the section' (*per* Lord Diplock at 57). The House of Lords reversed the decision of the Court of Appeal which had applied a more objective test. The subjective test was also applied by the House of Lords in *Duport Steels Ltd v Sirs* [1980] IRLR 116. It is sufficient if one purpose of the strike is the furtherance of the dispute, even though there may be other purposes not within the immunity (*Associated British Ports v TGWU* [1989] 1 WLR 939, a point not argued on appeal).

43.6 LIMITS IMPOSED ON SECONDARY ACTION

In non-legal language, 'secondary action' is the term used to describe industrial action taken by workers where the real dispute is not between themselves and their own employer. The typical example is the 'sympathy strike'.

Nothing in *TULRCA 1992, s 219* prevents an act from being actionable in tort where one of the facts relied upon for the purpose of establishing liability is that there has been secondary action which is not lawful picketing (*TULRCA 1992, s 224(1)*). Lawful picketing means acts done in the course of such attendance as is declared lawful by *TULRCA 1992, s 220* by a worker employed or last employed by the employer who is party to the dispute, or by a trade union official whose attendance is lawful by virtue of *s 220(1)(b)*. There is secondary action in relation to a trade dispute when, and only when, a person:

(a)   induces another to break a contract of employment or interferes with or induces another to interfere with its performance, or

(b)   threatens that a contract of employment under which he or another is employed will be broken or its performance interfered with, or that he will induce another to break a contract of employment or to interfere with its performance,

and the employer under the contract of employment is not the employer party to the dispute (*TULRCA 1992, s 224(2)*). An employer cannot be party to a dispute between another employer and his workers, and if more than one employer is in dispute with his workers, each dispute is to be treated as separate (*TULRCA 1992, s 224(4)*). A contract of employment is defined to include any contract for personal service, and is thus not confined to the contracts of those who are employees in the strict sense (*TULRCA 1992, s 224(6)*; cf EMPLOYEE, SELF-EMPLOYED OR WORKER? (14)).

The effect of *TULRCA 1992, ss 220* and *224(1)* is that it will not be actionable if, for example, strikers in dispute with their own employer and picketing their workplace induce a lorry-driver not to cross the picket-line, and thus to breach his contract of employment with his own employer who is not a party to the dispute. Subject to this limited type of exception, however, it will be tortious to organise any form of secondary action, including secondary picketing. Unlike under earlier legislation, there is no exception where the aim of the secondary action is to disrupt the supply of goods and services to or from the employer who is party to the dispute or an associated employer of that party.

However, if a particular act constitutes primary action in relation to a trade dispute, the same act may not be relied upon as constituting secondary action so as to evade the immunity in tort. Primary action means the same as secondary action but where the employer under the contract of employment *is* party to the dispute (*TULRCA 1992, s 224(5)*).

43.7   PRESSURE TO IMPOSE UNION MEMBERSHIP OR RECOGNITION

Under *TULRCA 1992, ss 222* and *225*, certain industrial action taken to impose union membership or recognition requirements does not have the protection of *s 219* and will therefore be unlawful. Specifically, there is no immunity from actions in tort for individuals who induce or attempt to induce another:

(a)   to incorporate in a contract to which that other person is a party, or proposed contract to which that other person intends to be a party, a term or conditions which would require that a party to the contract should recognise one or more trade unions for the purpose of negotiating on behalf of workers employed by him, or that he should negotiate with or consult with an official of one or more trade unions;

(b)   on grounds of union exclusion (that is, that the supplier or prospective supplier does not or is not likely to recognise, negotiate or consult as set out in (*a*) above), to:

  (i)   exclude a person from a list of approved suppliers of goods and services or persons from whom tenders for the supply of goods or services are invited;

  (ii)   exclude a person from the group of persons from whom tenders for the supply of goods or services are invited;

  (iii)   fail to permit a particular person to submit such a tender; or

  (iv)   terminate or determine not to enter into a contract with a particular person for the supply of goods or services.

(*TULRCA 1992, ss 186, 187, 225.*)

Nor is there any immunity where the act concerned is done because, or partly because, a particular employer is employing, has employed or might employ a person who is not a member of any, or any particular, trade union, or because a particular employer refrains from discriminating against such a person, or because it is believed that any of these things has occurred (*TULRCA 1992, s 222(1)*).

Nor is there any immunity where the act concerned is, or is part of, an inducement or an attempted inducement of a person:

(a)   to incorporate in a contract to which that person is party or intends to be party a term or condition which would require that the whole, or some part, of the work done for the purposes of the contract be done only by persons who are or are not members of trade unions or a particular trade union; or

(b)   on union membership grounds (that is, that if the proposed contract were entered into with the person concerned, work for the purposes of the contract would be or would be likely to be done by persons who were or were not members of trade unions or a particular trade union; or in the case of the termination of a contract that such work has been or is likely to be done by such persons), to

(i)   exclude a person from a list of approved suppliers of goods and services or persons from whom tenders for the supply of goods and services may be invited;

(ii)   exclude a person from the group of persons from whom tenders for the supply of goods or services are invited;

(iii)   fail to permit a particular person to submit such a tender;

(iv)   determine not to enter into a contract with a particular person for the supply of goods or services; or

(v)   terminate a contract with a particular person for the supply of goods or services.

(TULRCA 1992, ss 144, 145, 222(3).)

See also **49.19** TRADE UNIONS – **II**.

43.8   Action in response to dismissal of unofficial strikers

The immunity under *TULRCA 1992, s 219* is lost where the reason, or one of the reasons, for doing the act in question (such as an inducing of breaches of contract by organising a strike) is the fact or belief that an employer has dismissed one or more employees in circumstances such that by virtue of *TULRCA 1992, s 237* they have no right to complain of unfair dismissal (*TULRCA 1992, s 223*).

TULRCA 1992, s 237, which is discussed in detail in **51.18** UNFAIR DISMISSAL – **I**, provides that an employee has no right to complain of unfair dismissal if at the time of dismissal he was taking part in an unofficial strike or other unofficial industrial action.

43.9   PICKETING

As noted above, any successful picket will be liable to involve the commission of a tort. The statutory immunity for picketing is contained in *TULRCA 1992, s 220*. A person acts lawfully if he attends:

(a)   in contemplation or furtherance of a trade dispute; *and*

(b)   at a specified place, namely:

(i)   at or near his own place of work; or

(ii)   if he is unemployed and either his last employment was terminated in connection with a trade dispute or if the termination was one of the circumstances giving rise to a trade dispute, at or near his former place of work; or

(iii)   if he does not work or normally work at any one place or if the place where he works or normally works is in a location such that attendance there for picketing is impracticable, at any premises of his employer from which he works or from which his work is administered; or

(iv)   if he is an official of a trade union, at or near the place of work or former place of work of a member of that union whom he is accompanying and whom he represents; and

(c)   for the purpose only of peacefully obtaining or communicating information or peacefully persuading any person to work or abstain from working.

Any person who pickets outside these limits will lose the immunity from actions in tort. By reason of *TULRCA 1992, s 219(3)* he cannot rely upon the general immunity conferred by *s 219* upon acts done in contemplation or furtherance of a trade dispute unless *s 220* is also satisfied. Accordingly, he will be liable to a claim for an injunction and/or damages if, in the course of such picketing, he commits a tort.

The purpose of condition (*b*) above is to remove the immunity from 'flying pickets'. The Court of Appeal considered its effects in *Union Traffic Ltd v Transport and General Workers Union* [1989] ICR 98 in which it was held that lorry drivers were not entitled to picket depots at which they frequently called for deliveries, repairs and the like, because they were not the bases from which the drivers worked. In *Rayware Ltd v Transport and General Workers Union* [1989] ICR 457 a gate leading to a private trading estate but some way from the employer's premises on that estate was held to be 'near' the place of work since it was the nearest the pickets could get to their place of work without committing a trespass.

Further, *s 220* only serves to give immunity from actions in tort where the tort arises out of the mere act of attendance at the place concerned. If the picket commits further torts, such as inducing breaches of the contracts of employment of those whom he seeks to dissuade from crossing the picket line, he will be liable unless he has the protection of *s 219*, which is discussed more fully elsewhere in this chapter.

One of the circumstances in which the protection of *TULRCA 1992, s 219* is lost is where one of the facts relied on for the purpose of establishing liability is that there has been secondary action which is not lawful picketing (*TULRCA 1992, s 224(1)*) (see **43.6** above). Any picket is liable to involve secondary action, because the pickets will try to turn back the employees of third parties, hence the exception in *s 224(1)* for lawful picketing. Lawful picketing is defined in *TULRCA 1992, s 224(3)* as acts done, in the course of attendance declared lawful by *s 220*, by a worker employed (or, if not in employment, last employed) by the employer party to the dispute or by a trade union official whose attendance is lawful by virtue of *TULRCA 1992, s 220(1)(b)*. The effect of these provisions is to remove the immunity from secondary picketing whilst retaining it for direct picketing of the employer who is a party to the dispute, even if that involves pickets trying to turn back the employees of third parties.

43.10   Broome's case

In *Broome v DPP* [1974] ICR 84, the defendant, a picket during an industrial dispute, stood holding a placard in front of a vehicle on a highway, urging the driver not to go to a nearby site and preventing him from so doing for some nine minutes. The Divisional Court reversed the decision of the Stockport magistrates acquitting the defendant and convicted him of obstructing the highway. The House of Lords affirmed the conviction. The law which their Lordships had to consider was *Industrial Relations Act 1971, s 134* (which was framed, for these purposes, in similar terms to the present *TULRCA 1992, s 220*). Lord Reid said of the defendant's conduct (at 89):

> ' . . . his attendance there is only made lawful by subsection (2) if he attended only for the purpose of obtaining or communicating information or "peacefully persuading" the lorry driver. Attendance for that purpose must I think include the right to try to persuade anyone who chooses to stop and listen, at least in so far as this is done in a reasonable way with due consideration for the rights of others. A right to attend for the purpose of peaceful persuasion would be meaningless unless this were implied.

> But I see no ground for implying any right to require the person whom it is sought to persuade to submit to any kind of constraint or restriction of his personal freedom.'

Lord Salmon made similar observations.

Thus, police officers acted within their powers when they prevented pickets from approaching a lorry carrying 'strike breakers' during an industrial dispute because they feared an obstruction or a breach of the peace (*Kavanagh v Hiscock* [1974] ICR 282).

43.11   Code of Practice

The Secretary of State for Employment has issued a Code of Practice on picketing under his statutory powers (see **4.4 CODES OF PRACTICE**). The original Code was revised and reissued by virtue of the *Employment Code of Practice (Picketing) Order 1992 (SI 1992/476)*.

The most notable provisions of the *Code* include the recommendation that there should not generally be more than six pickets at any one entrance (*para 51*), recommendations as to the functions of the picket organiser (*paras 54 to 57*), and recommendations concerning avoiding impediments to the movement of essential supplies, services and operations (*paras 62 to 64*).

43.12   CRIMINAL LIABILITY

Action taken by pickets may give rise to criminal liability. For example, they may be prosecuted under *TULRCA 1992, s 241(1)(d)*, which provides that a person who:

> ' . . . with a view to compelling another person to abstain from doing or to do any act which that person has a legal right to do or abstain from doing, wrongfully and without legal authority . . . watches or besets the house or other place where that person resides, or works, or carries on business, or happens to be, or the approach to such house or place',

shall, on summary conviction, be liable to a fine not exceeding level 5 on the Standard Scale, or up to six months' imprisonment, or both (*TULRCA 1992, s 241(2)*; see **1.10 INTRODUCTION**).

However, compulsion of the other person, and not mere persuasion of him, must be the object of the watching and besetting (*DPP v Fidler* [1992] 1 WLR 91). The watching and besetting is not wrongful unless tortious (*Thomas v National Union of Mineworkers (South Wales Area)* [1985] ICR 886), but it appears that it may be wrongful even if no action in tort could be brought because of the statutory immunity (*Galt v Philp* [1984] IRLR 156). Other criminal charges for assault, criminal damage and offences under the *Public Order Act 1986* (especially *ss 1–5*) may arise if the pickets behave unlawfully. In such cases *TULRCA 1992, s 220* cannot provide them with a defence. *Public Order Act 1986, Part II* gives the police certain powers to impose conditions upon public processions and assemblies, in addition to their common law powers to take such action as may be necessary to prevent a breach of the peace.

The House of Lords held in *DPP v Jones* [1999] 2 AC 240 that the public have the right to use the highway for such reasonable and usual activities, including peaceful assembly, as are consistent with the primary right of passage. This important decision was plainly influenced by *art 11* of the European Convention on Human Rights (the right to freedom of peaceful assembly).

Any action which does not fall within the provisions of *TULRCA 1992, s 220* constitutes an offence if the obstruction takes place on the public highway, since the *Highways Act 1980, s 137(1)* provides:

> 'If a person, without lawful authority or excuse, in any way wilfully obstructs the free passage along a highway he is guilty of an offence . . . '.

For the definition of obstruction, see *Cooper v Metropolitan Police Comr* (1985) 82 Cr App Rep 238. However, picketing may take place outside factory gates which are on private property. In such a case, the pickets cannot be guilty of obstructing the highway but may be liable for a private trespass or nuisance.

43.13 Strikes and Industrial Action

43.13 THE LIABILITY OF TRADE UNIONS

Trade unions are no longer, as they once were, immune from all proceedings in tort arising from industrial action. They are now liable for tortious acts which they are taken to have authorised or endorsed (see **48.16 TRADE UNIONS – I**). They enjoy the same statutory immunity as individuals, but only if they fulfil the ballot requirements of *TULRCA 1992*. The liability of trade unions in actions in tort is subject to statutory financial limits (see **48.17 TRADE UNIONS – I**).

43.14 BALLOTS BEFORE INDUSTRIAL ACTION

In order to enjoy immunity from actions in tort for acts inducing persons to take part or continue to take part in industrial action, trade unions must be supported by a ballot (*TULRCA 1992, s 226(1)*). The ballot must comply with the complex procedural obligations contained in *Part V* of *TULRCA 1992*. Notwithstanding the onerous nature of these requirements, the Court of Appeal held in *Metrobus Ltd v Unite the Union* [2009] EWCA Civ 829, [2010] ICR 173 that they were not incompatible with the right to freedom of association contained in *Article 11* of the *European Convention on Human Rights*. The following are the prerequisites of a ballot before industrial action.

(a)   All of those members whom it is reasonable for the union to believe will be called upon to take part in the industrial action, and no others, must be balloted (*TULRCA 1992, s 227(1)*). Those "taking part" in the industrial action are not confined to members who will in fact be called upon to breach their contracts of employment; they may participate in other ways: see *London Underground Ltd v ASLEF* [2011] EWHC 3506. Moreover, since 18 September 2000, this requirement has been mitigated by a new *TULRCA 1992, s 232B* which provides that a failure to comply which is accidental and on a scale which is unlikely to affect the result of the ballot will be disregarded. In *British Airways plc v Unite the Union* [2009] EWHC 3541, [2010] IRLR 423, the High Court held that the union had failed to comply with the requirement to ballot only those whom it reasonably believed would be called upon to take action, in circumstances where several hundred members had been balloted whom the union knew would no longer be employed by the employer at the time of the ballot. The union could gain no assistance from *TULRCA 1992, s 232B*, since the failure, though unintentional, could not properly be described as accidental. The Court of Appeal considered the requirement that a relevant failure must be "accidental" for *s 232B* to come into play in *London & Birmingham Railway Ltd v ASLEF; Serco Ltd v RMT* [2011] EWCA Civ 226, [2011] ICR 849, and held that the union's actions in permitting two members to vote who should not have been should be disregarded. The mistake was due to human error, and it did not matter that it could have been avoided if reasonable steps had been taken to keep the union's records up to date. Moreover, the Court of Appeal went on to express the view that a general de minimis principle applies in the context of the balloting procedures. By virtue of *TULRCA 1992, s 232A*, industrial action will not be regarded as having the support of a ballot if any member whom it was reasonable at the time of the ballot for the union to believe would be induced to take part in the action is induced to take part. However, the union is not confined to balloting and inducing to take part in the action only those who will be directly affected by the subject matter of the trade dispute: see *United Closures and Plastics Ltd* [2012] IRLR 29. It was held by the Court of Appeal in *London Underground Ltd v National Union of Rail, Maritime and Transport Workers* [1996] ICR 170 that the defendant union could induce members who had not been balloted to take part in industrial action if those members had joined the union since the ballot. It was also recognised that a union may induce non-members to participate, even though they will not have been balloted. In *P (a minor) v National Association of School Masters/Union of Women*

Teachers [2003] UKHL 8, [2003] ICR 386 the House of Lords held that the union's failure to send ballot papers to two teachers who had recently joined the staff did not invalidate the ballot. In particular, the failure to send those teachers ballot papers did not necessarily mean that they had not been accorded entitlement to vote within the meaning of *TULRCA 1992, s 232A(c)*. The requirement to send out ballot papers to those defined as entitled to vote in *s 227(1)* is subject to the caveat 'so far as is reasonably practicable' in *s 230(2)*. Further, *s 232B* makes the requirement to send out ballot papers subject to the disregard of small accidental errors. Accordingly, the ballot was valid. By contrast, in *Midline Mainline Ltd v National Union of Rail, Maritime and Transport Workers* [2001] EWCA Civ 1206, [2001] IRLR 813 the failure to ballot 25 union members in a ballot of 91 members was held by the Court of Appeal to be too significant to be disregarded.

If the persons balloted have different places of work, *TULRCA 1992, s 228* requires a separate ballot for each workplace, unless those balloted share a common feature of terms and conditions of employment or occupational description which is not shared by other members with the same employer who are not balloted and, in a case where there are such other members, is not a factor which employees of that employer have in common by virtue of having the same place of work. A new *TULRCA 1992, ss 228* and *228A*, enable unions to hold a ballot across separate workplaces if the dispute affects at least one member of the union in each workplace, or if the ballot is limited to all members whom the union reasonably believes to have particular kinds of occupation and are employed by a particular employer or employers with whom the union is in dispute, or if entitlement to vote is given to only to members of the union who are employed by an employer or employers with whom the union is in dispute. 'Workplace' is defined as the premises at which an employee works or, where an employee does not work at a particular premises, the premises with which his employment has the closest connection (*TULRCA 1992, s 228(4)*). Where separate workplace ballots are not required, the ballot may legitimately include employees of more than one employer, if a number of employers are party to the dispute (*University of Central England v NALGO* [1993] IRLR 81). Employees of different employers may be held to have the same place of work even if their respective employers each have only a licence over the premises at which they work (*Intercity West Coast Ltd v National Union of Rail, Maritime and Transport Workers* [1996] IRLR 583).

(b)   So far as is reasonably practicable, every person entitled to vote must have a voting paper sent to him by post at his home address (or other address which he has requested the union to treat as his postal address), and must be given a convenient opportunity to vote by post (*TULRCA 1992, s 230(2)*). Special provisions apply to merchant seamen. It was held in *British Railways Board v National Union of Railwaymen* [1989] ICR 678 that the words 'reasonably practicable' mean that inadvertent errors such as missing some members off the list will not necessarily invalidate the ballot. This principle was given statutory force by *TULRCA 1992, s 232B* which provides for small-scale, accidental failures to be disregarded (see (*a*) above).

(c)   The voting paper must contain at least one of the following questions –

(i)   a question which requires the voter to say, by answering 'Yes' or 'No' whether he is prepared to take part, or to continue to take part, in a strike;

(ii)   a question which requires the voter to say, by answering 'Yes' or 'No', whether he is prepared to take part, or as the case may be to continue to take part, in industrial action falling short of a strike.

(*TULRCA 1992, s 229(2)*.)

This means that a strike and action short of a strike must be the subject of separate questions on the ballot paper (*Post Office v Union of Communications Workers* [1990] ICR 258).

TULRCA 1992, s 229 provides that an overtime ban and a call-out ban constitute action short of a strike for the purposes of the strike ballot provisions.

(d)   The following statement must appear without comment on every voting paper:

'If you take part in a strike or other industrial action, you may be in breach of your contract of employment.

However, if you are dismissed for taking part in strike or other industrial action which is called officially and is otherwise lawful, the dismissal will be unfair if it takes place fewer than twelve weeks after you started taking part in the action, and depending on the circumstances may be unfair if it takes place later.'

(*TULRCA 1992, s 229(4)*.)

(e)   The voting paper must clearly specify the address to which, and the date by which, it is to be returned, and must be numbered (*TULRCA 1992, s 229(1A)*).

(f)   The voting paper must specify who, in the event of a vote in favour of action, is authorised for the purposes of *TULRCA 1992, s 233* (see **43.15** below) to call upon members to take part or continue to take part in the industrial action (*TULRCA 1992, s 229(3)*). The specified person need not be authorised under the rules of the union, but must be within *TULRCA 1992, s 20(2)* (ie a person empowered by the rules to call for the action, or the principal executive committee, president or general secretary, or any other committee or official of the union; see also TRADE UNIONS – I **(48)**). It is thought that the voting paper may specify alternative persons as having the authority to call for action. Further, in a case where an independent scrutineer is required (see (*k*) below), the ballot paper must state his name (*TULRCA 1992, s 229(1A)(a)*).

(g)   So far as is reasonably practicable those voting must vote in secret (*TULRCA 1992, s 230(4)(a)*). They must be allowed to vote without interference from the union, and so far as reasonably practicable, without incurring direct costs to themselves (this presumably means that reply-paid envelopes must be used for the postal ballot) (*TULRCA 1992, s 230(1)*). For reasonable practicability, see (*b*) above.

(h)   The votes must be fairly and accurately counted, although an inaccuracy in counting is to be disregarded if it is accidental and on a scale which could not affect the result of the ballot (*TULRCA 1992, s 230(4)*).

(i)   The majority of those voting in the ballot must have answered 'Yes' to the appropriate question (*TULRCA 1992, s 226(2)(b)*). Where a ballot poses two separate questions, one relating to strike action and the other to industrial action short of a strike, the relevant majority is a majority of those voting on the specific question. It is not necessary that the majority voting 'Yes' in response to the particular question also comprise a majority of those taking part in the ballot (*West Midlands Travel Ltd v Transport and General Workers' Union* [1994] ICR 978).

(j)   In a case where the number of members entitled to vote in the ballot (the aggregated number is taken where there are separate workplace ballots in accordance with (*a*) above) exceeds 50, a qualified scrutineer must be appointed. The union must ensure that he duly carries out his functions without interference, and must comply with all his reasonable requests. The scrutineer will make a report as soon as reasonably practicable after the ballot, and in any event within four weeks, stating whether he is satisfied that there are no reasonable grounds for believing that there was any contravention of statutory requirements, that the ballot arrangements included all reasonably practicable security arrangements to minimise the risk of unfairness or malpractice, and that he has been able to carry out his functions without interference from the union. Any person entitled to vote in the ballot, and the employer of any such person, is entitled (upon request made within six months of the ballot and upon payment of any reasonable fee specified by the union) to be provided with a copy of the report (*TULRCA 1992, ss 226B, 226C, 231B*). The persons qualified to be scrutineers are those satisfying the requirements of the *Trade Union Ballots and Elections (Independent Scrutineer Qualifications) Order 1993 (SI 1993/1909)*.

(k)   The union must take such steps as are reasonably necessary to secure that every person whom it is reasonable for the union to believe will be the employer of persons entitled to vote in the ballot receives both notice that the ballot will take place, and a sample voting paper. In *English, Welsh & Scottish Railway Ltd v National Union of Rail, Maritime and Transport Workers* [2004] EWCA Civ 1539, 148 Sol Jo LB 1246 the Court of Appeal held that, where a notice of intention to hold an industrial action ballot was addressed to only one of two very closely related employers involved in an industrial dispute with the union, the notice should be treated as having been given to both companies. The notice must be received not later than the seventh day before the opening of the ballot, and must specify the anticipated opening day and identify the categories of employees of that employer whom the union believes will be entitled to vote. The sample voting paper must be received not later than the third day before the opening day (*TULRCA 1992, s 226A*). Under the legislation prior to its amendment, in *Blackpool and the Fylde College v National Association of Teachers in Further and Higher Education* [1994] ICR 648, it was held that the notice must enable the employer readily to ascertain which individual employees were to be balloted, and so in some cases would require individuals to be named in the notice. However, this requirement was amended by *ERA 1999, Sch 3* with effect from 18 September 2000, by virtue of which the union was required to provide such information as is in its possession as would help the employer to make plans and bring information to the attention of the employees.

With effect from 1 October 2005, the notice provisions contained in *TULRCA 1992, s 226A* were amended yet again by *s 22* of the *Employment Relations Act 2004*. A valid notice must now contain lists of the categories of employee whom the union reasonably believes will be entitled to vote in the ballot and the workplaces at which they work. The notice must also state the total number of employees to be balloted and the number in each category, together with an explanation of how those figures were arrived at. The Court of Appeal held in *National Union of Rail, Maritime & Transport Workers v Serco Ltd* [2011] EWCA Civ 226, [2011] IRLR 399 that the duty to provide such an explanation is not an onerous one, usually requiring only an indication of the sources of the information and highlighting any major known deficiencies. Unions are expressed not to be under a duty to supply an employer with the names of the employees concerned. By *s 226(2D)*, the lists and figures supplied must be as accurate as is reasonably practicable in the light of the information in the possession of the union. In *London & Birmingham Railway Ltd v ASLEF; Serco Ltd v RMT* [2011] EWCA Civ 226, [2011] ICR 849 the Court of Appeal held that this obligation does not require unions to seek out additional information or set up systems to improve their record keeping. In *British Airways plc v Unite the Union* [2009] EWHC 3541, [2010] IRLR 423, the High Court held that the union had failed to comply with the notice provisions in circumstances where it had included in the ballot notice a substantial number of employees whom it could not reasonably have believed would be entitled to vote in the ballot, since they would no longer be employed by the employer by the time the strike was called. In *Metrobus Ltd v Unite the Union* [2009] EWCA Civ 829, [2010] ICR 173, a majority of the Court of Appeal held that, in respect of non-check off employees, the union is obliged to provide a list of the numbers of employees who will be entitled to vote, the numbers in each workplace, the numbers in each category of worker and an explanation of how the figures were worked out. However, a misstatement of the number of relevant check off employees (by 10 out of nearly 800) was held not to be sufficiently material to invalidate the ballot. As noted above, in *London & Birmingham Railway Ltd v ASLEF; Serco Ltd v RMT* [2011] EWCA Civ 226, [2011] ICR 849, the Court of Appeal endorsed the view (obiter) that a general de minimis principle applies in the context of the balloting notification procedures, such that a very small error in the notice will not generally invalidate a ballot. By contrast, in *Metroline Travel Ltd v Unite the Union* [2012] EWHC 1778 (QB), [2012] IRLR 749 a notice was held to be invalid when it referred to balloting certain grades of employee working on the contract for a particular client "on a full time or part basis". This was too imprecise, as it was unclear whether this included employees who might be expected to work for the client, or who were associated with the client, and whether they had to be working for the client directly or indirectly.

(l) As soon as is reasonably practicable after the holding of the ballot, the union must take such steps as are reasonably necessary to ensure that all persons entitled to vote, and their employers, are informed of the number of votes cast, the number of 'Yes' and 'No' votes, and the number of spoiled voting papers (*TULRCA 1992, s 231, s 231A*). These requirements have been interpreted relatively strictly by the courts. In *Metrobus Ltd v Unite the Union* [2009] EWCA Civ 829, [2010] ICR 173 the Court of Appeal held that the union had acted in breach of *TULRCA 1992, s 231A(1)* by delaying just two days in notifying the employer of the result of a strike ballot. It further held that the duty to provide such information applies irrespective of whether the union proposes to initiate industrial action. However, not every technical challenge will succeed. In *British Airways plc v Unite the Union* [2010] EWCA Civ 669, [2010] ICR 1316, a majority of the Court of Appeal held that the trade union had taken such steps as were reasonably necessary to comply with the duty to inform members of the results of the ballot by providing them on its website, on union notice boards and via news sheets, even though each member had not been sent an individual email or text message with the results.

Where there are separate ballots for different workplaces, paras (*b*) to (*m*) are to be tested in relation to the ballot for the workplace of the person whose inducement to take part in the action is relied upon to found the liability in tort (*TULRCA 1992, s 226(3)*). This means in particular that a 'Yes' vote is required at every workplace where the members are to be called upon to take action.

If there is a suspension of industrial action for negotiations, a further ballot need not be held before industrial action is resumed, provided that the terms of the original ballot cover the reason for the resumed action (*Monsanto plc v Transport and General Workers Union* [1987] ICR 269). However, this will not apply where there is a substantial interruption of the action as opposed to a mere suspension; where the action is irregular and spasmodic, it is a question of fact and degree whether it is sufficiently continuous and self-contained to be covered by a single ballot (*Post Office v Union of Communications Workers* [1990] ICR 258).

In *London Underground Ltd v National Union of Railwaymen* [1989] IRLR 341 it was held that at the time of the ballot there must be a genuine, definite, substantial dispute (actual or reasonably foreseeable) between the parties, and that the ballot question must relate wholly to matters capable of constituting a trade dispute. However, in *Associated British Ports v TGWU* [1989] 1 WLR 939 it was held that there was no need for the ballot information to describe or define every issue with which the dispute was concerned, provided that it was possible to identify the strike which was called with the strike which was voted for (the point was not argued on appeal).

Special provisions apply to overseas members and to members in Northern Ireland (*TULRCA 1992, s 232*). A union which is a federation, and which does not have individual members whom it will call out on strike, cannot comply with the relevant provisions of *TULRCA 1992* and therefore will enjoy no immunity from action when calling a strike (*Shipping Co Uniform Inc v International Transport Workers Federation* [1985] ICR 245).

The Secretary of State is empowered by *TULRCA 1992, ss 203, 204* to issue codes of practice relating to the conduct by trade unions of ballots and elections (see CODES OF PRACTICE (4)). The original *Code on Trade Union Ballots on Industrial Action* has been revised and reissued (*Employment Code of Practice (Industrial Action Ballots and Notice to Employers) Order 2005 (SI 2005/2420)*). The *Code* deals with, among other things, the situations in which an industrial action ballot is appropriate, establishment of the balloting 'constituency', preparation and distribution of voting papers, and the conduct and counting of the ballot.

43.15 CALLING FOR INDUSTRIAL ACTION

In order for the action to be treated as supported by the ballot, there must have been no call by the union to take part in or continue to take part in the action to which the ballot relates, or any authorisation or endorsement of such action (see **48.16 TRADE UNIONS – I**), *before* the date of the ballot (*TULRCA 1992, s 233(3)(a)*).

The call for industrial action must be made by the person specified on the ballot paper (see **43.14**(*f*) above). It is permissible for the specified person to call for action subject to some condition whose fulfilment is a matter for the judgment of local officials, although he may not simply delegate his authority (*Tanks and Drums Ltd v TGWU* [1992] ICR 1).

The call for action must be made, and the action must commence, before the end of the period of four weeks beginning with the date of the ballot (*TULRCA 1992, ss 233, 234(1)*). However, *TULRCA 1992, s 234(1)* provides that this period may be extended up to a maximum of eight weeks by agreement between the union and the employers. There are provisions which enable the union to apply to the court for an extension of time, up to a maximum of 12 weeks from the date of the ballot, where for the whole or part of that period action is prohibited by a court order or an undertaking given to the court which subsequently ceases to have effect (*TULRCA 1992, s 234(2)–(6)*).

The union must take such steps as are reasonably necessary to give notice to an employer whose employees it reasonably believes will be or have been induced to take part in the action, describing the categories of employees concerned and specifying whether the action is intended to be continuous (in which case it must state the intended commencement date for any of those employees) or discontinuous (in which case it must state the intended dates for any of them to take part). As with the notice of ballot, until 18 September 2000 it was necessary for the notice to enable the employer readily to ascertain which individual employees were to be called upon to take industrial action, and this in some cases required individuals' names to be given (*Blackpool and the Fylde College v National Association of Teachers in Further and Higher Education* [1994] ICR 648). However, again, as with the notice of ballot, this latter requirement was amended by *ERA 1999, Sch 3*, pursuant to which the union was required to provide only such information as would help the employer to make plans and bring information to the attention of the employees. With effect from 1 October 2005, these notice provisions were amended yet again by section 25 of the *Employment Relations Act 2004*. A valid notice must now contain lists of the categories of employee whom the union reasonably believes will be induced to take part in industrial action. The notice must also state the total number of employees to be induced to participate and the number in each category. Unions are expressed not to be under a duty to supply an employer with the names of the employees concerned. The notice must be received within the period beginning with the day when the requirement to notify employers of the ballot result is

43.15   Strikes and Industrial Action

satisfied (see **43.14(M)** above) and ending with the seventh day before the first day specified in the notice (*TULRCA 1992, s 234A*). Thus the union is effectively required to give an employer at least a week's notice of industrial action.

43.16   EMPLOYER'S RIGHTS AND REMEDIES

The withdrawal of labour will usually amount to a breach of the contracts of employment of the individuals concerned. A strike notice may, however, at least in theory, be construed as due notice to *terminate* the contracts of employment of the strikers. Whether this is so depends upon the words used and on the circumstances (*Boxfoldia Ltd v National Graphical Association* [1988] ICR 752). Action taken in a go-slow or work-to-rule may also be considered a breach by each individual participant of his contract of employment. In *Secretary of State for Employment v Associated Society of Locomotive Engineers and Firemen* [1972] ICR 7 at 56 Lord Denning MR said:

> 'If [an employee] with . . . others, takes steps wilfully to disrupt the undertaking, to produce chaos so that it will not run as it should, then each one who is a party to those steps is guilty of a breach of his contract. It is no answer for any one of them to say "I am only obeying the rule book", or "I am not bound to do more than a 40-hour week". That would be all very well if done in good faith without any wilful disruption of services; but what makes it wrong is the object with which it is done.'

See also *British Telecommunications plc v Ticehurst* [1992] ICR 383.

The courses of action open to an employer, and others affected by industrial action, include the following:

(a)   An employer may try to conciliate, if necessary with the assistance of the ADVISORY, CONCILIATION AND ARBITRATION SERVICE (2).

(b)   If employees are on strike or their work is disruptive within the meaning of Lord Denning's statement above, they do not have to be paid for the period during which industrial action persists. If employees are refusing to perform part of their contractual duties, employers may deduct an appropriate sum from their salaries (*Sim v Rotherham Metropolitan Borough Council* [1986] ICR 897; *Miles v Wakefield Metropolitan District Council* [1987] ICR 368; *Wiluszynski v Tower Hamlets London Borough Council* [1989] ICR 493; and see PAY – I (32)). In *Spackman v London Metropolitan University* [2007] IRLR 744 the claimant complained at having been paid only 70% of her contractual salary in respect of a period during which she had been performing only some of her contractual duties as part of industrial action being taken against her employer. The county court rejected her argument that she was entitled to a *quantum meruit* payment for some or all of the balance of her salary. Such an approach was inappropriate in circumstances where the contract of employment continued to govern the relationship between the parties. Moreover, it was held that employees participating in this type of industrial action are taking the risk of recovering no pay at all when they carry out only some of their contractual duties.

(c)   If employees or unions are taking disruptive industrial action which is not in contemplation or furtherance of a trade dispute or is unprotected secondary action or action for a purpose not within the statutory immunities, or is action by trade unions taken without a ballot, an employer affected may apply to the High Court for an *injunction* to prevent them from continuing such action. He may sue either the individuals involved or the union responsible, or both. Note that *TULRCA 1992, s 221(1)* requires that any application for an injunction must be brought to the attention of the other party if it seems likely that he may claim that he is acting in contemplation or furtherance of a trade dispute. Unless the court is satisfied that all reasonable steps have been taken, an injunction will not be granted. However, it is important to apply to the court speedily.

In deciding whether or not to grant the injunction, a court must have regard to the likelihood of the defendant succeeding in establishing a defence under *TULRCA 1992, s 219* or *s 220 (TULRCA 1992, s 221(2))*. Although the likelihood of establishing the defence is only one factor to be considered in deciding where the 'balance of convenience' lies (that being the test of whether to grant an interim injunction if the plaintiff has an arguable case and an ultimate award of damages would not be an adequate remedy for either party), the injunction will normally be refused if it appears more likely than not that the statutory defence will be made out (*NWL Ltd v Woods* [1979] ICR 867). The court will also have regard to whether it is likely that in practice the grant or refusal of the injunction will be decisive in determining the legal proceedings for an injunction (if so, it becomes more important to try to form a view of the ultimate chances of success); it will compare the disadvantage to the workers in being unable to strike while the iron is hot with the potential losses to the employer. In a proper case it may have regard to the public interest, and if all other considerations are evenly balanced it will usually attempt to preserve the status quo (see, eg *Dimbleby & Sons Ltd v NUJ* [1984] ICR 386; *Union Traffic Ltd v TGWU* [1989] ICR 98; *Associated British Ports v TGWU* [1989] 1 WLR 939 (point not argued in the House of Lords)). The court will, however, under no circumstances grant an injunction if its effect would be to compel the employees to work (*TULRCA 1992, s 236*).

In proceedings arising out of an act which is by virtue of *TULRCA 1992, s 20* taken to have been one by a trade union (as to which see **48.16** TRADE UNIONS – I), the court's power to grant an injunction includes power to require the union to take such steps as the court considers appropriate for ensuring that there is no, or no further, inducement of persons to take part in industrial action or to continue to do so, and that no person engages in any conduct after the granting of the injunction by virtue of such inducement prior to the injunction (*TULRCA 1992, s 20(6)*). This represents a statutory development of the decision in *Solihull Metropolitan Borough v National Union of Teachers* [1985] IRLR 211, that where industrial action was called without a ballot, union leaders could be required to rescind the instruction.

If the union or the individuals against whom a court order is obtained act in breach of the order, proceedings may be taken for contempt of court (see, eg *Richard Read (Transport) Ltd v National Union of Mineworkers (South Wales Area)* [1985] IRLR 67; *Express and Star Ltd v NGA* [1986] ICR 589; *Kent Free Press v NGA* [1987] IRLR 267). The penalties which a court may impose if it finds a contempt proved are a fine, sequestration and imprisonment. A writ of sequestration will not affect the separate funds of a branch which is an unincorporated association (see *News Group Newspapers Ltd v Society of Graphical and Allied Trades 1982* [1986] ICR 716). Note that the union will not be able to use its funds to indemnify individuals penalised for contempt of court, nor for certain criminal offences (*TULRCA 1992, s 15*; and see **48.18** TRADE UNIONS – I).

(d)   The employer may also claim damages against those taking part in or organising the industrial action, or against the union (see **48.16** TRADE UNIONS – I). A claim in *tort* for inducing breaches of contract (the most common cause of action) will only succeed if the statutory immunity does not apply. However, the immunity does not extend to straightforward actions for *breach of contract*, and individual strikers may be sued on that basis. In practice, this is rarely likely to be worthwhile for an employer. Notwithstanding the absence of a statutory immunity for breach of contract, an employer is precluded from obtaining an injunction to restrain a breach of contract where the effect of the order would be to compel the employee to work (*TULRCA 1992, s 236*). Damages are limited to the loss actually caused by the individual striker (*National Coal Board v Galley* [1958] 1 WLR 16), which may be difficult to prove, or confined to the extra cost of hiring a substitute; and to seek to enforce a substantial award of damages against ordinary employees, even if practicable, will clearly have industrial relations implications. In certain circumstances it may also be possible to recover money which the employer has been forced to pay under duress of unlawful industrial action (see, eg *Dimskal Shipping Co SA v ITWF* [1992] IRLR 78). The damages which may be awarded against a trade union in tort are limited (by reference to the number of members) by *TULRCA 1992, s 22*.

(e)   If necessary, an employer may in limited circumstances dismiss all employees on strike (or taking other industrial action) and try to engage a new labour force. In the case of unofficial action, he may dismiss selectively. The employment tribunal's unfair dismissal jurisdiction is also *prima facie* excluded in respect of workers dismissed during official industrial action (subject to the significant exception contained in *s 238A* – see below) if two conditions are met: *first*, all the employees in the employer's establishment who were taking part in the industrial action at the date when the complainant was dismissed must also be dismissed; *second*, none of those employees can be offered re-engagement by the employer until *after* the expiry of the period of three months beginning with the date of the dismissal, or else all of them must be offered re-engagement within that period (see further **51.17 UNFAIR DISMISSAL – I**) (*TULRCA 1992, ss 237, 238*).

However, the exclusion from the right to claim unfair dismissal contained in *TULRCA 1992, s 238* does not apply where the employee is taking part in 'protected industrial action' and if certain other conditions are satisfied (*TULRCA 1992, s 238A*). 'Protected industrial action' is defined as action which was induced by an act protected by *TULRCA 1992, s 219*. An employee will be treated as having been automatically unfairly dismissed if the reason or principal reason for his dismissal was that the employee has taken part in protected industrial action and:

(i)   the dismissal took place within twelve weeks of the start of the protected industrial action by the employee (or within such further period as falls to be added to the twelve weeks to reflect any period during which the employee was locked out by his employer); or

(ii)   the dismissal took place more than twelve weeks (or such longer period as results from a lock-out period) after the start of the protected industrial action and the employee had ceased taking part in the industrial action within the twelve-week period; or

(iii) the dismissal took place more than twelve weeks (or such longer period as results from a lock-out period) after the start of the protected industrial action, the employee had not ceased to take part in the industrial action within the first twelve weeks but the employer had failed to take such procedural steps as would have been reasonable for the purposes of resolving the dispute.

(See further **52.3 UNFAIR DISMISSAL – II**.)

43.17 UNION MEMBERS' RIGHT TO A BALLOT

TULRCA 1992, s 62 gives a remedy to a trade union member whose union seeks to involve him in industrial action without the support of a ballot. This includes all those members who work under contracts for personal services, and not merely those who are employees in the strict sense (*TULRCA 1992, s 62(8)*). Such a person may apply to the High Court (or the Court of Session in Scotland), which will make an order (see below) if he can demonstrate that:

(a)   the union has, without the support of a ballot, authorised or endorsed any industrial action; and

(b)   that members of the union, including the applicant, have been or are likely to be
         induced by the union to take part in or continue to take part in that action.

Again, any application should be made without undue delay.

For the purpose of deciding whether the members are induced by the union and whether
action is authorised or endorsed by the union, reference is made to the test of liability of
unions for official action contained in *TULRCA 1992, s 20 (TULRCA 1992, s 62(5)* and see
48.16 TRADE UNIONS – I). The fact that the inducement is ineffective is immaterial (*TULRCA
1992, s 62(6)*).

The action is authorised or endorsed without the support of a ballot unless, not more than
four weeks (or such longer period as may be agreed in accordance with *TULRCA 1992,
s 234(1)*) before the commencement of the action, there has been a ballot complying with
TULRCA 1992, ss 226B to *233* (see **43.14** and **43.15** above) in respect of the action, in which
the applicant was entitled to vote. The majority of those voting must have answered 'Yes'
to a question asking them whether they are prepared to strike or take part in the industrial
action concerned (*TULRCA 1992, s 62(2)*).

If the court upholds the complaint, it will make such order as it considers appropriate for
requiring the union to take steps to ensure that there is no further inducement of members
to take part in the action and that no member engages in any further conduct resulting from
the prior inducement. The steps so required may include the withdrawal of any relevant
authorisation or endorsement (*TULRCA 1992, s 62(3)*). Disobedience to such an
order will, of course, be a contempt of court.

43.18 THIRD PARTIES' RIGHTS AND REMEDIES

At common law, parties whose contracts were interfered with by unlawful industrial action
could apply to the High Court for an injunction and damages, provided that the loss caused
was not too remote or unforeseeable. The holder of a train ticket was able to recover damages
from the rail unions for wrongfully interfering with his contract with British Rail (*Falconer
v ASLEF and NUR* [1986] IRLR 331).

There is a statutory right under *TULRCA 1992, s 235A*, for an individual to apply to the
High Court where he claims that any trade union or other person has done or is likely to
do an unlawful act to induce any person to take part or continue to take part in industrial
action, if a likely effect of the industrial action is to prevent or delay the supply of goods or
services to the applicant, or to reduce the quality of goods or services supplied to him
(*TULRCA 1992, s 235A(1)*). For these purposes an act is unlawful if it is actionable in tort
by any one or more persons (which need not include the applicant himself), or in the case
of an act by a trade union, if it could form the basis of an application by a member under
TULRCA 1992, s 62 (see **43.17** above) (*TULRCA 1992, s 235A(2)*). It is immaterial whether
the applicant has any entitlement to be supplied with the goods or services in question
(*TULRCA 1992, s 235A(3)*).

If the court is satisfied that the claim is well founded, it must make such order as it
considers appropriate for requiring the person by whom the act of inducement has been or
is likely to be done to take steps for ensuring that no or no further act of inducement is done
by him, and that no person engages in further conduct by virtue of his prior inducement
(cf **43.16**(*c*) above) (*TULRCA 1992, s 235A(4)*). The court also has power to grant
interlocutory relief (*TULRCA 1992, s 235A(5)*).

43.19 CONSEQUENCES FOR EMPLOYEES

For any industrial action, whether or not in contemplation or furtherance of a trade dispute:

43.19   Strikes and Industrial Action

(a)   the employee loses his right to pay during the industrial action (see **43.16**(b) above and PAY – I **(32)**);

(b)   he is not entitled to receive jobseeker's allowance or income support, although his family may in some circumstances receive income support (see *Cartlidge v Chief Adjudication Officer* [1986] ICR 256) subject to the deduction of a prescribed sum in respect of notional strike pay (see *Tolley's Social Security and State Benefits Handbook* for further details);

(c)   he is not entitled to any guarantee payment in respect of the days on which he is engaged in industrial action;

(d)   if dismissed during a strike, a participant in that strike may not be able to claim compensation for unfair dismissal (although he will be treated as automatically unfairly dismissed in the circumstances outlined in **43.16**(e) above);

(e)   so far as the computation of periods of continuous employment is concerned (for example, for redundancy and unfair dismissal claims), absence due to participation in a strike will not break continuity, but the period of absence is not counted in the computation. The start of the period of employment will be deemed to be postponed by the appropriate number of days (see **6.11** CONTINUOUS EMPLOYMENT).

43.20 EMPLOYEES WHO MAY NOT STRIKE

Some employees are forbidden by law to strike. These include members of the armed services, prison officers and police officers. In *Ministry of Justice v Prison Officers Association* [2008] EWHC 239 (QB), [2008] ICR 702 Wyn Williams J rejected an argument by the Prison Officers' Union that he should refused to grant an injunction to restrain strike action on the basis of the right to freedom of association conferred by *Article 11(1)* of the Convention. That article, as he found, does not confer any right to strike. Attempts have been made to argue that, given that inducement of a breach of statutory duty does not fall within the *TULRCA 1992, s 219* immunity (see **43.3** above), such provisions effectively prohibit organised strike action. But the decisions of the House of Lords in *Associated British Ports v TGWU* [1989] 1 WLR 939 at 970 and of Mantell J in *Wandsworth London Borough Council v NASUWT* [1994] ICR 81 (the point was not argued on appeal), suggest that the courts will be reluctant to construe the relevant statutes so as to reach such a result.

It is a criminal offence for a person 'wilfully and maliciously [to break] a contract of service or of hiring, knowing or having reasonable cause to believe that the probable consequences of his so doing, either alone or in combination with others, will be to endanger human life, or cause serious bodily injury, or to expose valuable property whether real or personal to destruction or serious injury' (*TULRCA 1992, s 240(1)*). The penalty is a fine not exceeding level 2 on the Standard Scale (see **1.10** INTRODUCTION) or imprisonment for not more than three months (*TULRCA 1992, s 240(3)*).

44 Taxation

44.1 OUTLINE

ITEPA 2003

The employment tax legislation is contained in the main in the *Income Tax (Earnings and Pensions) Act 2003* which is referred to in this chapter as *ITEPA 2003*. This is supported by various regulations, including the *Income Tax (Pay As You Earn) Regulations 2003 (SI 2003/2682)*.

44.2 Employment income

For income tax purposes, income from employment includes 'general earnings' and 'specific employment income'.

(a)   General earnings include (in each case, excluding exempt amounts):

    (i)   earnings which are defined by *ITEPA 2003, s 62* as including any salary, wage or fee, gratuities or other profit or benefit obtained if it is money or money's worth, or anything else constituting an emolument of employment ('money's worth' means something of direct monetary value to the employee or capable of being converted into money or something of direct monetary value to the employee); and

    (ii)   amounts treated as earnings which include amounts paid to agency workers (*ss 44–47*), amounts paid through intermediaries (*ss 48–61*), benefits in kind (*ss 63–220*), sickness and disability pay (*s 221*), payments of tax by the employer (*ss 222, 223*), payments to non-approved personal pension arrangements (*ss 44–47*), payments or valuable consideration given for restrictive undertakings (*ss 225, 226*), or balancing charges treated as earnings (*Capital Allowances Act 2001, s 262*).

(b)   Specific employment income includes (in each case, excluding exempt amounts):

    (i)   other non-share related income including payments to and benefits from non-approved pension schemes (*ss 386–400*) or payments on termination of employment (*ss 401–416*);

    (ii)   share related payments and benefits (*ss 417–554*); and

    (iii)   payments which count as employment income under any other enactment.

(*ITEPA 2003, s 7.*)

General earnings include 'benefits in kind' as per (*a*)(ii) above (see **44.21** et seq below). Such benefits are taxable where they are received by employees or directors but there are certain exclusions in the case of 'lower-paid' employees (see **44.3** and **44.23** below). In general terms, the amount assessable on the P11D employee or director in respect of a benefit is its cash equivalent value. Unless specific rules apply to determine the calculation of the cash equivalent value of the benefit (as, for example in the case of company cars and fuel, living accommodation etc), the cash equivalent value is simply the cost to the employer less any amount made good by the employee (*ITEPA 2003, ss 203–206*) (see **44.28** below). Where a benefit is taxable on a lower-paid employee, such an employee will (subject to special rules for particular benefit, for example living accommodation) be taxed on its second-hand value.

44.3 Taxation

44.3 'Directors and lower-paid employees'

The rules governing the taxability of benefits in kind recognise two categories of employers – directors and employees earnings at the rate of at least £8,500 a year (P11D employees) and lower-paid employees.

As far as directors are concerned, the rules for P11D employees and directors apply to all 'directors', irrespective of the level of their earnings unless they:

(a)   earn less than £8,500 per year (including all benefits in kind and before deduction of any necessary expenses of the employment); and

(b)   have no material interest (ie the interest does not exceed 5% with or without associates) in the company; and

(c)   are either working full-time as a director or the company is non-profit making and does not hold investments, or is a charity.

The charging provisions apply equally to directors and employees, with specific exclusions for 'lower-paid' employees. These are employees whose earnings are at the rate of less than £8,500 per year, including all benefits in kind and before deduction of any necessary expenses of the employment.

The charging provisions also cover the provision of benefits to the family or household of the employee or director. The benefit is essentially taxed in the same way as if were provided to the employee.

(*ITEPA 2003, ss 63, 67, 68, 216–220.*)

For the purpose of this chapter, a director who is not excluded by virtue of (*a*)–(*c*) above or an employee who is not a 'lower-paid employee' is referred to as a 'P11D employee'. Lower paid employees are referred to as P9D employees.

44.4 PAY AS YOU EARN (PAYE)

Definition and earnings limits

PAYE is the statutory system of deducting income tax from the employment income (see **44.2** above) of an employee at the time that the employee is paid by the employer so as to secure, as far as possible, that the income tax liability in respect of the employment income is satisfied by the deductions made. The employer effectively acts as a tax collector for HM Revenue and Customs. In addition, the PAYE system collects National Insurance contributions of both employee and employer. It is also used for the operation of Statutory Sick Pay (SSP). Statutory Maternity Pay (SMP), Ordinary Statutory Paternity Pay (OSPP), Additional Statutory Paternity Pay (ASPP) and Statutory Adoption Pay (SAP), to collect student loan repayments and to collect charitable donations under Payroll Giving (see **44.33** below).

Under Real Time Information (RTI) employers are required to send details of pay and deductions to HMRevenue and Customs electronically each time that an employer is paid. RTI applies generally from 6 April 2013 and all employers must operate in real time from October 2013.

The PAYE system applies to all payments of employment income assessable to income tax in excess of certain defined limits. These limits (the 'PAYE thresholds') are as laid down from time to time by HM Revenue and Customs. For a person with one employment only, the PAYE threshold is broadly aligned with the weekly/monthly equivalent of the personal allowance for income tax.

For 2013/14 the PAYE thresholds are as follows:

Weekly	£156
Monthly	£675
Annual	£8,105

The regulations governing the operation of PAYE are the *Income Tax (Pay As You Earn) Regulations 2003 (SI 2003/2682)*. (*ITEPA 2003, ss 684, 686, 708; Income Tax (Pay As You Earn) Regulations (SI 2003/2682*, as amended by *SI 2004/85* (before 6 April 2004, *Income Tax (Employments) Regulations (SI 1993/744)*))

44.5 Sources of information

Guidance on PAYE is available on both the HMRC website (www.hmrc.gov.uk) and the Business Link website (www.businesslink.gov.uk). HMRC publish a range of forms and publications for employers, which are available to download from the 'Forms and publications for employers' section of the HMRC website (www.hmrc.gov.uk/payerti/forms -updates/forms-publications.htm). Detailed instructions on the operation of PAYE are contained in the HM Revenue and Customs booklet 'Employer's Further Guide to PAYE and NICs' (CWG2). This guide is available to download from the HM Revenue and Customs' website (see (www.hmrc.gov.uk/paye/forms-publications.htm). Detailed instructions on the operation of PAYE are contained in the HM Revenue and Customs booklet 'Employer 's Further Guide to PAYE and NICs' (CWG2). This guide is available to download from the HM Revenue and Customs' website (see www.hmrc.gov.uk/guidance/cwg2.pdf). Paper copies can be ordered from the employer orderline. In addition, HM Revenue and Customs publish various 'Employer Help Books' (E10 to E19), which contain all the relevant information most employers will need to operate PAYE and National Insurance contributions and which can be downloaded from the 'Forms and Publications for employers' section of the HMRC website. The section also contains tax and National Insurance tables for calculating tax and National Insurance. HM Revenue and Customs also operates 'Employer Helplines' and provides support services including one-to-one visits.

Guidance on the operation of PAYE is also contained in the HM Revenue and Customs guidance manuals – PAYE Instructions (collection) manual and PAYE Online Manual. Guidance on employment income generally is found in the Employment Income Manual.

HMRC also publish an online magazine for employers, Employer Bulletin, which is available to download from the HMRC website at www.hmrc.gov.uk/paye/employer -bulletin/index.htm. The bulletin is published three times a year and aims to provide employers and agents with the latest information on payroll topics and other issues that affect them.

To help employers to work out their PAYE and NIC liabilities, HMRC also publish a free software package, Basic PAYE Tools which is available to download from the HMRC website. The package, which comprises:

- an employer database on which employers can record employee details;

- a P11 calculator that can be used to work out employee's tax and National Insurance contributions and any student loan deductions;

- the ability to file forms P45, P46, P35 and P14 online;

- a P32 payment record;

- a range of calculators;

- interactive forms; and

- a learning zone.

Is designed for employers with nine or fewer employees. A RTI version is available for 2013/14 to enable employers to report pay and deductions information to HMRC in real time.

Employers can register with HMRC for an employer email alert service (see www.hmrc.gov.uk/paye/forms-publications/register.htm). By registering for the service, employers will receive email alerts to remind them when the latest employer information is available on the HMRC website.

See also the *Payroll Management Handbook 2008* (or later edition).

44.6 Method of deduction

Employers must maintain (among other documents) a deductions working sheet (P11 or equivalent) for each employee known to be earning amounts above the PAYE threshold. The employee's tax code determines the amount that the employee is able to earn before paying tax and is used to work out the appropriate amount of tax to be deducted from that employee's wages. The employee's tax code must be recorded on the P11 or equivalent. A tax code will vary to reflect the circumstances of the employee and will be the appropriate amount of personal allowances less the final digit. For example, an employee who receives the basic personal allowance for 2013/14 of £9,440 would result in a code of 944. A suffix or prefix is then added to the code.

The suffix code letter indicates how the code should be updated to reflect changes announced in the Budget. The suffix code letters in use are as follows:

L = Personal allowance (born after 6 April 1948)

P = Personal allowance (born between 6 April 1938 and 5 April 1948)

Y = Personal allowance (born before 6 April 1938)

T = Specific notification required from HM Revenue and Customs.

Sometimes a code will have a prefix instead of a suffix:

D0 = Higher rate tax and no personal allowances)

D1 = Additional rate (and no personal allowances)

K = Where state pension or benefits in kind exceed personal allowances

BR = Basic rate tax and no personal allowances

0T = No personal allowances

NT = No tax to be deducted

Therefore, a person who receives the basic personal allowance for 2013/14 for persons born before 6 April 1948 and who has no other adjustments to his or her code has a tax code for 2013/14 of 944L.

A K code requires an addition to be made to the employee's pay (or to a pension) in order to arrive at taxable pay. This enables the correct amount of tax to be deducted where emoluments such as benefits in kind exceed personal allowances. There is an overriding regulatory limit to ensure that the maximum amount deducted from emoluments in any pay period does not exceed 50% of cash pay after allowing for deductions such as pension contributions and payroll giving.

The calculation of tax due is generally performed using computerised payroll systems. However, the correct results will only be obtained if the software is up to date and reflects current tax rates. The introduction of RTI and the requirement to report pay and deductions details to HMRC electronically means that manual payrolls are no longer an option. However, employers with only a few employees can use HMRC's free Basic PAYE Tools software package, an RTI version of which is available.

Contributions to registered pension schemes and charitable donations through Payroll Giving (see **44.33** below) are deducted from the gross pay before calculation of tax due.

44.7   Employees joining after 6 April

Employees joining after 6 April:

(a)   *Employees holding form P45 from previous employer.* The form P45 will show details of total pay and tax paid to the date of leaving the last employment, and the employee's code. These figures are entered on a deductions working sheet for the employee and the normal procedure is followed from the first pay day in the new employment with these figures incorporated into the totals on that day.

(b)   *New employees, with no form P45, earning in excess of the PAYE threshold (including existing employees earning over this threshold for the first time).* The employer must operate the code specified for Emergency use on the non-cumulative (Week or Month 1) basis until he is notified by the tax office of the correct code. The employer must notify the tax office as soon as possible after taking on such new employees. Employees taking up employment for the first time following full-time education are dealt with on a cumulative, rather than non-cumulative, Emergency coding basis. On the other hand, employees having other employment should have basic rate tax deducted from earnings. In either case, deductions must continue to be made on the appropriate basis until the correct code is notified. Any pension received by such employees must be brought to HM Revenue and Customs' attention to ensure the correct code is used.

Under RTI, employers must supply details of new starters to HM Revenue and Customs electronically as part of the Full Payment Submission (FPS). Where an employee joins without a form P45, the employer will need to collect the information required for the FPS from the employer. Form P46 or P46 (short) can be used for this purpose.

Employers not within RTI must send form P45, or form P46 where the employee has not provided a P45, to HMRC electronically. Penalties may be charged for a failure to file electronically.

44.8   Employee leaving or dismissed

Form P45 must be issued to an employee who leaves the employer's employment. This applies equally whether or not the employer is within RTI. Form P45 is the mechanism by which details of the employee's pay to date and tax deducted are transferred from one employer to the next.

Under RTI the employer is not required to send form P45 to HMRevenue and Customs. Instead, leaver details notified to HM Revenue and Customs as part of the FPS.

Employers who are not within RTI must send part 1 of form P45 to HM Revenue and Customs electronically using PAYE Online. The employee is given parts 1A, 2 and 3 and must pass parts 2 and 3 over to his or her new employer or, if unemployed, to the Jobseeker Plus.

Where payments are made to the former employee after the form P45 has been issued, tax must be deducted using the OT code rather than by reference to the employee's normal tax code.. Where payments are made after the P45 has been issued, under no circumstances should a further form P45 should be issued. From 6 April 2012 code OT must also be used for share-based payments made after the issue of form P45, rather than code BR as previously.

If the amount of the payment made after the leaving date is known before the employee leaves, it must be entered on the deductions working sheet by reference to the date of the future payment. In this situation, the amount is therefore included within the amount shown on form P45.

Pay in lieu of notice. Where an employee is dismissed with pay in lieu of notice, the taxation treatment is dependent on the nature of the payment. The tax treatment of pay in lieu of notice is complex and the term is often used to describe payments with varying characteristics. As a general rule, pay in lieu of notice is treated in the same way as a payment of wages or salary if the employee was contractually entitled to it or had an expectation of receiving it. A contractual PILON is one which has its source in the contractual arrangements between the employer and the employee. For a PILON to be contractual, it does not have to be set out in the main employment contract. It may be contained in another document, such as a side letter to the contract, the staff handbook, the letter of appointment, a redundancy agreement or an agreement with the relevant union. In determining whether a PILON is contractual (and therefore the appropriate tax treatment) it is important to check all relevant documents, not just the main contract of employment. However, HM Revenue and Customs accepts that where a contract or other supporting documentation makes no reference to pay in lieu of notice and the employee has no expectation of receiving pay in lieu of notice, a payment of such compensation would generally be for an employer's breach of contract. In that case, the payment will come within the charging provisions relating to termination payments (*ITEPA 2003, ss 401–403*) and so the first £30,000 of the payment would be exempt from tax. HM Revenue and Customs' views on what constitutes a contractual payment are set out in HM Revenue and Customs' Employment Income Manual EIM 12975ff.

In *Delaney v Staples* [1992] 1 All ER 944 it was held that *non-contractual* payments in lieu of notice were not to be regarded as wages for the purposes of what is now *ERA 1996, s 27*. However, HM Revenue and Customs takes the view that 'what constitutes wages under employment law is not the same as what constitutes emoluments under tax law'.

In *Richardson v Delaney* [2001] STC 1328 it was held that a discretionary PILON was taxable as earnings. The contract was brought to an end by mutual consent and a payment agreed in lieu of notice. The court found that there was no breach of earnings and consequently the payment was taxable as earnings.

In *EMI Group Electronics Ltd v Coldicott* [1999] STC 803 the Court of Appeal confirmed the HM Revenue and Customs' long-standing practice that *contractual* payments in lieu of notice are assessable as employment income but it was accepted that payments made to junior employees were not taxable since those employees had no contractual right to them. See HM Revenue and Customs' Employment Income Manual EIM 12977

Care should be taken when drafting termination letters and ambiguous language can cause confusion as to the correct tax treatment. This was illustrated in the decision in *Ibe v McNally (Inspector of Taxes)* [2005] EWHC 1551 (Ch), [2005] STC 1426.

44.9   Employee retiring on pension from employer

The employer must notify the tax office within 14 days and continue operating the code but on the non–cumulative basis until revised instructions are received from the tax office. However, if the pension is to be paid by the trustees of a pension scheme etc, the employee should be treated as leaving (see **44.8** above).

44.10   Death of employee

If an employee dies the employer must complete a form P45. Under RTI, the death of an employee is notified to HM Revenue and Customs electronically as for starters and leavers as part of the FPS. Employers not within RTI indicate that the employee has died (by an entry in the appropriate box) and file part 1 online to HM Revenue and Customs. If the software package automatically produces Parts 1A, 2 and 3 these should be destroyed as only Part 1 need to filed online. The same procedure applies if a pensioner dies.

The same rules apply in the case of payments made after the date of death as for payments made after the date an employee leaves (see **44.8** above).

44.11   Students employed during vacation

From 6 April 2013 the special P38(S) procedures that previously applied to students no longer apply and a student is treated in the same way as any other employee, even if the student only works during the holidays.

For 2012/13 and earlier tax years special arrangements existed which enabled students who work only during holiday time to be paid without the deduction of PAYE and NICs, provided that their earnings remain below the level of their personal allowance for that tax year. Normal PAYE procedures applied to students who worked throughout the year.

The special arrangements were known as the P38(S) procedures. Under the arrangements, form P38(S) was completed for each tax year for which the student was employed. The student's statement on form P38(S) was completed when the employment ends or, if relevant, at the end of the tax year. The statement confirmed that the individual is a student and that his or her total earnings for the tax year will not exceed the personal allowance for that year.

If the student's earnings exceeded their personal allowance, the employer was required to operate PAYE and NICs as for other employees.

The abolition of the P38(S) procedures from 6 April 2013 coincide with the introduction of Real Time Information (RTI).

44.12   Employees working abroad

The general rule is an employer must continue to operate PAYE in the normal way in respect of payments made to employees who go abroad to work. An employee who works abroad for a year or more may be able to obtain UK tax relief on their earnings and the employer may be permitted to use special PAYE arrangements. Where an employee has an overseas contract, tax may be deducted in that country. The employer is advised to contact both HM Revenue and Customs and the overseas authority to ensure that he is clear as to his obligations.

A new statutory residence test applies from 6 April 2103 to determine the residence status of an individual. The concept of ordinary residence is abolished.

An employer who has a place of business in the UK must pay Class 1 National Insurance contributions on all earnings paid during the first 52 weeks that an employee is working abroad where the employee is ordinarily resident in the UK and was resident in the UK immediately before starting the employment abroad.

44.12　Taxation

Further guidance on the procedures that should be followed in respect of employees going abroad to work can be found on the HMRC website at www.hmrc.gov.uk/paye/employees/changes/work-abroad.htm.

44.13　Refunds of tax when employee is away from work

Because of the cumulative nature of the PAYE system, periods during which no emoluments are received may give rise to a right to repayments of tax. In the case of such an absence, eg unpaid leave, a repayment may be made by the employer to the employee. This procedure is unlikely to apply to short absences caused by sickness as any statutory sick pay (see **42.6** SICKNESS AND SICK PAY) paid to the employee is taxable in the usual way. Tax is also chargeable on any payment made by the employer (or by a third party under arrangements made by the employer) through a sick pay scheme.

An employer must not refund tax to an employee who is absent from work in consequence of a trade dispute in which the employee is involved, until the dispute has ended unless the employer is authorised to make a tax refund on form P48, or the employee leaves during a trade dispute.

Where an employee becomes unemployed (see **44.8**) and claims jobseekers' allowance or employment support allowance or receives universal credit, any tax refund due to him will be made by the Jobcentre Plus. However, because these benefits are taxable, payment of any refund will be withheld until the person obtains a new job or, if earlier, until the end of the tax year. Where the employee does not claim either jobseekers allowance or income support and sends Part 2 and 3 of form P45 to HM Revenue and Customs with a declaration that he/she will remain unemployed for the rest of the tax year, any tax refund due will be paid by HM Revenue and Customs.

44.14　PAYE – PAYMENT OF TAX BY EMPLOYER

The employer must pay to the Collector of Taxes, within 17 days (ie by the 22nd of each month) where the payment is made by an approved electronic method or within 14 days of the end of every tax month (ie by the 19th of each month) where payment is made by post, all tax and National Insurance contributions deducted together with the employer's National Insurance contributions; plus any student loan deductions; less any recoveries of statutory sick pay, statutory maternity pay, statutory paternity pay and statutory adoption pay (see **31.15** MATERNITY AND PARENTAL RIGHTS and **42.6** SICKNESS AND SICK PAY) (where applicable including an amount to compensate for employer's National Insurance contributions thereon). A single remittance is sufficient. Failure to remit amounts due may result in proceedings for recovery against the employer. Where the deadline falls on a non-banking day, such as weekend or bank holiday, postal payments must reach HM Revenue and Customs on the previous banking day and in the case of electronic payment, cleared funds must reach HM Revenue and Customs's bank account on the previous banking day. If these deadlines are missed the payment will be treated as being made late.

Since 6 April 2004 employers with 250 or more employees have been required to make monthly payments of PAYE electronically. Penalties are charged for late payment of PAYE (see **44.14A**).

Employers who have reasonable grounds for believing that the average monthly total tax and National Insurance to be paid to the Collector will be less than £1,500 are able to make payments quarterly instead of monthly (*reg 70* (before 6 April 2004, *regs 41, 42*)). New employers must notify HM Revenue and Customs if they wish to make quarterly payments, but existing employers need not do so unless a demand is received from HMRC.

Employers with no PAYE or NIC to pay for a particular month or quarter must make a nil declaration. This can be done either by sending in a nil payslip or by making a nil declaration online (see www.hmrc.gov.uk/howtopay/paye_nil.htm).

HM Revenue and Customs has the power under *reg 80* of the PAYE regulations to determine the amount of tax payable where it appears to it that tax may have been payable but has not been paid; and interest at the prescribed rate on unpaid tax in respect of *reg 80* determinations can be charged under *reg 82*.

Interest at the prescribed rate is charged automatically on late payments of PAYE where tax is outstanding by more than 14 days after the end of the tax year, or by more than 17 days where the payment is made by an approved method of electronic communication. A repayment supplement at the prescribed rate is also available where overpaid deductions are later refunded (*regs 82, 83*).

The procedures for paying over PAYE and other deductions to HM Revenue and Customs remains the same under Real Time Information.

44.14A PENALTIES FOR LATE PAYMENT OF PAYE

For 2010/11 and subsequent tax years employers may suffer a penalty if they do not pay the PAYE they owe on time and in full on more than one occasion in the tax year. The penalty regime applies to all employers including large employers who are required to make payments of PAYE electronically. The late payment penalties replaced the mandatory electronic payment surcharge, which applied for 2009/10 and earlier years where a large employer fails to pay PAYE electronically.

The penalty amount is a percentage of the amount of PAYE that is owed. No penalty is charged if payment is made late only on one occasion in the tax year. Thereafter, the penalty rate depends on the number of occasions on which payment is made late. The penalty rate starts at 1% (2 to 4 defaults), rising to 2% (5 to 7 defaults) then to 3% (8 to 10 defaults) with a top penalty rate of 4% applying to 11 or more defaults. A further penalty of 5% will apply if the any of the PAYE remains unpaid after six months and again after 12 months.

Penalties will not be charged if HMRC accept that the employer had a reasonable excuse for the late payment.

44.15 PAYE – END OF YEAR PROCEDURE

The PAYE end of year procedures depend on whether the employer is within Real Time Information (RTI) or not..

PAYE – end of year procedure: non RTI-employers

The following procedures apply to employers who are not within RTI. Most employers will migrate to RTI from 6 April 2013 and in the majority of cases the following procedures will apply for 2012/13 and earlier tax years.

(a)   *Employee's certificates.* By 31 May following the end of the tax year, the employer must give each employee in office on 5 April a certificate (P60 or P60 (substitute)) showing the following details: the tax year to which the certificate applies, total taxable emoluments, net tax deducted, the code in use on 5 April, the employer's PAYE reference, the employee's name and National Insurance number, and the employer's name and address.

In the case of an employee engaged after 6 April, the certificate should include details of pay and tax of the previous employment, insofar as they were taken into account in computing the tax due under this employment. P60s can be given to the employee electronically.

(b)   *Returns.* By 19 May following the end of the tax year, the employer must give to HM Revenue and Customs the End of Year Return (P14 or substitute) which for each employee (including any employee who has left during the year) gives details of the total earnings, total net tax deducted, and National Insurance contributions together with amounts of any statutory sick pay, maternity pay, paternity pay or adoption pay (see **44.13** and **44.14** above) included in total earnings and details of any student loan deductions or payments of tax credits (see **44.35** below). This form must be accompanied by the employer's end of year return, form P35, containing a declaration and statement by the employer. All employers who are required to file year-end returns (P35 and P14)are required to file electronically and penalties are charged for a failure to file in this way.

PAYE – end of year procedures: RTI employers

Employers who are within RTI supply pay and deductions information to HM Revenue and Customs progressively throughout the tax year. As a result there is no need for them to complete annual returns after the end of the tax year and forms P35 and P14 are redundant under RTI. Instead, once within RTI, employers simply need to indicate on their final Full Payment Submission (FPS) for the tax year that it is the last FPS for the tax year. However, the employer is still required to provide an employee with a certificate of pay and tax deducted (form P60) by 31 May following the end of the tax year.

For most employers, the RTI year-end procedures will apply for the first time for the 2013/14 tax year. However, employers who joined RTI in 2012/13 will be subject to the RTI year end procedures in respect of that tax year.

44.16 Forms P11D, P9D and P11D(b)

Where non-cash benefits and expenses have been provided to employees or directors, a return of those benefits must be made to HM Revenue and Customs by 6 July after the end of the tax year. Form P11D is the return of benefits for employees earning at a rate of at least £8,500 a year (including the value of any benefits in kind provided) and for directors, irrespective of their earnings level. Form P9D is used for employees who earn at a rate of less than £8,500. The different forms reflect the different tax regimes that apply in relation to taxing benefits provided to employees earning at least £8,500 a year and those earning below this level. In determining whether the employee earns at a rate of at least £8,500 a year it is necessary to take into account the cash equivalent of any benefits provided, even if the benefit is not taxable on lower paid employees.

The employer must also submit form P11D(b) by 6 July following the end of the tax year to which it relates. Form P11D is a return of 'Expenses and Benefits' and return P11D(b) is a 'Return of Class 1A National Insurance Contributions' which declares the total amount of Class 1A contributions due to be paid on P11D benefits (see **44.17** below) and includes a declaration that all the required forms P11D and P11D(b) have been completed and submitted to HM Revenue and Customs.

For self-assessment purposes, employers must provide to each employee or director either a copy of the form P11D or P9D or a statement of their benefits by 6 July after the end of the tax year.

Items covered by a dispensation or included within a PAYE settlement agreement do not need to be returned on form P11D or P9D. See **44.28** below with respect to dispensations and **44.18** in relation to PAYE settlement agreements.

The procedure for making returns of benefits and expenses is the same following the introduction of RTI as before and applies equally to RTI and non-RTI employers.

44.17 Class 1A National insurance contributions

Class 1A National Insurance contributions are employer-only contributions payable on most benefits in kind provided to P11D employees and directors. No Class 1A National Insurance liability arises in respect of benefits provided to P9D employees, even if the benefit is taxable.

Class 1A National Insurance contributions must be paid by 22 July following the end of the tax year to which they relate if paid electrically (or by 19 July otherwise) and must be reported to HMRC on form P11D(b) (see **44.16** above). Returns P11D(b) not submitted by 6 July following the end of the tax year attract a penalty and interest is charged on Class 1A National Insurance contributions paid late. As with PAYE, if the deadline falls on a non-banking day, payment must reach HMRC by the previous banking day.

Class 1A National Insurance contributions are employer-only contributions chargeable at the Class 1A rate (13.8% for 2012/13 and for 2013/14). Where an item that would otherwise attract a Class 1A charge is included within a PAYE settlement agreement (see **44.18**), Class 1B contributions are payable instead.

(*Social Security Contributions and Benefits Act 1992, ss 10, 10ZA; Child Support, Pensions and Social Security Act 2000, ss 74, 75*). For further details of Class 1A contributions, see *Tolley's National Insurance Contributions 2006/07* (or later edition).

44.18 PAYE Settlement Agreements

A PAYE Settlement Agreements is an agreement with HMRC whereby the employer can settle, in a single payment, the income tax and National Insurance liability on certain expenses payments and benefits provided to employees. Such expenses payments and benefits do not then need to be processed through the PAYE system or recorded on forms P11D or P9D. A formal written agreement to make such a payment must be made with HM Revenue and Customs by 6 July following the end of the tax year.

The benefits which are covered by the agreement are subject to tax and Class 1B National Insurance contributions which must be paid by 19 October following the end of the tax year, or by 22 October where payment is made electronically. Class 1B National Insurance contributions are payable on the benefits that would otherwise be subject to Class 1 or Class 1A contributions if they were not included in the agreement. The tax payable must be 'grossed-up' at either the basic or higher rate of tax depending on the liability of the employees concerned since the payment of the tax liability is itself a benefit subject to tax.

Class 1B National Insurance contributions are payable on the aggregate of the total value of the benefits and the grossed-up amount of income tax due.

A PAYE Settlement Agreement is not suitable for all benefits in kind. The items which may be included within a PAYE Settlement Agreement are set out in HM Revenue and Customs Statement of Practice 5/96.

44.19 PAYE ONLINE

Prior to migrating to Real Time Information (RTI: see **44.19c**) employers are required to make annual returns to HM Revenue and Customs and to file their year-end returns (P35 and P14s) online. Penalties are charged for a failure to file the returns in this way (see **44.19A**). The introduction of RTI renders employer annual returns (and the associated requirement to file online) redundant. However, the procedures continue to apply to employers not within RTI (non-RTI employers).

Approved methods of electronic filing are the PAYE online service and electronic data interchange (EDI).

Prior to migrating to RTI employers are also required to file certain in-year information online. Compulsory online in-year filing applies to:

(a)   P45(1): details of employee leaving;

(b)   P45(3): new employee details;

(c)   P46: employee without a form P45; and

(d)   similar information for people receiving a pension.

Once an employer has migrated to RTI, this information is provided by means of the Full Payment Submission and the requirement to file in-year returns online no longer applies.

Penalties are charged for a failure to supply information electronically where required to do so (see **44.19**A).

The PAYE online service can be used to send and receive payroll information. It can be used by employers, agents and payroll bureaux alike. The use of the service is not limited to year-end returns. It can also be used for P11Ds, P9Ds, P11D(b)s and a range of other forms, notices and reminders.

Before using the service, employers and agents must register on the HM Revenue and Customs' web page and then activate the service using the activation PIN that is sent through the post. Employers must be registered for PAYE Online in order to be able to send pay and deductions information to HMRC electronically under Real Time Information.

HM Revenue and Customs is keen that the PAYE service is widely used and have publicised the benefits. See also www.hmrc.gov.uk.

44.19A ONLINE FILING PENALTIES

Prior to the migration to RTI employers are required to file year-end returns (P35 and P14s) electronically and to submit certain in-year information online.

Employers who fail to file electronically will be subject to penalties. The penalties depend on the number of employees for whom particulars should have been supplied electronically and are as follows:

Number of employees	Penalty: Year ending 5 April 2010	Penalty: Year ending 5 April 2011 and subsequent years
1 – 5	£0	£100
6 – 49	£100	£300
50 – 249	£600	£600
250 – 399	£900	£900
400 – 499	£1200	£1200
500 – 599	£1500	£1500
600 – 699	£1800	£1800
700 – 799	£2100	£2100
800 – 899	£2400	£2400
900 – 999	£2700	£2700
1,000 or more	£3000	£3000

However, where a deferred payment agreement has been reached with HMRC, penalties will be suspended.

44.19B SECURITY FOR PAYE

Since 6 April 2012, HMRevenue and Customs have been to ask employers to pay a security where there is a serious risk that the employer in question will not pay over PAYE and NIC to HMRC. The required security will usually take the form of a cash deposit from the business or director, which will be held in a joint taxpayer/HMRC bank account, or in the form of a bond from an approved financial institution which is payable on demand.

The power to require a security will only be exercised for employers who deliberately seek to defraud the Government. This includes employers who deliberately choose not to pay, who engage in pheonixism (whereby the business evades tax by becoming insolvent and then setting up a new company almost immediately to continue trading), companies that have no qualms about building up large PAYE and NIC debts and companies that do not respond to HMRC's attempts contact them to address their tax issues.

The amount of security required will be calculated on a case-by-case basis depending on the amount of tax that is at risk and the previous behaviour of the employer, Employers who are asked for a security for PAYE can appeal against this decision. Employers who are asked for a security and who fail to provide it risk prosecution by HMRC and may be fined.

44.19C REAL TIME PAYE INFORMATION

Real Time Information (RTI) requires employers to submit pay and deductions information to HMRC electronically each time that an employee is paid. RTI was introduced following a review of the PAYE system and a period of consultation.

A pilot exercise was undertaken from April 2012 and RTI is being rolled out to employers progressively from April 2013 such that all employers are within the scheme by October 2013. Most employers will migrate to RTI from the start of the 2013/14 tax year.

Prior to the introduction of RTI, employers will need to check that their payroll data is correct and that it is in the right format. Employers currently using payroll software will need to ensure that it is up to date and capable of submitting RTI data. Employers who do not currently use payroll software will need to plan ahead for its introduction so that they are able to submit RTI data to HMRC electronically when required to do so. Employers with nine or fewer employees can use HMRC's Basic PAYE Tools, which is free and available to download from the HMRC website.

Under RTI employers will report payments to HMRC as part of their normal payroll activity. The same procedure applies irrespective of whether the payments made via the payroll of payments of pay or pension. The legislation imposes a requirement on employers to report pay and deductions details to HM Revenue and Customs 'at or before' the time at which payment is made to the employee.

Under RTI the main submission that employers need to make to HM Revenue and Customs is the Full Payment Submission (FPS), which is made when payments are made to employees. The submission of the FPS should form a seamless part of the payroll procedures under RTI. Prior to, or at the same time as, making their first FPS, employers must undergo a payroll alignment process to ensure that the data held on their employees matches that held by HM Revenue and Customs. This can be carried out either by submitting a FPS which includes details of all employees, even if they have not been paid in the period or have left since the start of the tax year. Alternatively, the alignment process can be carried out by means of a separate Employer Alignment Submission (EAS). Employers with 250 or more employees must undertake the payroll alignment process via the EAS route.

Once the alignment process has been completed successfully, employers must provide pay and deductions information to HM Revenue and Customs by means of a FPS. Post-alignment, the FPS need only include details of employees who have been paid in the pay period. The employer may need to complete an Employer Payment Submission (EPS) in addition to or instead of the FPS. An EPS is made in various circumstances including where no payments are made to employees in the period or where the employee have received funding from HM Revenue and Customs.

Under RTI, employers supply starter and leaver details as part of the FPS and as such are not required to file forms P45 and P46 online. However, they must still provide an employee who leaves with a P45 as this remains the mechanism by which pay and tax details are transferred from one employer to another. If an employee joins without a form P45 the employer will need to collate the starter details required for the FPS submission. Form P46 or the shorter form P46(short) can be used for this purposes.

Under RTI employers do not need to complete and submit year end forms P14 and P35, or the supplementary form P38A. Instead the information is provided to HMRC progressively throughout the tax year each time that an employee is paid. However, employers will be required to indicate on their last payment on or before 5 April that this is their last submission for the tax year, provide each employee and pensioner on the payroll at 5 April with a P60 and complete any expenses and benefits forms (P11D and P11D(b)) and file them in accordance with the existing PAYE arrangements.

To ensure compliance with RTI, late filing penalties will apply from 6 April 2014.

44.20 RECORDS

The PAYE regulations stipulate various records that employers must keep for PAYE purposes. The records that the employer is required to maintain, but which do not need to be sent to HM Revenue and Customs, must be retained for not less than three years after the end of the year to which they relate. Under self-assessment, regulations require employees to keep sufficient records to enable them to make a correct and complete return.

44.21 TAXABLE BENEFITS – GENERAL RULES

Detailed information on the tax treatment of benefits in kind is to be found in *Tolley's Income Tax 2012/13*. Concise factual information, in tabular form, is contained in *Tolley's Tax Data 2012/13*. A brief account of general principles in relation to those benefits most commonly derived from employment is given in this paragraph and in **44.22–44.28** below. Special rules applying to employee share schemes are outlined briefly in **44.29–44.33** below.

The main taxable benefits are as follows.

(a) Expense payments and allowances – taxable subject to relief for actual expenses incurred in the performance of the duties; see **44.28** below (*ITEPA 2003, ss 70–72*).

(b) Cash vouchers – taxed on their redemption value.

Non-cash vouchers and transport vouchers – taxed on the cost to the employer of providing them less any contribution from employee (unless used to obtain certain non-taxable benefits).

Credit tokens – taxed on the cost to the employer of the money, goods or services obtained less any contribution from employee (unless used to obtain certain non-taxable benefits).

(*ITEPA 2003, ss 73–96.*)

(c) 'Living accommodation' – taxed on the annual value (as defined) or the actual rent paid by the employer if greater, subject to exemptions (eg where the employee is a representative occupier). For accommodation costing in excess of £75,000 made available to a P11D employee or a director, an additional charge is made on the excess value over £75,000 (*ITEPA 2003, ss 97–113*).

(d) Cars, vans and related expenses – taxed on the cash equivalent values, see **44.24** to **44.27** below (*ITEPA 2003, ss 114–172*). For cars the cash equivalent depends on the level of CO2 emissions and the list price, and for car fuel, the determinant is the level of $CO2$ emissions (which determines the appropriate percentage) and the multiplier set by HMRC. Vans are taxed by reference to a scale charge. A separate fuel charge also applies to vans.

(e) Interest-free or reduced interest employment-related loans – the taxable benefit is the difference between the interest paid (if any) and the 'official rate' of interest at a rate prescribed by the Treasury. There are certain reliefs for loans made at fixed rates not below market value when made, and loans for some specified purposes. No tax charge arises on loans made to employees on commercial terms where the employer lends to the general public. Nor is there any charge where the aggregate value of beneficial loans does not exceed £5,000 at any time in the tax year.

Loans written off are taxed on the amount written off.

(*ITEPA 2003, ss 173–191*)

(f) Shares and securities – an employee who is given shares or securities or options over shares and securities, or is allowed to acquire them on terms more favourable than those available to the public, is taxed on the value of the benefit he receives. Tax and National Insurance advantages are available in relation to certain approved share option and share incentive schemes (*ITEPA 2003, ss 192–200*).

(g) Assets gifted – if new, charged at cost to employer and if used, generally taxed at market value. See **44.22**(f) below in the case of P9D employees (*ITEPA 2003, ss 203, 204*).

(h) Mileage allowances – taxed on excess over approved amounts (*ITEPA 2003, ss 229–232, 235, 236*).

(i) Medical treatment or insurance premiums, unless for treatment outside the UK while the employee is working abroad (*ITEPA 2003, s 325*).

(j) Relocation expenses – non-qualifying expenses and benefits and qualifying expenses and benefits exceeding £8,000 per move (*ITEPA 2003, ss 271–289*).

(k) Use of employer's assets – land taxable at annual value, other assets at 20% of market value when first lent or rental charge if higher (*ITEPA 2003, ss 203–205*). Exemptions are available for computers loaned prior to 6 April 2006 (costing up to £2,500) and bicycles. Special rules apply to company cars, company vans, and living accommodation. No charge arises in respect of employer-provided mobile phones (limited to one per employee).

(l) Services supplied by employer, such as in-house goods or services provided at less than cost – taxed on the direct extra (marginal) cost the employer incurs, less any payments made by the employee or director. This was found to be the correct way of computing such benefits in *Pepper (Inspector of Taxes) v Hart* [1993] AC 593, [1993] ICR 291, HL.

44.22 Taxation

44.22 Benefits taxable on 'lower-paid' employees

The majority of benefits that may be provided to an employee are not taxable when provided to those employees in an excluded employment, ie employees who are not directors and who earn at a rate of less than £8,500 per annum including expenses payments and benefits. However, some benefits are taxable on all employees irrespective of the level of the employee's earnings. The benefits falling into this category are as follows:

(a)   Vouchers and credit tokens – as per **44.21**(b) above.

(b)   'Living accommodation' – as per **44.21**(c) above.

(c)   Loans written off – taxed on amount written off.

(d)   Non-business related expenses and personal expenses paid on the employee's behalf – expenses under £25 can be ignored.

(e)   Relocation expenses – as per **44.21**(j) above.

(f)   Assets gifted to employee – taxed at second hand value.

Where these benefits are provided to an employee earning at a rate of less than £8,500 a year, they must be returned to HM Revenue and Customs on form P9D by 6 July following the end of the tax year to which they relate (see **44.16**).

44.23 Tax-free benefits

A number of exemptions exist which enable a benefit to be provided free of tax. However, in the majority of cases, the exemption is conditional on certain conditions being met

(a)   Meals provided in a canteen – not assessable, but taxable on directors and P11D employees if not provided for the staff generally (*ITEPA 2003, s 317*). From 6 April 2011 the exemption does not apply if the meals are made available under salary sacrifice arrangements. Prior to 6 April 2013 separate exemptions applied to meals provided to employees who cycled to work on designated cycle to work days and to luncheon vouchers up to the value of 15p per day.

(b)   Contributions to registered pension schemes – contributions by an employer are not taxable.

(c)   Medical insurance premiums or medical treatment outside the UK where the employee performs duties abroad but not including the cost of an air ambulance back to or treatment in the UK (*ITEPA 2003, s 325*). Medical check-up, health screening, eye tests and corrective appliances (such as glasses) can also be provided tax-free as long as certain conditions are met.

(d)   Childcare facilities, such as workplace nurseries, for employees' children under 18 provided by the employer alone or with other employers, local authorities etc. Since 6 April 2005 the exemption has also applied (subject to qualifying conditions) to the provision of childcare at or away from the workplace at registered, non-residential facilities provided by the employer (either alone or in partnership with other parties but financed and managed wholly by the employer). Care provided by means of a workplace nurseries is tax-free without limit as long as the associated conditions are met. Employers can also provide childcare vouchers tax-free and/or employer supported childcare tax-free up to certain limits. Certain conditions must be met. The exemption applies (subject to the conditions) to the provision of childcare vouchers up to the weekly limit(plus the cost of supplying the vouchers) used to obtain qualifying childcare and to the provision of employer-supported childcare. (*ITEPA 2003, ss 84(2A), 270A, 318–318D; FA 2004, s 78, Sch 13*). The tax-free weekly limit depends on the date that the employee joined the childcare or voucher scheme and the employee's marginal rate of tax. The limit for employees who joined before 6 April 2011 is set at £55 per week, regardless of their marginal rate of tax. For 2011/12 and 2012/13 the limit is £55 per week for a basic rate taxpayer, £28 per week for a higher rate taxpayer and £22 per week for an additional rate tax payer. For 2013/14 the limits remain unchanged for basic and higher rate taxpayers but the limit for additional rate taxpayers is increased to £35 per week reflecting the reduction in the additional rate of tax to 45% from 6 April 2013. The relief is worth £11 per week to all employees who join after 6 April 2011 regardless of their marginal rate of tax.

(e)   Work-related training (*ITEPA 2003, ss 250–260*) and outplacement counselling services for employees who are or become redundant. Also welfare counselling (*SI 2000/2080*).

(f)   For employees starting a new job or moving with their existing employer, qualifying relocation expenses and benefits up to the value of £8,000 per move (*ITEPA 2003, ss 271–289*).

(g)   In-house workplace sports and recreational facilities provided by employers for use by the staff generally, provided overnight accommodation is not available and the facilities are not on domestic premises. The exemption does not cover the use of assets such as yachts, cars and aircraft for private use (*ITEPA 2003, ss 261–263*).

(h)   The provision of living accommodation for employees (but not directors) in certain circumstances where it is necessary for their job. This exemption extends to the employer's payment of employees' council tax. Accommodation provided as a result of a security threat is also exempt (*ITEPA 2003, ss 99, 100*).

(i)   The provision of accommodation, supplies or services used by the employee in performing the duties of the employment, provided that any private use is insignificant, and that the sole purpose of providing the benefit is to enable the employee to perform the duties (from 6 April 2000) (*ITEPA 2003, s 316*).

(j)   Alterations and additions to premises of a structural nature or landlord's repairs to premises of living accommodation which is provided by reason of a person's employment (*ITEPA 2003, s 313*).

(k)   The provision of parking facilities at or near the workplace for a car, cycle or motorcycle (*ITEPA 2003, s 237*).

(l)   Provision of travel, accommodation and subsistence during public transport disruption caused by industrial action (*ITEPA 2003, s 245*).

(m)   Provision of transport between home and place of employment or the provision of cars for severely disabled employees (*ITEPA 2003, ss 246, 247*).

(n)   Provision of transport for occasional late night journeys from work to home (*ITEPA 2003, s 248*).

(o)   Private use of mobile phones provided by the employer (from 6 April 1999) – limited to one phone per employee from 6 April 2006 (*ITEPA 2003, s 319*). The exemption applies equally to smartphones (Business Brief 02/12).

(p)   The loan of certain computer equipment provided prior to 6 April 2006 with a value not exceeding £2,500 (equating to a cash equivalent of £500) by the employer to the employee (providing that loans are not restricted to senior employees) (from 6 April 1999). The exemption does not apply to computer equipment loaned to the employee after 5 April 2006.

(q)   Provision of works buses with a seating capacity of nine or more, provided for employees to travel to and from work. Additionally, (from 6 April 2002) where employees benefit from their employer's subsidy of a bus service by receiving free or reduced-price travel, there is no tax charge on this benefit (*ITEPA 2003, ss 242, 243*). Also (from 6 April 2002) there is an exemption for the provision of buses for local shopping services (*SI 2002/205*).

(r)   The loan of bicycles and cycling safety equipment provided for employees to travel from home to work (from 6 April 1999) (*ITEPA 2003, s 244*).

(s)   The cost of an annual Christmas party or similar event, providing that it is open to all staff generally and the cost per person attending does not exceed £150. (*ITEPA 2003, s 264*).

44.24 COMPANY CARS, VANS AND FUEL

The provision of company cars, vans and fuel are taxable benefits for directors and 'P11D' employees (ie they are not taxable on 'lower-paid employees as defined, see **44.3** above). However, the cash equivalent of the benefit must be taken into account in determining whether the employee is 'lower paid' and in the case of a company car this may be sufficient to breach the £8,500 threshold.

44.25 Company cars

The cash equivalent of the benefit derived from the private use of a company car is based on a percentage of the car's list price, graduated according to the level of the vehicle's carbon dioxide (CO_2) emissions.

From 6 April 2012, the graduated bands start at 10%. The 10% rate applies to cars with CO_2 emissions below the relevant threshold. The relevant threshold is set at 95g/km for 2013/14 onwards and at 100g/km for 2012/13. Where the CO_2 emissions figure is equal to the relevant threshold, the appropriate percentage is set at 11% for 2012/13 and at 2013/14. Thereafter, the appropriate percentage is increased by 1% for every 5g/km increase in carbon dioxide emissions until the maximum appropriate percentage is reached (35% for 2013/14 and 2012/13). The actual CO_2 emissions are rounded down to the nearest 5g/km for the purposes of determining the appropriate percentage.

Diesel cars are subject to an additional 3% charge but are still subject to the 35% maximum.

For five years from 5 April 2010, no charge applies in respect of cars not capable of producing zero engine emissions (including electric cars). Cars with actual unrounded CO_2 emissions of 75g/km are subject to a lower charge of 5% for five years from 6 April 2010.

Cars which have no CO_2 emissions are charged as follows:

Engine size	Registration pre 1 January 1998	Registration 1 January 1998 to 30 September 1999
1400cc or less	15%	15%
1401cc to 2000cc	22%	25%
2001cc or more	32%	35%
N0 cylinder capacity	15% if electric; 32% otherwise	15% electric, 32% otherwise

For 2014/15 the appropriate percentage is to be increased by 1% for all cars with CO_2 emissions in excess of 75g/km, subject to a maximum charge of 35%.

In both 2016/16 and 2016/17 the appropriate percentage will increase by 2%. The maximum charge is increased from 25% to 37% from 6 April 2016.

From 6 April 2010 for five years, a zero charge applies to zero-emission cars. These are cars, including electric-only cars, which are not capable of producing CO_2 engine emissions in any circumstances. The zero rate comes to an end on 5 April 2015. Two new lower appropriate percentage bands for company car tax purposes are introduced from 2015/16. The two new bands will cover CO_2 emissions of 0–50g/km and 51–75g/km. The appropriate percentage for the lowest band will be set at five per cent in 2015/16 and at seven per cent in 2016/17. The appropriate percentage for the 51–75g/km band will be set at nine per cent in 2015/16 and at 11 per cent in 2016/17. The government have also provided a commitment to three percentage point differential between each of the lowest three bands in 2017/18 and a two percentage point differential between those bands in 2018/19 and 2019/20.

Diesel cars attract a supplement of 3%, subject to the maximum charge of 35%. The supplement is to be removed from 6 April 2016 such that for 2016/17 and subsequent tax years the appropriate percentage for diesel car will be the same as a petrol car with the same level of CO_2 emissions.

From 6 April 2010 for a period of five years, a lower charge of 5% applies to ultra-low emission cars, These are cars with actual (unrounded) CO_2 emissions of 75g/km or less. The 5% rate comes to an end on 5 April 2015. For 2015/16 the appropriate percentage for all cars with CO_2 emissions of less than 95g/km (including very low emission cars) is set at 13%. This is increased to 15% from 2016/17.

The 'list price' (subject to an overall limit of £80,000 for years prior to 2011/12) is the price published by the manufacturer, importer or distributor (inclusive of delivery charges and taxes) at the time of registration. It is important to note that this is unlikely to be the price actually paid by the employer for the car. The list price for the car includes any standard accessories provided with the car, but the price of any optional extras supplied with the car when first made available to the employee, together with any further accessory costing £100 or more must be added in. Where an employee makes a capital contribution to the initial cost of the car, the price of the car for the year of contribution and subsequent years is reduced by that contribution or £5,000 if less.

The value of the benefit is reduced proportionately if the car is 'unavailable' for part of the year. The benefit is further reduced (or extinguished) by the amount of contributions which an employee is required to make for private use. Cars more than 15 years old and worth over £15,000 are taxed by reference to their open market value in accordance with special rules for classic cars.

(*ITEPA 2003, ss 114–148.*)

44.26 Car fuel

Since 2003/04, the benefit on car fuel provided for private motoring in a company car is calculated by applying the car benefit appropriate percentage ascertained in **44.25** above to a multiplier. For 2013/14 the multiplier is set at £21,100 (for 2012/13 the multiplier was set at £20,200). The multiplier is increased annually by 2% more than inflation.

The value of the benefit is proportionately reduced if the car is not available for part of the year. No charge applies if the employee is required to, and does, make good to the employer the cost of all fuel used for private purposes (including travel between home and work). The charge is proportionately reduced if the employee begins to meet the cost of the fuel provided for private use, or fuel ceases to be provided for private use, from a date part way through the year, provided this condition continues to be met for the rest of the year. However, if the provision of fuel is withdrawn and then reinstated before the end of the year, the charge applies in full.

Before providing fuel for private motoring in a company car, employers and employees should consider whether this is a worthwhile benefit. At current levels of taxation it is unlikely to be a tax-efficient benefit unless private mileage is very high.

Where the employer does not provide a company car driver with fuel and the company car driver uses the company car for business purposes, the employer will usually reimburse the cost of that fuel. HM Revenue and Customs publish 'advisory' fuel rates for company cars which can be used to negotiate dispensations for mileage payments for business motoring in company cars. The figures may also be used for reimbursement by employers of fuel used for private motoring. The advisory rates will not be binding where the employer can demonstrate that the cost of business motoring is higher than the advisory rates. With effect from 1 March 2013, the rates are as follows:

Engine size	Petrol	LPG
1,400cc or less	15p	10p
1,401 to 2,000cc	18p	12p
Over 2,000cc	26p	18p

Engine size	Diesel
1,600cc or less	13p
1601cc to 2000cc	15p
Over 2,000cc	18p

The rates are revised quarterly (*ITEPA 2003, ss 149–153.*)

44.27 Vans

The provision of a company van weighing no more than 3.5 tonnes for the private use of employees is taxed by reference to an annual scale charge. Since 6 April 2007, the charge is £3,000 per tax year, regardless of the age of the van. The charge is reduced proportionately if the van is not available for the whole year, or is unavailable for 30 consecutive days or more. Payments by an employee towards private use of the van will also reduce the tax charge. Special provisions apply where vans are shared between several employees. Since 6 April 2005, no charge has applied to employees who have to take their van home and are not allowed, and do not make, any private use of the van (insignificant use being disregarded).

Since 6 April 2007, a separate fuel scale charge applies where fuel is provided for private mileage in the company van. For 2013/14 the charge is set at £564 (for 2012/13 the charge was £550 (*ITEPA 2003, ss 155–170*).

Since 6 April 2004, no charge has applied where emergency service workers in the fire, police and ambulance services have to take their emergency vehicle home when on call (*ITEPA 2003, s 248A*).

44.28 TAX RELIEF FOR EXPENSES AND DISPENSATIONS

Tax relief is available for expenses incurred wholly, exclusively and necessarily in the performance of the duties. This is an especially difficult test to satisfy and it must be shown that the employee is obliged to incur and pay the expense as the office holder. Similarly, reimbursements to employees (other than employees in an excluded employment, as defined in **44.3** above) in respect of expenses, or any sum put at their disposal to cover expenses (such as for business travel and subsistence), are treated as earnings and relief can be claimed for the allowable part (*ITEPA 2003, ss 333–336*, previously *ICTA 1988, s 198*).

The relief is given by deduction and must be claimed by the employee. If the employee reimburses expenses, the amount reimbursed is taxable on the employee. However, to the extent that the expenses are wholly, exclusively and necessarily incurred in the performance of the duties, the employee can claim a deduction, which will effectively offset the tax liability arising in respect of the reimbursed expense.

To avoid unnecessary administration, where expenses payments or benefits do no more than cover expenses incurred wholly, exclusively and necessarily in the performance of the duties, the employer can obtain a dispensation from HM Revenue and Customs. Such a dispensation would avoid the employer having to include the expenses payments and benefits on the employee's form P11D for tax and Class 1A National Insurance purposes or the expenses payments in the employee's gross pay for tax and Class 1 National Insurance purposes. The employee is relieved from the need to make an associated claim for relief to offset the taxable benefit that would otherwise arise.

44.29   EMPLOYEE SHARE SCHEMES

Tax advantages are available where employees are provided with shares or share options via an approved share or share option scheme. As part of their remit to provide the Government with advice on simplifying the tax system, the Office of Tax Simplification undertook a review into tax-advantaged share schemes and published a report of their findings on 6 March 2012. The Government consulted on the recommendations and published a summary of responses in December 2012, together with draft legislation for inclusion in the 2013 Finance Bill. Further changes, including the replacement of the current approvals process for SIP, SAYE and CSOP schemes with a self-certification process and the introduction of online filing of share scheme returns, are to be introduced in 2014.

Shares and share options can also be made available to employees by means of unapproved schemes. Although these lack the tax advantages available to approved schemes, they are not bound by the associated conditions and offer more flexibility. The Office of Tax Simplification has also undertaken a review of unapproved share schemes.

Savings-related share option schemes

Savings-related share option schemes are tax-advantaged schemes established in accordance with *ITEPA 2003 ss 516–520, Sch 3* (amended by *FA 2003, Schs 21, 22*) whereby a company may establish a scheme for its employees to obtain options to acquire the company's shares without charge to income tax either on the value of the options or on any subsequent increase in the value of the shares before the options are exercised. The scheme must be linked to an approved savings scheme (subject to a monthly limit of £250) to provide the funds for the acquisition of the shares when the option is exercised. For capital gains tax purposes, the market value is not substituted for the consideration given so the base cost is the amount paid for both the shares and the option. For further details of the scheme rules, see *Tolley's Income Tax 2005/06* (or later edition).

44.30   Company share option schemes

A company share option plan (CSOP) is a tax advantaged share option plan set up in accordance with *ITEPA 2003, ss 521–526, Sch 4* (as amended by *FA 2003, Sch 21 para 16*). The scheme applies to options granted from 17 July 1995 (before that date, options were granted under what was known as the 'executive share option scheme' which provided more generous tax relief). The aggregate market value of shares acquired under the option and any other approved options held by the employee (other than savings-related schemes) must not exceed £30,000. There is no tax charge when the options are granted, if all the conditions have been complied with. Options under the scheme have to be exercised between three and ten years after being granted but may be exercised within three years of the grant where the individual ceases to be an employee due to injury, disablement redundancy or retirement. Options granted before 9 April 2003 must be exercised between three and ten years after being granted (without exception), and not more frequently than once in every three years. For capital gains tax purposes, the base cost is the amount paid for both the shares and the option. For further details of the plan rules, see *Tolley's Income Tax 2005/06* (or later edition).

44.31   Share incentive plans

Share incentive plans were introduced by *FA 2000, s 47, Sch 8*, then known as the all-employee share ownership plan. The legislation is now found in *ITEPA 2003, ss 418, 488–515, Sch 2* (amended by *FA 2003, Schs 21, 22*). Share Incentive Plans (SIPs) are intended to be available to all employees, and were designed to replace profit-sharing schemes. Employees can receive up to £3,000 worth of free shares per year, with the option of purchasing shares up to £1,500 per year by deductions from salary. For every share purchased, the employee can be given two free shares. To remain free of tax and National Insurance, all shares acquired must be held in the plan for a specified period of time, normally at least three years. Dividends of up to £1,500 per employee per tax year can be reinvested tax-free in additional shares in the company. Withdrawals of shares from the plan are not subject to capital gains tax and they are treated as acquired by the employee at their market value at that time. For further details of the plan rules, see *Tolley's Income Tax 2005/06* (or later edition).

44.32   Enterprise management incentives

The 'enterprise management incentive scheme' was introduced by *FA 2000, s 62, Sch 14* and amended by *FA 2001, s 62, Sch 14*. The legislation is now contained within *ITEPA 2003, ss 527–541, Sch 5*. The scheme allows small independent trading companies to reward employees with tax-advantaged share options worth up to £120,000 per employee (£100,000 before 6 April 2008). Any gain on the sale of such shares is chargeable to capital gains tax. The company must be an independent UK company carrying on a qualifying trade, and its gross assets must not exceed £15,000,000. For further details *Tolley's Income Tax 2005/06* (or later edition).

The availability of enterprise management incentives is now limited to companies with fewer than 250 employees.

For a thorough discussion of the schemes outlined in **44.29–44.32**, see *Tolley's Tax Planning 2005/06* (or later edition).

44.33   PAYROLL GIVING SCHEME

Employees can authorise their employers to deduct charitable donations from their earnings before tax, for passing on to nominated charities approved through agency charities with which the employer has made arrangements. Deductions must be made under a scheme authorised by HM Revenue and Customs and subject to regulations made by Statutory Instrument. National Insurance contributions remain payable on the gross earnings.

44.34 PROVISION OF SERVICES THROUGH AN INTERMEDIARY

Provisions were introduced with effect from 6 April 2000 by *FA 2000, Sch 12* which are designed to counter what the Government considers to be tax avoidance where services are provided through an intermediary, ie typically single workers contracting out their services to a client via their own company. The provisions are generally referred to as IR35 after the Budget Press Release in which they were announced. The legislation is now found within *ITEPA 2003, ss 48–61* (as amended by *FA 2003, s 136*).

The measures were introduced following 'concern about the hiring of individuals through their own service companies so that they can exploit the fiscal advantages offered by a corporate structure'. The rules were extended from 10 April 2003 so they not only apply to services provided for another person's business but now also to those engaged in a domestic capacity, such as nannies. For an example of a case where, before the enactment of these provisions, personal service companies were used to avoid PAYE, see *Sports Club v HM Inspector of Taxes (and related appeals)* (Sp C 253) [2000] STC (SCD) 443.

The rules are designed to ensure that a comparable amount of PAYE is payable on contractors' income in circumstances where, if the service company did not exist, the worker would be an employee of the client as would be payable if the contractor were employed directly by the client. There are corresponding NIC provisions, contained in the *Welfare Reform and Pensions Act 1999, s 75 (SI 1999/3420)* and the *Social Security Contributions (Intermediaries) Regulations 2000*.

The provisions apply to 'relevant engagements'. To be a relevant engagement, the terms of all the contracts applying to the engagement will be reviewed, including the contract between an agency and the client, and between the worker's personal service company and the agency. If the terms of the contracts would have created a contract of employment had they been entered into directly between the client and the worker, the IR35 rules apply. The provisions do not introduce any statutory definition of employment or self-employment, so the existing case law will still apply to decide employment status.

For further details of the provisions, see *Tolley's Income Tax 2010/11*. HM Revenue and Customs has a substantial library of information about these provisions on its website at www.hmrc.gov.uk/ir35/index.htm.

The Court of Appeal confirmed the legality of the provisions in the judicial review case of *R (on the application of Professional Contractors Group Ltd) v IRC* [2001] EWCA Civ 1945, [2002] STC 165 employee-like services will be taxed as if there was a real employment situation.

The corresponding NIC provisions (contained in the *Social Security Contributions (Intermediaries) Regulations 2000 (SI 2000/727)*) were held to apply in *Battersby v Campbell (Inspector of Taxes)* (Sp C 287) [2001] STC (SCD) 189 and *FS Consulting Ltd v McCaul* (Sp C 305) [2002] STC (SCD) 138.

Following recommendations made by the Office of Tax Simplification, the Government has committed to a review of the IR35 provisions with a review to introducing administrative simplifications. Since April 2012 HM Revenue and Customs have been piloting a number of changes. Proposals to treat 'controlling persons' as employees for PAYE and NIC purposes have been abandoned following a consultation process.

44.35 MANAGED SERVICE COMPANIES

Managed service companies are intermediary companies through which the services of a worker are provided to an end client. They are not the same as personal service companies and in contrast to a personal service company the worker is not usually in business on his own account and does not exercise control over the business. The control is with the provider of the managed service company.

Legislation was introduced to counter the use of managed service companies to avoid tax and National Insurance contributions. The tax legislation, which is contained in *FA 2007, s 25* and *Sch 3*, applies from 6 April 2007. Corresponding National Insurance provisions, contained in the *Social Security Contributions (Managed Service Companies) Regulations 2007 (SI 2007/2070)*, apply from 6 August 2007.

Under the rules all payments made by a managed service company to a worker are treated as payments of employment income, regardless or the nature of the payment or how it is described. This means that PAYE and NIC must be applied, even if the payment is described as a dividend. The managed service company is responsible for the operation of PAYE and NIC.

The managed service company rules also reduced the scope for the worker to claim deductible travel expenses.

From 6 August 2007, where the PAYE and NIC debts of a managed service company cannot be recovered from the company, HMRC may transfer the debt personally to the company director or to the managed service company provider. Debts may be transferred to third parties from 6 January 2008

44.36 DISGUISED REMUNERATION

Provisions introduced from 6 April 2011 (*ITEPA 2003, Pt 7A*) tackle arrangements that use trusts and other vehicles to reward employees in a way that is designed to avoid, defer or reduce tax and National Insurance liabilities by disguising what is in effect remuneration. The rules also target arrangements that are designed to be used as a tax-advantaged way to save for retirement by using an employer financed retirement benefit scheme as an alternative to, or a top up to, savings in a registered pension scheme.

The rules provide for an income tax charge to apply where trusts or other intermediate vehicles are used in arrangements aimed at providing value to an individual in what is in substance a reward or recognition in connection with the individual's employment. Although the rules are not limited to arrangements involving employee benefit trusts (EBTs), in practice many of the arrangements that fall within their scope will feature EBTs. A charge will also apply where a loan is provided in connection with the employee's arrangement. The tax charge will operate in the following ways.

- Sums or assets that are earmarked for employees by trusts or other intermediaries will be treated as if the amount of the sum or the value of the asset earmarked for the employee is a payment of PAYE income provided by the employer's employee to the employee.

- Loans provided to employees by trusts and other intermediaries will be treated as if the value of the loan is a payment of PAYE income provided by the employee's employer to the employee.

- Assets provided to employees by trusts or other intermediaries will be regarded for tax purposes as a payment of PAYE income by the employer where certain conditions (as specified in the legislation) are met.

- Sums or assets that are earmarked by the employer with a view to a trust to other intermediary providing retirement benefits to the employee are treated as if the amount of the sum or value of the asset earmarked for the employee is a payment of PAYE income provided by the employee's employer to the employee.

The disguised remuneration rules apply from 6 April 2011 in relation to rewards which are earmarked for an individual employee or otherwise made available on or after that date. Anti-forestalling rules applied in certain situations in relation to sums paid or assets provided between 9 December 2010 and 6 April 2011, where if provision had been made on or after 6 April 2011, the new rules would be in point.

Regulations impose a National Insurance charge on the amounts chargeable to tax from the same date.

45   Temporary and Seasonal Employees

Cross-references. See 14.3 EMPLOYEE, SELF-EMPLOYED OR WORKER? for the distinction between a contract for services and a contract of service/employment. See TAXATION (44) for vacation employment of students. See also ENGAGEMENT OF EMPLOYEES (20) and PROBATIONARY EMPLOYEES (34).

45.1   An employer may sometimes engage workers on a temporary basis. This might be to take over work while a permanent employee is away or to cope with fluctuating work loads (eg due to seasonal work requirements). In this chapter, the description 'temporary' is applied to a worker who is referred to an employer by an employment agency (the kind of worker commonly referred to as a 'temp') and also to an employee who is employed for a limited period. 'Seasonal worker' is applied to a person who enters into the direct employment of the employer for a limited period at a busy time of the year. Employees who are engaged for a limited period (including seasonal workers) may be fixed-term employees and accordingly will qualify for protection under the provisions of the *Fixed-Term Employees (Prevention of Less Favourable Treatment) Regulations 2002 (SI 2002/2034)* (these *Regulations* are considered below at **45.14**).

As to employment of part-time workers or job-sharers, their employment rights are not dependent on their working a specified number of hours in a week: see CONTINUOUS EMPLOYMENT (6). See also the *Part-time Workers (Prevention of Less Favourable Treatment) Regulations 2000 (SI 2000/ 1551)* as amended by *SI 2002/2035* (see 21.12 EQUAL PAY).

45.2   TEMPORARY WORKERS

Employment agencies

Employment agencies fulfil two main functions: they effect introductions of permanent staff to employers and they supply temporary staff for a short period of time. So far as the first category is concerned, after the introduction has been made, the employment agency drops out of the picture, and the employer enters into a direct relationship with the employee with all the attendant duties and responsibilities of a normal employment contract. If, however, the worker is supplied on a temporary basis – the agency charging its client a weekly fee out of which it pays the worker – the client is more accurately to be regarded in most circumstances as a user of that worker's services and not his employer (here called the 'quasi employer'). Because the quasi employer controls not only what the agency worker does but how he does it, the quasi employer may be vicariously liable for any wrong done by the worker while working for him (see VICARIOUS LIABILITY (54)) and be liable to the worker for any claim by him for damages for personal injuries (*Mersey Docks and Harbour Board v Coggins and Griffiths (Liverpool) Ltd* [1947] AC 1; *Denham v Midland Employers' Mutual Assurance Ltd* [1955] 2 QB 437). However, it was for a considerable period doubtful whether the quasi employer would be liable to the worker for unfair dismissal or redundancy if the employment agency could be regarded as the primary employer who lends the worker's services to other employers (*Cross v Redpath Dorman Long (Contracting) Ltd* [1978] ICR 730, EAT). In *Ironmonger v Movefield Ltd* [1988] IRLR 461, it was held that the contract with the employment agency was one *sui generis*, somewhere between a contract of employment and a contract for services. A similar approach was taken in *Wickens v Champion Employment* [1984] ICR 365 where there was held to be no contract of employment between a worker and an employment agency.

In *McMeechan v Secretary of State for Employment* [1997] IRLR 353 the Court of Appeal held that an agency worker *may* have the status of an employee in relation to a *particular engagement* actually worked even if there is no such status as an employee under the *general terms of engagement* between the worker and the employment agency. In this case, the appellant's claim to employee status was limited to a specific contract in relation to which he was owed money. The Court of Appeal held, despite an express term describing the appellant as 'a self-employed worker' that he was in fact an employee in relation to the specific engagement under consideration. It was, accordingly, unnecessary for the Court of Appeal to determine whether the appellant was to be considered an employee under the general terms of the engagement with the employment agency.

The issue of the employment status of temporary and agency workers has been a difficult and ongoing problem with conflicting judicial decision and bursts of judicial activism and then retreat as the cases summarised below illustrate. What is clear is that it will be a matter for Parliament to address ultimately and not the courts – a point made with particular clarity by the Court of Appeal in *James v Greenwich London Borough Council* [2008] EWCA Civ 35, [2008] ICR 545, [2008] IRLR 302 (below).

45.3   *Similar facts different results*

In *Costain Building and Civil Engineering Ltd v Smith* [2000] ICR 215, the EAT had reversed a finding by an Employment Tribunal that a worker supplied by an agency and appointed by a trade union as a safety representative was an employee. The worker was paid without deduction of tax or National Insurance. The EAT held that the only contracts were between the employment agency and the worker and between the employment agency and the company. By way of contrast, in *Motorola Ltd v Davidson* [2001] IRLR 4, the EAT held that a worker supplied by an agency was an employee of the hiring company (Motorola) and could, accordingly, present a complaint of unfair dismissal. The EAT held that Motorola exercised sufficient control in reality over the worker to give rise to employee status, rejecting Motorola's argument that the worker was controlled by the agency. This was a significant decision in that there was no express contract between the worker and Motorola, a factor which had previously been fatal to the contention that the worker was an employee of the quasi employer. The facts of the case should also be noted in that the employee was specifically selected to work at Motorola and had done so permanently for over two years.

While each case may turn upon its own facts, in the area of employment status of agency workers even on similar facts, wholly different conclusions have been reached by different courts. This left agency workers in a very unsatisfactory and uncertain position with regard to employment protection rights. A clear illustration of the problem was provided by *Johnson Underwood Ltd v Montgomery* [2001] EWCA Civ 318, [2001] IRLR 269. In that case the claimant had worked for the client of the employment business for some two and a half years. Upon the termination of her 'employment' she presented a claim for unfair dismissal. The issue of who was the employer arose as a preliminary issue. The case eventually reached the Court of Appeal which concluded, applying the tests of control and mutuality of obligation, that, on the particular facts, the claimant was not an employee of the employment business. The unfortunate consequence of this decision was that the claimant was left without a remedy as the original employment tribunal decision (to the effect that she was not an employee of the client business at which she had worked for two and a half years) had not been appealed. A striking example of very long term agency workers being found not to have employment status was provided by *Esso Petroleum Co Ltd v Jarvis* [2002] All ER (D) 112 (Jan). In that case, agency workers who had worked for the same client for 9 and 11 years, respectively, were found not to be employees of the client on the basis of the absence of a contractual relationship between the workers and the client. This may be contrasted with the *Motorola* decision above. In *Hewlett Packard Ltd v O'Murphy* [2002] IRLR 4 it was held that there was no contractual nexus between the worker (who had worked for six years) and the appellant client. Accordingly, he was not an employee. *Motorola* was not, however, referred to in the *Hewlett Packard* case.

45.4   *Activism – the search for an implied contract of employment*

The lack of certainty in this area of the law and the apparently conflicting decisions at EAT level lead to a trilogy of decisions of the Court of Appeal which developed the concept of an *implied contract of employment* arising between the worker and the client using his services. In *Franks v Reuters Ltd* [2003] EWCA Civ 417, [2003] IRLR 423 the claimant entered into a temporary worker agreement with an employment agency and was supplied to Reuters where he worked for five years working hours fixed by Reuters but paid by the employment agency. The Court of Appeal held that the worker was an employee of Reuters. The question to be addressed by an employment tribunal was whether a contract of employment could be implied between the worker and Reuters from the circumstances of his work and what was said by the parties at the time work commenced and subsequently. The Court of Appeal explained that although a person cannot become an employee simply by reason of length of the time which they have worked, the length of 'service' was not irrelevant evidence in the context of a person who was allowed to stay working in the same place for the same client for over five years because dealings between parties over a period of years, as distinct from weeks or months, are capable of generating implied contractual relationships.

The principles in *Franks* were developed in *Dacas v Brook Street Bureau (UK) Ltd* [2004] EWCA Civ 217, [2004] IRLR 358. In *Dacas* the applicant had worked exclusively as a cleaner at a hostel run by Wandsworth Council for at least four years until the engagement was terminated. Mrs Dacas brought proceedings for unfair dismissal against the supplying agency and, alternatively, the Council. In a striking illustration of the unsatisfactory nature of the law in this area the Employment Tribunal concluded that she was employed by neither the agency not the council. This result – that Mrs Dacas was employed by nobody – was described in the Court of Appeal (by Sedley LJ) as 'simply not credible'. The Court of Appeal concluded that the agency was not the employer of the claimant as the necessary mutuality of obligation or control was not present. As to the Council, Mummery LJ concluded that employment by that body would accord with 'practical reality and commonsense' and in Sedley LJ's view there was an inference to be drawn that the Council was the employer. The Court of Appeal in *Dacas* stressed that, in proceedings before an Employment Tribunal where the status of a claimant is in issue, the Tribunal is required as a matter of law to consider whether there is an *implied* contract between the parties who are not in an express contractual relationship with each other. (On the facts of *Dacas* there was a contract between Mrs Dacas and the agency and between the agency and the Council. The relationship between Mrs Dacas and the Council was considered by the majority (Munby J dissenting) to be an *implied* contract of employment).

In *Cable and Wireless plc v Muscat* [2006] EWCA Civ 220, [2006] IRLR 354 the implied contract approach was again considered but on somewhat atypical facts. The Court of Appeal held for the first (and only) time that there was *in fact* an implied contract of employment between the worker and the client end-user (in *Franks* the issue had been remitted to the Employment Tribunal and the observations in *Dacas* as to implied contract status of the claimant were, on the particular facts of that appeal, *obiter*). The facts of *Muscat* were complicated and somewhat unusual. The worker had originally been an employee who was then required to go to agency provided services followed by a TUPE transfer. As such, the case did not illustrate the more common factual circumstances of a worker providing services to a client consistently through an agency for a period of time in excess of, say, one year. Further the Court held that the guidance of the majority in *Dacas* was to be applied and followed by Employment Tribunals in future cases. On the issue of the fact that payment of the worker was made by the agency rather than the client end user (which factor was one of the main reasons for Munby J's dissent in *Dacas*), the Court held that this is not a particularly strong factor against employee status if the other factors point to employment by the end user client.

45.5   Temporary and Seasonal Employees

45.5   *The retreat from the implied contract: the need for 'necessity'*

The later authorities show that an implied contract will rarely be found and it appears that *Cable & Wireless plc v Muscat* is likely to be a case confined to its own facts. In a number of EAT decision culminating with an important test case decision of the Court of Appeal in *James v Greenwich London Borough Council* [2008] IRLR 302 it has been made clear that an implied contract between the worker and the end user will only arise when it is <u>necessary</u> to imply such a contract. In *James v Greenwich London Borough Council* [2007] ĪCR 577, [2007] IRLR 168 the claimant was an agency worker who had worked for the local authority for a number of years acting under the direction of the council without intervention from the employment agency. She was treated like a permanent member of staff on the staff rota. When she went off work by reason of sickness the agency replaced her with another worker. On her return the claimant was informed her services were no longer required and she brought a claim for unfair dismissal. The EAT ([2007] ICR 577, [2007] IRLR 168) held that the issue is whether it is *'necessary'* to imply a contract of employment between the worker and the end-user. The EAT (Elias P) held that it was not sufficient that the arrangements are *consistent* with a contract of employment as in order to imply such a contract it must be necessary in that the way in which the contract is performed is only consistent with an implied contact between the worker and the end-user and not consistent with another contractual relationship. The EAT held that mere passage of time will not justify such an implication but that there must be some words or conduct after commencement of the working relationship entitling the Tribunal to conclude that the agency relationship no longer adequately reflects the reality of the relationship. The EAT observed that 'we suspect that it will be a rare case where there will be evidence entitling the tribunal to imply a contract between the worker and end user'. In *Cairns v Visteon UK Ltd* [2007] IRLR 175 the facts engaged were somewhat unusual in that there *was* a contract of employment between the worker and the employment agency. The issue before the EAT was whether, in such circumstances, a contract of employment could nevertheless also be implied between the worker and the end-user client as well. The EAT held, following *James*, that there was no business necessity to make such an implication (nor any policy reason) to extend parallel protection under the *ERA* to an employee who was already protected by the employment relationship between the employer and the employment agency employer. Similar decisions of differently constituted EAT's followed in *Astbury v Gist Ltd* [2007] All ER (D) 480 (Mar), EAT, *Heatherwood and Wexham Park Hospitals NHS Trust v Kulubowila* [2007] All ER (D) 496 (Mar), EAT and *Wood Group Engineering Ltd v Robertson* UKEAT0081/06 (6 July 2007, unreported) and see *Wood v National Grid Electricity Transmission plc* [2007] All ER (D) 358 (Oct), EAT.

The Court of Appeal in *James v Greenwich London Borough Council* [2008] IRLR 302 has now confirmed the correctness of the EAT's approach in that case. The crucial test in relation to the end use is whether it is necessary to imply a contract of employment in order to explain the relationship. It is not enough for the claimant to show that the relationship looks like that of employer and employee. The guidance given by the EAT in James ([2007] IRLR 168) was specifically approved by the Court of Appeal. In *Dacas*, Sedley LJ had stated that conduct which was maintained over 'weeks or months' as opposed to 'a brief time' might rise to a finding that there was an implied contract of employment between the client and the worker which had appeared to suggest that a agency worker providing services for a substantial period of time to one end user would be likely to be considered an employee on the basis of an implied contract of employment. The EAT in *James* had disagreed with Sedley LJ on this point and the Court of Appeal in *James* firmly agrees with the EAT that mere length of time does not justify implication of a contact of employment. See also, on the proper approach to the test of necessity, *Cave v Portsmouth City Council* [2008] All ER (D) 313 (May), EAT.

The effect of *James v Greenwich London Borough Council* is that it will be very difficult for a claimant to show that it is necessary to imply a contract of employment between the worker and the end user as the relationship is explicable by the contract of agency between the agency and the worker which of course may not be a contact of employment between the worker and the agency. Whilst this is a substantial limitation upon atypical workers obtaining employment protection rights the judgment of the Court of Appeal (Mummery LJ and see Thomas LJ) concludes with express recognition of compelling policy arguments favouring agency workers having employment rights against the end user but emphasises that it is unrealistic, absent Parliament legislating on the issue, for litigants to hope or expect the Courts to be able to create such rights. By way of illustration, in *Muschett v HM Prison Service* [2010] IRLR 451 the Court of Appeal applying James, held that a temporary agency worker was unable to being a claim for discrimination and unfair dismissal against either the end user client or the supplying agency. This represents a considerable gap in the protection against discrimination which might be expected to apply to agency workers both as a matter of general principle and as a matter of European law. More recently in *Tilson v Alstom Transport* [2010] EWCA Civ 1308, [2011] IRLR 169, CA, it was held applying *James* that a senior manager engaged by the end user for two years through a third parry contractor was unable to claim unfair dismissal against the end user as he was not an employee. On the facts it was simply not necessary to imply a contract of employment. The Court of Appeal observed that the use of agencies was not contrary to public policy even if the aim was to avoid employment rights and "disapproval" of the arrangements by a tribunal could not justify implication of a contract of employment. Further, the conduct of the parties may be relevant in determining mutual expectations and the legal relationship subsisting. In *Tilson* the fact that the claimant had refused permanent employment because the agency work was more remunerative was a powerful factor against the implication of an employment contract. A further appeal in *Tilson* will be heard by the Supreme Court.

The *James v Greenwich London Borough Council* line of cases considers the possibility of employment by the client end-user. The issue of employment by the employment agency was revisited by the Court of Appeal in *Bunce v Postworth Ltd (t/a Skyblue)* [2005] EWCA Civ 490, [2005] IRLR 557. In that case the Court of Appeal held that an agency welder was not employed by the agency who supplied him. In this case the worker did not work for only one end user and a claim against the end user was not pursued. The absence of control exercised by the agency was held to be fatal to the claim against the agency and the Court of Appeal distinguished its earlier decision in *McMeechan* (above) in relation to the possibility of an overall contract with the agency and separate contracts in relation to each assignment. The legal position of such workers remains uncertain and unsatisfactory with a large number of people not enjoying the full range of employment rights solely because of their agency work arrangements as opposed to more typical 'employment'; a point stressed by Keene LJ in the Court of Appeal. The answer, however, was said to lie in the need for new legislation and not judicial creativity.

In a series of cases it has been made clear by the courts that the parties may not avoid employee status by the use of contractual definitions even if apparently unequivocal and recorded in a written agreement. In *Royal National Lifeboat Institution v Bushaway* [2005] IRLR 674, the EAT held that a written agreement, which defined the claimant as a 'temporary worker' supplied by an employment agency, was not conclusive as to the relationship between the parties notwithstanding a provision that the written agreement constituted the entire agreement between the parties. The EAT considered that as the relationship was not accurately reflected in the contractual document it was permissible to go beyond the terms of the document and examine the employment status of the claimant. On the facts the claimant was found to be an employee even though engaged on quite different terms and conditions to those of other employees.

In *Protectacoat Firthglow Ltd v Szilagyi* [2009] IRLR 365 and in *Autoclenz Ltd v Belcher & Others* [2010] IRLR 70 the Court of Appeal held that it was not necessary for a term to be properly characterised as a "sham" before it could be not applied. *Protectacoat* and *Autoclenz* established that where there is a dispute as to the genuineness of an express term there is no need to show a common intention to mislead. Instead it is enough if the written term did not represent the intentions or expectations of the parties. The court or tribunal was to consider whether or not the words of the written contract represented the true intentions or expectations of the parties (and therefore their implied agreement and contractual obligations) not only at the inception of the contract but at any later stage where the evidence shows that the parties have expressly or impliedly varied the agreement between them. The focus of the enquiry had to be to discover the actual legal obligations of the parties and to carry out that exercise the tribunal had to examine all the relevant evidence including the written term itself as read in the context of the whole agreement. It would include evidence of how the parties conducted themselves in practice and what their expectations of each other were. This approach gave rise to what was perceived to be a conflict with the earlier Court of Appeal decision in *Consistent Group Limited v Kalwak* [2008] IRLR 505 which had suggested that the term must be a "sham" before it could be disapplied.

The matter has now been resolved beyond doubt by the decision of the Supreme Court in *Autoclenz Ltd v Belcher* [2011] UKSC 41. The Supreme Court approved the judgments of the Court of Appeal in *Autoclenz* and *Protectacoat* (as well as that of the EAT in *Kalwak* so that the decision of the Court of Appeal in *Kalwak* is, effectively, overruled). The real question for the court is what was the true agreement between the parties? The concept or requirement of "a sham" was unhelpful in the employment context where a broader enquiry was required into the true terms of the agreement as the agreements in issue were frequently drafted by the employer and where inequality of bargaining power was present. The enquiry permitted consideration to be given to the subsequent conduct of the parties as evidence of what was originally agreed between them. The court must consider the relative bargaining power of the parties in deciding whether the terms of any written agreement in truth represented what was agreed and this required a purposive approach to the problem.

45.6   *The Temporary Agency Work Directive (2008/104/EC) and the Agency Worker Regulations 2010 (SI 2010/93)*

In May 2008 the then Government announced that it had reached agreement with the TUC and the CBI on legislating to give agency workers the right to terms and conditions of employment comparable to those enjoyed by permanent employees.

Under the agreement, agency workers were to be entitled to equal treatment with comparable permanent workers after 12 weeks of employment. The agreement defines equal treatment as 'at least the basic working and employment conditions that would apply to the workers concerned if they had been recruited directly by that undertaking to occupy the same job'. The agreement does not cover occupational social security schemes. The agreement also requires that these arrangements be reviewed after a suitable period to establish how they are working in practice.

In June 2008 the Council of the European Union announced that a common position had been reached on the draft Directive on agency work resulting in the *Temporary Agency Work Directive* (2008/104/EC). The Directive is limited to temporary *agency* workers and thus does not affect the employment status of temporary workers but permits the UK to implement the agreement between the Government, the CBI and the TUC.

The purpose of the Directive is to ensure the protection of temporary agency workers by applying the principle of equal treatment (*art 5*) so that, after 12 weeks in a given job, the basic working and employment conditions (duration of working time, overtime, breaks, rest periods, night work, holidays and public holidays and pay) of temporary agency workers shall be, for the duration of their assignment at a hirer, at least those that would apply if they had been recruited directly by that undertaking to occupy the same job. There are also other entitlements that aim to improve the situation for agency workers in other areas, for example, in terms of improved access to permanent employment and training. Member states had until 5 December 2011 to implement the Directive.

The Agency Worker Regulations 2010 (SI 2010/93)

Following consultation in relation to the implementation of the Directive the *Agency Worker Regulations 2010 (SI 2010/93)* were passed by the previous Government and were due to come into force on 1 October 2011. The *Regulations* were, however, further amended prior to their coming into force by the *Agency Workers (Amendment) Regulations 2011 (SI 2011/1941)*. Accordingly, particular care should be taken to ensure that the most up to date version of the *Regulations* is consulted. References to the *Regulations* below are to the amended *Regulations*. In May 2011 the Government's 51 page guidance document on the *Regulations* and their effect was published. See the "Agency Workers Regulations Guidance" which may be obtained from www.bis.gov.uk/assets/biscore/employment-matters/docs/a/11-949-agency-workers-regulations-guidance pdf The Guidance is not a Code of Practice and does not, accordingly, have any specific legal status but it is likely that it will be used by the employment tribunals in interpreting and applying the Regulations as a body of relevant case law is developed.

In summary, the *Regulations* introduce, with effect from 1 October 2011, a right to equal treatment in relation to terms and conditions of employment for agency workers in comparison to the permanent employees and workers of the hirer.

Definitions

Under the *Regulations* (*reg 3*) an "agency worker" means an individual who is supplied by a "temporary work agency" to work temporarily for and under the supervision and direction of "a hirer" and who has a contract with the temporary work agency which is a contract of employment or any other contract to perform work and services personally for the agency. "Worker" (as opposed to an agency worker) is subject to the usual statutory definition of a person who has entered into or works under (or where the employment has ceased, worked under) a contract of employment, or any other contract, whether express or implied and (if it is express) whether oral or in writing, whereby the individual undertakes to do or perform personally any work or services for another party to the contract whose status is not by virtue of the contract that of a client or customer of any profession or business undertaking carried on by the individual (*Reg 2*). The Guidance addresses "agency worker" at page 7 with examples of those who are considered to fall inside and outside that definition.

Reg 4 defines "temporary work agency" as a person engaged in the economic activity, public or private, whether or not operating for profit, and whether or not carrying on such activity in conjunction with others, of supplying individuals to work temporarily for and under the supervision and direction of hirers or paying for, or receiving or forwarding payment for, the services of individuals who are supplied to work temporarily for and under the supervision and direction of hirers. A "hirer" (*reg 2*) means a person engaged in "economic activity, public or private, whether or not operating for profit, to whom individuals are supplied, to work temporarily for and under the supervision and direction of that person".

The Rights

Under *reg 5(1)* the agency worker is entitled to the same basic working and employment conditions as he would be entitled to for doing the same job had he been recruited by the hirer. The "relevant terms and conditions" which must be provided equally are terms as to (a) pay; (b) the duration of working time; (c) night work; (d) rest periods; (e) rest breaks; and (f) annual leave (*reg 6(1)*). "Pay" (*reg 6(2)*) means any sums payable to a worker of the hirer in connection with the worker's employment, including any fee, bonus, commission, holiday pay or other emolument referable to the employment, whether payable under contract or otherwise but excludes the "payments or rewards" listed in *reg 6(3)*. The excluded payments include sick pay, pension payments, maternity payments, redundancy payments, any payment or reward made pursuant to a financial participation scheme (as defined in *reg 6(5)* as profit share and share option schemes), loyalty and long service bonuses, statutory time off payments for trade union duties, guarantee payments, any payment by way of an advance under an agreement for a loan or by way of an advance of pay, payment in respect of expenses incurred by the worker in carrying out the employment and any payment to the worker otherwise than in that person's capacity as a worker.

The rights under *reg 5* do not arise until the agency worker has completed the qualifying period (*reg 7*) whereby he must work in "the same role" with the same hirer for 12 continuous calendar weeks, during one or more assignments. The agency worker will be considered to work in the same role (*reg 7(3)*) unless he starts a new role with the hirer in relation to which the work making up the whole or main part of the new roles is "substantively different" from the previous role and the agency has informed the worker in writing of the type of work required in the new role. By *reg 7(3)* any week during the whole or part of which an agency worker works during an assignment is counted as a calendar week. *Regs 7(4)–(12)* make provision for determination if the work is executed for 12 continuous weeks and makes provision in *Reg 7(8)* for the effect of breaks in work by reason of sickness or injury, jury service, strike or lockout or maternity absence. If the qualifying period is satisfied the worker acquires the *reg 5* rights until the worker is no longer working in the same role, within the meaning of *reg 7(3)*, with that hirer (*reg 8(a)*) or there is a break between assignments, or during an assignment, when the agency worker is not working, to which *reg 7(8)* does not apply. *Reg 9* is an anti avoidance measure which provides that the agency worker will be treated as having satisfied the qualifying period if she or he is prevented from otherwise satisfying the requirements of *reg 7* by reason of "structure of assignments". Where the worker has worked in two or more substantively different roles for the hirer, if the most likely explanation for the adoption of that arrangement was to avoid the worker acquiring the qualifying period (and hence rights under *reg 5*), then the worker shall be treated by *reg 9* as having completed the qualifying period. Thus shifting workers around without legitimate purpose will not prevent the rights accruing and, if a hirer or temporary work agency is found to be engaged in such avoidance practices, the Regulations make provision for an additional award of up to £5000 (*reg 18(14)*).

Under *reg 10*, headed "Permanent contracts providing for pay between assignments", there is an important exception to the operation of at least part of the Regulations. To the extent to which it relates to pay, *reg 5* does not have effect in relation to an agency worker who has a permanent contract of employment with a temporary work agency if certain specific and stringent conditions set out in *reg 10* are satisfied (in summary, where the written contract provides for terms as to remuneration, location and hours of work and as to the type of work as may be offered and express exclusion of *reg 5* and where the agency is obliged to take reasonable steps to seek and provide work to the agency worker and where the agency is obliged during periods where the worker is not working for a hirer to make payment of a minimum amount). This is the so called "Swedish Derogation" as it was introduced into the *Temporary Agency Work Directive* (2008/104/EC) at the request of the Swedish government. By *reg 10(1)(a)* the relevant contract must be entered into before the first assignment and must include terms and conditions in writing relating to:

(i)   the minimum scale or rate of remuneration or the method of calculating remuneration;

(ii)   the location or locations where the agency worker may be expected to work;

(iii)   the expected hours of work during any assignment;

(iv)   the maximum number of hours of work that the agency worker may be required to work each week during any assignment;

(v)   the minimum hours of work per week that may be offered to the agency worker during any assignment, provided that it is a minimum of at least one hour; and

(vi)   the nature of the work that the agency worker may expect to be offered, including any relevant requirements relating to qualifications or experience.

Further, the relevant contract of employment must contain a statement that the effect of entering into it is that the employee does not, during the currency of the contract, have any entitlement to the rights conferred by *reg 5* insofar as they relate to pay. In addition, by *reg 10(c)*, the temporary work agency must take reasonable steps to seek suitable work for the agency worker, to provide suitable work as available and to pay minimum remuneration. The contract is not terminable unless the temporary work agency has complied with its obligations under *reg 10(c)* for not less than an aggregate of 4 weeks. These provisions have been considered at tribunal level in *Bray and others v Monarch Personnel Refuelling (UK) Ltd* ET/1801581/2012. That case considered agency workers who had undertaken the same work (tanker driving for BP) prior to the introduction of the Regulations but who entered into new contracts starting on 1 December 2011. The claimants contended that the new contracts did not comply with *reg 10* as they had not been entered into "before the first assignment". Rejecting the claims, the tribunal concluded that the contracts had been entered into before the beginning of the first assignment under the contract, even though the agency workers had actually worked for BP throughout a longer period. The assignment which started on 1 December 2011 was the "first assignment" under the new contract. The tribunal considered that "assignment" did not mean the entire continuous period that an agency worker works for a hirer and the absence of a gap in provision of the work did not prevent the workers being engaged on separate assignments. Accordingly, the contracts were compliant with *reg 10* and the workers were not entitled to the same rate of pay pursuant to *reg 5*.

Reg 11 makes provision for the calculation of the minimum amount of payment required under *reg 10(1)(c)*. It is important to note that even where a contract satisfying reg 10 exists, the agency worker is still entitled to the protection afforded by *reg 5* in relation to working time, night work, rest periods and holidays and the rights to access to collective facilities and job information.

In contrast to the *reg 5* rights which are subject to the *reg 7* qualifying period, all agency worker during an assignment are entitled to immediate equal access to "collective facilities and amenities" provided by the hirer *(reg 12)* as are available to a comparable worker. The facilities include canteen, childcare and transport services *(reg 12(3))* and a "comparable worker" is and employee or worker of the hirer engaged in broadly similar work for the hirer with (where relevant) a similar level of qualification and skills working at the same establishment *(reg 12(4))*. Agency workers also have the right to be informed by the hirer of any relevant vacant posts with the hirer, to give that agency worker the same opportunity as a comparable worker to find permanent employment with the hirer *(reg 13)*.

Liability for Breach

Under *reg 14* breach of *reg 5* will lead to liability in the temporary work agency and/or the hirer to the extent each is liable for breach. Under *reg 16* an agency worker may make a written request to the temporary work agency for a written statement containing information relating to a suspected breach of *reg 5* and a similar right exists in relation to a hirer in suspected breach of *reg 12* or *reg 13*. Failure to provide the information will permit adverse inferences to be drawn by an employment tribunal *(reg 16(9))*. Where the agency worker is an employee the usual protection against detriment in employment is provided along with provision for automatically unfair dismissal if the reason for the detriment or dismissal was the doing of any of a number of protected acts (see *reg 17*). The rights under the *Regulations* may be enforced in the employment tribunal subject to the normal time limits *(reg 18)* and just and equitable extension *(regs 18(4)* and *(5))*. Compensation is assessed on the just and equitable basis and is not subject to a statutory limit but excludes an injury to feelings award *(reg 18(15)* but an additional sum of up to £5000 may be awarded for seeking to avoid the rights under the Regulations accruing *(reg 18(14)* and *reg 9(4))*.

45.6 Temporary and Seasonal Employees

The *Regulations* make provision for consequential amendment to the relevant primary (principally *TULR(C)A* and *ERA*) and secondary legislation as set out in *Sch 2* to the *Regulations*.

45.7 Statutory control of employment agencies

Persons who carry on employment agencies or employment businesses had formerly to be licensed by the Secretary of State. The licensing provisions have now been replaced by a system under which the Secretary of State may apply to an Employment Tribunal for an order prohibiting a person from carrying on, or being concerned with the carrying on, of any employment agency or employment business or any specified description of such agency or business. The Tribunal may make the order if it is satisfied that the person concerned is unsuitable, on account of misconduct or for other sufficient reason, to do what the order prohibits; there are detailed provisions concerning the application of this test to companies and partnerships. There is an appeal on a question of law to the Employment Appeal Tribunal.

The prohibition, which may be for a maximum period of 10 years, may be absolute or it may be on carrying on the business otherwise than in accordance with specified conditions. Non-compliance with a prohibition order without reasonable excuse is an offence punishable by a fine. The person to whom the order applies may apply to the tribunal to have it varied or revoked where there has been a material change in circumstances.

(*Employment Agencies Act 1973, ss 3–3D*, as inserted by *Deregulation and Contracting Out Act 1994, Sch 10 para 1*.)

It is a criminal offence to charge a person a fee for finding or seeking to find him employment, save in such cases as the Secretary of State prescribes (*Employment Agencies Act 1973, s 6*). The classes which have been prescribed relate to occupations in the entertainment industry, to modelling and to *au pairs*.

The *Employment Act 2008* introduced with effect from 6 April 2009 a strengthening of the enforcement regime. Certain offences under the Act are now triable on indictment as well as summarily (*s 15* of the *Employment Act 2008*). The offences affected are those of: (i) failure to comply with a prohibition order, (ii) contravention of any regulations made under the 1973 Act and (iii) requesting or receiving a fee for providing work-finding services (except in those sectors such as entertaining and modelling where agencies are entitled to charge for these services under certain circumstances). As a result of the option of trial on indictment the Employment Agency Standards Inspectorate ('EAS') will be able to prosecute for 'attempting' to commit offences under the 1973 Act (eg attempting to obtain money for providing work-finding services). The EAS will be able to bring a prosecution for attempting to commit one of these offences on the basis of evidence obtained from the agency's records, without the need for agency workers to give evidence as witnesses.

If tried on indictment the penalty is a fine but may exceed that which may be imposed on summary conviction (see **1.10** INTRODUCTION for the Standards Scale of fines applicable to summary offences). In addition, significant amendments are made to *s 9* of the *Employment Agencies Act 1973* in relation to rights of inspection and disclosure of documents to officers by *s 16* of the *Employment Act 2008*. The EAS is now able to require a person carrying on an agency to provide financial records and documents and information at such time and place as the inspector may specify. In addition, banks may be required to provide financial information regarding agencies (where the agency has been asked to provide the information specified and has not done so). The inspectors are also given powers to remove documents from an agency in order to take copies. By *s 18* of the *Employment Act 2008* enforcement of the National Minimum Wage and employment agency standards is enabled by allowing officers appointed under the relevant legislation to share information with each other for the purpose of their respective enforcement functions. *Section 18* now allows minimum wage and employment agency officers to pass information about an employer's compliance to each other for the purposes of their enforcement functions.

In *First Point International Ltd v Department of Trade and Industry* (1999) 164 JP 89 the Court of Appeal, considered the scope of the unamended *s 6*. The section provides that a person 'shall not demand or directly or indirectly receive from any person a fee for finding him employment or seeking to find him employment'. The facts of *First Point International* were as follows. A person interested in work in Thailand contacted First Point International which sent him promotional materials and details of a 'personal client appraisal service' which required payment of almost £100 for an 'appraisal pack' containing appraisal questionnaires to be completed by the potential employee. The potential employee duly paid the fee, completing the questionnaires. First Point International then offered to identify suitable employment for him, for which service they would charge £3,150. The potential employee did not avail himself of this opportunity but First Point International was convicted of two offences under *s 6*. The £100 payment was found to be a fee for seeking to find employment; the £3,150 was found to be a 'demand' for payment for seeking to find employment. On appeal, the Court of Appeal upheld the convictions concluding that the fee for the appraisal documents was, as a matter of law, part of the 'seeking of employment'. As to the invitation to pay £3,150, the Court of Appeal concluded that *s 6* was not limited to cases where there was an enforceable legal right to payment but extended to invitations to make payments.

The *Employment Relations Act 1999* clarifies the application of *s 6* by providing that the prohibition on the charging of fees will extend to 'requests' for payment or the provision of information. The relevant amendments came into force on 25 October 1999.

The conduct of employment agencies was further regulated by the *Conduct of Employment Agencies and Employment Businesses Regulations 1976 (SI 1976/715)*. These Regulations have now been replaced with the *Conduct of Employment Agencies and Employment Businesses Regulations 2003 (SI 2003/3319)* with effect from 6 April 2004 (as amended) (see below **45.9**).

45.8   Statutory control of employment agencies: the 2003 reforms

As far back as 1999, the Government published a consultation paper, 'Regulation of the Private Recruitment Industries', proposing the replacement of, *inter alia*, the *Conduct of Employment Agencies and Employment Businesses Regulations 1976 (SI 1976/715)*. The key proposals in that document sought to clarify the legal rights and obligations of agencies, their workers and clients, to require checks to be made upon the relevant qualifications of workers and, in certain cases, to require references and to prevent workers engaging in hazardous work for which they were not qualified. Consultation of the proposed changes had a lengthy history continuing into 2002–2003. From 6 April 2004 the *Conduct of Employment Agencies and Employment Business Regulations 2003 (SI 2003/3319)* ('the *2003 Regulations*') have been in force.

The Department for Trade and Industry (now BIS) consulted on new measures to protect vulnerable agency workers in 2007. As a consequence of the responses to that consultation the Government made amendments to the *Regulations* by the *Conduct of Employment Agencies and Employment Businesses (Amendment) Regulations 2007 (SI 2007/3575)* ('the *2007 Regulations*') which came into force on 6 April 2008.

The government engaged in further consultation which closed in June 2009 in relation to the *Regulations* with particular regard to vulnerable categories of agency workers in the entertainment and modelling field and the use of upfront fees and umbrella companies in the employment of temporary workers. New regulations, the *Conduct of Employment Agencies and Employment Business Regulations (Amendment) Regulations 2010 (SI 2010/1782)*, came into force on 1 October 2010. The *2010 Regulations* take effect by

45.8 Temporary and Seasonal Employees

amendment to the *2003 Regulations*. The amendments increase the protection of performers seeking work through employment agencies and employment businesses by limiting when upfront fees can be charged and by extending cooling off periods. In addition the changes made by the amendments in the *2010 Regulations* purport to reduce the administrative burden placed on employment agencies and business expect in situations where the person seeking work will be working with or caring for vulnerable groups.

The *2003 Regulations* as amended by the *2010 Regulations* are considered below. BIS guidance on the *Regulations* is available on the BIS website at www.bis.gov.uk/policies/employment-matters/eas.

45.9 The Conduct of Employment Agencies and Employment Businesses Regulations 2003 (SI 2003/3319) (as amended)

The majority of provisions of the *2003 Regulations* came into force with effect from 6 April 2004 Transitional provisions dealt with engagements which were in place prior to the coming into force of the *2003 Regulations*.

At the outset it is important to identify the precise terminology used by the *Regulations*. Under the *2003 Regulations* a person seeking work through an agency or employment business is a 'work-seeker'. The client to whom the services are supplied is the 'hirer' (*reg 2*). As to the agencies, the relevant definitions are found in the *Employment Agencies Act 1973* as follows. An 'employment agency' finds work-seekers employment with hirers or supplies hirers with work-seekers for employment (*s 13(2)*). An 'employment business' engages work seekers directly and supplies them on a temporary basis to the hirer (*s 13(3)*). Thus in ordinary usage headhunters are employment *agencies* and temping agencies are employment *businesses*.

Under the *2003 Regulations*, an employment agency or business (as the case may be) must on the first occasion of offering to provide or arrange the provision of a service to a work-seeker provide certain notice to the work seeker in relation to the service and fee calculations (*reg 13(1)*). However, it is important to note that *reg 13(1)* only applies where one or more services or goods referred to in *reg 13(1)(b)* for which the work-seeker will or may be charged a fee may be provided to the work-seeker. By *reg 13(1)(b)* (as amended by the *2007 Regulations* and the *2010 Regulations*) where an employment agency or business offers to provide or arrange additional charged for services they are required to provide (i) the amount or method of calculation of the fee (ii) the identity of the person to whom the fee is or will be payable(iii) a description of the services or goods to which the fee relates and a statement of the work-seeker's right to cancel or withdraw from the service and the notice period required and (iv) the circumstances, if any, in which refunds or rebates are payable to the work-seeker, the scale of such refunds or rebates, and if no refunds or rebates are payable, a statement to that effect.

By *reg 12* there are prohibitions on employment businesses withholding payment to work-seekers on certain grounds. By *reg 14* employment businesses are required to obtain agreement to terms with work-seekers, which terms must be recorded in documentary form. In relation to a work-seeker, terms must be agreed in advance of provision of services in one document or a number of documents given at the same time (*reg 14(2)*). The terms of engagement can only be varied with the work-seeker's consent and the variation must be agreed in writing (*reg 14(4), (5)*). When terms have been agreed, the employment business cannot threaten to withdraw its services in order to induce the work-seeker to accept a variation to the terms of business (*reg 14(6)*). It should be noted that the obligations under *reg 14* no longer apply to employment agencies after 1 October 2010. This was one of the amendments to ease administrative burdens introduced by the *2010 Regulations*.

Also in the case of employment businesses, the written terms must state whether the work-seeker is to be an employee of the business (*reg 15*). The terms must also specify the terms of employment, including notice periods, holidays and holiday pay and remuneration intervals. There must be an undertaking from the employment business to pay the agreed rate of pay (even if the hirer does not pay) and the level of remuneration must be specified (or at least the minimum rate expected to be obtained) (*reg 15*).

By *reg 16* employment agencies are required to obtain agreement from the work-seeker as to the terms which will apply, including details of services to be provided, the agency's authority to act for the work-seeker and details of fees. It should be noted that this provision only applies to any work-finding services for which the employment agency is permitted by *reg 26(1)* to charge a fee.

In relation to the hirer, the written terms with an employment business are governed by *reg 17*. The terms must be agreed in advance and must include a statement that the employment business is operating as an employment business with the hirer. Variations must be recorded in writing and details of fees payable, refund provisions and refund scales must be set out. For employment businesses a procedure to cover the situation of unsatisfactory workers must be specified. Again it should be noted that *reg 17* no longer applies to employment agencies by the amendments made by the *2010 Regulations*.

The *2003 Regulations* (as amended) contain detailed provisions in relation to the charging for the services of an employment agency or employment business. In general, employment agencies and businesses are prohibited from charging a fee to work-seekers for finding a job. Under the *Employment Agencies Act 1973* it is not unlawful to charge for certain services such as training or assistance with CV drafting and the like. By *reg 5* it is, however, unlawful to insist that a work-seeker avails themselves of such additional services as a condition for the provision of employment business services. Where the worker uses such services as are not unlawful under the *Act* by *reg 5(2)* (added by the *2007 Regulations*), the agency or business must ensure that the work-seeker is able to cancel or withdraw from those services at any time without incurring any detriment or penalty, subject to the work-seeker giving to the provider of those services in paper form or by electronic means notice of five business days or, for services relating to the provision of living accommodation, notice of ten business days. In the case of employment as an actor, background artist, dancer, extra, musician, singer or other performer or as a photographic or fashion model, where that work-seeker uses a service for which the *Act* does not prohibit the charging of a fee, then *reg 5(3)* provides for a 30 day cooling off period during which the agency or the employment business shall not charge a fee to a work-seeker for that part of the service which consists of providing photographs, audio or video recording of the work-seeker. Further, the work-seeker shall be entitled without detriment or penalty to cancel or withdraw from any contract with the agency or employment business for such a service with immediate effect by informing the agency or employment business of cancellation or withdrawal. Where the work-seeker informs the agency or employment business of cancellation or withdrawal the work-seeker has no obligation to make any payment under the contract.

Reg 6 restricts an employment business or agency from taking detrimental action relating to work-seekers working elsewhere and *reg 7* restricts employment businesses from providing work-seekers in cases of industrial disputes. *Reg 8* restricts agencies and employment businesses from purporting to act on a different basis (eg purporting to be an agency when in fact acting as a business). *Reg 10* restricts the charging of certain fees to hirers and *reg 11* limits the entering into of contracts on behalf of clients.

Limited exceptions to the general principles apply in relation to employment agencies who deal with actors, musicians, models, sportspersons and those engaged in the creative arts, film or theatrical businesses such as composers, writers, artists, directors, production managers and the like (see *Sch 3* to the *Regulations* as amended). Even in these categories, the practice of demanding payment of fees in advance of securing an engagement is, in the main, prohibited (see *regs 26(3), (5)* and *(6)* as amended) along with the practice of charging both the work-seeker and the hirer a fee. The *2007 Regulations* add a seven day 'cooling off period' in which work seekers may cancel or withdraw from any contract to include their details in a publication without detriment or penalty. Agencies thus cannot take a fee for including a work seeker in a publication until after seven days from the work seeker entering into a contract with the agency (*reg 26(5)(d)*).

The *2003 Regulations* permit charges to be made to hirers on a broader basis. One important area of limitation is, however, in relation to 'transfer fees' (ie where a hirer wishes to permanently engage a temporary worker supplied by an employment business or where the hirer wishes to re-engage the worker through a different employment business). In the light of concerns about such fees being an unhelpful restriction on the provision of labour, the *Regulations* limit transfer fees as follows: in cases of workers becoming permanent employees, transfer fees may only be charged if the hirer employs the worker within eight weeks of the end of the engagement or within 14 weeks of the start of the assignment. Further, the contract between the employment business and the hirer must provide the option for the hirer to extend the period of the original hire on no less favourable terms (*reg 10*).

Part IV of the *2003 Regulations* makes provision for requirements to be satisfied in relation to the introduction or supply of a work-seeker to a hirer (see *regs 18–22*). The *Regulations* impose minimum obligations on the employment agency or employment business to take steps to ensure that the work-seeker is suitable and also that the hirer is suitable (see *reg 20*). In relation to the work-seeker the employment business or agency must obtain confirmation of identity and willingness to perform the role (*regs 19, 21(1)(a)(i)*). Where an employment business receives information relevant to the suitability of a worker supplied it must inform the hirer or terminate the engagement (*reg 20(2), (3), (4)*). Similar provisions apply in relation to an employment agency (*reg 20(5), (6)*). Further obligations arise in relation to checking professional qualifications (*reg 22*) and in relation to suitability for working with vulnerable persons (*reg 22*). Information about the post, health and safety risks, qualifications required and rates payable and other terms of engagement must be obtained by the agency or employment business from the hirer (*reg 18*) and the employment business or agency should ensure that the hirer has carried out an adequate risk assessment for health and safety purposes. In relation to assignments of five consecutive days or less the administrative burden in relation to provision of information is reduced (*regs 21(4)* and *(5)*). Written notifications must still however be provided to the hirer in relation to the name of the work-seeker and confirmation of identity and experience and to the work-seeker in relation to the identity of the hirer, the nature of the business and the duration or likely duration of the work.

Further, an employment business or agency must not withhold pay due to a work-seeker in a number of circumstances (including that the hirer has not paid the employment business) (see *reg 12*) and must not disclose information relating to the work-seeker without prior consent, save for the purposes of providing the job finding services or for legal proceedings or to professional bodies relevant to the work-seeker (*reg 28*). An employment agency or business may not subject a work-seeker to any detriment on the ground that the work-seeker has terminated the contract or given notice to terminate the contract and cannot require a work-seeker to provide information as to the identity of future employers (*reg 6*).

As to work-seekers who provide their services via limited companies, the provisions of the *Regulations* were, by *reg 32(1)*, extended to this category of work-seeker with effect from 6 July 2004. The work-seeker is the limited company providing the individual's services and the individual is termed the 'person supplied by the work-seeker to carry out the work'. In this category the worker with a service company may opt out of the application of the *Regulations*. Any such opt out must be signed by the individual and the company before any assignment starts (*reg 32(9)*). By an amendment made by the *2007 Regulations* the agency or employment business must inform the hirer that such an opt-out agreement exists so that the *Regulations* do not apply. The opt-out option does not apply to engagements which involve working with vulnerable groups such as children and the elderly (*reg 32(12)*).

Breach of the *Regulations* (or breach of the *Employment Agencies Act 1973*) resulting in damage is actionable in the civil courts (*reg 30(1)*) and an employment agency or employment business which breaches the *Regulations* may be liable to prosecution and a fine (*Employment Agencies Act 1973, s 5(2)*). By *reg 31(1), (2)* contractual terms in agreements with work-seekers or hirers which are prohibited by the *Regulations* are unenforceable and transfer fees which are in breach of the *Regulations* are liable to be repaid.

45.10 Further likely reform

On 17 January 2013 the government commenced consultation on further reform to the regulatory framework applying to employment agencies and employment businesses. The consultation document "Recruitment Sector Legislation: Consultation on reforming the regulatory framework for employment agencies and employment business" (www.gov.uk/government/uploads/system/uploads/attachment_data/file/52049/
13-530-recruitment-sector-legislation-consultation-on-reforming-regulatory
-framework.pdf) records that the government consider the existing *Regulations* and the *Employment Agencies Act 1973* to be complicated and difficult for businesses and individuals to understand and proposes a new system with minimum regulation and increased sector self regulation. It is proposed that four key aims should guide new legislation, namely (i) that restrictions on employment agencies and employment businesses charging fees to work seekers be retained, (ii) that there be clarity on who is responsible for paying temporary workers, (iii) contracts with recruitment firms should not hinder freedom of movement between jobs and (iv) that work seekers have confidence in the sector and are able to assert their rights. Consultation closed on 11 April 2013 and a response to the consultation is expected twelve weeks thereafter.

45.11 The application of the National Minimum Wage

The *National Minimum Wage Act 1998*, applies to all workers (as defined in *s 54(3)*). By *s 34* of the *National Minimum Wage Act 1998*, agency workers shall have the right to the National Minimum Wage in relation to whichever of the parties (agent or principal) is responsible for paying or actually pays the worker (see further PAY – I **(32)**). On the new power to share relevant information between enforcement officers under the Employment Agency and NMW regimes see *s 18* of the *Employment Act 2008* and **45.7** above.

45.12 Employees

A temporary employee may accrue sufficient qualifying employment to present a complaint of unfair dismissal. If at the outset of his employment it was made clear to him that he was only engaged on a temporary basis, the employer's refusal to renew his temporary contract should be considered to be for a substantial reason falling within *ERA 1996, s 98(1)(b)* and may well be considered fair. (See *Fay v North Yorkshire County Council* [1986] ICR 133 approving *Terry v East Sussex County Council* [1977] 1 All ER 567.) The dismissal of replacement employees, taken on in place of permanent employees on medical suspension or absent because of pregnancy or confinement, will be considered to be for a reason falling within *s 98(1)(b)* provided that the dismissal is effected so as to allow the permanent employee to resume his original work, and provided that the dismissed employee was informed in writing at the time of the engagement that the employment was temporary and would be terminated when the permanent employee returned (*ERA 1996, s 106*). The Tribunal will then go on to decide whether the dismissal was fair within the meaning of *ERA 1996, s 98(4)(b)*. See also the provisions of the *Fixed-Term Employees (Prevention of Less Favourable Treatment) Regulations 2002 (SI 2002/2034)* (below at **45.14**).

45.13 SEASONAL WORKERS

Workers taken on for a limited period of time, such as seasonal sales staff or extra staff taken on to deal with the tourist season, are considered to be employees for all purposes. They enjoy all the normal employment protection rights provided that they have the necessary qualifying periods of employment.

Where such an employee is dismissed when the seasonal demand has ended, the fact that he was only taken on as a seasonal worker will not automatically make the dismissal fair. It is merely one of the circumstances which must be taken into account by an Employment Tribunal in deciding whether the employer acted reasonably (see UNFAIR DISMISSAL – II (52)). Also, a seasonal worker must be given at least the statutory minimum period of notice to terminate his contract of employment, unless the contract was for a fixed term (see **46.7** TERMINATION OF EMPLOYMENT).

If the period of unemployment between seasons is short and the employee is habitually re-engaged, his continuity of employment may be preserved during the period of his absence due to the temporary cessation of work (*ERA 1996, s 212(3)(b)*). (See **7.6** CONTINUOUS EMPLOYMENT, *Fitzgerald v Hall, Russell & Co Ltd* [1970] AC 984, *Ford v Warwickshire County Council* [1983] ICR 273 *Sillars v Charringtons Fuels Ltd* [1989] ICR 475, *Prater v Cornwall County Council* [2006] EWCA Civ 102, [2006] IRLR 362 and see also *Hellyer Bros Ltd v McLeod* [1987] ICR 526.)

Employers should therefore take just as much care to comply with all the applicable employment rules regarding seasonal staff as they do in the case of their permanent staff. See also the provisions of the *Fixed-Term Employees (Prevention of Less Favourable Treatment) Regulations 2002 (SI 2002/2034)* (below at **45.14**).

45.14 FIXED-TERM EMPLOYEES (PREVENTION OF LESS FAVOURABLE TREATMENT) REGULATIONS 2002 (SI 2002/2034)

In the case of employees who are engaged for a fixed period or for a particular task the *Fixed-Term Employees (Prevention of Less Favourable Treatment) Regulations 2002 (SI 2002/2034) ('the Regulations')* provide important rights to ensure that these employees are not less favourably treated than employees who are permanent or employed for an unlimited duration. The provisions of the Regulations came into force on 1 October 2002 and are derived from the *Fixed-Term Work Directive 99/70/EC*. Current guidance may be found at www.businesslink.gov.uk/bdotg/action/layer?topicId=1081853623&r.lc=en&r.s=sl and www.direct.gov.uk/en/Employment/Understandingyourworkstatus. The guidance, unfortunately, is not as detailed as the previous BERR guidance referenced in earlier editions.

A fixed term contract is defined under the *Regulations (reg 1)* as a contract of employment that under its provisions will terminate (a) on the expiry of a specific term (b) on the completion of a particular task or (c) on the occurrence or non occurrence of any other specific event other than the attainment by the employee of any normal and bona fide retirement age. Thus (a) covers, say, an engagement for six months, (b) covers engagement to undertake a specific task (cf **45.12** above) and (c) is apt to cover the situation where an employee is engaged to cover for an absent employee until their return to work (eg following, say, a period of maternity absence). If a contract is to terminate on expiry of a specific term then the fact that there is also provision for earlier termination by notice does not prevent the contract being a fixed term contract for the purpose of the Regulations (*Allen v National Australia Group Europe Ltd* [2004] IRLR 847, EAT).

Certain employments are excluded from the protection afforded by the *Regulations* including apprentices, those on work experience and the armed forces (*regs 14, 18, 20*). The most significant exclusion, perhaps, is contained in *reg 19* whereby 'agency workers' are excluded from the protection of the *Regulations*. Agency worker means any person who is supplied by an employment business to do work for another person under a contract or other arrangements made between the employment business and the other person. 'Employment Business' for the purpose of the *Regulations* means 'the business . . . of supplying persons in the *employment* of the person carrying on the business, to act for, and under the control of, other persons in any capacity' (emphasis added (*reg 19(3)*). In the light of the complexity of the law relating to the issue of when an agency worker is employed by the agency (see **45.2** above) it appears likely that the ambit of this exclusion will be uncertain and highly likely to lead to continued litigation of the issue of who in fact employs an agency worker. In relation to agency workers the extent of the exclusion and its relationship with rights to statutory sick pay (SSP) was considered by the Court of Appeal in *Revenue and Customs Comrs v Thorn Baker Ltd* [2007] EWCA Civ 626, [2008] ICR 46. In the result agency workers engaged on a contract for less than three months continue to be excluded from the right to SSP.

The *Regulations* introduce the concept of a 'comparable permanent employee' (*reg 2*) who is, in relation to the fixed term employee, employed by the same employer and engaged in the same or broadly similar work having regard, where relevant, to whether they have a similar level of qualification or skill. The comparable permanent employee is to be employed at the same establishment as the fixed term employee or, if no suitable comparator exists at the establishment at which the fixed term employee is engaged, at another of the employer's establishments.

By *reg 3* the fixed term employee has the right not to be treated less favourably than a comparable permanent employee as regards terms of the contract or by being subjected to any detriment by the employer. The right includes the right not to be less favourably treated in relation to any period of service qualification relating to any particular condition of service, any opportunity to receive training or the opportunity to secure any permanent position in the establishment (*reg 3(2)*). The Court of Appeal in *Department of Work and Pensions v Webley* [2004] EWCA Civ 1745, [2005] IRLR 288 held that the non-renewal of a fixed-term contract, of itself, is not capable of involving less favourable treatment for the purpose of the Regulations. In that case fixed term workers had their contracts terminated after 51 weeks as a matter of policy regardless of whether there was an ongoing need for work or not.

Guidance on the structured approach to be taken by employment tribunals under the *Regulations* is provided by *Manchester College v Cocliff* (UKEAT/0035/10/CEA) [2010] All ER (D) 92 (Sep). The claimant employee had worked as a part-time lecturer at the employer college on a succession of fixed-term contracts since March 2005. He claimed that the terms of his employment were less favourable than those of a comparator employed on a permanent basis. The EAT held that an employment tribunal must first determine if the claimant and comparator were engaged in the same or broadly similar work. If so, it must then consider whether the less favourable treatment was on the ground that the claimant was a fixed term employee. Only if the second question is answered affirmatively is there a need to consider objective justification. In *Cocliff* the tribunal erred in considering the question of whether the less favourable treatment was justified before it had considered the reason for the treatment. Further the tribunal erred in rejecting justification based on differences in the jobs. The finding that the work was broadly similar does not preclude justification based upon such differences as do exist. The question is whether they are sufficient to justify the different treatment.

In relation to the opportunity to secure permanent positions, the fixed term employee has the right to be informed of available vacancies in the establishment by the employer (*reg 3(6), (7)*). The protection against less favourable treatment applies only if the treatment in issue is on the grounds that the employee is a fixed term employee and the treatment is not justified on objective grounds (*reg 3(3)*). Thus, for example, if an employer pays a fixed term employee at a lower rate than comparable permanent employees by reason of the fixed term status, this may (but not must) be less favourable treatment which the employer may have to objectively justify. On the application of the *Fixed-Term Work Directive 99/70/EC* and, hence, the *Regulations* (as a matter of purposive construction) to issues of inequality of pay see the ECJ's decision in *Del Cerro Alonso v Osakidetza-Servicio Vasco de Salud*: C-307/05 [2007] 3 CMLR 1492, [2008] ICR 145. In *Impact v Minister for Agriculture and Food*: C-268/06 [2008] IRLR 552 ECJ the principles in *Del Cerro* are developed, holding that *cl 4* of the Directive must be interpreted to cover not only pay but also pensions and thus exclusion from such rights will require objective justification. The ECJ in *Impact* (and in *Zentralbetriebsrat der Landeskrankenhäuser Tirols v Land Tirol*: C-486/08 [2010] IRLR 631) also held that *cl 4* was precise enough to be directly effective at national level but *cl 5* (on successive contracts) was not directly effective but nevertheless provided a guide to interpretation. Also, the ECJ held that employment adjudicating bodies (ie the employment tribunals in the UK) must have jurisdiction to hear directly arguments based on the Directive. See also *Gavieiro v Conselleria de Educacion e Ordinacion Universitaria del la Xunta de Galicia*: C-444/09 [2011] IRLR 504 (ECJ) in which an argument that the inevitably temporary nature of fixed term employment could itself objectively justify unequal treatment was (unsurprisingly) rejected but which also upheld the direct effect of *art 4* of the Framework Agreement on fixed term work so that it could be relied upon during a period of failure to implement the Directive.

Similarly, if, say, the employer limits certain facilities to permanent staff such as health care or other benefits, this may (but not must) be less favourable treatment of the fixed term employee which may require objective justification if it is to be permissible. It is not every difference in treatment, however, that will amount to less favourable treatment. *Regulation 3(5)* is an important provision which provides that, in order to determine whether a fixed term employee has been treated less favourably than a comparator, the 'pro rata' principle shall be applied unless it is inappropriate. The pro rata principle is defined in *reg 1* as follows:

> "where a comparable permanent employee receives or is entitled to pay or any other benefit, a fixed term employee is to receive or be entitled to such proportion of that pay or other benefit as is reasonable in the circumstances having regard to the length of his contract of employment and to the terms on which the pay or other benefit is offered."

Regulation 4 provides an important gloss on objective justification providing that, in the event of less favourable treatment of a fixed term employee as regards any term in his contract, that treatment is to be regarded as objectively justified if the terms of the fixed term employee's contract 'taken as a whole' are at least as favourable as the comparator's contract of employment. Thus it is appropriate to look at the whole employment package afforded to the fixed term employee and not to concentrate on any single term when considering objective justification of contractual differences.

By *reg 5* a fixed term employee has the right to request in writing a statement from the employer setting out the reasons for any treatment in issue. That statement is to be provided within 21 days of the request (*reg 5(1)*). The statement is admissible in evidence before an employment tribunal (*reg 5(2)*) and failure to provide a statement without reasonable excuse or provision of an evasive or equivocal statement permits the tribunal to draw such inferences as appear just and equitable including an inference that the right in question has been infringed (*reg 5(3)*).

By *reg 6* a fixed term employee who is dismissed by reason of (i) bringing proceedings or (ii) giving evidence in relation to proceedings under the *Regulations*, or (iii) requesting a statement of reasons or (iv) alleging that the employer had contravened the *Regulations* or (v) doing anything under the *Regulations* or (vi) refusing forego a right conferred by the *Regulations*, is to be regarded as having been unfairly dismissed for the purposes of *Part 10* of the *ERA*. (See *reg 6(3)*). If the fixed term employee is dismissed in contravention of *reg 6*, then no qualifying period of service applies for the purposes of the *ERA*: see *ERA s 108(3)(j)*. By *reg 6(2)* a fixed term worker has the right not to be subjected to any detriment for like reasons to those applying to dismissal (see *reg 6(3)*).

The right to present complaints to the employment tribunal is set out in *reg 7* and the normal three month time limit subject to just and equitable extension applies (*reg 7(2), (3)*). By *reg 7(6)* it is for the employer to identify the ground for the less favourable treatment or detriment. If an employment tribunal finds a complaint well founded it may provide a declaration as to the claimant's right and may award compensation assessed on the just and equitable basis including compensation for any loss suffered by the claimant (*reg 7(8), (9)*). Infringement of *reg 3* (Less favourable treatment) shall not, however, include an injury to feelings award (*reg 7(10)*). The employment tribunal also has power to make recommendations for the purpose of obviating or reducing the adverse effect on the complainant (*reg 7(7)(c)*). Failure without reasonable justification to comply with such recommendations may lead to an increase in the award of compensation (*reg 7(13)*).

An important right arises under *reg 8* to deal with the situation of persons employed on a succession of purported fixed-term contracts or a lengthy fixed term contract which is renewed. *Regulation 8* provides that, where a fixed term employee has been continuously employed under (i) a single fixed-term contract which is renewed or (ii) a number of fixed term contracts for a total period of four years or more and where continuity of employment is preserved, then the employee will become a permanent employee unless the employer can show objective justification (*reg 8(2)*). For the purposes of determining continuous employment *Chapter 1* of *Part 14* of the *ERA* is applied (*reg 8(4)*) (See also CONTINUOUS EMPLOYMENT (6)).

In *Duncombe and Fletcher v Secretary of State for Children Schools and Families* [2011] UKSC 14 the Supreme Court considered the applicability and effect of reg 8 of the Regulations. The case involved employment at European Schools in other member States. Such schools have a rule that teachers may only be employed for 9 years (a two year contract followed by contracts of three and four years). In the EAT and Court of Appeal the decision of the tribunal that objective justification for the 9 year rule was not made out was upheld on appeal. In the Supreme Court it was held that the case had proceeded on the wrong basis. The purpose of the Regulations was not to prevent fixed term contracts but to prevent discrimination against fixed term workers. The focus of *reg 8* was whether the use of the current fixed term contract (if that current contract took the overall period of employment over four years) was objectively justifiable. The issue was not whether the "nine year rule" as a maximum period for employment of the teachers was objectively justified. Indeed it would have been wholly permissible to have engaged the teachers on one nine year fixed term contract from the outset. Understood in this way objective justification of the final (current contract) was made out: "It is not [the nine year rule] which requires to be justified, but the use of the latest fixed-term contract bringing the total period up to nine years. And that can readily be justified by the existence of the nine year rule. The teachers were employed to do a particular job which could only last for nine years. The Secretary of State could not foist those teachers on the schools for a longer period, no matter how unjustifiable either he or the employment tribunals of this country thought the rule to be" (per Baroness Hale at para 25). Given this finding it was not necessary to determine the subsidiary issue as to whether the Regulations in fact could apply to employees engaged in other member States, although Baroness Hale stated (para 33) that she "would be inclined to agree with the Tribunals and the Court of Appeal that Mr Duncombe and other teachers employed by the Secretary of State in European schools abroad are covered by the Fixed-term Regulations". Finally, the case raised issues of unfair dismissal jurisdiction and the application of *Lawson v Serco* principles and on these issues the Supreme Court reserved judgment.

45.14 Temporary and Seasonal Employees

It should be noted, in the context of the application of *reg 8*, that any period of continuous employment prior to 10 July 2002 does not count for the purposes of *reg 8*. The effect is that from 10 July 2006 and thereafter those who have been employed on two or more successive fixed term contracts for four or more years will be deemed to be permanent employees absent objective justification. On objective justification see the judgment of the ECJ in *Adeneler v Ellinikos Organismos Galaktos*: C-212/04 [2006] IRLR 716 in which the compatibility of Greek legislation on fixed–term work with the *Fixed-Term Work Directive 99/70/EC* and Framework Agreement was considered. The ECJ held that 'objective reasons' requiring the use of fixed-term contacts required justification by specific factors relating to the particular activity carried out and the conditions under which it is carried out. What is required is 'precise and concrete circumstances characterising a given activity, which are therefore capable in that particular context of justifying the use of successive fixed term contracts'. The ECJ explained that these 'circumstances' may arise from the specific nature of the tasks undertaken or their inherent characteristics or from the pursuit of a legitimate social policy objective of a Member State. See also *Zentralbetriebsrat der Landeskrankenhäuser Tirols v Land Tirol*: C-486/08 [2010] IRLR 631. In *Secretary of State for Children, Schools and Families v Fletcher* [2008] 3 CMLR 1462, [2009] ICR 102 the issue of objective justification was considered in relation to *reg 8* in a domestic context where a teacher at a European School succeeded in establishing permanent status by the use of *reg 8* despite provisions to the effect that, under the relevant treaty provisions setting up the school, a teacher's secondment could not exceed nine years. In *Hudson v Department for Work and Pension* [2013] IRLR 32 (CA) the claimant relied on a series of fixed term contracts with the DWP in order to claim a declaration in accordance with *reg 8* that she had become a permanent employee. The final contract in the series was not covered by *reg 18* (which disapplies the *Regulations* in cases of employment on a scheme to provide training) but the earlier contracts fell within the *reg 18* exclusion. The EAT had held that, as *reg 18* used the present tense, it only applied to a current contract and not the earlier ones with the result that they could count towards the requisite four year period of service for the purposes of *reg 8*. Reversing the EAT ([2012] IRLR 900) the Court of Appeal by majority held that that *reg 18* when engaged totally disapplies the *Regulations* so that any period of employment falling under *reg 18* cannot count towards the period of four years continuous employment required to convert the contract into a permanent one under *reg 8*.

Reg 8 may be modified or excluded by a collective agreement or workforce agreement *(reg 8(5))*. A fixed term worker, however, may not individually contract out of his rights under the Regulations save as is permitted under *s 203* of the *ERA*.

By *reg 9* an employee who considers that by application of *reg 8* he is a permanent employee may request a written statement from the employer confirming his permanent employee status. Such a statement is to be provided within 21 days and must either confirm the change in status or provide reasons why it is said the employee remains a fixed term employee *(reg 9(1), (2))*. If the employer intends to rely upon objective justification the grounds must be specified in the statement *(reg 9(2))*. The statement is admissible in any court proceedings *(reg 9(3))* and failure to provide a statement or evasive or equivocal replies permit adverse inferences to be drawn *(reg 9(4))*. An employee who considers himself to be a permanent employee by virtue of *reg 8* may apply to the employment tribunal for a declaration to that effect *(reg 9(5))* but prior to making an application for the declaration the employee must have sought or obtained a statement pursuant to *reg 9(1) (reg 9(6)(a))*. Finally, at the time of the application for the declaration the employee must be employed by the employer and accordingly 'historical' applications for a declaration by former employees are not to be entertained *(reg 9(6)(b))*.

The *Regulations* make provision for vicarious liability of the employer for the acts of its employees and agents *(reg 12(1), (2))* subject to a defence for the employer to prove that it took such steps as were reasonably practicable to prevent the employee doing the act or acts of that description in the course of his employment *(reg 12(3))*.

46   Termination of Employment

46.1   A contract of employment may be terminated in several ways: by mutual agreement; by frustration; by expiry; by dismissal by the employer; by notice given by the employee; or by acceptance of a fundamental repudiatory breach of contract by the employer or the employee. The distinction between these different modes of termination may be of importance in determining whether the employee may bring a claim for UNFAIR DISMISSAL – I (51), WRONGFUL DISMISSAL (56) or REDUNDANCY – I (36).

The death of either party terminates the contract of employment, unless the contract expressly or impliedly provides otherwise. The bankruptcy of the employer does not operate as a dissolution of the contracts of employment between himself and his employees, but in general the winding-up of a company and the dissolution of a partnership do operate to terminate the contract (see, eg *Briggs v Oates* [1990] ICR 473, holding that the expiration of the partnership represented a breach of the employee's contract, but suggesting that mere departures from, and additions to, a body of partners would not have such an effect). This is subject to the effect of the *Transfer of Undertakings (Protection of Employment) Regulations 2006 (SI 2006/246)* (see TRANSFER OF UNDERTAKINGS (50)).

It may be held in a particular case that, where an employee starts to work for his old employer in a new capacity, then the old contract has come to an end and has been replaced by a new one. Whether or not this is so is a question of degree (*Hogg v Dover College* [1990] ICR 39; *Alcan Extrusions v Yates* [1996] IRLR 327; and, more recently, *Smith v Trafford Housing Trust* [2013] IRLR 86 where the demotion of an employee, and a reduction in his salary, as a disciplinary sanction for posting a comment about gay marriage on his Facebook wall was held to be a (wrongful) termination of the earlier contract).

46.2   MUTUAL AGREEMENT

Termination by agreement between employer and employee may be effected either orally or in writing. The agreement to terminate may take effect on any day in the month or year, and does not have to coincide with a pay-day.

The courts will scrutinise an apparent agreement to terminate if the employee alleges that he was given no choice but to consent to the ending of his employment. The general principle which the courts will apply is that if the cause of the employee's willingness to agree to the termination of his employment is the threat of dismissal, he will be held to have been dismissed. If, however, other additional factors, such as financial inducements, affected his decision he will be taken to have resigned by mutual agreement. He will then not be entitled to bring any claim for unfair or wrongful dismissal.

In *Sheffield v Oxford Controls Co Ltd* [1979] ICR 396, the employee was told that if he did not resign he would be dismissed. He signed an agreement to resign in return for certain financial benefits. The Employment Appeal Tribunal found that he had resigned and had not been dismissed because his resignation had been brought about not by the threat of dismissal but by other factors such as the offer of financial benefits. See also *Birch v University of Liverpool* [1985] ICR 470, *Scott v Coalite Fuels and Chemicals Ltd* [1988] ICR 355, *Hellyer Bros Ltd v Atkinson and Dickinson* [1992] IRLR 540 and *Optare Group Ltd v Transport and General Workers' Union* [2007] IRLR 931.

The authorities were reviewed in *Sandhu v Jan de Rijk Transport Ltd* [2007] ICR 1137. On the facts of that case, the Court of Appeal held that the employee had not resigned even though he had entered into a severance agreement. The employee had been invited to a meeting at which he was told, without prior warning, that he was being dismissed. During the course of the meeting, the parties agreed severance terms. However, the employee had not received any legal advice and had no opportunity to reflect on matters. In reaching an agreement, he had simply done his best to 'salvage what he could from the inevitable fact that he was going to be dismissed'. Furthermore, the severance terms were not particularly favourable to him (three months' salary, and the short term retention of the use of the employer's car and mobile phone).

Also, in *Caledonian Mining Co Ltd v Bassett* [1987] ICR 425, an employer who dishonestly persuaded his employees to resign was treated as having dismissed them. The dishonesty in that case was held by the employment tribunal to consist of a preconceived arrangement designed by the employers to avoid liability for redundancy payments.

An agreement for the automatic termination of a contract of employment on the occurrence of a certain event may be ineffective to exclude entitlement to statutory employment protection rights because of *ERA 1996, s 203(1)* (see **51.19** UNFAIR DISMISSAL – I).

46.3   FRUSTRATION

Frustration occurs where the performance of the contract of employment becomes impossible or substantially different from that which the parties contemplated at the time of entering into the agreement by reason of an unforeseen and unprovided for event which has occurred without the fault or default of either party to the contract (*Paal Wilson & Co A/S v Partenreederei Hannah Blumenthal* [1983] 1 AC 854 at 909). A contract will be terminated by frustration if performance becomes unlawful (eg by the passing of a statute after the contract is made). The question of termination of a contract of employment by reason of frustration most frequently arises in cases of absence of the employee because of illness or imprisonment. Where the contract is frustrated, there is no dismissal (the essence of frustration is that in law termination is *automatic*), and hence no possible claim for wrongful or unfair dismissal or redundancy. The employee will be able to recover for services rendered prior to the frustrating event, relying if necessary upon *Law Reform (Frustrated Contracts) Act 1943, s 1(3)*.

In *Williams v Watsons Luxury Coaches Ltd* [1990] ICR 536, the EAT drew together the principles of the doctrine of frustration as they apply to contracts of employment. At 541, Wood J held that the following principles applied to cases of frustration by reason of illness:

> 'First, that the court must guard against too easy an application of the doctrine, more especially when redundancy occurs and also when the true situation may be a dismissal by reason of disability. Secondly, that although it is not necessary to decide that frustration occurred on a particular date, nevertheless an attempt to decide the relevant date is far from a useless exercise as it may help to determine in the mind of the court whether it really is a true frustration situation. Thirdly, that there are a number of factors which may help to decide the issue as they may each point in one or other direction. These we take from the judgment of Phillips J in *Egg Stores (Stamford Hill) Ltd v Leibovici* [1977] ICR 260, 265:

" . . . Among the matters to be taken into account in such a case in reaching a decision are these: (1) the length of the previous employment; (2) how long it had been expected that the employment would continue; (3) the nature of the job; (4) the nature, length and effect of the illness or disabling event; (5) the need of the employer for the work to be done, and the need for a replacement to do it; (6) the risk to the employer of acquiring obligations in respect of redundancy payments or compensation for unfair dismissal to the replacement employee; (7) whether wages have continued to be paid; (8) the acts and the statements of the employer in relation to the employment, including the dismissal of, or failure to dismiss, the employee; and (9) whether in all the circumstances a reasonable employer could be expected to wait any longer."

To these we would add the terms of the contract as to the provisions for sickness pay, if any, and also, a consideration of the prospects of recovery. Fourthly – see *FC Shepherd & Co Ltd v Jerrom* [1986] ICR 802 – the party alleging frustration should not be allowed to rely upon the frustrating event if that event was caused by that party – at least where it was caused by its fault.'

For earlier cases of frustration of the contract due to illness, see *Marshall v Harland and Wolff Ltd* [1972] ICR 101; *Hart v AR Marshall & Sons (Bulwell) Ltd* [1977] ICR 539; *Egg Stores (Stamford Hill) Ltd v Leibovici* [1977] ICR 260; and *Notcutt v Universal Equipment Co (London) Ltd* [1986] ICR 414. For frustration of the contract of employment due to imprisonment, see *FC Shepherd & Co Ltd v Jerrom* [1986] ICR 802, in which the Court of Appeal held that a contract of employment was capable of being frustrated by the imposition of a custodial sentence.

In *Four Seasons Healthcare Ltd (formerly Cotswold Spa Retirement Hotels Ltd) v Maughan* [2005] IRLR 324, on the other hand, the EAT held that bail conditions which effectively prevented a registered mental nurse from attending work at a care home did not constitute a 'frustrating event'. The EAT noted that it was unaware of similar cases which supported an argument for 'frustration', and further that the employer had the opportunity, of dismissing the employee, if it so wished.

The rule that frustration could not be induced by a party's own default applied only to the party alleging that frustration had occurred.

The doctrine of frustration was analysed by Gray J in *Gryf-Lowczowski (Jan) v Hinchingbrooke Healthcare NHS Trust* [2005] EWHC 2407 (QB), [2006] IRLR 100. The case concerned a consultant general and colorectal surgeon who, following a referral to the National Clinical Assessment Authority, had been on special leave from work for almost two years and could not resume his duties at the employing trust until he had undergone a period of training at another trust. The employer sought to argue that the contract of employment had been frustrated. This was rejected by Gray J who stressed that, in looking at point (9) (in the *Leibovici*) case, where the employment was of such a nature that its termination by frustration would have a 'catastrophic' effect on the employee of making it highly unlikely that he would find work again as a medical practitioner within the NHS, it would be reasonable to expect an employer to wait rather longer than might be the case in other circumstances before the contract was held to be frustrated.

On the facts of that case, Gray J held that the crucial question for the Court was whether there remained a realistic possibility that a placement could be found to enable the employee to be re-skilled and thereafter to resume his former duties with the employer. Gray J held that there was such a possibility, and so the contract was not frustrated.

Where a contract of employment has been brought to an end by reason of 'frustration' (ie performance of the contract becomes impossible or substantially different from that contemplated by the parties at inception without fault on either side), the parties cannot thereafter agree that the contract continues to subsist: see *G F Sharp & Co Ltd v McMillan* [1998] IRLR 632. In that case, a joiner lost the use of his left hand and could never work for his employer in that capacity again. Although the parties agreed to keep the employee 'on the books' so that he could gain access to greater pension benefits, the EAT held that this did not amount to a continuation of the contract of employment. The contract had been nullified by the employee's injury. As a consequence, the employee was not entitled to notice of termination of his employment or payment in lieu.

46.4   EXPIRY

If a contract is for a fixed period, it will automatically terminate at the end of that period. No notice need be given. It should be noted that, for the purposes of a claim for redundancy pay or in respect of unfair dismissal, the expiry of a fixed-term contract may nevertheless constitute a dismissal (see **36.7** REDUNDANCY – I and **51.4–51.6** UNFAIR DISMISSAL – I). If an employee remains in his employment after the expiry of the term, he will be considered to be working under the same terms and conditions as before, save only that his employment is subject to an implied term that it can be terminated by either party upon giving reasonable notice (see **46.6** below).

46.5 DISMISSAL BY THE EMPLOYER

'Dismissal' is here used in its popular sense, to mean termination of a contract of employment by the employer. For the purposes of the unfair dismissal and redundancy payments legislation, the concept of dismissal is given a special statutory meaning which includes both the expiry of a fixed-term contract without its renewal and 'constructive dismissal' (see **36.7** REDUNDANCY – I and **51.4** UNFAIR DISMISSAL – I).

Sometimes there may be a dispute as to whether the words used by the employer (or the employee in the case of a resignation) in fact amount to a dismissal. Where those words are ambiguous, the court or tribunal should ask how they would have been understood by a reasonable listener in the circumstances (*Sothern v Franks Charlesly & Co* [1981] IRLR 278).

A party who has used unambiguous words cannot normally be heard to say that he did not mean what he appeared to mean. There are 'special circumstances', however, in which the words used will not be treated as definitive. In those circumstances, the person purportedly giving notice should be given an opportunity to satisfy the recipient that he did not intend to bring the employment relationship to an end (*Willoughby v CF Capital Ltd* [2011] IRLR 985). See, for instance, *Barclay v City of Glasgow District Council* [1983] IRLR 313, where a mentally handicapped employee purported to resign and the EAT held that there are circumstances where words are spoken under emotional stress, which the other party ought to know are not meant to be taken seriously. Similarly, where words are spoken in the heat of the moment: see *Sovereign House Security Services Ltd v Savage* [1989] IRLR 115. See also *Kwik-Fit (GB) Ltd v Lineham* [1992] ICR 183.

Dismissal may be either *summary* or with *notice*. At common law, either party to the contract of employment is always free to terminate the relationship by giving the proper notice provided that the contract is one which, whether expressly or impliedly, is terminable upon giving notice. Thus, if such notice is given, there can be no claim for WRONGFUL DISMISSAL **(56)**. To be effective in law, the notice must expire on a certain specified day (*Morton Sundour Fabrics Ltd v Shaw* (1966) 2 ITR 84), or upon the occurrence of a specified event (*Burton Group Ltd v Smith* [1977] IRLR 351). There is no dismissal on notice where an employer informs an absent employee that if he does not return to work by a particular date he will be treated as having terminated his employment, even if the employee does not turn up on that date and the employer treats the employment as having been terminated (*Rai v Somerfield Stores Ltd.* [2004] ICR 656).

For the date at which termination takes effect, see **51.13** UNFAIR DISMISSAL – I. The parties may by agreement either advance or postpone the date of termination (*Mowlem Northern Ltd v Watson* [1990] ICR 751; and see also *Palfrey v Transco plc* [2004] IRLR 916).

The contract of employment may provide for summary termination in certain circumstances. Summary dismissal in other circumstances is *prima facie* a breach of contract, unless the employee is in fundamental breach of the contract (see **46.13** below). Whether the dismissal is or is not fair is an entirely separate question. A dismissal may be fair even though proper notice is not given, and a dismissal on notice may nonetheless be unfair (see *Treganowan v Robert Knee & Co Ltd* [1975] ICR 405; *BSC Sports and Social Club v Morgan* [1987] IRLR 391; and UNFAIR DISMISSAL – II **(52)**).

Where an employer is expressly permitted to terminate the contract of employment by making a payment in lieu of notice, there is an implied obligation on the employer to notify the employee in clear and unambiguous terms that such payment has been made and that it is made in the exercise of the contractual right to terminate the employment with immediate effect (*Société Générale v Geys* [2013] ICR 117).

Where an employer exercises the power to terminate the contract of employment by making a payment in lieu, a debt will accrue, and it will not be open to the employer to resile from making the necessary payment on discovering conduct which would otherwise have justified a wrongful dismissal. There has been no wrongful dismissal, but a termination in accordance with the contract's own terms: see *Cavenagh v William Evans Ltd* [2012] ICR 1231. The principle set out in *Boston Deep Sea Fishing and Ice Co v Ansell* 39 Ch D 339 did not go as far as to say that after-discovered misconduct provided an employer with a defence to an action for payment of an accrued debt.

A 'dismissal' by the employer can result from the termination of one contract and its replacement by another: see *Hogg v Dover College* [1990] ICR 39; and *Smith v Trafford Housing Trust* [2013] IRLR 86 (see **46.1**).

46.6   Termination on notice – the contractual notice period

The contract of employment will usually specify the period of notice to be given to terminate the contract; indeed, the written particulars given to the employee must include the length of notice which the employee is obliged to give or entitled to receive (see **7.7** CONTRACT OF EMPLOYMENT).

If the contract is not for a fixed term and the notice period has not been expressly agreed, there is an implied term that it may be terminated upon reasonable notice (see *Reda v Flag Ltd* [2002] UKPC 38, [2002] IRLR 747). The court will determine what amounts to reasonable notice. Factors taken into account include the seniority and remuneration of the employee, his age, his length of service and what is usual in the particular trade. As a very rough guide, a period of two weeks or one month might be appropriate in the case of a manual worker, three months in the case of senior skilled workers or middle management, and between three months and one year in the case of more senior managers. However, the period of notice must be determined on the particular facts of each case. (For a discussion of the factors, see *Clarke v Fahrenheit 451 (Communications) Ltd* (EAT 591/99) (1999) IDS Brief 666, p 11.)

46.7   Termination on notice – statutory minimum notice

Whatever may be the contractual provisions – whether express or implied – for termination of the contract, the notice actually given must not be less than the statutory minimum period of notice. The contractual notice must be given if that is longer. The statutory rules are as follows:

(a)   an employee who has been continuously employed for one month or more but less than two years is entitled to not less than one week's notice;

(b)   an employee who has been continuously employed for two years or more but less than 12 years is entitled to one week's notice for each year of continuous employment;

(c)   any employee who has been employed for 12 years or more is entitled to not less than 12 weeks' notice.

(*ERA 1996, s 86(1)*.)

This results in the following:

46.7   Termination of Employment

Table of statutory minimum notice

Period of continuous employment (years)	Minimum period (weeks)
Less than 2 (but 1 month or more)	1
At least 2 but less than 3	2
At least 3 but less than 4	3
At least 4 but less than 5	4
At least 5 but less than 6	5
At least 6 but less than 7	6
At least 7 but less than 8	7
At least 8 but less than 9	8
At least 9 but less than 10	9
At least 10 but less than 11	10
At least 11 but less than 12	11
12 or more	12

For example, if a clerk has been employed for 12 years under a contract which does not specify the period of notice to which he is entitled, a term of reasonable notice would be implied which in his case may well be one month. However, his length of service entitled him to 12 weeks' notice and that is the minimum notice he must be given.

An employee cannot contract out of his right to the statutory minimum period of notice (*ERA 1996, s 203*). However, he may waive his right to notice on a particular occasion, or accept a payment in lieu of notice (*ERA 1996, s 86(3)*; *Trotter v Forth Ports Authority* [1991] IRLR 419).

46.8   Exceptions

The following employees do not have the right to be given the statutory minimum period of notice:

(a)   employees engaged in work wholly or mainly outside Great Britain, unless the employee ordinarily works in Great Britain and the work outside Great Britain is for the same employer (*ERA 1996, s 196(1)*; cf **51.15**(b) UNFAIR DISMISSAL – I);

(b)   employees in employment under a contract made in contemplation of the performance of a specific task which is not expected to last for more than three months, unless they have been continuously employed for more than three months (*ERA 1996, s 86(5)*);

(c)   certain seamen (*ERA 1996, s 199*).

46.9   Pay in lieu of notice

An employer who intends to dismiss an employee may consider it desirable that the employee should cease work immediately and not work out his notice period. For example, some employers consider it unwise to let a sales representative, who knows that he is to be dismissed, have any further contact with the employer's customers, for fear of endangering their goodwill. If an employee is dismissed without notice or with short notice it is usual to give him pay in lieu of notice. It would be possible, although unusual, to give an employee notice to expire halfway through the contractual or statutory notice period and to make a payment in lieu of notice in respect of the remainder of the period. Another possibility is to continue to pay the employee as usual, but to ask him to remain at home. This will not normally represent a breach of contract by the employer (but see **7.13** CONTRACT OF

EMPLOYMENT). Even if he makes a payment in lieu of notice, an employer will nevertheless in theory be guilty of a breach of contract (unless the contract provides for this possibility – as, for example, in *Cavenagh v William Evans Ltd* [2012] ICR 1231). However, the employee will not normally have a right of action in damages unless, through the premature determination of his contract, he has been deprived of valuable statutory rights. (See observations in *Robert Cort & Son Ltd v Charman* [1981] ICR 816; *Delaney v Staples* [1992] IRLR 191; and *Abrahams v Performing Rights Society* [1995] IRLR 486, CA.) However, in certain circumstances, the employee may be able to obtain an injunction to restrain a termination before the expiry of the contractual notice period. Such relief may be obtained where, by the employer's breach, the employee will suffer loss for which he cannot be compensated in damages, as where during the notice period the employee would have been able to exercise a share option in respect of which a claim in damages has been excluded.

The practice of giving pay in lieu of notice is virtually universal, but it does not fit easily into the traditional legal framework. Two connected problem areas are:

(a)   whether pay in lieu of notice is taxable (see **46.10** below);

(b)   if tax-free, whether it should be paid gross or net (see **46.11** below).

46.10

Taxation of pay in lieu of notice. The contract of employment may expressly empower the employer to dismiss the employee summarily on making a payment in lieu of notice. If the contract does set out such a right then the payment in lieu constitutes an 'emolument' of the employment, and tax should be deducted under PAYE in the usual way (see *EMI Group Electronics Ltd v Coldicott (Inspector of Taxes)* [1999] IRLR 630). The employee is not entitled to the benefit of the £30,000 exemption referred to below. It is probable that any appropriate National Insurance contributions should be paid as well.

Normally, there is no express contractual term relating to the making of payments in lieu of notice, but the employer may have an almost invariable custom of giving pay in lieu of notice. The House of Lords has held that such a payment is a payment of compensation for the employer's breach of contract in not giving due notice (*Delaney v Staples* [1992] ICR 483). Accordingly, the payment escapes the general Schedule E charge. It follows that neither the frequency with which such payments are made nor any expectation on the part of the employee would affect this. Since a non-contractual payment in lieu of notice falls to be regarded as compensation, it will be tax-free under the general rules. It may nevertheless be taxable under the special rules on compensation payments for loss of office (eg 'golden handshakes'), but only if the *total* amount paid to the employee, including any redundancy payment and any other termination payments, exceeds £30,000 (*Income Tax (Earnings and Pensions) Act 2003, ss 401, 403*). A non-contractual payment in lieu of notice is not subject to National Insurance contributions.

Where the employer and employee genuinely negotiate an agreement to terminate the employment contract, and no question of breach of contract by the employer arises, then any lump sum payable as part of the agreement will be treated as an 'emolument' from employment and will be taxable under Schedule E. The £30,000 exemption will not apply: see *Richardson (HM Inspector of Taxes) v Delaney* [2001] IRLR 663.

46.11 *Payment gross or net?* Most employers who make a payment in lieu of notice which is tax-free, pay over to the employee his full gross wages or salary. Legally, however, if pay in lieu of notice is to be regarded as compensation for breach of contract (see above), it would follow that the employer is only liable to pay the net amount that the employee would have received after deduction of tax and National Insurance. This is because the measure of damages for breach of contract is calculated on the basis of *the amount lost* by the employee in not being allowed to work his notice. However, there is nothing to prevent an employer from paying the gross amount and there may be sound reasons for doing so, eg to maintain good industrial relations or public relations. It is also conceivable, although unlikely, that an employer who had a consistent practice of making payments gross might be held liable to pay the gross amount to an employee on the ground that the consistent practice had given rise to an implied contractual term (see, eg *Gothard v Mirror Group Newspapers Ltd* [1988] ICR 729). (To avoid the tax charge it would be necessary to establish that this term related only to the manner of calculating pay in lieu and not to the employer's liability to make the payment.) Pay in lieu of notice does not amount to wages for the purposes of the provisions relating to protection of wages (*ERA 1996, ss 13–27*) (see **32.6 PAY – I**).

46.12 Employee's rights during period of notice

Where an employee has been continuously employed for one month or more (see CONTINUOUS EMPLOYMENT (6)), and his employment is terminated either by the employer giving notice, or by notice given by himself, the employee is given certain rights during the statutory minimum notice period, ie the period shown in **46.7** above where the employer gives notice, and one week where the employee gives notice (*ERA 1996, s 87(1), (2)*). This does not apply, however, where notice is given by the employer and the contractual notice period exceeds the statutory minimum by at least one week (*ERA 1996, s 87(4)*), as illustrated in the case of *Budd v Scotts Co (UK) Ltd* [2004] ICR 299, [2003] IRLR 145, EAT.

The rights in question are set out in *ERA 1996, ss 87–91*. Although it will not be possible to rely upon them directly if the statutory minimum notice is not given by the employer, they are to be taken into account in assessing damages in a WRONGFUL DISMISSAL (56) action (*ERA 1996, s 91(5)*).

The principal right conferred is to be paid in cases where the employee is ready and willing to work, but no work is provided for him by his employer, or where the employee is incapable of work because of sickness or injury, or where the employee is absent from work wholly or partly because of pregnancy or childbirth, or is absent in accordance with the terms of his employment relating to holidays. Where there are normal working hours, the amount payable is arrived at by taking the number of hours covered by the above situations and applying to them the hourly rate of remuneration produced by dividing a week's pay by the number of normal working hours (*ERA 1996, s 88*). Where there are no normal working hours, the employer must pay a week's pay in each week of the notice period, provided that the employee is ready and willing to do work of a reasonable nature and amount to earn a week's pay (*ERA 1996, s 89*). In each case, any payments in fact made (including holiday pay and sick pay) go towards meeting the employer's liability.

Accordingly, an employee who has been dismissed on account of prolonged sickness absence is entitled to receive full salary during his notice period if his sickness continues during that period. This is the case even if the employee had by the time of his dismissal exhausted his rights to sick pay, and would have received no payment from his employer if his contract had not been terminated.

The employer is not liable to make payments in respect of a period during which the employee is on leave at his own request (*ERA 1996, s 91(1)*), nor where the employee has given notice and thereafter takes part in a strike (*ERA 1996, s 91(2)*).

Where the employer breaks the contract during the notice period, payments made under *ERA 1996, ss 87–91* go to mitigate the damage suffered (*ERA 1996, s 91(3)*). Where the employer terminates the contract during the notice period and is entitled to do so because of the employee's breach of contract (see **46.13** below), there is no liability under *ERA 1996, s 88* or *s 89* in respect of the subsequent part of the full notice period (*ERA 1996, s 91(4)*).

46.13 Summary dismissal

If the employee acts in a way which is incompatible with the faithful discharge of his duty to his employer he may be dismissed instantly, without notice or wages in lieu of notice. Examples of misconduct which can in certain circumstances give rise to the right to dismiss summarily are wilful disobedience of a lawful order from the employer, theft of the employer's property, and drunkenness such as to impair the performance of his duties. The misconduct must be gross or grave, seen in the light of all the circumstances of the case. In general, employees should be given a clear indication of the type of conduct which the employer regards as warranting summary dismissal (*ACAS Code of Practice 1, para 23*).

Summary dismissal for misconduct which is not gross is a breach of contract rendering the employer liable in damages for WRONGFUL DISMISSAL (**56**).

For a discussion of the exact moment when a dismissal without notice takes effect, see *Octavius Atkinson & Sons Ltd v Morris* [1989] ICR 431.

46.14 Written statement of reasons for dismissal

An employee is entitled to be provided by his employer, on request, within 14 days of that request, with a written statement giving particulars of the reasons for his dismissal if:

(a)   he is given by his employer notice of termination of his contract of employment; or

(b)   his contract of employment is terminated by his employer without notice; or

(c)   where he is employed under a contract for a fixed term, that term expires without being renewed under the same contract.

(ERA 1996, s 92(1).)

The reasons given by an employer are admissible in evidence in any proceedings. The employer's reply to a request may refer to full reasons given in an earlier written communication, a copy of which should be sent with the reply. Where a legal adviser is appointed by the employee, as a duly authorised agent to receive the information, it is sufficient to communicate the information to the legal adviser (*Kent County Council v Gilham* [1985] ICR 227).

An employee is not normally entitled to written reasons unless he has been continuously employed for a period of two years ending with the effective date of termination (*Unfair Dismissal and Reasons for Dismissal (Variation of Qualifying Period) Order 2012 (SI 2012/989)*) (an exception is made for employees whose continuous period of employment commenced before 6th April 2012: for these employees, only one year's continuous employment is required).

Special rules apply if an employee is dismissed at any time while she is pregnant, or after childbirth in circumstances in which her maternity leave period ends by reason of her dismissal (for the maternity leave period, see **31.24** MATERNITY AND PARENTAL RIGHTS). She is entitled to a written statement of reasons for the dismissal, irrespective of the length of her employment, and without having to make any request (*ERA 1996, s 92(4)*).

46.15 Remedy for failure to give reasons

A complaint may be made by the employee to an industrial tribunal on the grounds:

(a)   that his employer unreasonably failed to provide a written statement under *ERA 1996, s 92* of the reason for dismissal; or

(b)   that the particulars given in purported compliance with that section are inadequate or untrue.

46.15   Termination of Employment

(*ERA 1996, s 93(1)*.)

The obligation is, of course, to give the actual reason for dismissal; the question is not whether that reason is in fact well-founded.

In *Daynecourt Insurance Brokers Ltd v Iles* [1978] IRLR 335, the company failed to answer an employee's request for written reasons for his dismissal. Its justification for doing so was a general request by the police officer who investigated the alleged theft of company funds by the employee, that the company should not answer any correspondence or deal with any matter that related to the police investigations of the company's records. The EAT held that the industrial tribunal's finding, that the company should not have simply ignored the employee's statutory request but should have sought further advice of the police officer, was not wrong in law. A failure to provide written reasons may be unreasonable even if the employee knows perfectly well why he has been dismissed, since one purpose of the provision is that the employee should be able to show the reasons to third parties (*McBrearty v Thomson*, IDS Brief 450, p 15).

Except in maternity cases (see **46.14** above), there cannot be a complaint to the tribunal that the reasons given are inadequate if there has been no request for proper reasons by the employee pursuant to *ERA 1996, s 92(1)* (*Catherine Haigh Harlequin Hair Design v Seed* [1990] IRLR 175).

In *Banks v Lavin*, IDS Brief 410, p 6, the EAT held that the statement 'many jobs not being done' was an inadequate reason, because it was not sufficiently specific.

The time limit for presentation of the complaint is three months from the effective date of termination of employment. This period can be extended if the industrial tribunal is satisfied that it was not reasonably practicable to present it within the three-month period (*ERA 1996, s 93(3)*; and see **17.25** EMPLOYMENT TRIBUNALS – I).

If the tribunal finds the complaint well-founded, it will make an award that the employer pay to the employee a sum equal to the amount of two weeks' pay. It may also make a declaration as to what it finds that the employer's reasons were for dismissing the employee (*ERA 1996, s 93(2)*). A week's pay is calculated in accordance with the provisions of *ERA 1996, ss 221–229*, formerly *EPCA 1978, Sch 14* and the calculation date is:

(i)   where the dismissal was with notice, the date on which the employer's notice was given; or

(ii)   in any other case, the effective date of termination.

(*ERA 1996, s 226(2)*.)

(See further REDUNDANCY – I (36).)

The amount of a week's pay is not subject to a statutory maximum for this purpose.

46.16   RESIGNATION BY THE EMPLOYEE

As in the case of dismissal by the employer, the employee may resign with or without notice. For the question of whether the words used will amount to a resignation, see **46.5** above. No particular terms of art are required for resignations (*Walmsley v C&R Ferguson Ltd* [1989] IRLR 112). A failure to give due notice is *prima facie* a breach of contract, but may be justified where the employee resigns in response to a repudiatory breach of contract by the employer (see **46.18** below).

A failure by an employee to give proper notice of resignation is *prima facie* a breach of contract. The more difficult question will usually be what, if any, are the damages payable by the employee. In *Giraud UK Ltd v Smith* [2000] IRLR 763, the Employment Appeal

Tribunal struck down a clause in an employment contract which provided that 'failure to give the proper notice and work it out will result in a reduction from your final payment equivalent to the number of days short'. This was held to be an unlawful penalty clause rather than a lawful liquidated damages clause. There was evidence to suggest that the employer could easily find replacements for the employee in question (he worked as a driver), so that it was not a genuine pre-estimate of loss. Furthermore, the clause was oppressive, as there was no limitation on the right of the employers to recover damages for actual loss if this was greater than that specified in the clause. Therefore, the employee was in a position where if the actual loss turned out to be nil, he would be liable for the sum set out in the clause, but if the actual loss was greater than the sum set out in the clause, he could face an unlimited claim for the balance. The clause enabled the employer to say, 'Heads I win, tails you lose'.

46.17 Termination by the employee giving notice

The statutory minimum period of notice to be given by an employee, who has been continuously employed for one month or more, is one week (*ERA 1996, s 86(2)*). However, the contractual period of notice to be given will, in many cases, be longer. The contractual notice may be either expressly agreed upon or implied. If it is implied, the notice to be given is that which is a reasonable period in all the circumstances (see **46.6** above).

46.18 Summary termination by the employee

If an employer is in breach of a fundamental term of the contract of employment, the employee is entitled to leave the employment forthwith. Leaving the employment in these circumstances is known as 'constructive dismissal' for redundancy payments and unfair dismissal purposes, since although the employee takes the initiative in leaving his employment he will be considered to have been dismissed within the meaning of *ERA 1996, s 136(1)* (see **36.6** REDUNDANCY – I) and *ERA 1996, s 95(1)* (see **51.4** UNFAIR DISMISSAL – I). In such circumstances, the employee would also be able to claim damages for WRONGFUL DISMISSAL (**56**).

46.19 REPUDIATORY CONDUCT

It has already been seen (see **46.13** and **46.18** above) that a repudiatory breach of contract by either the employer or the employee entitles the other party to terminate the relationship without giving notice or by giving short notice. A dismissal in such circumstances is not necessarily fair, nor a constructive dismissal following the employer's breach necessarily unfair, although they often will be.

The courts have sometimes gone further, and suggested that a repudiatory breach *automatically* brings a contract of employment to an end (see, eg *Marriott v Oxford and District Co-operative Society Ltd (No 2)* [1970] 1 QB 186). The 'automatic' theory has now been rejected by the Supreme Court in *Société Générale v Geys* [2013] ICR 117. This means that (leaving aside questions of frustration and expiry at a specified time or upon the occurrence of a specified event) there is no such thing as an automatic termination because of one party's conduct. There must always be an acceptance of the breach constituting a dismissal by the employer or a resignation by the employee.

However, it is of the nature of the employment relationship that, where one party is unwilling to perform the contract, it will be very difficult for the other party to say that the relationship remains alive. An acceptance of the breach by the innocent party will readily be inferred from his conduct. See also *Marsh v National Autistic Society* [1993] ICR 453.

The Court of Appeal in *Weathersfield Ltd (t/a Van & Truck Rentals) v Sargent* [1999] IRLR 94 overruled the decision of the EAT in *Holland v Glendale Industries Ltd* [1998] ICR 493 that an employee must make plain to his employer the reason for leaving if he is to rely upon his employer's repudiatory conduct as justifying his resignation and subsequent claim of constructive dismissal. The court held that whether there has been an 'acceptance' of the employer's repudiatory conduct is for the employment tribunal (or court) to determine on the facts and evidence in each case. On the facts of that case (where an employee had been instructed to discriminate against black and Asian customers), the employee had been put in 'an outrageous and embarrassing position', and so did not want to confront her employers with the reason for leaving. She just left the job a few days after being issued with the instruction. This did not prevent her from claiming successfully that she had been constructively dismissed on the grounds of the instruction.

It is always a question of fact for the court or tribunal as to whether the employee resigned in consequence of the employer's repudiatory breach of contract. In *TSB Bank plc v Harris* [2000] IRLR 157, the Employment Appeal Tribunal upheld a finding of constructive dismissal where the employee was considering leaving her job in any case before the repudiatory breach of contract occurred (the breach arose out of the contents of a reference supplied to a prospective employer). See also *White v Bristol Rugby Ltd* [2002] IRLR 204. In *Da'Bell v NSPCC* [2010] IRLR 19, the Employment Appeal Tribunal observed that where a person reacts to offensive conduct by writing a letter the next day, this will easily lead to a finding that he resigned in response to that conduct. If he leaves the matter for a year, however, and digs it up again, his resignation at that point is less likely to be treated as directly related to the breach.

46.20 RETRACTION OF RESIGNATION OR DISMISSAL

The general rule is that words of resignation or dismissal, once communicated to the other party and accepted by him, cannot unilaterally be withdrawn (*Riordan v War Office* [1959] 3 All ER 552, *Willoughby v CF Capital plc* [2011] IRLR 985). However, the EAT has suggested that good industrial relations practice requires that an employer should be able to withdraw words of dismissal provided that he does so almost immediately (*Martin v Yeoman Aggregates Ltd* [1983] ICR 314). If this view is correct, it should apply equally to a case of resignation by the employee.

46.21 REMEDIES FOR WRONGFUL TERMINATION

An employee who has been dismissed, or who has resigned in circumstances amounting to a constructive dismissal, may complain of UNFAIR DISMISSAL – I (51) to an employment tribunal, whether or not proper notice was given to him. If proper notice was not given, or if he resigned summarily in response to the employer's repudiatory breach, he may bring a claim for WRONGFUL DISMISSAL (56) in the ordinary courts. Where the employee fails to give proper notice, the employer may also in principle sue for damages. Also, either party may in certain, limited circumstances be able to obtain an injunction restraining an unlawful termination. See further 7.23 CONTRACT OF EMPLOYMENT.

47   Time Off Work

Cross references. See CHILDREN AND YOUNG PERSONS (3.8), EDUCATION AND TRAINING (13), HOLIDAYS (27), MATERNITY AND PARENTAL RIGHTS (31), SICKNESS AND SICK PAY (42) and STRIKES AND INDUSTRIAL ACTION (43).

47.1   In addition to the rights to take time off work covered elsewhere in this book, there are several distinct rights in exercise of which an employee may take time off work in specific circumstances.

 Trade union officials and members may take time off work for certain duties and activities (see **47.2–47.5** below).

—   Employees have the right to take time off work to perform certain public duties (see **47.4–47.5** below).

—   An employee under notice of redundancy may take time off to look for work, etc (see **47.6–47.7** below).

—   Safety representatives, and elected representatives, must be given time off to perform their duties (see **47.8–47.9** below).

—   Employees who are trustees of occupational pension schemes have a right to time off for performing their duties (see **47.10–47.11** below).

—   Employee representatives must be given time off to perform their functions (see **47.12–47.13** below).

—   Employees have the right to time off for European Works Council duties (see **47.14** below).

—   Employees have the right to time off to care for dependants (see **47.15–47.16** below).

—   Employees have the right to request flexible working to care for children (see **47.17** below).

This chapter also considers the obligation to reinstate members of the reserve forces in employment after military service (see **47.18** below).

47.2   TRADE UNION OFFICIALS

An employer is obliged to permit an employee, who is an official of an independent trade union recognised by the employer, to take time off during working hours to:

(a)   carry out duties, as such an official, which are concerned with:

(i)   negotiations with the employer that are related to or connected with any matters that fall within *TULRCA 1992, s 178(2)* (see **37.4** REDUNDANCY – II) and in relation to which the trade union is recognised by the employer, or

(ii)   the performance, on behalf of employees of the employer, of any functions that are related to or connected with any matters falling within *TULRCA 1992, s 178(2)* that the employer has agreed may be so performed by the trade union, or

(iii)   receipt of information from the employer and consultation with the employer under *TULRCA 1992, s 188* or under the *Transfer of Undertakings (Protection of Employment) Regulations 2006 (SI 2006/246)* (see REDUNDANCY – II (37) and TRANSFER OF UNDERTAKINGS (50));

(b)   undergo training in aspects of industrial relations which is:

  (i)   relevant to the carrying out of any such duties as are mentioned in (a); and

  (ii)   approved by the Trades Union Congress or by the independent trade union of which he is an official.

(TULRCA 1992, s 168(1), (2).)

The Court of Appeal in *British Bakeries (Northern) Ltd v Adlington* [1989] ICR 438 held that it was a question of fact, dependent on the particular circumstances of the case, whether a preparatory meeting was sufficiently proximate to carrying out duties concerned with (at that time) industrial relations to come within the statutory predecessor of *s 168, TULRCA 1992*. Although the section has been amended since *Adlington*, it is thought that the decision is equally applicable to whether attendance at a meeting is sufficiently proximate to carrying out the duties now specified in *s 168*. See also *London Ambulance Service v Charlton* [1992] ICR 773.

It is to be noted that the right accrues only to officials of independent trade unions recognised by the employer (see **48.19** TRADE UNIONS – I). There is no right to time off if, for example, the purpose is to attend a demonstration in support of a dispute with another employer or to carry out internal union duties. Nor would *s 168* extend to, say, taking part in a course on pension schemes if the employer does not consult or bargain with the union about pensions and has not agreed to it performing any pension-related functions on behalf of his employees.

In *Ashley v Ministry of Defence* [1984] ICR 298, the EAT held that unless it can be shown that the recognised union expressly or impliedly required the attendance of its official at a meeting, the attendance of the official at such a meeting cannot constitute the carrying out by the official of a duty within the meaning of *s 168*. The EAT further held that attendance at an advisory meeting could be a duty within the meaning of *s 168*; whether it is, is a question of fact.

In deciding whether the right to time off is being exercised reasonably within the meaning of *s 168(3)*, the EAT in *Depledge v Pye Telecommunications Ltd* [1981] ICR 82, considered that where comprehensive arrangements existed for the discussion of industrial relations matters it would be reasonable for trade union officials to use them.

The amount of time a trade union official is permitted to take off in the exercise of his statutory right, the purposes for which, the occasions on which, and any conditions subject to which, time off may be so taken are those that are reasonable in all the circumstances, having regard to any relevant provisions in the ACAS Code of Practice (*TULRCA 1992, s 168(3)*).

In considering whether the request for time off is reasonable in all the circumstances, tribunals will take into account such matters as the nature, extent and purpose of time off already being taken by that employee (*Wignall v British Gas Corpn* [1984] ICR 716; *Borders Regional Council v Maule* [1993] IRLR 199). *Section 168(3)* assumes that a request for time off has been made and that such request has come to the notice of the employer. It is only if these two conditions are satisfied that the employee can have a remedy for an employer's failure to permit him to take time off (see *Ryford Ltd v Drinkwater* [1996] IRLR 16 and **47.6** below).

An employee who is a member of an independent trade union recognised by the employer and who is a learning representative of the trade union is entitled to time off under *s 168A, TULRCA 1992*. An employee who is a learning representative is entitled to time off in order to undertake, in relation to qualifying members of the trade union, the analysis of learning and training needs, the provision of information and advice on learning and training matters, the promotion of the values of learning and training, the consultation of the employer on learning and training activities, and preparation for the learning representative's activities. The right to time off arises only where the trade union has provided the employer with written notice that the employee is a learning representative and that (a) he has undergone sufficient training for his learning representative activities within the last six months and the trade union has given the employer notice in writing of this fact; (b) the trade union has given the employer notice in the last six months that the employee will be undergoing such training; or (c) within six months of such notice, the employee has undergone the training and the trade union has given the employer notice of that fact. The employer is also required the permit the employee time off for training that is relevant to his functions as a learning representative. The employer's obligation to permit time off is subject to a reasonableness test.

The trade union official who is entitled to take time off work to perform his duties under *section 168* or *168A, TULRCA 1992* is entitled to be paid for the period of his absence. Where his pay does not vary with the amount of work done, he is paid as if he had worked during the period of absence. Where his pay does vary according to the amount of work done, the amount he is to be paid during his absence is calculated by reference to the average hourly earnings for that work. The average hourly earnings are those of the employee concerned unless they cannot fairly be estimated, in which case the tribunal will take the average earnings of persons in comparable employment with the same employer or (if there are no such persons) a reasonable figure (*TULRCA 1992, s 169*).

The employee is entitled to paid time off only at a time when he would otherwise be working, and not to paid time off in lieu if the trade union duties are performed at a time when he would not otherwise be working (*Hairsine v Kingston upon Hull City Council* [1992] IRLR 211 and *Diamond v Park Lane College* UKEAT/0249/05/LA). However, a part time worker is entitled to receive pay for the actual hours attended on a training course, rather than just for the part time hours that they normally worked; a failure to pay for the actual hours worked would be unjustifiable indirect sex discrimination: *Davies v Neath Port Talbot County Borough Council* [1999] ICR 1132, [1999] IRLR 769, EAT.

If an employer is obliged under a contract of employment to pay an employee for time off taken to perform trade union duties, then those payments will go to discharge any statutory liability he may have to make such payments, and vice versa (*TULRCA 1992, s 169(4)*).

Trade union officials are statutorily entitled to a reasonable amount of paid time off to accompany a worker at a disciplinary or grievance hearing, provided that they are certified by the union as being capable of acting as the worker's companion (*ERA 1999, s 10(6)*). This right applies whether or not the union is recognised by the employer, but the worker must be employed by the same employer as the union official.

See also the ACAS Code of Practice 3: Time off for trade union duties and activities which lays down guidelines. The Code is to be taken into account in determining what is reasonable and the current version came into force on 1 January 2010.

It should be noted that in October 2012 the Cabinet Office announced reforms to ensure that civil servants who are trade union representatives spend at least 50% of their working hours delivering their civil service role, with any exemptions requiring specific agreement.

47.3   TRADE UNION ACTIVITIES

An employer is obliged to permit an employee of his, who is a member of an independent trade union recognised by him, to take part in certain trade union activities during working hours. The activities are defined as:

(a)   any activities of the trade union of which the employee is a member; and

(b)   any activities in relation to which the employee is acting as a representative of such union;

(*TULRCA 1992, s 170(1)*). This excludes activities which themselves consist of industrial action whether or not in contemplation or furtherance of a trade dispute (*TULRCA 1992, s 170(2)*).

The right in *section 170(1), TULRCA 1992* does not include a right to time off for the purpose of acting as, or having access to services provided by, a learning representative of a trade union (*TULRCA 1992, s 170(2A)*). However, where the trade union learning representative in question is carrying out activities for which he is entitled to time off under *section 68A, TULRCA 1992*, the employer is obliged to permit an employee to take time off in his working hours to access those services (*TULRCA 1992, s 170(2B)–(2C)*).

In *Luce v Bexley London Borough Council* [1990] ICR 591, the EAT held that whether trade union activity fell within the definition was a matter of fact and degree, but that it must in a broad sense be linked to the employment relationship; the tribunal had been entitled to hold that teachers were not entitled to time off to lobby Parliament against the *Education Reform Bill*. See also **52.3**(a) Unfair Dismissal – II.

The amount of time that may be taken, and the purposes for which and the occasions on which it may be taken, are those that are reasonable in all the circumstances; the same test applies to the imposition of conditions by the employer (*TULRCA 1992, s 170(3)*). The employee is not entitled to be paid for time he takes off to participate in trade union activities unless he is a trade union official and the time is taken in accordance with **47.2** above.

47.4 PUBLIC DUTIES

An employer is obliged to permit an employee of his who is:

(a)   a justice of the peace;

(b)   a member of a local authority (within the meaning of the *Local Government Act 1972*), the Common Council of the City of London, a National Park Authority or the Broads Authority;

(c)   a member of any statutory tribunal;

(d)   a member of an independent monitoring board for a prison;

(e)   a member of the National Health Service Commissioning Board, a clinical commissioning group, a National Health Service Trust, an NHS foundation trust, the National Institute for Health and Care Excellence, the Health and Social Care Information Centre, a Strategic Health Authority, a Local Health Board, a Special Health Authority, or a Primary Care Trust;

(f)   a member of the managing or governing body of an educational establishment maintained by a local education authority, the governing body of a further education corporation, sixth form college corporation or higher education corporation, or the General Teaching Council for England or Wales;

(g)   a member of the Environment Agency;

(h)   various similar bodies in Scotland.

to take time off work during the employee's contractual working hours for certain specified purposes (*ERA 1996, s 50*). There is no right to be paid for this time off work.

The right does not extend to specified classes of employees (*ERA 1996, ss 191–195, 199* and *200*). Clergy of the Church of England also have a right to time off work for public duties by virtue of the *Ecclesiastical Offices (Terms of Service) Regulations 2009 (SI 2009/2108)*.

In deciding when and how much time is to be taken off, regard will be paid to:

(i)   how much time off is required for the performance of the duties of the office, or as a member of the body in question, and how much time off is required for the performance of the particular duty;

(ii)   how much time off has already been permitted for the performance of any relevant public duty, union duty or activity;

(iii)   the circumstances of the employer's business and the effect of the employee's absence on the running of that business;

and these considerations will be applied in deciding what is reasonable in the circumstances (*ERA 1996, s 50(4)*). (See *Borders Regional Council v Maule* [1993] IRLR 199 and *Riley-Williams v Argos Ltd* EAT/811/02, (2003) 147 SJLB 695.)

Local authorities may not allow their employees more than 208 hours' paid time off in any financial year for the purpose of performing duties as councillors (other than council chairmen) (*Local Government and Housing Act 1989, s 10*).

Although there is no statutory provision entitling an employee to time off for jury service, prevention of a person from attending as a juror is a contempt of court and employees are protected from being subjected to a detriment or dismissal as a result of jury service (*ERA 1996, ss 43M, 98B*).

47.5   EMPLOYEE'S REMEDIES IN RESPECT OF TIME OFF FOR TRADE UNION AND PUBLIC DUTIES

An employee may present a complaint to an employment tribunal that (*a*) he has not been allowed time off to carry out public duties or trade union duties or activities, or (*b*) in the case of a trade union official's duties that he has not been paid for time he has been permitted to take off (*ERA 1996, s 51(1); TULRCA 1992, ss 168(4), 168A(9), 169(5), 170(4)*). An employee can only bring a complaint under *TULRCA 1992, s 168(4)* that an employer has failed to permit him to take time off, in circumstances where a request for time off has been made by the employee and that request has come to the notice of the employer (see *Ryford Ltd v Drinkwater* [1996] IRLR 16).

If it finds such a complaint well-founded, the tribunal will make a declaration to that effect and may order the employer to pay the employee compensation for the default and for any loss caused thereby (*ERA 1996, s 51(3); TULRCA 1992, s 172(1), (2)*). In the case of a union official who has not been paid for time taken off, the tribunal will order the employer to make the appropriate payment (*TULRCA 1992, s 172(3)*; see **47.2** above). In *Skiggs v South West Trains Ltd* [2005] IRLR 459 a union official was prevented by his employer from attending meetings in the capacity of union representative pending the outcome of a grievance investigation into his behaviour. The EAT held that although he had suffered no financial loss nor injury to feelings, he was entitled to recover compensation to reflect the fact that a wrong was done to him, because *TULRCA 1992, s 172(2)* makes reference to both the employer's default and any loss sustained by the employee.

An employment tribunal does not have the power to impose conditions upon the parties as to the way in which the time off shall be taken or to specify the amount of time off which should be allowed (*Corner v Buckinghamshire County Council* [1978] IRLR 320).

The time limit for presenting such complaints is three months from the date of the failure complained of. If the tribunal is satisfied that it was not reasonably practicable for the complaint to be presented within the period of three months (see **17.2** EMPLOYMENT

47.5 Time Off Work

TRIBUNALS – I), then this time limit may be extended (*ERA 1996, s 51(2); TULRCA 1992, s 171*). Time is automatically extended in specified circumstances where there is mediation in certain cross-border disputes (*ERA 1996, s 207A*).

In *Gayle v Sandwell and West Birmingham Hospitals NHS Trust* [2011] EWCA Civ 924, [2012] ICR Digest D3, the statutory rights to unpaid time off for trade union activities were not relied upon but the employer had a recognition agreement whereby it would permit accredited representatives such time off for trade union activities as was reasonable and subject to the needs of the service. The employee attended a trade union meeting without complying a management instruction to resolve the issue of time off under the recognition agreement and was disciplined. The Court of Appeal upheld the tribunal's finding that this was on the basis of her failure to comply with the management request and not her trade union activities therefore there was no breach of *section 146, TULRCA 1992*.

47.6 TIME OFF TO LOOK FOR WORK OR MAKE ARRANGEMENTS FOR TRAINING

An employee who has been given notice of dismissal by reason of redundancy must be allowed reasonable time off by his employer, during his working hours before the end of his notice period, to look for new employment or to make arrangements for training for future employment (*ERA 1996, s 52(1)*). In order to qualify for this right, the employee must have been continuously employed for a period of at least two years, by the date on which (*a*) the notice is due to expire, or (*b*) the date on which it would expire had the statutory minimum period of notice been given, whichever is the longer (*ERA 1996, s 52(2)*). (See CONTINUOUS EMPLOYMENT (6).) For an employee's general rights relating to education and training, see EDUCATION AND TRAINING (13).)

An employee who is so allowed time off is entitled to be paid for the time taken off at the appropriate hourly rate, which is calculated by the amount of one week's pay divided by the number of normal working hours in a week or, where the number of those hours varies, by taking the average of the 12 weeks ending with the last complete week before the notice was given (*ERA 1996, s 53(1)–(3)*). The maximum amount payable cannot exceed 40% of a week's pay (*ERA 1996, s 53(5)*). The right to be paid is dependent upon the right to take time off. Thus, if an employee with less than two years' continuous service is given time off to seek other employment, there is no statutory obligation on the employer to pay him for time so taken.

An employee who is under notice of redundancy is entitled to time off to look for work irrespective of whether he has an appointment to attend a specific interview (*Dutton v Hawker Siddeley Aviation Ltd* [1978] IRLR 390).

47.7 Remedy

If an employer has unreasonably refused the employee time off or has failed to pay him, the employee may present a complaint to an employment tribunal (*ERA 1996, s 54(1)*). The time limit for the presentation of such a complaint is three months beginning with the day on which it is alleged that time off should have been allowed. If the tribunal is satisfied that it was not reasonably practicable for the complaint to be presented within the period of three months (see **18.2** EMPLOYMENT TRIBUNALS – I), then this time may be extended (*ERA 1996, s 54(2)*). Time is automatically extended in specified circumstances where there is mediation in certain cross-border disputes (*ERA 1996, s 207A*).

The employer may be made liable to pay (i) remuneration for the period of absence or (ii) remuneration for the period during which he should have allowed time off, or both. The maximum amount, where both these provisions are applicable together, cannot exceed 40% of a week's pay (*ERA 1996, s 54(4)*).

If an employer unreasonably refuses to allow an employee time off work when statutorily obliged to do so, the employee is entitled to be paid the remuneration to which he would have been entitled if he had been allowed time off, in addition to his normal pay (*ERA 1996, s 53(4)–(6)*).

Any contractual remuneration paid to an employee for a period of time which he takes off to seek or train for new employment when he is under notice of dismissal for redundancy goes towards discharging the employer's statutory liability, and vice versa (*ERA 1996, s 53(7)*).

47.8 SAFETY REPRESENTATIVES AND ELECTED REPRESENTATIVES

The *Safety Representatives and Safety Committees Regulations 1977 (SI 1977/500)*, as amended, impose a duty upon employers to allow safety representatives time off with pay for the performance of their duties as safety representatives, and to undergo training in health and safety matters. There are guidelines for the exercise of the latter right; the 1978 Code of Practice approved by the Health and Safety Commission on time off for the training of safety representatives remains in force. The two questions are (1) whether the proposed training was reasonable in all the circumstances, and (2) whether it was necessary for the employee to take paid time off work: *Duthie v Bath and North East Somerset Council* [2003] ICR 1405 and *Walker v North Tees and Hartlepool NHS Trust* UKEAT/0563/07/RN. Also see *Coats v Strathclyde Fire Board* UKEATS/0022/09/BI, where an employee failed to establish that it was necessary for him to take time off to perform any of the specified health and safety functions on the dates and at the times in relation to which he was refused permission. On the rights of part-time employees, see *Calder v Secretary of State for Work and Pensions* UKEAT/0512/08/LA.

The *Health and Safety (Consultation with Employees) Regulations 1996 (SI 1996/1513)* impose a similar duty upon employers who, pursuant to those *Regulations* (see **26.22** HEALTH AND SAFETY AT WORK – II), consult with elected employee representatives. In addition to the duty to allow such representatives time off with pay to perform their duties as such and to undergo training, an employer must also permit a candidate for election as such a representative time off with pay to perform his functions as such a candidate.

47.9 Remedy

If an employer refuses a safety representative or elected representative time off for these purposes or if he does not pay him for the time taken, the safety representative or elected representative may present a complaint to an employment tribunal (*1977 Regulations, reg 11(1); 1996 Regulations, Sch 2 para 2*). The time limit within which a complaint must be presented is three months from the date where the failure occurred, or within such further period as the tribunal considers reasonable in a case where it is satisfied that it was not reasonably practicable for the complaint to be presented within the period of three months (*1977 Regulations, reg 11(2); 1996 Regulations, Sch 2 para 3*; see **17.21** EMPLOYMENT TRIBUNALS – I). Where an employment tribunal finds the complaint well-founded, it may make an award of such an amount as the tribunal considers just and equitable in all the circumstances, having regard to the employer's default in failing to permit time off to be taken by the employee and to any loss sustained by the employee which is attributable to the employee's complaint (*1977 Regulations, reg 11(3); 1996 Regulations, Sch 2 para 4*). Where the complaint is based upon the failure of the employer to pay remuneration due, the employment tribunal will order that sum to be paid to the employee (*1977 Regulations, reg 11(4); 1996 Regulations, Sch 2 para 5*).

47.10 TIME OFF FOR OCCUPATIONAL PENSION SCHEME TRUSTEES

Employees who are trustees of an occupational pension scheme, or directors of trustee companies, have a right to time off during working hours (*ERA 1996, ss 58–60* and also see the *Occupational Pension Schemes (Member-Nominated Trustees and Directors) Regulations*

2006, SI 2006/714). Such employees will have a right to time off for the purpose of performing any of their duties as trustees or undergoing training relevant to such performance (*ERA 1996, s 58(1)*). This right is not subject to a period of continuous employment which an employee may have with an employer. The amount of time off which an employee is to be permitted to take and the conditions under which time off may be taken are those that are reasonable in all the circumstances having regard, in particular, to (*a*) the amount of time off required for the performance of the duties of a trustee of the scheme and undergoing training, and (*b*) the circumstances of the employer's business and the effect of the employee's absence on the running of that business (*ERA 1996, s 58(2)*).

An employee who is so allowed time off is entitled to be paid for the time taken off. The amount to be paid is the amount which he would have been paid if he had worked during the time taken off or, if his remuneration varies with the amount of work done, an amount calculated by reference to his average hourly earnings (*ERA 1996, s 59(1)–(3)*). If the work is such that no fair estimate can be made of the employee's average hourly earnings, then the amount to be paid will be calculated by reference to the average hourly earnings of similar work of a person in comparable employment with the same employer as the employee in question, or if there are no such persons, a figure of average hourly earnings which is reasonable in the circumstances (*ERA 1996, s 59(3)(4)*).

47.11 Remedy

If an employer has failed to permit the employee to take time off, or has failed to pay him, the employee may present a complaint to an employment tribunal (*ERA 1996, s 60(1)*). Note that there is no requirement for an unreasonable refusal by the employer (in contrast to the position under the *Safety Representatives and Safety Committees Regulations 1977*, discussed at **47.9** above). The time limit for the presentation of such a complaint is three months beginning with the date when the failure occurred. If the tribunal is satisfied that it was not reasonably practicable for the complaint to be presented within the period of three months (see **18.2** EMPLOYMENT TRIBUNALS), then this period may be extended (*ERA 1996, s 60(2)*). Time is automatically extended in specified circumstances where there is mediation in certain cross-border disputes (*ERA 1996, s 207A*).

Where an employment tribunal finds the complaint as to failure to permit time off to be well-founded, it will make an order to that effect and may award such an amount as the tribunal considers just and equitable in all the circumstances, having regard to the employer's default in so failing and any loss sustained by the employee which is attributable to the complaint (*ERA 1996, s 60(3), (4)*). Where the complaint is that the employer has failed to pay the employee for time taken off, the employment tribunal will order the employer to pay the sum found to be due (*ERA 1996, s 60(5)*).

Any contractual remuneration paid to an employee for a period of time off for the purpose of performing his duties as a trustee of an occupational pension scheme or for related training, goes towards discharging the employer's statutory liability, and vice versa (*ERA 1996, s 59(6)*).

47.12 TIME OFF FOR EMPLOYEE REPRESENTATIVES

An employee who is an employee representative for the purposes of *TULRCA 1992, Part IV Chapter II* (see **37.4** REDUNDANCY – **II**) or *Transfer of Undertakings (Protection of Employment) Regulations 2006 (SI 2006/246), regs 9, 12* and *15* (see TRANSFER OF UNDERTAKINGS (**50**)), or a candidate in an election for such an employee representative, has the right to reasonable time off during contractual working hours in order to perform his functions as such an employee representative or candidate, or in order to undergo training to perform such functions (*ERA 1996, s 61*).

This right is not subject to a period of continuous employment which the employee may have with an employer. The employee is entitled to be paid for time taken off during working hours. The amount of pay is calculated in accordance with the provisions governing a week's pay and *Part XIV* of *ERA 1996* (*ERA 1996, s 62(1)*) (see P<small>AY</small> – I (32)).

An employee who is a negotiating representative or an information and consultation representative is entitled to take reasonable time off during his working hours in order to perform his representative functions (*Information and Consultation of Employees Regulations 2004, reg 27 (SI 2004/3426)*). He is entitled to be paid remuneration for the time off at the appropriate hourly rate (*reg 28*).

An employee who is a member of a special negotiating body, a member of a representative body, an information and consultation representative, an employee member on a supervisory or administrative organ, or a candidate in an election in which any person elected will, on being elected, be such a member or representative, is entitled to take reasonable time off during working hours in order to perform the functions of member, representative or candidate (the *European Public Limited-Liability Company (Employee Involvement) (Great Britain) Regulations 2009 (SI 2009/2401), reg 26*). Where an employee takes time off in this way, he is entitled to be paid remuneration at the appropriate hourly rate (*reg 27*).

The *Occupational and Personal Pension Schemes (Consultation by Employers and Miscellaneous Amendment) Regulations 2006 (SI 2006/349)* provide (*para 2, Sch*) that an employee who is a representative falling within *reg 12(2)(a)* or *(3)* or *13(2)*, and is consulted under the *Regulations* about a listed change by a relevant employer is entitled to be permitted by his employer to take reasonable time off during the employee's contractual working hours in order to perform his functions as such a representative. He is entitled to be paid for such time off at the appropriate hourly rate (*para 3, Sch*).

The *European Cooperative Society (Involvement of Employees) Regulations 2006 (SI 2006/2059)* give under *reg 28* a right to reasonable time off to an employee who is a member of a special negotiating body or representative body, an information and consultation representative, an employee member of a supervisory or administrative organ, an election candidate or meeting participant under *reg 17(2)(h)* or *para 11(2)(h)* of *Sch 1* or *para 7(4)* of *Sch 2*. *Regulation 29* entitles the employee to payment at the appropriate hourly rate and *reg 30* gives the employee the right to present an employment tribunal claim where time off or payment are denied.

The *Companies (Cross-Border Mergers) Regulations 2007 (SI 2007/2974)* give an employee who is a member of a special negotiating body, a director of a transferee company, or a candidate in an election for a director or member, a right to take reasonable time off during working hours in order to perform his functions as such a member, director or candidate (*reg 43*). The right to remuneration at the appropriate hourly rate is provided by *reg 44*. The right to present a claim to an employment tribunal where time off or payment are denied is provided by *reg 45*.

Note that some of the above rights only apply where there is a minimum number of employees.

47.13 Remedy

If an employer unreasonably fails to allow an employee to take time off or fails to pay him for time off, the employee may complain to an employment tribunal. The claim must be presented within three months of the day on which time off was taken, or which it is alleged time off should have been allowed. The tribunal may extend time if it was not reasonably practicable to present the claim within three months. Time is automatically extended in specified circumstances where there is mediation in certain cross-border disputes (*ERA 1996, s 207A*). Where the complaint is that time off has unreasonably been denied, the tribunal may order payment at the appropriate rate for the period which should have been allowed.

47.14 TIME OFF FOR EUROPEAN WORKS COUNCIL DUTIES

An employee who is a member of a European Works Council, a member of a special negotiating body, an information and consultation representative, or a candidate for election to be such a representative, is entitled to paid time off in order to carry out his or her duties (*Transnational Information and Consultation of Employees Regulations 1999, regs 25 and 26 (SI 1999/3323)*). The right has recently been extended so that an employee who is a member of a special negotiating board or a European Works Council has the right to take reasonable time off during working hours to undertake training (*regs 19B* and *25*). An employee who is unreasonably refused such time off, or denied payment in accordance with the formula contained in *reg 26*, may bring a complaint to an employment tribunal under *reg 27*.

47.15 TIME OFF FOR DEPENDANTS

Under *ERA 1996, s 57A* employees are entitled to be permitted by their employer to take a reasonable amount of time off during working hours in order to take action which is necessary:

(a)   to provide assistance when a dependant falls ill, gives birth, is injured or assaulted;

(b)   to make arrangements for the provision of care for a dependant who is ill or injured;

(c)   in consequence of the death of a dependant;

(d)   because of the unexpected disruption or termination of arrangements for the care of a dependant; or

(e)   to deal with an incident which involves the employee's child which occurs unexpectedly in a period during which an educational establishment which the child attends is responsible for him.

(*ERA 1996, s 57A(1)*.) Any disruption caused to the employer is irrelevant in determining whether the employee's circumstances trigger the right: *Qua v John Ford Morrison Solicitors* [2003] ICR 482.

An employee must inform his employer as soon as reasonably practicable of the reason for his absence, and, where he is able to inform his employer in advance of his absence, how long he expects to be absent (*ERA 1996, s 57A(2)*).

"Dependant' is defined as a spouse or civil partner, child or parent of the employee, or a person who lives in the same household as the employee (excluding live-in employees, tenants, lodgers and boarders). In addition, for the purposes of (*a*), (*b*) and (*d*) above, a dependant includes any person who reasonably relies on the employee to assist him if ill or injured, or who reasonably relies on the employee to make arrangements to provide care for him (*ERA 1996, s 57A(3), (4)* and *(5)*). Illness and injury are defined to include mental illness and injury (*ERA 1996, s 57A(6)*).

In a case concerning a childminder's unavailability, of which the employee had 16 days' notice during which period she had tried and failed to make alternative childcare arrangements, the EAT considered whether, given the length of time, she had been entitled to take a day off and provide childcare herself (*Harrison v Royal Bank of Scotland plc* [2009] IRLR 28). The EAT held that the relevant question was whether the action taken by the employee was necessary because of the unexpected disruption or termination in the care of her dependant. The length of notice of the disruption was significant, because it enabled the employee to explore alternative arrangements, however, there were no hard and fast rules.

A period of a month or more for a parent to care for a child would almost never fall within *ERA 1996, s 57A*: *Cortest Ltd v O'Toole* UKEAT/0470/07/LA.

Sick leave taken because of a bereavement reaction does not qualify as time off in consequence of the death of a dependant (*Forster v Cartwright Black* [2004] IRLR 781).

47.16 Remedy

An employee who has unreasonably been refused permission to take time off in accordance with his right under *s 57A* may complain to an employment tribunal (*ERA 1996, s 57B(1)*). The time limit for such complaints is three months beginning with the date the refusal occurred. The tribunal has a discretion to extend time where it was not reasonably practicable for the employee to present his claim in the three-month period (*ERA 1996, s 57B(2)*). Time is automatically extended in specified circumstances where there is mediation in certain cross-border disputes (*ERA 1996, s 207A*). If a tribunal finds the complaint well-founded, it may make a declaration to that effect, and may award such compensation as it considers just and equitable, having regard to the employer's default in refusing to permit time off to be taken by the employee, and any loss sustained by the employee (*ERA 1996, s 57B(3) and (4)*).

47.17 TIME OFF TO CARE FOR CHILDREN

Maternity, paternity, adoption leave and leave for ante-natal care are covered in detail in MATERNITY AND PARENTAL RIGHTS (31).

Flexible working

An employee who has been continuously employed for 26 weeks may formally apply in writing to his or her employer to request a change in hours, times or location of work for the purpose of enabling the employee to care for a child under the age of 17, or a disabled child under 18 or certain adults (*Employment Rights Act 1996, ss 80F–80I; Flexible Working ('Procedural Requirements) Regulations 2002 (SI 2002/3207)*; and *Flexible Working (Eligibility, Complaints and Remedies) Regulations 2002 (SI 2002/3236)*). An employee is eligible to request flexible working if he or she is, or is the partner of, the mother, father, adopter, guardian or foster parent of the child, and expects to have responsibility for the upbringing of the child. The employer may refuse such an application only on grounds of the burden of additional costs, detrimental effect on the ability to meet customer demand, inability to re-organise work among existing staff, inability to recruit additional staff, detrimental impact on quality, detrimental impact on performance, insufficiency of work during the periods during which the employee proposes to work, or planned structural changes.

An employer must hold a meeting with the employee to discuss the request for flexible working within 28 days from the making of the application. The employer must notify the employee in writing of the decision on the application within 14 days of the meeting. An employee has a right of appeal against the decision within 14 days of the decision. An appeal meeting must be held within 14 days of the employee's notice of appeal and the employer must notify the employee of the appeal decision within 14 days of the appeal meeting. The employee has a right to be accompanied at the meetings to discuss flexible working and is protected against detriment or dismissal on the ground that he or she exercised or sought to exercise the right to be accompanied or to accompany in such a situation. An employee is protected against detriment (*Employment Rights Act 1996, s 47E*) and dismissal (*Employment Rights Act 1996, s 104C*) on the ground that he or she exercised or sought to exercise the rights to apply for, take, or enforce the right to request flexible working.

An employee may complain to an employment tribunal that an employer has failed to deal with his or her request for flexible working properly or has rejected the application on the basis of incorrect facts (*ERA 1996, s 80H* and see eg *Commotion Ltd v Rutty* [2006] IRLR

171). If the complaint is upheld the employment tribunal may order the employer to reconsider the application and may award compensation of up to eight weeks' pay. The employment tribunal does not have the power to order the employer to implement the employee's request for flexible working.

It should be noted that the current version of the Children and Families Bill extends the right to request flexible working from certain parents and carers (see **47.17** below) to all employees with more than 26 weeks continuous employment and simplifies employers' duties by imposing only a general obligation to deal with such requests in a reasonable manner and within a reasonable period of time.

It should be noted that the current version of the Children and Families Bill 2013 extends this right to all employees with 26 weeks' continuous employment and simplifies employers' duties by imposing only a general obligation to deal with such requests in a reasonable manner and within a reasonable period.

47.18 REINSTATEMENT AFTER MILITARY SERVICE

The *Reserve Forces (Safeguard of Employment) Act 1985* provides two basic types of employment protection for reservists in the armed forces: (1) protection (on pain not just of liability to pay compensation but also of criminal prosecution) against dismissal on account of the reservist's liability to be mobilised, and (2) a right to reinstatement when the reservist returns to his civilian job after a period of mobilisation. In November 2012 the government published a consultation paper, "Future Reserves 2020: Delivering the Nation's Security Together" setting out its plans for reform of reserve forces, including "a more open relationship" with employers underpinned by "a greater predictability of reservists' training and deployment and a greater emphasis on mutual benefit in the development and transfer of skills."

So far as the right of reinstatement is concerned, the following is a short summary of the main provisions in the *1985 Act*.

Where a person has entered upon a period of whole-time service in the armed forces of the Crown, and has done so in pursuance of a notice or directions for the calling out of reserve or auxiliary forces, or for the recall of service pensioners, or in pursuance of an obligation or undertaking to serve as a commissioned officer, then he has certain rights to be reinstated in employment by his former employer.

The former employee must apply in writing to his former employer after the period of military service ends and not later than the third Monday after the end of that period, or as soon afterwards as reasonably possible (*s 3*). He must also notify the employer of a date, not later than 21 days after the latest date allowed for the application, when he will be available for employment (*s 4*).

The employer must then reinstate the former employee in his old occupation on terms no less favourable than would have applied but for the military service, or (if that is not reasonable and practicable – as to which, see *s 5*), in the most favourable occupation and on the most favourable terms and conditions which are reasonable and practicable in his case (*s 1(2)*). The person concerned must then be employed for at least 13, 26 or 52 weeks, depending on the length of his continuous employment prior to the military service, or for so much of that time as is reasonable and practicable (*s 7*; see *Slaven v Thermo Engineers Ltd* [1992] ICR 295).

Complaints that a person's statutory rights have been infringed may be made to a Reinstatement Committee, which may order employment to be made available to the applicant, and order the payment of compensation to him (*s 8*). There are rights of appeal in certain circumstances to an umpire sitting with assessors (*s 9*). Non-compliance with an order is a criminal offence (*s 10*). The procedure upon applications and appeals is governed by the *Reinstatement in Civil Employment (Procedure) Regulations 1944 (SR & O 1944/880)*.

48   Trade Unions – I: Nature and Liabilities

Cross-references. See also STRIKES AND INDUSTRIAL ACTION **(43)**; TIME OFF WORK **(47)** for time off for trade union duties or activities; TRADE UNIONS – **II (49)** for individual rights and union membership; **52.3** UNFAIR DISMISSAL – **II** for dismissal for participation in union activities.

48.1   THE STATUS OF A TRADE UNION

The present law on the status and liability of trade unions is governed by the *Trade Union and Labour Relations (Consolidation) Act 1992* ('*TULRCA 1992*'). 'Trade union' is statutorily defined in *TULRCA 1992, s 1* as an organisation (whether permanent or temporary) which either –

(a)   consists wholly or mainly of workers of one or more descriptions and is an organisation whose principal purposes include the regulation of relations between workers of that description or those descriptions and employers or employers' associations; or

(b)   consists wholly or mainly of –

(i)   constituent or affiliated organisations which fulfil the conditions specified in para (*a*) above (or themselves consist wholly or mainly of constituent or affiliated organisations which fulfil those conditions), or

(ii)   representatives of such constituent or affiliated organisations;

and in either case is an organisation whose principal purposes include the regulation of relations between workers and employers or between workers and employers' associations, or include the regulation of relations between its constituent or affiliated organisations.

In *British Association of Advisers and Lecturers in Physical Education v National Union of Teachers* [1986] IRLR 497, the Court of Appeal construed this definition broadly so as to include an association 'concerned with the professional interests of its members'.

Several of the larger trade unions are made up of a number of constituent sections. The definition in *TULRCA 1992, s 1* ensures that both the conglomerate organisation and its constituent parts are considered to be trade unions. The National Union of Mineworkers is made up of a number of areas such as the National Union of Mineworkers (South Wales area), all of which are, under *TULRCA 1992*, to be considered trade unions. Similarly, a branch of a trade union may be held to be a trade union (see *News Group Newspapers Ltd v Society of Graphical and Allied Trades '82 (No 2)* [1987] ICR 181).

48.2   Legal capacity

Unless a trade union is a special registered body as defined by *TULRCA 1992, s 117* (such bodies are mostly incorporated professional associations), it is not, nor to be treated as if it were, a corporate entity (*TULRCA 1992, s 10*). However, *TULRCA 1992, s 10(1)* gives a trade union a statutory legal personality which it would otherwise lack so that it can:

(a)   make contracts;

(b)   sue or be sued in its own name (see **48.16** and **48.17** below for certain immunities enjoyed by trade unions); and

(c)   be a defendant in criminal proceedings.

All property belonging to a trade union must be vested in trustees in trust for the union (*TULRCA 1992, s 12(1)*).

48.3   CERTIFICATION OFFICER

The Secretary of State appoints a Certification Officer in consultation with ACAS under *TULRCA 1992, s 254*. He makes an annual report to the Secretary of State, who presents it to Parliament and publishes it (*TULRCA 1992, s 258*). His functions include:

(a)   dealing with complaints relating to the keeping of the register of a union's members (see **48.13** below);

(b)   dealing with complaints relating to trade union internal elections (see **48.14** below);

(c)   dealing with complaints relating to political fund ballots (see **48.15** below);

(d)   maintaining a list of trade unions (see **48.21** below);

(e)   certifying whether trade unions are independent (see **18.22** below);

(f)   certain supervisory functions in relation to trade union amalgamations (see **48.39** below); and

(g)   administering the scheme for financial contributions towards trade union ballots.

The Certification Officer may at any time, if he thinks there is good reason to do so, require a trade union (or any person who appears to be in possession of the documents) to produce specified documents which are accounting documents or which may be relevant in considering the union's financial affairs (*TULRCA 1992, s 37A*). He may also appoint inspectors to investigate and report upon a union's financial affairs if there are circumstances suggesting fraud, misconduct or a breach of statutory obligations or union rules in relation to those affairs, and all past and present officials and agents of the union and other persons appearing to be in possession of relevant information must then co-operate with the investigation, including by producing documents and attending before the inspectors (*TULRCA 1992, s 37B*). Reports made will be published by the Certification Officer, and there are various other administrative provisions, as well as criminal sanctions for contravention of statutory requirements (*TULRCA 1992, ss 37C–37E; TULRCA 1992, ss 45, 45A*).

The Certification Officer has jurisdiction to consider applications by members or former members of a trade union claiming that there has been a breach or threatened breach of the union's rules, pursuant to a new *TULRCA 1992, s 108A*. The Certification Officer may consider such a claim only if it relates to:

(a)   the appointment or election of a person to, or their removal from, any office;

(b)   disciplinary proceedings (including expulsion);

(c)   the balloting of members on any issue other than industrial action;

(d)   the constitution or proceedings of any executive committee or of any decision-making meeting; and

(e)   such other matters as the Secretary of State may specify.

In *UNISON v Gallagher* (2005) IDS Brief No 791 the Employment Appeal Tribunal found that the Certification Officer had exceeded his jurisdiction in holding that the appellant union had breached its disciplinary rules by excluding a member, who had previously been disciplined and debarred from holding office for five years, from is annual delegate conference. The exclusion followed a decision by the union that all those who had been expelled or debarred from holding office should no longer be allowed to attend the conference. Although the exclusion was consequent upon the previous disciplinary determination, it was held to be administrative in nature, and therefore fell outside the Certification Officer's jurisdiction.

The limited nature of the Certification Officer's jurisdiction was again emphasised in *Irving v GMB* [2008] IRLR 202. In that case, the EAT upheld the decision of the Certification Officer that he had no jurisdiction to consider the applicant's complaint about the way in which a complaint against him had been handled. This was because the matter was dealt with by way of grievance proceedings rather than disciplinary proceedings, and so fell outside the Certification Officer's jurisdiction.

The complaint must be made within six months of either the alleged breach or threatened breach, the conclusion of an internal complaints procedure relating to the breach or the expiry of one year from such a complaints procedure being invoked. *TULRCA 1992, s 108B* provides that the Certification Officer must accept an application only if satisfied that the applicant has taken all reasonable steps to resolve the claim through internal complaints procedures. If he accepts an application, he may make a declaration and an enforcement order requiring steps to be taken to remedy the breach. By *TULRCA 1992, s 108C* an appeal lies on points of law to the Employment Appeal Tribunal.

48.4   CENTRAL ARBITRATION COMMITTEE

The Central Arbitration Committee ('CAC') was established pursuant to the *Employment Protection Act 1975* and continues by virtue of *s 259* of the *Trade Union and Labour Relations (Consolidation) Act 1992* ('*TULRCA 1992*').

48.5   Constitution

The Secretary of State for Trade and Industry is responsible for appointing members of the CAC whom he selects from persons nominated by ACAS as being experienced in industrial relations and who include both employers' and workers' representatives. In addition, the Secretary of State appoints a chairman and may appoint one or more deputy chairmen after consultation with ACAS (*TULRCA 1992, s 260*).

48.6   Functions

These are:

(a)   Arbitration in trade disputes (see **48.7** below).

(b)   Resolution of complaints that an employer has failed to disclose information which he was required to disclose by *TULRCA 1992, s 181* (*TULRCA 1992, s 183*) (see **48.8** below).

(c)   Determination of questions previously referred to the Industrial Arbitration Board (*TULRCA 1992, Sch 3 para 7*). (The Board was the successor of the Industrial Court created by the *Industrial Courts Act 1919*, to which trade disputes of various kinds could be referred.)

(d)   Union recognition disputes (see **48.11** below).

(e)   Resolution of complaints that an employer has failed to comply with its duty to provide data requested under the *Information and Consultation of Employees Regulations 2004 (SI 2004/3426)* (see EMPLOYEE PARTICIPATION (15)).

48.7 Arbitration

The CAC may arbitrate on trade disputes at the request of one or more parties to the dispute, provided that all parties consent to the arbitration. The request for arbitration is made to ACAS in the first instance, which may refer the matter to the CAC (*TULRCA 1992, s 212(1)(b)*; and see **2.6** ADVISORY, CONCILIATION AND ARBITRATION SERVICE).

48.8 Complaint of failure to disclose information

The CAC may hear and determine complaints made by an independent trade union recognised for collective bargaining purposes that the employer by whom it is recognised has not disclosed information to which the union is statutorily entitled (see **9.3** DISCLOSURE OF INFORMATION) (*TULRCA 1992, ss 181, 183*). The CAC is only empowered to make a declaration if the union is recognised by the employer for the particular purpose to which the information relates (*R v Central Arbitration Committee, ex p BTP Tioxide Ltd* [1981] ICR 843). The CAC will refer the complaint for conciliation by ACAS if it considers that it is reasonably likely to be settled in that way (*TULRCA 1992, s 183(2)*). Any person with a proper interest in the complaint is entitled to be heard by the CAC (*TULRCA 1992, s 183(1)*). If the CAC finds the complaint well-founded, it will make a declaration specifying the information which must be disclosed, the date upon which the employer refused or failed to disclose it and the period within which it must be disclosed (*TULRCA 1992, s 183(3), (5)*).

If the employer fails to comply with the order of the CAC, the union may present a further complaint which may be coupled with, or followed by, a claim that certain terms and conditions should be included in the contracts of one or more descriptions of employees in respect of whom the union is recognised by the employer (*TULRCA 1992, ss 184, 185*).

If the CAC finds the further complaint wholly or partly well-founded, it may make an award that, in respect of any description of employees specified in a claim for the inclusion of terms and conditions, the employer shall from a certain date observe either the terms and conditions specified in the claim or other terms and conditions which the CAC considers appropriate (*TULRCA 1992, ss 184(2), (4), 185(3)*). These terms and conditions have effect as part of the contract of employment of any such employee, unless superseded or varied by a further award, a collective agreement, or an agreement with the employee which improves those terms (*TULRCA 1992, s 185(5)*).

An award may only be made in respect of a description of employees, and may only comprise terms and conditions relating to matters in respect of which the trade union making the claim is recognised by the employer (*TULRCA 1992, s 185(4)*). The right to present a claim for terms and conditions expires if the employer discloses, or confirms in writing, the information specified in the declaration, and a claim presented shall be treated as withdrawn if the employer does so before the CAC makes an award on the claim (*TULRCA 1992, s 185(2)*).

48.9 No contracting out

Any provision in an agreement is void insofar as it purports to prevent a person from bringing proceedings before the CAC, unless a conciliation officer has taken action pursuant to his statutory duties or unless the agreement varies or supersedes an award under *TULRCA 1992, s 185* (*TULRCA 1992, s 288*).

48.10 Appeal

There is no appeal against an award of the CAC, but its decision may be challenged by judicial review proceedings in the High Court (or, in Scotland, the Court of Session) and set aside if it can be shown that the CAC:

(a)   misdirected itself in law or exceeded its jurisdiction;

(b)   failed to take into account relevant considerations or took into account irrelevant ones; or

(c)   acted unreasonably or in breach of natural justice.

For an example of the very limited basis on which the Court of Session was prepared to intervene in a decision of the CAC, see *Fullarton Computer Industries Ltd v Central Arbitration Committee* [2001] IRLR 752.

48.11   Statutory trade union recognition

With the coming into force of *s 70A* and *Sch A1* of *TULRCA 1992*, introduced by the *Employment Relations Act 1999* ('*ERA 1999*'), the role of the CAC was considerably expanded and enhanced. With effect from 6 June 2000, trade unions gained a statutory right to be recognised by employers for collective bargaining purposes. See further **48.19–48.38**.

The CAC, under the chairmanship of Sir Michael Burton, plays a central role in relation to the recognition procedures. Applications to the CAC in relation to recognition are heard by a panel of three members, including the chairman or a deputy chairman.

48.12   OBLIGATIONS

Trade unions have statutory obligations to keep accounting records (for members' rights of inspection, see **49.2** TRADE UNIONS – II), to make annual returns, to appoint auditors and to make arrangements for the inspection of their members' superannuation schemes (*TULRCA 1992, ss 28, 32, 32A, 33, 40*). They must keep an up-to-date register of members (see **48.13** below), hold periodic elections for membership of the principal executive committee and for certain other positions (see **48.14** below), and hold ballots on the continued application of trade union funds for political purposes (see **48.15** below) (*TULRCA 1992, ss 24, 46, 71*). In *Paul v NALGO* [1987] IRLR 43 the Certification Officer considered several of these obligations. A trade union must, at the request of any person, supply him with a copy of its rules either free or on payment of a reasonable charge (*TULRCA 1992, s 27*).

48.13   Register of members

Every trade union is obliged by *TULRCA 1992, s 24* to compile and keep up to date a register of members. A member has a right to a copy of any register entry relating to him (*TULRCA 1992, s 24(3)*).

A member of the union may apply to the Certification Officer, or to the High Court in England or the Court of Session in Scotland, for a declaration that these requirements have not been complied with (*TULRCA 1992, ss 25, 26*). The court or (since 25 October 1999) the Certification Officer may also make an enforcement order requiring the union to compile or update the register (*TULRCA 1992, ss 25(5A), 26(4)*). There is a right of appeal against this Certification Officer's decisions under this section to the Employment Appeal Tribunal on any question of law pursuant to *TULRCA 1992, s 45D*.

48.14   Elections and disqualification from office

Trade unions are obliged to secure that, with certain exceptions, all members of its principal executive committee, and its president and general secretary, stand for election at least every five years (*TULRCA 1992, ss 46(1), 119*). Members of the principal executive committee are those who, under the rules or practice of the union, may attend at some or all of its meetings (other than merely to provide factual information or professional advice) (*TULRCA 1992, s 46(3)*). The position of president or general secretary is exempted from the election requirement if its holder is not an employee of the union, is not a voting member of the executive and holds the position for not more than 13 months (*TULRCA 1992, s 46(4)*). The position of president is also exempted if the incumbent was appointed or elected in accordance with the union's rules, at the time of such appointment or election he or she held a designated executive position by virtue of having been elected in accordance with the election requirements under the section and continues to hold such a designated position, and has held such a position for no more than five years (*TULRCA 1992, s 46(4A)*).

In *GMB Union v Corrigan* [2008] ICR 197 the claimant alleged that *TULRCA 1992, s 46* had been breached because, following the suspension of its general secretary, the union had appointed an acting general secretary but failed to hold an election for over a year, pending the completion of an internal investigation. The EAT held that there had been no breach of the statutory duty, since the acting general secretary continue to play an acting role only, and the investigation was a legitimate reason for postponing the election of a new general secretary.

The ballot must, as far as is reasonably practicable, be secret. An independent scrutineer must be appointed to oversee the ballot, and his name must appear on the voting paper. Among his other duties, the scrutineer is obliged to make a report on the ballot to the union which must send it or notify its contents to members. Handling of voting papers and counting of votes must also be independently undertaken. Candidates must, so far as reasonably practicable, be enabled to distribute election addresses without cost to themselves. The members entitled to vote must, so far as is reasonably practicable, be given a convenient opportunity to vote by post. Members may not be unreasonably excluded from standing as candidates, and may not be required, directly or indirectly, to belong to a political party. There are detailed provisions governing the circumstances in which particular classes of members may be excluded from voting (*TULRCA 1992, ss 47–52; Trade Union Ballots and Elections (Independent Scrutineer Qualifications) Order 1993 (SI 1993/1909)*).

Although *TULRCA 1992, s 51(6)* requires the election result to be determined solely by counting the number of votes cast, this did not invalidate a rule limiting the number of members of the National Executive Council ('NEC') who could be elected from any one geographical division (*R v Certification Officer for Trade Unions and Employers' Associations, ex p Electrical Power Engineers' Association* [1990] ICR 682, HL). The House of Lords took the view that the statutory provision was intended only to exclude weighted or block votes and electoral colleges.

The Certification Officer has held that it is permissible for ballot papers to contain information, such as the names of nominating branches, other than that prescribed by the statute (*Decision D/3/89*).

A person who claims that his union is in breach of the election provisions may apply to the Certification Officer, or to the High Court in England or to the Court of Session in Scotland. He must have been a member of the union at the date of the election, and at the date of the application. The application must be made within one year of the date on which the result of the election was announced (*TULRCA 1992, s 54*). The Certification Officer or the court may make a declaration specifying the provisions with which the trade union has failed to comply (*TULRCA 1992, ss 55(2), (3), 56(3)*). If it makes a declaration, the court or the Certification Officer must also, unless it is considered that to do so would be inappropriate, make an enforcement order to secure the holding of an election specified in the order (*TULRCA 1992, ss 55(5A), 56(4)*). There is a right of appeal to the Employment Appeal Tribunal against a decision of the Certification Officer, or a question of law, under *TULRCA 1992, s 56A*.

The Secretary of State is empowered by *TULRCA 1992, ss 203* and *204* to issue a Code of Practice relating to the conduct by trade unions of ballots and elections (see CODES OF PRACTICE (4)). Codes of Practice have been issued, which deal with ballots on industrial action (see STRIKES AND INDUSTRIAL ACTION (43)) and access to workers during recognition and derecognition ballots.

In the event that the executive council of a union seeks to breach the union's election rules, individual members of the union have a contractual right by virtue of their contracts of membership to challenge the validity of the council's decision (*Wise v Union of Shop, Distributive and Allied Workers* [1996] ICR 691). It was held by the High Court in *Ecclestone v National Union of Journalists* [1999] IRLR 166 that a union's exclusion of a candidate for election on the basis that he did not have the confidence of the NEC was both a breach of the union's rules and contrary to the prohibition on unreasonably excluding candidates within *TULRCA 1992, s 47*.

Persons who have previously been convicted of certain offences under *TULRCA 1992, s 45* as amended (which deals in particular with failure to comply with statutory obligations, and with dishonest falsification or destruction of documents) are disqualified from membership of the principal executive committee and from being president or general secretary (subject to the same exemptions as set out above). The disqualification is for five or ten years, depending upon the offence committed (*TULRCA 1992, s 45B*). If a union allows a disqualified person to hold office, a member of the union may apply to the Certification Officer or to the court for a declaration to that effect. They have the power to require the union to take steps to remedy the position (*TULRCA 1992, s 45C, 45C(5A)*). There is a right of appeal against the Certification Officer's decisions under this section to the Employment Appeal Tribunal on any question of law, under *TULRCA 1992, s 45D*.

In *AB v CD* [2001] IRLR 808, the Court of Appeal considered the appropriate mechanism for resolving a tied vote in the second round of the election, by single transferable vote, of a regional union representative. The rules of the union, the RMT, were silent as to how such a tie should be resolved. In the absence of any express rule, the candidate who had received the most votes in the first round was declared elected.

The Court of Appeal upheld this decision. A term was to be implied into the union rules that a tie would be resolved in this way, in order to give efficacy to the contract, as an obvious inference from the express terms of the rules and in order to complete the contract between the members. However, such a term was not to be implied from custom and practice. In order for custom and practice to warrant the implication of a contractual term in the rules of a trade union, the relevant custom must be known, or at least readily ascertainable, by all members.

48.15 Political levy

A trade union may not apply its ordinary funds in the furtherance of political objects as defined by *TULRCA 1992, s 72*, which deals mainly with support for political parties and with attempts to influence the outcome of elections. Payments for such purposes may only be made out of a separate political fund, and then only if there is a political resolution in force approving the furtherance of those objects (*TULRCA 1992, s 71*). Union members have a right to apply to the Certification Officer for a decision that funds have been applied in breach of *s 71* (*TULRCA 1992, s 72A*). Such a resolution must be passed at least every 10 years by a ballot held in accordance with union rules which have been approved by the Certification Officer as complying with the relevant statutory requirements (*TULRCA 1992, ss 73, 74*). Those requirements, found in *TULRCA 1992, ss 75–78* are very similar to those which apply to ballots for union elections (see **48.14** above). Complaints of non-compliance with the ballot requirements may be made either to the Certification Officer or to the court within a year after the announcement of the result (*TULRCA 1992, ss 79–81*).

A union member is entitled to give notice that he objects to contributing to the political fund, and he is then to be exempted from making such contributions, and must not be put at any disadvantage or excluded from the union as a result (*TULRCA 1992, s 82*). A member who complains of a breach of these requirements may complain to the Certification Officer, who may make such order for remedying the breach as he thinks just under the circumstances (*TULRCA 1992, s 82(2), (3)*). A notice of objection should be in the form set out in *TULRCA 1992, s 84(1)* or to like effect. When a political resolution is adopted, members must be notified of their right to object and be given the opportunity to obtain exemption notice forms from union offices or from the Certification Officer (*TULRCA 1992, s 84(2)*).

If a union member certifies to his employer that he is exempt from making political contributions, the employer must ensure that they are not deducted from his wages (*TULRCA 1992, s 86*). There is a right to apply to an employment tribunal for a declaration that the employer has breached this obligation, and for an order that the employer repay sums deducted and, if considered appropriate, require the employer to take specified steps in relation to emoluments payable to the union member. If the member considers that the employer has failed to comply with an order to take such specified steps, he may present a further complaint to the tribunal (*TULRCA 1992, ss 86, 87*; and see PAY – I **(32)**).

48.16 LIABILITY IN TORT

The immunity of trade unions in proceedings in tort arising out of strikes or industrial action is now similar to that of individuals (see STRIKES AND INDUSTRIAL ACTION **(43)**). Such immunity only applies to action taken in contemplation or furtherance of a trade dispute. With certain narrowly defined exceptions, it does not protect secondary action or action taken to enforce trade union membership. Further, a trade union does not enjoy immunity from liability in tort for inducing breaches of contracts of employment unless its action has the support of a ballot (see **43.14** STRIKES AND INDUSTRIAL ACTION). However, where proceedings in tort are brought against a trade union:

(a)   for a reason specified in *TULRCA 1992, s 219* (inducing breach of, and interference with, contracts; see **43.2** STRIKES AND INDUSTRIAL ACTION); or

(b)   in respect of an agreement or combination by two or more persons to induce or do an unlawful act;

then that act will only be taken to have been done by the union if it is taken to have been authorised or endorsed by the union (*TULRCA 1992, s 20(1)*). An act will only be taken to have been authorised or endorsed if it was done, authorised or endorsed by one of the following:

(i)   the principal executive committee; or

(ii) any person who is empowered by the rules to do, authorise or endorse acts of the kind in question; or

(iii) the president or general secretary as defined in *TULRCA 1992, s 119*; or

(iv) any other official of the union (whether employed by it or not), or by any member of a group to which such an official belongs and whose purposes include organising or co-ordinating industrial action; or

(v)   any other committee of the union, by which is meant any group of persons constituted in accordance with the rules of the union.

(*TULRCA 1992, s 20(2), (3)*).

An act will not be taken to have been endorsed by a person in category (iv) or (v) above if it was repudiated by the principal executive committee or the president or general secretary as soon as reasonably practicable after coming to the knowledge of any of them (*TULRCA 1992, s 21(1)*).

In order to be effective, written notice of the repudiation must be given without delay to the committee or official in question, and the union must also do its best to give individual written notice without delay to every member who it has reason to believe is taking part in, or might otherwise take part in, industrial action as a result of the repudiated act, and to the employer of every such member. The written notice must contain a statement in statutorily prescribed form (*TULRCA 1992, s 21(2)–(4)*).

The union will not be able to rely upon such a repudiation if the principal executive committee, or president or general secretary, has subsequently behaved in a way which is inconsistent with the purported repudiation (*TULRCA 1992, s 21(5)*). They will be treated as so behaving if, upon a request made within three months of the purported repudiation by a party to a commercial contract whose performance has been or may have been interfered with by the repudiated act and to whom written notice of the repudiation has not been given, they do not forthwith confirm in writing that the act has been repudiated (*TULRCA 1992, s 21(6)*). (See also *Express and Star Ltd v National Graphical Association* [1985] IRLR 455; upheld on other grounds, [1986] ICR 589.)

The liability of trade unions in such actions in tort is subject to financial limits, considered below.

48.17 Limits on damages awarded against a trade union, enforcement of judgments and protected property

With the exception of amounts awarded in actions for personal injury or for breach of duty in connection with the ownership, occupation, possession, control or use of property, the amount of damages awarded (not including interest; see *Boxfoldia Ltd v National Graphical Association* [1988] ICR 752) in any proceedings in tort brought against a trade union must not exceed the following limits:

(i)   £10,000, if the union has fewer than 5,000 members;

(ii)   £50,000, if it has 5,000 or more members but fewer than 25,000 members;

(iii)   £125,000, if it has 25,000 or more members but fewer than 100,000 members;

(iv)   £250,000, if it has 100,000 or more members.

(*TULRCA 1992, s 22(2)*.)

The Secretary of State may by order vary any of these sums (*TULRCA 1992, s 22(3)*).

A judgment, order or award made in proceedings of any description brought against a trade union is enforceable against any property held in trust for the union (see **48.2** above) to the same extent and in the same manner as if it were a body corporate (*TULRCA 1992, s 12(2)*). However, no award of damages, costs or expenses is recoverable by enforcement against protected property (*TULRCA 1992, s 23(1)*). Protected property includes the property of individual members, officials and trustees, the contents of a political fund which cannot, under the rules, be used to finance industrial action (see **48.15** above), and the contents of separate provident benefit funds (*TULRCA 1992, s 23(2)*).

48.18 LIABILITY OF INDIVIDUAL MEMBERS

The individual participants in industrial action have the same immunity as trade unions. Such immunity only applies to action taken in contemplation or furtherance of a trade dispute. There is, however, no limit on the damages which may be awarded if an individual is found liable. With certain narrowly defined exceptions, secondary industrial action is not protected. (See **43.6** STRIKES AND INDUSTRIAL ACTION.)

TULRCA 1992, s 15 renders unlawful the application of the property of a trade union towards the payment of any penalty imposed upon an individual for an offence or for contempt of court, or towards any indemnity in respect of such liabilities. This applies to all kinds of offences unless designated otherwise by order made by the Secretary of State (*TULRCA 1992, s 15(5)*). However, the prohibition does not extend to civil liabilities, provided that the indemnity or contribution is otherwise lawful and *intra vires* the union. The union is given the right to recover property or its value applied in contravention of these provisions from the individual concerned (*TULRCA 1992, s 15(2)*), and in the event of its unreasonable failure to take proceedings to this end, the court may order, upon application by a union member, that that member shall be authorised to do so in the union's name and at its expense (*TULRCA 1992, s 15(3)*).

48.19 RECOGNITION, INDEPENDENCE AND RIGHTS

The most far-reaching change in the law brought about by the *Employment Relations Act 1999* was the new recognition machinery for collective bargaining purposes contained in *Sch 1* to that *Act*. The relevant provisions, which are now contained in *Sch A1* to *TULRCA 1992*, confer a right upon trade unions to be recognised by employers for collective bargaining purposes, provided various (extremely complex) conditions are fulfilled. Thus, whilst the new procedures encourage employers and unions to agree on recognition wherever possible, they bring about a fundamental change in the law in providing for compulsory recognition in certain circumstances. The new provisions came into force on 6 June 2000. The principal features of the recognition machinery are summarised at **48.25–48.38** below.

The European Court of Human Rights held in *Wilson and National Union of Journalists v United Kingdom* (Applications 30668/96, 30679/61 and 30678/96) [2002] IRLR 568 that *art 11* of the European Convention of Human Rights did not impose a requirement for compulsory collective bargaining. However, in *Demir v Turkey* (Application No 34503/97) (2008) 48 EHRR 1272, [2009] IRLR 766, the European Court held for the first time that the right to bargain collectively is one of the essential elements of the right to form and join trade unions for the protection of workers' interests and so should in general (and subject to any lawful restrictions) be recognised as forming part of the right to freedom of association.

Previous provisions in the *Employment Protection Act 1975* ('*EPA 1975*'), covering the statutory procedure by which independent trade unions could refer recognition issues to ACAS, were repealed in 1980.

Although the previous statutory recognition machinery in the *EPA 1975* was repealed, the concepts of 'independence' and 'recognition' discussed below continue to be relevant for some purposes. One is the procedure for handling redundancies laid down in *TULRCA 1992, Part IV* (see **37.2** REDUNDANCY – II). Others are disclosure of information for collective bargaining purposes under *TULRCA 1992, s 181* (see **9.2** DISCLOSURE OF INFORMATION), the information and consultation requirements contained in the *Transfer of Undertakings (Protection of Employment Regulations 2006 (SI 2006/246)* (see **50.22** TRANSFER OF UNDERTAKINGS) and the right to time off for trade union duties and activities (see **47.2, 47.3** TIME OFF WORK). In addition, the concept of 'independence' is central to the new procedures for recognition for collective bargaining purposes (see below).

48.20 Voluntary recognition

The recognition provisions contained in *TULRCA 1992, Sch A1* provide specifically for voluntary recognition. Even before those provisions came into effect, however, an employer could voluntarily agree to recognise a trade union. Recognition can be express or implied. An employer need not have entered into a formal recognition agreement in order to be considered to have recognised a particular trade union. 'Recognition' is defined in *TULRCA 1992, s 178(3)* as 'the recognition of the union by an employer . . . to any extent, for the purpose of collective bargaining', and 'collective bargaining' means negotiations relating to or connected with: terms and conditions of employment; physical conditions of work; recruitment, dismissal and suspension; allocation of work; matters of discipline; union membership; facilities for officials of trade unions; and bargaining machinery and other procedures (*TULRCA 1992, s 178(1)(2)*). A different definition of collective bargaining applies under the new recognition machinery (see below).

If management in fact consult a trade union about some or all of these matters they may be taken to have recognised that trade union (*Joshua Wilson & Bros Ltd v Union of Shop, Distributive and Allied Workers* [1978] IRLR 120). In *National Union of Gold, Silver and Allied Trades v Albury Bros Ltd* [1979] ICR 84, the Court of Appeal held that an act of recognition is such an important matter that it should not be held to be established unless the evidence is clear, either by actual agreement for recognition or clear and distinct conduct showing an implied agreement to recognise the trade union for the purposes of collective bargaining. In that case, the Court of Appeal held that an attempt by the union to negotiate with the management increased wages for one man did not establish recognition by the employer. Recognition will not be inferred from the fact that a union has been given a right of representation in pay bargaining where that right is given by a third party over whom the employer has no control (*Cleveland County Council v Springett* [1985] IRLR 131).

48.21 Listing

A list of trade unions is maintained by the Certification Officer (*TULRCA 1992, s 2*). Any trade union whose name is entered on the list may apply to the Certification Officer for a certificate that it is independent (*TULRCA 1992, s 6(1)*). A union which is not on the list maintained by the Certification Officer will automatically be refused a certificate of independence (*TULRCA 1992, s 6(3)*).

48.22 Independence

If the union is listed, the Certification Officer will proceed to determine whether the applicant is an independent trade union. An independent trade union is defined in *TULRCA 1992, s 5* as:

' . . . a trade union which –

(a)   is not under the domination or control of an employer or a group of employers or of one or more employers' associations; and

(b)   is not liable to interference by an employer or any such group or association (arising out of the provision of financial or material support or by any other means whatsoever) tending towards such control.'

In *Squibb UK Staff Association v Certification Officer* [1979] ICR 235, CA, the Certification Officer refused to grant a certificate of independence to a staff association which relied to a considerable extent upon facilities provided by the employers. He considered that the association could not be said to be free from liability to interference by the employers. The Court of Appeal upheld the refusal of the grant of the certificate. For a more recent example, see *Government Communications Staff Federation v Certification Officer* [1993] ICR 163.

48.23 Factors implying independence

In *Blue Circle Staff Association v Certification Officer* [1977] 1 WLR 239, some of the principles upon which the Certification Officer acts are set out (at 245–246):

'1   *Finance*: If there is any evidence that a union is getting a direct subsidy from an employer, it is immediately ruled out.

2   *Other assistance*: The Certification Officer's inspectors see what material support, such as free premises, time off work for officials, or office facilities a union is getting from an employer, and attempt to cost them out.

3   *Employer interference*: If a union is very small and weak and gets a good deal of help, then on the face of it its independence will be considered to be in danger and liable to employer interference.

4   *History*: The recent history of a union . . . is considered. It was not unusual for a staff association to start as a "creature of management and grow into something independent".

5   *Rules*: The applicant union's rule book is scrutinised to see if the employer can interfere with or control it, and if there are any restrictions on membership. If a union is run by people near the top of a company it could be detrimental to rank and file members.

6   *Single company unions*: While they are not debarred from getting certificates, because such a rule could exclude unions like those of miners and railwaymen, they are considered to be more liable to employer interference. Broadly based multi-company unions are considered more difficult to influence.

7   *Organisation*: The Certification Officer's inspectors then examine the applicant union in detail, its size and recruiting ability, whether it is run by competent and experienced officers, the state of its finance, and its branch and committee structure. Again, if the union was run by senior men in a company, employer interference was a greater risk.

8   *Attitude*: Once the other factors have been assessed, inspectors looked for a "robust attitude in negotiation" as a sign of genuine independence, backed up by a good negotiating record . . . '

Before making a determination on the question of independence, the Certification Officer makes such inquiries as he sees fit and takes into account any relevant information submitted to him (*TULRCA 1992, s 6(4)*). In general, he should not be cross-examined upon his reasons for his decision (*Squibb* at **48.22** above).

48.24 Withdrawal of certificate of independence and appeals against Certification Officer's decision

The Certification Officer may at any time withdraw a certificate, after giving notice to the trade union affected and determining the relevant questions, if he is of the opinion that the trade union in question is no longer independent (*TULRCA 1992, s 7(1)*).

A trade union aggrieved by the refusal of the Certification Officer to issue it with a certificate, or by a decision of his to withdraw its certificate, may appeal to the Employment Appeal Tribunal. If the appeal is successful the Employment Appeal Tribunal will give directions to the Certification Officer to act according to its findings (*TULRCA 1992, s 9*).

48.25 RECOGNITION FOR COLLECTIVE BARGAINING PURPOSES

The current procedure for the recognition of trade unions by employers for the purposes of collective bargaining was introduced by *ERA 1999, Sch 1*. This recognition machinery came into effect on 6 June 2000 and is contained in *TULRCA 1992, Sch A1*. The new law represented a fundamental change in industrial relations in the United Kingdom, since it conferred upon trade unions a right to be recognised by employers for collective bargaining purposes, provided various conditions are satisfied. The new regime does, however, seek to promote voluntary recognition wherever possible. Also significant is the enhanced role for the Central Arbitration Committee ('CAC') (see **48.4**) in determining a range of issues relating to recognition. In carrying out these functions, the CAC is under a duty to have regard to the object of encouraging and promoting fair and efficient practices in the workplace. The provisions relating to the membership of the CAC contained in *TULRCA 1992, s 260* were amended by *ERA 1999, s 24* so as to require the Secretary of State to appoint only persons experienced in industrial relations, having first consulted with ACAS and such other persons as he may choose to consult (*TULRCA 1992, Sch A1 para 171*) (see **48.11** above). The new recognition procedures are extremely complex. Below is set out a summary of the principal provisions.

48.26   The scope of the new procedure

The recognition procedures apply only to employers which, taken with any associated employers, employ either at least 21 workers on the day on which a request for recognition is received, or have employed an average of at least 21 workers in the 13 preceding weeks (*TULRCA 1992, Sch A1 para 7(1)*). For this purpose, the definition of 'worker' contained in *TULRCA 1992, s 296(1)* applies. In *R (on the application of the BBC) v Central Arbitration Committee* [2003] EWHC 1375 (Admin), [2003] ICR 1542 it was held that an application for recognition should not have been entertained by the CAC in respect of freelance cameramen and women working for the BBC, since they were excluded from the definition of 'workers' as 'professionals'. The CAC had erred in finding that the cameramen and women were not 'professionals' merely because they had no regulatory body.

Only unions which have been certified as independent under *TULRCA 1992, s 6* may make a request for recognition.

The territorial reach of the CAC union recognition procedures was considered in *Netjets Management Ltd v CAC* [2012] EWHC 2685 (Admin), [2012] IRLR 986. The employer, which ran private business flights throughout Europe, sought to argue that the union's application for recognition in respect of all pilots fell outside the CAC's remit because most of the pilots were based outside the United Kingdom. The High Court upheld the CAC's decision that it had jurisdiction. There were "sufficiently strong" connections with Great Britain. In particular, the pilots' contracts were governed by English law and subject to the exclusive jurisdiction of the English Courts. No other EU states have been put forward as a more appropriate forum for collective bargaining. Moreover, if there was no collective bargaining on pay, hours and holidays in Great Britain, the pilots would be prevented from exercising their right to collective bargaining under Article 11 of the Convention.

48.27   Collective bargaining

The definition of collective bargaining contained in *TULRCA 1992, s 178* does not apply to the new recognition provisions. Instead, collective bargaining is defined as negotiations relating to pay, hours and holidays, subject to the parties agreeing that additional matters may also be the subject of collective bargaining (*Sch A1, paras 1–4*). For the purposes of this provision, the CAC has held that pension benefits fall within the definition of pay (see *UNIFI v Union Bank of Nigeria* [2001] IRLR 713).

48.28   The request for recognition

A union or unions seeking recognition must apply first to the employer. The request must be made in writing, identify the relevant unions and bargaining unit and state that it is made under *TULRCA 1992, Sch A1 para 8*. If the parties agree within 10 working days on the appropriate bargaining unit and further agree that the union is (or unions are) to be recognised to conduct collective bargaining on behalf of that unit, then the union is (or unions are) deemed to be recognised, and no further steps need be taken. If the employer does not accept the request, but agrees to negotiate, then the union will be deemed to be recognised if the parties are able to agree within a further 20-day period. The parties may request ACAS to assist in conducting such negotiations (*Sch A1, para 10*).

48.29 Reference to the CAC

If the employer either rejects or fails to respond to the request within 10 days, or if negotiations break down during the subsequent 20-day period, the union may apply to the CAC to decide on the appropriate bargaining unit and whether the union has the support of a majority of workers within that unit. The union may ask the CAC to determine the question of majority support if the parties have agreed on the appropriate bargaining unit, but have not agreed on whether the union should be entitled to conduct collective bargaining on its behalf. However, the union may not apply to the CAC if it has rejected or failed to respond to a proposal by the employer that ACAS be requested to assist in negotiations (*Sch A1, paras 11, 12*).

TULRCA 1992, Sch A1 sets out a detailed procedure for the various sequential steps that must be taken by the CAC once it has received an application for union recognition. This procedure is subject to a relatively strict timetable, with the CAC generally being given 10 days to reach a determination at each stage of the procedure. The time limits within the recognition procedure are subject to extension by the CAC in most cases, although in some circumstances the CAC is under a duty to give reasons for such an extension to the parties.

The CAC must decide whether any application for recognition is 'valid' within the meaning of *TULRCA 1992, Sch A1 paras 5–9* and 'admissible' within the meaning of *TULRCA 1992, Sch A1 paras 33–42*, having considered any evidence provided by the employer or the union (*Sch A1, para 15*). The criteria of 'validity' are essentially the requirements as to union independence and number of workers employed referred to above. An application may be 'inadmissible' if there is already in force a collective agreement under which a union is recognised for collective bargaining purposes (*Sch A1, para 35*). This exclusion can have far-reaching consequences. In *R (on the application of National Union of Journalists) v Central Arbitration Committee* [2005] EWCA Civ 1309, [2006] ICR 1 the Court of Appeal upheld the decision of the High Court that the NUJ's application to the CAC was inadmissible, because the employer already had a recognition agreement with another union. This was the case notwithstanding that that agreement had not been used to determine the terms and conditions of workers within the bargaining unit and the other union had at most one member working in the relevant division of the employer's business. Similarly, in *Transport and General Workers' Union v Asda* [2004] IRLR 836 the CAC held the union's application inadmissible because the employer had a 'partnership agreement' in place with another union. This was despite the fact that the 'partnership agreement' provided for only limited representational rights, and specifically excluded collective bargaining on terms and conditions of employment, including pay.

However, these decisions now need to be read in the light of the CAC's important decision in *Pharmacists' Defence Association v Boots Management Services Ltd* [2013] IRLR 262. The employer had a long-standing relationship with a listed trade union, but the union was not recognised for the purposes of collective bargaining in relation to terms and conditions of employment. On the literal wording of *Sch A1, para 35*, the application by a rival union for recognition was precluded, because another union was already recognised for some collective bargaining purposes. The CAC held that a literal reading of the paragraph would be incompatible with Article 11 of the Convention. Accordingly, it re-wrote *Sch A1, para 35*, so that a recognition application by another union will be precluded only if another union is already recognised as entitled to conduct collective bargaining *"in respect of pay, hours and holidays"*.

An application will be inadmissible unless members of the relevant union (or unions) constitute at least 10% of workers within the bargaining unit and a majority of the workers within that unit are likely to favour recognition (*Sch A1, para 36*). Further, where an application is made by more than one union, the application will be inadmissible unless they show that they will co-operate with each other so as to secure and maintain a stable and effective collective bargaining arrangement, and further that they will act together for collective bargaining purposes if the employer wishes (*Sch A1, para 37*). An application will also be inadmissible if brought within three years of a previous application by the same union or unions in respect of the same or substantially the same bargaining unit (*Sch A1, paras 39–40*). If the application does not fulfil the criteria of 'validity' and 'admissibility', it must not be accepted by the CAC.

If the CAC accepts an application, it must first try to assist the parties in seeking to agree on the appropriate bargaining unit within a period of 20 working days (which may be extended). In the absence of agreement, the CAC must decide on the appropriate bargaining unit (*Sch A1, paras 18, 19*).

In *Prison Officers' Association and Securicor Custodial Services Ltd*, Re (2000) IDS Brief 670, the CAC accepted that the employer's recognition of a non-independent staff association precluded the application by an independent trade union for recognition pursuant to *Sch A1, para 35*. Where such an association is recognised, therefore, the independent union may well have to seek to initiate derecognition proceedings.

48.30 The appropriate bargaining unit

In deciding on the appropriate bargaining unit, the CAC must take into account the need for the unit to be compatible with effective management and, in so far as they do not conflict with that primary need, the following additional factors:

(a)   the views of the parties;

(b)   existing national and local bargaining arrangements;

(c)   the desirability of avoiding small fragmented bargaining units within an undertaking;

(d)   the characteristics of the workforce falling within and outside of the unit; and

(e)   the location of workers (*Sch A1, para 19*).

In *R (on the application of Kwik-Fit (GB) Ltd) v Central Arbitration Committee* [2002] EWCA Civ 512, [2002] ICR 1212, the Court of Appeal considered the approach to be adopted by the CAC when considering competing contentions by the union and employer as to the appropriate bargaining unit. Buxton LJ rejected the employer's contention that the CAC has a duty to treat on equal terms the unit proposed by the union and any alternative proposed by the employer. The recognition machinery is put in motion by a request from the union. Provided the CAC finds that the unit put forward by the union is 'appropriate', it need not go further and consider whether there is a more appropriate unit that might be identified. It must take into account the employer's views, but should not weigh up whether an alternative unit put forward by the employer might be better than that proposed by the union, provided that that proposed by the union meets the requirement of being 'appropriate'. The decision highlights the way in which the recognition process is essentially union-driven.

In *Re Benteler Automotive UK and ISTC* (Central Arbitration Committee, 17 October 2000) (IDS Brief 677), the CAC broadly accepted the union's argument that the relevant bargaining unit was shop-floor employees only. Although the employer argued that supervisory, technical and administrative staff should be included, so as to reflect their 'whole company' ethos, the CAC noted that this did not reflect the existing management organisation and practice at the company. Although the CAC did not wish to impede the employers in achieving a 'whole company' approach, existing economic realities determined the appropriate bargaining unit.

In *Graphical Paper and Media Union v Derry Print Ltd* [2002] IRLR 380, the CAC considered the proper approach to determining the appropriate bargaining unit where a single business was run through two separate companies, with members of the workforce being allocated to one business or the other. The CAC concluded that, under the recognition machinery in *TULRCA 1992, Sch A1*, a bargaining unit could not include the employees of more than one employer. The language and scheme of the recognition provisions envisaged the determination of a bargaining unit by reference to a single employer.

However, the CAC went on to hold that, on the facts of the case, it was permissible to treat the two companies in question as a single employer. A more liberal approach to lifting the corporate veil in this way was appropriate here than in some other legal contexts. The CAC accordingly determined that the appropriate bargaining unit comprised the production workers of both companies. The CAC thereby recognised the importance of determining the bargaining unit by reference to the economic realities on the shop floor.

In *R (on the application of Cable & Wireless Services UK Ltd) v Central Arbitration Committee* [2008] EWHC 115 (Admin), [2008] IRLR 425, [2008] ICR 693 Collins J upheld a decision of the CAC that the smallness of a bargaining unit would not in itself necessary lead to fragmentation. Whilst small fragmented bargaining units were undesirable, the mischief underlying this criterion was avoiding the proliferation of such units resulting from the creation of a unit lacking in any obviously identifiable boundary.

If the parties have agreed, or the CAC has decided on, a bargaining unit which differs from that originally proposed, the CAC must consider whether the application is valid by reference to further criteria of 'validity' set out in *paras 43–50 (Sch A1, para 20)*. These further criteria of validity closely mirror those of 'admissibility' set out above (see *paras 33–42*). Where there is no such disparity, and where the CAC is satisfied that the criteria of validity are satisfied, the CAC must proceed with the application for union recognition.

48.31 Union recognition

The central provisions of the new recognition procedure are those which provide for the compulsory recognition of unions for collective bargaining purposes. Such recognition may or may not be preceded by a secret ballot of the workers within the relevant bargaining unit. Where the CAC is satisfied that a majority of the workers within the bargaining unit are members of the union, it must issue a declaration that the union is recognised as entitled to conduct collective bargaining on behalf of the workers within the bargaining unit, unless:

(a)   it is satisfied that a ballot should be held in the interests of good industrial relations; or

(b)   there is credible evidence from a significant number of union members within the bargaining unit that they do not want the union to conduct collective bargaining on their behalf; or

(c)   evidence about the circumstances in which members joined the union or about the length of time they have been members is produced, which leads the CAC to conclude that there are doubts about whether a significant number of members wish the union to conduct collective bargaining on their behalf.

If any of those circumstances apply, the CAC must give notice that it intends to arrange for the holding of a secret ballot in which the workers will be asked whether they want the union to be recognised. Equally, the CAC must give notice of its intention to arrange for the holding of a secret ballot if it is not satisfied that a majority of workers within the bargaining unit are members of the union. The CAC must then arrange for the holding of a ballot unless it receives notification within 10 working days (or such longer period as the CAC specifies) from the union (or from the union and employer jointly) that they do not want a ballot to take place (*Sch A1, paras 20–24*).

In *Fullarton Computer Industries Ltd v Central Arbitration Committee* [2001] IRLR 752, the Court of Session upheld the CAC's decision that a trade union should be recognised without a ballot on the grounds that a ballot would not be in the interests of good industrial relations. The Court of Session approached the case on the basis that the CAC was under no obligation to give reasons for its decision. (The CAC is obliged by the statute to give reasons for some of its decisions, particularly those relating to the extension of time limits within the recognition procedure, but not, ironically, for those substantive decisions, such as this one, which are likely to be determinative of the outcome of the recognition application.) If reasons were given, the decision could be set aside only if they disclosed some manifest error or flaw on the face of the record. This case highlights the difficulty inherent in challenging the CAC's decision as to whether a ballot is likely to be in the interests of good industrial relations.

48.32   The recognition ballot

The recognition ballot, which must be conducted by a qualified independent person appointed by the CAC, may be conducted in the workplace, by post or, exceptionally, by some combination of the two. A 'qualified independent person' is defined for these purposes as someone who fulfils the conditions of either being a practicing solicitor or being eligible for appointment as a company auditor. In addition, a number of organisations providing electoral services are specified by name to be such persons (*Recognition and Derecognition Ballots (Qualified Persons) Order 2000 (SI 2000/1306)*). The costs of the ballot are divided equally between the employer on the one hand and the union (or unions) on the other. In deciding on the appropriate method, the CAC must take into account the risk of unfairness or malpractice if the ballot is conducted in the workplace, costs and practicality, and such other matters as it considers appropriate (*Sch A1, paras 25, 28*).

The employer is placed under five duties in relation to a recognition ballot:

(a)   it must co-operate generally with both the union and the person appointed to conduct the ballot;

(b)   it must give the union such reasonable access to the workers within the bargaining unit as will enable it to inform the workers of its object and seek their support and opinions;

(c)   it must give the CAC the names and home addresses of the workers within the bargaining unit, including any workers who join the unit after the initial list has been provided, and must further inform the CAC if any such workers have ceased to be within the unit. The CAC passes this information on to the person appointed to conduct the ballot;

(d)   it must refrain from unreasonably seeking to induce workers to refrain from attending meetings with a union regarding recognition;

(e)   it must refrain from taking or threatening action against a worker because he has attended or intends to attend a meeting with a union regarding recognition

A new code of practice on access to workers during recognition and derecognition ballots came into effect on 1 October 2005 pursuant to *TULRCA 1992, ss 203–204* and the *Employment Code of Practice (Access to Workers during Recognition and Derecognition Ballots) Order 2005 (SI 2005/2421)*.

It the employer fails to comply with any of these duties, the CAC may order the employer to take remedial steps. If the employer fails to comply with such an order, the CAC may cancel the ballot (or ignore it if it has taken place) and make a declaration of recognition (*Sch A1, paras 26, 27*).

The person appointed to conduct the ballot must send all relevant workers any information supplied by the union, provided that the union bears the cost of sending such information.

The most important (and controversial) provision in the union recognition procedure is that which determines the effect of the outcome of the recognition ballot. If union recognition for collective bargaining purposes is supported by:

(a)   a majority of the workers voting, and

(b)   at least 40% of the workers within the bargaining unit,

then the CAC must issue a declaration that the union is recognised for collective bargaining purposes. If those conditions are not satisfied, then the CAC must declare that the union is not so recognised. The Secretary of State may by order amend this provision so as to specify a different degree of requisite support (*Sch A1, para 29*). It follows that, even if a majority of those voting support recognition, the union will not be recognised if a low turnout entails that those in favour constitute less than 40% of the workforce within the bargaining unit.

In *R (on the application of Ultraframe (UK) Ltd) v Central Arbitration Committee* [2005] EWCA Civ 560 [2005] ICR 1194 the Court of Appeal upheld a decision of the CAC directing a re-run of a recognition ballot. Although a majority of those voting had supported recognition, the 40% requirement had not been achieved by four votes. The unions complained that a number of employees had not received ballot papers, and the CAC concluded that five employees, who would have voted in favour of recognition, had not been given a reasonable opportunity to vote. The Court of Appeal concluded that the CAC had jurisdiction to investigate and, if appropriate, to annul the ballot, and so had acted within its powers in ordering a re-run.

All parties informed by the CAC of a recognition ballot must refrain from using unfair practices in relation to such a ballot (*Sch A1, para 27A*). 'Unfair practices' are defined so as to include; making inducements to vote in a particular way; coercion; undue influence; and dismissal, disciplinary action or detriment, or threats of such actions, aimed at influencing the outcome of the ballot. A party may complain to the CAC if it believes that unfair practices have been used (*Sch A1, para 27C*). If the CAC finds a complaint well-founded, it must make a declaration to that effect, and may order the party concerned to take specified action, or give notice that it intends to arrange a secret ballot in which the workers are asked whether they want the union to conduct collective bargaining on their behalf (*Sch A1, para 27C*). The CAC's further powers upon such a finding also include a power in certain circumstances to cancel or annul a ballot.

48.33   The method of collective bargaining

Once a declaration of recognition has been made, the parties may seek to negotiate an agreement as to the method by which they will conduct collective bargaining during a 30-day period or such longer period as they agree. If no agreement is reached, the parties may apply to the CAC for assistance. The CAC must try to help the parties to reach an agreement. If after a further 20 days (or such further period as the CAC agrees with the parties) still no agreement has been reached, the CAC must specify the method by which the parties will conduct collective bargaining. A detailed 'specified method' is set out in the *Trade Union Recognition (Method of Collective Bargaining) Order 2000 (SI 2000/1300)*. This must be taken into account by the CAC when specifying a method of collective bargaining for the parties. In those circumstances, unless the parties agree otherwise, the specified method has effect as if made in a legally enforceable contract between parties. However, specific performance will be the only remedy available for any breach of the specified method. If the parties have agreed the method by which they will conduct collective bargaining, but one or more of the parties fails to carry it out, the parties may apply to the CAC for assistance (*Sch A1, paras 30–32*).

48.34 Voluntary recognition

TULRCA 1992, Sch A1 Part II contains additional provisions relating specifically to voluntary recognition. These provisions apply where the parties reach agreement that the union should be recognised as entitled to conduct collective bargaining at some point before the compulsory recognition procedure summarised above has been exhausted. Agreement may have been reached either before or after an application to the CAC has been made (*Sch A1, para 52*). Any party to such an agreement may apply to the CAC for a decision whether or not the agreement is indeed an 'agreement for recognition' as defined (*Sch A1, para 55*).

If the CAC decides that the agreement is an 'agreement for recognition', the employer may not terminate the agreement for a period of three years. The union, however, may terminate such an agreement at any time, with or without the consent of the employer. It follows that an employer, but not a union, who enters into a recognition agreement may be bound by that agreement for up to three years (but see below for the provisions relating to changes in the bargaining unit and derecognition) (*Sch A1, para 56*).

Where the parties have entered into a recognition agreement, but have failed to agree on a method for conducting collective bargaining, they may apply to the CAC for assistance. Equally, if the parties have agreed on a method, but one or more of the parties fails to carry it out, they may apply to the CAC for assistance. The CAC must not accept either type of application unless the requirements as to number of workers employed and union certification are satisfied. Once it has decided that an application is admissible, the CAC must try to help the parties to reach an agreement. If after a period of 20 days (or such further period as the parties agree) still no agreement has been reached, the CAC must specify the method by which the parties will conduct collective bargaining, taking into account the 'specified method' set out in the *Trade Union Recognition (Method of Collective Bargaining) Order 2000 (SI 2000/1300)*. As in the case of compulsory recognition, unless the parties agree otherwise, the specified method has effect as if made in a legally enforceable contract between parties. Again, however, specific performance is the only remedy available for any breach of the specified method (*Sch A1, paras 58–63*).

48.35 Changes in the bargaining unit

If either party believes that the original bargaining unit is no longer appropriate, it may apply to the CAC for a decision as to the appropriate bargaining unit. Such an application is admissible only if the CAC decides that the original unit is likely to be no longer appropriate, either because the organisation or structure of the employer's business or the employer's business activities have changed, or because there has been a substantial change in the number of workers employed in the original unit (*Sch A1, paras 64–68*). Once the CAC has accepted the application, the parties may agree on a new bargaining unit. If no such agreement is reached, the CAC must decide whether the original unit is appropriate and, if not, decide on a new unit or units. Again, in deciding whether the original unit is appropriate, the CAC must take into account only changes in the organisation or structure of the employer's business or the employer's business activities, or any substantial change in the number of workers employed in the original unit. In deciding what new unit might be appropriate, the CAC must adopt similar criteria to those outlined above in respect of an initial application for recognition (*Sch A1, paras 69–73*).

If an employer believes that the original bargaining unit has ceased to exist and wishes the collective bargaining arrangements to cease to have effect, it must give notice to the union, copied to the CAC. Provided proper notice is given, the collective bargaining arrangements will cease to have effect unless the union applies to the CAC within 10 days for a decision on whether the original unit has ceased to exist and whether it is no longer appropriate in any event. If such an application is made, the CAC must determine these questions, having given the employer and the unions an opportunity to put forward their views on whether the unit has ceased to exist or is no longer appropriate. Again, in deciding whether the original unit is no longer appropriate, the CAC must take into account only any changes in the organisation or structure of the employer's business or the employer's business activities, or any substantial change in the number of workers employed in the original unit. If the CAC decides that the original unit has ceased to exist, the collective bargaining arrangements cease to have effect. If it decides that it has not ceased to exist and remains an appropriate bargaining unit, the collective bargaining arrangements remain in place. If, however, the CAC decides that the original unit has not ceased to exist, but that it is no longer an appropriate unit, it must decide what other bargaining unit is (or units are) appropriate by reference to the same criteria as apply when initially deciding on the appropriate bargaining unit (see above) (*Sch A1, paras 74–81*).

The CAC must further decide whether the difference between the original unit and the new unit is such that the level of support for the union within the new unit needs to be assessed. If not, then the CAC simply issues a declaration that the union is recognised as entitled to conduct collective bargaining on behalf of the new unit. If, however, the CAC decides that the level of support needs to be assessed, it must carry out a procedure similar to that in respect of an initial application for recognition before determining whether to make a recognition declaration. This procedure may require the holding of a secret ballot. The threshold for recognition is the same as in the case of an initial application for recognition (ie a majority of those voting and 40% of workers within the unit voting in favour of union recognition) (*Sch A1, paras 85–89*).

48.36 Derecognition

The procedure set out in *TULRCA 1992, Sch A1* also contains detailed provisions relating to the derecognition of unions for collective bargaining purposes. Following the expiry of three years from a declaration of recognition by the CAC, the employer may apply for derecognition if he believes that he (taken with any associated employers) has employed an average of fewer than 21 workers over a period of 13 weeks (*Sch A1, paras 99–103*). Further, an employer may issue a request to the unions to agree to end the collective bargaining arrangements, again following the expiry of three years from a declaration of recognition. If the union rejects or fails to respond to such a request, or the parties enter negotiations but fail to reach agreement, the employer may apply to the CAC with a view to a secret ballot being held to decide whether the bargaining arrangements should be ended (*Sch A1, paras 104–111*). A specific derecognition procedure applies where a declaration of recognition has been made automatically by the CAC on the basis that it is satisfied that a majority of the workers within the bargaining unit are members of the union, and the basis of the employer's request for an end to the bargaining arrangements is that fewer than half of the workers within the unit are, in fact, union members (*Sch A1, paras 122–133*).

Any worker falling within the bargaining unit similarly may apply to the CAC to have collective bargaining arrangements ended once three years have expired after a declaration of recognition. However, such an application is inadmissible unless the CAC decides that at least 10% of the workers within the bargaining unit favour ending the collective bargaining arrangements *and* that a majority of the workers within the unit would be *likely* to favour ending the arrangements. In the absence of agreement through negotiation (or withdrawal of the application), the CAC must arrange for the holding of a secret ballot to decide whether the bargaining arrangements should be ended (*Sch A1, paras 112–116*). A specific derecognition procedure applies where an employer and a union which has not been certified as independent have agreed that the union should be recognised as entitled to conduct collective bargaining purposes and a worker wishes to apply to the CAC to have the bargaining arrangements ended (*Sch A1, paras 134–147*).

The provisions relating to the conduct of a derecognition ballot mirror closely the provisions summarised above in relation to a recognition ballot (*Sch A1, paras 117–121*).

If a union which the CAC has declared to be recognised as entitled to conduct collective bargaining has its certificate of independence withdrawn (or, where, several unions are parties, they all have their certificates withdrawn), the relevant bargaining arrangements shall cease to have effect and the parties shall be taken to have agreed that the union is entitled to conduct collective bargaining on behalf of the bargaining unit concerned. However, if the union (or one of the unions) succeeds in an appeal against the decision to withdraw its certificate, the bargaining arrangements are reinstated (*Sch A1, paras 149–153*).

48.37 Detriment

TULRCA 1992, Sch A1 Part VIII creates a right on the part of workers not to be subjected to a detriment on union recognition-related grounds. In particular, a worker has a right not to be subjected to a detriment by any act, or any deliberate failure to act, by his employer on grounds that the worker:

(a)   sought to obtain or prevent recognition of a union;

(b)   indicated support for, or opposition to, recognition;

(c)   sought to secure or prevent the ending of collective bargaining arrangements;

(d)   indicated support for, or opposition to, the ending of collective bargaining arrangements;

(e)   influenced or sought to influence the way in which votes would be cast in a recognition ballot;

(f)   influenced or sought to influence other workers to vote or abstain in such a ballot;

(g)   voted in such a ballot;

(h)   proposed to do, failed to do, or proposed to decline to do, any of the matters set out above.

However, an unreasonable act or omission by the worker is not capable of falling within these grounds. If subjected to such a detriment, the worker may complain to an employment tribunal (*Sch A1, para 156*).

There is a parallel right not to be dismissed on union recognition-related grounds. Such dismissal will be automatically unfair (see **52.3 Unfair Dismissal – II**) (*Sch A1, paras 161–165*).

The worker may make a complaint to an employment tribunal within three months of the act or failure to act complained of, or within such further period as the tribunal considers reasonable in a case where it is satisfied that it was not reasonably practicable for the complaint to be presented within three months (*Sch A1, para 157*).

It is for the employer to show the ground on which he acted or failed to act (*Sch A1, para 158*). If the tribunal finds the complaint well-founded, it will make a declaration to that effect and may order compensation to be paid. The compensation will be such amount as it considers just and equitable in all the circumstances, having regard to the infringement complained of and any loss sustained by the complainant. Compensation may be reduced on account of a failure to mitigate, or on account of the applicant's contributory fault (*Sch A1, para 159*). By analogy with the principles applied to action short of dismissal on trade union grounds (see **49.18 TRADE UNIONS – II**), it is likely that such compensation may include an award in respect of injury to feelings (compare *Adams v Hackney London Borough Council* [2003] IRLR 402).

48.38 Training

The *Employment Relations Act 1999* also imposed training obligations upon employers where a union is recognised for collective bargaining purposes in accordance with *TULRCA 1992, Sch A1* in circumstances where the CAC has specified to the parties the method for conducting collective bargaining (*ERA 1999, s 5*). In those circumstances, an employer is under a duty to invite trade union representatives to meetings, to be held at least once every six months, for the purpose of:

(a)   consulting about the employer's policy on training workers within the bargaining unit;

(b)   consulting about the employer's plans for such training in the following six months; and

(c)   reporting about training provided since the previous meeting.

The employer must provide to the union any information without which the union representatives would be materially impeded in participating, and which it would be in accordance with good industrial relations practice to provide, at least two weeks before such a meeting. The employer must also take into account any written representations submitted by the union within four weeks of a meeting (*TULRCA 1992, s 70B*).

A trade union may complain to an employment tribunal if an employer fails to comply with the obligation to consult on training. Such a complaint must be presented within three months of the alleged failure complained of, or within such further period as the tribunal considers reasonable in a case where it is satisfied that it was not reasonably practicable for the complaint to be presented within three months. Where a complaint is upheld, the tribunal shall make a declaration to that effect and may award compensation to each person who was, at the time when the failure occurred, a member of the bargaining unit. The maximum amount of compensation is two weeks' pay per worker (subject to the limit on a week's pay set out in *ERA 1996, s 227(1)*, currently £450).

48.39 AMALGAMATIONS AND TRANSFERS OF ENGAGEMENTS

One trade union may amalgamate with or transfer its engagements to another trade union. However, it may not do so unless a resolution which approves the amalgamation or transfer, in a form approved by the Certification Officer, has been passed by a vote of members. The right to be balloted may not extend to members who are not full members of the union (see *National Union of Mineworkers (Yorkshire Area) v Millward* [1995] ICR 482). *TULRCA 1992, ss 97–105* and the *Trade Unions and Employers' Associations (Amalgamations, etc) Regulations 1975 (SI 1975/536)*, as amended, regulate amalgamations and specify the information which must be given to union members and the manner in which the ballot must be taken. *TULRCA 1992, s 103* provides a remedy, by way of complaint to the Certification Officer, to a union member dissatisfied with the way in which the vote on the resolution was taken.

49   Trade Unions – II: Individual Rights and Union Membership

49.1   RIGHTS OF UNION MEMBERS IN RELATION TO EMPLOYER

An employee who is a member of a trade union has the following rights in relation to his employer.

(a)   He may not be refused employment because of his membership of a trade union (see **49.3** below).

(b)   Dismissal for membership of, or for taking part in the activities of, an independent trade union is automatically unfair, as is dismissal on union recognition-related grounds (see **52.3** Unfair Dismissal – **II**).

(c)   Subjection to detriment by his employer for membership of, or for taking part in the activities of, or using the services of, an independent trade union, or on union recognition-related grounds, gives the employee the right to complain to an employment tribunal which may award him compensation (see **49.18** below).

(d)   The right to time off from work to take part in trade union activities (see **47.3** Time off Work).

(e)   The right not to suffer the deduction of unauthorised or excessive union subscriptions from his wages (see **49.21** below).

(f)   Where a trade union is recognised for collective bargaining purposes within *TULRCA 1992, Sch A1, TULRCA 1992, s 70B* imposes upon the employer a duty to consult with trade union representatives on training for workers within the bargaining unit (see Trade Unions **I (48)**);

(g)   A worker who is required or invited to attend a disciplinary or grievance hearing by his employer has the right to be accompanied by a trade union official (see **49.22** below).

In addition, a trade union *official* has the right to take time off with pay for his trade union duties (see **47.2** Time off Work).

49.2   RIGHTS OF UNION MEMBERS OR INTENDING MEMBERS IN RELATION TO UNION

A trade union member or would-be member has the following rights in relation to his union.

(a)   The right not to be excluded or expelled save on certain specified grounds and in accordance with the rules of the union (see **49.11** to **49.14** below).

(b)   The right under *TULRCA 1992, s 69* to terminate his membership with the union on giving reasonable notice and complying with any reasonable conditions.

(c)   The right not to have disciplinary action taken against him by the union save in accordance with the rules of the union and to be protected from disciplinary action taken on certain grounds (see **49.15** and **49.16** below).

(d)   The right under *TULRCA 1992, s 62* to apply to the High Court (or, in Scotland, the Court of Session) if members of his union, including himself, have been called on to take industrial action which has not received prior ballot approval (see **43.18** Strikes and Industrial Action).

(e)   The right under *TULRCA 1992, s 30* to inspect the union's accounting records, in the company of an accountant if he so desires.

(f)   The right under *TULRCA 1992, s 16* to apply for relief to the High Court (or, in Scotland, the Court of Session) where the trustees of the union's property permit it to be applied unlawfully or comply with unlawful directions from the union.

He or she is also protected against unlawful discrimination (see **11.29 DISCRIMINATION AND EQUAL OPPORTUNITIES – II**). For example, in *Allen v GMB* [2008] EWCA Civ 810, [2008] ICR 1407, [2008] IRLR 690 the Court of Appeal held a trade union to be liable to affected members when it negotiated a pay deal the effect of which was indirectly discriminatory against women members. Nationals of other EU member states are entitled to equal rights as members of trade unions (*Regulation 1612/68/EEC, art 8*; and see **EUROPEAN UNION LAW (22)**).

An attempt to bring a common law claim against a union which had not achieved a result favouring a particular member was struck out as having no prospect of success in *Iwanuszezak v General Municipal Boilermakers and Allied Trades Union* [1988] IRLR 219. The union had to put the collective interests of its whole membership first.

49.3   CLOSED SHOP

The *Industrial Relations Act 1971* gave the right to employees to belong to the trade union of their choice or not to belong to a trade union at all. That *Act* was repealed by the *Trade Union and Labour Relations Act 1974* ('*TULRA 1974*'), which enabled an employer lawfully to enforce a closed shop by a 'union membership agreement' made with a trade union or trade unions. The *Employment Acts 1980* and *1982* subsequently imposed certain restrictions and conditions on the closed shop. The *Employment Act 1988* effectively outlawed dismissals to enforce a closed shop. Dismissals to enforce a union membership agreement are automatically unfair. The *Employment Act 1990* made it unlawful to refuse a person employment on grounds of membership or non-membership of a trade union. The relevant provisions are now all to be found in the *Trade Union and Labour Relations (Consolidation) Act 1992* ('*TULRCA 1992*').

(See also **28.4 HUMAN RIGHTS**.)

49.4   The pre-entry closed shop

Where an employer has a policy of offering employment only to members of a particular trade union, this is known as a pre-entry closed shop. Until 1991 such a policy remained lawful.

TULRCA 1992, s 137(1) now provides that it is unlawful to refuse a person employment because he is, or is not, a member of a trade union. The refusal is also unlawful if it is because the person is unwilling to accept a requirement to become or remain (or to cease to be or not to become) a member, or to make payments or suffer deductions in the event of his not being a member. References in this context to being or not being a member of a trade union are to being or not being a member of any trade union, of a particular trade union or of one of a number of particular trade unions, or of a particular branch or section of a trade union (*TULRCA 1992, s 143(3)*). In *Harrison v Kent County Council* [1995] ICR 434, it was held that an employer's refusal to employ an applicant because of his previous union *activities* could amount to an unlawful refusal of employment on grounds of union membership. In *Miller v Inserverve Industrial Services Ltd* (UKEAT/0244/12/SM) the EAT held that there had been no breach of *TULRCA 1992, s 137(1)* where a trade union official had pressurised an employer to recruit three named employees, with a view to their acting as shop stewards. The relevant manager declined to recruit them because he resented being "bullied" by the union. It was not the individuals' trade union membership *per se* that led him to refuse to recruit them, but his dislike of the union's approach.

These provisions do not apply where the employee would ordinarily work outside Great Britain (*TULRCA 1992, s 285(1)*; **51.15**(e) UNFAIR DISMISSAL – I). Nor do they apply to cases where a person may not be considered for appointment to an office in a trade union unless he is a member of the union, even though as a holder of the office he would be employed by the union (*TULRCA 1992, s 137(7)*). For the meaning of 'office', see *TULRCA 1992, s 137(7)(a), (b)*.

A deliberate omission to offer employment is considered to be a refusal for these purposes, as are a refusal or deliberate omission to deal with the application or the causing of its withdrawal, a spurious offer of employment (that is, one the terms of which are such as no reasonable employer who wished to fill the post would offer and which is not accepted) and an offer of employment which is withdrawn or which the offeror causes the prospective employee not to accept, or an offer which is not accepted because it includes a requirement of union membership or non-membership (*TULRCA 1992, s 137(5), (6)*).

There are two situations where the refusal of employment is deemed to have been on union membership grounds:

(a)   where an advertisement is published which indicates or might reasonably be understood as indicating that the employment is only open to union members or non-members, or that a requirement of the sort referred to in *s 137(1)(b)* will be imposed, and a person who does not satisfy that condition or is unwilling to accept that requirement is refused employment to which the advertisement relates (*TULRCA 1992, s 137(3)*); or

(b)   where there is an arrangement or practice under which employment is offered only to persons put forward or approved by a union which puts forward or approves only its members, and a person who is not a member of the union is refused employment in pursuance of the arrangement or practice (*TULRCA 1992, s 137(4)*).

A person who is refused employment on unlawful grounds has a right of complaint to an employment tribunal, and no other remedy (*TULRCA 1992, s 143(4)*). The complaint must be presented within three months of the refusal or other conduct complained of, unless the tribunal considers that it was not reasonably practicable to do so (*TULRCA 1992, s 139(1)*; and see **17.25** EMPLOYMENT TRIBUNALS – I). Where the respondent has acted under pressure from a third party such as a trade union, there is provision for that third party to be joined into the proceedings and to be ordered to pay all or part of any compensation awarded (*TULRCA 1992, s 142*).

If the tribunal finds the complaint well-founded, it will make a declaration to that effect, and may (if it considers it just and equitable to do so) order the respondent to pay compensation assessed on the same basis as damages for breach of statutory duty, which may include compensation for injury to feelings (*TULRCA 1992, s 140(1), (2)*). The tribunal will presumably ask itself whether the applicant would have obtained the job had it not been for his membership or non-membership of a union, or the percentage chance of his doing so, and will compensate him for lost earnings if so. The maximum award of compensation is the same as for unfair dismissal, currently £74,200 (*ERA 1999, s 34*; *Employment Rights (Increase of Limits) Order 2012 (2012/3007)*).

The tribunal may also, or alternatively, make a recommendation that the respondent take within a specified period action appearing to the tribunal to be practicable for the purpose of obviating or reducing the adverse effect on the applicant of the conduct complained of, and may make or increase an award of compensation (up to the statutory maximum) if the respondent fails without reasonable justification to comply (*TULRCA 1992, s 140(1)(b), (3)*).

An appeal on a question of law lies from the decision of the tribunal to the Employment Appeal Tribunal (*TULRCA 1992, s 291(2)*).

Any agreement purporting to exclude the right to complain under these provisions is void, unless reached as part of a settlement after a conciliation officer has taken action, or where the statutory conditions governing compromise contracts have been satisfied, including that the complainant should have had advice from a relevant independent advisor (*TULRCA 1992, s 288*; and see **2.4** ADVISORY, CONCILIATION AND ARBITRATION SERVICE and **17.27** EMPLOYMENT TRIBUNALS – I).

There are also provisions dealing similarly with cases where an employment agency acts on behalf of an employer, or where such an agency refuses its services on unlawful grounds (*TULRCA 1992, s 138*; see also *TULRCA 1992, ss 141* and *143(2)*).

49.5   Dismissal and the closed shop

The dismissal of an employee or his selection for redundancy will automatically be regarded as unfair if the principal reason for the dismissal or selection was that he was not a member of any trade union, or of a particular trade union, or of one of a number of particular trade unions, or had refused or proposed to refuse to become or remain a member (*TULRCA 1992, ss 152(1)(c), 153*) (see **52.3** UNFAIR DISMISSAL – II). References to trade union membership include membership of any trade union, or of a particular trade union or one of a number of particular trade unions, or of a particular branch or section of a trade union (*TULRCA 1992, s 152(4)*).

'Proposing to refuse to remain a member' covers the situation where the proposed refusal is contingent upon a particular event (*Crosville Motor Services Ltd v Ashfield* [1986] IRLR 475).

For the relevance of the employer's belief in the employee's membership or non-membership, see *Leyland Vehicles Ltd v Jones* [1981] ICR 428.

Compensation for the dismissal is assessed as described in **49.7** below.

Note that there is no minimum qualifying period of employment before an employee is entitled to make such a complaint of unfair dismissal, nor is there any upper age limit (*TULRCA 1992, s 154*).

49.6   FAILURE TO MAKE PAYMENTS

Instead of being a member of a trade union, an employee may be subject to a requirement to make a payment, eg to a charity. If such an employee who is not or ceases to be a union member refuses, in breach of a requirement, to make such a payment and is dismissed for that reason, he will be treated as dismissed for failure to become or remain a member of a trade union. The same is true if he is dismissed for objecting to a provision which entitles his employer to deduct such a payment from his wages (*TULRCA 1992, s 152(3)*). A dismissal for failure to make such a payment or for objecting to such a provision will be regarded as automatically unfair, and will be compensated as described in **49.7** below.

An employer may only deduct a trade union subscription from an employee's pay if certain statutory requirements are complied with (see **49.21** below).

49.7   COMPENSATION FOR CLOSED SHOP DISMISSALS

For the detailed rules on compensation, see **53.6–53.19** UNFAIR DISMISSAL – III. Note in particular, however, that *in addition* to the general rules governing unfair dismissal awards, the following apply to 'automatically' unfair dismissals to enforce a closed shop.

(a)   There is a minimum basic award of £5,500, although the compensatory award is calculated in the normal way.

(b)   There is provision that conduct of the employee in refusing to join a union or to make payments in lieu of joining, or in objecting to such payments, should be disregarded in assessing contributory fault for possible reduction of any part of the award (*TULRCA 1992, s 155*). However, it seems that confrontational conduct by the employee could form the basis for a finding of contributory fault provided that the immediate circumstances constituting the principal reason for dismissal are excluded from consideration (*TGWU v Howard* [1992] ICR 106).

(c)   The employee may request that a third party (eg a union) be joined in the unfair dismissal proceedings if pressure by it has induced the dismissal and the award may be made wholly or partly against that third party.

(*TULRCA 1992, ss 155–156, 160.*)

49.8   DETRIMENT

Every worker has the right not to be subjected to detriment by his employer for the purpose of compelling him to be or become a member of a trade union or a particular trade union, or for the purpose of enforcing a requirement that in the event of his failing to become or ceasing to be a member he must make one or more payments (*TULRCA 1992, s 146(1)(c), (3)*). Infringement of this right entitles the employee to complain to an industrial tribunal and seek a declaration and compensation (*TULRCA 1992, s 146(5)*; and see **49.18, 49.19** below).

49.9   INDUSTRIAL ACTION, TRADE UNION DISCIPLINE AND THE CLOSED SHOP

The statutory immunity for industrial action is inapplicable where the purpose of the action is to impose union membership requirements or to enforce a closed shop. For a more detailed account of the relevant provisions, see **43.7** STRIKES AND INDUSTRIAL ACTION.

An individual member of a trade union may not be disciplined either for proposing to resign from the union, or for working with non-union members or for an employer who employs non-union labour (*TULRCA 1992, s 65(2)* as amended; for further details, see **49.16** below).

49.10   TRADE UNION 'BLACKLISTS'

The *ERA 1999* contains provisions to prohibit the compilation of trade union 'blacklists'. The Secretary of State is empowered to make regulations prohibiting the making of lists which relate to trade union members or those who have taken part in trade union activities with a view to such lists being used by employers or employment agencies for discriminating in relation to recruitment or treatment of workers. The Secretary of State may further make regulations prohibiting the use, sale and supply of such lists. (*ERA 1999, ss 3, 4*). The *Employment Relations Act 1999 (Blacklists) Regulations 2010 (SI 2010/493)* came into force on 2 March 2010, prohibiting the use of blacklists to deny employment to or dismiss or cause detriment to employees as a result of their trade union membership or activities. These regulations introduced a general prohibition on compiling, using, selling or supplying lists which contain details of union members or participants in trade union activities, and are compiled with a view to being used by employers or employment agencies for the purposes of discrimination in relation to the recruitment or treatment of workers (*reg 3*). A person who has been refused employment has a right to complain to the employment tribunal against another person who has refused him employment if that other person has contravened the prohibition contained in *reg 3* or has relied on information provided by a person in contravention of *reg 3*, in circumstances where he knows or ought reasonably to know that the information relied upon is supplied in contravention of that regulation (*reg 5*). In *Miller v Inserverve Industrial Services Ltd* (UKEAT/0244/12/SM) the EAT held that there had no breach of *reg 5* where a trade union official had pressurised an employer to recruit three named employees, with a view to their acting as shop stewards, but the relevant manager had declined to recruit them because he resented being "bullied" by the union. Even if it could be said that the manager had compiled a "mental list" of the three individuals, it was not a prohibited list because it had not been prepared for the purposes of discriminating against the individuals on grounds of their trade union membership or activities. His disinclination to recruit them arose from his dislike of the union's approach.

There is an equivalent right to complain against an employment agency which refuses to provide its services on such grounds (*reg 6*). If the claim is upheld, the tribunal must make a declaration to that effect, and make order compensation and make recommendations (reg 8). Where an award of compensation is made, the amount shall be not less than £5,500 (subject to certain increases and deductions) (*reg 8(3)*). An equivalent right to bring a claim before the employment tribunal is given to any person who is subjected to a detriment for a reason relating to a prohibited list (*reg 9*). In addition, *reg 12* amends the *ERA 1996* so as render it automatically unfair to dismiss an employee for a reason related to a prohibited list (*ERA 1996, s 104F*). In those circumstances, the minimum basic award again shall not be less than £5,500 (*ERA 1996, s 120(1C)*).

49.11 EXCLUSION OR EXPULSION FROM A UNION – GENERAL

TULRCA 1992, s 174 confers upon persons seeking or in employment, in respect of which a closed shop agreement is in force, the right not to be unreasonably excluded or expelled from a trade union. However, since it is unlawful for an employer to refuse employment on grounds of non-membership of a trade union, this provision is of little practical importance. *TURERA 1993, s 14* introduced a new right not to be excluded or expelled, save on certain grounds, which is not dependent upon the existence of a closed shop. This right is considered in **49.13** below.

The common law also provides a remedy for members expelled from a trade union in breach of an express or implied provision of the rules (see **49.12** below).

49.12 The common law

Since there is no contract in existence between an applicant for membership and a trade union, the only right he may have in certain circumstances at common law is not to have his application rejected arbitrarily or capriciously (see *Nagle v Feilden* [1966] 2 QB 633). However, this right was developed in cases where a closed shop or the equivalent was in force (which is no longer likely to be a practical problem, for the reasons given in **49.3** above), and there may be little need to invoke it in future in view of the new statutory right discussed in **49.13** below.

Once a person has been accepted as a member of a union he may not be expelled except in accordance with the rules (see, for example, *Edwards v Society of Graphical and Allied Trades* [1971] Ch 354). In *Goring v British Actors Equity Association* [1987] IRLR 122, the court took the view that the sole common law rights of a union member against the union were those conferred by its rules (including the implied obligation not to act capriciously or arbitrarily). Further, in *Hamlet v General Municipal Boilermakers and Allied Trades Union* [1987] ICR 150, the court held that where a member of a union complained of the decision of a union, the court's function was not to review that decision but merely to ensure that the internal procedures of the union had been complied with. However, in addition to any implied term that a member is not to be expelled arbitrarily or capriciously, a member whose expulsion is being considered is entitled to be dealt with in accordance with the rules of natural justice (*Lee v Showmen's Guild of Great Britain* [1952] 2 QB 329 and see also *Hudson v GMB* [1990] IRLR 67). See also **49.15** below.

The common law remains important in relation to expulsions because, unlike the statutory right (see **49.13** below), it provides a means of controlling the procedure which is followed. Further, the common law right may be used, by means of an application for an injunction, to prevent the expulsion taking place at all.

49.13 The statutory right

A union member has a statutory right not to be excluded or expelled from a trade union except on certain specified grounds (*TULRCA 1992, ss 174–177*) (see **49.3** above).

The exclusion or expulsion of an individual from a union is only permissible in the following circumstances:

(a)   he does not satisfy an enforceable membership requirement contained in the rules (ie one which restricts membership solely by reference to one or more of the following criteria: employment in a specified trade, industry or profession; occupational description; or possession of specified qualifications or work experience);

(b)   he does not qualify for membership because the union only operates in particular parts of Great Britain;

(c)   the union's purpose is to regulate relations between its members and a particular employer (or particular associated employers; for associated employers see **6.9**(a) CONTINUOUS EMPLOYMENT), and he is not employed by such an employer;

(d)   the exclusion or expulsion is entirely attributable to his conduct, provided such conduct does not include either conduct consisting of being, ceasing to be or having been or ceased to be a member of another trade union or employed by a particular employer or at a particular place or conduct to which *TULRCA 1992, s 65* applies (see **49.16** below); and the conduct to which his exclusion or expulsion is wholly or mainly attributable is not conduct consisting of being or ceasing to be or having been or ceased to be a member of a political party, unless membership of that party is contrary to the rules or objectives of the trade union (provided that the relevant objective is reasonable ascertainable). However, exclusion or expulsion for membership of a political party will not be permissible if it was done contrary to the union's rules, if the decision was taken unfairly, or if the individual would lose his livelihood or suffer exceptional hardship by reason of not being, or ceasing to be, a member of the union.

(*TULRCA 1992, s 174(1)–(4)*.)

The earlier provision in *s 174* preventing a trade union from excluding or expelling a member for being or ceasing to be a member of a political party was held by the European Court of Human Rights in *Associated Society of Locomotive Engineers & Firemen v United Kingdom (Application No 11002/05)* [2007] IRLR 361, ECtHR to infringe the right to freedom of association under Article 11 of the European Convention. The Court found that the UK law did not strike the right balance between the member's rights and those of the union in so far as it prevented the union from expelling the member on grounds of his membership of the British National Party. As a result, with effect from 6 April 2009 *s 174* was amended by *EA 2008, s 19* so as to permit expulsion on grounds of membership of a political party in the circumstances set out in the legislation.

For these purposes, if an application for membership of a trade union is neither granted nor rejected, it will be treated as having been refused on the expiry of the period within which it might reasonably have been expected to have been granted or refused. In addition, if under the rules of a trade union any person ceases to be a member of the trade union on the happening of an event specified in the rules, he will be treated as having been expelled from the union (*TULRCA 1992, s 177(2)*).

An employee, who had voluntarily surrendered his membership of a union, could not make a complaint under the predecessor of *s 174* on the basis that his resignation had been forced on him by the conduct of union officials, although there might be cases where the resignation was not truly voluntary (*McGhee v Midlands British Road Services Ltd* [1985] ICR 503). Furthermore, an employee who had been suspended from a union beyond the six-month period allowed in the union's rule book was held to have been neither excluded nor expelled within the meaning of *s 174* (*NACODS v Gluchowski* [1996] IRLR 252).

These rights are additional to common law rights in relation to expulsion or exemptions (see **49.12** above) (*TULRCA 1992, s 177(5)*).

49.14 The remedy

TULRCA 1992 provides for a two-stage remedy for an employee who complains that he has been expelled or excluded in breach of *s 174*. He must begin by presenting a complaint to an employment tribunal against the union in question, within the period of six months from the refusal or expulsion. Applications outside this time limit can only be heard if the tribunal is satisfied that it was not reasonably practicable to present the complaint in time and the complaint was presented within such further period as the tribunal considers reasonable (*TULRCA 1992, ss 174(4), 175*; and see **17.25** EMPLOYMENT TRIBUNALS – I).

At the first stage, the tribunal's function is limited to rejecting the application or finding that it is well-founded, and, if the latter, making a declaration to that effect (*TULRCA 1992, s 176(1)*).

Where the tribunal declares that the applicant has been wrongly refused or expelled from union membership, he will be entitled to compensation. However, he cannot apply for compensation until four weeks have elapsed after the declaration. This four-week period is designed to give the trade union an opportunity of admitting or readmitting the applicant to membership. The application must be made to an employment tribunal, however, within six months of the declaration. (*TULRCA 1992, s 176(2), (3)*).

Amount of compensation. Compensation will be of such amount as is considered just and equitable in all the circumstances, but the minimum award is £8,100. The maximum award of compensation is equal to the aggregate of:

(a)   30 times the current limit on the amount of a week's pay for the purposes of calculating the basic award in unfair dismissal cases, which is at present £450; and

(b)   the current maximum compensatory award in unfair dismissal cases, which is at present £74,200.

(See UNFAIR DISMISSAL – III (53).) Thus the present maximum award is £87,700. Since it will now be unusual, because the closed shop has been outlawed, for the inability to belong to a union to cause financial loss, it is unclear how the assessment of compensation should be approached. In *Bradley v NALGO* [1991] ICR 359, the EAT indicated that, assuming compensation for injury to feelings to be available, it should be on a modest scale. However, in *Adams v Hackney London Borough Council* [2003] IRLR 402 the EAT held, in the context of action short of dismissal by an employer on trade union grounds, that in principle awards for injury to feelings should not be approached any differently whatever the ground of discrimination relied upon, although each case will depend on its own facts. (See also *Beaumont v Amicus MSF* (2004) 148 Sol Jo LB 1063 in which an award for injury to feelings was made in a claim for unjustifiable discipline by a trade union).

Compensation may be reduced where the exclusion or expulsion was, to any extent, caused or contributed to by the action of the applicant (*TULRCA 1992, s 176(5)*). It appears that this step should precede the application of the statutory maximum or minimum.

Where a complaint of expulsion under *s 174* succeeds, the applicant cannot also complain of the expulsion under *TULRCA 1992, s 66* (unjustifiable disciplining; see **49.16** below).

49.15 DISCIPLINING BY A TRADE UNION – COMMON LAW

A member of a trade union has a right to be dealt with in accordance with the rules of his union and in accordance with natural justice (see also **49.12** above). If a union acts in breach of the rules or in breach of natural justice, the member affected may apply to the High Court for an injunction and a declaration of his rights. Members of the National Union of Mineworkers ('NUM'), disciplined for breach of a union instruction given in breach of the rules, were held to be entitled to a declaration of the invalidity of the instruction and the unlawfulness of the disciplinary action (*Taylor v National Union of Mineworkers (Derbyshire Area)* [1984] IRLR 440). Injunctions were granted to NUM members to restrain their union from instructing or seeking to persuade them or others not to work. The NUM had described the strike as official, where it had been called without a ballot as required by the rules, and had threatened disciplinary action. However, the courts will not review a decision of a trade union which is taken in accordance with the rules but which is attacked on the basis that it is one which no reasonable trade union could have reached in the circumstances (*Hamlet v General Municipal Boilermakers and Allied Trades Union* [1987] ICR 150). Nevertheless, the rules may be subject to an implied obligation not to act capriciously or arbitrarily (*Goring v British Actors Equity Association* [1987] IRLR 122). For examples of the courts intervening where there has been a breach of natural justice (ie the right to a fair hearing before an unbiased decision-maker), see *Roebuck v National Union of Mineworkers (Yorkshire Area)* [1977] ICR 573 and *Stevenson v United Road Transport Union* [1977] ICR 893. However, the rules of natural justice are not generally applicable in the context of a union's contractual relations with its officials, in its capacity as an employer (*Meacham v Amalgamated Engineering and Electrical Union* [1994] IRLR 218). The court may imply into a union's rule-book a power to discipline its members where no express power exists (*McVitae v UNISON* [1996] IRLR 33).

The court will ignore any provision of the union's rules which purports to provide that his only remedy is by way of some form of determination or conciliation in accordance with the rules (*TULRCA 1992, s 63(1)*). It will also ignore any provision which requires or permits such determination or conciliation, provided that the member has made a valid application to the union for determination or conciliation more than six months before bringing court proceedings (*TULRCA 1992, s 63(2)*), unless the member has himself unreasonably delayed matters (*TULRCA 1992, s 63(4)*). Applications are deemed valid unless the union informs the member of invalidity within 28 days of receipt (*TULRCA 1992, s 63(3)*).

49.16 DISCIPLINING BY A TRADE UNION – STATUTORY PROVISIONS

TULRCA 1992, s 64(1) confers an important right 'not to be unjustifiably disciplined' by a union of which a person is or has at any time been a member. This right is conferred in addition to any existing rights and the only remedies for any infringement are those conferred by *ss 66* and *67* (*TULRCA 1992, s 64(4), (5)*). In *Unison v Kelly* (UKEAT/0188/11/SM) the EAT rejected an argument put forward by the union that the statutory right not to be unjustifiably disciplined amounted to an unlawful interference with Article 11 of the Convention. Union members have a right to hold their unions to account in this regard.

A person is unjustifiably disciplined if the conduct or supposed conduct for which he is disciplined falls within, or is believed by the union to amount to conduct which falls within, any of the 12 categories which may be summarised as follows:

(a)   failing to participate in or support, or opposing, any industrial action;

(b)   failing to break a contract of employment or other agreement with the employer for the purposes of industrial action;

(c)   asserting, including by bringing proceedings, that the union or any of its officials or representatives is in breach of its obligations under the general law, its rules or any agreement (although false assertions made in bad faith are excluded by *s 65(6)*);

(d)   encouraging or assisting another person to fulfil obligations to the employer or to make or to attempt to vindicate assertions of the kind described in para (*c*);

(e)   failing to comply with any requirement imposed as a result of unjustifiable disciplinary action taken against himself or another;

(f)   failing to agree to the deduction of union dues from his wages,

(g)   resigning or proposing to resign from the union or another union, or being or becoming, or proposing or refusing to become, a member of another union;

(h)   working or proposing to work with individuals who do not belong to the union, or who are or are not members of another union;

(i)   working or proposing to work for an employer of such individuals;

(j)   requiring the union to do an act which any provision of *TULRCA 1992* requires it to do on a member's requisition;

(k)   consulting or requesting assistance from the Certification Officer (see **48.3** TRADE UNIONS – I), or from any other person in relation to assertions of the kind described in para (*c*);

(l)   proposing to do any of these things, or doing acts which are preparatory or incidental to them,

unless that conduct would independently and justifiably lead to disciplinary action (*TULRCA 1992, s 65(2)–(5)*).

The disciplinary action against which members are protected includes expulsion, fines, deprivation of benefits or facilities, encouragement to another union not to accept him as a member, or subjection to any other detriment (*TULRCA 1992, s 64(2)*). This extends to suspension from membership, and to naming a strike-breaker in a branch circular with the intention of causing embarrassment (*NALGO v Killorn and Simm* [1991] ICR 1).

Complaints of unjustifiable disciplinary action are to be made to an employment tribunal within three months of the determination complained of (*TULRCA 1992, s 66(1), (2)*). A mere recommendation is not a determination (*TGWU v Webber* [1990] ICR 711). Time may be extended for such period as the tribunal considers reasonable, either where it was not reasonably practicable to present the complaint within three months (see **17.25** EMPLOYMENT TRIBUNALS – I), or where any delay is wholly or partly attributable to a reasonable attempt to pursue an appeal or otherwise to have the decision reconsidered (see *NALGO v Killorn and Simm*, above). If the complaint is well-founded, the tribunal will make a declaration to that effect (*TULRCA 1992, s 66(3)*). If such a declaration is made, the complainant may make an application to the employment tribunal to seek compensation and/or the repayment of any sums paid by him as the result of the disciplinary action (*TULRCA 1992, s 67(1)*). Applications for compensation are to be made not less than four weeks or more than six months after the disciplinary action is declared unjustifiable (*TULRCA 1992, s 67(3)*).

The compensation awarded will be that sum which is just and equitable in all the circumstances, taking account of the duty to mitigate loss and of any contributory fault (*TULRCA 1992, s 67(5)–(7)*). The Court of Appeal considered the principles to be applied in awarding compensation for unjustified discipline by a trade union in *Massey v Unifi* [2007] EWCA Civ 800, [2008] ICR 62. Among other matters, the approach to injury to feelings in *Vento v Chief Constable of West Yorkshire Police* [2002] EWCA Civ 1871, [2003] ICR 318 was applied and it was accepted in principle (although not on the facts of the case) that aggravated damages could be awarded. Before dealing with mitigation or contribution, however, the tribunal is required by *TULRCA 1992, s 67(9)* to apply the statutory maxima and minima contained in *s 67(8)*. The maximum is the aggregate of (*a*) 30 times the maximum week's pay for calculating the basic award in unfair dismissal cases (*ERA 1996, s 227*), and (*b*) the maximum compensatory award in such cases (*ERA 1996, s 124*). These figures are at present £450 and £74,200, respectively, giving a maximum award under *s 67(8)* of £87,700. If the determination has not been revoked, or the union has failed to take all reasonable steps to reverse the determination, the minimum award is the amount for the time being specified in *TULRCA 1992, s 176(6A)*, which is at present £8,400. (See also **53.14** UNFAIR DISMISSAL – **III**.)

49.17 DETRIMENT ON GROUNDS OF UNION MEMBERSHIP OR ACTIVITIES

TULRCA 1992, s 146 concerns detriment caused by an employer against a worker as an individual:

(a)   to prevent or deter him from, or to penalise him for, belonging to an independent trade union; or

(b)   to prevent him or deter him from taking part in the activities of an independent union at an appropriate time (ie a time outside working hours or a time when the employer has consented to him taking part in union activities), or to penalise him for doing so; or

(c)   from 1 October 2004, to prevent him or deter him from making use of trade union services at an appropriate time, or to penalise him for doing so; or

(d)   to compel him to join any trade union.

There was previously considerable doubt as to whether omissions could constitute 'action' for those purposes. In *Associated Newspapers Ltd v Wilson; Associated British Ports v Palmer* [1995] ICR 406, a majority of the House of Lords held that withholding a salary increase from employees who refused to sign personal contracts and give up collectively bargained terms and conditions did not amount to a breach of *s 146*.

However, the *ERA 1999, Sch 2* had the effect of reversing this aspect of the House of Lords' decision in *Wilson/Palmer* with effect from 25 October 1999. In particular, *TULRCA 1992, s 146(1)* now prohibits subjecting an individual to a detriment by any act, or any deliberate failure to act, by the employer on grounds of trade union membership or activities.

Wilson/Palmer subsequently went to the European Court of Human Rights in *Wilson and National Union of Journalists v United Kingdom* (Applications 30668/96, 30679/61 and 30678/96) [2002] IRLR 568. The Court held that, by permitting employers to use financial incentives to induce employees to surrender the right to union representation (as opposed to deterring union membership altogether), the United Kingdom had failed in its positive duty to secure the enjoyment of the right to freedom of association under *art 11* of the *European Convention on Human Rights*. In response to that decision, *s 29* of the *Employment Rights Act 2004* inserted new *ss 145A–145F* into *TULRCA 1992* which from 1 October 2004 conferred upon workers a right not to have an offer made to them by their employer for the sole or main purpose of inducing the worker:

(a)   not to be or seek to become a member of a trade union;

(b)   not to take part, at an appropriate time, in trade union activities;

(c)   not to make use, at an appropriate time, of trade union services; or

(d)   to be or become a member of a trade union (*s 145A*).

In addition, a worker who is a member of an independent trade union which is recognised, or is seeking to be recognised, by his employer, has the right not to have an offer made to him by his employer if:

(a)   acceptance of that offer, together with other workers' acceptance of similar offers, would result in the workers' terms and conditions no longer being determined by collective bargaining with the union; and

(b)   the employer's sole or main purpose in making the offers is to achieve that result (*s 145B*).

In *Davies v Asda Stores Ltd* (IDS Brief 801) an employment tribunal held that the employer had breached *s 145B* of *TULRCA 1992* by offering new terms and conditions to union members provided they relinquished collective bargaining. The 340 members were each awarded £2,500.

In *Department of Transport v Gallacher* [1994] ICR 967, the Court of Appeal held that an employer's advice that an employee's prospects of promotion would be improved if he returned to a line management position, instead of engaging in full-time trade union duties, was not given for the purpose of deterring the employee from taking part in union activities within the meaning of *TULRCA 1992, s 146*. The relevant purpose is the object which the employer desires or seeks to achieve – in *Gallacher*, his purpose was to assist the employee in obtaining promotion.

In *FW Farnsworth Ltd v McCoid* [1998] IRLR 362, it was held that the derecognition of a shop steward by an employer could amount to action taken against the shop steward as an individual for the purpose of preventing or deterring him from taking part in trade union activities or penalising him for doing so within the meaning of *TULRCA 1992, s 148*.

A worker also has the right not to be subjected to a detriment in order to require him to make payments in lieu of union subscriptions when he is not (or is no longer) a union member (*TULRCA 1992, s 146(3)*). In addition, *ERA 1999, Sch 1* introduced a new right not to be subjected to a detriment on union recognition-related grounds (see **48.37** TRADE UNIONS – I).

See also **51.3** UNFAIR DISMISSAL – II.

49.18   The remedy

The employee may make a complaint to an employment tribunal within three months of the action complained of, or within such further period as the tribunal considers reasonable in a case where it is satisfied that it was not reasonably practicable for the complaint to be presented within three months (see **17.25** EMPLOYMENT TRIBUNALS – I) (*TULRCA 1992, ss 146(5), 147*).

It is for the employer to show the purpose for which action was taken against the employee (*TULRCA 1992, s 148(1)*). If the tribunal finds the complaint well-founded, it will make a declaration to that effect and may order compensation to be paid. The compensation will be such amount as it considers just and equitable in all the circumstances, having regard to the right infringed and any loss sustained by the complainant. Compensation may be reduced on account of the applicant's contributory fault (*TULRCA 1992, s 149*). It would appear that compensation for an action short of dismissal may include an award in respect of injury to feelings (*Cleveland Ambulance NHS Trust v Blane* [1997] ICR 851). In *Adams v Hackney London Borough Council* [2003] IRLR 402 the EAT held that in principle awards for injury to feelings should not be approached any differently in cases of discrimination on trade union grounds than in other cases of discrimination. However, the level of award will depend on the individual applicant. Some may feel deeply hurt by trade union discrimination, whilst other more robust characters may suffer little, if any, distress. Since the aim is to compensate and not to punish, the compensation ought not to be the same in each case.

Joinder of third parties. Where the employer was induced to take the action complained of by industrial action or threat of such action, although no account is to be taken by the tribunal of such pressure when deciding the complaint, the union (or unions) may be joined as a third party to the proceedings and may be ordered to pay all or part of the compensation as the tribunal considers just in the circumstances (*TULRCA 1992, ss 148(2), 150*).

49.19 PROHIBITION ON UNION MEMBERSHIP AND UNION RECOGNITION REQUIREMENTS IN CONTRACTS FOR GOODS OR SERVICES

Any term or condition of a contract for the supply of goods or services is void insofar as it purports:

(a)   to require that the whole, or some part, of the work done for the purposes of the contract is to be done only by persons who are or who are not members of trade unions or of a particular trade union (*TULRCA 1992, s 144*);

(b)   to require any party to the contract to recognise one or more trade unions (whether or not named in the contract) for the purpose of negotiating on behalf of workers, or any class of worker, employed by him or to negotiate or consult with, or with any official of, one or more trade unions (whether or not so named) (*TULRCA 1992, s 186*).

(For the prohibition of industrial action to impose union membership or recognition requirements, see **43.7 STRIKES AND INDUSTRIAL ACTION.**)

Further, it is unlawful for a person to refuse to deal with a supplier or prospective supplier of goods or services on union membership grounds (*TULRCA 1992, s 145(1)*). Refusing to deal with a person means excluding that person's name from a list of approved suppliers or of persons from whom tenders may be or are invited, or if he fails to permit that person to submit a tender, decides not to enter into a contract with that person, or terminates an existing contract (*TULRCA 1992, s 145(2), (3), (4)*). Such a refusal is on union membership grounds if the ground or one of the grounds for it is that work done for the purposes of any contract would be done, or would be likely to be done, by persons who were or were not members of a trade union or of a particular union (*TULRCA 1992, s 145(2)*).

It is also unlawful to refuse to deal with such a person on the ground that he does not, or is not likely to, recognise one or more trade unions for negotiating purposes or negotiate or consult with one or more trade unions or their officials (*TULRCA 1992, s 187*).

In the case of an unlawful refusal to deal, an action for breach of statutory duty may be brought by the person with whom the defendant has refused to deal or by any other person adversely affected (*TULRCA 1992, ss 145(5), 187(3)*).

49.20 DEDUCTION OR SUBSCRIPTIONS: THE 'CHECK-OFF'

The following provisions are to be found in *TULRCA 1992, ss 68 and 68A* as amended by the *Deregulation (Deduction from Pay of Union Subscriptions) Order 1998 (SI 1998/1529)*.

Where arrangements exist between an employer and a union relating to the making of deductions from wages in respect of union subscriptions (commonly known as the 'check-off'), the employer must ensure that deductions are only made in accordance with an authorisation signed and dated by the worker concerned (*TULRCA 1992, s 68(1), (2)*). A worker has the same meaning as in *Part II* of the *Employment Rights Act 1996* (see Pay – I (32)), and is thus not confined to employees in the strict sense (*TULRCA 1992, s 68(4)*). If the worker subsequently withdraws the authorisation in writing, the employer must cease to make deductions as soon as is reasonably practicable (*TULRCA 1992, s 68(2)*).

The signing of an authorisation does not oblige the employer to maintain or continue to maintain the arrangements for making deductions (*TULRCA 1992, s 68(3)*).

If the employer makes a deduction in contravention of these provisions, the worker may present a complaint to an employment tribunal within the period of three months beginning with the date of payment of the wages from which the deduction (or the last deduction, if the complaint relates to more than one) was made (*TULRCA 1992, s 68A(1)*). If the tribunal is satisfied that it was not reasonably practicable for the complaint to be presented within that period, it may extend time for such further period as it considers reasonable.

Where the tribunal finds a complaint well-founded, it will make a declaration to that effect, and will order the employer to repay the amount improperly deducted and not already repaid (*TULRCA 1992, s 68A(2)*). Provision is made to avoid double recovery where the same deduction also contravenes other statutory provisions (*TULRCA 1992, s 68A(3)*). It is not clear whether, if the sums deducted had already been paid by the employer to the union, the employer would be able to recover them from the union in a common law claim for restitution.

Prior to 23 June 1998, the 'check-off' provisions further required that the worker's authorisations must have been signed within the last three years. They also required that an increased subscription could only be deducted if the employer had given the worker at least one month's written notice. These requirements were removed by the *Deregulation (Deduction from Pay of Union Subscriptions) Order 1998 (SI 1998/1529)* made under the *Deregulation and Contracting Out Act 1994*.

The repealed requirements continue to apply to authorisations given before 23 June 1998 (*reg 3(1)*). However, by *reg 3(2), (3)*, an employer may give a worker notice in a form prescribed in the *Schedule* to the *Regulations* that such an authorisation is to be treated as having been given under the new provisions (and so will be treated as of unlimited duration until withdrawal, and as not requiring advance notice of any increase in the amount deducted). Provided the worker does not object by written notice within 14 days, the new provisions will apply.

49.21   THE RIGHT TO BE ACCOMPANIED

A new right to be accompanied by a trade union official (or a fellow employee) was introduced by *s 10* of the *Employment Relations Act 1999*. Any worker who is required or invited to attend a disciplinary or grievance hearing by his employer is now entitled to be accompanied either by a trade union official (as defined in *TULRCA 1992, ss 1, 119*) or fellow worker of his choice. The employer must permit the companion to put the worker's case, respond to any views expressed and confer with the worker during the hearing. However, the employer is not required to permit the companion to answer questions on the worker's behalf (*ERA 1999, s 10(2B), (2C)*). If the worker's chosen companion is not available at the time of the hearing, and the worker proposes a reasonable alternative time within the subsequent period of five working days, the employer must postpone the hearing to the time proposed (*ERA 1999, s 10(4), (5)*). The employer must also give the worker's companion time off for the purpose of accompanying the worker to the meeting (*ERA 1999, s 10(6)*). Guidance on the application of this right is given in the ACAS Code of Practice on Disciplinary and Grievance Procedures (2009).

A 'disciplinary hearing' is defined for these purposes so as to include a hearing which could result in a formal warning (*ERA 1999, s 13(4)*). For these purposes, the test of whether a warning is 'formal' is one of substance. If the warning will become part of the worker's disciplinary record, then the right to be accompanied applies (*Ferenc-Batchelor v London Underground Ltd* [2003] ICR 656). However, the right is confined to disciplinary or grievance matters. It therefore did not apply to a meeting which led to an employee's dismissal on grounds of redundancy: see *Heathmill Multimedia ASP Ltd v Jones* [2003] IRLR 856. The EAT held in *Skiggs v South West Trains Ltd* [2005] IRLR 459 that an investigative interview regarding a grievance raised by another employee against the claimant was not a disciplinary hearing at which the claimant had a right to be accompanied.

This new statutory right does not require a union to provide representation to an employee. However, a member may have a contractual right to representation deriving from the union rule-book. In *English v UNISON* (2000) IDS Brief 668, the county court held that a qualified right to representation arose as a matter of contract from the union's guide to disciplinary hearings.

A worker denied the right to be accompanied may complain to the employment tribunal within three months of the employer's failure (or such further period as is considered reasonable where it was not reasonably practicable to present the complaint within three months) (*ERA 1999, s 11(1), (2)*). Where a complaint is upheld, the tribunal may make an award of up to two weeks' pay, subject to the statutory maximum contained in *ERA 1996, s 227(1)*, currently £450. In addition, a worker has a right not to be subjected to a detriment or dismissed for seeking to exercise the right to be accompanied. Dismissal on this ground will be automatically unfair (*ERA 1999, s 12*).

49.22 ADVICE BY TRADE UNIONS TO MEMBERS

The scope of a trade union's duty of care towards its members in giving advice was considered by the High Court in *Friend v Institution of Professional Managers and Specialists* [1999] IRLR 173. It was held that a trade union advising or acting for a member in an employment dispute owed the member a duty of care in tort to use ordinary skill and care. However, once solicitors had been engaged on the member's behalf, any duty there might previously have been on the union to advise on the dispute came to an end.

50   Transfer of Undertakings

50.1   Far-reaching rules for the protection of employees' rights on the transfer of an undertaking are contained in the *Transfer of Undertakings (Protection of Employment) Regulations 2006 (SI 2006/246)* ('the *Regulations*'). These came into force on 6 April 2006. They replace entirely the previous legislation, the *Transfer of Undertakings (Protection of Employment) Regulations 1981 (SI 1981/1794)* as amended by the *Transfer of Undertakings (Protection of Employment) (Amendment) Regulations 1987 (SI 1987/442)*, by the *Trade Union Reform and Employment Rights Act 1993*, by the *Collective Redundancies and Transfer of Undertakings (Protection of Employment) (Amendment) Regulations 1995 (SI 1995/2587)* and by the *Collective Redundancies and Transfer of Undertakings (Protection of Employment) (Amendment) Regulations 1999 (SI 1999/1925.)*

The purpose of the original 1981 Regulations was to fulfil the United Kingdom's obligations under European Community law to give effect to *EC Council Directive 77/187*, generally known as the *Acquired Rights Directive*. A new *Directive* was adopted on 29 June 1998 which amends *Directive 77/187* by wholly replacing the texts of *arts 1–7*. Member states had three years within which to bring into force measures which implement the amended *Directive*. See *Official Journal, 17 July 1998 (L201/88)*. The provisions of the original and the amending *Directive* have been consolidated in a further *Directive* adopted on 12 March 2001: *Directive 2001/23/EC*, Official Journal, 22 March 2001 (L82/16). It was the need to transpose the new provisions into UK law which prompted the introduction of the *Regulations*. However, the *Regulations* go further than is required by European law and introduce an additional concept, that of 'a service provision change'. That they go further than European law is emphasised by the fact that the *Regulations* are made not only under *s 2(2)* of the *European Communities Act 1972* but also under *s 38* of the *Employment Relations Act 1999*, which empowered the Secretary of State to make regulations in circumstances other than those to which the Community obligation applies. In addition, the *Regulations* seek to clarify the meaning of certain terms by incorporating concepts developed by the courts.

Historically, English courts and tribunals have so far as possible construed the *Regulations* consistently with the *Directive*, even to the extent of reading in additional words (see **50.10** below, and **22.2 EUROPEAN UNION LAW**). However, when considering the meaning of a service provision change, they may not feel obliged so to do, although the concepts of 'service provision change' and 'transfer of an undertaking' are not mutually exclusive.

Note that the Government is consulting on proposed changes to the *Regulations*, in particular to remove the concept of a service provision change. If this were implemented, there would no doubt be renewed focus on the extensive jurisprudence concerning the meaning of a "transfer of an undertaking", as to which see in particular **50.5** below.

References below are to provisions of the *Regulations* unless stated otherwise.

50.2   Where there is a 'relevant transfer', that is either where there is a 'service provision change' (see **50.3** below) from person *A* to person *B*, or where an 'undertaking' (see **50.4** below) is 'transferred' (see **50.5** below) from person *A* to person *B:*

(a)   individuals who are employed by *A* 'immediately before the transfer' (see **50.14** and **50.12** below) automatically become the employees of *B* from the time of the transfer, on the terms and conditions they previously held with *A* (see **50.13** below);

(b)   *B* inherits *A's* rights and liabilities in relation to those individuals (see **50.18** below);

(c)   collective agreements, made by or on behalf of *A* with a trade union recognised by *A*, are inherited by *B* (see **50.20** below);

(d)   where *A* recognises a union in respect of employees in the undertaking to be transferred and, following the transfer, the undertaking transferred maintains an identity distinct from any other undertaking owned by *B*, *B* must recognise the union in respect of those employees (see **50.21** below);

(e)   *A* must inform recognised trade unions or employee representatives about the consequences of the transfer, and *B* must provide *A* with sufficient information in this regard (see **50.22** below);

(f)   in certain circumstances, it may be necessary for *A* or *B* to consult with recognised trade unions or elected employee representatives concerning the transfer (see **50.23** below); and

(g)   dismissal of any employee (whether before or after the transfer) for any reason connected with the transfer is automatically unfair unless the reason is 'an economic, technical or organisational reason entailing changes in the workforce' in which case the dismissal is for a fair reason and the question is whether it is fair in all the circumstances, applying the normal principles of unfair dismissal (see **50.24** below).

50.3   WHAT IS A 'RELEVANT TRANSFER'?

Service provision change

There are three situations which may amount to a service provision change (*reg 3(1)(b)*):

(a)   Activities cease to be carried out by a person ('a client') on his own behalf and are carried out instead by another person on the client's behalf ('a contractor'). This situation is sometimes referred to as contracting out or outsourcing.

(b)   Activities cease to be carried out by a contractor on a client's behalf (whether or not those activities had previously been carried out by the client on his own behalf) and are carried out instead by another person ('a subsequent contractor') on the client's behalf. This situation is sometimes referred to as reassigning.

(c)   Activities cease to be carried out by a contractor or a subsequent contractor on a client's behalf (whether or not those activities had previously been carried out by the client on his own behalf) and are carried out instead by the client on his own behalf. This situation is sometimes referred to as contracting in or insourcing.

In any of these three situations there will be a relevant transfer if immediately before the service provision change:

(a)   There is an organised grouping of employees situated in Great Britain which has as its principal purpose the carrying out of the activities concerned on behalf of the client; and

(b)   The client intends that the activities will, following the service provision change, be carried out by the transferee other than in connection with a single specific event or task of short-term duration (*reg 3(3)(a)*). The focus here is on the intention of the client, rather than on that of the transferee: *SNR Denton UK LLP v Kirwan* [2013] ICR 101. There are conflicting views on whether activities are excluded if they relate to either a single specific event or task of short-term duration or whether they must relate to both: see *SNR Denton and Liddell's Coaches v Cook* (UKEATS/0025/12, 9 October 2012).

However, a service provision change will not be a relevant transfer if the activities concerned consist wholly or mainly of the supply of goods for the client's use (*reg 3(3)(b)*). The application of this exception is essentially one of fact: the supply of sandwiches and drinks to a client's canteen for sale to its staff would fall within the exception, but if the supplier also provided the canteen staff to dispense the goods, then this might not fall within the exception: *Pannu v Geo W King Ltd* [2012] IRLR 193.

There is no service provision change where there is a change of both contractor and of client; the activities carried out by different contractors before and after the transfer must be carried out for the same client: *Hunter v McCarrick* [2012] EWCA Civ 1399, [2013] ICR 235.

The requirement for an organised grouping of employees connotes that the employees be organised in some sense by reference to the requirements of the client in question, a deliberate putting together of a group of employees for the purpose of the relevant client work: *Seawell Ltd v Ceva Freight (UK) Ltd* [2012] IRLR 802). The client work need not be the sole purpose, provided it is the principal purpose: *Argyll Coastal Services Ltd v Stirling* (UKEATS/0012/11, 15 February 2012). There is no such grouping where a group of employees happen to work mostly on tasks for a particular client only from a combination of circumstances such as shift patterns and working practices, where there was no deliberate planning or intent: *Eddie Stobart Ltd v Moreman* [2012] ICR 919. A director involved in a mainly strategic role and spending little time on actual service delivery may not be part of an organised grouping: *Edinburgh Home-Link Partnership v The City of Edinburgh Council* (UKEATS/0061/11, 10 July 2012).

The EAT has considered the question of service provision change in three cases in particular: *Kimberley Group Housing Ltd v Hambley* [2008] ICR 1030; *Churchill Dulwich Ltd (in liq) v Metropolitan Resources Ltd* [2009] ICR 1380; and *OCS Group Ltd v Jones* (UKEAT/0038/09). From these cases, the following principles can be drawn:

(a)   Service provision change is a wholly new statutory concept. The circumstances in which one is established are comprehensively and clearly set out in *reg 3(1)(b)* itself and *reg 3(3)*. The new provisions appear straightforward and their application to an individual case is essentially a question of fact.

(b)   There is no need to adopt a purposive construction as opposed to a straightforward and common sense application of the relevant statutory words. See also *Hunter v McCarrick* [2012] EWCA Civ 1399, [2013] ICR 235.

(c)   Under *reg 3(1)(b)*, the first question for the Tribunal is to identify the relevant activity or activities, since only then can one consider whether those activities cease to be carried on by the contractor on a client's behalf and are carried out instead by another person on the client's behalf. See further *SNR Denton UK LLP v Kirwan* [2013] ICR 101.

(d)   The conditions in *reg 3(3)* cannot be considered until a decision is made as to whether or not there is a service provision change falling within *reg 3(1)(b)*.

(e)   Whether the activities carried out by the putative transferee are fundamentally or essentially the same as those carried out by the putative transferor is a question of fact and degree. Some minor differences between the nature of the tasks carried on after what is said to have been a service provision change as compared with before it, or in the way in which they are performed as compared with the nature or mode of performance of those tasks in the hands of the alleged transferor, does not mean that there is no service provision change. Further, a substantial change in the amount of the particular activity required by the client could show that the post-transfer activity was not the same as it was pre-transfer: *Department for Education v Huke* (UKEAT/0080/12, 17 October 2012).

(f)   It is possible for a transferor to transfer the provision of a service to more than one transferee.

(g)   However, there may be some circumstances in which a service which is being provided by one contractor to a client is in the event so fragmented that nothing which one can properly determine as being a service provision change has taken place.

(h)   In considering whether an employee is assigned to the part of the provision of the service transferred to a particular transferee, the tribunal applies the same approach as to a transfer under *reg 3(1)(a)*.

In *Ankers v Clearsprings Management Ltd* [2009] All ER (D) 261 (Feb) the tribunal found that there was no discernible pattern in the transfer of accommodation services to asylum seekers from one service provider to another. The EAT determined that where the service provided is so fragmented, a tribunal may be entitled to find that no relevant transfer took place. The EAT subsequently rejected a tribunal's finding that there was no service provision change based upon a combination of 'fragmentation' and a finding that 15% of the work done by the original contractor would not be required by the new contractor and so the "activities" undertaken before and after the contract would not be essentially or fundamentally the same: *Enterprise Management Services Ltd v Connect-Up Ltd* [2012] IRLR 190.

In *Ward Hadaway Solicitors v Love* (UKEAT/0471/09) the EAT refused to interfere with a tribunal's judgment that there was no service provision change following a competitive tender for future solicitors' regulatory services in circumstances in which none of the work in progress was handed over and no employee transferred. Similarly, in *Johnson Controls Ltd v Campbell* (UKEAT/0041/12) the EAT refused to interfere with a tribunal's judgment that there was no service provision change where a client ceased to use a centralised taxi administration service, but instead arranged for its secretaries to book taxis with taxi firms directly, since the activity undertaken by the contractor was not continued by the client.

Where there is a service provision change which is a relevant transfer, 'the transferor' means the person who carried out the activities prior to the service provision change and 'the transferee' means the person who carries out the activities as a result of the service provision change (*reg 2(1)*).

50.4   Transfer of an undertaking or business

Undertaking or business

The *Regulations* apply to the transfer of an undertaking or of a business situated immediately before the transfer in the United Kingdom.

The *Regulations* also cover the transfer of part of an undertaking or business. A 'part' of an 'undertaking' means a unit which is to some extent separate and self-contained from the remainder of the enterprise such as an operating division which is autonomous from the remainder of the business by virtue, for example, of having its own accounts, management structure, and product specialisation. However, the *Regulations* may apply even where the part does not retain its organisational autonomy, provided that the functional link between the various elements of production transferred is preserved and that functional link enables the transferee to use those elements to pursue an identical or analogous economic activity: see *Klarenberg v Ferrotron Technologies GmbH*: C-466/07 [2009] ICR 1263.

In *Fairhurst Ward Abbotts Ltd v Botes Building Ltd* [2004] EWCA Civ 83, [2004] ICR 919 the Court of Appeal ruled that, provided that there is an identifiable stable economic entity before the transfer takes place, the law does not require that the particular part transferred should itself, before the date of the transfer, exist as a discrete and identifiable economic entity: it is sufficient if a part of the larger entity becomes identified for the first time as a separate economic entity on the occasion of the transfer separating a part from the whole. This approach was applied in *Transport & General Workers Union v Swissport (UK) Ltd (in administration)* [2007] ICR 1593.

'Undertaking' would appear to include a professional practice, such as that of an NHS doctor (see *Jeetle v Elster* [1985] ICR 389), the activities of a charitable foundation (*Redmond (Dr Sophie) Stichting v Bartol*: C-29/91 [1992] ECR I-3189, [1992] IRLR 366), and the carrying out of an activity pursuant to a contract (see **50.5** below). An undertaking which is carried out on a non-profit making basis but is contracted out to be carried out on a commercial basis may still transfer where all the other characteristics of the activity remained the same before and after the alleged transfer: *Alderson v Secretary of State for Trade and Industry* [2003] EWCA Civ 1767, [2004] ICR 512.

However, an economic entity is not defined only by the employment status of a group of employees, but also by the function which that group undertakes: *Wynnwith Engineering Co Ltd v Bennett* [2002] IRLR 170. In *Wain v Guernsey Ship Management Ltd* [2007] EWCA Civ 294, [2007] ICR 1350 the Court of Appeal rejected the contention that a group of short-term contract employees comprised an economic entity.

50.5 *Transfer*

A relevant transfer occurs where there is a transfer of an economic identity which retains its identity *(reg 3(1)(a))*.

Thus, in deciding whether there has been a transfer of an undertaking, the critical question is whether the undertaking retains its identity and is carried on by the transferee. In answering that question, all the factual circumstances must be considered, but particular factors include: the type of undertaking or business concerned; whether tangible assets such as buildings and moveable property are transferred; the value of intangible assets at the time of the transfer; whether the majority of employees are taken over by the new employer; whether customers are transferred; the degree of similarity between the activities carried on before and after the alleged transfer; and the period, if any, for which those activities are suspended (*Spijkers v Gebroeders Benedik Abbatoir CV*: 24/85 [1986] 2 CMLR 296; *Redmond (Dr Sophie) Stichting v Bartol*: C-29/91 [1992] ECR I-3189, [1992] IRLR 366; *Rask and Christensen v ISS Kantineservice A/S*: C-209/91 [1993] IRLR 133, ECJ).

The ECJ has considered the application of this test in a number of cases involving the contracting out of services and changes of contractors. The importance within the UK of this line of authority is likely to be limited in the future since such cases are likely to constitute service provision changes, whether or not there is a transfer of an undertaking.

In *Schmidt v Spar und Leihkasse der Früheren Ämter Bordersholm, Kiel und Cronshagen*: C-392/92 [1995] ICR 237 it was held that there could be a transfer of contracted-out cleaning services, even where the services are performed by a single employee and there is no transfer of tangible assets; and *Merckx v Ford Motors Co Belgium SA*: C-171/94 and C-172/94 [1996] IRLR 467. The ECJ held in *Ledernes Hovedorganisation (acting for Rygard) v Dansk Arbejdsgiverforening (acting for Sto Molle Akustik A/S)*: C-48/94 [1995] ECR I-2745, [1996] ICR 333, however, that the transfer of an undertaking must involve the transfer of a 'stable economic entity' and went on to hold in *Süzen v Zehnacker Gebäudereingung GmbH Krankenhausservice*: C- 13/95 [1997] ICR 662 that an activity does not, in itself, constitute such an entity. It follows, the ECJ stated, that the mere fact that a similar activity is carried on before and after a change of contractors does not mean there is a transfer of an undertaking. In the case of a labour-intensive undertaking with no significant assets (eg contract cleaning), there will generally be no transfer unless the new contractor takes on a majority of the old contractor's staff. This approach was reinforced in *Vidal (Francisco Hernandez) SA v Gomez Perez*: C-127/96, C-229/96 and C-74/97 [1999] IRLR 132, ECJ and in *Sánchez Hidalgo v Asociación de Servicios Aser*: C-173/96 [2002] ICR

73. The ECJ again emphasised the requirement for a stable economic entity, adding that 'an organised group of wage earners who are specifically and permanently assigned to a common task may, in the absence of other factors of production, amount to an economic entity'. Examples of the application of this approach include *Oy Liikenne Ab v Liskojarvi*: C-172/99 [2002] ICR 155 (the absence of a transfer of assets conclusive where the activity required substantial tangible assets) and *Jouini v Princess Personal Service GmbH*: C-458/05 [2008] ICR 128 (the possibility of a transfer of a part of a temporary employment agency).

The importance of the distinction between a labour-intensive undertaking and an asset reliant undertaking was crucial in *Abler v Sodexho MM Catering Betriebsgesellschaft mbH*: C-340/01 [2004] IRLR 168, in which the ECJ found that the catering sector was based essentially on equipment. Thus, where a new contractor took over the use of that equipment then there was a transfer, even though the equipment was in fact owned by neither the transferor nor the transferee but by the party contracting out the activity. The ECJ specifically held that the degree of importance to be attached to each factor will vary according to the activity carried on. (See also *Guney-Gorres v Securicor Aviation (Germany) Ltd*: C-232/04 and C-233/04 [2006] IRLR 305.) The ECJ's most recent pronouncement, again in relation to the cleaning of premises, was in *CLECE SA v Valor* C-463/09 [2011] ICR 1319.

The Court of Appeal has emphasised that the correct approach is 'multi-factorial': *Balfour Beatty Power Networks Ltd v Wilcox* [2006] EWCA Civ 1240, [2007] IRLR 63. No single aspect need determine the question. All factors must be balanced before a decision is reached. The CA considered that there could be a relevant transfer even in an industry which was asset reliant and where there was no transfer of tangible assets: the ECJ had not, the CA considered, laid down any stark rule to the contrary in *Oy Liikenne*. On the facts, the assets were in any event leased and so they could be better characterised as tools and equipment. The CA also observed that an enterprise may be 'stable' as a matter of practical and industrial reality, even though its long-term future is not assured. A similar, multi-factorial approach had been followed by the EAT in *P & O Trans European Ltd v Initial Transport Service Ltd* [2003] IRLR 128 and in *NUMAST v P&O Scottish Ferries Ltd* [2005] ICR 1270.

A number of cases involving contracting out and changes of contractors have also come before the UK courts, many arising out of local government compulsory competitive tendering. The courts have held in this context that if similar activities are carried on before and after a change of service provider, there can be a transfer of an undertaking notwithstanding that no assets are transferred (*Dines v Initial Health Care Services Ltd* [1995] ICR 11) or that neither assets nor staff are transferred (*BSG Property Services v Tuck* [1996] IRLR 134). See also *Kenny v South Manchester College* [1993] IRLR 265, *Isles of Scilly Council v Brintel Helicopters Ltd* [1995] ICR 249 and *Kelman v Care Contract Services Ltd* [1995] ICR 260. The reasoning of these cases must now, however, be reconsidered in the light of *Betts v Brintel Helicopters Ltd* [1997] IRLR 361, in which the Court of Appeal followed *Süzen* (see above) and held that there was no transfer on a change of contractor providing helicopter services to a company, where the new contractor took over no staff, and only a limited part of the old contractor's assets. The court distinguished labour intensive undertakings, where the key factor is whether the majority of employees are taken over by the new employer, and other types of undertaking, where a broader range of factors must be considered.

The Court of Appeal reconsidered the scope of *Süzen* (with express reference to *Sánchez Hidalgo*) in *ECM (Vehicle Delivery Service) v Cox* [1999] IRLR 559. The court stated that the importance of *Süzen* had been overstated: the ECJ had not overruled its previous interpretive rulings. It is for the national court to make the necessary factual appraisal, considering in particular the factors identified in *Spijkers*. One relevant factor is whether the majority of employees are taken over by the new employer to enable it to carry on the activities of the undertaking on a regular basis. The mere loss of a service contract to a competitor does not of itself indicate the existence of a transfer. This appeal was followed by Lindsay J in *RCO Support Services Ltd v Unison* [2000] ICR 1502 and in *Cheesman v R Brewer Contracts Ltd* [2001] IRLR 144.

The Court of Appeal's judgment in *RCO Support Services Ltd v Unison* [2002] EWCA Civ 464, [2002] ICR 751 appeared to accept that *Süzen* represented a shift on the previous position, such that a mere similarity in the activities of the entity before and after the transfer cannot be enough to establish a transfer. However, the additional factors required need not amount to a transfer of a majority of the workforce (in terms of numbers and skills) as had been the case in *Süzen*. On the facts of *RCO* a similarity in operating methods and training within the activities was found to be enough, even where the location of the activity had moved.

As to the question of the relevance of an intention of the transferee to avoid the application of TUPE, the Court of Appeal in *RCO* stated that a subjective motive of the putative transferee to avoid the application of TUPE is not the real point. However, in deciding whether or not there is a transfer, it may be relevant to take into account the objective circumstances surrounding a decision not to take on the workforce. It is far from clear how that distinction will be drawn in practice. Some guidance is to be found in the decision in *Astle v Cheshire County Council* [2005] IRLR 12. The EAT held that if a tribunal finds that the reason or principal reason of the transferee was to avoid the application of TUPE then it is a relevant factor to take into account in the *Spijkers* exercise, and may be decisive.

In *RCO* the Court of Appeal made reference to its earlier decision in *ADI (UK) Ltd v Willer* [2001] EWCA Civ 971, [2001] IRLR 542 in which it had recognised that *Süzen* represented something of a retreat by the ECJ from its earlier decisions. In *ADI* it concluded that, in a labour-intensive operation, the absence of a transfer of staff from the outgoing contractor to the incoming contractor should lead to the conclusion that there is no transfer of an undertaking, even though the work, the equipment used, the location and the ultimate customers are the same. However, in such cases, the balance would be tipped the other way if the reason why there was no transfer of staff was that the parties wished to avoid the application of the *Regulations*. If such an intention is established, then there will be deemed to have been a transfer. This ruling substantially supersedes the decisions in *Whitewater Leisure Management Ltd v Barnes* [2000] ICR 1049, EAT and *Lightways (Contractors) Ltd v Associated Holdings Ltd* [2000] IRLR 247, Ct of Sess.

In *Rygaard v Stro Molle Akustik* [1996] IRLR 51, the ECJ held that existing authorities presuppose that the transfer relates to a stable economic entity whose activity is not limited to one specific works contract. However, the scope of this ruling was restricted to its facts (ie single contracts for building works) by the EAT in *Argyll Training Ltd v Sinclair* [2000] IRLR 630, in which it stated that there is no basis for automatically excluding all single-contract undertakings from the possibility of being transferred. Indeed, it is possible (though not common) for a single employee to constitute a stable economic entity, provided that the entity can be said to be sufficiently structured and autonomous: *Dudley Bower Building Services Ltd v Lowe* [2003] ICR 843.

50.6   Other concepts defining 'relevant transfer'

General

The *Regulations* apply to public and private undertakings engaged in economic activities, whether or not they are operating for gain (*reg 3(4)(a)*).

The *Regulations* apply even if the transfer is governed or effected by foreign law, or if the employees in the undertaking, business or activities work outside the UK or if their employment is governed by foreign law (*reg 3(4)(b)*). The *Regulations* have the potential to

50.6 Transfer of Undertakings

apply to a transfer from the UK to a non-EU entity in the event that on the transfer the undertaking did not remain within the jurisdiction: *Holis Metal Industries Ltd v GMB and Newell Ltd* [2008] ICR 464, [2008] IRLR 187, EAT.

In *Allen v Amalgamated Construction Co Ltd*: C-234/98 [1999] ECR I-8643, [2000] ICR 119, the ECJ held that the *Acquired Rights Directive* can apply to a transfer between two subsidiary companies in the same group, provided that they are distinct legal persons each with specific employment relationships with their employees. This was so even though the two companies had the same management, were in the same premises, and were engaged in the same works.

On the other hand, where an individual is employed by one group company but works on a permanent basis in an undertaking run by another company within the group, the latter company may be the 'transferor' for the purposes of the *Directive*, even though there is no contractual relationship between that company and the individual: *Albron Catering BV v FNV Bondgenoten*: C-242/09 [2011] ICR 373.

In *Foreningen af Arbejdsledere i Danmark v Daddy's Dance Hall A/S*: 324/86 [1988] IRLR 315 the European Court of Justice held that there was a relevant transfer where a lessee of restaurant premises gave notice to its employees upon the determination of the lease, and the lessor then granted a new lease to a third party which continued to run the business without any interruption. Where the identity of the economic unit was retained, it did not matter that the transfer took place in two phases. The same result was reached on similar facts in *Litster v Forth Dry Dock and Engineering Co Ltd* [1989] ICR 341 and in *P Bork International A/S v Foreningen af Arbejdsledere i Danmark*: 101/87 [1989] IRLR 41 (owner of leased undertaking repossessed it after forfeiture of the lease and then sold it on to a third party who resumed operation of the business). These decisions will be important where businesses are operated on a franchise (see also *LMC Drains Ltd v Waugh* [1991] 3 CMLR 172).

If the agreement pursuant to which the transfer occurred is rescinded, there may be a relevant 'retransfer' back to the original transferor (*Berg and Busschers v Besselsen*: 144/87 and 145/87 [1990] ICR 396).

50.7 *More than one transaction*

A relevant transfer may be affected by a series of two or more transactions (*reg 3(6)(a)*). In construing the *1981 Regulations* purposively, it has been held that the court will seek to identify whether there is in truth a single transfer and will look beyond an 'ingenious device' whereby an intermediary company is introduced for the sole purpose of achieving the contracting parties' mutual wish to transfer an undertaking between them which is stripped of liability to the employees (see *Re Maxwell Fleet and Facilities Management Ltd (No 2)* [2000] ICR 717). In *Temco Service Industries SA v Imzilyen*: C-51/00 [2002] IRLR 214 the ECJ confirmed that the absence of a contractual link does not in itself prevent the application of the *Directive*; it was enough if the transferor and transferee were part of the web of contractual relations.

50.8 *Transfer of property*

A transfer may take place whether or not any property is transferred to the transferee by the transferor (*reg 3(6)(b)*).

50.9 *Administrative functions carried out by a public body*

'A relevant transfer' does not include an administrative reorganisation of public administrative authorities, or the transfer of administrative functions between public administrative authorities (*reg 3(5)*). This limited exclusion was originally explained by the European Court of Justice in *Henke v Gemeinde Schierke*: C-298/94 [1996] IRLR 701 and was then recognised in *art 1(1)(c)* of *Directive 2001/23*. It was further clarified in two subsequent decisions of the European Court of Justice: *Mayeur v Association Promotion de l'Information Messine*: C-175/99 [2002] ICR 1316 (transfer where the work of a non-profit making tourist agency was taken over by the municipality); and *Collino v Telecom Italia SpA*: C-343/98 [2002] ICR 38 (transfer on a reorganisation of telephone service providers). In *Viggosdottir v Islandspostur HF* [2002] IRLR 425, the EFTA Court held that the *Directive* could apply to the conversion of a state entity into a wholly state-owned limited liability company, and that it is for the national court to decide whether the individuals fall under the protection of national employment law in accordance with the principles set out by the ECJ in *Collino*. The *Henke* exception was applied by the High Court in *Law Society of England and Wales v Secretary of State for Justice* [2010] EWHC 352 (QB), [2010] IRLR 407, [2010] All ER (D) 10 (Mar) to extend to the Legal Complaints Service on the basis that it was a body which had exercised public authority in that it carried out regulatory and quasi-judicial functions which are subject to judicial review. However, the exception did not apply to auxiliary services within Italian State schools, such as cleaning, caretaking and administrative assistance: *Scattolon v Ministero dell'Istruzione, dell'Università e della Ricerca*: C-108/10 [2012] ICR 740.

50.10 *Share transfers*

The *Regulations* apply only to the transfer of an undertaking from one legal person to another. They do not apply, for example, to the transfer of shares in a company which carries on the undertaking (*Initial Supplies Ltd v McCall* 1992 SLT 67). This is so even though this form of transaction was adopted with the purpose of avoiding the *Regulations* (*Brookes v Borough Care Services* [1998] IRLR 636).

In *Millam v Print Factory (London) 1991 Ltd* [2007] EWCA Civ 322, [2007] ICR 1331 the Court of Appeal reiterated this principle, but went on to uphold a tribunal's conclusion that the business nevertheless transferred to the acquiring company. The CA also rejected the EAT's analysis that it could pierce the corporate veil. An issue of piercing the corporate veil arises only when it is established that activity X is carried on by company A, but for policy reasons it is sought to show that in reality the activity is the responsibility of the owner of company A, company B, to pierce the corporate veil it must generally be shown that the subsidiary company is a sham or façade. In the present case, the activity was in fact carried on by company B, and so there was a relevant transfer from A to B.

50.11 *Insolvency*

The ECJ held in *Abels v Administrative Board of the Bedrijfsvereniging voor de Metaalindustrie en de Electrotechnische Industrie*: 135/83 [1985] ECR 469 that the *Directive* does not apply to the transfer of an undertaking, business or part of a business in the course of insolvency proceedings. In *Jules Dethier Equipment SA v Dassy*: C-319/94 [1998] ICR 541, it ruled that it does apply in the event of the transfer of an undertaking which is being wound up by a court if the undertaking continues to trade. It also applies where the undertaking transferred is being wound up voluntarily (*Europièces SA (in liq) v Sanders*: C-399/96 [1998] ECR I-6965, ECJ). The distinction drawn in *Donaldson v Perth & Kinross Council* [2004] ICR 667 was between an 'irretrievable insolvency and cessation of business' and 'the sale of the business as a going concern', but this was not followed in *Transport & General Workers Union v Swissport (UK) Ltd (in administration)* [2007] ICR 1593.

Clarification is now given in *reg 8(7)*, which provides that *reg 4* (effect of relevant transfer on contracts of employment) and *reg 7* (dismissal of employee because of relevant transfer) do not apply to any relevant transfer where the transferor is the subject of 'bankruptcy proceedings or any analogous insolvency proceedings which have been instituted with a view to the liquidation of the assets of the transferor and are under the supervision of an insolvency practitioner'.

Furthermore, *regs 8(1)* to *(6)* apply to 'relevant insolvency proceedings', that is insolvency proceedings which have been opened in relation to the transferor not with a view to the liquidation of the assets of the transferor and which are under the supervision of an insolvency practitioner. They extend the statutory regimes for payments by the Secretary of State (under chapter VI of *Part XI* and *Part XII* of the *Employment Rights Act 1996*) to transfers in such cases. The relevant debts (those falling within *s 184* of the *Employment Rights Act 1996*) have to arise before the transfer in order to come within that state guarantee: *Pressure Coolers Ltd v Molloy* [2012] ICR 51.

In order to determine whether 'insolvency proceedings' had commenced, it is necessary to identify the particular proceedings and then determine, in accordance with the statutory provisions relating to those proceedings, whether they had commenced or not at the time of the transfer: *Secretary of State for Trade and Industry v Slater* [2008] ICR 54. The Court of Appeal has confirmed that the directive requires an 'absolute approach' such that administration proceedings under *Schedule B1* of the *Insolvency Act 1986* can never constitute "insolvency proceedings" within the meaning of *Regulation 8(7)*: *Key2Law (Surrey) LLP v De'Antiquis* [2011] EWCA Civ 1567, [2012] ICR 881.

50.12 Time of the transfer

It may be important to identify the precise time of the transfer, because of the requirement (see **50.13** below) that the employee be employed by his old employer immediately before the transfer. However, following the decision of the House of Lords in *Litster v Forth Dry Dock and Engineering Co Ltd* [1989] ICR 341, a gloss is effectively put on that requirement if the employee is dismissed for a reason connected with the transfer, and some of the reported cases would now be decided differently as a result (a principle now enshrined in *reg 4(3)*; see **50.14** below).

A number of cases have arisen where, for example, the employee has been dismissed between the exchange of contracts for the sale of the business and the completion date (*Wheeler v Patel* [1987] ICR 631), or joined the new employers after they were let into possession under a deed of assignment but before completion (*Brook Lane Finance Co Ltd v Bradley* [1988] ICR 423). In these cases it was held that the contract of employment was not automatically continued by virtue of the *Regulations*. In both *Wheeler* and *Brook Lane* the EAT considered that it was bound by the decision of the Court of Appeal in *Secretary of State for Employment v Spence* [1986] ICR 651 to hold that a transfer was only capable of taking place at a particular moment, and not over a period of time. However, after the judgment of the House of Lords in *Litster*, the EAT in *Macer v Abafast Ltd* [1990] ICR 234 did not follow the approach adopted in *Brook Lane*.

In *Celtec Ltd v Astley* C-478/03 [2005] ICR 1409 the ECJ considered a reference from the House of Lords which raised this issue. It recognised that a transfer may take place over a period of time. However, there is a 'date of a transfer' and this must be understood a referring to the date on which responsibility as employer for carrying on the business of the unit in question moves from the transferor to the transferee. The ECJ was clear that the date of the transfer cannot be postponed to another date at the will of either party. This judgment was applied by the House of Lords at [2006] ICR 992. This was applied (and *Wheeler v Patel* distinguished) by the EAT in *Commercial Motors (Wales) Ltd v M Howley* (UKEAT/0491/11).

50.13 THE AUTOMATIC ASSIGNMENT OF CONTRACTS OF EMPLOYMENT AND ASSOCIATED RIGHTS AND LIABILITIES

The most drastic consequences of a transfer of an undertaking are specified in *reg 4*. Those of the transferor's employees:

(i)   who were employed by the transferor immediately before the transfer; and

(ii)   who were assigned to the organised grouping of resources or employees that is subject to the relevant transfer; and

(iii)   whose contracts would otherwise have been terminated by the transfer,

automatically become, from the moment of the transfer, employed by the transferee on the terms and conditions which they enjoyed with the transferor. This is subject only to an employee's right of objection (see **50.16** below); it cannot be prevented by an intention on the part of the transferor and transferee, or agreement between them, to the contrary (*Hertaing v Benoidt*: C-305/94 [1997] IRLR 127), nor by ignorance on the part of the employee of the transfer or identity of the transferee (*Secretary of State for Trade and Industry v Cook* [1997] ICR 288) disapproving the decision of the EAT to the contrary in *Photostatic Copiers (Southern) Ltd v Okuda* [1995] IRLR 11. A failure to comply with the duty to provide information (see 50.23 below) cannot of itself lead to the avoidance of a transfer: *Marcroft v Heartland (Midlands) Ltd* [2011] EWCA Civ 438, [2011] IRLR 599. With certain specified exceptions, all the transferor's rights and liabilities connected with their contracts of employment are likewise assigned to the transferee, and anything done by the transferor prior to the transfer in relation to those employees or their contracts is deemed to have been done by the transferee.

Under the *Regulations*, an 'employee' covers an individual who works for another person under a contract of employment or apprenticeship, or otherwise, but does not include an independent contractor (*reg 2(1)*). The words 'or otherwise' in the definition do not exclude the fact that there must be a contract between the individual and the transferor. Thus, the *Regulations* did not apply on the reorganisation of a school by its governing body since the teacher was employed by the local education authority and not the governing body (*Clifton Middle School Governing Body* [2000] ICR 286, CA). In *Morris Angel & Son Ltd v Hollande* [1993] ICR 71 Dillon LJ queried whether the unique nature of a managing director's position might mean that employment in that capacity was incapable of being transferred, but the correctness of this suggestion is doubted.

Reg 2(1) defines "assigned" as "assigned other than on a temporary basis". An individual is not assigned on a temporary basis simply because he is serving notice: *Marcroft v Heartland (Midlands) Ltd* [2011] EWCA Civ 438, [2011] IRLR 599.

50.14 Immediately before the transfer

Regulation 4(1) applies to a person employed in an undertaking or part of one transferred, provided that he is so employed immediately before the transfer or would have been so employed if he had not been dismissed in the circumstances described in *reg 7*, that is for a reason which is the transfer itself or a reason connected with the transfer (*reg 4(3)*). This enshrines the approach adopted by the House of Lords in *Litster v Forth Dry Dock and Engineering Co Ltd* [1989] ICR 341: if the dismissal in fact took place solely or principally because of the prospective transfer, then the employee would be deemed to have been employed immediately before the transfer. Their Lordships accepted the reasoning of the European Court of Justice in *P Bork International A/S v Foreningen af Arbejdslederen i Danmark*: 101/87 [1989] IRLR 41, namely, that the fact that *Directive 77/187* prohibited dismissal because of a transfer (see **50.25** below) meant that a dismissal in breach of that prohibition could not effectively exclude the operation of the *Regulations*. See also *Macer v Abafast Ltd* [1990] ICR 234, where the EAT warned in a similar context that the courts would lean against artificial attempts to break continuity; and *Harrison Bowden Ltd v Bowden* [1994] ICR 186 and *A & G Tuck Ltd v Bartlett* [1994] ICR 379. However, contrast *Longden v Ferrari Ltd* [1994] ICR 443, where the EAT held that a succession of events over a period of a few weeks, causally connected to one another, were not a series of transactions by which a transfer of the employers' undertaking was 'effected' and that the transfer was effected only by the final act, a single agreement for sale. As a consequence, the employees (dismissed nearly two weeks before the agreement) were not employed 'immediately before the transfer', even though they were dismissed after the agreement had been submitted in draft.

50.14   Transfer of Undertakings

Regulation 4(3) also deals with cases where there is more than one transaction by which the transfer is effected, and provides that *reg 4* catches any person employed immediately before any of the transactions in question.

Where an employee has been dismissed at the time of the transfer but is subsequently reinstated on appeal, he is deemed to have been employed immediately before the transfer and so transfer to the transferee: *Anstey v G4S Justice Services (UK) Ltd* [2006] IRLR 588.

50.15 'Would otherwise have been terminated'

Regulation 4 transfers the contracts of employment of those, and only those, whose contracts of employment would otherwise have been terminated by the transfer. The contracts of employment of individuals employed in a part of the undertaking which is not being transferred will not be assigned by the *Regulations* to the transferee. If the employee is employed at the time of the transfer in the business transferred then he will automatically transfer to the transferee. That is so even where the employer has the power to transfer the employee away from the business transferred so that he is not assigned to it at the point of transfer; if that is not in fact done, then the transfer takes effect: *Communication Workers Union v Royal Mail Group Ltd* [2009] ICR 357 (this aspect of the judgment was not the subject of the appeal to the Court of Appeal reported at [2010] ICR 83).

A difficult question may arise if the employee divides his time between two or more parts of the undertaking, some but not all of which are transferred. In *Botzen v Rotterdamsche Droogdok Maatschappij BV*: 186/83 [1986] 2 CMLR 50 the Advocate General of the ECJ suggested that an employee could only be transferred if he worked wholly or almost wholly in the part transferred, but it is also possible that the court would apply a test of where the employee was predominantly employed. See also *Northern General Hospital NHS Trust Ltd v Gale* [1994] ICR 426; *Sunley Turriff Holdings Ltd v Thomson* [1995] IRLR 184; *Michael Peters Ltd v Farnfield* [1995] IRLR 190; *Duncan Web Offset (Maidstone) Ltd v Cooper* [1995] IRLR 633; and *Buchanan-Smith v Schleicher & Co International Ltd* [1996] ICR 613. In *CPL Distribution Ltd v Todd* [2002] EWCA Civ 1481, [2003] IRLR 28, the Court of Appeal upheld a decision that a personal assistant was not assigned to the part of an undertaking transferred, even though the majority of her work related to the contract transferred. The employee was effectively assigned to a particular manager and there was no evidence that the manager was assigned to the undertaking transferred since a substantial part of his time was involved in other activities. The same approach is to be applied in cases of a service provision change, for example where overlapping activities were outsourced to two contractors: see *Kimberley Group Housing Ltd v Hambley* [2008] ICR 1030, applying *Botzen* and *Duncan Webb Offset*.

50.16 The employee's right of objection

In *Katsikas v Konstantinidis* [1993] IRLR 179 the ECJ held that an employee could not be transferred to the employment of a new employer against his will. As a result, *reg 4(7)* provides that the transfer of the contract of employment and rights, powers, duties and liabilities under and in connection with it will not occur if the employee informs the transferor or the transferee that he objects to becoming employed by the transferee. In that event, the transfer will terminate the employee's contract of employment with the transferor, but he will not be treated for any purpose as having been dismissed by the transferor (*reg 4(8)*).

Indeed, where the employee is not told of the identity of the new employer until after the transfer, *reg 4(7)* must be purposively construed in order to allow the employee to object: *New ISG Ltd v Vernon* [2007] EWHC 2665 (Ch), [2008] ICR 319.

The question of whether an employee has objected is an objective one. Thus, where an individual purported to object but then worked for the transferee for a period of six weeks after the transfer, she had not in fact objected. The parties cannot consistently with an objection agree that an individual's employment continues even for a limited period after the transfer: *Capita Health Solutions v McLean* [2008] IRLR 595.

The ECJ held, however, in *Merckx v Ford Motors Co Belgium* [1997] ICR 352 that where an employee resigns prior to a transfer because the transferee refuses to guarantee his level of remuneration after the transfer, his 'employer' is to be treated, under *art 4(2)* of the *Directive*, as having dismissed him. In *P & O Property Ltd v Allen* [1997] ICR 436 the EAT held that the 'employer' responsible for the dismissal in these circumstances is the transferee. The EAT has held that an employee objects to his employment being transferred if he refuses to give his consent to the transfer, and that refusal is communicated to the transferor or transferee prior to the transfer (*Hay v George Hanson (Building Contractors) Ltd* [1996] IRLR 427).

In *Senior Heat Treatment Ltd v Bell* [1997] IRLR 614 an employee who 'opted out' of the transfer and accepted a severance payment from the transferor was found not to have objected within the meaning of the *Regulations*. He had accepted employment with the transferee from the date of transfer and so his contract of employment had not terminated.

Under the *Regulations*, where a relevant transfer involves or would involve a substantial change in the working conditions to the material detriment of a person whose employment contract is or would be transferred, such an employee may treat the contract as having been terminated. If he does so, the employee shall be treated for any purpose as having been dismissed by the employer, although no damages are payable by the employer in respect of wages otherwise payable in respect of a notice period which the employee has failed to work (*reg 4(9)* and *(10)*). The meaning of 'substantial change' was considered by the EAT in *Tapere v South London and Maudsley NHS Trust* [2009] ICR 1563. It is a factual matter for the tribunal, focusing on the nature as well as the degree of the change and considering the impact of the proposed change from the employee's point of view. The requirement is for a substantial change in working conditions, a phrase which is wider than "contractual conditions" and so may apply to the physical conditions of work (such as the place from which the work is based): see *Abellio London Ltd v Musse* [2012] IRLR 360.

In any event, an employee retains the right to resign in response to a repudiatory breach of contract by his employer (*reg 4(11)*).

Relying upon the decision in *Merckx*, the Court of Appeal in *University of Oxford (Chancellor, Master and Scholars) v Humphreys* [2000] ICR 405 emphasised that it is necessary to distinguish the case where an employee objects to his transfer under what is now *reg 4(7)* and will not then be able to claim that he has been dismissed, from the case where an employee treats his contract as terminated by the employer. In the latter case, the employee could seek compensation.

50.17 What the transferee acquires

As noted above, the transferee inherits those employees employed by the transferor immediately before the transfer on their existing terms and conditions, assuming that they do not object in accordance with **50.16** above. He has no power to impose, without the agreement of the individual employee (see **50.28** below), any different terms and conditions from those he has inherited from the transferor (see **50.26** below). Equally, the transferred employee has no right to insist that he be given the benefit of any superior terms and conditions enjoyed by the transferee's existing staff (see *Jackson v Computershare Investor Services plc* [2007] EWCA Civ 1065, [2008] ICR 341) (except possibly by means of a claim for EQUAL PAY (21)).

50.17 Transfer of Undertakings

For the effect of a transfer upon restrictive covenants expressed in terms of the transferor's customers, see *Morris Angel & Son Ltd v Hollande* [1993] ICR 71; see also **50.29** below and RESTRAINT OF TRADE, CONFIDENTIALITY AND EMPLOYEE INTERVENTIONS **(39)**. For the effect of a transfer on the question whether employees are redundant, see *Chapman and Elkin v CPS Computer Group plc* [1987] IRLR 462. For the effect of a transfer on an employee's normal retiring age, see *Cross v British Airways* [2006] EWCA Civ 549, [2006] ICR 1239.

50.18 The transferee inherits all accrued rights and liabilities connected with the contract of employment of the transferred employee. This includes liability for negligence and breach of statutory duty (*Taylor v Serviceteam Ltd* [1998] PIQR P201). If, for example, the transferor was in arrears with wages at the time of the transfer, the employee can sue the transferee as if the original liability had been the transferee's. The transferor is relieved of his former obligations without any need for the employee's consent (*Berg and Busschers v Besselsen* [1990] ICR 396). Equally, the transferee can sue an employee for a breach of contract committed against the transferor prior to transfer. The transferee will also inherit all the statutory rights and liabilities which are connected with the individual contract of employment. The transferred employee's period of continuous employment will date from the beginning of his period of employment with the transferor, and the statutory particulars of terms and conditions of employment, which every employer is obliged to issue, must take account of any continuity enjoyed by virtue of the *Regulations*. (As to continuity of employment when a school transfers to grant-maintained status, see *Pickwell v Lincoln-shire County Council* [1993] ICR 87.)

Liability for (for example) sex discrimination transfers to the transferee, even though the employee was employed part-time at the time of the transfer and the discrimination concerned the termination of a previous full-time contract (*DJM International Ltd v Nicholas* [1996] IRLR 76). In *Bernadone v Pall Mall Services Group* [2001] ICR 197, the Court of Appeal held that an employee's claim for personal injuries against his former employer was transferred to the new employer, together with the right of the former employer to an indemnity from its insurers: it was an implied term of the employee's contract of employment that he would be protected by insurance, as required by statute and that right to an indemnity fell within *reg 4(2)*. It did not matter whether the employee's claim was pleaded in contract, tort or breach of statutory duty.

Where a contract provides that nationally agreed pay rates will normally be paid by an employer, it is an implied term that the employer must give notice if it intends to depart from that normal situation. That implied term will transfer, so that if a transferee employer fails to give such notice it will be bound to pay a nationally agreed pay increase, even though it is not itself part of the transferor's bargaining structure: *Glendale Managed Services v Graham* [2003] EWCA Civ 773, [2003] IRLR 465.

However, in *French v MITIE Management Services Ltd* [2002] IRLR 512 the EAT accepted the transferee's argument that the employees' right to benefit from a profit sharing or share option scheme required only that the transferee provide the right to participate in a scheme of 'substantial equivalence', but one which is free from unjust, absurd or impossible features'. That concept cannot be applied to a mobility clause which operates within a defined geographic area: *Tapere v South London and Maudsley NHS Trust* [2009] ICR 1563.

50.19 Rights and liabilities which are not assigned under the Regulations

The *Regulations* do not have the effect of assigning:

(a)   criminal liabilities (*reg 4(6)*); or

(b)   rights and liabilities relating to provisions of occupational pension schemes which relate to benefits for old age, invalidity or survivors (*reg 10*).

In *Walden Engineering Co Ltd v Warrener* [1993] ICR 967, the EAT rejected arguments that employees should be entitled to equivalent pension benefits after the transfer. Moreover, it was held by the Court of Appeal in *Adams v Lancashire County Council* [1997] ICR 834 that the *Regulations* and the *Directive* do not cover transfer of future pension rights, that the exclusion of pension rights from the *Regulations* is consistent with the *Directive*, and that therefore there was no duty on a private contractor to provide an occupational pension scheme for former local government catering workers; see *Eidesund v Stavanger Catering A/S*: C-2/95 [1996] IRLR 684. Since the term relating to pension does not transfer under the *Regulations*, time to bring a claim under the *Equal Pay Act 1970* starts to run from the time of the transfer: *Preston v Wolverhampton Healthcare NHS Trust (No 3); Powerhouse Retail Ltd v Burroughs* [2004] EWCA Civ 1281, [2005] ICR 222 (applied to all pay terms in *Gutridge v Sodexo Ltd* [2009] EWCA Civ 729, [2009] ICR 1486, [2009] IRLR 721).

However, these exceptions are to be interpreted strictly: *Beckmann v Dynamco Whicheloe Macfarlane Ltd*: C-164/00 [2003] ICR 50. The ECJ ruled that early retirement benefits and benefits intended to enhance the conditions of such retirement did not fall within the meaning of rights to old-age pension schemes and so the obligation to pay such benefits did transfer to the new employer. These principles were applied by the ECJ in *Martin v South Bank University*: C-4/01 [2004] IRLR 74.

Moreover, *ss 257* and *258* of the *Pensions Act 2004* (together with the *Transfer of Employment (Pension Protection) Regulations 2005 (SI 2005/649)*) require a transferee to provide certain pension benefits to employees for whom there was an occupational pension scheme with the transferor.

The application of the distinction as to what does and does not transfer is illustrated by *Procter & Gamble Co v Svenska Cellulosa Aktiebolaget SCA* [2012] IRLR 733: the High Court held that the employees' right to be considered for early retirement benefits transferred under TUPE, whereas benefits payable after normal retirement age (including those first triggered as early retirement benefits) do not transfer.

50.20   TRANSFER OF AN UNDERTAKING AND THE TRADE UNION

Collective agreements

Under *reg 5*, a collective agreement, which:

(a)   is made between the transferor and a union recognised by the transferor; and

(b)   applies to an employee whose contract has become automatically assigned to the transferee by virtue of the transfer,

is automatically transferred to the transferee in its application to that employee. Further, anything done by or under or in connection with that agreement by the transferor before the transfer is deemed to have been done by the transferee.

The practical effect of this provision is probably minimal, since collective agreements are in English law presumed to be unenforceable (see *TULRCA 1992, s 179* and **5.2 COLLECTIVE AGREEMENTS**) unless, which is rare, the contrary is stated in the agreement. It is only in this rare case where a binding agreement is entered into that *reg 5* will pass any legal obligation to the transferee. If the terms of a collective agreement are incorporated into the contract of employment of an individual, whose service is automatically assigned on the transfer, then its terms will bind the transferee simply by virtue of the general rule that the transferee inherits the rights and liabilities in the individual's contract: *Whent v T Cartledge Ltd* [1997] IRLR 153. However, a contract which incorporates a collective agreement may not necessarily also incorporate the mechanism for incorporating subsequent agreements: *Ackinclose v*

50.20   Transfer of Undertakings

Gateshead Metropolitan Borough Council [2005] IRLR 79. The ECJ has ruled that any changes made after the transfer are not binding on the transferee if it is not itself a part of the collective bargaining machinery: *Werhof v Freeway Traffic Systems GmbH & Co KG*: Case C-499/04 [2006] IRLR 400. In *Alemo-Herron v Parkwood Leisure Ltd* [2010] EWCA Civ 24, [2010] ICR 793 the Court of Appeal applied Werhof to determine that a 'dynamic' wage-fixing clause would not be protected on transfer, disapproving the contrary approach in *Whent*. However, the Supreme Court took the view that the position was not *acte clair* and so referred the question to the ECJ: [2011] ICR 920. The Advocate General has proposed (in an opinion delivered on 19 February 2013) that the ECJ should hold that EU law does not preclude national courts from allowing a dynamic interpretation of clauses referring to collectively-agreed terms.

Regulation 5(b) provides that any order made in respect of a collective agreement transferred under *reg 5* takes effect as if the transferee were a party to the agreement. In effect, this means that awards of the Central Arbitration Committee ('CAC') made against the transferor are binding against the transferee to the extent that they previously bound the transferor.

50.21 Recognition

Where the transferor recognises a union in respect of employees in the undertaking or part of the undertaking to be transferred and, following the transfer, the undertaking or part of the undertaking transferred maintains an identity distinct from the rest of the transfer-ee's business or businesses, the transferee must recognise the union in respect of those employees (*reg 6*). The underlying provision within the *Directive* was considered by the ECJ in *Federación de Servicios Públicos de la UGT (UGT-FSP) v Ayuntamiento de La Línea de la Concepción*: C-151/09 [2010] ICR 1248.

Although machinery for enforcing trade union recognition has now been repealed and there is no penalty under the *Regulations* for refusal to recognise, or for withdrawal of recognition, the transfer of recognition may be significant when a transferred employee seeks to invoke against the transferee a right which is dependent on the existence of a recognised union, eg the right to take time off for trade union activities under *TULRCA 1992, s 170* (see **47.3** TIME OFF WORK).

50.22 Information and consultation

Employee Liability Information

Regulations 11 to 16 provide an important code for the provision of information by the transferor to the transferee, and by employers to affected employees.

Regulation 11 imposes a duty on the transferor to notify the transferee of certain information relating to any person employed by him who is assigned to the activity which is the subject of the relevant transfer. The information must be in writing or some other readily accessible form.

That information, defined as 'employee liability information' is:

(a)   the identity and age of the employee;

(b)   the information specified in *s 1* of the *Employment Rights Act 1996* (see **7.6** CONTRACT OF EMPLOYMENT);

(c)   information of any disciplinary action taken against the employee and of any grievance raised by them within the previous two years to which a Code of Practice issued under *Part IV* of the *TULR(C)A 1992* applies;

(d)   information relating to actual or potential claims against the transferor;

1134

(e)   information of any collective agreement which will apply to the employee pursuant
         to *reg 5.*

This information must also be provided in relation to an employee who has resigned because
of the transfer (or for a reason connected to it): *reg 11(4).*

This information must be provided not less than fourteen days before the relevant transfer,
unless there are special circumstances which mean that this is not reasonably practicable, in
which case it must be given as soon as reasonably practicable thereafter: *reg 11(6).*

If the transferor fails to comply with this obligation, the transferee may present a complaint
to an employment tribunal. If successful, the tribunal may make an award of compensation
to the transferee, such as is just and equitable in particular having regard to any loss
sustained by the transferor which is attributable to the breach and the terms of any contract
between transferor and transferee which provide for the payment of such a sum in any event.
The minimum level of such an award is, however, fixed at £500 per employer (subject to a
discretion to award a lower figure if the tribunal considers that just and equitable).

50.23 *Information and consultation of employees*

Under *reg 13*, the employer of employees affected by the transfer, whether he is the
transferor or transferee, must inform all the appropriate representatives of any of the
affected employees, long enough before the transfer to enable consultations to take place
between the employer and those representatives, of the following:

(a)   the fact that a relevant transfer is to take place;

(b)   when it is to take place;

(c)   the reasons for it;

(d)   the legal, economic and social implications of the transfer for affected employees;

(e)   the measures which he envisages taking in relation to those employees (and if no
         measures are envisaged, that fact);

(f)   if the employer is the transferor, the measures which the transferee envisages that he
         will take in relation to those employees who are to be automatically assigned to him
         on the transfer (or if no measures are envisaged, that fact).

Where such information is provided, the employer must also include specified information
relating to the use of agency workers (if any) by that employer: *reg 13(2A).*

The obligation under sub-para (*d*) is satisfied where the employer states a genuine belief,
even if that belief is wrong in law: *Communication Workers Union v Royal Mail Group Ltd*
[2010] ICR 83.

Appropriate representatives are representatives of an independent trade union recognised
by the employer for employees of that description. If there is no such union then the
appropriate representatives are, at the employer's choice, either (i) employee representatives
elected by the affected employees for this purpose in an election complying with the
requirements of *reg 14*, or (ii) employee representatives appointed or elected by the affected
employees for some other purpose but who have authority from those employees to receive
information and to be consulted about the proposed dismissals on their behalf
(*reg 13(3)(b)*). If there are no appropriate representatives at the relevant time, the employer
is under a positive duty to invite the affected employees to elect employee representatives
for this purpose: *Howard v Millrise Ltd* [2005] ICR 435.

If a question arises as to whether or not any employee representative was an appropriate
representative, it is for the employer to show that the employee representative had the
necessary authority to represent the affected employees (*reg 15(3)*).

Regulation 14 sets out the requirements for the election of employee representatives under *reg 13(3)*. In particular, all affected employees on the date of the election are entitled to vote for employee representatives and so far as reasonably practicable the vote should be in secret. It is for the employer to show that the requirements of *reg 14* have been satisfied (*reg 15(4)*). If the employer has invited affected employees to elect representatives and they fail to do so within a reasonable time, then the employer must give the information required by *reg 13(2)* to each affected employee (*reg 13(11)*).

Employee representatives are afforded special protection in certain circumstances. They have the right not to be subjected to any detriment on the ground that they perform or propose to perform any function or activity as an employee representative (*ERA 1996, s 47*, as amended by *SI 1999/1925*) and any dismissal of an employee representative on that ground is automatically unfair (*ERA 1996, s 103*, as amended by *SI 1999/1925*). They have the right to take reasonable time off (which is paid) in order to perform their functions as an employee representative (*ERA 1996, ss 61–63*).

Where assurances are given by the transferee employer in the course of the consultation process and those assurances are accepted by employee representatives, that alone cannot constitute an independent contractual commitment. Thus, a non-contractual bonus scheme could not be elevated to a contractual entitlement simply because the transferee had given assurances about the continuation of the scheme: *Small v Boots Co plc* [2009] IRLR 328.

These provisions (as enacted in another context) were extensively discussed in *Institution of Professional Civil Servants v Secretary of State for Defence* [1987] IRLR 373, which is authority for several of the propositions referred to below, although not all of them were essential to the decision.

The transferee must give the transferor the information necessary to enable him to comply in time with sub-para (*f*) above (*reg 13(4)*). But the transferee is under no *obligation* to envisage any measures, and sometimes he may envisage them too late for there to be compliance with sub-para (*f*). Note that the duty to inform arises independently of the obligation to consult: even where there is no duty to consult, there will be a duty to inform under *reg 13(2)* since that duty is intended to anticipate both compulsory and voluntary consultation (*Cable Realisations Ltd v GMB Northern* [2010] IRLR 42 and *Todd v Strain* [2011] IRLR 11).

There is no obligation to consult post-transfer concerning measures in connection with the transfer: *Amicus v City Building (Glasgow) LLP* [2009] IRLR 253.

The information to be given to the representatives is to be delivered to them personally or (in the case of union representatives) sent by post to the union's head office or other address notified by the representatives (*reg 13(5)*).

If either the transferor or the transferee envisages that he will take measures in relation to any of the affected employees, he must enter into consultation with their appropriate representatives with a view to seeking their agreement to measures to be taken. (This is the only *obligation* to consult. Although, as stated above, there are other obligations to give information in time for consultation, consultation itself is voluntary in those cases.) The measures referred to must be definite plans or proposals, not mere hopes or possibilities, and must be such as would not have happened but for the transfer; they do not need to be disadvantageous in order to trigger the requirement to consult: *Todd v Strain* [2011] IRLR 11. The information to be disclosed does not include the calculations and assumptions underlying those plans. Consultation involves considering and replying to representations made by the representatives and, insofar as representations are rejected, stating the reasons for the rejection. Reasons need not be given in writing, though this may be advisable. It is as yet unclear how the content of the obligation has been affected by the addition of the stipulation that the consultation must be with a view to seeking agreement (*reg 13(6)*).

In *Unison v Somerset County Council* [2010] ICR 498 the EAT considered that the category of 'affected employees' (identified in *reg 13(1)*) extends not only to those who are to transfer, but to those who will be or may be transferred or whose jobs are in jeopardy by reason of the proposed transfer, or who have job applications with the organisation pending at the time of the transfer.' It does not extend to employees of the transferor whose future career opportunities might be diminished by a change in the recruitment arrangements in the part transferred.

If an employer fails to inform or consult, then a complaint may be made to an employment tribunal by the trade union (where the failure relates to trade union representatives) or by the employee representatives or any of them (where the failure relates to employee representatives) or by any of his employees who are affected employees (where the failure relates to the election of employee representatives and in any other case) (*reg 15(1)*). If it is not reasonably practicable to bring the complaint within three months, it may be presented within a reasonable time thereafter (*reg 15(12)*; and see **17.25** EMPLOYMENT TRIBUNALS – I). There is no need to wait for the transfer to take place before presenting the complaint (*South Durham Health Authority v Unison* [1995] ICR 495), and it appears that the complaint may proceed even if in fact the transfer never takes place (*Banking Insurance and Finance Union v Barclays Bank plc* [1987] ICR 495).

Where a complaint succeeds, the tribunal must make a declaration to this effect and may order the employer to pay compensation to affected employees (*reg 15(7)*). The maximum payable is 13 weeks' pay for each employee affected (*reg 16(3)*). The amount of a week's pay is not capped: *Zaman v Kozee Sleep Products Ltd* [2011] IRLR 196. The transferee is jointly and severally liable with the transferor in respect of compensation payable (*reg 15(9)*). In determining the amount of an award, the tribunal must apply the same approach as it does to protective awards in redundancy cases and in particular follow the guidance of the Court of Appeal in *Susie Radin Ltd v GMB* [2004] IRLR 400 (see *Sweetin v Coral Racing* [2006] IRLR 252; and see **37.6** REDUNDANCY – II). The approach in *Susie Radin* was applied in *Todd v Strain* [2011] IRLR 11.

It is a defence for the employer to show that there were special circumstances which rendered it not reasonably practicable to perform the duty in question, provided that he took whatever steps to perform that duty as were reasonably practicable in the circumstances (*reg 13(9)*). By analogy with the case law on *TULRCA 1992, s 188* (see **37.5** REDUNDANCY – II), an employer is unlikely to show that a failure to inform or consult was due to 'special circumstances' unless the transfer has to be arranged or expedited because of a sudden and unforeseen emergency. However, the tribunal should look at the matter broadly, and ought not ordinarily to grant relief unless the employer has plainly been recalcitrant or neglectful of his obligations.

If a transferor wishes to allege that the reason for his default is the failure of the transferee to supply him with information, he must give the transferee notice of that fact and the transferee must be made a party to the proceedings (*reg 15(5)*).

If an employer fails to pay compensation ordered to be paid by the tribunal, the employee concerned may present a complaint to an employment tribunal (*reg 15(10)*). This is subject to the same time limits as the original complaint under *reg 15(12)*.

50.24 DISMISSAL ON THE TRANSFER OF AN UNDERTAKING

If an individual employed in an undertaking is dismissed:

(a)   by the transferor in advance of the transfer of that undertaking; or

(b)   by the transferee after the transfer,

he may wish to bring a claim for unfair dismissal, a redundancy payment or wrongful dismissal.

50.25 Unfair dismissal and transfer of an undertaking

Dismissal

In order to complain of unfair dismissal the individual must first show that he has been dismissed within the statutory definition, that is to say:

(a)   that his contract of employment has been terminated by the employer (direct dismissal);

(b)   that he was employed for a fixed term which has expired and not been renewed; or

(c)   that he resigned in circumstances where he was entitled to do so without notice on account of his employer's conduct (constructive dismissal).

(*ERA 1996, s 95.*)

(For a discussion of the statutory definition of dismissal see **51.4–51.10** UNFAIR DISMISSAL – I.)

The *Regulations* affect the operation of this definition in a number of ways.

First, the transfer itself cannot be treated as a dismissal. As can be seen from **50.9** above, the transfer operates to assign to the transferee the contracts of employment of those who would otherwise have been dismissed upon the transfer. An employee who exercises his right of objection to the transfer (see **50.16** above) will not be treated as having been dismissed. Nor is a transfer a repudiatory breach of contract by the transferor which the employee can obtain an injunction to restrain, at least where the transferor is acting in good faith (*Newns v British Airways plc* [1992] IRLR 575); and see *Sita (GB) Ltd v Burton* [1998] ICR 17.

Second, if the transferor refrains from dismissing employees before the transfer so that they are automatically assigned to the transferee, but the transferee indicates – before the transfer – that he is unwilling to employ them, it appears that the employees will be treated as dismissed by the transferee immediately after the transfer (see *Premier Motors (Medway) Ltd v Total Oil (Great Britain) Ltd* [1984] ICR 58).

Third, if the transferee substantially changes the terms and conditions of employment previously enjoyed by the transferred staff to their detriment, the staff may resign and treat themselves as constructively dismissed. For this purpose, the change must amount to a repudiatory breach of contract (*reg 4(11)*).

Where an employee treats himself as constructively dismissed on the grounds that the transfer will involve a substantial and detrimental change in his terms and conditions of employment the employee's right lies against the transferor (*University of Oxford (Chancellor, Master and Scholars) v Humphreys* [2000] ICR 405). In that case, the Court of Appeal said that it would be inconsistent with the scheme of the *Directive* and the *1981 Regulations* for existing rights and liabilities to pass to the transferee when existing contracts of employment did not.

Fourth, where a relevant transfer involves or would involve a substantial change in working conditions to the material detriment of a person whose contract of employment is or would be transferred, such an employee may treat the contract as having been terminated and the employee shall be treated for any purpose as having been dismissed by the employer (*reg 4(9)*). "Working conditions" includes contractual terms and conditions, as well as physical conditions; whether or not there has been a "substantial change" is a factual matter for the tribunal focusing on the nature as well as the degree of the change; what has to be considered was the impact of the proposed change from the employee's point of view: *Tapere v South London and Maudsley NHS Trust* [2009] ICR 1563; *Abelio London Ltd v Musse* [2012] IRLR 360 and see **50.16** above. However, no damages are payable by the employer in respect of any failure by the employer to pay wages to an employee in respect of a notice period which the employee has failed to work.

50.26   *The fairness of the dismissal*

If an employee has been dismissed by either the transferee or the transferor and the reason for the dismissal is he transfer, the dismissal is automatically unfair (*reg 7(1)(a)*). (The normal conditions to bringing a claim for unfair dismissal, including the qualifying period of service, apply.)

If an employee has been dismissed by either the transferee or the transferor and the reason for the dismissal is a reason connected with the transfer, the dismissal is automatically unfair unless it qualifies as an 'economic, technical or organisational reason entailing changes in the workforce' of either the transferor or the transferee (*reg 7(1)(b)*). If the reason falls within this category ('an ETO reason') it will be held to be for a fair reason, either by reason of redundancy or for some other substantial reason justifying dismissal (*reg 7(3)* and see UNFAIR DISMISSAL – II (52)). The employee's remedy for a breach of *reg 7(1)* is to complain of unfair dismissal. Both transferee and transferor may dismiss employees for an economic, technical or organisational reason (*Jules Dethier Equipement v Dassy* [1998] ICR 541).

Regulation 7(1) must be read in sequence. Consider first whether the transfer was the reason for the dismissal. If so, the dismissal is unfair. Then consider whether the reason for the dismissal was connected with the transfer. If not, there is no need to enquire further; if so, it may be necessary to consider whether the reason for dismissal was an economic, technical or organisational reason. See *Warner v Adnet Ltd* [1998] IRLR 394 and *Collins v John Ansell & Partners Ltd*, IDS Brief 659.

In *Kerry Foods Ltd v Creber* [2000] ICR 556, receivers dismissed all of the employees of an undertaking prior to its transfer. The employment tribunal found that the reason for this dismissal was the transfer. The EAT ruled that the tribunal should then have concluded that (by reason of the *Litster* principle – see **50.10** above) the employees were employed in the undertaking immediately before the transfer, that their employment was transferred and the transferee was then treated as having dismissed them. However, if the main reason for the dismissal is an ETO reason within *reg 7(1)(b)*, then the employee is not deemed to have been employed immediately before the transfer, his employment docs not transfer and his only remedy for unfair dismissal is against the transferor. If the dismissal is in fact effected by the transferee, then the employee's remedy lies against the transferee, which may itself invoke an ETO reason.

In *Wilson v St Helens Borough Council* [1999] 2 AC 52 the House of Lords (reversing the decision of the Court of Appeal) held that an actual dismissal before, on or after the transfer is effective, even where the transfer (or a reason connected with it) was the reason for the dismissal. The dismissal is not a nullity and the employee cannot compel the transferee to employ him on the same terms and conditions as those on which the transferor employed him.

For the transfer or a reason connected with it to be the reason for dismissal within *reg 7(1)*, it is not necessary that the employer had in mind a specific transferee at the time of the dismissal (*Morris v John Grose Group Ltd* [1998] ICR 655, an approach approved in *Spaceright Europe Ltd v Baillavoine* [2011] EWCA Civ 1656, [2012] ICR 520).

The passage of time may increase the chances that the chain of causation between the transfer and the reason for the dismissal has been broken; however, the mere passage of time without anything happening does not in itself constitute a weakening to the point of dissolution of the chain of causation: *Taylor v Connex South Eastern Ltd*, IDS Brief 670, p 10.

The reason for dismissal may be connected with the transfer, even though the employee dismissed was never employed in the undertaking or part transferred (*reg 7(4)*). If, for example, the transferee dismisses his existing staff to accommodate the employees he is to inherit from the transferor, or if the job of an existing employee disappears following a reorganisation consequent upon the transfer, the dismissal will nonetheless be connected with the transfer.

It appears that a transferor may not invoke the defence of an 'organisational' or 'economic' reason where a transferee is willing to acquire the undertaking only on terms that the transferor's staff are first dismissed, because the reason must relate to the conduct of the business for those words to apply (*Wheeler v Patel* [1987] ICR 631 and *Gateway Hotels Ltd v Stewart* [1988] IRLR 287, not following *Anderson v Dalkeith Engineering Ltd* [1985] ICR 66, EAT. See also *Ibex Trading Co Ltd v Walton* [1994] ICR 907).

Whitehouse v Blatchford & Sons Ltd [2000] ICR 542 concerned a transfer following the award of a new contract for the provision of services to a hospital. It was a stipulation of that contract that the number of employees be reduced. The applicant was dismissed following the transfer. The Court of Appeal held that the employment tribunal had been entitled to find that the applicant's dismissal was for an economic, technical or organisational reason. If the transferee had not complied with the stipulation then it would not have won the contract. The court followed *Wheeler v Patel*: the reason must be connected with the future conduct of the business as a going concern. See also *Thompson v SCS Consulting Ltd* [2001] IRLR 801. A transferor cannot dismiss and then rely upon the future conduct of the business by the transferee after the transfer in an attempt to establish an ETO reason; the transferor itself has no intention of continuing the business and so the reason for the dismissal does not relate to its future conduct of the business: *Hynd v Armstrong* [2007] CSIH 16, [2007] IRLR 338 (Court of Session, Inner House). Similarly, an administrator may not rely upon an ETO reason where it dismisses an employee to make the business of the company a more attractive proposition to prospective transferees as a going concern, since here the intention is not to continue to conduct the business but to sell it: *Spaceright Europe Ltd v Baillavoine* [2011] EWCA Civ 1656, [2012] ICR 520, applied in *Kavanagh v Crystal Palace FC (2000) Ltd* [2013] IRLR 291.

The EAT has held that when a transferor gives notice of termination to employees before a transfer takes place and the notice expires after the transfer, it is the transferor's reasons for the dismissals which should be examined in determining whether the transferee can be held to have unfairly dismissed the employees (*BSG Property Services v Tuck* [1996] IRLR 134).

The words 'entailing changes in the workforce' impose important limitations on the defence of 'economic, technical or organisational reason'. It is only when the employer sets out to change the structure of his workforce, by reducing numbers or changing the functions which individuals perform, that the reason will entail a change in the workforce. Hence, the employer cannot fairly dismiss transferred employees who will not agree to changes in their old terms and conditions of employment (see *Berriman v Delabole Slate Ltd* [1985] ICR 546; *Crawford v Swinton Insurance Brokers Ltd* [1990] ICR 85; *Porter and Nanayakkara v Queen's Medical Centre (Nottingham University Hospital)* [1993] IRLR 486). It is not a requirement that the whole workforce be affected (see *Nationwide Building Society v Benn* [2010] IRLR 922, a case which also makes it clear that an employer can raise the ETO defence even in cases of constructive dismissal). A change from using employees to franchisees who were limited companies to carry out meter reading work entailed changes to the workforce; the word 'workforce' connotes the whole body of employees as an entity and does not include limited companies: *Meter U Ltd v Ackroyd* [2012] ICR 834.

There is, however, no limitation on the defence of 'economic, technical or organisational reason' that the dismissal would have been made in any case, for instance pursuant to a decision taken before there was any question of transferring the undertaking (*Trafford v*

Sharpe & Fisher (Building Supplies) Ltd [1994] IRLR 325, not following Advocate-General Van Gerven in *D'Urso v Ercole Marelli Elettromeccanica Generale SpA*: C-362/89 [1992] IRLR 136, ECJ).

In determining the reason for dismissal, the tribunal must consider the reasons of the employer. Where an administrator has been appointed, it is his reasons which are relevant and any earlier stratagem of a director cannot be attributed to the administrator: *Amicus v Dynamex Friction Ltd* [2008] EWCA Civ 381, [2009] ICR 511. It is necessary to consider whether the dismissal of the particular employee was for an ETO reason, rather than simply whether there were changes to the workforce: *The Manchester College v Hazel* (UKEAT/0642/11), a case which is the subject of an appeal to the Court of Appeal.

If an employer brings the case within the category of economic, technical or organisational reason entailing changes in the workforce, it will remain to be considered whether he acted reasonably in the circumstances (applying the ordinary approach to unfair dismissal cases). The considerations which will be relevant must vary with the circumstances of the individual case. It is fair to assume, however, that a failure to offer the employee an available job in some part of the business not affected by the economic technical or organisational problem in question, or a failure to consult the employee, will be grounds on which such dismissals may sometimes be considered unfair.

Whilst each case turns on its facts, it is unlikely to be unreasonable for an employee to refuse an offer from a transferee who refuses to acknowledge the effect of TUPE, but offers engagement on a self-employed basis or on less favourable terms: *F&G Cleaners Ltd v Saddington* [2012] IRLR 892.

50.27 Redundancy payments

An employee dismissed by reason of redundancy is, subject to various qualifying conditions, entitled to a redundancy payment (see REDUNDANCY – I (36)). He is dismissed by reason of redundancy if the principal reason is that his employer has ceased or intends to cease carrying on business in the place where the employee was employed or if there is a diminution in the requirements of the employer's business for the work of the particular kind for which the employee is employed.

An employee whose contract is automatically assigned under the *Regulations* will not be dismissed by the transferor and cannot therefore become entitled to a redundancy payment unless and until he is dismissed by the transferee by reason of redundancy.

If, however:

(a)   an employee is dismissed by the transferor in advance of the transfer by reason of the fact that the transferor is to go out of business in the place where the employee was employed or no longer requires work of the particular kind done by the employee; or

(b)   following the transfer, the transferee dismisses the employee for either of these reasons,

the employee is, on the face of it, entitled to a redundancy payment.

Despite decisions of the EAT in Scotland to the contrary, the Employment Appeal Tribunal in England has now confirmed that the employee will, in these circumstances, qualify for a redundancy payment even though the reason for his dismissal may qualify as an economic, technical or organisational reason entailing changes in the workforce. In *Gorictree Ltd v Jenkinson* [1985] ICR 51, it was held that the dismissal does not cease to be by reason of redundancy merely because it also qualifies as an economic, technical or organisational reason under the *Regulations*. It is likely that this decision, and not the earlier Scottish decisions, will be followed in future.

50.28 AVOIDING THE REGULATIONS AND THEIR CONSEQUENCES

An agreement to exclude or limit the application of the *Regulations* is invalid (*reg 18*). The transferor and transferee may, however, validly agree that one shall indemnify the other for sums payable in consequence of the operation of the *Regulations*. In practice, it is quite common for transferees to take such indemnities from transferors.

The principle of automatic transfer may not be derogated from by a collective agreement with a trade union (*D'Urso v Ercole Marelli Elettromeccanica Generale SpA*: C-362/89 [1992] IRLR 136, ECJ), nor on account of the business being in critical difficulties (*Spano v Fiat Geotech SpA*: C-472/93 [1995] ECR I-4321, ECJ).

Where an employee's employment contract is brought to an end, a compromise agreement will be effective and is not an agreement which purports to exclude or limit the operation of the *Regulations*: *Solectron Scotland Ltd v Roper* [2004] IRLR 4.

50.29 Variation of employees' contracts after transfer of an undertaking

Although an employee cannot waive the benefit of the *Regulations*, there may be an agreed variation to the terms and conditions of employment following the transfer provided that the reason for the change is not the transfer itself or is a reason connected with the transfer that is an economic, technical or organisation reason entailing changes in the workforce (*reg 4(4)* and *(5)* developing principles established in *Martin v South Bank University*: C-4/01 [2004] IRLR 74; *Foreningen af Arbejdsledere i Danmark v Daddy's Dance Hall A/S*: 324/86 [1988] IRLR 315); cf the judgment of the CA in *Power v Regent Security Services Ltd* [2007] EWCA Civ 1188, [2008] ICR 442, applying the *1981 Regulations*, which did not have provisions equivalent to *reg 4(4)* and *(5)*).

The ECJ has ruled that the *Directive* does not preclude a public body, as a transferee, from reducing the pay of its incoming staff where it is necessary to do so in order to comply with national rules in force for public employees. However, if the variation is sufficiently detrimental, then the employees will be entitled to resign and claim that the employer was responsible for their dismissal (under *art 4(2)*).

In *Cornwall County Care Ltd v Brightman* [1998] ICR 529, employees were dismissed by the transferee after the transfer and re-employed on less favourable terms and conditions. The EAT held that they had been unfairly dismissed since the reason for the dismissals had been the transfer. However, the employees had 'accepted' the new terms and conditions by continuing to work for the transferee. They were unable to continue to claim a right to their original terms and conditions – that claim was 'bought out' by the compensation for unfair dismissal. A change in terms and conditions brought about merely because of the expiry of employees' fixed-term contract may be effective: *Ralton v Havering College of Further and Higher Education* [2001] IRLR 738. The tribunal had been right to apply the test of whether the variation was solely by reason of the transfer. In *Enterprise Managed Services Ltd v Dance* (UKEAT/0200/11) a variation in terms was effective where it was introduced in order to achieve improved performance and efficiency, and so the harmonisation of terms amongst employees was simply a by-product of the variation, rather than the principal reason for it. The question is not whether the variation would not have happened 'but for' the transfer, but what the operative reason in fact was and so where the reason was a mistaken view that the employee was being overpaid, then this was not a reason connected with the transfer: *Smith v Trustees of Brooklands College* (UKEAT/0128/11).

51   Unfair Dismissal – I: The Right to Make a Claim

Cross-references. See TERMINATION OF EMPLOYMENT **(46)** for the various ways of terminating the contract at common law; UNFAIR DISMISSAL – II **(52)** for whether the dismissal was fair; UNFAIR DISMISSAL – III **(53)** for remedies for unfair dismissal; WRONGFUL DISMISSAL **(56)** for dismissals in breach of contract.

51.1   The *Industrial Relations Act 1971* originally created the right not to be unfairly dismissed. The right was then re-enacted in the *Employment Protection (Consolidation) Act 1978* and then in the *Employment Rights Act 1996* (*'ERA 1996'*). *ERA 1996* is a consolidation Act, so the rights thereunder are exactly the same as those which previously existed under the earlier statutes and the old case law remains relevant.

An employer who dismisses an employee without good reason or without following a fair procedure lays itself open to a claim for unfair dismissal. When such a claim is brought, the employer bears the burden of proof in establishing the reason for the dismissal. The employment tribunal will then consider whether the dismissal was fair in all the circumstances, neither party having the evidential burden in this enquiry. If the dismissal is held to be unfair, the employer can be ordered to re-engage, reinstate or to pay compensation to the ex-employee. The parties to a claim for unfair dismissal are known as the *claimant* (employee) and the *respondent* (employer). The claimant was formerly called the applicant.

51.2   PRE-CONDITIONS OF A CLAIM

A complaint of unfair dismissal must be presented to an employment tribunal before the end of the period of three months beginning with the effective date of termination of the employment (or within such further period as the tribunal considers reasonable in a case where it is satisfied that it was not reasonably practicable for the complaint to be presented within the period of three months) (*ERA 1996, s 111(2)*).

Prior to 6 April 2009, an employee benefited from a limitation period of six months from the effective date of termination of the employment (*EA 2002, s 32* and *Employment Act 2002 (Dispute Resolution) Regulations 2004, reg 15*) in certain circumstances. The provisions for the extension of time in this way were repealed by the *Employment Act 2008, s 1*. (See further **17.19–17.20** EMPLOYMENT TRIBUNALS-I and also **51.13** below for effective date of termination.)

A claimant must also satisfy the conditions set out below if he wishes to bring a claim for unfair dismissal. If these conditions are not disputed by the respondent, no evidence need be brought by the claimant to establish them. If, however, there are grounds for suspecting that any of those necessary prerequisites is absent, the employment tribunal will inquire into the matter, as it affects their jurisdiction to hear the case. The burden is on the claimant to show that he satisfies those conditions. The conditions are:

(a)   that the claimant was employed by the respondent under a contract of employment (see **51.3** below);

(b)   that the claimant was dismissed, as defined (see **51.4** below);

(c)   in most cases, that the claimant was employed for the necessary qualifying period (see **51.11** below). (The employer may sometimes argue that a claim cannot be brought because the employee did not work for the qualifying period under a *lawful* contract (see **51.16** below).); and

(d)   (only where the trigger event occurred prior to 6 April 2009) that the claimant has met the requirements of *s 32* of the *Employment Act 2002*.

51.2 Unfair Dismissal – I: The Right to Make a Claim

The exclusion of employees over retirement age from the right to complain of unfair dismissal was removed on 1 October 2006. Special rules apply to dismissals by reason of retirement (see **51.14**).

Certain employees are excluded from the right not to be unfairly dismissed:

(i) certain specified classes of employees (see **51.15** below);

(ii) those dismissed in connection with a lock-out or unofficial strike and, in some cases, persons dismissed in connection with an official strike, provided certain conditions are satisfied (see **51.17–51.18** below).

51.3 EMPLOYMENT BY THE RESPONDENT

In order to bring a claim for unfair dismissal, a claimant must show that he was employed by the respondent under a contract of employment (*ERA 1996, ss 94(1), 230(1)*). Therefore, sub-contractors or consultants under contracts for services are not protected by the unfair dismissal provisions even though they may work regularly for one person or organisation. See EMPLOYEE, SELF-EMPLOYED OR WORKER? **(14)**.

The *Employment Relations Act 1999, s 23* gives the Secretary of State the power to extend the right not to be unfairly dismissed to individuals who do not fit the current definition of 'employee'.

51.4 DISMISSAL BY THE RESPONDENT

An employee is treated as having been dismissed if, but only if:

(a) the contract under which he is employed by the employer is terminated by the employer, whether it is so terminated by notice or without notice;

(b) where he is employed under a limited-term contract, and the contract terminates by virtue of the limiting event without being renewed under the same contract; or

(c) the employee terminates that contract with or without notice in circumstances such that he is entitled to terminate it without notice by reason of the employer's conduct (usually called 'constructive dismissal').

(*ERA 1996, s 95(1)*.)

The contract of employment of an employee who is on ordinary or additional maternity leave or parental leave is deemed to continue whilst he or she is on leave, with appropriate amendments (*ERA 1996, s 71* and *Maternity and Parental Leave, etc Regulations 1999 (SI 1999/3312), reg 17*). It follows that if an employer does not permit the employee to return at the end of the leave or acts in repudiatory breach of contract during the leave period (and the employee accepts the repudiation), the employee will be treated as having been dismissed (see further **31.18** MATERNITY AND PARENTAL RIGHTS).

51.5 Termination by the employer

Notice of dismissal, once accepted, cannot generally be withdrawn (*Riordan v War Office* [1959] 1 WLR 1046). Thus, an employer who gives notice to an employee which is accepted cannot thereafter withdraw that notice without the consent of the employee. The same principle applies to notice of resignation given by the employee. In *Willoughby v CF Capital* [2011] EWCA Civ 1115; [2011] IRLR 985 the Court of Appeal discussed the so called 'special circumstances exception' to the rule in *Riordan* and concluded that it was not truly an exception to the rule but rather "*a cautionary reminder to the recipient of the notice that, before accepting or otherwise acting upon it, the circumstances in which it is given may require him first to satisfy himself that the giver of the notice did in fact really intend what he had apparently said by it.*"

Where an employer gives notice to an employee to terminate his contract of employment and, at a time within the period of that notice, the employee gives notice to the employer to terminate the contract of employment on a date earlier than the date on which the employer's notice is due to expire, the employee will nevertheless be taken to have been dismissed by his employer for the purposes of an unfair dismissal claim. The reasons for the dismissal are then taken to be the reasons for which the employer's notice was given (*ERA 1996, s 95(2)*). According to the EAT, an employer may vary the notice of dismissal which determines the effective day of termination, with the effect of bringing forward that date (*Palfrey v Transco plc* [2004] IRLR 916). If an employee gives notice to terminate his employment and, during that period of notice, the employer summarily dismisses him, the employee will be considered to have been dismissed despite the fact that he first gave notice to terminate his contract (*Harris and Russell Ltd v Slingsby* [1973] 3 All ER 31). However, if, after the employee has given notice, the employer takes advantage of a contractual right to make a payment in lieu of notice, there is no dismissal (even if the employee is thereby deprived of commission income) (*Marshall (Cambridge) Ltd v Hamblin* [1994] ICR 362, [1994] IRLR 260).

A contract of employment is only terminated by an employer if there is a specified or ascertainable date on which the contract is to cease (*Haseltine Lake & Co v Dowler* [1981] ICR 222). Dismissal, to be effective, must be communicated to the employee (*Hindle Gears Ltd v McGinty* [1985] ICR 111 and *Gisda Cyf v Barratt* [2010] UKSC 41, [2010] ICR 1475, contrasted with *Kirklees MBC v Radecki* [2009] EWCA Civ 298, [2009] IRLR 555).

An employer is not entitled to deny that there was a dismissal merely because the individual who dismissed the employee did not in fact have the authority to do so (*Warnes v Trustees of Cheriton Oddfellows Social Club* [1993] IRLR 58).

A very substantial departure by an employer from an original contract of employment may amount to termination of that contract of employment and its replacement by the offer of a different and inferior contract. In such cases, there is a termination by the employer, rather than a constructive dismissal (see **51.7** below; *Alcan Extrusions v Yates* [1996] IRLR 327; but see *Robinson v Tescom Corp* [2008] IRLR 408 for circumstances in which a contract remains extant although the employee works under protest).

51.6   Expiry of a fixed-term contract

It used to be thought that a fixed-term contract was one which did not contain a provision for prior determination by notice. However, in *Dixon v BBC* [1979] ICR 281, the Court of Appeal held that the words 'a fixed term' include a specified stated term even though the contract is determinable by notice within its term. *Regulation 1* of the *Fixed-term Employees (Prevention of Less Favourable Treatment) Regulations 2002 (SI 2002/2034)* provides that a fixed-term contract is a contract of employment that, under its provisions determining how it will terminate in the normal course, will terminate – (a) on the expiry of a specific term, (b) on the completion of a particular task, or (c) on the occurrence or non-occurrence of any other specific event other than the attainment by the employee of any normal and *bona fide* retiring age in the establishment for an employee holding the position held by him. (see Less Favourable Treatment of Part-Time Workers (30)).

51.7   Constructive dismissal

In order to establish that he has been constructively dismissed, an employee must show the following:

51.7   Unfair Dismissal – I: The Right to Make a Claim

(i)   His employer has committed a repudiatory breach of contract. A repudiatory breach is a significant breach going to the root of the contract (*Western Excavating (ECC) Ltd v Sharp* [1978] ICR 221). In *Tullett Prebon Plc v BGC Brokers LP* [2011] EWCA Civ 131, [2011] IRLR 420 the Court of Appeal applied the orthodox contractual test for a repudiatory breach in holding that it is one in which the contract-breaker has shown an intention, objectively judged, to abandon and altogether refuse to perform the contract. It is not enough to show merely that the employer has behaved unreasonably although "*reasonableness is one of the tools in the employment tribunal's factual analysis kit for deciding whether there has been a fundamental breach*" (*Buckland v Bournemouth University Higher Education Corporation* [2010] EWCA Civ 121, [2010] IRLR 445). The line between serious unreasonableness and a breach of the implied term of trust and confidence (see **5.13** CONTRACT OF EMPLOYMENT) is a fine one (see eg *Sheridan v Stanley Cole (Wainfleet) Ltd* [2003] ICR 297, [2003] IRLR 52). For example, in *Brown v Merchant Ferries Ltd* [1998] IRLR 682, the Northern Ireland Court of Appeal said that, although the correct approach to constructive dismissal is to ask whether the employer was in breach of contract and not whether the employer acted unreasonably, if the employer's conduct is seriously unreasonable, that may provide sufficient evidence that there has been a breach of contract. Likewise, there is no rule that an act of direct or indirect discrimination by an employer will constitute a repudiatory breach, but the line between repudiatory and non-repudiatory acts of discrimination is narrow (see eg *Shaw v CCL Ltd* [2008] IRLR 284). Every breach of the implied term of trust and confidence is a repudiatory breach of contract (*Morrow v Safeway Stores* [2002] IRLR 9, *Ahmed v Amnesty International* [2009] ICR 1450). The breach of contract may be an *anticipatory* rather than an *actual* one, i.e. even though no breach has yet occurred, it is sufficient if the employer has indicated a clear intention not to fulfil the terms of the contract in the future, and the employee accepts that intention to commit a breach as bringing the contract to an end (*Norwest Holst Group Administration Ltd v Harrison* [1985] ICR 668; *Greenaway Harrison Ltd v Wiles* [1994] IRLR 380). However, in *Kerry Foods Ltd v Lynch* [2005] IRLR 680 the EAT held that an employee had resigned prematurely in response to his employer's notice that it intended to terminate his employment and re-engage him on varied terms to which he had refused to agree. The EAT considered that the giving of lawful notice of termination could not by itself constitute a repudiatory breach of contract.

(ii)   He has left because of the breach (*Walker v Josiah Wedgwood & Sons Ltd* [1978] ICR 744; *Holland v Glendale Industries Ltd* [1998] ICR 493). It was also suggested in *Walker* that the employee must make clear when he resigns that he regards himself as having been constructively dismissed.

(iii)   He has not waived the breach (also known as 'affirming' the contract). In other words, he must not delay his resignation too long, or do anything else which indicates acceptance of the changed basis of his employment. See the discussion in *WE Cox Toner (International) Ltd v Crook* [1981] ICR 823, [1981] IRLR 443. Merely to protest at the time will not prevent such acceptance being inferred. An express reservation of rights may in certain circumstances be effective (see *Bliss v South East Thames Regional Health Authority* [1987] ICR 700; *Waltons & Morse v Dorrington* [1997] IRLR 488) but not in others (see *Robinson v Tescom Corp* [2008] IRLR 408). Where there has been a repudiatory breach of contract by a party to a contract of employment, the breach is not capable of remedy in such a way as to preclude acceptance by the other party (*Buckland v Bournemouth University Higher Education Corporation* [2010] EWCA Civ 121, [2010] IRLR 445). The wronged party has an unfettered choice whether to accept the breach or not, whatever his motives. All the defaulting party can do is to invite affirmation of the contract by making amends.

Examples of breaches of contract upon which a complaint of constructive dismissal might be founded include: a reduction in pay (*Industrial Rubber Products v Gillon* [1977] IRLR 389); a complete change in the nature of the job (*Ford v Milthorn Toleman Ltd* [1980] IRLR 30; *Pedersen v Camden London Borough Council* [1981] ICR 674; *Land Securities Trillium Ltd v Thornley* [2005] IRLR 765); a failure to follow the prescribed disciplinary procedure (*Post Office v Strange* [1981] IRLR 515); an act of sex discrimination (*Shaw v CCL Ltd* [2008] IRLR 284). In *Crawford v Suffolk Mental Health Partnership* [2012] EWCA Civ 138, [2012] IRLR 402 Elias LJ observed, *obiter*, that suspending an employee as a 'knee-jerk' reaction would be a breach of the implied term of mutual trust and confidence. See also CONTRACT OF EMPLOYMENT (7).

A complaint of constructive dismissal may be based upon the conduct of a fellow employee even though that employee would not have had the authority to dismiss the complainant; the test is whether the employer is vicariously liable for the conduct complained of (*Hilton International Hotels (UK) Ltd v Protopapa* [1990] IRLR 316; see also *Warnes v Trustees of Cheriton Oddfellows Social Club* [1993] IRLR 58; and VICARIOUS LIABILITY (54)).

The employer may be held to be in repudiatory breach of contract not only if he breaks an express term but also if he infringes an implied term. Thus, an employer will be held guilty of a breach which entitles an employee to resign and claim that he has been constructively dismissed if the employer behaves in a way which destroys the relationship of trust and confidence with his employee (*Bliss*, above) (see also *Wigan Borough Council v Davies* [1979] ICR 411; *Woods v WM Car Services (Peterborough) Ltd* [1982] ICR 693; *Morrow v Safeway Stores* (above); see also *Horkulak v Cantor Fitzgerald International* [2004] IRLR 942). Even if the employer's act which was the proximate cause of an employee's resignation was not by itself a fundamental breach of contract, the employee may be able to rely upon the employer's course of conduct considered as a whole in establishing that he was constructively dismissed. The 'last straw' must contribute, however slightly, to the breach of trust and confidence (*Omilaju v Waltham Forest London Borough Council* [2004] EWCA Civ 1493, [2005] IRLR 35). Glidewell LJ conveniently summarised some of the relevant principles in *Lewis v Motorworld Garages Ltd* [1986] ICR 157 at 169D–170A:

> "If the employer is in breach of an express term of a contract of employment, of such seriousness that the employee would be justified in leaving and claiming constructive dismissal, but the employee does not leave and accepts the altered terms of employment, and if subsequently a series of actions by the employer might constitute together a breach of the implied obligation of trust and confidence, the employee is entitled to treat the original action by the employer which was a breach of the express terms of the contract as a part – the start – of the series of actions which, taken together with the employer's other actions, might cumulatively amount to a breach of the implied terms."

In *BG plc v O'Brien* [2001] IRLR 496, the EAT rejected an argument that the implied duty of trust and confidence could not impose a positive obligation upon an employer; it held that the employer in that case had breached the duty of trust and confidence by failing to offer him a revised contract of employment when all his colleagues were offered a revised contract. This is a somewhat surprising decision, because it means that the duty of trust and confidence can impose a contractual obligation to vary a contract, but it was upheld by the Court of Appeal ([2002] IRLR 444). In *Visa International Service Association v Paul* [2004] IRLR 42 the duty of trust and confidence was breached by a failure to notify an employee on maternity leave of a new post, for which she was not shortlistable but for which she would have applied.

There is a line of demarcation, however, between an employee's common law cause of action for breach of contract through destroying the relationship of trust and confidence and the employee's statutory complaint of unfair dismissal (see further *Eastwood v Magnox*

Electric plc [2004] UKHL 35, [2004] IRLR 733; *Triggs v GAB Robins (UK) Ltd* [2008] EWCA Civ 17, [2008] IRLR 317, and *Edwards v Chesterfield Royal Hospital NHS Foundation Trust* [2011] UKSC 58, [2012] ICR 201 and **7.13** CONTRACT OF EMPLOYMENT).

Where there is a genuine dispute between parties about the terms of a contract of employment, it is not an *anticipatory breach* of the contract for one party to do no more than argue his point of view (*Financial Techniques (Planning Services) Ltd v Hughes* [1981] IRLR 32; see also *Bridgen v Lancashire County Council* [1987] IRLR 58).

However, there can be a constructive dismissal even where the employer acts on a genuine, although mistaken, belief. So, for example, an employer's action in appointing a replacement for the claimant and in telling customers that the claimant was no longer employed is capable of amounting to a constructive dismissal, even in circumstances where the employer genuinely, although mistakenly, believed that the employee had left (*Brown v JBD Engineering Ltd* [1993] IRLR 568).

The offer of a new contract on less favourable terms upon the expiry of a fixed-term contract cannot amount to a constructive dismissal, because when the offer is made, there is no contract in existence (*Pfaffinger v City of Liverpool Community College* [1997] ICR 142).

A constructive dismissal is not necessarily unfair (*Savoia v Chiltern Herb Farms Ltd* [1982] IRLR 166, *Buckland v Bournemouth University Higher Education Corporation* [2010] EWCA Civ 121, [2010] IRLR 445). In practice, however, it will be harder to demonstrate that a particular action is reasonable where it contravenes the contract of employment. The tribunal will look at the conduct of the employer which amounted to the breach of contract, at which stage the test is objective and the range of reasonable responses test should not be used; and then tribunal will ask whether the employer acted reasonably, in the same way as any other case of unfair dismissal (see UNFAIR DISMISSAL II (52)). The Court of Appeal clarified the correct test in *Buckland*: (i) in determining whether or not the employer is in fundamental breach of the implied term of trust and confidence the unvarnished *Malik* test applies; (ii) if acceptance of that breach entitled the employee to leave, he has been constructively dismissed; (iii) it is open to the employer to show that such dismissal was for a potentially fair reason; and (iv) if he does so, it will then be for the employment tribunal to decide whether the dismissal for that reason, both substantively and procedurally, fell within the range of reasonable responses and was fair.

For dismissals prior to 6 April 2009, it was vital to note the statutory dismissal and disciplinary and grievance procedures contained in *EA 2002, Sch 2, paras 6–9* and *EA (Dispute Resolution) Regulations 2004, regs 6–10*. In nearly all cases, it was relevant to ask whether and to what extent an employee had invoked the statutory grievance procedure, and to what extent the employer had complied, when assessing whether or not there had been a constructive dismissal and whether or not such a dismissal had been unfair. These matters remain relevant, not in regard to the employment tribunal's jurisdiction, but as important aspects of the evidence.

51.8   Forced resignation

If an employee resigns in circumstances where he is given no alternative but to resign or be dismissed, he will be considered to have been dismissed for the purposes of unfair dismissal. The question of whether the conduct of the employer caused the employee to leave is one of fact for the employment tribunal (*Martin v Glynwed Distribution Ltd* [1983] ICR 511, CA). However, telling an employee that he will be dismissed at some unspecified date in the future does not give the employee the right to resign and claim that he has been constructively dismissed if the employer is guilty of no anticipatory breach of contract – the employer may intend to give due notice, and a dismissal giving contractual notice is not, of course, a breach of contract (*Haseltine Lake & Co v Dowler* [1981] ICR 222; see also *Norwest Holst Group Administration Ltd v Harrison* [1985] ICR 668).

If an employee decides to leave because he has negotiated satisfactory terms for his departure, he will be considered to have resigned. Nevertheless, in *Sheffield v Oxford Controls Co Ltd* [1979] ICR 396, Arnold J said, at 402:

> "It is plain, we think, that there must exist a principle . . . that where an employee resigns and that resignation is determined upon by him because he prefers to resign rather than to be dismissed (the alternative having been expressed to him by the employer in the terms of the threat that if he does not resign he will be dismissed), the mechanics of the resignation do not cause that to be other than a dismissal. The cases do not in terms go further than that. We find the principle to be one of causation."

Sheffield v Oxford Controls was endorsed by the Court of Appeal in *Jones v Mid-Glamorgan County Council* [1997] ICR 815. Again, in *Sandhu v Jan de Rijk Transport Ltd* [2008] EWCA Civ 430, [2007] IRLR 519, the Court of Appeal construed a forced resignation during one meeting as a dismissal, holding that resignation implies some form of negotiation and discussion and must be a genuine choice on the part of the employee. The Court of Appeal observed that none of the authorities treated as a resignation a decision made during a single meeting, and placed weight on the facts that the employee had had no warning that the purpose of the meeting was to dismiss him, had had no advice, and had had no time to reflect.

The Court of Appeal in *Birch v University of Liverpool* [1985] ICR 470 held that an employee who took advantage of an early retirement scheme was not dismissed, in a case that predated the introduction of statutory protection from unlawful age discrimination. Dismissal does not include termination by mutual consent, however, special rules apply to dismissal by reason of retirement.

51.9 Repudiatory conduct by the employee

Employers sometimes consider that an employee has 'dismissed himself' by breaching some fundamental term of his contract of employment, such as failing to attend work. This is almost certainly not a correct approach. In *Thomas Marshall (Exports) Ltd v Guinle* [1978] ICR 905, Megarry VC held that an employee's repudiation of his contract of employment had to be accepted by the employer to bring the contract to an end. This 'acceptance' view was approved by a majority of the Court of Appeal in *Gunton v Richmond-upon-Thames London Borough Council* [1980] ICR 755, and by a majority of the Court of Appeal in *London Transport Executive v Clarke* [1981] ICR 355. Similarly, in *Boyo v Lambeth London Borough Council* [1994] ICR 727, the Court of Appeal endorsed the 'acceptance' view of the termination of a contract of employment. The Court of Appeal took this approach in *Triggs v GAB Robins (UK) Ltd* [2008] EWCA Civ 17, [2008] IRLR 317 in respect of a requirement for an employee to accept an employer's repudiatory breach, making a conceptual distinction between the repudiatory breach and the acceptance which effects the dismissal (see TERMINATION OF EMPLOYMENT (46)).

There is now an authoritative exposition of the law in this area in the Supreme Court's decision in *Société Générale v Geys* [2012] UKSC 63, [2013] ICR 117. By a majority, the Supreme Court approved the *Gunton/Boyo* 'acceptance' approach which it described as the 'elective theory' (as opposed to the 'automatic theory'). It remains the case, therefore, that an unaccepted repudiatory breach of contract by an employee remains a 'thing writ in water'.

51.10 Situations of no dismissal

There is *no dismissal* in the following cases.

(a)   *Termination of the contract of employment by consent of both parties* (see **51.8** above).

(b)   *Termination by the employee whether with or without notice* in the absence of 'constructive dismissal' or forced resignation (see **51.7** and **51.8** above). A valid notice given by an employee cannot usually be withdrawn without the employer's consent (*Riordan v War Office* [1959] 3 All ER 552, [1960] 3 All ER 774; *Sothern v Franks Charlesly & Co* [1981] IRLR 278). However, it may be that words of resignation (or dismissal) spoken in the heat of the moment can be regarded as not being a true resignation, or else can be withdrawn if this is done very quickly (*Martin v Yeoman Aggregates Ltd* [1983] ICR 314; *Barclay v City of Glasgow District Council* [1983] IRLR 313 and *Willoughby v CF Capital* [2011] EWCA Civ 1115, [2011] IRLR 985 (above **51.5**)).

(c)   *Termination of employment by 'frustration'*. If the contract of employment cannot be performed or if its performance becomes radically different from that contemplated when the contract was entered into, it may be considered to have been terminated by frustration (see further **46.3** TERMINATION OF EMPLOYMENT).

(d)   *Termination on the occurrence of an external event*. A contract for a voyage may be terminated 'automatically' when the voyage is completed (*Ryan v Shipboard Maintenance Ltd* [1980] ICR 88). An appointment for 'as long as sufficient funds are provided either by the Manpower Services Commission or by other firms/sponsors to fund it' was held to come to an end automatically when the specified event took place (*Brown v Knowsley Borough Council* [1986] IRLR 102). See also **51.6** above.

51.11 EMPLOYMENT FOR QUALIFYING PERIOD

From 1 June 1999, the qualifying period for claims of unfair dismissal was reduced from two years to one year (*ERA 1996, s 108(1)* and the *Unfair Dismissal and Statement of Reasons for Dismissal (Variation of Qualifying Period) Order 1999 (SI 1999/1436)*). For persons whose period of continuous employment begins on or after 6th April 2012, the qualifying period is once again two years (*Unfair Dismissal and Statement of Reasons for Dismissal (Variation of Qualifying Period) Order 2012 (SI 2012/989)*).

In *Seymour-Smith (R v Secretary of State for Employment, ex p Seymour-Smith (No 2)* [2000] IRLR 263), the applicants had argued that the two-year qualifying period for unfair dismissal claims then in force had a disproportionately adverse effect on women and was inconsistent with the *EC Treaty, art 119*, now *157 TFEU* (equal pay). The European Court of Justice had held that the two-year qualifying period for unfair dismissal claims could be struck down only if there was a considerable difference in the ability of men and women to comply with it, and if the period could not be justified by the Government. The House of Lords in the light of the guidance (such as it was) given by the ECJ ([1999] IRLR 253) decided that the date by reference to which the comparison should be made was the date of the applicants' dismissal in 1991. At that time, 74.5% of men could comply, as against 67.4% of women. Notwithstanding the hint given by the European court that the statistics provided to the court did not, on the face of it, show that a considerably smaller percentage of women than men were able to comply, the House of Lords, by a 3–2 majority, held that, since there had been a constant disparity since the two-year limit was introduced in 1985, the necessary disparate impact existed. However, the House of Lords held that the Government had justified the discriminatory effect of the limit, because it had been entitled to decide that the requirement was a suitable method of achieving its stated end of increasing employment opportunities in 1985, and six years was a reasonable period to wait to see if the policy was working. Accordingly, the appeals of Mrs Seymour-Smith and Mrs Perez failed. It remains to be seen if any similar litigation will follow the recent return to a two-year qualifying period.

The qualifying period is calculated from the beginning of the employee's employment under the relevant contract of employment. This could be earlier than the date the employee starts performing duties under the contract (*General of the Salvation Army v Dewsbury* [1984] ICR

498; but in *Wood v Cunard Line Ltd* [1991] ICR 13 the Court of Appeal expressed some doubt as to whether *Dewsbury* was correctly decided). The first day on which the employee started work is included, so that an employee who has worked 365 days (and whose period of continuous employment commenced prior to 6th April 2012) is protected against unfair dismissal (*O'Brien v Pacitti Jones (a firm)* [2005] CSIH 56, [2005] IRLR 888).

If an employee is dismissed on medical grounds in compliance with any law, regulation or code of practice providing for health and safety at work, the qualifying period for a claim is only one month (*ERA 1996, s 108(2)*).

An employee who is wrongfully dismissed in breach of the contractual notice entitlements and whose dismissal has the effect of preventing him or her from attaining the qualifying period for a complaint of unfair dismissal may not in an action for wrongful dismissal recover damages representing the loss of the chance to bring unfair dismissal proceedings (*Harper v Virgin Net Ltd* [2004] EWCA Civ 271, [2004] IRLR 390).

In certain other cases, no qualifying period is necessary. Generally speaking, the cases in which no qualifying period of employment is necessary in order to acquire the right to complain of unfair dismissal also involve reasons for dismissal which are automatically unfair (see UNFAIR DISMISSAL II, 52.3). These are where the reason or principal reason for the dismissal:

(a)   was that the employee was summoned for jury service or was absent from work because he attended at any place in pursuance of being summoned for jury service, unless the employee's absence was likely to cause substantial injury to the employer's undertaking, the employer brought those circumstances to the employee's attention, and the employee unreasonably refused or failed to apply to the appropriate officer for excusal from or deferral of the obligation to attend (*ERA 1996, s 108(3)(aa)*);

(b)   was a prescribed reason in connection with leave for family reasons (*ERA 1996, s 108(3)(b)*);

(c)   was a health and safety-related reason (*ERA 1996, s 108(3)(c)*;

(d)   was a reason connected with the refusal of Sunday work by a shop worker or betting worker (*ERA 1996, s 108(3)(d)*;

(e)   was a reason related to working time (*ERA 1996, s 108(3)(dd)*;

(f)   was a reason related to participation in education or training (*ERA 1996, s 108(3)(de)*)

(g)   was a reason connected with the performance by an employee who is a pension scheme trustee of his functions as such a trustee (*ERA 1996, s 108(3)(e)*;

(h)   was a reason connected with the performance by an employee representative (see 37.4 REDUNDANCY – II and 50.23 TRANSFER OF UNDERTAKINGS), or a candidate in an election for such an employee representative, or of his functions as such an employee representative or candidate in a redundancy or transfer of undertakings context (*ERA 1996, s 108(3)(f)*,

(i)   was a reason connected with the making of a protected disclosure under *ERA 1996, ss 43A–43L* (*ERA 1996, s 108(3)(ff)*;

(j)   was the assertion of a statutory right (*ERA 1996, s 108(3)(g)*;

(k)   was a reason connected with the assertion of rights under the *National Minimum Wage Act 1998* (*ERA 1996, s 108(3)(gg)*;

(l)   was that the worker took, or proposed to take, action with a view to enforcing or securing the benefit of a right under the *Tax Credits Act 2002*, or a penalty was imposed upon the employer as a result of action taken by, or on behalf of, the employee for the purpose of enforcing his or her rights under the *Act* (*ERA 1996, s 108(3)(gh)*, under the *Tax Credits Act 1999* and substituted by the *Tax Credits Act 2002*);

(m)   was a prescribed reason in connection with flexible working (*ERA 1996, s 108(3)(gi)*);

(n)   was a prescribed reason in connection with pension enrolment (*ERA 1996, s 108(3)(gj)*);

(o)   was a prescribed reason in connection with applications for study and training (*ERA 1996, s 108(3)(gk)*);

(p)   was a prescribed reason in connection with blacklists (*ERA 1996, s 108(3)(gl)*);

(q)   was a selection for redundancy for a reason which would have been automatically unfair if it had been the reason for dismissal (*ERA 1996, s 108(3)(h)*);

(r)   was that the worker had carried out activities as a member of a special negotiating body, a European Works Council, as an information and consultation representative, or as a candidate in an election for such a position, or that the employee exercised the specific rights relevant to the above bodies which are listed in the *Transnational Information and Consultation of Employees Regulations 1999, reg 28* (*ERA 1996, s 108(3)(hh)*;

(s)   was that the worker has brought proceedings against his employer under the *Part-time Workers (Prevention of Less Favourable Treatment) Regulations 2000* or has otherwise done anything under the *Regulations* in relation to the employer or any other person (*ERA 1996, s108(3)(i)*);

(t)   was that the employee brought proceedings against his employer under the *Fixed-term Employees (Prevention of Less Favourable Treatment) Regulations 2002* or has otherwise done anything under the *Regulations* in relation to the employer or any other person (*ERA 1996, s 108(3)(j)*);

(u)   was the performance or attempted performance by an employee representative or election candidate in the context of the *European Public Limited-Liability Company Regulations 2004* (*ERA 1996, s 108(3)(k)*);

(v)   was the performance or attempted performance by an employee representative or election candidate in the context of the *Information and Consultation of Employees Regulations 2004* (*ERA 1996, s 108(3)(l)*);

(w)   was the performance or attempted performance of functions or activities as a representative or candidate under the *Occupational and Personal Pension Schemes (Consultation by Employers and Miscellaneous Amendment) Regulations 2006* (*ERA 1996, s 108(3)(m)*);

(x)   was that the employee exercised or sought to exercise his right to be accompanied at a meeting to consider his request not to retire, or that the employee accompanied or sought to accompany another employee who sought to exercise the right to be accompanied at such a meeting (*ERA 1996, s 108(3)(n)*);

(y)   was that the employee performed or proposed to perform any functions or activities as a member, representative, candidate or participant under the *European Cooperative Society (Involvement of Employees) Regulations 2006* (*SI 2006/2059*) or that the employee or a person on his behalf made or proposed to make a request for time off or remuneration for time off under the Regulations (*ERA 1996, s 108(3)(o)*);

(z)   was that the employee took or proposed to take any proceedings to enforce a right conferred by the *Companies (Cross-Border Mergers) Regulations 2007*, exercised or proposed to exercise any entitlement to apply, complain or appeal to the CAC or Appeal Tribunal, acted with a view to securing that a special negotiating body did or did not come into existence, indicated whether he did or did not support the coming into existence of a special negotiating body, stood for election as a member of a special negotiating body or director of UK transferee company, canvassed lawfully before a ballot under the Regulations, voted, expressed doubts about the proper conduct of a ballot, or proposed to do, failed to do, or proposed to decline to do, various acts in relation to such a ballot; and in respect of an employee who is a member of a special negotiating body, a director of a transferee company or a candidate in an election to such a position, that the reason is: that the employee performed or proposed to perform any functions or activities as a member, director or candidate, or the employee or someone on his behalf made or proposed to make a request for time off work or remuneration for time off work (*ERA 1996, s 108(3)(p)*);

(A)   was that the employee did a protected act under the *Agency Workers Regulations 2010, reg 17* (*ERA 1996, s 108(3)(q)*);

(B)   was a union-related reason (or where selection for redundancy was for a union-related reason) (*TULRCA 1992, s 154*;

(C)   was a reason connected with trade union recognition or bargaining arrangements (*TULRCA 1992, Sch A1, para 162* inserted by *Employment Relations Act 1999, s 1(2)* and *Sch 1*;

(D)   was that the employee exercised or sought to exercise the right, pursuant to *Employment Relations Act 1999, s 10*, to be accompanied to a disciplinary or grievance hearing or that the employee accompanied or sought to accompany another worker to such a hearing (*Employment Relations Act 1999, s 12(4)*);

(E)   was that the employee was dismissed for taking part in protected industrial action in the circumstances set out in *TULRCA 1992, s 138A*, introduced by *Employment Relations Act 1999, s 16* and *Sch 5*. See **51.17** below.

Clause 13 of the *Enterprise and Regulatory Reform Bill* will, if enacted, provide that no qualifying period is necessary in a case where the reason for dismissal is or relates to an employee's political beliefs or affiliation. This provision was introduced into the bill to take account of the decision of the European Court of Human Rights in *Redfearn v United Kingdom* [2013] IRLR 51.

51.12 Calculation of period of continuous employment

The detailed provisions relating to the calculation of a period of continuous employment are set out in *ERA 1996, ss 210–219*. They are considered fully in CONTINUOUS EMPLOYMENT (6). They provide, for example, that there is continuity of employment when the business in which an employee works is transferred from one owner to another (see *Oakland v Wellswood (Yorkshire) Ltd* [2009] EWCA Civ 1094, [2010] IRLR 82, in which the Court avoided deciding the question whether the situation involved "analogous insolvency proceedings" and the fact of the transfer was conceded), when the employee is incapable of work because of sickness or injury, or absent from work wholly or partly because of pregnancy or childbirth or family-related leave.

51.13 Effective date of termination

The qualifying period is calculated up to and including the effective date of termination. The effective date of termination is defined as:

51.13   Unfair Dismissal – I: The Right to Make a Claim

(a)   in relation to an employee whose contract of employment is *terminated by notice*, whether given by his employer or by the employee, the date on which that notice expires;

(b)   in relation to an employee whose contract of employment is terminated *without notice*, the date on which the termination takes effect; and

(c)   in relation to an employee who is employed under a *contract for a fixed term*, where that term expires without being renewed under the same contract, the date on which that term expires.

(ERA 1996, s 97(1).)

The effective date of termination is an objectively determined statutory construct, which it is not open to the employer and employee to agree between themselves (*Fitzgerald v University of Kent at Canterbury* [2004] EWCA Civ 143, [2004] IRLR 300). It is possible therefore for the EDT not to coincide with when an employment contract terminates at common law (see for example *Geys v Société Générale* [2011] EWCA Civ 307, [2011] IRLR 482). In most cases, the effective date of termination is the date on which the employee ceases work. If an employer makes it clear to an employee that he is terminating his employment forthwith and pays him a sum of money in lieu of notice, the effective date of termination is the actual date of termination of the employment whether or not the employee was dismissed in breach of contract (*Dedman v British Building and Engineering Appliances Ltd* [1974] ICR 53; *Robert Cort and Son Ltd v Charman* [1981] ICR 816; see also *Stapp v Shaftesbury Society* [1982] IRLR 326; *Leech v Preston Borough Council* [1985] ICR 192; *Batchelor v British Railways Board* [1987] IRLR 136; *Octavius Atkinson & Sons Ltd v Morris* [1989] ICR 431). If, however, the contract continues although the employee stays away from work, the effective date of termination will be the date upon which the contract comes to an end in accordance with the notice.

The Court of Appeal in *Kirklees Metropolitan Borough Council v Radecki* [2009] EWCA Civ 298, [2009] IRLR 555 held that the effective date of termination is the date of summary dismissal, as long as the summary dismissal is known to the employee. The question of the effective date of termination should, however, be freed from the niceties of contract law concerning acceptance of a repudiatory breach, so that ordinary employees are able to understand when employment has come to an end and time starts running for the purposes of presenting employment tribunal claims. Where, after protracted compromise discussions, the local authority had informed the employee that it would cease to pay him on a particular date, the cessation of payment unequivocally and unilaterally ended the employment. In *Gisda Cyf v Barratt*, [2010] UKSC 41, [2010] ICR 1475, however, the Supreme Court held that the effective date of termination was the date on which the employee actually read the letter of summary dismissal, or had had a reasonable opportunity to read it. The letter had been sent on 29 November, but the employee had left home before the post arrived on 30 November in order to visit her sister who had just had a baby in another city. The employee did not return home until late on 3 December, and she did not enquire about her post until 4 December, when she read the letter dismissing her. The 'general law of contract' the Court held, should not even provide a preliminary guide to the proper interpretation of *ERA 1996, s 97* as it is part of a charter protecting employee's rights, and an interpretation that promotes those rights is to be preferred.

In *West v Kneels Ltd* [1987] ICR 146, the EAT held that 'seven days' notice', used on dismissal, meant seven *clear* days. The contract cannot be terminated until the employee receives notification of the dismissal (*Brown v Southall and Knight* [1980] IRLR 130 and *McMaster v Manchester Airport plc* [1998] IRLR 112). Where an employee exercises a right of appeal against his dismissal but his appeal is not allowed, in the absence of any contrary contractual provision the effective date of termination will be the date of the original dismissal (*J Sainsbury Ltd v Savage* [1981] ICR 1, approved in *West Midlands Co-operative Society Ltd v Tipton* [1986] ICR 192).

For the purpose of deciding whether the employee had the necessary qualifying period of employment, if an employer dismisses an employee giving him no notice or less notice than that required by *ERA 1996, s 86*, the effective date will be the date on which the statutory minimum period of notice would have expired had it been given (*ERA 1996, s 97(2)*). Thus, if an employer dismisses an employee without notice after 51 weeks, the effective date of termination will be taken to be one week later, as the minimum period of notice after more than one month's employment is one week (see **46.7** TERMINATION OF EMPLOYMENT). The employee will thus be entitled to claim compensation for unfair dismissal. However, the extra time will not be added where an employee is summarily dismissed in circumstances where the employer is entitled to dismiss summarily, eg for gross misconduct (see **46.13** TERMINATION OF EMPLOYMENT). An employer is not entitled simply to define a dismissal as being for gross misconduct without the tribunal investigating whether that description is justified (*Lanton Leisure Ltd v White and Gibson* [1987] IRLR 119). The statutory extension of the effective date of termination applies even where the employee waives his right to notice (*Secretary of State for Employment v Staffordshire County Council* [1989] IRLR 117, the Court of Appeal holding that the fact that an employee has waived his right to notice or has accepted a payment in lieu of notice under *ERA 1996, s 97(4)* is relevant only to his rights in contract).

For the purpose of calculating the qualifying period of employment where an employee terminates his contract of employment in circumstances in which he is entitled to do so by reason of his employer's conduct, the effective date of termination will be considered to be the date on which the statutory minimum notice required of the employer would have expired (*ERA 1996, s 97(4)*).

51.14 RETIRING AGE

The *Employment Equality (Age) Regulations 2006 (SI 2006/1031)* came into force on 1 October 2006 and were largely repealed with effect from 1st October 2010 by *Equality Act 2010, s 211(2), Schedule 27, Part 2*.

The upper age limit for complaining of unfair dismissal, contained in *ERA 1996, s 109*, was removed and was replaced by a byzantine statutory process contained in *ERA 1996, sections 98ZA–98ZH*. With effect from 6th April 2011 however, those provisions were repealed and the concept of default retirement age abolished by the *Employment Equality (Repeal of Retirement Age Provisions) Regulations 2011 (SI 2011/1069)* (subject to savings in *regulation 5*). See **52.4** UNFAIR DISMISSAL II (52), RETIREMENT (40). Retirement is no longer a potentially fair reason for dismissal under *ERA 1996, section 98*.

51.15 EXCLUDED CLASSES OF EMPLOYEES

Certain classes of employment are excluded from the protection of the unfair dismissal provisions. If a respondent wishes to show that a claimant falls within an excluded class, the burden of proof is on him to do so (*Kapur v Shields* [1976] ICR 26). The excluded cases are defined by *ERA 1996, ss 199* and *200*.

(a)   Dismissal from any employment as a master or as a member of the crew of a *fishing vessel* where the employee is not remunerated otherwise than by a share in the profits or gross earnings of the vessel (*ERA 1996, s 199(2)*).

(b)   Dismissal from employment in respect of which the employee has validly contracted out of his right to claim compensation for unfair dismissal (*ERA 1996, s 203(2)* and see **51.19, 51.20** below).

51.15 Unfair Dismissal – I: The Right to Make a Claim

(c) Dismissal from employment under a contract of employment in police service or to persons engaged in such employment (*ERA 1996, s 200* and see *Spence v British Railways Board* [2001] ICR 232), except for unfair dismissals on health and safety grounds (contrary to *ERA 1996, s 100*), or because the employee has made a protected disclosure (contrary to *ERA 1996, s 103A*).

(d) *Where the trigger event was prior to 6 April 2009:* Dismissal from employment in circumstances in which the employee failed to make use of the statutory grievance procedure (*Employment Act 2002, s 32* and *Sch 2*).

An employee or ex-employee is barred from bringing a claim for unfair dismissal in three circumstances:

(i) the grievance concerned a matter to which the requirement in *Sch 2* to set out the grievance in writing applied and the requirement had not been complied with; or

(ii) the employee had not waited 28 days after serving his or her grievance in writing; or

(iii) the employee had not set out and serve the grievance in writing until more than one month after the end of the original time limit for making the tribunal complaint in question (*s 32(2)– (4)*).

In each of the three cases, the tribunal was prevented from considering the complaint only if the breach was apparent to the tribunal from the information supplied to it by the employee in connection with the bringing of the proceedings, or the tribunal was satisfied of the breach as a result of the employer raising the matter in accordance with the *Rules of Procedure Regulations* (*s 32(6)*).

(e) *Section 196* of the *ERA 1996* was repealed in its entirety by s *32(3)* of the *Employment Relations Act 1999* and so, with effect from 25 October 1999, the territorial limits were removed. For those dismissed before 25 October 1999, any employment where under his contract of employment *the employee ordinarily worked outside Great Britain* was an excluded case.

The House of Lords gave guidance in *Lawson v Serco Ltd* [2006] UKHL 3, [2006] IRLR 289 on the circumstances in which the right not to be unfairly dismissed applies. A claimant will generally be protected if he was working in Great Britain at the time of his dismissal and peripatetic employees are subject to a 'base' test. It is a question of law where an employee is based. The EAT applied the *Serco* test in *Williams v University of Nottingham* [2007] IRLR 660, *Bleuse v MBT Transport Ltd* [2008] IRLR 264, *Ministry of Defence v Wallis* [2010] ICR 1301 (and see [2011] EWCA Civ 231) and *Pervez v Macquarie* [2011] ICR 266. See also the Supreme Court's recent revisitation of the *Serco* test in *Duncombe v Secretary of State for Children, Schools and Families (No 2)* [2011] ICR 1312 and *Ravat v Halliburton & Manufacturing & Services Ltd* [2012] ICR 389. These cases have considerably softened the edges of the *Serco* test. The factual examples within the case law on *ERA 1996, s 196* remain of relevance to cases where it is asserted that an employment tribunal has jurisdiction over certain employment, even though the legal test for jurisdiction over unfair dismissal claims changed with the repeal of *s 196*. Where an employee worked both inside and outside Great Britain, one would look at the terms of the contract, express or implied, and how the contract operated in practice, in order to ascertain where the employee's base was (cf *Wilson v Maynard Shipbuilding Consultants AB* [1978] ICR 376, and *per* Lord Denning MR and Sir David Cairns in *Todd v British Midland Airways Ltd* [1978] ICR 959. See also *Jackson v Ghost Ltd* [2003] IRLR 824, *Crofts v Cathay Pacific Airways Ltd* [2005] EWCA Civ 599, [2005] IRLR 624 and *Diggins v Condor Marine Crewing Services Ltd* [2009] EWCA Civ 1133, [2010] IRLR 119.

The contract to be considered is that subsisting at the time of dismissal, and not any previous contract between the parties (*Weston v Vega Space Systems Engineering Ltd* [1989] IRLR 429). Where the contract of employment is of little assistance, the tribunal should go by the conduct of the parties and the way they have operated the contract (*per* Lord Denning MR in *Todd* at 964).

The relevant location used to be the employer's operational base, not the actual place of work (*Addison v Denholm Ship Management (UK) Ltd* [1997] IRLR 389).

A person employed to work on board a ship registered in the United Kingdom (not being a ship registered at a port outside Great Britain) used to be regarded as a person who under his contract ordinarily worked in Great Britain unless:

(i)   the employment was wholly outside Great Britain; or

(ii)   the employee was not ordinarily resident in Great Britain.

(*ERA 1996, s 196(5)*; see, eg *Wood v Cunard Line Ltd* [1991] ICR 13.)

Employees engaged upon certain activities connected with offshore drilling were given employment protection rights by the *Employment Protection (Offshore Employment) Order 1976 (SI 1976/766)*. See *Addison*, above, and *ERA 1996, s 201*.

(f)   *Section 197* of the *ERA 1996* excluded certain cases of dismissal occurring prior to October 1999 on expiry of fixed term contracts of one year or more where the employee had contracted out of unfair dismissal protection. It was repealed in its entirety by the *Fixed-term Employees (Prevention of Less Favourable Treatment) Regulations 2002 (SI 2002/2034), reg 11, Sch 2, Pt 1, para 3(1)* and *(15)*, (subject to *Sch 2, Pt 2, para 5*) with effect from 1 October 2002.

51.16 EMPLOYEE CANNOT ENFORCE RIGHTS IF CONTRACT ILLEGAL

The courts will not enforce an illegal contract. Thus, if it appears to an employment tribunal that, for example, a contract of employment was entered into with an agreement that no tax be paid on some part or all of the remuneration, the tribunal may consider the agreement to be a fraud on the Inland Revenue and may dismiss the claim. The position will normally be different if the employee was innocent of any wrongdoing, or if he merely performed some unlawful act in the course of an otherwise lawful employment. The leading case is *Colen v Cebrian (UK) Ltd* [2004] IRLR 210. For a fuller discussion, see **7.24** CONTRACT OF EMPLOYMENT.

51.17 DISMISSAL IN CONNECTION WITH A LOCK-OUT OR STRIKE

Official action

The law relating to unfair dismissals in the context of official industrial action was changed substantially by *Employment Relations Act 1999, s 16* and *Sch 5*, which introduced a new *TULCRA 1992, s 238A* from 24 April 2000. (See *Employment Relations Act 1999 (Commencement No 5 and Transitional Provision) Order 2000, art 3 (SI 2000/875)*) (*TULRCA 1992, s 238*, as amended by *TURERA 1993, Sch 8 para 77* and *ERA 1996, Sch 1 para 56*). Section 238A was amended further by the *Employment Relations Act 2004*.

Prior to the changes introduced by *Sch 5* and the *Employment Relations Act 2004*, employees who took part in lawful industrial action lost their right to claim unfair dismissal if they were dismissed whilst the industrial action was taking place and all other employees who were taking part in the industrial action were similarly dismissed. The main consequences of the changes were that:

51.17   Unfair Dismissal – I: The Right to Make a Claim

(a)   the right to claim unfair dismissal is restored for many employees who are taking part in lawful, official, industrial action, provided that the reason for their dismissal is their participation in the industrial action; and

(b)   dismissal for such a reason will, in such cases, be automatically unfair.

TULRCA 1992, s 238, as amended by *Sch 5*, provides that the exclusion from the right to claim unfair dismissal if dismissal takes place during industrial action will not apply where the employee is regarded as unfairly dismissed by reason of *TULRCA 1992, s 238A*. An employee will be treated as being unfairly dismissed by reason of *s 238A* if the employee is taking part in protected industrial action and if certain other conditions (set out below) are satisfied.

Section 238A defines 'protected industrial action' as meaning action which was induced by an act protected by *TULRCA 1992, s 219* (see **43.3 STRIKES AND INDUSTRIAL ACTION**). In effect, 'protected industrial action' is official industrial action in respect of which the trade union concerned and its officials enjoy immunity from suit.

An employee will be treated as having been automatically unfairly dismissed if the reason or principal reason for dismissal was that the employee has taken part in protected industrial action and:

(i)   the date of dismissal is within the protected period; or

(ii)   the date of dismissal is after the end of protected period and the employee had stopped taking protected industrial action before the end of that period; or

(iii)   the date of dismissal is after the end of the protected period, the employee had not stopped taking protected industrial action before the end of that period, and the employer had not taken such procedural steps as would have been reasonable for the purposes of resolving the dispute to which the protected industrial action relates.

An employee may be taking part in industrial action even though he is not in breach of his contract of employment, eg by refusing to work overtime (*Power Packing Casemakers Ltd v Faust* [1983] ICR 292). Industrial action will generally exist where there is concerted action involving the application of pressure in the search for some advantage (*Glenrose (Fish Merchants) Ltd v Chapman*, IDS Brief 438, p 5). One person may be involved in industrial action on his own (*Lewis and Britton v E Mason & Sons* [1994] IRLR 4).

In deciding whether the employer has taken reasonable procedural steps, the tribunal must consider whether the employer complied with procedures set out in any relevant collective bargaining agreement, whether the employer or the union agreed to take part in negotiations after the industrial action had commenced, and whether the employer or the union had unreasonably refused to take part in conciliation or mediation. *TULCRA 1992, s 238A(7)* provides that in deciding whether the employer has taken reasonable procedural steps, the tribunal should take no account of the merits of the dispute which gave rise to the industrial action.

The above provisions represented a major change in the law relating to unfair dismissal in the context of official industrial action. It should be emphasised that not that every employee who is dismissed whilst taking part in official industrial action will be deemed to be unfairly dismissed. It is only if the reason for dismissal is that the employee was taking part in the protected industrial action that the dismissal will be automatically unfair. If the employee is dismissed for some other reason, such as misconduct or redundancy, during the relevant period, the dismissal will not be automatically unfair; rather, the tribunal will consider whether the dismissal was fair applying normal principles. Similarly, if the employee is dismissed for inducing the industrial action, rather than being induced, the dismissal will not be automatically unfair under s *238A*.

There may still be cases in which the right to claim unfair dismissal will be excluded, namely, if the whole of the part of the workforce which is taking part in industrial action is dismissed and the conditions set out in *s 238A* are not satisfied, for example because the industrial action has lasted for more than the protected period and the employer has taken reasonable procedural steps to resolve the dispute. In practice, however, *TULRCA 1992, s 238A* is likely to deter employers from dismissing all employees who are taking part in industrial action, because of the risk that this will lead to a finding that each of the employees concerned has been automatically unfairly dismissed.

TULRCA 1992, s 239(4) provides that if a claim for unfair dismissal arising out of protected industrial action succeeds, a tribunal should not consider the question of reinstatement or re-engagement until after the end of the employee's participation in the protected industrial action.

51.18 Unofficial action

TULRCA 1992, s 237 provides that an employee has no right to complain of unfair dismissal if at the time of dismissal he was taking part in an unofficial strike or other unofficial industrial action (see *Sehmi v Gate Gourmet* [2009] IRLR 807). This bar to jurisdiction is different from that contained in *TULRCA 1992, s 238*. The effect of the change is that, where the employees take part in unofficial industrial action, the employer can dismiss selectively without the tribunal thereby acquiring jurisdiction to hear a complaint of unfair dismissal. It is immaterial whether participation in the unofficial action was in fact the reason for the dismissal.

The time of dismissal means:

(a)   where the employee's contract is terminated by notice, when the notice is given;

(b)   where the contract is terminated without notice, when the termination takes effect; and

(c)   where the employee is employed under a fixed-term contract which expires without renewal, when that term expires.

(TULRCA 1992, s 237(5).)

The test of whether a person is taking part in unofficial action at a particular time will presumably be the same as in cases under *TULRCA 1992, s 238* (see **51.17** above).

Industrial action will be unofficial in relation to the dismissed employee unless:

(i)   that employee is a member of a union which has authorised or endorsed the action;

(ii)   the employee is not a union member, but those taking part in the action include members of a union which has authorised or endorsed it; or

(iii)   none of those taking part in the action are union members.

(TULRCA 1992, s 237(2).)

Thus, if the employee is a union member, his own union *must* have authorised or endorsed the action if it is not to be unofficial. If he is not, then if there are *any* union members among the participants, at least one union whose members are involved must have authorised or endorsed the action if it is not to be unofficial.

For the purposes of determining whether industrial action is to be taken to have been endorsed by a union, *TULRCA 1992, s 20(2)* is to be applied, by reference to the facts as at the time of dismissal (see **46.16** TRADE UNIONS – I). However, a repudiation under *TULRCA 1992, s 21* does not make action unofficial before the end of the next working day *(TULRCA 1992, s 237(3), (4))*.

For the purposes of *s 237*, membership of a union for purposes unconnected with the employment in question shall be disregarded. But an employee who is a union member when he starts to take part in action will be treated as such throughout the action even if he ceases to be a member (*TULRCA 1992, s 237(6)*).

Again, the exclusion of jurisdiction does not apply if the reason for the dismissal is one specified in *ERA 1996, ss 98B,99, 100, 101A(d), 103, 103A, 104, or 104C* (jury service, family, health and safety, working time or redundancy or transfer of undertaking employee representative, protected disclosure cases, or assertion of statutory right to take time off work for dependants).

51.19 NO CONTRACTING OUT

With certain exceptions (see **51.20** below), any agreement to prevent any person from presenting or pursuing a complaint of unfair dismissal is void (*ERA 1996, s 203(1)*). A clause in a contract of employment purporting to exclude this right will be ineffective, leaving the employee free to pursue a claim for unfair dismissal in the employment tribunal. In *Igbo v Johnson Matthey Chemicals Ltd* [1986] ICR 505, the Court of Appeal held that a variation of an employment contract which provided that if an employee failed to return from a period of leave on a certain date, her contract would be automatically terminated, converted a right not to be unfairly dismissed into a conditional right not to be dismissed; accordingly, it was void by reason of *EPCA 1978, s 140(1)* (the predecessor section of *ERA 1996, s 203(1)*). However, in *Scott v Coalite Fuels and Chemicals Ltd* [1988] ICR 355, an employee who had agreed to accept voluntary retirement as an alternative to redundancy was not successful in putting forward a similar argument. In *Salton (Logan) v Durham County Council* [1989] IRLR 99, EAT, a case where an employee under threat of dismissal agreed terms for termination, *Igbo* was distinguished on the grounds that this was a separate contract from the contract of employment, entered into without duress, after proper advice and for good consideration, and that termination was not contingent upon the happening of future events in circumstances which the parties might not have envisaged.

Similarly, any agreement to pay an ex-employee money in consideration for his refraining from presenting or pursuing a complaint in an employment tribunal is normally unenforceable, subject to the exceptions considered in **51.20** below.

51.20 Exceptions

An agreement restricting the right to claim for unfair dismissal is enforceable if it is contained in the following agreements:

(a)   a valid compromise contract satisfying the statutory conditions, including that the employee should have taken independent legal advice (see **18.27** EMPLOYMENT TRIBUNALS – I and note *Hinton v University of East London* [2005] EWCA Civ 532, [2005] IRLR 552 and *Industrious Ltd v Horizon Recruitment Ltd (in liq)* [2010] IRLR 204) (*ERA 1996, s 203(2)*);

(b)   a dismissal procedure agreement reached between employers and one or more independent trade unions which has been approved by the Secretary of State;

(c)   any agreement to refrain from presenting a complaint that he was unfairly dismissed where the conciliation officer has taken action in accordance with his statutory duties (see **2.3** ADVISORY, CONCILIATION AND ARBITRATION SERVICE (ACAS));

(d)   any agreement to refrain from proceeding with a complaint where the conciliation officer has taken action in accordance with his statutory duties (see **2.3** ADVISORY, CONCILIATION AND ARBITRATION SERVICE (ACAS)). Where there has been a transfer of an undertaking for the purposes of the *Transfer of Undertakings (Protection of*

Employment) Regulations 2006 (SI 2006/246), such an agreement if made by the transferor and not finalised until after the transfer will not prevent an employee from claiming against the transferee (*Thompson v Walon Car Delivery* [1997] IRLR 343).

52   Unfair Dismissal – II: The Fairness of the Dismissal

Cross-references. See Unfair Dismissal – I (51) for the right to make a claim; Unfair Dismissal – III (53) for remedies for unfair dismissal.

52.1   REASONS FOR DISMISSAL

Once the fact of dismissal has been established, it is for the employer to show (*ERA 1996, s 98(1)*):

(a)   what was the reason (or, if there was more than one, the principal reason) for the dismissal; and

(b)   that it was one of the reasons set out in **52.2** below.

An employment tribunal will investigate the real reason for the dismissal of the employee. The fact that an employer told an employee that the reason for his dismissal was redundancy will not preclude the tribunal from deciding that, for example, the real reason for dismissal was lack of capability (*Abernethy v Mott, Hay and Anderson* [1974] ICR 323). However, the tribunal should not find for the employer on a ground not argued before it if this would prejudice the employee who, for example, might have put his case differently if he was aware that the argument was being run (*Hannan v TNT-Ipec (UK) Ltd* [1986] IRLR 165). The facts which cause the employer to act as he does are to be treated as the reason for the dismissal even if the employer does not realise that his actions amount to a dismissal (*Ely v YKK Fasteners (UK) Ltd* [1994] ICR 164).

If there is a dispute over the reason for the dismissal, the burden of proving which one of the competing reasons for the dismissal was the principal reason is on the employer (*Maund v Penwith District Council* [1984] ICR 143). Additionally, the employer will only be allowed to rely upon facts known to him at the time of the dismissal to establish what the reason for the dismissal was. Thus, facts which come to light after the dismissal cannot be relied upon to justify the dismissal, although they may affect the level of compensation (*W Devis & Sons Ltd v Atkins* [1977] ICR 662; and see **53.13** Unfair Dismissal – III).

When a dismissal is by notice, the employer's reason for the dismissal must be determined both by reference to the reason for giving the notice to terminate and by reference to the reason when dismissal occurs (*Parkinson v Marc Consulting Ltd* [1998] ICR 276).

52.2   Acceptable reasons for dismissal

The following are acceptable reasons for dismissal (*ERA 1996, s 98(1), (2)*):

(a)   reasons related to the capability or qualifications of the employee for performing work of the kind which he was employed to do;

(b)   reasons related to the conduct of the employee;

(c)   that the employee was redundant (for the definition of 'redundancy' see **36.7** Redundancy – I);

(d)   that the employee could not continue to work in the position which he held without contravention (either on his part or on that of his employer) of a duty or restriction imposed by or under an enactment; or

(e)   some other substantial reason of a kind such as to justify the dismissal of an employee holding the position which that employee held.

Until 6th April 2011, retirement was an additional potentially fair reason for dismissal under *ERA 1996, s 98(2)(ba)*. This has been repealed by the *Employment Equality (Repeal of Retirement Age Provisions) Regulations 2011*. Retirement will no longer be a potentially fair reason for dismissal and will have to be brought under one of the other headings (most likely the "some other substantial reason" category). This will be considered further at **52.4** below.

It is a question for the tribunal to determine under which, if any, of the acceptable reasons the reason for dismissal given by the employer falls. This was recently emphasised by the EAT in *UPS Ltd v Harrison* (UKEAT/0038/11/RN) (16 January 2012, unreported). The tribunal should first make findings as to the employer's own reasons for dismissal. It should then ask itself how those reasons are best characterised in terms of *ERA 1996, s 98*. However, whilst the tribunal is not bound by the employer's label, it must seek to characterise the employer's own reasons (i.e. the reasons which the tribunal finds, as a matter of fact, led the employer to dismiss), rather than substitute its own view as to the reason for the dismissal. To take an example of this approach in practice, where the reason for dismissal put forward by the employer was 'incapability by reason of unsatisfactory attendance record' but it was clear that the reason for the dismissal was the claimant's poor attendance and not the ill health which caused this attendance, the tribunal erred in law in characterising the reason for the dismissal as 'capability' rather than 'some other substantial reason' (*Wilson v Post Office* [2000] IRLR 834).

If a claimant positively asserts a different and inadmissible reason for dismissal, he must produce some evidence to support his case (see *Kuzel v Roche Products Ltd* [2008] ICR 799 where the claimant asserted that he had been dismissed because he made a protected disclosure). The claimant does not bear the burden of proving that reason, but some evidence must be put before the tribunal in support of his assertion. As the Court of Appeal stated in *Kuzel*, if the tribunal finds that the reason put forward by the employer was not, in fact, the reason for the dismissal, it is not correct to say, as a matter of law or logic, that it must find that the reason was that asserted by the employee (though as the court also noted, this will often be the case). The tribunal should first consider the potentially fair reason being advanced by the employer, since it bears the primary burden, before considering the alternative reasons for dismissal, including those advanced by the employee (*Whitelock and Storr v Khan* (UKEAT/0017/10/RN) (26 October 2010, unreported)), though note the view of the EAT in *Governing Body of John Loughborough School v Alexis* (UKEAT/0583/10/JOJ) (16 December 2011, unreported) to the effect that if an employer's reason is rejected, it has failed to discharge the burden placed upon it by *ERA, s 98(1)* and the dismissal must therefore be unfair (see also *Earl v Slater and Wheeler (Airlyne) Ltd* [1973] 1 WLR 51, observation of Sir John Donaldson *obiter* at 149).

The fact that an employer has a prior reason for wishing to dismiss an employee (such as poor performance) does not by itself mean that, if a different ground for dismissal arises (such as the employee commits an act of gross misconduct), this cannot be the reason or principal reason for a subsequent dismissal. The fact that the employer welcomes the opportunity to dismiss does not mean that misconduct was not the reason for the dismissal having occurred (*Governing Body of John Loughborough School v Alexis* (UKEAT/0583/10/JOJ) (16 December 2011, unreported), following *ASLEF v Brady* [2006] IRLR 576). However, in such a case determining the reason or principal reason is likely to be a complex factual question for the tribunal. This is illustrated by the facts in *Governing Body of John Loughborough School v Alexis*, where the EAT upheld the tribunal's finding that the principal reason for the dismissal was not misconduct as alleged by the employer, but the employer's pre-existing views about the claimant's inadequate performance.

This chapter first considers the unacceptable reasons for dismissal (see **52.3** below), followed by the criteria for assessment of the fairness of a dismissal where the reason is acceptable (see **52.4** below). Finally, each of the acceptable reasons listed above are addressed in more detail in turn (see **52.5** and onwards below).

52.3   DISMISSALS WHICH ARE DEEMED UNFAIR

The *Employment Rights Act 1996* sets out a number of circumstances in which a dismissal will be deemed to be unfair automatically. Additionally, most of the following automatically unfair reasons for dismissal will render the dismissal unfair if they constitute the reason for which an employee was selected for redundancy (see **52.11**(a) below). In most cases, where an employee has been dismissed for an automatically unfair reason it will also be possible for the tribunal to hear the claim and pronounce the dismissal unfair when it would not normally have jurisdiction to do so because the employee lacked sufficient continuous service though significantly, this is not the case in relation to dismissals rendered unfair by the *Transfer of Undertakings (Protection of Employment) Regulations 2006 (SI 2006/246)* (see Unfair Dismissal – I **(51)**)

(a) Employer's failure to follow statutory dismissal and disciplinary procedures

The *Employment Act 2002, s 34* inserted a new *s 98A* into the *Employment Rights Act 1996*, concerning statutory dismissal and disciplinary procedures. These procedures were repealed on 6 April 2009. They continued to apply, during a transitional period, to cases where the trigger event occurred prior to the date of repeal. The number of cases to which they are relevant is now low, although there continue to be some, mostly at appellate level, where they fall to be considered.

Section 98A(1) rendered a dismissal automatically unfair if: (i) one of the statutory disciplinary procedures set out in Sch 2 applied in relation to the dismissal; (ii) the procedure had not been completed; and (iii) the non-completion of the procedure was wholly or mainly attributable to failure by the employer to comply with its requirements. The *Employment Act 2002 (Dispute Resolution) Regulations 2004 (SI 2004/752)* ("the **Dispute Resolution Regulations**") described the circumstances and manner in which the statutory dismissal and disciplinary procedures applied. These procedures will not be considered further in this chapter due to their diminishing significance in practice. Previous editions may be referred to for a detailed discussion of their operation.

(b) Union-membership, participation and non-membership dismissals

The dismissal of an employee will automatically be regarded as unfair if the reason or principal reason for it was that the employee (*TULRCA 1992, s 152*):

(i)   was, or proposed to become, a member of an independent trade union;

(ii)   had taken part, or proposed to take part, in the activities of an independent trade union at an appropriate time;

(iii)   had made use, or proposed to make use, of trade union services at an appropriate time;

(iv)   had failed to accept an inducement contrary to *TULRCA 1992, s 145A* or *145B;* or

(v)   was not a member of any trade union, or of a particular trade union, or of one of a number of particular trade unions, or had refused, or proposed to refuse, to become or remain a member.

There is no need for an employee to have been employed for any qualifying period to present a complaint on this ground (*TULRCA 1992, s 154*). Where the employee has not been employed for the qualifying period, the burden of proving that the reason for dismissal was union-related is upon the employee. In other cases, it is for the employer to prove the reason for dismissal in the usual way (*Smith v Hayle Town Council* [1978] ICR 996; *Maund v Penwith District Council* [1984] ICR 143).

An 'independent trade union' is defined as any union which is not under the control or domination of an employer (*TULRCA 1992, s 5*) (see **48.22** TRADE UNIONS – I).

'Membership of a trade union' within the meaning of *TULRCA 1992, s 152* was construed broadly by the EAT in *Discount Tobacco and Confectionery Ltd v Armitage* [1995] ICR 431 to include approaching a trade union officer to enlist his help in elucidating and attempting to negotiate terms and conditions of employment. *Discount Tobacco v Armitage* was followed by the EAT in *Speciality Care plc v Pachela* [1996] ICR 633.

Such action may, alternatively, be considered to be taking part in the activities of a trade union (*Dixon and Shaw v West Ella Developments* [1978] ICR 856; see also *British Airways Engine Overhaul Ltd v Francis* [1981] ICR 278). For an employee to be taking part in the activities of a trade union, the activity must be that of the union and not merely that of an individual who happens to belong to a union (*Drew v St Edmundsbury Borough Council* [1980] ICR 513, holding also that trade union activity within *s 152* did not include the taking of industrial action). The dismissal of an employee because of union activities with a previous employer can come within *s 152*, although dismissing an employee for failing to tell the truth about past activities would not (*Fitzpatrick v British Railways Board* [1992] ICR 221).

'An appropriate time', in relation to an employee taking part in the activities of a trade union, means a time which either (*TULRCA 1992, s 152(2)*):

(A)   is outside his working hours; or

(B)   is a time within his working hours at which, in accordance with arrangements agreed with or consent given by his employers, it is permissible for him to take part in those activities or make use of trade union services.

'Working hours', in relation to an employee, means any time when, in accordance with his contract of employment, he is required to be at work (*TULRCA 1992, s 152(2)*). Consent for these purposes may be express or implied (*Marley Tile Co Ltd v Shaw* [1980] ICR 72).

It is not necessary for the employee to show that the employer's actions were motivated by malice or anti-union hostility (*Dundon v GPT Ltd* [1995] IRLR 403).

Dismissal for conduct which on its own would justify dismissal, such as assault, may not become automatically unfair simply because it took place in the course of union activities, though in *Bass Taverns v Burgess* [1995] IRLR 596 the Court of Appeal held a dismissal to be automatically unfair under *s 152* even though the employee had gone 'over the top' in making critical remarks about the employer.

Closed shop. Under the relevant provisions of *TULRCA 1992*, all dismissals to enforce a closed shop are now automatically unfair (see TRADE UNIONS – II (49) for more detail on the issue of closed shops).

(c) Health and safety-related dismissals

The dismissal of an employee will automatically be regarded as unfair if the reason or principal reason for it was that the employee (*ERA 1996, s 100(1)*, as amended):

(i)   having been designated by the employer to carry out activities in connection with preventing or reducing risks to health and safety at work, carried out, or proposed to carry out, any such activities;

(ii)   being a representative of workers on matters of health and safety at work, or a member of a safety committee in accordance with arrangements established under or by virtue of any enactment, or by reason of being acknowledged as such by the employer, performed or proposed to perform any functions as such a representative or a member of such a committee;

(iii) took part (or proposed to take part) in consultation with the employer pursuant to the *Health and Safety (Consultation with Employees) Regulations 1996 (SI 1996/1513)* (see **26.22** HEALTH AND SAFETY AT WORK – **II**) or in an election of representatives within the meaning of those *Regulations*, whether as a candidate or otherwise;

(iv) being an employee at a place where there was no such representative or safety committee, or where it was not reasonably practicable for the employee to raise the matter by means of the representative or safety committee, brought to his employer's attention by reasonable means circumstances connected with his work which he reasonably believed were harmful or potentially harmful to health or safety;

(v) in circumstances of danger which he reasonably believed to be serious and imminent and which he could not reasonably have been expected to avert, left or proposed to leave or (while the danger persisted) refused to return to his place of work or any dangerous part of his place of work; or

(vi) in circumstances of danger which he reasonably believed to be serious and imminent, took or proposed to take appropriate steps to protect himself or other persons from the danger.

In the case of (vi) above, whether the steps in question were appropriate will be judged by reference to all the circumstances, including in particular the employee's knowledge and the facilities and advice available to him at the time. The dismissal will not be unfair if the employer shows that it was or would have been so negligent for the employee to take those steps that a reasonable employer might have dismissed him for taking or proposing to take them (*ERA 1996, s 100(2), (3)*).

In *Goodwin v Cabletel UK Ltd* [1998] ICR 112, the EAT applied by analogy the approach adopted by the Court of Appeal in *Bass Taverns Ltd v Burgess* [1995] IRLR 596 in holding that the manner in which an activity is carried out may be protected, as well as the actual doing of it. The protection afforded to the way in which a protected employee carries out his health and safety activities must not be diluted too easily by finding that acts done for that purpose in fact justify dismissal. On the other hand, not every act should be treated as a protected act, however malicious or irrelevant to the task in hand.

For a claim under (iv) above to succeed the tribunal must find that: (i) it was not reasonably practicable for the employee to raise the health and safety matters through a safety representative or committee; (ii) he brought to the employer's attention by reasonable means the circumstances that he reasonably believed were harmful or potentially harmful to health or safety; and (iii) the principal reason for his dismissal was the fact the employee was exercising his rights under *ERA 1996, s 100(1)(c)* (*Balfour Kilpatrick Ltd v Acheson & Ors* [2003] IRLR 683). As such, *ERA 1996, s 100(1)(c)* only applies if there is no safety representative/committee or it is not reasonably practicable for the employee to raise matters through those channels (*Balfour Kilpatrick* above). Where the matters raised relate to a serious and imminent danger, however, the employee who does not go through those channels may be able to rely instead upon *ERA 1996, s 100(1)(e)*, following the construction of that subsection adopted by the EAT in *Balfour Kilpatrick* (above), which was approved in *Oudahar v Esporta Group Ltd* [2011] ICR 1406.

In determining whether an employee's belief that circumstances connected with his work were harmful or potentially harmful to health or safety, the tribunal should focus upon what is in his mind and determine whether that constituted reasonable grounds for holding that belief. An employee might, for example, reasonably believe that his employer is acting in breach of a legislative provision designed to protect health and safety, even though there is in fact no such breach (*Joao v Jurys Hotel Management UK Ltd* (UKEAT/0210/11/SM) (11 October 2011, unreported)).

52.3   Unfair Dismissal – II

In *Harvest Press Ltd v McCaffrey* [1999] IRLR 778, a night-shift worker walked out because he was frightened of the abusive behaviour of his co-worker and was dismissed for leaving his post. The EAT upheld the finding of the tribunal that Mr McCaffrey was automatically unfairly dismissed because he was dismissed for leaving his post in circumstances of danger (*s 100(1)(d), ERA 1996*), even though the danger was caused by his co-worker and did not arise from the workplace itself.

ERA 1996, s 100(1)(e) should be applied in two stages. First, the tribunal should consider whether, as a matter of fact: (i) there were circumstances of danger which the employee reasonably believed to be serious and imminent and; (ii) the employee took or proposed to take appropriate steps to protect himself or others from danger. Secondly, if those criteria are met, the tribunal should consider whether the sole or principal reason for the dismissal was that the employee took or proposed to take such steps. If it was, the dismissal will be unfair. The fact that the employer disagreed with the employee's view as to whether there were circumstances of danger, or whether the steps taken were appropriate, is irrelevant. An employer who is indifferent to the reason for an employee's absence, or does not bother to ascertain that reason, is equally liable (*Oudahar v Esporta Group Ltd* [2011] ICR 1406).

In *Masiak v City Restaurants (UK) Ltd* [1999] IRLR 780, a chef left his employment after refusing to cook food which he considered to be a hazard to public health. The EAT held that Mr Maziak was automatically unfairly dismissed, under *s 100(1)(e)*, because he had been dismissed for 'taking steps to protect other persons from danger' and it was not necessary, for *s 100(1)(e)* to apply, that the 'other persons' were co-workers.

For safety representatives and safety committees, see **26.20** HEALTH AND SAFETY AT WORK – II. For the right not to suffer detriment short of dismissal on these grounds, see **26.9** HEALTH AND SAFETY AT WORK – II.

Since 25 October 1999, there has been no statutory maximum upon compensation in automatically unfair health and safety unfair dismissal cases (*ERA 1996, s 124(1A)*).

(d) Dismissals for asserting statutory rights

The dismissal of an employee will automatically be regarded as unfair if the reason or principal reason for it was that the employee brought proceedings against the employer to enforce a right of his which is a relevant statutory right, or alleged that the employer had infringed a right of his which is a relevant statutory right (*ERA 1996, s 104(1)*).

The relevant statutory rights are:

(i)   any right conferred by the *ERA 1996* for which the remedy for its infringement is by way of complaint or reference to an employment tribunal;

(ii)   the right to statutory minimum notice under *ERA 1996, s 86* (see **46.7** TERMINATION OF EMPLOYMENT);

(iii) the rights conferred by *ss 68, 86, 145 A, 145B, 146, 168, 168A, 169* and *170* of *TULRCA 1992* (deductions from pay, union activities and time off);

(iv)   the rights conferred by the *Working Time Regulations 1998*, the *Merchant Shipping (Working Time: Inland Waterways) Regulations 2003*, the *Fishing Vessels (Working Time: Sea-fishermen) Regulations 2004*, or the *Cross-border Railway Services (Working Time) Regulations 2008*; and

(v)   the rights conferred by the *Transfer of Undertakings (Protection of Employment) Regulations 2006*.

Provided that the employee's claim is made in good faith, it does not matter whether he in fact had the right or whether it was in fact infringed (*ERA 1996, s 104(2)*; and see *Mennell v Newell & Wright (Transport Contractors) Ltd* [1997] ICR 1039). The employee need not have specified the right concerned if he made it reasonably clear to the employer what the right claimed to have been infringed was (*ERA 1996, s 104(3)*).

The statutory rights whose assertion is protected under *ERA 1996, s 104* do not include the rights protecting against unlawful discrimination. The various anti-discrimination legislation contain their own anti-victimisation provisions (see DISCRIMINATION AND EQUAL OPPORTUNITIES – I (10)); in any event, the dismissal of an employee who had asserted such rights would probably be unfair on normal principles (see **52.4** below).

(e) Family-related dismissals

ERA 1996, s 99 provides that an employee's dismissal will automatically be unfair if the reason or principal reason for the dismissal was a reason relating to:

(i)   pregnancy, childbirth or maternity;

(ii)   ordinary, compulsory or additional maternity leave;

(iii)   ordinary or additional adoption leave;

(iv)   parental leave;

(v)   ordinary or additional paternity leave; or

(vi)   time off for dependants under *ERA 1996, s 57A*.

and which reason has been prescribed by the Secretary of State in regulations.

Pursuant to the Maternity and Parental Leave, etc Regulations 1999 (SI 1999/3312), reg 20 and the *Paternity Leave and Adoption Leave Regulations 2002 (SI 2002/2788), reg 29*, a reason is of a prescribed kind if it is: (i) the employee's pregnancy; (ii) the fact that she has given birth; (iii) the application of a relevant health and safety requirement or recommendation because of maternity (see *ERA 1996, s 66(2)*); (iv) the fact that the employee has taken (or sought to take) ordinary or additional maternity leave, parental leave or time off for dependants under *ERA 1996, s 57A*; (v) the fact that she failed to return to work after ordinary or additional maternity leave where either the employer failed to notify her of the return date and she reasonably believed her maternity leave had not ended or the employer gave her less than 28 days' notice of the return date and it was not reasonably practicable for her to return on that date; (vi) the fact that the employee undertook, considered undertaking, or refused to undertake work during maternity leave (see *reg 12A*); (vii) the fact that she has declined to sign a workforce agreement for the purposes of the regulations; or (viii) the fact that the employee has performed any functions or activities as an employee representative (or candidate for employee representative).

A full discussion of these provisions appears at **31.7** MATERNITY AND PARENTAL RIGHTS.

(f) Pension scheme trustees

An employee's dismissal will automatically be regarded as unfair if the reason or principal reason for it is that, being a trustee of a trust scheme which relates to his employment, the employee performed (or proposed to perform) any functions as such a trustee (*ERA 1996, s 102*).

(g) Employee representatives

An employee's dismissal will automatically be regarded as unfair if the reason or principal reason for it is that the employee, being (*ERA 1996, s 103*):

(i)   an employee representative for the purposes of *TULRCA 1992, Part IV Chapter 2* (see **37.4** Redundancy – **II**) or *Transfer of Undertakings (Protection of Employment) Regulations 1981 (SI 1981/1794)*, and from 6 April 2006 the *2006 Regulations (SI 2006/246)* (see **50.18** Transfer of Undertakings); or

(ii)   a candidate in an election for such an employee representative,

performed, or proposed to perform, any functions or activities as such an employee representative or candidate. A dismissal will also be automatically unfair if the reason or principal reason is the employee's participation in an election for employee representatives in a redundancy or transfer of undertakings context.

Similarly, dismissals of employee representatives contrary to the *Occupational and Personal Pension Schemes (Consultation by Employers and Miscellaneous Amendment) Regulations 2006 (SI 2006/349) (para 5, Sch)* are automatically unfair, as are dismissals contrary to the *European Cooperative Society (Involvement of Employees) Regulations 2006 (SI 2006/2059) (reg 31)*.

(h) Shop workers and betting workers who refuse Sunday work

These provisions were introduced by the *Sunday Trading Act 1994* (shop workers) and the *Deregulation and Contracting Out Act 1994* (betting workers) and are now contained in *ERA 1996, s 101* (see **7.48** Contract of Employment). The dismissal of an employee who is a shop worker or betting worker will automatically be regarded as unfair if the reason or principal reason for the dismissal is that the employee:

(i)   being a protected shop worker or an opted-out shop worker, or a protected betting worker or an opted-out betting worker, refused (or proposed to refuse) to do shop work, or betting work, on Sunday or on a particular Sunday, except (in the case of an opted-out shop worker or an opted-out betting worker) in respect of any Sunday or Sundays falling before the opting-out notice expired; or

(ii)   gave (or proposed to give) an opting-out notice to the employer.

(j) Working time cases

An employee's dismissal will automatically be regarded as unfair if the reason or principal reason for the dismissal is that the employee (*ERA 1996, s 101A*):

(i)   refused (or proposed to refuse) to comply with a requirement which the employer imposed (or proposed to impose) in contravention of the *Working Time Regulations 1998* or the *Merchant Shipping (Working Time: Inland Waterways) Regulations 2003*;

(ii)   refused (or proposed to refuse) to forgo a right conferred on him by those regulations;

(iii)   failed to sign a workforce agreement for the purposes of those regulations, or to enter into, or agree to vary or extend, any other agreement with his employer which is provided for in those *Regulations*; or

(iv)   being a representative of members of the workforce for the purposes of *Sch 1* to those regulations, or a candidate in an election for such a representative, performed (or proposed to perform) any functions or activities as such a representative or candidate.

(k) Unfair selection for redundancy

A dismissal for redundancy will be unfair if the selection was made upon any of the grounds which would render a dismissal automatically unfair. Prohibited reasons for redundancy selection are set out in *ERA 1996, s 105* (see below).

(l) Dismissals on a transfer of an undertaking

Where either before or after a relevant transfer, any employee of the transferor or transferee is dismissed, that employee shall *prima facie* be treated as unfairly dismissed if the transfer or a reason connected with it is the reason or principal reason for his dismissal (*Transfer of Undertakings (Protection of Employment) Regulations 2006 (SI 2006/246), reg 7(1(a))*). However, the dismissal is not *automatically* unfair if the reason for it falls within *reg7(1)(b)*, that is if it is for an economic, technical or organisational reason entailing changes in the workforce. See TRANSFER OF UNDERTAKINGS (50).

(m) Spent convictions

A spent conviction or a failure to disclose it is not a proper ground for dismissal (see 16.3 EMPLOYEE'S PAST CRIMINAL CONVICTIONS).

(n) National Minimum Wage cases

This provision was inserted into *ERA 1996* by the *National Minimum Wage Act 1998, s 25* (see 32.9 PAY – I). A dismissal will automatically be regarded as unfair if the reason or principal reason for the dismissal is that (*ERA 1996, s 104A*):

(i)   any action was taken, or was proposed to be taken, by or on behalf of the employee with a view to enforcing, or otherwise securing the benefit of, specified rights granted under the *National Minimum Wage Act 1998*;

(ii)   the employer was prosecuted for any offence under the *National Minimum Wage Act 1998, s 31*, by reason of any action taken by or on behalf of the employee; or

(iii)   the employee qualifies, or will or might qualify, for the National Minimum Wage or for a particular rate of the National Minimum Wage.

It is immaterial whether the employee in fact has the right to the National Minimum Wage or that right has been infringed, provided that the claim made by or on behalf of the employee was made in good faith.

(o) Public interest disclosure cases

This provision was inserted into *ERA 1996, ss 103A and 105(6A)* by the *Public Interest Disclosure Act 1998, s 5* (see 9.17 DISCLOSURE OF INFORMATION). An employee's dismissal will automatically be regarded as unfair if the reason or principal reason for the dismissal is that the employee made a protected disclosure as defined in *ERA 1996, ss 43A–43L* (*ERA 1996, s 103A*). There is no statutory maximum cap upon compensation in public interest disclosure cases (*ERA 1996, s 124(1A)*). In *Stolt Offshore Ltd v Miklaszewicz* [2002] IRLR 344, the Scottish Court of Session upheld the EAT's ruling that it was possible to bring a claim under *ERA 1996, ss 103* and *105(6A)* even if the disclosure itself took place many years before the *Public Interest Disclosure Act 1998* came into force, provided that the dismissal itself took place after 2 July 1999.

(p) Dismissals connected with union recognition

Dismissals connected with union recognition are automatically unfair (*TULRCA 1992, Sch A1, para 161*, inserted by *Employment Relations Act 1999, s 1(2)* and *Sch 1*). This applies to dismissals where the reason or principal reason is that: (i) the employee acted with a view to obtaining or preventing recognition; (ii) indicated that he supported or did not support recognition; (iii) acted with a view to securing or preventing the ending of bargaining arrangements; (iv) indicated that he supported or did not support the ending of bargaining arrangements; (v) influenced or sought to influence whether other employees voted or how they voted; (vi) voted in such a ballot; or (vii) proposed to do or failed to do or proposed to decline to do, any of the above acts. A dismissal for one of the above reasons will not be automatically unfair, however, if the reason was an unreasonable act or omission by the employee.

(q) Right to be accompanied at disciplinary and grievance hearings

This set of automatically unfair dismissals consists of dismissals of employees because they exercised or sought to exercise the right under *s 10* of the *ERA 1999* to be accompanied at disciplinary and grievance hearings, or because they accompanied a fellow worker to such a hearing (*Employment Relations Act 1999, s 12*). *Sections 10–12* do not apply only to employees in the normal sense used for the purposes of the *ERA 1996* (*ERA 1996, s 230(3)*), but to a wider group of workers set out in *Employment Relations Act 1999, s 13* and include agency workers and home workers.

(r) Protected industrial action

Employment Relations Act 1999, s 16 and *Sch 5* provide that the dismissal of employees who are taking part in protected (ie official) industrial action will be automatically unfair if the conditions set out in the new *TULRCA 1992, s 238A* are satisfied.

(s) Dismissals for asserting the rights of part-time workers

Regulation 7 of the *Part-time Workers (Prevention of Less Favourable Treatment) Regulations 2000* provides that an employee who is dismissed for any of the following reasons will automatically be regarded as having been unfairly dismissed:

(i)   if the employee has brought proceedings against his employer under the *Regulations* or requested a written statement of reasons under the *Regulations*;

(ii)   if the employee has given evidence or information in connection with such proceedings brought by a worker or otherwise done anything under the *Regulations* in relation to the employer or any other person, or alleged that the employer had infringed the *Regulations*;

(iii)   if the employee refused (or proposed to refuse) to forgo a right conferred on him by the *Regulations*; or

(iv)   if the employer believes or suspects that the employee has done or intends to do any of the above things.

(See Less Favourable Treatment of Part-Time Workers (30))

(t) Action to enforce rights under the Tax Credits Act 1999

ERA 1996, s 104B provides that a dismissal will be automatically unfair if the reason, or principal reason, is that the employee took, or proposed to take, action with a view to enforcing or securing the benefit of a right under the *Tax Credits Act 1999*, or that a penalty was imposed upon the employer as a result of action taken by or on behalf of the employee for the purpose of enforcing his or her rights under the *Act*, or that the employee is entitled, or will or may be entitled to working families' tax credit or disabled persons tax credit.

(u) Activities as a member of special negotiating body, European Works Council, etc

The *Transnational Information and Consultation of Employees Regulations 1999, reg 28* provides that a worker will be automatically unfairly dismissed if the reason or principal reason for the employee's dismissal was that:

(i)   the employee had performed any functions or activities as a member or representative of, or a candidate for, a special negotiating body, a European Works Council, or as an information and consultation representative or as a candidate for such a position; or

(ii)   the employee or a person acting on his behalf asked for time off in relation to such activities; or

(iii)   the employee took specific steps in relation to such activities specified in *reg 28(6)*, including taking proceedings before the Employment Tribunal, the Employment Appeal Tribunal or the CAC, acting with a view to securing that a relevant body did or did not come into existence, voting in a ballot, or seeking to influence others' votes.

The *European Public Limited-Liability Company Regulations 2004, reg 42* and the *Information and Consultation of Employees Regulations 2004, reg 30* create similar protections for employee representatives and candidates, as do the *Companies (Cross-Border) Mergers Regulations 2007*.

(v) Dismissals for asserting the rights of fixed-term employees

Regulation 6 of the *Fixed-term Employees (Prevention of Less Favourable Treatment) Regulations 2002* provides that a dismissal will be automatically unfair if the reason or principal reason was that:

(i)   the employee brought proceedings against his employer under the *Regulations* or requested a written statement of reasons under the *Regulations;*

(ii)   the employee gave evidence or information in connection with such proceedings brought by an employee or otherwise did anything under the *Regulations* in relation to the employer or any other person, or alleged that the employer had infringed the *Regulations*;

(iii)   the employee refused (or proposed to refuse) to forgo a right conferred on him by the *Regulations*;

(iv)   the employee declined to sign a workforce agreement for the purpose of the *Regulations;*

(v)   the employee, being a workforce representative or candidate for the purpose of the *Regulations*, performed (or proposed to perform) any functions or activities in that capacity; or

(vi)   the employer believes or suspects that the employee has done or intends to do any of the above things.

(w) Dismissals for asserting the right to request flexible working

Section 104C of the *ERA 1996* renders a dismissal automatically unfair where the reason (or if more than one, the principal reason) was that the employee:

(i)   made (or proposed to make) an application for a contract variation (see *ERA 1996, s 80F*);

(ii)   exercised (or proposed to exercise) a right conferred on him by *ERA 1996, s 80G* (procedural entitlements);

(iii)   brought proceedings against his employer to enforce the right to request flexible working under *ERA 1996, s 80H*; or

(iv)   alleged the existence of any circumstance which would constitute a ground for bringing such proceedings against his employer.

(See **47 17 TIME OFF WORK**)

(x) Jury service

ERA 1996, s 98B makes a dismissal automatically unfair where the reason or principal reason was that the employee was summoned to do jury service, or was absent from work because he attended at any place in pursuance of being called to perform jury service. The dismissal is not unfair if the employer shows that the circumstances were such that the employee's absence in pursuance of being summoned was likely to cause substantial injury to the employer's undertaking, that the employer brought those circumstances to the attention of the employee, and the employee unreasonably failed or refused to apply to the appropriate officer for excusal from or deferral of the obligation to attend in pursuance of being so summoned.

(y) Participation in Education or Training

ERA 1996, s 101B makes a dismissal automatically unfair where the reason or principal reason was that, being entitled to be permitted to participate in education or training by the *Education and Skills Act 2008, s 27* or *s 28*, the employees exercised or proposed to exercise that right.

(z) Pension Enrolment

ERA 1996, s 104D makes a dismissal automatically unfair where the reason or principal reason was that:

(i)   any action was taken or was proposed to be taken with a view to enforcing in favour of the employee a requirement to which *ERA 1996, s 104D* applied;

(ii)   the employer was prosecuted for an offence under *Pensions Act 1998, s 45* as a result of action taken for the purpose of enforcing in favour of the employee a requirement to which *ERA 1996, s 104D* applied; or

(iii)   any provision of *Chapter 1* of *Part 1* of the *Pensions Act 1998* applied to the employee or would apply or might have applied.

It is immaterial whether or not the statutory requirement applied in the favour of the employee or whether or not the requirement had been contravened, but the claim that the requirement applied or had been contravened must have been made in good faith.

(A) Study and Training

ERA 1996, s 104E makes a dismissal automatically unfair where the reason or principal reason was that the employee:

(i)   made (or proposed to make) an application for time off for study and training under *ERA 1996, s 63D*,

(ii)   exercised (or proposed to exercise) a right conferred on the employee under *ERA 1996, s 63F*,

(iii)   brought proceedings against the employer under *ERA 1996, s 63I*, or

(iv)   alleged the existence of any circumstance which would constitute a ground for bringing such proceedings.

(See EDUCATION AND TRAINING (14))

(B) Blacklists

ERA 1996, s 104F makes a dismissal automatically unfair where the reason or principal reason relates to a prohibited list and either:

(i)   the employer contravenes *Employment Relations Act 1999 (Blacklists) Regulations 2010, reg 3* in relation to that prohibited list, or

(ii)   the employer—

(a)   relies on information supplied by a person who contravenes that regulation in relation to that list, and

(b)   knows or ought reasonably to know that the information relied on is supplied in contravention of that regulation.

(See **49.10** TRADE UNIONS II: INDIVIDUAL RIGHTS AND UNION MEMBERSHIP)

If there are facts from which the tribunal could conclude, in the absence of any other explanation, that the employer:

(i)   contravened *Employment Relations Act 1999 (Blacklists) Regulations 2010, reg 3*, or

(ii)   relied on information supplied in contravention of that *Regulation*,

the tribunal must find that such a contravention or reliance on information occurred, unless the employer shows that it did not.

(C) Agency Workers

Under the *Agency Workers Regulations 2010, reg 17*, a dismissal will be unfair where the reason or principal reason is that:

(i)   the agency worker brought proceedings under the *Agency Workers Regulations 2010*,

(ii)   the agency worker gave evidence or information in connection with such proceedings brought by any agency worker,

(iii)   the agency worker made a request for a written statement under *Agency Workers Regulations, reg 16*,

(iv)   the agency worker otherwise did anything under the *Regulations* in relation to a temporary work agency, hirer or any other person,

(v)   the agency worker alleged that a temporary work agency or hirer had breached the *Regulations*, provided that the allegation is not false and is made in good faith; or

(vi)   the agency worker refused or proposed to refuse to forgo a right conferred by the *Regulations*,

(vii)   the agency worker that the hirer or a temporary work agency believes or suspects that the agency worker has done or intends to do any of the above protected acts.

(See 45 Temporary And Seasonal Employees)

52.4   FAIRNESS IN THE CIRCUMSTANCES

If the employer establishes that the reason for the dismissal is an acceptable reason other than retirement, the tribunal will proceed to determine whether the dismissal was fair or unfair in all the circumstances (which expressly include the size and administrative resources of the employer's undertaking), having regard to equity and the substantial merits of the case (*ERA 1996, s 98(4)*). Whereas the burden of establishing the reason for the dismissal rests on the employer, the burden in relation to this second limb of the tribunal's inquiry is neutral.

A number of principles apply to tribunals' assessment of whether an employer has acted reasonably in dismissing an employee regardless of the reason for dismissal relied upon. This will be discussed in this section. The chapter will then go on to consider the issues which commonly arise when assessing reasonableness in relation to each of the acceptable reasons for dismissal.

Previously, where an employer could show that the reason for dismissal was retirement, the dismissal was presumed to be fair provided that the employer had followed the procedure set out in *Schedule 6* to the *Employment Equality (Age) Regulations 2006 (ERA 1996, s 98(3A) and 98ZG)*. Subject to transitional provisions applicable to employees to whom notice of retirement was given prior to 6th April 2011, these provisions have now been repealed by the *Employment Equality (Repeal of Retirement Age Provisions) Regulations 2011*. Employers continuing to operate a retirement age in their workplace will now need to objectively justify the policy, to avoid the dismissal being an act of age discrimination. Further, for the purposes of unfair dismissal, it seems likely that employers will rely upon the dismissal being for "some other substantial reason". If that dismissal is to be fair, it must be procedurally and substantively reasonable. Whilst awaiting authority on the question of what is required in such circumstances, the consultation provisions detailed in *Schedule 6* to the *Employment Equality (Age) Regulations 2006* would seem to be a sensible place for an employer to start.

When addressing fairness in the circumstances, the tribunal will consider whether the employer acted reasonably or unreasonably in treating the reason for the dismissal as a sufficient reason for dismissing the employee. If *part* of the reason or principal reason was not reasonably relied upon, the dismissal will be unfair (*Smith v City of Glasgow District Council* [1987] ICR 796). The EAT has recently reiterated that the tribunal must focus on whether the employer acted reasonably in dismissing for the reason(s) for which the tribunal has found that the employee has been dismissed. The tribunal should not add or exclude certain reasons which it has found formed part of the employer's reason to dismiss when it comes to consider whether the employer acted reasonably in dismissing for those reasons for the purposes of *ERA 1996, s 98(4)* (*O'Hanlon v Post Office Ltd* UKEAT/0202/12/LA (15 October 2012, unreported) and *Nejjary v Aramark Ltd* UKEAT/0054/12/CEA (31 May 2012, unreported)).

The tribunal will take into account not only whether the employer had reasonable grounds for dismissing the employee, but also whether it adopted a fair procedure in dismissing him. The correct approach for a tribunal, when applying *ERA 1996, s 98(4)*, is to consider whether the employer's actions, including its decision to dismiss, fell within the band of responses which a reasonable employer could adopt (*Iceland Frozen Foods Ltd v Jones* [1983] ICR 17; *British Leyland (UK) Ltd v Swift* [1981] IRLR 91, CA; *Gilham v Kent County Council (No 2)* [1985] ICR 233; *Neale v Hereford and Worcester County Council* [1986] ICR 471). The tribunal must not substitute its view for that of the employer and judge whether the employer has taken the "correct" approach. Rather it should recognise that different employers may reasonably react in different ways to a particular situation. A finding of unfair dismissal should only be made where an employer's conduct and decision making fell outside the range of reasonable responses.

The 'band of reasonable responses' test does not apply solely to the decision to dismiss. It applies also to the procedure followed by the employer (*Whitbread plc v Hall* [2001] ICR 699; *Sainsbury's Supermarkets Ltd v Hitt* [2003] ICR 111).

Doubt was cast upon the correctness of the band of reasonable responses approach by the EAT in *Haddon v Van den Bergh Foods Ltd* [1999] ICR 1150. However, the matter was reconsidered by the Court of Appeal in *Foley v Post Office and HSBC Bank (formerly Midland Bank) v Madden* [2000] ICR 1283 and the orthodox position was restored. The Court of Appeal held that tribunals were not to approach the issue of reasonableness by reference to their own judgment of what would have been done if they had been the employer. The test has been applied consistently since Foley (see, for example, *Sarkar v West London Mental Health NHS Trust* [2010] IRLR 508). In *Tuner v East Midlands Trains Ltd* [2013] IRLR 107 the Court of Appeal recently confirmed that the range of reasonable responses test is compatible with *ECHR, Art 8* and reiterated that it should not be equated with the *Wednesdbury* unreasonable test applied in administrative law.

Before deciding to dismiss, the employer must have investigated the relevant facts adequately. The reason for, and the fairness of, the action taken is determined by examining the circumstances known to the employer at the time of the dismissal or when he maintains that decision at the conclusion of an internal appeal (*West Midlands Co-operative Society Ltd v Tipton* [1986] ICR 192). In *Orr v Milton Keynes Council* [2011] ICR 704, the Court of Appeal (Sedley LJ dissenting) held that the knowledge of an employee is not to be attributed to the dismissing officer for the purposes of deciding whether or not dismissal was fair in the circumstances (though the claimant employee is likely to argue that the employer would have uncovered that knowledge had it conducted a reasonable investigation) (see also **52.10**, **52.15** below). An employer cannot be criticised for failing to have regard to material which came to light for the first time as evidence during the tribunal hearing (*Dick v Glasgow University* [1993] IRLR 581).

With regards procedural matters, even if the employer has complied with its own dismissal procedures, or the ACAS Code, the tribunal may nevertheless consider that the employer did not adopt a fair procedure in dismissing the employee. It is therefore important to consider in each case what procedural requirements fairness called for. In this context, the paragraphs in the *ACAS Code of Practice* relating to disciplinary practice and procedures provide useful guidelines but are not prescriptive or exhaustive (*Lock v Cardiff Rly Co* [1998] IRLR 358). The main point of these provisions is that *there should be a known disciplinary procedure which should be followed.* If there is a complaint against an employee, he should be informed in detail and preferably in writing of the complaint, and be given an opportunity to make representations, if necessary through, or in the presence of, an employee representative. (If the employee is a union member, his representative may be his shop steward.) In *Clark v Civil Aviation Authority* [1991] IRLR 412 at para 20, the EAT gave guidance as to how a disciplinary hearing should be conducted. Although a failure to follow the ACAS Codes of Practice, or internal procedures, is not determinative of the fairness of a dismissal (see *UPS Ltd v Harrison* (UKEAT/0038/11/RN) (16 January 2012, unreported) emphasising that the tribunal must address whether the procedure followed, overall, was reasonable, it being insufficient to simply find that the employer did not follow its own policy). That said, it is important to bear in mind that such a failure can affect the outcome, and, with the shift of the burden of proof in discrimination cases, a failure to follow a relevant Code of Practice or internal procedure may lead an employment tribunal to infer unlawful discrimination **10.21 DISCRIMINATION AND EQUAL OPPORTUNITIES – I**).

The employee should also be given the opportunity, where practicable, to appeal to a level of management not previously involved (although cf *Robinson v Ulster Carpet Mills Ltd* [1991] IRLR 348). The tribunal must have regard to the appeal process when considering the unfair dismissal claim before it. The Court of Appeal has emphasised that there is no rule of law that earlier unfairness can be cured only by an appeal by way of a rehearing and not by way of a review. The Tribunal should examine the fairness of the disciplinary process as a whole and each case will depend upon its own facts (*Taylor v OCS Group Ltd* [2006] ICR 1602). Two recent examples illustrate the important role which an appeal can play depending on those facts. In *Scott v Northumbria Probation Board* UKEAT/0451/11/RN (22 May 2012, unreported) a substantial aspect of the original decision to dismiss was overturned by an internal appeal board, but the dismissal was upheld. The EAT held that in such circumstances the individual hearing the appeal necessarily puts itself in the position of being the principal decision-maker and the tribunal must focus carefully upon its decision. The EAT reiterated that whether the appeal was classified as a review or a re-hearing is irrelevant in this regard. In *First Hampshire & Dorset Ltd v Parhar* UKEAT/0643/11/LA (10 May 2012, unreported), the EAT reminded tribunals to consider the whole process, including the appeal, when examining ill-health capability dismissals, particularly where new facts or evidence were available by the time of the appeal. This applies whether the new facts or evidence assist the employee or, as they did on the facts of *Parhar* (above), the employer.

In general, whether a dismissal has been carried out in breach of contract is a relevant factor in assessing its fairness, but is not conclusive (*Hooper v British Railways Board* [1988] IRLR 517; *Post Office v Marney* [1990] IRLR 170; and see *Stoker v Lancashire County Council* [1992] IRLR 75). However, see *Johnston v Welsh National Opera Ltd* [2012] EWCA Civ 1046 for a recent example of a case where a failure to follow a contractual disciplinary procedure played a very significant role in a finding of unfair dismissal which was upheld by the Court of Appeal. It is important to note that not every procedural defect will make a dismissal unfair; the seriousness of the defect must be considered in deciding whether the overall result was a dismissal which was unfair (*Fuller v Lloyds Bank plc* [1991] IRLR 336).

Although notice once given cannot unilaterally be withdrawn, it may be withdrawn by agreement. The result is that the tribunal has regard, in appropriate cases, to what takes place between the giving of notice and the ultimate termination of employment in determining whether a dismissal was reasonable in all the circumstances. Dismissal is better analysed as a process than an event as highlighted, for example, by the fact that tribunals take internal appeals into account in assessing fairness (*South Tyneside Council v Ward* (UKEAT/0358/10/RN) (12 July 2011, unreported)).

The most common procedural failings in practice include: a failure to give warnings when shortcomings in an employee's performance first emerge, or to record them properly in writing; failure to give adequate advance notice of a disciplinary hearing, or to inform the employee before the hearing of the substance of the complaint to be considered or the fact that, if the complaint is found proved, the employee may be dismissed; failure to inform the employee of or to permit him to exercise the right to be accompanied to a disciplinary hearing; managers acting on evidence on which the employee has had no chance to comment; decisions being taken or influenced by persons other than those who have considered what the employee has to say; and appeals being determined by persons with a prior involvement in the matter. Procedural requirements in particular contexts are dealt with in more detail in **52.6–52.14** below.

For several years it was thought that if an employer had adopted an unfair procedure in dismissing an employee, but established that if he had adopted a fair procedure the employee would still have been dismissed, the dismissal could be held to be fair. However, in *Polkey v A E Dauton (or Dayton) Services Ltd* [1988] ICR 142, the House of Lords confirmed that the sole question for the tribunal was whether the employer acted reasonably at the time. In the vast majority of cases, there was no scope to consider what might have happened if the employer had acted differently, except at the stage of assessing compensation (see **53.13** Unfair Dismissal – III). However, the House of Lords also stated that where the employer could reasonably have concluded in the light of circumstances known to him at the time of dismissal that it would have been utterly useless to follow the normal procedure, he might well have acted reasonably if he did not follow the procedure. In *Duffy v Yeomans & Partners Ltd* [1995] ICR 642, the Court of Appeal said that it was not necessary, in order to come within this exception, that the employer actually applied his mind to the question whether normal procedures would be utterly useless. It will, however, be an unusual case where following procedures would meet this high threshold.

EA 2002, s 34, introduced a new *s 98A(2)* into *ERA 1996* which had the effect of overturning *Polkey*. Failure to follow a procedure in relation to the dismissal of an employee was not regarded – by itself – as making the employer's action unreasonable if he showed that he would have decided to dismiss the employee if he had followed the procedure. This provision was repealed with effect from 6 April 2009.

52.5 GROUNDS FOR DISMISSAL – LACK OF CAPABILITY OR QUALIFICATIONS

Capability means capability assessed by reference to skill, aptitude, health, or any other physical or mental quality. *Qualifications* means any degree, diploma or other academic, technical or professional qualification, *relevant to the position which the employee held* (*ERA 1996, s 98(3)*).

52.6 Capability

As with other reasons for dismissal, the employer is not required to prove that the employee was incapable of performing his job in order to defeat a claim for unfair dismissal. The employer need only establish an honest belief on reasonable grounds that the employee was incapable (*Taylor v Alidair Ltd* [1978] ICR 445).

In cases of lack of capability, it has long been established that before dismissal an employer should inform the employee what is required, inform the employee of the ways in which he is failing to perform his job adequately, warn him of the possibility that he may be dismissed because of this, and provide him with an opportunity to improve (see, for example, *James v Waltham Holy Cross UDC* [1973] ICR 398).

There are some cases where a tribunal might be prepared to accept that a warning was not required. For example, in *James v Waltham Holy Cross UDC* itself, it was suggested that a capability defect may be so extreme that there is an irredeemable incapability, with the result that a warning would be of no benefit to the employee. Equally, in *Taylor v Alidair Ltd* (above), the Court of Appeal stated that the potential consequences of incompetence may be so serious that one failure to perform may justify dismissal e.g. a failure committed by a passenger-carrying airline pilot. However, in practice such cases are likely to be very rare, and should be treated as exceptional departures from the general rule that a warning, and time for improvement, are required.

52.6A Procedure for capability dismissals

(See also **52.10** below.) In regard to capability and performance management, employers should follow procedures agreed with or notified to their employees. Such procedures may include the following steps.

52.6A   Unfair Dismissal – II

(i)   If an employee falls short of the performance required of him, a meeting (of which the employee is given prior written notice containing an outline of the matters to be considered) should be arranged with him and his representative at which he is informed of:

    (a)   the respects (in detail) in which he falls short of the required standards;

    (b)   the time within which his performance must improve; and

    (c)   the fact that if he fails to improve he will receive a written warning and if he still fails to improve within a reasonable time he may be dismissed.

    If possible, a note taker should attend this meeting and take a contemporaneous note of what is said. If this cannot be done, a written record of what was said should be made as soon as possible after the meeting. The employee and his representative/companion (if appropriate) should be sent a letter setting out a brief summary of the meeting and of the conclusions reached, including any warning given.

(ii)   If the employee's performance fails to improve, he should be sent a letter:

    (a)   setting out the respects in which he has failed to improve; and

    (b)   inviting him and his representative to another meeting to explain this failure.

(iii)   At the second meeting, at which again there should be a witness and a record kept:

    (a)   the complaints against the employee should be reiterated; and

    (b)   he should be given an opportunity to explain.

    If he has no satisfactory explanation for his failure to improve, he should be informed that:

    (c)   he has a further time in which to improve; and

    (d)   failure to improve within this time will result in dismissal.

    The employee and his representative should again be sent a summary of the meeting.

(iv)   If there is no improvement, repeat step (ii), warning him that his dismissal will be considered.

(v)   At the third meeting, repeat steps (iii)(*a*) and (*b*) and if no satisfactory explanation is given, give notice of dismissal if the circumstances warrant such a sanction.

(vi)   If practicable, and in any event if the contract or any disciplinary or grievance procedure requires it, if the employee wishes to challenge his dismissal, a manager or managers not involved in the original decision to dismiss should conduct an appeal hearing.

Other steps which may be taken are the offer of training to assist the employee's performance, and consultation with his union representative. Consideration should be given to whether the employer has other work available to which the employee would be better suited.

The importance of these steps will vary according to the circumstances. For example, it may be that a senior employee ought to be well aware of what is required of him and the consequences of failing to perform his duties adequately. However, it is best to give formal warnings in cases of incapability, irrespective of the seniority of the employee.

52.7   Qualifications

Dismissal for lack of qualifications is not common since an employer will have difficulty in convincing a tribunal that an employee whom he engaged with full knowledge of his qualifications is not qualified for the job. If, however, the employee misled the employer into believing that he possessed certain qualifications which were essential for the performance of the task to which he was appointed, he may be dismissed for his lack of qualifications. Some of the cases on lack of qualifications have arisen where a man employed as a driver is disqualified from driving and therefore is no longer able to perform his duties (see, for example, *Appleyard v F M Smith (Hull) Ltd* [1972] IRLR 19). Consideration should be given to offering a disqualified employee suitable alternative employment.

52.8   Lack of capability due to ill-health

In cases of ill-health which make future performance of the contract of employment impossible, the contract may be considered to have been frustrated and the employee not to have been dismissed (see **46.3** TERMINATION OF EMPLOYMENT). However, instances of frustration of the contract of employment are extremely rare.

Before dismissing an employee for reasons of ill-health, an employer should find out the current medical position. This will involve obtaining, with the employee's consent, a report from the employee's general practitioner and, if appropriate, his consultant (see **9.15** DISCLOSURE OF INFORMATION for the *Access to Medical Reports Act 1988* and the *Access to Health Records Act 1990*). In some cases, it may be thought necessary to have the employee examined, with his consent, by a doctor appointed by the employer.

In *D B Schenker Rail (UK) Ltd v Doolan* (UKEATS/0053/09/BI) (13 April 2011, unreported), the Scottish EAT reiterated that whilst employers were obliged to take steps to inform themselves of the employee's medical position, this should be judged against a standard of reasonableness. The Scottish EAT, by analogy with the *Burchell* test applied to cases of misconduct, considered that a tribunal should ask whether a reasonable employer could find, from the material before it that the employee was not capable of returning to his post. The tribunal was not to substitute its own answer to that question for that given by the employer. The Scottish EAT further emphasised that whilst medical and expert reports may assist the employer, the question is ultimately managerial rather than medical.

Once the employer has properly informed himself of the employee's state of health and the prognosis, he should consider the requirements of his business, the employee's past sickness record and whether the employee could be offered an alternative position more suitable to his state of health (*Spencer v Paragon Wallpapers Ltd* [1977] ICR 301). The employer should also consider whether the employee should be regarded as disabled and, if so, whether any reasonable adjustments should be made for the employee. The employer should consult the employee and any representative before dismissing him (*East Lindsay District Council v Daubney* [1977] ICR 566; *Merseyside and North Wales Electricity Board v Taylor* [1975] ICR 185).

Having properly informed itself of the position and consulted with the employee, the employer must decide what action to take. The EAT in *Lynock v Cereal Packaging Ltd* [1988] ICR 670 stated that whilst each case will turn on its facts, some factors which may be important include: (i) the nature of the illness; (ii) the likelihood of it recurring or some other illness arising; (iii) the length of the various absences and the spaces of good health between them; (iv) the need of the employer for the work done by the particular employee; (v) the impact of the absences on others who work with the employee; (vi) the adoption and the carrying out of the policy; (vii) the emphasis on a personal assessment in the ultimate decision and of course, (viii) the extent to which the difficulty of the situation and the position of the employer has been made clear to the employee so that the employee realises that the point of no return, the moment when the decision was ultimately being made may be approaching. The EAT also held that the mere fact that an employee is fit at the time of dismissal will not render the dismissal unfair, as the tribunal has to look at the history as a whole.

Whilst it is important to consider whether an employee can be offered an alternative position, an employer will not act unreasonably if he offers the employee alternative employment at a reduced rate of pay where this is the only suitable alternative employment which is available for him (*British Gas Services Ltd v McCaull* [2001] IRLR 60). Fairness requires the employer to consider eligibility under an ill-health early retirement scheme before dismissing an employee for long-term ill-health (*First West Yorkshire Ltd t/a First Leeds v Haigh* [2008] IRLR 182). The employee, on the other hand, has no duty to volunteer information about his prospects of recovery to his employer (*Mitchell v Arkwood Plastics (Engineering) Ltd* [1993] ICR 471), though this may reduce the information which the employer has to take into account if it is to have acted reasonably.

Where the problem consists not of a long absence but of persistent short absences caused by unconnected minor ailments, a medical examination has little purpose. The employee should be told what level of attendance he is expected to attain, the period within which that is to be achieved and that dismissal may follow if there is no sufficient improvement. The situation should then be monitored to see whether absence is reduced below a reasonable level. A second warning would be appropriate in borderline cases (see *International Sports Co Ltd v Thomson* [1980] IRLR 340; *Rolls-Royce Ltd v Walpole* [1980] IRLR 343; *Lynock v Cereal Packaging Ltd* [1988] ICR 670).

Whether the ill health was caused by the employer's actions will not determine fairness. The issue of responsibility for the illness or injury is tangential to the question of fairness of the dismissal (*London Fire and Civil Defence Authority v Betty* [1994] IRLR 384; *Edwards v Governors of Hanson School* [2001] IRLR 733; *McAdie v Royal Bank of Scotland* [2008] ICR 1087).

In *H J Heinz Co Ltd v Kenrick* [2000] IRLR 144, the EAT held that it would be an error of law for a tribunal to proceed on the basis that a disability-related dismissal which is not 'justified' under the *Disability Discrimination Act 1995* is, without more, automatically unfair under the *ERA 1996*. Separate consideration must be given to the question of unfairness.

52.9   GROUNDS FOR DISMISSAL – CONDUCT

It is worth noting that in order to prove a potentially fair reason for dismissal, an employer need only show that the reason for the dismissal related to the employee's conduct. Tribunals should not be drawn into the trap of construing the concept of conduct too narrowly. This point has been reiterated by the Scottish EAT, stating that the conduct need not be of any particular character, and finding that the tribunal had erred by asking whether the conduct was "reprehensible" (*Royal Bank of Scotland v Donaghay* (UKEATS/0049/10/BI) (11 November 2011, unreported)). This was an impermissible gloss on the statutory language.

The starting point in most cases where misconduct is the reason for dismissal is the approach formulated by Arnold J in *British Home Stores Ltd v Burchell* [1980] ICR 303n. At 304 he stated:

> 'What the tribunal have to decide every time is, broadly expressed, whether the employer who discharged the employee on the grounds of misconduct in question (usually, though not necessarily, dishonest conduct) entertained a reasonable suspicion amounting to a belief in the guilt of the employee of that misconduct at that time. That is really stating shortly and compendiously what is in fact more than one

element. First of all, there must be established by the employer the fact of that belief; that the employer did believe it. Secondly, that the employer had in his mind reasonable grounds upon which to sustain that belief. And thirdly, we think, that the employer, at the stage at which he formed that belief on those grounds, at any rate at the final stage at which he formed that belief on those grounds, had carried out as much investigation into the matter as was reasonable in all the circumstances of the case.'

In *Boys and Girls Welfare Society v McDonald* [1997] ICR 693, the EAT pointed out that *Burchell* had been decided when the burden of proving reasonableness rested with the employer rather than neutrally as is the position today. The above passage must be read subject to this qualification to avoid the tribunal falling into error and requiring the employer to prove reasonableness. The EAT in *McDonald* added that (i) in any event, *Burchell* may not be appropriate where there is no real conflict on the facts; and (ii) *Burchell* does not mean that an employer who fails one or more of the three tests is, without more, guilty of unfair dismissal. The tribunal should focus upon the question whether the employer's action fell within the range of reasonable responses open to a reasonable employer. Notwithstanding the comments made by the EAT in *McDonald*, the *Burchell* test was approved by the *Court of Appeal in Foley v Post Office, HSBC Bank (formerly Midland Bank) v Madden* [2000] ICR 1283 (amongst other cases), and is applied almost as a matter of course by tribunals in practice.

In addition to the three tests set out in *Burchell*, if the dismissal is to be fair it must have been reasonable for the employer to have dismissed the employee for the misconduct in question. In other words, dismissal must be a fair sanction. As with other aspects of the law on unfair dismissal, the tribunal will again focus on whether or not the sanction imposed fell within the band of responses which a reasonable employer might have adopted (see *Foley* above) (the same test will be applied when the tribunal assesses the reasonableness of the investigation undertaken by the employer (see *Sainsbury's Supermarkets Ltd v Hitt* [2003] ICR 111 above)).

The consequence of the range of reasonable responses test is that the tribunal should not substitute its own factual findings about events giving rise to the dismissal for those of the dismissing officer, nor should it impose its view of the appropriate sanction for those of the employer. Instead that tribunal should ask (i) whether there were reasonable grounds upon which the employer could believe that the employee had committed the misconduct in question; (ii) whether the employer completed a reasonable investigation prior to dismissal; and (iii) whether the decision to dismiss for the misconduct in question fell within the band of reasonable responses (*London Ambulance Service NHS Trust v Small* [2009] IRLR 563). The Court of Appeal has recently emphasised this principle in *Boardman v Nugent Care Society* [2013] EWCA Civ 198, in which the Court drew a clear distinction between the tribunal's fact-finding role in unfair and wrongful dismissal claims. An example of this principle in practice is *Quadrant Catering Ltd v Smith* (UKEAT/0362/10/RN) (10 December 2010, unreported), where the EAT held that the tribunal erred by suggesting that dismissal should have been used only as a last resort, and substituting its view of the facts for those of the employer. In *Tayeh v Barchester Healthcare Ltd* [2013] EWCA Civ 29 the Court of Appeal recently emphasised that it is for the employer to judge the severity of offence. In that case the tribunal's decision was overturned as it had substituted its own mistaken view of the severity of the offence for that of the employer. Equally, the EAT should not substitute its view for that of the employment tribunal, and should avoid an overly "pernickety" scrutiny of the tribunal's reasons (*Fuller v Brent London Borough Council* [2011] ICR 806).

When deciding what sanction to impose, it is important to consider the circumstances of the individual case, and not simply to apply an inflexible policy (*Post Office v Marney* [1990] IRLR 170; *Rentokil Ltd v Mackin* [1989] IRLR 286, EAT). For example, even where an employee is dismissed for misconduct such as dishonesty which is referred to in the employer's disciplinary code as being misconduct which would normally lead to dismissal, the duty on an employer to act fairly and reasonably requires that they should investigate the seriousness of the offence in the particular case (*John Lewis plc v Coyne* [2001] IRLR 139). In particular, it is important to consider any mitigating features which might justify a lesser sanction for reasons specific to the employee, or the incident in question. The ACAS Guidance on disciplinary proceedings suggests the following factors may be relevant when determining what, if any, disciplinary penalty to impose: whether the employer's rules indicate the likely penalty; the penalty imposed in similar cases in the past; the employee's disciplinary record, work record, experience and length of service; whether there are any special mitigating circumstances which might make it appropriate to adjust the severity of the penalty; and whether the proposed penalty is reasonable in all the circumstances. An employment tribunal is likely to have similar factors in mind when determining whether or not dismissal was a reasonable sanction in the circumstances of the case.

Although employers should consider each disciplinary case on its individual merits, on occasion a dismissal may be held unfair on the ground that the dismissed employee has been treated inconsistently, in that the employer has on other occasions dealt more leniently with similar instances of misconduct (*Cain v Leeds Western Health Authority* [1990] ICR 585, *Post Office v Fennell* [1981] IRLR 221). In *Hadjioannous v Coral Casinos Ltd* [1981] IRLR 352, the EAT held that evidence of inconsistency is relevant in a limited range of circumstances, namely: (i) it may be evidence as to how an employee has been led to be believe that certain categories of conduct will be viewed by his employer; (ii) it may suggest that the purported reason for dismissal advanced by the employer is not real or genuine; and (iii) it may support an argument that the sanction of dismissal was unreasonable. However, this should only be the case if the two cases in question were, to adopt the language used by the EAT in *Hadjioannous*, "truly parallel", as the emphasis should be on the individual employee's case. Tribunals should generally be cautious in finding a dismissal to have been unfair on grounds of inconsistent treatment (*Hadjioannous* (above); *Paul v East Surrey District Health Authority* [1995] IRLR 305; *Harrow London Borough Council v Cunningham* [1996] IRLR 256, EAT). The EAT continues to apply a test of strict parity in cases where comparators are relied upon (see *Honey v City and County of Swansea* (UKEAT/0465/09/JOJ) (16 April 2010, unreported) where a difference in seniority and job description justified a difference in sanction). The EAT has emphasised that the appropriate question remains whether a reasonable employer could properly, within the bounds of a range of reasonable responses, have decided to deal with the two cases differently. Where the tribunal accepts the employer's reason for having treated the two cases differently, the dismissal will only be unfair if that reason can be said to have been outside the range of responses open to the employer (*General Mills (Berwick) Ltd v Glowacki* (UKEAT/0139/11/ZT) (22 September 2011, unreported) and see also *SPS Technologies Ltd v Chughtai* UKEAT/0204/12/SM (3 December 2012, unreported) where the employer was held to have drawn a reasonable distinction between two cases because it reasonably found on the evidence that charges were made out against one employee but not another).

Whilst the employer's policy on conduct which will and will not be treated as gross misconduct is of course relevant to the reasonableness of the dismissal, the fact that the employee is dismissed for conduct not set out in a handbook or similar document will not inevitably lead to a finding that the dismissal is unfair. For example, the tribunal is entitled to take into account whether the employee should have been aware of the gravity of the misconduct in question in determining whether a reasonable employer would necessarily have warned the employee of the consequences of his actions (*Royal Bank of Scotland v Nwosuagwe-Ibe* (UKEAT/0594/10/ZT) (February 2010, unreported) provides an example of such reasoning).

If an employee has recently been given a disciplinary warning (especially if it was for a similar offence), this may make it more reasonable to dismiss for the act of misconduct. The EAT in *Auguste Noel Ltd v Curtis* [1990] ICR 604 confirmed that previous warnings for dissimilar conduct may also be relevant. In *Wincanton Group Plc v Stone & Ors* [2013] IRLR 178 the EAT emphasised that the misconduct for which the employee is dismissed need not necessarily be of the same nature as the conduct which led to the warning being imposed. The EAT further noted that a final written warning always implies, subject only to the individual terms of a contract, that any misconduct of whatever nature will often, and usually, be met with dismissal, and it is likely to be by way of exception that that will not occur. Where an appeal against a prior warning is pending, the employer should take into account both the warning and the fact that it is subject to an undetermined appeal in considering whether to dismiss, although he is not precluded from dismissing before the appeal is heard (*Tower Hamlets Health Authority v Anthony* [1989] ICR 656, see also *Wincanton Group Plc v Stone & Ors* [2013] IRLR 178 in which the EAT further suggested that an employer ought to take account of any challenge to the warning being made in legal proceedings). In *Davies v Sandwell Metropolitan Borough Council* [2013] EWCA Civ 135 the Court of Appeal doubted, albeit *obiter*, whether the EAT had been correct in that case to suggest that it was unreasonable for the employer to take into account the fact that an appeal against historic disciplinary sanction had been abandoned.

In *Diosynth Ltd v Thomson* [2006] CSIH 5, [2006] IRLR 284 the Court of Session concluded that it had been unreasonable for an employer to dismiss an employee for breaches of safety procedures after a fatality, because the employer had treated an expired warning for breach of safety procedures as a determining factor in the decision to dismiss. In *Webb v Airbus UK Ltd* [2008] ICR 561, however, the Court of Appeal held that it is open to an employment tribunal to find a dismissal fair even where an employer has taken into account a spent warning. Diosynth was distinguished on the basis that in that case the expired warning tipped the balance towards the decision to dismiss, but in *Airbus* the employer had shown that the reason for dismissal was the later misconduct, and the previous misconduct affected the decision as to what sanction to impose.

There has recently been a great deal of litigation concerning the circumstances in which it will be appropriate for a tribunal to consider the reasonableness of an earlier written warning during an unfair dismissal hearing. In *Nunn v Royal Mail Group* [2011] ICR 162 the EAT considered a case where an employee was dismissed because he failed to accept a demotion sanction imposed on him following disciplinary proceedings. The EAT held that unless there is a glaringly obvious reason why the demotion (or, presumably, any other previous sanction) was unfair, the tribunal is not required to examine in detail the precise nature of the allegations and procedure involved. If the employee is dissatisfied with the demotion, his proper remedy is a claim for constructive unfair dismissal. In *Davies v Sandwell Metropolitan Borough Council* [2013] EWCA Civ 135 the Court of Appeal considered in detail the approach employers and tribunals should take to previous warnings in unfair dismissal cases. The Court of Appeal approved the central principle laid down in earlier authorities to the effect that it is legitimate for an employer to rely on a final warning, provided that it was issued in good faith, that there were at least prima facie grounds for imposing it and that it was not manifestly inappropriate to issue it. The Court of Appeal added that in answering that question it is not for the tribunal to re-open the warning and consider the adequacy of the evidence in detail. There need to be exceptional circumstances before a tribunal should go behind an earlier disciplinary process (see also *Wincanton Group Plc v Stone & Ors* [2013] IRLR 178). Whilst the issue for the tribunal is therefore relatively narrow, it remains necessary for the tribunal to apply its mind to that question and consider and decide whether the warning given was manifestly inappropriate (*Simmonds v Milford Club* UKEAT/0323/12/KN (6 December 2012, unreported). In *Simmonds*, the EAT held that if an Employment Tribunal has cause on the facts to consider that a previous disciplinary sanction may have been manifestly inappropriate, it should hear evidence and decide on the relevant facts whether the sanction applied was manifestly inappropriate.

If the employer reasonably believes that one of a number of employees is guilty of dishonesty and, despite proper investigation, cannot identify the culprit, it may be reasonable to dismiss all those who could have been responsible (*Monie v Coral Racing Ltd* [1981] ICR 109; *Whitbread & Co plc v Thomas* [1988] ICR 135; *Parr v Whitbread & Co plc* [1990] ICR 427; *Frames Snooker Centre v Boyce* [1992] IRLR 472). In *John Lewis plc v Coyne* [2001] IRLR 139, the EAT gave useful guidance on what type of misconduct can be said to amount to 'dishonesty', holding that the best working test is that set out in *R v Ghosh* [1982] QB 1053. In summary, there are two aspects to dishonesty – the objective and the subjective – and judging whether or not there has been dishonesty involves going through a two-stage process. First, it must be decided whether according to the ordinary standards of reasonable and honest people, what was done was dishonest. If so, then second, consideration must be given to whether the person concerned must have realised that what he or she was doing was by those standards dishonest. See also *Panama v Hackney London Borough Council* [2003] IRLR 278 on proof of fraudulent conduct.

An employer is entitled to take into account both the actual impact of the impugned conduct, and the potential impact of that conduct when determining whether dismissal was a reasonable sanction (*Wincanton Plc v Atkinson* (UKEAT/0040/11/DM) (19 July 2011, unreported)). In that case, two employees failed to renew their HGV licences with the effect that they had been driving the employer's vehicles in breach of regulations and without valid insurance. The tribunal took the view that as they had not caused an accident, and the employer had not been subject to regulatory sanctions, no harm had resulted and their dismissals were unfair. The EAT overturned the tribunal on the grounds that insufficient weight have been given to the very serious potential consequences of the misconduct.

Where an employer relies upon the employee's conduct in refusing to obey an instruction, the lawfulness of that instruction was not decisive when considering the reasonableness of the dismissal under ERA 1996, s 98(4), although it is a relevant factor: *Farrant v Woodroffe School* [1998] ICR 184. The same principle applies where an employee is dismissed for breach of an absence policy (*Sakharkar v Northern Foods Grocery Group Ltd* (UKEAT/0442/10/ZT) (8 March 2011, unreported)).

Length of service is a factor which an employment tribunal may properly take into account in deciding whether the decision of an employer to dismiss in reaction to the employee's conduct was an appropriate one (*Strouthos v London Underground Ltd* [2004] IRLR 636).

The conduct for which an employee is dismissed usually relates to behaviour during working hours, but in certain cases an employee may be dismissed fairly for other behaviour, if it is likely to affect the performance of his contract. If, for example, a playgroup leader is convicted of an indecent assault on a child outside his hours of work, his conviction for such an offence may make him unsuitable for carrying on his employment (eg *Nottinghamshire County Council v Bowly* [1978] IRLR 252, in which the EAT held to be fair the dismissal of a teacher after his conviction for an offence of gross indecency with a man and similarly the Court of Appeal in *X v Y* [2004] ICR 1634 including consideration of *art 8* of the *ECHR*).

Even in a case of misconduct justifying dismissal from the employee's existing job, it may sometimes be necessary to consider whether the employee could still be employed in some other capacity. However, it may be reasonable to leave investigation of that possibility until after the time when notice is given (*P v Nottinghamshire County Council* [1992] ICR 706). The EAT gave further consideration to this point in *Wincanton Group Plc v Stone & Ors* [2013] IRLR 178. The EAT consider it "highly arguable" that when an employee is dismissed from a job he has been employed to do in circumstances in which he cannot be expected legally to continue doing it, the employer may owe no duty to seek alternative employment. However, as both sides accepted that was such a duty in that case the EAT declined to resolve the point conclusively.

Cases in which an employee is arrested by the police and charged with theft of his employer's property pose particular difficulties. Even if the employee may be charged with a criminal offence, he must be given an opportunity by his employer to state his case (*Read v Phoenix Preservation Ltd* [1985] ICR 164). In *Leach v Office of Communications* [2012] ICR 1269 the Court of Appeal upheld the EAT's decision to the effect that an employer which receives information from a third party must, as far as practicable, assess for itself the reliability of the information. For example, it should check the integrity of the informant body and the safeguards within the body's internal processes to assess the accuracy of the information supplied. The employer should not simply take an uncritical view of the information provided. However, the Court acknowledged that there will be cases where an employer cannot be expected to carry out his own independent investigation in order to test the reliability of the information provided by a responsible public authority.

Is it proper for the employer to conduct his own investigation and question the employee whilst the police investigations are proceeding? In *Harris v Courage (Eastern) Ltd* [1982] ICR 530, the Court of Appeal approved the decision of the EAT that there is no absolute rule that once an employee had been charged with an offence and advised to say nothing until his criminal trial, an employer could not dismiss him for the alleged offence. Because of the long delay before a criminal prosecution is finally disposed of, it will often be necessary or desirable for the employer to act before its conclusion. Employers frequently carry out their own investigations and dismiss for dishonest conduct before a prosecution is concluded. If the employer awaits the outcome of a criminal trial and the employee is acquitted, he may find it harder to justify a subsequent dismissal, although the burden on the prosecution at the criminal trial is heavier than upon the employer in showing that he acted reasonably. The evidence which it is permissible for the employer to rely upon is less restricted than that which is admissible in the criminal trial, but how far it is reasonable for the employer to rely upon evidence which has been ruled inadmissible in a criminal trial depends on the facts in each case (*Dhaliwal v British Airways Board* [1985] ICR 513). In *Close v Rhondda Cynon Taff Borough Council* [2008] IRLR 868, the EAT held that it was not outside the range of reasonable responses for the employer to choose not to conduct its own independent questioning of witnesses during its disciplinary process but instead to rely on statements given by the witnesses to the police, even though the statements had been given in a police investigation into different allegations against the employee. According to the EAT, the focus of the police investigation was irrelevant and there was no duty on the employer to allow cross examination of the witnesses.

52.10 Procedure for misconduct dismissals

Employers are no longer under a legal obligation to follow the statutory dismissal procedures but they are advised to adopt and use rigorous internal procedures instead. It is important to have a known disciplinary procedure. Employers are also advised to consult the ACAS Code of Practice. The statutory dismissal and disciplinary procedures, although repealed from 6 April 2009, may still affect some ongoing cases.

If an employee is suspected of misconduct, the employer should investigate the matter fully and give the employee an opportunity to explain himself.

An employer will often wish to suspend an employee during the course of an investigation, for example where it suspects that an employee has engaged in dishonest or fraudulent conduct. However, as Elias LJ has recently pointed out in *obiter* remarks, employers should not automatically suspend employees and assume that this action will be justified. A suspension which amounts to nothing more than a knee jerk reaction will be a breach of the implied term of mutual trust and confidence. Elias LJ further doubted the cogency of the widely expressed view that suspension is in the best interest of both the employer and the employee (*Crawford & Ors v Suffolk Mental Health Partnership NHR Trust* [2012] IRLR 402). However, in both *Graham v Secretary of State for Work and Pensions* [2012] IRLR 759 and *Tayeh v Barchester Healthcare Ltd* [2013] EWCA Civ 29 the Court of Appeal was of the view that a tribunal could take into account the fact that an employee had not been suspended promptly when assessing the reasonableness of the employer's decision to dismiss for misconduct. This places employers in a difficult position where, on the one hand, any suspension should not be a knee jerk reaction on their part but, on the other, the decision not to suspend might later be taken to indicate that they did not regard the offence as serious.

An employer has no right to suspend an employee without pay unless this is expressly provided for in the contract of employment. A suspension without pay in the absence of a contractual right to do so may be a serious breach of contract enabling the employee to resign and claim constructive dismissal (*Morrison v Amalgamated Transport and General Workers Union* [1989] IRLR 361). It is also important to make sure that the employee understands that the suspension is not a disciplinary sanction, and that the employer has not yet decided whether he committed the alleged acts.

The extent of the investigation will depend on the circumstances. In *Royal Society for the Protection of Birds v Croucher* [1984] ICR 604, the EAT held that in a case in which an employee admitted offences of dishonesty there was very little scope for the kind of investigation referred to in *Burchell* (see **54.9** above). The employer does not have to prove beyond reasonable doubt that the employee was guilty of the misconduct, but merely that he had acted reasonably in treating the misconduct as sufficient for dismissing the employee in the circumstances known to him at the time. Where, however, the facts are disputed, it is of great importance that employers take seriously their responsibility to conduct a fair investigation where the employee's ability to work in his/her chosen career could be blighted by a finding of misconduct (*Salford Royal NHS Foundation Trust v Roldan* [2010] ICR 1457). Serious allegations of criminal misbehaviour should also be investigated very carefully and conscientiously, albeit tribunals should remember that the investigation is being conducted by an employer and it is inappropriate to require the safeguards found in a criminal trial (*A v B* [2003] IRLR 405). The Court of Appeal applied the decisions in *Roldan* and *A v B* in *Crawford v Suffolk Mental Health Partnership NHS Trust* [2012] IRLR 402. Most recently, in *Tuner v East Midlands Trains Ltd* [2013] IRLR 107, the Court of Appeal again reiterated that when determining whether an employer has acted as the hypothetical reasonable employer would do, it will be relevant to have regard to the nature and consequences of the allegations as a reasonable employer should have regard to the gravity of those consequences when determining the nature and scope of the appropriate investigation. The Court of Appeal went on to hold that where an employee's rights under *ECHR, Art 8* are engaged, matters bearing on the culpability of the employee must be investigated with a full appreciation of the potentially adverse consequences to the employee and that the band of reasonable responses test allows for a heightened standard to be adopted where those consequences are particularly grave. In *Stuart v London City Airport* UKEAT/0273/12/BA (9 November 2012, unreported) (in which permission to appeal has been granted) the EAT rejected an argument that the "heightened scrutiny" test set out in *A v B* did not apply to a case where an employee was alleged to have dishonestly taken goods from premises without paying for them. The EAT considered that such an allegation was always serious and required careful investigation which includes gathering evidence which might potentially be viewed as exculpatory or consistent with the Claimant's explanation. The EAT overturned the Tribunal's decision on the basis that it had failed in a number of respects to investigate the Claimant's explanations or exculpatory information.

For certain professions, where internal disciplinary procedures are likely to lead to external statutory procedures, the standards of procedural fairness required for the internal disciplinary process may be higher than in the general case, in order to ensure that the employee's rights under *ECHR, Art 6* are respected. In *Kulkarni v Milton Keynes Hospital NHS Trust* [2010] ICR 101 the Court of Appeal held that a doctor facing allegations of sexual misconduct was entitled to legal representation during his internal disciplinary hearing. Likewise, in *R(G) v Governors of X School* [2010] 1 WLR 2218, which involved a teaching assistant at a primary school who was accused of sexual misconduct, the Court of Appeal held that he was entitled to legal representation at the school's disciplinary hearing, because *ECHR, Art 6* applied to an internal disciplinary process which was determinative of the employee's civil right to practise his profession. In *Mattu v University Hospitals of Coventry and Warwickshire NHS Trust* [2012] IRLR 661 the Court of Appeal again considered the impact of *Art 6* to disciplinary proceedings, concluding that the *NHS Trusts'* decision to dismiss an employee under his contract of employment did not determine his civil rights as defined in *Art 6* (see HUMAN RIGHTS (28.7(a)) for a more detailed discussion of the authorities in this area).

The circumstances known to the employer for these purposes are those known to the dismissing officer, and those known to other senior officers who are not party to the decision to dismiss will not be attributed to that office (*Orr v Milton Keynes Council* [2011] ICR 704 (Sedley LJ dissenting)), though the employee might argue that an investigation which failed to uncover those facts was unreasonable. It does not matter if the employer's view, if reasonable at the time, is subsequently found to be mistaken (*St Anne's Board Mill Co Ltd v Brien* [1973] ICR 444; *British Home Stores Ltd v Burchell* [1980] ICR 303n). Equally, if the employer did not have reasonable grounds to dismiss at the time, the dismissal will be considered to be unfair even if evidence subsequently comes to light which proves him right (*W Devis & Sons Ltd v Atkins* [1977] ICR 662). In such a case, however, the employee may be awarded little or no compensation (see UNFAIR DISMISSAL – III (53)). The reasonableness of the decision will be scrutinised at the time of the final decision to dismiss, namely, at the conclusion of any appeal hearing (*West Midland Co-operative Society Ltd v Tipton* [1986] ICR 192).

In *Salford Royal NHS Foundation Trust* [2010] ICR 1457, Elias LJ gave guidance, albeit *obiter*, about the approach an employer should take to allegations of misconduct where the evidence consists of diametrically conflicting accounts of an alleged incident with little other evidence to provide corroboration to either account. Employers are not obliged to believe one employee and disbelieve the other. It may be, for example, that the parties are both seeking to be truthful, but perceive events differently. Alternatively, in some cases the employer will be entitled to find that they are not satisfied that they can resolve the conflict of evidence and simply find the case not proved and give the employee the benefit of the doubt. This need not mean that they do not believe the complainant.

It is important to frame the disciplinary charge carefully in order to ensure that a misconduct dismissal is for a matter charged, which has been fully investigated and to which the employee has had a proper opportunity to respond (*Strouthos v London Underground Ltd* [2004] IRLR 636). Whilst in some cases it might be arguable that the employee knows the essence of the case against him, and the dismissal is accordingly fair, an employee is entitled to know the specific charge against him. For example, where money has gone missing, an employee is entitled to know whether the employer is alleging fraud or mere incompetence, as these are likely to lead to different reactions from the employee (*Celebi v Scolarest Compass Group UK & Ireland Ltd* (UKEAT/0032/10/LA) [2010] All ER (D) 136 (Sep), where additional matters came to light during the process, and allegations were added to the charge with the employee's consent). A further example of this principle is found in *Royal Mail Group Ltd v Lall* UKEAT/0228/12/ZT (15 October 2012, unreported) in which the employee was disbelieved as to his integrity without being given the opportunity to address the allegation.

An employer's disciplinary procedures should follow the principles of natural justice, although a breach of the rules of these principles does not automatically make a dismissal unfair (*Slater v Leicestershire Health Authority* [1989] IRLR 16). Each case will turn on its facts and, as with the extent of the investigation, what is required will depend upon the relevant circumstances, such as the resources of the employer and the nature of the allegation. In *Khanum v Mid-Glamorgan Area Health Authority* [1979] ICR 40, it was held that natural justice required that the employee should know the accusations made against her, that she should be given an opportunity to state her case and that the members of the management team and the appeals panel should act in good faith. Further, in *Bentley Engineering Co Ltd v Mistry* [1979] ICR 47, the EAT held that natural justice required not merely that a man should have a chance to state his own case but that he must know sufficiently what was being said against him so that he could put forward his own case properly. This principle was reaffirmed in *Louies v Coventry Hood and Seating Co Ltd* [1990] ICR 54: if heavy reliance is placed upon the statements of witnesses, the dismissal will almost always be unfair unless the employee has sight of the statements or is told exactly what is in them. However, in *Hussain v Elonex plc* [1999] IRLR 420, the Court of Appeal stressed that there is no hard and fast rule that in all cases an employee must be shown copies of witness statements obtained by an employer about the employee's conduct. Nor is there a rule obliging an employer to make witnesses available for cross examination by the employee (*Santamera v Express Cargo Forwarding* [2003] IRLR 273). It is a matter of what is fair and reasonable in each case; the gravity of the allegation and the consequences for the employee might allow a tribunal to find that an employer's refusal to allow the employee to question a witness was unreasonable (*TDG Chemical Ltd v Benton* (UKEAT/0166/10/DM) (10 September 2010, (unreported). For guidance in cases where an informant does not wish to be identified, see *Linfood Cash and Carry Ltd v Thomson* [1989] ICR 518 and *Asda Stores Ltd v Thompson (No 2)* [2004] IRLR 598. The EAT has held that unjustifiable delay in carrying out disciplinary proceedings can render unfair a dismissal which would otherwise have been held fair (*Royal Society for the Prevention of Cruelty to Animals v Cruden* [1986] ICR 205). If possible, the employer should avoid a situation where the same members of management act as witnesses or complainants and as judges (Slater, above, but the Court of Appeal recognised that avoidance of this might sometimes prove impractical, especially where the employer is a very small organisation).

Other points to bear in mind are: that the employee should be given reasonable advance warning of the hearing and that disciplinary action is under consideration; that the employee should be given the opportunity to call witnesses if appropriate; and that the decision to dismiss should be taken by those who conduct the hearing, and not by someone who had only received a report of the disciplinary hearing (this was held to be an essential requirement of fairness by the EAT in *Budgen & Co v Thomas* [1976] ICR 344 though see *Parker v Clifford Dunn Ltd* [1979] ICR 463 to the effect that that will not inevitably be the case). A failure to keep adequate notes of a disciplinary hearing may amount to a procedural defect (*Vauxhall Motors Ltd v Ghafoor* [1993] ICR 376). A clandestine recording of a disciplinary hearing may be admissible evidence during an unfair dismissal claim, as in *Chairman and Governors of Amwell View School v Dagherty* [2007] ICR 135, although the EAT held that those parts of the secret recording which contained the disciplinary panel's private deliberations were not admissible.

In *Bailey v BP Oil (Kent Refinery) Ltd* [1980] ICR 642, the Court of Appeal held that the failure by employers to comply with a disciplinary procedure agreement was a factor to be taken into account, but that the weight to be given to it depended upon the circumstances; see also *Stoker v Lancashire County Council* [1992] IRLR 75. Similarly, in *Westminster City Council v Cabaj* [1996] ICR 960, the Court of Appeal held that failure by an employer to follow its own contractually enforceable disciplinary procedure does not inevitably mean that the dismissal was unfair. In *Sarkar v West London Mental Health NHS Trust* [2010] IRLR 508 an employee's misconduct was initially dealt with under one procedure (under which an employee could receive, at most, a written warning) but it was later dealt with by a disciplinary panel when the more informal procedure broke down, and the employee was dismissed. The Court of Appeal held that the employer had not fettered its disciplinary options by using the first procedure, and was entitled to revise its approach to the misconduct following a detailed assessment of the evidence of the employee's conduct and its impact. However, the tribunal had been entitled to conclude that the use of the first procedure indicated a view on the employer's part that the misconduct alleged was relatively minor, and that it was inconsistent with this approach to later make a finding of gross misconduct based on the same matters.

Defects in the original procedure may be capable of being cured by a fair appeal, depending upon the seriousness of any allegations made against the employee, how bad the initial unfairness was and whether the appeal takes the form of a complete rehearing. The Court of Appeal has emphasised that there is no rule of law that earlier unfairness can be cured only by an appeal by way of a rehearing and not by way of a review, because the examination should be of the fairness of the disciplinary process as a whole. Each case will depend upon its own facts (*Taylor v OCS Group Ltd* [2006] ICR 1602)

Section 10 of the *Employment Relations Act 1999* gives an employee a right to be accompanied at a disciplinary hearing by a trade union official or another of the employer's workers. If the employee is denied this right, he may present a claim to the employment tribunal and may be awarded up to two weeks' pay (*ERA 1999, s 11*).

52.11 GROUNDS FOR DISMISSAL – REDUNDANCY

Redundancy is a potentially fair reason for dismissal. However, where the reason or the principal reason for the dismissal of an employee was that he was redundant (see REDUNDANCY – I (36)), the dismissal may be automatically unfair under *ERA 1996, s 105*. The dismissal will be automatically unfair if the circumstances constituting the redundancy applied equally to one or more employees in the same undertaking who held positions similar to that held by the dismissed employee and who have not been dismissed by the employer, and the reason for dismissed employee's selection was an automatically-unfair reason. The automatically unfair reasons for redundancy selection are in largely similar terms to the automatically unfair reasons for dismissal (see 52.3 above) and so are summarised in relatively brief fashion here:

(i)   the reason (or if more than one, the principal reason) for which the employee was selected was one of the reasons related to jury service specified in *ERA 1996, s 98B(1)*, provided that *s 98B(2)* does not apply;

(ii)   the reason (or, if more than one, the principal reason) for which he was selected was one of the health and safety-related reasons specified in *ERA 1996, s 100*;

(iii)   the reason (or, if more than one, the principal reason) for which he was selected was one of those related to shop/betting shop workers refusing to work Sundays set out in *ERA 1996, s 101*;

(iv)   the reason (or, if more than one, the principal reason) for which he was selected was one of those related to working time set out in *ERA 1996, s 101A*;

(v)   the reason (or, if more than one, the principal reason) for which he was selected was related to his role as a trustee of an occupational pension scheme, as specified in *ERA 1996, s 102(1)*;

(vi)   the reason (or, if more than one, the principal reason) for which he was selected related to his work as an employee representative (see 37.4 REDUNDANCY – II) as specified in *ERA 1996, s 103*;

(vii)   the reason (or, if more than one, the principal reason) for which he was selected was that he had made a protected disclosure, as specified in *ERA 1996, s 103A*;

(viii) the reason (or, if more than one, the principal reason) for which he was selected related to his assertion of a statutory right as specified in *ERA 1996, s 104(1)*;

(ix)   the reason (or, if more than one, the principal reason) for which he was selected was one of those relating to the national minimum wage set out in *ERA 1996, s 104A*;

(x)   the reason (or, if more than one, the principal reason) for which he was selected was one of those relating to tax credit specified in *ERA, s 104B*;

(xi)   the reason (or, if more than one, the principal reason) for which he was selected related to a flexible working request as specified in *ERA, s 104C*;

(xii)   the reason (or, if more than one, the principal reason) for which he was selected was one of those related to studying and training specified in *ERA, s 104E*;

(xiii) the reason (or, if more than one, the principal reason) for which he was selected was one of those relating to official industrial action mentioned in *Trade Union and Labour Relations (Consolidation) Act 1992 s 238A(2)*, and *s 238A(3), (4)* or *(5)* applies to the dismissal;

(xiv)   the reason (or, if more than one, the principal reason) for which he was selected was one related to his activities as a member of a special negotiating body as specified in *regulation 28(3)* or *(6)* of the *Transnational Information and Consultation of Employees Regulations 1999*;

(xv)   the reason (or, if more than one, the principal reason) for which he was selected was one related to his assertion of his rights as a part-time worker, as detailed in *reg 7(3)* of the *Part-time Workers (Prevention of Less Favourable Treatment) Regulations 2000*;

(xvi)   the reason (or, if more than, the principal reason) for which he was selected was one related to his assertion of his rights as a fixed-term employee as specified in *reg 6(3)* of the *Fixed-term Employees (Prevention of Less Favourable Treatment) Regulations 2002*;

(xvii) the reason (or, if more than, the principal reason) for which he was selected was one specified in the *European Public Limited-Liability Company Regulations 2004, reg 42(3)* or *(6)*;

(xviii) the reason (or, if more than one, the principal reason) for which he was selected related to his activities as an employee representative (see **49.18 TRANSFER OF UNDERTAKINGS**) as detailed in *Information and Consultation of Employees Regulations 2004, reg 30*;

(xix)   the reason (or, if more than one, the principal reason) for which he was selected was one specified in *paragraph 5(3)* or *(5)* of the *Schedule* to the *Occupational and Personal Pension Schemes (Consultation by Employers and Miscellaneous Amendment) Regulations 2006*;

(xx)   the reason (or, if more than one, the principal reason) for which the employee was selected was one specified in *para (3)* or *(6)* of *regulation 31* of the *European Cooperative Society (Involvement of Employees) Regulations*;

(xxi)   the reason (or, if more than one, the principal reason) for which the employee was selected was one specified in the *Companies (Cross-Border Mergers) Regulations 2007, reg 46(2)* or *47(2)*;

(xxii) the reason (or, if more than one, the principal reason) for which the employee was selected was one specified in *European Public Limited-Liability Company (Employee Involvement) (Great Britain) Regulations 2009, reg 29(3)* or *(6)*;

(xxiii) the reason (or, if more than one, the principal reason) for which the employee was selected related to a prohibited black list as specified in *ERA, s 104F(1)* and the condition in either 104F(1)(a) or (b) is met;

(xxiv) the reason (or, if more than one, the principal reason) for which the employee was selected was one specified in the *Agency Workers Regulations 2010, reg 17(3)*.

(xxv) the reason (or, if more than one, the principal reason) for which he or she was selected related to pregnancy, maternity leave etc within the meaning of *ERA 1996, s 99* and the *Maternity and Parental Leave etc Regulations 1999, reg 20*.

(xxvi) the reason (or, if more than one, the principal reason) for which the employee was selected for dismissal related to trade union membership or activities under the *Trade Union and Labour Relations (Consolidation) Act 1992, s 153*.

An employer should not, however, give preferential consideration to an employee in a redundancy selection process on the ground that he or she is a health and safety representative (*Smiths Industries Aerospace and Defence Systems v Rawlings* [1996] IRLR 656).

A redundancy dismissal which is not automatically unfair may nevertheless be unfair 'in all the circumstances' within the meaning of *ERA 1996, s 98(4)*. Whilst a tribunal will not investigate the commercial merits of an employer's decision that redundancies were required (*James W Cook & Co (Wivenhoe) Ltd (in liq) v Tipper* [1990] ICR 716, CA; *Campbell v Dunoon and Cowal Housing Association* [1993] IRLR 496), there are other ways in which a dismissal by reason of redundancy might be found to be unfair. The position was summarised by Lord Bridge in *Polkey v A E Dayton Services Ltd* [1988] ICR 142 at 162–163:

" . . . in the case of redundancy, the employer will normally not act reasonably unless he warns and consults any employees affected or their representative, adopts a fair basis on which to select for redundancy and takes such steps as may be reasonable to avoid or minimise redundancy by redeployment within his own organisation . . . It is quite a different matter if the tribunal is able to conclude that the employer himself, at the time of dismissal, acted reasonably in taking the view that, in the exceptional circumstances of the particular case, the procedural steps normally appropriate would have been futile, could not have altered the decision to dismiss and therefore could be dispensed with."

TULRCA 1992, s 188 (as amended by *TURERA 1993, s 34* and *SI 1995/2587*) imposes a duty on employers to consult appropriate representatives of the employees concerned. A failure to comply with that requirement will probably – although not necessarily – render the dismissal unfair (*Hough v Leyland DAF Ltd* [1991] ICR 696). In order to comply with the requirements of *s 188*, the employer must begin consultations before giving individual notices of dismissal (*National Union of Teachers v Avon County Council* [1978] ICR 626). See **37.2–37.5** REDUNDANCY – **II** for further details. Even where no trade union is recognised for bargaining purposes, in respect of dismissals taking effect on or after 1 March 1996, employers must (by virtue of *SI 1995/2587*) consult with employee representatives before deciding which employees should be made redundant, where at least 20 or more employees are proposed to be made redundant at one establishment within 90 days or less (see **37.2** et seq REDUNDANCY – **II**).

The EAT in *Williams v Compair Maxam Ltd* [1982] ICR 156 listed the principles which, in the experience of the two lay members, reasonable employers adopted when dismissing for redundancy employees who are represented by an independent trade union recognised by them. The EAT stressed that the principles would not stay unaltered forever, and that they are not principles of law, but standards of behaviour. However, the principles outlined in *Williams* have been adopted by employment tribunals and the EAT as standards by which to judge the fairness of dismissals for redundancy where a trade union is recognised by an employer.

(i) The employer will seek to give as much warning as possible of impending redundancies so as to enable the union and the employees who may be affected to take early steps to inform themselves of the relevant facts, consider possible alternative solutions and, if necessary, find alternative employment in the undertaking or elsewhere.

(ii)   The employer will consult the union as to the best means by which the desired management result can be achieved fairly and with as little hardship to the employees as possible. In particular, the employer will seek to agree with the union the criteria to be applied in selecting the employees to be made redundant. When a selection has been made, the employer will consider with the union whether the selection has been made in accordance with those criteria.

(iii)   Whether or not an agreement as to the criteria to be adopted has been agreed with the union, the employer will seek to establish criteria for selection which so far as possible do not depend solely upon the opinion of the person making the selection but can be objectively checked against such things as attendance record, efficiency at the job, experience, or length of service.

(iv)   The employer will seek to ensure that the selection is made fairly in accordance with these criteria and will consider any representations the union may make as to such selection.

(v)   The employer will seek to see whether instead of dismissing an employee he could offer him alternative employment.

The extent to which any one or more of these principles apply depends on the circumstances of the particular case, and an employer's failure to adopt any one or more of these practices will not necessarily lead to a finding of unfair dismissal (*Grundy (Teddington) Ltd v Plummer* [1983] ICR 367). Moreover, the principles set out in *Williams* should not be treated as if they were a statute or check list (*Rolls-Royce Motors Ltd v Dewhurst* [1985] ICR 869). In particular, it is now a common and accepted practice for employers to adopt a system of selection for redundancy which relies upon managerial assessment of employees' ability and performance as well as upon more purely objective criteria (see the EAT's recent summary of the authorities to this effect in *Mitchells of Lancaster v Tattersall* UKEAT/0605/11/SM (29 May 2012, unreported)). However, it remains the case that a simple subjective judgement by line managers about 'who should stay and who should go' is unlikely to be a fair method of selection (see, by way of example, the EAT's consideration of a "requirements of the business" criterion in *Watkins v Crouch (t/a Temple Bird Solicitors)* [2011] IRLR 382.

Where redundancy arises in consequence of a re-organisation and there are new roles to be filled, the employer's decision is likely to centre upon the assessment of the ability of the individual to perform in the new role. The *Williams* criteria are unlikely to be useful in such cases, as appointment to the new role is likely to involve something more akin to an interview than a traditional selection process. The tribunal remains entitled to consider how far the process was objective, but should recognise that the decision as to which candidate will perform best in the new role will involve a substantial element of judgment (*Morgan v Welsh Rugby Union* [2011] IRLR 376). Further, the information which a reasonable employer must have provided an employee in advance of such an interview may differ from what an employee would need to be told about a traditional scoring exercise (*Samsung Electronics (UK) Ltd v Monte-D'cruz* (UKEAT/0039/DM) (1 March 2012, unreported), though see also *Cumbria Partnership NHS Foundation Trust v Steel* UKEAT/0635/11/JOJ (17 May 2012, unreported) in which the EAT upheld the tribunal's decision that the employer had acted unfairly in requiring employees to meet a competency bar as part of its process of "slotting them" into other roles, albeit the EAT emphasised the significance of the employer's policies and past practice in its decisions).

When consulting, it is not enough for an employer to warn of impending redundancies and then to announce the result; the employer must consult and consider the employees' views properly and genuinely (*Rowell v Hubbard Group Services Ltd* [1995] IRLR 195). Consultation may be necessary at a number of separate stages: when the overall need for redundancies is being considered; when the *s 188* notice is issued (see **37.4 REDUNDANCY**

– II); when employees are being selected for redundancy; and upon the giving of notice or during the notice period (*Dyke v Hereford and Worcester County Council* [1989] ICR 800). Fair consultation will usually require the body consulted to be given a fair and proper opportunity to understand fully the matters about which it is being consulted, to express its views on those subjects, with the employer thereafter considering those views properly and genuinely (*R v British Coal Corporation ex p Price & Ors* [1994] IRLR 72, applied by the EAT in *Pinewood Repro Ltd v Page* [2011] ICR 508). For an example of a case where the time allowed for consultation was found to be insufficient see *Flintshire County Council v Moore* (UKEAT/0379/11/DA) (15 September 2011, unreported).

Where an employee has no representative, good industrial relations practice requires consultation with the employee before dismissing him as redundant, except in special circumstances (*Freud v Bentalls Ltd* [1983] ICR 77; *Ferguson v Prestwick Circuits Ltd* [1992] IRLR 266). Indeed, a tribunal may hold a redundancy dismissal to be unfair for lack of consultation with individual employees even where their union has been consulted (*Walls Meat Co Ltd v Selby* [1989] ICR 601; *Rolls-Royce Motor Cars Ltd v Price* [1993] IRLR 203), though a dismissal may be fair where there was consultation with a trade union, even if there was no consultation with the individual employees (*Mugford v Midland Bank plc* [1997] ICR 399). The fact that the employer is a small company does not remove the obligation to consult, although it may affect the nature or formality of the consultation process which it must undertake in order to have acted reasonably (*De Grasse v Stockwell Tools Ltd* [1992] IRLR 269). If a company is in dire financial straits and in desperate need of a purchaser, the normal requirement of consultation does not apply (*Warner v Adnet Ltd* [1998] ICR 1056). Such a situation will, however, be rare in practice. In *Mental Health Care (UK) Ltd v Biluan & Ors* UKEAT/0248/12/SM (28 February 2013, unreported) the EAT drew a distinction between collective consultation seen in cases where trade union or other representatives are involved and that held with individual employees. The EAT accepted that where the consultation is with individuals the scope for useful consultation on issues such as avoiding the redundancy situation altogether or the choice of selection criteria is likely to be reduced and the focus instead will be on the circumstances affecting the individual's case, in particular, though not necessarily only, the chances of alternative employment. This is a distinction of which Tribunals should take account.

Although individual consultation is not always necessary (whether it is required is a question of fact, see *Mugford* (above)), employees should have the opportunity to contest their selection, either themselves or through their trade union. This may involve showing employees the marks given to them in the selection process (*John Brown Engineering Ltd v Brown* [1997] IRLR 90). In *Davies v Farnborough College of Technology* [2008] IRLR 14 the EAT explained that an employee must be given sufficient information so that he may understand the dismissal and be placed in a position to challenge the accuracy of markings, correct them, and provide supplemental information; this may be something short of disclosing actual markings to the employee. What the employer must disclose in order to have acted within the range of reasonable responses will turn upon the facts of the case, with factors of particular relevance being what the employee asked for and whether he/she challenged the scores awarded to him/her (*Camelot Group Plc v Hogg* (UKEATS/0019/10/BI) (13 October 2011, unreported)).

However, the tribunal will not usually undertake a review of the marks employees received. It will usually be sufficient for the employer to show that he set up a good system of selection and that it was fairly administered. There will ordinarily be no need for the employer to justify all the assessment on which the selection was based. In general, if the employer sets up a system of selection which can reasonably be described as fair and applies it without any overt signs of conduct which mars its fairness, it will have satisfied the requirements of *ERA s 98(4)*. This does not, however, mean that a marking system renders the dismissal automatically fair. The tribunal should evaluate the fairness of the system, the criteria, and the methods of marking, but the system should not be subjected to an over-minute analysis

(*British Aerospace v Green* [1995] ICR 1006 and *Bascetta v Santander UK Plc* [2010] EWCA Civ 351). This point was recently confirmed in *Nicholls v Rockwell Automation Ltd* UKEAT/0540/11/SM (25 June 2012, unreported). The EAT held that whilst to some extent it might be permissible to look at the way scores were reached (in that case to see if the employee's challenge to the employer's motivation was made out), but the tribunal should not embark upon a detailed critique of individual items of scoring to determine if an employee's selection was reasonable. In that case, having found the system of selection to be reasonable, the Tribunal should not have gone on to examine in detail the actual scores awarded, nor should it have substituted its view of the score which should have been given to the employee for that awarded by the employer without assessing the reasonableness of the score.

That said, in cases of glaring inconsistency or bad faith, a finding of unfairness might be made (*Northgate HR Ltd v Mercy* [2008] ICR 410). Such a case was *Carclo Technical Plastics Ltd v Jeyanthikumar* (UKEAT/0129/10/CEA) (3 August 2010, unreported) where the EAT described the employer as having made a fundamental and obvious error in the application of the procedure. Equally, an employee might be able to show that the scoring criteria or system of selection were unreasonable in themselves (*Flintshire County Council v Moore* (UKEAT/0379/11/DA) (15 September 2011, unreported) and *Mental Health Care (UK) Ltd v Biluan & Ors* UKEAT/0248/12/SM (28 February 2013, unreported).

As with the scoring exercise, determining the pool from which those employees to be made redundant are selected is principally a matter for the employer and it will be *difficult* for an employee to challenge it when the employer has genuinely applied his mind to the question (*Taymech Limited v Ryan* (UKEAT/663/94) (15 November 1994, unreported), *Capita Hartshead Ltd v Byard* [2012] ICR 1256) where the EAT emphasised the italicised words above and stated the tribunal is entitled, if not obliged, to consider with care and scrutinise carefully the reasoning of the employer to determine if he has genuinely applied his mind to the issue of who should be in the pool for consideration for redundancy). The question for the Tribunal is whether the pool adopted by the employer was one which a reasonable employer could have adopted. However, where the employer fails to consider the applicable pool the employee will be able to argue that his dismissal is unfair. This sometimes occurs in cases where one job is redundant and the employer simply assumes that it will make the current holder of that position redundant, without considering placing other employees into a pool. In *Fulcrum Pharma (Europe) Ltd v Bonassera* (UKEAT/0198/10/DM) (22 October 2010, unreported), the EAT approved the tribunal's finding that the employer erred in automatically assuming that because an employee's role had to go, the pool should include that employee alone, without further consideration or consultation on the issue of the appropriate pool (see also *Mitchells of Lancaster v Tattersall* UKEAT/0605/11/SM (29 May 2012, unreported). In Fulcrum, the EAT also approved guidance given earlier by another division of the EAT in *Lionel Leventhal Ltd v North* (UKEAT/0265/04) (27 October 2004, unreported) on the factors which an employer should consider when deciding whether or not subordinate employees ought to be brought into the pool. These include: (i) whether or not there is a vacancy; (ii) how different the two jobs are; (iii) the difference in remuneration between them; (iv) the relative length of service of the two employees; and (v) the qualifications of the employee in danger of redundancy. However, the EAT in *Wrexham Golf Co Ltd v Ingham* UKEAT/0190/12/RN (10 July 2012, unreported) reiterated that there will be cases, of which that was one, where it was reasonable for the employer to focus upon a single employee without developing or even considering the development of a pool. Until case law provides further guidance on those circumstances in which that will be the case, however, it is suggested that it is sensible for the employer to give the pool careful consideration so that it can justify its position if challenged at a later date.

A dismissal of an employee may be considered unfair if no consideration is given to finding him another job within that company, or if the company is a member of a group, within that group (*Vokes Ltd v Bear* [1974] ICR 1; *Euroguard Ltd v Rycroft*, IDS Brief 498, p 2). The redundant employee should be offered an available vacancy even if it is at a lower salary or is of lower status than the post from which he is being made redundant (*Avon-mouth Construction Co Ltd v Shipway* [1979] IRLR 14). In some cases, it may be necessary to consider dismissing some other (perhaps less long-serving) employee to make way for the employee whose job has disappeared (*Thomas and Betts Manufacturing Ltd v Harding* [1980] IRLR 255). This is known as 'bumping'. However, the Court of Appeal in *Samels v University of Creative Arts* [2012] EWCA Civ 1152 suggested that it is not compulsory for an employer to consider whether he should bump another employee. It is permissible to take 'spent' convictions into account when considering whether a redundant employee is suitable for alternative positions (*Wood v Coverage Care Ltd* [1996] IRLR 264).

When an employee is interviewed for an alternative role, the tribunal remains entitled to consider how far the process was objective, but should recognise that the decision as to which candidate will perform best in the new role will involve a substantial element of judgment. There is no obligation to always use objective criteria (*Samsung Electronics (UK) Ltd v Mote-D'cruz* (UKEAT/0039/11/DM) (1 March 2012, unreported)). In the same case the EAT emphasised that terms used in such processes may appear to lawyers to be nebulous and vague, but might have a clearer meaning to managers who utilise them on a regular basis. The assessment tools used are, in the first instance, a matter for the employer. Nor, the EAT held, should a finding of unfair dismissal in such a case turn upon the minutiae of good interview practice.

The fairness of a dismissal for redundancy will be judged not simply at the date on which notice is given but also with regard to events up to the date on which it takes effect (*Stacey v Babcock Power Ltd* [1986] ICR 221; see also *Dyke*, above, and *White v South London Transport Ltd* [1998] ICR 293). Hence, if a suitable vacancy arises during the notice period it should be offered to the otherwise redundant employee.

In *Lloyd v Taylor Woodrow Construction* [1999] IRLR 782, the EAT held that, as with conduct and capability cases, a defect in a redundancy consultation process could be cured on appeal, provided that the appeal is a rehearing and not merely a review of the original decision. The Court of Appeal, however, has ruled that the appeal need not take the form of a rehearing (see *Taylor v OCS Group Ltd* above).

> 'If the employer can establish that had he taken reasonable steps to consult with the employee or find him other employment, he would still have been dismissed, an employment tribunal may find the dismissal to be unfair but award no compensation, or compensate only for the wages and benefits which would have been received while consultation was taking place. (See also **52.4** above; and **53.13** Unfair Dismissal – III.) The question to be asked in the exceptional case contemplated by *Polkey* (above) where consultation would be pointless is not whether the employer in fact made a conscious decision not to consult, but whether a reasonable employer could have decided not to consult in the light of the facts that were known at the time (*Duffy v Yeomans & Partners Ltd* [1993] IRLR 368; cf *Dick v Boots the Chemists Ltd* IDS Brief 451, p 12; see also *Heron v Citylink – Nottingham* [1993] IRLR 372).'

It is worth noting that the significance of *Polkey* was changed for a period by *EA 2002, s 34*, which introduced a new *s 98A(2)* into *ERA 1996*. This provision, however, was repealed in April 2009. *Section 98A(2)* provided that failure to follow a procedure in relation to the dismissal of an employee should not be regarded as, by itself, making the employer's action unreasonable if he showed that he would have decided to dismiss the employee if he had followed the procedure. The purpose of the subsection was to deter employees from bringing unfair dismissal claims if they were relying upon a technical breach of procedure by the employer, which had no effect on the outcome (see further *Kelly-Madden* above).

52.12 Dismissal procedure

From decided cases (see **52.11** above) the following guidelines emerge,:

(a)   consult with employee representatives;

(b)   consider possible alternatives to redundancies, eg short-time working, work sharing, other costs savings, etc;

(c)   if redundancy becomes necessary, in consultation with employee representatives, agree objective criteria for selection for redundancy;

(d)   apply the criteria objectively;

(e)   inform the employees affected at the earliest opportunity and give the employees an opportunity to contest the scores they are given;

(f)   investigate the possibilities of offering them alternative employment within the company or group, continuing the investigation until the employment has come to an end;

(g)   give them time off to seek employment;

(h)   pay all moneys due;

(i)   conduct an appeal; and

(j)   keep careful records and minutes of these steps.

Whilst the failure to follow the above will not necessarily render a dismissal unfair, they provide a useful starting point for an employer undertaking a redundancy exercise.

52.13 GROUNDS FOR DISMISSAL – CONTRAVENTION OF ANY ENACTMENT

If an employer dismisses an employee because the employee could not continue to work in the position which he held without contravention (either on his part or on that of his employer) of a duty or restriction imposed by or under an enactment, the reason for the dismissal falls within *ERA 1996, s 98(2)(d)*.

The fact that an employer genuinely but erroneously believes that he would be breaking the law by continuing to employ an employee does not make the reason for the dismissal of that employee a reason falling within *ERA 1996, s 98(2)(d)*, but it could be 'some other substantial reason' justifying the dismissal within *ERA 1996, s 98(1)(b)* (see **52.14** below) (*Bouchaala v Trusthouse Forte Hotels Ltd* [1980] ICR 721).

Procedure. In these cases employers should:

(a)   arrange a formal meeting at which the employee (ideally with an accompanying person) should be informed of the situation and invited (himself or through a representative) to express his views; and

(b)   in appropriate cases, find out if the company or an associated company has a suitable vacancy which the employee can be offered instead.

52.14 GROUNDS FOR DISMISSAL – 'SOME OTHER SUBSTANTIAL REASON'

These reasons need not be of the same type as those that are specified in the *Act*. If the reason for dismissal is not one of those set out in *ERA 1996, s 98(2)* (see **52.2** above), it may nevertheless be an acceptable reason if the employer can show that it was 'some other substantial reason of a kind such as to justify the dismissal of an employee holding the position which that employee held' (*ERA 1996, s 98(1)(b)*). Examples of such reasons are the following.

(a)   *Necessary re-organisation of the business* (*Hollister v National Farmers' Union* [1979] ICR 542; *Richmond Precision Engineering Ltd v Pearce* [1985] IRLR 179; *Catamaran Cruisers Ltd v Williams* [1994] IRLR 386; *Cobley v Forward Technology Industries plc* [2003] ICR 1050). This may also apply in cases where changes in terms and conditions have led the employee to claim constructive dismissal (*Genower v Ealing, Hammersmith and Hounslow Area Health Authority* [1980] IRLR 297). But note that the employee must be fairly considered for any new job created by the reorganisation (*Oakley v Labour Party* [1988] ICR 403). An employer does not need to establish that the change in terms of employment in such cases is essential in order to show that the reason falls within *ERA, s 98(1)(b)*. There is no principle of law that the survival of the business must depend upon the adoption of the terms (*Garside and Laycock Ltd v Booth* (UKEAT/0003/11/CEA) (27 May 2011, unreported)). If ostensibly the reason could justify the dismissal, it is a substantial reason and the enquiry moves to the fairness of the dismissal. It is at this later stage when the balancing exercise between the needs of the employer and the detriment to the employee falls to be considered (*Roberts v Acumed Ltd* (UKEAT/0466/09/DA) (25 November 2010, unreported). This balancing exercise requires a focus on the words "in accordance with equity" in *ERA 1996, s 98(4)*, as well as a careful scrutiny of the procedure followed (*Garside and Laycock v Booth* (above)). For an example of a successful dismissal followed by re-engagement on new terms, see *Slade & Ors v TNT (UK) Ltd* (UKEAT/0113/11/DA) (13 September 2011, unreported).

(b)   *Economic, technical or organisational reasons entailing changes in the workforce* of the transferor or the transferee before or after a relevant transfer within the meaning of the *Transfer of Undertakings (Protection of Employment) Regulations 2006 (SI 2006/246), reg 7(3)(b)* (see **50.26** TRANSFER OF UNDERTAKINGS).

(c)   Reasons of *necessary economies* such as in *Durrant and Cheshire v Clariston Clothing Co Ltd* [1974] IRLR 360 in which a tribunal held that it was reasonable for a company to dismiss two employees who were earning £25.87 per week each but for whom they had to provide transport costing the company £24 per week each. See also *Buckland v Bournemouth University Higher Education Corporation* [2010] IRLR 445, in which the Court of Appeal speculated about a case of constructive dismissal which could be characterised as a fair dismissal for some other substantial reason, where a major customer of the employer had defaulted on a payment with the consequence that the employer had an unexpected lack of funds and had, in repudiatory breach of contract, failed to pay the employee.

(d)   *Protection of the interest of the business* such as in *RS Components Ltd v Irwin* [1974] 1 All ER 41 in which the company was held to have fairly dismissed an employee for refusing to sign a reasonable restrictive covenant which was considered necessary. In considering the fairness of a dismissal for a refusal to accept new terms and conditions, it is material to consider what proportion of the workforce had accepted the change when the decision to dismiss was taken (*St John of God (Care Services) Ltd v Brooks* [1992] ICR 715). The Court of Appeal has now gone further in *Willow Oak Developments Ltd (t/a Windsor Recruitment) v Silverwood* [2006] EWCA Civ 660, [2007] IRLR 607 and held a dismissal lawful for refusal to sign restrictive covenants, where the new covenants were provided to the employee earlier on the same day and were unreasonably wide, on the basis that the employer's reliance on the refusal to sign was lawful because the reliance was on a reason of the 'kind' capable of justifying dismissal.

(e)   *An employee's personality* cannot, by itself, be a fair reason for dismissal, however, in certain circumstances the manifestations of that personality can give rise to 'some other substantial reason' for dismissal (*Perkin v St George's Healthcare NHS Trust* [2005] EWCA Civ 1174, [2005] IRLR 934).

(f)   *Expiry of a fixed-term contract* when it is shown that the contract was adopted for a genuine purpose and that fact was known to the employee, and it is also shown that the specific purpose for which the contract was adopted has ceased to be applicable (*North Yorkshire County Council v Fay* [1986] ICR 133. See also *Terry v East Sussex County Council* [1976] ICR 536 and *Tasneem v Dudley Group of Hospitals NHS Trust* (UKEAT/0232/10/CEA) (29 June 2011, unreported)). Note, however, the *Fixed-term Employees (Prevention of Less Favourable Treatment) Regulations 2002*.

(g)   The imposition of a *sentence of imprisonment* (*Kingston v British Railways Board* [1984] ICR 781). In some cases, this may have the effect of *frustrating* the contract, thus bringing it to an end without a dismissal (see **46.3** TERMINATION OF EMPLOYMENT).

(h)   *Dismissal of the replacement of an employee suspended on medical or maternity grounds (ERA 1996, s 106(3))*. Where an employer suspends an employee on medical grounds in compliance with a statutory requirement and engages another in his place, he should inform the replacement employee in writing when engaging him that his employment will be terminated at the end of the suspension of the original employee. If he dismisses the replacement employee in order to allow the original employee to resume work, the dismissal will be regarded as having been for a reason falling within *ERA 1996, s 98(1)(b)*.

(i)   *Dismissal of the replacement of an employee absent due to pregnancy or childbirth (ERA 1996, s 106(2))*. Where an employer engages an employee to replace another employee who is absent due to pregnancy and on engaging the replacement employee the employer informs him in writing that his employment will be terminated on the return to work of the pregnant employee, a dismissal of the replacement employee to give work to the original employee will be considered as a dismissal for a reason falling within *ERA 1996, s 98(1)(b)*.

(j)   *Relationship breakdown*. In *Ezsias v North Glamorgan NHS Trust* [2011] IRLR 550 the EAT accepted the employment tribunal's finding that the employer had dismissed the employee because of a breakdown in relationship, rather than the employee's conduct which led to that breakdown. The result was that the employer was not required to follow a contractual disciplinary hearing. However, the EAT noted that tribunals would be on the lookout for an employer using the rubric of "some other substantial reason" as a pretext to conceal the real reason for dismissal. This was recently reiterated by the Court of Appeal in *Leach v Office of Communications* [2012] ICR 1269 which stated that "breakdown of trust" is not a mantra that can be mouthed by an employer faced with difficulties in establishing a more conventional conduct reason for dismissal.

As usual, dismissal for such a reason will be fair if it was within the 'range of reasonable responses' (see **52.4** above) and a fair procedure was followed. In *Alboni v Ind Coope Retail Ltd* [1998] IRLR 131, the Court of Appeal held that an employment tribunal is bound to have regard to events between notice of dismissal and the date that dismissal took effect, both in determining the reason for dismissal and whether the employers acted reasonably in the circumstances in treating it as a sufficient reason for dismissal.

When breakdown of trust and confidence is given as the reason for the dismissal, what is the scope of the tribunal's examination of the facts which resulted in that position having been reached? This was considered by the EAT in *Governing Body of Tubbenden Primary School v Sylvester* UKEAT/0527/11/RN (25 April 2012, unreported). The EAT held that where, as in that case, the reason was essentially a consequence of conduct, it made sense for the tribunal to have regard to the immediate history leading up to the dismissal when assessing reasonableness. The EAT made it clear that it was not holding that in every case in which there is a dismissal because of a breakdown of trust and confidence the tribunal must have regard to how that situation came about. Tribunals are, however, entitled to do so in an appropriate case, of which that was an example.

The fact that a client which procures the dismissal of an employee may have acted unfairly does not mean the dismissal is unfair (*Henderson v Connect (South Tyneside) Ltd* [2010] IRLR 468). If the employer has done everything he reasonably can to avoid or mitigate the injustice brought about by the stance of the client, most obviously by trying to get the client to change his mind and, if that is impossible, by trying to find alternative work for the employee, but has failed, the eventual dismissal will be fair. The employer does, however, need to take into account the injustice and take the steps which it can to remedy it. See *Dobie v Burns International Security Services (UK) Ltd* [1984] ICR 812 for a discussion of factors to be considered when assessing the question of injustice for these purposes. *Bancroft v Interserve (Facilities Management) Ltd* UKEAT/0329/12/KN (13 December 2012, unreported) is a recent example of such a case. The employee in that case was dismissed because of third party pressure from a client. The EAT applied Henderson and found that the tribunal had failed to grapple properly with the question of whether or not the employer had done everything it could to mitigate the injustice caused by the third party's request. The EAT also raised an interesting question as to whether the employer was required to have taken steps earlier in the employment history to seek to remedy a problem before it became an insuperable problem leading to dismissal at the behest of the client, but did not find it necessary to resolve the issue in its decision.

In *Jefferson (Commercial) LLP v Westgate* UKEAT/0128/12/SM (19 July 2012, unreported) the EAT considered the question of procedural fairness in the context of an SOSR dismissal. In that case both the employer and employee were found to have lost trust and confidence in each other, the employee having stated that he did not intend to return to work. The EAT overturned the tribunal's finding that the resulting dismissal was unfair because of a failure on the employer's part to hold a meeting. The EAT held that whilst the ACAS Code might extend beyond pure misconduct and poor performance scenarios, it had little to say in the present context of an irretrievable breakdown, where a further meeting would not have achieved anything. The EAT reiterated that in every case it is necessary for the tribunal to consider *ERA, s 98(4)* and apply it sensibly to the facts of the case.

52.15 DISMISSAL FOLLOWING AN INTERNAL APPEAL

If an employee uses an internal appeal procedure to challenge a decision to dismiss him, and his appeal is rejected, he will be regarded as having been dismissed from the date of his original dismissal, unless his contract provides otherwise (see, eg *J Sainsbury Ltd v Savage* [1981] ICR 1, approved in *West Midlands Co-operative Society Ltd v Tipton* [1986] ICR 192).

In *Tipton*, the House of Lords decided that the fairness of a dismissal is judged at the time of the final decision to dismiss, which, if there is an internal appeal, will be at the conclusion of such an appeal. Lord Bridge said at 204D:

'A dismissal is unfair if the employer unreasonably treats his real reasons as a sufficient reason to dismiss the employee, either when he makes his original decision to dismiss, or when he maintains that decision at the conclusion of an internal appeal.'

In other words, facts and matters that come to light during the appeal hearing, whether in favour of the employee or against him, ought to be taken into account (see 52.4 above for a detailed discussion about the role of the appeal).

52.16 PRESSURE ON AN EMPLOYER TO DISMISS UNFAIRLY

In determining the reason for a dismissal, or whether it was fair in the circumstances, no account is taken of any pressure which by calling, organising, procuring or financing a strike or other industrial action, or threatening to do so, was exercised on the employer to dismiss the employee. Any question relating to dismissal will be determined as if no such pressure had been exercised (*ERA 1996, s 107*).

However, a trade union or an individual who induced the employer to dismiss an employee may, in certain circumstances, be joined in the proceedings and be ordered to pay all or part of any compensation awarded for unfair dismissal (*TULRCA 1992, s 160*). (See **53.17** UNFAIR DISMISSAL – III.)

53   Unfair Dismissal – III: Remedies

53.1   When an employment tribunal finds that a complaint of unfair dismissal is well-founded, it may make an order for the reinstatement or re-engagement of the complainant, or an order for compensation. This chapter deals with the remedies for unfair dismissal and the settlement of claims, as follows.

—   Reinstatement (see **53.2** below) and re-engagement (see **53.3** below) and related rules (see **53.4**, **53.5** below).

—   Awards of compensation (see **53.6**–**53.16** below), comprising the following:

•   Basic award (see **53.7**–**53.9** below).

•   Compensatory award (see **53.10**–**53.13** below).

•   Additional award in case of non-compliance with order for reinstatement or re-engagement (except union-related, health and safety, pension scheme trustee and employee representative cases) (see **53.14** below).

•   Maximum awards (see **53.16** below).

•   Union-related, health and safety, pension scheme trustees and employee representative dismissals – special award (see **53.16**–**53.18** below) and reduction of total award (see **53.19** below).

—   Joinder of parties (see **53.17** below).

—   Interim relief (see **53.18** below).

—   Settlement (see **53.19** below).

For the enforcement of, and interest upon, tribunal awards, see **18.66** and **18.67** EMPLOYMENT TRIBUNALS – II.

In practice, a successful complainant will in most cases receive an award of compensation which is made up of a basic award and a compensatory award. Orders for reinstatement and re-engagement are rare. Other payments are restricted to special circumstances as indicated in the relevant paragraphs.

The tribunal's first step on finding a dismissal to be unfair should be to explain to the employee the possibility of an order for reinstatement or re-engagement, and to ask him whether he wishes such an order to be made (*ERA 1996, s 112(1)*). This question should be asked even if the employee has indicated his preferred remedy in his originating application. Although the tribunal's failure to ask the claimant whether he wishes to be reinstated or re-engaged does not render its decision on remedies a nullity, at least where the claimant was legally represented (*Cowley v Manson Timber Ltd* [1995] ICR 367), an appeal tribunal should be very ready to remit a case for further consideration of remedy in these circumstances (*Constantine v McGregor Cory Ltd* [2000] ICR 938).

Even where an employer has offered to pay the maximum possible award of compensation, but has not admitted that the dismissal was unfair, the employee is entitled to proceed with his complaint (*Telephone Information Services Ltd v Wilkinson* [1991] IRLR 148; see also *NRG Victory Reinsurance Ltd v Alexander* [1992] ICR 675).

53.2   REINSTATEMENT

An order for reinstatement is defined as *an order that the employer shall treat the complainant in all respects as if he had not been dismissed.* In deciding whether to make such an order, the tribunal must consider:

(a)   whether the complainant wishes to be reinstated;

(b)   whether it is practicable for an employer to comply with an order for reinstatement; and

(c)   (in a case where the complainant wholly or partially caused or contributed to the dismissal) whether it would be just to order his reinstatement.

(*ERA 1996, s 116(1)*.)

In deciding whether to make an order for reinstatement, the tribunal will consider the effect that such an order would have on the respondent's business. If, as in *Coleman and Stephenson v Magnet Joinery Ltd* [1974] ICR 25, such an order would inevitably lead to industrial unrest, it should not be made. Nor should it be considered practicable where it would lead to a redundancy situation or to significant overmanning (*Cold Drawn Tubes Ltd v Middleton* [1992] ICR 318; see also *Port of London Authority v Payne* [1994] ICR 555). A finding on the practicality or otherwise of ordering re-employment is one which is obviously within the tribunal's exclusive territory as an 'industrial jury' and an appeal against such a finding on grounds of perversity alone was described as 'virtually impossible' in *Clancy v Cannock Chase Technical College* [2001] IRLR 331. If the tribunal orders reinstatement, it must specify:

(i)   any amount payable by the employer in respect of any benefit which the complainant might reasonably be expected to have received but for the dismissal, including arrears of pay, for the period between the date of termination of employment and the date of reinstatement;

(ii)   any rights and privileges, including seniority and pension rights, which must be restored to the employee; and

(iii)   the date by which the order must be complied with.

(*ERA 1996, s 114(1)*.)

Moreover, if the complainant would have benefited from an improvement in his terms and conditions of employment had he not been dismissed, the order for reinstatement will require him to be treated as if he had benefited from that improvement from the date on which he would have done so had he not been dismissed. Thus, if an order for reinstatement is made, the claimant must be restored to his original job and receive back pay and benefits from the date of his dismissal (*ERA 1996, s 114(3)*).

Where an employee's appeal against dismissal is successful and he is reinstated, he cannot pursue any claim of unfair dismissal which he has already presented (*Roberts v West Coast Trains Ltd* [2004] EWCA Civ 900, [2004] IRLR 788).

Where there is a breakdown in trust and confidence, the remedy of reinstatement of re-engagement has very limited scope and will only be practicable in the rarest of cases. In *Wood Group Heavy Industrial Turbines Ltd v Crossan* [1998] IRLR 680, the Scottish EAT overturned an order for re-engagement made by a tribunal in a case in which the employee had been unfairly dismissed for dealing in drugs in the workplace and the employer genuinely believed in the guilt of the employee.

53.3 RE-ENGAGEMENT

If an employment tribunal decides not to order reinstatement, it must go on to consider re-engagement (*ERA 1996, s 116(2)*). An order for re-engagement is defined as *an order that the complainant be engaged by the employer*, or by a successor of the employer or by an associated employer, *in employment comparable to that from which he was dismissed or other suitable employment* (ie not in the same job) (*ERA 1996, s 115(1)*). For associated employers, see **6.9**(a) CONTINUOUS EMPLOYMENT. 'Successor' is defined by *ERA 1996, s 235(1)*.

In deciding whether to order re-engagement, the tribunal will take into consideration the same factors as for reinstatement above. The tribunal must specify the terms on which re-engagement will take place and, unless it considers that the complainant contributed to the dismissal, the terms of the re-engagement must be, as far as is reasonably practicable, as favourable as if reinstatement had been ordered (*ERA 1996, s 116(4)*).

In particular, the tribunal will specify:

(a)   the identity of the employer;

(b)   the nature of the employment;

(c)   the remuneration for the employment;

(d)   any amount payable by the employer in respect of any benefit which the complainant might reasonably be expected to have received but for the dismissal, including arrears of pay, for the period between the date of termination of employment and the date of re-engagement;

(e)   any rights and privileges including seniority and pension rights which must be restored; and

(f)   the date by which the order must be complied with.

(*ERA 1996, s 115(2)*.)

The tribunal will not discharge its statutory obligations if it simply orders re-engagement on terms to be agreed between the parties: *Pirelli General Cable Works Ltd v Murray* [1979] IRLR 190. An employment tribunal may not, however, order re-engagement on terms substantially more favourable than the terms of the former job (*Rank Xerox (UK) Ltd v Stryczek* [1995] IRLR 568). In *Stryczek*, the EAT added that it was generally inadvisable for the employment tribunal to order re-engagement to a specific job, as distinct from identifying the nature of the proposed employment.

53.4   GENERAL RULES ON REINSTATEMENT AND RE-ENGAGEMENT

The EAT's decision in *King v Royal Bank of Canada (Europe) Ltd* [2012] IRLR 280 emphasises the importance of tribunals complying with *ERA 1996, s 112(2)* and not overlooking the question of reinstatement or re-engagement as it proceeds to assess compensation.

For the purpose of deciding whether it is practicable to make an order for reinstatement or re-engagement, the tribunal will not take into account the fact that the employer has engaged a permanent replacement for the dismissed employee unless he can show *either* that it was not practicable for him to arrange for the dismissed employee's work to be done without engaging a permanent replacement, *or* that he engaged the replacement after the lapse of a reasonable period of time, without having heard from the dismissed employee that he wished to be reinstated or re-engaged, and that when the employer engaged the replacement it was no longer reasonable for him to arrange for the dismissed employee's work to be done except by a permanent replacement (*ERA 1996, s 116(5), (6)*).

Where the employee has indicated at least seven days before the hearing of his complaint of unfair dismissal that he will seek such an order, the employer must come ready with evidence as to the availability of the old job or comparable or suitable employment, or else bear the costs of any adjournment in the absence of a special reason for the failure (*Employment Tribunals (Constitution and Rules of Procedure) Regulations 2004 (SI 2004/1861), rule 39*).

53.4 Unfair Dismissal – III: Remedies

The continuity of employment of the employee is preserved, and any week falling between the effective date of termination and his re-employment counts towards his period of continuous employment (*ERA 1996, s 219; Employment Protection (Continuity of Employment) Regulations 1996 (SI 1996/3147)*). The *Regulations* deal not only with cases where the tribunal orders reinstatement or re-engagement, but also where that is part of an agreed settlement (see **17.26 EMPLOYMENT TRIBUNALS – I**).

In calculating the amount payable on account of arrears of pay and benefits, the tribunal will take into account, so as to reduce the employer's liability, any sums received by the complainant in respect of the period between the date of termination of employment and the date of reinstatement or re-engagement by way of:

(a)   wages in lieu of notice or *ex gratia* payments paid by the employer;

(b)   remuneration paid in respect of employment with another employer;

and such other benefits as the tribunal thinks appropriate in the circumstances (*ERA 1996, ss 114(4), 115(3)*). It is not permissible to reduce the award of arrears on the ground of delay in asserting the employee's rights in relation to re-engagement (*City and Hackney Health Authority v Crisp* [1990] ICR 95).

If an order for reinstatement or re-engagement is made but the terms of the order are not fully complied with, the tribunal will make an award of compensation of such an amount as it thinks fit having regard to the loss sustained by the complainant as a result of the employer's failure to comply with the particular terms in question (*ERA 1996, s 117(1), (2)*). This is subject to the same statutory maximum as the compensatory award, save that the usual maximum may be exceeded to the extent necessary to enable the award fully to reflect any sums which ought to have been paid pursuant to the original order (*ERA 1996, s 124(3)*; and see **53.10** below). A purported reinstatement which is on much inferior terms will be treated as a refusal to reinstate at all, so that additional compensation may be awarded in accordance with *ERA, s 117(3), (4)* (see **53.5** below) (*Artisan Press Ltd v Srawley and Parker* [1986] IRLR 126).

53.5 REFUSAL TO REINSTATE OR RE-ENGAGE

If an order for reinstatement or re-engagement is made but the employer refuses to comply with it, the tribunal will award the complainant additional compensation over and above the basic and compensatory awards (see **53.15** below), unless the employer can satisfy the tribunal that it was not practicable to comply with the order (*ERA 1996, s 117(3), (4)*). Although the tribunal should carefully scrutinise the reasons advanced by the employer, it should give due weight to the commercial judgment of the employer unless the employer was to be disbelieved. The tribunal should not set the standard of proof too high, since the test is practicability, not possibility (*Port of London Authority v Payne* [1994] ICR 555).

For the purpose of deciding whether it was practicable for the employer to comply with the order, the tribunal will not take into account the fact that he has engaged a permanent replacement unless the employer can show that it was not practicable for the dismissed employee's work to be done without engaging a permanent replacement (*ERA 1996, s 117(7)*).

The employee's only remedy for the employer's failure to reinstate or to re-engage in breach of an order to do so is to obtain compensation under *s 117(3)*, comprising a compensatory, basic and additional award (see **53.7–53.15** below). The calculation under *s 117(3)* must have regard to the loss sustained by the employee and the tribunal can have regard to the amount of lost benefit even in the period between dismissal and the date set for reinstatement (*Awotona v South Tyneside Healthcare NHS Trust* [2005] EWCA Civ 217, [2005] ICR 958).

The employee cannot ask for a renewed order that he be reinstated or re-engaged (*Mabirizi v National Hospital for Nervous Diseases* [1990] ICR 281, EAT). However, in awarding the additional compensation, the tribunal will be able to reflect any amounts which should have been paid to the employee under the reinstatement or re-engagement order (see *Selfridges Ltd v Malik* [1998] ICR 268 and **53.10** below). The employer will not be permitted to obtain a financial advantage through non-compliance with an order for reinstatement. The statutory cap on compensation for unfair dismissal may be disapplied, if the amount of back pay due to an employee exceeds that cap and the employer has refused to comply with an order for reinstatement (*Parry v National Westminster Bank plc* [2004] EWCA Civ 1563, [2005] IRLR 193).

If the employer reinstates or re-engages an employee following an order, but the terms of the order are not fully complied with, then, subject to the upper limit on compensatory awards (see **53.14** below), the employee will be awarded compensation of such amount as the tribunal thinks fit having regard to the loss sustained by the complainant in consequence of the failure to comply fully with the terms of the order (*ERA 1996, s 117(2)*).

In practice, the employee rarely desires reinstatement or re-engagement and, even if he does, it is rarely ordered. If no such order is made, the amount of compensation will be calculated as set out below.

On the other hand, the employee's duty to mitigate encompasses reasonable acceptance of an offer of reinstatement or re-engagement (*Wilding v British Telecommunications plc* [2002] EWCA Civ 349, [2002] IRLR 524).

53.6   COMPENSATION

When a tribunal makes an award of compensation for unfair dismissal, the award must consist of a *basic award* and a *compensatory award* (*ERA 1996, s 118(1)*). These awards are the most common and are often the only categories of award. They are considered first (see **53.7–53.13** below). There are statutory maxima for nearly all the awards and these are set out for reference in **53.14** below.

Some awards are made only in certain circumstances: these are the 'additional award' where there has been non-compliance with an order for reinstatement or re-engagement (see **53.15** below) and, in similar circumstances for union-related dismissals, health and safety-related dismissals, pension scheme trustee dismissals and employee representative dismissals only, the 'special award' (see **53.16–53.18** below).

Recoupment provisions. Where the claimant has received statutory benefits, the respondent will be ordered to pay part of the compensation awarded not to the claimant but to the authority which paid the benefit, so that it recovers the money paid. This procedure, known as 'recoupment', is initiated by the service on the respondent of a 'recoupment notice' issued pursuant to the *Employment Protection (Recoupment of Jobseeker's Allowance and Income Support) Regulations 1996 (SI 1996/2349)*. It does not apply where a sum is paid by way of settlement of a dispute, before or after a finding of unfair dismissal is made.

A recoupment order will be made only in respect of that period before the hearing for which the tribunal concludes that the claimant has suffered loss. So, where the hearing took place ten months after dismissal, but compensation for loss of earnings was restricted to six months, recoupment should be ordered only in respect of six months' benefits (*Homan v A1 Bacon Co Ltd* [1996] ICR 721).

53.7 BASIC AWARD

Amount

The amount of the basic award will, in most cases, be the same as that of a statutory redundancy payment (see REDUNDANCY – I (36) and the ready reckoner at the end of that chapter.

The maximum amount of a week's pay for the purpose of the calculation is £450 (for dismissals taking place on or after 1st February 2013, see *ERA 1996, s 227(1)* and *Employment Rights (Increase of Limits) Order 2012 (SI 2012/3007)*) and the maximum number of years to be taken into account is 20 (*ERA 1996, s 119(3)*). A week's pay is calculated in accordance with *ERA 1996, ss 221–229* and is based on gross pay. The *Employment Relations Act 1999, s 34* provides that the maximum amount of a week's pay will be revised annually and linked to the retail prices index (see a week's pay). Subject to the exceptions set out below, the amount of the basic award is calculated by reference to the period, ending with the effective date of termination, during which the employee was continuously employed, by starting at the end of that period and reckoning backwards the number of complete years of employment falling within that period and allowing:

(a)   one and a half week's pay for each year of employment in which the employee was not below the age of 41;

(b)   one week's pay for each year of employment not falling within (*a*) in which the employee was not below the age of 22; and

(c)   half a week's pay for each such year of employment not falling within either (*a*) or (*b*).

(*ERA 1996, s 119(2).*)

Where an employer is obliged but fails to give the statutory minimum period of notice, the effective date of termination for the purposes of calculating the basic award is taken as that upon which the notice would have expired had it been given (*ERA 1996, s 92(7)*). Similarly, if the employee is constructively dismissed, and the employer has not given notice, the effective date of termination for the purposes of calculating the basic award is taken as that upon which the statutory minimum period of notice would have expired had it been given by the employer (*ERA 1996, s 97(4)*).

Where an employee is unfairly dismissed both by the transferor and then (after being re-engaged) again by the transferee of a business, the transferee may be liable to pay two basic awards because of the provisions of the *Transfer of Undertakings (Protection of Employment) Regulations 2006 (Fenton v Stablegold Ltd (t/a Chiswick Court Hotel)* [1986] ICR 236) (see also TRANSFER OF UNDERTAKINGS (50)).

53.8 Exceptions

The amount of the basic award is *two weeks' pay* where the tribunal finds that the reason or the principal reason for the dismissal of the employee was that he was redundant and that:

(a)   he unreasonably refused or left suitable alternative employment (contrary to *ERA 1996, s 141)*; or

(b)   his employment was renewed or he was re-engaged and he was therefore not considered dismissed under *ERA 1996, s 138(1)*.

(*ERA 1996, s 121.*)

The above provision has the curious effect that an employee is entitled to a basic award of compensation notwithstanding the fact that he is not considered as dismissed for the purposes of claiming a redundancy payment (see **37.6** REDUNDANCY – I).

Where a dismissal is to be regarded as unfair by virtue of:

(i)   *TULRCA 1992, s 152 or 153* (ie for a 'union-related' reason); or

(ii)   *ERA 1996, s 100(1)(a)* or *(b)* (health and safety activities as a representative, committee member or designated employee; note that this does not apply to all the circumstances in which a health and safety dismissal is automatically unfair); or

(iii)   *ERA 1996, s 101A(1)(d)* (activities as a workforce representative in a 'working time' case; note that this does not apply to all the circumstances in which a 'working time' dismissal is automatically unfair); or

(iv)   *ERA 1996, s 102(1)* (activities as a pension scheme trustee); or

(v)   *ERA 1996, s 103* (activities as an employee representative),

then the amount of any basic award (before any reduction) will be not less than £5,500 (TULRCA 1992, s 156(1); ERA 1996, s 120(1)).

The provisions in *s 120(1A)* and *(1B)*, introduced by *EA 2002, s 34(6)* which provided for an increase to the basic award in certain cases of unfair retirement dismissal were repealed, subject to transitional provisions, with effect from 6th April 2011 by *Employment Equality (Repeal of Retirement Age Provisions) Regulations (SI 2011/1069)*.

53.9   Reduction of basic award

Where the tribunal considers that any conduct of the complainant before the dismissal (or, where the dismissal was with notice, before the notice was given) was such that it would be just and equitable to reduce or further reduce the amount of the basic award to any extent, the tribunal will so reduce the award (*ERA 1996, s 122(2); TULRCA 1992, s 156(2)*). See also **53.13** below. However, a basic award can never be reduced on the basis of a failure to mitigate (*Lock v Connell Estate Agents* [1994] IRLR 444).

The amount of the basic award will not be reduced by virtue of the above provisions where the reason or principal reason for the dismissal was that the employee was redundant, unless the dismissal is to be regarded as unfair (*a*) by virtue of *TULRCA 1992, s 153* (selection for redundancy for a 'union-related' reason), or (*b*) because the reason for selecting the employee for dismissal was one of those specified in *ERA 1996, s 100(1)(a)* or *(b)*, *101A(1)(d)*, *102(1)* or *103* (see (ii)–(v) in **53.8** above). In that event, the reduction will apply only to so much of the basic award as is payable because of *TULRCA 1992, s 156(1)* or *ERA 1996, s 120* (see **53.8** above) (*ERA 1996, s 122(3); TULRCA 1992, s 156(2)*).

Where the tribunal finds that the complainant has unreasonably refused an offer by the employer which, if accepted, would have the effect of reinstating the complainant in his employment in all respects as if he had not been dismissed, the tribunal will reduce or further reduce the amount of the basic award to such extent as it considers just and equitable having regard to that finding (*ERA 1996, s 122(1)*).

The basic award may also be reduced where the employee has been awarded any amount in respect of the dismissal under a designated dismissal procedures agreement, to such extent as the tribunal considers it just and equitable having regard to that award (*ERA 1996, s 122(3A)* inserted by the *Employment Rights (Dispute Resolution) Act 1998, s 15, Sch 1, para 22*).

The amount of the basic award will be reduced or, as the case may be, further reduced, by the amount of any redundancy payment awarded by the tribunal in respect of the same dismissal or of any payment made by the employer to the employee on the ground that the dismissal was by reason of redundancy, whether in pursuance of statutory provisions or otherwise (*ERA 1996, s 122(4)*). No reduction of the basic award will be made, however, when the employer makes a payment in respect of redundancy but, objectively viewed, the employee was not redundant (*Boorman v Allmakes Ltd* [1995] IRLR 553).

Note that, where an employee had received an *ex gratia* payment from his former employers which included his statutory entitlement and which was sufficient to cover any basic or compensatory award, the EAT held that an employment tribunal was not obliged to make a basic award (*Chelsea Football Club and Athletic Co Ltd v Heath* [1981] ICR 323; cf *Barnsley Metropolitan Borough Council v Prest* [1996] ICR 85).

See also **53.14** below for reduction in union-related cases.

53.10 COMPENSATORY AWARD

The compensation recoverable on a complaint of unfair dismissal increased dramatically in 1999, but, in the current job market, the maximum award is often criticised as being unrealistically low. There are some calls to increase or even remove the cap, though such calls have certainly fallen on deaf ears in the present government which plans to implement a cap on the compensatory award of 12 months' pay (through the mechanism in clause 15 of the Enterprise and Regulatory Reform Bill). It is presently expected that the cap will come into force some time in Summer 2013. It appears that the intention is for a successful complainant to be entitled to the lower figure of either 12 months' pay or the numerical capped figure set out below.

For dismissals before 25 October 1999, the maximum amount of the compensatory award was £12,000. With effect from 25 October 1999, the maximum amount of the compensatory award was increased to £50,000, and was abolished altogether in a small number of cases (*Employment Relations Act 1999, ss 34(4) and 37(1); SI 1992/2830*). For dismissals on or after 1 February 2013, the maximum compensatory award has again increased from £72,300 to £74,200 (*SI 2012/3007*). There is no maximum compensatory award in health and safety cases (*ERA 1996, s 100*), protected disclosure cases (*ERA 1996, s 103A*), selection for redundancy on health and safety grounds (*ERA 1996, s 105(3)*), and selection for redundancy on protected disclosure grounds (*ERA 1996, s 105(6A)*). In the case of a refusal to reinstate or re-engage (see **53.5** above), the tribunal may exceed the normal maximum to the extent necessary fully to reflect the sums which would have been payable under its original order (*ERA 1996, s 124(4)*).

The application of the statutory limit is the last step in the calculation, applied after assessing the amount of loss and after taking into account any payments made by the respondent to the claimant and after any increase or reduction required by any statute or rule of law (*ERA 1996, s 124(5)*). For example, if a claimant's loss was assessed at £90,000 after making an adjustment under the *Employment Act 2002*, and the tribunal found that he was 50% to blame for the dismissal, he would be awarded £45,000 and not 50% of the statutory maximum (*Walter Braund (London) Ltd v Murray* [1991] ICR 327). Similarly, an employment tribunal must first deduct an *ex gratia* payment and then apply the statutory maximum (*McCarthy v British Insulated Callenders Cables plc* [1985] IRLR 94).

The order in which deductions should be made is further considered at **53.13** below.

For the relationship between compensation for unfair and wrongful dismissal, see **56.33** WRONGFUL DISMISSAL.

53.11 Amount

The amount of compensation is such amount as the tribunal considers just and equitable in all the circumstances, having regard to the loss sustained by the complainant in consequence of the dismissal insofar as that loss is attributable to action taken by the employer (*ERA 1996, s 123(1)*).

The loss shall be taken to include:

(a)   any expenses reasonably incurred by the complainant in consequence of the dismissal; and

(b)   loss of any benefit save for the contingent right to a redundancy payment which he might reasonably be expected to have had but for the dismissal.

(ERA 1996, s 123(2), (3).)

53.12 Assessment of compensatory award

Since the decision in *Norton Tool Co Ltd v Tewson* [1972] ICR 501, the tribunal has a duty to show how compensation is made up. The most common heads of compensation are those set out below. Whereas the basic award is based upon *gross* pay, the compensatory award depends upon the *net* value of wages and other benefits.

Immediate loss of wages. This is the sum of the loss of wages from the date of termination until the date of the hearing. Account will be taken of wages paid in lieu of notice and earnings in other employments (see also **53.13** below). If the employee has obtained new permanent employment, but has then lost it again, the original employer should not be taken as having caused the loss of earnings after the second dismissal (*Mabey Plant Hire Ltd v Richens*, IDS Brief 495, p 13).

In *Burlo v Langley* [2006] EWCA Civ 1178, [2007] IRLR 145 the Court of Appeal confirmed that *Norton Tool* is authority only for the proposition that compensation for unfair summary dismissal should include full pay for the notice period, without any requirement for the claimant to mitigate his loss during the notice period or to give account of earnings from other employers during the notice period. The observation in *Norton Tool* that it was good industrial relations practice to pay full notice pay whenever an employee was dismissed without notice had to be considered in the light of the House of Lords judgment in *Dunnachie v Kingston-Upon-Hull City Council* [2004] UKHL 26, [2005] 1 AC 226, and a claimant was only entitled to receive compensation for his actual losses. This meant that the claimant nanny was not entitled to receive full pay in respect of the notice period following her unfair dismissal during which she was in fact unable to work after accidental injury; her loss during the notice period was her sick pay entitlement only.

In *Stuart Peters Ltd v Bell* [2009] EWCA Civ 938, [2009] IRLR 941, the Court of Appeal explained that *Norton Tool* principle does not apply to cases of constructive unfair dismissal. They held that good industrial relations practice requires that an employer who chooses to bring a contract of employment to an end without a notice period should, in the absence of gross misconduct by the employee, offer the employee pay in lieu of notice, and the *Norton Tool* principle ensures that an employer who fails to comply with that good practice is not in a better position than the employer who does comply, since the employee need not give credit for sums earned in mitigation during the notice period. In cases of constructive dismissal, however, there is no principle of industrial relations requiring the employer to offer a payment in lieu. Indeed, the employer may wish to retain the services of the employee and be hoping that the employee will affirm the contract. The employee may also wish to remain in employment but claim damages for the repudiatory breach of contract. Therefore, in cases of constructive unfair dismissal, an employee must give credit for sums earned in mitigation during the notice period.

Future loss of earnings. If the claimant is unemployed at the time of the hearing or is in less remunerative employment than that from which he was dismissed, he will be awarded a sum for future loss of earnings. The award will be based upon the claimant's net loss of earnings for such period as the tribunal considers reasonable, bearing in mind such matters as the length of time he may be unemployed. Compensation must be assessed on the basis of what has actually occurred by the time of the hearing, rather than what might have been expected to occur at the time of the dismissal (*Gilham v Kent County Council (No 3)* [1986] ICR 52). Nevertheless, the exercise of assessing future loss involves predicting what might have happened if the Claimant had not been dismissed and what might happen in the future, and the tribunal will have to make an assessment based on uncertainties and sometimes speculation (*Scope v Thornett* [2006] EWCA Civ 1600, [2007] IRLR 155). Future loss of earnings does not necessarily cease when an employee obtains employment of a permanent nature at an equivalent or higher salary than he previously enjoyed. If the employee obtains another job but then loses the new job within a short time with no right to compensation, the loss from the first dismissal may continue (*Dench v Flynn & Partners* [1998] IRLR 653, overruling *Whelan (t/a Cheers Off Licence) v Richardson* [1998] IRLR 114, EAT). In *Wardle v Crédit Agricole Corporate and Investment Bank* [2011] EWCA Civ 545, [2011] ICR 1290 the Court of Appeal, overturning a tribunal's decision to award career-long loss to the Claimant, held that it would be a rare case in which awarding compensation for such a period would be appropriate. The rare case would be one where the evidence showed that there was no real prospect of the employee obtaining another job. In other cases – which would be the vast majority – the tribunal should only award damages to the time when the employee was "likely to obtain an equivalent job".

The award will take into account any increase in salary or any other benefit the claimant would have enjoyed had he not been dismissed, even beyond his contractual entitlements (*York Trailer Co Ltd v Sparkes* [1973] ICR 518). It will take account not only of regular wage or salary payments but also, for example, commission or bonus payments.

If the employee has obtained new employment which is more remunerative than the original job, it may be that the overall result by the time of the hearing is that he has suffered no loss at all (*Ging v Ellward Lancs Ltd* [1991] ICR 222). But where there has been a great delay in assessing the loss suffered, it may not be just and equitable to apply *Ging* (*Fentiman v Fluid Engineering Products Ltd* [1991] ICR 570; *Lytlarch Ltd v Reid* [1991] ICR 216).

The tribunal may award damages for loss of earnings in relation to a period in which the claimant is unfit for work and in receipt of invalidity benefit, if the inability to work is itself attributable to the actions of the employer in unfairly dismissing him. So, for example, if the claimant is receiving invalidity benefit because of depression caused by unemployment, which in turn was caused by the unfair dismissal, the claimant may receive compensation for the period in which he was unfit to work (*Hilton International Hotels (UK) Ltd v Faraji* [1994] ICR 259; *Devine v Designer Flowers Wholesale Florists Sundries Ltd* [1993] IRLR 517). The invalidity benefit received will, however, be taken into account (*Puglia v C James & Sons* [1996] ICR 301). Where there has been a constructive dismissal, however, losses flowing from repudiatory breach of contract are not recoverable in unfair dismissal proceedings, even where the repudiatory breach reduced the employee's earning capacity post-dismissal (*Triggs v GAB Robbins (UK) Ltd* [2008] EWCA Civ 17, [2008] IRLR 317).

Loss of use of a company car. If the employee had the use of a company car not only for the purposes of his employment but also for private use, he will be compensated for the loss of that benefit. The tribunal will take into account whether or not the employer paid for the petrol for private motoring. The incidence of tax will be taken into account as it is in the assessment of loss of all benefits in kind. In assessing the value of a car, petrol and running costs, reference is sometimes made to annual estimates published by the AA (*Shove v Downs Surgical plc* [1984] ICR 532).

Loss of benefits in kind. In assessing compensation, the tribunal will take into account other benefits in kind such as free accommodation, medical insurance and subsidised meals. It may do so even where there was no strict contractual entitlement to such benefits. A claimant is not entitled to receive compensation in respect of life insurance (and, logically, any other insurance) for a period following dismissal during which he did not take out replacement cover and the risks insured did not occur (*Knapton v ECC Card Clothing Ltd* [2006] IRLR 756). This is because to make a payment in respect of that period would give the claimant a windfall.

Loss of reputation. It had long been believed that the claimant is not entitled to damages for the loss to his reputation which has resulted from the dismissal (*Addis v Gramophone Co Ltd* [1909] AC 488). However in *Malik v BCCI* [1997] ICR 606, the House of Lords held that the claimant will be entitled to 'stigma damages' to compensate for difficulties in finding work which may result from the poor reputation of the employer at the time of dismissal, on the basis that the employer breached its duty of trust and confidence to the employee by acting in a manner which gave rise to its poor reputation. A claimant may not receive damages for the stress or injury to feelings resulting from the manner of dismissal (*Bliss v South-East Thames Regional Health Authority* [1987] ICR 700, *French v Barclays Bank plc* [1998] IRLR 646, CA and *Dunnachie v Kingston-Upon-Hull City Council* [2004] UKHL 36, [2004] IRLR 727 in which the HL ended the uncertainty created by Lord Hoffman's comments in *Johnson v Unisys Ltd* [2001] UKHL 13, [2001] IRLR 279 and the CA's decision [2004] EWCA Civ 84, [2004] IRLR 287). If an employee suffers from a reactive depression following a dismissal, which renders him unfit for employment between the date of dismissal and the date on which compensation is determined, the employment tribunal must ask what caused his loss. It may be just and equitable to compensate him for all or part of his loss of earnings, despite his unfitness for work, depending on the degree to which the dismissal caused his loss (*Dignity Funerals v Bruce* [2005] IRLR 189).

Pension rights. If, prior to his dismissal, the complainant was a member of a company pension scheme, and fails to obtain new employment, or obtains new employment where there is no company pension scheme, he will almost certainly suffer financial loss because any deferred pension payable will be based on the employee's salary at the date of dismissal (subject to statutory uplifting) instead of on the salary he would have received at normal retiring age. Even if he has obtained employment in another company which operates such a scheme, so that he is able to transfer his accrued rights under the previous scheme to the new scheme, it is likely that this will still involve a degree of loss because the transfer value will only reflect the value of those accrued rights at the date of leaving rather than reflecting the enhanced value which would have been added to those accrued rights, had the complainant remained with the previous company until retirement age instead of being dismissed. In any of these circumstances, the task of assessing compensation for loss of pension rights is a hard one. Some guidance is provided by a booklet prepared by a committee of employment tribunal chairmen in consultation with the Government Actuary's Department ('Employment Tribunals – Compensation for Loss of Pension Rights', 3rd ed. TSO, 2003),. The booklet is not binding upon tribunals (*Bingham v Hobourn Engineering Ltd* [1992] IRLR 298; see also *Manpower Ltd v Hearne* [1983] ICR 567; *Tradewinds Airways Ltd v Fletcher* [1981] IRLR 272; *Willmont Bros Ltd v Oliver* [1979] ICR 378; *Mono Pumps Ltd v Froggatt and Radford* [1987] IRLR 368). An alternative approach may be for the tribunal to assess the period for which the employee should be compensated for loss of pension rights, and to make an award based upon the cost of purchasing a policy to make up the difference between the pension which he will receive and the amount he would have received had he remained in employment until the end of the period. An award for loss of pension rights which is based solely on the value of the employer's contributions is not appropriate in assessing loss of pension rights under a scheme which yields not only an income benefit but also a lump sum arising as of right rather than by commutation. In *Bentwood Bros (Manchester) Ltd v Shepherd* [2003] EWCA Civ 380, [2003] IRLR 364 the Court of Appeal held that an employment tribunal had erred in applying only a 5% discount for accelerated receipt, even though the sum represented two and a half years' future earnings and ten years' pension payments.

Payments received by an employee under an occupational or private pension scheme, whether contributory or not, should not be offset against compensation awarded for unfair dismissal. This is because pensions are deferred pay and a decision by an employee to take an early pension after unfair dismissal is a personal decision about money management, rather than a factor which reduces the loss suffered in consequence of the unfair dismissal (*Knapton v ECC Card Clothing Ltd* [2006] IRLR 756).

Loss of statutory rights. The tribunal will assess a nominal figure for loss of protection from unfair dismissal for the first two years (the period for acquiring unfair dismissal protection) of any new employment. A few years ago, the appropriate figure was normally £100 (*SH Muffett Ltd v Head* [1987] ICR 1). It is now common for tribunals to award £250–£350.

It will also award compensation for loss of the accrued right to the statutory minimum period of notice. The loss was assessed in *Daley v AE Dorsett (Almar Dolls) Ltd* [1982] ICR 1 as half the wages due during that period, but it is thought that this may be too high in the ordinary case. See also *Arthur Guinness Son & Co (Great Britain) Ltd v Green* [1989] ICR 241.

Frequently, employment tribunals will award just one sum for loss of statutory rights, commonly in the region of £250–£350, to cover loss of protection from unfair dismissal and loss of accrued right to statutory notice.

53.13 FACTORS REDUCING OR INCREASING THE COMPENSATORY AWARD

Just and equitable. The tribunal has a discretion to make an award which is less than the full amount of the claimant's loss if the tribunal considers it just and equitable to do so (*ERA 1996, s 123(1)*). Thus, if the employee has been guilty of misconduct which was only discovered after the dismissal, and therefore could not be relied upon to establish contributory fault (see below), a reduced award or no award may be made (*W Devis & Sons Ltd v Atkins* [1977] ICR 662; *Tele-Trading Ltd v Jenkins* [1990] IRLR 430; *Chaplin v H J Rawlinson Ltd* [1991] ICR 553). See *Slaughter v C Brewer & Sons Ltd* [1990] ICR 730 for reductions under *s 123(1)* in cases of ill-health.

The fact that an employer could have dismissed an employee fairly for poor attendance when he dismissed her unfairly for ill-health was held by the Court of Appeal not to justify a reduction in the compensatory award on just and equitable grounds where the employer, in full knowledge of the facts, chose not to dismiss her on grounds of poor attendance (*Devonshire v Trico-Folberth Ltd* [1989] ICR 747).

It is only events which took place before dismissal which can render it just and equitable to reduce the compensatory award. A tribunal may not, for example, take account of a breach of a duty of confidentiality which took place after dismissal (*Soros v Davison* [1994] ICR 590).

In *Simrad Ltd v Scott* [1997] IRLR 147, the EAT held that it was not just and equitable to assess the compensatory award by reference to the lower rate of pay which the applicant was receiving because of her decision to change career and train as a nurse. The change of career was too remote to be linked to the dismissal.

Contributory fault. Where the tribunal finds that the dismissal was to any extent caused or contributed to by any action of the complainant, it will reduce the amount of the compensatory award by such proportion as it considers just and equitable having regard to that finding (*ERA 1996, s 123(6)*). The same percentage of deduction will usually apply to both basic and compensatory awards.

If, therefore, an employee was guilty of misconduct which was grave, but did not justify dismissal, or if the procedures used to dismiss him were unfair, but his own conduct to a certain extent contributed to his misfortune, the amount of compensation may be reduced. The reduction may be as much as 100% in an appropriate case (*W Devis & Sons Ltd v Atkins* [1977] ICR 662). See also **53.19** below for reduction in union-related cases.

In order for a deduction for contributory fault to be made for the employee's misconduct, that conduct must be culpable or blameworthy in the sense that, whether or not it amounted to a breach of contract or tort, it was foolish or perverse or unreasonable in the circumstances (*Nelson v BBC (No 2)* [1980] ICR 110).

Where the tribunal has jurisdiction in the case of a dismissal for taking part in industrial action (see **51.17** UNFAIR DISMISSAL – I), it is not open to the tribunal to hold that participation in the industrial action in itself amounts to contributory fault: *Crossville Wales Ltd v Tracey* [1997] ICR 862, overruling *TNT Express Ltd v Downes* [1994] ICR 1.

Lack of capability is unlikely to be blameworthy in the *Nelson* sense unless it involves, for example, laziness or obstructive behaviour. However, in a case, say, of incapability due to ill-health, it may be appropriate to make a reduction under the general 'just and equitable' formulation referred to above (*Slaughter*, above).

A reduction for contributory fault may be made in the case of constructive dismissal and where the employer has failed to establish an acceptable reason for the dismissal (*Morrison v Amalgamated Transport and General Workers Union* [1989] IRLR 361; *Polentarutti v Autokraft Ltd* [1991] ICR 757).

In *Optikinetics Ltd v Whooley* [1999] ICR 984, the EAT held that where a tribunal found that there was contributory fault on the part of a claimant, it was obligatory for the tribunal to make a reduction in the compensatory award by such proportion as it considered just and equitable, but there was no similar obligation in respect of the basic award.

The Court of Appeal in *London Ambulance Service NHS Trust v Small* [2009] EWCA Civ 220, [2009] IRLR 563 advised employment tribunals that it was desirable to keep separate their findings of fact on the fairness of the dismissal from their findings on other questions, such as contributory fault, constructive dismissal, discrimination and victimisation. This is because the fairness of the dismissal is decided on the basis of an objective view of the employer's decision making process, without the need for a rehearing on the question of misconduct. By contrast, other disputed facts, such as whether the employee's fault had contributed to the dismissal, required a decision by the tribunal based upon the evidence which it had heard.

The Court of Session in Scotland has held that it is an error of law for a tribunal to fail to give reasons for a reduction in an award for contributory fault (*Nairne v Highlands and Islands Fire Brigade* [1989] IRLR 366).

Failure to follow statutory procedures: reduction or increase in compensation. Dismissals for which the 'trigger event' occurred between 1 October 2004 and 6 April 2009 were subject to the statutory minimum disciplinary and grievance procedures which were introduced by the *EA 2002* (see **52.3(a)** UNFAIR DISMISSAL – II, **7.5** CONTRACT OF EMPLOYMENT and **17.18** EMPLOYMENT TRIBUNALS – I). The employee's failure to comply with the procedures may result in the compensatory award being reduced, and the employer's failure to comply may result in the compensatory award being increased.

(A) Reduction in compensation: *EA 2002, s 31(2)* provides that an award to an employee may be reduced if the claim to which the proceedings relate concerns a matter to which one of the statutory procedures applies, the statutory procedure was not completed before the proceedings were begun and the non-completion of the statutory procedure was wholly or mainly attributable to a failure by the employee to comply with a requirement of the procedure or to exercise a right of appeal under it.

Section 31(2) says that the tribunal must reduce the award in such circumstances by 10% and may, if it considers it just and equitable to do so, reduce it by a further amount, up to a total of 50%. *Section 31(4)* provides that the tribunal has a discretion not to make a reduction, or to make a reduction of less than 10% if there are exceptional circumstances which would make a larger deduction unjust or inequitable.

The reduction in the compensatory award is made before both the reduction for contributory fault and the reduction to take account of the extent to which a contractual or *ex gratia* redundancy payment exceeds the statutory redundancy payment *(ERA 1996, s 124A)*.

(B) Increase in compensation: *Section 31(3)* provides that if the non-completion of the statutory procedure was wholly or mainly attributable to the failure by the employer to comply with a requirement of the procedure, the tribunal may increase the award by the same percentages as it may reduce the award if the fault lies with the employee.

In *Wardle v Crédit Agricole Corporate and Investment Bank* [2011] EWCA Civ 545, [2011] ICR 1290 the Court of Appeal held that the size of the award is relevant to the uplift to be applied under *section 31(3)*. The intention behind *s 31(3)* was that a tribunal was enjoined to start at a 10 per cent uplift and it then had to consider whether it was just and equitable on the particular circumstances to increase that percentage. Elias LJ stated that an increase to the maximum of 50 per cent should be very rare indeed and given only in the most egregious of cases.

The Secretary of State has made regulations in relation to the circumstances in which compensation should be increased or reduced, such as specifying what constitutes compliance with a requirement of a statutory procedure *(EA 2002, s 31(6)* and *EA 2002 (Dispute Resolution) Regulations 2004 (SI 2004/752))*.

In *McKindless Group v McLaughlin* [2008] IRLR 678 the EAT reduced to 10% a statutory uplift of 50% in compensation for unfair dismissal, where the employer had conceded the unfairness on the eve of the hearing. The EAT held that a tribunal may award an uplift greater than 10% only by reference to some particular facts and circumstances which make it just and equitable to do so, and may not take account of conduct or events which occurred during the hearing, rather than during the process of dismissal.

Under *EA 2002, s 38*, an employment tribunal which finds in favour of an employee after hearing a complaint of unfair dismissal but makes no award to the employee, and which has noticed that when the proceedings began the employer was in breach of its duty to provide the employee with a written statement of initial employment particulars or particulars of change, must make an award of at least two weeks' pay (up to £760) and may, if it considers it just and equitable in all the circumstances, make an award of four weeks' pay *(EA 2002, s 38(2))* (up to £1,520). Where the employment tribunal makes an award to the employee for unfair dismissal in such a case, that award must be increased by at least two and up to four weeks' pay *(EA 2002, s 38(3))*. The duty to award at least two and up to four week's pay in such a case does not arise if there are exceptional circumstances which would make the award or increase unjust or inequitable *(EA 2002, s 38(5))*.

Failure to follow 2009 ACAS Code of Practice 1 on Disciplinary and Grievance Procedures. Section 1 of the *Employment Act 2008* repealed *ss 29–33* of the *EA 2002*, namely the statutory dispute resolution provisions, with effect from 6 April 2009. *Section 3* of the *EA 2008* inserted a new *s 207A* into *TULRCA 1992* which came into force on 6 April 2009. The effect in unfair dismissal cases to which the new rules apply is that where an employment tribunal concludes that an employer has unreasonably failed to comply with the 2009 ACAS Code of Practice 1 on disciplinary and grievance procedures, it may increase any award which it makes to the employee by up to 25%, if it is just and equitable in all the circumstances. Conversely, if the employee has unreasonably failed to comply with the ACAS Code, the tribunal may reduce the award by up to 25%, if it considers it to be just and equitable in all the circumstances.

Whether the unfairness made any difference. It was initially thought that, if the employee would have been dismissed even if the employer had done all that he ought to have done, the dismissal ought not to be regarded as unfair. That approach was held to be wrong in

Polkey v AE Dayton Services Ltd [1988] ICR 142 (see **52.4** UNFAIR DISMISSAL – II) which introduced an approach requiring the tribunal to reduce compensation by a percentage to take account of the possibility that the employee would have been dismissed even if a fair procedure had been followed.

Subsequently, *ERA 1996, s 98A* (as introduced by *EA 2002, s 34*) came into force and in general there were fewer cases in which tribunals found dismissals to be procedurally unfair but went on to award no compensation because the unfairness made no difference. That was because where an employer failed to comply with the statutory dismissal procedures, the dismissal was automatically unfair under *s 98A(1)*, *ERA* 1996. In some cases, there remained, however, the question under *s 98A(2)* whether the employer could show that the decision to dismiss was not unreasonable because he would have decided to dismiss even if he had followed a fair procedure. Note that *ERA 1996, s 98A* has now been repealed, although it may apply in cases for which the trigger event preceded the repeal.

The Scottish Court of Session in *King v Eaton (No 2)* [1998] IRLR 686 said that it was open to a tribunal to decline to permit an employer at a remedies hearing to lead additional evidence to show that the result would have been the same even if fair procedures had been followed. If it is not realistic or practicable to embark upon such an exercise or the exercise would be highly speculative, the tribunal should not do so. The EAT held in *Kelly-Madden v Manor Surgery* [2007] IRLR 17 that *s 98A(2)* applies to the failure to follow any procedure with which the employment tribunal considers that the employer should in fairness have complied. To ask what would have happened if the employer had acted fairly is still relevant to compensation. For example, if the company shut down and all the employees were made redundant a few weeks after the claimant was unfairly dismissed, his compensatory award ought not to run beyond that date (see *James W Cook & Co (Wivenhoe) Ltd v Tipper* [1990] ICR 716, holding also that the tribunal cannot investigate the commercial and economic reasons behind the closure). The tribunal may take account of the fact that an employee with a short period of service is more at risk of being selected for redundancy if job losses occur (*Morris v Acco Ltd* [1985] ICR 306). Again, it may be that the tribunal considers that an employee dismissed for misconduct without a hearing could not, in fact, have said anything effective in his own defence, or that an employee dismissed without warning for lack of capability was not capable of improvement in any event. In a different context, it has been suggested that it ought not to be assumed too readily that a failure to observe the principles of natural justice made no difference to the result (*John v Rees* [1970] Ch 345 at 402).

The tribunal ought also to consider *when* that dismissal would have taken place, eg even if it is certain that a fair procedure would have led to the same result, it may be that its adoption would have prolonged the period of earning for a number of weeks (see *Mining Supplies (Longwall) Ltd v Baker* [1988] ICR 676) or perhaps not at all (*Robertson v Magnet Ltd (Retail Division)* [1993] IRLR 512). If the employee could only have hoped for continued employment in a different and less well-paid job, the calculation of his loss ought to be based upon those lower earnings (*Red Bank*, above).

In *O'Donoughue v Redcar and Cleveland Borough Council* [2001] EWCA Civ 701, [2001] IRLR 615, the Court of Appeal made it clear that it was not always necessary or appropriate to make a percentage assessment as to whether the claimant would have been dismissed fairly if there had been no unfair dismissal. This was especially the case if the tribunal was assessing the likelihood that the claimant might have been fairly dismissed, not at the time of dismissal, but at some time in the future. In such circumstances, it may not be possible to identify an overall percentage risk, because there may be, say, a 20% chance of dismissal in six months but a 30% chance in a year. In Miss O'Donoughue's case the tribunal concluded that her divisive and antagonistic approach was such that she would have been bound to be dismissed fairly within six months, and so the tribunal limited compensation for future loss to the six-month period. The Court of Appeal held that the tribunal had approached the matter correctly and that it had been appropriate to assess a safe date by which the tribunal was certain that that dismissal would take place and then to make an award of full compensation in respect of the period prior thereto. See also *Scope v Thornett* [2006] EWCA Civ 1600, [2007] IRLR 155.

The approach taken by the EAT in *Mining Supplies (Longwall) v Baker* was not followed by the EAT in *Elkouil v Coney Island Ltd* [2002] IRLR 174. In *Elkouil*, the tribunal held that redundancy consultation should have begun some 10 weeks before dismissal, and that consultation would have prolonged employment by two weeks. The tribunal made a compensatory award of two weeks' pay. The EAT held that the tribunal should have awarded 10 weeks' pay, because if consultation had taken place at the right time, the applicant would have had the opportunity of looking for another job some 10 weeks earlier than he could. Accordingly, he lost the chance of being re-employed substantially earlier than he was.

The EAT in *Chagger v Abbey National plc* [2009] IRLR 86 advised tribunals that even where the dismissal was unfair because of discriminatory grounds, it is necessary to conduct a *Polkey* exercise, to consider what would have happened if the claimant had not been dismissed for discriminatory reasons and whether there would have been a lawful dismissal for a fair reason. The Court of Appeal [2009] EWCA Civ 1202, [2010] IRLR 47, however, held that the EAT had erred in limiting the future loss to that period during which the claimant would have been employed by the respondent, observing that an employee's success in finding new employment is influenced by the particular job market at the time when he finds himself seeking work and that it is generally easier for someone who is still working to find a new job than someone who has been unemployed or out of the industry. Most notably, the Court held that a discriminatory dismissal can alter someone's career path, by necessitating his bringing an employment tribunal claim against the employer, which can create a stigma making him unattractive to future employers, for which the original employer must remain liable. Such future loss flowing from stigma would be equally recoverable in a general unfair dismissal claim as in a claim of a discriminatory dismissal.

In *Andrews v Software 2000 Ltd* [2007] IRLR 568 the EAT explained that s 98A(2) (which was then in force) should be applied first, and then *Polkey* questions fall to be addressed. The following principles emerged from the relevant case law:

(a)   In assessing compensation the task of the tribunal is to assess the loss flowing from the dismissal, using its common sense, experience and sense of justice. In the normal case, that requires it to assess for how long the employee would have been employed but for the dismissal.

(b)   If the employer seeks to contend that the employee would or might have ceased to be employed in any event had fair procedures been followed, or alternatively would not have continued in employment indefinitely, it is for him to adduce any relevant evidence on which he wishes to rely. However, the tribunal must have regard to all the evidence when making that assessment, including any evidence from the employee himself.

(c)   There will, however, be circumstances where the nature of the evidence which the employer wishes to adduce, or on which he seeks to rely, is so unreliable that the tribunal may take the view that the whole exercise of seeking to reconstruct what might have been is so riddled with uncertainty that no sensible prediction based on that evidence can properly be made.

(d)   Whether that is the position is a matter of impression and judgment for the tribunal; but in reaching that decision the tribunal must direct itself properly. It must recognise that it should have regard to any material and reliable evidence which might assist it in fixing just compensation, even if there are limits to the extent to which it can confidently predict what might have been; and it must appreciate that a degree of uncertainty is an inevitable feature of the exercise. The mere fact that an element of speculation is involved is not a reason for refusing to have regard to the evidence.

(e)   An appellate court must be wary about interfering with the tribunal's assessment that the exercise is too speculative. However, it must interfere if the tribunal has not directed itself properly and has taken too narrow a view of its role.

(f)   The *s 98A(2)* and *Polkey* exercises run in parallel and will often involve consideration of the same evidence, but they must not be conflated. It follows that even if a tribunal considers some of the evidence or potential evidence to be too speculative to form any sensible view as to whether dismissal would have occurred on the balance of probabilities, it must nevertheless take into account any evidence on which it considers it can properly rely and from which it could in principle conclude that the employment may have come to an end when it did, or alternatively would not have continued indefinitely.

(g)   Having considered the evidence, the tribunal may determine:

(i)   that if fair procedures had been complied with, the employer has satisfied it – the onus being firmly on the employer – that on the balance of probabilities the dismissal would have occurred when it did in any event. The dismissal is then fair by virtue of *s 98A(2)*;

(ii)   that there was a chance of dismissal but less than 50%, in which case compensation should be reduced accordingly;

(iii)   that employment would have continued but only for a limited fixed period. The evidence demonstrating that may be wholly unrelated to the circumstances relating to the dismissal itself, as in the *O'Donoghue* case; or

(iv)   employment would have continued indefinitely.

However, this last finding should be reached only where the evidence that it might have been terminated earlier is so scant that it can effectively be ignored.

In *Eversheds v De Belin* [2011] ICR 1137 the EAT followed *Andrews v Software 2000* and *Scope v Thornett* [2006] EWCA Civ 1600, [2007] IRLR 155 in holding that tribunals should not decline to undertake a *Polkey* exercise merely because it involves 'speculation'. It is only in circumstances where the evidence is 'so scant that it can effectively be ignored' that the tribunal could safely hold that the exercise would be too speculative. Note that in *Ministry of Justice v Parry* [2013] ICR 311 the EAT pointed out that the part of the *Software 2000* guidance relating to *section 98A(2)* should no longer be followed in light of the repeal of that subsection. In *Compass Group v Ayodele* [2011] IRLR 802 the EAT held that although the primary burden of proving loss lies on a Claimant, that would initially be discharged by showing that he has been unfairly dismissed. If an employer seeks to argue a *Polkey* point it must be properly raised and supported by evidence.

If a percentage reduction is being made on the basis that employment may have terminated fairly during the period for which compensation is being assessed and also on account of contributory fault, the two reductions should be applied sequentially (*Rao v Civil Aviation Authority* [1994] ICR 495). Thus, if there was a 50% chance that the employee would have been dismissed in any event, and he was 30% to blame for his dismissal, he should be awarded only 35% of his actual loss (ie half of 70%). If the employee receives a termination payment, the payment should be deducted after this process has been carried out (*Digital Equipment Co Ltd v Clements (No 2)* [1998] ICR 258; *Heggie v Uniroyal Englebert Tyres Ltd* [1998] IRLR 425).

In *Steel Stockholders (Birmingham) Ltd v Kirkwood* [1993] IRLR 515, the EAT held that it was only where the defect was procedural rather than substantive that a percentage reduction may be made. The distinction between procedural and substantive defects was however easier to state than to apply and in *O'Dea v ISC Chemicals Ltd (t/a as Rhône-Poulenc Chemicals)* [1995] IRLR 599, the Court of Appeal held that employment tribunals should not attempt to categorise defects in this manner.

Mitigation of loss. The employee is under a duty to mitigate his loss. He must take reasonable steps to obtain alternative employment. A compensatory award is intended to compensate the employee for loss and is not a penal award against the employer. What employment he will be under a duty to accept is a matter to be determined by the tribunal. He must be realistic in his job expectations. He may not demand a salary or status higher than that which he previously enjoyed, and may have to accept some reduction. If the employee has not made reasonable efforts to find other work, his compensation will be reduced to reflect the tribunal's view of what would have happened if he *had* mitigated his loss. However, the burden of proving a failure to mitigate is on the employer, and the standard of what is reasonably required of the employee should not be set too high (*Fyfe v Scientific Furnishings Ltd* [1989] ICR 648).

Where an unfairly dismissed employee had unreasonably refused an employer's offer of reinstatement, he was rightly held only to be entitled to a basic award (*Sweetlove v Redbridge and Waltham Forest Area Health Authority* [1979] ICR 477). In *Wilding v British Telecommunications plc* [2002] EWCA Civ 349, [2002] IRLR 524, the Court of Appeal held that the duty to mitigate which is imposed on an employee requires him when considering an offer of re-employment to act as a reasonable person unaffected by the prospect of compensation, that the onus is on the employer to show that the employee had failed in that duty, that the test of reasonableness was objective, that the circumstances in which an offer of re-employment was made and refused, the attitude of the employer, the way in which the employee had been treated, and all the surrounding circumstances should be taken into account by the tribunal, and that the tribunal must not be too stringent in its expectations of the injured party.

There is no duty to mitigate until the dismissal has actually taken place (*Trimble v Supertravel Ltd* [1982] IRLR 451). Failure by the employee to activate the internal appeals procedure after the dismissal cannot, as a matter of law, amount to a failure to mitigate (*Lock v Connell Estate Agents* [1994] IRLR 444, not following *Hoover Ltd v Forde* [1980] ICR 239). Under *EA 2002, s 31(2)* a claimant will be penalised by a reduction in compensation if he fails to exhaust internal procedures (see '*Failure to follow statutory procedures: reduction or increase in compensation*' above).

In *Daley v AE Dorsett (Almar Dolls) Ltd* [1982] ICR 1, the EAT did not interfere with an employment tribunal's finding that an employee's decision not to accept full-time employment at a rate of earnings less than the amount of unemployment benefit was reasonable. It stressed, however, that employment tribunals should be very slow indeed in finding reasonable a decision of a dismissed employee not to accept subsequent employment because he would be receiving less than unemployment benefit.

Expenses incurred in seeking to mitigate the loss suffered (eg the cost of travelling to job interviews) are recoverable as part of the compensatory award. That could include the cost of starting up a business of the employee's own, if that was a reasonable thing to do (see *Aon Training Ltd (formerly Totalamber plc) v Dore* [2005] EWCA Civ 411, [2005] IRLR 891; *Gardiner-Hill v Roland Beiger Technics Ltd* [1982] IRLR 498). Legal expenses incurred in pursuing the unfair dismissal claim are not recoverable (for the award of costs see **17.35** EMPLOYMENT TRIBUNALS – I).

Payments made by the employer. Payments made by the claimant's former employer, whether under a contractual liability or *ex gratia*, will generally be taken into account (*Rushton v Harcros Timber and Building Supplies Ltd* [1993] ICR 230). In *Simrad Ltd v Scott* [1997]

IRLR 147, however, the EAT held that a loan which was to be repaid by way of work need not be taken into account for these purposes as it would not be just and equitable to do so since the employee had been deprived of the opportunity to carry on working.

It was formerly understood that the employee must give credit for pay in lieu of notice and other benefits received from the old employer during the notice period (*Addison v Babcock FATA Ltd* [1987] ICR 805) and for earnings from any new employment during the notice period, because the contractual right to notice pay does not create a debt owed by the employer which must be paid irrespective of the employee's real loss, but gives rise merely to a claim in damages or compensation where the employer breaches his contractual or statutory notice obligations (*Rowley v Cerberus Software Ltd* [2001] EWCA Civ 78, [2001] IRLR 160). Similarly, neither pension payments (*Hopkins v Norcros plc* [1994] ICR 11), nor an educational grant received in connection with a course embarked upon after dismissal (*Justfern Ltd v D'Ingerthorpe* [1994] ICR 286) were taken into account. The full amount of invalidity benefit was deducted in *Puglia v James & Sons* ([1996] IRLR 70), which did not follow *Hilton International Hotels (UK) Ltd v Faraji* ([1994] ICR 259). *Puglia v James* was itself not followed in *Rubenstein and Roskin (t/a McGuffies Dispensing Chemists) v McGloughlin* [1996] IRLR 557, in which the EAT deducted only half the amount of invalidity benefit. In a further variation, the EAT in *Sheffield Forgemasters International Ltd v Fox* [2009] ICR 333, [2009] IRLR 192 held that receipt of incapacity benefit did not preclude a claimant from obtaining compensation for loss of earnings during such a period, because some people can lawfully claim incapacity benefit while performing light work.

There were subsequently conflicting decisions at EAT level concerning the deductibility from the compensatory award of monies which the employee earns or receives during the notice period. In *Hardy v Polk (Leeds) Ltd* [2004] IRLR 420 the EAT held that the same duty to mitigate arises as there is at common law and account should be taken of earnings from new employment. A differently-constituted EAT in *Voith Turbo Ltd v Stowe* [2005] IRLR 228 held that it was open to an employment tribunal not to deduct earnings from new employment from the pay in lieu of notice, in accordance with good industrial practice. A more recent EAT decision, however, in *Morgans v Alpha Plus Security* [2005] IRLR 234, held that incapacity benefit received following a dismissal was properly deducted from the compensatory award, in order to ensure that the employee was compensated for his actual loss only. The Court of Appeal has now concluded that an employee is not required to give credit against his unfair dismissal compensatory award for earnings from another employer during the notice period, when unfairly dismissed without pay in lieu of notice, but that his entitlement for compensation in respect of the notice period is limited to his actual loss (see *Burlo v Langley* above [2006] EWCA Civ 1178, [2007] IRLR 145).

Jobseeker's allowance received will not be taken into account (but see **53.6** above for the rules on recoupment).

The payments made by the employer are deducted by the employment tribunal from the gross sum after compensation has been reduced to take account of contributory fault and/or the fact that dismissal might have taken place anyway: *Digital Equipment Co Ltd v Clements (No 2)* [1998] IRLR 134.

Delayed Payment. In *Melia v Magna Kansei Ltd* [2005] EWCA Civ 1547, [2006] IRLR 117, the Court of Appeal held that when assessing a claimant's loss, an employment tribunal may make an allowance for delayed payment. According to the Court, this is distinct from a tribunal awarding interest, which it may not do.

The order in which deductions should be made. The Court of Appeal in *Digital Equipment v Clements (No 2)* [1998] IRLR 134 and the Scottish Court of Session in *Leonard v Strathclyde Buses Ltd* [1998] IRLR 693 have considered the order in which deductions should be made from the compensatory award. The position is now clear, except where non-statutory redundancy payments are concerned. The order of deduction is as follows:

(a)   calculate the total loss actually suffered by the claimant;

(b)   deduct amounts received in mitigation and any payment made by the former employer (other than a non-statutory redundancy payment);

(c)   make any adjustment for failure on the part of the employee or employer to follow statutory procedures;

(d)   make any reduction for contributory fault;

(e)   apply the statutory maximum.

The controversy as regards non-statutory redundancy payments is as to whether the effect of *ERA 1996, s 123(7)* is that such payments should be deducted after the reduction for contributory fault but before the statutory maximum is applied, or whether they should only be deducted after the statutory maximum is applied. It is not clear from the judgments in *Digital Equipment v Clements (No 2)* which of the two alternative approaches should be followed. In *Leonard v Strathclyde Buses*, however, the Court of Session held that non-statutory redundancy payments should be deducted before the statutory maximum is applied and said that there was nothing in *Digital Equipment v Clements (No 2)* which points to any different view.

The approach taken by the Court of Appeal in *Digital Equipment v Clements (No 2)* was adopted once again by the Scottish Court of Session in *Heggie v Uniroyal Englebert Tyres Ltd* [1999] IRLR 802.

53.14   ADDITIONAL AWARD – NON-COMPLIANCE WITH AN ORDER

Additional compensation in cases where an order for reinstatement or re-engagement is made but not complied with (see **53.5** above) consisting of not less than 26 weeks' and not more than 52 weeks' pay (except union-related, health and safety, pension scheme trustee and employee representative cases where a special award may be made, see **53.16** below) (*ERA 1996, s 117*).

The tribunal may not simply make the maximum award in order to force compliance with its order. It must consider factors such as the employer's conduct and the extent to which the compensatory award has met the actual loss suffered (*Morganite Electrical Carbon Ltd v Donne* [1988] ICR 18).

Where the employer has made an *ex gratia* payment which exceeds the amount of any loss suffered, it may be possible to set off the surplus against any additional award (*Darr v LRC Products Ltd* [1993] IRLR 257).

53.15   REDUCTION OF AWARD – 'UNION-RELATED' CASES

Where an award of compensation is made in respect of a dismissal which is to be regarded as unfair by virtue of *TULRCA 1992, s 152* or *s 153*, a tribunal, in considering whether it would be just and equitable to reduce or further reduce the amount of *any part* of the award, will disregard any conduct or action which constitutes:

(a)   a breach or proposed breach of a requirement that the complainant should:

    (i)   be or become a member;

    (ii)   cease to be or refrain from becoming a member; or

    (iii)   not take part in the activities; or

(iv)   not make use of the services which are made available to him

of any trade union or a particular trade union or one of a number of particular trade unions;

(b)   acceptance of or failure to accept an offer by the employer made to induce the employee not to become a member or participate in activities of a trade union (contrary to *TULRCA 1992, s 145A*) or not to participate in collective bargaining (contrary to *TULRCA 1992, s 145B*); or

(c)   an objection or proposed objection (however expressed) to the operation of a provision for the deduction of union subscriptions from his remuneration (under *TULRCA 1992, s 152(3)*).

(*TULRCA 1992, s 153.*)

However, it seems that confrontational conduct by the employee could form the basis for a finding of contributory fault provided that the immediate circumstances constituting the principal reason for dismissal are excluded from consideration (*Transport and General Workers' Union v Howard* [1992] ICR 106).

53.16 MAXIMUM AWARDS

Maximum awards:

(i)   The maximum amount of a 'week's pay', which determines the maximum amount of a basic award, is reviewed annually and linked to the RPI (*ERelA 1999, s 34(1)*) (but see *SI 2009/1903, Art 3*, which excluded the operation of *ERelA 1999, s 34* following the increase to £380 from 1 October 2009) (see PAY– I (32)). The current maximum is £450.

(ii)   The minimum basic award in a case of dismissal unfair under *TULRCA 1992, s 152* or *s 153* or *ERA 1996, s 100(1)(a)* and *(b)*, *101A(d)*, *102(1)* or *103* is £5,500.

(iii)   The maximum basic award is $20 \times 1\frac{1}{2} \times £450 = £13,500$.

(iv)   An employee may also receive an award in respect of unfair dismissal which is increased by £900–£1,800 under *EA 2002, s 38* (see **53.13** above).

(v)   The maximum compensatory award is £74,200 (see **53.10** above).

(vi)   Note the exceptions in which the ceiling on compensation does not apply (*ERA 1996, s 124(1A)*). There is no statutory maximum compensatory award in cases in which a person is regarded as automatically unfairly dismissed by reason of *ERA 1996, s 100* (health and safety cases), *s 103A* (public interest disclosure cases), *s 105(3)* (selection for redundancy on grounds of health and safety activity) or *s 105(6A)* (selection for redundancy on the ground of public interest disclosure) (*ERelA 1999, s 37(1)*).

(vii)   The additional award will, in all cases, be not less than 26 and not more than 52 weeks' pay, giving a maximum of £23,400 (see **53.14**).

53.17 JOINDER OF THIRD PARTIES

If, in any proceedings before an employment tribunal on a complaint of unfair dismissal, either the employer or the complainant claims:

(a)   that the employer was induced to dismiss the complainant by the actual or threatened calling, organising, procuring or financing of a strike or other industrial action; and

(b)   that such pressure was exercised because the complainant was not a member of any trade union or of a particular trade union or of one of a number of particular trade unions,

the employer or the complainant may request the tribunal to direct that the person whom he claims exercised the pressure, be joined as a party to the proceedings (*TULRCA 1992, s 160(1)*).

A tribunal must grant such a request if it is made before the hearing of the complaint begins, but it may be refused if it is made after that time. The tribunal will refuse to hear such a request if it is made after the tribunal has made an award of compensation (*TULRCA 1992, s 160(2)*).

If the tribunal makes an award of compensation and considers that the complaint of pressure is well-founded, it may make an order that the third party (joined according to the procedure outlined above) pay all or such part of the award as the tribunal may consider just and equitable in the circumstances (*TULRCA 1992, s 160(3)*).

53.18   INTERIM RELIEF IN RESPECT OF CERTAIN DISMISSALS

An employee who complains that he has been dismissed for:

(a)   being or proposing to become a member of an independent trade union;

(b)   taking part or proposing to take part in the activities of an independent trade union at an appropriate time;

(c)   not being a member of any trade union, or of a particular trade union, or of one of a number of particular trade unions, or refusing or proposing to refuse to become or remain a member;

(d)   carrying out, or proposing to carry out, activities which he has been designated by the employer to carry out in connection with preventing or reducing risks to health and safety at work;

(e)   performing or proposing to perform any functions as a representative of workers on matters of health and safety at work, or as a member of a safety committee;

(f)   performing or proposing to perform any functions or activities as (i) a representative of members of the workforce for the purposes of *Sch 1* to the *Working Time Regulations 1998* or (ii) a candidate for election as such a representative;

(g)   performing or proposing to perform any functions as a trustee of a relevant occupational pension scheme which relates to his employment;

(h)   performing or proposing to perform any functions as (i) an employee representative for the purposes of *TULRCA 1992, Part IV, Chapter II* (redundancies) or *regs 10 and 11* of *Transfer of Undertakings (Protection of Employment) Regulations 1981* or (ii) a candidate for election as such a representative;

(i)   activities relating to union recognition or bargaining arrangements; or

(j)   exercising his or her right to be accompanied to disciplinary or grievance hearings, or to accompany a fellow employee to such a hearing; or

(k)   making a protected disclosure;

may apply to an employment tribunal for an order for interim relief (*TULRCA 1992, s 161(1); ERA 1996, s 128;* and see **52.3 Unfair Dismissal – II**). Note that this does not apply to all the cases where a health and safety dismissal or 'working time' dismissal is automatically unfair. In *Bombardier Aerospace/Short Brothers Plc v McConnell* [2007] NICA 27, [2008] IRLR 51, the Northern Ireland Court of Appeal held that interim relief was not available where the true reason for dismissal was redundancy, but there was an unlawful union-related reason for the selection. This is because interim relief in the form of reinstatement or re-engagement would be of no value where the employer had ceased to carry on business due to redundancy. If an employer dismissed the employee for a reason in respect of which interim relief was available and then created a spurious redundancy in order to mask the real reason for dismissal, then interim relief would be available. The case returned to the tribunal, at which the claimants conceded that there was a genuine redundancy situation, although arguing that the principal reason for their own dismissals was their trade union and health and safety activities. The tribunal denied them interim relief, and the case again returned to the NICA ([2008] NICA 50; [2009] IRLR 201). The NICA agreed with the tribunal that interim relief was not available, because there was a true redundancy situation, which made it unlikely that the tribunal would conclude that the sole or principal reason for the dismissals was trade union or health and safety activities. On the other hand, the tribunal might find that there had been unfair selection for redundancy, but interim relief was not available for such a claim.

An order for interim relief may be made pending a substantive hearing where the tribunal considers that the complainant will succeed. The order is either for reinstatement or re-engagement, or for continuation of the terms of the contract.

An application for interim relief will only be entertained if it is presented to the tribunal within seven days following the effective date of termination and (where the complainant relies on (*a*) or (*b*) above) if there is also presented within that time a certificate from an authorised official of the union that the complainant was, or proposed to become, a member of the union and that there are good grounds for supposing that the reason or principal reason for the dismissal was one alleged in the complaint (*TULRCA 1992, s 161(2),(3)*; *ERA 1996, s 128(2)*). The tribunal should deal with the interim application as soon as possible (*TULRCA 1992, s 162(1)*; *ERA 1996, s 128(3)*). Both parties may be present at the hearing, the employer having had at least seven days' notice of the application (*TULRCA 1992, s 162(2)*; *ERA 1996, s 128(4)*). A party who has been joined to the proceedings in accordance with a request made under *TULRCA 1992, s 160* made at least three days before the hearing (see **53.20** above), must have as much notice as is reasonably practicable (*TULRCA 1992, s 162(3)*). The hearing may only be postponed in special circumstances (*TULRCA 1992, s 162(4)*; *ERA 1996, s 128(5)*). Guidance as to the procedure to be followed in interim relief cases was given by the EAT in *Derby Daily Telegraph Ltd v Foss*, IDS Brief 471, p 15.

If it appears likely to the tribunal that the complaint is well-founded (in *Taplin v C Shippam Ltd* [1978] ICR 1068, the EAT said that the test should be whether there was 'a pretty good chance' of success. That test remains good law: *Dandpat v University of Bath* UKEAT/0408/09), it will ask the employer, if he is present, whether he is willing to reinstate or re-engage the complainant pending the full hearing or settlement of the matter. If the employer states that he is willing to reinstate the employee, the tribunal will make an order to that effect.

If the employer states that he is willing to re-engage the employee in another job and specifies the terms and conditions on which he is willing to do so, the tribunal will ask the employee whether he is willing to accept the job on those terms and conditions, and:

(i)   if he is willing, make an order to that effect; and

(ii)   if he is unwilling to accept the job on those terms and conditions, then if the tribunal is of the opinion that the refusal is reasonable, it will make an order for the *continuation* of his contract of employment (a 'continuation order').

53.18   Unfair Dismissal – III: Remedies

If the employer has failed to attend the hearing before the tribunal or states that he is unwilling either to reinstate the employee or re-engage him, the tribunal will make a continuation order.

(*TULRCA 1992, s 163*; *ERA 1996, s 129*.)

A continuation order is an order that, until the complaint has been dealt with, the employee's contract will be treated as continuing for the purposes of his entitlement to benefits, including pay, and for the purposes of determining the length and continuity of his employment. If an employer fails to comply with a continuation order, compensation for such non-compliance may also be awarded if the complainant has thereby suffered loss, and the employer will be ordered to pay any amount of wages due under the continuation order (*TULRCA 1992, ss 164, 166*; *ERA 1996, ss 130, 132*).

At any time between the making of an order by an employment tribunal under these interim provisions and the determination or settlement of the complaint to which it relates, the employer or the employee may apply to the tribunal for the revocation of the order on the ground of a relevant change of circumstances which has occurred since the making of the order (*TULRCA 1992, s 165; ERA 1996, s 131*).

53.19   SETTLEMENT

Employers may wish to settle a claim or a potential claim for unfair dismissal rather than proceed to a hearing. The tribunals have a duty to encourage settlement and may do so at the hearing. If settlement is reached, one of two courses must be followed for any agreement reached with the employee to be binding. Either a conciliation offer must be involved (see **2.4 Advisory, Conciliation and Arbitration Service** and note *BNP Paribas v Mezzotero* [2004] IRLR 508, EAT and *Hinton v University of East London* [2005] EWCA Civ 532, [2005] IRLR 552) or the conditions of a statutorily valid compromise agreement must be fulfilled, including that the employee has had independent advice (*ERA 1996, s 203*). In *Industrious Ltd v Horizon Recruitment Ltd* [2010] IRLR 204, the EAT held that an employment tribunal was empowered to decide whether a compromise agreement ought to be set aside for misrepresentation.

If this is not done, an employee will be free to bring a claim notwithstanding that he has received a sum in settlement. Although this amount may be taken into account in assessing compensation (as in the example at **53.10** above), nevertheless it may not be sufficient to extinguish the employer's liability. If a compromise is reached after a tribunal has held a dismissal to be unfair but before making an award of compensation, the same is required in order for the agreement to be binding (see *Courage Take Home Trade Ltd v Keys* [1986] ICR 874). It was also held in *Courage* that where a settlement was fairly reached, but was not binding because of what is now *ERA 1996, s 203*, it might well not be 'just and equitable' to award any further compensation.

In the light of the increasing exercise of the employment tribunal's power to award costs, note *Kopel v Safeway Stores plc* [2003] IRLR 753 with regard to 'Calderbank' letters in the tribunal context, and see further **18.36 Employment Tribunals – II**.

Sums paid by an employer to an employee under a compromise of tribunal proceedings may be subject to different tax liabilities and recoupment rules from sums payable by order of a tribunal or sums payable under the contract of employment itself, therefore care is needed in negotiating and concluding settlements (see eg *Wilson (HM Inspector of Taxes) v Clayton* [2004] EWHC 898 (Ch), [2004] IRLR 611).

54   Vicarious Liability

54.1   'Vicarious liability' describes the principle of law which allows an employer to be held liable for the tortious acts of his employees committed in the course of their employment. Such liability would extend, for example, to the case of a van driver who drives negligently in the normal course of his duties and causes an accident; his employer will be held liable for any resulting injury. The employer may also be held vicariously liable where one employee injures another at work, or where an employee steals from a customer, again providing that the act is done in the course of employment.

There are some instances of vicarious liability imposed by statute, eg by the *Equality Act 2010, s 109(1)* *(see* **11.26** DISCRIMINATION AND EQUAL OPPORTUNITIES – II).

The common law tests (see below) for vicarious liability are not applicable where there is express statutory provision in relation to vicarious liability (*Jones v Tower Boot Co Ltd* [1997] IRLR 168). This principle finds illustration in the case of *Mahood v Irish Centre Housing* (2011) (appeal no UKEAT/0228/10/ZT). In *Mahood*, the Employment Appeal held that an employer was not vicariously liable for the alleged harassment of an employee by a temporary agency worker under the *RRA 1976*. Even if the employer exerted a sufficient degree of control over the agency worker to render the employer tortiously liable at common law for his actions, that did not impact on the question of whether the employer was vicariously liable under statutory provisions contained in the *RRA 1976*. The relevant provisions on vicarious liability did not create liability for third parties. If, however, the tribunal found that the agency worker, as a matter of implication, could be deemed to be an employee of the employer or alternatively, if the harassment occurred in circumstances where the agency worker was exercising authority conferred on him by the employer, and therefore was acting as the employer's agent, then the employer may yet be vicariously liable for the agency worker's actions. However, the common law tests remain relevant to whether or not an employer may be vicariously liable for an employee's contravention of a statute that does not make any express provision as to vicarious liability: *Majrowski v Guys and St Thomas' NHS Hospital Trust* [2006] UKHL 34, [2006] 3 WLR 125, [2006] ICR 1199. In that case, the House of Lords held that an employer may be vicariously liable for harassment committed by its employee that was unlawful by virtue of s 3 of the Protection from Harassment Act 1997 (a provision that on its face only applies to individuals). The judgment in *Majrowski* should be compared with the judgment of the Court of Appeal in *NHS Manchester v Fecitt & Ors* [2011] EWCA Civ 1190. In *Fecitt*, an employee had been subject to victimising behaviour on the part of her colleagues in response to the fact she had made a protected disclosure. The Court of Appeal held that the employer was not liable for the acts of victimisation. This was because the *Employment Rights Act 1996*, which affords protection to employees who have made protected disclosures, does not prohibit victimisation of a whistle-blower by co-workers (cf. *s 39* of the *Equality Act 2010* which prohibits victimisation of an employee who complains of discrimination). In the circumstances, the co-workers victimisation of the employee, whilst being morally repugnant, was not unlawful per se. It followed that there was no unlawful act in respect of which the employer could be held vicariously liable (*Cumbria CC v Carlisle-Morgan* [2007] IRLR 314 overruled)

A key consideration when applying the doctrine of vicarious liability is the degree of connection which the wrongful act has with the particular employment. In *Gravil v Carroll* [2008] EWCA Civ 689, [2008] ICR 1222, [2008] IRLR 829 the Court of Appeal concluded that a rugby club was vicariously liable when one of its players assaulted another player. The Court of Appeal found that the club was liable because the assault was so closely connected to the player's employment with the club that it would be fair and just to hold the club liable. More recently, the Court of Appeal held that church trustees were vicariously liable for the sexual abuse of a minor by an assistant priest: *Maga v Birmingham*

Vicarious Liability

Roman Catholic Archdiocese Trustees [2010] EWCA Civ 256, [2010] 1 WLR 1441 (overturning the judgment of the High Court ([2009] EWHC 780 (QB)). In *Maga*, the Court of Appeal concluded it was fair and just to impose vicarious liability for the sexual abuse on the trustees because there were a number of factors which, when taken together, showed that there was a sufficiently close connection between the employment at the church of the assistant priest (C) and the abuse which C had inflicted on M. The factors relied upon by the Court of Appeal included in particular that: through being employed by the church as a priest, C had been able to hold himself out to M as being particularly trustworthy and authoritative; C had also used his functions as a priest, including his duty to evangelize, to get to know M; the church had given C particular responsibilities for youth work and C had been able to 'groom' M through that work; moreover, C had developed his relationship with M in the course of a disco which had been organised by the church, took place on church premises and which C attended as a priest. It is clear that central to the Court of Appeal's analysis was the fact that it was C's role as a priest in the archdiocese which gave him the status, authority and opportunity to draw M into his sexually abusive orbit. The Supreme Court then took a similar approach in *Catholic Child Welfare Society & Ors v Institute of the Brothers of Christian Schools* [2012] UKSC 56, [2012] 3 WLR 1319, [2013] IRLR 219. In that case, a lay Roman Catholic order provided education to children. The diocesan bodies responsible for the Institute and the Institute itself were found vicariously liable for sexual abuse by the teachers. Having reviewed the cases on vicarious liability, the Court took the view that establishing vicarious liability required the application of a two stage test. At the first stage, the question was whether the relationship between the defendant and the tortfeasor was one which was capable of giving rise to vicarious liability, for example was it akin to an employer/employee relationship. At the second stage, the question was whether the defendant had not only used the tortfeasor to carry on its own business but had done so in a manner which created or significantly increased the risk that the victims would be subject to the relevant unlawful act. In other words, there had to be a strong causative link between the relationship between the defendant and the tortfeasor on the one hand and the unlawful act on the other. It was this 'close connection' which was required between the relationship and the unlawful act which established the defendant's vicarious liability. The Court held that, on the facts of the case before it, the element of vicarious liability was made out. The judgment in Catholic Child Welfare should be compared with the Court of Appeal's judgment in *Brink's Global Services Inc v Igrox Ltd* [2010] EWCA Civ 1207. In *Brink's* the Court of Appeal held that an employer was liable for the acts of an employee who had stolen silver bars from a container awaiting fumigation. The Court held that the theft from the very container which he had been instructed to fumigate was reasonably incidental to the purpose for which he was employed and it was otherwise fair and just to hold the employer liable (compare *Wilson v Excel UK Ltd* [2010] CSIH 35).

In the conjoined cases of *Richard Weddall v Barchester Healthcare Ltd: Wallbank v Wallbank Fox Designs Ltd* [2012] EWCA Civ 25, the Court of Appeal highlighted the essentially fact-sensitive nature of the assessment which must be undertaken in order to determine whether an employer is vicariously liable for the acts of its employee. In the *Weddall* case, an employee of a care home had attended at his place of work and assaulted a co-worker. The assault had taken place shortly after the co-worker had, on instructions from his employer, rung the employee in order to inform him that he needed come into work in order cover a shift. The Court of Appeal held that the employer was not vicariously liable for the assault as it amounted to an independent venture which was separate and distinct from the employee's employment; the instruction by the co-worker was merely a pretext for violence which was entirely unconnected to the employee's employment. By way of contrast, in *Wallbank*, a junior employee had spontaneously and immediately assaulted the managing director of the employing company in response to a verbal instruction. The Court of Appeal held that the company was vicariously liable for the assault as it was essentially a spontaneous reaction to the instruction per se. The judgment indicates that the courts may be more willing to accept that an employer is vicariously liable for the assault of an employee in circumstances where the conditions of the employment themselves tend to increase friction between employees (e.g. in a factory).

In the case of *Hawley v Luminar Leisure Ltd* [2006] EWCA Civ 18, [2006] IRLR 817, the Court of Appeal decided that the owners of a nightclub could be held vicariously liable for an assault carried out by a doorman on a member of the public, even though the doorman had been supplied to the nightclub by a third party company. Though the doorman was not directly employed by the nightclub, he could properly be deemed to be an employee of the nightclub for the purposes of vicarious liability principles. See also on the question of dual vicarious liability, *Viasystems (Tyneside) Ltd v Thermal Transfer (Northern) Ltd* [2005] EWCA Civ 1151, [2006] 2 WLR 428, [2006] ICR 327. In this case, the Court of Appeal held that both the employer and the third party exercising day-to-day control over the employee could be vicariously liable for the employee's negligence. The *Viasystems* decision was considered by the Court of Appeal in *Hawley*. The Court of Appeal concluded that, on the facts of the *Hawley* case, only the nightclub and not the doorman's employer should be liable for the assault on the basis that there had been a total transfer of control to the nightclub. In *Colour Quest Ltd v Total Downstream UK plc* [2009] EWHC 540 (Comm), [2009] 2 Lloyd's Rep 1, the High Court considered questions of vicarious liability in connection with the widely reported explosions at the Buncefield oil storage depot. In that case, the oil tank which caused the explosion was part of the operations of a particular oil storage company (H). The explosion had been caused by the negligence of an employee (N) who had been seconded to H by an oil company (T). T sought to argue that it was not vicariously liable for the explosion and that vicarious liability lay with H as the company to which N had been seconded and, further, as the company which directed and controlled tank filling operations. The court held that T was vicariously liable for N's negligence because, as a matter of fact, it was T rather than H which controlled both tank filling operations and the activities of on-site staff. These conclusions were not challenged when the case went on appeal to the Court of Appeal: [2010] EWCA Civ 180, [2010] QB 86.

In general, there is no vicarious liability for the torts of persons other than employees, such as independent contractors engaged by the employer (but see **54.3** below). Provided that the employer has exercised due care in the choice of the contractor, he should not be held liable for acts of negligence committed by that contractor. This principle was confirmed in by the Court of Appeal in *Biffa Waste Services Ltd v Maschinenfabrik Ernst Hese GMBH* [2008] EWCA Civ 1257, [2009] BLR 1. In that case, the Court of Appeal held that the appellant company (B) was not vicariously liable for the negligence of a sub-contractor (P) who had negligently caused a fire in part of a recycling plant which B was contracted to provide. In reaching this conclusion, the court took into account in particular that: P's men were skilled workers; B did not exercise control over the way they worked; the men had not become part of B's business; their work had been temporary (taking place over a couple of days); and B was not based in the UK and had no presence at the site. The fact that B had supervisory rights in respect of the work did not mean it exercised control in respect of the work, particularly as the right to supervise did not, by itself, carry with it the entitlement to instruction how to do the work. The court emphasised that the burden to show transfer of liability for an employee was a heavy one. The court also rejected arguments that B should be held vicariously liable for P's negligence because the work in question was extra-hazardous. The court held that such an argument would only succeed where the work was exceptionally dangerous whatever precautions were taken. The Court of Appeal thereby distinguishing the earlier and much criticised Court of Appeal judgment in *Honeywill & Stein Ltd v Larkin Bros (London's Commercial Photographers) Ltd* [1934] 1 KB 191. However, where the employer owes a personal duty to safeguard others from harm (as he does in relation to the safety of his employees), he may not escape responsibility by delegating that duty, and will thus have to answer for harm caused by the negligent act of a contractor engaged for the purpose of discharging the duty (see, eg *McDermid v Nash Dredging and Reclamation Co Ltd* [1987] ICR

917; although, this is a case not so much of vicarious liability as a failure to discharge the employer's own primary duty). See also the statutory occupier's liability for independent contractors. (**25.15** HEALTH AND SAFETY AT WORK – I) and statutory liability under *HSWA 1974* (**25.16** HEALTH AND SAFETY AT WORK – I).

For a case in which a town council was held vicariously liable for the behaviour of a councillor towards a council employee, see *Moores v Bude Stratton Town Council* [2000] IRLR 676. The reasoning in *Moores* was applied by the EAT in *De Clare Johnson v MYA Consulting Ltd* [2007] All ER (D) 58 (Dec), EAT. In that case, the EAT found that a company was vicariously liable for the acts of the managing director's partner where the partner lived in the business premises.

An employer which is liable to a third party for damages resulting from the negligence of its employee may seek to recover those damages from the negligent employee. See for example: *Lister v Romford Ice and Cold Storage Co Ltd* [1957] AC 555, HL.

54.2 'IN THE COURSE OF HIS EMPLOYMENT'

The essential precondition of vicarious liability is that the act complained of should have been done in the course of the employment. This concept extends beyond, although it will almost invariably also include, acts which the employee is in fact instructed or authorised to perform. In 2001, the principle was refined by the House of Lords in *Lister v Hesley Hall Ltd* [2001] UKHL 22, [2002] 1 AC 215, [2001] IRLR 472 (see below).

In *Aldred v Nacanco* [1987] IRLR 292, the Court of Appeal approved the following test (taken from *Salmond on Torts*, 18th edn, p 437):

> 'If a servant does negligently that which he was authorised to do carefully, or if he does fraudulently that which he was authorised to do honestly, or if he does mistakenly that which he was authorised to do correctly, his master will answer for that negligence, fraud or mistake. On the other hand, if the unauthorised and wrongful act of the servant is not so connected with the authorised act as to be a mode of doing it, but is an independent act, the master is not responsible; for in such a case the servant is not acting in the course of his employment but has gone outside of it.'

Thus, there may be vicarious liability for the consequences of an act which has been expressly forbidden, eg *Rose v Plenty* [1976] 1 WLR 141 (milk roundsman allowing boy to help with deliveries despite contrary instruction, and boy injured through roundsman's negligence), or which is clearly unauthorised, eg *Morris v CW Martin & Sons Ltd* [1966] 1 QB 716 (dry-cleaning company held liable to owner of fur coat stolen by employee to whom the goods had been entrusted); see also *Brink's Global Services Inc v Igrox Ltd* [2010] EWCA Civ 1207 discussed above. The employer may be vicariously liable for fraud even where the employee acts purely for his own benefit and not to advance the interests of the employer, if the employee is ostensibly authorised to act on the employer's behalf (*Lloyd v Grace, Smith & Co* [1912] AC 716).

In *Lister v Hesley Hall Ltd* [2001] UKHL 22, [2002] 1 AC 215, [2001] IRLR 472, the House of Lords pointed out that the *Salmond* test also states that an employer:

> '. . . is liable even for acts which he has not authorised, provided they are so *connected* with acts which he has authorised that they may rightly be regarded as modes – although improper modes – of doing them.'

The *Lister* case concerned acts of sexual abuse committed by a school warden on boys in his care. Previously, in *Trotman v North Yorkshire County Council* [1999] IRLR 98, a case with similar facts, the Court of Appeal had held that acts of indecent assault on a pupil were too far removed from being an unauthorised mode of carrying out a teacher's duties as to make the employer vicariously liable. This had been followed by the lower courts in *Lister*. However, the House of Lords in *Lister* held that this was the wrong approach. The correct test is to ask whether the employee's torts were so closely connected with the employment that it would be fair and just to hold the employer vicariously liable. On the facts in *Lister* the answer was that they were. See also *Fennelly v Connex South Eastern Ltd* [2001] IRLR 390, CA; *Mattis v Pollock (t/a Flamingo Nightclub)* [2003] EWCA Civ 887, [2003] 1 WLR 2158, CA; *Bernard v A-G of Jamaica* [2004] UKPC 47, [2005] IRLR 398. *Sidhu v Aerospace Composite Technology Ltd* [2000] IRLR 602; *Wilson v Exel UK Ltd (t/a Exel)* [2010] CSIH 35; *Brink's Global Services Inc v Igrox Ltd* [2010] EWCA Civ 1207; *Maga v Birmingham Roman Catholic Archdiocese Trustees* [2010] EWCA Civ 256 and *Richard Weddall v Barchester Healthcare Ltd: Wallbank v Wallbank Fox Designs Ltd* [2012] EWCA Civ 25, discussed above. *Lister* indicates that the details of the relationship between employer and victim, not the precise terms of the tortfeasor employee's employment, will determine whether vicarious liability exists. If the employee's torts took place in the discharge of the employer's duties to the victim, the employer will be vicariously liable: see *Balfron Trustees Ltd v Peterson* [2001] IRLR 758. In *Catholic Child Welfare Society & Ors v Institute of the Brothers of Christian* (see above), the Supreme Court considered the test in Lister. Lord Phillips, giving the judgment of the Court, commented that Lister had not given clear guidance on the nature of the 'close connection' which was required in order to establish vicarious liability. He stressed that the creation of a risk that the unlawful act would take place was likely to be an important element in the facts which gave rise to vicarious liability, although it would not be sufficient to establish vicarious liability without more. This explained why many of the cases where vicarious liability had been established involved employment relationships where the tortfeasor was responsible for care of the victim.

In *Sidhu*, the employer was not vicariously liable for direct racial discrimination for a racist attack on Mr Sidhu which was carried out by a fellow employee out of hours at a racetrack. The attack took place during a social event organised by the company. The Court of Appeal held that the Tribunal had been entitled to find that such behaviour did not fall within the 'course of employment' for the purposes of s 32(1) of the *Race Relations Act 1976*. The fact that the majority of those attending the event were friends and family rather than employees was a significant factual consideration in the case. In *Wilson v Exel UK Ltd (t/a Exel)*, the Scottish Court of Session held that a company was not vicariously liable for a personal injury which had been sustained by an employee following an assault by a colleague. The assault had taken place at the company's offices and during working hours. The Court held that these facts alone were not sufficient to establish liability and that the company was not vicariously liable for the assault as the employee had been acting on a frolic of his own (cf. *Richard Weddall v Barchester Healthcare Ltd: Wallbank v Wallbank Fox Designs Ltd* [2012] EWCA Civ 25, discussed above).

There may be vicarious liability for acts done even whilst the employee is not working, if at the time that employee is being paid for his time, is carrying out the instructions of his employer or is subject to the employer's directions. In *Smith v Stages* [1989] ICR 272, the House of Lords held an employer vicariously liable for injuries sustained in a crash caused by the negligent driving of an employee driving his workmate (the injured claimant) home to Staffordshire after completing a job in Pembroke. The speeches of Lord Goff and Lord Lowry contain extensive analyses of vicarious liability for the acts of employees travelling to and from work. Generally, an employer will not be held vicariously liable for any accident caused by the negligent driving of an employee travelling between his home and his regular place of work, because such a journey is not 'in the course of employment'. However, liability for an accident may be established where the employee is travelling in the employer's time in the course of the employer's business (as in *Smith v Stages*). This will depend on the employee's status, and the nature of his occupation; employees in peripatetic occupations (such as engineers or sales representatives) are likely to come within this category.

54.2   Vicarious Liability

It is a different matter if the tortious act is so far removed from what the employee is in fact authorised to do that he can be said to be on 'a frolic of his own'. Thus, there was no vicarious liability where firemen pursuing a go-slow drove at a snail's pace to a fire (*General Engineering Services Ltd v Kingston and St Andrew Corpn* [1989] ICR 88: their act was not a mere mode of performance, but was the very antithesis of what they were engaged to do). Nor was a contract cleaning company vicariously liable when its employee made international telephone calls from the offices of clients (*Heasmans v Clarity Cleaning Co Ltd* [1987] ICR 949: there was not sufficient nexus with the employment, which had merely provided the opportunity for the criminal act).

In two cases involving police officers, the courts have found the relevant authority to be vicariously liable for the acts of police officers on the basis that the officers in question had, at the time of the unlawful act, held themselves out to the complainant as being police officers. The first of those cases, *Weir v Bettison (sued as Chief Constable of Merseyside Police)* [2003] EWCA Civ 111, [2003] ICR 708, concerned the vicarious liability of the Chief Constable under *s 88* of the *Police Act 1996*. In that case an off-duty police officer had told the claimant he was a police officer before violently assaulting him and locking him in a police van (taken by the officer without authority). The Court of Appeal held that the Chief Constable was vicariously liable: at the time of the incident the police officer was 'apparently acting as a constable, albeit one behaving very badly'. The second case, *Bernard v A-G of Jamaica* [2004] UKPC 47, [2005] IRLR 398, concerned the Attorney General's vicarious liability at common law. Applying the principles enunciated in *Lister*, the Privy Council held that the Attorney-General was vicariously liable for the acts of a police officer who, after announcing that he was a policeman, shot the claimant and subsequently purported to arrest the claimant for interfering with his duties as a policeman. Compare *Hartnell v A-G of the British Virgin Islands* [2004] UKPC 12, [2004] 1 WLR 1273 in which the Privy Council held that the Attorney-General was not vicariously liable where a police officer had used his police gun to open fire, without warning, in a bar. The Privy Council did, however, hold that the Attorney General was primarily liable in negligence for entrusting someone of Mr Hartwell's character and disposition with a gun. See also *N v Chief Constable of Merseyside Police* [2006] EWHC 3041 (QB), [2006] All ER (D) 421 (Nov), the Chief Constable was not vicariously liable where a police officer wearing his uniform and holding himself out as a police officer took an intoxicated woman to his home and raped her. The fact that the officer had used his uniform and position to secure the trust of the woman in question did not by itself render the Chief Constable vicariously liable. The Chief Constable was not liable from the point where the officer put the woman in his car. The judge made clear that the circumstances as whole must be looked at and that the result may have been different if he had been exercising a police functions such as making an arrest.

As will be seen from the above examples, the dividing line between what is and what is not within the course of employment is a fine one, and will often depend upon what the court considers that justice requires in the particular case.

54.3   'PRO HAC VICE' EMPLOYMENT

Sometimes an employer (the general employer) may lend or hire his employee to another employer (the special employer) for a particular task or transaction. Although the employee continues to be employed by the general employer under his contract of employment, he may in certain circumstances be treated as the employee of the special and not of the general employer for the purposes of establishing vicarious liability. One term for this situation is *pro hac vice* ('for this occasion') employment.

Whether the potential liability has in fact been transferred from the general to the special employer must depend upon the arrangements that exist between them, and in particular upon which of them has the right to control the way in which the work is done. It will not be easy to show such a transfer (see, eg *Mersey Docks and Harbour Board v Coggins and Griffith (Liverpool) Ltd* [1947] AC 1), but it was established in the case of *Sime v Sutcliffe Catering Scotland Ltd* [1990] IRLR 228 where the special employer had complete control over day-to-day management and the way the work was carried out. The question of whether potential liability has transferred from the general employer to the special employer was considered by the Court of Appeal in *Hawley v Luminar Leisure Ltd* [2006] EWCA Civ 18, [2006] IRLR 817. In that case, a company which owned a nightclub ('L') contracted with a third party supplier of personnel ('S') for the supply of a doorman. The doorman went on to assault a member of the public whilst working at the nightclub. The Court of Appeal found that the doorman should be deemed to be a temporary employee of L for the purposes of determining vicarious liability. The Court of Appeal went on to find that vicarious liability should be attributed to L rather than S even though S employed the doorman. The Court of Appeal concluded that L, and not S, should be held vicariously liable for the assault, first, because, in obtaining the doorman's services, L had not been seeking to gain access to trained specialists on whose skill and expertise it depended and, second, because control of the doorman had rested with L; thus, there had been an effective transfer of both control and responsibility from S to L. Note, however, that while control is the paramount test, 'entire and absolute control' is not a necessary precondition of vicarious liability in such cases: *Viasystems (Tyneside) Ltd v Thermal Transfer (Northern) Ltd* [2005] EWCA Civ 1151, [2006] 2 WLR 428, [2005] IRLR 983. In the case of *Biffa Waste Services Ltd v Maschinenfabrik Ernst Hese GMBH* [2008] EWCA Civ 1257 [2009] BLR 1, the Court of Appeal held that a contractor (B) who enjoyed supervisory rights in respect of work done by a sub-contractor (P) lacked the necessary control over the sub-contractor's employees to be vicariously liable for their negligence. Factors influencing the Court of Appeal's conclusion on this issue included that the contractor was not present at the site where the negligence occurred (*Viasystems* distinguished); P's workers were skilled workers; B did not control the way they worked; and the work was done over a very short period (a couple of days).

Where it is the subcontracted employee himself who is injured, the 'pro hac vice' doctrine does not apply and there is a right of action against the general employer. The question of who controls the subcontracted employee is only relevant to the issue of liability if the subcontracted employee injures a third party (*Morris v Breaveglen Ltd* [1993] IRLR 350).

It was, until the decision of the Court of Appeal in the *Viasystems* case, generally assumed that it was not possible for both the general employer and the special employer to be vicariously liable for the same act of the same employee. *Viasystems* concerned the installation of air conditioning in a factory. The first defendants were engaged to do the work. They subcontracted ducting work to the second defendants, who in turn contracted with the third defendants for the provision of fitters and fitters' mates. A fitters' mate (S) negligently damaged part of the ducting system, causing the factory to flood. At the time he was under the supervision of both the fitter (employed, like S, by the third defendants) and the second defendants' supervisor. At first instance, the County Court found the third defendants alone to be vicariously liable for the negligence of S. It was assumed (apparently by all parties) that it was not possible to have dual vicarious liability. On appeal to the Court of Appeal, however, the Court reviewed the authorities that were said to support that assumption. They found that, in most of those cases, the possibility of dual vicarious liability had not been argued or considered (as, indeed, it had not in *Viasystems* at first instance). May LJ observed that 'the core question is who was entitled, and in theory obliged, to control the employee's relevant negligent act so as to prevent it'. He concluded that, if there were (as there were in *Viasystems*) genuinely two 'employers' who could have controlled the employee, then both could be vicariously liable. Rix LJ agreed that two 'employers' could be vicariously liable, but he put the test slightly differently. He said dual vicarious liability would be found in a 'situation where the employee in question, at any rate for relevant purposes, is so much a part of the work, business or organisation of both employers that it is just to make both employers answer for his negligence'. The Court noted that such situations would be rare, and that dual vicarious liability would be redundant where one of the 'employers' was itself primarily liable. The Court determined that the second and third defendants were equally responsible and that the second and third defendants should each contribute 50% of the damages awarded to the claimant pursuant to *ss 1(1)* and *2* of the *Civil Liability (Contribution) Act 1978* (which provide, respectively, that 'any person liable in respect of any damage suffered by another person may recover contribution from any other person liable in respect of the same damage (whether jointly with him or otherwise)' and that the amount of recoverable contribution 'shall be such as may be found by the court to be just and equitable having regard to the extent of the person's responsibility for the damage in question'.

The Supreme Court has now approved Rix LJ's approach and disapproved that of May LJ. It found two 'employers' vicariously liable in *Catholic Child Welfare Society & Ors v Institute of the Brothers of Christian Schools* (see above). In that case, the institute was a Roman Catholic order providing education to children. The diocesan bodies with statutory responsibility for managing a school left it to the institute to nominate a brother to act as headmaster and appoint other brothers to teach there. The question was whether the Diocesan bodies or the institute itself should be held liable for sexual abuse by the brothers teaching in the institute. The Supreme Court held them both liable. In doing so, it expressly preferred Rix LJ's approach. It found that: 'where two defendants were potentially vicariously liable for the act of a tortfeasor, it was necessary to give independent consideration to the relationship between the tortfeasor and each defendant in order to decide whether that defendant was vicariously liable. The test for liability was not whether both defendants had exercised control over the tortfeasor but whether the tortfeasor had been so much a part of the work, business or organisation of both defendants that it was fair to make both answer for his acts. In considering that question in relation to each defendant the approach of Rix LJ is to be preferred to that of May LJ.'

55   Working Time

55.1   THE WORKING TIME DIRECTIVE

Until relatively recently working hours were not regulated by statute for the vast majority of workers in the UK. Special provisions have applied to specific groups in the past but most were swept away in the 1980s and 1990s. For example, restrictions on the employment of retail workers contained in the *Shops Act 1950* were repealed by the *Deregulation and Contracting Out Act 1994*, although some protection against enforced Sunday working has remained (now contained in ss *36–43 Employment Rights Act 1996*).

This situation changed in 1998 as a result of European legislation, but only after a protracted battle. In November 1993 *EC Directive 93/104* 'concerning certain aspects of the organisation of working time' ('the *Working Time Directive*') was adopted; it came into force in member states on 23 November 1996. The legal basis for the *Directive* was as a health and safety measure under *art 118A* of the *Treaty of Rome* (the current equivalent is *art 154* of the *Treaty on the Functioning of the European Union*), which requires only qualified majority voting. Hence it could be, and was, adopted without the assent of the UK Government. However, the Conservative Government of the day refused to accept the legitimacy of the *Directive* on the grounds that it could not be categorised as health and safety legislation. No attempt was made by the UK to comply with the 1996 deadline for implementation, pending the outcome of a challenge to the *Directive* in the CJEU.

In the event the Court ruled, in *United Kingdom v EU Council*: C-84/94 [1997] ICR 443, that (with one minor exception) the UK's objections should be rejected. Following a change of government, implementation of the *Directive* eventually took place on 1 October 1998, by means of the *Working Time Regulations 1998 (SI 1998/1833)*. The *1998 Regulations* have been supplemented by guidance published by the Department of Trade and Industry (now the Department for Business, Innovation and Skills (BIS)), in accordance with a duty imposed on the Secretary of State by *reg 35A* (a provision added in 1999). It should, however, be noted that this guidance has no formal legal status as an interpretation of the *Regulations*. For further details see **55.26**.

The *Directive*, which covers working hours, rest breaks and holidays, initially did not apply to a number of sectors of activity. The exceptions were: air, rail, road, sea, inland waterway and lake transport, sea fishing, other work at sea and the activities of doctors in training. (For the scope of these exceptions see further **55.3** below.)

However, agreement was reached in 2000 on the extension of the *Directive* to excluded sectors and activities. The *Working Time Directive* was amended by *Directive 2000/34* to cover all non-mobile workers in the excluded sectors, doctors in training, and offshore and railway workers (including mobile railway workers). The *Directive* was implemented domestically by amendments to the *Working Time Regulations* with effect from 1 August 2003, with implementation for doctors in training phased over several years but finally completed from 1 August 2011. The *Directive*, as amended by the *2000 Directive*, was in turn replaced by *Directive 2003/88/EC*, a purely consolidating measure, which came into force on 2 August 2004. References in this chapter to the *Directive* apply equally to the 2003 version.

In addition to this general extension of the original *Directive*, further *Directives* have been adopted for those specific categories of workers still not covered by the principal provisions. The working time of seafarers engaged on merchant ships was covered in *Directive 99/63*, which was given effect in the UK by the *Merchant Shipping (Hours of Work) Regulations 2002*; see **55.31** below for more details. Comparable provisions covering workers on sea fishing vessels, and on inland waterway and lake transport, are summarised at **55.31** and **55.32**.

Mobile workers in the civil aviation sector were covered by a separate *Directive, 2000/79*, in turn implemented domestically by the *Civil Aviation (Working Time) Regulations 2004, SI 2004/756*, discussed at **55.33** below.

A further *Directive, 2002/15* 'on the organisation of working time of persons performing mobile road transport activities', which applies to drivers covered by *Regulation EEC 3820/85* (now *Regulation 561/2006*) or the AETR agreement, was implemented by the *Road Transport (Working Time) Regulations 2005, SI 2005/639*. For further details see **55.34** and **55.35** below. Self-employed owner-drivers were not initially covered by the *Regulations*. However in April 2012 amendments were made to the *2005 Regulations* by the *Road Transport (Working Time) (Amendment) Regulations 2012, SI 2012/991*, extending the application of the *2005 Regulations* to self-employed drivers, with effect from 11 May 2012.

The provisions of the original *Working Time Directive* permitting derogations from its provisions, in particular those permitting individual opt-outs from the 48 hour week, were expressly made subject to a review by the European Council on a report from the Commission. The principal areas considered for amendment of the *Directive* were a tightening up (or the removal) of the provision permitting member states to allow individual opt-outs from the maximum 48 hour working week (a provision the UK has adopted: see **55.7** below) and a change in the status under the *Directive* of time spent on call but not actually working.

The Commission's initial report was issued in December 2003. This was then followed by various rounds of consultations on proposals and counter-proposals, eventually ending in April 2009 in deadlock between the Parliament, the Council and the Commission, and abandonment of the attempt to amend the *Directive*.

A fresh initiative by the Commission to secure agreement to amendments to the *Directive* was announced in March 2010. After an initial decision by the Social Partners not to attempt to produce a Framework Agreement, their agreement to negotiate a Framework Agreement was eventually announced in November 2011, but these negotiations failed to produce an agreed proposal, and there is currently no immediate prospect of any agreement being reached on changes to the *Directive*.

55.2 WORKING TIME REGULATIONS 1998

As noted above, the *Working Time Directive* was implemented in Great Britain by the *Working Time Regulations 1998 (SI 1998/1833)*, which came into force on 1 October 1998. The *1998 Regulations* also brought into force certain provisions in the EC *Directive on the Protection of Young People at Work (94/33)* ('the *Young Workers' Directive*) relating to rest periods, breaks and night work in respect of young people. See also **3.6** CHILDREN AND YOUNG PERSONS. The *1998 Regulations* have subsequently been amended several times; details are given below. The *1998 Regulations*, as amended, govern hours of work, night work, breaks and holidays.

Since the *1998 Regulations* (as amended) are the domestic implementation of the *Directive*, courts and tribunals will approach the interpretation of the *Regulations* on the basis that they should so far as possible be so interpreted as to give effect to the stated purposes of the *Directive*. In this context it is important to appreciate that the *Directive* was adopted as a health and safety measure, as one of the 'daughter' directives under the 1989 *Framework Health and Safety Directive 89/391*. It should therefore be interpreted so as to promote the protection of workers' health and safety whenever such an interpretation is possible. In addition, of course, the case law of the CJEU on the interpretation and application of the *Directive* is likely to be a decisive guide to the interpretation of equivalent provisions in the *1998 Regulations*.

The CJEU has held that *art 7* of the *Directive*, which gives workers the right to paid annual leave, is sufficiently unconditional and precise to be directly enforceable in national courts, against state authorities in their capacity as employers: *Dominguez v Centre informatique du*

Cente Ouest Atlantique: C-282/10 [2012] IRLR 321. This means that in claims made under the *Regulations* against those public sector employers which are, in EU terms, state authorities, the *Directive* can be relied on as a source of rights if the *Regulations* cannot be interpreted to give full effect to the equivalent provision of the *Directive*. The CJEU has also held that *art 6(b)* of the *Directive*, which sets a limit on the working week of an average of 48 hours, is directly enforceable in national courts and tribunals against state authorities as employers: see *Pfeiffer v Deutsches Rotes Kreuz, Kreisverband Waldshut eV*: C-397/01 to 403/01 [2005] IRLR 137.

An example of the general approach of the CJEU to the interpretation of the *Working Time Directive* is its decision in *European Commission v United Kingdom*: C-484/04 [2006] IRLR 888. In this case, the European Commission had issued a Reasoned Opinion that the United Kingdom had failed fully to implement the *Directive* in two respects. The first complaint related to *reg 20(2)*, which gave exemptions from the *Regulations* for the unmeasured part of partly unmeasured working time. The second related not to the wording of the *Regulations* themselves but to the accompanying Guidance issued by the Department of Trade and Industry, which (at that time) stated that 'employers must make sure that workers *can* take [rest breaks and rest periods], but are not required to make sure that they *do* take their rest' (the emphasis was in the original text). The UK Government declined to act on the Reasoned Opinion, and the Commission brought enforcement proceedings.

The United Kingdom formally conceded the first point, on partly unmeasured working time, at the hearing of the case in January 2006, and subsequently introduced the *Working Time (Amendment) Regulations 2006 (SI 2006/99)*, which removed the offending provision. The Court however addressed the issue in its decision, finding that there was no room in the *Directive* for partial exemptions for those whose working time was partly unmeasured. On the second point, the Court also found against the UK. Whilst accepting that the *Directive* did not require member states to go so far as requiring employers to force their workers to take rest entitlements, the Guidance was 'liable to render the rights [to rest periods and rest breaks] meaningless' and was thus incompatible with the objective of the directive, which required minimum rest periods to be treated as 'essential for the protection of workers' health and safety'. The Court added that 'Member States are under an obligation to guarantee that each of the minimum requirements laid down by the directive is observed'. The DTI amended the passage in the Guidance criticised by the Court, by deleting the second half of the quoted passage.

55.3   Coverage

Workers covered by the *1998 Regulations* include employees working under a contract of employment and other individuals who work under a contract personally to perform work or provide services for the 'employer' (except for people genuinely in business on their own account who are in a client or customer relationship with the 'employer') (*reg 2(1)*). *Regulation 36* provides that an agency worker who would not otherwise fall within the definition of a worker under these provisions will be treated as being employed by whichever of the agent or principal is responsible for paying him or her or, if that is not ascertainable, by whichever in fact pays the worker (see further for the position of agency workers generally **55.37** below). The extended definition of 'worker' has been held to include self-employed building subcontractors who in practice worked exclusively for one employer: *Byrne Bros (Formwork) Ltd v Baird* [2002] IRLR 96. (See further on this *Wright v Redrow Homes (Yorkshire) Ltd* [2004] EWCA Civ 469, [2004] IRLR 720, and, for a fuller discussion of these and subsequent cases on this much-litigated issue, see EMPLOYEE, SELF-EMPLOYED OR WORKER? **14.9**.)

The *Regulations* also apply, by express provision, to those in Crown service and the armed forces, and to police officers (who would otherwise fall outside the definition of 'workers'): *regs 37–41*. Certain non-employed trainees are also covered by the *Regulations* (*reg 42*). The breadth of the application of the Regulations reflects the point that the CJEU has repeatedly held that the term 'worker', 'has an autonomous meaning specific to European Union Law' applicable to the scope of the *Working Time Directive*, which 'may not be interpreted differently according to the law of member States': see most recently *Union syndicale Solidaires Isère v Premier Ministre*: C-428/09 [2011] 1 CMLR 1206, [2011] IRLR 84, para 28. The CJEU in that case went on to reject an argument that casual or seasonal workers, restricted to working no more than 80 days a year, could be regarded as outside the scope of the *Directive*.

Those requirements of the *Young Workers' Directive* which were not implemented by the *1998 Regulations* were implemented by amendments to the *1998 Regulations* introduced by the *Working Time (Amendment) Regulations 2002*. The principal changes are the imposition of a maximum working day of 8 hours, and a maximum working week of 40 hours (neither of which is subject to averaging over a longer period) for workers below the age of 18 (but above compulsory school age: see below). See further **55.6**.

In addition, the *2002 Regulations* restrict the employment of a young worker during the 'restricted period', which is normally 10 pm to 6 am, but 11 pm to 7 am if the worker is contractually required to work later than 10 pm: for details of these restrictions see **55.10** below.

There are separate provisions in the *Children and Young Persons Act 1933, s 18(1)*, as amended in compliance with *Directive 94/33*, which regulate the working hours and holiday entitlements of children below the maximum compulsory school age. (For Scotland, the equivalent provisions are in the *Children and Young Persons (Scotland) Act 1937*.) The EAT has held, by reference to these provisions, that such children are not 'workers' for the purposes of the *1998 Regulations*, and accordingly not covered by them: *Ashby v Addison (t/a Brayton News)* [2003] ICR 667, a case involving a claim for holiday pay by a 15 year old paper boy.

Following amendments made by the *Working Time (Amendment) Regulations 2003*, the *1998 Regulations* now apply to all workers (with the exclusion of school age children) other than those mobile workers in certain transport sectors, who are now all covered by separate legislation. Doctors in training were brought fully within the scope of the *Regulations* with effect from August 2009, subject to limited and specific exemptions from the 48 hour working week the last of which expired on 31 July 2011.

The *Regulations* do not apply to 'certain activities of the armed forces, police or other civil protection services', but only to the extent that certain characteristics of the particular service concerned 'inevitably conflict' with the *Regulations: reg 18*. This exception mirrors a provision in *art 1(3)* of the *Directive*, which was narrowly construed by the CJEU in *Pfeiffer v Deutsches Rotes Kreuz, Kreisverband Waldshut eV*: C-397/01 to C-403/01 [2005] IRLR 137 as applying to the emergency services only in the context of the provision of services essential for the protection of public health, safety or order in situations of exceptional gravity, and thus not excluding from the *Directive* the routine operation of a public ambulance service. The same conclusion was reached in relation to a public fire service in *Personalrat der Feuerwehr Hamburg v Leiter der Feuerwehr Hamburg*: C-52/04, unreported, with the proviso that the 48 hour limit on weekly working time could be exceeded 'in exceptional circumstances of such gravity and scale that the aim of ensuring the proper functioning of services essential for the protection of public interests, such as public order, health and safety, must temporarily prevail over the aim of guaranteeing the health and safety of workers assigned to intervention and rescue teams'. This interpretation is very likely to be followed in the construction of the exception in the *1998 Regulations*.

With regard to the former exclusion of transport workers, the position initially was that all workers, whether mobile or non-mobile, within undertakings in the excluded sectors, were excluded from the *Directive*: *Bowden v Tuffnells Parcels Express Ltd*: C-133/00 [2001] IRLR

838. This is still relevant to the exclusion of mobile workers in the civil aviation and road transport sectors referred to at (i) and (iii) below, but non-mobile workers in these sectors were brought within the scope of the *Regulations* by the amendments made in 2003. The Court in *Pfeiffer*, above, held that emergency ambulance services were outside the road transport sector. It was accepted that bus drivers engaged in the provision of scheduled services fall within the provisions of the *1998 Regulations*, rather than the *Road Transport (Working Time) Regulations 2005*, in *Feist v First Hampshire & Dorset Ltd* [2007] All ER (D) 180 (Feb), EAT.

In summary, the position as to the coverage of the *1998 Regulations* is now as follows:

(a)   all workers in Great Britain are covered save for those in exempted categories listed below; see below for the application of the *Regulations* outside Great Britain;

(b)   the *Regulations* do not apply to those of compulsory school age;

(c)   the *Regulations* do not apply to merchant seafarers to whom *Directive 99/63* applies;

(d)   the *Regulations* do not apply to workers on board sea-going fishing vessels or ships or hovercraft operating inland waterway or lake transport (of goods or passengers); see further below.

In addition, the provisions of the *Regulations* limiting working time and night work, relating to monotonous work, and conferring rights to rest periods and rest breaks, do not apply:

(i)   to mobile workers in the civil aviation sector who are covered by the legislation implementing *Directive 2000/79;*

(ii)   to the extent that characteristics peculiar to the armed forces, the police and civil protection services inevitably conflict with any such provisions;

(iii)   to mobile workers in the road transport sector, who are covered by legislation under *Directive 2002/15*

(For those in categories (i) and (ii), but not (iii), entitlements regarding health assessments and paid annual leave are also excluded.)

For the specific application of the *1998 Regulations* to mobile workers on railways see **55.29**; for scafarers see further **55.31**, for mobile workers in the lake and inland waterway transport sectors see further **55.32**, for the aviation sector see further **55.33** and for mobile workers in road transport see **55.34** and **55.35**. One further exclusion, in respect of hours of work, restrictions on night work, rights to health assessments and protection from monotonous work, but not in respect of rest breaks, rest periods or rights to annual leave, is for workers employed as domestic servants in a private household: *reg 19*. See further **55.30** below.

The *1998 Regulations* apply to Great Britain. The territorial scope of the *Regulations* was extended by the *Working Time (Amendment) Regulations 2003 (SI 2003/1684)* to 'offshore work', as defined, and from 1 October 2006 their territorial scope was further extended to cover workers on oil and gas rigs in UK territorial waters and the UK and cross-border oil and gas fields within the UK sector of the Continental Shelf (see the *Working Time (Amendment No 2) Regulations 2006, SI 2006/2389)*; the EAT has since confirmed the view of the DTI (as it then was) that this amendment was simply declaratory of the effect of the *2003 Regulations*: *Transocean International Resources Ltd v Russell* (UKEATS/0074/05) (4 October 2006, unreported).

In *Bleuse v MBT Transport Ltd* [2008] IRLR 264, the EAT had to consider whether the *1998 Regulations* can apply outside Great Britain and its associated waters. The claim in issue was brought by a German national, resident in Germany, who worked as a lorry driver, principally in Austria, for a company registered in the UK but owned by an Austrian national. The Claimant never worked within Britain, but his contract of employment was expressed to be governed by English law. In the context of a claim for holiday pay, the EAT held that the claim could be maintained in an employment tribunal as this was necessary in order to give effect to a directly enforceable EU right.

The status and scope of what has become known as the '*Bleuse* principle' is however far from clear. It is unclear from the EAT's reasoning in *Bleuse* itself whether the decision would apply equally to other rights under the *1998 Regulations*, or what difference it would make if there was a clear right to pursue the claim in another EU member state, if the Respondent was not a UK company, or the contract was not governed by English law (or some combination of these factors). The Court of Appeal in *Duncombe v Secretary of State for Children, Schools and Families* [2009] EWCA Civ 1355, [2010] IRLR 331 held that *Bleuse* was correctly decided, and enunciated a general principle that tribunals have jurisdiction under statutory provisions implementing EU Directives in any case where it is necessary to assume jurisdiction to give effect to an EU right, at least where the contract in issue is governed by English (or Scots) law.

However when the case reached the Supreme Court (under the name *Secretary of State for Children, Schools and Families v Fletcher* [2011] UKSC 14, [2011] ICR 495), it was decided on a different point, making it unnecessary to decide the correctness of the *Bleuse* principle. Lady Hale, giving the only reasoned judgment, indicated that the Court was favourably inclined to the principle, but that had it been necessary to decide whether the claimants could rely on rights conferred by a Directive in relation to employment in another EU member state, the Court would have considered it necessary to refer the point to the CJEU for an opinion. The applicability of the '*Bleuse* principle' is therefore unclear pending a decision on the point by the CJEU.

It is in any case clear that the *Bleuse* principle does not confer rights under the *1998 Regulations* on a worker outside the EU; this was confirmed by the EAT in *Dhunna v Creditsights Ltd* (UKEAT/0246/12) (3 April 2013, unreported) in relation to a worker based in Dubai.

55.4   Agreements: definition

Where flexibility and modifications are permitted under the *Working Time Regulations*, employers may conclude agreements to cover the situation. Depending on the circumstances, these may take the form of a collective agreement, a workforce agreement or a relevant agreement.

Regulation 2(1) provides that a *collective agreement* is an agreement or arrangement made by or on behalf of one or more independent trade unions and one or more employers or employers' associations relating to matters set out in *TULRCA 1992, s 178(2)*; see 5 COLLECTIVE AGREEMENTS. For the purposes of the Working Time Regulations, a collective agreement may include an award made under a collective agreement providing for binding third party arbitration: *Bewley v HM Prison Service* [2004] ICR 422.

A *workforce agreement* means an agreement between an employer and its workers or their elected representatives in respect of which certain conditions are satisfied as set out in *Sch 1*:

(a)   the agreement is in writing;

(b)   it has effect for a specified period of five years or less;

(c)   it applies to all the relevant members of the workforce or to all of the relevant members who belong to a particular group (eg who undertake a particular function, work at a particular workplace or belong to a particular department);

(d)   it is signed by representatives of the workforce (or particular group, as applicable). If the employer has 20 or fewer workers, the agreement may be signed either by appropriate representatives or by the majority of workers employed by the employer, but note that the limit is on the total number of workers employed, not the number covered by the agreement, if that is only a section of the workforce;

(e)   before the agreement was signed, the employer provided all workers to whom the agreement applies with copies and such guidance as is reasonable to understand it fully.

Requirements concerning the election of representatives are set out at *Sch 1 para 3*.

A *relevant agreement* includes both collective and workforce agreements and, in addition, any other agreement in writing which is legally enforceable as between worker and employer. This definition may therefore include the written terms of a contract of employment.

Where a provision of the *Regulations* is modified or excluded by a workforce or collective agreement and a worker is thereby required to work during what would be a rest period or break, the employer must allow, where possible, an equivalent period of compensatory rest. In exceptional cases where it is not possible for objective reasons to grant compensatory rest, the employer must provide appropriate protection to safeguard the worker's health and safety (*reg 24*). The scope of the concept of compensatory rest is considered more fully at **55.29** below.

55.5   WORKING TIME

In relation to a worker, 'working time' is defined in *reg 2(1)* as:

(a)   any period during which the individual is working, at the employer's disposal and carrying out his or her activity or duties;

(b)   any period during which he or she is receiving 'relevant training'; and

(c)   any additional period which is to be treated as working time for the purpose of the *Regulations* under a relevant agreement.

'Relevant training' means work experience or training provided on a training course or programme of training for employment, other than courses run by educational institutions or organisations whose main business is the provision of training.

According to the BIS Guidance for employers, the definition of working time includes: working lunches, business travel time, job-related training, and time spent abroad working for an employer in Great Britain. It does not include: home-to-work travel, rest breaks when no work is done, time spent travelling outside normal working time or non job-related training.

There is no corresponding definition of 'rest', and a rest period is defined in such a way as to exclude any period of working time from being treated as a rest period, but not otherwise more specifically. In effect the two concepts are mutually exclusive, and any time that is not working time can be attributed as part of an entitlement to a rest period, including time spent on such activities as travel between the workplace and the worker's home. See further **55.14–55.17**, below.

One important issue as to the ambit of the definition of working time is the status of time 'on call'. This has been the subject of three decisions of the CJEU, to the effect that 'on-call' time constitutes working time where the worker is required to be at his or her place of work during this period. If the worker is away from the workplace when on call and can pursue leisure activities, on–call time is not working time (*Sindicato de Médicos de Asistencia Pública (Simap) v Conselleria de Sanidad y Consumo de la Generalidad Valenciana*: C-303/98 [2000] IRLR 845). The Court has subsequently confirmed that time spent on call and at the workplace, but not actually performing the worker's duties, was to be regarded as working time in circumstances where the worker (a hospital doctor) was permitted to rest when his services were not required, and rest facilities were provided for this purpose by the employer: *Landeshauptstadt Kiel v Jaeger*, above: C-151/02 [2003] IRLR 804.

This conclusion was reiterated in *Vorel v Nemocnice Český Krumlov*: C-437/05 [2007] ECR-I 331, but with the important additional qualification that this did not prevent national law from providing for a lower rate of pay for the inactive parts of periods on–call (as the Czech law under reference did).

However, in *Dellas v Premier Ministre*: C-14/04 [2006] IRLR 225 the CJEU held to be incompatible with the *Directive* a French law which provided for time spent on call and at the employer's premises, but not actually working, to count at the rate of only a half or a third of actual time; the principal objection of the Court was that it was (at least theoretically) possible for workers subject to this law to work in excess of the 48 hour week, although France has adopted a lower maximum of 44 hours. Thus whilst the rate of pay for time on call may be lower (subject, in the UK context, to the application of the National Minimum Wage), time on call itself must be taken into account fully.

These decisions of the CJEU have been controversial for their implications for the staffing of emergency medical services in particular, and would have been affected by the implementation of the Commission's proposals for revision of the *Directive*, referred to at **55.1** above. The failure of negotiations between the Social Partners on amendments to the *Directive* however precludes any immediate change in the position.

The EAT has held that the effect of the decision in *Jaeger* is that a warden employed at a sheltered housing complex on 24 hour call is to be regarded as working throughout the period on call although she was provided with a flat to occupy at the premises, and was free to use her time as she pleased subject to remaining in the vicinity to be available for call-outs. Accordingly the employer was in breach of the requirement to permit a daily rest period for the warden: *MacCartney v Oversley House Management* [2006] ICR 510, EAT, not following the earlier case of *Stamp v South Holland District Council* [2003] All ER (D) 19 (Jun), which the EAT regarded as inconsistent with the reasoning and decision in *Jaeger*. *MacCartney* has since been followed in a further EAT decision on similar facts, *Hughes v Graham (t/a Graylyns Residential Home)* [2008] All ER (D) 137 (Oct), EAT. However not all time spent on call is working time, as confirmed by the decision of the Northern Ireland Court of Appeal in *Blakley v South Eastern Health & Social Services Trust* [2009] NICA 62 that time spent on call by an Estates Officer, who was required to be contactable to be called out but not required to be at his workplace, or at home, was not 'working time'; only the time during which he was actually on a call-out met the requirements of the definition.

The English Court of Appeal has also considered the application of the definition of 'working time' to 'down time': *Gallagher v Alpha Catering Services Ltd* [2004] EWCA Civ 1559, [2005] IRLR 102. The employees delivered catering supplies to aircraft at Gatwick Airport. They often had to wait for an aircraft to be ready for servicing; during these periods they had to remain at the airport and in radio contact with the employer, but could use the time eg to take refreshment. It was held that all three limbs of the definition of 'working time' were satisfied on these facts, and the down time or waiting time counted as working time.

On the other hand, an employment tribunal in a test case on the rights of workers on North Sea oil rigs has held that the time between each working shift whilst the worker is offshore is not working time, and accordingly can constitute a rest period, despite the necessary restrictions on what activities can be undertaken whilst on the oil rig and the fact that the worker cannot in practice leave the oil rig between shifts: *Russell v Transocean International Resources Ltd* (Case S/104056/04) (May 2005, unreported). This point was not directly in issue in the subsequent appeals to the EAT, Court of Session and Supreme Court in this case (see *Russell v Transocean International Resources Ltd* [2011] UKSC 57, [2012] IRLR 149), but the tribunal's view was implicitly endorsed in the approach to the case adopted by Lord Hope in the Supreme Court.

The issue of what constitutes 'working time' may also arise as a matter of contract. An example is *Alexander v Jarvis Hotels plc* (EATS/0062/05) (30 May 2006, unreported) where the EAT held that time spent by a hotel manager overnight at the hotel was working time, although he was free to sleep. His work consisted of being present at the hotel to respond to any emergency, an arrangement required of the hotel for health and safety reasons. There have also been a number of cases about what constitutes time for which payment is due under the *National Minimum Wage Act 1998*, but these relate to different definitions and do not necessarily assist in interpreting the definition of 'working time' in the *1998 Regulations* (and nor do decisions on the meaning of 'working time' under the *Working Time Regulations* assist in the interpretation of the *National Minimum Wage Regulations*: see *Wray v J W Lees & Co (Brewers) Ltd* [2012] IRLR 43, EAT).

55.6   Maximum weekly working time

An employer is required to take all reasonable steps, in keeping with the need to protect health and safety, to ensure that each adult worker works no more than 48 hours on average in each working week, averaged over reference periods of 17 weeks. Such periods are extended to 26 weeks for certain workers – see 'special case' exemptions at 55.29 below. The reference period may also be extended to a maximum of 52 weeks where a collective or workforce agreement so provides, on the basis of objective or technical reasons concerning the organisation of work (*regs 4(1), (2), (5), 23(b)*). The possible extension to 52 weeks is the technical basis on which 'annualised hours' agreements are most appropriately made. *Regulations 25A* and *25B* of the *1998 Regulations* make specific provision for the reference periods applicable respectively to doctors in training (26 weeks) and offshore workers (52 weeks).

A relevant agreement may stipulate when the reference period begins. Otherwise, the reference period will be a rolling 17–week (or 26 or up to 52 week) period (*reg 4(3)*). Where a worker has been employed for less than 17 weeks, the reference period will be the number of weeks which have elapsed since he or she started work (*reg 4(4)*).

Average working time is calculated according to the formula:

$$\frac{A+B}{C}$$

where:

'A' is the total number of hours of working time in the reference period;

'B' is the total number of hours worked immediately after the reference period during extra days equivalent to the number of 'excluded days' (see below for this) in the reference period; and

'C' is the number of weeks in the reference period (*reg 4(6)*).

For the purpose of calculating average hours, certain days are to be excluded: days taken as basic statutory annual leave under the *1998 Regulations* (but not days of annual leave taken under a contractual provision over and above the statutory entitlement, or days taken as part of the additional statutory entitlement introduced by the *Working Time (Amendment)*

Regulations 2007; periods of sick leave and maternity, paternity, adoption or parental leave; and any hours in respect of which an individual opt-out agreement (see **55.7** below) is in force (*reg 4(7)*). The effect of the exclusions is in broad terms intended to ensure that the average is accurate, but because not all periods of leave are excluded, the formula will in some cases understate the actual average of the hours normally worked.

Steps reasonably taken by an employer to ensure that it complies with the duty imposed by *reg 4* in relation to a particular worker will not constitute a detriment to that worker for the purposes of a claim under the *Employment Rights Act 1996: Arriva London South Ltd v Nicolaou (No 2)* [2012] ICR 510, EAT. See further **55.23** below.

The weekly limit is disapplied in the case of workers whose time is 'unmeasured' (see **55.28** below). Following the revocation of *reg 20(2)*, this only applies to workers the *whole* of whose working time is unmeasured.

Young workers (ie those under 18 but above compulsory school age) are subject to stricter limits on working hours. There is a maximum working day of 8 hours, and a maximum working week of 40 hours; in neither case is there provision for averaging over a longer period: see *reg 5A*.

The restrictions on the working week for adult workers apply in relation to a particular employer. There is no provision in the *1998 Regulations* imposing any specific duty on employers to limit the aggregate working hours of those workers who work for more than one employer, and no mechanism for enabling employers to police such arrangements. The sole exceptions to this are the provisions relating to young workers: see *reg 5A(2)*, which specifically limits the total working time which may be undertaken for *all* employers; and *reg 12(5)*, which requires the aggregation of working time for different employers in calculating young workers' rest break entitlements. Whilst the absence of any equivalent provisions for adult workers is a significant weakness in the protection of workers from excessive hours, it is not considered to be contrary to the *Working Time Directive*. One of the amendments to the *Directive* proposed by the Parliament would have applied the 48 hour maximum to the aggregate time worked for all employers, but this proposal fell with the breakdown of negotiations over the proposed amended *Directive* in April 2009, and is unlikely to feature in any future amendment to the *Directive*.

55.7 Opt-out agreements

It is permissible to disapply the 48-hour weekly maximum if the employer obtains the worker's written agreement to exceed these hours (*reg 4(1)*). Any such opt-out agreement may relate to a specified period or apply indefinitely. Agreements are to be terminable by the worker giving not less than seven days' notice in writing. The employer may not require more than three months' notice (*reg 5(2), (3)*). Employers are required to maintain up-to-date records of all workers who have signed an opt-out agreement (*reg 4(2)*). However, following amendment of the *1998 Regulations* in 1999 it is no longer necessary to maintain records of hours actually worked by a worker who has opted out; this was raised by the Commission as a potential breach of the *Directive* in 2002, but the point has not been pursued further. Opt-outs must be made voluntarily. It is unlawful to victimise or dismiss a worker for refusing to sign an opt-out.

The consent of each individual worker to an opt-out agreement is required. Consent given by trade union representatives in the context of a collective agreement is not equivalent to that given by the worker (*SIMAP* [2000] IRLR 845). There is no specific provision in either the *1998 Regulations* or the *Directive* restricting the way in which consent may be recorded, and in practice it is not uncommon for employers to incorporate a requirement for consent in the offer of employment, so that agreement to opt out is tied in to the acceptance of the job offered. The validity of such agreements may be open to challenge on the basis that, giving effect to the approach of the CJEU to construe exemptions from the Directive narrowly, such an arrangement does not ensure that genuine consent is freely given. As at April 2013, there is no reported authority on this point.

The principal issue in the lengthy process of considering proposals for the reform of the *Directive* was whether the facility to legislate to allow individual opt-outs should be phased out, or continue under tighter restrictions. The collapse of negotiations in late April 2009 means that the facility to permit opt-outs will remain available to the UK government for the foreseeable future; it is likely that any fresh proposal to amend the *Directive* that does not preserve in some form the possibility of individual opt-outs will not command sufficiently wide support to be adopted.

In addition to recording the names of workers who have opted out, employers are required to keep records for two years to show that they have complied with the provisions on maximum weekly working time (*reg 9*). The *Regulations* do not specify the format of such records; in particular, there is no requirement for records of the working hours of opted-out workers (as distinct from records of opt-out agreements) to be maintained.

55.8   Enforcement

The right not to have to work more than a 48 hour week is not one of the rights in respect of which the Regulations confer a right for individual workers to complain to an employment tribunal; the *Regulations* instead provide for enforcement by the authorities responsible for enforcing health and safety legislation for whichever sector of employment is involved. However the High Court has held that *reg 4(1)* creates contractual rights not to have to work in excess of the limits on working time: *Barber v RJB Mining (UK) Ltd* [1999] IRLR 308 and the corresponding provision in the *Working Time Directive, art 6(2)*, has been held by the CJEU to be directly enforceable against employers which are state authorities (*Pfeiffer v Deutsches Rotes Kreuz, Kreisverband Waldshut eV*: C-397/01 to 401/01 [2005] IRLR 137). The CJEU has subsequently held that member states must provide a means for individual workers to obtain reparation for breaches of the right conferred by *art 6(2)*: *Fuss v Stadt Halle (No 2)*: C-429/09 [2011] IRLR 176. Whether this entails that such claims may be considered by employment tribunals despite the absence of any provision in the *Working Time Regulations* conferring jurisdiction is a matter which will require to be determined by further case law; the point is discussed more fully (together with the rights, which are enforceable by way of individual complaint to a tribunal, not to be dismissed or suffer detriment for insisting on the right not to work more than 48 hours a week) at **55.20–55.22** below. Steps reasonably taken by an employer to ensure that a worker who has not opted out does not exceed the 48 hour working week will not normally constitute detriments to that worker: *Arriva London South Ltd v Nicolaou (No 2)* [2012] ICR 510, discussed at **55.23** below.

55.9   NIGHT WORK

In the *1998 Regulations* 'night time' means a period of not less than seven hours which includes the period between midnight and 5 am (*reg 2(1)*). The precise period may be determined by a relevant agreement (see **55.4** above). Where it has not been so agreed, the period will be 11 pm to 6 am. A 'night worker' is an individual who, as a normal course, works at least three hours of daily working time during night time or who is likely during night time to work at least such proportion of annual working time as may be specified for these purposes in a collective or workforce agreement. The definition provides that someone works hours 'as a normal course' if he or she works those hours on the majority of his or her working days, but this does not mean that other patterns of work do not qualify as being 'in the normal course'. In *R v A-G for Northern Ireland, ex p Burns* [1999] IRLR 315, the Northern Ireland

High Court held that 'as a normal course' means simply that night work should be a regular feature of employment. Therefore, a worker who spent one week in three of a rotating shift working at least three hours during the night was a night worker for the purposes of the *Directive*.

55.10   Length of night work

Employers are required to take all reasonable steps, in keeping with the need to protect workers' health and safety, to ensure that night workers' normal hours of work do not exceed an average of eight in each 24 hours during a 17-week reference period (*reg 6(1)*, *(2)*). This will be a rolling 17-week period unless a relevant agreement specifies successive periods (*reg 6(3)*). For individuals who have worked for less than 17 weeks, the average is calculated over the period since they started work for the employer (*reg 6(4)*).

Regulation 6(5) provides that average normal hours of work for a night worker are calculated according to the formula:

$$\frac{A}{B - C}$$

where:

'A' is the number of normal working hours during the reference period;

'B' is the number of days during the reference period; and

'C' is the total number of hours during the reference period spent by the worker in statutory weekly rest periods (see **55.17** below) divided by 24. The effect of the formula is to create a maximum of 48 hours a week (8 hours in each of the 6 days a week, excluding one weekly rest day).

Normal hours of work do not include overtime hours unless overtime is guaranteed; therefore it is not a breach of the *Regulations* if a night worker exceeds the permissible maximum hours only by virtue of working voluntary overtime (subject to compliance with the general 48-hour week, if the worker has not opted out of this limit). Further restrictions on working hours for night work involving special hazards or heavy mental or physical strain are summarised in **55.11** below.

Limits on the length of night work and the 17-week reference period may be excluded or modified by collective or workforce agreement (*reg 23*). Exclusions also apply to workers whose working time is 'unmeasured' and those covered by the 'special case' exceptions (see **55.28**, **55.29** below).

The foregoing restrictions on night work apply to adult workers. For young workers under 18, there are much stricter restrictions, introduced by the *2002 Regulations*. Young workers are prohibited from working at all between midnight and 4 am, with very limited exceptions applicable to workplaces such as hospitals, or in connection with cultural, artistic, sporting or advertising activities, where the work is required to provide continuity of service, and no adult worker is available to perform the work. For most young workers there is a restricted period, which is either 10 pm to 6 am, or, if the worker is contractually required to work later than 10 pm, 11 pm to 7 am. Young workers are not permitted to work at all during this period, except as mentioned above, and subject to further exceptions in relation to work in agriculture, retail trading, postal and newspaper delivery, catering, hotels, restaurants and similar establishments, and bakeries; workers in these sectors are permitted to work during the restricted period, but not between midnight and 4 am, in the same limited circumstances of necessity mentioned above. These provisions are contained in *regs 6A* and *27A* of the *1998 Regulations*.

55.11   Special hazards

Where a night worker's job involves special hazards or heavy physical or mental strain, no averaging of hours is permitted. The employer must ensure that the worker does not work for more than eight hours in any 24-hour period which includes night work (*reg 6(7)*). This maximum applies separately to each 24-hour period, without averaging, and includes all hours actually worked.

Regulation 6(8) provides that work will be regarded as involving special hazards or heavy strain if it is identified as such in a collective or workforce agreement which takes account of the specific effects and hazards of night work, or alternatively if it has been recognised as involving significant risk in a risk assessment made under the *Management of Health and Safety at Work Regulations 1999 (SI 1999/3242)*: see **26.17** HEALTH AND SAFETY AT WORK – **II**. A collective or workforce agreement may modify or exclude the application of *reg 6(7)* (*reg 23*). Exceptions apply as for length of night work (see **55.10** above).

55.12   Health assessments

Before assigning an adult worker to night work, the employer must ensure that the worker has the opportunity of a free health assessment (*reg 7(1)*). However, if the worker has previously had an assessment and there is no reason to believe that it is no longer valid, a further assessment is not necessary. Free assessments must also be offered at regular intervals thereafter. The length of time between assessments should be whatever is appropriate to the particular circumstances. The BIS Guidance suggests that a yearly assessment will often be appropriate.

Young persons are to have the opportunity for a free assessment of health and capacities before being assigned to work during the restricted period (see **55.10**) and at regular intervals (*reg 7(2)*). It is not necessary to offer a further assessment if the young person has previously had an assessment and there is no reason to believe that it is no longer valid. BIS advises that special consideration should be given to young workers' suitability for night work, taking account of physique, level of maturity and experience. The requirement to offer an assessment to a young worker does not apply where the work is of an exceptional nature (*reg 7(4)*).

An assessment, whether of an adult or young worker, does not necessarily entail a full medical examination. BIS suggests that employers ask workers to complete a questionnaire which asks about health issues which are relevant to the particular type of night work. If the employer is then unsure about a worker's fitness for night work, he or she should be asked to undergo a medical examination.

Regulation 7(5) provides that the assessment may not be disclosed, except to the worker in question, unless he or she has given consent in writing to the disclosure. This may cause difficulties for the employer if a medical adviser identifies that a worker has a medical condition which could expose him or her to a risk to health. It would be the duty of the employer to safeguard the worker against such a risk, but the employer has no practical means of knowing of the risk unless the information is volunteered by the worker or there is consent to disclosure of the medical assessment. The medical adviser who has evaluated the information supplied or conducted the examination can however make a simple statement (if applicable) to the effect that the assessment shows the worker to be fit, or not fit, to take up, or continue, a night work assignment.

55.13   Transfer to day work

If an employer is advised by a registered medical practitioner that a worker is suffering from health problems which are connected with night working, the employer is required to transfer the worker, if possible, to work which does not qualify as 'night work' (see **55.9** above) (*reg 7(6)*). Normally this will be day work but could involve some night work, provided this is less than 3 hours in any 24 hours. Such work must be work 'to which the worker is suited'. Unlike the comparable provisions in relation to pregnant employees (under *s 6 of ERA 1996* and *reg 17* of the *Management of Health and Safety at Work Regulations 1999*), there is no provision for the protection of enhanced rates of pay for night work for a worker who is transferred to other work under *reg 7(6)*. However, employers may also need to take into consideration their obligations under the *Equality Act 2010* where a worker's lack of fitness amounts to a disability.

Employers are required to maintain, and retain for two years, records which are adequate to show compliance with the provisions on length of night work and health assessments (*reg 9*).

55.14   REST PERIODS AND REST BREAKS

Under the *1998 Regulations* workers are entitled to daily and weekly rest periods totalling 90 hours per week and to rest breaks during the working day. A 'rest period' is defined in *reg 2(1)* as a period which is not working time, other than a rest break or statutory annual leave. It therefore includes time spent in travelling between a worker's home and the normal workplace. However it does not include time spent on call at the employer's premises, even if the worker is in fact able to rest between times when his or her services are required, and is provided with facilities for resting: *Landeshauptstadt Kiel v Jaeger*: C-151/02 [2003] IRLR 804, CJEU. See further the discussion of what constitutes 'working time' at **55.5** above.

The Supreme Court has confirmed that there is no qualitative requirement for rest periods other than the absence of a requirement to work: see *Russell v Transocean International Resources Ltd* [2011] UKSC 57, [2012] IRLR 149, a case holding that it was permissible for employers to require oil rig workers, who worked a pattern of two weeks offshore and two weeks onshore, to take their annual leave entitlement during the periods onshore, notwithstanding that these were periods during which they would not otherwise be required to work, and provided that there was also sufficient time during onshore 'field breaks' for rest periods and any compensatory rest.

55.15   Daily rest periods

Adult workers are entitled to a rest period of at least 11 consecutive hours in each 24-hour working period (*reg 10(1)*). It is not necessary for the 11 hours to fall within the same calendar day provided they are consecutive.

The 11-hour rule does not apply to shift workers when they change shifts and cannot take a daily rest period between the end of one shift and the start of the next (*reg 22(1)(a)*). Similarly it does not apply to workers whose activities involve periods of work split up over the day, such as cleaning or catering staff working split shifts (*reg 22(1)(c)*). 'Shift work' means 'any method of organising work in shifts whereby workers succeed each other at the same workstations according to a certain pattern, including a rotating pattern, and which may be continuous or discontinuous, entailing the need for workers to work at different times over a given period of days or weeks'.

Compensatory rest must normally be offered to shift workers who have to work during what would otherwise be a rest period. If this is not possible, 'appropriate protection' is required to safeguard health and safety (*reg 24*). The CJEU has held (*Landeshauptstadt Kiel v Jaeger*: C-151/02 [2003] IRLR 804; *Union syndicale Solidaires Isère v Premier Ministre*: C-428/09 [2011] 1 CMLR 1206, [2011] IRLR 84) that compensatory rest must be provided immediately following the period of work without a rest period or rest break for which it compensates. See further the discussion of compensatory rest in relation to rest breaks at **55.17** below.

There is a separate provision in *reg 24A* for those mobile workers not excluded from the right to rest periods generally (see as to this **55.33–55.36** below), excluding the right to rest periods provided that 'adequate rest' is afforded, the requirements of which are defined in *reg 24A(3)*. The right to adequate rest in such cases is in substitution for, not cumulative with, the right to compensatory rest under *Reg 24*: *Feist v First Hampshire & Dorset Ltd* [2007] All ER (D) 180 (Feb), EAT.

Adult workers whose time is 'unmeasured' (see **55.28** below) and those who are considered 'special case' exceptions under *reg 21* (subject to certain conditions, see **55.29** below) are not covered by the entitlement to daily rest. The entitlement may also be modified or excluded by collective or workforce agreement under *reg 23*. The second and third of these exceptions are subject to the provision of compensatory rest, or 'appropriate protection' in default.

For young workers (ie those over compulsory school age but under 18) the requirement is to provide not less than 12 consecutive hours' rest in any 24-hour period (*reg 10(2)*). Where activities involve periods of work that are split up over the day or are of short duration, the 12-hour rest period may be interrupted (*reg 10(3)*). In addition a *force majeure* clause applies, which gives the employer leeway to require a young worker to work during the 12-hour minimum where work has to be done which no adult worker is available to do and the requirement:

(a)   is due to unusual and unforeseeable circumstances beyond the employer's control or exceptional events which could not have been avoided despite all due care by the employer;

(b)   is of a temporary nature; and

(c)   must be carried out straight away.

An equivalent period of compensatory rest must be allowed within the following three weeks (*reg 27*). This concession is designed to cope with exceptional circumstances which cannot be handled in any other way.

Entitlement to rest periods entails at the least that the employer must *allow* employees who wish to do so to take their rest period. The extent to which it also entails an obligation on the employer to *ensure* that rest periods are *taken* is more contentious. The DTI (as BIS then was) view, as expressed in the original Guidance on the *Regulations*, was that it does not. This view was, however, successfully challenged by the Commission in proceedings before the European Court (*European Commission v United Kingdom*: C-484/04 [2006] IRLR 888). (For further details see **55.2** above.) Despite this, the EAT has since twice held that there is no breach of *reg 10* until the worker requests that he or she be allowed rest periods and the employer refuses: *Miles v Linkage Community Trust Ltd* [2008] IRLR 602 and *Carter v Prestige Nursing Ltd* (UKEAT/0014/12) (11 May 2012, unreported). However the authority of these cases must be regarded as doubtful, particularly following the decision of the CJEU in *Fuss v Stadt Halle (No 2)*: C-429/09 [2011] IRLR 176 that the right to reparation for an infringement of the right not to work more than 48 hours a week could not be made to depend on the worker having applied to the employer for a reduction in working hours: it is at least arguable that the same approach should be applied to the entitlement to rest periods. *Carter* was decided after *Fuss (No 2)* but that decision was not cited and appears not to have been drawn to the attention of the EAT.

55.16 Weekly rest periods

Adult workers are normally entitled (as to the meaning of this see the final paragraph of **55.15**) to an uninterrupted rest period of at least 24 hours in each seven-day period of working. This may be arranged as two uninterrupted rest periods of not less than 24 hours in each 14-day period, or one uninterrupted period of not less than 48 hours in each 14-day period (*reg 11(1)*,

(2)). The minimum weekly rest period must not run concurrently with any part of a daily rest period (see **55.15** above) except where this is justified by objective or technical reasons, or reasons 'concerning the organisation of work' *(reg 11(7))*. Thus the combined effect of the daily and weekly rest entitlements is to create a minimum entitlement of 35 consecutive hours each week, or 59 hours in each 14–day period.

For young workers the minimum weekly rest period is 48 hours. This may be interrupted where activities involve periods of work that are split up over the day or are of short duration, and may be reduced where this is justified by technical or organisational reasons. However the period may not be reduced to less than 36 consecutive hours *(reg 11(3), (8))*.

A seven or 14-day period for these purposes begins on the day provided for in a relevant agreement (see **55.4** above) or, failing this, at the start of each week (or every other week, as the case may be). A 'week' for this purpose starts at midnight between Sunday and Monday *(reg 11(4), (6))*.

In the case of shift workers, the weekly rest requirement in respect of adults does not apply when workers change shift and cannot take a weekly rest period between the end of one shift and the start of another. Neither does it apply to workers whose activities involve periods of work split up over the day *(reg 22(1))*. Cleaning and catering staff may provide examples. For the definition of 'shift working' see **55.15** above. Compensatory rest must normally be offered to shift workers who have to work during what would otherwise be a rest period. If this is not possible, 'appropriate protection' is required to safeguard the worker's health and safety *(reg 24)*. (See as to these concepts the discussion at **55.17** below.)

The right to rest periods may also be modified or excluded by a collective or workforce agreement, but subject to the workers concerned being afforded compensatory rest: *regs 23, 24*. The right is also excluded, subject to the same conditions as to compensatory rest, for certain categories of work: see *reg 21*, discussed at **55.29**. The position for mobile workers not excluded from the *Regulations* altogether is the same in relation to weekly rest periods as for daily rest periods: see *reg 24A* and **55.15** above.

Adult workers whose time is 'unmeasured' (see **55.28** below) are not subject to the weekly rest requirements.

55.17 Rest breaks

After a working period of six hours, an adult worker is entitled to a rest break *(reg 12(1))*. The length of the break and any conditions which apply to it are to be determined by collective or workforce agreement. In the absence of such an agreement, the break is to be at least an uninterrupted period of 20 minutes which the worker is entitled to take away from the workstation where applicable *(reg 12(2), (3))*. If a worker works a single shift of 12 hours, the entitlement is still to one rest break, not two: *Hughes v Corps of Commissionaires Management Ltd (No 1)* [2009] ICR 345, [2009] IRLR 122, EAT.

Regulation 12(1) may be modified or excluded by collective or workforce agreement, subject to the provision of compensatory rest *(regs 23, 24)*. The right is also excluded, subject to the same conditions as to compensatory rest, for certain categories of work: see *reg 21*, discussed at **55.29** below. Those mobile workers not excluded altogether from the *1998 Regulations*, as summarised in **55.15** above, are subject to the same limitations on the right to rest breaks as described above. Adult workers whose time is 'unmeasured' are not entitled to rest breaks (see **55.28** below).

It has been held that for a period to count as a rest break, the worker must be able to know at the beginning of the period that it will not be interrupted by the demands of work. Accordingly, 'down time', and periods during time on call, at least where the worker is required to be at his or her workplace, cannot be counted as a rest period, even if it transpires that there was a continuous period of at least 20 minutes during which the worker was not called on to perform any work: *Gallagher v Alpha Catering Services Ltd* [2004] EWCA Civ 1559, [2005] IRLR 102; *MacCartney v Oversley House Management* [2006] ICR 510, EAT. A case the other side of the line is *Martin v Southern Health & Social Care Trust* [2010] NICA 31, [2010] IRLR 1048; the claimant, a nurse, was expressly entitled to an uninterrupted (and unpaid) break unless an emergency arose, in which case she was entitled to claim time off in lieu by way of compensation. The Northern Ireland Court of Appeal held that this was sufficient to constitute the breaks as 'rest breaks' despite relatively frequent interruptions in practice (but for which compensatory time off was always given if claimed). The crucial distinction from the facts in *Gallagher* was that in that case there was no presumption that there would be an uninterrupted break. As to the meaning of 'entitled', see the final paragraph of **55.15**.

As to compensatory rest, the CJEU has twice held that this must be afforded immediately after the period of work without the required rest period or rest break for which it is intended to compensate: *Landeshuptstadt Kiel v Jaeger*: C-151/02, [2003] IRLR 804, and *Union syndicale Solidaires Isère v Premier Ministre*: C-428/09 [2011] 1 CMLR 1206, [2011] IRLR 84. In the latter case the Court observed that in order to be effective to enable the worker to rest effectively, the compensatory rest must entail the worker 'being able to remove himself from his working environment for a specific number of hours' immediately following the period of work in issue.

The application of the requirement to afford compensatory rest has been considered domestically in a number of cases. The first case was *Hughes (No 1)*, above. The EAT held that compensatory rest must be of equivalent length to the break foregone, and afforded at a time which would otherwise be part of the worker's working time. Such compensatory rest must be offered if at all possible, and it is only if it is not possible for 'objective reasons' that the employer may instead provide 'appropriate protection' to the employee. The precise scope of 'appropriate protection' is a matter of considerable uncertainty, and the EAT did not find it necessary to set out further what the concept requires.

Hughes (No 1) also raised the question whether the worker is entitled to be paid for any period of compensatory rest. The EAT concluded that this was not required by the *Regulations*, and whether it was required as a matter of contract would depend on the terms of the worker's contract; this was remitted to the tribunal to consider, but with the EAT indicating a provisional view that generally there would be an entitlement to be paid. This however is far from clear, since there is no requirement for rest breaks themselves to be paid – this too is a matter of contract between the parties – and if payment for compensatory rest was required where the break compensated for would not have attracted a right to be paid, it could be said that the worker would be overcompensated for the loss of the break.

The second case, *Hughes v Corps of Commissionaires Management Ltd (No 2)* [2011] EWCA Civ 1061, [2011] IRLR 915, was an appeal from the decision of the tribunal hearing the remission of certain issues in *Hughes (No 1)*, which had rejected Mr Hughes' claims. The EAT upheld that decision, but on different grounds; it decided that on the facts compensatory rest had been granted: Mr Hughes, a security guard, was permitted to re-commence any rest break which had been interrupted by a requirement to resume his duties (the risk of which had led to the finding that he had not been permitted to take the required rest breaks). Compensatory rest did not have to mirror exactly the requirements of the break for the denial of which it compensated, provided the arrangements were 'equivalent'. As the alternative arrangements were within the time for which he was in any case paid, the issue whether there is any separate right to be paid for compensatory rest did not in the event arise. The case then proceeded to the Court of Appeal, which upheld the EAT's decision. An equivalent period of compensatory rest had to have the characteristics of rest, in the sense of being a break from work, and as far as possible must ensure that the period free from work was at least the 20 minutes required for a rest break; however on the facts these requirements had been met.

The issue of compensatory rest did not fall directly for decision in *Martin*, above, but it is implicit in the decision in that case that a right to claim time off in lieu (it appears without loss of pay) for any break which in the event was interrupted did satisfy the requirements for compensatory rest. The judgment does not indicate when time off in lieu was in practice taken. As noted above, the ECJ has twice held that compensatory rest must be afforded immediately following the period of work without the required rest break for which it is compensation; however as the point did not arise directly in the light of its decision on what constitutes a rest break, the Court in *Martin* did not have to consider whether the requirements of timing of the compensatory rest were met by these arrangements.

If in exceptional cases it is not possible 'for objective reasons' to afford compensatory rest, 'appropriate protection' must if possible be offered instead (*reg 24(b)*; the phrase is taken directly from the wording of the *Directive*). This provision was considered, obiter, in *Hughes (No 2)*; the EAT suggested that it could include a range of measures other than the provision of rest such as the way that work is organised or health checks for affected workers. The CJEU subsequently expressed the view in *Union syndicale*, above, that 'only in absolutely exceptional circumstances' could resort be had to 'appropriate protection', and that limiting the number of days in a year that seasonal workers could work to a maximum of 80 was not a permissible means of affording 'appropriate protection' for the denial of daily rest periods. This judgment was not cited to the Court of Appeal when the appeal in *Hughes (No 2)* reached the Court, which rejected the argument that there must be 'exceptional circumstances' in addition to objective reasons for not providing compensatory rest: it would be exceptional that there were objective reasons, and that was sufficient. Whether the Court would have reached this conclusion if it had been aware of the decision in *Union syndicale* is unclear. The Court of Appeal did not consider in any detail the range of what could constitute protection under *reg 24(b)*, as it was satisfied that the arrangements for a deferred break were sufficient; but it did reject, as had the EAT, a submission that the employer would have to conduct a risk assessment to assess the sufficiency of the protection afforded.

In the case of young workers, there is an entitlement to a break of at least 30 minutes, consecutive if possible, if the individual's daily working time exceeds four and a half hours. The worker is entitled to take the break away from the workstation if applicable. When a young worker has more than one employment, the daily working time must be calculated by aggregating the number of hours worked for each employer (*reg 12(4), (5)*). There is an exception to the entitlements of young workers under a *force majeure* clause (*reg 27*). This specifies that *reg 12(4)* does not apply where work has to be done which no adult worker is available to do and:

(a)   the requirement is due to unusual and unforeseeable circumstances beyond the employer's control or exceptional events which could not have been avoided despite all due care by the employer;

(b)   is of a temporary nature; and

(c)   must be carried out straight away.

An equivalent period of compensatory rest must be allowed within the following three weeks.

55.18   Monotonous work

Apart from the specific obligations to provide rest breaks described in **55.17**, an employer is required to ensure that workers are given adequate rest breaks where the work pattern puts workers' health and safety at risk, in particular because the work is monotonous or the work rate pre-determined (*reg 8*). This appears to be a requirement which is additional to the basic entitlement to rest breaks set out in *reg 12*. The wording of the regulation is a paraphrase of *art 13* of the *Directive*, and it has not to date been the subject of judicial interpretation. Apart from those in excluded sectors to whom the *Regulations* do not apply at all, there are no exceptions to the application of *reg 8*.

55.19 ANNUAL LEAVE

Workers within the *1998 Regulations* are entitled to a total of 5.6 weeks' statutory holiday in respect of each leave year (subject to a maximum entitlement of 28 working days (*regs 13* and *13A*). This entitlement was increased from the original three weeks to four weeks in 1999, to 4.8 weeks from 1 October 2007, and to 5.6 weeks from 1 April 2009; the latter increases were made by the *Working Time (Amendment) Regulations 2007, SI 2007/2079*, which give workers a separate right to the additional annual leave under slightly different conditions, rather than simply increasing the basic entitlement. The *Regulations* also cover statutory holiday pay, notice requirements in respect of taking annual leave, and pay in lieu on termination. Full details of the annual leave provisions in the *1998 Regulations* are set out in 27 - HOLIDAYS. Special rules apply to agricultural workers (reg 43, Sch 2) and the equivalent Regulations for workers in civil aviation also have different provisions as to the computation of holiday pay: see *British Airways plc v Williams* [2012] UKSC 43, [2012] IRLR 1014, [2012] ICR 1375.

55.20 ENFORCEMENT AND REMEDIES

Different enforcement arrangements operate according to the nature of the breach of the *1998 Regulations*. Working time limits are enforced by the Health and Safety Executive ('HSE') and local authorities, and within their areas of responsibility the Civil Aviation Authority ('CAA') and the Vehicle and Operator Services Agency ('VOSA') and the Office of Rail Regulation ('ORR'). The HSE enforces the limits in factories, building sites, mines, farms, fairgrounds, quarries, chemical plants, nuclear installations, schools and hospitals. Local authority officers have the same role in respect of shops and retailing, offices, hotels and catering, sports, leisure and consumer services. The enforcement powers of the various agencies are essentially the same as those provided for in the *Health and Safety at Work etc Act 1974*. For technical reasons the addition of the CAA and VOSA to the list of enforcing authorities was considered to necessitate the restatement of the enforcement powers within the *1998 Regulations*, and these can be found in *regs 28–29E* and *Sch 3*. These provisions were then applied to the ORR when it was given enforcement responsibilities in relation to rail staff by the *Railways Act 2005* and regulations made under that Act. For further details of enforcement powers and penalties see **55.21** below and **25.29–25.41** HEALTH AND SAFETY AT WORK – I.

The other method of enforcement is that workers who are not receiving their entitlements or are penalised for insisting on their rights can pursue claims in employment tribunals: see **55.22–55.24** below.

55.21 Health and safety

Regulation 28 provides that the relevant enforcing authority, ie the HSE, local authority or the CAA, VOSA or ORR, is responsible for enforcing the following provisions: weekly working time (*reg 4(2)*); length of night work (*reg 6(2)*, *(7)*); health assessments for night workers (*reg 7(1)*, *(2)*) and transfers to day work (*reg 7(6)*); rest breaks for monotonous work (*reg 8*); record-keeping (*reg 9*); and compensatory rest in relation to night work (*reg 24*). Enforcing authorities are also responsible for the enforcement of the additional restrictions on working hours and night work for young workers in *regs 5A(4)* and *27A(4)(a)*, and for the provisions on adequate rest for mobile workers under *reg 24A*.

An employer who fails to comply with any of these requirements commits an offence (*reg 29*). The offences are punishable on summary conviction by a fine not exceeding £5,000 (the limit on the maximum fine will be removed when the relevant parts of the *Legal Aid, Sentencing and Punishment of Offenders Act 2012* comes into force). On conviction on indictment the punishment is an unlimited fine. *Regulations 29A–29E* contain provisions equivalent to those in the *Health and Safety at Work etc Act 1974* in relation to offences due to the default, etc of another person, offences by bodies corporate, powers to prosecute and powers of courts to require the remedying of causes of offences. Provisions as to the appointment and powers of inspectors, including the making of improvement and prohibition notices and rights of appeal against such notices, and restrictions on disclosure of information, are contained in *Sch 3*.

Additionally, the High Court has held that *reg 4(1)*, which specifies that a worker's average hours per week should not exceed 48, imposes a contractual obligation on an employer. Contracts should therefore be read as providing that an employee should work no more than an average of 48 hours during the reference period (*Barber v RJB Mining (UK) Ltd* [1999] IRLR 308). Consequently, employees who are asked to work over the 48-hour limit without their agreement may be able to bring proceedings in the civil courts for a declaration of rights and seek an injunction barring the employer from requiring them to work additional hours. However, this does not confer any right to claim compensation in an employment tribunal for being required to work more than 48 hours a week: the jurisdiction of the tribunals does not extend to claims for breach of *reg 4* (see **55.22** below). It remains to be determined judicially whether the position thus summarised sufficiently meets the requirements of EU law, in the light of the judgment of the CJEU in *Fuss v Stadt Halle (No 2)*: C-429/09 [2011] IRLR 176 that the right not to work more than a 48 hour week conferred by *art 6(b)* of the *Working Time Directive* is directly enforceable domestically, at least as against those employers which are state authorities, so that a worker whose right has been infringed must have the right to secure reparation for any infringement once the scope of the law has been made clear at CJEU level (as was the case on the facts, which related to time spent on call at the workplace). It may be that the remedy of an action for breach of contract would be regarded in EU law as sufficient to meet the requirements of the Court in *Fuss (No 2)*, but if not, it is considered that a claim against a state authority as employer based on the *Directive* rather than the *Regulations* could be brought in an employment tribunal despite the lack of jurisdiction to hear such claims under the *Regulations* themselves, by analogy with equal pay claims.

There is as yet no reported case in which a worker has successfully claimed damages for personal injury resulting directly from being made to work hours in excess of those permitted under the *Regulations*, but in two cases in which the Court of Appeal has upheld awards of damages for psychiatric injury, the fact that the employee had worked well in excess of the 48 hour limit without his agreement was regarded as an evidentially relevant factor in favour of the point that the damage ought to have been foreseen by the employer: *Hone v Six Continents Retail Ltd* [2005] EWCA Civ 922, [2006] IRLR 49; *Pakenham-Walsh v Connell Residential* [2006] EWCA Civ 90, [2006] 11 LS Gaz R 25. However, in *Sayers v Cambridgeshire County Council* [2006] EWHC 2029 (QB), [2007] IRLR 29 (a case where a claim for damages for personal injury failed on the facts) the High Court held that a breach of *reg 4* by the employer does not confer a right for the worker to sue for damages for breach of statutory duty.

55.22 Individual remedies

Under *reg 30(1)(a)* a complaint may be made to an employment tribunal that the employer has refused to permit a worker to exercise his or her rights in connection with: daily rest (*reg 10(1), (2)*); weekly rest (*reg 11(1), (2), (3)*); rest breaks (*reg 12(1), (4)*); entitlement to annual leave (*reg 13(1)*); entitlement to compensatory rest (except in relation to night work) (*regs 24, 25, 27*) or to adequate rest (*reg 24A*).

Reg 30(1)(b) makes similar provision for complaints of failure to pay any sums due as payments in respect of annual leave entitlement or accrued holiday pay on termination under *reg 16(1)* or *14(2)* respectively. The House of Lords has ruled that claims for holiday pay can in the alternative be brought as claims for unlawful deductions from wages under *Part II* of the *Employment Rights Act 1996*, which are subject to somewhat less strict time limits (*Stringer v HM Revenue and Customs* [2009] UKHL 31, [2009] IRLR 677, reversing the decision of the Court of Appeal (*IRC v Ainsworth* [2005] EWCA Civ 441, [2005] IRLR 465). However this is only possible for claims for unpaid holiday pay or pay in lieu; other claims can in their nature only be brought under *reg 30*.

It should be noted that (apart from complaints of failure to pay sums due), the basis for complaints is of a refusal to permit the worker to exercise a relevant right. It is not enough that the right was not in fact exercised, unless this was attributable to the employer.

Tribunals have no express jurisdiction to hear claims by individuals for breach of the 48-hour limit on weekly working time. (See **55.20** above as to possible claims under the Directive itself for infringement of a worker's right not to work more than 48 hours a week). Following the lead given by the High Court in *Barber v RJB Mining (UK) Ltd* [1999] IRLR 308 (see **55.21**), tribunals may accept that a term is implied into a contract of employment that the employer must not require the employee to work more than 48 hours a week in the reference period. The effect of this is, however, limited. An employee complaining of constructive dismissal could rely on being required to work excessive hours as a breach of contract, but the tribunal has no power to award compensation for excessive hours as such, unless overtime is required under the terms of the employee's contract to be paid, in which case a claim for unlawful deductions could be made (*Forbouys Ltd v Rich* [2002] All ER (D) 156 (Apr), EAT), or there is a claim under the *National Minimum Wage Act 1998*.

Claims brought under *reg 30* must normally be presented within three months of the date on which the right should have been permitted or the payment should have been made. This period is extended to six months for complaints by members of the armed forces (who are required to utilise internal redress procedures before commencing tribunal proceedings). Where a tribunal is satisfied that it was not reasonably practicable to present a claim within the time limit, it may extend the period to a date it considers reasonable. In relation to claims for refusal to permit the claimant to take rest breaks or rest periods, the time limit for making a complaint runs from the date of each refusal: *Scottish Ambulance Service v Truslove* (UKEATS/0028/11), 12 January 2012, unreported. The EAT in that case rejected an argument that where the employee had raised a grievance, time ran from the date on which the grievance was rejected, or on the date (if later, of the first refusal of a rest period, holding that each refusal was a fresh cause of action with its own time limit (and thus the claims were in time so far as relating to refusals occurring within three months prior to the claims being presented). It follows that claims presented more than three months after any particular refusal of rest will be out of time (subject to any extension of time); there is no provision in reg 30 for time not to run during a series of refusals.

Following an amendment to the *Employment Tribunals Act 1996, s 4*, claims for holiday pay, and for pay in lieu of holiday not taken prior to the termination of employment, may be heard by an employment judge sitting alone: see *SI 2009/789*. This amendment is intended to facilitate tribunals dealing with claims for holiday pay speedily together with claims for unpaid wages, as the two are often brought together, and frequently not defended (usually because the employer is insolvent). Other claims made under *reg 30* of the *Working Time Regulations* require to be heard by a full tribunal of three.

Where a complaint is considered to be well-founded, the tribunal will make a declaration to that effect and may make an award of such compensation (if any) as it considers to be just and equitable in all the circumstances, having regard to the employer's default and any loss sustained by the worker. It should be emphasised that the award of compensation is discretionary, and a nil award is permissible; such an award was upheld by the EAT in *Miles v Linkage Community Trust Ltd* [2008] IRLR 602. However, insofar as the reasoning in that case is based on the claimant's failure to complain for some time about the denial of his rights, it is of doubtful authority following the subsequent decision of the CJEU in *Fuss v Stadt Halle (No 2)*: C-429/09 [2011] IRLR 176 that a right to reparation for an infringement of rights under the Directive (in that case by a requirement to work more than 48 hours a week) could not be made conditional on the worker having first complained about the continuing infringement of rights. Despite this, in a subsequent case (in which *Fuss (No 2)* appears not to have been drawn to the attention of the EAT), Miles was endorsed and followed: *Carter v Prestige Nursing Ltd* (UKEAT/0014/12) (11 May 2012, unreported). Where the complaint involves failure to pay holiday pay (the issue arising in the vast majority of claims under the *1998 Regulations*), the tribunal will order the employer to pay the amount owed.

55.23   Victimisation

ERA 1996, s 45A (as inserted by *reg 31* of the *1998 Regulations*) provides that a worker has the right not to be subjected to any detriment by any act, or any deliberate failure to act, by his or her employer on the ground that the worker:

(a)   refused (or proposed to refuse) to comply with a requirement of the employer imposed in contravention of the *Regulations*;

(b)   refused (or proposed to refuse) to forgo a right conferred by the *Regulations*;

(c)   failed to sign a workforce agreement, or to enter into or agree to vary or extend any other agreement provided for in the *Regulations*;

(d)   being a representative of members of the workforce for the purposes of *Sch 1* or a candidate in an election for such a representative, performed (or proposed to perform) any functions or activities as such a representative or candidate;

(e)   brought proceedings against the employer to enforce a right conferred by the *Regulations*; or

(f)   alleged that the employer had infringed such a right.

So far as (*e*) and (*f*) are concerned, it is immaterial whether or not the worker has the right or whether or not the right has been infringed, but the claim must be made in good faith. In respect of (*f*), it is sufficient for the worker to make it reasonably clear to the employer what the right was that he or she alleges has been infringed.

There is separate protection, for employees only, from unfair dismissal (see **55.24** below) and dismissal is excluded from the definition of detriment for employees; for a worker who is not an employee, a complaint of subjection to detriment can be brought to cover the comparable situation of termination of his or her contract. It is at least arguable that *s 45A* covers detriments suffered after the termination of employment, by analogy with the Court of Appeal's reasoning in *Woodward v Abbey National plc* [2006] EWCA Civ 822, [2006] ICR 1436 on the equivalent provision in relation to 'whistleblowers' (*ERA 1996, s 47B*).

The remedy for a contravention of *s 45A* is a complaint to an employment tribunal under *s 48*. Normally the complaint must be presented within three months of the act or failure to act the subject of the complaint but tribunals have discretion to extend the time limit where it was not reasonably practicable to present the claim in time. Where the complaint is of an act or omission 'extending over a period', time does not start to run until the last day of the period.

It is for the employer to show the reason for any detriment to which the worker was subjected: *s 48(2)*. The EAT in *Fecitt v NHS Manchester* [2011] IRLR 111 held that the standard of proof thus placed on the employer is the same as in discrimination cases where the burden of proof has been reversed in accordance with *Igen Ltd v Wong* [2005] EWCA Civ 142, [2005] IRLR 258. On a further appeal to the Court of Appeal ([2011] EWCA Civ 1190, [2012] IRLR 64), the Court acknowledged that strictly *Igen v Wong* had no application as no EU derived right was involved, but nevertheless upheld the correctness of the general approach, noting that this created an anomaly by comparison with the burden of proof in a claim for automatically unfair dismissal under *Employment Rights Act 1996, s 103A*.

An example of a claim based on detriment under *s 45A* is *Arriva London South Ltd v Nicolaou* (UKEAT/0280/10), where the claimant, a bus driver, was denied access to lucrative rest day working because he had refused to opt out of the 48 hour week. The EAT remitted the case to the tribunal to consider whether the employer had acted reasonably in the light of its explanation that it was concerned to comply with its duty under *reg 4(2)* not, so far as reasonably practicable, to permit a worker who had not opted out to work more than 48 hours a week, a point not fully addressed by the tribunal. In a second appeal, *Arriva London South Ltd v Nicolaou (No 2)* [2012] ICR 510, the EAT upheld the tribunal's second rejection of Mr Nicolaou's complaint. The tribunal had held that the employer had been acting reasonably to ensure that it complied with its duty not to permit an employee who has not opted out to work more than an average of 48 hours a week. The EAT accepted the argument that any resulting disadvantage to the employee was not a detriment, because it did not entail a legitimate sense of grievance, and that the reason for denying the claimant access to rest day working was not causally connected to his having opted out, but rather to the employer's desire to take steps to ensure compliance with its statutory obligations.

In well-founded cases, the tribunal will make a declaration to that effect and may also award such compensation as it considers just and equitable. The amount of compensation which may be awarded is unlimited, except that where the detrimental action suffered by a worker (who is not working under a contract of employment) is termination of contract, the compensation must not exceed the maximum amount which could be awarded to an employee who has been unfairly dismissed for a similar reason (*ERA 1996, s 49*). Compensation may include compensation for injury to feelings.

For workers in sectors covered by specific regulations, and who are either wholly or partially excluded from the application of the *1998 Regulations*, the position is inconsistent. *Section 45A* also applies in the same way in relation to the equivalent provisions of the *Merchant Shipping (Working Time: Inland Waterways) Regulations 2003* and the *Fishing Vessels (Working Time: Sea-fishermen) Regulations 2004*, but not (either through legislative oversight or to reflect differences in the parent *Directives*) to the comparable provisions for workers in civil aviation and road transport: see further 55.33 and 55.34. Merchant seamen (see 55.31) are also not covered by the provisions of *s 45A*.

55.24   Unfair dismissal

It is automatically unfair to dismiss an employee for certain reasons connected with rights and entitlements under the *1998 Regulations* (*ERA 1996, s 101A*, as inserted by *reg 32(1)*). Employees may present a claim under this provision regardless of length of service. *Section 101A* does not cover employees asserting the equivalent rights under the *Road Transport (Working Time) Regulations 2005*: see *Ross v Eddie Stobart Ltd* (UKEAT/0085/10), 16 May 2011, unreported. An alternative basis of claim may be that the employee has raised concerns about health and safety in relation to working time: see *ERA 1996 s 100*, and *Joao v Jurys Hotel Management UK Ltd* (UKEAT/0210/11), 11 October 2011, unreported (reasonableness of employee's objection to working nine successive night shifts not dependent on the shift pattern being a breach of the *Working Time Regulations*). For further details see 52.3(h) UNFAIR DISMISSAL – II.

It is also automatically unfair to dismiss an employee for 'asserting a statutory right' (*ERA 1996, s 104*). The rights conferred by the *1998 Regulations* are included within the definition of 'statutory rights' under *s 104* (as amended by *reg 32(2)*). Therefore where an employee has been dismissed for bringing proceedings to enforce a working time right, or for alleging that the employer has infringed such a right, this will be considered automatically unfair. Employees may present a claim under this provision also regardless of length of service. In *Ajayi v Aitch Care Homes (London) Ltd* (UKEAT/0464) (3 February 2012, unreported), the EAT held that the assertion of a statutory right such as the right to take a rest break had to be communicated to the employer, so that employees dismissed for sleeping on duty could not claim that they were thereby asserting their right to a rest break. See also **52.3(c)** Unfair Dismissal – II.

The points made in **55.23** above about the application of *s 45A* to workers covered by equivalent legislation for particular sectors apply equally to protection from unfair dismissal.

55.25   Restrictions on contracting out

A provision in an agreement which purports to exclude or limit the operation of any part of the *1998 Regulations* or to prevent a person from making a tribunal claim connected with the *Regulations* will be void, except, of course, where the *Regulations* themselves permit exclusion or modification (*reg 35*). The general rule does not apply where worker and employer have entered into an ACAS-conciliated settlement or a compromise agreement. For comments on the potential breadth of the restrictions on contracting out, see the contrasting reasoning of the Court of Session in *MPB Structure Ltd v Munro* [2003] IRLR 350 and the Court of Appeal in *Caulfield v Marshalls Clay Products Ltd* [2004] EWCA Civ 422, [2004] IRLR 564, and the views of the CJEU in *Robinson-Steele v RD Retail Services Ltd*: C-131/04 [2006] IRLR 386, broadly endorsing the approach of the Court of Session.

55.26   GUIDANCE

The Secretary of State for Business,Innovation and Skills is responsible for arranging publication of information and advice on the *1998 Regulations* after consultation with both sides of industry (*reg 35A*). The Guidance was updated in August 2003 to reflect the changes made in the *Regulations* by the *2003 Amendment Regulations*, and was further amended following the decision of the CJEU in *European Commission v United Kingdom*: C-484/04 [2006] IRLR 888 that the guidance on workers' rights to rest periods and rest breaks put the UK in breach of its obligations to implement the *Directive* (see **55.2**). The guidance has now been replaced by separate versions for employers (see www.businesslink.co.uk/btodg/action/layer?topicId=1073858926) and workers (see www.gov.uk/browse/working/time-off). It should be noted that the Guidance does not have the force of law, and is not necessarily entirely accurate (both because of brevity and specific inaccuracies, such as the statement in the Direct.gov version that the 48 hour limit on the working week applies to the total working time of those who work for more than one employer, a statement not included in the Business Link advice). Useful additional guidance for enforcing authorities has been issued by the Health and Safety Executive: see www.hse.gov.uk/lau/lacs/95-1.htm.

55.27   EXCEPTIONS

In addition to sectors of activity wholly excluded from the ambit of the *1998 Regulations* (see **55.3** above) various categories of worker are excepted from the full scope of the *Regulations*.

55.28   Unmeasured working time

The limit on the average working week, requirements as to daily and weekly rest periods and breaks for adults, and restrictions on hours of work for night workers are disapplied for workers whose working time is not measured or pre-determined or can be determined by the workers themselves, on account of the specific characteristics of their job (*reg 20(1)*). *Regulation 20* suggests that this may be the case for:

(a)   managing executives or other persons with autonomous decision-taking powers;

(b)   family workers; or

(c)   workers officiating at religious ceremonies in churches and religious communities.

(Annual leave entitlements nevertheless apply to workers within the exemptions created by *reg 20*.)

Following the enforcement proceedings by the Commission described in **55.2** above, the partial exemption from *reg 20* for those whose working time is partially unmeasured (*reg 20(2)*) was revoked by the *Working Time (Amendment) Regulations 2006 (SI 2006/99)* with effect from 6 April 2006.

There have as yet been no reported cases in the UK courts on the scope of the exception. The scope of the exception was briefly considered by the CJEU in *Union syndicale Solidaires Isère v Premier Ministre*: C–428/09 [2011] 1 CMLR 1206, [2011] IRLR 84, but the Court went no further than concluding that as there was no indication in the papers before it that the workers concerned could decide the number of hours they worked, they did not fall within the exception. In some other EU member states the domestic legislation specifies particular categories or levels of management as being within the exemption, but in the UK the approach has been simply to reproduce the rather imprecise wording of the *Directive* itself. In consequence the contractual arrangements in each case, and not just the individual's job title, would need to be considered to determine whether the individual falls within the exemption.

55.29 Special cases

Regulation 21 provides that in relation to certain specified situations or types of activity, the *Regulations* relating to daily and weekly rest periods and breaks (in respect of adults only) and hours of work for night workers are disapplied. This is subject to workers being permitted to take compensatory rest or, if that is not possible, being provided with appropriate protection; see for a discussion of this **55.17** above. The following groups fall within the *reg 21* exception:

(a)   where the worker's activities are such that the place of work and home are distant from one another or different places of work are distant from one another, including cases where the worker is involved in offshore work;

(b)   where the worker is engaged in security and surveillance activities requiring a permanent presence in order to protect property and persons, as may be the case for security guards and caretakers or security firms;

(c)   where the worker's activities involve the need for continuity of service or production, as may be the case in relation to:

> (i)   services relating to the reception, treatment or care provided by hospitals or similar establishments (including the activities of doctors in training), residential institutions and prisons;

> (ii)   work at docks or airports;

> (iii)   press, radio, television, cinematographic production, postal and telecommunications services and civil protection services;

> (iv)   gas, water and electricity production, transmission and distribution, household refuse collection and incineration;

> (v)   industries in which work cannot be interrupted on technical grounds;

> (vi)   research and development activities;

(vii)   agriculture;

(viii)   the carriage of passengers on regular urban passenger services;

(d)   where there is a foreseeable surge of activity, as may be the case in relation to agriculture, tourism and postal services;

(e)   where the worker's activities are affected by:

(i)   an occurrence due to unusual and unforeseeable circumstances, beyond the control of the worker's employer;

(ii)   exceptional events, the consequences of which could not have been avoided despite the exercise of all due care by the employer; or

(iii)   an accident or the imminent risk of an accident;

(f)   where the worker works in railway transport and –

(i)   his or her activities are intermittent;

(ii)   he or she spends his working time on board trains; or

(iii)   his or her activities are linked to transport timetables and to ensuring the continuity and regularity of traffic.

Additionally, for workers falling within these categories the reference period for the weekly working time limit is extended from 17 weeks to 26 weeks (*reg 4(5)*).

The list of exclusions, which the regulation has copied largely verbatim from the *Directive*, is open to differences of interpretation. In particular, it should be noted that the categories listed in (*c*) are neither necessarily within the exemption (the wording is 'as may be the case in relation to') nor exhaustive of possible exempt activities.

The application of these exceptions was considered by the Court of Appeal in *Gallagher v Alpha Catering Ltd* [2004] EWCA Civ 1559, [2005] IRLR 102, a case concerning workers engaged in delivering and uplifting catering supplies to and from aircraft at Gatwick Airport, whose complaint was that they were refused rest breaks during the working day in breach of *reg 12*. The employers relied on two points in *reg 21* as providing exemption from their liability to afford rest breaks. These points were (*c*)(ii) and (*d*) above. As to the first, the Court emphasised that the emphasis in (*c*) was placed squarely on the activity of the worker, not of the employer, so that the test was not whether the employer had to maintain continuity of service but whether the particular worker's activity involved such continuity; on the facts it did not. The same approach was applied by the Court of Appeal to the work of security guards under (*b*) in *Hughes v Corps of Commissionaires Management (No 2)* [2011] EWCA Civ 1190, [2011] IRLR 915, but on the facts it was held that the work did require a continuous presence of the worker. In *Martin v Southern Health & Social Care Trust* [2010] NICA 31, [2010] IRLR 1048, the work of nurses providing care to in-patients in a hospital were held to fall within the exception at (c) above.

Subsequently, in *Associated British Ports v Bridgeman* [2012] IRLR 639, the EAT referred to the CJEU the question whether the *Directive* requires a separate assessment of whether continuity of service is required with respect to rest breaks and to daily rest periods, or a single assessment covering both. The point arose in a case brought by a ship's pilot, the employment tribunal having held that the need for continuity of service was made out for rest breaks (since the pilot could not take a break whilst piloting a ship) but not daily rest periods between duties. The case was however settled before the CJEU could rule on the point.

The Court in *Gallagher* also rejected an argument that the variations in the numbers of aircraft requiring servicing at different times of the week, and increases in numbers during holiday periods, amounted to a 'foreseeable surge of activity'. (For a discussion of the requirement for compensatory rest when one of the exceptions in *reg 21* applies, see **55.17** above.

The exception for the carriage of passengers on urban bus services was considered in *Feist v First Hampshire & Dorset Ltd* [2007] All ER (D) 180 (Feb), EAT, where it was held that the entitlement to compensatory rest attaching to the exemptions under *reg 21* applied only where the workers concerned were excluded from the right to rest solely by *reg 21*. In the case of bus drivers, who are also excluded as mobile workers by the effect of *reg 24A*, the corresponding right is limited to the right to 'adequate' rest conferred by *reg 24A*; the rights are not cumulative.

55.30 Domestic servants

Workers who are employed as domestic servants in a private household are excluded from the scope of the *Regulations* relating to: the 48-hour week; length of night work; health assessments and transfers to day work; and breaks for monotonous work. Such domestic workers are, however, covered by provisions on rest periods, breaks and annual leave (*reg 19*). The basis in the *Directive* for this exclusion appears to be that workers in domestic service are specifically excluded from the definition of 'worker' in the framework *Health and Safety Directive 89/391, art 3(a)*, and it appears that this limitation is considered to be incorporated by reference into the *Working Time Directive* itself by *art 1(4)*. However it is not entirely clear whether this is in fact the position; the point has yet (as at 1 April 2013) to be tested.

55.31 SEAFARERS AND WORKERS ON INLAND WATERWAYS

A separate set of rules regulating the working time of seafarers on sea going United Kingdom flagged vessels is laid down by the *Merchant Shipping (Hours of Work) Regulations 2002*. These implement EC *Directive 99/63*, which was adopted to fill one of the gaps in the coverage of the *Working Time Directive*. (Equivalent legislation is required of other member states in relation to the crews of ships flying their respective flags, but the inspection and enforcement provisions of the *2002 Regulations* extend to such vessels whilst in a UK port or UK waters: *reg 3(1)*). The *2002 Regulations* do not apply to fishing vessels, pleasure vessels, static offshore installations or most tug boats, or their respective crews. The *1998 Regulations* do not apply at all to those seafarers covered by *Directive 99/63*, or to the crews of fishing vessels: *reg 18(1)*.

The principal features of the *Merchant Shipping Regulations* are:

(a)   a minimum of 10 hours' daily rest (divided into not more than two periods);

(b)   a minimum of 77 hours' rest in any seven-day period;

(c)   provision for (a) and/or (b) to be made subject to exceptions by way of a collective or workforce agreement;

(d)   provision for the suspension of scheduled working hours and rest periods in an emergency;

(e)   maintenance of records of hours worked;

(f)   a prohibition on night work for those under 18;

(g)   entitlement to four weeks' paid annual leave (which may be taken in instalments);

(h)   powers of inspection and enforcement, including penalties.

55.31 Working Time

Directive 99/95 provides a mechanism for the verification and enforcement of compliance with *Directive 99/63* by ships calling at ports of member states. *Directive 99/63* has been extensively amended by a later *Directive, 2009/13*, which gives effect to the *International Labour Organisation Maritime Labour Convention 2006*, which is due to come into force in August 2013. Further legislation to give effect to the *2009 Directive* will then be required (although the UK has not yet ratified the Convention).

Neither the *Directive* nor the *Merchant Shipping Regulations* apply to the crews of vessels registered in non-EU states. This has the (surprising) consequence that the *1998 Regulations* apply to some such seafarers, such as those based in the UK and working on vessels operating from British ports: see by way of analogy *Diggins v Condor Marine Crewing Services Ltd* [2009] EWCA Civ 1133, [2010] IRLR 119.

Separate regulations, the *Fishing Vessels (Working Time: Sea-fishermen) Regulations 2004 (SI 2004/1713)* apply to the crews of UK registered fishing vessels; these *Regulations* came into force on 16 August 2004. The *1998 Regulations* do not apply at all to those workers covered by the *2004 Regulations: 1998 Regulations, reg 18(1)(b)*.

The *2004 Regulations* apply to those employed on non fishing vessels registered in the UK, wherever the vessel may be, and also (but in relation only to rights to rest periods and certain enforcement provisions) to those working on vessels registered in an EU member state whilst in UK waters. They apply only to those employed under a contract of employment, not to workers in the wider sense; that point apart, the definitions used are essentially the same as those used in the *1998 Regulations*. The principal rights conferred are:

(a)   a maximum 48 hour working week (averaged over 52 weeks, but with no facility for individual opt-outs);

(b)   adequate rest (with minimum entitlements of 10 hours in 24, in no more than two separate periods, and 77 hours in any week);

(c)   health assessments, and transfer from night work if the health assessment discloses health problems associated with night work;

(d)   paid annual leave; and

(e)   to make a complaint to an employment tribunal if denied adequate rest or paid leave.

The rights not to be subjected to detriment, or dismissed, for asserting rights under the *Regulations*, are conferred by amendments to the *ERA 1996*. Other enforcement provisions include powers for the Maritime and Coastguard Agency to inspect records and detain vessels. The Secretary of State has a limited power to grant exemptions from the limits on working time and the minimum required periods of rest, and there is a general exemption for emergencies.

55.32   Workers employed on UK vessels operating under certificates limiting the vessel to inland waterways and lakes, or not requiring to be certificated, or on non-UK registered vessels operating solely within such waters, are covered by the *Merchant Shipping (Hours of Work: Inland Waterways) Regulations 2003 (SI 2003/3049)*, made under *s 85* of the *Merchant Shipping Act 1995*. In summary, these *Regulations* provide for a maximum of 48 hours working time a week, averaged in the same way as under the *1998 Regulations*, rights for night workers to free health assessments and to be transferred to other work if available if the worker's health is prejudiced by night working, rights to adequate rest, which must be of at least 77 hours in total in any week, and to four weeks' paid annual leave in each leave year. Other rights conferred by the *1998 Regulations* are however not mirrored in these *Regulations*.

There are limited exceptions for workers whose working time is unmeasured, and in certain cases the averaging period for the 48 hour week is extended to 26 weeks and may be further extended by a collective or workforce agreement. Employers are under a duty to maintain records. Breach of the provisions relating to maximum working time, health assessments and record keeping are offences, whilst the remedy for breaches of the provisions on rest periods and annual leave is by way of complaint to an employment tribunal. The *2003 Regulations* contain the usual prohibition on contracting out, except by way of a compromise agreement. The *2003 Regulations* mirror the *1998 Regulations* very closely in terminology; the *1998 Regulations* are excluded completely for those workers covered by the *2003 Regulations: 1998 Regulations, reg 18(1)(c)*.

In February 2012 a Framework Agreement was made by the sectoral social partners which will form the basis of a revised Directive for the Inland Waterways sector, likely to be adopted later in 2012. This will when implemented domestically increase the minimum entitlement to daily and weekly rest and further restrict maximum hours of night working.

55.33 AVIATION SECTOR

In November 2000 the Social Affairs Council formally adopted a *Directive* implementing the social partners' agreement on working time in the aviation sector, *Directive 2000/79* on the organisation of working time of mobile workers in civil aviation. The domestic implementation of this *Directive* has been effected by the *Civil Aviation (Working Time) Regulations 2004 (SI 2004/756)*. The *2004 Regulations* apply to crew members of civil aircraft flying for the purposes of public transport, and confer the following rights:

(a)   paid annual leave of at least four weeks, as to which see *British Airways plc v Williams* [2012] UKSC 43, [2012] IRLR 1014, [2012] ICR 1375;

(b)   free health assessments;

(c)   right of transfer from night work to day work where possible if health problems are caused by night work;

(d)   appropriate health and safety protection;

(e)   maximum working time of 2,000 hours a year, calculated on a rolling basis;

(f)   a maximum of 900 hours block flying time in any one (rolling) year;

(g)   at least seven local days (ie days at the crew member's home base) each month and at least 96 local days each year free of all duty and standby.

Infringements of the rights at (a), (b) and (c) may be made the subject of a complaint to an employment tribunal; however there is no equivalent to the protection from detriment or dismissal for asserting rights under the *1998 Regulations* for workers covered by the *Civil Aviation Regulations*; the reason for this omission is unclear. In other respects the *Regulations* are enforceable by the Civil Aviation Authority, following the model of the *1998 Regulations*.

Workers covered by *Directive 2000/79* are excluded from the operative provisions of the *1998 Regulations* governing adult workers: *reg 18(2)(b)*. However, unlike those in the sectors discussed in **55.31** and **55.32** above, this is not an exclusion of the *Regulations* in their entirety; the principal practical difference appears to be that specific provisions on young workers' hours in the *1998 Regulations* and the provisions for their enforcement by the CAA, do apply to the civil aviation sector. One issue which has arisen under the *2004 Regulations* is the treatment in calculating an individual's total annual working time (see (e) above) of standby duty. The *Regulations* were amended, following consultations by the Department for Transport, by the *Civil Aviation (Working Time) (Amendment) Regulations 2010, SI 2010/1226*, to provide that standby time counts in full towards the permitted annual working hours, subject to certain exceptions the effect of which is that time counts at half the rate of actual time. The amendments came into effect on 28 June 2010.

55.34 MOBILE WORKERS IN ROAD AND RAIL TRANSPORT

Mobile workers are defined as 'any worker employed as a member of travelling or flying personnel by an undertaking which operates transport services for passengers or goods by road or air': *1998 Regulations, reg 2(1)*.

Most such mobile workers are excluded from the application of the *1998 Regulations* by *reg 18*, by virtue of their falling within the terms of either *Directive 2000/79* (as to which, see **55.33** above) or *Directive 2002/15*, which requires member states to enact parallel provisions as to working time, etc for mobile workers in road transport. Any mobile workers (as defined above) who fall outside these categories are subject to *reg 24A*, which excludes the provisions of the *Regulations* as to night work, rest breaks and rest periods, but not those relating to the working week, health assessments, monotonous work, or paid annual leave. The exclusions are subject to rights to periods of adequate rest, which are required to be sufficiently long and continuous to ensure that the worker's health is protected. The EAT has held that the right to adequate rest is in effect in substitution for rights under *reg 24* to compensatory rest, rather than cumulative with that right: *Feist v First Hampshire & Dorset Ltd* [2007] All ER (D) 180 (Feb), EAT.

55.35   *Directive 2002/15* applies to mobile workers employed in the road transport industry who are covered by the *Drivers' Hours Regulations (Regulation 3820/85)*, which cover maximum driving hours for drivers of most commercial freight and passenger vehicles within the EU or the European Economic Area, or by the AETR Agreement 1970, which makes equivalent provisions covering road transport across the outer boundaries of the EU and EEA. (Note that following the introduction of *Directive 2002/15*, the *Drivers' Hours Regulations* were replaced by an updated equivalent, *Regulation 561/2006*, which came into force on 11 April 2007.) The *Directive* covers maximum working hours, breaks, rest periods and restrictions on night work, and the maintenance of records. It does not cover annual leave entitlement or rights to health assessments, or the rights in relation to working time, daily rest periods and rest breaks of young workers, in respect of which the *1998 Regulations* apply equally to workers otherwise governed by the *2002 Directive* (insofar as those provisions affecting only young workers are capable of applying to mobile workers in road transport).

The implementation of this *Directive* was effected, with effect from 4 April 2005, by the *Road Transport (Working Time) Regulations 2005 (SI 2005/639)*. The *2005 Regulations* apply to those mobile workers who in the course of their work drive, or travel in vehicles to which either the *Drivers' Hours Regulations* or the AETR agreement apply. They are thus not limited in their application to drivers as such, but may cover, for instance, attendants on long distance coaches. However, in line with the *Directive*, *Regulations* did not initially cover self-employed owner-drivers. Under *Art 2(1)* of the *Directive* the exclusion of self-employed drivers was due to lapse on 23 March 2009, but the *Directive* also made provision for the Parliament to decide, on the basis of a report by the Commission, whether the exemption should continue. Initially in September 2009 the Parliament rejected a report by the Commission which would have had the effect of extending the *Directive* to self-employed drivers; however, the Parliament subsequently reversed its position on the point, and the *2005 Regulations* have been amended accordingly, with effect from 11 May 2012, to apply to self-employed drivers in accordance with the *Directive*: see the *Road Transport (Working Time) (Amendment) Regulations 2012, SI 2012/991*.

The *2005 Regulations* impose a limit on working time of an average of 48 hours a week, averaged over either rolling or fixed periods of 17 weeks, with an absolute limit of 60 hours in any week. In limited circumstances the averaging period may be extended to 26 weeks. Working time is broadly defined to include all working time, not just the time spent driving or travelling, but excluding breaks and certain periods on standby (referred to as 'periods of availability'). See further *Vehicle and Operator services Agency v Wright* [2011] EWHC

1389, 27 May 2011, unreported, Div Ct (driving a 23-seat coach for private purposes counted as 'driving'). The *2012 Regulations* include an extended definition of 'working time' which makes it clear that the performance of general administration by self-employed drivers does not count as working time.

The *Regulations* do not contain any provision for individual opt-outs from the limits on working hours. In addition to limits on working hours, there are provisions for rest breaks and rest periods, and additional limits on night working. However the *Regulations* do not confer entitlements to paid annual leave. This is because the *1998 Regulations* apply in this respect; enforcement of rights to paid leave is by way of individual complaint to an employment tribunal under *reg 30* of the *1998 Regulations* or *Part II* of the *ERA 1996*.

Employers (and self employed drivers, from 11 May 2012) are required to ensure compliance with the *Regulations*, and enforcement is by inspectors appointed by the Department for Transport, using sanctions similar to those under the equivalent provisions of the *1998 Regulations*. The *2005 Regulations* do not make provision for individual workers to complain to an employment tribunal if not afforded the required rest breaks or rest periods, or dismissed or subjected to detriment for asserting their rights. This omission was challenged by way of Judicial Review in *R (oao United Road Transport Union) v Secretary of State for Transport* [2012] IRLR 941 (HCt). The challenge was rejected on the ground that the Regulations are intended to impose an obligation on drivers to take the specified breaks; this reflected the purpose of the *Regulations*, which was to promote the safe operation of road transport. Drivers' interests were in the Court's view protected by the fact that they could not be required to work without the mandatory breaks, and any attempt by an employer to require them to do so would be a breach of an implied term of their employment.

The *Drivers' Hours Regulations* apply directly as part of domestic law without the need for separate implementing legislation. The restrictions on the maximum permitted hours of work, and minimum rest periods, for drivers covered by the *Regulations*, are underpinned by criminal liability: an example of a successful prosecution for taking an insufficiently long rest break between shifts is *Harding v Vehicle and Operator Services Agency* [2010] EWHC 713 (Admin).

55.36   Mobile workers in the rail sector are covered by the *1998 Regulations*, and fall outside the exclusions applied by *reg 24A*, as they are outside the definition of 'mobile workers' quoted above; however they are subject to the effects of *reg 21*: see **55.29** above for this. Separate Regulations govern various aspects of the working time of rail workers working on services through the Channel Tunnel: see the *Cross-Border Railway Services (Working Time) Regulations 2008, SI 2008/1660*.

55.37   AGENCY WORKERS

Agency workers are covered by the *1998 Regulations* whether or not they satisfy the test to be workers under the *Regulations*: see *reg 36*. In addition, with effect from 1 October 2011, the *Agency Workers Regulations 2010 (SI 2010/93)*, which implement the EU *Agency Workers Directive 2009*, confer on agency workers (within the definition in *reg 3*) rights to equality of treatment with comparable directly employed staff of the end user of their services: *reg 5*. This right applies to contractual terms relating to working time, including night work, rest periods, rest breaks and annual leave (*reg 6(1)*). Thus if a comparable directly employed employee is entitled to an hour's paid break during a shift, the agency worker will have the same entitlement, although this is more generous than the statutory minimum stipulated by the *Working Time Regulations*. The entitlement is to the terms and conditions that would have applied to the agency worker had he or she been directly recruited to do the same job as an employee of the end user, and is subject to a number of conditions, of which the most significant is a qualifying period of 12 weeks working for the end user (*reg 7*).

55.38 CHURCH OF ENGLAND CLERGY

By virtue of the *Ecclesiastical Offices (Terms of Service) Regulations 2009*, which came into force on 1 January 2010, the holders of certain ecclesiastical offices in the Church of England (who are neither employees nor workers for the purposes of the *1998 Regulations*) are given rights to a weekly rest day (but it may be stipulated by the relevant Church authorities that this must not be taken on a Sunday or any of the principal feast days of the Church of England) and to annual leave without loss of stipend. Enforcement of these rights is a matter of internal Church procedures: there is no right of recourse to an employment tribunal. The rights conferred by the *2009 Regulations* do not apply to ministers of any church other than the Church of England; the position in other cases will therefore depend on whether the individual is held to be a worker within the *1998 Regulations*.

56   Wrongful Dismissal

56.1   INTRODUCTION

A wrongful dismissal occurs when an employer dismisses an employee in a way which is in breach of the employee's contract of employment. Most commonly, this arises when the employer dismisses the employee summarily (ie without any notice at all) or with short notice, and has no sufficient justification for doing so. However, there may also be a wrongful dismissal in other situations: for example, if the employer terminates the employment without following some procedure prescribed by the contract. Further, if the employee resigns in response to some repudiatory breach of contract by the employer, that will give rise to a claim which is in effect for wrongful dismissal.

Thus, wrongful dismissal is a common law cause of action based upon a breach of contract. The right not to be wrongfully dismissed, unlike the right not to be unfairly dismissed, is not one which depends upon statute. A dismissal which is wrongful need not necessarily be unfair, and vice versa. This is because an employer may behave unreasonably in dismissing an employee even though he has observed the letter of their contract, whilst a decision to dismiss may be reasonable even if it involves a breach of contract (although failure to comply with contractual procedures is one factor to be taken into account in deciding whether a dismissal is unfair). See *Treganowan v Robert Knee & Co Ltd* [1975] ICR 405; *BSC Sports and Social Club v Morgan* [1987] IRLR 391 and *Westminster City Council v Cabaj* [1996] ICR 960.

The primary remedy for an employee who is wrongfully dismissed is an action for damages for breach of contract. In certain circumstances, however, the employee may seek the assistance of the court in keeping the contract of employment alive.

56.2   Contracts whose breach may give rise to wrongful dismissal claims

The wrongful termination of any normal contract of employment will give rise to an action for wrongful dismissal. Certain special categories of employment are dealt with below (see **56.43** and **56.44**). Where the contract pursuant to which a self-employed person provides services is wrongfully terminated, the action for breach of contract is not strictly speaking one for wrongful dismissal but similar principles will apply.

56.3   WHAT CONSTITUTES A DISMISSAL

The fundamental precondition for a wrongful dismissal claim is that the employee should have been dismissed. This will usually occur in one of the following ways:

(a)   dismissal upon notice by the employer (see **56.5** below), although there will normally be no wrongful dismissal if full notice has been given;

(b)   summary dismissal by the employer; and

(c)   constructive dismissal (see **56.6** below).

However, there may also be a deemed dismissal in certain other circumstances (see **56.8–56.10** below).

1267

56.4 Wrongful Dismissal

56.4 Dismissal contrasted with other modes of termination

The employee will have no right to claim damages if the contract is brought to an end by mutual agreement or by his own resignation (unless in response to the employer's repudiatory breach), by frustration, or through the automatic operation of provisions in the contract (for example, expiry of a fixed term contract, or a provision that the employment will end as soon as the employee reaches a certain age).

For a fuller discussion of these possible modes of termination, see UNFAIR DISMISSAL – I (51). Note that expiry of a fixed term contract without renewal constitutes a deemed dismissal for the purposes of unfair dismissal but not for the purposes of wrongful dismissal.

56.5 Dismissal upon notice

Unless the contract otherwise provides, an effective notice may be given either orally or in writing. However, a notice is of no effect unless and until it is communicated to the employee (*Brown v Southall and Knight* [1980] ICR 617; *Hindle Gears Ltd v McGinty* [1985] ICR 111).

A purported notice is ineffective unless it is expressed to expire on a certain specified or ascertainable day, or upon the occurrence of a specified event (*Morton Sundour Fabrics Ltd v Shaw* (1966) 2 ITR 84; *Burton Group Ltd v Smith* [1977] IRLR 351). Accordingly, there will be no dismissal if the employee is merely warned that his job will come to an end at some point in the future (*Devon County Council v Cook* [1977] IRLR 188; *International Computers Ltd v Kennedy* [1981] IRLR 28), or if it is not possible to tell from the notice when the employment will end (*Haseltine Lake & Co v Dowler* [1981] ICR 222).

Usually, the employer's intention to dismiss will be clear. Sometimes, however, the language of a letter or conversation may leave room for doubt as to whether the employer is actually dismissing the employee, or whether he is merely warning or threatening that he may do so, or indeed whether he is simply expressing frustration or anger. In such circumstances, the court will consider, not the employer's subjective intention, but rather the objective meaning of the words used, considered against the background of the circumstances in which they are used. The ultimate question is how the words should reasonably have been regarded by the other party to the contract (*Tanner v DT Kean Ltd* [1978] IRLR 110; *Sovereign House Security Services Ltd v Savage* [1989] IRLR 115).

In order to decide whether due notice has been given, or whether the employee has been wrongfully dismissed, it may be important to decide on what date the notice takes effect. The day on which the notice is given will not normally be counted in calculating any period to which the notice refers (*West v Kneels Ltd* [1987] ICR 146).

Once notice has been given by one party to the contract, it may not be withdrawn except by mutual consent (*Riordan v War Office* [1959] 1 WLR 1046). Therefore, if an employer gives short notice to an employee, and later realises his mistake and seeks to retract that notice, the employee is entitled to refuse to agree to the retraction and to sue for wrongful dismissal (although the employer might then argue that the employee had failed to mitigate his loss).

56.6 Constructive dismissal

The employee will be treated as having been constructively dismissed if he resigns in response to a repudiatory breach of contract by the employer. This means that the employer must have breached some term of the contract, whether express or implied (or have indicated a clear intention to do so – see **56.22** below), and the breach must be sufficiently serious to 'go to the root of the contract'. (This will be the case if, for instance, the employer has breached the duty of trust and confidence: see *Morrow v Safeway Stores plc* [2002] IRLR 9). The employee must accept the breach by resigning, and he must not take so long to do so that he is deemed to have affirmed the contract or waived the employer's breach.

1268

For a full discussion of the different factual circumstances which may amount to a constructive dismissal, see UNFAIR DISMISSAL – I (51). Note, however, that in the unfair dismissal context it has been held to be necessary for the employer's breach of contract to be the true cause of the resignation. It is not thought that this applies to an action for wrongful dismissal (cf *Boston Deep Sea Fishing and Ice Co v Ansell* (1888) 39 Ch D 339; and see *RDF Media Group plc v Clements* [2007] EWHC 2892 (QB), [2008] IRLR 207).

56.7 Need for employer's breach of contract to be accepted

Where one party commits a repudiatory breach of contract, it is necessary for that breach to be 'accepted' by the other, innocent party before the contract can be brought to an end. That is because the innocent party may instead choose to keep the contract in existence, and simply to sue for damages if the breach of contract has caused him loss.

This rule applies to a contract of employment where the employer's breach of contract consists of some act or omission falling short of a purported dismissal. For instance, if the employer persists in withholding some significant benefit in kind, the employee may choose whether to resign and bring the contract to an end (thereafter suing for wrongful dismissal), or whether to remain in employment and simply sue for damages for the loss of the benefit.

This rule also applies where the employer purports to dismiss the employee in breach of contract (for example, in breach of a contractual procedure, or by purporting to dismiss summarily where there is no justification for doing so). In such a situation, the employee will normally simply accept his dismissal and sue for damages for wrongful dismissal. However, in some cases, the employee may wish to keep the contract alive — perhaps because there is an advantage to him in still being employed at a particular date (eg to receive a bonus or to invoke the benefits of an insurance policy), or because he hopes for a different outcome if the employer is obliged to go through a proper disciplinary procedure.

The Supreme Court has rejected the proposition that the act of wrongful dismissal brings the employment to an end without any need for acceptance of the breach by the employee: the 'automatic termination' theory (see *Société Générale v Geys* [2013] ICR 117).

Nonetheless, it is clear that in the employment context such acceptance will be readily inferred from the employee's words or conduct. For instance, an employee who seeks other work, or signs on for jobseeker's allowance, or even one who simply does not return to work and says nothing, will very probably be held to have ceased to be employed. (However, see *Brompton v AOC International Ltd* (above) where, on the facts of that case, the employee's request for his P45 did not amount to acceptance of the repudiatory breach; and see *Geys v Société Générale, London Branch* [2010] EWHC 648 (Ch), [2010] IRLR 950, where a request by an employee's solicitors for delivery of 'termination documentation' was treated by the Court as the employee keeping his options open, rather than affirmation of the breach.) To be on the safe side, an employee who wishes to argue that his employment continues should assert clearly and quickly that he regards himself as still employed, and that he is available for work if required.

56.8 Employer changing identity or ceasing to exist

If the employer is an individual, the death of that individual will bring the contract to an end. However, it appears that this will be regarded as a case of termination pursuant to an implied term of the contract, and not of wrongful dismissal (see *Farrow v Wilson* (1869) LR 4 CP 744).

If the employer is a partnership, then the dissolution of that partnership or a major change in its composition amounts to a dismissal of the employee (*Tunstall v Condon* [1980] ICR 786; *Briggs v Oates* [1990] ICR 473). It was held in *Brace v Calder* [1895] 2 QB 253 that the same applied when there was any change in the identity of the partners. However, it is not

56.8   Wrongful Dismissal

thought that this approach would be taken by the courts in modern cases of large partnerships whose membership frequently fluctuates. Firms should insert appropriate express terms into their contracts of employment to deal with this situation.

The permanent closure of the workplace amounts to a termination of the contracts of those employed there (*Glenboig Union Fireclay Co Ltd v Stewart* (1971) 6 ITR 14). This is not true of a temporary shutdown, although that might, depending upon the circumstances, amount to a repudiatory breach of contract.

56.9   Insolvency

Where the employer is a company, then an order for the compulsory winding up of that company has the immediate effect of terminating the contracts of employment of the company's employees (*Re General Rolling Stock Co* (1866) LR 1 Eq 346; *Measures Bros Ltd v Measures* [1910] 2 Ch 248, CA). However, contracts of employment continue during a voluntary winding up (*Midland Counties District Bank Ltd v Attwood* [1905] 1 Ch 357).

Again, contracts of employment are treated as coming immediately to an end if the employing company is put into receivership by an order of the court (*Reid v Explosives Co Ltd* (1887) 19 QBD 264; *Re Foster Clark Ltd's Indenture Trusts* [1966] 1 WLR 125). By contrast, the employment continues if the receiver is appointed otherwise by the court and as agent for the company, as typically occurs under, say, a creditor bank's debenture (*Hopley-Dodd v Highfield Motors (Derby) Ltd* (1969) 4 ITR 289; *Griffiths v Secretary of State for Social Services* [1974] QB 468). However, even a receivership of this latter kind may have the effect of terminating the contract of employment of a senior manager, if there is a fundamental inconsistency between the continuation of that individual's employment and the receiver's power and duty to conduct the business of the company (*Re Mack Trucks (Britain) Ltd* [1967] 1 WLR 780).

(See INSOLVENCY OF EMPLOYER (29).)

56.10   Removal from board of directors

In principle, a person's status as a director of the company and his status as an employee of that company are separate and distinct. Accordingly, the employee may cease to be a director without any impact upon his contract of employment.

Sometimes, however, it may be an express or implied term of the contract of employment that the employee is to be a director, either of the employing company itself, or of some associated company. In such a case, removal from the board will amount to a repudiation of the contract of employment, allowing the employee to sue for wrongful dismissal (*Shindler*, below).

However, even in a case where removal from the board brings the employment to an end, it may be contended that the company's articles of association were incorporated into the contract of employment when it was made, and have the effect of ending the employment without any breach on the company's part (see eg *Read v Astoria Garage (Streatham) Ltd* [1952] Ch 637; cf *Southern Foundries (1926) Ltd v Shirlaw* [1940] AC 701; *Shindler v Northern Raincoat Co Ltd* [1960] 1 WLR 1038).

(See DIRECTORS (8).)

56.11 DISMISSAL WITHOUT DUE NOTICE

Express notice periods

There will usually be a written contract of employment which stipulates expressly the period of notice to which the employee is entitled. Indeed, in most cases, the employer will be under a statutory obligation to provide this information as part of the written particulars of employment (see CONTRACT OF EMPLOYMENT (7)).

56.12 Fixed term contracts

Where the contract is for a fixed term, rather than one which contains a provision for the employer to give notice, damages for early termination will be awarded so as to put the employee in the same position as if the contract had continued until the end of that term. There is no need for the employer to give any advance notice that the contract will terminate at the end of the fixed term (although it may be sensible to do so), because it will do so automatically.

A contract which is for a fixed term, in that it will expire automatically on a given date, may also include provisions enabling either party to give notice to take effect at some earlier date.

Analogous to the fixed term contract is the contract which is expressed to terminate upon the occurrence of a specified event, such as the completion of a particular task.

56.13 Rolling contracts

A 'rolling contract' is not a precisely defined legal concept. However, the term is in general used to describe a contract which is of a length (say, two years) generally associated with a fixed term contract, but where the unexpired term always remains the same unless notice has been given. There is no difference in substance between a two-year rolling contract and a contract incorporating a two year notice period.

56.14 Directors' notice periods

A restriction upon the length of notice periods in directors' contracts of employment is contained in *s 188* of the *Companies Act 2006*. Save with the approval by resolution of the members of the company, a company cannot validly enter into contracts with its directors which it cannot terminate by notice, or which it can terminate only in specified circumstances, for a period exceeding two years. The same applies to directors of holding companies employed within the group. For the purpose of calculating the period within which the company can terminate the contract, the unexpired period of any preceding contract will be added to the term of the new contract if the latter is concluded more than six months before the expiry of the formers.

Any term which infringes this rule is void, and is replaced by a deemed term entitling the company to terminate the director's employment upon reasonable notice (see 56.15 below).

For other relevant principles, see DIRECTORS (8).

56.15 Implied notice periods

If the contract does not contain any expressly agreed notice period, and it is not a fixed term contract, then the court will generally imply a term that either party may bring the contract to an end by giving reasonable notice (*Richardson v Koefod* [1969] 1 WLR 1812. Cf *Reda v Flag Ltd* [2002] UKPC 38, [2002] IRLR 747, in which case the Privy Council held that there was no need to imply a term giving reasonable notice into a fixed term contract). It is most unusual for a contract to be construed as giving a right to a 'job for life', although in *McClelland v Northern Ireland General Health Services Board* [1957] NI 100, [1957] 2 All ER 129, HL the contract was held to be terminable only in the limited circumstances specified within it.

What constitutes a reasonable notice period must be decided by the court having regard to all the circumstances of the case. Such circumstances include the seniority and remuneration of the employee, his age and length of service, and what is usual in the particular trade. Very broadly speaking, the courts tend to approach such questions by adopting in most cases a period of one, three or six months or one year, with manual employees at one end of the range and senior executives at the other. The reasonable notice required to be given by the employer is not necessarily the same as that required to be given by the employee (cf *Libyan Arab Foreign Bank v Bankers Trust Co* [1989] QB 728 at 756G).

Where there is a training component to a contract of employment (eg in a Modern Apprenticeship type situation), then this will affect the period of notice that would be implied by the Courts. In *Flett v Matheson* [2005] ICR 1134, the EAT observed that reasonable notice would be geared towards the time in which it would be reasonable for arrangements to be made to place the apprentice with another employer.

56.16 Statutory minimum notice periods

Whatever the parties may have agreed in the contract, an employee who has worked for over a month is normally entitled at least to the statutory minimum period of notice prescribed by s 86 of the *ERA 1996* (essentially, one week for each year's completed service up to a maximum of twelve weeks; see further CONTRACT OF EMPLOYMENT (7)) (see eg *Masiak v City Restaurants (UK) Ltd* [1999] IRLR 780). It is not possible to override this statutory right by a provision in the contract of employment, but the employee may waive his right to notice on any given occasion or accept a payment in lieu of notice (*ERA 1996, s 86(3)*). The Employment Appeal Tribunal has questioned whether waiver of statutory notice rights can take place at the outset of a contract by means of a contractual payment in lieu clause (*Cerberus Software Ltd v Rowley* [2000] ICR 35). This point was not specifically addressed by the Court of Appeal [2001] EWCA Civ 78, [2001] ICR 376. However, it must be doubted, as the Court did not find that a payment in lieu clause was invalid.

The existence of the statutory minimum period does not prevent the implication of some longer reasonable period as a term of the contract (see **56.15** above).

56.17 Justification for summary dismissal

An employee may be summarily dismissed if he is guilty of a repudiatory breach of the contract of employment. As in the converse case of constructive dismissal, this means a breach which is sufficiently fundamental (see eg *Laws v London Chronicle (Indicator Newspapers) Ltd* [1959] 1 WLR 698; *Jupiter General Insurance Co Ltd v Shroff* [1937] 3 All ER 67).

The most frequent example of a repudiatory breach of contract by the employee is misconduct sufficiently serious to be regarded as gross misconduct. There is no rigid definition of what amounts to gross misconduct but, by way of example, the courts would normally be expected to treat summary dismissal as justified in any case of dishonesty, in cases of deliberate and inexcusable failure to comply with lawful instructions, and in cases where the misconduct is repeated or otherwise particularly flagrant. See the discussion in *Wilson v Racher* [1974] ICR 428 and the decision of Lord Jauncey in the Westminster Abbey organist case (*Neary v Dean of Westminster* [1999] IRLR 288). See also the curious case of *Briscoe v Lubrizol Ltd* [2002] EWCA Civ 508, [2002] IRLR 607, where an employee's behaviour in refusing to adhere to his employer's instructions during a lengthy period of sickness absence was held to justify his summary dismissal.

If the misconduct occurs outside the scope of the employment (eg an employee caught stealing from his local shop), it may still in principle be such as to justify summary dismissal. However, this will be so only if it is so serious as to strike at the root of the confidence which must exist for the contract of employment to be effective (*Jackson v Invicta Plastics Ltd* [1987] BCLC 329).

Sometimes the contract of employment will give a list of cases in which the employee may be summarily dismissed. Subject to the possible effect of the *Unfair Contract Terms Act 1977* (see **56.37** below), the court should probably uphold a dismissal carried out pursuant to such a clause, even if the conduct in question would not otherwise be considered sufficiently gross to merit summary dismissal. However, the danger which the employer runs in including such a clause in the contract is that the court may hold that it is intended as a complete and exhaustive list of the situations in which summary dismissal may be justified (see eg *Dietman v Brent London Borough Council* [1987] ICR 737, affirmed [1988] ICR 842; but see *Macari v Celtic Football & Athletic Co Ltd* [1999] IRLR 787, where the failure to follow a contractual dismissal procedure did not prevent the employer from relying on his common law right to dismiss summarily). Accordingly, from the employer's point of view, any clause of this kind must always be carefully drafted so as to make clear that it does not prejudice any right to dismiss summarily that would otherwise exist.

It is possible in principle to dismiss an employee summarily (and lawfully) for incompetence. This is because there is an implied term in the contract of employment that the employee is reasonably competent to do the job (*Harmer v Cornelius* (1858) 5 CBNS 236). However, *Jackson* (above) suggests that a summary dismissal on grounds of competence will be justified only in fairly extreme cases. A summary dismissal may also be justified on grounds of extreme carelessness (*Savage v British India Steam Navigation Co Ltd* (1930) 46 TLR 294). Mere illness disabling the employee from performance through no fault of his own is not a breach of contract.

All-out strike action will almost certainly amount to a repudiatory breach of contract entitling the employer to dismiss summarily (see *Simmons v Hoover Ltd* [1977] ICR 61), although it is possible that a very short walk-out might be considered insufficiently serious to have this consequence. Lesser forms of industrial action may or may not amount to a breach of contract at all (for example, an overtime ban is only a breach of contract if the contract provides for compulsory overtime) and may or may not be fundamental enough to be considered repudiatory.

56.18   DISMISSAL IN BREACH OF OTHER CONTRACTUAL REQUIREMENTS

Dismissal procedures

If the contract of employment stipulates that a particular procedure must be followed before an employee is dismissed, then a dismissal which is carried out without that procedure having been followed is necessarily wrongful (see, eg *Gunton v Richmond-upon-Thames London Borough Council* [1980] ICR 755; *R v BBC, ex p Lavelle* [1983] ICR 99; and *Dietman v Brent London Borough Council* [1988] ICR 842; but cf *Boyo v Lambeth London Borough Council* [1994] ICR 727).

However, it will be a question of fact in every case as to whether any disciplinary or similar procedure has in fact been incorporated into the contract of employment, or whether it merely represents a statement of the employer's current policy. If it is the latter, then breach of the procedure may well have the effect of making the dismissal unfair but it will not render it wrongful so far as the law of contract is concerned.

In *Johnson v Unisys Ltd* [2001] UKHL 13, [2001] ICR 480, the House of Lords rejected the contention that there could be implied into a contract of employment a provision that the employer would not dismiss save for good cause, and after giving the employee a reasonable opportunity to demonstrate that no such cause existed, in circumstances where there was an express term entitling the employer to dismiss on notice without any cause. In other words, the courts will not readily imply any procedural safeguards against dismissal into a contract of employment.

56.19   Other requirements

A dismissal might also be wrongful because, for example, it was carried out in contravention of a contractual term concerning the manner in which employees would be selected for redundancy. Such an argument was rejected on the facts in *Alexander v Standard Telephones and Cables Ltd (No 2)* [1991] IRLR 286.

Also, where the contract of employment contains the right to receive benefits under a permanent health insurance scheme, the court may imply a term preventing an employer from dismissing the employee (in the absence of conduct amounting to a repudiatory breach or for other cause, such as redundancy) during the period in which that employee is incapacitated from work. Dismissal in breach of this implied term would be wrongful, and may entitle the employee to recover damages reflecting the loss of permanent health benefits to which he would otherwise have been entitled (compare *Aspden v Webbs Poultry and Meat Group (Holdings) Ltd* [1996] IRLR 521 and *Hill v General Accident Fire and Life Assurance Corpn plc* [1998] IRLR 641; see also *Villella v MFI Furniture Centres Ltd* [1999] IRLR 468).

Similarly, if an employer decides to make an employee redundant, it cannot subsequently deny the employee of the benefits of the contractual redundancy scheme by dismissing him for another reason where it had no cause to do so. This would be a breach of an implied term of the employee's contract of employment, allowing the employee to claim damages to be assessed on the basis of the contractual redundancy scheme: see *Jenvey v Australian Broadcasting Corp* [2003] ICR 79.

56.20   RELEVANCE OF ACTUAL REASON FOR DISMISSAL

In a complaint of unfair dismissal, the reason for which the employer actually chose to dismiss the employee is of central importance. But in an action for wrongful dismissal, it is possible to justify the dismissal by reference to conduct of the employee of which the employer was unaware at the time of the dismissal, and which may have happened a considerable time prior to the dismissal (*Boston Deep Sea Fishing and Ice Co v Ansell* (1888) 39 Ch D 339; *Cyril Leonard & Co v Simo Securities Trust Ltd* [1972] 1 WLR 80; *Item Software (UK) Ltd v Fassihi* [2003] IRLR 769).

In principle, it should also be possible for the employer to rely upon conduct of which he was aware at the time of the dismissal, but was not in fact his reason for dismissing the employee. However, unless that conduct occurred or was discovered only a short time prior to the dismissal, the employer is likely to be held to have waived his right to terminate the contract on account of it.

Where an employee's misconduct was well known to the employer and it was not treated by them as justifying his dismissal, it will not be open to new owners or managers to seek to rely on that earlier misconduct on the grounds that they were not aware of it themselves. The issue is tested by reference to the legal personality of the employer, and by its actions and knowledge from time to time (*Welsh v Cowdenbeath Football Club Ltd* [2009] IRLR 362).

56.21   WAIVER OF NOTICE, PAY IN LIEU OF NOTICE AND GARDEN LEAVE

Frequently, an employer who has resolved to dismiss an employee will not wish that employee to continue working for him until the notice period has expired. It may, for example, be thought that the disgruntled employee's presence will be disruptive or bad for morale, or that there is a threat to confidential information, or simply that the employee will be unproductive and that a replacement should start work at the earliest opportunity.

In this situation, there are three principal options open to the employer (assuming that there are no grounds for a summary dismissal). The first is to negotiate an early termination with the employee. Some financial incentive may be offered, or the employee may simply be happy to be released from his obligations sooner rather than later. There is no legal obstacle to this course, because *s 86(3)* of the *ERA 1996* permits the employee to waive his right even to the statutory minimum period of notice (or to accept a payment in lieu of notice).

The second option is for the employer to pay the employee wages in lieu of notice. This course is frequently adopted. However, it should be borne in mind that to dismiss an employee with pay in lieu rather than to give due notice is in fact to dismiss wrongfully. The true legal analysis of this situation is that there is a summary dismissal carried out in breach of contract, and the wages paid in lieu in fact represent a payment of damages for that breach of contract (see *Gothard v Mirror Group Newspapers Ltd* [1988] IRLR 396). In some cases, the fact that the dismissal is theoretically wrongful may be of no practical significance. But that will not always be so. For instance, the dismissed employee may have a residual claim for the value of lost benefits in kind during the notice period. (See, for example, *Silvey v Pendragon plc* [2001] IRLR 685, where the early termination deprived an employee of enhanced pension rights. Even though the employee had accepted pay in lieu of notice, the Court of Appeal held that the loss of these pension rights was recoverable as damages for wrongful dismissal). The wrongful dismissal may also prevent the employer from relying upon restrictive covenants in the contract of employment (see **56.34** below).

An employee has no statutory or common law right to be paid in lieu of notice (*Rowley v Cerberus Software Ltd* [2001] EWCA Civ 78, [2001] ICR 376; *Hardy v Polk (Leeds) Ltd* [2004] IRLR 420. However, provision may be made by contract. In order to avoid the problems of the 'theoretically wrongful' dismissal described above, many service agreements now incorporate a clause which gives the employer the option of terminating the contract lawfully by making a payment in lieu of notice instead of actually giving notice. Such a clause ought to define clearly whether the payment is to be based upon basic pay only, or whether the calculation is also to have regard to other elements of the remuneration package, and whether the payment is to be made gross or net of tax. Where the contract of employment does not expressly define the payment that will be made in lieu of notice the Court will interpret the contract 'holistically', without any preconception that it necessarily seeks to give the employee what he would have earned had he remained in employment during the notice period (*Locke v. Candy & Candy Ltd* [2010] EWCA Civ 1350, [2011] IRLR 163.

Summary termination pursuant to a payment in lieu (PILON) provision does not constitute a breach of contract (*Rex Stewart Jeffries Parker Ginsberg Ltd v Parker* [1988] IRLR 483). Where payment in lieu has been made in accordance with a PILON provision, this will bring the contract of employment to an end, so long as the employer notifies the employee in clear and unambiguous terms that such payment has been made and that it is made in the exercise of the contractual right to terminate the employment with immediate effect (*Société Générale v Geys* [2013] ICR 117).

Where the employer exercises the right to terminate the contract with a payment in lieu of notice, the employee is under no obligation to give credit for actual or imputed earnings during what would have been the notice period. In other words, there is no duty on the employee to mitigate loss (as to which, see **56.30** below). He is entitled to claim for the full sum due to him under the contract as a debt (*Abrahams v Performing Rights Society* [1995] ICR 1028).

The sum paid to the employee in lieu of notice will be taxable in his hands under Schedule E (*EMI Group Electronics Ltd v Coldicott (Inspector of Taxes)* [1999] IRLR 630).

Merely because a contract of employment contains a payment in lieu clause, however, does not mean that every termination will be treated as if the employer exercised the right to dismiss and then make the payment in lieu without any deduction for mitigation. Much will depend on the precise wording of the contract. In *Gregory v Wallace* [1998] IRLR 387, the Court of Appeal held that, on the facts, the employer did not exercise the right to make a payment in lieu, where notice of termination had to be in writing and termination had been oral. Instead, the employer was treated as having dismissed the employee wrongfully and in breach of contract.

In *Cerberus Software Ltd v Rowley* [2001] ICR 376, on the other hand, where the contract stated that the employer 'may' make a payment in lieu of notice to the employee. The Court of Appeal held that this gave the employer the choice whether or not to make the payment.

There is no breach of contract even if it is the employee who has originally given notice, and the employer who then brings the employment to an immediate end with a payment in lieu (*Marshall (Cambridge) Ltd v Hamblin* [1994] IRLR 260). In *Hamblin* it was also held that the employment could be lawfully terminated with a payment in lieu of salary only, notwithstanding that the employee typically received a high proportion of his remuneration from commission; however, the EAT's reasoning is hard to follow and may depend upon the fact that the payment of commission was held to be discretionary and not a contractual right.

The third option is for the employee to be put on so-called 'garden leave'. This means that notice is duly given and the employee continues to be paid and to receive his full contractual benefits but he is not required or permitted to attend for work. This may be achieved by an express garden leave clause or, in certain circumstances, by 'implying' such a clause into the contract.

The power to place an employee on garden leave will not be implied if the refusal to provide work would constitute a repudiatory breach of contract. There will be a repudiatory breach if the contractual consideration moving from the employer includes an obligation to permit the employee to perform work but not if the contractual consideration is confined to payment of remuneration only (*Collier v Sunday Referee Publishing Co Ltd* [1940] 2 KB 647).

The Court of Appeal has acknowledged that employees increasingly regard work itself as important to them, and not just remuneration (*William Hill Organisation Ltd v Tucker* [1999] ICR 291). Moreover, it held that whether there is an obligation to provide work, rather than merely pay, will depend on a careful construction of the contractual arrangements. Of particular importance will be whether the position of the employee was 'specific and unique'; and whether the employee has some skill which will be lost if not practised. Other factors may be whether the contractual remuneration consists in part of a commission which depends upon work actually done (see eg *Devonald v Rosser & Sons* [1906] 2 KB 728). See also *Langston v Amalgamated Union of Engineering Workers* [1974] ICR 180, 510, CA; *Breach v Epsylon Industries Ltd* [1976] ICR 316; *Spencer v Marchington* [1988] IRLR 392; *SBJ Stephenson Ltd v Mandy* [2000] IRLR 233 (no obligation to provide work to a divisional director of an insurance brokerage).

In the recent case of *SG&R Valuation Service Co LLC v Boudrais* [2008] EWHC 1340 (QB), [2008] IRLR 770, the court held that the Defendant employees had a right to work, based on the *Tucker* analysis. However, this right was qualified, and was subject to the employees being ready and willing to work. The employees' wrongdoing (removal of confidential information, solicitation of staff and diversion of business opportunities) demonstrated that they were not ready and willing to work, and so the employer was entitled to withhold work from them during their notice period.

It should be borne in mind, however, that the existence of an express garden leave clause may be taken into account by a court in determining the validity of any post-termination restraints on the employee (*Credit Suisse Asset Management Ltd v Armstrong* [1996] ICR 882; see further RESTRAINT OF TRADE (39)).

56.22 ANTICIPATORY BREACHES OF CONTRACT

It is important to remember that a breach of contract, in this as in other contexts, may be either *actual* or *anticipatory*. An anticipatory breach of contract occurs where there has not yet been any actual breach, because the time for performance of the relevant obligation has not yet arrived, but one party has indicated a clear refusal to perform the contract, or has made it impossible for himself to fulfil his obligations when the time comes. In the case of an employment contract, this might occur, for example, if the employer announced that the employee's salary would be unilaterally reduced by a significant amount the following month.

Where an anticipatory breach of contract occurs, and it is sufficiently serious to be repudiatory, the innocent party is faced with a choice. First, he may immediately accept the breach as bringing the contract to an end, and sue for damages. Secondly, he may keep the contract alive, and continue to call for performance by the other party. Thus, in the example above, the employee could immediately resign and sue for damages for wrongful dismissal. Alternatively, he could continue to assert his right to be paid a full salary the following month, which would give the employer an opportunity to change his mind; if the salary was indeed reduced, then the employee would at that point have to choose between resigning and affirming the contract, as discussed in **56.6** above. In the latter event, he might also be able to sue in debt for arrears of salary, as discussed in **56.24** below.

It has been suggested that an anticipatory breach, as opposed to an actual breach of contract, will not be repudiatory if it stems from an innocent mistake on the part of the party in breach as to what the contract requires of him (see *Frank Wright & Co (Holdings) Ltd v Punch* [1980] IRLR 217, EAT; *United Bank Ltd v Akhtar* [1989] IRLR 507; and *Brown v JBD Engineering Ltd* [1993] IRLR 568).

56.23 REMEDIES FOR WRONGFUL DISMISSAL

Remedies other than claims for damages

Injunctions

If the employee moves swiftly, he may be able to obtain an injunction restraining the employer from dismissing him wrongfully. However, it is unusual for the court to agree to insist upon performance of a contract of employment, because of the personal relationship between employer and employee without which the contract cannot properly function. Nevertheless, the breakdown of the relationship of trust and confidence will not automatically prevent an employee from obtaining injunctive relief (see *Gryf-Lowczowski (Jan) v Hinchingbrooke Healthcare NHS Trust* [2005] EWHC 2407 (QB), [2006] IRLR 100 (see further CONTRACT OF EMPLOYMENT (7)).

56.24 *Claims in debt*

If the employer's breach of contract consists of the failure to pay a sum of money that is due, for example by imposing a reduction in salary, the employee's sole choice is not between resigning and claiming to have been wrongfully dismissed on the one hand, and accepting the reduced salary on the other. Rather, he may choose to affirm the contract of employment despite the employer's breach, yet continue to assert his entitlement to the unpaid moneys, and sue in debt for those moneys if they remain unpaid. For examples, see the decisions of the House of Lords in *Rigby v Ferodo Ltd* [1988] ICR 29 and the EAT in *Bruce v Wiggins Teape (Stationery) Ltd* [1994] IRLR 536.

56.25 Wrongful Dismissal

56.25 Actions for damages for wrongful dismissal

General approach to assessment of damages

The basic principle in assessing the damages payable for wrongful dismissal is that the employee must be put into the same position as if the employer had properly performed the contract. However, it is to be assumed for these purposes that the employer would have performed the contract in the way least burdensome to himself, and would have minimised his obligations to the employee by giving due notice to terminate the contract at the earliest opportunity (see *Lavarack v Woods of Colchester Ltd* [1967] 1 QB 278 and *Clark v BET plc* [1997] IRLR 348, though see *Horkulak v Cantor Fitzgerald International* [2004] EWCA Civ 1287, [2005] ICR 402. In that case, the Court of Appeal held that the rule did not apply to the failure to make discretionary bonus payments where the employer is contractually obliged to exercise his discretion rationally and in good faith. In those circumstances, the Court will look to see what bonus the employee probably would have received if he had continued in employment, rather than the minimum sum that his employer might have awarded him consistent with his contractual obligation to act rationally and in good faith).

Two main consequences follow from this basic principle. First, the court will have to ask itself how much better off the employee would have been if he had been given proper notice on the date when he was wrongfully dismissed (or if notice which had already been given had been allowed to run its course). This will normally mean that the *prima facie* measure of the damages is the net amount of the employee's salary and benefits for the notice period. In the case of a fixed term contract, the equivalent period is of course the unexpired portion of the term remaining as at the date of dismissal.

Second, the court (unlike an employment tribunal assessing compensation for unfair dismissal) will only compensate the employee for the loss of benefits to which he was contractually entitled, and not for those which he would probably have received in practice but to which he had no legal right (*Laverack*, above). It may also be necessary to consider questions of causation arising upon the particular facts of a given case. For example, the employer may be able to prove upon a balance of probabilities that the employee would have left his job voluntarily within the notice period in any event, or that an employee dismissed because of long-term absence through sickness would have remained off work throughout the notice period and would therefore have earned nothing during that period.

Where the wrongfulness of the dismissal stems from a failure to follow a proper procedure (see **56.18** above), the traditional view has been that damages should be awarded on the basis that notice could lawfully have been given on the day when the necessary procedures, if followed, could have been concluded (*Gunton v Richmond-upon-Thames London Borough Council* [1980] ICR 755; see also *Alexander v Standard Telephones and Cables Ltd (No 2)* [1991] IRLR 286 and *Boyo v Lambeth London Borough Council* [1994] ICR 727). The court will not speculate as to whether or not the employee would have remained in employment if the disciplinary procedure had been followed (*Focsa Services (UK) Ltd v Birkett* [1996] IRLR 325; *Janciuk v Winerite Ltd* [1998] IRLR 63; *Wise Group v Mitchell* [2005] ICR 896). The Supreme Court in *Edwards v Chesterfield Royal Hospital NHS Foundation Trust* [2012] ICR 201 declined to consider whether *Gunton* was properly decided.

56.26 'Liquidated damages' clauses and other provisions for termination payments

Sometimes a service agreement may contain a provision that the employer is to pay a specified sum, or a sum calculated in a specified way, to the employee if the employment comes to an end in particular circumstances.

If the employee seeks to enforce such a provision, a basic question which may arise is whether the clause is a penalty clause. If so, the court will not give effect to it, and the employee will simply have to sue for damages in the normal way (assuming that he has been wrongfully dismissed). In order to decide whether a particular provision is indeed a penalty clause, it is necessary to apply a two-stage test.

First, does the clause apply where there has been a breach of contract? A provision which provides for a particular sum to be payable upon an occurrence which does *not* amount to a breach of contract cannot be a penalty clause. If the triggering event may or may not amount to a breach of contract depending upon the circumstances, the court will ask whether there was a breach of contract in the case in question. Thus, a provision in a contract of employment that, if the employer gave due notice to terminate the contract, he would pay £1,000 to the employee could not be a penalty clause, because there would be no breach of contract in circumstances to which it applied. If the contract provided for the employer to pay £1,000 if he dismissed *without* due notice, then that could be a penalty clause, depending upon the application of the second stage of the test (see below). If the provision was for £1,000 to be paid in any case in which the employee was dismissed, then that might amount to a penalty clause, but only in a case in which the dismissal was in fact wrongful. For these somewhat anomalous distinctions, see *Export Credit Guarantee Department v Universal Oil Products Co* [1983] 1 WLR 399.

Assuming that the provision operates upon a breach of contract (as will be the case if one is dealing with a wrongful dismissal), the second stage of the test is to ask whether it represents a genuine pre-estimate of the loss suffered (in which case it is a valid liquidated damages clause, and will be enforced), or whether it is in effect designed to terrorise the other party into performing the contract (see *Dunlop Pneumatic Tyre Co Ltd v New Garage and Motor Co Ltd* [1915] AC 79). A comparison between the amount that would be payable on breach with the loss which might be sustained is, however, merely a 'guide' as to whether the clause is penal. Thus, in *Murray v Leisureplay plc* [2005] EWCA Civ 963, [2005] IRLR 946, the Court of Appeal overturned the trial judge's finding that a clause requiring the payment of one year's gross salary in the event of wrongful termination was a 'penalty', emphasising Lord Dunedin's approach in *Dunlop* that a clause 'will be held to be a penalty if the sum stipulated for is extravagant and unconscionable in amount in comparison with the greatest loss that could conceivably be provided to have followed from the breach.' On the facts of the case, the Court held that the clause was 'generous' but 'not unconscionable', and did not meet the test of 'extravagance'. The Court held that it was appropriate for the remuneration package to provide 'generous reassurance against the consequences of dismissal.'

The difference between a liquidated damages clause and a penalty clause was considered in *Giraud UK Ltd v Smith* [2000] IRLR 763, a case that illustrates that an employee may be liable for damages if he gives short notice. In that case, the contract of employment provided that if an employee failed to give his contractual notice when resigning, it would result in a deduction from his wages equivalent to the number of days short. The EAT upheld the decision of the employment tribunal that this was a penalty clause (and thus invalid). It was not a liquidated damages clause because it was not a genuine pre-estimate of the loss to the employer if the employee failed to give proper notice. Further, it did not prohibit the employer from seeking further damages through the courts greater than that specified in the clause. There was evidence to suggest that the employer could easily find replacements for the employee in question (he was a lorry driver). In the circumstances, therefore, the clause enabled the employer to say 'Heads I win, tails you lose!'

The advantage of a valid liquidated damages clause is that, in a case where liability for wrongful dismissal is accepted, it may enable the parties to avoid costly and lengthy litigation involving disputes about the precise valuation of benefits and the adequacy of attempts at mitigation (cf *Abrahams* above).

56.27 *Rights of employee in period of notice*

As set out in **56.16** above, *s 86* of the *ERA 1996* provides for statutory minimum notice periods. *Section 87(1), ERA 1996* provides that, if an employer gives notice of dismissal to an employee who has been continuously employed for at least one month, then during the statutory minimum period, the employee will enjoy the rights conferred by *ss 88 to 91, ERA 1996*.

The importance for present purposes of the rights conferred by these provisions is that they are to be taken into account in assessing any claim for damages for wrongful dismissal (*ERA 1996, s 91(5)*). In other words, when assessing what the employee would have received if the employer had performed his minimum obligations, it is necessary to take account not only of his contractual obligations, but of these statutory obligations as well.

The principal right conferred by these statutory provisions is for the employee to be paid in cases where he is ready and willing to work, but no work is provided for him by his employer, or where the employee is absent from work through sickness, pregnancy or being on holiday. This would include employees absent on long-term ill-health grounds. The precise qualifications for payment, and the amount to which the employee is entitled, are the subject of detailed provisions.

Where sums which should have been payable pursuant to these provisions fall to be taken into account in assessing damages, they are subject to reduction for mitigation in the usual way (*Westwood v Secretary of State for Employment* [1985] ICR 209).

It is significant to note that these rights do not apply where the contractual period of notice exceeds the statutory minimum period by at least one week (*ERA 1996, s 87(4)*). This point was highlighted in *Budd v Scotts Co (UK) Ltd* [2003] IRLR 145, where the employee's contractual notice period exceeded the statutory period. The EAT held that the employee was not entitled to be paid for his contractual notice period as he was sick throughout and was not capable of working. By contrast, he would have been paid for the entire period if the contractual notice period had been the same or less than the statutory period.

56.28 *Valuation of particular benefits*

Salary. This will normally be straightforward to calculate, since it will simply be a question of applying the rate of pay enjoyed by the claimant at the date of dismissal to the length of the notice period. Sometimes the employee is entitled to an annual increase either of a set amount, or related to the prevailing rate of inflation, and such an entitlement must of course be built into the calculation if the notice period extends beyond the date upon which the next increase was due (*Re Crowther & Nicholson Ltd* (1981) Times, 10 June).

Where the contract provides for an annual increase but the amount of the increase is in the absolute discretion of the employer, the employer will be obliged to exercise that discretion in good faith and not capriciously (*Clark*, above). Perhaps more commonly, the contract may stipulate that salary will be reviewed on an annual basis. However, in *Runciman v Walter Runciman plc* [1992] BCLC 1084 the court refused to award any damages to represent the loss of a chance that such a review would have led to a salary increase.

Bonuses and commission. Where the employee was entitled to receive a bonus or commission as part of his remuneration, the court will have to assess what the value of that entitlement would have been if the employee had remained employed through the notice period. Sometimes an exact figure will be readily ascertainable, as where the bonus depends upon the pre-tax profits of a large company, whose profits for the relevant period have already been declared and cannot have been significantly affected by the absence of the claimant. In other cases, such as where the employee was entitled to a percentage of the value of sales which he himself achieved, the court will have to make the best estimate possible of what would have happened if due notice had been given. It will consider, for example, evidence of past performance by that employee, and performance by other employees during the relevant period as compared with their own past performance. In yet other cases, the court may be required to assess the employer's likely profits in years which are yet to come, in which case expert evidence is likely to be required if the claim is of any size. Where an employer operates a discretionary bonus scheme an employee who has a contractual entitlement to participate in that scheme is entitled to a bona fide and rational exercise of discretion by his employer as to whether or not he receives his bonus and in what sum (*Clark v Nomura International plc* [2000] IRLR 766, EAT; *Horkulak v Cantor Fitzgerald International* [2004] EWCA Civ 1287, [2005] ICR 402). In deciding how much compensation to award an employee where his employer has failed to exercise its discretion rationally and in good faith, the court may take into account the range of bonus payments made to other employees. The court is not obliged to award the employee the minimum bonus that the employer could lawfully have paid if it is not fair and reasonable to do so (see *Horkulak*).

Share options. The effect of dismissal may be that the employee loses the right to exercise share options which he holds, or that he is compelled to exercise them within a shorter timescale than would otherwise have been the case, with adverse implications for the differential between the exercise price and the market price of the shares. Where this is so, and where there is no valid exclusion clause in respect of liability for such loss (see 56.37 below), the court will have to assess the value of the shares which the employee could otherwise have obtained, less what it would have cost him to acquire them.

Cars. Company cars often represent a substantial head of loss, although for any damages to be recoverable it is obviously essential that the claimant should have been permitted to make some personal use of the car.

There are a number of possible ways in which the loss may be assessed. If the employee has actually had to hire a replacement car, and has acted reasonably in doing so, then the hire charges should be recoverable. Alternatively, a fairly rough and ready lump sum may be awarded.

More commonly, however, the court will be invited to have regard either to the value which the Inland Revenue places upon the car for tax purposes, or to the AA's estimated running costs. The Revenue scales, which are based on size or value, age and mileage, were formerly not much relied upon by employees, because the tax treatment of such benefits was generous, and did not reflect their true value. More recently, changes in policy have made the Revenue scales a better and fairer guide.

The AA estimates provided the basis of valuation adopted by the court in *Shove v Downs Surgical plc* [1984] ICR 532. They are annual figures comprising standing charges and running costs per mile for various sizes of car and a given annual mileage.

Clearly, whatever basis of valuation is adopted, it is necessary to examine the terms of the contract (either express, or implied through practice) as to what costs associated with running the car were to be met by the employer, and which by the employee. In particular, it is necessary to know which party was responsible for meeting the cost of petrol for private use.

Pensions. The loss of pension contributions, or pension rights, is also in many cases an extremely important head of damages.

Insurance cover. It is commonplace for employees to be contractually entitled to the benefit of free medical insurance, permanent health insurance and the like, both for themselves and for their families.

The value of such benefits is frequently assessed as if it could be equated with the cost to the employer of providing the insurance cover, and this may be convenient when the sums at stake are small. However, it is not a strictly accurate approach. If the employee has in fact obtained replacement cover, then the loss suffered is the reasonable cost to him of doing so (and an individual may have to pay more than a company purchasing the same cover on a group basis). However, if the employee has chosen not to take out such insurance himself, then he suffers no loss (save, perhaps for the 'peace of mind' which the employee previously enjoyed, knowing that insurance coverage was in place) unless during the relevant period some event occurs which would have led to the making of a payment under the policy, had it still been in force. In that event, there may be arguments as to whether the whole amount of the lost payment is recoverable, or whether the employee should have mitigated his loss by obtaining replacement cover.

It is also necessary to bear in mind that, depending upon the basis on which the insurance is arranged and paid for, the period for which cover is lost through the wrongful dismissal (or replacement cover has to be purchased) may not exactly correspond to the period between the dismissal and the date when due notice would have expired.

Holidays. The conventional view is that the right to paid holiday is not a separate compensatable head of loss, since the pay which would have been received is covered by the claim for lost salary. However, it is at least arguable that the opportunity to receive that salary, without having to work for it, is itself a valuable benefit, and that the salary payable in respect of the relevant period is the appropriate measure of that value. The counter-argument is that the wrongfully dismissed employee in effect finds himself enjoying a good deal of holiday time, whether he likes it or not. On the other hand, he is not truly on holiday (because he has a continuing duty to look for ways of mitigating his loss), and he may find other employment which offers the same pay but less generous holiday arrangements.

Accommodation. If it was a contractual benefit that the employee should be provided with free or cheap accommodation, and the employee has had to vacate that accommodation as a result of the dismissal, then the cost of finding alternative accommodation for the duration of the notice period is a recoverable head of loss.

Sometimes employees who have lost accommodation seek to claim for their removal expenses. However, it is unlikely that such expenses are properly recoverable in most cases, since the employee would have had to leave the accommodation in due course even if proper notice had been given.

Miscellaneous. In advising employees with wrongful dismissal claims, it is important to ensure that all contractual benefits have been identified and claims made for their value. Other than the common and valuable benefits discussed above, benefits in kind may include, for example, meals, payment of telephone bills and the use of a mobile phone, discounts on particular products (such as mortgages for bank employees), and personal use of credit cards offering preferential interest rates. See also **56.33** below for loss of the right to complain of unfair dismissal.

However, a right to reimbursement of expenses only represents a head of loss if the expenses in question were not confined to expenditure incurred for the purposes of the job (the point being that such expenditure will cease to be incurred once the job is lost).

In all cases, it is wise to be sure that benefits have been properly declared to tax before they are introduced into the calculation of loss, lest an argument be put forward that the contract is void for illegality (see **56.35** below).

A claim for damages for wrongful dismissal will often be combined with a claim in debt for wages accrued to the date of dismissal, and for accrued holiday pay if that is a contractual right. Claims in debt are not subject to the obligation to mitigate. Nor can the employer avoid paying accrued wages even if there was misconduct prior to the dismissal which justified summary termination (*Healey v Française Rubastic SA* [1917] 1 KB 946). Wages accrue on a daily basis and an employee will normally be entitled to claim an apportionment of wages for a period worked even where he has been summarily dismissed before his salary became due under the terms of his contract: *Item Software (UK) Ltd v Fassihi* [2002] EWHC 3116 (Ch), [2003] IRLR 769.

56.29   *Compensation for distress and other intangible loss*

The normal rule is that in an action for breach of contract, including an action for wrongful dismissal, it is not possible to recover damages for distress or injured feelings for the manner of the breach (*Addis v Gramophone Co Ltd* [1909] AC 488; *Johnson v Unisys Ltd* [2001] UKHL 13, [2001] ICR 480).

Further, while an employee may recover damages at common law for a breach of the implied term of trust and confidence occurring prior to a dismissal, the House of Lords has held that such a claim cannot be made in respect of the dismissal itself, for this would impinge on the statutory right not to be unfairly dismissed, the jurisdictional and compensatory limits for which have been determined by Parliament (*Johnson*, ibid). Their Lordships considered this boundary, which they called 'the *Johnson* exclusionary area', again in *McCabe v Cornwall County Council* [2004] UKHL 35; [2004] IRLR 733. Their Lordships affirmed the decision in *Johnson*, but expressed dissatisfaction with the boundary line drawn. Lord Steyn, noting that the reasoning of a number of their Lordships in *Johnson* had been underpinned by an assumption that compensation for non-pecuniary loss was available in unfair dismissal, suggested that the issue ought to be revisited in the light of the decision of the House in *Dunnachie v Kingston-Upon-Hull City Council* [2004] UKHL 36, [2004] IRLR 727. (In *Dunnachie*, their Lordships ruled that compensation for unfair dismissal was strictly limited to compensation for pecuniary loss: see generally **53.12** UNFAIR DISMISSAL – III.) Lord Nicholls, however, observed (at para 33) that the whole issue required the 'urgent attention' of Parliament.

In *Gibb v Maidstone & Tunbridge Wells NHS Trust* [2009] IRLR 707, the Court held that the employing trust had been in breach of the implied term of trust and confidence in giving assurances to its former chief executive that the necessary approvals were or would be in place for the compromise agreement that they were entering into. However, the Court held that this did not give rise to a cause of action in damages, as it fell within 'the Johnson exclusion area'. The inaccurate assurances had been given by the employer as part of the steps leading up to the employee's dismissal. The case has recently been considered by the Court of Appeal ([2010] EWCA Civ 678, [2010] IRLR 786), and the decision overturned on other grounds. On this point, however, Laws LJ held that if he was required to decide it, he would have held that the breach did not fall within 'the Johnson exclusion area', as the employee entered into the compromise agreement before the termination of her contract, and the fact that the loss fell in after it does not show that the termination caused the loss.

It is possible, however, to recover damages for loss of reputation or future prospects on the labour market (in actions for wrongful dismissal or breach of contract – where the breach is not known until after termination) where the employer is in breach of the duty of trust and confidence: so-called 'stigma damages' (*Malik v BCCI SA* [1997] ICR 606). Recovery of stigma damages will probably be rare, however, as the employee is required to establish not only that there was a breach of the duty, but that the requirements of causation and remoteness are also satisfied. In the *Malik* case it was assumed for the purposes of argument that the employer bank operated its business in a corrupt and dishonest way; that its corruption and dishonesty were widely known; and that the employees were at a handicap on the labour market as they were tainted by their connection with the employer. At trial, however, none of the former employees were able to establish that the employer's breach caused them any financial loss, as they could not demonstrate that the bank's wrongdoing blighted their job prospects (*Bank of Credit and Commerce International SA v Ali* [1999] IRLR 508).

Damages for the loss of future employment prospects may be more readily available where the contract is one of apprenticeship (*Dunk v George Waller & Son Ltd* [1970] 2 QB 163), or where (as with the engagement of an actor) part of its purpose is to provide publicity for the employee (*Clayton (Herbert) and Jack Waller Ltd v Oliver* [1930] AC 209, HL).

56.30 *Mitigation and collateral benefits*

An employee who has been wrongfully dismissed is under a duty to mitigate his loss by seeking alternative sources of income. Any other income received during the notice period in relation to which the employee is being compensated will normally have to be taken into account so as to reduce the loss suffered.

The dismissed employee's obligation is to act reasonably. The principles applied in wrongful dismissal cases are very similar to those applicable in assessing compensation for unfair dismissal, and reference should also be made to the discussion in UNFAIR DISMISSAL – III (53).

The claimant's obligation to mitigate ought not to be treated as imposing too heavy an obligation upon him, and the burden of proving a failure to mitigate is upon the defendant (*Fyfe v Scientific Furnishings Ltd* [1989] ICR 648). In the first instance, it will probably (depending upon all the circumstances) be reasonable for the employee to seek to find employment of a status and at a salary commensurate with that which he lost upon being dismissed. However, if time goes by without other work being found, the court will expect him to lower his sights. Employees must certainly expect to provide cogent justification for refusing any jobs which are actually offered to them. How far afield in geographical terms a dismissed employee must seek for work in order to be acting reasonably will depend upon his age, the nature of his work, and his personal and domestic circumstances.

It is often advisable for the claimant employee to be able to show that he has pursued all the available avenues of job-seeking, such as registration with agencies and Jobcentres, perusal of job advertisements in general and specialist publications, and use of consultants or outplacement services; not all these possibilities will be appropriate in all cases, however. Copies of all letters written and other relevant documents should be retained, and a record kept of relevant telephone conversations.

It has become increasingly common in large wrongful dismissal claims for expert evidence to be given by recruitment consultants, who use their experience of the relevant industrial sectors to estimate when, and with what remuneration package, a person in the claimant's position should have been able to obtain alternative employment (see, for example, *Clark*, above).

Seeking employment is not the only reasonable means by which a dismissed employee may seek to mitigate his loss. In an appropriate case he may seek to set up his own business or to work in a self-employed or freelance capacity (*Gardiner-Hill v Roland Beiger Technics Ltd* [1982] IRLR 498). Only in an exceptional case, however, would it be held that a claimant had acted unreasonably in *failing* to go into business on his own account. It is more doubtful that there has been proper mitigation where a claimant chooses to undertake further education or retraining instead of seeking work, unless his or her existing skills are very unlikely to lead to a new job.

If the circumstances of the dismissal have been acrimonious, or have involved bad faith or unreasonable conduct on the part of the employer, it is unlikely that the employee will be held to have acted unreasonably if he rejects an offer of new employment made by that employer (see eg *Shindler v Northern Raincoat Co Ltd* [1960] 1 WLR 1038). Nor, it appears, is it an unreasonable failure to mitigate if the employee fails to invoke an internal appeal procedure (*Lock v Connell Estate Agents* [1994] IRLR 444). However, a failure to complete the statutory grievance procedure in Sch 2 to the *Employment Act 2002* will mean that a tribunal will reduce any damages awarded (*s 31*) or even prevent the employee from bringing a claim altogether (*s 32*). See generally **53.9** Unfair Dismissal – III.

Expenses reasonably incurred in attempting to mitigate loss may be deducted from the fruits of the mitigation or added to the loss suffered as the case may be.

Moneys received during the notice period which have to be deducted from wrongful dismissal damages include not only income from a new job, but also any payments already made by the defendant on account of the dismissal, and state benefits (*Parsons v BNM Laboratories Ltd* [1964] 1 QB 95; but it was held in *Westwood v Secretary of State for Employment* [1985] ICR 209 that unemployment benefit should not be taken into account if the entitlement to it runs out whilst the employee is still out of work after the end of the notice period). However, the employee does not have to give credit for any benefits received from insurance policies which pay out in the event of unemployment, or for a pension which becomes payable upon the dismissal (*Hopkins v Norcros plc* [1994] ICR 11). Nor does the employee have to give credit for the fact that he works shorter hours in his new job, or receives longer holidays than beforehand (*Potter v Arafa* [1995] IRLR 316).

56.31 *Interest and accelerated receipt*

Depending upon the length of the notice period or fixed term contract, and how long it takes for the wrongful dismissal claim to be brought to trial, the claimant may find either that he has suffered a loss through being deprived of the use and benefit of his salary for the period between the dismissal and the trial, or that he gains because the award of damages is in his pocket much sooner than the salary which it represents would have been paid.

Accordingly, that part of the award of damages which represents salary which ought to have been paid in the past will normally carry an award of interest. The discretionary power of the High Court to award interest is found in *s 35A* of the *Supreme Court Act 1981*, and that of the county court in *s 69* of the *County Courts Act 1984*. The rate and period of interest, as well as whether to award it at all, are in the court's discretion. However, the award will always be of simple interest; it will generally run from the date when payment should have been made until the date of judgment, unless the claimant has been culpably slow in prosecuting the proceedings; and it will frequently reflect the judgment rate of interest over the relevant period (currently 8%).

Where damages are being received earlier than the payments for whose loss they compensate were due, it is normal for a percentage discount to be applied on account of accelerated receipt, generally reflecting the anticipated rate of inflation over the relevant period.

Sometimes, where the award of damages covers a very long period, the percentage discount may be increased (or a further discount applied) to take account of the so called 'vicissitudes of life' – in other words, the intangible chance that the claimant might never have served the full notice period because he fell ill, chose to depart, or encountered the proverbial number 57 bus. It is not thought that any very large discount is generally appropriate on this score.

56.32 *Taxation of damages*

The ultimate objective of the award of damages, as explained above, is to put the claimant into exactly the same position as if the contract had been duly performed. In that event, he would of course have been paid his salary net of tax and national insurance contributions, and would have had to pay tax upon most benefits in kind. However, simply to deduct tax and national insurance from the gross loss would be too simplistic an approach, because the award of damages will itself be subject to tax in the hands of the employee. A further complication is that the damages will only be taxed insofar as they exceed the tax-free allowance of £30,000 which applies to compensation payments for loss of office. The principal relevant taxing provisions are contained in *Part 6* of the *Income tax (Earnings and Pensions) Act 2003*. Employers are required to report to the Inland Revenue details of any award of payment and/or benefits upon termination of an employment contract where the total amount of the award exceeds £30,000 (*Income Tax (Pay as You Earn) Regulations 2003 (SI 2003/2682), regs 91 to 93*).

The correct approach is therefore for the court to ascertain the net sum which the employee ought ultimately to receive, and to gross that amount up until it has arrived at a grossed-up sum which, when the damages are taxed, will reduce again to the correct net sum. Authority for this grossing-up procedure is to be found in *Stewart v Glentaggart* 1963 SLT 119 and *Shove v Downs Surgical plc* [1984] ICR 532. In order to ensure the correct application of tax rates, bands and allowances, it may be necessary to have details of the employee's income from all sources.

Similar principles should apply where one is calculating a settlement figure rather than an award of damages. It will be necessary to look at each element that makes up the overall settlement sum.

An employer who pays a grossed-up sum by way of settlement should first ensure either that the Inland Revenue is content for moneys to be paid gross and taxed in the employee's hands, or that the employee has agreed as part of the settlement to reimburse the employer for any demand for tax upon the sums paid which may subsequently be made.

56.33   Wrongful Dismissal

56.33   Relationship with compensation for unfair dismissal

An employee who has been both wrongfully and unfairly dismissed cannot be compensated twice for the same loss. However, there are a number of important respects in which the rules governing the compensatory award for unfair dismissal differ from those governing damages for wrongful dismissal. In particular: damages for wrongful dismissal are essentially limited to the notice period, whereas compensation for unfair dismissal may in principle extend indefinitely; in wrongful dismissal only strict contractual rights are taken into account, whereas the employment tribunal may allow for other benefits and heads of loss (eg likely future pay increases, discretionary bonuses, loss of statutory rights); and the compensatory award in unfair dismissal may not exceed a statutory maximum.

Therefore, if an employee who has already received damages for wrongful dismissal goes on to obtain a ruling from an employment tribunal that he has been unfairly dismissed, he may ask for compensation (up to the statutory maximum) representing his loss beyond the notice period and his non-contractual benefits within the notice period.

If an employee who has already been compensated for unfair dismissal brings an action for wrongful dismissal, the court must examine the way in which that compensation has been calculated, and deduct from the wrongful dismissal damages those elements already covered by the tribunal award. The same will apply where the unfair dismissal claim has been settled by payment of a sum to the former employee (*Aspden* — see **56.19** above). However, if the sum actually awarded by the tribunal has been capped at the statutory maximum, it will frequently not be possible to say whether the award actually received represents one sort of loss rather than another. In that situation, the court will therefore not make any deduction from the damages which it awards (*O'Laoire v Jackel International Ltd (No 2)* [1991] ICR 718).

A summary dismissal, albeit wrongful, is nonetheless effective to terminate the employment at once (subject to the question of acceptance of the breach, as to which see **56.7** above). It is not generally possible for an employee to complain of unfair dismissal unless he has been continuously employed for two years prior to the effective date of termination (see UNFAIR DISMISSAL – I (51)). Hence it is possible that the effect of a wrongful dismissal may be to deprive the employee of an unfair dismissal claim, if the absence of due notice or proper application of contractual disciplinary procedures makes the difference to whether there is the necessary period of service prior to termination. However, an employee cannot claim that lost right of complaint as a head of damages in the wrongful dismissal proceedings (*Harper v Virgin Net Ltd* [2004] EWCA Civ 271, [2005] ICR 921; applied in *Wise Group v Mitchell* [2005] ICR 896).

56.34   EFFECT OF A WRONGFUL DISMISSAL UPON OTHER CONTRACTUAL OBLIGATIONS

If the employee is wrongfully dismissed, the effect will normally be to release him from any further performance of his own contractual obligations, even those which are expressed to continue after the termination of the employment. In particular, this means that the employer will be unable to enforce any restrictive covenants contained in the contract of employment (*General Billposting Co Ltd v Atkinson* [1909] AC 118; *Rock Refrigeration Ltd v Jones* [1996] IRLR 675).

However, an arbitration clause will normally remain enforceable even after a wrongful dismissal.

56.35 POSSIBLE DEFENCES TO A WRONGFUL DISMISSAL CLAIM

Illegality

No action may be brought upon a contract which is treated as illegal upon grounds of public policy. In the employment context, this most frequently applies to situations where the employer and employee have colluded to evade the payment of income tax. For a fuller account, see CONTRACTS OF EMPLOYMENT (7) and UNFAIR DISMISSAL – I (51).

56.36 Invalidity of contract

The employer may seek to argue that the contract, or some of its terms, were never validly entered into. This might arise, for example, if the employer was a local authority, and contended that entry into the contract had for some reason been *ultra vires*. Alternatively, a limited company might contend that a director's contract of employment had been concluded in a way which was not in accordance with the company's articles of association, or that the contract had been concluded for an improper purpose (for example, if members of the board of directors voted to grant each other long fixed term contracts in order to protect their own positions in advance of an anticipated takeover). See *Re W and M Roith Ltd* [1967] 1 WLR 432; *Guinness plc v Saunders* [1990] 2 AC 663; and *Runciman v Walter Runciman plc* [1992] BCLC 1084.

56.37 Exclusion clauses

It is not common to find in a contract of employment provisions purporting to exclude or limit the employer's liability for wrongful dismissal (although share option schemes often provide that no sum in respect of lost opportunities under the scheme is to be awarded by way of compensation for dismissal). Although no such provision could effectively exclude compensation for statutory rights (see UNFAIR DISMISSAL – I (51)), there is no reason in principle why a contract should not seek to exclude or limit liability for wrongful dismissal or other possible contractual claims.

An employee faced with such an exclusion clause, however, might seek to argue that it was subject to the controls laid down by the *Unfair Contract Terms Act 1977* (*UCTA*). If *UCTA* applied, then the clause would be upheld only insofar as it satisfied the requirement of reasonableness at the time when the contract was made. Nevertheless, in *Commerzbank AG v Keen* [2007] ICR 623, the Court of Appeal held that *UCTA* did not apply to contracts for the remuneration of employees.

56.38 PROCEDURAL ASPECTS OF WRONGFUL DISMISSAL CLAIMS

Choice of court

Until recently, and subject to the possibility of arbitration, it has been necessary to bring an action for wrongful dismissal in the ordinary courts – that is, the High Court (in London or in a district registry) or the county court. Those courts remain the primary forum for such actions, certainly those of substantial value. However, as discussed below, employment tribunals also now have a contractual jurisdiction which extends to wrongful dismissal claims.

The choice of whether to proceed in the High Court or county court depends principally upon the value of the claim. In a wrongful dismissal action, there is no absolute bar to commencing proceedings in either court. However, the trial of the action will normally take place in the county court if the value of the action (ie the amount, exclusive of interest, which the claimant reasonably expects to recover) is less than £50,000, and will normally take place in the High Court if that value is £50,000 or more.

56.38   Wrongful Dismissal

Employees are also able to bring proceedings in the employment tribunal in respect of claims for (inter alia) damages for breach of a contract of employment arising or outstanding on the termination of employment, which would of course include claims for wrongful dismissal (*Employment Tribunals Act 1996, s 3; Employment Tribunals Extension of Jurisdiction (England and Wales) Order 1994 (SI 1994/1623)* – see *SI 1994/1624* in relation to Scotland). However, the tribunal is not empowered in such proceedings to order the payment of an amount exceeding £25,000. Nor does the tribunal have any jurisdiction to award interest (although the award once made will carry interest if not satisfied within 42 days). Employees should bear in mind that where wrongful dismissal (or any breach of contract) proceedings are issued in the employment tribunal, the employer is entitled to counterclaim for any breach of contract committed by the employee which arises or is outstanding on the termination of employment (*art 4* of the *1994 Order*).

Occasionally, a contract of employment may contain an arbitration clause capable of applying to a wrongful dismissal claim. In such a case, the employee is entitled to refer the claim to arbitration rather than commencing proceedings in the ordinary courts or the employment tribunal. If the employee instead chooses to begin proceedings in the High Court or county court, the employer may seek to have those proceedings stayed under *s 94* of the *Arbitration Act 1996* so that the matter can be referred to arbitration. The court is obliged to grant a stay unless satisfied that the arbitration agreement is null and void, inoperative, or incapable of being performed (*section 9(4)*).

It would appear that wrongful dismissal proceedings brought in the employment tribunal could also be stayed so as to give effect to an arbitration clause. Although any provision in an agreement purporting to preclude the presentation of a complaint to a tribunal is normally void, this does not apply where (as here) the tribunal's jurisdiction is founded upon an order made under *s 3* of the *Employment Tribunals Act 1996*.

56.39   Relationship with tribunal proceedings

Where a claim for wrongful dismissal is commenced in the High Court or county court, and at the same time a complaint of unfair dismissal is presented to an employment tribunal, an application may be made for one or other set of proceedings (usually the tribunal claim) to be stayed pending the outcome of the other litigation.

Where the claim of wrongful dismissal has been brought in the employment tribunal and judgment has been reached by the tribunal, it is not open to the employee to recover damages in excess of the tribunal's jurisdiction (£25,000) by proceedings in the county court or High Court. The common law doctrine of merger of causes of action will be held to apply (see *Fraser v HLMAD Ltd* [2006] EWCA Civ 738, [2006] IRLR 687). Therefore, where the employee's potential recovery is greater than £25,000, the appropriate forum in which to proceed with an action must be thought through with some care.

An employee may be able to withdraw an employment tribunal claim for wrongful dismissal, however, and proceed instead in the county court or High Court without being barred by the operation of the principle of cause of action estoppel, if it is made clear that the withdrawal from the employment tribunal is for this very purpose (see *Sajid v Sussex Muslim Society* [2001] EWCA Civ 1684, [2002] IRLR 113).

56.40   Limitation periods

A wrongful dismissal action in the High Court or county court is a claim for breach of contract, and as such is subject to a limitation period of six years from the accrual of the cause of action (*Limitation Act 1980, s 5*). Hence, proceedings must be commenced before the sixth anniversary of the dismissal.

In the employment tribunal, the complaint will have to be presented within the period of three months beginning with the effective date of termination of the contract of employment, or (where the tribunal is satisfied that it was not reasonably practicable for the complaint to be presented within that period) within such further period as the tribunal considers reasonable (*Employment Tribunals Extension of Jurisdiction (England and Wales) Order 1994 (SI 1994/1623)*, *art 7* – see *art 7* of *SI 1994/1624* in relation to Scotland).

56.41 Summary judgment, interim payments, payments into court, and hearings on liability and quantum

In the High Court and county court, although not the employment tribunal, the claimant employee who considers that the defendant employer has no real prospect of successfully defending the claim may apply for summary judgment on written evidence alone (*Civil Procedure Rules 1998, Part 24*). This is particularly important in wrongful dismissal claims, where the true issue between the parties is often not whether the employer was entitled to dismiss without due notice, but what loss the employee has suffered, and in particular the extent to which that loss could or should have been mitigated. In such a case the court may be persuaded to enter judgment for damages to be assessed, or at least to make the granting of leave to defend the action conditional upon the defendant making a payment into court (which will act as an incentive to settlement of the claim, and should ensure that the claimant is able to enforce any judgment ultimately obtained).

The application for summary judgment will often be combined with an application for an interim payment (*CPR 1998, rule 25.6*), which will also be appropriate in a case where the employer has admitted liability but contests the amount of damages.

If the defendant employer believes that the claimant is likely to succeed on the issue of whether he was wrongfully dismissed, but that he is claiming damages substantially in excess of those to which he is truly entitled, then it may be appropriate for that defendant to make a payment into court in satisfaction of the claimant's cause of action (*CPR 1998, Part 36*). If the claimant accepts the payment in within a specified period, the proceedings will come to an end, and the claimant will automatically be entitled to his costs up until the date of payment in. If the claimant does not do so, and ultimately recovers less at trial than the sum paid in, then he will have to pay the defendant's costs since payment in.

Where both liability and quantum are in dispute, the parties will wish to consider (especially where the calculation of loss raises complex points of detail) whether liability should be tried as a preliminary issue, with a hearing on quantum to follow only if the claimant establishes that he has been wrongfully dismissed and the parties are still unable to compromise their differences at that point.

Save for the possibility of separate hearings on liability and quantum, none of these procedural opportunities will be available if the claim is brought in the employment tribunal.

56.42 Compromise of claims

The various statutory restrictions, which prescribe that an employee may compromise claims based upon his statutory rights only in certain specified ways, do not apply to wrongful dismissal claims (*Sutherland v Network Appliance Ltd* [2001] IRLR 12). Any compromise contained in a binding contract will do, and a binding contract requires only offer and acceptance, an intention to create legal relations and consideration. There is good consideration for a contract of compromise even if the claimant's claim is in fact ill-founded, because the defendant is spared the expense and vexation of resisting it. However, it may in certain circumstances be possible to set aside a compromise on the grounds of mistake or misrepresentation (see eg *Bell v Lever Bros Ltd* [1932] AC 161).

Once High Court or county court proceedings have actually been commenced, it is not unusual for terms of settlement to be incorporated into an order of the court. In particular, the order may give the parties liberty to apply to the court for the purpose of enforcing those terms.

56.43 SPECIAL CATEGORIES OF EMPLOYMENT

Crown servants

This category covers, principally, civil servants and (probably) NHS employees. Although Crown servants have the right to complain of unfair dismissal (*ERA 1996, s 191*), it does not appear that it is possible for them to bring an action for wrongful dismissal. This is because it is a rule of law that Crown service is determinable by the Crown at will (*Riordan v War Office* [1959] 1 WLR 1046). Consistently with this principle, Crown servants do not enjoy the right to a statutory minimum period of notice.

56.44 Apprentices

The employer's right of summary dismissal is more restricted in a contract of apprenticeship than in a normal contract of employment. It appears that nothing short of conduct which makes it impossible for the employer to carry out the essential purpose of the contract (to teach the apprentice his trade) will justify termination without notice (see *Learoyd v Brook* [1891] 1 QB 431; *Newell v Gillingham Corpn* [1941] 1 All ER 552).

By the same token, an employer will generally be precluded from terminating a contract of apprenticeship solely on the ground of redundancy where the business is not closed down, or there is no change in the character of the business (*Wallace v CA Roofing Services Ltd* [1996] IRLR 435).

For special considerations applying to the assessment of damages for wrongful dismissal of an apprentice, see **56.29** above. For Modern Apprenticeships, see generally **13 EDUCATION AND TRAINING**.

Index

[all references are to paragraph number]

Absence from work,
annual leave entitlement, 27.3A
sabbatical, 27.3B
unpaid leave, 27.3B
Abuse of process
tribunal procedure, and, 18.26
ACAS
advisory function, 2.9
arbitration function
generally, 18.37
introduction, 2.7
arbitration scheme, 2.8
Codes of Practice
disclosure of information, 2.11
introduction, 2.11
legal effect, 4.3
power to issue, 4.2
revision, 4.17
revocation, 4.17
compromise agreements, and, 17.27
conciliation function
CAC complaints, in, 2.6
compulsory early, 2.5
employment tribunal complaints, in, 2.4
generally, 18.29–18.32
introduction, 2.3
constitution, 2.2
contact details, 2.12
disclosing information, prohibition, 2.5
flexible working requests, 2.5
functions
advice, 2.9
arbitration, 2.7
conciliation, 2.3–2.6
inquiry, 2.10
inquiry function, 2.10
introduction, 2.1
prescribed information, 2.5
unfair dismissal claims, 2.5
Accelerated receipt
wrongful dismissal, and, 56.31
Acceptance of employer's breach
wrongful dismissal, and, 56.7
Access to medical reports
disclosure of information, and, 9.14
Access to records
criminal convictions, and, 16.7
Access to training
positive discrimination, and, 11.10

Accident reporting
health and safety, and, 26.1
Accommodation
wrongful dismissal, and, 56.28
Accompanied at disciplinary hearings, right to be
generally, 49.21
unfair dismissal, and, 52.3
Account of profits
contracts of employment, and, 7.47d
restraint of trade covenants, and, 39.20
Accounts and records
trade unions, and, 48.12
Acquisitions,
restraint of trade, and, 39.1
Addition of new claims
tribunal procedure, and, 18.10
Additional award
unfair dismissal, and, 53.14
Additional maternity leave
generally, 31.28–31.33
redundancy, and, 31.34
Additional paternity leave
benefits during, 31.58
entitlement, 31.56
generally, 31.57
Adjournment application
tribunal procedure, and, 18.54
Administrative receivers, liability of
insolvency of employer, and, 29.11
Adopted children
adoption leave, and, 31.59
paternity leave, and, 31.59
Adoption leave
Children and Families Bill, 31.4A
fostering to adopt system, 31.4A
generally, 31.59
introductory meetings, 31.4A
payments from National Insurance Fund, and, 29.8
protection against detriment, 31.60
statutory pay, 31.61
time off work, and, 47.17
unfair dismissal, and, 52.3
Advertisements
employment, in, 10.43
injunctions, 12.30
introduction, 20.1

Index

Advisory, Conciliation and Arbitration Service (ACAS)
advisory function, 2.9
arbitration function
  generally, 18.37
  introduction, 2.7
Codes of Practice
  disclosure of information, 2.11
  introduction, 2.11
  legal effect, 4.3
  power to issue, 4.2
  revision, 4.17
  revocation, 4.17
compromise agreements, and, 17.27
conciliation function
  CAC complaints, in, 2.6
  compulsory early, 2.5
  employment tribunal complaints, in, 2.4
  generally, 18.29–18.32
  introduction, 2.3
constitution, 2.2
contact details, 2.12
disclosing, prohibition, 2.5
flexible working requests, 2.5
functions
  advice, 2.9
  arbitration, 2.7
  conciliation, 2.3–2.6
  inquiry, 2.10
inquiry function, 2.10
introduction, 2.1
prescribed information, 2.5
unfair dismissal claims, 2.5
Advocates
discrimination, and, 11.27
Age
see also AGE DISCRIMINATION
advertising, and, 20.1
interview and selection, 20.2–20.4
retirement
  age, 50.14
  change, 40.7
  discrimination regulations, 40.3–40.4
  employment protection, and, 40.2
  generally, 40.1
  justifying dismissals, 40.5
Age discrimination
advertisements
  employment, in, 10.43
  injunctions, 12.30
  introduction, 20.1
advocates, 11.27
agent's acts, 10.56
aiding unlawful acts, 10.58

Age discrimination – *cont.*
applications to Employment Tribunal
  burden of proof, 12.3
  compensation, 12.13–12.20
  conciliation, 12.10
  disclosure, 12.9
  extension of time, 12.7
  formulation of complaint, 12.8
  generally, 12.2
  publicity, 12.11
  questionnaire, 12.9
  recommendations, 12.21
  remedies, 12.12–12.22
  time limits, 12.4–12.7
assistance for persons discriminated
    against, 12.31
barristers, 11.27
'because of the protected characteristic', 10.25
benefits provided to public, 11.20
burden of proof, 12.3
careers guidance, 11.32
Codes of Practice, and
  legal effect, 4.11
  power to issue, 4.11
  revision, 4.17
  revocation, 4.17
combined discrimination, 10.29
comparators, 10.15
compensation
  aggravated damages, 12.18
  discrimination, 12.19
  exemplary damages, 12.18
  general principles, 12.13
  indirect discrimination, 12.14
  injury to feelings, 12.16
  interest, 12.20
  introduction, 12.12
  pecuniary loss, 12.15
  personal injury, 12.17
  unfair dismissal, 12.19
compliance with law, 11.21
conciliation, 12.10
contract workers, 11.24
Crown, 11.36
detriment, 10.50
direct discrimination
  'because of the protected
      characteristic', 10.25
  generally, 10.13
  less favourable treatment, 10.14–10.16
disclosure, 12.9
dismissal, 10.49
duty to make reasonable adjustments, 10.37
education needs, 11.10

Index

Age discrimination – *cont.*

employed at establishment in GB, 10.42

employment agencies, 11.32

employment, in

advertisements, 10.43

dismissal, 10.49

'employment', 10.41

engagement, 10.44–10.46

harassment, 10.51

introduction, 10.40

opportunities, 10.47–10.48

post-employment behaviour, 10.52

subjection to other detriment, 10.50–10.51

territorial jurisdiction, 10.42

employment outside Great Britain, 11.18

employment-related services, 11.33

employment service-providers, 11.34

enforcement

applications to Employment
    Tribunal, 12.2–12.22

assistance for persons discriminated
    against, 12.31

EHRC, by, 12.23–12.24

injunctions, 12.29–12.30

introduction, 12.1

settlement, 12.33

void contract terms, 12.32

enforcement by the EHRC

formal inquiries and
    investigations, 12.25–12.27

generally, 12.23–12.24

introduction, 11.38

unlawful act notices, 12.28

engagement, 10.44

equal opportunities, and

enforcement, 11.38

general exceptions, 11.17–11.23

genuine occupational requirement or
    qualification, 11.2–11.8

introduction, 11.1

justification, 11.9

non-employees/employers
    covered, 11.24–11.36

positive discrimination, 11.10

public authorities, and, 11.37

specific exceptions, 11.11–11.16

Equality Act 2010, 10.331

exceptions

genuine occupational requirement, 11.8

length of service, 11.15

life assurance cover to retired workers, 11.15

national minimum wage, 11.15

pension schemes, 11.15, 11.35

redundancy benefits, 11.15

retirement, 11.15

Age discrimination – *cont.*

extension of time, 12.7

foreign employees, and, 23.9

formulation of complaint, 12.8

general exceptions

benefits provided to public, 11.20

compliance with law, 11.21

employment outside Great Britain, 11.18

illegal contracts, 11.19

introduction, 11.17

national security, 11.22

State immunity, 11.23

genuine occupational requirement or
    qualification, 11.8

harassment

generally, 10.39

partnerships, 11.28

trade organisations, 11.29

illegal contracts, 11.19

indirect discrimination

application of the test, 10.34

discriminatory measure, 10.34

disparity of effect, 10.34

generally, 10.34

personal disadvantage, 10.34

sex discrimination, and, 10.35

sexual orientation discrimination, and, 10.36

test, 10.34

injunctions

advertisements, 12.30

instructions to discriminate, 12.30

persistent discrimination, 12.29

pressure to discriminate, 12.30

instructions to commit unlawful acts

enforcement by EHRC, 11.38

generally, 10.53

injunctions, 12.30

interview and selection, 20.2–20.4

introduction, 10.331

justification, 11.9

legal sources, 10.10

legitimate aim, 11.9

length of service, 11.15

less favourable treatment,

comparators, 10.15

introduction, 10.14

positive discrimination, 10.16

life assurance cover to retired workers, 11.15

meaning

combined discrimination, 10.29

direct discrimination, 10.13–10.27

harassment, 10.39

indirect discrimination, 10.34–10.36

introduction, 10.12

Index

Age discrimination – *cont.*
meaning – *cont.*
   perceived discrimination, 10.28
   victimisation, 10.38
national minimum wage, 11.15
national security, 11.22
non-employees/employers covered, 11.24–11.36
occupational pension schemes, 11.35
office holders, 11.25
opportunities in employment
   generally, 10.47
   sex discrimination, 10.48
overview, 10.331
partnerships, 11.28
pension schemes, 11.15, 11.35
perceived discrimination, 10.28
personal disadvantage, 10.34
police, 11.26
positive discrimination,
   access to training, 11.10
   childbirth, 11.10
   EU law, under, 11.10
   generally, 11.10
   introduction, 10.16
   membership of trade organisation, 11.10
   pregnancy, 11.10
   Sikhs on construction sites, 11.13
post-employment behaviour,, 10.52
pressure to commit unlawful acts
   enforcement by EHRC, 11.38
   generally, 10.53
   injunctions, 12.30
prohibited grounds
   combined discrimination, 10.29
   direct discrimination, 10.13–10.27
   harassment, 10.39
   indirect discrimination, 10.34–10.36
   introduction, 10.12
   perceived discrimination, 10.28
   victimisation, 10.38
protected characteristics, 10.10
public authorities, and, 11.37
publicity, 12.11
pupillage, 11.27
qualifications bodies, 11.30
questionnaire, 12.9
reasonable adjustments, 10.37
recommendations, 12.21
redundancy benefits, 11.15
redundancy payments, and, 36.10
remedies
   compensation, 12.13–12.20
   introduction, 12.12
   pension rights, 12.22

Age discrimination – *cont.*
remedies – *cont.*
   recommendations, 12.21
retirement, 11.15
retirement dismissals
   generally, 40.2
   justifying, 40.5
   pension benefits, 40.14
   summary of regulations 40.6
settlement of claim, 12.33
specific exceptions, 11.16
State immunity, 11.23
state provision of facilities and services, 11.33
territorial jurisdiction, 10.42
third party acts, 10.57
time limits for claims, and
   generally, 12.4–12.7
   introduction, 17.29
trade organisations, 11.29
training needs, 11.10
trustees of occupational pension schemes, 11.35
unfavourable treatment, 10.14
unlawful act notices, 12.28
unlawful acts
   agent's acts, 10.56
   aiding unlawful acts, 10.58
   employee's acts, 10.54–10.55
   enforcement by EHRC, 11.38
   instructions to commit unlawful acts, 10.53
   pressure to commit unlawful acts, 10.53
   third party acts, 10.57
   vicarious liability, 10.54–10.55
unlawful instructions
   enforcement only by Commissions, 11.38
   generally, 10.53
   injunctions, 12.30
unlawful pressure
   enforcement only by Commissions, 11.38
   generally, 10.53
   injunctions, 12.30
vicarious liability
   defence, 10.55
   generally, 10.54
vocational training providers, 11.31
welfare needs, 11.10
Agencies
see also **AGENCY WORKERS**
Conduct Regulations, 45.5
discrimination, and, 11.32
EC Directive, 45.2d
engagement of employees, and, 20.6
generally, 45.2–45.2c
harassment, and, 11.32
reforms, 45.4

Agencies – *cont.*
  Regulations, 45.2d
  statutory control, 45.3
Agency workers
  see also **AGENCIES**
  ante-natal care, 31.10
  employment agencies, and
    Conduct Regulations, 45.5
    EC Directive, 45.2d
    generally, 45.2–45.2c
    reforms, 45.4
    Regulations, 45.2d
    statutory control, 45.3
  EU law, and, 22.13
  less favourable treatment, 45.9
  maternity rights
    ante-natal care, 31.10
    suspension on maternity grounds, 31.14
  national minimum wage
    generally, 45.6
    introduction, 32.10
  Regulations, 45.2d
  suspension on maternity grounds, 31.14
  unfair dismissal
    generally, 52.3
    introduction, 45.7
  working time, and, 55.37
Agents
  discrimination by, 10.56
Aggravated damages
  discrimination compensation, and, 12.18
Agricultural tied houses
  service lettings, and, 41.9
Agricultural workers
  equal pay, and, 21.20
  holidays, and, 27.7
Aiding unlawful acts
  generally, 10.58
Air crew
  holidays, and, 27.8
  working time, and, 55.33
Alcohol misuse
  health and safety, and, 26.2
Alterations
  contracts of employment, and
    agreement, by, 7.32
    breach of contract, and, 7.34
    express variation clause, by, 7.33
    generally, 7.31
    introduction, 7.9
    termination of contract, and, 7.34
  written particulars, and, 7.9
Alternative employment, refusal of
  redundancy payments, and, 36.12

Amalgamations
  trade unions, and, 48.39
Amendment of claims
  generally, 18.10
  introduction, 17.15
Annual Christmas party
  tax-free benefits, and, 44.23
Annual leave
  agricultural workers, 27.7
  additional annual leave, 27.3A
  annual leave
    illness, 27.3A
    part-time workers, 30.10
    payment, 27.4
    working time, 55.19
  civil aviation workers, 27.8
  contractual entitlement, 27.9
  entitlement
    Community social law principle, 27.3A
    illness, 27.3A
    opportunity to take, 27.3A
    sabbatical, 27.3B
    unpaid leave, 27.3B
    generally, 27.2
  illness, and
    annual leave, 27.3A
    generally, 27.3
  insolvency of employer, and
    generally, 29.2
    payments from National Insurance
      Fund, 29.5
  introduction, 27.1
  notice requirements, 27.5
  part-time workers, and, 30.10
  payment
    calculating a week's pay, 27.4
    generally, 27.4
    termination of employment, on, 27.4A
  period of leave, 27.3
  remedies, 27.6
  sick leave, and, 27.3
  statutory entitlement, 27.2
  termination of employment, 27.4A
  timing, 27.5
  'workers', 27.2
  Working Time Regulations, and, 27.2, 55.19
  wrongful dismissal, and, 56.28
Anonymity orders
  EAT procedures, and, 19.26
Ante-natal care, time off for
  agency workers, 31.10
  generally, 31.6
  insolvency of employer, and, 29.2
  qualifying requirements, 31.7

Index

Ante-natal care, time off for – *cont.*
remedies for refusal, 31.9
right to remuneration, 31.8
Anticipatory breach of contract
wrongful dismissal, and, 56.22
Appeals
Central Arbitration Committee,
   and, 48.10–48.11
Court of Appeal, to, 19.47
EAT, to
   amendments to notices of appeal, 19.27
   anonymity orders, 19.26
   bias allegation, 19.23–19.25
   conduct of, 19.28–19.40
   content, 19.13
   costs, 19.42–19.45
   disposal of appeal, 19.38–19.40
   EAT, 19.1–19.8
   error of law, 19.35–19.37
   EU law issues, 19.48
   fees, 19.9
   fresh evidence, 19.34
   generally, 19.4
   grounds, 19.16
   inadequacy of reasons, 19.36
   institution, 19.13
   notes of evidence, 19.21
   other powers, 19.41
   perverse decision, 19.35–19.37
   preliminary hearing, 19.19–19.20
   preliminary sifting, 19.17–19.18
   procedural failures, 19.37
   raising points not taken at tribunal
      hearing, 19.33
   reference back for clarification of
      reasons, 19.22
   response to notice of appeal, 19.15
   restricted reporting orders, 19.26
   review of order, 19.46
   supporting documentation, 19.12–19.13
   time limits, 19.14
   wasted costs orders, 19.45
improvement notices, and
   cost of remedy required, 25.36
   effect, 25.35
   introduction, 25.34
prohibition notices, and
   cost of remedy required, 25.36
   effect, 25.35
   introduction, 25.34
Applicable law
foreign employees, and
   contract and tort, 23.7
   generally, 23.6

Applications to Employment Tribunal
abuse of process, 18.26
ACAS, and
   arbitration schemes, 18.37
   conciliation, 18.29–18.32
   introduction, 2.4
adding new claims, 18.10
adjournment application, 18.54
administration, 17.6
amendment of claims
   generally, 18.10
   introduction, 17.15
bias, 18.50
breach of contracts of employment, and, 7.44
'Calderbank' offers, 18.36
case management
   case management discussions, 18.2–18.5
   interim hearings, 18.6
   powers in practice, 18.7–18.14
   overriding objective, and, 18.1
   pre-hearing reviews, 18.6
   tribunal's powers, 18.2
case management discussions
   application for orders, 18.3
   background, 17.5
   introduction, 18.2
   non-compliance with orders, 18.4
   orders not available, 18.5
claims
   default judgments, 17.38
   extension of time, 17.22–17.33
   post-presentation action, 17.34
   presentation, 17.21
   response by respondent, 17.35–17.37
   time limits, 17.18–17.20
commencing proceedings, 17.15–17.17
composition
   employment judge sitting alone, 17.9–17.10
   generally, 17.7–17.8
compromise agreements, 18.33–18.35
conciliation
   'Calderbank' offers, 18.36
   compromise agreements, 18.33–18.35
   discrimination complaints, 12.10
   generally, 18.29–18.31
   settlements, 18.32
conduct of hearing, 18.52
conflict of interest, 18.50
contracts of employment, and, 7.44
costs
   generally, 18.69–18.70
   orders, 18.71–18.72
   preparation time orders, 18.73
   wasted costs orders, 18.74

Applications to Employment Tribunal – *cont.*
costs warning, 18.15
default judgments, 17.38
deposit orders, 18.15
disclosure
    discrimination complaints, 12.9
    generally, 18.11–18.12
    privileged documents, 18.13
discrimination complaints
    compensation, 12.13–12.20
    conciliation, 12.10
    disclosure, 12.9
    extension of time, 12.7
    formulation of complaint, 12.8
    generally, 12.2
    publicity, 12.11
    questionnaire, 12.9
    recommendations, 12.21
    remedies, 12.12–12.22
    time limits, 12.4–12.7
discrimination questionnaires, 12.9
dismissal of claims, 18.28
dismissal of party, 18.23
employment judges
    appointment, 17.4
    generally, 17.7
    sitting alone, 17.9–17.10
    tenure, 17.4
estoppel, 18.26
extension of time
    contract claims, 17.32
    discrimination complaints, 12.4
    effective date of termination, 17.23–17.24
    equal pay, 17.28
    generally, 17.22
    introduction, 18.21
    'just and equitable, 17.30
    'not reasonably practicable' to present in
        time, 17.25–17.26
    other claims, 17.33
    redundancy payments, 17.27
    response by respondent, and, 17.36
    unlawful deductions from wages, 17.31
    unlawful discrimination, 17.29
fees, 19.9
further information
    generally, 18.8
    questionnaires, 18.9
hearing
    adjournment application, 18.54
    bias, 18.50
    conduct, 18.52
    conflict of interest, 18.50
    control of procedure, 18.56

Applications to Employment Tribunal – *cont.*
hearing – *cont.*
    generally, 18.49
    listing, 18.39–18.48
    non-attendance of parties, 18.54
    order of evidence, 18.53
    other procedural points, 18.58–18.61
    preparation, 18.38
    private hearing, 18.51
    representation, 18.55
    witnesses, 18.57
historical background, 17.1–17.2
interest, 18.67
interim hearings, 18.6
introduction, 17.1–17.2
itemised pay statements, and
    generally, 32.19
    order, 32.20
joinder of parties, 18.23
judgments
    adequacy of reasons, 18.63
    corrections and changes, 18.64
    generally, 18.62
    register, 18.65
jurisdiction
    breach of contracts of employment, 7.44
    EU law, over, 17.12
    generally, 17.11
    Human Rights Act, under, 17.13
listing arrangements, 18.39–18.48
miscellaneous powers, 18.20
multiple claims, 18.24
non-attendance of parties, 18.54
order of evidence, 18.53
overriding objective
    background, 17.2
    case management, 18.1
    generally, 17.14
part-time workers, and,
    introduction, 30.26
    remedies, 30.28
    time limits, 30.27
post-presentation action, 17.34
pre-hearing reviews
    background, 17.5
    generally, 18.6
preparation for hearing
    general, 18.38
    listing arrangements, 18.39–18.48
preparation time orders, 18.73
presentation of claim, 17.21
private hearing, 18.51
privileged documents, 18.13
questionnaires, 18.9

Index

Applications to Employment Tribunal – *cont.*
reasons for decision
  adequacy, 18.63
  generally, 18.62
recoupment of benefits, 18.68
references, and, 38.8
register of judgments, 18.65
remedies
  costs, 18.69–18.74
  generally, 18.66
  interest, 18.67
  recoupment of benefits, 18.68
representation, 18.55
response by respondent
  extensions of time, 17.36
  failure to respond in time, 17.36–17.37
  generally, 17.35
restricted reporting orders, 18.18–18.19
review of judgment, 18.75–18.76
Rules of Procedure, 17.4–17.5
settlement
  conciliation, 18.32
  generally, 18.29–18.31
specialist jurisdictions, 18.78
statutory provision, 17.3
stay of proceedings, 18.22
striking out, 18.16–18.17
time limits for claims
  contract claims, 17.32
  discrimination complaints, 12.4–12.7
  equal pay, 17.28
  generally, 17.18
  'just and equitable', 17.30
  'not reasonably practicable' to present in
    time, 17.25–17.26
  other claims, 17.33
  post-EA 2002, 17.19–17.20
  redundancy payments, 17.27
  unlawful deductions from wages, 17.31
  unlawful discrimination, 17.29
transfer of proceedings, 18.25
vexatious litigants, 18.77
wasted costs orders, 18.74
withdrawal of claims, 18.28
witness orders, 18.14
witnesses, 18.57
Appointment of directors
introduction, 8.2
relationship between articles and contracts, 8.3
scope of employment, 8.5
status, 8.4
terms, 8.4
written particulars, 8.6

Apprenticeships
apprenticeship agreement, 13.11
'apprenticeship offer', 13.10
certificate, 13.11
contract of service, 13.2
legislation, 13.9
Sector Skills Councils, 13.7
standard completion conditions, 13.11
structural changes, 13.10
study and training
  complaint to tribunal, 13.17
  detriment, and, 13.19
  employee's duties, 13.16
  employer's duties, 13.15
  generally, 13.12
  remedies, 13.18
  right to request, 13.13
  supplementary provisions, 13.14
  unfair dismissal, and, 13.19
wrongful dismissal, 56.44
Appropriate bargaining unit
collective bargaining, and, 48.30
Appropriate representatives
election, 37.5
generally, 37.4
Arbitration
ACAS, and, 2.7
Central Arbitration Committee, and, 48.7
Armed forces personnel
EU law, 35.8
equal pay, and, 21.4
generally, 35.3
introduction, 35.1
judicial review as to rights, 35.6
national minimum wage, and, 32.10
national security, 35.7
part-time workers, and, 30.4
public interest immunity, 35.7
sex discrimination, and, 11.11
strikes, and, 43.20
working time, and, 55.3
Arrangements for training
generally, 47.6
remedies, 47.7
Arrears of pay
payments from National Insurance Fund,
  and, 29.5
Articles of association
directors, and, 8.3
Assertion of statutory rights
unfair dismissal, and, 52.3
Assistance
discrimination, and, 12.31

Association, freedom of
  human rights, and, 28.4
Associated company, offer by
  redundancy payments, and, 36.6
Associative discrimination
  generally, 10.27
Assured tenancies
  generally, 41.5
  recovery of possession, 41.6
  rent control, 41.8
Assured shorthold tenancies
  generally, 41.5
  recovery of possession, 41.6
  rent control, 41.8
Attachment of earnings
  attachable earnings
    deductions, 33.3
    generally, 33.2
  child support maintenance, 33.11
  clerical costs, 33.9
  Council Tax, 33.10
  deduction from attachable earnings
    calculation, 33.4
    introduction, 33.3
    priority of orders, 33.5
    time limits, 33.6
  employer's obligations, 33.7
  introduction, 33.1
  itemised pay statements, 33.9
  other issues, 33.9
  penalties for non-compliance, 33.8
  priority of orders, 33.5
  protected earnings, 33.3
Attendance of witnesses
  tribunal procedure, and, 17.17
Automatic enrolment
  pensions, and, 40.11
Aviation sector
  holidays, and, 27.8
  working time, and, 55.33
Ballots before strike action
  Codes of Practice, and
    legal effect, 4.5
    power to issue, 4.4
  generally, 43.14
  members' right, 43.1
Bankers
  capping bonuses, 22.17
Barring-out orders
  confidential information, 39.13
Barristers
  discrimination, and, 11.27
Basic award
  amount, 53.7

Basic award – cont.
  exceptions, 53.8
  maximum award, 53.16
  reduction, 53.9
'Because of the protected characteristic'
  age, 10.25
  disability, 10.26
  gender reassignment, 10.21
  general principles, 10.17
  marital or civil partnership status, 10.19
  pregnancy or maternity leave, 10.24
  racial grounds, 10.20
  religion or belief, 10.22
  sex, 10.18
  sexual orientation, 10.23
Beginning of employment
  generally, 6.3
  postponement, 6.11
Belief
  and see RELIGIOUS AND BELIEF DIS-
    CRIMINATION
  manifesting, 10.22
  meaning, 10.22
Benefits in kind
  meaning of 'wages', and, 32.6
  taxation, and, 44.2
  unfair dismissal, and, 53.12
Benefits provided to the public
  discrimination, and, 11.20
Bias
  EAT procedure, and, 19.23–19.25
  tribunal procedure, and, 18.50
Bicycles, loans for
  tax-free benefits, and, 44.23
BIS see DEPARTMENT FOR BUSINESS, IN-
    NOVATION & SKILLS
'Blacklists'
  trade union members, and, 49.10
  unfair dismissal, and, 52.3
'Blue pencil' test
  restraint of trade covenants, and, 39.7
Bonuses
  wrongful dismissal, and, 56.28
Border and Immigration Agency,
  Codes of Practice,
    illegal working, 4.6
    race discrimination prohibition, 4.6
Breaks
  children, and, 3.6
Bullying
  health and safety, and, 26.28
'Calderbank' offer
  tribunal procedure, and, 18.36

Index

Calls for action
strike action, and, 43.15
Capability
generally, 52.6
ill–health, 52.8
introduction, 52.5
procedure, 52.6A
qualifications, 52.7
summary, 52.2
Capping bonuses
bankers, 22.17
Car fuel
taxation, and, 44.26
Care in performance of duties
implied contract terms, and, 7.18
Care for children
time off work, and, 47.17
Careers guidance
discrimination, and, 11.32
Cars
taxation, and, 44.25
wrongful dismissal, and, 56.28
Case management
addition of new claims, 18.10
amendment of claims, 18.10
case management discussions
application for orders, 18.3
background, 17.5
introduction, 18.2
non-compliance with orders, 18.4
orders not available, 18.5
overview, 17.5
disclosure
discrimination complaints, 12.9
generally, 18.11–18.12
privileged documents, 18.13
dismissal of party, 18.23
further information
generally, 18.8
questionnaires, 18.9
interim hearings, 18.6
powers in practice, 18.7
overriding objective, and, 18.1
pre-hearing reviews
generally, 18.6
overview, 17.5
questionnaires, 18.9
tribunal's powers, 18.2
witness orders, 18.14
Cash vouchers
taxable benefits, and, 44.21–44.22
Casual workers
part-time workers, and, 30.4

Central Arbitration Committee (CAC)
ACAS's role, 2.6
appeals against awards, 48.10–48.11
arbitration, 48.7
collective bargaining, and, 48.29
complaint of failure to disclose information, 48.8
constitution, 48.5
contracting out, and, 48.9
establishment, 48.4
functions, 48.6–48.9
Certification officer
trade unions, and, 48.3
Change of employer
continuous employment, and, 6.9
redundancy payments, and, 36.5
wrongful dismissal, and, 56.8
Charities
positive discrimination, 11.1, 11.10A
'Check-off'
deduction of union subscriptions, and, 49.20
Child care facilities
tax-free benefits, and, 44.23
Child support maintenance
attachment of earnings, and, 33.11
Childbirth
and see PREGNANCY
positive discrimination, and, 11.10
unfair dismissal, and, 52.3
Children and Families Bill
adopters, 31.4A
ante-natal, 31.4A
shared parental leave, 31.4A
surrogacy, 31.4A
Children, employment of
breaks, 3.6
contracts of employment, 3.11
definitions, 3.1
detriment, 3.10
health and safety
breaks, 3.6
introduction, 3.5
night work, 3.6
rest periods, 3.6
local authority powers, 3.3
night work, 3.6
rest periods, 3.6
restrictions
generally, 3.2
local authority powers, 3.3
other provisions, 3.4
time off for study or training
introduction, 3.8
remedy for refusal, 3.9
right not to suffer detriment, 3.10

Children, employment of – *cont.*
work experience, 3.7
working time, and, 55.3
Christmas party
tax-free benefits, and, 44.23
Church of England clergy
working time, and, 55.38
Civil aviation workers
holidays, and, 27.8
Civil liability
health and safety, and, 25.43
Civil partnership status
and see **DISCRIMINATION**
'because of the protected characteristic', 10.19
direct discrimination, 10.13
discrimination in employment
advertisements, 10.43
dismissal, 10.49
'employment', 10.41
engagement, 10.44
introduction, 10.40
opportunities, 10.47
post-employment behaviour, 10.52
subjection to other detriment, 10.51
territorial jurisdiction, 10.42
harassment, 10.39
indirect discrimination, 10.34
legal sources, 10.4
protected characteristics, 10.4
sexual orientation, and, 11.14
Civil servants
EU law, 35.8
generally, 35.2
introduction, 35.1
judicial review as to rights, 35.6
national security, 35.7
public interest immunity, 35.7
redundancy payments, and, 36.10
Clergy
working time, and, 55.38
Clerical costs
attachment of earnings, and, 33.9
Closed shop
dismissal, and
compensation, 49.7
generally, 49.5
industrial action, and, 49.9
introduction, 49.3
pre-entry, 49.4
Codes of Practice
ACAS, by
introduction, 2.11
legal effect, 4.3
power to issue, 4.2

Codes of Practice – *cont.*
ACAS, by – *cont.*
revision and revocation, 4.17
ballots
legal effect, 4.5
power to issue, 4.4
Border and Immigration Agency, by
illegal working, 4.6
race discrimination prohibition, 4.6
collective bargaining
generally, 9.4
legal effect, 4.3
power to issue, 4.2
Commission for Racial Equality, by
legal effect, 4.8
power to issue, 4.7
Department of Trade and Industry, by (now BIS)
legal effect, 4.5
power to issue, 4.4
revision and revocation, 4.17
disability discrimination
legal effect, 4.11
power to issue, 4.11
Disability Rights Commission, by
legal effect, 4.11
power to issue, 4.11
revision and revocation, 4.17
discipline and grievance procedures
introduction, 2.11
legal effect, 4.3
power to issue, 4.2
disclosure of information
trade unions, to, 2.11, 4.2
Equal Opportunities Commission, by
legal effect, 4.10
power to issue, 4.9
employment, 4.13
equal pay
generally, 4.13
introduction, 21.2
prior to Equality Act 2010, 4.9–4.10
Equality Act 2010, under
employment, 4.13
equal pay, 4.13
grievance procedures, 4.2
Health and Safety Commission, by
introduction, 25.28
legal effect, 4.15
power to issue, 4.14
Industrial Relations Code
generally, 4.2
legal effect, 4.3
Information Commissioner, by, 4.16

Index

Codes of Practice – *cont.*
introduction, 4.1
part time workers, and, 30.2
picketing, and
generally, 43.11
legal effect, 4.5
power to issue, 4.4
racial equality
legal effect, 4.8
power to issue, 4.7
revision, 4.17
revocation, 4.17
safety representatives
legal effect, 4.15
power to issue, 4.14
sex discrimination
legal effect, 4.10
power to issue, 4.9
time off for trade union duties and activities
legal effect, 4.3
power to issue, 4.2
working time, and, 55.26
Collateral benefits
wrongful dismissal, and, 56.30
Collective agreements
amendments, 5.11–5.12
contracts of employment, and, 5.5–5.10
definition, 5.2
discriminatory agreements, 5.15
equal pay, and, 21.23
introduction, 5.1
legal status, 5.3–5.4
'no strike' clauses, 5.13
status, 5.3
transfer of undertakings, and, 50.20
workforce agreements, 5.14
working time, and, 55.4
Collective bargaining
Code of Practice
disclosure of information, 9.4
legal effect, 4.3
power to issue, 4.2
derecognition for, 48.36
disclosure of information
Code of Practice, 9.4
exceptions to duty, 9.3
failure to comply with request, 9.5
general duty, 9.3
introduction, 9.2
recognition for
appropriate bargaining unit, 48.30
ballot, 48.31–48.32
changes in bargaining unit, 48.35
'collective bargaining', 48.27

Collective bargaining – *cont.*
recognition for – *cont.*
introduction, 48.25
method of bargaining, 48.33
reference to CAC, 48.29
request for recognition, 48.28
voluntary, 48.34
scope of procedure, 48.26
Collective redundancies
consultation, and, 15.61
Employment Law Review, and, 24.7
Colour
And see DISCRIMINATION
advertisements, 10.43
applicable test, 10.34
disparity of effect, 10.34
harassment, 10.39
indirect discrimination, 10.34
meaning of 'because of race', 10.20
nationality, 10.34
pressure to commit unlawful acts, 10.53
Combined discrimination
generally, 10.29
Commencement of proceedings
tribunal procedure, and, 17.15–17.17
Commission
wrongful dismissal, and, 56.28
Commission for Equality and Human Rights (EHRC)
Code of Practice, 4.11
formal inquiries and investigations
Commissioner's report, 12.27
generally, 12.25
information, 12.26
generally, 12.23–12.24
introduction, 12.1
unlawful act notices, 12.28
Commission for Racial Equality (CRE)
And see COMMISSION FOR EQUALITY AND HUMAN RIGHTS
Code of Practice
legal effect, 4.8
power to issue, 4.7
generally, 12.23
Communal accommodation
discrimination, and, 11.11
Company cars
taxation, and, 44.25
unfair dismissal, and, 53.12
Company share option schemes
generally, 44.30
Comparators
discrimination, and, 10.15
equal pay, and, 21.9

Comparators – *cont.*
part-time workers, and,
actual comparator, 30.13
circumstances where comparator not
required, 30.19
'comparable full time worker', 30.15–30.18
'full time worker', 30.14
introduction, 30.12
'part time worker', 30.14
'same or broadly similar work', 30.17
'same type of contract', 30.16
scope of comparison, 30.18
Compensation
aggravated damages, 12.18
discrimination, 12.19
equal pay, 21.19B
exemplary damages, 12.18
general principles, 12.13
indirect discrimination, 12.14
injury to feelings, 12.16
interests, 12.20
introduction, 12.12
pecuniary loss, 12.15
personal injury, 12.17
unfair dismissal, 12.19
Compensation for unfair dismissal
additional award, 53.14
basic award
amount, 53.7
exceptions, 53.8
maximum award, 53.16
reduction, 53.9
compensatory award
amount, 53.11
heads of loss, 53.12
increase, 53.13
introduction, 53.10
loss of benefits, 53.12
loss of earnings, 53.12
loss of statutory rights, 53.12
maximum award, 53.16
pension rights, 53.12
reduction, 53.13, 53.15
union-related cases, 53.15
introduction, 53.6
maximum amounts, 53.16
recoupment of statutory benefits, 53.5
union-related cases, 53.15
Compensatory award
amount, 53.11
heads of loss, 53.12
increase, 53.13
introduction, 53.10
loss of benefits, 53.12

Compensatory award – *cont.*
loss of earnings, 53.12
loss of statutory rights, 53.12
maximum award, 53.16
pension rights, 53.12
reduction
generally, 53.13
union-related cases, 53.15
union-related cases, 53.15
Competent fellow workers
health and safety, and, 25.7
Compliance with the law
discrimination, and, 11.21
Composition of tribunals
Chairmen sitting alone, 17.9–17.10
generally, 17.7–17.8
Compromise agreements
Employment Law Review, and, 24.5
tribunal procedure, and, 18.33–18.35
Compromise of claims
wrongful dismissal, and, 56.42
Compulsory maternity leave
generally, 31.27
Computation of periods of employment
beginning of period
generally, 6.3
postponement, 6.11
end of period, 6.3
generally, 6.2
Conciliation
CAC complaints, in, 2.6
'Calderbank' offers, 18.36
compromise agreements, 18.33–18.3
discrimination complaints, and, 12.10
Employment Law Review, and, 24.5
employment tribunal complaints, in, 2.4
generally, 18.29–18.31
introduction, 2.3
settlements, 18.32
Conditional employment
references, and, 38.9
Conduct dismissals
generally, 52.9
procedure, 52.10
summary, 52.2
Confidential information
'barring-out' orders, 39.13
cross border mergers, and, 15.59
disclosure of information, and, 9.15
European co-operative societies (SCEs),
and, 15.47
European Works Councils, and, 15.28
ICE Regulations 2004, and, 15.19
implied contract terms, and, 7.15

Index

Confidential information – *cont.*
  information and consultation rights, and, 15.19
  restraint of trade covenants, and
    generally, 39.13
    remedies, 39.19
Confinement
  statutory maternity pay, and, 31.39
Conflict of interest
  tribunal procedure, and, 18.50
Conflict of laws
  restraint of trade covenants, and, 39.12
Consideration
  restraint of trade covenants, and, 39.10
Conspiracy
  strike action, and, 43.1
Construction site management
  health and safety, and, 26.4
Constructive dismissal
  dismissal by employer, and, 46.5
  summary termination by employee, and, 46.18
  unfair dismissal, and, 51.7
  wrongful dismissal, and, 56.6
Consultation
  collective redundancies, 15.61
  cross border mergers
    application of requirements, 15.51–15.52
    complaints, 15.58
    confidential information, 15.59
    definition, 15.50
    disputes, 15.58
    duty of merging company to provide
      information, 15.54
    employment protection, 15.60
    introduction, 15.49
    meaning, 15.50
    negotiated agreements, 15.56
    pre-merger process, 15.53
    special negotiating body, 15.55
    standard rules, 15.57
  directors' obligations
    directors' reports, 15.3
    regard for interests of employees, 15.2
  directors' reports, 15.3
  disclosure of information, and, 9.10
  employee participation, and,
    generally, 15.28
    training, on, 15.63
  EU law, 15.1
  European companies (SEs)
    alternative arrangements, 15.36
    complaints, 15.37
    disputes, 15.37
    employer's duty to provide information, 15.32
    employment protection, 15.38

Consultation – *cont.*
  European companies (SEs) – *cont.*
    implementation in UK, 15.31
    introduction, 15.30
    negotiated agreements, 15.34
    special negotiating body, 15.33
    standard rules, 15.34
  European co-operative societies (SCEs),
    alternative arrangements, 15.45
    complaints, 15.46
    confidential information, 15.47
    disputes, 15.46
    duty to provide information, 15.41
    employment protection, 15.48
    implementation in UK, 15.40
    introduction, 15.39
    negotiated agreements, 15.43
    special negotiating body, 15.42
    standard rules, 15.44
  European Works Councils
    amending Regulations, 15.29A
    confidential information, 15.28
    employment protection, 15.29
    establishment, 15.27
    introduction, 15.22
    number of employees, 15.24
    requests, 15.25
    special negotiating body, 15.26
  health and safety issues, 15.61
  ICE Regulations 2004,
    application, 15.6
    background, 15.4
    complaints, 15.20
    confidential information, 15.19
    co-operation, 15.14
    election or appointment of
      representatives, 15.13
    employee data requests, 15.7
    employment protection, 15.21
    initiation of obligations, 15.8–15.11
    introduction, 15.4–15.5
    negotiated agreements, 15.12
    overview, 9.10
    pre-existing agreements, 15.17–15.18
    standard information and consultation
      provisions, 15.15–15.16
    'undertakings', 15.6
  interests of employees, 15.2
  introduction, 15.1
  Partnership at Work Fund, 15.64
  redundancy, and,
    appropriate representatives, 37.4–37.5
    introduction, 37.2
    meaning of 'redundancy', 37.3

Consultation – *cont.*
redundancy, and, – *cont.*
protective award, 37.6
time off for representatives, and,
generally, 47.12
remedies, 47.13
training, 15.63
transfer of undertakings, and, 50.22
Continuous employment
beginning of employment,
generally, 6.3
postponement, 6.11
change of employer, 6.9
computation of periods of employment,
beginning and end of period, 6.3
generally, 6.2
end, 6.3
events affecting,
change of employer, 6.9
introduction, 6.4
preliminary points, 6.5
weeks which count, 6.6–6.8
weeks which do not count, 6.10–6.11
events breaking continuity, 6.12
introduction, 6.1
part timers, 6.8
postponement of start of employment, 6.11
presumption, 6.5
qualifying periods, 6.13
redundancy payments, and
changes in ownership, 36.5
generally, 36.4
start of employment
generally, 6.3
postponement, 6.11
statutory concept, 6.5
unfair dismissal, and
calculation, 51.12
effective date of termination, 51.13
introduction, 51.11
'week', 6.5
weeks which count
introduction, 6.6
'no employment' periods, 6.7
part timers, 6.8
weeks which do not count
introduction, 6.10
postponement of start of employment, 6.11
Contract claims
time limits for claims, and, 17.32
Contracts for services
generally, 14.3
Contracts of employment
acceptance of fundamental breach, 7.47a

Contracts of employment – *cont.*
account of profits, 7.47d
alterations
agreement, by, 7.32
breach of contract, and, 7.34
express variation clause, by, 7.33
generally, 7.31
introduction, 7.9
termination of contract, and, 7.34
breach
changes to terms, and, 7.34
employee's remedies, 7.35–7.46
employer's remedies, 7.47–7.47d
care in performance of duties, and, 7.18
changes to terms
agreement, by, 7.32
breach of contract, and, 7.34
express variation clause, by, 7.33
generally, 7.31
introduction, 7.9
termination of contract, and, 7.34
children, and, 3.11
collective agreements, and, 5.5–5.10
continuation of employment during ill-
health, 7.22b
contracts for services, distinction from
distinction from contracts for
services, 14.3–14.8
generally, 14.2
contracting out of certain provisions, 7.26
damages for breach
employee's remedies, 7.36–7.41
employer's remedies, 7.47b
damages for breach (employee's remedies)
express terms, 7.41
extent, 7.36
loss of chance to claim unfair dismissal, 7.37
loss of reputation, 7.38
pecuniary loss, 7.39
stigma, 7.40
deduction of wages, 7.47
discretionary benefits and payments, 7.22c
discriminatory terms, 7.27
economic well-being of employee, 7.22a
employee's duties
care in performance of duties, 7.18
fidelity, 7.16
obey employer's instructions, 7.17
employee's remedies for breach
damages, 7.36–7.41
disclosure, 7.45
injunctions, 7.42 7.43
introduction, 7.35
jurisdiction, 7.44

Index

Contracts of employment – *cont.*
employer handbooks and policies, 7.13
employer's duties
  continuation of employment during ill-health, 7.22b
  discretionary benefits and payments, 7.22c
  economic well-being of employee, 7.22a
  health and safety, 7.19
  place of work, 7.22e
  provision of work, 7.21
  redress for grievances, 7.20
  suspension on reasonable grounds, 7.22
  termination of contract, 7.22f
  trust and confidence, 7.22d
employer's remedies for breach
  acceptance of fundamental breach, 7.47a
  account of profits, 7.47d
  damages, 7.47b
  deduction of wages, 7.47
  injunctions, 7.47c
  specific performance, 7.47c
  withholding of wages, 7.47
express terms, 7.14
fidelity, and, 7.16
form, 7.3
formation, 7.2
generally, 7.1
health and safety, 7.19
holidays, and, 27.9
implied terms
  employee's duties, 7.16–7.18
  employer's duties, 7.19–7.22f
  generally, 7.14–7.15
incorporated terms, 7.22g
industrial action restrictions, 7.29
injunctions (employee's remedies)
  circumstances of grant, 7.42
  interlocutory, 7.43
injunctions (employer's remedies), 7.47c
introduction, 1.3
obeying employer's instructions, and, 7.17
parties, 7.4–7.5
provision of work, 7.21
redress for grievances, 7.20
remedies for breach
  employee, for, 7.35–7.46
  employer, for, 7.47
restraint of trade, 7.28
sources of law, and, 1.5
specific performance, 7.47c
Sunday trading, and, 7.48
suspension on reasonable grounds, 7.22
terms
  changes, 7.9, 7.31–7.34

Contracts of employment – *cont.*
terms – *cont.*
  contrary to public policy, 7.24
  employee's duties, 7.16–7.18
  employer handbooks, 7.13
  express terms, 7.14
  freedom to agree, 7.12
  implied terms, 7.14–7.18
  incorporated terms, 7.22g
  unenforceable terms, 7.23–7.30
  unlawful terms, 7.24
  variation by statute, 7.25
trust and confidence, 7.22d
unenforceable terms
  contracting out of certain provisions, 7.26
  contrary to public policy, 7.24
  discriminatory terms, 7.27
  industrial action restrictions, 7.29
  introduction, 7.23
  restraint of trade, 7.28
  UCTA 1977, and, 7.30
unfair terms, 7.30
unlawful terms, 7.24
variation by statute, 7.25
withholding of wages, 7.47
written particulars
  alternatives to inclusion, 7.8
  changes, 7.9
  excepted employees, 7.10
  introduction, 7.6
  remedies for failure to provide, 7.11
  requirements, 7.7
Contract of service
and see CONTRACTS OF EMPLOYMENT
generally, 14.2
Contract workers
discrimination 11.24
Contracting out
Central Arbitration Committee, and, 48.9
part time workers, and, 30.29
redundancy payments, and, 36.14
unfair dismissal, and
  exceptions, 51.20
  generally, 51.19
working time, and, 55.25
Contractual notice period
dismissal, and, 46.6
Contrary to public policy
contracts of employment, and, 7.24
Contravention of any enactment, dismissal for
generally, 52.13
summary, 52.2
Contributory fault
unfair dismissal, and, 53.13

Contributory negligence
health and safety, and, 25.44
Convictions
access to records, 16.7
Disclosure and Barring Service (DBS), 16.9
effect of provisions, 16.5
engagement of employees, 20.4
recording, 16.10
rehabilitation periods, 16.6
removal from certificate, 16.7
spent convictions
dismissal, and, 16.3
exceptions, 16.4
introduction, 16.1
non-disclosure, 16.2
vulnerable groups, and, 16.8**Coroner's inquests**
findings, 25.46
generally, 25.47
"interested persons", 25.48
introduction, 25.45
Corporate governance
directors' service contracts, 8.15
remuneration, 8.28
UK Corporate Governance Code, 8.15
Corporate killing
health and safety, and, 25.42
Costs
EAT procedure, and
amount, 19.44
generally, 19.42
grounds for orders, 19.43
means, 19.44
wasted costs orders, 19.45
generally, 18.69–18.70
orders, 18.71–18.72
preparation time orders, 18.73
warning, 18.15
wasted costs orders, 18.74
Council Tax
attachment of earnings, and, 33.10
Credit tokens
taxable benefits, and, 44.21
Criminal convictions
access to records, 16.7
Disclosure and Barring Service (DBS), 16.9
effect of provisions, 16.5
engagement of employees, 20.4
recording, 16.10
rehabilitation periods, 16.6
removal from certificate, 16.7
spent convictions
dismissal, and, 16.3
exceptions, 16.4
introduction, 16.1

Criminal convictions – *cont.*
spent convictions – *cont.*
non-disclosure, 16.2
vulnerable groups, and, 16.8
Criminal liability
strike action, and, 43.12
Criminal proceedings
health and safety, and
corporate killing, 25.42
defence, 25.41
directors' liability, 25.38
generally, 25.37
order to remedy default, 25.39
time for commencing proceedings, 25.40
strike action, and, 43.12
Cross border mergers
consultation, and
application of requirements, 15.51–15.52
complaints, 15.58
confidential information, 15.59
definition, 15.50
disputes, 15.58
duty of merging company to provide
information, 15.54
employment protection, 15.60
introduction, 15.49
meaning, 15.50
negotiated agreements, 15.56
pre-merger process, 15.53
special negotiating body, 15.55
standard rules, 15.57
Crown
discrimination, and, 11.36
Crown servants
EU law, 35.8
generally, 35.2
introduction, 35.1
judicial review as to rights, 35.6
minimum wage, and, 32.10
national security, 35.7
public interest immunity, 35.7
wrongful dismissal, and, 56.43
Daily rest periods
working time, and, 55.15
Damages
breach of contracts of employment
(employee's remedies), and
express terms, 7.41
extent, 7.36
loss of chance to claim unfair dismissal, 7.37
loss of reputation, 7.38
pecuniary loss, 7.39
stigma, 7.40

Index

Damages – *cont.*
breach of contracts of employment
(employer's remedies), and, 7.47b
wrongful dismissal, and
accelerated receipt, 56.31
accommodation, 56.28
assessment approach, 56.25
bonuses, 56.28
cars, 56.28
collateral benefits, 56.30
commission, 56.28
distress, 56.29
holidays, 56.28
insurance cover, 56.28
intangible loss, 56.29
interest, 56.31
'liquidated damages' clauses, 56.26
mitigation, 56.30
pensions, 56.28
rights in period of notice, 56.27
salary, 56.28
share options, 56.28
taxation, 56.32
unfair dismissal compensation, and, 56.33
valuation of benefits, 56.28
Data protection
background, 9.11
Codes of Practice, 4.16
engagement of employees, 20.7
generally, 9.12
overview, 9.13
references, 9.13, 38.6
Death of employee
pay as you earn, and, 44.10
sex discrimination, and, 11.11
Deduction from wages
attachment of earnings, and
calculation, 33.4
introduction, 33.3
priority of orders, 33.5
time limits, 33.6
breach of contracts of employment, and, 7.47
generally, 32.6
introduction, 32.2
minimum wage, and, 32.9–32.13
other, 32.14
remedies for breach, 32.8
retail employment, 32.7
time limits for claims, and, 17.31
trade union members, and
generally, 49.20
introduction, 32.6
workers in retail employment, 32.7

Default judgments
tribunal procedure, and, 17.38
Defences
wrongful dismissal, and
exclusion clauses, 56.37
illegality, 56.35
invalidity of contract, 56.36
Defined benefit pension schemes
generally, 40.9
**Department for Business Innovation and
Skills (BIS)**
Codes of Practice, and, 4.4
Department of Trade and Industry (now BIS)
Codes of Practice, and
legal effect, 4.5
power to issue, 4.4
revision, 4.17
Dependants, time off work for
generally, 47.15
remedies, 47.16
unfair dismissal, and, 52.3
Deposit orders
tribunal procedure, ands, 18.15
Detriment
children, and, 3.10
discrimination, and, 10.51
part-time workers, and, 30.24
study and training, and, 13.19
trade union members, and
generally, 49.17
remedy, 49.18
summary, 49.8
trade unions, and, 48.37
Direct discrimination
age, 10.25
associative discrimination, and, 10.27
'because of the protected characteristic'
age, 10.25
disability, 10.26
gender reassignment, 10.21
general principles, 10.17
marital or civil partnership status, 10.19
pregnancy or maternity leave, 10.24
racial grounds, 10.20
religion or belief, 10.22
sex, 10.18
sexual orientation, 10.23
civil partnership status, 10.19
disability, 10.26
gender reassignment, 10.21
generally, 10.13
less favourable treatment
'because of the protected
characteristic', 10.17–10.26

Direct discrimination – *cont.*
less favourable treatment – *cont.*
comparators, 10.15
generally, 10.14
positive discrimination, 10.16
marital or civil partnership status, 10.19
maternity leave, 10.24
perceived discrimination, 10.28
pregnancy leave, 10.24
race, 10.20
religion or belief, 10.22
sex, 10.18
sexual orientation, 10.23
Direction of third party
health and safety, and, 25.10
Directors
act within powers, 8.18
appointment
introduction, 8.2
relationship between articles and
contracts, 8.3
scope of employment, 8.5
status, 8.4
terms, 8.4
written particulars, 8.6
avoid conflict of interests, 8.22
care, skill and diligence, 8.21
Companies Act 2006, and
duties, 8.17
introduction, 8.1
conflicts of interest, 8.22
consultation obligations, and
directors' reports, 15.3
regard for interests of employees, 15.2
duties
act within powers, 8.18
avoid conflict of interests, 8.22
Companies Act 2006, and, 8.17
continuing obligations, 8.24
fiduciary, 8.19
indemnity, 8.25
independent judgment, 8.20
introduction, 8.16
not to accept benefits from third parties, 8.23
promote success of company, 8.19
reasonable care, skill and diligence, 8.21
relief from liability, 8.26
duration of service contracts
introduction, 8.13
recommendations, 8.15
section 188 restrictions, 8.14
indemnity, 8.25
independent judgment, 8.20
introduction, 8.1

Directors – *cont.*
non-executive, 22.6
not to accept benefits from third parties, 8.23
pensions, 8.35
promote success of company, 8.19
property transfer, 8.40
reasonable care, skill and diligence, 8.21
relief from liability, 8.26
remuneration
disclosure, 8.31
introduction, 8.27
Listing Rules requirements, 8.34
pensions, 8.35
quoted companies, developments 8.33
recommendations, 8.28
Remuneration Code, 8.30
remuneration policy, 8.33
remuneration report, 8.33
small company provisions, 8.32
Stewardship Code, 8.29
service contracts
disclosure, 8.12
duration, 8.13–8.15
inspection, 8.8
introduction, 8.7
Listing Rules requirements, 8.10
sole members also directors, with, 8.9
Take-over Code requirements, 8.11
takeovers, 8.11
taxation, and, 44.3
termination of office
generally, 8.36
Listing Rules requirements, 8.39
property transfer, 8.38
recommendations, 8.36
takeovers, 8.41
termination payments, 8.37
transfer of undertakings, 8.42
written particulars, 8.6
Directors' liability
health and safety, and, 25.38
Directors' reports
employee participation, and, 15.3
Disability discrimination
adjustments by employer, 10.37
advertisements
employment, in, 10.43
injunctions, 12.30
introduction, 20.1
advocates, 11.27
agent's acts, 10.56
aiding unlawful acts, 10.58
applications to Employment Tribunal
burden of proof, 12.3

Index

Disability discrimination – *cont.*
applications to Employment Tribunal – *cont.*
  compensation, 12.13–12.20
  conciliation, 12.10
  disclosure, 12.9
  extension of time, 12.7
  formulation of complaint, 12.8
  generally, 12.2
  publicity, 12.11
  questionnaire, 12.9
  recommendations, 12.21
  remedies, 12.12–12.22
  time limits, 12.4–12.7
armed forces, 11.16
assistance for persons discriminated
  against, 12.31
barristers, 11.27
'because of the protected characteristic', 10.26
benefits provided to public, 11.20
burden of proof, 12.3
careers guidance, 11.32
charities, 11.10A, 11.16
Codes of Practice, and
  legal effect, 4.11
  power to issue, 4.11
  revision, 4.17
  revocation, 4.17
combined discrimination, 10.29
comparators, 10.15
compensation
  aggravated damages, 12.18
  discrimination, 12.19
  exemplary damages, 12.18
  general principles, 12.13
  indirect discrimination, 12.14
  injury to feelings, 12.16
  interest, 12.20
  introduction, 12.12
  pecuniary loss, 12.15
  personal injury, 12.17
  unfair dismissal, 12.19
compliance with law, 11.21
conciliation, 12.10
contract workers, 11.24
Crown, 11.36
detriment, 10.50
direct discrimination
  'because of the protected
    characteristic', 10.26
  generally, 10.13
  less favourable treatment, 10.14–10.16
disability
  definition, 4.12
  guidance, 4.12

Disability discrimination – *cont.*
disclosure, 12.9
dismissal, 10.49
duty to make reasonable adjustments, 10.37
education needs, 11.10
employed at establishment in GB, 10.42
employment agencies, 11.32
employment, in
  advertisements, 10.43
  dismissal, 10.49
  'employment', 10.41
  engagement, 10.44–10.46
  harassment, 10.51
  introduction, 10.40
  opportunities, 10.47–10.48
  post-employment behaviour, 10.52
  subjection to other detriment, 10.50–10.51
  territorial jurisdiction, 10.42
employment outside Great Britain, 11.18
employment-related services, 11.33
employment service-providers, 11.34
enforcement
  applications to Employment
    Tribunal, 12.2–12.22
  assistance for persons discriminated
    against, 12.31
  EHRC, by, 12.23–12.24
  injunctions, 12.29–12.30
  introduction, 12.1
  settlement, 12.33
  void contract terms, 12.32
enforcement by the EHRC
  formal inquiries and
    investigations, 12.25–12.27
  generally, 12.23–12.24
  introduction, 11.38
  unlawful act notices, 12.28
engagement, 10.44
equal opportunities, and
  enforcement, 11.38
  general exceptions, 11.17–11.23
  genuine occupational requirement or
    qualification, 11.2–11.8
  introduction, 11.1
  justification, 11.9
  non-employees/employers
    covered, 11.24–11.36
  positive discrimination, 11.10
  public authorities, and, 11.37
  specific exceptions, 11.11–11.16
Equality Act 2010, 10.331
exceptions
  armed forces, 11.16
  charities, 11.16
  public facilities, 11.16

Index

Disability discrimination – *cont.*
extension of time, 12.7
fire officers, 11.16
foreign employees, and, 23.9
formulation of complaint, 12.8
general exceptions
  benefits provided to public, 11.20
  compliance with law, 11.21
  employment outside Great Britain, 11.18
  illegal contracts, 11.19
  introduction, 11.17
  national security, 11.22
  State immunity, 11.23
generally, 10.33
genuine occupational requirement or
    qualification, 11.2
harassment
  generally, 10.39
  partnerships, 11.28
  trade organisations, 11.29
illegal contracts, 11.19
indirect discrimination
  application of the test, 10.34
  discriminatory measure, 10.34
  disparity of effect, 10.34
  generally, 10.34
  personal disadvantage, 10.34
  sex discrimination, and, 10.35
  sexual orientation discrimination, and, 10.36
  test, 10.34
injunctions
  advertisements, 12.30
  instructions to discriminate, 12.30
  persistent discrimination, 12.29
  pressure to discriminate, 12.30
instructions to commit unlawful acts
  enforcement by EHRC, 11.38
  generally, 10.53
  injunctions, 12.30
interview and selection, 20.2–20.4
introduction, 10.331
justification, 11.9
legal sources, 10.3311
less favourable treatment,
  comparators, 10.15
  introduction, 10.14
  positive discrimination, 10.16
meaning
  combined discrimination, 10.29
  direct discrimination, 10.13–10.27
  generally, 10.33
  harassment, 10.39
  indirect discrimination, 10.34–10.36
  introduction, 10.12

Disability discrimination – *cont.*
meaning – *cont.*
  perceived discrimination, 10.28
  victimisation, 10.38
national security, 11.22
non-employees/employers covered, 11.24–11.36
occupational pension schemes, 11.35
office holders
  exceptions, 11.16
  generally, 11.25
opportunities in employment
  generally, 10.47
  sex discrimination, 10.48
partnerships, 11.28
perceived discrimination, 10.28
personal disadvantage, 10.34
police
  exceptions, 11.16
  generally, 11.26
positive discrimination,
  access to training, 11.10
  childbirth, 11.10
  EU law, under, 11.10
  generally, 11.10
  introduction, 10.16
  membership of trade organisation, 11.10
  pregnancy, 11.10
  Sikhs on construction sites, 11.13
post-employment behaviour,, 10.52
pressure to commit unlawful acts
  enforcement by EHRC, 11.38
  generally, 10.53
  injunctions, 12.30
prison officers, 11.16
prohibited grounds
  combined discrimination, 10.29
  direct discrimination, 10.13–10.27
  disability-related discrimination, 10.33
  harassment, 10.39
  indirect discrimination, 10.34–10.36
  introduction, 10.12
  perceived discrimination, 10.28
  victimisation, 10.38
protected characteristics, 10.11
public authorities, and, 11.37
public facilities, 11.16
publicity, 12.11
pupillage, 11.27
qualifications bodies, 11.30
questionnaire, 12.9
reasonable adjustments, 10.37
recommendations, 12.21
remedies
  compensation, 12.13–12.20

Index

Disability discrimination – *cont.*
  remedies – *cont.*
    introduction, 12.12
    pension rights, 12.22
    recommendations, 12.21
  selection, 20.2–20.4
  settlement of claim, 12.33
  small business, no exemption, 11.16
  specific exceptions, 11.16
  State immunity, 11.23
  state provision of facilities and services, 11.33
  third party acts, 10.57
  time limits for claims, and
    generally, 12.4–12.7
    introduction, 17.29
  trade organisations, 11.29
  training needs, 11.10
  trustees of occupational pension schemes, 11.35
  unfavourable treatment, 10.14
  unlawful act notices, 12.28
  unlawful acts
    agent's acts, 10.56
    aiding unlawful acts, 10.58
    employee's acts, 10.54–10.55
    enforcement by EHRC, 11.38
    instructions to commit unlawful acts, 10.53
    pressure to commit unlawful acts, 10.53
    third party acts, 10.57
    vicarious liability, 10.54–10.55
  unlawful instructions
    enforcement only by Commissions, 11.38
    generally, 10.53
    injunctions, 12.30
  unlawful pressure
    enforcement only by Commissions, 11.38
    generally, 10.53
    injunctions, 12.30
  vicarious liability
    defence, 10.55
    generally, 10.54
  vocational training providers, 11.31
  welfare needs, 11.10
Disciplinary action against trade union members
  common law, 49.15
  right to be accompanied
    generally, 49.21
    unfair dismissal, and, 52.3
  statutory provisions, 49.16
  summary, 49.9
Disciplinary procedures
  Codes of Practice, and
    generally, 10.331
    legal effect, 4.3

Disciplinary procedures – *cont.*
  Codes of Practice, and – *cont.*
    power to issue, 4.2
  trade union members, and
    and see above
    common law, 49.15
    right to be accompanied, 49.21
    statutory provisions, 49.16
    summary, 49.9
Disclosure
  and see **DISCLOSURE** OF INFORMATION
  breach of contracts of employment, and, 7.46
  Code of Practice, 2.11
  criminal convictions, 16.1-16.7
    Disclosure and Barring Service (DBS), 16.9
    removal from certificate, 16.7
  directors' remuneration, and
    generally, 8.31
    Listing Rules requirements, 8.34
    small companies, 8.32
  directors' service contracts, and
    generally, 8.12
    Listing Rules requirements, 8.10
    Take-over Code, 8.11
  discrimination complaints, and, 12.9
  tribunal procedure, and
    discrimination complaints, 12.9
    generally, 18.11–18.12
    privileged documents, 18.13
Disclosure of information
  collective bargaining, for
    Code of Practice, 9.4
    exceptions to duty, 9.3
    failure to comply with request, 9.5
    general duty, 9.3
    introduction, 9.2
  confidential information, and, 9.15
  data protection, and
    background, 9.11
    generally, 9.12
    overview, 9.13
  economic situation of undertakings, 9.10
  employees, by
    generally, 9.16
    protected disclosures, 9.17
  employment prospects, 9.10
  health and safety, for
    introduction, 9.7
    safety representatives, 9.8
  ICE Regulations 2004, 9.10
  introduction, 9.1
  medical reports, and, 9.14
  occupational pension schemes, by, 9.9

Index

Disclosure of information – *cont.*

public interest, in
  generally, 9.16
  protected disclosures, 9.17–9.18
transfer of undertakings, for, 9.6
whistleblowing, and
  generally, 9.16
  protected disclosures, 9.17
'worker', definition, 9.18

Discrimination

advertisements
  employment, in, 10.43
  injunctions, 12.30
  introduction, 20.1
advocates, 11.27
age
  'because of', 10.25
  generally, 10.10
  legitimate aim, 11.9
agent's acts, 10.56
aiding unlawful acts, 10.58
applications to Employment Tribunal
  burden of proof, 12.3
  compensation, 12.13–12.20
  conciliation, 12.10
  disclosure, 12.9
  extension of time, 12.7
  formulation of complaint, 12.8
  generally, 12.2
  publicity, 12.11
  questionnaire, 12.9
  recommendations, 12.21
  remedies, 12.12–12.22
  time limits, 12.4–12.7
assistance for persons discriminated
    against, 12.31
barristers, 11.27
'because of the protected characteristic'
  age, 10.25
  disability, 10.26
  gender reassignment, 10.21
  general principles, 10.17
  marital or civil partnership status, 10.19
  pregnancy or maternity leave, 10.24
  racial grounds, 10.20
  religion or belief, 10.22
  sex, 10.18
  sexual orientation, 10.23
benefits provided to public, 11.20
burden of proof, 12.3
careers guidance, 11.32
charities, 11.10A
civil partnership status,
  'because of', 10.19

Discrimination – *cont.*

civil partnership status, – *cont.*
  direct discrimination, 10.13
  generally 10.332
  harassment, 10.39
  indirect discrimination, 10.34
Codes of Practice, and
  disability discrimination, 4.11
  race discrimination, 4.6–4.8
  sex discrimination, 4.9–4.10
collective agreements, and, 5.15
colour, and
  advertisements, 10.43
  applicable test, 10.34
  disparity of effect, 10.34
  harassment, 10.39
  indirect discrimination, 10.34
  meaning of 'because of race', 10.20
  nationality, 10.34
  pressure to commit unlawful acts, 10.53
combined discrimination, 10.29
comparators, 10.15
compensation
  aggravated damages, 12.18
  discrimination, 12.19
  exemplary damages, 12.18
  general principles, 12.13
  indirect discrimination, 12.14
  injury to feelings, 12.16
  interest, 12.20
  introduction, 12.12
  pecuniary loss, 12.15
  personal injury, 12.17
  unfair dismissal, 12.19
compliance with law, 11.21
conciliation, 12.10
contract workers, 11.24
Crown, 11.36
detriment, 10.50
direct discrimination
  'because of the protected
    characteristic', 10.17–10.26
  generally, 10.13
  less favourable treatment, 10.14–10.16
disability
  'because of', 10.26
  duty to make reasonable adjustments, 10.37
  generally, 10.332
  introduction, 10.33
disclosure, 12.9
dismissal, 10.49
duty to make reasonable adjustments, 10.37
education needs, 11.10
employed at establishment in GB, 10.42

Index

Discrimination – *cont.*
  employment agencies, 11.32
  employment, in
    advertisements, 10.43
    dismissal, 10.49
    'employment', 10.41
    engagement, 10.44–10.46
    harassment, 10.51
    introduction, 10.40
    opportunities, 10.47–10.48
    post-employment behaviour, 10.52
    subjection to other detriment, 10.50–10.51
    territorial jurisdiction, 10.42
  employment outside Great Britain, 11.18
  employment-related services, 11.33
  employment service-providers, 11.34
  enforcement
    applications to Employment
        Tribunal, 12.2–12.22
    assistance for persons discriminated
        against, 12.31
    EHRC, by, 12.23–12.24
    injunctions, 12.29–12.30
    introduction, 12.1
    settlement, 12.33
    void contract terms, 12.32
  enforcement by the EHRC
    formal inquiries and
        investigations, 12.25–12.27
    generally, 12.23–12.24
    introduction, 11.38
    unlawful act notices, 12.28
  engagement
    generally, 10.44
    race discrimination, 10.45
    sex discrimination, 10.46
  equal opportunities, and
    enforcement, 11.38
    general exceptions, 11.17–11.23
    genuine occupational requirement or
        qualification, 11.2–11.8
    introduction, 11.1
    justification, 11.9
    non-employees/employers
        covered, 11.24–11.36
    positive discrimination, 11.10
    public authorities, and, 11.37
    specific exceptions, 11.11–11.16
  Equality Act 2010, 10.1
  exceptions
    age, 11.15
    civil partnership status, 11.14
    disability, 11.16
    general, 11.17–11.23
    marital status, 11.14

Discrimination – *cont.*
  exceptions – *cont.*
    race, 11.12
    religion or belief, 11.13
    sex, 11.11
    sexual orientation, 11.14
  extension of time, 12.7
  foreign employees, and, 23.9
  formulation of complaint, 12.8
  gender reassignment, 10.6
  general exceptions
    benefits provided to public, 11.20
    compliance with law, 11.21
    employment outside Great Britain, 11.18
    illegal contracts, 11.19
    introduction, 11.17
    national security, 11.22
    State immunity, 11.23
  genuine occupational requirement or
        qualification
    age, 11.8
    gender reassignment, 11.5
    generally, 11.2
    partnerships, 11.28
    race, 11.4
    religion or belief, 11.6
    sex, 11.3
    sexual orientation, 11.7
  guidance material, 10.2
  harassment
    generally, 10.39
    partnerships, 11.28
    trade organisations, 11.29
  illegal contracts, 11.19
  indirect discrimination
    application of the test, 10.34
    discriminatory measure, 10.34
    disparity of effect, 10.34
    generally, 10.34
    personal disadvantage, 10.34
    sex discrimination, and, 10.35
    sexual orientation discrimination, and, 10.36
    test, 10.34
  injunctions
    advertisements, 12.30
    instructions to discriminate, 12.30
    persistent discrimination, 12.29
    pressure to discriminate, 12.30
  instructions to commit unlawful acts
    enforcement by EHRC, 11.38
    generally, 10.53
    injunctions, 12.30
  interview and selection, 20.2–20.4
  introduction, 10.1

Discrimination – *cont.*
   justification, 11.9
   legal sources
      age discrimination, 10.10
      civil partnership status, 10.4
      disability discrimination, 10.3311
      gender reassignment, 10.6
      introduction, 10.332
      marital status, 10.4
      maternity leave, 10.9
      pregnancy, 10.9
      race discrimination, 10.5
      religion or belief discrimination, 10.7
      sex discrimination, 10.333
      sexual orientation discrimination, 10.8
      transsexuals, 10.6
   less favourable treatment,
      comparators, 10.15
      generally, 10.14
      positive discrimination, 10.16
   local authority members, 11.35A
   marital status,
      'because of', 10.19
      direct discrimination, 10.13
      generally 10.332
      harassment, 10.39
      indirect discrimination, 10.34
   maternity leave,
      'because of', 10.24
      direct discrimination, 10.13
      generally 10.332
      harassment, 10.39
   meaning
      combined discrimination, 10.29
      direct discrimination, 10.13–10.27
      disability-related discrimination, 10.33
      harassment, 10.39
      indirect discrimination, 10.34–10.36
      introduction, 10.12
      perceived discrimination, 10.28
      victimisation, 10.38
   national security, 11.22
   non-employees/employers covered, 11.24–11.36
   occupational pension schemes, 11.35, 40.12
   office holders, 11.25
   opportunities in employment
      generally, 10.47
      sex discrimination, 10.48
   part time workers, and,
      comparators, 30.12–30.19
      direct effect, 30.2
      less favourable treatment, 30.7–30.9
      objective justification, 30.21

Discrimination – *cont.*
   part time workers, and, – *cont.*
      'on the ground that the worker is a part-time worker', 30.20
   partnerships, 11.28
   pensions, and,
      age discrimination, 40.2
      introduction, 11.11
      sex discrimination, 40.13
   perceived discrimination, 10.28
   personal disadvantage, 10.34
   police, 11.26
   positive discrimination,
      access to training, 11.10
      childbirth, 11.10
      EU law, under, 11.10
      generally, 11.10
      introduction, 10.16
      membership of trade organisation, 11.10
      pregnancy, 11.10
      Sikhs on construction sites, 11.13
   post-employment behaviour,, 10.52
   pregnancy,
      'because of', 10.24
      direct discrimination, 10.13
      generally, 10.332
      harassment, 10.39
      positive discrimination, 11.10
   pressure to commit unlawful acts
      enforcement by EHRC, 11.38
      generally, 10.53
      injunctions, 12.30
   prohibited grounds
      combined discrimination, 10.29
      direct discrimination, 10.13–10.27
      disability-related discrimination, 10.33
      harassment, 10.39
      indirect discrimination, 10.34–10.36
      introduction, 10.12
      perceived discrimination, 10.28
      victimisation, 10.38
   proportionality, 11.9
   protected characteristics
      age discrimination, 10.10
      civil partnership status, 10.4
      disability discrimination, 10.3311
      gender reassignment, 10.6
      marital status, 10.4
      maternity leave, 10.9
      pregnancy, 10.9
      race discrimination, 10.5
      religion or belief discrimination, 10.7
      sex discrimination, 10.333
      sexual orientation discrimination, 10.8

Index

Discrimination – *cont.*
protected characteristics – *cont.*
transsexuals, 10.6
public authorities, and, 11.37
publicity, 12.11
pupillage, 11.27
qualifications bodies, 11.30
questionnaire, 12.9
race, 10.332
reasonable adjustments, 10.37
recommendations, 12.21
religion or belief, 10.332
remedies
compensation, 12.13–12.20
introduction, 12.12
pension rights, 12.22
recommendations, 12.21
selection, 20.2–20.4
settlement of claim, 12.33
sex, 10.332
sexual orientation, 10.332
specific exceptions
age, 11.15
civil partnership status, 11.14
disability, 11.16
marital status, 11.14
race, 11.12
religion or belief, 11.13
sex, 11.11
sexual orientation, 11.14
sports and competitions,
race discrimination, 11.12
sex discrimination, 11.11
State immunity, 11.23
state provision of facilities and services, 11.33
territorial jurisdiction, 10.42
territorial jurisdiction, 10.42
third party acts, 10.57
time limits for claims, and
generally, 12.4–12.7
introduction, 17.29
trade organisations, 11.29
training needs, 11.10
transsexuals, 10.332
trustees of occupational pension schemes, 11.35
unfavourable treatment, 10.14
unlawful act notices, 12.28
unlawful acts
agent's acts, 10.56
aiding unlawful acts, 10.58
employee's acts, 10.54–10.55
enforcement by EHRC, 11.38
instructions to commit unlawful acts, 10.53
pressure to commit unlawful acts, 10.53

Discrimination – *cont.*
unlawful acts – *cont.*
third party acts, 10.57
vicarious liability, 10.54–10.55
unlawful instructions
enforcement only by Commissions, 11.38
generally, 10.53
injunctions, 12.30
unlawful pressure
enforcement only by Commissions, 11.38
generally, 10.53
injunctions, 12.30
vicarious liability
defence, 10.55
generally, 10.54
victimisation, 10.38
vocational training providers, 11.31
welfare needs, 11.10
work permits, persons requiring, 11.9
Discrimination questionnaires
generally, 12.9
tribunal procedure, and, 17.18
Discriminatory terms
unenforceable terms, and, 7.27
Disguised remuneration
taxation, and, 44.36
Dismissal
and see **REDUNDANCY**
and see **UNFAIR** DISMISSAL
and see **WRONGFUL** DISMISSAL
Codes of Practice, and
legal effect, 4.3
power to issue, 4.2
discrimination, and, 10.49
dismissal and disciplinary procedures
Codes of Practice, and, 4.2–4.3
introduction, 46.5
notice, by,
contractual notice period, 46.6
employee, by, 46.17
introduction, 46.5
pay in lieu of notice, 46.9–46.10
rights during notice period, 46.12
statutory minimum notice, 46.7–46.8
pay as you earn, and, 44.8
probationary employees, and, 34.2
retraction of, 46.20
spent convictions, and, 16.3
summary, 46.13
transfer of undertakings, and,
introduction, 50.24
redundancy, 50.27
unfair dismissal, 50.25–50.26

Dismissal – *cont.*
written statement of reasons,
generally, 46.14
remedy for failure to give, 46.15
wrongful dismissal, and,
acceptance of employer's breach, 56.7
cessation of existence of employer, 56.8
change of employer's identity, 56.8
constructive dismissal, 56.6
contrast with other modes of
termination, 56.4
dismissal with notice, 56.5
dismissal without notice, 56.11–56.17
insolvency of employer, 56.9
introduction, 56.3
removal of director from board, 56.10
Dismissal and disciplinary procedures
Codes of Practice, and
legal effect, 4.3
power to issue, 4.2
Dismissal notices
redundancy, and, 37.9
Dismissal of claims
tribunal procedure, and, 18.28
Dismissal with notice
wrongful dismissal, and, 56.5
Dismissal without notice
directors' notice periods, 56.14
express notice periods, 56.11
fixed term contracts, 56.12
implied notice periods, 56.15
justification, 56.17
rolling contracts, 56.13
statutory minimum notice, 56.16
Display screen equipment
health and safety, and, 26.5
Dispute resolution
disciplinary or grievance process,
transitional, 2.11
sick pay, and, 42.8
Disqualification from office
trade unions, and, 48.14
Distress
wrongful dismissal, and, 56.29
Doctors in training
working time, and, 55.3
Domestic legislation
sources of law, and, 1.6
Domestic servants
redundancy payments, and, 36.10
working time, and, 55.30
Drug misuse
generally, 26.2
testing, 26.3

Due diligence and care
implied contract terms, and, 7.15
Duration of directors' service contracts
introduction, 8.13
recommendations, 8.15
section 188 restrictions, 8.14
Duty of care for advice given
trade unions, and, 49.22
Early conciliation
Employment Law Review, and, 24.5
Early retirement
generally, 40.6
Earnings limits
taxation, and, 44.4
Earnings, loss of
unfair dismissal, and, 53.12
Economic situation of undertakings
information and consultation, and, 9.10
Economic, technical or organisational reasons
unfair dismissal, and, 52.14
Economic torts
strike action, and, 43.1
Education and training
apprenticeships
generally, 13.2
statutory provisions, 13.11
Apprenticeships, Skills, Training and Children
Act 2009
apprenticeships, 13.11
introduction, 13.9
structural changes, 13.10
study and training, 13.12–13.19
DCELLS, 13.8
discrimination, and, 11.10
employee participation in consultation,
and, 15.63
industrial training boards, 13.4
introduction, 13.1
learndirect, 13.8
Learning and Skills Council, 13.10
local enterprise companies, 13.8
New Deal, 13.6
positive discrimination, and, 11.10
recovery of costs, 13.3
school-leavers, for, 13.5
Skills Funding Agency, 13.8
study and training
complaint to tribunal, 13.17
detriment, and, 13.19
employee's duties, 13.16
employer's duties, 13.15
generally, 13.12
remedies, 13.18
right to request, 13.13

Index

Education and training – *cont.*
study and training – *cont.*
supplementary provisions, 13.14
unfair dismissal, and, 13.19
tax-free benefits, and, 44.23
time off from work, and
generally, 47.6
remedies, 47.7
trade unions, and, 48.38
unfair dismissal, and, 52.3
work-based training, 13.7
Education workers
continuous employment, and, 6.9
EU law, 35.8
generally, 35.5
introduction, 35.1
judicial review as to rights, 35.6
national security, 35.7
public interest immunity, 35.7
EEA nationals
foreign workers, and
generally, 23.2
posted workers, 23.3
Effective date of termination
unfair dismissal, and, 51.13
Effluxion of time
termination, and, 46.4
Elections
trade unions, and, 48.14
Electricity
health and safety, and, 26.6
Emoluments
taxation, and, 44.2
Employee participation
collective redundancies, 15.61
cross border mergers
application of requirements, 15.51–15.52
complaints, 15.58
confidential information, 15.59
definition, 15.50
disputes, 15.58
duty of merging company to provide
information, 15.54
employment protection, 15.60
introduction, 15.49
meaning, 15.50
negotiated agreements, 15.56
pre-merger process, 15.53
special negotiating body, 15.55
standard rules, 15.57
directors' obligations
directors' reports, 15.3
regard for interests of employees, 15.2
directors' reports, 15.3

Employee participation – *cont.*
EU law, 15.1
European companies (SEs)
alternative arrangements, 15.36
complaints, 15.37
disputes, 15.37
employer's duty to provide information, 15.32
employment protection, 15.38
implementation in UK, 15.31
introduction, 15.30
negotiated agreements, 15.34
special negotiating body, 15.33
standard rules, 15.34
European co-operative societies (SCEs),
alternative arrangements, 15.45
complaints, 15.46
confidential information, 15.47
disputes, 15.46
duty to provide information, 15.41
employment protection, 15.48
implementation in UK, 15.40
introduction, 15.39
negotiated agreements, 15.43
special negotiating body, 15.42
standard rules, 15.44
European Works Councils
amending Regulations, 15.29A
confidential information, 15.28
employment protection, 15.29
establishment, 15.27
introduction, 15.22
number of employees, 15.24
requests, 15.25
special negotiating body, 15.26
health and safety issues, 15.61
ICE Regulations 2004,
application, 15.6
background, 15.4
complaints, 15.20
confidential information, 15.19
co-operation, 15.14
election or appointment of
representatives, 15.13
employee data requests, 15.7
employment protection, 15.21
initiation of obligations, 15.8–15.11
introduction, 15.4–15.5
negotiated agreements, 15.12
overview, 9.10
pre-existing agreements, 15.17–15.18
standard information and consultation
provisions, 15.15–15.16
'undertakings', 15.6
interests of employees, 15.2

Index

Employee participation – *cont.*
introduction, 15.1
other consultation rights, 15.61–15.62
Partnership at Work Fund, 15.64
training, 15.63
transfer of undertakings, and, 50.22
Employee representatives
generally, 47.12
remedies, 47.13
unfair dismissal, and, 52.3
Employee share schemes
company share option, 44.30
enterprise management incentives, 44.32
incentive plans, 44.31
savings-related share option, 44.29
Employee trustees
pensions, and, 40.15
Employees
disclosure, and,
  generally, 9.16
  protected disclosures, 9.17
excluded employment, and, 44.22
generally, 14.2–14.3
obligation of fidelity, 8.19
  office-holders, distinction, 14.8
pension trustees, and, 40.15
rights and obligations, 14.4–14.5
taxable benefits, and, 44.22
Employee's certificates
pay as you earn, and, 44.15
Employee's duties
fidelity, of, 7.16
obey employer's instructions, to, 7.17
take care in performance of duties, to, 7.18
Employer handbooks and policies
contracts of employment, and, 7.13
Employment
meaning, 1.2–1.3
sources of law, 1.4–1.7
stages, 1.9
Employment agencies
Conduct Regulations, 45.5
EC Directive, 45.2D
discrimination, and, 11.32
engagement of employees, and, 20.6
generally, 45.2–45.2C
harassment, and, 11.32
reforms, 45.4
Regulations, 45.2D
statutory control, 45.3
Employment agency workers
employee status, 14.3
employment agencies, and
  Conduct Regulations, 45.5

Employment agency workers – *cont.*
employment agencies, and – *cont.*
  EC Directive, 45.2D
  generally, 45.2–45.2C
  reforms, 45.4
  Regulations, 45.2D
  statutory control, 45.3
less favourable treatment, 45.9
national minimum wage
  generally, 45.6
  introduction, 32.10
Regulations, 45.2D
unfair dismissal, 45.7
working time, and, 55.3
Employment Appeal Tribunal
administration, 19.8
composition, 19.4–19.5
jurisdiction, 19.3
introduction, 19.1
practice, 19.6–19.7
status, 19.2
Employment Appeal Tribunal procedure
anonymity orders, 19.26
appellants, 19.10
bias allegation, 19.23–19.25
conduct of,
  disposal of appeal, 19.38–19.40
  error of law, 19.35–19.37
  fresh evidence, 19.34
  hearing, 19.32
  introduction, 19.11
  preparation for the hearing, 19.29–19.30
  raising points not taken at tribunal
    hearing, 19.33
  representation, 19.28
  skeleton arguments, 19.31
content, 19.13
costs
  amount, 19.44
  generally, 19.42
  grounds for orders, 19.43
  means, 19.44
  wasted costs orders, 19.45
disposal of appeal, 19.38–19.40
error of law
  generally, 19.35
  inadequacy of reasons, 19.36
  procedural failures, 19.37
EU law issues, 19.48
extensions of time, 19.14
fees, 19.9
fresh evidence, 19.34
generally, 19.4
grounds, 19.16

Index

Employment Appeal Tribunal procedure – *cont.*
hearing
  generally, 19.32
  preparation, 19.29–19.30
inadequacy of reasons, 19.36
institution, 19.11
notes of evidence, 19.21
other powers, 19.41
perverse decision
  generally, 19.35
  inadequacy of reasons, 19.36
  procedural failures, 19.37
preliminary hearing, 19.19–19.20
preliminary sifting, 19.17–19.18
preparation for the hearing, 19.29–19.30
procedural failures, 19.37
raising points not taken at tribunal
  hearing, 19.33
reference back for clarification of reasons, 19.22
response to notice of appeal, 19.15
representation, 19.28
restricted reporting orders, 19.26
review of order, 19.46
skeleton arguments, 19.31
time limits, 19.14
wasted costs orders, 19.45
Employment income
taxation, and, 44.2
Employment Law Review
changes in force from April 2012, 24.3
collective redundancies, 24.7
compromise agreements, 24.5
early conciliation, 24.5
employment tribunal rules, 24.4
fees, 24.6
generally, 24.1
historical background, 24.2
mediation, 24.5
other issues, 24.7
penalties, 24.6
protected conversations, 24.5
rapid resolution scheme, 24.7
TUPE, 24.7
whistleblowing, 24.7
Employment law sources
domestic legislation, 1.6
European law, 1.7
introduction, 1.4
terms of contracts of employment, 1.5
Employment outside GB
discrimination, and, 11.18
Employment prospects
information and consultation, and, 9.10

Employment protection
cross border mergers, and, 15.60
European companies, and, 15.38
European co-operative societies, and, 15.48
European Works Councils, and, 15.29
health and safety, and
  breach of safety regulations, 26.11
  detriment, 26.8
  introduction, 26.7
  remedy, 26.10
  whistleblowing, 26.9
information and consultation rights, and, 15.21
Employment-related services
discrimination, and, 11.33
Employment service-providers
age discrimination, and, 11.34
Employment status
employees
  generally, 14.2–14.3
  office-holders, 14.8
  rights and obligations, 14.4–14.5
introduction, 14.1
office-holders, 14.8
partners, 14.3
self-employed
  generally, 14.2–14.3
  rights and obligations, 14.6–14.7
workers, 14.9
Employment tribunals
abuse of process, 18.26
ACAS, and
  arbitration schemes, 18.37
  conciliation, 18.29–18.32
  introduction, 2.4
adding new claims, 18.10
adjournment application, 18.54
administration, 17.6
amendment of claims
  generally, 18.10
  introduction, 17.15
appeals
  amendments to notices of appeal, 19.27
  anonymity orders, 19.26
  bias allegation, 19.23–19.25
  conduct of, 19.28–19.40
  costs, 19.42–19.45, 19.47
  Court of Appeal, to, 19.47
  disposal, 19.38–19.40
  document sending, 19.14
  EAT, 19.1–19.3
  error of law, 19.35–19.37
  EU law issues, 19.48
  fresh evidence, 19.34
  generally, 19.4

Employment tribunals – *cont.*
appeals – *cont.*
grounds, 19.16
inadequacy of reasons, 19.36
hearing, 19.32
institution, 19.13
notes of evidence, 19.21
other powers, 19.41
perverse decision, 19.35
preliminary hearing, 19.19–19.20
preliminary sifting, 19.17–19.18
preparation for the hearing, 19.29–19.30
procedural failures, 19.37
raising points not taken at tribunal
hearing, 19.33
reference back for clarification of
reasons, 19.22
representation, 19.28
restricted reporting orders, 19.26
review of order, 19.46
skeleton arguments, 19.31
supporting documentation, 19.12–19.13
time limits, 19.14
wasted costs orders, 19.45
bias, 18.50
breach of contracts of employment, and, 7.44
'Calderbank' offers, 18.36
case management
case management discussions, 18.2–18.5
interim hearings, 18.6
powers in practice, 18.7–18.14
overriding objective, and, 18.1
pre-hearing reviews, 18.6
tribunal's powers, 18.2
case management discussions
application for orders, 18.3
introduction, 18.2
non-compliance with orders, 18.4
orders not available, 18.5
claims
default judgments, 17.38
extension of time, 17.22–17.33
post-presentation action, 17.34
presentation, 17.21
response by respondent, 17.35–17.37
time limits, 17.18–17.20
commencing proceedings, 17.15–17.17
composition
Chairmen sitting alone, 17.9–17.10
generally, 17.7–17.8
compromise agreements, 18.33–18.35
conciliation
'Calderbank' offers, 18.36
compromise agreements, 18.33–18.35

Employment tribunals – *cont.*
conciliation – *cont.*
discrimination complaints, 12.10
generally, 18.29–18.31
settlements, 18.32
conduct of hearing, 18.52
conflict of interest, 18.50
costs
generally, 18.69–18.70
orders, 18.71–18.72
preparation time orders, 18.73
wasted costs orders, 18.74
costs warning, 18.15
default judgments, 17.38
deposit orders, 18.15
disclosure
discrimination complaints, 12.9
generally, 18.11–18.12
privileged documents, 18.13
discrimination complaints
compensation, 12.13–12.20
conciliation, 12.10
disclosure, 12.9
extension of time, 12.7
formulation of complaint, 12.8
generally, 12.2
publicity, 12.11
questionnaire, 12.9
recommendations, 12.21
remedies, 12.12–12.22
time limits, 12.4–12.7
discrimination questionnaires, 12.9
dismissal of claims, 18.28
dismissal of party, 18.23
Employment Law Review, and, 24.4
estoppel, 18.26
extension of time
contract claims, 17.32
discrimination complaints, 12.7
effective date of termination, 17.23–17.24
equal pay, 17.28
generally, 17.22
introduction, 18.21
'just and equitable, 17.30
'not reasonably practicable' to present in
time, 17.25–17.26
other claims, 17.33
redundancy payments, 17.27
unlawful deductions from wages, 17.31
unlawful discrimination, 17.29
further information
generally, 18.8
questionnaires, 18.9

Index

Employment tribunals – *cont.*
  hearing
    adjournment application, 18.54
    bias, 18.50
    conduct, 18.52
    conflict of interest, 18.50
    control of procedure, 18.56
    generally, 18.49
    non-attendance of parties, 18.54
    order of evidence, 18.53
    other procedural points, 18.58–18.61
    private hearing, 18.51
    representation, 18.55
    witnesses, 18.57
  historical background, 17.1–17.2
  interest, 18.67
  interim hearings, 18.6
  introduction, 17.1–17.2
  itemised pay statements, and
    generally, 32.19
    order, 32.20
  joinder of parties, 18.23
  judgments
    adequacy of reasons, 18.63
    corrections and changes, 18.64
    generally, 18.62
    register, 18.65
  jurisdiction
    breach of contracts of employment, 7.44
    EU law, over, 17.12
    generally, 17.11
    Human Rights Act, under, 17.13
  listing arrangements, 18.39–18.48
  miscellaneous powers, 18.20
  multiple claims, 18.24
  non-attendance of parties, 18.54
  order of evidence, 18.53
  overriding objective
    case management, 18.1
    generally, 17.14
  post-presentation action, 17.34
  pre-hearing reviews, 18.6
  preparation for hearing
    general, 18.38
    listing arrangements, 18.39–18.48
  preparation time orders, 18.73
  presentation of claim, 17.21
  private hearing, 18.51
  questionnaires, 18.9
  reasons for decision
    adequacy, 18.63
    generally, 18.62
  recoupment of benefits, 18.68
  references, and, 38.8

Employment tribunals – *cont.*
  register of judgments, 18.65
  remedies
    costs, 18.69–18.74
    generally, 18.66
    interest, 18.67
    recoupment of benefits, 18.68
  representation, 18.55
  response by respondent, 17.35–17.37
  restricted reporting orders, 18.18–18.19
  review of judgment, 18.75–18.76
  Rules of Procedure, 17.4–17.5
  settlement
    conciliation, 18.32
    generally, 18.29–18.31
  specialist jurisdictions, 18.78
  statutory provision, 17.3
  stay of proceedings, 18.22
  striking out, 18.16–18.17
  time limits for claims
    contract claims, 17.32
    discrimination claims, 12.4–12.7
    equal pay, 17.28
    generally, 17.18
    'just and equitable, 17.30
    'not reasonably practicable' to present in
      time, 17.25–17.26
    other claims, 17.33
    post-EA 2002, 17.19–17.20
    redundancy payments, 17.27
    unlawful deductions from wages, 17.31
    unlawful discrimination, 17.29
  transfer of proceedings, 18.25
  vexatious litigants, 18.77
  wasted costs orders, 18.74
  withdrawal of claims, 18.28
  witness orders, 18.14
  witnesses, 18.57
End of year PAYE procedure
  certificates, 44.15
  Class 1A NICs, 44.17
  P9D, 44.16
  P11D, 44.16
  P11D(b), 44.16
  returns, 44.15
Enforcement
  Commission for Equality and Human Rights, by
    formal inquiries and
      investigations, 12.25–12.27
    generally, 12.23–12.24
    unlawful act notices, 12.28
  discrimination, and
    applications to Employment
      Tribunal, 12.2–12.22

Enforcement – *cont.*
discrimination, and – *cont.*
assistance for persons discriminated
against, 12.31
EHRC, by, 12.23–12.28
injunctions, 12.29–12.30
introduction, 12.1
settlement, 12.33
void contract terms, 12.32
formal inquiries and investigations
Commissioner's report, 12.27
generally, 12.25
information, 12.26
gender equality duty, 11.38
health and safety, and
appeals against notices, 25.34–25.36
enforcing authorities, 25.29
improvement notices, 25.31
inspectors, 25.31
prohibition notices, 25.32
withdrawal of notices, 25.33
unlawful act notices, 12.28
working time, and
health and safety authorities, by, 55.21
individual, by, 55.22
introduction, 55.20
Enforcing authorities
health and safety, and, 25.29
Engagement of employees
advertising, 20.1
agencies, and, 20.6
data protection, 20.7
disclosure of convictions, 20.4
discrimination, and
generally, 10.44
race discrimination, 10.45
sex discrimination, 10.46
employment agencies, 20.6
interview, 20.2–20.4
notification of terms and conditions, 20.5
race discrimination, 10.45
selection, 20.2–20.4
sex discrimination, 10.46
withdrawal of offers, 20.8
Enterprise and Regulatory Reform Act 2013
employer liability
direct fault, 25.1
equal pay audits, 21.19C
Enterprise management incentives
generally, 44.32
Equal access to social security benefits
European law, and, 22.5

Equal Opportunities Commission
And see **COMMISSION FOR EQUALITY
AND HUMAN RIGHTS**
Code of Practice
legal effect, 4.10
power to issue, 4.9
generally, 12.23
Equal pay
after-the-event justification, 21.12
Agricultural Wages Orders, and, 21.20
armed forces personnel, 21.4
associated employers, 21.9
attendance allowances, 21.12
background, 21.1
burden of proof, 21.21
civil courts, 21.19E
Code of Practice, 21.2
collective agreements, 21.23
comparators, 21.9
contractual effect, 21.22
cost, 21.12
different establishments, 21.9
direct discrimination
generally, 21.5
'material factor' defence, and, 21.12
effect on contracts, 21.22
eligible employees, 21.4
Equality Act 2010, 10.1, 21.18A
equality clause
comparator, 21.9
introduction, 21.5
like work, 21.6
work of equal value, 21.8
work rated as equivalent, 21.7
'Equality of Terms', 10.1
equivalence, 21.9
expert evidence, 21.21
foreign employees, and, 23.9
'genuine material factor' defence
direct discrimination, and, 21.12
generally, 21.11
hours worked, 21.12
indirect discrimination, 21.10
pool, selection of 21.11
provision, criterion or practice (PCP) 21.11
industrial relations, 21.12
introduction, 21.1
legislative framework
domestic legislation, 21.2
EU provisions, 21.3
length of service, 21.12
like work, 21.6

Index

Equal pay – *cont.*
  'material factor' defence
    direct discrimination, and, 21.12
    generally, 21.11
  maternity pay, 21.14
  maternity suspension, and, 21.4
  mistake, 21.12
  office-holders, 21.4
  part-time workers
    introduction, 21.2
    pensions, 21.18
  pay protection arrangements, 21.12
  pensions, and
    Barber claims, 21.17
    Equality Act 2010, and, 21.18A
    introduction, 21.15
    part-time workers, 21.18
    statutory regime prior to EA 2010, 21.16
  posted employees, 21.4
  procedure, 21.21
  productivity bonuses, 21.12
  qualifications, 21.12
  remedies
    Agricultural Wages Orders, 21.20
    compensation, 21.19B
    employer penalties, 21.19D
    employment tribunals, 21.19
    equal pay audits, 21.19C
    time limits, 21.19A
  right to, 21.4
  same establishment, 21.9
  seniority, 21.12
  'single source' test, 21.9
  time limits for claims, and, 17.28
  trade union representation, and, 21.12
  training, 21.12
  transparency, and, 21.12
  transsexuals, and
    generally, 21.13
    introduction, 21.2
  work of equal value, 21.8
  work rated as equivalent, 21.7
Equal treatment
  European law, and, 22.6
Equality Act 2010
  introduction, 10.331
Equality and Human Rights Commission
  Code of Practice, 4.11
  formal inquiries and investigations
    Commissioner's report, 12.27
    generally, 12.25
    information, 12.26
  generally, 12.23–12.24
  introduction, 12.1

Equality and Human Rights Commission –
  cont.
  unlawful act notices, 12.28
Equality of terms
  after-the-event justification, 21.12
  Agricultural Wages Orders, and, 21.20
  armed forces personnel, 21.4
  associated employers, 21.9
  attendance allowances, 21.12
  background, 21.1
  burden of proof, 21.21
  civil courts, 21.19E
  Codes of Practice, and
    introduction, 21.2
    prior to Equality Act 2010, 4.9–4.10
  collective agreements, 21.23
  comparators, 21.9
  contractual effect, 21.22
  cost, 21.12
  different establishments, 21.9
  direct discrimination
    generally, 21.5
    'material factor' defence, and, 21.12
  effect on contracts, 21.22
  eligible employees, 21.4
  Equality Act 2010, 10.1, 21.18A
  equality clause
    comparator, 21.9
    introduction, 21.5
    like work, 21.6
    work of equal value, 21.8
    work rated as equivalent, 21.7
  equivalence, 21.9
  expert evidence, 21.21
  foreign employees, and, 23.9
  'genuine material factor' defence
    direct discrimination, and, 21.12
    generally, 21.11
  hours worked, 21.12
  indirect discrimination, 21.10
    pool, selection of 21.11
    provision, criterion or practice (PCP) 21.11
  industrial relations, 21.12
  introduction, 21.1
  legislative framework
    domestic legislation, 21.2
    EU provisions, 21.3
  length of service, 21.12
  like work, 21.6
  'material factor' defence
    direct discrimination, and, 21.12
    generally, 21.11
  maternity pay, 21.14
  maternity suspension, and, 21.4

Equality of terms – *cont.*
mistake, 21.12
office-holders, 21.4
part-time workers
introduction, 21.2
pensions, 21.18
pay protection arrangements, 21.12
pensions, and
Barber claims, 21.17
Equality Act 2010, and, 21.18A
introduction, 21.15
part-time workers, 21.18
statutory regime prior to EA 2010, 21.16
posted employees, 21.4
procedure, 21.21
productivity bonuses, 21.12
qualifications, 21.12
remedies
Agricultural Wages Orders, 21.20
compensation, 21.19B
employer penalties, 21.19D
employment tribunals, 21.19
time limits, 21.19A
same establishment, 21.9
seniority, 21.12
'single source' test, 21.9
time limits for claims, and, 17.28
trade union representation, and, 21.12
training, 21.12
transparency, and, 21.12
transsexuals, and
generally, 21.13
introduction, 21.2
work of equal value, 21.8
work rated as equivalent, 21.7
Equipment and materials
health and safety, and, 25.6
Equipment for work
health and safety, and, 26.12
Error of law
generally, 19.35
inadequacy of reasons, 19.36
procedural failures, 19.37
Estoppel
tribunal procedure, and, 18.26
EU law
agency workers, 22.13
bankers' bonuses, 22.17
consultation, 22.12
direct effect, 22.2
disclosure of information, and, 9.10
effect, 22.2
employment law requirements, 22.3
enforcement, 22.2

EU law – *cont.*
equal access to benefits, 22.5
equal pay
generally, 22.6
introduction, 21.3
equal treatment, 22.6
fixed-term workers, 22.16
Francovich claims, 22.2
free movement of labour, 22.4
health and safety, and
generally, 25.25
introduction, 22.10
information, 22.12
insolvent employers, 22.15
introduction, 22.1
non-executive directors, 22.6
posted workers, 22.14
redundancy, 22.8
sources of law, and, 1.7
supremacy, 22.2
terms of employment, 22.7
transfer of undertakings, 22.9
working time, 22.11
works councils, 22.12
written particulars of terms, 22.7
European companies/Societas Euopaea (SEs)
alternative arrangements, 15.36
complaints, 15.37
disputes, 15.37
employer's duty to provide information, 15.32
employment protection, 15.38
implementation in UK, 15.31
introduction, 15.30
negotiated agreements, 15.34
special negotiating body, 15.33
standard rules, 15.34
European Convention on Human Rights
effect, 28.2
introduction, 28.1
pre-HRA 1998, 28.5
rights, 28.7
European co-operative societies (SCEs)
alternative arrangements, 15.45
complaints, 15.46
confidential information, 15.47
disputes, 15.46
duty to provide information, 15.41
employment protection, 15.48
implementation in UK, 15.40
introduction, 15.39
negotiated agreements, 15.43
special negotiating body, 15.42
standard rules, 15.44

Index

European law
  agency workers, 22.13
  bankers' bonuses, 22.17consultation,22.12
  direct effect, 22.2
  disclosure of information, and, 9.10
  effect, 22.2
  employment law requirements, 22.3
  enforcement, 22.2
  equal access to benefits, 22.5
  equal pay
    generally, 22.6
    introduction, 21.3
  equal treatment, 22.6
  fixed-term workers, 22.16
  Francovich claims, 22.2
  free movement of labour, 22.4
  health and safety, and
    generally, 25.25
    introduction, 22.10
  information, 22.12
  insolvent employers, 22.7
  introduction, 22.1
  non-executive directors, 22.6
  posted workers, 22.14
  redundancy, 22.8
  sources of law, and, 1.7
  supremacy, 22.2
  terms of employment, 22.7
  transfer of undertakings, 22.9
  working time, 22.11
  works councils, 22.12
  written particulars of terms, 22.7
European Social Charter
  human rights, and, 28.8
European Works Councils
  amending Regulations, 15.29A
  confidential information, 15.28
  employment protection, 15.29
  establishment, 15.27
  European law, and, 22.12
  introduction, 15.22
  number of employees, 15.24
  requests, 15.25
  special negotiating body, 15.26
  time off work, and, 47.14
  unfair dismissal, and, 52.3
Excluded employment, employees in
  taxable benefits, 44.22
Exclusion and expulsion from trade union
  common law, 49.12
  introduction, 49.11
  remedy, 49.14
  statutory provisions, 49.13

Exclusions
  wrongful dismissal, and, 56.37
Exemplary damages
  discrimination compensation, and, 12.18
Expenses incurred in the performance of duties
  generally, 44.21
  relief, 44.28
Express terms
  contracts of employment, and, 7.14
  contract claims, 17.32
  discrimination complaints, 12.4
  effective date of termination, 17.23–17.24
  equal pay, 17.28
  generally, 17.22
  introduction, 18.21
  'just and equitable, 17.30
  'not reasonably practicable' to present in
    time, 17.25–17.26
  other claims, 17.33
  redundancy payments, 17.27
  unlawful deductions from wages, 17.31
  unlawful discrimination, 17.29
Expression, freedom of
  human rights, and, 28.7
Extensions of time
  appeals to EAT, and, 19.14
  applications to Employment Tribunal, and
    contract claims, 17.32
    discrimination complaints, 12.4
    effective date of termination, 17.23–17.24
    equal pay, 17.28
    generally, 17.22
    introduction, 18.21
    'just and equitable, 17.30
    'not reasonably practicable' to present in
      time, 17.25–17.26
    other claims, 17.33
    redundancy payments, 17.27
    response by respondent, and, 17.36
    unlawful deductions from wages, 17.31
    unlawful discrimination, 17.29
  discrimination complaints, and, 12.7
Failure to follow statutory disciplinary procedures
  unfair dismissal, and, 52.3
Failure to make payments
  trade union members, and, 49.6
Fair hearing, right to
  human rights, and, 28.7
Fairness of dismissal
  acceptable reasons for dismissal
    any other substantial reason, 52.14
    capability, 52.5–52.8
    contravention of any enactment, 52.13

Fairness of dismissal – *cont.*
  acceptable reasons for dismissal – *cont.*
    ill-health, 52.8
    introduction, 52.1
    misconduct, 52.9–52.10
    qualifications, 52.7
    redundancy, 52.11–52.12
    summary, 52.2
  deemed unfair dismissals, 52.3
  'in the circumstances', 52.4
  redundancy, and, 37.8
  transfer of undertakings, and, 50.26
Family and private life, right to
  human rights, and, 28.7
Family-related dismissal
  unfair dismissal, and, 52.3
Fee-paid holders of judicial office
  part-time workers, and, 30.5
Fees
  Employment Law Review, and, 24.6
Fidelity
  employee obligation, 8.19
  implied contract terms, and, 7.16
Fiduciary duty
  director, 8.19
Financial Conduct Authority (FCA)
  Listing Rule requirements, 8.10
Fines
  standard scale, 1.10
Fire precautions
  health and safety, and, 26.13
First aid
  health and safety, and, 26.14
Fixed-term contracts
  dismissal on expiry of
    generally, 51.6
    some other substantial reason, 52.14
  termination, and, 46.4
Fixed-term employees
  European law, 22.16
  less favourable treatment, and, 45.9
  unfair dismissal, and, 52.3
Flexible working
  ACAS, 2.5
  generally, 47.17
  unfair dismissal, and, 52.3
Forced resignation
  unfair dismissal, and, 51.8
Foreign employees
  applicable law
    contract and tort, 23.7
    generally, 23.6
  discrimination claims, 23.9

Foreign employees – *cont.*
  EEA nationals
    generally, 23.2
    posted workers, 23.3
  employment-related offences, 23.5–23.6
  Equality Act 2010, and, 23.9
  introduction, 23.1
  jurisdiction
    common law claims, 23.8
    statutory claims, 23.9
  non-EEA nationals, 23.4
  points-based system
    generally, 23.4
    introduction, 23.1
  posted workers, 23.3
  statutory claims, 23.9
  work permits, 23.4
Forfeiture
  service lettings, and, 41.5
Fostering-to-adopt system
  Children and Families Bill, 31.4A
Free movement of labour
  European law, and, 22.4
Freedom of association
  human rights, and, 28.4
Freedom to agree
  terms of contract, and, 7.12
Fresh evidence
  EAT procedure, and, 19.34
Frustration
  termination, and, 46.3
  unfair dismissal and, 51.10
Further information
  generally, 18.8
  questionnaires, 18.9
Future loss of earnings
  unfair dismissal, and, 53.12
'Garden leave'
  restraint of trade covenants, and, 39.14
  wrongful dismissal, and, 56.21
Gender equality duty
  enforcement, 11.38
  introduction, 11.1
Gender reassignment
  and see SEX DISCRIMINATION
  'because of the protected characteristic', 10.21
  comparators, 10.15
  equal pay, and
    generally, 21.13
    introduction, 21.2
  generally, 10.6
  genuine occupational requirement or
    qualification, 11.5

Index

Gender reassignment – *cont.*
less favourable treatment
'because of the protected
characteristic', 10.21
comparators, 10.15
generally, 10.14
positive discrimination, 10.16
protected characteristics, 10.6
General earnings
taxation, and, 44.2
'Genuine material factor' defence
direct discrimination, and, 21.12
generally, 21.11
**Genuine occupational requirement or
qualification**
age, 11.8
gender reassignment, 11.5
generally, 11.2
partnerships, 11.28
race, 11.4
religion or belief, 11.6
sex, 11.3
sexual orientation, 11.7
Gifted assets
taxable benefits, and, 44.21–44.22
Goods or services contracts
trade union members, and, 49.12
**Governance Code (UK Corporate
Governance Code)**
directors' service contracts, 8.15
remuneration, 8.28
Governing law
foreign employees, and
contract and tort, 23.7
generally, 23.6
Government proposals
collective redundancies, 24.7
compromise agreements, 24.5
early conciliation, 24.5
Employment Law Review
changes in force from April 2012, 24.3
generally, 24.1
historical background, 24.2
employment tribunal rules, 24.4
fees, 24.6
mediation, 24.5
other issues, 24.7
penalties, 24.6
protected conversations, 24.5
rapid resolution scheme, 24.7
TUPE, 24.7
whistleblowing, 24.7
Gratuities
national minimum wage, and, 32.9

Gratuities – *cont.*
pay, and, 32.21
Grievance procedures
Codes of Practice, and, 4.2
implied contract terms, and, 7.15
Grounds of appeal
EAT procedure, and, 19.16
Guaranteed debts
insolvency of employer, and, 29.5
Guarantee payments
amount, 32.27
exclusions, 32.26
insolvency of employer, and, 29.2
introduction, 32.23
qualifying period, 32.25
remedy for failure to make payment, 32.28
'workless days', 32.24
Guidance
part time workers, and, 30.2
working time, and, 55.26
Handbooks and policies
contracts of employment, and, 7.13
Harassment
barristers, 11.27
employment, in
generally, 10.50
grounds of marriage, civil partnership,
pregnancy or maternity, on, 10.51
employment agencies, 11.32
generally, 10.39
office holders, 11.25
partnerships, 11.28
trade organisations, 11.29
trustees of occupational pension schemes, 11.35
Hazardous substances
health and safety, and, 26.26
Health and safety
accident reporting, 26.1
alcohol misuse, 26.2
appeals against notices
cost of remedy required, 25.36
effect, 25.35
introduction, 25.34
bullying, 26.28
children, and
breaks, 3.6
introduction, 3.5
night work, 3.6
rest periods, 3.6
civil liability, 25.43
Codes of Practice, and
generally, 25.28
legal effect, 4.15
power to issue, 4.14

Health and safety – *cont.*
  common law duty
    competent fellow workers, 25.7
    independent contractors, 25.11
    introduction, 25.2
    protection from risk of injury, 25.8
    safe equipment and materials, 25.6
    safe means of access, 25.4
    safe place of work, 25.3
    safe system of work, 25.5
    vicarious liability for acts of employees, 25.9
    working under direction of third party, 25.10
  competent fellow workers, 25.7
  construction site management, 26.4
  contracts of employment, and, 7.16
  contributory negligence, 25.44
  coroner's inquests
    findings, 25.46
    generally, 25.47
    "interested persons", 25.48
    introduction, 25.45
  corporate killing, 25.42
  criminal proceedings
    corporate killing, 25.42
    defence, 25.41
    directors' liability, 25.38
    generally, 25.37
    order to remedy default, 25.39
    time for commencing proceedings, 25.40
  direction of third party, 25.10
  directors' liability, 25.38
  disclosure of information, and
    introduction, 9.7
    safety representatives, 9.8
  display screen equipment, 26.5
  drug misuse
    generally, 26.2
    testing, 26.3
  electricity, 26.6
  employees' duties, 25.22
  employer
    liability, 25.1
    obligations, 25.18
  employment protection
    breach of safety regulations, 26.11
    detriment, 26.8
    introduction, 26.7
    remedy, 26.10
    whistleblowing, 26.9
  enforcement
    appeals against notices, 25.34–25.36
    enforcing authorities, 25.29
    improvement notices, 25.31
    inspectors, 25.31

Health and safety – *cont.*
  enforcement – *cont.*
    prohibition notices, 25.32
    withdrawal of notices, 25.33
  enforcing authorities, 25.29
  Enterprise and Regulatory Reform Act 2013,
    direct fault, 25.1
  equipment and materials, 25.6
  equipment for work, 26.12
  European law, and
    generally, 25.25
    introduction, 22.10
  fire precautions, 26.13
  first aid, 26.14
  hazardous substances, 26.26
  Health and Safety Commission
    Codes of Practice, 25.28
    enforcement policy, 25.29
    establishment, 25.26
    information, 25.27
  Health and Safety Executive, 25.26
  hours of work, 26.15
  implied contract terms, and, 7.19
  improvement notices
    appeals, 25.34–25.36
    generally, 25.31
    withdrawal, 25.33
  independent contractors
    faulty work by, 25.15
    generally, 25.11
  inspectors' powers, 25.31
  insurance against liability, 26.16
  interference with safety measures, 25.23
  introduction, 25.1
  management, 26.17
  manual handling of loads, 26.18
  manufacturer's duties, 25.21
  means of access, 25.4
  miners' knee, 26.31
  noise levels, 26.19
  occupier's duties, 25.20
  occupiers' liability
    faulty work by independent contractor, 25.15
    introduction, 25.12
    'occupier', 25.13
    occupier's duty, 25.14
  prohibition notices
    appeals, 25.34–25.36
    generally, 25.32
    withdrawal, 25.33
  place of work, 25.3
  protection from risk of injury, 25.8
  religious belief, conflict, 28.7
  repetitive strain injury, 26.31

Index

Health and safety – *cont.*
reporting of accidents, 26.1
safe equipment and materials, 25.6
safe means of access, 25.4
safe place of work, 25.3
safe system of work, 25.5
safety measures
  charges for, 25.24
  interference with, 25.23
safety representatives
  Codes of Practice, and, 4.14–4.15
  disclosure of information, and, 9.8
  introduction, 26.20
  non-unionised workers, 26.22
  time off work, and, 47.8–47.9
  union-appointees, 26.21
safety signs, 26.30
self-employed persons, 25.19
smoking, 26.23
statutory provisions
  employees' duties, 25.22
  employer's obligations, 25.18
  health, safety and welfare, 25.17
  interference with safety measures, 25.23
  introduction, 25.16
  manufacturer's duties, 25.21
  occupier's duties, 25.20
  self-employed, 25.19
stress
  common law liability, 26.25
  generally, 26.24
substances hazardous to health, 26.26
system of work, 25.5
time off work for safety representatives, and
  Codes of Practice, and, 4.14–4.15
  generally, 47.8
  remedies, 47.9
unfair dismissal
  breach of safety regulations, 26.11
  detriment, 26.8
  generally, 52.3
  introduction, 26.7
  remedy, 26.10
vibration, 26.27
vicarious liability for acts of employees, 25.9
violence, 26.28
volunteers, 25.7
whistleblowing, 26.9
working under direction of third party, 25.10
workplace standards
  generally, 26.29
  safety signs, 26.30
work-related upper limb disorders, 26.31

Health and Safety Commission
Codes of Practice
  introduction, 25.28
  legal effect, 4.15
  power to issue, 4.14
enforcement policy, 25.29
establishment, 25.26
information, 25.27
Health and Safety Executive
generally, 25.26
Health and safety representatives
disclosure of information, and, 9.8
introduction, 26.20
non-unionised workers, 26.22
time off work, and
  generally, 47.8
  remedies, 47.9
union-appointees, 26.21
Health assessment
night work, and, 55.12
Hearing
adjournment application, 18.54
bias, 18.50
conduct, 18.52
conflict of interest, 18.50
control of procedure, 18.56
EAT procedure, and, 19.32
generally, 18.49
non-attendance of parties, 18.54
order of evidence, 18.53
other procedural points, 18.58–18.61
private hearing, 18.51
representation, 18.55
witnesses, 18.57
Hearings on liability and quantum
wrongful dismissal, and, 56.41
Holidays
agricultural workers, 27.7
additional annual leave, 27.3A
annual leave
  illness, 27.3A
  part-time workers, 30.10
  payment, 27.4
  working time, 55.19
civil aviation workers, 27.8
contractual entitlement, 27.9
entitlement
  Community social law principle, 27.3A
  illness, 27.3A
  opportunity to take, 27.3A
  sabbatical, 27.3B
  unpaid leave, 27.3Bgenerally,27.2
illness, and
  annual leave, 27.3A

Holidays – *cont.*
illness, and – *cont.*
generally, 27.3
insolvency of employer, and
generally, 29.2
payments from National Insurance
Fund, 29.5
introduction, 27.1
notice requirements, 27.5
part-time workers, and, 30.10
payment
calculating a week's pay, 27.4
generally, 27.4
termination of employment, on, 27.4A
period of leave, 27.3
remedies, 27.6
sick leave, and, 27.3
statutory entitlement, 27.2
termination of employment, 27.4A
timing, 27.5
'workers', 27.2
Working Time Regulations, and, 27.2, 55.19
wrongful dismissal, and, 56.28
Home workers
national minimum wage, and, 32.10
Hours of work
agricultural workers, 27.7
contract, under, 27.9
health and safety, and, 26.15
introduction, 27.2
notice requirements, 27.5
payment, 27.4
period of leave, 27.3
remedies, 27.6
Human rights
European Convention
effect, 28.2
implementation in UK, 28.6
introduction, 28.1
pre-HRA 1998, 28.5
rights, 28.7
European Social Charter, 28.8
freedom of association, 28.4
freedom of expression, 28.8
freedom of thought, conscience and
religion, 28.7
health and safety
religious belief conflict, 28.7
Human Rights Act 1998
application, 28.7
generally, 28.6
introduction, 28.1
petition by individual, 28.3
political affiliation, 28.4

Human rights – *cont.*
pre-Convention position, 28.5
right to fair hearing, 28.7
right to respect for private and family life
application in employment, 28.7
generally, 28.4
whistleblowing, 28.4
ICE Regulations 2004
application, 15.6
background, 15.4
complaints, 15.20
confidential information, 15.19
co-operation, 15.14
election or appointment of representatives, 15.13
employee data requests, 15.7
employment protection, 15.21
initiation of obligations
employee requests, 15.10
employer, by, 15.9
general considerations, 15.11
introduction, 15.8
introduction, 15.4–15.5
negotiated agreements, 15.12
overview, 9.10
pre-existing agreements, 15.17–15.18
standard information and consultation
provisions, 15.15–15.16
transfer of undertakings, and, 50.22
'undertakings', 15.6
Illegal contracts
discrimination, and, 11.19
unfair dismissal, and, 51.16
wrongful dismissal, and, 56.35
Ill-health dismissals
generally, 52.8
introduction, 52.5
retirement, and, 40.6
summary, 52.2
Illness
holidays, and, 27.3
carry-over period, 27.6
termination of employment, 27.4A
Immunity from liability for strike action
background, 43.1
'in contemplation or furtherance', 43.5
introduction, 43.3
'trade dispute', 43.4
Implied terms
contracts of employment, and, 7.14–7.15
Imprisonment
unfair dismissal, and, 52.14
Improvement notices
appeals
cost of remedy required, 25.36

Index

Improvement notices – *cont.*
appeals – *cont.*
effect, 25.35
introduction, 25.34
generally, 25.31
withdrawal, 25.33
Incentive plans
generally, 44.31
Indemnity
directors' duties, and, 8.25
Independence of trade unions
factors, 48.23
introduction, 48.22
withdrawal of certificate, 48.24
Independent contractors
health and safety, and
faulty work by, 25.15
generally, 25.11
Indirect discrimination
application of the test, 10.34
compensation, 12.14
discriminatory measure, 10.34
disparity of effect, 10.34
generally, 10.34
equal pay, and, 21.10
pool, selection of 21.11
provision, criterion or practice
(PCP) 21.11generally,10.34
legitimate aim, 11.9
personal disadvantage, 10.34
sex discrimination, and, 10.35
sexual orientation discrimination, and, 10.36
Inducement of breach of contract
strike action, and, 43.2
Industrial action
armed forces, 43.20
ballots before action
Codes of Practice, and, 4.4–4.5
generally, 43.14
members' right, 43.17
calls for action, 43.15
Codes of Practice, and
legal effect, 4.5
power to issue, 4.4
common law liability, 43.2
consequences for employers, 43.19
criminal liability, 43.12
deductions from wages, and, 32.6
employer's rights and remedies, 43.16
immunity from liability for
background, 43.1
'in contemplation or furtherance', 43.5
introduction, 43.3
'trade dispute', 43.4

Industrial action – *cont.*
liability for
background, 43.1
common law, at, 43.2
statutory immunity, 43.3–43.5
trade unions, 43.13–43.15
picketing
case law, 43.10
Code of Practice, 4.4–4.5, 43.11
generally, 43.9
police officers, 43.20
pressure to impose union membership or
recognition, 43.7
prohibited employees, 43.20
remedies
employers, 43.16
third parties', 43.18
restricted employees, 43.20
restrictions, 7.29
secondary action, limits on
dismissal of unofficial strikers, 43.8
generally, 43.6
pressure to impose membership or
recognition, 43.7
third parties' rights and remedies, 43.18
time off work for trade union officials, and, 47.2
trade union, liability of
ballots before action, 43.14
calls for action, 43.15
generally, 43.13
introduction, 49.9
unfair dismissal, and
introduction, 52.3
official action, 51.17
unofficial action, 51.18
Industrial Relations Act 1971
Codes of Practice, and, 4.2
Industrial Relations Code of Practice
generally, 4.2
Industrial training boards
education and training, and, 13.4
Information and con sultation
see also INFORMATION DISCLOSURE
European law, and, 22.12
transfer of undertakings, and
advance notification, 50.23
employee liability information, 50.22
**Information and Consultation Regulations
2004**
and see EMPLOYEE PARTICIPATION
application, 15.6
background, 15.4
complaints, 15.20
confidential information, 15.19

Information and Consultation Regulations 2004 – *cont.*
co-operation, 15.14
election or appointment of representatives, 15.13
employee data requests, 15.7
employment protection, 15.21
initiation of obligations
employee requests, 15.10
employer, by, 15.9
general considerations, 15.11
introduction, 15.8
introduction, 15.4–15.5
negotiated agreements, 15.12
overview, 9.10
pre-existing agreements, 15.17–15.18
standard information and consultation
provisions, 15.15–15.16
'undertakings', 15.6
transfer of undertakings, and, 50.22

Information Commissioner
archived sources, 4.16
Codes of Practice, and, 4.16
personal devices 4.16
subject access requests, 4.16

Information disclosure
collective bargaining, for
Code of Practice, 9.4
exceptions to duty, 9.3
failure to comply with request, 9.5
general duty, 9.3
introduction, 9.2
confidential information, and, 9.15
data protection, and
background, 9.12
overview, 9.13
employees, by
generally, 9.16
protected disclosures, 9.17
economic situation of undertaking, 9.10
employment prospects, 9.10
health and safety, for
introduction, 9.7
safety representatives, 9.8
introduction, 9.1
medical reports, and, 9.14
occupational pension schemes, by, 9.9
participation in company affairs, 9.10
public interest, in
generally, 9.16
protected disclosures, 9.17
transfer of undertakings, and
advance notification, 50.23
employee liability information, 50.22
introduction, 9.6

Information disclosure – *cont.*
whistleblowing, and
generally, 9.16
protected disclosures, 9.17

Injunctions
breach of contracts of employment, and
employee's remedies, 7.42–7.43
employer's remedies, 7.47c
discrimination, and
advertisements, 12.30
instructions to discriminate, 12.30
persistent discrimination, 12.29
pressure to discriminate, 12.30
restraint of trade covenants, and, 39.17
wrongful dismissal, and, 56.23

Injury to feelings
discrimination compensation, and, 12.16

Inquests
findings, 25.46
generally, 25.47
"interested persons", 25.48
introduction, 25.45

Inspection
directors' service contracts, and, 8.8

Inquiries
ACAS, and, 2.10

Insolvency of employer
administrative receivers' liability, 29.11
European law, 22.15
introduction, 29.1
other consequences, 29.10
payments from National Insurance Fund
adoption pay, 29.8
apprentices' fees, 29.5
arrears of pay, 29.5
guaranteed debts, 29.5
holiday pay, 29.5
introduction, 29.3
maternity pay, 29.8
notice pay, 29.5
paternity pay, 29.8
redundancy payments, 29.4
remedy for non-payment, 29.6
sick pay, 29.8
unfair dismissal compensation, 29.5
unpaid pension contributions, 29.7
pensions, and
Pensions Act 2004, 29.9
unpaid contributions, 29.7
preferential debts, 29.2
transfer of undertakings, and
generally, 50.11
introduction, 29.10
wrongful dismissal, and, 56.9

Index

Inspectors' powers
health and safety, and, 25.31
Instructions to discriminate
enforcement only by Commissions, 11.38
generally, 10.53
injunctions, 12.30
Insurance against liability
health and safety, and, 26.17
Insurance cover
wrongful dismissal, and, 56.28
Intangible loss
wrongful dismissal, and, 56.29
Interest
discrimination, and, 12.20
generally, 18.67
wrongful dismissal, and, 56.31
Interest-free loans
taxable benefits, and, 44.21
Interests of the parties
restraint of trade covenants, and, 39.4
Interim payments
wrongful dismissal, and, 56.41
Interim hearings
case management, and, 18.6
Interim relief
unfair dismissal, and, 53.18
Internal appeals
unfair dismissal, and, 52.15
Interviews
engagement of employees, and, 20.2–20.4
Intimidation
strike action, and, 43.1
Invalidity of contract
wrongful dismissal, and, 56.36
Itemised pay statements
application to tribunal
generally, 32.19
order, 32.20
attachment of earnings, and, 33.9
exclusions, 32.18
fixed deductions, 32.17
generally, 32.16
Joinder of parties
tribunal procedure, and, 18.23
unfair dismissal, and, 53.17
Joining after 6 April
pay as you earn, and, 44.7
Judgments
adequacy of reasons, 18.63
corrections and changes, 18.64
generally, 18.62
register, 18.65
Judicial office holders
part-time workers, and, 30.5

Judicial review
public sector employees, and, 35.6
Jurisdiction of tribunals
breach of contracts of employment, 7.44
EU law, over, 17.12
foreign employees, and
common law claims, 23.8
statutory claims, 23.9
generally, 17.11
Human Rights Act, under, 17.13
Jury service
unfair dismissal, and, 52.3
Just and equitable
time limits for claims, and, 17.30
Justices of the Peace
time off work, and, 47.4
Justification
discrimination, and, 11.9
Lay-off
redundancy payments, and
counter-notice, 36.9
generally, 36.8
Learndirect
education and training, and, 13.8
Learning and Skills Council
education and training, and, 13.10
Legal capacity
trade unions, and, 48.2
Legal representation
tribunal procedure, and, 18.55
Legitimate aim
discrimination, and, 11.9
Less favourable treatment
comparators, 10.15
discrimination, and
comparators, 10.15
generally, 10.14
positive discrimination, 10.16
fixed-term employees, and, 45.9
part time workers, and,
introduction, 30.7
overtime, 30.9
paid annual leave, 30.10
pro rata principle, 30.8
written statement of reasons, and, 30.23
positive discrimination, 10.16
Licence
service lettings, and, 41.4
Life assurance cover to retired workers
age discrimination, and, 11.15
Like work
equal pay, and, 21.6
Limitation periods
and see TIME LIMITS ON CLAIMS

Limitation periods – *cont.*
  wrongful dismissal, and, 56.40
'Liquidated damages' clauses
  wrongful dismissal, and, 56.26
Listing
  trade unions, and, 48.21
Listing arrangements
  tribunal procedure, and, 18.39–18.48
Listing Rules requirements
  directors remuneration, 8.34
  service contracts, 8.10
  termination of office, 8.39
Living accommodation
  and see SERVICE LETTINGS
  taxable benefits, and, 44.21–44.23
Loans
  taxable benefits, and, 44.21–44.22
Local authority members
  discrimination, 11.35A
Local authority powers
  children, and, 3.3
  litigation, and, 35.7
Local enterprise companies
  education and training, and, 13.8
Local government employees
  EU law, 35.8
  generally, 35.5
  introduction, 35.1
  judicial review as to rights, 35.6
  national security, 35.7
  public interest immunity, 35.7
Lock-outs
  and see STRIKES
  unfair dismissal, and
    official action, 51.17
    unofficial action, 51.18
Look for work, time off to
  generally, 47.6
  remedies, 47.7
Loss of benefits
  unfair dismissal, and, 53.12
Loss of earnings
  unfair dismissal, and, 53.12
Loss of pension rights
  unfair dismissal, and, 53.12
"Lower-paid" employees
  generally, 44.3
  taxable benefits, 44.22
Managed service companies
  taxation, and, 44.35
Manual handling of loads
  health and safety, and, 26.18
Marital status
  and see DISCRIMINATION

Marital status – *cont.*
  'because of the protected characteristic', 10.19
  direct discrimination, 10.13
  discrimination in employment
    advertisements, 10.43
    dismissal, 10.49
    'employment', 10.41
    engagement, 10.44
    introduction, 10.40
    opportunities, 10.47
    post-employment behaviour, 10.52
    subjection to other detriment, 10.51
    territorial jurisdiction, 10.42
  generally 10.332
  harassment, 10.39
  indirect discrimination, 10.34
  legal sources, 10.4
  protected characteristics, 10.4
  sexual orientation, and, 11.14
'Material factor' defence
  direct discrimination, and, 21.12
  generally, 21.11
Maternity allowance
  generally, 31.45
Maternity leave
  additional leave
    generally, 31.28–31.33
    redundancy, and, 31.34
  'because of the protected characteristic', 10.24
  compulsory leave, 31.27
  discrimination, and,
    and see DISCRIMINATION
    'because of', 10.24
    comparators, 10.15
    generally 10.332
    harassment, 10.39
  dismissal of replacement, 31.35
  equal pay, and, 21.4
  introduction, 31.20
  legal sources, 10.9
  ordinary leave
    generally, 31.21–31.26
    redundancy, and, 31.34
  protected characteristics, 10.9
  redundancy, and, 31.34
  statement of reasons for dismissal, 31.36
  time off work, and, 47.17
  unfair dismissal, and, 52.3
  working during, 31.37
Maternity pay
  amount, 31.42
  claim procedure, 31.40
  'confinement', 31.39
  insolvency of employer, and, 29.8

Index

Maternity pay – *cont.*
introduction, 31.38
payments from National Insurance Fund,
    and, 29.8
period of entitlement, 31.41
qualifying requirements, 31.39
recoupment by employer, 31.44
remedy for non-payment, 31.43
sick pay, and, 42.4
Maternity rights
additional maternity leave, 31.28–31.33
agency workers
    ante-natal care, 31.10
    suspension on maternity grounds, 31.14
ante-natal care, time off for
    introduction, 31.6
    qualifying requirements, 31.7
    remedies for refusal, 31.9
    right to remuneration, 31.8
compulsory maternity leave, 31.27
Equality Act 2010, and, 31.5
equal pay
    generally, 21.14
    suspension, 21.4
insolvency of employer, and, 29.2
introduction, 31.1–31.4
keeping in touch days 31.37
    payment for work, 31.37
leave
    additional leave, 31.28–31.33
    compulsory leave, 31.27
    dismissal of replacement, 31.35
    introduction, 31.20
    ordinary leave, 31.21–31.26
    working during, 31.37
maternity allowance, 31.45
ordinary maternity leave
    generally, 31.21–31.26
    redundancy, and, 31.34
pregnancy, detriment by reason of
    introduction, 31.18
    remedies, 31.19
pregnancy reasons, dismissal for
    generally, 31.16
    qualifying period, 31.17
    statement of reasons, 31.36
statement of reasons for dismissal, 31.36
statutory maternity pay
    amount, 31.42
    claim procedure, 31.40
    'confinement', 31.39
    insolvency of employer, and, 29.8
    introduction, 31.38
    period of entitlement, 31.41

Maternity rights – *cont.*
statutory maternity pay – *cont.*
    qualifying requirements, 31.39
    recoupment by employer, 31.44
    remedy for non-payment, 31.43
suspension on maternity grounds
    allowances, 31.15
    ante-natal care, 31.14
    alternative work, 31.19
    introduction, 31.11
    remuneration, 31.13
time off for ante-natal care
    introduction, 31.6
    qualifying requirements, 31.7
    remedies for refusal, 31.9
    right to remuneration, 31.8
unfair dismissal, and, 52.3
working during leave, 31.37
    payment, 31.37
Maximum weekly time
working time, and, 55.6
Meals in canteen
tax-free benefits, and, 44.23
Means of access
health and safety, and, 25.4
Mediation
Employment Law Review, and, 24.5
Medical insurance premiums
taxable benefits, and, 44.21
Medical reports
disclosure of information, and, 9.14
Medical suspension, pay during
amount, 32.32
equal pay, and, 21.4
exclusions, 32.31
generally, 32.29
insolvency of employer, and, 29.2
qualifying conditions, 32.30
remedy for failure to make payment, 32.33
Medical treatment
taxable benefits, and, 44.21
Merchant seamen
working time, and, 55.31–55.32
Mergers
and see **CROSS BORDER MERGERS**
restraint of trade, and, 39.1
Method of payment
generally, 32.3
Migrant workers
applicable law
    contract and tort, 23.7
    generally, 23.6
EEA nationals
    generally, 23.2

Migrant workers – *cont.*
  EEA nationals – *cont.*
    posted workers, 23.3
  employment-related offences, 23.5–23.6
  introduction, 23.1
  jurisdiction
    common law claims, 23.8
    statutory claims, 23.9
  non-EEA nationals, 23.4
  points-based system
    generally, 23.4
    introduction, 23.1
  posted workers, 23.3
  statutory claims, 23.9
  work permits, 23.4
Mileage allowances
  taxable benefits, and, 44.21
Military service
  reinstatement after, 47.18–47.19
Miners' knee
  health and safety, and, 26.31
Minimum wage
  age discrimination, and, 11.15
  agency workers
    generally, 45.6
    introduction, 32.10
  coverage, 32.10
  introduction, 32.9
  records, 32.11
  relevant workers, 32.10
  remedies for failure to pay, 32.12–32.13
  statements, 32.11
  unfair dismissal, and, 52.3
Ministers of religion
  employees and office holders, 14.8
  sex discrimination, and, 11.11
Minors, employment of
  breaks, 3.6
  contracts of employment, 3.11
  definitions, 3.1
  health and safety
    breaks, 3.6
    introduction, 3.5
    night work, 3.6
    rest periods, 3.6
  local authority powers, 3.3
  night work, 3.6
  rest periods, 3.6
  restrictions
    generally, 3.2
    local authority powers, 3.3
    other provisions, 3.4
  time off for study or training
    introduction, 3.8

Minors, employment of – *cont.*
  time off for study or training – *cont.*
    remedy for refusal, 3.9
    right not to suffer detriment, 3.10
    work experience, 3.7
  working time, and, 55.3
Misconduct dismissals
  generally, 52.9
  procedure, 52.10
  redundancy payments, and, 36.10
  summary, 52.2
Mitigation
  wrongful dismissal, and, 56.30
Mitigation of loss
  unfair dismissal, and, 53.13
Mobile workers
  working time, and, 55.34–55.36
Money purchase pension schemes
  generally, 40.9
Money's worth
  taxation, and, 44.2
Monotonous work
  working time, and, 55.18
Multiple claims
  tribunal procedure, and, 18.24
Mutual agreement
  termination, and, 46.2
Mutual trust and confidence
  implied contract terms, and, 7.15
National Health Service
  continuous employment, and, 6.9
National insurance contributions
  pay as you earn, and, 44.17
National Insurance Fund, payments from
  adoption pay, 29.8
  apprentices' fees, 29.5
  arrears of pay, 29.5
  guaranteed debts, 29.5
  holiday pay, 29.5
  introduction, 29.3
  maternity pay, 29.8
  notice pay, 29.5
  paternity pay, 29.8
  redundancy payments, 29.4
  remedy for non-payment, 29.6
  sick pay, 29.8
  unfair dismissal compensation, 29.5
  unpaid pension contributions, 29.7
National minimum wage
  age discrimination, and, 11.15
  agency workers
    generally, 45.6
    introduction, 32.10
  coverage, 32.10

Index

National minimum wage – *cont.*
introduction, 32.9
records, 32.11
relevant workers, 32.10
remedies for failure to pay, 32.12–32.13
statements, 32.11
unfair dismissal, and, 52.3
National security
discrimination, and, 11.22
public sector employees, and, 35.7
Nationality
and see **RACE** DISCRIMINATION
generally, 10.34
Necessary economies
unfair dismissal, and, 52.14
New Deal
education and training, and, 13.6
Night work
children, and, 3.6
duration, 55.10
health assessments, 55.12
introduction, 55.9
special hazards, 55.11
transfer to day work, 55.13
'No employment' periods
continuous employment, and, 6.7
'No strike' clauses
collective agreements, and, 5.13
Noise levels
health and safety, and, 26.19
Non-attendance of parties
tribunal procedure, and, 18.54
Non-cash vouchers
taxable benefits, and, 44.21–44.22
Non-competition covenants
restraint of trade, and, 39.1
Non-contractual bonus
meaning of 'wages', and, 32.6
Non-dealing covenants
restraint of trade, and, 39.1
Non-discrimination notices
See UNLAWFUL ACT NOTICES
Non-EEA nationals
foreign workers, and, 23.4
Non-executive directors
gender balance, 22.6
Non-membership of union
unfair dismissal, and, 52.3
Non-solicitation covenants
restraint of trade, and, 39.1
'Normal retiring age'
retirement, and, 40.2
'Not reasonably practicable'
time limits for claims, and, 17.25–17.26

Notes of evidence
EAT procedure, and, 19.21
Notice, termination by
contractual notice period, 46.6
employee, by, 46.17
introduction, 46.5
pay in lieu of notice
generally, 46.9
gross or net, 46.11
taxation, 46.10
payments from National Insurance Fund,
and, 29.5
rights during notice period, 46.12
statutory minimum notice
exceptions, 46.8
generally, 46.7
Notice to quit
service lettings, and, 41.5
Notification requirements
redundancy, and, 37.7
Notification of terms and conditions
engagement of employees, and, 20.5
Nurseries
tax-free benefits, and, 44.23
Obedience
implied contract terms, and, 7.17
Occupational pension scheme trustees
discrimination, and, 11.35
introduction, 40.15
time off work, and
generally, 47.10
remedies, 47.11
unfair dismissal, and, 52.3
Occupational pension schemes
see also **PENSIONS**
disclosure of information, and, 9.9
discrimination, and, 11.35, 40.12
employee trustees
generally, 40.15
time off work, 47.10–47.11
generally, 40.9
part-time workers, and
generally, 21.18
less favourable treatment, 30.11
retirement, and, 40.1
Occupiers' liability
faulty work by independent contractor, 25.15
introduction, 25.12
'occupier', 25.13
occupier's duty, 25.14
Occurrence of external event
unfair dismissal, and, 51.10
Offers of employment
advertising, 20.1

Index

Offers of employment – *cont.*
agencies, and, 20.6
data protection, 20.7
discrimination, and
generally, 10.44
race discrimination, 10.45
sex discrimination, 10.46
employment agencies, 20.6
interview, 20.2–20.4
notification of terms and conditions, 20.5
race discrimination, 10.45
selection, 20.2–20.4
sex discrimination, 10.46
withdrawal of offers, 20.8
Office-holders
directors, and, 8.1
discrimination, and, 11.25
equal pay, and, 21.4
generally, 14.4
Offsetting sick pay
contributory pension schemes, 42.11
contributory sickness schemes, 42.10
introduction, 42.9
Offshore workers
national minimum wage, and, 32.10
Online services
pay as you earn, and
generally, 44.19
penalties, 44.19a
real time information, 44.19c
security, 44.19b
Opportunities in employment
discrimination, and, 10.47
Opt-out agreements
working time, and, 55.7
Order of evidence
tribunal procedure, and, 18.53
Ordinary maternity leave
generally, 31.21–31.26
redundancy, and, 31.34
Ordinary paternity leave
benefits during, 31.55
entitlement, 31.53
generally, 31.54
Overpayment
deductions from wages, and, 32.6
pay, and, 32.15
Overriding objective
case management, 18.1
generally, 17.14
Overtime
part-time workers, and, 30.9
'week's pay', and, 32.36

P9D
pay as you earn, and, 44.16
P11D
pay as you earn, and, 44.16
"P11D" employees
generally, 44.3
P11D(b)
pay as you earn, and, 44.16
Parental leave
Children and Families Bill, 31.4A
generally, 31.46–31.51
paternity leave
additional leave, 31.56–31.58
adopted children, and, 31.59
generally, 31.52
ordinary leave, 31.53–31.55
payments from National Insurance Fund,
and, 29.8
protection against detriment, 31.60
statutory pay, 31.61
time off work, and, 47.17
unfair dismissal, and, 52.3
Parking facilities
tax-free benefits, and, 44.23
Part time workers
annual leave, 30.10
applications to Employment Tribunal,
introduction, 30.26
remedies, 30.28
time limits, 30.27
armed forces personnel, 30.4
casual workers, 30.4
comparators,
actual comparator, 30.13
circumstances where comparator not
required, 30.19
'comparable full time worker', 30.15–30.18
'full time worker', 30.14
introduction, 30.12
'part time worker', 30.14
'same or broadly similar work', 30.17
'same type of contract', 30.16
scope of comparison, 30.18
continuous employment, and, 6.8
contracting out, 30.29
detriment, 30.24
direct effect, 30.2
discrimination,
comparators, 30.12–30.19
less favourable treatment, 30.7–30.11
objective justification, 30.21
'on the ground that the worker is a part-time
worker', 30.20
employers' liability, 30.30

Index

Part time workers – *cont.*
equal pay, and
introduction, 21.2
pensions, 21.18
fee-paid holders of judicial office, 30.5
'full time worker', 30.14
generally, 45.1
guidance, 30.2
introduction, 30.1
judicial office holders, 30.5
legal sources, 30.1
less favourable treatment,
introduction, 30.7
occupational pension, 30.11
overtime, 30.9
paid annual leave, 30.10
pro rata principle, 30.8
written statement of reasons, and, 30.23
objective justification, 30.21
'on the ground that the worker is a part-time
worker', 30.20
overtime, 30.9
'part time worker', 30.14
pensions, and
generally, 21.18
less favourable treatment, 30.11
qualifying period, 30.6
relevant persons
armed forces personnel, 30.4
casual workers, 30.4
fee-paid holders of judicial office, 30.5
service personnel, 30.4
workers, 30.3
remedies, 30.28
'same or broadly similar work', 30.17
'same type of contract', 30.16
service personnel, 30.4
time limits for applications, 30.27
unfair dismissal, and,
generally, 30.25
introduction, 52.3
victimisation, 30.26
workers, 30.3
written statement of reasons, 30.23
Partnership at Work Fund
employee participation, 15.64
Partnerships
discrimination, and, 11.28
partners, employment status, 11.3
Past criminal convictions
access to records, 16.7
Disclosure and Barring Service (DBS), 16.9
effect of provisions, 16.5
recording, 16.10

Past criminal convictions – *cont.*
rehabilitation periods, 16.6
removal from certificate, 16.7
spent convictions
dismissal, and, 16.3
exceptions, 16.4
introduction, 16.1
non-disclosure, 16.2
vulnerable groups, and, 16.8
Paternity leave
additional leave
benefits during, 31.58
entitlement, 31.56
generally, 31.57
adopted children, and, 31.59
Children and Families Bill, 31.4A
generally, 31.52
ordinary leave
benefits during, 31.55
entitlement, 31.53
generally, 31.54
payments from National Insurance Fund,
and, 29.8
protection against detriment, 31.60
statutory pay, 31.61
time off work, and, 47.17
unfair dismissal, and, 52.3
Pay
and see **EQUAL PAY**
attachment of earnings, and
attachable earnings, 33.2
child support maintenance, 33.11
Council Tax, 33.10
deductions, 33.3–33.6
employer's obligations, 33.7
introduction, 33.1
other issues, 33.9
penalties for non-compliance, 33.8
deductions from wages
generally, 32.6
introduction, 32.2
minimum wage, and, 32.9–32.13
other, 32.14
remedies for breach, 32.8
retail employment, 32.7
discrimination, and, 11.11
fixed deductions, 32.17
generally, 32.3
gratuities, 32.21
guarantee payments
amount, 32.27
exclusions, 32.26
introduction, 32.23
qualifying period, 32.25

Pay – *cont.*
guarantee payments – *cont.*
remedy for failure to make payment, 32.28
'workless days', 32.24
holidays, and, 27.4
implied contract terms, and, 7.15
introduction, 32.1
itemised statements
application to tribunal, 32.19–32.20
exclusions, 32.18
fixed deductions, 32.17
generally, 32.16
medical suspension, and
amount, 32.32
exclusions, 32.31
generally, 32.29
qualifying conditions, 32.30
remedy for failure to make payment, 32.33
method of payment, 32.3
national minimum wage
coverage, 32.10
introduction, 32.9
records, 32.11
relevant workers, 32.10
remedies for failure to pay, 32.12–32.13
statements, 32.11
normal working hours, 32.35
overpayment, 32.15
overtime, 32.36
pre-1987 position
exceptions, 32.5
generally, 32.4
records, 32.11
statement of fixed deductions, 32.17
termination of employment, and, 32.22
troncs, 32.21
'week's pay'
amount, 32.39
calculation date, 32.38
introduction, 32.34
no normal working hours, 32.37
normal working hours, 32.35
overtime, 32.36
'worker', 32.6
workless days, and, 32.23
Pay as you earn (PAYE)
death of employee, 44.10
definition, 44.4
dismissal, 44.8
earnings limits, 44.4
end of year procedure
certificates, 44.15
Class 1A NICs, 44.17
P9D, 44.16

Pay as you earn (PAYE) – *cont.*
end of year procedure – *cont.*
P11D, 44.16
P11D(b), 44.16
real time information (RTI), 44.19
returns, 44.15
joining after 6 April, 44.7
method of deduction, 44.6
online services
generally, 44.19
penalties, 44.19a
real time information (RTI), 44.19c
registration, 44.19
security, 44.19b
payment by employer, 44.14
penalties for late payment, 44.14a
real time information (RTI),
Full Payment Submission (FPS), 44.19c
requirement, 44.4
refunds, 44.13
retirement, 44.9
security, 44.19b
settlement agreements, 44.18
sources of information, 44.5
students during vacation, 44.11
working abroad, 44.12
Pay in lieu of notice
generally, 46.9
gross or net, 46.11
taxation, 44.8, 46.10
wrongful dismissal, and, 56.21
Payments into court
wrongful dismissal, and, 56.41
Payroll giving scheme
taxation, and, 44.33
Pecuniary loss
discrimination compensation, and, 12.15
Penalties
Employment Law Review, and, 24.6
Enterprise and Regulatory Reform Act
2013, 21.19D
late payment, for
pay as you earn, 44.14a
non-compliance, for
attachment of earnings, 33.8
Pension contributions
age discrimination, and, 11.15
insolvency of employer, and, 29.7
tax-free benefits, and, 44.23
Pension enrolment
unfair dismissal, and, 52.3
Pension Protection Fund (PPF)
generally, 29.9

Index

Pension rights
unfair dismissal, and, 53.12
Pension scheme trustees
discrimination, and, 11.35
introduction, 40.15
time off work, and
generally, 47.10
remedies, 47.11
unfair dismissal, and, 52.3
Pensions and pension benefits
age discrimination, 40.14
exceptions, 11.15, 11.35
automatic enrolment, 40.11
claims and disputes, 40.17
directors, and, 8.35
discrimination, and,
age discrimination, 40.14
introduction, 11.35
occupational pension schemes, 40.12
sex discrimination, 40.13
employee trustees
generally, 40.15
time off work, 47.10–47.11
employers' duties, 40.16
equal pay, and
Barber claims, 21.17
introduction, 21.15
part-time workers, 21.18
statutory regime prior to EA 2010, 21.16
generally, 40.9
insolvency, and, 29.9
unpaid contributions, 29.7
introduction, 40.7
part-time workers, and
generally, 21.18
less favourable treatment, 30.11
sex discrimination, 40.13
single-tier, 40.9
stakeholder pensions, 40.10
unfair dismissal, and, 53.12
wrongful dismissal, and, 56.28
Pensions Regulator
generally, 29.9
Perceived discrimination
generally, 10.28
Performance of duties
implied contract terms, and, 7.18
Permanent health benefits
effect
calculation of damages, on, 42.14
termination of employment contract,
on, 42.13
generally, 42.12
'unable to follow any occupation', 42.15

Permits for foreign workers
generally, 23.4
Personal disadvantage
discrimination, and, 10.34
Personal injury
discrimination compensation, and, 12.17
Perverse decision
generally, 19.35
inadequacy of reasons, 19.36
procedural failures, 19.37
Petition by individual
human rights, and, 28.3
Philosophical belief
and see **RELIGIOUS** AND BELIEF DIS-
CRIMINATION
meaning, 10.22
Picketing
case law, 43.10
Codes of Practice, and
generally, 43.11
legal effect, 4.5
power to issue, 4.4
generally, 43.9
Place of work
health and safety, and, 25.3
Points-based system
generally, 23.4
introduction, 23.1
Police officers
discrimination, and, 11.26
EU law, 35.8
generally, 35.4
introduction, 35.1
judicial review as to rights, 35.6
national security, 35.7
office holders, 11.26
public interest immunity, 35.7
sex discrimination, and, 11.11
strikes, and, 43.20
working time, and, 55.3
Political levy
trade unions, and, 48.15
Political party
association, 11.30
unfair dismissal, 28.4
victimisation, 11.30
Positive action
access to training, 11.10
childbirth, 11.10
EU law, under, 11.10
generally, 11.10
introduction, 10.16
membership of trade organisation, 11.10
pregnancy, 11.10

Positive action – *cont.*
Sikhs on construction sites, 11.13
Posted workers
equal pay, and, 21.4
European law, and, 22.14
foreign workers, and, 23.3
Postponement of start of employment
continuous employment, and, 6.11
Pre-entry closed shop
trade union members, and, 49.4
Preferential debts
insolvency of employer, and, 29.2
Pregnancy
ante-natal appointments, 31.4A
'because of the protected characteristic', 10.24
detriment by reason of
introduction, 31.18
remedies, 31.19
discrimination, and
and see **DISCRIMINATION**
'because of', 10.24
comparators, 10.15
generally 10.332
harassment, 10.39
positive discrimination, 11.10
dismissal for reasons of
generally, 31.16
qualifying period, 31.17
equal pay, and, 21.4
legal sources, 10.9
protected characteristics, 10.9
sick pay, and, 42.4
unfair dismissal, and, 52.3
written statement of reasons for dismissal,
and, 46.14
Pre-hearing reviews
and see **TRIBUNAL PROCEDURE**
generally, 18.6
overview, 17.5
Preparation for tribunal hearing
EAT procedure, and, 19.29–19.30
general, 18.38
listing arrangements, 18.39–18.48
Preparation time orders
tribunal procedure, and, 18.73
Prerequisites
taxation, and, 44.2
Presentation of claim
tribunal procedure, and, 17.21
**Pressure to commit unlawful discriminatory
acts**
enforcement only by Commissions, 11.38
generally, 10.53
injunctions, 12.30

Pressure to dismiss unfairly
unfair dismissal, and, 52.16
**Pressure to impose union membership or
recognition**
secondary action, and, 43.7
Previous convictions
access to records, 16.7
Disclosure and Barring Service (DBS), 16.9
effect of provisions, 16.5
recording, 16.10
rehabilitation periods, 16.6
removal from certificate, 16.7
spent convictions
dismissal, and, 16.3
exceptions, 16.4
introduction, 16.1
non-disclosure, 16.2
vulnerable groups, and, 16.8
Prison officers
sex discrimination, and, 11.11
Prisoners
national minimum wage, and, 32.10
sick pay, and, 42.4
Private hearing
tribunal procedure, and, 18.51
Private households
race discrimination, and, 11.12
Private and family life, right to
application in employment, 28.7
generally, 28.4
'Pro hac vice'
vicarious liability, and, 54.3
Probationary employees
dismissal, 34.2
extension, 34.3
status, 34.1
Prohibition notices
appeals
cost of remedy required, 25.36
effect, 25.35
introduction, 25.34
generally, 25.31
withdrawal, 25.33
Property transfers
directors, and, 8.40
Proportionality
discrimination, and, 11.9
Protected conversations
Employment Law Review, and, 24.5
Protected shorthold tenancies
generally, 41.5
recovery of possession, 41.6
rent control, 41.8

Index

Protected tenancies
generally, 41.5
recovery of possession, 41.6
rent control, 41.8
Protection of interests of business
unfair dismissal, and, 52.14
Protective award
consultation on redundancy, and, 37.6
insolvency of employer, and, 29.2
Public authorities
gender equality duty, 11.37
litigation, and, 35.7
Public authority tenants
service lettings, and, 41.7
Public duties, time off for
generally, 47.4
remedies, 47.5
Public interest
disclosure, and,
generally, 9.16
protected disclosures, 9.17
unfair dismissal, 52.3
restraint of trade covenants, and, 39.5
Public interest immunity
public sector employees, and, 35.7
Public policy
contracts of employment, and, 7.24
restraint of trade covenants, and, 39.1
Public sector employees
armed forces, 35.3
Crown servants, 35.2
EU law, 35.8
education workers, 35.5
introduction, 35.1
judicial review as to rights, 35.6
local government employees, 35.5
national security, 35.7
police, 35.4
public interest immunity, 35.7
redundancy payments, and, 36.10
status, 35.2
Publicity
discrimination complaints, and, 12.11
Pupillage
discrimination, and, 11.27
Qualifications bodies
discrimination, and, 11.30
political parties, position of, 11.30
Qualifications-related dismissal
generally, 52.7
introduction, 52.5
summary, 52.2
Qualifying period of employment
calculation of continuous employment, 51.12

Qualifying period of employment – *cont.*
effective date of termination, 51.13
introduction, 51.11
part time workers, and, 30.6
Questionnaires
generally, 18.9
Race discrimination
advertisements
employment, in, 10.43
injunctions, 12.30
introduction, 20.1
advocates, 11.27
age, and, 10.331
agent's acts, 10.56
aiding unlawful acts, 10.58
applications to Employment Tribunal
burden of proof, 12.3
compensation, 12.13–12.20
conciliation, 12.10
disclosure, 12.9
extension of time, 12.7
formulation of complaint, 12.8
generally, 12.2
publicity, 12.11
questionnaire, 12.9
recommendations, 12.21
remedies, 12.12–12.22
time limits, 12.3
assistance for persons discriminated
against, 12.31
barristers, 11.27
'because of the protected characteristic', 10.20
benefits provided to public, 11.20
Border and Immigration Agency, 4.6
burden of proof, 12.3
careers guidance, 11.32
Codes of Practice, and
Border and Immigration Agency, 4.6
legal effect, 4.8
power to issue, 4.7
colour, and
advertisements, 10.43
applicable test, 10.34
disparity of effect, 10.34
harassment, 10.39
indirect discrimination, 10.34
meaning of 'because of race', 10.20
nationality, 10.34
pressure to commit unlawful acts, 10.53
comparators, 10.15
compensation
aggravated damages, 12.18
discrimination, 12.19
exemplary damages, 12.18

Race discrimination – *cont.*
  compensation – *cont.*
    general principles, 12.13
    indirect discrimination, 12.14
    injury to feelings, 12.16
    interests, 12.20
    introduction, 12.12
    pecuniary loss, 12.15
    personal injury, 12.17
    unfair dismissal, 12.19
  compliance with law, 11.21
  conciliation, 12.10
  contract workers, 11.24
  Crown, 11.36
  detriment, 10.50
  direct discrimination
    'because of the protected
      characteristic', 10.20
    generally, 10.13
    less favourable treatment, 10.14–10.16
  disclosure, 12.9
  dismissal, 10.49
  employed at establishment in GB, 10.42
  employment agencies, 11.32
  employment, in
    advertisements, 10.43
    dismissal, 10.49
    'employment', 10.41
    engagement, 10.45
    introduction, 10.40
    opportunities, 10.47
    post-employment behaviour, 10.52
    subjection to other detriment, 10.50
    territorial jurisdiction, 10.42
  employment outside Great Britain, 11.18
  employment-related services, 11.33
  employment service-providers, 11.34
  enforcement
    applications to Employment
      Tribunal, 12.2–12.22
    assistance for persons discriminated
      against, 12.31
    EHRC, by, 12.23–12.28
    injunctions, 12.29–12.30
    introduction, 12.1
    settlement, 12.33
    void contract terms, 12.32
  enforcement by the EHRC
    formal inquiries and
      investigations, 12.25–12.27
    generally, 12.23–12.24
    introduction, 11.38
    unlawful act notices, 12.28
  engagement, 10.45

Race discrimination – *cont.*
  equal opportunities, and
    enforcement, 11.38
    general exceptions, 11.17–11.23
    genuine occupational requirement or
      qualification, 11.4
    introduction, 11.1
    justification, 11.9
    non-employees/employers
      covered, 11.24–11.36
    positive discrimination, 11.10
    public authorities, and, 11.37
    specific exceptions, 11.12
  extension of time, 12.7
  foreign employees, and, 23.9
  formal inquiries and investigations
    Commissioner's report, 12.27
    generally, 12.25
    information, 12.26
  formulation of complaint, 12.8
  general exceptions
    benefits provided to public, 11.20
    compliance with law, 11.21
    employment outside Great Britain, 11.18
    illegal contracts, 11.19
    introduction, 11.17
    national security, 11.22
    State immunity, 11.23
  genuine occupational requirement or
    qualification
    generally, 11.4
    introduction, 11.2
  harassment
    generally, 10.39
    partnerships, 11.28
    trade organisations, 11.29
  illegal contracts, 11.19
  indirect discrimination
    application of the test, 10.34
    discriminatory measure, 10.34
    disparity of effect, 10.34
    generally, 10.34
  injunctions
    advertisements, 12.30
    instructions to discriminate, 12.30
    persistent discrimination, 12.29
    pressure to discriminate, 12.30
  instructions to commit unlawful acts
    enforcement only by Commissions, 11.38
    generally, 10.53
    injunctions, 12.30
  interview and selection, 20.2–20.4
  introduction, 10.331
  justification, 11.9

Index

Race discrimination – *cont.*
legal sources, 10.5
less favourable treatment
'because of the protected
characteristic', 10.20
comparators, 10.15
generally, 10.14
positive discrimination, 10.16
meaning
direct discrimination, 10.20
harassment, 10.39
indirect discrimination, 10.34
introduction, 10.12
victimisation, 10.38
national security, 11.22
non-employees/employers covered, 11.24–11.36
occupational pension schemes, 11.35
office holders, 11.25
opportunities in employment, 10.47
partnerships, 11.28
personal disadvantage, 10.34
police, 11.26
positive discrimination
access to training, 11.10
childbirth, 11.10
EU law, under, 11.10
generally, 11.10
introduction, 10.16
membership of trade organisation, 11.10
pregnancy, 11.10
Sikhs on construction sites, 11.13
post-employment, 10.52
pressure to commit unlawful acts
enforcement only by Commissions, 11.38
generally, 10.53
injunctions, 12.30
prohibited grounds
combined discrimination, 10.29
direct discrimination, 10.13–10.27
disability-related discrimination, 10.33
harassment, 10.39
indirect discrimination, 10.34–10.36
introduction, 10.12
perceived discrimination, 10.28
victimisation, 10.38
protected characteristics, 10.5
public authorities, and, 11.37
publicity, 12.11
pupillage, 11.27
qualifications bodies, 11.30
questionnaire, 12.9
recommendations, 12.21
remedies
compensation, 12.13–12.20

Race discrimination – *cont.*
remedies – *cont.*
introduction, 12.12
pension rights, 12.22
recommendations, 12.21
selection, 20.2–20.4
settlement of claim, 12.33
specific exceptions, 11.12
sports and competitions, 11.12
State immunity, 11.23
state provision of facilities and services, 11.33
territorial jurisdiction, 10.42
third party acts, 10.57
time limits
acts extending over a period, 12.6
extension of time, 12.7
generally, 12.4
omissions, 12.5
trade organisations, 11.29
trustees of occupational pension schemes, 11.35
unfavourable treatment, 10.14
unlawful act notices, 12.28
unlawful acts
agent's acts, 10.56
aiding unlawful acts, 10.58
employee's acts, 10.54–10.55
enforcement by EHRC, 11.38
instructions to commit unlawful acts, 10.53
pressure to commit unlawful acts, 10.53
third party acts, 10.57
vicarious liability, 10.54–10.55
unlawful instructions
enforcement only by Commissions, 11.38
generally, 10.53
injunctions, 12.30
unlawful pressure
enforcement only by Commissions, 11.38
generally, 10.53
injunctions, 12.30
vicarious liability
defence, 10.55
generally, 10.54
victimisation, 10.38
vocational training providers, 11.31
Rail workers
working time, and, 55.36
Rapid resolution scheme
Employment Law Review, and, 24.7
Real time information (RTI)
Employer Alignment Submission (EAS), 44.19c
Employer Payment Submission (EPS), 44.19c
Full Payment Submission (FPS), 44.19cPay As
You Earn (PAYE),44.4
PAYE Online registration, 44.19

Reasonableness
restraint of trade covenants, and, 39.6–39.9
Reasons for decision
adequacy, 18.63
generally, 18.62
Reasons for dismissal
unfair dismissal, and, 52.1
wrongful dismissal, and, 56.20
Recognition of trade unions
collective bargaining, for
appropriate bargaining unit, 48.30
ballot, 48.31–48.32
changes in bargaining unit, 48.35
'collective bargaining', 48.27
introduction, 48.25
method of bargaining, 48.33
reference to CAC, 48.29
request for recognition, 48.28
scope of procedure, 48.26
voluntary, 48.34
independence, 48.22–48.24
introduction, 48.19
listing, 48.21
transfer of undertakings, and, 50.21
unfair dismissal, and, 52.3
voluntary, 48.20
Recommendations
discrimination remedies, and, 12.21
Records
Codes of Practice, and, 4.16
pay, and, 32.11
pay as you earn, and, 44.20
sick pay, and, 42.7
trade unions, and, 48.12
working time, and, 55.8
Recoupment of benefits
tribunal procedure, and, 18.68
unfair dismissal, and, 53.5
Recovery of costs
education and training, and, 13.3
Recovery of possession
generally, 41.3
grounds, 41.6
public authority tenants, 41.7
service licence, 41.4
service tenancy, 41.5
Recreational facilities
tax-free benefits, and, 44.23
Redundancy
and see **REDUNDANCY** PAYMENTS
checklist, 37.9
consultation requirements
appropriate representatives, 37.4–37.5
introduction, 37.2

Redundancy – *cont.*
consultation requirements – *cont.*
meaning of 'redundancy', 37.3
protective award, 37.6
dismissal notices, 37.9
employee representatives, and, 37.4–37.5
'establishment', meaning, 37.4
European law, and, 22.8
fairness of dismissal, 37.8
introduction, 37.1
maternity leave, and, 31.34
meaning, 37.3
notification to BIS, 37.7
preliminary procedure, 37.9
protective awards, 37.6
transfer of undertakings, and, 50.27
unfair dismissal, and
generally, 52.11
procedure, 52.12
summary, 52.2
unfair selection, 52.3
Redundancy payments
age discrimination, and
generally, 11.15
introduction, 36.10
amount, 36.13
continuous employment for requisite period
changes in ownership, 36.5
generally, 36.4
contracting out, 36.14
'dismissal'
generally, 36.6
reason, 36.7–36.9
excluded persons, 36.10
insolvency of employer, and, 29.4
introduction, 36.1
lay off, and
counter-notice, 36.9
generally, 36.8
payments from National Insurance Fund,
and, 29.4
pension contributions, and, 29.6
pre-conditions
applicant an employee, 36.3
continuous employment for requisite
period, 36.4–36.5
dismissal, 36.6
introduction, 36.2
reason for dismissal, 36.7–36.9
ready reckoner, 36.15
redundancy as reason for dismissal, and, 36.7
references to tribunal, 36.14
short time working, and
counter-notice, 36.9

Index

Redundancy payments – *cont.*
short time working, and – *cont.*
generally, 36.8
time limits for claims, 17.27, 36.11
transfer of undertakings, and
generally, 50.27
introduction, 36.5
unreasonable refusal of alternative
employment, 36.12
Re-engagement
general rules, 53.4
generally, 53.3
redundancy payments, and, 36.6
refusal to re-engage, 53.5
References
conditional employment, and, 38.9
contents, 38.3
data protection, and, 38.6
employer liabilities
employee, to, 38.4
recipient, to, 38.5
employer's obligation, 38.2
introduction, 38.1
third party liabilities, 38.7
tribunals, and, 38.8
References to CJEU
tribunal procedure, and, 19.48
Refunds
pay as you earn, and, 44.13
Refusal of alternative employment
redundancy payments, and, 36.12
Refusal to work on Sunday
unfair dismissal, and, 52.3
Register of judgments
tribunal procedure, and, 18.65
Register of members
trade unions, and, 48.13
Rehabilitation periods
criminal convictions, and, 16.6
Reinstatement
general rules, 53.4
generally, 53.2
military service, and, 47.18–47.19
refusal to reinstate, 53.5
Relief for assessable benefits
taxation, and, 44.28
Relief from liability
directors, and, 8.26
Religion or belief discrimination
advertisements
employment, in, 10.43
injunctions, 12.30
introduction, 20.1
advocates, 11.27

Religion or belief discrimination – *cont.*
age, and, 10.331
agent's acts, 10.56
aiding unlawful acts, 10.58
applications to Employment Tribunal
burden of proof, 12.3
compensation, 12.13–12.20
conciliation, 12.10
disclosure, 12.9
extension of time, 12.7
formulation of complaint, 12.8
generally, 12.2
publicity, 12.11
questionnaire, 12.9
recommendations, 12.21
remedies, 12.12–12.22
time limits, 12.4–12.7
assistance for persons discriminated
against, 12.31
barristers, 11.27
'because of the protected characteristic', 10.22
benefits provided to public, 11.20
careers guidance, 11.32
comparators, 10.15
compensation
aggravated damages, 12.18
discrimination, 12.19
exemplary damages, 12.18
general principles, 12.13
indirect discrimination, 12.14
injury to feelings, 12.16
interests, 12.20
introduction, 12.12
pecuniary loss, 12.15
personal injury, 12.17
unfair dismissal, 12.19
compliance with law, 11.21
conciliation, 12.10
contract workers, 11.24
Crown, 11.36
detriment, 10.50
direct discrimination
'because of the protected
characteristic', 10.22
generally, 10.13
disclosure, 12.9
dismissal, 10.49
employed at establishment in GB, 10.42
employment agencies, 11.32
employment, in
advertisements, 10.43
dismissal, 10.49
'employment', 10.41
engagement, 10.44

Religion or belief discrimination – *cont.*
 employment, in – *cont.*
  introduction, 10.40
  opportunities, 10.47
  post-employment behaviour, 10.52
  subjection to other detriment, 10.50
  territorial jurisdiction, 10.42
 employment outside Great Britain, 11.18
 employment-related services, 11.33
 employment service-providers, 11.34
 enforcement
  applications to Employment
   Tribunal, 12.2–12.22
  assistance for persons discriminated
   against, 12.31
  EHRC, by, 12.23–12.28
  injunctions, 12.29–12.30
  introduction, 12.1
  settlement, 12.33
  void contract terms, 12.32
 enforcement by the EHRC
  formal inquiries and
   investigations, 12.25–12.27
  generally, 12.23–12.24
  introduction, 11.38
  unlawful act notices, 12.28
 engagement, 10.44
 equal opportunities, and
  enforcement, 11.38
  general exceptions, 11.17–11.23
  genuine occupational requirement or
   qualification, 11.5
  introduction, 11.1
  justification, 11.9
  non-employees/employers
   covered, 11.24–11.36
  positive discrimination, 11.10
  public authorities, and, 11.37
  specific exceptions, 11.13
 extension of time, 12.7
 foreign employees, and, 23.9
 formulation of complaint, 12.8
 general exceptions
  benefits provided to public, 11.20
  compliance with law, 11.21
  employment outside Great Britain, 11.18
  illegal contracts, 11.19
  introduction, 11.17
  national security, 11.22
  State immunity, 11.23
 genuine occupational requirement or
  qualification, 11.6
 harassment
  generally, 10.39
  partnerships, 11.28

Religion or belief discrimination – *cont.*
 harassment – *cont.*
  trade organisations, 11.29
 health and safety conflict, 28.7
 illegal contracts, 11.19
 indirect discrimination
  application of the test, 10.34
  discriminatory measure, 10.34
  disparity of effect, 10.34
  generally, 10.34
 injunctions
  advertisements, 12.30
  instructions to discriminate, 12.30
  persistent discrimination, 12.29
  pressure to discriminate, 12.30
 instructions to commit unlawful acts
  enforcement only by Commissions, 11.38
  generally, 10.53
  injunctions, 12.30
 interview and selection, 20.2–20.4
 introduction, 10.331
 justification, 11.9
 legal sources, 10.7
 manifesting a religious belief, 10.22
 meaning
  direct discrimination, 10.22
  harassment, 10.39
  indirect discrimination, 10.34
  introduction, 10.12
  religious
   victimisation, 10.38
 national security, 11.22
 non-discrimination notices, 12.28
 non-employees/employers covered, 11.24–11.36
 occupational pension schemes, 11.35
 office holders, 11.25
 opportunities in employment, 10.47
 partnerships, 11.28
 personal disadvantage, 10.34
 police, 11.26
 positive discrimination
  access to training, 11.10
  childbirth, 11.10
  EU law, under, 11.10
  generally, 11.10
  membership of trade organisation, 11.10
  pregnancy, 11.10
  Sikhs on construction sites, 11.13
 post-employment, 10.52
 pressure to commit unlawful acts
  enforcement only by Commissions, 11.38
  generally, 10.53
  injunctions, 12.30

Index

Religion or belief discrimination – *cont.*
  prohibited grounds
    combined discrimination, 10.29
    direct discrimination, 10.13–10.27
    disability-related discrimination, 10.33
    harassment, 10.39
    indirect discrimination, 10.34–10.36
    introduction, 10.12
    perceived discrimination, 10.28
    victimisation, 10.38
  protected characteristics, 10.7
  public authorities, and, 11.37
  publicity, 12.11
  pupillage, 11.27
  qualifications bodies, 11.30
  questionnaire, 12.9
  recommendations, 12.21
  remedies
    compensation, 12.13–12.20
    introduction, 12.12
    pension rights, 12.22
  selection, 20.2–20.4
  settlement of claim, 12.33
  specific exceptions, 11.13
  State immunity, 11.23
  state provision of facilities and services, 11.33
  third party acts, 10.57
  time limits
    acts extending over a period, 12.6
    extension of time, 12.7
    generally, 12.4
    omissions, 12.5
  trade organisations, 11.29
  trustees of occupational pension schemes, 11.35
  unlawful act notices, 12.28
  unlawful acts
    agent's acts, 10.56
    aiding unlawful acts, 10.58
    employee's acts, 10.54–10.55
    enforcement by EHRC, 11.38
    instructions to commit unlawful acts, 10.53
    pressure to commit unlawful acts, 10.53
    third party acts, 10.57
    vicarious liability, 10.54–10.55
  unlawful instructions
    enforcement only by Commissions, 11.38
    generally, 10.53
    injunctions, 12.30
  unlawful pressure
    enforcement only by Commissions, 11.38
    generally, 10.53
    injunctions, 12.30
  vicarious liability
    defence, 10.55

Religion or belief discrimination – *cont.*
  vicarious liability – *cont.*
    generally, 10.54
  victimisation, 10.38
  vocational training providers, 11.31
Religious communities
  national minimum wage, and, 32.10
Relocation expenses
  taxable benefits, and, 44.21–44.23
Remedies
  breach of contracts of employment
      (employee's remedies), and
    damages, 7.36–7.41
    disclosure, 7.45
    injunctions, 7.42–7.43
    introduction, 7.35
    jurisdiction, 7.44
  breach of contracts of employment
      (employer's remedies), and
    acceptance of fundamental breach, 7.47a
    account of profits, 7.47d
    damages, 7.47b
    deduction of wages, 7.47
    injunctions, 7.47c
    specific performance, 7.47c
    withholding of wages, 7.47
  compensation for discrimination
    aggravated damages, 12.18
    discrimination, 12.19
    exemplary damages, 12.18
    general principles, 12.13
    indirect discrimination, 12.14
    injury to feelings, 12.16
    interests, 12.20
    introduction, 12.12
    pecuniary loss, 12.15
    personal injury, 12.17
    unfair dismissal, 12.19
  costs, 18.69–18.74
  deductions from wages, and, 32.8
  detriment by reason of pregnancy, and, 31.19
  discrimination complaints, and
    compensation, 12.13–12.20
    introduction, 12.12
    pension schemes, 12.22
    recommendations, 12.21
  equal pay, and
    Agricultural Wages Orders, 21.20
    compensation, 21.19B
    employer penalties, 21.19D
    employment tribunals, 21.19
    equal pay audits, 21.19C
    time limits, 21.19A
  guarantee payments, and, 32.28

Remedies – *cont.*
holidays, and, 27.6
interest, 18.67
medical suspension, and, 32.33
national minimum wage, and
individual remedies, 32.12
state remedies, 32.13
non-payment of statutory maternity pay,
and, 31.43
pension schemes, and, 12.22
recommendations, 12.21
recoupment of benefits, 18.68
restraint of trade covenants, and,
account of profits, 39.20
damages, 39.19
declaration, 39.18
injunctions, 39.17
pleading, 39.16
strike action, and
employers', 43.16
third parties', 43.18
time off work, and
ante-natal care, 31.9
arrangements for training, 47.7
dependants, 47.16
employee representatives, 47.13
look for work, 47.7
pension scheme trustees, 47.11
public duties, 47.5
safety representatives, 47.9
trade union activities, 47.5
tribunal procedure, and
costs, 18.69–18.74
generally, 18.66
interest, 18.67
recoupment of benefits, 18.68
unfair dismissal, and
compensation, 53.6–53.16
interim relief, 53.18
introduction, 53.1
joinder of third parties, 53.17
re-engagement, 53.3–53.5
reinstatement, 53.2–53.5
settlement, 53.19
written statements of reasons for dismissal,
and, 46.15
wrongful dismissal, and
claims in debt, 56.24
damages, 56.25–56.33
injunctions, 56.23
wrongful termination, and, 46.21
Remuneration of directors
Code, 9.29
disclosure, 8.31

Remuneration of directors – *cont.*
Governance Code, 8.28
introduction, 8.27
Listing Rules requirements, 8.34
pensions, 8.35
quoted companies, developments
remuneration policy 8.33
remuneration report, 8.33
recommendations, 8.28
Remuneration Code, 8.30
small company provisions, 8.32
termination of office, on
generally, 8.36
Listing Rules requirements, 8.39
property transfer, 8.40
recommendations, 8.38
takeovers, 8.41
termination payments, 8.37
transfer of undertakings, 8.42
Remuneration of employees
And see **PAY**
implied contract terms, and, 7.15
Renewal of contract
redundancy payments, and, 36.6
Rent control
service lettings, and, 41.8
Reorganisation of business
unfair dismissal, and, 52.14
Repetitive strain injury (RSI)
health and safety, and, 26.31
Replacement employee
unfair dismissal, and, 52.14
Reporting of accidents
health and safety, and, 26.1
Representation
EAT procedure, and, 19.28
tribunal procedure, and, 18.55
Repudiatory conduct
restraint of trade covenants, and, 39.11
termination, and, 46.19
unfair dismissal, and, 51.9
Reputation, loss of
unfair dismissal, and, 53.12
Resignation
generally, 46.16
notice by employee, 46.17
retraction of resignation, 46.20
summary termination by employee, 46.18
Response by respondent
tribunal procedure, and, 17.35–17.37
Rest breaks
generally, 55.17
monotonous work, 55.18

Index

Rest periods
children, and, 3.6
daily, 55.15
introduction, 55.14
weekly, 55.16
Restraint of trade covenants
ambit of restraint, 39.8
'blue pencil' test, 39.7
common law doctrine, 39.2
confidential information, 39.13
conflict of laws, 39.12
consequence of finding of
    unreasonableness, 39.9
consideration, 39.10
construction, 39.6
coverage, 39.3
duration of restraint, 39.8
'garden leave' injunctions, and, 39.14
geographical scope, 39.8
interests of the parties, 39.4
introduction, 39.1
nature of restraint, 39.8
procedural matters,
    account of profits, 39.20
    damages, 39.19
    declaration, 39.18
    injunctions, 39.17
    pleading, 39.16
proscribed actions, 39.8
public interest, 39.5
reasonableness
    ambit of restraint, 39.8
    consequences, 39.9
    duration of restraint, 39.8
    general approach, 39.8
    geographical scope, 39.8
    introduction, 39.6
    nature of restraint, 39.8
    proscribed actions, 39.8
    severance, 39.7
    test, 39.8
repudiatory breach, 39.11
severance, 39.7
'springboard' relief, and, 39.15
testing reasonableness, 39.8
trade secrets, 39.13
Restricted reporting orders
EAT procedure, and, 19.26
tribunal procedure, and, 18.18–18.19
Retail employment
deductions from wages, and, 32.7
Retirement
age discrimination, and,
    generally, 11.15

Retirement – *cont.*
age discrimination, and, – *cont.*
    pension benefits, 40.14
    summary of regulations 40.6
age, 50.14
    changing, 40.7
    discrimination regulations, 40.3–40.4
    employment protection, and, 40.2
    generally, 40.1
    justifying dismissals, 40.5
benefits, 40.8
discrimination, and,
    age discrimination, 40.14
    introduction, 11.11
    sex discrimination, 40.13
early, 40.6
effect on protected rights, 40.2
introduction, 40.1
justifying retirement dismissals, 40.5
pensions,
    age discrimination, and, 40.14
    claims and disputes, 40.17
    employee trustees, 40.15
    employers' duties, 40.16
    generally, 40.9
    sex discrimination, 40.13
    stakeholder, 40.10
persons over retirement age
    redundancy payments, 36.10
    sick pay, 42.4
    unfair dismissal, 51.12
post-retirement benefits, 40.7
pay as you earn, and, 44.9
sex discrimination, and
    generally, 11.11
    pension benefits, 40.13
unfair dismissal, and, 52.4
Retirement age
changing, 40.7
employment protection, and, 40.2
equalisation, 40.1
generally, 40.1
labour market and younger workers, 40.5
unfair dismissal, 52.4
Retirement age, persons over
redundancy payments, and, 36.10
sick pay, and, 42.4
unfair dismissal, and, 51.12
Returns
pay as you earn, and, 44.15
Review of order
EAT procedure, and, 19.46
tribunal procedure, and, 18.75–18.76

Right to respect for private and family life
application in employment, 28.7
generally, 28.4
Risk of injury, protection from
health and safety, and, 25.8
Road transport workers
working time, and, 55.34–55.35
Sabbatical
annual leave entitlement, 27.3B
Safe equipment and materials
health and safety, and, 25.6
Safe means of access
health and safety, and, 25.4
Safe place of work
health and safety, and, 25.3
Safe system of work
health and safety, and, 25.5
Safety measures
charges for, 25.24
interference with, 25.23
Safety representatives
Codes of Practice, and
legal effect, 4.15
power to issue, 4.14
disclosure of information, and, 9.8
introduction, 26.20
non-unionised workers, 26.22
time off work, and
Codes of Practice, and, 4.14–4.15
generally, 47.8
remedies, 47.9
union-appointees, 26.21
Safety signs
health and safety, and, 26.30
Salary
attachment of earnings, and
attachable earnings, 33.2
child support maintenance, 33.11
Council Tax, 33.10
deductions, 33.3–33.6
employer's obligations, 33.7
introduction, 33.1
other issues, 33.9
penalties for non-compliance, 33.8
deductions from wages
generally, 32.6
minimum wage, and, 32.9–32.13
other, 32.14
remedies for breach, 32.8
retail employment, 32.7
fixed deductions, 32.17
generally, 32.2
gratuities, 32.21

Salary – *cont.*
guarantee payments
amount, 32.27
exclusions, 32.26
introduction, 32.23
qualifying period, 32.25
remedy for failure to make payment, 32.28
'workless days', 32.24
holidays, and, 27.4
insolvency of employer, and, 29.2
introduction, 32.1
itemised statements
application to tribunal, 32.19–32.20
exclusions, 32.18
fixed deductions, 32.17
generally, 32.16
medical suspension, and
amount, 32.32
exclusions, 32.31
generally, 32.29
qualifying conditions, 32.30
remedy for failure to make payment, 32.33
method of payment, 32.3
national minimum wage
coverage, 32.10
introduction, 32.9
records, 32.11
relevant workers, 32.10
remedies for failure to pay, 32.12–32.13
statements, 32.11
overpayment, 32.15
pre-1987 position
exceptions, 32.5
generally, 32.4
records, 32.11
statement of fixed deductions, 32.17
termination of employment, and, 32.22
troncs, 32.21
'week's pay'
amount, 32.39
calculation date, 32.38
introduction, 32.34
no normal working hours, 32.37
normal working hours, 32.35
overtime, 32.36
workless days, and, 32.23
wrongful dismissal, and, 56.28
Salary continuance benefits
effect
calculation of damages, on, 42.14
termination of employment contract, on, 42.13
generally, 42.12
'unable to follow any occupation', 42.15

Index

Same work
equal pay, and, 21.6
Savings-related share option schemes
generally, 44.29
School-leavers
education and training, and, 13.5
School workers
continuous employment, and, 6.9
EU law, 35.8
generally, 35.5
introduction, 35.1
judicial review as to rights, 35.6
national security, 35.7
public interest immunity, 35.7
Seafarers
working time, and, 55.31–55.32
Seamen recruited abroad
race discrimination, and, 11.12
Seasonal workers
generally, 45.8
less favourable treatment, 45.9
unfair dismissal, and, 45.8
Secondary action, limits on
dismissal of unofficial strikers, 43.8
generally, 43.6
pressure to impose membership or
recognition, 43.7
Security
pay as you earn, and, 44.19b
Selection
engagement of employees, and, 20.2–20.4
Self-employed
generally, 14.2–14.3
rights and obligations, 14.6–14.7
SERPS
generally, 40.9
Service contracts for directors
disclosure, 8.12
duration, 8.13–8.15
inspection, 8.8
introduction, 8.7
Listing Rules requirements, 8.10
sole members also directors, with, 8.9
Take-over Code requirements, 8.11
Service lettings
agricultural tied houses, 41.9
introduction, 41.1
licence, 41.4
nature of occupancy, 41.2
public authority tenants, 41.7
recovery of possession
generally, 41.3
grounds, 41.6
public authority tenants, 41.7

Service lettings – *cont.*
recovery of possession – *cont.*
service licence, 41.4
service tenancy, 41.5
rent control, 41.8
tenancy, 41.5
Service licence
generally, 41.4
Service provision change
background, 50.1
introduction, 50.2
relevant activities, 50.3
Service tenancy
See also **Service lettings**
generally, 41.5
Services personnel
EU law, 35.8
equal pay, and, 21.4
generally, 35.3
introduction, 35.1
judicial review as to rights, 35.6
national minimum wage, and, 32.10
national security, 35.7
part-time workers, and, 30.4
public interest immunity, 35.7
sex discrimination, and, 11.11
strikes, and, 43.20
working time, and, 55.3
Services through an intermediary
taxation, and, 44.34
Settlement agreements
pay as you earn, and, 44.18
Settlement of claim
conciliation, 18.32
discrimination, and, 12.33
generally, 18.29–18.31
unfair dismissal, and, 53.19
Severance
restraint of trade covenants, and, 39.7
Sex discrimination
advertisements
employment, in, 10.43
injunctions, 12.30
introduction, 20.1
advocates, 11.27
age, and, 10.331
agent's acts, 10.56
aiding unlawful acts, 10.58
applications to Employment Tribunal
burden of proof, 12.3
compensation, 12.13–12.20
conciliation, 12.10
disclosure, 12.9
extension of time, 12.7

Sex discrimination – *cont.*

applications to Employment Tribunal – *cont.*

formulation of complaint, 12.8

generally, 12.2

publicity, 12.11

questionnaire, 12.9

recommendations, 12.21

remedies, 12.12–12.22

time limits, 12.4–12.7

assistance for persons discriminated
against, 12.31

barristers, 11.27

'because of the protected characteristic', 10.18

benefits provided to public, 11.20

burden of proof, 12.3

careers guidance, 11.32

comparators, 10.15

compensation

aggravated damages, 12.18

discrimination, 12.19

exemplary damages, 12.18

general principles, 12.13

indirect discrimination, 12.14

injury to feelings, 12.16

interests, 12.20

introduction, 12.12

pecuniary loss, 12.15

personal injury, 12.17

unfair dismissal, 12.19

compliance with law, 11.21

conciliation, 12.10

contract workers, 11.24

Crown, 11.36

detriment, 10.50

direct discrimination

generally, 10.13

less favourable treatment, 10.14 10.16

prohibited grounds, 10.18

disclosure, 12.9

dismissal, 10.49

employed at establishment in GB, 10.42

employment agencies, 11.32

employment, in

advertisements, 10.43

dismissal, 10.49

employed at establishment in GB, 10.42

'employment', 10.41

engagement, 10.46

introduction, 10.40

opportunities, 10.48

post-employment behaviour, 10.52

subjection to other detriment, 10.50

territorial jurisdiction, 10.42

employment outside Great Britain, 11.18

Sex discrimination – *cont.*

employment-related services, 11.33

employment service-providers, 11.34

enforcement

applications to Employment
Tribunal, 12.2–12.22

assistance for persons discriminated
against, 12.31

EHRC, by, 12.23–12.28

injunctions, 12.29–12.30

introduction, 12.1

settlement, 12.33

void contract terms, 12.32

enforcement by the EHRC

formal inquiries and
investigations, 12.25–12.27

generally, 12.23–12.24

introduction, 11.38

unlawful act notices, 12.28

engagement, 10.46

equal opportunities, and

enforcement, 11.38

general exceptions, 11.17–11.23

genuine occupational requirement or
qualification, 11.3

introduction, 11.1

justification, 11.9

non-employees/employers
covered, 11.24 11.36

positive discrimination, 11.10

public authorities, and, 11.37

specific exceptions, 11.11

extension of time, 12.7

foreign employees, and, 23.9

formulation of complaint, 12.8

gender reassignment, 10.6

general exceptions

benefits provided to public, 11.20

compliance with law, 11.21

employment outside Great Britain, 11.18

illegal contracts, 11.19

introduction, 11.17

national security, 11.22

State immunity, 11.23

genuine occupational requirement or
qualification

generally, 11.3

introduction, 11.2

harassment

generally, 10.39

partnerships, 11.28

trade organisations, 11.29

illegal contracts, 11.19

indirect discrimination

application of the test, 10.34

Index

Sex discrimination – *cont.*
  indirect discrimination – *cont.*
    discriminatory measure, 10.34
    disparity of effect, 10.34
    full-time work, 10.35
    generally, 10.34
  injunctions
    advertisements, 12.30
    instructions to discriminate, 12.30
    persistent discrimination, 12.29
    pressure to discriminate, 12.30
  instructions to commit unlawful acts
    enforcement only by Commissions, 11.38
    generally, 10.53
    injunctions, 12.30
  interview and selection, 20.2–20.4
  introduction, 10.331
  justification, 11.9
  legal sources, 10.3
  less favourable treatment
    'because of the protected
      characteristic', 10.18
    comparators, 10.15
    generally, 10.14
    positive discrimination, 10.16
  marital status, 10.4
  meaning
    direct discrimination, 10.14–10.16
    harassment, 10.39
    indirect discrimination, 10.34–10.35
    introduction, 10.12
    victimisation, 10.38
  national security, 11.22
  non-discrimination notices, 12.28
  non-employees/employers covered, 11.24–11.36
  occupational pension schemes, 11.35
  office holders, 11.25
  opportunities in employment, 10.48
  partnerships, 11.28
  pension benefits, 40.13
  personal disadvantage, 10.34
  police, 11.26
  positive discrimination
    access to training, 11.10
    childbirth, 11.10
    EU law, under, 11.10
    generally, 11.10
    introduction, 10.16
    membership of trade organisation, 11.10
    pregnancy, 11.10
    Sikhs on construction sites, 11.13
  post-employment, 10.52
  pressure to commit unlawful acts
    enforcement only by Commissions, 11.38

Sex discrimination – *cont.*
  pressure to commit unlawful acts – *cont.*
    generally, 10.53
    injunctions, 12.30
  prohibited grounds
    combined discrimination, 10.29
    direct discrimination, 10.13–10.27
    disability-related discrimination, 10.33
    harassment, 10.39
    indirect discrimination, 10.34–10.36
    introduction, 10.12
    perceived discrimination, 10.28
    victimisation, 10.38
  protected characteristics, 10.3
  public authorities, and, 11.37
  publicity, 12.11
  pupillage, 11.27
  qualifications bodies, 11.30
  questionnaire, 12.9
  recommendations, 12.21
  remedies
    compensation, 12.13–12.20
    introduction, 12.12
    pension rights, 12.22
    recommendations, 12.21
  retirement, and
    generally, 11.11
    pension benefits, 40.13
  selection, 20.2–20.4
  settlement of claim, 12.33
  specific exceptions, 11.11
  sports and competitions, 11.11
  State immunity, 11.23
  state provision of facilities and services, 11.33
  territorial jurisdiction, 10.42
  third party acts, 10.57
  time limits
    acts extending over a period, 12.6
    extension of time, 12.7
    generally, 12.4
    omissions, 12.5
  trade organisations, 11.29
  transsexuals, 10.6
  trustees of occupational pension schemes, 11.35
  unlawful act notices, 12.28
  unlawful acts
    agent's acts, 10.56
    aiding unlawful acts, 10.58
    employee's acts, 10.54–10.55
    enforcement by EHRC, 11.38
    instructions to commit unlawful acts, 10.53
    pressure to commit unlawful acts, 10.53
    third party acts, 10.57
    vicarious liability, 10.54–10.55

Sex discrimination – *cont.*
  unlawful instructions
    enforcement only by Commissions, 11.38
    generally, 10.53
    injunctions, 12.30
  unlawful pressure
    enforcement only by Commissions, 11.38
    generally, 10.53
    injunctions, 12.30
  vicarious liability
    defence, 10.55
    generally, 10.54
  victimisation, 10.38
  vocational training providers, 11.31
Sexual orientation discrimination
  advertisements
    employment, in, 10.43
    injunctions, 12.30
    introduction, 20.1
  advocates, 11.27
  age, and, 10.331
  agent's acts, 10.56
  aiding unlawful acts, 10.58
  applications to Employment Tribunal
    burden of proof, 12.3
    compensation, 12.13–12.20
    conciliation, 12.10
    disclosure, 12.9
    extension of time, 12.7
    formulation of complaint, 12.8
    generally, 12.2
    publicity, 12.11
    questionnaire, 12.9
    recommendations, 12.21
    remedies, 12.12–12.22
    time limits, 12.4–12.7
  assistance for persons discriminated
      against, 12.31
  barristers, 11.27
  'because of the protected characteristic', 10.23
  benefits provided to public, 11.20
  burden of proof, 12.3
  careers guidance, 11.32
  civil partnership status, 11.14
  comparators, 10.15
  compensation
    aggravated damages, 12.18
    discrimination, 12.19
    exemplary damages, 12.18
    general principles, 12.13
    indirect discrimination, 12.14
    injury to feelings, 12.16
    interests, 12.20
    introduction, 12.12

Sexual orientation discrimination – *cont.*
  compensation – *cont.*
    pecuniary loss, 12.15
    personal injury, 12.17
    unfair dismissal, 12.19
  compliance with law, 11.21
  conciliation, 12.10
  contract workers, 11.24
  Crown, 11.36
  detriment, 10.50
  direct discrimination
    'because of the protected
        characteristic', 10.23
    generally, 10.13
  disclosure, 12.9
  dismissal, 10.49
  employed at establishment in GB, 10.42
  employment agencies, 11.32
  employment, in
    advertisements, 10.43
    dismissal, 10.49
    'employment', 10.41
    engagement, 10.44
    harassment, 10.51
    introduction, 10.40
    opportunities, 10.47
    post-employment behaviour, 10.52
    subjection to other detriment, 10.50
    territorial jurisdiction, 10.42
  employment outside Great Britain, 11.18
  employment-related services, 11.33
  employment service-providers, 11.34
  enforcement
    applications to Employment
        Tribunal, 12.2–12.22
    assistance for persons discriminated
        against, 12.31
    EHRC, by, 12.23–12.28
    injunctions, 12.29–12.30
    introduction, 12.1
    settlement, 12.33
    void contract terms, 12.32
  enforcement by the EHRC
    formal inquiries and
        investigations, 12.25–12.27
    generally, 12.23–12.24
    introduction, 11.38
    unlawful act notices, 12.28
  engagement, 10.44
  equal opportunities, and
    enforcement only by Commissions, 11.38
    general exceptions, 11.17–11.23
    genuine occupational requirement or
        qualification, 11.7
    introduction, 11.1

Index

Sexual orientation discrimination – *cont.*
equal opportunities, and – *cont.*
 justification, 11.9
 non-employees/employers
  covered, 11.24–11.36
 positive discrimination, 11.10
 relationships terminated, 11.37
 specific exceptions, 11.14
extension of time, 12.7
foreign employees, and, 23.9
formulation of complaint, 12.8
general exceptions
 benefits provided to public, 11.20
 compliance with law, 11.21
 employment outside Great Britain, 11.18
 illegal contracts, 11.19
 introduction, 11.17
 national security, 11.22
 State immunity, 11.23
genuine occupational requirement or
 qualification, 11.7
harassment
 generally, 10.39
 partnerships, 11.28
 trade organisations, 11.29
illegal contracts, 11.19
indirect discrimination
 application of the test, 10.34
 discriminatory measure, 10.34
 disparity of effect, 10.34
 generally, 10.34
 particular cases, 10.36
injunctions
 advertisements, 12.30
 instructions to discriminate, 12.30
 persistent discrimination, 12.29
 pressure to discriminate, 12.30
instructions to commit unlawful acts
 enforcement only by Commissions, 11.38
 generally, 10.53
 injunctions, 12.30
interview and selection, 20.2–20.4
introduction, 10.331
justification, 11.9
legal sources, 10.8
marital status, 11.14
meaning
 direct discrimination, 10.23
 harassment, 10.39
 indirect discrimination, 10.34–10.36
 introduction, 10.12
 victimisation, 10.38
national security, 11.22
non-employees/employers covered, 11.24–11.36

Sexual orientation discrimination – *cont.*
occupational pension schemes, 11.35
office holders, 11.25
opportunities in employment, 10.47
partnerships, 11.28
personal disadvantage, 10.34
police, 11.26
positive discrimination
 access to training, 11.10
 childbirth, 11.10
 EU law, under, 11.10
 generally, 11.10
 membership of trade organisation, 11.10
 pregnancy, 11.10
post-employment, 10.52
pressure to commit unlawful acts
 enforcement only by Commissions, 11.38
 generally, 10.53
 injunctions, 12.30
prohibited grounds
 combined discrimination, 10.29
 direct discrimination, 10.13–10.27
 disability-related discrimination, 10.33
 harassment, 10.39
 indirect discrimination, 10.34–10.36
 introduction, 10.12
 perceived discrimination, 10.28
 victimisation, 10.38
protected characteristics, 10.8
publicity, 12.11
pupillage, 11.27
qualifications bodies, 11.30
questionnaire, 12.9
recommendations, 12.21
relationships terminated, 11.37
remedies
 compensation, 12.13–12.20
 introduction, 12.12
 pension rights, 12.22
 recommendations, 12.21
selection, 20.2–20.4
settlement of claim, 12.33
specific exceptions, 11.14
State immunity, 11.23
state provision of facilities and services, 11.33
territorial jurisdiction, 10.42
third party acts, 10.57
time limits
 acts extending over a period, 12.6
 extension of time, 12.7
 generally, 12.4
 omissions, 12.5
trade organisations, 11.29
transsexuals, 10.6

Sexual orientation discrimination – *cont.*
trustees of occupational pension schemes, 11.35
unlawful act notices, 12.28
unlawful acts
  agent's acts, 10.56
  aiding unlawful acts, 10.58
  employee's acts, 10.54–10.55
  enforcement by EHRC, 11.38
  instructions to commit unlawful acts, 10.53
  pressure to commit unlawful acts, 10.53
  third party acts, 10.57
  vicarious liability, 10.54–10.55
unlawful instructions
  enforcement only by Commissions, 11.38
  generally, 10.53
  injunctions, 12.30
unlawful pressure
  enforcement only by Commissions, 11.38
  generally, 10.53
  injunctions, 12.30
vicarious liability
  defence, 10.55
  generally, 10.54
victimisation, 10.38
vocational training providers, 11.31
Share fishermen
national minimum wage, and, 32.10
redundancy payments, and, 36.10
Share incentive plans
generally, 44.31
Share options
taxable benefits, and, 44.21
wrongful dismissal, and, 56.28
Share schemes
company share option, 44.30
enterprise management incentives, 44.32
incentive plans, 44.31
savings–related share option, 44.29
Share transfers
transfer of undertakings, and, 50.10
Ship-board workers
national minimum wage, and, 32.10
Short time working
redundancy payments, and
  counter-notice, 36.9
  generally, 36.8
Sick leave
annual leave entitlement, 27.3A
holidays, and, 27.3
Sick pay
amount, 42.6
contractual provisions, and
  generally, 42.2
  offsetting against SSP, 42.9–42.11

Sick pay – *cont.*
disputes, 42.8
excluded employees, 42.4
generally, 42.3
holidays, and, 27.3
insolvency of employer, and
  generally, 29.2
  payments from National Insurance
    Fund, 29.8
introduction, 42.1
offsetting
  contributory pension schemes, 42.11
  contributory sickness schemes, 42.10
  introduction, 42.9
payment period, 42.5
permanent health benefits, and
  effect on calculation of damages, 42.14
  effect on termination of employment
    contract, 42.13
  generally, 42.12
  'unable to follow any occupation', 42.15
records, 42.7
recoverable amount, 42.6
requirements, 42.3
salary continuance benefits, and
  effect on calculation of damages, 42.14
  effect on termination of employment
    contract, 42.13
  generally, 42.12
  'unable to follow any occupation', 42.15
statutory framework, 42.3
Sikhs on construction sites
discrimination, and, 11.13
Skeleton arguments
EAT procedure, and, 19.31
Skills Funding Agency
education and training, and, 13.8
Smoking
health and safety, and, 26.23
"Some other substantial reason"
generally, 52.14
summary, 52.2
Sources of law
domestic legislation, 1.6
European law, 1.7
introduction, 1.4
terms of contracts of employment, 1.5
Special hazards
night work, and, 55.11
Special negotiating body
cross border mergers, and, 15.55
European companies, and, 15.33
European co-operative societies, and, 15.42
European Works Councils, and, 15.26

Index

Special negotiating body – *cont.*
  unfair dismissal, and, 52.3
Specific employment income
  taxation, and, 44.2
Specific performance
  employer's remedies, and, 7.47c
Spent convictions
  dismissal, and, 16.3
  effect, 16.5
  exceptions, 16.4
  introduction, 16.1
  non-disclosure, 16.2
  rehabilitation periods, 16.6
  unfair dismissal, and, 52.3
Sports and competitions
  race discrimination, and, 11.12
  sex discrimination, and, 11.11
Sports facilities
  tax-free benefits, and, 44.23
Springboard relief
  restraint of trade, 39.15
Stakeholder pensions
  generally, 40.10
Start of employment
  generally, 6.3
  postponement, 6.11
State earnings related pension scheme
    (SERPS)
  generally, 40.9
State immunity
  discrimination, and, 11.23
State provision of facilities and services
  discrimination, and, 11.33
Statement of fixed deductions
  itemised pay statements, and, 32.17
Statements of reasons for dismissal
  generally, 46.14
  remedy for failure to give, 46.15
Status of employment
  employees
    generally, 14.2–14.3
    office-holders, 14.8
    rights and obligations, 14.4–14.5
  introduction, 14.1
  office-holders, 14.8
  self-employed
    generally, 14.2–14.3
    rights and obligations, 14.6–14.7
  workers, 14.9
Statutory adoption pay
  generally, 31.61
Statutory dismissal and disciplinary
    procedures
  Codes of Practice, and, 4.2

Statutory dismissal and disciplinary procedures
  – *cont.*
  unfair dismissal, and, 52.3
Statutory maternity pay
  amount, 31.42
  claim procedure, 31.40
  'confinement', 31.39
  insolvency of employer, and, 29.8
  introduction, 31.38
  payments from National Insurance Fund,
    and, 29.8
  period of entitlement, 31.41
  qualifying requirements, 31.39
  recoupment by employer, 31.44
  remedy for non-payment, 31.43
  sick pay, and, 42.4
Statutory paternity pay
  generally, 31.61
Statutory minimum notice
  exceptions, 46.8
  generally, 46.7
Statutory rights, loss of
  unfair dismissal, and, 53.12
Stay of proceedings
  tribunal procedure, and, 18.22
Stewardship Code
  company's remuneration, 8.29
Stoppage at work
  sick pay, and, 42.4
Stress
  health and safety, and
    common law liability, 26.25
    generally, 26.24
Strike action
  armed forces, 43.20
  ballots before action
    Codes of Practice, and, 4.4–4.5
    generally, 43.14
    members' right, 43.17
  calls for action, 43.15
  Codes of Practice, and
    generally, 43.11
    legal effect, 4.5
    power to issue, 4.4
  common law liability, 43.2
  consequences for employers, 43.19
  criminal liability, 43.12
  deductions from wages, and, 32.6
  employer's rights and remedies, 43.16
  immunity from liability for
    background, 43.1
    'in contemplation or furtherance', 43.5
    introduction, 43.3
    'trade dispute', 43.4

Strike action – *cont.*
  liability for
    background, 43.1
    common law, at, 43.2
    statutory immunity, 43.3–43.5
    trade unions, 43.13–43.15
  picketing
    case law, 43.10
    Code of Practice, 4.4–4.5, 43.11
    generally, 43.9
  police officers, 43.20
  pressure to impose union membership or
    recognition, 43.7
  prohibited employees, 43.20
  remedies
    employers, 43.16
    third parties', 43.18
  restricted employees, 43.20
  restrictions, 7.29
  secondary action, limits on
    dismissal of unofficial strikers, 43.8
    generally, 43.6
    pressure to impose membership or
      recognition, 43.7
  third parties' rights and remedies, 43.18
  time off work for trade union officials, and, 47.2
  trade union, liability of
    ballots before action, 43.14
    calls for action, 43.15
    generally, 43.13
    introduction, 49.9
  unfair dismissal, and
    introduction, 52.3
    official action, 51.17
    unofficial action, 51.18
Striking out
  tribunal procedure, and, 18.16–18.17
Students during vacation
  pay as you earn, and, 44.11
Study and training
  complaint to tribunal, 13.17
  detriment, and, 13.19
  employee's duties, 13.16
  employer's duties, 13.15
  generally, 13.12
  remedies, 13.18
  right to request, 13.13
  supplementary provisions, 13.14
  unfair dismissal, and, 13.19, 52.3
Substances hazardous to health
  health and safety, and, 26.26
Suitable alternative employment
  redundancy payments, and, 36.10

Summary dismissal
  directors' notice periods, 56.14
  express notice periods, 56.11
  fixed term contracts, 56.12
  implied notice periods, 56.15
  justification, 56.17
  rolling contracts, 56.13
  statutory minimum notice, 56.16
  termination, and, 46.13
Summary judgment
  wrongful dismissal, and, 56.41
Sunday trading
  contracts of employment, and, 7.48
Sunday work
  unfair dismissal, and, 52.3
Surrogacy
  Children and Families Bill, 31.4A
Suspension on maternity grounds
  allowances, 31.15
  alternative work, 31.19
  ante-natal care, 31.14
  introduction, 31.11
  remuneration, 31.13
System of work
  health and safety, and, 25.5
Take-over Code
  directors' service contracts, and, 8.11
Takeovers
  directors' compensation, and, 8.41
Tax credits
  unfair dismissal, and, 52.3
Taxable benefits
  car fuel, 44.26
  company cars, 44.25
  generally, 44.21
  lower-paid employees, 44.22
  vans, 44.27
Taxation
  benefits in kind, 44.2
  car fuel, 44.26
  company cars, 44.25
  company share option schemes, 44.30
  death of employee, 44.10
  directors, 44.3
  disguised remuneration, 44.36
  dismissal of employee, 44.8
  dispensations for expenses, 44.28
  earnings limits, 44.4
  employee share schemes
    company share option, 44.30
    enterprise management incentives, 44.32
    incentive plans, 44.31
    savings-related share option, 44.29
    share incentive plans, 44.31

Index

Taxation – *cont.*
  employment income, 44.2
  end of year procedure
    certificates, 44.15
    Class 1A NICs, 44.17
    P9D, 44.16
    P11D, 44.16
    P11D(b), 44.16
    real time information (RTI), 44.15
    returns, 44.15
  enterprise management incentives, 44.32
  expenses incurred in the performance of
    duties, 44.28
  Full Payment Submission (FPS), 44.7, 44.15
  introduction, 44.1
  joining after 6 April, 44.7
  lower-paid employees
    generally, 44.3
    taxable benefits, 44.22
  managed service companies, 44.35
  national insurance contributions, 44.17
  online services
    generally, 44.19
    penalties, 44.19a
    security, 44.19b
    real time information (RTI), 44.19c
  P9D, 44.16
  P11D, 44.16
  P11D(b), 44.16
  pay as you earn (PAYE)
    death of employee, 44.10
    definition, 44.4
    dismissal, 44.8
    earnings limits, 44.4
    end of year procedure, 44.15–44.17
    joining after 6 April, 44.7
    method of deduction, 44.6
    online, 44.19–44.19c
    payment by employer, 44.14
    penalties for late payment, 44.14a
    refunds, 44.13
    retirement, 44.9
    settlement agreements, 44.18
    sources of information, 44.5
    students during vacation, 44.11
    working abroad, 44.12
  PAYE Online
    registration, 44.19
  pay in lieu of notice (PILON), 44.8
  payroll giving scheme, 44.33
  real time information (RTI), 44.4
    Employer Alignment Submission
      (EAS), 44.19c
    Employer Payment Submission (EPS), 44.19c

Taxation – *cont.*
  real time information (RTI), – *cont.*
    Full Payment Submission (FPS), 44.19c
  records, 44.20
  refunds, 44.13
  relief for assessable benefits, 44.28
  retirement of employee, 44.9
  savings-related share option, 44.29
  security for PAYE, 44.19b
  services through an intermediary, 44.34
  settlement agreements, 44.18
  share incentive plans, 44.31
  software, HMRC, 44.5-44.6
  statutory residence test, 44.12
  students during vacation, 44.11
  taxable benefits
    car fuel, 44.26
    company cars, 44.25
    generally, 44.21
    lower-paid employees, 44.22
    vans, 44.27
  tax-free benefits, 44.23
  vans, 44.27
  working abroad, 44.12
  wrongful dismissal, and, 56.32
  year-end information
    on-line, 44.19
Tax-free benefits
  taxation, and, 44.23
Temporary employees
  employment agencies, and
    Conduct Regulations, 45.5
    EC Directive, 45.2d
    generally, 45.2–45.2c
    national minimum wage, 45.6
    reforms, 45.4
    Regulations, 45.2d
    statutory control, 45.3
    unfair dismissal, 45.7
  introduction, 45.1
  less favourable treatment, 45.9
  seasonal workers, 45.8
  unfair dismissal, and, 45.7
Tenancy
  service lettings, and, 41.5
Termination of employment
  accrued but untaken leave, 27.4A
  constructive dismissal, by, 46.18
  contractual notice period, 46.6
  dismissal, by
    introduction, 46.5
    notice, 46.6–46.12
    retraction of, 46.20
    summary, 46.13

Termination of employment – *cont.*
  dismissal, by – *cont.*
    written statement of reasons, 46.14–46.15
    effluxion of time, by, 46.4
    expiry, by, 46.4
    frustration, by, 46.3
    holidays, and, 27.4A
    implied contract terms, and, 7.15
    introduction, 46.1
    mutual agreement, by, 46.2
    notice, by
      contractual notice period, 46.6
      employee, by, 46.17
      introduction, 46.5
      pay in lieu of notice, 46.9–46.10
      rights during notice period, 46.12
      statutory minimum notice, 46.7–46.8
    pay, and, 32.22
    pay in lieu of notice
      generally, 46.9
      gross or net, 46.11
      taxation, 46.10
    reasons for dismissal
      generally, 46.14
      remedy for failure to give, 46.15
    remedies, 46.21
    repudiatory conduct, by, 46.19
    resignation, by
      generally, 46.16
      notice by employee, 46.17
      retraction of, 46.20
      summary termination by employee, 46.18
    statutory minimum notice
      exceptions, 46.8
      generally, 46.7
    summary dismissal, by, 46.13
    written statements of reasons for dismissal
      generally, 46.14
      remedy for failure to give, 46.15
    wrongful termination, 46.21
Termination of office
  generally, 8.36
  Listing Rules requirements, 8.39
  property transfer, 8.38
  recommendations, 8.38
  takeovers, 8.41
  termination payments, 8.37
Terms of contracts of employment
  changes, 7.9
  contrary to public policy, 7.24
  employer handbooks, 7.13
  express, 7.14
  freedom to agree, 7.12
  implied, 7.14–7.15

Terms of contracts of employment – *cont.*
  unenforceable
    contracting out of certain provisions, 7.26
    discriminatory terms, 7.27
    industrial action restrictions, 7.29
    introduction, 7.23
    restraint trade, 7.28
    UCTA 1977, and, 7.30
    unlawful, 7.24
    variation by statute, 7.25
Terms of employment
  written particulars, 22.7
Terms of engagement
  temporary workers, and, 45.2–45.2c
Territorial scope
  discrimination, 10.42
  equality legislation, 11.17
  generally, 1.8
Third parties
  discriminatory acts, 10.57
Time limits for proceedings
  contract claims, 17.32
  discrimination complaints, and
    acts extending over a period, 12.6
    extension of time, 12.7
    generally, 12.4
    omissions, 12.5
  EAT, and, 19.14
  equal pay, 17.28
  generally, 17.18
  'just and equitable, 17.30
  'not reasonably practicable' to present in
    time, 17.25–17.26
  other claims, 17.33
  post-EA 2002, 17.19–17.20
  redundancy payments, 17.27
  unlawful deductions from wages, 17.31
  unlawful discrimination, 17.29
  redundancy payments, and, 36.11
Time off work
  adoption leave, 47.17
  ante-natal care, and
    generally, 31.6
    qualifying requirements, 31.7
    remedies for refusal, 31.9
    right to remuneration, 31.8
  arrangements for training
    generally, 47.6
    remedies, 47.7
  care for children, 47.17
  consultation representatives
    generally, 47.12
    remedies, 47.13

Index

Time off work – *cont.*
dependants, for
generally, 47.15
remedies, 47.16
employee representatives
generally, 47.12
remedies, 47.13
European Works Council duties, 47.14
flexible working, 47.17
health and safety representatives
generally, 47.8
remedies, 47.9
insolvency of employer, and, 29.2
introduction, 47.1
look for work
generally, 47.6
remedies, 47.7
maternity leave, 47.17
military service
reinstatement after 47.18–47.19
occupational pension scheme trustees
generally, 47.10
remedies, 47.11
parental leave, 47.17
paternity leave, 47.17
pension scheme trustees
generally, 47.10
remedies, 47.11
public duties
generally, 47.4
remedies, 47.5
safety representatives
Codes of Practice, and, 4.14–4.15
generally, 47.8
remedies, 47.9
study and training, and
introduction, 3.8
remedy for refusal, 3.9
right not to suffer detriment, 3.10
trade union activities
Codes of Practice, and, 4.2–4.3
generally, 47.3
remedies, 47.5
trade union officials, 47.2
unfair dismissal, and, 52.3
Tips and gratuities
national minimum wage, and, 32.9
pay, and, 32.21
Tortious liability of trade unions
generally, 48.16
limits on damages, 48.17
Trade dispute
strike action, and, 43.4

Trade organisations
discrimination, and, 11.29
Trade secrets
implied contract terms, and, 7.15
restraint of trade covenants, and, 39.13
Trade union activities
civil servants, 47.2
Codes of Practice, and
legal effect, 4.3
power to issue, 4.2
generally, 47.3
insolvency of employer, and, 29.2
remedies, 47.5
unfair dismissal, and, 52.3
Trade union dues
deductions from wages, and, 32.6
Trade union membership
advice from unions, 49.22
'blacklists', 49.10
'check-off', 49.20
closed shop
dismissal, and, 49.5
industrial action, and, 49.9
introduction, 49.3
pre-entry, 49.4
closed shop dismissals
compensation, 49.7
generally, 49.5
contracts for goods and services, and, 49.19
deductions from wages
generally, 49.20
introduction, 32.6
detriment
generally, 49.17
remedy, 49.18
summary, 49.8
disciplinary action
common law, 49.15
right to be accompanied, 49.21
statutory provisions, 49.16
summary, 49.9
exclusion from union
common law, 49.12
introduction, 49.11
remedy, 49.14
statutory provisions, 49.13
expulsion from union
common law, 49.12
introduction, 49.11
remedy, 49.14
statutory right, 49.13
failure to make payments, 49.6
goods or services contracts, 49.19
industrial action, 49.9

Trade union membership – *cont.*
pre-entry closed shop, 49.4
rights
employer, in relation to, 49.1
union, in relation to, 49.2
time off work, and
Codes of Practice, 4.2–4.3
generally, 47.3
remedies, 47.5
tortious liability, 48.18
unfair dismissal, and, 52.3
Trade union officials
time off work, and
Codes of Practice, 4.2–4.3
generally, 47.2
unfair dismissal, and, 52.3
Trade unions
accounts and records, 48.12
amalgamations, 48.39
Central Arbitration Committee
appeals against awards, 48.10–48.11
arbitration, 48.7
complaint of failure to disclose
information, 48.8
constitution, 48.5
contracting out, and, 48.9
establishment, 48.4
functions, 48.6–48.9
certification officer, 48.3
collective bargaining, and
derecognition, 48.36
recognition, 48.26–48.35
detriment, 48.37
disqualification from office, 48.14
duty of care for advice given, 49.22
elections, 48.14
independence
factors, 48.23
introduction, 48.22
withdrawal of certificate, 48.24
legal capacity, 48.2
listing, 48.21
membership rights
and see **TRADE** UNION MEMBERS
generally, 49.1–49.22
obligations
accounts and records, 48.12
disqualification from office, 48.14
elections, 48.14
introduction, 48.12
political levy, 48.15
register of members, 48.13
political levy, 48.15

Trade unions – *cont.*
pressure to impose membership or recognition,
and, 43.7
recognition
collective bargaining, for, 48.25–48.35
independence, 48.22–48.24
introduction, 48.19
listing, 48.21
unfair dismissal, and, 52.3
voluntary, 48.20
recognition for collective bargaining
appropriate bargaining unit, 48.30
ballot, 48.31–48.32
changes in bargaining unit, 48.35
'collective bargaining', 48.27
introduction, 48.25
method of bargaining, 48.33
reference to CAC, 48.29
request for recognition, 48.28
scope of procedure, 48.26
voluntary, 48.34
records, 48.12
register of members, 48.13
status
generally, 48.1
legal capacity, 48.2
strike action, and
ballots before action, 43.14
calls for action, 43.15
generally, 43.13
tortious liability
generally, 48.16
limits on damages, 48.17
training, 48.38
transfer of engagements, 48.39
transfer of undertakings, and
collective agreements, 50.20
employee liability information, 50.22
information and consultation, 50.22–50.23
recognition, 50.21
unfair dismissal, and, 52.3
voluntary recognition
collective bargaining, for, 48.34
generally, 48.20
Training and education
and see **TIME** OFF
apprenticeships, 13.2
Apprenticeships, Skills, Training and Children
Bill, 13.9
DELLS, 13.8
discrimination, and, 11.10
employee participation in consultation,
and, 15.63
industrial training boards, 13.4

Index

Training and education – *cont.*
introduction, 13.1
Learning and Skills Council, 13.8
New Deal, 13.6
positive discrimination, and, 11.10
recovery of costs, 13.3
school-leavers, for, 13.5
tax-free benefits, and, 44.23
time off from work, and
generally, 47.6
remedies, 47.7
trade unions, and, 48.38
unfair dismissal, and, 52.3
work-based training, 13.7
Work Programme, 13.6
Transfer of engagements
trade unions, and, 48.39
Transfer of proceedings
tribunal procedure, and, 18.25
Transfer of undertakings (TUPE)
administrative functions carried out by public
body, 50.9
applications to Employment Tribunals, 18.25
assignment of employment contracts
employee's right of objection, 50.16
exclusions, 50.19
'immediately before the transfer', 50.14
introduction, 50.13
nature of acquisition by
transferee, 50.17–50.18
'would otherwise have been
terminated', 50.15
avoidance of, 50.28
background, 50.1
change of employer, 6.9
collective agreements, 50.20
consultation of employees, 50.23
directors, and, 8.42
disclosure of information, and, 9.6
dismissal, and
introduction, 50.24
redundancy, 50.27
unfair dismissal, 50.25–50.26
employee liability information, 50.22
Employment Law Review, and, 24.7
European law, and, 22.9
excluded rights and liability, 50.19
information and consultation
advance notification, 50.23
employee liability information, 50.22
introduction, 9.6
insolvency of employer
generally, 50.11
introduction, 29.10

Transfer of undertakings (TUPE) – *cont.*
introduction, 50.1–50.2
legislative background, 50.1
meaning
introduction, 50.1–50.2
"service provision change", 50.3
"transfer", 50.5
"undertaking", 50.4
more than one transaction, 50.7
payments from National Insurance Fund, and
generally, 50.11
introduction, 29.10
recognition of trade unions, and, 50.21
redundancy payments
generally, 50.27
introduction, 36.5
"relevant transfer"
administrative functions carried out by public
body, 50.9
introduction, 50.2
more than one transaction, 50.7
other concepts, 50.6–50.10
service provision change, 50.3
share transfers, 50.10
transfer, 50.5
transfer of property, 50.8
undertaking or business, 50.4
rights and liabilities assigned
employee's right of objection, 50.16
exclusions, 50.19
'immediately before the transfer', 50.14
introduction, 50.13
nature of acquisition by
transferee, 50.17–50.18
'would otherwise have been
terminated', 50.15
rights and liabilities not assigned, 50.19
"service provision change"
background, 50.1
introduction, 50.2
relevant activities, 50.3
share transfers, and, 50.10
timing, 50.12
trade unions, and
collective agreements, 50.20
employee liability information, 50.22
information and consultation, 50.22–50.23
recognition, 50.21
"transfer", 50.5
transfer of property, 50.8
"undertaking or business", 50.4
unfair dismissal, and
dismissal, 50.25
fairness of dismissal, 50.26

Transfer of undertakings (TUPE) – *cont.*
  unfair dismissal, and – *cont.*
    generally, 52.3
    variation of employees' contracts, 50.29
Transport vouchers
  taxable benefits, and, 44.21
Transport workers
  working time, and, 55.3
Transsexuals
  and see DISCRIMINATION
  comparators, 10.15
  equal pay, and
    generally, 21.13
    introduction, 21.2
  generally, 10.6
  genuine occupational requirement or
      qualification, 11.5
  less favourable treatment
    comparators, 10.15
    generally, 10.14
    positive discrimination, 10.16
  protected characteristics, 10.6
Travel expenses
  tax-free benefits, and, 44.23
Troncs
  pay, and, 32.21
Trust and confidence
  implied contract terms, and, 7.15
Trustees of pension schemes
  discrimination, and, 11.35
  introduction, 40.15
  time off work, and
    generally, 47.10
    remedies, 47.11
  unfair dismissal, and, 52.3
TUPE
  and see TRANSFER OF UNDERTAKINGS
  change of employer, 6.9
  directors, 8.42
  Employment Law Review, and, 24.7
UK Corporate Governance Code
  directors' service contracts, 8.15
  remuneration, 8.28
Undertaking
  and see TRANSFER OF UNDERTAKINGS
  meaning, 50.4
Unenforceable terms of contract
  contracting out of certain provisions, 7.26
  discriminatory terms, 7.27
  industrial action restrictions, 7.29
  introduction, 7.23
  restraint trade, 7.28
  UCTA 1977, and, 7.30

Unfair Contract Terms Act 1977
  unenforceable terms, and, 7.30
Unfair dismissal
  ACAS, 2.5
  acceptable reasons for dismissal
    capability, 52.5–52.8
    contravention of any enactment, 52.13
    ill-health, 52.8
    introduction, 52.1
    misconduct, 52.9–52.10
    qualifications, 52.7
    redundancy, 52.11–52.12
    some other substantial reason, 52.14
    summary, 52.2
  accompanied at disciplinary hearings, and, 52.3
  additional award, 53.14
  adoption leave, and, 52.3
  agency workers, and
    generally, 52.3
    introduction, 45.7
  assertion of statutory rights, 52.3
  basic award
    amount, 53.7
    exceptions, 53.8
    maximum award, 53.16
    reduction, 53.9
  'blacklists', 52.3
  capability
    generally, 52.6
    ill-health, 52.8
    introduction, 52.5
    procedure, 52.6A
    qualifications, 52.7
    summary, 52.2
  childbirth, and, 52.3
  compensation
    additional award, 53.14
    basic award, 53.7–53.9
    compensatory award, 53.10–53.13
    introduction, 53.6
    maximum amounts, 53.16
    recoupment of statutory benefits, 53.5
    union-related cases, 53.15
  compensatory award
    amount, 53.11
    heads of loss, 53.12
    increase, 53.13
    introduction, 53.10
    loss of benefits, 53.12
    loss of earnings, 53.12
    loss of statutory rights, 53.12
    maximum award, 53.16
    pension rights, 53.12
    reduction, 53.13, 53.15

Index

Unfair dismissal – *cont.*
compensatory award – *cont.*
union-related cases, 53.15
conduct
generally, 52.9
procedure, 52.10
summary, 52.2
constructive dismissal, 51.7
continuous employment
calculation, 51.12
effective date of termination, 51.13
introduction, 51.11
contracting out
exceptions, 51.20
generally, 51.19
contravention of any enactment
generally, 52.13
summary, 52.2
deemed unfair dismissals, 52.3
disciplinary hearings, and, 52.3
dismissal by respondent
constructive dismissal, 51.7
excepted terminations, 51.10
expiry of fixed-term contract, 51.6
forced resignation, 51.8
introduction, 51.4
repudiatory conduct by employee, 51.9
termination by employer, 51.5
economic, technical or organisational
reasons, 52.14
education and training, and, 52.3
effective date of termination, 51.13
employee representatives, and, 52.3
employment by respondent, 51.3
European Works Council, and, 52.3
excluded employees, 51.15
expiry of fixed-term contract
generally, 51.6
some other substantial reason, 52.14
failure to follow statutory disciplinary
procedures, 52.3
fairness
acceptable reasons for dismissal, 52.1–52.2
deemed unfair dismissals, 52.3
'in the circumstances', 52.4
family-related reasons, 52.3
fixed-term employees, and, 52.3
flexible working, and, 52.3
forced resignation, 51.8
frustration, and, 51.10
grounds
capability, 52.5–52.6A
conduct, 52.9–52.10
contravention of enactment, 52.13

Unfair dismissal – *cont.*
grounds – *cont.*
ill-health, 52.8
qualifications, 52.7
redundancy, 52.11–52.12
some other substantial reason, 52.14
health and safety, and
breach of safety regulations, 26.11
detriment, 26.8
generally, 52.3
introduction, 26.7
whistleblowing, 26.9
remedy, 26.10
illegal contracts, 51.16
ill-health
generally, 52.8
introduction, 52.5
summary, 52.2
imprisonment, 52.14
industrial action, and, 52.3
insolvency of employer, and, 29.5
interim relief, 53.18
internal appeals, and, 52.15
introduction, 51.1
joinder of third parties, 53.17
jury service, and, 52.3
lock-outs, and
official action, 51.17
unofficial action, 51.18
maternity leave, and, 52.3
minimum wage, and, 52.3
misconduct
generally, 52.9
procedure, 52.10
summary, 52.2
national minimum wage, and, 52.3
necessary economies, 52.14
non-membership of union, 52.3
occurrence of external event, and, 51.10
parental leave, and, 52.3
part-time workers, and,
generally, 30.25
introduction, 52.3
paternity leave, and, 52.3
payments from National Insurance Fund,
and, 29.5
pension enrolment, and, 52.3
pension scheme trustees, and, 52.3
pre-conditions of claim
dismissal by respondent, 51.4–51.10
employment by respondent, 51.3
introduction, 51.2
qualifying period of employment, 51.11–51.13
pregnancy, and, 52.3

Unfair dismissal – *cont.*
pressure on employer to dismiss unfairly, 52.16
protection of interests of business, 52.14
public interest disclosure, and, 52.3
qualifications
  generally, 52.7
  introduction, 52.5
  summary, 52.2
qualifying period of employment
  calculation of continuous employment, 51.12
  effective date of termination, 51.13
  human rights, and, 28.4
  introduction, 51.11
reasons for dismissal, 52.1
redundancy
  generally, 52.11
  procedure, 52.12
  summary, 52.2
  unfair selection, 52.3
re-engagement
  general rules, 53.4
  generally, 53.3
  refusal to reinstate, 53.5
refusal to work on Sunday, and, 52.3
reinstatement
  general rules, 53.4
  generally, 53.2
  refusal to reinstate, 53.5
remedies
  compensation, 53.6–53.16
  interim relief, 53.18
  introduction, 53.1
  joinder of third parties, 53.17
  re-engagement, 53.3–53.5
  reinstatement, 53.2–53.5
  settlement, 53.19
reorganisation of business, 52.14
replacement employee, 52.14
repudiatory conduct by employee, 51.9
retirement, and, 52.4
seasonal workers, and, 45.8
settlement, 53.19
some other substantial reason
  generally, 52.14
  summary, 52.2
special negotiating bodies, and, 52.3
spent convictions, and, 52.3
strikes, and
  official action, 51.17
  unofficial action, 51.18
study, and, 52.3
Sunday work, and, 52.3
tax credits, and, 52.3
temporary workers, and, 45.7

Unfair dismissal – *cont.*
termination by employer, 51.5
time off for dependants, and, 52.3
training, and, 52.3
transfer of undertakings, and
  dismissal, 50.25
  fairness of dismissal, 50.26
  generally, 52.3
union membership, and, 52.3
union recognition, and, 52.3
working time, and
  generally, 55.24
  introduction, 52.3
works councils, and, 52.3
wrongful dismissal, and, 56.33
Unfair terms
contracts of employment, and, 7.30
Unfavourable treatment
discrimination, and, 10.14
Union membership
and see **TRADE UNIONS**
unfair dismissal, and, 52.3
Union recognition
and see **TRADE UNIONS**
unfair dismissal, and, 52.3
Unlawful act notices
generally, 12.28
Unlawful acts
discrimination, and, 10.54–10.55
Unlawful deductions from wages
time limits for claims, and, 17.31
Unlawful instructions to discriminate
enforcement only by Commissions, 11.38
generally, 10.53
injunctions, 12.30
Unlawful pressure to discriminate
enforcement only by Commissions, 11.38
generally, 10.53
injunctions, 12.30
Unlawful terms
contracts of employment, and, 7.24
Unmeasured working time
working time, and, 55.28
Unofficial workers, dismissal of
strike action, and, 43.8
Unpaid leave
annual leave entitlement, 27.3B
**Unreasonable refusal of alternative
employment**
redundancy payments, and, 36.12
Use of employer's assets
taxable benefits, and, 44.21
Vacation work
taxation, and, 44.11

Index

Valuation of benefits
wrongful dismissal, and, 56.28
Vans
taxation, and, 44.27
Variation of contracts of employment
generally, 7.25
transfer of undertakings, and, 50.29
Vexatious litigants
tribunal procedure, and, 18.77
Vibration
health and safety, and, 26.27
Vicarious liability
'close connection', 54.2
common law, and, 54.1
discrimination, and
defence, 10.55
generally, 10.54
health and safety, and, 25.9
fellow workers, 25.7
introduction, 54.1
meaning
generally, 54.1
'in the course of his employment', 54.2
part-time workers, and, 30.30
'pro hac vice' employment, 54.3
temporary workers, and, 45.2–45.2c
Victimisation
discrimination, and, 10.38
employee, claim against, 10.54
part time workers, and, 30.26
working time, and, 55.23
Violence
health and safety, and, 26.28
Vocational training providers
discrimination, and, 11.31
Voluntary recognition of trade unions
collective bargaining, for, 48.34
generally, 48.20
Voluntary workers
employer, vicarious liability 25.7
national minimum wage, and, 32.10
status, 14.9
Vouchers
taxable benefits, and, 44.21–44.22
Vulnerable groups
criminal convictions, and, 16.8
Wages
attachment of earnings, and
attachable earnings, 33.2
child support maintenance, 33.11
Council Tax, 33.10
deductions, 33.3–33.6
employer's obligations, 33.7
introduction, 33.1

Wages – cont.
attachment of earnings, and – cont.
other issues, 33.9
penalties for non-compliance, 33.8
breach of contracts of employment, and, 7.47
deductions from wages
generally, 32.6
minimum wage, and, 32.9–32.13
other, 32.14
remedies for breach, 32.8
retail employment, 32.7
fixed deductions, 32.17
generally, 32.2
gratuities, 32.21
guarantee payments
amount, 32.27
exclusions, 32.26
introduction, 32.23
qualifying period, 32.25
remedy for failure to make payment, 32.28
'workless days', 32.24
holidays, and, 27.4
insolvency of employer, and, 29.2
introduction, 32.1
itemised statements
application to tribunal, 32.19–32.20
exclusions, 32.18
fixed deductions, 32.17
generally, 32.16
meaning, 32.6
medical suspension, and
amount, 32.32
exclusions, 32.31
generally, 32.29
qualifying conditions, 32.30
remedy for failure to make payment, 32.33
method of payment, 32.3
national minimum wage
coverage, 32.10
introduction, 32.9
records, 32.11
relevant workers, 32.10
remedies for failure to pay, 32.12–32.13
statements, 32.11
overpayment, 32.15
pre-1987 position
exceptions, 32.5
generally, 32.4
records, 32.11
statement of fixed deductions, 32.17
termination of employment, and, 32.22
troncs, 32.21
'week's pay'
amount, 32.39

Wages – *cont.*
  'week's pay' – *cont.*
    calculation date, 32.38
    introduction, 32.34
    no normal working hours, 32.37
    normal working hours, 32.35
    overtime, 32.36
    workless days, and, 32.23
Waiver
  wrongful dismissal, and, 56.21
Wasted costs orders
  tribunal procedure, and, 18.74, 19.45
Weekly rest periods
  working time, and, 55.16
Weeks
  continuous employment, and
    meaning, 6.5
    weeks which count, 6.6–6.8
    weeks which do not count, 6.10–6.11
  working time, and, 55.6
'Week's pay'
  amount, 32.39
  calculation date, 32.38
  introduction, 32.34
  no normal working hours, 32.37
  normal working hours, 32.35
  overtime, 32.36
  unfair dismissal, and, 53.7
Welfare
  discrimination, and, 11.10
Whistleblowing
  Employment Law Review, and, 24.7
  generally, 9.16
  health and safety, and, 26.9
  human rights, and, 28.4
  protected disclosures, 9.17
Withdrawal of claims
  tribunal procedure, and, 18.28
Withdrawal of offer of employment
  engagement of employees, and, 20.8
Withholding wages
  breach of contracts of employment, and, 7.47
Witness orders
  tribunal procedure, and, 18.14
  witnesses, 18.57
Women suspended on medical grounds
  equal pay, and, 21.4
Work-based training
  generally, 13.7
Work experience
  generally, 3.7
Work of equal value
  equal pay, and, 21.8

Work permits
  generally, 23.4
Work Programme
  education and training, and, 13.6
Work rated as equivalent
  equal pay, and, 21.7
Workers
  holiday, and, 27.2
  meaning, 14.9
  part-time workers, and, 30.3
Workforce agreements
  generally, 5.14
  working time, and, 55.4
Working abroad
  statutory residence test, 44.12
  taxation, and, 44.12
Working time
  agency workers, 55.37
  annual leave, 55.19
  armed forces personnel, 55.3
  aviation sector, 55.33
  children, 55.3
  Church of England clergy, 55.38
  collective agreements, 55.4
  contracting out, 55.25
  daily rest periods, 55.15
  definition, 55.5
  doctors in training, 55.3
  domestic service, 55.30
  EC Directive, 55.1
  enforcement
    health and safety authorities, by, 55.21
    individual, by, 55.22
    introduction, 55.20
  European law, and, 22.11
  exceptions
    domestic service, 55.30
    introduction, 55.27
    special cases, 55.29
    unmeasured working time, 55.28
  Guidance, 55.26
  holidays, and
    agricultural workers, 27.7
    introduction, 27.2
    notice requirements, 27.5
    payment, 27.4
    period of leave, 27.3
    remedies, 27.6
    sick leave, and, 27.3
    timing, 27.5
    'workers', 27.2
  introduction, 55.1
  maximum weekly time, 55.6
  merchant seamen, 55.31–55.32

Index

Working time – *cont.*
mobile workers, 55.34–55.36
monotonous work, 55.18
night work
duration, 55.10
health assessments, 55.12
introduction, 55.9
special hazards, 55.11
transfer to day work, 55.13
offshore workers, 55.1
opt-out agreements, 55.7
police, 55.3
railway workers, 55.36
records, 55.8
Regulations
coverage, 55.3
definitions, 55.4
introduction, 55.2
relevant agreement, 55.4
relevant workers, 55.3
rest breaks
generally, 55.17
monotonous work, 55.18
rest periods
daily, 55.15
introduction, 55.14
weekly, 55.16
road transport workers, 55.34–55.35
seafarers, 55.31–55.32
transport workers, 55.34–55.35
unfair dismissal, and
generally, 55.24
introduction, 52.3
unmeasured working time, 55.28
victimisation, 55.23
weekly rest periods, 55.16
workforce agreement, 55.4
young persons, 55.3
Working under direction of third party
health and safety, and, 25.10
Working with due diligence and care
implied contract terms, and, 7.15
'Workless days'
guarantee payments, and, 32.24
Workplace nurseries
tax-free benefits, and, 44.23
Workplace standards
health and safety, and, 26.29
Work-related training
tax-free benefits, and, 44.23
Work-related upper limb disorders
health and safety, and, 26.31
Works councils
amending Regulations, 15.29A

Works councils – *cont.*
confidential information, 15.28
employment protection, 15.29
establishment, 15.27
European law, and, 22.12
introduction, 15.22
number of employees, 15.24
requests, 15.25
special negotiating body, 15.26
time off work, and, 47.14
unfair dismissal, and, 52.3
Written particulars of contract
alternatives to inclusion, 7.8
changes, 7.9
directors, and, 8.6
European law, and, 22.7
excepted employees, 7.10
introduction, 7.6
remedies for failure to provide, 7.11
requirements, 7.7
Written statements of reasons
dismissal, and,
generally, 46.14
remedy for failure to give, 46.15
part time workers, and, 30.23
Wrongful dismissal
acceptance of employer's breach, 56.7
anticipatory breaches of contract, 56.22
apprentices, and, 56.44
cessation of existence of employer, 56.8
change of employer's identity, 56.8
choice of court, 56.38
claims procedure
choice of court, 56.38
compromise of claims, 56.42
hearings on liability and quantum, 56.41
interim payments, 56.41
limitation periods, 56.40
payments into court, 56.41
relationship with tribunal proceedings, 56.39
summary judgment, 56.41
compromise of claims, 56.42
constructive dismissal, 56.6
contrast with other modes of termination, 56.4
Crown servants, and, 56.43
damages
accelerated receipt, 56.31
accommodation, 56.28
assessment approach, 56.25
bonuses, 56.28
cars, 56.28
collateral benefits, 56.30
commission, 56.28
distress, 56.29

Wrongful dismissal – *cont.*
  damages – *cont.*
    holidays, 56.28
    insurance cover, 56.28
    intangible loss, 56.29
    interest, 56.31
    'liquidated damages' clauses, 56.26
    mitigation, 56.30
    pensions, 56.28
    rights in period of notice, 56.27
    salary, 56.28
    share options, 56.28
    taxation, 56.32
    unfair dismissal compensation, and, 56.33
    valuation of benefits, 56.28
  defences
    exclusion clauses, 56.37
    illegality, 56.35
    invalidity of contract, 56.36
  'dismissal'
    acceptance of employer's breach, 56.7
    cessation of existence of employer, 56.8
    change of employer's identity, 56.8
    constructive dismissal, 56.6
    contrast with other modes of
      termination, 56.4
    dismissal with notice, 56.5
    dismissal without notice, 56.11–56.17
    insolvency of employer, 56.9
    introduction, 56.3
    removal of director from board, 56.10
  dismissal in breach of other requirements, 56.19
  dismissal in breach of procedures, 56.18
  dismissal with notice, 56.5
  dismissal without notice
    directors' notice periods, 56.14
    express notice periods, 56.11
    fixed term contracts, 56.12
    implied notice periods, 56.15
    justification, 56.17
    rolling contracts, 56.13
    statutory minimum notice, 56.16
  effect on other obligations, 56.34
  exclusion clauses, 56.37
  garden leave, 56.21
  hearings on liability and quantum, 56.41
  illegality, 56.35

Wrongful dismissal – *cont.*
  injunctions, 56.23
  insolvency of employer, 56.9
  interim payments, 56.41
  introduction, 56.1–56.2
  invalidity of contract, 56.3
  limitation periods, 56.40
  pay in lieu of notice, 56.21
  payments into court, 56.41
  reason for dismissal, and, 56.20
  remedies
    claims in debt, 56.24
    damages, 56.25–56.33
    injunctions, 56.23
  removal of director from board, 56.10
  summary dismissal
    directors' notice periods, 56.14
    express notice periods, 56.11
    fixed term contracts, 56.12
    implied notice periods, 56.15
    justification, 56.17
    rolling contracts, 56.13
    statutory minimum notice, 56.16
  summary judgment, 56.41
  waiver of notice, 56.21
Young persons, employment of
  breaks, 3.6
  contracts of employment, 3.11
  definitions, 3.1
  health and safety
    breaks, 3.6
    introduction, 3.5
    night work, 3.6
    rest periods, 3.6
  local authority powers, 3.3
  night work, 3.6
  rest periods, 3.6
  restrictions
    generally, 3.2
    local authority powers, 3.3
    other provisions, 3.4
  time off for study or training
    introduction, 3.8
    remedy for refusal, 3.9
    right not to suffer detriment, 3.10
  work experience, 3.7
  working time, and, 55.3